Pocket Oxford American Dictionary and Thesaurus

Pocket Oxford American Dictionary and Thesaurus

THIRD EDITION

OXFORD
UNIVERSITY PRESS

Oxford University Press, Inc., publishes works that further
Oxford University's objective of excellence
in research, scholarship, and education.

Oxford New York

Auckland Cape Town Dar es Salaam Hong Kong Karachi
Kuala Lumpur Madrid Melbourne Mexico City Nairobi
New Delhi Shanghai Taipei Toronto

With offices in

Argentina Austria Brazil Chile Czech Republic France Greece
Guatemala Hungary Italy Japan Poland Portugal Singapore
South Korea Switzerland Thailand Turkey Ukraine Vietnam

First edition 2002
Second edition 2006
Third edition 2010

Published by Oxford University Press, Inc.
198 Madison Avenue, New York, NY 10016
www.oup.com

The Library of Congress Cataloging-in-Publication Data

Data available

ISBN 978-0-19-972995-1

1 3 5 7 9 8 6 4 2

Printed in the United States of America
on acid-free paper

Contents

Contributors

Project Manager
Maurice Waite

Senior Editor
Christine A. Lindberg

Lexicographers
Carol Braham
Elizabeth J. Jewell

Preface

The *Pocket Oxford American Dictionary and Thesaurus* is an all-in-one reference book. In one single entry you will find the spelling, syllabification, pronunciation, and meanings of a word, as well as any derived words, phrases containing the word, and, where appropriate, synonyms (similar-meaning words) and antonyms (opposites).

This Third Edition is completely new. It has been created from Oxford's most up-to-date dictionaries and thesauruses, which are compiled using information from the Oxford English Corpus, a two-billion-word database of all types of English. The *Pocket Oxford American Dictionary and Thesaurus* therefore includes many recent coinages and new senses such as *biofuel*, *bipolar*, *carbon footprint*, *cybercrime*, *ringtone*, and *social networking*.

The 9,500 boxed sections of synonyms work just like a thesaurus to help you express yourself more accurately and in more interesting and varied ways. By listing groups of words that have similar meanings to each other, they offer a choice of alternative words that can be used in place of one that you already have in mind. They can provide the answer when a word is on the tip of your tongue, as well as expanding your vocabulary or helping to solve crossword puzzles and many other word games.

Many entries also give clear guidance to help you write better English: usage notes on points of good English (for example, whether to say *disinterested* or *uninterested*) and spelling notes to help you remember how to spell tricky words such as *embarrass* and *sacrilege*.

The central reference supplement contains a selection of handy information including US Presidents, Countries of the World, and a guide to using punctuation.

Guide to the Dictionary

1. Structure of entries

Here are examples of the major types of information in entries:

headword: **leaf** /lēf/ ▶ n. (plural **leaves** /lēvz/) **1** a flat green part of a plant that is attached to a stem. **2** a single sheet of paper in a book. **3** gold or silver in the form of a very thin sheet. **4** a hinged or detachable part of a tabletop. **5** the state of having leaves: *the trees were in leaf.* ▶ v. (**leaf through**) turn over pages or papers, reading quickly or casually.

SYNONYMS ▶ n. **1** (**leaves**) **foliage**, greenery. **2 page**, sheet, folio. ▶ v. *I leafed through a magazine* **flip through**, flick through, thumb through, skim through/over, browse through, glance through/over, riffle through, scan, run your eye over, peruse.

□ **leaf peeper** a person who views autumn foliage, especially in New England. **turn over a new leaf** start to behave in a better way.

Annotations: part of speech (word class); plural form; example of use, to help distinguish different senses; a use or form of the headword that has its own definition; words that can be used as alternatives to the headword; phrase for which synonyms are given; phrases.

de·sert¹ /də'zərt/ ▶ v. **1** leave someone without help or support. **2** leave a place, making it seem empty. **3** illegally leave the armed forces.

SYNONYMS **1 abandon**, leave, jilt, leave high and dry, leave in the lurch, leave behind, strand, maroon; informal walk/run out on, dump, ditch; literary forsake. **2** (**deserted**) **abandoned**, jilted, cast aside, neglected, stranded, marooned, forlorn; literary forsaken. **3** (**deserted**) **empty**, uninhabited, unoccupied, abandoned, evacuated, desolate, lonely, godforsaken. **4 abscond**, defect, run away, decamp, flee, turn tail, take French leave; Military go AWOL.

■ **de·sert·er** n. **de·ser·tion** n.

de·sert² /'dezərt/ ▶ n. an empty, waterless area of land with very few plants.

SYNONYMS **wasteland**, wastes, wilderness, dust bowl.

□ **desert island** an uninhabited tropical island.

USAGE

Don't confuse **desert** (a waterless area) with **dessert** (the sweet course eaten at the end of a meal).

Annotations: numbered sense of the headword; register label indicating the style of English in which the following synonym(s) are used (see section 3 for explanations); different words with the same spelling, numbered; a form of the headword for which the following synonym(s) can be substituted; derivatives (words derived from the headword); compound; note giving help with using the headword.

ad·duce /ə'd(y)o͞os/ ▶ v. (**adduces**, **adducing**, **adduced**) formal refer to something as evidence.

Annotations: pronunciation (see section 5 for key); verb forms (inflections).

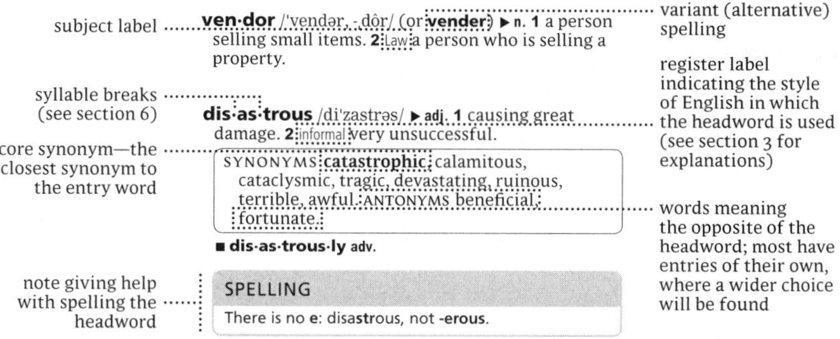
subject label
ven·dor /ˈvendər, -dôr/ (or vender) ▶ n. 1 a person selling small items. 2 Law a person who is selling a property.
variant (alternative) spelling
register label indicating the style of English in which the headword is used (see section 3 for explanations)
syllable breaks (see section 6)
dis·as·trous /diˈzastrəs/ ▶ adj. 1 causing great damage. 2 informal very unsuccessful.
core synonym—the closest synonym to the entry word
SYNONYMS catastrophic, calamitous, cataclysmic, tragic, devastating, ruinous, terrible, awful. ANTONYMS beneficial, fortunate.
■ dis·as·trous·ly adv.
words meaning the opposite of the headword; most have entries of their own, where a wider choice will be found
note giving help with spelling the headword
SPELLING
There is no e: disastrous, not -erous.

2. Spelling and forms of nouns and verbs

Alternative spellings

The main form of each word given in the dictionary is the accepted American spelling. Although there is only one way that most words can be spelled, sometimes other spellings (called *variants*) are also acceptable. Such spellings are given after the headword, e.g., **flier** (or **flyer**), or before a particular sense if the spelling variant is only used in that sense. In all such cases the spelling given as the headword is the one that most people use.

Hyphenation

Although standard spelling in English is fixed, the use of hyphens is not. There are a few general rules that should be followed, and these are outlined below.

Noun compounds: there are no set rules as to whether a compound (such as **airstream**) should be written as one word, as two words, or with a hyphen (unless the hyphen is used to show the word's grammatical function; see the next section): **airstream**, **air stream**, and **air-stream** are all acceptable. However, more compounds are being written as either one word or two words, rather than with a hyphen.

To save space and avoid confusion, the dictionary gives only the standard form. This does not, however, mean that other forms are incorrect or not used.

Grammatical information: hyphens are also used to show a word's grammatical function. When a noun compound made up of two separate words (e.g. **credit card**) is placed before another noun, the rule is that the compound has a hyphen, so you should write, for example, *I used my credit card* but *credit-card debt*. You will see this in some example phrases and sentences, but it is not otherwise mentioned.

There is a similar rule with compound adjectives such as **well-known**. When they are placed after the verb (in the *predicative* position) such adjectives are written with or without a hyphen (*he is well-known* or *he is well known*), but when they are placed before the noun (in the *attributive* position) they should have a hyphen (*he is a well-known painter*).

If a noun compound that is two words (e.g. **hero worship**) is used as a verb, it should normally be written with a hyphen (to **hero-worship**). Compound verbs of this type are always shown in the dictionary entries.

Forms of nouns and verbs (inflections)

Plurals of nouns

The plurals of most nouns are formed by adding *-s*, or *-es* when they end in *-s*, *-x*, *-z*, *-sh*, or *-ch* (as in *church*). These kinds of plural are not shown in the dictionary.

Irregular and difficult plural forms are shown, for example: **fly** (plural **flies**), **foot** (plural **feet**).

Verbs

Most verbs change their form (inflect) by adding *-s*, *-ing*, and *-ed* to the infinitive (the basic unchanged part of the verb), e.g. **jump → jumps, jumping, jumped**. Verbs of this type do not have their different forms shown in the dictionary.

Irregular and difficult verb forms are shown, e.g., **bake** (**bakes**, **baking**, **baked**); **sing** (**sings**, **singing**, past **sang**; past participle **sung**), **bat** (**bats**, **batting**, **batted**).

Adjectives

Most adjectives form their comparatives and superlatives in the following ways, and these are not shown in the dictionary:

- words of one syllable adding *-er* and *-est*, e.g., **great → greater**, **greatest**
- words of one syllable ending in silent (unspoken) *-e*, which drop the *-e* and add *-er* and *-est*, e.g., **brave → braver**, **bravest**
- words that form the comparative and superlative by adding "more" and "most," e.g., *more beautiful, most beautiful.*

In all other cases the forms are shown in the dictionary, e.g., **hot** (**hotter**, **hottest**); **happy** (**happier**, **happiest**).

3. Labels

The majority of the words and senses in this dictionary are part of standard English, which means that they are the kind of words we use in every type of situation, whether at home, with friends, or in a formal work situation. Some words, however, are suitable only for certain situations or are found only in certain types of writing, and where this is the case a label (or a combination of labels) is used.

Register labels

Register labels refer to the particular level of use in the language—indicating whether a term is informal, formal, historical, and so on.

- **formal:** normally used only in writing, such as in official documents (e.g., **missive**)
- **informal:** normally used only in speaking or writing to friends (e.g., **cornball**)
- **dated:** no longer used by most English speakers, but still used by older people or to give a humorous or other effect (e.g., **confounded**)
- **old use:** old-fashioned language, not in ordinary use today, though sometimes used to give an old-fashioned or humorous effect and also found in the literature of the past (e.g., **damsel**)
- **historical:** only used today to refer to something that is no longer part of modern life (e.g., **blunderbuss**)
- **literary:** found only or mainly in literature (e.g., **foe**)

- **technical:** normally used only in technical language, though not restricted to a particular subject field (e.g., **dorsal**)
- **humorous:** used to sound funny or playful (e.g., **discombobulate**)
- **euphemistic:** used instead of a more direct or rude term (e.g., **powder room** instead of “women’s toilet”)
- **dialect:** only used in certain local regions of the English-speaking world (e.g., **y’all**)
- **disapproving:** deliberately intended to express a low opinion or insult someone else (e.g., **bureaucrat**)
- **offensive:** likely to cause offence, especially racial offence, whether the person using it means to or not

Subject labels

Subject labels are used to show that a word or sense is associated with a particular subject field or specialist activity, such as Music, Chemistry, or Baseball.

4. Cross References

A cross reference is a pointer to another entry, where full information on a word will be found. An equals sign (as in **swop** = **SWAP**) will take you to a different spelling, while an arrow (as in **puma** ⇒**COUGAR**) will take you to a different word that means the same.

5. Pronunciations

This dictionary uses a simple respelling system to show how entries are pronounced, using the symbols listed below. If two or more identical headwords are pronounced identically, only the first has a pronunciation given. Where a derivative simply adds a common suffix such as **-less**, **-ness**, or **-ly** to the headword, the derivative may not have a pronunciation shown unless some other element of the pronunciation also changes.

Symbol	Example	Symbol	Example	Symbol	Example
a	**hat** /hat/	ī	**time** /tīm/	p	**put** /po͝ot/,
ā	**day** /dā/	i(ə)r	**beer** /bi(ə)r/		**cap** /kap/
ä	**lot** /lät/	j	**judge** /jəj/	r	**run** /rən/, **fur** /fər/
b	**big** /big/	k	**cut** /kət/	s	**sit** /sit/
CH	**church** /CHərCH/	l	**lap** /lap/	SH	**shut** /SHət/
d	**dog** /dôg/	m	**main** /mān/	t	**top** /täp/
e	**men** /men/	n	**need** /nēd/	TH	**thin** /THin/
ē	**feet** /fēt/	NG	**sing** /siNG/,	T͟H	**then** /T͟Hen/
e(ə)r	**care** /ke(ə)r/		**anger** /'aNGgər/	v	**very** /'verē/
ə	**about** /ə'bout/,	ō	**go** /gō/	w	**wait** /wāt/
	curt /kərt/	ô	**law** /lô/	y	**yet** /yet/,
f	**free** /frē/	oi	**boy** /boi/		**accuse** /ə'kyo͞oz/
g	**get** /get/	o͝o	**wood** /wo͝od/,	z	**zipper** /'zipər/
h	**her** /hər/		**sure** /SHo͝or/	ZH	**measure** /'meZHər/
(h)w	**when** /(h)wen/	o͞o	**food** /fo͞od/		
i	**fit** /fit/	ou	**mouse** /mous/		

Foreign Sounds

KH **chutzpah** /'KHo͝otspə/ A "guttural" consonant pronounced with the tongue in the same position as for /k/, as in German *Buch*, or Scottish *loch*.

N **tranche** /tränSH/ The /N/ does not represent a separate sound: it indicates that the preceding vowel is nasalized, as in French *bon*.

œ **adieu** /ä'dyœ/ A vowel made by rounding the lips as with /o͞o/ while saying /e/, as in French *feu* or German *Höhle*.

Y **couture** /ko͞o'tYr/ A vowel made by rounding the lips as with /o͞o/ while saying /ē/, as in French *rue* or German *fühlen*.

Stress Marks

Stress (or accent) is indicated by the mark ' before the syllable with the heaviest stress, and by ˌ before a syllable with weaker stress, e.g., **oversee** /ˌōvər'sē/.

Variant Pronunciations

There are several ways in which variant pronunciations are indicated in the respellings.

Some respellings show a pronunciation symbol within parentheses to indicate a possible variation in pronunciation; for example, in **sandwich** /'san(d)wiCH/ sometimes the /d/ is pronounced, while sometimes it is not.

Variant pronunciations may be respelled in full, separated by commas. The more common pronunciation is listed first, if this can be determined, but it many cases it cannot.

Variant pronunciations may be indicated by respelling only the part of the word that changes; then a hyphen replaces the part of the pronunciation that remains the same, as in **adhesive** /əd'hēsiv, -ziv/

A hyphen is sometimes used to separate syllables because the respelling might otherwise look confusing, as in **adrenalin** /ə'drenl-in/.

6. Syllable breaks

Syllable breaks are shown for headwords and derivatives, e.g. **de·flect**, **de·flec·tion**. They can be used as a guide for dividing words at the end of lines, but it is best **not** to divide:

- a word of five or fewer letters, e.g., **mor·al**
- a proper name, e.g., **Al·ex·an·der**
- a contraction, e.g., **could·n't**
- after the first letter of a word, e.g., **a·float**
- before the last letter of a word, e.g., **catch·y**
- anywhere other than at the hyphen in a word that is already hyphenated, e.g., **self-con·trol**
- if the result would be misleading or distracting, e.g., **leg·end**

7. Abbreviations used in the dictionary

abbr.	abbreviation	exclam.	exclamation	usu.	usually
adj.	adjective	n.	noun	v.	verb
adv.	adverb	prep.	preposition		
conj.	conjunction	pron.	pronoun		

Abbreviations in general use (such as e.g., cm, and UK) are explained in their own entries.

A (or **a**) ▶ **n.** (plural **As** or **A's**) the first letter of the alphabet. ▶ **abbr.** **1** (**Å**) angstroms. **2** (**A**) ampere(s). ☐ **A-bomb** an atom bomb.

a /ā, ə/ ▶ **determiner** **1** used when mentioning someone or something for the first time; the indefinite article. **2** one single: *a hundred*. **3** per: *typing 60 words a minute*.

A1 ▶ **adj.** informal excellent.

AA ▶ **abbr.** Alcoholics Anonymous.

aard·vark /ˈärdˌvärk/ ▶ **n.** a long-snouted African animal that eats ants and termites.

a·back /əˈbak/ ▶ **adv.** (**be taken aback**) be shocked or surprised.

ab·a·cus /ˈabəkəs/ ▶ **n.** (plural **abacuses**) a frame with rows of wires along which you slide beads, used for counting.

a·baft /əˈbaft/ ▶ **adv. & prep.** at the back of or behind a ship.

ab·a·lo·ne /ˌabəˈlōnē, ˈabəˌlōnē/ ▶ **n.** an edible sea creature that has a shell lined with mother-of-pearl.

a·ban·don /əˈbandən/ ▶ **v.** **1** leave a place or person permanently. **2** give up a practice completely. **3** (**abandon yourself to**) give in to a desire. ▶ **n.** complete lack of self-consciousness or self-control.

> SYNONYMS ▶ **v.** **1** *he abandoned his wife* **desert**, leave, turn your back on, cast aside, finish with, jilt, throw over; informal walk/run out on, dump, ditch; literary forsake. **2** *she had abandoned painting* **give up**, stop, be done with; informal quit. **3** *they abandoned the car* **leave (behind)**, vacate, dump, quit, evacuate, discard, jettison. **4** *the party abandoned those policies* **renounce**, relinquish, dispense with, discard, give up, drop; informal ditch, scrap, junk; formal forswear. ANTONYMS keep. ▶ **n.** **uninhibitedness**, recklessness, lack of restraint, lack of inhibition. ANTONYMS self-control.

■ **a·ban·doned** **adj.** **a·ban·don·ment** **n.**

a·base /əˈbās/ ▶ **v.** (**abases**, **abasing**, **abased**) (**abase yourself**) behave in a very humble way. ■ **a·base·ment** **n.**

a·bashed /əˈbasht/ ▶ **adj.** embarrassed or ashamed.

a·bate /əˈbāt/ ▶ **v.** (**abates**, **abating**, **abated**) become less severe or widespread.

> SYNONYMS **subside**, die down/away/out, lessen, ease (off/up), let up, decrease, diminish, fade, weaken. ANTONYMS intensify.

■ **a·bate·ment** **n.**

ab·at·toir /ˈabəˌtwär/ ▶ **n.** a slaughterhouse.

ab·bess /ˈabis/ ▶ **n.** a woman who is the head of an abbey of nuns.

ab·bey /ˈabē/ ▶ **n.** (plural **abbeys**) a building occupied by a community of monks or nuns.

ab·bot /ˈabət/ ▶ **n.** a man who is the head of an abbey of monks.

ab·bre·vi·ate /əˈbrēvēˌāt/ ▶ **v.** (**abbreviates**, **abbreviating**, **abbreviated**) shorten a word or phrase.

> SYNONYMS **shorten**, reduce, cut, contract, condense, compress, abridge, summarize, précis. ANTONYMS lengthen, expand.

ab·bre·vi·a·tion /əˌbrēvēˈāshən/ ▶ **n.** a shortened form of a word or phrase.

> SYNONYMS **short form**, contraction, acronym, initialism.

ABC /ˌābēˈsē/ ▶ **n.** **1** the alphabet. **2** (also **the ABCs**) the basic facts of a subject.

ab·di·cate /ˈabdiˌkāt/ ▶ **v.** (**abdicates**, **abdicating**, **abdicated**) **1** give up being king or queen. **2** fail to carry out a duty.

> SYNONYMS **resign**, retire, stand down, step down, renounce the throne.

■ **ab·di·ca·tion** /ˌabdiˈkāshən/ **n.**

ab·do·men /ˈabdəmən, abˈdōmən/ ▶ **n.** **1** the part of the body that contains the organs used for digestion and reproduction. **2** the rear part of the body of an insect, spider, or crustacean.

> SYNONYMS **stomach**, belly, gut, middle; informal tummy, guts.

ab·dom·i·nal /abˈdämənl/ ▶ **adj.** relating to the abdomen.

> SYNONYMS **gastric**, intestinal, stomach, duodenal, visceral, celiac, ventral.

ab·duct /abˈdəkt/ ▶ **v.** take someone away, especially by force.

> SYNONYMS **kidnap**, carry off, seize, capture, run away/off with, take hostage; informal snatch.

■ **ab·duc·tion** **n.** **ab·duc·tor** **n.**

ab·er·rant /ˈabərənt, əˈber-/ ▶ **adj.** not normal or acceptable.

ab·er·ra·tion /ˌabəˈrāshən/ ▶ **n.** **1** an action or event that is not normal or acceptable. **2** an unexpected silly mistake.

> SYNONYMS **anomaly**, deviation, abnormality, irregularity, variation, freak, oddity, peculiarity, curiosity, mistake.

a·bet /əˈbet/ ▶ **v.** (**abets**, **abetting**, **abetted**) encourage or help someone to do something wrong. ■ **a·bet·tor** (or **abetter**) **n.**

a·bey·ance /əˈbāəns/ ▶ **n.** (**in** or **into abeyance**) temporarily not occurring or in use.

ab·hor /abˈhôr/ ▶ **v.** (**abhors**, **abhorring**, **abhorred**) feel strong hatred for.

SYNONYMS **hate**, detest, loathe, despise, shudder at; formal abominate. ANTONYMS love, admire.

ab·hor·rent /ab'hôrənt, -'här-/ ▶ **adj.** disgusting or hateful.

SYNONYMS **hateful**, detestable, loathsome, abominable, repellent, repugnant, repulsive, revolting, vile, odious, disgusting, horrible, horrid, horrifying, awful, heinous. ANTONYMS admirable.

■ **ab·hor·rence** **n.**

a·bide /ə'bīd/ ▶ **v.** (**abides**, **abiding**, **abided**) **1** (**abide by**) accept or obey a rule or decision. **2** (**cannot abide**) dislike very much. **3** (of a feeling or memory) last for a long time.

SYNONYMS **1** *I can't abide smoke* **stand**, bear, tolerate; formal brook. **2** *one memory will abide* **continue**, remain, survive, last, persist, live on.

a·bid·ing /ə'bīdiNG/ ▶ **adj.** lasting; enduring.

SYNONYMS **enduring**, lasting, everlasting, perpetual, eternal, unending, permanent.

■ **a·bid·ing·ly** **adv.**

a·bil·i·ty /ə'bilitē/ ▶ **n.** (plural **abilities**) **1** the power or capacity to do something. **2** skill or talent.

SYNONYMS **1 capacity**, capability, power, potential, faculty, facility, wherewithal, means. **2 talent**, skill, aptitude, expertise, savoir faire, prowess, accomplishment, competence, proficiency, flair, gift, knack, genius; informal know-how. ANTONYMS inability.

ab·ject /'abˌjekt, ab'jekt/ ▶ **adj.** **1** very unpleasant and humiliating: *abject poverty*. **2** completely without pride or dignity: *an abject apology*. ■ **ab·ject·ly** **adv.**

ab·jure /ab'jo͝or/ ▶ **v.** (**abjures**, **abjuring**, **abjured**) formal swear that you will give up a belief or claim.

ab·la·tive /'ablətiv/ ▶ **n.** (in Latin, German, etc.) the case of nouns indicating an agent, instrument, or location of an action, expressed by "by," "with," or "from" in English.

a·blaze /ə'blāz/ ▶ **adj.** burning fiercely.

a·ble /'ābəl/ ▶ **adj.** (**abler**, **ablest**) **1** having the power, skill, or means to do something. **2** skillful and capable.

SYNONYMS **intelligent**, clever, talented, skillful, skilled, expert, accomplished, gifted, proficient, apt, adroit, adept, capable, competent. ANTONYMS incompetent.

□ **able-bodied** physically fit and healthy. ■ **a·bly** **adv.**

ab·lu·tions /ə'blo͞osHənz/ ▶ **pl.n.** the act of washing yourself.

ab·ne·ga·tion /ˌabni'gāsHən/ ▶ **n.** formal the giving up of something wanted or valuable. ■ **ab·ne·gate** /'abniˌgāt/ **v.**

ab·nor·mal /ab'nôrməl/ ▶ **adj.** different from what is usual or expected in a bad or worrying way.

SYNONYMS **unusual**, uncommon, atypical, untypical, unexpected, unrepresentative, irregular, anomalous, deviant, aberrant, freak, strange, odd, peculiar, eccentric, bizarre, weird, unnatural, perverted, twisted, warped; informal funny, freaky, kinky. ANTONYMS normal.

■ **ab·nor·mal·ly** **adv.**

ab·nor·mal·i·ty /ˌabnôr'malitē/ ▶ **n.** (plural **abnormalities**) **1** a feature or event that is not normal: *babies with congenital abnormalities*. **2** the state of being abnormal.

SYNONYMS **deformity**, defect, malformation, oddity, strangeness, irregularity, anomaly, deviation, aberration.

a·board /ə'bôrd/ ▶ **adv. & prep.** on or into a ship, train, or other vehicle.

a·bode /ə'bōd/ ▶ **n.** a house or home.

a·bol·ish /ə'bälisH/ ▶ **v.** put an end to a custom or law.

SYNONYMS **put an end to**, get rid of, scrap, cancel, end, remove, dissolve, stop, ban; informal do away with, ax, ditch.

ab·o·li·tion /ˌabə'lisHən/ ▶ **n.** the abolishing of a custom or law.

ab·o·li·tion·ist /ˌabə'lisHənist/ ▶ **n.** historical a person who supported the abolition of slavery.

a·bom·i·na·ble /ə'bäm(ə)nəbəl/ ▶ **adj.** **1** very unpleasant and causing disgust. **2** informal very bad.

SYNONYMS **loathsome**, detestable, hateful, obnoxious, despicable, contemptible, disgusting, revolting, repellent, repulsive, repugnant, abhorrent, reprehensible, atrocious, execrable, foul, vile, wretched, horrible, awful, dreadful, appalling, nauseating; informal terrible, shocking, God-awful, beastly. ANTONYMS good, admirable.

□ **Abominable Snowman** ⇨ **YETI**.
■ **a·bom·i·na·bly** **adv.**

a·bom·i·nate /ə'bäməˌnāt/ ▶ **v.** (**abominates**, **abominating**, **abominated**) feel strong hatred for.

a·bom·i·na·tion /əˌbämə'nāsHən/ ▶ **n.** **1** something that you hate or find disgusting. **2** a feeling of hatred.

ab·o·rig·i·nal /ˌabə'rijənl/ ▶ **adj.** **1** existing in a country from the earliest times. **2** (**Aboriginal**) having to do with the Australian Aborigines. ▶ **n.** (**Aboriginal**) an Australian Aborigine.

Ab·o·rig·i·ne /ˌabə'rijənē/ ▶ **n.** a member of one of the original peoples of Australia.

a·bort /ə'bôrt/ ▶ **v.** **1** end a pregnancy early to stop the baby from developing and being born. **2** undergo a natural abortion. **3** end something early because of a problem or fault.

SYNONYMS *the crew aborted the takeoff* **halt**, stop, end, call off, abandon, discontinue, terminate; informal pull the plug on.

a·bor·tion /ə'bôrsHən/ ▶ **n.** **1** the deliberate ending of a human pregnancy. **2** the natural ending of a pregnancy before the fetus is able to survive on its own.

a·bor·tion·ist /ə'bôrsHənist/ ▶ **n.** often disapproving a person who carries out abortions.

a·bor·tive /ə'bôrtiv/ ▶ **adj.** failing to achieve the intended result; unsuccessful.

SYNONYMS **unsuccessful**, failed, vain, ineffective, ineffectual, unproductive, futile, useless, unavailing. ANTONYMS successful.

a·bound /ə'bound/ ▶ **v.** **1** exist in large numbers or amounts. **2** (**abound in** or **with**) have a large number or amount of something.

SYNONYMS **be plentiful**, be abundant, be numerous, be thick on the ground; informal grow on trees, be a dime a dozen.

a·bout /ə'bout/ ▶ **prep. & adv. 1** on the subject of. **2** here and there within a particular area: *rugs strewn about the hall.* **3** approximately.

SYNONYMS **1 regarding**, concerning, referring to, with regard to, with respect to, relating to, on, dealing with, on the subject of. **2 approximately**, roughly, around, in the region of, circa, of the order of, or so, or thereabouts, more or less; informal in the ballpark of.

□ **about-face 1** Military a turn made so as to face the opposite direction. **2** a complete change of opinion or policy. **be about to** be on the point of.

a·bove /ə'bəv/ ▶ **prep. & adv. 1** at a higher level (than). **2** rather or more than: *he valued safety above comfort.* **3** (in printed writing) mentioned earlier.

SYNONYMS **1 over**, higher (up) than, on top of, on. **2 superior to**, senior to, over, higher (up) than, more powerful than, in charge of, commanding. **3 overhead**, on/at the top, high up, on high, up above, (up) in the sky. ANTONYMS below.

□ **not be above** be capable of doing (something unworthy).

a·bove·board /ə'bəv,bôrd/ ▶ **adj.** legitimate, honest, and open. ▶ **adv.** legitimately, honestly, and openly.

ab·ra·ca·dab·ra /,abrəkə'dabrə/ ▶ **exclam.** a word said by magicians when performing a trick.

a·brade /ə'brād/ ▶ **v.** (**abrades**, **abrading**, **abraded**) scrape or wear away.

a·bra·sion /ə'brāzʜən/ ▶ **n. 1** the process of scraping or wearing away. **2** an area of scraped skin.

SYNONYMS **1 erosion**, wearing away/down. **2 graze**, cut, scrape, scratch, gash, laceration.

a·bra·sive /ə'brāsiv, -ziv/ ▶ **adj. 1** able to polish or clean a surface by rubbing or grinding. **2** harsh or unkind.

SYNONYMS **1 rough**, coarse, harsh, scratchy, chafing. **2 curt**, brusque, sharp, harsh, caustic, grating. ANTONYMS gentle.

■ **a·bra·sive·ly adv. a·bra·sive·ness n.**

a·breast /ə'brest/ ▶ **adv. 1** side by side and facing the same way. **2** (**abreast of**) up to date with.

a·bridge /ə'brij/ ▶ **v.** (**abridges**, **abridging**, **abridged**) shorten a book or movie.

SYNONYMS **shorten**, cut (down), edit, abbreviate, condense, compress, truncate, prune, summarize, précis, synopsize; (**abridged**) concise. ANTONYMS extend.

a·bridg·ment /ə'brijmənt/ (or **abridgement**) ▶ **n.** a shortened version of a larger work.

SYNONYMS **summary**, synopsis, précis, abstract, outline, résumé, digest, cut-down version.

a·broad /ə'brôd/ ▶ **adv. 1** in or to a foreign country or countries. **2** felt or talked about by many people: *there is a new spirit abroad.* **3** over a wide area; in different directions: *millions of seeds are annually scattered abroad.*

SYNONYMS **overseas**, out of the country, to/in foreign parts, to/in a foreign country/land.

ab·ro·gate /'abrə,gāt/ ▶ **v.** (**abrogates**, **abrogating**, **abrogated**) formal cancel or do away with a law or agreement. ■ **ab·ro·ga·tion** /,abrə'gāsʜən/ **n.**

ab·rupt /ə'brəpt/ ▶ **adj. 1** sudden and unexpected. **2** brief to the point of rudeness.

SYNONYMS **1 sudden**, rapid, quick, hasty, unexpected, unanticipated, unforeseen, precipitate. **2 curt**, brusque, blunt, short, rude, sharp, terse, brisk, unceremonious. ANTONYMS gradual, gentle.

■ **ab·rupt·ly adv. ab·rupt·ness n.**

abs /abz/ ▶ **pl.n.** informal the abdominal muscles.

ab·scess /'ab,ses/ ▶ **n.** a swelling that contains pus.

SPELLING

Remember the **s** and **c**: abs**c**ess.

ab·scond /ab'skänd/ ▶ **v.** leave quickly and secretly to escape from custody or avoid arrest.

SYNONYMS **run away**, run off, escape, bolt, flee, make off, take flight, take off, decamp; informal vamoose.

■ **ab·scond·er n.**

ab·sence /'absəns/ ▶ **n. 1** the state of being away from a place or person. **2** (**absence of**) the lack of.

SYNONYMS **1 nonattendance**, absenteeism, truancy, leave, vacation, sabbatical. **2 lack**, want, nonexistence, unavailability, scarcity, shortage, dearth. ANTONYMS presence.

ab·sent ▶ **adj.** /'absənt/ **1** not present. **2** not paying attention. ▶ **v.** /ab'sənt/ (**absent yourself**) go away.

SYNONYMS ▶ **adj. 1 away**, off, out, elsewhere, off duty, on leave, playing truant; informal AWOL, playing hooky. **2 nonexistent**, lacking, missing. **3 distracted**, preoccupied, inattentive, vague, absorbed, dreamy, faraway, blank, empty, vacant. ANTONYMS present.

■ **ab·sent·ly** /'absəntlē/ **adv.**

ab·sen·tee /,absən'tē/ ▶ **n.** a person who is absent.

ab·sen·tee·ism /,absən'tē,izəm/ ▶ **n.** frequent absence from work or school without good reason.

ab·sent·mind·ed /'absənt,mīndid/ ▶ **adj.** forgetful or tending not to pay attention.

SYNONYMS **forgetful**, distracted, scatterbrained, preoccupied, inattentive, vague; informal with a mind/memory like a sieve.

ab·sinthe /'ab,sinтн/ ▶ **n.** a green aniseed-flavored liqueur.

ab·so·lute /'absə,lo͞ot, ,absə'lo͞ot/ ▶ **adj. 1** complete; total. **2** having unlimited power. **3** not related or compared to anything else.

SYNONYMS **1** *absolute silence* | *an absolute disgrace* **complete**, total, utter, out-and-out, outright, perfect, pure, thorough, unqualified, unreserved, downright, unmitigated, sheer, unadulterated. **2** *absolute power* **unlimited**, unrestricted, unrestrained, infinite, total, supreme, unconditional. **3** *an absolute ruler* **autocratic**, dictatorial, all-powerful, omnipotent, supreme. ANTONYMS partial, qualified, limited.

□ **absolute majority** a majority over all rivals considered as a group; more than half. **absolute**

pitch Music **1** the ability to recognize the pitch of a note or produce any given note; perfect pitch. **2** a fixed standard of pitch defined by the frequency of the sound vibration. **absolute temperature** a temperature measured from absolute zero in kelvins. **absolute zero** the lowest temperature theoretically possible (−273.15°C or −459.67°F).

ab·so·lute·ly /ˌabsəˈlo͞otlē/ ▶ **adv. 1** completely; entirely: *she trusted him absolutely*. **2** used for emphasis or to express agreement.

> SYNONYMS **completely**, totally, utterly, perfectly, entirely, wholly, fully, quite, thoroughly, unreservedly, definitely, certainly, unquestionably, undoubtedly, without (a) doubt, without question, in every way/respect, one hundred percent.

ab·so·lu·tion /ˌabsəˈlo͞osʜən/ ▶ **n.** formal forgiveness of a person's sins.

ab·so·lut·ism /ˈabsəlo͞oˌtizəm/ ▶ **n.** the principle that the government or ruler should have unlimited power. ■ **ab·so·lut·ist n. & adj.**

ab·solve /əbˈzälv, -ˈsälv/ ▶ **v.** (**absolves**, **absolving**, **absolved**) formally declare that someone is free from guilt, blame, or sin.

ab·sorb /əbˈzôrb, -ˈsôrb/ ▶ **v. 1** soak up liquid or another substance. **2** take in information. **3** take over something less powerful. **4** use up time or resources. **5** reduce the effect or strength of sound or an impact: *buffers absorbed most of the shock*. **6** hold someone's attention.

> SYNONYMS **1 soak up**, suck up, draw up/in, take up/in, mop up. **2 engross**, captivate, occupy, preoccupy, engage, rivet, grip, hold, immerse, involve, enthrall, spellbind, fascinate.

■ **ab·sorb·er n.**

ab·sorb·ent /əbˈzôrbənt, -ˈsôr-/ ▶ **adj.** able to soak up liquid easily.

> SYNONYMS **spongy**, spongelike, porous, permeable.

■ **ab·sorb·en·cy n.**

ab·sorb·ing /əbˈzôrbiɴɢ, -ˈsôr-/ ▶ **adj.** holding someone's interest completely; very interesting.

> SYNONYMS **fascinating**, interesting, captivating, gripping, engrossing, compelling, compulsive, enthralling, riveting, spellbinding; informal unputdownable. ANTONYMS boring.

ab·sorp·tion /əbˈzôrpsʜən, -ˈsôrp-/ ▶ **n.** the process of absorbing, or of being absorbed.

> SYNONYMS **1 soaking up**, sucking up. **2 involvement**, immersion, raptness, preoccupation, captivation, fascination, enthrallment.

ab·stain /əbˈstān/ ▶ **v. 1** (**abstain from**) stop yourself from doing something pleasant. **2** formally choose not to vote.

> SYNONYMS **refrain**, desist, forbear, give up, renounce, avoid, eschew, forgo, go/do without, refuse, decline; informal cut out.

■ **ab·stain·er n.**

ab·ste·mi·ous /əbˈstēmēəs/ ▶ **adj.** not letting yourself have much food, alcohol, or enjoyment.

> SYNONYMS **moderate**, restrained, temperate, self-disciplined, self-restrained, self-denying, sober, austere, ascetic, puritanical, spartan. ANTONYMS self-indulgent.

■ **ab·ste·mi·ous·ly adv. ab·ste·mi·ous·ness n.**

ab·sten·tion /əbˈstensʜən/ ▶ **n. 1** a deliberate decision not to vote. **2** abstinence.

ab·sti·nence /ˈabstənəns/ ▶ **n.** the avoidance of something enjoyable, such as food or alcohol.

> SYNONYMS **self-denial**, self-restraint, teetotalism, temperance, sobriety, abstemiousness.

■ **ab·sti·nent adj.**

ab·stract ▶ **adj.** /abˈstrakt, ˈabˌstrakt/ **1** having to do with ideas or qualities rather than physical or concrete things. **2** (of art) using color and shapes to create an effect rather than attempting to represent real life accurately. ▶ **v.** /abˈstrakt/ take out or remove. ▶ **n.** /ˈabˌstrakt/ a summary of a book or article.

> SYNONYMS ▶ **adj. theoretical**, conceptual, intellectual, metaphysical, philosophical, academic. ANTONYMS actual, concrete. ▶ **n. summary**, synopsis, précis, résumé, outline, abridgment, wrap-up.

■ **ab·stract·ly adv.** /abˈstraktlē, ˈabˌstraktlē/.

ab·stract·ed /abˈstraktid/ ▶ **adj.** not paying attention to what is happening; preoccupied. ■ **ab·stract·ed·ly adv.**

ab·strac·tion /abˈstraksʜən/ ▶ **n. 1** the quality of being abstract. **2** something that exists only as an idea. **3** the state of being preoccupied.

ab·struse /abˈstro͞os/ ▶ **adj.** difficult to understand.

> SYNONYMS **obscure**, arcane, esoteric, rarefied, recondite, difficult, hard, cryptic, over/above your head, incomprehensible, unfathomable, impenetrable.

ab·surd /əbˈsərd, -ˈzərd/ ▶ **adj.** completely unreasonable or inappropriate.

> SYNONYMS **irrational**, illogical, inappropriate, ridiculous, ludicrous, farcical, comical, stupid, idiotic, asinine, harebrained, foolish, silly, pointless, senseless, preposterous; informal crazy, cockeyed, daft. ANTONYMS sensible.

■ **ab·surd·i·ty n. ab·surd·ly adv.**

a·bun·dance /əˈbəndəns/ ▶ **n.** a very large quantity or amount of something; plentifulness.

> SYNONYMS **plenty**, plentifulness, plethora, profusion, exuberance, riot, cornucopia, superabundance. ANTONYMS scarcity.

a·bun·dant /əˈbəndənt/ ▶ **adj. 1** existing in large quantities; plentiful. **2** (**abundant in**) having plenty of.

> SYNONYMS **plentiful**, copious, ample, profuse, large, huge, great, bumper, prolific, overflowing, teeming, superabundant; informal galore. ANTONYMS scarce.

■ **a·bun·dant·ly adv.**

a·buse ▶ **v.** /əˈbyo͞oz/ (**abuses**, **abusing**, **abused**) **1** use something to bad effect or for a bad purpose. **2** treat someone cruelly or violently. **3** speak to someone in an insulting way. ▶ **n.** /əˈbyo͞os/ **1** the wrong or harmful use of something. **2** cruel and violent treatment. **3** insulting language.

> SYNONYMS ▶ **v. 1 misuse**, exploit, take advantage of. **2 mistreat**, maltreat, ill-treat, hurt, harm, beat, molest, interfere with. **3 insult**, be rude to, swear at, shout at, vilify, curse. ▶ **n. 1 misuse**, exploitation. **2 mistreatment**, maltreatment, ill-treatment,

molestation. **3 insults**, expletives, swear words, swearing, name-calling, invective, vilification, curses.

■ **a·bus·er** n.

a·bu·sive /ə'byo͞osiv, -ziv/ ▶ adj. **1** very insulting. **2** involving cruelty and violence.

SYNONYMS **1 insulting**, rude, offensive, derogatory, defamatory, slanderous, libelous. **2 violent**, brutal, cruel, harsh, oppressive. ANTONYMS polite.

■ **a·bu·sive·ly** adv.

a·but /ə'bət/ ▶ v. (**abuts**, **abutting**, **abutted**) be next to or touching.

a·bys·mal /ə'bizməl/ ▶ adj. very bad; terrible.

SYNONYMS **terrible**, dreadful, awful, appalling, frightful, atrocious, disgraceful, deplorable, lamentable; informal rotten, pathetic, pitiful, woeful, useless, lousy, shocking, dire, the pits.

■ **a·bys·mal·ly** adv.

a·byss /ə'bis/ ▶ n. a very deep hole.

SYNONYMS **chasm**, crevasse, gulf, pit, void.

AC ▶ abbr. **1** alternating current. **2** air conditioning.

a/c ▶ abbr. **1** account. **2** air conditioning.

a·ca·cia /ə'kāshə/ ▶ n. a tree or shrub with yellow or white flowers.

ac·a·de·mi·a /ˌakə'dēmēə/ ▶ n. the world of higher education.

ac·a·dem·ic /ˌakə'demik/ ▶ adj. **1** having to do with education or study. **2** not related to a real situation; theoretical. ▶ n. a teacher or scholar at a university or college.

SYNONYMS ▶ adj. **1 educational**, scholastic. **2 scholarly**, learned, literary, intellectual, erudite, high-brow, bookish, studious. **3 theoretical**, hypothetical, notional, speculative, conjectural, irrelevant, beside the point. ▶ n. **scholar**, intellectual, professor, man/woman of letters, thinker; informal egghead.

■ **ac·a·dem·i·cal·ly** adv.

a·cad·e·my /ə'kadəmē/ ▶ n. (plural **academies**) **1** a place where people study or are trained in a particular field. **2** a society of scholars, artists, or scientists.

SYNONYMS **school**, college, university, institute.

□ **Academy Award** an Oscar.

a·can·thus /ə'kanthəs/ ▶ n. a plant or shrub with spiny leaves.

a cap·pel·la /ˌä kə'pelə/ ▶ adj. & adv. (of music) sung without being accompanied by instruments.

ac·cede /ak'sēd/ ▶ v. (**accedes**, **acceding**, **acceded**) (usually **accede to**) formal **1** agree to a demand or request. **2** take up a role or position: *accede to the throne.*

ac·cel·er·ate /ak'seləˌrāt/ ▶ v. (**accelerates**, **accelerating**, **accelerated**) **1** begin to move more quickly. **2** begin to happen more quickly.

SYNONYMS **1 speed up**, go faster, gain momentum, increase speed, pick up speed, gather speed. **2 hasten**, quicken, speed up, further, advance, expedite; informal crank up. ANTONYMS decelerate, delay.

■ **ac·cel·er·a·tion** /akˌselə'rāshən/ n.

ac·cel·er·a·tor /ak'seləˌrātər/ ▶ n. **1** a foot pedal that controls the speed of a vehicle. **2** Physics a machine that makes charged particles move at high speeds.

ac·cent ▶ n. /'akˌsent/ **1** a way of pronouncing a language. **2** an emphasis given to a syllable, word, or musical note. **3** a mark on a letter or word that shows how a sound is pronounced or stressed. **4** a particular emphasis: *the accent is on participation.* ▶ v. /'akˌsent/ **1** (**accented**) spoken with a particular accent: *accented English.* **2** stress or emphasize.

SYNONYMS ▶ n. **1 pronunciation**, intonation, enunciation, articulation, inflection. **2 emphasis**, stress, priority, importance, prominence.

ac·cen·tu·ate /ak'senchooˌāt/ ▶ v. (**accentuates**, **accentuating**, **accentuated**) make more noticeable or prominent.

SYNONYMS **focus attention on**, draw attention to, point up, underline, underscore, accent, highlight, spotlight, foreground, bring to the fore, emphasize, stress.

■ **ac·cen·tu·a·tion** n.

ac·cept /ak'sept/ ▶ v. **1** agree to receive or do something that is offered or suggested. **2** believe that something said is true or correct. **3** admit responsibility for something. **4** come to terms with something unwelcome. **5** make someone welcome.

SYNONYMS **1 receive**, take, get, obtain, acquire, pick up. **2 agree to**, accede to, consent to, acquiesce in, concur with, endorse, comply with, go along with, defer to, put up with, recognize, acknowledge, admit. **3 believe**, trust, credit, be convinced of, have faith in; informal buy, swallow. **4** (**accepted**) **recognized**, acknowledged, established, traditional, orthodox, agreed, approved, customary, normal, standard. ANTONYMS reject, unorthodox.

■ **ac·cep·tor** n.

USAGE

Don't confuse **accept** with **except**, which means 'not including.'

ac·cept·a·ble /ak'septəbəl/ ▶ adj. **1** able to be accepted. **2** good enough; adequate.

SYNONYMS **satisfactory**, adequate, reasonable, fair, good enough, sufficient, tolerable, passable.

■ **ac·cept·a·bil·i·ty** /akˌseptə'bilitē/ n. **ac·cept·a·bly** adv.

ac·cept·ance /ak'septns/ ▶ n. **1** the action of agreeing to receive or do something. **2** the action of being received as adequate or suitable. **3** agreement with or belief in an idea, opinion, or explanation. **4** willingness to tolerate a difficult or unpleasant situation.

SYNONYMS **1 receipt**, receiving, taking. **2 respect**, acknowledgment, belief, toleration, consent, agreement, assent, compliance, acquiescence.

ac·cess /'akˌses/ ▶ n. **1** a way of approaching or entering a place. **2** the right or opportunity to use something or see someone. ▶ v. **1** approach or enter a place. **2** obtain information stored in a computer.

SYNONYMS ▶ n. **1** *a side access* **entrance**, entry, approach, path, drive, way in. **2** *they were denied access* **admission**, admittance, entry.

ac·ces·si·ble /ak'sesəbəl/ ▶ **adj.** **1** able to be reached or used. **2** friendly and easy to talk to. **3** easily understood or enjoyed.

SYNONYMS **approachable**, attainable, reachable, obtainable, available, understandable, comprehensible, intelligible; informal get-at-able.

■ **ac·ces·si·bil·i·ty** /-ˌsesə'bilitē/ **n.** **ac·ces·si·bly adv.**

ac·ces·sion /ak'sesHən/ ▶ **n.** **1** the gaining of an important position or rank. **2** a new item added to a library or museum collection.

ac·ces·so·rize /ak'sesəˌrīz/ ▶ **v.** (**accessorizes**, **accessorizing**, **accessorized**) add a fashion accessory to a garment; wear or carry an accessory.

ac·ces·so·ry /ak'ses(ə)rē/ ▶ **n.** (plural **accessories**) **1** a thing that can be added to or worn with something else to make it more useful or attractive. **2** Law a person who helps someone commit a crime without taking part in it.

SYNONYMS **1 extra**, add-on, addition, supplement, attachment, fitment. **2 accomplice**, abettor, collaborator, co-conspirator, henchman, associate.

ac·ci·dent /'aksidənt/ ▶ **n.** **1** something harmful that happens unexpectedly or without being intended. **2** an incident that happens by chance or without apparent cause.

SYNONYMS **1 mishap**, misadventure, disaster, tragedy, catastrophe, calamity. **2 crash**, collision, wreck, smash, bump, derailment; informal smash-up, pile-up. **3 chance**, fate, fortune, luck, good luck, fluke, coincidence.

ac·ci·den·tal /ˌaksi'dentl/ ▶ **adj.** happening by chance.

SYNONYMS **1 chance**, coincidental, unexpected, incidental, fortuitous, serendipitous. **2 unintentional**, unintended, unplanned, inadvertent, unwitting, unpremeditated. ANTONYMS intentional.

■ **ac·ci·den·tal·ly adv.**

ac·claim /ə'klām/ ▶ **v.** praise enthusiastically and publicly. ▶ **n.** enthusiastic public praise.

SYNONYMS ▶ **v. praise**, applaud, cheer, commend, approve, welcome, hail, celebrate, eulogize; formal laud. ANTONYMS criticize. ▶ **n. praise**, applause, tributes, plaudits, approval, admiration, congratulations, commendation, eulogies. ANTONYMS criticism.

ac·cla·ma·tion /ˌaklə'māsHən/ ▶ **n.** enthusiastic approval or praise.

ac·cli·ma·tize /ə'klīməˌtīz/ ▶ **v.** (**acclimatizes**, **acclimatizing**, **acclimatized**) get used to a new climate or new conditions.

SYNONYMS **adjust**, adapt, acclimate, get used, familiarize yourself, find your feet, get your bearings.

■ **ac·cli·ma·ti·za·tion** /əˌklīmətə'zāsHən/ **n.**

ac·co·lade /'akəˌlād, -ˌläd/ ▶ **n.** something given as a special honor or as a reward for excellence.

SYNONYMS **tribute**, honor, compliment, prize.

ac·com·mo·date /ə'käməˌdāt/ ▶ **v.** (**accommodates**, **accommodating**, **accommodated**) **1** provide a room or rooms for someone, or space for something. **2** adapt to or fit in with.

SYNONYMS **1** *refugees were accommodated in army camps* **lodge**, house, put up, billet, board. **2** *the cottages accommodate six people* **hold**, take, have room for, sleep, seat. **3** *we tried to accommodate her* **help**, assist, oblige, cater to, fit in with, satisfy, meet the needs of.

SPELLING
Double **c**, double **m**: a**cc**o**mm**odate.

ac·com·mo·dat·ing /ə'käməˌdātiNG/ ▶ **adj.** willing to fit in with someone's wishes.

SYNONYMS **obliging**, cooperative, helpful, amenable, hospitable, flexible.

ac·com·mo·da·tion /əˌkämə'dāsHən/ ▶ **n.** (usually **accommodations**) a room or building where someone may live or stay.

SYNONYMS (**accommodations**) **housing**, homes, lodging(s), (living) quarters, rooms, billet, shelter, a roof over your head; informal digs, pad; formal residence, dwelling, abode.

ac·com·pa·ni·ment /ə'kəmp(ə)nimənt/ ▶ **n.** **1** a musical part that accompanies an instrument, voice, or group. **2** something that adds to or improves something else, typically food.

SYNONYMS **1** *a musical accompaniment* **backing**, support, background, soundtrack. **2** *wine is a good accompaniment to cheese* **complement**, addition, adjunct, accessory, companion.

ac·com·pa·nist /ə'kəmpənist/ ▶ **n.** a person who plays a musical accompaniment.

ac·com·pa·ny /ə'kəmp(ə)nē/ ▶ **v.** (**accompanies**, **accompanying**, **accompanied**) **1** go somewhere with someone. **2** be present or happen at the same time as. **3** play musical backing for an instrument or voice.

SYNONYMS **1 escort**, go with, travel with, keep someone company, chaperone, partner, show, see, usher, conduct. **2 occur with**, go along with, go together with, attend, be linked with, go hand in hand with. **3** *he accompanied the choir on the piano* **back**, play along with, support.

ac·com·plice /ə'kämplis/ ▶ **n.** a person who helps another commit a crime.

SYNONYMS **partner in crime**, abettor, accessory, collaborator, co-conspirator, henchman, associate; informal sidekick.

ac·com·plish /ə'kämplisH/ ▶ **v.** achieve or complete something successfully.

SYNONYMS **achieve**, succeed in, realize, attain, manage, bring off, carry through, execute, effect, perform, complete.

ac·com·plished /ə'kämplisHt/ ▶ **adj.** highly trained or skilled.

SYNONYMS **expert**, skilled, skillful, masterly, virtuoso, master, proficient, polished, practiced, consummate, talented, gifted, able, capable; informal crack, ace.

ac·com·plish·ment /ə'kämplisHmənt/ ▶ **n.** **1** an activity that you can do well. **2** something that has been achieved successfully. **3** the successful achievement of a task.

SYNONYMS **1 achievement**, success, act, deed, exploit, effort, feat, coup. **2 talent**, skill, gift, ability.

ac·cord /ə'kôrd/ ▶ **v. 1** give power or recognition to. **2** (**accord with**) be consistent or in agreement with. ▶ **n. 1** agreement in opinion or feeling. **2** an official agreement or treaty.

SYNONYMS ▶ **v. 1 give**, grant, present, award, confer on, bestow on. **2 correspond**, agree, tally, match, concur, be in harmony, be in tune. ANTONYMS disagree, differ. ▶ **n. 1** *a peace accord* **pact**, treaty, agreement, settlement, deal, entente, protocol. **2** *the two sides failed to reach accord* **agreement**, consensus, unanimity, harmony. ANTONYMS disagreement.

□ **of your own accord** willingly.

ac·cord·ance /ə'kôrdns/ ▶ **n.** (**in accordance with**) in a way that fits in with.

ac·cord·ing /ə'kôrdiNG/ ▶ **adv.** (**according to**) **1** as stated by. **2** in a way that corresponds to: *cook the rice according to the instructions*. **3** (**according as**) depending on whether.

ac·cord·ing·ly /ə'kôrdiNGlē/ ▶ **adv. 1** appropriately. **2** therefore.

ac·cor·di·on /ə'kôrdēən/ ▶ **n.** a musical instrument that you play by stretching and squeezing it with your hands and pressing buttons or keys. ■ **ac·cor·di·on·ist n.**

ac·cost /ə'kôst, ə'käst/ ▶ **v.** approach someone and speak to them, often in a rude or aggressive way.

SYNONYMS **confront**, approach, stop, detain, speak to; informal buttonhole, collar.

ac·count /ə'kount/ ▶ **n. 1** a description of an event. **2** a record of money that has been spent and received. **3** an arrangement by which you can keep money in a bank or buy things from a business on credit. **4** importance: *fame was of no account to her*. ▶ **v.** consider in a particular way.

SYNONYMS ▶ **n. 1 description**, report, version, story, statement, explanation, tale, chronicle, narrative, history, record, log. **2 financial record**, ledger, balance sheet, financial statement; (**accounts**) books. **3** *his background is of no account* **importance**, import, significance, consequence, value.

□ **account for 1** supply or make up an amount. **2** give an explanation of. **call someone to account** ask someone to explain a mistake or a poor performance. **on someone's account** for someone's benefit. **on account of** because of. **on no account** under no circumstances. **take account of** take into consideration.

ac·count·a·bil·i·ty /ə,kountə'bilitē/ ▶ **n.** the state of being accountable for something.

SYNONYMS **responsibility**, liability, answerability.

ac·count·a·ble /ə'kountəbəl/ ▶ **adj.** expected to explain your actions or decisions.

SYNONYMS **responsible**, liable, answerable, to blame.

ac·count·ant /ə'kount(ə)nt/ ▶ **n.** a person who keeps or inspects financial accounts. ■ **ac·count·an·cy n.**

ac·count·ing /ə'kountiNG/ ▶ **n.** the keeping of financial accounts.

ac·cou·ter·ment /ə'ko͞otərmənt/ (or **accoutrement**) ▶ **n.** an extra item of clothing or equipment.

ac·cred·it /ə'kredit/ ▶ **v.** (**accredits**, **accrediting**, **accredited**) **1** (**accredit something to**) give someone the credit for something. **2** give official authorization to. ■ **ac·cred·i·ta·tion** /ə,kredi'tāSHən/ **n.**

ac·cre·tion /ə'krēSHən/ ▶ **n. 1** growth or increase by a gradual buildup. **2** something formed or added gradually.

ac·crue /ə'kro͞o/ ▶ **v.** (**accrues**, **accruing**, **accrued**) **1** (of money) be received in regular or increasing amounts. **2** collect or receive payments or benefits. ■ **ac·cru·al n.**

ac·cu·mu·late /ə'kyo͞omyə,lāt/ ▶ **v.** (**accumulates**, **accumulating**, **accumulated**) **1** gather together a number or quantity of. **2** increase.

SYNONYMS **gather**, collect, amass, stockpile, pile up, build up, store (up), hoard, lay in/up, increase, accrue, run up. ANTONYMS disperse.

■ **ac·cu·mu·la·tive** /-lətiv, -,lātiv/ **adj.**

SPELLING

Two **cs**, one **m**: accumulate.

ac·cu·mu·la·tion /ə,kyo͞omyə'lāSHən/ ▶ **n. 1** the gradual gathering of something. **2** a mass of something that has gradually gathered or been acquired.

SYNONYMS **mass**, buildup, pile, collection, stock, store, stockpile, hoard.

ac·cu·mu·la·tor /ə'kyo͞omyə,lātər/ ▶ **n.** a person or thing that accumulates things.

ac·cu·ra·cy /'akyərəsē/ ▶ **n.** the quality or state of being correct or precise.

SYNONYMS **correctness**, precision, exactness, fidelity, truth, truthfulness, authenticity, realism.

ac·cu·rate /'akyərit/ ▶ **adj. 1** correct in all details. **2** reaching an intended target.

SYNONYMS **1 correct**, precise, exact, right, factual, literal, faithful, true, truthful, on the mark, authentic, realistic; informal on the money, on the button, on the nose. **2 well-aimed**, on target, unerring, deadly, true.

■ **ac·cu·rate·ly adv.**

ac·curs·ed /ə'kərst, ə'kərsid/ ▶ **adj.** literary under a curse.

ac·cu·sa·tion /,akyə'zāSHən, ,akyo͞o-/ ▶ **n.** a claim that someone has done something illegal or wrong.

SYNONYMS **allegation**, charge, indictment, impeachment, claim, assertion, imputation.

ac·cu·sa·tive /ə'kyo͞ozətiv/ ▶ **n.** Grammar (in some languages) the case used for the object of a verb.

ac·cu·sa·to·ry /ə'kyo͞ozə,tôrē/ ▶ **adj.** suggesting that you believe a person has done something wrong: *an accusatory stare*.

ac·cuse /ə'kyo͞oz/ ▶ **v.** (**accuses**, **accusing**, **accused**) (often **accuse someone of**) claim that someone has done something wrong or illegal.

SYNONYMS **1 charge**, indict, impeach, prefer charges against, arraign. **2 blame**, hold responsible, condemn, criticize, denounce; informal point the finger at.

■ **ac·cus·er n.**

ac·cus·tom /ə'kəstəm/ ▸ v. **1** (**accustom someone/thing to**) make someone or something used to: *tried to accustom him to their lighthearted ways.* **2** (**be accustomed to**) be used to.

SYNONYMS **adapt**, adjust, acclimate, acclimatize, habituate, familiarize, become reconciled, get used to, come to terms with, learn to live with.

ac·cus·tomed /ə'kəstəmd/ ▸ adj. usual or habitual.

SYNONYMS **customary**, established, habitual, usual, normal, regular, routine; literary wonted.

AC/DC ▸ adj. alternating-current/direct-current.

ace /ās/ ▸ n. **1** a playing card with a single spot on it, the highest card in its suit in most games. **2** informal a person who is very good at a particular activity. **3** Tennis a service that an opponent is unable to return. ▸ adj. informal very good. ▫ **an ace up your sleeve** a plan or piece of information that you keep secret until it is needed. **hold all the aces** have all the advantages.

a·cel·lu·lar /ā'selyələr/ ▸ adj. Biology **1** not divided into or containing cells. **2** consisting of one cell only.

a·cer·bic /ə'sərbik/ ▸ adj. sharp and direct. ▪ **a·cer·bi·cal·ly** adv. **a·cer·bi·ty** n.

ac·e·tate /'asi,tāt/ ▸ n. **1** a kind of chemical compound made from acetic acid. **2** fiber or plastic made of cellulose acetate.

a·ce·tic ac·id /ə'sētik/ ▸ n. the acid that gives vinegar its taste.

ac·e·tone /'asi,tōn/ ▸ n. a colorless liquid used as a solvent.

a·cet·y·lene /ə'setlən, -,ēn/ ▸ n. a gas that burns with a bright flame, used in welding.

ache /āk/ ▸ n. a continuous or long-lasting dull pain. ▸ v. (**aches**, **aching**, **ached**) **1** suffer from an ache. **2** (**ache for** or **to do**) want very much to have or do something.

SYNONYMS ▸ n. **pain**, twinge, pang, soreness, tenderness, irritation, discomfort, burning, throbbing, cramp. ▸ v. **hurt**, be sore, be painful, be tender, burn, be in pain, throb.

▪ **ach·ing** adj.

a·chieve /ə'CHēv/ ▸ v. (**achieves**, **achieving**, **achieved**) manage to do something by effort, skill, or courage.

SYNONYMS **attain**, reach, realize, bring off, pull off, accomplish, carry through, fulfill, complete, succeed in, manage, effect; informal wrap up, swing.

▪ **a·chiev·a·ble** adj. **a·chiev·er** n.

SPELLING

The usual rule is **i** before **e**, when the sound is *ee*, except after **c**: achieve.

a·chieve·ment /ə'CHēvmənt/ ▸ n. **1** a thing that is achieved. **2** the process of achieving something.

SYNONYMS **1 attainment**, realization, accomplishment, fulfillment, implementation, completion. **2 feat**, exploit, triumph, coup, accomplishment, act, action, deed, effort, work, handiwork.

A·chil·les heel /ə'kilēz/ ▸ n. a weak point.

A·chil·les ten·don /ə'kilēz/ ▸ n. the tendon connecting calf muscles to the heel.

ach·ro·mat·ic /,akrə'matik, ,ākrə-/ ▸ adj. **1** transmitting light without separating it into colors. **2** without color.

ach·y /'ākē/ ▸ adj. (**achier**, **achiest**) suffering from an ache or aches.

ac·id /'asid/ ▸ n. **1** a substance that turns litmus red, neutralizes alkalis, and dissolves some metals. **2** informal the drug LSD. ▸ adj. **1** sharp-tasting or sour. **2** (of a remark) bitter or cutting.

SYNONYMS ▸ adj. **1 sour**, acidic, tart, sharp, vinegary. **2 sharp**, sharp-tongued, catty, sarcastic, scathing, cutting, biting, stinging, caustic; informal bitchy. ANTONYMS sweet.

▫ **acid rain** rainfall that has been made acidic by pollution. **acid reflux** /'rē,fləks/ a condition in which gastric acid is regurgitated. **acid test** a decisive test of something. ▪ **a·cid·ic** /ə'sidik/ adj. **a·cid·i·ty** /ə'siditē/ n. **ac·id·ly** adv. **ac·id·y** adj.

a·cid·i·fy /ə'sidə,fī/ ▸ v. (**acidifies**, **acidifying**, **acidified**) make or become acid.

ac·knowl·edge /ak'nälij/ ▸ v. (**acknowledges**, **acknowledging**, **acknowledged**) **1** accept that something exists or is true. **2** confirm that you have received something. **3** greet someone with words or gestures.

SYNONYMS **1 admit**, accept, grant, agree, own, allow, concede, confess, recognize. **2 answer**, reply to, respond to. **3 greet**, salute, address, nod to, wave to, say hello to. ANTONYMS deny, ignore.

ac·knowl·edg·ment /ak'nälijmənt/ (or **acknowledgement**) ▸ n. **1** the action of acknowledging. **2** something done or given as thanks to someone. **3** a mention of someone in a book thanking them for work they have done or help they have given.

ac·me /'akmē/ ▸ n. the highest point of achievement or excellence.

ac·ne /'aknē/ ▸ n. a skin condition causing red pimples.

ac·o·lyte /'akə,līt/ ▸ n. an assistant or follower.

a·corn /'ā,kôrn/ ▸ n. the fruit of the oak tree, a smooth oval nut in a cuplike base.

a·cous·tic /ə'ko͞ostik/ ▸ adj. **1** having to do with sound or hearing. **2** not electrically amplified: *an acoustic guitar.* ▸ n. (**acoustics**) **1** the aspects of a room or building that affect how well it transmits sound. **2** the branch of physics concerned with sound. ▪ **a·cous·ti·cal** adj. **a·cous·ti·cal·ly** adv.

ac·quaint /ə'kwānt/ ▸ v. **1** (**acquaint someone with**) make someone aware of or familiar with. **2** (**be acquainted with**) know someone personally.

SYNONYMS *our job is to* ***acquaint*** *you* ***with*** *the facts* **familiarize with**, make aware of, inform of, advise of, brief on; informal fill in on, clue in on.

SPELLING

Acquaint, **acquiesce**, **acquire**, **acquit**, and related words have a **c** before the **qu**: acquaint.

ac·quaint·ance /ə'kwāntns/ ▸ n. **1** familiarity with someone or something. **2** a person you know slightly.

SYNONYMS **1** *a business acquaintance* **contact**, associate, colleague. **2** *my acquaintance with George* **association**, relationship. **3** *some acquaintance with the language* **familiarity** with, knowledge of, experience with/of, awareness of, understanding of, grasp of.

ac·qui·esce /ˌakwē'es/ ▶ v. (**acquiesces, acquiescing, acquiesced**) accept something without protest.

ac·qui·es·cent /ˌakwē'esənt/ ▶ adj. ready to accept or do something without protest. ■ **ac·qui·es·cence** n.

ac·quire /ə'kwī(ə)r/ ▶ v. (**acquires, acquiring, acquired**) **1** buy or obtain an article. **2** learn or develop a skill or quality.

SYNONYMS **get**, obtain, come by, receive, collect, gain, buy, earn, win, come into, secure, pick up, procure; informal get your hands on, get hold of, land, bag, score. ANTONYMS lose.

■ **ac·quir·er** n.

ac·qui·si·tion /ˌakwə'zisʜən/ ▶ n. **1** something that you have recently obtained. **2** the action of obtaining or learning something.

SYNONYMS **purchase**, addition, investment, possession, accession; informal buy.

ac·quis·i·tive /ə'kwizitiv/ ▶ adj. too interested in gaining money or material things. ■ **ac·quis·i·tive·ly** adv. **ac·quis·i·tive·ness** n.

ac·quit /ə'kwit/ ▶ v. (**acquits, acquitting, acquitted**) **1** formally state that someone is not guilty of a criminal charge. **2** (**acquit yourself**) behave or perform in a particular way.

SYNONYMS **1 clear**, exonerate, find innocent, absolve, discharge, free, release; informal let off (the hook). **2** *the boys acquitted themselves well* **behave yourself**, conduct yourself, perform, act. ANTONYMS convict.

■ **ac·quit·tal** n.

a·cre /'ākər/ ▶ n. a unit of land area equal to 4,840 square yards (0.405 hectare). ■ **a·cre·age** /'āk(ə)rij/ n.

ac·rid /'akrid/ ▶ adj. unpleasantly bitter or sharp.

SYNONYMS **pungent**, bitter, sharp, harsh, stinging, burning.

ac·ri·mo·ni·ous /ˌakrə'mōnēəs/ ▶ adj. angry and bitter.

SYNONYMS **bitter**, angry, rancorous, harsh, vicious, nasty, bad-tempered, ill-natured.

■ **ac·ri·mo·ni·ous·ly** adv.

ac·ri·mo·ny /'akrəˌmōnē/ ▶ n. feelings of anger and bitterness.

ac·ro·bat /'akrəˌbat/ ▶ n. an entertainer who performs spectacular gymnastic feats.

ac·ro·bat·ic /ˌakrə'batik/ ▶ adj. involving or performing spectacular gymnastic feats. ▶ n. (**acrobatics**) spectacular gymnastic feats.

ac·ro·nym /'akrəˌnim/ ▶ n. a word formed from the first letters of other words (e.g., *radar*).

a·crop·o·lis /ə'kräpəlis/ ▶ n. the citadel of an ancient Greek city, built on high ground.

a·cross /ə'krôs, ə'kräs/ ▶ prep. & adv. from one side to the other of something: *the bridge runs across the river*. □ **across the board** applying to all.

a·cros·tic /ə'krôstik, ə'kräs-/ ▶ n. a poem or puzzle in which certain letters in each line form a word or words.

a·cryl·ic /ə'krilik/ ▶ adj. (of paint, fabric, etc.) made using **acrylic acid** (an organic acid).

ACT /ˌāsē'tē/ ▶ n. trademark a US college entrance test.

act /akt/ ▶ v. **1** do something. **2** have a particular effect. **3** behave in a particular way. **4** (**act as**) perform the function of. **5** (**acting**) temporarily doing the duties of another person. **6** perform a role in a play or film. ▶ n. **1** a thing done. **2** a law passed formally by a legislative body. **3** a pretense: *putting on an act*. **4** a main division of a play, ballet, or opera. **5** a set performance, or a performing group.

SYNONYMS ▶ v. **1 take action**, take steps, take measures, move. **2 behave**, conduct yourself, react. **3** *I'll act as lookout* **function**, work, serve, operate. **4** (**acting**) **temporary**, interim, caretaker, pro tem, provisional, stopgap; informal pinch-hitting. **5 perform**, play, appear; informal tread the boards. ANTONYMS permanent. ▶ n. **1 deed**, action, step, move, gesture, feat, exploit. **2 law**, decree, statute, bill, edict, ruling, order. **3 pretense**, show, front, facade, masquerade, charade, pose; informal put-on. **4 performance**, turn, routine, number, sketch.

□ **act of God** an event caused by natural forces beyond human control. **act up** informal behave badly. **get in on the act** informal become involved in a particular activity to share its benefits.

ac·tion /'aksʜən/ ▶ n. **1** the process of doing something to achieve an aim. **2** a thing done. **3** the effect of something such as a chemical. **4** a lawsuit. **5** fighting in a battle or war. **6** the way in which something works or moves. **7** informal exciting activity. ▶ v. deal with a particular matter.

SYNONYMS ▶ n. **1 deed**, act, undertaking, feat, exploit, behavior, conduct, activity. **2 measures**, steps, initiatives, activism, campaigning, pressure. **3 operation**, working, effect, influence, process, power. **4 battle**, combat, hostilities, fighting, conflict, active service. **5 lawsuit**, suit, case, prosecution, litigation, proceedings.

ac·tion·a·ble /'aksʜənəbəl/ ▶ adj. giving someone grounds to take legal action.

ac·ti·vate /'aktəˌvāt/ ▶ v. (**activates, activating, activated**) make something start working.

SYNONYMS **start (up)**, switch on, turn on, trigger (off), set off, energize.

■ **ac·ti·va·tion** /ˌaktə'vāsʜən/ n. **ac·ti·va·tor** n.

ac·tive /'aktiv/ ▶ adj. **1** moving about often or energetically. **2** regularly taking part in something. **3** working; functioning. **4** (of a volcano) erupting or having erupted in the past. **5** Grammar (of a verb) having as its subject the person or thing doing the action (e.g., *she loved him* as opposed to the passive form *he was loved*).

SYNONYMS **1 busy**, lively, dynamic, vigorous, sprightly, spry, mobile; informal on the go, full of beans. **2 hard-working**, industrious, tireless, energetic, diligent, enthusiastic, keen, committed, devoted, zealous. **3 working**, operative, functioning, operational, in action, in operation, in force; informal (up and) running. ANTONYMS inactive.

□ **active service** military service in wartime. ■ **ac·tive·ly** adv.

ac·tiv·ist /'aktəˌvist/ ▶ n. a person who campaigns for political or social change. ■ **ac·tiv·ism** n.

ac·tiv·i·ty /ak'tivitē/ ▶ n. (plural **activities**) **1** a condition in which things are happening or being done. **2** busy or energetic action or movement. **3** an action, especially one done for interest or pleasure: *vacation activities*.

> SYNONYMS **1 action**, bustle, movement, life, hurly-burly; informal comings and goings. **2 pursuit**, occupation, hobby, pastime, recreation, diversion, venture, undertaking, enterprise, project, scheme.

ac·tor /'aktər/ ▶ **n.** a person whose profession is acting.

> SYNONYMS **performer**, player, thespian, star, starlet.

ac·tress /'aktris/ ▶ **n.** a female actor.

> SYNONYMS **performer**, player, thespian, star, starlet.

ac·tu·al /'akCHo͞oəl/ ▶ **adj.** existing in fact or reality.

> SYNONYMS **real**, true, genuine, authentic, bona fide, confirmed, definite, hard, concrete; informal real live. ANTONYMS imaginary.

ac·tu·al·i·ty /ˌakCHo͞o'alitē/ ▶ **n.** (plural **actualities**) actual reality or fact.

ac·tu·al·ize /'akCHo͞oəˌlīz/ ▶ **v.** (**actualizes**, **actualizing**, **actualized**) make something real or actual.

ac·tu·al·ly /'akCHo͞oəlē/ ▶ **adv.** in truth; in reality.

> SYNONYMS **really**, in (actual) fact, in point of fact, as a matter of fact, in reality, in truth, if truth be told, to tell the truth.

ac·tu·ar·y /'akCHo͞oˌerē/ ▶ **n.** (plural **actuaries**) a person who calculates insurance risks. ■ **ac·tu·ar·i·al** /ˌakCHo͞o'e(ə)rēəl/ **adj.**

ac·tu·ate /'akCHo͞oˌāt/ ▶ **v. 1** cause a machine to function. **2** motivate someone to act in a particular way.

a·cu·i·ty /ə'kyo͞oitē/ ▶ **n.** sharpness of thought, vision, or hearing.

a·cu·men /ə'kyo͞omən, 'akyə-/ ▶ **n.** the ability to make good judgments and quick decisions.

> SYNONYMS **astuteness**, shrewdness, acuity, sharpness, smartness, brains; judgment, canniness, insight; informal savvy, know-how, smarts; formal perspicuity.

ac·u·punc·ture /'akyəˌpəNGkCHər/ ▶ **n.** a medical treatment in which very thin needles are inserted into the skin. ■ **ac·u·punc·tur·ist n.**

a·cute /ə'kyo͞ot/ ▶ **adj. 1** (of something bad) very serious. **2** intelligent and shrewd. **3** (of a physical sense or faculty) highly developed. **4** (of an angle) less than 90°.

> SYNONYMS **1 severe**, dire, terrible, grave, serious, desperate, urgent, pressing. **2 excruciating**, sharp, severe, stabbing, agonizing, racking, searing. **3 quick**, astute, shrewd, sharp, keen, penetrating, razor-sharp, quick-witted, agile, nimble, intelligent, canny, discerning, perceptive. ANTONYMS mild, dull.

□ **acute accent** a mark (´) placed over certain letters in some languages to show pronunciation (e.g., in *fiancée*). ■ **a·cute·ly adv. a·cute·ness n.**

AD ▶ **abbr.** Anno Domini, used to indicate that a date comes a particular number of years after the traditional date of Jesus's birth: *AD 400*.

> USAGE
> If a date is written in figures, AD should be placed **before** the numerals, e.g., AD *375*, but when the date is spelled out, AD should be placed after it, as in *the third century* AD.

ad /ad/ ▶ **n.** informal an advertisement.

ad·age /'adij/ ▶ **n.** a popular saying expressing something that most people accept as true.

a·da·gio /ə'däjō, ə'däZHēˌō/ ▶ **adj. & adv.** Music in slow time.

ad·a·mant /'adəmənt/ ▶ **adj.** refusing to be persuaded or to change your mind.

> SYNONYMS **unshakable**, unwavering, unswerving, immovable, resolute, resolved, determined, firm, dead set.

■ **ad·a·mant·ly adv.**

Ad·am's ap·ple /'adəmz/ ▶ **n.** a projection at the front of the neck, more prominent in men than women.

a·dapt /ə'dapt/ ▶ **v. 1** make something suitable for a new use or purpose. **2** become adjusted to new conditions.

> SYNONYMS **1** *the policy can be adapted* **modify**, alter, change, adjust, remodel, reorganize, customize, tailor; informal tweak. **2** *he adapts well to new surroundings* **adjust**, conform, acclimatize, accommodate, get used, get accustomed, habituate yourself.

■ **a·dap·tive adj.**

a·dapt·a·ble /ə'daptəbəl/ ▶ **adj.** able to adjust to, or be altered for, new conditions or uses. ■ **a·dapt·a·bil·i·ty** /əˌdaptə'bilitē/ **n.**

ad·ap·ta·tion /ˌadap'tāSHən, ˌadəp-/ (or **adaption**) ▶ **n. 1** the process of adapting. **2** a movie or play adapted from a written work.

a·dapt·er /ə'daptər/ (or **adaptor**) ▶ **n. 1** a device for connecting pieces of equipment. **2** a person who adapts a text to make it suitable for filming, broadcasting, or the stage.

ADD ▶ **abbr.** attention deficit disorder.

add /ad/ ▶ **v. 1** put something together with something else. **2** put together two or more numbers or amounts to find their total value. **3** (**add up**) increase in amount or number. **4** say as a further remark. **5** (**add up**) informal make sense.

> SYNONYMS **1 attach**, append, tack on, join on. **2** *they added the figures up* **total**, count (up), reckon up, tally. ANTONYMS subtract.

ad·den·dum /ə'dendəm/ ▶ **n.** (plural **addenda** /-də/) an extra item added at the end of a book or other publication.

ad·der /'adər/ ▶ **n.** a poisonous snake of Europe and Asia with a dark zigzag pattern on its back.

ad·dict /'adikt/ ▶ **n. 1** a person who is addicted to something. **2** informal an enthusiast of something.

> SYNONYMS **1 abuser**; informal junkie, druggie, -head, freak, hophead. **2 enthusiast**, fan, lover, devotee, aficionado; informal buff, freak, nut, fanatic.

ad·dict·ed /ə'diktid/ ▶ **adj.** (usu. **addicted to**) **1** physically dependent on a particular substance. **2** very enthusiastic about a particular interest or activity.

> SYNONYMS *they seem* ***addicted to*** *their cell phones* **dependent on**, obsessed with, fixated

on, fanatical about, passionate about, a slave to; informal hooked on.

ad·dic·tion /ə'dikSHən/ ▶ **n.** the condition of being addicted to something.

SYNONYMS **dependency**, dependence, habit, obsession, infatuation, passion, love, mania, enslavement.

ad·dic·tive /ə'diktiv/ ▶ **adj.** (of a substance or activity) causing someone to become addicted to it.

SYNONYMS **habit-forming**, addicting, compulsive.

ad·di·tion /ə'disHən/ ▶ **n. 1** the action of adding. **2** a person or thing that is added.

SYNONYMS **1 adding**, inclusion, incorporation, introduction. **2 add-on**, extra, adjunct, appendage, supplement, rider, addendum, postscript, appendix. ANTONYMS subtraction.

ad·di·tion·al /ə'disHənl/ ▶ **adj.** added; extra.

SYNONYMS **extra**, added, supplementary, further, more, spare, other, new, fresh.

ad·di·tion·al·ly /ə'disHən(ə)lē/ ▶ **adv.** as an extra factor or circumstance.

SYNONYMS **also**, in addition, besides, too, as well, on top (of that), furthermore, moreover, into the bargain, to boot, to say nothing of.

ad·di·tive /'aditiv/ ▶ **n.** a substance added to improve or preserve something.

ad·dled /'adld/ ▶ **adj. 1** humorous confused or puzzled. **2** old use (of an egg) rotten.

SYNONYMS **muddled**, confused, muzzy, fuddled, befuddled, dazed, disoriented, disorientated, fuzzy; informal woozy.

ad·dress /ə'dres, 'a,dres/ ▶ **n. 1** the details of where a building is or where someone lives. **2** a string of characters identifying a destination for email messages. **3** a formal speech. ▶ **v. 1** write a name and address on an envelope or parcel. **2** make a speech or remark to. **3** think about a task and begin to deal with it.

SYNONYMS ▶ **n. 1 house**, home, apartment, location, whereabouts; formal residence, dwelling, domicile. **2 speech**, lecture, talk, presentation, dissertation, sermon, oration. ▶ **v. speak to**, talk to, give a talk to, lecture, make a speech to, hold forth to.

■ **ad·dress·ee** /,adre'sē, ə,dre'sē/ **n. ad·dress·er n.**

SPELLING

Two **d**s: a**dd**ress.

ad·duce /ə'd(y)o͞os/ ▶ **v.** (**adduces**, **adducing**, **adduced**) formal refer to something as evidence.

ad·e·noids /'adn,oidz/ ▶ **pl.n.** a mass of tissue between the back of the nose and the throat.

a·dept ▶ **adj.** /ə'dept/ very skilled or able. ▶ **n.** /'adept/ an adept person.

SYNONYMS ▶ **adj. expert**, proficient, accomplished, skillful, practiced, masterly, consummate. ANTONYMS inept.

■ **a·dept·ly adv. a·dept·ness n.**

ad·e·quate /'adikwit/ ▶ **adj.** satisfactory or acceptable; good enough.

SYNONYMS **1** *he has adequate financial resources* **sufficient**, enough. **2** *an adequate service* **satisfactory**, acceptable, passable, reasonable, tolerable, fair, average, not bad, all right, middling; informal OK. ANTONYMS insufficient, inadequate.

■ **ad·e·qua·cy** /-kwəsē/ **n. ad·e·quate·ly adv.**

ADHD ▶ **abbr.** attention deficit hyperactivity disorder.

ad·here /ad'hi(ə)r/ ▶ **v.** (**adheres**, **adhering**, **adhered**) (**adhere to**) **1** stick firmly to. **2** follow or observe.

SYNONYMS **1 stick**, cling, bond, hold. **2** (**adhere to**) **abide by**, stick to, hold to, comply with, conform to, follow, obey, heed, observe, respect, uphold, fulfill.

■ **ad·her·ence n.**

ad·her·ent /ad'hi(ə)rənt, -'her-/ ▶ **n.** a person who supports a particular party, person, or set of ideas. ▶ **adj.** sticking firmly to an object or surface.

SYNONYMS ▶ **n. follower**, supporter, upholder, defender, advocate, disciple, devotee, member. ANTONYMS opponent.

ad·he·sion /ad'hēzHən/ ▶ **n.** the process of adhering.

ad·he·sive /ad'hēsiv, -ziv/ ▶ **n.** a substance used to stick things together. ▶ **adj.** sticky.
■ **ad·he·sive·ly adv. ad·he·sive·ness n.**

ad hoc /'ad 'häk, 'hōk/ ▶ **adj. & adv.** created or done for a particular purpose only.

a·dieu /ə'd(y)o͞o, ä'dyœ/ ▶ **exclam.** old use goodbye.

ad in·fi·ni·tum /,ad infə'nītəm/ ▶ **adv.** endlessly; forever.

ad·i·pose /'adə,pōs/ ▶ **adj.** technical having to do with fatty body tissue.

ad·ja·cent /ə'jāsənt/ ▶ **adj.** near or next to something else.

SYNONYMS **adjoining**, neighboring, next-door, abutting; formal contiguous.

ad·jec·tive /'ajiktiv/ ▶ **n.** Grammar a word used to describe a noun or to make its meaning clearer, such as *sweet* or *red*. ■ **ad·jec·ti·val** /,ajik'tīvəl/ **adj.**

ad·join /ə'join/ ▶ **v.** be next to and joined with.

SYNONYMS (**adjoining**) **connecting**, connected, interconnecting, bordering, abutting, attached, adjacent, neighboring, next-door.

ad·journ /ə'jərn/ ▶ **v. 1** break off a meeting until later. **2** postpone a decision.

SYNONYMS **suspend**, break off, discontinue, interrupt, recess, postpone, put off/back, defer, delay, hold over.

■ **ad·journ·ment n.**

ad·judge /ə'jəj/ ▶ **v.** (**adjudges**, **adjudging**, **adjudged**) (of a court of law or judge) formally decide.

ad·ju·di·cate /ə'jo͞odi,kāt/ ▶ **v.** (**adjudicates**, **adjudicating**, **adjudicated**) **1** make a formal judgment. **2** judge a competition.
■ **ad·ju·di·ca·tion** /ə,jo͞odi'kāsHən/ **n. ad·ju·di·ca·tor** /-,kātər/ **n.**

ad·junct /'ajəNGkt/ ▶ **n.** an additional part or thing.

ad·jure /ə'jo͝or/ ▶ **v.** (**adjures**, **adjuring**, **adjured**) formal urge someone to do something.

ad·just /ə'jəst/ ▶ **v. 1** alter something slightly. **2** become used to a new situation. **3** decide the amount to be paid when settling an insurance claim.

SYNONYMS **1 modify**, alter, regulate, tune, fine-tune, balance, tailor, customize, rearrange, change, reshape; informal tweak. **2** *she adjusted to her new life* **adapt to**, become accustomed to, get used to, accommodate yourself to, acclimate to, acclimatize to, habituate yourself to, assimilate to, come to terms with, fit in with.

■ **ad·just·er** n.

ad·just·a·ble /ə'jəstəbəl/ ▸ adj. able to be adjusted.

SYNONYMS **alterable**, adaptable, modifiable, variable, convertible, multiway, versatile.

■ **ad·just·a·bil·i·ty** /əˌjəstə'bilitē/ n.

ad·just·ment /əjəstmənt/ ▸ n. **1** a minor change made so as to correct or improve something: *the company will make adjustments to its packaging.* **2** the action of adjusting.

ad·ju·tant /'ajətənt/ ▸ n. a military officer who helps a senior officer with administrative work.

ad-lib /'ad'lib/ ▸ v. (**ad-libs**, **ad-libbing**, **ad-libbed**) speak or perform in public without preparing first. ▸ n. an unprepared remark or speech.

ad·min·is·ter /əd'minəstər/ ▸ v. (**administers**, **administering**, **administered**) **1** organize or put into effect. **2** give out or apply a drug or remedy.

SYNONYMS **1 manage**, direct, control, operate, regulate, coordinate, conduct, handle, run, organize, govern, steer. **2 dispense**, issue, give out, provide, apply, offer, distribute, deliver, hand out, deal out, dole out.

ad·min·is·trate /əd'minəˌstrāt/ ▸ v. (**administrates**, **administrating**, **administrated**) manage the affairs of a business or organization.

ad·min·is·tra·tion /ədˌminə'strāsʜən/ ▸ n. **1** the running of a business or system. **2** the action of giving out or applying something. **3** the government in power.

SYNONYMS **1 management**, direction, control, conduct, operation, running, coordination, governance, supervision, regulation. **2 government**, regime, executive, cabinet, authority, directorate, council, leadership, management, incumbency, term of office.

ad·min·is·tra·tive /əd'miniˌstrātiv, -strətiv/ ▸ adj. relating to the running of a business, organization, etc.

SYNONYMS **managerial**, executive, operational, organizational, supervisory, directorial, governmental, regulatory.

ad·min·is·tra·tor /əd'minəˌstrātər/ ▸ n. a person responsible for managing an organization.

SYNONYMS **manager**, director, executive, controller, official, coordinator, supervisor.

ad·mi·ra·ble /'admərəbəl/ ▸ adj. deserving respect and approval.

SYNONYMS **commendable**, praiseworthy, laudable, creditable, exemplary, worthy, deserving, respectable, worthwhile, good, sterling, fine, excellent. ANTONYMS deplorable.

■ **ad·mi·ra·bly** adv.

ad·mi·ral /'admərəl/ ▸ n. **1** a commander of a fleet or naval squadron. **2** a naval officer of very high rank.

ad·mi·ra·tion /ˌadmə'rāsʜən/ ▸ n. respect and warm approval.

SYNONYMS **respect**, approval, appreciation, (high) regard, esteem, recognition. ANTONYMS scorn.

ad·mire /əd'mī(ə)r/ ▸ v. (**admires**, **admiring**, **admired**) **1** respect or approve of. **2** look at with pleasure.

SYNONYMS **1 respect**, think highly of, look up to, have a high opinion of, hold in high regard, rate highly, esteem, prize, approve of. **2 adore**, love, worship, be taken with, be attracted to, idolize, hero-worship; informal carry a torch for, have a thing about. ANTONYMS despise.

■ **ad·mir·ing** adj.

ad·mir·er /əd'mī(ə)rər/ ▸ n. **1** a person who admires something or someone. **2** a man who is attracted to a particular woman.

SYNONYMS **fan**, devotee, enthusiast, aficionado, supporter, adherent, follower, disciple.

ad·mis·si·ble /əd'misəbəl/ ▸ adj. **1** acceptable or valid. **2** allowed to enter a place.

ad·mis·sion /əd'misʜən/ ▸ n. **1** the process of being allowed in to a place. **2** a confession.

SYNONYMS **1 admittance**, entry, entrance, access, entrée, acceptance, initiation. **2 confession**, acknowledgment, acceptance, concession, disclosure, divulgence.

ad·mit /əd'mit/ ▸ v. (**admits**, **admitting**, **admitted**) **1** confess that something is true or is the case. **2** allow someone to enter a place. **3** accept that something is valid.

SYNONYMS **1** *Paul admitted that he was angry* **confess**, acknowledge, concede, grant, accept, allow, own, reveal, disclose, divulge. **2** *he admitted the offense* **confess (to)**, plead guilty to, own up to. **3 let in**, accept, receive, initiate, take on. ANTONYMS deny.

ad·mit·tance /əd'mitns/ ▸ n. the process of entering, or of being allowed to enter.

SYNONYMS **entry**, admission, entrance, access, entrée. ANTONYMS exclusion.

ad·mix /ad'miks/ ▸ v. chiefly technical mix with something else. ■ **ad·mix·ture** n.

ad·mon·ish /əd'mänisʜ/ ▸ v. **1** firmly express disapproval. **2** seriously urge or warn.

SYNONYMS **reprimand**, rebuke, scold, reprove, reproach, upbraid, chastise, chide, berate, criticize, take to task, read the Riot Act to, haul over the coals; informal tell off, dress down, bawl out, rap on the knuckles, give hell, chew out; formal castigate.

■ **ad·mon·ish·ment** n. **ad·mon·i·to·ry** /əd'mänəˌtôrē/ adj.

ad·mo·ni·tion /ˌadmə'nisʜən/ ▸ n. a firm warning.

ad nau·se·am /ad 'nôzēəm/ ▸ adv. to an annoying or boring extent.

a·do /ə'do͞o/ ▸ n. trouble; fuss.

a·do·be /ə'dōbē/ ▸ n. a kind of clay used to make sun-dried bricks.

ad·o·les·cence /ˌadl'esəns/ ▸ n. the period during which a young person develops from a child into an adult.

SYNONYMS **teenage years**, teens, youth, later childhood.

ad·o·les·cent /ˌadl'esənt/ ▶ adj. in the process of developing from a child into an adult. ▶ n. an adolescent boy or girl.

SYNONYMS ▶ adj. **teenage**, young, pubescent, immature, childish, juvenile, infantile, puerile; informal teen. ANTONYMS mature. ▶ n. **teenager**, youth, juvenile; informal teen, teeny-bopper.

A·don·is /ə'dänis/ ▶ n. a very handsome young man.

a·dopt /ə'däpt/ ▶ v. **1** legally take someone else's child and bring it up as your own. **2** choose an option or course of action.

SYNONYMS **take on**, embrace, take up, espouse, assume, follow, choose, endorse, approve. ANTONYMS abandon.

■ **a·dopt·a·ble** adj. **a·dopt·ee** /ədäpt'tē/ n. **a·dopt·er** n. **a·dop·tion** n.

a·dop·tive /ə'däptiv/ ▶ adj. (of a parent) having adopted a child.

a·dor·a·ble /ə'dôrəbəl/ ▶ adj. very lovable or charming.

SYNONYMS **lovable**, appealing, charming, cute, sweet, enchanting, bewitching, captivating, engaging, endearing, dear, delightful, lovely, beautiful, attractive, gorgeous, winsome, winning, fetching. ANTONYMS repulsive, hateful.

■ **a·dor·a·bly** adv.

a·dore /ə'dôr/ ▶ v. (**adores**, **adoring**, **adored**) love deeply.

SYNONYMS **love**, be devoted to, dote on, cherish, treasure, prize, think the world of, admire, look up to, revere, worship. ANTONYMS hate.

■ **ad·o·ra·tion** /ˌadə'rāsʜən/ n. **a·dor·er** n. **a·dor·ing** adj.

a·dorn /ə'dôrn/ ▶ v. make more attractive; decorate.

SYNONYMS **decorate**, embellish, array, ornament, bedeck, trim, enhance. ANTONYMS disfigure.

■ **a·dorn·ment** n.

ad·re·nal /ə'drēnl/ ▶ adj. having to do with the **adrenal glands**, a pair of glands above the kidneys.

a·dren·a·line /ə'drenl-in/ (or **adrenalin**) ▶ n. a hormone produced by the adrenal glands in response to stress that makes the body's natural processes work more quickly; epinephrine.

A·dri·at·ic /ˌādrē'atik/ ▶ adj. having to do with the region of the **Adriatic Sea**, the arm of the Mediterranean between Italy and the Balkans.

a·drift /ə'drift/ ▶ adj. & adv. **1** (of a boat) drifting without control. **2** no longer fixed in position.

SYNONYMS **1 lost**, off course, drifting, disorientated, confused, (all) at sea, rootless, unsettled. **2 loose**, free, detached, unsecured, unfastened.

a·droit /ə'droit/ ▶ adj. clever or skillful.

SYNONYMS **skillful**, adept, dexterous, deft, nimble, able, capable, skilled, expert, masterly, masterful, practiced, polished, slick, proficient, accomplished, gifted, talented; quick-witted, quick-thinking, clever, smart, sharp, cunning, wily, resourceful, astute, shrewd, canny; informal nifty. ANTONYMS inept, clumsy.

ad·sorb /ad'zôrb, -'sôrb/ ▶ v. (of a solid) hold molecules of a gas or liquid in a layer on its surface. ■ **ad·sorb·a·ble** adj. **ad·sorb·ent** adj. **ad·sorp·tion** n.

ad·u·la·tion /ˌajə'lāsʜən/ ▶ n. excessive admiration. ■ **ad·u·la·to·ry** /'ajələˌtôrē/ adj.

a·dult /ə'dəlt, 'adˌəlt/ ▶ n. a person who is fully grown and developed. ▶ adj. **1** fully grown and developed. **2** suitable for or typical of adults.

SYNONYMS ▶ adj. **mature**, grown-up, fully grown, fully developed, of age. ANTONYMS immature.

■ **a·dult·hood** n.

a·dul·ter·ate /ə'dəltəˌrāt/ ▶ v. (**adulterates**, **adulterating**, **adulterated**) make something worse in quality by adding another substance. ■ **a·dul·ter·a·tion** /əˌdəltə'rāsʜən/ n.

a·dul·ter·er /ə'dəltərər/ ▶ n. (feminine **adulteress**) a person who has committed adultery.

a·dul·ter·y /ə'dəlt(ə)rē/ ▶ n. sex between a married person and a person who is not their spouse. ■ **a·dul·ter·ous** adj.

ad·um·brate /'adəmˌbrāt, ə'dəm-/ ▶ v. (**adumbrates**, **adumbrating**, **adumbrated**) formal give a faint or general idea of.

ad·vance /əd'vans/ ▶ v. (**advances**, **advancing**, **advanced**) **1** move forward. **2** put forward a theory or suggestion. **3** hand over payment to someone as a loan or before it is due. ▶ n. **1** a forward movement. **2** a development or improvement. **3** an amount of money advanced. **4** an approach made with the aim of beginning a romantic relationship. ▶ adj. done, sent, or supplied beforehand.

SYNONYMS ▶ v. **1 move forward**, press on, push on, attack, make progress, make headway, gain ground, forge ahead. **2** *the move advanced his career* **promote**, further, forward, help, aid, assist, boost. **3** *technology has advanced* **progress**, develop, evolve, make strides, move forward (in leaps and bounds), move on. **4 lend**, loan, put up, come up with. ANTONYMS retreat. ▶ n. **1 progress**, (forward) movement, attack. **2 breakthrough**, development, step forward, (quantum) leap. ▶ adj. **early**, prior.

ad·vanced /əd'vanst/ ▶ adj. **1** far on or ahead in progress or life. **2** complex; not basic.

SYNONYMS **1 state-of-the-art**, modern, sophisticated, up to date, up to the minute, cutting-edge, new, the latest, pioneering, innovative, progressive, trendsetting. **2 higher-level**, higher, tertiary. ANTONYMS primitive, elementary.

ad·vance·ment /əd'vansmənt/ ▶ n. **1** the process of helping a cause or plan to develop or succeed. **2** the raising of a person to a higher rank or status. **3** a development or improvement.

ad·van·tage /əd'vantij/ ▶ n. **1** something that puts you in a good position. **2** Tennis a score marking a point between deuce and winning the game. ▶ v. (**advantages**, **advantaging**, **advantaged**) be of benefit to.

SYNONYMS ▶ n. **1 upper hand**, edge, lead, sway, whip hand, superiority, dominance, supremacy. **2 benefit**, value, good/strong point, asset, plus, bonus, boon, blessing, virtue, profit, good. ANTONYMS disadvantage.

□ **take advantage of 1** make unfair use of someone. **2** make good use of an opportunity.

ad·van·ta·geous /ˌadvənˈtājəs, -van-/ ▶ **adj.** good or useful in a particular situation.

SYNONYMS **1 superior**, dominant, powerful, fortunate, lucky, favorable. **2 beneficial**, of benefit, helpful, of assistance, useful, of value, profitable, in someone's interests. ANTONYMS disadvantageous.

■ **ad·van·ta·geous·ly adv.**

ad·vent /ˈadˌvent/ ▶ **n. 1** the arrival of an important person or thing. **2** (**Advent**) (in Christian belief) the coming or second coming of Jesus. **3** (**Advent**) the time leading up to Christmas.

Ad·vent·ist /ˈadˌventist/ ▶ **n.** a member of a Christian sect that focuses on the belief that the second coming of Christ is about to happen.

ad·ven·ti·tious /ˌadvenˈtisʜəs/ ▶ **adj.** formal happening by chance. ■ **ad·ven·ti·tious·ly adv.**

ad·ven·ture /adˈvencʜər, əd-/ ▶ **n. 1** an unusual, exciting, and daring experience. **2** excitement resulting from danger or risk.

SYNONYMS **1 exploit**, escapade, undertaking, experience, incident. **2 excitement**, thrills, action, stimulation, risk, danger.

ad·ven·tur·er /adˈvencʜərər, əd-/ ▶ **n. 1** a person willing to take risks or do dishonest things for personal gain: *a political adventurer*. **2** a person who looks for adventure.

ad·ven·ture·some /adˈvencʜərsəm, əd-/ ▶ **adj.** fond of adventures or of taking risks; adventurous.

ad·ven·tur·ous /adˈvencʜərəs, əd-/ ▶ **adj. 1** involving new or daring methods or experiences. **2** willing to take risks and try new things.

SYNONYMS **1 risky**, dangerous, perilous, hazardous, exciting. **2 intrepid**, daring, daredevil, bold, fearless, brave; informal gutsy. ANTONYMS cautious, safe.

■ **ad·ven·tur·ous·ly adv. ad·ven·tur·ous·ness n.**

ad·verb /ˈadˌvərb/ ▶ **n.** Grammar a word that gives more information about an adjective, verb, or other adverb (e.g., *gently*, *very*). ■ **ad·ver·bi·al** /adˈvərbēəl/ **adj.**

ad·ver·sar·i·al /ˌadvərˈse(ə)rēəl/ ▶ **adj.** having to do with conflict or opposition.

ad·ver·sar·y /ˈadvərˌserē/ ▶ **n.** (plural **adversaries**) an opponent or enemy.

SYNONYMS **opponent**, rival, enemy, antagonist, challenger, contender, competitor, opposition, competition; literary foe. ANTONYMS ally.

ad·verse /adˈvərs, ˈadvərs/ ▶ **adj.** harmful or unfavorable.

SYNONYMS **1** *adverse weather* **unfavorable**, inclement, bad, poor, untoward, inauspicious, unpropitious. **2** *adverse side effects* **harmful**, dangerous, injurious, detrimental, deleterious, inimical. **3** *an adverse response* **hostile**, unfavorable, antagonistic, unfriendly, negative. ANTONYMS favorable, beneficial.

■ **ad·verse·ly adv.**

USAGE

Don't confuse **adverse** with **averse**, which means 'strongly disliking or opposed to,' as in *I am not averse to helping out.*

ad·ver·si·ty /adˈvərsitē/ ▶ **n.** (plural **adversities**) a difficult or unpleasant situation; misfortune.

SYNONYMS **misfortune**, bad luck, trouble, difficulty, hardship, disaster, suffering, sorrow, misery, woe, trials and tribulations.

ad·ver·tise /ˈadvərˌtīz/ ▶ **v.** (**advertises, advertising, advertised**) **1** describe a product, service, or event in a publication or on television or radio in order to increase sales or attendance. **2** try to fill a housing vacancy or job opening by publishing details of it. **3** make a fact known.

SYNONYMS **publicize**, make public, announce, broadcast, proclaim, trumpet, promote, market; informal push, plug, hype, ballyhoo.

■ **ad·ver·tis·er n. ad·ver·tis·ing n.**

ad·ver·tise·ment /ˈadvərˌtīzmənt, ədˈvərtiz-/ ▶ **n.** a notice or display advertising something.

SYNONYMS **announcement**, commercial, promotion, blurb, write-up; informal ad, push, plug.

ad·vice /ədˈvīs/ ▶ **n.** guidance or recommendations about what someone should do in the future.

SYNONYMS **guidance**, counseling, counsel, help, direction, recommendations, guidelines, suggestions, hints, tips, pointers.

USAGE

Don't confuse the noun **advice** and the verb **advise**.

ad·vis·a·ble /ədˈvīzəbəl/ ▶ **adj.** sensible; to be recommended.

SYNONYMS **wise**, sensible, prudent, expedient, politic, in your (best) interests.

■ **ad·vis·a·bil·i·ty** /-ˌvīzəˈbilitē/ **n.**

ad·vise /ədˈvīz/ ▶ **v.** (**advises, advising, advised**) **1** recommend that someone should do something; suggest. **2** tell someone about a fact or situation. **3** offer advice to.

SYNONYMS **1 recommend**, advocate, suggest, urge. **2 counsel**, give guidance, guide, offer suggestions, give hints/tips/pointers. **3 inform**, notify, give notice, apprise, warn.

ad·vised /ədˈvīzd/ ▶ **adj.** behaving as someone would recommend; sensible. ■ **ad·vis·ed·ly** /ədˈvīzidlē/ **adv.**

ad·vis·er /ədˈvīzər/ (also **advisor**) ▶ **n. 1** a person whose job is to give advice. **2** a school or college teacher or counselor who helps a student plan a course of study.

SYNONYMS **counselor**, aide, mentor, guide, consultant, confidant, confidante, guru.

ad·vi·so·ry /ədˈvīzərē/ ▶ **adj.** having the power to make recommendations but not to make sure that they are carried out.

ad·vo·cate ▶ **n.** /ˈadvəkit/ **1** a person who publicly supports or recommends a cause or policy. **2** a person who argues a case on someone else's behalf. ▶ **v.** /ˈadvəˌkāt/ (**advocates, advocating, advocated**) publicly recommend or support.

SYNONYMS ▶ **n. champion**, upholder, supporter, apologist, backer, promoter, booster, proponent, campaigner, lobbyist. ANTONYMS critic. ▶ **v. recommend**, champion, uphold, support, back, promote, campaign for, urge, subscribe to, speak for, argue for, lobby for. ANTONYMS oppose.

■ **ad·vo·ca·cy** /ˈadvəkəsē/ **n.**

adz /adz/ (or **adze**) ▶ n. a tool like an ax, with an arched blade.

Ae·ge·an /i'jēən/ ▶ adj. referring to the region of the **Aegean Sea**, the part of the Mediterranean between Greece and Turkey.

ae·gis /'ējis/ ▶ n. the protection, backing, or support of someone.

aer·ate /'e(ə)rāt/ ▶ v. bring air into something. ■ **aer·a·tion** /e(ə)r'āsHən/ n. **aer·a·tor** n.

aer·i·al /'e(ə)rēəl/ ▶ n. a wire, rod, etc., that sends out or receives radio or television signals; an antenna. ▶ adj. **1** existing or taking place in the air. **2** involving the use of aircraft.

aer·ie /'e(ə)rē, 'i(ə)rē/ (or **eyrie**) ▶ n. a nest of an eagle or other bird of prey, typically built high in a tree or on a cliff.

aer·o·bat·ics /ˌe(ə)rə'batiks/ ▶ n. exciting and daring flying performed for display. ■ **aer·o·bat·ic** adj.

aer·o·bic /ə'rōbik, e(ə)'rō-/ ▶ adj. (of exercise) intended to increase the amount of oxygen you breathe in and make it move around the body more quickly. ■ **aer·o·bi·cal·ly** adv.

aer·o·bics /ə'rōbiks, e(ə)'rō-/ ▶ n. exercises intended to strengthen the heart and lungs.

aer·o·dy·nam·ic /ˌe(ə)rōdī'namik/ ▶ adj. **1** relating to aerodynamics. **2** having a shape that moves through the air quickly. ▶ n. (**aerodynamics**) the science concerned with the movement of objects through the air. ■ **aer·o·dy·nam·i·cal·ly** adv.

aer·o·nau·tics /ˌe(ə)rə'nôtiks/ ▶ n. the study or practice of travel through the air. ■ **aer·o·nau·tic** adj. **aer·o·nau·ti·cal** adj.

aer·o·sol /'erəˌsôl, -ˌsäl/ ▶ n. a substance sealed in a container under pressure and released as a fine spray.

aer·o·space /'e(ə)rōˌspās/ ▶ n. the technology and industry concerned with flight.

aes·thete /'esˌTHēt/ (or **esthete**) ▶ n. a person who appreciates art and beauty.

aes·thet·ic /es'THetik/ (or **esthetic**) ▶ adj. **1** concerned with beauty. **2** having a pleasant appearance. ▶ n. a set of principles behind the work of an artist or artistic movement. ■ **aes·thet·i·cal·ly** adv.

aes·thet·ics /es'THetiks/ (or **esthetics**) ▶ n. **1** a set of principles concerned with beauty. **2** the branch of philosophy that deals with questions of beauty and artistic taste.

a·far /ə'fär/ ▶ adv. at or to a distance.

AFB ▶ abbr. Air Force Base.

AFC ▶ abbr. American Football Conference.

af·fa·ble /'afəbəl/ ▶ adj. good-natured and friendly.

> SYNONYMS **friendly**, amiable, genial, congenial, cordial, warm, pleasant, nice, likable, personable, charming, agreeable, sympathetic, good-humored, good-natured, kindly, kind, approachable, accessible, amenable, sociable, outgoing, gregarious, neighborly, welcoming, hospitable, obliging. ANTONYMS unfriendly.

■ **af·fa·bil·i·ty** /ˌafə'bilitē/ n. **af·fa·bly** adv.

af·fair /ə'fe(ə)r/ ▶ n. **1** an event or series of events. **2** a matter that is a particular person's responsibility. **3** a love affair. **4** (**affairs**) matters of public interest and importance.

> SYNONYMS **1 event**, incident, episode, case, matter, business. **2 business**, concern, matter, responsibility, problem. **3 relationship**, romance, fling, dalliance, liaison, involvement, amour; informal hanky-panky. **4** (**affairs**) **transactions**, activities, dealings, undertakings, ventures, business.

af·fect /ə'fekt/ ▶ v. **1** make a difference to. **2** make someone feel sadness, pity, etc. **3** pretend to have a particular feeling. **4** wear something or behave in a particular way in an attempt to impress people.

> SYNONYMS **1 influence**, have an effect on, have an impact on, act on, change, alter, modify. **2 move**, touch, hit (hard), make an impression on, upset, trouble, distress, disturb, shake (up). **3 put on**, assume, take on, adopt, feign.

> USAGE
> Don't confuse **affect** and **effect**. **Affect** chiefly means 'make a difference to,' as in *the changes will affect everyone*. **Effect** is chiefly a noun meaning 'a result,' as in *the effects of aging*.

af·fec·ta·tion /ˌafek'tāsHən/ ▶ n. behavior that is designed to impress people.

> SYNONYMS **pretension**, pretentiousness, affectedness, artificiality, posturing, airs.

af·fect·ed /ə'fektid/ ▶ adj. designed to impress people. ■ **af·fect·ed·ly** adv.

af·fec·tion /ə'feksHən/ ▶ n. a feeling of fondness or liking.

> SYNONYMS **fondness**, love, liking, soft spot, tenderness, warmth, devotion, caring, attachment, friendship.

af·fec·tion·ate /ə'feksHənit/ ▶ adj. readily showing affection.

> SYNONYMS **fond**, loving, adoring, devoted, caring, tender, warm, friendly, demonstrative; informal touchy-feely, lovey-dovey. ANTONYMS cold.

■ **af·fec·tion·ate·ly** adv.

af·fi·da·vit /ˌafi'dāvit/ ▶ n. a written statement that a person swears is true and that can be used as evidence in a court of law.

af·fil·i·ate ▶ v. /ə'filēˌāt/ (**affiliates**, **affiliating**, **affiliated**) officially link a person or group to an organization. ▶ n. /ə'filēit/ an affiliated person or group.

> SYNONYMS ▶ v. **associate**, unite, combine, join (up), join forces, link up, ally, align, amalgamate, merge.

■ **af·fil·i·a·tion** /əˌfilē'āsHən/ n.

af·fin·i·ty /ə'finitē/ ▶ n. (plural **affinities**) **1** a natural liking or understanding. **2** a close relationship between people or things with similar qualities.

> SYNONYMS **empathy**, rapport, sympathy, accord, harmony, similarity, relationship, bond, closeness, understanding; informal chemistry. ANTONYMS aversion.

af·firm /ə'fərm/ ▶ v. state firmly or publicly.

> SYNONYMS **declare**, state, assert, proclaim, pronounce, attest, swear, maintain, avow. ANTONYMS deny.

af·firm·a·tion /ˌafər'māsHən/ ▶ n. **1** the action or process of affirming or being affirmed. **2** Law a formal declaration by a person who declines to take an oath for reasons of conscience.

af·firm·a·tive /ə'fərmətiv/ ▶ **adj.** agreeing with a statement, or consenting to a request.

> SYNONYMS **positive**, assenting, consenting, approving, favorable. ANTONYMS negative.

□ **affirmative action** action favoring people who are often discriminated against. ■ **af·firm·a·tive·ly** adv.

af·fix ▶ **v.** /ə'fiks/ attach or fasten something to something else. ▶ **n.** /'a,fiks/ Grammar a prefix or suffix.

af·flict /ə'flikt/ ▶ **v.** cause pain or suffering to.

> SYNONYMS **trouble**, burden, distress, beset, harass, worry, oppress, torment, plague, bedevil.

■ **af·flic·tion** /ə'flikSHən/ **n.**

af·flu·ent /'aflo͞oənt, ə'flo͞o-/ ▶ **adj.** wealthy; rich.

> SYNONYMS **wealthy**, rich, prosperous, well off, well-to-do, of means; informal well-heeled, rolling in it, made of money, loaded. ANTONYMS poor.

■ **af·flu·ence** **n.**

af·ford /ə'fôrd/ ▶ **v. 1** have enough money or time for. **2** provide an opportunity or facility: *the rooftop terrace affords beautiful views.*

> SYNONYMS **1 pay for**, find the money for, run to, stand, manage, spare. **2 give**, offer, supply, provide, furnish, yield.

■ **af·ford·a·bil·i·ty** /ə,fôrdə'bilitē/ **n.** **af·ford·a·ble** adj.

af·fray /ə'frā/ ▶ **n.** Law, dated a breach of the peace by fighting in a public place.

af·front /ə'frənt/ ▶ **n.** an action or remark that offends someone. ▶ **v.** offend someone.

> SYNONYMS ▶ **n.** *an affront to public morality* **insult**, offense, slight, snub, put-down, provocation, injury; outrage, atrocity, scandal; informal slap in the face, kick in the teeth. ▶ **v.** *she was affronted by his familiarity* **insult**, offend, provoke, pique, wound, hurt; put out, irk, displease, bother, rankle, vex, gall; outrage, scandalize; informal needle.

Af·ghan /'af,gan/ ▶ **n.** a person from Afghanistan. ▶ **adj.** relating to Afghanistan.

a·fi·ci·o·na·do /ə,fisH(ē)ə'nädō, ə,fisyə-/ ▶ **n.** (plural **aficionados**) a person who knows a lot about an activity or subject and is very enthusiastic about it.

> SYNONYMS **connoisseur**, expert, authority, specialist, pundit; enthusiast, devotee; informal buff, freak, nut, fiend, maniac, fanatic, addict.

a·field /ə'fēld/ ▶ **adv.** to or at a distance: *competitors from as far afield as Hong Kong.*

a·flame /ə'flām/ ▶ **adj.** in flames.

a·float /ə'flōt/ ▶ **adj. & adv. 1** floating in water. **2** out of debt or difficulty.

a·foot /ə'fo͝ot/ ▶ **adv. & adj.** happening; in preparation or progress.

a·fore·men·tioned /ə'fôr,mensHənd/ ▶ **adj.** previously mentioned.

a·fraid /ə'frād/ ▶ **adj.** feeling fear.

> SYNONYMS **1 frightened**, scared, terrified, fearful, nervous, petrified, intimidated, cowardly, faint-hearted; informal scared stiff, chicken, spooked. **2 reluctant**, hesitant, unwilling, slow, shy. **3** *I'm afraid I'm late* **sorry**. ANTONYMS brave, confident.

□ **I'm afraid** expressing polite regret.

a·fresh /ə'fresH/ ▶ **adv.** in a new or different way.

Af·ri·can /'afrikən/ ▶ **n.** a person from Africa. ▶ **adj.** relating to Africa or Africans. □ **African American** **1** a black American. **2** relating to black Americans.

Af·ri·kaans /,afri'känz/ ▶ **n.** a language of southern Africa that developed from Dutch.

Af·ri·ka·ner /,afri'känər/ ▶ **n.** an Afrikaans-speaking white person in South Africa.

Af·ro /'afrō/ ▶ **n.** a hairstyle that consists of a mass of very tight curls all round the head.

Af·ro-A·mer·i·can ▶ **n. & adj.** ⇒ **AFRICAN AMERICAN.**

aft /aft/ ▶ **adv. & adj.** at or toward the rear of a ship or an aircraft.

af·ter /'aftər/ ▶ **prep. 1** in the time following an event or another period of time: *shortly after Christmas.* **2** next to and following in order or importance: *in their order of priorities, health comes after housing.* **3** behind: *she went out, shutting the door after her.* **4** trying to find or get: *most of them are after money.* **5** in reference to: *they named her Pauline, after Barbara's mother.* ▶ **conj. & adv.** in the time following an event: *bathtime ended in a flood after the faucets were left running.*

> SYNONYMS ▶ **prep. following**, subsequent to, at the end of, in the wake of.

□ **after all** in spite of any suggestion otherwise. **after hours** after normal working or opening hours.

af·ter·birth /'aftər,bərTH/ ▶ **n.** the placenta and other material that passes out of the mother's uterus after a birth.

af·ter·care /'aftər,ke(ə)r/ ▶ **n.** care of a person after a stay in the hospital or on release from prison.

af·ter·ef·fect /'aftəri,fekt/ ▶ **n.** an effect that happens some time after its cause.

af·ter·glow /'aftər,glō/ ▶ **n.** light remaining in the sky after the sun has set.

af·ter·life /'aftər,līf/ ▶ **n.** life after death.

af·ter·math /'aftər,maTH/ ▶ **n.** the situation that exists as a result of an unpleasant or disastrous event.

> SYNONYMS **consequences**, after-effects, results, repercussions, upshot.

af·ter·noon /,aftər'no͞on/ ▶ **n.** the time from noon or lunchtime to evening.

af·ter·shave /'aftər,sHāv/ ▶ **n.** a scented liquid for men to apply to their skin after shaving.

af·ter·shock /'aftər,sHäk/ ▶ **n.** a smaller earthquake following the main shock of a large earthquake.

af·ter·taste /'aftər,tāst/ ▶ **n.** a strong or unpleasant taste lingering in the mouth after eating or drinking.

af·ter·thought /'aftər,THôt/ ▶ **n.** something that is thought of or added later.

af·ter·ward /'aftərwərd/ (or **afterwards**) ▶ **adv.** at a later or future time.

> SYNONYMS **later**, later on, subsequently, then, next, after this/that, in due course.

af·ter·word /'aftər,wərd/ ▶ **n.** a section at the end of a book, usually by a person other than the author.

Ag ▶ **symbol** the chemical element silver.

a·gain /ə'gen, ə'gān/ ▶ **adv.** **1** once more: *it was great to meet old friends again.* **2** returning to a previous position or condition: *he rose, made the bed, and sat down again.* **3** in addition: *the wages were low, but they made half as much again in tips.*

SYNONYMS **once more**, another time, afresh, anew.

a·gainst /ə'genst, ə'gānst/ ▶ **prep.** **1** in opposition to: *the fight against crime.* **2** in resistance to: *he turned up his collar against the wind.* **3** in contrast to: *the benefits must be weighed against the costs.* **4** in or into contact with: *she stood with her back against the door.*

SYNONYMS **opposed to**, in opposition to, hostile to, antagonistic toward, unsympathetic to, at odds with, in disagreement with; informal anti.

□ **have something against** dislike or bear a grudge against.

a·gape /ə'gāp/ ▶ **adj.** (of a person's mouth) wide open.

ag·ate /'agit/ ▶ **n.** an ornamental stone marked with bands of color.

age /āj/ ▶ **n.** **1** the length of time that a person or thing has existed. **2** a particular stage in someone's life: *children of elementary school age.* **3** old age. **4** a distinct period of history: *the Elizabethan age.* ▶ **v.** (**ages**, **ageing** or **aging**, **aged**) grow old or older.

SYNONYMS ▶ **n.** **1 old age**, maturity, advancing years, elderliness, seniority, senescence. **2 era**, epoch, period, time, generation. ▶ **v.** **1 mature**, mellow, ripen, soften, season, weather. **2 grow old**, decline, wither, fade.

□ **age-old** having existed for a very long time. **come of age** become an adult.

aged ▶ **adj.** **1** /ājd/ of a specified age. **2** /'ājid/ old.

age·ism /'āj,izəm/ ▶ **n.** prejudice or discrimination on the grounds of a person's age. ■ **age·ist adj.** & **n.**

age·less /'ājlis/ ▶ **adj.** not aging or appearing to age.

a·gen·cy /'ājənsē/ ▶ **n.** **1** an organization providing a particular service. **2** action or intervention: *canals carved by the agency of running water.*

SYNONYMS **business**, organization, company, firm, office, bureau.

a·gen·da /ə'jendə/ ▶ **n.** **1** a list of items to be discussed at a meeting. **2** a list of matters to be dealt with.

SYNONYMS **program**, schedule, to-do list, timetable, plan.

a·gent /'ājənt/ ▶ **n.** **1** a person who provides a particular service: *a travel agent.* **2** a spy. **3** a person or thing that takes an active role or produces a particular effect.

SYNONYMS **1 representative**, intermediary, middleman, negotiator, go-between, proxy, broker, emissary, envoy, spokesperson, delegate; informal rep. **2 spy**, secret agent, operative, mole; informal G-man.

a·gent pro·vo·ca·teur /ä,zнän(t) prə,väkə'tər/ ▶ **n.** (plural **agents provocateurs**) a person who tempts suspected criminals to commit a crime and therefore be convicted.

ag·glom·er·a·tion /ə,glämə'rāsнən/ ▶ **n.** a mass or collection of things.

ag·glu·ti·nate /ə'glōōtn,āt/ ▶ **v.** (**agglutinates**, **agglutinating**, **agglutinated**) firmly stick together to form a mass. ■ **ag·glu·ti·na·tion** /ə,glōōtn'āsнən/ **n.**

ag·gran·dize /ə'gran,dīz/ ▶ **v.** (**aggrandizes**, **aggrandizing**, **aggrandized**) make more powerful, important, or impressive. ■ **ag·gran·dize·ment** /-,dīzmənt, -diz-/ **n.**

ag·gra·vate /'agrə,vāt/ ▶ **v.** (**aggravates**, **aggravating**, **aggravated**) **1** make worse. **2** informal annoy or exasperate.

SYNONYMS **1 worsen**, make worse, exacerbate, inflame, compound. **2 annoy**, antagonize, irritate, exasperate, nettle, provoke, get on someone's nerves, rub the wrong way; informal needle, tick off, get someone's goat. ANTONYMS alleviate, improve.

■ **ag·gra·va·tion** /,agrə'vāsнən/ **n.**

ag·gre·gate ▶ **n.** /'agrigit/ **1** a whole formed by combining several different elements. **2** pieces of hard material such as stone, gravel, and sand, used to make concrete. **3** the total score of a player or team in a series of sporting contests. ▶ **adj.** /'agrigit/ formed by combining many separate items. ▶ **v.** /'agri,gāt/ (**aggregates**, **aggregating**, **aggregated**) combine into a whole.

SYNONYMS ▶ **n.** **total**, sum, grand total, combined score.

ag·gres·sion /ə'gresнən/ ▶ **n.** hostile or violent behavior or attitudes.

SYNONYMS **hostility**, belligerence, force, violence, attack.

ag·gres·sive /ə'gresiv/ ▶ **adj.** **1** very angry or hostile. **2** too forceful.

SYNONYMS **1** *aggressive behavior* **violent**, confrontational, antagonistic, combative, pugnacious. **2** *aggressive foreign policy* **warmongering**, warlike, warring, belligerent, bellicose, hawkish, militaristic, expansionist; informal gung-ho. **3** *an aggressive campaign* **assertive**, forceful, pushy, vigorous, energetic, dynamic, audacious; informal in-your-face, feisty. ANTONYMS peaceable, peaceful.

■ **ag·gres·sive·ly adv.** **ag·gres·sive·ness n.**

SPELLING
Double **g**, double **s**: aggre**ss**ive.

ag·gres·sor /ə'gresər/ ▶ **n.** a person or country that attacks another without being provoked.

ag·grieved /ə'grēvd/ ▶ **adj.** resentful because you feel you have been treated unfairly.

SPELLING
Remember, the rule is **i** before **e**, when the sound is *ee*, except after **c**: aggrieved.

a·ghast /ə'gast/ ▶ **adj.** filled with horror or shock.

SYNONYMS **horrified**, appalled, dismayed, thunderstruck, stunned, shocked, staggered; informal flabbergasted.

ag·ile /'ajəl/ ▶ **adj.** **1** able to move quickly and easily. **2** able to think quickly and intelligently.

SYNONYMS **1 nimble**, lithe, supple, graceful, fit, acrobatic, sprightly, spry. **2 alert**, sharp, acute, shrewd, astute, perceptive, quick. ANTONYMS clumsy.

■ **ag·ile·ly** adv. **a·gil·i·ty** /əˈjilitē/ n.

ag·i·tate /ˈajiˌtāt/ ▶ v. (**agitates**, **agitating**, **agitated**) **1** make someone troubled or nervous. **2** try to arouse public concern about an issue. **3** stir or shake a liquid.

SYNONYMS **1 upset**, fluster, ruffle, disconcert, unnerve, disquiet, disturb, distress, unsettle, worry, perturb, trouble; informal rattle, faze. **2 shake**, whisk, beat, stir.

ag·i·ta·tion /ˌajiˈtāsнən/ ▶ n. **1** a state of anxiety or nervous excitement. **2** the action of agitating to arouse concern about something.

ag·i·ta·tor /ˈajiˌtātər/ ▶ n. a person who urges other people to protest or rebel.

ag·nos·tic /agˈnästik/ ▶ n. a person who believes it is impossible to know whether or not God exists. ■ **ag·nos·ti·cism** /-təˌsizəm/ n.

a·go /əˈgō/ ▶ adv. before the present; earlier: *he left five minutes ago.*

a·gog /əˈgäg/ ▶ adj. very eager to hear or see something.

ag·o·nize /ˈagəˌnīz/ ▶ v. (**agonizes**, **agonizing**, **agonized**) **1** worry about something very much. **2** (**agonizing**) very painful or worrying.

SYNONYMS (**agonizing**) **excruciating**, painful, acute, searing, severe, harrowing, torturous.

ag·o·ny /ˈagənē/ ▶ n. (plural **agonies**) extreme suffering.

SYNONYMS **suffering**, torture, pain, torment, anguish.

ag·o·ra /ˈagərə/ ▶ n. (plural **agorae** /-rē/ or **agoras**) (in ancient Greece) a public open space used for meetings and markets.

ag·o·ra·pho·bi·a /ˌagərəˈfōbēə/ ▶ n. abnormal fear of open or public places. ■ **ag·o·ra·pho·bic** adj. & n.

a·grar·i·an /əˈgre(ə)rēən/ ▶ adj. having to do with agriculture.

a·gree /əˈgrē/ ▶ v. (**agrees**, **agreeing**, **agreed**) **1** have the same opinion about something. **2** (**agree to**) say that you will do something that has been suggested by someone else. **3** (**agree with**) be consistent with: *your body language does not agree with what you are saying.* **4** (**agree with**) be good for: *she ate something which didn't agree with her.*

SYNONYMS **1 concur**, see eye to eye, be in sympathy, be as one, be unanimous. **2** *they agreed to a ceasefire* **consent to**, assent to, acquiesce to, allow, approve; formal accede to. **3 match** (**up**), correspond, conform, coincide, fit, tally, be consistent; informal square. **4** *can we agree on a price?* **decide on**, settle on, arrive at, negotiate, shake hands on. ANTONYMS disagree.

a·gree·a·ble /əˈgrēəbəl/ ▶ adj. **1** pleasant. **2** willing to agree to something. **3** acceptable.

SYNONYMS **1** *an agreeable atmosphere* **pleasant**, pleasing, enjoyable, pleasurable, nice, appealing, relaxing, friendly, congenial. **2** *an agreeable man* **likable**, amiable, affable, pleasant, nice, friendly, good-natured, sociable, genial. **3 willing**, amenable, in agreement. ANTONYMS unpleasant.

■ **a·gree·a·ble·ness** n. **a·gree·a·bly** adv.

a·gree·ment /əˈgrēmənt/ ▶ n. **1** the state of sharing the same opinion or feeling. **2** an arrangement that has been made between people. **3** consistency between two things.

SYNONYMS **1 accord**, concurrence, consensus, assent, acceptance, consent, acquiescence. **2 contract**, treaty, pact, concordat, accord, settlement, understanding, bargain. **3 correspondence**, consistency, compatibility, accord, similarity, resemblance, likeness. ANTONYMS discord, dissimilarity.

ag·ri·cul·tur·al /ˌagriˈkəlcнərəl/ ▶ adj. relating to agriculture.

SYNONYMS **farm**, farming, agrarian, rural, rustic, countryside. ANTONYMS urban.

■ **ag·ri·cul·tur·al·ly** adv.

ag·ri·cul·ture /ˈagriˌkəlcнər/ ▶ n. the science or practice of farming.

SYNONYMS **farming**, cultivation, husbandry, agribusiness, agronomy.

a·gron·o·my /əˈgränəmē/ ▶ n. the science of soil management and crop production. ■ **ag·ro·nom·ic** /ˌagrəˈnämik/ adj. **a·gron·o·mist** n.

a·ground /əˈground/ ▶ adj. & adv. (of a ship) touching the bottom in shallow water.

a·gue /ˈāˌgyo͞o/ ▶ n. old use malaria or some other illness involving fever and shivering.

a·head /əˈhed/ ▶ adv. **1** further forward: *he had to pay attention to the road ahead.* **2** in the lead: *the Yankees were ahead by four.* **3** in advance: *we have to plan ahead.* □ **ahead of 1** before. **2** earlier than planned or expected.

a·hoy /əˈhoi/ ▶ exclam. a call used by people in ships or boats to attract attention.

AI ▶ abbr. artificial intelligence.

aid /ād/ ▶ n. **1** help or support. **2** food or money given to a country in need of help. ▶ v. give help to.

SYNONYMS ▶ n. **1** *with the aid of his colleagues* **assistance**, support, help, backing, cooperation, a helping hand. **2** *humanitarian aid* **relief**, assistance, support, subsidy, funding, donations, grants; historical alms. ANTONYMS hindrance. ▶ v. **help**, assist, be of service, support, encourage, further, boost, promote, facilitate. ANTONYMS hinder.

aide /ād/ ▶ n. an assistant to a political leader.

SYNONYMS **assistant**, helper, adviser, supporter, right-hand man/woman, adjutant, deputy, second (in command), lieutenant.

aide-de-camp /ˈād də ˈkamp/ ▶ n. (plural **aides-de-camp**) a military officer acting as a personal assistant to a senior officer.

AIDS /ādz/ ▶ n. a disease, caused by the HIV virus and transmitted in body fluids, that breaks down the sufferer's natural defenses against infection.

ai·ki·do /ˌīkēˈdō, īˈkēdō/ ▶ n. a Japanese martial art.

ail /āl/ ▶ v. old use cause someone to suffer or have problems.

ail·ing /ˈāliɴɢ/ ▶ adj. in bad health.

SYNONYMS **1 ill**, sick, unwell, sickly, poorly, weak, in poor/bad health, infirm. **2 failing**, weak, poor, fragile, unstable. ANTONYMS healthy.

ail·ment /ˈālmənt/ ▶ n. a minor illness.

SYNONYMS **illness**, disease, disorder, affliction, malady, complaint, infirmity; informal bug, virus.

aim /ām/ ▶ **v. 1** point a weapon, camera, etc., at a target. **2** try to achieve something. ▶ **n. 1** a purpose or intention. **2** the aiming of a weapon or missile.

> SYNONYMS ▶ **v. 1** *he aimed the rifle* **point**, direct, train, sight, line up. **2** *she* ***aimed at*** *the target* **take aim at**, fix on, zero in on, draw a bead on. **3** *this food is* ***aimed at*** *children* **target at**, intend for, direct at, design for, tailor for, market to, pitch to/at. **4 intend**, mean, hope, want, plan, propose. ▶ **n. objective**, object, goal, end, target, design, desire, intention, intent, plan, purpose, ambition, aspiration, wish, dream, hope.

□ **take aim** point a weapon or camera at a target.

aim·less /ˈāmlis/ ▶ **adj.** having no direction or purpose.

> SYNONYMS **purposeless**, pointless, directionless, undirected, random. ANTONYMS purposeful.

■ **aim·less·ly adv.**

ain't /ānt/ ▶ **contr.** informal **1** am not; are not; is not. **2** has not; have not.

> **USAGE**
> Do not use **ain't** when writing or speaking in a formal situation.

air /e(ə)r/ ▶ **n. 1** the invisible mixture of gases surrounding the earth. **2** the open space above the surface of the earth. **3** (**an air of**) an impression of: *she answered with a faint air of boredom.* **4** (**airs**) a pretentious or condescending way of behaving. **5** a tune. ▶ **v. 1** express an opinion or complaint publicly. **2** broadcast a program on radio or television. **3** expose something to fresh or warm air.

> SYNONYMS ▶ **n. 1 breeze**, draft, wind, gust/puff of wind; literary zephyr. **2** *an air of defiance* **look**, appearance, impression, aspect, manner, tone, feel, atmosphere, mood. ▶ **v. 1 express**, voice, make public, articulate, give vent to, state, declare. **2 ventilate**, freshen, refresh, cool.

□ **air conditioner** a device for air conditioning. **air conditioning** a system that cools the air in a building or vehicle. **air force** the branch of the armed forces concerned with fighting in the air. **air gun** a gun that uses compressed air to fire pellets. **air traffic control** the people on the ground who control the movements of aircraft within a particular area. **in the air** noticeable all around. **on the air** being broadcast on radio or television. **up in the air** unresolved. **walk on air** feel extremely pleased or happy.

air·bag /ˈe(ə)rˌbag/ ▶ **n.** a safety device that inflates rapidly when there is a sudden impact, so protecting a vehicle's occupants in a collision.

air·base /ˈe(ə)rˌbās/ ▶ **n.** a base for military aircraft.

air·borne /ˈe(ə)rˌbôrn/ ▶ **adj. 1** carried or spread through the air. **2** (of an aircraft) in the air; flying.

air·brush /ˈe(ə)rˌbrəsʜ/ ▶ **n.** a device for spraying paint by means of compressed air. ▶ **v.** paint a picture or alter a photograph with an airbrush.

air·craft /ˈe(ə)rˌkraft/ ▶ **n.** (plural **aircraft**) a plane, helicopter, or other machine that can fly. □ **aircraft carrier** a large warship from which aircraft can take off and land.

air·crew /ˈe(ə)rˌkro͞o/ ▶ **n.** the crew of an aircraft.

Aire·dale /ˈe(ə)rˌdāl/ ▶ **n.** a large rough-coated black-and-tan breed of terrier.

air·fare /ˈe(ə)rˌfe(ə)r/ ▶ **n.** the price to be paid by an aircraft passenger for a journey.

air·field /ˈe(ə)rˌfēld/ ▶ **n.** an area of ground where aircraft can take off and land.

air·foil /ˈe(ə)rˌfoil/ ▶ **n.** a curved structure, such as a wing, designed to give an aircraft lift.

air·head /ˈe(ə)rˌhed/ ▶ **n.** informal a stupid person.

air·ing /ˈe(ə)rɪɴɢ/ ▶ **n. 1** an act of exposing laundry or a place to warm or fresh air. **2** a public expression of an opinion or discussion of a subject.

air·less /ˈe(ə)rlis/ ▶ **adj.** stuffy; not ventilated.

> SYNONYMS **stuffy**, close, muggy, humid, stifling, suffocating, oppressive, unventilated. ANTONYMS airy.

air·lift /ˈe(ə)rˌlift/ ▶ **n.** an act of transporting supplies by aircraft.

air·line /ˈe(ə)rˌlīn/ ▶ **n.** a company that provides regular flights for the public to use.

air·lin·er /ˈe(ə)rˌlīnər/ ▶ **n.** a large passenger aircraft.

air·lock /ˈe(ə)rˌläk/ ▶ **n. 1** a bubble of air that stops the flow in a pump or pipe. **2** a compartment that allows people to move between areas that are at different pressures.

air·mail /ˈe(ə)rˌmāl/ ▶ **n.** a system of transporting mail overseas by air.

air·man /ˈe(ə)rmən/ ▶ **n.** (plural **airmen**) a pilot or crew member in a military aircraft.

air·plane /ˈe(ə)rˌplān/ ▶ **n.** a powered flying vehicle with fixed wings.

air·play /ˈe(ə)rˌplā/ ▶ **n.** broadcasting time devoted to a particular record, performer, or type of music.

air·port /ˈe(ə)rˌpôrt/ ▶ **n.** an area consisting of a set of runways and buildings where nonmilitary aircraft can take off and land.

air·ship /ˈe(ə)rˌsʜip/ ▶ **n.** a large aircraft filled with gas that is lighter than air.

air·space /ˈe(ə)rˌspās/ ▶ **n.** the part of the air above a particular country.

air·speed /ˈe(ə)rˌspēd/ ▶ **n.** the speed of an aircraft in relation to the air through which it is moving.

air·stream /ˈe(ə)rˌstrēm/ ▶ **n.** a current of air.

air·strip /ˈe(ə)rˌstrip/ ▶ **n.** a strip of ground where aircraft can take off and land.

air·tight /ˈe(ə)rˌtīt/ ▶ **adj. 1** not allowing air to escape or pass through. **2** unable to be proved false: *an airtight alibi.*

air·time /ˈe(ə)rˌtīm/ ▶ **n.** time during which a broadcast is being transmitted.

air·waves /ˈe(ə)rˌwāvz/ ▶ **pl.n.** the radio frequencies used for broadcasting.

air·way /ˈeərˌwā/ ▶ **n. 1** the passage by which air reaches the lungs. **2** a recognized route followed by aircraft.

air·wor·thy /ˈe(ə)rˌwərᴛʜē/ ▶ **adj.** (of an aircraft) safe to fly.

air·y /ˈe(ə)rē/ ▶ **adj.** (**airier**, **airiest**) **1** spacious and having plenty of fresh air. **2** showing that you feel something is not worth serious consideration: *her airy unconcern for budgeting.* **3** light as air; delicate.

> SYNONYMS **spacious**, uncluttered, light, bright, well-ventilated, fresh. ANTONYMS airless, stuffy.

■ **air·i·ly adv. air·i·ness n.**

aisle /īl/ ▶ **n.** a passage between rows of seats in a public building, aircraft, or train or between shelves in a store.

SYNONYMS **passage**, passageway, lane, path, gangway, walkway.

aitch /āCH/ ▶ **n.** the letter H.

a·jar /ə'jär/ ▶ **adv. & adj.** (of a door or window) slightly open.

aka ▶ **abbr.** also known as: *John Merrick, aka the Elephant Man.*

a·kim·bo /ə'kimbō/ ▶ **adv.** with hands on the hips and elbows turned outward.

a·kin /ə'kin/ ▶ **adj. 1** similar in nature or type. **2** related by blood.

SYNONYMS **similar**, related, close, near, comparable, equivalent, connected, alike, analogous. ANTONYMS unlike.

Al ▶ **symbol** the chemical element aluminum.

al·a·bas·ter /'alə,bastər/ ▶ **n.** a white, semitransparent mineral that is carved into ornaments.

à la carte /,ä lä 'kärt, lə/ ▶ **adj. & adv.** (of a menu) offering dishes that are separately priced, rather than part of a set meal.

a·lac·ri·ty /ə'lakritē/ ▶ **n.** great eagerness or enthusiasm.

à la mode /,ä lä 'mōd/ ▶ **adv. & adj. 1** up to date; fashionable. **2** served with ice cream.

a·larm /ə'lärm/ ▶ **n. 1** anxiety or fear caused by being aware of danger. **2** a warning of danger. **3** a sound or device that gives a warning of danger. ▶ **v. 1** frighten or disturb. **2** (**be alarmed**) (of a car or building) be fitted with an alarm.

SYNONYMS ▶ **n. 1 fear**, anxiety, apprehension, distress, agitation, consternation, fright, panic, trepidation. **2 warning**, danger signal, siren, bell, detector, sensor. ANTONYMS calmness, composure. ▶ **v. frighten**, scare, panic, unnerve, distress, agitate, upset, disconcert, shock, disturb; informal rattle, spook.

□ **alarm clock** a clock set to sound at a particular time to wake you up.

a·larm·ist /ə'lärmist/ ▶ **n.** a person who exaggerates a danger and causes unnecessary alarm. ▶ **adj.** causing needless alarm.

a·las /ə'las/ ▶ **exclam.** literary or humorous an expression of grief, pity, or concern.

al·ba·core /'albə,kôr/ ▶ **n.** a tuna of warm seas that travels in large schools and is an important food fish.

Al·ba·ni·an /al'bānēən, ôl-/ ▶ **n. 1** a person from Albania. **2** the language of Albania. ▶ **adj.** relating to Albania.

al·ba·tross /'albə,trôs, -,träs/ ▶ **n.** (plural **albatrosses**) a very large white seabird with long, narrow wings.

al·be·it /ôl'bē-it, al-/ ▶ **conj.** though: *he was making progress, albeit rather slowly.*

al·bi·no /al'bīnō/ ▶ **n.** (plural **albinos**) a person or animal born with white skin and hair and pink eyes. ■ **al·bi·nism** /'albə,nizəm/ **n.**

al·bum /'albəm/ ▶ **n. 1** a blank book for displaying photographs, stamps, etc. **2** a collection of musical recordings issued as a single item.

al·bu·men /al'byo͞omən/ ▶ **n.** egg white.

al·bu·min /al'byo͞omən/ ▶ **n.** Biochemistry a water-soluble form of protein found especially in blood and egg white.

al·che·my /'alkəmē/ ▶ **n.** a medieval form of chemistry that was chiefly concerned with trying to convert ordinary metals into gold. ■ **al·chem·i·cal** /al'kemikəl/ **adj. al·che·mist n.**

al·co·hol /'alkə,hôl, -,häl/ ▶ **n. 1** drinks containing a colorless liquid that can make people drunk, such as wine, beer, and liquor. **2** this liquid.

al·co·hol·ic /,alkə'hôlik, -'häl-/ ▶ **adj.** relating to alcohol. ▶ **n.** a person suffering from alcoholism.

SYNONYMS ▶ **adj. intoxicating**, strong, hard, stiff, fermented, brewed, distilled. ▶ **n. drunkard**, dipsomaniac, drunk, heavy drinker, problem drinker, alcohol abuser; informal lush, alky, dipso, wino.

al·co·hol·ism /'alkəhô,lizəm, -hä-/ ▶ **n.** addiction to alcoholic drink.

al·cove /'al,kōv/ ▶ **n.** a recess in the wall of a room.

al·de·hyde /'aldə,hīd/ ▶ **n.** Chemistry a kind of compound made by oxidation of an alcohol.

al den·te /äl 'dentā, al/ ▶ **adj. & adv.** (of food) cooked so as to be still firm when bitten.

al·der /'ôldər/ ▶ **n.** a tree of the birch family, which produces catkins and woody cones.

al·der·man /'ôldərmən/ ▶ **n.** (plural **aldermen**) an elected member of a municipal council.

ale /āl/ ▶ **n.** a fermented beverage similar to beer with a bitter flavor and higher alcoholic content.

a·le·a·to·ry /'ālēə,tôrē, 'al-/ (also **aleatoric** /,ālēə'tôrik, ,al-/) ▶ **adj.** depending on the throw of a dice or on chance.

a·lert /ə'lərt/ ▶ **adj. 1** quick to notice and respond to danger or change. **2** quick-thinking; intelligent. ▶ **n. 1** a watchful state. **2** a warning of danger. ▶ **v.** warn someone of a danger or problem.

SYNONYMS ▶ **adj. 1 vigilant**, watchful, attentive, observant, wide awake, on the lookout, on your guard/toes; informal keeping your eyes open/peeled. **2 quick-witted**, sharp, bright, quick, perceptive, on your toes; informal on the ball, quick on the uptake, all there, with it. ANTONYMS inattentive. ▶ **n. 1 vigilance**, watchfulness, attentiveness, alertness. **2 warning**, notification, notice, siren, alarm, signal. ▶ **v. warn**, notify, inform, apprise, forewarn, put someone on their guard; informal tip off.

■ **a·lert·ly adv. a·lert·ness n.**

Al·ex·an·der tech·nique /,alig'zandər/ ▶ **n.** a system designed to promote well-being through the control of posture.

al·ex·an·drine /,alig'zandrin, -,drēn/ ▶ **adj.** Poetry (of a line of verse) having six iambic feet.

al·fal·fa /al'falfə/ ▶ **n.** a plant with bluish flowers, used as food for animals.

al·fres·co /al'freskō, äl-/ ▶ **adv. & adj.** in the open air.

al·gae /'aljē/ ▶ **pl.n.** simple plants that do not have true stems, roots, and leaves, such as seaweed.

al·ge·bra /'aljəbrə/ ▶ **n.** the branch of mathematics in which letters and other symbols are used to represent numbers and quantities. ■ **al·ge·bra·ic** /,aljə'brā-ik/ **adj.**

Al·ge·ri·an /al'ji(ə)rēən/ ▶ **n.** a person from Algeria. ▶ **adj.** relating to Algeria.

Al·gon·quin /al'gäNGk(w)in/ (also **Algonkin** /-kin/) ▶ **n. 1** a member of an American Indian people living in Canada in the region of the Ottawa River. **2** the language of this people. ▶ **adj.** relating to this people.

al·go·rithm /ˈalgəˌriTHəm/ ▶ **n.** a process or set of rules used in calculations.

a·li·as /ˈālēəs/ ▶ **adv.** also known as. ▶ **n.** a false identity.

al·i·bi /ˈaləˌbī/ ▶ **n.** (plural **alibis**) a piece of evidence that a person was somewhere else when a crime was committed.

a·li·en /ˈālyən, ˈālēən/ ▶ **adj. 1** belonging to a foreign country. **2** unfamiliar and unappealing: *principles that are alien to them.* **3** from another world. ▶ **n. 1** a foreigner. **2** a being from another world.

SYNONYMS ▶ **adj. foreign**, unfamiliar, unknown, peculiar, exotic, strange. ANTONYMS native, familiar. ▶ **n. 1 foreigner**, non-native, immigrant, émigré, stranger. **2 extraterrestrial**, ET; informal little green man.

■ **al·ien·ness n.**

al·ien·ate /ˈālēəˌnāt, ˈālyə-/ ▶ **v.** (**alienates**, **alienating**, **alienated**) **1** make someone feel isolated. **2** lose the support or sympathy of.

SYNONYMS **isolate**, distance, estrange, cut off, turn away, drive apart, set at variance/odds, drive a wedge between.

al·ien·a·tion /ˌālēəˈnāSHən, ˌālyə-/ ▶ **n.** the state of being alienated.

SYNONYMS **isolation**, detachment, estrangement, distance, separation.

a·light¹ /əˈlīt/ ▶ **v. 1** get off a train or bus. **2** (of a bird) land on something. **3** (**alight on**) happen to notice.

a·light² /əˈlīt/ ▶ **adv. & adj. 1** on fire. **2** shining brightly.

SYNONYMS **burning**, ablaze, on fire, in flames, blazing, lit.

a·lign /əˈlīn/ ▶ **v. 1** place something in a straight line or in the right position in relation to other things. **2** (**align yourself with**) be on the side of.

SYNONYMS **1 line up**, range, rank, straighten, even up, arrange, coordinate. **2** *he aligned himself with the workers* **ally**, affiliate, associate, side, join forces, team up, band together, throw in your lot.

a·lign·ment /əˈlīnmənt/ ▶ **n. 1** arrangement in a straight line or in the correct position. **2** the route or course of a road or railroad.

a·like /əˈlīk/ ▶ **adj.** similar: *the houses all looked alike.* ▶ **adv.** in a similar way: *the girls dressed alike in black pants and white blouses.*

SYNONYMS ▶ **adj. similar**, (much) the same, analogous, corresponding, indistinguishable, identical, uniform, interchangeable. ANTONYMS different. ▶ **adv.** *great minds think alike* **similarly**, the same way, correspondingly, analogously, identically. ANTONYMS differently.

al·i·men·ta·ry ca·nal /ˌaləˈment(ə)rē/ ▶ **n.** the passage along which food passes through the body.

al·i·mo·ny /ˈaləˌmōnē/ ▶ **n.** financial support for a husband or wife after separation or divorce.

A-line /ˈā ˌlīn/ ▶ **adj.** (of a garment) slightly flared.

al·i·quot /ˈalikwət/ ▶ **n.** a portion or sample taken for analysis or treatment.

A-list /ˈā ˌlist/ ▶ **n.** a list of the most famous or sought-after people, especially in show business.

a·live /əˈlīv/ ▶ **adj. 1** living; not dead. **2** continuing in existence or use: *keeping hope alive.* **3** alert and active. **4** (**alive with**) full of: *in spring those cliffs are alive with gulls.* **5** (**alive to**) aware of and willing to respond to: *the manager is always alive to new ideas.*

SYNONYMS **1 active**, in existence, functioning, in operation, operative, on the map. **2 alert**, awake, aware, conscious, mindful, heedful, sensitive. ANTONYMS dead, unaware.

al·ka·li /ˈalkəˌlī/ ▶ **n.** (plural **alkalis**) a substance whose chemical properties include turning litmus blue and neutralizing acids. ■ **al·ka·line** /ˈalkəlin, -ˌlīn/ **adj.**

al·kane /ˈalˌkān/ ▶ **n.** Chemistry any of the series of saturated hydrocarbons whose simplest members are methane and ethane.

al·kene /ˈalˌkēn/ ▶ **n.** Chemistry any of the series of unsaturated hydrocarbons containing a double bond, of which the simplest member is ethylene.

all /ôl/ ▶ **determiner 1** the whole quantity or extent of: *all her money.* **2** any whatever: *he denied all knowledge.* **3** the greatest possible: *with all speed.* ▶ **pron.** everything or everyone. ▶ **adv. 1** completely. **2** indicating an equal score: *one-all.* □ **all along** from the beginning. **all and sundry** everyone. **all around 1** in all respects. **2** for or by each person. **all-around 1** having a great many abilities or uses. **2** in all respects. **all but 1** very nearly: *the subject was all but forgotten.* **2** all except: *we have support from all but one of the networks.* **the all clear** a signal that danger is over. **all for** informal strongly in favor of. **all in** informal exhausted. **all in all** on the whole. **all out** trying as hard as you can. **all over** informal **1** everywhere. **2** informal typical of the person mentioned. **all over the place** informal **1** everywhere. **2** in a state of disorder. **all right 1** satisfactory; acceptable. **2** safe; unharmed. **3** able to be done or to happen; allowable. **4** fairly well. **All Saints' Day** a Christian festival in honor of all the saints, held (in the Western Church) on November 1. **All Souls' Day** a Catholic festival with prayers for the souls of the dead in purgatory, held on November 2. **all told** in total. **at all** in any way. **in all** in total. **on all fours** on hands and knees. **your all** your fullest effort.

Al·lah /ˈälə, ˈalə/ ▶ **n.** the Arabic name of God.

al·lay /əˈlā/ ▶ **v.** reduce or end fear, concern, or difficulty.

SYNONYMS **reduce**, diminish, decrease, lessen, alleviate, assuage, ease, relieve, soothe, soften, calm. ANTONYMS increase, intensify.

al·le·ga·tion /ˌaliˈgāSHən/ ▶ **n.** a claim that someone has done something illegal or wrong.

SYNONYMS **claim**, assertion, charge, accusation, contention.

al·lege /əˈlej/ ▶ **v.** (**alleges**, **alleging**, **alleged**) **1** claim that someone has done something illegal or wrong. **2** (**alleged**) declared but not proved.

SYNONYMS **1 claim**, assert, accuse, contend, state, declare, maintain. **2** (**alleged**) **reported**, supposed, so-called, claimed, professed, purported, ostensible, unproven.

■ **al·leg·ed·ly** /-idlē/ **adv.**

al·le·giance /əˈlējəns/ ▶ **n.** loyalty to a person, group, or cause.

SYNONYMS **loyalty**, faithfulness, fidelity, obedience, adherence, devotion; historical fealty. ANTONYMS disloyalty, treachery.

al·le·go·ry /ˈaləˌgôrē/ ▶ **n.** (plural **allegories**) a story, poem, or picture that contains a hidden meaning. ■ **al·le·gor·i·cal** /ˌaliˈgôrikəl, -ˈgär-/ **adj.**

al·le·gret·to /ˌaliˈgretō/ ▶ **adv. & adj.** Music at a fairly brisk speed.

al·le·gro /əˈlegrō/ ▶ **adj. & adv.** Music at a brisk speed.

al·le·lu·ia /ˌaləˈlo͞oyə/ (or **hallelujah** /ˌhaləˈlo͞oyə/) ▶ **exclam.** God be praised.

Al·len screw /ˈalən/ ▶ **n.** trademark a screw with a hexagonal socket in the head.

Al·len wrench /ˈalən/ ▶ **n.** trademark a wrench designed to turn an Allen screw.

al·ler·gen /ˈalərjən/ ▶ **n.** a substance that causes an allergic reaction.

al·ler·gen·ic /ˌalərˈjenik/ ▶ **adj.** likely to cause an allergic reaction.

al·ler·gic /əˈlərjik/ ▶ **adj. 1** caused by an allergy: *an allergic reaction.* **2** having an allergy.

al·ler·gy /ˈalərjē/ ▶ **n.** (plural **allergies**) a medical condition that makes you feel ill when you eat or come into contact with a particular substance.

al·le·vi·ate /əˈlēvēˌāt/ ▶ **v.** (**alleviates**, **alleviating**, **alleviated**) make a pain or problem less severe.

SYNONYMS **ease**, relieve, take the edge off, deaden, dull, lessen, reduce, moderate, allay, assuage, soothe, help, soften. ANTONYMS aggravate.

■ **al·le·vi·a·tion** /əˌlēvēˈāsHən/ **n.**

al·ley /ˈalē/ ▶ **n.** (plural **alleys**) **1** (also **alleyway** /ˈalēˌwā/) a narrow passageway between or behind buildings. **2** a path in a park or garden. **3** a long, narrow area used in the game of bowling.

SYNONYMS **passage**, passageway, alleyway, backstreet, lane, path, pathway, walk.

al·li·ance /əˈlīəns/ ▶ **n. 1** the state of being joined or associated. **2** an agreement made between countries or organizations to work together. **3** a relationship or connection: *an alliance between medicine and morality.*

SYNONYMS **association**, union, league, confederation, federation, syndicate, consortium, cartel, coalition, partnership, relationship, marriage, cooperation.

al·lied /əˈlīd, ˈalˌīd/ ▶ **adj. 1** joined by an alliance. **2** (**Allied**) relating to the United States and its allies in World War I and World War II. **3** (**allied to** or **with**) combined with.

SYNONYMS **associated**, united, related, connected, interconnected, linked, cooperating, in league, affiliated, combined, coupled, married. ANTONYMS unrelated, independent.

al·li·ga·tor /ˈaliˌgātər/ ▶ **n.** a large reptile similar to a crocodile but with a broader and shorter head. □ **alligator pear** ⇨ **AVOCADO**.

al·lit·er·a·tion /əˌlitəˈrāsHən/ ▶ **n.** the occurrence of the same letter or sound at the beginning of words that are next to or close to each other. ■ **al·lit·er·a·tive** /əˈlitərətiv, -ˌrātiv/ **adj.**

al·lo·cate /ˈaləˌkāt/ ▶ **v.** (**allocates**, **allocating**, **allocated**) assign or give to.

SYNONYMS **allot**, assign, set aside, earmark, consign, distribute, apportion, share out, dole out, give out.

al·lo·ca·tion /ˌaləˈkāsHən/ ▶ **n. 1** the action of allocating something. **2** an amount of a resource given to someone.

SYNONYMS **1 allotment**, assignment, distribution, sharing out, doling out, giving out. **2 allowance**, allotment, consignment, quota, share, ration; informal cut.

al·lot /əˈlät/ ▶ **v.** (**allots**, **allotting**, **allotted**) give out something as a share or assign as a task.

al·lot·ment /əˈlätmənt/ ▶ **n. 1** the action of allotting something. **2** an amount of something allotted to someone.

al·lo·trope /ˈaləˌtrōp/ ▶ **n.** Chemistry each of two or more different physical forms in which a particular element exists. ■ **al·lo·trop·ic** /ˌaləˈträpik, -ˈtrō-/ **adj.**

al·low /əˈlou/ ▶ **v. 1** let someone do something. **2** (**allow for**) take into consideration. **3** provide or set aside: *allow an hour or so for driving.* **4** admit that something is true.

SYNONYMS **1 permit**, let, enable, authorize, give leave, license, entitle, consent to, assent to, acquiesce in, agree to, approve; informal give the go-ahead to, give the thumbs up to, OK, give the green light to; formal accede to. **2 set aside**, allocate, allot, earmark, designate, reserve. ANTONYMS prevent, forbid.

■ **al·low·a·ble** **adj.**

USAGE

Don't confuse **allowed**, meaning 'permitted,' with **aloud**, meaning 'out loud.'

al·low·ance /əˈlou-əns/ ▶ **n. 1** the amount of something that is allowed. **2** a sum of money paid regularly to a person, usually for expenses. **3** a reduction in price: *a trade-in allowance on our old car.*

SYNONYMS **1 allocation**, allotment, quota, share, ration, grant, limit. **2 payment**, contribution, grant, handout, subsidy, maintenance.

□ **make allowances for 1** take into consideration. **2** treat someone less harshly because they are in difficult circumstances.

al·loy ▶ **n.** /ˈaˌloi/ **1** a mixture of two or more metals. **2** an inferior metal mixed with a precious one. ▶ **v.** /ˈaˌloi, əˈloi/ mix metals to make an alloy.

all·spice /ˈôlˌspīs/ ▶ **n.** the dried fruit of a Caribbean tree, used as a spice in cooking.

al·lude /əˈlo͞od/ ▶ **v.** (**alludes**, **alluding**, **alluded**) (**allude to**) **1** mention in passing. **2** hint at.

SYNONYMS *I have **alluded to** that possibility* **refer to**, touch on, suggest, hint at, imply, make an allusion to, mention (in passing), intimate.

al·lure /əˈlo͝or/ ▶ **n.** the quality of being very attractive or appealing.

al·lur·ing /əˈlo͝oriNG/ ▶ **adj.** very attractive or tempting.

SYNONYMS **enticing**, tempting, attractive, appealing, inviting, captivating, seductive; enchanting, charming, fascinating.

■ **al·lur·ing·ly** **adv.**

al·lu·sion /ə'lo͞ozнən/ ▶ **n.** an indirect reference to something.

SYNONYMS **reference**, mention, suggestion, intimation, hint.

■ **al·lu·sive** /ə'lo͞osiv/ **adj.**

al·lu·vi·al /ə'lo͞ovēəl/ ▶ **adj.** made of clay, silt, and sand that is left by floodwater.

al·ly ▶ **n.** /'alī/ (plural **allies**) **1** a person, organization, or country that cooperates with another. **2** (**the Allies**) the countries that fought with the United States in World War I and World War II. ▶ **v.** /ə'lī/ (**allies, allying, allied** /ə'līd, 'al,īd/) **1** (**ally something to** or **with**) combine one resource with another in a way that benefits both: *he allied his racing experience with his father's business skills.* **2** (**ally yourself with**) side with.

SYNONYMS ▶ **n. associate**, colleague, friend, confederate, partner, supporter. ANTONYMS enemy, opponent. ▶ **v. unite**, combine, join (up), join forces, band together, team up, collaborate, side, align yourself.

al·ma ma·ter /'älmə 'mätər, 'almə/ ▶ **n.** the school, college, or university that a person once attended.

al·ma·nac /'ôlmə,nak, 'al-/ (or **almanack**) ▶ **n.** **1** a calendar that gives important dates and also information about the sun, moon, tides, etc. **2** a book published yearly and containing useful information for that year.

al·might·y /ôl'mītē/ ▶ **adj.** **1** having unlimited or very great power. **2** informal enormous. ▶ **n.** (**the Almighty**) God.

al·mond /'ä(l)mənd, 'a(l)-/ ▶ **n.** an oval nut with a woody shell, growing on a tree found in warm climates.

al·most /ôl'mōst, 'ôl,mōst/ ▶ **adv.** very nearly.

SYNONYMS **nearly**, (just) about, practically, virtually, all but, as good as, close to, not quite; informal pretty nearly/much/well; literary well nigh, nigh on.

alms /ä(l)mz/ ▶ **pl.n.** money or goods given to the poor.

alms·house /'ä(l)mz,hous/ ▶ **n.** (in the past) a house built for poor people to live in.

al·oe /'alō/ ▶ **n.** a tropical plant with succulent leaves, whose bitter juice is used in medicine.

al·oe ver·a /'verə, 'vi(ə)rə/ ▶ **n.** a jellylike substance obtained from a kind of aloe, used to soothe the skin.

a·loft /ə'lôft/ ▶ **adj. & adv.** up in or into the air.

a·lo·ha /ə'lō,hä/ ▶ **exclam. & n.** a Hawaiian word used when greeting or parting from someone.

a·lone /ə'lōn/ ▶ **adj. & adv.** **1** on your own. **2** isolated and lonely. **3** only; exclusively.

SYNONYMS **by yourself**, on your own, unaccompanied, solo, single, isolated, solitary, lonely, deserted, abandoned, friendless. ANTONYMS accompanied.

□ **leave** (or **let**) **someone/something alone** **1** abandon or desert someone or something. **2** stop disturbing or interfering with someone or something.

a·long /ə'lônɢ, ə'länɢ/ ▶ **prep. & adv.** **1** moving on a surface in a constant direction: *we were driving along a narrow road.* **2** extending on a surface in a horizontal line: *the path along the cliff.* **3** in company with other people: *he had brought along a friend of his.* □ **along with** in company with, or at the same time as. **come along** arrive.

a·long·side /ə'lônɢ'sīd, ə'länɢ-/ ▶ **prep.** **1** close to the side of; next to. **2** at the same time as.

a·loof /ə'lo͞of/ ▶ **adj.** not friendly or showing an interest in other people.

SYNONYMS **distant**, detached, unfriendly, remote, unapproachable, reserved, unforthcoming, uncommunicative; informal standoffish. ANTONYMS friendly.

■ **a·loof·ness** **n.**

al·o·pe·ci·a /,alə'pēsн(ē)ə/ ▶ **n.** abnormal loss of hair.

a·loud /ə'loud/ ▶ **adv.** not silently; out loud.

USAGE

Don't confuse **aloud**, meaning 'out loud,' with **allowed**, meaning 'permitted.'

alp /alp/ ▶ **n.** **1** a high mountain. **2** (**the Alps**) a high range of mountains in Switzerland and adjoining countries.

al·pac·a /al'pakə/ ▶ **n.** (plural **alpaca** or **alpacas**) a long-haired South American animal related to the llama.

al·pha /'alfə/ ▶ **n.** the first letter of the Greek alphabet (Α, α). ▶ **adj.** referring to the dominant animal or person in a group: *the alpha male.* □ **alpha and omega** the beginning and the end. **alpha particle** Physics a helium nucleus, emitted by some radioactive substances.

al·pha·bet /'alfə,bet, -bit/ ▶ **n.** a set of letters or symbols used to represent the basic speech sounds of a language.

al·pha·bet·i·cal /,alfə'betikəl/ ▶ **adj.** in the order of the letters of the alphabet. ■ **al·pha·bet·i·cal·ly** **adv.**

al·pha·bet·ize /'alfəbi,tīz/ ▶ **v.** arrange words in alphabetical order.

al·pha·nu·mer·ic /,alfən(y)o͞o'merik/ ▶ **adj.** using both letters and numerals.

al·pine /'al,pīn/ ▶ **adj.** **1** relating to or found on high mountains. **2** (**Alpine**) relating to the Alps.

al·read·y /ôl'redē/ ▶ **adv.** **1** before the time in question. **2** as surprisingly soon or early as this.

al·right /ôl'rīt/ see ALL RIGHT.

al·so /'ôlsō/ ▶ **adv.** in addition.

SYNONYMS **too**, as well, besides, in addition, additionally, furthermore, further, moreover, into the bargain, on top (of that), what's more, to boot.

□ **also-ran** a loser in a race or contest.

al·tar /'ôltər/ ▶ **n.** **1** the table in a Christian church at which bread and wine are made sacred. **2** a table or block on which offerings are made to a god or goddess.

al·tar·piece /'ôltər,pēs/ ▶ **n.** a work of art set above and behind an altar.

al·ter /'ôltər/ ▶ **v.** make or become different; change.

SYNONYMS **change**, make/become different, adjust, adapt, amend, modify, revise, rework, redo, transform; informal tweak.

al·ter·a·tion /,ôltə'rāsнən/ ▶ **n.** a change or modification.

SYNONYMS **change**, adjustment, adaptation, modification, amendment, transformation.

al·ter·ca·tion /ˌôltərˈkāsʜən/ ▶ **n.** a noisy argument or disagreement.

al·ter e·go /ˈôltər ˈēgō/ ▶ **n.** **1** another side to a person's normal personality. **2** a close friend who is very like yourself.

al·ter·nate ▶ **v.** /ˈôltərˌnāt/ (**alternates, alternating, alternated**) **1** (of two things or people) repeatedly follow one another in turn. **2** keep changing between two states. ▶ **adj.** /ˈôltərnit/ **1** every other. **2** (of two things) each following and succeeded by the other in a regular pattern.

> SYNONYMS ▶ **v. 1 be interspersed**, follow one another, take turns, oscillate, seesaw. **2 rotate**, swap, exchange, interchange. ▶ **adj. every other**, every second, alternating.

□ **alternating current** an electric current that reverses its direction many times a second.
■ **al·ter·nate·ly adv. al·ter·na·tion** /ˌôltərˈnāsʜən/ **n.**

al·ter·na·tive /ôlˈtərnətiv/ ▶ **adj. 1** (of one or more things) available as another possibility. **2** different from what is usual or traditional: *alternative therapy*. ▶ **n.** one of two or more available possibilities.

> SYNONYMS ▶ **adj. 1 different**, other, second, substitute, alternate, replacement, standby, emergency, reserve, backup, auxiliary, fallback. **2 unorthodox**, unconventional, nonconformist, radical, revolutionary, avant-garde; informal offbeat, way-out. ▶ **n.** (**other**) **option**, (other) choice, substitute, replacement.

■ **al·ter·na·tive·ly adv.**

al·ter·na·tor /ˈôltərˌnātər/ ▶ **n.** a generator that produces an alternating current.

al·though /ôlˈᴛʜō/ ▶ **conj. 1** in spite of the fact that. **2** but.

al·tim·e·ter /alˈtimitər/ ▶ **n.** an instrument that indicates the altitude that has been reached.

al·ti·tude /ˈaltiˌt(y)o͞od/ ▶ **n.** the height of an object or point above sea level or ground level.

al·to /ˈaltō/ ▶ **n.** (plural **altos**) the highest adult male or lowest female singing voice.

al·to·geth·er /ˌôltəˈgeᴛʜər/ ▶ **adv. 1** completely. **2** in total. **3** on the whole.

> SYNONYMS **1 completely**, totally, entirely, absolutely, wholly, fully, thoroughly, utterly, perfectly, one hundred percent, in all respects. **2 in all**, all told, in total.

□ **in the altogether** informal naked.

al·tru·ism /ˈaltro͞oˌizəm/ ▶ **n.** unselfish concern for other people. ■ **al·tru·ist n. al·tru·is·tic** /ˌaltro͞oˈistik/ **adj.**

a·lum /ˈaləm/ ▶ **n.** a compound of aluminum and potassium, used in dyeing and in making leather.

a·lu·mi·nize /əˈlo͞oməˌnīz/ ▶ **v.** (**aluminizes, aluminizing, aluminized**) coat with aluminum.

a·lu·mi·num /əˈlo͞omənəm/ ▶ **n.** a lightweight silvery-gray metal.

a·lum·nus /əˈləmnəs/ ▶ **n.** (plural **alumni** /-nī, -nē/) a former student of a particular school, college, or university.

al·ways /ˈôlˌwāz, -wēz/ ▶ **adv. 1** at all times. **2** forever. **3** repeatedly. **4** failing all else.

> SYNONYMS **1** *he's always late* **every time**, all the time, without fail, consistently, invariably, regularly, habitually, unfailingly. **2** *she's always complaining* **continually**, continuously, constantly, forever, all the time, day and night; informal 24-7. **3** *the place will always be dear to me* **forever**, for good, for evermore, for ever and ever, until the end of time, eternally. ANTONYMS never, seldom.

Alz·hei·mer's dis·ease /ˈältsˌhīmərz, ˈôlts-, ˈälz-, ˈôlz-/ ▶ **n.** a disease of the brain that can affect older people, causing memory loss and confusion.

AM ▶ **abbr.** amplitude modulation.

am /am/ 1st person singular present of **BE**.

a.m. ▶ **abbr.** before noon.

AMA ▶ **abbr.** American Medical Association.

a·mal·gam /əˈmalgəm/ ▶ **n. 1** a mixture or blend of things. **2** an alloy of mercury with another metal.

a·mal·ga·mate /əˈmalgəˌmāt/ ▶ **v.** (**amalgamates, amalgamating, amalgamated**) combine two or more things to form one organization or structure.

> SYNONYMS **combine**, merge, unite, join, fuse, blend, meld, mix, incorporate. ANTONYMS separate.

■ **a·mal·ga·ma·tion** /əˌmalgəˈmāsʜən/ **n.**

a·man·u·en·sis /əˌmanyo͞oˈensis/ ▶ **n.** (plural **amanuenses**) a person who helps a writer with their work, especially by taking dictation or copying manuscripts.

am·a·ryl·lis /ˌaməˈrilis/ ▶ **n.** a plant with large trumpet-shaped flowers.

a·mass /əˈmas/ ▶ **v.** build up over time.

> SYNONYMS **gather**, collect, assemble, accumulate, stockpile, hoard.

am·a·teur /ˈamətər, -ˌtər, -ˌcʜo͝or, -cʜər/ ▶ **n. 1** a person who takes part in a sport or other activity without being paid. **2** a person who is not skilled at an activity. ▶ **adj. 1** non-professional. **2** not skillful.

> SYNONYMS ▶ **n. nonprofessional**, nonspecialist, layman, layperson, dilettante, dabbler. ▶ **adj. nonprofessional**, unpaid, nonspecialist, lay, unqualified, inexperienced. ANTONYMS professional, expert.

■ **am·a·teur·ism n.**

> SPELLING
> Write **-eur**, not **-uer**: amateur.

am·a·teur·ish /ˌaməˈtərisʜ, -ˈt(y)o͝or-, -ˈcʜo͝or-/ ▶ **adj.** not done or made very well; unskillful.

> SYNONYMS **incompetent**, inept, inexpert, unprofessional, amateur, clumsy, crude, second-rate.

am·a·to·ry /ˈaməˌtôrē/ ▶ **adj.** having to do with love or desire.

a·maze /əˈmāz/ ▶ **v.** (**amazes, amazing, amazed**) make someone feel very surprised.

> SYNONYMS **astonish**, astound, surprise, stun, stagger, nonplus, shock, startle, stop someone in their tracks, leave open-mouthed, dumbfound; informal bowl over, flabbergast; (**amazed**) thunderstruck, at a loss for words, speechless.

a·maze·ment /əˈmāzmənt/ ▶ **n.** a feeling of great surprise or wonder.

> SYNONYMS **astonishment**, surprise, shock, speechlessness, awe, wonder.

a·maz·ing /əˈmāziNG/ ▶ **adj.** **1** causing great surprise or wonder; astonishing: *an amazing number of people registered.* **2** informal very good or impressive: *she makes the most amazing cakes.*

SYNONYMS **astonishing**, astounding, surprising, stunning, staggering, breathtaking, awesome, awe-inspiring, sensational, remarkable, spectacular, stupendous, phenomenal, extraordinary, incredible, unbelievable; informal mind-blowing; literary wondrous.

■ **a·maz·ing·ly** **adv.**

Am·a·zon /ˈaməˌzän, -zən/ ▶ **n.** **1** a member of a legendary race of female warriors. **2** a very tall, strong woman. ■ **Am·a·zo·ni·an** /ˌaməˈzōnēən/ **adj.**

am·bas·sa·dor /amˈbasədər, -ˌdôr/ ▶ **n.** **1** a person sent by a state as its representative in a foreign country. **2** a person who represents or promotes a particular activity: *he is a good ambassador for the industry.*

SYNONYMS **envoy**, emissary, representative, diplomat, minister, consul, attaché.

am·ber /ˈambər/ ▶ **n.** **1** a hard, clear yellowish substance used in jewelry. **2** a yellowish color.

am·ber·gris /ˈambərˌgris, -ˌgrē(s)/ ▶ **n.** a wax-like substance produced by sperm whales, used in making perfume.

am·bi·dex·trous /ˌambiˈdekst(ə)rəs/ ▶ **adj.** able to use the right and left hands equally well.

am·bi·ence /ˈambēəns, ˈämbēäns/ (or **ambiance**) ▶ **n.** the character and atmosphere of a place.

SYNONYMS **atmosphere**, air, aura, climate, mood, feel, feeling, vibrations, character, quality, impression, flavor, look, tone; informal vibe(s).

am·bi·ent /ˈambēənt/ ▶ **adj.** **1** relating to the surroundings of something: *the liquid is stored at below ambient temperature.* **2** (of music) quiet and relaxing.

am·bi·gu·i·ty /ˌambiˈgyo͞o-itē/ ▶ **n.** (plural **ambiguities**) the quality of having more than one possible meaning.

am·big·u·ous /amˈbigyo͞oəs/ ▶ **adj.** **1** having more than one possible meaning. **2** not clear or decided.

SYNONYMS **vague**, unclear, ambivalent, double-edged, equivocal, inconclusive, enigmatic, cryptic. ANTONYMS clear.

■ **am·big·u·ous·ly** **adv.**

am·bit /ˈambit/ ▶ **n.** the scope or extent of something.

am·bi·tion /amˈbisHən/ ▶ **n.** **1** a strong desire to do or achieve something. **2** desire for success, wealth, or fame.

SYNONYMS **1 drive**, determination, enterprise, initiative, eagerness, motivation, a sense of purpose; informal get-up-and-go. **2 aspiration**, desire, dream, intention, goal, aim, objective, plan.

am·bi·tious /amˈbisHəs/ ▶ **adj.** **1** having or showing determination to succeed. **2** intended to reach a high standard and therefore difficult to achieve: *an ambitious enterprise.*

SYNONYMS **1 aspiring**, determined, motivated, energetic, committed, purposeful, power-hungry; informal go-ahead, go-getting. **2 challenging**, exacting, demanding, formidable, difficult, hard, tough.

■ **am·bi·tious·ly** **adv.**

am·biv·a·lent /amˈbivələnt/ ▶ **adj.** having mixed feelings about something or someone. ■ **am·biv·a·lence** **n.** **am·biv·a·lent·ly** **adv.**

am·ble /ˈambəl/ ▶ **v.** (**ambles**, **ambling**, **ambled**) walk at a leisurely pace. ▶ **n.** a leisurely walk.

am·bro·sia /amˈbrōzH(ē)ə/ ▶ **n.** **1** Greek & Roman Mythology the food of the gods. **2** something very pleasing to taste or smell.

am·bu·lance /ˈambyələns/ ▶ **n.** a vehicle for taking sick or injured people to and from a hospital.

am·bu·la·to·ry /ˈambyələˌtôrē/ ▶ **adj.** **1** relating to walking. **2** able to walk or move.

am·bush /ˈamˌbo͝osH/ ▶ **n.** a surprise attack by people lying in wait in a hidden position. ▶ **v.** make a surprise attack on someone from a hidden position.

SYNONYMS ▶ **v. surprise**, waylay, trap, ensnare, attack, jump on, pounce on, bushwhack.

a·me·ba /əˈmēbə/ (or **amoeba**) ▶ **n.** (plural **amebas** or **amebae**) a microscopic creature that is made up of a single cell and can change its shape.

a·me·lio·rate /əˈmēlyəˌrāt, əˈmēlēə-/ ▶ **v.** (**ameliorates**, **ameliorating**, **ameliorated**) formal make something better.

a·men /äˈmen, āˈmen/ ▶ **exclam.** a word said at the end of a prayer or hymn, meaning "so be it."

a·me·na·ble /əˈmēnəbəl, əˈmen-/ ▶ **adj.** **1** willing to be persuaded. **2** (**amenable to**) able to be affected by.

a·mend /əˈmend/ ▶ **v.** change or make minor improvements to.

SYNONYMS **revise**, alter, change, modify, adapt, adjust, edit, rewrite, redraft, rephrase, reword.

a·mend·ment /əˈmen(d)mənt/ ▶ **n.** a change or minor improvement.

a·mends /əˈmendz/ ▶ **pl.n.** (**make amends**) make up for a wrongdoing.

SYNONYMS (**make amends for**) **make up for**, atone for, pay for, make good.

a·men·i·ty /əˈmenitē, əˈmē-/ ▶ **n.** (plural **amenities**) a useful or desirable feature of a place.

SYNONYMS **facility**, service, resource, convenience, comfort.

A·mer·i·can /əˈmerikən/ ▶ **adj.** relating to the United States or to the continents of America. ▶ **n.** a person from the United States or any of the countries of North, South, or Central America. □ **American Indian** a member of one of the original peoples of America. ■ **A·mer·i·can·ize** /əˈmerikəˌnīz/ **v.**

A·mer·i·can·ism /əˈmerikəˌnizəm/ ▶ **n.** a word or phrase originating in the United States.

Am·er·in·di·an /ˌaməˈrindēən/ (also **Amerind** /ˈamərind/) ⇒ **AMERICAN INDIAN**.

am·e·thyst /ˈaməTHəst/ ▶ **n.** a violet or purple precious stone.

a·mi·a·ble /ˈāmēəbəl/ ▶ **adj.** friendly and pleasant.

SYNONYMS **friendly**, affable, amicable, cordial, good-natured, nice, pleasant, agreeable, likable, genial, good-humored, companionable. ANTONYMS unfriendly, disagreeable.

■ **a·mi·a·bil·i·ty** /ˌāmēəˈbilitē/ **n.** **a·mi·a·bly** **adv.**

am·i·ca·ble /ˈamikəbəl/ ▶ **adj.** friendly and without disagreement: *the meeting was relatively amicable.*

■ **am·i·ca·bly** adv.

a·mid /ə'mid/ (or **amidst** /ə'midst/) ▶ prep. in the middle of: *our dream home, set amid magnificent rolling countryside.*

a·mid·ships /ə'mid,sHips/ ▶ adv. & adj. in the middle of a ship.

a·mi·go /ə'mēgō/ ▶ n. (plural **amigos**) informal a friend.

a·mine /ə'mēn, 'amēn/ ▶ n. Chemistry an organic compound derived from ammonia by replacement of one or more hydrogen atoms by organic radicals.

a·mi·no ac·id /ə'mēnō/ ▶ n. any of the natural substances that combine to form proteins.

a·mir /ə'mi(ə)r/ (or **emir**) ▶ n. a title of some Muslim rulers.

A·mish /'ämisH/ ▶ pl.n. a strict Protestant sect living mainly in Pennsylvania and Ohio.

a·miss /ə'mis/ ▶ adj. not quite right; inappropriate. □ **take something amiss** be offended by something.

am·i·ty /'amitē/ ▶ n. formal friendly relations between people or countries.

am·me·ter /'a(m),mētər/ ▶ n. an instrument for measuring electric current.

am·mo /'amō/ ▶ n. informal ammunition.

am·mo·nia /ə'mōnyə, -nēə/ ▶ n. a colorless, strong-smelling gas that can be used to make a cleaning fluid.

am·mo·nite /'amə,nīt/ ▶ n. an extinct sea creature with a spiral shell.

am·mu·ni·tion /,amyə'nisHən/ ▶ n. **1** a supply of bullets and shells. **2** points used to support your case in an argument.

am·ne·sia /am'nēzHə/ ▶ n. loss of memory. ■ **am·ne·si·ac** /am'nēzē,ak, -zHē,ak/ adj.

am·nes·ty /'amnistē/ ▶ n. (plural **amnesties**) **1** a pardon given to people who have committed an offense against the government. **2** a period during which people who admit to committing an offense are not punished.

SYNONYMS **pardon**, reprieve, forgiveness, release, discharge.

am·ni·o·cen·te·sis /,amnē-ōsen'tēsis/ ▶ n. (plural **amniocenteses**) a medical procedure in which a sample of amniotic fluid is taken to check for possible abnormalities in the unborn baby.

am·ni·ot·ic flu·id /,amnē'ätik/ ▶ n. the fluid surrounding an unborn baby in the uterus.

a·moe·ba /ə'mēbə/ ▶ n. (plural **amoebas** or **amoebae** /-bē/) ⇨ AMEBA.

a·mok /ə'mək, ə'mäk/ (or **amuck** /ə'mək/) ▶ adv. (**run amok**) behave in an uncontrolled way.

a·mong /ə'məNG/ ▶ prep. **1** surrounded by: *you're among friends.* **2** included or occurring in: *a drop in tooth decay among children.* **3** shared by; between: *members of the club bickered among themselves.*

a·mor·al /ā'môrəl/ ▶ adj. not concerned with doing what is right. ■ **a·mo·ral·i·ty** /,āmə'ralitē/ n.

am·o·rous /'amərəs/ ▶ adj. showing or feeling romantic desire.

SYNONYMS **lustful**, sexual, erotic, amatory, ardent, passionate, impassioned; in love, enamored, lovesick; informal lovey-dovey, kissy, smoochy, hot. ANTONYMS unloving.

■ **am·o·rous·ly** adv.

a·mor·phous /ə'môrfəs/ ▶ adj. without a clear shape or form.

am·or·tize /'amər,tīz/ ▶ v. (**amortizes**, **amortizing**, **amortized**) gradually pay off a debt.

a·mount /ə'mount/ ▶ n. **1** the total number, size, or value of something. **2** a quantity. ▶ v. (**amount to**) **1** add up to. **2** be the same as.

SYNONYMS ▶ n. **quantity**, number, total, aggregate, sum, quota, size, mass, weight, volume.

amp /amp/ ▶ n. short for AMPERE.

am·per·age /'amp(ə)rij/ ▶ n. the strength of an electric current, measured in amperes.

am·pere /'am,pi(ə)r/ ▶ n. a basic unit of electric current.

am·per·sand /'ampər,sand/ ▶ n. the sign &, which means *and.*

am·phet·a·mine /am'fetə,mēn, -min/ ▶ n. a drug used as a stimulant.

am·phib·i·an /am'fibēən/ ▶ n. an animal such as a frog or toad, which lives in the water when young and on the land as an adult. ■ **am·phib·i·ous** adj.

am·phi·the·a·ter /'amfə,THēətər/ ▶ n. a round building without a roof, in which tiers of seats surround a central space used for performing plays or for sports.

am·ple /'ampəl/ ▶ adj. (**ampler**, **amplest**) **1** enough or more than enough; plentiful. **2** large.

SYNONYMS **1 enough**, sufficient, adequate, plenty of, more than enough, abundant, copious, profuse, lavish, liberal, generous; informal galore. **2 spacious**, full, capacious, roomy, voluminous, loose-fitting, baggy, sloppy. ANTONYMS insufficient.

■ **am·ply** adv.

am·pli·fi·er /'amplə,fīər/ ▶ n. a device that makes sounds or radio signals louder.

am·pli·fy /'amplə,fī/ ▶ v. (**amplifies**, **amplifying**, **amplified**) **1** increase the strength of a sound or an electrical signal. **2** explain something in more detail.

SYNONYMS **1 make louder**, turn up, increase, raise. **2 expand**, enlarge on, elaborate on, develop, flesh out.

■ **am·pli·fi·ca·tion** /,ampləfi'kāsHən/ n.

am·pli·tude /'ampli,t(y)o͞od/ ▶ n. **1** the maximum amount by which a vibration such as an alternating current varies from its average level. **2** great size, range, or extent.

am·poule /'am,p(y)o͞ol/ (also **ampule**) ▶ n. a small glass capsule containing liquid used in giving an injection.

am·pu·tate /'ampyə,tāt/ ▶ v. (**amputates**, **amputating**, **amputated**) cut off a limb in a surgical operation. ■ **am·pu·ta·tion** /,ampyə'tāsHən/ n.

am·pu·tee /,ampyə'tē/ ▶ n. a person who has had a limb amputated.

Am·trak /'am,trak/ ▶ n. trademark the national passenger railroad service in the US, a government-subsidized corporation.

a·muck /ə'mək/ = AMOK.

am·u·let /'amyəlit/ ▶ n. a small piece of jewelry worn as protection against evil.

a·muse /ə'myo͞oz/ ▶ v. (**amuses**, **amusing**, **amused**) **1** make someone laugh or smile. **2** give someone something enjoyable to do.

SYNONYMS **1 make someone laugh**, entertain, delight, divert, cheer (up), please, charm, tickle; informal crack up. **2 occupy**, engage, busy, absorb, engross, entertain. ANTONYMS bore.

a·muse·ment /ə'myo͞ozmənt/ ▶ **n. 1** the feeling that you have when something is funny. **2** a game or activity that provides entertainment and pleasure.

SYNONYMS **1 mirth**, merriment, hilarity, glee, delight. **2 entertainment**, pleasure, leisure, relaxation, fun, enjoyment, interest. **3 activity**, entertainment, diversion, pastime, recreation, game, sport.

□ **amusement park** a large outdoor area with rides and other entertainments.

a·mus·ing /ə'myo͞oziNG/ ▶ **adj.** causing laughter or providing entertainment.

SYNONYMS **funny**, comical, humorous, lighthearted, jocular, witty, droll, entertaining, diverting.

an /an/ ▶ **determiner** the form of the indefinite article "a" used before words beginning with a vowel sound: *the teacher assigned an essay to her class.*

An·a·bap·tist /ˌanə'bapˌtist/ ▶ **n.** a member of a Protestant religious group believing that only adults should be baptized.

an·a·bol·ic ste·roid /ˌanə'bälik/ ▶ **n.** a synthetic hormone used to build up muscle.

a·nab·o·lism /ə'nabəˌlizəm/ ▶ **n.** the formation of complex molecules from simpler ones in living organisms. ■ **an·a·bol·ic** /ˌanə'bälik/ **adj.**

a·nach·ro·nism /ə'nakrəˌnizəm/ ▶ **n. 1** something that seems to belong to another time. **2** something that is wrongly placed in a particular period. ■ **a·nach·ro·nis·tic** /əˌnakrə'nistik/ **adj.**

an·a·con·da /ˌanə'kändə/ ▶ **n.** a very large snake of the boa family, found in South America.

an·aer·o·bic /ˌane(ə)'rōbik, ˌanə-/ ▶ **adj.** not using oxygen from the air.

an·a·gram /'anəˌgram/ ▶ **n.** a word or phrase formed by rearranging the letters of another.

a·nal /'ānl/ ▶ **adj.** having to do with the anus.

an·al·ge·sic /ˌanl'jēzik, -sik/ ▶ **n.** a pain-relieving drug.

an·a·log /'anlˌôg, -ˌäg/ (or **analogue**) ▶ **adj.** using a variable physical effect, such as voltage or the position of a pointer, to represent information, rather than a digital display. ▶ **n.** something that is similar to and can be compared with something else.

a·nal·o·gous /ə'naləgəs/ ▶ **adj.** similar to and able to be compared with something else.

a·nal·o·gy /ə'naləjē/ ▶ **n.** (plural **analogies**) a way of explaining something by comparing it to something else.

SYNONYMS **similarity**, parallel, correspondence, likeness, resemblance, correlation, relation, comparison. ANTONYMS dissimilarity.

■ **an·a·log·i·cal** /ˌanə'läjikəl/ **adj.**

a·nal·y·sis /ə'naləsis/ ▶ **n.** (plural **analyses**) **1** a detailed examination of the elements or structure of something. **2** psychoanalysis.

SYNONYMS **examination**, inspection, study, scrutiny, breakdown, investigation, exploration, evaluation.

an·a·lyst /'anl-ist/ ▶ **n.** a person who carries out analysis.

an·a·lyt·i·cal /ˌanl'itikəl/ (or **analytic** /ˌanl'itik/) ▶ **adj.** using analysis.

SYNONYMS **systematic**, logical, scientific, methodical, precise, meticulous, rigorous, investigative, inquiring.

■ **an·a·lyt·i·cal·ly adv.**

an·a·lyze /'anlˌīz/ ▶ **v.** (**analyzes**, **analyzing**, **analyzed**) **1** examine something in detail to explain it or to find out its structure or composition. **2** psychoanalyze someone.

SYNONYMS **examine**, inspect, survey, study, scrutinize, investigate, probe, explore, evaluate, break down.

an·ar·chic /ə'närkik/ ▶ **adj.** not controlled or governed by any rules or principles.

an·ar·chist /'anərkist/ ▶ **n.** a person who believes that all government and laws should be abolished. ■ **an·ar·chism** /'anərˌkizəm/ **n. an·ar·chis·tic** /ˌanər'kistik/ **adj.**

an·ar·chy /'anərkē/ ▶ **n. 1** a situation in which no rules or principles are being followed and there is complete disorder. **2** a society with no government.

SYNONYMS **lawlessness**, disorder, chaos, pandemonium, mayhem, riot, revolution. ANTONYMS order.

a·nath·e·ma /ə'naTHəmə/ ▶ **n.** something that you hate: *racism was anathema to her.*

a·nath·e·ma·tize /ə'naTHəməˌtīz/ ▶ **v.** (**anathematizes**, **anathematizing**, **anathematized**) curse; condemn.

a·nat·o·mize /ə'natəˌmīz/ ▶ **v.** (**anatomizes**, **anatomizing**, **anatomized**) examine in detail.

a·nat·o·my /ə'natəmē/ ▶ **n.** (plural **anatomies**) **1** the scientific study of the structure of the human body. **2** the structure of a person, animal, or plant. **3** a detailed examination or analysis.

SYNONYMS **structure**, makeup, composition, constitution, form, body, physique.

■ **an·a·tom·i·cal** /ˌanə'tomikəl/ **adj. an·a·tom·i·cal·ly** /ˌanə'tomik(ə)lē/ **adv. a·nat·o·mist n.**

an·ces·tor /'anˌsestər/ ▶ **n. 1** a person from whom you are descended. **2** something from which a later species or version has developed.

SYNONYMS **forefather**, forebear, predecessor, antecedent, progenitor, parent, grandparent. ANTONYMS descendant.

an·ces·tral /an'sestrəl/ ▶ **adj.** inherited from your ancestors: *their ancestral home.*

an·ces·try /'anˌsestrē/ ▶ **n.** (plural **ancestries**) your ancestors or ethnic origins.

SYNONYMS **ancestors**, forebears, forefathers, progenitors, antecedents, family tree, lineage, genealogy, parentage, blood.

an·chor /'aNGkər/ ▶ **n.** a heavy object that is attached to a boat by a rope or chain and dropped to the seabed to stop the boat from drifting. ▶ **v. 1** hold with an anchor. **2** secure or fix firmly in position.

an·chor·age /'aNGk(ə)rij/ ▶ **n.** a place where ships may anchor safely.

an·cho·rite /'aNGkəˌrīt/ ▶ **n.** (in the past) a person who lived alone for religious reasons.

an·chor·man /ˈanGkər,man/ (or **anchorwoman** /ˈanGkər,wo͝omən/) ▶ n. (plural **anchormen** or **anchorwomen**) a person who presents a live television or radio program.

an·cho·vy /ˈan,CHōvē, anˈCHōvē/ ▶ n. (plural **anchovies**) a small fish of the herring family, with a strong flavor.

an·cien ré·gime /änˈsyaN rāˈZHēm/ ▶ n. (plural **anciens régimes**) a political or social system that has been replaced by a more modern one.

an·cient /ˈānCHənt/ ▶ adj. **1** belonging to the very distant past. **2** very old. ▶ n. (**the ancients**) the people of ancient times.

> SYNONYMS ▶ adj. **1** *ancient civilizations* **early**, prehistoric, primeval, primordial, primitive, bygone. **2** *an ancient custom* **old**, age-old, venerable, time-worn, time-honored, archaic, antique, obsolete. **3** *I feel ancient* **antiquated**, antediluvian, geriatric; informal as old as the hills. ANTONYMS contemporary, recent.

an·cil·lar·y /ˈansə,lerē/ ▶ adj. **1** providing support. **2** additional; extra: *laboratories with ancillary rooms*.

and /and/ ▶ conj. **1** used to connect words, clauses, or sentences. **2** (connecting two numbers) plus.

an·dan·te /änˈdän,tā/ ▶ adv. & adj. Music at a moderately slow pace.

an·drog·y·nous /anˈdräjənəs/ ▶ adj. partly male and partly female. ■ **an·drog·y·ny** n.

an·droid /ˈan,droid/ ▶ n. (in science fiction) a robot with a human appearance.

an·ec·do·tal /,anikˈdōtl/ ▶ adj. (of a story) not backed up by facts.

an·ec·dote /ˈanik,dōt/ ▶ n. a short entertaining story about a real incident or person.

> SYNONYMS **story**, tale, urban myth, narrative, reminiscence; informal yarn.

a·ne·mi·a /əˈnēmēə/ ▶ n. a shortage of red cells or hemoglobin in the blood, making a person pale and tired. ■ **a·ne·mic** adj.

an·e·mom·e·ter /,anəˈmämitər/ ▶ n. an instrument for measuring the speed of the wind.

a·nem·o·ne /əˈnemənē/ ▶ n. **1** a plant of the buttercup family with brightly colored flowers. **2** a sea anemone.

an·er·oid ba·rom·e·ter /ˈanə,roid/ ▶ n. a barometer that measures air pressure by the action of air on the flexible lid of a box containing a vacuum.

an·es·the·sia /,anəsˈTHēZHə/ ▶ n. insensitivity to pain, especially as artificially induced by the injection of drugs before surgery.

an·es·thet·ic /,anəsˈTHetik/ ▶ n. a drug or gas that makes you unable to feel pain.

an·es·the·tize /əˈnesTHi,tīz/ ▶ v. (**anesthetizes**, **anesthetizing**, **anesthetized**) give an anesthetic to. ■ **an·es·the·tist** n.

an·eu·rysm /ˈanyə,rizəm/ (or **aneurism**) ▶ n. a swelling of the wall of an artery.

a·new /əˈn(y)o͞o/ ▶ adv. **1** in a new or different way. **2** once more; again.

an·gel /ˈānjəl/ ▶ n. **1** a messenger of God, pictured as being of human form but with wings. **2** a very beautiful or good person. □ **angel food cake** a very light, pale sponge cake made with no egg yolks.

an·gel·fish /ˈānjəl,fiSH/ ▶ n. a tropical fish with large translucent fins.

an·gel·ic /anˈjelik/ ▶ adj. **1** relating to angels. **2** very beautiful, innocent, or kind: *his small, angelic face*.

> SYNONYMS **innocent**, pure, virtuous, saintly, cherubic, adorable.

■ **an·gel·i·cal·ly** adv.

an·gel·i·ca /anˈjelikə/ ▶ n. **1** a tall aromatic plant of the parsley family. **2** the stalk of this plant, preserved in sugar and used in cake decoration.

an·ge·lus /ˈanjələs/ ▶ n. **1** a Roman Catholic prayer said at morning, noon, and sunset. **2** a ringing of bells announcing this.

an·ger /ˈaNGgər/ ▶ n. a strong feeling of extreme displeasure. ▶ v. (**angers**, **angering**, **angered**) make someone angry.

> SYNONYMS ▶ n. **annoyance**, vexation, temper, indignation, rage, fury, wrath, outrage; literary ire. ▶ v. **annoy**, irk, vex, enrage, incense, infuriate, rile, provoke, outrage. ANTONYMS pacify, placate.

an·gi·na /anˈjīnə/ (or **angina pectoris** /ˈpektərəs/) ▶ n. severe pain in the chest caused by an inadequate supply of blood to the heart.

an·gi·o·sperm /ˈanjēə,spərm/ ▶ n. a plant of a large group that has flowers and produces seeds enclosed in a carpel, including herbaceous plants, shrubs, grasses, and most trees.

An·gle /ˈaNGgəl/ ▶ n. a member of a people originally from north and west Europe who came to England in the 5th century AD and founded kingdoms in the north and east of the country.

an·gle¹ /ˈaNGgəl/ ▶ n. **1** the space between two lines or surfaces that meet. **2** a position from which something is viewed: *he was filmed from a variety of camera angles*. **3** a way of thinking about something: *a fresh angle on life*. ▶ v. (**angles**, **angling**, **angled**) **1** place something in a slanting position. **2** present information from a particular point of view.

> SYNONYMS ▶ n. **1** **gradient**, slope, slant, inclination. **2** **corner**, point, fork, nook, crook, edge. **3** **perspective**, point of view, viewpoint, standpoint, position, aspect, slant, direction, approach, tack. ▶ v. **tilt**, slant, twist, swivel, lean, tip, turn.

an·gle² /ˈaNGgəl/ ▶ v. (**angles**, **angling**, **angled**) **1** fish with a rod and line. **2** try to get something without asking for it directly: *she was angling for sympathy*. ■ **an·gler** /ˈaNGglər/ n.

an·gler·fish /ˈaNGglər,fiSH/ ▶ n. (plural **anglerfish** or **anglerfishes**) a sea fish that lures prey with a fleshy attachment that projects from its snout.

An·gli·can /ˈaNGglikən/ ▶ adj. relating to the Church of England. ▶ n. a member of the Church of England. ■ **An·gli·can·ism** n.

An·gli·cism /ˈaNGglə,sizəm/ ▶ n. a word or phrase that is peculiar to British English.

an·gli·cize /ˈaNGglə,sīz/ ▶ v. (**anglicizes**, **anglicizing**, **anglicized**) make something English. ■ **an·gli·ci·za·tion** /,aNGgləsəˈzāSHən/ n.

An·glo·phile /ˈaNGglə,fīl/ ▶ n. a person who admires England or Britain.

An·glo-Sax·on /,aNGglōˈsaksən/ ▶ n. **1** a person living in England between the 5th century and the Norman Conquest, whose ancestors came from north and west Europe. **2** the Old English language.

an·go·ra /aNG'gôrə/ ▶ **n.** **1** a breed of cat, goat, or rabbit with long, soft hair. **2** fabric made from the hair of the angora goat or rabbit.

an·gos·tu·ra /ˌaNGgə'st(y)o͝orə/ ▶ **n.** the bitter bark of a South American tree, used as a flavoring.

an·gry /'aNGgrē/ ▶ **adj.** (**angrier**, **angriest**) **1** feeling or showing anger. **2** (of a wound or sore) red and swollen.

SYNONYMS **furious**, irate, vexed, wrathful, irked, enraged, incensed, seething, infuriated, in a temper, fuming, apoplectic, outraged, cross; informal (hopping) mad, up in arms, foaming at the mouth, steamed, sore. ANTONYMS pleased.

■ **an·gri·ly** **adv.**

angst /aNG(k)st, äNG(k)st/ ▶ **n.** a strong feeling of anxiety about life in general.

SYNONYMS **anxiety**, fear, worry, trepidation, malaise, disquiet, unease, anguish.

ang·strom /'aNGstrəm/ ▶ **n.** a unit of length equal to one hundred-millionth of a centimeter.

an·guish /'aNGgwisH/ ▶ **n.** severe pain or suffering.

SYNONYMS **agony**, pain, torment, torture, suffering, distress, woe, misery, sorrow, heartache. ANTONYMS happiness.

an·guished /'aNGgwisHt/ ▶ **adj.** feeling or expressing severe pain or distress.

an·gu·lar /'aNGgyələr/ ▶ **adj.** **1** having angles or sharp corners. **2** (of a person) lean and bony. **3** placed or directed at an angle. ■ **an·gu·lar·i·ty** **n.**

an·hy·drous /an'hīdrəs/ ▶ **adj.** Chemistry containing no water.

an·i·line /'anl-in/ ▶ **n.** an oily liquid found in coal tar, used in making dyes, drugs, and plastics.

an·i·mad·vert /ˌanəmad'vərt/ ▶ **v.** (**animadvert on** or **against**) formal speak out against; criticize. ■ **an·i·mad·ver·sion** **n.**

an·i·mal /'anəməl/ ▶ **n.** **1** a living being that can move about of its own accord and has specialized sense organs and a nervous system. **2** a mammal, as opposed to a bird, reptile, fish, or insect. ▶ **adj.** **1** having to do with animals. **2** physical rather than spiritual or intellectual.

SYNONYMS ▶ **n.** **1** **creature**, beast, (living) thing; (**animals**) wildlife, fauna. **2** *the man was an animal* **beast**, brute, monster, devil, fiend; informal swine, bastard, pig.

an·i·mal·ism /'anəməˌlizəm/ ▶ **n.** behavior that is characteristic of or appropriate to animals.

an·i·mate ▶ **v.** /'anəˌmāt/ (**animates**, **animating**, **animated**) **1** bring life or energy to. **2** make drawings or models into an animated movie. ▶ **adj.** /-mit/ living.

SYNONYMS ▶ **v.** **enliven**, energize, invigorate, liven up, inspire, fire, rouse, stir, galvanize, stimulate, excite, move, revitalize, revive, rejuvenate. ▶ **adj.** **living**, alive, live, breathing, sentient. ANTONYMS inanimate.

■ **an·i·ma·tor** /'anəˌmātər/ **n.**

an·i·mat·ed /'anəˌmātid/ ▶ **adj.** **1** lively. **2** (of a movie) made using animation.

SYNONYMS **lively**, spirited, energetic, full of life, excited, enthusiastic, eager, alive, vigorous, vibrant, vivacious, exuberant, ebullient, bouncy, bubbly, perky; informal bright-eyed and bushy-tailed, full of beans, chirpy, chipper. ANTONYMS lethargic, lifeless.

■ **an·i·mat·ed·ly** **adv.**

an·i·ma·tion /ˌanə'māsHən/ ▶ **n.** **1** liveliness. **2** the technique of filming a sequence of drawings or positions of models to give the appearance of movement. **3** the creation of moving images by means of a computer.

an·i·me /'anəˌmā/ ▶ **n.** Japanese animated films, typically having a science fiction theme.

an·i·mism /'anəˌmizəm/ ▶ **n.** the belief that all things in nature have a soul. ■ **an·i·mist** **n.**

an·i·mos·i·ty /ˌanə'mäsitē/ ▶ **n.** (plural **animosities**) hatred or strong dislike.

SYNONYMS **hostility**, antipathy, antagonism, rancor, enmity, resentment, hatred, loathing, ill feeling/will, dislike, bad blood, animus. ANTONYMS goodwill, friendship.

an·i·mus /'anəməs/ ▶ **n.** hatred or dislike.

an·i·on /'anˌīən/ ▶ **n.** an ion with a negative charge.

an·i·seed /'anə(s)ˌsēd/ ▶ **n.** the seed of the **anise plant**, used as a flavoring.

an·kle /'aNGkəl/ ▶ **n.** the joint connecting the foot with the leg.

an·klet /'aNGklit/ ▶ **n.** **1** a sock that reaches just above the ankle. **2** a chain or band worn around the ankle.

an·nals /'anəlz/ ▶ **pl.n.** a historical record of events made year by year.

an·neal /ə'nēl/ ▶ **v.** heat metal or glass and allow it to cool slowly, so as to toughen it.

an·ne·lid /'anlˌid/ ▶ **n.** a worm with a body made up of segments, such as an earthworm.

an·nex ▶ **v.** /ə'neks, 'aneks/ **1** take possession of another country's land. **2** add something as an extra part. ▶ **n.** /'aneks, -iks/ (plural **annexes**) **1** a building attached to or near a main building. **2** an addition to a document. ■ **an·nex·a·tion** /ˌanek'sāsHən, ˌanik-/ **n.**

an·ni·hi·late /ə'nī-əˌlāt/ ▶ **v.** (**annihilates**, **annihilating**, **annihilated**) destroy completely.

SYNONYMS **destroy**, obliterate, eradicate, wipe out, wipe off the face of the earth; informal rub out, snuff out. ANTONYMS create.

■ **an·ni·hi·la·tion** /əˌnīə'lāsHən/ **n.**

an·ni·ver·sa·ry /ˌanə'vərsərē/ ▶ **n.** (plural **anniversaries**) the date on which an event took place in a previous year.

An·no Dom·i·ni /'anō 'dämənē, -nī, 'änō/ full form of **AD**.

an·no·tate /'anəˌtāt/ ▶ **v.** (**annotates**, **annotating**, **annotated**) add explanatory notes to. ■ **an·no·ta·tion** /ˌanə'tāsHən/ **n.**

an·nounce /ə'nouns/ ▶ **v.** (**announces**, **announcing**, **announced**) **1** make a public statement about. **2** be a sign of: *lilies announce the arrival of summer*.

SYNONYMS **make public**, make known, report, declare, state, publicize, broadcast, publish, advertise, circulate, proclaim, release, disclose, divulge.

an·nounce·ment /ə'nounsmənt/ ▶ **n.** a public statement.

SYNONYMS **1** **statement**, declaration, proclamation, pronouncement, bulletin, advisory, communiqué. **2** **declaration**, notification, reporting, publishing, broadcasting, disclosure.

an·nounc·er /ə'nounsər/ ▶ **n.** a person who announces something, especially someone who introduces or gives information about programs on radio or television.

an·noy /ə'noi/ ▶ **v.** make someone slightly angry.

SYNONYMS **1 irritate**, bother, vex, exasperate, irk, anger, antagonize, nettle, rankle with, rub the wrong way; informal aggravate, peeve, miff, rile, needle, get (to), bug, tee off, tick off. **2** (**annoyed**) **irritated**, cross, angry, vexed, exasperated, irked, piqued, displeased, put out, disgruntled, nettled; informal aggravated, peeved, miffed, riled, hot under the collar, teed off, ticked off, sore. **3** (**annoying**) **irritating**, infuriating, exasperating, maddening, trying, tiresome, troublesome, irksome, vexing, galling; informal aggravating. ANTONYMS please.

an·noy·ance /ə'noi-əns/ ▶ **n. 1** the feeling or state of being annoyed. **2** a thing that annoys someone.

SYNONYMS **irritation**, exasperation, vexation, indignation, anger, displeasure, chagrin.

an·nu·al /'anyo͞oəl/ ▶ **adj. 1** happening once a year. **2** calculated over or covering a year: *his annual income*. **3** (of a plant) living for a year or less. ▶ **n.** a book published once a year.

SYNONYMS ▶ **adj. yearly**, once-a-year, year-long, twelve-month.

an·nu·al·ly /'anyo͞oəlē/ ▶ **adv.** once a year.

SYNONYMS **yearly**, once a year, each year, per annum.

an·nu·i·ty /ə'n(y)o͞oitē/ ▶ **n.** (plural **annuities**) a fixed sum of money paid to someone each year.

an·nul /ə'nəl/ ▶ **v.** (**annuls, annulling, annulled**) declare a law, marriage, or other legal contract to be no longer valid.

SYNONYMS **declare invalid**, declare null and void, nullify, invalidate, void, repeal, revoke.

■ **an·nul·ment n.**

an·nu·lar /'anyələr/ ▶ **adj.** technical ring-shaped.

an·nun·ci·a·tion /əˌnənsē'āsʜən/ ▶ **n.** (**the Annunciation**) (in Christian belief) the announcement by the angel Gabriel to the Virgin Mary that she was to be the mother of Jesus.

an·ode /'anōd/ ▶ **n.** an electrode with a positive charge.

an·o·dized /'anəˌdīzd/ ▶ **adj.** (of metal) coated with a protective layer by the action of an electric current.

an·o·dyne /'anəˌdīn/ ▶ **adj.** not likely to cause offense or disagreement. ▶ **n.** a painkilling drug.

a·noint /ə'noint/ ▶ **v.** dab or smear water or oil on someone as part of a religious ceremony.

a·nom·a·lous /ə'nämələs/ ▶ **adj.** differing from what is standard or normal.

a·nom·a·ly /ə'nämәlē/ ▶ **n.** (plural **anomalies**) something that is different from what is normal or expected.

SYNONYMS **oddity**, peculiarity, abnormality, irregularity, inconsistency, aberration, quirk.

an·o·mie /'anəˌmē/ (or **anomy**) ▶ **n.** lack of the usual standards of good or acceptable behavior.

a·non /ə'nän/ ▶ **adv.** old use soon; shortly.

anon. ▶ **abbr.** anonymous.

a·non·y·mous /ə'nänəməs/ ▶ **adj. 1** having a name that is not publicly known. **2** having no outstanding or individual features: *her anonymous dorm room.*

SYNONYMS **unnamed**, nameless, unidentified, unknown, incognito, unsigned.

■ **an·o·nym·i·ty** /ˌanə'nimitē/ **n. a·non·y·mous·ly adv.**

an·o·rak /'anəˌrak/ ▶ **n.** a waterproof jacket with a hood.

an·o·rex·i·a /ˌanə'reksēə/ (or **anorexia nervosa** /ˌnərv'ōsə/) ▶ **n.** a disorder in which a person refuses to eat because they are afraid of becoming fat. ■ **an·o·rex·ic adj. & n.**

an·oth·er /ə'nəT͟Hər/ ▶ **determiner & pron. 1** one more. **2** different from the one already mentioned: *come back another day.*

an·swer /'ansər/ ▶ **n. 1** something said or written in reaction to a question or statement. **2** the solution to a problem. ▶ **v.** (**answers, answering, answered**) **1** give an answer. **2** (**answer back**) give a impudent reply. **3** (**answer to**) have to explain your actions or decisions to someone. **4** (**answer for**) be responsible for the things you do.

SYNONYMS ▶ **n. 1 reply**, response, rejoinder, reaction, retort, riposte; informal comeback. **2 solution**, remedy, way out, explanation. ANTONYMS question. ▶ **v. reply**, respond, rejoin, retort, riposte.

□ **answering machine** a machine that gives a prerecorded reply to a telephone call and can record a message from the caller.

an·swer·a·ble /'ansərəbəl/ ▶ **adj. 1** (**answerable to**) having to explain to someone why you have done the things you have done. **2** (**answerable for**) responsible for something.

SYNONYMS **accountable**, responsible, liable.

ant /ant/ ▶ **n.** a small insect that lives with many others in an organized group.

ant·ac·id /ant'asid/ ▶ **adj.** (of a medicine) reducing excess acid in the stomach.

an·tag·o·nism /an'tagəˌnizəm/ ▶ **n.** the expression of hostile feelings.

an·tag·o·nist /an'tagənist/ ▶ **n.** an opponent or enemy.

an·tag·o·nis·tic /anˌtagə'nistik/ ▶ **adj.** showing or feeling opposition or hostility.

SYNONYMS **hostile**, opposed, antipathetic, ill-disposed, resistant, in disagreement; informal anti.

an·tag·o·nize /an'tagəˌnīz/ ▶ **v.** (**antagonizes, antagonizing, antagonized**) make someone feel hostile.

SYNONYMS **provoke**, intimidate, alienate, anger, annoy, irritate. ANTONYMS pacify.

Ant·arc·tic /ant'är(k)tik/ ▶ **adj.** relating to the region surrounding the South Pole.

SPELLING

Remember the **c** after the **r**: Antarctic.

an·te /'antē/ ▶ **n.** a stake put up by a player in poker or similar games before receiving cards. □ **up** (or **raise**) **the ante** increase what is at stake.

ant·eat·er /'ant,ētər/ ▶ **n.** an animal with a long snout and sticky tongue that feeds on ants and termites.

an·te·ced·ent /,antə'sēdnt/ ▶ **n. 1** a thing that exists or comes before another. **2** (**antecedents**) a person's ancestors. ▶ **adj.** coming before in time or order.

an·te·date /'anti,dāt/ ▶ **v.** (**antedates, antedating, antedated**) come or exist before something else.

an·te·di·lu·vi·an /,antēdə'lo͞ovēən/ ▶ **adj. 1** belonging to the time before the biblical Flood. **2** very old-fashioned.

an·te·lope /'antl,ōp/ ▶ **n. 1** a swift deerlike animal found in Africa and Asia. **2** (also **pronghorn** /'prôNG,hôrn/ or **pronghorn antelope**) a deerlike North American mammal with black horns.

an·te·na·tal /,antē'nātl/ ▶ **adj.** before birth; during pregnancy.

an·ten·na /an'tenə/ ▶ **n. 1** (plural **antennae** /-'tenē/) each of a pair of long, thin feelers on the heads of some insects and shellfish. **2** (plural **antennas** or **antennae**) a rod, wire, or other device used to transmit or receive radio or television signals.

an·te·pe·nul·ti·mate /,antēpə'nəltəmit/ ▶ **adj.** last but two in a series.

an·te·ri·or /an'ti(ə)rēər/ ▶ **adj.** at or near the front.

an·te·room /'antē,ro͞om, -,ro͝om/ ▶ **n.** a small room leading to a more important one.

an·them /'anTHəm/ ▶ **n. 1** a song chosen by a country to express patriotic feelings. **2** a musical setting of a religious work that is sung by a choir during a church service.

> SYNONYMS **hymn**, song, chorale, chant, psalm, canticle.

an·ther /'anTHər/ ▶ **n.** the part of a flower's stamen that contains the pollen.

ant·hill /'ant,hil/ ▶ **n.** a mound of earth made by ants when they build a nest.

an·thol·o·gy /an'THäləjē/ ▶ **n.** (plural **anthologies**) a collection of poems or other pieces of writing or music.

> SYNONYMS **collection**, selection, compendium, compilation, miscellany, treasury.

an·thra·cite /'anTHrə,sīt/ ▶ **n.** hard coal that burns without producing much flame and smoke.

an·thrax /'an,THraks/ ▶ **n.** a serious disease of sheep and cattle that can be passed to humans.

an·thro·poid /'anTHrə,poid/ ▶ **adj.** having to do with apes that resemble human beings in form, such as gorillas or chimpanzees.

an·thro·pol·o·gy /,anTHrə'päləjē/ ▶ **n.** the study of human origins, societies, and cultures. ■ **an·thro·po·log·i·cal** /-pə'läjikəl/ **adj. an·thro·pol·o·gist n.**

an·thro·po·mor·phic /,anTHrəpə'môrfik/ ▶ **adj.** treating a god, animal, or object as if they were human.

an·ti·bi·ot·ic /,antēbī'ätik, ,antī-/ ▶ **n.** a medicine that kills bacteria.

an·ti·bod·y /'anti,bädē/ ▶ **n.** (plural **antibodies**) a protein produced in the blood to react against harmful substances.

An·ti·christ /'antē,krīst, 'antī-/ ▶ **n.** an enemy of Christ that some people believe will appear before the end of the world.

an·tic·i·pate /an'tisə,pāt/ ▶ **v.** (**anticipates, anticipating, anticipated**) **1** be aware of and prepared for a future event. **2** look forward to. **3** do something earlier than someone else.

> SYNONYMS **1 expect**, foresee, predict, be prepared for, bargain on, reckon on; informal figure on. **2 look forward to**, await, long for, can't wait for.

■ **an·tic·i·pa·to·ry** /an'tisəpə,tôrē/ **adj.**

an·tic·i·pa·tion /an,tisə'pāSHən/ ▶ **n.** the action of anticipating something.

> SYNONYMS **expectation**, expectancy, prediction, hope, excitement, suspense.

an·ti·cli·max /,antē'klī,maks, ,antī-/ ▶ **n.** a disappointing end to an exciting series of events.

> SYNONYMS **letdown**, disappointment, comedown, nonevent, disillusionment; informal washout; literary bathos.

■ **an·ti·cli·mac·tic** /,antēklī'maktik, ,antī-/ **adj.**

an·tics /'antiks/ ▶ **pl.n.** silly or amusing behavior.

> SYNONYMS **capers**, pranks, larks, high jinks, skylarking, horseplay, clowning; informal monkey business.

an·ti·cy·clone /,antē'sīklōn, ,antī-/ ▶ **n.** an area of high atmospheric pressure around which air slowly circulates, usually resulting in calm, fine weather.

an·ti·dote /'anti,dōt/ ▶ **n.** a medicine taken to undo the effect of a poison.

> SYNONYMS **remedy**, cure, solution, countermeasure, corrective.

an·ti·freeze /'anti,frēz/ ▶ **n.** a liquid added to water to prevent it from freezing, used in car radiators.

an·ti·gen /'antijən/ ▶ **n.** a harmful substance that causes the body to produce antibodies.

an·ti·he·ro /'antē,hi(ə)rō, 'antī-/ ▶ **n.** a central character in a story, movie, or play who is either ordinary or unpleasant.

an·ti·his·ta·mine /,antē'histəmin, -mēn/ ▶ **n.** a drug that is used in treating allergies.

an·ti·log·a·rithm /,antē'lôgə,riTHəm, -'läg-, ,antī-/ ▶ **n.** the number of which a given number is the logarithm.

an·ti·ma·cas·sar /,antēmə'kasər/ ▶ **n.** a decorative piece of cloth put over the back of a chair to protect it from grease and dirt.

an·ti·mat·ter /'antē,matər, 'antī-/ ▶ **n.** Physics matter consisting of particles with the same mass as those of normal matter but opposite electric or magnetic properties.

an·ti·mo·ny /'antə,mōnē/ ▶ **n.** a brittle silvery-white metallic element.

an·ti·no·mi·an /,anti'nōmēən/ ▶ **adj.** believing that Christians do not need to obey moral laws.

an·tin·o·my /an'tinəmē/ ▶ **n.** (plural **antinomies**) a paradox.

an·ti·ox·i·dant /,antē'äksidənt, ,antī-/ ▶ **n.** a substance that undoes the effect of oxidation.

an·ti·par·ti·cle /'antē,pärtikəl, 'antī-/ ▶ **n.** a subatomic particle with the same mass as a corresponding particle but an opposite electric charge or magnetic effect.

an·tip·a·thy /an'tipəTHē/ ▶ **n.** (plural **antipathies**) a strong feeling of dislike.

> SYNONYMS **hostility**, antagonism, animosity, aversion, animus, distaste, dislike, hatred, abhorrence, loathing. ANTONYMS affinity, liking.

■ **an·ti·pa·thet·ic** /anˌtipəˈᴛʜetik/ **adj.**

an·ti·per·spi·rant /ˌantiˈpərspərənt/ ▶ **n.** a substance applied to the skin to prevent or reduce sweating.

an·ti·phon /ˈantəˌfän/ ▶ **n.** a short sentence sung or recited before or after a psalm or canticle.

an·tiph·o·nal /anˈtifənl/ ▶ **adj.** sung or recited alternately by two groups.

an·ti·quar·i·an /ˌantiˈkwe(ə)rēən/ ▶ **adj.** relating to the collection or study of antiques or rare books.

an·ti·quat·ed /ˈantiˌkwātid/ ▶ **adj.** very old-fashioned or out of date.

> SYNONYMS **outdated**, outmoded, outworn, behind the times, old, old-fashioned, anachronistic, antediluvian; informal superannuated. ANTONYMS modern.

an·tique /anˈtēk/ ▶ **n.** an object or piece of furniture that is valuable because of its age. ▶ **adj.** having value because of its age.

> SYNONYMS ▶ **n. collector's item**, museum piece, period piece, antiquity. ▶ **adj. antiquarian**, old, collectable, vintage, classic. ANTONYMS modern.

an·tiq·ui·ty /anˈtikwitē/ ▶ **n.** (plural **antiquities**) **1** the distant past. **2** an object from the distant past.

> SYNONYMS **1** *the civilizations of antiquity* **long ago**, the past, prehistory, classical/ancient times. **2** *Inuit antiquities* **antique**, artifact, treasure, object, collector's piece.

an·ti-Sem·i·tism ▶ **n.** hostility to or prejudice against Jews. ■ **an·ti-Sem·ite n. an·ti-Se·mit·ic adj.**

an·ti·sep·tic /ˌantiˈseptik/ ▶ **adj.** preventing the growth of germs that cause disease or infection. ▶ **n.** an antiseptic substance.

an·ti·so·cial /ˌantēˈsōsʜəl, ˌantī-/ ▶ **adj. 1** behaving in a way that is unacceptable or annoying to other people. **2** not wanting to mix with other people.

> SYNONYMS **1** *antisocial behavior* **objectionable**, offensive, unacceptable, disruptive, rowdy. **2** *I'm feeling a bit antisocial* **unsociable**, unfriendly, uncommunicative, reclusive, misanthropic. ANTONYMS acceptable, sociable.

an·tith·e·sis /anˈtiᴛʜəsis/ ▶ **n.** (plural **antitheses**) **1** a person or thing that is the direct opposite of another. **2** the putting together of contrasting ideas or words to produce an effect in writing or speaking.

an·ti·thet·i·cal /ˌantəˈᴛʜetikəl/ ▶ **adj.** opposed to each other.

an·ti·vi·ral /ˌantēˈvīrəl, ˌantī-/ ▶ **n.** (of a medicine or a computer program) effective against viruses.

an·ti·viv·i·sec·tion·ist /ˌantēˌviviˈseksʜənist, ˌantī-/ ▶ **n.** a person who is opposed to using live animals for scientific research.

ant·ler /ˈantlər/ ▶ **n.** each of a pair of branched horns on the head of an adult male deer.

an·to·nym /ˈantəˌnim/ ▶ **n.** a word opposite in meaning to another.

ant·sy /ˈantsē/ ▶ **adj.** agitated, impatient, or restless.

a·nus /ˈānəs/ ▶ **n.** the opening through which solid waste matter leaves the body.

an·vil /ˈanvil/ ▶ **n.** an iron block on which metal is hammered and shaped.

anx·i·e·ty /aɴɢˈzī-itē/ ▶ **n.** (plural **anxieties**) an anxious feeling or state.

> SYNONYMS **worry**, concern, apprehension, unease, fear, disquiet, doubts, nervousness, nerves, tension, stress, angst; informal butterflies (in your stomach), the jitters.

anx·ious /ˈaɴɢ(k)sʜəs/ ▶ **adj. 1** feeling worried or nervous. **2** very eager.

> SYNONYMS **1 worried**, concerned, apprehensive, fearful, uneasy, disturbed, fretful, agitated, nervous, on edge, worked up, jumpy, tense, distraught; informal uptight, with butterflies in one's stomach, jittery, twitchy, antsy. **2** *she was anxious for news* **eager**, keen, itching, impatient, desperate. ANTONYMS unconcerned.

■ **anx·ious·ly adv.**

an·y /ˈenē/ ▶ **determiner & pron. 1** one or some, no matter how much or how many. **2** whichever or whatever you choose. ▶ **adv.** at all: *he wasn't any good at football.*

an·y·bod·y /ˈenēˌbädē, -ˌbədē/ ▶ **pron.** anyone.

an·y·how /ˈenēˌhou/ ▶ **adv. 1** anyway. **2** in a careless or haphazard way.

an·y·more /ˌenēˈmôr/ (or **any more**) ▶ **adv.** to any further extent; any longer: *she refused to listen anymore.*

an·y·one /ˈenēˌwən/ ▶ **pron.** any person or people.

an·y·place /ˈenēˌplās/ ▶ **adv.** informal ⇒ **ANYWHERE.**

an·y·thing /ˈenēˌᴛʜiɴɢ/ ▶ **pron.** a thing of any kind. □ **anything but** not at all.

an·y·time /ˈenētīm/ (also **any time**) ▶ **adv.** at whatever time; whenever necessary.

an·y·way /ˈenēˌwā/ ▶ **adv. 1** said to emphasize something just said or to change the subject. **2** nevertheless.

an·y·ways /ˈenēˌwāz/ ▶ **adv.** informal or dialect form of **ANYWAY.**

an·y·where /ˈenēˌ(h)we(ə)r/ ▶ **adv.** in or to any place. ▶ **pron.** any place.

a·or·ta /āˈôrtə/ ▶ **n.** the main artery supplying blood from the heart to the rest of the body.

a·pace /əˈpās/ ▶ **adv.** literary quickly.

A·pach·e /əˈpacʜē/ ▶ **n.** (plural **Apache** or **Apaches**) a member of an American Indian people living chiefly in New Mexico and Arizona.

a·part /əˈpärt/ ▶ **adv. 1** separated by a distance. **2** into pieces. **3** (**apart from**) except for. **4** (**apart from**) as well as.

> SYNONYMS (**apart from**) **except for**, but for, aside from, with the exception of, excepting, excluding, bar, barring, besides, other than; informal outside of.

a·part·heid /əˈpärtˌ(h)āt, -ˌ(h)īt/ ▶ **n.** the official system of racial segregation formerly in force in South Africa.

a·part·ment /əˈpärtmənt/ ▶ **n.** a suite of rooms forming one residence, typically in a building containing a number of these.

> SYNONYMS efficiency (unit), loft, studio apartment, walk-up, penthouse; informal pad.

> **SPELLING**
>
> Only one **p**: apartment.

ap·a·thet·ic /ˌapəˈTHetik/ ▶ **adj.** not interested or enthusiastic.

SYNONYMS **uninterested**, indifferent, unenthusiastic, unconcerned, unmoved, uninvolved, unemotional, lukewarm, halfhearted, unresponsive, lethargic; informal couldn't-care-less. ANTONYMS enthusiastic.

ap·a·thy /ˈapəTHē/ ▶ **n.** general lack of interest or enthusiasm.

ap·a·to·sau·rus /əˌpatōˈsôrəs/ ▶ **n.** a huge plant-eating dinosaur with a long neck and tail. Formerly called **brontosaurus**.

APB ▶ **abbr.** all-points bulletin.

ape /āp/ ▶ **n.** an animal related to the monkeys but with no tail, such as a chimpanzee or gorilla. ▶ **v.** (**apes**, **aping**, **aped**) imitate someone.

a·pe·ri·tif /äˌperiˈtēf, -əˌper-/ ▶ **n.** an alcoholic drink taken before a meal.

ap·er·ture /ˈapərˌCHər/ ▶ **n. 1** an opening, hole, or gap. **2** the variable opening by which light enters a camera.

SYNONYMS **opening**, hole, gap, slit, slot, vent, crevice, chink, crack; technical orifice.

a·pex /ˈāpeks/ ▶ **n.** (plural **apexes** or **apices** /ˈāpəˌsēz, ˈapə-/) the top or highest point of something.

a·phid /ˈāfid, ˈaf-/ ▶ **n.** a small insect that feeds on the sap of plants.

aph·o·rism /ˈafəˌrizəm/ ▶ **n.** a short clever phrase that makes a true point.

aph·ro·dis·i·ac /ˌafrəˈdizēˌak, -ˈdēzē-, -ˈdēzHē-/ ▶ **n.** a food, drink, or other thing that arouses sexual desire.

a·pi·ar·y /ˈāpēˌerē/ ▶ **n.** (plural **apiaries**) a place where bees are kept.

a·pi·cal /ˈāpikəl, ˈap-/ ▶ **adj.** technical relating to or forming an apex.

a·piece /əˈpēs/ ▶ **adv.** for or by each one: *tickets were a dollar apiece.*

a·plen·ty /əˈplentē/ ▶ **adj.** in large amounts: *he has work aplenty.*

a·plomb /əˈpläm, əˈpləm/ ▶ **n.** calm self-confidence.

APO ▶ **abbr.** Army and Air Force Post Office.

a·poc·a·lypse /əˈpäkəˌlips/ ▶ **n.** a terrible event in which everything is destroyed.

a·poc·a·lyp·tic /əˌpäkəˈliptik/ ▶ **adj.** having to do with or resembling the destruction of the world.

A·poc·ry·pha /əˈpäkrəfə/ ▶ **n.** those books of the Old Testament not accepted as part of Hebrew scripture and excluded from the Protestant Bible at the Reformation.

a·poc·ry·phal /əˈpäkrəfəl/ ▶ **adj.** (of a story or piece of information) widely known but unlikely to be true.

ap·o·gee /ˈapəjē/ ▶ **n. 1** the highest point reached: *his creative activity reached its apogee in 1910.* **2** the point in the orbit of the moon or a satellite at which it is furthest from the earth.

a·po·lit·i·cal /ˌāpəˈlitikəl/ ▶ **adj.** not interested or involved in politics.

a·pol·o·get·ic /əˌpäləˈjetik/ ▶ **adj.** showing that you are sorry for making a mistake or doing something wrong.

SYNONYMS **sorry**, regretful, contrite, remorseful, penitent, repentant. ANTONYMS unrepentant.

■ **a·pol·o·get·i·cal·ly adv.**

ap·o·lo·gi·a /ˌapəˈlōj(ē)ə/ ▶ **n.** a formal defense of opinions or actions.

a·pol·o·gist /əˈpäləjist/ ▶ **n.** a person who defends something controversial.

a·pol·o·gize /əˈpäləˌjīz/ ▶ **v.** (**apologizes**, **apologizing**, **apologized**) say that you are sorry for making a mistake or doing something wrong.

SYNONYMS **say (you are) sorry**, express regret, ask forgiveness, ask for pardon, eat humble pie.

a·pol·o·gy /əˈpäləjē/ ▶ **n.** (plural **apologies**) **1** a statement in which someone apologizes for a mistake made or for harm done. **2** (**an apology for**) a very bad example of.

SYNONYMS **regrets**, expression of regret.

ap·o·plec·tic /ˌapəˈplektik/ ▶ **adj. 1** very angry. **2** old use relating to apoplexy (a stroke).

ap·o·plex·y /ˈapəˌpleksē/ ▶ **n.** (plural **apoplexies**) old use a stroke.

a·pos·ta·sy /əˈpästəsē/ ▶ **n.** the abandoning of a belief or principle.

a·pos·tate /əˈpäsˌtāt, -tit/ ▶ **n.** a person who abandons a belief or principle.

a·pos·tle /əˈpäsəl/ ▶ **n. 1** (**Apostle**) each of the twelve chief disciples of Jesus. **2** a person who strongly supports a policy, cause, etc.

ap·os·tol·ic /ˌapəˈstälik/ ▶ **adj. 1** relating to the Apostles. **2** relating to the pope, seen as the successor to St. Peter.

a·pos·tro·phe /əˈpästrəfē/ ▶ **n.** a punctuation mark (') used to show that something belongs to someone or to show that letters or numbers have been left out.

a·poth·e·car·y /əˈpäTHiˌkerē/ ▶ **n.** (plural **apothecaries**) old use a person who prepared and sold medicines.

ap·o·thegm /ˈapəˌTHem/ ▶ **n.** a concise saying stating a general truth.

a·poth·e·o·sis /əˌpäTHēˈōsis, ˌapəˈTHēəsis/ ▶ **n.** (plural **apotheoses**) the highest level in the development of something: *some believe that science is the apotheosis of the intellect.*

ap·pall /əˈpôl/ ▶ **v.** make someone feel horror and dismay.

SYNONYMS **horrify**, shock, dismay, distress, outrage, scandalize, disgust, revolt, sicken, nauseate, offend, make someone's blood run cold.

ap·pall·ing /əˈpôliNG/ ▶ **adj. 1** causing horror and dismay. **2** informal very bad.

SYNONYMS **1** *an appalling crime* **horrific**, shocking, horrible, terrible, awful, dreadful, ghastly, hideous, horrendous, frightful, atrocious, abominable, outrageous. **2** *your schoolwork is appalling* **dreadful**, terrible, atrocious, deplorable, hopeless, lamentable; informal rotten, crummy, woeful, useless, lousy, abysmal, dire, shocking.

■ **ap·pall·ing·ly adv.**

Ap·pa·loo·sa /ˌapəˈlo͞osə/ ▶ **n.** a horse of a breed having dark spots on a light background.

ap·pa·rat·chik /ˌäpəˈräCHik/ ▶ **n.** (plural **apparatchiks** or **apparatchiki** /-ˌkē/) **1** chiefly historical a member of the administrative system of a communist party. **2** disapproving or humorous an official in a large political organization.

ap·pa·rat·us /ˌapəˈratəs, -ˈrātəs/ ▶ **n.** (plural **apparatuses**) the equipment needed for a particular activity or task.

SYNONYMS **equipment**, gear, tackle, mechanism, appliance, device, instrument, machine, tool.

ap·par·el /əˈparəl/ ▶ **n.** formal clothing.

ap·par·ent /əˈparənt, əˈpe(ə)r-/ ▶ **adj. 1** clearly seen or understood; obvious. **2** seeming real, but not necessarily so.

SYNONYMS **1 evident**, plain, obvious, clear, manifest, visible, discernible, noticeable, perceptible, unmistakable, patent. **2 seeming**, ostensible, outward, superficial. ANTONYMS unclear, real.

SPELLING

Write **-ent**, not **-ant**: appar**ent**.

ap·par·ent·ly /əˈparəntlē, əˈpe(ə)rəntlē/ ▶ **adv. 1** as far as you know or can see. **2** used to avoid committing yourself to the truth of what you are saying: *foreign ministers met but apparently failed to make progress.*

ap·pa·ri·tion /ˌapəˈrisʜən/ ▶ **n.** a remarkable thing making a sudden appearance, especially a ghost.

SYNONYMS **ghost**, phantom, specter, spirit, wraith; informal spook; literary phantasm.

ap·peal /əˈpēl/ ▶ **v. 1** ask earnestly or formally for something. **2** be attractive or interesting. **3** ask a higher court of law to reverse the decision of a lower court. ▶ **n. 1** an act of appealing. **2** the quality of being attractive or interesting.

SYNONYMS ▶ **v. 1 ask**, request, call, petition, plead, entreat, beg, implore, beseech. **2** (**appeal to**) **attract**, interest, fascinate, please, tempt, lure, draw; informal float someone's boat. ▶ **n. 1 plea**, request, petition, entreaty, cry, call, cri de coeur. **2 attraction**, allure, charm, fascination, magnetism, pull.

ap·peal·ing /əˈpēliɴɢ/ ▶ **adj.** attractive or interesting.

SYNONYMS **attractive**, engaging, alluring, enchanting, captivating, bewitching, fascinating, tempting, enticing, irresistible, charming.

■ **ap·peal·ing·ly adv.**

ap·pear /əˈpi(ə)r/ ▶ **v. 1** come into view or start to exist: *smoke appeared on the horizon.* **2** seem. **3** present yourself as a performer or in a court of law.

SYNONYMS **1 become visible**, come into view, materialize, turn up, show up. **2** *differences were beginning to appear* **be revealed**, emerge, surface, manifest itself, become apparent/evident, come to light, arrive, arise, crop up, show up. **3** *they appeared completely devoted* **seem**, look, give the impression of being, come across as, strike someone as. ANTONYMS vanish.

ap·pear·ance /əˈpi(ə)rəns/ ▶ **n. 1** the way that someone or something looks or seems. **2** an act of appearing.

SYNONYMS **1** *her disheveled appearance* **look**, air, aspect, looks, mien, expression, behavior. **2** *an appearance of respectability* **impression**, air, (outward) show, semblance, illusion, facade, front, pretense. **3 occurrence**, manifestation, emergence, arrival, development, materialization.

ap·pease /əˈpēz/ ▶ **v.** (**appeases**, **appeasing**, **appeased**) make someone calm or less hostile by agreeing to their demands.

SYNONYMS **placate**, conciliate, pacify, mollify, reconcile, win over; informal sweeten. ANTONYMS provoke.

■ **ap·pease·ment n.**

ap·pel·la·tion /ˌapəˈlāsʜən/ ▶ **n.** formal a name or title.

ap·pend /əˈpend/ ▶ **v.** add something to the end of a document.

ap·pend·age /əˈpendij/ ▶ **n.** a thing that is attached to something larger or more important.

ap·pen·di·ci·tis /əˌpendəˈsītis/ ▶ **n.** inflammation of the appendix.

ap·pen·dix /əˈpendiks/ ▶ **n.** (plural **appendices** /-diˌsēz/ or **appendixes**) **1** a small tube of tissue attached to the lower end of the large intestine. **2** a section of additional information at the end of a book.

SYNONYMS **supplement**, addendum, postscript, codicil, coda, epilogue, afterword, tailpiece.

ap·per·tain /ˌapərˈtān/ ▶ **v.** (**appertain to**) formal **1** relate to. **2** be applicable.

ap·pe·tite /ˈapiˌtīt/ ▶ **n. 1** a natural desire and physical need for food. **2** a liking or desire for something.

SYNONYMS **1 hunger**, taste, palate, stomach. **2** *my appetite for learning* **desire**, liking, hunger, thirst, longing, yearning, passion, enthusiasm, keenness, eagerness; informal yen.

ap·pe·tiz·er /ˈapiˌtīzər/ ▶ **n.** a small dish of food or a drink taken before a meal to stimulate the appetite.

ap·pe·tiz·ing /ˈapiˌtīziɴɢ/ ▶ **adj.** stimulating the appetite.

SYNONYMS **mouthwatering**, inviting, tempting, tasty, delicious, flavorsome, toothsome, delectable; informal scrumptious, yummy.

ap·plaud /əˈplôd/ ▶ **v. 1** show approval by clapping. **2** say that you approve of or admire something: *the world applauded his courage.*

SYNONYMS **1 clap**, give a standing ovation, put your hands together; informal give someone a big hand. **2 praise**, congratulate, commend, salute, welcome, celebrate, approve of. ANTONYMS boo, criticize.

ap·plause /əˈplôz/ ▶ **n.** clapping.

ap·ple /ˈapəl/ ▶ **n.** a round fruit with green or red skin and crisp flesh. □ **apple-pie order** perfect neatness and order. **the apple of your eye** a person who you are very fond and proud of. **a rotten** (or **bad**) **apple** informal a corrupt person in a group, likely to have a bad influence on the others. **upset the apple cart** spoil a plan.

ap·pli·ance /əˈplīəns/ ▶ **n.** an electrically operated machine for use in the home.

SYNONYMS **device**, machine, instrument, gadget, tool, contraption, apparatus, mechanism, contrivance, labor-saving device; informal gizmo.

ap·pli·ca·ble /'aplikəbəl, ə'plik-/ ▶ **adj.** relevant to someone or something.

SYNONYMS **relevant**, appropriate, pertinent, apposite, material, fitting, suitable, apt. ANTONYMS inappropriate, irrelevant.

■ **ap·pli·ca·bil·i·ty** /ˌaplikə'bilitē/ **n.**

ap·pli·cant /'aplikənt/ ▶ **n.** a person who applies for something.

SYNONYMS **candidate**, interviewee, contender, entrant, claimant, petitioner, prospective student/employee, job-seeker.

ap·pli·ca·tion /ˌapli'kāsʜən/ ▶ **n. 1** a formal request to an authority. **2** the action of applying something. **3** practical use or relevance. **4** continued effort. **5** a computer program designed to fulfill a particular purpose.

SYNONYMS **1 request**, appeal, petition, approach, claim, demand. **2 implementation**, use, exercise, employment, execution, enactment. **3 hard work**, diligence, industry, effort, commitment, dedication, devotion, perseverance, persistence, concentration.

ap·pli·ca·tor /'apliˌkātər/ ▶ **n.** a device for putting something into or on to something.

ap·plied /ə'plīd/ ▶ **adj.** (of a subject of study) used in a practical way: *applied chemistry*.

ap·pli·qué /ˌapli'kā/ ▶ **n.** decorative needlework in which fabric shapes are sewn or stuck on to a background.

ap·ply /ə'plī/ ▶ **v.** (**applies**, **applying**, **applied**) **1** make a formal request for something: *he applied for a job as a carpenter*. **2** bring into operation or use. **3** be relevant. **4** put a substance on a surface. **5** (**apply yourself**) concentrate on what you are doing.

SYNONYMS **1** *300 people **applied for** the job* **put in**, bid for, try (out) for, audition for, seek, solicit (for), claim, request, ask for, petition for, make a bid for. **2** *the law does not **apply to** students* **be relevant to**, pertain to, appertain to, relate to, concern, affect, involve, cover, touch, deal with, have a bearing on. **3 implement**, put into practice, introduce. **4 put on**, rub in/on, work in, spread, smear on, slap on. **5 exert**, administer, use, exercise, employ, utilize, bring to bear.

ap·point /ə'point/ ▶ **v. 1** give someone a job or role. **2** decide on a time for something. **3** (**appointed**) equipped or furnished in a particular way: *a luxuriously appointed bathroom*.

SYNONYMS **1 nominate**, name, designate, install, commission, engage, co-opt, select, choose, elect, vote in. **2 schedule**, arrange, prearrange, specify, agree, designate, set, allot, fix. **3** (**appointed**) **furnished**, decorated, fitted out, supplied.

ap·point·ment /ə'pointmənt/ ▶ **n. 1** an arrangement to meet. **2** the appointing of someone to a job. **3** (**appointments**) furniture or fittings.

SYNONYMS **1 meeting**, engagement, interview, consultation, rendezvous, date, assignation; literary tryst. **2 nomination**, naming, designation, installation, commissioning, engagement, co-option, selection, election. **3 job**, post, position, situation, place, office.

ap·por·tion /ə'pôrsʜən/ ▶ **v.** share out; divide and allocate. ■ **ap·por·tion·ment n.**

ap·po·site /'apəzit/ ▶ **adj.** appropriate.

ap·po·si·tion /ˌapə'zisʜən/ ▶ **n.** Grammar a relationship in which a word or phrase is placed next to another that it is equivalent to, so as to qualify or explain it (e.g., *our first president, George Washington*).

ap·prais·al /ə'prāzəl/ ▶ **n.** an assessment of the quality or value of something.

SYNONYMS **assessment**, evaluation, estimation, judgment, summing-up, consideration.

ap·praise /ə'prāz/ ▶ **v.** (**appraises**, **appraising**, **appraised**) assess the quality or value of something.

ap·pre·ci·a·ble /ə'prēsʜ(ē)əbəl/ ▶ **adj.** large or important enough to be noticed.

SYNONYMS **considerable**, substantial, significant, sizable, goodly, fair, reasonable, marked; perceptible, noticeable, visible; informal tidy. ANTONYMS negligible.

■ **ap·pre·ci·a·bly adv.**

ap·pre·ci·ate /ə'prēsʜēˌāt/ ▶ **v.** (**appreciates**, **appreciating**, **appreciated**) **1** recognize the value of something. **2** understand a situation fully. **3** be grateful for. **4** rise in value or price.

SYNONYMS **1 value**, admire, respect, think highly of, think much of, be grateful for, be glad of. **2 recognize**, realize, know, be aware of, be conscious of, be sensitive to, understand, sympathize with. **3 increase**, gain, grow, rise, go up, soar. ANTONYMS disparage, depreciate.

ap·pre·ci·a·tion /əˌprēsʜē'āsʜən/ ▶ **n. 1** recognition of the value of something. **2** gratitude for something. **3** a piece of writing in which the qualities of a person or their work are discussed. **4** an increase in value.

SYNONYMS **1 knowledge**, awareness, enjoyment, love, feeling, discrimination, sensitivity. **2 gratitude**, thanks, gratefulness. **3 acknowledgment**, recognition, realization, knowledge, awareness, consciousness, understanding. **4 review**, critique, criticism, analysis, assessment, evaluation, judgment. **5 increase**, gain, growth, rise, inflation, escalation. ANTONYMS ingratitude, depreciation.

ap·pre·cia·tive /ə'prēsʜ(ē)ətiv/ ▶ **adj.** feeling or showing gratitude or pleasure.

SYNONYMS **1** *we are **appreciative of** your support* **grateful for**, thankful for, obliged for, indebted for. **2** *an appreciative audience* **admiring**, enthusiastic, approving, complimentary.

■ **ap·pre·cia·tive·ly adv.**

ap·pre·hend /ˌapri'hend/ ▶ **v. 1** arrest someone for doing something wrong. **2** understand something.

SYNONYMS **1** *the thieves were apprehended* **arrest**, catch, capture, seize; take prisoner, take into custody; informal collar, nab, nail, run in, bust, pick up, pull in. **2** *they are slow to apprehend danger* **appreciate**, recognize, discern, perceive, grasp, understand, comprehend; informal get the picture about.

ap·pre·hen·sion /ˌapri'hensʜən/ ▶ **n. 1** a feeling of worry or fear about what might happen. **2** understanding. **3** the act of arresting someone.

SYNONYMS **1 anxiety**, worry, unease, nervousness, nerves, misgivings, disquiet, concern, trepidation. **2 arrest**, capture, seizure, detention. ANTONYMS confidence.

ap·pre·hen·sive /ˌapriˈhensiv/ ▶ **adj.** worried or afraid about what might happen.

SYNONYMS **anxious**, worried, uneasy, nervous, concerned, fearful. ANTONYMS confident.

■ **ap·pre·hen·sive·ly** **adv.**

ap·pren·tice /əˈprentis/ ▶ **n.** a person learning a skilled trade from an employer. ▶ **v.** (**be apprenticed**) be employed as an apprentice.

SYNONYMS ▶ **n. trainee**, learner, novice, beginner, tyro, student, pupil; informal rookie, tenderfoot, greenhorn. ANTONYMS veteran.

■ **ap·pren·tice·ship** **n.**

ap·prise /əˈprīz/ ▶ **v.** (**apprises**, **apprising**, **apprised**) (**apprise someone of**) make someone aware of: *I apprised him of what had happened.*

ap·proach /əˈprōcH/ ▶ **v. 1** come near to. **2** go to someone with a proposal or request. **3** deal with something in a certain way. ▶ **n. 1** a way of dealing with something. **2** a proposal or request. **3** the action of approaching. **4** a way leading to a place.

SYNONYMS ▶ **v. 1 move toward**, near, come near, close in on, close with, gain on. **2 speak to**, talk to, sound out, make a proposal to, proposition, appeal to. **3 tackle**, address, manage, set about, go about, start work on. ANTONYMS leave. ▶ **n. 1 method**, procedure, technique, modus operandi, style, way, strategy, tactic, system, means, line of action. **2 proposal**, submission, application, appeal, plea, request, overture, proposition. **3 advance**, arrival, appearance. **4 driveway**, road, path, entry, way.

ap·proach·a·ble /əˈprōcHəbəl/ ▶ **adj. 1** friendly and easy to talk to. **2** able to be reached from a particular direction.

SYNONYMS **1 friendly**, welcoming, pleasant, agreeable, affable, sympathetic, congenial. **2 accessible**, reachable, attainable; informal get-at-able. ANTONYMS aloof, inaccessible.

ap·pro·ba·tion /ˌaprəˈbāsHən/ ▶ **n.** approval.

ap·pro·pri·ate ▶ **adj.** /əˈprōprē-it/ suitable or right in the circumstances. ▶ **v.** /əˈprōprēˌāt/ (**appropriates**, **appropriating**, **appropriated**) **1** take something for your own use without permission. **2** set money aside for a special purpose.

SYNONYMS ▶ **adj. suitable**, proper, fitting, seemly, apt, right, convenient, opportune, relevant, apposite. ANTONYMS inappropriate. ▶ **v. seize**, commandeer, requisition, expropriate, usurp, take over, hijack, steal; informal swipe, nab.

■ **ap·pro·pri·ate·ly** /-itlē/ **adv.** **ap·pro·pri·a·tion** /-ˈāsHən/ **n.**

ap·prov·al /əˈpro͞ovəl/ ▶ **n. 1** a feeling that something is good or acceptable. **2** official permission or agreement.

SYNONYMS **1 favor**, liking, appreciation, admiration, regard, esteem, respect. **2 acceptance**, agreement, consent, assent, permission, rubber stamp, sanction, blessing, endorsement, ratification, authorization; informal the go-ahead, the green light, the OK, the thumbs up. ANTONYMS disapproval, refusal.

□ **on approval** (of goods) able to be returned to a supplier if not satisfactory.

ap·prove /əˈpro͞ov/ ▶ **v.** (**approves**, **approving**, **approved**) **1** feel that something is good or acceptable: *he approved of harsh punishments for criminals.* **2** officially accept something as satisfactory.

SYNONYMS **agree to**, accept, consent to, assent to, give your blessing to, bless, ratify, sanction, endorse, authorize, validate, pass, rubber-stamp; informal give the go-ahead to, give the green light to, give the OK to, give the thumbs up to. ANTONYMS refuse.

ap·prox·i·mate ▶ **adj.** /əˈpräksəmit/ almost but not completely accurate. ▶ **v.** /əˈpräksəˌmāt/ (**approximates**, **approximating**, **approximated**) come close or be similar to.

SYNONYMS ▶ **adj. estimated**, rough, imprecise, inexact, broad, loose; informal ballpark. ANTONYMS precise.

■ **ap·prox·i·ma·tion** /əˌpräksəˈmāsHən/ **n.**

ap·prox·i·mate·ly /əˈpräksəmitlē/ ▶ **adv.** near to but not exactly.

SYNONYMS **roughly**, about, around, circa, round/around about, more or less, nearly, almost, approaching; informal pushing, in the ballpark of.

ap·pur·te·nan·ces /əˈpərtn-ənsiz/ ▶ **pl.n.** the things you need for a particular activity.

APR ▶ **abbr.** annual (or annualized) percentage rate.

a·près-ski /ˌäprā ˈskē/ ▶ **n.** parties and other entertainment that take place after a day's skiing.

ap·ri·cot /ˈapriˌkät, ˈāpri-/ ▶ **n.** an orange-yellow fruit resembling a small peach.

A·pril /ˈāprəl/ ▶ **n.** the fourth month of the year.
□ **April Fool's Day** April 1, traditionally an occasion for playing tricks.

a pri·o·ri /ˈä prēˈôrē, prīˈôrī, ˈā/ ▶ **adj. & adv.** using facts that are known to be true in order to decide what an unknown effect or result will be.

a·pron /ˈāprən/ ▶ **n. 1** a garment tied over the front of clothes to keep them clean. **2** an area on an airfield used for maneuvering or parking aircraft. **3** a strip of stage extending in front of the curtain.
□ **tied to someone's apron strings** be dominated or excessively influenced by someone.

ap·ro·pos /ˌaprəˈpō/ ▶ **prep.** (**apropos of**) with reference to.

apse /aps/ ▶ **n.** a recess with a domed or arched roof in a church, usually at one end and containing the altar.

apt /apt/ ▶ **adj. 1** suitable for the occasion; appropriate. **2** (**apt to**) tending to. **3** quick to learn.

SYNONYMS **1 suitable**, fitting, appropriate, relevant, apposite, felicitous. **2 inclined**, given, likely, liable, prone. **3 clever**, quick, bright, sharp, smart, able, gifted, talented. ANTONYMS inappropriate.

■ **apt·ly** **adv.**

ap·ti·tude /ˈaptiˌt(y)o͞od/ ▶ **n.** a natural ability.

SYNONYMS **talent**, gift, flair, bent, skill, knack, facility, ability, capability, potential, capacity, faculty.

aq·ua·ma·rine /ˌäkwəməˈrēn, ˌak-/ ▶ **n.** **1** a bluish-green precious stone. **2** a light bluish-green color.

aq·ua·plane /ˈäkwəˌplān, ˈak-/ ▶ **n.** a board for riding on water, pulled by a speedboat. ▶ **v.** (**aquaplanes**, **aquaplaning**, **aquaplaned**) (of a vehicle) slide uncontrollably on a wet surface.

a·quar·i·um /əˈkwe(ə)rēəm/ ▶ **n.** (plural **aquariums** or **aquaria** /-ēə/) a water-filled glass tank in which fish and other water creatures are kept.

A·quar·i·us /əˈkwe(ə)rēəs/ ▶ **n.** a sign of the zodiac (the Water Carrier), January 21–February 20.

a·quat·ic /əˈkwätik, əˈkwat-/ ▶ **adj.** **1** relating to water. **2** living in or near water.

aq·ue·duct /ˈäkwəˌdəkt, ˈak-/ ▶ **n.** a long channel or bridgelike structure for carrying water across country.

SPELLING

Write **aque-**, not **aqua-**: **aque**duct.

a·que·ous /ˈākwēəs, ˈak-/ ▶ **adj.** relating to or containing water.

a·que·ous hu·mor ▶ **n.** the clear fluid in the eyeball in front of the lens.

aq·ui·fer /ˈäkwəfər, ˈak-/ ▶ **n.** a body of rock that holds water or through which water flows.

aq·ui·line /ˈakwəˌlīn, -lin/ ▶ **adj.** **1** (of a person's nose) curved like an eagle's beak. **2** like an eagle.

Ar·ab /ˈarəb/ ▶ **n.** a member of a people inhabiting much of the Middle East and North Africa.

ar·a·besque /ˌarəˈbesk/ ▶ **n.** **1** a ballet position in which one leg is extended horizontally backward and the arms are outstretched. **2** an ornamental design of intertwined flowing lines.

A·ra·bi·an /əˈrābēən/ ▶ **adj.** relating to Arabia or its people. ▶ **n.** old use an Arab.

Ar·a·bic /ˈarəbik/ ▶ **n.** the language of the Arabs, written from right to left. ▶ **adj.** relating to the Arabs or Arabic. □ **Arabic numeral** any of the numerals 0, 1, 2, 3, 4, 5, 6, 7, 8, and 9.

ar·a·ble /ˈarəbəl/ ▶ **adj.** (of land) able to be used for growing crops.

a·rach·nid /əˈraknid/ ▶ **n.** a creature of a class including spiders, scorpions, mites, and ticks.

a·rach·no·pho·bi·a /əˌraknəˈfōbēə/ ▶ **n.** extreme fear of spiders.

Ar·a·ma·ic /ˌarəˈmāik/ ▶ **n.** an ancient Semitic language still spoken in parts of the Middle East.

ar·bi·ter /ˈärbitər/ ▶ **n.** **1** a person who settles a dispute. **2** a person who has influence in a particular area: *an arbiter of fashion.*

ar·bi·trar·y /ˈärbiˌtr(ə)rē/ ▶ **adj.** **1** not seeming to be based on any plan or system. **2** (of power) used without restraint.

SYNONYMS **random**, unpredictable, capricious, subjective, whimsical, wanton, motiveless, irrational, groundless, unjustified.

■ **ar·bi·trar·i·ly** /ˌärbiˈtre(ə)rəlē/ **adv.**

ar·bi·trate /ˈärbiˌtrāt/ ▶ **v.** (**arbitrates**, **arbitrating**, **arbitrated**) act as an arbitrator to settle a dispute.

ar·bi·tra·tion /ˌärbiˈtrāsʜən/ ▶ **n.** the use of an arbitrator to settle a dispute.

SYNONYMS **adjudication**, judgment, mediation, conciliation, intervention.

ar·bi·tra·tor /ˈärbiˌtrātər/ ▶ **n.** a person or organization appointed to settle a dispute.

SYNONYMS **adjudicator**, arbiter, judge, referee, umpire, mediator, go-between.

ar·bor /ˈärbər/ ▶ **n.** a shady place in a garden, with a canopy of trees or climbing plants trained over a wooden framework.

ar·bo·re·al /ärˈbôrēəl/ ▶ **adj.** **1** living in trees. **2** relating to trees.

ar·bo·re·tum /ˌärbəˈrētəm/ ▶ **n.** (plural **arboretums** or **arboreta** /-tə/) a garden in which trees are grown for study and display to the public.

arc /ärk/ ▶ **n.** **1** a curve forming part of the circumference of a circle. **2** a curving movement through the air. **3** a glowing electrical discharge between two points. ▶ **v.** (**arcs**, **arcing**, **arced**) move in an arc.

SYNONYMS ▶ **n.** **curve**, arch, bow, curl, crescent, semicircle, half-moon.

ar·cade /ärˈkād/ ▶ **n.** **1** a series of arches supporting a roof or wall. **2** a covered walk with stores along the sides. **3** an indoor area with video games operated by coins, tickets, or tokens.

Ar·ca·di·an /ärˈkādēən/ ▶ **adj.** literary relating to a perfect country scene or way of life.

ar·ca·na /ärˈkānə/ ▶ **pl.n.** (singular **arcanum**) hidden things; mysteries.

ar·cane /ärˈkān/ ▶ **adj.** secret and mysterious.

arch¹ /ärcʜ/ ▶ **n.** **1** a curved structure spanning an opening or supporting the weight of a bridge or roof. **2** the inner side of the foot. ▶ **v.** form an arch.

SYNONYMS ▶ **n.** **archway**, vault, span. ▶ **v.** **curve**, arc, bend, bow, crook, hunch.

arch² /ärcʜ/ ▶ **adj.** suggesting in a playful way that you know more than you are revealing. ■ **arch·ly** **adv.**

ar·chae·ol·o·gy /ˌärkēˈäləjē/ (or **archeology**) ▶ **n.** the study of ancient history through the examination of objects, structures, and materials dug up from old sites. ■ **ar·chae·o·log·i·cal** /-əˈläjikəl/ **adj.** **ar·chae·ol·o·gist** **n.**

ar·chae·op·ter·yx /ˌärkēˈäptəriks/ ▶ **n.** the oldest known fossil bird, which had teeth like a dinosaur.

ar·cha·ic /ärˈkāik/ ▶ **adj.** **1** very old or old-fashioned. **2** belonging to an earlier period. ■ **ar·cha·ism** /ˈärkēˌizəm, ˈärkā-/ **n.**

arch·an·gel /ˈärkˌānjəl/ ▶ **n.** an angel of high rank.

arch·bish·op /ˈärcʜˈbisʜəp/ ▶ **n.** a bishop of the highest rank.

arch·dea·con /ˈärcʜˈdēkən/ ▶ **n.** (in the Anglican church) a senior Christian priest.

arch·duke /ˈärcʜˈd(y)o͞ok/ ▶ **n.** a chief duke, especially (historical) a son of the emperor of Austria.

arch·en·e·my /ˈärcʜˈenəmē/ ▶ **n.** a chief enemy.

arch·er /ˈärcʜər/ ▶ **n.** a person who shoots with a bow and arrows.

ar·cher·y /ˈärcʜərē/ ▶ **n.** the activity or sport of shooting with a bow and arrows.

ar·che·type /ˈärk(i)ˌtīp/ ▶ **n.** **1** a very typical example: *he looked the archetype of the old sailor.* **2** an original model that others follow. ■ **ar·che·typ·al** /ˌärk(i)ˈtīpəl/ **adj.**

ar·chi·pel·a·go /ˌärkəˈpeləˌgō/ ▶ **n.** (plural **archipelagos** or **archipelagoes**) a group of many islands and the sea surrounding them.

ar·chi·tect /ˈärkiˌtekt/ ▶ **n.** **1** a person who designs buildings. **2** the person responsible for something:

the architect of the reforms.

SYNONYMS **designer**, planner, originator, author, creator, founder, inventor.

ar·chi·tec·ton·ic /ˌärkitek'tänik/ ▶ **adj.** relating to architecture or architects. ▶ **n.** (**architectonics**) the scientific study of architecture.

ar·chi·tec·ture /'ärkiˌtekCHər/ ▶ **n. 1** the design and construction of buildings. **2** the complex structure of something.

SYNONYMS **building**, planning, design, construction.

■ **ar·chi·tec·tur·al** /ˌärki'tekCHərəl/ **adj.**

ar·chi·trave /'ärkiˌtrāv/ ▶ **n. 1** (in classical architecture) a beam resting across the tops of columns. **2** the frame around a doorway or window.

ar·chive /'ärˌkīv/ ▶ **n. 1** a collection of historical documents or records. **2** a complete record of the data in a computer system. ▶ **v.** (**archives**, **archiving**, **archived**) put something in an archive.

SYNONYMS ▶ **n. 1** *the family archives* **records**, papers, documents, files, annals, chronicles, history. **2** *the Institute's archive* **record office**, registry, repository, museum, library. ▶ **v. file**, log, catalog, document, record, register, store.

■ **ar·chi·val** /är'kīvəl/ **adj.**

ar·chi·vist /'ärkəvist, -ˌkī-/ ▶ **n.** a person who is in charge of archives of historical material.

arch·way /'ärCHˌwā/ ▶ **n.** a curved structure forming a passage or entrance.

Arc·tic /'ärktik, 'ärtik/ ▶ **adj.** relating to the regions around the North Pole.

SPELLING

Remember the first **c**: Arctic.

ar·dent /'ärdnt/ ▶ **adj. 1** feeling passionate about something. **2** old use burning; glowing.

SYNONYMS **passionate**, fervent, zealous, wholehearted, intense, fierce, enthusiastic, keen, eager, avid, committed, dedicated. ANTONYMS apathetic.

■ **ar·dent·ly adv.**

ar·dor /'ärdər/ ▶ **n.** passionate feelings.

ar·du·ous /'ärjo͞oəs/ ▶ **adj.** difficult and tiring.

SYNONYMS **tough**, difficult, hard, heavy, laborious, onerous, taxing, strenuous, back-breaking, demanding, challenging, punishing, grueling; informal killing. ANTONYMS easy.

■ **ar·du·ous·ly adv.**

are /är/ 2nd person singular present and 1st, 2nd, and 3rd person plural present of **BE**.

USAGE

Don't confuse **are** with **our**.

ar·e·a /'e(ə)rēə/ ▶ **n. 1** a part of a place, object, or surface. **2** the extent or measurement of a surface. **3** a subject or range of activity.

SYNONYMS **1 district**, zone, region, sector, quarter, locality, neighborhood; informal neck of the woods, turf. **2** *the dining area* **space**, section, part, place, room. **3** *specific areas of knowledge* **field**, sphere, realm, domain, sector, province, territory.

□ **area code** a telephone dialing code.

a·re·na /ə'rēnə/ ▶ **n. 1** a level area surrounded by seating, in which sports and other events are held. **2** an area of activity: *conflicts within the political arena.*

SYNONYMS **1 stadium**, amphitheater, ground, field, ring, rink, court, bowl, park. **2 scene**, sphere, realm, province, domain, forum, territory, world.

aren't /är(ə)nt/ ▶ **contr. 1** are not. **2** am not (only in questions): *I'm right, aren't I?*

a·re·o·la /ə'rēələ/ ▶ **n.** (plural **areolae** /-ˌlē/) the circular area of darker skin surrounding a human nipple.

a·rête /ə'rāt/ ▶ **n.** a sharp mountain ridge.

Ar·gen·tin·i·an /ˌärjən'tinēən/ (or **Argentine** /'ärjənˌtīn, -ˌtēn/) ▶ **n.** a person from Argentina. ▶ **adj.** relating to Argentina.

ar·gon /'ärˌgän/ ▶ **n.** an inert gaseous element, present in small amounts in the air.

ar·got /'ärgō, -gət/ ▶ **n.** the jargon or slang of a particular group.

ar·gu·a·ble /'ärgyo͞oəbəl/ ▶ **adj.** able to be argued or disagreed with. ■ **ar·gu·a·bly adv.**

ar·gue /'ärgyo͞o/ ▶ **v.** (**argues**, **arguing**, **argued**) **1** discuss something in a serious or angry way with someone who disagrees with you. **2** make statements in support of an action or opinion.

SYNONYMS **1 quarrel**, disagree, dispute, squabble, bicker, have words, cross swords, fight, wrangle, row. **2 claim**, maintain, insist, contend, assert, hold, reason, allege.

ar·gu·ment /'ärgyəmənt/ ▶ **n. 1** a serious or angry discussion between people who disagree with each other. **2** a set of reasons given in support of an action or opinion.

SYNONYMS **1 quarrel**, disagreement, difference of opinion, squabble, dispute, altercation, fight, wrangle, row; informal tiff, set-to. **2 reasoning**, justification, explanation, case, defense, vindication, evidence, reasons, grounds.

SPELLING

No **e** in the middle: **argu**ment, not **argue-**.

ar·gu·men·ta·tion /ˌärgyəmən'tāSHən/ ▶ **n.** systematic reasoning in support of something.

ar·gu·men·ta·tive /ˌärgyə'mentətiv/ ▶ **adj.** tending to argue.

a·ri·a /'ärēə/ ▶ **n.** a song for a solo voice in an opera.

ar·id /'arid/ ▶ **adj. 1** very dry because of having little or no rain. **2** dull and boring: *arid verse.*

SYNONYMS **dry**, waterless, parched, scorched, desiccated, desert, barren, infertile. ANTONYMS wet, fertile.

■ **a·rid·i·ty** /ə'riditē/ **n.**

Ar·ies /'e(ə)rēz, 'e(ə)rē-ēz/ ▶ **n.** a sign of the zodiac (the Ram), March 20–April 20.

a·rise /ə'rīz/ ▶ **v.** (**arises**, **arising**, **arose** /ə'rōz/; past participle **arisen** /ə'rizən/) **1** start to exist or be noticed. **2** (**arise from** or **out of**) happen as a result of. **3** formal stand up.

SYNONYMS **1** *many problems arose* **come about**, happen, occur, come into being, emerge, crop up, come to light, become apparent, appear, turn up, surface, spring up. **2** *injuries arising from defective products* **result**, stem, originate, proceed, follow, ensue, be caused by.

ar·is·toc·ra·cy /ˌari'stäkrəsē/ ▶ **n.** (plural **aristocracies**) the highest social class in some societies, consisting of people whose families hold a title such as *Lord* or *Duke*.

a·ris·to·crat /ə'ristəˌkrat/ ▶ **n.** a member of the aristocracy.

SYNONYMS **nobleman**, noblewoman, lord, lady, peer (of the realm), patrician. ANTONYMS commoner.

a·ris·to·crat·ic /əˌristə'kratik/ ▶ **adj.** relating to or typical of the aristocracy.

SYNONYMS **noble**, titled, upper-class, blue-blooded, high-born, patrician; informal upper-crust, top-drawer. ANTONYMS common.

■ **a·ris·to·crat·i·cal·ly adv.**

a·rith·me·tic /ə'riTHməˌtik/ ▶ **n.** the use of numbers in counting and calculation. ■ **ar·ith·met·i·cal** /ˌariTH'metikəl/ **adj. ar·ith·met·i·cal·ly adv.**

ark /ärk/ ▶ **n. 1** (in the Bible) the ship built by Noah to save two of every kind of animal from the Flood. **2** a chest or cupboard in a synagogue in which the holy scrolls are kept. **3** (**Ark of the Covenant**) the chest that contained the laws of the ancient Israelites.

arm[1] /ärm/ ▶ **n. 1** each of the two upper limbs of the human body from the shoulder to the hand. **2** a side part of a chair supporting a sitter's arm. **3** a strip of water or land. **4** a branch or division of a company or organization. □ **arm in arm** with arms linked. **cost an arm and a leg** informal be very expensive. **keep someone/something at arm's length** avoid close contact with someone or something. **with open arms** with great warmth or enthusiasm.

arm[2] /ärm/ ▶ **v. 1** supply with weapons. **2** provide with essential equipment or information. **3** make a bomb ready to explode.

SYNONYMS **equip**, provide, supply, furnish, issue, fit out.

ar·ma·da /är'mädə/ ▶ **n.** a fleet of warships.

ar·ma·dil·lo /ˌärmə'dilō/ ▶ **n.** (plural **armadillos**) an omnivorous animal of Central America, South America, and the southern United States, with a body covered in bony plates and sharp claws for burrowing.

Ar·ma·ged·don /ˌärmə'gedn/ ▶ **n. 1** (in the Bible) the final battle between good and evil before the Last Judgement. **2** a terrible war with a catastrophic ending.

ar·ma·ment /'ärməmənt/ ▶ **n. 1** (also **armaments**) military weapons and equipment. **2** the equipping of military forces.

SYNONYMS **arms**, weapons, weaponry, firearms, guns, ordnance, artillery, munitions, materiel.

ar·ma·ture /'ärməCHər, -ˌCHo͝or/ ▶ **n. 1** the rotating coil of a dynamo or electric motor. **2** a piece of iron placed across the poles of a magnet to preserve its power.

arm·chair /'ärmˌCHe(ə)r/ ▶ **n.** a comfortable chair with padded sides on which to rest your arms.

armed /ärmd/ ▶ **adj.** carrying a weapon. □ **armed forces** a country's army, navy, and air force.

ar·mi·stice /'ärməstis/ ▶ **n.** an agreement to stop fighting.

SYNONYMS **truce**, ceasefire, peace, suspension of hostilities.

arm·load /'ärmˌlōd/ ▶ **n.** the amount that can be carried with one arm or in both arms.

ar·mor /'ärmər/ ▶ **n. 1** (also **body armor**) coverings worn to protect the body in battle. **2** (also **armor plate**) the tough metal layer covering a military vehicle or ship. **3** (**armored**) covered with armor.

SYNONYMS (**armored**) **armor-plated**, steel-plated, ironclad, bulletproof, bombproof, reinforced, toughened.

ar·mor·er /'ärmərər/ ▶ **n.** a person who makes, supplies, or looks after weapons or armor.

ar·mo·ri·al /är'môrēəl/ ▶ **adj.** relating to coats of arms.

ar·mor·y /'ärmərē/ ▶ **n.** (plural **armories**) **1** a stored supply of arms. **2** the place where a supply of arms is kept.

arm·pit /'ärmˌpit/ ▶ **n.** a hollow under the arm at the shoulder.

arms /ärmz/ ▶ **pl.n. 1** guns and other weapons. **2** the emblems on a coat of arms.

SYNONYMS **weapons**, weaponry, firearms, guns, ordnance, artillery, armaments, munitions.

□ **up in arms** protesting strongly.

ar·my /'ärmē/ ▶ **n.** (plural **armies**) **1** a military force that fights on land. **2** a large number of people or things.

SYNONYMS **1 armed force**, military force, land force(s), military, soldiery, infantry, militia, troops, soldiers. **2** *an army of tourists* **crowd**, swarm, horde, mob, gang, throng, mass, flock, herd, pack.

a·ro·ma /ə'rōmə/ ▶ **n.** a pleasant smell.

SYNONYMS **smell**, odor, fragrance, scent, perfume, bouquet, nose.

a·ro·ma·ther·a·py /əˌrōmə'THerəpē/ ▶ **n.** the use of aromatic oils for healing or to give pleasant feelings. ■ **a·ro·ma·ther·a·pist n.**

ar·o·mat·ic /ˌarə'matik/ ▶ **adj. 1** having a pleasant and distinctive smell. **2** (of an organic compound such as benzene) containing a flat ring of atoms in its molecule. ▶ **n.** an aromatic plant, substance, or compound.

SYNONYMS ▶ **adj. fragrant**, scented, perfumed, fragranced.

■ **ar·o·mat·i·cal·ly adv.**

a·rose /ə'rōz/ past of **ARISE**.

a·round /ə'round/ ▶ **adv. 1** located or situated on every side. **2** so as to surround someone or something. **3** so as to rotate or cause rotation. **4** so as to cover the whole area surrounding a particular center. **5** so as to turn and face in the opposite direction. **6** used in describing the position of something: *the wrong way around*. **7** about; approximately. **8** so as to reach a new place or position. **9** available or present. ▶ **prep. 1** so as to encircle or embrace someone or something. **2** on every side of something. **3** in or to many places throughout an area.

SYNONYMS ▶ **prep. 1 surrounding**, enclosing, on all sides of. **2 approximately**, about, around about, circa, roughly, more or less, nearly, almost, approaching; informal in the ballpark of.

a·rouse /ə'rouz/ ▶ **v.** (**arouses, arousing, aroused**) **1** bring about a feeling or response in someone.

2 awaken someone from sleep.

SYNONYMS **1 provoke**, trigger, stir up, engender, cause, whip up, rouse, inflame, agitate, incite, galvanize, electrify, stimulate, inspire, fire up. **2 wake (up)**, awaken, bring to/around, rouse. ANTONYMS allay.

■ **a·rous·al** n.

ar·peg·gi·o /är'pejē,ō/ ▶ n. (plural **arpeggios**) the notes of a musical chord played in rapid succession.

ar·raign /ə'rān/ ▶ v. call someone before a court to answer a criminal charge. ■ **ar·raign·ment** n.

ar·range /ə'rānj/ ▶ v. (**arranges**, **arranging**, **arranged**) **1** put in a neat or a particular order. **2** organize or plan. **3** adapt a piece of music for performance.

SYNONYMS **1 set out**, (put in) order, lay out, align, position, present, display, exhibit, group, sort, organize, tidy. **2 organize**, fix (up), plan, schedule, contrive, determine, agree. **3** *he arranged the piece for a full orchestra* **adapt**, set, score, orchestrate.

■ **ar·rang·er** n.

ar·range·ment /ə'rānjmənt/ ▶ n. **1** a plan for a future event. **2** something made up of things arranged in a particular way. **3** an arranged piece of music.

SYNONYMS **1 preparation**, plan, provision, planning. **2 agreement**, deal, understanding, bargain, settlement, pact. **3 positioning**, presentation, grouping, organization, alignment. **4** *an arrangement of Beethoven's symphonies* **adaptation**, orchestration, scoring, interpretation.

ar·rant /'arənt/ ▶ adj. dated complete; absolute: *arrant nonsense*.

ar·ray /ə'rā/ ▶ n. **1** an impressive display or range. **2** an ordered arrangement of troops. **3** literary elaborate clothing. ▶ v. **1** (**be arrayed**) be displayed or arranged in a neat or impressive way. **2** (**be arrayed in**) be dressed in.

SYNONYMS ▶ n. **range**, collection, selection, assortment, variety, arrangement, lineup, display, exhibition. ▶ v. **arrange**, assemble, group, order, range, place, position, set out, lay out, spread out, display, exhibit.

ar·rears /ə'ri(ə)rz/ ▶ pl.n. money owed that should already have been paid. □ **in arrears 1** behind with paying money that is owed. **2** (of wages or rent) paid at the end of each period of work or occupation.

ar·rest /ə'rest/ ▶ v. **1** seize someone and take them into custody. **2** stop the progress of something. **3** (**arresting**) attracting attention. ▶ n. **1** the action of arresting someone. **2** a sudden stop: *a cardiac arrest*.

SYNONYMS ▶ v. **1 detain**, apprehend, seize, capture, take into custody; informal pick up, pull in, collar, nab. **2 stop**, halt, check, block, curb, prevent, obstruct, stem, slow, interrupt, delay. **3** (**arresting**) **striking**, eye-catching, conspicuous, impressive, imposing, spectacular, dramatic, breathtaking, stunning, awe-inspiring. ANTONYMS release, inconspicuous. ▶ n. **detention**, apprehension, seizure, capture. ANTONYMS release.

ar·ri·val /ə'rīvəl/ ▶ n. **1** the process of arriving somewhere. **2** a person or thing that has just arrived.

SYNONYMS **coming**, appearance, entrance, entry, approach, advent. ANTONYMS departure.

ar·rive /ə'rīv/ ▶ v. (**arrives**, **arriving**, **arrived**) **1** reach a destination. **2** (of a particular moment) come about. **3** (**arrive at**) reach a conclusion or decision.

SYNONYMS **come**, turn up, get here/there, make it, appear; informal show (up), roll in/up, blow in. ANTONYMS depart, leave.

ar·ri·viste /,ärē'vēst/ ▶ n. often disapproving a person who has recently become wealthy or risen in social status.

ar·ro·gant /'arəgənt/ ▶ adj. behaving in an unpleasant way because you think that you are better than other people.

SYNONYMS **haughty**, conceited, self-important, cocky, supercilious, condescending, full of yourself, overbearing, imperious, proud; informal high and mighty, too big for your britches. ANTONYMS modest.

■ **ar·ro·gance** n. **ar·ro·gant·ly** adv.

ar·ro·gate /'arə,gāt/ ▶ v. (**arrogates**, **arrogating**, **arrogated**) formal take or claim something that you have no right to.

ar·row /'arō/ ▶ n. **1** a stick with a sharp point, shot from a bow. **2** a symbol resembling this, used to show direction or position.

ar·row·root /'arō,ro͞ot, -,ro͝ot/ ▶ n. a starch obtained from a plant and used as a thickener in cooking.

ar·roy·o /ə'roi,ō/ ▶ n. (plural **arroyos**) a deep gully cut by the action of fast-flowing water in an arid area.

ar·se·nal /'ärs(ə)-nl/ ▶ n. a store of weapons and ammunition.

ar·se·nic /'ärs(ə)nik/ ▶ n. a brittle gray element from which a highly poisonous white powder is obtained.

ar·son /'ärsən/ ▶ n. the criminal act of deliberately setting fire to property. ■ **ar·son·ist** n.

art /ärt/ ▶ n. **1** the expression of creative skill in a visual form such as painting or sculpture. **2** paintings, drawings, and sculpture as a whole. **3** (**the arts**) creative activities such as painting, music, and drama. **4** (**arts**) subjects of study concerned with human culture. **5** a skill.

SYNONYMS **1 fine art**, design, artwork, aesthetics. **2 skill**, craft, technique, knack, facility, aptitude, talent, flair, mastery, expertise.

art dec·o /'dekō/ ▶ n. a decorative style of the 1920s and 1930s, featuring geometric shapes.

ar·te·ri·o·scle·ro·sis /är,ti(ə)rēōsklə'rōsis/ ▶ n. Medicine thickening and hardening of the walls of the arteries.

ar·ter·y /'ärtərē/ ▶ n. (plural **arteries**) **1** any of the tubes through which blood flows from the heart around the body. **2** an important transport route. ■ **ar·te·ri·al** /är'ti(ə)rēəl/ adj.

ar·te·sian well /är'tēzʜən/ ▶ n. a well in which water comes to the surface through natural pressure.

art·ful /'ärtfəl/ ▶ adj. clever in a cunning way. ■ **art·ful·ly** adv.

ar·thri·tis /är'ᴛʜrītis/ ▶ n. painful inflammation and stiffness of the joints. ■ **ar·thrit·ic** /-'ᴛʜritik/ adj. & n.

ar·thro·pod /ˈärᴛʜrəˌpäd/ ▶ **n.** an animal with a body that is divided into segments, such as an insect, spider, crab, etc.

ar·ti·choke /ˈärtiˌᴄʜōk/ ▶ **n.** a vegetable consisting of the unopened flower head of a thistlelike plant.

ar·ti·cle /ˈärtikəl/ ▶ **n. 1** a particular object. **2** a piece of writing in a newspaper or magazine. **3** an item in a legal document.

SYNONYMS ▶ **n. 1 object**, thing, item, piece, artifact, device, implement. **2 report**, account, story, essay, feature, item, piece (of writing), column. **3 clause**, section, paragraph, point, item.

□ **article of faith** a firmly held belief.

ar·tic·u·lar /ärˈtikyələr/ ▶ **adj.** Anatomy relating to a joint.

ar·tic·u·late ▶ **adj.** /ärˈtikyəlit/ **1** fluent and clear in speech. **2** having joints or jointed segments. ▶ **v.** /ärˈtikyəˌlāt/ (**articulates**, **articulating**, **articulated**) **1** pronounce words distinctly. **2** clearly express an idea or feeling. **3** (**articulated**) having sections connected by a flexible joint or joints.

SYNONYMS ▶ **adj. eloquent**, fluent, effective, persuasive, lucid, expressive, silver-tongued, clear, coherent. ANTONYMS unintelligible. ▶ **v. express**, voice, vocalize, put in words, communicate, state.

■ **ar·tic·u·late·ly** **adv.** **ar·tic·u·la·tion** /ärˌtikyəˈlāsʜən/ **n.**

ar·ti·fact /ˈärtəˌfakt/ ▶ **n.** a useful or decorative man-made object.

ar·ti·fice /ˈärtəfis/ ▶ **n.** the clever use of tricks to deceive someone.

ar·tif·i·cer /ärˈtifəsər/ ▶ **n.** a person skilled in making or planning things.

ar·ti·fi·cial /ˌärtəˈfisʜəl/ ▶ **adj. 1** made as a copy of something natural. **2** not sincere: *she gave an artificial smile.*

SYNONYMS **1 synthetic**, fake, imitation, mock, ersatz, man-made, manufactured, plastic, simulated, faux; informal pretend. **2 insincere**, feigned, false, unnatural, contrived, put-on, forced, labored, hollow; informal pretend, phony. ANTONYMS natural, genuine.

□ **artificial horizon** an aircraft instrument that shows the angle of the aircraft to the earth. **artificial insemination** the injection of semen through a syringe into the vagina or uterus. **artificial intelligence** the performance by computers of tasks that normally need human intelligence. **artificial respiration** the forcing of air into and out of a person's lungs to make them begin breathing again. ■ **ar·ti·fi·ci·al·i·ty** /-ˌfisʜēˈalitē/ **n.** **ar·ti·fi·cial·ly** **adv.**

ar·til·ler·y /ärˈtilərē/ ▶ **n. 1** large guns used in warfare on land. **2** a branch of the armed forces that uses artillery.

ar·ti·san /ˈärtizən/ ▶ **n.** a skilled worker who makes things by hand. ■ **ar·ti·san·al** **adj.**

art·ist /ˈärtist/ ▶ **n. 1** a person who paints or draws. **2** a person who practices or performs any of the creative arts.

ar·tiste /ärˈtēst/ ▶ **n.** a professional singer or dancer.

ar·tis·tic /ärˈtistik/ ▶ **adj. 1** having creative skill. **2** having to do with art or artists: *an artistic temperament.*

SYNONYMS **1 creative**, imaginative, inventive, sensitive, perceptive, discerning. **2 attractive**, aesthetic, beautiful, stylish, ornamental, decorative, graceful, subtle, expressive.

■ **ar·tis·ti·cal·ly** **adv.**

art·ist·ry /ˈärtistrē/ ▶ **n.** creative skill or ability.

art·less /ˈärtlis/ ▶ **adj.** straightforward and sincere. ■ **art·less·ly** **adv.**

art nou·veau /är(t) nōōˈvō/ ▶ **n.** a style of art and architecture of the late 19th and early 20th centuries, having intricate designs and flowing curves.

art·sy /ˈärtsē/ (or **arty** /ˈärtē/) ▶ **adj.** informal displaying an obvious interest in the arts. ■ **art·si·ness** **n.**

art·work /ˈärtˌwərk/ ▶ **n.** illustrations to be included in a publication.

a·ru·gu·la /əˈrōōgələ/ ▶ **n.** a plant similar to lettuce, eaten in salads.

Ar·y·an /ˈe(ə)rēən, ˈar-, -yən/ ▶ **n. 1** a member of an ancient people of Europe and Asia. **2** (in Nazi thinking) a white person not of Jewish descent. ▶ **adj.** relating to Aryans.

as /az/ ▶ **adv.** used in comparisons to refer to extent or amount. ▶ **conj. 1** while. **2** in the way that: *dress as you would if guests were coming.* **3** because. **4** even though. ▶ **prep. 1** in the role of; being: *a job as a cook.* **2** while; when. □ **as for** with regard to. **as yet** until now or that time.

ASAP (or **asap**) ▶ **abbr.** as soon as possible.

as·bes·tos /asˈbestəs, az-/ ▶ **n.** a fibrous gray-white mineral that does not burn.

as·bes·to·sis /ˌasbesˈtōsis, ˌaz-/ ▶ **n.** a serious lung disease caused by breathing asbestos dust.

as·cend /əˈsend/ ▶ **v.** go up; climb or rise.

as·cend·ant /əˈsendənt/ ▶ **adj. 1** rising in power or status. **2** (of a planet or sign of the zodiac) just above the eastern horizon. ■ **as·cend·an·cy** **n.**

as·cen·sion /əˈsensʜən/ ▶ **n. 1** the action of reaching a higher position or status. **2** (**the Ascension**) the ascent of Jesus into heaven after the Resurrection.

as·cent /əˈsent/ ▶ **n. 1** the action of going up. **2** an upward slope.

SYNONYMS **1** *the ascent of the Matterhorn* **climbing**, scaling, conquest. **2** *the ascent grew steeper* **slope**, incline, gradient, grade, hill, climb. ANTONYMS descent, drop.

as·cer·tain /ˌasərˈtān/ ▶ **v.** find something out for certain.

SYNONYMS **find out**, discover, get to know, work out, make out, fathom, learn, deduce, divine, establish, determine; informal figure out.

■ **as·cer·tain·a·ble** **adj.**

as·cet·ic /əˈsetik/ ▶ **adj.** choosing to live without pleasures and luxuries. ▶ **n.** an ascetic person. ■ **as·cet·i·cism** /-ˌsizəm/ **n.**

ASCII /ˈaskē/ ▶ **abbr.** Computing American Standard Code for Information Interchange.

a·scor·bic ac·id /əˈskôrbik/ ▶ **n.** vitamin C.

as·cot /ˈasˌkät, -kət/ ▶ **n.** a man's broad silk necktie.

as·cribe /əˈskrīb/ ▶ **v.** (**ascribes**, **ascribing**, **ascribed**) (**ascribe something to**) say or believe that something is caused by: *he ascribed his breakdown to exhaustion.* ■ **as·crip·tion** **n.**

ASEAN /ˈäsēˌän, ˈas-/ ▶ **abbr.** Association of Southeast Asian Nations.

a·sep·tic /āˈseptik/ ▶ **adj.** free from germs.

a·sex·u·al /āˈsekshōōəl/ ▶ **adj. 1** without sex or sexual organs. **2** not having sexual feelings. ■ **a·sex·u·al·ly adv.**

ash¹ /ash/ ▶ **n. 1** the powder remaining after something has been burned. **2** (**ashes**) the remains of a human body after cremation. □ **Ash Wednesday** the first day of Lent.

ash² ▶ **n.** a tree with silver-gray bark, compound leaves, and hard pale wood.

a·shamed /əˈshāmd/ ▶ **adj.** feeling embarrassed or guilty.

SYNONYMS **1 sorry**, shamefaced, sheepish, guilty, contrite, remorseful, regretful, apologetic, mortified, red-faced, repentant, penitent, rueful, chagrined. **2 reluctant**, loath, unwilling, afraid, embarrassed. ANTONYMS proud.

ash·en /ˈashən/ ▶ **adj.** very pale from shock, fear, or illness.

Ash·ke·naz·i /ˌashkəˈnazē, ˌäshkəˈnäzē/ ▶ **n.** (plural **Ashkenazim** /-ˈnazim, -ˈnäzim/) a Jew of central or eastern European descent. ■ **Ash·ke·naz·ic adj.**

ash·lar /ˈashlər/ ▶ **n.** large square-cut stones used as the surface layer of a wall.

a·shore /əˈshôr/ ▶ **adv.** to or on the shore or land.

ash·ram /ˈäshrəm, ˈashˌram/ ▶ **n.** a Hindu religious retreat or community.

ash·tray /ˈashˌtrā/ ▶ **n.** a small container for tobacco ash and cigarette ends.

A·sian /ˈāzhən/ ▶ **n.** a person from Asia, or whose family originally came from Asia. ▶ **adj.** relating to Asia.

A·si·at·ic /ˌāzhēˈatik, ˌāzē-/ ▶ **adj.** relating to Asia.

a·side /əˈsīd/ ▶ **adv. 1** to one side; out of the way. **2** in reserve. ▶ **n. 1** an actor's remark spoken to the audience. **2** a remark not directly related to the subject being discussed. □ **aside from** apart from.

as·i·nine /ˈasəˌnīn/ ▶ **adj.** very foolish.

ask /ask/ ▶ **v. 1** say something so as to get an answer or some information. **2** say that you want someone to do, give, or allow something. **3** (**ask for**) say that you want to speak to. **4** expect something of someone. **5** invite someone to a social occasion.

SYNONYMS **1 inquire**, want to know, question, interrogate, quiz. **2** *they'll ask a few questions* **put** (**forward**), pose, raise, submit. **3 request**, demand, seek, solicit, apply, petition, call, appeal. ANTONYMS answer.

□ **for the asking** for little or no effort or cost.

a·skance /əˈskans/ ▶ **adv.** with a suspicious or disapproving look.

a·skew /əˈskyōō/ ▶ **adv. & adj.** not straight or level.

a·slant /əˈslant/ ▶ **adv. & prep.** at a slant or crossing something at a slant.

a·sleep /əˈslēp/ ▶ **adj. & adv. 1** in or into a state of sleep. **2** (of a limb) numb. **3** not alert.

SYNONYMS **sleeping**, napping, dozing, drowsing; informal snoozing, dead to the world; humorous in the land of Nod. ANTONYMS awake.

asp /asp/ ▶ **n.** a small southern European viper.

as·par·a·gus /əˈsparəgəs/ ▶ **n.** a vegetable consisting of the tender young shoots of a tall plant.

as·par·tame /ˈaspärˌtām/ ▶ **n.** a low-calorie artificial sweetener.

ASPCA ▶ **abbr.** American Society for the Prevention of Cruelty to Animals.

as·pect /ˈaspekt/ ▶ **n. 1** a particular part or feature of something. **2** a particular appearance or quality: *the air of desertion lent the place a sinister aspect.* **3** the side of a building facing a particular direction.

SYNONYMS **1 feature**, facet, side, characteristic, particular, detail. **2 point of view**, position, standpoint, viewpoint, perspective, angle, slant. **3** *his face had a sinister aspect* **appearance**, look, air, mien, demeanor, expression.

as·pen /ˈaspən/ ▶ **n.** a poplar tree with small rounded leaves.

as·per·i·ty /əˈsperitē/ ▶ **n.** harshness in the way you speak to or treat someone.

as·per·sions /əˈspərzhənz/ **pl.n.** (**cast aspersions on**) attack someone's character or reputation.

as·phalt /ˈasfôlt/ ▶ **n.** a tarlike substance used in surfacing roads or roofs.

SPELLING
Just **as-**, not **ash-**: **as**phalt.

as·pho·del /ˈasfəˌdel/ ▶ **n.** a plant with clusters of yellow or white flowers on a long stem.

as·phyx·i·a /asˈfiksēə/ ▶ **n.** a condition in which someone cannot get enough oxygen and becomes unconscious or dies.

as·phyx·i·ate /asˈfiksēˌāt/ ▶ **v.** (**asphyxiates**, **asphyxiating**, **asphyxiated**) die or cause to die from lack of oxygen. ■ **as·phyx·i·a·tion** /asˌfiksēˈāshən/ **n.**

as·pic /ˈaspik/ ▶ **n.** a savory jelly made with meat stock.

as·pi·dis·tra /ˌaspiˈdistrə/ ▶ **n.** a plant with broad tapering leaves.

as·pir·ant /ˈaspərənt, əˈspī-/ ▶ **n.** a person with ambitions to do or be something.

as·pi·rate ▶ **v.** /ˈaspəˌrāt/ **1** pronounce a word with the sound of *h* at the start. **2** inhale; draw something into the lungs. **3** Medicine remove a liquid from a vessel or cavity by using a suction device. ▶ **n.** /ˈasp(ə)rit/ the sound of *h*.

as·pi·ra·tion /ˌaspəˈrāshən/ ▶ **n.** a hope or ambition.

SYNONYMS **desire**, hope, dream, wish, longing, yearning, aim, ambition, expectation, goal, target.

■ **as·pi·ra·tion·al adj.**

as·pire /əˈspī(ə)r/ ▶ **v.** (**aspires**, **aspiring**, **aspired**) have a strong desire to achieve or become something: *she aspired to be an actress.*

SYNONYMS (**aspiring**) **would-be**, hopeful, budding, potential, prospective; informal wannabe.

as·pi·rin /ˈasp(ə)rin/ ▶ **n.** (plural **aspirin** or **aspirins**) a medicine used to relieve pain and reduce fever and inflammation.

ass /as/ ▶ **n. 1** a donkey or related small wild horse. **2** informal a stupid person.

as·sail /əˈsāl/ ▶ **v. 1** attack someone violently. **2** (of an unpleasant feeling) come upon someone strongly.

as·sail·ant /ə'sālənt/ ▶ **n.** an attacker.

as·sas·sin /ə'sasin/ ▶ **n.** a person who assassinates someone.

> SYNONYMS **murderer**, killer, gunman, executioner; informal hit man.

as·sas·si·nate /ə'sasə,nāt/ ▶ **v.** (**assassinates**, **assassinating**, **assassinated**) murder a political or religious leader.

> SYNONYMS **murder**, kill, eliminate, liquidate, execute, terminate; informal hit, whack.

■ **as·sas·si·na·tion** /ə,sasə'nāsHən/ **n.**

as·sault /ə'sôlt/ ▶ **n.** **1** a violent attack. **2** a determined attempt: *an assault on Mt. Everest.* ▶ **v.** make an assault on.

> SYNONYMS ▶ **n.** **1 violence**, battery. **2 attack**, strike, onslaught, offensive, charge, push, thrust, raid. ▶ **v.** **attack**, hit, strike, beat up; informal lay into, rough up.

as·say /'a,sā, a'sā/ ▶ **n.** the testing of a metal to see how pure it is. ▶ **v.** test a metal.

as·se·gai /'asə,gī/ ▶ **n.** (plural **assegais**) an iron-tipped spear used by southern African peoples.

as·sem·blage /ə'semblij/ ▶ **n.** **1** a collection or gathering of things or people. **2** something made of pieces fitted together.

as·sem·ble /ə'sembəl/ ▶ **v.** (**assembles**, **assembling**, **assembled**) **1** come or bring together. **2** construct something by fitting parts together.

> SYNONYMS **1 gather**, collect, get together, congregate, convene, meet, muster, rally, round up, marshal. **2 construct**, build, erect, set up, make, manufacture, fabricate, put together, connect. ANTONYMS disperse, dismantle.

as·sem·bly /ə'semblē/ ▶ **n.** (plural **assemblies**) **1** a group of people gathered together. **2** a group of people with powers to make decisions and laws. **3** the action of fitting the parts of something together.

> SYNONYMS **1 gathering**, meeting, congregation, convention, council, rally, group, crowd; informal get-together. **2 construction**, manufacture, building, fabrication, erection.

□ **assembly line** a series of workers and machines in a factory along which identical products pass to be assembled in stages.

as·sent /ə'sent/ ▶ **n.** approval or agreement. ▶ **v.** agree to a request or suggestion: *she assented to the change.*

as·sert /ə'sərt/ ▶ **v.** **1** confidently state that something is true. **2** (**assert yourself**) be confident and forceful.

> SYNONYMS **1 declare**, state, maintain, contend, argue, claim, insist. **2** *you should assert your rights* **insist on**, stand up for, uphold, defend, press/push for.

as·ser·tion /ə'sərsHən/ ▶ **n.** a confident and forceful statement.

> SYNONYMS **declaration**, contention, statement, claim, opinion, protestation.

as·ser·tive /ə'sərtiv/ ▶ **adj.** speaking and doing things in a confident and forceful way.

> SYNONYMS **confident**, self-confident, bold, decisive, forceful, insistent, emphatic, determined, strong-willed, commanding, pushy; informal feisty. ANTONYMS timid.

■ **as·ser·tive·ly adv. as·ser·tive·ness n.**

as·sess /ə'ses/ ▶ **v.** make a judgment about the value or quality of something.

> SYNONYMS **evaluate**, judge, gauge, rate, estimate, appraise, weigh up, calculate, value, work out, determine; informal size up.

■ **as·sess·ment n. as·ses·sor n.**

as·set /'aset/ ▶ **n.** **1** a useful or valuable thing or person. **2** (**assets**) property owned by a person or company.

> SYNONYMS **1 benefit**, advantage, blessing, good/strong point, strength, forte, virtue, recommendation, attraction, resource. **2** *the seizure of all their assets* **property**, resources, estate, holdings, funds, valuables, possessions, effects, belongings. ANTONYMS liability.

as·sev·er·a·tion /ə,sevə'rāsHən/ ▶ **n.** formal a solemn or emphatic declaration. ■ **as·sev·er·ate** /ə'sevə,rāt/ **v.**

as·sid·u·ous /ə'sijəwəs/ ▶ **adj.** showing great care and thoroughness. ■ **as·si·du·i·ty** /,asi'd(y)o͞oitē/ **n.** **as·sid·u·ous·ly adv.**

as·sign /ə'sīn/ ▶ **v.** **1** give someone a task or duty. **2** set something aside for a purpose.

> SYNONYMS **1 allocate**, give, set, charge with, entrust with. **2 appoint**, promote, delegate, nominate, commission, post, co-opt; Military detail. **3 earmark**, designate, set aside, reserve, appropriate, allot, allocate.

as·sig·na·tion /,asig'nāsHən/ ▶ **n.** a secret meeting, especially between lovers.

> SYNONYMS **rendezvous**, date, appointment, meeting; literary tryst.

as·sign·ment /ə'sīnmənt/ ▶ **n.** a piece of work that someone has been asked to do as part of a job or course of study.

> SYNONYMS **task**, job, duty, responsibility, mission, errand, undertaking, commission.

as·sim·i·late /ə'simə,lāt/ ▶ **v.** (**assimilates**, **assimilating**, **assimilated**) **1** take in and understand information. **2** absorb people or ideas into a society or culture. ■ **as·sim·i·la·tion** /ə,simə'lāsHən/ **n.**

as·sist /ə'sist/ ▶ **v.** help someone.

> SYNONYMS **1 help**, aid, lend a (helping) hand to, support, back (up), work with, cooperate with. **2** *the aim was to assist cashflow* **facilitate**, aid, ease, promote, boost, speed, benefit, encourage, further. ANTONYMS hinder.

as·sis·tance /ə'sistəns/ ▶ **n.** help or support.

> SYNONYMS **help**, aid, a (helping) hand, support, backing, reinforcement. ANTONYMS hindrance.

as·sis·tant /ə'sistənt/ ▶ **n.** a person employed to help someone more senior.

> SYNONYMS **helper**, aide, deputy, second (in command), number two, right-hand man/woman, personal assistant, PA, auxiliary, attendant, henchman; informal sidekick, gofer.

as·size /ə'sīz/ (or **assizes**) ▶ **n.** historical a court that sat at intervals in each county of England and Wales.

as·so·ci·ate ▶ v. /əˈsōsēˌāt, -SHē-/ (**associates**, **associating**, **associated**) **1** (**associate something with**) mentally connect something with something else. **2** (**associate with**) frequently meet or have dealings with. **3** (**associate yourself with**) be involved with. ▶ n. /-it/ a work or business partner or colleague. ▶ adj. /-it/ **1** connected with an organization. **2** belonging to an association but not having full membership.

SYNONYMS ▶ v. **1 link**, connect, relate, bracket, identify, equate. **2 mix**, keep company, mingle, socialize, go around, have dealings; informal hobnob, hang out/around. **3** (**associated**) *two associated events* **related**, connected, linked, similar, corresponding, attendant, accompanying, incidental. ANTONYMS avoid, unrelated. ▶ n. **partner**, colleague, coworker, workmate, collaborator, comrade, ally; informal crony.

as·so·ci·a·tion /əˌsōsēˈāSHən, -SHē-/ ▶ n. **1** a group of people organized for a joint purpose. **2** a connection or link.

SYNONYMS **1 alliance**, consortium, coalition, union, league, guild, syndicate, federation, confederation, cartel, cooperative, partnership. **2 relationship**, relation, interrelation, connection, interconnection, interdependence, link, bond.

as·so·nance /ˈasənəns/ ▶ n. a rhyming of vowel sounds.

as·sort·ed /əˈsôrtid/ ▶ adj. made up of various sorts.

SYNONYMS **various**, miscellaneous, mixed, varied, diverse, different, sundry. ANTONYMS uniform.

as·sort·ment /əˈsôrtmənt/ ▶ n. a varied collection.

SYNONYMS **variety**, mixture, array, mix, miscellany, selection, medley, melange, ragbag, potpourri.

as·suage /əˈswāj/ ▶ v. (**assuages**, **assuaging**, **assuaged**) **1** make an unpleasant feeling less strong. **2** relieve thirst or an appetite or desire.

as·sume /əˈso͞om/ ▶ v. (**assumes**, **assuming**, **assumed**) **1** think that something must be true but have no proof. **2** take responsibility or control. **3** begin to have: *the island has recently assumed increased importance as a tourist destination.* **4** take on a manner or identity, sometimes falsely.

SYNONYMS **1 presume**, suppose, take it (as given), take for granted, conclude, infer, think, fancy, imagine, surmise, believe, understand, gather, suspect, figure. **2 affect**, adopt, put on. **3 accept**, shoulder, bear, undertake, take on/up. **4 seize**, take (over), appropriate, wrest, usurp. **5** (**assumed**) **false**, fictitious, fake, bogus, invented, made-up; informal pretend, phony. ANTONYMS genuine.

as·sum·ing /əˈso͞omiNG/ ▶ conj. based on the assumption that.

as·sump·tion /əˈsəm(p)SHən/ ▶ n. **1** a feeling that something must be true. **2** the taking on of responsibility or control.

SYNONYMS **supposition**, presumption, inference, conjecture, belief, surmise, hypothesis, theory, suspicion, guess.

as·sur·ance /əˈSHo͝orəns/ ▶ n. **1** something said to make someone feel confident about something. **2** self-confidence.

SYNONYMS **1 promise**, word (of honor), pledge, vow, oath, undertaking, guarantee, commitment. **2 confidence**, self-confidence, self-assurance, self-possession, nerve, poise; informal cool. **3 insurance**, indemnity, protection, security, cover.

as·sure /əˈSHo͝or/ ▶ v. (**assures**, **assuring**, **assured**) **1** make someone feel confident about something. **2** make certain.

SYNONYMS **1 reassure**, convince, satisfy, persuade. **2 promise**, guarantee, swear, confirm, certify, vow, give your word. **3 ensure**, secure, guarantee, seal, clinch; informal sew up.

as·sured /əˈSHo͝ord/ ▶ adj. **1** confident in yourself and your abilities. **2** certain; guaranteed; protected against change: *assured healthcare.*

SYNONYMS **1 confident**, self-confident, self-assured, self-possessed, poised, composed, imperturbable, unruffled; informal unflappable, together. **2 guaranteed**, certain, sure, secure, reliable, dependable; informal surefire. ANTONYMS nervous, uncertain.

■ **as·sur·ed·ly** /əˈSHo͝oridlē/ adv.

as·ter·isk /ˈastəˌrisk/ ▶ n. a symbol (*) used as a pointer to a note.

SPELLING

Asteri**sk**, not -**ix**.

a·stern /əˈstərn/ ▶ adv. behind or toward the rear of a ship or aircraft.

as·ter·oid /ˈastəˌroid/ ▶ n. a small rocky planet orbiting the sun.

asth·ma /ˈazmə/ ▶ n. a medical condition that causes difficulty in breathing. ■ **asth·mat·ic** /azˈmatik/ adj. & n.

a·stig·ma·tism /əˈstigməˌtizəm/ ▶ n. a fault in the shape of the eye that prevents clear vision.

a·stir /əˈstər/ ▶ adj. **1** in a state of excited movement. **2** awake and out of bed.

as·ton·ish /əˈstäniSH/ ▶ v. surprise someone very much.

SYNONYMS **1 amaze**, astound, stagger, startle, stun, surprise, confound, dumbfound, nonplus, take aback, leave open-mouthed; informal flabbergast, bowl over, blow away, floor, throw/knock for a loop. **2** (**astonishing**) **amazing**, astounding, staggering, surprising, breathtaking, remarkable, extraordinary, incredible, unbelievable, phenomenal; informal mind-boggling. ANTONYMS unremarkable.

■ **as·ton·ish·ment** n.

as·tound /əˈstound/ ▶ v. shock or surprise someone very much.

SYNONYMS **1 amaze**, astonish, stagger, surprise, startle, stun, confound, dumbfound, take aback, leave open-mouthed; informal flabbergast, bowl over, blow away, floor, throw/knock for a loop. **2** (**astounding**) **amazing**, astonishing, staggering, surprising, breathtaking, remarkable, extraordinary, incredible, unbelievable, phenomenal; informal mind-boggling. ANTONYMS unremarkable.

as·tral /ˈastrəl/ ▶ adj. relating to the stars.

a·stray /əˈstrā/ ▶ adv. away from the correct course.

a·stride /ə'strīd/ ▶ **prep. & adv.** with a leg on each side of. ▶ **adv.** (of a person's legs) apart.

as·trin·gent /ə'strinjənt/ ▶ **adj. 1** causing body tissue to contract. **2** sharp or severe. ▶ **n.** an astringent lotion. ■ **as·trin·gen·cy n.**

as·tro·labe /'astrə,lāb/ ▶ **n.** an instrument formerly used in navigation and for measuring the altitude of the stars.

as·trol·o·gy /ə'strälәjē/ ▶ **n.** the study of the supposed influence of the stars and planets on human affairs. ■ **as·trol·o·ger n. as·tro·log·i·cal** /,astrə'läjikəl/ **adj.**

as·tro·naut /'astrə,nôt/ ▶ **n.** a person trained to travel in a spacecraft.

as·tro·nom·i·cal /,astrə'nämikəl/ ▶ **adj. 1** relating to astronomy. **2** informal very large: *astronomical fees*. ■ **as·tro·nom·ic adj. as·tro·nom·i·cal·ly adv.**

as·tron·o·my /ə'stränəmē/ ▶ **n.** the scientific study of stars, planets, and the universe. ■ **as·tron·o·mer n.**

as·tro·phys·ics /,astrō'fiziks/ ▶ **n.** the study of the physical nature of stars and planets. ■ **as·tro·phys·i·cist** /-isist/ **n.**

as·tute /ə'st(y)o͞ot/ ▶ **adj.** good at making accurate judgements.

> SYNONYMS **shrewd**, sharp, acute, quick, clever, intelligent, bright, smart, canny, perceptive, perspicacious; informal quick on the uptake. ANTONYMS stupid.

■ **as·tute·ly adv.**

a·sun·der /ə'səndər/ ▶ **adv.** apart or into pieces.

a·sy·lum /ə'sīləm/ ▶ **n. 1** protection from danger. **2** protection given to someone who has fled their country for political reasons. **3** dated an institution for people who are mentally ill.

> SYNONYMS **refuge**, sanctuary, shelter, protection, immunity, a safe haven.

a·sym·met·ri·cal /,āsə'metrikəl/ ▶ **adj.** not symmetrical. ■ **a·sym·met·ric adj.**

a·sym·me·try /ā'simitrē/ ▶ **n.** (plural **asymmetries**) lack of symmetry.

a·syn·chro·nous /ā'siNGkrənəs/ ▶ **adj.** not existing or occurring at the same time.

at /at/ ▶ **prep.** used chiefly to express location, arrival, or time. □ **at that** in addition.

at·a·vis·tic /,atə'vistik/ ▶ **adj.** inherited from the earliest human beings: *atavistic fears*. ■ **at·a·vism** /'atə,vizəm/ **n.**

ate /āt/ past of **EAT**.

at·el·ier /,atl'yā/ ▶ **n.** a workshop or studio, especially one used by an artist.

a·the·ism /'āTHē,izəm/ ▶ **n.** the belief that God does not exist. ■ **a·the·ist n. a·the·is·tic** /,āTHē'istik/ **adj.**

ath·lete /'aTH,lēt/ ▶ **n.** a person who is good at sports. □ **athlete's foot** a form of ringworm infection affecting the feet.

ath·let·ic /aTH'letik/ ▶ **adj. 1** physically fit and good at sports. **2** relating to athletics.

> SYNONYMS **muscular**, fit, strapping, well-built, strong, sturdy, powerful, brawny, burly.

■ **ath·let·i·cal·ly adv. ath·let·i·cism** /-,sizəm/ **n.**

a·thwart /ə'THwôrt/ ▶ **prep.** across, from side to side.

At·lan·tic /ət'lantik, at-/ ▶ **adj.** having to do with the Atlantic Ocean.

at·las /'atləs/ ▶ **n.** a book of maps or charts.

ATM ▶ **abbr.** automated teller machine.

atm ▶ **abbr.** Physics atmosphere(s), as a unit of pressure.

at·mos·phere /'atməs,fi(ə)r/ ▶ **n. 1** the gases surrounding the earth or another planet. **2** the quality of the air in a place. **3** an overall tone or mood: *the hotel has a friendly atmosphere*. **4** a unit of pressure equal to the pressure of the atmosphere at sea level.

> SYNONYMS **1 air**, sky; literary the heavens, the ether. **2** *a relaxed atmosphere* **ambience**, spirit, air, mood, feel, feeling, character, tone, aura, quality, environment, climate; informal vibe.

at·mos·pher·ic /,atməs'fi(ə)rik, -'ferik/ ▶ **adj. 1** relating to the atmosphere of a planet. **2** creating a distinctive mood: *atmospheric lighting*. ▶ **n.** (**atmospherics**) electrical disturbances in the atmosphere.

at·oll /'at,ôl, 'at,äl, 'ā,tôl, 'ā,täl/ ▶ **n.** a ring-shaped coral reef or chain of islands.

at·om /'atəm/ ▶ **n. 1** the smallest particle of a chemical element that can exist. **2** a very small amount: *she did not have an atom of strength left*. □ **atom bomb** (or **atomic bomb**) a bomb whose explosive power comes from the fission (splitting) of the nuclei of atoms.

a·tom·ic /ə'tämik/ ▶ **adj. 1** relating to an atom or atoms. **2** relating to nuclear energy or weapons.

at·om·ize /'atə,mīz/ ▶ **v.** (**atomizes**, **atomizing**, **atomized**) convert something into very fine particles or droplets. ■ **at·om·iz·er n.**

a·ton·al /ā'tōnl/ ▶ **adj.** not written in any musical key.

a·tone /ə'tōn/ ▶ **v.** (**atones**, **atoning**, **atoned**) (**atone for**) do something to show you are sorry for something that happened in the past. ■ **a·tone·ment n.**

a·top /ə'täp/ ▶ **prep.** literary on the top of.

a·tri·um /'ātrēəm/ ▶ **n.** (plural **atria** /'ātrēə/ or **atriums**) **1** a central hall rising through several stories. **2** an open entrance hall or central court in an ancient Roman house. **3** each of the two upper cavities of the heart.

a·tro·cious /ə'trōSHəs/ ▶ **adj. 1** horrifyingly wicked. **2** very bad or unpleasant.

> SYNONYMS **1 wicked**, cruel, brutal, barbaric, vicious, monstrous, vile, inhuman, fiendish. **2 appalling**, awful, dreadful, terrible, miserable; informal abysmal, dire, shocking, rotten, lousy. ANTONYMS admirable, superb.

■ **a·tro·cious·ly adv.**

a·troc·i·ty /ə'träsitē/ ▶ **n.** (plural **atrocities**) a very wicked or cruel act.

> SYNONYMS **1** *a number of atrocities* **outrage**, horror, violation, abuse, crime. **2** *scenes of hardship and atrocity* **wickedness**, cruelty, brutality, barbarity, viciousness, savagery, inhumanity.

at·ro·phy /'atrəfē/ ▶ **v.** (**atrophies**, **atrophying**, **atrophied**) (of a part of the body) waste away. ▶ **n.** the condition or process of atrophying.

at·tach /ə'taCH/ ▶ **v. 1** fasten; join. **2** believe that something has significance or importance: *the country attaches importance to human rights*. **3** (**be attached to**) be working with a group of people. **4** (**attached to**) very fond of.

SYNONYMS **1 fasten**, fix, affix, join, secure, stick, connect, tie, link, couple, pin, hitch. **2** *they attach importance to research* **ascribe**, assign, attribute, accredit, impute. **3** (**attached to**) *the medical officer attached to HQ* **assigned**, appointed, allocated, seconded. **4** (**attached to**) *he was very attached to her* **fond of**, devoted to, keen on; informal mad about, crazy about. ANTONYMS detach.

■ **at·tach·a·ble** adj.

SPELLING

There is no **t** before the **ch** in att**ach**.

at·ta·ché /ˌatəˈshā, ˌata-/ ▶ n. a person on an ambassador's staff: *a military attaché.* □ **attaché case** a small, flat briefcase for carrying documents.

at·tach·ment /əˈtachmənt/ ▶ n. **1** an extra part that is attached to something. **2** a computer file sent with an email. **3** affection or fondness for someone or something.

SYNONYMS **1 accessory**, fitting, extension, add-on. **2 bond**, closeness, devotion, loyalty, fondness for, love for, affection for, feeling for, sympathy for.

at·tack /əˈtak/ ▶ v. **1** violently hurt or attempt to hurt. **2** have a harmful effect on. **3** fiercely criticize. **4** tackle something with determination. **5** (in sports) try to score goals or points. ▶ n. **1** an instance of attacking. **2** a sudden period of illness.

SYNONYMS ▶ v. **1 assault**, beat up, set upon, mug, charge, pounce on, raid, rush, storm; informal lay into, work over, rough up. **2 criticize**, censure, condemn, denounce, revile, vilify, impugn, disparage; informal knock, slam, lay into. ANTONYMS defend, praise. ▶ n. **1 assault**, onslaught, offensive, strike, blitz, raid, incursion, sortie, foray, charge, invasion. **2 criticism**, censure, condemnation, vilification, disparagement. **3 fit**, seizure, spasm, convulsion, paroxysm, bout, episode. ANTONYMS defense, praise.

at·tack·er /əˈtakər/ ▶ n. a person that attacks someone or something.

SYNONYMS **assailant**, assaulter, mugger, aggressor, raider, invader. ANTONYMS victim.

at·tain /əˈtān/ ▶ v. **1** succeed in doing. **2** reach: *he attained the grand old age of 47.*

SYNONYMS **achieve**, accomplish, reach, obtain, gain, secure, get, win, earn, realize, fulfill; informal clinch, bag, wrap up.

■ **at·tain·a·ble** adj.

at·tain·ment /əˈtānmənt/ ▶ n. **1** the achieving of something. **2** an achievement.

at·tar /ˈatər/ ▶ n. a sweet-smelling oil made from rose petals.

at·tempt /əˈtem(p)t/ ▶ v. make an effort to do something. ▶ n. an effort to do something.

SYNONYMS ▶ v. **try**, strive, aim, venture, endeavor, seek, have a go. ▶ n. **try**, effort, endeavor, venture, bid, go; informal crack, shot, stab.

at·tend /əˈtend/ ▶ v. **1** be present at or go regularly to. **2** (**attend to**) deal with or pay attention to. **3** happen at the same time as or as a result of. **4** escort and help someone.

SYNONYMS **1 be present at**, sit in on, take part in, appear at, turn up at, visit, go to; informal show up at. **2 pay attention**, listen, be attentive, concentrate.

at·tend·ance /əˈtendəns/ ▶ n. **1** the action of attending. **2** the number of people present.

SYNONYMS **1 presence**, appearance, attention. **2 audience**, turnout, house, gate, crowd. ANTONYMS absence.

at·tend·ant /əˈtendənt/ ▶ n. **1** a person employed to help people in a public place. **2** an assistant to an important person. ▶ adj. accompanying: *the sea and its attendant attractions.*

SYNONYMS ▶ n. **assistant**, aide, companion, escort, steward, servant, retainer, valet, maid. ▶ adj. **accompanying**, associated, concomitant, related, connected, resulting, consequent.

at·ten·tion /əˈtenshən/ ▶ n. **1** special care, notice, or consideration. **2** (**attentions**) things done to help someone or to express romantic interest. **3** a straight standing position taken by soldiers.

SYNONYMS **1 consideration**, contemplation, deliberation, thought, study, observation, mind, investigation, action. **2 awareness**, notice, scrutiny, eye, gaze. **3** *medical attention* **care**, ministrations, treatment, therapy, relief, aid, assistance.

at·ten·tive /əˈtentiv/ ▶ adj. **1** paying close attention. **2** considerate and helpful.

SYNONYMS **1** *an attentive student* **alert**, perceptive, observant, acute, aware, heedful, focused, studious, diligent, conscientious, earnest. **2** *the most attentive of husbands* **considerate**, conscientious, thoughtful, kind, caring, solicitous, understanding, sympathetic. ANTONYMS inattentive.

■ **at·ten·tive·ly** adv.

at·ten·u·ate /əˈtenyoo͞ˌāt/ ▶ v. (**attenuates**, **attenuating**, **attenuated**) **1** make something weaker. **2** make something thin or thinner. ■ **at·ten·u·a·tion** /əˌtenyoo͞ˈāshən/ n.

at·test /əˈtest/ ▶ v. **1** provide or act as clear evidence of something. **2** declare something to be true: *I can attest to his tremendous energy.* ■ **at·tes·ta·tion** /ˌateˈstāshən/ n.

at·tic /ˈatik/ ▶ n. a space or room inside the roof of a building.

SYNONYMS **loft**, roof space, garret.

at·tire /əˈtī(ə)r/ formal ▶ n. clothes of a particular kind. ▶ v. (**be attired**) be wearing clothes of a particular kind.

at·ti·tude /ˈatiˌt(y)o͞od/ ▶ n. **1** a way of thinking. **2** a position of the body. **3** informal self-confident or aggressive behavior.

SYNONYMS **1 view**, viewpoint, outlook, perspective, stance, standpoint, position, frame of mind, approach, opinion. **2** *an attitude of prayer* **posture**, position, pose, stance.

at·ti·tu·di·nize /ˌatiˈt(y)o͞odnˌīz/ ▶ v. (**attitudinizes**, **attitudinizing**, **attitudinized**) adopt an attitude just for effect.

at·tor·ney /əˈtərnē/ ▶ n. (plural **attorneys**) a person who is appointed to act for someone else in legal matters; a lawyer. □ **attorney general** (plural **attorneys general**) **1** the chief legal officer in some countries. **2** the head of the US Department of Justice.

at·tract /ə'trakt/ ▶ **v. 1** draw someone in by offering something interesting or appealing. **2** cause a particular reaction. **3** draw something closer by an unseen force.

SYNONYMS **1 appeal to**, fascinate, charm, captivate, interest, tempt, entice, lure, bewitch, beguile, seduce. **2 draw**, pull, magnetize. ANTONYMS repel.

at·trac·tion /ə'traksHən/ ▶ **n. 1** the action or power of attracting. **2** something interesting or appealing.

SYNONYMS **1 appeal**, attractiveness, pull, desirability, fascination, allure, charisma, charm. **2** *the town's main attractions* **entertainment**, activity, diversion, amenity, service. **3** *magnetic attraction* **pull**, draw, force. ANTONYMS repulsion.

at·trac·tive /ə'traktiv/ ▶ **adj. 1** very pleasing to look at. **2** arousing interest.

SYNONYMS **1 good-looking**, beautiful, pretty, handsome, lovely, stunning, striking, desirable, gorgeous, prepossessing, fetching; informal cute, drop-dead gorgeous, hunky; old use comely. **2 appealing**, inviting, tempting, pleasing, interesting. ANTONYMS unattractive, ugly.

■ **at·trac·tive·ly adv. at·trac·tive·ness n.**

at·trib·ute ▶ **v.** /ə'tri͵byo͞ot/ (**attributes, attributing, attributed**) (**attribute something to**) say or believe that something is the result of or belongs to: *the moth's scarcity is attributed to pollution.* ▶ **n.** /'atrə͵byo͞ot/ a quality or feature.

SYNONYMS ▶ **v. ascribe**, assign, accredit, credit, put down, chalk up, pin on. ▶ **n. quality**, characteristic, trait, feature, element, aspect, property, sign, hallmark, mark.

■ **at·trib·ut·a·ble** /ə'tribyətəbəl/ **adj. at·tri·bu·tion** /͵atrə'byo͞osHən/ **n.**

at·trib·u·tive /ə'tribyətiv/ ▶ **adj.** Grammar (of an adjective) coming before the word that it describes, as *old* in *the old dog.*

at·tri·tion /ə'trisHən/ ▶ **n.** gradual wearing down through prolonged attack, pressure, or friction.

at·tune /ə't(y)o͞on/ ▶ **v.** (**be attuned**) be receptive to and able to understand someone or something.

Atty. ▶ **abbr.** attorney.

a·typ·i·cal /ā'tipikəl/ ▶ **adj.** not typical.

Au ▶ **symbol** the chemical element gold.

au·brie·tia /ô'brēsH(ē)ə/ (also **aubretia**) ▶ **n.** a trailing plant with purple, pink, or white flowers.

au·burn /'ôbərn/ ▶ **n.** a reddish-brown color.

auc·tion /'ôksHən/ ▶ **n.** a public sale in which each item is sold to the person who offers most for it. ▶ **v.** sell something at an auction.

auc·tion·eer /͵ôksHə'ni(ə)r/ ▶ **n.** a person who conducts auctions.

au·da·cious /ô'dāsHəs/ ▶ **adj.** very confident and daring. ■ **au·da·cious·ly adv.**

au·dac·i·ty /ô'dasitē/ ▶ **n. 1** the willingness to take risks: *a traveler of extraordinary audacity.* **2** rude or disrespectful behavior: *he had the audacity to contradict me.*

SYNONYMS **1 boldness**, daring, pluck; recklessness; spirit; informal guts, gutsiness, spunk, moxie. **2 impudence**, impertinence, insolence, presumption, cheek, effrontery, nerve, gall, defiance, temerity; informal brass, chutzpah.

au·di·ble /'ôdəbəl/ ▶ **adj.** able to be heard.

SYNONYMS **perceptible**, discernible, detectable, distinct, clear. ANTONYMS inaudible, faint.

■ **au·di·bil·i·ty** /͵ôdə'bilitē/ **n. au·di·bly adv.**

au·di·ence /'ôdēəns/ ▶ **n. 1** the people gathered to see or listen to a play, concert, movie, etc. **2** a formal interview with a person in authority.

SYNONYMS **1 spectators, listeners**, viewers, onlookers, crowd, throng, gallery, congregation, turnout. **2 meeting**, interview, consultation, conference, hearing, reception.

au·di·o fre·quen·cy /'ôdē͵ō/ ▶ **n.** a frequency that can be heard by the human ear.

au·di·o·tape /'ôdē-ō͵tāp/ ▶ **n.** magnetic tape on which sound can be recorded.

au·di·o·vis·u·al /͵ôdē-ō'vizHo͞oəl/ ▶ **adj.** using both sight and sound.

au·dit /'ôdit/ ▶ **n.** an official inspection of an organization's accounts. ▶ **v.** (**audits, auditing, audited**) inspect the accounts of. ■ **au·di·tor n.**

au·di·tion /ô'disHən/ ▶ **n.** an interview for a performer in which they give a practical demonstration of their skill. ▶ **v.** assess or be assessed by an audition.

au·di·to·ri·um /͵ôdi'tôrēəm/ ▶ **n.** (plural **auditoriums** or **auditoria** /-rēə/) the part of a theater or hall in which the audience sits.

au·di·to·ry /'ôdi͵tôrē/ ▶ **adj.** relating to hearing.

au fait /͵ō 'fe/ ▶ **adj.** (**au fait with**) completely familiar with.

au·ger /'ôgər/ ▶ **n.** a tool for boring holes.

aught /awt/ ▶ **pron.** old use anything at all.

aug·ment /ôg'ment/ ▶ **v.** increase the amount or value of.

SYNONYMS **increase**, add to, supplement, enhance, build up, raise, boost, up, hike up, enlarge, swell, expand, extend. ANTONYMS decrease, reduce.

■ **aug·men·ta·tion** /͵ôgmen'tāsHən/ **n.**

au grat·in /͵ō 'grätn, 'gratn, gra'taN/ ▶ **adj.** sprinkled with breadcrumbs or grated cheese and browned: *crab au gratin.*

au·gur /'ôgər/ ▶ **v.** be a sign of a likely outcome.

au·gu·ry /'ôg(y)ərē/ ▶ **n.** (plural **auguries**) a sign of what will happen in the future.

Au·gust /'ôgəst/ ▶ **n.** the eighth month of the year.

au·gust /ô'gəst/ ▶ **adj.** inspiring respect and admiration.

SYNONYMS **distinguished**, respected, eminent, venerable, illustrious, prestigious, renowned, celebrated, honored, acclaimed, esteemed.

auk /ôk/ ▶ **n.** a black and white seabird.

auld lang syne /ôld laNG 'zīn/ ▶ **n.** times long past.

aunt /ant, änt/ ▶ **n.** the sister of your father or mother, or the wife of your uncle.

aunt·ie /'antē, 'än-/ (also **aunty**) ▶ **n.** (plural **aunties**) informal an aunt.

au pair /͵ō 'pe(ə)r/ ▶ **n.** a foreign girl employed to look after children and help with housework.

au·ra /'ôrə/ ▶ **n.** (plural **auras**) the distinctive feeling that seems to surround a particular place or person.

SYNONYMS **atmosphere**, ambience, air, quality, character, mood, feeling; informal vibe.

au·ral /'ôrəl/ ▶ **adj.** having to do with the ear or hearing. ■ **au·ral·ly adv.**

au·re·ole /'ôrē,ōl/ ▶ **n.** a circle of light around the sun or moon.

au re·voir /,ō rəv'wär/ ▶ **exclam.** goodbye.

au·ri·cle /'ôrikəl/ ▶ **n. 1** the external part of the ear. **2** either of the upper two cavities of the heart.

au·ror·a bo·re·a·lis /ə'rôrə ,bôrē'alis, ô'rôrə, ,bôrē'ālis/ ▶ **n.** streamers of light sometimes seen in the sky near the North Pole; the Northern Lights.

aus·pice /'ôspis/ ▶ **n.** old use an omen. □ **under the auspices of** with the support or protection of.

aus·pi·cious /ô'spishəs/ ▶ **adj.** suggesting that there is a good chance of success.

SYNONYMS **favorable**, promising, encouraging, fortunate, opportune, timely, advantageous, good. ANTONYMS inauspicious, unfavorable.

■ **aus·pi·cious·ly adv.**

Aus·sie /'ôsē/ informal ▶ **n.** (plural **Aussies**) an Australian. ▶ **adj.** Australian.

aus·tere /ô'sti(ə)r/ ▶ **adj. 1** without luxuries or decoration; very simple and plain. **2** severe or strict in appearance or behavior.

SYNONYMS **1 severe**, stern, strict, harsh, dour, grim, cold, frosty, unfriendly. **2 spartan**, frugal, ascetic, puritanical, abstemious, strict, simple, hard. **3** *an austere building* **plain**, simple, basic, functional, unadorned, bleak, bare, clinical. ANTONYMS easygoing, ornate.

■ **aus·tere·ly adv. aus·ter·i·ty** /ô'steritē/ **n.**

Aus·tral·a·sian /,ôstrə'lāzhən/ ▶ **adj.** relating to Australasia, a region made up of Australia, New Zealand, and neighboring islands.

Aus·tral·ian /ô'strālyən/ ▶ **n.** a person from Australia. ▶ **adj.** relating to Australia.

Aus·tri·an /'ôstrēən/ ▶ **n.** a person from Austria. ▶ **adj.** relating to Austria.

au·tar·chy /'ô,tärkē/ ▶ **n.** (plural **autarchies**) **1** (or **autocracy** /ô'täkrəsē/) a system of government in which one person has total power. **2** (or **autarky**) economic independence or self-sufficiency. **3** (or **autarky**) an economically independent state or society.

au·tar·ky /'ô,tärkē/ (also **autarchy**) ▶ **n. 1** economic independence or self-sufficiency. **2** an economically independent state or society.

au·then·tic /ô'thentik/ ▶ **adj.** known to be real; genuine.

SYNONYMS **1 genuine**, real, bona fide, true, legitimate; informal kosher. **2 accurate**, factual, true, truthful, reliable, trustworthy, honest, faithful. ANTONYMS fake, unreliable.

■ **au·then·ti·cal·ly adv. au·then·tic·i·ty** /,ôthen'tisitē/ **n.**

au·then·ti·cate /ô'thenti,kāt/ ▶ **v.** (**authenticates**, **authenticating**, **authenticated**) prove or show that something is real and genuine.

SYNONYMS **verify**, validate, prove, substantiate, corroborate, confirm, support, back up. ANTONYMS disprove.

■ **au·then·ti·ca·tion** /ô,thenti'kāshən/ **n.**

au·thor /'ôthər/ ▶ **n. 1** a writer of a book or article. **2** the inventor of something.

SYNONYMS **1 writer**, novelist, poet, playwright, dramatist, columnist, reporter, wordsmith; informal scribe, scribbler. **2 creator**, originator, founder, father, architect, designer, producer.

■ **au·thor·ship n.**

au·thor·i·tar·i·an /ə,thôri'te(ə)rēən, ô,thär-/ ▶ **adj.** demanding strict obedience to authority and rules. ▶ **n.** an authoritarian person.

SYNONYMS ▶ **adj. strict**, autocratic, dictatorial, despotic, tyrannical, domineering, imperious, illiberal, undemocratic; informal bossy. ANTONYMS democratic, liberal. ▶ **n. disciplinarian**, autocrat, dictator, despot, tyrant. ANTONYMS democrat, liberal.

au·thor·i·ta·tive /ə'thôri,tātiv, ə'thär-/ ▶ **adj. 1** true or accurate and so able to be trusted. **2** commanding and self-confident. **3** official.

SYNONYMS **1 reliable**, dependable, trustworthy, accurate, authentic, valid, definitive, classic. **2 commanding**, masterful, assertive, self-assured, self-confident. ANTONYMS unreliable.

■ **au·thor·i·ta·tive·ly adv.**

au·thor·i·ty /ə'thôritē, ô'thär-/ ▶ **n.** (plural **authorities**) **1** the power to give orders and make people obey you. **2** a person or organization that has official power. **3** recognized knowledge or expertise. **4** a person or book that is trusted as a source of knowledge.

SYNONYMS **1** *a rebellion against those in authority* **power**, command, control, charge, dominance, jurisdiction, rule. **2** *the authority to arrest drug traffickers* **right**, authorization, power, mandate, prerogative, license. **3** *they need congressional authority* **permission**, authorization, consent, sanction, assent, agreement, approval, clearance; informal the go-ahead. **4** (**the authorities**) **officials**, officialdom, government, administration, establishment, police; informal the powers that be. **5 expert**, specialist, professional, master, connoisseur, pundit, doyen/doyenne, guru.

au·thor·ize /'ôthə,rīz/ ▶ **v.** (**authorizes**, **authorizing**, **authorized**) give official permission to or for.

SYNONYMS **1** *they authorized further action* **permit**, sanction, allow, approve, consent to, assent to; informal give the go-ahead for, OK. **2** *the troops were authorized to fire* **empower**, give authority, mandate, commission, entitle. **3** (**authorized**) **approved**, sanctioned, accredited, recognized, licensed, certified, official, legal, legitimate. ANTONYMS forbid, unauthorized, unofficial.

■ **au·thor·i·za·tion** /,ôthərə'zāshən/ **n.**

au·tism /'ô,tizəm/ ▶ **n.** a mental condition in which a person has great difficulty in communicating with other people. ■ **au·tis·tic** /ô'tistik/ **adj.**

au·to /'ôtō/ ▶ **adj. & n. 1** automatic. **2** automobile.

au·to·bi·og·ra·phy /,ôtəbī'ägrəfē/ ▶ **n.** (plural **autobiographies**) an account of a person's life written by that person. ■ **au·to·bi·o·graph·i·cal** /,ôtəbīə'grafikəl/ **adj.**

au·toc·ra·cy /ô'täkrəsē/ ▶ **n.** (plural **autocracies**) a system of government in which one person has total power.

au·to·crat /'ôtə,krat/ ▶ **n. 1** a ruler who has total power. **2** a person who expects obedience.

■ **au·to·crat·ic** /ˌôtə'kratik/ adj.

au·to·di·dact /ˌôtō'dīˌdakt/ ▶ n. a self-taught person.

au·to·graph /'ôtəˌgraf/ ▶ n. a signature, especially a celebrity's signature written for an admirer. ▶ v. write an autograph on something.

au·to·mate /'ôtəˌmāt/ ▶ v. (**automates, automating, automated**) convert a process or machine so that it can operate automatically. □ **automated teller machine** a machine that provides banking services when a special card is inserted. ■ **au·to·ma·tion** /ˌôtə'māsHən/ n.

au·to·mat·ic /ˌôtə'matik/ ▶ adj. 1 operating by itself without human control. 2 (of a gun) able to fire continuously until the bullets run out. 3 done without conscious thought. 4 (of a punishment) applied without question because of a fixed rule. ▶ n. 1 an automatic gun. 2 an automatic vehicle.

> SYNONYMS ▶ adj. 1 **mechanized**, powered, mechanical, automated, computerized, electronic, robotic. 2 **instinctive**, involuntary, unconscious, reflex, knee-jerk, subconscious, spontaneous, impulsive, unthinking, mechanical; informal gut. 3 **inevitable**, unavoidable, inescapable, certain. ANTONYMS manual, conscious, deliberate.

□ **automatic pilot** a device for keeping an aircraft on course without the pilot having to control it. ■ **au·to·mat·i·cal·ly** adv.

au·tom·a·ton /ô'tämətən, -ˌtän/ ▶ n. (plural **automata** /-tə/ or **automatons**) a mechanical device that looks like a human being.

au·to·mo·bile /ˌôtəmō'bēl/ ▶ n. a car.

au·to·mo·tive /ˌôtə'mōtiv/ ▶ adj. having to do with motor vehicles.

au·ton·o·mous /ô'tänəməs/ ▶ adj. self-governing or independent.

> SYNONYMS **self-governing**, independent, sovereign, free. ANTONYMS dependent.

■ **au·ton·o·mous·ly** adv.

au·ton·o·my /ô'tänəmē/ ▶ n. 1 self-government. 2 freedom of action.

> SYNONYMS **self-government**, self-rule, home rule, self-determination, independence, sovereignty, freedom. ANTONYMS dependence.

au·to·pi·lot /'ôtōˌpīlət/ ▶ n. a device for keeping an aircraft on course without the pilot having to control it.

au·top·sy /'ôˌtäpsē/ ▶ n. (plural **autopsies**) an examination of a dead body to discover the cause of death.

auto·work·er /'ôtōˌwərkər/ ▶ n. a worker in the motor vehicle manufacturing industry.

au·tumn /'ôtəm/ ▶ n. ⇒ FALL (sense 6 of the noun). ■ **au·tum·nal** /ô'təmnəl/ adj.

aux·il·ia·ry /ôg'zilyərē, -'zil(ə)rē/ ▶ adj. providing extra help and support. ▶ n. (plural **auxiliaries**) an auxiliary person or thing.

> SYNONYMS ▶ adj. **additional**, supplementary, extra, reserve, backup, emergency, fallback, second.

□ **auxiliary verb** a verb such as *be*, *do*, and *have* that is used to form tenses of other verbs.

a·vail /ə'vāl/ ▶ v. (**avail yourself of**) formal use or take advantage of. ▶ n. use or benefit: *his protests were to no avail.*

a·vail·a·ble /ə'vāləbəl/ ▶ adj. 1 able to be used or obtained. 2 not occupied.

> SYNONYMS **obtainable**, accessible, at hand, to be had, on sale, untaken, unsold, free, vacant, unoccupied; informal up for grabs, on tap.

■ **a·vail·a·bil·i·ty** /əˌvālə'bilitē/ n.

av·a·lanche /'avəˌlancH/ ▶ n. 1 a mass of snow and ice falling rapidly down a mountainside. 2 an overwhelming amount of something.

> SYNONYMS *an avalanche of inquiries* **barrage**, flood, deluge, torrent, wave, onslaught.

a·vant-garde /'ävänt 'gärd, ˌävän/ ▶ adj. (in the arts) new and experimental.

> SYNONYMS **experimental**, modern, cutting-edge, progressive, unorthodox, unconventional; informal edgy, offbeat, way-out. ANTONYMS conservative, traditional.

av·a·rice /'avəris/ ▶ n. extreme greed for money or material things.

> SYNONYMS **greed**, acquisitiveness, covetousness, materialism. ANTONYMS generosity.

av·a·ri·cious /ˌavə'risHəs/ ▶ adj. very greedy for money or material things.

av·a·tar /'avəˌtär/ ▶ n. 1 Hinduism a god or goddess appearing in bodily form on earth. 2 Computing an image representing a person on a website or in a computer game.

A·ve Ma·ri·a /'ävā mə'rēə/ ▶ n. a prayer to the Virgin Mary used in Catholic worship.

a·venge /ə'venj/ ▶ v. (**avenges, avenging, avenged**) repay something bad that has been done to you by harming the person who did it.

> SYNONYMS **requite**, punish, repay, pay back, take revenge for, get even for.

■ **a·veng·er** n.

av·e·nue /'avəˌn(y)o͞o/ ▶ n. 1 a broad road or path. 2 a way of making progress toward achieving something: *all these avenues have been tried over the years.*

a·ver /ə'vər/ ▶ v. (**avers, averring, averred**) formal declare that something is the case.

av·er·age /'av(ə)rij/ ▶ n. 1 the result obtained by adding several amounts together and then dividing the total by the number of amounts. 2 a usual amount or level. ▶ adj. 1 being an average: *the average temperature in May was 8° below normal.* 2 usual or ordinary. ▶ v. (**averages, averaging, averaged**) 1 amount to a particular figure as an average: *annual inflation averaged 5 percent.* 2 calculate the average of several amounts.

> SYNONYMS ▶ n. **mean**, median, mode, norm, standard, rule, par. ▶ adj. 1 *the average temperature* **mean**, median. 2 *a woman of average height* **normal**, standard, typical, ordinary, common, regular. ANTONYMS abnormal, unusual.

a·verse /ə'vərs/ ▶ adj. (**averse to**) strongly disliking or opposed to.

> SYNONYMS **opposed**, hostile, antagonistic, resistant, disinclined, reluctant, loath; informal anti. ANTONYMS keen.

USAGE

Don't confuse **averse** with **adverse**, which means 'harmful or unfavorable.'

a·ver·sion /ə'vərzʜən/ ▶ **n.** a strong dislike.

SYNONYMS **dislike**, hatred, loathing, abhorrence, distaste, antipathy, hostility, reluctance, disinclination. ANTONYMS liking.

a·vert /ə'vərt/ ▶ **v. 1** turn away your eyes. **2** prevent something unpleasant from happening.

SYNONYMS **1 turn aside**, turn away, shift, redirect. **2 prevent**, avoid, stave off, ward off, head off, forestall.

a·vi·an /'āvēən/ ▶ **adj.** having to do with birds.

a·vi·ar·y /'āvē,erē/ ▶ **n.** (plural **aviaries**) a large enclosure for keeping birds in.

a·vi·a·tion /,āvē'āsʜən/ ▶ **n.** the activity of operating and flying aircraft.

a·vi·a·tor /'āvē,ātər/ ▶ **n.** dated a pilot.

av·id /'avid/ ▶ **adj.** very interested or enthusiastic.

SYNONYMS **keen**, eager, enthusiastic, ardent, passionate, zealous, devoted. ANTONYMS apathetic.

■ **av·id·ly adv.**

a·vi·on·ics /,āvē'äniks/ ▶ **pl.n.** electronics used in aviation.

av·o·ca·do /,avə'kädō, ,ävə-/ ▶ **n.** (plural **avocados**) a pear-shaped fruit with pale green flesh and a large stone.

av·o·cet /'avə,set/ ▶ **n.** a wading bird with long legs and an upturned bill.

a·void /ə'void/ ▶ **v. 1** keep away from, or stop yourself from doing. **2** prevent something from happening. **3** manage not to collide with.

SYNONYMS **1 keep away from**, steer clear of, give a wide berth to. **2 evade**, dodge, sidestep, escape, run away from; informal duck, wriggle out of, get out of. **3** *book early to avoid disappointment* **prevent**, preclude, stave off, forestall, head off, ward off. **4** *avoid alcohol* **refrain from**, abstain from, desist from, steer clear of, eschew. ANTONYMS confront, face.

■ **a·void·a·ble adj. a·void·ance n.**

av·oir·du·pois /,ävərdə'poiz/ ▶ **n.** the system of weights based on a pound of 16 ounces.

a·vow /ə'vou/ ▶ **v.** openly state or confess.
■ **a·vowed adj.**

a·vun·cu·lar /ə'vəɴɢkyələr/ ▶ **adj. 1** of or relating to an uncle. **2** kind and friendly toward a younger person.

a·wait /ə'wāt/ ▶ **v.** wait for.

SYNONYMS **1 wait for**, expect, look forward to, anticipate. **2 be in store for**, lie ahead of, be waiting for, be (right/just) around the corner.

a·wake /ə'wāk/ ▶ **v.** (**awakes**, **awaking**, **awoke** /ə'wōk/; past participle **awoken** /ə'wōkən/) **1** stop sleeping. **2** make or become active again. ▶ **adj.** not asleep.

SYNONYMS ▶ **v. wake up**, wake, awaken, waken, stir, come to, come around, rouse, call. ▶ **adj. 1 sleepless**, wide awake, restless, insomniac. **2** *too few are awake to the dangers* **aware of**, conscious of, mindful of, alert to. ANTONYMS asleep, oblivious.

a·wak·en /ə'wākən/ ▶ **v. 1** awake. **2** stir up a feeling.

SYNONYMS **1** see **AWAKE** (verb). **2 arouse**, kindle, bring out, trigger, stir up, stimulate, revive.

■ **a·wak·en·ing n. & adj.**

a·ward /ə'wôrd/ ▶ **v.** give an official prize or reward to. ▶ **n. 1** an official prize or reward. **2** the action of awarding.

SYNONYMS ▶ **v. give**, grant, accord, confer on, bestow on, present to, decorate with. ▶ **n. 1 prize**, trophy, medal, decoration, reward. **2 grant**, scholarship, endowment.

a·ware /ə'we(ə)r/ ▶ **adj.** (usually **aware of** or **that**) knowing about a situation or fact.

SYNONYMS **1** *she is aware of the dangers* **conscious of**, mindful of, informed about, acquainted with, familiar with, alive to, alert to; informal wise to, in the know about. **2** *environmentally aware* **sensitive**, enlightened, knowledgeable, (well-)informed; informal clued in. ANTONYMS ignorant.

a·ware·ness /ə'we(ə)rnəs/ ▶ **n.** the state of knowing about a situation or fact.

SYNONYMS **consciousness**, recognition, realization, perception, understanding, grasp, appreciation, knowledge, familiarity.

a·wash /ə'wôsʜ, ə'wäsʜ/ ▶ **adj.** covered or flooded with water.

a·way /ə'wā/ ▶ **adv. 1** to or at a distance. **2** into a place for storage. **3** out of existence. **4** constantly or continuously. ▶ **adj.** (of a sports competition) played at the opponents' grounds.

SYNONYMS ▶ **adv. elsewhere**, abroad, gone, off, out, absent, on vacation.

awe /ô/ ▶ **n.** a feeling of great respect mixed with fear. ▶ **v.** (**awes**, **awing**, **awed**) fill someone with awe.

SYNONYMS ▶ **n. wonder**, wonderment, admiration, reverence, respect, fear, dread.

awe·some /'ôsəm/ ▶ **adj. 1** inspiring awe. **2** informal excellent.

SYNONYMS **breathtaking**, awe-inspiring, magnificent, amazing, stunning, staggering, imposing, formidable, intimidating; informal mind-boggling, mind-blowing, brilliant. ANTONYMS unimpressive.

aw·ful /'ôfəl/ ▶ **adj. 1** very bad or unpleasant. **2** used to emphasize something: *an awful lot.*

SYNONYMS **1** *the place smells awful* **disgusting**, terrible, dreadful, ghastly, horrible, vile, foul, revolting, repulsive, repugnant, sickening, nauseating; informal gross. **2** *an awful book* **dreadful**, terrible, frightful, atrocious, lamentable; informal crummy, pathetic, rotten, woeful, lousy, appalling, abysmal, dismal, dire. **3** *I feel awful* **ill**, unwell, sick, nauseous, poorly. ANTONYMS delightful, excellent, well.

■ **aw·ful·ness n.**

aw·ful·ly /'ôf(ə)lē/ ▶ **adv. 1** informal very or very much. **2** very badly or unpleasantly.

SYNONYMS **1** *an awfully nice man* **very**, extremely, really, immensely, exceedingly, thoroughly, dreadfully, terrifically, terribly, exceptionally, remarkably, extraordinarily;

informal real, mighty, seriously; informal, dated frightfully. **2** *we played awfully* **terribly**, dreadfully, atrociously, appallingly; informal abysmally.

a·while /ə'(h)wīl/ ▶ **adv.** for a short time.

awk·ward /'ôkwərd/ ▶ **adj.** **1** hard to do or deal with. **2** causing or feeling embarrassment. **3** uncomfortable or abnormal. **4** clumsy; not graceful.

SYNONYMS **1 difficult**, tricky, cumbersome, unwieldy. **2 unreasonable**, uncooperative, unhelpful, difficult, obstructive, contrary, perverse, obstinate, stubborn; informal balky. **3** *an awkward time* **inconvenient**, inappropriate, inopportune, difficult. **4** *he put her in an awkward position* **embarrassing**, uncomfortable, unenviable, delicate, tricky, problematic, troublesome, humiliating, compromising; informal sticky. **5** *she felt awkward* **uncomfortable**, uneasy, tense, nervous, edgy, self-conscious, embarrassed. **6** *his awkward movements* **clumsy**, ungainly, uncoordinated, graceless, inelegant, gauche, gawky, stiff, unskillful, inept, blundering; informal all thumbs, ham-fisted, cack-handed. ANTONYMS easy, amenable, convenient, graceful.

■ **awk·ward·ly** **adv.**

awl /ôl/ ▶ **n.** a small pointed tool used for making holes.

awn /ôn/ ▶ **n.** Botany a stiff bristle growing from the ear or flower of barley, rye, and grasses.

awn·ing /'ôniNG/ ▶ **n.** a sheet of canvas on a frame, used for shelter.

a·woke /ə'wōk/ past of **AWAKE**.

a·wo·ken /ə'wōkən/ past participle of **AWAKE**.

AWOL /'ā,wôl/ ▶ **adj.** informal absent from where you should be: *he went AWOL.*

a·wry /ə'rī/ ▶ **adv. & adj.** away from the expected course or position.

ax /aks/ (or **axe**) ▶ **n.** a tool with a heavy blade, used for chopping wood. ▶ **v.** (**axes, axing, axed**) suddenly and ruthlessly cancel or dismiss.

SYNONYMS ▶ **n. hatchet**, chopper, cleaver; historical battleax. ▶ **v. 1 cancel**, withdraw, drop, scrap, cut, discontinue, end; informal ditch, dump, pull the plug on. **2 dismiss**, lay off, get rid of; informal sack, fire, can.

□ **have an ax to grind** have a private reason for doing something.

ax·il /'aksəl/ ▶ **n.** Botany the upper angle where a leaf joins a stem.

ax·i·om /'aksēəm/ ▶ **n.** a statement regarded as being obviously true. ■ **ax·i·o·mat·ic** /,aksēə'matik/ **adj.**

ax·is /'aksis/ ▶ **n.** (plural **axes** /'ak,sēz/) **1** an imaginary line around which an object or shape rotates. **2** a fixed line against which points on a graph are measured. **3** (**the Axis**) Germany and its allies in World War II.

ax·le /'aksəl/ ▶ **n.** a rod passing through the center of a wheel or group of wheels.

SYNONYMS **shaft**, spindle, rod.

a·ya·tol·lah /,äyə'tōlə, ,īyə-/ ▶ **n.** a religious leader in Iran.

aye /ī/ ▶ **exclam.** old use or dialect yes. ▶ **n.** an affirmative answer, especially in voting.

a·zal·ea /ə'zālyə/ ▶ **n.** a shrub with brightly colored flowers.

az·i·muth /'azəməTH/ ▶ **n.** Astronomy the direction of a star measured horizontally as an angle from due north or south.

Az·tec /'az,tek/ ▶ **n.** a member of an American Indian people that ruled Mexico before the Spanish conquest of the 16th century.

az·ure /'azHər/ ▶ **n.** a bright blue color like a cloudless sky.

Bb

B (or **b**) ▶ **n.** (plural **Bs** or **B's**) the second letter of the alphabet. ▫ **B-movie** a low-budget movie, originally one supporting a main movie in a theater program.

B & B (or **b & b**) ▶ **abbr.** bed and breakfast.

BA ▶ **abbr.** Bachelor of Arts.

baa /bä/ ▶ **v.** (**baas, baaing, baaed**) (of a sheep or lamb) bleat. ▶ **n.** the cry of a sheep or lamb.

baba[1] /ˈbäˌbä/ ▶ **n.** a small rich sponge cake soaked in rum-flavored syrup.

baba[2] ▶ **n.** Indian informal **1** a respectful form of address for a father or an older man. **2** (often **Baba**) a holy man.

bab·ble /ˈbabəl/ ▶ **v.** talk quickly in a foolish, confused, or incomprehensible way. ▶ **n.** foolish, confused, or incomprehensible talk.

SYNONYMS ▶ **v. prattle**, rattle on, gabble, chatter, jabber, twitter, burble, blather; informal yatter, blabber, jaw, gas, shoot your mouth off.

babe /bāb/ ▶ **n. 1** literary a baby. **2** informal an attractive young woman.

ba·bel /ˈbabəl, ˈbā-/ ▶ **n.** a confused noise made by many people speaking together.

ba·boon /baˈbo͞on/ ▶ **n.** a large monkey with a long snout and a pink rump.

ba·bush·ka /bəˈbo͝oshkə/ ▶ **n. 1** (in Russia) an old woman or grandmother. **2** a headscarf tied under the chin.

ba·by /ˈbābē/ ▶ **n.** (plural **babies**) **1** a child or animal that has recently been born. **2** a timid or childish person. ▶ **adj.** small or very young: *baby carrots*. ▶ **v.** (**babies, babying, babied**) treat someone too protectively.

SYNONYMS ▶ **n. infant**, newborn, child; technical neonate; informal tot; literary babe. ▶ **adj. miniature**, mini, little, toy, pocket, midget, dwarf, vest-pocket; informal teeny, teensy, bite-sized.

▫ **baby boom** a temporary sharp rise in the birth rate, especially the one following World War II. **baby boomer** a person born during a baby boom. ▪ **ba·by·hood n.**

ba·by·ish /ˈbābēish/ ▶ **adj.** childish and immature.

SYNONYMS **childish**, infantile, juvenile, puerile, immature. ANTONYMS mature.

Bab·y·lo·ni·an /ˌbabəˈlōnēən/ ▶ **n.** a person from Babylon or Babylonia, an ancient city and kingdom in Mesopotamia (part of modern Iraq). ▶ **adj.** relating to Babylon or Babylonia.

ba·by·sit /ˈbābēˌsit/ ▶ **v.** (**babysits, babysitting, babysat**) look after a child or children while the parents are out. ▪ **ba·by·sit·ter n.**

bac·ca·lau·re·ate /ˌbakəˈlôrēit/ ▶ **n. 1** a university bachelor's degree. **2** an exam taken in some countries to qualify for higher education.

bac·ca·rat /ˈbäkəˌrä, ˌbakəˈrä/ ▶ **n.** a gambling card game.

bac·cha·na·li·an /ˌbakəˈnālyən/ ▶ **adj.** (of a party or celebration) drunken and wild.

bach·e·lor /ˈbach(ə)lər/ ▶ **n. 1** a man who has never been married. **2** a person who holds an undergraduate degree from a university.

bach·e·lor·ette /ˌbach(ə)ləˈret/ ▶ **n.** a young unmarried woman.

ba·cil·lus /bəˈsiləs/ ▶ **n.** (plural **bacilli** /-ˈsilī/) a type of bacterium.

back /bak/ ▶ **n. 1** the rear surface of a person's body, or the upper part of an animal's body. **2** the side or part of something that is furthest from the front. **3** a defending player in a team game. ▶ **adv. 1** in the opposite direction from the one in which you are facing or traveling. **2** so as to return to an earlier or normal position or state. **3** into the past. **4** in return. ▶ **adj. 1** at or toward the back. **2** in a remote or less important position. **3** relating to the past. ▶ **v. 1** give support to. **2** walk or drive backwards. **3** bet money on a person or animal to win a race or contest. **4** (**back on to**) (of a building) have its back facing or next to. **5** cover the back of an object. **6** provide musical backing for a singer or musician.

SYNONYMS ▶ **n. 1 spine**, backbone, spinal column, vertebrae, vertebral column. **2 rear**, end, rear end, tail end; Nautical stern. **3 reverse**, other side, underside; informal flip side. ANTONYMS front. ▶ **adj. 1 rear**, rearmost, hind, hindmost, posterior. **2 past**, old, previous, earlier. ANTONYMS front, future. ▶ **v. 1 sponsor**, finance, fund, subsidize, underwrite; informal pick up the bill for. **2 support**, endorse, sanction, approve of, give your blessing to, smile on, favor, advocate, promote, champion; informal throw your weight behind. **3 bet on**, gamble on, stake money on. **4 reverse**, draw back, step back, pull back, retreat, withdraw. ANTONYMS oppose, advance.

▫ **back and forth** to and fro. **back-breaking** (of manual labor) physically demanding. **the back of beyond** a very remote place. **back down** give in. **back off** stop opposing someone. **back out** withdraw from something you have promised to do. **back-to-back 1** following one after the other. **2** (of two people) facing in opposite directions with backs touching. **3** consecutively; in succession. **back someone/something up 1** support someone or something. **2** Computing make a spare copy of data or a disk. **behind someone's back** without a person knowing. **put someone's back up** annoy someone. **put your back into** tackle a task in a determined and energetic way. **turn your back on** ignore or reject. **with**

your back to (or **up against**) **the wall** in a very difficult situation.

back·ache /ˈbakˌāk/ ▶ **n.** prolonged pain in your back.

back·bit·ing /ˈbakˌbītiNG/ ▶ **n.** spiteful talk about a person who is not present.

back·board /ˈbakˌbôrd/ ▶ **n.** Basketball an upright board behind the basket, off which the ball may rebound.

back·bone /ˈbakˌbōn/ ▶ **n.** **1** the spine. **2** strength of character.

> SYNONYMS **1 spine**, spinal column, vertebrae, vertebral column. **2 mainstay**, cornerstone, foundation. **3 strength of character**, strength of will, firmness, resolution, resolve, grit, determination, fortitude, mettle, spirit.

back·coun·try /ˈbakˌkəntrē/ ▶ **n.** sparsely inhabited rural areas; wilderness.

back·date /ˈbakˌdāt/ ▶ **v.** (**backdates**, **backdating**, **backdated**) make something valid from an earlier date.

back·door /ˈbakˌdôr/ ▶ **adj.** done in an underhand or secret way.

back·drop /ˈbakˌdräp/ ▶ **n.** **1** a painted cloth hung at the back of a theater stage as part of the scenery. **2** the setting or background for a scene or event.

back·er /bakər/ ▶ **n.** a person, institution, or country that supports something, especially financially.

> SYNONYMS **1 sponsor**, investor, underwriter, financier, patron, benefactor; informal angel. **2 supporter**, defender, advocate, promoter, booster.

back·field /ˈbakˌfēld/ ▶ **n.** Football the area of play behind either the offensive or defensive line.

back·fire /ˈbakˌfī(ə)r/ ▶ **v.** (**backfires**, **backfiring**, **backfired**) **1** (of an engine) make a banging sound as a result of fuel igniting incorrectly. **2** produce an effect that is the opposite of what was intended.

> SYNONYMS **rebound**, boomerang, come back, fail; informal blow up in someone's face.

back·gam·mon /ˈbakˌgamən/ ▶ **n.** a board game for two players who move their pieces according to throws of the dice.

back·ground /ˈbakˌground/ ▶ **n.** **1** the part of a scene or picture behind the main figures. **2** information or circumstances that influence or explain something. **3** a person's education, experience, and early life.

> SYNONYMS **1 backdrop**, surrounding(s), setting, scene, framework. **2 social circumstances**, family circumstances, environment, class, culture, tradition. **3 experience**, record, history, past, training, education. ANTONYMS foreground.

back·hand /ˈbakˌhand/ ▶ **n.** (in tennis and similar games) a stroke played with the back of the hand facing in the direction of the stroke.

back·hand·ed /ˈbakˌhandid/ ▶ **adj.** expressed in a way that is indirect or has more than one meaning: *a backhanded compliment*.

back·hand·er /ˈbakˌhandər/ ▶ **n.** a backhand stroke or blow.

back·hoe /ˈbakˌhō/ ▶ **n.** a mechanical digger with a bucket attached to a hinged pole.

back·ing /ˈbakiNG/ ▶ **n.** **1** support. **2** a layer of material that forms or strengthens the back of something. **3** music or singing accompanying a main singer, especially in popular music.

> SYNONYMS **1 support**, endorsement, approval, blessing, assistance, aid, help. **2 sponsorship**, financing, funding, subsidy, patronage.

back·lash /ˈbakˌlasH/ ▶ **n.** an angry reaction by a large number of people.

> SYNONYMS **adverse reaction**, counterblast, repercussion, comeback, retaliation, reprisal.

back·log /ˈbakˌlôg, -ˌläg/ ▶ **n.** a buildup of things needing to be dealt with.

back·lot /ˈbakˌlät/ ▶ **n.** an outdoor area in a movie studio where large sets are made and some outside scenes are filmed.

back·pack /ˈbakˌpak/ ▶ **n.** a bag with two shoulder straps, carried on the back. ▶ **v.** travel carrying your belongings in a backpack. ■ **back·pack·er n.**

back·ped·al /ˈbakˌpedl/ ▶ **v.** reverse a previous action or opinion.

back·side /ˈbakˌsīd/ ▶ **n.** informal a person's bottom; the part of your body that you sit on.

back·slap·ping /ˈbakˌslapiNG/ ▶ **n.** the offering of hearty congratulations or praise.

back·slid·ing /ˈbakˌslīdiNG/ ▶ **n.** a return to bad behavior after an attempt to improve.

back·spin /ˈbakˌspin/ ▶ **n.** a backward spin given to a moving ball, making it stop more quickly or bounce back at a steeper angle.

back·stage /ˈbakˈstāj/ ▶ **adv. & adj.** behind the stage in a theater.

back·sto·ry /ˈbakˌstôrē/ ▶ **n.** (plural **backstories**) a history or background created for a fictional character in a movie or television program.

back·street /ˈbakˌstrēt/ ▶ **n.** a less important street in a town or city.

back·stroke /ˈbakˌstrōk/ ▶ **n.** a swimming stroke in which you lie on your back and lift your arms out of the water in a backward circular movement.

back·talk /ˈbakˌtôk/ ▶ **n.** informal rude or impertinent remarks made in reply to someone in authority.

back·track /ˈbakˌtrak/ ▶ **v.** **1** retrace your steps. **2** change your opinion to the opposite of what it was.

back·up /ˈbakˌəp/ ▶ **n.** **1** support. **2** a person or thing kept ready to be used when needed. **3** Computing a copy of computer data made in case the original is lost or damaged. ▶ **adj.** kept ready to be used when needed.

> SYNONYMS ▶ **n. help**, support, assistance, aid, reserve, reinforcements. ▶ **adj. reserve**, spare, substitute, replacement, standby, fallback, emergency.

back·ward /ˈbakwərd/ ▶ **adj.** **1** directed toward the back. **2** having made less progress than is normal or expected. ▶ **adv.** (also **backwards**) **1** toward the back, or back toward the starting point. **2** opposite to the usual direction or order.

> SYNONYMS ▶ **adj. 1 rearward**, toward the rear, behind you, reverse. **2 retrograde**, regressive, for the worse, in the wrong direction, downhill, negative. **3 underdeveloped**, undeveloped, primitive. **4 hesitant**, reticent, reluctant, shy, diffident, timid, self-effacing, unassertive. ANTONYMS forward, advanced. ▶ **adv. backwards**, toward the rear, rearward, behind you. ANTONYMS forward.

□ **bend over backward** informal try your hardest to be fair or helpful. **know something backward and forward** know something very fully.

back·wash /ˈbakˌwôsʜ, -ˌwäsʜ/ ▶ **n.** waves flowing outward behind a ship.

back·wa·ter /ˈbakˌwôtər, -ˌwätər/ ▶ **n. 1** a stretch of stagnant water on a river. **2** a place where change happens very slowly.

back·woods /ˈbakˈwo͝odz/ ▶ **pl.n.** a remote area or region.

back·yard /ˈbakˈyärd/ ▶ **n. 1** a yard at the back of a house. **2** informal the area close to where you live.

ba·con /ˈbākən/ ▶ **n.** salted or smoked meat from the back or sides of a pig. □ **bring home the bacon** informal make money or achieve success.

bac·te·ri·a /bakˈti(ə)rēə/ ▶ **pl.n.** (singular **bacterium**) a group of microscopic organisms, many kinds of which can cause disease. ■ **bac·te·ri·al adj.**

USAGE

Bacteria is actually a plural (the singular is **bacterium**), and should always be used with a plural verb, e.g., *the bacteria were multiplying*.

bac·te·ri·ol·o·gy /bakˌti(ə)rēˈäləjē/ ▶ **n.** the study of bacteria. ■ **bac·te·ri·o·log·i·cal** /bakˌti(ə)rēəˈläjikəl/ **adj. bac·te·ri·ol·o·gist n.**

Bac·tri·an cam·el /ˈbaktrēən/ ▶ **n.** a camel with two humps, found in central Asia.

bad /bad/ ▶ **adj.** (**worse** /wərs/, **worst** /wərst/) **1** low in quality; well below standard. **2** unpleasant. **3** severe; serious. **4** wicked or evil. **5** (**bad for**) harmful to. **6** injured, ill, or diseased. **7** (of food) decayed. **8** informal good; excellent.

SYNONYMS **1** *bad workmanship* **unsatisfactory**, substandard, poor, inferior, second-rate, second-class, inadequate, deficient, imperfect, defective, faulty, shoddy, negligent, disgraceful, awful, terrible, appalling, dreadful, frightful, atrocious, abysmal; informal crummy, rotten, pathetic, useless, woeful, lousy. **2** *the alcohol had a bad effect* **harmful**, damaging, detrimental, injurious, hurtful, destructive, deleterious, inimical. **3** *the bad guys* **wicked**, evil, sinful, criminal, immoral, corrupt, villainous; informal crooked. **4** *you bad girl!* **naughty**, badly behaved, disobedient, wayward, willful, defiant, unruly, undisciplined. **5** *bad news* **unpleasant**, disagreeable, unwelcome, unfavorable, unfortunate, grim, distressing, gloomy. **6** *a bad time to arrive* **unfavorable**, inauspicious, unpropitious, inopportune, unfortunate, disadvantageous, inappropriate, unsuitable. **7** *a bad accident* **serious**, severe, grave, critical, acute. **8** *the meat's bad* **rotten**, decayed, putrid, rancid, curdled, sour, moldy, off. **9** *a bad knee* **injured**, wounded, diseased; dated game. ANTONYMS good, beneficial, virtuous, favorable.

□ **bad debt** a debt that will not be repaid. **bad-mouth** informal criticize spitefully. **bad-tempered** easily angered or annoyed. **too bad** informal said when something is not what you want but cannot be changed. ■ **bad·ness n.**

bade /bad, bād/ past of **BID**[2].

badge /baj/ ▶ **n.** a small flat object that a person pins to their clothing to show that they belong to an organization, have a particular rank, hold an office, etc.

SYNONYMS **1 brooch**, pin, button, emblem, crest, insignia. **2** *a badge of success* **sign**, symbol, indication, signal, mark, hallmark, trademark.

badg·er /ˈbajər/ ▶ **n.** an animal with a black and white striped head that lives underground and is active at night. ▶ **v.** (**badgers**, **badgering**, **badgered**) pester someone to do something.

SYNONYMS ▶ **v. pester**, harass, hound, harry, nag, bother; informal hassle, bug.

bad·i·nage /ˌbadnˈäzʜ/ ▶ **n.** witty conversation.

bad·lands /ˈbadˌlandz/ ▶ **pl.n.** land where plants or crops will not grow.

bad·ly /ˈbadlē/ ▶ **adv.** (**worse** /wərs/, **worst** /wərst/) **1** in a way that is not acceptable or satisfactory. **2** severely; seriously. **3** very much.

SYNONYMS **1 poorly**, unsatisfactorily, inadequately, incorrectly, faultily, defectively, shoddily, amateurishly, carelessly, incompetently, inexpertly. **2 unfavorably**, ill, critically, disapprovingly. **3 naughtily**, disobediently, willfully, mischievously. **4 cruelly**, wickedly, unkindly, harshly, shamefully, unfairly, unjustly, wrongly. **5 unfavorably**, unsuccessfully, adversely, unfortunately. **6 severely**, seriously, gravely, acutely, critically. ANTONYMS well.

□ **badly off** poor.

bad·min·ton /ˈbadmintn/ ▶ **n.** a game in which the players hit a shuttlecock back and forth across a high net with rackets.

baf·fle /ˈbafəl/ ▶ **v.** (**baffles**, **baffling**, **baffled**) make someone feel puzzled. ▶ **n.** a device for controlling the flow of sound, light, gas, or fluid.

SYNONYMS ▶ **v. puzzle**, perplex, bewilder, mystify, confuse; informal flummox, stump.

■ **baf·fle·ment n.**

bag /bag/ ▶ **n. 1** a flexible container with an opening at the top. **2** (**bags**) loose folds of skin under a person's eyes. **3** informal an unpleasant or unattractive woman. ▶ **v.** (**bags**, **bagging**, **bagged**) **1** put something in a bag. **2** manage to catch an animal. **3** informal manage to get.

SYNONYMS ▶ **n. suitcase**, case, valise, carryall, grip, rucksack, haversack, satchel, handbag. ▶ **v. 1 catch**, land, capture, trap, net, snare. **2 get**, secure, obtain, acquire, pick up, win, achieve; informal land, net.

□ **bag lady** informal a homeless woman who carries her possessions in shopping bags. **in the bag** informal sure to be gained.

bag·a·telle /ˌbagəˈtel/ ▶ **n. 1** a game in which you hit small balls into numbered holes on a board. **2** something unimportant or of little value.

ba·gel /ˈbāgəl/ ▶ **n.** a ring-shaped bread roll with a heavy texture, made by boiling dough and then baking it.

bag·gage /ˈbagij/ ▶ **n.** luggage packed with belongings for traveling.

SYNONYMS **luggage**, suitcases, bags, belongings.

bag·gy /ˈbagē/ ▶ **adj.** (**baggier**, **baggiest**) loose and hanging in folds.

SYNONYMS **loose**, roomy, generously cut, sloppy, voluminous, full. ANTONYMS tight.

bag·pipes /ˈbag,pīps/ ▶ **pl.n.** a musical instrument with pipes that are sounded by wind squeezed from a bag. ■ **bag·pip·er n.**

ba·guette /baˈget/ ▶ **n.** **1** a long, narrow loaf of French bread. **2** a gem, especially a diamond, cut into a long rectangular shape.

Ba·ha·mi·an /bəˈhāmēən, -ˈhäm-/ ▶ **n.** a person from the Bahamas. ▶ **adj.** relating to the Bahamas.

bail[1] /bāl/ ▶ **n.** **1** the release of an accused person on condition that a sum of money is left with the court, which will be returned as long as the person attends their trial. **2** money paid to release an accused person. ▶ **v.** release an accused person on payment of bail.

SYNONYMS ▶ **n.** **surety**, security, indemnity, bond, guarantee, pledge.

bail[2] ▶ **v.** **1** scoop water out of a ship or boat. **2** (**bail out**) make an emergency jump out of an aircraft, using a parachute. **3** (**bail someone out**) rescue someone who is in difficulties.

bai·le /ˈbīlā/ ▶ **n.** (in the south-western US) a gathering for dancing.

bai·ley /ˈbālē/ ▶ **n.** (plural **baileys**) the outer wall of a castle.

bail·iff /ˈbālif/ ▶ **n.** an official in a court of law who keeps order, looks after prisoners, etc.

bail·i·wick /ˈbālə,wik/ ▶ **n.** **1** a district over which a bailiff has authority. **2** a person's area of activity or interest.

bail·out /ˈbāl,out/ ▶ **n.** an act of giving financial assistance to a failing business or economy to save it from collapse.

bait /bāt/ ▶ **n.** food put on a hook or in a trap to attract fish or other animals. ▶ **v.** **1** taunt or tease. **2** (**baiting**) the activity of setting dogs on an animal that is trapped or tied up. **3** put bait on a hook or in a trap.

SYNONYMS ▶ **n.** **enticement**, lure, decoy, snare, trap, inducement, siren, carrot, attraction; informal come-on. ▶ **v.** **taunt**, tease, goad, pick on, torment, persecute, harass; informal needle.

□ **rise to the bait** react to being teased or tempted exactly as someone planned.

baize /bāz/ ▶ **n.** a thick green material used for covering billiard and card tables.

bake /bāk/ ▶ **v.** (**bakes**, **baking**, **baked**) **1** cook food in an oven. **2** heat something to dry or harden it. **3** (**baking**) informal (of weather) very hot. □ **baking soda** sodium bicarbonate used in cooking, for cleaning, or in toothpaste. **baking powder** a mixture of sodium bicarbonate and cream of tartar, used to make cakes rise.

bak·er /ˈbākər/ ▶ **n.** a person whose job is making bread and cakes. □ **baker's dozen** a group of thirteen.

bak·er·y /ˈbākərē/ ▶ **n.** (plural **bakeries**) a place where bread and cakes are made or sold.

bak·sheesh /ˈbakSHēSH, bakˈSHēSH/ ▶ **n.** (in India and some other eastern countries) money given as charity, a tip, or a bribe.

bal·a·cla·va /,baləˈklävə/ ▶ **n.** a close-fitting woolen hat covering the head and neck except for the face.

bal·a·lai·ka /,baləˈlīkə/ ▶ **n.** a Russian musical instrument like a guitar, with a triangular body.

bal·ance /ˈbaləns/ ▶ **n.** **1** a state in which weight is evenly distributed, so that a person or object does not wobble or fall over. **2** a situation in which different parts are in the right proportions: *political balance in broadcasting.* **3** a piece of equipment for weighing. **4** an amount that is the difference between money received and money spent in an account: *a healthy bank balance.* **5** an amount still owed when part of a debt has been paid. ▶ **v.** (**balances**, **balancing**, **balanced**) **1** put your body, or an object, in a steady position. **2** compare the value of one thing with another. **3** give equal importance to two or more things: *she managed to balance work and family life.*

SYNONYMS ▶ **n.** **1** **stability**, equilibrium, steadiness, footing. **2** **fairness**, justice, impartiality, parity, equity, evenness, uniformity, comparability. **3** **remainder**, outstanding amount, rest, residue, difference. ANTONYMS instability, bias. ▶ **v.** **1** **steady**, stabilize, poise, level. **2** **counterbalance**, balance out, offset, counteract, compensate for, make up for. **3** **correspond**, agree, tally, match up, coincide. **4** **weigh** (**up**), compare, evaluate, consider, assess.

□ **balance of payments** the difference between payments into and out of a country over a period of time. **balance of power** a situation in which states of the world have roughly equal power. **balance of trade** the difference in value between a country's imports and exports. **balance sheet** a written statement of what a business owns and what it owes. **be** (or **hang**) **in the balance** be in an uncertain state. **on balance** when everything is taken into account.

bal·bo·a /balˈbōə/ ▶ **n.** the basic unit of money of Panama.

bal·co·ny /ˈbalkənē/ ▶ **n.** (plural **balconies**) **1** a platform with a railing or low wall, projecting from the outside of a building. **2** the highest level of seats in a theater.

bald /bôld/ ▶ **adj.** **1** having no hair on the head. **2** (of a tire) having the tread worn away. **3** plain or blunt: *the bald facts.*

SYNONYMS **1** **hairless**, smooth, shaven, depilated. **2** **plain**, simple, direct, blunt, unadorned, unvarnished, unembellished, stark; informal upfront. ANTONYMS hairy.

■ **bald·ly adv. bald·ness n.**

bal·der·dash /ˈbôldər,daSH/ ▶ **n.** nonsense.

bald·ing /bôldiNG/ ▶ **adj.** going bald.

bale /bāl/ ▶ **n.** a large bundle of paper, hay, or cloth. ▶ **v.** (**bales**, **baling**, **baled**) make paper, hay, or cloth into bales.

ba·leen /bəˈlēn/ ▶ **n.** whalebone.

ba·leen whale ▶ **n.** any of the kinds of whale that have plates of whalebone in the mouth for straining plankton from the water.

bale·ful /ˈbālfəl/ ▶ **adj.** threatening to cause harm. ■ **bale·ful·ly adv.**

balk /bôk/ ▶ **v.** **1** (**balk at**) hesitate to accept an idea. **2** prevent from getting or doing something.

Bal·kan /ˈbôlkən/ ▶ **adj.** relating to the countries on the peninsula in SE Europe surrounded by the Adriatic, Ionian, Aegean, and Black Seas.

Bal·kan·ize /ˈbôlkə,nīz/ ▶ **v.** (**Balkanizes**, **Balkanizing**, **Balkanized**) divide (a region or body) into smaller states or groups who oppose each other. ■ **Bal·kan·i·za·tion** /,bôlkənəˈzāSHən/ **n.**

ball[1] /bôl/ ▶ **n.** **1** a rounded object that is kicked, thrown, or hit in a game. **2** a game played with a ball, especially baseball. **3** a single throw or kick of the ball in a game. **4** a rounded part or thing:

the ball of the foot. ▶ **v.** squeeze or form something into a ball.

SYNONYMS ▶ **n. sphere**, globe, orb, globule, spheroid.

□ **ball bearing 1** a ring of small metal balls that separate moving parts to reduce rubbing. **2** one of these balls. **ball-and-socket joint** a joint in which a rounded end lies in a socket, allowing movement in all directions. **ball game** a game played with a ball. **the ball is in your court** it is up to you to make the next move. **keep your eye on** (or **take your eye off**) **the ball** concentrate (or fail to concentrate) on what you are doing. **on the ball** alert. **play ball** informal cooperate. **start the ball rolling** make a start.

ball² ▶ **n.** a formal gathering for dancing and meeting people. □ **have a ball** informal really enjoy yourself.

bal·lad /ˈbaləd/ ▶ **n. 1** a poem or song telling a story. **2** a slow, sentimental song.

bal·last /ˈbaləst/ ▶ **n. 1** a heavy substance carried by a ship or hot-air balloon to keep it stable. **2** stones used to form the base of a railroad track or road.

ball·boy /ˈbôlˌboi/ (or **ballgirl** /ˈbôlˌgərl/) ▶ **n.** a boy (or girl) who fetches balls that go out of play during a tennis match or baseball game.

ball·cock /ˈbôlˌkäk/ ▶ **n.** a valve that automatically fills a water tank when liquid is drawn from it.

bal·le·ri·na /ˌbaləˈrēnə/ ▶ **n.** a female ballet dancer.

bal·let /baˈlā/ ▶ **n.** an artistic form of dancing performed to music, using set steps and gestures. ■ **bal·let·ic** /baˈletik, bə-/ **adj.**

bal·lis·tic /bəˈlistik/ ▶ **adj.** having to do with the flight of missiles, bullets, or similar objects. □ **ballistic missile** a missile that is fired into the air and falls onto its target. **go ballistic** informal fly into a rage.

bal·loon /bəˈlo͞on/ ▶ **n. 1** a small rubber bag that is blown up and used as a toy or decoration. **2** (also **hot-air balloon**) a large bag filled with hot air or gas to make it rise in the air, with a basket for passengers attached to it. **3** a rounded outline in which the words of characters in a cartoon are written. ▶ **v. 1** swell outward. **2** increase quickly. **3** (**ballooning**) traveling by hot-air balloon.

bal·lot /ˈbalət/ ▶ **n. 1** a way of voting on something secretly by putting paper slips in a box. **2** (**the ballot**) the total number of votes recorded. **3** (**the ballot**) the right to vote. ▶ **v.** (**ballots, balloting, balloted**) ask people to vote by ballot.

SYNONYMS ▶ **n. vote**, poll, election, referendum, show of hands, plebiscite.

ball·park /ˈbôlˌpärk/ ▶ **n. 1** a baseball stadium or field. **2** informal a particular area or range. ▶ **adj.** informal approximate: *a ballpark figure.*

ball·point pen /ˈbôlˌpoint/ ▶ **n.** a pen with a tiny ball as its writing point.

ball·room /ˈbôlˌro͞om, -ˌro͝om/ ▶ **n.** a large room for formal dancing. □ **ballroom dancing** formal dancing for couples.

balls·y /ˈbôlzē/ ▶ **adj.** (**ballsier, ballsiest**) informal bold and confident.

bal·ly·hoo /ˈbalēˌho͞o/ ▶ **n.** informal a lot of fuss.

balm /bä(l)m/ ▶ **n. 1** a sweet-smelling ointment used to heal or soothe the skin. **2** something that soothes or heals.

balm·y /ˈbä(l)mē/ ▶ **adj.** (**balmier, balmiest**) (of the weather) pleasantly warm.

ba·lo·ney /bəˈlōnē/ ▶ **n.** informal nonsense.

bal·sa /ˈbôlsə/ ▶ **n.** very lightweight wood from a tropical American tree, used for making models.

bal·sam /ˈbôlsəm/ ▶ **n.** a scented substance obtained from some trees and shrubs, used in perfumes and medicines.

bal·sam·ic vin·e·gar /bôlˈsamik, -ˈsäm-/ ▶ **n.** dark, sweet Italian vinegar.

Bal·tic /ˈbôltik/ ▶ **adj.** relating to the Baltic Sea or the states on its eastern shores.

bal·us·ter /ˈbaləstər/ ▶ **n.** a short pillar or column forming part of a series supporting a rail.

bal·us·trade /ˈbaləˌstrād/ ▶ **n.** a railing supported by balusters.

bam·boo /ˌbamˈbo͞o/ ▶ **n.** a giant tropical grass with hollow woody stems.

bam·boo·zle /bamˈbo͞ozəl/ ▶ **v.** (**bamboozles, bamboozling, bamboozled**) informal cheat or deceive.

ban /ban/ ▶ **v.** (**bans, banning, banned**) **1** officially forbid something. **2** forbid someone to do something. ▶ **n.** an official order forbidding something.

SYNONYMS ▶ **v. prohibit**, forbid, veto, proscribe, outlaw, make illegal, bar, debar, prevent, exclude, banish. ANTONYMS permit, admit. ▶ **n. prohibition**, embargo, veto, boycott, bar, proscription, moratorium, injunction.

ba·nal /ˈbānl, bəˈnal, -ˈnäl/ ▶ **adj.** boring through being too ordinary and predictable.

SYNONYMS **unoriginal**, unimaginative, uninspired, trite, hackneyed, clichéd, platitudinous, commonplace, stereotyped, overused, stale, boring, dull, obvious, predictable, tired, pedestrian; informal corny, old hat. ANTONYMS original.

■ **ba·nal·i·ty** /bəˈnalitē/ **n.** (plural **banalities**) **ba·nal·ly adv.**

ba·nan·a /bəˈnanə/ ▶ **n.** a long curved fruit of a tropical tree, with yellow skin. □ **go bananas** informal become mad or angry.

band¹ /band/ ▶ **n. 1** a flat, thin strip or loop of material used for fastening, strengthening, or decoration. **2** a stripe or strip that is different from its surroundings: *adding a band of bright color fabric to the edge of your throw pillows.*

SYNONYMS **1 loop**, wristband, headband, ring, circlet, belt, sash, girdle, strap, strip, tape, circle. **2 stripe**, strip, line, belt, bar, streak, border, swathe.

□ **Band-Aid** trademark an adhesive bandage with a gauze pad in the center, used to cover minor wounds. **band saw** a power saw consisting of a moving steel belt with a toothed edge. ■ **band·ed adj.**

band² ▶ **n. 1** a small group of musicians and singers who play pop, jazz, or rock music. **2** a group of musicians who play brass, wind, or percussion instruments. **3** a group of people with the same aim or a shared feature. ▶ **v.** form a group with other people.

SYNONYMS ▶ **n. 1 (musical) group**, pop group, rock group, ensemble, orchestra; informal combo. **2 gang**, group, mob, pack, troop, troupe, company, set, party, crew, body, team; informal bunch.

band·age /ˈbandij/ ▶ **n.** a strip of material tied around a wound or an injury. ▶ **v.** (**bandages**, **bandaging**, **bandaged**) tie a bandage around.

SYNONYMS ▶ **n.** **dressing**, covering, plaster, compress, gauze. ▶ **v.** **bind**, dress, cover.

ban·dan·na /banˈdanə/ (also **bandana**) ▶ **n.** a square of brightly colored fabric worn on the head or around the neck.

ban·deau /banˈdō/ ▶ **n.** (plural **bandeaux**) **1** a narrow band worn around the head to hold the hair in position. **2** a woman's strapless top formed from a band of fabric.

ban·di·coot /ˈbandiˌko͞ot/ ▶ **n.** an insect-eating animal (a marsupial) found in Australia and New Guinea.

ban·dit /ˈbandit/ ▶ **n.** a member of a gang of armed robbers.

SYNONYMS **robber**, thief, raider, mugger, pirate, outlaw, hijacker, looter, marauder, gangster; literary brigand; historical rustler, highwayman, footpad.

■ **ban·dit·ry** **n.**

ban·do·lier /ˌbandəˈli(ə)r/ ▶ **n.** a belt with loops or pockets for carrying bullets, worn over the shoulder.

band·stand /ˈbandˌstand/ ▶ **n.** a covered outdoor platform for a band to play on.

band·wag·on /ˈbandˌwagən/ ▶ **n.** an activity or cause that has suddenly become fashionable or popular: *the company is jumping on the Green bandwagon.*

band·width /ˈbandˌwidᴛʜ/ ▶ **n.** **1** a range of frequencies used in telecommunications. **2** the ability of a computer network to transmit signals.

ban·dy[1] /ˈbandē/ ▶ **adj.** (**bandier**, **bandiest**) (of a person's legs) curved outward so that the knees are wide apart.

ban·dy[2] ▶ **v.** (**bandies**, **bandying**, **bandied**) use an idea or word frequently in casual talk. □ **bandy words** exchange angry remarks.

bane /bān/ ▶ **n.** a cause of great distress or annoyance.

bang /baɴɢ/ ▶ **n.** **1** a sudden loud noise. **2** a sudden painful blow. ▶ **v.** **1** hit or put down forcefully and noisily. **2** make a bang.

SYNONYMS ▶ **n.** **1** **crash**, crack, thud, thump, bump, boom, blast, clap, report, explosion. **2** **blow**, bump, knock, hit, smack, crack, thump; informal bash, whack. ▶ **v.** **1** **hit**, strike, beat, thump, hammer, knock, rap, pound, thud, punch, bump, smack, crack, slap, slam; informal bash, whack, clobber, clout, wallop. **2** **crash**, boom, pound, explode, detonate, burst, blow up.

□ **bang for your** (or **the**) **buck** informal value for money; performance for cost. **bang-up** informal excellent. **get a bang out of** informal derive excitement or pleasure from. **go off with a bang** go successfully. **with a bang** impressively or spectacularly.

Bang·la·desh·i /ˌbäɴɢgləˈdesʜē, ˌbaɴɢlə-/ ▶ **n.** (plural **Bangladeshis**) a person from Bangladesh. ▶ **adj.** relating to Bangladesh.

ban·gle /ˈbaɴɢgəl/ ▶ **n.** a bracelet of rigid material worn loosely on the wrist.

ban·ish /ˈbanisʜ/ ▶ **v.** **1** make someone leave a place as a punishment. **2** get rid of; drive away.

SYNONYMS **1** **exile**, expel, deport, eject, repatriate, transport, extradite, evict, throw out, exclude, shut out, ban. **2** **dispel**, dismiss, disperse, scatter, dissipate, drive away, chase away, shut out.

■ **ban·ish·ment** **n.**

ban·is·ter /ˈbanəstər/ (or **bannister**) ▶ **n.** **1** the upright posts and handrail at the side of a staircase. **2** a single upright post at the side of a staircase.

ban·jo /ˈbanjō/ ▶ **n.** (plural **banjos** or **banjoes**) a stringed musical instrument with a long neck and a round body.

bank[1] /baɴɢk/ ▶ **n.** **1** the land alongside a river or lake. **2** a long, high slope, mound, or mass: *mud banks.* **3** a set of similar things grouped together in rows. ▶ **v.** **1** form into a bank. **2** (of an aircraft) tilt sideways in making a turn.

SYNONYMS ▶ **n.** **1** **edge**, shore, side, embankment, levee, margin, verge, brink. **2** **slope**, rise, incline, gradient, grade, ramp, mound, pile, heap, ridge, hillock, knoll, bar, shoal, mass, drift. **3** **array**, row, line, tier, group, series. ▶ **v.** **1** **pile up**, heap up, stack up, amass. **2** **tilt**, lean, tip, slant, incline, angle, list, camber, pitch.

bank[2] ▶ **n.** **1** an organization that makes loans and keeps customers' money for them. **2** a stock or supply of something: *a blood bank.* ▶ **v.** **1** put money in a bank. **2** have an account at a bank. **3** (**bank on**) rely on.

SYNONYMS ▶ **n.** **store**, reserve, stock, stockpile, supply, pool, fund, cache, hoard, deposit. ▶ **v.** **deposit**, pay in, save.

□ **bank rate** the interest rate set by a central bank. **break the bank** informal **1** cost more than you can afford. **2** (in gambling) win more money than is held by the bank. ■ **bank·ing** **n.**

bank·a·ble /ˈbaɴɢkəbəl/ ▶ **adj.** certain to bring profit and success.

bank·er /ˈbaɴɢkər/ ▶ **n.** **1** a person who manages or owns a bank. **2** the person who keeps the bank in some gambling or board games.

bank·note /ˈbaɴɢkˌnōt/ ▶ **n.** a piece of paper money.

bank·roll /ˈbaɴɢkˌrōl/ ▶ **v.** informal give money to. ▶ **n.** a roll of banknotes.

bank·rupt /ˈbaɴɢkˌrəpt, -rəpt/ ▶ **adj.** officially declared not to have enough money to pay your debts. ▶ **n.** a bankrupt person. ▶ **v.** make someone bankrupt.

SYNONYMS ▶ **adj.** **insolvent**, ruined, in receivership; informal bust, broke, belly up, wiped out. ANTONYMS solvent.

■ **bank·rupt·cy** /ˈbaɴɢkˌrəp(t)sē, -rəp(t)sē/ **n.** (plural **bankruptcies**).

ban·ner /ˈbanər/ ▶ **n.** a long strip of cloth with a slogan or design, hung up or carried on poles.

SYNONYMS **1** **placard**, sign, poster, notice. **2** **flag**, standard, ensign, color(s), pennant, pennon, banderole.

banns /banz/ ▶ **pl.n.** an announcement of an intended marriage read out in a church.

ban·quet /ˈbaɴɢkwit/ ▶ **n.** an elaborate formal meal for many people. ▶ **v.** (**banquets**, **banqueting**, **banqueted**) attend a banquet.

SYNONYMS ▶ n. **feast**, dinner; informal spread, blowout.

ban·quette /baNG'ket/ ▶ n. a padded bench along a wall.

ban·shee /'banSHē/ ▶ n. (in Irish legend) a female spirit whose wailing warns of a death.

ban·tam /'bantəm/ ▶ n. a kind of small chicken.

ban·tam·weight /'bantəm,wāt/ ▶ n. a weight in boxing between flyweight and featherweight.

ban·ter /'bantər/ ▶ n. friendly teasing. ▶ v. (**banters**, **bantering**, **bantered**) make friendly teasing remarks.

SYNONYMS ▶ n. **repartee**, witty conversation, raillery, wordplay, badinage, persiflage. ▶ v. **joke**, jest; informal josh, wisecrack.

Ban·tu /'bantoo/ ▶ n. (plural **Bantu** or **Bantus**) **1** a member of a large group of peoples living in central and southern Africa. **2** the group of languages spoken by these peoples.

USAGE

Bantu is a very offensive word in South African English, especially when used to refer to individual people.

ban·yan /'banyən/ ▶ n. an Indian fig tree with spreading branches from which roots grow downward to the ground and form new trunks.

ban·zai /'ban'zī/ ▶ exclam. a cry used by the Japanese when going into battle or in greeting their emperor. ▶ adj. informal fierce and reckless.

ba·o·bab /'bāō,bab, 'bä-ō-/ ▶ n. a short African tree with a very thick trunk and large fruit.

bap·tism /'bap,tizəm/ ▶ n. the Christian ceremony of sprinkling a person with water or dipping them in it to show that they have entered the church. □ **baptism of fire** a difficult new experience. ■ **bap·tis·mal** /bap'tizməl/ adj.

Bap·tist /'baptist/ ▶ n. a member of a Christian group believing that only adults, not babies, should be baptized.

bap·tis·tery /'baptəstrē/ (also **baptistry**) ▶ n. (plural **baptisteries**) a building or part of a church used for baptism.

bap·tize /'bap,tīz, bap'tīz/ ▶ v. (**baptizes**, **baptizing**, **baptized**) **1** perform the baptism ceremony on someone. **2** give someone a name or nickname.

SYNONYMS **1 christen**. **2** *they were baptized into the church* **admit**, initiate, enroll, recruit. **3 name**, call, dub.

bar /bär/ ▶ n. **1** a long rigid piece of wood, metal, etc. **2** food or another substance formed into a regular narrow block. **3** a counter, room, or place where alcohol is served. **4** something that stops or delays progress. **5** any of the short units into which a piece of music is divided. **6** (**the bar**) the place in a courtroom where an accused person stands during a trial. **7** (**the Bar**) the legal profession. ▶ v. (**bars**, **barring**, **barred**) **1** fasten with a bar or bars. **2** forbid or prevent. ▶ prep. except for.

SYNONYMS ▶ n. **1 rod**, stick, pole, batten, shaft, rail, spar, strut, crosspiece, beam. **2 block**, slab, cake, tablet, wedge, ingot. **3 counter**, table, buffet. **4 tavern**, barroom, taproom, pub, club, sports bar, cocktail lounge, lounge, roadhouse, saloon; informal watering hole, nineteenth hole. **5 obstacle**, impediment, hindrance, obstruction, block, hurdle, barrier. ANTONYMS aid. ▶ v. **1 bolt**, lock, fasten, secure, block, barricade, obstruct. **2 prohibit**, debar, preclude, forbid, ban, exclude, obstruct, prevent, hinder, block, stop.

□ **bar code** a row of printed stripes identifying a product and its price, able to be read by a computer. **bar chart** (or **bar graph**) a diagram in which different quantities are shown by rectangles of varying height. **behind bars** in prison.

barb /bärb/ ▶ n. **1** the backward-pointing part of a fish hook, the tip of an arrow, etc. **2** a spiteful remark.

bar·bar·i·an /bär'be(ə)rēən/ ▶ n. **1** (in ancient times) a person who did not belong to the Greek, Roman, or Christian civilizations. **2** a very uncivilized or cruel person.

SYNONYMS **savage**, heathen, brute, beast, philistine, boor, yahoo, oaf, lout, vandal.

bar·bar·ic /bär'barik/ ▶ adj. **1** savagely cruel. **2** not cultured or civilized.

SYNONYMS **1 cruel**, brutal, barbarous, brutish, savage, vicious, wicked, ruthless, vile, inhuman. **2 uncultured**, uncivilized, barbarian, philistine, boorish, loutish. ANTONYMS civilized.

bar·ba·rism /'bärbə,rizəm/ ▶ n. **1** great cruelty. **2** an uncivilized or primitive state. ■ **bar·bar·i·ty** /bär'baritē/ n. (plural **barbarities**).

bar·ba·rous /'bärbərəs/ ▶ adj. **1** very cruel. **2** uncivilized or uncultured.

bar·be·cue /'bärbi,kyoo/ ▶ n. **1** an outdoor meal at which food is grilled over an open fire or on a portable grill. **2** a grill used at a barbecue. ▶ v. (**barbecues**, **barbecuing**, **barbecued**) cook food on a barbecue.

barbed /bärbd/ ▶ adj. **1** having a barb or barbs. **2** (of a remark) spiteful. □ **barbed wire** (or **barbwire**) wire with clusters of short, sharp spikes along it.

bar·bel /'bärbəl/ ▶ n. **1** a long, thin growth hanging from the mouth or snout of some fish. **2** a freshwater fish with barbels.

bar·bell /'bär,bel/ ▶ n. a long metal bar with disks of different weights attached at each end, used for weightlifting.

bar·ber /'bärbər/ ▶ n. a person whose job is cutting men's hair and shaving or trimming their beards.

bar·bi·can /'bärbikən/ ▶ n. a double tower above a gate or drawbridge of a castle or fortified city.

bar·bi·tu·rate /bär'biCHərit, -ə,rāt/ ▶ n. a kind of drug used as a sedative.

bard /bärd/ ▶ n. **1** old use a poet. **2** (**the Bard**) Shakespeare.

bare /be(ə)r/ ▶ adj. **1** not wearing clothes. **2** without the usual covering or contents: *a big, bare room*. **3** without detail; basic. **4** only just enough: *a bare majority*. ▶ v. (**bares**, **baring**, **bared**) uncover or reveal.

SYNONYMS ▶ adj. **1 naked**, unclothed, undressed, uncovered, stripped, with nothing on, nude; informal without a stitch on, in the altogether, buck naked, in your birthday suit. **2 empty**, unfurnished, clear, undecorated, unadorned, bleak, austere. **3 basic**, essential, fundamental, plain, straightforward, simple, unembellished, pure, stark, bald, cold, hard. ANTONYMS dressed.

□ **with your bare hands** without using tools or weapons. ■ **bare·ness** n.

bare·back /ˈbe(ə)rˌbak/ ▶ **adv. & adj.** on a horse without a saddle.

bare·faced /ˈbe(ə)rˌfāst/ ▶ **adj.** done openly and without shame: *a barefaced lie.*

bare·foot /ˈbe(ə)rˌfo͝ot/ (or **barefooted** /-ˌfo͝otid/) ▶ **adj. & adv.** wearing nothing on your feet.

bare·ly /ˈbe(ə)rlē/ ▶ **adv. 1** only just; almost not: *she nodded, barely able to speak.* **2** only a short time before: *they had barely sat down when forty policemen swarmed in.* **3** in a simple and sparse way: *their barely furnished house.*

> SYNONYMS **hardly**, scarcely, only just, narrowly, by the skin of your teeth, by a hair's breadth; informal by a whisker.

barf /bärf/ ▶ **v.** informal vomit.

bar·gain /ˈbärgən/ ▶ **n. 1** an agreement made between people to do something for each other. **2** a thing sold at a low price. ▶ **v. 1** discuss the terms of an agreement. **2** (**bargain for** or **on**) expect.

> SYNONYMS ▶ **n. 1 agreement**, arrangement, understanding, deal, contract, pact. **2 good value**; informal good buy, steal, giveaway. ▶ **v. haggle**, negotiate, discuss terms, deal, barter.

□ **drive a hard bargain** press hard for a deal in your favor. **into the bargain** as well.

> SPELLING
> Remember the second a: barg**a**in.

barge /bärj/ ▶ **n.** a long flat-bottomed boat for carrying goods on canals and rivers. ▶ **v.** (**barges**, **barging**, **barged**) **1** move forcefully or roughly. **2** (**barge in**) burst in on someone rudely.

ba·ri·sta /bəˈrēstə/ ▶ **n.** a person whose job is to make and serve coffee drinks.

bar·i·tone /ˈbariˌtōn/ ▶ **n.** a man's singing voice between tenor and bass.

bar·i·um /ˈbe(ə)rēəm, ˈbar-/ ▶ **n.** a chemical element that is a soft white metal.

bark[1] /bärk/ ▶ **n.** the sharp sudden cry of a dog, fox, or seal. ▶ **v. 1** give a bark. **2** say a command or question suddenly or fiercely.

> SYNONYMS ▶ **v. 1 woof**, yap. **2 shout**, snap, bawl, yell, roar, bellow, thunder; informal holler.
> ANTONYMS whisper.

□ **your bark is worse than your bite** you are not as fierce as you seem. **be barking up the wrong tree** informal be doing or thinking something that is incorrect.

bark[2] ▶ **n.** the tough outer covering of the trunk and branches of a tree. ▶ **v.** scrape the skin off your shin by accidentally hitting it.

> SYNONYMS ▶ **n. rind**, skin, peel, covering.

bark[3] /bärk/ (or **barque**) ▶ **n. 1** a sailing ship with three masts. **2** literary a boat.

bark·er /ˈbärkər/ ▶ **n.** informal a person at a fair who calls out to passersby to persuade them to visit a sideshow.

bar·ley /ˈbärlē/ ▶ **n.** a type of cereal plant with a bristly head.

bar mitz·vah /ˌbär ˈmitsvə/ ▶ **n.** a religious ceremony in which a Jewish boy aged 13 takes on the responsibilities of an adult.

barn /bärn/ ▶ **n.** a large farm building used for storing hay or grain or keeping livestock. □ **barn dance** a party with square dancing, originally held in a barn. **barn owl** a pale-colored owl with a heart-shaped face.

bar·na·cle /ˈbärnəkəl/ ▶ **n.** a small shellfish that fixes itself to things.

barn·storm /ˈbärnˌstôrm/ ▶ **v. 1** tour country districts putting on shows or giving displays of flying. **2** make a rapid tour as part of a political campaign. **3** tour rural districts giving theatrical performances.

barn·yard /ˈbärnˌyärd/ ▶ **n.** the area of open ground around a barn.

ba·rom·e·ter /bəˈrämitər/ ▶ **n.** an instrument that measures the pressure of the atmosphere, used to forecast the weather.

bar·on /ˈbarən/ ▶ **n. 1** a man belonging to the lowest rank of the British nobility. **2** (in the Middle Ages) a man who held lands or property granted to him by the king or queen or a lord. **3** a powerful person in business or industry. ■ **ba·ro·ni·al** /bəˈrōnēəl/ **adj.**

bar·on·ess /ˈbarənis/ ▶ **n. 1** the wife or widow of a baron. **2** a woman holding the rank of baron.

bar·on·et /ˈbarənit, ˌbarəˈnet/ ▶ **n.** a man who holds a title below that of baron.

bar·on·et·cy /ˈbarənitsē/ ▶ **n.** (plural **baronetcies**) the rank of a baronet.

bar·o·ny /ˈbarənē/ ▶ **n.** (plural **baronies**) the rank and lands of a baron.

ba·roque /bəˈrōk/ ▶ **adj.** in a highly decorated style of European architecture, art, and music popular during the 17th and 18th centuries.

bar·racks /ˈbarəks/ ▶ **n.** a building or set of buildings for soldiers to live in.

> SYNONYMS **garrison**, camp, encampment, depot, billet, quarters, fort, cantonment.

bar·ra·cu·da /ˌbarəˈko͞odə/ ▶ **n.** (plural **barracuda** or **barracudas**) a large predatory fish found in tropical seas.

bar·rage /bəˈräzн/ ▶ **n. 1** a continuous attack by heavy guns. **2** an overwhelming number of questions or complaints. **3** a barrier used to hold back river water.

> SYNONYMS **1 bombardment**, gunfire, shelling, salvo, volley, fusillade; historical broadside. **2 deluge**, stream, storm, torrent, onslaught, flood, spate, tide, avalanche, hail, blaze. **3 dam**, barrier, weir, dike, embankment, wall.

barre /bär/ ▶ **n.** a horizontal bar at waist level used by ballet dancers during exercises.

bar·rel /ˈbarəl/ ▶ **n. 1** a large cylindrical container bulging out in the middle and with flat ends. **2** a tube forming part of a gun, pen, etc.

> SYNONYMS **cask**, keg, butt, vat, tun, drum, hogshead, firkin.

□ **barrel organ** a small organ that plays a tune when you turn a handle. **over a barrel** informal at a great disadvantage.

bar·ren /ˈbarən/ ▶ **adj. 1** (of land) not good enough to produce plants or crops. **2** unable to produce children or young animals. **3** bleak.

> SYNONYMS **unproductive**, infertile, unfruitful, sterile, arid, desert, waste, lifeless, empty.
> ANTONYMS fertile.

bar·rette /bəˈret/ ▶ **n.** a typically bar-shaped clip or ornament for the hair.

bar·ri·cade /ˈbariˌkād/ ▶ **n.** a makeshift barrier used to block a road or entrance. ▶ **v.** (**barricades**,

barricading, **barricaded**) block or defend with a barricade.

SYNONYMS ▶ n. **barrier**, roadblock, blockade, obstacle, obstruction. ▶ v. **seal up**, close up, block off, shut off/up, defend, protect, fortify, occupy.

bar·ri·er /ˈbarēər/ ▶ n. something that stops people entering a place or making progress.

SYNONYMS **1 fence**, railing, barricade, hurdle, bar, blockade, roadblock. **2** *a barrier to international trade* **obstacle**, obstruction, hurdle, stumbling block, bar, impediment, hindrance, curb.

□ **barrier reef** a coral reef close to the shore but separated from it by a channel of deep water.

bar·ring /ˈbäriNG/ ▶ prep. except for; if not for.

bar·ri·o /ˈbärēˌō/ ▶ n. (plural **barrios**) **1** (in a Spanish-speaking country) a district of a town. **2** (in the US) the Spanish-speaking quarter of a town or city.

bar·room /ˈbärˌro͞om, -ˌro͝om/ ▶ n. a room where alcoholic drinks are served over a counter.

bar·row[1] /ˈbarō/ ▶ n. **1** a metal frame with two wheels used for transporting luggage, etc. **2** = **WHEELBARROW**.

bar·row[2] ▶ n. a mound of earth built over a grave in ancient times.

bar·tend·er /ˈbärˌtendər/ ▶ n. a person mixing and serving drinks at a bar.

bar·ter /ˈbärtər/ ▶ v. (**barters**, **bartering**, **bartered**) exchange goods or services for other goods or services. ▶ n. trade by bartering.

SYNONYMS ▶ v. **1 swap**, trade, exchange, sell. **2 haggle**, bargain, negotiate, deal.

ba·sal /ˈbāsəl, -zəl/ ▶ adj. forming or belonging to a base.

ba·salt /bəˈsôlt/ ▶ n. a dark volcanic rock.

base[1] /bās/ ▶ n. **1** the lowest or supporting part of something. **2** the main place where a person works or stays. **3** a center of operations: *a military base*. **4** a main element to which others are added. **5** Chemistry a substance able to react with an acid to form a salt and water. **6** Baseball each of the four points that you must reach in turn to score a run. ▶ v. (**bases**, **basing**, **based**) **1** (**base something on**) use something as the foundation for something else. **2** station someone or something at a particular base.

SYNONYMS ▶ n. **1 foundation**, bottom, foot, support, stand, pedestal, plinth, rest. **2 basis**, foundation, bedrock, starting point, source, origin, root(s), core, key component. **3 headquarters**, camp, site, station, settlement, post, center. ANTONYMS top. ▶ v. **1 found**, build, construct, form, ground; (**be based on**) derive from, spring from, stem from, depend on. **2 locate**, situate, position, install, station, site.

□ **base hit** Baseball a fair ball hit such that a batter can advance safely to first base.

base[2] ▶ adj. **1** bad or immoral. **2** old use of low social class.

SYNONYMS **sordid**, ignoble, low, mean, immoral, unscrupulous, unprincipled, dishonest, dishonorable, shameful, shabby, contemptible, despicable. ANTONYMS noble.

□ **base metal** a common non-precious metal.

base·ball /ˈbāsˌbôl/ ▶ n. a game played with a bat and ball on a diamond-shaped circuit of four bases, which a batter must run around to score. □ **baseball cap** a cotton cap with a large peak.

base·less /ˈbāslis/ ▶ adj. not based on fact; untrue.

base·line /ˈbāsˌlīn/ ▶ n. **1** a starting point for comparisons. **2** (in tennis, volleyball, etc.) the line marking each end of a court. **3** Baseball the line between bases, which a runner must stay close to.

base·man /ˈbāsmən/ ▶ n. (plural **basemen**) Baseball a fielder designated to cover first, second, or third base.

base·ment /ˈbāsmənt/ ▶ n. a room or floor below ground level.

ba·ses plural of **BASE[1]** and **BASIS**.

bash /basH/ informal ▶ v. hit hard and violently. ▶ n. **1** a heavy blow. **2** a party.

bash·ful /ˈbasHfəl/ ▶ adj. shy and easily embarrassed.

SYNONYMS **shy**, reserved, diffident, inhibited, retiring, reticent, reluctant, shrinking, self-effacing, unassertive, timid, nervous, self-conscious. ANTONYMS bold, confident.

■ **bash·ful·ly** adv.

ba·sic /ˈbāsik/ ▶ adj. **1** forming an essential foundation; fundamental. **2** of the simplest or lowest kind or standard: *a basic wage*. ▶ n. (**basics**) essential facts or principles.

SYNONYMS ▶ adj. **1 fundamental**, essential, vital, primary, principal, cardinal, elementary, intrinsic, central, pivotal, critical, key, focal. **2 plain**, simple, unsophisticated, straightforward, adequate, spartan, stark, severe, austere, limited, meager, rudimentary, patchy, sketchy, minimal, crude, makeshift. ANTONYMS unimportant, luxurious. ▶ n. (**basics**) **fundamentals**, essentials, first principles, foundations, preliminaries, groundwork, essence, basis, core; informal nitty-gritty, brass tacks, nuts and bolts, ABCs.

ba·si·cal·ly /ˈbāsik(ə)lē/ ▶ adv. **1** in the most fundamental respects. **2** used to sum up a more complex situation: *I basically did the same thing*.

SYNONYMS **fundamentally**, essentially, first and foremost, primarily, at heart, intrinsically, inherently, principally, chiefly, above all, mostly, mainly, on the whole, by and large; informal at the end of the day.

bas·il /ˈbāzəl, ˈbazəl/ ▶ n. an herb used in cooking.

ba·sil·i·ca /bəˈsilikə/ ▶ n. a large church or hall with two rows of columns inside and a curved end with a dome.

bas·i·lisk /ˈbasəˌlisk, ˈbaz-/ ▶ n. a mythical reptile that could kill people by looking at or breathing on them.

ba·sin /ˈbāsən/ ▶ n. **1** a large bowl or open container for holding liquid. **2** a circular valley. **3** an area drained by a river. **4** an enclosed area of water for mooring boats.

SYNONYMS **bowl**, dish, pan, container, receptacle, vessel.

ba·sis /ˈbāsis/ ▶ n. (plural **bases** /ˈbāsēz/) **1** the foundation of a theory or process. **2** the reasons why something is done.

SYNONYMS **1** *the basis of his method* **foundation**, support, base, reasoning, rationale, defense, reason, grounds, justification. **2** *the basis of discussion* **starting**

point, base, point of departure, beginning, premise, fundamental point/principle, cornerstone, core, heart. **3** *on a part-time basis* **footing**, condition, status, position, arrangement.

bask /bask/ ▶ v. **1** lie in the sun for pleasure. **2** (**bask in**) take great pleasure in.

SYNONYMS **1 laze**, lie, lounge, relax, sprawl, loll, luxuriate. **2 revel**, wallow, delight, take pleasure, enjoy, relish, savor.

□ **basking shark** a large shark that feeds on plankton and swims slowly close to the surface.

bas·ket /'baskit/ ▶ n. **1** a container for carrying things, made from strips of cane or wire. **2** a net fixed on a hoop, used as the goal in basketball. □ **basket case** informal a person or thing regarded as useless or unable to cope.

bas·ket·ball /'baskit,bôl/ ▶ n. a team game in which goals are scored by throwing a ball through a hoop.

bas·ma·ti rice /bäs'mätē/ ▶ n. a kind of long-grain Indian rice with a delicate aroma.

Basque /bask/ ▶ n. **1** a member of a people living in the western Pyrenees in France and Spain. **2** the language of this people.

bas-re·lief /,bä rə'lēf/ ▶ n. Art low relief.

bass¹ /bās/ ▶ n. **1** the lowest adult male singing voice. **2** a bass guitar or double bass. **3** the deep, low-frequency part of sound. ▶ adj. making a deep sound.

SYNONYMS ▶ adj. **low**, deep, resonant, sonorous, rumbling, booming, resounding. ANTONYMS high.

■ **bass·ist** n.

bass² /bas/ ▶ n. (plural **bass** or **basses**) a fish related to the perch, used for food.

bass clef /bās klef/ ▶ n. Music a clef placing F below middle C on the second-highest line of the stave.

bas·set hound /'basit/ ▶ n. a breed of hunting dog with a long body, short legs, and long, drooping ears.

bas·soon /bə'sōōn, ba-/ ▶ n. a large low-pitched woodwind instrument. ■ **bas·soon·ist** n.

bas·tard /'bastərd/ ▶ n. **1** old use a person who was born when their parents were not married. **2** informal a nasty person. ▶ adj. no longer in its pure or original form.

bas·tard·ize /'bastər,dīz/ ▶ v. (**bastardizes**, **bastardizing**, **bastardized**) make something less good by adding new elements.

baste /bāst/ ▶ v. (**bastes**, **basting**, **basted**) pour fat or juices over meat while it cooks.

bas·tion /'basCHən/ ▶ n. **1** a part of a fortified building that sticks out. **2** something that protects or preserves particular principles or activities: *the town was a bastion of conservative politics*.

bat¹ /bat/ ▶ n. an implement with a handle and a solid surface, usually made of wood but sometimes of aluminum or another material, used in sports for hitting the ball. ▶ v. (**bats**, **batting**, **batted**) **1** (in sports) take the role of hitting rather than throwing the ball. **2** hit with the flat of your hand. □ **bat a thousand** informal produce consistently favorable outcomes; be consistently correct.

bat² ▶ n. **1** a flying animal that is active at night. **2** (**old bat**) informal an unpleasant woman. □ **have bats in the belfry** informal be eccentric or crazy.

bat³ ▶ v. (**bats**, **batting**, **batted**) flutter your eyelashes. □ **not bat an eyelid** informal show no surprise or concern.

batch /baCH/ ▶ n. a quantity of goods produced or dispatched at one time.

SYNONYMS **group**, quantity, lot, bunch, cluster, raft, set, collection, bundle, pack, consignment, shipment.

bat·ed /'bātid/ ▶ adj. (**with bated breath**) in great suspense.

SPELLING

Bated, not baited.

bath /baTH, bäTH/ ▶ n. **1** an act or process of immersing and washing your body in a large container of water. **2** such a container and its contents; a bathtub. **3** (also **baths**) a building containing a swimming pool or washing facilities. ▶ v. wash someone in a bath. □ **bath salts** crystals that are dissolved in bathwater to soften or perfume it.

bathe /bā<u>TH</u>/ ▶ v. (**bathes**, **bathing**, **bathed**) **1** wash by putting your body in water. **2** soak or wipe gently with liquid.

SYNONYMS **1 swim**, take a dip. **2 clean**, wash, rinse, wet, soak, steep. **3 envelop**, cover, flood, fill, wash, pervade, suffuse.

□ **bathing suit** a swimsuit. ■ **bath·er** n.

ba·thos /'bāTHäs/ ▶ n. (in literature) an unintentional change from a serious mood to something trivial.

bath·robe /'baTH,rōb/ ▶ n. a robe, usually made of terrycloth, worn before or after bathing.

bath·room /'baTH,rōōm, -,rŏŏm/ ▶ n. **1** a room containing a bathtub or shower and usually also a sink and toilet. **2** a room containing a toilet and usually a sink.

SYNONYMS **restroom**, washroom, toilet, men's/ladies' room, powder room, lavatory, comfort station, urinal; Military latrine, head; informal facilities, little boys'/girls' room, can, john; old use commode, privy, outhouse.

bath·tub /'baTH,təb/ ▶ n. a tub in which to bathe.

ba·tik /bə'tēk/ ▶ n. a method of producing colored designs on cloth using wax to cover the areas not to be dyed.

bat mitz·vah /bät 'mitsvə/ ▶ n. a religious ceremony in which a Jewish girl aged 12 takes on the responsibilities of an adult.

ba·ton /bə'tän/ ▶ n. **1** a thin stick used to conduct an orchestra or choir. **2** a short stick passed from runner to runner in a relay race. **3** a police officer's club.

SYNONYMS **stick**, rod, staff, wand, truncheon, club, mace.

□ **pass** (or **take up**) **the baton** hand over (or take up) a duty or responsibility.

bat·tal·ion /bə'talyən/ ▶ n. an army unit forming part of a brigade.

SPELLING

Two t's, one l: battalion.

bat·ten /'batn/ ▶ n. a long wooden or metal strip used for strengthening or securing something. □ **batten down the hatches** prepare for a crisis.

bat·ter¹ /'batər/ ▶ v. (**batters**, **battering**, **battered**) hit repeatedly with hard blows.

SYNONYMS **beat up**, hit repeatedly, pummel, pound, rain blows on, buffet, belabor, thrash; informal knock about/around, lay into.

bat·ter² ▶ n. a mixture of flour, egg, and milk or water, used for making cakes or coating food before frying.

bat·ter³ ▶ n. a player who bats in baseball.

bat·tered /ˈbatərd/ ▶ adj. (of food) coated in batter and fried.

bat·ter·y /ˈbatərē/ ▶ n. (plural **batteries**) **1** a device containing one or more electrical cells, used as a source of power. **2** an extensive series: *a battery of tests.* **3** Law an unlawful physical attack on another person.

bat·tle /ˈbatl/ ▶ n. **1** a prolonged fight between organized armed forces. **2** a long and difficult struggle or conflict: *a battle of wits.* ▶ v. (**battles**, **battling**, **battled**) fight or struggle with determination.

SYNONYMS ▶ n. **1** *he was killed in the battle* **fight**, engagement, armed conflict, clash, struggle, skirmish, fray, war, campaign, crusade, warfare, combat, action, hostilities; informal scrap, dogfight, shoot-out. **2** *a legal battle* **conflict**, clash, struggle, disagreement, argument, dispute, tussle. ▶ v. **fight**, combat, contend with, resist, withstand, stand up to, confront, war, feud, struggle, strive, work.

bat·tle·ax /ˈbatl,aks/ (or **battleaxe**) ▶ n. **1** a large ax used in ancient warfare. **2** informal an aggressive older woman.

bat·tle·dress /ˈbatl,dres/ ▶ n. clothing worn by soldiers for fighting.

bat·tle·field /ˈbatl,fēld/ ▶ n. the piece of ground where a battle is fought.

SYNONYMS **battleground**, field of battle, field of operations, combat zone, lines, front, theater of war.

bat·tle·ment /ˈbatlmənt/ ▶ n. a wall at the top of a castle with gaps for firing through.

bat·tle·ship /ˈbatl,sHip/ ▶ n. a heavily armored warship with large guns.

bat·ty /ˈbatē/ ▶ adj. (**battier**, **battiest**) informal crazy; insane.

bau·ble /ˈbôbəl/ ▶ n. a small, showy trinket or decoration.

baux·ite /ˈbôksīt/ ▶ n. a claylike rock from which aluminum is obtained.

bawd·y /ˈbôdē/ ▶ adj. (**bawdier**, **bawdiest**) humorously indecent.

SYNONYMS **ribald**, indecent, risqué, racy, earthy, rude, suggestive, titillating, naughty, improper, indelicate, vulgar, crude, smutty; informal raunchy.

bawl /bôl/ ▶ v. **1** shout out noisily. **2** cry noisily. **3** (**bawl someone out**) informal criticize someone angrily. ▶ n. a loud shout.

SYNONYMS ▶ v. **1 shout**, yell, roar, bellow, screech, scream, shriek, bark, thunder; informal yammer, holler. **2 cry**, sob, weep, wail, whine, howl. ANTONYMS whisper.

bay¹ /bā/ ▶ n. an area of sea and coast forming a broad curve.

SYNONYMS **cove**, inlet, gulf, sound, bight, basin, fjord.

bay² ▶ n. a Mediterranean shrub whose leaves are used in cooking.

bay³ ▶ n. **1** a window area that sticks out from a wall. **2** an area for a particular purpose: *a loading bay.*

SYNONYMS **alcove**, recess, niche, nook, opening, inglenook.

□ **bay window** a window sticking out from a wall.

bay⁴ ▶ adj. (of a horse) mainly reddish-brown in color.

bay⁵ ▶ v. (of a dog) bark or howl loudly. □ **at bay** trapped or cornered. **hold** (or **keep**) **someone/something at bay** prevent someone or something from approaching or having an effect.

bay·ber·ry /ˈbā,berē/ ▶ n. (plural **bayberries**) a shrub with aromatic leathery leaves and waxy berries.

bay·o·net /ˈbāənit, ˌbāəˈnet/ ▶ n. a long blade fixed to a rifle for hand-to-hand fighting. ▶ v. (**bayonets**, **bayoneting**, **bayoneted**) stab someone with a bayonet.

bay·ou /ˈbīo͞o, ˈbīō/ ▶ n. (plural **bayous**) (in the southern US) a marshy outlet of a lake or river.

ba·zaar /bəˈzär/ ▶ n. **1** a market in a Middle Eastern country. **2** a sale of goods to raise funds.

SYNONYMS **1 market**, marketplace, mart. **2 fete**, fair, fund-raiser, rummage sale, tag sale, flea market.

ba·zoo·ka /bəˈzo͞okə/ ▶ n. a short-range rocket launcher used against tanks.

b-ball /ˈbē,bôl/ ▶ n. informal basketball.

BBQ ▶ abbr. barbecue.

BC ▶ abbr. before Christ (used to show that a date is before the traditional date of Jesus's birth).

USAGE

Write BC *after* the numerals, as in *72* BC.

BCE ▶ abbr. before the Common Era (used instead of BC, especially by non-Christians).

BE ▶ abbr. **1** Bachelor of Education. **2** Bachelor of Engineering.

be /bē/ ▶ v. (singular present **am** /am/; **are** /är/; **is** /iz/; plural present **are**; 1st and 3rd singular past **was** /wəz/; 2nd singular past and plural past **were** /wər/; present participle **being** /ˈbēiNG/; past participle **been** /bin/) **1** exist; be present. **2** happen. **3** have the specified state, nature, or role: *I want to be a teacher.* **4** come or go: *have you been to Chicago?* ▶ auxiliary v. **1** used with a present participle to form continuous tenses: *they are coming.* **2** used with a past participle to form the passive voice: *it is said.* **3** used to show something that is due to, may, or should happen.

SYNONYMS ▶ v. **1 exist**, live, be alive, breathe, be extant. **2 occur**, happen, take place, come about, arise, fall; literary come to pass, befall, betide. **3 be situated**, be located, be found, be present, be set, be positioned, be placed, be installed, sit, lie.

□ **the be-all and end-all** informal the most important aspect of something.

beach /bēCH/ ▶ n. a shore of sand or pebbles at the edge of the sea. ▶ v. bring something on to a beach from the water.

SYNONYMS ▶ n. **sands**, seaside, seashore, coast; literary strand, littoral. ▶ v. **1 land**, ground, strand, run ashore. **2** (**beached**) **stranded**, run aground, ashore, marooned, high and dry, stuck.

beach·comb·er /ˈbēcʜˌkōmər/ ▶ **n.** a person who searches beaches for valuable things.

bea·con /ˈbēkən/ ▶ **n. 1** a fire lit on the top of a hill as a signal. **2** a light acting as a signal for ships or aircraft.

SYNONYMS **signal**, light, fire, danger signal, bonfire, lighthouse.

bead /bēd/ ▶ **n. 1** a small piece of glass, stone, etc., threaded with others to make a necklace. **2** a drop of a liquid on a surface.

SYNONYMS **1 ball**, pellet, pill, globule, sphere, spheroid, orb, round; (**beads**) necklace, rosary, chaplet. **2** *beads of sweat* **droplet**, drop, drip, blob, pearl, dot.

■ **bead·ed** **adj.**

bead·y /ˈbēdē/ ▶ **adj.** (of a person's eyes) small, round, and observant.

bea·gle /ˈbēgəl/ ▶ **n.** a small short-legged breed of hound.

beak /bēk/ ▶ **n.** a bird's hard projecting jaws.

SYNONYMS **bill**, nib, mandible.

beak·er /ˈbēkər/ ▶ **n. 1** a cylindrical glass container used in laboratories. **2** old use a large drinking container with a wide mouth.

SYNONYMS **cup**, tumbler, glass, mug, drinking vessel.

beam /bēm/ ▶ **n. 1** a long piece of wood or metal used as a support in building. **2** a narrow length of wood for balancing on in gymnastics. **3** a ray of light or particles. **4** a wide, happy smile. **5** the width of a ship. ▶ **v. 1** transmit a radio signal. **2** shine brightly. **3** smile broadly.

SYNONYMS ▶ **n. 1 plank**, timber, joist, rafter, lintel, spar, girder, support. **2 ray**, shaft, stream, streak, pencil, flash, gleam, glint. **3 grin**, smile. ANTONYMS frown. ▶ **v. 1 broadcast**, transmit, relay, disseminate, direct, send, aim. **2 shine**, radiate, glare, gleam. **3 grin**, smile. ANTONYMS frown.

bean /bēn/ ▶ **n. 1** an edible seed growing in long pods on certain plants. **2** the hard seed of a coffee or cocoa plant. **3** informal a very small amount: *there is not a bean of truth in the report.* □ **bean sprouts** the edible sprouting seeds of certain beans. **full of beans** informal in high spirits.

bean·bag /ˈbēnˌbag/ ▶ **n. 1** a small bag filled with dried beans and used in children's games. **2** a large cushion filled with polystyrene beads, used as a seat.

bear¹ /be(ə)r/ ▶ **v.** (**bears**, **bearing**, **bore** /bôr/; past participle **borne** /bôrn/) **1** carry. **2** have a particular quality or visible mark. **3** support a weight. **4** (**bear yourself**) behave in a particular way. **5** tolerate. **6** give birth to a child. **7** (of a tree or plant) produce fruit or flowers. **8** turn and go in a particular direction: *bear left.*

SYNONYMS **1 carry**, bring, transport, move, convey, take, fetch; informal tote. **2 display**, be marked with, show, carry, exhibit. **3 withstand**, support, sustain, stand, take, carry, hold up, cope with, handle. **4 harbor**, foster, entertain, cherish, nurse. **5** *I can't bear his arrogance* **endure**, tolerate, put up with, stand, abide, countenance, stomach; informal hack, swallow; formal brook. **6 give birth to**, bring forth, deliver, have, produce, spawn. **7 produce**, yield, give, provide, supply.

□ **bear down on** approach someone in a determined or threatening way. **bear on** be evidence of. **bear something out** support or confirm something. **bear up** remain cheerful in difficult circumstances. **bear with** be patient with. **bear witness** (or **testimony**) **to** testify to. **bring to bear** prepare and use effectively.

bear² ▶ **n.** a large, heavy animal with thick fur. □ **bear hug** a rough, tight embrace. **bear market** Stock Exchange a market in which share prices are falling.

bear·a·ble /ˈbe(ə)rəbəl/ ▶ **adj.** able to be endured.

SYNONYMS **tolerable**, endurable, supportable, sustainable.

■ **bear·a·bly** **adv.**

beard /bi(ə)rd/ ▶ **n.** a growth of hair on a man's chin and lower cheeks. ▶ **v.** boldly confront or challenge an important or powerful person. ■ **beard·ed** **adj.**

bear·er /ˈbe(ə)rər/ ▶ **n. 1** a person or thing that carries something. **2** a person who presents a check or other order to pay money.

SYNONYMS **carrier**, porter; **bringer**, messenger, agent, conveyor, emissary.

bear·ing /ˈbe(ə)rɪɴɢ/ ▶ **n. 1** a person's way of standing, moving, or behaving. **2** relevance: *the case has no bearing on the issues.* **3** a part of a machine that allows one part to rotate or move in contact with another. **4** direction or position in relation to a fixed point. **5** (**your bearings**) awareness of where you are.

SYNONYMS **1 posture**, stance, carriage, gait, demeanor, deportment, manner, mien, air, aspect, attitude, style. **2** *this has no bearing on the matter* **relevance**, pertinence, connection, relation, relationship, import, significance, application. **3 direction**, orientation, course, trajectory, heading, tack, path. **4** *I lost my bearings* **orientation**, sense of direction, whereabouts, location, position. ANTONYMS irrelevance.

beast /bēst/ ▶ **n. 1** an animal, especially a large or dangerous mammal. **2** a very cruel or wicked person.

SYNONYMS **1 creature**, animal; informal critter. **2 monster**, brute, savage, barbarian, animal, swine, ogre, fiend, sadist, demon, devil.

□ **beast of burden** an animal used for carrying loads.

beast·ly /ˈbēstlē/ ▶ **adj.** informal very unpleasant. ■ **beast·li·ness** **n.**

beat /bēt/ ▶ **v.** (**beats**, **beating**, **beat**; past participle **beaten**) **1** hit someone repeatedly and violently. **2** hit something repeatedly to flatten it or make a noise. **3** defeat or be better than. **4** informal baffle someone. **5** (of the heart) throb. **6** (of a bird) move its wings up and down. **7** stir cooking or baking ingredients vigorously. ▶ **n. 1** an act of beating. **2** the main rhythm, or a unit of rhythm, in music or poetry. **3** a brief pause. **4** an area patrolled by a police officer. ▶ **adj.** informal completely exhausted.

SYNONYMS ▶ **v. 1 hit**, strike, batter, thump, bang, hammer, punch, knock, thrash, pound, pummel, slap, rain blows on, assault; informal wallop, belt, bash, whack, clout, clobber. **2 throb**, pulse, pulsate, pump, palpitate, pound, thump, thud, hammer, drum. **3 flap**, flutter, thrash, wave, vibrate. **4 whisk**, mix, blend, whip. **5 defeat**, conquer, vanquish, trounce, rout, overpower, overcome; informal lick, thrash, whip. **6 exceed**, surpass, better, improve on, eclipse, transcend, top, trump, cap. ▶ **n. 1 rhythm**, pulse, meter, time, measure, cadence, stress, accent. **2 pounding**, banging, thumping, thudding, hammering, crashing. **3 pulse**, pulsation, vibration, throb, palpitation, reverberation, pounding, thump, thud, hammering, drumming. **4 circuit**, round, route, path.

□ **beat around** (or **about**) **the bush** discuss something without coming to the point. **beat it** informal leave. **beat someone up** (or **beat up on someone**) hit or kick someone repeatedly. **off the beaten track** isolated.

be·a·tif·ic /ˌbēəˈtifik/ ▶ **adj.** feeling or expressing blissful happiness. ■ **be·a·tif·i·cal·ly adv.**

be·at·i·fy /bēˈatəˌfī/ ▶ **v.** (**beatifies**, **beatifying**, **beatified**) state officially that a dead person is very holy (the first step toward making them a saint).

beat·nik /ˈbētnik/ ▶ **n.** a young person in the 1950s and early 1960s who rejected conventional society.

beau /bō/ ▶ **n.** (plural **beaux** /bōz/ or **beaus**) dated **1** a young woman's boyfriend or male admirer. **2** a rich, fashionable young man; a dandy.

Beau·fort scale /ˈbōfərt/ ▶ **n.** a scale of wind speed ranging from force 0 to force 12.

beau·ti·cian /byo͞oˈtisHən/ ▶ **n.** a person whose job is to give beauty treatments.

beau·ti·ful /ˈbyo͞otəfəl/ ▶ **adj. 1** very pleasing to the senses. **2** of a very high standard; excellent.

SYNONYMS **attractive**, pretty, handsome, good-looking, fetching, lovely, charming, graceful, elegant, appealing, winsome, ravishing, gorgeous, stunning, glamorous; informal knockout, drop-dead gorgeous, cute, foxy; old use comely. ANTONYMS ugly.

■ **beau·ti·ful·ly adv.**

SPELLING

Remember the **u** before the **t**: beau**t**iful.

beau·ti·fy /ˈbyo͞otəˌfī/ ▶ **v.** (**beautifies**, **beautifying**, **beautified**) make someone or something look more attractive.

SYNONYMS **adorn**, embellish, enhance, decorate, ornament, prettify, glamorize; informal do up, spruce up.

beau·ty /ˈbyo͞otē/ ▶ **n.** (plural **beauties**) **1** the quality of being very pleasing to the senses. **2** a beautiful woman. **3** an excellent example of something. **4** an attractive feature or advantage.

SYNONYMS **1 attractiveness**, prettiness, good looks, loveliness, appeal, winsomeness, charm, grace, elegance, exquisiteness, glamour; literary pulchritude. **2 belle**, vision, goddess, picture, Venus; informal babe, looker, lovely, stunner, knockout, bombshell. ANTONYMS ugliness.

□ **beauty queen** the winner of a competition to be judged the most beautiful woman. **beauty salon** (or **beauty parlor**) a place in which hairdressing and cosmetic treatments are carried out.

beaux /bōz/ plural of BEAU.

bea·ver /ˈbēvər/ ▶ **n.** (plural **beaver** or **beavers**) a large rodent that lives partly in water. ▶ **v.** (**beavers**, **beavering**, **beavered**) (**beaver away**) informal work hard.

be·calmed /biˈkä(l)md/ ▶ **adj.** (of a sailing ship) unable to move because there is no wind.

be·came /biˈkām/ past of BECOME.

be·cause /biˈkôz, -ˈkəz/ ▶ **conj.** for the reason that; since.

SYNONYMS **since**, as, seeing that, in view of the fact that, in that.

□ **because of** by reason of.

beck /bek/ ▶ **n.** (**at someone's beck and call**) always having to be ready to obey someone's orders.

beck·on /ˈbekən/ ▶ **v. 1** make a movement encouraging someone to approach or follow. **2** seem appealing: *the wide open spaces of Australia beckoned.*

SYNONYMS **1 gesture**, signal, wave, gesticulate, motion. **2 entice**, invite, tempt, lure, charm, attract, draw, call.

be·come /biˈkəm/ ▶ **v.** (**becomes**, **becoming**, **became** /biˈkām/, past participle **become**) **1** begin to be. **2** turn into. **3** (**become of**) happen to. **4** suit or be appropriate to. **5** (**becoming**) (of clothing) looking good on someone.

SYNONYMS **1** *she became rich* **grow**, get, turn, come to be, get to be. **2** *he became a tyrant* **turn into**, change into, be transformed into, be converted into. **3** *he became foreign secretary* **be appointed**, be assigned as, be nominated, be elected. **4** (**become of**) **happen to**, be the fate of, be the lot of, overtake. **5 suit**, flatter, look good on, set off; informal do something for. **6** (**becoming**) **flattering**, fetching, attractive, pretty, elegant, handsome, well-chosen, stylish, fashionable, tasteful.

bec·que·rel /ˌbek(ə)ˈrel/ ▶ **n.** a unit of radioactivity.

BEd /ˌbē ˈed/ ▶ **abbr.** Bachelor of Education.

bed /bed/ ▶ **n. 1** a piece of furniture for sleeping on. **2** an area of ground where flowers and shrubs are grown. **3** a flat base. ▶ **v.** (**beds**, **bedding**, **bedded**) **1** (**bed down**) sleep in a place where you do not usually sleep. **2** (**bed something in**) fix something firmly.

SYNONYMS ▶ **n. 1 cot**, bunk bed, futon, daybed, sofa bed, four-poster, berth, crib, cradle; informal the sack. **2** *a flower bed* **patch**, plot, border, strip. **3 base**, foundation, footing, support, basis. ▶ **v. embed**, set, fix, insert, inlay, implant, bury, plant.

□ **bed and breakfast 1** sleeping accommodations and breakfast in a guest house or hotel. **2** a guest house offering this. **bedding plant** a plant produced for planting in a bed in the spring. **bed linen** sheets, pillowcases, and duvet covers. **a bed of roses** a comfortable or easy situation or activity. **bed-wetting** urinating while asleep.

bed·bug /ˈbedˌbəg/ ▶ **n.** a bug that sucks the blood of sleeping humans.

bed·clothes /ˈbedˌklō(TH)z/ ▶ **pl.n.** coverings for a bed, such as sheets and blankets.

bed·ding /ˈbediNG/ ▶ **n. 1** bedclothes. **2** straw for animals to sleep on.

be·dev·il /biˈdevəl/ ▶ **v.** (**bedevils**, **bedeviling**, **bedeviled**) cause continual trouble to.

bed·lam /ˈbedləm/ ▶ **n.** a scene of great confusion and noise.

Bed·ou·in /'bed(ə)win, 'bedo͞oin/ (also **Beduin**) ▶ **n.** (plural **Bedouin**) an Arab living as a nomad in the desert.

bed·pan /'bed,pan/ ▶ **n.** a container used as a toilet by a bedridden patient.

bed·post /'bed,pōst/ ▶ **n.** any of the four upright supports of a bedstead.

be·drag·gled /bi'dragəld/ ▶ **adj.** untidy.

SYNONYMS **disheveled**, disordered, untidy, unkempt, tousled; informal mussed. ANTONYMS neat.

bed·rid·den /'bed,ridn/ ▶ **adj.** unable to get out of bed because of illness or old age.

bed·rock /'bed,räk/ ▶ **n.** **1** a layer of solid rock under soil. **2** the central principles on which something is based.

bed·room /'bed,ro͞om, -,ro͝om/ ▶ **n.** a room for sleeping in. ▫ **bedroom community** a town from which people travel to work in a nearby city.

bed·side man·ner /'bed,sīd/ ▶ **n.** the way in which a doctor acts toward a patient: *he has a perfect bedside manner.*

bed·sore /'bed,sôr/ ▶ **n.** a sore caused by lying in bed in one position for a long time.

bed·spread /'bed,spred/ ▶ **n.** a decorative cloth used to cover a bed.

bed·stead /'bed,sted/ ▶ **n.** the framework of a bed.

bed·time /'bed,tīm/ ▶ **n.** the usual time when someone goes to bed.

bee /bē/ ▶ **n.** a winged insect that collects nectar and pollen from flowers and makes wax and honey.

beech /bēCH/ ▶ **n.** a large tree with gray bark and pale wood.

beef /bēf/ ▶ **n.** the flesh of a cow, bull, or ox, used as food. ▶ **v.** (**beef something up**) informal make something stronger or larger.

beef·steak /'bēf,stāk/ ▶ **n.** a thick slice of steak.

beef·y /'bēfē/ ▶ **adj.** (**beefier**, **beefiest**) informal muscular or strong.

bee·hive /'bē,hīv/ ▶ **n.** a structure in which bees are kept.

bee·keep·ing /'bē,kēpiNG/ ▶ **n.** the owning and breeding of bees for their honey. ■ **bee·keep·er n.**

bee·line /'bē,līn/ ▶ **n.** (**make a beeline for**) hurry straight to.

Be·el·ze·bub /bē'elzə,bəb/ ▶ **n.** the Devil.

been /bin/ past participle of **BE**.

beep /bēp/ ▶ **n.** a short, high-pitched sound made by electronic equipment or the horn of a vehicle. ▶ **v.** produce a beep.

beep·er /'bēpər/ ▶ **n.** a small device that bleeps or vibrates to inform you that it has received a message; a pager.

beer /bi(ə)r/ ▶ **n.** an alcoholic drink made from fermented malt flavored with hops. ▫ **beer belly** (or **beer gut**) informal a man's stomach that sticks out because of excessive drinking of beer.

bees·wax /'bēz,waks/ ▶ **n.** **1** wax produced by bees to make honeycombs, used for wood polishes and candles. **2** informal a person's concern or business: *that's none of your beeswax.*

beet /bēt/ ▶ **n.** a plant with a fleshy root, grown as food and for making into sugar.

bee·tle /'bētl/ ▶ **n.** an insect with hard, shiny covers over its wings.

beet·root /'bēt,ro͞ot/ ▶ **n.** the edible dark-red root of a kind of beet.

be·fall /bi'fôl/ ▶ **v.** (**befalls**, **befalling**, **befell**; past participle **befallen**) literary (of something bad) happen to someone.

be·fit /bi'fit/ ▶ **v.** (**befits**, **befitting**, **befitted**) be appropriate for. ■ **be·fit·ting adj.**

be·fore /bi'fôr/ ▶ **prep., conj., & adv.** **1** during the time preceding. **2** in front of. **3** rather than.

SYNONYMS **1 prior to**, previous to, earlier than, preparatory to, in advance of, ahead of, pre-. **2 in front of**, in the presence of. **3 in preference to**, rather than, sooner than. ANTONYMS after.

be·fore·hand /bi'fôr,hand/ ▶ **adv.** in advance.

SYNONYMS **in advance**, in readiness, ahead of time, before, before now/then, earlier (on), previously, already, sooner. ANTONYMS afterward.

be·friend /bi'frend/ ▶ **v.** become a friend to.

be·fud·dled /bi'fədld/ ▶ **adj.** confused.

beg /beg/ ▶ **v.** (**begs**, **begging**, **begged**) **1** humbly ask someone for something. **2** ask for food or money as charity.

SYNONYMS **1 ask for money**, seek charity; informal sponge, cadge, scrounge, bum. **2** *we begged for mercy* **plead for**, request, ask for, appeal for, call for, sue for, solicit, seek. **3** *he begged her not to go* **implore**, entreat, plead with, appeal to, pray to, call on, petition; literary beseech.

▫ **beg the question** **1** (of a fact or action) invite a question or point that has not been dealt with. **2** assume that something is true without discussing it. **go begging** be available because other people do not want it.

be·gan /bi'gan/ past of **BEGIN**.

be·get /bi'get/ ▶ **v.** (**begets**, **begetting**, **begot** /bi'gät/ or **begat** /bi'gat/; past participle **begotten** /bi'gätn/) old use **1** cause something. **2** become the father of a child.

beg·gar /'begər/ ▶ **n.** **1** a person who lives by begging for food or money. **2** informal a particular type of person: *lucky beggar!* ▶ **v.** (**beggars**, **beggaring**, **beggared**) make someone very poor.

SYNONYMS ▶ **n. tramp**, hobo, vagrant, vagabond, mendicant; informal scrounger, sponger, freeloader, bum.

▫ **beggar description** (or **belief**) be too extraordinary to be described (or believed). ■ **beg·gar·ly adj.**

be·gin /bi'gin/ ▶ **v.** (**begins**, **beginning**, **began** /bi'gan/, past participle **begun** /bi'gən/) **1** carry out or experience the first part of an action or activity. **2** come into being. **3** have a particular starting point. **4** (**begin on**) set to work on.

SYNONYMS **1 start**, commence, set about, go about, embark on, launch into, get down to, take up, initiate, set in motion, get going, get off the ground, lead off, institute, inaugurate, open; informal get cracking on, kick off. **2 appear**, arise, become apparent, spring up, crop up, turn up, come into existence, originate, start, commence, develop. ANTONYMS finish, end.

be·gin·ner /bi'ginər/ ▶ **n.** a person just starting to learn a skill or take part in an activity.

SYNONYMS **novice**, learner, starter, (raw) recruit, newcomer, tyro, apprentice, trainee; informal rookie, new kid (on the block), tenderfoot, greenhorn. ANTONYMS expert, veteran.

□ **beginner's luck** good luck supposedly experienced by a beginner at a particular activity.

be·gin·ning /bi'giniNG/ ▶ **n.** the point in time or space at which something starts: *he left at the beginning of February.* ▶ **adj.** new or inexperienced.

SYNONYMS ▶ **n. 1 start**, commencement, creation, birth, inception, conception, origination, origin, genesis, germ, emergence, rise, dawn, launch, onset, outset, day one; informal kickoff. **2 opening**, start, commencement, first part, introduction, preamble. ANTONYMS end, conclusion.

□ **the beginning of the end** the event to which ending or failure can be traced.

be·go·nia /bi'gōnyə, -nēə/ ▶ **n.** a plant with brightly colored flowers.

be·got /bi'gät/ past of **BEGET**.

be·got·ten /bi'gätn/ past participle of **BEGET**.

be·grudge /bi'grəj/ ▶ **v. 1** feel envious that someone possesses something. **2** give something resentfully.

SYNONYMS **envy**, resent, grudge, be jealous of, be envious of, mind, object to.

be·guile /bi'gīl/ ▶ **v.** charm or trick.

be·gun /bi'gən/ past participle of **BEGIN**.

be·half /bi'haf/ ▶ **n.** (**on behalf of** or **on someone's behalf**) **1** in the interests of a particular person, group, or principle. **2** as a representative of.

SYNONYMS **1 in the interests of**, in support of, for, for the benefit of, for the good of, for the sake of. **2 representing**, as a representative of, as a spokesperson for, for, in the name of, in place of, on the authority of.

be·have /bi'hāv/ ▶ **v. 1** act in a certain way. **2** (also **behave yourself**) act in a polite or proper way.

SYNONYMS **1** *she behaved badly* **act**, conduct **yourself**, acquit yourself. **2** *the children behaved for once* **act correctly**, be good, be well-behaved, mind your manners; informal mind your Ps and Qs. ANTONYMS misbehave.

be·haved /bi'hāvd/ ▶ **adj.** acting in a certain way: *a well-behaved child.*

be·hav·ior /bi'hāvyər/ ▶ **n.** the way in which someone or something behaves.

SYNONYMS **conduct**, actions, manners, ways, deportment, bearing, etiquette.

■ **be·hav·ior·al adj.**

be·head /bi'hed/ ▶ **v.** execute someone by cutting off their head.

be·held /bi'held/ past and past participle of **BEHOLD**.

be·he·moth /bi'hēməTH, 'bēəməTH/ ▶ **n. 1** a huge creature. **2** something enormous, especially a big and powerful organization.

be·hest /bi'hest/ ▶ **n.** (**at someone's behest**) in response to someone's order.

be·hind /bi'hīnd/ ▶ **prep. & adv. 1** at or to the back or far side of. **2** further back than other members of a group. **3** in support of. **4** responsible for an event or plan. **5** late in doing something.

SYNONYMS **1 at the back of**, at the rear of, in back of, beyond, on the far side of. **2 after**, following, at the back/rear of, hard on the heels of, in the wake of. **3 responsible for**, at the bottom of, the cause of, the perpetrator of, the organizer of, to blame for, guilty of. **4 supporting**, backing, for, on the side of, in agreement with; informal rooting for.

be·hold /bi'hōld/ ▶ **v.** (**beholds**, **beholding**, **beheld** /bi'held/) old use see or look at.

be·hold·en /bi'hōldən/ ▶ **adj.** (**beholden to**) owing something to someone because they have done you a favor.

be·hoove /bi'hōōv/ ▶ **v.** (**it behooves someone to do**) formal it is right or appropriate for someone to do.

beige /bāZH/ ▶ **n.** a pale sandy color.

be·ing /'bēiNG/ ▶ **n. 1** existence. **2** the nature of a person. **3** a living creature: *alien beings.*

SYNONYMS **1 existence**, living, life, reality, lifeblood, vital force. **2 soul**, spirit, nature, essence, psyche, heart, bosom, breast. **3 creature**, life form, organism, living thing, individual, person, human.

be·jew·eled /bi'jōōəld/ ▶ **adj.** decorated with jewels.

be·lat·ed /bi'lātid/ ▶ **adj.** coming late or too late.

SYNONYMS **late**, overdue, behindhand, delayed, tardy, unpunctual. ANTONYMS early.

■ **be·lat·ed·ly adv.**

belch /belCH/ ▶ **v. 1** noisily expel gas from the stomach through the mouth. **2** send smoke or flames out or up with great force. ▶ **n.** an act of belching.

be·lea·guered /bi'lēgərd/ ▶ **adj. 1** in difficulties. **2** under siege.

SYNONYMS **1 besieged**, blockaded, surrounded, encircled, hemmed in, under attack. **2 troubled**, harassed, hard-pressed, in difficulties, under pressure, in a tight corner; informal up against it.

bel·fry /'belfrē/ ▶ **n.** (plural **belfries**) the place in a bell tower or steeple in which the bells are situated.

Bel·gian /'beljən/ ▶ **n.** a person from Belgium. ▶ **adj.** relating to Belgium.

be·lie /bi'lī/ ▶ **v.** (**belies**, **belying**, **belied**) **1** fail to give a true idea of. **2** show that something is not true.

be·lief /bi'lēf/ ▶ **n. 1** a feeling that something exists or is true. **2** a firmly held opinion. **3** (**belief in**) trust or confidence in. **4** religious faith.

SYNONYMS **1 opinion**, view, conviction, judgment, thinking, idea, theory, thought, feeling. **2 faith**, trust, reliance, confidence, credence. **3 ideology**, principle, ethic, tenet, doctrine, teaching, dogma, creed, credo. ANTONYMS disbelief, doubt.

□ **beyond belief** astonishing; incredible.

be·liev·a·ble /bi'lēvəbəl/ ▶ **adj. 1** able to be believed; credible. **2** (of a fictional character or situation) convincing or realistic. ■ **be·liev·a·bly adv.**

be·lieve /bi'lēv/ ▶ **v.** (**believes**, **believing**, **believed**) **1** accept that something is true or someone is telling the truth. **2** (**believe in**) have faith that something is true or exists. **3** think or suppose. **4** have a religious faith.

SYNONYMS **1** *I don't believe you* **trust**, have confidence in, consider honest, consider truthful. **2** *do you believe that story?* **accept**, be convinced by, give credence to, credit, trust, put confidence in; informal swallow, buy, go for. **3 think**, be of the opinion that, have an idea that, imagine, assume, presume, take it, understand, gather; informal reckon, figure. ANTONYMS doubt.

SPELLING

Write **i** before **e** except after **c**, when the sound is 'ee': bel**ie**ve.

be·liev·er /bi'lēvər/ ▶ **n. 1** a person who believes in the truth or existence of something. **2** someone with religious faith.

SYNONYMS **disciple**, follower, supporter, adherent, devotee, upholder, worshiper. ANTONYMS infidel, skeptic.

be·lit·tle /bi'litl/ ▶ **v.** (**belittles**, **belittling**, **belittled**) dismiss as unimportant.

SYNONYMS **disparage**, denigrate, run down, deprecate, play down, trivialize, minimize; informal pooh-pooh.

bell /bel/ ▶ **n. 1** a deep metal cup that sounds a clear musical note when struck. **2** a device that buzzes or rings to give a signal. □ **bell-ringing** the activity or hobby of ringing church bells or handbells. **ring a bell** informal sound vaguely familiar.

bel·la·don·na /ˌbelə'dänə/ ▶ **n. 1** another name for deadly nightshade. **2** a drug made from deadly nightshade.

belle /bel/ ▶ **n.** a beautiful woman.

bell·hop /'belˌhäp/ (also **bellboy** /'belˌboi/) ▶ **n.** a person employed to carry luggage in a hotel.

bel·li·cose /'beliˌkōs/ ▶ **adj.** aggressive and ready to fight.

bel·lig·er·ence /bə'lijərəns/ ▶ **n.** aggressive or warlike behavior.

bel·lig·er·ent /bə'lijərənt/ ▶ **adj. 1** hostile and aggressive. **2** taking part in a war or conflict.

SYNONYMS **1 hostile**, aggressive, threatening, antagonistic, pugnacious, bellicose, truculent, confrontational, contentious, militant, combative, argumentative; informal scrappy, spoiling for a fight. **2** *the belligerent states* **warring**, combatant, fighting, battling. ANTONYMS peaceable.

■ **bel·lig·er·ent·ly adv.**

bel·low /'belō/ ▶ **v. 1** give a deep roar of pain or anger. **2** shout or sing very loudly. ▶ **n.** a deep shout or noise.

SYNONYMS ▶ **v. roar**, shout, bawl, thunder, boom, bark, yell, shriek, howl, scream; informal holler. ANTONYMS whisper.

bel·lows /'belōz/ ▶ **pl.n.** a device consisting of a bag with two handles, used for blowing air into a fire.

bel·ly /'belē/ ▶ **n.** (plural **bellies**) **1** the front part of the body below the ribs, containing the stomach and bowels. **2** a person's stomach.

SYNONYMS **stomach**, abdomen, paunch, middle, midriff, girth; informal tummy, gut, insides.

□ **go belly up** informal go bankrupt. **belly button** informal a person's navel. **belly laugh** a loud unrestrained laugh.

bel·ly·ache /'belēˌāk/ informal ▶ **n.** a stomach pain. ▶ **v.** complain noisily or often.

bel·ly·flop /'belēˌfläp/ ▶ **n.** informal a dive into water in which you land flat on your front.

be·long /bi'lôNG/ ▶ **v. 1** (**belong to**) be the property of. **2** (**belong to**) be a member of. **3** be rightly put into a particular position or class. **4** feel at ease in a particular place or situation.

SYNONYMS **1 be owned by**, be the property of, be held by, be in the hands of. **2 be a member of**, be in, be affiliated with, be allied to, be associated with. **3 be part of**, be attached to, go with. **4 fit in**, be suited to; informal go, click.

be·long·ings /bi'lôNGiNGz/ ▶ **pl.n.** a person's movable possessions.

SYNONYMS **possessions**, effects, worldly goods, chattels, property; informal gear, tackle, things, stuff, bits and pieces.

be·lov·ed /bi'ləv(i)d/ ▶ **adj.** dearly loved. ▶ **n.** a much loved person.

SYNONYMS ▶ **adj. darling**, dear, precious, adored, cherished, treasured, prized, valued, idolized. ▶ **n. sweetheart**, love, darling, dearest, lover, girlfriend, boyfriend; informal steady, baby, angel, honey, pet.

be·low /bi'lō/ ▶ **prep. & adv. 1** at a lower level than. **2** (in printed writing) mentioned further down.

SYNONYMS **1 beneath**, under, underneath, lower than. **2 less than**, lower than, under, not as much as, smaller than. **3 inferior to**, subordinate to, under, beneath. ANTONYMS above, over.

belt /belt/ ▶ **n. 1** a strip of leather or fabric worn around the waist. **2** a continuous band in machinery that connects two wheels. **3** a strip or encircling area: *the asteroid belt*. ▶ **v. 1** fasten with a belt. **2** hit very hard. **3** (**belt something out**) informal sing or play something loudly.

SYNONYMS ▶ **n. 1 sash**, girdle, band, strap, cummerbund. **2 region**, strip, stretch, zone, area, district, sector, territory.

□ **below the belt** against the rules; unfair. **tighten your belt** spend less money. **under your belt** achieved or acquired.

belt·way /'beltˌwā/ ▶ **n.** a highway encircling an urban area.

be·lu·ga /bə'lo͞ogə/ ▶ **n.** (plural **beluga** or **belugas**) **1** a small white whale of Arctic waters. **2** a very large sturgeon from which caviar is obtained.

be·ly·ing /bi'lī-iNG/ present participle of **BELIE**.

be·moan /bi'mōn/ ▶ **v.** express sadness or regret about something.

be·mused /bi'myo͞ozd/ ▶ **adj.** confused or bewildered.

SYNONYMS **bewildered**, confused, puzzled, perplexed, baffled, mystified, nonplussed, dumbfounded, at sea, at a loss; informal flummoxed, bamboozled, fazed.

■ **be·muse·ment n.**

bench /benCH/ ▶ **n. 1** a long seat for more than one person. **2** a long table for working at in a workshop or laboratory. **3** (**the bench**) the office of judge. **4** (**the bench**) a seat at the side of a sports field for coaches and reserve players.

SYNONYMS **1 seat**, form, pew, stall, settle. **2 workbench**, worktop, counter.

□ **bench press** an exercise in which you lie on a bench with your feet on the floor and raise a weight with both arms.

bench·mark /ˈbencн,märk/ ▶ n. a standard against which things may be compared.

SYNONYMS **standard**, point of reference, guide, guideline, norm, touchstone, yardstick, barometer, model, gauge, criterion, specification.

bend /bend/ ▶ v. (**bends**, **bending**, **bent**) **1** change from being straight; make or become curved or angled. **2** lean or curve the body downward. **3** change a rule to suit yourself. ▶ n. **1** a place where something bends; a curve or turn. **2** (**the bends**) decompression sickness.

SYNONYMS ▶ v. **1 curve**, crook, flex, angle, hook, bow, arch, buckle, warp, contort, distort, deform, twist. **2 turn**, curve, incline, swing, veer, fork, change course, curl, loop. **3 stoop**, bow, crouch, hunch, lean down/over. ANTONYMS straighten. ▶ n. **curve**, turn, corner, kink, angle, arc, twist.

□ **around the bend** informal insane; crazy.

bend·er /ˈbendər/ ▶ n. informal a drinking bout.

be·neath /biˈnēтн/ ▶ prep. & adv. extending or directly underneath. ▶ prep. of lower status or worth than.

SYNONYMS ▶ prep. & adv. **under**, underneath, below, at the foot of, at the bottom of, lower than; further down, lower down. ANTONYMS above. ▶ prep. **1 inferior to**, below, lower than, subordinate to. **2 unworthy of**, unbecoming to, degrading to. ANTONYMS above.

Ben·e·dic·tine /ˌbeniˈdikˌtēn, -tin/ ▶ n. a monk or nun of a Christian religious order following the rule of St. Benedict.

ben·e·dic·tion /ˌbeniˈdiksнən/ ▶ n. the speaking of a blessing.

ben·e·fac·tor /ˈbenəˌfaktər, ˌbenəˈfaktər/ ▶ n. a person who gives money or other help.

SYNONYMS **patron**, supporter, backer, sponsor, donor, contributor, subscriber; informal angel.

ben·e·fice /ˈbenəfis/ ▶ n. an arrangement by which a Christian priest is paid and given accommodations for being in charge of a parish.

be·nef·i·cent /bəˈnefəsənt/ ▶ adj. doing or resulting in good. ■ **be·nef·i·cence** n.

ben·e·fi·cial /ˌbenəˈfisнəl/ ▶ adj. having a good effect.

SYNONYMS **advantageous**, favorable, helpful, useful, of assistance, valuable, salutary, worthwhile, fruitful, productive, profitable, rewarding, gainful. ANTONYMS disadvantageous.

■ **ben·e·fi·cial·ly** adv.

ben·e·fi·ci·ar·y /ˌbenəˈfisнēˌerē/ ▶ n. (plural **beneficiaries**) a person who benefits from something, especially a trust, will, or insurance policy.

SYNONYMS **recipient**, payee, heir, heiress, inheritor.

ben·e·fit /ˈbenəfit/ ▶ n. **1** advantage or profit. **2** payment made by the state to someone in need: *unemployment benefit*. **3** a public performance to raise money for a charity. ▶ v. (**benefits**, **benefiting** or **benefitting**; **benefited** or **benefitted**) **1** get an advantage; profit. **2** bring advantage to.

SYNONYMS ▶ n. **1 good**, sake, welfare, well-being, advantage, comfort, ease, convenience, help, aid, assistance, service. **2 advantage**, profit, plus point, boon, blessing, reward; informal perk. **3 social security payment**, welfare, charity; informal the dole. ANTONYMS detriment, disadvantage. ▶ v. **1 help**, be advantageous to, be beneficial to, profit, do good to, be of service to, serve, be useful to, be helpful to, aid, assist. **2 profit**, gain, reap rewards, make the most of, exploit, turn to your advantage, put to good use. ANTONYMS disadvantage, harm.

□ **give someone the benefit of the doubt** accept that someone must be regarded as right or innocent if the opposite has not been proven.

be·nev·o·lent /bəˈnevələnt/ ▶ adj. **1** well-meaning and kindly. **2** (of an organization) charitable rather than profit-making.

SYNONYMS **kind**, kindly, kindhearted, good-natured, compassionate, caring, altruistic, humanitarian, philanthropic, beneficent, well-meaning, benign. ANTONYMS unkind.

■ **be·nev·o·lence** n.

Ben·ga·li /ˌbenGˈgälē/ ▶ n. (plural **Bengalis**) **1** a person from Bengal in the Indian subcontinent. **2** the language of Bangladesh and West Bengal. ▶ adj. relating to Bengal.

be·night·ed /biˈnītid/ ▶ adj. ignorant or primitive.

be·nign /biˈnīn/ ▶ adj. **1** cheerful and kindly. **2** favorable; not harmful. **3** (of a tumor) not malignant.

SYNONYMS **1 kindly**, kind, warmhearted, good-natured, friendly, genial, tenderhearted, gentle, sympathetic, compassionate, caring, well-disposed, benevolent. **2 mild**, temperate, gentle, balmy, soft, pleasant, favorable, healthy. **3 harmless**, nonmalignant, noncancerous. ANTONYMS unkind, malignant.

bent /bent/ past and past participle of **BEND** ▶ adj. **1** informal dishonest or corrupt. **2** (**bent on**) determined to do. ▶ n. a natural talent.

SYNONYMS ▶ adj. **1 twisted**, crooked, warped, contorted, deformed, misshapen, out of shape, bowed, arched, curved, angled, hooked, kinked; informal pretzeled. **2 corrupt**, dishonest, fraudulent, criminal, untrustworthy. ANTONYMS straight. ▶ n. **1 inclination**, leaning, tendency, talent, gift, flair, aptitude, facility, skill. **2** (**bent on**) **intent on**, determined on, set on, insistent on, resolved on.

ben·zene /ˈbenˌzēn, benˈzēn/ ▶ n. a liquid present in coal tar and petroleum.

ben·zine /ˈbenˌzēn, benˈzēn/ ▶ n. a mixture of liquid hydrocarbons obtained from petroleum.

be·queath /biˈkwēтн, -ˈkwē<u>тн</u>/ ▶ v. **1** leave property to someone by a will. **2** hand down or pass on.

SYNONYMS **leave**, will, hand down, pass on, entrust, make over, grant, transfer, give, bestow on, confer on.

be·quest /biˈkwest/ ▶ n. **1** something that is left to someone by a will. **2** the action of bequeathing.

SYNONYMS **legacy**, estate, inheritance, endowment, settlement.

be·rate /biˈrāt/ ▶ v. (**berates**, **berating**, **berated**) angrily scold or criticize.

SYNONYMS **scold**, rebuke, reprimand, reproach, reprove, admonish, chide, criticize, upbraid, take to task; informal tell off, give someone a talking-to, read someone the riot act, give someone a dressing-down, bawl out, come down on, tear into, chew out, ream (out), blast; formal castigate. ANTONYMS praise.

Ber·ber /'bərbər/ ▶ **n.** a member of people native to North Africa.

be·reave /bi'rēv/ ▶ **v.** (**be bereaved**) be deprived of a close relation or friend through their death.

be·reave·ment /bi'rēvmənt/ ▶ **n.** an instance of being bereaved.

SYNONYMS **death in the family**, loss, passing (away), demise; formal decease.

be·reft /bi'reft/ ▶ **adj. 1** (**bereft of**) deprived of; without. **2** lonely and abandoned.

SYNONYMS **deprived**, robbed, stripped, devoid, bankrupt; (**bereft of**) wanting, in need of, lacking, without; informal minus, clean out of; literary sans.

be·ret /bə'rā/ ▶ **n.** a flat round cap of felt or cloth.

ber·ga·mot /'bərgə,mät/ ▶ **n.** an oily substance found in some oranges, used as a flavoring.

ber·i·ber·i /'berē'berē/ ▶ **n.** a disease caused by a lack of vitamin B_1.

Ber·mu·da shorts /bər'myōōdə/ ▶ **pl.n.** casual knee-length shorts.

ber·ry /'berē/ ▶ **n.** (plural **berries**) a small, juicy round fruit without a stone.

ber·serk /bər'zərk, -'sərk/ ▶ **adj.** out of control; wild and frenzied.

SYNONYMS **mad**, crazy, insane, out of your mind, hysterical, frenzied, crazed, demented, maniacal, manic, frantic, raving, wild, out of control, amok, on the rampage; informal off the deep end, ape, bananas, bonkers, postal.

berth /bərTH/ ▶ **n. 1** a place in a harbor where a boat can stay. **2** a bunk on a ship or train. ▶ **v.** moor a boat in a berth.

SYNONYMS ▶ **n. 1 mooring**, dock, pier, jetty, quay. **2 bunk**, bed, cot, couch, hammock. ▶ **v. dock**, moor, land, tie up, make fast.

□ **give a wide berth to** stay well away from.

ber·yl /'berəl/ ▶ **n.** a transparent pale green, blue, or yellow gemstone.

be·ryl·li·um /bə'rilēəm/ ▶ **n.** a hard, gray, lightweight metallic element.

be·seech /bi'sēCH/ ▶ **v.** (**beseeches**, **beseeching**, **besought** /bi'sôt/ or **beseeched**) ask in a pleading way.

SYNONYMS **implore**, beg, entreat, plead with, appeal to, call on, importune, pray to, ask, petition.

be·set /bi'set/ ▶ **v.** (**besets**, **besetting**, **beset**) continually trouble or worry.

be·side /bi'sīd/ ▶ **prep. 1** at the side of. **2** compared with. **3** (also **besides**) as well as.

SYNONYMS **alongside**, by/at the side of, next to, parallel to, abreast of, adjacent to, next door to, neighboring.

□ **beside yourself** frantic with worry.

be·sides /bi'sīdz/ ▶ **prep.** in addition to; apart from. ▶ **adv.** as well.

SYNONYMS ▶ **prep. in addition to**, as well as, over and above, on top of, apart from, other than, aside from, not counting, excluding, leaving aside; informal outside of.

be·siege /bi'sēj/ ▶ **v.** (**besieges**, **besieging**, **besieged**) **1** surround a place so that no one can come or go. **2** overwhelm someone with requests or complaints.

SYNONYMS **1 lay siege to**, beleaguer, blockade. **2 surround**, mob, harass, pester, badger. **3 overwhelm**, bombard, inundate, deluge, flood, swamp, snow under.

SPELLING

Remember, **i** before **e**, when the sound is *ee*, except after **c**: besiege.

be·smirch /bi'smərCH/ ▶ **v.** damage someone's reputation.

be·som /'bēzəm/ ▶ **n.** a broom made of twigs tied around a stick.

be·sot·ted /bi'sätid/ ▶ **adj.** so much in love that you stop acting sensibly.

be·sought /bi'sôt/ past and past participle of **BESEECH**.

be·speak /bi'spēk/ ▶ **v.** (**bespeaks**, **bespeaking**, **bespoke** /bi'spōk/; past participle **bespoken** /bi'spōkən/) **1** be evidence of. **2** formal order or reserve in advance.

best /best/ ▶ **adj. 1** of the highest quality. **2** most suitable or sensible. ▶ **adv. 1** to the highest degree; most. **2** most suitably or sensibly. ▶ **n.** (**the best**) something that is of the highest quality.

SYNONYMS ▶ **adj. finest**, premier, greatest, top, foremost, leading, preeminent, supreme, superlative, unrivaled, second to none, without equal, unsurpassed, unparalleled, unbeatable, optimum, ultimate, incomparable, record-breaking; informal star, number-one, a cut above the rest, top-drawer. ▶ **n.** *only the best will do* **finest**, choicest, top, cream, choice, prime, elite, crème de la crème, flower, jewel in the crown; informal tops, pick of the litter. ANTONYMS worst.

□ **at best** taking the most optimistic view. **best man** a male friend or relative who helps a bridegroom at his wedding. **the best of three** (or **five**, etc.) victory achieved by winning the majority of a specified odd number of games. **the best part of** most of. **get the best of** overcome. **had best** find it most sensible to. **make the best of** get what advantage you can from.

bes·tial /'bēsCHəl, 'bes-/ ▶ **adj.** savagely cruel.

bes·ti·al·i·ty /,bēsCHē'alitē, ,bes-/ ▶ **n.** savagely cruel behavior.

be·stir /bi'stər/ ▶ **v.** (**bestirs**, **bestirring**, **bestirred**) (**bestir yourself**) make yourself start to do something.

be·stow /bi'stō/ ▶ **v.** give an honor, right, or gift.

SYNONYMS **confer on**, grant, accord, afford, endow with, present, award, give, donate, entrust with, vouchsafe.

be·stride /bi'strīd/ ▶ **v.** (**bestrides**, **bestriding**, **bestrode** /bi'strōd/; past participle **bestridden** /bi'stridən/) put a leg on either side of.

best·sell·er /,best'selər/ ▶ **n.** a book or other product that sells in very large numbers. ■ **best·sell·ing adj.**

bet /bet/ ▶ v. (**bets, betting, bet** or **betted**) **1** risk money against someone else's on the basis of the outcome of an unpredictable event such as a race. **2** informal feel sure. ▶ n. an act of betting or the money betted.

> SYNONYMS ▶ v. **1 wager**, gamble, stake, risk, venture, hazard, chance. **2 be certain**, be sure, be convinced, be confident, expect, predict, guess. ▶ n. **1 wager**, gamble, stake, ante. **2** *your best bet is to go early* **option**, choice, alternative, course of action, plan.

□ **you bet** informal certainly.

be·ta /'bātə/ ▶ n. the second letter of the Greek alphabet (Β, β). □ **beta blocker** a drug used to treat high blood pressure and angina. **beta particle** a fast-moving electron given off by some radioactive substances. **beta test** a trial of software in the final stages of development, carried out by selected users.

be·take /bi'tāk/ ▶ v. (**betakes, betaking, betook** /bi'to͝ok/; past participle **betaken**) (**betake yourself to**) literary go to.

be·tel /'bētl/ ▶ n. the leaf of an Asian plant, chewed as a mild stimulant.

be·tel nut ▶ n. the seed of a tropical palm, chewed with betel leaves.

bête noire /ˌbāt 'nwär, ˌbet/ ▶ n. (plural **bêtes noires**) a person or thing that you greatly dislike.

be·think /bi'THiNGk/ ▶ v. (**bethinks, bethinking, bethought** /bi'THôt/) (**bethink yourself**) formal come to think.

be·tide /bi'tīd/ ▶ v. (**betide, betiding, betided**) literary happen or happen to.

be·times /bi'tīmz/ ▶ adv. in good time; early.

be·to·ken /bi'tōkən/ ▶ v. be a sign of.

be·took /bi'to͝ok/ past of **BETAKE**.

be·tray /bi'trā/ ▶ v. **1** harm someone or something by giving information to an enemy. **2** be disloyal to someone. **3** reveal a secret without meaning to.

> SYNONYMS **1 be disloyal to**, be unfaithful to, break faith with, inform on/against, give away, denounce, sell out, stab in the back; informal rat on/out, snitch on, finger, sell down the river. **2 reveal**, disclose, divulge, tell, give away, leak, bring out into the open.

be·tray·al /bi'trāəl/ ▶ n. the act of being disloyal.

> SYNONYMS **disloyalty**, treachery, bad faith, breach of faith, breach of trust, faithlessness, duplicity, deception, double-dealing, stab in the back, double-cross, sellout. ANTONYMS loyalty.

be·troth·al /bə'trōT͟Həl, -'trôTHəl/ ▶ n. the act of becoming engaged to be married; a marriage engagement.

be·trothed /bə'trōT͟Hd, -'trôTHd/ ▶ adj. engaged to be married.

bet·ter /'betər/ ▶ adj. **1** of a higher standard or quality. **2** partly or fully recovered from illness or injury. ▶ adv. **1** in a more satisfactory way. **2** to a greater degree; more. ▶ n. (**your betters**) people who have greater ability or are more important than you. ▶ v. **1** improve on something. **2** (**better yourself**) improve your social position.

> SYNONYMS ▶ adj. **1 superior**, finer, of higher quality, preferable; informal a cut above, head and shoulders above, ahead of the pack/field. **2 healthier**, fitter, stronger, well again, cured, healed, recovered, recovering, on the road to recovery, on the mend. ANTONYMS worse, inferior. ▶ v. **1 surpass**, improve on, beat, exceed, top, cap, trump, eclipse. **2 improve**, ameliorate, raise, advance, further, lift, upgrade, enhance. ANTONYMS worsen.

□ **better off** having more money or being in a more desirable situation. **better half** informal a person's husband or wife. **the better part of** most of. **get the better of** defeat. **had better** would find it wiser to.

bet·ter·ment /'betərmənt/ ▶ n. improvement.

be·tween /bi'twēn/ ▶ prep. & adv. **1** at, into, or across the space separating two things. **2** in the period separating two points in time. **3** indicating a connection or relationship. **4** shared by two or more people or things.

> SYNONYMS **1 in the middle of**, with one on either side, among; old use betwixt. **2 connecting**, linking, joining, uniting, allying.

□ **between you and me** (or **ourselves**) in confidence.

be·twixt /bi'twikst/ ▶ prep. & adv. old use between. □ **betwixt and between** informal neither one thing nor the other.

bev·el /'bevəl/ ▶ n. an edge cut at an angle in wood or glass. ▶ v. (**bevels, beveling, beveled**) cut the edge of wood or glass at an angle.

bev·er·age /'bev(ə)rij/ ▶ n. a drink.

bev·y /'bevē/ ▶ n. (plural **bevies**) a large group.

be·wail /bi'wāl/ ▶ v. express regret, disappointment, or bitterness about something by complaining to others about it.

be·ware /bi'we(ə)r/ ▶ v. be aware of and alert to danger.

> SYNONYMS **watch out**, look out, mind, be alert, be on your guard, keep your eyes open/peeled, keep an eye out, take care, be careful, be cautious, watch your step, guard against.

be·wil·der /bi'wildər/ ▶ v. (**bewilders, bewildering, bewildered**) puzzle or confuse.

> SYNONYMS **1 baffle**, mystify, bemuse, perplex, puzzle, confuse; informal flummox, faze, stump, beat. **2** (**bewildered**) **baffled**, mystified, bemused, perplexed, puzzled, confused, nonplussed, at sea, at a loss, disorientated; informal flummoxed, discombobulated, bamboozled.

■ **be·wil·der·ment** n.

be·witch /bi'wiCH/ ▶ v. **1** put a magic spell on. **2** attract and delight.

> SYNONYMS **captivate**, enchant, entrance, enrapture, charm, beguile, delight, fascinate, enthrall, cast a spell on.

be·yond /bē'änd, bi'yänd/ ▶ prep. & adv. **1** at or to the further side of. **2** outside the range or limits of. **3** happening or continuing after. **4** except.

> SYNONYMS **1 on the far side of**, on the other side of, further away than, behind, past, after. **2 later than**, past, after. **3 greater than**, more than, exceeding, in excess of, above, upwards of.

be·zique /bə'zēk/ ▶ n. a card game for two, played with a double deck of 64 cards that includes only the seven to ace of each suit.

b.h.p. ▶ abbr. brake horsepower.

bi·an·nu·al /bī'anyo͞oəl/ ▶ **adj.** happening twice a year. ■ **bi·an·nu·al·ly adv.**

bi·as /'bīəs/ ▶ **n. 1** a feeling for or against a person or thing that is based on prejudice rather than reason. **2** a direction diagonal to the grain of a fabric. ▶ **v.** cause someone to have a prejudice in favour of or against.

> SYNONYMS ▶ **n. prejudice**, partiality, favoritism, partisanship, unfairness, one-sidedness, discrimination, leaning, tendency, inclination. ANTONYMS impartiality. ▶ **v. prejudice**, influence, color, sway, predispose, distort, skew, slant.

bi·ased /'bīəsd/ ▶ **adj.** having a bias; prejudiced.

> SYNONYMS **prejudiced**, partial, partisan, one-sided, bigoted, discriminatory, distorted, warped, twisted, skewed. ANTONYMS impartial.

bi·ath·lon /bī'aᴛʜlän/ ▶ **n.** an athletic contest combining cross-country skiing and rifle shooting.

bib /bib/ ▶ **n. 1** a piece of cloth or plastic fastened under a baby's chin to protect its clothes when it is being fed. **2** the part of an apron or pair of overalls that covers the chest.

Bi·ble /'bībəl/ ▶ **n.** the book containing the writings of the Christian Church. □ **Bible Belt** the areas of the southern and midwestern US where many Protestants believe in a literal interpretation of the Bible. **King James Bible** an English translation of the Bible made in 1611 at the order of King James I of England. ■ **bib·li·cal** /'biblikəl/ **adj.**

bib·li·og·ra·phy /ˌbiblē'ägrəfē/ ▶ **n.** (plural **bibliographies**) **1** a list of books on a particular subject. **2** a list of the books referred to in a scholarly work, usually printed as an appendix. ■ **bib·li·og·ra·pher n. bib·li·o·graph·ic** /ˌbiblēə'grafik/ **adj.**

bib·li·o·phile /'biblēəˌfīl/ ▶ **n.** a person who collects books.

bib·u·lous /'bibyələs/ ▶ **adj.** fond of drinking alcohol.

bi·cam·er·al /bī'kamərəl/ ▶ **adj.** (of a legislative body) having two separate parts.

bi·car·bo·nate /bī'kärbəˌnāt, -nit/ ▶ **n.** a compound containing HCO_3 negative ions together with a metallic element. □ **bicarbonate of soda** a soluble white powder used in effervescent drinks, in baking, and in fire extinguishers; baking soda.

bi·cen·ten·ar·y /ˌbīsen'tenərē/ ▶ **n.** (plural **bicentenaries**) a two-hundredth anniversary. ■ **bi·cen·ten·ni·al** /ˌbīsen'tenēəl/ **n. & adj.**

bi·ceps /'bīˌseps/ ▶ **n.** (plural **biceps**) a large muscle in the upper arm that flexes the arm and forearm.

bick·er /'bikər/ ▶ **v.** (**bickers**, **bickering**, **bickered**) argue about unimportant things.

bi·cus·pid /bī'kəspid/ ▶ **adj.** having two cusps or points. ▶ **n.** a tooth with two cusps.

bi·cy·cle /'bīsikəl/ ▶ **n.** a two-wheeled vehicle that you ride by pushing the pedals with your feet. ▶ **v.** (**bicycles**, **bicycling**, **bicycled**) ride a bicycle.

bid¹ /bid/ ▶ **v.** (**bids**, **bidding**, **bid**) **1** offer a price for something. **2** (**bid on** (or **for**)) offer to do work for a stated price. **3** (**bid for**) try to get. ▶ **n.** an act of bidding.

> SYNONYMS ▶ **v. offer**, put up, tender, proffer, propose. ▶ **n. 1 offer**, tender, proposal. **2 attempt**, effort, endeavor, try; informal crack, go, shot, stab.

■ **bid·der n.**

bid² ▶ **v.** (**bids**, **bidding**, **bid** or **bade** /bad, bād/; past participle **bid**) **1** say a greeting. **2** old use command.

bid·da·ble /'bidəbəl/ ▶ **adj.** obedient.

bid·ding /'bidiɴɢ/ ▶ **n.** an authoritative instruction to do something.

> SYNONYMS **command**, order, direction, instruction, decree, injunction, demand, beck and call.

bid·dy /'bidē/ ▶ **n.** (plural **biddies**) informal an old woman, especially one thought of as annoying or interfering.

bide /bīd/ ▶ **v.** (**bides**, **biding**, **bided**) old use or dialect stay in a place. □ **bide your time** wait patiently for an opportunity to do something.

bi·en·ni·al /bī'enēəl/ ▶ **adj. 1** taking place every other year. **2** (of a plant) living for two years.

bier /bi(ə)r/ ▶ **n.** a platform on which a coffin or dead body is placed before burial.

bi·fo·cal /'bīˌfōkəl/ ▶ **adj.** (of a lens) made in two sections, one for distant and one for close vision. ▶ **n.** (**bifocals**) a pair of glasses with bifocal lenses.

big /big/ ▶ **adj.** (**bigger**, **biggest**) **1** large in size, amount, or extent. **2** very important or serious. **3** informal (of a brother or sister) older: *my big sister*.

> SYNONYMS **1 large**, sizable, substantial, considerable, great, huge, immense, enormous, extensive, colossal, massive, mammoth, vast, gigantic, giant, spacious; informal jumbo, whopping, bumper, mega, ginormous; formal commodious. **2 well-built**, sturdy, brawny, burly, broad-shouldered, muscular, bulky, hulking, strapping, hefty, tall, huge, fat, stout; informal hunky, beefy. **3 elder**, older, grown-up, adult, mature, grown. **4 important**, significant, major, momentous, weighty, far-reaching, key, vital, crucial. **5** *that was big of you* **generous**, kind, kindly, caring, compassionate, loving. ANTONYMS small, minor.

□ **Big Bang** the rapid expansion of dense matter that is thought to have started the formation of the universe. **Big Brother** a person or organization that has total control over other people's lives. **Big Dipper** a prominent formation of seven stars in the constellation Ursa Major (the Great Bear). **big end** the larger end of the connecting rod in a piston engine. **big mouth 1** a person who boasts about things. **2** a person who cannot keep secrets. **the big screen** the movies. **big top** the main tent in a circus. **in a big way** informal to a great extent or high degree. **talk big** informal talk confidently or boastfully. **think big** informal be ambitious.

big·a·my /'bigəmē/ ▶ **n.** the crime of marrying someone when you are already married to someone else. ■ **big·a·mist n. big·a·mous adj.**

Big·foot /'bigˌfo͝ot/ ▶ **n.** a large, hairy apelike creature said by some people to live in remote parts of northwestern America.

big·head·ed /'bigˌhedid/ ▶ **adj.** informal conceited.

bight /bīt/ ▶ **n.** a long inward curve in a coastline.

big·ot /'bigət/ ▶ **n.** a prejudiced and intolerant person. ■ **big·ot·ry n.**

big·ot·ed /'bigətid/ ▶ **adj.** unreasonably intolerant.

> SYNONYMS **prejudiced**, biased, partial, one-sided, sectarian, discriminatory, opinionated, dogmatic, intolerant, narrow-minded, blinkered, illiberal. ANTONYMS open-minded.

big·wig /'bigˌwig/ ▶ **n.** informal an important person.

bi·jou /ˈbēzhoo/ ▶ **adj.** small and elegant. ▶ **n.** a small and finely wrought trinket or jewel.

bike /bīk/ informal ▶ **n.** a bicycle or motorcycle. ▶ **v.** (**bikes**, **biking**, **biked**) ride a bicycle or motorcycle. ■ **bik·er n.**

bi·ki·ni /biˈkēnē/ ▶ **n.** (plural **bikinis**) a woman's very brief two-piece swimsuit.

bi·lat·er·al /bīˈlatərəl/ ▶ **adj.** involving two countries or groups of people.

bile /bīl/ ▶ **n. 1** a bitter fluid that is produced by the liver and helps digestion. **2** anger. □ **bile duct** the tube that conveys bile from the liver and the gall bladder to the duodenum.

bilge /bilj/ ▶ **n.** the bottom of a ship's hull. □ **bilge water** dirty water that collects in the bilge.

bi·lin·gual /bīˈlinggwəl/ ▶ **adj. 1** speaking two languages fluently. **2** expressed in two languages.

bil·ious /ˈbilyəs/ ▶ **adj. 1** affected by or associated with nausea or vomiting. **2** relating to bile.

bilk /bilk/ ▶ **v.** informal cheat someone.

bill[1] /bil/ ▶ **n. 1** a note saying how much a person owes for something. **2** a written proposal for a new law, presented to Congress for discussion. **3** a program of entertainment at a theater. **4** an advertising poster. **5** a banknote. ▶ **v. 1** send someone a bill saying what they owe. **2** list someone in a program of entertainment. **3** (**bill someone/thing as**) describe someone or something as.

> SYNONYMS ▶ **n. 1 invoice**, account, statement, check, list of charges; humorous damage; informal tab. **2 draft law**, proposal, measure. **3 program**, lineup, playbill. **4** *Jefferson is on the $2 bill* **banknote**, note; informal greenback. **5 poster**, advertisement, notice, announcement, flyer, leaflet, handbill; informal ad. ▶ **v. 1 invoice**, charge, debit. **2 advertise**, announce, schedule, program, slate. **3** *he was billed as the new Sean Connery* **describe as**, call, style, label, dub, promote as, talk up as; informal hype as.

□ **a clean bill of health** confirmation that you are healthy. **bill of rights** a statement of the rights of a country's citizens, especially the first ten amendments to the US Constitution. **fit the bill** be suitable. ■ **bill·ing n.**

bill[2] ▶ **n.** a bird's beak. □ **bill and coo** informal behave in a loving and sentimental way; kiss and hug.

bill·board /ˈbilˌbôrd/ ▶ **n.** a large board for displaying advertising.

bil·let /ˈbilit/ ▶ **n.** a private house where soldiers live temporarily. ▶ **v.** (**be billeted**) (of a soldier) stay in a particular place.

bil·let-doux /ˈbilā ˈdoo, ˈbēyā-/ ▶ **n.** (plural **billets-doux**) a love letter.

bill·fold /ˈbilˌfōld/ ▶ **n.** a man's wallet.

bill·hook /ˈbilˌhook/ ▶ **n.** a tool with a curved blade, used for pruning.

bil·liards /ˈbilyərdz/ ▶ **n.** a game played on a table with pockets at the sides and corners, into which balls are struck with a cue.

bil·lion /ˈbilyən/ ▶ **cardinal number** (plural **billions** or (with another word or number) **billion**) a billion; 1,000,000,000. ■ **bil·lionth ordinal number.**

bil·lion·aire /ˈbilyəˌne(ə)r/ ▶ **n.** a person owning money and property worth at least a billion dollars (or pounds, euros, etc.).

bil·low /ˈbilō/ ▶ **v. 1** (of smoke, cloud, or steam) roll outward. **2** fill with air and swell out: *her dress billowed out behind her.* ▶ **n. 1** a large rolling mass of cloud, smoke, or steam. **2** literary a large sea wave.

> SYNONYMS ▶ **v. 1 swirl**, spiral, roll, undulate, eddy, pour, flow. **2 puff out**, balloon (out), swell, fill (out).

bil·ly goat /ˈbilēˌgōt/ ▶ **n.** a male goat.

bim·bo /ˈbimbō/ ▶ **n.** (plural **bimbos**) informal an attractive but unintelligent young woman.

bin /bin/ ▶ **n. 1** a container for trash. **2** a large storage container. ▶ **v.** (**bins**, **binning**, **binned**) put something in a bin.

bi·na·ry /ˈbīˌnerē, -nərē/ ▶ **adj. 1** composed of or involving two things. **2** relating to a system of numbers that has two as its base and uses only the digits 0 and 1.

bind /bīnd/ ▶ **v.** (**binds**, **binding**, **bound** /bound/) **1** firmly tie, wrap, or fasten. **2** hold together in a united group or mass: *a society of equals bound by a common spirit.* **3** (**be bound by**) be hampered or restricted by. **4** require someone to do something by law or because of a contract. **5** (**bind someone over**) (of a court of law) require someone to do something: *he was bound over for trial.* **6** enclose the pages of a book in a cover. **7** trim the edge of a piece of material with a fabric strip. ▶ **n.** informal an annoying or difficult situation.

> SYNONYMS ▶ **v. 1 tie up**, fasten together, secure, make fast, attach, rope, lash, tether. **2 bandage**, dress, cover, wrap, strap up, tape up. **3 trim**, hem, edge, border, fringe.
> ANTONYMS untie.

bind·er /ˈbīndər/ ▶ **n. 1** a cover for holding loose papers together. **2** a machine that binds grain into sheaves. **3** a person who binds books. ■ **bind·er·y n.** (plural **binderies**).

bin·di /ˈbindē/ ▶ **n.** (plural **bindis**) a decorative mark worn in the middle of the forehead by some Indian women.

bind·ing /ˈbīnding/ ▶ **n. 1** a strong covering holding the pages of a book together. **2** fabric in a strip, used for binding the edges of material. ▶ **adj.** (of an agreement) legally compelling someone to do what is stated.

> SYNONYMS ▶ **adj. irrevocable**, unalterable, inescapable, unbreakable, contractual, compulsory, obligatory, mandatory, incumbent.

bind·weed /ˈbīndˌwēd/ ▶ **n.** a plant that twines itself around things.

binge /binj/ informal ▶ **n.** a short period of uncontrolled eating or drinking. ▶ **v.** (**binges**, **binging**, **binged**) eat or drink in an uncontrolled way.

> SYNONYMS ▶ **n. bout**, spell, fling, spree, orgy, drinking bout; informal bender, session, jag.

bin·go /ˈbinggō/ ▶ **n.** a game in which players mark off on a card numbers called at random, the winner being the first to mark off five numbers in a row or another required pattern. ▶ **exclam. 1** a call by someone who wins a game of bingo. **2** said to express satisfaction at a sudden good event.

bin·na·cle /ˈbinəkəl/ ▶ **n.** a casing to hold a ship's compass.

bin·oc·u·lar /bīˈnäkyələr/ ▶ **adj.** for or using both eyes. ▶ **n.** (**binoculars**) an instrument with a separate lens for each eye, for viewing distant objects.

bi·no·mi·al /bīˈnōmēəl/ ▶ **n.** Math an algebraic expression consisting of two terms linked by a plus or minus sign.

bi·o·chem·is·try /ˌbīōˈkeməstrē/ ▶ **n.** the study of the chemical processes that take place within living things. ■ **bi·o·chem·i·cal** /ˌbīōˈkemikəl/ **adj. bi·o·chem·ist n.**

bi·o·de·grad·a·ble /ˌbīōdiˈgrādəbəl/ ▶ **adj.** able to be decomposed by bacteria or other living things.

bi·o·di·ver·si·ty /ˌbīōdiˈvərsitē/ ▶ **n.** the variety of plant and animal life in the world or in a particular environment.

bi·o·en·gi·neer·ing /ˌbīōˌenjəˈni(ə)riNG/ ▶ **n.** **1** genetic engineering. **2** the use of artificial tissues or organs in the body. **3** the use of organisms or biological processes in industry.

bi·o·fu·el /ˈbīōˌfyo͞oəl/ ▶ **n.** fuel obtained directly from living matter.

bi·og·ra·phy /bīˈägrəfē/ ▶ **n.** (plural **biographies**) an account of a person's life written by someone else. ■ **bi·og·ra·pher n. bi·o·graph·i·cal** /ˌbīəˈgrafikəl/ **adj.**

bi·o·haz·ard /ˈbīōˌhazərd/ ▶ **n.** a risk to human health or the environment arising from biological research.

bi·o·log·i·cal /ˌbīəˈläjikəl/ ▶ **adj. 1** relating to biology or living things. **2** (of a parent or child) related by blood. **3** relating to the use of germs as a weapon in war. □ **biological clock** a process in plants and animals that controls the rhythm of certain processes, such as sleeping. ■ **bi·o·log·i·cal·ly adv.**

bi·ol·o·gy /bīˈäləjē/ ▶ **n.** the scientific study of the life and structure of plants and animals. ■ **bi·ol·o·gist n.**

bi·on·ic /bīˈänik/ ▶ **adj. 1** (of an artificial body part) electronically powered. **2** informal having superhuman powers.

bi·op·sy /ˈbīˌäpsē/ ▶ **n.** (plural **biopsies**) an examination of tissue taken from the body to discover the presence or cause of a disease.

bi·o·rhythm /ˈbīōˌriT͟Həm/ ▶ **n.** a recurring cycle in the functioning of an animal or plant.

bi·o·se·cur·i·ty /ˌbīōsiˈkyo͝oritē/ ▶ **n.** procedures intended to protect humans or animals against disease or harmful substances.

bi·o·sphere /ˈbīəˌsfi(ə)r/ ▶ **n.** the parts of the earth occupied by living organisms.

bi·o·syn·the·sis /ˌbīōˈsinTHəsis/ ▶ **n.** the production of complex molecules within living organisms or cells. ■ **bi·o·syn·thet·ic** /-ˌsinˈTHetik/ **adj.**

bi·o·tech·nol·o·gy /ˌbīōtekˈnäləjē/ ▶ **n.** the use of living cells and bacteria in industry and medicine.

bi·o·ter·ror·ism /ˌbīōˈterəˌrizəm/ ▶ **n.** the use of harmful organisms such as viruses or bacteria as weapons of terrorism.

bi·ot·ic /bīˈätik/ ▶ **adj.** relating to living things and the effect they have on each other.

bi·o·tin /ˈbīətin/ ▶ **n.** a vitamin of the B complex, found in egg yolk, liver, and yeast.

bi·par·ti·san /bīˈpärtəzən/ ▶ **adj.** involving the cooperation of two political parties.

bi·par·tite /bīˈpärˌtīt/ ▶ **adj.** involving two separate groups or parties.

bi·ped /ˈbīped/ ▶ **n.** an animal that walks on two feet.

bi·plane /ˈbīˌplān/ ▶ **n.** an early type of aircraft with two pairs of wings, one above the other.

bi·po·lar /bīˈpōlər/ ▶ **adj.** having two poles or outer limits. □ **bipolar disorder** a mental disorder with alternating periods of elation and depression.

birch /bərCH/ ▶ **n. 1** a slender tree with thin peeling bark. **2** (**the birch**) (in the past) the punishment of being beaten with a bundle of birch twigs.

bird /bərd/ ▶ **n.** an animal with feathers, wings, and a beak, that lays eggs and is usually able to fly.

SYNONYMS fowl, chick, fledgling, nestling.

□ **bird of paradise** (plural **birds of paradise**) **1** a brightly colored tropical bird. **2** an African plant that bears a showy irregular flower with a long projecting tongue. **bird of prey** (plural **birds of prey**) a bird that eats small animals or birds, such as an eagle or hawk. **bird's-eye view** a view of something from high above.

bird·brain /ˈbərdˌbrān/ ▶ **n.** informal a stupid person.

bird·ie /ˈbərdē/ ▶ **n.** (plural **birdies**) Golf a score of one stroke under par at a hole.

bird·lime /ˈbərdˌlīm/ ▶ **n.** a sticky substance spread on to twigs to trap small birds.

bird·watch·ing /ˈbərdˌwäCHiNG/ ▶ **n.** the hobby of observing birds in their natural environment.

bi·ret·ta /bəˈretə/ ▶ **n.** a square cap worn by Roman Catholic clergymen.

birth /bərTH/ ▶ **n. 1** the process by which a baby or other young animal comes out of its mother's body. **2** the beginning of something. **3** a person's family origins: *he is of noble birth.*

SYNONYMS **1 childbirth**, delivery, nativity. **2 beginning(s)**, emergence, genesis, dawn, dawning, rise, start. **3 ancestry**, lineage, blood, descent, parentage, family, extraction, origin, stock. ANTONYMS death, end.

□ **birth certificate** an official document recording a person's name, their place and date of birth, and the names of their parents. **birth control** the use of contraceptives to prevent unwanted pregnancies. **birth rate** the number of babies born each year for every thousand people in the population. **birth sign** the sign of the zodiac through which the sun is passing when someone is born. **give birth** produce a baby or young animal.

birth·day /ˈbərTHˌdā/ ▶ **n.** the day in each year which is the same as the day on which a person was born.

birth·mark /ˈbərTHˌmärk/ ▶ **n.** an unusual mark on the body that is there from birth.

birth·place /ˈbərTHˌplās/ ▶ **n.** the place where a person was born.

birth·right /ˈbərTHˌrīt/ ▶ **n. 1** a right or privilege that a person inherits. **2** a basic right belonging to all human beings.

bis·cuit /ˈbiskit/ ▶ **n. 1** a small round cake of bread leavened with baking powder, baking soda, or sometimes yeast. **2** a light brown color.

SPELLING

Don't forget the **u**: bisc**u**it.

bi·sect /bīˈsekt, ˈbīˌsekt/ ▶ **v.** divide into two parts.

bi·sex·u·al /bīˈsekSHo͞oəl/ ▶ **adj. 1** sexually attracted to both men and women. **2** Biology having both male and female organs.

bish·op /ˈbiSHəp/ ▶ **n.** (in the Christian Church) a senior minister who is in charge of a diocese (a district).

bish·op·ric /ˈbisHəprik/ ▶ **n.** the office or diocese of a bishop.

bis·muth /ˈbizməTH/ ▶ **n.** a brittle reddish-gray metallic element resembling lead.

bi·son /ˈbīsən, -zən/ ▶ **n.** (plural **bison**) a wild ox with a humped back and shaggy hair.

bisque[1] /bisk/ ▶ **n.** a rich soup made from lobster or other shellfish.

bisque[2] ▶ **n.** **1** fired unglazed pottery. **2** a light brown color.

bis·tro /ˈbistrō, ˈbē-/ ▶ **n.** (plural **bistros**) a small, informal or unpretentious restaurant.

bit[1] /bit/ ▶ **n.** **1** a small piece or quantity. **2** (**a bit**) a short time or distance. **3** (**a bit**) rather; slightly.

> SYNONYMS **piece**, portion, section, part, chunk, lump, hunk, fragment, scrap, shred, crumb, grain, speck, spot, drop, pinch, dash, morsel, mouthful, bite, sample, iota, jot, whit, atom, particle, trace, touch, suggestion, hint, tinge; informal smidgen, tad.

□ **bit by bit** gradually. **bit part** a small acting role in a play or a film. **do your bit** informal make a useful contribution. **to bits 1** into pieces. **2** informal very much.

bit[2] ▶ **n.** **1** a metal mouthpiece attached to a bridle, used to control a horse. **2** a tool or piece for boring or drilling. □ **get the bit between your teeth** make a determined effort.

bit[3] ▶ **n.** Computing the smallest unit of information, expressed as either a 0 or 1.

bit[4] past of **BITE**.

bitch /bicH/ ▶ **n.** **1** a female dog. **2** informal a spiteful or unpleasant woman. ▶ **v.** informal grumble; complain.

bitch·y /ˈbicHē/ ▶ **adj.** (**bitchier**, **bitchiest**) informal spiteful. ■ **bitch·i·ness n.**

bite /bīt/ ▶ **v.** (**bites**, **biting**, **bit** /bit/; past participle **bitten** /ˈbitn/) **1** cut into something with your teeth. **2** (of a tool, tire, etc.) grip a surface. **3** take effect in an unwelcome way: *the cuts in education were starting to bite.* ▶ **n.** **1** an act of biting or a piece bitten off. **2** informal a quick snack. **3** a feeling of cold in the air.

> SYNONYMS ▶ **v.** **1 chew**, sink your teeth into, munch, crunch, chomp, champ. **2 grip**, hold, get a purchase on. **3 take effect**, work, act, have results. ▶ **n.** **1 chew**, munch, nibble, gnaw, nip. **2 mouthful**, piece, bit, morsel, snack. **3 piquancy**, pungency, spiciness, tang, zest; informal kick, punch, zing.

□ **bite the bullet** make yourself do something that is difficult or unpleasant. **bite the dust** informal die or be killed. **bite the hand that feeds you** deliberately hurt or offend a person who is trying to help. **bite off more than you can chew** try to do something that turns out to be too difficult or complicated. **bite your tongue** try hard to stop yourself saying something.

bit·ing /ˈbītiNG/ ▶ **adj.** **1** (of a wind) painfully cold. **2** (of something said) cruel.

> SYNONYMS **1 freezing**, icy, arctic, bitter, piercing, penetrating, raw. **2 vicious**, harsh, cruel, savage, cutting, sharp, bitter, scathing, caustic, acerbic, acid, acrimonious, spiteful, venomous, vitriolic; informal bitchy, catty. ANTONYMS mild.

bit·map /ˈbit,map/ ▶ **n.** a display of all the separate bits, or tiny units of information, that go to make up an image on a computer screen.

bit·ten /ˈbitn/ past participle of **BITE**.

bit·ter /ˈbitər/ ▶ **adj.** **1** having a sharp or sour taste or smell; not sweet. **2** feeling or causing resentment or unhappiness. **3** (of a conflict) intense and full of hatred: *a bitter argument broke out.* **4** very cold. ▶ **n.** (**bitters**) bitter liquor used in cocktails.

> SYNONYMS ▶ **adj.** **1 sharp**, acid, acrid, tart, sour, vinegary. **2 acrimonious**, hostile, angry, rancorous, spiteful, vicious, vitriolic, savage, ferocious, nasty. **3 resentful**, embittered, aggrieved, spiteful, jaundiced, sullen, sour. **4 freezing**, icy, arctic, biting, piercing, penetrating, raw. ANTONYMS sweet, mild.

□ **to the bitter end** to the very end, in spite of harsh difficulties. ■ **bit·ter·ly adv. bit·ter·ness n.**

bit·tern /ˈbitərn/ ▶ **n.** a marshland bird of the heron family with a booming call.

bit·ter·sweet /ˈbitər,swēt/ ▶ **adj.** **1** sweet with a bitter aftertaste. **2** bringing pleasure mixed with sadness.

bit·ty /ˈbitē/ ▶ **adj.** (**bittier**, **bittiest**) informal tiny.

bi·tu·men /biˈt(y)o͞omən, bī-/ ▶ **n.** a black sticky substance obtained from oil, used for covering roads and roofs. ■ **bi·tu·mi·nous** /biˈt(y)o͞omənəs, bī-/ **adj.**

bi·valve /ˈbī,valv/ ▶ **n.** a creature that has a shell divided into two parts, such as an oyster or mussel.

biv·ou·ac /ˈbivo͞o,ak, ˈbivwak/ ▶ **n.** a makeshift open-air camp without tents. ▶ **v.** (**bivouacs**, **bivouacking**, **bivouacked**) stay overnight in such a camp.

bi·zarre /biˈzär/ ▶ **adj.** very strange or unusual.

> SYNONYMS **strange**, peculiar, odd, funny, fantastic, extraordinary, curious, outlandish, eccentric, unconventional, unorthodox, weird, outré, surreal; informal wacky, wacko, oddball, way out, freaky. ANTONYMS normal.

■ **bi·zarre·ly adv.**

> SPELLING
> One **z**, two **r**s: bizarre.

blab /blab/ ▶ **v.** (**blabs**, **blabbing**, **blabbed**) informal give away a secret.

blab·ber /ˈblabər/ ▶ **v.** (**blabbers**, **blabbering**, **blabbered**) informal talk in a silly or annoying way.

blab·ber·mouth /ˈblabər,mouTH/ ▶ **n.** informal a person who talks excessively or indiscreetly.

black /blak/ ▶ **adj.** **1** of the very darkest color. **2** relating to people who have dark-colored skin. **3** (of coffee or tea) without milk. **4** indicating that bad or unwelcome things are likely to happen: *the future looks black.* **5** (of a joke) making something bad or unwelcome seem funny. **6** full of anger or hatred. ▶ **n.** **1** black color. **2** a black person. ▶ **v.** **1** make something black. **2** (**black out**) faint. **3** (**black something out**) make a building dark by switching off lights and covering windows.

> SYNONYMS ▶ **adj.** **1 dark**, pitch-black, coal-black, jet-black, ebony, inky, sable. **2** *a black day* **tragic**, dark, disastrous, calamitous, catastrophic, cataclysmic, fateful. **3** *a black mood* **miserable**, unhappy, sad, wretched, heartbroken, grief-stricken, sorrowful, anguished, desolate, despairing, disconsolate, downcast, dejected, gloomy; informal blue.

4 **macabre**, cynical, unhealthy, ghoulish, weird, morbid, gruesome; informal sick. ANTONYMS white, bright.

□ **black and white** involving issues or choices that differ in a clear, straightforward way. **black art** (or **arts**) black magic. **black belt** a black belt awarded to an expert in judo, karate, and other martial arts. **black box** a machine that records what is happening to the controls in an aircraft during a flight. **black currant** a small round edible purple-black berry. **black eye** an area of bruising around the eye. **black-eyed pea** a plant of the pea family, cultivated for food and forage. **black hole** an area in space where gravity is so strong that nothing, not even light, can escape. **black ice** a transparent coating of ice on a road. **black magic** magic in which evil spirits are called on. **black mark** a note that someone has behaved badly. **black market** the illegal trade in goods that are officially controlled or hard to obtain. **black sheep** a person who is considered bad or embarrassing by the rest of their family. **black widow** a very poisonous spider with a black body and red markings. **black tie** semiformal evening wear. **in the black** not owing any money. ■ **black·ly adv. black·ness n.**

black·ball /'blak,bôl/ ▶ **v.** prevent someone from joining a club.

black·ber·ry /'blak,berē/ ▶ **n.** (plural **blackberries**) a soft purple-black fruit that grows on a prickly bush.

black·bird /'blak,bərd/ ▶ **n.** a bird with black feathers and a yellow beak.

black·board /'blak,bôrd/ ▶ **n.** a board with a black surface for writing on with chalk.

black·en /'blakən/ ▶ **v. 1** make or become black. **2** damage someone's reputation.

black·fly /'blak,flī/ ▶ **n.** (plural **blackflies**) **1** a small black fly, the female of which sucks blood and can transmit a number of serious human and animal diseases. **2** a black or dark green aphid that eats the young shoots of plants.

black·guard /'blagərd, 'blak,gärd/ ▶ **n.** dated a man who is dishonest or treats other people badly.

black·head /'blak,hed/ ▶ **n.** a lump of oily matter blocking a pore in the skin.

black·jack /'blak,jak/ ▶ **n. 1** a gambling card game in which players try to acquire cards with a face value as close as possible to 21 without going over. **2** a flexible lead-filled club.

black·list /'blak,list/ ▶ **n.** a list of people who cannot be trusted or who are out of favor. ▶ **v.** put someone on a blacklist.

SYNONYMS ▶ **v. boycott**, ostracize, avoid, embargo, ignore, refuse to employ.

black·mail /'blak,māl/ ▶ **n. 1** the demanding of money from someone in return for not giving away secret information about them. **2** the use of threats or other pressure to influence someone: *emotional blackmail*. ▶ **v.** use blackmail on someone.

SYNONYMS ▶ **n. extortion**, threats, intimidation. ▶ **v. 1 extort money from**, threaten, hold for ransom, intimidate. **2 coerce**, pressure, force, dragoon; informal lean on, twist someone's arm.

Black Ma·ri·a /mə'rīə/ ▶ **n.** informal a police vehicle for transporting prisoners.

black·out /'blak,out/ ▶ **n. 1** a period when all lights must be turned off or covered during an enemy air raid. **2** a sudden failure of electric lights. **3** a short loss of consciousness. **4** an official restriction on the publishing of news: *a total news blackout*.

black·shirt /'blak,sHərt/ ▶ **n.** a member of a Fascist organization, especially in Italy before and during World War II.

black·smith /'blak,smiTH/ ▶ **n.** a person who makes and repairs things made of iron.

black·thorn /'blak,THôrn/ ▶ **n.** a thorny bush that has blue-black fruits (called sloes).

blad·der /'bladər/ ▶ **n.** a baglike organ in the abdomen in which urine collects before it is passed from the body.

blade /blād/ ▶ **n. 1** the flat cutting edge of a knife or other tool or weapon. **2** the broad flat part of an oar, leaf, or other object. **3** a long, narrow leaf of grass.

blame /blām/ ▶ **v.** (**blames**, **blaming**, **blamed**) say that someone is responsible for something bad: *the terrorists were blamed for the bombings*. ▶ **n. 1** responsibility for something bad. **2** criticism for doing something badly or wrongly.

SYNONYMS ▶ **v. 1 hold responsible**, hold accountable, condemn, accuse, find/consider guilty. **2** *they* ***blame*** *the economic decline* ***on*** *this administration* **attribute to**, ascribe to, impute to, lay at the door of, put down to; informal pin on. ANTONYMS absolve. ▶ **n. responsibility**, guilt, accountability, liability, culpability, fault.

■ **blame·wor·thy** /'blām,wərTHē/ **adj.**

blame·less /'blāmlis/ ▶ **adj.** having done nothing bad; innocent.

SYNONYMS **innocent**, guiltless, above reproach, irreproachable, unimpeachable, in the clear, exemplary, impeccable, unblemished; informal squeaky clean. ANTONYMS guilty.

blanch /blancH/ ▶ **v. 1** become white or pale. **2** prepare vegetables by putting them briefly in boiling water.

blanc·mange /blə'mänj, -'mänzH/ ▶ **n.** a dessert like milky jell-o, made with cornstarch and milk.

bland /bland/ ▶ **adj. 1** not having any interesting features or qualities: *the pasta tasted a little bland*. **2** showing no emotion or excitement: *bland assurances that things were going well*.

SYNONYMS **1 uninteresting**, dull, boring, tedious, monotonous, ordinary, run-of-the-mill, drab, dreary, unexciting, lackluster, flat, stale, trite. **2 tasteless**, flavorless, plain, insipid, weak, watery, thin, wishy-washy. ANTONYMS interesting, tangy.

bland·ish·ments /'blandisHmənts/ ▶ **pl.n.** nice things said to someone in order to persuade them to do something.

blank /blaNGk/ ▶ **adj. 1** not marked or decorated. **2** not understanding or reacting. ▶ **n. 1** a space in a form left to be filled in. **2** a state in which you cannot understand or remember something. **3** a gun cartridge containing gunpowder but no bullet. ▶ **v.** (**blank something out**) hide or block out something: *she blanked out her memories of him*.

SYNONYMS ▶ **adj. 1 empty**, unmarked, unused, clear, free, bare, clean, plain. **2 expressionless**, deadpan, wooden, stony, impassive, inscrutable, glazed, fixed, lifeless. ANTONYMS expressive. ▶ **n. space**, gap, void.

□ **blank verse** poetry that has a regular rhythm but does not rhyme. **draw a blank** fail to get a result or reply that you want. ■ **blank·ly** adv. **blank·ness** n.

blan·ket /ˈblaNGkit/ ▶ n. **1** a large piece of woolen material or similar material used as a warm covering. **2** a thick mass or layer: *a blanket of cloud.* ▶ v. (**blankets**, **blanketing**, **blanketed**) cover with a thick layer.

> SYNONYMS ▶ n. *a blanket of cloud* **covering**, layer, coating, carpet, cloak, mantle, veil, pall, shroud. ▶ v. **cover**, coat, carpet, cloak, shroud, swathe, envelop.

□ **blanket stitch** a looped stitch used on the edges of material too thick to be hemmed.

blare /ble(ə)r/ ▶ v. (**blares**, **blaring**, **blared**) make a loud, harsh sound. ▶ n. a loud, harsh sound.

blar·ney /ˈblärnē/ ▶ n. talk that is friendly and charming but that may not be truthful.

bla·sé /bläˈzā/ ▶ adj. not impressed by something because you have experienced it often before.

> SYNONYMS **indifferent**, unconcerned, casual, nonchalant, offhand, uninterested, unimpressed, unmoved, uncaring; informal laid-back.

blas·pheme /blasˈfēm, ˈblasˌfēm/ ▶ v. (**blasphemes**, **blaspheming**, **blasphemed**) speak irreverently about God or use the name of God as a swear word.

blas·phe·mous /ˈblasfəməs/ ▶ adj. disrespectful toward God or sacred things.

> SYNONYMS **sacrilegious**, profane, irreligious, irreverent, impious, ungodly, godless. ANTONYMS reverent.

blas·phe·my /ˈblasfəmē/ ▶ n. (plural **blasphemies**) disrespectful talk about God or sacred things.

> SYNONYMS **profanity**, sacrilege, irreligion, irreverence, taking the Lord's name in vain, impiety, desecration. ANTONYMS reverence.

blast /blast/ ▶ n. **1** an explosion, or the rush of compressed air spreading outward from it. **2** a strong gust of wind. **3** a single loud note of a horn or whistle. ▶ v. **1** blow something up with explosives. **2** (**blast off**) (of a rocket or spacecraft) take off. **3** produce loud music or noise. **4** informal criticize fiercely.

> SYNONYMS ▶ n. **1 explosion**, detonation, discharge, burst. **2 gust**, rush, gale, squall, flurry. **3** *the shrill blast of the trumpets* **blare**, wail, roar, screech, shriek, hoot, honk, beep. ▶ v. **1 blow up**, bomb, blow (to pieces), dynamite, explode, fire, shoot, blaze, let fly, discharge. **2 blare**, boom, roar, thunder, bellow, shriek, screech.

□ **at full blast** at maximum power or intensity. **blast furnace** a furnace for extracting metal from ore, using blasts of hot compressed air. ■ **blast·er** n.

blast·off /ˈblastˌôf, -ˌäf/ ▶ n. the launching of a rocket or spacecraft.

bla·tant /ˈblātnt/ ▶ adj. done in an open and unashamed way: *a blatant act of racism.*

> SYNONYMS **flagrant**, glaring, obvious, undisguised, open, overt, outright, naked, shameless, barefaced, unashamed, brazen. ANTONYMS discreet, inconspicuous.

■ **bla·tan·cy** n. **bla·tant·ly** adv.

> **SPELLING**
> Write **-ant**, not **-ent**: blatant.

blath·er /ˈblaTHər/ ▶ v. (**blathers**, **blathering**, **blathered**) talk without making much sense. ▶ n. rambling talk.

> SYNONYMS ▶ v. **prattle**, babble, chatter, twitter, prate, go on, run on, rattle on, yap, ramble, drivel; informal yak, yatter.

blaze /blāz/ ▶ n. **1** a very large or fierce fire. **2** a very bright light or display of color. **3** a conspicuous display or outburst of something: *a blaze of publicity.* **4** a white stripe down the face of a horse. ▶ v. (**blazes**, **blazing**, **blazed**) **1** burn or shine fiercely or brightly. **2** shoot repeatedly or wildly.

> SYNONYMS ▶ n. **1 fire**, flames, conflagration, inferno, holocaust. **2** *a blaze of light* **glare**, flash, burst, flare, streak, radiance, brilliance, beam, glitter. ▶ v. **1 burn**, be alight, be on fire, be in flames. **2 shine**, flash, flare, glare, gleam, glitter, glisten. **3 fire**, shoot, blast, let fly.

□ **blaze a trail 1** mark out a path. **2** be the first to do something.

blaz·er /ˈblāzər/ ▶ n. **1** a jacket worn by schoolchildren or sports players as part of a uniform. **2** a plain jacket, often dark blue, not forming part of a suit but considered appropriate for semiformal wear.

bla·zon /ˈblāzən/ ▶ v. display or proclaim something in a way that catches people's attention: *their company name was blazoned all over the media.*

bleach /blēCH/ ▶ v. lighten something by using a chemical or leaving it in sunlight. ▶ n. a chemical used to remove stains and also to sterilize sinks or other materials.

> SYNONYMS ▶ v. **turn white**, whiten, turn pale, blanch, lighten, fade. ANTONYMS darken.

bleach·ers /ˈblēCHərz/ ▶ pl.n. cheap bench seats in an uncovered part of a sports arena.

bleak /blēk/ ▶ adj. **1** bare and exposed to the weather. **2** dreary and unwelcoming: *a bleak little room.* **3** (of a situation) not hopeful.

> SYNONYMS **1 bare**, exposed, desolate, stark, desert, lunar, open, empty, windswept. **2 unpromising**, unfavorable, dim, gloomy, black, grim, discouraging, disheartening, depressing, dismal. ANTONYMS lush, promising.

■ **bleak·ly** adv. **bleak·ness** n.

blear·y /ˈbli(ə)rē/ ▶ adj. (**blearier**, **bleariest**) (of the eyes) tired and not focusing properly.

> SYNONYMS **blurry**, unfocused, fogged, clouded, misty, watery, rheumy. ANTONYMS clear.

■ **blear·i·ly** adv.

bleat /blēt/ ▶ v. **1** (of a sheep or goat) make a weak, wavering cry. **2** speak or complain in a weak or silly way. ▶ n. a bleating sound.

bleed /blēd/ ▶ v. (**bleeds**, **bleeding**, **bled**) **1** lose blood from the body. **2** informal drain someone of money or resources. **3** (of dye or color) seep into an adjoining color or area. **4** allow fluid or gas to escape from a closed system through a valve. **5** (in the past) take blood from someone as a medical treatment. ▶ n. an instance of bleeding.

> SYNONYMS ▶ v. **1 lose blood**, hemorrhage. **2** *one color bled into another* **flow**, run, seep, filter, percolate, leach. **3** *sap bleeding from the trunk* **flow**, run, ooze, seep, exude, weep. **4** *my heart bleeds for them* **grieve for**, ache for, sorrow for, mourn for, lament for, feel for, suffer for; sympathize with, pity.

□ **bleeding heart** informal, disapproving a person considered to be too liberal or softhearted.

bleep /blēp/ ▶ n. a short, high-pitched sound made by an electronic device. ▶ v. make a bleep.

blem·ish /'blemisн/ ▶ n. a small mark or flaw. ▶ v. spoil the appearance of.

> SYNONYMS ▶ n. **imperfection**, flaw, defect, fault, discoloration, stain, scar, mark, spot. ▶ v. **mar**, spoil, impair, disfigure, deface, mark, stain, scar, blight, tarnish. ANTONYMS enhance.

blench /blencн/ ▶ v. flinch suddenly out of fear or pain.

blend /blend/ ▶ v. **1** mix and combine one thing with something else. **2** (**blend in**) become unnoticeable: *a bodyguard has to blend in.* ▶ n. a mixture.

> SYNONYMS ▶ v. **1 mix**, mingle, combine, merge, fuse, amalgamate, stir, whisk, fold in. **2 harmonize**, go (well), fit (in), be in tune, be compatible, coordinate, match, complement, suit. ▶ n. **mixture**, mix, melange, combination, synthesis, compound, amalgam, fusion, alloy.

blend·er /'blendər/ ▶ n. an electric device for liquefying or chopping food.

blen·ny /'blenē/ ▶ n. (plural **blennies**) a small coastal fish with scaleless skin and spiny fins.

bless /bles/ ▶ v. **1** make something holy by saying a prayer over it. **2** ask God to protect a person or thing. **3** (**be blessed with**) have or be given something that is desired.

> SYNONYMS **1 consecrate**, sanctify, dedicate to God, make holy; formal hallow. **2 endow**, bestow, furnish, give, favor, confer on. **3 sanction**, consent to, endorse, agree to, approve, back, support; informal give the green light to, OK. ANTONYMS curse, oppose.

□ **bless you!** said to a person who has just sneezed.

bless·ed /blest, 'blesid/ ▶ adj. **1** holy and protected by God. **2** bringing welcome pleasure or relief: *blessed sleep.*

> SYNONYMS **holy**, sacred, hallowed, consecrated, sanctified, ordained, canonized, beatified. ANTONYMS cursed.

■ **bless·ed·ly** /'blesidlē/ adv.

bless·ing /'blesiNG/ ▶ n. **1** God's approval and protection. **2** a prayer asking for God's approval and protection. **3** something for which you are very grateful: *it's a blessing we're alive.* **4** a person's approval or support.

> SYNONYMS **1 benediction**, dedication, consecration, grace, invocation, intercession. **2 sanction**, endorsement, approval, consent, assent, agreement, backing, support; informal the green light, OK. **3 advantage**, godsend, boon, benefit, help, bonus, plus, stroke of luck, windfall. ANTONYMS condemnation.

blew /blo͞o/ past of BLOW[1].

blight /blīt/ ▶ n. **1** a plant disease caused by fungi. **2** a thing that spoils or damages something: *divorce is a great blight on your life.* ▶ v. **1** spoil or damage something. **2** infect with blight.

> SYNONYMS ▶ n. **1** *potato blight* **disease**, canker, infestation, fungus, mildew, mold. **2** *the blight of aircraft noise* **curse**, scourge, affliction, plague, menace, misfortune, bane, trouble, nuisance, pest. ▶ v. **ruin**, wreck, spoil, mar, frustrate, disrupt, undo, scotch, destroy, shatter, devastate, demolish; informal mess up, foul up, put paid to, put the kibosh on, stymie.

blimp /blimp/ ▶ n. informal **1** a small nonrigid airship. **2** an obese person.

blind /blīnd/ ▶ adj. **1** not able to see. **2** done without being able to see or without certain information. **3** without awareness or judgment: *blind acceptance.* **4** concealed, closed, or blocked off: *a blind alley.* ▶ v. **1** make someone blind. **2** stop someone thinking clearly or sensibly: *he was blinded by rage.* ▶ n. a screen for a window.

> SYNONYMS ▶ adj. **1 sightless**, unsighted, visually impaired, unseeing. **2 uncritical**, unreasoned, unthinking, unquestioning, mindless, undiscerning, indiscriminate. **3** ***blind to*** *the realities of the situation* **unaware of**, oblivious to, ignorant of, unmindful of, heedless of, insensible to, indifferent to. ▶ n. **screen**, shade, sunshade, curtain, awning, canopy, louver, jalousie, shutter.

□ **blind date** a meeting with a person you have not met before, arranged in the hope of starting a romantic relationship. **blind man's bluff** (or **blind man's buff**) a game in which a player tries to catch people while wearing a blindfold. **blind spot 1** an area where someone's view is obstructed. **2** an inability to understand something: *he had a blind spot where ethics were concerned.* **3** a small area in the retina of the eye that is insensitive to light. **turn a blind eye** pretend not to notice. ■ **blind·ness** n.

blind·ers /'blīndərz/ ▶ pl.n. a pair of small flaps attached to a horse's bridle to prevent it from seeing sideways.

blind·fold /'blīnd,fōld/ ▶ n. a piece of cloth covering someone's eyes, so that they cannot see. ▶ v. cover someone's eyes with a blindfold.

blind·ing /'blīndiNG/ ▶ adj. **1** (of light) very bright. **2** (of pain) very severe. ■ **blind·ing·ly** adv.

blind·ly /blīndlē/ ▶ adv. **1** as if blind. **2** without reasoning or questioning.

> SYNONYMS **1 impetuously**, impulsively, recklessly, heedlessly. **2 uncritically**, unquestioningly, unthinkingly, mindlessly, indiscriminately.

bling /'bliNG /▶ n. informal showy, expensive jewelry and clothing.

blink /bliNGk/ ▶ v. **1** shut and open the eyes quickly. **2** (of a light) flash on and off. ▶ n. an act of blinking. □ **on the blink** informal (of a machine) no longer working properly.

blink·er /'bliNGkər/ ▶ pl.n. **1** a device that blinks, especially a vehicle's turn signal. **2** (**blinkers**) ⇒ BLINDERS.

blink·ered /'bliNGkərd/ ▶ adj. having a limited point of view.

blip /blip/ ▶ n. **1** a short, high-pitched sound made by an electronic device. **2** a small flashing point of light on a radar screen. **3** a temporary change in a situation or process that is generally steady: *a minor blip in the company's growth rate.* ▶ v. (**blips**, **blipping**, **blipped**) make a blip.

bliss /blis/ ▶ n. perfect happiness.

> SYNONYMS **joy**, happiness, pleasure, delight, ecstasy, elation, rapture, euphoria, seventh heaven. ANTONYMS misery.

bliss·ful /ˈblisfəl/ ▶ **adj.** full of joy and happiness. ■ **bliss·ful·ly adv.**

blis·ter /ˈblistər/ ▶ **n. 1** a small bubble on the skin filled with watery liquid. **2** a similar bubble on a surface. ▶ **v.** (**blisters, blistering, blistered**) form blisters.

blis·ter·ing /ˈblistəriNG/ ▶ **adj. 1** (of heat) very strong. **2** very fierce or forceful.

blithe /blīTH, blīTH/ ▶ **adj. 1** without thought or care: *a blithe ignorance of the facts.* **2** very happy.

> SYNONYMS **casual**, indifferent, unconcerned, unworried, untroubled, uncaring, careless, heedless, thoughtless; nonchalant, blasé. ANTONYMS thoughtful.

■ **blithe·ly adv.**

blith·er·ing /ˈbliTHəriNG/ ▶ **adj.** informal thoroughly stupid: *a blithering idiot.*

blitz /blits/ ▶ **n. 1** a sudden fierce military attack. **2** informal a sudden and concentrated effort. **3** (in football) a charge of the passer by the defensive linebackers just after the ball is snapped. ▶ **v.** make a sudden fierce attack on.

> SYNONYMS ▶ **n. bombing**, air raid, air strike, bombardment, barrage, attack, assault.

bliz·zard /ˈblizərd/ ▶ **n.** a snowstorm with high winds.

bloat /blōt/ ▶ **v.** cause something to swell with fluid or gas.

bloat·ed /blōtid/ ▶ **adj. 1** (of part of the body) swollen with fluid or gas. **2** excessive in size or amount: *the company trimmed its bloated labor force.*

> SYNONYMS **swollen**, distended, bulging, puffed out, inflated, dilated.

blob /bläb/ ▶ **n. 1** a drop of a thick or sticky liquid. **2** a roundish mass or shape.

> SYNONYMS **drop**, droplet, globule, bead, bubble, spot, dab, blotch, blot, dot, smudge.

bloc /bläk/ ▶ **n.** a group of allied countries with similar political systems.

> SYNONYMS **group**, alliance, coalition, federation, confederation, league, union, axis, association.

block /bläk/ ▶ **n. 1** a large solid piece of material. **2** a group of buildings with streets on all four sides. **3** an obstacle. ▶ **v. 1** prevent movement or flow in something. **2** prevent the progress of something.

> SYNONYMS ▶ **n. 1 chunk**, hunk, lump, wedge, cube, brick, ingot, slab, piece. **2 building**, complex, structure, development. **3 obstacle**, bar, barrier, impediment, hindrance, check, hurdle. ▶ **v. 1 clog**, stop up, choke, plug, bung up, obstruct, gum up, dam up, congest, jam. **2 hinder**, hamper, obstruct, impede, inhibit, halt, stop, bar, check, prevent, fend off, hold off, repel. ANTONYMS clear, aid.

□ **block capitals** plain capital letters. **block and tackle** a lifting mechanism consisting of ropes, a pulley block, and a hook. **knock someone's block off** informal hit someone on the head.

block·ade /bläˈkād/ ▶ **n.** a blocking of the way in or out of a place to prevent people or goods from entering or leaving it. ▶ **v.** (**blockades, blockading, blockaded**) block the way in or out of a place. □ **run a blockade** (of a ship) manage to enter or leave a blockaded port.

block·age /ˈbläkij/ ▶ **n.** an obstruction.

> SYNONYMS **obstruction**, stoppage, block, jam, congestion, bottleneck.

block·bust·er /ˈbläk,bəstər/ ▶ **n.** informal a movie or book that is very successful.

block·head /ˈbläk,hed/ ▶ **n.** informal a stupid person.

block·house /ˈbläk,hous/ ▶ **n.** a reinforced concrete shelter used as an observation point.

blog /bläg/ ▶ **n.** a personal website on which someone regularly writes about their experiences, interests, etc. ▶ **v.** (**blogs, blogging, blogged**) regularly update a blog. ■ **blog·ger n.**

blonde /bländ/ (also **blond**) ▶ **adj. 1** (of hair) pale yellow. **2** having pale yellow hair. ▶ **n.** a woman with blonde hair.

> SYNONYMS ▶ **adj. fair**, light, yellow, flaxen, golden. ANTONYMS dark.

blood /bləd/ ▶ **n. 1** the red liquid that flows through the arteries and veins. **2** family background: *she must have Irish blood.* ▶ **v.** give someone their first experience of an activity.

> SYNONYMS ▶ **n. 1 lifeblood**, gore, vital fluid. **2 ancestry**, lineage, descent, parentage, family, birth, extraction, origin, stock.

□ **blood brother** a man who has sworn to treat another man as a brother. **blood group** any of the various types into which human blood is classified for medical purposes. **blood feud** a lengthy conflict between families involving a cycle of revenge killings. **blood money** money paid to compensate the family of someone who has been killed. **blood pressure** the pressure created by blood as it moves around the body. **blood poisoning** a diseased state that results when harmful microorganisms have infected the blood. **blood relation** someone who is related to another by birth rather than marriage. **blood sport** a sport involving the hunting or killing of animals. **blood sugar** the concentration of glucose in the blood. **blood vessel** a vein, artery, or capillary carrying blood through the body. **first blood 1** the first shedding of blood in a fight. **2** the first point or advantage gained in a contest. **have blood on your hands** be responsible for someone's death. **in your blood** part of your character. **make someone's blood boil** make someone very angry. **make someone's blood run cold** horrify someone. **new** (or **fresh**) **blood** people who join a group and give it new ideas.

blood·bath /ˈbləd,baTH/ ▶ **n.** an event in which many people are violently killed.

blood·cur·dling /ˈbləd,kərd(ə)liNG/ ▶ **adj.** horrifying; causing great terror.

blood·hound /ˈbləd,hound/ ▶ **n.** a large hound used for following scents.

blood·less /ˈblədlis/ ▶ **adj. 1** without violence or killing: *a bloodless coup.* **2** (of the skin) drained of color. **3** lacking emotion or vitality.

blood·let·ting /ˈbləd,letiNG/ ▶ **n. 1** violent conflict. **2** (in the past) the removal of some of a patient's blood as a medical treatment.

blood·line /ˈbləd,līn/ ▶ **n.** a pedigree or set of ancestors.

blood·shed /ˈbləd,SHed/ ▶ **n.** the killing or wounding of people.

> SYNONYMS **slaughter**, massacre, killing, wounding, carnage, butchery, bloodletting, bloodbath.

blood·shot /'bləd,sʜät/ ▶ **adj.** (of the eyes) having tiny red blood vessels visible in the whites.

blood·stream /'bləd,strēm/ ▶ **n.** the blood circulating through the body.

blood·thirst·y /'bləd,ᴛʜərstē/ ▶ **adj.** (**bloodthirstier**, **bloodthirstiest**) taking pleasure in killing and violence.

> SYNONYMS **murderous**, homicidal, violent, vicious, barbarous, barbaric, savage, brutal, cutthroat.

blood·y /'blədē/ ▶ **adj.** (**bloodier**, **bloodiest**) **1** covered with or containing blood. **2** involving violence or cruelty. ▶ **v.** (**bloodies**, **bloodying**, **bloodied**) cover or stain with blood.

> SYNONYMS ▶ **adj. 1 bloodstained**, blood-soaked, gory, bleeding. **2 vicious**, ferocious, savage, fierce, brutal, cruel, murderous.

bloom /blo͞om/ ▶ **v. 1** produce flowers; be in flower. **2** be healthy and happy. ▶ **n. 1** a flower. **2** a state or period of blooming: *the apples trees were in bloom.* **3** a healthy glow in a person's complexion. **4** a powdery coating on the surface of some fruit.

> SYNONYMS ▶ **v. 1 flower**, blossom, open, mature. **2 flourish**, thrive, prosper, progress, burgeon; informal be in the pink. ANTONYMS wither, decline.

bloo·mers /'blo͞omərz/ ▶ **pl.n. 1** women's baggy knee-length underpants. **2** historical women's loose-fitting trousers.

bloop·er /'blo͞opər/ ▶ **n.** informal an embarrassing mistake.

blos·som /'bläsəm/ ▶ **n.** a flower or a mass of flowers on a tree. ▶ **v. 1** produce blossom. **2** mature or develop in a promising or healthy way: *our friendship blossomed into love.*

> SYNONYMS ▶ **n. flower**, bloom, bud. ▶ **v. 1 bloom**, flower, open, mature. **2 develop**, grow, mature, progress, evolve, burgeon, flourish, thrive, prosper, bloom. ANTONYMS wither, decline.

blot /blät/ ▶ **n. 1** a spot of ink. **2** a thing that spoils something good: *the hotel is a blot on the coastline.* ▶ **v.** (**blots**, **blotting**, **blotted**) **1** dry something with an absorbent material. **2** mark or spoil. **3** (**blot something out**) hide something. **4** (**blot out**) keep from your mind: *they wanted to blot out the bad news.*

> SYNONYMS ▶ **n. 1 patch**, dab, smudge, blotch, mark, dot, spot. **2 blemish**, taint, stain, blight, flaw, fault. **3** *a blot on the landscape* **eyesore**, monstrosity, mess; informal sight.

□ **blotting paper** absorbent paper used for drying ink when writing.

blotch /bläcʜ/ ▶ **n.** an irregular mark. ▶ **v.** mark something with blotches.

blotch·y /bläcʜē/ ▶ **adj.** marked with blotches.

> SYNONYMS **patchy**, smudged, dappled, mottled, spotty, marked.

blot·ter /'blätər/ ▶ **n.** a pad of blotting paper.

blouse /blous, blouz/ ▶ **n.** a woman's top that is similar to a shirt.

blous·on /'blou,sän, 'blo͞o-, ,zän/ ▶ **n.** a short loose-fitting jacket.

blow¹ /blō/ ▶ **v.** (**blows**, **blowing**, **blew** /blo͞o/; past participle **blown** /blōn/) **1** (of the wind) move. **2** send out air through pursed lips. **3** force air into an instrument through the mouth. **4** sound a horn. **5** break something open with explosives: *the blast blew the windows out of the van.* **6** burst through pressure or overheating. **7** informal spend money recklessly. **8** informal waste an opportunity. ▶ **n.** an act of blowing.

> SYNONYMS ▶ **v. 1 gust**, puff, flurry, blast, roar, bluster, rush, storm. **2 sweep**, carry, toss, drive, push, force, drift, flutter, waft, float, glide, whirl. **3** *he blew the trumpet* **sound**, blast, toot, play, pipe, trumpet.

□ **blow a fuse** informal lose your temper. **blow-dry** style the hair while drying it with a hand-held dryer. **blow hot and cold** keep changing your mind. **blow someone's mind** informal impress or affect someone very strongly. **blow your nose** clear your nose of mucus by blowing through it. **blow over** (of trouble) fade away. **blow your top** informal lose your temper. **blow up** explode. **blow something up 1** make something explode. **2** inflate something.

blow² ▶ **n. 1** a powerful stroke with a hand or weapon. **2** a sudden shock or disappointment.

> SYNONYMS **1 stroke**, knock, bang, hit, punch, thump, smack, crack, rap; informal whack, bash, clout, wallop. **2 upset**, disaster, setback, misfortune, disappointment, calamity, catastrophe, thunderbolt, bombshell, shock, surprise, jolt.

□ **blow-by-blow** giving every detail. **come to blows** start arguing or fighting about something.

blow·er /'blōər/ ▶ **n.** a device that creates a current of air to dry or heat something.

blow·fish /'blō,fisʜ/ ▶ **n.** (plural **blowfish** or **blowfishes**) a fish that is able to inflate its body when alarmed.

blow·fly /'blō,flī/ ▶ **n.** (plural **blowflies**) a large fly that lays its eggs in meat.

blow·hard /'blō,härd/ ▶ **n.** informal a boastful or pompous person.

blow·hole /'blō,hōl/ ▶ **n.** the nostril of a whale or dolphin on the top of its head.

blown /blōn/ past participle of **BLOW¹**.

blow·out /'blō,out/ ▶ **n.** the release of air or gas from a tire, oil well, etc.

blow·pipe /'blō,pīp/ ▶ **n.** a weapon consisting of a long tube through which an arrow or dart is blown.

blows·y /'blouzē/ (or **blowzy**) ▶ **adj.** (of a woman) plump and untidy.

blow·torch /'blō,tôrcʜ/ ▶ **n.** a portable device producing a hot flame, used to burn off paint.

blow·y /'blō-ē/ ▶ **adj.** windy or windswept.

BLT /,bēel'tē/ ▶ **n.** a bacon, lettuce, and tomato sandwich.

blub·ber¹ /'bləbər/ ▶ **n.** the fat of whales and seals. ■ **blub·ber·y adj.**

blub·ber² ▶ **v.** (**blubbers**, **blubbering**, **blubbered**) informal cry noisily.

bludg·eon /'bləjən/ ▶ **n.** a thick, heavy stick used as a weapon. ▶ **v. 1** hit someone with a thick, heavy stick. **2** bully someone into doing something.

> SYNONYMS ▶ **n. cudgel**, club, stick, truncheon, nightstick, blackjack, baton. ▶ **v. 1 batter**, cudgel, club, beat, thrash; informal clobber. **2 coerce**, force, compel, pressurize, pressure, bully, browbeat, hector, dragoon, steamroller; informal strong-arm, railroad.

blue /blo͞o/ ▶ **adj.** (**bluer**, **bluest**) **1** of the color of the sky on a sunny day. **2** informal sad or depressed. **3** informal indecent or pornographic: *a blue movie*. ▶ **n.** a blue color.

SYNONYMS ▶ **adj.** azure, cobalt, sapphire, navy, indigo, sky-blue, ultramarine, aquamarine, turquoise, cyan.

□ **blue-blooded** from a royal or aristocratic family. **blue cheese** cheese having veins of mold in it. **blue-chip** (of an investment) safe and reliable. **blue-collar** relating to manual work. **blue-eyed boy** informal, disapproving a person held in high regard and treated with special favor. **blue ribbon 1** a blue ribbon given to the winner of a competition. **2** (**blue-ribbon**) of the highest quality; first-class. **blue-sky** informal not yet capable of being achieved or making a profit. **blue tit** a common titmouse with a blue cap and yellow underparts. **blue whale** a bluish-gray whale that is the largest living animal. **once in a blue moon** informal very rarely. **out of the blue** unexpectedly.

blue·bell /ˈblo͞oˌbel/ ▶ **n.** a woodland plant with clusters of blue bell-shaped flowers.

blue·ber·ry /ˈblo͞oˌberē/ ▶ **n.** (plural **blueberries**) **1** a hardy dwarf shrub of the heath family, with small, whitish drooping flowers and dark blue edible berries. **2** the small, sweet edible berry of this plant.

blue·bird /ˈblo͞oˌbərd/ ▶ **n.** a songbird, the male of which has a blue head, back, and wings.

blue·bot·tle /ˈblo͞oˌbätl/ ▶ **n.** a large fly with a bluish body.

blue·grass /ˈblo͞oˌgras/ ▶ **n.** a kind of traditional American country music played on banjos and guitars.

blue·print /ˈblo͞oˌprint/ ▶ **n. 1** a technical drawing or plan. **2** a model or prototype.

SYNONYMS **plan**, design, diagram, drawing, sketch, layout, model, template, pattern, example, guide, prototype, pilot.

blues /blo͞oz/ ▶ **n. 1** slow, sad music of black American folk origin. **2** (**the blues**) informal feelings of sadness or depression. ■ **blues·y adj.**

blue·stock·ing /ˈblo͞oˌstäkiNG/ ▶ **n.** a serious intellectual woman.

bluff[1] /bləf/ ▶ **n.** a pretense that you know or can do something when this is not true. ▶ **v.** pretend in this way.

SYNONYMS ▶ **n. trick**, deception, fraud, ruse, pretense, sham, fake, hoax, charade; informal put-on. ▶ **v. pretend**, sham, fake, feign, lie, deceive, delude, mislead, trick, fool, hoodwink, dupe, hoax; informal con, kid, put on.

□ **call someone's bluff** challenge someone to do something in the belief that they will not be able to.

bluff[2] ▶ **adj.** frank and direct in a good-natured way.

bluff[3] ▶ **n.** a steep cliff or bank.

SYNONYMS **cliff**, promontory, headland, crag, bank, peak, escarpment, scarp.

blu·ish /ˈblo͞oiSH/ (or **blueish**) ▶ **adj.** having a blue tinge.

blun·der /ˈbləndər/ ▶ **n.** a clumsy mistake. ▶ **v.** (**blunders**, **blundering**, **blundered**) **1** make a blunder. **2** move clumsily or as if unable to see.

SYNONYMS ▶ **n. mistake**, error, gaffe, slip, oversight, faux pas; informal slip-up, boo-boo, blooper. ▶ **v. 1 make a mistake**, err, miscalculate, bungle, trip up; informal slip up, screw up, blow it, goof. **2 stumble**, lurch, stagger, flounder, grope.

blun·der·buss /ˈbləndərˌbəs/ ▶ **n.** historical a gun with a short, wide barrel.

blunt /blənt/ ▶ **adj. 1** not having a sharp edge or point. **2** frank and direct: *a blunt statement of fact*. ▶ **v.** make or become blunt.

SYNONYMS ▶ **adj. 1** *a blunt knife* **dull**, worn. **2** *a broad leaf with a blunt tip* **rounded**, flat, stubby. **3 straightforward**, frank, plain-spoken, candid, direct, bluff, forthright, unequivocal, brusque, abrupt, curt, bald, brutal, harsh, stark; informal upfront. ANTONYMS sharp, subtle. ▶ **v. dull**, deaden, dampen, numb, take the edge off, weaken, allay, diminish, lessen. ANTONYMS intensify.

■ **blunt·ly adv.**

blur /blər/ ▶ **v.** (**blurs**, **blurring**, **blurred**) make or become unclear or less distinct. ▶ **n.** something that cannot be seen, heard, or remembered clearly.

SYNONYMS ▶ **v. 1 cloud**, fog, obscure, dim, make hazy, make fuzzy, soften, dull, numb, deaden, mute. **2** (**blurred**) **indistinct**, fuzzy, hazy, misty, foggy, clouded, cloudy, faint, unclear, vague, indefinite, unfocused. ANTONYMS sharpen, clear, sharp.

■ **blur·ry adj.**

blurb /blərb/ ▶ **n.** a short description written to promote a book, movie, or other product.

blurt /blərt/ ▶ **v.** (**blurt something out**) say something suddenly and without thinking.

SYNONYMS **burst out with**, exclaim, call out, divulge, disclose, reveal, betray, let slip, give away; informal blab, spill the beans.

blush /bləSH/ ▶ **v.** become red in the face from shyness or embarrassment. ▶ **n.** a reddening of the face from shyness or embarrassment.

SYNONYMS ▶ **v. redden**, go pink, go red, flush, color, burn up. ▶ **n. flush**, rosiness, redness, pinkness, bloom, glow.

blush·er /ˈbləSHər/ ▶ **n.** a cosmetic used to give a warm pink, red, peach, or bronze tinge to the cheeks.

blus·ter /ˈbləstər/ ▶ **v.** (**blusters**, **blustering**, **blustered**) **1** talk loudly or aggressively but without having any effect. **2** (of wind or rain) blow or beat fiercely and noisily. ▶ **n.** loud and aggressive talk that does not have much effect.

blus·ter·y /ˈbləstərē/ ▶ **adj.** (of weather) featuring strong winds.

SYNONYMS **stormy**, gusty, blowy, windy, squally, wild. ANTONYMS calm.

blvd. ▶ **abbr.** boulevard.

BM ▶ **abbr. 1** Bachelor of Medicine. **2** Bachelor of Music.

BMI ▶ **abbr.** body mass index, a measure of whether someone is over- or underweight.

BMX ▶ **abbr.** a sturdy bicycle for cross-country riding or racing.

bo·a /ˈbōə/ ▶ **n. 1** a large snake that winds itself around and crushes its prey. **2** a long, thin scarf of feathers or fur.

boar /bôr/ ▶ **n.** (plural **boar** or **boars**) **1** (also **wild boar**) a wild pig with tusks. **2** a male pig.

board /bôrd/ ▶ n. **1** a long, narrow, flat piece of wood used in building. **2** a rectangular piece of stiff material used as a surface for a particular purpose. **3** the people who control and direct an organization. **4** regular meals provided in return for payment. ▶ v. **1** get on a ship, aircraft, or other passenger vehicle. **2** (**board something up** or **over**) seal something in with pieces of wood. **3** have a bedroom and receive meals in return for payment. **4** (of a pupil) live at school during the semester in return for payment.

SYNONYMS ▶ n. **1 plank**, beam, panel, slat, batten, timber. **2 committee**, council, panel, directorate, commission. ▶ v. **1 get on**, go on board, go aboard, enter, mount, ascend, embark, catch. **2 lodge**, live, reside, stay, room, be housed. **3 accommodate**, take in, put up, house, keep, billet.

□ **board game** a game in which counters are moved around a board. **boarding house** a private house providing rooms and meals for paying guests. **boarding school** a school at which the students live during the semester. **go by the board** (of a plan or principle) be rejected or abandoned. **on board** on or in a ship, aircraft, or other vehicle.

board·er /ˈbôrdər/ ▶ n. a student who lives at school during the semester.

board·room /ˈbôrdˌro͞om, -ˌro͝om/ ▶ n. a room in which a board of directors regularly meets.

board·walk /ˈbôrdˌwôk/ ▶ n. a promenade along a beach or waterfront.

boast /bōst/ ▶ v. **1** talk about yourself with too much pride. **2** (of a place or organization) have something as an impressive feature: *the hotel boasts high standards of comfort.* ▶ n. an act of boasting.

SYNONYMS ▶ v. **1 brag**, crow, swagger, swank, show off, blow your own horn, sing your own praises; informal talk big, lay it on thick. **2** *the hotel boasts a fine restaurant* **have**, possess, own, enjoy, pride yourself/itself on, offer. ▶ n. **1 brag**, exaggeration, overstatement. **2 pride**, joy, pride and joy, apple of someone's eye, wonder, delight.

boast·ful /ˈbōstfəl/ ▶ adj. showing excessive pride in yourself.

SYNONYMS **bragging**, swaggering, bumptious, swell-headed, swollen-headed, puffed up, full of yourself, cocky, conceited, arrogant; informal swanky, bigheaded. ANTONYMS modest.

■ **boast·ful·ly** adv.

boat /bōt/ ▶ n. **1** a vehicle that travels on water and is smaller than a ship. **2** a flattish jug for sauce or gravy.

SYNONYMS **vessel**, craft, watercraft, ship; literary keel, barque.

□ **be in the same boat** informal be in the same difficult situation as other people. **boat people** refugees who have left a country by sea. **miss the boat** informal be too slow to take advantage of something. **rock the boat** informal make a situation unsettled.

boat·er /ˈbōtər/ ▶ n. a flat-topped straw hat with a brim.

boat·hook /ˈbōtˌho͝ok/ ▶ n. a long pole with a hook and a spike at one end, used for fending off or pulling a boat.

boat·man /ˈbōtmən/ ▶ n. (plural **boatmen**) a person who provides transport by boat.

boat·swain /ˈbōsən/ (or **bo'sun** or **bosun**) ▶ n. an officer in charge of equipment and the crew on a ship.

bob[1] /bäb/ ▶ v. (**bobs**, **bobbing**, **bobbed**) **1** make a quick, short movement up and down. **2** curtsy briefly. ▶ n. a bobbing movement.

SYNONYMS ▶ v. **move up and down**, bounce, toss, skip, dance, wobble, jiggle, joggle, jolt, jerk.

bob[2] ▶ n. **1** a short hairstyle that hangs evenly all around. **2** a weight on a pendulum or plumb line. ▶ v. (**bobs**, **bobbing**, **bobbed**) cut hair in a bob.

bob·bin /ˈbäbin/ ▶ n. a reel for holding thread.

bob·ble /ˈbäbəl/ ▶ n. a small ball made of strands of wool, used as a decoration on a hat or on furnishings.

bob·by pin /ˈbäbēˌpin/ ▶ n. a sprung hairpin.

bob·sled /ˈbäbˌsled/ ▶ n. a mechanically steered and braked sled, used for racing down an ice-covered run.

bode /bōd/ ▶ v. (**bodes**, **boding**, **boded**) (**bode well** or **ill**) be a sign of a good or bad outcome: *the movie's success bodes well for similar projects.*

bo·de·ga /bōˈdāgə/ ▶ n. (in Spanish-speaking communities) a grocery store.

bod·ice /ˈbädis/ ▶ n. **1** the part of a dress above the waist. **2** a woman's sleeveless undergarment.

bod·i·ly /ˈbädl-ē/ ▶ adj. relating to the body. ▶ adv. by taking hold of a person's body with force: *he hauled her bodily from the van.*

SYNONYMS ▶ adj. **physical**, corporeal, corporal, mortal, material, tangible, concrete, real, actual, incarnate. ANTONYMS spiritual, mental. ▶ adv. **forcefully**, forcibly, violently, completely, entirely.

bod·kin /ˈbädkin/ ▶ n. a thick needle with a blunt, rounded end.

bod·y /ˈbädē/ ▶ n. (plural **bodies**) **1** a person's or animal's physical structure. **2** the main part of the body, apart from the head and limbs. **3** the main or central part of something: *the body of the aircraft was filled to capacity.* **4** a mass or collection. **5** a group of people organized for a particular purpose: *a regulatory body.*

SYNONYMS **1 figure**, frame, form, physique, anatomy, skeleton. **2 torso**, trunk. **3 corpse**, carcass, skeleton, remains; informal stiff; Medicine cadaver. **4 main part**, core, heart, hub. **5 association**, organization, assembly, delegation, committee, executive, company, society, corporation, group.

□ **body clock** a person's biological clock. **body language** the showing of your feelings through the way in which you move or hold your body. **body politic** the people of a nation or society considered as an organized group of citizens. **body stocking** an all-in-one stretchy garment that covers the body. **keep body and soul together** stay alive in difficult circumstances. **over my dead body** informal used to express strong opposition.

bod·y·build·er /ˈbädēˌbildər/ ▶ n. a person who enlarges their muscles through exercise.

bod·y·guard /ˈbädēˌgärd/ ▶ n. a person paid to protect someone rich or famous.

bod·y·suit /ˈbädēˌso͞ot/ ▶ n. a woman's close-fitting one-piece stretch garment for the torso.

bod·y·work /ˈbädēˌwərk/ ▶ **n.** the metal outer shell of a vehicle.

Boer /bôr, bo͝or/ ▶ **n.** a member of the Dutch people who settled in southern Africa.

bog /bäg, bôg/ ▶ **n.** an area of soft, wet ground. ▶ **v.** (**be/get bogged down**) be prevented from making progress.

> SYNONYMS ▶ **n.** **marsh**, swamp, mire, quagmire, morass, slough, fen, wetland.

■ **bog·gy adj.**

bo·gey¹ /ˈbōgē/ Golf ▶ **n.** (plural **bogeys**) a score of one stroke over par at a hole. ▶ **v.** (**bogeys**, **bogeying**, **bogeyed**) play a hole in one stroke over par.

bo·gey² /ˈbōgē, ˈbo͝ogē/ (or **bogy**) ▶ **n.** (plural **bogeys** or **bogies**) an evil or mischievous spirit.

bo·gey·man /ˈbo͝ogēˌman, ˈbō-/ (or **bogyman**) ▶ **n.** (plural **bogeymen**) an evil spirit.

bog·gle /ˈbägəl/ ▶ **v.** (**boggles**, **boggling**, **boggled**) informal **1** be astonished or baffled: *the mind boggles at the complexity of the system.* **2** (**boggle at**) hesitate to do.

bo·gus /ˈbōgəs/ ▶ **adj.** not genuine or true.

> SYNONYMS **fake**, spurious, false, fraudulent, sham, counterfeit, forged, feigned; informal phony, pretend. ANTONYMS genuine.

Bo·he·mi·an /bōˈhēmēən/ ▶ **n.** **1** a native or inhabitant of Bohemia. **2** (also **bohemian**) an artistic and unconventional person. ▶ **adj.** unconventional.

> SYNONYMS ▶ **n.** **nonconformist**, avant-gardist, free spirit, dropout; hippie, beatnik. ANTONYMS conservative. ▶ **adj.** **unconventional**, nonconformist, unorthodox, avant-garde, irregular, alternative; artistic; informal artsy-fartsy, way-out, offbeat. ANTONYMS conventional.

bo·ho /ˈbōˌhō/ ▶ **n. & adj.** (plural **bohos**) informal ⇨ **BOHEMIAN n. sense 2 & adj.**

boil¹ /boil/ ▶ **v.** **1** (of a liquid) reach a temperature where it bubbles and turns to vapor. **2** cook food in boiling water. **3** (**boil down to**) amount to. ▶ **n.** the process of boiling.

> SYNONYMS ▶ **v.** **simmer**, bubble, stew, seethe, froth, foam.

□ **boiling point** the temperature at which a liquid boils.

boil² ▶ **n.** an inflamed pus-filled swelling on the skin.

> SYNONYMS **swelling**, spot, pimple, blister, gathering, pustule, carbuncle, abscess.

boil·er /ˈboilər/ ▶ **n.** a device for heating water.

boil·ing /ˈboiliNG/ ▶ **adj.** **1** (of a liquid) at or near the temperature at which it boils. **2** informal very hot.

bois·ter·ous /ˈboist(ə)rəs/ ▶ **adj.** lively and high-spirited.

> SYNONYMS **lively**, animated, exuberant, spirited, noisy, loud, rowdy, unruly, wild, uproarious, unrestrained, uninhibited, uncontrolled, rough, disorderly, riotous; informal rambunctious. ANTONYMS restrained.

■ **bois·ter·ous·ly adv.**

bold /bōld/ ▶ **adj.** **1** brave and confident. **2** (of a color or design) strong or vivid. **3** (of printed words or letters) in thick, dark type.

> SYNONYMS **1** **daring**, intrepid, brave, courageous, valiant, valorous, fearless, dauntless, audacious, daredevil, adventurous, heroic, plucky; informal gutsy, spunky. **2** **striking**, vivid, bright, strong, eye-catching, prominent, gaudy, lurid, garish. ANTONYMS timid, faint.

□ **as bold as brass** too confident; not showing enough respect. ■ **bold·ly adv.** **bold·ness n.**

bole /bōl/ ▶ **n.** a tree trunk.

bo·le·ro /bəˈle(ə)rō/ ▶ **n.** (plural **boleros**) **1** a Spanish dance in simple triple time. **2** a woman's short open jacket.

Bo·liv·i·an /bəˈlivēən/ ▶ **n.** a person from Bolivia. ▶ **adj.** relating to Bolivia.

boll /bōl/ ▶ **n.** the rounded seed capsule of plants such as cotton or flax.

bol·lard /ˈbälərd/ ▶ **n.** a short post on a ship or quayside for securing a rope.

Bol·ly·wood /ˈbälēˌwo͝od/ ▶ **n.** informal the Indian popular film industry, based in Bombay.

bo·lo·gna /bəˈlōnē/ ▶ **n.** a large smoked, seasoned sausage.

Bol·she·vik /ˈbōlsHəˌvik/ ▶ **n.** a member of the group that seized power in the Russian Revolution of 1917. ■ **Bol·she·vism** /-ˌvizəm/ **n.**

bol·ster /ˈbōlstər/ ▶ **n.** a long, firm pillow. ▶ **v.** (**bolsters**, **bolstering**, **bolstered**) support or strengthen: *campaigns to bolster the president's image.*

> SYNONYMS ▶ **v.** **strengthen**, reinforce, boost, fortify, support, prop up, buoy up, shore up, buttress, maintain, help, augment, increase.

bolt /bōlt/ ▶ **n.** **1** a heavy metal pin with a head that screws into a nut, used to fasten things together. **2** a bar that slides into a socket to fasten a door or window. **3** a short, heavy arrow shot from a crossbow. **4** a flash of lightning. **5** a roll of fabric. ▶ **v.** **1** fasten with a bolt. **2** run away suddenly. **3** eat food quickly. **4** (of a plant) grow quickly upwards and stop flowering as seeds develop.

> SYNONYMS ▶ **n.** **1** *the bolt on the door* **bar**, lock, catch, latch, fastener. **2** *nuts and bolts* **pin**, rivet, peg, screw. ▶ **v.** **1** *he bolted the door* **lock**, bar, latch, fasten, secure. **2** *the lid was bolted down* **pin**, rivet, peg, screw, fasten, fix. **3** **dash**, dart, run, sprint, hurtle, rush, fly, shoot; informal tear, scoot. **4** **gobble**, gulp, wolf, guzzle, devour; informal demolish, polish off, scarf (down), shovel in.

□ **a bolt from** (or **out of**) **the blue** a sudden and unexpected event. **bolt upright** with the back very straight.

bomb /bäm/ ▶ **n.** **1** a device designed to explode and cause damage. **2** (**the bomb**) nuclear weapons. **3** (**the bomb**) informal very good; excellent: *that song is the bomb.* ▶ **v.** **1** attack with a bomb or bombs. **2** informal fail badly.

> SYNONYMS ▶ **n.** **explosive**, incendiary (device), missile, projectile. ▶ **v.** **blow up**, blast, shell, blitz, strafe, pound, bombard, attack, assault, destroy, demolish.

bom·bard /bämˈbärd/ ▶ **v.** **1** attack continuously with bombs or other missiles. **2** direct a continuous flow of questions or information at.

> SYNONYMS **1** **shell**, pound, blitz, strafe, bomb, batter, blast, pelt. **2** **swamp**, inundate, flood, deluge, snow under, overwhelm.

bom·bar·dier /ˌbämbə(r)ˈdi(ə)r/ ▶ **n.** **1** a member of a bomber crew in the US Air Force who is responsible for releasing the bombs. **2** a rank of noncommissioned officer in certain Canadian and British artillery regiments, equivalent to corporal.

bom·bard·ment /bämˈbärdmənt/ ▶ **n.** an act of bombarding.

SYNONYMS **assault**, attack, bombing, shelling, strafing, blitz, air raid, cannonade, fusillade, barrage, broadside.

bom·bast /ˈbämbast/ ▶ **n.** language that sounds impressive but has little meaning.

bom·bas·tic /bämˈbastik/ ▶ **adj.** using inflated language.

SYNONYMS **pompous**, blustering, turgid, verbose, orotund, high-flown, high-sounding, overwrought, pretentious, ostentatious, grandiloquent; informal highfalutin.

bom·ba·zine /ˌbämbəˈzēn, ˈbämbəˌzēn/ ▶ **n.** a twill dress fabric of worsted and silk or cotton.

bombed /bämd/ ▶ **adj.** informal intoxicated by drink or drugs.

bomb·er /ˈbämər/ ▶ **n.** **1** an aircraft designed for dropping bombs. **2** a person who plants bombs. □ **bomber jacket** a short zipped jacket, usually leather, that is gathered at the waist and cuffs.

bomb·shell /ˈbämˌsнel/ ▶ **n.** **1** a great surprise or shock. **2** informal a very attractive woman.

bo·na fide /ˈbōnə ˌfīd, ˈbänə/ ▶ **adj.** genuine; real.

SYNONYMS **authentic**, genuine, real, true, actual; legal, legitimate, lawful, valid, proper; informal legit, the real thing, the real McCoy, the genuine article. ANTONYMS bogus.

bo·na fi·des /ˈbōnə ˌfīdz, ˈfīdēz, ˈbänə/ ▶ **n.** **1** honesty and trustworthiness. **2** informal evidence proving that a person is what they claim to be; credentials.

bo·nan·za /bəˈnanzə/ ▶ **n.** **1** a situation creating wealth or success. **2** a large amount of something desirable.

SYNONYMS **windfall**, godsend, blessing, bonus, stroke of luck; informal jackpot.

bon·bon /ˈbänˌbän/ ▶ **n.** a piece of candy, especially one covered with chocolate.

bond /bänd/ ▶ **n.** **1** a thing used to tie or fasten things together. **2** (**bonds**) ropes or chains used to hold someone prisoner. **3** an instinct or feeling that draws people together: *the bonds between mother and daughter*. **4** a legally binding agreement. **5** a certificate issued by a government or public company promising to repay money lent to it at a fixed rate of interest and at a particular time. ▶ **v.** **1** join or be joined securely to something else. **2** feel connected to someone.

SYNONYMS ▶ **n.** **1 friendship**, relationship, fellowship, partnership, association, affiliation, alliance, attachment, tie, connection, link. **2 promise**, pledge, vow, oath, word (of honor), guarantee, assurance, agreement, contract, pact, deal. ▶ **v. join**, fasten, fix, affix, attach, secure, bind, stick, fuse.

□ **bond paper** high-quality writing paper.

bond·age /ˈbändij/ ▶ **n.** the state of being a slave or of having no freedom.

bone /bōn/ ▶ **n.** **1** any of the pieces of hard material that make up the skeleton in vertebrates. **2** the hard material of which bones are made. ▶ **v.** (**bones**, **boning**, **boned**) remove the bones from meat or fish before cooking. □ **bone china** white porcelain that contains a mineral obtained from bone. **bone dry** completely dry. **bone of contention** something argued about. **close to the bone** (of a remark) accurate to the point of making you feel uncomfortable. **have a bone to pick with** informal have reason to quarrel with someone or to tell them off. **in your bones** felt or believed deeply or instinctively. **make no bones about** be direct in stating or dealing with. **work your fingers to the bone** work very hard. ■ **bone·less** adj.

bone·head /ˈbōnˌhed/ ▶ **n.** informal a stupid person.

bone·meal /ˈbōnˌmēl/ ▶ **n.** ground bones used as a fertilizer.

bon·fire /ˈbänˌfīr/ ▶ **n.** an open-air fire lit to burn trash or as a celebration.

bon·go /ˈbänɢgō, ˈbôɴɢ-/ ▶ **n.** (plural **bongos**) each of a pair of small drums that are held between the knees.

bon·ho·mie /ˈbänəˌmē, ˌbänəˈmē/ ▶ **n.** good-natured friendliness.

bo·ni·to /bəˈnētō/ ▶ **n.** (plural **bonitos**) a small tuna with dark stripes.

bonk /bäɴɢk/ ▶ **v.** informal hit or knock. ▶ **n.** a hit or knock.

bon·kers /ˈbäɴɢkərz/ ▶ **adj.** informal crazy; insane.

bon mot /ˌbän ˈmō, ˌbôɴ ˈmō/ ▶ **n.** (plural **bons mots** same pronunciation or /ˈmōz/) a clever or witty remark.

bon·net /ˈbänit/ ▶ **n.** a woman's or child's hat tied under the chin.

bon·sai /bänˈsī, ˈbänsī/ ▶ **n.** the art of growing miniature ornamental trees.

bo·nus /ˈbōnəs/ ▶ **n.** **1** a sum of money added to a person's wages for good performance. **2** an unexpected extra benefit.

SYNONYMS **1 gratuity**, handout, gift, present, reward, prize, incentive; informal perk, sweetener. **2 advantage**, plus, benefit, extra, boon, blessing, godsend, stroke of luck, attraction. ANTONYMS disadvantage.

bon vi·vant /ˈbän vēˈvänt, ˌbôɴ vēˈväɴ/ ▶ **n.** (plural **bon vivants** or **bons vivants**) a person who enjoys a sociable and luxurious lifestyle.

bon vo·yage /ˈbän voiˈäzн, ˈbōn, bôɴ/ ▶ **exclam.** have a good journey.

bon·y /ˈbōnē/ ▶ **adj.** (**bonier**, **boniest**) **1** containing or resembling bones. **2** so thin that the bones can be seen.

SYNONYMS **skinny**, thin, lean, gaunt, scrawny, spare, skin and bones, skeletal, emaciated, underweight. ANTONYMS plump.

boo /bo͞o/ ▶ **exclam.** **1** said suddenly to surprise someone. **2** said to show disapproval or contempt. ▶ **v.** (**boos**, **booing**, **booed**) say "boo" to show disapproval or contempt.

boob /bo͞ob/ ▶ **n.** informal a foolish or stupid person. □ **boob tube** informal television or a television set.

boo-boo ▶ **n.** informal a mistake.

boo·by /ˈbo͞obē/ ▶ **n.** (plural **boobies**) informal a stupid person. □ **booby prize** a prize given to someone who comes in last in a contest. **booby trap** an object containing a hidden explosive device.

boo·dle /ˈbo͞odl/ ▶ **n.** informal money, especially that gained illegally or spent foolishly.

boo·ger /ˈbo͝ogər, ˈbo͝ogər/ ▶ n. **1** ⇒ **BOGEYMAN**. **2** informal a piece of dried nasal mucus.

boog·ie /ˈbo͝ogē/ ▶ n. (or **boogie-woogie** /-ˈwo͝ogē/) a style of blues played on the piano with a strong, fast beat. ▶ v. (**boogies**, **boogieing**, **boogied**) informal **1** dance to pop music. **2** move or leave somewhere fast.

book /bo͝ok/ ▶ n. **1** a written or printed work consisting of pages fastened together along one side and bound in covers. **2** a main division of a literary work or of the Bible. **3** (**books**) a record of financial transactions. ▶ v. **1** reserve accommodations or a ticket. **2** engage a performer or guest for an event. **3** (**be booked up**) have all places or dates reserved. **4** make an official note of the name of someone who has broken a law or rule.

> SYNONYMS ▶ n. **1 volume**, tome, publication, title, novel, treatise, manual. **2 notepad**, notebook, pad, scratch pad, exercise book, logbook, ledger, journal, diary. ▶ v. **reserve**, prearrange, order.

□ **book club** a group of people who discuss books together. **by the book** strictly according to the rules. **on the books** contained in a list of members, employees, or clients. **throw the book at** informal reprimand or punish as severely as possible.

book·case /ˈbo͝okˌkās/ ▶ n. a cabinet containing shelves on which books are kept.

book·end /ˈbo͝okˌend/ ▶ n. a support placed at the end of a row of books to keep them upright.

book·ie /ˈbo͝okē/ ▶ n. (plural **bookies**) informal a bookmaker.

book·ing /ˈbo͝okiNG/ ▶ n. **1** an act of reserving accommodations, a ticket, etc. **2** Soccer an instance of a player being cautioned by the referee for foul play.

book·ish /ˈbo͝okisH/ ▶ adj. very interested in reading and studying.

book·keep·ing /ˈbo͝okˌkēpiNG/ ▶ n. the keeping of records of financial transactions.

book·let /ˈbo͝oklit/ ▶ n. a small, thin book with paper covers.

> SYNONYMS **pamphlet**, brochure, folder, mailer, leaflet, tract.

book·mak·er /ˈbo͝okˌmākər/ ▶ n. a person who takes bets and pays out winnings.

book·mark /ˈbo͝okˌmärk/ ▶ n. **1** a strip of leather, cardboard, fabric, or other material used to mark a place in a book. **2** a record of the address of a computer file, Internet page, etc., enabling a user to return to it quickly. ▶ v. record the address of a computer file, Internet page, etc.

book·worm /ˈbo͝okˌwərm/ ▶ n. informal a person who loves reading.

Bool·e·an /ˈbo͞olēən/ ▶ adj. Computing (of a system of notation) used to represent logical operations by means of the binary digits 0 (false) and 1 (true).

boom¹ /bo͞om/ ▶ n. a deep, loud sound. ▶ v. make a boom.

> SYNONYMS ▶ n. **roar**, rumble, thunder, crashing, drumming, pounding, echoing, resonance, reverberation. ▶ v. **1 roar**, rumble, thunder, crash, roll, clap, explode, bang, resound, blare, echo, resonate, reverberate. **2 shout**, yell, bellow, roar, thunder, bawl; informal holler.

boom² ▶ n. **1** a movable pole to which the bottom of a sail is attached. **2** a movable arm carrying a microphone or movie camera. **3** a beam used to form a barrier across the mouth of a harbor.

boom³ ▶ n. a period of great prosperity or rapid economic growth: *a boom in precious metal mining.* ▶ v. enjoy a period of great prosperity or rapid economic growth.

> SYNONYMS ▶ n. **increase**, growth, advance, boost, escalation, improvement, upsurge, upturn. ANTONYMS slump. ▶ v. **flourish**, thrive, prosper, burgeon, progress, improve, pick up, expand.

boom·er /ˈbo͞omər/ ▶ n. informal **1** (also **baby boomer**) a person born in the period after World War II. **2** something large or notable of its kind.

boo·mer·ang /ˈbo͞oməˌraNG/ ▶ n. a curved flat piece of wood that follows a circle through the air and returns to you when you throw it.

boon /bo͞on/ ▶ n. a very helpful thing.

> SYNONYMS **blessing**, godsend, bonus, plus, benefit, advantage, help, aid, asset; stroke of luck; informal perk; formal perquisite. ANTONYMS curse.

□ **boon companion** a close friend.

boon·docks /ˈbo͞onˌdäks/ ▶ pl.n. (**the boondocks**) informal rough or isolated country.

boon·dog·gle /ˈbo͞onˌdägəl, -ˌdôgəl/ ▶ n. informal an unnecessary, wasteful, or fraudulent project.

boon·ies /ˈbo͞onēz/ ▶ pl.n. short for **BOONDOCKS**.

boor /bo͝or/ ▶ n. a rough and bad-mannered person.

> SYNONYMS **lout**, oaf, ruffian, thug, barbarian, Neanderthal, brute, beast; informal yahoo, clod, roughneck, pig.

boor·ish /ˈbo͝orisH/ ▶ adj. rude and ill-mannered.

> SYNONYMS **coarse**, uncouth, rude, vulgar, uncivilized, unrefined, oafish, ignorant, uncultured, philistine, rough, thuggish, loutish, Neanderthal. ANTONYMS refined.

boost /bo͞ost/ ▶ v. help or encourage: *a range of measures to boost tourism.* ▶ n. a source of help or encouragement.

> SYNONYMS ▶ v. **increase**, raise, escalate, improve, strengthen, inflate, push up, promote, advance, foster, stimulate, encourage, facilitate, help, assist, aid; informal hike, bump up. ANTONYMS decrease. ▶ n. **1** *a boost to your morale* **uplift**, lift, spur, encouragement, help, inspiration, stimulus, fillip; informal shot in the arm. **2** *a boost in sales* **increase**, expansion, upturn, upsurge, rise, escalation, improvement, advance, growth, boom; informal hike. ANTONYMS decrease.

boost·er /ˈbo͞ostər/ ▶ n. **1** a dose of a vaccine that increases or renews the effect of an earlier one. **2** the part of a rocket or spacecraft used to give acceleration after liftoff.

boot /bo͞ot/ ▶ n. **1** an item of footwear covering the foot and the ankle or lower leg. **2** informal a hard kick. **3** = **DENVER BOOT**. **4** (**the boot**) informal dismissal from a job. ▶ v. **1** informal kick someone hard. **2** (**boot someone out**) informal force someone to leave. **3** (**boot up**) start a computer and make it ready to operate.

> SYNONYMS ▶ v. **kick**, punt, tap, propel, drive, knock.

□ **boot camp** a military training camp with very

harsh discipline. **give** (or **get**) **the boot** informal dismiss (or be dismissed) from a job. **to boot** as well.

booth /bo͞oTH/ ▶ **n. 1** an enclosed compartment that gives you privacy when telephoning, voting, etc. **2** a small temporary structure used for selling goods or staging shows at a market or fair.

> SYNONYMS **1** *a phone booth* **cubicle**, kiosk, box, compartment, enclosure, cabin. **2 stall**, stand, kiosk.

boot·ie /ˈbo͞otē, bo͞oˈtē/ (or **bootee**) ▶ **n. 1** a baby's woolen sock. **2** a woman's short boot.

boot·leg /ˈbo͞otˌleg/ ▶ **adj.** made or distributed illegally. ■ **boot·leg·ger n. boot·leg·ging n.**

boot·lick·er /ˈbo͞otˌlikər/ ▶ **n.** informal a person who tries to gain favor by servile behavior.

boot·strap /ˈbo͞otˌstrap/ ▶ **n.** a loop at the back of a boot, used to pull it on. ▫ **pull yourself up by your bootstraps** improve your position by your own efforts.

boo·ty /ˈbo͞otē/ ▶ **n.** valuable stolen goods.

> SYNONYMS **loot**, plunder, haul, spoils, ill-gotten gains, pickings; informal swag.

booze /bo͞oz/ informal ▶ **n.** alcoholic drink. ▶ **v.** (**boozes**, **boozing**, **boozed**) drink a lot of alcohol. ■ **booz·er n. booz·y adj.**

bop¹ /bäp/ (or **bebop** /ˈbēˌbäp/) informal ▶ **n.** a dance to pop music. ▶ **v.** (**bops**, **bopping**, **bopped**) **1** dance to pop music. **2** move or travel energetically. ■ **bop·per n.**

bop² ▶ **v.** (**bops**, **bopping**, **bopped**) informal hit or punch someone.

bo·rac·ic /bəˈrasik/ ▶ **adj.** having to do with boric acid.

bor·age /ˈbôrij, ˈbär-/ ▶ **n.** a plant with bright blue flowers and hairy leaves.

bo·rax /ˈbôraks/ ▶ **n.** a white mineral used in making glass and ceramics, as a metallurgical flux, and as an antiseptic.

bor·del·lo /bôrˈdelō/ ▶ **n.** (plural **bordellos**) literary a brothel.

> SYNONYMS **brothel**, whorehouse; informal cathouse; euphemistic massage parlor; old use bawdy house, house of ill repute.

bor·der /ˈbôrdər/ ▶ **n. 1** a boundary between two countries, states, or areas. **2** a decorative band around the edge of something. **3** a strip of ground along the edge of a lawn where flowers or shrubs are planted. ▶ **v.** (**borders**, **bordering**, **bordered**) **1** form a border around or along. **2** (of a country, state, or area) be next to. **3** (**border on**) come near to: *his demands bordered on the impossible*.

> SYNONYMS ▶ **n. 1 edge**, margin, perimeter, circumference, periphery, rim, fringe, verge, sides. **2 frontier**, boundary, borderline, perimeter. ▶ **v. 1 surround**, enclose, encircle, edge, fringe, bound, flank. **2 edge**, fringe, hem, trim, pipe, finish. **3 adjoin**, abut, be next to, be adjacent to, touch.

bor·der·line /ˈbôrdərˌlīn/ ▶ **n.** a boundary. ▶ **adj.** on the boundary between two qualities or categories: *the borderline area between sleep and waking*.

> SYNONYMS ▶ **n. dividing line**, division, line, cutoff point; threshold, margin, border, boundary. ▶ **adj.** *borderline cases* **marginal**, uncertain, indefinite, unsettled, undecided, doubtful, indeterminate, unclassifiable, equivocal; questionable, debatable, controversial, contentious, problematic; informal iffy.

bore¹ /bôr/ ▶ **v.** (**bores**, **boring**, **bored**) make a hole in something with a drill or other tool. ▶ **n.** the hollow part inside a gun barrel or other tube.

> SYNONYMS ▶ **v. drill**, pierce, perforate, puncture, punch, tunnel, burrow, mine, dig, gouge, sink.

bore² ▶ **n.** a dull person or activity. ▶ **v.** (**bores**, **boring**, **bored**) make someone feel tired and unenthusiastic by being dull.

> SYNONYMS ▶ **n. tedious person/thing**, tiresome person/thing, bother, nuisance, pest, annoyance, trial, thorn in your flesh/side; informal drag, pain (in the neck), headache, hassle. ▶ **v. weary**, pall on, tire, fatigue, put to sleep, leave cold; informal turn off. ANTONYMS interest.

bore³ past of BEAR¹.

bore⁴ ▶ **n.** a high wave caused by the meeting of two tides or by a tide rushing up a narrow estuary.

bored /bôrd/ ▶ **adj.** feeling tired and unenthusiastic because you have nothing interesting to do.

> USAGE
> Use **bored by** or **bored with** rather than **bored of**.

bore·dom /ˈbôrdəm/ ▶ **n.** the state of feeling bored.

> SYNONYMS **tedium**, ennui, apathy, weariness, dullness, monotony, repetitiveness, flatness, dreariness. ANTONYMS interest, excitement.

bore·hole /ˈbôrˌhōl/ ▶ **n.** a deep hole in the ground made to find water or oil.

bo·ric ac·id /ˈbôrik ˈasid/ ▶ **n.** a substance made from boron, used as an antiseptic.

bor·ing /ˈbôriNG/ ▶ **adj.** dull and uninteresting.

> SYNONYMS **tedious**, dull, dreary, monotonous, repetitive, uneventful, unimaginative, characterless, featureless, colorless, lifeless, uninteresting, unexciting, lackluster, humdrum, mind-numbing, soul-destroying, wearisome, tiresome; informal deadly, dullsville. ANTONYMS interesting, exciting.

born /bôrn/ ▶ **adj. 1** having come out of your mother's body; having started life. **2** having a particular natural ability: *a born engineer*. **3** (**born of**) existing as a result of a situation or feeling. ▫ **born-again** newly converted to Christianity or some other cause. **born and bred** by birth and upbringing. **in all your born days** throughout your life (used for emphasis). **I** (or **he, she**, etc.) **wasn't born yesterday** I am (or he, she, etc., is) not easily deceived.

> USAGE
> Don't confuse **born** with **borne**, which is the past participle of **bear** and means 'carried.'

borne /bôrn/ past participle of BEAR¹.

bo·ron /ˈbôrän/ ▶ **n.** a chemical element used in making alloy steel and in nuclear reactors.

bor·ough /ˈbərō/ ▶ **n. 1** a town or district that is an administrative unit. **2** an incorporated municipality in some US states. **3** each of five divisions of New York City. **4** in Alaska, a district corresponding to a county elsewhere in the United States.

bor·row /'bärō, 'bôrō/ ▶ **v.** take and use something belonging to someone else with the intention of returning it.

SYNONYMS **1 loan**, lease, hire; informal mooch, cadge, scrounge, bum, hit someone up for. **2 adopt**, take on, acquire, embrace, copy, imitate. ANTONYMS lend.

□ **be living on borrowed time 1** still be alive after the time when you were expected to die. **2** be doing something that other people will soon stop you doing.

bor·zoi /'bôrzoi/ ▶ **n.** (plural **borzois**) a breed of large Russian dog with a narrow head and silky coat.

bosh /bäsн/ ▶ **n.** informal nonsense.

Bos·ni·an /'bäznēən/ ▶ **n.** a person from Bosnia. ▶ **adj.** relating to Bosnia.

bos·om /'bo͝ozəm/ ▶ **n. 1** a woman's breast or chest. **2** loving care: *he went home to the bosom of his family.* ▶ **adj.** (of a friend) very close.

SYNONYMS ▶ **n. 1 bust**, chest; breasts; informal boobs, knockers, bazooms. **2 heart**, breast, soul, core, spirit. ▶ **adj.** *bosom friends* **close**, boon, intimate, inseparable, faithful, constant, devoted; good, best, firm, favorite.

boss[1] /bôs, bäs/ informal ▶ **n.** a person who is in charge of other people at work. ▶ **v.** tell someone what to do in an arrogant or annoying way.

SYNONYMS ▶ **n. head**, chief, principal, director, president, chief executive, chair, manager, supervisor, foreman, overseer, controller, employer, owner, proprietor; informal head honcho. ▶ **v. order around**, dictate to, bully, push around/about, call the shots, lay down the law; informal bulldoze, walk all over, railroad.

boss[2] ▶ **n.** a knob at the center of a shield, propeller, or similar object.

bos·sa no·va /'bäsə 'nōvə, 'bô-/ ▶ **n.** a dance like the samba, from Brazil.

boss·y /'bôsē, 'bäs-/ ▶ **adj.** (**bossier**, **bossiest**) tending to tell people what to do in an arrogant or annoying way.

SYNONYMS **domineering**, pushy, overbearing, imperious, officious, high-handed, authoritarian, dictatorial, autocratic; informal high and mighty. ANTONYMS submissive.

■ **boss·i·ness n.**

bot /bät/ ▶ **n.** an autonomous program on a computer network that can interact with systems or users.

bot·a·ny /'bätn-ē/ ▶ **n.** the scientific study of plants. □ **botanical garden** a place where plants are grown for scientific study and display to the public. ■ **bo·tan·i·cal** /bə'tanikəl/ (or **botanic** /bə'tanik/) **adj. bot·a·nist n.**

botch /bäcн/ ▶ **v.** informal do something badly or carelessly.

both /bōтн/ ▶ **determiner & pron.** two people or things, considered together. ▶ **adv.** applying to each of two alternatives: *it won favor with both young and old.*

both·er /'bäт͟нər/ ▶ **v.** (**bothers**, **bothering**, **bothered**) **1** take the trouble to do something: *the driver didn't bother to ask why.* **2** annoy, worry, or upset someone. **3** (**bother with** or **about**) feel concern about or interest in. ▶ **n. 1** trouble and fuss. **2** (**a bother**) a cause of trouble or fuss.

SYNONYMS ▶ **v. 1** *no one bothered her* **disturb**, trouble, inconvenience, pester, badger, harass, molest, plague; informal hassle, bug, ride. **2** *don't bother about me* **concern yourself**, worry, trouble yourself, care. **3** *something was bothering him* **worry**, trouble, concern, perturb, disturb, disquiet; informal rattle. ▶ **n. 1 trouble**, effort, exertion, inconvenience, fuss, pains; informal hassle. **2 nuisance**, pest, rigmarole, trial, bore, drag, inconvenience, trouble; informal hassle, headache, pain (in the neck).

both·er·some /'bäт͟нərsəm/ ▶ **adj.** troublesome.

bot·tle /'bätl/ ▶ **n.** a container with a narrow neck, used for storing liquids. ▶ **v.** (**bottles**, **bottling**, **bottled**) **1** place in bottles for storage. **2** (**bottle something up**) hide your feelings.

SYNONYMS ▶ **n. flask**, carafe, decanter, pitcher, flagon, magnum, demijohn, vial.

□ **bottle green** dark green.

bot·tle·neck /'bätl,nek/ ▶ **n.** a narrow section of road where the flow of traffic is restricted.

SYNONYMS **1 traffic jam**, congestion, holdup, gridlock, bumper-to-bumper traffic; informal snarl. **2** constriction, narrowing, restriction, obstruction, blockage.

bot·tom /'bätəm/ ▶ **n. 1** the lowest or furthest point or part of something. **2** the lowest position in a competition or ranking: *life at the bottom of society.* **3** a person's buttocks. **4** (also **bottoms**) the lower half of a two-piece garment. ▶ **adj.** in the lowest or furthest position. ▶ **v. 1** (**bottom out**) (of a situation) reach the lowest point before becoming stable or improving. **2** (of a ship) touch the bottom of the sea.

SYNONYMS ▶ **n. 1 foot**, lowest part, base, foundation. **2 underside**, underneath, undersurface, underbelly. **3 floor**, bed, depths. **4 farthest point**, extremity, far end. **5 buttocks**, rear (end), rump, seat, derrière; informal behind, backside, butt, fanny; humorous posterior. ANTONYMS top, surface. ▶ **adj. lowest**, last, bottommost. ANTONYMS top.

□ **get to the bottom of** find an explanation for. **the bottom falls** (or **drops**) **out of something** something suddenly fails or collapses. **the bottom line** informal the most important factor. **bottoms up!** informal said as a toast before drinking.

bot·tom·less /'bätəmlis/ ▶ **adj. 1** without a bottom. **2** very deep. **3** inexhaustible: *I don't have a bottomless pit of money.*

bot·u·lism /'bäcнə,lizəm/ ▶ **n.** a dangerous form of food poisoning.

bou·clé /,bo͞o'klā/ ▶ **n.** yarn with a looped or curled strand.

bou·doir /'bo͞o,dwär/ ▶ **n.** a woman's bedroom or small private room.

bouf·fant /bo͞o'fänt/ ▶ **adj.** (of hair) styled so as to stand out from the head in a rounded shape.

bou·gain·vil·le·a /,bo͞ogən'vilēə, -vilyə, -'vēə, ,bō-/ ▶ **n.** a tropical climbing plant with brightly colored flowerlike leaves (called bracts).

bough /bou/ ▶ **n.** a large branch.

bought /bôt/ past and past participle of **BUY**.

USAGE

Don't confuse **bought** with **brought**, which is the past of **bring**.

bouil·lon /'bo͞olyən, -yän/ ▶ **n.** thin soup or stock made by stewing meat, fish, or vegetables in water.

boul·der /'bōldər/ ▶ **n.** a large rock.

boule /bo͞ol/ (also **boules**) ▶ **n.** a French lawn game, played on rough ground with metal balls.

boul·e·vard /'bo͞olə,värd/ ▶ **n.** a wide street.

bounce /bouns/ ▶ **v.** (**bounces**, **bouncing**, **bounced**) **1** move quickly up or away from a surface after hitting it. **2** move or jump up and down repeatedly. **3** informal (of a check) be returned by a bank when there is not enough money in an account for it to be paid. ▶ **n. 1** an act of bouncing. **2** lively confidence: *the bounce was back in Jenny's step.* **3** body in a person's hair.

SYNONYMS ▶ **v. 1 rebound**, spring back, ricochet, carom. **2 bound**, leap, jump, spring, bob, hop, skip, gambol, trip, prance. ▶ **n. 1 springiness**, resilience, elasticity, give. **2 vitality**, vigor, energy, vivacity, liveliness, animation, sparkle, verve, spirit; informal get-up-and-go, pep, zing.

bounc·er /'bounsər/ ▶ **n.** a person employed by a bar or nightclub to control or keep out troublemakers.

bounc·ing /'bounsiNG/ ▶ **adj.** (of a baby) vigorous and healthy.

bounc·y /'bounsē/ ▶ **adj.** (**bouncier**, **bounciest**) **1** able to bounce, or making something bounce. **2** confident and lively.

SYNONYMS **1 springy**, flexible, resilient, elastic, stretchy, rubbery. **2** *a bouncy ride* **bumpy**, jolting, jerky, jumpy, jarring, rough. **3 lively**, energetic, perky, frisky, jaunty, dynamic, vital, vigorous, vibrant, animated, spirited, buoyant, bubbly, sparkling, vivacious; enthusiastic, upbeat; informal peppy, zingy, chirpy.

bound¹ /bound/ ▶ **v.** move with long, leaping strides. ▶ **n.** a leaping movement.

SYNONYMS ▶ **v. leap**, jump, spring, vault, bounce, hop, skip, dance, prance, gambol, gallop.

bound² ▶ **v. 1** form the boundary of. **2** restrict. ▶ **n.** a boundary or restriction.

SYNONYMS ▶ **v. 1 enclose**, surround, encircle, circle, border, close in/off, hem in. **2 limit**, restrict, confine, circumscribe, demarcate, delimit.

□ **out of bounds 1** (in sports) beyond the field of play. **2** beyond where you are allowed to go.

bound³ past and past participle of **BIND**. ▶ **adj. 1** restricted to or by a place or situation: *his job kept him city-bound.* **2** going toward somewhere: *a train bound for Chicago.* **3** (**bound to**) certain to be, do, or have: *there is bound to be a change of plan.* **4** (**bound to**) obliged to do.

SYNONYMS **1 tied**, restrained, fixed, fastened, secured. **2 certain**, sure, very likely, destined. **3** *bound by secrecy* **constrained**, obliged, compelled, required, obligated. ANTONYMS free.

bound·a·ry /'bound(ə)rē/ ▶ **n.** (plural **boundaries**) a line marking the limits of an area.

SYNONYMS **1 border**, frontier, borderline, partition, dividing line. **2** *the boundary of his estate* **limits**, confines, bounds, margins, edges, fringes, border, periphery, perimeter.

bound·en /'boundən/ ▶ **adj.** (in phr. **your bounden duty**) a duty that you feel is morally right.

bound·er /'boundər/ ▶ **n.** informal, dated a man who behaves in a dishonest or unacceptable way; a cad.

bound·less /'boundlis/ ▶ **adj.** unlimited.

SYNONYMS **limitless**, untold, immeasurable, abundant, inexhaustible, endless, infinite, interminable, unfailing, ceaseless, everlasting. ANTONYMS limited.

boun·te·ous /'bountēəs/ ▶ **adj.** given or giving generously.

boun·ti·ful /'bountəfəl/ ▶ **adj. 1** existing in large quantities. **2** giving generously.

SYNONYMS **1 abundant**, plentiful, ample, copious, bumper, superabundant, inexhaustible, prolific, profuse; lavish, generous, handsome, rich; informal whopping; literary plenteous. **2 generous**, magnanimous, munificent, open-handed, unselfish, unstinting, lavish; benevolent, beneficent, charitable. ANTONYMS meager, mean.

boun·ty /'bountē/ ▶ **n.** (plural **bounties**) **1** literary generosity, or something given in generous amounts: *people along the Nile depend on its bounty.* **2** a reward paid for killing or capturing someone.

SYNONYMS **reward**, prize, award, commission, premium, dividend, bonus, gratuity, tip, donation, handout; incentive, inducement; informal perk, sweetener; formal perquisite.

bou·quet /bō'kā, bo͞o-/ ▶ **n. 1** a bunch of flowers. **2** the pleasant smell of a particular wine or perfume.

SYNONYMS **1 posy**, nosegay, spray, corsage, buttonhole, garland, wreath, arrangement. **2 aroma**, nose, smell, fragrance, perfume, scent, odor.

bour·bon /'bərbən/ ▶ **n.** an American whiskey made from corn and rye.

bour·geois /bo͝or'zHwä, 'bo͝orzHwä/ ▶ **adj.** having to do with the middle class, especially in being concerned with wealth and social status.

SYNONYMS **middle-class**, conservative, conformist, conventional, propertied, provincial, suburban, small-town. ANTONYMS proletarian.

bour·geoi·sie /,bo͝orzHwä'zē/ ▶ **n.** the middle class.

bout /bout/ ▶ **n. 1** a short period of great activity. **2** a short period of illness. **3** a wrestling or boxing match.

SYNONYMS **1 spell**, period, stretch, stint, session, burst, flurry, spurt. **2 attack**, fit, spasm. **3 contest**, fight, match, round, competition, meeting, encounter.

bou·tique /bo͞o'tēk/ ▶ **n.** a small shop selling fashionable clothes.

bo·vine /'bōvīn, -vēn/ ▶ **adj. 1** having to do with cattle. **2** rather slow and stupid. ▶ **n.** an animal of the cattle group.

bow¹ /bō/ ▶ **n. 1** a knot tied with two loops and two loose ends. **2** a weapon for shooting arrows, consisting of a string held taut by a strip of bent wood. **3** a rod with horsehair stretched along its length, used for playing some stringed instruments. □ **bow-legged** having legs that curve outward at the knee. **bow tie** a man's tie that is tied in a bow. **bow window** a curved bay window.

bow² /bou/ ▶ v. **1** bend the head and upper body as a sign of respect. **2** bend with age or under a heavy weight. **3** give in to pressure. **4** (**bow out**) withdraw from an activity. ▶ n. an act of bowing.

SYNONYMS ▶ v. **1 incline your head**, bend, stoop, bob, curtsy, kneel, genuflect. **2** *the mast bowed in the wind* **bend**, buckle, curve, flex. **3** *they bowed to foreign pressure* **give in**, submit, yield, surrender, succumb, capitulate. ▶ n. **nod**, bob, obeisance, curtsy, genuflection, salaam.

□ **bow and scrape** try too hard to please someone. **take a bow** acknowledge applause by bowing.

bow³ /bou/ (or **bows**) ▶ n. the front end of a ship.

SYNONYMS **prow**, front, stem, nose, head.

bowd·ler·ize /ˈbōdləˌrīz, ˈboud-/ ▶ v. (**bowdlerizes**, **bowdlerizing**, **bowdlerized**) remove parts of a written work that might shock or offend people.

bow·el /ˈbou(ə)l/ ▶ n. **1** (also **bowels**) the intestine. **2** (**bowels**) the innermost parts of something.

SYNONYMS **1 intestines**, entrails, viscera, innards, digestive system, gut; informal guts, insides. **2** (**bowels**) **interior**, inside, core, belly, depths, recesses; informal innards.

□ **bowel movement** an act of emptying waste matter from the bowels.

bow·er /ˈbou(-ə)r/ ▶ n. a pleasant shady place under trees.

bow·er·bird /ˈbou(-ə)rˌbərd/ ▶ n. an Australasian bird noted for the male's habit of building an elaborate bower to attract the female.

bow·ie knife /ˈbo͞oē, ˈbōē/ ▶ n. a long knife with a blade double-edged at the point.

bowl¹ /bōl/ ▶ n. **1** a round, deep dish or basin. **2** a rounded, hollow part of an object.

SYNONYMS **dish**, basin, pot, crock, vessel, receptacle.

bowl² ▶ v. roll a round object along the ground. ▶ n. a heavy ball used in lawn bowling. □ **bowl someone over 1** knock someone down. **2** informal surprise or impress someone very much.

bowl·er¹ /ˈbōlər/ ▶ n. a player at lawn bowling or tenpin bowling.

bowl·er² ▶ n. a man's hard black felt hat that is rounded at the top and has a rim.

bow·line /ˈbōlin, ˈbōˌlīn/ ▶ n. a simple knot for forming a nonslipping loop at the end of a rope.

bowl·ing /ˈbōliNG/ ▶ n. **1** the game of tenpin, candlepin, or duckpin bowling. **2** the game of lawn bowling. □ **bowling alley 1** a long lane along which balls are rolled in bowling. **2** a building containing such lanes. **bowling green** an area of cut grass for playing a bowling game on.

bow·sprit /ˈbouˌsprit, ˈbō-/ ▶ n. a pole projecting from a ship's bow, to which the ropes supporting a ship's front mast are fastened.

box¹ /bäks/ ▶ n. **1** a square or rectangular container with a lid. **2** an enclosed area reserved for a group of people in a theater or sports arena. **3** (**the box**) informal television. ▶ v. **1** put something in a box. **2** (**box someone in**) restrict or confine someone.

SYNONYMS ▶ n. **carton**, pack, packet, case, crate, chest, coffer, casket. ▶ v. **pack**, package, parcel, encase, bundle, crate.

□ **box number 1** a number identifying an advertisement in a newspaper, used as an address for replies. **2** a number of a box at the post office from which mail can be collected. **box office** the place at a theater where tickets are sold. **box pleat** a pleat consisting of two parallel creases forming a raised band. **box set** a set of related recordings or books sold as a unit.

box² ▶ v. take part in boxing. ▶ n. a slap on the side of a person's head.

SYNONYMS ▶ v. **fight**, spar, battle, brawl; informal scrap.

□ **box someone's ears** slap someone on both sides of the head.

box³ ▶ n. a shrub with small, round glossy leaves.

box·car /ˈbäksˌkär/ ▶ n. an enclosed railroad freight car.

box·er /ˈbäksər/ ▶ n. **1** a person who boxes as a sport. **2** a breed of dog with a smooth brown coat and a flattened face.

SYNONYMS **fighter**, pugilist, prizefighter; informal bruiser, scrapper.

□ **boxer shorts** men's underpants that look like shorts.

box·ing /ˈbäksiNG/ ▶ n. a sport in which contestants fight each other wearing big padded gloves.

box·y /ˈbäksē/ ▶ adj. **1** roughly square in shape. **2** (of a room or space) cramped.

boy /boi/ ▶ n. a male child or youth.

SYNONYMS **lad**, youth, young man, stripling.

□ **Boy Scout** a member of an organization for boys, especially the **Boy Scouts of America**, that promotes character, outdoor activities, good citizenship, and service to others. ■ **boy·hood** n. **boy·ish** adj.

boy·cott /ˈboiˌkät/ ▶ v. **1** refuse to have dealings with. **2** refuse to buy goods as a protest. ▶ n. an act of boycotting someone or something.

SYNONYMS ▶ v. **shun**, snub, spurn, avoid, ostracize, blacklist, blackball, reject, veto. ▶ n. **ban**, veto, embargo, prohibition, moratorium, sanction, restriction, avoidance, rejection.

boy·friend /ˈboiˌfrend/ ▶ n. a person's regular male companion in a romantic relationship.

SYNONYMS **lover**, sweetheart, beloved, darling, partner; informal fella, (main) squeeze; dated beau; literary swain.

boy·sen·ber·ry /ˈboizənˌberē/ ▶ n. (plural **boysenberries**) a large red fruit similar to a blackberry.

bo·zo /ˈbōzō/ ▶ n. (plural **bozos**) informal a stupid or insignificant person.

BP ▶ abbr. **1** before the present (era). **2** blood pressure.

bra /brä/ ▶ n. a woman's undergarment worn to support the breasts.

brace /brās/ ▶ n. **1** a part that strengthens or supports something. **2** (usually **braces**) a wire or plastic device used to straighten the teeth. **3** (plural **brace**) a pair: *a brace of grouse*. **4** (also **brace and bit**) a drilling tool with a crank handle and a socket to hold a bit. ▶ v. (**braces**, **bracing**, **braced**) **1** make something stronger or firmer with a brace. **2** press your body firmly against something to stay balanced. **3** (**brace yourself**) prepare for something difficult or unpleasant.

SYNONYMS ▶ n. **prop**, strut, stay, support, bracket. ▶ v. **1 support**, shore up, prop up, hold up, buttress, reinforce. **2 steady**, secure, stabilize, poise, fix. **3** ***brace yourself for disappointment*** **prepare**, get ready, gear up, nerve, steel, fortify; informal psych (yourself) up.

brace·let /ˈbrāslit/ ▶ n. an ornamental band or chain worn on the wrist or arm.

brac·ing /ˈbrāsiNG/ ▶ adj. refreshing; making you feel full of energy.

SYNONYMS **invigorating**, refreshing, stimulating, energizing, exhilarating, restorative, rejuvenating.

brack·en /ˈbrakən/ ▶ n. a tall fern.

brack·et /ˈbrakit/ ▶ n. **1** each of a pair of marks ( ) [ ] { } ⟨ ⟩ used to enclose words or figures. **2** a category of similar people or things: *a high income bracket*. **3** a right-angled support that sticks out from a wall. ▶ v. (**brackets**, **bracketing**, **bracketed**) **1** enclose in brackets. **2** place in the same category.

SYNONYMS ▶ n. **1 support**, prop, stay, batten, rest, mounting, rack, frame. **2 group**, category, grade, classification, division.

brack·ish /ˈbrakisH/ ▶ adj. (of water) slightly salty.

bract /brakt/ ▶ n. a leaf with a flower in the angle where it meets the stem.

brad /brad/ ▶ n. a nail with a rectangular cross section and a small head.

brag /brag/ ▶ v. (**brags**, **bragging**, **bragged**) speak boastfully. ▶ n. a simplified form of the card game poker.

SYNONYMS ▶ v. **boast**, crow, swagger, swank, show off, blow your own horn, sing your own praises; informal talk big.

brag·gart /ˈbragərt/ ▶ n. a boastful person.

Brah·man /ˈbrämən/ ▶ n. (plural **Brahmans**) (also **Brahmin** /-min/) a member of the highest Hindu caste, that of the priesthood.

braid /brād/ ▶ n. **1** threads woven into a decorative band. **2** a length of hair made up of strands plaited together. ▶ v. **1** form hair into a braid. **2** trim something with braid.

Braille /brāl/ ▶ n. a written language for blind people, using raised dots.

brain /brān/ ▶ n. **1** an organ contained in the skull that controls thought and feeling and is the center of the nervous system. **2** (usually **brains**) intellectual ability: *success requires brains as well as brawn*. **3** (**the brains**) informal the main organizer within a group. ▶ v. informal hit someone hard on the head.

SYNONYMS ▶ n. **intelligence**, intellect, brainpower, cleverness, wit(s), reasoning, wisdom, judgment, understanding, sense, nous; informal gray matter, smarts.

□ **brain-dead** suffering from brain death. **brain death** irreversible brain damage causing the end of independent breathing. **brain-teaser** informal a problem or puzzle. **have something on the brain** informal be obsessed with something.

brain·child /ˈbrān,cHīld/ ▶ n. informal an idea or invention thought up by a particular person.

brain·less /ˈbrānlis/ ▶ adj. very stupid.

brain·storm /ˈbrān,stôrm/ ▶ v. hold a group discussion to solve a problem or produce new ideas.

brain·wash /ˈbrān,wôsH, -,wäsH/ ▶ v. force someone to accept an idea or belief by putting pressure on them or repeating the same thing over and over again.

SYNONYMS **indoctrinate**, condition, re-educate, persuade, influence.

brain·wave /ˈbrān,wāv/ ▶ n. **1** an electrical impulse in the brain. **2** informal a sudden clever idea.

brain·y /ˈbrānē/ ▶ adj. (**brainier**, **brainiest**) informal intelligent.

braise /brāz/ ▶ v. (**braises**, **braising**, **braised**) fry food lightly and then stew it slowly in a closed container.

brake /brāk/ ▶ n. a device for slowing or stopping a moving vehicle. ▶ v. (**brakes**, **braking**, **braked**) slow or stop a vehicle with a brake.

SYNONYMS ▶ n. **curb**, check, restraint, constraint, control, limit. ▶ v. **slow (down)**, decelerate, reduce speed. ANTONYMS accelerate.

□ **brake drum** a broad, short cylinder attached to a wheel, against which the brake shoes press to cause braking. **brake shoe** a long curved block that presses on to a brake drum.

USAGE

Don't confuse **brake** with **break**, which mainly means 'separate into pieces' or 'a pause or short rest.'

bram·ble /ˈbrambəl/ ▶ n. a blackberry bush or similar prickly shrub.

bran /bran/ ▶ n. pieces of the outer husk left when grain is made into flour.

branch /brancH/ ▶ n. **1** a part of a tree that grows out from the trunk. **2** a river, road, or railroad extending out from a main one. **3** a division of a larger group. ▶ v. **1** divide into one or more branches. **2** (**branch out**) start doing a different sort of activity.

SYNONYMS ▶ n. **1 bough**, limb, arm, offshoot, twig. **2 division**, subdivision, section, subsection, department, unit, sector, wing, office, bureau, agency, subsidiary. ▶ v. **1 fork**, divide, split, bifurcate. **2** ***narrow paths branched off the road*** **diverge from**, deviate from, split off from, fan out from, radiate from.

brand /brand/ ▶ n. **1** a type of product made by a company under a particular name. **2** (also **brand name**) a name given to a product by its maker. **3** a mark burned on farm animals with a piece of hot metal. **4** a piece of smoldering wood. ▶ v. **1** mark with a piece of hot metal. **2** mark someone out as being bad in a particular way: *she was branded a liar*. **3** give a brand name to.

SYNONYMS ▶ n. **1 make**, line, label, marque, trademark, trade name, proprietary name. **2 type**, kind, sort, variety, class, category, genre, style, ilk, stripe. ▶ v. **1 mark**, stamp, burn, sear. **2 stigmatize**, characterize, label, mark out, denounce, discredit, vilify.

□ **brand new** completely new.

bran·dish /ˈbrandiSH/ ▶ **v.** wave something as a threat or in anger or excitement.

> SYNONYMS **flourish**, wave, shake, wield, swing, swish.

bran·dy /ˈbrandē/ ▶ **n.** (plural **brandies**) a strong alcoholic drink made from wine or fermented fruit juice.

brash /braSH/ ▶ **adj.** confident in a rather rude or aggressive way.

> SYNONYMS **1 self-assertive**, pushy, cocky, self-confident, arrogant, bold, audacious, brazen. **2 garish**, gaudy, loud, flamboyant, showy, tasteless; informal flashy, tacky. ANTONYMS meek.

■ **brash·ly** **adv.** **brash·ness** **n.**

brass /bras/ ▶ **n.** **1** a yellowish metal made by mixing copper and zinc. **2** brass wind instruments forming a section of an orchestra. □ **get down to brass tacks** informal start to consider the basic facts. **brass band** a group of musicians playing brass instruments. **top brass** informal people in authority.

bras·se·rie /ˌbrasəˈrē/ ▶ **n.** (plural **brasseries**) an inexpensive French or French-style restaurant.

bras·siere /brəˈzi(ə)r/ ▶ **n.** a bra.

brass·y /ˈbrasē/ ▶ **adj.** (**brassier**, **brassiest**) **1** resembling brass in color. **2** unpleasantly bright or showy. **3** harsh or blaring like a brass instrument.

brat /brat/ ▶ **n.** informal a badly behaved child.

> SYNONYMS **spoiled child**, scamp, rascal, imp; informal monster, horror, hellion, whippersnapper, rotten kid.

bra·va·do /brəˈvädō/ ▶ **n.** confidence or a show of confidence that is intended to impress.

> SYNONYMS **boldness**, swaggering, bluster; machismo; boasting, bragging, bombast, braggadocio; informal showing off.

brave /brāv/ ▶ **adj.** willing to do something that is dangerous or frightening; not afraid. ▶ **n.** dated an American Indian warrior. ▶ **v.** (**braves**, **braving**, **braved**) face or deal with something frightening or unpleasant.

> SYNONYMS ▶ **adj. courageous**, intrepid, bold, plucky, heroic, fearless, daring, audacious, dauntless, valiant, valorous, doughty, indomitable, stouthearted; informal game, gutsy. ANTONYMS cowardly. ▶ **v. endure**, put up with, bear, withstand, weather, suffer, face, confront, defy.

■ **brave·ly** **adv.**

brav·er·y /ˈbrāvərē/ ▶ **n.** courageous behavior or character.

> SYNONYMS **courage**, boldness, heroism, intrepidity, nerve, daring, fearlessness, audacity, pluck, mettle, valor; informal guts.

bra·vo /bräˈvō, ˈbrävō/ ▶ **exclam.** shouted to express approval for a performer.

bra·vu·ra /brəˈv(y)o͞orə/ ▶ **n.** **1** great skill; brilliance. **2** the display of great daring.

brawl /brôl/ ▶ **n.** a noisy fight or quarrel. ▶ **v.** take part in a brawl.

> SYNONYMS ▶ **n. fight**, skirmish, scuffle, tussle, fray, melee, fracas, fisticuffs; informal scrap, set-to.

brawn /brôn/ ▶ **n.** physical strength.

brawn·y /ˈbrônē/ ▶ **adj.** physically strong; muscular.

> SYNONYMS **strong**, muscular, muscly, well-built, powerful, strapping, burly, sturdy; informal beefy, hulking. ANTONYMS puny, weak.

bray /brā/ ▶ **v.** (of a donkey) make a loud, harsh cry. ▶ **n.** the loud, harsh cry of a donkey.

braze /brāz/ ▶ **v.** (**brazes**, **brazing**, **brazed**) join metal parts together using an alloy of copper and zinc. ▶ **n.** a brazed joint.

bra·zen /ˈbrāzən/ ▶ **adj.** not caring if other people think you are behaving badly; shameless. ▶ **v.** (**brazen it out**) endure an awkward situation without seeming ashamed or embarrassed.

> SYNONYMS ▶ **adj. bold**, shameless, unashamed, unrepentant, unabashed, defiant, impudent, impertinent, cheeky, barefaced, blatant, flagrant.

■ **bra·zen·ly** **adv.**

bra·zier /ˈbrāZHər/ ▶ **n.** a portable heater holding lighted coals.

Bra·zil·ian /brəˈzilēən/ ▶ **n.** a person from Brazil. ▶ **adj.** relating to Brazil.

Bra·zil nut /brəˈzil ˌnət/ ▶ **n.** the large three-sided nut of a South American forest tree.

breach /brēCH/ ▶ **v.** **1** make a hole in; break through. **2** break a rule or agreement. ▶ **n.** **1** a gap made in a wall or barrier. **2** an act that breaks a rule or agreement. **3** a quarrel or disagreement.

> SYNONYMS ▶ **v. 1 break (through)**, burst, rupture. **2 contravene**, break, violate, infringe, defy, disobey, flout. ▶ **n. 1 contravention**, violation, infringement, infraction, transgression. **2 break**, rupture, split, crack, fracture, opening, gap, hole, fissure. **3 rift**, severance, estrangement, parting, parting of the ways, split, falling-out, schism.

□ **breach of promise** the breaking of a sworn promise. **step into the breach** replace someone who is suddenly unable to do a job.

bread /bred/ ▶ **n.** **1** food made of flour, water, and yeast mixed together and baked. **2** informal money. □ **bread and butter** a person's main source of income. **know which side your bread is buttered (on)** informal know where your advantage lies.

bread·crumb /ˈbredˌkrəm/ ▶ **n.** a very small fragment of bread.

bread·ed /ˈbredid/ ▶ **adj.** (of food) coated with breadcrumbs and fried.

bread·line /ˈbredˌlīn/ ▶ **n.** a line of people waiting to receive free food.

breadth /bredTH/ ▶ **n.** **1** the distance from side to side of something. **2** wide range: *breadth of experience.*

> SYNONYMS **1 width**, broadness, thickness, span, diameter. **2 range**, extent, scope, depth, reach, compass, scale.

bread·win·ner /ˈbredˌwinər/ ▶ **n.** a person who supports their family with the money they earn.

break /brāk/ ▶ **v.** (**breaks**, **breaking**, **broke** /brōk/; past participle **broken** /ˈbrōkən/) **1** separate into pieces as a result of a blow or strain. **2** stop working. **3** interrupt a sequence or course. **4** fail to obey a rule or agreement. **5** beat a record. **6** work out a code. **7** make a rush or dash. **8** soften a fall. **9** suddenly become public. **10** (of a person's voice) falter and change tone. **11** (of a teenage boy's voice) become deeper. **12** (of the weather) change suddenly. ▶ **n. 1** a pause or gap. **2** a short rest. **3** an instance of breaking, or the point where something is broken. **4** a sudden rush or dash. **5** informal a chance: *his big break had finally come*. **6** Tennis the winning of a game against an opponent's serve. **7** a player's turn to start a game of pool, snooker, or billiards. **8** a short solo in music.

SYNONYMS ▶ **v. 1 shatter**, smash, crack, snap, fracture, fragment, splinter, split, burst; informal bust. **2 stop working**, break down, give out, go wrong, malfunction, crash; informal go kaput, conk out. **3 violate**, contravene, infringe, breach, defy, flout, disobey. **4** *the movie broke box-office records* **beat**, surpass, exceed, better, cap, top, outdo, outstrip. **5** *he tried to break the news gently* **reveal**, disclose, divulge, impart, tell, announce, release. ANTONYMS repair, obey. ▶ **n. 1 interval**, interruption, gap, disruption, stoppage, cessation, halt, stop. **2 rest**, respite, recess, pause, intermission; informal breather, time out. **3 gap**, opening, space, hole, breach, chink, crack, fracture, fissure, tear, split.

□ **break away** escape. **break your back** work hard to achieve something. **break down 1** stop working. **2** lose control of your emotions when upset. **break in 1** force your way into a building. **2** make new shoes comfortable by wearing them. **break-in** an illegal forced entry made in order to steal something. **break a horse** make a horse used to being ridden. **break into** burst forth into (laughter, song, a run, etc.). **break off** stop suddenly. **break out 1** (of something unwelcome) start suddenly. **2** escape. **break out in** suddenly be affected by: *break out in hives*. **break up 1** (of a gathering) end. **2** (of a couple) end a relationship. **break with 1** quarrel with. **2** go against a tradition. **give someone a break** informal stop putting pressure on someone. ■ **break·a·ble adj.**

break·age /ˈbrākij/ ▶ **n. 1** the action of breaking something. **2** a thing that has been broken.

break·a·way /ˈbrākəˌwā/ ▶ **n. 1** a major change from something established: *rock was a breakaway from pop*. **2** (in sports) a sudden attack or forward movement.

break·dan·cing /ˈbrākˌdansiNG/ ▶ **n.** an energetic and acrobatic style of street dancing.

break·down /ˈbrākˌdoun/ ▶ **n. 1** a failure or collapse. **2** a careful analysis of costs or figures: *a detailed cost breakdown*.

SYNONYMS **1 failure**, collapse, disintegration, foundering. **2 nervous breakdown**, collapse. **3 malfunction**, failure, crash. **4 analysis**, itemization, classification, examination, investigation, explanation.

break·er /ˈbrākər/ ▶ **n. 1** a heavy sea wave that breaks on the shore. **2** a person that breaks something.

break·fast /ˈbrekfəst/ ▶ **n.** the first meal of the day. ▶ **v.** eat breakfast.

break·neck /ˈbrākˌnek/ ▶ **adj.** dangerously fast.

break·through /ˈbrākˌTHro͞o/ ▶ **n.** a sudden important development or success.

SYNONYMS **advance**, development, step forward, success, improvement, discovery, innovation, revolution, quantum leap. ANTONYMS setback.

break·wa·ter /ˈbrākˌwôtər, -ˌwätər/ ▶ **n.** a barrier built out into the sea to protect a coast or harbor from waves.

bream /brim, brēm/ ▶ **n.** (plural **bream**) a greenish-bronze freshwater fish.

breast /brest/ ▶ **n. 1** either of the two soft organs on a woman's chest that produce milk when she has had a baby. **2** a person's or animal's chest. ▶ **v.** move forward while pushing against something: *I watched him breast the wave*.

SYNONYMS ▶ **n. chest**, bosom, bust; informal boobs, knockers.

breast·bone /ˈbrestˌbōn/ ▶ **n.** a bone running down the center of the chest and connecting the ribs.

breast·feed /ˈbrestˌfēd/ ▶ **v.** (**breastfeeds, breastfeeding, breastfed**) feed a baby with milk from the breast.

breast·plate /ˈbrestˌplāt/ ▶ **n.** a piece of armor covering the chest.

breast·stroke /ˈbrestˌstrōk/ ▶ **n.** a swimming stroke in which you push your arms forward and then sweep them back while kicking your legs out.

breath /breTH/ ▶ **n. 1** air taken into or sent out of the lungs. **2** an instance of breathing in or out. **3** a slight movement of air. **4** a sign or hint: *he avoided the slightest breath of scandal*.

SYNONYMS **inhalation**, exhalation, gulp of air, puff, gasp; Medicine respiration.

□ **breath of fresh air** a refreshing change. **breath test** a test in which a driver is made to blow into a Breathalyzer. **draw breath** breathe in. **hold your breath** stop breathing temporarily. **out of breath** gasping for air. **take someone's breath away** astonish or inspire someone. **under your breath** in a very quiet voice.

breath·a·ble /ˈbrēT͟Həbəl/ ▶ **adj. 1** (of air) fit to breathe. **2** (of clothing or material) allowing air to the skin so that sweat may evaporate. ■ **breath·a·bil·i·ty** /ˌbrēT͟Həˈbilitē/ **n.**

Breath·a·lyz·er /ˈbreTHəˌlīzər/ ▶ **n.** trademark a device for measuring the amount of alcohol in a driver's breath.

breathe /brēT͟H/ ▶ **v.** (**breathes, breathing, breathed**) **1** take air into the lungs and send it out again. **2** say quietly. **3** let air or moisture in or out.

SYNONYMS **1 inhale**, exhale, respire, draw breath, puff, pant, blow, gasp, wheeze; Medicine inspire, expire. **2 whisper**, murmur, purr, sigh.

□ **breathe down someone's neck 1** follow closely behind someone. **2** constantly check up on someone. **breathe your last** die. **breathing space** an opportunity to relax or decide what to do next.

breath·er /ˈbrēT͟Hər/ ▶ **n.** informal a brief pause for rest.

breath·less /ˈbreTHlis/ ▶ **adj. 1** gasping for breath. **2** feeling or causing great excitement.

SYNONYMS **1 out of breath**, panting, puffing, gasping, wheezing, winded; informal out of wind. **2 eager**, agog, open-mouthed, excited, on the edge of your seat, on tenterhooks.

■ **breath·less·ly adv.**

breath·tak·ing /ˈbreTHˌtākiNG/ ▶ **adj.** astonishing or awe-inspiring.

SYNONYMS **spectacular**, magnificent, awe-inspiring, awesome, astonishing, amazing, stunning, thrilling; informal sensational, out of this world.

■ **breath·tak·ing·ly adv.**

breath·y /ˈbreTHē/ ▶ **adj.** (of speech or singing) having a noticeable sound of breathing: *a breathy laugh*.

bred /bred/ past and past participle of BREED.

breech /brēCH/ ▶ n. the back part of a rifle or gun barrel. ◻ **breech birth** a birth in which the baby's buttocks or feet are delivered first.

breech·es /'briCHiz, 'brē-/ ▶ pl.n. short trousers fastened just below the knee.

breed /brēd/ ▶ v. (**breeds**, **breeding**, **bred**) **1** (of animals) mate and then produce young. **2** keep animals for the young that they produce. **3** produce or cause: *familiarity breeds contempt*. ▶ n. a particular type of domestic or farm animal that has been specially developed.

SYNONYMS ▶ v. **1 reproduce**, produce offspring, procreate, multiply, mate. **2 bring up**, rear, raise, nurture. **3 cause**, produce, bring about, give rise to, occasion, arouse, stir up, generate, foster. ▶ n. **1** *a breed of cow* **variety**, stock, strain, race, species. **2** *a new breed of journalist* **type**, kind, sort, variety, class, genre, generation.

■ **breed·er** n.

breed·ing /'brēdiNG/ ▶ n. good manners regarded as characteristic of the upper class and conferred by heredity.

SYNONYMS (**good**) **manners**, gentility, refinement, cultivation, polish, urbanity; informal class.

breeze /brēz/ ▶ n. **1** a gentle wind. **2** informal something easy to do. ▶ v. (**breezes**, **breezing**, **breezed**) informal come or go casually.

SYNONYMS ▶ n. **gentle wind**, gust, draft; literary zephyr.

breez·y /'brēzē/ ▶ adj. (**breezier**, **breeziest**) **1** pleasantly windy. **2** relaxed and cheerfully brisk: *a breezy matter-of-fact manner*.

SYNONYMS **1 windy**, fresh, brisk, blowy, blustery, gusty. **2 jaunty**, cheerful, cheery, brisk, carefree, easy, casual, relaxed, informal, lighthearted, upbeat.

breth·ren /'breTH(ə)rin/ ▶ pl.n. **1** dated plural of BROTHER. **2** fellow Christians or members of a group.

Bret·on /'bretn/ ▶ n. **1** a person from Brittany. **2** the language of Brittany.

bre·vi·ar·y /'brēvē,erē, 'brev-/ ▶ n. (plural **breviaries**) a book containing the service for each day, used in the Roman Catholic Church.

brev·i·ty /'brevitē/ ▶ n. **1** economical and exact use of words. **2** the fact of lasting a short time.

SYNONYMS **conciseness**, concision, succinctness, pithiness, incisiveness, shortness, compactness.

brew /bro͞o/ ▶ v. **1** make beer. **2** make tea or coffee by mixing it with hot water. **3** begin to develop: *trouble is brewing*. ▶ n. something brewed.

SYNONYMS ▶ v. **1 ferment**, make, prepare, infuse, steep. **2 develop**, loom, be imminent, be on the horizon, be in the offing, be just around the corner. ▶ n. **1** *home brew* **beer**, ale. **2** *a hot brew* **drink**, beverage, infusion. **3 mixture**, mix, blend, combination, amalgam, cocktail.

■ **brew·er** n.

brew·er·y /'bro͞oərē/ ▶ n. (plural **breweries**) a place where beer is made.

bribe /brīb/ ▶ v. (**bribes**, **bribing**, **bribed**) pay someone to do something dishonest that helps you. ▶ n. an amount of money offered in an attempt to bribe someone.

SYNONYMS ▶ v. **buy off**, pay off, suborn; informal grease someone's palm. ▶ n. **inducement**; informal payoff, kickback, sweetener, hush money.

brib·er·y /'brībərē/ ▶ n. the giving or offering of a bribe: *he was convicted of racketeering and bribery*.

SYNONYMS **corruption**, payola; informal palm-greasing, graft.

bric-a-brac /'brik ə ,brak/ ▶ n. various small ornamental objects of little value.

brick /brik/ ▶ n. a small rectangular block of fired clay, used in building. ▶ v. (**brick something up**) block or enclose something with a wall of bricks. ◻ **brick red** a deep brownish red. **bricks and mortar** buildings, especially as the location of a business when compared with a similar business on the Internet. **like a ton of bricks** informal with crushing weight or force.

brick·bat /'brik,bat/ ▶ n. a critical remark.

brick·lay·er /'brik,lāər/ ▶ n. a person whose job is to build structures with bricks.

brid·al /'brīdl/ ▶ adj. relating to a bride or a newly married couple.

bride /brīd/ ▶ n. a woman at the time of her wedding.

bride·groom /'brīd,gro͞om/ ▶ n. a man at the time of his wedding.

brides·maid /'brīdz,mād/ ▶ n. a girl or woman who accompanies a bride at her wedding.

bridge /brij/ ▶ n. **1** a structure that allows people or vehicles to cross a river, road, etc. **2** the platform on a ship where the captain and officers stand. **3** the upper bony part of a person's nose. **4** the part on a stringed instrument over which the strings are stretched. **5** a card game played by two teams of two players. ▶ v. (**bridges**, **bridging**, **bridged**) be or make a bridge over.

SYNONYMS ▶ n. **1 viaduct**, overpass, aqueduct. **2 link**, connection, bond, tie. ▶ v. **span**, cross (over), extend across, traverse, arch over, straddle.

◻ **bridge loan** a sum of money lent by a bank to cover the period of time between the buying of one thing and the selling of another.

bridge·head /'brij,hed/ ▶ n. a strong position gained by an army inside enemy territory.

bri·dle /'brīdl/ ▶ n. the harness used to control a horse. ▶ v. (**bridles**, **bridling**, **bridled**) **1** put a bridle on. **2** show resentment or anger. ◻ **bridle path** a path or track used for horseback riding.

Brie /brē/ ▶ n. a kind of soft, mild, creamy cheese.

brief /brēf/ ▶ adj. **1** lasting a short time. **2** using few words. **3** (of clothing) not covering much of the body. ▶ n. a summary of the facts in a case given to a lawyer to argue in court. ▶ v. give someone information to prepare them for a task.

SYNONYMS ▶ adj. **1 concise**, succinct, short, pithy, compact, thumbnail, potted, condensed, to the point, terse, summary. **2 short**, flying, fleeting, hasty, hurried, quick, cursory, perfunctory, temporary, short-lived, ephemeral, transient, transitory. ANTONYMS long. ▶ n. **1 instructions**, directions, directive, remit, mandate. **2** *a lawyer's brief* **case**, summary, argument, contention, dossier. ▶ v. **inform**, tell, update, notify, advise, prepare, prime, instruct; informal fill in.

brief·case /ˈbrēfˌkās/ ▶ n. a flat rectangular case for carrying documents.

brief·ing /ˈbrēfiNG/ ▶ n. a meeting for giving information or instructions.

brief·ly /ˈbrēflē/ ▶ adv. **1** for a short time. **2** in a few words.

SYNONYMS **1 concisely**, succinctly, tersely. **2 momentarily**, temporarily, fleetingly. **3** *briefly, the plot is as follows* **in short**, to make a long story short, in brief, in a word, in a nutshell, in essence.

briefs /brēfs/ ▶ pl.n. short, close-fitting underpants.

SYNONYMS **underpants**, underwear, shorts, bikini briefs; informal panties.

bri·er /ˈbrī(ə)r/ (or **briar**) ▶ n. a prickly shrub.

brig /brig/ ▶ n. a sailing ship with two masts.

bri·gade /briˈgād/ ▶ n. **1** a large army unit, forming part of a division. **2** disapproving a particular group of people: *the anti-smoking brigade*.

SYNONYMS **squad**, team, group, band, party, crew, force, outfit.

brig·a·dier gen·er·al /ˈbrigəˌdi(ə)r ˈjenərəl/ ▶ n. a military officer ranking above colonel and below major general.

brig·and /ˈbrigənd/ ▶ n. a member of a gang of bandits.

brig·an·tine /ˈbrigənˌtēn/ ▶ n. a sailing ship with two masts.

bright /brīt/ ▶ adj. **1** giving out light, or filled with light. **2** (of color) strong and eye-catching. **3** intelligent and quick-witted. **4** (of sound) clear and high-pitched. **5** cheerfully lively. **6** (of prospects) good.

SYNONYMS **1 shining**, brilliant, dazzling, glaring, sparkling, flashing, glittering, gleaming, glistening, shimmering, radiant, glowing, luminous, shiny, glossy, lustrous. **2 sunny**, cloudless, clear, fair, fine. **3** *bright colors* **vivid**, brilliant, intense, strong, vibrant, bold, gaudy, lurid, garish. **4 clever**, intelligent, quick-witted, smart, canny, astute, perceptive, ingenious; informal brainy. ANTONYMS dull, cloudy, dark, stupid.

□ **bright-eyed and bushy-tailed** informal alert and lively. ■ **bright·ly** adv. **bright·ness** n.

bright·en /ˈbrītn/ ▶ v. make or become brighter or more cheerful.

SYNONYMS **1 illuminate**, light up, lighten. **2 cheer up**, perk up, liven up, rally, hearten; informal buck up.

brill /bril/ ▶ n. a flatfish similar to the turbot.

bril·liance /ˈbrilyəns/ ▶ n. **1** intense brightness of light. **2** exceptional talent or intelligence.

SYNONYMS **1 brightness**, vividness, intensity, sparkle, glitter, blaze, luminosity, radiance. **2 genius**, intelligence, talent, ability, prowess, skill, expertise, aptitude, flair, wisdom, intellect. **3 splendor**, magnificence, grandeur, resplendence, glory. ANTONYMS dullness, stupidity.

bril·liant /ˈbrilyənt/ ▶ adj. **1** (of light or color) very bright or vivid. **2** very clever or talented.

SYNONYMS **1 bright**, shining, sparkling, blazing, dazzling, vivid, intense, glaring, luminous, radiant. **2 clever**, bright, intelligent, smart, able, talented, gifted, skillful, astute; informal brainy. **3** *her brilliant career* **superb**, glorious, illustrious, successful, impressive, remarkable, exceptional, excellent, outstanding, distinguished. ANTONYMS dim, stupid, undistinguished.

■ **bril·liant·ly** adv.

bril·lian·tine /ˈbrilyənˌtēn/ ▶ n. **1** dated scented oil used on men's hair to make it look glossy. **2** a kind of shiny dress fabric. ■ **bril·lian·tined** adj.

brim /brim/ ▶ n. **1** the projecting edge around the bottom of a hat. **2** the lip of a cup, bowl, etc. ▶ v. (**brims**, **brimming**, **brimmed**) be full to the point of overflowing.

SYNONYMS ▶ n. **1** peak, visor, shield. **2 rim**, lip, brink, edge. ▶ v. **be full** (**up**), overflow, run over, well over.

■ **brimmed** adj.

brim·ful /ˈbrimˌfo͝ol/ ▶ adj. filled to the point of overflowing.

brim·stone /ˈbrimˌstōn/ ▶ n. old use sulfur.

brin·dle /ˈbrindl/ (or **brindled**) ▶ adj. (of an animal) brownish with streaks of gray or black.

brine /brīn/ ▶ n. water that contains dissolved salt.

bring /briNG/ ▶ v. (**brings**, **bringing**, **brought** /brôt/) **1** take someone or something to a place. **2** cause to be in a particular position or state. **3** cause someone to receive something: *his first novel brought him a great deal of money*. **4** (**bring yourself to do**) force yourself to do something unpleasant. **5** begin legal action.

SYNONYMS **1 fetch**, carry, bear, take, convey, transport, shift. **2 escort**, conduct, guide, lead, usher. **3 cause**, produce, create, bring about, generate, precipitate, occasion, provoke, lead to, give rise to, result in.

□ **bring something about** cause something to happen. **bring something forward** move something planned to an earlier time. **bring the house down** make an audience laugh or applaud very enthusiastically. **bring something off** achieve something successfully. **bring something on** cause something unpleasant to develop. **bring something out 1** produce and launch a new product: *the band are bringing out a video*. **2** emphasize a feature. **bring someone around 1** make someone conscious again. **2** persuade someone to agree to something. **bring something to bear** put something into effect. **bring someone up** look after a child until it is an adult. **bring something up** mention something in order to discuss it. ■ **bring·er** n.

brink /briNGk/ ▶ n. **1** the edge of land before a steep slope or an area of water. **2** the stage just before a new situation.

SYNONYMS **1 edge**, verge, margin, rim, lip, border, boundary. **2** *on the brink of war* **verge**, threshold, point, edge.

brink·man·ship /ˈbriNGkmənˌSHip/ ▶ n. the practice of continuing with a dangerous course of action to the limits of safety before stopping.

brin·y /ˈbrīnē/ ▶ adj. salty.

bri·o /ˈbrēō/ ▶ n. energy or liveliness of style or performance.

bri·oche /brēˈōsh, -ˈôsh/ ▶ **n.** a soft, sweet French roll.

bri·quette /briˈket/ (also **briquet**) ▶ **n.** a block of compressed charcoal, coal dust, or peat used as fuel.

brisk /brisk/ ▶ **adj. 1** quick, active, or energetic. **2** (of a person's manner) practical and efficient: *a brisk, businesslike tone.*

> SYNONYMS **1 quick**, rapid, fast, swift, speedy, hurried, energetic, lively; informal zippy. **2 no-nonsense**, businesslike, decisive, brusque, abrupt, short, sharp, curt, blunt, terse; informal snappy. ANTONYMS leisurely.

■ **brisk·ly adv.**

bris·ket /ˈbriskit/ ▶ **n.** meat from the chest of a cow.

bris·tle /ˈbrisəl/ ▶ **n.** a short, stiff hair. ▶ **v.** (**bristles, bristling, bristled**) **1** (of hair or fur) stand upright away from the skin. **2** react angrily or defensively. **3** (**bristle with**) be covered with.

> SYNONYMS ▶ **n. 1 hair**, whisker; (**bristles**) stubble, five o'clock shadow. **2 spine**, prickle, quill, barb. ▶ **v. 1 rise**, stand up, stand on end. **2 take offense**, bridle, take umbrage, be offended. **3 be crowded**, be full, be packed, be jammed, be covered, overflow; informal be thick, be chock-full.

■ **bris·tly adj.**

Brit /brit/ ▶ **n.** informal a British person.

Bri·tan·ni·a /briˈtanyə, -ˈtanēə/ ▶ **n.** the personification of Britain, usually a helmeted woman with a shield and trident.

Brit·ish /ˈbritish/ ▶ **adj.** relating to Great Britain.

Brit·ish·er /ˈbritishər/ ▶ **n.** informal (especially in North America) a British person.

Brit·on /ˈbritn/ ▶ **n.** a British person.

brit·tle /ˈbritl/ ▶ **adj. 1** hard but likely to break easily. **2** sharp or artificial: *a brittle laugh.* ▶ **n.** a candy made from nuts and set melted sugar.

> SYNONYMS ▶ **adj. breakable**, fragile, crisp, crumbly, delicate. ANTONYMS flexible.

bro /brō/ ▶ **n.** informal **1** short for **BROTHER**. **2** a friendly greeting or form of address: *"Yo bro!"*

broach /brōch/ ▶ **v. 1** raise a subject for discussion. **2** pierce a container such as a cask to draw liquor. **3** open and start using the contents of a bottle or other container.

> SYNONYMS **bring up**, raise, introduce, mention, touch on, air.

broad /brôd/ ▶ **adj. 1** larger than usual from side to side; wide. **2** large in area or range: *a broad expanse of corn fields.* **3** without detail; general: *a broad outline.* **4** (of a hint) clear and unmistakable. **5** (of an accent) very strong. ▶ **n.** informal a woman.

> SYNONYMS ▶ **adj. 1 wide**, extensive, vast, immense, great, spacious, expansive, sizable, sweeping. **2 comprehensive**, inclusive, extensive, wide, all-embracing, unlimited. **3** *a broad outline* **general**, nonspecific, rough, approximate, basic, loose, vague. ANTONYMS narrow, limited.

□ **broad bean** a large flat green bean. **broad daylight** full daylight; day. **broad-minded** not easily shocked; tolerant. ■ **broad·ly adv.**

broad·band /ˈbrôd,band/ ▶ **n.** a telecommunications technique that uses a wide range of frequencies, enabling messages to be sent at the same time.

broad·cast /ˈbrôd,kast/ ▶ **v.** (**broadcasts, broadcasting, broadcast**) **1** transmit on radio or television or the Internet. **2** tell to a lot of people. ▶ **n.** a radio or television or Internet program.

> SYNONYMS ▶ **v. 1 transmit**, relay, air, beam, show, televise, screen. **2 report**, announce, publicize, advertise, make public, proclaim, spread, circulate, promulgate. ▶ **n. transmission**, program, show, telecast, production.

■ **broad·cast·er n.**

broad·cloth /ˈbrôd,klôth/ ▶ **n.** a fine cloth of wool or cotton.

broad·en /ˈbrôdn/ ▶ **v.** make or become broader.

> SYNONYMS **1** *her smile broadened* **widen**, expand, stretch (out), spread. **2** *the government tried to broaden its political base* **expand**, enlarge, extend, widen, swell, increase, add to, develop. ANTONYMS narrow, restrict.

broad·loom /ˈbrôd,lo͞om/ ▶ **n.** carpet woven in wide widths.

broad·sheet /ˈbrôd,shēt/ ▶ **n.** a newspaper printed on large sheets of paper.

broad·side /ˈbrôd,sīd/ ▶ **n. 1** a fierce verbal or written criticism. **2** historical a firing of all the guns from one side of a warship. **3** a sheet of paper printed on one side only, forming one large page.

bro·cade /brōˈkād/ ▶ **n.** a rich fabric woven with a raised pattern.

broc·co·li /ˈbräk(ə)lē/ ▶ **n.** a vegetable with heads of small green or purplish flower buds.

> SPELLING
> Two cs, one l: broccoli.

bro·chure /brōˈsho͝or/ ▶ **n.** a booklet or magazine containing information about a product or service.

> SYNONYMS **booklet**, prospectus, catalog, pamphlet, leaflet, circular, mailer.

bro·de·rie an·glaise /ˌbrōdəˈrē äNGˈglez, -ˈglāz/ ▶ **n.** open embroidery on fine white cotton or linen.

brogue /brōg/ ▶ **n. 1** a strong outdoor shoe with perforated patterns in the leather. **2** a strong regional accent, especially an Irish or Scottish accent when speaking English.

broil /broil/ ▶ **v.** cook meat or fish using direct heat.

broil·er /ˈbroilər/ ▶ **n.** a young chicken suitable for roasting, grilling, or barbecuing.

broke /brōk/ past of **BREAK** ▶ **adj.** informal having no money. □ **go for broke** informal risk everything in an all-out effort.

bro·ken /ˈbrōkən/ past participle of **BREAK** ▶ **adj.** (of a language) spoken hesitantly and with many mistakes.

> SYNONYMS **1 smashed**, shattered, fragmented, splintered, crushed, snapped, in bits, in pieces, cracked, split, fractured; informal in smithereens. **2 faulty**, damaged, defective, not working, malfunctioning, out of order, broken down, down; informal kaput, busted, acting up. **3 interrupted**, disturbed, fitful, disrupted, discontinuous, intermittent. **4 halting**, hesitating, disjointed, faltering, imperfect.

□ **broken home** a family in which the parents are divorced or separated. **broken-down 1** worn out and run down. **2** (of a machine) not working.

broken-hearted overwhelmed by grief or disappointment.

bro·ker /ˈbrōkər/ ▶ **n.** a person who buys and sells things for other people. ▶ **v.** arrange a deal or plan.

SYNONYMS ▶ **n. dealer**, agent, middleman, intermediary, mediator, factor, liaison, stockbroker. ▶ **v. arrange**, organize, orchestrate, work out, settle, clinch, negotiate, mediate.

bro·mide /ˈbrōmīd/ ▶ **n.** a compound of bromine, used in medicine.

bro·mine /ˈbrōmēn/ ▶ **n.** a dark red toxic liquid chemical element.

bron·chi /ˈbrängkī, -kē/ plural of **BRONCHUS**.

bron·chi·al /ˈbrängkēəl/ ▶ **adj.** relating to the tubes leading to the lungs.

bron·chi·tis /brängˈkītis/ ▶ **n.** inflammation of the tubes that lead to the lungs.

bron·chus /ˈbrängkəs/ ▶ **n.** (plural **bronchi** /ˈbrängkī, -kē/) any of the major air passages of the lungs that spread out from the windpipe.

bron·co /ˈbrängkō/ ▶ **n.** (plural **broncos**) a wild or half-tamed horse of the western United States.

bron·to·sau·rus /ˌbräntəˈsôrəs/ ▶ **n.** former name of a huge plant-eating dinosaur with a long neck and tail. Now called **apatosaurus**.

bronze /bränz/ ▶ **n. 1** a yellowish-brown metal made by mixing copper and tin. **2** a yellowish-brown color. **3** (also **bronze medal**) a medal given for third place in a competition. ▶ **v.** (**bronzes**, **bronzing**, **bronzed**) **1** give something a bronze surface. **2** make someone suntanned. □ **Bronze Age** an ancient period when weapons and tools were made of bronze, following the Stone Age.

brooch /brōch, bro͞och/ ▶ **n.** an ornament fastened to clothing with a hinged pin.

brood /bro͞od/ ▶ **n.** a family of young animals born or hatched at one time. ▶ **v. 1** think deeply about an unpleasant subject. **2** (**brooding**) appearing mysterious or menacing: *the brooding castle*. **3** (of a bird) sit on eggs to hatch them.

SYNONYMS ▶ **n. offspring**, young, family, litter, clutch, progeny. ▶ **v. think**, ponder, contemplate, meditate, ruminate, muse, worry, dwell on, fret, agonize.

brook¹ /bro͝ok/ ▶ **n.** a small stream.

SYNONYMS **stream**, creek, streamlet, rivulet, rill.

brook² ▶ **v.** formal tolerate: *she would brook no criticism*.

SYNONYMS **tolerate**, allow, stand, bear, abide, put up with, endure; accept, permit, countenance; informal stomach, hack.

broom /bro͞om, bro͝om/ ▶ **n. 1** a long-handled brush used for sweeping. **2** a shrub with yellow flowers.

broom·stick /ˈbro͞omˌstik, ˈbro͝om-/ ▶ **n.** a brush with twigs at one end and a long handle, on which witches are said to fly.

Bros. ▶ **abbr.** brothers.

broth /bräth, brôth/ ▶ **n.** thin soup or stock, sometimes with chunks of meat or vegetables.

broth·el /ˈbräthəl, ˈbrôthəl/ ▶ **n.** a house where men visit prostitutes.

SYNONYMS **whorehouse**, bordello; informal cathouse; euphemistic massage parlor; old use bawdy house, house of ill repute.

broth·er /ˈbrəthər/ ▶ **n. 1** a man or boy in relation to other children of his parents. **2** a male colleague or friend. **3** (plural **brothers** or **brethren** /ˈbreth(ə)rin/) a male fellow Christian or member of a religious order: *a Benedictine brother*. □ **brother-in-law** (plural **brothers-in-law**) **1** the brother of a person's wife or husband. **2** the husband of a person's sister or sister-in-law.

broth·er·hood /ˈbrəthərˌho͝od/ ▶ **n. 1** the relationship between brothers. **2** a feeling of friendliness and understanding between people. **3** a group of people linked by a shared interest: *a religious brotherhood*.

broth·er·ly /ˈbrəthərlē/ ▶ **adj. 1** relating to a brother. **2** kind and affectionate.

SYNONYMS **fraternal**, friendly, comradely, affectionate, amicable, kind, devoted, loyal.

brough·am /ˈbro͞oəm, ˈbrōəm/ ▶ **n.** historical **1** a horse-drawn carriage with a roof and an open driver's seat in front. **2** a car with an open driver's seat.

brought /brôt/ past and past participle of **BRING**.

USAGE

Don't confuse **brought** with **bought**, which is the past and past participle of **buy**.

brou·ha·ha /ˈbro͞ohäˌhä, bro͞oˈhähä/ ▶ **n.** a noisy and overexcited reaction.

brow /brou/ ▶ **n. 1** a person's forehead. **2** an eyebrow. **3** the highest point of a hill.

SYNONYMS **1 forehead**, temple. **2 summit**, peak, top, crest, crown, head, pinnacle, apex.

brow·beat /ˈbrouˌbēt/ ▶ **v.** (**browbeats**, **browbeating**, **browbeat**; past participle **browbeaten**) bully someone with aggressive or threatening words.

SYNONYMS **bully**, intimidate, force, coerce, compel, dragoon, bludgeon, pressure, pressurize, tyrannize, terrorize; informal bulldoze, railroad.

brown /broun/ ▶ **adj. 1** of a color produced by mixing red, yellow, and blue. **2** dark-skinned or suntanned. ▶ **n.** a brown color. ▶ **v.** make or become brown by cooking.

SYNONYMS ▶ **adj. 1** hazel, chestnut, chocolate, coffee, brunette, sepia, mahogany, tan, café au lait, caramel. **2 tanned**, suntanned, bronzed, swarthy. ▶ **v. grill**, toast, singe, sear, barbecue, sauté.

□ **brownnose** (also **brownnoser**) a person who behaves in an ingratiating way toward someone in order to gain their approval. **brown rice** unpolished rice with only the husk of the grain removed. **brown sugar** unrefined or partially refined sugar. **brown trout** the common trout of European lakes and rivers. ■ **brown·ish adj.**

brown·field /ˈbrounˌfēld/ ▶ **adj.** (of a piece of land) having had buildings on it already.

Brown·i·an mo·tion /ˈbrounēən/ ▶ **n.** Physics the irregular movement of tiny particles in a fluid, caused by the surrounding molecules striking against them.

Brown·ie /ˈbrounē/ ▶ **n.** (plural **Brownies**) **1** a member of the junior branch of the Girl Scouts. **2** (**brownie**) a small square of rich chocolate cake. **3** (**brownie**) a kind elf believed to do people's housework secretly.

brown·out /ˈbrounˌout/ ▶ **n.** a partial blackout.

Brown·shirt /'broun,sʜərt/ ▶ **n.** a member of a Nazi military force with brown uniforms.

brown·stone /'broun,stōn/ ▶ **n.** **1** a kind of reddish-brown sandstone used for building. **2** a building faced with such sandstone.

browse /brouz/ ▶ **v.** (**browses**, **browsing**, **browsed**) **1** read or look at something in a leisurely way. **2** look at information on a computer. **3** (of an animal) feed on leaves, twigs, etc. ▶ **n.** an act of browsing.

> SYNONYMS ▶ **v.** ***browsing through the want ads*** **look through**, scan (through), skim (through), glance through, peruse, thumb through, leaf through, flick through, dip into.

brows·er /'brouzər/ ▶ **n.** **1** a person or animal that browses. **2** a computer program for navigating the World Wide Web.

bruise /bro͞oz/ ▶ **n.** **1** an area of discolored skin on the body, caused by a blow. **2** a damaged area on a fruit or vegetable. ▶ **v.** (**bruises**, **bruising**, **bruised**) make a bruise appear on.

> SYNONYMS ▶ **n.** **contusion**, bump, swelling, lump, mark, injury, welt. ▶ **v.** **contuse**, injure, mark, discolor, make black and blue, blemish, damage, spoil.

bruis·er /'bro͞ozər/ ▶ **n.** informal a tough, aggressive person.

bruit /bro͞ot/ ▶ **v.** spread a report or rumor widely.

brunch /brənʜ/ ▶ **n.** a late-morning meal eaten instead of breakfast and lunch.

bru·nette /bro͞o'net/ ▶ **n.** a woman or girl with dark brown hair.

brunt /brənt/ ▶ **n.** the chief impact of something bad.

brush[1] /brəsʜ/ ▶ **n.** **1** an object with a handle and a block of bristles, hair, or wire. **2** an act of brushing. **3** a slight, brief touch. **4** a brief encounter with something bad. **5** the bushy tail of a fox. ▶ **v.** **1** clean, smooth, or apply with a brush. **2** touch lightly. **3** (**brush someone or something off**) dismiss someone or something abruptly.

> SYNONYMS ▶ **n.** **1** hairbrush, toothbrush, paintbrush, scrub brush, whisk broom. **2** *give it a brush* **sweep**, wipe, dust. **3** *a brush with the law* **encounter**, clash, confrontation, conflict, altercation, incident; informal run-in, to-do. ▶ **v.** **1** *brush your hair* **groom**, comb, neaten, tidy, smooth, arrange. **2** *his lips brushed her cheek* **touch**, stroke, caress, skim, sweep, graze, contact, kiss.

□ **brush up on** work to improve a skill you have not used for a long time.

brush[2] ▶ **n.** undergrowth, small trees, and shrubs.

> SYNONYMS **undergrowth**, scrub, underbrush, chaparral, brushwood, shrubs, bushes.

brushed /brəsʜt/ ▶ **adj.** (of fabric) having soft raised fibers.

brush·wood /'brəsʜ,wo͝od/ ▶ **n.** undergrowth, twigs, and small branches.

brusque /brəsk/ ▶ **adj.** rather rude and abrupt.

> SYNONYMS **curt**, abrupt, blunt, short, sharp, brisk, peremptory, gruff, discourteous, impolite, rude. ANTONYMS polite.

■ **brusque·ly** **adv.**

Brus·sels sprout /'brəsəl(z)/ ▶ **n.** a small green vegetable, the bud of a variety of cabbage.

brut /bro͞ot/ ▶ **adj.** (of sparkling wine) very dry.

bru·tal /'bro͞otl/ ▶ **adj.** **1** savagely violent. **2** not attempting to hide something unpleasant: *brutal honesty*.

> SYNONYMS **savage**, violent, cruel, vicious, ferocious, barbaric, wicked, murderous, bloodthirsty, cold-blooded, callous, ruthless, heartless, merciless, sadistic, inhuman. ANTONYMS gentle.

■ **bru·tal·i·ty** /bro͞o'talitē/ **n.** **bru·tal·ly** **adv.**

bru·tal·ize /'bro͞otl,īz/ ▶ **v.** (**brutalizes**, **brutalizing**, **brutalized**) **1** make someone cruel or violent by frequently exposing them to violence: *he had been brutalized in prison and had become cynical*. **2** treat someone in a violent way.

brute /bro͞ot/ ▶ **n.** **1** a violent or savage person. **2** a large and uncontrollable animal. ▶ **adj.** involving physical strength rather than reasoning: *brute force*.

> SYNONYMS ▶ **n.** **savage**, beast, monster, animal, barbarian, fiend, ogre; sadist; thug, lout, ruffian; informal swine, pig. ▶ **adj.** *brute strength* **physical**, bodily; crude, violent.

■ **brut·ish** **adj.**

BS ▶ **abbr.** Bachelor of Science.

BSE ▶ **abbr.** bovine spongiform encephalopathy, a fatal brain disease in cattle. Popularly called **mad cow disease**.

B-side /'bē,sīd/ ▶ **n.** the less important side of a pop single recording.

btw ▶ **abbr.** by the way.

bub·ble /'bəbəl/ ▶ **n.** **1** a thin ball of liquid enclosing a gas. **2** a ball filled with gas in a liquid or a material such as glass. **3** a transparent dome. ▶ **v.** (**bubbles**, **bubbling**, **bubbled**) **1** (of a liquid) contain rising bubbles of gas. **2** (**bubble with**) be filled with: *she was bubbling with enthusiasm*. □ **bubble bath** fragrant-smelling liquid added to bathwater to make it foam.

bub·ble·gum /'bəbəl,gəm/ ▶ **n.** chewing gum that can be blown into bubbles.

bub·bly /'bəb(ə)lē/ ▶ **adj.** (**bubblier**, **bubbliest**) **1** containing bubbles. **2** cheerful and high-spirited. ▶ **n.** informal champagne.

> SYNONYMS ▶ **adj.** **1** **fizzy**, sparkling, effervescent, gassy, aerated, carbonated, frothy, foamy. **2** **vivacious**, animated, ebullient, lively, high-spirited, bouncy, merry, happy, cheerful, sunny; informal chirpy. ANTONYMS still.

bu·bon·ic plague /b(y)o͞o'bänik/ ▶ **n.** a form of plague that is passed on by rat fleas and includes fever, delirium, and swollen lymph nodes.

buc·ca·neer /,bəkə'ni(ə)r/ ▶ **n.** **1** historical a pirate. **2** a recklessly adventurous person. ■ **buc·ca·neer·ing** **adj.**

buck[1] /bək/ ▶ **n.** **1** the male of some animals, e.g., deer and rabbits. **2** a vertical jump performed by a horse. **3** old use a fashionable young man. ▶ **v.** **1** (of a horse) perform a buck. **2** go against something: *don't try to buck the system*. **3** (**buck up** or **buck someone up**) informal become or make someone more cheerful. □ **buck teeth** teeth that stick out.

buck[2] ▶ **n.** informal a dollar.

buck[3] ▶ **n.** an object placed in front of a poker player whose turn it is to deal. □ **the buck stops here** informal the responsibility for something cannot be avoided. **pass the buck** informal shift responsibility to someone else.

buck·et /'bəkit/ ▶ n. 1 an open container with a handle, used to carry liquids. 2 (**buckets**) informal large quantities. ■ **buck·et·ful** n.

buck·le /'bəkəl/ ▶ n. a flat frame with a hinged pin, used as a fastener. ▶ v. (**buckles**, **buckling**, **buckled**) 1 fasten with a buckle. 2 bend and give way under pressure. 3 (**buckle down**) tackle a task with determination.

SYNONYMS ▶ n. **clasp**, clip, catch, hasp, fastener. ▶ v. 1 **fasten**, do up, hook, secure, clasp, clip. 2 **bend**, warp, twist, distort, contort, deform, crumple, collapse, give way.

buck·ram /'bəkrəm/ ▶ n. coarse cloth stiffened with paste, used in binding books.

buck·shot /'bək,shät/ ▶ n. coarse lead shot used in shotgun shells.

buck·skin /'bək,skin/ ▶ n. 1 the skin of a male deer. 2 grayish leather with a suede finish, traditionally made from the skin of a deer but now more commonly made from sheepskin. 3 thick smooth cotton or woolen fabric.

buck·thorn /'bək,thôrn/ ▶ n. a thorny shrub that bears black berries.

buck·wheat /'bək,(h)wēt/ ▶ n. a grain used for flour or animal feed.

bu·col·ic /byo͞o'kälik/ ▶ adj. relating to country life: *the church is lovely for its bucolic setting.*

bud /bəd/ ▶ n. a growth on a plant that develops into a leaf, flower, or shoot. ▶ v. (**buds**, **budding**, **budded**) form a bud or buds.

Bud·dhism /'bo͞odizəm, 'bo͝od-/ ▶ n. a religion based on the teachings of Buddha (real name Siddartha Gautama, *c.*563–*c.*460 BC). ■ **Bud·dhist** n. & adj.

bud·ding /'bədiNG/ ▶ adj. beginning and showing signs of promise: *their budding relationship.*

SYNONYMS **promising**, up-and-coming, rising, in the making, aspiring, future, fledgling, developing.

bud·dy /'bədē/ ▶ n. (plural **buddies**) informal a close friend.

budge /bəj/ ▶ v. (**budges**, **budging**, **budged**) 1 move very slightly. 2 change an opinion.

SYNONYMS 1 **move**, shift, stir, go. 2 **persuade**, convince, influence, sway, bend.

budg·er·i·gar /'bəjərē,gär/ ▶ n. a small Australian parakeet.

budg·et /'bəjit/ ▶ n. 1 an estimate of income and spending for a set period of time. 2 the amount of money needed or available for a purpose. 3 a regular estimate of national income and spending put forward by the government. ▶ v. (**budgets**, **budgeting**, **budgeted**) plan to spend a particular amount of money. ▶ adj. inexpensive.

SYNONYMS ▶ n. 1 **financial plan**, forecast. 2 *the defense budget* **allowance**, allocation, quota, funds, resources, capital. ▶ v. **allocate**, allot, allow, earmark, designate, set aside.

■ **budg·et·ar·y** adj.

budg·ie /'bəjē/ ▶ n. informal a budgerigar; a small Australian parakeet.

buff¹ /bəf/ ▶ n. a yellowish-beige color. ▶ v. polish something with a soft cloth.

SYNONYMS ▶ v. **polish**, burnish, shine, smooth, rub.

□ **in the buff** informal naked.

buff² ▶ n. informal a person who knows a lot about a particular subject: *a movie buff.*

SYNONYMS **enthusiast**, fan, devotee, lover, admirer, expert, aficionado, authority; informal freak, nut, addict.

buf·fa·lo /'bəfə,lō/ ▶ n. (plural **buffalo** or **buffaloes**) 1 a heavily built wild ox with backward-curving horns. 2 the North American bison.

buff·er /'bəfər/ ▶ n. a person or thing that lessens the impact of harmful effects: *family and friends can provide a buffer against stress.*

SYNONYMS **cushion**, bulwark, shield, barrier, guard, safeguard.

buf·fet¹ /bə'fā/ ▶ n. 1 a meal made up of several dishes from which you serve yourself. 2 a counter at which snacks are sold. 3 a cabinet with shelves and drawers for keeping dinnerware and table linens.

SYNONYMS 1 **smorgasbord**, self-service meal, spread. 2 **sideboard**, cabinet, cupboard.

buf·fet² /'bəfit/ ▶ v. (**buffets**, **buffeting**, **buffeted**) (especially of wind or waves) strike repeatedly.

SYNONYMS **batter**, pound, lash, strike, hit, beat.

buf·foon /bə'fo͞on/ ▶ n. a ridiculous but amusing person. ■ **buf·foon·er·y** n.

bug /bəg/ ▶ n. 1 a small insect. 2 informal a germ, or an illness caused by one. 3 informal an enthusiasm for something: *the sailing bug.* 4 a microphone used for secret recording. 5 an error in a computer program or system. ▶ v. (**bugs**, **bugging**, **bugged**) 1 hide a microphone in a room or telephone. 2 informal annoy someone.

SYNONYMS ▶ n. 1 **insect**, arachnid; informal creepy-crawly. 2 **illness**, disease, sickness, disorder, upset, ailment, infection, virus. 3 **listening device**, hidden microphone, wire, wiretap, tap. 4 **fault**, error, defect, flaw, virus; informal glitch, gremlin. ▶ v. **eavesdrop on**, spy on, wiretap, tap, monitor.

□ **bug-eyed** with bulging eyes.

bug·a·boo /'bəgə,bo͞o/ ▶ n. a cause of fear.

bug·bear /'bəg,be(ə)r/ ▶ n. something that causes anxiety or irritation.

bug·gy /'bəgē/ ▶ n. (plural **buggies**) 1 a baby carriage. 2 a small motor vehicle, often with an open top. 3 historical a light horse-drawn vehicle.

bu·gle /'byo͞ogəl/ ▶ n. a brass instrument like a small trumpet. ■ **bu·gler** n.

build /bild/ ▶ v. (**builds**, **building**, **built**) 1 make something by putting parts together. 2 (**build up**) increase over time. 3 (**build on**) use as a basis for further development. ▶ n. the size or form of someone or something: *she was of slim build.*

SYNONYMS ▶ v. **construct**, erect, put up, assemble, make, create, fashion, model, shape. ANTONYMS demolish, dismantle. ▶ n. **physique**, frame, body, figure, form, shape, stature, proportions; informal vital statistics.

■ **build·er** n.

build·ing /'bildiNG/ ▶ n. 1 a structure with a roof and walls. 2 the process or trade of building houses and other structures.

SYNONYMS **structure**, construction, edifice, pile, property, premises, establishment.

build·up /ˈbildˌəp/ ▶ **n. 1** a gradual increase. **2** a period of preparation before an event.

SYNONYMS **increase**, growth, expansion, enlargement, escalation, accumulation, development.

built /bilt/ past and past participle of **BUILD**. ▶ **adj.** of a particular physical build: *a slightly built woman.* ◻ **built-in** included as part of a larger structure: *a kitchen with a built-in stove.* **built-up** covered by many buildings.

bulb /bəlb/ ▶ **n. 1** the rounded base of the stem of some plants, from which the roots grow. **2** ⇒ **LIGHT BULB**.

bul·bous /ˈbəlbəs/ ▶ **adj. 1** round or bulging in shape. **2** (of a plant) growing from a bulb.

SYNONYMS **bulging**, round, fat, rotund, swollen, distended, bloated.

Bul·gar·i·an /ˌbəlˈge(ə)rēən, ˌbo͝ol-/ ▶ **n. 1** a person from Bulgaria. **2** the language of Bulgaria. ▶ **adj.** relating to Bulgaria.

bulge /bəlj/ ▶ **n. 1** a rounded swelling on a flat surface. **2** informal a temporary increase: *a bulge in the birth rate.* ▶ **v.** (**bulges**, **bulging**, **bulged**) **1** swell or stick out unnaturally. **2** (**bulge with**) be full of: *a briefcase bulging with documents.*

SYNONYMS ▶ **n. swelling**, bump, lump, hump, protrusion, protuberance. ▶ **v. swell**, stick out, project, protrude, stand out, puff out, balloon (out), fill out, distend.

bu·lim·i·a /bo͞oˈlimēə, ˈlē-/ ▶ **n.** a disorder marked by bouts of overeating, followed by fasting or vomiting. ■ **bu·lim·ic adj. & n.**

bulk /bəlk/ ▶ **n. 1** the mass or size of something large. **2** the greater part of something. **3** a large mass or shape. **4** roughage in food. ▶ **adj.** large in quantity: *bulk orders.*

SYNONYMS ▶ **n. 1 size**, volume, dimensions, proportions, mass, scale. **2 majority**, mass, generality, main part, lion's share, preponderance.

◻ **in bulk** (of goods) in large quantities.

bulk·head /ˈbəlkˌhed/ ▶ **n.** an internal wall or barrier in a ship or aircraft.

bulk·y /ˈbəlkē/ ▶ **adj.** (**bulkier**, **bulkiest**) large and unwieldy.

SYNONYMS **unwieldy**, cumbersome, unmanageable, awkward, ponderous, outsize, oversized; informal hulking.

bull¹ /bo͝ol/ ▶ **n. 1** an adult male animal of the cattle group. **2** a large male animal, e.g., a whale or elephant. ◻ **bull terrier** a dog that is a crossbreed of bulldog and terrier. **like a bull in a china shop** behaving clumsily in a delicate situation. **take the bull by the horns** deal decisively with a difficult situation.

bull² ▶ **n.** an order or announcement issued by the pope.

bull·dog /ˈbo͝olˌdôg/ ▶ **n.** a breed of dog with a flat wrinkled face and a broad chest.

bull·doze /ˈbo͝olˌdōz/ ▶ **v.** (**bulldozes**, **bulldozing**, **bulldozed**) clear or destroy with a bulldozer.

bull·doz·er /ˈbo͝olˌdōzər/ ▶ **n.** a tractor with a broad curved blade at the front for clearing ground.

bul·let /ˈbo͝olit/ ▶ **n.** a small piece, usually of metal, fired from a gun.

SYNONYMS **ball**, shot, pellet; informal slug; (**bullets**) lead.

bul·le·tin /ˈbo͝olitn, -ˌtin/ ▶ **n. 1** a short official statement or summary of news. **2** a regular newsletter or report.

SYNONYMS **1 report**, dispatch, story, newsflash, statement, announcement, message, communication, communiqué. **2 newsletter**, proceedings, newspaper, magazine, gazette, review.

◻ **bulletin board 1** a board for displaying notices. **2** a site on a computer system where any user can read or write messages.

bull·fight·ing /ˈbo͝olˌfītiNG/ ▶ **n.** the sport of baiting and killing bulls as a public entertainment. ■ **bull·fight n. bull·fight·er n.**

bull·finch /ˈbo͝olˌfinCH/ ▶ **n.** a finch (songbird) with a reddish breast.

bull·frog /ˈbo͝olˌfrôg, -ˌfräg/ ▶ **n.** a very large frog with a deep croak.

bul·lion /ˈbo͝olyən/ ▶ **n.** gold or silver in bulk before being made into coins.

bull·ish /ˈbo͝olisH/ ▶ **adj.** aggressively confident.

bul·lock /ˈbo͝olək/ ▶ **n.** ⇒ **STEER²**.

bull·ring /ˈbo͝olˌriNG/ ▶ **n.** an arena where bullfights are held.

bulls·eye /ˈbo͝olsˌī/ ▶ **n.** the center of the target in sports such as archery and darts.

bul·ly /ˈbo͝olē/ ▶ **n.** (plural **bullies**) a person who frightens or persecutes weaker people. ▶ **v.** (**bullies**, **bullying**, **bullied**) frighten or persecute a weaker person.

SYNONYMS ▶ **n. persecutor**, oppressor, tyrant, tormentor, intimidator, thug. ▶ **v. 1** *the others bully him* **persecute**, oppress, tyrannize, browbeat, intimidate, dominate, terrorize; informal push around/about. **2** *she was bullied into helping* **coerce**, pressure, press, push, prod, browbeat, dragoon, strong-arm; informal bulldoze, railroad, lean on.

◻ **bully for you!** often ironic an expression of admiration or approval.

bul·rush /ˈbo͝olˌrəsH/ (or **bullrush**) ▶ **n.** a tall reedlike waterside plant.

bul·wark /ˈbo͝olˌwərk/ ▶ **n. 1** a defensive wall. **2** a person or thing that acts as a defense. **3** an extension of a ship's sides above deck level.

bum /bəm/ informal ▶ **n. 1** a homeless person or beggar. **2** a lazy or worthless person. ▶ **v.** (**bums**, **bumming**, **bummed**) **1** get something by asking or begging. **2** (**bum around**) laze about. ▶ **adj.** bad: *not one bum note was played.*

bum·ble /ˈbəmbəl/ ▶ **v.** (**bumbles**, **bumbling**, **bumbled**) act or speak in an awkward or confused way.

bum·ble·bee /ˈbəmbəlˌbē/ ▶ **n.** a large hairy bee with a loud hum.

bum·mer /ˈbəmər/ ▶ **n.** informal an annoying or disappointing thing.

bump /bəmp/ ▶ **n. 1** a light blow or collision. **2** a hump or projection on a level surface. ▶ **v. 1** knock or run into with a jolt. **2** move with a lot of jolting. **3** (**bump into**) meet by chance. **4** (**bump someone off**) informal murder someone. **5** (**bump something up**) informal increase something.

SYNONYMS ▶ **n. 1 jolt**, crash, smash, smack, crack, bang, thud, thump, clang, knock, clunk, boom; informal whack, wallop. **2 swelling**, lump, bulge, injury, contusion, hump, knob. ▶ v. **1** *their car **bumped into** our mailbox* **hit**, crash into, smash into, slam into, bang (into), knock (into), run into, plow into, ram (into), collide with, strike. **2 bounce**, jolt, jerk, rattle, shake.

bump·er /ˈbəmpər/ ▶ n. a bar fixed across the front or back of a vehicle to reduce damage in a collision. ▶ adj. exceptionally large or successful: *a bumper crop.*

SYNONYMS ▶ adj. **exceptional**, large, abundant, rich, bountiful, good, plentiful, record, successful; informal whopping. ANTONYMS meager.

□ **bumper car** a small electric car with rubber bumpers all around, driven at an amusement park with the aim of bumping other such cars.

bump·kin /ˈbəmpkin/ ▶ n. an unsophisticated person from the countryside.

bump·tious /ˈbəmpshəs/ ▶ adj. irritatingly confident and self-important.

bump·y /ˈbəmpē/ ▶ adj. (**bumpier**, **bumpiest**) **1** (of a surface) uneven, with many patches raised above the rest. **2** involving sudden jolts and jerks because of an uneven surface.

SYNONYMS **1 uneven**, rough, rutted, pitted, potholed, lumpy, rocky. **2 bouncy**, rough, uncomfortable, jolting, lurching, jerky, jarring, bone-shaking. ANTONYMS smooth.

bun /bən/ ▶ n. **1** a bread roll. **2** a tight coil of hair at the back of the head. □ **have a bun in the oven** informal be pregnant.

bunch /bənch/ ▶ n. **1** a number of things grouped or held together. **2** informal a group of people. ▶ v. **1** collect or form into a bunch. **2** gather cloth into close folds.

SYNONYMS ▶ n. **1 bouquet**, posy, nosegay, spray, wreath, garland. **2 cluster**, clump, knot, group, bundle. ▶ v. **cluster**, huddle, gather, congregate, collect, amass, group, crowd.

bun·dle /ˈbəndl/ ▶ n. **1** a group of things tied or wrapped up together. **2** informal a large amount of money. ▶ v. (**bundles**, **bundling**, **bundled**) **1** tie or roll up in a bundle. **2** (**be bundled up**) be dressed in a lot of warm clothes. **3** informal push or carry forcibly.

SYNONYMS ▶ n. **collection**, roll, clump, wad, parcel, sheaf, bale, pile, stack, heap, mass, bunch; informal load. ▶ v. **1 tie**, parcel, wrap, swathe, roll, fold, bind, pack. **2** *he was **bundled** into a van* **push**, shove, thrust, throw, propel, jostle, manhandle.

bung /bəng/ ▶ n. a stopper for a hole in a container. ▶ v. (**bung something up**) block something up.

bun·ga·low /ˈbənggəˌlō/ ▶ n. a low house of only one story and with a broad front porch.

bun·gee /ˈbənjē/ (also **bungee cord**) ▶ n. a strong nylon-cased elastic band used for securing luggage and in the sport of bungee jumping.

bun·gee jump·ing ▶ n. the sport of jumping from a high place to which you are attached with a long bungee cord tied to your ankles.

bun·gle /ˈbənggəl/ ▶ v. (**bungles**, **bungling**, **bungled**) fail in performing a task. ▶ n. a mistake or failure.

SYNONYMS ▶ v. **1 mishandle**, mismanage, mess up, spoil, ruin; informal blow, botch, fluff, make a mess of, screw up, goof up. **2** (**bungling**) **incompetent**, blundering, amateurish, inept, unskillful, clumsy, awkward, bumbling; informal ham-fisted.

■ **bun·gler** n.

bun·ion /ˈbənyən/ ▶ n. a painful swelling on the big toe.

bunk¹ /bəngk/ ▶ n. a narrow shelflike bed. □ **bunk bed** a structure made up of two beds, one above the other.

bunk² ▶ n. informal nonsense: *anyone with a brain would never believe such bunk.*

bun·ker /ˈbəngkər/ ▶ n. **1** a large container for storing fuel. **2** an underground shelter for use in wartime. **3** a hollow filled with sand on a golf course.

bun·kum /ˈbəngkəm/ ▶ n. informal, dated nonsense.

bun·ny /ˈbənē/ ▶ n. (plural **bunnies**) informal a rabbit.

Bun·sen burn·er /ˈbənsən/ ▶ n. a small gas burner used in laboratories.

bunt /bənt/ ▶ v. **1** Baseball (of a batter) gently tap a pitched ball without swinging in order to make it more difficult to field. **2** (of a person or animal) butt with the head or horns. ▶ n. Baseball an act or result of tapping a pitched ball in such a way.

bunt·ing¹ /ˈbənting/ ▶ n. a small songbird with brown streaked feathers.

bunt·ing² ▶ n. flags and streamers used as decorations.

bu·oy /ˈbo͞o-ē, boi/ ▶ n. an anchored float used to mark an area of water. ▶ v. (**be buoyed** or **buoyed up**) be cheered up and made more confident.

SYNONYMS ▶ n. **float**, marker, beacon.

SPELLING

The **u** comes before the **o** in bu**o**y and bu**o**yant.

buoy·ant /ˈboi-ənt, ˈbo͞oyənt/ ▶ adj. **1** able to keep afloat. **2** cheerful and optimistic.

SYNONYMS **1 floating**, floatable. **2 cheerful**, cheery, happy, lighthearted, carefree, joyful, bubbly, bouncy, sunny, upbeat. ANTONYMS gloomy.

■ **buoy·an·cy** n.

bur·ble /ˈbərbəl/ ▶ v. (**burbles**, **burbling**, **burbled**) **1** make a continuous murmuring noise. **2** speak for a long time in a way that is hard to understand. ▶ n. a continuous murmuring noise.

bur·bot /ˈbərbət/ ▶ n. the only freshwater fish of the cod family.

bur·den /ˈbərdn/ ▶ n. **1** a heavy load. **2** something that causes hardship, worry, or grief. **3** the main responsibility for a task. ▶ v. **1** load heavily. **2** cause someone worry, hardship, or grief.

SYNONYMS ▶ n. **responsibility**, onus, obligation, duty, liability, trouble, care, problem, difficulty, worry, strain. ▶ v. **oppress**, trouble, worry, weigh down, overload, encumber, saddle, tax, afflict.

bur·den·some /ˈbərdnˈsəm/ ▶ adj. causing worry or difficulty.

bur·dock /ˈbərdäk/ ▶ n. a plant with large leaves and prickly flowers.

bu·reau /'byŏŏrō/ ▶ **n.** (plural **bureaus** or **bureaux**) **1** a chest of drawers. **2** an office for carrying out particular business: *a news bureau*. **3** a government department.

SYNONYMS **1 dresser**, chest of drawers, tallboy, highboy, cabinet. **2 department**, agency, office, division, branch, section, station, unit.

bu·reauc·ra·cy /byŏŏ'räkrəsē/ ▶ **n.** (plural **bureaucracies**) **1** administrative procedures that are too complicated. **2** a system of government in which most decisions are made by state officials.

SYNONYMS **1 red tape**, rules and regulations, protocol, officialdom, paperwork. **2 civil service**, government, administration, establishment, system, powers that be, authorities.

bu·reau·crat /'byŏŏrə,krat/ ▶ **n.** a government official, especially one who follows guidelines rigidly.

SYNONYMS **official**, administrator, civil servant, minister, functionary, mandarin; disapproving apparatchik.

■ **bu·reau·crat·ic** /,byŏŏrə'kratik/ **adj.**

bu·reau de change /'byŏŏrō də 'SHänZH/ ▶ **n.** (plural **bureaux de change** same pronunciation) a place where you can exchange foreign money.

bu·rette /byŏŏ'ret/ (also **buret**) ▶ **n.** a graduated glass tube with a tap at one end, for delivering known volumes of a liquid.

burg /bərg/ ▶ **n. 1** informal a town or city. **2** an ancient or medieval fortress or walled town.

bur·geon /'bərjən/ ▶ **v.** grow or increase rapidly.

SYNONYMS **grow**, increase, rocket, mushroom, expand, escalate, swell, boom, flourish, thrive, prosper.

burg·er /'bərgər/ ▶ **n.** a hamburger.

burgh·er /'bərgər/ ▶ **n.** old use a citizen of a town or city.

bur·glar /'bərglər/ ▶ **n.** a person who burgles a building.

SYNONYMS **robber**, thief, intruder, housebreaker, raider, looter, cat burglar.

bur·glar·ize /'bərglə,rīz/ ▶ **v.** enter a building illegally with the intention of committing a crime.

bur·gla·ry /'bərglərē/ ▶ **n.** (plural **burglaries**) the action of burgling a building.

SYNONYMS **housebreaking**, breaking and entering, break-in, theft, raid, stealing, robbery, larceny, looting; informal heist.

bur·gle /'bərgəl/ ▶ **v.** (**burgles**, **burgling**, **burgled**) go into a building illegally to steal its contents.

SYNONYMS **rob**, loot, steal from, raid.

bur·gun·dy /'bərgəndē/ ▶ **n.** (plural **burgundies**) **1** a red wine from Burgundy in France. **2** a deep red color.

bur·i·al /'berēəl/ ▶ **n.** the burying of a dead body.

SYNONYMS **funeral**, interment, committal, inhumation, entombment, obsequies, exequies. ANTONYMS exhumation.

burl /bərl/ ▶ **n. 1** a lump in wool or cloth. **2** a rounded knotty growth on a tree, giving an attractive figure when polished and used to make decorative objects or veneer for furniture.

bur·lap /'bərlap/ ▶ **n.** coarse canvas woven from jute or hemp.

bur·lesque /bər'lesk/ ▶ **n. 1** a comically exaggerated imitation of something. **2** a variety show.

bur·ly /'bərlē/ ▶ **adj.** (**burlier**, **burliest**) (of a man) large and strong.

SYNONYMS **strapping**, well-built, strong, muscular, muscly, hefty, sturdy, brawny; informal hunky, beefy. ANTONYMS puny.

Bur·mese /bər'mēz, -'mēs/ ▶ **n.** (plural **Burmese**) **1** a member of the largest ethnic group of Burma (now Myanmar) in Southeast Asia. **2** a person from Burma. **3** (also **Burmese cat**) a cat of a short-coated breed originating in Asia. ▶ **adj.** relating to Burma or the Burmese.

burn[1] /bərn/ ▶ **v.** (**burns**, **burning**, **burned** or **burnt**) **1** (of a fire) produce flames and heat while using up a fuel. **2** harm or damage by fire. **3** (**be burning with**) experience a very strong desire or emotion. **4** (**burn out**) become exhausted through working too hard. **5** produce a CD by copying from an original or master copy. ▶ **n.** an injury caused by burning.

SYNONYMS ▶ **v. 1 be on fire**, be alight, blaze, go up in flames/smoke, be in flames, smolder, glow. **2 set fire to**, set alight, kindle, ignite, touch off, incinerate, cremate; informal torch. **3 scorch**, singe, sear, char, blacken, brand.

□ **burn your bridges** do something that makes turning back impossible. **burn the candle at both ends** go to bed late and get up early. **burn a hole in your pocket** (of money) tempt you to spend it. **burn the midnight oil** work late into the night. **burn rubber** informal drive very quickly.

burn[2] ▶ **n.** Scottish a small stream.

burn·er /'bərnər/ ▶ **n.** a part of a stove, lamp, etc., that produces a flame. □ **on the back burner** given a low priority.

burn·ing /'bərniNG/ ▶ **adj. 1** very hot. **2** deeply felt. **3** important and urgent: *the burning issues of the day*.

SYNONYMS **1 on fire**, blazing, flaming, fiery, glowing, red-hot, smoldering. **2** *a burning desire* **intense**, passionate, deep-seated, profound, strong, ardent, fervent, urgent, fierce, consuming. **3** *burning issues* **important**, crucial, critical, vital, essential, pivotal, urgent, pressing, compelling.

bur·nish /'bərniSH/ ▶ **v.** polish something by rubbing it.

burn·out /'bərn,out/ ▶ **n.** physical or mental collapse.

burp /bərp/ informal ▶ **v. 1** noisily expel gas from the stomach through the mouth; belch. **2** pat a baby on its back to help it bring up air swallowed while feeding. ▶ **n.** a belch.

burr /bər/ ▶ **n. 1** a strong pronunciation of the letter *r*. **2** a prickly seed case or flower head that clings to clothing and animal fur.

bur·ri·to /bə'rētō/ ▶ **n.** (plural **burritos**) a Mexican dish consisting of a tortilla rolled around a filling of beans or chopped or shredded beef.

bur·ro /'bərō, 'bŏŏrō/ ▶ **n.** (plural **burros**) a small donkey used as a pack animal.

bur·row /'bərō/ ▶ **n.** a hole or tunnel dug by a small animal to live in. ▶ **v. 1** make a burrow. **2** hide underneath something. **3** search inside something.

SYNONYMS ▶ n. **hole**, tunnel, warren, dugout, lair, set, den, earth. ▶ v. **tunnel**, dig, excavate, mine, bore, channel.

bur·sar /ˈbərsər/ ▶ n. a person who manages the financial affairs of a college or school.

burst /bərst/ ▶ v. (**bursts**, **bursting**, **burst**) **1** break suddenly and violently apart. **2** (**be bursting**) be very full. **3** move or be opened suddenly and forcibly. **4** (**be bursting with**) feel full of an emotion. **5** (**burst out** or **into**) suddenly do something as a result of strong emotion: *she burst out crying.* ▶ n. **1** an instance of bursting. **2** a sudden brief outbreak: *a burst of activity.* **3** a period of continuous effort: *he did it all in one 24-hour burst.*

SYNONYMS ▶ v. **1** *one balloon burst* **split (open)**, rupture, break, tear. **2** *a shell burst* **explode**, blow up, detonate, go off. **3** *smoke burst through the hole* **gush**, erupt, surge, rush, stream, flow, pour, spurt, jet. **4** *he burst into the room* **charge**, plunge, barge, plow, hurtle, careen, rush, dash, tear. ▶ n. **1** **rupture**, puncture, breach, split, blowout. **2** **explosion**, detonation, blast, eruption, bang. **3** *a burst of gunfire* **volley**, salvo, barrage, hail, rain. **4** *a burst of activity* **outbreak**, eruption, flare-up, blaze, attack, fit, rush, storm, surge, spurt.

□ **burst someone's bubble** shatter someone's illusions.

bur·y /ˈberē/ ▶ v. (**buries**, **burying**, **buried**) **1** place or hide something underground. **2** make something disappear or be hidden. **3** (**bury yourself**) involve yourself deeply in something.

SYNONYMS **1** **inter**, lay to rest, entomb. **2** **hide**, conceal, cover, enfold, sink. **3** *the bullet buried itself in the wood* **embed**, sink, implant, submerge, lodge. ANTONYMS exhume.

bus /bəs/ ▶ n. (plural **buses** or **busses**) a large motor vehicle that carries customers along a fixed route. ▶ v. (**buses**, **busing**, **bused** or **busses**, **bussing**, **bussed**) transport or travel in a bus.

bus·boy /ˈbəsˌboi/ ▶ n. a young man who clears tables in a restaurant or cafeteria.

bush /bo͝osн/ ▶ n. **1** a shrub or clump of shrubs. **2** (**the bush**) (in Australia and Africa) wild or uncultivated country.

SYNONYMS **1** **shrub**, thicket; (**bushes**) undergrowth, shrubbery. **2** *the bush* **wilds**, wilderness, backwoods, backcountry; informal boondocks, boonies.

bush·ba·by /ˈbo͝osнˌbābē/ ▶ n. (plural **bushbabies**) a small African tree-dwelling primate with very large eyes.

bushed /bo͝osнt/ ▶ adj. informal exhausted.

bush·el /ˈbo͝osнəl/ ▶ n. a measure of capacity equal to 64 pints (35.2 liters).

Bush·man /ˈbo͝osнmən/ ▶ n. (plural **Bushmen**) **1** a member of an aboriginal people of southern Africa. **2** (**bushman**) a person who lives or travels in the Australian bush.

bush·y /ˈbo͝osнē/ ▶ adj. (**bushier**, **bushiest**) **1** growing thickly. **2** covered with bushes.

SYNONYMS **thick**, shaggy, curly, fuzzy, bristly, fluffy, woolly.

busi·ness /ˈbiznis/ ▶ n. **1** a person's regular occupation. **2** commercial activity. **3** a commercial organization. **4** work to be done or things to be attended to. **5** a person's concern: *it's none of your business.*

SYNONYMS **1** **work**, occupation, profession, career, employment, job, position. **2** **trade**, commerce, dealing, traffic, dealings, transactions, negotiations. **3** **firm**, company, concern, enterprise, venture, organization, operation, undertaking; informal outfit. **4** *it's none of your business* **concern**, affair, responsibility, duty. **5** *an odd business* **affair**, matter, case, circumstance, situation, event, incident.

□ **in business** informal able or beginning to function. **mind your own business** avoid meddling in other people's affairs.

SPELLING

Remember the **i**: business.

busi·ness·like /ˈbiznisˌlīk/ ▶ adj. efficient and practical.

SYNONYMS **professional**, efficient, organized, slick, methodical, systematic, orderly, structured, disciplined, practical, pragmatic.

busi·ness·man /ˈbiznisˌman, -mən/ (or **businesswoman**) ▶ n. (plural **businessmen** or **businesswomen**) a person who works in business.

SYNONYMS **executive**, entrepreneur, industrialist, merchant, dealer, trader, manufacturer, tycoon, employer, broker, buyer, seller, tradesman, retailer, supplier.

busk /bəsk/ ▶ v. play music or otherwise perform in the street in the hope of being given money by passersby. ■ **busk·er** n.

bust[1] /bəst/ ▶ n. **1** a woman's breasts. **2** a sculpture of a person's head, shoulders, and chest.

SYNONYMS **1** **bosom**, breasts, chest; informal boobs, knockers. **2** **sculpture**, carving, effigy, statue, head and shoulders.

bust[2] informal ▶ v. (**busts**, **busting**, **busted** or **bust**) **1** break, split, or burst. **2** raid or search a building, or arrest someone. **3** strike violently. ▶ n. **1** a period of economic difficulty. **2** a police raid. ▶ adj. bankrupt.

bus·tard /ˈbəstərd/ ▶ n. a large swift-running bird of open country.

bust·er /ˈbəstər/ ▶ n. informal a form of address to a man or boy.

bus·tier /bo͞osˈtyā/ ▶ n. a close-fitting strapless top for women.

bus·tle[1] /ˈbəsəl/ ▶ v. (**bustles**, **bustling**, **bustled**) **1** move energetically or noisily. **2** (of a place) be full of activity. ▶ n. excited activity and movement.

SYNONYMS ▶ v. **1** **rush**, dash, hurry, scurry, scuttle, scamper, scramble; informal scoot, beetle, buzz. **2** (**bustling**) **busy**, crowded, swarming, teeming, humming, buzzing, hectic, lively. ▶ n. **activity**, action, liveliness, excitement, tumult, commotion, hubbub, hurly-burly, whirl.

bus·tle[2] ▶ n. a pad or frame formerly worn by women under a skirt to puff it out behind.

bus·y /ˈbizē/ ▶ adj. (**busier**, **busiest**) **1** having a lot to do. **2** occupied with an activity. **3** crowded or full of activity. **4** (of a telephone line) unavailable because already in use. ▶ v. (**busies**, **busying**, **busied**) (**busy yourself**) keep yourself occupied.

> SYNONYMS ▶ **adj.** **1** *I'm very busy* **hard at work**, involved, hard-pressed; informal on the go, hard at it. **2** *I'm sorry, she's busy* **unavailable**, engaged, occupied, absorbed, engrossed, immersed, preoccupied, working; informal tied up. **3** *a busy day* **hectic**, active, lively, full, eventful, energetic, tiring. ANTONYMS idle, free, quiet. ▶ **v.** **occupy**, involve, engage, concern, absorb, engross, immerse, distract.

□ **busy signal** a repeating sound indicating that a telephone line is in use. ■ **bus·i·ly** **adv.**

bus·y·bod·y /ˈbizēˌbädē/ ▶ **n.** (plural **busybodies**) an interfering or nosy person.

> SYNONYMS **meddler**, interferer, troublemaker; gossip, scandalmonger; eavesdropper, gawker; informal snoop, buttinsky.

but /bət/ ▶ **conj.** **1** nevertheless. **2** on the contrary. **3** other than; otherwise than: *one cannot but sympathize.* **4** old use without it being the case that: *it never rains but it pours.* ▶ **prep.** except; apart from: *the last but one.* ▶ **adv.** only.

> SYNONYMS ▶ **conj.** **1** **however**, nevertheless, nonetheless, even so, yet, still. **2** **whereas**, conversely. ▶ **prep.** **except** (**for**), apart from, other than, besides, aside from, with the exception of, bar.

□ **but for** **1** except for. **2** if it were not for. **but then** on the other hand.

bu·tane /ˈbyo͞oˌtān/ ▶ **n.** a flammable gas present in petroleum and natural gas and used as a fuel.

butch /bo͝ocн/ ▶ **adj.** informal aggressively masculine.

butch·er /ˈbo͝ocнər/ ▶ **n.** **1** a person who cuts up and sells meat as a trade. **2** a person who kills animals for food. **3** a person who kills brutally. ▶ **v.** (**butchers**, **butchering**, **butchered**) **1** kill or cut up an animal for food. **2** kill someone brutally. **3** ruin something: *the movie was butchered by the studio that released it.* ■ **butch·er·y** **n.**

but·ler /ˈbətlər/ ▶ **n.** the chief male servant of a house.

butt[1] /bət/ ▶ **v.** **1** hit with the head or horns. **2** (**butt in**) interrupt a conversation. ▶ **n.** a rough push with the head.

> SYNONYMS ▶ **v.** **ram**, headbutt, bump, poke, prod, push, shove, thrust.

butt[2] ▶ **n.** **1** an object of criticism or ridicule. **2** a target in archery or shooting.

> SYNONYMS **target**, victim, object, dupe, laughingstock.

butt[3] ▶ **n.** **1** the thicker end of a tool or a weapon. **2** the stub of a cigar or a cigarette. **3** informal a person's buttocks. ▶ **v.** meet end to end.

> SYNONYMS ▶ **n.** **1** **stock**, end, handle, hilt, haft. **2** **stub**, end, stump.

butt[4] ▶ **n.** a cask used for wine, beer, or water.

butte /byo͞ot/ ▶ **n.** a hill with steep sides and a flat top.

but·ter /ˈbətər/ ▶ **n.** a pale yellow fatty substance made by churning cream. ▶ **v.** (**butters**, **buttering**, **buttered**) **1** spread with butter. **2** (**butter someone up**) informal flatter someone. □ **butter bean** a large flat edible bean; a lima bean. **look as if butter wouldn't melt in your mouth** informal appear innocent while being the opposite.

but·ter·cream /ˈbətərˌkrēm/ ▶ **n.** a mixture of butter and confectioners' sugar used to ice cakes.

but·ter·cup /ˈbətərˌkəp/ ▶ **n.** a plant with small bright yellow flowers.

but·ter·fat /ˈbətərˌfat/ ▶ **n.** the natural fat found in milk and dairy products.

but·ter·fin·gers /ˈbətərˌfiNGgərz/ ▶ **n.** (plural **butterfingers**) informal a person who often drops things.

but·ter·fly /ˈbətərˌflī/ ▶ **n.** (plural **butterflies**) **1** an insect with two pairs of large wings, which feeds on nectar. **2** (**butterflies**) informal a fluttering sensation in the stomach when you are nervous. **3** a stroke in swimming in which you raise both arms out of the water together. **4** a showy or frivolous person: *a social butterfly.*

but·ter·milk /ˈbətərˌmilk/ ▶ **n.** the slightly sour liquid left after butter has been churned.

but·ter·nut /ˈbətərˌnət/ ▶ **n.** a walnut tree valued for its nuts and wood.

but·ter·scotch /ˈbətərˌskäcн/ ▶ **n.** a candy made with butter and brown sugar.

but·ter·y /ˈbətərē/ ▶ **adj.** containing, resembling, or covered with butter.

but·tock /ˈbətək/ ▶ **n.** either of the two round fleshy parts of the human body that you sit on.

> SYNONYMS (**buttocks**) **rear** (**end**), rump, seat, bottom, derrière, cheeks; informal behind, backside, butt, fanny, ass; humorous posterior.

but·ton /ˈbətn/ ▶ **n.** **1** a small disk or knob sewn on to a garment to fasten it by being pushed through a buttonhole. **2** a knob on a piece of equipment that is pressed to operate it. ▶ **v.** fasten a garment with buttons. □ **button your lip** informal stop yourself from talking. **button mushroom** a young unopened mushroom. **on the button** informal precisely. ■ **but·toned** **adj.**

but·ton·hole /ˈbətnˌhōl/ ▶ **n.** a slit in a piece of clothing through which a button is pushed to fasten it. ▶ **v.** (**buttonholes**, **buttonholing**, **buttonholed**) informal stop someone and hold them in conversation.

but·tress /ˈbətris/ ▶ **n.** **1** a projecting support built against a wall. **2** a projecting part of a hill or mountain. ▶ **v.** support or strengthen.

> SYNONYMS ▶ **v.** **strengthen**, shore up, reinforce, fortify, support, bolster, underpin, cement, uphold, defend, back up.

bux·om /ˈbəksəm/ ▶ **adj.** (of a woman) attractively plump with a large bosom.

> SYNONYMS **large-breasted**, bosomy, big-bosomed; shapely, ample, plump, rounded, full-figured, voluptuous, curvaceous, Rubenesque; informal busty, chesty, well-endowed, curvy.

buy /bī/ ▶ **v.** (**buys**, **buying**, **bought** /bôt/) **1** get something in return for payment. **2** informal accept that something is true. **3** get something by sacrifice or great effort. ▶ **n.** informal something that has been bought.

> SYNONYMS ▶ **v.** **purchase**, acquire, obtain, get, pick up, snap up, invest in; informal get hold of, score. ANTONYMS sell. ▶ **n.** **purchase**, deal, bargain, investment, acquisition.

□ **buy it** (or **the farm**) informal be killed. **buy someone out** pay someone to give up a share in something. **buy time** delay an event so as to have longer to improve your own position.

buy·er /'bīər/ ▶ **n.** **1** a person who buys something. **2** a person employed to buy stock for a retail or manufacturing business.

SYNONYMS **purchaser**, customer, consumer, shopper, investor; (**buyers**) clientele, market.

buy·er's mar·ket ▶ **n.** a situation in which goods or shares are plentiful and buyers can keep prices down.

buy·out /'bī,out/ ▶ **n.** the purchase of a controlling share in a company.

buzz /bəz/ ▶ **n.** **1** a low continuous humming sound. **2** the sound of a buzzer or telephone. **3** an atmosphere of excitement and activity. **4** informal a thrill. ▶ **v.** **1** make a humming sound. **2** call someone with a buzzer. **3** move quickly. **4** (**buzz off**) informal go away. **5** have an air of excitement or activity.

SYNONYMS ▶ **n.** **hum**, murmur, drone, whirr.

□ **buzz cut** a haircut in which the hair is clipped very close to the head.

buz·zard /'bəzərd/ ▶ **n.** a large bird of prey.

buzz·er /'bəzər/ ▶ **n.** an electrical device that makes a buzzing noise to attract attention.

buzz·word /'bəz,wərd/ ▶ **n.** informal a technical word or phrase that has become fashionable.

by /bī/ ▶ **prep.** **1** through the action of. **2** indicating an amount or the size of a margin: *the shot missed her by miles.* **3** indicating the end of a time period. **4** beside. **5** past and beyond. **6** during. **7** according to: *it is all right by me.* ▶ **adv.** so as to go past. □ **by and by** before long. **by the by** in passing. **by and large** on the whole.

bye¹ /bī/ ▶ **n.** the moving of a competitor straight to the next round of a competition because they have no opponent.

bye² (also **bye-bye**) ▶ **exclam.** informal goodbye.

by·gone /'bī,gôn/ ▶ **adj.** belonging to an earlier time. □ **let bygones be bygones** decide to forget past disagreements.

by·law /'bī,lô/ ▶ **n.** a rule made by a company or society.

by·line /'bī,līn/ ▶ **n.** **1** a line in a newspaper naming the writer of an article. **2** (in soccer) the part of the goal line to either side of the goal.

by·pass /'bī,pas/ ▶ **n.** **1** a road passing around a town or its center. **2** an operation to help the circulation of blood by directing it through a new passage. ▶ **v.** go past or around.

SYNONYMS ▶ **n.** **detour**, alternate route, diversion, shortcut. ▶ **v.** **1** **go around**, go past, make a detour around, avoid. **2** **avoid**, sidestep, evade, escape, elude, skirt, dodge, circumvent, get around, pass over, ignore; informal duck.

by·prod·uct /'bī,prädəkt/ ▶ **n.** a product produced in the process of making something else.

by·stand·er /'bī,standər/ ▶ **n.** a person who is present at an event but does not take part.

SYNONYMS **onlooker**, passerby, observer, spectator, eyewitness.

byte /bīt/ ▶ **n.** a unit of information stored in a computer, equal to eight bits.

by·way /'bī,wā/ ▶ **n.** a minor road or path.

by·word /'bī,wərd/ ▶ **n.** **1** a notable example of something. **2** a saying.

Byz·an·tine /'bizən,tēn, bə'zan-, -,tīn/ ▶ **adj.** **1** relating to Byzantium (now Istanbul). **2** relating to the Eastern Orthodox Church. **3** very complicated and detailed. **4** very devious or underhand.

Cc

C (or **c**) ▶ n. (plural **Cs** or **C's**) **1** the third letter of the alphabet. **2** the Roman numeral for 100. ▶ abbr. **1** Celsius or centigrade. **2** (©) copyright. **3** (**c**) cent(s). **4** (**c** or **ca.**) circa. **5** (**c.**) century or centuries.

Ca ▶ symbol the chemical element calcium.

cab /kab/ ▶ n. **1** a taxi. **2** the driver's compartment in a truck, bus, or train.

SYNONYMS **taxi**, taxicab, hack; pedicab.

ca·bal /kə'bäl, -'bal/ ▶ n. a secret political group.

cab·a·ret /ˌkabə'rā, 'kabəˌrā/ ▶ n. entertainment held in a nightclub or restaurant while the audience members sit at tables.

cab·bage /'kabij/ ▶ n. a vegetable with thick green or purple leaves.

cab·bie /'kabē/ (also **cabby**) ▶ n. (plural **cabbies**) informal a taxi driver.

cab·in /'kabən/ ▶ n. **1** a private compartment on a ship. **2** the passenger compartment in an aircraft. **3** a small wooden shelter or house, usually in a remote or wild area.

SYNONYMS **1 berth**, stateroom, compartment. **2 cottage**, log cabin, shanty, hut, shack; chalet; cabana.

□ **cabin cruiser** a motorboat with a living area.

cab·i·net /'kabənit/ ▶ n. **1** a cupboard with drawers or shelves for storing things. **2** a box or piece of furniture enclosing a radio, speaker, etc. **3** a body of advisers to the president, composed of the heads of the executive departments of the government.

SYNONYMS **1 cupboard**, wall unit, bookcase; china cabinet, file cabinet, medicine cabinet; sideboard, credenza, buffet. **2 council**, administration, ministry.

cab·i·net·mak·er /'kabənitˌmākər/ ▶ n. a person who makes fine wooden furniture as a job.

ca·ble /'kābəl/ ▶ n. **1** a thick rope of wire or fiber. **2** a wire for transmitting electricity or telecommunication signals.

SYNONYMS **1** *a thick cable moored the ship* **rope**, cord, line, guy; Nautical hawser. **2** *electric cables* **wire**, lead, cord, power line.

□ **cable car** a small carriage that travels on a cable railway or that hangs from a moving cable and travels up and down the side of a mountain. **cable television** a system in which programs are transmitted by cable.

ca·boo·dle /kə'bo͞odl/ ▶ n. (**the whole (kit and) caboodle**) informal the whole number of people or things in question.

ca·boose /kə'bo͞os/ ▶ n. a railroad car with accommodations for the train crew, typically attached to the end of the train.

cab·ri·o·let /ˌkabrēə'lā/ ▶ n. **1** a car with a roof that folds down. **2** a horse-drawn carriage with a hood.

ca·ca·o /kə'kou, kə'kāō/ ▶ n. (plural **cacaos**) a seed of a tropical American tree, from which cocoa and chocolate are made.

cache /kasʜ/ ▶ n. a hidden store of things.

SYNONYMS **hoard**, store, stockpile, stock, supply, reserve, arsenal; informal stash.

ca·chet /ka'sʜā/ ▶ n. the state of being respected or admired; prestige.

cack·le /'kakəl/ ▶ v. (**cackles**, **cackling**, **cackled**) **1** laugh noisily. **2** (of a hen) make a noisy clucking cry. ▶ n. a noisy cry or laugh.

ca·coph·o·ny /kə'käfənē/ ▶ n. (plural **cacophonies**) a mixture of loud and unpleasant sounds. ■ **ca·coph·o·nous** adj.

cac·tus /'kaktəs/ ▶ n. (plural **cacti** /-tī, -tē/ or **cactuses**) a succulent plant with a thick fleshy stem that has spines but no leaves.

cad /kad/ ▶ n. dated or humorous a man who is dishonest or treats other people, especially women, badly. ■ **cad·dish** adj.

ca·dav·er /kə'davər/ ▶ n. Medicine a dead body.

ca·dav·er·ous /kə'davərəs/ ▶ adj. resembling a corpse in being very pale and thin.

cad·die /'kadē/ (or **caddy**) ▶ n. (plural **caddies**) a person who carries a golfer's clubs. ▶ v. (**caddies**, **caddying**, **caddied**) work as a caddie.

cad·dy /'kadē/ ▶ n. (plural **caddies**) a small storage container.

ca·dence /'kādns/ ▶ n. **1** the rise and fall in pitch of the voice. **2** the close of a musical phrase.

SYNONYMS **modulation**, intonation, inflection, lilt; rhythm, tempo, meter, beat, pulse.

ca·den·za /kə'denzə/ ▶ n. a difficult solo passage in a concerto or other piece of music.

ca·det /kə'det/ ▶ n. a young trainee in the armed services or police.

cadge /kaj/ ▶ v. (**cadges**, **cadging**, **cadged**) informal ask for or get something without paying or working for it.

cad·mi·um /'kadmēəm/ ▶ n. a silvery-white metallic element.

ca·dre /'kadrē, 'käd-, -ˌrā, -rə/ ▶ n. a small group of people trained for a particular purpose or at the center of a political organization.

Cae·sar /'sēzər/ ▶ n. a title of Roman emperors.

SPELLING

Write -ae-, not -ea-: Caesar.

cae·su·ra /si'zʜo͝orə, -'zo͝orə/ ▶ n. **1** (in Greek and Latin verse) a break between words within a metrical foot. **2** (in modern verse) a pause near the middle of a line.

ca·fe /ka'fā, kə-/ ▶ **n.** a small restaurant selling light meals and drinks.

SYNONYMS **bistro**, restaurant, coffee shop, tea room; diner, snack bar, cafeteria, lunchroom.

caf·e·te·ri·a /ˌkafi'ti(ə)rēə/ ▶ **n.** a restaurant or a school's dining room at which people serve themselves or are served as they walk past a counter where food is available.

SYNONYMS **lunchroom**, canteen, luncheonette, buffet, cafe, snack bar, mess hall; informal caf.

caf·feine /ka'fēn, 'kafˌēn/ ▶ **n.** a stimulating substance found in tea and coffee.

caf·tan ⇒ **KAFTAN.**

cage /kāj/ ▶ **n.** a structure of bars or wires used for confining animals. ▶ **v.** (**cages**, **caging**, **caged**) confine an animal in a cage.

SYNONYMS ▶ **n.** **enclosure**, pen, pound, coop, hutch, birdcage, aviary. ▶ **v.** **confine**, shut in/up, fence in, pen, coop up, enclose, impound.

cag·ey /'kājē/ ▶ **adj.** informal cautiously reluctant to speak.

SYNONYMS **secretive**, guarded, tight-lipped, reticent, evasive; informal playing your cards close to your chest.

■ **cag·i·ly** /'kājilē/ **adv.**

ca·hoots /kə'ho͞ots/ ▶ **pl.n.** (**in cahoots**) informal making secret plans together.

cai·man /'kāmən/ ▶ **n.** a tropical American reptile similar to an alligator but with a heavily armored belly.

Cain /kān/ ▶ **n.** (**raise Cain**) informal create trouble or a commotion.

cairn /ke(ə)rn/ ▶ **n.** a mound of rough stones built as a memorial or landmark.

ca·jole /kə'jōl/ ▶ **v.** (**cajoles**, **cajoling**, **cajoled**) persuade someone to do something by flattering them.

SYNONYMS **persuade**, wheedle, coax, talk into, prevail on; informal sweet-talk, soft-soap.

Ca·jun /'kājən/ ▶ **n.** a member of a French-speaking community in areas of southern Louisiana. ▶ **adj.** relating to the Cajuns.

cake /kāk/ ▶ **n.** **1** an item of soft sweet food made from baking a mixture of flour, fat, eggs, and sugar. **2** a flat round item of savory food: *crab cakes*. ▶ **v.** (**cakes**, **caking**, **caked**) (of a thick or sticky substance) cover and become encrusted on something.

SYNONYMS ▶ **n.** **1** *chocolate cake* gateau, torte, layer cake, sheet cake, petit four. **2** *a cake of soap* **bar**, brick, block, slab, lump. ▶ **v.** *boots caked with mud* **coat**, encrust, plaster, cover.

□ **a piece of cake** informal something easily achieved. **take the cake** informal surpass or exceed all others.

cake·walk /'kākˌwôk/ ▶ **n.** informal a very easy task.

Cal ▶ **abbr.** large calorie(s).

cal ▶ **abbr.** small calorie(s).

cal·a·brese /'kaləˌbrēz/ ▶ **n.** a bright green variety of broccoli.

cal·a·mine /'kaləˌmīn/ ▶ **n.** a pink powder used to make a soothing lotion or ointment.

ca·lam·i·ty /kə'lamitē/ ▶ **n.** (plural **calamities**) an event causing great and sudden damage or distress.

SYNONYMS **disaster**, catastrophe, tragedy, cataclysm, accident, misfortune, misadventure.

■ **ca·lam·i·tous adj.**

cal·car·e·ous /kal'ke(ə)rēəs/ ▶ **adj.** containing calcium carbonate; chalky.

cal·cif·er·ol /kal'sifəˌrôl, -ˌrōl/ ▶ **n.** vitamin D_2, essential for the storing of calcium in bones.

cal·ci·fied /'kalsəˌfīd/ ▶ **adj.** hardened by the addition of calcium salts.

cal·cine /'kalˌsīn/ ▶ **v.** (**calcines**, **calcining**, **calcined**) reduce, oxidize, or dry a substance by strong heat.

cal·cite /'kalˌsīt/ ▶ **n.** a white or colorless mineral consisting of calcium carbonate.

cal·ci·um /'kalsēəm/ ▶ **n.** a soft gray metallic substance. □ **calcium carbonate** a white compound found as chalk, limestone, and marble.

cal·cu·late /'kalkyəˌlāt/ ▶ **v.** (**calculates**, **calculating**, **calculated**) **1** work out a number or amount using mathematics. **2** intend an action to have a particular effect.

SYNONYMS **1** **compute**, work out, reckon, figure, add up/together, count up, tally, total, tote, tot up. **2** **intend**, mean, design.

■ **cal·cu·la·ble** /'kalkyələbəl/ **adj.**

cal·cu·lat·ed /'kalkyəˌlātid/ ▶ **adj.** done with awareness of the likely effect.

SYNONYMS **deliberate**, premeditated, planned, preplanned, preconceived, intentional, intended. ANTONYMS unintentional.

cal·cu·lat·ing /'kalkyəˌlātiNG/ ▶ **adj.** craftily planning things so as to benefit yourself.

SYNONYMS **cunning**, crafty, wily, sly, scheming, devious, disingenuous.

cal·cu·la·tion /ˌkalkyə'lāSHən/ ▶ **n.** **1** a count or assessment done using mathematics. **2** an assessment of the risks or effects of a course of action.

SYNONYMS **1** **computation**, reckoning, adding up, counting up, working out. **2** **assessment**, judgment, forecast, projection, prediction.

cal·cu·la·tor /'kalkyəˌlātər/ ▶ **n.** a small electronic device used for making mathematical calculations.

cal·cu·lus /'kalkyələs/ ▶ **n.** (plural **calculi** /-ˌlī, -ˌlē/ or **calculuses**) the branch of mathematics concerned with problems involving rates of change.

Cal·e·do·ni·an /ˌkalə'dōnēən/ ▶ **adj.** relating to Scotland or the Scottish Highlands.

cal·en·dar /'kaləndər/ ▶ **n.** **1** a chart showing the days, weeks, and months of a particular year. **2** a system by which the beginning and end of a year are fixed. **3** a list of special days or events.

SYNONYMS **schedule**, agenda, timetable, diary, program.

calf[1] /kaf/ ▶ **n.** (plural **calves** /kavz/) **1** a young cow or bull. **2** the young of some other large animals, e.g., elephants.

calf[2] ▶ **n.** (plural **calves**) the fleshy part at the back of a person's leg below the knee.

cal·i·ber /'kaləbər/ ▶ **n.** **1** the diameter of the inside of a gun barrel, or of a bullet or shell. **2** a person's quality or ability: *a man of high caliber*.

SYNONYMS **1** **bore**, diameter, gauge. **2** **quality**, standard, level, merit, distinction, stature, excellence, ability, expertise, talent, capability.

cal·i·brate /'kaləˌbrāt/ ▶ **v.** (**calibrates**, **calibrating**, **calibrated**) **1** mark a gauge or instrument with units of measurement. **2** compare the readings of an instrument with those of a standard. ■ **cal·i·bra·tion** /kalə'brāSHən/ **n.**

cal·i·co /'kali,kō/ ▶ **n.** (plural **calicoes** or **calicos**) printed cotton fabric.

cal·i·per /'kaləpər/ (or **calliper**) ▶ **n. 1** (also **calipers**) a measuring instrument with two hinged legs. **2** (also **caliper splint**) a metal support for a person's leg.

ca·liph /'kālif, 'kal-/ ▶ **n.** (in the past) the chief Muslim ruler.

cal·is·then·ics /,kaləs'THeniks/ ▶ **pl.n.** gymnastic exercises.

call /kôl/ ▶ **v. 1** shout to someone to attract their attention or ask them to come somewhere. **2** telephone someone. **3** (of a bird or animal) make its characteristic cry. **4** pay a brief visit. **5** name or describe someone or something. **6** predict the result of a vote or contest. ▶ **n. 1** an act of calling someone. **2** an act of telephoning someone. **3** the cry of a bird or animal. **4** a brief visit. **5** (**call for**) demand or need for: *there is little call for antique furniture.*

> SYNONYMS ▶ **v. 1 cry**, cry out, shout, yell, sing out, exclaim, shriek, scream, roar; informal holler. **2 phone**, telephone, give someone a call; informal call up, give someone a ring, give someone a buzz. **3 summon**, send for, order. **4 convene**, summon, assemble. **5 name**, christen, baptize, designate, style, term, dub. **6 describe as**, regard as, look on as, think of as, consider to be. ▶ **n. 1 cry**, shout, yell, exclamation, shriek, scream, roar; informal holler. **2** *the call of the barn owl* **cry**, song. **3 phone call**, telephone call. **4 appeal**, plea, request. **5** *there's no call for that kind of language* **need**, necessity, reason, justification, excuse. **6** *there's no call for expensive wine* **demand**, desire, market. **7 attraction**, appeal, lure, allure, pull, draw.

□ **call center** an office in which large numbers of telephone calls are handled for an organization. **call for** require. **call something in** demand payment of a loan. **call-in** a radio or television program during which you can telephone the studio to make comments or ask questions. **call something off** cancel something. **call on** turn to for help. **call sign** (also **call signal**) **1** a message or tune broadcast on radio to identify the sender. **2** the sequence of letters identifying a radio station. **call the shots** (or **tune**) be in charge of how something should be done. **call someone up** summon someone to serve in the army or to play in a team. **on call** available to provide a service if necessary. ■ **call·er n.**

call·back /'kôl,bak/ ▶ **n. 1** an invitation to return for a second audition or interview. **2** a telephone call made to return a call.

cal·lig·ra·phy /kə'ligrəfē/ ▶ **n.** decorative handwriting. ■ **cal·lig·ra·pher n.**

call·ing /'kôliNG/ ▶ **n. 1** a profession or occupation. **2** a strong feeling that you are suitable for a particular occupation; a vocation.

> SYNONYMS **profession**, occupation, job, vocation, career, métier, work, line of work, employment, trade, craft.

cal·lous /'kaləs/ ▶ **adj.** insensitive and cruel.

> SYNONYMS **heartless**, unfeeling, uncaring, cold, cold-hearted, hard, hardbitten, as hard as nails, hard-hearted, insensitive, unsympathetic. ANTONYMS kind, compassionate.

■ **cal·lous·ly adv.**

cal·low /'kalō/ ▶ **adj.** young and inexperienced.

> SYNONYMS **immature**, inexperienced, naive, green, raw, untried, unworldly, unsophisticated; informal wet behind the ears. ANTONYMS mature.

cal·lus /'kaləs/ (or **callous**) ▶ **n.** an area of thickened and hardened skin.

calm /kä(l)m/ ▶ **adj. 1** not nervous, angry, or excited. **2** peaceful and undisturbed. ▶ **n.** a calm state or period. ▶ **v.** (often **calm down** or **calm someone down**) become or make someone calm.

> SYNONYMS ▶ **adj. 1 relaxed**, composed, self-possessed, serene, tranquil, unruffled, unperturbed, unflustered, untroubled, unexcitable, levelheaded, unemotional, phlegmatic, imperturbable; informal unflappable, laid-back. **2 windless**, still, quiet, tranquil, smooth. ANTONYMS excited, nervous, stormy. ▶ **n. 1** *his usual calm deserted him* **composure**, coolness, calmness, self-possession, sangfroid, serenity, tranquility; informal cool, unflappability. **2** *calm prevailed* **tranquility**, stillness, quiet, peace.

■ **calm·ly adv. calm·ness n.**

ca·lor·ic /kə'lôrik, -'lär-/ ▶ **adj.** technical relating to heat.

cal·o·rie /'kal(ə)rē/ ▶ **n.** (plural **calories**) **1** a unit for measuring how much energy food will produce. **2** a unit of heat.

cal·o·rif·ic /,kalə'rifik/ ▶ **adj.** relating to the amount of energy contained in food or fuel.

cal·o·rim·e·ter /,kalə'rimitər/ ▶ **n.** a device for measuring the amount of heat involved in a chemical reaction or other process.

ca·lum·ni·ate /kə'ləmnē,āt/ ▶ **v.** (**calumniates**, **calumniating**, **calumniated**) formal make false and damaging statements about.

cal·um·ny /'kaləmnē/ ▶ **n.** (plural **calumnies**) formal the making of false and damaging statements about someone.

calve /kav/ ▶ **v.** (**calves**, **calving**, **calved**) give birth to a calf.

calves /kavz/ plural of CALF[1], CALF[2].

Cal·vin·ism /'kalvə,nizəm/ ▶ **n.** the form of Protestantism of John Calvin (1509–64) and his successors, centering on the belief that God has ordained everything that happens. ■ **Cal·vin·ist n. Cal·vin·is·tic** /,kalvə'nistik/ **adj.**

ca·lyp·so /kə'lipsō/ ▶ **n.** (plural **calypsos**) a kind of West Indian song with improvised words on a topical theme.

ca·lyx /'kāliks, 'kal-/ (or **calix**) ▶ **n.** (plural **calyces** /'kālə,sēz, 'kal-/ or **calyxes**) the ring of small leaves (sepals) that form a layer around the bud of a flower.

cam /kam/ ▶ **n. 1** a projecting part on a wheel or shaft, which comes into contact with another part while rotating and makes it move. **2** a camshaft.

ca·ma·ra·de·rie /,käm(ə)'rädərē, ,kam-, -'rad-/ ▶ **n.** trust and friendship between people.

cam·ber /'kambər/ ▶ **n.** a slightly curved shape of a horizontal surface such as a road.

cam·bi·um /'kambēəm/ ▶ **n.** (plural **cambia** /-bēə/ or **cambiums**) Botany a layer of cells in a plant stem from which new tissue grows by the division of cells.

Cam·bo·di·an /kam'bōdēən/ ▶ **n.** a person from Cambodia. ▶ **adj.** relating to Cambodia.

Cam·bri·an /'kambrēən, 'kām-/ ▶ **adj. 1** Welsh. **2** Geology relating to the first period in the Paleozoic era (about 570 million to 510 million years ago).

cam·bric /'kāmbrik/ ▶ n. a lightweight white linen or cotton fabric.

cam·cord·er /'kam,kôrdər/ ▶ n. a portable combined video camera and video recorder.

came /kām/ past tense of COME.

cam·el /'kaməl/ ▶ n. a large long-necked animal with either one or two humps on its back.

ca·mel·lia /kə'mēlyə/ ▶ n. an evergreen shrub with white, pink, or red flowers and shiny leaves.

Cam·em·bert /'kaməm,be(ə)r/ ▶ n. a kind of rich, soft, creamy cheese originally made near Camembert in Normandy, France.

cam·e·o /'kamē,ō/ ▶ n. (plural **cameos**) **1** a piece of jewelry consisting of a carving of a head against a differently colored background. **2** a short piece of writing giving a good description of a person or thing. **3** a small part played by a well-known actor.

cam·er·a /'kam(ə)rə/ ▶ n. a device for taking photographs or recording moving images. □ **in camera** Law in a judge's private rooms, without the press and public being present.

cam·er·a·man /'kam(ə)rə,man/ ▶ n. (plural **cameramen**) a man whose job is operating a television or movie camera.

cam·er·a ob·scu·ra /əb'skyŏŏrə/ ▶ n. a darkened box or building with a lens or opening for casting the image of an outside object onto a screen inside.

cam·i·sole /'kamə,sōl/ ▶ n. a woman's loose-fitting undergarment for the upper body.

cam·ou·flage /'kamə,fläzH, -,fläj/ ▶ n. **1** the painting or covering of soldiers and military equipment to make them blend in with their surroundings. **2** clothing or materials used for this purpose. **3** the natural appearance of an animal that allows it to blend in with its surroundings. ▶ v. (**camouflages**, **camouflaging**, **camouflaged**) disguise using camouflage.

> SYNONYMS ▶ n. **disguise**, mask, screen, cover, cloak, front, facade, blind, concealment, subterfuge. ▶ v. **disguise**, hide, conceal, mask, screen, cover (up).

camp¹ /kamp/ ▶ n. **1** a place where soldiers, refugees, etc., live temporarily in tents, huts, or cabins. **2** a recreational institution providing facilities for outdoor activities, sports, crafts, and other special interests and typically featuring rustic overnight accommodations. **3** the supporters of a particular party or set of beliefs. ▶ v. live in a tent while on vacation.

> SYNONYMS ▶ n. **1 campsite**, encampment, camping ground, bivouac, base, settlement. **2 faction**, wing, group, lobby, caucus, bloc.

□ **camp follower 1** a person who associates with a group without being a full member. **2** a civilian attached to a military camp.

camp² informal ▶ adj. deliberately exaggerated and theatrical in style. □ **camp it up** behave in a camp way.

cam·paign /kam'pān/ ▶ n. **1** a series of military operations in a particular area. **2** an organized course of action to achieve a goal. ▶ v. work toward a goal.

> SYNONYMS ▶ n. **1** *Napoleon's Russian campaign* **operation**(s), maneuver(s), offensive, attack, war, battle, crusade. **2** *the campaign to reduce vehicle emissions* **effort**, drive, push, struggle, movement, crusade, operation, strategy. ▶ v. **fight**, battle, push, press, strive, struggle, lobby, agitate.

■ **cam·paign·er** n.

cam·pa·ni·le /,kampə'nēlē, -'nēl/ ▶ n. a bell tower.

cam·pa·nol·o·gy /,kampə'näləjē/ ▶ n. the art of bell-ringing.

camp·er /'kampər/ ▶ n. **1** a person who spends a vacation in a tent or camp. **2** a large motor vehicle with facilities for sleeping and cooking while camping. □ **happy camper** a comfortable, contented person.

camp·fire /'kamp,fī(ə)r/ ▶ n. an open-air fire in a camp.

cam·phor /'kamfər/ ▶ n. a strong-smelling white substance, used in medicine and in insect repellents.

camp·site /'kamp,sīt/ ▶ n. a place used for camping.

cam·pus /'kampəs/ ▶ n. (plural **campuses**) the grounds and buildings of a university, college, or high school.

cam·shaft /'kam,sHaft/ ▶ n. a shaft with one or more cams attached to it.

can¹ /kan/ ▶ modal v. (3rd singular present **can**; past **could** /kŏŏd/) **1** be able to. **2** be allowed to.

> USAGE
>
> When you're asking to be allowed to do something, it is more polite to say **may** rather than **can** (*may we leave now?* rather than *can we leave now?*).

can² ▶ n. a cylindrical metal container. ▶ v. (**cans**, **canning**, **canned**) preserve food in a can. □ **a can of worms** a complicated matter that will prove difficult to manage.

Can·a·da goose /'kanədə/ ▶ n. a brownish-gray goose with a black head and neck.

Ca·na·di·an /kə'nādēən/ ▶ n. a person from Canada. ▶ adj. relating to Canada.

Ca·na·di·an·ism /kə'nādēə,nizəm/ ▶ n. a word or phrase used or originating in Canada.

ca·nal /kə'nal/ ▶ n. **1** a water-filled channel made for boats to travel on or to convey water to fields. **2** a passage in a plant or animal carrying food, liquid, or air: *the ear canal*.

can·al·ize /'kanəl,īz/ ▶ v. (**canalizes**, **canalizing**, **canalized**) **1** convert a river into a canal. **2** convey through a duct or channel. **3** give a direction or purpose to.

can·a·pé /'kanə,pā, -pē/ ▶ n. a small piece of bread or pastry with a savory topping.

ca·nard /kə'när(d)/ ▶ n. a false rumor or story.

ca·nar·y /kə'ne(ə)rē/ ▶ n. (plural **canaries**) a small bright yellow bird with a tuneful song.

ca·nas·ta /kə'nastə/ ▶ n. a card game using two packs and usually played by two pairs of partners.

can·can /'kan,kan/ ▶ n. a lively, high-kicking stage dance.

can·cel /'kansəl/ ▶ v. (**cancels**, **canceling**, **canceled**) **1** decide that a planned event will not take place. **2** withdraw from or end an arrangement. **3** (**cancel something out**) (of one thing) have an equal but opposite effect on another thing. **4** mark a stamp, ticket, etc., to show that it has been used.

> SYNONYMS **1 call off**, abandon, scrap, drop, ax; informal scrub, nix, redline. **2 annul**, invalidate, declare null and void, void, revoke, rescind, retract, withdraw. **3** (**cancel out**) **nullify**, negate, neutralize, wipe out, balance (out), make up for, compensate for, offset.

■ **can·cel·la·tion** /,kansə'lāsHən/ n.

Can·cer /'kansər/ ▶ **n.** a sign of the zodiac (the Crab), June 21–July 22.

can·cer /'kansər/ ▶ **n. 1** a disease caused by an uncontrolled growth of abnormal cells in a part of the body. **2** a tumor. **3** something evil or destructive that is hard to contain or destroy.

SYNONYMS (**malignant**) **growth**, tumor, malignancy; technical carcinoma, sarcoma.

■ **can·cer·ous adj.**

can·de·la /kan'dēlə, -'delə/ ▶ **n.** the basic unit of luminous intensity.

can·de·la·brum /ˌkandə'läbrəm, -'lab-/ ▶ **n.** (plural **candelabra** /-brə/) a large branched holder for several candles or lamps.

can·did /'kandid/ ▶ **adj.** truthful and straightforward; frank.

SYNONYMS **frank**, forthright, direct, blunt, outspoken, plain-spoken, open, honest, truthful, sincere; informal upfront, on the up and up. ANTONYMS guarded.

■ **can·did·ly adv.**

can·di·date /'kandiˌdāt, -dit/ ▶ **n. 1** a person who applies for a job or is nominated for election. **2** a student who has nearly completed the requirements for a degree. **3** a person or thing seen as suitable for a particular treatment or position: *she was the perfect candidate for a biography.*

SYNONYMS **applicant**, interviewee, examinee; contender, competitor, nominee, entrant, hopeful.

■ **can·di·da·cy** /'kandidəsē/ **n.**

can·died /'kandēd/ ▶ **adj.** (of fruit) preserved in a sugar syrup.

can·dle /'kandl/ ▶ **n.** a stick of wax with a central wick that is lit to produce light as it burns.

can·dle·stick /'kandlˌstik/ ▶ **n.** a support or holder for a candle.

can·dle·wick /'kandlˌwik/ ▶ **n.** a thick, soft cotton fabric with a tufted pattern.

can·dor /'kandər, -ˌdôr/ ▶ **n.** the quality of being open and honest.

SYNONYMS **frankness**, openness, honesty, candidness, truthfulness, sincerity, forthrightness, directness, bluntness; informal telling it like it is.

can·dy /'kandē/ ▶ **n.** (plural **candies**) a small item of sweet food made with sugar, chocolate, etc. □ **candy-striped** patterned with alternating stripes of white and another color.

cane /kān/ ▶ **n. 1** the hollow stem of tall reeds, grasses, etc. **2** a length of cane used as a walking stick, for beating someone, etc. ▶ **v.** (**canes**, **caning**, **caned**) beat someone with a cane as a punishment.

ca·nine /'kāˌnīn/ ▶ **adj.** relating to or resembling a dog. ▶ **n.** a pointed tooth next to the incisors.

can·is·ter /'kanəstər/ ▶ **n.** a round or cylindrical container.

SPELLING

One **n**: canister.

can·ker /'kaNGkər/ ▶ **n. 1** a disease of trees and plants. **2** a condition in animals that causes open sores.

can·na·bis /'kanəbəs/ ▶ **n.** a drug made from the hemp plant.

canned /kand/ ▶ **adj.** preserved in a sealed can.

can·nel·li·ni bean /ˌkanl'ēnē/ ▶ **n.** a kidney-shaped bean of a creamy-white variety.

can·nel·lo·ni /ˌkanl'ōnē/ ▶ **pl.n.** rolls of pasta stuffed with a meat or vegetable mixture and cooked in a cheese sauce.

can·ner·y /'kanərē/ ▶ **n.** (plural **canneries**) a factory where food is canned.

can·ni·bal /'kanəbəl/ ▶ **n.** a person who eats the flesh of human beings. ■ **can·ni·bal·ism n. can·ni·bal·is·tic** /ˌkanəbə'listik/ **adj.**

can·ni·bal·ize /'kanəbəˌlīz/ ▶ **v.** (**cannibalizes**, **cannibalizing**, **cannibalized**) use a machine as a source of spare parts for others.

can·non /'kanən/ ▶ **n.** (plural **cannon** or **cannons**) **1** a large, heavy gun formerly used in warfare. **2** an automatic heavy gun that fires shells from an aircraft or tank. □ **cannon fodder** soldiers seen merely as a resource to be used up in war.

can·non·ade /ˌkanə'nād/ ▶ **n.** a period of continuous heavy gunfire.

can·non·ball /'kanənˌbôl/ ▶ **n.** a metal or stone ball fired from a cannon.

can·not /kə'nät, 'kanˌät/ ▶ **contr.** can not.

can·ny /'kanē/ ▶ **adj.** (**cannier**, **canniest**) shrewd, especially in financial matters.

SYNONYMS **shrewd**, astute, smart, sharp, discerning, discriminating, perceptive, clever, judicious, wise. ANTONYMS foolish.

■ **can·ni·ly adv.**

ca·noe /kə'nōō/ ▶ **n.** a narrow boat with pointed ends, propelled with a paddle. ▶ **v.** (**canoes**, **canoeing**, **canoed**) travel in a canoe. ■ **ca·noe·ist n.**

can·o·la /kə'nōlə/ ▶ **n.** the seed of the rape plant, which yields a valuable cooking oil.

can·on /'kanən/ ▶ **n. 1** a general rule or principle by which something is judged: *his designs break the canons of fashion.* **2** a church decree or law. **3** the works of a particular author or artist that are recognized as genuine. **4** a list of literary works considered as being of the highest quality. **5** a member of the clergy on the staff of a cathedral. **6** a piece of music in which a theme is taken up by two or more parts that overlap. □ **canon law** the laws of the Christian Church.

ca·non·i·cal /kə'nänikəl/ ▶ **adj. 1** accepted as authentic or as a standard: *the canonical works of modern science fiction.* **2** according to the laws of the Christian Church.

can·on·ize /'kanəˌnīz/ ▶ **v.** (**canonizes**, **canonizing**, **canonized**) officially declare a dead person to be a saint. ■ **can·on·i·za·tion** /ˌkanənə'zāSHən/ **n.**

ca·noo·dle /kə'nōōdl/ ▶ **v.** (**canoodles**, **canoodling**, **canoodled**) informal kiss and cuddle lovingly.

can·o·py /'kanəpē/ ▶ **n.** (plural **canopies**) **1** a cloth covering over a throne or bed. **2** a rooflike covering or shelter. **3** the expanding, umbrella-like part of a parachute.

SYNONYMS **awning**, shade, sunshade, covering.

■ **can·o·pied adj.**

cant[1] /kant/ ▶ **n. 1** insincere talk about moral or religious matters. **2** disapproving the language typical of a particular group: *thieves' cant.*

cant[2] ▶ **v.** tilt or slope. ▶ **n.** a slope or tilt.

can't /kant/ ▶ **contr.** cannot.

can·ta·bi·le /kän'täbəˌlā/ ▶ **adv. & adj.** Music in a smooth singing style.

can·ta·loupe /ˈkantlˌōp/ ▶ **n.** a small melon with orange flesh.

can·tan·ker·ous /kanˈtaNGkərəs/ ▶ **adj.** bad-tempered and uncooperative.

> SYNONYMS **grumpy**, grouchy, irritable, crotchety, testy, curmudgeonly, ill-tempered, ill-humored, crabby; cranky, ornery. ANTONYMS affable.

can·ta·ta /kənˈtätə/ ▶ **n.** a musical work with a solo voice and usually a chorus and orchestra.

can·teen /kanˈtēn/ ▶ **n. 1** a restaurant in a workplace or military base. **2** a small water bottle used by soldiers, campers, or hikers.

can·ter /ˈkantər/ ▶ **n.** a pace of a horse between a trot and a gallop. ▶ **v.** (**canters**, **cantering**, **cantered**) move at this pace.

can·ti·cle /ˈkantikəl/ ▶ **n.** a hymn or chant forming part of a church service.

can·ti·le·ver /ˈkantlˌēvər, -ˌevər/ ▶ **n.** a long beam or girder fixed at only one end, used for supporting a bridge. ■ **can·ti·le·vered adj.**

can·to /ˈkanˌtō/ ▶ **n.** (plural **cantos**) a division of a long poem.

can·ton /ˈkantn, ˈkanˌtän/ ▶ **n.** a political or administrative subdivision of a country, especially in Switzerland.

Can·ton·ese /ˌkantnˈēz, -ˈēs/ ▶ **n.** (plural **Cantonese**) **1** a person from Canton (another name for Guangzhou), a city in China. **2** a form of Chinese spoken mainly in SE China and Hong Kong. ▶ **adj.** relating to Canton or Cantonese.

can·tor /ˈkantər/ ▶ **n. 1** an official who leads the prayers in a synagogue. **2** a person who sings solo verses to which the choir or congregation respond in a Christian service.

can·vas /ˈkanvəs/ (or **canvass**) ▶ **n. 1** a strong, coarse cloth used to make sails, tents, etc. **2** an oil painting on canvas. **3** (**the canvas**) the floor of a boxing or wrestling ring, having a canvas covering.

can·vass /ˈkanvəs/ ▶ **v. 1** visit someone to ask for their vote in an election. **2** question someone to find out their opinion.

> SYNONYMS **1 campaign**, electioneer. **2 poll**, question, survey, interview, consult.

■ **can·vass·er n.**

can·yon /ˈkanyən/ ▶ **n.** a deep gorge, usually with a river flowing through it.

> SYNONYMS **ravine**, gorge, gully, chasm, abyss, gulf, gulch, coulee.

cap /kap/ ▶ **n. 1** a soft flat hat without a brim and sometimes having a visor. **2** a protective lid or cover. **3** an upper limit on spending or borrowing. **4** a small amount of explosive powder in a case that explodes when you hit it. ▶ **v.** (**caps**, **capping**, **capped**) **1** put a cap on. **2** be a fitting end to. **3** put a limit on.

> SYNONYMS ▶ **n. 1 hat**, baseball cap, ski cap, stocking cap, beanie, yarmulke; mortarboard. **2 lid**, top, stopper, cork, bung, stopple. **3 limit**, ceiling, curb, check. ▶ **v. 1 top**, crown, cover, coat, tip. **2 limit**, restrict, curb, control, peg.

□ **cap in hand** humbly asking for a favor.

ca·pa·bil·i·ty /ˌkāpəˈbilitē/ ▶ **n.** (plural **capabilities**) the power or ability to do something.

> SYNONYMS **ability**, capacity, power, potential, competence, aptitude, faculty, skill, talent, flair; informal know-how. ANTONYMS inability.

ca·pa·ble /ˈkāpəbəl/ ▶ **adj. 1** (**capable of**) having the ability to do something. **2** able to achieve what you need to do; competent.

> SYNONYMS **able**, competent, effective, proficient, accomplished, experienced, skillful, talented, gifted; informal useful. ANTONYMS incapable, incompetent.

■ **ca·pa·bly adv.**

ca·pa·cious /kəˈpāsHəs/ ▶ **adj.** having a lot of space inside; roomy.

ca·pac·i·tance /kəˈpasitəns/ ▶ **n.** the ability to store electric charge.

ca·pac·i·tor /kəˈpasitər/ ▶ **n.** a device used to store electric charge.

ca·pac·i·ty /kəˈpasitē/ ▶ **n.** (plural **capacities**) **1** the maximum amount that something can contain or produce. **2** the ability or power to do something. **3** a role or position: *working in a voluntary capacity.*

> SYNONYMS **1 volume**, size, dimensions, measurements, proportions. **2 ability**, capability, power, potential, competence, aptitude, faculty, skill, talent, flair. **3 role**, function, position, post, job, office.

ca·par·i·son /kəˈparəsən/ ▶ **v.** (**be caparisoned**) be clothed in rich decorative coverings.

cape[1] /kāp/ ▶ **n.** a short cloak.

> SYNONYMS **cloak**, mantle, shawl, poncho, pashmina.

cape[2] ▶ **n.** a piece of land that sticks out into the sea.

> SYNONYMS **headland**, promontory, point, head, horn, peninsula.

ca·per[1] /ˈkāpər/ ▶ **v.** (**capers**, **capering**, **capered**) skip or dance about in a lively or playful way. ▶ **n.** informal **1** a lighthearted or dishonest activity. **2** a playful skipping movement.

ca·per[2] ▶ **n.** the flower bud of a bramblelike shrub, pickled and used in cooking.

cap·il·lar·i·ty /kapəˈlaritē/ ▶ **n.** capillary action.

cap·il·lar·y /ˈkapəˌlerē/ ▶ **n.** (plural **capillaries**) **1** a very small blood vessel. **2** a tube with a very narrow diameter. □ **capillary action** the force that acts on a liquid in a narrow tube to push it up or down.

cap·i·tal /ˈkapitl/ ▶ **n. 1** the most important city or town of a country or region. **2** wealth that is owned or invested, lent, or borrowed. **3** a capital letter. **4** the top part of a pillar. ▶ **adj.** informal, dated excellent.

> SYNONYMS ▶ **n. money**, finance(s), funds, cash, wherewithal, means, assets, wealth, resources.

□ **capital gain** a profit from the sale of property or an investment. **capital goods** goods that are used in producing other goods. **capital letter** a large size of letter used to begin sentences and names. **capital offense** an offense that is punished by death. **capital punishment** the punishment of a crime by death. **capital sum** a lump sum of money payable to an insured person or paid as an initial fee or investment. **make capital out of** use to your own advantage.

cap·i·tal·ism /ˈkapətlˌizəm/ ▶ **n.** a system in which a country's trade and industry are controlled by private owners for profit.

> SYNONYMS **private enterprise**, free enterprise, the free market, private ownership. ANTONYMS communism.

■ **cap·i·tal·ist n. & adj.**

cap·i·tal·ize /ˈkapətl͵īz/ ▶ **v.** (**capitalizes**, **capitalizing**, **capitalized**) **1** (**capitalize on**) take advantage of. **2** convert into or provide with financial capital. **3** write in capital letters or with a capital first letter.

SYNONYMS (**capitalize on**) **take advantage of**, profit from, make the most of, exploit, develop; informal cash in on.

■ **cap·i·tal·i·za·tion** /͵kapətl-əˈzāsʜən/ **n.**

cap·i·ta·tion /͵kapiˈtāsʜən/ ▶ **n.** the payment of a fee or grant to a doctor, school, etc., the amount being determined by the number of patients, pupils, or customers involved.

cap·i·tol /ˈkapitl/ ▶ **n.** **1** a building housing a lawmaking body. **2** (**the Capitol**) the seat of the US Congress in Washington, DC.

ca·pit·u·late /kəˈpicʜə͵lāt/ ▶ **v.** (**capitulates**, **capitulating**, **capitulated**) give in to an opponent.

SYNONYMS **surrender**, give in, concede defeat, yield, give up (the struggle), submit, lay down your arms, throw in the towel. ANTONYMS resist.

■ **ca·pit·u·la·tion** **n.**

cap'n /ˈkapn/ ▶ **n.** informal captain.

ca·po /ˈkäpō/ ▶ **n.** (plural **capos**) the head or a branch head of the Mafia.

ca·pon /ˈkā͵pän, -pən/ ▶ **n.** a male chicken that has been fattened up for eating.

cap·puc·ci·no /͵käpəˈcʜēnō, ͵kap-/ ▶ **n.** (plural **cappuccinos**) coffee made with milk that has been made frothy by pressurized steam.

SPELLING

Double **p**, double **c**: cap**p**uc**c**ino.

ca·price /kəˈprēs/ ▶ **n.** a sudden change of mood or behavior.

ca·pri·cious /kəˈprisʜəs, -ˈprē-/ ▶ **adj.** having sudden changes of mood.

SYNONYMS **fickle**, volatile, unpredictable, temperamental, mercurial, impulsive, changeable, unreliable, erratic, wayward, whimsical, flighty. ANTONYMS consistent.

■ **ca·pri·cious·ly** **adv.**

Cap·ri·corn /ˈkapri͵kôrn/ ▶ **n.** a sign of the zodiac (the Goat), December 21–January 20.

ca·pri pants /kəˈprē/ (also **capris**) ▶ **pl.n.** close-fitting calf-length tapered trousers for women.

cap·si·cum /ˈkapsikəm/ ▶ **n.** (plural **capsicums**) a sweet pepper or chili pepper.

cap·size /ˈkap͵sīz, kapˈsīz/ ▶ **v.** (**capsizes**, **capsizing**, **capsized**) (of a boat) overturn in the water.

SYNONYMS **overturn**, turn over, turn upside down, upend, flip/tip over, keel over, turn turtle.

cap·stan /ˈkapstən/ ▶ **n.** a broad revolving cylinder for winding a heavy rope or cable.

cap·sule /ˈkapsəl, ˈkap͵so͞ol/ ▶ **n.** **1** a small gelatin container with a dose of medicine inside, swallowed whole. **2** a small case or compartment. **3** (also **space capsule**) a small spacecraft or the part of a larger one that contains the instruments or crew.

SYNONYMS **1 pill**, tablet, lozenge, pastille; informal tab. **2 module**, craft, probe.

cap·tain /ˈkaptən/ ▶ **n.** **1** the person in command of a ship or commercial aircraft. **2** the rank of naval officer above commander. **3** the rank of army officer above lieutenant. **4** the leader of a team. ▶ **v.** be the captain of.

SYNONYMS ▶ **n.** **1** *the ship's captain* **commander**, master; informal skipper. **2** *the team captain* **leader**, head, chief; informal boss.

■ **cap·tain·cy** **n.**

cap·tion /ˈkapsʜən/ ▶ **n.** **1** a title or explanation accompanying an illustration or cartoon. **2** a piece of writing appearing as part of a movie or television broadcast. ▶ **v.** provide a caption for.

SYNONYMS ▶ **n.** **title**, heading, legend, description.

cap·tious /ˈkapsʜəs/ ▶ **adj.** formal prone to petty fault-finding.

cap·ti·vate /ˈkaptə͵vāt/ ▶ **v.** (**captivates**, **captivating**, **captivated**) attract and hold the interest of; charm.

SYNONYMS **enthrall**, charm, enchant, bewitch, fascinate, beguile, entrance, delight, attract, allure. ANTONYMS bore.

cap·tive /ˈkaptiv/ ▶ **n.** a person who has been captured. ▶ **adj.** unable to escape.

SYNONYMS ▶ **n.** **prisoner**, convict, detainee, hostage, prisoner of war, internee. ▶ **adj.** **confined**, caged, incarcerated, locked up, jailed, imprisoned, interned, detained. ANTONYMS free.

cap·tiv·i·ty /kapˈtivitē/ ▶ **n.** the condition of being imprisoned or confined.

SYNONYMS **imprisonment**, incarceration, confinement, detention, internment. ANTONYMS freedom.

cap·tor /ˈkaptər, -͵tôr/ ▶ **n.** a person who captures another.

cap·ture /ˈkapcʜər/ ▶ **v.** (**captures**, **capturing**, **captured**) **1** take prisoner. **2** forcibly get possession of. **3** record accurately in words or pictures. **4** cause data to be stored in a computer. ▶ **n.** the action of capturing.

SYNONYMS ▶ **v.** **1 catch**, apprehend, seize, arrest, take prisoner, take into custody, detain. **2 occupy**, invade, conquer, seize, take. ANTONYMS release, liberate. ▶ **n.** **arrest**, apprehension, detention, seizure.

Cap·u·chin /ˈkap(y)əsʜən, kəˈp(y)o͞o-/ ▶ **n.** **1** a friar belonging to a strict branch of the Franciscan order. **2** (**capuchin**) a South American monkey with a hoodlike cap of hair on the head.

cap·y·ba·ra /͵kapə͵berə, -͵bärə/ ▶ **n.** (plural **capybara** or **capybaras**) a large South American rodent.

car /kär/ ▶ **n.** **1** a powered road vehicle designed to carry a small number of people. **2** a railroad carriage or wagon.

SYNONYMS **1 automobile**, motor vehicle, vehicle; dated motorcar; informal auto, wheels, jalopy. **2** *the dining car* **railroad car**, coach.

car·a·bi·ner /͵karəˈbēnər/ (or **karabiner**) ▶ **n.** a coupling link with a safety closure, used by rock climbers.

ca·rafe /kəˈraf, -ˈräf/ ▶ **n.** a wide-necked glass bottle for serving wine.

ca·ram·bo·la /͵karəmˈbōlə/ ▶ **n.** a golden-yellow fruit that is shaped like a star when cut through.

car·a·mel /ˈkarəməl, -ˌmel, ˈkärməl/ ▶ **n.** **1** sugar or syrup heated until it turns brown. **2** a soft candy made with sugar and butter.

car·a·pace /ˈkarəˌpās/ ▶ **n.** the hard upper shell of a tortoise, lobster, etc.

car·at /ˈkarət/ ▶ **n.** a unit of weight for precious stones and pearls.

car·a·van /ˈkarəˌvan/ ▶ **n.** historical a group of people traveling together across a desert.

car·a·van·sa·ry /ˌkarəˈvansərē/ (or **caravanserai** /-səˌrī/) ▶ **n.** (plural **caravansaries** or **caravanserais**) **1** historical an inn with a central courtyard in the desert regions of Asia or North Africa. **2** a group of people traveling together; a caravan.

car·a·vel /ˈkarəˌvel, -vəl/ (also **carvel** /ˈkärvel/) ▶ **n.** historical a small, fast Spanish or Portuguese ship of the 15th–17th centuries.

car·a·way /ˈkarəˌwā/ ▶ **n.** a plant whose seeds are used as a spice.

car·bide /ˈkärˌbīd/ ▶ **n.** a compound of carbon with a metal or other element.

car·bine /ˈkärˌbīn, -ˌbēn/ ▶ **n.** a light automatic rifle.

car·bo·hy·drate /ˌkärbəˈhīˌdrāt/ ▶ **n.** a substance (e.g., sugar or starch) containing carbon, hydrogen, and oxygen, found in food and used to give energy.

car·bol·ic /kärˈbälik/ (or **carbolic acid**) ▶ **n.** a kind of disinfectant.

car·bon /ˈkärbən/ ▶ **n.** a chemical element with two main pure forms (diamond and graphite), found in all organic compounds. □ **carbon capture** the process of trapping carbon dioxide produced by burning fossil fuels, to prevent it from entering the atmosphere. **carbon copy 1** a copy made with carbon paper. **2** a person or thing identical to another. **carbon dating** a method of finding out how old something is by measuring the amount of radioactive carbon-14 in it. **carbon dioxide** a gas produced by people and animals breathing out, and also by burning carbon, which is absorbed by plants in photosynthesis. **carbon fiber** a material consisting of thin, very strong filaments of carbon. **carbon footprint** the amount of carbon dioxide emitted by the activities of a particular person or organization. **carbon monoxide** a poisonous gas formed when carbon is not completely burned. **carbon-neutral** making no overall release of carbon dioxide into the atmosphere, through doing things like planting trees to offset emissions. **carbon paper** thin paper coated with carbon, used for making a copy of a document.

car·bo·na·ceous /ˌkärbəˈnāsнəs/ ▶ **adj.** consisting of or containing carbon or its compounds.

car·bo·nate /ˈkärbənət, -ˌnāt/ ▶ **n.** a compound containing carbon and oxygen together with a metal.

car·bo·nat·ed /ˈkärbəˌnātid/ ▶ **adj.** (of a drink) fizzy because it contains small bubbles of carbon dioxide.

car·bon·ic ac·id /kärˈbänik/ ▶ **n.** a very weak acid formed from carbon dioxide and water.

Car·bon·if·er·ous /ˌkärbəˈnifərəs/ ▶ **adj.** Geology relating to the fifth period in the Paleozoic era (about 363 to 290 million years ago).

car·bon·ize /ˈkärbəˌnīz/ ▶ **v.** (**carbonizes**, **carbonizing**, **carbonized**) convert into carbon, by heating or burning. ■ **car·bon·i·za·tion** /ˌkärbənəˈzāsнən/ **n.**

car·bo·run·dum /ˌkärbəˈrəndəm/ ▶ **n.** a very hard black substance used for grinding and polishing.

car·boy /ˈkärˌboi/ ▶ **n.** a large rounded glass or plastic bottle with a narrow neck, used for holding acids.

carbs /kärbz/ ▶ **pl.n.** informal dietary carbohydrates.

car·bun·cle /ˈkärˌbəngkəl/ ▶ **n.** **1** a large abscess or boil in the skin. **2** a polished red gem.

car·bu·re·tor /ˈkärb(y)əˌrātər/ ▶ **n.** a device in an engine that mixes the fuel with air.

car·cass /ˈkärkəs/ ▶ **n.** the dead body of an animal.

> SYNONYMS **corpse**, dead body, remains; Medicine cadaver; informal stiff.

car·cin·o·gen /kärˈsinəjən, ˈkärsənəˌjen/ ▶ **n.** a substance that can cause cancer. ■ **car·cin·o·gen·ic** /ˌkärsənəˈjenik/ **adj.**

car·ci·no·ma /ˌkärsəˈnōmə/ ▶ **n.** (plural **carcinomas**) a cancer of the skin or of the internal organs.

card[1] /kärd/ ▶ **n.** **1** thick, stiff paper or thin cardboard. **2** a piece of card printed with information, greetings, etc. **3** a small rectangular piece of plastic used for obtaining money from a bank or paying for goods. **4** a playing card. **5** (**cards**) a game played with playing cards. □ **card-carrying** registered as a member of a political party or labor union. **card sharp** a person who cheats at cards. **in the cards** possible or likely. **play your cards right** use your assets and opportunities well to get what you want. **put your cards on the table** state your plans openly.

card[2] ▶ **v.** disentangle the fibers of raw wool by combing it with a sharp-toothed instrument.

car·da·mom /ˈkärdəməm/ ▶ **n.** the seed and pods of a Southeast Asian plant, used as a spice.

card·board /ˈkärdˌbôrd/ ▶ **n.** thin board made from paper pulp.

car·di·ac /ˈkärdēˌak/ ▶ **adj.** having to do with the heart.

car·di·gan /ˈkärdigən/ ▶ **n.** a sweater with buttons down the front.

car·di·nal /ˈkärd-nl, ˈkärdn-əl/ ▶ **n.** an important Roman Catholic priest, having the power to elect the pope. ▶ **adj.** most important; chief. □ **cardinal number** a number expressing quantity (one, two, three, etc.). **cardinal point** each of the four main points of the compass (north, south, east, and west).

car·di·o·graph /ˈkärdēəˌgraf/ ▶ **n.** an instrument for recording heart movements.

car·di·ol·o·gy /ˌkärdēˈäləjē/ ▶ **n.** the branch of medicine concerned with the heart.

car·di·o·vas·cu·lar /ˌkärdēōˈvaskyələr/ ▶ **adj.** having to do with the heart and blood vessels.

car·doon /kärˈdo͞on/ ▶ **n.** a tall thistlelike plant related to the globe artichoke, with edible leaves and roots.

care /ke(ə)r/ ▶ **n.** **1** special attention or effort made to avoid damage, risk, or error. **2** the process of looking after and protecting someone or something. **3** a cause for anxiety, or a worried feeling. ▶ **v.** (**cares**, **caring**, **cared**) **1** feel concern or interest. **2** feel affection or liking. **3** (**care for** or **to do**) like to have or be willing to do. **4** (**care for**) look after.

> SYNONYMS ▶ **n.** **1 safekeeping**, supervision, custody, charge, protection, responsibility, guardianship. **2 discretion**, caution, sensitivity, thought, regard, consideration. **3 worry**, anxiety, trouble, concern, stress, pressure, strain. ANTONYMS neglect, carelessness. ▶ **v.** **be concerned**, worry (yourself), trouble/concern yourself, bother, mind, be interested; informal give a damn/hoot.

□ **care of** at the address of someone who will look after or pass on mail. **take care 1** be careful.

2 make sure to do a particular thing. **take care of** look after or deal with.

ca·reen /kə'rēn/ ▶ v. **1** (of a ship) tilt to one side. **2** move in an uncontrolled way; career.

ca·reer /kə'ri(ə)r/ ▶ n. an occupation that is undertaken for a long period of a person's life. ▶ v. (**careers**, **careering**, **careered**) move very fast and in an uncontrolled way.

SYNONYMS ▶ n. **profession**, occupation, vocation, calling, life's work, employment. ▶ v. **hurtle**, rush, shoot, race, speed, charge, fly; informal belt, tear.

ca·reer·ist /kə'ri(ə)rist/ ▶ n. a person whose only concern is to make progress in their career. ■ **ca·reer·ism** n.

care·free /'ke(ə)r,frē/ ▶ adj. free from anxiety or responsibility.

SYNONYMS **unworried**, untroubled, blithe, nonchalant, happy-go-lucky, free and easy, easygoing, relaxed; informal laid-back. ANTONYMS troubled.

care·ful /'ke(ə)rfəl/ ▶ adj. **1** taking care to avoid harm; cautious. **2** showing a lot of thought and attention.

SYNONYMS **1** *be careful on the stairs* **cautious**, alert, attentive, watchful, vigilant, wary, on your guard, circumspect. **2** *careful with money* **prudent**, thrifty, economical, sparing, frugal. **3** *careful consideration of the facts* **attentive**, conscientious, painstaking, meticulous, diligent, assiduous, scrupulous, methodical. ANTONYMS careless.

■ **care·ful·ly** adv. **care·ful·ness** n.

care·giv·er /'ke(ə)r,givər/ ▶ n. someone who takes care of a child or a sick or disabled adult.

care·less /'ke(ə)rlis/ ▶ adj. not giving enough attention to avoiding harm or mistakes.

SYNONYMS **1** *careless drivers* **inattentive**, negligent, heedless, irresponsible, impetuous, reckless. **2** *careless work* **shoddy**, slapdash, slipshod, scrappy, slovenly, sloppy, negligent, lax, slack, disorganized, hasty, hurried. **3** *a careless remark* **thoughtless**, insensitive, indiscreet, unguarded, incautious, inadvertent. ANTONYMS careful.

■ **care·less·ly** adv. **care·less·ness** n.

ca·ress /kə'res/ ▶ v. touch or stroke gently or lovingly. ▶ n. a gentle or loving touch.

SYNONYMS ▶ v. **stroke**, touch, fondle, brush, feel, skim.

car·et /'karit/ ▶ n. a mark (‸, ⁁) placed below a line of text to indicate an insertion.

care·tak·er /'ke(ə)r,tākər/ ▶ n. a person employed to look after a building.

SYNONYMS **custodian**, janitor, maintenance man/woman, superintendent; curator; attendant, porter, concierge; informal super.

care·worn /'ke(ə)r,wôrn/ ▶ adj. showing signs of prolonged worry.

car·go /'kärgō/ ▶ n. (plural **cargoes** or **cargos**) goods carried on a ship, aircraft, etc.

SYNONYMS **freight**, load, haul, consignment, delivery, shipment, goods, merchandise.

Car·ib /'karib/ ▶ n. **1** a member of a South American people living mainly in coastal regions of French Guiana, Suriname, Guyana, and Venezuela. **2** the language of the Carib.

Car·ib·be·an /,karə'bēən, kə'ribēən/ ▶ adj. relating to the Caribbean Sea and its islands.

SPELLING

One **r** and two **bs**: Ca**r**i**bb**ean.

car·i·bou /'karə,bo͞o/ ▶ n. (plural **caribou** or **caribous**) a reindeer.

car·i·ca·ture /'karikəCHər, -,CHo͝or/ ▶ n. a picture in which a person's distinctive features are amusingly exaggerated. ▶ v. (**caricatures**, **caricaturing**, **caricatured**) make a caricature of.

SYNONYMS ▶ n. **cartoon**, parody, satire, lampoon, burlesque; informal sendup, takeoff. ▶ v. **parody**, satirize, lampoon, make fun of, mock, ridicule; informal send up, take off.

car·ies /'kerēz/ ▶ n. decay of a tooth or bone.

car·il·lon /'karə,län, -lən/ ▶ n. a set of bells sounded from a keyboard or by an automatic mechanism.

car·ing /'ke(ə)riNG/ ▶ adj. showing kindness and concern for others: *a caring and invaluable friend.* ▶ n. the work of looking after those unable to care for themselves.

Car·mel·ite /'kärmə,līt/ ▶ n. a friar or nun of an order founded at Mount Carmel in Israel during the Crusades.

car·mine /'kärmən, -,mīn/ ▶ n. a vivid crimson color.

car·nage /'kärnij/ ▶ n. the killing of a large number of people.

SYNONYMS **slaughter**, massacre, murder, butchery, bloodbath, bloodletting, holocaust.

car·nal /'kärnl/ ▶ adj. relating to sexual needs and activities. ■ **car·nal·i·ty** /kär'nalitē/ n.

car·na·tion /kär'nāSHən/ ▶ n. a double-flowered cultivated plant with pink, white, or red flowers.

car·nel·ian /kär'nēlyən/ ▶ n. a dull red or pink semiprecious stone.

car·ni·val /'kärnəvəl/ ▶ n. a festival involving processions, music, and dancing, especially that held during the week before Lent in Roman Catholic countries.

SYNONYMS **festival**, fiesta, fete, fair, gala, Mardi Gras.

car·ni·vore /'kärnə,vôr/ ▶ n. an animal that eats meat.

car·niv·o·rous /kär'nivərəs/ ▶ adj. eating a diet of meat.

car·ob /'karəb/ ▶ n. a substitute for chocolate, made from the pod of an Arabian tree.

car·ol /'karəl/ ▶ n. a religious song associated with Christmas. ▶ v. (**carols**, **caroling**, **caroled**) **1** sing carols in the streets. **2** sing or say happily.

car·om /'karəm/ ▶ n. a stroke in billiards or pool in which the cue ball strikes two balls successively. ▶ v. make a carom.

car·o·tene /'karə,tēn/ ▶ n. an orange or red substance found in carrots and other plants, important in the formation of vitamin A.

ca·rot·id ar·ter·y /kə'rätid/ ▶ n. either of two main arteries carrying blood to the head.

ca·rouse /kə'rouz/ ▶ v. (**carouses**, **carousing**, **caroused**) drink alcohol and enjoy yourself with other people in a noisy, lively way.

SYNONYMS **revel**, celebrate, roister; drink and make merry, go on a drinking bout/spree; informal booze (it up), go boozing, paint the town red, party, whoop it up.

car·ou·sel /ˌkarəˈsel, ˈkarəˌsel/ ▶ **n.** **1** a merry-go-round at a fair. **2** a rotating device for baggage collection at an airport.

carp¹ /kärp/ ▶ **n.** (plural **carp**) an edible freshwater fish.

carp² ▶ **v.** complain or find fault.

SYNONYMS **complain**, find fault, quibble, grumble, grouse, whine; informal nitpick, gripe, moan, bitch.

car·pal /ˈkärpəl/ ▶ **adj.** relating to the bones in the wrist.

car·pel /ˈkärpəl/ ▶ **n.** the female reproductive organ of a flower.

car·pen·ter /ˈkärpəntər/ ▶ **n.** a person who makes objects and structures out of wood.

SYNONYMS **woodworker**, cabinetmaker; dated joiner.

■ **car·pen·try** **n.**

car·pet /ˈkärpit/ ▶ **n.** **1** a floor covering made from thick woven fabric. **2** a thick or soft layer of something. ▶ **v.** (**carpets**, **carpeting**, **carpeted**) cover with a carpet. □ **carpet-bomb** bomb an area intensively. **carpet slipper** a soft slipper with an upper of wool or thick cloth. **on the carpet** informal being told off by someone in authority.

car·pet·bag /ˈkärpitˌbag/ ▶ **n.** a traveling bag of a kind originally made of carpet fabric.

car·pet·bag·ger /ˈkärpitˌbagər/ ▶ **n.** **1** informal a politician who tries to get elected in an area where they have no local connections. **2** historical a person from the northern states who went to the South after the Civil War to profit from the Reconstruction.

car·pet·ing /ˈkärpitiNG/ ▶ **n.** material for carpets or carpets as a whole.

car·pool /ˈkärˌpo͞ol/ ▶ **n.** an arrangement among people to make a regular trip in a single vehicle, with each person taking turns as the driver. ▶ **v.** participate in a carpool.

car·port /ˈkärˌpôrt/ ▶ **n.** a shelter for a parked car with at least one open side, usually attached to a house.

car·pus /ˈkärpəs/ ▶ **n.** (plural **carpi** /-ˌpī, -ˌpē/) the group of small bones in the wrist.

car·ra·geen /ˈkarəˌgēn/ ▶ **n.** an edible red seaweed.

car·rel /käˈrel/ ▶ **n.** a small cubicle with a desk for a reader in a library.

car·riage /ˈkarij/ ▶ **n.** **1** a four-wheeled horse-drawn vehicle for passengers. **2** the carrying of goods from one place to another. **3** a person's way of standing or moving. **4** a wheeled support for moving a gun.

car·ri·er /ˈkarēər/ ▶ **n.** **1** a person or thing that carries or holds something. **2** a company that transports goods or people for payment. □ **carrier pigeon** a homing pigeon trained to carry messages.

car·ri·on /ˈkarēən/ ▶ **n.** the decaying flesh of dead animals.

car·rot /ˈkarət/ ▶ **n.** **1** a tapering orange root vegetable. **2** something tempting offered as a means of persuasion. The opposite of STICK¹.

car·rot·y /ˈkarətē/ ▶ **adj.** (of a person's hair) orange-red.

car·ry /ˈkarē/ ▶ **v.** (**carries**, **carrying**, **carried**) **1** move or take from one place to another. **2** support the weight of. **3** take on or accept responsibility or blame. **4** have a particular feature or result. **5** approve a proposal by a majority of votes. **6** publish or broadcast something. **7** (of a sound or voice) travel a long way. **8** (**carry yourself**) stand and move in a particular way. **9** be pregnant with.

SYNONYMS **1 convey**, transfer, transport, move, haul, take, bring, bear, fetch; informal cart, lug. **2 transmit**, conduct, relay, communicate, convey, beam, send. **3 approve**, pass, accept, endorse, ratify. **4 be audible**, travel, reach, be heard.

□ **be** (or **get**) **carried away** lose self-control. **carry something forward** transfer figures to a new page or account. **carrying-on** improper behavior. **carry something off** succeed in doing something. **carry on 1** continue with something. **2** informal have a love affair. **carry-on** a bag or suitcase compact enough for you to carry onto an airplane. **carry something out** perform a task. **carry something through** manage to complete something. **carry weight** be influential.

cart /kärt/ ▶ **n.** **1** an open horse-drawn vehicle for carrying goods or people. **2** a shallow open container on wheels, pulled or pushed by hand. ▶ **v.** **1** carry in a cart or similar vehicle. **2** informal carry a heavy object with difficulty. □ **put the cart before the horse** reverse the proper order of doing something.

carte blanche /ˈkärt ˈbläNSH, ˈblänCH/ ▶ **n.** complete freedom to act as you wish.

car·tel /kärˈtel/ ▶ **n.** an association of manufacturers or suppliers formed to keep prices high.

Car·te·sian /kärˈtēZHən/ ▶ **adj.** relating to the French philosopher René Descartes (1596–1650) and his ideas. □ **Cartesian coordinates** a system for locating a point by reference to its distance from axes intersecting at right angles.

cart·horse /ˈkärtˌhôrs/ ▶ **n.** a large, strong horse suitable for heavy work.

Car·thu·sian /kärˈTH(y)o͞oZHən/ ▶ **n.** a monk or nun of a strict order founded at Chartreuse in France in 1084.

car·ti·lage /ˈkärtl-ij/ ▶ **n.** firm, flexible tissue that covers the ends of joints and forms structures such as the external ear. ■ **car·ti·lag·i·nous** /ˌkärtlˈajənəs/ **adj.**

car·tog·ra·phy /kärˈtägrəfē/ ▶ **n.** the science or practice of drawing maps. ■ **car·tog·ra·pher** **n.** **car·to·graph·ic** /ˌkärtəˈgrafik/ **adj.**

car·ton /ˈkärtn/ ▶ **n.** a light cardboard box or container.

SYNONYMS **box**, package, cardboard box, case, container, pack, packet.

car·toon /kärˈto͞on/ ▶ **n.** **1** a humorous drawing in a newspaper or magazine. **2** (also **cartoon strip**) a sequence of cartoon drawings that tell a story. **3** a movie made from a sequence of drawings, using animation techniques to give the appearance of movement. **4** a full-size drawing made as a preliminary design for a work of art.

SYNONYMS **1 animation**, animated film, comic strip, graphic novel. **2 caricature**, parody, lampoon, satire; informal takeoff, sendup.

■ **car·toon·ist** **n.**

car·touche /kär'to͞osh/ ▶ **n.** **1** a carved decoration or drawing in the form of a scroll with rolled-up ends. **2** an oval or oblong containing Egyptian hieroglyphs representing the name and title of a monarch.

car·tridge /'kärtrij/ ▶ **n.** **1** a container holding film, ink, etc., designed to be inserted into a mechanism such as a camera or printer. **2** a casing containing explosives and a bullet or shot for a gun.

> SYNONYMS **cassette**, magazine, canister, case, container.

cart·wheel /'kärt,(h)wēl/ ▶ **n.** a sideways somersault performed with the arms and legs extended. ▶ **v.** perform cartwheels.

carve /kärv/ ▶ **v.** (**carves**, **carving**, **carved**) **1** cut into a hard material to produce an object or design. **2** cut cooked meat into slices for eating. **3** (**carve something out**) develop a career, reputation, etc., through great effort. **4** (**carve something up**) divide something up ruthlessly.

> SYNONYMS **1 sculpt**, cut, hew, whittle, chisel, shape, fashion. **2 engrave**, incise, score, cut. **3 slice**, cut up, chop.

carv·ing /'kärviNG/ ▶ **n.** an object or design carved from wood or stone.

cas·bah /'kaz,bä, 'kaz-/ (or **kasbah**) ▶ **n.** the citadel of a North African city, and the area surrounding it.

cas·cade /kas'kād/ ▶ **n.** **1** a small waterfall. **2** a mass of something falling or hanging down. ▶ **v.** (**cascades**, **cascading**, **cascaded**) pour downward in large quantities.

> SYNONYMS ▶ **n.** **waterfall**, cataract, falls, rapids, whitewater, flood, torrent. ▶ **v.** **pour**, gush, surge, spill, stream, flow, issue, spurt, jet.

case¹ /kās/ ▶ **n.** **1** an instance of something happening. **2** an incident being investigated by the police. **3** a legal action decided in a court of law. **4** a set of facts or arguments supporting one side of a debate or lawsuit. **5** a person or problem being given the attention of a doctor, social worker, etc. **6** Grammar a form of a noun, adjective, or pronoun expressing the relationship of the word to others in the sentence.

> SYNONYMS **1** *a classic case of overreaction* **instance**, example, occurrence, occasion, demonstration, illustration. **2** *is that the case?* **situation**, position, state of affairs, circumstances, conditions, facts; informal score. **3 assignment**, job, project, investigation, exercise. **4** *he lost his case* **lawsuit**, legal action, trial, legal proceedings, litigation. **5** *the case against animal testing* **argument**, defense, justification, vindication, exposition, thesis.

□ **case history** a record of a person's background or medical history kept by a doctor or social worker. **case study** **1** a particular instance used to illustrate a general principle. **2** a detailed study of the development of a person, group, or situation over a period of time. **in case** so as to allow for the possibility of something happening.

case² ▶ **n.** **1** a container or protective covering. **2** a box containing bottles or cans of a beverage, sold as a unit. ▶ **v.** (**cases**, **casing**, **cased**) **1** enclose in a case. **2** informal examine a place before robbing it.

> SYNONYMS ▶ **n.** **1 container**, box, carton, canister, holder. **2 casing**, cover, sheath, envelope, sleeve, jacket, shell.

ca·sein /kā'sēn, 'kāsēən/ ▶ **n.** the main protein present in milk and cheese.

case·ment /'kāsmənt/ ▶ **n.** a window hinged at the side so that it opens like a door.

cash /kaSH/ ▶ **n.** **1** money in coins or notes. **2** money available for use. ▶ **v.** **1** give or receive notes or coins for a check or money order. **2** (**cash something in**) convert an insurance policy, savings account, etc., into money. **3** (**cash in on**) informal take advantage of.

> SYNONYMS ▶ **n.** **1 money**, currency, banknotes, bills, coins, change; informal dough, loot, dinero, moolah, bucks, bread. **2 finance**, money, resources, funds, assets, means, wherewithal.

□ **cash and carry** a system of wholesale trading whereby goods are paid for in full and taken away by the purchaser. **cash book** a book in which receipts and payments of money are recorded. **cash crop** a crop produced for sale rather than for use by the grower. **cash flow** the total amount of money passing into and out of a business. **cash in your chips** informal die. **cash register** a machine used in shops for adding up and recording the amount of each sale and storing the money received.

cash·ew /'kaSH,o͞o, kə'SHo͞o/ ▶ **n.** an edible kidney-shaped nut.

cash·ier /ka'SHi(ə)r/ ▶ **n.** a person responsible for paying out and receiving money in a store, bank, etc. ▶ **v.** (**cashiers**, **cashiering**, **cashiered**) dismiss someone from the armed forces.

> SYNONYMS ▶ **n.** **clerk**, teller, banker, treasurer, bursar, purser.

cash·mere /'kaZH,mi(ə)r, 'kaSH-/ ▶ **n.** fine, soft wool from a breed of Himalayan goat.

cas·ing /'kāsiNG/ ▶ **n.** **1** a cover that protects or encloses something. **2** the frame around a door or window.

ca·si·no /kə'sēnō/ ▶ **n.** (plural **casinos**) a public building or room for gambling.

cask /kask/ ▶ **n.** a large barrel for storing alcoholic drinks.

> SYNONYMS **barrel**, keg, butt, tun, vat, drum, hogshead; historical firkin.

cas·ket /'kaskit/ ▶ **n.** **1** a small ornamental box or chest for holding valuable objects. **2** a coffin.

Cas·san·dra /kə'sandrə, -'sän-/ ▶ **n.** a person who makes gloomy predictions.

cas·sa·va /kə'sävə/ ▶ **n.** the root of a tropical tree, used as food.

cas·se·role /'kasə,rōl/ ▶ **n.** **1** a large dish with a lid, used for cooking food slowly in an oven. **2** a kind of stew cooked slowly in an oven. ▶ **v.** (**casseroles**, **casseroling**, **casseroled**) cook food in a casserole.

cas·sette /kə'set/ ▶ **n.** a sealed plastic case containing audiotape, videotape, film, etc., designed to be inserted into a player or camera.

cas·sock /'kasək/ ▶ **n.** a long garment worn by Christian priests and members of church choirs.

cas·so·war·y /'kasə,werē/ ▶ **n.** (plural **cassowaries**) a very large bird that cannot fly, found in New Guinea.

cast /kast/ ▶ **v.** (**casts**, **casting**, **cast**) **1** throw forcefully. **2** make light or shadow appear on a surface. **3** direct your eyes or thoughts. **4** give a vote. **5** make a magic spell take effect. **6** throw a fishing line out into the water. **7** shed or discard. **8** shape metal by pouring it into a mold while molten. **9** give a part to an actor, or allocate parts in a play or movie. ▶ **n. 1** the actors taking part in a play or movie. **2** (also **casting**) an object made by casting metal. **3** a bandage stiffened with plaster of Paris to support and protect a broken limb. **4** the appearance or character of a person or thing. **5** a slight squint.

SYNONYMS ▶ **v. 1 throw**, toss, fling, pitch, hurl, lob; informal chuck, sling. **2 direct**, shoot, throw, fling, send. **3** *cast your vote* **register**, record, enter, file. **4 emit**, give off, throw, send out, radiate. **5 mold**, fashion, form, shape, forge. ▶ **n. 1 mold**, die, matrix, shape, casting, model. **2 actors**, performers, players, company, troupe, dramatis personae, characters.

□ **be cast down** feel depressed. **cast about** (or **around**) search far and wide. **casting vote** an extra vote used by a chairperson to decide an issue when votes on each side are equal. **cast iron** a hard alloy of iron and carbon that can be cast in a mold. **cast off 1** Knitting take the stitches off the needle by looping each over the next. **2** release a boat or ship from its moorings. **cast on** Knitting make the first row of loops on the needle.

cas·ta·nets /ˌkastəˈnets/ ▶ **pl.n.** a pair of small curved pieces of wood, clicked together by the fingers to accompany Spanish dancing.

cast·a·way /ˈkastəˌwā/ ▶ **n.** a person who has been shipwrecked in an isolated place.

caste /kast/ ▶ **n.** each of the classes of Hindu society.

SYNONYMS **class**, rank, level, order, stratum, echelon, status.

cas·tel·lat·ed /ˈkastəˌlātid/ ▶ **adj.** having battlements.

cast·er /ˈkastər/ ▶ **n. 1** a small swiveling wheel fixed to the legs or base of a piece of furniture. **2** a small container with holes in the top, used for sprinkling salt, sugar, etc.

cas·ti·gate /ˈkastəˌgāt/ ▶ **v.** (**castigates**, **castigating**, **castigated**) tell someone off severely. ■ **cas·ti·ga·tion** /ˌkastəˈgāsʜən/ **n.**

cast·ing /ˈkastiɴɢ/ ▶ **n.** an object made by pouring molten metal or other material into a mold.

cas·tle /ˈkasəl/ ▶ **n. 1** a large fortified building of the medieval period. **2** Chess a rook.

SYNONYMS **fortress**, fort, stronghold, fortification, keep, citadel, palace, chateau, tower.

□ **castles in the air** dreams or plans that will never be achieved.

cast·off /ˈkastˌôf/ ▶ **adj.** abandoned or discarded. ▶ **n.** a garment that is no longer wanted.

cas·tor oil /ˈkastər/ ▶ **n.** a pale yellow oil obtained from castor beans, used as a purgative and a lubricant.

cas·trate /ˈkasˌtrāt/ ▶ **v.** (**castrates**, **castrating**, **castrated**) **1** remove the testicles of. **2** make something less powerful or strong. ■ **cas·tra·tion** /kaˈstrāsʜən/ **n.**

cas·u·al /ˈkazʜo͞oəl/ ▶ **adj. 1** relaxed and unconcerned. **2** done without enough attention or proper planning. **3** occasional or temporary: *casual work*. **4** happening by chance; accidental. **5** (of clothes) informal.

SYNONYMS **1** *a casual attitude* **unconcerned**, uncaring, indifferent, lackadaisical, nonchalant, offhand, flippant, easy-going, free and easy, blithe, carefree, devil-may-care; informal laid-back. **2** *a casual remark* **offhand**, spontaneous, unthinking, unconsidered, impromptu, throwaway, unguarded; informal off-the-cuff. **3** *a casual glance* **cursory**, perfunctory, superficial, passing, fleeting. **4** *casual work* **temporary**, freelance, irregular, occasional. **5** *a casual meeting* **chance**, accidental, unplanned, unintended, unexpected, unforeseen. **6** *a casual atmosphere* **relaxed**, friendly, informal, easygoing, free and easy; informal laid-back.
ANTONYMS serious, deliberate, formal.

■ **cas·u·al·ly adv.**

cas·u·al·ty /ˈkazʜ(o͞o)əltē/ ▶ **n.** (plural **casualties**) **1** a person killed or injured in a war or accident. **2** a person or thing badly affected by an event or situation.

SYNONYMS **victim**, sufferer, fatality, death, loss, wounded person, injured person.

cas·u·ist·ry /ˈkazʜo͞oəstrē/ ▶ **n.** the use of clever but false reasoning.

CAT /kat/ ▶ **abbr.** Medicine computerized axial tomography.

cat /kat/ ▶ **n. 1** a small furry animal kept as a pet. **2** a wild animal related to this, such as a lion or tiger. **3** informal a spiteful woman.

SYNONYMS **feline**, tomcat, tom, kitten; informal pussy (cat), puss, kitty.

□ **cat burglar** a thief who enters a building by climbing to an upper story. **cat-o'-nine-tails** historical a whip consisting of nine knotted ropes. **cat's cradle** a game in which patterns are formed in a loop of string held between the fingers of each hand. **cat's paw** a person used by another to carry out an unpleasant task. **let the cat out of the bag** reveal a secret by mistake. **like a cat on a hot tin roof** very agitated or anxious.

ca·tab·o·lism /kəˈtabəˌlizəm/ ▶ **n.** the breakdown of complex molecules in living organisms to form simpler ones, together with the release of energy. ■ **cat·a·bol·ic** /ˌkatəˈbälik/ **adj.**

cat·a·clysm /ˈkatəˌklizəm/ ▶ **n.** a violent upheaval or disaster. ■ **cat·a·clys·mic** /ˌkatəˈklizmik/ **adj.**

cat·a·comb /ˈkatəˌkōm/ ▶ **n.** an underground cemetery consisting of tunnels with recesses for tombs.

cat·a·falque /ˈkatəˌfô(l)k, -ˌfalk/ ▶ **n.** a decorated wooden framework to support a coffin.

Cat·a·lan /ˈkatlˌan, ˈkatl-ən/ ▶ **n. 1** a person from Catalonia in northeastern Spain. **2** the language of Catalonia. ▶ **adj.** relating to Catalonia.

cat·a·lep·sy /ˈkatlˌepsē/ ▶ **n.** a condition in which a person becomes unconscious and goes rigid.

cat·a·log /ˈkatlˌôg, -ˌäg/ (or **catalogue**) ▶ **n. 1** a list of items arranged in order. **2** a publication containing details of items for sale. **3** a series of bad things: *a catalog of failures*. ▶ **v.** (**catalogs** or **catalogues**, **cataloging** or **catalogued**, **cataloged** or **cataloguing**) list in a catalog.

SYNONYMS ▶ **n. 1 directory**, register, index, list, listing, record, schedule, archive, inventory. **2 brochure**, mailer, magazine, wish book. ▶ **v. classify**, categorize, index, list, archive, record, itemize.

ca·tal·y·sis /kəˈtaləsis/ ▶ **n.** the speeding up of a chemical reaction by a catalyst. ■ **cat·a·lyt·ic** /ˌkatlˈitik/ **adj.**

cat·a·lyst /ˈkatl-ist/ ▶ **n. 1** a substance that increases the rate of a chemical reaction while remaining unchanged itself. **2** a person or thing that causes something to happen.

cat·a·lyt·ic con·vert·er /ˌkatl'itik kən'vərtər/ ▶ **n.** a device in a motor vehicle that converts pollutant exhaust gases into less harmful ones.

cat·a·lyze /'katlˌīz/ ▶ **v.** (**catalyzes**, **catalyzing**, **catalyzed**) cause or speed up a reaction by acting as a catalyst.

cat·a·ma·ran /ˌkatəmə'ran, 'katəməˌran/ ▶ **n.** a boat with twin parallel hulls.

cat·a·mount /'katəˌmount/ ▶ **n.** a medium-sized or large wild cat, especially a cougar.

cat·a·pult /'katəˌpəlt, -ˌpo͝olt/ ▶ **n.** **1** a device for launching a glider or aircraft. **2** a military machine formerly used for hurling large stones. ▶ **v.** **1** throw forcefully. **2** move suddenly or very fast.

cat·a·ract /'katəˌrakt/ ▶ **n.** **1** a large waterfall. **2** a condition in which the lens of the eye becomes cloudy, resulting in blurred vision.

ca·tarrh /kə'tär/ ▶ **n.** excessive mucus in the nose or throat.

ca·tas·tro·phe /kə'tastrəfē/ ▶ **n.** a sudden event that causes great damage or suffering.

> SYNONYMS **disaster**, calamity, cataclysm, ruin, tragedy, fiasco, debacle.

cat·a·stroph·ic /ˌkatə'sträfik/ ▶ **adj.** **1** involving or causing sudden great damage or suffering. **2** extremely unfortunate or unsuccessful.
■ **cat·a·stroph·i·cal·ly** **adv.**

cat·a·to·ni·a /ˌkatə'tōnēə/ ▶ **n.** a condition in which a person experiences both periods of near unconsciousness and periods of overactivity.
■ **cat·a·ton·ic** /ˌkatə'tänik/ **adj.**

cat·call /'katˌkôl/ ▶ **n.** a shrill whistle or shout of mockery or disapproval. ▶ **v.** make a catcall.

catch /kacʜ, kecʜ/ ▶ **v.** (**catches**, **catching**, **caught** /kôt/) **1** seize and hold something moving. **2** capture a person or animal. **3** be in time to get on a vehicle or to see a person or event. **4** entangle or become entangled. **5** surprise someone in the act of doing something wrong or embarrassing. **6** (**be caught in**) unexpectedly find yourself in an unwelcome situation. **7** see, hear, or understand. **8** hit or strike. **9** become infected with an illness. **10** (**catching**) (of a disease) infectious. ▶ **n.** **1** an act of catching. **2** a device for fastening a door, window, etc. **3** a hidden problem. **4** a break in a person's voice caused by emotion. **5** an amount of fish caught.

> SYNONYMS ▶ **v.** **1** **seize**, grab, snatch, grasp, grip, clutch, intercept, trap, receive, get. **2** **capture**, apprehend, seize, arrest, take prisoner, trap, snare, net; informal nab, collar. **3** **become trapped**, become entangled, snag, jam, wedge, lodge, get stuck. **4** **discover**, find, come across, stumble on, chance on, surprise. **5** **contract**, go/come down with, be taken ill with, develop, pick up, succumb to. **6** (**catching**) **infectious**, contagious, communicable; dated infective. ANTONYMS drop, release. ▶ **n.** **1** **haul**, net, bag, yield. **2** **latch**, lock, fastener, clasp, hasp. **3** **snag**, disadvantage, drawback, stumbling block, hitch, complication, problem, trap, trick.

□ **catch-all** a term or category intended to cover all possibilities. **catch on** informal **1** become popular. **2** understand. **catch-22** a difficult situation from which there is no escape because it involves conditions that conflict with each other. **catch up** do tasks that you should have done earlier. **catch someone up** update someone. **play catch-up** try to overcome a disadvantage or surpass a competitor who is ahead.

catch·er /'kacʜər, 'kecʜ-/ ▶ **n.** Baseball a fielder positioned behind home plate mainly to catch pitches not hit by the batter.

catch·ment area /'kacʜmənt, 'kecʜ-/ ▶ **n.** **1** the area from which a hospital's patients or a school's pupils are drawn. **2** the area from which rainfall flows into a river, lake, or reservoir.

catch·pen·ny /'kacʜˌpenē, 'kecʜ-/ ▶ **adj.** outwardly attractive so as to sell quickly.

catch·phrase /'kacʜˌfrāz, 'kecʜ-/ ▶ **n.** a well-known sentence or phrase.

catch·word /'kacʜˌwərd, 'kecʜ-/ ▶ **n.** a word or phrase frequently used to sum something up.

catch·y /'kacʜē, 'kecʜē/ ▶ **adj.** (**catchier**, **catchiest**) (of a tune or phrase) appealing and easy to remember.

> SYNONYMS **memorable**, unforgettable, haunting, appealing, popular. ANTONYMS forgettable.

cat·e·chism /'katəˌkizəm/ ▶ **n.** a summary of the principles of Christian religion in the form of questions and answers, used for teaching.

cat·e·chist /'katəkist/ ▶ **n.** a teacher of the Christian religion.

cat·e·chize /'katəˌkīz/ ▶ **v.** (**catechizes**, **catechizing**, **catechized**) teach by using a catechism.

cat·e·go·ri·cal /ˌkatə'gôrikəl/ ▶ **adj.** completely clear and direct.

> SYNONYMS **unqualified**, unconditional, unequivocal, absolute, explicit, unambiguous, definite, direct, emphatic, positive, out-and-out.

■ **cat·e·gor·i·cal·ly** **adv.**

cat·e·go·rize /'katəgəˌrīz/ ▶ **v.** (**categorizes**, **categorizing**, **categorized**) place in a category.
■ **cat·e·go·ri·za·tion** /ˌkatəgərə'zāsʜən/ **n.**

cat·e·go·ry /'katəˌgôrē/ ▶ **n.** (plural **categories**) a class or group of people or things with shared characteristics.

> SYNONYMS **class**, classification, group, grouping, bracket, heading, set, type, sort, kind, grade, order, rank.

ca·ter /'kātər/ ▶ **v.** **1** provide food and drink at a social event. **2** (**cater to**) provide someone with what is needed. **3** (**cater to**) satisfy a need or demand.

> SYNONYMS **1** **provide** (**food**) **for**, feed, serve, cook for. **2** (**cater to**) *a resort catering to the rich* **serve**, provide for, meet the needs/wants of, accommodate. **3** (**cater to**) *we cater to all tastes* **take into account**, take into consideration, allow for, consider, bear in mind, make provision for, have regard for.

■ **ca·ter·er** **n.**

cat·er-cor·nered /'katər ˌkôrnərd/ (or **kitty-corner** /'kitē/) ▶ **adj.** situated diagonally opposite. ▶ **adv.** diagonally.

cat·er·pil·lar /'katə(r)ˌpilər/ ▶ **n.** a creature like a small worm with legs, which develops into a butterfly or moth.

cat·er·waul /'katərˌwôl/ ▶ **v.** make a shrill howling or wailing noise.

cat·fish /'katˌfisʜ/ ▶ **n.** a fish with growths resembling whiskers around the mouth.

cat·gut /'katˌgət/ ▶ **n.** material used for the strings of musical instruments, made of the dried intestines of sheep or horses.

ca·thar·sis /kəˈTHärsis/ ▶ **n.** the process of releasing strong but pent-up emotions in such a way as to free yourself of them. ■ **ca·thar·tic adj.**

ca·the·dral /kəˈTHēdrəl/ ▶ **n.** the most important church of a diocese (district).

cath·e·ter /ˈkaTHətər/ ▶ **n.** a tube that is inserted into a body cavity to drain fluid.

cath·ode /ˈkaTHˌōd/ ▶ **n.** an electrode with a negative charge. □ **cathode ray tube** a tube in which beams of electrons produce a luminous image on a screen, as in a television.

cath·o·lic /ˈkaTH(ə)lik/ ▶ **adj. 1** including a wide variety of things: *catholic tastes.* **2** (**Catholic**) Roman Catholic. ▶ **n.** (**Catholic**) a Roman Catholic. ■ **Ca·thol·i·cism** /kəˈTHäləˌsizəm/ **n.**

cat·i·on /ˈkatˌīən, -ˌīän/ ▶ **n.** an ion with a positive charge.

cat·kin /ˈkatkin/ ▶ **n.** a spike of small, soft flowers hanging from trees such as willow and hazel.

cat·nap /ˈkatˌnap/ ▶ **n.** a short sleep during the day.

cat·sup /ˈkecHəp, ˈkacHəp, ˈkatsəp/ ▶ **n.** ⇒ **KETCHUP.**

cat·tle /ˈkatl/ ▶ **pl.n.** cows, bulls, and oxen.

> SYNONYMS **cows**, oxen, herd, livestock.

cat·ty /ˈkatē/ ▶ **adj.** (**cattier**, **cattiest**) spiteful.

cat·walk /ˈkatˌwôk/ ▶ **n. 1** a narrow platform along which models walk to display clothes. **2** a narrow raised walkway.

Cau·ca·sian /kôˈkāzHən/ ▶ **adj. 1** relating to peoples from Europe, western Asia, and parts of India and North Africa. **2** white-skinned. ▶ **n.** a Caucasian person.

cau·cus /ˈkôkəs/ ▶ **n.** (plural **caucuses**) **1** a meeting of a policymaking group of a political party. **2** a group of people within a larger organization who have similar interests.

cau·dal /ˈkôdl/ ▶ **adj.** having to do with the tail or the rear part of the body.

caught /kôt/ past and past participle of **CATCH.**

caul /kôl/ ▶ **n.** a membrane that encloses an unborn baby in the womb.

caul·dron /ˈkôldrən/ (or **caldron**) ▶ **n.** a large metal cooking pot.

cau·li·flow·er /ˈkôliˌflou(-ə)r, ˈkäli-/ ▶ **n.** a vegetable with a large white edible flower head.

caulk /kôk/ (or **calk**) ▶ **n.** a waterproof substance used to fill cracks and seal joints.

caus·al /ˈkôzəl/ ▶ **adj.** relating to or being a cause: *a causal connection between smoking and lung cancer.* ■ **caus·al·ly adv. cau·sal·i·ty** /kôˈzalətē/ **n.**

cau·sa·tion /kôˈzāsHən/ ▶ **n.** the process of causing an effect. ■ **caus·a·tive** /ˈkôzətiv/ **adj.**

cause /kôz/ ▶ **n. 1** a person or thing that produces an effect. **2** a good reason for thinking or doing something: *cause for concern.* **3** a principle or movement. ▶ **v.** (**causes**, **causing**, **caused**) make something happen.

> SYNONYMS ▶ **n. 1** *the cause of the fire* **source**, root, origin, beginning(s), starting point, originator, author, creator, agent. **2** *there is no cause for alarm* **reason**, grounds, justification, call, need, necessity, occasion, excuse. **3** *raising money for good causes* **principle**, ideal, belief, conviction, object, aim, objective, purpose, charity. ▶ **v. bring about**, give rise to, lead to, result in, create, produce, generate, engender, spawn, bring on, precipitate, prompt, provoke, trigger, make happen, induce, inspire, promote, foster.

cause cé·lè·bre /ˈkôz səˈleb(rə), ˈkōz/ ▶ **n.** (plural **causes célèbres**) a matter causing great public interest and discussion.

cause·way /ˈkôzˌwā/ ▶ **n.** a raised road or track across low or wet ground.

caus·tic /ˈkôstik/ ▶ **adj. 1** able to burn through or wear away something by chemical action. **2** sarcastic in a hurtful way.

> SYNONYMS **1 corrosive**, acid, burning. **2 sarcastic**, cutting, biting, mordant, sharp, scathing, sardonic, scornful, trenchant, acerbic, vitriolic.

□ **caustic soda** sodium hydroxide, used in industrial processes, such as soap-making. ■ **caus·ti·cal·ly adv.**

cau·ter·ize /ˈkôtəˌrīz/ ▶ **v.** (**cauterizes**, **cauterizing**, **cauterized**) burn the area round a wound to stop bleeding or prevent infection.

cau·tion /ˈkôsHən/ ▶ **n. 1** care taken to avoid danger or mistakes. **2** a warning to the public. ▶ **v.** warn or advise someone.

> SYNONYMS ▶ **n. care**, attention, attentiveness, vigilance, carefulness, alertness, circumspection, discretion, prudence. ▶ **v. advise**, warn, counsel; admonish, exhort.

□ **throw caution to the wind** act in a reckless way.

cau·tion·ar·y /ˈkôsHəˌnerē/ ▶ **adj.** acting as a warning.

cau·tious /ˈkôsHəs/ ▶ **adj.** taking care to avoid possible problems or dangers.

> SYNONYMS **careful**, attentive, alert, judicious, circumspect, prudent, tentative, guarded. ANTONYMS reckless.

■ **cau·tious·ly adv.**

cav·al·cade /ˌkavəlˈkād/ ▶ **n.** a procession of vehicles or people on horseback.

cav·a·lier /ˌkavəˈli(ə)r/ ▶ **n.** (**Cavalier**) a supporter of King Charles I in the English Civil War. ▶ **adj.** showing a lack of proper concern: *the cavalier treatment of mental illness.*

cav·al·ry /ˈkavəlrē/ ▶ **n.** (plural **cavalries**) (in the past) the part of the army that fought on horseback. ■ **cav·al·ry·man n.**

cave /kāv/ ▶ **n.** a large natural hollow in the side of a hill or cliff, or underground. ▶ **v.** (**caves**, **caving**, **caved**) **1** (**cave in**) give way or collapse. **2** (**cave in**) give in to demands. **3** explore caves as a sport.

> SYNONYMS ▶ **n. cavern**, grotto, underground chamber.

ca·ve·at /ˈkavēˌät, ˈkäv-/ ▶ **n.** a warning.

cav·ern /ˈkavərn/ ▶ **n.** a large cave.

cav·ern·ous /ˈkavərnəs/ ▶ **adj.** huge, spacious, or gloomy.

cav·i·ar /ˈkavēˌär/ (or **caviare**) ▶ **n.** the pickled roe of the sturgeon (a large fish).

cav·il /ˈkavəl/ ▶ **v.** (**cavils**, **caviling**, **caviled**) make unnecessary complaints. ▶ **n.** an unnecessary complaint.

cav·i·ty /ˈkavitē/ ▶ **n.** (plural **cavities**) **1** a hollow space inside something solid. **2** a decayed part of a tooth.

> SYNONYMS **space**, chamber, hollow, hole, pocket, gap, crater, pit.

cav·ort /kəˈvôrt/ ▶ **v.** jump or dance around excitedly.

ca·vy /'kāvē/ ▶ **n.** (plural **cavies**) a kind of guinea pig from South America.

caw /kô/ ▶ **v.** make a harsh cry.

cay·enne /kī'en, kā'en/ ▶ **n.** a hot-tasting red powder made from dried chili peppers.

CB ▶ **abbr.** Citizens' Band.

cc ▶ **abbr.** **1** carbon copy. **2** cubic centimeter(s).

CCTV ▶ **abbr.** closed-circuit television.

CD ▶ **abbr.** **1** certificate of deposit. **2** compact disc.

cd ▶ **abbr.** candela.

CD-ROM /ˌsē ˌdē 'räm/ ▶ **abbr.** a compact disc storing large amounts of information, used in a computer (*ROM* stands for "read-only memory").

CDT ▶ **abbr.** Central Daylight Time.

CE ▶ **abbr.** Church of England.

cease /sēs/ ▶ **v.** (**ceases**, **ceasing**, **ceased**) come or bring to an end; stop.

> SYNONYMS **stop**, come/bring to an end, come/bring to a halt, end, halt, conclude, terminate, finish, wind up, discontinue, suspend, break off. ANTONYMS start, continue.

□ **without cease** without stopping.

cease·fire /'sēsˌfīr/ ▶ **n.** a temporary period during a conflict when fighting stops.

cease·less /'sēslis/ ▶ **adj.** not stopping.

> SYNONYMS **continual**, constant, continuous, incessant, unending, endless, never-ending, interminable, nonstop, unremitting, relentless, unrelenting, sustained, persistent, eternal, perpetual. ANTONYMS intermittent.

■ **cease·less·ly adv.**

ce·cum /'sēkəm/ ▶ **n.** (plural **ceca** /'sēkə/) a pouch connected to the join between the small and large intestines. ■ **ce·cal adj.**

ce·dar /'sēdər/ ▶ **n.** a tall evergreen tree with sweet-smelling wood.

cede /sēd/ ▶ **v.** (**cedes**, **ceding**, **ceded**) give up power or territory.

ce·dil·la /sə'dilə/ ▶ **n.** a mark (̧) written under the letter *c* to show that it is pronounced like an *s* (e.g., *soupçon*).

cei·lidh /'kālē/ ▶ **n.** a party with Scottish or Irish folk music and dancing.

ceil·ing /'sēliNG/ ▶ **n.** **1** the top surface of a room. **2** a top limit set on prices, wages, or spending.

> SPELLING
>
> Write **i** before **e**, when the sound is *ee*, except after **c**: ceiling.

cel·an·dine /'selənˌdīn, -ˌdēn/ ▶ **n.** a yellow flower related to the buttercup.

cel·e·brant /'seləbrənt/ ▶ **n.** a priest who performs the service of Holy Communion in a church.

cel·e·brate /'seləˌbrāt/ ▶ **v.** (**celebrates**, **celebrating**, **celebrated**) **1** mark an important occasion by doing something special. **2** honor or praise someone publicly. **3** perform a religious ceremony.

> SYNONYMS **1 have a party**, make merry, enjoy yourself, have fun, have a good time; informal party, whoop it up, have a ball, step out. **2 commemorate**, observe, mark, keep, honor, remember. **3 acclaim**, admire, rate highly, esteem, exalt, vaunt; (**celebrated**) **acclaimed**, eminent, great, distinguished, prestigious, illustrious, notable. **4 perform**, observe, officiate at, preside at.

■ **cel·e·bra·to·ry** /sə'lebrəˌtôrē, 'seləbrə-/ **adj.**

cel·e·bra·tion /ˌselə'brāsHən/ ▶ **n.** the action of celebrating an important event or occasion: *a birthday celebration.*

> SYNONYMS **1 party**, merrymaking, festivities, revelry, festival, fete, carnival, jamboree; informal do, bash, partying. **2 commemoration**, observance, marking, keeping; officiation, solemnization.

ce·leb·ri·ty /sə'lebrətē/ ▶ **n.** (plural **celebrities**) **1** a famous person. **2** the state of being famous.

> SYNONYMS **1 famous person**, VIP, personality, big name, household name, star, superstar; informal celeb, megastar. **2 fame**, prominence, renown, stardom, popularity, distinction, prestige, stature, repute, reputation. ANTONYMS obscurity.

ce·ler·i·ac /sə'lerēˌak/ ▶ **n.** a vegetable with a large edible root.

ce·ler·i·ty /sə'leritē/ ▶ **n.** old use speed of movement.

cel·er·y /'sel(ə)rē/ ▶ **n.** a vegetable with crisp juicy stalks.

ce·les·tial /sə'lescHəl/ ▶ **adj.** **1** relating to heaven. **2** relating to the sky or outer space.

> SYNONYMS **1 heavenly**, holy, saintly, divine, godly, godlike, ethereal, angelic. **2 (in) space**, heavenly, astronomical, extraterrestrial, stellar, planetary.

cel·i·bate /'seləbət/ ▶ **adj.** not married or in a sexual relationship.

> SYNONYMS **unmarried**, single, chaste, pure, virginal.

■ **cel·i·ba·cy n.**

cell /sel/ ▶ **n.** **1** a small room for a prisoner, monk, or nun. **2** the smallest structural and functional unit of a living thing. **3** a small political group that is part of a larger organization. **4** a device for producing electricity by chemical action or light. **5** a cell phone.

> SYNONYMS **1 room**, cubicle, chamber, dungeon, compartment, lockup. **2 unit**, squad, detachment, group.

□ **cell phone** a portable telephone using a cellular radio system.

cel·lar /'selər/ ▶ **n.** **1** a room below ground level, used for storage. **2** a stock of wine.

> SYNONYMS **basement**, vault, crypt.

cel·lo /'cHelō/ ▶ **n.** (plural **cellos**) an instrument like a large violin, held upright on the floor between the legs of the seated player. ■ **cel·list n.**

Cel·lo·phane /'seləˌfān/ ▶ **n.** trademark a thin transparent wrapping material.

cel·lu·lar /'selyələr/ ▶ **adj.** **1** relating to or made up of cells. **2** (of a cell phone system) using a number of short-range radio stations to cover the area it serves.

cel·lu·lite /'selyəˌlīt/ ▶ **n.** fat that builds up under the skin, causing a dimpled effect.

cel·lu·loid /'selyəˌloid/ ▶ **n.** a kind of transparent plastic formerly used for movie film.

cel·lu·lose /'selyəˌlōs, -ˌlōz/ ▶ **n.** a substance found in all plant tissues, used in making paint, plastics, and fibers.

Cel·si·us /ˈselsēəs, ˈselsHəs/ ▶ **n.** a scale of temperature on which water freezes at 0° and boils at 100°.

Celt /kelt, selt/ ▶ **n.** a member of a people who lived in Britain and elsewhere in Europe before the Romans arrived.

Celt·ic /ˈkeltik, ˈsel-/ ▶ **n.** a group of languages including Irish, Scottish Gaelic, and Welsh. ▶ **adj.** relating to Celtic languages or to the Celts.

ce·ment /siˈment/ ▶ **n.** a powdery substance made by heating lime and clay, used in making mortar and concrete. ▶ **v.** **1** fix with cement. **2** make something stronger: *the occasion cemented our friendship.*

> SYNONYMS ▶ **n.** **adhesive**, glue, fixative, gum, paste.

cem·e·ter·y /ˈseməˌterē/ ▶ **n.** (plural **cemeteries**) a large burial ground.

> SYNONYMS **graveyard**, churchyard, burial ground, necropolis, memorial park; informal boneyard; historical potter's field; archaic God's acre.

> **SPELLING**
> Write **-tery**, not **-try** or **-tary**: **cemetery**.

ce·no·taph /ˈsenəˌtaf/ ▶ **n.** a monument built to honor soldiers killed in a war.

Ce·no·zo·ic /ˌsenəˈzōik/ ▶ **adj.** Geology having to do with the era following the Mesozoic era (from about 65 million years ago to the present).

cen·ser /ˈsensər/ ▶ **n.** a container in which incense is burned.

cen·sor /ˈsensər/ ▶ **n.** a person who examines movies, books, or documents and bans unacceptable parts. ▶ **v.** ban unacceptable parts of a movie, book, or document.

> SYNONYMS ▶ **v.** **cut**, edit, expurgate, sanitize, clean up, ban, delete.

■ **cen·sor·ship** **n.**

cen·so·ri·ous /senˈsôrēəs/ ▶ **adj.** very critical.

> SYNONYMS **critical**, overcritical, hypercritical, disapproving, condemnatory, judgmental, moralistic, fault-finding, reproachful.

cen·sure /ˈsensHər/ ▶ **v.** (**censures**, **censuring**, **censured**) criticize strongly. ▶ **n.** strong disapproval or criticism.

> SYNONYMS ▶ **v.** **condemn**, criticize, attack, reprimand, rebuke, admonish, upbraid, reproach. ANTONYMS defend, praise. ▶ **n.** **condemnation**, criticism, attack, reprimand, rebuke, admonishment, reproof, disapproval, reproach. ANTONYMS approval, praise.

> **USAGE**
> Don't confuse **censure** with **censor**.

cen·sus /ˈsensəs/ ▶ **n.** (plural **censuses**) an official count of a population.

cent /sent/ ▶ **n.** a unit of money equal to one hundredth of a dollar, euro, or other decimal currency unit.

cen·taur /ˈsenˌtôr/ ▶ **n.** (in Greek mythology) a creature with a man's head, arms, and upper body and a horse's lower body and legs.

cen·ta·vo /senˈtävō/ ▶ **n.** (plural **centavos**) a unit of money of Mexico, Brazil, and certain other countries, equal to one hundredth of the basic unit.

cen·te·nar·i·an /ˌsentnˈe(ə)rēən/ ▶ **n.** a person who has reached one hundred years of age.

cen·ten·ar·y /senˈtenərē, ˈsentnˌerē/ ▶ **n.** (plural **centenaries**) the hundredth anniversary of an event.

cen·ten·ni·al /senˈtenēəl/ ▶ **adj.** relating to a hundredth anniversary. ▶ **n.** a hundredth anniversary.

cen·ter /ˈsentər/ ▶ **n.** **1** a point in the middle of something. **2** a place where a particular activity takes place: *a conference center.* **3** a point from which something spreads or to which something is directed: *the city was a center of discontent.* ▶ **v.** (**centers**, **centering**, **centered**) **1** place in the center. **2** (**center on** or **around**) have as a main concern or theme.

> SYNONYMS ▶ **n.** **middle**, nucleus, heart, core, hub. ANTONYMS edge. ▶ **v.** **focus**, concentrate, pivot, revolve, be based.

□ **center field** Baseball the central part of the outfield, behind second base. **center of gravity** the central point in an object, around which its mass is evenly distributed.

cen·ter·board /ˈsentərˌbôrd/ ▶ **n.** a board lowered through the keel of a sailboat to reduce sideways movement.

cen·ter·fold /ˈsentərˌfōld/ ▶ **n.** the two middle pages of a magazine, usually containing a special feature.

cen·ter·piece /ˈsentərˌpēs/ ▶ **n.** **1** a decorative piece or display placed in the middle of a dining or serving table. **2** an item that is designed to have people's attention focused on it.

cen·ti·grade /ˈsentəˌgrād/ ▶ **adj.** measured by the Celsius scale of temperature.

cen·ti·li·ter /ˈsentəˌlētər/ ▶ **n.** a metric unit equal to one hundredth of a liter.

cen·time /ˈsänˌtēm, ˈsent-/ ▶ **n.** a unit of money equal to one hundredth of a franc.

cen·ti·me·ter /ˈsentəˌmētər, ˈsän-/ ▶ **n.** a metric unit equal to one hundredth of a meter.

cen·ti·mo /ˈsentəmō/ ▶ **n.** (plural **centimos**) a unit of money of certain Latin American countries (and formerly of Spain), equal to one hundredth of the basic unit.

cen·ti·pede /ˈsentəˌpēd/ ▶ **n.** an insectlike creature with a long, thin body and many legs.

cen·tral /ˈsentrəl/ ▶ **adj.** **1** in or near the center. **2** very important.

> SYNONYMS **1** **middle**, center, halfway, midway, mid; inner, innermost. **2** **main**, chief, principal, primary, foremost, key, crucial, vital, essential, basic, fundamental, core; informal number-one. ANTONYMS side, outer.

□ **central bank** a national bank that provides services for its country's government and commercial banking system, and issues currency. **central heating** heating conducted from a boiler through pipes and radiators. **central nervous system** the system of nerve tissues in the brain and spinal cord in vertebrates. **central processing unit** the part of a computer in which operations are controlled and carried out. **Central time** the standard time in a zone that includes the central states of the US and parts of central Canada.

■ **cen·tral·ly** **adv.**

cen·tral·ize /'sentrə,līz/ ▶ v. (**centralizes**, **centralizing**, **centralized**) bring under the control of a central authority.

SYNONYMS **concentrate**, consolidate, amalgamate, condense, unify, focus. ANTONYMS devolve.

■ **cen·tral·ist** n. & adj. **cen·tral·i·za·tion** /,sentrələ'zāsHən/ n.

cen·trif·u·gal /sen'trif(y)əgəl/ ▶ adj. moving away from a center. □ **centrifugal force** a force that appears to cause something traveling around a central point to fly outward from its circular path.

cen·tri·fuge /'sentrə,fyo͞oj/ ▶ n. a machine with a rapidly rotating container, used to separate liquids from solids.

cen·trip·e·tal /sen'tripətl/ ▶ adj. moving toward a center. □ **centripetal force** a force that causes something traveling around a central point to move inward from its circular path.

cen·trist /'sentrəst/ ▶ n. a person having moderate political views or policies.

cen·tu·ri·on /sen't(y)o͝orēən/ ▶ n. a commander of one hundred men in the army of ancient Rome.

cen·tu·ry /'sencH(ə)rē/ ▶ n. (plural **centuries**) **1** a period of one hundred years. **2** a unit of a hundred men in the army of ancient Rome.

CEO ▶ abbr. chief executive officer.

ce·phal·ic /sə'falik/ ▶ adj. relating to the head.

ceph·a·lo·pod /'sefələ,päd/ ▶ n. the name in zoology for an octopus or squid.

ce·ram·ic /sə'ramik/ ▶ adj. made of fired clay. ▶ n. (**ceramics**) the art of making ceramic articles.

ce·re·al /'si(ə)rēəl/ ▶ n. **1** a grass producing an edible grain, such as wheat, oats, corn, or rye. **2** a breakfast food made from the grain of cereals.

cer·e·bel·lum /,serə'beləm/ ▶ n. (plural **cerebellums** or **cerebella** /-'belə/) the part of the brain at the back of the skull.

ce·re·bral /sə'rēbrəl, 'serəbrəl/ ▶ adj. **1** relating to the brain. **2** intellectual rather than emotional or physical: *cerebral pursuits such as chess.* □ **cerebral palsy** a condition in which a person has difficulty controlling their muscles.

cer·e·bra·tion /,serə'brāsHən/ ▶ n. formal the working of the brain; thinking.

ce·re·bro·spi·nal /sə,rēbrō'spīnl, ,serəbrō-/ ▶ adj. relating to the brain and spine.

ce·re·brum /sə'rēbrəm, 'serə-/ ▶ n. (plural **cerebra** /-brə/) the main part of the brain, in the front of the skull.

cer·e·mo·ni·al /,serə'mōnēəl/ ▶ adj. relating to or used in ceremonies.

SYNONYMS **formal**, official, state, public, ritual, ritualistic, stately, solemn. ANTONYMS informal.

■ **cer·e·mo·ni·al·ly** adv.

cer·e·mo·ni·ous /,serə'mōnēəs/ ▶ adj. done in a formal and grand way. ■ **cer·e·mo·ni·ous·ly** adv.

cer·e·mo·ny /'serə,mōnē/ ▶ n. (plural **ceremonies**) a formal occasion during which a set of special acts are performed.

SYNONYMS **1 rite**, ritual, observance, service, event, function. **2 pomp**, protocol, formality, formalities, niceties, decorum, etiquette, pageantry, ceremonial.

□ **stand on ceremony** behave formally.

ce·rise /sə'rēs, -'rēz/ ▶ n. a light pinkish-red color.

ce·ri·um /'si(ə)rēəm/ ▶ n. a silvery-white metallic element.

cer·tain /'sərtn/ ▶ adj. **1** able to be relied on to happen or be the case. **2** completely sure about something. **3** specific but not directly named or stated: *he mentioned certain personal problems.* ▶ pron. some but not all.

SYNONYMS ▶ adj. **1** *I'm certain he's guilty* **sure**, confident, positive, convinced, in no doubt, satisfied. **2** *it is certain that more changes are in the offing* **unquestionable**, sure, definite, beyond question, indubitable, undeniable, indisputable. **3** *they are certain to win* **sure**, bound, destined. **4** *certain defeat* **inevitable**, assured, unavoidable, inescapable, inexorable. **5** *there is no certain cure* **reliable**, dependable, foolproof, guaranteed, sure, infallible; informal sure-fire. ANTONYMS doubtful, unlikely, possible.

cer·tain·ly /'sərtnlē/ ▶ adv. **1** without doubt; definitely. **2** yes.

SYNONYMS **definitely**, surely, assuredly, unquestionably, beyond/without question, undoubtedly, without doubt, indubitably, undeniably, irrefutably, indisputably.

cer·tain·ty /'sərtntē/ ▶ n. (plural **certainties**) **1** the state of being certain. **2** a fact that is true or an event that is definitely going to take place.

SYNONYMS **1 confidence**, sureness, conviction, assurance. **2 inevitability**, foregone conclusion; informal sure thing. ANTONYMS doubt, possibility.

cer·ti·fi·a·ble /,sərtə'fīəbəl/ ▶ adj. able or needing to be officially declared insane.

cer·tif·i·cate /sər'tifikit/ ▶ n. **1** an official document recording a particular fact, event, or achievement. **2** an official classification given to a movie, saying that age group it is suitable for.

SYNONYMS **guarantee**, document, authorization, authentication, accreditation, credentials, testimonial.

■ **cer·ti·fi·ca·tion** /,sərtəfi'kāsHən/ n.

cer·ti·fy /'sərtə,fī/ ▶ v. (**certifies**, **certifying**, **certified**) **1** declare or confirm in a certificate or other official document. **2** officially declare someone insane.

SYNONYMS **1 verify**, guarantee, attest, validate, confirm, endorse. **2 accredit**, recognize, license, authorize, approve.

cer·ti·tude /'sərtə,t(y)o͞od/ ▶ n. a feeling of complete certainty.

ce·ru·le·an /sə'ro͞olēən/ ▶ adj. deep blue like a clear sky.

cer·vi·cal /'sərvikəl/ ▶ adj. relating to the cervix.

cer·vix /'sərviks/ ▶ n. (plural **cervices** /-və,sēz/) the narrow necklike passage between the lower end of the uterus and the vagina.

ce·sar·e·an /si'ze(ə)rēən/ (or **cesarean section**) ▶ n. an operation for delivering a child by cutting through the wall of the mother's abdomen.

ces·sa·tion /se'sāsHən/ ▶ n. the stopping of something.

SYNONYMS **end**, termination, halt, finish, stoppage, conclusion, winding up, pause, suspension. ANTONYMS start, resumption.

ces·sion /ˈsesHən/ ▶ **n.** the giving up of rights or territory by a state.

cess·pool /ˈses,po͞ol/ (or **cesspit** /ˈses,pit/) ▶ **n.** an underground tank or covered pit where sewage is collected.

ce·ta·cean /siˈtāsHən/ ▶ **n.** the name in zoology for a whale or dolphin.

cf. ▶ **abbr.** compare with.

CFC ▶ **abbr.** chlorofluorocarbon, a gas used in refrigerators and aerosols that is harmful to the ozone layer.

ch. ▶ **abbr.** chapter.

Cha·blis /sHaˈblē, sHə-, sHä-/ ▶ **n.** a dry white wine from Chablis in France.

cha-cha /ˈcHä ˌcHä/ ▶ **n.** a dance performed to a Latin American rhythm.

cha·conne /sHäˈkôn, -ˈkän, -ˈkən/ ▶ **n.** a musical composition in a series of varying sections in slow triple time.

chad·or /ˈcHədər, ˈcHäd,ôr/ ▶ **n.** a piece of dark cloth worn by Muslim women around the head and upper body.

chafe /cHāf/ ▶ **v.** (**chafes**, **chafing**, **chafed**) **1** make something sore or worn by rubbing against it. **2** rub a part of the body to warm it. **3** become impatient because of restrictions.

chaf·er /ˈcHāfər/ ▶ **n.** a large flying beetle.

chaff¹ /cHaf/ ▶ **n.** husks of grain that have been separated from the seed. ▫ **separate the wheat from the chaff** pick out what is valuable from what is worthless.

chaff² ▶ **v.** tease someone.

chaf·finch /ˈcHaf,incH/ ▶ **n.** a small finch (songbird) with a pink breast.

cha·grin /sHəˈgrin/ ▶ **n.** a feeling of disappointment or annoyance. ▶ **v.** (**be chagrined**) feel disappointed or annoyed.

chain /cHān/ ▶ **n.** **1** a series of connected metal links. **2** a connected series, set, or sequence: *a chain of superstores.* ▶ **v.** fasten or restrain with a chain.

> SYNONYMS ▶ **n.** **1 fetters**, shackles, irons, manacles, handcuffs; informal cuffs, bracelets. **2 series**, succession, string, sequence, train, course. ▶ **v.** **secure**, fasten, tie, tether, hitch, restrain, shackle, fetter, manacle, handcuff.

▫ **chain gang** a group of convicts chained together while working outside the prison. **chain letter** a letter sent to a number of people, all of whom are asked to make copies and send these to other people, who then do the same. **chain mail** armor made of small metal rings linked together. **chain reaction 1** a series of events, each caused by the previous one. **2** a chemical reaction in which the products of the reaction cause further changes. **chain-smoke** smoke cigarettes one after the other. **chain store** each of a series of stores owned by one company.

chain·saw /ˈcHān,sô/ ▶ **n.** a power-driven saw with teeth set on a moving chain.

chair /cHe(ə)r/ ▶ **n.** **1** a seat for one person, usually with a back and four legs. **2** a person in charge of a meeting or an organization. **3** a post as professor. ▶ **v.** be in charge of a meeting.

chair·lift /ˈcHe(ə)r,lift/ ▶ **n.** a lift for carrying skiers up and down a mountain, consisting of a series of chairs hung from a moving cable.

chair·man /ˈcHe(ə)rmən/ (or **chairwoman** /-,wo͝omən/) ▶ **n.** (plural **chairmen** or **chairwomen**) a person in charge of a meeting or organization.

> SYNONYMS **chair**, chairperson, president, chief executive, leader, master of ceremonies, emcee, MC.

chair·per·son /ˈcHe(ə)r,pərsən/ ▶ **n.** a person in charge of a meeting.

chaise /sHāz/ ▶ **n.** historical a two-wheeled horse-drawn carriage for one or two people.

chaise longue /ˈsHāz ˈlôNG/ ▶ **n.** (plural **chaises longues**) a sofa with a backrest at only one end.

chal·ced·o·ny /kalˈsedn,ē, cHal-, ˈkalsə,dōnē, ˈcHalsə-/ ▶ **n.** (plural **chalcedonies**) a type of quartz with very small crystals, such as onyx and agate.

cha·let /sHaˈlā, ˈsHa,lā/ ▶ **n.** **1** a wooden house with overhanging eaves, found in the Swiss Alps. **2** a wooden cabin used by vacationers.

chal·ice /ˈcHaləs/ ▶ **n.** a large cup or glass for wine.

chalk /cHôk/ ▶ **n.** **1** a soft white limestone. **2** a similar substance made into sticks and used for drawing or writing. ▶ **v.** draw or write with chalk. ▫ **chalk something up 1** achieve something noteworthy. **2** (**chalk up to**) associate something with a particular cause. ■ **chalk·i·ness n.** **chalk·y adj.**

chal·lenge /ˈcHalənj/ ▶ **n.** **1** an interesting but difficult task or situation. **2** an invitation to someone to take part in a contest or to prove something. ▶ **v.** (**challenges**, **challenging**, **challenged**) **1** raise doubt as to whether something is true or genuine. **2** call on someone to fight or do something difficult: *I challenged him to a fight.* **3** (of a guard) call on someone to prove their identity.

> SYNONYMS ▶ **n.** **1 problem**, difficult task, test, trial. **2 dare**, provocation, offer. ▶ **v.** **1 question**, dispute, take issue with, call into question, protest against, oppose. **2 dare**, defy, invite, throw down the gauntlet to. **3 test**, tax, strain, make demands on, stretch.

■ **chal·leng·er n.**

chal·leng·ing /ˈcHalənjiNG/ ▶ **adj.** testing your abilities in an interesting way: *the most challenging job in medicine.*

> SYNONYMS **demanding**, testing, taxing, exacting, hard, difficult, stimulating.
> ANTONYMS easy.

cham·ber /ˈcHāmbər/ ▶ **n.** **1** a large room used for formal or public events. **2** each of two houses of a legislature. **3** old use a bedroom. **4** a hollow space inside something. **5** the part of a gun bore that contains the explosive. ▫ **chamber music** classical music played by a small group of musicians. **Chamber of Commerce** a local association to promote the interests of the business community. **chamber pot** a bowl kept in a bedroom and used as a toilet.

cham·ber·lain /ˈcHāmbərlən/ ▶ **n.** (in the past) a person who looked after the household of a king or queen, or a noble.

cham·ber·maid /ˈcHāmbər,mād/ ▶ **n.** a woman who cleans rooms in a hotel.

cham·bray /ˈsHam,brā, -brē/ ▶ **n.** a cotton fabric with white weft threads and colored warp threads.

cha·me·le·on /kəˈmēlyən, -lēən/ ▶ **n.** a small lizard that is able to change color to fit in with its surroundings.

cham·fer /ˈcHamfər/ ▶ **v.** (**chamfers**, **chamfering**, **chamfered**) (in carpentry) cut an angled edge on a piece of wood.

cham·ois /'sHamē/ ▶ n. (plural **chamois**) **1** an antelope that lives in the mountains of southern Europe. **2** (also **chamois leather**) very soft leather made from the skin of sheep, goats, or deer.

cham·o·mile /'kamə,mēl, -,mīl/ (or **camomile**) ▶ n. a plant with white and yellow flowers, used in herbal preparations.

champ[1] /cHamp/ ▶ v. munch noisily; chomp. ▫ **champ at the bit** be very impatient.

champ[2] ▶ n. informal short for CHAMPION.

cham·pagne /sHam'pān/ ▶ n. a white sparkling wine from the Champagne region of France.

cham·pi·on /'cHampēən/ ▶ n. **1** a person who has won a contest. **2** a person who argues or fights for a cause. ▶ v. argue or fight in support of a cause: *priests who championed human rights.*

SYNONYMS ▶ n. **1 winner**, title-holder, gold medalist, prizewinner; informal champ, number one. **2 advocate**, proponent, promoter, supporter, defender, upholder, backer, booster. ▶ v. **advocate**, promote, defend, uphold, support, espouse, stand up for, campaign for, lobby for, fight for. ANTONYMS oppose.

cham·pi·on·ship /'cHampēən,sHip/ ▶ n. a competition for the position of champion.

chance /cHans/ ▶ n. **1** (also **chances**) a possibility of something happening. **2** an opportunity. **3** the way that things happen without any obvious plan or cause: *they met by chance.* ▶ v. (**chances**, **chancing**, **chanced**) **1** happen to do something. **2** informal do something even though it is risky. ▶ adj. happening without any obvious plan or cause.

SYNONYMS ▶ n. **1 possibility**, prospect, probability, likelihood, risk, threat, danger. **2** *I gave her a chance to answer* **opportunity**, opening, occasion, window. **3** *he took an awful chance* **risk**, gamble, leap in the dark. **4 coincidence**, accident, fate, destiny, providence, happenstance, good fortune, luck, fluke. ANTONYMS certainty. ▶ adj. **accidental**, fortuitous, fluky, coincidental.

▫ **by any chance** possibly. **on the off chance** just in case. **stand a chance** have the possibility of succeeding. **take a chance** (or **chances**) take a risk.

chan·cel /'cHansəl/ ▶ n. the part of a church near the altar, where the choir sits.

chan·cel·ler·y /'cHans(ə)lərē/ ▶ n. (plural **chancelleries**) the post or department of a chancellor.

chan·cel·lor /'cHans(ə)lər/ ▶ n. **1** a senior state or legal official. **2** the head of the government in some European countries. **3** the president or chief administrative officer of a college or university.

chanc·y /'cHansē/ ▶ adj. (**chancier**, **chanciest**) informal uncertain and risky.

chan·de·lier /,sHandə'li(ə)r/ ▶ n. an ornamental hanging light with holders for several candles or light bulbs.

chan·dler /'cHan(d)lər/ ▶ n. a person who buys and sells supplies and equipment for ships and boats. ■ **chan·dler·y** n.

change /cHānj/ ▶ v. (**changes**, **changing**, **changed**) **1** make or become different. **2** exchange one thing for something else. **3** (**change over**) move from one system or situation to another. **4** exchange a sum of money for the same sum in a different currency or different units. ▶ n. **1** a process through which something becomes different. **2** money returned as the balance of the amount paid or given in exchange for the same amount in larger units. **3** coins as opposed to banknotes. **4** a clean set of clothes.

SYNONYMS ▶ v. **1 alter**, make/become different, adjust, adapt, amend, modify, revise, vary, transform, metamorphose, evolve. **2 exchange**, substitute, swap, switch, replace, alternate. ▶ n. **1 alteration**, modification, variation, revision, amendment, adjustment, adaptation, metamorphosis, transformation, evolution. **2 replacement**, exchange, substitution, swap, switch.

▫ **change hands** pass to a different owner. **change your tune** express an opinion that is different from one you have expressed before. ■ **change·less** adj. **chang·er** n.

change·a·ble /'cHānjəbəl/ ▶ adj. **1** likely to change in an unpredictable way. **2** able to be changed.

SYNONYMS **variable**, varying, changing, fluctuating, irregular, erratic, inconsistent, unstable, unsettled, inconstant, fickle, capricious, temperamental, volatile, mercurial, unpredictable. ANTONYMS constant.

change·ling /'cHānjliNG/ ▶ n. a child believed to have been left by fairies in exchange for the parents' real child.

change·o·ver /'cHānj,ōvər/ ▶ n. a change from one system or situation to another.

chan·nel /'cHanl/ ▶ n. **1** a band of frequencies used in radio and television broadcasting. **2** a means of communication: *they didn't apply through the proper channels.* **3** a wide stretch of water joining two seas: *the English Channel.* **4** a passage along which liquid flows. **5** a passage that boats can pass through in a stretch of water. **6** an electric circuit that acts as a path for a signal. ▶ v. (**channels**, **channeling**, **channeled**) **1** direct something toward a particular purpose. **2** pass along or through a particular channel.

SYNONYMS ▶ n. **1 strait(s)**, sound, narrows, passage. **2 duct**, gutter, conduit, trough, sluice, drain. **3 means**, medium, instrument, mechanism, agency, vehicle, route, avenue. ▶ v. **convey**, transmit, conduct, direct, relay, pass on, transfer.

chant /cHant/ ▶ n. **1** a repeated rhythmic phrase that is called out or sung to music. **2** a tune to which the words of psalms are fitted by singing several syllables or words to the same note. ▶ v. say, shout, or sing in a chant.

SYNONYMS ▶ n. **shout**, cry, call, slogan, chorus, refrain. ▶ v. **shout**, chorus, repeat, call.

Cha·nu·kah /'KHänəkə, 'hänəkə/ ▶ n. ⇒ HANUKKAH.

cha·os /'kā,äs/ ▶ n. complete confusion and disorder.

SYNONYMS **disorder**, disorganization, confusion, mayhem, bedlam, pandemonium, havoc, turmoil, a shambles, anarchy, lawlessness; informal all hell broken loose. ANTONYMS order.

cha·ot·ic /kā'ätik/ ▶ adj. in a state of complete confusion and disorder.

SYNONYMS **disorderly**, disorganized, in confusion, in turmoil, topsy-turvy, anarchic, lawless.

■ **cha·ot·i·cal·ly** adv.

chap /CHap/ ▶ **n.** informal a man or boy.

chap·el /ˈCHapəl/ ▶ **n. 1** a small building or room used for prayers. **2** a part of a large church with its own altar.

chap·er·one /ˈSHapəˌrōn/ ▶ **n. 1** a person who accompanies and looks after another person or group of people. **2** dated an older woman in charge of an unmarried girl at social occasions. ▶ **v.** (**chaperones**, **chaperoning**, **chaperoned**) go with and look after.

chap·lain /ˈCHaplən/ ▶ **n.** a minister of the church, attached to a chapel in an institution or military unit, or a private house. ■ **chap·lain·cy n.**

chap·let /ˈCHaplət/ ▶ **n.** an ornamental circular band worn on the head.

chapped /CHapt/ ▶ **adj.** (of the skin) cracked and sore through exposure to cold weather.

chaps /CHaps, SHaps/ ▶ **pl.n.** leather pants without a seat, worn by a cowboy over ordinary pants to protect the legs.

chap·ter /ˈCHaptər/ ▶ **n. 1** a main division of a book. **2** a particular period in history or in a person's life. **3** the group of people in charge of a cathedral or other religious community. **4** a local branch of a society, club, or organization.

> SYNONYMS **1 section**, part, division, topic, stage, episode. **2 period**, phase, page, stage, epoch, era.

□ **chapter and verse** an exact reference or authority.

char[1] /CHär/ ▶ **v.** (**chars**, **charring**, **charred**) partially burn something so as to blacken the surface.

char[2] (also **charr**) ▶ **n.** (plural **char** or **charr**) a freshwater or sea fish resembling a trout.

char·ac·ter /ˈkariktər/ ▶ **n. 1** the particular qualities that make a person or thing an individual and different from others: *running away was not in keeping with her character.* **2** strong personal qualities such as courage and determination. **3** a person's good reputation. **4** a person in a novel, play, or movie. **5** informal an eccentric or amusing person. **6** a printed or written letter or symbol.

> SYNONYMS **1 personality**, nature, quality, disposition, temperament, mentality, makeup, spirit, identity, tone, feel. **2 integrity**, honor, moral strength/fiber, strength, backbone, resolve, grit, will power; informal guts. **3 reputation**, (good) name, standing, position, status. **4 eccentric**, oddity, crank, original, individualist, madcap, nonconformist; informal oddball. **5 person**, man, woman, soul, creature, individual, customer; informal guy. **6 letter**, figure, symbol, mark, device, sign, hieroglyph.

■ **char·ac·ter·less adj.**

char·ac·ter·is·tic /ˌkariktəˈristik/ ▶ **n.** a quality typical of a person or thing. ▶ **adj.** typical of a particular person or thing: *he began with a characteristic attack on extremism.*

> SYNONYMS ▶ **n. attribute**, feature, quality, property, trait, aspect, idiosyncrasy, peculiarity, quirk. ▶ **adj. typical**, usual, normal, distinctive, representative, particular, special, peculiar, idiosyncratic. ANTONYMS abnormal.

■ **char·ac·ter·is·ti·cal·ly adv.**

char·ac·ter·ize /ˈkariktəˌrīz/ ▶ **v.** (**characterizes**, **characterizing**, **characterized**) **1** describe the character of. **2** be typical of: *the rugged hills that characterize this part of West Virginia.*

> SYNONYMS **1 portray**, depict, present, represent, describe, categorize, class, brand. **2 distinguish**, mark, typify, set apart.

■ **char·ac·ter·i·za·tion** /ˌkariktərəˈzāSHən/ **n.**

cha·rade /SHəˈrād/ ▶ **n. 1** a pretense that something is true when it is clearly not. **2** (**charades**) a game of guessing a word or phrase from clues that are acted out.

> SYNONYMS **pretense**, act, masquerade, show, facade, pantomime, farce, travesty, mockery, parody.

char·broil /ˈCHärˌbroil/ ▶ **v.** grill food, especially meat on a rack over charcoal.

char·coal /ˈCHärˌkōl/ ▶ **n. 1** a form of carbon obtained when wood is burned slowly with little air. **2** a dark gray-black color.

chard /CHärd/ (also **Swiss chard**) ▶ **n.** a vegetable with large leaves and thick leaf stalks.

charge /CHärj/ ▶ **v.** (**charges**, **charging**, **charged**) **1** ask an amount as a price. **2** formally accuse someone of something. **3** rush forward in an attack. **4** (**charge someone with**) give someone a task or responsibility. **5** store electrical energy in a battery. **6** load or fill a container, gun, etc. **7** fill with an emotion or quality: *the air was charged with menace.* ▶ **n. 1** a price asked. **2** a formal accusation. **3** responsibility for the care or control of a person or thing. **4** a person or thing handed over to someone's care. **5** a headlong rush forward. **6** the electricity naturally existing in a substance. **7** energy stored chemically in a battery. **8** a quantity of explosive needed to fire a gun.

> SYNONYMS ▶ **v. 1 ask**, demand, bill, invoice. **2 accuse**, indict, arraign, prosecute, try, put on trial, impeach. **3 entrust**, burden, encumber, saddle, tax. **4 attack**, storm, assault, assail, descend on; informal lay into, tear into. **5 rush**, storm, stampede, push, plow, go headlong; informal barrel, steam. ▶ **n. 1 fee**, payment, price, rate, tariff, fare, levy. **2 accusation**, allegation, indictment, impeachment, arraignment. **3 attack**, assault, offensive, onslaught, drive, push. **4** *the child was in her charge* **care**, protection, safekeeping, control, custody, hands.

□ **charge card** a kind of credit card for which the balance must be paid in full each month.
■ **charge·a·ble adj.**

char·gé d'af·faires /SHärˌZHā däˈfer/ ▶ **n.** (plural **chargés d'affaires** same pronunciation) **1** an ambassador's deputy. **2** the diplomatic representative in a country to which an ambassador has not been sent.

charg·er /ˈCHärjər/ ▶ **n. 1** a device for charging a battery. **2** a strong horse formerly ridden by a knight or mounted soldier.

char·i·ot /ˈCHarēət/ ▶ **n.** a two-wheeled horse-drawn vehicle, used in ancient warfare and racing.
■ **char·i·ot·eer** /ˌCHarēəˈti(ə)r/ **n.**

cha·ris·ma /kəˈrizmə/ ▶ **n.** attractiveness that inspires admiration or enthusiasm in other people.

> SYNONYMS **charm**, presence, (force of) personality, strength of character, (animal) magnetism, appeal, allure.

char·is·mat·ic /ˌkarizˈmatik/ ▶ **adj. 1** having a charm that can inspire admiration in other people. **2** relating to a Christian movement that emphasizes special gifts from God, such as the healing of the sick.

SYNONYMS **charming**, magnetic, compelling, inspiring, captivating, mesmerizing, appealing, alluring, glamorous.

char·i·ta·ble /ˈCHaritəbəl/ ▶ **adj.** **1** relating to help given to people in need. **2** showing kindness and understanding when judging other people.

SYNONYMS **1 philanthropic**, generous, open-handed, giving, munificent, benevolent, altruistic, unselfish, public-spirited, humanitarian, non-profit-making. **2 magnanimous**, generous, liberal, tolerant, sympathetic, understanding, lenient, indulgent, forgiving. ANTONYMS commercial, mean.

■ **char·i·ta·bly** **adv.**

char·i·ty /ˈCHaritē/ ▶ **n.** (plural **charities**) **1** an organization set up to help people in need. **2** the giving of money or other help to people in need. **3** kindness and understanding shown when judging other people.

SYNONYMS **1 nonprofit organization**, charitable institution, fund, trust, foundation. **2 aid**, financial assistance, welfare, relief, donations, handouts, gifts, largesse, alms. **3 philanthropy**, humanitarianism, altruism, public-spiritedness, social conscience, benevolence. **4 goodwill**, compassion, consideration, concern, kindness, sympathy, indulgence, tolerance, leniency.

char·la·tan /ˈSHärlətən, ˈSHärlətn/ ▶ **n.** a person who claims to have skills or knowledge that they do not really have.

SYNONYMS **quack**, sham, fraud, fake, impostor, hoodwinker, double-dealer, swindler, fraudster; informal phony, shark, con man/artist, bunco artist, chiseler.

charles·ton /ˈCHärlstən/ ▶ **n.** a dance of the 1920s that involved turning the knees inward and kicking out the lower legs.

charm /CHärm/ ▶ **n.** **1** the power or quality of delighting or fascinating other people: *he was captivated by her youthful charm.* **2** a small ornament worn on a necklace or bracelet. **3** an object or saying believed to have magic power. ▶ **v.** **1** make someone feel great pleasure or delight. **2** use your charm in order to influence someone: *he charmed her into going out.* **3** (**charmed**) unusually lucky as if protected by magic: *a charmed life.*

SYNONYMS ▶ **n.** **1 appeal**, attraction, fascination, beauty, loveliness, allure, seductiveness, magnetism, charisma. **2 spell**, incantation, formula; mojo, hex. **3 talisman**, trinket, amulet, mascot, fetish. ▶ **v.** **1 delight**, please, win (over), attract, captivate, lure, fascinate, enchant, beguile. **2 coax**, cajole, wheedle; informal sweet-talk, soft-soap.

■ **charm·er** **n.** **charm·less** **adj.**

charm·ing /ˈCHärmiNG/ ▶ **adj.** **1** delightful; attractive. **2** very likable.

SYNONYMS **delightful**, pleasing, endearing, lovely, adorable, appealing, attractive, good-looking, alluring, winning, fetching, captivating, enchanting, entrancing.

■ **charm·ing·ly** **adv.**

char·nel house /ˈCHärnl/ ▶ **n.** a place formerly used for keeping dead bodies and bones in.

chart /CHärt/ ▶ **n.** **1** a sheet of paper on which information is displayed in the form of a table, graph, or diagram. **2** a map used for navigation by sea or air. **3** (**the charts**) a weekly listing of the current best-selling pop records. ▶ **v.** **1** make a map of. **2** follow progress or record something on a chart.

SYNONYMS ▶ **n.** **graph**, table, diagram, plan, map; Computing graphic. ▶ **v.** **1 plot**, tabulate, graph, record, register, represent. **2 follow**, trace, outline, describe, detail, record, document.

char·ter /ˈCHärtər/ ▶ **n.** **1** an official document stating that a ruler or government allows an institution to exist and setting out its rights. **2** a document listing and describing the functions of an organization. **3** the hiring of an aircraft, ship, or vehicle. ▶ **v.** **1** hire an aircraft, ship, or vehicle. **2** grant a charter to an institution.

SYNONYMS ▶ **n.** **1** *a royal charter* **authority**, authorization, sanction, dispensation, permit, license, warrant. **2** *the UN Charter* **constitution**, code, principles. ▶ **v.** **hire**, lease, rent, book.

□ **charter flight** a flight by an aircraft that has been hired for a specific journey.

char·treuse /SHärˈtro͞oz, -ˈtro͞os/ ▶ **n.** **1** a pale green or yellow liqueur. **2** a pale green or yellow color resembling this liqueur.

char·y /ˈCHe(ə)rē/ ▶ **adj.** (**charier**, **chariest**) cautious about doing something: *leaders are chary of reform.*

chase¹ /CHās/ ▶ **v.** (**chases**, **chasing**, **chased**) **1** go after someone in order to catch them. **2** rush or hurry. **3** try to make contact with or get hold of: *the company employs people to chase down debtors.* ▶ **n.** **1** an act of chasing. **2** (**the chase**) hunting as a sport.

SYNONYMS ▶ **v.** **1 pursue**, run after, follow, hunt, track, trail; informal tail. **2** *she chased away the dogs* **drive**, send, scare; informal send packing. **3** *she chased away all thoughts of him* **dispel**, banish, dismiss, drive away, shut out, put out of your mind. ▶ **n.** **pursuit**, hunt, trail.

□ **give chase** go after someone.

chase² ▶ **v.** (**chases**, **chasing**, **chased**) engrave metal.

chas·er /ˈCHāsər/ ▶ **n.** informal a mild alcoholic drink taken after a stronger one.

chasm /ˈkazəm/ ▶ **n.** **1** a deep crack in the earth. **2** a very big difference between two people or their opinions.

SYNONYMS **1** *a deep chasm* **gorge**, abyss, canyon, ravine, gully, gulch, gulf, crevasse, fissure, crevice. **2** *the chasm between their views* **breach**, gulf, rift; difference, separation, division, schism.

chas·sis /ˈCHasē, ˈSHasē/ ▶ **n.** (plural **chassis**) the framework forming the base of a vehicle.

chaste /CHāst/ ▶ **adj.** **1** having sex only with your husband or wife, or not at all. **2** not expressing sexual interest; demure and modest. ■ **chaste·ly** **adv.**

chas·ten /ˈCHāsən/ ▶ **v.** make someone feel subdued and less confident about something: *they were chastened by the bitter lessons of life.*

chas·tise /CHasˈtīz/ ▶ **v.** (**chastises**, **chastising**, **chastised**) tell someone off in a very strict way.

chas·ti·ty /ˈCHastətē/ ▶ **n.** the practice of having sex only with your husband or wife, or not at all.

chas·u·ble /ˈCHazəbəl, ˈCHazH-, ˈCHas-/ ▶ **n.** a long sleeveless garment worn by a priest over other robes.

chat /CHat/ ▶ **v.** (**chats, chatting, chatted**) **1** talk informally. **2** exchange messages in real time with other users of the Internet. ▶ **n. 1** an informal conversation. **2** the exchange of messages in real time with other users of the Internet.

SYNONYMS ▶ **v. talk**, gossip; informal jaw, yammer, chew the fat, shoot the breeze. ▶ **n. talk**, conversation, gossip; informal rap/bull session, confab, chinwag.

□ **chat line** a telephone service that allows conversation among a number of people who call in separately. **chat room** an area on the Internet where users can communicate.

cha·teau /SHaˈtō/ ▶ **n.** (plural **chateaux** /-ˈtō/ or **chateaus** /-ˈtōz/) a large French country house or castle.

cha·teau·bri·and /SHa,tōbrēˈôn/ ▶ **n.** a thick tenderloin of beef.

chat·e·laine /ˈSHatl,ān/ ▶ **n.** dated a woman in charge of a large house.

chat·tel /ˈCHatl/ ▶ **n.** a personal possession.

chat·ter /ˈCHatər/ ▶ **v.** (**chatters, chattering, chattered**) **1** talk informally about unimportant things. **2** (of a person's teeth) click together continuously from cold or fear. ▶ **n.** informal or unimportant talk.

SYNONYMS ▶ **v. blather**, prattle, chat, gossip, jabber, babble; informal yatter. ▶ **n. prattle**, chat, gossip, patter, jabber, babble; informal chitchat, yammering, yattering.

chat·ter·box /ˈCHatər,bäks/ ▶ **n.** informal a person who likes to chatter.

chat·ty /ˈCHatē/ ▶ **adj.** (**chattier, chattiest**) **1** fond of chatting. **2** (of a letter) informal and lively.

SYNONYMS **talkative**, communicative, effusive, gossipy, loquacious, voluble; informal mouthy, gabby. ANTONYMS taciturn.

■ **chat·ti·ly adv. chat·ti·ness n.**

chauf·feur /ˈSHōfər, SHōˈfər/ ▶ **n.** a person who is employed to drive someone around in a car. ▶ **v.** be a driver for someone.

chau·vin·ism /ˈSHōvə,nizəm/ ▶ **n. 1** a strong and unreasonable belief that your own country or group is better than others. **2** the belief held by some men that men are superior to women: *the club is a bastion of male chauvinism.* ■ **chau·vin·ist adj. & n. chau·vin·is·tic** /,SHōvəˈnistik/ **adj.**

cheap /CHēp/ ▶ **adj. 1** low in price, or charging low prices. **2** low in price and of bad quality. **3** having no value because achieved in a bad way: *her moment of cheap triumph.*

SYNONYMS **1 inexpensive**, low-priced, low-cost, economical, competitive, affordable, reasonable, budget, economy, bargain, reduced, discounted; informal dirt cheap. **2 poor-quality**, second-rate, substandard, inferior, vulgar, shoddy, trashy, tawdry; informal tacky. **3 despicable**, contemptible, immoral, unscrupulous, unprincipled, cynical. ANTONYMS expensive.

■ **cheap·ly adv. cheap·ness n.**

cheap·en /ˈCHēpən/ ▶ **v.** lower the quality or value of something.

cheap·skate /ˈCHēp,skāt/ ▶ **n.** informal a person who hates to spend money.

cheat /CHēt/ ▶ **v. 1** act dishonestly or unfairly to gain an advantage. **2** deprive someone of something by tricking them. ▶ **n.** a person who cheats.

SYNONYMS ▶ **v. swindle**, defraud, deceive, trick, dupe, hoodwink, double-cross, gull; informal rip off, con, pull a fast one on, sucker. ▶ **n. swindler**, fraudster, confidence trickster, double-dealer, double-crosser, fraud, fake, charlatan; informal con artist.

check[1] /CHek/ ▶ **v. 1** examine the accuracy, quality, or condition of. **2** make sure that something is the case. **3** stop or slow the progress of. ▶ **n. 1** an act of checking accuracy, quality, or condition. **2** a control or restraint. **3** Chess a position in which a king is directly threatened. **4** the bill in a restaurant.

SYNONYMS ▶ **v. 1 examine**, inspect, look at/over, scrutinize, study, investigate, probe, look into, inquire into; informal check out, give something a/the once-over. **2 make sure**, confirm, verify. **3 halt**, stop, arrest, bar, obstruct, foil, thwart, curb, block. ▶ **n. 1 examination**, inspection, scrutiny, perusal, study, investigation, test, checkup; informal once-over. **2 control**, restraint, constraint, curb, limitation.

□ **check in** register at a hotel or airport. **check mark** a mark (✓) used to indicate that a written item is correct or has been chosen. **check out 1** pay your hotel bill before leaving. **2** informal die. **check something out** find out about something. **check up on** investigate. **in check** under control.

check[2] ▶ **n.** a pattern of small squares. ▶ **adj.** (also **checked**) having a pattern of small squares.

check[3] ▶ **n.** a written order to a bank to pay a stated sum from an account to a named person.

check·er·board /ˈCHekər,bôrd/ ▶ **n.** a board for playing checkers and similar games, having a checkered pattern in black and white.

check·ered /ˈCHekərd/ ▶ **adj. 1** divided into or marked with checks. **2** having successful and unsuccessful periods: *a checkered career.*

check·ers /ˈCHekərz/ ▶ **n. 1** a game for two players, with twelve pieces each, played on a checkerboard. **2** a pattern of alternately colored squares.

check·list /ˈCHek,list/ ▶ **n.** a list of items to be considered or things to be done.

check·mate /ˈCHek,māt/ Chess ▶ **n.** a position of check from which a king cannot escape. ▶ **v.** put a king into checkmate.

check·out /ˈCHek,out/ ▶ **n.** a point at which goods are paid for in a supermarket or large store.

check·point /ˈCHek,point/ ▶ **n.** a barrier where security checks are carried out on travelers.

check·up /ˈCHek,əp/ ▶ **n.** an examination by a doctor or dentist.

ched·dar /ˈCHedər/ ▶ **n.** a kind of firm, smooth cheese.

cheek /CHēk/ ▶ **n. 1** the area on either side of the face below the eye. **2** either of the buttocks. **3** rude or disrespectful behavior: *he had the cheek to complain.* □ **cheek by jowl** close together. **turn the other cheek** stop yourself from fighting back.

cheek·bone /ˈCHēk,bōn/ ▶ **n.** the rounded bone below the eye.

cheek·y /ˈCHēkē/ ▶ **adj.** (**cheekier, cheekiest**) showing a cheerful lack of respect. ■ **cheek·i·ly adv.**

cheep /CHēp/ ▶ **n.** a squeaky cry made by a young bird. ▶ **v.** make a cheep.

cheer /CHi(ə)r/ ▶ **v. 1** shout for joy or in praise or encouragement. **2** praise or encourage a person or group. **3** (**cheer up** or **cheer someone up**) become or make someone less miserable. **4** give comfort to someone. ▶ **n. 1** a shout of joy, encouragement, or praise. **2** (also **good cheer**) cheerfulness; optimism. **3** (**cheers**) informal said before having an alcoholic drink with other people. **4** (**cheers**) informal said on parting, or written in closing; goodbye, or good wishes.

> SYNONYMS ▶ **v. 1 applaud**, hail, salute, shout for, clap, put your hands together for; informal holler for, give someone a big hand, ballyhoo. **2 please**, raise/lift someone's spirits, brighten, buoy up, hearten, gladden, perk up, encourage; informal buck up. ANTONYMS boo, depress. ▶ **n. hurrah**, hurray, whoop, bravo, shout; (**cheers**) acclaim, applause, ovation. ANTONYMS boo.

cheer·ful /ˈCHi(ə)rfəl/ ▶ **adj. 1** noticeably happy and optimistic. **2** bright and pleasant: *a cheerful, flower-filled garden.*

> SYNONYMS **1 happy**, jolly, merry, bright, sunny, joyful, in good/high spirits, buoyant, cheery, animated, smiling, good-humored; informal chipper, chirpy, full of beans. **2 pleasant**, agreeable, bright, sunny, friendly, welcoming. ANTONYMS sad, gloomy.

■ **cheer·ful·ly adv. cheer·ful·ness n.**

cheer·lead·er /ˈCHi(ə)rˌlēdər/ ▶ **n.** a person belonging to a group that performs organized chanting and dancing at sports events.

cheer·less /ˈCHi(ə)rlis/ ▶ **adj.** gloomy; depressing.

> SYNONYMS **gloomy**, dreary, dull, dismal, bleak, drab, somber, dark, dim, dingy, funereal, austere, stark, unwelcoming, uninviting, depressing.

cheer·y /ˈCHi(ə)rē/ ▶ **adj.** (**cheerier**, **cheeriest**) happy and optimistic. ■ **cheer·i·ly adv.**

cheese /CHēz/ ▶ **n.** a food made from the pressed curds of milk.

cheese·cake /ˈCHēzˌkāk/ ▶ **n.** a rich, sweet kind of dessert cake having a thick filling made with cream cheese and a bottom crust of graham crackers, cookie crumbs, or pastry.

cheese·cloth /ˈCHēzˌklôTH/ ▶ **n.** thin, loosely woven cotton cloth.

chees·y /ˈCHēzē/ ▶ **adj.** (**cheesier**, **cheesiest**) **1** like cheese. **2** informal sentimental or of bad quality: *a big cheesy grin.*

chee·tah /ˈCHētə/ ▶ **n.** a large spotted cat that can run very fast, found in Africa and parts of Asia.

chef /SHef/ ▶ **n.** a professional cook in a restaurant or hotel.

chem·i·cal /ˈkemikəl/ ▶ **adj.** relating to chemistry or chemicals. ▶ **n.** a substance that has been artificially prepared or purified. □ **chemical engineering** the branch of engineering concerned with the design and operation of industrial chemical plants. ■ **chem·i·cal·ly adv.**

che·mise /SHəˈmēz, -ˈmēs/ ▶ **n.** a woman's loose-fitting dress, nightdress, or petticoat.

chem·ist /ˈkemist/ ▶ **n.** an expert in chemistry; a person engaged in chemical research or experiments.

chem·is·try /ˈkeməstrē/ ▶ **n. 1** the branch of science concerned with the nature of substances and how they react with each other. **2** attraction or interaction between two people.

che·mo /ˈkēmō/ ▶ **n.** informal chemotherapy.

che·mo·ther·a·py /ˌkēmōˈTHerəpē, ˌkemō-/ ▶ **n.** the treatment of cancer with drugs.

che·nille /SHəˈnēl/ ▶ **n.** a fabric with a thick velvety pile.

cher·ish /ˈCHeriSH/ ▶ **v. 1** protect and care for someone lovingly. **2** keep a thought or memory in your mind: *I will always cherish memories of those days.*

> SYNONYMS **1 adore**, love, dote on, be devoted to, revere, think the world of, care for, look after, protect, keep safe. **2 treasure**, prize, hold dear. **3 harbor**, entertain, nurse, cling to, foster. ANTONYMS hate.

Cher·o·kee /ˈCHerəkē/ ▶ **n.** (plural **Cherokee** or **Cherokees**) a member of an American Indian people formerly living in the southeastern United States.

che·root /SHəˈro͞ot/ ▶ **n.** a cigar with both ends open.

cher·ry /ˈCHerē/ ▶ **n.** (plural **cherries**) **1** a small, round red fruit with a stone. **2** a bright red color. □ **cherry-pick** choose the best things or people from those available. **cherry tomato** a miniature tomato.

cher·ub /ˈCHerəb/ ▶ **n. 1** (plural **cherubim** /ˈCHer(y)əbim/ or **cherubs**) a type of angel, shown in art as a plump child with wings. **2** (plural **cherubs**) a beautiful or innocent-looking child. ■ **che·ru·bic** /CHəˈro͞obik/ **adj.**

cher·vil /ˈCHərvəl/ ▶ **n.** an herb with an aniseed flavor.

Chesh·ire /ˈCHeSHər, ˈCHeSHˌir/ ▶ **n.** a kind of pale crumbly cheese.

chess /CHes/ ▶ **n.** a board game for two players, the object of which is to put the opponent's king under a direct attack, leading to checkmate.

chess·board /ˈCHesˌbôrd/ ▶ **n.** a square board divided into sixty-four checkered squares, used for playing chess or checkers.

chest /CHest/ ▶ **n. 1** the front of a person's body between the neck and the stomach. **2** a large, strong box for storing or transporting things.

> SYNONYMS **1 breast**, upper body, torso, trunk, front. **2 box**, case, crate, trunk, coffer, strongbox, casket.

□ **chest of drawers** a piece of furniture fitted with a set of drawers. **get something off your chest** informal say something that you have wanted to say for a long time. **keep your cards close to your chest** informal be secretive about your plans.

ches·ter·field /ˈCHestərˌfēld/ ▶ **n.** a sofa with a back of the same height as the arms.

chest·nut /ˈCHes(t)ˌnət/ ▶ **n. 1** an edible nut with a glossy brown shell. **2** a deep reddish-brown color. **3** (**old chestnut**) a joke, story, or subject that has become boring through being repeated too often.

> SPELLING
>
> Remember the **t** in the middle: chestnut.

chev·a·lier /SHəˈvalˌyā, SHəvalˈyā/ ▶ **n. 1** historical a knight. **2** a member of the French Legion of Honor.

chev·ron /ˈSHevrən/ ▶ **n.** a V-shaped line or stripe, worn on the sleeve of a military uniform to show rank or length of service.

chew /CHōō/ ▶ v. **1** grind food with the teeth to make it easier to swallow. **2** (**chew something over**) discuss or consider something at length. ▶ n. a candy meant for chewing.

SYNONYMS ▶ v. **munch**, champ, chomp, crunch, gnaw, bite, masticate.

□ **chewing gum** flavored gum for chewing. **chew the fat** informal chat with someone in a leisurely way.

chew·y /'CHōōē/ ▶ adj. needing a lot of chewing.

Chi·an·ti /kē'äntē, -'antē/ ▶ n. (plural **Chiantis**) a dry red Italian wine.

chi·a·ro·scu·ro /kē,ärə'sk(y)ōōrō, kē,arə-/ ▶ n. the treatment of light and shade in drawing and painting.

chic /SHēk/ ▶ adj. (**chicer**, **chicest**) neat and fashionable in appearance.

SYNONYMS **stylish**, smart, elegant, sophisticated, fashionable; informal trendy, kicky, tony. ANTONYMS unfashionable.

chi·cane /SHi'kān, CHi-/ ▶ n. a sharp double bend in a road-racing track.

chi·can·er·y /SHi'kānərē, CHi-/ ▶ n. the use of cunning tricks to get what you want.

Chi·ca·no /CHi'känō, SHi-/ (or **Chicana** /-nə/) ▶ n. (plural **Chicanos** or **Chicanas**) (in North America) a person of Mexican origin or descent.

chick /CHik/ ▶ n. **1** a newly hatched young bird. **2** informal a young woman.

chick·en /'CHikən/ ▶ n. **1** a large domestic bird kept for its eggs or meat. **2** informal a coward. ▶ adj. informal cowardly. ▶ v. (**chicken out**) informal be too scared to do something. □ **chicken feed** informal a very small sum of money.

chick·en·pox /'CHikən,poks/ ▶ n. a disease causing itchy inflamed pimples.

chick·pea /'CHik,pē/ ▶ n. a yellowish seed eaten as a vegetable.

chick·weed /'CHik,wēd/ ▶ n. a small white-flowered plant that grows as a garden weed.

chic·o·ry /'CHikərē/ ▶ n. (plural **chicories**) a plant whose leaves are eaten and whose root can be roasted and ground to use as a substitute for coffee.

chide /CHīd/ ▶ v. (**chides**, **chiding**, **chided**) tell someone off.

chief /CHēf/ ▶ n. a leader or ruler. ▶ adj. **1** having the highest rank or authority. **2** most important: *the chief reason*.

SYNONYMS ▶ n. **1** *an Iroquois chief* **leader**, chieftain, head, ruler, master, commander. **2** *the chief of the central bank* **head**, chief executive, chief executive officer, CEO, president, chairman, chairwoman, principal, governor, director, manager; informal boss, (head) honcho. ▶ adj. **1** **head**, leading, principal, premier, highest, supreme, arch. **2** **main**, principal, primary, prime, first, cardinal, central, key, crucial, essential; informal number-one. ANTONYMS subordinate, minor.

□ **chief of staff** the senior staff officer of an armed service, military command, or government official.

chief·ly /'CHēflē/ ▶ adv. mainly; mostly.

SYNONYMS **mainly**, in the main, primarily, principally, predominantly, mostly, for the most part, usually, typically, commonly, generally, on the whole, largely.

chief·tain /'CHēftən/ ▶ n. the leader of a people or clan.

chif·fon /SHi'fän, 'SHif,än/ ▶ n. a light, see-through fabric.

chi·gnon /'SHēn,yän, SHēn'yän/ ▶ n. a knot or coil of hair arranged on the back of a woman's head.

chi·hua·hua /CHə'wäwə, SHə-/ ▶ n. a very small breed of dog with smooth hair.

chil·blain /'CHil,blān/ ▶ n. a painful, itchy swelling on a hand or foot caused by exposure to cold.

child /CHīld/ ▶ n. (plural **children** /'CHildrən/) **1** a young human being below the age of full physical development. **2** a son or daughter of any age.

SYNONYMS **youngster**, baby, infant, toddler, minor, juvenile, junior, descendant; informal kid, kiddie, nipper, rugrat, tyke, tot; derogatory brat.

□ **child's play** a task that is easily accomplished. **with child** old use pregnant. ■ **child·less** adj.

child·birth /'CHīld,bərTH/ ▶ n. the process of giving birth to a baby.

SYNONYMS **labor**, delivery, birthing; formal parturition; old use confinement.

child·hood /'CHīld,hŏŏd/ ▶ n. the state or period of being a child.

SYNONYMS **youth**, early years/life, infancy, babyhood, boyhood, girlhood, minority. ANTONYMS adulthood.

child·ish /'CHīldisH/ ▶ adj. **1** silly and immature. **2** like a child.

SYNONYMS **immature**, babyish, infantile, juvenile, puerile, silly. ANTONYMS mature.

child·like /'CHīld,līk/ ▶ adj. (of an adult) innocent and unsuspecting like a child.

SYNONYMS **youthful**, innocent, unsophisticated, naive, trusting, artless, unaffected, uninhibited, natural, spontaneous. ANTONYMS adult.

chil·dren /'CHildrən/ plural of **CHILD**.

Chil·e·an /'CHilēən, CHə'lāən/ ▶ n. a person from Chile. ▶ adj. relating to Chile.

chil·i /'CHilē/ ▶ n. (plural **chilies**) a small hot-tasting pepper, used in cooking and as a spice. □ **chili con carne** a stew of pieces of beef or pork, ground beef, or sausage, and usually beans and tomatoes, flavored with chili.

chill /CHil/ ▶ n. **1** an unpleasant feeling of coldness. **2** a feverish cold. ▶ v. **1** make cold. **2** frighten or horrify. **3** (usually **chill out**) informal relax: *chilling out in a hammock*. ▶ adj. unpleasantly cold.

SYNONYMS ▶ n. **coldness**, chilliness, coolness, nip. ANTONYMS warmth. ▶ v. **scare**, frighten, petrify, terrify, alarm, make someone's blood run cold; informal scare the pants off. ANTONYMS warm. ▶ adj. **cold**, chilly, cool, fresh, wintry, frosty, icy, arctic, bitter, freezing; informal nippy.

chill·er /'CHilər/ ▶ n. **1** a cold cabinet or refrigerator for keeping stored food a few degrees above freezing point. **2** short for **SPINE-CHILLER**.

chill·y /'CHilē/ ▶ adj. (**chillier**, **chilliest**) **1** too cold to be comfortable. **2** unfriendly.

SYNONYMS **1** **cold**, cool, crisp, fresh, wintry, frosty, icy; informal nippy. **2** **unfriendly**, unwelcoming, cold, cool, frosty; informal standoffish. ANTONYMS warm.

chime /CHīm/ ▶ n. **1** a tuneful ringing sound. **2** a bell, bar, or tube used in a set to produce chimes when struck. ▶ v. (**chimes**, **chiming**, **chimed**) **1** (of a bell or clock) make a tuneful ringing sound. **2** (**chime in**) interject a remark into a conversation.

chi·me·ra /kī'mi(ə)rə, kə-/ (or **chimaera**) ▶ n. **1** (in Greek mythology) a female monster with a lion's head, a goat's body, and a snake's tail. **2** an unrealistic hope or dream.

chi·mer·i·cal /kī'mi(ə)rikəl, kə-/ ▶ adj. not real or possible.

chim·ney /'CHimnē/ ▶ n. (plural **chimneys**) a pipe or channel that takes smoke and gases up from a fire or furnace.

chimp /CHimp/ ▶ n. informal a chimpanzee.

chim·pan·zee /ˌCHimˌpan'zē, -pən'zē, -'panzē/ ▶ n. an ape native to west and central Africa.

chin /CHin/ ▶ n. the part of the face below the mouth. □ **keep your chin up** informal remain cheerful in difficult circumstances. **take it on the chin** informal accept misfortune without complaint.

chi·na /'CHīnə/ ▶ n. **1** a delicate white ceramic material. **2** household objects made from china.

> SYNONYMS **dishes**, plates, cups and saucers, tableware, porcelain, dinnerware, dinner service, tea service.

□ **china clay** a soft white clay used for making porcelain and china.

chin·chil·la /CHin'CHilə/ ▶ n. a small South American rodent with soft gray fur and a long bushy tail.

chine /CHīn/ ▶ n. the backbone of an animal, or a joint of meat containing part of it.

Chi·nese /CHī'nēz, -'nēs/ ▶ n. (plural **Chinese**) **1** the language of China. **2** a person from China. ▶ adj. relating to China.

chink¹ /CHiNGk/ ▶ n. **1** a narrow opening or crack. **2** a beam of light entering through a chink.

> SYNONYMS **gap**, crack, space, hole, aperture, fissure, cranny, cleft, split, slit.

chink² ▶ v. make a high-pitched ringing sound. ▶ n. a high-pitched ringing sound.

chin·less /'CHinlis/ ▶ adj. lacking a well-defined chin.

chi·noi·se·rie /ˌSHēnˌwäz(ə)'rē, ˌSHēn'wäzərē/ ▶ n. **1** the use of Chinese styles in Western art, furniture, and architecture. **2** objects or decorations in this style.

chinos /'CHēnōz/ ▶ pl.n. casual trousers made from a smooth cotton fabric.

chintz /CHints/ ▶ n. patterned cotton fabric with a glazed finish, used for curtains and upholstery.

chintz·y /'CHintsē/ ▶ adj. **1** like chintz. **2** colorful but fussy and tasteless.

chip /CHip/ ▶ n. **1** a small piece cut or broken off from something hard. **2** (also **potato chip**) a wafer-thin slice of potato fried until crisp and eaten as a snack. **3** a microchip. **4** a counter used in some gambling games to represent money. ▶ v. (**chips**, **chipping**, **chipped**) **1** cut or break off a small piece from something hard. **2** (**chip away**) gradually make something smaller or weaker. **3** (**chip in**) add a contribution.

> SYNONYMS ▶ n. **1 fragment**, sliver, splinter, shaving, shard, flake. **2 nick**, crack, scratch. **3 counter**, token. ▶ v. **1 nick**, crack, scratch. **2** *chip off the old plaster* **cut**, hack, chisel, carve, hew, whittle.

□ **a chip off the old block** informal someone who resembles their parent in character. **a chip on your shoulder** informal a long-held feeling of resentment. **when the chips are down** informal when a very serious situation arises.

chip·board /'CHipˌbôrd/ ▶ n. ⇒ PARTICLEBOARD.

chip·munk /'CHipˌməNGk/ ▶ n. a burrowing squirrel with light and dark stripes running down the body.

chip·per /'CHipər/ ▶ adj. informal cheerful and lively.

chip·ping /'CHipiNG/ ▶ n. a small fragment of stone, wood, or similar material.

chi·rop·o·dy /kə'räpədē, SHə-/ ▶ n. dated care and treatment of the feet. ■ **chi·rop·o·dist** n.

chi·ro·prac·tic /ˌkīrə'praktik/ ▶ n. a system of complementary medicine based on the manipulation of the joints, especially those of the spinal column. ■ **chi·ro·prac·tor** /'kīrəˌpraktər/ n.

chirp /CHərp/ ▶ v. (of a small bird) make a short, high-pitched sound. ▶ n. a chirping sound.

chirp·y /'CHərpē/ ▶ adj. (**chirpier**, **chirpiest**) informal cheerful and lively.

chis·el /'CHizəl/ ▶ n. a hand tool with a narrow blade, used with a hammer to cut or shape wood, stone, or metal. ▶ v. (**chisels**, **chiseling**, **chiseled**) **1** cut or shape something with a chisel. **2** (**chiseled**) (of a man's facial features) clear and strong.

chit /CHit/ ▶ n. a short note recording a sum of money owed.

chit·chat /'CHitˌCHat/ informal ▶ n. trivial conversation. ▶ v. (**chitchats**, **chitchatting**, **chitchatted**) talk about trivial things.

chi·tin /'kītn/ ▶ n. Biochemistry a fibrous substance that forms the external skeletons of some insects, spiders, and crustaceans.

chiv·al·rous /'SHivəlrəs/ ▶ adj. acting in a polite and charming way toward women.

> SYNONYMS **gallant**, gentlemanly, honorable, respectful, considerate, courteous, polite, gracious, well-mannered. ANTONYMS rude.

■ **chiv·al·rous·ly** adv.

chiv·al·ry /'SHivəlrē/ ▶ n. **1** an honorable code of behavior that knights in medieval times were expected to follow. **2** polite behavior by a man toward women.

chives /CHīvz/ ▶ pl.n. a plant with long, thin leaves that are used as an herb.

chlo·ral /'klôrəl/ ▶ n. Chemistry a liquid used as a sedative.

chlo·rate /'klôrˌāt/ ▶ n. Chemistry a compound containing ClO_3 negative ions together with a metallic element: *sodium chlorate*.

chlo·ride /'klôrˌīd/ ▶ n. a compound of chlorine with another substance.

chlo·ri·nate /'klôrəˌnāt/ ▶ v. (**chlorinates**, **chlorinating**, **chlorinated**) treat water with chlorine. ■ **chlo·ri·na·tion** /ˌklôrə'nāSHən/ n.

chlo·rine /'klôrˌēn/ ▶ n. a chemical element in the form of a green gas, sometimes added to water as a disinfectant.

chlo·ro·fluor·o·car·bon /ˌklôrōˌflo͝orō'kärbən/ ▶ n. any of a class of compounds of carbon, hydrogen, chlorine, and fluorine, typically gases used chiefly in refrigerants and aerosol propellants.

chlo·ro·form /'klôrəˌfôrm/ ▶ n. a liquid used to dissolve things; formerly used as an anesthetic. ▶ v. use chloroform to make someone unconscious.

chlo·ro·phyll /ˈklôrəˌfil/ ▶ **n.** a green pigment in plants that allows them to absorb sunlight and use it in photosynthesis.

chlo·ro·plast /ˈklôrəˌplast/ ▶ **n.** a structure in green plant cells that contains chlorophyll and in which photosynthesis takes place.

chock /CHäk/ ▶ **n.** a wedge or block placed against a wheel to prevent it from moving. □ **chock-a-block** (or **chock-full**) informal filled to overflowing.

choc·o·hol·ic /ˌCHäkəˈhôlik, ˌCHô-, -ˈhälik/ (also **chocaholic**) ▶ **n.** informal a person who is very fond of chocolate.

choc·o·late /ˈCHäk(ə)lit, ˈCHôk-/ ▶ **n.** **1** a dark brown sweet food made from roasted cacao seeds. **2** a drink made by mixing milk or water with powdered chocolate.

choice /CHois/ ▶ **n.** **1** an act of choosing. **2** the right or ability to choose. **3** a range from which to choose. **4** something that has been chosen. ▶ **adj.** of very good quality.

> SYNONYMS ▶ **n.** **1** *freedom of choice* **selection**, choosing, picking, pick, preference, decision, say, vote. **2** *you have no other choice* **option**, alternative, course of action. **3** *an extensive choice* **range**, variety, selection, assortment. ▶ **adj.** **superior**, first-class, first-rate, prime, premier, grade A, best, finest, select, quality, top, top-quality, high-grade, prize; informal A1, top-notch. ANTONYMS inferior.

choir /kwīr/ ▶ **n.** **1** an organized group of singers. **2** the part of a church between the altar and the nave, used by the choir.

choir·boy /ˈkwīrˌboi/ ▶ **n.** a boy who sings in a church choir.

choke /CHōk/ ▶ **v.** (**chokes**, **choking**, **choked**) **1** prevent someone from breathing by blocking their throat or depriving them of air. **2** have trouble breathing. **3** (**be choked with**) be blocked or filled with. ▶ **n.** a valve used to reduce the amount of air in the fuel mixture of a gas engine.

> SYNONYMS ▶ **v.** **1 suffocate**, asphyxiate, smother, stifle, strangle, throttle; informal strangulate. **2 gag**, retch, cough, fight for breath. **3 clog (up)**, bung up, stop up, block, obstruct.

chok·er /ˈCHōkər/ ▶ **n.** a close-fitting necklace.

cho·le·cal·cif·er·ol /ˌkōləˌkalˈsifəˌrôl, -ˌrōl/ ▶ **n.** a form of vitamin D (vitamin D_3), produced naturally in the skin by the action of sunlight.

chol·er·a /ˈkälərə/ ▶ **n.** an infectious disease causing severe vomiting and diarrhea.

chol·er·ic /ˈkälərik, kəˈlerik/ ▶ **adj.** literary bad-tempered.

cho·les·ter·ol /kəˈlestəˌrôl, -ˌrōl/ ▶ **n.** a substance in the body that is believed to cause disease of the arteries when there is too much of it in the blood.

chomp /CHämp, CHômp/ ▶ **v.** munch or chew food noisily.

choose /CHo͞oz/ ▶ **v.** (**chooses**, **choosing**, **chose** /CHōz/; past participle **chosen** /ˈCHōzən/) pick something out as being the closest to what you want or need.

> SYNONYMS **1 select**, pick (out), opt for, settle on, prefer, decide on, fix on, elect, adopt. **2 wish**, want, desire, please, like.

choos·y /ˈCHo͞ozē/ ▶ **adj.** (**choosier**, **choosiest**) informal very careful in making a choice.

> SYNONYMS **fussy**, finicky, fastidious, overparticular, hard to please; informal picky, persnickety.

chop /CHäp/ ▶ **v.** (**chops**, **chopping**, **chopped**) **1** cut something into pieces with a knife or ax. **2** hit with a short downward stroke. ▶ **n.** **1** a thick slice of meat cut from or including the rib bone. **2** a downward cutting movement.

> SYNONYMS ▶ **v.** **cut (up)**, cube, dice, hash, hew, split, fell.

chop·per /ˈCHäpər/ ▶ **n.** **1** a short ax with a large blade. **2** informal a helicopter.

chop·py /ˈCHäpē/ ▶ **adj.** (of the sea) having many small waves.

> SYNONYMS **rough**, turbulent, heavy, heaving, stormy, tempestuous, squally. ANTONYMS calm.

chops /CHäps/ ▶ **pl.n.** informal **1** a person's or animal's mouth, jaws, or cheeks. **2** the technical skill of a musician, especially one who plays jazz.

chop·stick /ˈCHäpˌstik/ ▶ **n.** each of a pair of thin sticks used by the Chinese and Japanese to eat with.

chop su·ey /ˌCHäp ˈso͞oē/ ▶ **n.** a Chinese-style dish of meat with bean sprouts, bamboo shoots, and onions.

cho·ral /ˈkôrəl/ ▶ **adj.** sung by a choir or chorus.

cho·rale /kəˈral, -ˈräl/ ▶ **n.** a simple, stately hymn tune.

chord /kôrd/ ▶ **n.** a group of three or more musical notes sounded together in harmony.

> USAGE
> Don't confuse **chord** with **cord**, which means 'thin string or rope.'

chore /CHôr/ ▶ **n.** a boring or routine job or task.

> SYNONYMS **task**, job, duty, errand, burden; informal hassle.

cho·re·o·graph /ˈkôrēəˌgraf/ ▶ **v.** compose the sequence of steps for a ballet or dance routine. ■ **cho·re·og·ra·phy** /ˌkôrēˈägrəfē/ **n.**

cho·re·og·ra·pher /ˌkôrēˈägrəfər/ ▶ **n.** a person who designs the steps and movements for a ballet or other dance.

chor·is·ter /ˈkôrəstər, ˈkär-/ ▶ **n.** a member of a church choir.

chor·tle /ˈCHôrtl/ ▶ **v.** (**chortles**, **chortling**, **chortled**) chuckle happily.

cho·rus /ˈkôrəs/ ▶ **n.** (plural **choruses**) **1** a part of a song that is repeated after each verse. **2** a group of singers or dancers performing together in a supporting role in an opera, musical, etc. **3** something said at the same time by many people. ▶ **v.** (**choruses**, **chorusing**, **chorused**) (of a group of people) say the same thing at the same time. □ **chorus girl** a young woman who sings or dances in the chorus of a musical.

chose /CHōz/ past of **CHOOSE**.

cho·sen /ˈCHōzən/ past participle of **CHOOSE**.

chough /CHəf/ ▶ **n.** a black bird of the crow family with a red or yellow bill.

choux past·ry /SHo͞o/ ▶ **n.** very light pastry made with egg.

chow /CHou/ ▶ **n.** informal food.

chow·der /ˈCHoudər/ ▶ **n.** a soup containing fish, clams, or corn with potatoes.

chow mein /ˈCHou ˈmān/ ▶ **n.** a Chinese-style dish of fried noodles served with shredded meat or seafood and vegetables.

Christ /krīst/ ▶ **n.** the title given to Jesus.

chris·ten /ˈkrisən/ ▶ **v.** give a name to a baby while it is being baptized.

SYNONYMS **1** *she was christened Sara* **baptize**, name, give the name of, call. **2** *a group christened "The Magic Circle"* **call**, name, dub, style, term, label, nickname.

■ **chris·ten·ing** **n.**

Chris·ten·dom /ˈkrisəndəm/ ▶ **n.** dated the worldwide body of Christians.

Chris·tian /ˈkrisCHən/ ▶ **adj.** based on or believing in Christianity. ▶ **n.** a person who believes in Christianity. □ **Christian Era** the period of time that begins with the traditional date of Christ's birth. **Christian name** a person's first name. **Christian Science** the beliefs and practices of the Church of Christ Scientist, a Christian sect. **Christian Scientist** an adherent of Christian Science.

Chris·ti·an·i·ty /ˌkrisCHēˈanitē/ ▶ **n.** the religion based on the life and teaching of Jesus.

Christ·mas /ˈkrisməs/ ▶ **n.** (plural **Christmases**) the annual Christian festival celebrating the birth of Jesus, held on December 25. □ **Christmas rose** a winter-blooming evergreen of the buttercup family with white flowers. **Christmas tree** an evergreen tree decorated with lights and ornaments at Christmas.

chro·mat·ic /krōˈmatik/ ▶ **adj.** **1** Music using notes that do not belong to the key in which the passage is written. **2** Music going up or down by semitones. **3** relating to or produced by color.

chro·ma·tog·ra·phy /ˌkrōməˈtägrəfē/ ▶ **n.** Chemistry a technique for the separation of a mixture by passing it through a medium in which the components move at different rates.
■ **chro·mat·o·graph·ic** /krōˌmatəˈgrafik/ **adj.**

chrome /krōm/ ▶ **n.** a hard, bright metal coating made from chromium.

chro·mi·um /ˈkrōmēəm/ ▶ **n.** a hard white metallic element.

chro·mo·some /ˈkrōməˌsōm/ ▶ **n.** a threadlike structure found in the nuclei of most living cells, carrying genetic information in the form of genes.

chron·ic /ˈkränik/ ▶ **adj.** **1** (of an illness or problem) lasting for a long time. **2** having a long-lasting illness or bad habit.

SYNONYMS **1** *a chronic illness* **persistent**, long-standing, long-term, incurable. **2** *chronic economic problems* **constant**, continuing, persistent, long-lasting, severe, serious, acute, grave, dire. **3** *a chronic liar* **inveterate**, hardened, dyed-in-the-wool, incorrigible, compulsive; informal pathological. ANTONYMS acute, temporary.

■ **chron·i·cal·ly** **adv.**

chron·i·cle /ˈkränikəl/ ▶ **n.** a record of historical events made in the order in which they happened. ▶ **v.** (**chronicles**, **chronicling**, **chronicled**) record a series of events in detail.

SYNONYMS ▶ **n.** **record**, account, history, annals, archive(s), log, diary, journal. ▶ **v.** **record**, write down, set down, document, report.

■ **chron·i·cler** **n.**

chron·o·log·i·cal /ˌkränlˈäjikəl/ ▶ **adj.** (of a record of events) starting with the earliest and following the order in which they happened.
■ **chron·o·log·i·cal·ly** **adv.**

chro·nol·o·gy /krəˈnäləjē/ ▶ **n.** (plural **chronologies**) the arrangement of events or dates in the order in which they happened.

chro·nom·e·ter /krəˈnämətər/ ▶ **n.** an instrument for measuring time.

chrys·a·lis /ˈkrisələs/ ▶ **n.** (plural **chrysalises**) a butterfly or moth when it is changing from a larva to the adult form, inside a hard case.

chry·san·the·mum /kriˈsanTHəməm/ ▶ **n.** (plural **chrysanthemums**) a garden plant of the daisy family with brightly colored flowers.

chub /CHəb/ ▶ **n.** a thick-bodied river fish.

chub·by /ˈCHəbē/ ▶ **adj.** (**chubbier**, **chubbiest**) plump and rounded.

SYNONYMS **plump**, tubby, flabby, rotund, portly, chunky; informal zaftig, corn-fed. ANTONYMS skinny.

chuck[1] /CHək/ ▶ **v.** informal throw something carelessly or casually.

SYNONYMS **1** **throw**, toss, fling, hurl, pitch, cast, lob. **2** **throw away**, throw out, discard, dispose of, get rid of, dump, jettison; informal ditch, trash, junk. **3** **give up**, leave, resign from; informal quit, pack in.

chuck[2] ▶ **v.** touch someone playfully under the chin.

chuck[3] ▶ **n.** **1** a device for holding a workpiece in a lathe or a tool in a drill. **2** a cut of beef extending from the neck to the ribs.

chuck[4] ▶ **n.** food or provisions.

chuck·le /ˈCHəkəl/ ▶ **v.** (**chuckles**, **chuckling**, **chuckled**) laugh quietly. ▶ **n.** a quiet laugh.

SYNONYMS ▶ **v.** **laugh**, chortle, giggle, titter, snigger.

chuff /CHəf/ ▶ **v.** (of a steam engine) move with a regular puffing sound.

chug /CHəg/ ▶ **v.** (**chugs**, **chugging**, **chugged**) (of a vehicle) move slowly with a loud, regular sound.

chum /CHəm/ ▶ **n.** informal a close friend.

SYNONYMS **friend**, companion, playmate, classmate, schoolmate, workmate; informal pal, crony, buddy, bud. ANTONYMS enemy.

chum·my /ˈCHəmē/ ▶ **adj.** friendly and sociable.

chump /CHəmp/ ▶ **n.** informal **1** a silly person. **2** a person who is gullible and easily deceived.

chunk /CHəNGk/ ▶ **n.** a thick, solid piece.

SYNONYMS **lump**, hunk, wedge, block, slab, square, nugget, brick, cube; informal gob.

chunk·y /ˈCHəNGkē/ ▶ **adj.** (**chunkier**, **chunkiest**) **1** (of a person) short and sturdy. **2** bulky and thick. **3** containing chunks. ■ **chunk·i·ly** **adv.** **chunk·i·ness** **n.**

church /CHərCH/ ▶ **n.** **1** a building where Christians go to worship. **2** (**Church**) a particular Christian organization. **3** (**the Church**) people within the Christian faith. □ **Church of England** the English branch of the Western Christian Church, which has the British monarch as its head.

church·man /ˈCHərCHmən/ (or **churchwoman** /ˈCHərCHˌwo͝omən/) ▶ **n.** (plural **churchmen** or **churchwomen**) a minister of a Christian Church.

church·ward·en /'CHərCH,wôrdn/ ▶ **n.** either of two people in an Anglican parish who are elected to represent the congregation.

church·yard /'CHərCH,yärd/ ▶ **n.** an enclosed area surrounding a church.

churl /CHərl/ ▶ **n.** an unfriendly or rude person.

churl·ish /'CHərlisH/ ▶ **adj.** unfriendly and rude.

> SYNONYMS **rude**, ill-mannered, discourteous, ungracious, impolite, inconsiderate, surly, sullen. ANTONYMS polite.

■ **churl·ish·ly adv.**

churn /CHərn/ ▶ **n. 1** a machine for making butter by shaking milk or cream. **2** a large metal milk can. ▶ **v. 1** (of liquid) move about vigorously. **2** (**churn something out**) produce something in large quantities and without much thought. **3** shake milk or cream in a churn to produce butter.

> SYNONYMS ▶ **v. disturb**, stir up, agitate, beat.

chute /SHo͞ot/ ▶ **n. 1** a sloping channel for moving things to a lower level. **2** a slide into a swimming pool.

chut·ney /'CHətnē/ ▶ **n.** (plural **chutneys**) a spicy sauce made of fruits or vegetables with vinegar, spices, and sugar.

chutz·pah /'ho͝otspə, 'KHo͝otspə, -spä/ ▶ **n.** informal extreme self-confidence.

chyle /kīl/ ▶ **n.** Physiology a milky fluid that drains from the small intestine into the lymphatic system during digestion.

chyme /kīm/ ▶ **n.** Physiology the fluid that passes from the stomach to the small intestine, consisting of gastric juices and partly digested food.

CIA ▶ **abbr.** Central Intelligence Agency.

cia·bat·ta /CHə'bätə/ ▶ **n.** a flat Italian bread made with olive oil.

ciao /CHou/ ▶ **exclam.** informal used to say hello or goodbye.

ci·ca·da /sə'kādə, sə'kädə/ ▶ **n.** an insect that makes a shrill droning noise.

cic·e·ly /'sisilē/ (also **sweet cicely**) ▶ **n.** (plural **cicelies**) an aromatic white-flowered plant with fernlike leaves.

ci·der /'sīdər/ ▶ **n. 1** (also **sweet cider**) a drink made from apple juice. **2** (also **hard cider**) an alcoholic drink made from apple juice.

ci·gar /si'gär/ ▶ **n.** a cylinder of tobacco rolled in tobacco leaves for smoking.

cig·a·rette /,sigə'ret, 'sigə,ret/ ▶ **n.** a cylinder of finely cut tobacco rolled in paper for smoking.

cig·a·ril·lo /,sigə'rilō, -'rē(y)ō/ ▶ **n.** (plural **cigarillos**) a small cigar.

cil·i·um /'silēəm/ ▶ **n.** (plural **cilia** /'silēə/) a microscopic hairlike structure, found on the surface of certain cells.

cinch /sinCH/ ▶ **n.** informal **1** a very easy task. **2** a certainty.

cin·der /'sindər/ ▶ **n.** a piece of partly burned coal or wood. □ **cinder block** a lightweight building brick made from sand, cement, and pieces of partly burned coal or wood.

cin·e·ma /'sinəmə/ ▶ **n. 1** movies, collectively. **2** the production of movies as an art or industry.

cin·e·mat·ic /,sinə'matik/ ▶ **adj.** relating to the movies, or like a movie.

cin·e·ma·tog·ra·phy /,sinəmə'tägrəfē/ ▶ **n.** the skilled use of the camera in filmmaking.

■ **cin·e·ma·tog·ra·pher n.**

cin·na·bar /'sinə,bär/ ▶ **n.** a bright red mineral consisting of mercury sulfide.

cin·na·mon /'sinəmən/ ▶ **n.** a spice made from the bark of an Asian tree.

cinque·foil /'siNGk,foil, 'saNGk-/ ▶ **n.** a plant with leaves made up of five leaflets and five-petaled yellow flowers.

ci·pher /'sīfər/ (or **cypher**) ▶ **n. 1** a code. **2** a key to a code. **3** an unimportant person or thing. ▶ **v.** (**ciphers**, **ciphering**, **ciphered**) put a message into code.

cir·ca /'sərkə/ ▶ **prep.** (often preceding a date) approximately.

> SYNONYMS **approximately**, about, around, in the region of, roughly, something like, or so, or thereabouts, more or less; informal in the ballpark of. ANTONYMS exactly.

cir·ca·di·an /sər'kādēən/ ▶ **adj.** relating to processes in the body that happen regularly every twenty-four hours.

cir·cle /'sərkəl/ ▶ **n. 1** a round flat shape whose edge is at the same distance from the center all the way round. **2** a group of people with shared interests, friends, etc. ▶ **v.** (**circles**, **circling**, **circled**) **1** move or be placed all the way around. **2** draw a line around.

> SYNONYMS ▶ **n. 1 ring**, band, hoop, circlet, halo, disk/disc. **2 group**, set, crowd, band, company, clique, coterie, club, society; informal gang, bunch. ▶ **v. 1** *seagulls circled above* **wheel**, revolve, rotate, whirl, spiral. **2** *satellites circling the earth* **go around**, travel around, circumnavigate, orbit. **3** *the abbey was circled by a wall* **surround**, encircle, ring, enclose.

□ **come full circle** return to a previous position. **go** (or **run**) **around in circles** informal do something for a long time without achieving anything.

cir·clet /'sərklət/ ▶ **n.** a circular band worn on the head as an ornament.

cir·cuit /'sərkət/ ▶ **n. 1** a roughly circular line, route, or movement. **2** a system of components forming a complete path for an electric current. **3** a series of sports events or entertainments.

> SYNONYMS *two circuits of the track* **lap**, turn, round, circle.

□ **circuit breaker** an automatic safety device for stopping the flow of current in an electric circuit.

cir·cu·i·tous /sər'kyo͞oətəs/ ▶ **adj.** (of a route) long and indirect.

> SYNONYMS **roundabout**, indirect, winding, meandering, twisting, tortuous. ANTONYMS direct.

cir·cuit·ry /'sərkətrē/ ▶ **n.** (plural **circuitries**) a system of electric circuits.

cir·cu·lar /'sərkyələr/ ▶ **adj. 1** having the form of a circle. **2** (of a letter or advertisement) for distribution to a large number of people. ▶ **n.** a circular letter or advertisement.

> SYNONYMS ▶ **adj. round**, ring-shaped. ▶ **n. leaflet**, pamphlet, handbill, flyer, advertisement, notice.

□ **circular saw** a power saw with a quickly turning toothed disk.

cir·cu·late /'sərkyə,lāt/ ▶ **v.** (**circulates**, **circulating**, **circulated**) **1** move continuously through a system or area. **2** pass from place to place or person to person.

> SYNONYMS **1 spread**, communicate, disseminate, make known, make public, broadcast, publicize, distribute. **2 socialize**, mingle, mix, wander, stroll.

cir·cu·la·tion /ˌsərkyəˈlāsʜən/ ▶ **n. 1** movement through a system or area. **2** the continuous movement of blood around the body. **3** the spreading or passing of something from one person or place to another. **4** the number of copies of a newspaper or magazine sold.

cir·cum·am·bu·late /ˌsərkəmˈambyəˌlāt/ ▶ **v.** (**circumambulates**, **circumambulating**, **circumambulated**) formal walk all the way around.

cir·cum·cise /ˈsərkəmˌsīz/ ▶ **v.** (**circumcises**, **circumcising**, **circumcised**) **1** cut off a boy's or man's foreskin. **2** cut off a girl's or woman's clitoris. ■ **cir·cum·ci·sion** /ˌsərkəmˈsizʜən, ˈsərkəmˌsizʜən/ **n.**

cir·cum·fer·ence /sərˈkəmf(ə)rəns/ ▶ **n. 1** the boundary that encloses a circle. **2** the distance around something.

cir·cum·flex /ˈsərkəmˌfleks/ ▶ **n.** a mark (^) placed over a vowel in some languages to show a change in its sound.

cir·cum·lo·cu·tion /ˌsərkəmˌlōˈkyo͞osʜən/ ▶ **n.** a way of saying something that uses more words than are necessary.

cir·cum·nav·i·gate /ˌsərkəmˈnavəˌgāt/ ▶ **v.** (**circumnavigates**, **circumnavigating**, **circumnavigated**) sail all the way around. ■ **cir·cum·nav·i·ga·tion** /-ˌnavəˈgāsʜən/ **n.**

cir·cum·scribe /ˈsərkəmˌskrīb/ ▶ **v.** (**circumscribes**, **circumscribing**, **circumscribed**) restrict the freedom or power of.

cir·cum·spect /ˈsərkəmˌspekt/ ▶ **adj.** not wanting to take risks; cautious.

> SYNONYMS **cautious**, wary, careful, chary, guarded, on your guard; informal cagey.
> ANTONYMS unguarded.

cir·cum·stance /ˈsərkəmˌstans, -stəns/ ▶ **n. 1** a fact or condition that is connected with an event or action. **2** things that happen that are beyond your control: *a victim of circumstance.* **3** (**circumstances**) the practical things that affect a person's life.

> SYNONYMS (**circumstances**) **situation**, conditions, state of affairs, position, the lay of the land, (turn of) events, factors, facts, background, environment, context.

□ **under** (or **in**) **the circumstances** given the difficult nature of the situation. **under** (or **in**) **no circumstances** never.

cir·cum·stan·tial /ˌsərkəmˈstancʜəl/ ▶ **adj.** (of evidence) consisting of facts that make something seem likely but do not prove it. ■ **cir·cum·stan·tial·ly adv.**

cir·cum·vent /ˌsərkəmˈvent/ ▶ **v.** find a way of avoiding a problem or obstacle.

cir·cus /ˈsərkəs/ ▶ **n.** (plural **circuses**) a traveling group of entertainers, including acrobats, clowns, and people who perform with trained animals.

cir·rho·sis /səˈrōsəs/ ▶ **n.** a chronic disease of the liver.

cir·ro·cu·mu·lus /ˌsirōˈkyo͞omyələs/ ▶ **n.** cloud forming a layer of small fleecy clouds high in the sky.

cir·ro·stra·tus /ˌsirōˈstratəs, -ˈstrātəs/ ▶ **n.** cloud forming a uniform semitranslucent layer high in the sky.

cir·rus /ˈsirəs/ ▶ **n.** (plural **cirri** /ˈsirī/) cloud forming wispy streaks high in the sky.

CIS ▶ **abbr.** Commonwealth of Independent States.

Cis·ter·cian /sisˈtərsʜən/ ▶ **n.** a monk or nun of an order that is a stricter branch of the Benedictines.

cis·tern /ˈsistərn/ ▶ **n.** a tank connected to a toilet, in which the water used for flushing it is stored.

cit·a·del /ˈsitədl, -ˌdel/ ▶ **n.** a fortress protecting or overlooking a city.

ci·ta·tion /sīˈtāsʜən/ ▶ **n. 1** a quotation from a book or author. **2** an official mention of someone who has done something deserving praise.

cite /sīt/ ▶ **v.** (**cites**, **citing**, **cited**) quote a book or author as evidence for an argument.

> SYNONYMS **quote**, mention, refer to, allude to, instance, specify, name.

cit·i·zen /ˈsitizən, -sən/ ▶ **n. 1** a person who is legally recognized as being a member of a country. **2** an inhabitant of a town or city.

> SYNONYMS **1** *a US citizen* **subject**, national, passport holder. **2** *the citizens of Juneau* **inhabitant**, resident, native, townsman, townswoman, townsperson, taxpayer; formal denizen.

□ **Citizens' Band** a range of radio frequencies that are able to be used for local communication by private individuals. ■ **cit·i·zen·ship n.**

cit·ric ac·id /ˈsitrik/ ▶ **n.** a sharp-tasting acid present in the juice of lemons and other sour fruits.

cit·ron /ˈsitrən/ ▶ **n.** the lemonlike fruit of an Asian tree.

cit·ron·el·la /ˌsitrəˈnelə/ ▶ **n.** a fragrant natural oil used as an insect repellent and in perfume.

cit·rus /ˈsitrəs/ ▶ **n.** (plural **citruses**) a fruit of a group that includes the lemon, lime, orange, and grapefruit.

cit·y /ˈsitē/ ▶ **n.** (plural **cities**) **1** a large town. **2** an incorporated municipal center.

> SYNONYMS **town**, municipality, metropolis, megapolis, megacity, conurbation, urban area, borough, township; informal burg.

□ **city slicker** a person with the sophisticated tastes or values associated with people who live in a city. **city-state** chiefly historical a city that with its surrounding territory forms an independent state.

cit·y·scape /ˈsitēˌskāp/ ▶ **n.** a city landscape.

civ·et /ˈsivət/ ▶ **n. 1** a cat native to Africa and Asia. **2** a strong perfume obtained from the civet.

civ·ic /ˈsivik/ ▶ **adj.** having to do with a city or town.

> SYNONYMS **municipal**, city, town, urban, metropolitan, public, community.

□ **civic center** a building containing municipal offices and often with space for conventions, sports events, and entertainment.

civ·ics /ˈsiviks/ ▶ **pl.n.** the study of the rights and duties of citizenship.

civ·il /ˈsivəl/ ▶ **adj. 1** relating to the lives of ordinary people rather than to military or church matters. **2** (of a court) dealing with personal legal matters rather than criminal offenses: *a civil court.* **3** polite.

> SYNONYMS **1 secular**, nonreligious, lay. **2 nonmilitary**, civilian. **3 polite**, courteous,

well-mannered, gentlemanly, chivalrous, ladylike. ANTONYMS religious, military, rude.

□ **civil disobedience** the refusal to obey certain laws or to pay taxes, as a political protest. **civil engineer** an engineer who designs roads, bridges, dams, etc. **civil law** law concerned with ordinary citizens, rather than criminal, military, or religious affairs. **civil liberties** a person's rights to freedom of action and speech (while staying within the law). **civil rights** the rights of citizens to political and social freedom. **civil servant** a person who works in the civil service. **civil service** the departments that carry out the work of the government. **civil union** a legally recognized union of a couple of the same sex, with rights similar to those of marriage. **civil war** a war between groups of people within the same country. ■ **civ·il·ly** adv.

ci·vil·ian /sə'vilyən/ ▶ n. a person who is not a member of the armed services or the police force. ▶ adj. relating to a civilian.

ci·vil·i·ty /sə'vilətē/ ▶ n. (plural **civilities**) polite behavior or speech.

civ·i·li·za·tion /ˌsivələ'zāshən/ ▶ n. **1** an advanced stage of human development in which people in a society behave well toward each other and share a common culture. **2** the society, culture, and way of life of a particular area or period.

SYNONYMS **1 human development**, advancement, progress, enlightenment, culture, refinement, sophistication. **2 culture**, society, nation, people.

civ·i·lize /'sivəˌlīz/ ▶ v. (**civilizes**, **civilizing**, **civilized**) **1** bring a person or group to an advanced stage of social development. **2** (**civilized**) polite and good-mannered.

SYNONYMS **1 enlighten**, improve, educate, instruct, refine, cultivate, socialize. **2** (**civilized**) *civilized society* **advanced**, developed, sophisticated, enlightened, educated, cultured, cultivated. **3** (**civilized**) *civilized behavior* **polite**, courteous, well-mannered, civil, refined, polished. ANTONYMS unsophisticated, rude.

CJD ▶ abbr. Creutzfeldt–Jakob disease, a fatal disease affecting the brain, possibly linked to bovine spongiform encephalopathy.

Cl ▶ symbol the chemical element chlorine.

cl ▶ abbr. centiliter.

clack /klak/ ▶ v. make a sharp sound like that of one hard object hitting another. ▶ n. a clacking sound.

clad /klad/ ▶ adj. **1** clothed. **2** fitted with cladding.

clad·ding /'kladiNG/ ▶ n. a protective or insulating covering or coating.

claim /klām/ ▶ v. **1** say that something is true although you are not able to prove it. **2** request something that you believe you have a right to. **3** cause the loss of someone's life: *the war which followed claimed four million lives*. **4** ask for money under the terms of an insurance policy. **5** call for someone's attention. ▶ n. **1** a statement that something is true. **2** a statement requesting something that you believe you have a right to. **3** a request for compensation under the terms of an insurance policy.

SYNONYMS ▶ v. **1 assert**, declare, profess, protest, maintain, insist, contend, allege. **2 request**, ask for, apply for, demand. ▶ n. **1 assertion**, declaration, profession, protestation, insistence, contention, allegation. **2 application**, request, demand.

□ **lay claim to** assert your right to or possession of. ■ **claim·ant** n.

clair·voy·ant /kle(ə)r'voiənt/ ▶ n. a person who claims that they are able to see into the future or communicate mentally with people who are dead or far away. ▶ adj. able to see into the future. ■ **clair·voy·ance** n.

clam /klam/ ▶ n. a large shellfish with a hinged shell. ▶ v. (**clams**, **clamming**, **clammed**) (**clam up**) informal suddenly stop talking about something.

clam·bake /'klamˌbāk/ ▶ n. an outdoor social gathering at which clams and other seafood are baked.

clam·ber /'klambər, 'klamər/ ▶ v. (**clambers**, **clambering**, **clambered**) climb or move using your hands and feet.

clam·my /'klamē/ ▶ adj. (**clammier**, **clammiest**) **1** unpleasantly damp and sticky. **2** (of air) cold and damp.

clam·or /'klamər/ ▶ n. **1** a loud and confused noise. **2** a loud protest or demand. ▶ v. shout or demand something loudly.

SYNONYMS ▶ n. **noise**, din, racket, rumpus, uproar, shouting, commotion, hubbub; informal hullabaloo.

■ **clam·or·ous** adj.

clamp /klamp/ ▶ n. a brace, band, or clasp for holding something tightly. ▶ v. **1** fasten or hold with a clamp. **2** (**clamp down**) suppress or prevent something.

SYNONYMS ▶ v. **fasten**, secure, fix, attach, clench, grip, hold, press, clasp, screw, bolt.

clamp·down /'klampˌdoun/ ▶ n. informal an organized attempt to suppress something.

clan /klan/ ▶ n. a group of families, especially in the Scottish Highlands.

SYNONYMS **family**, house, dynasty, tribe.

clan·des·tine /klan'destən, -ˌtīn, -ˌtēn, 'klandəs-/ ▶ adj. done secretly.

SYNONYMS **secret**, covert, furtive, surreptitious, stealthy, cloak-and-dagger, underhanded/underhand; informal hush-hush.

■ **clan·des·tine·ly** adv.

clang /klaNG/ ▶ n. a loud metallic sound. ▶ v. make a clang.

clang·or /'klaNGər/ ▶ n. a continuous clanging sound.

clank /klaNGk/ ▶ n. a sharp sound like that of pieces of metal being struck together. ▶ v. make a clank.

clan·nish /'klanish/ ▶ adj. (of a group) tending to exclude people from outside the group.

clans·man /'klanzmən/ ▶ n. (plural **clansmen**) a male member of a clan.

clap /klap/ ▶ v. (**claps**, **clapping**, **clapped**) **1** bring the palms of your hands together loudly and repeatedly to show that you approve of something. **2** slap someone encouragingly on the back. **3** suddenly place a hand over a part of your face as a gesture of dismay. ▶ n. **1** an act of clapping. **2** a sudden loud sound of thunder.

SYNONYMS ▶ v. **applaud**, give someone a round of applause, put your hands together; informal give someone a (big) hand, give it up (for someone). ▶ n. **1 round of applause**, handclap; informal hand. **2 crack**, peal, crash, bang, boom.

clap·board /ˈklabərd, ˈklapˌbôrd/ ▶ n. one of a series of overlapping planks of wood, used to cover the outer walls of buildings.

clap·per /ˈklapər/ ▶ n. the moving part inside a bell.

clap·per·board /ˈklapərˌbôrd/ ▶ n. a pair of hinged boards that are struck together at the beginning of filming so that the picture and sound can be matched.

clap·trap /ˈklapˌtrap/ ▶ n. nonsense.

claque /klak/ ▶ n. **1** a group of people hired to applaud or heckle a performer. **2** a group of slavish followers.

clar·et /ˈklarit/ ▶ n. a red wine from Bordeaux in France.

clar·i·fy /ˈklarəˌfī/ ▶ v. (**clarifies**, **clarifying**, **clarified**) **1** make something easier to understand. **2** melt butter to separate out the impurities.

SYNONYMS **make clear**, shed/throw light on, illuminate, elucidate, explain, interpret, spell out, clear up. ANTONYMS confuse.

■ **clar·i·fi·ca·tion** /ˌklarəfiˈkāsнən/ n.

clar·i·net /ˌklarəˈnet/ ▶ n. a woodwind instrument with holes that are stopped by keys. ■ **clar·i·net·ist** n.

clar·i·on /ˈklarēən/ ▶ n. historical a war trumpet. □ **clarion call** a loud, clear call for action.

clar·i·ty /ˈklaritē/ ▶ n. **1** the quality of being clear and easily understood. **2** transparency or purity.

SYNONYMS **1** *the clarity of his explanation* **lucidity**, precision, coherence, transparency, simplicity. **2** *the clarity of the image* **sharpness**, clearness, crispness, definition. **3** *the clarity of the water* **transparency**, clearness, limpidity, translucence.

clash /klasн/ ▶ v. **1** come into violent conflict. **2** disagree or be at odds. **3** (of colors) look unpleasant together. **4** (of events) happen inconveniently at the same time. **5** strike metal objects together, producing a loud harsh sound. ▶ n. an act or sound of clashing.

SYNONYMS ▶ v. **1 fight**, battle, confront, skirmish, contend, come to blows. **2 disagree**, differ, wrangle, dispute, cross swords, lock horns, be at loggerheads. **3 conflict**, coincide, overlap. **4 bang**, strike, clang, crash. ▶ n. **1 fight**, battle, confrontation, skirmish, engagement, encounter, conflict. **2 argument**, altercation, confrontation, quarrel, disagreement, dispute; informal run-in. **3 crash**, clang, bang, clatter, clangor.

clasp /klasp/ ▶ v. **1** grasp tightly with your hand. **2** place your arms tightly around. **3** fasten with a clasp. ▶ n. **1** a device with interlocking parts used for fastening. **2** an act of clasping.

SYNONYMS ▶ v. **grasp**, grip, clutch, hold, squeeze, seize, grab, embrace, hug. ▶ n. **1 fastener**, catch, clip, pin, buckle. **2 grasp**, grip, squeeze, embrace, hug.

class /klas/ ▶ n. **1** a set or category of things that have something in common. **2** the division of people into different groups according to their social status. **3** a group of people of the same social status. **4** a group of students who are taught together. **5** a course of instruction in school or college. **6** informal impressive stylishness. ▶ v. place something in a particular category.

SYNONYMS ▶ n. **1 kind**, sort, type, variety, genre, category, grade, rating, classification. **2 group**, grouping, rank, stratum, level, echelon, status, caste. ▶ v. **classify**, categorize, group, grade, order, rate, bracket, designate, label, rank.

■ **class·less** adj.

clas·sic /ˈklasik/ ▶ adj. **1** judged over a period of time to be of the highest quality. **2** typical. ▶ n. (**Classics**) the study of ancient Greek and Latin language and culture.

SYNONYMS ▶ adj. **1 definitive**, authoritative, outstanding, first-rate, first-class, best, finest, excellent, superior, masterly. **2 typical**, archetypal, quintessential, model, representative, perfect, prime, textbook. **3 timeless**, traditional, simple, elegant, understated. ▶ n. **definitive example**, model, epitome, paradigm, exemplar, masterpiece, masterwork.

clas·si·cal /ˈklasikəl/ ▶ adj. **1** relating to the cultures of ancient Greece and Rome. **2** representing the highest standard within a long-established form. **3** (of music) written in the tradition of formal European music. ■ **clas·si·cal·ly** adv.

clas·si·cism /ˈklasəˌsizəm/ ▶ n. the use of a simple and elegant style characteristic of the art, architecture, or literature of ancient Greece and Rome.

clas·si·cist /ˈklasəsist/ ▶ n. a person who studies the Classics.

clas·si·fi·ca·tion /ˌklasəfəˈkāsнən/ ▶ n. **1** the arrangement of things in categories. **2** a category into which something is put.

SYNONYMS **categorization**, classifying, grouping, grading, ranking, organization, sorting, codification.

clas·si·fied /ˈklasəˌfīd/ ▶ adj. **1** (of newspaper or magazine advertisements) organized in categories. **2** (of information or documents) officially secret.

clas·si·fy /ˈklasəˌfī/ ▶ v. (**classifies**, **classifying**, **classified**) **1** arrange things in groups according to features that they have in common. **2** put in a particular class or category. **3** make documents or information officially secret.

SYNONYMS **categorize**, group, grade, rank, order, organize, sort, type, codify, bracket.

class·mate /ˈklasˌmāt/ ▶ n. a fellow member of your school or college class.

class·room /ˈklasˌro͞om, -ˌro͝om/ ▶ n. a room in which a class of students is taught.

class·y /ˈklasē/ ▶ adj. (**classier**, **classiest**) informal stylish and sophisticated.

SYNONYMS **stylish**, high-class, superior, exclusive, chic, elegant, smart, sophisticated, upscale, high-toned; informal posh, ritzy, plush, swanky.

clat·ter /ˈklatər/ ▶ n. a loud rattling sound like that of hard objects hitting each other. ▶ v. (**clatters**, **clattering**, **clattered**) make a clatter.

clause /klôz/ ▶ n. **1** a group of words that includes a subject and a verb and forms part of a sentence. **2** a part of a treaty, bill, or contract.

SYNONYMS **section**, paragraph, article, passage, subsection, chapter, condition, proviso, rider.

claus·tro·pho·bi·a /ˌklôstrəˈfōbēə/ ▸ **n.** an extreme fear of being in a small or enclosed space.

claus·tro·pho·bic /ˌklôstrəˈfōbik/ ▸ **adj. 1** (of a person) suffering from claustrophobia. **2** (of a place or situation) causing people to feel claustrophobia.

clav·i·cle /ˈklavikəl/ ▸ **n.** the collarbone.

claw /klô/ ▸ **n. 1** each of the horny nails on the feet of birds, lizards, and some mammals. **2** the pincer of a shellfish. ▸ **v.** scratch or tear at something with the claws or fingernails.

SYNONYMS ▸ **n. talon**, nail, pincer. ▸ **v. scratch**, lacerate, tear, rip, scrape, dig into.

□ **claw hammer** a hammer with one side of the head split and curved. **get your claws into** informal have a controlling influence over.

clay /klā/ ▸ **n.** sticky earth that can be molded when wet and baked to make bricks and pottery. □ **clay pigeon** a saucer-shaped piece of baked clay thrown up in the air as a target for shooting.

clean /klēn/ ▸ **adj. 1** free from dirt or harmful substances. **2** not yet used or marked. **3** not obscene. **4** having no record of offenses or crimes: *a clean driving record.* **5** (of an action) smoothly and skillfully done. ▸ **adv.** so as to be free from dirt. ▸ **v.** make something free from dirt or harmful substances. ▸ **n.** an act of cleaning.

SYNONYMS ▸ **adj. 1 washed**, scrubbed, cleansed, cleaned, laundered, spotless, unstained, unsullied, unblemished, immaculate, pristine, disinfected, sterilized, sterile, aseptic, decontaminated. **2 blank**, empty, clear, plain, unused, new, pristine, fresh, unmarked. **3 pure**, clear, fresh, unpolluted, uncontaminated. ANTONYMS dirty, polluted. ▸ **v. wash**, cleanse, wipe, sponge, scrub, mop, rinse, scour, swab, shampoo, launder, dry-clean. ANTONYMS dirty.

□ **clean-cut** (of a person) clean and neat. **clean-shaven** (of a man) without a beard or moustache. **come clean** informal fully confess something.
■ **clean·ly adv.**

clean·er /ˈklēnər/ ▸ **n.** a person or thing that cleans something. □ **take someone to the cleaners** informal **1** take all someone's money or possessions in a dishonest or unfair way. **2** inflict a crushing defeat on someone: *the Blue Jays were taken to the cleaners by the Red Sox.*

clean·li·ness /ˈklenlēnis/ ▸ **n.** the quality of being clean.

cleanse /klenz/ ▸ **v.** (**cleanses**, **cleansing**, **cleansed**) make something thoroughly clean or pure.

SYNONYMS **1 clean (up)**, wash, bathe, rinse, disinfect. **2** *cleansing the environment of traces of lead* **rid**, clear, free, purify, purge.

■ **cleans·er n.**

clean·up /ˈklēnˌəp/ ▸ **n. 1** an act of making a place clean or tidy. **2** an act of putting an end to disorder, immorality, or crime.

clear /kli(ə)r/ ▸ **adj. 1** easy to see, hear, or understand. **2** leaving or feeling no doubt. **3** transparent. **4** free of obstructions or unwanted objects. **5** (of a period of time) free of commitments. **6** free from disease or guilt. **7** (**clear of**) not touching. ▸ **adv.** so as to be out of the way of or uncluttered by something. ▸ **v. 1** make or become clear. **2** get past or over something safely or without touching it. **3** show or state that someone is innocent. **4** give official approval to. **5** make people leave a place. **6** (of a check) be paid into someone's account.

SYNONYMS ▸ **adj. 1 obvious**, evident, plain, sure, definite, unmistakable, manifest, indisputable, unambiguous, patent, incontrovertible, visible, conspicuous, overt, blatant, glaring. **2 understandable**, comprehensible, intelligible, plain, uncomplicated, explicit, lucid, coherent, simple, straightforward, unambiguous, clear-cut. **3 transparent**, limpid, translucent, crystal clear, pellucid. **4 bright**, cloudless, unclouded, blue, sunny, starry. **5 unobstructed**, passable, open, unrestricted, unhindered. ANTONYMS incoherent, vague, cloudy. ▸ **v. 1 disappear**, go away, stop, die away, fade, wear off, lift, settle, evaporate, dissipate, decrease, lessen, shift. **2 unblock**, unstop, clean out. **3 evacuate**, vacate, empty, leave. **4 remove**, strip, take away, carry away, tidy away/up. **5 go over**, pass over, sail over, jump (over), vault (over), leap (over). **6 acquit**, declare innocent, find not guilty, absolve, exonerate; informal let off (the hook).

□ **clear the air 1** make the air less sultry. **2** ease a tense situation by talking about things. **clear-cut** easy to see or understand. **clear out** informal go away. **clear-sighted** able to think clearly and make good judgments. **clear up 1** (of an illness) become cured. **2** stop raining. **clear something up 1** tidy something. **2** solve or explain a mystery or misunderstanding. **in the clear** no longer in danger or under suspicion.

clear·ance /ˈkli(ə)rəns/ ▸ **n. 1** the action of clearing. **2** official permission for something to take place. **3** clear space allowed for a thing to move past or under another.

SYNONYMS **1 removal**, clearing, demolition. **2 authorization**, permission, consent, approval, leave, sanction, license, dispensation; informal the go-ahead. **3 space**, room (to spare), headroom, margin, leeway.

clear·ing /ˈkli(ə)riNG/ ▸ **n.** an open space in a wood or forest.

clear·ing·house /ˈkli(ə)riNGˌhous/ ▸ **n.** a bankers' establishment where checks and bills from member banks are exchanged.

clear·ly /ˈkli(ə)rlē/ ▸ **adv. 1** in a clear way. **2** without doubt; obviously.

SYNONYMS **1 intelligibly**, plainly, distinctly, comprehensibly, legibly, audibly. **2 obviously**, evidently, patently, unquestionably, undoubtedly, without doubt, plainly, undeniably.

cleat /klēt/ ▸ **n. 1** a projection to which a rope may be attached. **2** a projecting wedge on a tool, the sole of a boot, etc., to prevent its slipping.

cleav·age /ˈklēvij/ ▸ **n. 1** the space between a woman's breasts. **2** a sharp difference or division between people.

cleave[1] /klēv/ ▸ **v.** (**cleaves**, **cleaving**, **clove** /klōv/ or **cleft** /kleft/ or **cleaved** /klēvd/; past participle **cloven** /ˈklōvən/ or **cleft** or **cleaved**) divide or split in two.

cleave[2] ▸ **v.** (**cleaves**, **cleaving**, **cleaved**) (**cleave to**) literary **1** stick to something. **2** become strongly involved with or emotionally attached to someone.

cleav·er /ˈklēvər/ ▸ **n.** a tool with a broad, heavy blade, used for chopping meat.

clef /klef/ ▶ **n.** Music a symbol placed next to the notes on a stave, to show their pitch.

cleft /kleft/ past and past participle of **CLEAVE**[1]. ▶ **adj.** split or divided into two. ▶ **n.** a split or indentation.

SYNONYMS ▶ **n. split**, crack, fissure, crevice.

□ **cleft lip** an upper lip with an abnormal split in the center. **cleft palate** a split in the roof of the mouth.

clem·a·tis /'klemətəs, klə'matəs/ ▶ **n.** an ornamental climbing plant.

clem·en·cy /'klemənsē/ ▶ **n.** kind or merciful treatment.

clem·ent /'klemənt/ ▶ **adj.** (of weather) mild.

clem·en·tine /'klemən,tīn, -,tēn/ ▶ **n.** a small citrus fruit with bright orange-red skin.

clench /klencH/ ▶ **v. 1** close your fist or hold your teeth or muscles together tightly in response to stress or anger. **2** grasp something tightly.

SYNONYMS **grip**, grasp, grab, clutch, clasp, clamp, hold tightly, seize, squeeze.

clere·sto·ry /'kli(ə)r,stôrē/ ▶ **n.** (plural **clerestories**) a row of windows in the upper part of the wall of a church or other large building.

cler·gy /'klərjē/ ▶ **n.** (plural **clergies**) the priests and ministers of a religion, especially those of the Christian Church.

cler·gy·man /'klərjēmən/ (or **clergywoman** /'klərjē,wŏŏmən/) ▶ **n.** (plural **clergymen** or **clergywomen**) a Christian priest or minister.

SYNONYMS **priest**, cleric, minister, preacher, chaplain, padre, father, pastor, vicar, rector, parson, curate.

cler·ic /'klerik/ ▶ **n.** a priest or religious leader.

cler·i·cal /'klerikəl/ ▶ **adj. 1** relating to the normal work of an office clerk. **2** relating to the priests and ministers of the Christian Church.

SYNONYMS **1 office**, desk, administrative, secretarial, white-collar. **2 ecclesiastical**, church, priestly, religious, spiritual, holy.

□ **clerical collar** a stiff white collar worn by the clergy in some churches.

clerk /klərk/ ▶ **n. 1** a person employed in an office or bank to keep records or accounts and do other routine work. **2** a person in charge of the records of a local council or court.

clev·er /'klevər/ ▶ **adj.** (**cleverer**, **cleverest**) **1** quick to understand and learn. **2** skilled at doing something.

SYNONYMS **1 intelligent**, bright, smart, astute, quick-witted, shrewd, talented, gifted, capable, able, competent; informal brainy. **2** *a clever scheme* **ingenious**, canny, cunning, crafty, artful, slick, neat. **3** *she was clever with her hands* **skillful**, dexterous, adroit, adept, deft, nimble, handy, skilled, talented, gifted. ANTONYMS stupid.

■ **clev·er·ly** adv. **clev·er·ness** n.

cli·ché /klē'sHā, kli-, 'klē,sHā/ ▶ **n.** a phrase or idea that has been used too much and is no longer fresh or interesting.

SYNONYMS **platitude**, hackneyed phrase, commonplace, banality, truism, stock phrase; informal old chestnut.

■ **cli·chéd** adj.

click /klik/ ▶ **n.** a short, sharp sound as of two hard objects coming into contact. ▶ **v. 1** make a click. **2** move or become secured with a click. **3** Computing press a mouse button. **4** informal become suddenly clear or understood.

SYNONYMS ▶ **v. 1 clack**, snap, pop, tick, clink. **2 become clear**, fall into place, make sense, dawn on someone, register, get through, sink in. **3 take to each other**, get along, be compatible, be like-minded, see eye to eye, be on the same wavelength; informal hit it off. **4 go down well**, prove popular, be a hit, succeed, resonate, work, take off.

cli·ent /'klīənt/ ▶ **n.** a person who uses the services of a professional person or organization.

SYNONYMS **customer**, buyer, purchaser, shopper, patient, patron.

cli·en·tele /,klīən'tel, ,klē-/ ▶ **n.** the clients or customers of a store, restaurant, or professional service.

cliff /klif/ ▶ **n.** a steep rock face at the edge of the sea.

SYNONYMS **precipice**, rock face, crag, bluff, ridge, escarpment, scar, scarp.

cliff·hang·er /'klif,haNGər/ ▶ **n.** a situation in a story that is exciting because you do not know what is going to happen next.

cli·mac·ter·ic /klī'maktərik, ,klīmak'terik/ ▶ **n.** the period in a person's life when their fertility has started to decline.

cli·mac·tic /klī'maktik, klə-/ ▶ **adj.** forming an exciting climax.

USAGE

Don't confuse **climactic**, 'forming a climax,' with **climatic**, which means 'relating to climate.'

cli·mate /'klīmit/ ▶ **n. 1** the general weather conditions in an area over a long period. **2** a general attitude or feeling among people.

SYNONYMS **1** (**weather**) **conditions**, weather. **2 atmosphere**, mood, spirit, ethos, feeling, ambience, environment.

□ **climate change** long-term, significant change in the climate of an area. ■ **cli·mat·ic** /klī'matik/ adj.

cli·max /'klī,maks/ ▶ **n.** the most intense, exciting, or important point of something. ▶ **v.** reach a climax.

SYNONYMS ▶ **n. peak**, pinnacle, height, high point, top, zenith, culmination. ANTONYMS anticlimax, nadir.

climb /klīm/ ▶ **v. 1** go or come up to a higher position. **2** go up a hill, rock face, etc. **3** move with effort or difficulty, especially into or out of a confined space. **4** increase in value or amount. **5** (of a plant) grow up a structure by clinging to or twining round it. ▶ **n. 1** an act of climbing. **2** a route up a mountain or cliff.

SYNONYMS ▶ **v. 1 ascend**, mount, scale, scramble up, clamber up, shinny up, conquer. **2 rise**, ascend, go up, gain height, soar, rocket. **3** *the road climbs steeply* **slope** (**upward**), rise, go uphill, incline. ANTONYMS descend.

□ **climb down** admit that you are wrong about something. ■ **climb·er** n.

clime /klīm/ ▶ **n.** literary a place considered in terms of its climate: *sunnier climes.*

clinch /klinCH/ ▶ **v. 1** settle a contract or contest. **2** settle something that has been uncertain or undecided. ▶ **n. 1** a tight hold in a fight or struggle. **2** informal a tight embrace.

> SYNONYMS ▶ **v. 1** *he clinched the deal* **secure**, settle, conclude, close, confirm, seal, finalize, wrap up; informal sew up. **2** *these findings clinched the matter* **settle**, decide, determine, resolve.

clinch·er /ˈklinCHər/ ▶ **n.** informal a fact, argument, or event that settles a matter conclusively.

cling /kliNG/ ▶ **v.** (**clings**, **clinging**, **clung** /kləNG/) (**cling to** or **on to**) **1** hold on tightly to. **2** stick to. **3** be unwilling to give up (a belief or hope). **4** be emotionally dependent on.

> SYNONYMS **stick**, adhere, hold.

cling·y /ˈkliNGē/ ▶ **adj.** (**clingier**, **clingiest**) **1** (of a garment) clinging to the body. **2** (of a person) too emotionally dependent on someone else.
■ **cling·i·ness n.**

clin·ic /ˈklinik/ ▶ **n.** a place where medical treatment or advice is given.

clin·i·cal /ˈklinikəl/ ▶ **adj. 1** relating to the observation and treatment of patients. **2** (of a place) very clean and plain. **3** efficient and showing no emotion.

> SYNONYMS **1 plain**, stark, austere, spartan, bleak, bare, functional, basic, institutional. **2 detached**, impersonal, dispassionate, indifferent, uninvolved, distant, remote, aloof, cold. ANTONYMS emotional.

■ **clin·i·cal·ly adv.**

clink /kliNGk/ ▶ **n.** a sharp ringing sound. ▶ **v.** make a clink.

clink·er /ˈkliNGkər/ ▶ **n.** the stony remains from burned coal or from a furnace.

clip¹ /klip/ ▶ **n. 1** a flexible or spring-loaded device for holding objects together or in place. **2** a piece of jewelry that is fastened with a clip. ▶ **v.** (**clips**, **clipping**, **clipped**) fasten with a clip.

> SYNONYMS ▶ **n. fastener**, clasp, hasp, catch, hook, buckle, lock. ▶ **v. fasten**, attach, fix, join, pin, staple, tack.

clip² ▶ **v.** (**clips**, **clipping**, **clipped**) **1** cut or trim with shears or scissors. **2** trim the hair or wool of an animal. **3** hit quickly or lightly. ▶ **n. 1** an act of clipping. **2** a short sequence taken from a movie or broadcast. **3** informal a quick or light blow.

> SYNONYMS ▶ **v. 1 trim**, prune, cut, snip, crop, shear, lop. **2 hit**, strike, graze, glance off, nudge, scrape. ▶ **n. 1 extract**, excerpt, snippet, fragment, trailer. **2 trim**, cut, crop, haircut.

□ **clip art** predrawn pictures and symbols, often provided with word-processing software and drawing packages, that users can add to their own documents.

clip·board /ˈklipˌbôrd/ ▶ **n.** a board with a clip at the top, for holding papers and writing on.

clipped /klipt/ ▶ **adj.** (of speech) having short, sharp vowel sounds and clear pronunciation.

clip·per /ˈklipər/ ▶ **n. 1** (**clippers**) an instrument for clipping. **2** (in the past) a type of fast sailing ship.

clip·ping /ˈklipiNG/ ▶ **n. 1** a small piece trimmed from something: *hedge clippings.* **2** an article cut from a newspaper or magazine.

clique /klēk, klik/ ▶ **n.** a small group of people who do not allow other people to join them.

> SYNONYMS **coterie**, set, circle, ring, in-crowd, group, gang, fraternity.

■ **cli·quey adj.**

clit·o·ris /ˈklitərəs/ ▶ **n.** the small sensitive organ just in front of the vagina.

cloak /klōk/ ▶ **n. 1** an outer garment that hangs loosely from the shoulders to the knees or ankles. **2** something that hides or covers: *a cloak of secrecy.* ▶ **v.** cover or hide something.

> SYNONYMS ▶ **n. 1 cape**, robe, wrap, mantle. **2** *a cloak of secrecy* **cover**, veil, mantle, shroud, screen, blanket. ▶ **v. conceal**, hide, cover, veil, shroud, mask, obscure, cloud, envelop, swathe, surround.

□ **cloak-and-dagger** involving secret activities.

cloak·room /ˈklōkˌro͞om, -ˌro͝om/ ▶ **n.** a room where coats and bags may be left.

clob·ber /ˈkläbər/ ▶ **v.** informal (**clobbers**, **clobbering**, **clobbered**) hit someone hard.

cloche /klōSH/ ▶ **n. 1** a small cover for protecting young or tender plants. **2** a woman's close-fitting bell-shaped hat.

clock /kläk/ ▶ **n. 1** an instrument that indicates the time. **2** informal a measuring device resembling a clock, such as a speedometer. ▶ **v.** informal **1** reach a particular speed or distance. **2** (**clock in** or **out**) register the time you are arriving at or leaving work. □ **around the clock** all day and all night. **turn** (or **put**) **back the clock** return to the past or to an earlier way of doing things.

clock·wise /ˈkläkˌwīz/ ▶ **adv. & adj.** in the direction of the movement of the hands of a clock.

clock·work /ˈkläkˌwərk/ ▶ **n.** a mechanism that has a spring and a system of interlocking wheels, used to make a mechanical clock or other device work. □ **like clockwork** very smoothly and easily.

clod /kläd/ ▶ **n. 1** a lump of earth. **2** informal a stupid person.

clod·hop·per /ˈklädˌhäpər/ ▶ **n.** informal **1** a large, heavy shoe. **2** a clumsy person.

clog /kläg, klôg/ ▶ **n.** a shoe with a thick wooden sole. ▶ **v.** (**clogs**, **clogging**, **clogged**) (often **clog something up**) block something up.

> SYNONYMS ▶ **v. block**, obstruct, congest, jam, choke, bung up, plug, stop up.

clois·ter /ˈkloistər/ ▶ **n.** a covered passage around an open courtyard in a convent, monastery, cathedral, etc.

clois·tered /ˈkloistərd/ ▶ **adj. 1** having a cloister. **2** protected from the outside world.

clomp /klämp, klômp/ ▶ **v.** walk with a heavy tread. ▶ **n.** the sound of a heavy tread.

clone /klōn/ ▶ **n.** an animal or plant created from the cells of another, to which it is genetically identical. ▶ **v.** (**clones**, **cloning**, **cloned**) **1** create something as a clone. **2** make an identical copy of something.

clop /kläp/ ▶ **n.** a sound made by a horse's hooves on a hard surface.

close¹ /klōs/ ▶ **adj. 1** only a short distance away or apart in space or time. **2** (of a connection or likeness) strong. **3** (of two people) very affectionate and friendly. **4** (of observation or examination) done in a careful and thorough way. ▶ **adv.** so as to be very near; with very little space between.

SYNONYMS ▶ **adj.** **1 near**, nearby, adjacent, neighboring, adjoining, abutting, at hand. **2 neck and neck**, even, nip and tuck. **3 intimate**, dear, bosom, close-knit, inseparable, devoted, faithful, special, firm. **4** *a close resemblance* **noticeable**, marked, distinct, pronounced, strong. **5 careful**, detailed, thorough, minute, searching, painstaking, meticulous, rigorous. **6 humid**, muggy, stuffy, airless, heavy, sticky, sultry, stifling. ANTONYMS far, distant.

□ **close-knit** (of a group of people) united by strong relationships. **at close quarters** (or **range**) from a position close to someone or something. **close-run** won or lost by a very small margin. **close shave** (or **close call**) informal a narrow escape from danger or disaster. **close-up** a photograph or sequence in a movie that is taken from a very short distance. ■ **close·ly adv.**

close[2] /klōz/ ▶ **v.** (**closes**, **closing**, **closed**) **1** move something so as to cover an opening. **2** (also **close something up**) bring two parts of something together. **3** (**close on** or **in on**) gradually surround or get nearer to. **4** (**close around** or **over**) encircle and hold. **5** come or bring something to an end. **6** finish speaking or writing. **7** (often **close down**) stop trading or working. **8** bring a deal or arrangement to a conclusion. ▶ **n.** the end of an event or of a period of time or activity.

SYNONYMS ▶ **v.** **1** *she closed the door* **shut**, pull (shut), push (shut), slam. **2** *close the hole* **block**, stop up, plug, seal, bung up, clog up, choke, obstruct. **3 end**, conclude, finish, terminate, wind up. **4 shut down**, close down, cease production, cease trading, be wound up, go out of business; informal fold, go to the wall, go bust. **5 clinch**, settle, secure, seal, confirm, pull off, conclude, finalize; informal wrap up. ANTONYMS open, start. ▶ **n. end**, finish, conclusion. ANTONYMS beginning.

□ **closed season** a period in the year when fishing or hunting is officially forbidden.

closed /klōzd/ ▶ **adj.** **1** not open or allowing people to go in. **2** not communicating with or influenced by other people. □ **behind closed doors** taking place secretly. **closed-circuit television** a television system used to watch people within a building, shopping center, etc. **closed shop** a place of work where all employees must belong to a particular labor union.

clos·et /ˈkläzit/ ▶ **n.** a small room or cupboard used for storing things. ▶ **v.** (**closets**, **closeting**, **closeted**) shut someone in a private room. ▶ **adj.** secret.

SYNONYMS ▶ **n. cupboard**, wardrobe, cabinet, locker. ▶ **v. shut away**, sequester, seclude, cloister, confine, isolate. ▶ **adj. secret**, covert, private, surreptitious, clandestine.

□ **in** (or **out of**) **the closet** not open (or open) about being homosexual.

clo·sure /ˈklōzhər/ ▶ **n.** **1** the closing of something. **2** a feeling that an upsetting experience has been resolved.

clot /klät/ ▶ **n.** a lump that is formed when a thick liquid substance dries or becomes thicker. ▶ **v.** (**clots**, **clotting**, **clotted**) form into clots.

SYNONYMS ▶ **n. lump**, clump, mass, thrombosis; informal glob. ▶ **v. coagulate**, set, congeal, thicken, solidify.

cloth /klôth/ ▶ **n.** (plural **cloths**) **1** fabric made from a soft fiber such as wool or cotton. **2** a piece of cloth used for a particular purpose. **3** (**the cloth**) ministers of the Church.

SYNONYMS **1 fabric**, material, textile(s), stuff. **2 rag**, wipe, duster, flannel.

clothe /klōth/ ▶ **v.** (**clothes** /klōthz/, **clothing**, **clothed**) **1** provide with clothes. **2** (**be clothed in**) be dressed in.

SYNONYMS **dress**, attire, robe, garb, costume, swathe, deck (out), turn out, fit out, rig (out); informal get up.

clothes /klō(th)z/ ▶ **pl.n.** things worn to cover the body.

SYNONYMS **clothing**, garments, attire, garb, dress, wear, costume, wardrobe; informal gear, togs, threads, getup; formal apparel.

□ **clothes horse 1** a frame on which washed clothes are hung to dry. **2** informal, often disapproving a person who is excessively concerned with wearing fashionable clothes.

clothes·line /ˈklō(th)zˌlīn/ ▶ **n.** a rope or wire on which washed clothes are hung to dry.

clothes·pin /ˈklō(th)zˌpin/ ▶ **n.** a wooden or plastic clip for securing clothes to a clothesline.

cloth·ier /ˈklōthyər, -thēər/ ▶ **n.** a person who makes or sells clothes or cloth.

cloth·ing /ˈklōthiNG/ ▶ **n.** clothes.

SYNONYMS see **CLOTHES**.

cloud /kloud/ ▶ **n.** **1** a mass of vapor floating in the atmosphere. **2** a mass of smoke, dust, etc., in the air. **3** a state or cause of gloom or anxiety. ▶ **v.** **1** (**cloud over**) (of the sky) become full of clouds. **2** become less clear. **3** (of someone's face or eyes) show sadness, anxiety, or anger.

SYNONYMS ▶ **n.** *a cloud of exhaust smoke* **mass**, billow, mantle, blanket, pall. ▶ **v. confuse**, muddle, obscure.

□ **have your head in the clouds** have a lot of fantasies and unrealistic thoughts. **on cloud nine** very happy. **under a cloud** out of favor or suspected of having done wrong. ■ **cloud·less adj.**

cloud·burst /ˈkloudˌbərst/ ▶ **n.** a sudden fall of very heavy rain.

cloud·y /ˈkloudē/ ▶ **adj.** **1** covered with clouds; having many clouds. **2** (of a liquid) not clear or transparent.

SYNONYMS **1 overcast**, dark, gray, black, leaden, murky, gloomy, sunless, starless. **2 murky**, muddy, milky, dirty, turbid. ANTONYMS clear, sunny.

clout /klout/ informal ▶ **n.** **1** a heavy blow. **2** influence or power. ▶ **v.** hit someone hard.

clove[1] /klōv/ ▶ **n.** the dried flower bud of a tropical tree, used as a spice.

clove[2] ▶ **n.** any of the segments making up a bulb of garlic.

clove[3] past of **CLEAVE[1]**. □ **clove hitch** a knot used to fasten a rope to a spar or another rope.

clo·ven /ˈklōvən/ past participle of **CLEAVE[1]**. □ **cloven hoof** the divided hoof of animals such as cattle, sheep, and deer.

clo·ver /ˈklōvər/ ▶ **n.** a plant with white or pink flowers and a leaf that usually has three lobes. □ **in clover** in ease and luxury.

clown /kloun/ ▶ n. 1 an entertainer, often in costume and with exaggerated makeup, who does silly things to make people laugh. 2 a playful or silly person. ▶ v. 1 perform as a clown. 2 behave in a funny or silly way.

SYNONYMS ▶ n. 1 **joker**, comedian, comic, wag, wit, jester. 2 **fool**, idiot, buffoon, dolt, ignoramus; informal moron, ass, numbskull, halfwit, fathead, twerp.

■ **clown·ish** adj.

clown·fish /ˈklounˌfisн/ ▶ n. (plural **clownfish** or **clownfishes**) a small brightly colored tropical sea fish.

cloy·ing /kloi-ɪɴɢ/ ▶ adj. 1 too sweet and making you feel slightly sick. 2 too sentimental.

club[1] /kləb/ ▶ n. 1 a group of people who meet regularly for a particular activity. 2 a place where members can relax, eat meals, or stay overnight. 3 a nightclub with dance music. ▶ v. (**clubs**, **clubbing**, **clubbed**) 1 (**club together**) combine with other people to do something. 2 informal go out to nightclubs.

SYNONYMS ▶ n. 1 **society**, association, group, circle, league, guild, union. 2 **nightclub**, bar, discotheque, disco. 3 **team**, squad, side.

■ **club·ber** n.

club[2] ▶ n. 1 a heavy stick used as a weapon. 2 a heavy stick with a thick head, used to hit the ball in golf. 3 (**clubs**) one of the four suits in a pack of playing cards, represented by a design of three black clover leaves on a short stem. ▶ v. (**clubs**, **clubbing**, **clubbed**) beat someone with a heavy stick.

SYNONYMS ▶ n. **stick**, cudgel, truncheon, bludgeon, baton, mace, bat, blackjack, nightstick. ▶ v. **hit**, beat, strike, cudgel, bludgeon, batter; informal clout, clobber.

□ **club foot** a deformed foot that is twisted so that the sole cannot be placed flat on the ground. **club sandwich** a sandwich consisting of three layers of bread, usually made with bacon, lettuce, and tomato, plus chicken or turkey or beef.

club·house /ˈkləbˌhous/ ▶ n. a building having a bar and other facilities for club members.

cluck /klək/ ▶ v. (of a hen) make a short, throaty sound. ▶ n. the short, throaty sound made by a hen.

clue /klo͞o/ ▶ n. a fact or piece of evidence that helps to clear up a mystery or solve a problem.

SYNONYMS **hint**, indication, sign, signal, pointer, lead, tip, evidence.

□ **not have a clue** informal have no idea about something. **clued into** informal well-informed about.

clue·less /ˈklo͞oləs/ ▶ adj. not able to understand or do something.

clump /kləmp/ ▶ n. 1 a small group of trees or plants growing closely together. 2 a mass or lump of something. 3 the sound of a heavy tread. ▶ v. 1 form into a clump or mass. 2 walk heavily.

SYNONYMS ▶ n. 1 *a clump of trees* **cluster**, thicket, group, bunch. 2 *a clump of earth* **lump**, clod, mass, chunk.

clump·y /ˈkləmpē/ ▶ adj. (of shoes or boots) thick and heavy.

clum·sy /ˈkləmzē/ ▶ adj. (**clumsier**, **clumsiest**) 1 awkward and badly coordinated. 2 tactless.

SYNONYMS 1 **awkward**, uncoordinated, ungainly, graceless, lumbering, inelegant, inept, unskillful, accident-prone, all thumbs; informal klutzy, having two left feet, ham-fisted, butterfingered. 2 **unwieldy**, cumbersome, bulky, awkward. ANTONYMS graceful.

■ **clum·si·ly** adv. **clum·si·ness** n.

clung /kləɴɢ/ past and past participle of **CLING**.

clunk /kləɴɢk/ ▶ n. a dull, heavy sound. ▶ v. make a clunk.

clus·ter /ˈkləstər/ ▶ n. a group of similar things placed or occurring closely together. ▶ v. (**cluster**, **clustering**, **clustered**) form a cluster.

SYNONYMS ▶ n. **bunch**, clump, mass, knot, group, clutch, huddle, crowd. ▶ v. **congregate**, gather, collect, group, assemble, huddle, crowd.

clutch[1] /kləcн/ ▶ v. grasp something tightly. ▶ n. 1 a tight grasp. 2 (**clutches**) power and control. 3 a mechanism in a vehicle that connects the engine with the axle and wheels.

SYNONYMS ▶ v. **grip**, grasp, clasp, cling to, hang on to, clench, hold, grab, snatch.

clutch[2] ▶ n. 1 a group of eggs fertilized at the same time and laid in a single session. 2 a group of chicks hatched from the same clutch of eggs.

clut·ter /ˈklətər/ ▶ v. (**clutters**, **cluttering**, **cluttered**) cover or fill with an untidy assortment of things. ▶ n. 1 things lying about untidily. 2 an untidy state.

SYNONYMS ▶ v. **litter**, mess up, be strewn, be scattered, cover, bury. ▶ n. **disorder**, chaos, mess, disarray, untidiness, confusion, litter, rubbish, junk.

cm ▶ abbr. centimeter(s).

c'mon /kəˈmän/ ▶ contr. come on: *c'mon, it'll be fun!*

CO ▶ abbr. Commanding Officer.

Co. ▶ abbr. 1 company. 2 county.

c/o ▶ abbr. care of.

coach[1] /kōcн/ ▶ n. 1 a comfortable bus used for longer journeys. 2 a railroad car for passengers. 3 a large horse-drawn carriage.

coach[2] ▶ n. 1 a person who trains someone in a sport. 2 a person who gives private lessons in a subject. ▶ v. give private lessons or training to someone.

SYNONYMS ▶ n. **instructor**, trainer, teacher, tutor, mentor, guru. ▶ v. **instruct**, teach, tutor, school, educate, drill, train.

co·ag·u·late /kōˈagyəˌlāt/ ▶ v. (**coagulates**, **coagulating**, **coagulated**) (of a liquid) thicken or become solid.

SYNONYMS **congeal**, clot, thicken, solidify, harden, set, dry.

■ **co·ag·u·lant** n. **co·ag·u·la·tion** /kōˌagyəˈlāsнən/ n.

coal /kōl/ ▶ n. a black rock used as fuel, consisting mainly of carbon formed from the remains of ancient plants. □ **coal tar** a thick black liquid produced when gas is made from coal. **haul over the coals** tell someone off harshly.

co·a·lesce /ˌkōəˈles/ ▶ v. (**coalesces**, **coalescing**, **coalesced**) come or bring together to form a single mass or whole.

coal·face /ˈkōlˌfās/ ▶ n. an exposed surface of coal in a mine.

coal·field /ˈkōlˌfēld/ ▶ n. a large area where there is a lot of coal underground.

co·a·li·tion /ˌkōəˈlisʜən/ ▶ n. an alliance for combined action, especially a government made up of two political parties who have agreed to work together.

SYNONYMS **alliance**, union, partnership, bloc, federation, league, association, confederation, consortium, syndicate, amalgamation, merger.

coarse /kôrs/ ▶ adj. **1** having a rough texture. **2** consisting of large grains or particles. **3** rude or vulgar.

SYNONYMS **1 rough**, scratchy, prickly, wiry, harsh. **2** *coarse manners* **uncouth**, oafish, loutish, boorish, rude, impolite, ill-mannered, vulgar, common, rough. **3** *a coarse remark* **vulgar**, crude, rude, off-color, lewd, smutty, indelicate. ANTONYMS soft, refined, polite.

■ **coarse·ly** adv.

USAGE

Don't confuse **coarse** with **course**, which means 'a direction,' as in *the plane changed course*.

coars·en /ˈkôrsən/ ▶ v. make or become coarse.

coast /kōst/ ▶ n. a stretch of land next to or near the sea. ▶ v. **1** move easily without using power. **2** do something without making much effort: *the Giants coasted to victory*.

SYNONYMS ▶ n. **shore**, coastline, seashore, seaboard, shoreline, seaside; literary strand. ▶ v. **freewheel**, cruise, taxi, drift, glide, sail.

□ **coast guard** an organization or person that keeps watch over coastal waters. **the coast is clear** there is no danger of being seen or caught. ■ **coast·al** adj.

coast·er /ˈkōstər/ ▶ n. **1** a small mat for a drinking glass, used to protect the surface of a table. **2** a ship that sails along the coast from port to port. **3** a sled, such as a toboggan.

coast·line /ˈkōstˌlīn/ ▶ n. the shape or appearance of the land along a coast: *a rugged coastline*.

coat /kōt/ ▶ n. **1** a full-length outer garment with sleeves. **2** an animal's covering of fur or hair. **3** an outer layer or covering. **4** a single layer of paint. ▶ v. form or provide with a layer or covering.

SYNONYMS ▶ n. **1 fur**, hair, wool, fleece, hide, pelt, skin. **2 layer**, covering, coating, skin, film, deposit. ▶ v. **cover**, surface, plate, spread, daub, smear, plaster, cake.

□ **coat of arms** a design used as a special symbol of a family, city, or organization. **coat of mail** a jacket composed of metal rings or plates, serving as armor.

coat·ing /ˈkōtiɴɢ/ ▶ n. a thin layer or covering.

coat·tail /ˈkōtˌtāl/ ▶ n. each of the flaps formed by the back of a tailcoat. □ **on someone's coattails** undeservedly benefiting from another's success.

coax /kōks/ ▶ v. **1** gently persuade someone to do something. **2** gently guide or move something.

SYNONYMS **persuade**, wheedle, cajole, get around, inveigle, maneuver; informal sweet-talk, soft-soap, twist someone's arm.

co·ax·i·al /kōˈaksēəl/ ▶ adj. (of a cable) having two wires, one wrapped around the other but separated by insulation.

cob /käb/ ▶ n. **1** the central part of an ear of corn. **2** (also **cobnut**) a hazelnut or filbert. **3** a sturdily built horse.

co·balt /ˈkōˌbôlt/ ▶ n. a silvery-white metallic element.

cob·ble¹ /ˈkäbəl/ (or **cobblestone** /ˈkäbəlˌstōn/) ▶ n. a small round stone used to cover road surfaces. ■ **cob·bled** adj.

cob·ble² ▶ v. (**cobbles**, **cobbling**, **cobbled**) (**cobble something together**) make up something roughly from materials that happen to be available.

cob·bler /ˈkäblər/ ▶ n. **1** a person whose job is mending shoes. **2** a fruit pie with a cakelike crust.

co·bra /ˈkōbrə/ ▶ n. a highly poisonous snake native to Africa and Asia.

cob·web /ˈkäbˌweb/ ▶ n. a spider's web.

co·ca /ˈkōkə/ ▶ n. a tropical American shrub grown for its leaves, which are the source of cocaine.

co·caine /kōˈkān, ˈkōˌkān/ ▶ n. an addictive drug made from the leaves of a tropical plant.

coc·cus /ˈkäkəs/ ▶ n. (plural **cocci** /ˈkäkˌ(s)ī, ˈkäkˌ(s)ē/) Biology a rounded bacterium.

coc·cyx /ˈkäksiks/ ▶ n. (plural **coccyges** /ˈkäksəˌjēz/ or **coccyxes**) a small triangular bone at the base of the spine.

coch·i·neal /ˈkäcʜəˌnēəl, ˈkō-/ ▶ n. a bright red dye used for coloring food.

coch·le·a /ˈkōklēə, ˈkäk-/ ▶ n. (plural **cochleae** /-lēˌē, -lēˌī/) the spiral cavity of the inner ear.

cock /käk/ ▶ n. a male chicken or game bird. ▶ v. **1** tilt or bend something in a particular direction. **2** raise the firing lever of a gun to make it ready to shoot. □ **cock and bull story** a very unlikely story.

cock·ade /käˈkād/ ▶ n. a rosette or knot of ribbons worn on a hat as part of a uniform.

cock-a-doo·dle-doo /ˌkäk ə ˌdo͞odl ˈdo͞o/ ▶ n. used to represent the sound made by a cock when it crows.

cock·a·tiel /ˈkäkəˌtēl/ ▶ n. a small Australian parrot with a crest.

cock·a·too /ˈkäkəˌto͞o/ ▶ n. a kind of parrot with a crest.

cock·crow /ˈkäkˌkrō/ ▶ n. literary dawn.

cock·er·el /ˈkäkərəl/ ▶ n. a young cock.

cock·er span·iel /ˈkäkər/ ▶ n. a small breed of spaniel with a silky coat.

cock·eyed /ˈkäkˈīd/ ▶ adj. informal **1** crooked. **2** stupid and impractical.

cock·fight·ing /ˈkäkˌfītiɴɢ/ ▶ n. the illegal sport of setting two cocks to fight each other.

cock·le /ˈkäkəl/ ▶ n. an edible shellfish with a ribbed shell. □ **warm the cockles of your heart** give you a feeling of contentment.

cock·ney /ˈkäknē/ ▶ n. (plural **cockneys**) **1** a person who was born in the East End of London. **2** the dialect or accent used in this area.

cock·pit /ˈkäkˌpit/ ▶ n. **1** a compartment for the pilot and crew in an aircraft or spacecraft. **2** the driver's compartment in a race car.

cock·roach /ˈkäkˌrōcʜ/ ▶ n. a beetlelike insect with long antennae and legs.

cock·sure /ˈkäkˈsʜo͝or/ ▶ adj. arrogantly confident.

cock·tail /ˈkäkˌtāl/ ▶ n. **1** an alcoholic drink consisting of a liquor mixed with other ingredients. **2** a mixture: *a cocktail of chemicals*.

cock·y /ˈkäkē/ ▶ adj. (**cockier**, **cockiest**) too self-confident.

SYNONYMS **arrogant**, conceited, overconfident, swollen-headed, self-important, full of yourself, egotistical, presumptuous, boastful; informal too big for your britches. ANTONYMS modest.

■ **cock·i·ly** adv. **cock·i·ness** n.

co·coa /'kōkō/ ▶ n. a drink made from powdered cacao seeds, mixed with hot milk or water. □ **cocoa butter** a fatty substance obtained from cocoa beans.

co·co·nut /'kōkə,nət/ ▶ n. **1** the large brown seed of a kind of palm tree, consisting of a woody husk lined with edible white flesh. **2** the white flesh of a coconut.

SPELLING
Just -o-, not -oa-: coconut.

co·coon /kə'ko͞on/ ▶ n. **1** a silky case spun by the larva of many insects, which protects it while it is turning into an adult. **2** something that envelops you in a protective or comforting way. ▶ v. wrap in a cocoon.

cod /käd/ ▶ n. (plural **cod**) a large sea fish used for food. □ **cod liver oil** oil obtained from the liver of cod, rich in vitamins D and A.

co·da /'kōdə/ ▶ n. an extra passage marking the end of a piece of music.

cod·dle /'kädl/ ▶ v. (**coddles**, **coddling**, **coddled**) give someone too much care and attention.

code /kōd/ ▶ n. **1** a system of words, figures, or symbols used to represent others secretly or briefly. **2** instructions for a computer program. **3** a set of laws or rules: *the penal code*. ▶ v. (**codes**, **coding**, **coded**) **1** convert into a code. **2** (**coded**) expressed in an indirect way.

SYNONYMS ▶ n. **1** **cipher**. **2** **convention**, etiquette, protocol, ethic. **3** **law(s)**, rules, regulations, constitution, system.

co·deine /'kō,dēn/ ▶ n. a painkilling drug obtained from morphine.

co·dex /'kō,deks/ ▶ n. (plural **codices** /'kōdə,sēz/ or **codexes**) an ancient manuscript text in book form.

codg·er /'käjər/ ▶ n. informal an elderly man.

cod·i·cil /'kädəsəl, -,sil/ ▶ n. a part added to a will that explains or alters an earlier part.

cod·i·fy /'kädə,fī, 'kōd-/ ▶ v. (**codifies**, **codifying**, **codified**) arrange a set of rules as a formal code. ■ **cod·i·fi·ca·tion** /,kädəfə'kāsHən, ,kōd-/ n.

cod·piece /'käd,pēs/ ▶ n. (in the past) a pouch worn by a man over his trousers, covering the groin.

co·ed·u·ca·tion /,kō,ejə'kāsHən/ ▶ n. the teaching of boys and girls together in the same schools. ■ **co·ed·u·ca·tion·al** adj.

co·ef·fi·cient /,kōə'fisHənt/ ▶ n. **1** Math a quantity that is placed before another that it multiplies (e.g., *4* in $4x^2$). **2** Physics a multiplier or factor that measures some property.

coe·la·canth /'sēlə,kanTH/ ▶ n. a large sea fish that was thought to have been extinct for millions of years until one was found alive in 1938.

coe·len·ter·ate /si'lentə,rāt, -rət/ ▶ n. Zoology a member of a group of aquatic invertebrate animals, including jellyfish, corals, and sea anemones.

co·erce /kō'ərs/ ▶ v. (**coerces**, **coercing**, **coerced**) force someone to do something.

SYNONYMS **pressure**, press, push, constrain, force, compel, oblige, browbeat, bully, threaten, intimidate, dragoon, twist someone's arm; informal railroad, lean on.

■ **co·er·cion** /kō'ərzHən, -sHən/ n. **co·er·cive** adj.

co·e·val /kō'ēvəl/ ▶ adj. having the same age or date of origin; contemporary. ▶ n. a person of roughly the same age as yourself; a contemporary.

co·ex·ist /,kō-ig'zist/ ▶ v. **1** exist at the same time or in the same place. **2** be together in harmony. ■ **co·ex·ist·ence** n.

cof·fee /'kôfē, 'käfē/ ▶ n. a hot drink made from the seeds of a tropical shrub. □ **coffee break** a short rest from work for coffee or a snack. **coffee cake** a cake with a drizzled white icing or crumb topping. **coffee table** a small low table for putting cups, books, etc., on. **coffee-table book** a large, lavishly illustrated book.

cof·fer /'kôfər, 'käfər/ ▶ n. a small chest for holding money or valuable items.

cof·fin /'kôfən, 'käf-/ ▶ n. a long box in which a dead body is buried or cremated.

cog /käg/ ▶ n. **1** (also **cogwheel** /'käg,(h)wēl/) a wheel or bar with projections on its edge, which transfers motion by engaging with projections on another wheel or bar. **2** a projection on a cog.

co·gent /'kōjənt/ ▶ adj. (of an argument) clear, logical, and convincing.

SYNONYMS **convincing**, persuasive, compelling, strong, forceful, powerful, potent, effective, sound, telling, coherent, clear, lucid, logical, well-argued.

■ **co·gen·cy** n. **co·gent·ly** adv.

cog·i·tate /'käjə,tāt/ ▶ v. (**cogitates**, **cogitating**, **cogitated**) formal think carefully about something. ■ **cog·i·ta·tion** /,käjə'tāsHən/ n.

co·gnac /'kōn,yak, 'kän-, 'kôn-/ ▶ n. brandy made in Cognac in western France.

cog·ni·tion /,käg'nisHən/ ▶ n. the process of gaining knowledge through thought, experience, and the senses. ■ **cog·ni·tive** /'kägnətiv/ adj.

cog·ni·zance /'kägnəzəns/ ▶ n. formal (**take cognizance of**) take notice or account of. ■ **cog·ni·zant** adj.

co·gno·scen·ti /,känyō'sHentē, ,kägnə-, -'sen-/ ▶ pl.n. people who are well-informed about a particular subject.

co·here /kō'hi(ə)r/ ▶ v. (**coheres**, **cohering**, **cohered**) hold firmly together; form a whole.

co·her·ent /kō'hi(ə)rənt/ ▶ adj. **1** (of an argument or theory) logical and consistent. **2** able to speak clearly and logically.

SYNONYMS **logical**, reasoned, rational, sound, cogent, consistent, clear, lucid, articulate, intelligible. ANTONYMS muddled.

■ **co·her·ence** n. **co·her·ent·ly** adv.

co·he·sion /kō'hēzHən/ ▶ n. the fact of holding firmly together.

co·he·sive /kō'hēsiv, -ziv/ ▶ adj. holding or making something hold together.

co·hort /'kō,hôrt/ ▶ n. **1** a large group of people. **2** an ancient Roman military unit equal to one tenth of a legion.

coif /koif/ ▶ n. a close-fitting cap worn by nuns under a veil. ▶ v. /kwäf, koif/ (**coifs**, **coiffing**, **coiffed**) arrange someone's hair.

coif·fure /kwä'fyo͝or/ ▶ n. a person's hairstyle. ■ **coif·fured** adj.

coil /koil/ ▶ n. a length of something wound in loops. ▶ v. arrange or form something into a coil.

SYNONYMS ▶ v. **wind**, loop, twist, curl, spiral, twine, wrap.

coin /koin/ ▶ n. a flat disk or piece of metal used as money. ▶ v. **1** invent a new word or phrase. **2** make coins by stamping metal.

SYNONYMS ▶ v. **invent**, create, make up, conceive, originate, think up, dream up.

coin·age /'koinij/ ▶ n. **1** coins of a particular type. **2** a newly invented word or phrase.

co·in·cide /ˌkōən'sīd, 'kōənˌsīd/ ▶ v. (**coincides**, **coinciding**, **coincided**) **1** happen at the same time or place. **2** be the same or similar; tally.

SYNONYMS **1 occur simultaneously**, happen together, co-occur, coexist. **2 tally**, correspond, agree, accord, match up, be compatible, dovetail, mesh; informal square. ANTONYMS differ.

co·in·ci·dence /kō'insədəns, -ˌdens/ ▶ n. **1** a remarkable instance of things happening at the same time by chance. **2** the fact of things being the same or similar.

SYNONYMS **accident**, chance, providence, happenstance, fate, luck, fortune, fluke.

co·in·ci·den·tal /kōˌinsə'dentl/ ▶ adj. resulting from a coincidence; not planned or intentional.

SYNONYMS **accidental**, chance, fluky, random, fortuitous, unintentional, unplanned.

■ **co·in·ci·den·tal·ly** adv.

coke[1] /kōk/ ▶ n. a solid fuel made by heating coal in the absence of air.

coke[2] ▶ n. informal cocaine.

col /käl/ ▶ n. the lowest point of a ridge or saddle between two peaks.

Col. ▶ abbr. Colonel.

col·an·der /'kələndər, 'käl-/ ▶ n. a bowl with holes in it, used to strain off liquid from food.

cold /kōld/ ▶ adj. **1** at a low temperature. **2** not feeling or showing emotion. **3** (of a color) containing a lot of blue or gray and giving no impression of warmth. **4** (of a scent or trail) no longer fresh and easy to follow. **5** without preparation: *going into the test cold.* ▶ n. **1** cold weather. **2** a viral infection causing a runny nose and sneezing.

SYNONYMS ▶ adj. **1 chilly**, chill, cool, freezing, icy, wintry, frosty, raw, bitter; informal nippy. **2 unfriendly**, inhospitable, unwelcoming, cool, frigid, frosty, distant, formal, stiff. ANTONYMS hot, warm.

□ **cold-blooded 1** (of reptiles and fish) having a body that is the same temperature as the surrounding air. **2** heartless and cruel. **cold-call** visit or telephone (someone) without their agreement in an attempt to sell goods or services. **cold cream** a cream for cleansing and softening the skin. **cold cuts** slices of cold cooked meats. **cold frame** a frame with a glass top in which small plants are grown and protected. **cold-hearted** unfeeling; unkind. **the cold shoulder** deliberately unfriendly behavior. **cold sore** an inflamed blister near the mouth, caused by a virus. **cold snap** a brief period of cold weather. **cold sweat** a state of sweating caused by nervousness or illness. **cold turkey** the abrupt and complete cessation of taking a drug to which someone is addicted. **the Cold War** a state of hostility between the Soviet Union and the United States (and their respective allies) after World War II. **get cold feet** lose your nerve. **in cold blood** deliberate or premeditated; without emotion. ■ **cold·ly** adv. **cold·ness** n.

cole·slaw /'kōlˌslô/ ▶ n. a dish of shredded raw cabbage mixed with a dressing.

col·ic /'kälik/ ▶ n. severe pain in the abdomen caused by gas or an obstruction in the intestines. ■ **col·ick·y** adj.

col·lab·o·rate /kə'labəˌrāt/ ▶ v. (**collaborates**, **collaborating**, **collaborated**) **1** work together on an activity. **2** cooperate with your country's enemy.

SYNONYMS **1 cooperate**, join forces, work together, combine, pool resources. **2 fraternize**, conspire, collude, cooperate, consort.

■ **col·lab·o·ra·tion** /kəˌlabə'rāsнən/ n. **col·lab·o·ra·tive** /kə'labərətiv/ adj.

col·lab·o·ra·tor /kə'labəˌrātər/ ▶ n. **1** a person who works with someone on an activity or project. **2** a person who betrays their country by cooperating with an enemy.

SYNONYMS **1 coworker**, partner, associate, colleague, confederate, assistant. **2 sympathizer**, traitor, quisling, fifth columnist.

col·lage /kə'läzн, kô-, kō-/ ▶ n. a form of art in which various materials are arranged and stuck to a backing.

col·la·gen /'käləjən/ ▶ n. a protein found in animal tissue.

col·lapse /kə'laps/ ▶ v. (**collapses**, **collapsing**, **collapsed**) **1** suddenly fall down or give way. **2** fail and come to a sudden end. ▶ n. **1** the falling down or giving way of a structure. **2** a sudden failure.

SYNONYMS ▶ v. **1 cave in**, fall in, subside, fall down, give (way), crumple, crumble, disintegrate. **2 faint**, pass out, black out, lose consciousness. **3 go to pieces**, break down, be overcome; informal crack up. **4 fail**, break down, fall through, fold, founder; informal flop, fizzle out. ▶ n. **1 cave-in**, disintegration. **2 breakdown**, failure.

col·laps·i·ble /kə'lapsəbəl/ ▶ adj. able to be folded down.

col·lar /'kälər/ ▶ n. **1** a band of material around the neck of a shirt or other garment. **2** a band put around the neck of a dog or cat. ▶ v. informal seize someone.

col·lar·bone /'kälərˌbōn/ ▶ n. either of the pair of bones joining the breastbone to the shoulder blades.

col·late /kə'lāt, 'kōˌlāt, 'kälˌāt/ ▶ v. (**collates**, **collating**, **collated**) collect and combine documents or information. ■ **col·la·tion** /kə'lāsнən, kō-, kä-/ n.

col·lat·er·al /kə'latərəl, kə'latrəl/ ▶ n. something that you promise to give to someone if you cannot repay a loan. ▶ adj. additional but less important; secondary.

col·league /'kälˌēg/ ▶ n. a person that you work with.

SYNONYMS **coworker**, fellow worker, workmate, teammate, associate, partner, collaborator, ally, confederate.

col·lect /kə'lekt/ ▶ v. **1** bring or gather things together. **2** come together and form a group. **3** go somewhere to fetch someone or something. **4** buy or find and keep items of a particular kind as a hobby.

SYNONYMS **1** *he collected the trash* **gather**, accumulate, assemble, amass, stockpile, pile up, heap up, store (up), hoard, save. **2 fetch**, pick up, go/come and get, call for. ANTONYMS distribute, disperse.

col·lect·ed /kə'lektid/ ▶ **adj. 1** calm. **2** brought together in one volume or edition.

SYNONYMS **calm**, cool, self-possessed, self-controlled, composed, poised, serene, tranquil, relaxed; informal laid-back. ANTONYMS excited.

col·lect·i·ble /kə'lektəbəl/ (also **collectable**) ▶ **adj.** (of an item) worth collecting. ▶ **n.** an item valued and sought by collectors.

col·lec·tion /kə'leksHən/ ▶ **n. 1** the action of collecting. **2** a group of things that have been collected. **3** a time when mail is picked up from a mailbox, or when trash is taken away.

SYNONYMS **1 hoard**, pile, heap, stock, store, stockpile, accumulation, reserve, supply, bank, pool, fund; informal stash. **2 group**, crowd, body, gathering, knot, cluster. **3 anthology**, selection, compendium, compilation, miscellany, treasury.

col·lec·tive /kə'lektiv/ ▶ **adj. 1** done by or belonging to all the members of a group. **2** taken as a whole. ▶ **n.** a small business or project owned by all the people who work for it.

SYNONYMS ▶ **adj. common**, shared, joint, combined, mutual, communal, pooled, united, allied, cooperative, collaborative. ANTONYMS individual.

□ **collective bargaining** negotiation of wages and other conditions of employment by an organized body of employees. ■ **col·lec·tive·ly adv.**

col·lec·tiv·ism /kə'lektə,vizəm/ ▶ **n. 1** the giving of priority to a group over each individual in it. **2** the ownership of land and the means of production by the people or the state.

col·lec·tor /kə'lektər/ ▶ **n. 1** a person who collects things of a specified type. **2** an official who is responsible for collecting money owed.

col·lege /'kälij/ ▶ **n. 1** a place providing higher education or specialized training. **2** (within a university) a school that offers a particular degree, such as engineering or medicine. **3** (within a university) a school that offers a liberal arts curriculum leading to a bachelor's degree.

col·le·giate /kə'lējət/ ▶ **adj. 1** having to do with a college or college students. **2** (of a university) composed of different colleges.

col·lide /kə'līd/ ▶ **v.** (**collides**, **colliding**, **collided**) move or bump into something.

SYNONYMS *they nearly **collided with** a bus* **crash into**, hit, strike, run into, bump into.

col·lie /'kälē/ ▶ **n.** (plural **collies**) a breed of sheepdog with long hair.

col·lier /'kälyər/ ▶ **n.** a coal miner.

col·lier·y /'kälyərē/ ▶ **n.** (plural **collieries**) a coal mine.

col·lin·e·ar /kə'linēər, kä-/ ▶ **adj.** Geometry (of points) lying in the same straight line.

col·li·sion /kə'lizHən/ ▶ **n.** an instance when two or more things collide.

SYNONYMS **crash**, accident, smash, wreck; informal smash-up, pile-up.

col·lo·ca·tion /,kälə'kāsHən/ ▶ **n. 1** the frequent occurrence of a word with another word or words. **2** a word or group of words that very often occur together (e.g., *heavy drinker*). ■ **col·lo·cate** /'kälə,kāt/ **v.**

col·loid /'käl,oid/ ▶ **n. 1** a homogeneous substance consisting of submicroscopic particles of one substance dispersed in another, as in an emulsion or gel. **2** a gluey substance. ■ **col·loi·dal** /kə'loidl/ **adj.**

col·lo·qui·al /kə'lōkwēəl/ ▶ **adj.** (of language) used in ordinary conversation.

SYNONYMS **informal**, conversational, everyday, familiar, popular, casual, idiomatic, slangy, vernacular. ANTONYMS formal.

■ **col·lo·qui·al·ism n. col·lo·qui·al·ly adv.**

col·lo·qui·um /kə'lōkwēəm/ ▶ **n.** (plural **colloquiums** or **colloquia** /-kwēə/) an academic conference or seminar.

col·lo·quy /'käləkwē/ ▶ **n.** (plural **colloquies**) formal a conference or conversation.

col·lude /kə'lo͞od/ ▶ **v.** (**colludes**, **colluding**, **colluded**) make a secret plan with someone to do something illegal or dishonest. ■ **col·lu·sion n.**

col·o·bus /'käləbəs/ ▶ **n.** (plural **colobus**) a slender African monkey with silky fur.

co·logne /kə'lōn/ ▶ **n.** a type of light perfume.

Co·lom·bi·an /kə'ləmbēən/ ▶ **n.** a person from Colombia. ▶ **adj.** relating to Colombia.

co·lon¹ /'kōlən/ ▶ **n.** a punctuation mark (:) used before a list of items, a quotation, or an expansion or explanation.

co·lon² ▶ **n.** the main part of the large intestine, which leads to the rectum. ■ **co·lon·ic** /kō'länik, kə-/ **adj.**

colo·nel /'kərnl/ ▶ **n.** a rank of officer in the army and the air force, above a lieutenant colonel and below a brigadier general.

co·lo·ni·al /kə'lōnyəl, -nēəl/ ▶ **adj. 1** having to do with a colony or with colonialism. **2** relating to the period of the British colonies in America before independence. ▶ **n.** a person who lives in a colony.

co·lo·ni·al·ism /kə'lōnēə,lizəm, kə'lōnyə,lizəm/ ▶ **n.** the practice of gaining control over other countries and occupying them with settlers. ■ **co·lo·ni·al·ist n. & adj.**

col·o·nist /'kälənist/ ▶ **n.** an inhabitant of a colony.

col·o·nize /'kälə,nīz/ ▶ **v.** (**colonizes**, **colonizing**, **colonized**) **1** make a colony in. **2** take over a place for your own use.

SYNONYMS **settle (in)**, people, populate, occupy, take over, invade.

■ **col·o·ni·za·tion** /,kälənə'zāsHən/ **n.**

col·on·nade /,kälə'nād/ ▶ **n.** a row of evenly spaced columns supporting a roof.

col·o·ny /'kälənē/ ▶ **n.** (plural **colonies**) **1** a country or area under the control of another country and occupied by settlers from that country. **2** a group of people of one nationality or race living in a foreign place. **3** a place where a group of people with a common interest live together: *an artists' colony*. **4** a community of animals or plants living close together.

SYNONYMS **territory**, dependency, protectorate, satellite, settlement, outpost, province.

col·or /'kələr/ ▶ **n. 1** an object's property of producing different sensations on the eye as a result of the way it reflects or gives out light. **2** one of the parts into which light can be separated. **3** the use of all colors in photography or television. **4** the natural coloring of the skin as an indication of someone's race. **5** redness of the complexion. **6** interest and excitement: *a town full of color and character.* ▶ **v. 1** change the color of something. **2** blush. **3** influence something: *the experiences had colored her whole existence.*

> SYNONYMS ▶ **n. 1 hue**, shade, tint, tone, coloration. **2 paint**, pigment, colorant, dye, stain. ▶ **v. 1 tint**, dye, stain, tinge. **2 influence**, affect, taint, warp, skew, distort.

□ **color-blind** not able to see certain colors. **color scheme** an arrangement or combination of colors.

Col·o·rad·o po·ta·to bee·tle /ˌkäləˈrädō, -ˈradō/ ▶ **n.** a beetle whose larvae destroy potato plants.

col·or·a·tion /ˌkələˈrāsʜən/ ▶ **n.** the colors and markings of a plant or animal.

col·o·ra·tu·ra /ˌkələrəˈt(y)o͝orə, ˌkäl-/ ▶ **n. 1** elaborate ornamentation of a vocal melody. **2** a soprano skilled in such singing.

col·ored /ˈkələrd/ ▶ **adj. 1** having a color or colors. **2** (also **Colored**) offensive wholly or partly of nonwhite descent. ▶ **n.** (also **Colored**) offensive a person who is wholly or partly of nonwhite descent.

col·or·fast /ˈkələrˌfast/ ▶ **adj.** dyed in colors that will not fade or be washed out.

col·or·ful /ˈkələrfəl/ ▶ **adj. 1** having many or varied colors. **2** lively and exciting; vivid.

> SYNONYMS **1 bright**, vivid, vibrant, brilliant, radiant, gaudy, garish, multicolored, psychedelic; informal jazzy. **2** *a colorful account* **vivid**, graphic, lively, animated, dramatic, fascinating, interesting, stimulating, scintillating, evocative. ANTONYMS drab, dull.

■ **col·or·ful·ly adv.**

col·or·ing /ˈkələriɴɢ/ ▶ **n. 1** the process or art of applying color. **2** visual appearance in terms of color. **3** a substance used to color something.

col·or·ist /ˈkələrist/ ▶ **n.** an artist or designer who uses color in a special or skillful way.

col·or·less /ˈkələrləs/ ▶ **adj. 1** without color. **2** without character or interest; dull.

co·los·sal /kəˈläsəl/ ▶ **adj.** very large.

> SYNONYMS **huge**, massive, enormous, gigantic, giant, mammoth, vast, immense, monumental, mountainous; informal monster, whopping, humongous, ginormous. ANTONYMS tiny.

■ **co·los·sal·ly adv.**

co·los·sus /kəˈläsəs/ ▶ **n.** (plural **colossi** /-sī/ or **colossuses**) a person or thing that is very important or large in size.

co·los·to·my /kəˈlästəmē/ ▶ **n.** (plural **colostomies**) a surgical operation in which the colon is shortened and the cut end is moved to a new opening made in the wall of the abdomen.

colt /kōlt/ ▶ **n.** a young male horse.

colt·ish /ˈkōltisʜ/ ▶ **adj.** energetic but awkward in movement or behavior.

colts·foot /ˈkōltsˌfo͝ot/ ▶ **n.** a plant with yellow flowers and heart-shaped leaves.

co·lum·bine /ˈkäləmˌbīn/ ▶ **n.** a plant with purplish-blue flowers.

col·umn /ˈkäləm/ ▶ **n. 1** an upright pillar supporting a structure or standing alone as a monument. **2** a line of people or vehicles moving in the same direction. **3** a vertical division of a page or piece of writing. **4** a regular section of a newspaper or magazine on a particular subject or by a particular person.

> SYNONYMS **1 pillar**, post, support, upright, pier, pile. **2 line**, file, queue, procession, convoy. **3 article**, piece, feature.

col·um·nist /ˈkäləmnist/ ▶ **n.** a journalist who writes a column in a newspaper or magazine.

co·ma /ˈkōmə/ ▶ **n.** a state of long-lasting deep unconsciousness.

Co·man·che /kəˈmancʜē/ ▶ **n.** (plural **Comanche** or **Comanches**) a member of an American Indian people of the southwestern United States.

com·a·tose /ˈkōməˌtōs, ˈkämə-/ ▶ **adj.** in a coma.

comb /kōm/ ▶ **n. 1** an object with a row of narrow teeth, used for smoothing and neatening the hair. **2** a device for separating and smoothing the fibers of raw wool or cotton. **3** the red fleshy crest on the head of a chicken. ▶ **v. 1** neaten the hair with a comb. **2** search systematically through something. **3** prepare wool or cotton for manufacture with a comb.

> SYNONYMS ▶ **v. 1 groom**, brush, untangle, smooth, straighten, neaten, tidy, arrange. **2 search**, scour, explore, sweep.

com·bat /ˈkämˌbat/ ▶ **n.** fighting, especially between armed forces. ▶ **v.** (**combats**, **combating**, **combated** or **combats**, **combatting**, **combatted**) take action to prevent something undesirable.

> SYNONYMS ▶ **n. battle**, fighting, action, hostilities, conflict, war, warfare. ▶ **v. fight**, battle, tackle, attack, counter, resist.

com·bat·ant /kəmˈbatnt, ˈkämbətənt/ ▶ **n.** a person or group that is fighting a battle or war. ▶ **adj.** engaged in fighting.

com·bat·ive /kəmˈbativ/ ▶ **adj.** ready or eager to fight or argue.

> SYNONYMS **aggressive**, pugnacious, antagonistic, quarrelsome, argumentative, hostile, truculent, belligerent; informal spoiling for a fight. ANTONYMS conciliatory.

com·bi·na·tion /ˌkämbəˈnāsʜən/ ▶ **n. 1** something that is made up of distinct parts. **2** the action of combining different things.

> SYNONYMS **mixture**, mix, blend, fusion, amalgamation, amalgam, merger, marriage, synthesis.

□ **combination lock** a lock that is opened using a sequence of letters or numbers.

com·bine ▶ **v.** /kəmˈbīn/ (**combines**, **combining**, **combined**) **1** join or mix together: *combine work and pleasure.* **2** join together to do something: *combine to fight evil.* ▶ **n.** /ˈkämˌbīn/ a group acting together for a commercial purpose.

> SYNONYMS ▶ **v. 1 mix**, blend, fuse, amalgamate, integrate, merge, marry. **2 unite**, collaborate, join forces, get together, team up.

□ **combine harvester** a farming machine that cuts a crop and separates out the grain in one process.

com·bo /ˈkämbō/ ▶ **n.** (plural **combos**) informal **1** a small jazz, rock, or pop band. **2** a combination.

com·bust /kəmˈbəst/ ▶ **v.** catch fire or burn.

com·bus·ti·ble /kəmˈbəstəbəl/ ▶ **adj.** able to catch fire and burn easily.

com·bus·tion /kəmˈbəsCHən/ ▶ **n. 1** the process of burning. **2** rapid chemical combination with oxygen, producing heat and light.

come /kəm/ ▶ **v.** (**comes**, **coming**, **came** /kām/; past participle **come**) **1** move toward or into a place near to the speaker: *Jess came into the kitchen.* **2** arrive. **3** happen; take place. **4** have or achieve a certain position: *she came in second.* **5** be sold or available in a particular form: *they come in three sizes.* **6** pass into a particular condition or state: *his shirt came undone.*

SYNONYMS **1** *come and listen* **approach**, advance, draw close/closer, draw near/nearer. **2** *they came last night* **arrive**, get here/there, make it, appear, turn up, materialize; informal show (up), roll in/up. **3** *they came to a stream* **reach**, arrive at, get to, come across, run across, happen on, chance on, come upon, stumble on, end up at; informal wind up at. **4** *she comes from Belgium* **be from**, be a native of, hail from, live in, reside in. **5 happen**, occur, take place, come about, fall, crop up. ANTONYMS go, leave.

□ **come about** happen. **come across 1** give a particular impression. **2** meet or find by chance. **come back** reply or respond vigorously. **come by** manage to get. **come down to** be dependent on (a factor). **come from** originate in. **come-hither** informal flirtatious. **come in** prove to be: *it came in handy.* **come into** inherit. **come of** result from. **come off** succeed. **come off it** informal said when expressing strong disbelief. **come on 1** (of a state or condition) begin. **2** (also **come upon**) meet or find by chance. **come out 1** (of a fact) become known. **2** say publicly that you are for or against something. **come out with** say in a sudden or incautious way. **come around 1** recover consciousness. **2** be converted to another person's opinion. **come to 1** recover consciousness. **2** (of an expense) amount to. **come up** happen. **come what may** no matter what happens. **have it coming (to you)** informal be due to face the unpleasant consequences of your behavior.

come·back /ˈkəmˌbak/ ▶ **n. 1** a return to fame or popularity. **2** informal a quick reply to a remark.

SYNONYMS **return**, recovery, resurgence, rally, upturn.

co·me·di·an /kəˈmēdēən/ (feminine **comedienne** /kəˌmēdēˈen/) ▶ **n.** an entertainer whose act is intended to make people laugh.

SYNONYMS **1 comic**, comedienne, funny man/woman, humorist, stand-up. **2 joker**, wit, wag, comic, clown; informal laugh, hoot.

come·down /ˈkəmˌdoun/ ▶ **n.** informal **1** a loss of status or importance. **2** a feeling of disappointment or depression.

com·e·dy /ˈkämədē/ ▶ **n.** (plural **comedies**) **1** a movie, play, or other entertainment intended to make people laugh. **2** a lighthearted play in which the characters find happiness after experiencing difficult situations.

SYNONYMS **humor**, fun, hilarity, funny side, laughs, jokes. ANTONYMS tragedy.

■ **co·me·dic** /kəˈmēdik/ **adj.**

come·ly /ˈkəmlē/ ▶ **adj.** (**comelier**, **comeliest**) old use pleasant to look at.

co·mes·ti·bles /kəˈmestəbəlz/ ▶ **pl.n.** formal items of food.

com·et /ˈkämit/ ▶ **n.** a mass of ice and dust with a long tail, moving around the solar system.

come·up·pance /kəˈməpəns/ ▶ **n.** (**get your comeuppance**) informal get the punishment or fate that you deserve.

com·fort /ˈkəmfərt/ ▶ **n. 1** a pleasant state of ease and relaxation. **2** (**comforts**) things that contribute to comfort. **3** consolation for unhappiness or anxiety: *a few words of comfort.* ▶ **v.** make someone less unhappy.

SYNONYMS ▶ **n. 1 ease**, repose, luxury, prosperity. **2 consolation**, condolence, sympathy, commiseration, support, reassurance, cheer. ANTONYMS discomfort. ▶ **v. console**, support, reassure, soothe, calm, cheer, hearten. ANTONYMS distress, depress.

■ **com·fort·er n.**

com·fort·a·ble /ˈkəmfərtəbəl, ˈkəmftərbəl/ ▶ **adj. 1** giving or enjoying physical comfort. **2** free from financial worry. **3** (of a victory) easily achieved.

SYNONYMS **1 affluent**, prosperous, well-to-do, pleasant, luxurious, opulent. **2 cozy**, snug, warm, pleasant, agreeable, homey, unpretentious; informal comfy. **3 loose**, loose-fitting, roomy, casual; informal comfy.

■ **com·fort·a·bly adv.**

com·frey /ˈkəmfrē/ ▶ **n.** (plural **comfreys**) a plant with clusters of purplish or white flowers.

com·fy /ˈkəmfē/ ▶ **adj.** (**comfier**, **comfiest**) informal comfortable.

com·ic /ˈkämik/ ▶ **adj. 1** making people laugh; amusing. **2** having to do with comedy: *a comic actor.* ▶ **n. 1** a comedian. **2** a magazine that contains comic strips, usually either amusing or adventurous.

SYNONYMS ▶ **adj. humorous**, funny, amusing, hilarious, comical, zany, witty, droll. ANTONYMS serious. ▶ **n. comedian**, comedienne, funny man/woman, humorist, wit, joker.

□ **comic strip** a sequence of drawings that tell an amusing story.

com·i·cal /ˈkämikəl/ ▶ **adj.** causing laughter, especially through being ridiculous.

SYNONYMS **1 funny**, humorous, droll, witty, comic, amusing, entertaining; informal wacky. **2 absurd**, silly, ridiculous, laughable, ludicrous, preposterous, foolish; informal crazy. ANTONYMS serious.

■ **com·i·cal·ly adv.**

coming /ˈkəmiNG/ ▶ **adj. 1** due to happen or just beginning: *the coming election.* **2** likely to be successful in the future: *a coming man.* ▶ **n.** an arrival or an approach: *the coming of spring.*

SYNONYMS ▶ **adj. forthcoming**, imminent, impending, approaching. ▶ **n. approach**, advance, advent, arrival, appearance, emergence.

com·i·ty /ˈkämitē/ ▶ **n.** (plural **comities**) **1** an association of nations for their mutual benefit. **2** (also **comity of nations**) the mutual recognition by nations of the laws of others.

com·ma /ˈkämə/ ▶ **n.** a punctuation mark (,) showing a pause between parts of a sentence or separating items in a list.

com·mand /kəˈmand/ ▶ **v. 1** give an order. **2** be in charge of a military unit. ▶ **n. 1** an order. **2** authority: *the officer in command.* **3** a group of officers in control of a particular group or operation. **4** the ability to use or control something: *his command of English.* **5** an instruction that makes a computer carry out one of its basic functions.

SYNONYMS ▶ **v. 1 order**, tell, direct, instruct, call on, require, charge, enjoin, ordain; old use bid. **2 be in charge of**, be in command of, head, lead, control, direct, manage, supervise, oversee; informal head up. ▶ **n. 1 order**, instruction, direction, directive, injunction, decree, edict, dictate, mandate, commandment, fiat. **2** *he had 160 men under his command* **authority**, control, charge, power, direction, dominion, guidance, leadership, rule, government, management, supervision, jurisdiction. **3 knowledge**, mastery, grasp, comprehension, understanding.

□ **command economy** an economy in which production, investment, prices, and incomes are determined centrally by a government. **command performance** a presentation of a play, concert, or movie at the request of a sovereign or head of state.

com·man·dant /'kämən,dant, -,dänt/ ▶ **n.** an officer in charge of a force or institution.

com·man·deer /,kämən'di(ə)r/ ▶ **v.** (**commandeers**, **commandeering**, **commandeered**) officially take possession of something for military purposes.

com·mand·er /kə'mandər/ ▶ **n. 1** a person in command. **2** the rank of naval officer below captain.

SYNONYMS **leader**, head, chief, overseer, director, controller; informal boss, skipper, head honcho.

□ **commander-in-chief** (plural **commanders-in-chief**) **1** an officer in charge of all of the armed forces of a country. **2** the president of the United States.

com·mand·ing /kə'mandiNG/ ▶ **adj. 1** having or showing authority: *her style is commanding.* **2** having greater strength: *a commanding lead in the polls.*

SYNONYMS **dominant**, controlling, superior, powerful, advantageous, favorable.

com·mand·ment /kə'mandmənt/ ▶ **n.** a divine rule, especially one of the Ten Commandments.

com·man·do /kə'mandō/ ▶ **n.** (plural **commandos**) a soldier trained for carrying out raids.

com·mem·o·rate /kə'memə,rāt/ ▶ **v.** (**commemorates**, **commemorating**, **commemorated**) honor the memory of.

SYNONYMS **celebrate**, remember, recognize, acknowledge, observe, mark, pay tribute to, pay homage to, honor, salute.

■ **com·mem·o·ra·tion** /kə,memə'rāSHən/ **n.** **com·mem·o·ra·tive** /kə'mem(ə)rətiv, kə'memə,rātiv/ **adj.**

SPELLING

The first **m** is double, but not the second: commemorate.

com·mence /kə'mens/ ▶ **v.** (**commences**, **commencing**, **commenced**) begin.

SYNONYMS **begin**, inaugurate, start, initiate, launch into, open, get the ball rolling, get going, get under way, get off the ground, set about, embark on; informal kick off. ANTONYMS conclude.

com·mence·ment /kə'mensmənt/ ▶ **n. 1** the beginning of something. **2** a ceremony at which degrees or diplomas are conferred on graduating students.

com·mend /kə'mend/ ▶ **v. 1** praise formally or officially. **2** recommend someone or something.

SYNONYMS **1 praise**, compliment, congratulate, applaud, salute, honor, sing the praises of, pay tribute to. **2 recommend**, endorse, vouch for, speak for, support, back. ANTONYMS criticize.

■ **com·men·da·tion** /,kämən'dāSHən, -,en-/ **n.**

com·mend·a·ble /kə'mendəbəl/ ▶ **adj.** deserving praise.

SYNONYMS **admirable**, praiseworthy, creditable, laudable, meritorious, exemplary, honorable, respectable. ANTONYMS reprehensible.

■ **com·mend·a·bly adv.**

com·men·sal /kə'mensəl/ ▶ **adj.** Biology (of two organisms) having an association in which one benefits and the other derives neither benefit nor harm.

com·men·su·ra·ble /kə'mensərəbəl, -'mensHə-/ ▶ **adj.** formal able to be measured by the same standard: *the finite is not commensurable with the infinite.*

com·men·su·rate /kə'mensərət, -'mensHə-/ ▶ **adj.** (often **commensurate with**) matching something else in size, value, etc.: *salary will be commensurate with experience.*

com·ment /'käm,ent/ ▶ **n. 1** a remark expressing an opinion or reaction. **2** discussion of an issue or event. ▶ **v.** express an opinion or reaction.

SYNONYMS ▶ **n. 1 remark**, observation, statement, pronouncement, judgment, reflection, opinion, view. **2 discussion**, debate, interest. **3 note**, annotation, commentary, footnote, gloss, explanation. ▶ **v. remark**, observe, say, state, note, point out, mention, interject; formal opine.

com·men·tar·y /'kämən,terē/ ▶ **n.** (plural **commentaries**) **1** a broadcast account of a sports contest or other event as it happens. **2** the expression of opinions about an event or situation. **3** a set of explanatory notes on a written work.

SYNONYMS **1 narration**, description, report, review, voice-over. **2 explanation**, elucidation, interpretation, analysis, assessment, review, criticism, notes, comments.

com·men·tate /'kämən,tāt/ ▶ **v.** (**commentates**, **commentating**, **commentated**) give a commentary on an event.

com·men·ta·tor /'kämən,tātər/ ▶ **n. 1** a person who comments on events, especially in the media. **2** a person who provides a commentary on a live event.

SYNONYMS **1 reporter**, narrator, journalist, newscaster. **2 analyst**, pundit, critic, columnist, leader-writer, monitor, observer.

com·merce /'kämərs/ ▶ **n.** the activity of buying and selling; trade.

SYNONYMS **trade**, trading, business, dealing, buying and selling, traffic, trafficking.

com·mer·cial /kə'mərSHəl/ ▶ **adj. 1** concerned with commerce. **2** making or intended to make a profit. ▶ **n.** a television or radio advertisement.

SYNONYMS ▶ **adj. 1 trade**, trading, business, mercantile, sales. **2 profit-making**, materialistic, mercenary.

■ **com·mer·cial·ly adv.**

com·mer·cial·ism /kə'mərsHə,lizəm/ ▶ n. emphasis on making as much profit as possible.

com·mer·cial·ize /kə'mərsHə,līz/ ▶ v. (**commercializes**, **commercializing**, **commercialized**) manage something in a way designed to make a profit. ■ **com·mer·cial·i·za·tion** /kə,mərsHələ'zāsHən/ n.

com·mie /'kämē/ ▶ n. (plural **commies**) informal, disapproving a communist.

com·min·gle /kə'miNGgəl, kä-/ ▶ v. (**commingles**, **commingling**, **commingled**) literary mix; blend.

com·mis·er·ate /kə'mizə,rāt/ ▶ v. (**commiserates**, **commiserating**, **commiserated**) express sympathy or pity; sympathize. ■ **com·mis·er·a·tion** /kə,mizə'rāsHən/ n.

com·mis·sar /'kämə,sär, ,kämə'sär/ ▶ n. an official of the Communist Party responsible for political education.

com·mis·sar·i·at /,kämə'se(ə)rēit/ ▶ n. a military department for the supply of food and equipment.

com·mis·sion /kə'misHən/ ▶ n. **1** an instruction, command, or duty. **2** a formal request for something to be produced. **3** a group of people given official authority to do something. **4** payment made to someone for selling goods or services. **5** the position of officer in the armed forces. ▶ v. **1** order something to be made or produced. **2** bring something into working order. **3** (**commissioned**) having the rank of a military officer.

> SYNONYMS ▶ n. **1 percentage**, share, premium, fee, bonus, royalty; informal cut, take, slice. **2 contract**, engagement, assignment, booking, job. **3 committee**, board, council, panel, body. ▶ v. **1 engage**, contract, book, employ, hire, recruit, take on, retain, appoint. **2 order**, place an order for, pay for.

□ **out of commission** not in working order.

com·mis·sion·er /kə'misH(ə)nər/ ▶ n. **1** a member of an official commission. **2** a representative of the highest authority in an area.

com·mit /kə'mit/ ▶ v. (**commits**, **committing**, **committed**) **1** do something wrong or bad. **2** set aside something for a particular use. **3** (**commit yourself**) say that you will definitely do something: *they were reluctant to commit themselves to any specific time*. **4** put something in a state or place: *the letter was committed to the flames*. **5** send someone to prison or a psychiatric hospital.

> SYNONYMS **1 entrust**, consign, assign, deliver, hand over. **2 consign**, send, confine. **3 carry out**, do, perpetrate, engage in, execute, accomplish, be responsible for; informal pull off.

com·mit·ment /kə'mitmənt/ ▶ n. **1** the time, work, and loyalty that someone devotes to a cause, activity, or job. **2** a promise. **3** an appointment or duty that limits your freedom of action: *business commitments*.

> SYNONYMS **1 responsibility**, obligation, duty, liability, engagement, tie. **2 dedication**, devotion, allegiance, loyalty. **3 promise**, vow, pledge, undertaking.

> **SPELLING**
> There is a single **t** in the middle: commitment.

com·mit·tal /kə'mitl/ ▶ n. the sending of someone to prison or a psychiatric hospital, or for trial.

com·mit·ted /kə'mitid/ ▶ adj. devoting a lot of time and hard work to a cause, activity, or job.

> SYNONYMS **devoted**, dedicated, staunch, loyal, faithful, devout, firm, steadfast, unwavering, passionate, ardent, sworn. ANTONYMS apathetic.

com·mit·tee /kə'mitē/ ▶ n. a group of people appointed for a particular function by a larger group.

> **SPELLING**
> Double **m**, double **t**: committee.

com·mode /kə'mōd/ ▶ n. a piece of furniture containing a concealed chamber pot.

com·mod·i·fy /kə'mädə,fī/ ▶ v. (**commodifies**, **commodifying**, **commodified**) turn into or treat as a mere commodity: *art has become commodified*. ■ **com·mod·i·fi·ca·tion** /kə,mädəfə'kāsHən/ n.

com·mo·di·ous /kə'mōdēəs/ ▶ adj. formal roomy and comfortable.

com·mod·i·ty /kə'mäditē/ ▶ n. (plural **commodities**) **1** a raw material or agricultural product that can be bought and sold. **2** something useful or valuable.

com·mo·dore /'kämə,dôr/ ▶ n. **1** the naval rank above captain. **2** the president of a yacht club.

com·mon /'kämən/ ▶ adj. (**commoner**, **commonest**) **1** happening, found, or done often; not rare. **2** without special qualities or position; ordinary. **3** of the most familiar type: *the common name*. **4** shared by two or more people or things. **5** belonging to or affecting the whole of a community: *common land*. **6** not well-mannered or tasteful, in a way supposedly typical of lower-class people. ▶ n. **1** a piece of open land for the public to use. **2** (**the Commons**) ⇒ **House of Commons**.

> SYNONYMS ▶ adj. **1** *a common occurrence* **frequent**, regular, everyday, normal, usual, ordinary, familiar, standard, commonplace, average, unexceptional, typical. **2** *a common belief* **widespread**, general, universal, popular, mainstream, prevalent, rife, established, conventional, accepted. **3 collective**, communal, shared, community, public, popular, general. **4 uncouth**, vulgar, coarse, rough, uncivilized, unsophisticated, unrefined, inferior, plebeian. ANTONYMS unusual, rare.

□ **common denominator 1** Math a number that can be divided exactly by all the numbers below the line in a set of fractions. **2** a feature shared by all members of a group. **Common Era** ⇒ **Christian Era**. **common fraction** a fraction expressed by a numerator and a denominator, not decimally. **common ground** views shared by each of two or more parties. **common law** law derived from custom and precedent rather than statutes. **the Common Market** the European Union. **common noun** a noun referring to a class of things (e.g., *plant*, *sea*) as opposed to a particular person or thing. **common room** a room in a school or college for students or staff to use outside teaching hours. **common sense** good sense and judgment in practical matters. **common time** a rhythm in which there are two or four beats in a bar. **in common** shared. ■ **com·mon·ly** adv.

com·mon·al·i·ty /'kämən,alitē/ ▶ n. (plural **commonalities**) the sharing of features.

com·mon·er /'kämənər/ ▶ n. an ordinary person as opposed to an aristocrat.

com·mon·place /ˈkämənˌplās/ ▶ **adj.** ordinary. ▶ **n.** a remark that is not new or interesting.

SYNONYMS ▶ **adj.** see **COMMON** (sense 1 of the adjective).

com·mon·sen·si·cal /ˌkämənˈsensikəl/ ▶ **adj.** having common sense.

com·mon·wealth /ˈkämənˌwelTH/ ▶ **n. 1** an independent country or community. **2** a self-governing unit voluntarily grouped with the United States, such as Puerto Rico. **3** a formal title of some of the states of the United States, especially Kentucky, Massachusetts, Pennsylvania, and Virginia. **4** (**the Commonwealth**) an association consisting of the United Kingdom together with countries that used to be part of the British Empire.

com·mo·tion /kəˈmōSHən/ ▶ **n.** a state of confused and noisy disturbance.

SYNONYMS **disturbance**, uproar, disorder, confusion, rumpus, fuss, furor, hue and cry, stir, storm, chaos, havoc, pandemonium.

com·mu·nal /kəˈmyo͞onl/ ▶ **adj.** shared or done by all members of a community.

SYNONYMS **1** *a communal kitchen* **shared**, joint, common, public, general. **2** *they farm on a communal basis* **collective**, cooperative, community. ANTONYMS private, individual.

■ **com·mu·nal·ly** adv.

com·mune¹ /ˈkämˌyo͞on/ ▶ **n.** a group of people living together and sharing possessions.

com·mune² /kəˈmyo͞on/ ▶ **v.** (**communes**, **communing**, **communed**) (**commune with**) **1** share your intimate thoughts or feelings with. **2** feel in close spiritual contact with: *he spent an hour communing with nature.*

com·mu·ni·ca·ble /kəˈmyo͞onikəbəl/ ▶ **adj.** (of a disease) able to be passed on to other people.

com·mu·ni·cant /kəˈmyo͞onikənt/ ▶ **n.** a person who receives Holy Communion.

com·mu·ni·cate /kəˈmyo͞onəˌkāt/ ▶ **v.** (**communicates**, **communicating**, **communicated**) **1** share or exchange information or ideas. **2** pass on or convey an emotion, disease, etc. **3** (**communicating**) (of two rooms) having a connecting door.

SYNONYMS **1 liaise**, be in touch, be in contact, have dealings, talk, speak, interface. **2 convey**, tell, relay, transmit, impart, pass on, report, recount, relate. **3 transmit**, spread, transfer, pass on.

com·mu·ni·ca·tion /kəˌmyo͞onəˈkāSHən/ ▶ **n. 1** the action of communicating. **2** a letter or message. **3** (**communications**) means of sending information or traveling.

SYNONYMS **1 contact**, dealings, relations, connection, correspondence, dialogue, conversation. **2 message**, statement, announcement, report, dispatch, bulletin, disclosure, communiqué, letter, correspondence.

com·mu·ni·ca·tive /kəˈmyo͞onəˌkātiv, -nikətiv/ ▶ **adj.** willing or eager to talk or pass on information.

SYNONYMS **forthcoming**, expansive, expressive, unreserved, vocal, outgoing, frank, open, candid, talkative, chatty.

com·mun·ion /kəˈmyo͞onyən/ ▶ **n. 1** the sharing of intimate thoughts and feelings. **2** (also **Holy Communion**) the service of Christian worship at which bread and wine are made holy and shared; the Eucharist.

com·mu·ni·qué /kəˌmyo͞onəˈkā, kəˈmyo͞onəˌkā/ ▶ **n.** an official announcement or statement.

com·mu·nism /ˈkämyəˌnizəm/ ▶ **n. 1** a political system in which all property is owned by the community. **2** a system of this kind based on Marxism.

com·mu·nist /ˈkämyəˌnist/ ▶ **n. & adj.** an adherent of communism; relating to communism.

SYNONYMS **collectivist**, Bolshevik, Marxist, Maoist, Soviet; informal, disapproving red, commie.

com·mu·ni·ty /kəˈmyo͞onitē/ ▶ **n.** (plural **communities**) **1** a group of people living together in one place or having the same religion, race, etc. **2** (**the community**) the people of an area or country considered as a group.

SYNONYMS **society**, population, populace, people, public, residents, inhabitants, citizens.

□ **community center** a place providing educational or recreational activities for a neighborhood. **community college** a nonresidential college offering courses to people living in the area. **community service 1** voluntary work intended to help people in a particular area. **2** socially useful work that an offender is sentenced to do instead of going to prison.

com·mu·tate /ˈkämyəˌtāt/ ▶ **v.** (**commutates**, **commutating**, **commutated**) regulate the direction of an alternating electric current, especially to make it a direct current.
■ **com·mu·ta·tion** /ˌkämyəˈtāSHən/ **n.**

com·mu·ta·tive /ˈkämyəˌtātiv, kəˈmyo͞otətiv/ ▶ **adj.** Math unchanged in result by altering the order of quantities, such that, for example $a \times b = b \times a$.

com·mu·ta·tor /ˈkämyəˌtātər/ ▶ **n.** an attachment that ensures that electric current flows as direct current.

com·mute /kəˈmyo͞ot/ ▶ **v.** (**commutes**, **commuting**, **commuted**) **1** regularly travel some distance between your home and place of work. **2** reduce a sentence given to an offender to a less severe one. ■ **com·mut·er** **n.**

com·pact¹ ▶ **adj.** /kəmˈpakt, käm-/ **1** closely and neatly packed together; dense. **2** having all the necessary parts fitted into a small space. ▶ **v.** /kəmˈpakt, käm-/ press something together into a small space. ▶ **n.** /ˈkämˌpakt/ **1** a small case containing face powder, a mirror, and a powder puff. **2** a medium-sized car.

SYNONYMS ▶ **adj. 1 dense**, tightly packed, compressed, thick, tight, firm, solid. **2 neat**, small, handy, portable. **3 concise**, succinct, condensed, brief, pithy, to the point, short and sweet; informal snappy. ANTONYMS loose, bulky, lengthy. ▶ **v. compress**, condense, pack down, tamp (down), flatten.

□ **compact disc** a small disc on which music or other digital information is stored.

com·pact² /ˈkämˌpakt/ ▶ **n.** a formal agreement between two or more parties.

SYNONYMS **treaty**, pact, accord, agreement, contract, bargain, deal, settlement.

com·pa·dre /kəmˈpädrā/ ▶ **n.** (plural **compadres**) informal a friend or companion.

com·pan·ion /kəm'panyən/ ▶ n. **1** a person that you spend time with or travel with. **2** each of a pair of things intended to match each other, or that can be used together.

SYNONYMS **comrade**, fellow, partner, associate, escort, compatriot, confederate, friend; informal pal, buddy, bud, chum, crony.

■ **com·pan·ion·ship** n.

com·pan·ion·a·ble /kəm'panyənəbəl/ ▶ adj. friendly and sociable. ■ **com·pan·ion·a·bly** adv.

com·pan·ion·way /kəm'panyən,wā/ ▶ n. a set of steps leading from a ship's deck down to a cabin or lower deck.

com·pa·ny /'kəmpənē/ ▶ n. (plural **companies**) **1** a commercial business. **2** the fact of being with other people: *she is excellent company*. **3** a guest or guests: *we're expecting company*. **4** a number of people gathered together. **5** a unit of soldiers. **6** a group of actors, singers, or dancers who perform together.

SYNONYMS **1 firm**, business, corporation, establishment, agency, office, house, institution, concern, enterprise, consortium, syndicate; informal outfit. **2 companionship**, fellowship, society, presence. **3 unit**, section, detachment, corps, squad, platoon.

□ **keep someone company** spend time with someone to prevent them feeling lonely or bored.

com·pa·ra·ble /'kämp(ə)rəbəl/ ▶ adj. similar to someone or something else and able to be compared.

SYNONYMS **1 similar**, close, near, approximate, equivalent, proportionate. **2** *nobody is comparable with him* **equal to**, as good as, in the same league as, on a level with, a match for. ANTONYMS incomparable.

■ **com·pa·ra·bly** adv.

com·par·a·tive /kəm'parətiv/ ▶ adj. **1** measured or judged by comparing one thing with another. **2** involving comparison between two or more subjects. **3** (of an adjective or adverb) expressing a higher degree of a quality, but not the highest possible (e.g., *braver*). ■ **com·par·a·tive·ly** adv.

SPELLING

Compar**ative**, not -**itive**.

com·par·a·tor /kəm'parətər/ ▶ n. **1** a device for comparing something measurable with a reference or standard. **2** something used as a standard for comparison.

com·pare /kəm'pe(ə)r/ ▶ v. (**compares**, **comparing**, **compared**) **1** (often **compare something to** or **with**) estimate or measure the ways in which one person or thing is similar to or unlike another. **2** (**compare something to**) point out the ways in which one person or thing is similar to another. **3** (usu. **compare with**) be similar to another thing or person.

SYNONYMS **1 contrast**, balance, set against, weigh up. **2 liken**, equate, class with. **3 be as good as**, be comparable to, bear comparison with, be the equal of, match up to, be on a par with, be in the same league as, come close to, rival.

com·par·i·son /kəm'parəsən/ ▶ n. **1** the action of comparing. **2** the quality of being similar.

SYNONYMS **resemblance**, likeness, similarity, correspondence.

com·part·ment /kəm'pärtmənt/ ▶ n. a separate section of a structure or container.

SYNONYMS **bay**, locker, recess, alcove, cell, cubicle, pod, pigeonhole, cubbyhole.

com·part·men·tal·ize /kəm,pärt'mentl,īz/ ▶ v. (**compartmentalizes**, **compartmentalizing**, **compartmentalized**) divide into categories or sections.

com·pass /'kəmpəs/ ▶ n. **1** an instrument containing a pointer that shows the direction of magnetic north. **2** (also **compasses**) an instrument for drawing circles, consisting of two arms linked by a movable joint. **3** range or scope.

SYNONYMS **scope**, range, extent, reach, span, breadth, ambit, limits, parameters, bounds.

com·pas·sion /kəm'pasʜən/ ▶ n. sympathetic pity and concern for the sufferings of other people.

SYNONYMS **sympathy**, empathy, understanding, fellow feeling, pity, care, concern, sensitivity, kindness. ANTONYMS indifference, cruelty.

com·pas·sion·ate /kəm'pasʜənət/ ▶ adj. feeling or showing compassion.

SYNONYMS **sympathetic**, understanding, pitying, caring, sensitive, warm, loving, kind. ANTONYMS unsympathetic, uncaring.

■ **com·pas·sion·ate·ly** adv.

com·pat·i·ble /kəm'patəbəl/ ▶ adj. **1** able to exist or be used together. **2** (of two people) able to have a good relationship; well-suited. **3** (usu. **compatible with**) consistent or in keeping.

SYNONYMS **well-matched**, (well-)suited, like-minded, in tune, in harmony, in keeping, consistent, consonant; informal on the same wavelength.

■ **com·pat·i·bil·i·ty** /kəm,patə'bilitē/ n.

SPELLING

Compat**ible**, not -**able**.

com·pa·tri·ot /kəm'pātrēət/ ▶ n. a person from the same country; a fellow citizen.

com·pel /kəm'pel/ ▶ v. (**compels**, **compelling**, **compelled**) **1** force someone to do something. **2** make something happen.

SYNONYMS **force**, pressure, coerce, dragoon, press, push, oblige, require, make; informal lean on, railroad, put the screws on.

com·pel·ling /kəm'pelɪɴɢ/ ▶ adj. powerfully gaining people's attention or admiration.

SYNONYMS **1 enthralling**, captivating, gripping, riveting, spellbinding, mesmerizing, absorbing. **2 convincing**, persuasive, cogent, irresistible, powerful, strong. ANTONYMS boring, weak.

■ **com·pel·ling·ly** adv.

com·pen·di·ous /kəm'pendēəs/ ▶ adj. formal comprehensive but concise.

com·pen·di·um /kəm'pendēəm/ ▶ n. (plural **compendiums** or **compendia** /-dēə/) **1** a collection of information about a subject. **2** a collection of similar items.

com·pen·sate /ˈkämpənˌsāt/ ▶ v. (**compensates**, **compensating**, **compensated**) **1** give someone something to reduce or balance the bad effect of loss, suffering, or injury. **2** (**compensate for**) reduce or balance something bad by having an opposite force or effect.

SYNONYMS **1 recompense**, repay, pay back, reimburse, remunerate, indemnify. **2 balance (out)**, counterbalance, counteract, offset, make up for, cancel out.

■ **com·pen·sa·to·ry** /kəmˈpensəˌtôrē/ adj.

com·pen·sa·tion /ˌkämpənˈsāsʜən/ ▶ n. **1** something given to compensate for loss, suffering, or injury. **2** something that compensates for something bad.

SYNONYMS **recompense**, repayment, reimbursement, remuneration, redress, amends, damages; informal comp.

com·pete /kəmˈpēt/ ▶ v. (**competes**, **competing**, **competed**) try to gain or win something by defeating other people.

SYNONYMS **1 take part**, participate, be a contestant, play, enter, go in for. **2** *they had to compete with other firms* **contend**, vie, battle, jockey, go head to head, pit yourself against, challenge, take on.

com·pe·tence /ˈkämpətəns/ ▶ n. **1** the ability to do something well. **2** the authority of a court or other body to deal with a particular matter.

SYNONYMS **1** *my technical competence* **ability**, capability, proficiency, accomplishment, expertise, skill, prowess; informal know-how. **2** *the competence of the system* **adequacy**, suitability, fitness.

com·pe·tent /ˈkämpətənt/ ▶ adj. **1** having the necessary skill or knowledge to do something successfully. **2** satisfactory, though not outstanding: *she spoke quite competent French.*

SYNONYMS **1 able**, capable, proficient, adept, accomplished, skillful, skilled, expert. **2 fit**, suitable, suited, appropriate, qualified, empowered, authorized.

■ **com·pe·tent·ly** adv.

com·pe·ti·tion /ˌkämpəˈtisʜən/ ▶ n. **1** the activity of competing against other people. **2** an event or contest in which people compete. **3** the person or people that you are competing against.

SYNONYMS **1 rivalry**, competitiveness, conflict; informal keeping up with the Joneses. **2 contest**, tournament, championship, match, game, heat. **3 opposition**, rivals, other side, field, enemy.

com·pet·i·tive /kəmˈpetətiv/ ▶ adj. **1** involving competition. **2** strongly wanting to be more successful than other people. **3** as good as or better than others of a similar nature.

SYNONYMS **1** *a competitive player* **ambitious**, zealous, keen, combative, aggressive. **2** *a highly competitive industry* **ruthless**, aggressive, fierce, cutthroat; informal dog-eat-dog. **3** *competitive prices* **reasonable**, moderate, keen, low, cheap, budget, bargain, rock-bottom, bargain-basement.

■ **com·pet·i·tive·ly** adv.

com·pet·i·tor /kəmˈpetətər/ ▶ n. **1** a person who takes part in a sports contest. **2** an organization that competes with others in business.

SYNONYMS **1 contestant**, contender, challenger, participant, entrant, player. **2 rival**, challenger, opponent, competition, opposition.

com·pi·la·tion /ˌkämpəˈlāsʜən/ ▶ n. **1** a book, recording, etc., compiled from different sources. **2** the process of compiling something.

com·pile /kəmˈpīl/ ▶ v. (**compiles**, **compiling**, **compiled**) produce a book, recording, etc., by bringing together material from different sources.

SYNONYMS **assemble**, put together, make up, collate, compose, organize, arrange, gather, collect.

■ **com·pil·er** n.

com·pla·cent /kəmˈplāsənt/ ▶ adj. smugly satisfied with yourself.

SYNONYMS **smug**, self-satisfied, self-congratulatory, resting on your laurels, pleased with yourself.

■ **com·pla·cen·cy** n. **com·pla·cent·ly** adv.

com·plain /kəmˈplān/ ▶ v. **1** express dissatisfaction or annoyance. **2** (**complain of**) state that you are suffering from a particular symptom.

SYNONYMS **protest**, grumble, whine, bleat, carp, cavil, grouse, make a fuss, object, find fault; informal gripe, moan, bitch.

com·plain·ant /kəmˈplānənt/ ▶ n. Law a plaintiff.

com·plaint /kəmˈplānt/ ▶ n. **1** an act of complaining. **2** a reason to be dissatisfied. **3** a minor illness or medical condition.

SYNONYMS **1 protest**, objection, grievance, grouse, grumble, criticism; informal gripe. **2 disorder**, disease, illness, sickness, ailment, infection, condition, problem, upset, trouble.

com·plai·sant /kəmˈplāsənt/ ▶ adj. willing to please other people or to accept their behavior without protest.

com·ple·ment /ˈkämpləmənt/ ▶ n. **1** a thing that contributes extra features to something else so as to improve it. **2** the number or quantity that makes something complete. **3** Grammar a word or words used with a verb to complete the meaning (e.g., *happy* in *we are happy*). ▶ v. add to something in a way that improves it.

SYNONYMS ▶ n. **1 accompaniment**, companion, addition, supplement, accessory, finishing touch. **2 amount**, contingent, capacity, allowance, quota. ▶ v. **accompany**, go with, round off, set off, suit, harmonize with, enhance, complete.

USAGE

Don't confuse **complement** and **compliment**. **Complement** means 'add to something in a way that improves it,' as in *pictures complement the written text*, while **compliment** means 'politely congratulate or praise,' as in *I complimented her on her work*.

com·ple·men·ta·ry /ˌkämpləˈment(ə)rē/ ▶ adj. combining so as to form a complete whole or to improve each other's qualities.

SYNONYMS **harmonious**, compatible, corresponding, matching, reciprocal.

□ **complementary angle** either of two angles whose sum is 90°. **complementary medicine** medical therapy that is not part of scientific medicine, e.g., acupuncture.

USAGE

Don't confuse **complementary** and **complimentary**. **Complementary** means 'added to something in a way that improves it,' as in *complementary flavors*, while **complimentary** means either 'politely congratulating or praising someone or something,' as in *complimentary remarks*, or 'provided free,' as in *complimentary drinks*.

com·plete /kəm'plēt/ ▶ **adj. 1** having all the necessary parts. **2** having run its course; finished. **3** to the greatest extent or degree; total. **4** skilled at every aspect of an activity: *the complete football player*. ▶ **v.** (**completes, completing, completed**) **1** finish making or doing something. **2** make something complete. **3** write the required information on a form.

SYNONYMS ▶ **adj. 1 entire**, whole, full, total, uncut, unabridged, unexpurgated. **2 finished**, ended, concluded, completed; informal wrapped up, sewn up. **3 absolute**, utter, out-and-out, total, downright, prize, perfect, unqualified, unmitigated, sheer, full-bore. ANTONYMS partial, unfinished. ▶ **v. 1 finish**, end, conclude, finalize, wind up, clinch; informal wrap up. **2 finish off**, round off, top off, crown, cap, add the finishing touch.

com·plete·ly /kəm'plētlē/ ▶ **adv.** totally; utterly: *the fire completely destroyed the building*.

SYNONYMS **totally**, entirely, wholly, thoroughly, fully, utterly, absolutely, perfectly, downright.

com·ple·tion /kəm'plēsнən/ ▶ **n. 1** the action of completing something or the state of being completed. **2** Football a successful forward pass.

com·ple·tist /kəm'plētist/ ▶ **n.** a fan who wants to own everything produced by a particular person or group.

com·plex ▶ **adj.** /käm'pleks, kəm'pleks, 'käm,pleks/ **1** consisting of many different and connected parts. **2** not easy to understand; complicated. ▶ **n.** /'käm,pleks/ **1** a group of similar buildings or facilities on the same site. **2** a network of linked things. **3** a group of subconscious ideas or feelings that influence a person's mental state or behavior.

SYNONYMS ▶ **adj. 1 compound**, composite, multiplex. **2 complicated**, involved, intricate, convoluted, elaborate, difficult. ANTONYMS simple. ▶ **n. 1 network**, system, nexus, web. **2 obsession**, fixation, preoccupation, neurosis; informal hang-up, thing.

□ **complex number** a number containing both a real and an imaginary part. ■ **com·plex·i·ty** /kəm'pleksitē/ **n.** (plural **complexities**).

com·plex·ion /kəm'pleksнən/ ▶ **n. 1** the natural condition of the skin of a person's face. **2** the general character of something.

SYNONYMS **1 skin**, skin color/tone, coloring. **2 kind**, nature, character, color, persuasion, outlook.

com·pli·ance /kəm'plīəns/ ▶ **n.** the action of complying.

com·pli·ant /kəm'plīənt/ ▶ **adj. 1** meeting rules or standards. **2** too ready to do what other people want.

com·pli·cate /'kämplə,kāt/ ▶ **v.** (**complicates, complicating, complicated**) make something less easy to understand or deal with.

SYNONYMS **make (more) difficult**, make complicated, mix up, confuse, muddle, obscure. ANTONYMS simplify.

com·pli·cat·ed /'kämplə,kātid/ ▶ **adj. 1** consisting of many connected elements; intricate. **2** involving many different and confusing aspects.

SYNONYMS **complex**, involved, intricate, convoluted, elaborate, difficult, knotty, tortuous, labyrinthine, Byzantine. ANTONYMS simple, straightforward.

com·pli·ca·tion /,kämplə'kāsнən/ ▶ **n. 1** a circumstance that complicates something; a difficulty. **2** an involved or confused state. **3** an extra disease or condition that makes an existing one worse.

SYNONYMS **difficulty**, problem, obstacle, hurdle, stumbling block, snag, catch, hitch; informal headache, fly in the ointment, monkey wrench in the works.

com·plic·it /kəm'plisit/ ▶ **adj.** involved with other people in an unlawful activity.

com·plic·i·ty /kəm'plisitē/ ▶ **n.** involvement with other people in an unlawful activity.

com·pli·ment /'kämpləmənt/ ▶ **n. 1** a remark that expresses praise or admiration. **2** (**compliments**) formal greetings. ▶ **v.** politely congratulate or praise.

SYNONYMS ▶ **n. tribute**, accolade, commendation, pat on the back; (**compliments**) praise, acclaim, admiration, flattery, congratulations. ANTONYMS criticism, insult. ▶ **v. praise**, pay tribute to, flatter, commend, acclaim, applaud, salute, congratulate. ANTONYMS criticize.

□ **with the compliments of someone** given without charge.

USAGE

Don't confuse **compliment** and **complement**: see the note at **COMPLEMENT**.

com·pli·men·ta·ry /,kämplə'mentərē, -'mentrē/ ▶ **adj. 1** praising or approving. **2** given free of charge.

SYNONYMS **1 flattering**, appreciative, congratulatory, admiring, approving, favorable, glowing. **2 free (of charge)**, gratis; informal on the house. ANTONYMS critical.

USAGE

Don't confuse **complimentary** and **complementary**: see the note at **COMPLEMENTARY**.

com·ply /kəm'plī/ ▶ **v.** (**complies, complying, complied**) (**comply with**) **1** do what someone wants or tells you to do. **2** meet specified standards.

SYNONYMS *I can't comply with those rules* **obey**, observe, abide by, adhere to, conform to, follow, respect, go along with. ANTONYMS disobey.

com·po·nent /kəm'pōnənt/ ▶ **n.** a part of a larger whole.

SYNONYMS **part**, piece, bit, element, constituent, ingredient, unit, module.

com·port /kəmˈpôrt/ ▶ v. (**comport yourself**) formal behave in a particular way.

com·pose /kəmˈpōz/ ▶ v. (**composes, composing, composed**) **1** make up a whole. **2** create a work of art, especially music or poetry. **3** arrange in an orderly or artistic way. **4** (**composed**) calm and in control of your feelings.

SYNONYMS **1 make up**, constitute, form, comprise. **2 write**, devise, make up, think up, produce, invent, pen, author. **3 organize**, arrange, construct, set out. **4** (**composed**) **calm**, collected, cool (as a cucumber), self-possessed, poised, serene, relaxed, at ease, unruffled, unperturbed; informal unflappable, together, laid-back.

com·pos·er /kəmˈpōzər/ ▶ n. a person who writes music.

com·pos·ite /kəmˈpäzət, käm-/ ▶ adj. made up of several parts. ▶ n. a thing made up of several parts.

com·po·si·tion /ˌkämpəˈzisHən/ ▶ n. **1** the way in which something is made up: *the molecular composition of cells*. **2** a work of music, literature, or art. **3** an essay written by a student. **4** the action of composing.

SYNONYMS **1 makeup**, constitution, configuration, structure, formation, anatomy, organization. **2 work** (**of art**), creation, opus, piece. **3 writing**, creation, formulation, compilation. **4 essay**, paper, study, piece of writing, theme. **5 arrangement**, layout, proportions, balance, symmetry.

com·pos·i·tor /kəmˈpäzitər/ ▶ n. a person who arranges type or keys material for printing.

com·pos men·tis /ˌkämpəs ˈmentəs/ ▶ adj. having full control of your mind.

com·post /ˈkämˌpōst/ ▶ n. decayed organic material added to soil as a fertilizer.

com·po·sure /kəmˈpōzHər/ ▶ n. the state of being calm and self-controlled.

SYNONYMS **self-control**, self-possession, calm, equanimity, equilibrium, serenity, tranquility, poise, presence of mind, sangfroid, placidness, impassivity; informal cool.

com·pound[1] ▶ n. /ˈkämˌpound/ **1** a thing made up of two or more separate elements. **2** a substance formed from two or more elements chemically united in fixed proportions. ▶ adj. /ˈkämˌpound, kämˈpound, kəmˈpound/ made up or consisting of several parts. ▶ v. /kəmˈpound, kämˈpound, ˈkämˌpound/ **1** make up a whole from several elements. **2** make something bad worse.

SYNONYMS ▶ n. **amalgam**, blend, mixture, mix, alloy. ▶ adj. **composite**, complex, multiple. ANTONYMS simple. ▶ v. **1 mix**, combine, blend. **2 aggravate**, exacerbate, worsen, add to, augment, intensify, heighten, increase.

□ **compound fracture** an injury in which a broken bone pierces the skin.

com·pound[2] /ˈkämˌpound/ ▶ n. a large open area, often containing buildings, enclosed by a fence.

com·pre·hend /ˌkämpriˈhend/ ▶ v. understand something.

SYNONYMS **understand**, grasp, see, take in, follow, make sense of, fathom; informal work out, figure out, get.

com·pre·hen·si·ble /ˌkämpriˈhensəbəl/ ▶ adj. able to be understood.

SYNONYMS **intelligible**, understandable, lucid, coherent, accessible, self-explanatory, clear, plain, straightforward. ANTONYMS incomprehensible.

com·pre·hen·sion /ˌkämpriˈhencHən/ ▶ n. **1** the action of understanding. **2** the ability to understand: *mysteries beyond human comprehension*.

SYNONYMS **understanding**, grasp, mastery, conception, knowledge, awareness. ANTONYMS ignorance.

com·pre·hen·sive /ˌkämpriˈhensiv/ ▶ adj. **1** including or dealing with all or nearly all aspects of something. **2** (of a victory or defeat) by a large margin.

SYNONYMS **inclusive**, all-inclusive, complete, full, thorough, extensive, all-embracing, blanket, exhaustive, detailed, sweeping, wholesale, broad, wide-ranging. ANTONYMS limited.

■ **com·pre·hen·sive·ly** adv.

com·press ▶ v. /kəmˈpres/ **1** flatten by pressure; force into less space. **2** squeeze or press two things together. **3** alter the form of computer data so that it takes up less space on a disk or magnetic tape. ▶ n. /ˈkämˌpres/ an absorbent pad pressed on to part of the body to relieve inflammation or stop bleeding.

SYNONYMS ▶ v. **1 squeeze**, press, squash, crush, compact. **2 shorten**, abridge, condense, abbreviate, contract, telescope, summarize, précis. ANTONYMS expand, pad out.

□ **compressed air** air that is at more than atmospheric pressure. ■ **com·pres·sion** n.

com·pres·sor /kəmˈpresər/ ▶ n. a machine used to supply air at increased pressure.

com·prise /kəmˈprīz/ ▶ v. (**comprises, comprising, comprised**) **1** be made up of; consist of. **2** (also **be comprised of**) make up a whole.

SYNONYMS **1** *the country comprises twenty states* **consist of**, be made up of, be composed of, contain. **2** *this breed comprises half the herd* **make up**, constitute, form, account for.

com·pro·mise /ˈkämprəˌmīz/ ▶ n. **1** an agreement reached by each side giving way on some points. **2** something that is midway between different or conflicting elements: *a compromise between price and quality of output*. ▶ v. (**compromises, compromising, compromised**) **1** give way on some points in order to settle a dispute. **2** accept something that is less good than you would like. **3** cause someone danger or embarrassment by behaving in an indiscreet or reckless way.

SYNONYMS ▶ n. **agreement**, understanding, settlement, terms, deal, trade-off, bargain, middle ground. ▶ v. **1 meet each other halfway**, come to an understanding, make a deal, make concessions, find a happy medium, strike a balance. **2 undermine**, weaken, damage, harm, jeopardize, prejudice.

com·pro·mis·ing /ˈkämprəˌmīzING/ ▶ adj. revealing an embarrassing or incriminating secret.

comp·trol·ler /kənˈtrōlər, ˌkäm(p)ˈtrōlər, ˈkäm(p)ˌtrōlər/ ▶ n. a person in charge of the financial affairs of an organization.

com·pul·sion /kəmˈpəlsHən/ ▶ n. **1** pressure to do something. **2** an irresistible urge to do something.

SYNONYMS **1** *he is under no compulsion to go* **obligation**, pressure, coercion. **2** **urge**, impulse, need, desire, drive, obsession, fixation, addiction.

com·pul·sive /kəm'pəlsiv/ ▶ **adj.** **1** done because of an irresistible urge. **2** unable to stop yourself doing something. **3** irresistibly exciting.

SYNONYMS **1** *a compulsive desire* **irresistible**, uncontrollable, compelling, overwhelming. **2** *compulsive eating* **obsessive**, obsessional, addictive, uncontrollable. **3** **inveterate**, chronic, incorrigible, incurable, hopeless, persistent, habitual; informal pathological. **4** **fascinating**, compelling, gripping, riveting, engrossing, enthralling, captivating.

■ **com·pul·sive·ly** **adv.**

com·pul·so·ry /kəm'pəlsərē/ ▶ **adj.** required by law or a rule; obligatory.

SYNONYMS **obligatory**, mandatory, required, requisite, necessary, binding, enforced, prescribed. ANTONYMS optional.

com·punc·tion /kəm'pəNG(k)SHən/ ▶ **n.** a feeling of guilt about doing something wrong: *he felt no compunction in letting her worry.*

com·pu·ta·tion /ˌkämpyŏŏ'tāSHən/ ▶ **n.** **1** mathematical calculation. **2** the use of computers. ■ **com·pu·ta·tion·al** **adj.**

com·pute /kəm'pyōōt/ ▶ **v.** (**computes**, **computing**, **computed**) calculate a figure or amount.

SYNONYMS **calculate**, work out, reckon, determine, evaluate, add up, total.

com·put·er /kəm'pyōōtər/ ▶ **n.** an electronic device capable of storing and processing information according to a set of instructions. □ **computer-literate** good at using computers. ■ **com·put·ing** **n.**

com·put·er·ize /kəm'pyōōtəˌrīz/ ▶ **v.** (**computerizes**, **computerizing**, **computerized**) convert to a system controlled by or stored on computer.

com·rade /'kämˌrad, 'kämrəd/ ▶ **n.** **1** (among people) a person who shares your activities or is a fellow member of an organization. **2** a fellow soldier.

SYNONYMS **companion**, friend, colleague, associate, partner, ally; informal buddy.

■ **com·rade·ship** **n.**

con¹ /kän/ informal ▶ **v.** (**cons**, **conning**, **conned**) deceive someone into doing or believing something. ▶ **n.** a deception of this kind. □ **con man** a man who cheats people after gaining their trust.

con² ▶ **n.** (usu. in **pros and cons**) a disadvantage of or argument against something.

con³ ▶ **n.** informal a convict: *the ex-con turned his life around and went back to college.*

con·cat·e·na·tion /kənˌkatn'āSHən/ ▶ **n.** a series of interconnected things.

con·cave /kän'kāv, 'känˌkāv/ ▶ **adj.** having an outline or surface that curves inward. ■ **con·cav·i·ty** /kän'kavitē/ **n.**

con·ceal /kən'sēl/ ▶ **v.** **1** stop someone or something being seen. **2** keep something secret.

SYNONYMS **1** *clouds concealed the sun* **hide**, screen, cover, obscure, block out, blot out, mask. **2** *he concealed his true feelings* **keep secret**, hide, disguise, mask, veil, bottle up; informal keep a/the lid on. ANTONYMS reveal, confess.

■ **con·ceal·ment** **n.**

con·cede /kən'sēd/ ▶ **v.** (**concedes**, **conceding**, **conceded**) **1** finally admit that something is true. **2** give up a possession, advantage, or right. **3** admit defeat in a game or contest. **4** fail to prevent an opponent scoring a goal or point.

SYNONYMS **1** **admit**, acknowledge, accept, allow, grant, recognize, own, confess, agree. **2** **surrender**, yield, give up, relinquish, hand over. ANTONYMS deny.

con·ceit /kən'sēt/ ▶ **n.** **1** too much pride in yourself. **2** an artistic effect. **3** a complicated metaphor.

SYNONYMS **vanity**, pride, arrogance, egotism, self-importance, narcissism, self-admiration. ANTONYMS humility.

con·ceit·ed /kən'sētid/ ▶ **adj.** too proud of yourself.

SYNONYMS **vain**, proud, arrogant, egotistic, self-important, narcissistic, full of yourself, swollen-headed, boastful, cocky, self-satisfied, smug; informal bigheaded, stuck-up.

con·ceiv·a·ble /kən'sēvəbəl/ ▶ **adj.** able to be imagined or understood.

SYNONYMS **imaginable**, possible, plausible, credible, believable, feasible.

■ **con·ceiv·a·bly** **adv.**

con·ceive /kən'sēv/ ▶ **v.** (**conceives**, **conceiving**, **conceived**) **1** become pregnant with a child. **2** form an idea in your mind.

SYNONYMS **1** **think up**, think of, dream up, devise, formulate, design, create, develop; informal cook up. **2** **imagine**, envisage, visualize, picture.

SPELLING

Remember **i** before **e**, when the sound is *ee*, except after **c**: conc**ei**ve.

con·cen·trate /'känsənˌtrāt/ ▶ **v.** (**concentrates**, **concentrating**, **concentrated**) **1** focus all your attention on something. **2** gather together in numbers or a mass at one point. **3** (**concentrated**) (of a liquid solution) strong. ▶ **n.** a concentrated substance or solution.

SYNONYMS ▶ **v.** **1** *she concentrated on the movie* **focus on**, pay attention to, give your attention to, put your mind to, keep your mind on, be absorbed in, be engrossed in, be immersed in. **2** **collect**, gather, congregate, converge, mass, rally. **3** (**concentrated**) **condensed**, reduced, undiluted, strong. ANTONYMS disperse, diluted.

con·cen·tra·tion /ˌkänsən'trāSHən/ ▶ **n.** **1** the action or power of concentrating. **2** a close gathering of people or things. **3** the amount of a particular substance in a solution or mixture.

SYNONYMS **close attention**, attentiveness, application, single-mindedness, absorption. ANTONYMS inattention.

□ **concentration camp** a camp for holding political prisoners or members of persecuted minorities.

con·cen·tric /kən'sentrik, kän-/ ▶ **adj.** (of circles or arcs) sharing the same center.

con·cept /'känˌsept/ ▶ **n.** an abstract idea.

SYNONYMS **idea**, notion, conception, abstraction, theory, hypothesis.

con·cep·tion /kən'sepshən/ ▶ **n.** **1** the conceiving of a child. **2** the forming of a plan or idea. **3** an idea or concept. **4** ability to imagine or understand.

SYNONYMS **1 pregnancy**, fertilization, impregnation, insemination. **2 inception**, genesis, origination, creation, invention, beginning, origin. **3 plan**, idea, notion, scheme, project, proposal, intention, aim.

con·cep·tu·al /kən'sepcho͞oəl/ ▶ **adj.** having to do with concepts. ■ **con·cep·tu·al·ly adv.**

con·cep·tu·al·ize /kən'sepcho͞oə͵līz/ ▶ **v.** (**conceptualizes**, **conceptualizing**, **conceptualized**) form an idea of something in your mind.

con·cern /kən'sərn/ ▶ **v.** **1** relate to; be about. **2** affect or involve: *many thanks to all concerned.* **3** make someone worried. ▶ **n.** **1** worry; anxiety. **2** a matter of interest or importance. **3** a business.

SYNONYMS ▶ **v.** **1** *the memo concerns health benefits* **be about**, deal with, cover, relate to, pertain to. **2** *does this concern you?* **affect**, involve, be relevant to, apply to, have a bearing on, impact (on). **3 worry**, disturb, trouble, bother, perturb, unsettle. ▶ **n.** **1 anxiety**, worry, disquiet, apprehensiveness, unease, misgiving. **2 care**, consideration, solicitude, sympathy. **3 responsibility**, business, affair, duty, job; informal bailiwick. **4** *issues of concern to women* **interest**, importance, relevance, significance. **5 firm**, business, company, enterprise, operation, corporation; informal outfit. ANTONYMS indifference.

□ **to whom it may concern** used to address a reader whose identity is unknown.

con·cerned /kən'sərnd/ ▶ **adj.** worried.

SYNONYMS **1 worried**, anxious, upset, troubled, uneasy, bothered. **2 interested**, involved, affected, implicated. ANTONYMS unconcerned.

con·cern·ing /kən'sərniNG/ ▶ **prep.** about.

SYNONYMS **about**, regarding, relating to, with reference to, referring to, with regard to, as regards, touching, in connection with, re, apropos.

con·cert /'kän͵sərt, 'känsərt/ ▶ **n.** a musical performance given in public. □ **in concert** acting together.

con·cert·ed /kən'sərtəd/ ▶ **adj.** **1** jointly arranged or carried out: *a concerted campaign.* **2** done in a determined way: *a concerted effort.*

SYNONYMS **1** *concerted action* **joint**, united, collaborative, collective, combined, cooperative. **2** *a concerted effort* **strenuous**, vigorous, intensive, all-out, intense, concentrated.

con·cer·ti·na /͵känsər'tēnə/ ▶ **n.** a small musical instrument that you play by stretching and squeezing it and pressing buttons. ▶ **v.** (**concertinas**, **concertinaing**, **concertinaed**) compress in folds like those of a concertina.

con·cer·to /kən'CHertō/ ▶ **n.** (plural **concertos** or **concerti** /-tē/) a musical work for an orchestra and one or more solo instruments.

con·ces·sion /kən'seshən/ ▶ **n.** **1** something done or given up in order to settle a dispute. **2** the right to use land or other property for a particular purpose. **3** a stall, bar, or small store selling things within a larger business or store.

SYNONYMS **1 compromise**, accommodation, trade-off, sop. **2 right**, privilege, license, permit, franchise, warrant.

■ **con·ces·sion·ar·y adj.**

conch /käNGk, käNCH, kôNGk/ ▶ **n.** (plural **conches**) a shellfish with a spiral shell.

con·cierge /kôN'syerzH, ͵känsē'erzH/ ▶ **n.** **1** (especially in France) a resident caretaker of an apartment complex or small hotel. **2** a hotel employee whose job is to assist guests by arranging tours, making theater and restaurant reservations, etc.

con·cil·i·ate /kən'silē͵āt/ ▶ **v.** (**conciliates**, **conciliating**, **conciliated**) **1** make someone calm and content. **2** try to bring the two sides in a dispute together. ■ **con·cil·i·a·tion** /kən͵silē'āshən/ **n.** **con·cil·i·a·to·ry** /kən'silēə͵tôrē/ **adj.**

con·cise /kən'sīs/ ▶ **adj.** giving a lot of information clearly and in few words.

SYNONYMS **succinct**, pithy, brief, abridged, condensed, abbreviated, compact. ANTONYMS lengthy.

■ **con·cise·ly adv.** **con·ci·sion** /-'sizHən/ **n.**

con·clave /'kän͵klāv/ ▶ **n.** **1** a private meeting. **2** (in the Roman Catholic Church) the assembly of cardinals for the election of a pope.

con·clude /kən'klo͞od/ ▶ **v.** (**concludes**, **concluding**, **concluded**) **1** bring or come to an end. **2** arrive at an opinion by reasoning. **3** formally settle or arrange a treaty or agreement.

SYNONYMS **1 finish**, end, come/bring to an end, draw to a close, close, wind up, terminate, stop, cease; informal wrap up. **2 settle**, clinch, finalize, tie up; informal sew up. **3 deduce**, infer, gather, judge, decide, surmise, figure. ANTONYMS begin.

con·clu·sion /kən'klo͞ozHən/ ▶ **n.** **1** an end or finish. **2** the summing up of an argument or written work. **3** a decision reached by reasoning.

SYNONYMS **1 end**, ending, finish, close. **2 settlement**, clinching, completion, arrangement. **3 deduction**, inference, interpretation, judgment, verdict. ANTONYMS beginning.

con·clu·sive /kən'klo͞osiv, -ziv/ ▶ **adj.** decisive or convincing.

SYNONYMS **incontrovertible**, undeniable, indisputable, irrefutable, unquestionable, convincing, certain, decisive, definitive, definite, positive, categorical, unequivocal. ANTONYMS unconvincing.

■ **con·clu·sive·ly adv.**

con·coct /kən'käkt/ ▶ **v.** **1** make a dish by combining ingredients. **2** think up a story or plan.

SYNONYMS **make up**, dream up, fabricate, invent, devise, formulate, hatch, brew; informal cook up.

■ **con·coc·tion n.**

con·com·i·tant /kən'kämitənt/ ▶ **adj.** formal naturally accompanying or connected with something else.

con·cord /'käNG,kôrd, 'kän-/ ▶ **n.** literary agreement; harmony.

con·cord·ance /kən'kôrdns/ ▶ **n.** an alphabetical list of the important words in a written work.

con·cor·dat /kən'kôr,dat/ ▶ **n.** an agreement or treaty.

con·course /'kän,kôrs, 'käNG-/ ▶ **n.** a large open area inside or in front of a public building, as in an airport or railroad station.

con·crete /kän'krēt, 'kän,krēt, kən'krēt/ ▶ **n.** a building material made from gravel, sand, cement, and water. ▶ **adj. 1** existing in a physical form; not abstract. **2** definite: *concrete proof.* ▶ **v.** (**concretes, concreting, concreted**) cover with concrete.

SYNONYMS ▶ **adj. 1 solid**, material, real, physical, tangible. **2 definite**, specific, firm, positive, conclusive, definitive. ANTONYMS abstract, imaginary.

con·cre·tion /kən'krēSHən, kän-/ ▶ **n.** a hard solid mass.

con·cu·bine /'käNGkyo͝o,bīn/ ▶ **n.** (in some societies) a woman who lives with a man but has lower status than his wife or wives.

con·cur /kən'kər/ ▶ **v.** (**concurs, concurring, concurred**) **1** (often **concur with**) agree. **2** happen at the same time.

SYNONYMS **agree**, be in agreement, accord, be in sympathy, see eye to eye, be of the same mind, be of the same opinion. ANTONYMS disagree.

con·cur·rent /kən'kərənt, -'kə-rənt/ ▶ **adj.** existing or happening at the same time. ■ **con·cur·rent·ly adv.**

con·cus·sion /kən'kəSHən/ ▶ **n.** temporary unconsciousness or confusion caused by a blow on the head. ■ **con·cussed adj.**

con·demn /kən'dem/ ▶ **v. 1** express complete disapproval of. **2** (usu. **condemn someone to**) sentence someone to a punishment. **3** (**condemn someone to**) force someone to endure something unpleasant. **4** officially declare something to be unfit for use.

SYNONYMS **1 censure**, criticize, denounce, deplore, decry; informal slam. **2** *his illness condemned him to a lonely childhood* **doom**, destine, damn, sentence. ANTONYMS praise.

■ **con·dem·na·tion** /,kändem'nāSHən, -dəm-/ **n.**

con·den·sa·tion /,kän,den'sāSHən, -dən-/ ▶ **n. 1** water from humid air collecting as droplets on a cold surface. **2** the conversion of a vapor or gas to a liquid.

con·dense /kən'dens/ ▶ **v.** (**condenses, condensing, condensed**) **1** change from a gas or vapor to a liquid. **2** make a liquid thicker or more concentrated. **3** express a piece of writing or a speech in fewer words.

SYNONYMS **abridge**, compress, summarize, shorten, cut, abbreviate, edit. ANTONYMS expand.

□ **condensed milk** milk that has been thickened and sweetened.

con·de·scend /,kändə'send/ ▶ **v. 1** behave as if you were better than someone else. **2** do something even though you think it is beneath your dignity: *he condescended to see me at my hotel.* **3** (**condescending**) behaving as if you are better than other people.

SYNONYMS **1 patronize**, talk down to, look down your nose at, look down on. **2** *he condescended to see us* **deign**, stoop, lower yourself, demean yourself, consent. **3** (**condescending**) **patronizing**, supercilious, superior, disdainful, lofty, haughty; informal snooty, stuck-up.

con·de·scen·sion /,kändə'senCHən/ ▶ **n.** a patronizing attitude or way of behaving.

con·di·ment /'kändəmənt/ ▶ **n.** something such as salt or mustard that is added to food to bring out its flavor.

con·di·tion /kən'diSHən/ ▶ **n. 1** the state that someone or something is in as regards appearance, fitness, or working order. **2** (**conditions**) circumstances that affect the way something works or exists. **3** a situation that must exist before something else is possible: *for a country to borrow money, three conditions must be met.* **4** an illness or medical problem. ▶ **v. 1** train or influence someone to behave in a certain way: *the child is conditioned to dislike certain foods.* **2** (**be conditioned by**) be influenced or determined by. **3** bring something into a good condition.

SYNONYMS ▶ **n. 1 state**, shape, order, fitness, health, form. **2 circumstances**, surroundings, environment, situation, state of affairs, position. **3 disorder**, problem, complaint, illness, disease, ailment, malady. **4 stipulation**, constraint, prerequisite, precondition, requirement, term, proviso. ▶ **v. train**, teach, educate, guide, accustom, adapt, habituate, mold.

□ **out of condition** unfit.

con·di·tion·al /kən'diSHənl/ ▶ **adj. 1** depending on one or more conditions being fulfilled. **2** Grammar expressing something that must happen or be true before something else can happen or be true.

SYNONYMS **qualified**, dependent, contingent, with reservations, limited, provisional, provisory.

■ **con·di·tion·al·ly adv.**

con·di·tion·er /kən'diSH(ə)nər/ ▶ **n.** a liquid added when washing hair or clothing, to make them softer.

con·do /'kändō/ ▶ **n.** (plural **condos**) short for CONDOMINIUM.

con·dole /kən'dōl/ ▶ **v.** (**condoles, condoling, condoled**) (**condole with**) express sympathy to.

con·do·lence /kən'dōləns/ ▶ **n.** an expression of sympathy.

con·do·min·i·um /,kändə'minēəm/ ▶ **n.** (plural **condominiums**) a building containing a number of individually owned apartments.

con·done /kən'dōn/ ▶ **v.** (**condones, condoning, condoned**) accept or forgive an offense or wrong.

SYNONYMS **disregard**, accept, allow, let pass, turn a blind eye to, overlook, forget, forgive, pardon, excuse. ANTONYMS condemn.

con·dor /'kän,dôr, -dər/ ▶ **n.** a very large South American vulture.

con·du·cive /kən'd(y)o͞osiv/ ▶ **adj.** (**conducive to**) contributing or helping toward.

SYNONYMS **favorable**, beneficial, advantageous, opportune, encouraging, promising, convenient, good, helpful, instrumental. ANTONYMS unfavorable.

con·duct ▶ **n.** /ˈkänˌdəkt/ **1** the way in which a person behaves. **2** management or direction: *the conduct of foreign affairs.* ▶ **v.** /kənˈdəkt/ **1** organize and carry out. **2** direct the performance of a piece of music. **3** guide or lead someone to a place. **4** (**conduct yourself**) behave in a particular way. **5** transmit heat or electricity directly through a substance.

> SYNONYMS ▶ **n. 1 behavior**, actions, deeds, doings, exploits. **2 management**, running, direction, control, supervision, regulation, administration, organization, coordination, handling. ▶ **v. 1 manage**, direct, run, administer, organize, coordinate, orchestrate, handle, carry out/on. **2 escort**, guide, lead, usher, steer. **3 transmit**, convey, carry, channel.

■ **con·duc·tion** /kənˈdəkshən/ **n.**

con·duct·ance /kənˈdəktəns/ ▶ **n.** the degree to which a material conducts electricity.

con·duc·tive /kənˈdəktiv/ ▶ **adj.** conducting heat or electricity. ■ **con·duc·tiv·i·ty** /ˌkänˌdəkˈtivitē, kən-/ **n.**

con·duc·tor /kənˈdəktər/ ▶ **n. 1** a person who conducts musicians. **2** a material or device that conducts heat or electricity. **3** a person who collects fares on a train.

con·duit /ˈkänˌd(y)o͞oət, ˈkänd(w)ət/ ▶ **n. 1** a channel for moving water from one place to another. **2** a tube protecting electric wiring.

cone /kōn/ ▶ **n. 1** an object that tapers from a circular base to a point. **2** the hard, dry fruit of a pine or fir tree.

con·fab /ˈkänˌfab, kənˈfab/ ▶ **n.** informal an informal conversation.

con·fab·u·late /kənˈfabyəˌlāt/ ▶ **v.** (**confabulates, confabulating, confabulated**) formal have a conversation. ■ **con·fab·u·la·tion** /-ˌfabyəˈlāshən/ **n.**

con·fect /kənˈfekt/ ▶ **v.** make something elaborate.

con·fec·tion /kənˈfekshən/ ▶ **n. 1** an elaborate sweet dish. **2** something put together in an elaborate or complicated way: *a confection of marble.*

con·fec·tion·er·y /kənˈfekshəˌnerē/ ▶ **n.** (plural **confectioneries**) candy and chocolates.

> SPELLING
> The ending is **-ery**, not **-ary**: confection**ery**.

con·fed·er·a·cy /kənˈfedərəsē/ ▶ **n.** (plural **confederacies**) **1** an alliance of states or groups. **2** (**the Confederacy**) the Confederate States of the United States, the 11 southern states (Alabama, Arkansas, Florida, Georgia, Louisiana, Mississippi, North Carolina, South Carolina, Tennessee, Texas, and Virginia) that seceded from the United States in 1860-61, thus precipitating the Civil War.

con·fed·er·ate ▶ **adj.** /kənˈfedərət/ **1** joined by an agreement or treaty. **2** (**Confederate**) having to do with the southern states that separated from the United States in 1860–61. ▶ **v.** /-ˌrāt/ (**confederates, confederating, confederated**) unite in an alliance.

con·fed·er·a·tion /kənˌfedəˈrāshən/ ▶ **n.** an alliance of states or groups.

con·fer /kənˈfər/ ▶ **v.** (**confers, conferring, conferred**) **1** formally give a title, benefit, or right to someone. **2** have discussions.

> SYNONYMS **1 bestow**, present, grant, award, honor with. **2 consult**, talk, speak, converse, have a chat, deliberate, compare notes.

■ **con·fer·ment** **n.**

con·fer·ence /ˈkänf(ə)rəns/ ▶ **n.** a formal meeting to discuss something.

> SYNONYMS **meeting**, congress, convention, seminar, discussion, council, forum, summit.

con·fess /kənˈfes/ ▶ **v. 1** admit that you have done something criminal or wrong. **2** acknowledge something reluctantly. **3** formally declare your sins to a priest.

> SYNONYMS **1 admit**, acknowledge, reveal, disclose, divulge, own up, plead guilty, accept the blame; informal come clean. **2** *I confess I don't know* **acknowledge**, admit, concede, grant, allow, own. ANTONYMS deny.

con·fes·sion /kənˈfeshən/ ▶ **n. 1** an act of confessing. **2** formal declaration of your sins to a priest.

con·fes·sion·al /kənˈfeshənl/ ▶ **n. 1** an enclosed box in a church, in which a priest sits to hear confessions. **2** a confession.

con·fes·sor /kənˈfesər/ ▶ **n.** a priest who hears confessions.

con·fet·ti /kənˈfetē/ ▶ **n.** small pieces of colored paper traditionally thrown over a bride and groom after a marriage ceremony or thrown in a celebration.

con·fi·dant /ˈkänfəˌdant, -ˌdänt/ ▶ **n.** (feminine **confidante**) a person you trust and confide in.

con·fide /kənˈfīd/ ▶ **v.** (**confides, confiding, confided**) (often **confide in**) tell someone about a secret or private matter.

> SYNONYMS **reveal**, disclose, divulge, impart, declare, vouchsafe, tell, confess.

con·fi·dence /ˈkänfədəns, -fəˌdens/ ▶ **n. 1** faith in someone or something. **2** a positive feeling gained from a belief in your own ability to do things well. **3** a feeling of certainty about something.

> SYNONYMS **1 trust**, belief, faith, credence. **2 self-assurance**, self-confidence, self-possession, assertiveness, self-belief, conviction. ANTONYMS distrust, doubt.

□ **confidence game** an act of cheating someone after gaining their trust. **in confidence** as a secret. **in someone's confidence** in a position of trust with someone. **take someone into your confidence** tell your secrets to someone.

con·fi·dent /ˈkänfədənt, -fəˌdent/ ▶ **adj. 1** feeling confidence in yourself. **2** feeling certain about something.

> SYNONYMS **1 self-assured**, assured, self-confident, positive, assertive, self-possessed. **2 sure**, certain, positive, convinced, in no doubt, satisfied.

■ **con·fi·dent·ly** **adv.**

con·fi·den·tial /ˌkänfəˈdenchəl/ ▶ **adj.** intended to be kept secret.

> SYNONYMS **private**, personal, intimate, quiet, secret, sensitive, classified, restricted; informal hush-hush.

■ **con·fi·den·ti·al·i·ty** /-ˌdenchēˈalitē/ **n.** **con·fi·den·tial·ly** **adv.**

con·fig·u·ra·tion /kənˌfig(y)əˈrāshən/ ▶ **n.** a particular arrangement of parts.

con·fig·ure /kənˈfigyər/ ▶ v. (**configures, configuring, configured**) **1** arrange or set up in a particular way. **2** arrange a computer system so that it is able to do a particular task.

con·fine ▶ v. /kənˈfīn/ (**confines, confining, confined**) **1** (**confine someone/thing to**) keep someone or something within certain limits. **2** (**be confined to**) be unable to leave a place because of illness or disability. ▶ n. /ˈkänˌfīn/ (**confines**) limits, boundaries, or restrictions.

> SYNONYMS ▶ v. **1 enclose**, incarcerate, imprison, intern, hold captive, cage, lock up, coop up. **2 restrict**, limit.

con·fined /kənˈfīnd/ ▶ adj. (of a space) small and enclosed.

con·fine·ment /kənˈfīnmənt/ ▶ n. **1** the state of being confined. **2** dated the time around which a woman gives birth to a baby.

con·firm /kənˈfərm/ ▶ v. **1** state or establish that something is definitely true or correct. **2** make something definite or valid. **3** (**be confirmed**) go through the religious ceremony of confirmation.

> SYNONYMS **1 corroborate**, verify, prove, substantiate, justify, vindicate, bear out. **2 affirm**, reaffirm, assert, assure someone, repeat. **3 ratify**, approve, endorse, validate, sanction, authorize. ANTONYMS contradict, deny.

con·fir·ma·tion /ˌkänfərˈmāshən/ ▶ n. **1** the action of confirming. **2** the ceremony at which a baptized person is admitted as a full member of the Christian Church.

con·firmed /kənˈfərmd/ ▶ adj. firmly established in a habit, belief, etc.: *a confirmed bachelor*.

con·fis·cate /ˈkänfəˌskāt/ ▶ v. (**confiscates, confiscating, confiscated**) officially take or seize someone's property.

> SYNONYMS **impound**, seize, commandeer, requisition, appropriate, expropriate, take, sequestrate.

con·fla·gra·tion /ˌkänfləˈgrāshən/ ▶ n. a large and destructive fire.

con·flate /kənˈflāt/ ▶ v. (**conflates, conflating, conflated**) combine into one. ■ **con·fla·tion** n.

con·flict ▶ n. /ˈkänˌflikt/ **1** a serious disagreement. **2** a long-lasting armed struggle. **3** a difference of opinions, principles, etc.: *a conflict of interests*. ▶ v. /kənˈflikt, ˈkänˌflikt/ (of opinions, stories, etc.) disagree or be different.

> SYNONYMS ▶ n. **1 dispute**, quarrel, squabble, disagreement, clash, feud, discord, friction, strife, antagonism, hostility. **2 war**, campaign, fighting, engagement, struggle, hostilities, warfare, combat. **3** *a conflict between work and home life* **clash**, incompatibility, friction, mismatch, variance, contradiction. ANTONYMS agreement, peace, harmony. ▶ v. **1 clash**, be incompatible, be at odds, differ, diverge, disagree, collide. **2** (**conflicting**) **contradictory**, incompatible, inconsistent, irreconcilable, contrary, opposite, opposing, clashing.

con·flu·ence /ˈkänˌflo͞oəns, kənˈflo͞oəns/ ▶ n. the junction of two rivers.

con·form /kənˈfôrm/ ▶ v. (often **conform to**) **1** obey a rule. **2** behave in an expected or conventional way. **3** be similar in form or type.

> SYNONYMS **1** *visitors have to* ***conform to*** *our rules* **comply with**, abide by, obey, observe, follow, keep to, stick to, adhere to, uphold, heed, accept, go along with. **2 fit in**, behave (yourself), toe the line, obey the rules; informal play by the rules. ANTONYMS flout, rebel.

■ **con·form·i·ty** n.

con·form·ist /kənˈfôrmist/ ▶ n. a person who behaves in an expected or conventional way.

con·found /kənˈfound/ ▶ v. **1** surprise or bewilder someone. **2** prove a person, theory, or expectation wrong. **3** (**confounded**) informal, dated used to express annoyance. **4** defeat a plan, aim, or hope.

> SYNONYMS **baffle**, bewilder, mystify, bemuse, perplex, puzzle, confuse, dumbfound, throw; informal flabbergast, flummox.

con·fra·ter·ni·ty /ˌkänfrəˈtərnitē/ ▶ n. (plural **confraternities**) a brotherhood, especially with a religious or charitable purpose.

con·front /kənˈfrənt/ ▶ v. **1** meet an enemy or opponent face to face. **2** face up to and deal with a problem. **3** make someone face up to a problem.

> SYNONYMS **1 challenge**, square up to, face (up to), come face to face with, meet, accost, stand up to, tackle. **2 face**, bedevil, beset, plague, bother, trouble, threaten. **3** *they must confront these issues* **tackle**, address, face (up to), come to grips with, grapple with, deal with, sort out. ANTONYMS evade.

con·fron·ta·tion /ˌkänfrənˈtāshən/ ▶ n. a situation of angry disagreement or hostility.

> SYNONYMS **conflict**, clash, fight, battle, encounter, head-to-head; informal set-to, run-in, dust-up, showdown.

■ **con·fron·ta·tion·al** adj.

Con·fu·cian /kənˈfyo͞oshən/ ▶ adj. relating to the Chinese philosopher Confucius.

con·fuse /kənˈfyo͞oz/ ▶ v. (**confuses, confusing, confused**) **1** make someone bewildered or puzzled. **2** make something less easy to understand. **3** mistake one thing or person for another.

> SYNONYMS **1 bewilder**, baffle, mystify, bemuse, perplex, puzzle, nonplus; informal flummox, faze. **2** (**confusing**) **puzzling**, baffling, perplexing, bewildering, mystifying, ambiguous, misleading, inconsistent, contradictory. **3** *the authors have confused the issue* **complicate**, muddle, blur, obscure, cloud. **4** *some confuse strokes with heart attacks* **mix up with**, muddle up with, mistake for. ANTONYMS enlighten, simplify.

con·fused /kənˈfyo͞ozd/ ▶ adj. **1** bewildered. **2** difficult to understand or distinguish.

> SYNONYMS **1 puzzled**, bemused, bewildered, perplexed, baffled, mystified; informal flummoxed. **2 disorientated**, bewildered, muddled, addled, befuddled, demented, senile. **3** *a confused recollection* **vague**, unclear, indistinct, imprecise, blurred, hazy, dim. **4 disorderly**, disorganized, untidy, jumbled, mixed up, chaotic, topsy-turvy, tangled; informal higgledy-piggledy. ANTONYMS clear, lucid.

con·fu·sion /kənˈfyo͞ozhən/ ▶ n. **1** uncertainty or bewilderment. **2** a situation of panic or disorder. **3** the mistaking of one person or thing for another.

> SYNONYMS **1 bewilderment**, bafflement, perplexity, puzzlement, bemusement,

mystification, befuddlement, disorientation, uncertainty. **2 disorder**, disarray, muddle, mess, chaos, mayhem, pandemonium, turmoil; informal shambles. ANTONYMS clarity, order.

con·fute /kən'fyo͞ot/ ▶ v. (**confutes, confuting, confuted**) formal prove a person or argument to be wrong.

con·ga /'käNGgə/ ▶ n. a Latin American dance performed by people in single file.

con·geal /kən'jēl/ ▶ v. become semi-solid.

SYNONYMS **coagulate**, clot, thicken, cake, set, gel.

con·gen·ial /kən'jēnyəl/ ▶ adj. suited or pleasing to your tastes.

SYNONYMS **agreeable**, pleasant, friendly, amicable, amiable, nice. ANTONYMS unfriendly, unpleasant.

■ **con·ge·ni·al·i·ty** /-,jēnē'alitē/ n.

con·gen·i·tal /kən'jenətl/ ▶ adj. **1** (of a disease or abnormality) present from birth. **2** having a particular characteristic as part of your character: *a congenital liar.* ■ **con·gen·i·tal·ly** adv.

con·ger eel /'käNGgər/ ▶ n. a large eel found in coastal waters.

con·gest·ed /kən'jestid/ ▶ adj. **1** so crowded that it is difficult to move freely. **2** abnormally full of blood. **3** blocked with mucus.

SYNONYMS **blocked**, clogged, choked, jammed, obstructed, crowded, overcrowded, overflowing, packed; informal snarled up, gridlocked. ANTONYMS clear.

■ **con·ges·tion** n.

con·glom·er·ate /kən'glämərət/ ▶ n. **1** a large corporation formed by the merging of separate companies. **2** something consisting of a number of different and distinct things. ■ **con·glom·er·a·tion** /kən,glämə'rāsHən/ n.

con·grats /kən'grats/ ▶ pl.n. informal congratulations.

con·grat·u·late /kən'gracHə,lāt, -'grajə-/ ▶ v. (**congratulates, congratulating, congratulated**) **1** tell someone that you are pleased at their success or good fortune. **2** (**congratulate yourself**) think that you are fortunate or clever.

SYNONYMS **compliment**, wish someone happiness, pay tribute to, pat on the back, take your hat off to, praise, applaud, salute, honor. ANTONYMS criticize.

■ **con·grat·u·la·to·ry** /-lə,tôrē/ adj.

con·grat·u·la·tion /kən,gracHə'lāsHən, -,grajə-/ ▶ n. **1** (**congratulations**) good wishes given to someone who has had success or good fortune. **2** the action of congratulating someone.

SYNONYMS (**congratulations**) **best wishes**, compliments, greetings, felicitations.

con·gre·gate /'käNGgrə,gāt/ ▶ v. (**congregates, congregating, congregated**) gather into a crowd or mass.

SYNONYMS **assemble**, gather, collect, come together, convene, rally, muster, meet, cluster, group. ANTONYMS disperse.

con·gre·ga·tion /,käNGgrə'gāsHən/ ▶ n. **1** a group of people assembled for religious worship. **2** a gathering or collection of people or things.

con·gress /'käNGgrəs, 'kän-/ ▶ n. **1** a formal meeting or series of meetings between representatives of different groups. **2** (**Congress**) (in the United States and some other countries) the group of people elected to pass laws. ■ **con·gres·sion·al** /kən'gresHənl/ adj.

con·gress·man /'käNGgrəsmən, 'kän-/ (or **congresswoman** /'käNGgrəs,wo͝omən, 'kän-/) ▶ n. (plural **congressmen** or **congresswomen**) a male (or female) member of the US Congress.

con·gru·ent /kən'gro͞oənt, 'käNGgro͞oənt/ ▶ adj. **1** in agreement or harmony. **2** Geometry (of figures) identical in form. ■ **con·gru·ence** n.

con·i·cal /'känikəl/ ▶ adj. shaped like a cone.

con·ic sec·tion /'känik/ ▶ n. the figure of a circle, ellipse, parabola, or hyperbola formed by the intersection of a plane and a circular cone.

co·ni·fer /'känəfər, 'kō-/ ▶ n. a tree that produces hard dry fruit (**cones**) and evergreen needlelike leaves. ■ **co·nif·er·ous** /kə'nifərəs, kō-/ adj.

con·jec·ture /kən'jekcHər/ ▶ n. an opinion based on incomplete information; a guess. ▶ v. (**conjectures, conjecturing, conjectured**) form a conjecture; guess. ■ **con·jec·tur·al** adj.

con·join /kən'join, kän-/ ▶ v. formal join; combine.

con·ju·gal /'känjəgəl/ ▶ adj. having to do with marriage.

con·ju·gate /'känjə,gāt/ ▶ v. (**conjugates, conjugating, conjugated**) Grammar give the different forms of a verb. ■ **con·ju·ga·tion** /,känjə'gāsHən/ n.

con·junc·tion /kən'jəNGksHən/ ▶ n. **1** Grammar a word used to connect words or clauses (e.g., *and*, *if*). **2** an instance of two or more things happening at the same time or being in the same place.

USAGE

A **conjunction** is used to connect words or clauses of a sentence together, as in the sentence *It was Monday morning and I was in bed.* Some people believe that it is wrong to start a sentence with a conjunction such as **and, because,** or **but**, but it is possible to do this as a way of creating a particular effect, for example: *What are the government's chances or winning in court? And what are the consequences?.*

con·junc·ti·vi·tis /kən,jəNG(k)tə'vītis/ ▶ n. inflammation of the eye.

con·jure /'känjər, 'kən-/ ▶ v. (**conjures, conjuring, conjured**) (usu. **conjure something up**) **1** make something appear by magic, or as if by magic. **2** make something appear as an image in your mind.

SYNONYMS **1 produce**, magic, summon. **2** *the picture that his words* ***conjured up*** **bring to mind**, call to mind, evoke, summon up, suggest.

con·jur·ing /'känjəriNG, 'kən-/ ▶ n. entertainment in the form of seemingly magical tricks. ■ **con·ju·ror** (or **conjurer**) n.

conk /käNGk, kôNGk/ ▶ v. (**conk out**) informal **1** (of a machine) break down. **2** faint or go to sleep.

con·nect /kə'nekt/ ▶ v. **1** join or bring together; link. **2** (**be connected**) be related in some way.

SYNONYMS **1 attach**, join, fasten, fix, link, hook (up), secure, hitch, stick. **2** *rituals* ***connected with*** *Easter* **associate with**, link to/with, couple with, identify with, relate to. ANTONYMS detach.

con·nec·tion /kə'neksHən/ ▶ n. **1** a link or relationship. **2** the action of linking one thing with another. **3** (**connections**) influential people that you know or are related to. **4** a train, bus, etc., that you can catch to continue a journey.

SYNONYMS **1 link**, relationship, relation, interconnection, interdependence, association, bond, tie, tie-in, correspondence. **2** *he has the right connections* **contacts**, friends, acquaintances, allies, colleagues, associates, relations.

□ **in connection with** concerning. **in this** (or **that**) **connection** with reference to this (or that).

con·nec·tive /kə'nektiv/ ▶ **adj.** connecting one thing to another. ▶ **n.** Grammar a word or phrase that links parts of a sentence. □ **connective tissue** bodily tissue that connects, supports, binds, or separates other tissues or organs.

con·nive /kə'nīv/ ▶ **v.** (**connives**, **conniving**, **connived**) **1** (**connive at** or **in**) secretly allow something wrong to be done. **2** (often **connive with**) conspire to do something wrong.

SYNONYMS **1 ignore**, overlook, disregard, pass over, take no notice of, turn a blind eye to. **2 conspire**, collude, collaborate, plot, scheme. **3** (**conniving**) **scheming**, cunning, calculating, devious, wily, sly, artful, manipulative, Machiavellian, deceitful.

■ **con·niv·ance** **n.**

con·nois·seur /ˌkänə'sər, -'so͝or/ ▶ **n.** a person with great knowledge and appreciation of something.

con·no·ta·tion /ˌkänə'tāsʜən/ ▶ **n.** an idea or feeling that is suggested by a word in addition to its main meaning.

SYNONYMS **overtone**, undertone, undercurrent, implication, nuance, hint, echo, association.

con·note /kə'nōt/ ▶ **v.** (**connotes**, **connoting**, **connoted**) (of a word) suggest something in addition to its main meaning.

con·nu·bi·al /kə'n(y)o͞obēəl/ ▶ **adj.** having to do with marriage.

con·quer /'käɴɢkər/ ▶ **v.** (**conquers**, **conquering**, **conquered**) **1** take control of a country or its people by military force. **2** successfully overcome a problem.

SYNONYMS **1 defeat**, beat, vanquish, triumph over, overcome, overwhelm, overpower, overthrow, subdue, subjugate. **2** *Peru was conquered by Spain* **seize**, take (over), appropriate, capture, occupy, invade, annex, overrun. **3 overcome**, get the better of, control, master, deal with, cope with, rise above; informal lick.

■ **con·quer·or** **n.**

con·quest /'kän͵kwest, 'käɴɢ-/ ▶ **n.** **1** the action of conquering. **2** a place that has been conquered. **3** a person whose affection you have won.

SYNONYMS **1 defeat**, overthrow, subjugation. **2 seizure**, takeover, capture, occupation, invasion, annexation.

con·quis·ta·dor /kôɴɢ'kēstə͵dôr, kän'k(w)istə-, kən-/ ▶ **n.** (plural **conquistadores** /-ēz, -ās/ or **conquistadors**) a Spanish conqueror of Mexico or Peru in the 16th century.

con·science /'känᴄʜəns/ ▶ **n.** a person's moral sense of right and wrong.

SYNONYMS **moral sense**, morals, sense of right and wrong, standards, values, principles, ethics, beliefs, scruples, qualms.

con·sci·en·tious /ˌkänᴄʜē'enᴄʜəs/ ▶ **adj.** careful and thorough in carrying out your work or duty.

SYNONYMS **diligent**, industrious, punctilious, painstaking, dedicated, careful, meticulous, thorough, attentive, hard-working, rigorous, scrupulous. ANTONYMS casual.

□ **conscientious objector** a person who refuses to serve in the armed forces for moral reasons. ■ **con·sci·en·tious·ly** **adv.**

con·scious /'känᴄʜəs/ ▶ **adj.** **1** aware of and responding to your surroundings. **2** (usu. **conscious of**) aware. **3** deliberate; intentional: *a conscious effort.*

SYNONYMS **1 aware**, awake, responsive; informal with us. **2 deliberate**, purposeful, knowing, considered, calculated, willful, premeditated. ANTONYMS unaware, unconscious.

■ **con·scious·ly** **adv.**

con·scious·ness /'känᴄʜəsnəs/ ▶ **n.** **1** the state of being conscious. **2** awareness or perception of something.

con·script ▶ **v.** /kən'skript/ call someone up for compulsory military service. ▶ **n.** /'kän͵skript/ a person who has been conscripted. ■ **con·scrip·tion** /kən'skripsʜən/ **n.**

con·se·crate /'känsi͵krāt/ ▶ **v.** (**consecrates**, **consecrating**, **consecrated**) **1** make or declare something holy. **2** officially make someone a bishop. ■ **con·se·cra·tion** /ˌkänsi'krāsʜən/ **n.**

con·sec·u·tive /kən'sekyətiv/ ▶ **adj.** following one after another in unbroken sequence.

SYNONYMS **successive**, succeeding, in succession, running, in a row, straight.

■ **con·sec·u·tive·ly** **adv.**

con·sen·su·al /kən'senᴄʜo͞oəl/ ▶ **adj.** relating to or involving consent or consensus.

con·sen·sus /kən'sensəs/ ▶ **n.** general agreement.

SYNONYMS **1 agreement**, unanimity, harmony, accord, unity, solidarity. **2** *the consensus was that they should act* **general opinion**, common view. ANTONYMS disagreement.

SPELLING

Consen**s**us, not -**cen**-.

con·sent /kən'sent/ ▶ **n.** permission or agreement. ▶ **v.** **1** give permission. **2** agree to do something.

SYNONYMS ▶ **n. agreement**, assent, acceptance, approval, permission, authorization, sanction; informal go-ahead, green light, OK, okay. ANTONYMS dissent. ▶ **v.** *she **consented to** surgery* **agree to**, assent to, submit to, allow, sanction, approve, go along with; informal give the go-ahead to, green-light, OK, okay. ANTONYMS forbid, refuse.

con·se·quence /'känsikwəns, -͵kwens/ ▶ **n.** **1** a result or effect. **2** importance or relevance: *the past is of no consequence.*

SYNONYMS **1 result**, upshot, outcome, effect, repercussion, ramification, product, end result. **2** *the past is of no consequence* **importance**, import, significance, account, value, concern. ANTONYMS cause.

con·se·quent /'känsikwənt, -͵kwent/ ▶ **adj.** following as a consequence.

SYNONYMS **resulting**, resultant, ensuing, consequential, following, subsequent.

con·se·quent·ly /'känsikwəntlē, -ˌkwentlē/ ▶ **adv.** as a result.

SYNONYMS **as a result**, as a consequence, so, thus, therefore, accordingly, hence, for this/that reason, because of this/that.

con·ser·va·tion /ˌkänsər'vāsʜən/ ▶ **n.** **1** preservation or restoration of the natural environment. **2** preservation of historical sites and objects. **3** careful use of a resource: *energy conservation.*

SYNONYMS **preservation**, protection, safekeeping, husbandry, upkeep, maintenance, repair, restoration.

■ **con·ser·va·tion·ist n.**

con·serv·a·tive /kən'sərvətiv/ ▶ **adj.** **1** opposed to change and holding traditional values. **2** (in politics) favoring free enterprise and private ownership. **3** (**Conservative**) relating to the Conservative Party, a political party in any of several countries of the world. **4** (of an estimate) deliberately low for the sake of caution. ▶ **n.** **1** a conservative person. **2** (**Conservative**) a supporter or member of a Conservative Party.

SYNONYMS ▶ **adj.** **1 right-wing**, reactionary, traditionalist, old-fashioned, dyed-in-the-wool, hidebound, unadventurous, set in your ways; informal stick-in-the-mud. **2 conventional**, sober, modest, sensible, restrained; informal square. ANTONYMS socialist, radical.

■ **con·serv·a·tism n. con·serv·a·tive·ly adv.**

con·ser·va·toire /kən'sərvəˌtwär/ ▶ **n.** another term for **CONSERVATORY** (sense 1).

con·serv·a·to·ry /kən'sərvəˌtôrē/ ▶ **n.** (plural **conservatories**) **1** a college for the study of classical music or other arts. **2** a room with a glass roof and walls, attached to a house.

con·serve ▶ **v.** /kən'sərv/ (**conserves**, **conserving**, **conserved**) protect something from being harmed or overused. ▶ **n.** /'känˌsərv/ fruit jam.

SYNONYMS ▶ **v. preserve**, protect, save, safeguard, keep, look after, sustain, husband. ANTONYMS squander.

con·sid·er /kən'sidər/ ▶ **v.** (**considers**, **considering**, **considered**) **1** think carefully about. **2** believe or think. **3** take into account when making a judgment.

SYNONYMS **1 think about**, contemplate, reflect on, mull over, ponder, deliberate on, chew over, meditate on, ruminate on, evaluate, appraise, take account of, bear in mind; informal size up. **2 deem**, think, believe, judge, rate, count, find, regard as, hold to be, reckon to be, view as, see as.

con·sid·er·a·ble /kən'sidər(ə)bəl, -'sidrəbəl/ ▶ **adj.** great in size, amount, or importance.

SYNONYMS **sizable**, substantial, appreciable, significant, plentiful, goodly; informal tidy. ANTONYMS paltry.

con·sid·er·a·bly /kən'sidər(ə)blē, -'sidrəblē/ ▶ **adv.** to a great extent: *alcoholic drinks vary considerably in strength.*

SYNONYMS **greatly**, (very) much, a great deal, a lot, lots, significantly, substantially, appreciably, markedly, noticeably; informal plenty.

con·sid·er·ate /kən'sidərət/ ▶ **adj.** careful not to harm or inconvenience other people.

SYNONYMS **attentive**, thoughtful, solicitous, kind, unselfish, caring, polite, sensitive.

■ **con·sid·er·ate·ly adv.**

con·sid·er·a·tion /kənˌsidə'rāsʜən/ ▶ **n.** **1** careful thought. **2** a fact taken into account when making a decision. **3** thoughtfulness toward other people.

SYNONYMS **1 thought**, deliberation, reflection, contemplation, examination, inspection, scrutiny, analysis, discussion, attention. **2 factor**, issue, matter, concern, aspect, feature. **3 attentiveness**, concern, care, thoughtfulness, solicitude, understanding, respect, sensitivity.

con·sid·er·ing /kən'sidəriɴɢ/ ▶ **prep. & conj.** taking something into account.

SYNONYMS **bearing in mind**, taking into consideration, taking into account, in view of, in light of.

con·sign /kən'sīn/ ▶ **v.** **1** deliver something to someone. **2** (**consign someone/thing to**) put someone or something in a place so as to be rid of them: *she consigned the letter to the wastebasket.*

con·sign·ment /kən'sīnmənt/ ▶ **n.** a batch of goods that are delivered.

con·sist /kən'sist/ ▶ **v.** **1** (**consist of**) be composed or made up of. **2** (**consist in**) have as an essential feature.

SYNONYMS (**consist of**) **be composed of**, be made up of, be formed of, comprise, include, contain.

con·sist·en·cy /kən'sistənsē/ ▶ **n.** (plural **consistencies**) **1** the state of being consistent. **2** the thickness of a liquid or semiliquid substance.

con·sist·ent /kən'sistənt/ ▶ **adj.** **1** always behaving in the same way; unchanging. **2** (usu. **consistent with**) in agreement.

SYNONYMS **1 constant**, regular, uniform, steady, stable, even, unchanging. **2** *her injuries were **consistent with** a knife attack* **compatible with**, in tune with, in line with, corresponding to, conforming to, consonant with. ANTONYMS irregular, incompatible.

■ **con·sist·ent·ly adv.**

con·sis·to·ry /kən'sistərē/ ▶ **n.** (plural **consistories**) (in the Roman Catholic Church) the council of cardinals.

con·so·la·tion /ˌkänsə'lāsʜən/ ▶ **n.** **1** comfort received after a loss or disappointment. **2** a source of such comfort.

SYNONYMS **comfort**, solace, sympathy, pity, commiseration, relief, encouragement, reassurance.

□ **consolation prize** a prize given to a competitor who just fails to win.

con·sole[1] /kən'sōl/ ▶ **v.** (**consoles**, **consoling**, **consoled**) comfort someone who is unhappy or disappointed about something.

SYNONYMS **comfort**, sympathize with, commiserate with, show compassion for, help, support, cheer (up), hearten, encourage, reassure, soothe. ANTONYMS upset.

con·sole² /ˈkänˌsōl/ ▸ n. **1** a panel or unit containing a set of controls for electronic or mechanical equipment. **2** a small machine for playing computerized video games.

con·sol·i·date /kənˈsäləˌdāt/ ▸ v. (**consolidates**, **consolidating**, **consolidated**) **1** make stronger or more solid. **2** combine into a single unit.

> SYNONYMS **1 strengthen**, secure, stabilize, reinforce, fortify. **2 combine**, unite, merge, integrate, amalgamate, fuse, synthesize.

■ **con·sol·i·da·tion** /-ˌsäləˈdāshən/ n.

con·som·mé /ˌkänsəˈmā/ ▸ n. a clear soup made with concentrated stock.

con·so·nance /ˈkänsənəns/ ▸ n. formal agreement or compatibility.

con·so·nant /ˈkänsənənt/ ▸ n. a letter of the alphabet representing a sound in which the breath is completely or partly obstructed. ▸ adj. (**consonant with**) formal in agreement or harmony with.

con·sort formal ▸ n. /ˈkänˌsôrt/ a wife, husband, or companion. ▸ v. /kənˈsôrt, ˈkänˌsôrt/ (**consort with**) habitually associate with.

> SYNONYMS ▸ v. *she is now consorting with the in-crowd* **associate**, keep company, mix, socialize, fraternize, have dealings.

con·sor·ti·um /kənˈsôrsh(ē)əm, -ˈsôrtēəm/ ▸ n. (plural **consortia** /-shēə, -tēə/ or **consortiums**) an association of several companies.

con·spic·u·ous /kənˈspikyōōəs/ ▸ adj. **1** clearly visible. **2** attracting notice: *conspicuous bravery*.

> SYNONYMS **obvious**, evident, apparent, visible, noticeable, clear, plain, marked, patent, blatant. ANTONYMS inconspicuous.

■ **con·spic·u·ous·ly** adv.

con·spir·a·cy /kənˈspirəsē/ ▸ n. (plural **conspiracies**) a secret plan by a group to do something unlawful or harmful.

> SYNONYMS **plot**, scheme, intrigue, plan, collusion.

con·spire /kənˈspīr/ ▸ v. (**conspires**, **conspiring**, **conspired**) **1** jointly make secret plans to commit a wrongful act. **2** (of circumstances) seem to be working together to bring about something bad.

> SYNONYMS **1 plot**, scheme, intrigue, maneuver, plan. **2 combine**, unite, join forces, work together.

■ **con·spir·a·tor** /kənˈspirətər/ n. **con·spir·a·to·ri·al** /kənˌspirəˈtôrēəl/ adj.

con·sta·ble /ˈkänstəbəl/ ▸ n. a peace officer with limited policing authority, typically in a small town.

con·stab·u·lar·y /kənˈstabyəˌlerē/ ▸ n. (plural **constabularies**) collectively, a town's constables.

con·stant /ˈkänstənt/ ▸ adj. **1** occurring continuously. **2** remaining the same. **3** faithful and dependable. ▸ n. **1** an unchanging situation. **2** Math & Physics a number or quantity that does not change its value.

> SYNONYMS ▸ adj. **1** *constant noise* **continuous**, persistent, sustained, ceaseless, unceasing, perpetual, incessant, never-ending, eternal, endless, nonstop. **2** *a constant speed* **consistent**, regular, steady, uniform, even, invariable, unvarying, unchanging. **3 faithful**, loyal, devoted, true, fast, firm, unswerving. ANTONYMS intermittent, variable, fickle.

■ **con·stan·cy** n. **con·stant·ly** adv.

con·stel·la·tion /ˌkänstəˈlāshən/ ▸ n. a group of stars forming a recognized pattern.

con·ster·na·tion /ˌkänstərˈnāshən/ ▸ n. anxiety or dismay.

> SYNONYMS **dismay**, distress, disquiet, discomposure, surprise, alarm, fear, fright, shock.

con·sti·pat·ed /ˈkänstəˌpātid/ ▸ adj. suffering from constipation.

con·sti·pa·tion /ˌkänstəˈpāshən/ ▸ n. difficulty in emptying the bowels.

con·stit·u·en·cy /kənˈstichōōənsē/ ▸ n. (plural **constituencies**) **1** a body of voters who elect a representative. **2** an area so represented.

con·stit·u·ent /kənˈstichōōənt/ ▸ adj. being a part of a whole. ▸ n. **1** a member of a constituency. **2** a part of a whole.

con·sti·tute /ˈkänstəˌt(y)ōōt/ ▸ v. (**constitutes**, **constituting**, **constituted**) **1** be a part of a whole. **2** be equivalent to. **3** establish by law.

> SYNONYMS **1 comprise**, make up, form, account for. **2 amount to**, be tantamount to, be equivalent to, represent. **3 establish**, inaugurate, found, create, set up.

con·sti·tu·tion /ˌkänstəˈt(y)ōōshən/ ▸ n. **1** a set of principles according to which a state or organization is governed. **2** (**the Constitution**) the basic written set of principles and precedents of federal government in the United States, which came into operation in 1789 and has since been modified by twenty-six amendments. **3** the composition or formation of something. **4** a person's physical or mental state.

> SYNONYMS **1 composition**, makeup, structure, construction, arrangement, configuration, formation, anatomy. **2 health**, condition, strength, stamina, build, physique.

con·sti·tu·tion·al /ˌkänstəˈt(y)ōōshənl/ ▸ adj. **1** relating or according to a constitution. **2** relating to a person's physical or mental state. ▸ n. dated a walk taken regularly so as to stay healthy.
■ **con·sti·tu·tion·al·ly** adv.

con·strain /kənˈstrān/ ▸ v. **1** force someone to do something. **2** (**constrained**) appearing forced or unnatural. **3** severely restrict or limit.

con·straint /kənˈstrānt/ ▸ n. a limitation or restriction.

> SYNONYMS **1 restriction**, limitation, curb, check, restraint, control. **2 inhibition**, uneasiness, embarrassment, self-consciousness, awkwardness. ANTONYMS freedom, ease.

con·strict /kənˈstrikt/ ▸ v. **1** make or become narrower; tighten. **2** stop someone moving or acting freely.

> SYNONYMS **narrow**, tighten, compress, contract, squeeze, strangle. ANTONYMS expand, dilate.

■ **con·stric·tion** n.

con·stric·tor /kənˈstriktər/ ▸ n. a snake that kills by squeezing and choking its prey.

con·struct ▸ v. /kənˈstrəkt/ build or put together. ▸ n. /ˈkänˌstrəkt/ an idea or theory containing various elements.

SYNONYMS ▶ v. **1 build**, erect, put up, set up, assemble, fabricate. **2 formulate**, create, form, put together, devise, compose, work out, frame. ANTONYMS demolish.

con·struc·tion /kənˈstrəksʜən/ ▶ n. **1** the process of constructing something. **2** a building or other structure. **3** an interpretation of something: *you could put an honest construction on their conduct.*

SYNONYMS **1 structure**, building, edifice, work. **2 interpretation**, explanation, analysis, reading, meaning; informal take.

con·struc·tive /kənˈstrəktiv/ ▶ adj. having a useful and helpful effect.

SYNONYMS **useful**, helpful, productive, positive, practical, valuable, profitable, worthwhile.

■ **con·struc·tive·ly** adv.

con·strue /kənˈstro͞o/ ▶ v. (**construes**, **construing**, **construed**) interpret something in a particular way.

con·sub·stan·ti·a·tion /ˌkänsəbˌstanchēˈāshən/ ▶ n. Christian Theology the doctrine that the substance of the bread and wine coexists with the body and blood of Christ in the Eucharist.

con·sul /ˈkänsəl/ ▶ n. **1** an official who is based in a foreign city and protects their country's citizens and interests there. **2** (in ancient Rome) each of two elected officials who ruled the republic jointly for a year. ■ **con·su·lar** /ˈkäns(y)ələr/ adj.

con·su·late /ˈkänsələt/ ▶ n. the place where a consul works.

con·sult /kənˈsəlt/ ▶ v. **1** try to get advice or information from. **2** have discussions or confer with someone, usually before undertaking a course of action.

SYNONYMS **1 seek advice from**, ask, call (on), turn to; informal pick someone's brain(s). **2 confer**, talk things over, communicate, deliberate, compare notes. **3 refer to**, look at, check.

■ **con·sul·ta·tive** adj.

con·sult·an·cy /kənˈsəltnsē/ ▶ n. (plural **consultancies**) a company that gives expert advice in a particular field.

con·sult·ant /kənˈsəltnt/ ▶ n. a person who provides expert advice professionally.

SYNONYMS **adviser**, expert, specialist, authority.

con·sul·ta·tion /ˌkänsəlˈtāshən/ ▶ n. **1** the process of consulting someone or discussing something. **2** a meeting to discuss something or to get advice or treatment.

SYNONYMS **1 discussion**, talk(s), dialogue, debate, negotiation, deliberation. **2 meeting**, talk, discussion, interview, audience, hearing.

con·sult·ing /kənˈsəltiɴɢ/ ▶ adj. giving specialist advice to others working in the same field: *a consulting engineer*. ▶ n. the business of giving specialist advice to others working in the same field.

con·sume /kənˈso͞om/ ▶ v. (**consumes**, **consuming**, **consumed**) **1** eat or drink. **2** use up. **3** (of a fire) completely destroy. **4** (of a feeling) absorb someone wholly: *she was consumed with guilt.*

SYNONYMS **1 eat**, devour, swallow, gobble up, wolf down, guzzle, drink. **2 use (up)**, expend, deplete, exhaust, spend. **3 destroy**, demolish, lay waste, raze, devastate, gut, ruin, wreck. **4 eat up**, devour, grip, overwhelm, absorb, obsess, preoccupy.

con·sum·er /kənˈso͞omər/ ▶ n. a person who buys a product or uses a service.

SYNONYMS **buyer**, purchaser, customer, shopper, user.

con·sum·er·ism /kənˈso͞oməˌrizəm/ ▶ n. the preoccupation of society with buying goods. ■ **con·sum·er·ist** adj.

con·sum·mate ▶ v. /ˈkänsəˌmāt/ (**consummates**, **consummating**, **consummated**) complete a transaction. ▶ adj. /ˈkänsəmət, kənˈsəmət/ showing great skill and flair. ■ **con·sum·ma·tion** /ˌkänsəˈmāshən/ n.

con·sump·tion /kənˈsəm(p)shən/ ▶ n. **1** the process of consuming, or an amount consumed. **2** dated tuberculosis. ■ **con·sump·tive** adj. (dated).

con·tact ▶ n. /ˈkänˌtakt/ **1** physical touching. **2** communicating or meeting. **3** a person whom you can ask for information or help. **4** a connection for an electric current to pass from one thing to another. ▶ v. /ˈkänˌtakt, kənˈtakt/ get in touch with.

SYNONYMS ▶ n. **1 communication**, correspondence, connection, relations, dealings, touch. **2 connection**, link, acquaintance, associate, friend. ▶ v. **get in touch with**, communicate with, approach, notify, speak to, write to, come forward; informal get (a) hold of.

□ **contact lens** a plastic lens placed on the surface of the eye to help you see better. **contact sport** a sport that must involve bodily contact between the participants.

con·ta·gion /kənˈtājən/ ▶ n. the passing of a disease from one person to another by close contact.

con·ta·gious /kənˈtājəs/ ▶ adj. **1** (of a disease) spread by contact between people. **2** having a contagious disease.

SYNONYMS **infectious**, communicable, transmittable, transmissible; informal catching.

con·tain /kənˈtān/ ▶ v. **1** have or hold something inside. **2** control or restrain. **3** prevent a problem from becoming worse.

SYNONYMS **1 hold**, carry, enclose, accommodate, have room for. **2 include**, comprise, incorporate, involve, consist of, be made up of, be composed of. **3 restrain**, control, curb, rein in, suppress, stifle, swallow, bottle up, keep in check.

con·tain·er /kənˈtānər/ ▶ n. **1** a box or similar object for holding something. **2** a large metal box for transporting goods.

SYNONYMS **receptacle**, vessel, holder, repository.

con·tain·ment /kənˈtānmənt/ ▶ n. the keeping of something harmful under control.

con·tam·i·nate /kənˈtaməˌnāt/ ▶ v. (**contaminates**, **contaminating**, **contaminated**) make something dirty or poisonous by allowing it to come into contact with harmful substances.

SYNONYMS **pollute**, taint, poison, stain, adulterate, defile, debase, corrupt. ANTONYMS purify.

■ **con·tam·i·na·tion** /-ˌtaməˈnāshən/ n.

con·tem·plate /ˈkäntəmˌplāt/ ▶ v. (**contemplates**, **contemplating**, **contemplated**) **1** look at thoughtfully. **2** think about. **3** think deeply and at length.

SYNONYMS **1 look at**, gaze at, stare at, view, regard, examine, inspect, observe, survey, study, eye. **2 think about**, ponder, reflect on, consider, mull over, muse on, dwell on, deliberate over, meditate on, ruminate on, chew over. **3 envisage**, consider, think about, have in mind, intend, plan, propose.

■ **con·tem·pla·tion** /ˌkäntəmˈplāsʜən/ **n.**

con·tem·pla·tive /kənˈtemplətiv/ ▶ **adj.** showing or involving contemplation: *a contemplative mood.* ▶ **n.** a person whose life is devoted to prayer, especially in a monastery or convent.

SYNONYMS ▶ **adj. thoughtful**, pensive, reflective, meditative, ruminative, introspective, brooding, deep/lost in thought.

con·tem·po·ra·ne·ous /kənˌtempəˈrānēəs/ ▶ **adj.** existing at or happening in the same period of time.

con·tem·po·rar·y /kənˈtempəˌrerē/ ▶ **adj. 1** living or happening at the same time. **2** belonging to or happening in the present. **3** modern in style. ▶ **n.** (plural **contemporaries**) a person living or working in the same period as another.

SYNONYMS ▶ **adj. 1** *contemporary sources* **of the time**, contemporaneous, concurrent, coexisting, coeval. **2** *contemporary society* **modern**, present-day, present, current. **3** *a very contemporary design* **modern**, up to date, up to the minute, fashionable, recent; informal trendy. ANTONYMS former, old-fashioned.

SPELLING

Contem**porary**, not -**pory**.

con·tempt /kənˈtem(p)t/ ▶ **n. 1** the feeling that someone or something is worthless. **2** (also **contempt of court**) the offense of disobeying or being disrespectful to a court of law.

SYNONYMS **scorn**, disdain, derision, disgust, disrespect. ANTONYMS respect.

□ **beneath contempt** completely worthless.

con·tempt·i·ble /kənˈtem(p)təbəl/ ▶ **adj.** deserving contempt.

SYNONYMS **despicable**, detestable, beneath contempt, reprehensible, deplorable, unspeakable, disgraceful, shameful, ignominious, abject, low, mean, cowardly, discreditable, worthless, shabby, cheap. ANTONYMS admirable.

■ **con·tempt·i·bly adv.**

con·temp·tu·ous /kənˈtem(p)ᴄʜo͞oəs/ ▶ **adj.** showing contempt.

SYNONYMS **scornful**, disdainful, derisive, mocking, sneering, scoffing, condescending, dismissive. ANTONYMS respectful.

■ **con·temp·tu·ous·ly adv.**

con·tend /kənˈtend/ ▶ **v. 1** (**contend with** or **against**) struggle to deal with a difficulty. **2** (**contend for**) struggle to achieve. **3** put forward a view in an argument.

SYNONYMS **1 compete**, vie, battle, tussle, struggle, jostle, strive. **2 assert**, maintain, hold, claim, argue, insist, allege.

■ **con·tend·er n.**

con·tent¹ /kənˈtent/ ▶ **adj.** peacefully happy or satisfied. ▶ **v.** satisfy or please. ▶ **n.** a state of happiness or satisfaction.

SYNONYMS ▶ **adj. satisfied**, contented, pleased, gratified, fulfilled, happy, glad, cheerful, at ease, at peace, relaxed, comfortable, untroubled. ANTONYMS dissatisfied. ▶ **v. satisfy**, comfort, gratify, gladden, please, soothe, placate, appease, mollify.

con·tent² /ˈkänˌtent/ ▶ **n. 1** (**contents**) the things that are contained in something. **2** the amount of a particular thing occurring in a substance: *soy milk has a low fat content.* **3** (**contents**) a list of chapters given at the front of a book or magazine. **4** the material in a piece of writing, as opposed to its form or style.

SYNONYMS **1 constituents**, ingredients, components. **2 amount**, proportion, level. **3 subject matter**, theme, argument, thesis, message, substance, material, ideas.

con·tent·ed /kənˈtentəd/ ▶ **adj.** happy or satisfied.

SYNONYMS see **CONTENT¹** (adjective).

■ **con·tent·ed·ly adv.**

con·ten·tion /kənˈtenᴄʜən/ ▶ **n. 1** heated disagreement. **2** a point of view that is expressed. □ **in contention** having a good chance of success in a contest.

con·ten·tious /kənˈtenᴄʜəs/ ▶ **adj.** causing disagreement or controversy; controversial.

SYNONYMS **controversial**, debatable, disputed, open to debate, moot, vexed.

con·tent·ment /kənˈtentmənt/ ▶ **n.** a state of happiness and satisfaction.

SYNONYMS **contentedness**, content, satisfaction, fulfillment, happiness, pleasure, cheerfulness, ease, comfort, well-being, peace.

con·test ▶ **n.** /ˈkänˌtest/ an event in which people compete to see who is the best. ▶ **v.** /kənˈtest, ˈkänˌtest/ **1** take part in a competition or election. **2** challenge or dispute a decision or theory.

SYNONYMS ▶ **n. 1 competition**, match, tournament, rally, race, game, bout. **2 fight**, battle, tussle, struggle, competition, race. ▶ **v. 1** *he will contest the seat* **compete for**, contend for, vie for, fight for. **2** *the parties contesting the election* **compete in**, take part in, fight, enter. **3 oppose**, challenge, take issue with, question, call into question, object to. ANTONYMS accept.

con·test·ant /kənˈtestənt/ ▶ **n.** a person who takes part in a contest.

SYNONYMS **competitor**, participant, player, contender, candidate, entrant.

con·text /ˈkänˌtekst/ ▶ **n. 1** the circumstances surrounding an event, statement, or idea. **2** the parts that come immediately before and after a word or passage and make its meaning clearer.

SYNONYMS **circumstances**, conditions, frame of reference, factors, state of affairs, situation, background, scene, setting.

■ **con·tex·tu·al** /kənˈteksᴄʜo͞oəl/ **adj.**

con·tig·u·ous /kənˈtigyo͞oəs/ ▶ **adj. 1** sharing a border. **2** next or together in sequence.

con·ti·nent¹ /ˈkäntn-ənt, ˈkäntnənt/ ▶ **n. 1** any of the world's main continuous expanses of land (Europe, Asia, Africa, North and South America, Australia, Antarctica). **2** (**the Continent**) the mainland of Europe.

con·ti·nent² ▶ adj. **1** able to control movements of the bowels and bladder. **2** restrained; self-disciplined. ▪ **con·ti·nence** n.

con·ti·nen·tal /ˌkäntn'entl/ ▶ adj. **1** forming or belonging to a continent. **2** coming from or like mainland Europe. **3** (also **Continental**) having to do with the 13 original colonies of the US. ▶ n. a person from mainland Europe. ▫ **continental breakfast** a light breakfast of coffee and bread rolls. **continental drift** the very gradual movement of the continents across the earth's surface through millions of years. **continental shelf** an area of seabed around a large landmass where the sea is relatively shallow.

con·tin·gen·cy /kən'tinjənsē/ ▶ n. (plural **contingencies**) **1** a future event that may happen but cannot be predicted with certainty. **2** a plan made in case a particular thing happens.

> SYNONYMS **eventuality**, possibility, chance event, incident, occurrence, accident, emergency.

con·tin·gent /kən'tinjənt/ ▶ n. a group of people forming part of a larger group. ▶ adj. **1** (**contingent on**) dependent on. **2** depending on chance.

con·tin·u·al /kən'tinyo͞oəl/ ▶ adj. happening constantly or often, with intervals in between: *he met with continual delays.*

> SYNONYMS **1** *continual breakdowns* **frequent**, regular, repeated, constant, recurrent, recurring, habitual. **2** *continual pain* **constant**, continuous, unremitting, unrelenting, nonstop, sustained, chronic, uninterrupted, incessant, ceaseless, unceasing, never-ending, unbroken, perpetual. ANTONYMS occasional, temporary.

▪ **con·tin·u·al·ly** adv.

> USAGE
>
> Note that **continual** and **continuous** don't mean exactly the same thing.

con·tin·u·a·tion /kənˌtinyə'wāsʜən/ ▶ n. **1** the action of continuing. **2** a part that is attached to something else and is an extension of it.

con·tin·ue /kən'tinyo͞o/ ▶ v. (**continues, continuing, continued**) **1** keep doing something; carry on with. **2** keep existing or happening. **3** carry on traveling in the same direction. **4** start doing something again.

> SYNONYMS **1 carry on**, go on, keep on, persist, persevere, proceed, pursue, keep at; informal stick at. **2** *we hope to continue this relationship* **maintain**, keep up, sustain, keep going, keep alive, preserve, perpetuate. **3** *his willingness to continue in office* **remain**, stay, carry on, keep going. **4** *we continued our conversation* **resume**, pick up, take up, carry on with, return to, revisit. ANTONYMS stop.

con·ti·nu·i·ty /ˌkäntn'(y)o͞oətē/ ▶ n. (plural **continuities**) **1** the fact of not stopping or changing. **2** an unbroken connection or line of development. **3** organization of a movie or television program so that the plot makes sense and clothing, scenery, etc., remain the same in different scenes.

con·tin·u·ous /kən'tinyo͞oəs/ ▶ adj. forming an unbroken whole or sequence without interruptions or exceptions: *a day of continuous rain.*

> SYNONYMS **continual**, persistent, sustained, ceaseless, unceasing, unremitting, unrelenting, perpetual, incessant, never-ending, eternal, endless, nonstop, unbroken, uninterrupted. ANTONYMS intermittent.

▪ **con·tin·u·ous·ly** adv.

con·tin·u·um /kən'tinyo͞oəm/ ▶ n. (plural **continua** /-yo͞oə/) a continuous sequence in which the elements change gradually.

con·tort /kən'tôrt/ ▶ v. twist or bend something out of its normal shape.

> SYNONYMS **twist**, bend out of shape, distort, misshape, warp, buckle, deform.

▪ **con·tor·tion** n.

con·tor·tion·ist /kən'tôrsʜənist/ ▶ n. an entertainer who twists and bends their body into unnatural positions.

con·tour /'känˌto͝or/ ▶ n. **1** an outline of the shape or form of something. **2** (also **contour line**) a line on a map joining points of equal height. ▪ **con·toured** adj.

con·tra·band /'käntrəˌband/ ▶ n. goods that have been imported or exported illegally.

con·tract ▶ n. /'känˌtrakt/ **1** an official, legally binding agreement. **2** informal an arrangement for someone to be murdered by a hired killer. ▶ v. /kən'trakt/ **1** make or become smaller. **2** become shorter and tighter. **3** shorten a word or phrase. **4** /'känˌtrakt, kən'trakt/ make a formal and legally binding agreement to do something. **5** /'känˌtrakt, kən'trakt/ catch or develop a disease.

> SYNONYMS ▶ n. **agreement**, arrangement, commitment, settlement, understanding, compact, covenant, deal, bargain. ▶ v. **1 shrink**, diminish, reduce, decrease, dwindle, decline. **2 tighten**, tense, flex, constrict, draw in. **3 engage**, take on, hire, commission, employ. **4 catch**, pick up, come/go down with, develop. ANTONYMS expand, relax, lengthen.

▫ **contract bridge** the standard form of the card game bridge. ▪ **con·trac·tu·al** /kən'trakcʜo͞oəl/ adj.

con·tract·i·ble /kən'traktəbəl/ ▶ adj. able to be shrunk or capable of contracting.

con·trac·tion /kən'traksʜən/ ▶ n. **1** the process of contracting. **2** a shortening of the muscles of the uterus happening at intervals during childbirth. **3** a shortened form of a word or words.

> SYNONYMS **1 shrinking**, shrinkage, decline, decrease, diminution, dwindling. **2 tightening**, tensing, flexing. **3 abbreviation**, short form, shortening.

con·trac·tor /'känˌtraktər/ ▶ n. a person or company that undertakes to provide materials or labor for a job, especially a construction job.

con·tra·dict /ˌkäntrə'dikt/ ▶ v. deny the truth of a statement made by someone by saying the opposite.

> SYNONYMS **1 deny**, refute, rebut, dispute, challenge, counter. **2 argue with**, go against, challenge, oppose. ANTONYMS confirm, agree with.

con·tra·dic·tion /ˌkäntrə'diksʜən/ ▶ n. **1** a combination of statements, ideas, or features that are opposed to one another. **2** saying the opposite to something already said.

> SYNONYMS **1 conflict**, clash, disagreement, inconsistency, mismatch. **2 denial**, refutation,

rebuttal, countering. ANTONYMS agreement, confirmation.

con·tra·dic·to·ry /ˌkäntrəˈdikt(ə)rē/ ▶ **adj.** **1** inconsistent with or opposing each other. **2** containing inconsistent elements.

SYNONYMS **inconsistent**, incompatible, irreconcilable, opposed, opposite, contrary, conflicting, at variance.

con·tra·dis·tinc·tion /ˌkäntrədəˈstiNGkSHən/ ▶ **n.** distinction made by contrasting two things.

con·tral·to /kənˈtraltō/ ▶ **n.** (plural **contraltos**) the lowest female singing voice.

con·trap·tion /kənˈtrapSHən/ ▶ **n.** a machine or device that appears strange or unnecessarily complicated.

SYNONYMS **device**, gadget, apparatus, machine, appliance, mechanism, invention, contrivance; informal gizmo, widget.

con·tra·pun·tal /ˌkäntrəˈpəntl/ ▶ **adj.** Music relating to or in counterpoint.

con·trar·i·wise /ˈkänˌtrerēˌwīz, kənˈtre(ə)rē-/ ▶ **adv.** in the opposite way.

con·trar·y ▶ **adj.** /ˈkänˌtre(ə)rē/ **1** opposite in nature, direction, or meaning. **2** (of two or more statements, beliefs, etc.) opposed to one another. **3** /kənˈtre(ə)rē/ deliberately inclined to do the opposite of what is expected or wanted. ▶ **n.** /ˈkänˌtre(ə)rē/ (**the contrary**) the opposite.

SYNONYMS ▶ **adj. 1 opposite**, opposing, contradictory, clashing, conflicting, antithetical, incompatible, irreconcilable. **2 perverse**, awkward, difficult, uncooperative, obstinate, pigheaded, intractable; informal balky. ANTONYMS compatible, accommodating. ▶ **n. opposite**, reverse, converse, antithesis.

■ **con·trar·i·ness** **n.**

con·trast ▶ **n.** /ˈkänˌtrast/ **1** the state of being noticeably different from something else. **2** a thing or person noticeably different from another. **3** the amount of difference between tones in a television picture, photograph, etc. ▶ **v.** /ˈkänˌtrast, kənˈtrast/ **1** be noticeably different. **2** compare two things to emphasize their differences.

SYNONYMS ▶ **n. 1 difference**, dissimilarity, disparity, divergence, variance, distinction, comparison. **2 opposite**, antithesis, foil, complement. ANTONYMS similarity. ▶ **v. 1** *a view that contrasts with his earlier opinion* **differ from**, be at variance with, be contrary to, conflict with, be at odds with, disagree with, clash with. **2** *they contrasted her with her sister* **compare with/to**, juxtapose with/to, measure against, distinguish from, differentiate from. ANTONYMS resemble, liken.

con·tra·vene /ˌkäntrəˈvēn/ ▶ **v.** (**contravenes**, **contravening**, **contravened**) **1** do something that breaks a law, treaty, etc. **2** conflict with a right, principle, etc. ■ **con·tra·ven·tion** /ˌkäntrəˈvenCHən/ **n.**

con·tre·temps /ˈkäntrəˌtäN, ˌkôNtrəˈtäN/ ▶ **n.** (plural **contretemps**) a minor disagreement.

con·trib·ute /kənˈtribyo͞ot, -byət/ ▶ **v.** (**contributes**, **contributing**, **contributed**) **1** give something in order to help an undertaking or effort. **2** (**contribute to**) help to cause or bring about.

SYNONYMS **give**, donate, put up, grant, provide, supply; informal chip in.

con·tri·bu·tion /ˌkäntrəˈbyo͞oSHən/ ▶ **n.** **1** a gift or payment to a common fund or collection. **2** the part played by a person or thing in causing or advancing something: *his contribution to 20th century music cannot be overstated.* **3** an item that forms part of a journal, book, broadcast, or discussion.

SYNONYMS **gift**, donation, offering, present, handout, grant, subsidy.

con·trib·u·tor /kənˈtribyo͞otər, -byətər/ ▶ **n.** a person who contributes something.

SYNONYMS **donor**, benefactor, supporter, backer, patron, sponsor.

con·trib·u·to·ry /kənˈtribyəˌtôrē/ ▶ **adj.** **1** playing a part in bringing something about. **2** (of a pension or insurance plan) operated by means of a fund into which people pay.

con·trite /kənˈtrīt/ ▶ **adj.** sorry for something that you have done.

SYNONYMS **remorseful**, repentant, penitent, regretful, sorry, apologetic, rueful, sheepish, hangdog, ashamed, shamefaced.

■ **con·trite·ly** **adv.** **con·tri·tion** /kənˈtriSHən/ **n.**

con·triv·ance /kənˈtrīvəns/ ▶ **n.** **1** a clever device or scheme. **2** the action of contriving something.

con·trive /kənˈtrīv/ ▶ **v.** (**contrives**, **contriving**, **contrived**) **1** plan or achieve something in a clever or skillful way. **2** manage to do something, especially something foolish.

SYNONYMS **1 create**, engineer, manufacture, devise, concoct, construct, fabricate, hatch. **2 manage**, find a way, engineer a way, arrange. ANTONYMS fail.

con·trived /kənˈtrīvd/ ▶ **adj.** deliberately created and seeming artificial; not natural or spontaneous.

SYNONYMS **forced**, strained, labored, overdone, unnatural, artificial, false, affected. ANTONYMS natural.

con·trol /kənˈtrōl/ ▶ **n.** **1** the power to influence people's behavior or the course of events. **2** the restriction of something: *pest control.* **3** a way of regulating or limiting something: *controls on local spending.* **4** a person or thing used as a standard of comparison for checking the results of a survey or experiment. ▶ **v.** (**controls**, **controlling**, **controlled**) **1** have control or command of. **2** limit or regulate.

SYNONYMS ▶ **n. 1 power**, authority, command, dominance, sway, management, direction, leadership, rule, government, sovereignty, supremacy. **2 limit**, limitation, restriction, restraint, check, curb, regulation. **3 self-control**, self-restraint, composure, calm; informal cool. ▶ **v. 1 run**, manage, direct, preside over, supervise, command, rule, govern, lead, dominate. **2** *she struggled to control her temper* **restrain**, keep in check, curb, hold back, suppress, repress. **3** *public spending was controlled* **limit**, restrict, curb, cap.

□ **control tower** a tall building at an airport from which the movements of aircraft are controlled. ■ **con·trol·la·ble** **adj.**

con·trol·ler /kənˈtrōlər/ ▶ **n.** a person in charge of an organization's finances.

con·tro·ver·sial /ˌkäntrəˈvərSHəl, -ˈvərsēəl/ ▶ **adj.** causing or likely to cause controversy.

SYNONYMS **disputed**, contentious, moot, debatable, arguable, vexed.

■ **con·tro·ver·sial·ly** adv.

con·tro·ver·sy /ˈkäntrəˌvərsē/ ▶ n. (plural **controversies**) debate or disagreement about a subject that arouses strong opinions.

SYNONYMS **dispute**, disagreement, argument, debate, contention, quarrel, war of words, storm.

con·tu·me·ly /kənˈt(y)o͞oməlē, ˈkänt(y)əˌmēlē, ˈkänˌt(y)o͞omlē/ ▶ n. (plural **contumelies**) old use insulting language or treatment.

con·tu·sion /kənˈto͞ozʜən/ ▶ n. a bruise.

co·nun·drum /kəˈnəndrəm/ ▶ n. (plural **conundrums**) **1** a difficult problem or question. **2** a riddle.

con·ur·ba·tion /ˌkänərˈbāsʜən/ ▶ n. an area consisting of several towns merging together or with a city.

con·va·lesce /ˌkänvəˈles/ ▶ v. (**convalesces**, **convalescing**, **convalesced**) gradually get better after an illness or injury.

SYNONYMS **recuperate**, get better, recover, get well, get back on your feet.

con·va·les·cent /ˌkänvəˈlesənt/ ▶ adj. recovering from an illness or injury. ■ **con·va·les·cence** n.

con·vec·tion /kənˈveksʜən/ ▶ n. the process by which heat moves through a gas or liquid as the warmer part rises and the cooler part sinks.

con·vec·tor /kənˈvektər/ ▶ n. a heater that circulates warm air by convection.

con·vene /kənˈvēn/ ▶ v. (**convenes**, **convening**, **convened**) **1** call people together for a meeting. **2** come together for a meeting.

SYNONYMS **1** *he convened a meeting* **summon**, call, order. **2** *the committee convened* **assemble**, gather, meet, come together; formal foregather.

■ **con·ven·er** (or **convenor**) n.

con·ven·ience /kənˈvēnyəns/ ▶ n. **1** freedom from effort or difficulty. **2** a useful or helpful device or situation.

SYNONYMS **1 advantage**, benefit, expedience, suitability. **2 ease of use**, usefulness, utility, accessibility, availability. ANTONYMS inconvenience.

□ **at your convenience** when or where it suits you. **convenience food** packaged food that needs little cooking.

con·ven·ient /kənˈvēnyənt/ ▶ adj. **1** fitting in well with a person's needs, activities, and plans. **2** involving little trouble or effort.

SYNONYMS **1 suitable**, favorable, advantageous, appropriate, opportune, timely, expedient. **2 nearby**, handy, well-situated, practical, useful, accessible.

■ **con·ven·ient·ly** adv.

con·vent /ˈkänˌvent/ ▶ n. a building where nuns live together.

con·ven·tion /kənˈvencʜən/ ▶ n. **1** a way in which something is usually done. **2** socially acceptable behavior. **3** a large meeting or conference, especially of members of a political party or a particular profession. **4** an agreement between countries.

SYNONYMS **1 custom**, usage, practice, tradition, etiquette, protocol. **2 agreement**, accord, protocol, pact, treaty. **3 conference**, meeting, congress, assembly, gathering.

con·ven·tion·al /kənˈvencʜənl/ ▶ adj. **1** based on or following what is generally done. **2** not individual or adventurous. **3** (of weapons or power) non-nuclear.

SYNONYMS **1 orthodox**, traditional, established, accepted, customary, received, prevailing, normal, standard, regular, ordinary, usual, typical. **2 conservative**, traditional, conformist, old-fashioned; informal square, stick-in-the-mud. **3 unoriginal**, formulaic, predictable, unadventurous, run-of-the-mill, routine, pedestrian. ANTONYMS unorthodox, original.

■ **con·ven·tion·al·ly** adv.

con·verge /kənˈvərj/ ▶ v. (**converges**, **converging**, **converged**) **1** come together from different directions. **2** (**converge on**) come from different directions and meet at.

SYNONYMS **meet**, intersect, cross, connect, link up, join, merge. ANTONYMS diverge.

■ **con·ver·gent** adj.

con·ver·sant /kənˈvərsənt/ ▶ adj. (**conversant with**) familiar with or knowledgeable about.

con·ver·sa·tion /ˌkänvərˈsāsʜən/ ▶ n. an informal talk between two or more people.

SYNONYMS **discussion**, talk, chat, gossip, tête-à-tête, exchange, dialogue; informal chinwag.

■ **con·ver·sa·tion·al** adj.

con·ver·sa·tion·al·ist /ˌkänvərˈsāsʜənl-ist/ ▶ n. a person who is good at or fond of engaging in conversation.

con·verse¹ /kənˈvərs/ ▶ v. (**converses**, **conversing**, **conversed**) hold a conversation.

con·verse² ▶ n. /ˈkänˌvərs/ something that is the opposite of another. ▶ adj. /ˈkänˌvərs, kənˈvərs/ opposite. ■ **con·verse·ly** adv.

con·ver·sion /kənˈvərzʜən/ ▶ n. **1** the action of converting. **2** the fact of changing your religion or beliefs. **3** the adaptation of a building for a new purpose. **4** Football the act of scoring an extra point or points after having scored a touchdown. **5** Rugby a successful kick at goal after a try.

SYNONYMS **change**, transformation, metamorphosis, alteration, adaptation, modification, redevelopment, rebuilding, remodeling.

con·vert ▶ v. /kənˈvərt/ **1** change the form, character, or function of something. **2** change money or units into others of a different kind. **3** adapt a building for a new purpose. **4** change your or someone else's religious faith. ▶ n. /ˈkänˌvərt/ a person who has changed their religious faith.

SYNONYMS ▶ v. **1 change**, transform, alter, adapt, turn, modify, redevelop, remodel, rebuild, reorganize, metamorphose. **2 win over**, convince, persuade, claim, redeem, save, reform, re-educate, proselytize, evangelize.

con·vert·i·ble /kənˈvərtəbəl/ ▶ adj. **1** able to be converted. **2** (of a car) having a folding or detachable roof. ▶ n. a convertible car.

con·vex /känˈveks, ˈkänˌveks, kənˈveks/ ▶ adj. having an outline or surface that curves outward.

con·vey /kənˈvā/ ▶ v. **1** transport or carry to a place. **2** communicate an idea or feeling.

SYNONYMS **1 transport**, carry, bring, take, fetch, move. **2 communicate**, pass on, impart, relate, relay, transmit, send. **3 express**, get across/over, put across/over, communicate, indicate.

con·vey·ance /kən'vāəns/ ▶ **n. 1** the action of conveying. **2** formal a means of transport. **3** the legal process of transferring property from one owner to another. ■ **con·vey·anc·ing n.**

con·vey·or /kən'vāər/ (also **conveyer**) ▶ **n. 1** a person or thing that transports or communicates something. **2** a conveyor belt. □ **conveyor belt** a continuous moving band used for transporting objects from one place to another.

con·vict ▶ **v.** /kən'vikt/ officially declare that someone is guilty of a criminal offense. ▶ **n.** /'kän,vikt/ a person in prison after being convicted of a criminal offense.

SYNONYMS ▶ **v. find guilty**, sentence. ANTONYMS acquit. ▶ **n. prisoner**, inmate, criminal, offender, felon; informal jailbird, con.

con·vic·tion /kən'vikSHən/ ▶ **n. 1** an instance of being convicted of a criminal offense. **2** a firmly held belief or opinion. **3** the quality of showing that you believe strongly in what you are saying or doing.

SYNONYMS **1 belief**, opinion, view, persuasion, ideal, position, stance, value. **2 assurance**, confidence, certainty. ANTONYMS diffidence.

con·vince /kən'vins/ ▶ **v.** (**convinces**, **convincing**, **convinced**) **1** cause someone to believe firmly that something is true. **2** persuade someone to do something.

SYNONYMS **1** *he convinced me I was wrong* **assure**, persuade, satisfy, prove to. **2** *I convinced her to marry me* **persuade**, induce, prevail on, talk into, win over, coax, cajole.

con·vinc·ing /kən'vinsiNG/ ▶ **adj. 1** able to convince someone. **2** (of a victory or a winner) leaving no margin of doubt.

SYNONYMS **1 persuasive**, powerful, strong, forceful, compelling, cogent, plausible, irresistible, telling. **2** *a convincing win* **resounding**, emphatic, decisive, conclusive. ANTONYMS unconvincing.

■ **con·vinc·ing·ly adv.**

con·viv·i·al /kən'vivēəl, kən'vivyəl/ ▶ **adj. 1** (of an atmosphere or event) friendly and lively. **2** (of a person) cheerfully sociable.

SYNONYMS **friendly**, genial, affable, amiable, congenial, agreeable, cordial, warm, sociable, outgoing, gregarious, cheerful.

■ **con·viv·i·al·i·ty** /kən,vivē'alitē/ **n.**

con·vo·ca·tion /,känvə'kāSHən/ ▶ **n.** a large formal assembly of people.

con·voke /kən'vōk/ ▶ **v.** (**convokes**, **convoking**, **convoked**) formal call together an assembly or meeting.

con·vo·lut·ed /'känvə,lo͞otid/ ▶ **adj. 1** (of an argument or account) very complex. **2** folded or twisted in an elaborate way.

con·vo·lu·tion /,känvə'lo͞oSHən/ ▶ **n. 1** a coil or twist. **2** (**convolutions**) something complex and difficult to follow.

con·vol·vu·lus /kən'välvyələs, -'vôl-/ ▶ **n.** (plural **convolvuluses**) a twining plant with trumpet-shaped flowers.

con·voy /'kän,voi/ ▶ **n.** a group of ships or vehicles traveling together under armed protection.

SYNONYMS **group**, fleet, cavalcade, motorcade, cortège, caravan, line.

con·vulse /kən'vəls/ ▶ **v.** (**convulses**, **convulsing**, **convulsed**) **1** suffer convulsions. **2** (**be convulsed**) make sudden, uncontrollable movements because of emotion, laughter, etc. ■ **con·vul·sive adj.**

con·vul·sion /kən'vəlSHən/ ▶ **n. 1** a sudden, irregular movement of the body caused by muscles contracting uncontrollably. **2** (**convulsions**) uncontrollable laughter. **3** a violent upheaval.

coo /ko͞o/ ▶ **v.** (**coos**, **cooing**, **cooed**) **1** (of a pigeon or dove) make a soft murmuring sound. **2** speak in a soft, gentle voice. ▶ **n.** a cooing sound.

cook /ko͝ok/ ▶ **v. 1** prepare food or a meal by heating the ingredients. **2** (of food) be heated so as to become edible. **3** informal alter accounts dishonestly. **4** (**cook something up**) informal invent a story or plan. ▶ **n.** a person who cooks.

SYNONYMS ▶ **v. prepare**, make, put together; informal fix, rustle up.

cook·book /'ko͝ok,bo͝ok/ ▶ **n.** a recipe book.

cook·er·y /'ko͝okərē/ ▶ **n.** the practice or skill of preparing and cooking food.

cook·ie /'ko͝okē/ ▶ **n.** (plural **cookies**) **1** a small, sweet cake, usually round, flat, and crisp. **2** informal a person of a particular kind: *she's a tough cookie.* **3** a packet of data stored on a computer, sent by an Internet server to a browser and returned by the browser each time it accesses the same server.

cook·ing /'ko͝okiNG/ ▶ **n. 1** the process or skill of preparing food by heating it. **2** food that has been prepared in a particular way: *authentic Italian cooking.*

cool /ko͞ol/ ▶ **adj. 1** fairly cold. **2** stopping you from becoming too hot. **3** unfriendly or unenthusiastic. **4** not anxious or excited: *he kept a cool head.* **5** informal fashionably attractive or impressive. **6** informal excellent. ▶ **n. 1** the state of being cold. **2** the state of being calm and self-controlled. ▶ **v.** (**cools**, **cooling**, **cooled**) make or become cool.

SYNONYMS ▶ **adj. 1 chilly**, chill, bracing, cold, brisk, crisp, fresh; informal nippy. **2 unenthusiastic**, lukewarm, tepid, indifferent, uninterested, apathetic. **3 unfriendly**, distant, remote, aloof, cold, chilly, frosty, unwelcoming; informal standoffish. **4 calm**, collected, composed, self-possessed, poised, serene, relaxed, at ease, unruffled, unperturbed; informal unflappable, together, laid-back. ANTONYMS warm, enthusiastic, friendly, panicky. ▶ **n. 1 chill**, chilliness, coldness, coolness. **2 self-control**, control, composure, self-possession, calmness, aplomb, poise. ANTONYMS warmth, panic. ▶ **v. chill**, refrigerate, freeze. ANTONYMS warm.

□ **cooling-off period 1** an interval during which the parties in a dispute can try to settle their differences before taking further action. **2** an interval after a sale contract is agreed on during which the purchaser can decide to cancel without loss. **cooling tower** an open-topped concrete tower, used for cooling water or condensing steam from an industrial process. ■ **cool·ly adv. cool·ness n.**

cool·ant /'ko͞olənt/ ▶ **n.** a fluid used to cool an engine or other device.

cool·er /'ko͞olər/ ▶ **n. 1** a device or container for keeping things cool. **2** (**the cooler**) informal prison.

coo·lie /'ko͞olē/ ▶ **n.** (plural **coolies**) dated, offensive an unskilled laborer in an Asian country.

coon /ko͞on/ ▶ **n.** a raccoon.

coop /ko͞op, ko͝op/ ▶ **n.** a cage or pen for poultry. ▶ **v.** (**coop someone/thing up**) confine a person or animal in a small space.

co-op /ˈkōˌäp, kōˈäp/ ▶ **n.** informal a cooperative.

coop·er /ˈko͞opər, ˈko͝opər/ ▶ **n.** a person who makes or repairs casks and barrels.

co·op·er·ate /kōˈäpəˌrāt/ ▶ **v.** (**cooperates, cooperating, cooperated**) **1** work together toward the same end. **2** do what someone wants.

> SYNONYMS **1 collaborate**, work together, pull together, join forces, team up, unite, combine, pool resources. **2 assist**, help, lend a hand, be of service, do your bit/part; informal play ball.

co·op·er·a·tion /kōˌäpəˈrāsʜən/ ▶ **n.** the process of working together to achieve something.

> SYNONYMS **1 collaboration**, joint action, combined effort, teamwork, give and take, compromise. **2 assistance**, help.

co·op·er·a·tive /kōˈäp(ə)rətiv/ (or **co-operative**) ▶ **adj. 1** involving cooperation. **2** willing to help. **3** (of a farm or other business) owned and run jointly by its members. ▶ **n.** a cooperative organization.

> SYNONYMS ▶ **adj. 1 collaborative**, collective, combined, joint, shared, united, concerted. **2 helpful**, eager to help, obliging, accommodating, willing.

■ **co·op·er·a·tive·ly** adv.

co-opt /kōˈäpt, ˈkōˌäpt/ ▶ **v. 1** appoint someone as a member of a committee or other body. **2** adopt an idea or policy for your own use.

co·or·di·nate (or **co-ordinate**) ▶ **v.** /kōˈôrdəˌnāt/ (**coordinates, coordinating, coordinated**) **1** bring the different elements of something together so that it works well. **2** (**coordinate with**) negotiate with other people to work together effectively. **3** (of different things) match or look attractive together. ▶ **n.** /kōˈôrdn-ət/ Math each of a group of numbers used to indicate the position of a point, line, or plane.

> SYNONYMS ▶ **v. organize**, arrange, order, synchronize, bring together, orchestrate.

■ **co·or·di·na·tor** n.

co·or·di·na·tion /kōˌôrdnˈāsʜən/ (or **co-ordination**) ▶ **n. 1** the process of coordinating. **2** the ability to move different parts of the body smoothly and at the same time.

coot /ko͞ot/ ▶ **n.** a waterbird with black feathers and a white bill.

cop /käp/ informal ▶ **n.** a police officer. ▶ **v.** (**cops, copping, copped**) **1** arrest an offender. **2** steal. **3** receive or experience something unwelcome. **4** (**cop out**) avoid doing something that you ought to do.

cope¹ /kōp/ ▶ **v.** (**copes, coping, coped**) deal effectively with something difficult.

> SYNONYMS **1 manage**, survive, look after yourself, fend for yourself, get by/through, hold your own. **2** *his inability to cope with the situation* **deal with**, handle, manage, address, face (up to), confront, tackle, come to grips with.

cope² ▶ **n.** a long cloak worn by a priest on ceremonial occasions.

Co·per·ni·can sys·tem /kəˈpərnikən/ (also **Copernican theory**) ▶ **n.** the theory proposed by the astronomer Nicolaus Copernicus that the sun is the center of the solar system, with the planets orbiting round it.

cop·i·er /ˈkäpēər/ ▶ **n.** a machine that makes exact copies of something.

co·pi·lot /ˈkōˌpīlət/ ▶ **n.** a second pilot in an aircraft.

cop·ing /ˈkōpiɴɢ/ ▶ **n.** the top line of bricks or stones in a wall.

co·pi·ous /ˈkōpēəs/ ▶ **adj.** in large amounts; plentiful.

> SYNONYMS **abundant**, plentiful, ample, profuse, extensive, generous, lavish, liberal, overflowing, in abundance, numerous, many; informal galore; literary plenteous. ANTONYMS sparse.

■ **co·pi·ous·ly** adv.

cop·per¹ /ˈkäpər/ ▶ **n. 1** a reddish-brown metal. **2** a reddish-brown color.

cop·per² ▶ **n.** informal a police officer.

cop·per·plate /ˌkäpərˈplāt, ˈkäpərˌplāt/ ▶ **n.** an elaborate style of handwriting.

cop·pice /ˈkäpəs/ ▶ **n.** an area of woodland in which the trees or shrubs are periodically cut back to ground level.

cop·ra /ˈkäprə/ ▶ **n.** dried coconut kernels, from which oil is obtained.

copse /käps/ ▶ **n.** a small group of trees.

Copt /käpt/ ▶ **n. 1** a native Egyptian in the periods of Greek and Roman domination. **2** a member of the Coptic Church, the native Christian Church in Egypt.

Cop·tic /ˈkäptik/ ▶ **n.** the language of the Copts.

cop·y /ˈkäpē/ ▶ **n.** (plural **copies**) **1** a thing made to be similar or identical to another. **2** a single example of a particular book, record, etc. **3** material for a newspaper or magazine article. ▶ **v.** (**copies, copying, copied**) **1** make a copy of. **2** imitate the behavior or style of.

> SYNONYMS ▶ **n. 1 duplicate**, facsimile, photocopy; trademark Xerox. **2 replica**, reproduction, imitation, likeness, forgery, fake, counterfeit. ▶ **v. 1 duplicate**, photocopy, xerox, photostat, reproduce. **2 reproduce**, replicate, forge, fake, counterfeit. **3 imitate**, reproduce, emulate, mimic; informal rip off.

■ **cop·y·ist** n.

cop·y·book /ˈkäpēˌbo͝ok/ ▶ **n.** a book containing models of handwriting for learners to imitate. ▶ **adj.** done in exactly in the proper way: *a copybook landing.*

cop·y·cat /ˈkäpēˌkat/ ▶ **n.** informal a person who copies another.

cop·y·ed·it /ˈkäpēˌedit/ ▶ **v.** edit text to be printed by checking its consistency and accuracy. ■ **cop·y·ed·i·tor** n.

cop·y·right /ˈkäpēˌrīt/ ▶ **n.** the exclusive right to publish, perform, film, or record literary, artistic, or musical material.

cop·y·writ·er /ˈkäpiˌrītər/ ▶ **n.** a person who writes advertisements or publicity material.

co·quette /kōˈket/ ▶ **n.** a flirtatious woman. ■ **co·quet·ry** /ˈkōkətrē, kōˈketrē/ n. **co·quet·tish** adj.

cor·a·cle /ˈkôrəkəl, ˈkär-/ ▶ **n.** a small round boat made of wickerwork covered with a watertight material.

cor·al /ˈkôrəl, ˈkär-/ ▶ **n. 1** a hard substance found in warm seas that consists of the skeletons of small animals living together as a stationary group. **2** a pinkish-red color.

cor·bel /ˈkôrbəl/ ▶ **n.** a projection jutting out from a wall to support a structure above it.

cord /kôrd/ ▶ **n. 1** thin string or rope made from several twisted strands. **2** a flexible insulated cable used for carrying electric current to an appliance. **3** corduroy. **4** (**cords**) trousers made of corduroy.

SYNONYMS **string**, thread, line, rope, cable, wire, twine, yarn.

USAGE

Don't confuse **cord** with **chord**, which means 'a group of musical notes.'

cor·dial /ˈkôrjəl/ ▶ **adj. 1** warm and friendly. **2** sincere. ▶ **n.** a liqueur. ■ **cor·dial·i·ty** /ˌkôrjēˈalitē/ **n. cor·dial·ly adv.**

cord·ite /ˈkôrˌdīt/ ▶ **n.** a kind of explosive.

cord·less /ˈkôrdləs/ ▶ **adj.** (of an electrical appliance) working without connection to a main supply or central unit.

cor·don /ˈkôrdn/ ▶ **n.** a line or circle of police, soldiers, or guards forming a barrier. ▶ **v.** (**cordon something off**) close a place off by means of a cordon.

SYNONYMS ▶ **n. barrier**, line, chain, ring, circle.

cor·don bleu /ˌkôrdôN ˈblœ/ ▶ **adj.** Cooking **1** of the highest class. **2** used to describe an escalope of veal or chicken rolled and filled with cheese and ham, and fried in breadcrumbs.

cor·du·roy /ˈkôrdəˌroi/ ▶ **n.** a thick cotton fabric with velvety ridges.

core /kôr/ ▶ **n. 1** the tough central part of a fruit. **2** the central or most important part of something. ▶ **v.** (**cores**, **coring**, **cored**) remove the core from a fruit.

SYNONYMS ▶ **n. 1** *the earth's core* **center**, interior, middle, nucleus. **2** *the core of the argument* **heart**, nucleus, nub, kernel, meat, essence, crux, pith, substance; informal nitty-gritty.

□ **to the core** to the depths of your being.

cor·gi /ˈkôrgē/ ▶ **n.** (plural **corgis**) a breed of dog with short legs and a pointed face.

co·ri·an·der /ˈkôrēˌandər, ˌkôrēˈandər/ ▶ **n.** a plant used as an herb in cooking.

cork /kôrk/ ▶ **n. 1** a light, soft brown substance obtained from the bark of a tree. **2** a bottle stopper made of cork. ▶ **v. 1** seal a bottle with a cork. **2** (**corked**) (of wine) spoiled by a faulty cork.

cork·age /ˈkôrkij/ ▶ **n.** a charge made by a restaurant for serving wine that has been brought in by a customer.

cork·er /ˈkôrkər/ ▶ **n.** informal an excellent person or thing. ■ **cork·ing adj.**

cork·screw /ˈkôrkˌskro͞o/ ▶ **n.** a device used for pulling corks from bottles. ▶ **v.** move or twist in a spiral.

corm /kôrm/ ▶ **n.** an underground part of certain plants, such as crocuses, gladioli, and cyclamens.

cor·mo·rant /ˈkôrmərənt/ ▶ **n.** a diving seabird with a long hooked bill and black feathers.

corn¹ /kôrn/ ▶ **n. 1** a cereal plant that yields large grains, or kernels, set in rows on a cob. **2** informal something sentimental or overused. □ **corned beef** beef preserved with salt. **corn on the cob** corn cooked and eaten straight from the cob.

corn² ▶ **n.** a painful area of thickened skin on the toes or foot.

corn·ball /ˈkôrnˌbôl/ ▶ **adj.** trite and sentimental. ▶ **n.** a person with trite or sentimental ideas.

corn·bread /ˈkôrnˌbred/ ▶ **n.** a type of bread made from cornmeal.

corn·cob /ˈkôrnˌkäb/ ▶ **n.** the central part of an ear of corn, to which the grains are attached.

corn·crake /ˈkôrnˌkrāk/ ▶ **n.** a crake inhabiting coarse grasslands, with a distinctive rasping call.

cor·ne·a /ˈkôrnēə/ ▶ **n.** the transparent layer forming the front of the eye.

cor·ner /ˈkôrnər/ ▶ **n. 1** a place or angle where two or more sides or edges meet. **2** a place where two streets meet. **3** a part, region, or area, especially one regarded as secluded or remote. **4** a difficult or awkward position. **5** Soccer a free kick taken by the attacking side from a corner of the field. ▶ **v.** (**corners**, **cornering**, **cornered**) **1** force someone into a place or situation from which it is hard to escape. **2** go around a bend in a road. **3** control the trade in a particular type of goods.

SYNONYMS ▶ **n. 1 bend**, curve, turn, junction, hairpin turn. **2 district**, region, area, quarter; informal neck of the woods. ▶ **v. 1 surround**, trap, hem in, pen in, cut off. **2 gain control of**, take over, dominate, monopolize, capture; informal sew up.

cor·ner·stone /ˈkôrnərˌstōn/ ▶ **n. 1** a vital part. **2** a stone that forms the base of a corner of a building.

cor·net /kôrˈnet/ ▶ **n.** a brass instrument resembling a trumpet but shorter and wider.

corn·flakes /ˈkôrnˌflāks/ ▶ **pl.n.** a breakfast cereal consisting of toasted flakes made from corn flour.

corn·flow·er /ˈkôrnˌflouər/ ▶ **n.** a plant with deep blue flowers.

cor·nice /ˈkôrnis/ ▶ **n.** a decorative border around the wall of a room just below the ceiling.

corn·meal /ˈkôrnˌmēl/ ▶ **n.** meal made from ground, dried corn.

corn·starch /ˈkôrnˌstärcʜ/ ▶ **n.** finely ground corn flour, used as a thickener in cooking.

cor·nu·co·pi·a /ˌkôrn(y)əˈkōpēə/ ▶ **n.** a plentiful supply of good things.

corn·y /ˈkôrnē/ ▶ **adj.** (**cornier**, **corniest**) informal sentimental or unoriginal.

co·rol·la /kəˈrälə, kəˈrōlə/ ▶ **n.** the petals of a flower.

cor·ol·lar·y /ˈkôrəˌlerē, ˈkärə-/ ▶ **n.** (plural **corollaries**) **1** a direct consequence or result. **2** a logical conclusion.

co·ro·na /kəˈrōnə/ ▶ **n.** (plural **coronae** /-nē, -nī/) **1** the gases surrounding the sun or a star. **2** a small circle of light around the sun or moon.

cor·o·nar·y /ˈkôrəˌnerē, ˈkär-/ ▶ **adj.** having to do with the heart, in particular with the arteries that supply it with blood. ▶ **n.** (plural **coronaries**) (also **coronary thrombosis**) a blockage of the flow of blood to the heart.

cor·o·na·tion /ˌkôrəˈnāsʜən, ˌkär-/ ▶ **n.** the ceremony of crowning a king or queen.

cor·o·ner /ˈkôrənər, ˈkär-/ ▶ **n.** an official who holds inquests into violent, sudden, or suspicious deaths.

cor·o·net /ˌkôrəˈnet, ˌkär-/ ▶ **n. 1** a small or simple crown. **2** a decorative band put around the head.

cor·po·ra /ˈkôrpərə/ plural of **corpus**.

cor·po·ral¹ /ˈkôrp(ə)rəl/ ▶ **n.** a rank of officer in the army, below sergeant.

cor·po·ral² ▶ adj. relating to the human body. □ **corporal punishment** physical punishment, such as caning.

cor·po·rate /ˈkôrp(ə)rət/ ▶ adj. **1** relating to a business corporation. **2** relating to or shared by all members of a group: *corporate responsibility.*

cor·po·ra·tion /ˌkôrpəˈrāsʜən/ ▶ n. a large company, or a group of companies acting as a single unit.

> SYNONYMS **company**, firm, business, concern, operation, conglomerate, group, chain, multinational.

cor·po·re·al /kôrˈpôrēəl/ ▶ adj. relating to a person's body; physical rather than spiritual.

corps /kôr/ ▶ n. (plural **corps**) **1** a large unit of an army. **2** a branch of an army with a particular kind of work. **3** a group of people involved in a particular activity: *the press corps.*

corps de bal·let /ˌkôr də baˈlā/ ▶ n. **1** the members of a ballet company who dance together as a group. **2** the lowest rank of dancers in a ballet company.

corpse /kôrps/ ▶ n. a dead body.

> SYNONYMS **dead body**, carcass, remains; informal stiff; Medicine cadaver.

cor·pu·lent /ˈkôrpyələnt/ ▶ adj. (of a person) fat. ■ **cor·pu·lence** n.

cor·pus /ˈkôrpəs/ ▶ n. (plural **corpora** /ˈkôrpərə/ or **corpuses**) a collection of written works.

cor·pus·cle /ˈkôrˌpəsəl/ ▶ n. a red or white blood cell.

cor·ral /kəˈral/ ▶ n. a pen for animals on a farm or ranch. ▶ v. (**corrals**, **corralling**, **corralled**) **1** drive animals into a corral. **2** gather a group together.

cor·rect /kəˈrekt/ ▶ adj. **1** free from mistakes; true or right. **2** following accepted social standards. ▶ v. **1** put something right. **2** mark the mistakes in a piece of writing. **3** tell someone that they are wrong.

> SYNONYMS ▶ adj. **1 right**, accurate, exact, true, perfect; informal spot on. **2 proper**, decent, right, respectable, decorous, seemly, suitable, appropriate, accepted. ANTONYMS wrong, improper. ▶ v. **rectify**, right, put right, set right, amend, remedy, repair, reform, cure.

■ **cor·rect·ly** adv. **cor·rect·ness** n.

cor·rec·tion /kəˈreksʜən/ ▶ n. **1** the process of correcting. **2** a change that corrects a mistake or inaccuracy.

> SYNONYMS **rectification**, righting, amendment, repair, remedy, cure.

cor·rec·tive /kəˈrektiv/ ▶ adj. designed to put something right.

cor·re·late /ˈkôrəˌlāt, ˈkär-/ ▶ v. (**correlates**, **correlating**, **correlated**) place things together so that one thing depends on another and vice versa.

cor·re·la·tion /ˌkôrəˈlāsʜən/ ▶ n. **1** a situation in which one thing depends on another and vice versa. **2** the process of correlating two or more things.

cor·re·spond /ˌkôrəˈspänd, ˌkär-/ ▶ v. **1** match or agree almost exactly. **2** be similar or the same. **3** communicate by exchanging letters.

> SYNONYMS **1 be consistent**, correlate, agree, accord, coincide, tally, tie in, match; informal square. **2** (**corresponding**) **equivalent**, related, parallel, matching, comparable, analogous. **3 exchange letters**, write, communicate.

cor·re·spond·ence /ˌkôrəˈspändəns, ˌkär-/ ▶ n. **1** letters sent or received. **2** a close connection or similarity.

> SYNONYMS **1 letters**, messages, mail, post, communication. **2 correlation**, parallel, agreement, consistency, conformity, similarity, resemblance, comparability.

□ **correspondence course** a course of study in which student and instructors communicate by mail.

> SPELLING
> The ending is **-ence**, not **-ance**: correspond**ence**.

cor·re·spond·ent /ˌkôrəˈspändənt, ˌkär-/ ▶ n. **1** a journalist who reports on a particular subject. **2** a person who writes letters.

> SYNONYMS **reporter**, journalist, columnist, writer, contributor, commentator.

cor·ri·dor /ˈkôrədər, ˈkär-, -ˌdôr/ ▶ n. **1** a passage in a building or train, with doors leading into rooms or compartments. **2** a strip of land linking two other areas. □ **the corridors of power** the senior levels of government or administration.

> SPELLING
> Write **-dor**, not **-door**: corri**dor**.

cor·rob·o·rate /kəˈräbəˌrāt/ ▶ v. (**corroborates**, **corroborating**, **corroborated**) confirm or give your support to a statement or theory. ■ **cor·rob·o·ra·tion** /kəˌräbəˈrāsʜən/ n.

cor·rode /kəˈrōd/ ▶ v. (**corrodes**, **corroding**, **corroded**) **1** slowly wear away a hard material by the action of a chemical. **2** gradually weaken or destroy: *the loss of her job corroded her self-esteem.*

cor·ro·sion /kəˈrōzʜən/ ▶ n. the process of corroding, or damage caused by it.

cor·ro·sive /kəˈrōsiv, -ziv/ ▶ adj. tending to cause corrosion.

cor·ru·gat·ed /ˈkôrəˌgātid, ˈkär-/ ▶ adj. shaped into alternate ridges and grooves. ■ **cor·ru·ga·tion** /ˌkôrəˈgāsʜən, ˌkär-/ n.

cor·rupt /kəˈrəpt/ ▶ adj. **1** willing to act dishonestly in return for money or other reward. **2** evil or immoral. **3** (of a written work or computer data) unreliable because of mistakes or alterations. ▶ v. make corrupt.

> SYNONYMS ▶ adj. **1 dishonest**, unscrupulous, criminal, fraudulent, illegal, unlawful; informal crooked. **2 immoral**, depraved, degenerate, debauched, vice-ridden, perverted, dissolute. ANTONYMS honest, ethical, pure. ▶ v. **deprave**, pervert, lead astray, debauch, defile, pollute, sully.

■ **cor·rupt·ly** adv.

cor·rup·tion /kəˈrəpsʜən/ ▶ n. **1** dishonest or illegal behavior. **2** the action of corrupting. **3** an alteration or error in a text or computer data.

> SYNONYMS **1 dishonesty**, unscrupulousness, double-dealing, fraud, misconduct, bribery, payola, venality; informal graft, sleaze. **2 immorality**, depravity, vice, degeneracy, perversion, debauchery, wickedness, evil, sin. ANTONYMS honesty, morality.

cor·sage /kôrˈsäzʜ, -ˈsäj/ ▶ n. a small bunch of flowers worn pinned to a woman's clothes or around her wrist.

cor·sair /ˈkôrˌse(ə)r/ ▶ **n.** old use a pirate.

cor·set /ˈkôrsət/ ▶ **n.** a tight-fitting undergarment worn to shape a woman's figure or to support a person's back.

cor·tège /kôrˈtezн, ˈkôrˌtezн/ ▶ **n.** a funeral procession.

cor·tex /ˈkôrˌteks/ ▶ **n.** (plural **cortices** /-təˌsēz/) the outer layer of an organ or structure, especially the outer layer of the brain.

cor·ti·sone /ˈkôrtəˌsōn/ ▶ **n.** a steroid hormone used to treat inflammation and allergy.

co·run·dum /kəˈrəndəm/ ▶ **n.** an extremely hard form of aluminum oxide, used for grinding, smoothing, and polishing.

cor·us·cat·ing /ˈkôrəˌskātiNG, ˈkär-/ ▶ **adj.** literary flashing or sparkling: *coruscating flashes of white energy.*

cor·vette /kôrˈvet/ ▶ **n.** a small warship designed for escorting convoys.

cos /käs, kôs/ ▶ **abbr.** cosine.

co·sec /ˈkōsek/ ▶ **abbr.** cosecant.

co·se·cant /kōˈsēˌkant, -kənt/ ▶ **n.** (in a right triangle) the ratio of the hypotenuse to the side opposite an acute angle.

cosh /käsн/ ▶ **n.** a thick, heavy stick or bar used as a weapon. ▶ **v.** hit someone on the head with a cosh.

co·sine /ˈkōˌsīn/ ▶ **n.** Math (in a right triangle) the ratio of the side next to a particular acute angle to the longest side.

cos·met·ic /käzˈmetik/ ▶ **adj.** **1** (of treatment) intended to improve a person's appearance. **2** improving something only outwardly: *a little paint provided a cosmetic change to the house.* ▶ **n.** (**cosmetics**) substances put on the face and body to make them more attractive.

> SYNONYMS ▶ **adj.** **superficial**, surface, skin-deep, outward, external. ANTONYMS fundamental.

cos·mic /ˈkäzmik/ ▶ **adj.** relating to the universe.

cos·mog·o·ny /käzˈmägənē/ ▶ **n.** (plural **cosmogonies**) the branch of science concerned with the origin of the universe, especially the solar system. ■ **cos·mo·gon·ic** /ˌkäzməˈgänik/ **adj.**

cos·mol·o·gy /käzˈmäləjē/ ▶ **n.** the science of the origin and development of the universe. ■ **cos·mo·log·i·cal** /ˌkäzməˈläjikəl/ **adj.** **cos·mol·o·gist** **n.**

cos·mo·naut /ˈkäzməˌnôt, -ˌnät/ ▶ **n.** a Russian astronaut.

cos·mo·pol·i·tan /ˌkäzməˈpälitn/ ▶ **adj.** **1** made up of people from many different countries and cultures: *Barcelona is one of Europe's most cosmopolitan cities.* **2** familiar with many different countries.

> SYNONYMS **1 multicultural**, multiracial, international, worldwide, global. **2 sophisticated**, cultivated, cultured, worldly, suave, urbane.

cos·mos /ˈkäzməs, -ˌmōs, -ˌmäs/ ▶ **n.** the universe.

Cos·sack /ˈkäsˌak, -ək/ ▶ **n.** a member of a people of Russia and Ukraine famous for being good horseback riders.

cos·set /ˈkäsət/ ▶ **v.** (**cossets**, **cosseting**, **cosseted**) look after and protect someone in a way that is too indulgent.

cost /kôst/ ▶ **v.** (**costs**, **costing**, **cost**) **1** be able to be bought or done for a specific price. **2** involve the loss of: *his heroism cost him his life.* **3** (**costs**, **costing**, **costed**) (often **cost something out**) estimate the cost of work that needs to be done. ▶ **n.** **1** an amount given or required as payment. **2** the effort or loss necessary to achieve something: *the cuts came at the cost of customer service.* **3** (**costs**) legal expenses.

> SYNONYMS ▶ **v.** **1 be priced at**, sell for, be valued at, fetch, come to, amount to; informal set someone back, go for. **2 price**, value, put a price/value/figure on. ▶ **n.** **1 price**, fee, tariff, fare, toll, levy, charge, payment, value, rate, outlay; humorous damage. **2 sacrifice**, loss, toll, harm, damage, price. **3** *we need to cover our costs* **expenses**, outgoings, overheads, expenditure, spend, outlay.

□ **at all costs** (or **at any cost**) regardless of the price or the effort needed. **cost-effective** effective or productive in relation to its cost.

co·star /ˈkōˌstär, kōˈstär/ ▶ **n.** a leading actor or actress appearing with another or others of equal importance. ▶ **v.** appear as a costar in a play, movie, etc.

Cos·ta Ri·can /ˌkōstə ˈrēkən, ˌkôstə, ˌkästə/ ▶ **n.** a person from Costa Rica. ▶ **adj.** relating to Costa Rica.

cost·ing /ˈkôstiNG/ ▶ **n.** the estimated cost of producing or undertaking something.

cost·ly /ˈkôstlē/ ▶ **adj.** (**costlier**, **costliest**) **1** expensive. **2** causing suffering, loss, or disadvantage: *the government's most costly mistake.*

> SYNONYMS **1 expensive**, dear, high-cost, overpriced; informal steep, pricey. **2 catastrophic**, disastrous, calamitous, ruinous, damaging, harmful, deleterious. ANTONYMS cheap.

■ **cost·li·ness** **n.**

cos·tume /ˈkäsˌt(y)o͞om, -təm/ ▶ **n.** **1** a set of clothes in a style typical of a particular country or historical period. **2** a set of clothes worn by an actor or performer for a role. ▶ **v.** (**be costumed**) be dressed in a costume.

> SYNONYMS ▶ **n.** **clothes**, garments, outfit, ensemble, dress, clothing, attire, garb, uniform, livery; formal apparel.

□ **costume jewelry** jewelry made with inexpensive materials or imitation gems.

cos·tu·mi·er /käsˈt(y)o͞omēər, -mēā/ ▶ **n.** a person who makes or supplies theatrical or fancy-dress costumes.

cot /kät/ ▶ **n.** **1** a portable bed that can be folded up, used for camping or for guests. **2** a plain narrow bed.

co·tan·gent /kōˈtanjənt/ ▶ **n.** (in a right triangle) the ratio of the side (other than the hypotenuse) adjacent to a particular acute angle to the side opposite the angle.

cote /kōt, kät/ ▶ **n.** a shelter for mammals or birds, especially pigeons.

co·te·rie /ˈkōtərē, ˌkōtəˈrē/ ▶ **n.** (plural **coteries**) a small, close-knit group of people.

cot·tage /ˈkätij/ ▶ **n.** a small house in the country.

> SYNONYMS **cabin**, lodge, bungalow, country house, chalet, shack, shanty.

□ **cottage cheese** soft, lumpy white cheese. **cottage industry** a business or manufacturing activity carried on in people's homes.

cot·ter pin /ˈkätər/ ▶ **n.** a metal pin used to fasten two parts of a mechanism together.

cot·ton /ˈkätn/ ▶ **n.** **1** soft white fibers surrounding the seeds of a plant that grows in warm climates. **2** cloth or thread made from these fibers.

▶ v. (**cotton on**) informal begin to understand. ▫ **absorbent cotton** fluffy soft material used for cleaning the skin or a wound. **cotton candy** a mass of artificially colored spun sugar wrapped around a stick.

cot·y·le·don /ˌkätlˈēdn/ ▶ n. the first leaf that grows from a seed.

couch /kouch/ ▶ n. a long padded piece of furniture for sitting or lying on. ▶ v. (**couch something in**) express something in language of a particular style: *some warnings are couched in general terms.*

SYNONYMS ▶ n. **sofa**, settee, divan, chaise longue, chesterfield, daybed, davenport, love seat, ottoman. ▶ v. **express**, phrase, word, frame, put, formulate, style, convey, say, state, utter.

▫ **couch potato** informal a person who watches a lot of television.

cou·gar /ˈkoogər/ ▶ n. **1** a large American wild cat with a plain tawny to grayish coat, found from Canada to Patagonia. **2** informal a mature woman who dates younger men.

cough /kôf/ ▶ v. **1** send out air from the lungs with a sudden sharp sound. **2** (**cough something up**) informal reluctantly give money or information. ▶ n. **1** an act of coughing. **2** an illness of the throat or lungs causing coughing.

SYNONYMS ▶ v. **hack**, hawk, bark, clear your throat. ▶ n. **bark**, hack; informal frog in your throat.

could /kood/ ▶ modal v. past of CAN[1].

could·n't /ˈkoodnt/ ▶ contr. could not.

cou·lomb /ˈkooˌläm, -ˌlōm/ ▶ n. a unit of electric charge.

coun·cil /ˈkounsəl/ ▶ n. **1** a group of people that meet regularly to discuss or organize something. **2** a group of people elected to manage the affairs of a city, county, or district.

SYNONYMS **1** *the Student Council* **committee**, board, commission, assembly, panel, synod. **2** *the town council* **authority**, government, administration, executive, chamber, assembly.

coun·cil·man /ˈkounsəlmən/ ▶ n. (plural **councilmen**) a person, especially a man, who is a member of a council.

coun·ci·lor /ˈkouns(ə)lər/ ▶ n. a member of a council.

USAGE

Note the difference between **councilor** and **counselor**.

coun·cil·wom·an /ˈkounsəlˌwoomən/ ▶ n. (plural **councilwomen**) a woman who is a member of a council.

coun·sel /ˈkounsəl/ ▶ n. **1** advice. **2** (plural **counsel**) a lawyer involved in a case. ▶ v. (**counsels**, **counseling**, **counseled**) **1** advise or recommend. **2** give professional help and advice to someone with psychological or personal problems.

SYNONYMS ▶ n. **1 advice**, guidance, counseling, recommendations, suggestions, direction. **2 lawyer**, attorney, attorney-at-law, counselor, advocate. ▶ v. **advise**, recommend, advocate, encourage, warn, caution, guide.

▫ **keep your own counsel** not reveal your plans or opinions.

coun·se·lor /ˈkouns(ə)lər/ ▶ n. a person trained to give advice on personal or psychological problems.

count[1] /kount/ ▶ v. **1** find the total number of. **2** recite numbers in ascending order. **3** take into account: *the staff has shrunk to five, if you count the director.* **4** regard as being: *people she counted as her friends.* **5** be important. **6** (**count on**) rely on. **7** (**count someone in** or **out**) include (or not include) someone in an activity. ▶ n. **1** an act of counting. **2** a total found by counting: *a low pollen count.* **3** a point to be discussed or considered. **4** Law each of the charges against an accused person.

SYNONYMS ▶ v. **1 add up**, reckon up, total, tally, calculate, compute. **2 include**, take into account/consideration, take account of, allow for. **3 consider**, think, feel, regard, look on as, view as, hold to be, judge, deem. **4 matter**, be important, be of consequence, be significant, signify, carry weight, rate.

▫ **down (or out) for the count 1** Boxing defeated by being knocked to the ground and unable to get up within ten seconds. **2** informal unconscious or asleep.

count[2] ▶ n. a European nobleman whose rank corresponds to that of an English earl.

count·down /ˈkountˌdoun/ ▶ n. **1** an act of counting backward to zero. **2** the final moments before a significant event.

coun·te·nance /ˈkountn-əns/ ▶ n. a person's face or expression. ▶ v. (**countenances**, **countenancing**, **countenanced**) tolerate or allow.

coun·ter[1] /ˈkountər/ ▶ n. **1** a long flat surface over which goods are sold or served or across which business is conducted with customers. **2** a small disk used in board games or to represent a coin. **3** a person or thing that counts something. ▫ **under the counter** bought or sold secretly and illegally.

coun·ter[2] ▶ v. (**counters**, **countering**, **countered**) **1** argue against or reply to. **2** try to stop or prevent: *he helped to counter an invasion.* ▶ adv. (**counter to**) **1** in the opposite direction to. **2** in opposition to.

SYNONYMS ▶ v. **1 respond to**, parry, hit back at, answer. **2 oppose**, dispute, argue against/with, contradict, challenge, contest. ANTONYMS support.

coun·ter·act /ˈkountərˌakt/ ▶ v. do something to reduce or prevent the bad effects of: *meditation can counteract the effects of stress.*

SYNONYMS **offset**, counterbalance, balance (out), cancel (out), work against, countervail, neutralize, nullify, prevent.

coun·ter·at·tack /ˈkountərəˌtak/ ▶ n. an attack made in response to an attack. ▶ v. attack in response.

coun·ter·bal·ance /ˈkountərˌbaləns/ ▶ n. **1** a weight that balances another. **2** something that has an equal but opposite effect to something else. ▶ v. /ˌkountərˈbaləns/ (**counterbalances**, **counterbalancing**, **counterbalanced**) have an equal but opposite effect to.

coun·ter·clock·wise /ˌkountərˈkläkˌwīz/ ▶ adv. & adj. in the opposite direction to the way in which a clock's hands move around.

coun·ter·es·pi·o·nage /ˌkountərˈespēəˌnäzh, -ˌnäj/ ▶ n. activities designed to prevent spying by an enemy.

coun·ter·feit /ˈkountərˌfit/ ▶ adj. made in exact imitation of something valuable so as to deceive or cheat people. ▶ n. a forgery. ▶ v. imitate something dishonestly.

SYNONYMS ▶ adj. **fake**, pirate, bogus, forged, imitation; informal phony. ANTONYMS genuine. ▶ n. **fake**, forgery, copy, reproduction, imitation, fraud, sham; informal phony. ANTONYMS original. ▶ v. **fake**, forge, copy, reproduce, imitate, falsify.

coun·ter·mand /ˌkountər'mand, 'kountərˌmand/ ▶ v. cancel an order.

coun·ter·meas·ure /'kountərˌmezHər/ ▶ n. something done to deal with a danger or threat.

coun·ter·pane /'kountərˌpān/ ▶ n. dated a bedspread.

coun·ter·part /'kountərˌpärt/ ▶ n. a person or thing that corresponds to another.

SYNONYMS **equivalent**, opposite number, peer, equal, parallel, complement, analog, match, twin, mate, fellow.

coun·ter·point /'kountərˌpoint/ ▶ n. **1** the playing of two or more tunes at the same time. **2** a tune played at the same time as another.

coun·ter·poise /'kountərˌpoiz/ ▶ n. a counterbalance. ▶ v. (**counterpoises**, **counterpoising**, **counterpoised**) counterbalance.

coun·ter·pro·duc·tive /ˌkountərprə'dəktiv/ ▶ adj. having the opposite effect to the one intended.

coun·ter·sign /'kountərˌsīn/ ▶ v. sign a document that has already been signed by another person.

coun·ter·sink /'kountərˌsiNGk/ ▶ v. (**countersinks**, **countersinking**, **countersunk** /-ˌsəNGk/) insert a screw or bolt so that the head lies flat with the surface.

coun·ter·ten·or /'kountərˌtenər/ ▶ n. the highest male adult singing voice.

coun·ter·ter·ror·ism /ˌkountər'terəˌrizəm/ ▶ n. political or military activities designed to prevent terrorism: *he specialized in counterterrorism, hostage rescue, and close-quarters combat.*

coun·ter·top /'kountərˌtäp/ ▶ n. a flat surface for working on in a kitchen.

coun·ter·vail·ing /ˌkountər'vāliNG/ ▶ adj. having an equal but opposite effect: *there are countervailing arguments.*

count·ess /'kountəs/ ▶ n. **1** the wife or widow of a count or earl. **2** a woman holding the rank of count or earl.

count·ing /'kountiNG/ ▶ prep. taking account of; including.

count·less /'kountləs/ ▶ adj. too many to be counted; very many.

SYNONYMS **innumerable**, numerous, untold, legion, numberless, limitless, incalculable; informal umpteen, gazillions of. ANTONYMS few.

coun·tri·fied /'kəntriˌfīd/ ▶ adj. characteristic of the country or country life.

coun·try /'kəntrē/ ▶ n. (plural **countries**) **1** a nation with its own government. **2** areas outside large towns and cities. **3** an area of land with particular physical features: *hilly country.*

SYNONYMS **1 nation**, (sovereign) state, kingdom, realm, land, territory, province. **2 people**, public, population, populace, citizens, nation; informal John Q. Public. **3 terrain**, land, territory, landscape, countryside, scenery, surroundings, environment. **4 countryside**, provinces, rural areas, backwoods, backcountry, hinterland; informal sticks, boondocks, boonies.

□ **country club** a club in a country or suburban area with sporting and social facilities, such as a golf course and a restaurant. **country dance** a traditional type of English dance, in particular one performed by couples facing each other in long lines. **country music** (or **country and western**) a kind of popular music from rural areas of the southern United States.

coun·try·man /'kəntrēmən/ (or **countrywoman**) ▶ n. (plural **countrymen** or **countrywomen**) **1** a person living or born in the country. **2** a person from the same country as someone else.

coun·try·side /'kəntrēˌsīd/ ▶ n. land and scenery outside towns and cities.

SYNONYMS see **COUNTRY** (senses 3 & 4)

coun·ty /'kountē/ ▶ n. (plural **counties**) **1** each of the main areas into which some countries are divided for the purposes of local government. **2** each of the main areas into which US states are divided for the purposes of government.

SYNONYMS **shire**, province, territory, region, district, area.

□ **county seat** the town that is the administrative center of a county.

coup /ko͞o/ ▶ n. (plural **coups** /ko͞oz/) **1** (also **coup d'état** /ˌko͞o dā'tä/) a sudden violent seizing of power from a government. **2** a successful move or action: *the deal is a major coup for the company.*

SYNONYMS **1 takeover**, coup d'état, overthrow, palace revolution, rebellion, uprising. **2 success**, triumph, feat, masterstroke, accomplishment, achievement, scoop.

coup de grâce /ˌko͞o də 'gräs/ ▶ n. (plural **coups de grâce** same pronunciation) a final blow or shot given to kill a wounded person or animal.

coupe /ko͞op/ ▶ n. a sports car with a fixed roof, two doors, and a sloping rear.

cou·ple /'kəpəl/ ▶ n. **1** two individuals of the same sort considered together. **2** two people who are married or in a romantic relationship. **3** informal an unspecified small number. ▶ v. (**couples**, **coupling**, **coupled**) connect or combine: *a sense of hope is coupled with a sense of loss.*

SYNONYMS ▶ n. **1 pair**, duo, twosome, two, brace. **2 husband and wife**, twosome, partners, lovers; informal item. ▶ v. **1** *the picnic was coupled with a nature walk* **combine with**, accompany with, ally with, mix with, incorporate with, add to, join to. **2 connect**, attach, join, fasten, fix, link, secure, hook (up). ANTONYMS detach.

cou·plet /'kəplət/ ▶ n. a pair of rhyming lines of poetry that form a unit.

cou·pling /'kəp(ə)liNG/ ▶ n. a device for connecting railroad vehicles or parts of machinery together.

cou·pon /'k(y)o͞oˌpän/ ▶ n. **1** a voucher that gives you the right to claim a discount or buy something. **2** a detachable portion of a bond that is given up in return for a payment of interest. **3** a form that can be sent off to ask for information or to enter a competition.

SYNONYMS **voucher**, token, ticket, slip, rain check.

cour·age /'kərij, 'kə-rij/ ▶ n. **1** the ability to do something frightening; bravery. **2** strength when faced with pain or grief.

SYNONYMS **bravery**, pluck, valor, fearlessness, nerve, daring, audacity, boldness, grit, heroism, gallantry; informal guts. ANTONYMS cowardice.

□ **have the courage of your convictions** be brave enough to do what you think is right.

cou·ra·geous /kə'rājəs/ ▶ **adj.** having courage; brave.

SYNONYMS **brave**, plucky, fearless, intrepid, valiant, heroic, undaunted, dauntless; informal gutsy. ANTONYMS cowardly.

■ **cou·ra·geous·ly** **adv.**

cour·i·er /'ko͝orēər, 'kərēər/ ▶ **n.** **1** a person employed to deliver goods or documents quickly. **2** a person employed to guide and help a group of tourists.

course /kôrs/ ▶ **n.** **1** a direction that is taken or intended: *the airplane changed course*. **2** the way in which something progresses or develops: *the course of history*. **3** (also **course of action**) a way of dealing with a situation. **4** a dish forming one of the stages of a meal. **5** a series of lectures or lessons in a particular subject. **6** a series of repeated treatments or doses of a drug. **7** an area prepared for racing, golf, or another sport. ▶ **v.** (**courses**, **coursing**, **coursed**) **1** (of liquid) flow. **2** (**coursing**) the activity of hunting animals, especially hares, with greyhounds.

SYNONYMS ▶ **n.** **1 route**, way, track, path, line, trail, trajectory, bearing, heading. **2 procedure**, plan (of action), course of action, practice, approach, technique, policy, strategy, tactic. **3 racecourse**, racetrack, track. **4 course of study**, curriculum, syllabus, classes, lectures, studies. **5 program**, series, sequence, system, schedule, regime. ▶ **v.** **flow**, pour, stream, run, rush, gush, cascade, flood, roll.

□ **of course** **1** as expected. **2** certainly; yes.

USAGE

Don't confuse **course** with **coarse**, which means 'having a rough texture.'

course·work /'kôrs,wərk/ ▶ **n.** work done during a course of study, counting toward a final mark.

court /kôrt/ ▶ **n.** **1** the judge, jury, and lawyers who sit and hear legal cases. **2** the place where a court of law meets. **3** an area marked out for ball games such as tennis. **4** a courtyard. **5** the home, advisers, and staff of a king or queen. ▶ **v.** **1** try to win someone's support. **2** behave in a way that might lead to something bad happening: *he often courted controversy*. **3** dated try to win the love of someone you want to marry.

SYNONYMS ▶ **n.** **1 court of law**, bench, bar, tribunal. **2 household**, retinue, entourage, train, courtiers, attendants. ▶ **v.** **1 cultivate**, flatter, curry favor with, wine and dine; informal butter up. **2 seek**, pursue, go after, strive for, solicit. **3 risk**, invite, attract, bring on yourself. **4 woo**, go out with, date, go steady with.

□ **court order** an instruction by a court or a judge requiring a person to do or not do something. **court shoe** a woman's plain shoe with a low-cut upper and no fastening. **hold court** be the center of attention. **pay court to** give someone a lot of flattering attention.

cour·te·ous /'kərtēəs/ ▶ **adj.** polite and considerate.

SYNONYMS **polite**, well-mannered, civil, respectful, well-behaved, gracious, obliging, considerate. ANTONYMS rude.

■ **cour·te·ous·ly** **adv.**

cour·te·sy /'kərtəsē/ ▶ **n.** (plural **courtesies**) **1** polite and considerate behavior. **2** a polite speech or action.

SYNONYMS **politeness**, good manners, civility, respect, grace, consideration, thought.

□ **courtesy of** given or allowed by.

court·house /'kôrt,hous/ ▶ **n.** a building in which a court of law is held.

cour·ti·er /'kôrtēər, 'kôrcнər/ ▶ **n.** a companion or adviser of a king or queen.

court·ly /'kôrtlē/ ▶ **adj.** (**courtlier**, **courtliest**) very dignified and polite.

court-mar·tial /'kôrt,märsнəl/ ▶ **n.** (plural **courts-martial** or **court-martials**) a court for trying people accused of breaking military law. ▶ **v.** (**court-martials**, **court-martialing**, **court-martialed**) try someone in a court-martial.

court·room /'kôrt,ro͞om, -,ro͝om/ ▶ **n.** the room or building in which a court of law meets.

court·ship /'kôrt,sнip/ ▶ **n.** **1** a period during which a couple develops a romantic relationship. **2** the process of trying to win someone's love or support.

court·yard /'kôrt,yärd/ ▶ **n.** an open area enclosed by walls or buildings.

cous·cous /'ko͞os,ko͞os/ ▶ **n.** a North African dish of steamed or soaked semolina.

cous·in /'kəzən/ ▶ **n.** (also **first cousin**) a child of your uncle or aunt. □ **second cousin** a child of your mother's or father's first cousin.

cou·ture /ko͞o'to͝or, -'tyr/ ▶ **n.** the design and making of fashionable clothes, especially for a particular customer.

cou·tu·ri·er /ko͞o'to͝orēər, -'to͝orē,ā/ ▶ **n.** a person who designs couture clothes.

cove /kōv/ ▶ **n.** a small sheltered bay.

SYNONYMS **bay**, inlet, fjord.

cov·en /'kəvən/ ▶ **n.** a group of witches who meet regularly.

cov·e·nant /'kəvənənt/ ▶ **n.** a formal agreement.

cov·er /'kəvər/ ▶ **v.** (**covers**, **covering**, **covered**) **1** put something over or in front of a person or thing so as to protect or hide them. **2** spread or extend over an area. **3** deal with a subject. **4** travel a particular distance. **5** (of money) be enough to pay for something. **6** (of insurance) protect against a loss or accident. **7** (**cover something up**) try to hide or deny a mistake or crime. **8** (**cover for**) temporarily take over someone's job. **9** (**cover for**) disguise the illicit absence or wrongdoing of someone in order to spare them punishment. **10** perform a cover version of a song. ▶ **n.** **1** something that covers or protects. **2** a thick protective outer part or page of a book or magazine. **3** shelter. **4** a means of hiding an illegal or secret activity. **5** (also **cover version**) a performance of a song previously recorded by a different artist. **6** a place setting in a restaurant.

SYNONYMS ▶ **v.** **1 protect**, shield, shelter, hide, conceal, mask, screen, veil, obscure, spread over, extend over, overlay. **2 cake**, coat, encrust, plaster, smother, blanket, carpet, shroud. **3 deal with**, consider, take in, include, involve, incorporate, embrace. ANTONYMS reveal. ▶ **n.** **1** *a protective cover* **covering**, sleeve, wrapping, wrapper, envelope, sheath, housing, jacket, casing, cowling, canopy. **2** *a manhole cover* **lid**, top, cap. **3** *a book cover* **binding**, jacket, dust jacket, dust cover, wrapper. **4** **coating**, coat, covering, layer, carpet, blanket, film, sheet, veneer, crust, skin, cloak, mantle, veil, pall, shroud. **5** **shelter**, protection, refuge, sanctuary.

□ **break cover** suddenly leave shelter when being chased. **cover charge** a charge per person added to the bill in a restaurant or paid for admission to a bar or club. **cover letter** a letter sent with a document or parcel to explain what it is.

cov·er·age /ˈkəv(ə)rij/ ▶ **n.** **1** the extent to which something is covered: *eighty transmitters would give nationwide coverage.* **2** protection by insurance.

cov·er·let /ˈkəvərlət/ ▶ **n.** a bedspread.

co·vert /ˈkōvərt, kōˈvərt, ˈkəvərt/ ▶ **adj.** not done openly; secret.

SYNONYMS **secret**, furtive, clandestine, surreptitious, stealthy, cloak-and-dagger, backstairs, hidden, concealed, private, undercover, underground; informal hush-hush. ANTONYMS overt.

cov·et /ˈkəvət/ ▶ **v.** (**covets**, **coveting**, **coveted**) long to possess something belonging to someone else.

SYNONYMS **desire**, yearn for, crave, have your heart set on, long for, hanker after/for, hunger after/for, thirst for.

■ **cov·et·ous** **adj.**

cov·ey /ˈkəvē/ ▶ **n.** (plural **coveys**) a small flock of game birds.

cow¹ /kou/ ▶ **n.** **1** a mature female animal of a domesticated breed of ox. **2** the female of certain other large animals.

cow² ▶ **v.** frighten someone so much that they do what you want: *the men were cowed by her presence.*

cow·ard /ˈkou-ərd/ ▶ **n.** a person who is too scared to do dangerous or unpleasant things.

SYNONYMS **mouse**, baby; informal chicken, scaredy-cat, yellow-belly, sissy, pantywaist, candy-ass.

cow·ard·ice /ˈkou-ərdəs/ ▶ **n.** lack of bravery.

cow·ard·ly /ˈkou-ərdlē/ ▶ **adj.** lacking courage.

SYNONYMS **faint-hearted**, lily-livered, spineless, craven, timid, timorous, fearful; informal yellow, chicken, gutless, yellow-bellied. ANTONYMS brave.

■ **cow·ard·li·ness** **n.**

cow·boy /ˈkouˌboi/ ▶ **n.** **1** a man on horseback who herds cattle in the western United States. **2** informal a person who is reckless, especially when driving an automobile. **3** informal a business person who ignores rules and conventions or who takes many risks.

cow·er /ˈkou(-ə)r/ ▶ **v.** (**cowers**, **cowering**, **cowered**) crouch down or shrink back in fear.

SYNONYMS **cringe**, shrink, flinch, crouch, blench.

cowgirl /ˈkouˌgərl/ ▶ **n.** a girl or woman on horseback who herds cattle in the western US.

cowl /koul/ ▶ **n.** **1** a large, loose hood forming part of a monk's garment. **2** a hood-shaped covering for a chimney or ventilation shaft.

cow·lick /ˈkouˌlik/ ▶ **n.** a lock of hair hanging over the forehead.

cowl·ing /ˈkouliNG/ ▶ **n.** a removable cover for a vehicle or aircraft engine.

co·work·er /ˌkōˈwərkər/ (also **co-worker**) ▶ **n.** a fellow worker.

cow·pat /ˈkouˌpat/ ▶ **n.** a flat, round piece of cow dung.

cow·pea /ˈkouˌpē/ ▶ **n.** a black-eyed pea.

cow·poke /ˈkouˌpōk/ ▶ **n.** informal a cowboy.

cow·rie /ˈkourē/ ▶ **n.** (plural **cowries**) a shellfish whose glossy shell has a long, narrow opening.

cow·slip /ˈkouˌslip/ ▶ **n.** **1** a name given to a number of North American plants, including the marsh marigold. **2** a wild European plant with clusters of yellow flowers.

cox /käks/ ▶ **n.** the person who steers a rowboat.

cox·comb /ˈkäksˌkōm/ ▶ **n.** old use a vain and conceited man.

cox·swain /ˈkäksən/ ▶ **n.** the person who steers a racing boat while motivating the crew, who are doing the rowing.

coy /koi/ ▶ **adj.** (**coyer**, **coyest**) **1** pretending to be shy or modest. **2** reluctant to give details about something: *he's coy about his age.*

SYNONYMS **demure**, shy, modest, bashful, diffident, self-effacing, shrinking. ANTONYMS brazen.

■ **coy·ly** **adv.** **coy·ness** **n.**

coy·o·te /ˈkīˌōt, kīˈōtē/ ▶ **n.** (plural **coyote** or **coyotes**) a wolflike wild dog found in North America.

coy·pu /ˈkoiˌpo͞o/ ▶ **n.** (plural **coypus**) a large South American rodent resembling a beaver.

coz·en /ˈkəzən/ ▶ **v.** literary trick or deceive.

co·zy /ˈkōzē/ ▶ **adj.** (**cozier**, **coziest**) **1** comfortable, warm, and secure. **2** not difficult or demanding: *the cozy belief that man is master.* ▶ **n.** (plural **cozies**) a cover to keep a teapot or a boiled egg hot.

SYNONYMS ▶ **adj.** **1** **snug**, comfortable, warm, homey, unpretentious, welcoming, safe, sheltered, secure; informal comfy. **2** **intimate**, relaxed, informal, friendly.

■ **co·zi·ly** **adv.** **co·zi·ness** **n.**

CPA ▶ **abbr.** certified public accountant.

CPR ▶ **abbr.** cardiopulmonary resuscitation.

cps (also **c.p.s.**) ▶ **abbr.** **1** Computing characters per second. **2** cycles per second.

CPU ▶ **abbr.** Computing central processing unit.

crab /krab/ ▶ **n.** a sea creature with a broad shell and five pairs of legs. □ **crab apple** a small, sour kind of apple.

crab·bed /ˈkrabəd/ ▶ **adj.** **1** (of writing) hard to read or understand. **2** bad-tempered.

crab·by /ˈkrabē/ ▶ **adj.** (**crabbier**, **crabbiest**) informal bad-tempered.

crab·wise /ˈkrabˌwīz/ ▶ **adv. & adj.** (of movement) sideways.

crack /krak/ ▶ **n.** **1** a narrow opening between two parts of something that has split or been broken. **2** a sudden sharp noise. **3** a sharp blow. **4** informal a joke. **5** informal an attempt to do something. **6** (also **crack cocaine**) a very strong form of cocaine. ▶ **v.** **1** break without dividing into separate parts: *take care not to crack the glass.* **2** give way under pressure or strain. **3** make a sudden sharp sound. **4** hit hard. **5** (of a person's voice) suddenly change in pitch. **6** informal solve or decipher: *the hint will help you crack the code.* ▶ **adj.** very good or skillful: *a crack shot.*

SYNONYMS ▶ **n.** **1** *a crack in the glass* **split**, break, chip, fracture, rupture. **2** *a crack between two rocks* **space**, gap, crevice, fissure, cleft, cranny, chink. **3** **bang**, report, explosion, detonation, clap, crash. **4** *a crack on the head* **blow**, bang, hit, knock, rap, bump, smack, slap; informal bash, whack, clout. ▶ **v.** **1** **break**, split, fracture, rupture, snap. **2** **break down**, give way, cave in, go to pieces, give in, yield, succumb. **3** **hit**, strike, smack, slap, beat, thump, knock, rap; informal bash, whack, clobber, clout, clip. **4** **decipher**, interpret, decode, break, solve.

□ **crack down on** informal deal severely with. **crack of dawn** daybreak. **crack a joke** tell a joke. **crack up** informal **1** suffer an emotional breakdown. **2** burst or cause to burst into laughter. **3** (**be cracked up to be**) be said to be: *acting isn't as glamorous as it's cracked up to be.* **get cracking** informal get busy on something that needs to be done.

crack·brained /ˈkrakˌbrānd/ ▶ **adj.** informal extremely foolish.

crack·down /ˈkrakˌdoun/ ▶ **n.** a series of severe measures against undesirable or illegal behavior.

crack·er /ˈkrakər/ ▶ **n.** **1** a thin, crisp wafer. **2** a firework that explodes with a crack. **3** a person who breaks into a computer system. **4** often offensive a poor white person regarded as socially inferior, especially one living in the southern United States.

crack·er·jack /ˈkrakərˌjak/ ▶ **adj.** exceptionally good.

crack·ers /ˈkrakərz/ (or **cracked** /krakt/) ▶ **adj.** informal insane; crazy.

crack·le /ˈkrakəl/ ▶ **v.** (**crackles**, **crackling**, **crackled**) make a series of slight cracking noises. ▶ **n.** a crackling sound. ■ **crack·ly** **adj.**

crack·ling /ˈkraklən, -liNG/ ▶ **n.** the crisp fatty skin of roast pork.

crack·pot /ˈkrakˌpät/ ▶ **n.** informal an eccentric or foolish person.

cra·dle /ˈkrādl/ ▶ **n.** **1** a baby's bed on rockers. **2** a place or period in which something originates or flourishes: *the cradle of civilization.* **3** a supporting framework. ▶ **v.** (**cradles**, **cradling**, **cradled**) hold gently and protectively.

SYNONYMS ▶ **n.** **1** **crib**, bassinet. **2** **birthplace**, fount, fountainhead, source, spring, origin. ▶ **v.** **hold**, support, cushion, pillow, nurse, rest.

craft /kraft/ ▶ **n.** **1** an activity involving skill in making things by hand. **2** skill in carrying out work. **3** (**crafts**) things made by hand. **4** (plural **craft**) a boat, ship, or aircraft. **5** skill in deceiving people. ▶ **v.** make something skillfully.

SYNONYMS ▶ **n.** **1** **activity**, occupation, trade, profession, work, line of work, job. **2** **vessel**, ship, boat, aircraft, spacecraft. **3** **cunning**, craftiness, guile, wiliness, artfulness, deviousness, slyness, trickery, duplicity, dishonesty, deceit, deceitfulness, deception, intrigue, subterfuge, wiles, ploys, ruses, schemes, tricks.

crafts·man /ˈkraf(t)smən/ ▶ **n.** (plural **craftsmen**) a worker who is skilled in a particular craft.

SYNONYMS **artisan**, artist, skilled worker, technician, expert, master.

■ **crafts·man·ship** **n.**

craft·y /ˈkraftē/ ▶ **adj.** (**craftier**, **craftiest**) **1** clever at deceiving people; cunning. **2** informal having to do with the making of decorative objects by hand.

SYNONYMS **cunning**, wily, sly, artful, devious, tricky, scheming, calculating, shrewd, canny, dishonest, deceitful. ANTONYMS honest.

■ **craft·i·ly** **adv.** **craft·i·ness** **n.**

crag /krag/ ▶ **n.** a steep or rugged cliff or rock face.

crag·gy /ˈkragē/ ▶ **adj.** (**craggier**, **craggiest**) **1** having many crags. **2** (of a man's face) attractively rugged.

cram /kram/ ▶ **v.** (**crams**, **cramming**, **crammed**) **1** force too many people or things into a space. **2** fill something to the point of overflowing. **3** study hard just before an exam.

SYNONYMS **1** *closets crammed with clothes* **fill**, stuff, pack, jam, fill to overflowing, overload, crowd, throng. **2** *he crammed his clothes into a case* **push**, thrust, shove, force, ram, jam, stuff, pack, pile, squash, squeeze, compress. **3** **study**, review; informal bone up.

cramp /kramp/ ▶ **n.** **1** pain caused by a muscle or muscles tightening. **2** a tool for clamping two objects together. ▶ **v.** restrict the development of: *tighter rules will cramp economic growth.*

SYNONYMS ▶ **n.** **spasm**, pain, shooting pain, twinge, pang, convulsion. ▶ **v.** **hinder**, impede, inhibit, hamper, constrain, hamstring, interfere with, restrict, limit, slow.

cramped /kram(p)t/ ▶ **adj.** **1** uncomfortably small or crowded. **2** (of handwriting) small and difficult to read.

SYNONYMS **1** **confined**, uncomfortable, restricted, constricted, small, tiny, narrow, crowded, congested. **2** *his cramped signature* **small**, crabbed, illegible, unreadable, indecipherable. ANTONYMS spacious.

cram·pon /ˈkramˌpän/ ▶ **n.** a spiked plate fixed to a boot for climbing on ice or rock.

cran·ber·ry /ˈkranˌberē, -bərē/ ▶ **n.** (plural **cranberries**) a small sour-tasting red berry.

crane /krān/ ▶ **n.** **1** a tall machine used for moving heavy objects by suspending them from a projecting arm. **2** a wading bird with long legs and a long neck. ▶ **v.** (**cranes**, **craning**, **craned**) stretch out your neck to see something. □ **crane fly** a flying insect with very long legs.

cra·ni·al /ˈkrānēəl/ ▶ **adj.** relating to the skull or cranium.

cra·ni·um /ˈkrānēəm/ ▶ **n.** (plural **craniums** or **crania** /-nēə/) the part of the skull that encloses the brain.

crank /kraNGk/ ▶ **n.** **1** a part of an axle or shaft that is bent at right angles, turned to produce motion. **2** an eccentric person. ▶ **v.** **1** start an engine by turning a crankshaft. **2** (**crank something up**) informal make something more intense or turn something up, especially volume. **3** (**crank something out**) informal produce something regularly and routinely: *an army of researchers cranked out worthy studies.*

crank·shaft /ˈkraNGkˌSHaft/ ▶ **n.** a shaft driven by a crank.

crank·y /ˈkraNGkē/ ▶ **adj.** (**crankier**, **crankiest**) informal **1** strange or eccentric. **2** bad-tempered.

cran·ny /ˈkranē/ ▶ **n.** (plural **crannies**) a small, narrow space or opening.

crap /krap/ ▶ **n.** **1** nonsense. **2** an item that is of extremely poor quality. ▶ **adj.** extremely poor in quality. ■ **crap·py** **adj.**

crape /krāp/ ▶ **n.** black silk, formerly used for mourning clothes.

craps /kraps/ ▶ **n.** a gambling game played with two dice.

crap·shoot /ˈkrap,sʜo͞ot/ ▶ **n. 1** a game of craps. **2** a risky or uncertain matter.

crap·u·lous /ˈkrapyələs/ (also **crapulent** /ˈkrapyələnt/) ▶ **adj.** literary relating to the drinking of alcohol or to drunkenness.

crash /krasʜ/ ▶ **v. 1** (of a vehicle) collide violently with an obstacle or another vehicle. **2** (of an aircraft) fall from the sky and hit the land or sea. **3** move or fall with a sudden loud noise: *huge waves crashed down on us*. **4** (of shares) fall suddenly in value. **5** Computing fail suddenly. **6** (also **crash out**) informal fall deeply asleep. **7** (**crashing**) informal complete; total: *a crashing bore*. ▶ **n. 1** an instance of crashing. **2** a sudden loud, deep noise. ▶ **adj.** rapid and concentrated: *a crash course in Italian*.

> SYNONYMS ▶ **v. 1** *the car crashed into a tree* **smash into**, collide with, be in a collision with, hit, strike, ram, impact, cannon into, plow into, meet head-on. **2** *he crashed his car* **smash**, wreck; informal total. **3 fall**, drop, plummet, plunge, sink, dive, tumble. **4 fail**, fold, collapse, go under, go bankrupt; informal go bust, go broke, go belly up. ▶ **n. 1 accident**, collision, wreck, smash; informal pile-up. **2 bang**, smash, smack, crack, bump, thud, explosion. **3 failure**, collapse, liquidation, bankruptcy.

□ **crash-dive** (of an aircraft or submarine) dive rapidly or uncontrollably. **crash helmet** a helmet worn by a motorcyclist to protect the head. **crash-land** (of an aircraft) land roughly in an emergency.

crass /kras/ ▶ **adj.** very thoughtless and stupid.

> SYNONYMS **stupid**, insensitive, thoughtless, witless, oafish, boorish, coarse, gross, graceless, tasteless, tactless, clumsy, blundering; informal ignorant. ANTONYMS intelligent.

■ **crass·ly adv.**

crate /krāt/ ▶ **n. 1** a wooden, metal, or plastic case for transporting goods. **2** a square container divided into individual units for holding bottles. **3** informal an old and ramshackle vehicle. ▶ **v.** (**crates, crating, crated**) pack in a crate.

> SYNONYMS ▶ **n. packing case**, chest, tea chest, box, container.

cra·ter /ˈkrātər/ ▶ **n.** a large hollow caused by an explosion or impact or forming the mouth of a volcano.

> SYNONYMS **hollow**, bowl, basin, hole, cavity, depression, dip; Geology caldera.

cra·vat /krəˈvat/ ▶ **n.** a strip of fabric worn by men around the neck and tucked inside a shirt.

crave /krāv/ ▶ **v.** (**craves, craving, craved**) **1** feel a very strong desire for. **2** old use ask for: *I must crave your indulgence*.

> SYNONYMS **long for**, yearn for, hanker after, desire, want, hunger for, thirst for, pine for; informal be dying for.

cra·ven /ˈkrāvən/ ▶ **adj.** cowardly.

crav·ing /ˈkrāviɴɢ/ ▶ **n.** a very strong desire for something.

> SYNONYMS **longing**, yearning, desire, hankering, hunger, thirst, appetite.

craw /krô/ ▶ **n.** dated the part of a bird's throat where food is prepared for digestion.

crawl /krôl/ ▶ **v. 1** move forward on the hands and knees or with the body close to the ground. **2** move very slowly along. **3** (**be crawling with**) be unpleasantly covered or crowded with: *the place was crawling with journalists*. **4** feel an unpleasant sensation like that of something moving over the skin. **5** informal be too friendly or obedient in order to make someone like you. ▶ **n. 1** an act of crawling. **2** a very slow rate of movement. **3** a swimming stroke involving alternate overarm movements and rapid kicks of the legs.

> SYNONYMS ▶ **v. 1 creep**, worm your way, go on all fours, wriggle, slither, squirm. **2** ***the arena was crawling with police*** **be full of**, overflow with, teem with, be packed with, be crowded with, be alive with. **3 grovel**, kowtow, pander, toady, bow and scrape, fawn; informal suck up, lick someone's boots.

cray·fish /ˈkrā,fisʜ/ ▶ **n.** (plural **crayfish** or **crayfishes**) a shellfish like a small lobster.

cray·on /ˈkrā,än, ˈkrāən/ ▶ **n.** a stick of colored chalk or wax, used for drawing. ▶ **v.** draw with a crayon or crayons.

craze /krāz/ ▶ **n.** a widespread but short-lived enthusiasm for something.

> SYNONYMS **fad**, fashion, trend, vogue, enthusiasm, mania, passion, rage; informal thing.

crazed /krāzd/ ▶ **adj. 1** behaving in a wild or insane way. **2** covered with fine cracks.

cra·zy /ˈkrāzē/ ▶ **adj.** (**crazier, craziest**) **1** insane. **2** (usu. **crazy about**) informal very enthusiastic about or fond of: *I'm crazy about Cindy*. **3** foolish or ridiculous.

> SYNONYMS **1 mad**, insane, out of your mind, deranged, demented, crazed, lunatic, unbalanced, unhinged; informal mental, nuts, nutty, batty, bonkers, cuckoo, loony, loco, off your rocker, round/around the bend. **2** ***he's crazy about her*** **passionate about**, (very) keen on, enamored of, infatuated with, smitten with, enthusiastic about, fanatical about; informal wild about, mad about, nuts about. **3** *a crazy idea* **stupid**, foolish, idiotic, silly, absurd, ridiculous, ludicrous, preposterous, asinine; informal cockeyed, half-baked, daft. ANTONYMS sane, sensible.

■ **cra·zi·ly adv. cra·zi·ness n.**

creak /krēk/ ▶ **v.** make a harsh, high sound. ▶ **n.** a creaking sound.

creak·y /krēkē/▶ **adj.** (**creakier, creakiest**) **1** making a harsh, high sound. **2** old-fashioned and inefficient: *the country's creaky legal system*.

cream /krēm/ ▶ **n. 1** the thick fatty liquid that rises to the top when milk is left to stand. **2** a sauce, soup, or dessert containing cream or having a creamy texture. **3** a thick liquid substance that is applied to the skin. **4** the very best of a group: *the club catered to the cream of New York society*. **5** a very pale yellow or off-white color. ▶ **v. 1** work butter, typically with sugar, to form a smooth soft paste. **2** mash a cooked vegetable with milk or cream, or combine it with a cream sauce.

> SYNONYMS ▶ **n. 1 lotion**, ointment, moisturizer, cosmetic, salve, rub. **2 best**, finest, pick, flower, crème de la crème, elite. **3 off-white**, ivory. ANTONYMS dregs.

□ **cream cheese** a soft, rich kind of cheese.

cream·er /'krēmər/ ▶ **n. 1** a substance for adding to coffee or tea instead of cream or milk. **2** a small jug for cream.

cream·er·y /'krēm(ə)rē/ ▶ **n.** (plural **creameries**) a factory where butter, cheese, and ice cream are produced.

cream·y /'krēmē/ ▶ **adj.** (**creamier**, **creamiest**) resembling or containing a lot of cream.

> SYNONYMS **smooth**, thick, velvety, rich, buttery.

■ **cream·i·ly adv. cream·i·ness n.**

crease /krēs/ ▶ **n.** a line or ridge produced on paper or cloth by folding or pressing it. ▶ **v.** (**creases**, **creasing**, **creased**) make creases in.

> SYNONYMS ▶ **n. fold**, line, crinkle, ridge, furrow, groove, corrugation, wrinkle, crow's foot. ▶ **v. crumple**, wrinkle, crinkle, line, scrunch up, rumple, ruck up, pucker.

cre·ate /krē'āt/ ▶ **v.** (**creates**, **creating**, **created**) **1** bring into existence. **2** cause something to happen: *he wanted to create a good impression.*

> SYNONYMS **1 produce**, generate, bring into being, make, fashion, build, construct. **2 bring about**, give rise to, lead to, result in, cause, breed, generate, engender, produce. **3 establish**, found, initiate, institute, constitute, inaugurate, launch, set up, form. ANTONYMS destroy, abolish.

cre·a·tion /krē'āsʜən/ ▶ **n. 1** the action of creating. **2** a thing that has been made or invented. **3** (**Creation**) literary the universe.

> SYNONYMS **1 establishment**, formation, foundation, initiation, institution, inauguration, constitution, setting up. **2 the world**, the universe, the cosmos, nature, the natural world. **3 work**, work of art, production, opus, oeuvre, achievement, concoction, invention; informal brainchild. ANTONYMS abolition, destruction.

cre·a·tive /krē'ātiv/ ▶ **adj.** involving the use of the imagination in order to create something.

> SYNONYMS **inventive**, imaginative, innovative, experimental, original, artistic, inspired, visionary. ANTONYMS unimaginative.

■ **cre·a·tive·ly adv. cre·a·tiv·i·ty** /ˌkrē-ā'tivitē/ **n.**

cre·a·tor /krē'ātər/ ▶ **n. 1** a person or thing that creates. **2** (**the Creator**) God.

> SYNONYMS **maker**, producer, author, designer, deviser, originator, inventor, architect.

crea·ture /'krēcʜər/ ▶ **n.** a living being, in particular an animal rather than a person.

> SYNONYMS **animal**, beast, brute, living thing, living being; informal critter.

□ **creature comforts** things that make life comfortable.

crèche /kresʜ, krāsʜ/ ▶ **n.** a model or tableau representing the scene of Jesus Christ's birth, displayed at Christmas.

cre·dence /'krēdns/ ▶ **n.** belief that something is true: *he gave no credence to the witness's statement.*

cre·den·tial /krə'dencʜəl/ ▶ **n. 1** a qualification, achievement, or quality used to indicate how suitable a person is for something: *his academic credentials cannot be doubted.* **2** (**credentials**) documents that prove a person's identity or qualifications.

> SYNONYMS **1** (**credentials**) **suitability**, eligibility, attributes, qualifications, record, experience, background. **2** (**credentials**) **documentation**, documents, ID, proof of identity, passport, testimonial, reference, certification.

cred·i·bil·i·ty /ˌkredə'bilitē/ ▶ **n. 1** the quality of being trusted or believable. **2** (also **street credibility**) acceptability among fashionable young urban people.

> SYNONYMS **plausibility**, believability, credence, trustworthiness, reliability, dependability, integrity.

cred·i·ble /'kredəbəl/ ▶ **adj.** able to be believed; convincing.

> SYNONYMS **believable**, plausible, conceivable, persuasive, convincing, tenable, probable, possible, feasible, reasonable.

■ **cred·i·bly adv.**

> **USAGE**
>
> Don't confuse **credible** with **creditable**: **credible** means 'believable or convincing,' whereas **creditable** means 'deserving recognition and praise.'

cred·it /'kredit/ ▶ **n. 1** the system of doing business by trusting that a customer will pay at a later date for goods or services supplied. **2** public recognition or praise given for an achievement or quality. **3** (**a credit to**) a source of pride to: *the boy is a credit to his parents.* **4** (**credits**) a list of the people who worked on a movie or television program, displayed at the end. **5** a unit of study counting toward a degree or diploma. **6** an entry in an account recording an amount received. ▶ **v.** (**credits**, **crediting**, **credited**) **1** (**credit someone with**) feel that someone is responsible for something good: *she has been credited with changing American cooking.* **2** believe something surprising. **3** add an amount of money to an account.

> SYNONYMS ▶ **n. praise**, commendation, acclaim, acknowledgment, recognition, kudos, glory, respect, appreciation. ▶ **v.** *we credit our success to one woman* **ascribe**, attribute, assign, put down.

□ **credit card** a plastic card that allows you to buy things and pay for them later. **do someone credit** make someone worthy of praise or respect.

cred·it·a·ble /'kreditəbəl/ ▶ **adj.** deserving recognition and praise. ■ **cred·it·a·bly adv.**

cred·i·tor /'kreditər/ ▶ **n.** a person or company to whom money is owed.

cred·it·worth·y /'kreditˌwərᴛʜē/ ▶ **adj.** considered suitable to receive financial credit.

cre·do /'krēdō, 'krādō/ ▶ **n.** (plural **credos**) a statement of a person's beliefs or aims.

cred·u·lous /'krejələs/ ▶ **adj.** too ready to believe things.

> SYNONYMS **gullible**, naive, easily taken in, impressionable, unsuspecting, unsuspicious, innocent, inexperienced, unsophisticated, wide-eyed. ANTONYMS suspicious.

■ **cre·du·li·ty** /krə'd(y)o͞olitē/ **n.**

creed /krēd/ ▶ **n. 1** a system of religious belief; a faith. **2** a set of beliefs or principles.

SYNONYMS **1** *people of many creeds* **faith**, religion, belief, religious persuasion. **2** *his political creed* **beliefs**, principles, articles of faith, tenets, ideology, credo, doctrines, teachings.

creek /krēk/ ▶ **n. 1** a narrow stretch of water running inland from the coast. **2** a stream or small river.

SYNONYMS **inlet**, bay, estuary, fjord.

□ **up the creek** informal in severe difficulty.

creel /krēl/ ▶ **n.** a large basket for carrying fish.

creep /krēp/ ▶ **v.** (**creeps, creeping, crept**) **1** move slowly and cautiously. **2** progress or develop gradually: *interest rates are creeping up.* ▶ **n. 1** informal an unpleasant person. **2** slow and gradual movement.

SYNONYMS ▶ **v. tiptoe**, steal, sneak, slink, edge, inch, skulk, prowl.

□ **give you the creeps** make you feel disgust or fear.

creep·er /ˈkrēpər/ ▶ **n.** a plant that grows along the ground or another surface.

creep·y /ˈkrēpē/ ▶ **adj.** (**creepier, creepiest**) informal causing an unpleasant feeling of fear or unease.

SYNONYMS **frightening**, eerie, disturbing, sinister, weird, menacing, threatening; informal spooky, scary.

cre·mate /ˈkrēˌmāt, kriˈmāt/ ▶ **v.** (**cremates, cremating, cremated**) dispose of a dead body by burning it. ■ **cre·ma·tion** /kriˈmāsʜən/ **n.**

cre·ma·to·ri·um /ˌkrēməˈtôrēəm, ˌkrem-/ ▶ **n.** (plural **crematoria** /-rēə/ or **crematoriums**) a building where dead people are cremated.

crème de la crème /ˌkrem də lə ˈkrem/ ▶ **n.** the best person or thing of a particular kind.

cren·el·la·tions /ˌkrenlˈāsʜənz/ ▶ **pl.n.** fortification consisting of a low protective wall along the top of a castle or fort, with openings for shooting through; battlements. ■ **cren·el·la·ted** /ˈkrenlˌātid/ **adj.**

Cre·ole /ˈkrēˌōl/ ▶ **n. 1** (in the Caribbean) a person of mixed European and black descent. **2** a descendant of French settlers in the southern United States. **3** a combination of a European language and an African language.

cre·o·sote /ˈkrēəˌsōt/ ▶ **n.** a dark brown oil painted on to wood to preserve it.

crepe /krāp/ (or **crêpe**) ▶ **n. 1** a light, thin fabric with a wrinkled surface. **2** hard-wearing wrinkled rubber used for the soles of shoes. **3** /krāp, krep/ a thin pancake. □ **crepe paper** thin, crinkled paper.

crept /krept/ past and past participle of **CREEP**.

cre·pus·cu·lar /krəˈpəskyələr/ ▶ **adj.** literary resembling twilight; dim and shadowy.

cre·scen·do /krəˈsʜendō/ ▶ **n.** (plural **crescendos** or **crescendi** /-dē/) **1** a gradual increase in loudness in a piece of music. **2** a climax: *the hysteria reached a crescendo around the spring festival.*

cres·cent /ˈkresənt/ ▶ **n.** a narrow curved shape tapering to a point at each end.

cress /kres/ ▶ **n.** a plant of the cabbage family with pungent, edible leaves.

crest /krest/ ▶ **n. 1** a tuft or growth of feathers, fur, or skin on the head of a bird or animal. **2** a plume of feathers on a helmet. **3** the top of a ridge, wave, etc. **4** a distinctive design in heraldry representing a family or organization. ▶ **v.** reach the top of: *she crested a hill and saw the valley.*

SYNONYMS ▶ **n. 1 tuft**, comb, plume, crown. **2 summit**, peak, top, ridge, pinnacle, brow, crown, apex. **3 insignia**, emblem, coat of arms, arms, badge, device, regalia.

■ **crest·ed adj.**

crest·fal·len /ˈkrestˌfôlən/ ▶ **adj.** sad and disappointed.

SYNONYMS **downhearted**, downcast, despondent, disappointed, disconsolate, disheartened, discouraged, dispirited, dejected, sad, dismayed, unhappy, forlorn. ANTONYMS cheerful.

Cre·ta·ceous /krəˈtāsʜəs/ ▶ **adj.** Geol. having to do with the last period of the Mesozoic era (about 146 to 65 million years ago), at the end of which dinosaurs and many other organisms died out.

cre·tin /ˈkrētn/ ▶ **n.** a stupid person. ■ **cre·tin·ous adj.**

cre·tonne /ˈkrēˌtän, kriˈtän/ ▶ **n.** a heavy cotton fabric with a floral pattern, used for upholstery.

Creutz·feldt–Ja·kob dis·ease /ˈkroitsˌfelt ˈyäkôb/ ▶ **n.** a fatal disease affecting the brain, a form of which is possibly linked to bovine spongiform encephalopathy.

cre·vasse /krəˈvas/ ▶ **n.** a deep open crack in a glacier.

crev·ice /ˈkrevəs/ ▶ **n.** a narrow opening or crack in a rock or wall.

SYNONYMS **crack**, fissure, interstice, cleft, chink, cranny, slit, split.

crew /kro͞o/ ▶ **n. 1** a group of people who work on a ship, aircraft, or train. **2** the members of a crew other than the officers. **3** a group of people who work together: *a film crew.* ▶ **v.** act as a member of a crew.

SYNONYMS ▶ **n. 1** *the ship's crew* **company**, complement, sailors, hands. **2** *a film crew* **team**, squad, company, unit, party, gang.

□ **crew cut** a very short haircut for men and boys. **crew neck** a close-fitting round neckline.

crib /krib/ ▶ **n. 1** a young child's bed with barred or latticed sides. **2** informal a list of answers or other information used, for example, by students to cheat in a test. **3** informal an apartment or house. **4** the discarded cards in a game of cribbage. ▶ **v.** (**cribs, cribbing, cribbed**) informal copy something dishonestly.

crib·bage /ˈkribij/ ▶ **n.** a card game for two players.

crick /krik/ ▶ **n.** a painful stiff feeling in the neck or back. ▶ **v.** twist or strain the neck or back.

crick·et[1] ▶ **n.** an insect like a grasshopper, the male of which produces a shrill chirping sound.

crick·et[2] /ˈkrikit/ ▶ **n.** a team game played with a bat, ball, and wickets. ■ **crick·et·er n.**

cri de cœur /ˌkrē də ˈkər/ ▶ **n.** (plural **cris de cœur** same pronunciation) a passionate appeal or complaint.

cried /krīd/ past and past participle of **CRY**.

crime /krīm/ ▶ **n. 1** an action that is against the law. **2** illegal actions as a whole: *the fight against organized crime.* **3** something disgraceful or very unfair: *it was a crime to wake them at that hour of the morning.*

SYNONYMS **1 offense**, unlawful act, illegal act, felony, violation, misdemeanor. **2 lawbreaking**, delinquency, wrongdoing, criminality, misconduct, illegality, villainy, vice.

crim·i·nal /ˈkrimənl/ ▶ **n.** a person who has committed a crime. ▶ **adj. 1** relating to crime or a crime. **2** informal disgraceful or very unfair.

SYNONYMS ▶ **n. lawbreaker**, felon, offender, malefactor, villain, delinquent, culprit, miscreant, wrongdoer; informal crook. ▶ **adj. 1 unlawful**, illegal, illicit, lawless, delinquent, corrupt, felonious, nefarious; informal crooked. **2 deplorable**, shameful, reprehensible, disgraceful, inexcusable, outrageous, scandalous. ANTONYMS lawful.

■ **crim·i·nal·i·ty** /ˌkriməˈnalitē/ **n. crim·i·nal·ly adv.**

crim·i·nol·o·gy /ˌkriməˈnäləjē/ ▶ **n.** the scientific study of crime and criminals. ■ **crim·i·nol·o·gist n.**

crimp /krimp/ ▶ **v.** press into small folds or ridges.

crim·son /ˈkrimzən/ ▶ **n.** a deep red color.

cringe /krinj/ ▶ **v.** (**cringes**, **cringing**, **cringed**) **1** shrink back or cower in fear. **2** have a sudden feeling of embarrassment or disgust.

SYNONYMS **1 cower**, shrink, recoil, shy away, flinch, quail, blench, tremble, quiver, quake. **2 wince**, shudder, squirm, feel embarrassed/mortified.

crin·kle /ˈkriNGkəl/ ▶ **v.** (**crinkle**, **crinkling**, **crinkled**) form small creases or wrinkles. ▶ **n.** a small crease or wrinkle. ■ **crin·kly adj.**

crin·o·line /ˈkrinl-in/ ▶ **n. 1** a petticoat stiffened with hoops, formerly worn to make a long skirt stand out. **2** a stiff underskirt.

crip·ple /ˈkripəl/ ▶ **n.** old use or offensive a person who is unable to walk or move properly because they are disabled or injured. ▶ **v.** (**cripples**, **crippling**, **crippled**) **1** make someone unable to move or walk properly. **2** severely damage or weaken.

SYNONYMS ▶ **v. 1 disable**, paralyze, immobilize, incapacitate, handicap. **2** (**crippled**) **disabled**, paralyzed, incapacitated, physically handicapped, lame, immobilized, bedridden, confined to a wheelchair; euphemistic physically challenged. **3 damage**, weaken, hamper, paralyze, ruin, destroy, wipe out, bring to a standstill, put out of action, put out of business.

cri·sis /ˈkrīsis/ ▶ **n.** (plural **crises** /-sēz/) **1** a time of severe difficulty or danger. **2** a time when a difficult decision must be made: *she's having a mid-life crisis.*

SYNONYMS **1 emergency**, disaster, catastrophe, calamity, meltdown, predicament, plight, dire straits. **2 critical point**, turning point, crossroads, head, point of no return, moment of truth; informal crunch.

crisp /krisp/ ▶ **adj. 1** firm, dry, and brittle. **2** (of the weather) cool and fresh. **3** brisk and decisive: *her answer was crisp.*

SYNONYMS **1 crunchy**, crispy, brittle, breakable, dry. **2 invigorating**, brisk, cool, fresh, refreshing, exhilarating. ANTONYMS soft.

■ **crisp·ly adv.**

crisp·y /ˈkrispē/ ▶ **adj.** (**crispier**, **crispiest**) (of food) having a pleasingly firm, dry, and brittle surface or texture: *crispy fried bacon.*

criss·cross /ˈkrisˌkrôs/ ▶ **adj.** with a pattern of crossing lines. ▶ **v. 1** form a crisscross pattern on: *the hill was crisscrossed with a network of tracks.* **2** repeatedly go back and forth around a place.

cri·te·ri·on /krīˈti(ə)rēən/ ▶ **n.** (plural **criteria** /-rēə/) a standard by which something may be judged.

SYNONYMS **standard**, measure, gauge, test, benchmark, yardstick, touchstone, barometer.

USAGE

The singular form is **criterion** and the plural form is **criteria**. It's wrong to use **criteria** as a singular: say *further criteria need to be considered* not *a further criteria needs to be considered.*

crit·ic /ˈkritik/ ▶ **n. 1** a person who finds fault with someone or something. **2** a person who assesses literary or artistic works.

SYNONYMS **1 detractor**, attacker, fault-finder. **2 reviewer**, commentator, analyst, judge, pundit, expert.

crit·i·cal /ˈkritikəl/ ▶ **adj. 1** expressing disapproval. **2** assessing a literary or artistic work. **3** very important in terms of the success or failure of something. **4** at a point of danger or crisis: *the floods were rising and the situation was critical.*

SYNONYMS **1 disapproving**, disparaging, scathing, fault-finding, judgemental, negative, unfavorable, censorious; informal nitpicking, picky. **2 serious**, grave, precarious, touch-and-go, in the balance, desperate, dire, acute, life-and-death. **3 crucial**, vital, essential, all-important, paramount, fundamental, key, pivotal. ANTONYMS complimentary.

■ **crit·i·cal·ly adv.**

crit·i·cism /ˈkritəˌsizəm/ ▶ **n. 1** expression of disapproval. **2** the assessment of literary or artistic works.

SYNONYMS **1 fault-finding**, censure, condemnation, disapproval, disparagement; informal flak, bad press, panning. **2 evaluation**, assessment, appraisal, appreciation, analysis, critique, judgment, commentary. ANTONYMS praise.

crit·i·cize /ˈkritəˌsīz/ ▶ **v.** (**criticizes**, **criticizing**, **criticized**) **1** express disapproval of. **2** assess a literary or artistic work.

SYNONYMS **find fault with**, censure, condemn, attack, disparage, denigrate, run down; informal knock, pan, pull to pieces, trash. ANTONYMS praise.

cri·tique /kriˈtēk/ ▶ **n.** a critical assessment.

crit·ter /ˈkritər/ ▶ **n.** informal or dialect a living creature.

croak /krōk/ ▶ **n.** a deep, hoarse sound, like that made by a frog. ▶ **v. 1** make a croak. **2** informal die. ■ **croak·y adj.**

Cro·a·tian /krōˈāsHən/ ▶ **n.** (also **Croat** /ˈkrōˌat, ˈkrōˌät, krōt/) **1** a person from Croatia. **2** the language of Croatia. ▶ **adj.** relating to Croatia or Croatian.

cro·chet /krōˈsHā/ ▶ **n.** a craft in which yarn is made into fabric with a hooked needle. ▶ **v.** (**crochets**, **crocheting** , **crocheted**) make an article by means of crochet.

crock[1] /kräk/ ▶ **n.** informal a feeble and useless old person.

crock[2] ▶ **n.** an earthenware pot or jar.

crock·er·y /ˈkräkərē/ ▶ **n.** plates, dishes, cups, etc., made of earthenware or china.

croc·o·dile /ˈkräkəˌdīl/ ▶ **n.** a large reptile with long jaws, a long tail, and a thick skin. ◻ **crocodile tears** insincere tears or sorrow.

cro·cus /ˈkrōkəs/ ▶ **n.** (plural **crocuses** or **croci** /ˈkrōˌkī, -ˌsī/) a small plant with bright yellow, purple, or white flowers.

Croe·sus /ˈkrēsəs/ ▶ **n.** a person of great wealth.

crois·sant /k(r)wäˈsänt, -ˈsäɴ/ ▶ **n.** a flaky crescent-shaped bread roll.

crone /krōn/ ▶ **n.** an ugly old woman.

cro·ny /ˈkrōnē/ ▶ **n.** (plural **cronies**) informal a close friend or companion.

cro·ny·ism /ˈkrōnēˌizəm/ ▶ **n.** the improper situation in which people in power give their friends positions of authority.

crook /kro͝ok/ ▶ **n. 1** a shepherd's or bishop's hooked staff. **2** a bend at a person's elbow. **3** informal a criminal or dishonest person. ▶ **v.** bend a finger or leg.

SYNONYMS ▶ **n.** see **CRIMINAL** (noun).

crook·ed /ˈkro͝okəd/ ▶ **adj. 1** bent or twisted out of shape or position. **2** informal dishonest or illegal.

SYNONYMS **1 winding**, twisting, zigzag, meandering, tortuous, serpentine. **2 bent**, twisted, misshapen, deformed, malformed, contorted, warped, bowed, distorted. **3 lopsided**, askew, awry, off-center, out of true, at an angle, slanting. **4 dishonest**, criminal, illegal, unlawful, nefarious, fraudulent, corrupt; informal shady. ANTONYMS straight.

croon /kro͞on/ ▶ **v.** hum, sing, or speak in a soft, low voice. ▪ **croon·er n.**

crop /kräp/ ▶ **n. 1** a plant grown in large quantities, especially as food. **2** an amount of a crop harvested at one time. **3** a very short hairstyle. **4** a pouch in a bird's throat where food is stored or prepared for digestion. **5** a short flexible whip used by horse riders. ▶ **v.** (**crops**, **cropping**, **cropped**) **1** cut something very short. **2** (of an animal) bite off and eat the tops of plants. **3** (**crop up**) appear or happen unexpectedly.

SYNONYMS ▶ **n. harvest**, yield, fruits, produce, vintage. ▶ **v. cut**, clip, trim, shear, shave, lop off, chop off, hack off, dock.

crop·per /ˈkräpər/ ▶ **n.** (**come a cropper**) informal fall or fail heavily.

cro·quet /krōˈkā/ ▶ **n.** a game in which wooden balls are hit through hoops with a mallet.

cro·quette /krōˈket/ ▶ **n.** a small cake or roll of vegetables, meat, or fish, covered in breadcrumbs and then fried.

cross /krôs/ ▶ **n. 1** a mark, object, or shape formed by two short intersecting lines or pieces (+ or ×). **2** a cross-shaped medal or monument. **3** (**the Cross**) the wooden cross on which Jesus was crucified. **4** an animal or plant resulting from crossbreeding. **5** a mixture of two things. ▶ **v. 1** go or extend across or to the other side of: *he started to cross the road*. **2** pass in an opposite or different direction. **3** place crosswise: *Michele crossed her legs*. **4** draw a line or lines across. **5** Soccer pass the ball across the field toward the center. **6** oppose or stand in the way of. **7** make an animal breed with another of a different species. ▶ **adj.** annoyed.

SYNONYMS ▶ **n. 1** *we all have our crosses to bear* **burden**, trouble, worry, trial, tribulation, affliction, curse, misfortune, woe; informal hassle, headache. **2** *a cross between a yak and a cow* **mixture**, blend, combination, amalgam, hybrid, crossbreed, mongrel. ▶ **v. 1 travel across**, traverse, negotiate, navigate, cover. **2 intersect**, meet, join, connect. **3 oppose**, resist, defy, obstruct, contradict, argue with, stand up to. **4 hybridize**, crossbreed, interbreed, cross-fertilize, cross-pollinate. ▶ **adj. angry**, annoyed, irate, vexed, irritated, in a bad mood, put out, exasperated; informal hot under the collar, sore, ticked off, peeved. ANTONYMS pleased.

◻ **at cross purposes** misunderstanding or having different aims from one another. **cross-check** check figures or information by using a different source or method. **cross-country 1** across fields or countryside. **2** across a region or country. **cross-examine** question a witness called by the other party in a court of law. **cross-eyed** having one or both eyes turned inward toward the nose. **cross-fertilize** fertilize a plant using pollen from another plant of the same species. **cross-legged** (of a seated person) with the legs crossed at the ankles and the knees bent outward. **cross something off** remove an item from a list. **cross something out** remove a word or phrase by drawing a line through it. **cross-pollinate** pollinate a flower or plant with pollen from another. **cross reference** a reference to another written work, or part of one, given to provide further information. **cross section 1** a surface exposed by making a straight cut through a solid object at right angles to its length. **2** a sample of a larger group. **cross swords** have an argument or dispute. **cross yourself** make the sign of the cross in front of your chest. **get your wires crossed** have a misunderstanding. ▪ **cross·ly adv.**

cross·bar /ˈkrôsˌbär/ ▶ **n. 1** a horizontal bar between two upright posts, particularly the bar between posts of a sports goal. **2** a bar between the handlebars and saddle on a bicycle.

cross·bow /ˈkrôsˌbō/ ▶ **n.** a bow with a mechanism for drawing and releasing the string.

cross·breed /ˈkrôsˌbrēd/ ▶ **n.** an animal or plant produced by mixing two different species, breeds, or varieties. ▶ **v.** produce an animal or plant in this way.

cross·fire /ˈkrôsˌfīr/ ▶ **n.** gunfire from two or more directions passing through the same area.

cross·hatch /ˈkrôsˌhaᴄʜ/ ▶ **v.** shade an area with many intersecting parallel lines.

cross·ing /ˈkrôsiɴɢ/ ▶ **n. 1** a place where roads or railroad lines cross. **2** a place to cross a street or railroad line.

SYNONYMS **1 junction**, crossroads, intersection, interchange, grade crossing, railroad crossing. **2 journey**, passage, voyage.

cross·o·ver /ˈkrôsˌōvər/ ▶ **n. 1** a point or place of crossing. **2** the process of achieving success in a different field or style, especially in popular music: *a perfect dance/soul crossover*.

cross·roads /ˈkrôsˌrōdz/ ▶ **n.** a place where two or more roads cross each other.

cross·talk /ˈkrôsˌtôk/ ▶ **n. 1** unwanted transfer of signals between communication channels. **2** witty conversation.

cross·walk /ˈkrôsˌwôk/ ▶ **n.** an area of road marked with broad white stripes, where pedestrians can cross.

cross·wind /ˈkrôsˌwind/ ▶ **n.** a wind blowing across your direction of travel.

cross·wise /'krôs,wīz/ (or **crossways**) ▶ **adv.** **1** in the form of a cross. **2** diagonally.

cross·word /'krôswərd/ ▶ **n.** a puzzle in which words crossing each other vertically and horizontally are written as answers to clues.

crotch /krăcH/ ▶ **n.** the part of the human body between the legs.

crotch·et·y /'krăcHətē/ ▶ **adj.** irritable.

crouch /kroucH/ ▶ **v.** bend the knees and bring the upper body forward and down. ▶ **n.** a crouching position.

SYNONYMS ▶ **v.** **squat**, bend (down), hunker down, hunch over, stoop, duck, cower.

croup¹ /kro͞op/ ▶ **n.** an illness of children, with coughing and breathing difficulties.

croup² ▶ **n.** a horse's hindquarters.

croup·i·er /'kro͞opē,ā, -pēər/ ▶ **n.** the person in charge of a gambling table in a casino.

crou·ton /'kro͞o,tän, kro͞o'tän/ ▶ **n.** a small piece of fried or toasted bread served with soup or on a salad.

crow¹ /krō/ ▶ **n.** a large black bird with a harsh call. □ **as the crow flies** in a straight line across country. **crow's feet** wrinkles at the outer corner of a person's eye. **crow's-nest** a platform at the top of a ship's mast to watch from.

crow² ▶ **v.** **1** (of a cock) make its loud, shrill cry. **2** boastfully express pride or triumph. ▶ **n.** the cry of a cock.

SYNONYMS ▶ **v.** **boast**, brag, blow your own horn, swagger, swank, gloat.

crow·bar /'krō,bär/ ▶ **n.** an iron bar with a flattened end, used as a lever.

crowd /kroud/ ▶ **n.** **1** a large number of people gathered together. **2** informal a group of people with a shared quality: *he hangs around with a wealthy crowd.* ▶ **v.** **1** fill a space almost completely. **2** move or come together as a crowd: *everyone crowded into the hall.* **3** move or stand too close to.

SYNONYMS ▶ **n.** **1** **horde**, throng, mass, multitude, host, army, herd, swarm, troop, mob, rabble; informal gaggle. **2** *they're a nice crowd* **group**, set, circle, clique; informal gang, bunch, crew, lot. **3** *a capacity crowd* **audience**, spectators, listeners, viewers, house, turnout, attendance, gate, congregation. ▶ **v.** **1** **cluster**, flock, swarm, mill, throng, huddle, gather, assemble, congregate, converge. **2** **surge**, throng, push, jostle, elbow your way, squeeze, pile, cram.

crowd·ed /'kroudid/ ▶ **adj.** (of a place) filled almost completely by a large number of people.

SYNONYMS **packed**, full, filled to capacity, full to bursting, congested, overflowing, teeming, swarming, thronged, populous, overpopulated, busy; informal jam-packed, stuffed, chock-a-block, chock-full, bursting at the seams, full to the gunwales, wall-to-wall, mobbed. ANTONYMS deserted.

crown /kroun/ ▶ **n.** **1** a circular headdress worn by a king or queen. **2** (**the Crown**) the reigning king or queen. **3** a wreath of leaves or flowers worn as an emblem of victory. **4** an award gained by a victory: *the world heavyweight crown.* **5** the top or highest part of something. **6** an artificial replacement or covering for the upper part of a tooth. ▶ **v.** **1** place a crown on the head of someone to declare them to be king or queen. **2** rest on or form the top of: *the knoll was crowned with trees.*

SYNONYMS ▶ **n.** **1** **coronet**, diadem, tiara, circlet. **2** **monarch**, sovereign, king, queen, emperor, empress, monarchy, royalty. **3** **top**, crest, summit, peak, pinnacle, tip, brow, apex. ▶ **v.** *the post at Harvard crowned his career* **round off**, cap, be the climax of, be the culmination of, top off, complete, perfect.

□ **crown jewels** the crown and other jewelry worn or carried by a sovereign on state occasions. **crown prince** (in some countries) a male heir to a throne. **crown princess** (in some countries) a female heir to a throne, or the wife of a crown prince.

cro·zier /'krōzHər/ ▶ **n.** a hooked staff carried by a bishop.

cru·cial /'kro͞osHəl/ ▶ **adj.** very important, especially in terms of the success or failure of something: *negotiations were at a crucial stage.*

SYNONYMS **1** **pivotal**, critical, key, decisive, life-and-death. **2** **all-important**, of the utmost importance, of the essence, critical, paramount, essential, vital. ANTONYMS insignificant, unimportant.

■ **cru·cial·ly** **adv.**

cru·ci·ble /'kro͞osəbəl/ ▶ **n.** a container in which metals or other substances may be melted or heated.

cru·cif·er·ous /kro͞o'sifərəs/ ▶ **adj.** Botany belonging to the cabbage family, with four equal petals arranged in a cross.

cru·ci·fix /'kro͞osə,fiks/ ▶ **n.** a small cross with a figure of Jesus on it.

cru·ci·fix·ion /,kro͞osə'fiksHən/ ▶ **n.** **1** the execution of a person by crucifying them. **2** (**the Crucifixion**) the crucifixion of Jesus.

cru·ci·form /'kro͞osə,fôrm/ ▶ **adj.** having the shape of a cross.

cru·ci·fy /'kro͞osə,fī/ ▶ **v.** (**crucifies**, **crucifying**, **crucified**) **1** kill someone by nailing or tying them to a cross. **2** informal criticize someone severely.

crud /krəd/ ▶ **n.** informal **1** an unpleasantly dirty or messy substance. **2** nonsense. ■ **crud·dy** **adj.**

crude /kro͞od/ ▶ **adj.** **1** in a natural state; not yet processed: *crude oil.* **2** rough or simple: *a pair of crude huts.* **3** coarse or vulgar.

SYNONYMS **1** **unrefined**, unpurified, unprocessed, untreated, coarse, raw, natural. **2** **primitive**, simple, basic, homespun, rudimentary, rough and ready, makeshift, improvised, unsophisticated. **3** **vulgar**, rude, dirty, naughty, smutty, indecent, obscene, coarse; informal blue. ANTONYMS refined.

■ **crude·ly** **adv.**

cru·di·tés /,kro͞odə'tā/ ▶ **pl.n.** mixed raw vegetables served with a sauce into which they may be dipped.

cru·el /'kro͞o(ə)l/ ▶ **adj.** (**crueler**, **cruelest**) **1** taking pleasure in the suffering of other people. **2** causing pain or suffering.

SYNONYMS **1** *a cruel man* **brutal**, savage, inhuman, barbaric, vicious, sadistic, monstrous, callous, ruthless, merciless, heartless, pitiless, implacable, unkind, inhumane. **2** *her death was a cruel blow* **harsh**, severe, bitter, heartbreaking, heart-rending, painful, agonizing, traumatic. ANTONYMS compassionate.

■ **cru·el·ly** adv.

cru·el·ty /ˈkro͞o(ə)ltē/ ▶ n. (plural **cruelties**) cruel behavior or treatment.

SYNONYMS **brutality**, savagery, inhumanity, barbarity, viciousness, sadism, callousness, ruthlessness.

cru·et /ˈkro͞oət/ ▶ n. a small container or set of containers for salt, pepper, oil, or vinegar.

cruise /kro͞oz/ ▶ v. (**cruises, cruising, cruised**) **1** move slowly around without a definite destination. **2** travel smoothly at a moderate speed. ▶ n. a voyage on a ship taken as a vacation.

SYNONYMS ▶ v. **1 sail**, voyage. **2 drive slowly**, drift; informal mosey, tootle. ▶ n. **(boat) trip**, voyage, sail.

□ **cruise missile** a low-flying missile fitted with a computer to guide it to its target.

cruis·er /ˈkro͞ozər/ ▶ n. **1** a large, fast warship. **2** a yacht or motorboat with passenger accommodations.

crumb /krəm/ ▶ n. **1** a small fragment of bread, cake, or cookie. **2** a very small amount: *the budget provided few crumbs of comfort.*

SYNONYMS **fragment**, bit, morsel, particle, speck, scrap, shred, atom, trace, mite, jot, ounce; informal smidgen, tad.

crum·ble /ˈkrəmbəl/ ▶ v. (**crumbles, crumbling, crumbled**) **1** break or fall apart into small fragments. **2** gradually decline or fall apart.

SYNONYMS **1 disintegrate**, fall apart, fall to pieces, collapse, decompose, break up, decay, become dilapidated, deteriorate, degenerate. **2 break up**, crush, fragment, pulverize.

crum·bly /ˈkrəmblē/ ▶ adj. easily breaking into small fragments.

crum·my /ˈkrəmē/ ▶ adj. (**crummier, crummiest**) informal bad or unpleasant.

crum·pet /ˈkrəmpət/ ▶ n. a soft, flat cake with an open texture, eaten toasted and buttered.

crum·ple /ˈkrəmpəl/ ▶ v. (**crumples, crumpling, crumpled**) **1** crease something by crushing it. **2** collapse: *she crumpled to the floor in a faint.*

SYNONYMS **1 crush**, scrunch up, screw up, squash, squeeze. **2 crease**, wrinkle, crinkle, rumple. **3 collapse**, give way, cave in, go to pieces, break down, crumble.

crunch /krənCH/ ▶ v. **1** crush something brittle or hard with the teeth. **2** move with a noisy grinding sound. **3** process large amounts of information or perform operations of great complexity, especially by computer. ▶ n. **1** a crunching sound. **2** (**the crunch**) informal the crucial point of a situation. **3** a physical exercise designed to strengthen the abdominal muscles; a sit-up.

SYNONYMS ▶ v. **munch**, chomp, champ, bite into, crush, grind.

crunch·y /ˈkrənCHē/ ▶ adj. (**crunchier, crunchiest**) **1** making a crunching noise when bitten or crushed. **2** informal politically and environmentally liberal. ■ **crunch·i·ness** n.

crup·per /ˈkrəpər/ ▶ n. a strap at the back of a saddle and looped under a horse's tail, to prevent the saddle or harness from slipping.

cru·sade /kro͞oˈsād/ ▶ n. **1** (**the Crusades**) a series of medieval military expeditions made by Europeans against Muslims in the Middle East. **2** an energetic organized campaign: *a crusade against crime.* ▶ v. (**crusades, crusading, crusaded**) take part in a crusade.

SYNONYMS ▶ n. **campaign**, drive, push, movement, effort, struggle, battle, war, offensive. ▶ v. **campaign**, fight, battle, do battle, strive, struggle, agitate, lobby.

■ **cru·sad·er** n.

crush /krəSH/ ▶ v. **1** squash, crease, or break up something by pressing it. **2** defeat completely: *he sent in the army to crush the militants.* ▶ n. **1** a crowd of people pressed closely together. **2** informal a strong, short-lived feeling of love for someone: *she had a crush on Dr. Jones.*

SYNONYMS ▶ v. **1 squash**, squeeze, press, pulp, mash, mangle, pulverize. **2 crease**, crumple, rumple, wrinkle, scrunch up. **3 suppress**, put down, quell, stamp out, repress, subdue, extinguish. **4 demoralize**, deflate, flatten, squash, devastate, shatter, mortify, humiliate. ▶ n. **crowd**, throng, horde, swarm, press, mob.

crust /krəst/ ▶ n. **1** the tough outer part of a loaf of bread. **2** a hardened layer, coating, or deposit. **3** the outermost layer of the earth. **4** a layer of pastry covering a pie. ▶ v. form into a crust, or cover with a crust.

SYNONYMS ▶ n. **covering**, layer, coating, surface, topping, sheet, film, skin, shell, scab.

crus·ta·cean /krəˈstāSHən/ ▶ n. a hard-shelled creature such as a crab or lobster, usually living in water.

crust·y /ˈkrəstē/ ▶ adj. (**crustier, crustiest**) **1** having or consisting of a crust. **2** easily irritated.

crutch /krəCH/ ▶ n. **1** a long stick with a bar at the top, used as a support by a lame person. **2** a person's crotch.

crux /krəks, kro͝oks/ ▶ n. (**the crux**) the most important point that is being discussed: *the crux of the matter is that attitudes have changed.*

cry /krī/ ▶ v. (**cries, crying, cried**) **1** shed tears. **2** shout or scream loudly. **3** (of an animal) make a distinctive call. **4** (**cry out for**) demand or need: *the plan cries out for reform.* **5** (**cry off**) informal fail to keep to an arrangement. ▶ n. (plural **cries**) **1** a period of shedding tears. **2** a loud shout or scream. **3** an animal's distinctive call.

SYNONYMS ▶ v. **1 weep**, shed tears, sob, wail, snivel, whimper; informal blubber. **2 call**, shout, exclaim, sing out, yell, bawl, bellow, roar; informal holler. ANTONYMS laugh. ▶ n. **call**, shout, exclamation, yell, bawl, bellow, roar; informal holler.

□ **a crying shame** a very unfortunate situation.

cry·o·gen·ics /ˌkrīəˈjeniks/ ▶ n. the branch of physics concerned with very low temperatures. ■ **cry·o·gen·ic** adj.

crypt /kript/ ▶ n. an underground room beneath a church, used as a chapel or burial place.

SYNONYMS **tomb**, vault, burial chamber, sepulcher, catacomb.

cryp·tic /ˈkriptik/ ▶ adj. mysterious or obscure in meaning: *he gave us a cryptic message to pass on.*

SYNONYMS **enigmatic**, mysterious, mystifying, puzzling, obscure, abstruse, arcane, unintelligible. ANTONYMS clear.

■ **cryp·ti·cal·ly** adv.

cryp·to·gram /ˈkriptəˌgram/ ▶ **n.** a text written in code.

cryp·tog·ra·phy /kripˈtägrəfē/ ▶ **n.** the art of writing or solving codes. ■ **cryp·tog·ra·pher n. cryp·to·graph·ic** /ˌkriptəˈgrafik/ **adj.**

crys·tal /ˈkristl/ ▶ **n. 1** a transparent mineral, especially quartz. **2** a piece of a solid substance that is formed naturally and has flat sides arranged symmetrically. **3** very clear glass. □ **crystal ball** a globe of glass or crystal, used for predicting the future.

crys·tal·line /ˈkristl-in, -tl-ˌīn, -tl-ˌēn/ ▶ **adj. 1** resembling a crystal. **2** literary very clear.

crys·tal·lize /ˈkristəˌlīz/ ▶ **v.** (**crystallizes, crystallizing, crystallized**) **1** form crystals. **2** become definite and clear: *his book helped me to crystallize my own thoughts.* **3** (**crystallized**) (of fruit) coated with and preserved in sugar.

crys·tal·log·ra·phy /ˌkristəˈlägrəfē/ ▶ **n.** the branch of science concerned with the structure and properties of crystals. ■ **crys·tal·log·ra·pher n.**

c/s ▶ **abbr.** cycles per second.

C-sec·tion ▶ **n.** ⇨ CESAREAN.

ct ▶ **abbr. 1** carat. **2** cent.

Cu ▶ **symbol** the chemical element copper.

cu. ▶ **abbr.** cubic.

cub /kəb/ ▶ **n. 1** the young of a fox, bear, lion, or other meat-eating mammal. **2** (also **Cub Scout**) a member of the junior branch of the Boy Scouts.

Cu·ban /ˈkyo͞obən/ ▶ **n.** a person from Cuba. ▶ **adj.** relating to Cuba.

cub·by /ˈkəbē/ ▶ **n.** (plural **cubbies**) a cubbyhole.

cub·by·hole /ˈkəbēˌhōl/ ▶ **n.** a small enclosed space or room.

cube /kyo͞ob/ ▶ **n. 1** a three-dimensional shape with six equal square faces. **2** the result obtained when a number is multiplied by itself twice. ▶ **v. 1** cut food into small cubes. **2** find the cube of a number. □ **cube root** the number that produces a given number when cubed.

cu·bic /ˈkyo͞obik/ ▶ **adj. 1** having the shape of a cube. **2** involving the cube of a quantity: *a cubic meter.*

cu·bi·cle /ˈkyo͞obikəl/ ▶ **n.** a small area of a room that is separated off for privacy.

cub·ism /ˈkyo͞oˌbizəm/ ▶ **n.** a style of painting featuring regular lines and shapes. ■ **cub·ist n. & adj.**

cu·bit /ˈkyo͞obit/ ▶ **n.** an ancient measure of length, approximately equal to the length of a forearm.

cu·boid /ˈkyo͞oˌboid/ ▶ **adj.** having the shape of a cube. ▶ **n.** a solid that has six rectangular faces at right angles to each other.

cuck·oo /ˈko͞oko͞o, ˈko͝oko͞o/ ▶ **n.** a bird known for laying its eggs in the nests of other birds. ▶ **adj.** informal crazy.

cu·cum·ber /ˈkyo͞oˌkəmbər/ ▶ **n.** a long green fruit with watery flesh, eaten in salads or pickled.

cud /kəd/ ▶ **n.** (usu. in **chew the cud**) partly digested food that cows and similar animals bring back from the first stomach to the mouth for further chewing. □ **chew the cud** think or talk reflectively.

cud·dle /ˈkədl/ ▶ **v.** (**cuddles, cuddling, cuddled**) **1** hold closely and lovingly in your arms. **2** (often **cuddle up to**) lie or sit close. ▶ **n.** an affectionate hug.

> SYNONYMS ▶ **v. 1 hug**, embrace, clasp, hold in your arms, caress, pet, fondle; informal canoodle, smooch. **2 snuggle**, nestle, curl up, nuzzle.

cud·dly /ˈkədlē, ˈkədl-ē/ ▶ **adj.** (**cuddlier, cuddliest**) pleasantly soft or plump.

cudg·el /ˈkəjəl/ ▶ **n.** a short, thick stick used as a weapon. ▶ **v.** (**cudgels, cudgeling, cudgeled**) beat with a cudgel.

> SYNONYMS ▶ **n. club**, truncheon, bludgeon, mace, blackjack, nightstick, baton. ▶ **v. club**, bludgeon, beat, batter, bash.

cue¹ /kyo͞o/ ▶ **n. 1** a signal to an actor to enter or to begin their speech or performance. **2** a signal or prompt for action. ▶ **v.** (**cues, cueing** or **cuing, cued**) **1** give a cue to. **2** set a piece of audio or video equipment to play a particular part of a recording.

> SYNONYMS ▶ **n. signal**, sign, indication, prompt, reminder.

□ **on cue** at the correct moment.

cue² ▶ **n.** a long rod for hitting the ball in pool, billiards, or snooker. □ **cue ball** the ball that is to be struck with the cue.

cuff¹ /kəf/ ▶ **n. 1** the end part of a sleeve, where the material of the sleeve is turned back or a separate band is sewn on. **2** a turned-up end of a trouser leg. □ **off the cuff** informal without preparation.

cuff² ▶ **v.** hit with an open hand. ▶ **n.** a blow with an open hand.

cuff·link /ˈkəfˌliNGk/ ▶ **n.** a device for fastening together the sides of a shirt cuff.

cui·rass /kwiˈras, kyo͝orˈas/ ▶ **n.** historical a piece of armor consisting of breastplate and a similar plate at the back.

cui·sine /kwiˈzēn/ ▶ **n.** a particular style of cooking: *classic French cuisine.*

cul-de-sac /ˈkəl di ˌsak/ ▶ **n.** (plural **cul-de-sacs**) a street or passage closed at one end.

cu·li·nar·y /ˈkələˌnerē, ˈkyo͞olə-/ ▶ **adj.** having to do with cooking.

cull /kəl/ ▶ **v. 1** kill a selected number of a certain kind of animal to reduce its population. **2** choose a few things from a wide range: *anecdotes culled from Roman history.* ▶ **n. 1** a selective killing of a certain kind of animal. **2** an inferior or surplus livestock animal selected for killing.

cul·mi·nate /ˈkəlməˌnāt/ ▶ **v.** (**culminates, culminating, culminated**) reach a climax or point of highest development: *the disorders which culminated in World War II.*

> SYNONYMS **come to a climax**, come to a head, climax, end, finish, conclude, build up to, lead up to.

cul·mi·na·tion /ˌkəlməˈnāSHən/ ▶ **n.** the highest or climactic point of something.

> SYNONYMS **climax**, peak, pinnacle, high point, height, summit, zenith, apotheosis, apex, apogee.

cu·lottes /ˈk(y)o͞oˌläts, k(y)o͞oˈläts/ ▶ **pl.n.** women's wide-legged knee-length trousers.

cul·pa·ble /ˈkəlpəbəl/ ▶ **adj.** deserving blame.

> SYNONYMS **to blame**, guilty, at fault, in the wrong, answerable, accountable, responsible. ANTONYMS innocent.

■ **cul·pa·bil·i·ty** /ˌkəlpəˈbilitē/ **n.**

cul·prit /ˈkəlprət, ˈkəlˌprit/ ▶ **n.** the person responsible for an offense.

> SYNONYMS **guilty party**, offender, wrongdoer, perpetrator, miscreant, criminal, lawbreaker,

felon, delinquent; informal baddy, bad guy, crook, perp.

cult /kəlt/ ▶ **n. 1** a system of religious worship directed toward a particular person or object. **2** a small, unconventional religious group. ▶ **adj.** attaining a popular or fashionable status among a particular group of people: *the series became a cult hit among teens.*

SYNONYMS ▶ **n. 1 sect**, group, movement. **2 obsession**, fixation, idolization, devotion, worship, veneration.

cul·ti·var /ˈkəltəˌvär/ ▶ **n.** a plant variety that has been produced by selective breeding.

cul·ti·vate /ˈkəltəˌvāt/ ▶ **v.** (**cultivates**, **cultivating**, **cultivated**) **1** prepare and use land for crops or gardening. **2** grow plants or crops. **3** try to develop or gain a particular quality: *he cultivated an air of detachment.* **4** try to win the friendship or support of. **5** (**cultivated**) well-educated and having good taste.

SYNONYMS **1 farm**, work, till, plow, dig. **2 grow**, raise, rear, tend, plant, sow. **3 woo**, court, curry favor with, ingratiate yourself with; informal get in good with someone. **4 improve**, better, refine, educate, develop, enrich. **5** (**cultivated**) see **CULTURED**.

■ **cul·ti·va·tion** /ˌkəltəˈvāsHən/ **n.** **cul·ti·va·tor n.**

cul·tur·al /ˈkəlcHərəl/ ▶ **adj. 1** relating to the culture of a society. **2** relating to the arts and intellectual achievements.

SYNONYMS **1 social**, lifestyle, sociological, anthropological, racial, ethnic. **2 aesthetic**, artistic, intellectual, educational, civilizing.

■ **cul·tur·al·ly adv.**

cul·ture /ˈkəlcHər/ ▶ **n. 1** the arts, customs, and institutions of a nation, people, or group: *the Americanization of French culture.* **2** the arts and intellectual achievements regarded as a whole: *museums of culture.* **3** a refined understanding or appreciation of culture. **4** a preparation of cells or bacteria grown for medical or scientific study.

SYNONYMS **1** *a lover of culture* **the arts**, high art. **2** *a man of culture* **education**, cultivation, enlightenment, discernment, discrimination, taste, refinement, sophistication. **3 civilization**, society, way of life, lifestyle, customs, traditions, heritage, values. **4 philosophy**, ethic, outlook, approach, rationale.

cul·tured /ˈkəlcHərd/ ▶ **adj. 1** well-educated and having good taste. **2** (of a pearl) formed around a foreign body inserted into an oyster.

SYNONYMS **cultivated**, artistic, enlightened, civilized, educated, well-read, learned, discerning, discriminating, refined, sophisticated; informal arty. ANTONYMS ignorant.

cul·vert /ˈkəlvərt/ ▶ **n.** a tunnel carrying a stream or open drain under a road or railroad.

cum /ko͝om, kəm/ ▶ **prep.** combined with: *a study-cum-bedroom.*

cum·ber·some /ˈkəmbərsəm/ ▶ **adj. 1** difficult to carry or use because of its size or weight. **2** complicated and time-consuming: *cumbersome business processes.*

cum·brous /ˈkəmbrəs/ ▶ **adj.** literary cumbersome.

cum·in /ˈkəmən, ˈk(y)o͞o-/ ▶ **n.** the seeds of a plant of the parsley family, used as a spice.

cum·mer·bund /ˈkəmərˌbənd/ ▶ **n.** a sash worn around the waist as part of a man's formal evening suit.

cu·mu·la·tive /ˈkyo͞omyələtiv, -ˌlātiv/ ▶ **adj.** increasing by successive additions: *the cumulative effect of years of drought.* ■ **cu·mu·la·tive·ly adv.**

cu·mu·lo·nim·bus /ˌkyo͞omyəlōˈnimbəs/ ▶ **n.** (plural **cumulonimbi** /-bī/) cloud forming a towering mass with a flat base, as in thunderstorms.

cu·mu·lus /ˈkyo͞omyələs/ ▶ **n.** (plural **cumuli** /-ˌlī, -lē/) cloud forming rounded masses heaped on a flat base.

cu·ne·i·form /kyo͞oˈnēəˌfôrm, ˈkyo͞on(ē)ə-/ ▶ **adj.** (of ancient writing systems) using wedge-shaped characters.

cun·ning /ˈkəniNG/ ▶ **adj. 1** skilled at deceiving people. **2** skillful or clever. ▶ **n.** craftiness.

SYNONYMS ▶ **adj. 1 crafty**, wily, artful, devious, Machiavellian, sly, scheming, canny, dishonest, deceitful. **2 clever**, shrewd, astute, canny, ingenious, imaginative, enterprising, inventive, resourceful, creative, original, inspired, brilliant. ANTONYMS honest, stupid. ▶ **n. 1 guile**, craftiness, deviousness, trickery, duplicity. **2 ingenuity**, imagination, inventiveness, enterprise, resourcefulness.

■ **cun·ning·ly adv.**

cup /kəp/ ▶ **n. 1** a small bowl-shaped drinking container with a handle. **2** a trophy in the shape of a cup on a stem, awarded as a prize in a sports contest. **3** a sports contest in which the winner is awarded a cup. **4** either of the two parts of a bra shaped to contain one breast. ▶ **v.** (**cups**, **cupping**, **cupped**) **1** form your hand or hands into the curved shape of a cup. **2** place your curved hand or hands around. □ **not your cup of tea** informal not what you like or find interesting.

cup·board /ˈkəbərd/ ▶ **n.** a piece of furniture, or a recess in a wall with a door, used for storage.

cup·cake /ˈkəpˌkāk/ ▶ **n.** a small iced cake baked in a cup-shaped container.

cu·pid·i·ty /kyo͞oˈpiditē/ ▶ **n.** greed for money or possessions.

cu·po·la /ˈkyo͞opələ/ ▶ **n.** a rounded dome that forms or decorates a roof.

cur /kər/ ▶ **n.** an aggressive mongrel dog.

cu·ra·re /k(y)o͝oˈrärē/ ▶ **n.** a paralysing poison obtained from South American plants.

cu·rate /ˈkyo͝orət, -ˌrāt/ ▶ **n.** an assistant to a parish priest.

cur·a·tive /ˈkyo͝orətiv/ ▶ **adj.** able to cure disease.

cu·ra·tor /ˈkyo͝orˌātər, kyo͝oˈrātər, ˈkyo͝orətər/ ▶ **n.** a keeper of a museum or other collection.

SYNONYMS **custodian**, keeper, conservator, guardian, caretaker.

curb /kərb/ ▶ **n. 1** a stone or concrete edging to a street or path. **2** a control or limit on something: *curbs on pollution.* **3** (also **curb bit**) a type of bit with a strap or chain that passes under a horse's lower jaw. ▶ **v.** control or put a limit on.

SYNONYMS ▶ **n. restraint**, restriction, check, brake, control, limit. ▶ **v. restrain**, hold back, keep in check, control, rein in, contain; informal keep a lid on.

curb·stone /ˈkərbˌstōn/ ▶ **n.** a long, narrow stone or concrete block, laid end to end with others to form a curb.

curd /kərd/ (or **curds**) ▶ **n.** a soft, white substance formed when milk coagulates.

cur·dle /ˈkərdl/ ▶ **v.** (**curdles**, **curdling**, **curdled**) form curds or lumps.

cure /kyo͝or/ ▶ **v.** (**cures**, **curing**, **cured**) **1** make a person who is ill well again. **2** end a disease, condition, or problem by treatment or appropriate action. **3** preserve meat, fish, etc., by salting, drying, or smoking. ▶ **n.** **1** something that cures; a remedy. **2** the healing of a person who is ill.

> SYNONYMS ▶ **v.** **1 heal**, restore to health, make well/better. **2 rectify**, remedy, put/set right, right, fix, mend, repair, solve, sort out, eliminate, end. **3 preserve**, smoke, salt, dry, pickle. ▶ **n.** **remedy**, medicine, medication, antidote, treatment, therapy.

■ **cur·a·ble** adj.

cur·few /ˈkərˌfyo͞o/ ▶ **n.** **1** a regulation requiring people to remain indoors between specific hours of the night. **2** the time at which a curfew begins.

Cu·ri·a /ˈkyo͝orēə/ ▶ **n.** the papal court at the Vatican, by which the Roman Catholic Church is governed.

cu·rie /kyo͝oˈrē, ˈkyo͝orē/ ▶ **n.** (plural **curies**) a unit of radioactivity.

cu·ri·o /ˈkyo͝orēˌō/ ▶ **n.** (plural **curios**) an object that is interesting because it is rare or unusual.

cu·ri·os·i·ty /ˌkyo͝orēˈäsitē/ ▶ **n.** (plural **curiosities**) **1** a strong desire to know or learn something. **2** an unusual or interesting object or fact.

> SYNONYMS **1 interest**, inquisitiveness, attention, spirit of inquiry; informal nosiness. **2 oddity**, curio, novelty, rarity.

cu·ri·ous /ˈkyo͝orēəs/ ▶ **adj.** **1** eager to know or learn something. **2** strange; unusual.

> SYNONYMS **1 intrigued**, interested, eager, inquisitive. **2 strange**, odd, peculiar, funny, unusual, queer, bizarre, weird, eccentric, extraordinary, abnormal, anomalous. ANTONYMS uninterested, normal.

■ **cu·ri·ous·ly** adv.

curl /kərl/ ▶ **v.** form a curved or spiral shape. ▶ **n.** something in the shape of a spiral or coil: *her hair was a mass of curls.*

> SYNONYMS ▶ **v.** **spiral**, coil, wreathe, twirl, swirl, wind, curve, twist (and turn), snake, corkscrew, twine, entwine, wrap. ▶ **n.** **1 ringlet**, corkscrew, kink, lock. **2** *a curl of smoke* **spiral**, coil, twirl, swirl, twist, corkscrew.

curl·er /ˈkərlər/ ▶ **n.** a roller or clasp around which you wrap hair to curl it.

cur·lew /ˈkərˌlo͞o, ˈkərlˌyo͞o/ ▶ **n.** (plural **curlew** or **curlews**) a large wading bird with a long curved bill.

curl·i·cue /ˈkərlēˌkyo͞o/ ▶ **n.** a decorative curl or twist.

curl·ing /ˈkərliNG/ ▶ **n.** a game played on ice, in which you slide large circular flat stones toward a mark.

curl·y /ˈkərlē/ ▶ **adj.** (**curlier**, **curliest**) having curls.

> SYNONYMS **wavy**, curling, curled, frizzy, kinky, corkscrew. ANTONYMS straight.

cur·mudg·eon /kərˈməjən/ ▶ **n.** a bad-tempered person. ■ **cur·mudg·eon·ly** adj.

cur·rant /ˈkərənt, ˈkə-rənt/ ▶ **n.** a dried fruit made from a small seedless variety of grape.

cur·ren·cy /ˈkərənsē, ˈkə-rənsē/ ▶ **n.** (plural **currencies**) **1** a system of money used in a country. **2** the state or period of being current: *the term has gained new currency.*

> SYNONYMS **1 money**, legal tender, cash, banknotes, notes, bills, coins. **2 popularity**, circulation, exposure, acceptance, prevalence.

cur·rent /ˈkərənt, ˈkə-rənt/ ▶ **adj.** **1** happening or being used or done now: *current events*. **2** in common or general use. ▶ **n.** **1** a flow of water or air in a particular direction. **2** a flow of electrically charged particles.

> SYNONYMS ▶ **adj.** **1 contemporary**, present-day, modern, topical, live, burning. **2 prevalent**, common, accepted, in circulation, popular, widespread. **3 valid**, usable, up to date. **4 incumbent**, present, in office, in power, reigning. ANTONYMS past, former. ▶ **n.** **1 flow**, stream, draught, jet, tide. **2 course**, progress, progression, flow, tide, movement.

> USAGE
> Don't confuse **current** with **currant**, which means 'a dried grape.'

cur·rent·ly /ˈkərəntlē, ˈkə-rəntlē/ ▶ **adv.** at the present time.

cur·ric·u·lum /kəˈrikyələm/ ▶ **n.** (plural **curricula** /-lə/ or **curriculums**) the subjects that make up a program of study in a school or college. □ **curriculum vitae** /ˈvēˌtī, ˈvītē/ a written account of a person's qualifications and previous jobs, sent with a job application. ■ **cur·ric·u·lar** adj.

cur·ried /ˈkərēd/ ▶ **adj.** made as a curry with a hot, spicy sauce.

cur·ry¹ /ˈkərē/ ▶ **n.** (plural **curries**) an Indian dish of meat, vegetables, or fish, cooked in a hot, spicy sauce.

cur·ry² ▶ **v.** (**curries**, **currying**, **curried**) **1** (**curry favor**) try to win someone's approval by flattering them and being very helpful. **2** groom a horse with a curry comb. □ **curry comb** a hand-held rubber device used for grooming horses.

curse /kərs/ ▶ **n.** **1** an appeal to a supernatural power to harm someone or something. **2** a cause of harm or misery: *impatience is the curse of our time.* **3** an offensive word or phrase used to express anger or annoyance. ▶ **v.** (**curses**, **cursing**, **cursed**) **1** use a curse against. **2** (**be cursed with**) continuously suffer from or be affected by. **3** say offensive words; swear.

> SYNONYMS ▶ **n.** **1 jinx**, malediction, hex; formal imprecation, anathema. **2 affliction**, burden, misery, ordeal, evil, scourge. **3 swear word**, expletive, oath, profanity, four-letter word, dirty word, obscenity; informal cuss word. ▶ **v.** **1 afflict**, trouble, plague, bedevil. **2 swear**, take the Lord's name in vain, blaspheme; informal cuss.

curs·ed /ˈkərsid, kərst/ ▶ **adj.** informal, dated used to express annoyance or irritation.

> SYNONYMS **damned**, doomed, ill-fated, ill-starred, jinxed.

cur·sive /ˈkərsiv/ ▶ **adj.** written with the characters joined.

cur·sor /ˈkərsər/ ▶ **n.** a mark on a computer screen identifying the point where typing or other input will take effect.

SPELLING
Write **-or** at the end, not **-er**: curs**or**.

cur·so·ry /ˈkərsərē/ ▶ **adj.** hasty and therefore not thorough.

SYNONYMS **brief**, hasty, hurried, quick, rapid, passing, perfunctory, desultory, casual. ANTONYMS thorough.

■ **cur·so·ri·ly** adv.

curt /kərt/ ▶ **adj.** (of a person's speech) rudely brief.

SYNONYMS **terse**, brusque, snappish, abrupt, clipped, blunt, short, sharp, rude, ungracious. ANTONYMS expansive.

■ **curt·ly** adv.

cur·tail /kərˈtāl/ ▶ **v.** cut short or restrict: *a movement to curtail the arms trade.*

SYNONYMS **reduce**, shorten, cut, cut down, decrease, trim, restrict, limit, curb, rein in, cut short, truncate; informal slash. ANTONYMS increase, extend.

■ **cur·tail·ment** n.

cur·tain /ˈkərtn/ ▶ **n.** **1** a piece of material hung up to form a screen at a window or between the stage and the audience in a theater. **2** (**curtains**) informal a disastrous end: *it's curtains for the bank.* ▶ **v.** provide or screen something with a curtain or curtains. □ **curtain call** the appearance of a performer on stage after a performance to acknowledge applause. **curtain-raiser** an event happening just before a longer or more important one.

curt·sy /ˈkərtsē/ (or **curtsey**) ▶ **n.** (plural **curtsies** or **curtseys**) a woman's or girl's respectful greeting, made by bending the knees with one foot in front of the other. ▶ **v.** (**curtsies**, **curtsying**, **curtsied** or **curtseys**, **curtseying**, **curtseyed**) perform a curtsy.

cur·va·ceous /kərˈvāsHəs/ ▶ **adj.** having an attractively curved shape.

cur·va·ture /ˈkərvəcHər, -ˌcHo͝or/ ▶ **n.** the fact of being curved; a curved shape: *curvature of the spine.*

curve /kərv/ ▶ **n.** a line that gradually turns from a straight course. ▶ **v.** (**curves**, **curving**, **curved**) form a curve.

SYNONYMS ▶ **n.** **bend**, turn, loop, arc, arch, bow, curvature. ▶ **v.** **bend**, turn, loop, wind, meander, snake, arc, arch.

cur·vet /kərˈvet/ ▶ **n.** a horse's short energetic leap. ▶ **v.** (**curvets**, **curveting**, **curveted**) (of a horse) make such a leap.

cur·vi·lin·e·ar /ˌkərvəˈlinēər/ ▶ **adj.** contained by or consisting of a curved line or lines: *a curvilinear building.*

curv·y /ˈkərvē/ ▶ **adj.** (**curvier**, **curviest**) **1** having many curves. **2** informal (of a woman's figure) curvaceous. ■ **curv·i·ness** n.

cush·ion /ˈko͝osHən/ ▶ **n.** **1** a bag of cloth stuffed with soft material, used to provide comfort when sitting. **2** something that gives protection against impact or something unpleasant. **3** the inner sides of a billiard table. ▶ **v.** **1** soften the effect of an impact on. **2** lessen the bad effects of: *he relied on his savings to cushion the blow of losing his job.*

SYNONYMS ▶ **n.** *a cushion against inflation* **protection**, buffer, shield, defense, bulwark. ▶ **v.** **1** *cushioned from the outside world* **protect**, shield, shelter, cocoon. **2** *cushion the blow* **soften**, lessen, diminish, mitigate, alleviate, take the edge off, dull, deaden.

cush·y /ˈko͝osHē/ ▶ **adj.** (**cushier**, **cushiest**) informal easy and undemanding: *a cushy job.*

cusp /kəsp/ ▶ **n.** **1** a pointed end where two curves meet. **2** a point in between two different states: *those on the cusp of adulthood.*

cuss /kəs/ informal ▶ **n.** an annoying or stubborn person or animal. ▶ **v.** swear or curse. □ **cuss word** a swear word.

cuss·ed /ˈkəsəd/ ▶ **adj.** informal stubborn and awkward. ■ **cuss·ed·ness** n.

cus·tard /ˈkəstərd/ ▶ **n.** **1** a sweet sauce made with milk and eggs, or milk and flavored cornstarch. **2** a baked dessert made from eggs and milk.

cus·to·di·an /kəsˈtōdēən/ ▶ **n.** a person responsible for looking after something.

cus·to·dy /ˈkəstədē/ ▶ **n.** **1** protective care or guardianship of someone or something. **2** Law parental responsibility, especially as allocated to one of two divorcing parents. **3** imprisonment: *he was taken into police custody.*

SYNONYMS **care**, guardianship, charge, supervision, safekeeping, responsibility, protection.

■ **cus·to·di·al** /ˌkəˈstōdēəl/ adj.

cus·tom /ˈkəstəm/ ▶ **n.** **1** a traditional way of behaving or doing something: *the English custom of dancing around the maypole.* **2** regular dealings with a store or business by customers.

SYNONYMS **1** *local customs* **tradition**, practice, usage, way, convention, formality, ritual, mores. **2** *it was his custom to sleep in a chair* **habit**, practice, routine, way; formal wont.

□ **custom-built** (or **custom-made**) made to a particular customer's order.

cus·tom·ar·y /ˈkəstəˌmerē/ ▶ **adj.** usual or habitual.

SYNONYMS **usual**, traditional, normal, conventional, habitual, familiar, accepted, accustomed, routine, established, time-honored, prevailing. ANTONYMS unusual.

■ **cus·tom·ar·i·ly** adv.

cus·tom·er /ˈkəstəmər/ ▶ **n.** **1** a person who buys goods or services from a store or business. **2** a person or thing that you have to deal with: *a tough customer.*

SYNONYMS **consumer**, buyer, purchaser, patron, client, shopper.

cus·tom·ize /ˈkəstəˌmīz/ ▶ **v.** (**customizes**, **customizing**, **customized**) modify something to suit a person or task: *each plan can be customized to suit your needs.*

cus·toms /ˈkəstəmz/ ▶ **pl.n.** **1** charges made by a government on imported goods. **2** the official department that administers and collects customs charges.

cut /kət/ ▶ **v.** (**cuts**, **cutting**, **cut**) **1** make an opening or wound with something sharp. **2** shorten, divide, or remove with something sharp. **3** make or design a garment in a particular way. **4** reduce the amount or quantity of. **5** go across or through an area:

we always cut through the neighbor's backyard. **6** stop filming or recording. **7** divide a pack of playing cards by lifting a portion from the top. ▶ **n. 1** a wound or opening resulting from cutting. **2** a reduction. **3** the style in which a garment or a person's hair is cut. **4** a piece of meat cut from a carcass. **5** informal a share of profits. **6** a version of a movie after editing.

SYNONYMS ▶ **v. 1 gash**, slash, lacerate, slit, wound, scratch, graze, nick. **2 slice**, chop, dice, cube, carve, hash. **3 carve**, engrave, incise, etch, score, chisel, whittle. **4 reduce**, cut back/down on, decrease, lessen, mark down, discount, lower; informal slash. **5 shorten**, abridge, condense, abbreviate, truncate, edit, censor. **6 delete**, remove, take out, excise. ▶ **n. 1 gash**, slash, laceration, incision, wound, scratch, graze, nick. **2 piece**, joint, fillet, section. **3 share**, portion, quota, percentage; informal slice (of the pie). **4 reduction**, cutback, rollback, decrease, lessening. **5 style**, design, line, fit.

□ **be cut from the same cloth** be of the same nature. **be cut out for** (or **to be**) informal have exactly the right qualities for a particular role. **a cut above** informal noticeably better than. **cut and dried** already decided. **cut and paste** (on a computer) move an item from one part of a file to another. **cut and run** informal quickly leave a difficult situation. **cut and thrust** a competitive atmosphere or environment. **cut both ways 1** (of a point) serve both sides of an argument. **2** have both good and bad effects. **cut corners** do something badly to save time or money. **cut someone dead** completely ignore someone. **cut glass** glass with decorative patterns cut into it. **cut in 1** interrupt. **2** pull in too closely in front of another vehicle. **3** (of a machine) begin operating automatically. **cut it out** informal stop it. **cut the mustard** informal reach the required standard. **cut someone/something off 1** make it impossible to reach a place. **2** deprive someone of a supply. **3** break a telephone connection with someone. **cut out** (of an engine) suddenly stop operating. **cut someone out** exclude someone. **cut your teeth** get initial experience of an activity. **cut a tooth** (of a baby) have a tooth appear through the gum. **cut up** informal behave in a mischievous or unruly manner.

cu·ta·ne·ous /kyo͞o'tānēəs/ ▶ **adj.** having to do with the skin.

cut·back /'kət,bak/ ▶ **n.** a reduction.

SYNONYMS **reduction**, cut, rollback, decrease, economy, saving. ANTONYMS increase.

cute /kyo͞ot/ ▶ **adj. 1** charmingly pretty; sweet. **2** clever; shrewd.

SYNONYMS **endearing**, adorable, lovable, sweet, lovely, appealing, engaging, delightful, dear.

■ **cute·ly adv.**

cu·ti·cle /'kyo͞otikəl/ ▶ **n.** the dead skin at the base of a fingernail or toenail.

cut·lass /'kətləs/ ▶ **n.** a short sword with a slightly curved blade, formerly used by sailors.

cut·ler /'kətlər/ ▶ **n.** a maker or seller of cutlery.

cut·ler·y /'kətlərē/ ▶ **n.** knives, forks, and spoons used for eating or serving food.

cut·let /'kətlət/ ▶ **n. 1** a lamb or veal chop from just behind the neck. **2** a flat cake of ground meat, nuts, etc., covered in breadcrumbs and fried.

cut·off /'kət,ôf/ ▶ **n. 1** a point or level marking a set limit. **2** a device for interrupting a power or fuel supply. **3** (**cutoffs**) shorts made by cutting off the legs of a pair of jeans.

cut·out /'kət,out/ ▶ **n. 1** a shape cut out of board or paper. **2** a hole cut for decoration or for something to be inserted. **3** a device that automatically breaks an electric circuit for safety.

cut·ter /'kətər/ ▶ **n. 1** a person or thing that cuts. **2** a light, fast patrol boat or sailboat. **3** a small boat carried by a ship.

cut·throat /'kət,THrōt/ ▶ **n.** murderer. ▶ **adj.** ruthless and fierce: *cutthroat competition.*

cut·ting /'kətiNG/ ▶ **n. 1** a piece cut from a plant to grow a new one. **2** a way dug through higher ground for a railroad, road, etc. ▶ **adj.** hurtful: *a cutting remark.*

SYNONYMS ▶ **adj. hurtful**, wounding, barbed, sharp, scathing, caustic, sarcastic, snide, spiteful, malicious, vicious, cruel; informal bitchy.

□ **the cutting edge** the most advanced or modern stage; the forefront.

cut·tle·fish /'kətl,fiSH/ ▶ **n.** (plural **cuttlefish** or **cuttlefishes**) a sea creature resembling a squid.

CV ▶ **abbr.** curriculum vitae.

cwt ▶ **abbr.** hundredweight.

cy·an /'sī,an, 'sīən/ ▶ **n.** a greenish-blue color.

cy·a·nide /'sīə,nīd/ ▶ **n.** a highly poisonous compound containing a metal combined with carbon and nitrogen atoms.

cy·a·no·co·bal·a·min /,sīənō,kō'baləmin, sī,anō-/ ▶ **n.** vitamin B_{12}, found in liver, fish, and eggs.

cy·a·no·sis /,sīə'nōsəs/ ▶ **n.** a bluish discoloration of the skin because of poor circulation or a lack of oxygen in the blood.

cy·ber·crime /'sībər,krīm/ ▶ **n.** criminal activities carried out by means of computers or the Internet.

cy·ber·net·ics /,sībər'netiks/ ▶ **n.** the science of communications and control in machines (e.g., computers) and living things (e.g., by the nervous system). ■ **cy·ber·net·ic adj.**

cy·ber·pho·bi·a /,sībər'fōbēə/ ▶ **n.** extreme or irrational fear of computers or technology.

cy·ber·space /'sībər,spās/ ▶ **n.** the hypothetical place in which communication over computer networks takes place.

cy·ber·squat·ting /'sībər,skwätiNG/ ▶ **n.** the registering of well-known names as Internet domain names, in the hope of selling them to the owner at a profit.

cy·borg /'sī,bôrg/ ▶ **n.** a fictional or hypothetical person having mechanical elements built into the body to extend their normal physical abilities.

cy·cla·men /'sīkləmən, 'sik-/ ▶ **n.** a plant having pink, red, or white flowers with backward-curving petals.

cy·cle /'sīkəl/ ▶ **n. 1** a series of events that are regularly repeated in the same order: *the cycle of birth and death.* **2** a complete sequence of changes associated with something recurring, such as an alternating electric current. **3** a series of musical or literary works composed around a particular theme. **4** a bicycle. ▶ **v.** (**cycles**, **cycling**, **cycled**) ride a bicycle.

SYNONYMS ▶ **n. 1** *the cycle of birth, death, and rebirth* **circle**, round, pattern, rhythm, loop. **2** *a cycle of three plays* **series**, sequence, set, succession, run.

■ **cy·clist** n.

cy·clic /'sīklik, 'sik-/ (or **cyclical** /-likl/) ▶ adj. happening in cycles.

cy·clone /'sī,klōn/ ▶ n. **1** a system of winds rotating inward to an area of low atmospheric pressure. **2** a violent tropical storm. ■ **cy·clon·ic** /sī'klänik/ adj.

cy·clo·pe·an /,sīklə'pēən, sī'klōpēən/ ▶ adj. having to do with a Cyclops.

Cy·clops /'sī,kläps/ ▶ n. (plural **Cyclops** or **Cyclopes** /sī'klōpēz/) Greek Mythology a member of a race of one-eyed giants.

cy·clo·tron /'sīklə,trän/ ▶ n. an apparatus for accelerating charged atomic and subatomic particles by making them move spirally in a magnetic field.

cyg·net /'signət/ ▶ n. a young swan.

cyl·in·der /'siləndər/ ▶ n. **1** a three-dimensional shape with straight parallel sides and circular or oval ends. **2** a chamber in which a piston moves in an engine. ■ **cy·lin·dri·cal** /sə'lindrikəl/ adj.

cym·bal /'simbəl/ ▶ n. a musical instrument consisting of a round brass plate that is either struck against another one or hit with a stick.

cyme /sīm/ ▶ n. a flower cluster with a central stem bearing a single flower on the end that develops first.

cyn·ic /'sinik/ ▶ n. **1** a person who believes that people always act from selfish motives. **2** a person who raises doubts about something: *the cynics were silenced when the factory opened.*

> SYNONYMS **skeptic**, doubter, doubting Thomas, pessimist, prophet of doom. ANTONYMS idealist, optimist.

■ **cyn·i·cism** n.

cyn·i·cal /'sinikəl/ ▶ adj. **1** believing that people always act from selfish motives. **2** doubtful or sneering. **3** concerned only with your own interests.

> SYNONYMS **skeptical**, doubtful, distrustful, suspicious, disbelieving, pessimistic, negative, world-weary, disillusioned, disenchanted, jaundiced. ANTONYMS idealistic, optimistic.

■ **cyn·i·cal·ly** adv.

cy·no·sure /'sīnə,shoor, 'sin-/ ▶ n. a person or thing that is the center of attention or admiration.

cy·press /'sīprəs/ ▶ n. an evergreen coniferous tree with small dark leaves.

Cyp·ri·ot /'siprēət, -,ät/ ▶ n. a person from Cyprus. ▶ adj. relating to Cyprus.

Cy·ril·lic /sə'rilik/ ▶ n. the alphabet used for Russian and related languages.

cyst /sist/ ▶ n. an abnormal cavity in the body that contains fluid.

cys·tic /'sistik/ ▶ adj. **1** having to do with cysts. **2** relating to the bladder or the gall bladder. □ **cystic fibrosis** an inherited disease that causes too much mucus to be produced and often leads to blockage of tubes in the body.

cys·ti·tis /sis'tītis/ ▶ n. inflammation of the bladder.

cy·tol·o·gy /sī'täləjē/ ▶ n. the branch of biology concerned with the structure and function of cells. ■ **cy·to·log·i·cal** /,sītl'äjikəl/ adj. **cy·tol·o·gist** n.

cy·to·plasm /'sītə,plazəm/ ▶ n. the material of a living cell, excluding the nucleus.

czar /zär, (t)sär/ ▶ n. **1** = TSAR. **2** a person with great authority or power in a particular area: *the government's new drug czar.*

Czech /chek/ ▶ n. **1** a person from the Czech Republic or (formerly) Czechoslovakia. **2** the language spoken in the Czech Republic.

Czech·o·slo·vak /,chekə'slō,väk, -,vak/ (also **Czechoslovakian** /,chekəslə'väkēən, -'vakēən/) ▶ n. a person from the former country of Czechoslovakia, now divided between the Czech Republic and Slovakia. ▶ adj. relating to Czechoslovakia.

Dd

D (or **d**) ▶ **n.** (plural **Ds** or **D's**) **1** the fourth letter of the alphabet. **2** the Roman numeral for 500. □ **D-Day** the day (June 6, 1944) in World War II on which Allied forces invaded northern France.

DA ▶ **abbr.** district attorney.

dab /dab/ ▶ **v.** (**dabs, dabbing, dabbed**) **1** press lightly with something absorbent. **2** apply with light, quick strokes. ▶ **n.** a small amount of something applied lightly.

SYNONYMS ▶ **v.** **pat**, press, touch, blot, swab, daub, wipe. ▶ **n.** **drop**, spot, smear, splash, bit.

dab·ble /ˈdabəl/ ▶ **v.** (**dabbles, dabbling, dabbled**) **1** gently move your hands or feet around in water. **2** take part in an activity in a casual way.

SYNONYMS **toy with**, dip into, flirt with, tinker with, play with.

■ **dab·bler n.**

dace /dās/ ▶ **n.** (plural **dace**) a small freshwater fish related to the carp.

dachs·hund /ˈdäksənd, ˈdäksˌho͝ont/ ▶ **n.** a breed of dog with a long body and very short legs.

dac·tyl /ˈdaktl/ ▶ **n.** Poetry a metrical foot consisting of one stressed syllable followed by two unstressed syllables.

dad /dad/ (or **daddy** /ˈdadē/) ▶ **n.** (plural **dads** or **daddies**) informal your father.

Da·da /ˈdädä/ ▶ **n.** an early 20th-century movement in the arts that mocked conventions and emphasized the illogical and absurd.

dad·dy long·legs /ˈläNGˌlegz/ ▶ **n.** **1** an arachnid with long thin legs, the harvestman. **2** a spider of the Pholcidae family with a small body and long legs.

daf·fo·dil /ˈdafəˌdil/ ▶ **n.** a plant that has bright yellow flowers with a long trumpet-shaped center.

daf·fy /ˈdafē/ ▶ **adj.** informal silly.

daft /daft/ ▶ **adj.** informal silly; foolish.

SYNONYMS **absurd**, preposterous, ridiculous, ludicrous, idiotic, stupid, foolish, asinine, senseless, inane; informal crazy, cockeyed, half-baked. ANTONYMS sensible.

dag·ger /ˈdagər/ ▶ **n.** a short pointed knife, used as a weapon.

da·guerre·o·type /dəˈge(ə)rəˌtīp/ ▶ **n.** an early kind of photograph produced using a silver-coated plate.

dahl·ia /ˈdalyə, ˈdäl-/ ▶ **n.** a garden plant of the daisy family with brightly colored flowers.

dai·ly /ˈdālē/ ▶ **adj.** done, happening, or produced every day or every weekday. ▶ **adv.** every day.

SYNONYMS ▶ **adj.** **everyday**, day-to-day; formal quotidian. ▶ **adv.** **every day**, once a day, day after day.

dain·ty /ˈdāntē/ ▶ **adj.** (**daintier, daintiest**) delicately small and pretty. ▶ **n.** (plural **dainties**) a small, tasty item of food.

SYNONYMS ▶ **adj.** **1** **delicate**, fine, elegant, exquisite, graceful. **2** **fastidious**, fussy, particular, finicky; informal choosy, picky. ANTONYMS unwieldy.

■ **dain·ti·ly adv.**

dair·y /ˈde(ə)rē/ ▶ **n.** (plural **dairies**) a building where milk and milk products are produced. ▶ **adj.** **1** made from milk. **2** involved in milk production: *a dairy farmer.*

da·is /ˈdāis, ˈdī-/ ▶ **n.** a low platform that supports a throne, or that people stand on to make a speech.

dai·sy /ˈdāzē/ ▶ **n.** (plural **daisies**) a small plant that has flowers with a yellow center and white petals.

Da·ko·ta /dəˈkōtə/ ▶ **n.** a member of a North American Indian people of the upper Mississippi valley and the surrounding plains.

Da·lai La·ma /ˈdälī ˈlämə/ ▶ **n.** the spiritual head of Tibetan Buddhism.

dale /dāl/ ▶ **n.** a valley, especially a broad one.

dal·li·ance /ˈdalēəns, ˈdalyəns/ ▶ **n.** a casual relationship.

dal·ly /ˈdalē/ ▶ **v.** (**dallies, dallying, dallied**) **1** do something in a leisurely way. **2** (**dally with**) have a casual relationship with.

Dal·ma·tian /dalˈmāSHən/ ▶ **n.** a breed of large dog with short white hair and dark spots.

dam¹ /dam/ ▶ **n.** a barrier constructed across a river to hold back water. ▶ **v.** (**dams, damming, dammed**) build a dam across.

SYNONYMS ▶ **n.** **barrage**, barrier, weir, wall, embankment, barricade, obstruction. ▶ **v.** **block (up)**, obstruct, bung up, close, hold back.

dam² ▶ **n.** the female parent of an animal.

dam·age /ˈdamij/ ▶ **n.** **1** physical harm that makes something less valuable or effective. **2** harmful effects. **3** (**damages**) money paid to compensate for a loss or injury. ▶ **v.** (**damages, damaging, damaged**) cause harm to.

SYNONYMS ▶ **n.** **1** **harm**, destruction, vandalism, injury, ruin, devastation. **2** *she won $4,000 in damages* **compensation**, recompense, restitution, redress, reparation(s); informal comp. ▶ **v.** **harm**, injure, deface, spoil, impair, vandalize, ruin, destroy, wreck; informal trash. ANTONYMS repair.

dam·ag·ing /ˈdamijiNG/ ▶ **adj.** harmful or undesirable: *the damaging effects of the sun.*

SYNONYMS **harmful**, detrimental, injurious, hurtful, destructive, ruinous, deleterious. ANTONYMS beneficial.

dam·ask /ˈdaməsk/ ▶ n. a rich, heavy fabric with a pattern woven into it.

dame /dām/ ▶ n. **1** (**Dame**) (in the UK) the title of a woman awarded a knighthood, equivalent to *Sir*. **2** informal a woman.

damn /dam/ ▶ v. **1** (**be damned**) (in Christian belief) be condemned by God to eternal punishment in hell. **2** harshly condemn. **3** curse.

SYNONYMS **condemn**, censure, criticize, attack, denounce. ANTONYMS praise.

□ **damn with faint praise** praise so unenthusiastically as to suggest condemnation.

dam·na·ble /ˈdamnəbəl/ ▶ adj. very bad or unpleasant.

dam·na·tion /damˈnāsʜən/ ▶ n. the fate of being condemned to eternal punishment in hell.

damned /damd/ ▶ adj. said to emphasize anger or frustration. □ **do your damnedest** do your utmost.

damn·ing /ˈdamiɴɢ/ ▶ adj. strongly suggesting guilt.

SYNONYMS **incriminating**, damaging, condemnatory, conclusive, irrefutable.

damp /damp/ ▶ adj. slightly wet. ▶ n. moisture in the air, on a surface, or in a solid substance. ▶ v. **1** make something damp. **2** (**damp something down**) control a feeling or situation.

SYNONYMS ▶ adj. **moist**, humid, muggy, clammy, sweaty, dank, wet, rainy, drizzly, showery, misty, foggy, dewy. ANTONYMS dry. ▶ n. **moisture**, liquid, wet, wetness, dampness, humidity.

damp·en /ˈdampən/ ▶ v. **1** make something damp. **2** make a feeling or reaction less strong or intense.

SYNONYMS **1 moisten**, damp, wet, soak. **2 lessen**, decrease, diminish, reduce, moderate, cool, suppress, stifle, inhibit. ANTONYMS dry, heighten.

damp·er /ˈdampər/ ▶ n. **1** a pad for silencing a piano string. **2** a movable metal plate for controlling the air flow in a chimney. □ **put a damper on** informal make something less enjoyable or lively.

dam·sel /ˈdamzəl/ ▶ n. old use a young unmarried woman.

dam·sel·fly /ˈdamzəlˌflī/ ▶ n. (plural **damselflies**) a slender insect resembling a dragonfly.

dam·son /ˈdamzən, -sən/ ▶ n. a small purple-black variety of plum.

dan /dan/ ▶ n. **1** any of ten degrees of advanced skill in judo or karate. **2** a person who has achieved a dan.

dance /dans/ ▶ v. (**dances**, **dancing**, **danced**) **1** move rhythmically to music. **2** move in a quick and lively way. ▶ n. **1** a series of steps and movements performed to music. **2** a social gathering at which people dance.

SYNONYMS ▶ v. **1 trip**, sway, twirl, whirl, pirouette, gyrate, jive; informal bop, get down, trip the light fantastic. **2** *the children danced around me* **caper**, cavort, frolic, skip, prance, gambol, leap, hop, jig, bounce. ▶ n. **ball**, prom, hoedown; informal disco, rave, hop.

□ **dance attendance on** try hard to please. **dance to someone's tune** go along with someone's demands. ■ **danc·er** n.

dan·de·li·on /ˈdandlˌīən/ ▶ n. a weed with large bright yellow flowers.

dan·der /ˈdandər/ ▶ n. (**get your dander up**) informal lose your temper.

dan·dle /ˈdandl/ ▶ v. (**dandles**, **dandling**, **dandled**) gently bounce a young child on your knees or in your arms.

dan·druff /ˈdandrəf/ ▶ n. flakes of dead skin on a person's scalp and in the hair.

dan·dy /ˈdandē/ ▶ n. (plural **dandies**) a man who is very concerned with looking stylish and fashionable. ▶ adj. (**dandier**, **dandiest**) excellent. ■ **dan·di·fied** adj.

Dane /dān/ ▶ n. a person from Denmark.

dang /daɴɢ/ ▶ adj., exclam., & v. informal a polite way of saying DAMN.

dan·ger /ˈdānjər/ ▶ n. **1** the possibility of suffering harm or of experiencing something unpleasant. **2** a cause of harm.

SYNONYMS **1 possibility**, chance, risk, probability, likelihood, threat. ANTONYMS safety. **2 peril**, hazard, risk, jeopardy, endangerment, menace.

dan·ger·ous /ˈdānjərəs/ ▶ adj. likely to cause harm or injury.

SYNONYMS **1 menacing**, threatening, treacherous. **2 hazardous**, perilous, risky, unsafe, unpredictable, precarious, insecure; informal dicey, hairy. ANTONYMS harmless, safe.

■ **dan·ger·ous·ly** adv.

dan·gle /ˈdaɴɢgəl/ ▶ v. (**dangles**, **dangling**, **dangled**) **1** hang or swing freely. **2** offer something to someone to persuade them to do something.

SYNONYMS **hang**, swing, droop, wave, trail, stream.

■ **dan·gly** adj.

Dan·ish /ˈdānisʜ/ ▶ adj. relating to Denmark or the Danes. ▶ n. the language of Denmark.

dank /daɴɢk/ ▶ adj. damp and cold.

SYNONYMS **damp**, musty, chilly, clammy. ANTONYMS dry.

dap·per /ˈdapər/ ▶ adj. (of a man) neat in appearance; smart.

SYNONYMS **smart**, spruce, trim, debonair, neat, well-dressed, elegant; informal snappy, natty, spiffy, fly. ANTONYMS scruffy.

dap·ple /ˈdapəl/ ▶ v. (**dapples**, **dappling**, **dappled**) mark with patches of color or of light and shadow. □ **dapple gray** (of a horse) gray with darker ring-shaped markings.

dare /de(ə)r/ ▶ v. (**dares**, **daring**, **dared**) **1** have the courage to do something. **2** challenge someone to do something. ▶ n. a challenge to do something brave or risky.

SYNONYMS ▶ v. **1 be brave enough**, have the courage, venture, have the nerve, risk, take the liberty of; informal stick your neck out. **2 challenge**, defy, invite, bid, provoke, goad. ▶ n. **challenge**, invitation, wager, bet.

dare·dev·il /ˈde(ə)rˌdevəl/ ▶ n. a person who enjoys doing dangerous things.

dar·ing /ˈde(ə)riɴɢ/ ▶ adj. willing to do dangerous or risky things. ▶ n. the courage to do dangerous or risky things.

SYNONYMS ▶ adj. **bold**, audacious, intrepid, fearless, brave, heroic, dashing; informal gutsy. ANTONYMS cowardly, timid. ▶ n. **boldness**, audacity, temerity, fearlessness, bravery, courage, pluck; informal nerve, guts, moxie. ANTONYMS cowardice.

■ **dar·ing·ly** adv.

dark /därk/ ▶ adj. **1** with little or no light. **2** of a deep color. **3** depressing or gloomy. **4** evil; wicked. **5** mysterious: *a dark secret.* ▶ n. **1** (**the dark**) the absence of light. **2** nightfall.

SYNONYMS ▶ adj. **1** *a dark room* **dingy**, gloomy, shadowy, murky, gray, poorly lit, inky, black. **2** *dark hair* **brunette**, dark brown, sable, jet-black, ebony. **3** *dark skin* **swarthy**, dusky, olive, black, ebony. **4** *dark thoughts* **gloomy**, dismal, negative, downbeat, bleak, grim, fatalistic, black. **5** *a dark look* **angry**, forbidding, threatening, ominous, moody, brooding, sullen, scowling, glowering. **6** *dark deeds* **evil**, wicked, sinful, bad, iniquitous, ungodly, vile, foul, monstrous; informal dirty, shady, crooked. ANTONYMS bright, light, blonde, pale. ▶ n. **night**, nighttime, nightfall, darkness, blackout.

□ **the Dark Ages** the period *c.*500–1100 in Europe, seen as lacking culture or learning. **dark horse** a person about whom little is known, especially someone whose abilities and potential for success are concealed. **in the dark** knowing nothing about a situation or matter. **a shot in the dark** a wild guess. ■ **dark·ly** adv.

dark·en /'därkən/ ▶ v. **1** make or become darker. **2** become unhappy or angry.

SYNONYMS **grow dark**, make dark, blacken, grow dim, cloud over, lour. ANTONYMS lighten.

□ **never darken someone's door** keep away from someone's home.

dark·ness /'därknis/ ▶ n. **1** the partial or total absence of light. **2** wickedness or evil: *the forces of darkness*. **3** secrecy or mystery. **4** unhappiness, distress, or gloom.

SYNONYMS **1** *lights shone in the darkness* **dark**, blackness, gloom, dimness, murk, shadow, shade, blackout. **2** *darkness fell* **night**, nighttime, dark. **3** *the forces of darkness* **evil**, wickedness, sin, ungodliness, the Devil, Satan.

dark·room /'därk,ro͞om, -,ro͝om/ ▶ n. a darkened room for developing photographs.

dar·ling /'därliNG/ ▶ n. **1** an affectionate form of address. **2** a lovable person. ▶ adj. **1** much loved. **2** charming.

SYNONYMS ▶ n. **1 dear**, dearest, love, sweetheart, beloved; informal honey, angel, pet, sweetie, baby. **2 favorite**, idol, hero, heroine. ▶ adj. **1 dear**, dearest, precious, beloved. **2 adorable**, charming, cute, sweet, enchanting, dear, delightful.

darn¹ /därn/ ▶ v. mend a hole in a knitted garment by weaving yarn across it. ■ **darn·ing** n.

darn² (or **darned**) ▶ adj. informal ⇨ DAMNED.

dart /därt/ ▶ n. **1** a small pointed missile fired as a weapon or thrown in the game of darts. **2** (**darts**) an indoor game in which you throw darts at a circular board marked with numbers. **3** a sudden rapid movement. **4** a tapered tuck stitched into a garment to make it fit better. ▶ v. move suddenly or rapidly.

SYNONYMS ▶ v. **1 dash**, rush, tear, shoot, sprint, bound, scurry, scamper; informal scoot, whip. **2 direct**, cast, throw, shoot, send, flash.

dart·board /'därt,bôrd/ ▶ n. a circular board used as a target in the game of darts.

Dar·win·ism /'därwə,nizəm/ ▶ n. the theory of the evolution of species by natural selection, advanced by the English natural historian Charles Darwin. ■ **Dar·win·i·an** /där'winēən/ n. & adj. **Dar·win·ist** n. & adj.

dash /dasH/ ▶ v. **1** run or travel in a great hurry. **2** hit or throw with great force. **3** destroy: *his hopes were dashed*. **4** (**dash something off**) write something hurriedly. ▶ n. **1** an act of dashing. **2** a small amount added to something: *a dash of salt*. **3** a horizontal stroke in writing (—). **4** impressive style and confidence. **5** a sprint.

SYNONYMS ▶ v. **1 rush**, race, run, sprint, careen, charge, shoot, hurtle, fly, speed, zoom; informal tear, belt, barrel. **2 hurl**, smash, fling, slam, throw, toss, cast. **3 shatter**, destroy, wreck, ruin, demolish, scotch, frustrate, thwart. ANTONYMS dawdle. ▶ n. **1 rush**, race, run, sprint, bolt, dart, leap, charge, bound. **2 pinch**, touch, sprinkle, taste, spot, drop, dab, splash; informal smidgen, tad.

dash·board /'dasH,bôrd/ ▶ n. the panel of instruments and controls facing the driver of a vehicle.

dash·ing /'dasHiNG/ ▶ adj. (of a man) attractive, stylish, and confident.

SYNONYMS **debonair**, stylish, dapper, devil-may-care, raffish, flamboyant, swashbuckling.

das·tard·ly /'dastərdlē/ ▶ adj. old use wicked and cruel.

DAT /dat, ,dēā'tē/ ▶ abbr. digital audiotape.

da·ta /'datə, 'dātə/ ▶ n. **1** facts, statistics, or other information. **2** information stored by a computer.

SYNONYMS **facts**, figures, statistics, details, particulars, information.

□ **data capture** Computing the process of gathering data and putting it into a form accessible by computer.

USAGE

data is the plural of the Latin word datum. Scientists use it as a plural noun, taking a plural verb (as in *the data were classified*). In everyday use, however, data is usually treated as a singular noun with a singular verb (as in *here is the data*).

da·ta·bank /'datə,baNGk, 'dā-/ ▶ n. a large store of data in a computer.

da·ta·base /'datə,bās, 'dā-/ ▶ n. a set of data held in a computer.

date¹ /dāt/ ▶ n. **1** the day of the month or year as specified by a number. **2** a day or year when a particular event happened or will happen. **3** a social or romantic appointment. **4** a person with whom you have a social or romantic appointment. **5** a musical or theatrical performance. ▶ v. (**dates, dating, dated**) **1** mark something with a date. **2** establish the date when something existed or was made. **3** (**date from** or **back to**) have existed since a particular time in the past. **4** informal go on a date or regular dates with.

SYNONYMS ▶ n. **1 day**, occasion, time, year, age, period, era, epoch. **2 appointment**, meeting, engagement, rendezvous, commitment, assignation; literary tryst. **3 partner**, escort, girlfriend, boyfriend. ▶ v. **1 age**, grow old, become dated, show its age, be of its time. **2 go out with**, take out, go with, see; informal go steady with; dated court, woo.

□ **to date** until now. ■ **dat·a·ble** (or **dateable**) adj.

date² ▶ n. the sweet, dark brown, oval fruit of a palm tree.

dat·ed /ˈdātid/ ▶ adj. old-fashioned.

SYNONYMS **old-fashioned**, outdated, outmoded, unfashionable, passé, behind the times, archaic, obsolete, antiquated; informal old hat, out of the Dark Ages. ANTONYMS modern.

da·tive /ˈdātiv/ ▶ n. Grammar (in Latin, Greek, German, etc.) the case of nouns and pronouns that indicates an indirect object or the person or thing affected by a verb.

da·tum /ˈdātəm, ˈdatəm/ ▶ n. (plural **data** /ˈdatə, ˈdātə/) a piece of information.

daub /dôb/ ▶ v. smear something with a thick substance. ▶ n. **1** plaster, clay, or a similar substance, used in building. **2** a smear of a thick substance.

daugh·ter /ˈdôtər, ˈdä-/ ▶ n. **1** a girl or woman in relation to her parents. **2** a female descendant. □ **daughter-in-law** (plural **daughters-in-law**) the wife of a person's son.

daunt /dônt, dänt/ ▶ v. **1** make someone feel nervous or discouraged. **2** (**daunting**) seemingly difficult in anticipation.

SYNONYMS **1 discourage**, deter, demoralize, put off, dishearten, intimidate, overawe, awe. **2** (**daunting**) **intimidating**, forbidding, challenging, formidable, unnerving, disconcerting, discouraging, disheartening, demoralizing, dismaying, scary, frightening, alarming.

daunt·less /ˈdôntlis, ˈdänt-/ ▶ adj. brave and determined.

dau·phin /ˈdôfin/ ▶ n. historical the eldest son of the king of France.

da·vit /ˈdavit, ˈdā-/ ▶ n. a small crane on a ship.

daw·dle /ˈdôdl/ ▶ v. (**dawdles**, **dawdling**, **dawdled**) move slowly; take your time.

SYNONYMS **linger**, take your time, be slow, waste time, dally, amble, stroll, trail, move at a snail's pace; informal dilly-dally. ANTONYMS hurry.

dawn /dôn, dän/ ▶ n. **1** the first appearance of light in the sky in the morning. **2** the beginning of something new: *the dawn of civilization*. ▶ v. **1** (of a day) begin. **2** come into existence. **3** (**dawn on**) (of a fact) become clear to: *the awful truth was beginning to dawn on him*.

SYNONYMS ▶ n. **1 daybreak**, sunrise, sunup, first light, daylight, crack of dawn. **2 beginning**, start, birth, inception, genesis, emergence, advent, appearance, arrival, rise, origin. ANTONYMS dusk. ▶ v. **1** *Thursday dawned crisp and sunny* **begin**, break, arrive, emerge. **2** *a bright new future has dawned* **begin**, start, commence, be born, appear, arrive, emerge, arise, rise, unfold, develop.

day /dā/ ▶ n. **1** a period of twenty-four hours, reckoned from midnight to midnight. **2** the time between sunrise and sunset. **3** (usu. **days**) a particular period of the past: *laws were strict in those days*. **4** (**the day**) the present time or the time in question.

SYNONYMS **1 daytime**, daylight (hours), waking hours. **2 period**, time, date, age, era, generation. ANTONYMS night.

□ **any day** informal at any time or under any circumstances. **call it a day** decide to stop doing something. **day-to-day 1** happening regularly every day. **2** ordinary. **day by day** gradually. **day in, day out** continuously over a long period. **day school** a school for pupils who live at home. **day trip** a journey or outing completed in one day. **day tripper** a person who makes a day trip. **that will be the day** informal that is very unlikely. **these days** at present.

day·break /ˈdāˌbrāk/ ▶ n. dawn.

day·care cen·ter /ˈdāˌke(ə)r/ ▶ n. a place providing daytime care for children or for elderly or disabled people.

day·dream /ˈdāˌdrēm/ ▶ n. a series of pleasant thoughts that distract your attention from the present. ▶ v. have a daydream.

day·light /ˈdāˌlīt/ ▶ n. **1** the natural light of the day. **2** dawn. □ **daylight saving** (or **savings**) **time** the time observed when clocks are set one hour ahead of standard time to achieve longer evening daylight.

day·time /ˈdāˌtīm/ ▶ n. **1** the time between sunrise and sunset. **2** the period of time corresponding to normal working hours.

daze /dāz/ ▶ n. a state of stunned confusion or bewilderment. ▶ v. make someone feel stunned or bewildered.

SYNONYMS ▶ n. **stupor**, trance, haze, spin, whirl, muddle, jumble. ▶ v. **dumbfound**, stupefy, stun, shock, stagger, bewilder, take aback, nonplus; informal flabbergast, knock for a loop.

■ **dazed** adj.

daz·zle /ˈdazəl/ ▶ v. (**dazzles**, **dazzling**, **dazzled**) **1** (of a bright light) blind someone temporarily. **2** amaze someone by being very impressive: *I was dazzled by her beauty*. ▶ n. blinding brightness.

SYNONYMS ▶ v. **1 blind**, confuse, disorient. **2 overwhelm**, overcome, impress, move, stir, touch, awe, overawe; informal bowl over, blow away, knock out.

■ **daz·zling** adj.

dB ▶ abbr. decibels.

DC ▶ abbr. **1** direct current. **2** District of Columbia.

DD ▶ abbr. Doctor of Divinity.

DDR ▶ abbr. historical German Democratic Republic.

DDT ▶ abbr. dichlorodiphenyltrichloroethane, a compound used as an insecticide but now banned in many countries.

dea·con /ˈdēkən/ ▶ n. **1** a Christian minister just below the rank of priest. **2** (in some Protestant Churches) a person who helps a minister but is not a member of the clergy. ■ **dea·con·ess** n.

de·ac·ti·vate /dēˈaktəvāt/ ▶ v. (**deactivates**, **deactivating**, **deactivated**) stop equipment from working by disconnecting or destroying it.

dead /ded/ ▶ adj. **1** no longer alive. **2** (of a part of the body) numb. **3** showing no emotion: *a cold, dead voice*. **4** without activity or excitement. **5** complete: *dead silence*. ▶ adv. absolutely, exactly, or directly: *you're dead right*.

SYNONYMS ▶ **adj.** **1 passed on**, passed away, departed, late, lost, perished, fallen, killed, lifeless, extinct; informal six feet under, pushing up daisies; formal deceased. **2 obsolete**, extinct, defunct, disused, abandoned, superseded, vanished, archaic, ancient. **3 not working**, out of order, inoperative, inactive, broken, defective; informal kaput, conked out, on the blink, bust. **4 boring**, uninteresting, unexciting, uninspiring, dull, flat, quiet, sleepy, slow, lifeless; informal one-horse, dullsville. ANTONYMS alive, living, lively. ▶ **adv.** **1 completely**, absolutely, totally, utterly, deadly, perfectly, entirely, quite, thoroughly. **2 directly**, exactly, precisely, immediately, right, straight, due.

□ **dead and buried** over; finished. **dead as a doornail** completely dead. **the dead of night** the quietest, darkest part of the night. **dead duck** informal an unsuccessful or useless person or thing. **dead end** a road or passage that is closed at one end. **dead heat** a result in a race in which two or more competitors finish at exactly the same time. **dead loss** a venture or situation that produces no profit at all. **the dead of winter** the coldest part of winter. **dead reckoning** a way of finding out your position by estimating the direction and distance traveled. **dead ringer** informal a person or thing very like another. **dead on your feet** informal extremely tired. **dead to the world** informal fast asleep. **from the dead** from being dead; from death.

dead·beat /ˈdedˌbēt/ ▶ **n.** informal a lazy or aimless person.

dead·bolt /ˈdedˌbōlt/ ▶ **n.** a bolt secured by turning a knob or key, rather than by spring action.

dead·en /ˈdedn/ ▶ **v.** **1** make a noise or sensation less strong or intense. **2** make something numb.

SYNONYMS **1 muffle**, mute, smother, stifle, damp (down), soften, cushion. ANTONYMS intensify, amplify. **2 numb**, dull, blunt, alleviate, mitigate, diminish, reduce, lessen, ease, soothe, relieve, assuage.

dead·head /ˈdedˌhed/ ▶ **v.** **1** remove dead flower heads from a plant to encourage further blooming. **2** informal (of a vehicle or driver) complete a trip without paying passengers or freight.

dead·line /ˈdedˌlīn/ ▶ **n.** the time or date by which you have to complete something.

SYNONYMS **time limit**, finishing date, target date, cutoff point.

dead·lock /ˈdedˌläk/ ▶ **n.** a situation in which no one can make any progress. ▶ **v.** (**be deadlocked**) be unable to make any progress.

SYNONYMS ▶ **n.** **stalemate**, impasse, checkmate, standoff, standstill, gridlock.

dead·ly /ˈdedlē/ ▶ **adj.** (**deadlier**, **deadliest**) **1** causing or able to cause death. **2** (of a voice, glance, etc.) filled with hate. **3** very accurate or effective. **4** informal very boring. ▶ **adv.** very: *she was deadly serious.*

SYNONYMS ▶ **adj.** **1 fatal**, lethal, mortal, life-threatening, noxious, toxic, poisonous. **2** *deadly enemies* **mortal**, irreconcilable, implacable, bitter, sworn. **3** *his aim is deadly* **unerring**, unfailing, perfect, true, accurate. ANTONYMS harmless.

□ **deadly nightshade** a plant with purple flowers and poisonous black berries. **deadly sin** (in Christian tradition) a sin seen as leading to damnation.

dead·pan /ˈdedˌpan/ ▶ **adj.** not showing any emotion; expressionless.

dead·weight /ˈdedˌwāt/ ▶ **n.** **1** the weight of a motionless person or thing. **2** the total weight that a ship can carry.

dead·wood /ˈdedˌwo͝od/ ▶ **n.** useless or unproductive people or things.

deaf /def/ ▶ **adj.** **1** unable to hear. **2** (**deaf to**) unwilling to listen to. □ **deaf mute** offensive a person who is deaf and unable to speak. **fall on deaf ears** be ignored. **turn a deaf ear** refuse to listen or respond. ■ **deaf·ness n.**

deaf·en /ˈdefən/ ▶ **v.** **1** make someone deaf. **2** (**deafening**) very loud.

SYNONYMS (**deafening**) **ear-splitting**, thunderous, crashing, uproarious, almighty, booming. ANTONYMS low, soft.

■ **deaf·en·ing·ly adv.**

deal[1] /dēl/ ▶ **v.** (**deals**, **dealing**, **dealt** /delt/) **1** (**deal something out**) distribute something. **2** buy and sell a product commercially. **3** buy and sell illegal drugs. **4** give out cards to players of a card game. ▶ **n.** **1** an agreement between two or more people or groups. **2** a particular form of treatment received: *working mothers get a bad deal.*

SYNONYMS ▶ **v.** **1 trade in**, buy and sell, purvey, supply, market, traffic in. **2 distribute**, give out, share out, divide out, hand out, pass out, pass around, dispense, allocate. ▶ **n.** **agreement**, understanding, pact, bargain, covenant, contract, treaty, arrangement, compromise, settlement, terms.

□ **a big deal** informal an important thing. **a deal of** a large amount of. **deal with 1** do business with. **2** do things to fix a problem. **3** cope with. **4** have something as a subject. **a good** (or **great**) **deal** a lot. **a square deal** a fair bargain or treatment.

deal[2] ▶ **n.** fir or pine wood.

deal·er /ˈdēlər/ ▶ **n.** **1** a person who buys and sells goods. **2** a person who buys and sells shares directly (rather than as a broker or agent). **3** a player who deals cards in a card game.

SYNONYMS **trader**, merchant, salesman, saleswoman, seller, vendor, purveyor, peddler, distributor, supplier, shopkeeper, retailer, wholesaler, tradesman, tradesperson.

■ **deal·er·ship n.**

deal·ing /ˈdēliNG/ ▶ **n.** **1** (usu. **dealings**) a business relation or transaction: *they had dealings with an insurance company.* **2** the particular way in which someone behaves toward others. **3** the activity of buying and selling a particular thing: *drug dealing.*

dean /dēn/ ▶ **n.** **1** the head of a college or university faculty or department. **2** the head of a cathedral's governing body.

dear /di(ə)r/ ▶ **adj.** **1** much loved. **2** used in the polite introduction to a letter: *dear sir.* **3** expensive. ▶ **n.** **1** a lovable person. **2** an affectionate form of address.

SYNONYMS ▶ **adj.** **1** *a dear friend* **beloved**, precious, close, intimate, bosom. **2** *her pictures were too dear to part with* **precious**, treasured, valued, prized, cherished, special. **3 endearing**, adorable, lovable, appealing, engaging, charming, captivating, lovely, delightful, sweet, darling. **4 expensive**, costly, high-priced, overpriced, exorbitant, extortionate; informal pricey. ANTONYMS disagreeable, cheap. ▶ n. **darling**, dearest, love, beloved, sweetheart, precious; informal sweetie, sugar, honey, baby, pet.

dear·est /ˈdi(ə)rist/ ▶ adj. **1** most loved or cherished. **2** most expensive. ▶ n. an affectionate form of address.

dear·ly /ˈdi(ə)rlē/ ▶ adv. **1** very much. **2** at great cost.

SYNONYMS **very much**, a great deal, greatly, profoundly, deeply.

dearth /dərTH/ ▶ n. a lack of something: *a dearth of evidence.*

SYNONYMS **lack**, scarcity, shortage, shortfall, deficiency, insufficiency, inadequacy, absence. ANTONYMS surfeit.

death /deTH/ ▶ n. **1** an instance of a person or an animal dying. **2** the end of life; the state of being dead. **3** the end of something.

SYNONYMS **1 dying**, demise, end, passing, loss of life; formal decease. **2 end**, finish, termination, extinction, extinguishing, collapse, destruction. ANTONYMS life, birth.

□ **at death's door** so ill that you may die. **catch your death of cold** informal catch a severe cold. **death certificate** an official statement of a person's death. **death knell 1** an event that signals the end of something. **2** the tolling of a bell to mark someone's death. **death penalty** punishment by being executed. **death rate** the number of deaths per one thousand people per year. **death row** a block of cells for prisoners who have been sentenced to death. **death tax** ⇒ INHERITANCE TAX. **death toll** the number of deaths resulting from a particular cause. **death trap** a dangerous building, vehicle, etc. **death-watch beetle** a beetle that makes a ticking sound that people used to think was an omen of death. **death wish** an unconscious desire for your own death. **do something to death** repeat something tediously. **like death warmed over** informal extremely tired or ill. **put someone to death** execute someone. **to death 1** until dead. **2** used for emphasis: *sick to death of him.*

death·ly /ˈdeTHlē/ ▶ adj. suggesting death: *a deathly hush.*

SYNONYMS **deathlike**, ghostly, ghastly, ashen, white, pale, pallid.

de·ba·cle /diˈbakəl, -ˈbäkəl/ ▶ n. an utter failure or disaster.

SYNONYMS **fiasco**, failure, catastrophe, disaster.

de·bar /dēˈbär/ ▶ v. (**debars**, **debarring**, **debarred**) officially prevent someone from doing something.

de·bark /dēˈbärk/ ▶ v. leave a ship or aircraft.

de·base /diˈbās/ ▶ v. (**debases**, **debasing**, **debased**) make something worse in quality, value, or character.

SYNONYMS **degrade**, devalue, demean, cheapen, prostitute, discredit, drag down, tarnish, blacken, disgrace, dishonor, shame. ANTONYMS enhance.

■ **de·base·ment** n.

de·bat·a·ble /diˈbātəbəl/ ▶ adj. open to discussion or argument.

SYNONYMS **arguable**, questionable, open to question, disputable, controversial, contentious, doubtful, dubious, uncertain, borderline, moot.

de·bate /diˈbāt/ ▶ n. **1** a formal discussion in which people present opposing arguments. **2** an argument. ▶ v. (**debates**, **debating**, **debated**) **1** discuss or argue about. **2** consider a possible course of action.

SYNONYMS ▶ n. **discussion**, argument, dispute, talks. ▶ v. **1 discuss**, talk over/through, talk about, thrash out, argue, dispute. **2 consider**, think over/about, chew over, mull over, weigh up, ponder, deliberate.

de·bauched /diˈbôCHt/ ▶ adj. indulging in a lot of pleasures in a way considered to be immoral.

SYNONYMS **dissolute**, dissipated, degenerate, decadent, profligate, immoral, lecherous, lewd, licentious. ANTONYMS wholesome.

■ **de·bauch·er·y** n.

de·bil·i·tate /diˈbiliˌtāt, dē-/ ▶ v. (**debilitates**, **debilitating**, **debilitated**) severely weaken.

de·bil·i·ty /diˈbilitē/ ▶ n. (plural **debilities**) physical weakness.

deb·it /ˈdebit/ ▶ n. **1** an entry in an account recording a sum owed. **2** a payment that has been made or that is owed. ▶ v. (**debits**, **debiting**, **debited**) (of a bank) remove money from a customer's account. □ **debit card** a card that lets you take money from your bank account electronically when buying something.

deb·o·nair /ˌdebəˈne(ə)r/ ▶ adj. (of a man) confident, stylish, and charming.

SYNONYMS **suave**, urbane, sophisticated, cultured, self-possessed, self-assured, confident, charming, gracious, courteous, gallant, gentlemanly, refined, polished, well-bred, genteel, dignified, courtly, well-groomed, elegant, stylish, smart, dashing; informal smooth, sharp. ANTONYMS unsophisticated.

de·bouch /diˈbouCH, -ˈbo͞oSH/ ▶ v. emerge from a confined space into a wide, open area.

de·brief /dēˈbrēf/ ▶ v. question someone in detail about a mission they have completed.

de·bris /dəˈbrē, ˌdā-/ ▶ n. **1** scattered items or pieces of trash. **2** loose broken pieces of rock.

SYNONYMS **ruins**, remains, rubble, wreckage, detritus, refuse, rubbish, waste, scrap, flotsam and jetsam.

debt /det/ ▶ n. **1** a sum of money owed. **2** a situation where you owe someone money. **3** gratitude for a favor or service.

SYNONYMS **1 bill**, account, dues, arrears, charges. **2 indebtedness**, obligation, gratitude, appreciation.

debt·or /ˈdetər/ ▶ n. a person who owes money.

de·bug /dēˈbəg/ ▶ v. (**debugs**, **debugging**, **debugged**) remove errors from computer hardware or software.

de·bunk /diˈbəNGk/ ▶ v. show that something believed in by many people is false or exaggerated.

de·burr /dēˈbər/ (also **debur**) ▶ v. (**deburs**, **deburring**, **deburred**) smooth the rough edges of an object, typically a metal one.

de·but /dāˈbyo͞o/ ▶ n. **1** a person's first appearance in a role. **2** old use the first appearance of a young woman in society. ▶ v. make a debut.

SYNONYMS ▶ n. **first appearance**, first performance, launch, entrance, premiere, introduction, inception, inauguration.

deb·u·tant /ˈdebyo͝oˌtänt, ˈdebyə-/ ▶ **n.** a person making a debut.

deb·u·tante /ˈdebyo͝oˌtänt, ˈdebyə-/ ▶ **n.** a young upper-class woman making her first appearance in society.

dec·ade /ˈdekād/ ▶ **n.** a period of ten years.

dec·a·dent /ˈdekədənt/ ▶ **adj. 1** immoral and interested only in pleasure. **2** luxuriously self-indulgent.

SYNONYMS **dissolute**, dissipated, degenerate, corrupt, depraved, sinful, unprincipled, immoral, amoral, licentious, abandoned, profligate, intemperate, sybaritic, hedonistic, pleasure-seeking, self-indulgent.

■ **dec·a·dence n. dec·a·dent·ly adv.**

de·caf·fein·a·ted /dēˈkafəˌnātəd/ ▶ **adj.** (of tea or coffee) having had most or all of its caffeine removed.

dec·a·gon /ˈdekəˌgän/ ▶ **n.** a figure with ten straight sides and angles.

dec·a·he·dron /ˌdekəˈhēdrən/ ▶ **n.** (plural **decahedrons** or **decahedra** /-drə/) a solid figure with ten sides.

dec·a·li·ter /ˈdekəˌlētər/ ▶ **n.** a unit of volume, equal to 10 liters.

Dec·a·logue /ˈdekəˌlôg, -ˌläg/ ▶ **n.** the Ten Commandments.

de·cam·e·ter /ˈdekəˌmētər/ ▶ **n.** a unit of length, equal to 10 meters.

de·camp /diˈkamp/ ▶ **v.** depart suddenly or secretly.

de·cant /diˈkant/ ▶ **v.** pour liquid (often wine or a solution) from one container into another.

de·cant·er /diˈkantər/ ▶ **n.** a glass container with a stopper, for wine or liquor.

de·cap·i·tate /diˈkapiˌtāt/ ▶ **v.** (**decapitates**, **decapitating**, **decapitated**) cut off the head of. ■ **de·cap·i·ta·tion** /diˌkapiˈtāsʜən/ **n.**

dec·a·pod /ˈdekəˌpäd/ ▶ **n.** a crustacean with five pairs of walking legs.

de·car·bon·ize /dēˈkärbəˌnīz/ ▶ **v.** (**decarbonizes**, **decarbonizing**, **decarbonized**) remove carbon deposits from an engine.

de·cath·lon /diˈkaᴛʜ(ə)ˌlän/ ▶ **n.** an athletic event in which each competitor takes part in the same ten events. ■ **de·cath·lete n.**

de·cay /diˈkā/ ▶ **v. 1** (of plant or animal material) rot. **2** become weaker or less good. ▶ **n. 1** the state or process of decaying. **2** rotten matter or tissue.

SYNONYMS ▶ **v. 1 decompose**, rot, putrefy, go bad, go off, spoil, fester, perish. **2 deteriorate**, degenerate, decline, go downhill, slump, slide, go to rack and ruin, go to seed; informal go to the dogs. ▶ **n. 1 decomposition**, putrefaction, rot. **2 deterioration**, degeneration, decline, weakening, crumbling, disintegration, collapse.

de·cease /diˈsēs/ ▶ **n.** formal or Law death.

de·ceased /diˈsēst/ formal or Law ▶ **n.** (**the deceased**) the recently dead person in question. ▶ **adj.** recently dead.

de·ceit /diˈsēt/ ▶ **n.** behavior intended to make someone believe something that is not true.

SYNONYMS **deception**, deceitfulness, duplicity, double-dealing, lies, fraud, cheating, trickery. ANTONYMS honesty.

de·ceit·ful /diˈsētfəl/ ▶ **adj.** deliberately deceiving other people.

SYNONYMS **dishonest**, untruthful, insincere, false, disingenuous, untrustworthy, unscrupulous, unprincipled, two-faced, duplicitous, fraudulent, double-dealing; informal sneaky, tricky, crooked. ANTONYMS honest.

■ **de·ceit·ful·ly adv.**

de·ceive /diˈsēv/ ▶ **v.** (**deceives**, **deceiving**, **deceived**) **1** deliberately make someone believe something that is not true. **2** (of a thing) give a mistaken impression.

SYNONYMS **trick**, cheat, defraud, swindle, hoodwink, hoax, dupe, take in, mislead, delude, fool; informal con, sucker, pull the wool over someone's eyes.

■ **de·ceiv·er n.**

SPELLING

Remember **i** before **e**, when the sound is *ee*, except after **c**: deceive.

de·cel·er·ate /dēˈseləˌrāt/ ▶ **v.** (**decelerates**, **decelerating**, **decelerated**) slow down. ■ **de·cel·er·a·tion** /-ˌseləˈrāsʜən/ **n.**

De·cem·ber /diˈsembər/ ▶ **n.** the twelfth month of the year.

de·cen·cy /ˈdēsənsē/ ▶ **n.** (plural **decencies**) **1** decent behavior. **2** (**decencies**) standards of acceptable behavior: *the common decencies.*

SYNONYMS **1 propriety**, decorum, good taste, respectability, morality, virtue, modesty. **2 courtesy**, politeness, good manners, civility, consideration, thoughtfulness.

de·cen·ni·al /diˈsenēəl/ ▶ **adj.** happening every ten years.

de·cent /ˈdēsənt/ ▶ **adj. 1** having good moral standards. **2** of an acceptable quality. **3** kind or generous.

SYNONYMS **1** *a decent burial* **proper**, correct, right, appropriate, suitable, respectable, decorous, modest, seemly, accepted. **2** *a job with decent pay* **satisfactory**, reasonable, fair, acceptable, adequate, sufficient, not bad, all right, tolerable, passable, suitable; informal OK. **3 kind**, generous, thoughtful, considerate, obliging, courteous, polite, well-mannered, neighborly, hospitable, pleasant, agreeable, amiable. ANTONYMS improper, unsatisfactory.

■ **de·cent·ly adv.**

de·cen·tral·ize /dēˈsentrəˌlīz/ ▶ **v.** (**decentralizes**, **decentralizing**, **decentralized**) transfer authority from central to local government. ■ **de·cen·tral·i·za·tion** /dēˌsentrəliˈzāsʜən/ **n.**

de·cep·tion /diˈsepsʜən/ ▶ **n. 1** the action of deceiving. **2** a thing that deceives.

SYNONYMS **1 deceit**, duplicity, double-dealing, fraud, cheating, trickery, guile, bluff, lying, pretense, treachery. **2 trick**, sham, fraud, pretense, hoax, ruse, scheme, dodge, cheat, swindle; informal con, setup, scam.

de·cep·tive /diˈseptiv/ ▶ **adj.** giving a false impression.

SYNONYMS **misleading**, confusing, illusory, distorted, ambiguous.

■ **de·cep·tive·ly adv.**

dec·i·bel /ˈdesəˌbel, -bəl/ ▶ **n.** a unit for measuring the loudness of a sound or the power of an electrical signal.

de·cide /di'sīd/ ▶ **v.** (**decides**, **deciding**, **decided**) **1** think about something and make a judgment or decision. **2** settle an issue or contest.

SYNONYMS **1 resolve**, determine, make up your mind, choose, opt, plan, aim, intend, have in mind, set your sights on. **2 settle**, resolve, determine, work out, answer; informal sort out. **3 adjudicate**, arbitrate, judge, pronounce on, give a verdict on, rule on.

de·cid·ed /di'sīdid/ ▶ **adj.** definite; clear: *a decided improvement.*

de·cid·ed·ly /di'sīdidlē/ ▶ **adv.** clearly and distinctly.

SYNONYMS **distinctly**, clearly, markedly, obviously, noticeably, unmistakably, patently, manifestly, definitely, positively.

de·cid·u·ous /di'sijo͞oəs/ ▶ **adj.** (of a tree or shrub) shedding its leaves annually.

dec·i·li·ter /'desəˌlētər/ ▶ **n.** a unit of volume, equal to one tenth of a liter.

dec·i·mal /'des(ə)məl/ ▶ **adj.** having to do with a system of numbers based on the number ten. ▶ **n.** a fractional number in the decimal system, written with figures on either side of a decimal point. □ **decimal place** the position of a digit to the right of a decimal point. **decimal point** a dot placed after the figure representing units in a decimal fraction.

dec·i·mate /'desəˌmāt/ ▶ **v.** (**decimates**, **decimating**, **decimated**) **1** kill or destroy a large proportion of. **2** drastically reduce in strength. ■ **dec·i·ma·tion** /ˌdesə'māsʜən/ **n.**

dec·i·me·ter /'desəˌmētər/ ▶ **n.** a unit of length, equal to one tenth of a meter.

de·ci·pher /di'sīfər/ ▶ **v.** (**deciphers**, **deciphering**, **deciphered**) **1** convert something from code into normal language. **2** succeed in understanding something that is hard to interpret.

de·ci·sion /di'sizʜən/ ▶ **n.** **1** a choice or judgment made after considering something. **2** the ability to decide things quickly.

SYNONYMS **1 resolution**, conclusion, settlement, choice, option, selection. **2 verdict**, finding, ruling, judgment, adjudication, sentence.

de·ci·sive /di'sīsiv/ ▶ **adj.** **1** having great importance for the outcome of a situation: *decisive evidence.* **2** able to make decisions quickly.

SYNONYMS **1 deciding**, conclusive, determining, key, pivotal, critical, crucial. **2 resolute**, firm, strong-minded, strong-willed, determined, purposeful.

■ **de·ci·sive·ly** **adv.** **de·ci·sive·ness** **n.**

deck /dek/ ▶ **n.** **1** a floor of a ship. **2** a floor or platform. **3** a set of playing cards. **4** a player or recorder for discs or tapes. ▶ **v.** decorate something. □ **hit the deck** informal fall to the ground.

deck·chair /'dekˌcʜe(ə)r/ ▶ **n.** a folding chair with a wooden frame and a canvas seat.

deck·ing /'dekiɴɢ/ ▶ **n.** material used in making a deck.

de·claim /di'klām/ ▶ **v.** speak or recite in a dramatic or passionate way.

SYNONYMS **make a speech**, give an address, give a lecture, speak, hold forth, orate, preach, lecture, deliver a sermon, sermonize, moralize; informal sound off, spout; speak out, rail, inveigh, fulminate, rage, rant, thunder.

dec·la·ma·tion /ˌdeklə'māsʜən/ ▶ **n.** the action of declaiming something. ■ **de·clam·a·to·ry** /di'klaməˌtôrē/ **adj.**

dec·la·ra·tion /ˌdeklə'rāsʜən/ ▶ **n.** **1** a formal statement or announcement. **2** the action of declaring.

SYNONYMS **1 announcement**, statement, communication, pronouncement, proclamation, advisory. **2 assertion**, profession, affirmation, acknowledgment, revelation, disclosure, confirmation, testimony, avowal, protestation.

de·clar·a·tive /di'kle(ə)rətiv, -'klar-/ ▶ **adj.** **1** of the nature of a declaration: *declarative statements.* **2** Grammar (of a sentence or phrase) taking the form of a simple statement.

de·clare /di'kle(ə)r/ ▶ **v.** (**declares**, **declaring**, **declared**) **1** announce something solemnly or officially. **2** (**declare yourself**) reveal your intentions or identity. **3** acknowledge that you have income or goods on which tax or duty should be paid.

SYNONYMS **1 announce**, proclaim, state, reveal, air, voice, articulate, express, vent, set forth, publicize, broadcast. **2 assert**, profess, affirm, maintain, state, contend, claim, argue, insist, avow.

de·clas·si·fy /dē'klasəˌfī/ ▶ **v.** (**declassifies**, **declassifying**, **declassified**) officially declare information or documents to be no longer secret.

de·clen·sion /di'klensʜən/ ▶ **n.** Grammar the changes in the form of a noun, pronoun, or adjective that identify its case, number, and gender.

dec·li·na·tion /ˌdeklə'nāsʜən/ ▶ **n.** **1** Astronomy the position of a point in the sky equivalent to latitude on the earth. **2** the angular deviation of a compass needle from true north.

de·cline /di'klīn/ ▶ **v.** (**declines**, **declining**, **declined**) **1** become smaller, weaker, or worse: *the birth rate continued to decline.* **2** politely refuse. **3** Grammar form a word according to its case, number, and gender. ▶ **n.** a gradual loss of strength, numbers, or value.

SYNONYMS ▶ **v.** **1 turn down**, reject, brush aside, refuse, rebuff, spurn, repulse, dismiss, pass up, say no (to). **2 decrease**, reduce, lessen, diminish, dwindle, contract, shrink, fall off, tail off, drop, fall, go down. **3 deteriorate**, degenerate, decay, crumble, collapse, slump, slip, slide, go downhill, worsen; informal go to the dogs. ANTONYMS accept, increase, improve. ▶ **n.** **1 reduction**, decrease, downturn, downswing, diminution, ebb, drop, slump, plunge. **2 deterioration**, degeneration, degradation, shrinkage, erosion. ANTONYMS rise, improvement.

de·cliv·i·ty /di'klivitē/ ▶ **n.** (plural **declivities**) formal a downward slope.

de·coc·tion /di'käksʜən/ ▶ **n.** the concentrated essence of a substance, produced by heating or boiling.

de·code /di'kōd/ ▶ **v.** (**decodes**, **decoding**, **decoded**) convert a coded message into understandable language.

SYNONYMS **decipher**, decrypt, work out, solve, interpret, translate, make sense of, get to the bottom of, unravel, find the key to; informal crack, figure out.

■ **de·cod·er** **n.**

dé·col·le·tage /dāˌkälə'täzн, ˌdekələ-/ ▶ n. a low neckline on a woman's dress or top.

dé·col·le·té /dāˌkälə'tā, ˌdekələ-/ ▶ adj. having a low neckline.

de·com·mis·sion /ˌdēkə'misнən/ ▶ v. take a nuclear reactor or weapon out of use and make it safe.

de·com·pose /ˌdēkəm'pōz/ ▶ v. (**decomposes**, **decomposing**, **decomposed**) decay; rot.

> SYNONYMS **decay**, rot, putrefy, go bad, go off, spoil, perish, deteriorate, degrade, break down.

■ **de·com·po·si·tion** /dēˌkämpə'zisнən/ n.

de·com·press /ˌdēkəm'pres/ ▶ v. **1** reduce the pressure on. **2** expand compressed computer data to its normal size.

de·com·pres·sion /ˌdēkəm'presнən/ ▶ n. **1** reduction in air pressure: *decompression of the aircraft cabin*. **2** the decompressing of computer data. □ **decompression sickness** a serious condition that results when a deep-sea diver surfaces too quickly.

de·con·ges·tant /ˌdēkən'jestənt/ ▶ n. a medicine used to relieve a blocked nose.

de·con·struct /ˌdēkən'strəkt/ ▶ v. reduce something to its basic elements in order to interpret it in a different way. ■ **de·con·struc·tion** n.

de·con·tam·i·nate /ˌdēkən'taməˌnāt/ ▶ v. (**decontaminates**, **decontaminating**, **decontaminated**) remove dangerous substances from. ■ **de·con·tam·i·na·tion** /-ˌtamə'nāsнən/ n.

de·cor /dā'kôr, di-/ ▶ n. the furnishing and decoration of a room.

> SYNONYMS **decoration**, furnishing, color scheme.

dec·o·rate /'dekəˌrāt/ ▶ v. (**decorates**, **decorating**, **decorated**) **1** make something more attractive by adding extra items. **2** give a room or house a color scheme. **3** give someone an award or medal.

> SYNONYMS **1 ornament**, adorn, trim, embellish, garnish, furnish, enhance. **2 design**, paint, wallpaper, paper, refurbish, renovate, redecorate; informal do up, give something a facelift, give something a makeover. **3 give a medal to**, honor, cite, reward.

dec·o·ra·tion /ˌdekə'rāsнən/ ▶ n. **1** the process or art of decorating. **2** a decorative object or pattern. **3** the way in which something is decorated. **4** a medal or award given as an honor.

> SYNONYMS **1 ornamentation**, adornment, trimming, embellishment, beautification. **2 ornament**, bauble, trinket, knick-knack. **3 medal**, award, prize.

dec·o·ra·tive /'dek(ə)rətiv, 'dekəˌrātiv/ ▶ adj. **1** making something look more attractive. **2** having to do with decoration: *a decorative artist*. **3** pretty or attractive.

> SYNONYMS **ornamental**, fancy, ornate, attractive, pretty, showy. ANTONYMS functional.

■ **dec·o·ra·tive·ly** adv.

dec·o·ra·tor /'dekəˌrātər/ ▶ n. a person who decorates, in particular a person who designs the interior of someone's home, by choosing colors, materials, and furnishings.

dec·o·rous /'dekərəs, di'kôrəs/ ▶ adj. in good taste; polite and restrained. ■ **dec·o·rous·ly** adv.

de·co·rum /di'kôrəm/ ▶ n. polite and socially acceptable behavior.

> SYNONYMS **1 propriety**, seemliness, decency, good taste, correctness, politeness, good manners. **2 etiquette**, protocol, good form, custom, convention. ANTONYMS impropriety.

dé·cou·page /ˌdākoo͞'päzн/ ▶ n. the decoration of a surface with paper cut-outs.

de·coy ▶ n. /'dēˌkoi/ **1** a real or imitation bird or animal, used by hunters to lure game. **2** a person or thing used to mislead or lure someone into a trap. ▶ v. /di'koi/ lure by means of a decoy.

de·crease /'dēˌkrēs, di'krēs/ ▶ v. (**decreases**, **decreasing**, **decreased**) make or become smaller or fewer. ▶ n. the process of decreasing, or the amount by which something decreases.

> SYNONYMS ▶ v. **lessen**, reduce, drop, diminish, decline, dwindle, fall off, plummet, plunge. ANTONYMS increase. ▶ n. **reduction**, drop, decline, downturn, cut, cutback, diminution. ANTONYMS increase.

de·cree /di'krē/ ▶ n. **1** an official order that has the force of law. **2** a judgment of certain law courts. ▶ v. (**decrees**, **decreeing**, **decreed**) order something officially.

> SYNONYMS ▶ n. **1** *a presidential decree* **order**, command, commandment, edict, proclamation, law, statute, act. **2** *a court decree* **judgment**, verdict, adjudication, finding, ruling, decision. ▶ v. **order**, direct, command, rule, dictate, pronounce, proclaim, ordain.

de·crep·it /di'krepit/ ▶ adj. **1** worn out or ruined because of age or neglect. **2** elderly and infirm.

> SYNONYMS **dilapidated**, rickety, run-down, tumbledown, ramshackle, derelict, ruined, in (a state of) disrepair, gone to rack and ruin, on its last legs, decayed, crumbling.

■ **de·crep·i·tude** n.

de·crim·i·nal·ize /dē'kriminlˌīz/ ▶ v. (**decriminalizes**, **decriminalizing**, **decriminalized**) change the law to make something no longer illegal. ■ **de·crim·i·nal·i·za·tion** /-ˌkriminl-i'zāsнən/ n.

de·cry /di'krī/ ▶ v. (**decries**, **decrying**, **decried**) publicly declare something to be wrong or bad.

> SYNONYMS **denounce**, condemn, criticize, censure, attack, rail against, run down, pillory, lambaste, vilify, revile; disparage, deprecate; informal slam, blast, knock. ANTONYMS praise.

de·crypt /di'kript/ ▶ v. convert a coded or unclear message into understandable language.

ded·i·cate /'dediˌkāt/ ▶ v. (**dedicates**, **dedicating**, **dedicated**) **1** give time or effort to a particular subject, task, or purpose. **2** address a book to someone as a sign of respect or affection.

> SYNONYMS **1 commit**, devote, pledge, give (up), sacrifice, set aside. **2 inscribe**, address, offer. **3 devote**, assign, bless, consecrate, sanctify.

ded·i·cat·ed /'dediˌkātid/ ▶ adj. **1** devoting a lot of time and attention to a particular task or subject. **2** exclusively given over to a particular purpose.

> SYNONYMS **1 committed**, devoted, enthusiastic, keen, staunch, firm, steadfast, loyal, faithful. **2 specialized**, custom-built, customized, purpose-built, exclusive. ANTONYMS halfhearted.

ded·i·ca·tion /ˌdediˈkāsʜən/ ▶ **n. 1** devotion to a particular task or subject. **2** the action of dedicating. **3** the words with which a book is dedicated to someone.

SYNONYMS **1 commitment**, devotion, loyalty, allegiance, application, resolve, conscientiousness, perseverance, persistence. **2 inscription**, message. ANTONYMS apathy.

de·duce /diˈd(y)o͞os/ ▶ **v.** (**deduces**, **deducing**, **deduced**) reach a conclusion by thinking about the information or evidence that is available.

SYNONYMS **conclude**, reason, work out, infer, understand, assume, presume, surmise, reckon; informal figure out, put two and two together.

de·duct /diˈdəkt/ ▶ **v.** take an amount away from a total.

SYNONYMS **subtract**, take away, take off, debit, dock, stop; informal knock off. ANTONYMS add.

■ **de·duct·i·ble adj.**

de·duc·tion /diˈdəksʜən/ ▶ **n. 1** the action of deducting something. **2** an amount that is or may be deducted. **3** the process of deducing something.

SYNONYMS **1 subtraction**, removal, debit. **2 stoppage**, tax, expenses, rebate, discount, concession. **3 conclusion**, inference, supposition, hypothesis, assumption, presumption, suspicion.

■ **de·duc·tive adj.**

deed /dēd/ ▶ **n. 1** something that is done deliberately. **2** a legal document, especially one regarding the ownership of property or legal rights.

SYNONYMS **1 act**, action, feat, exploit, achievement, accomplishment, endeavor. **2 document**, contract, instrument.

dee·jay /ˈdēˌjā/ ▶ **n.** informal a disc jockey.

deem /dēm/ ▶ **v.** formal consider in a particular way.

SYNONYMS **consider**, regard as, judge, hold to be, view as, see as, take for, class as, count, find, esteem, suppose, reckon.

deep /dēp/ ▶ **adj. 1** extending far down or in from the top or surface. **2** extending a specified distance from the top or surface. **3** (of sound) not shrill. **4** (of color) dark. **5** very intense or extreme: *he was in deep trouble*. **6** difficult to understand. **7** (in ball games) far down or across the field. ▶ **n.** (**the deep**) literary the sea.

SYNONYMS ▶ **adj. 1 cavernous**, yawning, gaping, huge, extensive, bottomless, fathomless. **2 intense**, heartfelt, wholehearted, deep-seated, sincere, genuine, earnest, enthusiastic, great. **3 profound**, serious, intelligent, intellectual, learned, wise, scholarly. **4** *he was deep in concentration* **rapt**, absorbed, engrossed, preoccupied, intent, immersed, lost, gripped. **5 obscure**, complex, mysterious, unfathomable, opaque, abstruse, esoteric, enigmatic. **6 low-pitched**, low, bass, rich, resonant, booming, sonorous. **7 dark**, intense, rich, strong, vivid. ANTONYMS shallow, superficial, high.

□ **be thrown into the deep end** informal have to face a difficult problem when you are new to something. **deep freeze** (or **deep freezer**) a freezer. **deep-fry** fry food in enough fat or oil to cover it completely. **deep-seated** (or **deep-rooted**) firmly established. **go off the deep end** informal give way immediately to an outburst of emotion. **in deep water** informal in trouble.

deep·en /ˈdēpən/ ▶ **v.** make or become deep or deeper.

deep·ly /ˈdēplē/ ▶ **adv. 1** far down or in. **2** intensely.

SYNONYMS **profoundly**, greatly, enormously, extremely, very, strongly, intensely, keenly, acutely, thoroughly, completely, entirely, seriously.

deer /di(ə)r/ ▶ **n.** (plural **deer**) a grazing animal with hooves, the male of which usually has antlers.

deer·stalk·er /ˈdi(ə)rˌstôkər/ ▶ **n.** a soft cloth cap, with peaks in front and behind and ear flaps that can be tied together over the top.

de·face /diˈfās/ ▶ **v.** (**defaces**, **defacing**, **defaced**) spoil the surface or appearance of.

SYNONYMS **vandalize**, disfigure, spoil, ruin, damage; informal trash.

de fac·to /di ˈfaktō, dā/ ▶ **adj. & adv.** existing or happening in fact, whether it is supposed to or not.

de·fame /diˈfām/ ▶ **v.** (**defames**, **defaming**, **defamed**) damage the good reputation of.

SYNONYMS **libel**, slander, malign, slur, cast aspersions on, smear, traduce, give someone a bad name, run down, speak ill of, vilify, besmirch, disparage, denigrate, discredit; informal bad-mouth, do a hatchet job on, drag through the mud. ANTONYMS compliment.

■ **def·a·ma·tion** /ˌdefəˈmāsʜən/ **n.** **de·fam·a·to·ry** /-ˈfaməˌtôrē/ **adj.**

de·fault /diˈfôlt/ ▶ **n. 1** failure to do something that is required by law. **2** an option adopted by a computer program or other mechanism when no alternative is specified. ▶ **v. 1** fail to do something that is required by law. **2** (**default to**) go back automatically to a default option. □ **by default** because there is no opposition or positive action.
■ **de·fault·er n.**

de·feat /diˈfēt/ ▶ **v. 1** win a victory against; beat. **2** prevent someone from achieving an aim. **3** reject or block a proposal or motion. ▶ **n.** an instance of defeating or of being defeated.

SYNONYMS ▶ **v. 1 beat**, conquer, win against, triumph over, get the better of, vanquish, rout, trounce, overcome, overpower; informal lick, thrash. **2 thwart**, frustrate, foil, ruin, scotch, derail; informal put paid to, stymie. ▶ **n. loss**, conquest, rout; informal thrashing, hiding, drubbing, licking. ANTONYMS victory.

de·feat·ist /diˈfētist/ ▶ **n.** a person who gives in to difficulty or failure too easily. ■ **de·feat·ism n.**

def·e·cate /ˈdefiˌkāt/ ▶ **v.** expel waste matter from the bowels. ■ **def·e·ca·tion n.**

de·fect¹ /ˈdēˌfekt/ ▶ **n.** a fault or imperfection.

SYNONYMS **fault**, flaw, imperfection, deficiency, deformity, blemish, mistake, error.

de·fect² /diˈfekt/ ▶ **v.** abandon your country or cause in favor of an opposing one. ■ **de·fec·tion n.** **de·fec·tor n.**

de·fec·tive /diˈfektiv/ ▶ **adj.** not perfect; faulty.

SYNONYMS **faulty**, flawed, imperfect, unsound, inoperative, malfunctioning, out of order, broken; informal on the blink. ANTONYMS perfect.

de·fend /di'fend/ ▶ **v. 1** protect from harm or danger. **2** argue in support of the person being accused or sued in a lawsuit. **3** attempt to justify. **4** compete to hold on to a title or seat in a contest or election. **5** (in sports) protect your goal rather than attempt to score against your opponents.

> SYNONYMS **1 protect**, guard, safeguard, secure, shield, fortify, watch over. **2 justify**, vindicate, explain, argue for, support, back, stand by, make a case for, stick up for. ANTONYMS attack, criticize.

de·fend·ant /di'fendənt/ ▶ **n.** a person sued or accused in a court of law.

de·fend·er /di'fendər/ ▶ **n.** a person who defends someone or something.

> SYNONYMS **1 protector**, guardian, guard, custodian. **2 supporter**, upholder, backer, champion, advocate, apologist.

de·fense /di'fens, 'dēˌfens/ ▶ **n. 1** the action of defending something. **2** something that protects a building, country, etc., against attack. **3** an attempt to justify something: *he spoke in defense of his actions*. **4** the case presented by the person being accused or sued in a lawsuit. **5** (**the defense**) the lawyer or lawyers acting for the person being accused or sued in a lawsuit. **6** (in sports) the action of defending the goal, or the players who perform this role.

> SYNONYMS **1 protection**, guarding, security, fortification, resistance. **2 armaments**, weapons, weaponry, arms, the military, the armed forces. **3 justification**, vindication, explanation, mitigation, excuse, alibi, denial, rebuttal, plea, pleading, argument, case. ANTONYMS attack, prosecution.

de·fense·less /di'fenslis/ ▶ **adj.** completely vulnerable.

> SYNONYMS **vulnerable**, helpless, powerless, weak, undefended, unprotected, unguarded, unarmed, exposed, open to attack.

de·fense·man /di'fensmən/ ▶ **n.** (plural **defensemen**) (in ice hockey and lacrosse) a player in a defensive position.

de·fen·si·ble /di'fensəbəl/ ▶ **adj. 1** able to be justified by argument. **2** able to be protected.

de·fen·sive /di'fensiv/ ▶ **adj. 1** used or intended to defend or protect. **2** very anxious to defend yourself against criticism.

> SYNONYMS **1 defending**, protective. **2 self-justifying**, oversensitive, prickly, paranoid, neurotic; informal twitchy.

□ **on the defensive** expecting or resisting criticism or attack. ■ **de·fen·sive·ly** adv. **de·fen·sive·ness** n.

de·fer¹ /di'fər/ ▶ **v.** (**defers**, **deferring**, **deferred**) put something off to a later time.

> SYNONYMS **postpone**, put off, table, delay, hold over/off, put back, shelve, suspend; informal put on ice, put on the back burner.

■ **de·fer·ment** n. **de·fer·ral** n.

de·fer² ▶ **v.** (**defers**, **deferring**, **deferred**) (**defer to**) give in to or agree to accept.

def·er·ence /'def(ə)rəns/ ▶ **n.** polite respect.

def·er·en·tial /ˌdefə'renchəl/ ▶ **adj.** polite and respectful. ■ **def·er·en·tial·ly** adv.

de·fi·ance /di'fīəns/ ▶ **n.** open refusal to obey someone or something.

> SYNONYMS **resistance**, opposition, noncompliance, disobedience, insubordination, rebellion, disregard, contempt, insolence. ANTONYMS obedience.

■ **de·fi·ant·ly** adv.

de·fi·ant /di'fīənt/ ▶ **adj.** openly refusing to obey someone or something.

> SYNONYMS **disobedient**, resistant, obstinate, uncooperative, noncompliant, recalcitrant, insubordinate. ANTONYMS cooperative.

de·fi·cien·cy /di'fishənsē/ ▶ **n.** (plural **deficiencies**) **1** a lack or shortage of something. **2** a failing or shortcoming.

> SYNONYMS **1 lack**, insufficiency, shortage, inadequacy, deficit, shortfall, scarcity, dearth. **2 defect**, fault, flaw, failing, weakness, shortcoming, limitation. ANTONYMS surplus, strength.

de·fi·cient /di'fishənt/ ▶ **adj. 1** not having enough of a particular quality or ingredient. **2** inadequate in amount or quantity: *the documentary evidence is deficient*.

def·i·cit /'defəsit/ ▶ **n. 1** the amount by which a total falls short of that required. **2** the amount by which money spent is greater than money earned in a particular period of time.

> SYNONYMS **shortfall**, deficiency, shortage, debt, arrears, loss. ANTONYMS surplus.

de·file¹ /di'fīl/ ▶ **v.** (**defiles**, **defiling**, **defiled**) **1** make dirty. **2** treat something sacred with disrespect. ■ **de·file·ment** n.

de·file² /di'fīl, 'dēˌfīl/ ▶ **n.** a narrow steep-sided gorge or mountain pass.

de·fine /di'fīn/ ▶ **v.** (**defines**, **defining**, **defined**) **1** describe the exact nature or scope of. **2** give the meaning of a word or phrase. **3** mark out the limits or outline of.

> SYNONYMS **1 explain**, give the meaning of, spell out, expound, interpret, describe. **2 determine**, establish, fix, specify, designate, decide, stipulate, set out.

■ **de·fin·a·ble** adj.

def·i·nite /'defənit/ ▶ **adj. 1** clearly stated or decided. **2** (of a person) certain about something. **3** known to be true or real. **4** having exact and measurable physical limits.

> SYNONYMS **specific**, explicit, express, precise, exact, clear, clear-cut, unambiguous, certain, sure, positive, conclusive, decisive, firm, unequivocal, unmistakable, proven, decided, marked, distinct, identifiable. ANTONYMS vague, ambiguous.

□ **the definite article** Grammar the word *the*.

> **SPELLING**
> The word ends with **-ite**, not **-ate**: defin**ite**.

def·i·nite·ly /'defənitlē/ ▶ **adv.** without doubt; certainly.

> SYNONYMS **certainly**, surely, for sure, unquestionably, without doubt, undoubtedly, undeniably, clearly, positively, absolutely, unmistakably.

def·i·ni·tion /ˌdefə'nishən/ ▶ **n. 1** a statement of the exact meaning of a word or the nature or scope of something. **2** the degree of sharpness in outline of an object or image.

SYNONYMS **1 meaning**, sense, interpretation, explanation, description. **2 clarity**, sharpness, focus, crispness, resolution.

□ **by definition** by its very nature.

de·fin·i·tive /di'finitiv/ ▶ **adj.** **1** (of a conclusion or agreement) final and not able to be changed. **2** (of a written work) the most accurate of its kind.

SYNONYMS **1 conclusive**, final, unqualified, absolute, categorical, positive, definite. **2 authoritative**, best, ultimate, classic, standard, recognized, accepted, exhaustive.

■ **de·fin·i·tive·ly** **adv.**

de·flate /di'flāt/ ▶ **v.** (**deflates**, **deflating**, **deflated**) **1** let air or gas out of a tire, balloon, etc. **2** make someone feel suddenly depressed. **3** reduce price levels in an economy.

de·fla·tion /di'flāsʜən/ ▶ **n.** **1** the action of deflating something. **2** reduction of the general level of prices in an economy. ■ **de·fla·tion·ar·y** **adj.**

de·flect /di'flekt/ ▶ **v.** **1** turn something aside from a straight course. **2** make someone change their mind about doing something.

SYNONYMS **divert**, turn away, draw away, distract, fend off, parry, stave off.

■ **de·flec·tion** **n.**

de·fo·li·ate /dē'fōlē,āt/ ▶ **v.** (**defoliates**, **defoliating**, **defoliated**) remove the leaves from trees or plants. ■ **de·fo·li·ant** /dē'fōlēənt/ **n.** **de·fo·li·a·tion** /dē,fōlē'āsʜən/ **n.**

de·for·est /dē'fôrist, -'fär-/ ▶ **v.** clear an area of trees. ■ **de·for·est·a·tion** /dē,fôrə'stāsʜən, -,fär-/ **n.**

de·form /di'fôrm/ ▶ **v.** change or spoil the usual shape of.

SYNONYMS (**deformed**) **misshapen**, distorted, malformed, contorted, out of shape, twisted, crooked, warped, buckled, gnarled, disfigured, mutilated, mangled.

de·form·i·ty /di'fôrmitē/ ▶ **n.** (plural **deformities**) **1** a deformed part. **2** the state of being deformed.

de·fraud /di'frôd/ ▶ **v.** illegally obtain money from someone by deception.

SYNONYMS **swindle**, cheat, rob, deceive, dupe, hoodwink, double-cross, trick; informal con, do, sting, diddle, rip off, shaft, pull a fast one on, put one over on, sucker, snooker, stiff.

de·fray /di'frā/ ▶ **v.** provide money to pay a cost.

de·frock /dē'fräk/ ▶ **v.** remove the official status of a Christian priest.

de·frost /di'frôst/ ▶ **v.** **1** remove ice from something. **2** thaw frozen food.

deft /deft/ ▶ **adj.** quick and neatly skillful.

SYNONYMS **skillful**, adept, adroit, dexterous, agile, nimble, handy, able, capable, skilled, proficient, accomplished, expert, polished, slick, professional. ANTONYMS clumsy.

■ **deft·ly** **adv.** **deft·ness** **n.**

de·funct /di'fəɴɢkt/ ▶ **adj.** no longer existing or functioning.

SYNONYMS **disused**, inoperative, nonfunctioning, unusable, obsolete, discontinued, no longer existing, extinct; discontinued. ANTONYMS working, extant.

de·fuse /di'fyo͞oz/ ▶ **v.** (**defuses**, **defusing**, **defused**) **1** make a situation less tense or difficult. **2** remove the fuse from an explosive device to prevent it from exploding.

USAGE

Don't confuse **defuse** with **diffuse**, which means 'spread over a wide area.'

de·fy /di'fī/ ▶ **v.** (**defies**, **defying**, **defied**) **1** openly resist or refuse to obey. **2** challenge someone to do or prove something.

SYNONYMS **disobey**, flout, disregard, ignore, break, violate, contravene, breach, challenge, fly in the face of, confront. ANTONYMS obey.

de·gen·er·ate ▶ **v.** /di'jenə,rāt/ (**degenerates**, **degenerating**, **degenerated**) deteriorate physically or morally; get worse. ▶ **adj.** /di'jenərit/ having very low moral standards. ▶ **n.** /di'jenərit/ a person with very low moral standards.

SYNONYMS ▶ **v.** **deteriorate**, decline, worsen, slip, slide, go downhill; informal go to the dogs. ANTONYMS improve. ▶ **adj.** **corrupt**, perverted, decadent, dissolute, dissipated, debauched, immoral, unprincipled, disreputable.

■ **de·gen·er·a·cy** **n.** **de·gen·er·a·tion** /di,jenə'rāsʜən/ **n.**

de·gen·er·a·tive /di'jenərətiv, -ə,rātiv/ ▶ **adj.** (of a disease) becoming progressively worse.

de·grade /di'grād/ ▶ **v.** (**degrades**, **degrading**, **degraded**) **1** cause someone to lose dignity or self-respect. **2** make worse in character or quality. **3** make something break down or deteriorate chemically.

SYNONYMS **demean**, debase, humiliate, humble, belittle, mortify, dehumanize, brutalize. ANTONYMS dignify.

■ **de·grad·a·ble** **adj.** **deg·ra·da·tion** /,degrə'dāsʜən/ **n.**

de·grad·ing /di'grādiɴɢ/ ▶ **adj.** causing a loss of self-respect; humiliating.

SYNONYMS **humiliating**, demeaning, shameful, mortifying, ignominious, undignified.

de·gree /di'grē/ ▶ **n.** **1** the amount, level, or extent to which something happens or is present. **2** a unit for measuring angles, equivalent to one ninetieth of a right angle. **3** a stage in a scale, e.g., of temperature or hardness. **4** a qualification awarded to someone who has successfully completed a program of study at a college or university.

SYNONYMS **level**, standard, grade, stage, mark, amount, extent, measure, intensity, strength, proportion.

□ **by degrees** gradually. **to a** (or **some**) **degree** to some extent.

de·hisce /di'his/ ▶ **v.** (**dehisces**, **dehiscing**, **dehisced**) technical gape or burst open.

de·hu·man·ize /dē'(h)yo͞omə,nīz/ ▶ **v.** (**dehumanizes**, **dehumanizing**, **dehumanized**) remove the positive human qualities from.

de·hu·mid·i·fy /,dē(h)yo͞o'midə,fī/ ▶ **v.** (**dehumidifies**, **dehumidifying**, **dehumidified**) remove moisture from the air or a gas. ■ **de·hu·mid·i·fi·er** **n.**

de·hy·drate /dē'hīdrāt/ ▶ **v.** (**dehydrates**, **dehydrating**, **dehydrated**) **1** make someone lose a lot of water from their body. **2** remove water from food to preserve it. ■ **de·hy·dra·tion** /,dēhī'drāsʜən/ **n.**

de-ice /dē'īs/ ▶ v. (**de-ices**, **de-icing**, **de-iced**) remove ice from. ■ **de-ic-er** n.

de·i·fy /'dēə,fī/ ▶ v. (**deifies**, **deifying**, **deified**) treat or worship someone as a god. ■ **de·i·fi·ca·tion** /,dēəfi'kāsʜən/ n.

deign /dān/ ▶ v. (**deign to do**) do something that you think you are too important to do.

SYNONYMS **condescend**, stoop, lower yourself, demean yourself, humble yourself, consent.

de·ism /'dēizəm/ ▶ n. belief in the existence of a supreme being who does not intervene in the universe. ■ **de·ist** n.

de·i·ty /'dēitē/ ▶ n. (plural **deities**) a god or goddess.

SYNONYMS **god**, goddess, divine being, supreme being, godhead, creator, divinity, immortal.

dé·jà vu /,dāzʜä 'vo͞o/ ▶ n. a feeling of having already experienced the present situation.

de·ject·ed /di'jektəd/ ▶ adj. sad and in low spirits.

SYNONYMS **downcast**, downhearted, despondent, disconsolate, dispirited, crestfallen, disheartened, depressed; informal down in the mouth, down in the dumps. ANTONYMS cheerful.

■ **de·jec·tion** n.

de ju·re /di 'jo͝orē, dā 'jo͝orā/ ▶ adv. rightfully; by right. ▶ adj. rightful.

de·lay /di'lā/ ▶ v. **1** make someone late or slow. **2** hesitate or be slow. **3** put off or postpone. ▶ n. the period or length of time that someone or something is delayed.

SYNONYMS ▶ v. **1 detain**, hold up, make late, slow up/down, bog down, hinder, hamper, impede, obstruct. **2 linger**, drag your feet, hold back, dawdle, waste time, stall, hesitate, dither, shilly-shally; informal dilly-dally. **3 postpone**, put off, defer, hold over, adjourn, reschedule. ANTONYMS hurry, advance. ▶ n. **1 holdup**, wait, interruption, stoppage. **2** *the delay of his trial* **postponement**, deferral, adjournment.

de·lec·ta·ble /di'lektəbəl/ ▶ adj. lovely, delightful, or delicious.

SYNONYMS **1 delicious**, mouthwatering, appetizing, flavorsome, toothsome, succulent, luscious, tasty; informal scrumptious, yummy, nummy. **2 delightful**, lovely, captivating, charming, enchanting, appealing, beguiling; informal divine, heavenly, dreamy. ANTONYMS unpalatable, unattractive.

■ **de·lec·ta·bly** adv.

de·lec·ta·tion /,dēlek'tāsʜən/ ▶ n. formal pleasure and delight.

del·e·gate ▶ n. /'deligit/ **1** a person sent to represent other people. **2** a member of a committee. ▶ v. /'delə,gāt/ (**delegates**, **delegating**, **delegated**) **1** give a task or responsibility to someone else, especially someone more junior. **2** authorize someone to act as a representative.

SYNONYMS ▶ n. **representative**, envoy, emissary, commissioner, agent, deputy. ▶ v. **assign**, entrust, pass on, hand on/over, turn over, devolve.

del·e·ga·tion /,deli'gāsʜən/ ▶ n. **1** a group of delegates. **2** the process of delegating something.

SYNONYMS **deputation**, mission, commission, contingent, legation.

de·lete /di'lēt/ ▶ v. (**deletes**, **deleting**, **deleted**) cross out or remove something written or printed or stored in a computer's memory.

SYNONYMS **remove**, cut (out), take out, edit out, excise, cancel, cross out, strike out, obliterate, rub out, erase. ANTONYMS add.

■ **de·le·tion** n.

del·e·te·ri·ous /,deli'ti(ə)rēəs/ ▶ adj. formal causing harm or damage.

delft /delft/ ▶ n. glazed earthenware, typically decorated in blue on a white background.

del·i /'delē/ ▶ n. (plural **delis**) informal a delicatessen.

de·lib·er·ate ▶ adj. /di'libərit/ **1** done on purpose; intentional. **2** careful and unhurried: *a deliberate worker*. ▶ v. /di'libə,rāt/ (**deliberates**, **deliberating**, **deliberated**) think about something carefully and for a long time.

SYNONYMS ▶ adj. **1 intentional**, calculated, conscious, intended, planned, willful, premeditated. **2 careful**, cautious, measured, regular, even, steady. **3 methodical**, systematic, careful, painstaking, meticulous, thorough. ANTONYMS accidental, hasty. ▶ v. **think**, think about/over/on, ponder, consider, contemplate, reflect on, muse on, meditate on, ruminate on, mull over.

de·lib·er·ate·ly /di'libəritlē/ ▶ adv. **1** intentionally; not accidentally. **2** slowly and carefully.

SYNONYMS **1 intentionally**, on purpose, purposely, by design, knowingly, wittingly, consciously, willfully. **2 carefully**, cautiously, slowly, steadily, evenly.

de·lib·er·a·tion /di,libə'rāsʜən/ ▶ n. **1** long and careful consideration. **2** slow and careful movement or thought.

SYNONYMS **thought**, consideration, reflection, contemplation, discussion.

de·lib·er·a·tive /di'libərətiv, -ə,rātiv/ ▶ adj. having to do with consideration or discussion: *a deliberative assembly*.

del·i·ca·cy /'delikəsē/ ▶ n. (plural **delicacies**) **1** intricate or fragile texture or structure. **2** discretion and tact. **3** a tasty, expensive food.

SYNONYMS **1 fineness**, delicateness, fragility, thinness, lightness, flimsiness. **2 difficulty**, trickiness, sensitivity, ticklishness, awkwardness. **3 care**, sensitivity, tact, discretion, diplomacy, subtlety. **4 treat**, luxury, tidbit, specialty.

del·i·cate /'delikit/ ▶ adj. **1** attractively light and intricate in texture or structure. **2** easily broken or damaged. **3** tending to become ill easily. **4** needing or showing careful handling: *a delicate issue*. **5** (of color or flavor) subtle and pleasant.

SYNONYMS **1** *delicate embroidery* **fine**, intricate, dainty, exquisite, graceful. **2** *a delicate shade of blue* **subtle**, soft, pale, muted, pastel, light. **3** *delicate china cups* **fragile**, dainty. **4** *his wife is very delicate* **sickly**, unhealthy, frail, feeble, weak. **5** *a delicate issue* **difficult**, tricky, sensitive, ticklish, awkward, touchy, embarrassing; informal sticky, dicey. **6** *the matter needs delicate handling* **careful**, sensitive, tactful, diplomatic, discreet, kid-glove, subtle. **7** *a delicate mechanism* **sensitive**, light, precision. ANTONYMS coarse, strong, robust.

■ **del·i·cate·ly** adv.

del·i·ca·tes·sen /ˌdelikə'tesən/ ▶ **n.** a store selling cold cuts, cheeses, and a variety of salads, as well as a selection of unusual or foreign prepared foods.

de·li·cious /di'lisʜəs/ ▶ **adj.** **1** having a very pleasant taste or smell. **2** delightful; very enjoyable: *a delicious irony*.

SYNONYMS **delectable**, mouthwatering, appetizing, tasty, flavorsome; informal scrumptious, finger-licking (good). ANTONYMS unpalatable.

■ **de·li·cious·ly** **adv.**

de·light /di'līt/ ▶ **v.** **1** please someone very much. **2** (**delight in**) take great pleasure in. ▶ **n.** great pleasure, or something that causes it.

SYNONYMS ▶ **v.** **charm**, enchant, captivate, entrance, thrill, entertain, amuse, divert; informal send, tickle pink, bowl over. ANTONYMS dismay, disgust. ▶ **n.** **pleasure**, happiness, joy, glee, excitement, amusement, bliss, ecstasy. ANTONYMS displeasure.

de·light·ed /di'lītid/ ▶ **adj.** very pleased.

SYNONYMS **pleased**, glad, happy, thrilled, overjoyed, ecstatic, elated, on cloud nine, walking on air, in seventh heaven, jumping for joy, gleeful; informal over the moon, tickled pink, as pleased as Punch, on top of the world.

■ **de·light·ed·ly** **adv.**

de·light·ful /di'lītfəl/ ▶ **adj.** causing delight; very pleasing.

SYNONYMS **1** *a delightful evening* **lovely**, enjoyable, amusing, entertaining, pleasant, pleasurable. **2** *a delightful girl* **charming**, enchanting, captivating, bewitching, appealing, sweet, endearing, cute, adorable, delectable.

■ **de·light·ful·ly** **adv.**

de·lim·it /di'limit/ ▶ **v.** (**delimits**, **delimiting**, **delimited**) determine the limits or boundaries of.

de·lin·e·ate /di'linēˌāt/ ▶ **v.** (**delineates**, **delineating**, **delineated**) describe or indicate something precisely. ■ **de·lin·e·a·tion** /-ˌlinē'āsʜən/ **n.**

de·lin·quen·cy /di'liɴɢkwənsē/ ▶ **n.** (plural **delinquencies**) minor crime.

de·lin·quent /di'liɴɢkwənt/ ▶ **adj.** tending to commit crime. ▶ **n.** a delinquent person.

SYNONYMS ▶ **adj.** **lawless**, lawbreaking, criminal; errant, badly behaved, troublesome, difficult, unruly, disobedient, uncontrollable. ▶ **n.** **offender**, wrongdoer, malefactor, lawbreaker, criminal, hooligan, vandal, ruffian, hoodlum.

del·i·quesce /ˌdeli'kwes/ ▶ **v.** (**deliquesces**, **deliquescing**, **deliquesced**) (of a solid) become liquid by absorbing moisture. ■ **del·i·ques·cence** **n.** **del·i·ques·cent** **adj.**

de·lir·i·ous /di'li(ə)rēəs/ ▶ **adj.** **1** suffering from delirium. **2** very excited or happy.

SYNONYMS **1** **incoherent**, raving, babbling, irrational, deranged, demented, out of your mind, feverish, frenzied. **2** *the crowd was delirious* **ecstatic**, elated, thrilled, overjoyed, beside yourself, walking on air, on cloud nine, in seventh heaven, transported, rapturous; hysterical, wild, frenzied; informal blissed out, over the moon. ANTONYMS lucid.

■ **de·lir·i·ous·ly** **adv.**

SPELLING

Note there's an **i**, not an **e**, in the middle: delirious.

de·lir·i·um /di'li(ə)rēəm/ ▶ **n.** a disturbed state of mind in which a person becomes very restless, has illusions, and is unable to think clearly.

de·liv·er /di'livər/ ▶ **v.** **1** bring something and hand it over to the person who is supposed to receive it. **2** provide something promised or expected. **3** give a speech. **4** launch or aim a blow or attack. **5** save or set free. **6** assist in the birth of a baby. **7** give birth to a baby.

SYNONYMS **1** **bring**, take, convey, carry, transport, send, distribute, dispatch, ship. **2** **state**, utter, give, read, broadcast, pronounce, announce, declare, proclaim, hand down, return. **3** **administer**, deal, inflict, give; informal land.

de·liv·er·ance /di'livərəns/ ▶ **n.** the process of being rescued or set free.

de·liv·er·y /di'livərē/ ▶ **n.** (plural **deliveries**) **1** the action of delivering something. **2** the process of giving birth. **3** an act of throwing or bowling a ball. **4** the manner or style of giving a speech.

SYNONYMS **1** **conveyance**, carriage, transportation, transport, distribution, dispatch, shipping. **2** **consignment**, load, shipment. **3** **speech**, pronunciation, enunciation, articulation, elocution.

dell /del/ ▶ **n.** literary a small valley.

Del·phic /'delfik/ ▶ **adj.** **1** having to do with the ancient Greek oracle at Delphi. **2** deliberately difficult to understand: *Delphic utterances*.

del·phin·i·um /del'finēəm/ ▶ **n.** (plural **delphiniums**) a garden plant of the buttercup family that has tall spikes of blue flowers.

del·ta /'deltə/ ▶ **n.** **1** an area of land where the mouth of a river has split into several channels. **2** the fourth letter of the Greek alphabet (Δ, δ).

de·lude /di'lo͞od/ ▶ **v.** (**deludes**, **deluding**, **deluded**) persuade someone to believe something that is not true.

SYNONYMS **mislead**, deceive, fool, take in, trick, dupe, hoodwink, gull, lead on; informal con, pull the wool over someone's eyes, sucker, snooker, lead up the garden path, take for a ride.

del·uge /'del(y)o͞oj/ ▶ **n.** **1** a severe flood or very heavy fall of rain. **2** a great quantity of something arriving at the same time: *a deluge of complaints*. ▶ **v.** (**deluges**, **deluging**, **deluged**) **1** overwhelm someone with a great quantity of something. **2** flood a place.

de·lu·sion /di'lo͞ozʜən/ ▶ **n.** a mistaken belief or impression.

SYNONYMS **misapprehension**, misconception, false impression, misunderstanding, mistake, error, misconstruction, illusion, fantasy, fancy.

■ **de·lu·sion·al** **adj.**

de·luxe /di'ləks/ ▶ **adj.** of a higher quality than usual.

delve /delv/ ▶ **v.** (**delves**, **delving**, **delved**) **1** reach inside a container and search for something. **2** research something very thoroughly. **3** literary dig.

SYNONYMS **1** **rummage**, search, hunt, scrabble about/around, root about/around, ferret (about/around), fish about/around, dig, rifle through. **2 investigate**, inquire, probe, explore, research, look into, go into.

de·mag·net·ize /dē'magni,tīz/ ▶ v. (**demagnetizes**, **demagnetizing**, **demagnetized**) remove magnetic properties from something.

dem·a·gogue /'demə,gäg/ ▶ n. a political leader who appeals to people's desires and prejudices rather than using reasoned arguments.

de·mand /di'mand/ ▶ n. **1** a very firm request for something. **2** (**demands**) tasks or requirements that are urgent or difficult. **3** the desire of consumers for a particular product or service. ▶ v. **1** ask very firmly. **2** insist on having. **3** require; need.

SYNONYMS ▶ n. **1** *I gave in to her demands* **request**, call, command, order, dictate. **2** *the demands of a young family* **requirement**, need, claim, commitment, imposition. **3 market**, call, appetite, desire. ▶ v. **1 call for**, ask for, request, push for, press for, seek, claim, insist on. **2 order**, command, enjoin, require. **3 ask**, inquire, question, query. **4 require**, need, necessitate, call for, involve, entail. **5 insist on**, stipulate, expect, look for.

□ **in demand** wanted by many people.

de·mand·ing /di'mandiNG/ ▶ adj. **1** (of a task) needing a lot of skill or effort. **2** (of a person) making others work hard or meet high standards.

SYNONYMS **1 difficult**, challenging, taxing, exacting, tough, hard, onerous, formidable, arduous, grueling, back-breaking, punishing. **2 nagging**, trying, tiresome, hard to please, high-maintenance. ANTONYMS easy.

de·mar·cate /di'mär,kāt, 'dēmär,kāt/ ▶ v. (**demarcates**, **demarcating**, **demarcated**) set the boundaries of. ■ **de·mar·ca·tion** /,dēmär'kāsHən/ n.

de·ma·te·ri·al·ize /,dēmə'ti(ə)rēə,līz/ ▶ v. (**dematerializes**, **dematerializing**, **dematerialized**) stop being physically present; disappear.

de·mean /di'mēn/ ▶ v. make someone lose dignity or respect.

SYNONYMS **1 discredit**, lower, degrade, debase, devalue, cheapen, abase, humiliate. **2** (**demeaning**) **degrading**, humiliating, shameful, undignified, menial. ANTONYMS dignify.

de·mean·or /di'mēnər/ ▶ n. the way a person behaves or appears to others.

SYNONYMS **manner**, air, attitude, appearance, look, mien, bearing, carriage, behavior, conduct.

de·ment·ed /di'mentid/ ▶ adj. **1** suffering from dementia. **2** informal wild and irrational.

SYNONYMS **mad**, insane, deranged, out of your mind, crazed, lunatic, unbalanced, unhinged, disturbed, non compos mentis; informal crazy, mental, raving mad, not all there. ANTONYMS sane.

de·men·tia /di'mensHə/ ▶ n. a disorder in which a person is unable to remember things or think clearly.

de·mer·it /di'merit/ ▶ n. a fault or disadvantage.

de·mer·sal /di'mərsəl/ ▶ adj. living close to the seabed.

de·mesne /di'mān/ ▶ n. **1** historical land attached to a manor. **2** old use a domain.

dem·i·god /'demē,gäd/ ▶ n. a being that is partly a god and partly a human.

dem·i·john /'demē,jän/ ▶ n. a narrow-necked bottle holding from 3 to 10 gallons of liquid.

de·mil·i·ta·rize /dē'militə,rīz/ ▶ v. (**demilitarizes**, **demilitarizing**, **demilitarized**) remove all military forces from an area. ■ **de·mil·i·ta·ri·za·tion** /-,militərə'zāsHən/ n.

dem·i·monde /'demē,mänd/ ▶ n. a group of people on the fringes of respectable society.

de·mise /di'mīz/ ▶ n. **1** a person's death. **2** the end or failure of something.

SYNONYMS **1 death**, dying, passing, end. **2 end**, break-up, disintegration, fall, downfall, collapse, overthrow. ANTONYMS birth.

dem·o /'demō/ ▶ n. (plural **demos**) informal a tape or disc containing a demonstration of a performer's music or a piece of software.

de·mo·bi·lize /dē'mōbə,līz/ ▶ v. (**demobilizes**, **demobilizing**, **demobilized**) take troops out of active service. ■ **de·mo·bi·li·za·tion** /-,mōbəli'zāsHən/ n.

de·moc·ra·cy /di'mäkrəsē/ ▶ n. (plural **democracies**) **1** a form of government in which the people can vote for representatives to govern the state on their behalf. **2** a state governed in this way.

dem·o·crat /'demə,krat/ ▶ n. **1** a supporter of democracy. **2** (**Democrat**) (in the United States) a member of the Democratic Party.

dem·o·crat·ic /,demə'kratik/ ▶ adj. **1** relating to or supporting democracy. **2** based on the principle that everyone in society is equal: *cycling is a very democratic activity*. **3** (**Democratic**) (in the United States) relating to or supporting the Democratic Party.

SYNONYMS **elected**, representative, parliamentary, popular, egalitarian, self-governing.

■ **dem·o·crat·i·cal·ly** adv.

de·moc·ra·tize /di'mäkrə,tīz/ ▶ v. (**democratizes**, **democratizing**, **democratized**) introduce a democratic system or democratic ideas to. ■ **de·moc·ra·ti·za·tion** /-,mäkrətə'zāsHən/ n.

de·mod·u·late /dē'mäjə,lāt/ ▶ v. (**demodulates**, **demodulating**, **demodulated**) Electronics reverse the modulation of.

de·mog·ra·phy /di'mägrəfē/ ▶ n. the study of changes in human populations using records of the numbers of births, deaths, etc., in a particular area. ■ **dem·o·graph·ic** /,demə'grafik/ adj.

de·mol·ish /di'mälisH/ ▶ v. **1** knock down a building. **2** show that a theory is completely wrong. **3** humorous eat up food quickly.

SYNONYMS **1 knock down**, pull down, tear down, destroy, flatten, raze (to the ground), dismantle, level, bulldoze, blow up. **2 destroy**, ruin, wreck, overturn, explode; informal shoot full of holes. ANTONYMS build.

dem·o·li·tion /,demə'lisHən/ ▶ n. the action of demolishing something.

de·mon /'dēmən/ ▶ n. an evil spirit or devil. ▶ adj. very forceful or skillful: *a demon cook*.

de·mon·e·tize /dē'mäni,tīz/ ▶ v. (**demonetizes**, **demonetizing**, **demonetized**) make a coin or precious metal no longer valid as money. ■ **de·mon·e·ti·za·tion** /-,mänitə'zāsHən/ n.

de·mo·ni·ac /di'mōnē,ak/ (or **demoniacal** /,dēmə'nīəkəl/) ▶ **adj.** demonic.

de·mon·ic /di'mänik/ ▶ **adj.** having to do with demons or evil spirits. ■ **de·mon·i·cal·ly adv.**

de·mon·ize /'dēmə,nīz/ ▶ **v.** (**demonizes, demonizing, demonized**) portray someone as wicked and threatening.

de·mon·ol·o·gy /,dēmə'näləjē/ ▶ **n.** the study of demons or belief in demons.

de·mon·stra·ble /di'mänstrəbəl/ ▶ **adj.** clearly apparent or able to be proved. ■ **de·mon·stra·bly adv.**

dem·on·strate /'demən,strāt/ ▶ **v.** (**demonstrates, demonstrating, demonstrated**) **1** clearly show that something exists or is true. **2** show and explain how something works. **3** express a feeling or quality by your actions. **4** take part in a public demonstration.

SYNONYMS **1 indicate**, prove, show, establish, confirm, verify. **2 reveal**, manifest, indicate, illustrate, signify, signal, denote, show, display, exhibit. **3 protest**, march, parade, picket, strike.

■ **dem·on·stra·tor n.**

dem·on·stra·tion /,demən'strāsʜən/ ▶ **n.** **1** the action of demonstrating. **2** a public meeting or march expressing an opinion on or protesting about an issue.

SYNONYMS **1 exhibition**, presentation, display. **2 manifestation**, indication, sign, mark, proof, testimony. **3 protest**, march, rally, sit-in.

de·mon·stra·tive /di'mänstrətiv/ ▶ **adj.** **1** tending to show your feelings openly. **2** demonstrating something.

SYNONYMS **expressive**, open, forthcoming, communicative, unreserved, emotional, effusive, affectionate, loving, warm, friendly, approachable; informal touchy-feely. ANTONYMS reserved.

■ **de·mon·stra·tive·ly adv.**

de·mor·al·ize /di'môrə,līz/ ▶ **v.** (**demoralizes, demoralizing, demoralized**) make someone lose confidence or hope.

SYNONYMS (**demoralized**) **dispirited**, disheartened, downhearted, dejected, downcast, low, depressed, dismayed, daunted, discouraged.

■ **de·mor·al·i·za·tion** /-,môrələ'zāsʜən/ **n.**

de·mote /di'mōt/ ▶ **v.** (**demotes, demoting, demoted**) move someone to a less senior position.

SYNONYMS **downgrade**, relegate, reduce, depose, unseat, displace, oust; Military cashier. ANTONYMS promote.

■ **de·mo·tion n.**

de·mot·ic /di'mätik/ ▶ **adj.** (of language) used by ordinary people.

de·mo·ti·vate /dē'mōtə,vāt/ ▶ **v.** make someone less eager to work or make an effort.

de·mur /di'mər/ ▶ **v.** (**demurs, demurring, demurred**) show reluctance. □ **without demur** without objecting or hesitating: *they accepted without demur.* ■ **de·mur·ral n.**

de·mure /di'myo͝or/ ▶ **adj.** (of a woman) reserved, modest, and shy.

SYNONYMS **modest**, reserved, shy, unassuming, decorous, decent, proper. ANTONYMS brazen.

■ **de·mure·ly adv.**

de·mys·ti·fy /dē'mistə,fī/ ▶ **v.** (**demystifies, demystifying, demystified**) make a subject less difficult to understand.

den /den/ ▶ **n.** **1** a wild animal's lair or home. **2** informal a person's private room. **3** a place where people meet to do something immoral or forbidden: *an opium den.*

SYNONYMS **1 lair**, burrow, hole, shelter, hiding place, hideout. **2 study**, studio, workshop, retreat, sanctuary, hideaway.

de·na·tion·al·ize /dē'nasʜənl,īz/ ▶ **v.** (**denationalizes, denationalizing, denationalized**) transfer an industry or business from public to private ownership.

de·na·ture /dē'nācʜər/ ▶ **v.** (**denatures, denaturing, denatured**) **1** alter the natural qualities of. **2** make alcohol unfit for drinking by adding poisonous or foul-tasting substances. ■ **de·na·tur·a·tion** /dē,nācʜə'rāsʜən/ **n.**

den·drite /'dendrīt/ ▶ **n.** a short outgrowth of a nerve cell that carries impulses to it. ■ **den·drit·ic** /den'dritik/ **adj.**

de·ni·a·ble /di'nīəbəl/ ▶ **adj.** able to be denied. ■ **de·ni·a·bil·i·ty** /-,nīə'bilitē/ **n.**

de·ni·al /di'nīəl/ ▶ **n.** **1** a statement that something is not true. **2** the refusal to acknowledge or accept something unpleasant: *he's still in denial.*

SYNONYMS **contradiction**, rebuttal, repudiation, refutation, disclaimer.

de·ni·er /'denēər/ ▶ **n.** a unit for measuring the fineness of nylon or silk.

den·i·grate /'deni,grāt/ ▶ **v.** (**denigrates, denigrating, denigrated**) criticize someone unfairly.

SYNONYMS **disparage**, belittle, deprecate, decry, cast aspersions on, criticize, attack, speak ill of, give someone a bad name, defame, slander, slur, libel, run down, abuse, insult, revile, malign, vilify; informal bad-mouth. ANTONYMS extol.

■ **den·i·gra·tion** /,deni'grāsʜən/ **n.**

den·im /'denəm/ ▶ **n.** **1** a hard-wearing cotton fabric. **2** (**denims**) jeans or other clothes made of denim.

den·i·zen /'denəzən/ ▶ **n.** formal an inhabitant or occupant.

SYNONYMS **inhabitant**, resident, townsman, townswoman, native, local, occupant, dweller.

de·nom·i·nate /di'nämə,nāt/ ▶ **v.** (**denominates, denominating, denominated**) formal call; name.

de·nom·i·na·tion /di,nämə'nāsʜən/ ▶ **n.** **1** a recognized branch of a church or religion. **2** the face value of a banknote, coin, postage stamp, etc. **3** formal a name or designation.

SYNONYMS **1 religious group**, sect, cult, movement, persuasion, order, creed, school, church. **2 value**, unit, size.

■ **de·nom·i·na·tion·al adj.**

de·nom·i·na·tor /di'nämə,nātər/ ▶ **n.** Math the number below the line in a fraction, for example, 4 in $^1/_4$.

de·note /di'nōt/ ▶ **v.** (**denotes, denoting, denoted**) **1** be a sign of. **2** (of a word) have something as a main meaning.

SYNONYMS **indicate**, be a mark of, signify, signal, designate, symbolize, represent.

de·noue·ment /ˌdānoo͞'mäɴ/ ▶ **n.** the final part of a play, movie, or story, in which matters are explained or settled.

de·nounce /di'nouns/ ▶ **v.** (**denounces**, **denouncing**, **denounced**) publicly declare that someone is wrong or evil.

SYNONYMS **1 condemn**, attack, censure, decry, stigmatize, deprecate, disparage, revile, damn. **2 expose**, betray, inform on, incriminate, implicate, cite, accuse.

dense /dens/ ▶ **adj. 1** containing many people or things crowded closely together: *an estuary dense with marine life.* **2** having a thick or closely packed texture. **3** informal stupid.

SYNONYMS **1** *a dense forest* **thick**, crowded, compact, solid, tight, overgrown, impenetrable, impassable. **2** *dense smoke* **thick**, heavy, opaque, murky. **3 stupid**, brainless, foolish, slow, simple-minded, empty-headed, obtuse; informal thick, dim, dopey. ANTONYMS sparse, thin.

■ **dense·ly adv.**

den·si·ty /'densitē/ ▶ **n.** (plural **densities**) **1** the degree to which something is dense. **2** the quantity of people or things in a given area.

SYNONYMS **solidity**, solidness, denseness, thickness, substance, mass, compactness, tightness, hardness.

dent /dent/ ▶ **n.** a slight hollow in a surface made by a blow or pressure. ▶ **v. 1** mark with a dent. **2** have a bad effect on: *the experience dented his enthusiasm.*

SYNONYMS ▶ **n. knock**, indentation, dint, depression, hollow, crater, pit; informal ding. ▶ **v. knock**, dint, mark; informal ding.

den·tal /'dentl/ ▶ **adj.** relating to the teeth or to dentistry.

den·tine /'denˌtēn/ ▶ **n.** the hard, bony tissue that teeth are made of.

den·tist /'dentist/ ▶ **n.** a person who is qualified to treat the diseases and conditions that affect the teeth and gums. ■ **den·tist·ry n.**

den·ti·tion /den'tisʜən/ ▶ **n.** the arrangement or condition of the teeth in a particular species or individual.

den·ture /'dencʜər/ ▶ **n.** a removable plate or frame fitted with one or more false teeth.

de·nude /di'n(y)o͞od/ ▶ **v.** (**denudes**, **denuding**, **denuded**) make something bare or empty; strip something of its covering.

de·nun·ci·a·tion /diˌnənsē'āsʜən/ ▶ **n.** the action of denouncing.

Den·ver boot /'denvər/ ▶ **n.** a clamp placed by the police on a wheel of an illegally parked vehicle to immobilize it.

de·ny /di'nī/ ▶ **v.** (**denies**, **denying**, **denied**) **1** state that something is not true. **2** refuse to admit something. **3** refuse to give someone a thing that they want. **4** (**deny yourself**) go without something you want.

SYNONYMS **1 contradict**, rebut, repudiate, refute, challenge, contest. **2 refuse**, turn down, reject, rebuff, decline, veto, dismiss; informal give the thumbs down to. ANTONYMS confirm, allow, accept.

de·o·dor·ant /dē'ōdərənt/ ▶ **n.** a substance that prevents unpleasant bodily odors.

de·o·dor·ize /dē'ōdəˌrīz/ ▶ **v.** (**deodorizes**, **deodorizing**, **deodorized**) prevent an unpleasant smell in.

deoxygenate /dē'äksijəˌnāt/ ▶ **v.** (**deoxygenates**, **deoxygenating**, **deoxygenated**) remove oxygen from.

de·ox·y·ri·bo·nu·cle·ic ac·id /dēˌäksēˌrībōn(y)o͞o'klēik/ ▶ **n.** a self-replicating material present in nearly all living organisms as the main constituent of chromosomes; it is the carrier of genetic information. Abbreviated **DNA**.

de·part /di'pärt/ ▶ **v. 1** leave; go away. **2** (**depart from**) do something different from the usual or accepted thing.

SYNONYMS **1 leave**, go away, withdraw, absent yourself, quit, exit, decamp, retreat, retire, make off; informal make tracks, take off, split. **2 deviate**, diverge, digress, stray, veer, differ, vary. ANTONYMS arrive.

de·part·ed /di'pärtid/ ▶ **adj.** deceased; dead.

de·part·ment /di'pärtmənt/ ▶ **n. 1** a division of a large organization such as a government, university, or business, or of a building. **2** an administrative district in some countries, e.g., France. **3** informal a person's area of special knowledge or responsibility.

SYNONYMS **division**, section, sector, unit, branch, wing, office, bureau, agency, ministry.

□ **department store** a large store that stocks many types of goods in different departments. ■ **de·part·men·tal** /diˌpärt'mentl, ˌdēpärt-/ **adj. de·part·men·tal·ly adv.**

de·par·ture /di'pärcʜər/ ▶ **n. 1** the action of leaving. **2** a change from the usual way of doing something.

SYNONYMS **1 leaving**, going, leave-taking, withdrawal, exit. **2 deviation**, divergence, digression, shift, variation. **3 change**, innovation, novelty.

de·pend /di'pend/ ▶ **v.** (**depend on**) **1** be determined by. **2** rely on.

SYNONYMS **1 be dependent**, hinge, hang, rest, rely. **2** *my family depends on me* **rely on**, lean on, count on, bank on, trust (in), pin your hopes on.

de·pend·a·ble /di'pendəbəl/ ▶ **adj.** trustworthy and reliable.

SYNONYMS **reliable**, trustworthy, trusty, faithful, loyal, stable, sensible, responsible.

■ **de·pend·a·bil·i·ty** /-ˌpendə'bilitē/ **n. de·pend·a·bly adv.**

de·pend·en·cy /di'pendənsē/ ▶ **n.** (plural **dependencies**) **1** a country or province controlled by another. **2** the state of being dependent.

de·pend·ent /di'pendənt/ ▶ **adj. 1** (**dependent on**) determined by. **2** relying on someone or something for support. **3** (**dependent on**) unable to do without. ▶ **n.** a person who relies on another for financial support.

SYNONYMS ▶ **adj. 1 reliant**, needy, helpless, infirm, invalid, incapable, debilitated, disabled. **2 addicted**, reliant; informal hooked. ANTONYMS independent.

■ **de·pend·ence n. de·pend·ent·ly adv.**

de·pict /di'pikt/ ▶ v. **1** represent something by a drawing, painting, or other art form. **2** portray in words.

> SYNONYMS **1 portray**, show, represent, picture, illustrate, reproduce, render. **2 describe**, detail, relate, present, set forth, set out, outline.

■ **de·pic·tion** n.

dep·i·late /'depə,lāt/ ▶ v. (**depilates**, **depilating**, **depilated**) remove the hair from. ■ **dep·i·la·tion** /,depə'lāsнən/ n. **de·pil·a·to·ry** /di'pilə,tôrē/ adj.

de·plane /dē'plān/ ▶ v. disembark from an aircraft.

de·plete /di'plēt/ ▶ v. (**depletes**, **depleting**, **depleted**) reduce the number or quantity of.

> SYNONYMS **reduce**, decrease, diminish, exhaust, use up, consume, expend, drain, empty. ANTONYMS augment.

de·ple·tion /di'plēsнən/ ▶ n. the action of decreasing something.

> SYNONYMS **exhaustion**, use, consumption, expenditure; reduction, decrease, diminution; impoverishment.

de·plor·a·ble /di'plôrəbəl/ ▶ adj. shockingly bad.

> SYNONYMS **1** *deplorable conduct* **disgraceful**, shameful, inexcusable, unpardonable, atrocious, awful, terrible, dreadful, diabolical, unforgivable, despicable, abominable, contemptible, beyond the pale. **2** *a deplorable state of neglect* **lamentable**, regrettable, unfortunate, wretched, atrocious, awful, terrible, dreadful, sorry, poor; informal appalling, dire, abysmal, woeful, lousy; formal grievous. ANTONYMS admirable.

■ **de·plor·a·bly** adv.

de·plore /di'plôr/ ▶ v. (**deplores**, **deploring**, **deplored**) strongly disapprove of.

> SYNONYMS **1 abhor**, find unacceptable, frown on, disapprove of, take a dim view of, take exception to, condemn, denounce. **2 regret**, lament, mourn, bemoan, bewail, complain about, grieve over, sigh over. ANTONYMS applaud.

de·ploy /di'ploi/ ▶ v. **1** bring or move forces into position for military action. **2** use a resource or quality effectively: *they are not always able to deploy this skill.*

> SYNONYMS **1 position**, station, post, place, install, locate, base. **2 use**, utilize, employ, take advantage of, exploit, call on.

■ **de·ploy·ment** n.

de·pop·u·late /dē'päpyə,lāt/ ▶ v. (**depopulates**, **depopulating**, **depopulated**) greatly reduce the population of a place. ■ **de·pop·u·la·tion** /-,päpyə'lāsнən/ n.

de·port /di'pôrt/ ▶ v. expel a foreigner or immigrant from a country.

> SYNONYMS **expel**, banish, extradite, repatriate. ANTONYMS admit.

■ **de·por·ta·tion** /,dēpôr'tāsнən/ n. **de·por·tee** /,dēpôr'tē/ n.

de·port·ment /di'pôrtmənt/ ▶ n. **1** the way a person stands and walks. **2** a person's behavior or manners.

de·pose /di'pōz/ ▶ v. (**deposes**, **deposing**, **deposed**) remove someone from office suddenly and forcefully.

> SYNONYMS **overthrow**, unseat, dethrone, topple, remove, supplant, displace, oust.

de·pos·it /di'päzit/ ▶ n. **1** a sum of money placed in an account. **2** a payment made as a first installment in buying something. **3** a returnable sum paid when renting something, to cover possible loss or damage. **4** a layer of a substance that has built up. ▶ v. (**deposits**, **depositing**, **deposited**) **1** put something down in a particular place. **2** store something somewhere for safekeeping. **3** pay a sum as a deposit. **4** lay down a layer of a substance: *salt is deposited by the tide.*

> SYNONYMS ▶ n. **1 layer**, covering, coating, blanket, accumulation, sediment. **2 seam**, vein, lode, layer, stratum, bed. **3 down payment**, advance payment, prepayment, instalment, retainer, security. ▶ v. **1 put down**, place, set down, unload, rest, drop; informal dump, park, plunk, plonk. **2 leave (behind)**, precipitate, dump, wash up, cast up. **3 lodge**, bank, house, store, stow.

de·pos·i·tar·y /di'päzi,terē/ (also **depository** /di'päzi,tôrē/) ▶ n. (plural **depositaries**) a person to whom something is entrusted.

dep·o·si·tion /,depə'zisнən/ ▶ n. **1** the action of deposing someone from office. **2** Law a sworn statement to be used as evidence in a court of law. **3** the action of depositing. **4** Law the giving of sworn evidence.

de·pos·i·tor·y /di'päzi,tôrē/ ▶ n. (plural **depositories**) a place where things are stored.

de·pot /'dēpō, 'de-/ ▶ n. **1** a place where large quantities of goods are stored. **2** a place where vehicles are kept and maintained. **3** a railroad or bus station.

> SYNONYMS **1 storehouse**, warehouse, store, repository, depository, cache, arsenal, armoury, dump. **2 terminal**, terminus, station, garage, headquarters, base.

de·prave /di'prāv/ ▶ v. (**depraves**, **depraving**, **depraved**) make someone morally bad; corrupt someone.

> SYNONYMS (**depraved**) **corrupt**, perverted, deviant, degenerate, debased, immoral, unprincipled, debauched, dissolute, licentious, lecherous, prurient, indecent, sordid, wicked, sinful, vile, iniquitous, nefarious; informal warped, twisted, sick.

de·prav·i·ty /di'pravitē/ ▶ n. immoral behavior or character.

dep·re·cate /'depri,kāt/ ▶ v. (**deprecates**, **deprecating**, **deprecated**) **1** express disapproval of. **2** dismiss something as being unimportant. ■ **dep·re·ca·tion** /,deprə'kāsнən/ n.

de·pre·ci·ate /di'prēsнē,āt/ ▶ v. (**depreciates**, **depreciating**, **depreciated**) **1** decrease in value over a period of time. **2** dismiss something as being unimportant. ■ **de·pre·ci·a·tion** /di,prēsнē'āsнən/ n.

dep·re·da·tions /,deprə'dāsнənz/ ▶ pl.n. acts that cause harm or damage.

de·press /di'pres/ ▶ v. **1** make someone feel very unhappy. **2** make something less active: *alcohol depresses the nervous system.* **3** push or pull down.

> SYNONYMS **1 sadden**, dispirit, cast down, get down, dishearten, demoralize, crush, weigh down on. **2 slow down**, weaken, impair, inhibit, restrict. **3 reduce**, lower, cut, cheapen,

discount, deflate, diminish, depreciate, devalue. **4 press**, push, hold down. ANTONYMS cheer, boost, raise.

de·pres·sant /di'presənt/ ▶ **n.** a drug or other substance that slows down the natural processes of the body.

de·pressed /di'prest/ ▶ **adj.** **1** feeling very unhappy and without hope. **2** suffering the damaging effects of an economic slump: *depressed rural areas.*

SYNONYMS **1 sad**, unhappy, miserable, gloomy, dejected, downhearted, downcast, down, despondent, dispirited, low, morose, dismal, desolate; informal blue, down in the dumps, down in the mouth. **2 weak**, inactive, flat, slow, slack, sluggish, stagnant. **3 poverty-stricken**, poor, disadvantaged, deprived, needy, distressed, run-down. ANTONYMS cheerful.

de·press·ing /di'presiNG/ ▶ **adj.** causing unhappiness or dejection.

SYNONYMS **dismal**, sad, unhappy, somber, gloomy, grave, bleak, black, melancholy, dreary, grim, cheerless.

de·pres·sion /di'presHən/ ▶ **n.** **1** a mental state in which a person has feelings of great unhappiness and hopelessness. **2** the medical condition of experiencing greater unhappiness and hopelessness than would seem justified by external circumstances, usually with a lack of energy and difficulty in maintaining concentration and interest in life. **3** a long and severe slump in an economy or market. **4** the action of depressing. **5** a sunken or hollow place. **6** an area of low pressure that may bring rain.

SYNONYMS **1 unhappiness**, sadness, melancholy, melancholia, misery, sorrow, gloom, despondency, low spirits. **2 recession**, slump, decline, downturn. **3 hollow**, indentation, dent, cavity, dip, pit, crater, basin, bowl.

de·pres·sive /di'presiv/ ▶ **adj.** tending to cause or feel depression.

dep·ri·va·tion /ˌdeprə'vāsHən/ ▶ **n.** **1** hardship resulting from not having enough of the things necessary for life. **2** the action of depriving someone of something.

SYNONYMS **1 poverty**, impoverishment, privation, hardship, destitution, need, want. **2 dispossession**, withholding, withdrawal, removal, seizure. ANTONYMS prosperity.

de·prive /di'prīv/ ▶ **v.** (**deprives**, **depriving**, **deprived**) prevent someone from having or using something: *the city was deprived of its water supply.*

SYNONYMS **dispossess**, strip, divest, relieve, rob, cheat out of.

de·prived /di'prīvd/ ▶ **adj.** not having enough of the things necessary for life: *the charity cares for deprived children.*

SYNONYMS **disadvantaged**, underprivileged, poverty-stricken, impoverished, poor, dirt poor, destitute, needy. ANTONYMS privileged.

de·pro·gram /dē'prōˌgram/ ▶ **v.** (**deprograms**, **deprogrammed**, **deprogramming** or **deprogramed**, **deprograming**) stop someone from being brainwashed or excessively influenced by a particular group.

Dept. ▶ **abbr.** Department.

depth /depTH/ ▶ **n.** **1** the distance from the top or surface down, or from front to back. **2** complex or meaningful thought: *the book has unexpected depth.* **3** extensive and detailed study. **4** strength of emotion: *depth of feeling.* **5** (**the depths**) the deepest, lowest, or innermost part of something: *the depths of the forest.*

SYNONYMS **1 deepness**, drop, height. **2 extent**, range, scope, breadth, width. **3 profundity**, wisdom, understanding, intelligence, discernment, penetration, insight, awareness. **4 intensity**, richness, vividness, strength, brilliance.

□ **depth charge** a device designed to explode under water, used for attacking submarines. **out of your depth 1** in water too deep to stand in. **2** in a situation that you are unable to cope with.

dep·u·ta·tion /ˌdepyə'tāsHən/ ▶ **n.** a group of people who are sent to do something on behalf of a larger group.

de·pute /di'pyo͞ot/ ▶ **v.** (**deputes**, **deputing**, **deputed**) instruct someone to do something that you are responsible for.

dep·u·tize /'depyəˌtīz/ ▶ **v.** (**deputizes**, **deputizing**, **deputized**) temporarily act on behalf of someone else.

SYNONYMS **stand in**, sit in, fill in, cover, substitute, replace, take someone's place, take over, hold the fort, step into the breach.

dep·u·ty /'depyətē/ ▶ **n.** (plural **deputies**) a person appointed to do the work of a more senior person in that person's absence.

SYNONYMS **second in command**, number two, assistant, aide, proxy, stand-in, replacement, substitute, representative, reserve.

de·rail /dē'rāl/ ▶ **v.** **1** make a train leave the tracks. **2** prevent a process from following its intended course: *an attempt to derail the negotiations.* ■ **de·rail·ment n.**

de·range /di'rānj/ ▶ **v.** (**deranges**, **deranging**, **deranged**) **1** make insane. **2** throw into disorder.

SYNONYMS (**deranged**) **insane**, mad, disturbed, unbalanced, unhinged, unstable, irrational, crazed, demented, berserk, frenzied, lunatic, non compos mentis; informal touched, crazy, mental. ANTONYMS rational.

Der·by /'dərbē/ ▶ **n.** (plural **Derbies**) **1** an annual flat race for three-year-old horses, founded by the Earl of Derby in 1780. **2** a similar race elsewhere, such as the Kentucky Derby. **3** (**derby**) a bowler hat.

de·reg·u·late /dē'regyəˌlāt/ ▶ **v.** (**deregulates**, **deregulating**, **deregulated**) remove regulations or restrictions from. ■ **de·reg·u·la·tion** /-ˌregyə'lāsHən/ **n.**

der·e·lict /'derəˌlikt/ ▶ **adj.** **1** in a very bad condition as a result of disuse and neglect. **2** failing to carry out your duties or obligations. ▶ **n.** a person without a home, job, or property.

SYNONYMS ▶ **adj. dilapidated**, ramshackle, run-down, tumbledown, in ruins, falling down, disused, abandoned, deserted. ▶ **n. tramp**, vagrant, down-and-out, homeless person, drifter, beggar; informal bag lady.

der·e·lic·tion /ˌderə'liksHən/ ▶ **n.** **1** an abandoned and run-down state. **2** (usu. **dereliction of**

duty) shameful failure to do something you are supposed to do.

de·ride /di'rīd/ ▶ v. (**derides**, **deriding**, **derided**) express contempt for; ridicule.

de ri·gueur /də ri'gər, rē'gœr/ ▶ adj. necessary if you want to be accepted socially: *large hotel suites are de rigueur.*

de·ri·sion /di'rizHən/ ▶ n. scornful ridicule or mockery.

SYNONYMS **mockery**, ridicule, jeers, sneers, taunts, disdain, disparagement, denigration, insults.

de·ri·sive /di'rīsiv/ ▶ adj. expressing contempt or ridicule. ■ **de·ri·sive·ly** adv.

de·ri·so·ry /di'rīsərē/ ▶ adj. **1** ridiculously small or inadequate. **2** expressing contempt or ridicule; derisive.

der·i·va·tion /ˌderə'vāsHən/ ▶ n. **1** the obtaining of something from a source. **2** the formation of a word from another word.

de·riv·a·tive /di'rivətiv/ ▶ adj. imitating the work of another artist, writer, etc.; not original. ▶ n. something that comes from or is based on another source.

de·rive /di'rīv/ ▶ v. (**derives**, **deriving**, **derived**) **1** (**derive something from**) obtain something from a source. **2** (**derive from**) originate or develop from.

der·ma·ti·tis /ˌdərmə'tītis/ ▶ n. inflammation of the skin as a result of irritation or an allergic reaction.

der·ma·tol·o·gy /ˌdərmə'täləjē/ ▶ n. the branch of medicine concerned with skin disorders. ■ **der·ma·to·log·i·cal** /-mətl'äjikəl/ adj. **der·ma·tol·o·gist** n.

der·mis /'dərmis/ ▶ n. Anatomy the thick layer of the skin below the epidermis.

der·o·gate /'derəˌgāt/ ▶ v. (**derogates**, **derogating**, **derogated**) formal **1** (**derogate from**) detract from. **2** (**derogate from**) deviate from a set of rules. **3** disparage. ■ **der·o·ga·tion** /ˌderə'gāsHən/ n.

de·rog·a·to·ry /di'rägəˌtôrē/ ▶ adj. critical or disrespectful.

SYNONYMS **disparaging**, disrespectful, demeaning, critical, pejorative, negative, unfavorable, uncomplimentary, unflattering, insulting, defamatory, slanderous, libelous. ANTONYMS complimentary.

der·rick /'derik/ ▶ n. **1** a type of crane. **2** the framework over an oil well for holding the drilling machinery.

der·ring-do /'deriNG 'dōō/ ▶ n. old use heroic actions.

der·vish /'dərvisH/ ▶ n. a member of a Sufi Muslim religious group, some orders of which are known for their ecstatic, wild rituals.

de·sal·i·nate /dē'saləˌnāt/ ▶ v. (**desalinates**, **desalinating**, **desalinated**) remove salt from seawater. ■ **de·sal·i·na·tion** /-ˌsalə'nāsHən/ n.

des·cant /'desˌkant/ ▶ n. an independent melody sung or played above a basic melody.

de·scend /di'send/ ▶ v. **1** move down or downward. **2** slope or lead downward. **3** (**descend to**) do something very shameful. **4** (**descend on**) make a sudden attack on or unwelcome visit to. **5** (**be descended from**) have a particular person as an ancestor.

SYNONYMS **1 go down**, come down, drop, fall, sink, dive, plummet, plunge, nosedive. **2 slope**, dip, slant, go down, fall away. **3 alight**, disembark, get down, get off, dismount. ANTONYMS climb, board.

de·scend·ant /di'sendənt/ ▶ n. a person that is descended from a particular ancestor.

SPELLING

The correct spelling of the noun **descendant** has **-ant**, not **-ent**, at the end.

de·scent /di'sent/ ▶ n. **1** an act of descending. **2** a downward slope. **3** a person's origin or nationality.

SYNONYMS **1 dive**, drop, fall, plunge, nosedive. **2 slope**, incline, dip, drop, gradient. **3 decline**, slide, fall, degeneration, deterioration. **4 ancestry**, parentage, ancestors, family, extraction, origin, derivation, birth, lineage, stock, blood, roots, origins.

de·scribe /di'skrīb/ ▶ v. (**describes**, **describing**, **described**) **1** give a detailed account of something in words. **2** mark out or draw a shape.

SYNONYMS **1 report**, recount, relate, narrate, tell of, set out, detail, give a rundown of. **2 portray**, depict, paint, define, characterize, call, label, class, brand. **3 mark out**, delineate, outline, trace, draw.

de·scrip·tion /di'skripsHən/ ▶ n. **1** a spoken or written account. **2** the process of describing. **3** a sort, kind, or class: *people of any description.*

SYNONYMS **1 account**, report, narrative, story, portrayal, portrait, sketch, details. **2 designation**, labeling, naming, dubbing, characterization, definition, classification, branding. **3 sort**, variety, kind, type.

de·scrip·tive /di'skriptiv/ ▶ adj. describing something, especially in a vivid style. ■ **de·scrip·tive·ly** adv.

de·scry /di'skrī/ ▶ v. (**descries**, **descrying**, **descried**) literary catch sight of.

des·e·crate /'desiˌkrāt/ ▶ v. (**desecrates**, **desecrating**, **desecrated**) damage something sacred or treat it with great disrespect.

SYNONYMS **violate**, profane, defile, debase, degrade, dishonor, vandalize, damage, destroy, deface.

■ **des·e·cra·tion** /ˌdesi'krāsHən/ n.

de·seg·re·gate /dē'segriˌgāt/ ▶ v. (**desegregates**, **desegregating**, **desegregated**) end a policy by which people of different races are kept separate. ■ **de·seg·re·ga·tion** /dēˌsegri'gāsHən/ n.

de·se·lect /ˌdēsə'lekt/ ▶ v. turn off a selected feature on a list of options on a computer menu. ■ **de·se·lec·tion** n.

de·sen·si·tize /dē'sensiˌtīz/ ▶ v. (**desensitizes**, **desensitizing**, **desensitized**) make less sensitive.

de·sert[1] /də'zərt/ ▶ v. **1** leave someone without help or support. **2** leave a place, making it seem empty. **3** illegally leave the armed forces.

SYNONYMS **1 abandon**, leave, jilt, leave high and dry, leave in the lurch, leave behind, strand, maroon; informal walk/run out on, dump, ditch; literary forsake. **2** (**deserted**) **abandoned**, jilted, cast aside, neglected, stranded, marooned, forlorn; literary forsaken. **3** (**deserted**) **empty**, uninhabited, unoccupied, abandoned, evacuated, desolate, lonely, godforsaken. **4 abscond**, defect, run away, decamp, flee, turn tail, take French leave; Military go AWOL.

■ **de·sert·er** n. **de·ser·tion** n.

de·sert² /'dezərt/ ▶ n. an empty, waterless area of land with very few plants.

SYNONYMS **wasteland**, wastes, wilderness, dust bowl.

□ **desert island** an uninhabited tropical island.

USAGE

Don't confuse **desert** (a waterless area) with **dessert** (the sweet course eaten at the end of a meal).

de·serts /də'zərts/ ▶ pl.n. (**get your just deserts**) get the reward or punishment that you deserve.

de·serve /də'zərv/ ▶ v. (**deserves**, **deserving**, **deserved**) do something worthy of a particular reward or punishment.

SYNONYMS **1 merit**, earn, warrant, rate, justify, be worthy of, be entitled to. **2** (**deserved**) **well-earned**, merited, warranted, justified, rightful, due, fitting, just, proper.

■ **de·serv·ed·ly** /-vidlē/ adv.

de·serv·ing /də'zərviNG/ ▶ adj. worthy of being treated well or helped.

SYNONYMS **worthy**, commendable, praiseworthy, admirable, estimable, creditable.

dés·ha·bil·lé /ˌdāzä'bēā/ ▶ n. the state of being only partly clothed.

des·ic·cate /'desiˌkāt/ ▶ v. (**desiccates**, **desiccating**, **desiccated**) remove the moisture from.
■ **des·ic·ca·tion** /-'kāSHən/ n.

de·sign /də'zīn/ ▶ n. **1** a plan or drawing produced before something is made. **2** the production of such plans or drawings. **3** purpose or deliberate planning: *we were seated together by design*. **4** a decorative pattern. ▶ v. **1** produce a design for. **2** (**be designed**) be intended for a purpose.

SYNONYMS ▶ n. **1 plan**, blueprint, drawing, sketch, outline, map, plot, diagram, draft. **2 pattern**, motif, device, style, theme, layout. ▶ v. **1 invent**, create, think up, come up with, devise, formulate, conceive; informal dream up. **2 intend**, aim, mean.

□ **have designs on** aim to obtain.

des·ig·nate ▶ v. /'dezigˌnāt/ (**designates**, **designating**, **designated**) **1** officially give a particular status or name to: *certain schools are designated "magnet schools."* **2** appoint someone to a job or position. ▶ adj. /'dezignit, 'dezigˌnāt/ appointed to a position but not yet having started it: *the Director designate*.

SYNONYMS ▶ v. **1 classify**, class, label, tag, name, call, term, dub. **2 appoint**, nominate, delegate, select, choose, pick, elect, name, identify, assign.

□ **designated driver** a person who abstains from alcohol in order to drive others home safely.

des·ig·na·tion /ˌdezig'nāSHən/ ▶ n. **1** the action of designating. **2** an official title or description.

de·sign·er /də'zīnər/ ▶ n. a person who designs things. ▶ adj. made by a famous fashion designer: *designer jeans*.

de·sir·a·ble /də'zī(ə)rəbəl/ ▶ adj. **1** wished for as being attractive, useful, or necessary. **2** (of a person) attractive as a boyfriend or girlfriend.

SYNONYMS **1 attractive**, sought-after, in demand, popular, enviable; informal to die for, must-have. **2 advantageous**, advisable, wise, sensible, recommended, beneficial, preferable. **3** (**sexually**) **attractive**, beautiful, pretty, appealing, seductive, alluring, irresistible; informal sexy. ANTONYMS unattractive.

■ **de·sir·a·bil·i·ty** /-ˌzī(ə)rə'bilitē/ n.

de·sire /də'zī(ə)r/ ▶ n. a strong feeling of wanting to have something or wishing for something to happen. ▶ v. (**desires**, **desiring**, **desired**) **1** strongly wish for or want. **2** find someone attractive.

SYNONYMS ▶ n. **1 wish**, want, aspiration, yearning, longing, craving, hankering, hunger; informal yen, itch. **2 lust**, passion, sensuality, sexuality, libido, lasciviousness. ▶ v. **want**, wish for, long for, yearn for, crave, hanker after, be desperate for, be bent on, covet, aspire to.

de·sir·ous /di'zīrəs/ ▶ adj. (**desirous of** or **to do**) wanting a particular thing: *the pope was desirous of peace in Europe*.

de·sist /di'sist/ ▶ v. stop doing something.

desk /desk/ ▶ n. **1** a piece of furniture with a flat or sloping surface for writing on. **2** a counter in a hotel, bank, etc.

desk·top /'deskˌtäp/ ▶ n. **1** a computer suitable to be used at a desk. **2** the area of a computer screen that you can work in. **3** the working surface of a desk.

des·o·late ▶ adj. /'desəlit/ **1** (of a place) bleak and empty. **2** very unhappy. ▶ v. /'desəˌlāt/ (**be desolated**) be very unhappy.

SYNONYMS ▶ adj. **1 bleak**, stark, bare, dismal, grim, wild, inhospitable, deserted, uninhabited, empty, abandoned, godforsaken, isolated, remote. **2 miserable**, unhappy, despondent, depressed, disconsolate, devastated, despairing, inconsolable, wretched, broken-hearted.

■ **des·o·la·tion** /ˌdesə'lāSHən/ n.

de·spair /di'spe(ə)r/ ▶ n. the complete loss or absence of hope. ▶ v. lose hope, or be without hope.

SYNONYMS ▶ n. **desperation**, anguish, unhappiness, despondency, depression, misery, wretchedness, hopelessness. ANTONYMS hope, joy. ▶ v. **lose hope**, give up, lose heart, be discouraged, be despondent, be demoralized.

SPELLING

Spell this word **des-**, not **dis-**: **des**pair.

des·per·a·do /ˌdespə'rädō/ ▶ n. (plural **desperadoes** or **desperados**) a reckless and dangerous criminal.

des·per·ate /'despərət/ ▶ adj. **1** feeling, showing, or involving despair. **2** done when everything else has failed: *a desperate bid to cut costs*. **3** very serious: *a desperate shortage*. **4** needing or wanting something very much. **5** very violent or dangerous: *a desperate struggle*.

SYNONYMS **1 despairing**, hopeless, anguished, distressed, wretched, desolate, forlorn, distraught, at your wits' end. **2 last-ditch**, last-gasp, eleventh-hour, do-or-die, final, frantic, frenzied, wild. **3 grave**, serious, critical, acute, urgent, pressing, drastic, extreme.

SPELLING

Write desperate, not -parate.

des·per·ate·ly /ˈdespərətlē/ ▶ **adv.** **1** in a way that shows despair. **2** used to emphasize how extreme something is: *he desperately needed a drink.*

des·per·a·tion /ˌdespəˈrāshən/ ▶ **n.** a state of despair, especially as resulting in extreme behavior.

SYNONYMS **hopelessness**, despair, distress, anguish, agony, torment, misery.

des·pi·ca·ble /diˈspikəbəl/ ▶ **adj.** deserving hatred and contempt.

SYNONYMS **contemptible**, loathsome, hateful, detestable, reprehensible, abhorrent, abominable, awful, heinous, odious, vile, low, mean, abject, shameful, ignominious, shabby, ignoble, disreputable, discreditable, unworthy; informal dirty, rotten, low-down. ANTONYMS admirable.

■ **des·pi·ca·bly** **adv.**

de·spise /diˈspīz/ ▶ **v.** (**despise**, **despising**, **despised**) hate or feel disgusted by.

SYNONYMS **detest**, hate, loathe, abhor, deplore, scorn, disdain, deride, sneer at, revile, spurn, shun. ANTONYMS adore, respect.

de·spite /diˈspīt/ ▶ **prep.** in spite of.

SYNONYMS **in spite of**, notwithstanding, regardless of, in the face of, in the teeth of, undeterred by, for all, even with.

de·spoil /diˈspoil/ ▶ **v.** literary steal valuable possessions from a place.

de·spond·ent /diˈspändənt/ ▶ **adj.** very sad and without much hope.

SYNONYMS **disheartened**, discouraged, dispirited, downhearted, downcast, crestfallen, down, low, disconsolate, despairing, wretched, melancholy, gloomy, morose, dismal, woebegone, miserable, depressed, dejected, sad; informal down in the mouth, down in the dumps. ANTONYMS hopeful, cheerful.

■ **de·spond·en·cy** **n.** **de·spond·ent·ly** **adv.**

des·pot /ˈdespət/ ▶ **n.** a ruler with unlimited power. ■ **des·pot·ism** **n.**

des·pot·ic /diˈspätik/ ▶ **adj.** ruling with absolute power; tyrannical.

SYNONYMS **autocratic**, dictatorial, totalitarian, absolutist, undemocratic, one-party, tyrannical, tyrannous, oppressive, repressive, draconian, illiberal. ANTONYMS democratic.

des·sert /diˈzərt/ ▶ **n.** the sweet course eaten at the end of a meal.

USAGE

Don't confuse **dessert** (the sweet course) with **desert** (a waterless area).

des·sert·spoon /diˈzərtˌspo͞on/ ▶ **n.** a spoon smaller than a tablespoon and larger than a teaspoon.

de·sta·bi·lize /dēˈstābəˌlīz/ ▶ **v.** (**destabilizes**, **destabilizing**, **destabilized**) **1** make or become less stable. **2** undermine a country or government.

des·ti·na·tion /ˌdestəˈnāshən/ ▶ **n.** the place to which someone or something is going or being sent.

des·tine /ˈdestin/ ▶ **v.** **1** (**be destined for** or **to**) be intended for a particular purpose, or certain to do or be a particular thing: *he was destined to be an engineer.* **2** (**be destined for**) be on the way to a particular place.

SYNONYMS **1** (**destined**) **fated**, ordained, predestined, doomed, meant, intended. **2** (**destined**) *computers destined for Pakistan* **heading**, bound, en route, scheduled, headed.

des·ti·ny /ˈdestinē/ ▶ **n.** (plural **destinies**) **1** the things that will happen to a person. **2** the hidden power believed to control what will happen in the future: *he believes in destiny.*

SYNONYMS **1 future**, fate, fortune, doom, lot. **2 providence**, fate, God, the stars, luck, fortune, chance, karma, kismet.

des·ti·tute /ˈdestiˌt(y)o͞ot/ ▶ **adj.** very poor and without a home or other things necessary for life.

SYNONYMS **penniless**, poor, dirt poor, impoverished, poverty-stricken, impecunious, indigent, down and out; informal (flat) broke; formal penurious. ANTONYMS rich.

■ **des·ti·tu·tion** /ˌdestiˈt(y)o͞oshən/ **n.**

de·stroy /diˈstroi/ ▶ **v.** **1** make something stop existing by damaging or attacking it. **2** defeat someone utterly. **3** kill a sick or unwanted animal using a humane method.

SYNONYMS **1 demolish**, knock down, level, raze (to the ground), fell, blow up. **2 spoil**, ruin, wreck, blight, devastate, wreak havoc on. **3 kill**, put down, put to sleep, slaughter, cull. **4 annihilate**, wipe out, obliterate, eliminate, eradicate, liquidate, exterminate; informal take out, waste. ANTONYMS build.

de·stroy·er /diˈstroiər/ ▶ **n.** **1** a person or thing that destroys. **2** a small, fast warship.

de·struct·i·ble /diˈstrəktəbəl/ ▶ **adj.** able to be destroyed.

de·struc·tion /diˈstrəkshən/ ▶ **n.** the destroying of something.

SYNONYMS **1 devastation**, carnage, ruin, chaos, wreckage. **2** *the destruction of the countryside* **wrecking**, ruining, annihilation, obliteration, elimination, eradication, devastation. **3 killing**, slaughter, extermination, culling. ANTONYMS preservation.

de·struc·tive /diˈstrəktiv/ ▶ **adj.** **1** causing destruction. **2** negative and unhelpful: *destructive criticism.*

SYNONYMS **devastating**, ruinous, damaging, harmful, detrimental, injurious, hurtful, deleterious.

■ **de·struc·tive·ly** **adv.**

des·ue·tude /ˈdeswiˌt(y)o͞od/ ▶ **n.** formal a state of disuse.

des·ul·to·ry /ˈdesəlˌtôrē/ ▶ **adj.** **1** lacking enthusiasm or a definite plan: *a few people were dancing in a desultory fashion.* **2** going constantly from one subject to another in a halfhearted way: *a desultory conversation.* ■ **des·ul·to·ri·ly** **adv.**

de·tach /diˈtach/ ▶ **v.** **1** remove something that is attached to something larger. **2** (**be detached**) Military be sent on a mission.

SYNONYMS **disconnect**, separate, unfasten, disengage, uncouple, isolate, remove, loose, unhitch, unhook, free, pull off, cut off, break off, split off, sever. ANTONYMS attach, join.

■ **de·tach·a·ble** adj.

SPELLING

Write **-ach**, not **-atch**: detach.

de·tached /di'tacHt/ ▶ adj. **1** separate or disconnected. **2** not involved or interested; aloof: *he remained detached from party politics.*

SYNONYMS **1 disconnected**, separated, separate, unfastened, disengaged, uncoupled, isolated, loosened, unhitched, unhooked, free, severed, cut off. **2 dispassionate**, disinterested, objective, outside, neutral, unbiased, impartial.

de·tach·ment /di'tacHmənt/ ▶ n. **1** a feeling of being uninvolved or aloof: *he felt a sense of detachment from what was going on.* **2** a group of troops, ships, etc., sent away on a mission.

SYNONYMS **1 objectivity**, dispassion, disinterest, neutrality, impartiality. **2 unit**, squad, detail, troop, contingent, task force, party, platoon.

de·tail /di'tāl, 'dētāl/ ▶ n. **1** a small individual item or fact. **2** small items or facts as a group: *attention to detail.* **3** a small part of a picture reproduced separately. **4** a small group of troops or police officers given a special duty. ▶ v. **1** describe something item by item. **2** instruct someone to undertake a particular task: *the ships were detailed to keep watch.*

SYNONYMS ▶ n. **1 feature**, respect, particular, characteristic, specific, aspect, fact, point, element. **2 triviality**, technicality, nicety, fine point. **3 unit**, detachment, squad, troop, contingent, outfit, task force, party, platoon. ▶ v. **describe**, relate, catalog, list, spell out, itemize, identify, specify.

de·tailed /di'tāld, 'dē,tāld/ ▶ adj. having many details.

SYNONYMS **comprehensive**, full, complete, thorough, exhaustive, all-inclusive, elaborate, minute, precise, itemized, blow-by-blow. ANTONYMS general.

de·tail·ing /'dētāliNG/ ▶ n. small decorative features on a building, garment, or work of art.

de·tain /di'tān/ ▶ v. **1** keep someone back: *she tried to open the door, but he detained her.* **2** keep someone in custody.

SYNONYMS **1 delay**, hold up, make late, keep, slow up/down, hinder. **2 hold**, take into custody, confine, imprison, intern, arrest, apprehend, seize; informal pick up. ANTONYMS release.

de·tain·ee /di,tā'nē, ,dētā'nē/ ▶ n. a person who is kept in custody.

de·tect /di'tekt/ ▶ v. **1** discover or notice that something is present: *we detected the faint scent of cinnamon.* **2** discover or investigate a crime or criminal.

SYNONYMS **1 notice**, perceive, discern, become aware of, note, make out, spot, recognize, identify, catch, sense. **2 discover**, uncover, turn up, unearth, dig up, root out, expose. **3 catch**, hunt down, track down, find out, expose, reveal, unmask, smoke out.

■ **de·tect·a·ble** adj. **de·tec·tion** n.

de·tec·tive /di'tektiv/ ▶ n. a person whose job is investigating crimes.

SYNONYMS **investigator**, police officer; informal private eye, sleuth, gumshoe.

de·tec·tor /di'tektər/ ▶ n. a device designed to detect that something, e.g., smoke or gas, is present.

dé·tente /dā'tänt/ ▶ n. the easing of hostility or strained relations between countries.

de·ten·tion /di'tensHən/ ▶ n. **1** the state of being kept in custody. **2** the punishment of being kept at school after hours.

SYNONYMS **custody**, imprisonment, incarceration, internment, captivity, remand, arrest, quarantine. ANTONYMS release.

□ **detention center** an institution where people are detained for short periods.

de·ter /di'tər/ ▶ v. (**deters**, **deterring**, **deterred**) **1** make someone decide not to do something because they are afraid of the consequences. **2** prevent something happening: *the policy did not deter war.*

SYNONYMS **1 discourage**, dissuade, put off, scare off, dishearten, demoralize, daunt, intimidate. **2 prevent**, stop, avert, stave off, ward off. ANTONYMS encourage.

de·ter·gent /di'tərjənt/ ▶ n. a chemical substance used for removing dirt and grease.

de·te·ri·o·rate /di'ti(ə)rēə,rāt/ ▶ v. (**deteriorates**, **deteriorating**, **deteriorated**) become gradually worse.

SYNONYMS **worsen**, decline, degenerate, fail, go downhill, wane. ANTONYMS improve.

■ **de·te·ri·o·ra·tion** /-,ti(ə)rēə'rāsHən/ n.

de·ter·mi·nant /di'tərminənt/ ▶ n. **1** a factor that determines the nature or outcome of something: *force of will was the main determinant of his success.* **2** Math a quantity obtained by adding products of the elements of a square matrix according to a given rule.

de·ter·mi·na·tion /di,tərmə'nāsHən/ ▶ n. **1** persistence in continuing to do something even when it is difficult. **2** the process of establishing something exactly: *accurate determination of the names of fossils.*

SYNONYMS **resolution**, resolve, willpower, strength of character, dedication, single-mindedness, perseverance, persistence, tenacity, staying power, doggedness; informal guts.

de·ter·mine /di'tərmin/ ▶ v. **1** make something develop in a particular way or be of a particular type: *it is biological age that determines our looks.* **2** discover the facts about something by research or calculation. **3** firmly decide.

SYNONYMS **1 control**, decide, regulate, direct, dictate, govern. **2 resolve**, decide, make up your mind, choose, elect, opt. **3 specify**, set, fix, decide on, settle, establish, ordain, prescribe, decree. **4 ascertain**, find out, discover, learn, establish, calculate, work out; informal figure out.

de·ter·mined /di'tərmind/ ▶ **adj.** persisting in doing something even when it is difficult; resolute.

SYNONYMS **resolute**, purposeful, adamant, single-minded, unswerving, unwavering, persevering, persistent, tenacious, dedicated, dogged. ANTONYMS irresolute.

■ **de·ter·mined·ly** adv.

de·ter·min·er /di'tərminər/ ▶ **n. 1** a person or thing that determines. **2** Grammar a word that comes before a noun to show how the noun is being used, e.g., *a, the, every*.

de·ter·rent /di'tərənt/ ▶ **n.** a thing that deters or is intended to deter.

SYNONYMS **disincentive**, discouragement, damper, curb, check, restraint, inhibition. ANTONYMS incentive.

■ **de·ter·rence** n.

de·test /di'test/ ▶ **v.** feel strong dislike for.

SYNONYMS **hate**, abhor, loathe, regard with disgust, be unable to bear, have an aversion to, find intolerable, disdain, despise. ANTONYMS love.

■ **de·test·a·ble** /di'testəbəl/ adj. **de·tes·ta·tion** /,dēte'stāsʜən/ n.

de·throne /dē'ᴛʜrōn/ ▶ **v.** (**dethrones**, **dethroning**, **dethroned**) remove a ruler from power.

det·o·nate /'detn,āt/ ▶ **v.** (**detonates**, **detonating**, **detonated**) explode, or make something explode. ■ **det·o·na·tion** /,detn'āsʜən/ n.

det·o·na·tor /'detn,ātər/ ▶ **n.** a device used to detonate an explosive.

de·tour /'dē,to͝or/ ▶ **n.** a long or indirect route taken to avoid something or to visit something along the way.

SYNONYMS **diversion**, roundabout route, indirect route, scenic route, bypass, digression, deviation.

de·tox·i·fy /dē'täksə,fī/ ▶ **v.** (**detoxifies**, **detoxifying**, **detoxified**) remove poisonous substances from.

de·tract /di'trakt/ ▶ **v.** (**detract from**) make something seem less valuable or impressive.

SYNONYMS **belittle**, take away from, diminish, reduce, lessen, minimize, play down, trivialize, decry, devalue.

de·trac·tor /di'traktər/ ▶ **n.** a person who is critical about someone or something.

det·ri·ment /'detrəmənt/ ▶ **n.** harm or damage: *she fasted to the detriment of her health.*

det·ri·men·tal /,detrə'mentl/ ▶ **adj.** causing harm or damage.

SYNONYMS **harmful**, damaging, injurious, hurtful, inimical, deleterious, destructive, pernicious, undesirable, unfavorable. ANTONYMS beneficial.

■ **det·ri·men·tal·ly** adv.

de·tri·tus /di'trītəs/ ▶ **n.** debris or waste material.

deuce /d(y)o͞os/ ▶ **n. 1** Tennis the score of 40 all in a game, at which two consecutive points are needed to win the game. **2** (**the deuce**) informal said instead of "devil" when making an exclamation.

de·us ex ma·chi·na /'dāəs eks 'mäkənə, -'mak-/ ▶ **n.** an unexpected event saving a seemingly hopeless situation.

deu·te·ri·um /d(y)o͞o'ti(ə)rēəm/ ▶ **n.** a stable isotope of hydrogen with a mass approximately twice that of the usual isotope.

Deutsch·mark /'doicʜ,märk/ ▶ **n.** the former basic unit of money in Germany.

de·val·ue /dē'valyo͞o/ ▶ **v.** (**devalues**, **devaluing**, **devalued**) **1** make something seem less important than it is: *people seem to devalue my achievement.* **2** reduce the value of a currency in relation to other currencies.

SYNONYMS **belittle**, disparage, denigrate, discredit, diminish, trivialize, reduce, undermine.

■ **de·val·u·a·tion** /,dēvalyo͞o'āsʜən/ n.

dev·as·tate /'devə,stāt/ ▶ **v.** (**devastates**, **devastating**, **devastated**) **1** destroy or ruin. **2** (**be devastated**) be overwhelmed with shock or grief: *she was devastated by the loss of Ryan.*

SYNONYMS **1 destroy**, ruin, wreck, lay waste, ravage, demolish, raze (to the ground), level, flatten. **2 shatter**, shock, stun, daze, dumbfound, traumatize, distress; informal knock for a loop, knock sideways.

dev·as·tat·ing /'devə,stātiɴɢ/ ▶ **adj. 1** highly destructive: *a devastating hurricane.* **2** very distressing: *a devastating blow.* **3** informal very impressive or attractive: *devastating wit.* ■ **dev·as·tat·ing·ly** adv.

dev·as·ta·tion /,devə'stāsʜən/ ▶ **n.** the action of destroying something or the state of being destroyed.

SYNONYMS **destruction**, ruin, desolation, wreckage, ruins.

de·vel·op /di'veləp/ ▶ **v.** (**develops**, **developing**, **developed**) **1** make or become larger or more advanced. **2** start to exist; come into being. **3** start to experience or possess something. **4** convert land to a new purpose. **5** treat a photographic film with chemicals to make a visible image.

SYNONYMS **1 grow**, expand, spread, advance, progress, evolve, mature. **2 initiate**, instigate, set in motion, originate, invent, form. **3 expand**, augment, broaden, supplement, reinforce, enhance, refine, improve, polish, perfect. **4 start**, begin, emerge, erupt, break out, arise, break, unfold.

□ **developing country** a poor agricultural country that is seeking to become more advanced. ■ **de·vel·op·er** n.

SPELLING

There is no **e** at the end: devel**op**.

de·vel·op·ment /di'veləpmənt/ ▶ **n. 1** the action of developing. **2** a new product or idea. **3** a new stage in a changing situation: *have there been any developments since yesterday?* **4** an area of land with new buildings on it.

SYNONYMS **1 evolution**, growth, expansion, enlargement, spread, progress. **2 event**, change, circumstance, incident, occurrence. **3 estate**, complex, site.

■ **de·vel·op·men·tal** /di,veləp'mentl/ adj.

de·vi·ant /'dēvēənt/ ▶ **adj.** different from what is considered normal. ▶ **n.** disapproving a deviant person.

SYNONYMS ▶ **adj. aberrant**, abnormal, atypical, anomalous, irregular, nonstandard;

nonconformist, perverse, uncommon, unusual, freakish, strange, warped, perverted, odd, peculiar, bizarre, eccentric, idiosyncratic, unorthodox, exceptional; informal kinky, quirky. ANTONYMS normal. ▶ n. **nonconformist**, eccentric, maverick, outsider, misfit, individualist; informal oddball, screwball, kook, weirdo, freak.

■ **de·vi·ance** n.

de·vi·ate /ˈdēvēˌāt/ ▶ v. (**deviates**, **deviating**, **deviated**) depart from an established course or from normal standards: *you must not deviate from the route you were given.*

SYNONYMS **diverge**, digress, drift, stray, veer, swerve, get sidetracked, branch off, differ, vary.

■ **de·vi·a·tion** /ˌdēvēˈāsʜən/ n.

de·vice /diˈvīs/ ▶ n. **1** a piece of equipment made for a particular purpose. **2** a plan or method with a particular aim: *a clever marketing device.* **3** an emblem or design.

SYNONYMS **1 implement**, gadget, utensil, tool, appliance, apparatus, instrument, machine, mechanism, contrivance, contraption; informal gizmo. **2 ploy**, tactic, move, stratagem, scheme, maneuver, plot, trick, ruse.

□ **leave someone to their own devices** leave someone to do as they wish.

dev·il /ˈdevəl/ ▶ n. **1** (**the Devil**) (in Christian and Jewish belief) the most powerful spirit of evil. **2** an evil spirit. **3** a very wicked or cruel person. **4** informal a person of a particular sort: *the poor devil.*

SYNONYMS **1 Satan**, Beelzebub, Lucifer, the Prince of Darkness; informal Old Nick. **2 evil spirit**, demon, fiend. **3 brute**, beast, monster, fiend, villain, sadist, barbarian, ogre.

□ **between the devil and the deep blue sea** caught in a dilemma. **devil-may-care** cheerful and reckless. **devil's advocate** a person who expresses an opinion that they do not really hold in order to provoke discussion. **the devil to pay** serious trouble to be dealt with. **speak** (or **talk**) **of the devil** said when a person appears just after being mentioned.

dev·iled /ˈdevəld/ ▶ adj. (of food) cooked with hot seasoning: *deviled eggs.*

dev·il·ish /ˈdevəlisʜ/ ▶ adj. **1** like a devil in evil and cruelty. **2** mischievous: *a devilish grin.* **3** very difficult to deal with. ■ **dev·il·ish·ly** adv.

dev·il·ment /ˈdevəlmənt/ ▶ n. mischievous behavior.

dev·il·ry /ˈdevəlrē/ ▶ n. **1** wicked activity. **2** mischievous behavior.

de·vi·ous /ˈdēvēəs/ ▶ adj. **1** behaving in a cunning way to get what you want. **2** (of a route or journey) indirect.

SYNONYMS **1 underhanded/underhand**, dishonest, crafty, cunning, conniving, scheming, sneaky, furtive; informal crooked, shady. **2 circuitous**, roundabout, indirect, meandering, tortuous. ANTONYMS honest, direct.

■ **de·vi·ous·ly** adv. **de·vi·ous·ness** n.

de·vise /diˈvīz/ ▶ v. (**devises**, **devising**, **devised**) plan or invent a complex procedure or device.

SYNONYMS **conceive**, think up, dream up, work out, formulate, concoct, hatch, contrive, design, invent, coin; informal cook up.

de·void /diˈvoid/ ▶ adj. (**devoid of**) entirely without: *her voice was devoid of emotion.*

SYNONYMS **empty of**, free of, bereft of, lacking, deficient in, without, wanting in; informal minus.

dev·o·lu·tion /ˌdevəˈlo͞osʜən/ ▶ n. the transfer of power by central government to local or regional governments.

de·volve /diˈvälv/ ▶ v. (**devolves**, **devolving**, **devolved**) **1** transfer power to a lower level. **2** (**devolve on** or **to**) (of responsibility) pass to: *his duties devolved on a friend.*

de·vo·ré /dəˈvôrā/ ▶ n. a velvet fabric with a pattern formed by burning the pile away with acid.

de·vote /diˈvōt/ ▶ v. (**devotes**, **devoting**, **devoted**) (**devote something to**) give time or resources to.

SYNONYMS **dedicate**, allocate, assign, allot, commit, give (over), consign, pledge, set aside, earmark, reserve.

de·vot·ed /diˈvōtid/ ▶ adj. very loving or loyal.

SYNONYMS **dedicated**, committed, devout, loyal, faithful, true, staunch, steadfast, fond, loving.

■ **de·vot·ed·ly** adv.

dev·o·tee /ˌdevəˈtē, -ˈtā/ ▶ n. **1** a person who is very enthusiastic about someone or something. **2** a follower of a particular religion or god.

SYNONYMS **enthusiast**, fan, lover, aficionado, admirer, supporter, disciple; informal buff, freak, nut, fanatic.

de·vo·tion /diˈvōsʜən/ ▶ n. **1** great love or loyalty. **2** religious worship. **3** (**devotions**) prayers or other religious practices.

SYNONYMS **1 loyalty**, fidelity, commitment, allegiance, dedication, fondness, love, care. **2 piety**, spirituality, godliness, holiness, sanctity.

■ **de·vo·tion·al** adj.

de·vour /diˈvou(ə)r/ ▶ v. **1** eat something greedily. **2** (of a force) destroy something completely: *fire devoured the old house.* **3** read something quickly and eagerly. **4** (**be devoured**) be totally absorbed by an emotion: *she was devoured by need.*

SYNONYMS **1 gobble**, guzzle, gulp down, bolt, wolf; informal polish off, scarf up/down. **2 consume**, engulf, envelop.

de·vout /diˈvout/ ▶ adj. **1** deeply religious. **2** earnestly sincere: *a devout hope.*

SYNONYMS **dedicated**, devoted, committed, loyal, sincere, fervent, pious, reverent, God-fearing, dutiful, churchgoing.

■ **de·vout·ly** adv.

dew /d(y)o͞o/ ▶ n. tiny drops of moisture that form on cool surfaces at night, when water vapor in the air condenses.

dew·ber·ry /ˈd(y)o͞oˌberē/ ▶ n. (plural **dewberries**) the edible blue-black fruit of a European trailing bramble.

dew·lap /ˈd(y)o͞oˌlap/ ▶ n. a fold of loose skin hanging from the neck or throat of an animal or bird.

dew·y /ˈd(y)o͞oē/ ▶ adj. covered with dew. □ **dewy-eyed** having eyes moist with tears because one is feeling nostalgic or sentimental.

dex·ter·i·ty /dekˈsteritē/ ▶ n. skill in performing tasks.

SYNONYMS **deftness**, adeptness, adroitness, agility, ability, talent, skill, proficiency, expertise, experience, efficiency, mastery, finesse.

dex·ter·ous /ˈdekst(ə)rəs/ (or **dextrous** /ˈdekstrəs/) ▶ **adj.** showing skill, especially with the hands. ■ **dex·ter·ous·ly adv.**

dhar·ma /ˈdärmə/ ▶ **n.** (in Indian religion) the eternal law of the universe.

dho·ti /ˈdōtē/ ▶ **n.** (plural **dhotis**) a long piece of cloth tied around the waist, worn by some Hindu men.

di·a·be·tes /ˌdīəˈbētēz, -tis/ ▶ **n.** an illness in which the body cannot absorb sugar and starch properly because it does not have enough of the hormone insulin.

di·a·be·tic /ˌdīəˈbetik/ ▶ **adj.** having to do with diabetes. ▶ **n.** a person with diabetes.

di·a·bol·i·cal /ˌdīəˈbälikəl/ ▶ **adj. 1** (also **diabolic**) relating to or like the Devil. **2** informal very bad: *a singer with an absolutely diabolical voice.*

SYNONYMS *diabolical forces* **devilish**, satanic, demonic, hellish, infernal, evil, wicked, ungodly, unholy.

■ **di·a·bol·i·cal·ly adv.**

di·ab·o·lism /dīˈabəˌlizəm/ ▶ **n.** worship of the Devil.

di·a·crit·ic /ˌdīəˈkritik/ ▶ **n.** a sign written above or below a letter to indicate a difference in pronunciation from the same letter when unmarked.

di·a·dem /ˈdīəˌdem/ ▶ **n.** a crown.

di·ag·nose /ˌdīəgˈnōs/ ▶ **v.** (**diagnoses, diagnosing, diagnosed**) identify that illness or problem a person is suffering from by examining the symptoms.

SYNONYMS **identify**, determine, distinguish, recognize, interpret, detect, pinpoint.

■ **di·ag·nos·tic** /ˌdīəgˈnästik/ **adj.**

di·ag·no·sis /ˌdīəgˈnōsis/ ▶ **n.** (plural **diagnoses**) the identification of which illness or problem a person is suffering from by examining the symptoms.

SYNONYMS **1 identification**, detection, recognition, determination, discovery, pinpointing. **2 opinion**, judgment, verdict, conclusion.

di·ag·o·nal /dīˈagənl/ ▶ **adj. 1** (of a straight line) joining opposite corners of a rectangle, square, or other figure. **2** straight and at an angle; slanting. ▶ **n.** a diagonal line.

SYNONYMS ▶ **adj. crosswise**, crossways, slanting, slanted, oblique, angled, cornerways, cornerwise.

■ **di·ag·o·nal·ly adv.**

di·a·gram /ˈdīəˌgram/ ▶ **n.** a simplified drawing showing the appearance or structure of something.

SYNONYMS **drawing**, representation, plan, outline, figure, chart, graph.

■ **di·a·gram·mat·ic** /ˌdīəgrəˈmatik/ **adj.**

di·al /ˈdī(ə)l/ ▶ **n. 1** a disk marked to show the time or to indicate a measurement. **2** a disk with numbered holes on a telephone, turned to make a call. **3** a disk turned to choose a setting on a radio, stove, etc. ▶ **v.** (**dials, dialing, dialed**) call a telephone number by turning a dial or pressing numbered keys. □ **dial tone** a sound produced by a telephone that indicates that you may start to dial.

di·a·lect /ˈdīəˌlekt/ ▶ **n.** a form of a language used in a particular region or by a particular social group. ■ **di·a·lec·tal** /ˌdīəˈlektəl/ **adj.**

di·a·lec·tic /ˌdīəˈlektik/ (or **dialectics**) ▶ **n.** a way of discovering whether ideas are true by discussion and logical argument. ■ **di·a·lec·ti·cal adj.**

di·a·logue /ˈdīəˌläg, -ˌlôg/ (also **dialog**) ▶ **n. 1** conversation between two or more people in a book, play, or movie. **2** a discussion intended to explore a subject or solve a problem.

SYNONYMS **conversation**, talk, discussion, chat, tête-à-tête, exchange, debate, conference, consultation; informal confab.

□ **dialog box** a small area on a computer screen in which the user is prompted to provide information or select commands.

di·al·y·sis /dīˈaləsis/ ▶ **n.** the use of a machine to purify the blood of a person whose kidneys do not work properly.

di·a·man·té /ˌdēəmänˈtā/ ▶ **adj.** decorated with glass that is cut to look like diamonds.

di·am·e·ter /dīˈamitər/ ▶ **n.** a straight line passing from side to side through the center of a circle or sphere.

di·a·met·ri·cal /ˌdīəˈmetrikəl/ ▶ **adj. 1** complete: *the diametrical opposite.* **2** having to do with a diameter. ■ **di·a·met·ri·cal·ly adv.**

dia·mond /ˈdī(ə)mənd/ ▶ **n. 1** a clear precious stone, the hardest naturally occurring substance. **2** a figure with four straight sides of equal length forming two opposite acute angles and two opposite obtuse angles. **3** (**diamonds**) one of the four suits in a pack of playing cards, represented by a red diamond shape. □ **diamond jubilee** the sixtieth anniversary of a notable event. **diamond wedding** (or **diamond wedding anniversary**) the sixtieth (or seventy-fifth) anniversary of a wedding.

dia·mond·back /ˈdī(ə)məndˌbak/ (also **diamondback rattlesnake**) ▶ **n.** a large rattlesnake with diamond-shaped markings.

di·a·pa·son /ˌdīəˈpāzən, -sən/ ▶ **n.** a stop controlling the tone of a pipe organ.

dia·per /ˈdī(ə)pər/ ▶ **n.** a piece of toweling or other absorbent material wrapped around a baby's bottom and between its legs to absorb and retain urine and feces.

di·aph·a·nous /dīˈafənəs/ ▶ **adj.** light, delicate, and semitransparent.

di·a·phragm /ˈdīəˌfram/ ▶ **n. 1** a layer of muscle between the lungs and the stomach. **2** a piece of flexible material in mechanical or sound systems.

di·a·rist /ˈdīərist/ ▶ **n.** a person who writes a diary.

di·ar·rhe·a /ˌdīəˈrēə/ ▶ **n.** a condition in which a person has frequent liquid bowel movements.

SPELLING

Two **rs**, and **-hea** at the end: dia**rrhea**.

di·a·ry /ˈdīərē/ ▶ **n.** (plural **diaries**) a book in which you keep a daily record of events and experiences, or note down future appointments.

SYNONYMS **1 appointment book**, engagement book, personal organizer. **2 journal**, memoir, chronicle, log, logbook, daybook, history, annal, record, weblog, blog.

di·as·po·ra /dīˈaspərə/ ▶ **n. 1** (**the diaspora**) the dispersion of the Jews beyond Israel, chiefly in the 8th to 6th centuries BC. **2** the dispersion of any people from their traditional homeland.

di·as·to·le /dī'astl-ē/ ▶ **n.** the phase of the heartbeat when the heart muscle relaxes and the chambers fill with blood. ■ **di·as·tol·ic** /ˌdīə'stälik/ **adj.**

di·a·tom /'dīəˌtäm/ ▶ **n.** a single-celled alga that has a cell wall of silica.

di·a·tom·ic /ˌdīə'tämik/ ▶ **adj.** Chemistry consisting of two atoms.

di·a·ton·ic /ˌdīə'tänik/ ▶ **adj.** Music involving only the notes of the appropriate major or minor scale.

di·a·tribe /'dīəˌtrīb/ ▶ **n.** a speech or piece of writing forcefully attacking someone.

SYNONYMS **tirade**, harangue, onslaught, attack, polemic, denunciation, broadside, fulmination; informal blast.

dib·ble /'dibəl/ ▶ **n.** a pointed hand tool for making holes in the ground for seeds or young plants.

dibs /dibz/ ▶ **pl.n.** informal money. □ **have first dibs on** have the first right to or choice of: *they never got first dibs on great prospects.*

dice /dīs/ ▶ **n.** (plural **dice**) a small cube whose sides are marked with one to six spots, used in games of chance. ▶ **v.** (**dices**, **dicing**, **diced**) **1** cut food into small cubes. **2** (**dice with**) take great risks with: *dicing with death.*

dic·ey /'dīsē/ ▶ **adj.** (**dicier**, **diciest**) informal difficult or risky.

di·chot·o·my /dī'kätəmē/ ▶ **n.** (plural **dichotomies**) a separation or contrast between two things: *the false dichotomy between education and entertainment.*

dick·ens /'dikənz/ ▶ **n.** informal used to express annoyance or surprise: *what the dickens is going on?*

Dick·en·si·an /di'kenzēən/ ▶ **adj.** like the novels of Charles Dickens, especially in terms of the urban poverty that they portray.

dick·er /'dikər/ ▶ **v.** (**dickers**, **dickering**, **dickered**) **1** argue or bargain in a petty way. **2** treat something casually; toy or fiddle with something.

di·cot·y·le·don /dīˌkätl'ēdn/ ▶ **n.** a plant with an embryo bearing two cotyledons (seed leaves).

dic·tate /'dikˌtāt/ ▶ **v.** (**dictates**, **dictating**, **dictated**) **1** give orders with great authority. **2** control or influence: *choice is often dictated by availability.* **3** speak words for someone else to type or write down. ▶ **n.** an order or principle that must be obeyed: *the dictates of fashion.*

SYNONYMS ▶ **v. 1 prescribe**, lay down, impose, set down, order, command, decree, ordain, direct. **2 determine**, control, govern, decide, influence, affect.

■ **dic·ta·tion** /dik'tāsʜən/ **n.**

dic·ta·tor /'dikˌtātər/ ▶ **n.** a ruler who has total power over a country.

SYNONYMS **autocrat**, despot, tyrant, absolute ruler. ANTONYMS democrat.

dic·ta·to·ri·al /ˌdiktə'tôrēəl/ ▶ **adj. 1** relating to or controlled by a dictator. **2** insisting on total obedience; domineering.

SYNONYMS **domineering**, autocratic, authoritarian, oppressive, imperious, overweening, overbearing, peremptory; informal bossy, high-handed.

dic·ta·tor·ship /dik'tātərˌsʜip, 'diktātər-/ ▶ **n. 1** government by a dictator. **2** a country governed by a dictator.

dic·tion /'diksʜən/ ▶ **n. 1** the choice and use of words in speech or writing: *they distanced their poetic diction from everyday speech.* **2** a person's way of pronouncing words.

dic·tion·ar·y /'diksʜəˌnerē/ ▶ **n.** (plural **dictionaries**) a book that lists the words of a language and gives their meaning, or their equivalent in a different language.

SYNONYMS **lexicon**, glossary, vocabulary.

dic·tum /'diktəm/ ▶ **n.** (plural **dicta** /-tə/ or **dictums**) **1** a formal announcement made by someone in authority. **2** a short statement that expresses a general principle.

did /did/ past of DO[1].

di·dac·tic /dī'daktik/ ▶ **adj.** intended to teach or give moral instruction. ■ **di·dac·ti·cal·ly adv.**

did·dle /'didl/ ▶ **v.** (**diddles**, **diddling**, **diddled**) informal cheat or swindle.

didg·er·i·doo /ˌdijərē'do͞o/ ▶ **n.** an Australian Aboriginal musical instrument in the form of a long wooden tube, which produces a deep sound when blown.

did·n't /'didnt/ ▶ **contr.** did not.

die[1] /dī/ ▶ **v.** (**dies**, **dying**, **died**) **1** stop living. **2** (**die out**) become extinct. **3** become less loud or strong: *the noise died down.* **4** (**be dying for** or **to do**) informal be very eager to have or do.

SYNONYMS **1 pass away**, pass on, perish; informal give up the ghost, kick the bucket, buy the farm, croak, bite the dust. **2 lessen**, subside, drop, ease (off), let up, moderate, abate, fade, peter out, wane, ebb. **3** *the engine died* **fail**, cut out, give out, break down, stop; informal conk out, go kaput. **4** (**dying**) **terminally ill**, at death's door, on your deathbed, fading fast, not long for this world, moribund, in extremis. **5** (**dying**) **declining**, vanishing, fading, waning; informal on the way out. ANTONYMS live.

□ **die hard** disappear or change very slowly. **never say die** do not give up hope. **to die for** informal very good or desirable.

die[2] ▶ **n. 1** (plural **dice**) a dice. **2** (plural **dies**) a device for cutting or molding metal or for stamping a design on to coins or medals. □ **die-cast** formed by pouring molten metal into a mold. **the die is cast** something has happened that cannot be changed.

die·hard /'dīˌhärd/ ▶ **n.** a person who stubbornly continues to support something in spite of opposition or changing circumstances.

SYNONYMS **reactionary**, ultraconservative, traditionalist; *diehard Marxists* hard-line, dyed-in-the-wool, intransigent, inflexible, uncompromising, rigid, staunch, entrenched.

di·e·lec·tric /ˌdīə'lektrik/ Physics ▶ **adj.** that does not conduct electricity; insulating. ▶ **n.** an insulator.

di·er·e·sis /dī'erəsis/ ▶ **n.** (plural **diereses** /-sēz/) a mark (¨) placed over a vowel to indicate that it is sounded separately, as in *naïve.*

die·sel /'dēzəl/ ▶ **n. 1** a type of engine in which heat produced by compressing air is used to ignite the fuel. **2** a form of petroleum used as fuel in diesel engines.

di·et /'dī-it/ ▶ **n. 1** the kinds of food that a person or animal usually eats. **2** a limited range or amount of food, eaten in order to lose weight or for medical reasons. ▶ v. (**diets**, **dieting**, **dieted**) keep to a special diet in order to lose weight.

> SYNONYMS ▶ n. 1 *a healthy diet* **food**, nutrition, eating habits. 2 *she's on a diet* **dietary regime**, regimen, restricted diet, fast. ▶ v. **be on a diet**, slim (down), reduce, lose weight, watch your weight, count calories; informal slenderize.

die·tar·y /ˈdī-iˌterē/ ▶ adj. 1 having to do with diets or dieting. 2 provided by the food you eat: *a regular intake of dietary fiber.*

di·e·tet·ics /ˌdī-iˈtetiks/ ▶ n. the branch of knowledge concerned with the diet and its effects on health. ■ **di·e·tet·ic** adj.

di·e·ti·tian /ˌdī-iˈtisʜən/ (or **dietician**) ▶ n. an expert on diet and nutrition.

dif·fer /ˈdifər/ ▶ v. (**differs**, **differing**, **differed**) 1 be different. 2 disagree.

> SYNONYMS 1 *the second set of data **differed from** the first* **contrast with**, be different to, vary from, deviate from, conflict with, run counter to, be at odds with, contradict. 2 **disagree**, conflict, be at variance/odds, be in dispute, not see eye to eye. ANTONYMS resemble, agree.

□ **agree to differ** stop arguing because agreement will not be reached.

dif·fer·ence /ˈdif(ə)rəns/ ▶ n. 1 a way in which people or things are unlike each other. 2 a disagreement or dispute. 3 what is left when one number or amount is subtracted from another.

> SYNONYMS 1 **dissimilarity**, contrast, distinction, differentiation, variance, variation, divergence, disparity, contradiction. 2 **disagreement**, difference of opinion, dispute, argument, quarrel. 3 *I'll pay the difference* **balance**, remainder, rest. ANTONYMS similarity.

□ **make a difference** have an effect.

dif·fer·ent /ˈdif(ə)rənt/ ▶ adj. 1 not the same as another or each other. 2 separate: *we talked on different occasions about dialects.* 3 informal new and unusual.

> SYNONYMS 1 **dissimilar**, unlike, contrasting, differing, varying, disparate, poles apart, incompatible, mismatched; informal like oil and water. 2 **changed**, altered, transformed, new, unfamiliar, unknown, strange. 3 **distinct**, separate, individual, independent. 4 **unusual**, out of the ordinary, unfamiliar, novel, new, fresh, original, unconventional, exotic. ANTONYMS similar, ordinary.

■ **dif·fer·ent·ly** adv.

dif·fer·en·tial /ˌdifəˈrencʜəl/ ▶ adj. involving a difference: *the differential achievements of boys and girls.* ▶ n. 1 Math a minute difference between successive values of a variable. 2 a gear that allows a vehicle's wheels to revolve at different speeds when going around corners. □ **differential calculus** the part of calculus concerned with the derivatives of functions. **differential equation** an equation involving derivatives of a function or functions.

dif·fer·en·ti·ate /ˌdifəˈrensʜēˌāt/ ▶ v. (**differentiates**, **differentiating**, **differentiated**) 1 recognize things as being different from each other; distinguish. 2 make things appear different from each other: *little differentiates the company's products from its rivals.* ■ **dif·fer·en·ti·a·tion** /-ˌrensʜēˈāsʜən/ n.

dif·fi·cult /ˈdifikəlt/ ▶ adj. 1 needing a lot of effort or skill to do or understand; hard. 2 causing or involving problems: *a difficult economic climate.* 3 not easy to please or satisfy; awkward.

> SYNONYMS 1 *a difficult job* **laborious**, strenuous, arduous, hard, tough, demanding, punishing, grueling, back-breaking, exhausting, tiring; informal hellish, no picnic. 2 *a difficult problem* **hard**, complicated, complex, puzzling, perplexing, baffling, problematic, thorny, ticklish. 3 *a difficult child* **troublesome**, tiresome, trying, exasperating, awkward, demanding, contrary, recalcitrant, uncooperative, fussy. ANTONYMS easy, simple, cooperative.

dif·fi·cul·ty /ˈdifikəltē/ ▶ n. (plural **difficulties**) 1 the state of being difficult. 2 a difficult or dangerous situation; a problem.

> SYNONYMS 1 **strain**, stress, trouble, problems, struggle; informal hassle. 2 **problem**, complication, snag, hitch, obstacle, hurdle, stumbling block, pitfall; informal headache. 3 *he got into **difficulties*** **trouble**, a predicament, a plight, hard times; informal a fix, a scrape, a jam. ANTONYMS ease.

dif·fi·dent /ˈdifidənt/ ▶ adj. not having much self-confidence.

> SYNONYMS **shy**, bashful, modest, self-effacing, unassuming, meek, unconfident, insecure, unassertive, timid, shrinking, reticent. ANTONYMS confident.

■ **dif·fi·dence** n. **dif·fi·dent·ly** adv.

dif·fract /diˈfrakt/ ▶ v. cause a beam of light to be spread out as a result of passing through a narrow opening or across an edge. ■ **dif·frac·tion** n.

dif·fuse ▶ v. /diˈfyo͞oz/ (**diffuses**, **diffusing**, **diffused**) 1 spread over a wide area: *technologies diffuse rapidly.* 2 (of a gas or liquid) become mingled with a substance. ▶ adj. /diˈfyo͞os/ 1 spread out over a large area; not concentrated. 2 not clearly or concisely expressed: *the second argument is more diffuse.* ■ **dif·fuse·ly** /-ˈfyo͞oslē/ adv. **dif·fu·sion** /-ˈfyo͞ozʜən/ n.

> USAGE
>
> Don't confuse **diffuse** with **defuse**, which means 'make a situation less tense or difficult' or 'remove the fuse from.'

dig /dig/ ▶ v. (**digs**, **digging**, **dug** /dəg/) 1 cut into earth in order to turn it over or move it. 2 remove or produce something by digging: *the workmen dug the cable up.* 3 push or poke sharply: *he dug his hands into his pockets.* 4 (**dig into** or **through**) search or rummage in. 5 (**dig something out** or **up**) discover facts. 6 (**dig in**) start eating heartily. 7 informal, dated like: *I really dig heavy rock.* ▶ n. 1 an act of digging. 2 an investigation of a site by archaeologists. 3 a sharp push or poke. 4 informal a critical remark. 5 (**digs**) informal temporary accommodations.

> SYNONYMS ▶ v. 1 *digging the soil* **turn over**, work, break up. 2 *he dug a hole* **excavate**, dig out, quarry, hollow out, scoop out, bore, burrow, mine. 3 **poke**, prod, jab, stab, shove, ram, push, thrust, drive, stick. 4 **delve**, probe, search, inquire, look, investigate, research. ▶ n. 1 **poke**, prod, jab, stab, shove, push. 2 **snide remark**, cutting remark, jibe, taunt, sneer, insult; informal wisecrack, put-down.

□ **dig in your heels** stubbornly refuse to do or agree to something.

di·gest ▶ **v.** /di'jest, dī-/ **1** break down food in the stomach and intestines so that it can be absorbed by the body. **2** reflect on and absorb information. ▶ **n.** /'dī,jest/ a summary or collection of material or information.

SYNONYMS ▶ **v. assimilate**, absorb, take in, understand, comprehend, grasp. ▶ **n. summary**, synopsis, abstract, précis, résumé, summation.

■ **di·gest·i·ble adj.**

di·ges·tion /di'jescʜən, dī-/ ▶ **n. 1** the process of digesting food. **2** a person's ability to digest food: *he suffered with his digestion.*

di·ges·tive /di'jestiv, dī-/ ▶ **adj.** relating to the digestion of food.

dig·ger /'digər/ ▶ **n.** a person, animal, or large machine that digs earth.

dig·i·cam /'diji,kam/ ▶ **n.** a digital camera.

dig·it /'dijit/ ▶ **n. 1** any of the numerals from 0 to 9. **2** a finger or thumb.

dig·it·al /'dijitl/ ▶ **adj. 1** having to do with information represented as a series of binary digits, as in a computer. **2** having to do with computer technology. **3** (of a clock or watch) showing the time by displaying numbers electronically, rather than having a clock face. **4** having to do with a finger or fingers. □ **digital audiotape** audiotape on which sound is recorded digitally. ■ **dig·it·al·ly adv.**

dig·i·tal·is /,diji'talis/ ▶ **n.** a drug prepared from foxglove leaves, used to stimulate the heart muscle.

dig·i·tize /'diji,tīz/ ▶ **v.** (**digitizes**, **digitizing**, **digitized**) convert pictures or sound into a digital form.

dig·ni·fied /'digni,fīd/ ▶ **adj.** having or showing dignity.

SYNONYMS **stately**, noble, majestic, distinguished, regal, imposing, impressive, grand, solemn, formal, ceremonious, decorous, sedate.

dig·ni·fy /'dignə,fī/ ▶ **v.** (**dignifies**, **dignifying**, **dignified**) make something impressive or worthy of respect: *they dignified their departure with a ceremony.*

dig·ni·tar·y /'digni,terē/ ▶ **n.** (plural **dignitaries**) a very important or high-ranking person.

dig·ni·ty /'dignitē/ ▶ **n.** (plural **dignities**) **1** the quality of being worthy of respect. **2** a calm or serious manner. **3** pride in yourself: *it was beneath his dignity to shout.*

SYNONYMS **1 stateliness**, nobility, majesty, impressiveness, grandeur, magnificence, ceremoniousness, formality, decorum, propriety, respectability, worthiness, integrity, solemnity, gravitas. **2 self-respect**, pride, self-esteem, self-worth.

□ **stand on your dignity** insist on being treated with respect.

di·graph /'dī,graf/ ▶ **n.** a combination of two letters representing one sound, as in *ph*.

di·gress /dī'gres/ ▶ **v.** temporarily leave the main subject in speech or writing. ■ **di·gres·sion n.**

di·he·dral /dī'hēdrəl/ ▶ **adj.** having or contained by two plane faces.

dike[1] /dīk/ (or **dyke**) ▶ **n. 1** a barrier built to prevent flooding from the sea. **2** a ditch or water-filled channel.

dike[2] ▶ **n.** DYKE[2].

dik·tat /dik'tät/ ▶ **n.** an order given by someone in power.

di·lap·i·dat·ed /di'lapi,dātid/ ▶ **adj.** old and in bad condition.

SYNONYMS **run-down**, tumbledown, ramshackle, in disrepair, shabby, battered, rickety, crumbling, in ruins, ruined, decaying, decrepit, neglected, uncared-for, gone to rack and ruin.

■ **di·lap·i·da·tion** /di,lapi'dāsʜən/ **n.**

SPELLING

Write **dil-**, not **del-**: **dil**apidated.

di·late /'dī,lāt, dī'lāt/ ▶ **v.** (**dilates**, **dilating**, **dilated**) become wider, larger, or more open: *her eyes dilated with horror.* ■ **di·la·tion** /dī'lāsʜən/ **n.**

dil·a·to·ry /'dilə,tôrē/ ▶ **adj. 1** slow to act. **2** intended to cause delay.

di·lem·ma /di'lemə/ ▶ **n.** a difficult situation in which you have to make a choice between alternatives.

SYNONYMS **quandary**, predicament, catch-22, vicious circle, plight, conflict; informal fix, tight spot/corner.

dil·et·tante /,dili'tänt/ ▶ **n.** (plural **dilettanti** /-'täntē/ or **dilettantes**) a person who does or studies something for enjoyment but does not take it very seriously.

SYNONYMS **dabbler**, amateur, nonprofessional, nonspecialist, layman, layperson.

dil·i·gent /'diləjənt/ ▶ **adj.** showing care and effort in a task or duty.

SYNONYMS **industrious**, hard-working, assiduous, conscientious, particular, punctilious, meticulous, painstaking, rigorous, careful, thorough, sedulous. ANTONYMS lazy.

■ **dil·i·gence n. dil·i·gent·ly adv.**

dill /dil/ ▶ **n.** an herb used in cooking and medicine.

dil·ly-dal·ly /'dilē,dalē/ ▶ **v.** (**dilly-dallies**, **dilly-dallying**, **dilly-dallied**) informal be slow or indecisive.

di·lute /di'lo͞ot, dī-/ ▶ **v.** (**dilutes**, **diluting**, **diluted**) **1** make a liquid thinner or weaker by adding water or other liquid. **2** weaken something by modifying it or adding other elements: *the breed had been diluted by the introduction of new strains.* ▶ **adj.** (of a liquid) diluted; weak.

SYNONYMS ▶ **v. 1** *dilute the bleach with water* **make weaker**, water down, thin, doctor, adulterate; informal cut. **2** *the original plans have been diluted* **tone down**, moderate, weaken, water down, compromise.

■ **di·lu·tion n.**

dim /dim/ ▶ **adj.** (**dimmer**, **dimmest**) **1** not bright or well-lit. **2** not clearly seen or remembered: *a dim figure in the dark kitchen.* **3** not able to see clearly: *his eyes became dim.* **4** informal stupid. ▶ **v.** (**dims**, **dimming**, **dimmed**) make or become dim.

SYNONYMS ▶ **adj. 1** *the dim light* **faint**, weak, feeble, soft, pale, dull, subdued, muted. **2** *long dim corridors* **dark**, badly lit, dingy, dismal, gloomy, murky. **3** *a dim figure* **indistinct**, ill-defined, vague, shadowy, nebulous, blurred, fuzzy. **4** *dim memories* **vague**, imprecise, imperfect, unclear, indistinct, sketchy, hazy. **5** see **STUPID** (sense 1). ANTONYMS bright, distinct, clear. ▶ **v. 1 turn down**, lower, soften, subdue. **2 fade**, dwindle, dull. ANTONYMS brighten.

□ **dim-witted** stupid or dull. **take a dim view of** disapprove of. ■ **dim·ly adv. dim·ness n.**

dime /dīm/ ▶ **n.** a ten-cent coin.

di·men·sion /di'menCHən/ ▶ **n. 1** a measure of how long, broad, high, etc., something is: *the dimensions of the pond were 14 ft x 8 ft.* **2** an aspect or feature: *we modern types lack a spiritual dimension.*

SYNONYMS **1** (**dimensions**) **size**, measurements, proportions, extent, length, width, breadth, depth. **2 aspect**, feature, element, angle, facet, side.

■ **di·men·sion·al adj.**

di·min·ish /di'minisH/ ▶ **v.** make or become smaller, weaker, or less.

SYNONYMS **1 subside**, lessen, decline, reduce, decrease, dwindle, fade, slacken off, let up. **2** *new laws diminished the courts' authority* **reduce**, decrease, lessen, curtail, cut, limit, curb. ANTONYMS increase.

di·min·u·en·do /di,minyōō'endō/ ▶ **adv. & adj.** Music with a decrease in loudness.

dim·i·nu·tion /,dimə'n(y)ōōSHən/ ▶ **n.** a reduction.

di·min·u·tive /di'minyətiv/ ▶ **adj.** very or unusually small. ▶ **n.** a shortened form of a person's name.

dim·mer /'dimər/ ▶ **n.** a device for varying the brightness of an electric light.

dim·ple /'dimpəl/ ▶ **n. 1** a small hollow formed in the cheeks when you smile. **2** a small depression in the flesh. ■ **dim·pled adj.**

dim·wit /'dim,wit/ ▶ **n.** informal a stupid person.

din /din/ ▶ **n.** a prolonged loud and unpleasant noise. ▶ **v.** (**dins, dinning, dinned**) (**din something into**) teach something to someone by constantly repeating it.

SYNONYMS ▶ **n. noise**, racket, rumpus, cacophony, hubbub, uproar, ruckus, commotion, clangor, clatter, clamor; informal hullabaloo. ANTONYMS silence.

di·nar /di'när/ ▶ **n.** the basic unit of money in the former country of Yugoslavia and certain Middle Eastern and North African countries.

dine /dīn/ ▶ **v.** (**dines, dining, dined**) eat dinner.

SYNONYMS **eat**, have dinner, have lunch.

□ **dining car** a railroad car equipped as a restaurant. **dining room** a room in which meals are eaten.

din·er /'dīnər/ ▶ **n. 1** a person who dines. **2** a small, inexpensive roadside restaurant, usually with a long counter and booths. **3** a dining car on a train.

di·nette /dī'net/ ▶ **n.** a small room or part of a room used for eating meals.

ding /diNG/ ▶ **v.** make a metallic ringing sound.

ding-dong /'diNG ,dôNG/ ▶ **n. 1** informal a silly or foolish person. **2** the sound of a bell ringing with alternate chimes.

din·ghy /'diNGē/ ▶ **n.** (plural **dinghies**) **1** a small open boat with a mast and sails. **2** a small inflatable rubber boat. **3** the smallest of a ship's boats, often used to reach shore from where the ship is moored.

din·go /'diNGgō/ ▶ **n.** (plural **dingoes** or **dingos**) a wild or partially domesticated Australian dog.

din·gy /'dinjē/ ▶ **adj.** (**dingier, dingiest**) gloomy and drab.

SYNONYMS **gloomy**, dark, dull, dim, dismal, dreary, drab, somber, grim, cheerless, dirty, grimy, shabby, seedy, run-down. ANTONYMS bright.

■ **din·gi·ness n.**

dink·y /'diNGkē/ ▶ **adj.** (**dinkier, dinkiest**) small and insignificant: *I can't believe the dinky salaries they pay here.*

din·ner /'dinər/ ▶ **n. 1** the main meal of the day, eaten either around midday or in the evening. **2** a formal evening meal.

SYNONYMS **main meal**, lunch, evening meal, supper, feast, banquet.

□ **dinner jacket** a black or white jacket worn by men for formal evening occasions.

di·no·saur /'dīnə,sôr/ ▶ **n.** an extinct reptile that lived millions of years ago, some kinds of which were very large.

dint /dint/ ▶ **n.** a dent. □ **by dint of** by means of.

di·o·cese /'dīəsis, -,sēz, -,sēs/ ▶ **n.** (plural **dioceses** /'dīəsēz/) a district under the control of a bishop in the Christian Church.

di·ode /'dī,ōd/ ▶ **n.** an electrical device that has two terminals and allows current to flow in one direction only.

Di·o·ny·sian /,dīə'nisHən, -'nisēən, -'nīsēən/ (also **Dionysiac** /-'nisēak, -'nīseak/) ▶ **adj. 1** relating to Dionysus, the Greek god of fertility and wine. **2** wild and uninhibited.

di·op·tric /dī'äptrik/ ▶ **adj.** of or relating to the refraction of light. ■ **di·op·trics pl.n.**

di·o·ram·a /,dīə'ramə, -'rä-/ ▶ **n.** a model representing a scene with three-dimensional figures against a painted background.

di·ox·ide /dī'äk,sīd/ ▶ **n.** an oxide with two atoms of oxygen to one of a metal or other element.

di·ox·in /dī'äksin/ ▶ **n.** a highly poisonous organic compound produced as a byproduct in some manufacturing processes.

dip /dip/ ▶ **v.** (**dips, dipping, dipped**) **1** (**dip something in** or **into**) put or lower something briefly in or into. **2** sink, drop, or slope downward: *the sun had dipped below the horizon.* **3** (of a level or amount) temporarily become lower or smaller. **4** lower something briefly: *the plane dipped its wings.* **5** (**dip into**) reach into a container to take something out. ▶ **n. 1** an act of dipping. **2** a thick sauce in which you dip pieces of food before eating them. **3** a brief swim. **4** a brief downward slope followed by an upward one.

SYNONYMS ▶ **v. 1 immerse**, submerge, plunge, dunk, bathe, sink. **2 sink**, set, drop, fall, descend. **3 decrease**, fall, drop, fall off, decline, diminish, dwindle, slump, plummet, plunge. **4 slope down**, descend, go down, drop (away), fall away. ANTONYMS rise, increase. ▶ **n. 1 swim**, wade. **2 slope**, incline, decline, descent, hollow, depression, basin. **3 decrease**, fall, drop, downturn, decline, falling-off, slump, reduction.

diph·the·ri·a /dif'THi(ə)rēə, dip-/ ▶ **n.** a serious, highly contagious illness that causes inflammation of the mucous membranes, especially in the throat.

diph·thong /ˈdifˌTHäNG, ˈdip-, -ˌTHôNG/ ▶ **n.** a sound formed by the combination of two vowels in a single syllable (as in *coin*).

dip·loid /ˈdipˌloid/ ▶ **adj.** Genetics (of a cell or nucleus) containing two complete sets of chromosomes, one from each parent.

di·plo·ma /diˈplōmə/ ▶ **n.** a certificate awarded to someone who has successfully completed a course of study.

di·plo·ma·cy /diˈplōməsē/ ▶ **n.** **1** the management of relations between countries. **2** skill and tact in dealing with people.

> SYNONYMS **1 statesmanship**, statecraft, negotiation(s), discussion(s), talks. **2 tact**, tactfulness, sensitivity, discretion.

dip·lo·mat /ˈdipləˌmat/ ▶ **n.** an official who represents a country abroad.

> SYNONYMS **ambassador**, attaché, consul, chargé d'affaires, envoy, emissary.

dip·lo·mat·ic /ˌdipləˈmatik/ ▶ **adj.** **1** having to do with diplomacy. **2** tactful.

> SYNONYMS **tactful**, sensitive, subtle, delicate, polite, discreet, judicious, politic. ANTONYMS tactless.

□ **diplomatic immunity** the exemption from certain laws granted to diplomats by the state in which they are working. ■ **dip·lo·mat·i·cal·ly** **adv.**

di·pole /ˈdīˌpōl/ ▶ **n.** **1** Physics a pair of equal and oppositely charged or magnetized poles separated by a distance. **2** an aerial consisting of a horizontal metal rod with a connecting wire at its center. ■ **di·po·lar** /dīˈpōlər/ **adj.**

dip·per /ˈdipər/ ▶ **n.** **1** a bird that dives into fast-flowing streams to feed. **2** a ladle.

dip·py /ˈdipē/ ▶ **adj.** informal foolish or eccentric.

dip·so·ma·ni·a /ˌdipsəˈmānēə/ ▶ **n.** alcoholism. ■ **dip·so·ma·ni·ac** **n.**

dip·stick /ˈdipˌstik/ ▶ **n.** a rod for measuring the depth of a liquid.

dip·tych /ˈdiptik/ ▶ **n.** a painting on two hinged wooden panels, typically forming an altarpiece.

dire /dīr/ ▶ **adj.** **1** very serious or urgent: *misuse of drugs can have dire consequences.* **2** informal of very bad quality.

> SYNONYMS **terrible**, dreadful, appalling, frightful, awful, grim, sore, alarming, acute, grave, serious, urgent, pressing, wretched, desperate, parlous.

di·rect /diˈrekt, dī-/ ▶ **adj.** **1** going from one place to another without changing direction or stopping. **2** with nothing or no one in between: *he relied on direct contact with the leaders.* **3** saying exactly what you mean; frank. **4** clear and explicit: *there is no direct evidence that they accepted bribes.* ▶ **adv.** in a direct way or by a direct route. ▶ **v.** **1** aim something toward: *comics directed at adolescent males.* **2** tell or show someone the way. **3** control the operations of. **4** supervise the production of a movie, play, etc. **5** give an order to.

> SYNONYMS ▶ **adj.** **1 straight**, short, quick. **2 nonstop**, through, unbroken, uninterrupted. **3 frank**, candid, straightforward, open, blunt, plain-spoken, outspoken, forthright, no-nonsense, matter-of-fact; informal upfront. ▶ **v.** **1 manage**, govern, run, administer, control, conduct, handle, be in charge of, preside over, lead, head, rule. **2 aim**, target, address to, intend for, mean for, design for. **3 give directions**, show the way, point someone in the direction of. **4 instruct**, tell, command, order, require; old use bid.

□ **direct current** an electric current that flows in one direction only. **direct mail** commercial literature mailed to prospective customers without them having asked for it. **direct object** a noun or noun phrase referring to a person or thing affected by the action of a transitive verb (e.g., *the dog* in *I fed the dog*). **direct speech** the actual words of a speaker quoted in writing. **direct tax** a tax, such as income tax, which is charged on the income or profits of the person who pays it, rather than on goods or services.

di·rec·tion /diˈrekSHən, dī-/ ▶ **n.** **1** a course along which someone or something moves, or which leads to a destination: *she set off in the opposite direction.* **2** a point to or from which someone or something moves or faces: *a house with views in all directions.* **3** the directing or managing of people. **4** (**directions**) instructions on how to reach a destination or how to do something.

> SYNONYMS **1 way**, route, course, line, bearing, orientation. **2 running**, management, administration, conduct, handling, supervision, superintendence, command, rule, leadership. **3 instruction**, order, command, rule, regulation, requirement.

■ **di·rec·tion·al** /diˈrekSHənl/ **adj.**

di·rec·tive /diˈrektiv/ ▶ **n.** an official instruction.

> SYNONYMS **instruction**, direction, command, order, injunction, decree, dictum, edict.

di·rect·ly /diˈrektlē/ ▶ **adv.** **1** in a direct way. **2** exactly in a particular position: *the house directly opposite.* **3** immediately.

> SYNONYMS **1** *they flew directly to New York* **straight**, as the crow flies. **2** *directly after breakfast* **immediately**, right (away), straight, straightaway, without delay, promptly. **3** *the houses directly opposite* **exactly**, right, immediately, diametrically; informal bang. **4 frankly**, candidly, openly, bluntly, forthrightly, without beating around/about the bush.

di·rec·tor /diˈrektər/ ▶ **n.** **1** a person who is in charge of an organization or activity. **2** a member of the board that manages a business. **3** a person responsible for directing a movie, play, etc.

> SYNONYMS **manager**, head, chief, principal, leader, governor, president, chair, chief executive; informal boss, gaffer.

■ **di·rec·to·ri·al** /diˌrekˈtôrēəl, ˌdīrek-/ **adj.**

di·rec·to·rate /diˈrektərit/ ▶ **n.** **1** the board of directors of a company. **2** a section of a government department in charge of a particular activity.

di·rec·to·ry /diˈrektərē/ ▶ **n.** (plural **directories**) a book that lists individuals or organizations and gives their addresses, telephone numbers, etc.

dirge /dərj/ ▶ **n.** **1** a piece of music expressing sadness for someone's death. **2** a slow, boring song or piece of music.

dir·i·gi·ble /ˈdirijəbəl, dəˈrijə-/ ▶ **n.** an airship.

dirk /dərk/ ▶ **n.** a kind of short dagger formerly carried by Scottish Highlanders.

dirt /dərt/ ▶ **n.** **1** a substance that makes something dirty. **2** soil or earth. **3** informal scandalous or damaging information about someone

SYNONYMS **1 grime**, filth, muck, dust, mud, pollution; informal grunge. **2** *a dirt road* **earth**, soil, clay, loam.

□ **dirt cheap** extremely cheap.

dirt·y /'dərtē/ ▶ adj. (**dirtier**, **dirtiest**) **1** covered or marked with mud, dust, grease, etc.; not clean. **2** obscene. **3** unfair or dishonest. ▶ v. (**dirties**, **dirtying**, **dirtied**) make something dirty.

SYNONYMS ▶ adj. **1 soiled**, grimy, grubby, filthy, mucky, stained, unwashed, greasy, muddy, dusty, polluted, contaminated, foul, unhygienic; informal grungy. **2 obscene**, indecent, rude, naughty, vulgar, smutty, coarse, crude, filthy, off color, pornographic, explicit, X-rated; informal blue; euphemistic adult. **3 dishonest**, deceitful, unscrupulous, dishonorable, unsporting, below the belt, unfair, unethical, unprincipled. ANTONYMS clean. ▶ v. **soil**, stain, muddy, blacken, mess (up), mark, spatter, smudge, smear, splatter, sully, pollute, foul.

□ **dirty look** informal a look expressing disapproval, disgust, or anger. **dirty word 1** an offensive or indecent word. **2** a reference to something regarded with dislike or disapproval. **get your hands dirty** (or **dirty your hands**) do manual, menial, or other hard work. **play dirty** informal act in a dishonest or unfair way.

dis·a·bil·i·ty /ˌdisə'bilitē/ ▶ n. (plural **disabilities**) **1** a physical or mental condition that restricts your movements, senses, or activities. **2** a disadvantage or handicap.

SYNONYMS **handicap**, incapacity, impairment, infirmity, defect, abnormality, condition, disorder, affliction.

dis·a·ble /dis'ābəl/ ▶ v. (**disables**, **disabling**, **disabled**) **1** cause someone to be disabled. **2** put something out of action.

SYNONYMS **1 incapacitate**, put out of action, debilitate, handicap, cripple, lame, maim, immobilize, paralyze. **2 deactivate**, defuse, disarm, make safe.

■ **dis·a·ble·ment** n.

dis·a·bled /dis'ābəld/ ▶ adj. having a disability.

SYNONYMS **handicapped**, incapacitated, infirm, crippled, lame, paralyzed, immobilized, bedridden; euphemistic physically challenged, differently abled. ANTONYMS able-bodied.

dis·a·buse /ˌdisə'byo͞oz/ ▶ v. (**disabuses**, **disabusing**, **disabused**) (**disabuse someone of**) persuade someone that an idea or belief is mistaken: *he disabused me of my fanciful notions*.

dis·ad·van·tage /ˌdisəd'vantij/ ▶ n. something that causes a problem or reduces the chances of success. ▶ v. (**disadvantages**, **disadvantaging**, **disadvantaged**) **1** put someone in an unfavorable position. **2** (**disadvantaged**) having less money and fewer opportunities than most people.

SYNONYMS ▶ n. **1 drawback**, snag, downside, fly in the ointment, catch, nuisance, handicap, trouble; informal minus. **2 detriment**, prejudice, harm, loss, hurt. ANTONYMS advantage.

■ **dis·ad·van·ta·geous** /disˌadvən'tājəs/ adj.

dis·af·fect·ed /ˌdisə'fektid/ ▶ adj. unhappy with the people in authority or with the organization you belong to, and no longer willing to support them.
■ **dis·af·fec·tion** n.

dis·a·gree /ˌdisə'grē/ ▶ v. (**disagrees**, **disagreeing**, **disagreed**) **1** have a different opinion. **2** be inconsistent: *results that disagree with the findings reported so far*. **3** (**disagree with**) make someone slightly unwell.

SYNONYMS **1 be of a different opinion**, not see eye to eye, take issue, challenge, contradict, differ, dissent, be in dispute, clash. **2 differ**, be dissimilar, be different, be at variance/odds, vary, contradict each other, conflict. **3** *the food disagreed with her* **make ill**, make unwell, upset, nauseate. ANTONYMS agree.

dis·a·gree·a·ble /ˌdisə'grēəbəl/ ▶ adj. **1** unpleasant. **2** bad-tempered.

SYNONYMS **unpleasant**, distasteful, off-putting, unpalatable, nasty, objectionable, disgusting, horrible, offensive, repulsive, obnoxious, odious, repellent, revolting, vile, foul. ANTONYMS pleasant.

dis·a·gree·ment /ˌdisə'grēmənt/ ▶ n. lack of consensus or approval.

SYNONYMS **dissent**, difference of opinion, controversy, discord, division, dispute, quarrel. ANTONYMS agreement.

dis·al·low /ˌdisə'lou/ ▶ v. declare that something is not valid.

dis·ap·pear /ˌdisə'pi(ə)r/ ▶ v. **1** stop being visible. **2** cease to exist.

SYNONYMS **1 vanish**, be lost to view/sight, recede, fade away, melt away, clear. **2 die out**, cease to exist, end, go, pass away, pass into oblivion, vanish, perish. ANTONYMS materialize.

■ **dis·ap·pear·ance** n.

SPELLING

Write one **s**, two **ps**: dis**app**ear.

dis·ap·point /ˌdisə'point/ ▶ v. **1** make someone sad or upset through failing to fulfill their hopes or expectations. **2** prevent hopes or expectations being fulfilled.

SYNONYMS **let down**, fail, dissatisfy, upset, dismay, sadden, disenchant, disillusion, shatter someone's illusions.

SPELLING

Write one **s**, two **ps**: dis**app**oint.

dis·ap·point·ed /ˌdisə'pointid/ ▶ adj. sad or displeased because your hopes have not been fulfilled.

SYNONYMS **upset**, saddened, let down, displeased, dissatisfied, disheartened, downhearted, discouraged, crestfallen, disenchanted, disillusioned; informal cut up. ANTONYMS delighted.

■ **dis·ap·point·ed·ly** adv.

dis·ap·point·ment /ˌdisə'pointmənt/ ▶ n. **1** sadness felt when hopes or expectations are not fulfilled. **2** a person or thing that causes disappointment: *the job proved a disappointment*.

SYNONYMS **1 sadness**, sorrow, regret, dismay, displeasure, dissatisfaction, disenchantment, disillusionment. **2 letdown**, nonevent, anticlimax; informal washout. ANTONYMS delight.

dis·ap·pro·ba·tion /disˌaprəˈbāsʜən/ ▶ **n.** strong disapproval.

dis·ap·prov·al /ˌdisəˈpro͞ovəl/ ▶ **n.** the possession or expression of an unfavorable opinion.

> SYNONYMS **disfavor**, objection, dislike, dissatisfaction, distaste, displeasure, criticism, censure, condemnation, denunciation. ANTONYMS approval.

dis·ap·prove /ˌdisəˈpro͞ov/ ▶ **v.** (**disapproves**, **disapproving**, **disapproved**) feel that someone or something is bad or immoral.

> SYNONYMS *Bob disapproved of drinking and driving* **object to**, have a poor opinion of, take exception to, dislike, take a dim view of, look askance at, frown on, be against, not believe in, deplore, censure, condemn, denounce.

dis·arm /disˈärm/ ▶ **v. 1** take a weapon or weapons away from someone. **2** (of a country) reduce the size of its armed forces or give up its weapons. **3** win over a hostile or suspicious person, especially through being charming. **4** remove the fuse from a bomb.

> SYNONYMS **1 lay down your arms**, demobilize, disband, demilitarize. **2 defuse**, disable, deactivate, make safe. **3 win over**, charm, persuade, soothe, mollify, appease, placate. ANTONYMS arm, antagonize.

dis·ar·ma·ment /disˈärməmənt/ ▶ **n.** the reduction or withdrawal of military forces and weapons.

> SYNONYMS **demilitarization**, demobilization, disbandment, decommissioning, arms reduction, arms limitation.

dis·arm·ing /disˈärmiɴɢ/ ▶ **adj.** removing suspicion or hostility, especially through charm.

> SYNONYMS **winning**, charming, irresistible, persuasive, soothing, conciliatory, mollifying.

dis·ar·range /ˌdisəˈrānj/ ▶ **v.** (**disarranges**, **disarranging**, **disarranged**) make something untidy or disordered.

dis·ar·ray /ˌdisəˈrā/ ▶ **n.** a state of disorder or confusion.

> SYNONYMS **disorder**, confusion, chaos, untidiness, disorganization, a mess, a muddle, a shambles. ANTONYMS tidiness.

dis·as·sem·ble /ˌdisəˈsembəl/ ▶ **v.** (**disassembles**, **disassembling**, **disassembled**) take apart.

dis·as·ter /diˈzastər/ ▶ **n. 1** a sudden accident or natural event that causes great damage or loss of life. **2** a sudden misfortune: *a string of personal disasters.*

> SYNONYMS **1 catastrophe**, calamity, cataclysm, tragedy, act of God, accident. **2 misfortune**, mishap, misadventure, setback, reversal, stroke of bad luck, blow. **3 failure**, fiasco, catastrophe; informal flop, washout, dead loss. ANTONYMS success.

dis·as·trous /diˈzastrəs/ ▶ **adj. 1** causing great damage. **2** informal very unsuccessful.

> SYNONYMS **catastrophic**, calamitous, cataclysmic, tragic, devastating, ruinous, terrible, awful. ANTONYMS beneficial, fortunate.

■ **dis·as·trous·ly adv.**

> SPELLING
> There is no **e**: disastrous, not **-erous**.

dis·a·vow /ˌdisəˈvou/ ▶ **v.** deny that you are responsible for or in favor of something.
■ **dis·a·vow·al n.**

dis·band /disˈband/ ▶ **v.** (of an organized group) break up: *the team was disbanded.*

> SYNONYMS **break up**, disperse, demobilize, dissolve, scatter, separate, go separate ways, part company. ANTONYMS assemble.

dis·bar /disˈbär/ ▶ **v.** (**disbars**, **disbarring**, **disbarred**) expel a lawyer from the Bar, so that they no longer have the right to practice law.

dis·be·lief /ˌdisbəˈlēf/ ▶ **n. 1** inability or refusal to accept that something is true or real. **2** lack of faith.

> SYNONYMS **incredulity**, incredulousness, skepticism, doubt, cynicism, suspicion, distrust, mistrust.

dis·be·lieve /ˌdisbəˈlēv/ ▶ **v.** (**disbelieves**, **disbelieving**, **disbelieved**) be unable to believe.

dis·burse /disˈbərs/ ▶ **v.** (**disburses**, **disbursing**, **disbursed**) pay out money from a fund.
■ **dis·burse·ment n.**

disc /disk/ ▶ **n.** = **DISK**.

dis·card ▶ **v.** /disˈkärd/ get rid of something useless or unwanted. ▶ **n.** /ˈdisˌkärd/ something that has been discarded.

> SYNONYMS ▶ **v. dispose of**, throw away/out, get rid of, toss out, jettison, dispense with, scrap, reject, drop; informal ditch, trash, junk. ANTONYMS keep.

dis·cern /diˈsərn/ ▶ **v. 1** recognize or be aware of: *I can discern no difference between the two policies.* **2** see or hear something with difficulty.

> SYNONYMS **perceive**, make out, pick out, detect, identify, determine, distinguish, recognize, notice, observe, see, spot; literary espy.

dis·cern·i·ble /diˈsərnəbəl/ ▶ **adj.** able to be discerned.

> SYNONYMS **visible**, detectable, noticeable, perceptible, observable, identifiable, apparent, evident, clear, obvious.

dis·cern·ing /diˈsərniɴɢ/ ▶ **adj.** having or showing good judgment.

> SYNONYMS **discriminating**, judicious, shrewd, astute, intelligent, sharp, selective, sophisticated, tasteful, sensitive, perceptive, knowing.

■ **dis·cern·ment n.**

dis·charge ▶ **v.** /disˈcʜärj/ (**discharges**, **discharging**, **discharged**) **1** dismiss or allow to leave: *he was discharged from the army.* **2** send out a liquid, gas, or other substance. **3** fire a gun or missile. **4** fulfill a responsibility. ▶ **n.** /ˈdisˌcʜärj/ **1** the action of discharging: *my discharge from the hospital.* **2** a substance that has been discharged.

> SYNONYMS ▶ **v. 1 dismiss**, eject, expel, throw out, make redundant, release, let go; Military cashier; informal sack, fire. **2 free**, set free, release, let out, liberate. **3 emit**, give off, let out, send out, exude, leak, secrete, excrete, release. **4 fire**, shoot, let off, set off, trigger, launch. **5 unload**, offload, put off, remove. **6 carry out**, perform, execute, conduct, fulfill, complete. ANTONYMS recruit, imprison.
> ▶ **n. 1 dismissal**, release, removal, ejection, expulsion; Military cashiering; informal the sack,

the boot. **2 leak**, leakage, emission, secretion, excretion, suppuration, pus. **3 carrying out**, performance, execution, conduct, fulfillment, accomplishment, completion.

dis·ci·ple /di'sīpəl/ ▶ **n. 1** a person who followed Jesus during his life, especially one of the twelve Apostles. **2** a follower of a teacher, leader, or philosophy.

SYNONYMS **follower**, adherent, believer, admirer, devotee, acolyte, apostle, supporter, advocate.

dis·ci·pli·nar·i·an /ˌdisəplə'nerēən/ ▶ **n.** a person who enforces firm discipline.

dis·ci·pli·nar·y /'disəpləˌnerē/ ▶ **adj.** having to do with discipline: *disciplinary action.*

dis·ci·pline /'disəplin/ ▶ **n. 1** the training of people to obey rules or a code of behavior. **2** controlled behavior resulting from such training: *he maintained discipline among his men.* **3** a branch of academic study. ▶ **v.** (**disciplines**, **disciplining**, **disciplined**) **1** train someone to be obedient or self-controlled. **2** formally punish someone for an offense. **3** (**disciplined**) behaving in a controlled way.

SYNONYMS ▶ **n. 1 control**, regulation, direction, order, authority, strictness. **2 good behavior**, order, control, obedience. **3 field (of study)**, branch of knowledge, subject, area, specialty. ▶ **v. 1 train**, drill, teach, school, coach. **2 punish**, penalize, reprimand, chastise, rebuke; informal throw the book at, call someone on the carpet.

SPELLING

There's a c in the middle: dis**c**ipline.

dis·claim /dis'klām/ ▶ **v.** refuse to acknowledge that you are responsible for or interested in something: *the school disclaimed any responsibility for the accident.*

dis·claim·er /dis'klāmər/ ▶ **n.** a statement disclaiming responsibility for something.

dis·close /dis'klōz/ ▶ **v.** (**discloses**, **disclosing**, **disclosed**) **1** make information known. **2** allow to be seen.

SYNONYMS **reveal**, make known, divulge, tell, impart, communicate, pass on, release, make public, broadcast, publish. ANTONYMS conceal.

dis·clo·sure /dis'klōzʜər/ ▶ **n. 1** the disclosing of information. **2** a secret that is disclosed.

SYNONYMS **1 revelation**, declaration, announcement, news, report, leak. **2** *the disclosure of official information* **publishing**, broadcasting, leaking, revelation, communication, release, uncovering, unveiling, exposure.

dis·co /'diskō/ (or **discotheque** /'diskəˌtek/) ▶ **n.** (plural **discos**) a club or party at which people dance to pop music.

dis·col·or /dis'kələr/ ▶ **v.** make something stained or unattractive in color.

SYNONYMS **stain**, mark, soil, dirty, streak, smear, tarnish, spoil.

■ **dis·col·or·a·tion** /-ˌkələ'rāsʜən/ **n.**

dis·com·bob·u·late /ˌdiskəm'bäbyəˌlāt/ ▶ **v.** humorous disconcert or confuse someone.

dis·com·fit /dis'kəmfit/ ▶ **v.** (**discomfits**, **discomfiting**, **discomfited**) make someone uneasy or embarrassed. ■ **dis·com·fi·ture n.**

dis·com·fort /dis'kəmfərt/ ▶ **n. 1** slight pain. **2** slight anxiety or embarrassment. ▶ **v.** cause someone discomfort.

SYNONYMS ▶ **n. 1 pain**, aches and pains, soreness, aching, twinge, pang, throb, cramp. **2 inconvenience**, difficulty, problem, trial, tribulation, hardship. **3 embarrassment**, discomfiture, unease, awkwardness, discomposure, confusion, nervousness, distress, anxiety.

dis·com·pose /ˌdiskəm'pōz/ ▶ **v.** (**discomposes**, **discomposing**, **discomposed**) make someone feel worried or disturbed.

dis·con·cert /ˌdiskən'sərt/ ▶ **v.** make someone feel worried, confused, or uneasy.

SYNONYMS (**disconcerting**) **unsettling**, unnerving, discomfiting, disturbing, perturbing, troubling, upsetting, worrying, alarming, confusing, bewildering, perplexing.

dis·con·nect /ˌdiskə'nekt/ ▶ **v. 1** break the connection between two things: *the sink should be disconnected from the drain.* **2** detach an electrical device from a power supply.

SYNONYMS **1 detach**, disengage, uncouple, unhook, unhitch, undo, unfasten, unyoke. **2 separate**, cut off, divorce, sever, isolate, dissociate, remove. **3 deactivate**, shut off, turn off, switch off, unplug. ANTONYMS attach, connect.

■ **dis·con·nec·tion n.**

dis·con·nect·ed /ˌdiskə'nektid/ ▶ **adj.** lacking a logical sequence.

dis·con·so·late /dis'känsəlit/ ▶ **adj.** very unhappy and unable to be consoled.

dis·con·tent /ˌdiskən'tent/ ▶ **n.** a feeling of unhappiness or dissatisfaction.

SYNONYMS **dissatisfaction**, disaffection, grievances, unhappiness, displeasure, resentment, envy, restlessness, unrest, unease. ANTONYMS satisfaction.

dis·con·tent·ed /ˌdiskən'tentəd/ ▶ **adj.** dissatisfied, especially with your circumstances.

SYNONYMS **dissatisfied**, disgruntled, disaffected, unhappy, aggrieved, displeased, resentful, envious, restless, frustrated; informal fed up. ANTONYMS satisfied.

■ **dis·con·tent·ment n.**

dis·con·tin·ue /ˌdiskən'tinyo͞o/ ▶ **v.** (**discontinues**, **discontinuing**, **discontinued**) stop doing, providing, or making: *he discontinued his visits.*

SYNONYMS **stop**, end, terminate, put an end/stop to, wind up, finish, call a halt to, cancel, drop, abandon, dispense with, do away with, get rid of, ax, abolish, suspend, interrupt, break off, withdraw; informal cut, pull the plug on, scrap.

■ **dis·con·tin·u·a·tion** /-ˌtinyo͞o'āsʜən/ **n.**

dis·con·tin·u·ous /ˌdiskən'tinyo͞oəs/ ▶ **adj.** having intervals or gaps; not continuous. ■ **dis·con·ti·nu·i·ty** /ˌdiskäntn'(y)o͞oitē/ **n.**

dis·cord /'diskôrd/ ▶ **n. 1** lack of agreement or harmony: *those who promote racial discord.* **2** lack of harmony between musical notes sounding together.

SYNONYMS **1 strife**, conflict, friction, hostility, antagonism, antipathy, enmity, bad feeling, ill feeling, bad blood, argument, quarreling, squabbling, bickering, wrangling, feuding, disagreement, dissension, dispute, disunity, division. **2** *the music faded in discord* **dissonance**, discordance, disharmony, cacophony. ANTONYMS accord, harmony.

dis·cord·ant /dis'kôrdnt/ ▶ **adj. 1** not in harmony or agreement: *discordant opinions*. **2** (of a sound or sounds) harsh and unpleasant.

SYNONYMS **tuneless**, inharmonious, off-key, dissonant, harsh, jarring, grating, jangly, jangling, strident, shrill, cacophonous. ANTONYMS harmonious.

dis·count ▶ **n.** /'diskount/ an amount by which the usual cost of something is reduced. ▶ **v.** /'diskount, dis'kount/ **1** reduce the usual price of something. **2** decide not to believe something because you think it is unlikely: *she'd heard rumors, but discounted them*.

SYNONYMS ▶ **n. reduction**, deduction, markdown, price cut, concession, rebate. ▶ **v. 1 disregard**, pay no attention to, take no notice of, dismiss, ignore, overlook; informal pooh-pooh. **2 reduce**, mark down, cut, lower; informal knock down.

dis·cour·age /dis'kərij, -'kə-rij/ ▶ **v.** (**discourages**, **discouraging**, **discouraged**) **1** cause someone to lose confidence or enthusiasm. **2** try to persuade someone not to do something: *we want to discourage children from smoking*.

SYNONYMS **1 dishearten**, dispirit, demoralize, disappoint, put off, unnerve, daunt, intimidate. **2** (**discouraged**) **disheartened**, dispirited, demoralized, deflated, disappointed, let down, disconsolate, despondent, dejected, cast down, downcast, crestfallen, dismayed, low-spirited, gloomy, glum, unenthusiastic, put off, daunted, intimidated, cowed, crushed; informal down in the mouth, down in the dumps, fed up, unenthused. **3 dissuade**, deter, put off, talk out of. **4 prevent**, deter, stop, avert, inhibit, curb. ANTONYMS encourage.

■ **dis·cour·age·ment n.**

dis·course ▶ **n.** /'dis,kôrs/ **1** written or spoken communication or debate. **2** a formal discussion of a topic. ▶ **v.** /dis'kôrs/ (**discourses**, **discoursing**, **discoursed**) speak or write about something with authority.

SYNONYMS ▶ **n. 1 discussion**, conversation, talk, dialogue, conference, debate, consultation, parley, powwow, chat; informal confab; formal confabulation, colloquy. **2 essay**, treatise, dissertation, paper, study, critique, monograph, disquisition, tract, lecture, address, speech, oration, sermon, homily. ▶ **v. 1 hold forth**, expatiate, pontificate, talk, give a talk, give a speech, lecture, sermonize, preach; informal spout, sound off. **2 converse**, talk, speak, debate, confer, consult, parley, chat.

dis·cour·te·ous /dis'kərtēəs/ ▶ **adj.** rude and without consideration for other people.

SYNONYMS **rude**, impolite, ill-mannered, bad-mannered, disrespectful, uncivil, ungentlemanly, unladylike, ill-bred, boorish, crass, ungracious, uncouth, insolent, impudent, impertinent, churlish, curt, brusque, blunt, abrupt, offhand, short, sharp; informal ignorant. ANTONYMS polite, courteous.

dis·cour·te·sy /dis'kərtəsē/ ▶ **n.** (plural **discourtesies**) behavior that is rude and inconsiderate.

dis·cov·er /dis'kəvər/ ▶ **v.** (**discovers**, **discovering**, **discovered**) **1** find something unexpectedly or in the course of a search. **2** gain knowledge about, or become aware of: *I am anxious to discover the truth*. **3** be the first to find or observe something.

SYNONYMS **1 find**, locate, come across/upon, stumble on, chance on, uncover, unearth, turn up. **2 find out**, learn, realize, ascertain, work out, recognize; informal figure out.

■ **dis·cov·er·er n.**

dis·cov·er·y /dis'kəvərē/ ▶ **n.** (plural **discoveries**) **1** the action of discovering. **2** a person or thing discovered.

SYNONYMS **1 finding**, location, uncovering, unearthing. **2 realization**, recognition, revelation, disclosure. **3 breakthrough**, finding, find, innovation.

dis·cred·it /dis'kredit/ ▶ **v.** (**discredits**, **discrediting**, **discredited**) **1** make someone seem less trustworthy or honorable. **2** make something seem false or unreliable: *his explanation was soon discredited*. ▶ **n.** damage to someone's reputation.

SYNONYMS ▶ **v. 1 bring into disrepute**, disgrace, dishonor, blacken the name of, show in a bad light, compromise, smear, slur, tarnish, sully. **2 disprove**, invalidate, explode, refute; informal debunk. ANTONYMS honor, prove. ▶ **n. dishonor**, disgrace, shame, humiliation, ignominy.

dis·cred·it·a·ble /dis'kreditəbəl/ ▶ **adj.** causing damage to someone's reputation; shameful.

dis·creet /dis'krēt/ ▶ **adj.** careful not to attract attention or give offense: *we made some discreet inquiries*.

SYNONYMS **tactful**, circumspect, diplomatic, judicious, sensitive, careful, cautious, strategic.

■ **dis·creet·ly adv.**

USAGE

Don't confuse **discreet** with **discrete**, which means 'separate.'

dis·crep·an·cy /dis'krepənsē/ ▶ **n.** (plural **discrepancies**) a difference between things that should be the same: *there's a discrepancy between your story and his*.

SYNONYMS **difference**, disparity, variation, deviation, divergence, disagreement, inconsistency, mismatch, conflict. ANTONYMS correspondence.

dis·crete /dis'krēt/ ▶ **adj.** separate and distinct.

dis·cre·tion /dis'kresʜən/ ▶ **n. 1** the quality of being discreet. **2** the freedom to decide what should be done in a particular situation: *scholarships will be awarded at the discretion of the committee*.

SYNONYMS **1 tact**, diplomacy, delicacy, sensitivity, good sense, prudence, circumspection. **2** *at the discretion of the council* **choice**, option, preference, disposition, pleasure, will, inclination.

dis·cre·tion·ar·y /dis'kresHə,nerē/ ▶ **adj.** done or used according to the judgment of a particular person.

dis·crim·i·nate /dis'krimə,nāt/ ▶ **v.** (**discriminates**, **discriminating**, **discriminated**) **1** recognize a difference between one thing and another. **2** treat people unfairly on the grounds of race, sex, or age.

> SYNONYMS **1 differentiate**, distinguish, draw a distinction, tell the difference, tell apart, separate. **2** *policies that* **discriminate against** *women* **be biased against**, be prejudiced against, treat differently, treat unfairly, put at a disadvantage, victimize, pick on.

dis·crim·i·nat·ing /dis'krimə,nātiNG/ ▶ **adj.** having or showing good taste or judgment.

> SYNONYMS **discerning**, perceptive, judicious, selective, tasteful, refined, sensitive, cultivated, cultured. ANTONYMS indiscriminate.

dis·crim·i·na·tion /dis,krimə'nāsHən/ ▶ **n.** **1** unfair treatment of people on the grounds of race, sex, or age. **2** recognition of the difference between one thing and another. **3** good judgment or taste.

> SYNONYMS **1 prejudice**, bias, bigotry, intolerance, favoritism, partisanship. **2 discernment**, judgment, perceptiveness, (good) taste, refinement, sensitivity, cultivation. ANTONYMS impartiality.

dis·crim·i·na·to·ry /dis'krimənə,tôrē/ ▶ **adj.** showing discrimination or prejudice.

dis·cur·sive /dis'kərsiv/ ▶ **adj.** (of writing) moving from subject to subject.

dis·cus /'diskəs/ ▶ **n.** (plural **discuses**) a heavy disk thrown in athletic contests.

dis·cuss /dis'kəs/ ▶ **v.** **1** talk about something in order to reach a decision. **2** talk or write about a topic in detail.

> SYNONYMS **1 talk over**, talk about, talk through, debate, confer about. **2 examine**, explore, study, analyze, go into, deal with, consider, tackle.

dis·cus·sion /dis'kəsHən/ ▶ **n.** **1** conversation or debate about something: *discussions about global warming.* **2** a detailed treatment of a topic in writing.

> SYNONYMS **1 conversation**, talk, chat, dialogue, conference, debate, exchange of views, consultation, deliberation; informal confab. **2 examination**, exploration, study, analysis, treatment, consideration.

dis·dain /dis'dān/ ▶ **n.** the feeling that someone or something does not deserve respect. ▶ **v.** treat with disdain.

> SYNONYMS ▶ **n. contempt**, scorn, derision, disrespect, condescension, superciliousness, hauteur, haughtiness. ANTONYMS respect. ▶ **v. scorn**, deride, regard with contempt, sneer at, look down your nose at, look down on, despise.

dis·dain·ful /dis'dānfəl/ ▶ **adj.** showing contempt or lack of respect. ■ **dis·dain·ful·ly** **adv.**

dis·ease /di'zēz/ ▶ **n.** an illness in a human, animal, or plant.

> SYNONYMS **illness**, sickness, ill health, infection, ailment, malady, disorder, condition, problem; informal bug, virus.

dis·eased /di'zēzd/ ▶ **adj.** suffering from disease.

> SYNONYMS **unhealthy**, ill, sick, unwell, ailing, infected, septic, rotten, bad.

dis·em·bark /,disem'bärk/ ▶ **v.** leave a ship, aircraft, or train. ■ **dis·em·bar·ka·tion** /dis,embär'kāsHən/ **n.**

dis·em·bod·ied /,disem'bädēd/ ▶ **adj.** **1** separated from the body, or existing without a body: *a disembodied head floating in space.* **2** (of a sound) not having any obvious physical source.

dis·em·bow·el /,disem'bouəl/ ▶ **v.** (**disembowels**, **disemboweling**, **disemboweled**) cut open and remove the internal organs of.

dis·em·pow·er /,disem'pouər/ ▶ **v.** (**disempowers**, **disempowering**, **disempowered**) make someone less powerful or confident.

dis·en·chant /,disen'cHant/ ▶ **v.** make someone disillusioned: *those who are disenchanted with science.* ■ **dis·en·chant·ment** **n.**

dis·en·fran·chise /,disen'francHīz/ ▶ **v.** (**disenfranchises**, **disenfranchising**, **disenfranchised**) **1** deprive someone of the right to vote. **2** deprive someone of a right or privilege.

dis·en·gage /,disen'gāj/ ▶ **v.** (**disengages**, **disengaging**, **disengaged**) **1** release or detach: *I disengaged his hand from mine.* **2** remove troops from an area of conflict. ■ **dis·en·gage·ment** **n.**

dis·en·tan·gle /,disen'taNGgəl/ ▶ **v.** (**disentangles**, **disentangling**, **disentangled**) stop something being tangled.

dis·es·tab·lish /,disi'stablisH/ ▶ **v.** end the official status of a national church.

dis·fa·vor /dis'fāvər/ ▶ **n.** disapproval or dislike.

dis·fig·ure /dis'figyər/ ▶ **v.** (**disfigures**, **disfiguring**, **disfigured**) spoil the appearance of.

> SYNONYMS **mar**, spoil, deface, scar, blemish, damage, mutilate, deform, maim, ruin; vandalize. ANTONYMS adorn.

■ **dis·fig·ure·ment** **n.**

dis·gorge /dis'gôrj/ ▶ **v.** (**disgorges**, **disgorging**, **disgorged**) **1** cause something to pour out: *a bus disgorged a group of youths.* **2** bring up food from the stomach.

dis·grace /dis'grās/ ▶ **n.** **1** the loss of other people's respect as the result of behaving badly. **2** a shamefully bad person or thing: *he's a disgrace to the legal profession.* ▶ **v.** (**disgraces**, **disgracing**, **disgraced**) bring disgrace to.

> SYNONYMS ▶ **n. 1 dishonor**, shame, discredit, ignominy, disrepute, infamy, scandal, stigma, humiliation, loss of face. **2 scandal**, discredit, reproach, stain, blemish, blot, black mark, outrage, affront. ANTONYMS honor, credit. ▶ **v. shame**, bring shame on, dishonor, discredit, stigmatize, taint, sully, tarnish, stain, blacken. ANTONYMS honor.

dis·grace·ful /dis'grāsfəl/ ▶ **adj.** shockingly unacceptable.

> SYNONYMS **shameful**, scandalous, contemptible, dishonorable, discreditable, disreputable, reprehensible, blameworthy, unworthy, ignoble. ANTONYMS admirable.

■ **dis·grace·ful·ly** **adv.**

dis·grun·tled /dis'grəntld/ ▶ **adj.** angry or dissatisfied.

> SYNONYMS **dissatisfied**, discontented, fed up, put out, aggrieved, resentful, displeased,

unhappy, disappointed, annoyed; informal sore, ticked off. ANTONYMS contented.

■ **dis·grun·tle·ment** n.

dis·guise /dis'gīz/ ▶ v. (**disguises, disguising, disguised**) **1** change the appearance of someone or something so they cannot be recognized: *he was disguised as a priest*. **2** hide a feeling or situation. ▶ n. **1** a way of disguising yourself. **2** the state of being disguised: *was she a man in disguise?*

SYNONYMS ▶ v. **camouflage**, conceal, hide, cover up, mask, screen, veil, paper over. ANTONYMS expose.

dis·gust /dis'gəst/ ▶ n. a strong feeling that something is unpleasant, offensive, or unacceptable. ▶ v. give someone a feeling of disgust.

SYNONYMS ▶ n. **revulsion**, repugnance, aversion, distaste, abhorrence, loathing, hatred. ANTONYMS delight. ▶ v. **revolt**, repel, repulse, sicken, nauseate, horrify, appall, shock, turn someone's stomach, scandalize, outrage, offend, affront; informal gross out. ANTONYMS delight.

dis·gust·ing /dis'gəstiNG/ ▶ adj. arousing revulsion or strong disapproval.

SYNONYMS **1** *the food was disgusting* **revolting**, repulsive, sickening, nauseating, stomach-turning; informal gross. **2** *I find racism disgusting* **outrageous**, objectionable, abhorrent, repellent, loathsome, offensive, appalling, shocking, horrifying, scandalous, monstrous, detestable; informal sick. ANTONYMS delightful.

■ **dis·gust·ing·ly** adv. **dis·gust·ing·ness** n.

dish /disH/ ▶ n. **1** a shallow container for cooking or serving food. **2** (**the dishes**) all the dishes and utensils used for a meal. **3** a particular kind of food: *a simple pork dish*. **4** a shallow concave object. **5** informal an attractive person. ▶ v. (**dish something out** or **up**) put food on to plates before a meal.

SYNONYMS ▶ n. **1 bowl**, plate, platter, salver, serving dish. **2 recipe**, meal, course, fare.

□ **dish the dirt** informal reveal or spread scandal.

dis·har·mo·ny /dis'härmənē/ ▶ n. lack of harmony.

dis·heart·en /dis'härtn/ ▶ v. make someone lose determination or confidence.

SYNONYMS **discourage**, dispirit, demoralize, cast down, depress, disappoint, dismay, put off, deter, unnerve, daunt. ANTONYMS encourage.

di·shev·eled /di'sHevəld/ ▶ adj. untidy in appearance: *a greasy, disheveled man*.

SYNONYMS **untidy**, unkempt, scruffy, messy, disarranged, rumpled, bedraggled, tousled, tangled, windswept; informal mussed (up). ANTONYMS tidy.

dis·hon·est /dis'änist/ ▶ adj. not honest, trustworthy, or sincere.

SYNONYMS **fraudulent**, cheating, underhanded/underhand, devious, treacherous, unfair, dirty, criminal, illegal, unlawful, false, untruthful, deceitful, lying, corrupt, dishonorable, untrustworthy, unscrupulous; informal crooked, shady, sharp. ANTONYMS honest.

■ **dis·hon·est·ly** adv. **dis·hon·es·ty** n.

dis·hon·or /dis'änər/ ▶ n. shame or disgrace. ▶ v. **1** bring shame or disgrace to. **2** fail to keep an agreement.

dis·hon·or·a·ble /dis'änərəbəl/ ▶ adj. bringing shame or disgrace.

SYNONYMS **disgraceful**, shameful, discreditable, ignoble, reprehensible, shabby, shoddy, despicable, contemptible, base, low.

dish·wash·er /'disH,wôsHər, -,wäsH-/ ▶ n. a machine for washing dishes automatically.

dish·y /'disHē/ ▶ adj. (**dishier, dishiest**) informal good-looking.

dis·il·lu·sion /,disə'lo͞ozHən/ ▶ v. make someone realize that a belief they hold is mistaken or unrealistic. ▶ n. disappointment caused by discovering that your beliefs are mistaken or unrealistic. ■ **dis·il·lu·sion·ment** n.

dis·in·cen·tive /,disin'sentiv/ ▶ n. a factor that discourages someone from doing a particular thing: *rising house prices are acting as a disincentive to development*.

dis·in·cli·na·tion /dis,inklə'nāsHən, dis,iNGklə-/ ▶ n. a reluctance to do something.

dis·in·clined /,disin'klīnd/ ▶ adj. reluctant; unwilling.

dis·in·fect /,disin'fekt/ ▶ v. clean with a disinfectant in order to destroy bacteria. ■ **dis·in·fec·tion** n.

dis·in·fect·ant /,disin'fektənt/ ▶ n. a chemical liquid that destroys bacteria.

dis·in·for·ma·tion /dis,infər'māsHən/ ▶ n. information that is intended to mislead people.

dis·in·gen·u·ous /,disin'jenyo͞oəs/ ▶ adj. not sincere, especially in pretending ignorance about something.

dis·in·her·it /,disin'herit/ ▶ v. (**disinherits, disinheriting, disinherited**) prevent a person from inheriting something.

dis·in·te·grate /dis'intə,grāt/ ▶ v. (**disintegrates, disintegrating, disintegrated**) break up into small parts as a result of impact or decay.

SYNONYMS **break up**, crumble, break apart, fall apart, fall to pieces, collapse, fragment, shatter, splinter.

■ **dis·in·te·gra·tion** /dis,intə'grāsHən/ n.

dis·in·ter /,disin'tər/ ▶ v. (**disinters, disinterring, disinterred**) dig up something buried.

dis·in·ter·est /dis'int(ə)rist/ ▶ n. **1** impartiality. **2** lack of interest.

dis·in·ter·est·ed /dis'intə,restid, -tristid/ ▶ adj. not influenced by personal feelings; impartial.

SYNONYMS **unbiased**, unprejudiced, impartial, neutral, detached, objective, dispassionate, nonpartisan.

USAGE

Don't confuse **disinterested** and **uninterested**. **Disinterested** means 'impartial,' while **uninterested** means 'not interested.'

dis·joint·ed /dis'jointid/ ▶ adj. not having a logical sequence or clear connection; disconnected.

dis·junc·tion /dis'jəNGksHən/ ▶ n. a difference or lack of agreement between things that you might expect to be the same: *the disjunction between what happened in France and her life at home*.

disk /disk/ (or **disc**) ▶ n. **1** a flat, thin, round object. **2** a device on which computer data is stored. **3** (**disc**) a layer of cartilage that separates vertebrae in the spine. **4** (**disc**) a compact disc or record. ◻ **disk drive** a device that allows a computer to read from and write onto computer disks. **disc** (or **disk**) **jockey** a person who introduces and plays recorded popular music, especially on radio or at a disco; a DJ.

disk·ette /dis'ket/ ▶ n. a floppy disk.

dis·like /dis'līk/ ▶ v. (**dislikes**, **disliking**, **disliked**) find someone or something unpleasant or offensive. ▶ n. **1** a feeling that someone or something is unpleasant or offensive. **2** a person or thing that you dislike.

> SYNONYMS ▶ v. **find distasteful**, regard with distaste, be averse to, have an aversion to, disapprove of, object to, take exception to, have no taste for, hate, despise. ANTONYMS like. ▶ n. **distaste**, aversion, disfavor, antipathy, disgust, abhorrence, hatred. ANTONYMS liking.

dis·lo·cate /dis'lōkāt, 'dislō,kāt/ ▶ v. (**dislocates**, **dislocating**, **dislocated**) **1** put a bone out of its proper position in a joint. **2** stop something from working properly; disrupt. ■ **dis·lo·ca·tion** /,dislō'kāsʜən/ n.

dis·lodge /dis'läj/ ▶ v. (**dislodges**, **dislodging**, **dislodged**) remove something from its position.

dis·loy·al /dis'loiəl/ ▶ adj. not loyal or faithful.

> SYNONYMS **unfaithful**, faithless, false, untrue, inconstant, two-faced, double-dealing, double-crossing, deceitful, treacherous, subversive, seditious, unpatriotic; informal backstabbing, two-timing; literary perfidious.

■ **dis·loy·al·ty** n.

dis·mal /'dizməl/ ▶ adj. **1** causing or showing gloom or depression. **2** informal disgracefully bad: *the team's dismal loss at home.*

> SYNONYMS **1** *a dismal look* **gloomy**, glum, melancholy, morose, doleful, woebegone, forlorn, dejected, downcast. **2** *a dismal hall* **dim**, dingy, dark, gloomy, dreary, drab, dull. ANTONYMS cheerful, bright.

■ **dis·mal·ly** adv.

dis·man·tle /dis'mantl/ ▶ v. (**dismantles**, **dismantling**, **dismantled**) take something to pieces.

> SYNONYMS **take apart**, take to pieces/bits, pull to pieces, disassemble, break up, strip (down). ANTONYMS build.

dis·may /dis'mā/ ▶ n. a feeling of unhappiness and discouragement. ▶ v. cause someone to feel dismay.

> SYNONYMS ▶ n. **alarm**, distress, concern, surprise, consternation, disquiet. ANTONYMS pleasure, relief. ▶ v. **concern**, distress, disturb, worry, alarm, disconcert, take aback, unnerve, unsettle. ANTONYMS encourage.

dis·mem·ber /dis'membər/ ▶ v. (**dismembers**, **dismembering**, **dismembered**) **1** tear or cut the limbs from. **2** divide up a territory or organization. ■ **dis·mem·ber·ment** n.

dis·miss /dis'mis/ ▶ v. **1** order or allow someone to leave. **2** order an employee to leave a job. **3** treat something as not being worthy of serious consideration: *the referee dismissed appeals for the goal to be disallowed.* **4** refuse to allow a legal case to continue. **5** (in sports) defeat or end an opponent's turn.

> SYNONYMS **1 give someone their notice**, discharge, lay off; informal sack, fire. **2 send away**, let go, release, disband, discharge. **3 banish**, set aside, put out of your mind, brush aside, reject, repudiate, spurn; informal pooh-pooh.

■ **dis·miss·al** n.

dis·mis·sive /dis'misiv/ ▶ adj. showing that you feel something is not worth serious consideration. ■ **dis·mis·sive·ly** adv.

dis·mount /dis'mount/ ▶ v. get off a horse or bicycle.

dis·o·be·di·ent /,disə'bēdēənt/ ▶ adj. failing or refusing to be obedient.

> SYNONYMS **naughty**, insubordinate, defiant, unruly, wayward, badly behaved, delinquent, rebellious, mutinous, troublesome, willful. ANTONYMS obedient.

■ **dis·o·be·di·ence** n.

dis·o·bey /,disə'bā/ ▶ v. fail or refuse to obey.

> SYNONYMS **defy**, go against, flout, contravene, infringe, transgress, violate, disregard, ignore, pay no heed to.

dis·or·der /dis'ôrdər/ ▶ n. **1** untidiness or disorganization. **2** the breakdown of peaceful and law-abiding behavior. **3** an illness or disease.

> SYNONYMS **1 untidiness**, mess, disarray, chaos, confusion, clutter, jumble, a muddle, a shambles. **2 unrest**, disturbance, turmoil, mayhem, violence, fighting, fracas, rioting, lawlessness, anarchy, breach of the peace. **3 disease**, infection, complaint, condition, affliction, malady, sickness, illness, ailment. ANTONYMS tidiness, peace.

■ **dis·or·dered** adj.

dis·or·der·ly /dis'ôrdərlē/ ▶ adj. **1** involving a breakdown of peaceful behavior. **2** untidy or disorganized.

> SYNONYMS **1 unruly**, riotous, disruptive, troublesome, disobedient, lawless. **2 untidy**, disorganized, topsy-turvy, at sixes and sevens, messy, jumbled, cluttered, in disarray, chaotic; informal like a bomb's hit it, higgledy-piggledy. ANTONYMS tidy, peaceful.

dis·or·gan·ized /dis'ôrgə,nīzd/ ▶ adj. **1** badly planned and controlled. **2** not able to plan your activities efficiently.

> SYNONYMS **unmethodical**, unsystematic, undisciplined, unstructured, haphazard, chaotic, muddled, hit-or-miss, sloppy, slapdash, slipshod. ANTONYMS organized.

■ **dis·or·gan·i·za·tion** /-,ôrgənə'zāsʜən/ n.

dis·o·ri·ent /dis'ôrē,ent/ (or **disorientate** /dis'ôrēən,tāt/) ▶ v. (**disorients**, **disorienting**, **disoriented**) make someone lose their bearings or feel confused. ■ **dis·o·ri·en·ta·tion** /dis,ôrēən'tāsʜən/ n.

dis·own /dis'ōn/ ▶ v. show or decide that you no longer want to have anything to do with someone.

> SYNONYMS **reject**, cast off/aside, abandon, renounce, repudiate, deny, turn your back on, wash your hands of, disinherit.

dis·par·age /di'sparij/ ▶ v. (**disparages**, **disparaging**, **disparaged**) speak critically or negatively about.

SYNONYMS **belittle**, denigrate, deprecate, play down, trivialize, ridicule, deride, demean, mock, scorn, scoff at, sneer at, run down, defame, slur, discredit, speak badly of, cast aspersions on, impugn, vilify, traduce, criticize; informal knock, slam, pan, bad-mouth, pooh-pooh. ANTONYMS praise.

dis·pa·rate /'dispərit, di'sparit/ ▶ **adj.** **1** very different from one another. **2** containing elements that are very different from one another: *a culturally disparate country.*

dis·par·i·ty /di'sparitē/ ▶ **n.** (plural **disparities**) a great difference.

SYNONYMS **discrepancy**, inconsistency, imbalance, variance, variation, divergence, gap, gulf, difference, dissimilarity, contrast. ANTONYMS similarity.

dis·pas·sion·ate /dis'pasHənit/ ▶ **adj.** not influenced by strong feelings; impartial. ■ **dis·pas·sion·ate·ly adv.**

dis·patch /dis'pacH/ (or **despatch**) ▶ **v.** **1** send to a destination, especially for a particular purpose. **2** send a letter or parcel somewhere. **3** deal with a task or problem quickly and efficiently. **4** kill a person or animal. ▶ **n.** **1** the action of dispatching. **2** a report on the latest situation in state or military affairs. **3** speed and efficiency: *proceed with dispatch.*

SYNONYMS ▶ **v.** **1 send (off)**, post, mail, forward. **2 deal with**, finish, conclude, settle, discharge, perform. **3 kill**, put to death, massacre, wipe out, exterminate, eliminate, murder, assassinate, execute. ▶ **n.** **message**, report, communication, communiqué, bulletin, statement, letter, news, intelligence.

dis·patch·er /dis'pacHər/ ▶ **n.** a person who works in communications, sending and receiving information to and from police, firefighters, train stations, trucking companies, etc.

dis·pel /dis'pel/ ▶ **v.** (**dispels**, **dispelling**, **dispelled**) make a doubt, feeling, or belief disappear.

SYNONYMS **banish**, drive away/off, chase away, scatter, eliminate, dismiss, allay, ease, quell.

dis·pen·sa·ble /dis'pensəbəl/ ▶ **adj.** able to be replaced or done without.

dis·pen·sa·ry /dis'pensərē/ ▶ **n.** (plural **dispensaries**) a room where medicines are prepared and provided.

dis·pen·sa·tion /ˌdispən'sāsHən, -pen-/ ▶ **n.** **1** special permission not to obey a rule. **2** a system of order, government, or organization of a nation, community, etc., of a particular time: *the capitalist dispensation.* **3** the action of dispensing.

dis·pense /dis'pens/ ▶ **v.** (**dispenses**, **dispensing**, **dispensed**) **1** distribute something to a number of people. **2** (of a pharmacist) prepare and supply medicine according to a prescription. **3** (**dispense with**) get rid of or manage without.

SYNONYMS **1 distribute**, pass around, hand out, dole out, dish out, share out. **2 administer**, deliver, issue, deal out, mete out. **3** *dispensing medicines* **prepare**, make up, supply, provide.

■ **dis·pens·er n.**

dis·perse /dis'pərs/ ▶ **v.** (**disperses**, **dispersing**, **dispersed**) **1** move apart and go in different directions: *the crowd dispersed.* **2** (of gas, smoke, etc.) thin out and eventually disappear.

SYNONYMS **1 break up**, split up, disband, scatter, leave, go their separate ways, drive away/off, chase away. **2 dissipate**, dissolve, melt away, fade away, clear, lift. **3 scatter**, distribute, spread, disseminate. ANTONYMS assemble, gather.

■ **dis·per·sal** /dis'pərsəl/ **n.** **dis·per·sion** /dis'pərzHən, -sHən/ **n.**

dis·pir·it·ed /di'spiritid/ ▶ **adj.** discouraged or depressed. ■ **dis·pir·it·ing adj.**

dis·place /dis'plās/ ▶ **v.** (**displaces**, **displacing**, **displaced**) **1** move something from its proper or usual position. **2** take over the position or role of: *machines are coming along to displace the typists.* **3** force someone to leave their home.

SYNONYMS **1 dislodge**, dislocate, move out of place/position, shift. **2 replace**, take the place of, supplant, supersede, oust, remove, depose.

dis·place·ment /dis'plāsmənt/ ▶ **n.** **1** the action of displacing something, or the amount by which something is displaced. **2** the volume or weight of water displaced by a floating ship, used as a measure of the ship's size.

dis·play /dis'plā/ ▶ **v.** **1** put something on show in a noticeable and attractive way. **2** show a quality or feeling: *both players displayed a great deal of spirit.* **3** show data or an image on a screen. ▶ **n.** **1** a performance, show, or event for public entertainment. **2** the displaying of a quality or feeling: *she was embarrassed at this display of emotion.* **3** a collection of objects being displayed. **4** the data or image shown on a screen.

SYNONYMS ▶ **v.** **1 exhibit**, show, arrange, array, present, lay out, set out. **2 show off**, parade, highlight, reveal, showcase. **3 manifest**, be evidence of, reveal, demonstrate, show. ANTONYMS conceal. ▶ **n.** **1 exhibition**, exposition, array, arrangement, presentation, demonstration, spectacle, show, parade. **2 manifestation**, expression, show, proof, demonstration, evidence.

dis·please /dis'plēz/ ▶ **v.** (**displeases**, **displeasing**, **displeased**) annoy or upset.

SYNONYMS **annoy**, irritate, anger, incense, irk, vex, nettle, put out, upset, exasperate.

dis·pleas·ure /dis'plezHər/ ▶ **n.** annoyance or dissatisfaction.

dis·port /dis'pôrt/ ▶ **v.** (**disport yourself**) old use enjoy yourself in an unrestrained way.

dis·pos·a·ble /dis'pōzəbəl/ ▶ **adj.** **1** intended to be used once and then thrown away. **2** (of money) available to be used.

dis·pos·al /dis'pōzəl/ ▶ **n.** the action of disposing of something. □ **at your disposal** available to be used whenever or however you wish.

dis·pose /dis'pōz/ ▶ **v.** (**disposes**, **disposing**, **disposed**) **1** (**dispose of**) get rid of. **2** (**be disposed to**) be inclined to do or think something: *I was disposed to quarrel with this.* **3** (**disposed**) having a particular attitude: *they were favorably disposed towards him.* **4** arrange something in a particular position.

SYNONYMS (**dispose of**) **throw away**, throw out, get rid of, discard, jettison, scrap; informal dump, trash, junk, ditch.

dis·po·si·tion /ˌdispə'zisHən/ ▶ **n.** **1** the natural qualities of a person's character: *a lady of a kindly disposition.* **2** an inclination or tendency. **3** the way in which something is arranged.

> SYNONYMS **1 temperament**, nature, character, constitution, makeup, mentality. **2 arrangement**, positioning, placement, configuration, setup, lineup, layout.

dis·pos·sess /ˌdispəˈzes/ ▶ **v.** deprive someone of a possession. ■ **dis·pos·ses·sion n.**

dis·pro·por·tion·ate /ˌdisprəˈpôrsʜənit/ ▶ **adj.** too large or too small in comparison with something else. ■ **dis·pro·por·tion·ate·ly adv.**

dis·prove /disˈpro͞ov/ ▶ **v.** (**disproves**, **disproving**, **disproved**) prove something to be false.

> SYNONYMS **refute**, prove false, rebut, debunk, invalidate, demolish; informal shoot full of holes, blow out of the water.

dis·pu·ta·tion /ˌdispyo͝oˈtāsʜən/ ▶ **n.** debate or argument.

dis·pu·ta·tious /ˌdispyo͝oˈtāsʜəs/ ▶ **adj.** fond of arguing.

dis·pute /disˈpyo͞ot/ ▶ **v.** (**disputes**, **disputing**, **disputed**) **1** argue about. **2** question whether something is true or valid. **3** compete for: *the drivers crashed while disputing the lead.* ▶ **n.** an argument or disagreement.

> SYNONYMS ▶ **v. 1 debate**, discuss, exchange views, quarrel, argue, disagree, clash, fall out, wrangle, bicker, squabble. **2 challenge**, contest, question, call into question, quibble over, contradict, argue about, disagree with, take issue with. ANTONYMS accept. ▶ **n. 1 debate**, discussion, argument, controversy, disagreement, dissent, conflict. **2 quarrel**, argument, altercation, squabble, falling-out, disagreement, difference of opinion, clash. ANTONYMS agreement.

■ **dis·put·a·ble adj.**

dis·qual·i·fy /disˈkwäləˌfī/ ▶ **v.** (**disqualifies**, **disqualifying**, **disqualified**) prevent someone performing an activity or taking an office because they have broken a rule or are not suitable.

> SYNONYMS **rule out**, bar, exclude, prohibit, debar, preclude.

■ **dis·qual·i·fi·ca·tion** /disˌkwäləfiˈkāsʜən/ **n.**

dis·qui·et /disˈkwī-it/ ▶ **n.** a feeling of anxiety. ■ **dis·qui·et·ing adj.**

dis·qui·si·tion /ˌdiskwəˈzisʜən/ ▶ **n.** a long or complex discussion of a topic.

dis·re·gard /ˌdisriˈgärd/ ▶ **v.** pay no attention to. ▶ **n.** the action of disregarding something: *his disregard for truth.*

> SYNONYMS ▶ **v. ignore**, take no notice of, pay no attention to, discount, overlook, turn a blind eye to, shut your eyes to, gloss over, brush off/aside, shrug off. ANTONYMS heed. ▶ **n. indifference**, nonobservance, inattention, heedlessness, neglect, contempt. ANTONYMS attention.

dis·re·pair /ˌdisriˈpe(ə)r/ ▶ **n.** (**in disrepair**) in a bad condition as a result of being neglected.

dis·rep·u·ta·ble /disˈrepyətəbəl/ ▶ **adj.** not respectable in appearance or character.

> SYNONYMS **bad**, unwholesome, villainous, unsavory, slippery, seedy, sleazy; informal crooked, shady, shifty. ANTONYMS respectable.

dis·re·pute /ˌdisrəˈpyo͞ot/ ▶ **n.** the state of having a bad reputation.

dis·re·spect /ˌdisriˈspekt/ ▶ **n.** lack of respect or courtesy. ■ **dis·re·spect·ful adj. dis·re·spect·ful·ly adv.**

dis·robe /disˈrōb/ ▶ **v.** (**disrobes**, **disrobing**, **disrobed**) take off your clothes.

dis·rupt /disˈrəpt/ ▶ **v.** interrupt or disturb an activity or process.

> SYNONYMS **interrupt**, disturb, interfere with, play havoc with, upset, unsettle, obstruct, impede, hold up, delay.

■ **dis·rup·tion n.**

dis·rup·tive /disˈrəptiv/ ▶ **adj.** causing disruption.

> SYNONYMS **troublesome**, disturbing, upsetting, unsettling, unruly, badly behaved, rowdy, disorderly, undisciplined, unmanageable, uncontrollable, uncooperative. ANTONYMS well behaved.

dis·sat·is·fac·tion /disˌsatisˈfaksʜən/ ▶ **n.** lack of satisfaction.

dis·sat·is·fied /disˈsatisˌfīd/ ▶ **adj.** not content or happy.

> SYNONYMS **discontented**, disappointed, disaffected, displeased, disgruntled, aggrieved, unhappy. ANTONYMS contented.

dis·sect /diˈsekt, dī-/ ▶ **v. 1** cut up the dead body of a person or animal to study its internal parts. **2** analyze in great detail. ■ **dis·sec·tion n.**

> SPELLING
>
> **Dissect** has a double **s**.

dis·sem·ble /diˈsembəl/ ▶ **v.** (**dissembles**, **dissembling**, **dissembled**) hide or disguise your motives or feelings.

dis·sem·i·nate /diˈseməˌnāt/ ▶ **v.** (**disseminates**, **disseminating**, **disseminated**) spread information widely. ■ **dis·sem·i·na·tion** /-ˌseməˈnāsʜən/ **n.**

dis·sen·sion /diˈsensʜən/ ▶ **n.** disagreement that causes trouble within a group.

dis·sent /diˈsent/ ▶ **v. 1** express disagreement with a widely held view. **2** disagree with the doctrine of an established church. **3** (in sports) disagree with the referee's decision. ▶ **n.** disagreement with a widely held view.

> SYNONYMS ▶ **v. disagree**, differ, demur, be at variance/odds, take issue, protest, object. ANTONYMS agree, conform. ▶ **n. disagreement**, difference of opinion, argument, dispute, resistance, objection, protest, opposition. ANTONYMS agreement, conformity.

■ **dis·sent·er n.**

dis·ser·ta·tion /ˌdisərˈtāsʜən/ ▶ **n.** a long essay, especially one written for the Doctor of Philosophy (PhD) degree.

dis·serv·ice /disˈsərvis/ ▶ **n.** a harmful action.

dis·si·dent /ˈdisidənt/ ▶ **n.** a person who opposes official policy. ▶ **adj.** opposing official policy.

> SYNONYMS ▶ **n. dissenter**, objector, protester, rebel, revolutionary, subversive, agitator, refusenik. ANTONYMS conformist. ▶ **adj. dissenting**, opposing, objecting, protesting, rebellious, revolutionary, subversive, nonconformist. ANTONYMS conformist.

■ **dis·si·dence n.**

dis·sim·i·lar /dis'similər/ ▶ **adj.** not similar; different.

SYNONYMS **different**, differing, unalike, variant, diverse, divergent, heterogeneous, disparate, unrelated, distinct, contrasting.

■ **dis·sim·i·lar·i·ty** /-ˌsimə'laritē/ **n.**

dis·sim·u·late /di'simyəˌlāt/ ▶ **v.** (**dissimulates, dissimulating, dissimulated**) hide or disguise your thoughts or feelings. ■ **dis·sim·u·la·tion** /-ˌsimyə'lāsʜən/ **n.**

dis·si·pate /'disəˌpāt/ ▶ **v.** (**dissipates, dissipating, dissipated**) **1** disappear or disperse: *the steam dissipated in the air.* **2** waste money, energy, or resources. **3** (**dissipated**) indulging too much in alcohol and other physical pleasures. ■ **dis·si·pa·tion** /ˌdisə'pāsʜən/ **n.**

SPELLING

Write two **s**'s, one **p**: dissipate.

dis·so·ci·ate /di'sōsʜēˌāt, -'sōsē-/ (or **disassociate** /ˌdisə'sōsʜēˌāt, -'sōsē-/) ▶ **v.** (**dissociates, dissociating, dissociated**) **1** disconnect or separate. **2** (**dissociate yourself from**) say publicly that you are not connected with.

SYNONYMS **separate**, detach, disconnect, sever, cut off, divorce, isolate, alienate. ANTONYMS associate.

■ **dis·so·ci·a·tion** /diˌsōsē'āsʜən/ **n.**

dis·so·lute /'disəˌlo͞ot/ ▶ **adj.** indulging too much in physical pleasures.

dis·so·lu·tion /ˌdisə'lo͞osʜən/ ▶ **n. 1** the formal closing down or ending of an official body or agreement. **2** the action of dissolving or decomposing.

dis·solve /di'zälv/ ▶ **v.** (**dissolves, dissolving, dissolved**) **1** (of a solid) mix with a liquid and form a solution. **2** close down or end an assembly or agreement. **3** (**dissolve into** or **in**) give way to strong emotion.

SYNONYMS **1 break down**, liquefy, melt, deliquesce, disintegrate. **2 disband**, disperse, bring to an end, end, terminate, discontinue, break up, close down, wind up/down, suspend, adjourn. **3 annul**, nullify, void, invalidate, revoke.

dis·so·nant /'disənənt/ ▶ **adj.** without harmony; discordant.

SYNONYMS **inharmonious**, discordant, unmelodious, atonal, off-key, cacophonous. ANTONYMS harmonious.

■ **dis·so·nance** **n.**

dis·suade /di'swād/ ▶ **v.** (**dissuades, dissuading, dissuaded**) persuade or advise someone not to do something: *they tried to dissuade him from going.*

SYNONYMS **discourage**, deter, prevent, stop, talk out of, persuade against, advise against, argue out of. ANTONYMS encourage.

■ **dis·sua·sion** **n.**

dis·taff /'distaf/ ▶ **n.** a stick or spindle on to which wool or flax is wound for spinning. □ **distaff side** the female side of a family.

dis·tance /'distəns/ ▶ **n. 1** the length of the space between two points: *I bicycled the short distance home.* **2** the state of being distant. **3** a far-off point or place: *she watched from a distance.* **4** the full length or time of a race. ▶ **v.** (**distances, distancing, distanced**) (**distance yourself**) become less friendly or supportive.

SYNONYMS ▶ **n. 1 interval**, space, span, gap, extent, length, range, reach. **2 aloofness**, remoteness, detachment, unfriendliness, reserve, reticence, formality; informal standoffishness. ANTONYMS proximity.

□ **distance learning** a method of studying in which lessons are conducted by correspondence or over the Internet.

dis·tant /'distənt/ ▶ **adj. 1** far away in space or time. **2** at a specified distance: *the star is 15 light years distant from Earth.* **3** far apart in terms of resemblance or relationship: *a distant acquaintance.* **4** aloof or reserved.

SYNONYMS **1 faraway**, far-off, far-flung, remote, out of the way, outlying. **2 bygone**, remote, ancient, prehistoric. **3 vague**, faint, dim, indistinct, sketchy, hazy. **4 aloof**, reserved, remote, detached, unapproachable, unfriendly; informal standoffish. **5 distracted**, absent, faraway, detached, vague. ANTONYMS near, close, recent.

■ **dis·tant·ly** **adv.**

dis·taste /dis'tāst/ ▶ **n.** the feeling that something is unpleasant or offensive.

dis·taste·ful /dis'tāstˌfəl/ ▶ **adj.** unpleasant or disliked.

SYNONYMS **unpleasant**, disagreeable, displeasing, undesirable, objectionable, offensive, unsavory, unpalatable. ANTONYMS agreeable.

■ **dis·taste·ful·ly** **adv.**

dis·tem·per /dis'tempər/ ▶ **n. 1** a kind of paint using glue or size instead of an oil base, used on walls or for scene-painting. **2** a viral disease of dogs, causing fever and coughing.

dis·tend /dis'tend/ ▶ **v.** swell because of internal pressure. ■ **dis·ten·sion** **n.**

dis·tend·ed /dis'tendid/ ▶ **adj.** swollen because of pressure from inside.

dis·till /dis'til/ ▶ **v.** (**distills, distilling, distilled**) **1** purify a liquid by heating it until it vaporizes, then condensing the vapor and collecting the resulting liquid. **2** make liquor such as whiskey in this way. **3** extract the most important aspects of: *my notes were distilled into a book.* ■ **dis·till·er** **n.** **dis·til·la·tion** /ˌdistə'lāsʜən/ **n.**

dis·till·er·y /dis'tilərē/ ▶ **n.** (plural **distilleries**) a factory that makes liquor.

dis·tinct /dis'tiɴɢkt/ ▶ **adj. 1** recognizably different: *there are two distinct types of the disease.* **2** able to be perceived clearly by the senses.

SYNONYMS **1** *two distinct categories* **discrete**, separate, different, unconnected, distinctive, contrasting. **2** *the tail has distinct black tips* **clear**, well-defined, unmistakable, easily distinguishable, recognizable, visible, obvious, pronounced, prominent, striking. ANTONYMS similar.

dis·tinc·tion /dis'tiɴɢksʜən/ ▶ **n. 1** a noticeable difference. **2** outstanding excellence. **3** a special honor or recognition.

SYNONYMS **1 difference**, contrast, variation, division, differentiation, discrepancy. **2 merit**, worth, greatness, excellence, quality, repute, renown, honor, credit. ANTONYMS similarity.

dis·tinc·tive /dis'tiNGktiv/ ▶ **adj.** characteristic of a person or thing and distinguishing them from others: *the car's distinctive design.*

SYNONYMS **distinguishing**, characteristic, typical, individual, particular, peculiar, unique, exclusive, special. ANTONYMS common.

■ **dis·tinc·tive·ly adv.**

dis·tinct·ly /dis'tiNGktlē/ ▶ **adv.** in a distinct way.

SYNONYMS **1 decidedly**, markedly, definitely, unmistakably, manifestly, patently. **2 clearly**, plainly, intelligibly, audibly.

dis·tin·guish /dis'tiNGgwisH/ ▶ **v. 1** recognize the difference between two people or things: *she can distinguish reality from fantasy.* **2** manage to see or hear. **3** be a characteristic that makes two people or things different: *what distinguishes friendship from love?* **4** (**distinguish yourself**) do something very well.

SYNONYMS **1 differentiate**, tell apart, discriminate between, tell the difference between. **2 discern**, see, perceive, make out, detect, recognize, identify. **3 separate**, set apart, make distinctive, make different, single out, mark off.

■ **dis·tin·guish·a·ble adj.**

dis·tin·guished /dis'tiNGgwisHt/ ▶ **adj. 1** successful and greatly respected. **2** having a dignified appearance.

SYNONYMS **eminent**, famous, renowned, prominent, well-known, great, esteemed, respected, notable, illustrious, acclaimed, celebrated. ANTONYMS unknown, obscure.

dis·tort /dis'tôrt/ ▶ **v. 1** pull or twist out of shape. **2** give a misleading account of.

SYNONYMS **1** (**distorted**) **twisted**, warped, contorted, buckled, deformed, malformed, misshapen, disfigured, crooked, out of shape. **2** (**distorted**) **misrepresented**, perverted, twisted, falsified, misreported, misstated, garbled, inaccurate, biased, prejudiced.

■ **dis·tor·tion n.**

dis·tract /dis'trakt/ ▶ **v. 1** prevent someone from giving their full attention to something. **2** take attention away from something.

SYNONYMS **divert**, sidetrack, draw away, lead astray, disturb, put off.

dis·tract·ed /dis'traktid/ ▶ **adj.** unable to concentrate on something.

SYNONYMS **preoccupied**, inattentive, vague, abstracted, absentminded, faraway, in a world of your own, troubled, harassed, worried; informal miles away, not with it. ANTONYMS attentive.

dis·trac·tion /dis'traksHən/ ▶ **n. 1** a thing that distracts someone's attention. **2** something that provides entertainment. **3** the state of being distracted.

SYNONYMS **1 diversion**, interruption, disturbance, interference. **2 amusement**, entertainment, diversion, recreation, pastime, leisure pursuit.

dis·traught /dis'trôt/ ▶ **adj.** very worried and upset.

SYNONYMS **distressed**, frantic, fraught, overcome, overwrought, beside yourself, out of your mind, desperate, hysterical, worked up, at one's wits' end; informal in a state. ANTONYMS calm.

dis·tress /dis'tres/ ▶ **n. 1** extreme unhappiness, pain, or suffering. **2** the state of a ship or aircraft when in danger or difficulty. ▶ **v.** cause distress to.

SYNONYMS ▶ **n. 1 anguish**, suffering, pain, agony, torment, heartache, heartbreak, sorrow, sadness, unhappiness. **2** *a ship in distress* **danger**, peril, difficulty, trouble, jeopardy, risk. ANTONYMS happiness. ▶ **v. upset**, pain, trouble, worry, perturb, disturb, disquiet, agitate, torment. ANTONYMS comfort.

dis·trib·ute /dis'tribyo͞ot/ ▶ **v.** (**distributes**, **distributing**, **distributed**) **1** hand or share out to a number of people. **2** (**be distributed**) be spread over an area. **3** supply goods to retailers.

SYNONYMS **1 give out**, deal out, pass out/around, dole out, dish out, hand out/around, share out, divide out/up, parcel out, apportion, allocate, allot. **2** *the newsletter is distributed free* **circulate**, issue, deliver, disseminate, publish. ANTONYMS collect.

dis·tri·bu·tion /ˌdistrə'byo͞osHən/ ▶ **n. 1** the action of distributing. **2** the way in which something is distributed: *the bird has a worldwide distribution.*

SYNONYMS **1** *the distribution of aid* **giving out**, dealing out, doling out, handing out/around, issuing, allocation, sharing out, dividing up/out, parceling out. **2** *centers of food distribution* **supply**, delivery, dispersal, transportation.

dis·trib·u·tor /dis'tribyətər/ ▶ **n. 1** a company that supplies goods to retailers. **2** a device in a gas engine for passing electric current to each spark plug in turn.

dis·trict /'distrikt/ ▶ **n.** a particular area of a town or region: *the heart of the banking district.*

SYNONYMS **area**, region, quarter, sector, zone, territory, locality, neighborhood, community.

□ **district attorney** a public official who acts as prosecutor for the state or the federal government in court in a particular district.

dis·trust /dis'trəst/ ▶ **n.** lack of trust. ▶ **v.** have little trust in.

SYNONYMS ▶ **n. mistrust**, suspicion, wariness, skepticism, doubt, cynicism, misgivings, qualms. ANTONYMS trust. ▶ **v. mistrust**, be suspicious of, be wary of, regard with suspicion, suspect, be skeptical of, question, doubt, be unsure of/about, have misgivings about. ANTONYMS trust.

■ **dis·trust·ful adj.**

dis·turb /dis'tərb/ ▶ **v. 1** interrupt the sleep, relaxation, or privacy of. **2** move something from its normal position: *do not disturb anything at the scene of the crime.* **3** make someone anxious. **4** (**disturbed**) having emotional or mental problems.

SYNONYMS **1 interrupt**, intrude on, butt in on, barge in on, distract, disrupt, bother, trouble, pester, harass. **2** (**disturbed**) *disturbed sleep* **disrupted**, interrupted, fitful, intermittent, broken. **3 move**, rearrange, mix up, interfere with, mess up. **4 perturb**, trouble, concern, worry, upset, fluster, disconcert, dismay, alarm, distress, unsettle. **5** (**disturbed**) **troubled**, distressed, upset, distraught, unbalanced, unstable, disordered, dysfunctional, maladjusted, neurotic, unhinged; informal screwed up. ANTONYMS calm, reassure.

dis·tur·bance /dis'tərbəns/ ▶ **n. 1** the interruption of a normal or settled condition. **2** a riot or other breakdown of peaceful behavior.

SYNONYMS **1 disruption**, distraction, interference, inconvenience, upset, annoyance, irritation, intrusion. **2 riot**, fracas, brawl, street fight, free-for-all, commotion, disorder. ANTONYMS order.

dis·u·nit·ed /ˌdisyo͞o'nītid/ ▶ **adj.** not united. ■ **dis·u·ni·ty** /dis'yo͞onitē/ **n.**

dis·use /dis'yo͞os/ ▶ **n.** the state of not being used; neglect. ■ **dis·used** /dis'yo͞ozd/ **adj.**

ditch /dich/ ▶ **n.** a narrow channel dug to hold or carry water. ▶ **v. 1** informal abandon or get rid of. **2** (of an aircraft) come down in a forced landing on the sea.

SYNONYMS ▶ **n. trench**, trough, channel, dike, drain, gutter, gully, watercourse.

dith·er /'diT͟Hər/ ▶ **v.** (**dithers**, **dithering**, **dithered**) be indecisive.

dit·to /'ditō/ ▶ **n. 1** the same thing again (used in lists). **2** a symbol consisting of two apostrophes (〃) placed under the item to be repeated.

dit·ty /'ditē/ ▶ **n.** (plural **ditties**) a short, simple song.

ditz /dits/ ▶ **n.** informal a scatterbrained person. ■ **ditz·i·ness n. ditz·zy adj.**

di·u·ret·ic /ˌdīyə'retik/ ▶ **adj.** (of a drug or natural substance) making you pass more urine.

di·ur·nal /dī'ərnl/ ▶ **adj. 1** relating to or during the daytime. **2** daily.

di·va /'dēvə/ ▶ **n. 1** a famous female opera singer. **2** a haughty, spoiled woman.

di·van /di'van, 'dīˌvan/ ▶ **n. 1** a long, low sofa without a back or arms. **2** (formerly) a legislative body, council, or court in some Middle Eastern countries.

dive /dīv/ ▶ **v.** (**dives**, **diving**, **dived**; past and past participle also **dove** /dōv/) **1** plunge head first into water. **2** (of a submarine or swimmer) go under water. **3** plunge steeply downward through the air. **4** move quickly or suddenly in a downward direction or under cover: *he dived into an office building to avoid the man following him.* ▶ **n. 1** an act of diving. **2** informal a disreputable nightclub or bar.

SYNONYMS ▶ **v. 1 plunge**, plummet, nosedive, jump, fall, drop, pitch. **2 leap**, jump, lunge, throw/fling yourself, go headlong. ▶ **n. 1 plunge**, nosedive, jump, fall, drop, swoop. **2 lunge**, spring, jump, leap.

□ **dive-bomb** bomb a target while diving steeply in an aircraft. **diving bell** an open-bottomed chamber supplied with air, in which a person can be let down under water. **diving board** a board projecting over a swimming pool, from which people dive in. **diving suit** a watertight suit with a helmet and an air supply, worn for working or exploring deep under water.

div·er /'dīvər/ ▶ **n. 1** a person who dives under water. **2** a large diving waterbird.

di·verge /di'vərj, dī-/ ▶ **v.** (**diverges**, **diverging**, **diverged**) **1** (of a route or line) separate from another route and go in a different direction. **2** be different: *I diverged from my prepared remarks.*

SYNONYMS **1 separate**, part, fork, divide, split, bifurcate, go in different directions. **2 differ**, be different, be dissimilar, disagree, be at variance/odds, conflict, clash. ANTONYMS converge, agree.

■ **di·ver·gence n. di·ver·gent adj.**

di·vers /'dīvərz/ ▶ **adj.** old use various; several: *in divers places.*

di·verse /di'vərs, dī-/ ▶ **adj.** widely varied.

SYNONYMS **various**, sundry, varied, varying, miscellaneous, assorted, mixed, diversified, divergent, different, differing, distinct, unlike, dissimilar. ANTONYMS similar.

di·ver·si·fy /di'vərsiˌfī, dī-/ ▶ **v.** (**diversifies**, **diversifying**, **diversified**) **1** make or become more varied. **2** (of a company) expand its range of products or area of operation. ■ **di·ver·si·fi·ca·tion** /-ˌvərsifi'kāshən/ **n.**

di·ver·sion /di'vərZHən, dī-/ ▶ **n. 1** the action of diverting something from its course: *the diversion of the country's largest river.* **2** something intended to distract attention. **3** a pastime or other pleasant activity.

SYNONYMS **1 detour**, deviation, alternative route, rerouting, redirection. **2 distraction**, disturbance, smokescreen; informal red herring. **3 entertainment**, amusement, pastime, delight, fun, recreation, pleasure.

■ **di·ver·sion·ar·y adj.**

di·ver·si·ty /di'vərsitē, dī-/ ▶ **n.** (plural **diversities**) **1** the state of being varied. **2** a range of different things.

SYNONYMS **variety**, miscellany, assortment, mixture, mix, range, array, multiplicity, variation, difference. ANTONYMS uniformity.

di·vert /di'vərt, dī-/ ▶ **v. 1** change the direction or course of: *a ditch designed to divert flood waters around the city.* **2** distract a person or their attention. **3** amuse or entertain.

SYNONYMS **1 reroute**, redirect, change the course of, deflect, channel. **2 distract**, sidetrack, disturb, draw away, put off. **3 amuse**, entertain, distract, delight, enchant, interest, fascinate, absorb, engross, rivet, grip.

di·ver·tisse·ment /di'vərtismənt/ ▶ **n.** a minor entertainment.

di·vest /di'vest, dī-/ ▶ **v. 1** (**divest someone/thing of**) deprive someone or something of: *they are unlikely to be divested of power.* **2** (**divest yourself of**) remove or get rid of.

di·vide /di'vīd/ ▶ **v.** (**divides**, **dividing**, **divided**) **1** separate into parts. **2** share out. **3** cause disagreement between people or groups: *the question had divided New Yorkers for years.* **4** form a boundary between. **5** find how many times one number contains another. ▶ **n.** a difference or disagreement between two groups: *the North-South divide.*

SYNONYMS ▶ **v. 1** *he divided his land among his heirs* **split** (**up**), cut up, carve up, dissect, bisect, halve, quarter. **2 share**, ration out, parcel out, deal out, dole out, dish out, distribute. **3 disunite**, drive apart, drive a wedge between, break up, split (up), separate, isolate, alienate. **4** *a curtain divided her cabin from the galley* **separate**, segregate, partition, screen off, section off, split off. **5 diverge**, separate, part, branch (off), fork, split (in two). ANTONYMS unify, converge, unite.

div·i·dend /ˈdiviˌdend/ ▶ **n. 1** a sum of money that is divided among a number of people, such as the part of a company's profits paid to its shareholders. **2** (**dividends**) benefits: *persistence pays dividends*.

di·vid·er /diˈvīdər/ ▶ **n. 1** a person or thing that divides a whole into parts. **2** a screen that divides a room into separate parts. **3** (**dividers**) a measuring compass.

div·i·na·tion /ˌdivəˈnāsʜən/ ▶ **n.** the use of supernatural means to find out about the future or the unknown.

di·vine[1] /diˈvīn/ ▶ **adj. 1** having to do with God or a god: *divine forces*. **2** informal excellent.

SYNONYMS **godly**, angelic, heavenly, celestial, holy, sacred. ANTONYMS mortal.

■ **di·vine·ly adv.**

di·vine[2] ▶ **v.** (**divines**, **divining**, **divined**) **1** discover by guesswork or intuition. **2** have supernatural insight into the future. **3** discover water by dowsing.

SYNONYMS **guess**, surmise, deduce, infer, discern, discover, perceive; informal **figure** (**out**).

■ **di·vin·er n.**

di·vin·i·ty /diˈvinitē/ ▶ **n.** (plural **divinities**) **1** the state of being divine. **2** a god or goddess. **3** the study of religion; theology.

di·vis·i·ble /diˈvizəbəl/ ▶ **adj. 1** capable of being divided. **2** (of a number) containing another number a number of times without a remainder.

di·vi·sion /diˈvizʜən/ ▶ **n. 1** the action of dividing, or the state of being divided. **2** each of the parts into which something is divided. **3** a major section of an organization. **4** a number of sports teams or competitors grouped to compete against each other. **5** a partition.

SYNONYMS **1** *the division of the island* **dividing** (**up**), breaking up, break-up, carving up, splitting, dissection, partitioning, separation, segregation. **2** *the division of his estates* **dividing up**, sharing, parceling out, dishing out, allocation, allotment, splitting up, carving up. **3 dividing line**, divide, boundary, border, demarcation line, gap, gulf. **4 section**, subsection, subdivision, category, class, group, grouping, set. **5 department**, branch, arm, wing. **6 disunity**, disunion, conflict, discord, disagreement, alienation, isolation. ANTONYMS unification.

□ **division sign** the sign ÷, placed between two numbers showing that the first is to be divided by the second, as in *6 ÷ 3 = 2*. ■ **di·vi·sion·al adj.**

di·vi·sive /diˈvīsiv/ ▶ **adj.** causing disagreement or hostility between people.

di·vi·sor /diˈvīzər/ ▶ **n.** Math a number by which another number is to be divided.

di·vorce /diˈvôrs/ ▶ **n.** the legal ending of a marriage. ▶ **v.** (**divorces**, **divorcing**, **divorced**) **1** legally end your marriage with. **2** (**divorce something from**) separate something from: *jazz has become divorced from its origins*.

SYNONYMS ▶ **n. 1 dissolution**, annulment, decree nisi, separation. **2** *the divorce between the church and people* **separation**, division, split, gulf, disunity, alienation, schism. ANTONYMS marriage. ▶ **v. 1 split up**, get a divorce, separate. **2** *religion cannot be divorced from morality* **separate**, divide, detach, isolate, alienate, set apart, cut off.

di·vor·cé /diˌvôrˈsā/ ▶ **n.** a divorced man.

di·vor·cée /divôrˈsā, -ˈsē/ ▶ **n.** a divorced woman.

div·ot /ˈdivət/ ▶ **n.** a piece of turf cut out of the ground, especially by a golf club making a stroke.

di·vulge /diˈvəlj, dī-/ ▶ **v.** (**divulges**, **divulging**, **divulged**) reveal information.

SYNONYMS **disclose**, reveal, tell, communicate, pass on, publish, give away, let slip. ANTONYMS conceal.

div·vy /ˈdivē/ informal ▶ **v.** (**divvies**, **divvying**, **divvied**) divide up and share: *they divvied up the proceeds*. ▶ **n.** (plural **divvies**) a portion or share.

Di·wa·li /diˈwälē/ (or **Divali**) ▶ **n.** a Hindu festival at which lights, candles, etc., are lit, held in October and November.

Dix·ie /ˈdiksē/ ▶ **n.** informal the Southern states of the United States.

Dix·ie·land /ˈdiksēˌland/ ▶ **n.** a kind of jazz with a strong two-beat rhythm.

DIY ▶ **abbr.** (of home repair) do it yourself.

diz·zy /ˈdizē/ ▶ **adj.** (**dizzier**, **dizziest**) having a sensation of spinning around and losing your balance. ▶ **v.** (**dizzies**, **dizzying**, **dizzied**) make unsteady or confused.

SYNONYMS ▶ **adj. giddy**, lightheaded, faint, unsteady, shaky, muzzy, wobbly; informal woozy.

■ **diz·zi·ly adv. diz·zi·ness n.**

DJ /ˈdēˌjā/ ▶ **n.** a person who introduces and plays recorded pop music on radio or at a club; a disc jockey.

djel·la·ba /jəˈläbə/ (also **djellabah**) ▶ **n.** a loose woolen hooded cloak traditionally worn by Arabs.

dl ▶ **abbr.** deciliter(s).

dm ▶ **abbr.** decimeter(s).

DMA ▶ **abbr.** Computing direct memory access.

DMZ ▶ **abbr.** demilitarized zone, an area from which warring parties agree to remove their military forces.

DNA ▶ **n.** a substance carrying genetic information that is found in the cells of nearly all animals and plants.

do[1] /do͞o/ ▶ **v.** (**does** /dəz/, **doing**, **did** /did/; past participle **done** /dən/) **1** carry out or complete an action, duty, or task. **2** have a specified amount of success: *the team did well*. **3** make or provide something. **4** have a particular result or effect on: *the walk will do me good*. **5** work at for a living or take as a subject of study: *what does she do?* **6** be suitable or acceptable: *if he's like you, he'll do*. **7** informal swindle someone. ▶ **auxiliary v. 1** used before a verb in questions and negative statements. **2** used to refer back to a verb already mentioned: *he looks better than he did before*. **3** used in commands, or to give emphasis to a verb: *do sit down*. ▶ **n.** (plural **dos** or **do's**) informal a party or other social event.

SYNONYMS ▶ **v. 1** *she does most of the work* **carry out**, undertake, discharge, execute, perform, accomplish, achieve, bring about, engineer; informal pull off. **2** *they can do as they please* **act**, behave, conduct yourself. **3 suffice**, be adequate, be satisfactory, fill/fit the bill, serve. **4** *a portrait I am doing* **make**, create, produce, work on, design, manufacture.

□ **be done up** be dressed elaborately. **do away with** informal put an end to or kill. **do-gooder** a well-meaning but unrealistic or interfering person. **do someone in** informal kill someone. **do-or-die** showing or requiring a great determination to succeed. **do someone out of** unfairly deprive someone of something. **dos and don'ts** rules of behavior. **do something up 1** fasten or wrap something. **2** informal renovate or redecorate a room or building.

do² /dō/ ▶ **n.** Music the first note of a major scale.

Do·ber·man /ˈdōbərmən/ (also **Doberman pinscher** /ˈpincʜər/) ▶ **n.** a large German breed of dog with powerful jaws and a smooth coat.

doc /däk/ ▶ **abbr.** informal **1** doctor. **2** Computing document.

do·cent /ˈdōsənt/ ▶ **n.** a guide in a museum, art gallery, or zoo.

doc·ile /ˈdäsəl/ ▶ **adj.** quiet and easy to control.

SYNONYMS **compliant**, obedient, pliant, submissive, deferential, unassertive, cooperative, amenable, accommodating, biddable. ANTONYMS disobedient, willful.

■ **doc·ile·ly adv. do·cil·i·ty** /däˈsilitē/ **n.**

dock¹ /däk/ ▶ **n.** an enclosed area of water in a port for loading, unloading, and repairing ships. ▶ **v. 1** (of a ship) come into a dock. **2** (of a spacecraft) join with a space station or another spacecraft in space.

SYNONYMS ▶ **n. harbor**, marina, port, wharf, quay, pier, jetty, landing stage. ▶ **v. moor**, berth, put in, tie up, anchor.

dock² ▶ **n.** the enclosure in a criminal court for a person on trial.

dock³ ▶ **n.** a coarse weed with broad leaves.

dock⁴ ▶ **v. 1** take away money from a person's wages before they are paid. **2** cut short an animal's tail.

SYNONYMS **1 deduct**, subtract, remove, debit, take off/away; Law garnish; informal knock off. **2 reduce**, cut, decrease. **3 cut off**, cut short, shorten, crop, lop.

dock·er /ˈdäkər/ ▶ **n.** a person employed in a port to load and unload ships.

dock·et /ˈdäkit/ ▶ **n. 1** a calendar or list of cases for trial or people having cases pending. **2** a document accompanying a batch of goods that lists its contents, shows that duty has been paid, etc.

dock·yard /ˈdäkˌyärd/ ▶ **n.** an area with docks and equipment for repairing and building ships.

doc·tor /ˈdäktər/ ▶ **n. 1** a person who is qualified to practice medicine. **2** (**Doctor**) a person who holds the highest university degree. ▶ **v. 1** change something in order to deceive people. **2** add a harmful or strong ingredient to food or drink.

SYNONYMS ▶ **n. physician**, medical practitioner, general practitioner, GP, clinician, consultant; informal doc, medic. ▶ **v. 1 adulterate**, tamper with, lace; informal spike. **2 falsify**, tamper with, interfere with, alter, change, forge, fake.

doc·tor·al /ˈdäktərəl/ ▶ **adj.** relating to a doctorate.

doc·tor·ate /ˈdäktərit/ ▶ **n.** the highest degree awarded by a university.

doc·tri·naire /ˌdäktrəˈner/ ▶ **adj.** very strict in applying beliefs or principles.

doc·trine /ˈdäktrin/ ▶ **n.** a set of beliefs or principles held by a religious or political group.

SYNONYMS **creed**, credo, dogma, belief, teaching, ideology, tenet, maxim, canon, principle.

■ **doc·tri·nal** /ˈdäktrənl/ **adj.**

doc·u·dra·ma /ˈdäkyəˌdrämə/ ▶ **n.** a television movie based on a dramatized version of real events.

doc·u·ment ▶ **n.** /ˈdäkyəment/ a piece of written, printed, or electronic material that provides information or evidence. ▶ **v.** /ˈdäkyəˌmənt/ record something in written or other form.

SYNONYMS ▶ **n. paper**, certificate, deed, form, contract, agreement, report, record. ▶ **v. record**, register, report, log, chronicle, authenticate, verify.

doc·u·men·ta·ry /ˌdäkyəˈmentərē/ ▶ **n.** (plural **documentaries**) a movie or television or radio program giving a factual report, using video, photographs, and sound recordings of real events. ▶ **adj.** consisting of documents: *documentary evidence.*

doc·u·men·ta·tion /ˌdäkyəmenˈtāsʜən/ ▶ **n.** documents providing official information, evidence, or instructions.

dod·der /ˈdädər/ ▶ **v.** be slow and unsteady.
■ **dod·der·y adj.**

do·dec·a·gon /dōˈdekəˌgän/ ▶ **n.** a figure with twelve straight sides and angles.

do·dec·a·he·dron /dōˌdekəˈhēdrən/ ▶ **n.** (plural **dodecahedrons** or **dodecahedra** /-drə/) a three-dimensional shape with twelve faces.

dodge /däj/ ▶ **v.** (**dodges**, **dodging**, **dodged**) **1** avoid something by a sudden quick movement. **2** avoid something in a cunning or dishonest way: *crooks who had dodged arrest warrants.* ▶ **n.** an act of avoiding something.

SYNONYMS ▶ **v. 1** *he dodged the police* **elude**, evade, avoid, escape, run away from, lose, shake (off); informal give someone the slip. **2** *the minister tried to dodge the debate* **avoid**, evade, get out of, back out of, sidestep; informal duck, wriggle out of. **3 dart**, duck, dive, swerve, veer. ▶ **n.** *a clever dodge* | *a tax dodge* **ruse**, scheme, tactic, stratagem, ploy, subterfuge, trick, hoax, cheat, deception, fraud; informal scam.

dodg·er /ˈdäjər/ ▶ **n.** a person who behaves in a cunning or dishonest way to avoid something undesirable: *tax dodgers.*

do·do /ˈdōdō/ ▶ **n.** (plural **dodos** or **dodoes**) a large extinct bird that could not fly, formerly found on Mauritius.

doe /dō/ ▶ **n. 1** a female deer or reindeer. **2** the female of some other animals, such as a rabbit or hare.

do·er /ˈdo͞oər/ ▶ **n. 1** the person who does something. **2** a person who acts rather than merely talking or thinking.

does /dəz/ 3rd person singular present of **DO¹**.

does·n't /ˈdəzənt/ ▶ **contr.** does not.

doff /däf, dôf/ ▶ **v.** remove your hat when greeting someone.

dog /dôg/ ▶ **n. 1** a four-legged meat-eating animal, kept as a pet or used for work or hunting. **2** any member of the dog family, such as the wolf or fox. **3** the male of an animal of the dog family. ▶ **v.** (**dogs**, **dogging**, **dogged**) **1** follow someone closely and persistently. **2** cause continual trouble for: *he was dogged by ankle problems.*

SYNONYMS ▶ n. **hound**, canine, man's best friend, mongrel; informal pooch, mutt. ▶ v. **plague**, beset, bedevil, blight, trouble.

□ **dog days** the hottest period of the year (formerly reckoned from the first time Sirius, the Dog Star, rose at the same time as the sun). **dog-eared** (of a book) having the corners of the pages curled or folded over from constant use. **dog paddle** a simple swimming stroke like that of a dog. **dog rose** a wild rose with pink or white flowers. **dog-tired** extremely tired. **go to the dogs** informal get much worse.

dog·catch·er /'dôg,kachər, -,kechər/ ▶ n. a person whose job is to round up stray dogs.

doge /dōj/ ▶ n. historical the chief magistrate of Venice or Genoa.

dog·fight /'dôg,fīt/ ▶ n. a close combat between military aircraft.

dog·fish /'dôg,fish/ ▶ n. (plural **dogfish** or **dogfishes**) a small shark with a long tail.

dog·ged /'dôgid/ ▶ adj. very persistent.

SYNONYMS **tenacious**, determined, resolute, stubborn, obstinate, purposeful, persistent, persevering, single-minded, tireless. ANTONYMS halfhearted.

■ **dog·ged·ly** adv.

dog·ger·el /'dôgərəl, 'däg-/ ▶ n. badly written verse.

dog·gone /'dôg'gôn/ ▶ adj. informal used to express surprise, annoyance, or pleasure.

dog·gy /'dôgē/ (or **doggie**) ▶ adj. **1** having to do with dogs. **2** fond of dogs. □ **doggy bag** a bag used to take home leftover food from a restaurant.

dog·house /'dôg,hous/ ▶ n. a dog's kennel. □ **in the doghouse** informal in disgrace.

dog·leg /'dôg,leg/ ▶ n. a sharp bend in a road.

dog·ma /'dôgmə/ ▶ n. a firm set of principles laid down by an authority as incontrovertibly true.

SYNONYMS **teaching**, belief, tenet, principle, precept, maxim, article of faith, canon, creed, credo, doctrine, ideology.

dog·mat·ic /dôg'matik/ ▶ adj. firmly putting forward your own opinions and not willing to accept those of other people.

SYNONYMS **opinionated**, assertive, insistent, emphatic, adamant, doctrinaire, authoritarian, imperious, dictatorial, uncompromising.

■ **dog·mat·i·cal·ly** adv.

dog·wood /'dôg,wo͝od/ ▶ n. a flowering shrub or small tree with red stems, colorful berries, and hard wood.

doi·ly /'doilē/ ▶ n. (plural **doilies**) a small decorative mat made of lace or paper.

do·ings /'do͞oiNGz/ ▶ pl.n. a person's actions or activities.

Dol·by /'dōlbē, 'dôl-/ ▶ n. trademark **1** a noise-reduction system used in tape recording. **2** an electronic system providing stereophonic sound for movie theaters and televisions.

dol·drums /'dōldrəmz, 'däl-, 'dôl-/ ▶ pl.n. (**the doldrums**) a state of being inactive or feeling depressed.

dole /dōl/ ▶ v. (**doles, doling, doled**) (**dole something out**) distribute something. ▶ n. informal unemployment benefits: *I ended up on the dole.*

SYNONYMS ▶ v. **deal out**, pass out, share, divide up, allocate, distribute, dispense, hand out, give out, dish out.

dole·ful /'dōlfəl/ ▶ adj. sad or depressing. ■ **dole·ful·ly** adv.

doll /däl/ ▶ n. **1** a small model of a human figure, used as a child's toy. **2** informal an attractive woman. ▶ v. (**be dolled up**) informal be dressed in attractive or fancy clothes.

dol·lar /'dälər/ ▶ n. the chief unit of money in the United States, Canada, Australia, and some other countries. □ **dollar sign** the sign $, representing a dollar.

dol·lop /'däləp/ informal ▶ n. a shapeless mass or lump. ▶ v. (**dollops, dolloping, dolloped**) casually add or serve out a mass of something.

dol·ly /'dälē/ ▶ n. (plural **dollies**) a child's word for a doll.

dol·man sleeve /'dōlmən/ ▶ n. a loose sleeve cut in one piece with the body of a garment.

dol·men /'dōlmən, 'däl-/ ▶ n. a prehistoric tomb with a large flat stone laid on upright ones.

do·lo·mite /'dälə,mīt, 'dō-/ ▶ n. a mineral or rock consisting chiefly of a carbonate of calcium and magnesium.

do·lor /'dōlər/ ▶ n. literary great sorrow or distress. ■ **dol·or·ous** adj.

dol·phin /'dälfin, 'dôl-/ ▶ n. a small whale with a beaklike snout and a curved fin on the back.

dol·phi·nar·i·um /,dälfi'ne(ə)rēəm, ,dôl-/ ▶ n. (plural **dolphinariums** or **dolphinaria** /-rēə/) an aquarium in which dolphins are kept and trained for public entertainment.

dolt /dōlt/ ▶ n. a stupid person.

do·main /dō'mān/ ▶ n. **1** an area controlled by a ruler or government. **2** an area of activity or knowledge. **3** a set of websites whose addresses end with the same group of letters.

SYNONYMS **1 realm**, kingdom, empire, dominion, province, territory, land. **2 field**, area, sphere, discipline, province, world.

dome /dōm/ ▶ n. **1** a rounded roof with a circular base. **2** a stadium or other building with a rounded roof. ■ **domed** adj.

do·mes·tic /də'mestik/ ▶ adj. **1** relating to a home or family. **2** for use in the home. **3** (of an animal) tame and kept by humans. **4** existing or occurring within a country; not foreign: *China's domestic affairs.*

SYNONYMS **1 family**, home, household. **2 domesticated**, homely, home-loving. **3 tame**, pet, domesticated. **4 national**, state, home, internal.

■ **do·mes·ti·cal·ly** adv.

do·mes·ti·cate /də'mesti,kāt/ ▶ v. (**domesticates, domesticating, domesticated**) tame an animal and keep it as a pet or on a farm. ■ **do·mes·ti·ca·tion** /-,mesti'kāshən/ n.

do·mes·tic·i·ty /,dōme'stisitē/ ▶ n. home life.

dom·i·cile /'dämə,sīl, 'dō-, 'däməsəl/ formal or Law ▶ n. **1** the country in which a person lives permanently. **2** a person's home. ▶ v. (**be domiciled**) be living in a particular country or place.

dom·i·cil·i·ar·y /,dämə'silē,erē, ,dō-/ ▶ adj. in someone's home: *a domiciliary visit.*

dom·i·nant /'dämənənt/ ▶ adj. **1** most important, powerful, or influential: *a dominant position in the market.* **2** (of a gene) appearing in offspring even if a contrary gene is also inherited. **3** (of a high place or object) overlooking others.

SYNONYMS **1 ruling**, governing, controlling, presiding, commanding. **2 assertive**, authoritative, forceful, domineering, commanding, controlling, pushy. **3 main**, principal, prime, chief, primary, central, key, crucial, core. ANTONYMS subservient, subsidiary.

■ **dom·i·nance** n. **dom·i·nant·ly** adv.

dom·i·nate /'dämə,nāt/ ▶ v. (**dominates, dominating, dominated**) **1** have a very strong influence over. **2** be the most important or noticeable person or thing in: *the race was dominated by the 2007 champion.*

SYNONYMS **1 control**, influence, command, be in charge of, rule, govern, direct. **2 overlook**, command, tower above/over, loom over.

dom·i·na·tion /,dämə'nāsHən/ ▶ n. the action of controlling someone or something.

SYNONYMS **control**, power, command, authority, dominion, rule, supremacy, superiority, ascendancy, sway, mastery.

dom·i·neer·ing /,dämə'ni(ə)riNG/ ▶ adj. arrogantly trying to control other people.

SYNONYMS **overbearing**, authoritarian, imperious, high-handed, peremptory, autocratic, dictatorial, despotic, strict, harsh; informal bossy.

Do·min·i·can /də'minikən/ ▶ n. a member of an order of friars founded by St. Dominic, or of a corresponding order of nuns.

do·min·ion /də'minyən/ ▶ n. **1** supreme power or control. **2** the territory of a ruler or government.

SYNONYMS **supremacy**, ascendancy, dominance, domination, superiority, predominance, preeminence, hegemony, authority, mastery, control, command, power, sway, rule, government, jurisdiction, sovereignty.

dom·i·no /'dämə,nō/ ▶ n. (plural **dominoes**) any of twenty-eight small oblong pieces marked with 0–6 dots in each half, used in the game of **dominoes**. □ **domino effect** an effect compared to a row of dominoes falling, when a political event in one country seems to cause similar events elsewhere.

don[1] /dän/ ▶ n. a university teacher, especially a senior member of a college at Oxford or Cambridge in the United Kingdom.

don[2] ▶ v. (**dons, donning, donned**) put on an item of clothing.

SYNONYMS **put on**, get dressed in, dress (yourself) in, get into, slip into/on, change into.

do·nate /'dōnāt, dō'nāt/ ▶ v. (**donates, donating, donated**) give something to a charity or other good cause.

SYNONYMS **give**, contribute, gift, subscribe, grant, present, endow; informal chip in.

do·na·tion /dō'nāsHən/ ▶ n. something given to a charity or other good cause.

SYNONYMS **gift**, contribution, subscription, present, handout, grant, offering.

done /dən/ past participle of **DO[1]** ▶ adj. **1** cooked thoroughly. **2** no longer happening or existing. **3** informal socially acceptable: *the done thing.* ▶ exclam. (in response to an offer) I accept! □ **done for** informal in serious trouble. **done in** informal extremely tired.

don·gle /'däNGgəl, 'dôNG-/ ▶ n. an electronic device that must be attached to a computer in order for protected software to be used.

don·key /'dôNGkē, 'däNG-/ ▶ n. (plural **donkeys**) a domesticated animal of the horse family with long ears and a braying call. □ **donkey's years** informal a very long time.

do·nor /'dōnər/ ▶ n. a person who donates something.

SYNONYMS **giver**, contributor, benefactor, subscriber, supporter, backer, patron, sponsor; informal angel. ANTONYMS beneficiary.

don't /dōnt/ ▶ contr. do not.

do·nut /'dō,nət/ ▶ n. = DOUGHNUT.

doo·dad /'dōō,dad/ ▶ n. informal **1** an object whose name is not known or has been forgotten. **2** a fancy article or trivial ornament.

doo·dle /'dōōdl/ ▶ v. (**doodles, doodling, doodled**) scribble absent-mindedly. ▶ n. a drawing made absentmindedly.

doom /dōōm/ ▶ n. death, destruction, or another terrible fate. ▶ v. (**be doomed**) be fated to fail or be destroyed.

SYNONYMS ▶ n. **destruction**, downfall, ruin, extinction, annihilation, death, nemesis. ▶ v. **1 destine**, fate, predestine, preordain, mean, condemn, sentence. **2** (**doomed**) **ill-fated**, ill-starred, cursed, jinxed, damned; literary star-crossed.

dooms·day /'dōōmz,dā/ ▶ n. **1** the last day of the world's existence. **2** (in religious belief) the day of the Last Judgment.

door /dôr/ ▶ n. a movable barrier at the entrance to a building, room, vehicle, etc. □ **lay something at someone's door** blame someone for something. **out of doors** in or into the open air.

door·bell /'dôr,bel/ ▶ n. a bell in a building that can be rung by visitors outside.

door·knob /'dôr,näb/ ▶ n. a rounded door handle.

door·man /'dôr,man, -mən/ ▶ n. (plural **doormen**) a man who is on duty at the entrance to a large building such as a hotel or apartment house to screen visitors, help people into cars or taxis, etc.

door·mat /'dôr,mat/ ▶ n. **1** a mat placed in a doorway for wiping your shoes. **2** informal a person who lets other people dominate them.

door·step /'dôr,step/ ▶ n. a step leading up to the outer door of a house.

door·stop /'dôr,stäp/ ▶ n. an object that keeps a door open or in place.

door·way /'dôr,wā/ ▶ n. an entrance with a door.

doo·zy /'dōōzē/ ▶ n. (plural **doo·zies**) informal something outstanding or unique of its kind.

dope /dōp/ ▶ n. **1** informal an illegal drug, especially cannabis. **2** a drug used to improve the performance of an athlete, racehorse, or greyhound. **3** informal a stupid person. ▶ v. (**dopes, doping, doped**) give a drug to.

dope·y /'dōpē/ (or **dopy**) ▶ adj. informal **1** in a semiconscious state from sleepiness or a drug. **2** stupid.

dop·pel·gäng·er /'däpəl,gaNGər/ ▶ n. a ghost or double of a living person.

Dop·pler ef·fect /'däplər/ ▶ n. an apparent change in the frequency of sound or light waves as the source and the observer move toward or away from each other.

dork /dôrk/ ▸ **n.** informal a dull, slow-witted, or socially inept person.

dorm /dôrm/ ▸ **n.** short for **DORMITORY**.

dor·mant /ˈdôrmənt/ ▸ **adj. 1** (of an animal) in a deep sleep. **2** (of a plant or bud) alive but not growing. **3** (of a volcano) temporarily inactive.

SYNONYMS **sleeping**, resting, **inactive**, hibernating, passive, inert, latent, idle, quiescent. ANTONYMS awake, active.

■ **dor·man·cy n.**

dor·mer /ˈdôrmər/ ▸ **n.** a window set vertically into a sloping roof.

dor·mi·to·ry /ˈdôrmiˌtôrē/ ▸ **n.** (plural **dormitories**) **1** a bedroom for a number of people in a school or other institution. **2** a hall of residence at a college or university.

dor·mouse /ˈdôrˌmous/ ▸ **n.** (plural **dormice**) a small mouselike rodent with a bushy tail.

dor·sal /ˈdôrsəl/ ▸ **adj.** relating to the upper side or back of an animal, plant, or organ.

do·ry /ˈdôrē/ ▸ **n.** (plural **dories**) a narrow sea fish with a large mouth.

DOS /dôs/ ▸ **abbr.** Computing disk operating system.

dose /dōs/ ▸ **n. 1** a quantity of a medicine taken at one time. **2** an amount of radiation absorbed at one time. ▸ **v.** (**doses**, **dosing**, **dosed**) give a dose of medicine to.

SYNONYMS ▸ **n. measure**, portion, draft, dosage.

■ **dos·age n.**

dos·si·er /ˈdôsēˌā, ˈdäs-/ ▸ **n.** a collection of documents about a person or subject.

DOT ▸ **abbr.** Department of Transportation.

dot /dät/ ▸ **n.** a small round mark or spot. ▸ **v.** (**dots**, **dotting**, **dotted**) **1** mark with a dot or dots. **2** cover an area with a scattering of something.

SYNONYMS ▸ **n. spot**, speck, fleck, speckle, period, decimal point. ▸ **v. 1 spot**, fleck, mark, spatter. **2 scatter**, pepper, sprinkle, strew, spread.

□ **dot-com** a company that carries out its business on the Internet. **on the dot** informal exactly on time.

dot·age /ˈdōtij/ ▸ **n.** the period of life in which a person is old and weak.

do·tard /ˈdōtərd/ ▸ **n.** a person who is weak or senile from old age.

dote /dōt/ ▸ **v.** (**dotes**, **doting**, **doted**) (**dote on**) love someone very much, ignoring their faults.

SYNONYMS **adore**, love dearly, be devoted to, idolize, treasure, cherish, worship.

dot·ty /ˈdätē/ ▸ **adj.** slightly crazy or eccentric.

dou·ble /ˈdəbəl/ ▸ **adj. 1** consisting of two equal, identical, or similar parts or things. **2** having twice the usual size, quantity, or strength: *a double latte.* **3** designed to be used by two people. **4** having two different roles or meanings: *she began a double life.* ▸ **adv.** twice the amount or quantity. ▸ **n. 1** a thing that is twice as large as usual or is made up of two parts. **2** a person who looks exactly like another. **3** Baseball a hit that allows the batter to reach second base safely. **4** (**doubles**) a game such as tennis involving sides made up of two players. ▸ **v.** (**doubles**, **doubling**, **doubled**) **1** make or become double. **2** fold or bend over on itself. **3** (**double up**) curl up with pain or laughter.

SYNONYMS ▸ **adj. dual**, duplex, twin, binary, duplicate, coupled, matching, twofold, in pairs. ANTONYMS single. ▸ **n. lookalike**, twin, clone, duplicate, exact likeness, replica, copy, facsimile, doppelgänger; informal spitting image, dead ringer.

□ **double agent** an agent who pretends to act as a spy for one country while in fact acting for its enemy. **double as** be used in a role different from its main one: *the van doubled as a mobile kitchen.* **double back** go back in the direction you have come from. **double-barreled** (of a gun) having two barrels. **double bass** the largest and lowest-pitched instrument of the violin family. **double-book** mistakenly reserve something for two different customers at the same time. **double-breasted** (of a jacket or coat) having a large overlap at the front and two rows of buttons. **double-check** check again. **double chin** a roll of flesh below a person's chin. **double-dealing** deceitful behavior. **double-decker** a bus with two levels. **double Dutch** a jump-rope game played with two long jump ropes swung in opposite directions so that they cross rhythmically. **double-edged 1** (of a blade) having two cutting edges. **2** having two contradictory aspects or possible outcomes. **double figures** a number from 10 to 99 inclusive. **double glazing** windows having two layers of glass with a space between them. **double helix** a pair of parallel helices with a common axis, especially that in the structure of DNA. **double-jointed** (of a person) having unusually flexible joints. **double play** Baseball a play in which two players are put out. **double pneumonia** pneumonia affecting both lungs. **double standard** a rule or principle applied unfairly in different ways to different people. **double take** a second reaction to something unexpected, immediately after your first one. **double time 1** a rate of pay equal to double the standard rate. **2** Music a rhythm that is twice as fast as an earlier one. **on the double** very fast. ■ **dou·bly adv.**

dou·ble en·ten·dre /ˈdo͞ob(ə)l änˈtändrə/ ▸ **n.** (plural **double entendres**) a word or phrase with two meanings, one of which is usually risqué.

dou·ble neg·a·tive ▸ **n.** Grammar a negative statement containing two negative elements (e.g., *didn't say nothing*).

USAGE

If you say *I don't know nothing*, this is not good English. The structure is called a **double negative** because it is the use of two negative words in the same clause to convey a single negative. This is incorrect because the two negative elements cancel each other out to give a positive statement, so that *I don't know nothing* would be taken to mean *I know something*; you should therefore say *I don't know anything* to avoid confusion.

dou·ble·speak /ˈdəbəlˌspēk/ ▸ **n.** language that is deliberately unclear or has more than one meaning.

dou·blet /ˈdəblət/ ▸ **n.** historical a man's short close-fitting padded jacket.

dou·ble·think /ˈdəbəlˌᴛʜɪɴɢk/ ▸ **n.** the acceptance of conflicting opinions or beliefs at the same time.

dou·bloon /dəˈblo͞on/ ▸ **n.** historical a Spanish gold coin.

doubt /dout/ ▸ **n.** a feeling of uncertainty. ▸ **v. 1** feel uncertain about something. **2** disbelieve or mistrust someone.

SYNONYMS ▸ **n. 1 uncertainty**, indecision, hesitation, irresolution, hesitancy, vacillation, lack of conviction. **2 skepticism**, distrust, mistrust, suspicion, cynicism, wariness, reservations, misgivings, suspicions. ANTONYMS certainty, trust. ▶ **v. disbelieve**, distrust, mistrust, suspect, be suspicious of, have misgivings about.

□ **doubting Thomas** a person who refuses to believe something without proof. **no doubt** certainly; probably.

doubt·ful /ˈdoutfəl/ ▶ **adj.** **1** feeling uncertain. **2** causing uncertainty. **3** not likely or probable: *it is doubtful whether the plan will have a lasting effect.*

SYNONYMS **1 hesitant**, in doubt, unsure, uncertain, of two minds, in a quandary, in a dilemma. **2 in doubt**, uncertain, open to question, unsure, debatable, up in the air, inconclusive, unconfirmed. **3 unlikely**, improbable. **4 distrustful**, mistrustful, skeptical, suspicious, having reservations, wary, leery. **5 questionable**, dubious, suspect, suspicious. ANTONYMS confident, certain.

■ **doubt·ful·ly** **adv.**

doubt·less /ˈdoutlis/ ▶ **adv.** very probably.

SYNONYMS **undoubtedly**, no doubt, unquestionably, indisputably, undeniably, certainly, surely, of course.

douche /do͞osʜ/ ▶ **n.** a jet of water applied to part of the body.

dough /dō/ ▶ **n.** **1** a thick mixture of flour and liquid, for baking into bread or pastry. **2** informal money. ■ **dough·y** **adj.**

dough·nut /ˈdōˌnət/ (or **donut**) ▶ **n.** a small fried cake of sweetened dough, typically in the shape of a ball or ring.

dough·ty /ˈdoutē/ ▶ **adj.** old use brave and determined.

dour /do͝or, dou(ə)r/ ▶ **adj.** very severe, stern, or gloomy.

SYNONYMS **stern**, unsmiling, unfriendly, severe, forbidding, gruff, surly, grim, sullen, solemn, austere, stony. ANTONYMS cheerful, friendly.

douse /dous/ (or **dowse**) ▶ **v.** (**douses**, **dousing**, **doused**) **1** drench with liquid. **2** extinguish a fire.

SYNONYMS **1 drench**, soak, saturate, wet. **2 extinguish**, put out, quench, smother.

dove[1] /dəv/ ▶ **n.** **1** a bird with a cooing voice, very similar to a pigeon. **2** (in politics) a person who is in favor of a policy of peace and negotiation. The opposite of HAWK[1].

dove[2] /dōv/ past and past participle of DIVE.

dove·cote /ˈdəvˌkōt/ (or **dovecot**) ▶ **n.** a shelter with nest holes for domesticated pigeons.

dove·tail /ˈdəvˌtāl/ ▶ **v.** **1** fit together neatly: *flights that dovetail with the working day.* **2** join by means of a dovetail. ▶ **n.** a wedge-shaped joint formed by interlocking two pieces of wood.

dow·a·ger /ˈdouəjər/ ▶ **n.** **1** a widow who holds a title that belonged to her late husband. **2** a dignified elderly woman.

dow·dy /ˈdoudē/ ▶ **adj.** unfashionable and dull in appearance.

SYNONYMS **unfashionable**, frumpy, old-fashioned, shabby, frowzy. ANTONYMS fashionable.

dow·el /ˈdouəl/ ▶ **n.** a peg used to hold together parts of a structure.

dow·er /ˈdou(-ə)r/ ▶ **n.** a widow's share for life of her late husband's estate.

down[1] /doun/ ▶ **adv.** **1** toward, in, or at a lower place, position, or level: *he put his glass down* | *output was down by 20 percent.* **2** to a smaller amount or size: *I must slim down a bit.* **3** in or into a weaker or worse position or condition. **4** away from a central place or the north: *they're living down south.* **5** from an earlier to a later point in time or order: *farms were passed down within the family.* **6** in or into writing. **7** (of a computer system) out of action. ▶ **prep.** **1** from a higher to a lower point of. **2** at or to a point further along the course of: *he lived down the street.* ▶ **adj.** **1** directed or moving downward. **2** unhappy or depressed. ▶ **v.** informal drink something quickly. □ **be down on** informal feel hostile toward. **down and out** homeless and without money. **down at the heels** shabby because of a lack of money. **down payment** an initial payment made when buying something on credit. **down-to-earth** practical and realistic. **Down Under** informal Australia and New Zealand. **down in the mouth** informal unhappy. **down with ...** expressing strong dislike.

down[2] ▶ **n.** fine, soft feathers or hairs.

down·beat /ˈdounˌbēt/ ▶ **adj.** **1** gloomy. **2** relaxed and low-key.

down·cast /ˈdounˌkast/ ▶ **adj.** **1** (of eyes) looking downward. **2** unhappy; discouraged.

down·er /ˈdounər/ ▶ **n.** informal **1** a tranquilizing or depressant drug. **2** a depressing experience.

down·fall /ˈdounˌfôl/ ▶ **n.** a loss of power, wealth, or status.

SYNONYMS **ruin**, ruination, undoing, defeat, overthrow, destruction, annihilation, end, collapse, fall, crash, failure. ANTONYMS rise.

down·grade /ˈdounˌgrād/ ▶ **v.** (**downgrades**, **downgrading**, **downgraded**) bring someone down to a lower rank or level of importance.

SYNONYMS **demote**, reduce, relegate. ANTONYMS promote.

down·heart·ed /ˈdounˈhärtid/ ▶ **adj.** unhappy; discouraged.

SYNONYMS **despondent**, disheartened, discouraged, dispirited, downcast, crestfallen, down, low, disconsolate, wretched, melancholy, gloomy, glum, doleful, dismal, woebegone, miserable, depressed, dejected, sorrowful, sad; informal blue, down in the mouth, down in the dumps. ANTONYMS elated.

down·hill /ˈdounˈhil/ ▶ **adv. & adj.** **1** toward the bottom of a slope. **2** into a steadily worsening situation: *the business is going downhill.*

down·load /ˈdounˌlōd/ ▶ **v.** copy data from one computer system to another. ▶ **n.** data that has been downloaded.

down·mar·ket /ˈdounˌmärkit/ ▶ **adj.** cheap and of low quality.

down·play /ˈdounˌplā/ ▶ **v.** make something appear less important than it really is.

down·pour /ˈdounˌpôr/ ▶ **n.** a heavy fall of rain.

down·right /ˈdounˌrīt/ ▶ **adj.** utter; complete. ▶ **adv.** extremely.

SYNONYMS ▶ **adj. complete**, total, absolute, utter, thorough, out-and-out, outright, sheer, pure; dated arrant. ▶ **adv. thoroughly**, utterly, positively, profoundly, really, completely, totally, entirely.

downs /dounz/ ▶ **n.** gently rolling hills.

down·scale /ˈdounˌskāl/ ▶ **v.** reduce the size or extent of something. ▶ **adj.** downmarket.

down·side /ˈdounˌsīd/ ▶ **n.** the negative aspect of something.

down·size /ˈdounˌsīz/ ▶ **v.** (**downsizes, downsizing, downsized**) **1** make (an organization) smaller by letting some personnel go. **2** (of an organization) let some personnel go.

down·stairs /ˈdounˈste(ə)rz/ ▶ **adv. & adj.** on or to a lower floor.

down·state /ˈdounˈstāt/ ▶ **adj. & adv.** of, in, or to the southern part of a state, especially a part remote from the state's large cities.

down·stream /ˈdounˈstrēm/ (or **downriver** /ˈdounˈrivər/) ▶ **adv.** in the direction in which a stream or river flows.

Down syn·drome /dounz/ (or **Down's syndrome**) ▶ **n.** a medical condition in which a person is born with physical abnormalities and an intellectual ability that is lower than average.

down·town /ˈdounˈtoun/ ▶ **adj. & adv.** in, to, or toward the central or main business area of a city.

down·trod·den /ˈdounˌträdn/ ▶ **adj.** treated badly by those in power.

down·turn /ˈdounˌtərn/ ▶ **n.** a decline in economic or other activity.

down·ward /ˈdounwərd/ ▶ **adj. & adv.** toward a lower point or level. ■ **down·wards adv.**

down·wind /ˈdounˈwind/ ▶ **adv.** in the direction in which the wind is blowing.

down·y /ˈdounē/ ▶ **adj.** covered with fine soft hair or feathers.

dow·ry /ˈdou(ə)rē/ ▶ **n.** (plural **dowries**) property or money brought by a bride to her husband on their marriage.

dowse /douz/ ▶ **v.** (**dowses, dowsing, dowsed**) search for underground water or minerals with a pointer that is supposedly moved by unseen influences.

dox·ol·o·gy /däkˈsäləjē/ ▶ **n.** (plural **doxologies**) a set form of prayer praising God.

doy·en /doiˈen, ˈdoi-en/ ▶ **n.** (feminine **doyenne** /doiˈen/) the most respected or prominent person in a field: *he became the doyen of physicists.*

doze /dōz/ ▶ **v.** (**dozes, dozing, dozed**) sleep lightly. ▶ **n.** a short, light sleep. ■ **do·zy adj.**

doz·en /ˈdəzən/ ▶ **n. 1** (plural **dozen**) a group or set of twelve. **2** (**dozens**) a lot.

DP ▶ **abbr.** data processing.

Dr. ▶ **abbr.** Doctor.

drab /drab/ ▶ **adj.** (**drabber, drabbest**) dull and uninteresting.

SYNONYMS **1 colorless**, gray, dull, washed out, dingy, dreary, dismal, cheerless, gloomy, somber. **2 uninteresting**, dull, boring, tedious, monotonous, dry, dreary. ANTONYMS bright, interesting.

■ **drab·ness n.**

drach·ma /ˈdräkmə/ ▶ **n.** (plural **drachmas** or **drachmae** /-mē/) the former basic unit of money in Greece.

dra·co·ni·an /drəˈkōnēən, drā-/ ▶ **adj.** (of laws) very harsh and severe.

draft /draft/ ▶ **n. 1** a preliminary version of a piece of writing. **2** compulsory recruitment for military service. **3** a current of cool air indoors. **4** the action or act of pulling something along, especially a vehicle or farm implement. **5** an act of drinking or breathing in. **6** a written order to pay a specified sum; a check. **7** old use a quantity of a medicinal liquid: *a sleeping draft.* **8** the depth of water needed to float a particular ship: *the shallow draft provides a flat cabin floor.* ▶ **v. 1** prepare a preliminary version of a text. **2** select a person or group of people for a certain purpose, such as military service or for a sports team. **3** pull or draw. ▶ **adj. 1** (of beer) served from a cask, barrel, or tank. **2** (of an animal) used for pulling heavy loads.

SYNONYMS ▶ **n. 1 version**, sketch, attempt, effort, outline, plan. **2 current of air**, wind, breeze, gust, puff, waft. **3 gulp**, drink, swallow, mouthful; informal swig. **4 check**, order, money order, bill of exchange.

■ **draft·er n.**

draft·ee /drafˈtē/ ▶ **n.** a person conscripted for military service.

drafts·man /ˈdraftsmən/ (or **draftswoman**) ▶ **n.** (plural **draftsmen** or **draftswomen**) **1** a person who makes detailed technical plans or drawings. **2** an artist skilled in drawing. **3** a person who drafts legal documents.

draft·y /ˈdraftē/ ▶ **adj.** uncomfortable because of drafts of cold air.

drag /drag/ ▶ **v.** (**drags, dragging, dragged**) **1** pull along forcefully, roughly, or with difficulty. **2** trail along the ground. **3** (of time) pass slowly. **4** (**drag something out**) make something last longer than necessary. **5** move an image across a computer screen using a mouse. **6** search the bottom of an area of water with hooks or nets. ▶ **n. 1** informal a boring or annoying person or thing. **2** a person or thing that makes progress difficult. **3** informal an act of inhaling smoke from a cigarette. **4** the force exerted by air or water to slow down a moving object.

SYNONYMS ▶ **v. haul**, pull, tug, heave, lug, draw, trail. ▶ **n. 1 bore**, nuisance, bother, trouble, pest, annoyance, trial; informal pain (in the neck), bind, headache, hassle. **2 pull**, resistance, tug.

□ **drag race** a short race between two cars from a standstill. **drag your feet** be slow or reluctant.

drag·net /ˈdragˌnet/ ▶ **n. 1** a net drawn through water or across ground to trap fish or game. **2** a systematic search for someone or something, especially criminals or criminal activity.

drag·on /ˈdragən/ ▶ **n.** a mythical monster that can breathe out fire.

drag·on·fly /ˈdragənˌflī/ ▶ **n.** (plural **dragonflies**) an insect with a long body and two pairs of large transparent wings.

dra·goon /drəˈgo͞on/ ▶ **n.** a member of any of several British cavalry regiments. ▶ **v.** force someone into doing something.

drain /drān/ ▶ **v. 1** make something empty or dry by removing the liquid from it. **2** (of liquid) run off or out. **3** make someone feel weak or tired. **4** use up a resource: *the hospital bills are draining my income.* **5** drink the entire contents of a glass or cup. ▶ **n. 1** a channel or pipe for carrying off rainwater or liquid waste. **2** a thing that uses up a resource or strength.

SYNONYMS ▶v. **1** *a valve for draining the tank* **empty (out)**, void, clear (out), evacuate, unload. **2** *drain off any surplus liquid* **draw off**, extract, siphon off, pour out, pour off, bleed, tap, filter, discharge. **3** *the water drained away* **flow**, pour, trickle, stream, run, rush, gush, flood, surge, leak, ooze, seep, dribble. **4 use up**, exhaust, deplete, consume, expend, get through, sap, milk, bleed. **5 drink**, gulp (down), guzzle, quaff, swallow, finish off, toss back; informal sink, down, swig, swill (down), knock back. ANTONYMS fill. ▶n. **1 sewer**, channel, ditch, culvert, duct, pipe, gutter. **2 strain**, pressure, burden, load, demand.

□ **go down the drain** informal be totally wasted.

drain·age /ˈdrānij/ ▶n. **1** the action or process of draining something. **2** a system of drains.

drain·board /ˈdrānˌbôrd/ ▶n. a surface next to a sink, on which washed dishes are left to drain.

drain·pipe /ˈdrānˌpīp/ ▶n. a pipe for carrying off rainwater from a building.

drake /drāk/ ▶n. a male duck.

DRAM /ˈdēˌram/ ▶abbr. Computing dynamic random-access memory.

dram /dram/ ▶n. a small drink of liquor.

dra·ma /ˈdrämə/ ▶n. **1** a play. **2** plays as a literary form. **3** an exciting or emotional series of events.

SYNONYMS **1 play**, show, piece, theatrical work, stage show, dramatization. **2 acting**, the theater, the stage, dramatic art, stagecraft, dramaturgy. **3 incident**, scene, spectacle, crisis, disturbance, row, commotion, excitement, thrill, sensation, dramatics, theatrics, histrionics.

dra·mat·ic /drəˈmatik/ ▶adj. **1** relating to drama. **2** sudden and striking: *a dramatic increase*. **3** exciting or impressive. ▶n. (**dramatics**) **1** the practice of acting in and presenting plays. **2** exaggerated or overemotional behavior.

SYNONYMS ▶adj. **1 theatrical**, thespian, dramaturgical. **2 considerable**, substantial, significant, remarkable, extraordinary, exceptional, phenomenal. **3 exciting**, stirring, action-packed, sensational, spectacular, startling, unexpected, tense, gripping, riveting, thrilling, hair-raising, lively. **4 striking**, impressive, imposing, spectacular, breathtaking, dazzling, sensational, awesome, awe-inspiring, remarkable. **5 exaggerated**, theatrical, ostentatious, overdone, stagy, showy, melodramatic. ANTONYMS unremarkable, boring.

■ **dra·mat·i·cal·ly** adv.

dram·a·tis per·so·nae /ˈdrämətis pərˈsōnē/ ▶pl.n. the characters of a play, novel, or narrative.

dram·a·tist /ˈdräməˌtist/ ▶n. a person who writes plays.

dram·a·tize /ˈdräməˌtīz/ ▶v. (**dramatizes**, **dramatizing**, **dramatized**) **1** present a novel or story as a play. **2** make something seem more exciting or serious than it really is.

SYNONYMS **1 adapt**, turn into a play/movie. **2 exaggerate**, overdo, overstate, magnify, amplify, inflate, sensationalize, embroider, color, aggrandize, embellish, elaborate; informal blow up (out of all proportion).

■ **dram·a·ti·za·tion** /ˌdrämətiˈzāsнən/ n.

drank /drangk/ past of DRINK.

drape /drāp/ ▶v. (**drapes**, **draping**, **draped**) **1** arrange cloth or clothing loosely on or around something. **2** rest part of your body on something in a relaxed way. ▶n. (**drapes**) long curtains.

SYNONYMS ▶v. **wrap**, cover, envelop, shroud, veil, cloak, wind, swathe, festoon, hang.

dra·per·y /ˈdrāpərē/ ▶n. (plural **draperies**) curtains or fabric hanging in loose folds.

dras·tic /ˈdrastik/ ▶adj. having a strong or far-reaching effect.

SYNONYMS **extreme**, serious, desperate, radical, far-reaching, momentous, substantial. ANTONYMS moderate.

■ **dras·ti·cal·ly** adv.

drat /drat/ ▶exclam. used to express mild annoyance.

draw /drô/ ▶v. (**draws**, **drawing**, **drew** /dro͞o/; past participle **drawn**) **1** produce a picture or diagram by making lines and marks on paper. **2** pull or drag a vehicle. **3** move in a particular direction: *the train drew into the station*. **4** pull curtains shut or open. **5** arrive at a point in time: *the campaign drew to a close*. **6** take from a container or source: *he drew his gun | she drew her savings out of the bank*. **7** be the cause of a particular response. **8** attract people to a place or an event. **9** persuade someone to reveal something: *he refused to be drawn about his future plans*. **10** reach a conclusion. **11** finish a contest or game with an even score. **12** take in a breath. ▶n. **1** a game or match that ends with the scores even. **2** an act of choosing names at random for prizes or to match competitors for games or sports, etc. **3** a person or thing that is very attractive or interesting. **4** an act of inhaling smoke from a cigarette.

SYNONYMS ▶v. **1 sketch**, outline, rough out, illustrate, render, represent, trace, portray, depict. **2 pull**, haul, drag, tug, heave, lug, tow; informal yank. **3 move**, go, come, proceed, progress, pass, drive, inch, roll, glide, cruise, sweep. **4 pull out**, take out, produce, fish out, extract, withdraw, unsheathe. **5 attract**, win, capture, catch, engage, lure, entice, bring in. ▶n. **1 tie**, dead heat, stalemate. **2 attraction**, lure, allure, pull, appeal, temptation, charm, fascination.

□ **draw someone's fire** attract hostile criticism away from a more important target. **draw in** (of successive days) become shorter. **draw the line at** refuse to do or tolerate. **draw something out** make something last longer. **draw something up** prepare a plan or document.

USAGE

Don't confuse **draw** with **drawer**, which means 'a sliding storage compartment.'

draw·back /ˈdrôˌbak/ ▶n. a disadvantage or problem.

SYNONYMS **disadvantage**, snag, downside, stumbling block, catch, hitch, pitfall, fly in the ointment, weak spot/point, weakness, imperfection; informal minus. ANTONYMS benefit.

draw·bridge /ˈdrôˌbrij/ ▶n. a bridge that is hinged at one end so that it can be raised.

draw·er /ˈdrô(ə)r/ ▶n. **1** a compartment for storage that slides horizontally in and out of a desk or chest or cabinet. **2** (**drawers**) dated underpants. **3** a person who draws something.

draw·ing /ˈdrô-iNG/ ▶ n. a picture or diagram made with a pencil, pen, or crayon.

SYNONYMS **1 sketch**, picture, illustration, representation, portrayal, depiction, diagram, outline. **2 raffle**, lottery, sweepstake.

□ **back to the drawing board** a plan has failed and a new one is needed. **drawing room** a sitting room; a room in a private house in which guests can be entertained.

drawl /drôl/ ▶ v. speak in a slow, lazy way with long vowel sounds. ▶ n. a drawling accent.

drawn /drôn/ past participle of DRAW ▶ adj. looking strained from illness or exhaustion. □ **drawn-out** lasting longer than is necessary.

draw·string /ˈdrôˌstriNG/ ▶ n. a string in the seam of a garment or bag, which can be pulled to tighten or close it.

dray /drā/ ▶ n. a low truck or cart for delivering barrels or other loads.

dread /dred/ ▶ v. think about something with great fear or anxiety. ▶ n. great fear or anxiety.

SYNONYMS ▶ v. **fear**, be afraid of, worry about, be anxious about, shudder at the thought of. ▶ n. **fear**, apprehension, trepidation, anxiety, panic, alarm, terror, disquiet, unease.

dread·ful /ˈdredfəl/ ▶ adj. **1** very bad or serious. **2** used for emphasis: *he's a dreadful flirt.*

SYNONYMS **1** *a dreadful accident* **terrible**, frightful, horrible, grim, awful, horrifying, shocking, distressing, appalling, harrowing, ghastly, gruesome, fearful, horrendous, tragic. **2** *a dreadful meal* **very bad**, frightful, shocking, awful, abysmal, wretched, dire, atrocious, disgraceful, deplorable; informal woeful, rotten, lousy. **3** *a dreadful flirt* **outrageous**, shocking, real, awful, terrible, inordinate, incorrigible. ANTONYMS wonderful, excellent.

■ **dread·ful·ly** adv.

dread·locks /ˈdredˌläks/ ▶ pl.n. a Rastafarian hairstyle in which the hair is twisted into tight braids or ringlets. ■ **dread·locked** adj.

dream /drēm/ ▶ n. **1** a series of images and feelings that happen in your mind while you are asleep. **2** an ambition or wish. **3** informal a wonderful or perfect person or thing. ▶ v. (**dreams**, **dreaming**, **dreamed** or **dreamt** /dremt/) **1** experience dreams during sleep. **2** have daydreams. **3** think of something as possible: *I never dreamed she'd take offense.* **4** (**dream something up**) imagine or invent something.

SYNONYMS ▶ n. **1 daydream**, reverie, trance, daze, stupor. **2 ambition**, aspiration, hope, goal, aim, objective, intention, desire, wish, daydream, fantasy. **3 delight**, joy, marvel, wonder, gem, treasure. ANTONYMS nightmare. ▶ v. **1 fantasize**, daydream, wish, hope, long, yearn, hanker. **2 daydream**, be in a trance, be lost in thought, be preoccupied, be abstracted, stare into space, be in la-la land.

□ **like a dream** informal very easily or successfully. ■ **dream·er** n.

dream·y /ˈdrēmē/ ▶ adj. **1** tending to daydream. **2** having a magical or pleasantly unreal quality. ■ **dream·i·ly** adv.

drear·y /ˈdri(ə)rē/ ▶ adj. (**drearier**, **dreariest**) dull, bleak, and depressing.

SYNONYMS **dull**, uninteresting, tedious, boring, unexciting, unstimulating, uninspiring, soul-destroying, monotonous, uneventful. ANTONYMS exciting.

■ **drear·i·ly** adv. **drear·i·ness** n.

dredge /drej/ ▶ v. (**dredges**, **dredging**, **dredged**) **1** use a machine to scoop out mud and objects from the bed of a river, canal, etc. **2** (**dredge something up**) mention something unpleasant that people have forgotten. ▶ n. a machine for dredging a river or seabed. ■ **dredg·er** n.

dregs /dregz/ ▶ n. **1** the last remaining amount of a liquid left in a cup, bottle, etc., together with any sediment. **2** the most worthless parts: *the dregs of society.*

drench /drencH/ ▶ v. wet thoroughly; soak.

SYNONYMS **soak**, saturate, wet through, douse, steep, flood, drown.

dress /dres/ ▶ v. **1** (also **get dressed**) put on your clothes. **2** put clothes on someone. **3** clean or apply a dressing to a wound. **4** prepare food (especially poultry or shellfish) for cooking or eating. **5** decorate or arrange in an artistic or attractive way. **6** wear clothes in a particular way or of a particular type: *she dresses well.* ▶ n. **1** a woman's garment that covers the body and extends down over the legs. **2** clothing of a particular kind: *formal dress.*

SYNONYMS ▶ v. **1 clothe**, attire, deck out, garb. **2 decorate**, trim, adorn, arrange, prepare. **3 bandage**, cover, bind, wrap. ANTONYMS undress. ▶ n. **1** *a long blue dress* gown, robe, shift, frock. **2** *full evening dress* **clothes**, clothing, garments, garb, attire, costume, outfit; informal getup, gear, threads; formal apparel.

□ **dress circle** the first level of seats above the ground floor in a theater. **dress down** informal **1** tell someone off. **2** wear informal clothes. **dress rehearsal** a final rehearsal in which costumes are worn and things are done as if it is a real performance. **dress shirt** a man's white shirt worn with a bow tie on formal occasions. **dress up** dress in fancy clothes or in a special costume.

dres·sage /drəˈsäzH/ ▶ n. the training of a horse to perform a series of precise movements at the rider's command.

dres·ser /ˈdresər/ ▶ n. **1** a chest of drawers. **2** a sideboard with shelves above it.

dress·ing /ˈdresiNG/ ▶ n. **1** a sauce for salads, usually consisting of oil and vinegar with flavorings. **2** a piece of material placed on a wound to protect it. □ **dressing-down** informal a severe reprimand or reprimand. **dressing gown** a long, loose garment worn after getting out of bed. **dressing room** a room in which performers change their clothes. **dressing table** a table with a mirror, used while dressing or putting on makeup.

dress·mak·er /ˈdresˌmākər/ ▶ n. a person who makes women's clothes. ■ **dress·mak·ing** n.

dress·y /ˈdresē/ ▶ adj. (**dressier**, **dressiest**) (of clothes) suitable for a festive or formal occasion.

drew /dro͞o/ past of DRAW.

drib·ble /ˈdribəl/ ▶ v. (**dribbles**, **dribbling**, **dribbled**) **1** (of a liquid) fall slowly in drops or a thin stream. **2** let saliva run from the mouth. **3** (in sports) take the ball forward with slight touches or continuous bouncing. ▶ n. a thin stream of liquid.

SYNONYMS ▶ v. **1 trickle**, drip, roll, run, drizzle, ooze, seep, leak. **2 drool**, slaver, slobber.

dribs and drabs /ˈdribz and ˈdrabz/ ▶ **pl.n.** (**in dribs and drabs**) informal in small amounts over a period of time.

dried /drīd/ past and past participle of **DRY**.

dri·er /ˈdrīər/ comparative of **DRY**.

drift /drift/ ▶ **v. 1** be carried slowly by a current of air or water. **2** walk or move slowly or casually. **3** (of snow, leaves, etc.) be blown into heaps by the wind. ▶ **n. 1** a continuous slow movement from one place to another. **2** the general meaning of someone's remarks: *he got her drift*. **3** a large mass of snow, leaves, etc., piled up by the wind.

SYNONYMS ▶ **v. 1 be carried**, be borne, float, bob, glide, coast, waft. **2 wander**, meander, stray, stroll, dawdle, float, roam. **3 stray**, digress, wander, deviate, get sidetracked. **4 pile up**, bank up, heap up, accumulate, gather, amass. ▶ **n. 1 movement**, shift, flow, transfer, gravitation. **2 gist**, meaning, sense, significance, thrust, import, tenor, intention, direction. **3 pile**, heap, bank, mound, mass, accumulation.

□ **drift net** a large fishing net kept upright and allowed to drift in the sea.

drift·er /ˈdriftər/ ▶ **n.** a person who moves from place to place, with no fixed home or job.

drift·wood /ˈdriftˌwo͝od/ ▶ **n.** pieces of wood floating on the sea or washed ashore.

drill /dril/ ▶ **n. 1** a tool or machine used for boring holes. **2** training in military exercises. **3** (**the drill**) informal the correct procedure. **4** a machine for sowing seed in rows. ▶ **v. 1** bore a hole with a drill. **2** give someone military training or other strict instruction.

SYNONYMS ▶ **n. 1 training**, instruction, coaching, teaching, (physical) exercises. **2 procedure**, routine, practice, program, schedule, method, system. ▶ **v. 1 bore**, pierce, puncture, perforate. **2 train**, instruct, coach, teach, discipline, exercise.

drink /driNGk/ ▶ **v.** (**drinks**, **drinking**, **drank** /draNGk/; past participle **drunk** /drəNGk/) **1** take a liquid into the mouth and swallow it. **2** drink alcohol. ▶ **n. 1** a liquid for drinking. **2** a quantity of liquid swallowed at one time. **3** alcohol, or an alcoholic drink.

SYNONYMS ▶ **v. 1 swallow**, gulp (down), quaff, guzzle, imbibe, sip, drain; informal swig, down, knock back. **2 drink alcohol**, tipple, indulge, carouse; informal hit the bottle, booze. ▶ **n. 1 beverage**, liquid refreshment. **2 alcohol**, liquor, spirits; informal booze, hooch, the hard stuff, the bottle. **3 swallow**, gulp, mouthful, draft, sip; informal swig, slug.

■ **drink·a·ble** adj. **drink·er** n.

drip /drip/ ▶ **v.** (**drips**, **dripping**, **dripped**) fall in small drops of liquid. ▶ **n. 1** a small drop of a liquid. **2** a device that slowly passes a liquid substance into a patient's body through a vein. **3** informal a weak person.

SYNONYMS ▶ **v. drop**, dribble, leak, trickle, run, splash, sprinkle. ▶ **n. drop**, dribble, spot, trickle, splash, bead.

□ **drip-feed** give a patient liquid nourishment or medicine through a drip.

drip·ping /ˈdripiNG/ ▶ **n.** (**drippings**) fat that has dripped from roasting meat. ▶ **adj.** very wet.

drip·py /ˈdripē/ ▶ **adj.** (**drippier**, **drippiest**) informal weak, ineffectual, or very sentimental.

drive /drīv/ ▶ **v.** (**drives**, **driving**, **drove** /drōv/; past participle **driven** /ˈdrivən/) **1** operate a motor vehicle. **2** take someone somewhere in a motor vehicle. **3** make someone or something move in a particular direction. **4** make someone behave in a particular way. **5** provide energy to make an engine or machine work. **6** Golf hit the ball from the tee. ▶ **n. 1** a journey in a car. **2** short for **DRIVEWAY**. **3** a natural urge. **4** an organized effort to achieve something. **5** determination and ambition.

SYNONYMS ▶ **v. 1 operate**, handle, manage, pilot, steer, work. **2 go by car**, motor. **3 run**, chauffeur, give someone a lift, take, ferry, transport, convey. **4 power**, propel, move, push. **5 hammer**, screw, ram, sink, plunge, thrust, knock. **6 force**, compel, prompt, precipitate, oblige, coerce, pressure, spur, prod. ▶ **n. 1 excursion**, outing, trip, jaunt, tour, ride, run, journey; informal spin. **2 motivation**, ambition, single-mindedness, determination, willpower, dedication, doggedness, tenacity, enthusiasm, zeal, commitment, energy, vigor; informal get-up-and-go. **3 campaign**, crusade, movement, effort, push, initiative.

□ **drive-in** referring to a movie theater, restaurant, etc. that you can visit without leaving your car. **drive-through** referring to a business or other place which you can drive to and be served without leaving your car.

driv·el /ˈdrivəl/ ▶ **n.** nonsense.

SYNONYMS **nonsense**, twaddle, claptrap, balderdash, gibberish, garbage, rubbish, mumbo-jumbo; informal rot, poppycock, phooey, piffle, tripe, bosh, bull, hogwash, baloney, flapdoodle, bushwa; informal, dated bunkum.

driv·en /ˈdrivən/ past participle of **DRIVE**.

driv·er /ˈdrīvər/ ▶ **n. 1** a person or thing that drives something. **2** a flat-faced golf club used for hitting the ball from the tee. □ **driver's license** an official document permitting a person to drive a motor vehicle. **in the driver's seat** in control.

drive·way /ˈdrīvˌwā/ ▶ **n.** a short private road leading from a public road to a house.

driz·zle /ˈdrizəl/ ▶ **n.** light rain falling in fine drops. ▶ **v.** (**drizzles**, **drizzling**, **drizzled**) **1** rain lightly. **2** pour a thin stream of liquid over a dish.
■ **driz·zly** adj.

droll /drōl/ ▶ **adj.** amusing in a strange or unusual way.

SYNONYMS **funny**, humorous, amusing, comic, comical, mirthful, hilarious, jocular, lighthearted, witty, whimsical, wry, tongue-in-cheek, zany, quirky; informal waggish, wacky, side-splitting, rib-tickling. ANTONYMS serious.

drom·e·dar·y /ˈdräməˌderē/ ▶ **n.** (plural **dromedaries**) a kind of camel with one hump.

drone /drōn/ ▶ **v.** (**drones**, **droning**, **droned**) **1** make a low continuous humming sound. **2** talk for a long time in a boring way. ▶ **n. 1** a low continuous humming sound. **2** a male bee that does no work but can fertilize a queen.

drool /dro͞ol/ ▶ **v.** (**drools**, **drooling**, **drooled**) **1** drop saliva uncontrollably from the mouth. **2** (often **drool over**) informal show great pleasure or desire. ▶ **n.** saliva falling from the mouth.

droop /dro͞op/ ▶ **v.** bend, hang, or sag downward limply or wearily. ▶ **n.** an instance of drooping.

SYNONYMS ▶ v. **hang down**, wilt, dangle, sag, flop, sink, slump, drop.

droop·y /ˈdro͞opē/ ▶ adj. (**droopier**, **droopiest**) **1** hanging down limply. **2** not having much strength or spirit.

drop /dräp/ ▶ v. (**drops**, **dropping**, **dropped**) **1** fall, or let something fall. **2** make or become lower or less: *he dropped his voice*. **3** abandon a course of action: *the charges against him were dropped*. **4** (often **drop someone/thing off**) set down or unload a passenger or goods. ▶ n. **1** a small round or pear-shaped amount of liquid. **2** a small drink: *a drop of water*. **3** an abrupt fall or slope. **4** a type of candy: *a lemon drop*.

SYNONYMS ▶ v. **1 let fall**, let go of, release. **2 fall**, descend, plunge, plummet, dive, sink, dip, tumble. **3 decrease**, lessen, reduce, fall, decline, dwindle, sink, slump. **4 abandon**, give up, discontinue, finish with, renounce, reject, forgo, relinquish, dispense with, leave out; informal dump, pack in. ANTONYMS rise, increase. ▶ n. **1 droplet**, blob, globule, bead. **2 small amount**, little, bit, dash, spot, dribble, sprinkle, trickle, splash, mouthful; informal smidgen, tad. **3 decrease**, reduction, decline, falloff, downturn, slump. **4 cliff**, precipice, slope, descent, incline.

□ **drop someone a line** informal send someone a note or letter. **drop by/in** visit informally and briefly. **drop cloth** a large sheet for covering furniture or flooring to protect it from dust or while painting. **drop goal** Rugby a goal scored by drop-kicking the ball over the crossbar. **drop kick** a kick made by dropping a ball and kicking it as it bounces. **drop off** fall asleep. **drop-off 1** a decline or decrease. **2** a sheer downward slope; a cliff. **drop out 1** stop taking part in something. **2** start living an alternative lifestyle. **drop shot** (in tennis or squash) a softly hit shot that drops abruptly to the ground.

drop·let /ˈdräplit/ ▶ n. a very small drop of a liquid.

drop·out /ˈdräpˌout/ ▶ n. a person who has started living an alternative lifestyle, or abandoned a course of study.

drop·pings /ˈdräpiNGz/ ▶ pl.n. the excrement of animals.

drop·sy /ˈdräpsē/ ▶ n. old-fashioned or nontechnical ⇒ **EDEMA**.

dross /drôs, dräs/ ▶ n. rubbish.

drought /drout/ ▶ n. a very long period of abnormally low rainfall.

drove[1] /drōv/ past of **DRIVE**.

drove[2] ▶ n. **1** a flock of animals being moved along. **2** a large number of people doing the same thing: *tourists arrived in droves*.

drown /droun/ ▶ v. **1** die through taking water into the lungs, or kill someone in this way. **2** flood an area. **3** (usu. **drown something out**) make something impossible to hear by being much louder.

drow·sy /ˈdrouzē/ ▶ adj. (**drowsier**, **drowsiest**) sleepy.

SYNONYMS **sleepy**, dozy, heavy-eyed, groggy, somnolent, tired, weary, fatigued, exhausted, yawning, nodding, lethargic, sluggish, torpid, listless, languid; informal snoozy, dopey, yawny, beat, all done, dog-tired. ANTONYMS alert.

■ **drow·si·ly** adv. **drow·si·ness** n.

drub /drəb/ ▶ v. (**drubs**, **drubbing**, **drubbed**) beat repeatedly. ■ **drub·bing** n.

drudge /drəj/ ▶ n. a person who is made to do hard or dull work.

drudg·er·y /ˈdrəjərē/ ▶ n. hard or dull work.

drug /drəg/ ▶ n. **1** a substance used as a medicine. **2** an illegal substance taken for the effects it has on the body. ▶ v. (**drugs**, **drugging**, **drugged**) make a person or animal unconscious or sleepy by giving them a drug.

SYNONYMS ▶ n. **1 medicine**, medication, remedy, cure, antidote. **2 narcotic**, stimulant, hallucinogen; informal dope, gear. ▶ v. **1 anesthetize**, poison, knock out; informal dope. **2 tamper with**, lace, poison; informal dope, spike, doctor.

drug·store /ˈdrəgˌstôr/ ▶ n. a pharmacy that also sells cosmetics and other articles.

Dru·id /ˈdro͞oid/ ▶ n. a priest in the ancient Celtic religion.

drum /drəm/ ▶ n. **1** a percussion instrument that you play by hitting it with sticks or the hands. **2** a cylindrical object or part. **3** a sound resembling that made by a drum. ▶ v. (**drums**, **drumming**, **drummed**) **1** play on a drum. **2** make a continuous rhythmic noise. **3** (**drum something into**) teach something to someone by constantly repeating it. **4** (**drum something up**) try hard to get support or business.

SYNONYMS ▶ n. **canister**, barrel, cylinder, tank, bin, can. ▶ v. **1 tap**, beat, rap, thud, thump, tattoo, thrum. **2 instill**, drive, impress, hammer, drill, implant, ingrain, inculcate.

□ **drum and bass** a type of dance music consisting largely of electronic drums and bass. **drum kit** a set of drums, cymbals, and other percussion instruments. **drum majorette 1** the female leader of a marching band. **2** a female member of such a band. **drum roll** a rapid succession of drumbeats.

drum·beat /ˈdrəmˌbēt/ ▶ n. a stroke or pattern of strokes on a drum.

drum·mer /ˈdrəmər/ ▶ n. a person who plays a drum or drums.

drum·stick /ˈdrəmˌstik/ ▶ n. **1** a stick used for beating a drum. **2** the lower joint of the leg of a cooked chicken or turkey.

drunk /drəNGk/ past participle of **DRINK** ▶ adj. having drunk so much alcohol that you cannot think or speak clearly. ▶ n. a person who is drunk or who often drinks too much.

SYNONYMS ▶ adj. **intoxicated**, inebriated, drunken, tipsy, under the influence; informal loaded, bombed, tight, plastered, sloshed, pickled, tanked (up), three sheets to the wind. ANTONYMS sober. ▶ n. **drunkard**, alcoholic, dipsomaniac, inebriate; informal boozer, wino, alky, lush.

□ **drunk driving** the crime of driving an automobile while under the influence of alcohol.

drunk·ard /ˈdrəNGkərd/ ▶ n. a person who is often drunk.

drunk·en /ˈdrəNGkən/ ▶ adj. **1** drunk. **2** caused by or showing the effects of drink: *a drunken stupor*. ■ **drunk·en·ly** adv. **drunk·en·ness** n.

drupe /dro͞op/ ▶ n. Botany a fruit with a central stone, e.g., a plum or olive.

dry /drī/ ▶ adj. (**drier**, **driest**) **1** free from moisture. **2** dull and serious. **3** (of humor) subtle and expressed in a matter-of-fact way. **4** (of wine) not sweet. ▶ **v.** (**dries**, **drying**, **dried**) **1** make or become dry. **2** preserve something by evaporating the moisture. **3** (**dry up**) (of a supply) decrease and stop.

> SYNONYMS ▶ **adj.** **1 arid**, parched, waterless, dehydrated, desiccated, withered, shriveled, wizened. **2 dull**, uninteresting, boring, unexciting, tedious, dreary, monotonous, unimaginative, sterile; informal deadly. **3 wry**, subtle, laconic, ironic, sardonic, sarcastic, cynical. ANTONYMS wet, moist. ▶ **v.** **1 parch**, scorch, bake, sear, dehydrate, desiccate, wither, shrivel. **2 wipe**, towel, rub dry, drain. ANTONYMS wet, moisten.

□ **dry-clean** clean a garment with a chemical rather than by washing it. **dry dock** a dock that be drained of water so that a ship can be repaired. **dry goods** fabric, clothing, etc., as distinct from hardware and groceries. **dry ice** white mist produced by solid carbon dioxide, used as a theatrical effect. **dry measure** a measure of volume for grains, fruit, etc. **dry rot** a fungus that causes wood to decay. **dry run** a rehearsal. ■ **dry·ness** n.

dry·er /'drīər/ (or **drier**) ▶ **n.** a machine or device for drying something.

dry·ly /'drīlē/ (or **drily**) ▶ **adv.** in a matter-of-fact or ironically humorous way.

dry·stone /'drīˌstōn/ ▶ **adj.** (of a stone wall) built without using mortar.

DSC ▶ **abbr.** Distinguished Service Cross.

DSL ▶ **abbr.** digital subscriber line, a method of routing digital data on telephone wires, allowing high-speed Internet access.

DSM ▶ **abbr.** Distinguished Service Medal.

DTP ▶ **abbr.** desktop publishing.

du·al /'d(y)o͞oəl/ ▶ **adj.** consisting of two parts or aspects.

> SYNONYMS **double**, twofold, duplex, binary, twin, matching, paired, coupled. ANTONYMS single.

du·al·ism /'d(y)o͞oəˌlizəm/ ▶ **n.** **1** division into two contrasted aspects, such as good and evil. **2** duality. ■ **du·al·ist** n. & adj.

du·al·i·ty /d(y)o͞o'alitē/ ▶ **n.** (plural **dualities**) the state of having two parts or aspects.

dub¹ /dəb/ ▶ **v.** (**dubs**, **dubbing**, **dubbed**) **1** give an unofficial name to. **2** knight someone by touching their shoulder with a sword in a special ceremony.

> SYNONYMS **name**, call, nickname, label, christen, term, tag.

dub² ▶ **v.** (**dubs**, **dubbing**, **dubbed**) **1** give a movie a soundtrack in a different language from the original. **2** add sound effects or music to a movie or recording.

du·bi·e·ty /d(y)o͞o'bī-itē/ ▶ **n.** formal uncertainty.

du·bi·ous /'d(y)o͞obēəs/ ▶ **adj.** **1** hesitating or doubting. **2** probably not honest. **3** of uncertain quality or value.

> SYNONYMS **1 doubtful**, uncertain, unsure, hesitant, skeptical, suspicious, mistrustful; informal iffy. **2 suspicious**, suspect, untrustworthy, unreliable, questionable; informal shady, fishy. ANTONYMS certain, trustworthy.

■ **du·bi·ous·ly** adv.

du·cal /'d(y)o͞okəl/ ▶ **adj.** relating to a duke or dukedom.

duc·at /'dəkət/ ▶ **n.** a gold coin formerly used in Europe.

duch·ess /'dəcнis/ ▶ **n.** **1** the wife or widow of a duke. **2** a woman holding a rank equivalent to duke.

duch·y /'dəcнē/ ▶ **n.** (plural **duchies**) the territory of a duke or duchess.

duck¹ /dək/ ▶ **n.** (plural **duck** or **ducks**) **1** a waterbird with a broad blunt bill, short legs, and webbed feet. **2** a female duck. □ **duck-billed platypus** a semiaquatic egg-laying mammal of Australia that has a bill like a duck, webbed feet, and fur. **like water off a duck's back** (of a critical remark) having no effect.

duck² ▶ **v.** **1** lower yourself quickly to avoid being hit or seen. **2** push someone under water. **3** informal avoid an unwelcome duty.

> SYNONYMS **1 bend down**, stoop, crouch, squat, hunch down, hunker down. **2 shirk**, dodge, evade, avoid, elude, escape, sidestep.

duck·boards /'dəkˌbôrdz/ ▶ **pl.n.** wooden slats joined together to form a path over muddy ground.

duck·ling /'dəkliɴɢ/ ▶ **n.** a young duck.

duct /dəkt/ ▶ **n.** **1** a tube or passageway for air, cables, etc. **2** a tube in the body through which fluid passes.

> SYNONYMS **tube**, channel, canal, vessel, conduit, pipe, outlet, inlet, flue, shaft, vent.

duc·tile /'dəktl, -ˌtīl/ ▶ **adj.** (of a metal) able to be drawn out into a thin wire.

duct·less /'dəktləs/ ▶ **adj.** Anatomy (of a gland) producing secretions directly into the bloodstream.

dud /dəd/ informal ▶ **n.** a thing that fails to work properly. ▶ **adj.** failing to work properly.

dude /do͞od/ ▶ **n.** informal a man.

dudg·eon /'dəjən/ ▶ **n.** deep resentment: *she returned home in high dudgeon.*

due /d(y)o͞o/ ▶ **adj.** **1** expected at a certain time. **2** owing; needing to be paid or given. **3** (of a person) owed or deserving something: *he was due for a raise.* **4** proper or adequate: *due process of law.* ▶ **n.** **1** (**someone's due** or **dues**) what someone deserves or is owed. **2** (**dues**) fees. ▶ **adv.** directly: *head due south.*

> SYNONYMS ▶ **adj.** **1** *their fees were due* **owing**, owed, payable, outstanding, overdue, unpaid, unsettled. **2** *the general's statement is due today* **expected**, anticipated, scheduled, awaited, required. **3 deserved**, merited, warranted, justified, owing, appropriate, fitting, right, rightful, proper. **4 proper**, correct, suitable, appropriate, adequate, sufficient. ▶ **n.** **fee**, subscription, charge, payment, contribution, levy. ▶ **adv.** **directly**, straight, exactly, precisely, dead.

□ **due to 1** caused by. **2** because of. **in due course** at the appropriate time.

du·el /'d(y)o͞oəl/ ▶ **n.** **1** historical a contest with deadly weapons between two people to settle a point of honor. **2** a contest between two parties. ▶ **v.** (**duels**, **dueling**, **dueled**) fight a duel.

> SYNONYMS ▶ **n.** **1 single combat**, fight, confrontation, head-to-head; informal shoot-out. **2 contest**, match, game, meet, encounter, clash.

■ **du·el·ist** n.

du·et /d(y)o͞o'et/ ▶ **n. 1** a performance by two singers or musicians. **2** a piece of music for two performers. ▶ **v.** (**duets**, **duetting**, **duetted**) perform a duet.

duf·fel /'dəfəl/ (also **duffle**) ▶ **n.** a coarse woolen cloth. ▫ **duffel bag** a cylinder-shaped canvas bag closed by a drawstring. **duffel coat** a hooded coat made of a rough woolen material.

duf·fer /'dəfər/ ▶ **n.** informal **1** an incompetent or stupid person. **2** a person inexperienced at something, especially at playing golf.

dug /dəg/ past and past participle of **DIG**.

du·gong /'do͞ogäNG, -gôNG/ ▶ **n.** (plural **dugong** or **dugongs**) a sea cow found in the Indian Ocean.

dug·out /'dəg,out/ ▶ **n. 1** a trench that is roofed over as a shelter for troops. **2** a low shelter at the side of a baseball field for a team's coaches and players. **3** a canoe made from a hollowed-out tree trunk.

duh /də, do͞o/ ▶ **exclam.** informal used to comment on an action perceived as foolish or stupid.

duke /d(y)o͞ok/ ▶ **n. 1** the highest rank of nobleman in Britain and certain other countries. **2** historical (in parts of Europe) a male ruler of a small independent state. ■ **duke·dom n.**

dul·cet /'dəlsit/ ▶ **adj.** (of a sound) sweet and soothing.

dul·ci·mer /'dəlsəmər/ ▶ **n.** a musical instrument that you play by hitting the strings with small hammers.

dull /dəl/ ▶ **adj. 1** not very interesting. **2** not vivid or bright. **3** (of the weather) overcast. **4** slow to understand. ▶ **v.** make or become dull.

> SYNONYMS ▶ **adj. 1 uninteresting**, boring, tedious, monotonous, unimaginative, uneventful, featureless, colorless, lifeless, unexciting, uninspiring, flat, bland, stodgy, dreary; informal deadly, dullsville. **2 overcast**, cloudy, gloomy, dark, dismal, dreary, somber, gray, murky, sunless. **3 drab**, dreary, somber, dark, subdued, muted. **4 muffled**, muted, quiet, soft, faint, indistinct, stifled. **5 unintelligent**, stupid, slow, brainless, mindless, foolish, idiotic; informal dense, dim, halfwitted, thick. ANTONYMS interesting, bright. ▶ **v. lessen**, decrease, diminish, reduce, dampen, blunt, deaden, allay, ease. ANTONYMS intensify.

■ **dull·ness n. dul·ly adv.**

dull·ard /'dələrd/ ▶ **n.** a slow or stupid person.

du·ly /'d(y)o͞olē/ ▶ **adv.** in the proper or expected way.

> SYNONYMS **1 properly**, correctly, appropriately, suitably, fittingly. **2 at the right time**, on time, punctually.

dumb /dəm/ ▶ **adj. 1** offensive unable to speak; not having the power of speech. **2** temporarily unable or unwilling to speak. **3** stupid. ▶ **v.** (**dumb something down**) informal make something less intellectually challenging.

> SYNONYMS ▶ **adj. 1 mute**, speechless, tongue-tied, silent, at a loss for words. **2 stupid**, unintelligent, ignorant, dense, brainless, foolish, slow, dull, simple; informal thick, dim, daft. ANTONYMS talkative, clever.

dumb·bell /'dəm,bel/ ▶ **n. 1** a short bar with a weight at each end, used typically in pairs for exercise or muscle-building. **2** informal a stupid person.

dumb·found·ed /,dəm'foundəd/ ▶ **adj.** greatly astonished.

> SYNONYMS **astonished**, astounded, amazed, staggered, startled, stunned, confounded, nonplussed, stupefied, dazed, dumbstruck, open-mouthed, speechless, thunderstruck, taken aback, disconcerted; informal flabbergasted, flummoxed.

dumb·struck /'dəm,strək/ ▶ **adj.** so shocked or surprised that you cannot speak.

dumb·wait·er /'dəm,wātər/ ▶ **n.** a small elevator for carrying food and dishes between floors.

dum·dum /'dəm,dəm/ ▶ **n.** a kind of soft-nosed bullet that expands on impact.

dum·my /'dəmē/ ▶ **n.** (plural **dummies**) **1** a model of a human being. **2** an object designed to resemble and take the place of the real one. **3** (in bridge) the declarer's partner, whose cards are exposed on the table after the opening lead and played by the declarer. **4** informal a stupid person. ▶ **adj.** resembling a real thing of the same kind.

> SYNONYMS ▶ **n. mannequin**, model, figure. ▶ **adj.** *a dummy warhead* **simulated**, practice, trial, mock, make-believe; informal pretend.

▫ **dummy run** a practice or trial.

dump /dəmp/ ▶ **n. 1** a place where garbage or waste is left. **2** a temporary store of weapons or military provisions. **3** informal an unpleasant or dreary place. ▶ **v. 1** get rid of something unwanted. **2** put down something carelessly. **3** informal abandon someone.

> SYNONYMS ▶ **n. hovel**, slum; informal hole, pigsty. ▶ **v. 1 put down**, set down, deposit, place, shove, unload, drop, throw down; informal stick, park, plunk, plonk. **2 dispose of**, get rid of, throw away/out, discard, jettison; informal ditch, junk.

▫ **dump truck** a truck with a body that tilts or opens at the back for unloading.

dump·ling /'dəmpliNG/ ▶ **n. 1** a small savory ball of dough boiled in water or in a soup or stew. **2** a dessert consisting of apples or other fruit encased in a sweet dough and baked.

dumps /dəmps/ ▶ **pl.n.** (**down in the dumps**) informal depressed or unhappy.

Dump·ster /'dəmpstər/ ▶ **n.** trademark a large trash receptacle designed to be hoisted and emptied into a truck.

dump·y /'dəmpē/ ▶ **adj.** short and stout.

> SYNONYMS **short**, squat, stubby; **plump**, stout, chubby, chunky, portly, fat, bulky; informal tubby, roly-poly, pudgy, porky. ANTONYMS tall, slender.

dun /dən/ ▶ **n.** a dull grayish-brown color.

dunce /dəns/ ▶ **n.** a person who is slow at learning. ▫ **dunce cap** a paper cone formerly put on the head of a dunce at school as a mark of disgrace.

dun·der·head /'dəndər,hed/ ▶ **n.** informal a stupid person.

dune /d(y)o͞on/ ▶ **n.** a mound or ridge of sand formed by the wind.

> SYNONYMS **bank**, mound, hillock, hummock, knoll, ridge, heap, drift.

dung /dəNG/ ▶ **n.** manure. ▫ **dung beetle** a beetle whose larvae feed on dung.

dun·ga·rees /ˌdəNGgəˈrēz/ ▶ **n.** blue jeans or overalls.

dun·geon /ˈdənjən/ ▶ **n.** a strong underground prison cell.

dung·hill /ˈdəNGˌhil/ ▶ **n.** a heap of dung or refuse.

dunk /dəNGk/ ▶ **v. 1** dip food into a drink or soup before eating it. **2** put something in water.

dun·lin /ˈdənlin/ ▶ **n.** (plural **dunlin** or **dunlins**) a sandpiper with a downcurved bill and (in winter) grayish-brown upper parts.

du·o /ˈd(y)o͞o-ō/ ▶ **n.** (plural **duos**) **1** a pair of people or things, especially in music or entertainment. **2** Music a duet.

du·o·dec·i·mal /ˌd(y)o͞oəˈdesəməl, ˌd(y)o͞o-ō-/ ▶ **adj.** (of a system of counting) having twelve as a base.

du·o·de·num /ˌd(y)o͞oəˈdēnəm, d(y)o͞oˈädn-əm/ ▶ **n.** (plural **duodenums**) the first part of the small intestine immediately beyond the stomach.

du·op·o·ly /d(y)o͞oˈäpəlē/ ▶ **n.** (plural **duopolies**) a situation in which two suppliers dominate a market.

dupe /d(y)o͞op/ ▶ **v.** (**dupes**, **duping**, **duped**) deceive; trick. ▶ **n.** a person who is tricked or deceived.

> SYNONYMS ▶ **v. deceive**, trick, hoodwink, hoax, swindle, defraud, cheat, double-cross; gull, mislead, take in, fool, inveigle; informal con, do, rip off, shaft, sucker, snooker, pull the wool over someone's eyes, pull a fast one on. ▶ **n. victim**, pawn, puppet, instrument, fool, innocent; informal sucker, pigeon, patsy, sap, stooge, fall guy.

du·ple /ˈd(y)o͞opəl/ ▶ **adj.** Music (of rhythm) based on two main beats to the bar.

du·plex /ˈd(y)o͞opleks/ ▶ **n. 1** a building divided into two apartments, with a separate entrance for each. **2** an apartment on two floors. ▶ **adj.** having two parts.

du·pli·cate ▶ **adj.** /ˈd(y)o͞opləkit/ **1** exactly like something else. **2** having two corresponding parts. ▶ **n.** /ˈd(y)o͞opləkit/ each of two or more identical things. ▶ **v.** /ˈd(y)o͞opləˌkāt/ (**duplicates**, **duplicating**, **duplicated**) **1** make or be an exact copy of. **2** multiply by two. **3** do something again unnecessarily.

> SYNONYMS ▶ **adj. matching**, identical, twin, corresponding, equivalent. ▶ **n. copy**, photocopy, facsimile, reprint, replica, reproduction, clone; trademark Xerox, Photostat. ▶ **v. 1 copy**, photocopy, photostat, xerox, reproduce, replicate, reprint, run off. **2 repeat**, do again, redo, replicate.

■ **du·pli·ca·tion** /ˌd(y)o͞opləˈkāSHən/ **n. du·pli·ca·tor** /ˈd(y)o͞opləˌkātər/ **n.**

du·plic·i·ty /d(y)o͞oˈplisitē/ ▶ **n.** deceitful behavior.

> SYNONYMS **deceitfulness**, deceit, deception, double-dealing, underhandedness, dishonesty, fraud, fraudulence, chicanery, trickery, subterfuge, skulduggery, treachery; informal crookedness, shadiness, dirty tricks, shenanigans, monkey business. ANTONYMS honesty.

■ **du·plic·i·tous adj.**

du·ra·ble /ˈd(y)o͝orəbəl/ ▶ **adj. 1** hard-wearing. **2** (of goods) not for immediate consumption and so able to be kept.

> SYNONYMS **1 hard-wearing**, wear-resistant, heavy-duty, tough, long-lasting, strong, sturdy, robust, utilitarian. **2 lasting**, long-lasting, long-term, enduring, persistent, abiding, permanent, undying, everlasting. ANTONYMS delicate, short-lived.

■ **du·ra·bil·i·ty** /ˌd(y)o͝orəˈbilitē/ **n.**

du·ra·tion /d(y)o͝orˈāSHən/ ▶ **n.** the time during which something continues.

> SYNONYMS **length**, time, period, term, span, extent, stretch.

du·ress /d(y)o͝oˈres/ ▶ **n.** threats or violence used to force a person to do something: *confessions extracted under duress.*

> SYNONYMS **coercion**, compulsion, force, pressure, intimidation, threats, constraint; informal arm-twisting.

dur·ing /ˈd(y)o͝oriNG/ ▶ **prep. 1** throughout the course of. **2** at a particular point in the course of.

du·rum wheat /ˈd(y)o͝orəm/ ▶ **n.** a kind of hard wheat, yielding flour that is used to make pasta.

dusk /dəsk/ ▶ **n.** the darker stage of twilight.

> SYNONYMS **twilight**, nightfall, sunset, sundown, evening, close of day, semidarkness; literary gloaming. ANTONYMS dawn.

dusk·y /ˈdəskē/ ▶ **adj.** dark, or darkish in color.

dust /dəst/ ▶ **n.** fine, dry powder, especially tiny particles of earth, sand, etc. ▶ **v. 1** remove dust from the surface of. **2** cover lightly with a powdered substance.

> SYNONYMS ▶ **n. dirt**, grime, grit, powder, particles. ▶ **v. 1 wipe**, clean, brush, sweep. **2** *dust the cake with powdered sugar* **sprinkle**, scatter, powder, dredge, sift, cover.

□ **dust bowl** an area where vegetation has been lost and soil reduced to dust and eroded. **the Dust Bowl** an area of Oklahoma, Kansas, and northern Texas affected by severe soil erosion caused by windstorms in the early 1930s, which obliged many people to move. **dust cover 1** a dust jacket for a book. **2** a drop cloth. **dust jacket** a removable paper cover on a book. **dust-up** informal a fight.

dust·er /ˈdəstər/ ▶ **n.** a cloth for dusting furniture.

dust·pan /ˈdəstˌpan/ ▶ **n.** a hand-held container into which you sweep dust and waste.

dust·y /ˈdəstē/ ▶ **adj.** (**dustier**, **dustiest**) **1** covered with or resembling dust. **2** (of a color) dull or muted. **3** staid and uninteresting: *the society has banished its dusty, fusty image.*

> SYNONYMS **1 dirty**, grimy, grubby. **2 powdery**, crumbly, chalky, granular, soft, gritty.

■ **dust·i·ly adv. dust·i·ness n.**

Dutch /dəCH/ ▶ **adj.** relating to the Netherlands or its language. ▶ **n.** the language of the Netherlands. □ **Dutch auction** a method of selling in which the price is reduced until a buyer is found. **Dutch courage** confidence gained from drinking alcohol. **Dutch door** a door horizontally divided, allowing one half to be shut and the other open. **Dutch elm disease** a disease of elm trees, caused by a fungus. **Dutch oven** a covered cooking pot for braising, etc. **Dutch treat** an outing, etc., at which people pay for themselves. **Dutch uncle** informal a kind but firm adviser. **go Dutch** share the cost of a meal equally.

Dutch·man /ˈdəCHmən/ (or **Dutchwoman** /ˈdəCHˌwo͝omən/) ▶ **n.** (plural **Dutchmen** or **Dutchwomen**) a person from the Netherlands.

du·ti·a·ble /ˈd(y)o͞otēəbəl/ ▶ **adj.** on which duty needs to be paid.

dut·i·ful /ˈd(y)o͞otəfəl/ ▶ **adj.** carrying out all your obligations; doing your duty.

> SYNONYMS **conscientious**, responsible, dedicated, devoted, attentive, obedient, deferential. ANTONYMS remiss.

■ **du·ti·ful·ly** **adv.**

du·ty /ˈd(y)o͞otē/ ▶ **n.** (plural **duties**) **1** a moral or legal obligation. **2** a person's regular work, or a task required as part of their job. **3** a charge made when some goods are imported, exported, or sold.

> SYNONYMS **1** *a sense of duty* **responsibility**, obligation, commitment, allegiance, loyalty. **2** *it was his duty to attend the king* **job**, task, assignment, mission, function, role. **3** **tax**, levy, tariff, excise, toll, rate.

□ **duty-bound** morally or legally obliged. **duty-free** not requiring duty to be paid. **on** (or **off**) **duty** engaged (or not engaged) in your regular work.

du·vet /ˌd(y)o͞oˈvā/ ▶ **n.** a thick quilt used instead of an upper sheet and blankets.

DVD ▶ **abbr.** digital video disc or digital versatile disc.

dwarf /dwôrf/ ▶ **n.** (plural **dwarfs** or **dwarves** /dwôrvz/) **1** a member of a mythical race of short humanlike creatures. **2** a person who is unusually small. ▶ **v.** make something seem small in comparison.

> SYNONYMS ▶ **v.** **1** **dominate**, tower over, loom over, overshadow. **2** **overshadow**, outshine, surpass, exceed, outclass, outstrip, outdo, top.

dwarf·ism /ˈd(w)ôrfizəm/ ▶ **n.** (in medical or technical contexts) the condition of being unusually short or small.

dweeb /dwēb/ ▶ **n.** informal a boring, studious, or socially awkward person.

dwell /dwel/ ▶ **v.** (**dwells**, **dwelling**, past and past participle **dwelt** or **dwelled**) **1** formal live in or at a place. **2** (**dwell on**) think about something at length.

> SYNONYMS **reside**, live, be housed, lodge, stay; informal put up; formal abide.

dwell·ing /ˈdweliNG/ ▶ **n.** formal a house or home.

dwin·dle /ˈdwindl/ ▶ **v.** (**dwindles**, **dwindling**, **dwindled**) gradually become smaller or weaker.

> SYNONYMS **diminish**, decrease, reduce, lessen, shrink, wane. ANTONYMS increase.

dye /dī/ ▶ **n.** a substance used to color something. ▶ **v.** (**dyes**, **dyeing**, **dyed**) make something a particular color with dye.

> SYNONYMS ▶ **n.** **coloring**, dyestuff, pigment, tint, stain, wash. ▶ **v.** **color**, tint, pigment, stain, wash.

□ **dyed in the wool** having firm beliefs that never change.

dye·stuff /ˈdīˌstəf/ ▶ **n.** a substance used as or yielding a dye.

dy·ing /ˈdī-iNG/ present participle of **DIE**[1].

dyke[1] /dīk/ **DIKE**[1].

dyke[2] (or **dike**) ▶ **n.** informal, disapproving a lesbian.

dy·nam·ic /dīˈnamik/ ▶ **adj.** **1** full of energy, enthusiasm, and new ideas. **2** (of a process or system) constantly changing and developing. **3** Physics relating to forces that produce motion.

> SYNONYMS **energetic**, spirited, active, lively, vigorous, forceful, high-powered, aggressive, enterprising; informal go-getting, zippy.

□ **dynamic range** the range of sound that occurs in a piece of music or that can be handled by a piece of equipment. ■ **dy·nam·i·cal·ly** **adv.**

dy·nam·ics /dīˈnamiks/ ▶ **pl.n.** **1** the study of the forces involved in movement. **2** forces that stimulate change. **3** the varying levels of sound in a musical performance.

dy·na·mism /ˈdīnəˌmizəm/ ▶ **n.** the quality of being full of energy, enthusiasm, and new ideas.

dy·na·mite /ˈdīnəˌmīt/ ▶ **n.** a kind of high explosive. ▶ **v.** (**dynamites**, **dynamiting**, **dynamited**) blow up something with dynamite.

dy·na·mo /ˈdīnəˌmō/ ▶ **n.** (plural **dynamos**) a machine for converting mechanical energy into electrical energy.

dy·nas·ty /ˈdīnəstē/ ▶ **n.** (plural **dynasties**) a series of rulers or powerful people who belong to the same family.

> SYNONYMS **family**, house, line, lineage, regime, empire.

dyne /dīn/ ▶ **n.** Physics force required to give a mass of one gram an acceleration of one centimeter per second per second.

dys·en·ter·y /ˈdisənˌterē/ ▶ **n.** a disease of the intestines that results in severe diarrhea.

dys·func·tion·al /disˈfəNGkSHənl/ ▶ **adj.** **1** not operating properly. **2** unable to deal with normal social relations.

dys·lex·i·a /disˈleksēə/ ▶ **n.** a disorder involving difficulty in learning to read words and letters. ■ **dys·lex·ic** **adj. & n.**

dys·pep·sia /disˈpepsēə, -ˈpepSHə/ ▶ **n.** indigestion.

dys·pep·tic /disˈpeptik/ ▶ **adj.** **1** suffering from indigestion. **2** irritable.

dys·prax·i·a /disˈpraksēə/ ▶ **n.** a disorder of the brain in childhood causing difficulty in activities requiring coordination and movement.

dys·to·pi·a /disˈtōpēə/ ▶ **n.** an imaginary place or society in which everything is bad. ■ **dys·to·pi·an** **adj. & n.**

dys·tro·phy /ˈdistrəfē/ ▶ **n.** Medicine a disorder in which an organ or tissue of the body wastes away.

Ee

E (or **e**) ▶ **n. 1** (plural **Es** or **E's**) the fifth letter of the alphabet. **2** (**€**) euro(s). ▶ **abbr. 1** (**E**) East or Eastern. **2** informal (**E**) the drug Ecstasy.

each /ēCH/ ▶ **determiner & pron.** every one of two or more people or things, regarded separately. ▶ **adv.** to, for, or by every one of a group.

SYNONYMS ▶ **adv. apiece**, per person, per head, per capita; informal a pop.

□ **each other** the other one or ones.

ea·ger /ˈēgər/ ▶ **adj.** very much wanting to do or have something.

SYNONYMS **1 keen**, enthusiastic, avid, ardent, zealous, highly motivated, committed, earnest. **2** *we were eager for news* **anxious**, impatient, agog, longing, yearning, wishing, hoping; informal itching, dying, raring. ANTONYMS apathetic.

■ **ea·ger·ly adv.**

ea·gle /ˈēgəl/ ▶ **n. 1** a large bird of prey with long, broad wings. **2** Golf a score of two strokes under par at a hole. **3** a gold US coin worth ten dollars. □ **bald eagle** a white-headed eagle, the national emblem of the US. **eagle-eyed** very observant. **eagle owl** a very large owl with ear tufts and a deep hoot.

ea·glet /ˈēglit/ ▶ **n.** a young eagle.

ear¹ /i(ə)r/ ▶ **n. 1** the organ of hearing in humans and animals. **2** an ability to recognize and appreciate music or language. **3** the spike of seeds at the top of the stalk of a cereal plant.

SYNONYMS *he has an ear for a good song* **appreciation**, feel, instinct, intuition, sense.

□ **ear-piercing 1** loud and shrill. **2** the piercing of the outside of the ears to allow the wearing of earrings. **ear-splitting** very loud. **ear trumpet** a trumpet-shaped device formerly used as a hearing aid.

ear² ▶ **n.** the seed-bearing head of a cereal plant.

ear·ache /ˈi(ə)rˌāk/ ▶ **n.** pain inside the ear.

ear·drum /ˈi(ə)rˌdrəm/ ▶ **n.** a membrane in the ear that vibrates in response to sound waves.

earl /ərl/ ▶ **n.** a British nobleman ranking above a viscount. □ **Earl Grey** a kind of China tea flavored with bergamot. ■ **earl·dom n.**

ear·lobe /ˈi(ə)rˌlōb/ ▶ **n.** the soft, fleshy lower part of the external ear.

ear·ly /ˈərlē/ (**earlier, earliest**) ▶ **adj. 1** done, happening, or produced before the usual or expected time. **2** belonging or happening at the beginning of a particular time or sequence. ▶ **adv. 1** before the usual or expected time. **2** at the beginning of a particular time or sequence.

SYNONYMS ▶ **adj. 1 advance**, initial, preliminary, first. **2 untimely**, premature, unseasonable. **3 primitive**, ancient, prehistoric, primeval. **4 prompt**, timely, quick, speedy. ANTONYMS late, overdue. ▶ **adv. 1 in advance**, in good time, ahead of schedule, with time to spare, before the last moment. **2 prematurely**, before the usual time, too soon, ahead of schedule. ANTONYMS late.

□ **at the earliest** not before the time or date specified. **early** (or **earlier**) **on** at an early (or earlier) stage.

ear·mark /ˈi(ə)rˌmärk/ ▶ **v.** choose or set aside for a particular purpose.

SYNONYMS **set aside**, keep (back), reserve, designate, assign, allocate.

ear·muffs /ˈi(ə)rˌməfs/ ▶ **pl.n.** a pair of fabric coverings worn over the ears to protect them from cold or noise.

earn /ərn/ ▶ **v. 1** be given money in return for work or services. **2** gain a reward for hard work or good qualities.

SYNONYMS **1 be paid**, take home, gross, receive, get, make, collect, bring in; informal pocket, bank. **2 deserve**, merit, warrant, justify, be worthy of, gain, win, secure, obtain. ANTONYMS lose.

■ **earn·er n.**

ear·nest /ˈərnist/ ▶ **adj.** very serious.

SYNONYMS **1 serious**, solemn, grave, sober, humorless, staid, intense. **2 devout**, heartfelt, wholehearted, sincere, impassioned, fervent, intense. ANTONYMS frivolous, halfhearted.

□ **in earnest** sincere and serious about your intentions. ■ **ear·nest·ly adv.**

earn·ings /ˈərniNGz/ ▶ **pl.n.** money or income earned.

SYNONYMS **income**, pay, wages, salary, stipend, remuneration, fees, revenue, yield, profit, takings, proceeds.

ear·phones /ˈi(ə)rˌfōnz/ ▶ **pl.n.** devices worn on the ears to listen to radio, recorded sound, etc.

ear·piece /ˈi(ə)rˌpēs/ ▶ **n.** the part of a telephone or other device that is held to or put inside the ear during use.

ear·plug /ˈi(ə)rˌpləg/ ▶ **n.** a piece of wax, rubber, absorbent cotton, etc., placed in the ear as protection against noise or water.

ear·ring /ˈi(ə)rˌ(r)iNG/ ▶ **n.** a piece of jewelry worn on the lobe or edge of the ear.

ear·shot /ˈi(ə)rˌSHät/ ▶ **n.** the range or distance over which you can hear or be heard. □ **within** (or **out of**) **earshot** near enough (or too far away) to be heard.

earth /ərTH/ ▶ **n.** **1** (also **Earth**) the planet on which we live. **2** the ground. **3** soil. **4** the underground lair of a badger or fox.

SYNONYMS **1 world**, globe, planet. **2 land**, ground, terra firma, floor. **3 soil**, clay, dust, dirt, loam, ground, turf.

□ **come back** (or **down**) **to earth** return to reality. **earth-shattering** informal very important or shocking. **earth sciences** the branches of science concerned with the physical composition of the earth and its atmosphere. **on earth** used for emphasis: *what on earth are you doing?*

earth·en /'ərTHən/ ▶ **adj.** made of earth or baked clay.

earth·en·ware /'ərTHən,wer/ ▶ **n.** pottery made of fired clay.

earth·ling /'ərTHliNG/ ▶ **n.** (in science fiction) a person from the earth.

earth·ly /'ərTHlē/ ▶ **adj.** **1** having to do with the earth or human life. **2** remotely possible: *no earthly reason.*

SYNONYMS **worldly**, temporal, mortal, human, material, carnal, fleshly, bodily, physical, corporeal, sensual. ANTONYMS spiritual, heavenly.

earth·quake /'ərTH,kwāk/ ▶ **n.** a sudden violent shaking of the ground, caused by movements within the earth's crust.

SYNONYMS (**earth**) **tremor**, shock, convulsion; informal quake.

earth·work /'ərTH,wərk/ ▶ **n.** a large man-made bank of soil.

earth·worm /'ərTH,wərm/ ▶ **n.** a burrowing worm that lives in the soil.

earth·y /'ərTHē/ ▶ **adj.** (**earthier**, **earthiest**) **1** like soil. **2** direct and uninhibited.

SYNONYMS **1 down-to-earth**, unsophisticated, unrefined, simple, plain, unpretentious, natural. **2 bawdy**, ribald, racy, rude, crude, coarse, indelicate, indecent; informal raunchy.

ear·wax /'i(ə)r,waks/ ▶ **n.** the protective waxy substance produced in the passage of the outer ear.

ear·wig /'i(ə)r,wig/ ▶ **n.** a small insect with a pair of pincers at its rear end. ▶ **v.** (**earwigs**, **earwigging**, **earwigged**) informal eavesdrop.

ease /ēz/ ▶ **n.** **1** lack of difficulty or effort. **2** freedom from problems. ▶ **v.** (**eases**, **easing**, **eased**) **1** make or become less serious or severe. **2** move carefully or gradually. **3** (**ease off** or **up**) do something in a less intense way.

SYNONYMS ▶ **n.** **1 effortlessness**, no trouble, simplicity. **2 naturalness**, casualness, informality, composure, nonchalance, insouciance. **3 affluence**, wealth, prosperity, luxury, plenty, comfort, enjoyment, well-being. ANTONYMS difficulty. ▶ **v.** **1 relieve**, alleviate, soothe, moderate, dull, deaden, numb. **2** *the rain eased off* **let up**, abate, subside, die down, slacken off, diminish, lessen. **3 calm**, quieten, pacify, soothe, comfort, console. **4 slide**, slip, squeeze, guide, maneuver, inch, edge. ANTONYMS aggravate, intensify.

ea·sel /'ēzəl/ ▶ **n.** a wooden frame on legs used by artists for holding the picture they are working on.

eas·i·ly /'ēz(ə)lē/ ▶ **adv.** **1** without difficulty or effort. **2** without doubt; definitely. **3** very probably.

SYNONYMS **effortlessly**, comfortably, simply, without difficulty, readily, without a hitch.

east /ēst/ ▶ **n.** **1** the direction in which the sun rises. **2** the eastern part of a place. ▶ **adj. & adv.** **1** toward or facing the east. **2** (of a wind) blowing from the east. ■ **east·ward** /'ēs(t)wərd/ **adj. & adv.** **east·wards** **adv.**

Eas·ter /'ēstər/ ▶ **n.** the Christian festival celebrating the resurrection of Jesus. □ **Easter egg** **1** an egg that is dyed and often decorated as part of the Easter celebration. **2** a chocolate egg given as a gift at Easter.

east·er·ly /'ēstərlē/ ▶ **adj. & adv.** **1** facing or moving toward the east. **2** (of a wind) blowing from the east.

east·ern /'ēstərn/ ▶ **adj.** **1** situated in or facing the east. **2** (**Eastern**) having to do with the part of the world to the east of Europe. □ **Eastern time** the standard time in a zone including the eastern states of the US and parts of Canada.

east·ern·er /'ēstərnər/ ▶ **n.** a person from the east of a region.

eas·y /'ēzē/ ▶ **adj.** (**easier**, **easiest**) **1** able to be done without great effort. **2** free from worry or problems. **3** not anxious or awkward: *his easy and agreeable manner.*

SYNONYMS **1 uncomplicated**, undemanding, effortless, painless, trouble-free, simple, straightforward, elementary, smooth sailing; informal a piece of cake, child's play, a cinch. **2 natural**, casual, informal, unceremonious, unreserved, unaffected, easygoing, amiable, affable, genial, good-humored, carefree, nonchalant, unconcerned; informal laid-back. **3 quiet**, tranquil, serene, peaceful, untroubled, contented, relaxed, comfortable, secure, safe. **4** *an easy pace* **leisurely**, unhurried, comfortable, undemanding, easygoing, gentle, sedate, moderate, steady. ANTONYMS difficult, demanding.

□ **easy chair** a comfortable armchair. **easy listening** popular music that is tuneful and undemanding. **easy street** informal a state of financial comfort. **take it easy** **1** proceed calmly. **2** make no unnecessary effort.

eas·y·go·ing /'ēzē,gōiNG/ ▶ **adj.** having a relaxed and tolerant attitude.

SYNONYMS **relaxed**, even-tempered, placid, happy-go-lucky, carefree, imperturbable, undemanding, patient, tolerant, lenient, broad-minded, understanding; informal laid-back, unflappable. ANTONYMS intolerant.

eat /ēt/ ▶ **v.** (**eats**, **eating**, **ate** /āt/; past participle **eaten** /'ētn/) **1** put food into the mouth and chew and swallow it. **2** (**eat something away**) gradually wear away or destroy something. **3** (**eat something up**) use resources in very large quantities.

SYNONYMS **1 consume**, devour, swallow, partake of, munch, chomp; informal tuck into, put away. **2 have a meal**, feed, snack, breakfast, lunch, dine; informal graze.

□ **eat your words** admit that what you previously said was wrong. ■ **eat·a·ble** **adj.**

eat·er /'ētər/ ▶ **n.** a person who consumes food in a specified way or of a specified kind.

eat·er·y /'ētərē/ ▶ **n.** (plural **eateries**) informal a restaurant or cafe.

eau de co·logne /ˌō də kəˈlōn/ ▶ **n.** a toilet water with a strong, characteristic scent, originally made in Cologne, Germany.

eaves /ēvz/ ▶ **pl.n.** the part of a roof that meets or overhangs the walls of a building.

eaves·drop /ˈēvzˌdräp/ ▶ **v.** (**eavesdrops, eavesdropping, eavesdropped**) secretly listen to a conversation.

SYNONYMS **listen in**, spy, overhear.

ebb /eb/ ▶ **n.** the movement of the tide out to sea. ▶ **v. 1** (of the tide) move away from the land. **2** (**ebb away**) gradually become less or weaker.

SYNONYMS ▶ **v. 1 recede**, go out, retreat. **2 diminish**, dwindle, wane, fade (away), peter out, decline, flag. ANTONYMS flow, increase.

□ **at a low ebb** in a weakened or depressed state.

eb·on·y /ˈebənē/ ▶ **n. 1** heavy dark wood from a tree of tropical and warm regions. **2** a very dark brown or black color.

e-book /ˈē ˌbo͝ok/ ▶ **n.** an electronic version of a printed book that can be read on a computer or hand-held device.

e·bul·lient /iˈbo͝olyənt, iˈbəlyənt/ ▶ **adj.** cheerful and full of energy.

SYNONYMS **exuberant**, buoyant, cheerful, cheery, merry, jolly, sunny, jaunty, animated, sparkling, vivacious, irrepressible; informal bubbly, bouncy, upbeat, chirpy, full of beans. ANTONYMS depressed.

■ **e·bul·lience n.**

EC ▶ **abbr.** European Community.

ec·cen·tric /ikˈsentrik/ ▶ **adj.** unconventional and slightly strange. ▶ **n.** an eccentric person.

SYNONYMS ▶ **adj. unconventional**, abnormal, anomalous, odd, strange, peculiar, weird, bizarre, outlandish, idiosyncratic, quirky; informal oddball, kooky, cranky. ANTONYMS conventional. ▶ **n. oddity**, free spirit, misfit; informal oddball, weirdo.

■ **ec·cen·tri·cal·ly adv. ec·cen·tric·i·ty** /ˌeksenˈtrisitē/ **n.**

ec·cle·si·as·ti·cal /iˌklēzēˈastikəl/ ▶ **adj.** relating to the Christian church or its clergy.

ECG ▶ **abbr.** electrocardiogram or electrocardiograph.

ech·e·lon /ˈeshəˌlän/ ▶ **n.** a level or rank in an organization, profession, or society.

echi·no·derm /iˈkīnəˌdərm, ˈekənəˌdərm/ ▶ **n.** Zoology a marine invertebrate of a large group including starfish, sea urchins, and sea cucumbers.

ech·o /ˈekō/ ▶ **n.** (plural **echoes**) **1** a sound caused by the reflection of sound waves from a surface back to the listener. **2** a reflected radio or radar beam. ▶ **v.** (**echoes, echoing, echoed**) **1** (of a sound) reverberate or be repeated after the original sound has stopped. **2** repeat someone's words or opinions: *these criticisms are echoed in a number of other studies.* **3** continue to have significance or influence.

SYNONYMS ▶ **n. reverberation**, reflection, ringing, repetition, repeat. ▶ **v. 1 reverberate**, resonate, resound, reflect, ring, vibrate. **2 repeat**, restate, reiterate, imitate, parrot, mimic, reproduce, recite.

□ **echo chamber** an enclosed space for producing echoes. **echo sounder** a device for determining the depth of the seabed or detecting objects in water by measuring the time taken for echoes to return to the listener. ■ **ech·o·ey adj.**

e·cho·ic /eˈkō-ik/ ▶ **adj.** of or like an echo.

ech·o·lo·ca·tion /ˌekōlōˈkāshən/ ▶ **n.** the location of objects by reflected sound, used by animals such as dolphins and bats.

e·clair /āˈkler, iˈkler/ ▶ **n.** a cake of light pastry filled with cream and topped with chocolate icing.

ec·lamp·si·a /iˈklam(p)sēə/ ▶ **n.** Medicine a condition in which convulsions occur in a pregnant woman suffering from high blood pressure.

é·clat /āˈklä/ ▶ **n.** a notably brilliant or successful effect.

ec·lec·tic /iˈklektik/ ▶ **adj.** taking ideas from a wide range of sources.

e·clipse /iˈklips/ ▶ **n. 1** an occasion when one planet, the moon, etc., passes between another and the observer, or in front of a planet's source of light. **2** a sudden loss of significance or power. ▶ **v.** (**eclipses, eclipsing, eclipsed**) **1** (of a planet, the moon, etc.) obscure the light coming from or shining on another. **2** make less significant or powerful.

SYNONYMS ▶ **v. outshine**, overshadow, surpass, exceed, outclass, outstrip, outdo, transcend.

e·clip·tic /iˈkliptik/ ▶ **n.** Astronomy a great circle on the celestial sphere representing the sun's apparent path during the year, so called because eclipses can only occur when the moon crosses it.

ec·logue /ˈekˌlôg, ˈekˌläg/ ▶ **n.** a short pastoral poem.

ec·o-friend·ly /ˈēkō-/ ▶ **adj.** not harmful to the environment.

E. co·li /ē ˈkōlī/ ▶ **n.** the bacterium *Escherichia coli,* commonly found in the intestines of humans, some strains of which can cause severe food poisoning.

e·col·o·gy /iˈkäləjē/ ▶ **n.** the study of how animals and plants relate to one another and to their surroundings. ■ **ec·o·log·i·cal** /ˌekəˈläjikəl, ˌēkə-/ **adj. ec·o·log·i·cal·ly** /ˌekəˈläjik(ə)lē, ˌēkə-/ **adv. e·col·o·gist n.**

e-com·merce ▶ **n.** commercial transactions conducted on the Internet.

ec·o·nom·ic /ˌekəˈnämik, ˌēkə-/ ▶ **adj. 1** relating to economics or the economy of a country or region. **2** profitable, or concerned with profitability: *organizations must become larger if they are to remain economic.*

SYNONYMS **1 financial**, monetary, budgetary, commercial, fiscal. **2 profitable**, moneymaking, lucrative, remunerative, fruitful, productive. ANTONYMS unprofitable.

ec·o·nom·i·cal /ˌekəˈnämikəl, ˌēkə-/ ▶ **adj. 1** giving good value in relation to the resources used or money spent. **2** careful in the use of resources or money.

SYNONYMS **1 cheap**, inexpensive, low-cost, budget, economy, cut-price, bargain. **2 thrifty**, provident, prudent, sensible, frugal. ANTONYMS expensive, spendthrift.

■ **ec·o·nom·i·cal·ly adv.**

ec·o·nom·ics /ˌekəˈnämiks, ˌēkə-/ ▶ **pl.n.** the study of the production, consumption, and transfer of wealth.

e·con·o·mist /iˈkänəmist/ ▶ **n.** an expert in economics.

e·con·o·mize /iˈkänəˌmīz/ ▶ v. (**economizes**, **economizing**, **economized**) spend less; be economical.

SYNONYMS **save** (**money**), cut costs, cut back, make cutbacks, retrench, scrimp.

e·con·o·my /iˈkänəmē/ ▶ n. (plural **economies**) **1** the state of a country or region in terms of the production and consumption of goods and services and the supply of money. **2** careful management of resources. **3** a financial savings. ▶ adj. offering good value for money: *an economy pack.*

SYNONYMS ▶ n. **1 wealth**, financial resources, financial management. **2 thrift**, thriftiness, prudence, careful budgeting, economizing, saving, restraint, frugality. ANTONYMS extravagance.

□ **economy of scale** a proportionate saving in costs gained by an increased level of production.

ec·o·sys·tem /ˈekōˌsistəm, ˈēkō-/ ▶ n. all the plants and animals of a particular area considered in terms of how they interact with their environment.

ec·o·tour·ism /ˌekōˈto͝orizəm, ˌēkō-/ ▶ n. tourism directed toward unspoiled natural environments and intended to support conservation efforts. ■ **ec·o·tour·ist** n.

ec·o-war·ri·or /ˈēkō-/ ▶ n. a person who engages in protest activities aimed at protecting the environment from damage.

ec·ru /ˈekro͞o/ ▶ n. the light cream or beige color of unbleached linen.

ec·sta·sy /ˈekstəsē/ ▶ n. (plural **ecstasies**) **1** an overwhelming feeling of great happiness. **2** (**Ecstasy**) an illegal drug that produces feelings of excitement and happiness. **3** an emotional or religious frenzy.

SYNONYMS **rapture**, bliss, joy, elation, euphoria, rhapsodies. ANTONYMS misery.

SPELLING

There is **cs** at the beginning, not **x**, and an **s** at the end: e**cs**ta**s**y.

ec·stat·ic /ekˈstatik/ ▶ adj. very happy or enthusiastic.

SYNONYMS **enraptured**, elated, euphoric, rapturous, joyful, overjoyed, blissful; informal over the moon, on top of the world.

■ **ec·stat·i·cal·ly** adv.

ec·top·ic /ekˈtäpik/ ▶ adj. Medicine in an abnormal place or position.

ec·to·plasm /ˈektəˌplazəm/ ▶ n. a substance that is thought by some people to come out of the body of a medium during a seance.

Ec·ua·dor·e·an /ˌekwəˈdôrēən/ (or **Ecuadorian**) ▶ n. a person from Ecuador. ▶ adj. relating to Ecuador.

ec·u·men·i·cal /ˌekyəˈmenikəl/ ▶ adj. **1** representing a number of different Christian churches. **2** wishing for the world's Christian churches to be united.

ec·ze·ma /ˈegzəmə, ˈeksə-, igˈzēmə/ ▶ n. a condition in which patches of skin become rough and inflamed.

E·dam /ˈēdəm/ ▶ n. a round yellow Dutch cheese with a red wax coating.

ed·dy /ˈedē/ ▶ n. (plural **eddies**) a circular movement of water causing a small whirlpool. ▶ v. (**eddies**, **eddying**, **eddied**) (of water, air, etc.) move in a circular way.

SYNONYMS ▶ n. **swirl**, whirlpool, vortex. ▶ v. **swirl**, whirl, spiral, wind, twist.

e·del·weiss /ˈādlˌwīs, -ˌvīs/ ▶ n. a European mountain plant with small flowers.

e·de·ma /iˈdēmə/ ▶ n. a buildup of watery fluid in the tissues of the body.

E·den /ˈēdn/ ▶ n. **1** (also **Garden of Eden**) the place where Adam and Eve lived in the story of the Creation in the Bible. **2** a place of happiness or unspoiled beauty.

edge /ej/ ▶ n. **1** the outside limit of an object, area, or surface. **2** the sharpened side of a blade. **3** the line along which two surfaces meet. **4** a slight advantage over close rivals: *his powerful serve gives him the edge over other players.* ▶ v. (**edges**, **edging**, **edged**) **1** provide with an edge. **2** move slowly and carefully.

SYNONYMS ▶ n. **1 border**, boundary, extremity, fringe, margin, side, lip, rim, brim, brink, verge, perimeter. **2 sharpness**, severity, bite, sting, sarcasm, malice, spite, venom. **3 advantage**, lead, head start, the whip hand, the upper hand, dominance. ANTONYMS middle. ▶ v. **1 border**, fringe, skirt, surround, enclose, encircle, bound. **2 trim**, decorate, finish, border, fringe. **3 creep**, inch, work your way, ease yourself, sidle, steal.

□ **on edge** tense or irritable.

edge·wise /ˈejˌwīz/ (or **edgeways** /-ˌwāz/) ▶ adv. with the edge uppermost or toward the viewer. □ **get a word in edgewise** manage to break into a conversation.

edg·ing /ˈejiNG/ ▶ n. something forming an edge or border.

edg·y /ˈejē/ ▶ adj. (**edgier**, **edgiest**) tense, nervous, or irritable.

SYNONYMS **tense**, nervous, on edge, anxious, apprehensive, uneasy, unsettled, twitchy, jumpy, nervy, keyed up, restive; informal uptight, wired. ANTONYMS calm.

ed·i·ble /ˈedəbəl/ ▶ adj. fit to be eaten.

e·dict /ˈēdikt/ ▶ n. an official order or announcement.

ed·i·fice /ˈedəfis/ ▶ n. formal a large, impressive building.

ed·i·fy /ˈedəˌfī/ ▶ v. (**edifies**, **edifying**, **edified**) teach someone something that is educational or morally improving.

SYNONYMS **educate**, instruct, teach, school, tutor, train, guide; enlighten, inform, cultivate, develop, improve, better.

■ **ed·i·fi·ca·tion** /ˌedəfiˈkāSHən/ n.

ed·it /ˈedit/ ▶ v. (**edits**, **editing**, **edited**) **1** prepare written material for publication by correcting or shortening it. **2** prepare material for a recording or broadcast. **3** be editor of a newspaper or magazine. ▶ n. a change made as a result of editing.

SYNONYMS ▶ v. **correct**, check, copy-edit, improve, polish, modify, adapt, revise, rewrite, reword, shorten, condense, cut, abridge.

e·di·tion /iˈdiSHən/ ▶ n. **1** a particular form of a published written work. **2** the total number of copies of a book, newspaper, etc., that are issued.

3 a particular example of a regular program or broadcast.

SYNONYMS **issue**, number, volume, printing, impression, publication, program, version.

ed·i·tor /ˈeditər/ ▶ **n. 1** a person who is in charge of a newspaper or magazine. **2** a person who prepares material for publication or broadcasting.

ed·i·to·ri·al /ˌediˈtôrēəl/ ▶ **adj.** relating to the editing of material. ▶ **n.** a newspaper article giving the editor's opinion.

ed·i·to·ri·al·ize /ˌediˈtôrēəˌlīz/ ▶ **v.** (**editorializes, editorializing, editorialized**) (of a newspaper or editor) express opinions rather than just report news.

EDT ▶ **abbr.** Eastern Daylight Time.

ed·u·cate /ˈejəˌkāt/ ▶ **v.** (**educates, educating, educated**) train or instruct someone to improve their mind or character.

SYNONYMS **1 teach**, school, tutor, instruct, coach, train, inform, enlighten. **2** (**educated**) **informed**, literate, schooled, tutored, well-read, learned, knowledgeable, enlightened, intellectual, academic, erudite, scholarly, cultivated, cultured.

□ **educated guess** a guess based on knowledge and experience.

ed·u·ca·tion /ˌejəˈkāshən/ ▶ **n. 1** the process of teaching or learning. **2** the theory and practice of teaching. **3** training in a particular subject.

SYNONYMS **1 teaching**, schooling, tuition, tutoring, instruction, coaching, training, guidance, enlightenment. **2 learning**, knowledge, literacy, scholarship, enlightenment.

ed·u·ca·tion·al /ˌejəˈkāshənl/ ▶ **adj. 1** of or relating to the provision of education. **2** intended or serving to educate or enlighten.

SYNONYMS **1 academic**, scholastic, learning, teaching, pedagogic. **2 instructive**, instructional, educative, informative, illuminating, enlightening; formal edifying.

■ **ed·u·ca·tion·al·ly adv.**

Ed·ward·i·an /edˈwôrdēən, -ˈwär-/ ▶ **adj.** relating to the reign of King Edward VII (1901–10) of the United Kingdom.

EEC ▶ **abbr.** European Economic Community.

eel /ēl/ ▶ **n.** a snakelike fish with a slender body.

e'er /e(ə)r/ literary form of **EVER**.

ee·rie /ˈi(ə)rē/ ▶ **adj.** (**eerier, eeriest**) strange and frightening.

SYNONYMS **uncanny**, sinister, ghostly, unnatural, unearthly, supernatural, otherworldly, strange, abnormal, weird, freakish; informal creepy, scary, spooky.

■ **ee·ri·ly adv.**

ef·face /iˈfās/ ▶ **v.** (**effaces, effacing, effaced**) **1** rub off a mark from a surface. **2** make something disappear. **3** (**efface yourself**) make yourself appear unimportant.

ef·fect /iˈfekt/ ▶ **n. 1** a change that something causes in something else; a result. **2** the state of being or becoming operative or effective: *the ban is to take effect in six months.* **3** the extent to which something succeeds: *wind power can be used to great effect.* **4** (**effects**) personal belongings. **5** (**effects**) the lighting, sound, or scenery used in a play or movie. ▶ **v.** make something happen.

SYNONYMS ▶ **n. 1** *the effect of these changes* **result**, consequence, upshot, outcome, repercussions, end result, aftermath. **2** *the effect of the drug* **impact**, action, effectiveness, power, potency, strength, success. **3** *the dead man's* ***effects*** **belongings**, possessions, worldly goods, chattels, property; informal things, stuff. ANTONYMS cause. ▶ **v. achieve**, accomplish, carry out, manage, bring off, execute, conduct, engineer, perform, do, cause, bring about, produce.

□ **in effect** in practice, even if not formally acknowledged.

USAGE

Don't confuse **effect** and **affect**. **Effect** chiefly means 'a result,' while **affect** is a verb whose main meaning is 'make a difference to.'

ef·fec·tive /iˈfektiv/ ▶ **adj. 1** producing a desired or intended result; successful. **2** (of a law or policy) in operation. **3** existing in fact, though not formally acknowledged as such: *under effective Soviet control.*

SYNONYMS **1 successful**, effectual, potent, powerful, helpful, beneficial, advantageous, valuable, useful. **2 convincing**, compelling, strong, forceful, persuasive, plausible, credible, logical, reasonable, cogent. **3 operative**, in force, in effect, valid, official, legal, binding. **4 virtual**, practical, essential, actual. ANTONYMS ineffective.

■ **ef·fec·tive·ly adv. ef·fec·tive·ness n.**

ef·fec·tu·al /iˈfekchoōəl/ ▶ **adj.** producing the intended result; effective.

ef·fem·i·nate /iˈfemənət/ ▶ **adj.** disapproving (of a man) looking, behaving, or sounding like a woman.

SYNONYMS **womanish**, effete, foppish, unmanly, feminine; informal camp, campy, limp-wristed. ANTONYMS manly.

■ **ef·fem·i·na·cy n.**

ef·fer·ves·cent /ˌefərˈvesənt/ ▶ **adj. 1** (of a liquid) giving off bubbles; fizzy. **2** lively and enthusiastic.

SYNONYMS **fizzy**, sparkling, carbonated, aerated, gassy, bubbly. ANTONYMS still.

■ **ef·fer·vesce** /ˌefərˈves/ **v. ef·fer·ves·cence n.**

ef·fete /iˈfēt/ ▶ **adj. 1** weak; feeble. **2** (of a man) effeminate.

ef·fi·ca·cious /ˌefiˈkāshəs/ ▶ **adj.** formal effective.

ef·fi·ca·cy /ˈefikəsē/ ▶ **n.** formal effectiveness.

ef·fi·cien·cy /iˈfishənsē/ ▶ **n.** (plural **efficiencies**) **1** the quality of being efficient. **2** a means of using resources in a less wasteful way. **3** (also **efficiency apartment**) an apartment in which one room contains the kitchen, living, and sleeping quarters.

SYNONYMS **1 economy**, productivity, cost-effectiveness, organization, order, orderliness, regulation. **2 competence**, capability, ability, proficiency, expertise, skill, effectiveness. ANTONYMS inefficiency, incompetence.

ef·fi·cient /iˈfishənt/ ▶ **adj.** working well with no waste of money or effort.

SYNONYMS **1 economic**, productive, effective, cost-effective, streamlined, organized, methodical, systematic, orderly. **2 competent**, capable, able, proficient, skillful, skilled, effective, productive, organized, businesslike. ANTONYMS inefficient, incompetent.

■ **ef·fi·cient·ly** adv.

ef·fi·gy /ˈefijē/ ▶ n. (plural **effigies**) a sculpture or statue of a person.

ef·flo·res·cence /ˌefləˈresəns/ ▶ n. literary a very high stage of development.

ef·flu·ence /ˈeflo͞oəns/ ▶ n. **1** a substance that flows out. **2** the action of flowing out.

ef·flu·ent /ˈeflo͞oənt/ ▶ n. liquid waste or sewage that flows into a river or the sea.

ef·flu·vi·um /iˈflo͞ovēəm/ ▶ n. (plural **effluvia** /-vēə/) an unpleasant or harmful smell.

ef·fort /ˈefərt/ ▶ n. **1** a determined attempt to do something. **2** the physical or mental energy needed to do something.

SYNONYMS **1 attempt**, try, endeavor; informal shot, stab, bash. **2 achievement**, accomplishment, feat, undertaking, enterprise, work, result, outcome. **3 exertion**, energy, work, application; informal elbow grease.

ef·fort·less /ˈefərtlis/ ▶ adj. done or achieved without effort; natural and easy.

SYNONYMS **easy**, undemanding, unchallenging, painless, simple, uncomplicated, straightforward, elementary; fluent, natural; informal as easy as pie, child's play, kids' stuff, a cinch, no sweat, a breeze, duck soup, a snap. ANTONYMS difficult.

■ **ef·fort·less·ly** adv.

ef·fron·ter·y /iˈfrəntərē/ ▶ n. rude and disrespectful behavior.

SYNONYMS **impudence**, impertinence, insolence, audacity, temerity, presumption, nerve, gall, cheek, shamelessness, impoliteness, disrespect, bad manners; informal brass, chutzpah.

ef·fu·sion /iˈfyo͞oZHən/ ▶ n. an act of talking or writing in an unrestrained or heartfelt way.

ef·fu·sive /iˈfyo͞osiv/ ▶ adj. expressing pleasure or approval in a warm and emotional way.

SYNONYMS **gushing**, gushy, unrestrained, extravagant, fulsome, demonstrative, lavish, enthusiastic, lyrical; expansive, wordy, verbose. ANTONYMS restrained.

■ **ef·fu·sive·ly** adv.

e.g. ▶ abbr. for example.

e·gal·i·tar·i·an /iˌgaləˈterēən/ ▶ adj. believing that all people are equal and deserve equal rights and opportunities. ▶ n. an egalitarian person. ■ **e·gal·i·tar·i·an·ism** n.

egg¹ /eg/ ▶ n. **1** a small oval or round object laid by a female bird, reptile, fish, etc., and containing a cell that can develop into a new creature. **2** a female reproductive cell; an ovum. **3** informal, dated a person of a specified kind.

SYNONYMS **ovum**, gamete; (**eggs**) roe, spawn.

□ **egg custard** a custard made with milk and eggs, typically sweetened and baked. **egg white** the clear substance around the yolk of an egg that turns white when cooked or beaten. **with egg on your face** informal appearing foolish.

egg² ▶ v. (**egg someone on**) urge someone to do something foolish.

egg·head /ˈegˌhed/ ▶ n. informal a very intelligent and academic person.

egg·plant /ˈegˌplant/ ▶ n. a large vegetable with purple skin.

egg·shell /ˈegˌSHel/ ▶ n. the fragile outer layer of an egg.

e·go /ˈēgō/ ▶ n. (plural **egos**) **1** a person's sense of their own value and importance. **2** the part of the mind that is responsible for a person's sense of who they are. □ **ego trip** informal something that a person does to make themselves feel important.

e·go·cen·tric /ˌēgōˈsentrik/ ▶ adj. self-centered.

e·go·ma·ni·a /ˌēgōˈmānēə/ ▶ n. an obsessive concern with yourself.

e·go·tism /ˈēgəˌtizəm/ (or **egoism** /ˈēgōˌizəm/) ▶ n. the quality of being very conceited or self-absorbed.

SYNONYMS **self-centeredness**, egomania, egocentricity, self-interest, selfishness, self-seeking, self-serving, self-regard, self-obsession; narcissism, vanity, conceit, self-importance; boastfulness.

■ **e·go·tis·ti·cal** /ˌēgəˈtistikəl/ adj.

e·go·tist /ˈēgəˌtist/ (or **egoist** /ˈēgōˌist/) ▶ n. an excessively conceited or self-centered person.

SYNONYMS **self-seeker**, egocentric, egomaniac, narcissist; boaster, braggart; informal swank, show-off, bighead, showboat.

e·go·tis·tic /ˌēgəˈtistik/ (or **egoistic** /ˌēgōˈistik/) ▶ adj. exhibiting egotism.

SYNONYMS **self-centered**, selfish, egocentric, self-interested, self-seeking, self-absorbed, self-obsessed, narcissistic, vain, conceited, self-important, boastful.

e·gre·gious /iˈgrējəs/ ▶ adj. formal very bad: *egregious abuses of the copyright law.*

e·gress /ˈēˌgres/ ▶ n. formal **1** the action of going out of a place. **2** a way out.

e·gret /ˈēgrit, ˈēˌgret, ˈegrit/ ▶ n. a kind of heron with white feathers.

E·gyp·tian /iˈjipSHən/ ▶ n. **1** a person from Egypt. **2** the language used in ancient Egypt. ▶ adj. relating to Egypt.

eh /ā, e/ ▶ exclam. used to ask for something to be repeated or explained or to elicit agreement.

Eid /ēd/ (or **Id**) ▶ n. **1** (in full **Eid ul-Fitr** /ēd o͝ol ˈfētr/) the Muslim festival marking the end of the fast of Ramadan. **2** (in full **Eid ul-Adha** /ēd o͝ol ˈädə/) the Muslim festival marking the end of the annual pilgrimage to Mecca.

ei·der /ˈīdər/ ▶ n. (plural **eider** or **eiders**) a black and white duck that lives in northern countries.

ei·der·down /ˈīdərˌdoun/ ▶ n. small, soft feathers from the breast of the female eider duck.

eight /āt/ ▶ cardinal number **1** one more than seven; 8. (Roman numeral: **viii** or **VIII**) **2** a racing shell (boat) with eight oars. **3** an eight-cylinder engine or a motor vehicle with such an engine.

eight·een /āˈtēn, ˈāˌtēn/ ▶ cardinal number one more than seventeen; 18. (Roman numeral: **xviii** or **XVIII**) ■ **eight·eenth** ordinal number.

eighth /ā(t)TH/ ▶ ordinal number **1** at number eight in a sequence; 8th. **2** (**an eighth** or **one eighth**) each of eight equal parts of something. □ **eighth note** Music a note having the time value of an eighth of a whole note or half a quarter note.

SPELLING

There are two hs: eighth.

eight·y /ˈātē/ ▶ **cardinal number** (plural **eighties**) ten less than ninety; 80. (Roman numeral: **lxxx** or **LXXX**) ■ **eight·i·eth ordinal number.**

ei·ther /ˈēT͟Hər, ˈīT͟Hər/ ▶ **conj. & adv. 1** used before the first of two alternatives specified. **2** used to indicate a similarity or link with a statement just made: *You don't like him, do you? I don't either.* **3** for that matter; moreover: *I was too tired to go. And I couldn't have paid my way, either.* ▶ **determiner & pron. 1** one or the other of two people or things. **2** each of two.

e·jac·u·late /iˈjakyəˌlāt/ ▶ **v.** (**ejaculates, ejaculating, ejaculated**) **1** (of a man or male animal) eject semen from the penis at the moment of orgasm. **2** dated say something suddenly. ■ **e·jac·u·la·tion** /iˌjakyəˈlāsHən/ **n.**

e·ject /iˈjekt/ ▶ **v. 1** force or throw out violently or suddenly. **2** force someone to leave a place. **3** (of a pilot) escape from an aircraft by means of an ejection seat.

> SYNONYMS **1 emit**, spew out, discharge, disgorge, give off, send out, belch, vent. **2 expel**, throw out, remove, oust, evict, banish; informal kick out, boot out.

□ **ejection seat** (or **ejector seat**) a seat that can throw the pilot out of the aircraft in an emergency. ■ **e·jec·tion n.**

eke /ēk/ ▶ **v.** (**ekes, eking, eked**) (**eke something out**) **1** make a supply of something last a long time. **2** make a living with difficulty.

EKG ▶ **abbr. 1** electrocardiogram. **2** electrocardiograph.

el /el/ ▶ **n.** informal an elevated railroad.

e·lab·o·rate ▶ **adj.** /iˈlab(ə)rit/ involving many carefully arranged parts; complicated. ▶ **v.** /iˈlabəˌrāt/ (**elaborates, elaborating, elaborated**) develop something in more detail.

> SYNONYMS ▶ **adj. 1 complicated**, complex, intricate, involved, detailed. **2 ornate**, decorated, embellished, adorned, ornamented, fancy, fussy, busy. ANTONYMS simple, plain. ▶ **v.** *please* ***elaborate on*** *your explanation* **expand on**, enlarge on, add to, flesh out, develop, fill out, amplify.

■ **e·lab·o·rate·ly adv. e·lab·o·ra·tion** /iˌlabəˈrāsHən/ **n.**

é·lan /āˈlän, āˈlan/ (also **elan**) ▶ **n.** energy and stylishness: *he played the march with great élan.*

e·land /ˈēlənd/ ▶ **n.** a spiral-horned African antelope.

e·lapse /iˈlaps/ ▶ **v.** (**elapses, elapsing, elapsed**) (of time) pass.

e·las·tic /iˈlastik/ ▶ **adj. 1** able to go back to its normal shape after being stretched or squeezed. **2** flexible. ▶ **n.** cord or fabric that returns to its original length or shape after being stretched.

> SYNONYMS ▶ **adj. 1 stretchy**, elasticated, springy, flexible, pliable, supple. **2 adaptable**, flexible, adjustable, accommodating, variable, fluid, versatile. ANTONYMS rigid.

□ **elastic band** a rubber band. ■ **e·las·tic·i·ty** /iˌlaˈstisitē, ēˌla-/ **n.**

e·las·to·mer /iˈlastəmər/ ▶ **n.** a natural or synthetic polymer having elastic properties, e.g., rubber.

e·lat·ed /iˈlātid/ ▶ **adj.** very happy and excited.

> SYNONYMS **thrilled**, delighted, overjoyed, ecstatic, euphoric, jubilant, rapturous, in raptures, walking on air, on cloud nine, in seventh heaven; informal on top of the world, over the moon, tickled pink. ANTONYMS miserable.

e·la·tion /iˈlāsHən/ ▶ **n.** great happiness and excitement.

el·bow /ˈelˌbō/ ▶ **n.** the joint between the forearm and the upper arm. ▶ **v.** push someone with your elbow. □ **elbow grease** informal hard work in cleaning something. **elbow room** informal enough space to move or work in.

eld·er¹ /ˈeldər/ ▶ **adj.** older. ▶ **n. 1** (**your elder**) a person who is older than you are. **2** a leader or senior figure in a tribe.

> SYNONYMS ▶ **adj. older**, senior. ▶ **n. leader**, patriarch, father.

eld·er² ▶ **n.** a small tree or shrub with white flowers and bluish-black or red berries (**elderberries**).

el·der·flow·er /ˈeldərˌflou(-ə)r/ ▶ **n.** the flower of the elder, used to make wines and cordials.

eld·er·ly /ˈeldərlē/ ▶ **adj.** old or aging.

> SYNONYMS **aged**, old, aging, long in the tooth, gray-haired, in your dotage; informal getting on, over the hill. ANTONYMS youthful.

eld·est /ˈeldəst/ ▶ **adj.** oldest.

e·lect /iˈlekt/ ▶ **v. 1** choose someone to hold a position by voting for them. **2** choose to do something. ▶ **adj. 1** elected to a position but not yet in office: *the president-elect.* **2** chosen or singled out.

> SYNONYMS ▶ **v. 1 vote in**, vote for, return, cast your vote for, choose, pick, select. **2 choose**, decide, opt, prefer, vote.

e·lec·tion /iˈleksHən/ ▶ **n. 1** a procedure by which a person is elected. **2** the action of electing.

> SYNONYMS **ballot**, vote, poll, primary.

e·lec·tion·eer·ing /iˌleksHəˈni(ə)riNG/ ▶ **n.** the action of campaigning to be elected.

e·lec·tive /iˈlektiv/ ▶ **adj. 1** using or chosen by election. **2** (of study, treatment, etc.) chosen; not compulsory.

e·lec·tor /iˈlektər, -ˌtôr/ ▶ **n. 1** a person who has the right to vote in an election. **2** a member of the Electoral College of the United States. **3** historical a German prince entitled to take part in the election of the Holy Roman Emperor.

e·lec·tor·al /iˈlektərəl/ ▶ **adj.** relating to elections or electors. □ **electoral college** an ad hoc assembly that casts votes for the election of the US president and vice president.

e·lec·tor·ate /iˈlektərət/ ▶ **n.** the people who are entitled to vote in an election.

e·lec·tric /iˈlektrik/ ▶ **adj. 1** of, worked by, or producing electricity. **2** very exciting. **3** (of a musical instrument) amplified through a loudspeaker.

> SYNONYMS *the atmosphere was electric* **exciting**, charged, electrifying, thrilling, dramatic, dynamic, stimulating, galvanizing.

□ **electric blanket** an electrically wired blanket used for heating a bed. **electric blue** a brilliant light blue. **electric chair** a chair in which convicted criminals are executed by electrocution. **electric eel** a large fish like an eel that uses pulses of electricity to kill prey and assist in navigation.

electric fence a fence through which an electric current can be passed, giving an electric shock to any person or animal touching it. **electric guitar** a guitar with a built-in pickup that converts sound vibrations into electrical signals. **electric shock** a sudden discharge of electricity through a part of the body.

e·lec·tri·cal /i'lektrikəl/ ▶ **adj.** concerned with, operating by, or producing electricity. □ **electrical storm** a thunderstorm. ■ **e·lec·tri·cal·ly adv.**

e·lec·tri·cian /ilek'trisʜən, ˌēlek-/ ▶ **n.** a person who installs and maintains electrical equipment.

e·lec·tric·i·ty /ilek'trisitē, ˌēlek-/ ▶ **n. 1** a form of energy resulting from charged particles. **2** the supply of electric current to a building for heating, lighting, etc.

e·lec·tri·fy /i'lektrəˌfī/ ▶ **v.** (**electrifies**, **electrifying**, **electrified**) **1** charge something with electricity. **2** convert something to use electrical power. **3** (**electrifying**) very exciting.

> SYNONYMS **excite**, thrill, stimulate, arouse, rouse, inspire, stir (up), exhilarate, galvanize, fire (with enthusiasm), fire (up) someone's imagination, invigorate, animate, light a fire under.

e·lec·tro·car·di·og·ra·phy /iˌlektrōˌkärdē'ägrəfē/ ▶ **n.** the measurement and recording of activity in the heart using electrodes placed on the skin. ■ **e·lec·tro·car·di·o·gram** /iˌlektrō'kärdēəˌgram/ **n.** **e·lec·tro·car·di·o·graph** /iˌlektrō'kärdiəˌgraf/ **n.**

e·lec·tro·con·vul·sive /iˌlektrōkən'vəlsiv/ ▶ **adj.** (of therapy for mental illness) using electric shocks applied to the brain.

e·lec·tro·cute /i'lektrəˌkyo͞ot/ ▶ **v.** (**electrocutes**, **electrocuting**, **electrocuted**) injure or kill by electric shock. ■ **e·lec·tro·cu·tion** /iˌlektrə'kyo͞osʜən/ **n.**

e·lec·trode /i'lektrōd/ ▶ **n.** a conductor through which electricity enters or leaves something.

e·lec·trol·y·sis /ilek'träləsis, ˌēlek-/ ▶ **n. 1** the separation of a liquid into its chemical parts by passing an electric current through it. **2** the removal of hair roots or small blemishes on the skin by means of an electric current.

e·lec·tro·lyte /i'lektrəˌlīt/ ▶ **n.** a liquid or gel that an electric current can pass through, e.g., in a battery.

e·lec·tro·mag·net /iˌlektrō'magnit/ ▶ **n.** a metal core made into a magnet by passing electric current through a surrounding coil.

e·lec·tro·mag·net·ic /iˌlektrōmag'netik/ ▶ **adj.** relating to electric currents and magnetic fields. □ **electromagnetic radiation** a kind of radiation in which electric and magnetic fields vary simultaneously. ■ **e·lec·tro·mag·net·ism** /iˌlektrō'magnəˌtizəm/ **n.**

e·lec·tro·mo·tive /iˌlektrə'mōtiv/ ▶ **adj.** tending to produce an electric current. □ **electromotive force** a difference in potential that tends to give rise to an electric current.

e·lec·tron /i'lekˌträn/ ▶ **n.** Physics a subatomic particle with a negative charge, found in all atoms. □ **electron microscope** a powerful microscope using electron beams instead of light.

e·lec·tron·ic /ilek'tränik, ˌēlek-/ ▶ **adj. 1** having parts such as microchips and transistors that control and direct electric currents. **2** relating to electrons or electronics. **3** carried out by means of a computer: *electronic shopping*. □ **electronic mail** email. **electronic publishing** the issuing of texts in machine-readable form rather than on paper. ■ **e·lec·tron·i·cal·ly adv.**

e·lec·tron·ics /ilek'träniks, ˌēlek-/ ▶ **pl.n. 1** the use or study of electronic devices. **2** the study of the behavior and movement of electrons. **3** circuits or devices using transistors, microchips, etc.

e·lec·tro·plate /i'lektrəˌplāt/ ▶ **v.** (**electroplates**, **electroplating**, **electroplated**) coat a metal object with another metal using electrolysis.

e·lec·tro·scope /i'lektrəˌskōp/ ▶ **n.** an instrument for detecting and measuring electric charge.

e·lec·tro·shock /i'lektrəˌsʜäk/ ▶ **adj.** ⇒ ELECTROCONVULSIVE.

e·lec·tro·stat·ic /iˌlektrə'statik/ ▶ **adj.** relating to stationary electric charges or fields as opposed to electric currents.

el·e·gance /'eləgəns/ ▶ **n.** the quality of being elegant.

> SYNONYMS **1 style**, grace, taste, sophistication, refinement, dignity, poise. **2 neatness**, simplicity, aptness.

el·e·gant /'eləgənt/ ▶ **adj. 1** attractive, graceful, and stylish. **2** pleasingly clever and simple.

> SYNONYMS **1 stylish**, graceful, tasteful, sophisticated, classic, chic, smart, poised, cultivated, polished, cultured. **2** *an elegant solution* **neat**, simple, apt. ANTONYMS inelegant.

■ **el·e·gant·ly adv.**

el·e·gi·ac /ˌelə'jīək, e'lējēˌak/ ▶ **adj.** expressing sadness, especially about the past or a person who has died.

el·e·gy /'eləjē/ ▶ **n.** (plural **elegies**) a poem expressing sadness, especially for a person who has died.

el·e·ment /'eləmənt/ ▶ **n. 1** a basic part of something. **2** each of more than one hundred substances that cannot be changed or broken down. **3** any of the four substances (earth, water, air, and fire) that were formerly believed to make up all matter. **4** a trace: *an element of danger*. **5** a distinct group within a larger group: *right-wing elements in the army*. **6** (**the elements**) weather conditions such as rain, wind, and cold. **7** a part in an electric device through which an electric current is passed to provide heat.

> SYNONYMS **1 component**, constituent, part, section, portion, piece, segment, aspect, factor, feature, facet, ingredient, strand, detail, member. **2 trace**, touch, hint, smattering, soupçon. **3** (**elements**) **weather**, climate, weather conditions.

□ **be in your element** be in your natural or preferred environment: *she was in her element*.

el·e·men·tal /ˌelə'mentl/ ▶ **adj. 1** fundamental. **2** having to do with or like the primitive forces of nature: *elemental hatred*.

el·e·men·ta·ry /ˌelə'ment(ə)rē/ ▶ **adj. 1** relating to the most basic aspects of a subject. **2** straightforward and uncomplicated.

> SYNONYMS **1** *an elementary astronomy course* **basic**, rudimentary, preparatory, introductory. **2** *a lot of the work is elementary* **easy**, simple, straightforward, uncomplicated, undemanding, painless, child's play, smooth sailing; informal a piece of cake. ANTONYMS advanced, difficult.

□ **elementary school** a school for the first four to six grades, and usually including kindergarten.

el·e·phant /ˈeləfənt/ ▶ **n.** (plural **elephant** or **elephants**) a very large animal with a trunk, long curved tusks, and large ears, found in Africa and Asia.

el·e·phan·tine /ˌeləˈfantēn, -ˌtīn, ˈeləfənˌtēn, -ˌtīn/ ▶ **adj.** resembling an elephant, especially in being large or clumsy.

el·e·vate /ˈeləˌvāt/ ▶ **v.** (**elevates**, **elevating**, **elevated**) **1** lift to a higher position. **2** raise to a higher level or status.

SYNONYMS **1 raise**, lift (up), raise up/aloft, hoist, hike up, haul up. **2 promote**, upgrade, move up, raise; informal kick upstairs. ANTONYMS lower, demote.

el·e·vat·ed /ˈeləˌvātid/ ▶ **adj.** of a high intellectual or moral level.

SYNONYMS **1 raised**, overhead, in the air, high up. **2 lofty**, grand, fine, sublime, inflated, pompous, bombastic. **3 high**, high-ranking, lofty, exalted, grand, noble.

el·e·va·tion /ˌeləˈvāsʜən/ ▶ **n.** **1** the action of elevating. **2** height above a given level, especially sea level. **3** the angle of something with the horizontal, especially of a gun or of the direction of a celestial object. **4** a particular side of a building or a drawing of a particular side of a building: *the architect included a drawing of the front elevation.*

el·e·va·tor /ˈeləˌvātər/ ▶ **n.** **1** a platform or compartment housed in a shaft for raising and lowering people or things to different floors or levels. **2** a machine consisting of an endless belt with scoops attached, used for lifting grain to a storage space. **3** a hinged flap on the horizontal stabilizer of an aircraft used to control its motion.

e·lev·en /iˈlevən/ ▶ **cardinal number 1** one more than ten; 11. (Roman numeral: **xi** or **XI**) **2** a sports team of eleven players.

e·lev·enth /iˈlevənᴛʜ/ ▶ **ordinal number 1** that is number eleven in a sequence; 11th. **2** (**an eleventh**/**one eleventh**) each of eleven equal parts into which something is divided. □ **the eleventh hour** the latest possible moment.

elf /elf/ ▶ **n.** (plural **elves** /elvz/) (in folk tales) a creature resembling a small human figure with pointed ears.

SYNONYMS **pixie**, fairy, sprite, imp, brownie; gnome, goblin, hobgoblin; leprechaun, puck, troll.

elf·in /ˈelfən/ ▶ **adj.** (of a person) small and delicate.

e·lic·it /iˈlisit/ ▶ **v.** (**elicits**, **eliciting**, **elicited**) produce or draw out a response or reaction.

SYNONYMS **obtain**, draw out, extract, bring out, evoke, induce, prompt, generate, trigger, provoke.

e·lide /iˈlīd/ ▶ **v.** (**elides**, **eliding**, **elided**) **1** omit a sound or syllable when speaking. **2** join together.

el·i·gi·ble /ˈeləjəbəl/ ▶ **adj.** **1** meeting the conditions to do or receive something: *you may be eligible for a refund.* **2** desirable as a husband or wife.

SYNONYMS **1 entitled**, permitted, allowed, qualified, able. **2 desirable**, suitable, available, single, unmarried, unattached.

■ **el·i·gi·bil·i·ty** /ˌeləjəˈbilitē/ **n.**

e·lim·i·nate /iˈliməˌnāt/ ▶ **v.** (**eliminates**, **eliminating**, **eliminated**) **1** completely remove or get rid of. **2** exclude someone from a competition by beating them.

SYNONYMS **1 remove**, get rid of, put an end to, do away with, end, stop, eradicate, destroy, stamp out. **2 knock out**, exclude, rule out, disqualify.

■ **e·lim·i·na·tion** /iˌliməˈnāsʜən/ **n.**

e·li·sion /iˈlizʜən/ ▶ **n.** the omission of a sound or syllable in speech.

e·lite /əˈlēt, āˈlēt/ ▶ **n.** a group of people regarded as the best in a particular society or organization.

SYNONYMS **best**, pick, cream, crème de la crème, flower, high society, beautiful people, aristocracy, ruling class. ANTONYMS dregs.

e·lit·ism /əˈlēˌtizəm, āˈlē-/ ▶ **n.** **1** the belief that a society should be run by an elite. **2** the superior attitude associated with an elite. ■ **e·lit·ist adj. & n.**

e·lix·ir /iˈliksər/ ▶ **n.** a drink believed to make people live for ever or have other magical effects.

E·liz·a·be·than /iˌlizəˈbēᴛʜən/ ▶ **adj.** relating to the reign of Queen Elizabeth I (1558–1603) of England.

elk /elk/ ▶ **n.** (plural **elk** or **elks**) a kind of large red deer native to North America.

el·lipse /iˈlips/ ▶ **n.** a regular oval shape.

el·lip·sis /iˈlipsis/ ▶ **n.** (plural **ellipses**) **1** the omission of words from speech or writing. **2** a set of dots (...) indicating such an omission.

el·lip·ti·cal /iˈliptikəl/ ▶ **adj.** **1** (of speech or writing) having a word or words deliberately left out. **2** (also **elliptic**) having the shape of an ellipse.

elm /elm/ ▶ **n.** a tall deciduous tree with rough leaves.

El Ni·ño /el ˈnēnyō/ ▶ **n.** (plural **El Niños**) a weather phenomenon occurring as often as every 4 years or as seldom as every 12 years, in which a warm ocean current creates a complex cycle of climatic changes affecting the Pacific region.

el·o·cu·tion /ˌeləˈkyo͞osʜən/ ▶ **n.** the skill of speaking clearly.

e·lon·gate /iˈlôɴɢˌgāt, iˈläɴɢ-/ ▶ **v.** (**elongates**, **elongating**, **elongated**) make or become longer. ■ **e·lon·ga·tion** /iˌlôɴɢˈgāsʜən, ēˌlôɴɢ-, iˌläɴɢ-, ēˌläɴɢ-/ **n.**

e·lope /iˈlōp/ ▶ **v.** (**elopes**, **eloping**, **eloped**) run away secretly to get married.

el·o·quence /ˈeləkwəns/ ▶ **n.** fluent or persuasive speaking or writing.

el·o·quent /ˈeləkwənt/ ▶ **adj.** **1** fluent or persuasive in speech or writing. **2** clearly expressive.

SYNONYMS **articulate**, fluent, expressive, persuasive, well-expressed, effective, lucid, vivid. ANTONYMS inarticulate.

■ **el·o·quent·ly adv.**

else /els/ ▶ **adv.** **1** in addition. **2** different; instead. □ **or else** if not; otherwise.

else·where /ˈelsˌ(h)wer/ ▶ **adv.** in, at, or to some other place or other places.

e·lu·ci·date /iˈlo͞osiˌdāt/ ▶ **v.** (**elucidates**, **elucidating**, **elucidated**) make clear; explain. ■ **e·lu·ci·da·tion** /iˌlo͞osiˈdāsʜən/ **n.**

e·lude /iˈlo͞od/ ▶ **v.** (**eludes**, **eluding**, **eluded**) **1** cleverly escape from or avoid. **2** fail to be understood or achieved by: *the logic of this eluded her.*

SYNONYMS **evade**, avoid, get away from, dodge, escape from, lose, shake off, give the slip to, slip away from, throw off the scent.

e·lu·sive /iˈlo͞osiv/ ▶ **adj.** difficult to find, catch, or achieve.

SYNONYMS **1 difficult to find**, evasive, slippery. **2 indefinable**, intangible, impalpable, fugitive, fleeting, transitory, ambiguous.

el·ver /ˈelvər/ ▶ **n.** a young eel.

elves /elvz/ plural of ELF.

E·ly·sian /iˈlizʜən, iˈlē-/ ▶ **adj. 1** relating to Elysium or the Elysian Fields, the place in Greek mythology where heroes were taken after death. **2** of or like paradise.

e·ma·ci·at·ed /iˈmāsʜēˌātid/ ▶ **adj.** abnormally thin and weak.

SYNONYMS **thin**, skeletal, bony, gaunt, wasted, thin as a rake, scrawny, skinny, scraggy, skin and bones, starved, cadaverous, shriveled, shrunken, withered. ANTONYMS fat.

■ **e·ma·ci·a·tion** /iˌmāsʜēˈāsʜən/ **n.**

e·mail /ˈē ˌmāl/ (or **e-mail**) ▶ **n.** the sending of electronic messages from one computer user to another via a network, or a message sent in this way. ▶ **v.** send someone a message using email.

em·a·nate /ˈeməˌnāt/ ▶ **v.** (**emanates**, **emanating**, **emanated**) **1** (**emanate from**) come out from a place or source. **2** give out a feeling or quality: *he emanated a brooding air.* ■ **em·a·na·tion** /ˌeməˈnāsʜən/ **n.**

e·man·ci·pate /iˈmansəˌpāt/ ▶ **v.** (**emancipates**, **emancipating**, **emancipated**) **1** set free from restrictions. **2** free from slavery.
■ **e·man·ci·pa·tion** /iˌmansəˈpāsʜən/ **n.**

e·mas·cu·late /iˈmaskyəˌlāt/ ▶ **v.** (**emasculates**, **emasculating**, **emasculated**) **1** make weaker or less effective. **2** deprive a man of his male role or identity. ■ **e·mas·cu·la·tion** /iˌmaskyəˈlāsʜən/ **n.**

em·balm /emˈbä(l)m/ ▶ **v.** treat a dead body to preserve it from decay.

em·bank·ment /emˈbaɴɢkmənt/ ▶ **n. 1** a wall or bank built to prevent flooding by a river. **2** a bank of earth or stone built to carry a road or railroad over an area of low ground.

em·bar·go /emˈbärgō/ ▶ **n.** (plural **embargoes**) an official ban, especially on trade with a particular country. ▶ **v.** (**embargoes**, **embargoing**, **embargoed**) put an embargo on.

SYNONYMS ▶ **n. ban**, bar, prohibition, stoppage, veto, moratorium, restriction, block, boycott. ▶ **v. ban**, bar, prohibit, stop, outlaw, blacklist, restrict, block, boycott. ANTONYMS allow.

em·bark /emˈbärk/ ▶ **v. 1** go on board a ship or aircraft. **2** (**embark on**) begin a new project or course of action.

SYNONYMS **board (ship)**, go on board, go aboard; informal hop on, jump on. ANTONYMS disembark.

■ **em·bar·ka·tion** /ˌembärˈkāsʜən/ **n.**

em·bar·rass /emˈbarəs/ ▶ **v. 1** make someone feel awkward or ashamed. **2** (**be embarrassed**) be in financial difficulties.

SYNONYMS **humiliate**, shame, put someone to shame, abash, mortify, fluster, discomfit; informal show up.

SPELLING

Double **r**, double **s**: embarrass.

em·bar·rassed /emˈbarəst/ ▶ **adj.** feeling or showing embarrassment.

SYNONYMS **humiliated**, mortified, red-faced, blushing, abashed, shamed, ashamed, shamefaced, self-conscious, uncomfortable, discomfited, disconcerted, flustered; informal with egg on your face.

em·bar·rass·ing /emˈbarəsiɴɢ/ ▶ **adj.** causing embarrassment: *an embarrassing muddle.*

SYNONYMS **humiliating**, shameful, mortifying, ignominious, awkward, uncomfortable, compromising; informal cringeworthy, toe-curling.

em·bar·rass·ment /emˈbarəsmənt/ ▶ **n. 1** a feeling of self-consciousness, shame, or awkwardness. **2** a cause of self-consciousness, shame, or awkwardness: *her extreme views might be an embarrassment to the movement.*

SYNONYMS **1 humiliation**, mortification, shame, shamefacedness, awkwardness, self-consciousness, discomfort, discomfiture. **2 difficulty**, predicament, plight, problem, mess; informal bind, pickle, fix.

em·bas·sy /ˈembəsē/ ▶ **n.** (plural **embassies**) the official residence or offices of an ambassador.

em·bat·tled /emˈbatld/ ▶ **adj. 1** facing a lot of difficulties: *the embattled senator.* **2** surrounded by enemy forces.

em·bed /emˈbed/ (or **imbed**) ▶ **v.** (**embeds**, **embedding**, **embedded**) fix something firmly in a surrounding mass.

em·bel·lish /emˈbelisʜ/ ▶ **v. 1** make more attractive; decorate. **2** add extra details to a story.

SYNONYMS **decorate**, adorn, ornament, beautify, enhance, trim, garnish, gild, deck, bedeck, festoon, emblazon.

em·ber /ˈembər/ ▶ **n.** a piece of burning wood or coal in a dying fire.

em·bez·zle /emˈbezəl/ ▶ **v.** (**embezzles**, **embezzling**, **embezzled**) steal money that you have been given responsibility for.

SYNONYMS **misappropriate**, steal, thieve, pilfer, purloin, appropriate, siphon off, pocket; informal filch, pinch.

■ **em·bez·zle·ment n.**

em·bit·tered /emˈbitərd/ ▶ **adj.** angry or resentful.

em·bla·zon /emˈblāzn/ ▶ **v.** display a design on something in a very noticeable way.

em·blem /ˈembləm/ ▶ **n.** a design or symbol as a badge of a nation, organization, or family.

SYNONYMS **symbol**, representation, token, image, figure, mark, sign, crest, badge, device, insignia, coat of arms, shield, logo, trademark.

em·blem·at·ic /ˌembləˈmatik/ ▶ **adj.** representing a particular quality or idea.

em·bod·y /emˈbädē/ ▶ **v.** (**embodies**, **embodying**, **embodied**) **1** give a tangible or visible form to an idea or quality. **2** include or contain.

SYNONYMS **1 personify**, manifest, symbolize, represent, express, epitomize, stand for, typify, exemplify. **2 incorporate**, include, contain.

■ **em·bod·i·ment**/ emˈbädēmənt, im-/ **n.**

em·bold·en /emˈbōldən/ ▶ **v.** make someone braver or more confident.

em·bo·lism /ˈembəˌlizəm/ ▶ **n.** obstruction of an artery by a clot of blood or an air bubble.

em·boss /emˈbôs, -ˈbäs/ ▶ **v.** carve a raised design on.

em·brace /emˈbrās/ ▶ **v.** (**embraces, embracing, embraced**) **1** hold someone closely in your arms. **2** include or contain. **3** willingly accept or support a belief or change. ▶ **n.** an act of embracing.

SYNONYMS ▶ **v. 1 hug**, take/hold in your arms, hold, cuddle, clasp/draw to your bosom, squeeze, clutch, enfold. **2 include**, take in, comprise, contain, incorporate, encompass, cover, subsume. **3 welcome**, welcome with open arms, accept, take on board, take up, take to your heart, adopt, espouse. ▶ **n. hug**, cuddle, squeeze, clinch, caress.

em·bro·ca·tion /ˌembrəˈkāsʜən/ ▶ **n.** a liquid medication rubbed on the body to relieve pain from sprains and strains.

em·broi·der /emˈbroidər/ ▶ **v.** (**embroiders, embroidering, embroidered**) **1** sew decorative needlework patterns on. **2** add false or exaggerated details to.

em·broi·der·y /emˈbroid(ə)rē/ ▶ **n.** (plural **embroideries**) **1** the art of embroidering. **2** embroidered cloth.

em·broil /emˈbroil/ ▶ **v.** (**embroil someone in**) involve someone in a conflict or difficult situation.

em·bry·o /ˈembrēˌō/ ▶ **n.** (plural **embryos**) an unborn or unhatched baby or animal in the early stages of development.

em·bry·on·ic /ˌembrēˈänik/ ▶ **adj. 1** relating to an embryo. **2** in a very early stage of development.

em·cee /ˌemˈsē/ ▶ **n.** informal a master of ceremonies; a host.

e·mend /iˈmend/ ▶ **v.** correct and revise a piece of writing.

USAGE

The words **emend** and **amend** both derive from Latin *emendare* 'to correct' and have similar, but not identical, meanings in English. **Emend** means 'correct and revise (a text),' while **amend** means 'make minor improvements to (a document, rule, or proposal).'

em·er·ald /ˈem(ə)rəld/ ▶ **n. 1** a green precious stone. **2** a bright green color.

e·merge /iˈmərj/ ▶ **v.** (**emerges, emerging, emerged**) **1** become gradually visible. **2** (of facts) become known. **3** recover from a difficult situation or experience.

SYNONYMS **1 appear**, come out, come into view, become visible, surface, materialize, issue, come forth. **2 become known**, become apparent, be revealed, come to light, come out, turn up, transpire, unfold, turn out, prove to be the case.

e·mer·gence /iˈmərjəns/ ▶ **n.** the process of coming into being.

SYNONYMS **appearance**, arrival, coming, materialization, advent, inception, dawn, birth, origination, start, development.

e·mer·gen·cy /iˈmərjənsē/ ▶ **n.** (plural **emergencies**) a serious and unexpected situation requiring immediate action. ▶ **adj.** caused by or used in an emergency.

SYNONYMS ▶ **n. crisis**, disaster, catastrophe, accident, calamity, plight. ▶ **adj. 1 urgent**, crisis, extraordinary. **2 reserve**, standby, backup, fallback.

□ **emergency room** the department of a hospital that provides immediate treatment for acute illnesses and trauma.

e·mer·gent /iˈmərjənt/ ▶ **adj.** new and still developing.

e·mer·i·tus /iˈmerətəs/ ▶ **adj.** having retired but allowed to keep a title as an honor: *an emeritus professor.*

em·er·y board /ˈem(ə)rē/ ▶ **n.** a strip of thin wood or cardboard coated with a rough material and used as a nail file.

e·met·ic /iˈmetik/ ▶ **adj.** causing vomiting.

EMF ▶ **abbr.** (**emf**) electromotive force.

em·i·grant /ˈemigrənt/ ▶ **n.** a person who emigrates.

em·i·grate /ˈemiˌgrāt/ ▶ **v.** (**emigrates, emigrating, emigrated**) leave your own country and settle permanently in another.

SYNONYMS **move abroad**, move overseas, leave your country, migrate, relocate, resettle. ANTONYMS immigrate.

■ **em·i·gra·tion** /ˌemiˈgrāsʜən/ **n.**

é·mi·gré /ˈeməˌgrā/ ▶ **n.** a person who has emigrated.

em·i·nence /ˈemənəns/ ▶ **n. 1** the quality of being very famous and respected in a particular area of activity. **2** an important or distinguished person. **3** (**His** or **Your Eminence**) a title given to a Roman Catholic cardinal, or used in addressing him: *His Eminence, Cardinal Thomas Wolsey.*

é·mi·nence grise /āmēnäɴs ˈgrēz/ ▶ **n.** (plural **éminences grises** same pronunciation) a person who has power or influence without holding an official position.

em·i·nent /ˈemənənt/ ▶ **adj. 1** very famous and respected; distinguished. **2** outstanding or obvious: *the eminent reasonableness of their claim.*

SYNONYMS **illustrious**, distinguished, renowned, esteemed, preeminent, notable, noted, noteworthy, great, prestigious, important, outstanding, celebrated, prominent, well-known, acclaimed, exalted. ANTONYMS unknown.

■ **em·i·nent·ly adv.**

e·mir /əˈmi(ə)r/ (or **amir**) ▶ **n.** a title of some Muslim rulers.

em·is·sar·y /ˈeməˌserē/ ▶ **n.** (plural **emissaries**) a person sent as a diplomatic representative on a mission.

e·mis·sion /iˈmisʜən/ ▶ **n. 1** the action of emitting. **2** a substance that is emitted.

SYNONYMS **discharge**, release, outpouring, outflow, outrush, leak.

e·mit /iˈmit/ ▶ **v.** (**emits, emitting, emitted**) **1** give out light, heat, gas, etc. **2** make a sound.

SYNONYMS **1 discharge**, release, give out/off, pour out, radiate, leak, ooze, disgorge, eject, belch, spew out, exude. **2 utter**, voice, let out, produce, give vent to, come out with.

Em·my /ˈemē/ ▶ **n.** (plural **Emmys**) a statuette awarded annually to an outstanding television program or performer.

e·mol·lient /iˈmälyənt/ ▶ **adj.** **1** softening or soothing the skin. **2** attempting to avoid conflict; calming.

e·mol·u·ment /iˈmälyəmənt/ ▶ **n.** formal a salary or fee.

e·mote /iˈmōt/ ▶ **v.** (**emotes**, **emoting**, **emoted**) show emotion in an exaggerated way.

e·mo·ti·con /iˈmōtəˌkän/ ▶ **n.** a textual representation of a facial expression, used in email or texting to show mood or feelings.

e·mo·tion /iˈmōSHən/ ▶ **n.** **1** a strong feeling, such as joy or anger. **2** instinctive feeling as opposed to reasoning.

SYNONYMS **1 feeling**, sentiment, reaction, response, instinct, intuition. **2 passion**, strength of feeling, heart.

e·mo·tion·al /iˈmōSHənəl/ ▶ **adj.** **1** relating to the emotions. **2** arousing or showing emotion.

SYNONYMS **1 passionate**, hot-blooded, ardent, fervent, warm, responsive, excitable, temperamental, demonstrative, sensitive. **2 poignant**, moving, touching, affecting, powerful, stirring, emotive, impassioned, dramatic; informal tear-jerking. ANTONYMS cold, clinical.

■ **e·mo·tion·al·ly** **adv.**

e·mo·tive /iˈmōtiv/ ▶ **adj.** arousing strong feeling.

em·pa·thize /ˈempəˌTHīz/ ▶ **v.** (**empathizes**, **empathizing**, **empathized**) understand and share the feelings of someone else.

SYNONYMS *I can* ***empathize with*** *her parents* **identify with**, sympathize with, understand, share the feelings of, be in tune with; relate to, feel for, have insight into; informal put yourself in the shoes of.

em·pa·thy /ˈempəTHē/ ▶ **n.** the ability to understand and share the feelings of someone else.

USAGE

Strictly, **empathy** does not mean the same thing as **sympathy**: if you have **empathy** for someone you understand and share their feelings, whereas if you have **sympathy** for them you feel sorry for them.

em·per·or /ˈemp(ə)rər/ ▶ **n.** the ruler of an empire. □ **emperor penguin** the largest kind of penguin, which has a yellow patch on each side of the head.

em·pha·sis /ˈemfəsis/ ▶ **n.** (plural **emphases**) **1** special importance or value given to something. **2** stress put on a word or words in speaking.

SYNONYMS **1 prominence**, importance, significance, value, stress, weight, accent, attention, priority. **2** *the emphasis is on the word "little"* **stress**, accent, weight, beat.

em·pha·size /ˈemfəˌsīz/ ▶ **v.** (**emphasizes**, **emphasizing**, **emphasized**) give special importance or prominence to.

SYNONYMS **stress**, underline, highlight, focus attention on, point up, lay stress on, draw attention to, spotlight, foreground. ANTONYMS understate.

em·phat·ic /emˈfatik/ ▶ **adj.** **1** showing or giving emphasis. **2** definite and clear: *an emphatic win.*

SYNONYMS **forceful**, firm, vehement, wholehearted, energetic, vigorous, direct, insistent, certain, definite, out-and-out, decided, categorical, unqualified, unconditional, unequivocal, unambiguous, absolute, explicit, downright, outright, clear.

■ **em·phat·i·cal·ly** **adv.**

em·phy·se·ma /ˌemfəˈsēmə, -ˈzēmə/ ▶ **n.** a condition that affects the lungs, causing breathlessness.

em·pire /ˈemˌpī(ə)r/ ▶ **n.** **1** a large group of countries under a single authority or ruler. **2** a large commercial organization under the control of one person or group.

SYNONYMS **1 kingdom**, realm, domain, territory, commonwealth, power. **2 business**, firm, company, corporation, multinational, conglomerate, group, consortium, operation.

em·pir·i·cal /emˈpirikəl/ ▶ **adj.** based on observation or experience rather than theory or logic. ■ **em·pir·i·cal·ly** **adv.** **em·pir·i·cism** /emˈpirəˌsizəm/ **n.** **em·pir·i·cist** **n.**

em·place·ment /emˈplāsmənt/ ▶ **n.** a structure or platform where a gun is placed for firing.

em·ploy /emˈploi/ ▶ **v.** **1** give work to someone and pay them for it. **2** make use of. **3** keep someone occupied.

SYNONYMS **1 hire**, engage, recruit, take on, sign up, appoint, retain. **2** (**employed**) **working**, in work, in employment, holding down a job, earning, salaried, waged. **3 occupy**, engage, involve, keep busy, tie up. **4 use**, utilize, make use of, apply, exercise, practice, put into practice, exert, bring into play, bring to bear, draw on, resort to, turn to, have recourse to. ANTONYMS dismiss.

em·ploy·ee /emˈploi-ē, ˌemploiˈē/ ▶ **n.** a person who is employed by a company or individual.

SYNONYMS **worker**, member of the staff, staff member, blue-collar worker, white-collar worker, workman, laborer, hand; (**employees**) personnel, staff, workforce.

em·ploy·er /emˈploi-ər/ ▶ **n.** a company or individual that employs people.

em·ploy·ment /emˈploimənt/ ▶ **n.** **1** the state of having paid work. **2** a person's work or profession.

SYNONYMS **work**, labor, service, job, post, position, situation, occupation, profession, trade, business, line of work.

em·po·ri·um /emˈpôrēəm/ ▶ **n.** (plural **emporiums** or **emporia** /-rēə/) a large store selling a wide variety of goods.

em·pow·er /emˈpou(-ə)r/ ▶ **v.** (**empowers**, **empowering**, **empowered**) **1** give authority or power to. **2** give strength and confidence to.

SYNONYMS **1 authorize**, entitle, permit, allow, license, enable. **2 emancipate**, unshackle, set free, liberate, enfranchise. ANTONYMS forbid.

■ **em·pow·er·ment** **n.**

em·press /ˈempris/ ▶ **n.** **1** a female emperor. **2** the wife or widow of an emperor.

emp·ty /ˈem(p)tē/ ▶ **adj.** (**emptier**, **emptiest**) **1** containing nothing; not filled or occupied. **2** (of words or gestures) having no real meaning: *empty promises.* ▶ **v.** (**empties**, **emptying**, **emptied**) **1** make or become empty. **2** (of a river) flow into the sea or a lake. **3** remove everything that is in a container.

SYNONYMS ▶ adj. **1 vacant**, unoccupied, uninhabited, bare, clear, free. **2 meaningless**, hollow, idle, vain, futile, worthless, useless, ineffectual. **3 futile**, pointless, purposeless, worthless, meaningless, fruitless, valueless, of no value, senseless. ANTONYMS full, occupied. ▶ v. **1 unload**, unpack, clear, evacuate, drain. **2 remove**, take out, extract, tip out, pour out. ANTONYMS fill, replace.

□ **empty-handed 1** having failed to get or achieve what you wanted. **2** having nothing in your hands: *guests who come to a birthday party empty-handed.* **empty-headed** foolish. ■ **emp·ti·ness** n.

em·py·re·an /em'pirēən, ˌempə'rēən/ literary ▶ n. (**the empyrean**) heaven or the sky. ▶ adj. relating to heaven.

EMT ▶ abbr. emergency medical technician.

e·mu /'ēm(y)o͞o/ ▶ n. a large Australian bird that is unable to fly, similar to an ostrich.

em·u·late /'emyəˌlāt/ ▶ v. (**emulates, emulating, emulated**) try to do as well as or be better than, usually by imitation.

SYNONYMS **imitate**, copy, mirror, echo, follow, model yourself on, take a page out of someone's book.

■ **em·u·la·tion** /ˌemyə'lāsʜən/ n.

e·mul·si·fy /i'məlsəˌfī/ ▶ v. (**emulsifies, emulsifying, emulsified**) combine two liquids into a smooth mixture. ■ **e·mul·si·fi·er** n.

e·mul·sion /i'məlsʜən/ ▶ n. **1** a mixture of two liquids in which particles of one are evenly distributed in the other. **2** a type of paint for walls and ceilings. **3** a light-sensitive coating for photographic film.

en·a·ble /en'ābəl/ ▶ v. (**enables, enabling, enabled**) **1** provide with the ability or means to do something. **2** make something possible.

SYNONYMS **allow**, permit, let, equip, empower, make able, fit, authorize, entitle, qualify. ANTONYMS prevent.

en·act /en'akt/ ▶ v. **1** pass a law. **2** act out a role or play.

SYNONYMS **1 make (into) law**, pass, approve, ratify, validate, sanction, authorize. **2 act out**, perform, appear in, stage, mount, put on, present. ANTONYMS repeal.

■ **en·act·ment** n.

e·nam·el /i'naməl/ ▶ n. **1** a colored glassy substance applied to metal, glass, or pottery for decoration or protection. **2** the hard substance that covers the crown of a tooth. **3** a paint that dries to give a hard coat. ▶ v. (**enamels, enameling, enameled**) coat or decorate with enamel.

en·am·or /i'namər/ ▶ v. (**be enamored of** or **with**) be filled with love or admiration for.

en bloc /äɴ 'bläk/ ▶ adv. all together, or all at once.

en·camp /en'kamp/ ▶ v. settle in or set up a camp.

en·camp·ment /en'kampmənt/ ▶ n. a place where a camp is set up.

en·cap·su·late /en'kaps(y)əˌlāt/ ▶ v. (**encapsulates, encapsulating, encapsulated**) summarize clearly and in few words.

en·case /en'kās/ ▶ v. (**encases, encasing, encased**) enclose or cover in a case.

en·ceph·a·li·tis /enˌsefə'lītis/ ▶ n. inflammation of the brain.

en·chant /en'cʜant/ ▶ v. **1** delight; charm. **2** put under a spell. ■ **en·chant·ment** n.

en·chant·er /en'cʜantər/ ▶ n. a man who uses magic or sorcery, especially to put someone or something under a spell.

en·chant·ing /en'cʜantiɴɢ/ ▶ adj. delightfully charming or attractive.

SYNONYMS **captivating**, charming, delightful, adorable, lovely, attractive, appealing, engaging, fetching, irresistible, fascinating.

en·chant·ress /en'cʜantris/ ▶ n. **1** a woman who uses magic or sorcery, especially to put someone under a spell. **2** a very attractive and seductive woman.

en·chi·la·da /ˌencʜə'lädə/ ▶ n. a rolled tortilla usually filled with meat and served with a chili sauce. □ **the big enchilada** informal a person or thing of great importance. **the whole enchilada** informal the whole situation; everything.

en·cir·cle /en'sərkəl/ ▶ v. (**encircles, encircling, encircled**) form a circle around.

en·clave /'enˌklāv, 'äɴɢ-/ ▶ n. **1** a small area of one country's territory that is surrounded by another country. **2** a place or group that is different in character from those surrounding it.

en·close /en'klōz/ ▶ v. (**encloses, enclosing, enclosed**) **1** surround or close off on all sides. **2** put a document or object in an envelope along with a letter.

SYNONYMS **1 surround**, circle, ring, encircle, bound, close in, wall in. **2 include**, insert, put in, send.

en·clo·sure /en'klōzʜər/ ▶ n. **1** an enclosed area. **2** a document or object put in an envelope along with a letter.

SYNONYMS **compound**, pen, corral, fold, stockade, ring, paddock, yard, run, coop.

en·code /en'kōd/ ▶ v. (**encodes, encoding, encoded**) convert into a coded form.

en·co·mi·um /en'kōmēəm/ ▶ n. (plural **encomiums** or **encomia** /-mēə/) formal a speech or piece of writing expressing praise.

en·com·pass /en'kəmpəs/ ▶ v. **1** include a wide range of things. **2** surround or cover.

SYNONYMS **include**, cover, embrace, incorporate, take in, contain, comprise, involve, deal with.

en·core /'änˌkôr/ ▶ n. a short extra performance given at the end of a concert in response to calls by the audience.

en·coun·ter /en'koun(t)ər/ ▶ v. (**encounters, encountering, encountered**) unexpectedly meet or be faced with. ▶ n. **1** an unexpected or casual meeting. **2** a confrontation.

SYNONYMS ▶ v. **1 experience**, run into, meet, come up against, face, be faced with, confront, suffer. **2 meet**, run into, come across/upon, stumble across/on, chance on, happen on; informal bump into. ▶ n. **1 meeting**, chance meeting. **2 battle**, fight, skirmish, clash, scuffle, confrontation, struggle; informal run-in, set-to, scrap.

en·cour·age /en'kərij, -'kə-rij/ ▶ v. (**encourages, encouraging, encouraged**) **1** give support, confidence, or hope to. **2** help the development of.

SYNONYMS **1 hearten**, cheer, buoy up, uplift, inspire, motivate, spur on, stir, fire up, stimulate, embolden; informal buck up. **2** (**encouraging**) **promising**, hopeful, auspicious, favorable, heartening, reassuring, cheering, comforting, welcome, pleasing, gratifying. **3** *she encouraged him to go* **persuade**, coax, urge, press, push, pressure, prod, egg on. **4 support**, back, promote, further, foster, nurture, cultivate, strengthen, stimulate. **5** (**encouraging**) **supportive**, understanding, helpful, positive, enthusiastic. ANTONYMS discourage.

en·cour·age·ment /en'kərijmənt, -'kə-rijmənt/ ▶ **n. 1** the action of encouraging someone to do something. **2** something that encourages someone: *his success served as an encouragement to younger artists.*

SYNONYMS **1 support**, cheering up, inspiration, motivation, stimulation, morale-boosting; informal a shot in the arm. **2 persuasion**, coaxing, urging, prodding, prompting, inducement, incentive, carrot. **3 backing**, sponsorship, support, promotion, furtherance, fostering, nurture, cultivation, stimulation.

en·croach /en'krōCH/ ▶ **v. 1** (**encroach on**) gradually intrude on a person's territory, rights, etc. **2** gradually advance beyond expected or acceptable limits: *the sea has encroached all around the coast.* ■ **en·croach·ment n.**

en croute /äN 'kro͞ot/ ▶ **adj.** in a pastry crust.

en·crust /en'krəst/ ▶ **v.** cover with a hard crust.

en·crypt /en'kript/ ▶ **v.** convert into code. ■ **en·cryp·tion n.**

en·cum·ber /en'kəmbər/ ▶ **v.** (**encumbers, encumbering, encumbered**) prevent someone from moving or acting freely.

en·cum·brance /en'kəmbrəns/ ▶ **n.** a thing that prevents someone from moving or acting freely.

en·cy·clo·pe·di·a /en,sīklə'pēdēə/ (or **encyclopaedia**) ▶ **n.** a book or set of books or a website giving information on many subjects, usually by presenting short articles in alphabetical order.

en·cy·clo·pe·dic /en,sīklə'pēdik/ ▶ **adj. 1** having detailed information on a wide variety of subjects: *an encyclopedic knowledge of food.* **2** relating to encyclopedias or information suitable for an encyclopedia.

end /end/ ▶ **n. 1** the final part of something. **2** the furthest or most extreme part. **3** the stopping of a state or situation: *they called for an end to violence.* **4** a person's death or downfall. **5** a goal or desired result. ▶ **v. 1** come or bring to an end. **2** (**end in**) have a particular result. **3** (**end up**) eventually reach or come to a particular state or place.

SYNONYMS ▶ **n. 1 conclusion**, termination, ending, finish, close, resolution, climax, finale, culmination, denouement. **2 extremity**, limit, edge, border, boundary, periphery, point, tip, head, top, bottom. **3 aim**, goal, purpose, objective, object, target, intention, aspiration, wish, desire, ambition. ANTONYMS beginning, means. ▶ **v. 1 finish**, conclude, terminate, close, stop, cease, culminate, climax. **2 break off**, call off, bring to an end, put an end to, stop, finish, terminate, discontinue, cancel. ANTONYMS begin.

□ **the end of the road** (or **line**) the point beyond which progress or survival cannot continue. **end-user** the person who uses a particular product. **in the end** eventually. **make ends meet** earn just enough money to live on. **on end** continuously: *sometimes they'll be gone for days on end.*

en·dan·ger /en'dānjər/ ▶ **v.** (**endangers, endangering, endangered**) put in danger.

SYNONYMS **jeopardize**, risk, put at risk, put in danger, be a danger to, threaten, compromise, imperil. ANTONYMS safeguard.

en·dan·gered /en'dānjərd/ ▶ **adj.** in danger of extinction.

en·dear /en'di(ə)r/ ▶ **v.** (**endear someone to**) make someone popular with or liked by.

en·dear·ing /en'di(ə)riNG/ ▶ **adj.** inspiring affection; lovable.

SYNONYMS **charming**, appealing, attractive, engaging, winning, captivating, enchanting, cute, sweet, delightful, lovely.

■ **en·dear·ing·ly adv.**

en·dear·ment /en'di(ə)rmənt/ ▶ **n. 1** a word or phrase expressing affection. **2** love or affection.

en·deav·or /en'devər/ ▶ **v.** try hard to achieve something. ▶ **n. 1** an attempt to achieve something. **2** concentrated hard work and effort.

SYNONYMS ▶ **v. try**, attempt, seek, strive, struggle, labor, toil, work. ▶ **n. 1 attempt**, try, bid, effort. **2 undertaking**, enterprise, venture, exercise, activity, exploit, deed, act, action, move.

en·dem·ic /en'demik/ ▶ **adj. 1** (of a disease or condition) regularly found among particular people or in a certain area. **2** (of a plant or animal) native to a certain area.

end·game /'en(d),gām/ ▶ **n.** the final stage of a game such as chess or bridge.

end·ing /'endiNG/ ▶ **n.** an end or final part.

SYNONYMS **end**, finish, close, conclusion, resolution, summing-up, denouement, finale. ANTONYMS beginning.

en·dive /'en,dīv, 'än,dēv/ ▶ **n.** a plant with bitter leaves, eaten in salads.

end·less /'en(d)ləs/ ▶ **adj.** having or seeming to have no end or limit.

SYNONYMS **1 unlimited**, limitless, infinite, inexhaustible, boundless, unbounded, ceaseless, unending, everlasting, constant, continuous, interminable, unfailing, perpetual, eternal, never-ending. **2 countless**, innumerable, numerous, a multitude of; informal umpteen, no end of; literary myriad. ANTONYMS limited, few.

■ **end·less·ly adv.**

en·do·crine /'endəkrin/ ▶ **adj.** (of a gland) secreting hormones or other products directly into the blood.

en·dor·phin /en'dôrfin/ ▶ **n.** a painkilling hormone within the brain and nervous system.

en·dorse /en'dôrs/ ▶ **v.** (**endorses, endorsing, endorsed**) **1** publicly state that you approve of something. **2** sign a check on the back so that it can be paid into an account.

SYNONYMS **support**, back, agree with, approve (of), favor, subscribe to, recommend, champion, uphold, sanction. ANTONYMS oppose.

en·dorse·ment /en'dôrsmənt/ ▶ **n.** **1** a declaration of approval: *the president's endorsement of the plan.* **2** the action of endorsing a check or bill of exchange.

SYNONYMS **support**, backing, approval, seal of approval, agreement, recommendation, patronage, sanction.

en·do·skel·e·ton /ˌendō'skelitn/ ▶ **n.** an internal skeleton.

en·do·sperm /'endəˌspərm/ ▶ **n.** Botany the part of a seed that acts as a food store for the developing plant embryo.

en·do·ther·mic /ˌendə'THərmik/ ▶ **n.** (of a reaction) absorbing heat.

en·dow /en'dou/ ▶ **v.** **1** give someone your property, or leave it to them in your will. **2** donate a large sum of money to an institution, from which they will be able to receive a regular income. **3** (**be endowed with**) have as a natural quality or characteristic: *he was endowed with tremendous physical strength.*

SYNONYMS **1 finance**, fund, pay for, subsidize, sponsor. **2** *he was endowed with great strength* **provide**, supply, furnish, equip, favor, bless, grace.

en·dow·ment /en'doumənt/ ▶ **n.** **1** property or a regular income that has been given or left to a person or an institution. **2** a quality or ability that you are born with.

SYNONYMS **gift**, present, grant, funding, award, donation, contribution, subsidy, sponsorship, bequest, legacy.

end·pa·per /'en(d)ˌpāpər/ ▶ **n.** a sheet of paper at the beginning or end of a book, fixed to the inside of the cover.

en·dur·ance /en'd(y)o͝orəns/ ▶ **n.** **1** the ability to do or cope with something painful or difficult for a long time. **2** the quality of lasting for a long time before wearing out.

SYNONYMS **1 toleration**, tolerance, forbearance, patience, acceptance, resignation, stoicism. **2 resistance**, durability, permanence, longevity, strength, toughness, stamina, staying power, fortitude.

en·dure /en'd(y)o͝or/ ▶ **v.** (**endures**, **enduring**, **endured**) **1** experience and be able to cope with prolonged pain or difficulty. **2** last for a long time: *these cities have endured through time.*

SYNONYMS **1 undergo**, go through, live through, experience, cope with, deal with, face, suffer, tolerate, put up with, brave, bear, withstand. **2 last**, live, live on, go on, survive, abide, continue, persist, remain.

end·wise /'en(d)ˌwīz/ (also **endways** /-ˌwāz/) ▶ **adv.** **1** with an end facing forward. **2** end to end.

en·e·ma /'enəmə/ ▶ **n.** a process in which liquid is injected into the rectum to clean it out.

en·e·my /'enəmē/ ▶ **n.** (plural **enemies**) **1** a person who is hostile to you. **2** (**the enemy**) a country that your own is fighting in a war.

SYNONYMS **opponent**, adversary, rival, antagonist, combatant, challenger, competitor, opposition, competition, the other side; literary foe. ANTONYMS friend, ally.

en·er·get·ic /ˌenər'jetik/ ▶ **adj.** having a lot of energy.

SYNONYMS **1** *an energetic woman* **active**, lively, dynamic, spirited, animated, bouncy, bubbly, sprightly, tireless, indefatigable, enthusiastic; informal full of beans. **2** *energetic exercises* **vigorous**, strenuous, brisk, hard, arduous, demanding, taxing, tough, rigorous. **3** *an energetic advertising campaign* **forceful**, vigorous, aggressive, hard-hitting, high-powered, all-out, determined, bold, intensive; informal in-your-face. ANTONYMS lethargic.

■ **en·er·get·i·cal·ly** **adv.**

en·er·gize /'enərˌjīz/ ▶ **v.** (**energizes**, **energizing**, **energized**) give energy and enthusiasm to: *people were energized by his ideas.*

en·er·gy /'enərjē/ ▶ **n.** (plural **energies**) **1** the strength and vitality that you need in order to be active. **2** (**energies**) a person's physical and mental powers: *I'll devote my energies to gardening this summer.* **3** power obtained from physical or chemical resources to provide light and heat or to work machines.

SYNONYMS **vitality**, vigor, strength, stamina, animation, spirit, verve, enthusiasm, zest, exuberance, dynamism, drive; informal punch, bounce, oomph, go, get-up-and-go.

en·er·vate /'enərˌvāt/ ▶ **v.** (**enervates**, **enervating**, **enervated**) cause someone to feel drained of energy.

en·fant ter·ri·ble /änˌfän te'rēbl(ə)/ ▶ **n.** (plural **enfants terribles**) a person who is known for behaving in an unconventional or controversial way.

en·fee·ble /en'fēbəl/ ▶ **v.** (**enfeebles**, **enfeebling**, **enfeebled**) make someone weak.

en·fi·lade /'enfəˌlād, -ˌläd/ ▶ **n.** a volley of gunfire directed along a line from end to end. ▶ **v.** (**enfilades**, **enfilading**, **enfiladed**) direct an enfilade at.

en·fold /en'fōld/ ▶ **v.** envelop someone: *silence enfolded them.*

en·force /en'fôrs/ ▶ **v.** (**enforces**, **enforcing**, **enforced**) **1** make sure a law or rule is obeyed. **2** force something to happen: *there is no outside agency to enforce cooperation between players.*

SYNONYMS **1 impose**, apply, administer, carry out, implement, bring to bear, put into effect. **2 force**, compel, coerce, exact.

■ **en·force·a·ble** **adj.** **en·force·ment** **n.** **en·forc·er** **n.**

en·fran·chise /en'franˌCHīz/ ▶ **v.** (**enfranchises**, **enfranchising**, **enfranchised**) **1** give a person or group the right to vote. **2** historical free a slave.
■ **en·fran·chise·ment** **n.**

en·gage /en'gāj/ ▶ **v.** (**engages**, **engaging**, **engaged**) **1** attract or involve someone's interest or attention. **2** (**engage in** or **with**) become involved in. **3** employ or hire someone. **4** move a part of a machine or engine into position: *the clutch will not engage.*

SYNONYMS **1 capture**, catch, arrest, grab, draw, attract, gain, hold, grip, absorb, occupy. **2** *the chance to engage in a wide range of pursuits* **participate in**, join in, take part in, partake in/of, enter into, embark on. **3 employ**, hire, recruit, take on, enroll, appoint. **4 attack**, fall on, take on, clash with, encounter, meet, fight, do battle with. ANTONYMS lose, dismiss.

en·gaged /en'gājd/ ▶ **adj.** **1** occupied: *I was otherwise engaged.* **2** having formally agreed to get married.

en·gage·ment /en'gājmənt/ ▶ n. **1** a formal agreement to get married. **2** an appointment. **3** the state of being involved in something. **4** fighting between armed forces.

SYNONYMS **1 appointment**, meeting, arrangement, commitment, date, assignation, rendezvous. **2 participation**, involvement. **3 battle**, fight, clash, confrontation, encounter, conflict, skirmish, action, hostilities.

en·gag·ing /en'gājiNG/ ▶ adj. charming and attractive.

SYNONYMS **charming**, attractive, appealing, pleasing, pleasant, agreeable, likable, lovable, sweet, winning, fetching. ANTONYMS unappealing.

■ **en·gag·ing·ly** adv.

en·gen·der /en'jendər/ ▶ v. (**engenders**, **engendering**, **engendered**) give rise to.

SYNONYMS **cause**, give rise to, bring about, occasion, lead to, result in, produce, create, generate, arouse, rouse, inspire, provoke, kindle, trigger, spark, stir up, whip up.

en·gine /'enjən/ ▶ n. **1** a machine with moving parts that converts power into motion. **2** a railroad locomotive.

SYNONYMS **motor**, generator, machine, turbine.

en·gi·neer /ˌenjə'ni(ə)r/ ▶ n. **1** a person who designs, builds, or maintains engines, machines, or public works. **2** a person who operates or controls an engine or machine. ▶ v. (**engineers**, **engineering**, **engineered**) **1** design and build. **2** arrange for something to happen: *she engineered another meeting with him.*

SYNONYMS ▶ n. **1** *a structural engineer* **designer**, planner, builder. **2** *a repair engineer* **mechanic**, repairer, technician, maintenance man, operator, driver. ▶ v. **bring about**, arrange, pull off, bring off, contrive, maneuver, negotiate, organize, orchestrate, plan, mastermind.

en·gi·neer·ing /ˌenjə'ni(ə)riNG/ ▶ n. the study of the design, building, and use of engines, machines, and structures.

Eng·lish /'iNG(g)lisH/ ▶ n. the language of England, used in many varieties throughout the world. ▶ adj. relating to England. ▫ **English breakfast** a substantial cooked breakfast, usually including bacon and eggs. **English horn** an alto woodwind instrument of the oboe family. **English muffin** a flat, round bread roll, eaten split, toasted, and buttered.

Eng·lish·man /'iNG(g)lisHˌmən/ (or **Englishwoman** /-ˌwo͝omən/) ▶ n. (plural **Englishmen** or **Englishwomen**) a person from England.

en·gorged /en'gôrjd/ ▶ adj. swollen.

en·grave /en'grāv/ ▶ v. (**engraves**, **engraving**, **engraved**) **1** carve words or a design on a hard surface or object. **2** (**be engraved on** or **in**) be fixed in a person's mind. ■ **en·grav·er** n.

en·grav·ing /en'grāviNG/ ▶ n. **1** a print made from an engraved plate or block. **2** the process of engraving.

SYNONYMS **etching**, print, plate, picture, illustration, inscription.

en·gross /en'grōs/ ▶ v. (often **be engrossed in**) absorb all of someone's attention.

SYNONYMS (**engrossed**) **absorbed**, involved, interested, occupied, preoccupied, immersed, caught up, riveted, gripped, rapt, fascinated, intent, captivated, enthralled.

en·gulf /en'gəlf/ ▶ v. (of a natural force) sweep over someone or something and completely surround or cover them.

SYNONYMS **swamp**, inundate, flood, deluge, immerse, swallow up, submerge, bury, envelop, overwhelm.

en·hance /en'hans/ ▶ v. (**enhances**, **enhancing**, **enhanced**) increase the quality, value, or extent of something.

SYNONYMS **improve**, add to, strengthen, boost, increase, intensify, heighten, magnify, amplify, inflate, build up, supplement, augment. ANTONYMS diminish.

■ **en·hance·ment** n.

e·nig·ma /i'nigmə/ ▶ n. a mysterious or puzzling person or thing.

SYNONYMS **mystery**, puzzle, riddle, conundrum, paradox.

■ **en·ig·mat·ic** /ˌenig'matik/ adj. **en·ig·mat·i·cal·ly** adv.

en·join /en'join/ ▶ v. instruct or urge someone to do something: *the code enjoined members to trade fairly.*

en·joy /en'joi/ ▶ v. **1** get pleasure from. **2** (**enjoy yourself**) have a good time. **3** have and benefit from: *these professions enjoy high status.*

SYNONYMS **1 like**, be fond of, take pleasure in, be keen on, delight in, relish, revel in, adore, lap up, savor, luxuriate in, bask in; informal get a thrill out of. **2 benefit from**, be blessed with, be favored with, be endowed with, possess, own, boast. ANTONYMS dislike, lack.

en·joy·a·ble /en'joi-əbəl/ ▶ adj. giving pleasure.

SYNONYMS **entertaining**, amusing, delightful, pleasant, congenial, convivial, agreeable, pleasurable, satisfying. ANTONYMS disagreeable.

■ **en·joy·a·bly** adv.

en·joy·ment /en'joimənt/ ▶ n. **1** the state or process of taking pleasure in something: *the weather didn't mar our enjoyment of the trip.* **2** a thing that gives pleasure. **3** the fact of having and benefiting from something.

SYNONYMS **pleasure**, fun, entertainment, amusement, recreation, relaxation, happiness, merriment, joy, satisfaction, liking.

en·large /en'lärj/ ▶ v. (**enlarges**, **enlarging**, **enlarged**) **1** make or become bigger. **2** (**enlarge on**) speak or write about something in greater detail.

SYNONYMS **1 extend**, expand, grow, add to, amplify, augment, magnify, build up, stretch, widen, broaden, lengthen, elongate, deepen, thicken. **2 swell**, distend, bloat, bulge, dilate, blow up, puff up. ANTONYMS reduce, shrink.

en·large·ment /en'lärjmənt/ ▶ n. **1** the state of being enlarged. **2** a photograph that is larger than the original negative or than an earlier print.

en·larg·er /en'lärjər/ ▶ n. a device for making a photographic print larger.

en·light·en /en'lītn/ ▶ **v. 1** give someone greater knowledge and understanding. **2** (**enlightened**) well-informed and able to make good judgments: *a most enlightened body of men.*

SYNONYMS **1 inform**, tell, make aware, open someone's eyes, illuminate; informal put someone in the picture. **2** (**enlightened**) **informed**, aware, sophisticated, liberal, open-minded, broad-minded, educated, knowledgeable, civilized, refined, cultured.

en·light·en·ment /en'lītnmənt/ ▶ **n. 1** the gaining of knowledge and understanding. **2** (**the Enlightenment**) a European intellectual movement of the late 17th and 18th centuries emphasizing reason and individualism rather than tradition.

SYNONYMS **insight**, understanding, awareness, education, learning, knowledge, illumination, awakening, instruction, teaching, open-mindedness, broad-mindedness, culture, refinement, cultivation, civilization.

en·list /en'list/ ▶ **v. 1** join the armed services. **2** ask for someone's help in doing something.

SYNONYMS **1 join up**, enroll, sign up, volunteer, register. **2 recruit**, call up, enroll, sign up, draft, conscript, mobilize. **3 obtain**, engage, secure, win, get. ANTONYMS discharge, demobilize.

□ **enlisted man** a member of the armed services below the rank of officer. ■ **en·list·ment n.**

en·liv·en /en'līvən/ ▶ **v. 1** make something more interesting. **2** make someone more cheerful or animated.

SYNONYMS **1** *a meeting enlivened by her wit* **liven up**, spice up; informal perk up, pep up. **2** *the visit had enlivened my mother* **cheer up**, brighten up, liven up, perk up, raise someone's spirits, uplift, gladden, buoy up, animate, vivify, vitalize, invigorate, restore, revive, refresh, stimulate, rouse, boost; informal buck up, pep up.

en masse /än 'mas/ ▶ **adv.** all together.

en·mesh /en'mesʜ/ ▶ **v.** (**be enmeshed in**) be involved in a complicated situation.

en·mi·ty /'enmitē/ ▶ **n.** (plural **enmities**) hostility.

SYNONYMS **hostility**, animosity, antagonism, friction, antipathy, animus, acrimony, bitterness, rancor, resentment, ill feeling, bad feeling, ill will, bad blood, hatred, loathing, odium. ANTONYMS friendship.

en·no·ble /en'nōbəl/ ▶ **v.** (**ennobles**, **ennobling**, **ennobled**) give greater dignity to: *ennoble the mind and uplift the spirit.*

en·nui /än'wē/ ▶ **n.** a feeling of listlessness, boredom, and dissatisfaction.

e·nor·mi·ty /i'nôrmitē/ ▶ **n.** (plural **enormities**) **1** (**the enormity of**) the extreme seriousness of something bad. **2** great size or scale: *the enormity of Einstein's intellect.* **3** a serious crime or sin.

SYNONYMS **1 wickedness**, vileness, heinousness, baseness, depravity, outrageousness. **2 immensity**, hugeness, size, extent, magnitude.

e·nor·mous /i'nôrməs/ ▶ **adj.** very large.

SYNONYMS **huge**, vast, immense, gigantic, giant, massive, colossal, mammoth, tremendous, extensive, mighty, monumental, mountainous; informal mega, monster, whopping, ginormous. ANTONYMS tiny.

■ **e·nor·mous·ly adv.**

e·nough /i'nəf/ ▶ **determiner & pron.** as much or as many as is necessary or desirable. ▶ **adv. 1** to the required degree. **2** to a moderate degree.

SYNONYMS ▶ **determiner & pron. 1** *enough food* **sufficient**, adequate, ample, abundant, the necessary; informal plenty of. **2** *there's enough for everyone* **sufficient**, plenty, an adequate amount, as much as necessary, a sufficiency, an ample supply, your fill. ANTONYMS insufficient.

□ **enough is enough** no more will be tolerated.

en·rage /en'rāj/ ▶ **v.** (**enrages**, **enraging**, **enraged**) make someone very angry.

SYNONYMS **1 anger**, infuriate, incense, madden, inflame, antagonize, provoke; informal drive mad/crazy, make someone see red, make someone's blood boil. **2** (**enraged**) **furious**, infuriated, irate, incensed, raging, incandescent, fuming, seething, beside yourself; informal mad, livid, foaming at the mouth. ANTONYMS placate.

en·rap·ture /en'rapcʜər/ ▶ **v.** (**enraptures**, **enrapturing**, **enraptured**) make someone feel great pleasure or joy.

en·rich/ en'ricʜ/ ▶ **v. 1** improve the quality or value of. **2** improve something by adding an extra item or ingredient.

SYNONYMS **enhance**, improve, better, add to, augment, supplement, complement, refine.

■ **en·rich·ment n.**

en·roll /en'rōl/ ▶ **v.** (**enrolls**, **enrolling**, **enrolled**) officially register or recruit someone as a member or student.

SYNONYMS **1 register**, sign on/up, put your name down, apply, volunteer, enter, join. **2 accept**, admit, take on, sign on/up, recruit, engage.

■ **en·roll·ment n.**

en route /än 'rōōt, en, äɴ/ ▶ **adv.** on the way.

en·sconce /en'skäns/ ▶ **v.** (**ensconces**, **ensconcing**, **ensconced**) establish in a comfortable, safe, or secret place.

en·sem·ble /än'sämbəl/ ▶ **n. 1** a group of musicians, actors, or dancers who perform together. **2** a group of items viewed as a whole: *an ensemble of curios showed that he had traveled widely.* **3** a set of clothes chosen to harmonize when worn together: *her ensemble of tweed and cashmere.*

SYNONYMS **1 group**, band, company, troupe, cast, chorus, corps; informal combo. **2 whole**, unit, body, set, collection, combination, composite, package. **3 outfit**, costume, suit; informal getup.

en·shrine /en'sʜrīn/ ▶ **v.** (**enshrines**, **enshrining**, **enshrined**) preserve a right, tradition, or idea in a form that ensures it will be respected: *rights enshrined in the constitution.*

en·shroud /en'sʜroud/ ▶ **v.** completely envelop something and hide it from view.

en·sign /'ensən, 'en,sīn/ ▶ **n.** a flag.

en·slave /en'slāv/ ▶ **v.** (**enslaves**, **enslaving**, **enslaved**) **1** make someone a slave. **2** make someone dependent on something: *youngsters enslaved by drugs.* ■ **en·slave·ment** n.

en·snare /en'sner/ ▶ v. (**ensnares**, **ensnaring**, **ensnared**) **1** catch an animal in a trap. **2** catch as if in a trap: *she ensnared men with her beauty.* **3** keep someone in a situation from which they cannot escape.

> SYNONYMS **capture**, catch, trap, entrap, snare, net; entangle, embroil, enmesh.

en·sue /en'so͞o/ ▶ v. (**ensues**, **ensuing**, **ensued**) happen afterward or as a result.

> SYNONYMS **result**, follow, develop, succeed, emerge, arise, proceed, stem.

en·sure /en'SHo͝or/ ▶ v. (**ensures**, **ensuring**, **ensured**) **1** make certain that something will turn out in a particular way. **2** (**ensure against**) make sure that a problem does not happen.

> SYNONYMS **1 make sure**, make certain, see to it, check, confirm, establish, verify. **2 secure**, guarantee, assure, certify.

ENT ▶ abbr. ear, nose, and throat (as a department in a hospital).

en·tail /en'tāl/ ▶ v. involve something as an inevitable part or result: *a situation which entails considerable risks.*

> SYNONYMS **involve**, necessitate, require, need, demand, call for, mean, imply, cause, give rise to, occasion.

en·tan·gle /en'taNGgəl/ ▶ v. (**entangles**, **entangling**, **entangled**) **1** cause something to become tangled. **2** involve someone in complicated circumstances.

> SYNONYMS **1** *their parachutes became entangled* **twist**, intertwine, entwine, tangle, snarl, knot, coil. **2** *he was entangled in a lawsuit* **involve**, embroil, mix up, catch up, bog down, mire.

■ **en·tan·gle·ment** n.

en·tente /än'tänt/ (or **entente cordiale**) ▶ n. a friendly understanding between people or countries.

en·ter /'entər/ ▶ v. (**enters**, **entering**, **entered**) **1** come or go into. **2** (often **enter into**) begin to be involved in or do. **3** join an institution or profession. **4** register as a participant in a competition or contest. **5** (**enter into**) undertake to be bound by an agreement: *he entered into an agreement with another company.* **6** record information in a book, computer, etc.

> SYNONYMS **1 go into**, come into, get into, set foot in, gain access to. **2 penetrate**, pierce, puncture, perforate. **3 join**, enroll in, enlist in, volunteer for, sign up for. **4 go in for**, register for, enroll for, sign on/up for, compete in, take part in, participate in. **5 record**, write, put down, take down, note, jot down, register, log. **6 key (in)**, type (in). ANTONYMS leave.

en·ter·prise /'entər,prīz/ ▶ n. **1** a business or company. **2** a large project. **3** the ability to think of and set up new projects: *success was the result of talent and enterprise.*

> SYNONYMS **1 business**, company, firm, venture, organization, operation, concern, establishment; informal outfit. **2 undertaking**, endeavor, venture, exercise, activity, operation, task, business, project, scheme. **3 initiative**, resourcefulness, imagination, ingenuity, inventiveness, originality, creativity.

en·ter·pris·ing /'entər,prīziNG/ ▶ adj. having the ability to think of and set up new projects.

> SYNONYMS **resourceful**, entrepreneurial, imaginative, ingenious, inventive, creative, adventurous, bold; informal go-ahead.

en·ter·tain /,entər'tān/ ▶ v. **1** provide someone with interest or amusement. **2** receive someone as a guest and provide them with food and drink. **3** give consideration to: *Washington entertained little hope of success.*

> SYNONYMS **1 amuse**, please, charm, cheer, interest, engage, occupy. **2 receive**, play host/hostess to, throw a party for, wine and dine, feed, fete. **3 consider**, contemplate, think of, countenance. ANTONYMS bore, reject.

■ **en·ter·tain·er** n.

en·ter·tain·ing /,entər'tāniNG/ ▶ adj. providing amusement or enjoyment. ■ **en·ter·tain·ing·ly** adv.

en·ter·tain·ment /,entər'tānmənt/ ▶ n. **1** the action of entertaining. **2** an event or activity designed to entertain other people.

> SYNONYMS **amusement**, pleasure, leisure, recreation, relaxation, fun, enjoyment, diversion, interest.

en·thrall /en'THrôl/ ▶ v. (**enthralls**, **enthralling**, **enthralled**) fascinate someone and hold their attention.

> SYNONYMS (**enthralling**) **fascinating**, entrancing, enchanting, bewitching, captivating, delightful, absorbing, engrossing, compelling, riveting, gripping, exciting; informal unputdownable.

en·throne /en'THrōn/ ▶ v. (**enthrones**, **enthroning**, **enthroned**) mark the new reign of a king or queen by a ceremony in which they sit on a throne. ■ **en·throne·ment** n.

en·thuse /en'THo͞oz/ ▶ v. (**enthuses**, **enthusing**, **enthused**) **1** express enthusiasm about something. **2** make someone enthusiastic: *the ringmaster must try hard to enthuse the crowd.*

en·thu·si·asm /en'THo͞ozē,azəm/ ▶ n. excited interest in and enjoyment of something.

> SYNONYMS **keenness**, eagerness, passion, fervor, zeal, zest, gusto, energy, vigor, fire, spirit, interest, commitment, devotion; informal get-up-and-go. ANTONYMS apathy.

en·thu·si·ast /en'THo͞ozē,ast/ ▶ n. a person who is very interested in a particular activity.

> SYNONYMS **fan**, devotee, supporter, follower, aficionado, lover, admirer; informal buff.

en·thu·si·as·tic /en,THo͞ozē'astik/ ▶ adj. feeling very interested in and happy about something.

> SYNONYMS **keen**, eager, avid, ardent, fervent, passionate, zealous, excited, wholehearted, committed, devoted, fanatical, earnest. ANTONYMS apathetic.

■ **en·thu·si·as·ti·cal·ly** adv.

en·tice /en'tīs/ ▶ v. (**entices**, **enticing**, **enticed**) attract someone by offering them something desirable.

> SYNONYMS **tempt**, lure, attract, appeal to, invite, persuade, beguile, coax, woo, lead on, seduce; informal sweet-talk.

en·tire /en'tīr/ ▶ adj. with no part left out; whole.

SYNONYMS **whole**, complete, total, full.

en·tire·ly /en'tīrlē/ ▶ **adv.** wholly; completely.

SYNONYMS **1 absolutely**, completely, totally, wholly, utterly, quite, altogether, thoroughly. **2 solely**, only, exclusively, purely, merely, just, alone.

en·tire·ty /en'tī(ə)rtē, -'tīritē/ ▶ **n.** (**the entirety**) the whole. ▫ **in its entirety** as a whole.

en·ti·tle /en'tītl/ ▶ **v.** (**entitles**, **entitling**, **entitled**) **1** give someone a right to do or have something. **2** give a title to a book, play, etc.

SYNONYMS **1 qualify**, make eligible, authorize, allow, permit, enable, empower. **2 name**, title, call, label, designate, dub.

en·ti·tle·ment /en'tītlmənt/ ▶ **n. 1** the fact of having a right to something. **2** the amount to which a person has a right.

en·ti·ty /'entitē/ ▶ **n.** (plural **entities**) a thing that exists independently.

SYNONYMS **being**, creature, individual, organism, life form, body, object, article, thing.

en·tomb /en'to͞om/ ▶ **v. 1** place someone in a tomb. **2** bury or completely cover.

en·to·mol·o·gy /ˌentə'mäləjē/ ▶ **n.** the study of insects. ■ **en·to·mo·log·i·cal** /-mə'läjikəl/ **adj.** **en·to·mol·o·gist n.**

en·tou·rage /ˌänto͞o'räzʜ/ ▶ **n.** a group of people who accompany and assist an important person.

en·trails /'entrālz, 'entrəlz/ ▶ **pl.n.** a person's or animal's intestines or internal organs.

en·trance¹ /'entrəns/ ▶ **n. 1** a door or passageway into a place. **2** an act of entering. **3** the right or opportunity to go into a place: *about fifty people attempted to gain entrance*.

SYNONYMS **1 entry**, entryway, way in, access, approach, door, portal, gate, opening, mouth, foyer, lobby, porch. **2 appearance**, arrival, entry, coming. **3 admission**, admittance, (right of) entry, entrée, access. ANTONYMS exit, departure.

en·trance² /en'trans/ ▶ **v.** (**entrances**, **entrancing**, **entranced**) **1** fill someone with wonder and delight. **2** cast a spell on.

SYNONYMS **enchant**, bewitch, beguile, captivate, mesmerize, hypnotize, spellbind, transfix, enthrall, engross, absorb, fascinate, stun, electrify, charm, delight; informal bowl over, knock out.

en·trant /'entrənt/ ▶ **n.** a person who joins or takes part in something.

SYNONYMS **competitor**, contestant, contender, participant, candidate, applicant.

en·trap /en'trap/ ▶ **v.** (**entraps**, **entrapping**, **entrapped**) **1** catch a person or animal in a trap. **2** trick someone into committing a crime in order to have them prosecuted. ■ **en·trap·ment n.**

en·treat /en'trēt/ ▶ **v.** ask someone earnestly or anxiously to do something.

SYNONYMS **implore**, beg, plead with, pray, ask, request, bid, enjoin, appeal to, call on; literary beseech.

en·treat·y /en'trētē/ ▶ **n.** (plural **entreaties**) an earnest request.

en·trée /'änˌtrā, ˌän'trā/ ▶ **n. 1** the main course of a meal. **2** the right to enter a place or social group: *an entrée into fashionable society*.

en·trench /en'trenCH/ ▶ **v. 1** establish a military force in fortified positions. **2** (**be entrenched**) be so firmly established that change is difficult: *prejudice is entrenched in our society*.

SYNONYMS (**entrenched**) **ingrained**, established, fixed, firm, deep-seated, deep-rooted, unshakable, ineradicable.

■ **en·trench·ment n.**

en·tre·pre·neur /ˌäntrəprə'no͝or, -'nər/ ▶ **n.** a person who is successful in setting up businesses.

SYNONYMS **businessman/businesswoman**; dealer, trader; promoter, impresario; informal wheeler-dealer, whiz kid, mover and shaker, go-getter.

■ **en·tre·pre·neur·i·al adj.**

en·tro·py /'entrəpē/ ▶ **n.** Physics a quantity expressing how much of a system's thermal energy is not available for conversion into mechanical work.

en·trust /en'trəst/ ▶ **v.** make someone responsible for doing or looking after something.

SYNONYMS **1** *he was entrusted with the job* **charge**, invest, endow; burden, encumber, saddle. **2** *the authority* ***entrusted to*** *our committee* **assign to**, confer on, bestow on, vest in, consign to, delegate to, give to, grant to, vouchsafe to.

en·try /'entrē/ ▶ **n.** (plural **entries**) **1** an act of entering. **2** a door or passageway into a place. **3** the right or opportunity to enter. **4** an item included in a list, reference book, etc.

SYNONYMS **1 appearance**, arrival, entrance, coming. **2 entrance**, entryway, way in, access, approach, door, portal, gate, entrance hall, foyer, lobby. **3 admission**, admittance, entrance, access. **4 item**, record, note, memo, memorandum. **5 submission**, application, entry form. ANTONYMS departure, exit.

▫ **entry-level** suitable for a beginner or first-time user.

en·twine /en'twīn/ ▶ **v.** (**entwines**, **entwining**, **entwined**) wind or twist together.

SYNONYMS **wind around**, twist around, coil around; weave, intertwine, interlace; entangle, tangle; twine.

e·nu·mer·ate /i'n(y)o͞oməˌrāt/ ▶ **v.** (**enumerates**, **enumerating**, **enumerated**) mention a number of things one by one.

SYNONYMS **list**, itemize, set out, give; cite, name, specify, identify, spell out, detail, particularize.

■ **e·nu·mer·a·tion** /iˌn(y)o͞omə'rāSHən/ **n.**

e·nun·ci·ate /i'nənsēˌāt/ ▶ **v.** (**enunciates**, **enunciating**, **enunciated**) **1** say or pronounce clearly. **2** set something out clearly and precisely: *a written document enunciating this policy*. ■ **e·nun·ci·a·tion** /iˌnənsē'āSHən/ **n.**

en·vel·op /en'veləp/ ▶ **v.** (**envelops**, **enveloping**, **enveloped**) wrap up, cover, or surround completely.

SYNONYMS **surround**, cover, enfold, engulf, encircle, cocoon, sheathe, swathe, enclose, cloak, veil, shroud.

SPELLING

Unlike the noun **envelope**, the verb **envelop** has no e on the end.

en·vel·ope /ˈenvəˌlōp, ˈänvə-/ ▶ **n. 1** a flat paper container with a flap, used to enclose a letter or document. **2** a covering or enclosing structure or layer.

en·vi·a·ble /ˈenvēəbəl/ ▶ **adj.** offering something desirable. ■ **en·vi·a·bly adv.**

en·vi·ous /ˈenvēəs/ ▶ **adj.** feeling discontented because you want something that someone else has.

SYNONYMS **jealous**, covetous, desirous, grudging, begrudging, resentful; informal green with envy.

■ **en·vi·ous·ly adv.**

en·vi·ron·ment /enˈvīrənmənt, -ˈvī(ə)rn-/ ▶ **n. 1** the surroundings in which a person, animal, or plant lives or operates. **2** (**the environment**) the natural world.

SYNONYMS **1 situation**, setting, milieu, background, backdrop, context, conditions, ambience, atmosphere. **2 the natural world**, nature, the earth, the ecosystem, the biosphere, Mother Nature, wildlife, flora and fauna, the countryside.

SPELLING

Remember the second **n**: environment.

en·vi·ron·men·tal /enˌvīrənˈmen(t)l, -ˌvī(ə)rn-/ ▶ **adj. 1** referring to the natural world. **2** designed to protect the natural world: *environmental tourism.* **3** of a person's surroundings: *environmental noise.* ■ **en·vi·ron·men·tal·ly adv.**

en·vi·ron·men·tal·ist /enˌvīrənˈmen(t)l-ist, -ˌvī(ə)rn-/ ▶ **n.** a person who is concerned with the protection of the environment.

SYNONYMS **conservationist**, ecologist, nature-lover, green; informal eco-warrior, tree-hugger.

■ **en·vi·ron·men·tal·ism n.**

en·vi·rons /enˈvīrənz, -ˈvī(ə)rnz/ ▶ **pl.n.** the surrounding area or district.

SYNONYMS **surroundings**, surrounding area, vicinity, vicinage; locality, neighborhood, district, region; precincts.

en·vis·age /enˈvizij/ ▶ **v.** (**envisages**, **envisaging**, **envisaged**) **1** see something as a possibility. **2** form a mental picture of.

SYNONYMS **1 foresee**, predict, forecast, anticipate, expect, think likely. **2 imagine**, contemplate, picture, conceive of, think of.

en·vi·sion /enˈvizHən/ ▶ **v.** visualize; envisage.

en·voy /ˈenˌvoi, ˈänˌvoi/ ▶ **n.** a messenger or representative.

SYNONYMS **ambassador**, emissary, diplomat, representative, delegate, spokesperson, agent, intermediary, mediator; informal go-between.

en·vy /ˈenvē/ ▶ **n.** (plural **envies**) **1** a feeling of wanting something that belongs to someone else. **2** (**the envy of**) a thing that is wanted by other people: *the Smiths' pool is the envy of the neighborhood.* ▶ **v.** (**envies**, **envying**, **envied**) wish that you had the same possessions or opportunities as someone else.

SYNONYMS ▶ **n. jealousy**, covetousness, resentment, bitterness. ▶ **v. 1 be envious of**, be jealous of, be resentful of. **2 covet**, desire, aspire to, wish for, want, long for, yearn for, hanker after, crave.

en·zyme /ˈenzīm/ ▶ **n.** a substance produced by an animal or plant that helps a chemical change happen without being changed itself.

e·on /ˈēən, ˈēˌän/ (or **aeon**) ▶ **n. 1** a very long period of time. **2** Geology a major division of geological time, subdivided into eras.

EPA ▶ **abbr.** Environmental Protection Agency.

ep·au·let /ˈepəˌlet, ˌepəˈlet/ (or **epaulette**) ▶ **n.** a flap attached to the shoulder of a coat or jacket.

e·phem·er·a /əˈfem(ə)rə/ ▶ **pl.n.** things that people use or are interested in for only a short time.

e·phem·er·al /əˈfem(ə)rəl/ ▶ **adj.** lasting only for a short time.

SYNONYMS **transitory**, transient, fleeting, passing, short-lived, momentary, brief, short, temporary, impermanent, short-term. ANTONYMS permanent.

ep·ic /ˈepik/ ▶ **n. 1** a long poem about the actions of great men or women or about a nation's history. **2** a long movie or book dealing with a long period of time or a major event such as a war. ▶ **adj. 1** having to do with an epic. **2** great and impressive in scale or character: *an epic journey around the world.*

SYNONYMS ▶ **adj.** *their epic journey* **ambitious**, heroic, grand, great; monumental.

ep·i·cen·ter /ˈepiˌsentər/ ▶ **n.** the point on the earth's surface where the effects of an earthquake are felt most strongly.

ep·i·cure /ˈepiˌkyo͝or/ ▶ **n.** a person who enjoys and is interested in good food and drink.

Ep·i·cu·re·an /ˌepikyəˈrēən, ˌepiˈkyo͝orēən/ ▶ **n. 1** a follower or student of the ancient Greek philosopher Epicurus. **2** (**epicurean**) a person who is very fond of pleasure, in particular of good food and drink. ▶ **adj. 1** of or concerning Epicurus or his ideas. **2** (**epicurean**) suitable for an epicure; very luxurious.

ep·i·dem·ic /ˌepiˈdemik/ ▶ **n.** a situation in which a large number of people have caught the same infectious disease.

SYNONYMS **1 outbreak**, plague, pandemic. **2 spate**, rash, wave, eruption, plague, outbreak, craze, upsurge.

ep·i·der·mis /ˌepiˈdərmis/ ▶ **n. 1** the surface layer of an animal's skin, on top of the dermis. **2** the outer layer of tissue in a plant. ■ **ep·i·der·mal adj.**

ep·i·du·ral /ˌepiˈd(y)o͝orəl/ ▶ **n.** an anesthetic injected into the space around the spinal cord, especially during childbirth.

ep·i·glot·tis /ˌepiˈglätəs/ ▶ **n.** a flap of cartilage in the throat that descends during swallowing to cover the opening of the windpipe.

ep·i·gram /ˈepiˌgram/ ▶ **n. 1** a concise and witty saying. **2** a short witty poem. ■ **ep·i·gram·mat·ic** /ˌepigrəˈmatik/ **adj.**

ep·i·graph /ˈepiˌgraf/ ▶ **n. 1** an inscription on a building, statue, or coin. **2** a short quotation introducing a book or chapter.

ep·i·la·tion /ˌepəˈlāsHən/ ▶ **n.** the removal of hair by the roots. ■ **ep·i·la·tor** /ˈepəˌlātər/ **n.**

ep·i·lep·sy /ˈepəˌlepsē/ ▶ **n.** a disorder of the nervous system that causes convulsions and loss of consciousness. ■ **ep·i·lep·tic** /ˌepəˈleptik/ **adj. & n.**

ep·i·logue /ˈepəˌlôg, -ˌläg/ (or **epilog**) ▶ **n.** a section at the end of a book or play that comments on what has happened.

e·piph·a·ny /iˈpifənē/ ▶ **n.** (plural **epiphanies**) **1** (**Epiphany**) (in the Bible) the time when the Magi visited the baby Jesus in Bethlehem. **2** a sudden and inspiring revelation.

e·pis·co·pa·cy /iˈpiskəpəsē/ ▶ **n.** (plural **episcopacies**) **1** government of a church by bishops. **2** (**the episcopacy**) the bishops of a region or church as a group.

e·pis·co·pal /iˈpiskəpəl/ ▶ **adj.** having to do with a bishop or bishops. □ **Episcopal Church** the Anglican Church in Scotland and the US, with elected bishops.

e·pis·co·pa·lian /iˌpiskəˈpālēən/ ▶ **adj. 1** relating to the government of a Church by bishops. **2** of or belonging to an episcopal Church. ▶ **n. 1** a supporter of the government of a Church by bishops. **2** (**Episcopalian**) a member of the Episcopal Church.

e·pis·co·pate /iˈpiskəpət, -ˌpāt/ ▶ **n. 1** the office or term of office of a bishop. **2** (**the episcopate**) the bishops of a church or region as a group.

ep·i·sode /ˈepiˌsōd/ ▶ **n. 1** an event or group of events happening as part of a sequence. **2** each of the separate parts into which a serialized story or program is divided.

SYNONYMS **1 incident**, event, occurrence, chapter, experience, occasion, interlude, adventure, exploit. **2 installment**, chapter, passage, part, portion, section, program, show. **3 period**, spell, bout, attack, phase; informal dose.

ep·i·sod·ic /ˌepəˈsädik/ ▶ **adj. 1** made up of a series of separate events. **2** happening at irregular intervals: *volcanic activity is highly episodic in nature.*

e·pis·te·mol·o·gy /iˌpistəˈmäləjē/ ▶ **n.** the branch of philosophy that deals with knowledge.

e·pis·tle /iˈpisəl/ ▶ **n. 1** formal a letter. **2** (**Epistle**) a book of the New Testament in the form of a letter from an apostle.

e·pis·to·lar·y /iˈpistəˌlerē/ ▶ **adj. 1** relating to the writing of letters. **2** (of a literary work) in the form of letters.

ep·i·taph /ˈepiˌtaf/ ▶ **n.** words written in memory of a person who has died.

ep·i·thet /ˈepəˌTHet/ ▶ **n.** a word or phrase describing someone or something's character or most important quality: *Alexander was given the epithet "the Great"*

e·pit·o·me /iˈpitəmē/ ▶ **n.** (**the epitome of**) a perfect example of something.

SYNONYMS **personification**, embodiment, incarnation, essence, quintessence, archetype, paradigm, exemplar, model.

e·pit·o·mize /iˈpitəˌmīz/ ▶ **v.** (**epitomizes, epitomizing, epitomized**) be a perfect example of.

ep·och /ˈepək/ ▶ **n. 1** a long and distinct period of time: *the Victorian epoch.* **2** Geology a division of time that is a subdivision of a period and is itself divided into ages: *the Pliocene epoch.*

SYNONYMS **era**, age, period, time, eon.

□ **epoch-making** of great importance and historical significance.

ep·o·nym /ˈepəˌnim/ ▶ **n. 1** a person after whom something is named. **2** a word or phrase based on someone's name.

e·pon·y·mous /əˈpänəməs/ ▶ **adj. 1** (of a person) giving their name to something. **2** (of a thing) named after a particular person.

Ep·som salts /ˈepsəm/ ▶ **pl.n.** crystals of magnesium sulfate used as a laxative or for other medicinal use.

eq·ua·ble /ˈekwəbəl/ ▶ **adj. 1** calm and even-tempered. **2** (of a climate) not changing very much.

SYNONYMS **1** *an equable man* **even-tempered**, calm, composed, collected, self-possessed, relaxed, easygoing; mellow, mild, tranquil, placid, stable, levelheaded; imperturbable, unexcitable, untroubled, well-balanced; informal unflappable, together, laid-back. **2** *an equable climate* **stable**, constant, uniform, unvarying, consistent, unchanging, changeless; moderate, temperate. ANTONYMS temperamental, extreme.

■ **eq·ua·bly adv.**

e·qual /ˈēkwəl/ ▶ **adj. 1** the same in quantity, size, value, or status. **2** evenly balanced. **3** (**equal to**) able to face a challenge. ▶ **n.** a person or thing that is equal to another. ▶ **v.** (**equals, equaling, equaled**) **1** be equal to. **2** be as good as.

SYNONYMS ▶ **adj. 1 identical**, uniform, alike, like, the same, matching, equivalent, corresponding. **2 impartial**, nonpartisan, fair, just, equitable, unprejudiced, nondiscriminatory. **3 evenly matched**, even, balanced, level, nip and tuck, neck and neck. ANTONYMS different, unequal. ▶ **n. equivalent**, peer, fellow, like, counterpart, match, parallel. ▶ **v. 1 be equal to**, be equivalent to, be the same as, come to, amount to, make, total, add up to. **2 match**, reach, parallel, be level with.

□ **equal opportunity** the policy of treating employees without discrimination. **equal sign** (or **equals sign**) the symbol =.

e·qual·i·ty /iˈkwälitē/ ▶ **n.** the state of having the same rights, opportunities, or advantages as others.

SYNONYMS **fairness**, equal rights, equal opportunities, impartiality, even-handedness, justice.

e·qual·ize /ˈēkwəˌlīz/ ▶ **v.** (**equalizes, equalizing, equalized**) **1** make things equal. **2** level the score in a game or match by scoring a goal. ■ **e·qual·i·za·tion** /ˌēkwəliˈzāSHən/ **n. e·qual·iz·er n.**

e·qual·ly /ˈēkwəlē/ ▶ **adv. 1** in an equal way or to an equal extent: *all children should be treated equally.* **2** to an equal extent: *follow-up discussion is equally important.* **3** in amounts or parts that are equal.

USAGE

The expression **equally as**, as in *follow-up discussion is equally as important* should be avoided: just use **equally** or **as** on its own.

e·qua·nim·i·ty /ˌēkwəˈnimitē, ˌekwə-/ ▶ **n.** calmness of temper.

SYNONYMS **composure**, calm, levelheadedness, self-possession, presence of mind, serenity, tranquility, imperturbability, equilibrium, poise, aplomb, sangfroid, nerve; informal cool. ANTONYMS anxiety.

e·quate /iˈkwāt/ ▶ v. (**equates**, **equating**, **equated**) consider one thing as equal to another.

SYNONYMS **1** *he equates criticism with treachery* **identify**, compare, bracket, class, associate, connect, link, relate. **2 equalize**, balance, even out/up, level, square, add up, tally, match.

e·qua·tion /iˈkwāZHən/ ▶ n. **1** the process of equating one thing with another. **2** Math a statement that the values of two mathematical expressions are equal (indicated by the sign =). **3** Chemistry a formula representing the changes that happen in a chemical reaction. **4** (**the equation**) a situation or problem in which several factors must be taken into account.

e·qua·tor /iˈkwātər/ ▶ n. an imaginary line around the earth at an equal distance from the two poles, dividing the earth into northern and southern hemispheres.

e·qua·to·ri·al /ˌekwəˈtôrēəl/ ▶ adj. having to do with the equator.

eq·uer·ry /ˈekwərē, əˈkwerē/ ▶ n. (plural **equerries**) a male officer of the British royal household who acts as an attendant to a member of the royal family.

e·ques·tri·an /iˈkwestrēən/ ▶ adj. relating to horse riding. ▶ n. a person on horseback.

e·ques·tri·an·ism /iˈkwestrēəˌnizəm/ ▶ n. the skill or sport of horse riding.

e·qui·dis·tant /ˌēkwiˈdistənt, ˌekwi-/ ▶ adj. at equal distances.

e·qui·lat·er·al /ˌēkwəˈlatərəl, ˌekwə-/ ▶ adj. having all its sides of the same length: *an equilateral triangle.*

e·qui·lib·ri·um /ˌēkwəˈlibrēəm, ˌekwə-/ ▶ n. (plural **equilibria** /-brēə/) **1** a state in which opposing forces are balanced. **2** the state of being physically balanced. **3** a calm state of mind.

SYNONYMS **balance**, stability, poise, symmetry, harmony. ANTONYMS imbalance.

e·quine /ˈekwīn, ˈēˌkwīn/ ▶ adj. **1** relating to horses. **2** resembling a horse: *her somewhat equine features.*

e·qui·noc·tial /ˌēkwəˈnäksHəl, ˌekwə-/ ▶ adj. **1** having to do with the equinox. **2** at or near the equator.

e·qui·nox /ˈekwəˌnäks, ˈēkwə-/ ▶ n. the time or date (twice each year, about September 22 and March 20) when day and night are of equal length.

e·quip /iˈkwip/ ▶ v. (**equips**, **equipping**, **equipped**) **1** supply someone with the things they need for a particular activity. **2** prepare someone for a situation or task: *he is not equipped for the modern age.*

SYNONYMS **1** *the boat was equipped with a flare gun* **provide**, furnish, supply, issue, stock, provision, arm. **2** *the course will equip them for the workplace* **prepare**, qualify, ready, suit, train.

e·quip·ment /iˈkwipmənt/ ▶ n. the items needed for a particular activity.

SYNONYMS **apparatus**, paraphernalia, tools, utensils, implements, hardware, gadgetry, things; informal stuff, gear.

e·qui·poise /ˈekwəˌpoiz/ ▶ n. balance of forces or interests: *this temporary equipoise of power.*

eq·ui·ta·ble /ˈekwitəbəl/ ▶ adj. fair and impartial.

SYNONYMS **fair**, just, impartial, even-handed, unbiased, unprejudiced, egalitarian; informal fair and square. ANTONYMS unfair.

■ **eq·ui·ta·bly** adv.

eq·ui·ta·tion /ˌekwiˈtāsHən/ ▶ n. formal the art and practice of horse riding.

eq·ui·ty /ˈekwitē/ ▶ n. (plural **equities**) **1** the quality of being fair and impartial. **2** the value of the shares issued by a company. **3** the value of a mortgaged property after all charges and debts have been paid. **4** a branch of law concerned with making fair judgments in situations not covered by existing laws.

e·quiv·a·lent /iˈkwivələnt/ ▶ adj. (often **equivalent to**) **1** equal in value, amount, function, meaning, etc. **2** having the same effect: *some regulations are equivalent to censorship.* ▶ n. a person or thing that is equivalent to another.

SYNONYMS ▶ adj. **comparable**, corresponding, commensurate, similar, parallel, analogous. ▶ n. **counterpart**, parallel, alternative, analog, twin.

■ **e·quiv·a·lence** n.

e·quiv·o·cal /iˈkwivəkəl/ ▶ adj. (of words or intentions) not clear because they can be interpreted in more than one way.

SYNONYMS **ambiguous**, indefinite, noncommittal, vague, imprecise, inexact, inexplicit, hazy, unclear, ambivalent, uncertain, unsure. ANTONYMS definite.

■ **e·quiv·o·cal·ly** adv.

e·quiv·o·cate /iˈkwivəˌkāt/ ▶ v. (**equivocates**, **equivocating**, **equivocated**) use language that can be interpreted in more than one way in order to hide the truth or avoid committing yourself. ■ **e·quiv·o·ca·tion** /iˌkwivəˈkāsHən/ n.

ER ▶ abbr. emergency room.

e·ra /ˈi(ə)rə, ˈerə/ ▶ n. **1** a long and distinct period of history. **2** Geology a major division of time that is a subdivision of an eon and is itself subdivided into periods: *the Mesozoic era.*

SYNONYMS **age**, epoch, period, time, date, day, generation.

e·rad·i·cate /iˈradiˌkāt/ ▶ v. (**eradicates**, **eradicating**, **eradicated**) remove or destroy completely.

SYNONYMS **eliminate**, get rid of, remove, obliterate, extinguish, exterminate, destroy, annihilate, kill, wipe out.

■ **e·rad·i·ca·tion** /iˌradiˈkāsHən/ n.

e·rase /iˈrās/ ▶ v. (**erases**, **erasing**, **erased**) **1** rub out something written. **2** remove all traces of something.

SYNONYMS **delete**, rub out, wipe off, blank out, expunge, excise, remove, obliterate.

e·ras·er /iˈrāsər/ ▶ n. a piece of rubber or plastic used to rub out something written.

ere /e(ə)r/ ▶ prep. & conj. old use before (in time).

e·rect /iˈrekt/ ▶ adj. rigidly upright. ▶ v. **1** put up a structure or object. **2** create or establish something: *the party that erected the welfare state.*

SYNONYMS ▶ adj. **upright**, straight, vertical, perpendicular, standing (on end), bristling, stiff. ▶ v. **build**, construct, put up, assemble, put together, fabricate, raise. ANTONYMS demolish, dismantle.

e·rec·tile /i'rektl, -ˌtīl/ ▶ **adj.** able to become erect.

e·rec·tion /i'reksʜən/ ▶ **n.** **1** the action of erecting a structure or object. **2** a building or other upright structure.

er·e·mite /'erəˌmīt/ ▶ **n.** a Christian hermit.

erg /ərg/ ▶ **n.** Physics a unit of work or energy.

er·go /'ərgō, 'ergō/ ▶ **adv.** therefore.

er·go·nom·ics /ˌərgə'nämiks/ ▶ **n.** the study of people's efficiency in their working environment. ■ **er·go·nom·ic** /ərgə'nämik/ **adj.**

Er·in /'erən/ ▶ **n.** old use or literary Ireland.

er·mine /'ərmən/ ▶ **n.** (plural **ermine** /'ərmən/ or **ermines**) **1** a stoat. **2** the white winter fur of the stoat.

e·rode /i'rōd/ ▶ **v.** (**erodes**, **eroding**, **eroded**) **1** gradually wear away. **2** gradually destroy: *this humiliation has eroded Jean's confidence.*

> SYNONYMS **wear away**, abrade, grind down, crumble, weather, undermine, weaken, deteriorate, destroy.

e·ro·sion /i'rōzʜən/ ▶ **n.** the process of eroding.

> SYNONYMS **wearing away**, abrasion, attrition, weathering, dissolution, deterioration, disintegration, destruction.

e·rot·ic /i'rätik/ ▶ **adj.** having to do with sexual desire or excitement.

> SYNONYMS **sexually arousing**, sexually stimulating, titillating, suggestive, pornographic, sexually explicit; informal steamy, blue, X-rated; euphemistic adult.

■ **e·rot·i·cal·ly** **adv.**

e·rot·i·ca /i'rätikə/ ▶ **n.** literature or art that is intended to make people feel sexually excited.

e·rot·i·cism /i'rätiˌsizəm/ ▶ **n.** **1** the use of images that are intended to be sexually exciting. **2** sexual desire or excitement.

err /ər, er/ ▶ **v.** **1** make a mistake. **2** do wrong: *he had erred as a husband.* □ **err on the side of** display more rather than less of (a specified quality) in your actions: *it is best to err on the side of caution.*

er·rand /'erənd/ ▶ **n.** a short journey made to deliver or pick up something.

> SYNONYMS **task**, job, chore, assignment, mission.

er·rant /'erənt/ ▶ **adj.** **1** doing something wrong or unacceptable. **2** old use traveling in search of adventure: *a knight errant.*

er·rat·ic /i'ratik/ ▶ **adj.** happening, moving, or acting in an irregular or uneven way.

> SYNONYMS **unpredictable**, inconsistent, changeable, variable, inconstant, irregular, fitful, unstable, varying, fluctuating, unreliable. ANTONYMS consistent.

■ **er·rat·i·cal·ly** **adv.**

er·ra·tum /i'rätəm, -'rā-, -'rat-/ ▶ **n.** (plural **errata** /-tə/) **1** a mistake in a book or printed document. **2** (**errata**) a list of corrected mistakes, added to a publication.

er·ro·ne·ous /i'rōnēəs/ ▶ **adj.** incorrect.

> SYNONYMS **wrong**, incorrect, mistaken, in error, inaccurate, untrue, false, fallacious; unsound, specious, faulty, flawed; informal off the beam, way out. ANTONYMS correct.

■ **er·ro·ne·ous·ly** **adv.**

er·ror /'erər/ ▶ **n.** **1** a mistake. **2** the state of being wrong: *human error.*

> SYNONYMS **mistake**, inaccuracy, miscalculation, blunder, slip, oversight, misconception, delusion, misprint; informal boo-boo, slip-up.

er·satz /'erˌsäts, -ˌzäts, er'zäts/ ▶ **adj.** **1** (of a product) artificial and not as good as the real thing. **2** not genuine: *ersatz emotion.*

erst·while /'ərstˌ(h)wīl/ ▶ **adj.** former: *the erstwhile president of the company.*

er·u·dite /'er(y)əˌdīt/ ▶ **adj.** having or showing knowledge gained from reading and study. ■ **er·u·di·tion** /'er(y)o͝oˌdisʜən/ **n.**

e·rupt /i'rəpt/ ▶ **v.** **1** (of a volcano) become active and eject lava, ash, and gases. **2** break out suddenly: *noise erupted from the conference room.* **3** show or express your feelings in a sudden and noisy way: *they erupted in fits of laughter.* **4** (of a blemish, rash, etc.) suddenly appear on the skin.

> SYNONYMS *fighting erupted* **break out**, flare up, blow up, explode, burst out.

e·rup·tion /i'rəpsʜən/ ▶ **n.** an act or instance of erupting.

> SYNONYMS **1 discharge**, explosion, lava flow, pyroclastic flow. **2 outbreak**, flare-up, upsurge, outburst, explosion, wave, spate.

e·ryth·ro·cyte /i'riтʜrəˌsīt/ ▶ **n.** technical a red blood cell.

es·ca·late /'eskəˌlāt/ ▶ **v.** (**escalates**, **escalating**, **escalated**) **1** increase rapidly. **2** become more serious.

> SYNONYMS **1 increase rapidly**, soar, rocket, shoot up, spiral; informal go through the roof. **2 grow**, develop, mushroom, increase, heighten, intensify, accelerate. ANTONYMS plunge, subside.

■ **es·ca·la·tion** /ˌeskə'lāsʜən/ **n.**

es·ca·la·tor /'eskəˌlātər/ ▶ **n.** a moving staircase consisting of a circulating belt of steps driven by a motor.

es·ca·lope /ˌeskə'lōp, i'skäləp, -'skal-/ ▶ **n.** a thin slice of meat coated in breadcrumbs and fried.

es·ca·pade /'eskəˌpād/ ▶ **n.** an adventure.

> SYNONYMS **exploit**, stunt, caper, antic(s); adventure, venture; deed, feat, experience; incident, occurrence, event.

es·cape /i'skāp/ ▶ **v.** (**escapes**, **escaping**, **escaped**) **1** break free from captivity or control. **2** succeed in avoiding something bad: *a boy narrowly escaped death.* **3** fail to be noticed or remembered by: *his name escapes me.* ▶ **n.** **1** an act of escaping. **2** a means of escaping.

> SYNONYMS ▶ **v.** **1 run away**, run off, get away, break out, break free, bolt, make your getaway, slip away, abscond; informal vamoose, skedaddle, fly the coop. **2** *he escaped his pursuers* **get away from**, elude, avoid, dodge, shake off; informal give someone the slip. **3** *they cannot escape their duties* **avoid**, evade, elude, cheat, sidestep, circumvent, steer clear of, shirk. **4 leak (out)**, spill (out), seep (out), discharge, flow (out), pour (out). ▶ **n.** **1 getaway**, breakout, flight. **2 leak**, spill, seepage, discharge, outflow, outpouring.

□ **escape clause** a clause in a contract which details the conditions under which one party can be freed from an obligation. ■ **es·cap·ee** /iˌskā'pē,

ˌeskāˈpē/ n. **es·cap·er** n.

es·cape·ment /iˈskāpmənt/ ▶ n. a mechanism that connects and regulates the movement of a clock or watch.

es·cap·ism /iˈskāpˌizəm/ ▶ n. the habit of doing enjoyable things to stop you thinking about unpleasant realities. ■ **es·cap·ist** n. & adj.

es·cap·ol·o·gist /iˌskāˈpäləjist, ˌeskā-/ ▶ n. an entertainer whose act consists of breaking free from ropes and chains. ■ **es·cap·ol·o·gy** n.

es·carp·ment /iˈskärpmənt/ ▶ n. a long, steep slope at the edge of an area of high land.

es·cha·tol·o·gy /ˌeskəˈtäləjē/ ▶ n. the part of theology concerned with death, judgment, and destiny.

es·chew /esˈCHo͞o/ ▶ v. deliberately avoid doing or having something.

es·cort ▶ n. /ˈesˌkôrt/ **1** a person, vehicle, or group accompanying someone to protect or honor them. **2** a person who accompanies a member of the opposite sex to a social event. ▶ v. /iˈskôrt/ accompany someone as an escort.

SYNONYMS ▶ n. **guard**, bodyguard, protector, minder, attendant, chaperone, entourage, retinue, protection, convoy. ▶ v. **1 conduct**, accompany, guide, usher, shepherd, take, lead. **2 partner**, accompany, chaperone.

es·cri·toire /ˌeskriˈtwär/ ▶ n. a small writing desk with drawers and compartments.

es·cu·do /iˈsko͞odō/ ▶ n. (plural **escudos**) the former basic unit of money in Portugal.

es·cutch·eon /iˈskəCHən/ ▶ n. a shield on which a coat of arms is depicted.

Es·ki·mo /ˈeskəˌmō/ ▶ n. (plural **Eskimo** or **Eskimos**) a member of a people inhabiting northern Canada, Alaska, Greenland, and eastern Siberia.

USAGE

Many of the peoples traditionally called **Eskimos** now prefer to call themselves **Inuit**.

ESL ▶ abbr. English as a second language.

ESOL /ˈēˌsäl/ ▶ abbr. English for speakers of other languages.

e·soph·a·gus /iˈsäfəgəs/ ▶ n. (plural **esophagi** /-ˌgī, -ˌjī/ or **esophaguses**) the muscular tube that connects the throat to the stomach.

es·o·ter·ic /ˌesəˈterik/ ▶ adj. intended for or understood by only a small number of people with a specialized knowledge.

SYNONYMS **abstruse**, obscure, arcane, rarefied, recondite, abstract, enigmatic, cryptic, complex, complicated, incomprehensible, impenetrable, mysterious.

ESP ▶ abbr. extrasensory perception.

es·pa·drille /ˈespəˌdril/ ▶ n. a light canvas shoe with a flexible sole made of rope or rubber.

es·pe·cial /iˈspeSHəl/ ▶ adj. **1** special: *it was of especial interest to me.* **2** for or belonging chiefly to one person or thing: *her outburst was for my especial benefit.*

es·pe·cial·ly /iˈspeSHəlē/ ▶ adv. **1** in particular. **2** to a great extent.

SYNONYMS **1 mainly**, mostly, chiefly, particularly, principally, largely, primarily. **2** *a committee formed especially for the purpose* **expressly**, specially, specifically, exclusively, just, particularly, explicitly. **3** *he is especially talented* **exceptionally**, particularly, unusually, extraordinarily, uncommonly, uniquely, remarkably, outstandingly.

Es·pe·ran·to /ˌespəˈräntō/ ▶ n. an artificial language devised in 1887 as an international medium of communication.

es·pi·o·nage /ˈespēəˌnäZH, -ˌnäj/ ▶ n. the practice of spying.

es·pla·nade /ˈespləˌnäd, -ˌnād/ ▶ n. a long, open, level area where people may walk for pleasure.

es·pouse /iˈspouz/ ▶ v. (**espouses**, **espousing**, **espoused**) support or choose a particular belief or way of doing things. ■ **es·pous·al** /iˈspouzəl, -səl/ n.

es·pres·so /eˈspresō/ ▶ n. (plural **espressos**) strong black coffee made by forcing steam through ground coffee beans.

SPELLING

Espresso is an Italian word (from *caffè espresso*, meaning 'pressed out coffee') and should be spelled the Italian way, with an **s**, not an **x**.

es·prit de corps /eˌsprē də ˈkôr/ ▶ n. a feeling of pride and loyalty that unites the members of a group.

es·py /iˈspī/ ▶ v. (**espies**, **espying**, **espied**) literary catch sight of.

Esq. ▶ abbr. Esquire.

Es·quire /ˈeskwīr, iˈskwīr/ ▶ n. a title added to a lawyer's surname: *my attorney, John Page, Esquire.*

es·say ▶ n. /ˈesā/ **1** a piece of writing on a particular subject. **2** formal an attempt. ▶ v. /eˈsā/ formal attempt to do something: *Donald essayed a smile.*

SYNONYMS ▶ n. **article**, composition, theme, paper, dissertation, thesis, discourse, study, assignment, treatise, piece, feature.

■ **es·say·ist** n.

es·sence /ˈesəns/ ▶ n. **1** the quality that is most important in making something what it is: *conflict is the essence of drama.* **2** an extract obtained from a plant or other substance and used for flavoring or scent.

SYNONYMS **1 nature**, heart, core, substance, basis, principle, quintessence, soul, spirit, reality; informal nitty-gritty. **2 extract**, concentrate, elixir, juice, oil.

□ **in essence** basically: *the theory is, in essence, very simple.* **of the essence** critically important.

es·sen·tial /iˈsenCHəl/ ▶ adj. **1** absolutely necessary. **2** relating to the most important part or basic nature of something: *the essential weakness of the case.* ▶ n. (**essentials**) **1** things that are absolutely necessary. **2** things that are part of the basic nature of something: *the essentials of the argument.*

SYNONYMS ▶ adj. **1 crucial**, key, vital, indispensable, all-important, critical, imperative. **2 basic**, inherent, fundamental, quintessential, intrinsic, underlying, characteristic, innate, primary. ANTONYMS unimportant, incidental. ▶ n. **1 necessity**, prerequisite; informal must. **2** (**essentials**) **fundamentals**, basics, rudiments, first principles, foundations, essence, basis, core, kernel, crux; informal nitty-gritty, nuts and bolts.

□ **essential oil** a natural oil extracted from a plant. ■ **es·sen·tial·ly** adv.

EST ▶ abbr. Eastern Standard Time.

es·tab·lish /iˈstablisн/ ▶ **v.** **1** set something up on a firm or permanent basis. **2** make someone or something accepted, recognized, or respected by other people. **3** show something to be true: *the police established that the passport was a forgery.*

SYNONYMS **1 set up**, start, initiate, institute, found, create, inaugurate. **2** (**established**) **accepted**, traditional, orthodox, set, fixed, official, usual, customary, common, normal, general, prevailing, accustomed, familiar, expected, conventional, standard. **3 prove**, demonstrate, show, indicate, determine, confirm.

es·tab·lish·ment /iˈstablisнmənt/ ▶ **n.** **1** the action of establishing something. **2** a business, public institution, or household. **3** (**the Establishment**) the group in society who have control over policy and resist change.

SYNONYMS **1 foundation**, institution, formation, inception, creation, installation, inauguration. **2 business**, firm, company, concern, enterprise, venture, organization, operation; informal outfit. **3 institution**, place, premises, institute. **4** *criticism of the Establishment* **the authorities**, the powers that be, the system, the ruling class.

es·tate /iˈstāt/ ▶ **n.** **1** a property consisting of a large house with grounds. **2** a property where crops such as coffee or grapes are grown. **3** all the money and property owned by a person at the time of their death.

SYNONYMS **1 property**, grounds, garden(s), park, parkland, land(s), territory. **2** *an industrial estate* **area**, development, complex. **3 plantation**, farm, ranch, holding, forest, vineyard. **4 assets**, capital, wealth, riches, holdings, fortune, property, effects, possessions, belongings.

es·teem /iˈstēm/ ▶ **n.** respect and admiration. ▶ **v.** respect and admire someone.

SYNONYMS ▶ **n. respect**, admiration, acclaim, appreciation, recognition, honor, reverence, estimation, regard. ▶ **v. respect**, admire, value, regard highly, appreciate, like, prize, treasure, revere.

es·ter /ˈestər/ ▶ **n.** Chemistry an organic compound formed by a reaction between an acid and an alcohol.

es·thete ▶ **n.** = **AESTHETE**.

es·thet·ic ▶ **adj.** = **AESTHETIC**.

es·ti·ma·ble /ˈestəməbəl/ ▶ **adj.** deserving respect and admiration.

es·ti·mate ▶ **v.** /ˈestəˌmāt/ (**estimates**, **estimating**, **estimated**) roughly calculate the value, number, or amount of something. ▶ **n.** /ˈestəmit/ **1** a rough calculation. **2** a written statement giving the likely price that will be charged for work. **3** an opinion: *his high estimate of the poem.*

SYNONYMS ▶ **v. 1 calculate**, approximate, guess, evaluate, judge, assess, weigh up. **2 consider**, believe, reckon, deem, judge, rate. ▶ **n. calculation**, approximation, estimation, guess, assessment, evaluation, quotation, valuation; informal guesstimate.

■ **es·ti·ma·tion** /ˌestəˈmāsнən/ **n.**

Es·to·ni·an /eˈstōnēən/ ▶ **n.** **1** a person from Estonia. **2** the native language of Estonia. ▶ **adj.** relating to Estonia.

es·tranged /iˈstrānjd/ ▶ **adj.** **1** no longer friendly or in contact with someone. **2** (of someone's husband or wife) no longer living with them.

es·trange·ment /iˈstrānjmənt/ ▶ **n.** the state of being estranged.

SYNONYMS **alienation**, disaffection, parting, separation, divorce, break-up, split, breach.

es·tro·gen /ˈestrəjən/ ▶ **n.** a hormone that produces female physical characteristics.

es·trus /ˈestrəs/ ▶ **n.** a recurring period of fertility in many female mammals.

es·tu·ar·y /ˈescнo͞oˌerē/ ▶ **n.** (plural **estuaries**) the mouth of a large river where it becomes affected by tides.

ET ▶ **abbr.** Eastern time.

ETA /ˈetə/ ▶ **abbr.** estimated time of arrival.

e-tail·er /ˈē ˌtālər/ ▶ **n.** a retailer who sells goods over the Internet.

et al. /ˌet ˈal, ˌet ˈäl/ ▶ **abbr.** and others.

etc. ▶ **abbr.** et cetera.

et cet·er·a /et ˈsetərə, ˈsetrə/ ▶ **adv.** and other similar things; and so on.

etch /ecн/ ▶ **v.** **1** engrave metal, glass, or stone by applying a coating, drawing on it with a needle, and then covering the surface with acid to attack the exposed parts. **2** cut words or a design on a surface. **3** (**be etched on** or **in**) be fixed permanently in someone's mind: *etched in the memory.*

SYNONYMS **engrave**, carve, inscribe, incise, score, mark, scratch.

etch·ing /ˈecнiNG/ ▶ **n.** **1** the process of etching. **2** a print produced by etching.

SYNONYMS **engraving**, print, plate.

e·ter·nal /iˈtərnl/ ▶ **adj.** lasting or existing forever.

SYNONYMS **everlasting**, never-ending, endless, perpetual, undying, immortal, abiding, permanent, enduring, constant, continual, continuous, sustained, uninterrupted, unbroken, nonstop, around/round-the-clock.

■ **e·ter·nal·ly** **adv.**

e·ter·ni·ty /iˈtərnitē/ ▶ **n.** (plural **eternities**) **1** unending time: *their love was sealed for eternity.* **2** (**an eternity**) informal an undesirably long period of time.

SYNONYMS **1 ever**, all time, perpetuity. **2 a long time**, an age, ages, a lifetime, hours, years, forever.

eth·ane /ˈetнˌān/ ▶ **n.** a flammable gas present in petroleum and natural gas.

eth·a·nol /ˈetнəˌnôl, -ˌnäl/ ▶ **n.** chemical name for **ethyl alcohol**.

e·ther /ˈētнər/ ▶ **n.** **1** a highly flammable liquid used as an anesthetic and a solvent. **2** literary the upper regions of the air.

e·the·re·al /iˈtнi(ə)rēəl/ ▶ **adj.** **1** very delicate and light: *she has a weirdly ethereal voice.* **2** heavenly or spiritual: *ethereal visions.*

SYNONYMS **1** *her ethereal beauty* **delicate**, exquisite; fragile, airy, fine, subtle. **2** *ethereal beings* **celestial**, heavenly, spiritual, otherworldly. ANTONYMS substantial, earthly.

E·ther·net /ˈētнərˌnet/ ▶ **n.** Computing a system for connecting a number of computer systems to form a local area network.

eth·ic /'eTHik/ ▶ **n. 1** (also **ethics**) a set of principles concerning right and wrong and how people should behave. **2** (**ethics**) the branch of philosophy concerned with moral principles.

> SYNONYMS **morals**, morality, values, principles, ideals, standards (of behavior).

eth·i·cal /'eTHikəl/ ▶ **adj. 1** having to do with principles about right and wrong: *ethical issues in nursing.* **2** morally correct.

> SYNONYMS **moral**, morally correct, right-minded, principled, good, just, honorable, fair.

■ **eth·i·cal·ly** **adv.**

E·thi·o·pi·an /,ēTHē'ōpēən/ ▶ **n.** a person from Ethiopia. ▶ **adj.** relating to Ethiopia.

eth·nic /'eTHnik/ ▶ **adj. 1** having to do with people from the same national or cultural background: *ethnic communities.* **2** referring to a person's origins rather than their present nationality: *ethnic Albanians.* **3** belonging to a non-Western cultural tradition: *ethnic music.*

> SYNONYMS **racial**, race-related, national, cultural, folk, tribal, ethnological.

□ **ethnic cleansing** the removal or killing of members of one ethnic or religious group in an area by those of another. **ethnic minority** a group that has a different ethnic origin from the main population. ■ **eth·ni·cal·ly** **adv.** **eth·nic·i·ty** /eTH'nisitē/ **n.**

eth·no·cen·tric /,eTHnō'sentrik/ ▶ **adj.** assessing other cultures according to the particular values or characteristics of your own.

eth·nog·ra·phy /eTH'nägrəfē/ ▶ **n.** the scientific description of peoples and cultures. ■ **eth·no·graph·ic** /,eTHnə'grafik/ **adj.**

eth·nol·o·gy /eTH'näləjē/ ▶ **n.** the study of the characteristics of different peoples and the differences and relationships between them. ■ **eth·no·log·i·cal** /,eTHnə'läjikəl/ **adj.**

e·thol·o·gy /ē'THäləjē/ ▶ **n.** the science of animal behavior.

e·thos /'ēTHäs/ ▶ **n.** the characteristic spirit of a culture, period, etc.

eth·yl /'eTHəl/ ▶ **n.** Chemistry a radical obtained from ethane, present in alcohol and ether. □ **ethyl alcohol** a colorless volatile flammable liquid that is the intoxicating constituent of wine, beer, and liquor, and is also used as an industrial solvent and as fuel.

eth·yl·ene /'eTHə,lēn/ ▶ **n.** Chemistry a flammable hydrocarbon gas of the alkene series, present in natural gas and coal gas.

e·ti·o·lat·ed /'ētēə,lātid/ ▶ **adj.** (of a plant) pale and weak due to a lack of light.

et·i·quette /'etikit, -,ket/ ▶ **n.** the rules of polite or correct behavior in a society.

> SYNONYMS **protocol**, manners, accepted behavior, the rules, decorum, good form; courtesy, propriety, formalities, niceties; custom, convention; informal the done thing, the thing to do.

E·trus·can /i'trəskən/ ▶ **n. 1** a person from Etruria, an ancient Italian state that was at its height *c.*500 BC. **2** the language of Etruria. ▶ **adj.** relating to Etruria.

et seq. /et sek/ ▶ **adv.** and what follows (used in page references).

et·y·mol·o·gy /,etə'mäləjē/ ▶ **n.** (plural **etymologies**) an account of the origins and the developments in meaning of a word. ■ **et·y·mo·log·i·cal** /-mə'läjikəl/ **adj.**

EU ▶ **abbr.** European Union.

eu·ca·lyp·tus /,yo͞okə'liptəs/ ▶ **n.** (plural **eucalyptuses** or **eucalypti** /-tī/) an evergreen Australasian tree whose leaves produce a strong-smelling oil.

Eu·cha·rist /'yo͞okərist/ ▶ **n. 1** the Christian ceremony commemorating the Last Supper, in which consecrated bread and wine are consumed. **2** the consecrated bread and wine used in this ceremony.

eu·gen·ics /yo͞o'jeniks/ ▶ **n.** the study of ways to increase the occurrence of desirable characteristics in a population by choosing which people become parents.

eu·lo·gize /'yo͞olə,jīz/ ▶ **v.** (**eulogizes**, **eulogizing**, **eulogized**) praise highly.

eu·lo·gy /'yo͞oləjē/ ▶ **n.** (plural **eulogies**) a speech or piece of writing that praises someone or something highly, typically someone who has just died.

eu·nuch /'yo͞onək/ ▶ **n.** a man who has had his testicles removed.

eu·phe·mism /'yo͞ofə,mizəm/ ▶ **n.** a less direct word used instead of one that is blunt or offensive. ■ **eu·phe·mis·tic** /,yo͞ofə'mistik/ **adj.** **eu·phe·mis·ti·cal·ly** **adv.**

eu·pho·ni·ous /yo͞o'fōnēəs/ ▶ **adj.** sounding pleasant. ■ **eu·pho·ni·ous·ly** **adv.**

eu·pho·ni·um /yo͞o'fōnēəm/ ▶ **n.** a brass musical instrument like a small tuba.

eu·pho·ny /'yo͞ofənē/ ▶ **n.** (plural **euphonies**) the quality of sounding pleasant.

eu·pho·ri·a /yo͞o'fôrēə/ ▶ **n.** a feeling of great happiness.

> SYNONYMS **elation**, happiness, joy, delight, glee, excitement, exhilaration, jubilation, exultation, ecstasy, bliss, rapture. ANTONYMS misery.

■ **eu·phor·ic** /yo͞o'fôrik, -'fär-/ **adj.**

Eur·a·sian /yo͝or'āZHən/ ▶ **adj. 1** of mixed European and Asian parentage. **2** relating to Eurasia (the landmass of Europe and Asia together).

eu·re·ka /yo͝o'rēkə, yə-/ ▶ **exclam.** a cry of joy or satisfaction when you discover something.

eu·ro /'yərō, 'yo͝orō/ ▶ **n.** the basic unit of money in sixteen member states of the European Union.

Eu·ro·cen·tric /,yərō'sentrik, ,yo͝orō-/ ▶ **adj.** seeing European culture as the most important. ■ **Eu·ro·cen·trism** **n.**

Eu·ro·pe·an /,yərə'pēən, ,yo͝orə-/ ▶ **n. 1** a person from Europe. **2** a person who is of European parentage. ▶ **adj.** having to do with Europe or the European Union. □ **European Union** an economic and political association of certain European countries.

Eu·ro·trash /'yərō,trasH, 'yo͝orō-/ ▶ **n.** informal rich European socialites.

Eu·sta·chian tube /yo͞o'stāSH(ē)ən, -kēən/ ▶ **n.** a narrow passage leading from the pharynx to the cavity of the middle ear.

eu·tha·na·sia /,yo͞oTHə'nāZHə/ ▶ **n.** the painless killing of a patient suffering from an incurable disease.

e·vac·u·ate /i'vakyə,wāt/ ▶ v. (**evacuates, evacuating, evacuated**) **1** remove someone from a place of danger to a safer place. **2** leave a dangerous place. **3** empty the bowels.

SYNONYMS **1 remove**, move out, take away. **2 leave**, vacate, abandon, move out of, withdraw from, retreat from, flee. **3** *police evacuated the area* **clear**, empty.

■ **e·vac·u·a·tion** /i,vakyoo'āshən/ n.

e·vac·u·ee /i,vakyoo'ē/ ▶ n. a person who is evacuated from a place of danger.

e·vade /i'vād/ ▶ v. (**evades, evading, evaded**) **1** escape or avoid. **2** avoid giving a direct answer to a question.

SYNONYMS **1 elude**, avoid, dodge, escape (from), steer clear of, sidestep, lose, leave behind, shake off; informal give someone the slip. **2 avoid**, dodge, sidestep, bypass, skirt around, fudge; informal duck (out of), cop out of. ANTONYMS confront.

e·val·u·ate /i'valyoo,āt/ ▶ v. (**evaluates, evaluating, evaluated**) form an idea of the amount or value of.

SYNONYMS **assess**, judge, gauge, rate, estimate, appraise, weigh up; informal size up.

■ **e·val·u·a·tion** /i,valyoo'āshən/ n. **e·val·u·a·tor** n.

ev·a·nes·cent /,evə'nesənt/ ▶ adj. soon passing out of existence; fleeting: *a shimmering evanescent bubble*. ■ **ev·a·nes·cence** n.

e·van·gel·i·cal /,ivan'jelikəl/ ▶ adj. **1** having to do with a tradition within Protestant Christianity that emphasizes the authority of the Bible and salvation through personal faith in Jesus. **2** having to do with the teaching of the gospel or Christianity. **3** showing passionate support for something: *evangelical feminists*. ▶ n. a member of the evangelical tradition in the Christian church. ■ **e·van·gel·i·cal·ism** n.

e·van·ge·list /i'vanjəlist/ ▶ n. **1** a person who sets out to convert other people to Christianity. **2** the writer of one of the four Gospels. **3** a passionate supporter of something. ■ **e·van·ge·lism** n. **e·van·ge·lis·tic** /i,vanjə'listik/ adj.

e·van·ge·lize /i'vanjə,līz/ ▶ v. (**evangelizes, evangelizing, evangelized**) **1** set out to convert people to Christianity. **2** preach the gospel.

e·vap·o·rate /i'vapə,rāt/ ▶ v. (**evaporates, evaporating, evaporated**) **1** turn from liquid into vapor. **2** cease to exist: *my goodwill evaporated*.

SYNONYMS **1 vaporize**, dry up. **2 end**, pass (away), fizzle out, peter out, wear off, vanish, fade, disappear, melt away. ANTONYMS condense, materialize.

□ **evaporated milk** thick sweetened milk from which some of the liquid has been evaporated. ■ **e·vap·o·ra·tion** /i,vapə'rāshən/ n.

e·va·sion /i'vāzhən/ ▶ n. the action of avoiding something.

e·va·sive /i'vāsiv/ ▶ adj. **1** avoiding committing yourself or revealing things about yourself. **2** (of an action) intended to avoid or escape something: *evasive action*.

SYNONYMS **equivocal**, prevaricating, elusive, ambiguous, noncommittal, vague, unclear, oblique.

■ **e·va·sive·ly** adv.

eve /ēv/ ▶ n. **1** the day or period of time immediately before an event or occasion. **2** evening.

e·ven[1] /'ēvən/ ▶ adj. **1** flat and smooth; level. **2** equal in number, amount, or value. **3** regular: *an even pace*. **4** equally balanced. **5** placid; calm: *an even temper*. **6** (of a number) able to be divided by two without a remainder. ▶ v. (**evens, evening** /'ēvniNG/, **evened**) make or become even. ▶ adv. used for emphasis: *he knows even less than I do*.

SYNONYMS ▶ adj. **1 flat**, smooth, uniform, level, plane. **2 uniform**, constant, steady, stable, consistent, unvarying, unchanging, regular. **3 tied**, drawn, all square, level, neck and neck, nip and tuck; informal even-steven(s). ANTONYMS bumpy, irregular, unequal.

□ **even as** at the very same time as. **evenhanded** fair and impartial. **even if** despite the possibility that. **even money** (in betting) odds offering an equal chance of winning or losing. **even now** (or **then**) **1** now (or then) as well as before. **2** in spite of what has (or had) happened. **3** at this (or that) very moment. **even so** nevertheless. **even though** despite the fact that. ■ **e·ven·ly** adv. **e·ven·ness** n.

e·ven[2] ▶ n. old use evening.

eve·ning /'ēvniNG/ ▶ n. the period of time at the end of the day.

SYNONYMS **dusk**, twilight, nightfall, sunset, sundown, night.

□ **evening primrose** a plant with pale yellow flowers that open in the evening, used for a medicinal oil. **evening star** the planet Venus, seen shining in the western sky after sunset.

e·ven·song /'ēvən,sôNG, 'evən,säNG/ ▶ n. a Christian service of evening prayers, psalms, and hymns.

e·vent /i'vent/ ▶ n. **1** a thing that happens or takes place. **2** a public or social occasion. **3** each of several contests making up a sports competition.

SYNONYMS **1 occurrence**, happening, incident, affair, occasion, phenomenon, function, gathering; informal do. **2 competition**, contest, tournament, match, fixture, race, game, meet, bout, sport, discipline.

□ **in any event** (or **at all events**) whatever happens or may have happened. **in the event 1** as it turned out. **2** (**in the event of** or **that**) if the specified thing happens.

e·vent·ful /i'ventfəl/ ▶ adj. marked by interesting or exciting events.

SYNONYMS **busy**, action-packed, full, lively, active, hectic. ANTONYMS dull.

e·ven·tide /'ēvən,tīd/ ▶ n. old use evening.

e·vent·ing /i'ventiNG/ ▶ n. an equestrian sport in which competitors must take part in each of several contests. ■ **e·vent·er** n.

e·ven·tu·al /i'venchooəl/ ▶ adj. occurring at the end of or resulting from a process or period of time.

SYNONYMS **final**, ultimate, resulting, ensuing, consequent, subsequent.

e·ven·tu·al·i·ty /i,venchoo'alitē/ ▶ n. (plural **eventualities**) a possible event or outcome.

e·ven·tu·al·ly /i'venchooəlē/ ▶ adv. in the end, especially after a long delay: *eventually, after midnight, I arrived at the hotel*.

SYNONYMS **in the end**, in due course, by and by, in time, after a time, finally, at last, ultimately, in the long run, at the end of the day, one day, some day, sometime, sooner or later.

ev·er /'evər/ ▶ **adv. 1** at any time. **2** used for emphasis in comparisons and questions: *better than ever.* **3** always. **4** increasingly: *ever larger sums.*

SYNONYMS **1 at any time**, at any point, on any occasion, under any circumstances, on any account, until now. **2 always**, forever, eternally, continually, constantly, endlessly, perpetually, incessantly.

ev·er·green /'evər,grēn/ ▶ **adj.** (of a plant) having green leaves throughout the year.

ev·er·last·ing /,evər'lastiNG/ ▶ **adj.** lasting forever or a very long time.

SYNONYMS **eternal**, endless, never-ending, perpetual, undying, abiding, enduring, infinite. ANTONYMS transient, occasional.

■ **ev·er·last·ing·ly adv.**

ev·er·more /,evər'môr/ ▶ **adv.** always; forever.

eve·ry /'evrē/ ▶ **determiner 1** used to refer to all the individual members of a set without exception. **2** used to indicate how often something happens: *every thirty minutes.* **3** all possible: *every effort was made.* □ **every now and then** (or **every so often**) occasionally. **every one** each one. **every other** each alternate one in a series. **every which way** informal **1** in all directions. **2** by all available means.

eve·ry·bod·y /'evrē,bädē, -,bədē/ ▶ **pron.** every person.

SYNONYMS **everyone**, all, one and all, all and sundry, the whole world, humanity, the public, the masses. ANTONYMS nobody.

eve·ry·day /'evrē,dā/ ▶ **adj. 1** daily. **2** happening regularly: *everyday activities.*

SYNONYMS **1 daily**, day-to-day, ongoing; formal quotidian. **2 commonplace**, ordinary, common, usual, regular, familiar, conventional, routine, run-of-the-mill, garden-variety, standard, stock, household, domestic. ANTONYMS unusual.

Eve·ry·man /'evrē,man/ ▶ **n.** an ordinary or typical human being.

eve·ry·one /'evrē,wən/ ▶ **pron.** every person.

SYNONYMS see **EVERYBODY**.

eve·ry·thing /'evrē,THiNG/ ▶ **pron. 1** all things, or all the things of a group. **2** the most important thing: *money isn't everything.*

eve·ry·where /'evrē,(h)wer/ ▶ **adv. 1** in or to all places. **2** in many places: *coffee bars are everywhere.*

SYNONYMS **all over**, all around, in every nook and cranny, far and wide, near and far, high and low, [here, there, and everywhere], the world over, worldwide; informal all over the place, all over the map. ANTONYMS nowhere.

e·vict /i'vikt/ ▶ **v.** legally force someone to leave a property.

SYNONYMS **expel**, eject, remove, dislodge, turn out, throw out, drive out, dispossess; informal chuck out, kick out, boot out, throw someone out on their ear.

■ **e·vic·tion n.**

ev·i·dence /'evədəns/ ▶ **n. 1** information indicating whether something is true or valid. **2** information used to establish facts in a legal investigation. ▶ **v.** (**evidences**, **evidencing**, **evidenced**) be or show evidence of: *popularity evidenced by a large turnout.*

SYNONYMS ▶ **n. 1 proof**, confirmation, verification, substantiation, corroboration. **2 testimony**, witness statement, declaration, submission; Law deposition, affidavit. **3 signs**, indications, marks, traces, suggestions, hints.

□ **in evidence** noticeable: *dirty dishes were in evidence, proving that housework wasn't on her mind.*

ev·i·dent /'evədənt/ ▶ **adj.** easily seen or understood; obvious.

SYNONYMS **obvious**, apparent, noticeable, conspicuous, visible, discernible, clear, plain, manifest, patent; informal as clear as day.

ev·i·den·tial /,evi'dencHəl/ ▶ **adj.** formal having to do with evidence.

ev·i·dent·ly /'evədəntlē/ ▶ **adv. 1** plainly or obviously. **2** it would seem that.

SYNONYMS **1 obviously**, clearly, plainly, unmistakably, manifestly, patently. **2 seemingly**, apparently, as far as you can tell, from all appearances, on the face of it, it seems, it appears.

e·vil /'ēvəl/ ▶ **adj. 1** deeply immoral and wicked. **2** very unpleasant: *an evil smell.* ▶ **n. 1** extreme wickedness. **2** something harmful or undesirable: *unpleasant social evils.*

SYNONYMS ▶ **adj. 1** *an evil deed* **wicked**, bad, wrong, immoral, sinful, vile, iniquitous, villainous, vicious, malicious, malevolent, demonic, diabolical, fiendish, dark, monstrous. **2** *an evil spirit* **harmful**, bad, malign. **3 unpleasant**, disagreeable, nasty, horrible, foul, filthy, vile. ANTONYMS good, virtuous. ▶ **n. 1** *the evil in our midst* **wickedness**, badness, wrongdoing, sin, sinfulness, immorality, vice, iniquity, corruption, villainy. **2** *nothing but evil will result* **harm**, pain, misery, sorrow, suffering, trouble, disaster, misfortune, woe. ANTONYMS good.

□ **the evil eye** a gaze superstitiously believed to cause harm. ■ **e·vil·ly adv.**

e·vince /i'vins/ ▶ **v.** (**evinces**, **evincing**, **evinced**) formal reveal the presence of: *his letters evince the excitement he felt.*

e·vis·cer·ate /i'visə,rāt/ ▶ **v.** (**eviscerates**, **eviscerating**, **eviscerated**) formal remove the intestines of. ■ **e·vis·cer·a·tion** /i,visə'rāsHən/ **n.**

e·voc·a·tive /i'väkətiv/ ▶ **adj.** bringing strong images, memories, or feelings to mind.

SYNONYMS **reminiscent**, suggestive, redolent; expressive, vivid, powerful, haunting, moving, poignant.

e·voke /i'vōk/ ▶ **v.** (**evokes**, **evoking**, **evoked**) **1** bring a feeling or memory into someone's mind. **2** obtain a response.

SYNONYMS **bring to mind**, put someone in mind of, conjure up, summon (up), invoke, elicit, induce, kindle, awaken, arouse.

■ **ev·o·ca·tion** /,ēvō'kāsHən, ,evə-/ **n.**

ev·o·lu·tion /,evə'lo͞osHən/ ▶ **n. 1** the process by which different kinds of animals and plants develop from earlier forms. **2** gradual development.

SYNONYMS **1 development**, progress, rise, expansion, growth. **2 natural selection**, Darwinism, adaptation, development.

■ **ev·o·lu·tion·ar·y adj.**

ev·o·lu·tion·ist /ˌevəˈlo͞oshənist/ ▶ **n.** a person who believes in the theories of evolution and natural selection.

e·volve /iˈvälv/ ▶ **v.** (**evolves**, **evolving**, **evolved**) **1** develop gradually. **2** (of an animal or plant) develop and change over many generations by evolution.

SYNONYMS **develop**, progress, advance, grow, expand, spread.

ewe /yo͞o/ ▶ **n.** a female sheep.

ew·er /ˈyo͞oər/ ▶ **n.** a large jug with a wide mouth.

ex /eks/ ▶ **n.** informal a former husband, wife, boyfriend, or girlfriend.

ex·ac·er·bate /igˈzasərˌbāt/ ▶ **v.** (**exacerbates**, **exacerbating**, **exacerbated**) make something that is already bad worse.

SYNONYMS **aggravate**, worsen, inflame, compound, intensify, increase, heighten, magnify, add to. ANTONYMS reduce.

■ **ex·ac·er·ba·tion** /igˌzasərˈbāshən/ **n.**

ex·act /igˈzakt/ ▶ **adj. 1** precise. **2** accurate in all details. ▶ **v. 1** demand and obtain something from someone. **2** take revenge on someone.

SYNONYMS ▶ **adj. 1** *an exact description* **precise**, accurate, correct, faithful, close, true, literal, strict, perfect. **2** *an exact record keeper* **careful**, meticulous, painstaking, punctilious, conscientious, scrupulous. ANTONYMS inaccurate, careless. ▶ **v. 1 demand**, require, impose, extract, compel, force, wring. **2 inflict**, impose, administer, mete out, wreak.

■ **ex·act·ness n.**

ex·act·ing /igˈzaktiNG/ ▶ **adj.** (of a task) making you concentrate or work very hard.

SYNONYMS **demanding**, stringent, testing, challenging, arduous, laborious, hard, taxing, grueling, punishing, tough. ANTONYMS easy, easygoing.

ex·ac·tion /igˈzakshən/ ▶ **n.** formal **1** the action of demanding something: *the exaction of payment from debtors*. **2** a sum of money demanded.

ex·ac·ti·tude /igˈzaktəˌt(y)o͞od/ ▶ **n.** the quality of being exact.

ex·act·ly /igˈzak(t)lē/ ▶ **adv. 1** in an exact way. **2** used to agree with what has just been said.

SYNONYMS **1 precisely**, entirely, absolutely, completely, totally, just, quite, in every respect. **2 accurately**, precisely, unerringly, faultlessly, perfectly, faithfully.

ex·ag·ger·ate /igˈzajəˌrāt/ ▶ **v.** (**exaggerates**, **exaggerating**, **exaggerated**) make something seem larger, more important, etc., than it really is.

SYNONYMS **overstate**, overemphasize, overestimate, inflate, embellish, embroider, elaborate, overplay, dramatize; informal blow all out of proportion. ANTONYMS understate.

■ **ex·ag·ger·a·tion** /igˌzajəˈrāshən/ **n.**

SPELLING

Two **g**s: exa**gg**erate.

ex·alt /igˈzôlt/ ▶ **v. 1** praise someone or something highly. **2** give someone or something a higher rank or status.

ex·al·ta·tion /ˌegzôlˈtāshən, ˌeksôl-/ ▶ **n. 1** extreme happiness. **2** the action of exalting.

ex·alt·ed /igˈzôltid, eg-/ ▶ **adj. 1** having high rank or status: *her exalted position*. **2** very grand or noble; lofty.

ex·am /igˈzam/ ▶ **n.** an examination in a subject or skill.

ex·am·i·na·tion /igˌzaməˈnāshən/ ▶ **n. 1** a detailed inspection. **2** a formal test of knowledge or ability in a subject or skill. **3** the action of examining.

SYNONYMS **1** *items spread out for examination* **scrutiny**, inspection, perusal, study, investigation, consideration, analysis. **2** *a medical examination* **inspection**, checkup, assessment, appraisal, test, scan. **3** *a school examination* **test**, exam, quiz, assessment.

ex·am·ine /igˈzamən/ ▶ **v.** (**examines**, **examining**, **examined**) **1** inspect something closely. **2** (of a doctor or dentist) look closely at a part of a person's body to detect any problems. **3** test someone's knowledge or ability.

SYNONYMS **1 inspect**, scrutinize, investigate, look at, study, appraise, analyze, review, survey; informal check out. **2 test**, quiz, question, assess, appraise.

■ **ex·am·i·nee** /igˌzaməˈnē/ **n. ex·am·in·er n.**

ex·am·ple /igˈzampəl/ ▶ **n. 1** a thing that is typical of or represents a particular group. **2** something that shows or supports a general rule. **3** a person or thing seen in terms of how suitable they are to be copied: *public figures should set an example*.

SYNONYMS **1 specimen**, sample, instance, case, illustration. **2 precedent**, lead, model, pattern, ideal, standard. **3 warning**, lesson, deterrent, disincentive.

□ **for example** used to introduce something chosen as a typical case. **make an example of** punish as a warning to others.

ex·as·per·ate /igˈzaspəˌrāt/ ▶ **v.** (**exasperates**, **exasperating**, **exasperated**) irritate someone very much.

SYNONYMS **infuriate**, anger, annoy, irritate, madden, provoke, irk, vex, gall, get on someone's nerves, rub the wrong way; informal aggravate, rile, bug, tee off, tick off.

■ **ex·as·per·a·tion** /igˌzaspəˈrāshən/ **n.**

ex·ca·vate /ˈekskəˌvāt/ ▶ **v.** (**excavates**, **excavating**, **excavated**) **1** make a hole by digging. **2** carefully remove earth from an area in order to find buried remains. **3** dig material out of the ground.

SYNONYMS **unearth**, dig up, uncover, reveal, disinter, exhume, dig out, quarry, mine.

■ **ex·ca·va·tion** /ˌekskəˈvāshən/ **n.**

ex·ceed /ikˈsēd/ ▶ **v. 1** be greater in number or size than. **2** go beyond a set limit. **3** go beyond what is expected: *they exceeded expectations*.

SYNONYMS **be more than**, be greater than, be over, go beyond, top, surpass.

SPELLING

The word is spelled **-eed**, not **-ede**: exc**eed**.

ex·ceed·ing·ly /ikˈsēdiNGlē/ ▶ **adv.** extremely.

ex·cel /ikˈsel/ ▶ **v.** (**excels**, **excelling**, **excelled**) **1** be very good at something. **2** be superior to.

SYNONYMS **shine**, be excellent, be outstanding, be skillful, be talented, stand out, be second to none.

ex·cel·lence /'eksələns/ ▶ **n.** the quality of being excellent.

> SYNONYMS **distinction**, quality, superiority, brilliance, greatness, caliber, eminence.

Ex·cel·len·cy /'eksələnsē/ ▶ **n.** (plural **Excellencies**) (**His**, **Her**, **Your**, etc., **Excellency**) a form of address for certain high officials of state or of the Roman Catholic Church.

ex·cel·lent /'eksələnt/ ▶ **adj.** very good; outstanding.

> SYNONYMS **very good**, first-class, superb, exceptional, marvelous, wonderful, splendid; informal terrific, fantastic. ANTONYMS inferior.

■ **ex·cel·lent·ly adv.**

ex·cept /ik'sept/ ▶ **prep.** not including. ▶ **conj.** used before a statement that forms an exception to one just made. ▶ **v.** exclude: *present company excepted.*

> SYNONYMS ▶ **prep. excluding**, not including, excepting, except for, omitting, not counting, but, besides, apart from, aside from, barring, bar, other than; informal outside of.

> **SPELLING**
> Don't forget the **c** in **except** and related words. Also, don't confuse **except** and **accept**, which means 'agree to receive or do something.'.

ex·cept·ing /ik'septiNG/ ▶ **prep.** except for.

ex·cep·tion /ik'sepSHən/ ▶ **n.** a person or thing that is excluded or that does not follow a rule.

> SYNONYMS **anomaly**, irregularity, deviation, special case, peculiarity, abnormality, oddity.

□ **take exception to** object strongly to.

ex·cep·tion·a·ble /ik'sepSHənəbəl/ ▶ **adj.** formal causing disapproval or offense.

ex·cep·tion·al /ik'sepSHənəl/ ▶ **adj. 1** unusual. **2** unusually good.

> SYNONYMS **1** *the drought was exceptional* **unusual**, abnormal, atypical, out of the ordinary, rare, unprecedented, unexpected, surprising. **2** *her exceptional ability* **outstanding**, extraordinary, remarkable, special, phenomenal, prodigious. ANTONYMS normal, average.

■ **ex·cep·tion·al·ly adv.**

ex·cerpt /'ek,sərpt/ ▶ **n.** a short extract from a movie or piece of music or writing.

> SYNONYMS **extract**, part, section, piece, portion, snippet, clip, citation, quotation, quote, line, passage, fragment.

ex·cess /ik'ses, 'ekses/ ▶ **n. 1** an amount that is too much. **2** (**excesses**) extreme or outrageous behavior: *the worst excesses of the French Revolution.* ▶ **adj.** going beyond an allowed or desirable amount: *excess fat.*

> SYNONYMS ▶ **n. 1 surplus**, surfeit, overabundance, superabundance, superfluity, glut. **2 remainder**, leftovers, extra, rest, residue. **3 overindulgence**, intemperance, immoderation, profligacy, extravagance, self-indulgence. ANTONYMS lack, restraint. ▶ **adj.** *excess oil* **surplus**, superfluous, redundant, unwanted, unneeded, excessive, extra.

□ **excess baggage 1** luggage weighing more than the limit allowed on an aircraft, for which a charge may be made. **2** a thing that is surplus to requirements, and therefore unwanted or inconvenient.

ex·ces·sive /ik'sesiv/ ▶ **adj.** more than is necessary, normal, or desirable.

> SYNONYMS **1 immoderate**, intemperate, overindulgent, unrestrained, uncontrolled, extravagant. **2 exorbitant**, extortionate, unreasonable, outrageous, uncalled for, inordinate, unwarranted, disproportionate; informal over the top.

■ **ex·ces·sive·ly adv.**

ex·change /iks'CHānj/ ▶ **n. 1** an act of giving something and receiving something else in return. **2** a short conversation or argument. **3** the changing of money to its equivalent in another currency. **4** a building used for financial trading. **5** a set of equipment that connects telephone lines during a call. ▶ **v.** (**exchanges**, **exchanging**, **exchanged**) give something and receive something else in return.

> SYNONYMS ▶ **n. 1 interchange**, trade, trading, swapping, traffic, trafficking. **2 conversation**, dialogue, chat, talk, discussion. ▶ **v. trade**, barter, swap, switch, change.

□ **exchange rate** the value at which one currency may be exchanged for another.

ex·cheq·uer /eks'CHekər, iks-/ ▶ **n.** a royal or national treasury.

ex·cise[1] /'ek,sīz/ ▶ **n.** a tax charged on certain goods produced or sold within a country.

ex·cise[2] /ik'sīz/ ▶ **v.** (**excises**, **excising**, **excised**) **1** cut something out surgically. **2** remove a section from a written work or piece of music. ■ **ex·ci·sion** /-'sizHən/ **n.**

ex·cit·a·ble /ik'sītəbəl/ ▶ **adj.** easily excited.

> SYNONYMS **temperamental**, volatile, mercurial, emotional, sensitive, highly strung, tempestuous, hotheaded, fiery. ANTONYMS placid.

■ **ex·cit·a·bil·i·ty** /ik,sītə'bilitē/ **n.** **ex·cit·a·bly adv.**

ex·cite /ik'sīt/ ▶ **v.** (**excites**, **exciting**, **excited**) **1** make someone feel very enthusiastic and eager. **2** give rise to: *the report excited great controversy in the press.* **3** increase the energy or activity in a physical or biological system.

> SYNONYMS **1 thrill**, exhilarate, animate, enliven, rouse, stir, stimulate, galvanize. **2 provoke**, stir up, rouse, arouse, kindle, trigger, spark, incite, cause. ANTONYMS bore.

■ **ex·ci·ta·tion** /ek,sī'tāsHən/ **n.**

> **SPELLING**
> Don't forget the **c**: excite.

ex·cite·ment /ik'sītmənt/ ▶ **n. 1** a feeling of great enthusiasm and eagerness. **2** something that arouses such a feeling: *the excitements of the previous night's fire.*

> SYNONYMS **1** *the excitement of seeing a leopard in the wild* **thrill**, pleasure, delight, joy; informal kick, buzz. **2** *the excitement in her eyes* **exhilaration**, elation, animation, enthusiasm, eagerness, anticipation.

ex·cit·ing /ik'sītiNG/ ▶ **adj.** causing great enthusiasm and eagerness.

> SYNONYMS **thrilling**, exhilarating, stirring, rousing, stimulating, intoxicating, electrifying,

invigorating, gripping, compelling, powerful, dramatic.

■ **ex·cit·ing·ly** adv.

ex·claim /ik'sklām/ ▶ v. cry out suddenly.

SYNONYMS **cry out**, declare, proclaim, blurt out, call out, shout, yell.

ex·cla·ma·tion /ˌekskləˈmāsʜən/ ▶ n. a sudden cry or remark. □ **exclamation point** a punctuation mark (!) indicating an exclamation. ■ **ex·clam·a·to·ry** /ik'sklaməˌtôrē/ adj.

ex·clude /ik'sklo͞od/ ▶ v. (**excludes**, **excluding**, **excluded**) **1** leave something out of consideration: *these figures exclude this month's sales*. **2** prevent someone from being a part of something.

SYNONYMS **1 be exclusive of**, not include. **2 rule out**, preclude. **3 keep out**, deny access to, shut out, bar, ban, prohibit. ANTONYMS admit, include.

ex·clud·ing /ik'sklo͞odiɴɢ/ ▶ prep. except.

ex·clu·sion /ik'sklo͞ozʜən/ ▶ n. the process of excluding, or the state of being excluded.

ex·clu·sive /ik'sklo͞osiv/ ▶ adj. **1** restricted to the person, group, or area concerned: *a problem not exclusive to Detroit*. **2** high-quality and expensive. **3** not including other things. **4** not published or broadcast elsewhere. ▶ n. a story or movie that has not been published or broadcast elsewhere.

SYNONYMS ▶ adj. **1 sole**, unshared, unique, individual, personal, private. **2 select**, chic, high-class, elite, fashionable, stylish, elegant, premier, upmarket, upscale; informal posh, classy, swish. **3** *prices **exclusive of** sales tax* **not including**, excluding, leaving out, omitting, excepting. ANTONYMS inclusive.

■ **ex·clu·sive·ly** adv. **ex·clu·siv·i·ty** /ˌekskloo͞'sivitē/ n.

ex·com·mu·ni·cate /ˌekskəˈmyo͞oniˌkāt/ ▶ v. (**excommunicates**, **excommunicating**, **excommunicated**) officially bar someone from membership of the Christian church. ■ **ex·com·mu·ni·ca·tion** /ˌekskəˌmyo͞oniˈkāsʜən/ n.

ex·co·ri·ate /ik'skôrēˌāt/ ▶ v. (**excoriates**, **excoriating**, **excoriated**) **1** formal criticize someone severely. **2** Medicine damage or remove part of the surface of the skin. ■ **ex·co·ri·a·tion** /ikˌskôrē'āsʜən/ n.

ex·cre·ment /'ekskrəmənt/ ▶ n. waste material passed from the body through the bowels.

SYNONYMS **feces**, stools, droppings, excreta; ordure, dung, manure, guano, scat; dirt, muck, mess; informal poop, poo, turds, doo-doo.

ex·cres·cence /ik'skresəns/ ▶ n. an abnormal growth or lump on a part of the body or a plant.

ex·cre·ta /ik'skrētə/ ▶ n. waste material that is passed out of the body.

ex·crete /ik'skrēt/ ▶ v. (**excretes**, **excreting**, **excreted**) pass waste material from the body. ■ **ex·cre·tion** /ik'skrēsʜən/ n. **ex·cre·to·ry** /'ekskriˌtôrē/ adj.

ex·cru·ci·at·ing /ik'skro͞osʜēˌātiɴɢ/ ▶ adj. **1** very painful. **2** very embarrassing, awkward, or boring.

SYNONYMS **agonizing**, severe, acute, intense, violent, racking, searing, piercing, stabbing, unbearable, unendurable; informal splitting, killing.

■ **ex·cru·ci·at·ing·ly** adv.

ex·cul·pate /'ekskəlˌpāt/ ▶ v. (**exculpates**, **exculpating**, **exculpated**) formal show or declare that someone is not guilty of doing something wrong.

ex·cur·sion /ik'skərzʜən/ ▶ n. a short journey or trip taken for pleasure.

SYNONYMS **outing**, trip, jaunt, expedition, journey, tour, day out, drive, run; informal spin.

ex·cuse ▶ v. /ik'skyo͞oz/ (**excuses**, **excusing**, **excused**) **1** give reasons why something that someone has done wrong may be justified. **2** forgive someone for something they have done wrong. **3** allow someone to not do something that is usually required. **4** allow someone to leave a room or meeting. **5** (**excuse yourself**) say politely that you are leaving. ▶ n. /ik'skyo͞os/ **1** a reason put forward to justify a fault or wrongdoing. **2** something said to conceal the real reason for an action. **3** informal a very bad example of something: *that pathetic excuse for a man*.

SYNONYMS ▶ v. **1 justify**, defend, condone, forgive, overlook, disregard, ignore, tolerate, explain, mitigate. **2 forgive**, pardon. **3 let off**, release, relieve, exempt, absolve, free. ANTONYMS punish, condemn. ▶ n. **1 justification**, defense, reason, explanation, mitigating circumstances, mitigation. **2 pretext**, pretense; informal story, alibi.

□ **excuse me** said as a polite apology. ■ **ex·cus·a·ble** /-zəbəl/ adj.

ex·e·cra·ble /'eksikrəbəl/ ▶ adj. very bad or unpleasant.

ex·e·crate /'eksiˌkrāt/ ▶ v. (**execrates**, **execrating**, **execrated**) feel or express great hatred for. ■ **ex·e·cra·tion** /ˌeksi'krāsʜən/ n.

ex·e·cute /'eksiˌkyo͞ot/ ▶ v. (**executes**, **executing**, **executed**) **1** carry out a plan, order, etc. **2** carry out an activity or maneuver. **3** kill a condemned person as a legal punishment.

SYNONYMS **1 carry out**, accomplish, bring off/about, implement, achieve, complete, engineer; informal pull off. **2 put to death**, kill, hang, behead, electrocute, shoot.

ex·e·cu·tion /ˌeksi'kyo͞osʜən/ ▶ n. **1** the carrying out of something. **2** the killing of a person who has been condemned to death.

SYNONYMS **1 implementation**, carrying out, performance, accomplishment, bringing off/about, attainment, realization. **2 killing**, capital punishment, the death penalty.

ex·e·cu·tion·er /ˌeksi'kyo͞osʜ(ə)nər/ ▶ n. an official who executes condemned criminals.

ex·ec·u·tive /ig'zekyətiv, eg-/ ▶ n. **1** a senior manager in a business. **2** a group of people who run an organization or business. **3** (**the executive**) the branch of a government responsible for putting plans, actions, or laws into effect. ▶ adj. having the power to put plans, actions, or laws into effect.

SYNONYMS ▶ n. **1 director**, manager, senior official, administrator; informal boss, exec, suit. **2 administration**, management, directorate, government, authority. ▶ adj. **administrative**, managerial, decision-making, lawmaking, governing, controlling.

ex·ec·u·tor /ig'zekyətər/ ▶ n. Law a person appointed by someone to carry out the terms of their will.

ex·ec·u·trix /igˈzekyəˌtriks/ ▶ **n.** Law a female executor.

ex·e·ge·sis /ˌeksiˈjēsis/ ▶ **n.** (plural **exegeses** /-sēz/) an explanation or interpretation of a written work.

ex·em·plar /igˈzemplər, -ˌplär/ ▶ **n.** a person or thing that is a good or typical example of something.

ex·em·pla·ry /igˈzemplərē/ ▶ **adj. 1** giving a good example to other people: *exemplary behavior.* **2** (of a punishment) acting as a warning.

SYNONYMS **perfect**, ideal, model, faultless, flawless, impeccable, irreproachable. ANTONYMS deplorable.

ex·em·pli·fy /igˈzempləˌfī/ ▶ **v.** (**exemplifies**, **exemplifying**, **exemplified**) be or give a typical example of.

SYNONYMS **typify**, epitomize, be an example of, be representative of, symbolize, illustrate, demonstrate.

■ **ex·em·pli·fi·ca·tion** /igˌzempləfiˈkāsʜən/ **n.**

ex·em·plum /igˈzempləm/ ▶ **n.** (plural **exempla** /-plə/) an example or model.

ex·empt /igˈzem(p)t/ ▶ **adj.** not having to do or pay something that other people have to do or pay. ▶ **v.** make someone exempt.

SYNONYMS ▶ **adj. free**, not liable, not subject, immune, excepted, excused, absolved. ▶ **v. excuse**, free, release, exclude, grant immunity, spare, absolve; informal let off.

ex·emp·tion /igˈzem(p)sʜən/ ▶ **n. 1** the process of exempting or state of being exempt from something: *exemption from antitrust laws.* **2** (also **personal exemption**) an amount of money that can be earned or received free of tax.

SYNONYMS **immunity**, exception, dispensation, indemnity, exclusion, freedom, release, relief, absolution.

ex·er·cise /ˈeksərˌsīz/ ▶ **n. 1** physical activity done to stay healthy or become stronger. **2** a set of movements, activities, or questions that test your ability or help you practice a skill. **3** an activity carried out for a specific purpose: *a public relations exercise.* **4** the putting into practice of a power or right: *the exercise of authority.* ▶ **v.** (**exercises**, **exercising**, **exercised**) **1** use or apply a power or right. **2** do physical exercise. **3** worry or puzzle someone: *the knowledge that a larger margin was possible still exercised him.*

SYNONYMS ▶ **n. 1 physical activity**, a workout, working out, movement, training. **2 task**, piece of work, problem, assignment, practice. **3 maneuver**, operation, deployment. ▶ **v. 1 use**, employ, make use of, utilize, practice, apply. **2 work out**, do exercises, train. **3 concern**, occupy, worry, trouble, bother, disturb, prey on someone's mind.

□ **exercise bike** (or **bicycle**) a stationary piece of exercise equipment like an ordinary bicycle.

ex·ert /igˈzərt/ ▶ **v. 1** use a force, influence, or quality to make something happen. **2** (**exert yourself**) make a physical or mental effort.

SYNONYMS **bring to bear**, apply, use, utilize, deploy.

ex·er·tion /igˈzərsʜən/ ▶ **n. 1** physical or mental effort. **2** the application of a force, influence, or quality.

ex·e·unt /ˈeksēənt, ˈeksēˌo͝ont/ ▶ **v.** (in a play) a stage direction telling actors to leave the stage.

ex·fo·li·ate /eksˈfōlēˌāt/ ▶ **v.** (**exfoliates**, **exfoliating**, **exfoliated**) **1** wash or rub the skin with a grainy substance to remove dead cells. **2** shed from a surface in scales or layers. ■ **ex·fo·li·a·tion** /eksˌfōlēˈāsʜən/ **n.**

ex·hale /eksˈhāl, ˈeksˌhāl/ ▶ **v.** (**exhales**, **exhaling**, **exhaled**) **1** breathe out. **2** give off vapor or fumes. ■ **ex·ha·la·tion** /ˌeks(h)əˈlāsʜən/ **n.**

ex·haust /igˈzôst/ ▶ **v. 1** tire someone out. **2** use up all of something. **3** talk about a subject so thoroughly that there is nothing left to say. ▶ **n. 1** waste gases that are expelled from the engine of a car or other machine. **2** the system through which these gases are expelled.

SYNONYMS ▶ **v. 1 tire out**, wear out, overtire, fatigue, weary, drain; informal take it out of someone, poop (out), tucker out. **2** (**exhausted**) **tired out**, worn out, weary, dog-tired, ready to drop, drained, fatigued; informal done in, all in, bushed, knocked out, wiped out, pooped, tuckered out, fried, zonked. **3** (**exhausting**) **tiring**, wearying, taxing, wearing, draining, arduous, strenuous, onerous, demanding, grueling; informal killing. **4 use up**, get through, consume, finish, deplete, spend, empty, drain; informal blow. **5** (**exhausted**) *exhausted reserves* **used up**, consumed, finished, spent, depleted; empty, drained. ANTONYMS invigorate, replenish.

■ **ex·haust·i·ble** **adj.**

ex·haus·tion /igˈzôscʜən/ ▶ **n.** the state of being exhausted.

SYNONYMS **tiredness**, fatigue, weariness, debility, enervation.

ex·haus·tive /igˈzôstiv/ ▶ **adj.** thoroughly covering all aspects of something.

SYNONYMS **comprehensive**, all-inclusive, complete, full, encyclopedic, thorough, in-depth; detailed, meticulous, painstaking. ANTONYMS perfunctory.

■ **ex·haus·tive·ly** **adv.**

ex·hib·it /igˈzibit/ ▶ **v. 1** display an item in an art gallery or museum. **2** show a particular quality: *they exhibited great humility.* ▶ **n. 1** an object or collection on display in an art gallery or museum. **2** an object produced in a court of law as evidence.

SYNONYMS ▶ **v. 1 put on display**, show, display, unveil, present. **2 show**, reveal, display, manifest, indicate, demonstrate, express, evince, evidence. ▶ **n. item**, piece, artifact, display, collection.

■ **ex·hib·i·tor** **n.**

ex·hi·bi·tion /ˌeksəˈbisʜən/ ▶ **n. 1** a public display of items in an art gallery or museum. **2** a display or demonstration of a skill or quality.

SYNONYMS **1 exposition**, display, show, showing, presentation. **2 display**, show, demonstration, manifestation, expression.

□ **make an exhibition of yourself** behave very foolishly in public.

ex·hi·bi·tion·ism /ˌeksəˈbisʜəˌnizəm/ ▶ **n.** behavior that is intended to make people notice you. ■ **ex·hi·bi·tion·ist** **n.**

ex·hil·a·rate /igˈziləˌrāt/ ▶ **v.** (**exhilarates**, **exhilarating**, **exhilarated**) make someone feel very happy and full of energy.

SYNONYMS (**exhilarating**) **thrilling**, exciting, invigorating, stimulating, intoxicating, electrifying.

■ **ex·hil·a·ra·tion** /igˌziləˈrāSHən/ **n.**

SPELLING

The middle is **-lar-**, not **-ler-**: exhi**lar**ate.

ex·hort /igˈzôrt/ ▶ **v.** strongly urge someone to do something.

SYNONYMS **urge**, encourage, call on, enjoin, charge, press, bid, appeal to, entreat, implore; literary beseech.

■ **ex·hor·ta·tion** /ˌegzôrˈtāSHən, ˌeksôr-/ **n.**

ex·hume /igˈz(y)o͞om, eksˈ(y)o͞om/ ▶ **v.** (**exhumes, exhuming, exhumed**) dig out from the ground something that has been buried, especially a corpse.

SYNONYMS **disinter**, dig up, disentomb. ANTONYMS bury.

■ **ex·hu·ma·tion** /ˌegz(y)o͞oˈmāSHən, ˌeks(h)yo͞o-/ **n.**

ex·i·gen·cy /ˈeksijənsē, igˈzijənsē/ ▶ **n.** (plural **exigencies**) formal an urgent need.

ex·i·gent /ˈeksijənt/ ▶ **adj.** formal needing urgent action; pressing: *exigent demands*.

ex·ig·u·ous /igˈzigyo͞oəs, ikˈsig-/ ▶ **adj.** formal very small.

ex·ile /ˈegˌzīl, ˈekˌsīl/ ▶ **n. 1** the state of being forbidden to live or spend time in your own country. **2** a person who lives in exile. ▶ **v.** (**exiles, exiling, exiled**) expel and bar someone from their own country.

SYNONYMS ▶ **n. 1 banishment**, expulsion, deportation, eviction, isolation. **2 expatriate**, émigré, deportee, displaced person, refugee.

ex·ist /igˈzist/ ▶ **v. 1** be present in a place or situation. **2** live.

SYNONYMS **1 live**, be alive, be, be present. **2 prevail**, occur, be found, be in existence, be the case; formal obtain. **3 survive**, subsist, live, support yourself, manage, make do, get by, scrape by, make ends meet, eke out a living.

ex·ist·ence /igˈzistəns/ ▶ **n. 1** the fact or state of existing. **2** a way of living: *a rural existence*.

SYNONYMS **1 survival**, continuation. **2 way of life**, life, lifestyle, situation.

SPELLING

Write **-ence**, not **-ance**: exist**ence**.

ex·ist·ent /igˈzistənt/ ▶ **adj.** existing.

ex·is·ten·tial /ˌegziˈstenCHəl/ ▶ **adj. 1** having to do with existence. **2** Philosophy concerned with existentialism.

ex·is·ten·tial·ism /ˌegziˈstenCHəˌlizəm/ ▶ **n.** a theory in philosophy that says that people are free individuals, responsible for their own actions. ■ **ex·is·ten·tial·ist n. & adj.**

ex·it /ˈegzit, ˈeksit/ ▶ **n. 1** a way out of a place. **2** an act of leaving. ▶ **v.** (**exits, exiting, exited**) go out of or leave a place.

SYNONYMS ▶ **n. 1 way out**, door, escape route, egress. **2 turning**, turnoff, junction. **3 departure**, leaving, withdrawal, going, retreat, flight, exodus, escape. ANTONYMS entrance, arrival. ▶ **v. leave**, go out, depart, withdraw, retreat. ANTONYMS enter.

□ **exit poll** an opinion poll in which people leaving a polling place are asked how they voted.

ex·o·crine /ˈeksəˌkrin, ˈeksəˌkrēn/ ▶ **adj.** (of a gland) secreting hormones through ducts rather than directly into the blood.

ex·o·dus /ˈeksədəs/ ▶ **n. 1** a mass departure of people. **2** (**the Exodus**) the departure of the Israelites from Egypt, as recounted in the second book of the Bible.

ex of·fi·ci·o /ˈeks əˈfiSHēō/ ▶ **adv. & adj.** as a result of your position or status: *an ex officio member of the committee*.

ex·on·er·ate /igˈzänəˌrāt/ ▶ **v.** (**exonerates, exonerating, exonerated**) officially state that someone has not done something wrong or illegal.

SYNONYMS **absolve**, clear, acquit, find innocent, discharge; formal exculpate. ANTONYMS convict.

■ **ex·on·er·a·tion** /igˌzänəˈrāSHən/ **n.**

ex·or·bi·tant /igˈzôrbitənt/ ▶ **adj.** (of an amount charged) unreasonably high.

SYNONYMS **extortionate**, excessive, prohibitive, outrageous, unreasonable, inflated; informal steep, stiff. ANTONYMS cheap.

■ **ex·or·bi·tant·ly adv.**

SPELLING

No **h**: exor**bi**tant.

ex·or·cise /ˈeksôrˌsīz, ˈeksər-/ (or **exorcize**) ▶ **v.** (**exorcises, exorcising, exorcises**) drive an evil spirit from a person or place. ■ **ex·or·cism n. ex·or·cist n.**

ex·o·skel·e·ton /ˌeksōˈskelitn/ ▶ **n.** Zoology the rigid outer covering of the body in some invertebrate animals.

ex·o·ther·mic /ˌeksəˈTHərmik/ ▶ **n.** (of a reaction) releasing heat.

ex·ot·ic /igˈzätik/ ▶ **adj. 1** coming from or characteristic of a distant foreign country. **2** strikingly colorful or unusual: *an exotic outfit*.

SYNONYMS **1** *exotic birds* **foreign**, nonnative, alien, tropical. **2** *exotic places* **foreign**, faraway, far-off, far-flung, distant. **3 striking**, colorful, eye-catching, unusual, unconventional, extravagant, outlandish.

■ **ex·ot·i·cal·ly adv. ex·ot·i·cism n.**

ex·pand /ikˈspand/ ▶ **v. 1** make or become larger or more extensive. **2** (**expand on**) give a fuller account of.

SYNONYMS **1** *metals expand when heated* **enlarge**, increase in size, swell, lengthen, stretch, spread, thicken, fill out. **2** *the company is expanding* **grow**, enlarge, increase in size, extend, augment, broaden, widen, develop, diversify, build up, branch out, spread. ANTONYMS contract.

■ **ex·pand·a·ble adj.**

ex·pand·ed /ikˈspandid/ ▶ **n. 1** (of a material) having a light structure: *expanded polystyrene*. **2** relatively broad in shape.

ex·panse /ikˈspans/ ▶ **n.** a wide continuous area of something: *the green expanse of forest*.

SYNONYMS **area**, stretch, sweep, tract, swathe, belt, region, sea, carpet, blanket, sheet.

ex·pan·sion /ik'spanshən/ ▶ n. **1** the action of becoming larger or more extensive. **2** the political strategy of extending a state's territory by encroaching on that of other nations.

> SYNONYMS **1** *expansion and contraction* **enlargement**, swelling, lengthening, elongation, stretching, thickening. **2** *the expansion of the company* **growth**, increase in size, enlargement, extension, development, diversification, spread. ANTONYMS contraction.

ex·pan·sive /ik'spansiv/ ▶ adj. **1** covering a wide area. **2** relaxed, friendly, and communicative.

> SYNONYMS **1** *expansive farmland* **extensive**, sweeping, rolling. **2** *expansive coverage* **wide-ranging**, extensive, broad, wide, comprehensive, thorough. **3** **communicative**, forthcoming, sociable, friendly, outgoing, affable, chatty, talkative.

■ **ex·pan·sive·ly** adv.

ex·pa·ti·ate /ik'spāshē,āt/ ▶ v. (**expatiates**, **expatiating**, **expatiated**) (**expatiate on**) speak or write in detail about something.

ex·pa·tri·ate /eks'pātrēit/ (or **expat** /eks'pat/) ▶ n. a person who lives outside their own country.

ex·pect /ik'spekt/ ▶ v. **1** think something is likely to happen. **2** think someone is likely to do or be something. **3** believe that someone will arrive soon. **4** assume or demand that someone will do something because it is their duty or responsibility: *we expect great things of you*. **5** (**be expecting**) informal be pregnant.

> SYNONYMS **1** **suppose**, presume, imagine, assume, surmise; informal guess, figure, reckon. **2** **anticipate**, envisage, await, look for, hope for, look forward to, contemplate, bargain for/on, predict, forecast. **3** **require**, ask for, call for, want, insist on, demand.

ex·pect·an·cy /ik'spektənsē/ ▶ n. (plural **expectancies**) the belief or hope that something will happen.

ex·pect·ant /ik'spektənt/ ▶ adj. **1** believing or hoping that something is about to happen. **2** (of a woman) pregnant. ■ **ex·pect·ant·ly** adv.

ex·pec·ta·tion /,ekspek'tāshən/ ▶ n. **1** belief that something will happen or be the case. **2** a thing that is expected to happen.

> SYNONYMS **1** **supposition**, assumption, presumption, conjecture, calculation, prediction, hope. **2** **anticipation**, expectancy, eagerness, excitement, suspense.

ex·pec·to·rant /ik'spektərənt/ ▶ n. a medicine that helps to bring up phlegm from the air passages, used to treat a cough.

ex·pec·to·rate /ik'spektə,rāt/ ▶ v. (**expectorates**, **expectorating**, **expectorated**) cough or spit out phlegm from the throat or lungs.

ex·pe·di·ent /ik'spēdēənt/ ▶ adj. **1** useful or helpful for a particular purpose. **2** useful in achieving something, rather than morally correct. ▶ n. a means of achieving something.

> SYNONYMS ▶ adj. **convenient**, advantageous, useful, beneficial, helpful, practical, pragmatic, politic, prudent, judicious. ▶ n. **measure**, means, method, stratagem, scheme, plan, move, tactic, maneuver, device, contrivance, ploy, ruse.

■ **ex·pe·di·en·cy** (or **expedience**) n.

ex·pe·dite /'ekspə,dīt/ ▶ v. (**expedites**, **expediting**, **expedited**) make something happen more quickly: *he promised to expedite economic reforms*.

ex·pe·di·tion /,ekspə'dishən/ ▶ n. a journey with a particular purpose, made by a group of people.

> SYNONYMS **journey**, voyage, tour, safari, trek, mission, quest, hike, trip.

■ **ex·pe·di·tion·ar·y** adj.

ex·pe·di·tious /,ekspə'dishəs/ ▶ adj. quick and efficient: *an expeditious investigation*. ■ **ex·pe·di·tious·ly** adv.

ex·pel /ik'spel/ ▶ v. (**expels**, **expelling**, **expelled**) **1** force someone to leave a school, organization, or place. **2** force something out, especially from the body: *she expelled a shuddering breath*.

> SYNONYMS **throw out**, bar, ban, debar, drum out, banish, exile, deport, evict; informal chuck out. ANTONYMS admit.

ex·pend /ik'spend/ ▶ v. spend or use up a resource.

ex·pend·a·ble /ik'spendəbəl/ ▶ adj. **1** able to be sacrificed in order to gain or achieve something: *the region is expendable in the wider context of national politics*. **2** suitable to be used once only.

> SYNONYMS **dispensable**, replaceable, disposable, nonessential, inessential, unnecessary, superfluous. ANTONYMS indispensable.

ex·pend·i·ture /ik'spendichər/ ▶ n. **1** the action of spending money. **2** the amount of money spent.

ex·pense /ik'spens/ ▶ n. **1** the amount something costs. **2** something on which money must be spent. **3** (**expenses**) money spent in doing a particular thing. **4** (**expenses**) money paid for meals, fares, etc., by an employee in the course of their work, which they can claim back from their employer.

> SYNONYMS **cost**, expenditure, spending, outlay, outgoings, payment, price, charge, fees, overhead, tariff, bill. ANTONYMS income, profit.

□ **at the expense of** **1** paid for by. **2** so as to cause harm to: *a joke at the expense of others*. **expense account** an arrangement under which money spent in the course of business is later repaid by your employer.

ex·pen·sive /ik'spensiv/ ▶ adj. costing a lot of money.

> SYNONYMS **costly**, high-priced, dear, overpriced, exorbitant, extortionate; informal steep, stiff, pricey. ANTONYMS cheap.

■ **ex·pen·sive·ly** adv.

ex·pe·ri·ence /ik'spi(ə)rēəns/ ▶ n. **1** the fact of being present at or taking part in something. **2** knowledge or skill gained over time. **3** an event that affects you in some way: *a learning experience*. ▶ v. (**experiences**, **experiencing**, **experienced** /ik'spi(ə)rēənst/) **1** be present at or be affected by something. **2** feel an emotion.

> SYNONYMS ▶ n. **1** **skill**, practical knowledge, understanding, familiarity, involvement, participation, contact, acquaintance, exposure, background, track record, history; informal know-how. **2** **incident**, occurrence, event, happening, episode, adventure. ▶ v. **undergo**, go through, encounter, face, meet, come across, come up against, come into contact with.

ex·pe·ri·enced /ik'spi(ə)rēənst/ ▶ adj. having gained a lot of knowledge or skill in a job or activity over time.

SYNONYMS **knowledgeable**, skillful, skilled, expert, proficient, trained, competent, capable, seasoned, practiced, mature, veteran.

ex·pe·ri·en·tial /ek,spi(ə)rē'encHəl/ ▶ **adj.** having to do with experience and observation: *experiential learning.*

ex·per·i·ment /ik'sperəmənt/ ▶ **n.** **1** a scientific procedure carried out to make a discovery, test a theory, or demonstrate a fact. **2** a new course of action that you try out without being sure of the outcome. ▶ **v.** **1** perform a scientific experiment. **2** try out new things.

SYNONYMS ▶ **n.** **test**, investigation, trial, examination, observation, research, assessment, evaluation, appraisal, analysis, study. ▶ **v.** **carry out experiments**, test, trial, try out, assess, appraise, evaluate.

■ **ex·per·i·men·ta·tion** /ik,sperəmən'tāsHən/ **n.**

ex·per·i·men·tal /ik,sperə'men(t)l/ ▶ **adj.** **1** based on a new idea and not yet fully tested. **2** having to do with scientific experiments. **3** (of art, music, etc.) new and unconventional.

SYNONYMS **1** **exploratory**, investigational, trial, test, pilot, speculative, tentative, preliminary. **2** **new**, innovative, creative, radical, avant-garde, alternative, unorthodox, unconventional, cutting-edge.

■ **ex·per·i·men·tal·ly** **adv.**

ex·pert /'ek,spərt/ ▶ **n.** a person who has great knowledge or skill in a particular field. ▶ **adj.** having or involving great knowledge or skill: *an expert witness.*

SYNONYMS ▶ **n.** **specialist**, authority, professional, pundit, maestro, virtuoso, master, wizard, connoisseur, aficionado; informal ace, pro, hotshot, dab hand, maven. ANTONYMS amateur. ▶ **adj.** **skillful**, skilled, adept, accomplished, experienced, practiced, knowledgeable, talented, masterly, virtuoso; informal ace, crack, mean. ANTONYMS incompetent.

■ **ex·pert·ly** **adv.**

ex·per·tise /,ekspər'tēz, -'tēs/ ▶ **n.** great skill or knowledge in a particular field.

SYNONYMS **skill**, prowess, proficiency, competence, knowledge, ability, aptitude, capability; informal know-how.

ex·pi·ate /'ekspē,āt/ ▶ **v.** (**expiates**, **expiating**, **expiated**) do something to make up for having done something wrong. ■ **ex·pi·a·tion** /,ekspē'āsHən/ **n.**

ex·pire /ik'spīr/ ▶ **v.** (**expires**, **expiring**, **expired**) **1** (of a document or agreement) cease to be valid. **2** (of a period of time) come to an end. **3** (of a person) die. **4** breathe out air from the lungs.

SYNONYMS **1** **run out**, become invalid, become void, lapse, end, finish, stop, terminate. **2** **die**, pass away, breathe your last; informal kick the bucket, croak, buy the farm.

ex·plain /ik'splān/ ▶ **v.** **1** describe something in a way that makes it easy to understand. **2** give a reason for something. **3** (**explain yourself**) say why you are doing something in order to justify or excuse it. **4** (**explain away**) give reasons why something is not your fault or why it is not serious.

SYNONYMS **1** **describe**, make clear, spell out, put into words, define, elucidate, expound, clarify, throw light on. **2** **account for**, give a reason for, excuse.

■ **ex·plain·er** **n.**

ex·pla·na·tion /,eksplə'nāsHən/ ▶ **n.** **1** a statement or description that makes something clear. **2** a reason or justification for an action or belief.

SYNONYMS **1** **clarification**, description, statement, interpretation, definition, commentary. **2** **account**, reason, justification, answer, excuse, defense, vindication.

ex·plan·a·to·ry /ik'splanə,tôrē/ ▶ **adj.** giving the reason for something, or making something clear.

ex·ple·tive /'eksplitiv/ ▶ **n.** a swear word.

SYNONYMS **swear word**, oath, curse, obscenity, profanity, four-letter word, dirty word; informal cuss word, cuss; formal imprecation; (**expletives**) bad language, foul language, strong language, swearing.

ex·pli·ca·ble /ek'splikəbəl, 'eksplik-/ ▶ **adj.** able to be explained.

ex·pli·cate /'ekspli,kāt/ ▶ **v.** (**explicates**, **explicating**, **explicated**) **1** analyze and develop (an idea) in detail. **2** analyze a literary work in order to reveal its meaning. ■ **ex·pli·ca·tion** /,ekspli'kāsHən/ **n.**

ex·plic·it /ik'splisit/ ▶ **adj.** clear, detailed, and easy to understand.

SYNONYMS **1** **clear**, plain, straightforward, crystal clear, precise, exact, specific, unequivocal, unambiguous, detailed. **2** **graphic**, candid, full-frontal, uncensored. ANTONYMS vague.

■ **ex·plic·it·ly** **adv.**

ex·plode /ik'splōd/ ▶ **v.** (**explodes**, **exploding**, **exploded**) **1** burst or shatter violently as a result of the release of internal energy. **2** show sudden violent emotion. **3** increase suddenly in number or extent: *the use of this drug exploded in the nineties.* **4** show a belief to be false.

SYNONYMS **1** **blow up**, detonate, go off, burst, erupt. **2** **lose your temper**, blow up; informal fly off the handle, hit the roof, blow your top/lid/stack. **3** **increase rapidly**, mushroom, snowball, escalate, burgeon, rocket. **4** **disprove**, refute, rebut, repudiate, debunk; informal shoot full of holes, blow out of the water.

ex·ploit ▶ **v.** /ik'sploit/ **1** make use of someone unfairly. **2** make good use of a resource. ▶ **n.** /'ek,sploit/ a daring act.

SYNONYMS ▶ **v.** **1** **take advantage of**, abuse, impose on, treat unfairly, misuse, ill-treat; informal walk (all) over. **2** **utilize**, make use of, put/turn to good use, make the most of, capitalize on, benefit from; informal cash in on. ▶ **n.** **feat**, deed, act, adventure, stunt, escapade, achievement.

■ **ex·ploi·ta·tion** /,eksploi'tāsHən/ **n.** **ex·ploit·a·tive** /ik'sploitətiv/ **adj.**

ex·plo·ra·tion /,eksplə'rāsHən/ ▶ **n.** **1** the action of traveling through an unfamiliar area in order to learn about it. **2** thorough analysis of a subject or theme.

SYNONYMS **investigation**, study, survey, research, inspection, examination, scrutiny, observation.

ex·plore /ik'splôr/ ▶ v. (**explores**, **exploring**, **explored**) **1** travel through an unfamiliar area in order to learn about it. **2** examine or discuss something in detail. **3** investigate.

SYNONYMS **1 travel through**, tour, survey, scout, reconnoiter. **2 investigate**, look into, consider, examine, research, survey, scrutinize, study, review; informal check out.

■ **ex·plor·a·to·ry** /ik'splôrə,tôrē/ **adj.** **ex·plor·er** **n.**

ex·plo·sion /ik'splōzhən/ ▶ n. an instance of exploding.

SYNONYMS **1 detonation**, eruption, bang, blast, boom. **2 outburst**, flare-up, outbreak, eruption, storm, rush, surge, fit, paroxysm. **3 sudden increase**, mushrooming, snowballing, escalation, multiplication, burgeoning, rocketing.

ex·plo·sive /ik'splōsiv/ ▶ adj. **1** able or likely to explode. **2** likely to cause anger or controversy: *the idea was politically explosive.* **3** (of an increase) sudden and dramatic. ▶ n. a substance that can be made to explode.

SYNONYMS ▶ adj. **1 volatile**, inflammable, flammable, combustible, incendiary. **2 fiery**, stormy, violent, volatile, passionate, tempestuous, turbulent, touchy, irascible. **3 tense**, highly charged, overwrought, dangerous, perilous, hazardous, sensitive, delicate, unstable, volatile. ▶ n. **bomb**, charge, incendiary (device).

■ **ex·plo·sive·ly** **adv.**

ex·po /'ekspō/ ▶ n. (plural **expos**) a large exhibition.

ex·po·nent /ik'spōnənt, 'ekspōnənt/ ▶ n. **1** a promoter of an idea or theory. **2** a person who does a particular thing skillfully. **3** Math a raised figure beside a number indicating how many times that number is to be multiplied by itself (e.g., ^{3} in $2^3 = 2 \times 2 \times 2$).

ex·po·nen·tial /,ekspə'nenchəl/ ▶ adj. **1** (of an increase) becoming more and more rapid. **2** Math having to do with a mathematical exponent.
■ **ex·po·nen·tial·ly** **adv.**

ex·port /ik'spôrt, 'ekspôrt/ ▶ v. **1** send goods or services to another country for sale. **2** introduce an idea or custom to another country. ▶ n. /'ek,spôrt/ **1** the exporting of goods or services. **2** an exported item. ■ **ex·por·ta·tion** /,ekspôr'tāshən/ **n.** **ex·port·er** **n.**

ex·pose /ik'spōz/ ▶ v. (**exposes**, **exposing**, **exposed**) **1** uncover something and make it visible. **2** show the true nature of someone or something. **3** (**exposed**) not protected from the weather. **4** (**expose someone to**) make someone vulnerable to: *expose colleagues to secondhand smoke.* **5** subject photographic film to light.

SYNONYMS **1** *at low tide the rocks are exposed* **reveal**, uncover, lay bare. **2** *he was exposed to radiation* **lay open**, subject, put at risk of, put in jeopardy of, leave unprotected from. **3** *they were exposed to new ideas* **introduce to**, bring into contact with, make aware of, familiarize with, acquaint with. **4 uncover**, reveal, unveil, unmask, detect, find out, denounce, condemn; informal blow the whistle on. ANTONYMS cover, protect.

ex·po·sé /,ekspō'zā/ ▶ n. a report in the news revealing shocking information about someone.

SYNONYMS **revelation**, disclosure, exposure; report, feature, piece, column; informal scoop, tell-all. ANTONYMS cover-up.

ex·po·si·tion /,ekspə'zishən/ ▶ n. **1** a careful setting out of the facts or ideas involved in something. **2** an exhibition. **3** Music the part of a movement in which the main themes are first presented.

ex·pos·i·tor /ik'späzitər/ ▶ n. a person or thing that explains complicated ideas or theories.
■ **ex·pos·i·to·ry** /ik'späzi,tôrē/ **adj.**

ex·pos·tu·late /ik'späschə,lāt/ ▶ v. (**expostulates**, **expostulating**, **expostulated**) express strong disapproval or disagreement. ■ **ex·pos·tu·la·tion** /ik,späschə'lāshən/ **n.**

ex·po·sure /ik'spōzhər/ ▶ n. **1** the state of being exposed to something harmful. **2** a physical condition resulting from being exposed to severe weather conditions. **3** the revealing of the true facts about someone or something. **4** the fact of being discussed or mentioned on television, in newspapers, etc.: *the meetings received regular exposure in the media.* **5** the quantity of light reaching a photographic film.

SYNONYMS **1 frostbite**, cold, hypothermia. **2 uncovering**, revelation, disclosure, unveiling, unmasking, discovery, detection. **3 publicity**, advertising, public attention, media interest; informal hype.

ex·pound /ik'spound/ ▶ v. set out and explain the facts or ideas involved in something.

SYNONYMS **present**, put forward, set forth, propose, propound; explain, give an explanation of, detail, spell out, describe.

ex·press¹ /ik'spres/ ▶ v. **1** show by words or actions what you are thinking or feeling. **2** squeeze out liquid or air.

SYNONYMS **communicate**, convey, indicate, show, demonstrate, reveal, put across/over, get across/over, articulate, put into words, voice, give voice to, state, air, give vent to.

ex·press² ▶ adj. operating or delivered very quickly. ▶ adv. by express train or delivery service. ▶ n. **1** a train that travels quickly and stops at few stations. **2** a special delivery service.

SYNONYMS ▶ adj. **rapid**, swift, fast, high-speed, nonstop, direct.

ex·press³ ▶ adj. **1** stated very clearly: *my express wish.* **2** excluding anything else: *the schools were for the express purpose of teaching deaf children.*

SYNONYMS **1 explicit**, clear, direct, plain, distinct, unambiguous, categorical. **2 sole**, specific, particular, special, specified. ANTONYMS vague.

■ **ex·press·ly** **adv.**

ex·pres·sion /ik'spreshən/ ▶ n. **1** the action of expressing. **2** the look on someone's face. **3** a word or phrase expressing an idea. **4** Math a collection of symbols expressing a quantity.

SYNONYMS **1 utterance**, uttering, voicing, declaration, articulation. **2 indication**, demonstration, show, exhibition, token, illustration. **3 look**, appearance, air, manner, countenance, mien. **4 idiom**, phrase, turn of phrase, term, proverb, saying, adage, maxim. **5 emotion**, feeling, spirit, passion, intensity, style.

■ **ex·pres·sion·less** **adj.**

ex·pres·sion·ism /ik'spreshə,nizəm/ ▶ n. a style in art, music, or drama in which the artist or writer shows the inner world of emotion rather than external reality. ■ **ex·pres·sion·ist** n. & adj.

ex·pres·sive /ik'spresiv/ ▶ adj. clearly showing thoughts or feelings.

SYNONYMS **1 eloquent**, meaningful, demonstrative, suggestive. **2 emotional**, passionate, poignant, moving, stirring, emotionally charged, lyrical. ANTONYMS undemonstrative.

■ **ex·pres·sive·ly** adv. **ex·pres·sive·ness** n.

ex·press·way /ik'spres,wā/ ▶ n. a highway designed for fast traffic, with controlled entrance and exit, a dividing strip between the traffic in opposite directions, and typically two or more lanes in each direction.

ex·pro·pri·ate /,eks'prōprē,āt/ ▶ v. (**expropriates**, **expropriating**, **expropriated**) (of the state or an authority) take property from its owner. ■ **ex·pro·pri·a·tion** /,eks,prōprē'āsHən/ n.

ex·pul·sion /ik'spəlsHən/ ▶ n. the action of expelling.

SYNONYMS **1 removal**, debarment, dismissal, exclusion, ejection, banishment, eviction. **2 discharge**, ejection, excretion, voiding, evacuation, elimination, passing. ANTONYMS admission.

ex·punge /ik'spənj/ ▶ v. (**expunges**, **expunging**, **expunged**) remove something completely.

SYNONYMS **erase**, remove, delete, rub out, wipe out, efface; cross out, strike out, blot out, blank out; destroy, obliterate, eradicate, eliminate.

ex·pur·gate /'ekspər,gāt/ ▶ v. (**expurgates**, **expurgating**, **expurgated**) remove unsuitable material from a written work.

SYNONYMS **censor**, bowdlerize, cut, edit; clean up, sanitize.

■ **ex·pur·ga·tion** /,ekspər'gāsHən/ n.

ex·quis·ite /ek'skwizit, 'ekskwizit/ ▶ adj. **1** very beautiful and delicate. **2** showing great sensitivity or refinement: *exquisite taste*. **3** strongly felt: *the most exquisite kind of agony*.

SYNONYMS **1 beautiful**, lovely, elegant, fine, delicate, fragile, dainty, subtle. **2** *exquisite taste* **discriminating**, discerning, sensitive, fastidious, refined.

■ **ex·quis·ite·ly** adv.

ex·tant /'ekstənt, ek'stant/ ▶ adj. still in existence.

ex·tem·po·ra·ne·ous /ik,stempə'rānēəs/ ▶ adj. spoken or done without preparation. ■ **ex·tem·po·ra·ne·ous·ly** adv.

ex·tem·po·rar·y /ik'stempə,rerē/ ▶ adj. spoken or done without preparation.

ex·tem·po·re /ik'stempərē/ ▶ adj. & adv. spoken or done without preparation: *extempore public speaking*.

ex·tem·po·rize /ik'stempə,rīz/ ▶ v. (**extemporizes**, **extemporizing**, **extemporized**) make something up as you go along: *he extemporized at the piano*.

ex·tend /ik'stend/ ▶ v. **1** make something larger in area. **2** make something last longer. **3** occupy a particular area or continue for a particular distance. **4** stretch out a part of your body. **5** offer something to someone: *she extended an invitation to her to stay*.

SYNONYMS **1 expand**, enlarge, increase, lengthen, widen, broaden. **2 continue**, carry on, stretch, reach. **3 widen**, expand, broaden, augment, supplement, increase, add to, enhance, develop. **4 prolong**, lengthen, increase, stretch out, protract, spin out, string out. **5 hold out**, reach out, hold forth, stretch out, outstretch, offer, give, proffer. ANTONYMS reduce, shorten.

□ **extended family** a family group consisting of parents and children and close relatives living nearby. ■ **ex·tend·a·ble** (or **extendible**) adj. **ex·ten·si·ble** adj.

ex·ten·sion /ik'stensHən/ ▶ n. **1** the action of extending something. **2** a part added to a building to make it bigger. **3** an additional period of time. **4** an extra telephone on the same line as the main one.

SYNONYMS **1 addition**, add-on, adjunct, annex, wing. **2 expansion**, increase, enlargement, widening, broadening, deepening, augmentation, enhancement, development, growth. **3 prolongation**, lengthening, increase.

□ **extension cord** a length of electric cord that can be plugged into a socket and has another socket on the end.

ex·ten·sive /ik'stensiv/ ▶ adj. **1** covering a large area. **2** large in amount or scale.

SYNONYMS **1 large**, sizable, substantial, considerable, ample, great, vast. **2 comprehensive**, thorough, exhaustive, broad, wide, wide-ranging, catholic.

■ **ex·ten·sive·ly** adv.

ex·ten·sor /ik'stensər, -sôr/ ▶ n. Anatomy a muscle that causes a part of the body to extend.

ex·tent /ik'stent/ ▶ n. **1** the area covered by something. **2** size or scale: *the extent of global warming*. **3** the degree to which something is the case: *everyone compromises to some extent*.

SYNONYMS **1 area**, size, expanse, length, proportions, dimensions. **2 degree**, scale, level, magnitude, scope, size, reach, range.

ex·ten·u·at·ing /ik'stenyoo͞,ātiNG/ ▶ adj. serving to make an offense less serious by partially excusing it: *extenuating circumstances*. ■ **ex·ten·u·a·tion** /ik,stenyoo͞'āsHən/ n.

ex·te·ri·or /ik'sti(ə)rēər/ ▶ adj. having to do with the outside of something. ▶ n. the outer surface or structure of something.

SYNONYMS ▶ adj. **outer**, outside, outermost, outward, external. ANTONYMS interior. ▶ n. **outside**, external surface, outward appearance, facade. ANTONYMS interior.

ex·ter·mi·nate /ik'stərmə,nāt/ ▶ v. (**exterminates**, **exterminating**, **exterminated**) destroy a group of people or animals completely.

SYNONYMS **kill**, destroy, wipe out, eliminate, eradicate, annihilate, extirpate.

■ **ex·ter·mi·na·tion** /ik,stərmə'nāsHən/ n.

ex·ter·nal /ik'stərnl/ ▶ adj. **1** having to do with the outside of something. **2** coming from outside an organization or situation: *external authority*. **3** having to do with another country or institution: *external affairs*. ▶ n. (**externals**) the outward aspects of something.

SYNONYMS ▶ adj. **outer**, outside, outermost, outward, exterior. ANTONYMS internal.

■ **ex·ter·nal·ly** adv.

ex·ter·nal·ize /ik'stərnə,līz/ ▶ v. (**externalizes**, **externalizing**, **externalized**) express a thought or feeling in words or actions.

ex·tinct /ik'stiNG(k)t/ ▶ adj. **1** no longer in existence. **2** (of a volcano) not having erupted in recorded history.

> SYNONYMS **1 vanished**, lost, gone, died out, wiped out, destroyed. **2 inactive**. ANTONYMS living, dormant.

ex·tinc·tion /ik'stiNG(k)SHən/ ▶ n. the state of being or process of becoming extinct.

> SYNONYMS **dying out**, disappearance, vanishing, extermination, destruction, elimination, eradication, annihilation.

ex·tin·guish /ik'stiNGgwiSH/ ▶ v. **1** put out a fire or light. **2** put an end to.

> SYNONYMS **douse**, quench, put out, stamp out, smother, snuff out. ANTONYMS light.

■ **ex·tin·guish·er** n.

ex·tir·pate /'ekstər,pāt/ ▶ v. (**extirpates**, **extirpating**, **extirpated**) search out and destroy something completely.

> SYNONYMS **weed out**, destroy, eradicate, stamp out, root out, wipe out, eliminate, suppress, crush, put down, put an end to, get rid of.

■ **ex·tir·pa·tion** /,ekstər'pāSHən/ n.

ex·tol /ik'stōl/ ▶ v. (**extols**, **extolling**, **extolled**) praise enthusiastically.

> SYNONYMS **praise**, wax lyrical about, sing the praises of, acclaim, applaud, celebrate, eulogize, rave about, enthuse over; formal laud. ANTONYMS criticize.

ex·tort /ik'stôrt/ ▶ v. obtain something by force, threats, or other unfair means.

> SYNONYMS **extract**, exact, wring, wrest, screw, squeeze.

■ **ex·tor·tion** n.

ex·tor·tion·ate /ik'stôrSHənit/ ▶ adj. (of a price) much too high.

> SYNONYMS **exorbitant**, excessive, outrageous, unreasonable, inordinate, inflated.

■ **ex·tor·tion·ate·ly** adv.

ex·tra /'ekstrə/ ▶ adj. added to an existing or usual amount or number. ▶ adv. **1** to a greater extent than usual. **2** in addition. ▶ n. **1** an additional item, for which an extra charge is made. **2** a person employed to take part in a crowd scene in a movie or play.

> SYNONYMS ▶ adj. **additional**, more, added, supplementary, further, auxiliary, ancillary, subsidiary, secondary. ▶ adv. **exceptionally**, particularly, specially, especially, extremely. ▶ n. **addition**, supplement, bonus, adjunct, addendum, add-on.

□ **extra virgin** referring to a particularly fine grade of olive oil made from the first pressing of the olives.

ex·tract ▶ v. /ik'strakt/ **1** remove something with care or effort. **2** obtain something from someone unwilling to give it: *I tried to extract a promise from him*. **3** separate out a substance by a special method: *lead was extracted from the copper*. ▶ n. /'ek,strakt/ **1** a short passage taken from a written work, movie, or piece of music. **2** an extracted substance.

> SYNONYMS ▶ v. **1 take out**, draw out, pull out, remove, withdraw, release, extricate. **2 wrest**, exact, wring, screw, squeeze, obtain by force, extort. **3 squeeze out**, press out, obtain. ANTONYMS insert. ▶ n. **1 excerpt**, passage, citation, quotation. **2 distillation**, distillate, concentrate, essence, juice.

ex·trac·tion /ik'strakSHən/ ▶ n. **1** the action of extracting. **2** the ethnic origin of someone's family.

ex·tra·cur·ric·u·lar /,ekstrəkə'rikyələr/ ▶ adj. (of an activity at a school or college) done in addition to the normal curriculum.

ex·tra·dite /'ekstrə,dīt/ ▶ v. (**extradites**, **extraditing**, **extradited**) hand over a person accused or convicted of committing a crime in a foreign state to the legal authority of that state. ■ **ex·tra·di·tion** /,ekstrə'diSHən/ n.

ex·tra·mar·i·tal /,ekstrə'maritl/ ▶ adj. happening outside marriage.

ex·tra·mu·ral /,ekstrə'myo͝orəl/ ▶ adj. **1** outside the walls or boundaries of a town, university, or institution. **2** additional to your work or course of study.

ex·tra·ne·ous /ik'strānēəs/ ▶ adj. **1** unrelated to the subject being dealt with. **2** of external origin: *extraneous noise*.

> SYNONYMS **irrelevant**, immaterial, beside the point, unrelated, unconnected, inapposite, inapplicable.

ex·tra·or·di·naire /,ekstrə,ôrdn'er/ ▶ adj. outstanding in a particular capacity: *she was a gardener extraordinaire*.

ex·traor·di·nar·y /ik'strôrdn,erē, ,ekstrə'ôrdn-/ ▶ adj. **1** very unusual or remarkable. **2** (of a meeting) held for a particular reason rather than being one of a regular series.

> SYNONYMS **1** *an extraordinary coincidence* **remarkable**, exceptional, amazing, astonishing, astounding, sensational, stunning, incredible, unbelievable, phenomenal; informal fantastic. **2** *extraordinary speed* **very great**, tremendous, enormous, immense, prodigious, stupendous, monumental. ANTONYMS unremarkable.

■ **ex·traor·di·nar·i·ly** adv.

> SPELLING
>
> The beginning is **extra-**, not just **extr-**: **extra**ordinary.

ex·trap·o·late /ik'strapə,lāt/ ▶ v. (**extrapolates**, **extrapolating**, **extrapolated**) use a fact or conclusion that is valid for one situation and apply it to a larger or different one. ■ **ex·trap·o·la·tion** /ik,strapə'lāSHən/ n.

ex·tra·sen·so·ry per·cep·tion /,ekstrə'sensərē/ ▶ n. the supposed ability to perceive things by means other than the known senses, e.g., by telepathy.

ex·tra·ter·res·tri·al /,ekstrətə'restrēəl/ ▶ adj. having to do with things that come from beyond the earth or its atmosphere. ▶ n. a fictional being from outer space.

ex·trav·a·gant /ik'stravəgənt/ ▶ adj. **1** spending or using more than is necessary or more than you can afford. **2** very expensive. **3** going beyond what is reasonable: *extravagant claims*.

SYNONYMS **1 spendthrift**, profligate, wasteful, prodigal, lavish. **2 excessive**, immoderate, exaggerated, gushing, unrestrained, effusive, fulsome. **3 ornate**, elaborate, fancy, overelaborate, ostentatious, exaggerated; informal flashy. ANTONYMS thrifty, moderate.

■ **ex·trav·a·gance** n. **ex·trav·a·gant·ly** adv.

ex·trav·a·gan·za /ikˌstravəˈganzə/ ▶ n. an elaborate and spectacular entertainment.

SYNONYMS **spectacular**, display, spectacle, show, pageant.

ex·treme /ikˈstrēm/ ▶ adj. **1** to the highest degree. **2** highly unusual: *extreme cases*. **3** very severe or serious. **4** not moderate: *extreme socialists*. **5** furthest from the center or a given point. ▶ n. **1** either of two abstract things that are as different from each other as possible. **2** the most extreme degree: *extremes of temperature*.

SYNONYMS ▶ adj. **1** *extreme danger* **utmost**, (very) great, greatest (possible), maximum, great, acute, enormous, severe, serious. **2** *extreme measures* **drastic**, serious, desperate, dire, radical, far-reaching, draconian. **3 radical**, extremist, immoderate, fanatical, revolutionary, subversive, militant. **4 dangerous**, hazardous, risky, high-risk; informal white-knuckle. **5 furthest**, farthest, utmost, remotest, ultra-. ANTONYMS slight, moderate. ▶ n. **extremity**, antithesis, opposite, (opposite) pole, limit, contrast.

□ **extreme unction** (in the Roman Catholic Church) a former name for the sacrament of anointing of the sick.

ex·treme·ly /ikˈstrēmlē/ ▶ adv. to a very high degree.

SYNONYMS **very**, exceptionally, especially, extraordinarily, tremendously, immensely, hugely, supremely, highly, mightily; informal awfully, terribly, seriously, mighty. ANTONYMS slightly.

ex·trem·ist /ikˈstrēmist/ ▶ n. a person who holds extreme political or religious views.

SYNONYMS **fanatic**, radical, zealot, fundamentalist, hardliner, militant, activist. ANTONYMS moderate.

■ **ex·trem·ism** n.

ex·trem·i·ty /ikˈstremitē/ ▶ n. (plural **extremities**) **1** the furthest point or limit. **2** (**extremities**) a person's hands and feet. **3** extreme hardship.

ex·tri·cate /ˈekstriˌkāt/ ▶ v. (**extricates**, **extricating**, **extricated**) **1** free someone from a difficult situation. **2** free something that is trapped.

SYNONYMS **extract**, free, release, disentangle, get out, remove, withdraw, disengage; informal get someone/yourself off the hook.

ex·trin·sic /ikˈstrinzik, -sik/ ▶ adj. coming from outside; not part of something's basic nature.

ex·tro·vert /ˈekstrəˌvərt/ ▶ n. an outgoing, lively person. ▶ adj. outgoing and lively: *his extrovert personality*.

SYNONYMS ▶ adj. **outgoing**, extroverted, sociable, gregarious, lively, ebullient, exuberant, uninhibited, unreserved. ANTONYMS introverted.

SPELLING

Write **extro-**, not **extra-**: **extro**vert.

ex·trude /ikˈstro͞od/ ▶ v. (**extrudes**, **extruding**, **extruded**) **1** thrust or force something out. **2** shape a material such as metal or plastic by forcing it through a die.

SYNONYMS **force out**, thrust out, squeeze out, express, eject, expel, release, emit.

ex·u·ber·ant /igˈzo͞obərənt/ ▶ adj. **1** lively and cheerful. **2** growing thickly: *exuberant foliage*.

SYNONYMS **ebullient**, buoyant, cheerful, high-spirited, cheery, lively, vivacious, enthusiastic, irrepressible, energetic, animated, full of life, sparkling; informal bubbly, bouncy, full of beans.

■ **ex·u·ber·ance** n. **ex·u·ber·ant·ly** adv.

ex·ude /igˈzo͞od/ ▶ v. (**exudes**, **exuding**, **exuded**) **1** send out or give off a liquid or a smell slowly and steadily: *the kitchen floor exuded the scent of a lemon cleaner*. **2** display an emotion or quality strongly and openly.

SYNONYMS **1** *milkweed exudes a milky sap* **give off/out**, discharge, release, emit, issue; ooze, secrete. **2** *he exuded self-confidence* **emanate**, radiate, ooze, emit; display, show, exhibit, manifest.

ex·ult /igˈzəlt/ ▶ v. show or feel triumphant joy.
■ **ex·ul·ta·tion** /ˌeksəlˈtāsнən, ˌegzəl-/ n.

ex·ult·ant /igˈzəltnt/ ▶ adj. triumphantly happy.

SYNONYMS **jubilant**, thrilled, triumphant, delighted, exhilarated, happy, overjoyed, joyous, joyful, gleeful, excited, rejoicing, ecstatic, euphoric, elated, rapturous, in raptures, enraptured, on cloud nine, in seventh heaven; informal over the moon.

■ **ex·ult·an·cy** n. **ex·ult·ant·ly** adv.

eye /ī/ ▶ n. **1** the organ of sight in humans and animals. **2** the small hole in a needle through which the thread is passed. **3** a small metal loop into which a hook is fitted as a fastener on a garment. **4** a person's opinion or feelings. **5** the calm region at the center of a storm. **6** a dark spot on a potato from which a new shoot grows. ▶ v. (**eyes**, **eyeing** or **eying**, **eyed**) look at closely or with interest.

SYNONYMS ▶ v. **look at**, observe, view, gaze at, stare at, regard, contemplate, survey, scrutinize, consider, glance at, watch; informal check out, size up, eyeball.

□ **an eye for an eye and a tooth for a tooth** doing the same thing in return is the appropriate way to deal with an offense or crime. **eye-catching** noticeable and attractive. **eye-opener** a revealing event or situation. **eye socket** a cavity in the skull that encloses the eye and its surrounding muscles. **have an eye for** be able to recognize and judge something wisely. **have your eye on** aim to acquire. **keep an eye out** (or **open**) **for** look out for something. **keep your eye on** watch something carefully. **only have eyes for** be interested only in. **open someone's eyes** cause someone to realize something. **see eye to eye** be in complete agreement. **a twinkle** (or **gleam**) **in someone's eye** something that is as yet no more than an idea or dream. **with an eye to** having a plan to. **with your eyes (wide) open** fully aware of possible difficulties.

eye·ball /'ī,bôl/ ▶ **n.** the round part of the eye of a vertebrate, within the eyelids. ▫ **eyeball to eyeball** face to face with someone. **up to your eyeballs** informal extremely busy.

eye·brow /'ī,brou/ ▶ **n.** the strip of hair growing on the ridge above a person's eye socket. ▫ **raise your eyebrows** show surprise or mild disapproval.

eye·ful /'ī,fo͝ol/ ▶ **n.** informal **1** a long, steady look. **2** an eye-catching person.

eye·glass /'ī,glas/ ▶ **n.** **1** a single lens for correcting eyesight. **2** (**eyeglasses**) a pair of lenses set in a frame resting on the nose and ears, used to correct or assist defective eyesight or protect the eyes.

eye·lash /'ī,lash/ ▶ **n.** each of the short hairs growing on the edges of the eyelids.

eye·let /'īlit/ ▶ **n.** a small round hole with a metal ring around it, for threading a lace or cord through.

eye·lid /'ī,lid/ ▶ **n.** each of the upper and lower folds of skin that cover the eye when it is closed.

eye·lin·er /'ī,līnər/ ▶ **n.** a cosmetic applied as a line around the eyes.

eye·piece /'ī,pēs/ ▶ **n.** the lens that is closest to the eye in a microscope or other optical instrument.

eye·shad·ow /'ī,shadō/ ▶ **n.** a cosmetic applied to the skin around the eyes.

eye·sight /'ī,sīt/ ▶ **n.** a person's ability to see.

eye·sore /'ī,sôr/ ▶ **n.** a thing that is very ugly.

eye·tooth /'ī',to͞oth/ ▶ **n.** a pointed tooth next to the incisors; a canine tooth. ▫ **give your eyeteeth for** (or **to be** or **to do**) do anything in order to have or to be or do.

eye·wit·ness /'ī'witnəs/ ▶ **n.** a person who has seen something happen, especially one who has seen a crime.

SYNONYMS **observer**, onlooker, witness, bystander, passerby.

eyr·ie /'e(ə)rē, 'i(ə)rē/ = **AERIE**.

e-zine /'ē ,zēn/ ▶ **n.** a magazine published only in electronic form on a computer network.

F (or **f**) ▶ **n.** (plural **Fs** or **F's**) the sixth letter of the alphabet. ▶ **abbr.** (**F**) Fahrenheit.

f ▶ **abbr.** Music forte.

fa /fä/ ▶ **n.** the fourth note of a major scale.

FAA ▶ **abbr.** Federal Aviation Administration.

fab /fab/ ▶ **adj.** informal fabulous.

Fa·bi·an /'fābēən/ ▶ **n.** a supporter of the Fabian Society, an organization aiming to achieve socialism by non-revolutionary methods. ▶ **adj. 1** relating to the Fabians. **2** employing cautious delaying tactics to wear out an enemy. ■ **Fa·bi·an·ism n. Fa·bi·an·ist n.**

fa·ble /'fābəl/ ▶ **n. 1** a short story, often about animals, which teaches about right and wrong behavior. **2** a story about mythical characters or events.

> SYNONYMS **parable**, allegory, myth, legend, story, tale.

fa·bled /'fābəld/ ▶ **adj. 1** famous: *a fabled art collection*. **2** described in myths and legends: *the fabled kingdom*.

fab·ric /'fabrik/ ▶ **n. 1** cloth. **2** the walls, floor, and roof of a building. **3** the basic structure of a system or organization: *the fabric of society*.

> SYNONYMS **1 cloth**, material, textile, stuff. **2 structure**, construction, makeup, organization, framework, essence.

fab·ri·cate /'fabrəˌkāt/ ▶ **v.** (**fabricates, fabricating, fabricated**) **1** make up facts that are not true: *fabricate evidence*. **2** make an industrial product.

> SYNONYMS **falsify**, fake, counterfeit, invent, make up.

■ **fab·ri·ca·tion** /ˌfabrə'kāsHən/ **n.**

fab·u·lous /'fabyələs/ ▶ **adj. 1** great; extraordinary. **2** informal wonderful. **3** existing in myths and legends.

> SYNONYMS **1 stupendous**, prodigious, phenomenal, exceptional, fantastic, breathtaking, staggering, unthinkable, unimaginable, incredible, undreamed of. **2** *a fabulous time* see **EXCELLENT**.

■ **fab·u·lous·ly adv.**

fa·cade /fə'säd/ ▶ **n. 1** the front of a building. **2** a misleading outward appearance.

> SYNONYMS **1 front**, frontage, face, elevation, exterior, outside. **2 show**, front, appearance, pretense, simulation, affectation, act, charade, mask, veneer.

face /fās/ ▶ **n. 1** the front part of the head from the forehead to the chin. **2** an expression on someone's face. **3** the surface of a thing. **4** a vertical or sloping side of a mountain or cliff. **5** an aspect of something: *the unacceptable face of social drinking*. ▶ **v.** (**faces, facing, faced**) **1** be positioned with the face or front toward something. **2** confront and deal with. **3** have a difficulty ahead of you. **4** cover the surface of something with a layer of material.

> SYNONYMS ▶ **n. 1 countenance**, physiognomy, features, profile; literary visage, lineaments. **2 expression**, look, appearance, mien, air. **3** *he made a face* **grimace**, scowl, wince, frown, pout. **4 side**, aspect, surface, plane, facet, wall, elevation. ▶ **v. 1 look out on**, front on to, look toward, look over/across, overlook, be opposite (to). **2 accept**, get used to, adjust to, learn to live with, cope with, deal with, come to terms with, become resigned to. **3 beset**, worry, trouble, confront, torment, plague, bedevil. **4 brave**, face up to, encounter, meet (head-on), confront. **5 cover**, clad, veneer, surface, dress, laminate, coat, line.

□ **face-saving** saving you from embarrassment. **face the music** be confronted with the unpleasant results of your actions. **face time** time you spend interacting with someone in their presence. **face value 1** the value stated on a coin or postage stamp. **2** the value that something seems to have before you look at it closely. **in the face of** when confronted with. **lose** (or **save**) **face** suffer (or avoid) humiliation. **on the face of it** apparently. **to your face** openly in your presence.

face·less /'fāsləs/ ▶ **adj.** without character or individuality; impersonal: *faceless bureaucrats*.

face·lift /'fāslift/ ▶ **n. 1** an operation to remove wrinkles in the face by tightening the skin. **2** work carried out to improve the appearance of something.

> SYNONYMS **renovation**, redecoration, refurbishment, revamp, makeover.

fac·et /'fasət/ ▶ **n. 1** one of the sides of a cut gemstone. **2** an aspect of something: *different facets of the truth*.

> SYNONYMS **aspect**, feature, factor, side, dimension, strand, component, element.

■ **fac·et·ed adj.**

fa·ce·tious /fə'sēsHəs/ ▶ **adj.** trying to be funny or clever about something that should be treated seriously.

> SYNONYMS **flippant**, flip, glib, frivolous, tongue-in-cheek, joking, jokey, jocular, playful.
> ANTONYMS serious.

■ **fa·ce·tious·ly adv.**

fa·cial /'fāsHəl/ ▶ **adj.** having to do with the face. ▶ **n.** a beauty treatment for the face. ■ **fa·cial·ly adv.**

fac·ile /'fasəl/ ▶ **adj. 1** produced without careful thought. **2** too simple, or too easily achieved.

fa·cil·i·tate /fə'siliˌtāt/ ▶ **v.** (**facilitates, facilitating, facilitated**) make something possible or easier.

SYNONYMS **make easier**, ease, make possible, smooth the way for, enable, assist, help (along), aid, promote, hasten, speed up. ANTONYMS impede.

■ **fa·cil·i·ta·tion** /fəˌsiliˈtāsнən/ **n.** **fa·cil·i·ta·tor** **n.**

fa·cil·i·ty /fəˈsilətē/ ▶ **n.** (plural **facilities**) **1** a building, service, or piece of equipment provided for a particular purpose. **2** a natural ability to do something well and easily.

SYNONYMS **1** *a wealth of local facilities* **amenity**, resource, service, benefit, convenience, equipment. **2** *a medical facility* **establishment**, center, station, location, premises, site, post, base. **3 ease**, effortlessness, skill, adroitness, smoothness, fluency, slickness.

fac·ing /ˈfāsiNG/ ▶ **n.** **1** a strip of material sewn inside the neck, armhole, etc., of a piece of clothing to strengthen it. **2** an outer layer covering the surface of a wall.

fac·sim·i·le /fakˈsiməlē/ ▶ **n.** **1** an exact copy of written or printed material. **2** a fax.

fact /fakt/ ▶ **n.** **1** a thing that is definitely the case. **2** (**facts**) information used as evidence or as part of a report.

SYNONYMS **1** *a fact we cannot ignore* **reality**, actuality, certainty, truth, verity, gospel. **2** *every fact was double-checked* **detail**, particular, finding, point, factor, feature, characteristic, aspect; (**facts**) information, data. ANTONYMS lie, fiction.

□ **before** (or **after**) **the fact** Law before (or after) the committing of a crime. **a fact of life** something that must be accepted, even if unpleasant. **the facts of life** information explaining things relating to sex. **in** (**point of**) **fact** in reality.

fac·tion /ˈfaksнən/ ▶ **n.** a small group within a larger one.

SYNONYMS **1 clique**, coterie, caucus, bloc, camp, group, grouping, splinter group. **2 infighting**, dissent, dispute, discord, strife, conflict, friction, argument, disagreement, disunity, schism.

■ **fac·tion·al** **adj.**

fac·tious /ˈfaksнəs/ ▶ **adj.** having opposing views.

fac·ti·tious /fakˈtisнəs/ ▶ **adj.** made up; not genuine: *a largely factitious national identity*.

fac·tor /ˈfaktər/ ▶ **n.** **1** a circumstance, fact, or influence that helps to bring about a result. **2** Math a number by which a larger number can be divided exactly. **3** the amount by which something increases or decreases. **4** any of a number of substances in the blood that are involved in clotting. **5** an agent who buys and sells goods on commission. ▶ **v.** (**factor something in** or **out**) consider (or ignore) something when making a decision.

SYNONYMS ▶ **n.** **element**, part, component, ingredient, strand, constituent, feature, facet, aspect, characteristic, consideration, influence, circumstance.

fac·to·ri·al /fakˈtôrēəl/ Math ▶ **n.** the product of a whole number and all the whole numbers below it, e.g., $4 \times 3 \times 2 \times 1$ (*factorial* 4, written as *4!* and equal to 24). ▶ **adj.** having to do with a factor or factorial.

fac·tor·ize /ˈfaktəˌrīz/ ▶ **v.** (**factorizes**, **factorizing**, **factorized**) Math break down or be able to be broken down into factors. ■ **fac·tor·i·za·tion** /ˌfaktərəˈzāsнən/ **n.**

fac·to·ry /ˈfakt(ə)rē/ ▶ **n.** (plural **factories**) a building where goods are made or assembled in large numbers.

SYNONYMS **plant**, works, yard, mill, facility, workshop, shop.

□ **factory farming** the rearing of poultry, pigs, or cattle indoors under strictly controlled conditions. **factory floor** the workers in a company or industry, rather than the management.

fac·to·tum /fakˈtōtəm/ ▶ **n.** (plural **factotums**) an employee who does all kinds of jobs.

fac·tu·al /ˈfakcнo͞oəl/ ▶ **adj.** based on or concerned with facts.

SYNONYMS **truthful**, true, accurate, authentic, historical, genuine, true-to-life, correct, exact. ANTONYMS fictitious.

■ **fac·tu·al·ly** **adv.**

fac·ul·ty /ˈfakəltē/ ▶ **n.** (plural **faculties**) **1** a basic mental or physical power. **2** a talent: *he had the faculty of appearing always cheerful*. **3** a department or group of related departments in a university. **4** the teaching or research staff of a school, university, or college.

SYNONYMS **1 power**, capability, capacity, facility; (**faculties**) senses, wits, reason, intelligence. **2 teaching staff**, teachers; department.

fad /fad/ ▶ **n.** a craze.

SYNONYMS **craze**, vogue, trend, fashion, mode, mania, rage.

■ **fad·dish** **adj.**

fade /fād/ ▶ **v.** (**fades**, **fading**, **faded**) **1** gradually grow faint and disappear. **2** lose color. **3** (**fade something in** or **out**) make a movie or video image or sound more or less clear or loud. ▶ **n.** an instance of fading.

SYNONYMS ▶ **v.** **1 grow pale**, become bleached, become washed out, lose color, discolor, blanch. **2** (**grow**) **dim**, grow faint, fail, dwindle, die away, wane, disappear, vanish, decline, melt away. **3 decline**, die out, diminish, decay, crumble, collapse, fail. ANTONYMS brighten.

fag /fag/ ▶ **n.** informal, disapproving a male homosexual. ■ **fag·gy** **adj.**

fag·got /ˈfagət/ ▶ **n.** informal, disapproving a homosexual man. ■ **fag·got·y** **adj.**

fag·ot /ˈfagət/ ▶ **n.** a bundle of sticks bound together as fuel.

Fahr·en·heit /ˈfarənˌhīt/ ▶ **n.** a scale of temperature on which water freezes at 32° and boils at 212°.

fail /fāl/ ▶ **v.** **1** not succeed in achieving something. **2** be unable to meet the standards set by a test. **3** not do something that you should have done: *the company failed to give adequate warnings*. **4** stop working properly. **5** become weaker or less good. **6** let someone down: *her nerve failed her*. ▶ **n.** a mark that is not high enough to pass an exam.

SYNONYMS ▶ **v.** **1 be unsuccessful**, fall through, fall flat, collapse, founder, backfire, miscarry, come unstuck; informal flop, bomb. **2 be unsuccessful in**, not make the grade; informal flunk. **3 let down**, disappoint, desert, abandon, betray, be disloyal to. **4 break** (**down**), stop working, cut out, crash, malfunction, go wrong; informal conk out. **5 deteriorate**, degenerate, decline, fade. **6 collapse**, crash, go under, go bankrupt, cease trading; informal fold, go bust. ANTONYMS succeed, pass, improve.

□ **fail-safe 1** (of machinery) going back to a safe condition if it is faulty. **2** unlikely or unable to fail. **without fail** whatever happens.

fail·ing /ˈfāliNG/ ▶ **n.** a weakness in a person's character. ▶ **prep.** if not.

SYNONYMS ▶ **n. fault**, shortcoming, weakness, imperfection, deficiency, defect, flaw, frailty. ANTONYMS strength.

fail·ure /ˈfālyər/ ▶ **n. 1** lack of success. **2** an unsuccessful person or thing. **3** a situation in which something stops working properly. **4** an instance of not doing something that is expected: *their failure to comply with the rules*.

SYNONYMS **1 lack of success**, defeat, collapse, foundering. **2 fiasco**, debacle, catastrophe, disaster; informal flop, washout, dead loss. **3 loser**, underachiever, ne'er-do-well, disappointment; informal no-hoper, dud. **4 negligence**, dereliction, omission, oversight. **5 breakdown**, malfunction, crash. **6 collapse**, crash, bankruptcy, insolvency, liquidation, closure. ANTONYMS success.

fain /fān/ old use ▶ **adj. 1** pleased or willing under the circumstances. **2** obliged. ▶ **adv.** gladly.

faint /fānt/ ▶ **adj. 1** not clearly seen, heard, or smelled. **2** slight: *a faint chance*. **3** close to losing consciousness. ▶ **v.** briefly lose consciousness. ▶ **n.** a sudden loss of consciousness.

SYNONYMS ▶ **adj. 1 indistinct**, vague, unclear, indefinite, ill-defined, imperceptible, pale, light, faded. **2 quiet**, muted, muffled, stifled, feeble, weak, low, soft, gentle. **3 slight**, slender, slim, small, tiny, remote, vague. **4 dizzy**, giddy, lightheaded, unsteady; informal woozy. ANTONYMS clear, loud, strong. ▶ **v. pass out**, lose consciousness, black out, keel over, swoon. ▶ **n. blackout**, fainting fit, loss of consciousness, coma, swoon.

□ **faint-hearted** timid.

faint·ly /ˈfāntlē/ ▶ **adv. 1** feebly, indistinctly. **2** very slightly.

SYNONYMS **1 indistinctly**, softly, gently, weakly, in a whisper. **2 slightly**, vaguely, somewhat, quite, fairly, rather, a little, a bit, a touch, a shade.

fair¹ /fe(ə)r/ ▶ **adj. 1** treating people equally. **2** reasonable or appropriate. **3** quite large in size or amount: *he did a fair bit of coaching*. **4** quite good. **5** (of hair or complexion) light; blonde. **6** (of weather) fine and dry. **7** old use beautiful.

SYNONYMS **1 just**, equitable, honest, impartial, unbiased, unprejudiced, neutral, evenhanded. **2 fine**, dry, bright, clear, sunny, cloudless. **3 blonde**, yellow, golden, flaxen, light. **4 pale**, light, pink, white, creamy. **5 reasonable**, passable, tolerable, satisfactory, acceptable, respectable, decent, all right, good enough, pretty good. ANTONYMS inclement, dark, poor.

□ **fair and square 1** with absolute accuracy. **2** honestly and straightforwardly. **fair enough** informal that is reasonable or acceptable. **fair game** a person or thing that people feel they can criticize or exploit. **fair is fair** informal used as a request for just treatment or an assertion that an arrangement is just. **Fair Isle** a traditional multicolored geometric design used in knitwear: *a beautiful Fair Isle sweater*. **fair play** respect for the rules or equal treatment for all. **the fair sex** (also **the fairer sex**) dated or humorous women. **fair-weather friend** a person who stops being a friend when you have problems. ■ **fair·ness n.**

fair² ▶ **n. 1** a gathering of sideshows, amusements, and rides for public entertainment. **2** (**agricultural fair**) a competitive exhibition of livestock, agricultural products, and household skills held annually by a town, county, or state, and also featuring entertainment and educational displays. **3** an event held to promote or sell goods: *an antiques fair*.

SYNONYMS **1 fete**, gala, festival, carnival. **2 market**, bazaar, exchange, sale. **3 exhibition**, display, show, exposition.

fair·ground /ˈfe(ə)rˌground/ ▶ **n.** an outdoor area where a fair is held.

fair·ly /ˈfe(ə)rlē/ ▶ **adv. 1** in a fair way. **2** to some extent; quite. **3** actually; really: *he fairly snarled at her*.

SYNONYMS **1 justly**, equitably, impartially, without bias, without prejudice, even-handedly, equally. **2 reasonably**, passably, tolerably, adequately, moderately, quite, relatively, comparatively; informal pretty. **3 positively**, really, simply, absolutely.

fair·way /ˈfe(ə)rˌwā/ ▶ **n. 1** the part of a golf course between a tee and a green. **2** a channel in a river or harbor that can be used by ships.

fair·y /ˈfe(ə)rē/ ▶ **n.** (plural **fairies**) a small imaginary being that has magical powers.

SYNONYMS **sprite**, pixie, elf, imp, brownie, puck, leprechaun.

□ **fairy godmother** a female character in fairy tales who brings good fortune to the hero or heroine. **fairy ring** a ring of dark grass caused by fungi, once believed to have been made by fairies dancing. **fairy tale** (or **fairy story**) **1** a children's story about magical beings and lands. **2** a lie.

fait ac·com·pli /ˈfet əkämˈplē, ˈfāt/ ▶ **n.** something that has been done and cannot be changed.

faith /fāTH/ ▶ **n. 1** complete trust or confidence. **2** belief in a religion. **3** a system of religious belief.

SYNONYMS **1 trust**, belief, confidence, conviction, reliance. **2 religion**, belief, creed, church, persuasion, ideology, doctrine. ANTONYMS mistrust.

□ **faith healing** healing achieved by religious faith, rather than by medical treatment.

faith·ful /ˈfāTHfəl/ ▶ **adj. 1** remaining loyal and committed. **2** accurate; true to the facts: *a faithful copy of a painting*. ▶ **n.** (**the faithful**) the people who believe in a particular religion.

SYNONYMS ▶ **adj. 1 loyal**, constant, true, devoted, staunch, steadfast, dedicated, committed, trusty, dependable, reliable. **2 accurate**, precise, exact, true, strict, realistic, authentic. ANTONYMS disloyal, treacherous.

■ **faith·ful·ly adv.**

faith·less /ˈfāTHlis/ ▶ **adj. 1** unable to be trusted; disloyal. **2** without religious faith.

fa·ji·tas /fə'hētəz/ ▶ **pl.n.** a Mexican dish consisting of strips of marinated meat with vegetables, wrapped in a tortilla.

fake /fāk/ ▶ **adj.** not genuine: *fake designer clothing.* ▶ **n.** a person or thing that is not genuine. ▶ **v.** (**fakes, faking, faked**) **1** make a copy or imitation of something in order to deceive. **2** pretend to have an emotion or illness.

SYNONYMS ▶ **adj. 1 counterfeit**, forged, fraudulent, sham, pirated, false, bogus; informal phony, dud. **2 imitation**, artificial, synthetic, simulated, reproduction, replica, ersatz, man-made, dummy, false, mock; informal pretend. **3 feigned**, faked, put-on, assumed, invented, affected. ANTONYMS genuine, real, authentic. ▶ **n. 1 forgery**, counterfeit, copy, sham, fraud, hoax, imitation; informal phony, rip-off. **2 charlatan**, quack, sham, fraud, impostor; informal phony. ▶ **v. 1 forge**, counterfeit, falsify, copy, pirate. **2 feign**, pretend, simulate, put on, affect.

fa·kir /fə'ki(ə)r, 'fākər/ ▶ **n.** a Muslim or Hindu holy man who lives by asking people for money or food.

fal·con /'falkən, 'fôl-/ ▶ **n.** a fast-flying bird of prey with long pointed wings.

fal·con·ry /'falkənrē, 'fôl-/ ▶ **n.** the keeping and training of birds of prey. ■ **fal·con·er n.**

fall /fôl/ ▶ **v.** (**falls, falling, fell** /fel/; past participle **fallen**) **1** move downward quickly and without control. **2** collapse to the ground. **3** slope down: *the land fell away in a steep bank.* **4** become less or lower. **5** become: *he fell silent.* **6** happen; come about. **7** (of someone's face) show dismay. **8** be captured or defeated. ▶ **n. 1** an act of falling. **2** a thing that falls or has fallen. **3** (**falls**) a waterfall. **4** a drop in size or number. **5** a defeat or downfall. **6** the season after summer and before winter.

SYNONYMS ▶ **v. 1 drop**, descend, plummet, plunge, sink, dive, tumble, cascade. **2 topple over**, tumble over, fall down/over, collapse. **3 subside**, recede, drop, retreat, fall away, go down, sink. **4 decrease**, decline, diminish, fall off, drop off, lessen, dwindle, plummet, plunge, slump, sink. **5 die**, perish, lose your life, be killed, be slain, be lost; informal bite the dust, buy it. **6 surrender**, yield, submit, give in, capitulate, succumb, be taken, be overwhelmed. **7 occur**, take place, happen, come about. ANTONYMS rise. ▶ **n. 1 tumble**, trip, spill, topple. **2 decline**, fall-off, drop, decrease, cut, dip, reduction, slump; informal crash. **3 downfall**, collapse, failure, decline, destruction, overthrow, demise. **4 surrender**, capitulation, yielding, submission, defeat. **5 descent**, slope, slant. ANTONYMS rise.

□ **fall back** retreat. **fall back on** turn to something for help. **fall for** informal **1** fall in love with. **2** be tricked by. **fall foul of** come into conflict with. **fall guy** informal a person who is blamed for something that is not their fault. **falling star** a meteor or shooting star. **fall in** (or **into**) **line** do what you are told or what others do. **fall into place** begin to make sense. **fall in with 1** meet by chance and become involved with. **2** agree to. **fall on 1** attack fiercely or unexpectedly. **2** be the duty of. **fall out** have an argument. **fall over yourself to do** informal be overeager to do. **fall short** fail to reach a required standard. **fall through** fail to happen or be completed. **fall to** become the duty of.

fal·la·cious /fə'lāshəs/ ▶ **adj.** based on a mistaken belief: *a fallacious explanation.*

fal·la·cy /'faləsē/ ▶ **n.** (plural **fallacies**) **1** a mistaken belief. **2** a false or misleading argument.

SYNONYMS **misconception**, misbelief, delusion, misapprehension, misinterpretation, misconstruction, error, mistake; untruth, inconsistency, myth.

fall·back /'fôl,bak/ ▶ **n.** an alternative plan for use in an emergency.

fall·en /'fôlən/ past participle of **FALL**.

fal·li·ble /'faləbəl/ ▶ **adj.** capable of making mistakes.

SYNONYMS **error-prone**, errant, liable to err, open to error; imperfect, flawed, weak.

■ **fal·li·bil·i·ty** /,falə'bilətē/ **n.**

Fal·lo·pi·an tube /fə'lōpēən/ ▶ **n.** either of a pair of tubes along which eggs travel from the ovaries to the uterus of a female mammal.

fall·out /'fôl,out/ ▶ **n. 1** radioactive particles that are spread over a wide area after a nuclear explosion. **2** the bad effects of a situation.

fal·low /'falō/ ▶ **adj.** (of farmland) plowed but left for a period without being planted with crops. □ **fallow deer** a small deer that has a white-spotted reddish-brown coat in summer.

false /fôls/ ▶ **adj. 1** not correct or true; wrong. **2** fake; artificial: *false eyelashes.* **3** based on something that is not true or correct: *a false sense of security.* **4** disloyal.

SYNONYMS **1 incorrect**, untrue, wrong, inaccurate, untruthful, fictitious, fabricated, invented, made up, trumped up, counterfeit, forged, fraudulent. **2 disloyal**, faithless, unfaithful, untrue, inconstant, treacherous, double-crossing, deceitful, dishonest, duplicitous. **3 fake**, artificial, imitation, synthetic, simulated, reproduction, replica, ersatz, man-made, dummy, mock; informal pretend. ANTONYMS correct, faithful, genuine.

□ **false alarm** a warning given about something that does not happen. **false move** an unwise action that could have dangerous consequences. **false pretenses** behavior that is intended to deceive. **false step 1** a slip or stumble. **2** a mistake. ■ **false·ly adv. fal·si·ty n.**

false·hood /'fôls,ho͝od/ ▶ **n. 1** the state of being untrue. **2** a lie.

SYNONYMS **1 lie**, untruth, fib, falsification, fabrication, invention, fiction. **2** *he accused me of falsehood* **lying**, untruthfulness, fabrication, invention, perjury, telling stories; deceit, deception, pretense, artifice, double-crossing, treachery. ANTONYMS truth, honesty.

fal·set·to /fôl'setō/ ▶ **n.** (plural **falsettos**) a high-pitched voice used by male singers.

fal·si·fy /'fôlsə,fī/ ▶ **v.** (**falsifies, falsifying, falsified**) alter something in order to mislead people: *they had falsified evidence.*

SYNONYMS **forge**, fake, counterfeit, fabricate, alter, change, doctor, tamper with, manipulate, misrepresent, misreport, distort.

■ **fal·si·fi·ca·tion** /,fôlsəfə'kāshən/ **n.**

fal·ter /'fôltər/ ▶ **v.** (**falters, faltering, faltered**) **1** lose strength or momentum. **2** move or speak hesitantly.

SYNONYMS **hesitate**, delay, drag your feet, stall, waver, vacillate, be indecisive, be irresolute; informal hem and haw, sit on the fence.

fame /fām/ ▶ **n.** the state of being famous.

> SYNONYMS **renown**, celebrity, stardom, popularity, prominence, distinction, esteem, eminence, repute. ANTONYMS obscurity.

famed /fāmd/ ▶ **adj.** famous; well-known.

fa·mil·ial /fə'milēəl, -'milyəl/ ▶ **adj.** having to do with a family.

fa·mil·iar /fə'milyər/ ▶ **adj. 1** well-known. **2** frequently encountered; common. **3** (**familiar with**) having a good knowledge of. **4** friendly or informal. ▶ **n.** a spirit believed to accompany a witch.

> SYNONYMS ▶ **adj. 1 well-known**, recognized, accustomed, everyday, day-to-day, habitual, customary, routine. **2** (**familiar with**) **acquainted with**, conversant with, versed in, knowledgeable of, well-informed in/of, au fait with; informal (well) up on. **3 overfamiliar**, presumptuous, disrespectful, forward, bold, impudent, impertinent.

■ **fa·mil·iar·ly** **adv.**

> SPELLING
> Remember that **familiar** is spelled with only one **l**.

fa·mil·iar·i·ty /fə,milē'aritē, -,mil'yar-/ ▶ **n. 1** good knowledge of something. **2** the quality of being well-known. **3** relaxed friendliness or informality between people. **4** inappropriately informal behavior or language.

> SYNONYMS **1** *a familiarity with politics* **acquaintance**, awareness, knowledge, experience, insight, understanding, comprehension. **2 overfamiliarity**, presumption, forwardness, boldness, cheek, impudence, impertinence, disrespect. **3 closeness**, intimacy, friendliness, friendship.

fa·mil·iar·ize /fə'milyə,rīz/ ▶ **v.** (**familiarizes, familiarizing, familiarized**) (**familiarize someone with**) give someone knowledge of something. ■ **fa·mil·iar·i·za·tion** /fə,milyərə'zāsʜən/ **n.**

fam·i·ly /'fam(ə)lē/ ▶ **n.** (plural **families**) **1** a group of parents and their children. **2** a group of people related by marriage or through having the same ancestors. **3** the children of a person or couple. **4** a group of things that are alike in some way. **5** a group of related plants or animals. ▶ **adj.** designed to be suitable for children as well as adults.

> SYNONYMS ▶ **n. 1 relatives**, relations, (next of) kin, clan, tribe; informal folks. **2 children**, little ones, youngsters; informal kids. **3 species**, order, class, genus, phylum.

□ **family name** a surname. **family room** a room in a house used for relaxation and recreation. **family tree** a diagram showing the relationship between people in a family.

fam·ine /'famən/ ▶ **n.** a period when there is a severe shortage of food in a region.

> SYNONYMS **1 food shortage**, hunger, starvation, malnutrition. **2 shortage**, scarcity, lack, dearth, deficiency, insufficiency, shortfall. ANTONYMS plenty.

fam·ished /'famisʜt/ ▶ **adj.** informal very hungry.

> SYNONYMS **ravenous**, hungry, starving, starved, empty, unfed; informal peckish. ANTONYMS replete.

fa·mous /'fāməs/ ▶ **adj. 1** known about by many people. **2** informal very good or impressive.

> SYNONYMS **well-known**, prominent, famed, popular, renowned, noted, eminent, distinguished, celebrated, illustrious, legendary. ANTONYMS unknown.

fa·mous·ly /'fāməslē/ ▶ **adv. 1** as is widely known: *they have famously reclusive lifestyles.* **2** excellently: *we got along famously.*

fan[1] /fan/ ▶ **n. 1** a device that uses rotating blades to create a current of air. **2** a semicircular flat object that you wave to cool yourself. ▶ **v.** (**fans, fanning, fanned**) **1** make a current of air blow toward: *he fanned himself with his hat.* **2** make a belief or emotion stronger. **3** (**fan out**) spread out from a central point.

□ **fan belt** a belt driving the fan that cools the radiator of a motor vehicle. **fan club** an organized group of fans of a famous person or team.

fan[2] ▶ **n.** a person who is very interested in a sport, celebrity, etc.

> SYNONYMS **enthusiast**, devotee, admirer, lover, aficionado, supporter, follower, disciple, adherent; informal buff.

fa·nat·ic /fə'natik/ ▶ **n.** a person who is too enthusiastic about something.

> SYNONYMS **extremist**, militant, dogmatist, fundamentalist, bigot, zealot, radical, diehard; informal maniac.

■ **fa·nat·i·cism** **n.**

fa·nat·ic·al /fə'natikəl/ ▶ **adj. 1** filled with excessive and single-minded zeal. **2** obsessively concerned with something.

> SYNONYMS **1 zealous**, extremist, extreme, militant, gung-ho, dogmatic, radical, diehard, intolerant, single-minded, blinkered, inflexible, uncompromising. **2 enthusiastic**, eager, keen, fervent, passionate, obsessive, obsessed, fixated, compulsive; informal wild, nuts, crazy.

■ **fa·nat·i·cal·ly** **adv.**

fan·ci·er /'fansēər/ ▶ **n.** a person who keeps or breeds a particular type of animal: *a pigeon fancier.*

fan·ci·ful /'fansəfəl/ ▶ **adj. 1** existing only in the imagination. **2** very unusual or creative: *lavish and fanciful costumes.* ■ **fan·ci·ful·ly** **adv.**

fan·cy /'fansē/ ▶ **v.** (**fancies, fancying, fancied**) imagine; think: *he fancied he could smell roses.* ▶ **adj.** (**fancier, fanciest**) elaborate or highly decorated. ▶ **n.** (plural **fancies**) **1** a brief feeling of attraction. **2** the ability to imagine things. **3** a belief or idea that may not be true.

> SYNONYMS ▶ **v. 1 imagine**, believe, think, be under the impression; informal reckon. **2 be attracted to**, find attractive, be infatuated with, be taken with; informal have a crush on, carry a torch for. ▶ **adj. elaborate**, ornate, ornamental, decorative, embellished, intricate, ostentatious, showy, flamboyant, lavish, expensive; informal flashy, snazzy, posh, classy. ANTONYMS plain. ▶ **n. 1 whim**, foible, urge, whimsy, fascination, fad, craze, enthusiasm, passion, caprice. **2 fantasy**, dreaming, imagination, creativity.

□ **fancy-free** not in a serious relationship. **take** (or **catch**) **someone's fancy** appeal to someone. **take a fancy to** become fond of.

fan·dan·go /fan'daNGgō/ ▶ **n.** (plural **fandangoes** or **fandangos**) a lively Spanish dance for two people.

fan·fare /'fan,fer/ ▶ **n.** a short tune played on brass instruments to announce someone or something.

fang /faNG, fäNG/ ▶ **n. 1** a long, pointed tooth of a dog or wolf. **2** a tooth with which a snake injects poison.

fan·light /'fan,līt/ ▶ **n.** a small semicircular window over a door or window.

fan·ta·sia /fan'tāzHə, fantə'zēə/ ▶ **n. 1** a musical composition that does not follow a conventional form. **2** a musical composition based on several familiar tunes.

fan·ta·size /'fantə,sīz/ ▶ **v.** (**fantasizes, fantasizing, fantasized**) daydream about something that you would like to do, or that you would like to happen: *he fantasized about traveling.*

fan·tas·tic /fan'tastik/ ▶ **adj. 1** hard to believe. **2** strange or exotic: *dancers dressed as fantastic animals.* **3** informal very good or large.

> SYNONYMS **1 fanciful**, extravagant, extraordinary, irrational, wild, absurd, far-fetched, unthinkable, implausible, improbable, unlikely; informal crazy. **2 strange**, weird, bizarre, outlandish, grotesque, surreal, exotic. **3 marvelous**, wonderful, sensational, outstanding, superb, excellent; informal terrific, fabulous. ANTONYMS ordinary.

■ **fan·tas·tic·al·ly adv.**

fan·ta·sy /'fantəsē/ ▶ **n.** (plural **fantasies**) **1** the imagining of things that do not exist in reality. **2** an imagined situation or event that is desirable but unlikely to happen: *making up fantasies about the lives we'd live.* **3** a type of fiction that involves magic and adventure.

> SYNONYMS **1 imagination**, fancy, invention, make-believe, creativity, vision, daydreaming, reverie. **2 dream**, daydream, pipe dream, fanciful notion, wish, fond hope, delusion; informal pie in the sky. ANTONYMS realism.

fan·zine /'fan,zēn, fan'zēn/ ▶ **n.** a magazine for fans of a particular performer, team, etc.

FAQ /fak/ ▶ **abbr.** frequently asked questions.

far /fär/ ▶ **adv.** (**further** /'fərTHər/, **furthest** /'fərTHist/ or **farther** /'färTHər/, **farthest** /'färTHist/) **1** at, to, or by a great distance in space or time. **2** by a great deal: *he's functioning far better than usual.* ▶ **adj. 1** distant in space or time. **2** extreme.

> SYNONYMS ▶ **adv. 1 a long way**, a great distance, a good way, afar. **2 much**, considerably, markedly, greatly, significantly, substantially, appreciably, by a long way, by a mile, easily. ▶ **adj. 1 distant**, faraway, far-off, remote, out of the way, far-flung, outlying. **2 further**, opposite. ANTONYMS near.

□ **as far as 1** for as great a distance as. **2** to the extent that. **be a far cry from** be very different from. **by far** by a great amount. **far and away** by a very large amount. **far and wide** over a large area. **far-fetched** exaggerated or unlikely: *a far-fetched plot.* **far-flung** spread out; scattered. **far gone** in a bad or worsening state. **far-reaching** having wide and important effects or implications. **go far 1** achieve a great deal. **2** be worth much: *your money won't go far in a place like that.* **go too far** go beyond what is reasonable or acceptable. **far out 1** unconventional. **2** informal, dated excellent. **the Far East** China, Japan, and other countries of east Asia. **far-off** distant in space or time.

far·ad /'farəd, -,ad/ ▶ **n.** the basic unit of electrical capacitance.

far·a·way /'färə,wā/ ▶ **adj. 1** remote or distant. **2** lost in thought; dreamy: *a faraway look.*

farce /färs/ ▶ **n. 1** a comedy based on situations that are ridiculous and improbable. **2** an absurd event.

> SYNONYMS **mockery**, travesty, parody, sham, pretense, charade, joke; informal shambles. ANTONYMS tragedy.

far·ci·cal /'färsikəl/ ▶ **adj.** absurd or ridiculous.
■ **far·ci·cal·ly adv.**

fare /fer/ ▶ **n. 1** the money that a passenger pays to travel on public transportation. **2** a range of food: *Italian fare.* ▶ **v.** (**fares, faring, fared**) perform in a specified way in a particular situation: *the party fared badly in the elections.*

> SYNONYMS ▶ **n. 1 price**, cost, charge, fee, toll, tariff. **2 food**, meals, cooking, cuisine. ▶ **v. get on**, get along, cope, manage, do, survive; informal make out.

fare·well /fer'wel/ ▶ **exclam.** old use goodbye. ▶ **n.** an act of leaving.

> SYNONYMS ▶ **exclam. goodbye**, adieu, au revoir, ciao, adios; informal bye, bye-bye, so long, see you later. ▶ **n. goodbye**, adieu, leave-taking, parting, departure, send-off.

far·i·na·ceous /,farə'nāsHəs/ ▶ **adj.** containing or resembling starch.

farm /färm/ ▶ **n. 1** an area of land and buildings used for growing crops and rearing animals. **2** a farmhouse. ▶ **v. 1** make a living by growing crops or keeping animals. **2** (**farm something out**) give work to other people to do.

> SYNONYMS ▶ **n. ranch**, farmstead, plantation, estate, farmland, dairy farm. ▶ **v. breed**, rear, keep, raise, tend.

farm·er /'färmər/ ▶ **n.** a person who owns or manages a farm.

farm·house /'färm,hous/ ▶ **n.** a house attached to a farm.

farm·ing /'färmiNG/ ▶ **n.** the activity or business of growing crops and raising livestock.

> SYNONYMS **agriculture**, cultivation, ranching, farm management, husbandry, agronomy, agribusiness.

farm·stead /'färm,sted/ ▶ **n.** a farm and its buildings.

farm·yard /'färm,yärd/ ▶ **n.** a yard or enclosure surrounded by farm buildings.

far·ra·go /fə'rägō, -'rā-/ ▶ **n.** (plural **farragos** or **farragoes**) a confused mixture.

far·ri·er /'fareēər/ ▶ **n.** a person who shoes horses.

far·row /'farō/ ▶ **n.** a litter of pigs. ▶ **v.** (of a sow) give birth to piglets.

far·see·ing /'fär,sē-iNG/ ▶ **adj.** having great foresight; farsighted.

Far·si /'färsē/ ▶ **n.** the modern form of the Persian language.

far·sight·ed /'fär,sītid, -'sītid/ ▶ **adj. 1** unable to see things clearly if they are relatively close to the eyes. **2** having great foresight.

far·thing /'färTHiNG/ ▶ **n.** a former British coin, worth a quarter of an old penny.

far·thin·gale /ˈfärᴛʜiɴɢˌgāl/ ▶ **n.** historical a hooped petticoat or circular pad of fabric around the hips, formerly worn under women's skirts to extend and shape them.

fas·ci·a /ˈfasʜ(ē)ə, ˈfā-/ (or **facia**) ▶ **n. 1** a board covering the ends of rafters or other fittings. **2** a detachable cover for the front of a cell phone.

fas·ci·nate /ˈfasəˌnāt/ ▶ **v.** (**fascinates**, **fascinating**, **fascinated**) interest or charm someone greatly.

SPELLING

Spell **fascinate** and **fascination** with an **s** before the **c**.

fas·ci·nat·ing /ˈfasəˌnātiɴɢ/ ▶ **adj.** extremely interesting.

SYNONYMS **interesting**, captivating, engrossing, absorbing, enchanting, enthralling, spellbinding, riveting, engaging, compelling, compulsive, gripping, charming, attractive, intriguing, diverting, entertaining. ANTONYMS boring.

fas·ci·na·tion /ˌfasəˈnāsʜən/ ▶ **n. 1** the state of being very attracted to and interested in someone or something. **2** the power of something to attract or interest someone.

SYNONYMS **interest**, preoccupation, passion, obsession, compulsion, allure, lure, charm, attraction, appeal, pull, draw.

USAGE

Be careful to distinguish between the expressions **fascination with** and **fascination for**. A person has a **fascination with** something they are very interested in (*her fascination with the British royal family*), whereas something interesting holds a **fascination for** a person (*circuses have a fascination for children*).

fas·cism /ˈfasʜˌizəm/ ▶ **n. 1** a right-wing system of government with extreme nationalistic beliefs. **2** an attitude that is very intolerant or right-wing. ■ **fas·cist n. & adj.**

SPELLING

There is an **s** before the **c**: fascism.

fash·ion /ˈfasʜən/ ▶ **n. 1** a popular style of clothes, way of behaving, etc. **2** a way of doing something: *the work was done in a casual fashion.* ▶ **v.** make or shape something: *the trio have fashioned a noisy album.*

SYNONYMS ▶ **n. 1 vogue**, trend, craze, rage, mania, fad, style, look, convention, mode; informal thing. **2 clothes**, clothing design, couture; the garment industry; informal the rag trade. **3 manner**, way, method, style, approach, mode. ▶ **v. construct**, build, make, manufacture, cast, shape, form, mold, sculpt, forge, hew, carve.

□ **after a fashion** to a certain extent but not perfectly.

fash·ion·a·ble /ˈfasʜ(ə)nəbəl/ ▶ **adj.** in a style that is currently popular.

SYNONYMS **in vogue**, in fashion, popular, up to date, up to the minute, modern, all the rage, trendsetting, stylish, chic, modish; informal trendy, classy, cool, tony.

■ **fash·ion·a·bly adv.**

fash·ion·is·ta /ˌfasʜəˈnēstə/ ▶ **n.** informal a devoted follower of fashion.

fast[1] /fast/ ▶ **adj. 1** moving or capable of moving very quickly. **2** taking place quickly. **3** (of a clock or watch) ahead of the correct time. **4** firmly fixed or attached: *he made a rope fast to each corner.* **5** (of a dye) not fading. ▶ **adv. 1** quickly. **2** firmly or securely.

SYNONYMS ▶ **adj. 1 speedy**, quick, swift, rapid, high-speed, accelerated, express, blistering, breakneck, hasty, hurried; informal zippy, scorching, supersonic. **2 secure**, fastened, tight, firm, closed, shut, immovable. **3 loyal**, devoted, faithful, firm, steadfast, staunch, true, boon, bosom, inseparable. ANTONYMS slow, loose. ▶ **adv. 1 quickly**, rapidly, swiftly, speedily, briskly, at full tilt, hastily, hurriedly, in a hurry; informal lickety-split. **2 securely**, firmly, tight. **3** *he's fast asleep* **deeply**, sound, completely.

□ **fast asleep** in a deep sleep. **fast breeder** a nuclear reactor using high-speed neutrons. **fast food** cooked food sold in snack bars and restaurants as a quick meal. **fast track** a rapid route or method. **fast-track** speed up the development or progress of. **pull a fast one** informal try to gain an unfair advantage.

fast[2] ▶ **v.** go without food or drink. ▶ **n.** a period of fasting.

SYNONYMS ▶ **v. eat nothing**, go without food, go hungry, starve yourself, go on a hunger strike.

fast·ball /ˈfas(t)ˌbôl/ ▶ **n.** a baseball pitch thrown at or near a pitcher's top speed.

fas·ten /ˈfasən/ ▶ **v. 1** close or do up securely. **2** fix or hold in place. **3** (**fasten on**) pick out and concentrate on: *critics fastened on two sections of the report.*

SYNONYMS **1 bolt**, lock, secure, make fast, chain, seal. **2 attach**, fix, affix, clip, pin, tack, stick, join. **3 tie** (**up**), tether, hitch, truss, fetter, lash, anchor, strap, rope. ANTONYMS unlock, untie.

■ **fas·ten·er n. fas·ten·ing n.**

fas·tid·i·ous /fasˈtidēəs/ ▶ **adj. 1** paying a lot of attention to detail. **2** very concerned about cleanliness. ■ **fas·tid·i·ous·ly adv.**

fast·ness /ˈfas(t)nəs/ ▶ **n. 1** a place that is secure and well-protected. **2** the ability of a dye to keep its color.

fat /fat/ ▶ **n. 1** an oily substance found in animals. **2** a substance used in cooking made from the fat of animals, or from plants. ▶ **adj.** (**fatter**, **fattest**) **1** having too much fat. **2** informal large; substantial: *fat profits.*

SYNONYMS ▶ **n. 1 blubber**, fatty tissue, adipose tissue, cellulite. **2 oil**, grease, lard, suet, butter, margarine. ▶ **adj. 1 obese**, overweight, plump, stout, chubby, portly, flabby, paunchy, potbellied, corpulent; informal tubby. **2 thick**, big, chunky, substantial, sizable. ANTONYMS thin, slim, lean.

□ **fat cat** disapproving a wealthy and powerful businessman. **fat chance** informal little or no chance. **live off the fat of the land** have the best of everything. ■ **fat·ness n.**

fa·tal /ˈfātl/ ▶ **adj. 1** causing death. **2** leading to disaster: *the strategy contained three fatal flaws.*

SYNONYMS **1 deadly**, lethal, mortal, death-dealing, terminal, incurable, untreatable, inoperable. **2 disastrous**, devastating, ruinous, catastrophic, calamitous, dire. ANTONYMS harmless, beneficial.

■ **fa·tal·ly** adv.

fa·tal·ism /ˈfātlˌizəm/ ▶ n. the belief that all events are decided in advance by a supernatural power. ■ **fa·tal·ist** n. **fa·tal·is·tic** /ˌfātlˈistik/ adj.

fa·tal·i·ty /fāˈtalətē, fə-/ ▶ n. (plural **fatalities**) a death occurring in a war, or caused by an accident or disease.

fate /fāt/ ▶ n. **1** a supernatural power believed to control all events. **2** the things that will inevitably happen to someone or something. ▶ v. (**be fated**) be destined to happen in a particular way: *they were fated to meet up again*.

SYNONYMS ▶ n. **1 destiny**, providence, the stars, chance, luck, serendipity, fortune, karma, kismet. **2 future**, destiny, outcome, end, lot. **3 death**, demise, end, sentence. ▶ v. **predestine**, preordain, destine, mean, doom.

□ **seal someone's fate** make it inevitable that something unpleasant will happen to someone.

fate·ful /ˈfātfəl/ ▶ adj. having important, often unpleasant, consequences.

fat·head /ˈfatˌhed/ ▶ n. informal a stupid person.

fa·ther /ˈfäT͟Hər/ ▶ n. **1** a male parent. **2** an important figure in the early history of something. **3** literary a male ancestor. **4** a priest. **5** (**the Father**) God. ▶ v. (**fathers**, **fathering**, **fathered**) be the father of.

SYNONYMS ▶ n. **1** informal **dad**, daddy, pop, pa, old man; informal, dated pater. **2 originator**, initiator, founder, inventor, creator, author, architect. ▶ v. **sire**, spawn, breed, give life to.

□ **father-in-law** (plural **fathers-in-law**) the father of a person's husband or wife. **Father's Day** the third Sunday in June, a day on which fathers are honored with greeting cards and gifts. ■ **fa·ther·hood** n.

fa·ther·land /ˈfäT͟Hərˌland/ ▶ n. a person's native country.

fa·ther·ly /ˈfäT͟Hərlē/ ▶ adj. protective and affectionate.

fath·om /ˈfaT͟Həm/ ▶ n. a measure of the depth of water, equal to six feet (1.8 meters). ▶ v. understand after a lot of thought: *I can't fathom his motives*.

fa·tigue /fəˈtēg/ ▶ n. **1** great tiredness. **2** weakness in metals caused by repeated stress. **3** (**fatigues**) loose-fitting clothing worn by soldiers. ▶ v. (**fatigues**, **fatiguing**, **fatigued**) make someone very tired.

SYNONYMS ▶ n. **tiredness**, weariness, exhaustion. ANTONYMS energy. ▶ v. **tire out**, exhaust, wear out, drain, weary, overtire; informal knock out, take it out of.

fat·ten /ˈfatn/ ▶ v. make or become fat or fatter.

fat·ty /ˈfatē/ ▶ adj. (**fattier**, **fattiest**) containing a lot of fat.

SYNONYMS **greasy**, fat, oily, creamy, rich.

□ **fatty acid** Chemistry an organic acid whose molecule contains a hydrocarbon chain.

fat·u·ous /ˈfaCHo͞oəs/ ▶ adj. silly and pointless.

SYNONYMS **silly**, foolish, stupid, inane, idiotic, vacuous, asinine; pointless, senseless, ridiculous, ludicrous, absurd. ANTONYMS sensible.

■ **fat·u·ous·ly** adv.

fat·wa /ˈfätwä/ ▶ n. a ruling on a point of Islamic law given by a recognized authority.

fau·cet /ˈfôsit, ˈfäs-/ ▶ n. a device by which a flow of liquid or gas from a pipe or container can be controlled.

fault /fôlt/ ▶ n. **1** a defect or mistake. **2** responsibility for an accident or unfortunate event: *it's not my fault that she left*. **3** (in tennis) a service of the ball that is against the rules. **4** a break in the layers of rock of the earth's crust. ▶ v. find a defect or mistake in someone or something.

SYNONYMS ▶ n. **1** *he has his faults* **defect**, failing, imperfection, blemish, flaw, shortcoming, weakness, weak point, vice. **2** *engineers have located the fault* **defect**, flaw, imperfection, bug, error, mistake, inaccuracy, oversight; informal glitch. **3 responsibility**, liability, culpability, guilt. ANTONYMS strength. ▶ v. **find fault with**, criticize, attack, condemn; informal knock.

□ **find fault** criticize unfairly. **to a fault** excessively: *you're generous to a fault*.

fault·less /ˈfôltlis/ ▶ adj. having no defects or errors.

SYNONYMS **perfect**, flawless, without fault, error-free, impeccable, accurate, precise, exact, correct, exemplary. ANTONYMS flawed.

■ **fault·less·ly**.

fault·y /ˈfôltē/ ▶ adj. (**faultier**, **faultiest**) having faults.

SYNONYMS **1 malfunctioning**, broken, damaged, defective, not working, out of order; informal on the blink, acting up. **2 flawed**, unsound, defective, inaccurate, incorrect, erroneous, wrong. ANTONYMS working, sound.

faun /fôn/ ▶ n. (in Roman mythology) a god of woods and fields, with a human body and a goat's horns, ears, legs, and tail.

fau·na /ˈfônə, ˈfänə/ ▶ n. the animals of a particular region or period.

faux /fō/ ▶ adj. artificial or imitation; false: *a string of faux pearls*.

faux pas /fō ˈpä, ˈfō ˌpä/ ▶ n. (plural **faux pas**) a mistake that causes embarrassment in a social situation.

fa·vor /ˈfāvər/ ▶ n. **1** approval or liking. **2** a kind or helpful act: *I've come to ask you a favor*. **3** special treatment of one person or group. ▶ v. **1** view or treat with favor: *few politicians favor a cut in public spending*. **2** work to the advantage of: *natural selection has favored bats*. **3** (**favor someone with**) give someone something they wish for.

SYNONYMS ▶ n. **1 approval**, approbation, goodwill, kindness, benevolence. **2 good turn**, service, good deed, act of kindness, courtesy. ANTONYMS disapproval, disservice. ▶ v. **1 advocate**, recommend, approve of, be in favor of, support, back, champion, campaign for, press for, lobby for, promote; informal push for. **2 prefer**, go for, choose, opt for, select, pick, like better, be biased toward. **3 benefit**, be to the advantage of, help, assist, aid, advance, be of service to. ANTONYMS oppose.

□ **in favor of 1** to be replaced by. **2** in support of.

fa·vor·a·ble /ˈfāv(ə)rəbəl/ ▶ **adj.** **1** expressing approval or consent. **2** advantageous or helpful: *favorable conditions for growth.*

> SYNONYMS **1 approving**, positive, complimentary, full of praise, flattering, glowing, enthusiastic, kind, good. **2 advantageous**, beneficial, in your favor, good, right, suitable, appropriate, auspicious, promising, encouraging. **3 positive**, affirmative, assenting, approving, encouraging, reassuring. ANTONYMS critical, unfavorable.

■ **fa·vor·a·bly** **adv.**

fa·vor·ite /ˈfāv(ə)rət/ ▶ **adj.** preferred to all other people or things of the same kind. ▶ **n.** **1** a favorite person or thing. **2** the competitor thought most likely to win. **3** a record of the address of a website, used for quick access.

> SYNONYMS ▶ **adj.** **favored**, preferred, chosen, choice, best-loved, dearest, pet. ▶ **n.** **first choice**, pick, preference, pet, darling, the apple of your eye; informal golden boy, teacher's pet; informal fair-haired boy/girl.

fa·vor·it·ism /ˈfāv(ə)rəˌtizəm/ ▶ **n.** the unfair favoring of one person or group.

fawn[1] /fôn, fän/ ▶ **n.** **1** a young deer. **2** a light brown color.

fawn[2] ▶ **v.** try to please someone by flattering them and being too attentive: *people fawn over you when you're famous.*

fax /faks/ ▶ **n.** **1** a copy of a document that has been scanned and transmitted electronically. **2** a machine for transmitting and receiving faxes. ▶ **v.** send a document by fax.

faze /fāz/ ▶ **v.** (**fazes**, **fazing**, **fazed**) informal shock or confuse.

FBI ▶ **abbr.** Federal Bureau of Investigation.

FDA ▶ **abbr.** Food and Drug Administration.

Fe ▶ **symbol** the chemical element iron.

fe·al·ty /ˈfēltē/ ▶ **n.** historical the loyalty sworn to a feudal lord by his tenant.

fear /fi(ə)r/ ▶ **n.** **1** an unpleasant emotion caused by the threat of danger. **2** the likelihood of something unwelcome happening: *she watched the other guests without fear of attracting attention.* ▶ **v.** **1** be afraid of. **2** (**fear for**) be anxious about.

> SYNONYMS ▶ **n.** **1 terror**, fright, fearfulness, horror, alarm, panic, trepidation, dread, anxiety, angst, apprehension, nervousness. **2 phobia**, aversion, antipathy, dread, nightmare, horror, terror; informal hang-up. ▶ **v.** **1 be afraid of**, be fearful of, be scared of, be apprehensive of, dread, live in fear of, be terrified of. **2 suspect**, be afraid, have a sneaking suspicion, be inclined to think, have a hunch.

fear·ful /ˈfi(ə)rfəl/ ▶ **adj.** **1** feeling afraid. **2** causing fear. **3** informal very great.

> SYNONYMS **1 afraid**, scared, frightened, scared stiff, scared to death, terrified, petrified, nervous, apprehensive, uneasy, anxious, timid; informal jittery. **2 terrible**, dreadful, awful, appalling, frightful, ghastly, horrific, horrible, shocking, gruesome. ANTONYMS unafraid.

■ **fear·ful·ly** **adv.**

fear·less /ˈfi(ə)rlis/ ▶ **adj.** having no fear; brave.

> SYNONYMS **brave**, courageous, bold, audacious, intrepid, valiant, plucky, heroic, daring, unafraid; informal gutsy. ANTONYMS timid, cowardly.

■ **fear·less·ly** **adv.**

fear·some /ˈfi(ə)rsəm/ ▶ **adj.** very impressive and frightening.

> SYNONYMS **frightening**, horrifying, terrifying, menacing, chilling, spine-chilling, alarming, unnerving, daunting, formidable, forbidding, dismaying, disquieting, disturbing; informal scary.

fea·si·ble /ˈfēzəbəl/ ▶ **adj.** **1** able to be done easily. **2** likely.

> SYNONYMS **practicable**, practical, workable, achievable, attainable, realizable, viable, realistic, possible; informal doable. ANTONYMS impracticable.

■ **fea·si·bil·i·ty** /ˌfēzəˈbilətē/ **n.** **fea·si·bly** **adv.**

> **USAGE**
>
> Some people say **feasible** should not be used to mean 'likely,' but this sense has been in the language for centuries and is generally considered to be acceptable.

feast /fēst/ ▶ **n.** **1** a large meal marking a special occasion. **2** an annual religious celebration. ▶ **v.** **1** have a feast. **2** (**feast on**) eat large quantities of.

> SYNONYMS ▶ **n.** **banquet**, dinner, treat; informal spread. ▶ **v.** **gorge**, dine, binge; (**feast on**) devour, consume, partake of, eat your fill of; informal stuff your face with, pig out on.

□ **feast your eyes on** gaze at with pleasure.

feat /fēt/ ▶ **n.** an achievement requiring great courage, skill, or strength.

> SYNONYMS **achievement**, accomplishment, coup, triumph, undertaking, enterprise, venture, exploit, operation, exercise, endeavor, effort.

feath·er /ˈfeT͟Hər/ ▶ **n.** any of the structures growing from a bird's skin, consisting of a hollow shaft fringed with fine strands. ▶ **v.** (**feathers**, **feathering**, **feathered**) turn an oar so that the blade passes through the air edgewise.

> SYNONYMS ▶ **n.** **plume**, quill; (**feathers**) plumage, down.

□ **a feather in your cap** an achievement to be proud of. **feather your nest** make money dishonestly. ■ **feath·er·y** **adj.**

feath·er·bed /ˈfeT͟Hərˌbed/ ▶ **n.** a bed with a mattress stuffed with feathers.

feath·er·brained /ˈfeT͟Hərˌbrānd/ ▶ **adj.** silly or absentminded.

feath·ered /ˈfeT͟Hərd/ ▶ **adj.** covered with feathers.

feath·er·weight /ˈfeT͟Hərˌwāt/ ▶ **n.** a weight in boxing between bantamweight and lightweight.

fea·ture /ˈfēCHər/ ▶ **n.** **1** a distinctive element or aspect: *the software has some welcome new features.* **2** a part of the face. **3** a special article in a newspaper or magazine. **4** (also **feature film**) a full-length movie intended as the main film showing at a movie theater. ▶ **v.** (**features**, **featuring**, **featured**) **1** have as a feature: *the hotel features a large pool and a sauna.* **2** have an important part in something: *relaxation did not feature in her busy day.*

SYNONYMS ▶ **n.** **1 characteristic**, attribute, quality, property, trait, hallmark, aspect, facet, factor, ingredient, component, element. **2** *her delicate features* **face**, countenance, physiognomy; informal mug; literary lineaments, visage. **3 centerpiece**, special attraction, highlight, focal point, focus, conversation piece. **4 article**, piece, item, report, story, column. ▶ **v.** **1 present**, promote, make a feature of, spotlight, highlight, showcase, foreground. **2 star**, appear, participate.

■ **fea·ture·less adj.**

Feb. ▶ **abbr.** February.

fe·brile /'feb,rīl, 'fē,brīl/ ▶ **adj.** **1** having the symptoms of a fever. **2** overactive and excitable: *her febrile imagination.*

Feb·ru·ar·y /'feb(y)o͞o,erē, 'febro͞o-/ ▶ **n.** (plural **Februaries**) the second month of the year.

SPELLING

Write **-ruary**, not **-uary**: Feb**ruary**.

fe·ces /'fēsēz/ ▶ **pl.n.** waste matter passed out of the body from the bowels. ■ **fe·cal** /fēkl/ **adj.**

feck·less /'fekləs/ ▶ **adj.** **1** lacking in efficiency or vitality. **2** unthinking and irresponsible: *the feckless exploitation of the world's natural resources.*

fe·cund /'fekənd, 'fē-/ ▶ **adj.** very fertile. ■ **fe·cun·di·ty** /fe'kəndətē, fi'kən-/ **n.**

Fed /fed/ ▶ **n.** informal a federal official, especially an FBI agent.

fed /fed/ past and past participle of **FEED**. □ **fed up** informal annoyed or bored.

fed·er·al /'fed(ə)rəl/ ▶ **adj.** **1** having a system of government in which several states unite under a central authority. **2** having to do with the central government of a federation. □ **Federal Reserve** the banking authority that has the functions of a central bank. ■ **fed·er·al·ly adv.**

fed·er·ate /'fedə,rāt/ ▶ **v.** (**federates**, **federating**, **federated**) join as a federation.

fed·er·a·tion /,fedə'rāsʜən/ ▶ **n.** **1** a group of states united under a central authority in which individual states keep control of their internal affairs. **2** a group organized like a federation.

SYNONYMS **confederation**, confederacy, association, league, alliance, coalition, union, syndicate, guild, consortium.

fe·do·ra /fə'dôrə/ ▶ **n.** a soft felt hat with a curled brim and the crown creased lengthwise.

fee /fē/ ▶ **n.** **1** a payment given for professional advice or services. **2** a sum paid to be allowed to do something: *the museum charges an admission fee.*

SYNONYMS **payment**, wage, salary, price, charge, bill, tariff, rate; (**fees**) remuneration, dues, earnings, pay; formal emolument.

fee·ble /'fēbəl/ ▶ **adj.** (**feebler**, **feeblest**) **1** weak. **2** not convincing or effective: *a feeble excuse.*

SYNONYMS **1 weak**, weakened, debilitated, enfeebled, frail, decrepit, infirm, delicate, sickly, ailing, unwell, poorly. **2 ineffective**, unconvincing, implausible, unsatisfactory, poor, weak, flimsy, lame. **3 cowardly**, faint-hearted, spineless, timid, timorous, fearful, unassertive, weak, ineffectual; informal sissy, chicken. **4 faint**, dim, weak, pale, soft, subdued, muted. ANTONYMS strong.

□ **feeble-minded** foolish; stupid. ■ **fee·ble·ness n.** **fee·bly adv.**

feed /fēd/ ▶ **v.** (**feeds**, **feeding**, **fed**) **1** give food to. **2** provide enough food for. **3** (of an animal or baby) eat. **4** supply with material or information. **5** pass something gradually through a confined space. ▶ **n.** **1** an act of feeding. **2** food for domestic animals.

SYNONYMS ▶ **v.** **1 provide for**, cook for, dine, nourish, cater. **2 eat**, graze, browse. **3 supply**, provide, give, deliver. ▶ **n.** **fodder**, food, provender.

feed·back /'fēd,bak/ ▶ **n.** **1** comments made in response to something you have done. **2** the return of part of the output of an amplifier to its input, causing a whistling sound.

feed·er /'fēdər/ ▶ **n.** **1** a person or thing that feeds or supplies something. **2** a person or animal that eats a particular food or in a particular manner. **3** a container filled with food for birds or mammals. **4** a tributary stream. **5** a minor road or railroad line that links outlying areas with the main route. **6** a cable carrying electricity to a distribution point.

feed·lot /'fēd,lät/ ▶ **n.** an enclosed area where livestock are fed and fattened for market.

feel /fēl/ ▶ **v.** (**feels**, **feeling**, **felt**) **1** be aware of, examine, or search by touch. **2** give a particular sensation when touched: *the wool feels soft.* **3** experience an emotion or sensation. **4** be affected by. **5** have a belief or opinion: *she felt that the woman disliked her.* ▶ **n.** **1** an act of feeling. **2** the sense of touch. **3** a sensation or impression: *the restaurant has a bistro feel.* **4** (**a feel for**) a sensitive appreciation of.

SYNONYMS ▶ **v.** **1 touch**, stroke, caress, fondle, finger, paw, handle. **2** *she felt a breeze on her back* **perceive**, sense, detect, discern, notice, be aware of, be conscious of. **3** *he will not feel any pain* **experience**, undergo, go through, bear, endure, suffer. **4 grope**, fumble, scrabble. **5 believe**, think, consider it right, be of the opinion, hold, maintain, judge; informal reckon, figure. ▶ **n.** **1 texture**, finish, touch, consistency. **2 atmosphere**, ambience, aura, mood, feeling, air, impression, spirit; informal vibes. **3 aptitude**, knack, flair, bent, talent, gift, ability.

□ **feel up to** have the strength or energy to. **get a feel for** become accustomed to. **make yourself** (or **your presence**) **felt** have a noticeable effect.

feel·er /'fēlər/ ▶ **n.** **1** an organ used by certain animals for testing things by touch. **2** a cautious proposal intended to find out someone's opinion.

feel·ing /'fēliɴɢ/ ▶ **n.** **1** an emotional state or reaction: *a feeling of joy.* **2** (**feelings**) the emotional side of a person's character. **3** strong emotion. **4** the ability to feel. **5** the sensation of touching or being touched: *the feeling of water against your skin.* **6** a belief or opinion. **7** (**feeling for**) an understanding of.

SYNONYMS **1 sensation**, sense, perception, awareness, consciousness. **2** (**sneaking**) **suspicion**, notion, inkling, hunch, impression, intuition, instinct, funny feeling, fancy, idea. **3 love**, affection, fondness, tenderness, warmth, emotion, passion, desire. **4 mood**, opinion, attitude, sentiment, emotion, belief, views, consensus. **5 compassion**, sympathy, empathy, fellow feeling, concern, pity, sorrow, commiseration. **6** (**feelings**) *he hurt her feelings* **sensibilities**, sensitivities, self-esteem, pride. **7 atmosphere**, ambience, aura, air, mood, impression, spirit; informal vibes. **8 aptitude**, knack, flair, bent, talent, feel, gift, ability.

feet /fēt/ plural of FOOT.

feign /fān/ ▶ v. pretend to feel or have: *she feigned nervousness.*

feint /fānt/ ▶ n. a movement made to deceive an opponent, especially in boxing or fencing. ▶ v. make a feint.

feist·y /ˈfīstē/ ▶ adj. (**feistier**, **feistiest**) lively and spirited.

feld·spar /ˈfel(d)ˌspär/ ▶ n. a mineral forming igneous rocks, consisting chiefly of aluminum silicates.

fe·lic·i·ta·tions /fəˌlisəˈtāsʜənz/ ▶ pl.n. formal congratulations.

fe·lic·i·tous /fəˈlisətəs/ ▶ adj. well-chosen or appropriate.

SYNONYMS **apt**, well-chosen, fitting, suitable, appropriate, apposite, pertinent, germane, relevant. ANTONYMS inappropriate.

fe·lic·i·ty /fəˈlisətē/ ▶ n. (plural **felicities**) **1** great happiness. **2** the ability to express yourself in an appropriate way. **3** a pleasing feature of an artistic work.

fe·line /ˈfēˌlīn/ ▶ adj. having to do with a cat or cats. ▶ n. a cat or other animal of the cat family.

fell¹ /fel/ past of FALL.

fell² ▶ v. **1** cut down a tree. **2** knock someone down.

SYNONYMS **1 cut down**, chop down, hack down, saw down, clear. **2 knock down**, knock to the ground, floor, strike down, knock out; informal deck, flatten, lay out.

fell³ ▶ adj. literary extremely evil or fierce. ▫ **in** (or **at**) **one fell swoop** all at one time.

fel·la /ˈfelə/ (or **fel·lah**) ▶ n. = FELLOW (used to represent speech in various dialects): *goodbye, young fella.*

fel·low /ˈfelō/ ▶ n. **1** a man or boy. **2** a person in the same situation as you: *the rebel was said to have been murdered by his fellows.* **3** a thing of the same kind as another. **4** a member of a learned society. **5** (or **research fellow**) a student or graduate receiving a fellowship for a period of research. ▶ adj. in the same situation: *a fellow sufferer.*

SYNONYMS ▶ n. **1 man**, boy, person, individual, character; informal guy, dude, lad. **2 companion**, friend, comrade, partner, associate, coworker, colleague; informal pal, buddy.

▫ **fellow feeling** sympathy based on shared experiences. **fellow traveler** a person who sympathizes with the Communist Party but is not a member of it.

fel·low·ship /ˈfelōˌsʜip/ ▶ n. **1** friendship between people who share an interest. **2** a group of people who share an interest. **3** the position of a fellow of a college or society.

SYNONYMS **1 companionship**, comradeship, camaraderie, friendship, sociability, solidarity. **2 association**, organization, society, club, league, union, guild, alliance, fraternity, brotherhood.

fel·on /ˈfelən/ ▶ n. a person who has committed a felony. ■ **fe·lo·ni·ous** /fəˈlōnēəs/ adj.

fel·o·ny /ˈfelənē/ ▶ n. (plural **felonies**) a serious crime, often involving violence.

felt¹ /felt/ ▶ n. cloth made from wool that has been rolled and pressed. ▫ **felt-tip pen** a pen with a writing point made of felt or tightly packed fibers.

felt² past and past participle of FEEL.

fe·male /ˈfēˌmāl/ ▶ adj. **1** of the sex that can give birth to offspring or produce eggs. **2** having to do with women: *a female name.* **3** (of a plant or flower) having a pistil but no stamens. **4** (of a fitting) having a hollow so that a corresponding part can be inserted. ▶ n. a female person, animal, or plant.

fem·i·nine /ˈfemənin/ ▶ adj. **1** having qualities associated with women. **2** female. **3** Grammar (of nouns and adjectives in some languages) having a gender regarded as female.

SYNONYMS **womanly**, ladylike, soft, gentle, tender, delicate, pretty. ANTONYMS masculine.

■ **fem·i·nin·i·ty** /ˌfeməˈninətē/ n.

fem·i·nism /ˈfeməˌnizəm/ ▶ n. a movement or theory that supports the rights of women. ■ **fem·i·nist** n. & adj.

fem·i·nize /ˈfeməˌnīz/ ▶ v. (**feminizes**, **feminizing**, **feminized**) make more feminine or female.

femme fa·tale /ˌfem fəˈtal, fəˈtäl/ ▶ n. (plural **femmes fatales**) an attractive and seductive woman.

fe·mur /ˈfēmər/ ▶ n. (plural **femurs** or **femora** /ˈfemərə/) the bone of the thigh. ■ **fem·o·ral** /ˈfemərəl/ adj.

fen /fen/ ▶ n. a low and marshy or frequently flooded area of land.

fence /fens/ ▶ n. **1** a barrier made of wire or wood that encloses an area of land. **2** an obstacle for horses to jump over in a competition. **3** informal a person who buys and resells stolen goods. ▶ v. (**fences**, **fencing**, **fenced**) **1** surround or protect with a fence. **2** take part in the sport of fencing. **3** informal buy and resell stolen goods.

SYNONYMS ▶ n. **barrier**, paling, railing, enclosure, barricade, stockade. ▶ v. **1 enclose**, surround, encircle. **2 confine**, pen in, coop up, shut in/up, corral.

▫ **sit on the fence** avoid making a decision. ■ **fenc·er** n.

fenc·ing /ˈfensiɴɢ/ ▶ n. **1** the sport of fighting with blunted swords. **2** fences or material for making fences.

fend /fend/ ▶ v. **1** (**fend for yourself**) look after yourself without help from other people. **2** (**fend someone/thing off**) defend yourself from an attack or attacker.

SYNONYMS **1** (**fend for yourself**) **take care of yourself**, look after yourself, cope alone, stand on your own two feet, get by. **2** (**fend off**) **ward off**, head off, stave off, hold off, repel, repulse, resist, fight off.

fend·er /ˈfendər/ ▶ n. **1** the mudguard or area around the wheel of a vehicle. **2** a low frame around a fireplace to stop coals from falling out. **3** a soft object that is hung over the side of a ship to protect it from collisions.

feng shui /ˈfəɴɢ ˈsʜwē, -sʜwā/ ▶ n. an ancient Chinese system of designing buildings and arranging objects in rooms to achieve a good flow of energy and so bring happiness or good luck.

fen·nel /ˈfenl/ ▶ **n.** a plant whose leaves and seeds are used as an herb and whose bulb is eaten as a vegetable.

fen·u·greek /ˈfenyəˌgrēk/ ▶ **n.** a plant with aromatic seeds that are used as a spice.

fe·ral /ˈfi(ə)rəl, ˈferəl/ ▶ **adj.** **1** (of an animal) wild, especially after having been tame or kept as a pet. **2** savage or fierce.

fer·ment ▶ **v.** /fərˈment/ **1** undergo a chemical change by the action of yeast or bacteria. **2** stir up disorder. ▶ **n.** /ˈfərment/ a state of widespread unrest or excitement. ■ **fer·men·ta·tion** /ˌfərmənˈtāsʜən/ **n.**

fern /fərn/ ▶ **n.** (plural **fern** or **ferns**) a plant that has feathery fronds and no flowers.

fe·ro·cious /fəˈrōsʜəs/ ▶ **adj.** very fierce or violent.

> SYNONYMS **1** *ferocious animals* **fierce**, savage, wild, predatory, ravening, aggressive, dangerous. **2** *a ferocious attack* **brutal**, vicious, violent, bloody, barbaric, savage, frenzied. ANTONYMS gentle, mild.

■ **fe·ro·cious·ly adv.**

fe·roc·i·ty /fəˈräsətē/ ▶ **n.** the state of being ferocious.

fer·ret /ˈferət/ ▶ **n.** a small, fierce animal with a long thin body, used for catching rabbits. ▶ **v.** (**ferrets**, **ferreting**, **ferreted**) **1** search among a lot of things. **2** (**ferret something out**) discover something by searching thoroughly. **3** (**ferreting**) hunting with ferrets.

fer·ric /ˈferik/ ▶ **adj.** Chemistry relating to iron with a valence of three.

Fer·ris wheel /ˈferis/ ▶ **n.** a fairground ride consisting of a large upright revolving wheel.

fer·rous /ˈferəs/ ▶ **adj.** (of a metal) containing iron.

fer·rule /ˈferəl/ ▶ **n.** a metal cap that protects the end of a stick or umbrella.

fer·ry /ˈferē/ ▶ **n.** (plural **ferries**) a boat or ship that transports passengers and goods as a regular service. ▶ **v.** (**ferries**, **ferrying**, **ferried**) carry by ferry or other transport.

> SYNONYMS ▶ **v.** **transport**, convey, carry, run, ship, shuttle.

fer·tile /ˈfərtl/ ▶ **adj.** **1** (of soil or land) producing a lot of plants or crops. **2** (of a person, animal, or plant) able to produce offspring or seeds. **3** producing a lot of good results or ideas: *a fertile debate*.

> SYNONYMS **1 productive**, fruitful, fecund, rich, lush. **2 creative**, inventive, innovative, visionary, original, ingenious, prolific. ANTONYMS barren.

■ **fer·til·i·ty** /fərˈtilitē/ **n.**

fer·ti·lize /ˈfərtlˌīz/ ▶ **v.** (**fertilizes**, **fertilizing**, **fertilized**) **1** introduce sperm or pollen into an egg or plant so that a new individual develops. **2** add fertilizer to soil to make it more productive. ■ **fer·til·i·za·tion** /ˌfərtl-iˈzāsʜən/ **n.**

fer·ti·liz·er /ˈfərtlˌīzər/ ▶ **n.** a chemical or natural substance added to soil to make it more fertile.

> SYNONYMS **plant food**, dressing, manure, muck, guano, compost.

fer·vent /ˈfərvənt/ ▶ **adj.** showing strong or passionate feeling.

> SYNONYMS **impassioned**, passionate, intense, vehement, ardent, sincere, heartfelt, enthusiastic, zealous, fanatical, wholehearted, avid, eager, keen, committed, dedicated, devout. ANTONYMS apathetic.

■ **fer·vent·ly adv.**

fer·vid /ˈfərvid/ ▶ **adj.** fervent.

fer·vor /ˈfərvər/ ▶ **n.** strong or passionate feeling.

> SYNONYMS **passion**, ardor, intensity, zeal, vehemence, emotion, warmth, avidity, eagerness, keenness, enthusiasm, excitement, animation, vigor, energy, fire, spirit. ANTONYMS apathy.

fes·tal /ˈfestəl/ ▶ **adj.** relating to a festival.

fes·ter /ˈfestər/ ▶ **v.** (**festers**, **festering**, **festered**) **1** (of a wound or sore) become septic. **2** become rotten. **3** become worse or more strongly felt: *tensions began to fester between Rose and Nick*.

fes·ti·val /ˈfestəvəl/ ▶ **n.** **1** a time when people celebrate a special occasion. **2** an organized series of concerts, movies, etc.: *the Sundance Film Festival*.

> SYNONYMS **celebration**, festivity, fete, fair, gala, carnival, fiesta, jamboree, feast day, holiday, holy day.

fes·tive /ˈfestiv/ ▶ **adj.** relating to a period of celebration: *the festive season*.

> SYNONYMS **jolly**, merry, joyous, joyful, happy, jovial, lighthearted, cheerful, jubilant, celebratory.

fes·tiv·i·ty /feˈstivətē/ ▶ **n.** (plural **festivities**) **1** joyful celebration. **2** (**festivities**) activities or events celebrating a special occasion.

fes·toon /fesˈto͞on/ ▶ **v.** decorate with chains of flowers, ribbons, etc. ▶ **n.** a decorative chain of flowers, ribbons, etc.

> SYNONYMS ▶ **v.** **decorate**, adorn, ornament, trim, deck (out), hang, drape, swathe, garland, wreathe, bedeck; informal do up/out, get up.

fet·a /ˈfetə/ ▶ **n.** a salty Greek cheese made from the milk of sheep or goats.

fe·tal /ˈfētl/ ▶ **adj.** relating to a fetus.

fetch /fecʜ/ ▶ **v.** **1** go for something and bring it back. **2** be sold for a particular price. **3** (**fetching**) attractive.

> SYNONYMS **1 go and get**, go for, call for, summon, pick up, collect, bring, carry, convey, transport. **2 sell for**, bring in, raise, realize, yield, make, command; informal go for. **3** (**fetching**) **attractive**, appealing, sweet, pretty, lovely, delightful, charming, captivating, enchanting, cute.

fete /fāt, fet/ (or **fête**) ▶ **n.** a celebration or festival. ▶ **v.** (**fetes**, **feting**, **feted**) praise or entertain someone lavishly.

fet·id /ˈfetid/ ▶ **adj.** smelling very unpleasant.

fet·ish /ˈfetisʜ/ ▶ **n.** an object worshiped for its supposed magical powers.

fet·lock /ˈfetˌläk/ ▶ **n.** a joint of a horse's leg between the knee and the hoof.

fe·tor /ˈfētər/ ▶ **n.** a strong, foul smell.

fet·ter /ˈfetər/ ▶ **v.** (**fetters**, **fettering**, **fettered**) **1** limit the freedom of. **2** restrain with chains or shackles. ▶ **n.** **1** (**fetters**) restraints or controls. **2** a chain placed around a prisoner's ankles.

fet·tle /ˈfetl/ ▶ **n.** physical, mental, or emotional condition: *the mare is in fine fettle*.

fet·tuc·ci·ne /ˌfetəˈCHēnē/ ▸ pl.n. pasta made in long flat strips.

fe·tus /ˈfētəs/ ▸ n. (plural **fetuses**) an unborn baby of a mammal.

feud /fyo͞od/ ▸ n. a long and bitter dispute. ▸ v. take part in a feud.

> SYNONYMS ▸ n. **vendetta**, conflict, quarrel, row, rivalry, hostility, strife. ▸ v. **quarrel**, fight, clash, argue, squabble, dispute.

feu·dal /ˈfyo͞odl/ ▸ adj. having to do with feudalism.

feu·dal·ism /ˈfyo͞odlˌizəm/ ▸ n. the social system in medieval Europe, in which people worked and fought for a nobleman in return for land.

fe·ver /ˈfēvər/ ▸ n. **1** an abnormally high body temperature. **2** a state of nervous excitement.

> SYNONYMS **1 feverishness**, high temperature; Medicine pyrexia; informal temperature. **2 excitement**, mania, frenzy, agitation, passion.

□ **fever pitch** a state of extreme excitement.

fe·vered /ˈfēvərd/ ▸ adj. **1** having a fever. **2** nervously excited: *my fevered imagination*.

fe·ver·few /ˈfēvərˌfyo͞o/ ▸ n. an aromatic plant with daisylike flowers, used as an herbal remedy for headaches.

fe·ver·ish /ˈfēvərisH/ ▸ adj. **1** having or showing the symptoms of a fever. **2** very excited or energetic: *the next couple of weeks were spent in a whirl of feverish activity*.

> SYNONYMS **1 febrile**, fevered, hot, burning. **2 frenzied**, frenetic, hectic, agitated, excited, restless, nervous, worked up, overwrought, frantic, furious, hysterical, wild, uncontrolled, unrestrained.

■ **fe·ver·ish·ly** adv.

few /fyo͞o/ ▸ determiner pron. & adj. **1** (**a few**) a small number of; some. **2** not many: *he had few friends*. ▸ n. (**the few**) a select minority.

> SYNONYMS ▸ determiner pron. & adj. **not many**, hardly any, scarcely any, a small number of, a handful of, a couple of, one or two. ANTONYMS many.

□ **few and far between** scarce. **not a few** a considerable number. **quite a few** a fairly large number.

> USAGE
>
> Make sure you distinguish between **fewer** and **less**. Use **fewer** with plural nouns, as in *there were fewer tourists this year*; use **less** with nouns referring to things that can't be counted, as in *there is less moss on this tree*. It's wrong to use **less** with a plural noun (as in *there were less tourists*).

fey /fā/ ▸ adj. **1** seeming vague or mysterious and unaware of the realities of life. **2** able to see into the future.

fez /fez/ ▸ n. (plural **fezzes**) a conical red hat with a flat top, worn by men in some Muslim countries.

ff. ▸ abbr. following pages.

fi·an·cé /ˌfēˌänˈsā, fēˈänsā/ ▸ n. (feminine **fiancée**) a person to whom you are engaged to be married.

fi·as·co /fēˈaskō/ ▸ n. (plural **fiascos**) a ridiculous or humiliating failure.

> SYNONYMS **failure**, disaster, catastrophe, debacle, farce, mess; informal flop, washout, shambles. ANTONYMS success.

fi·at /ˈfēət, ˈfēˌät/ ▸ n. an official order.

fib /fib/ ▸ n. a trivial lie. ▸ v. (**fibs**, **fibbing**, **fibbed**) tell a fib. ■ **fib·ber** n.

fi·ber /ˈfībər/ ▸ n. **1** each of the thin threads that form plant or animal tissue, cloth, or minerals. **2** a material made from fibers. **3** the part of some foods that is difficult to digest and that helps food to pass through the body. **4** strength of character: *he's lacking in moral fiber*.

> SYNONYMS **thread**, strand, filament, wisp, yarn.

□ **fiber optics** the use of glass fibers to send information in the form of light. ■ **fi·brous** /ˈfībrəs/ adj.

fiber·board /ˈfībərˌbôrd/ ▸ n. a building material made of compressed wood fibers.

fi·ber·glass /ˈfībərˌglas/ ▸ n. **1** a strong plastic material containing glass fibers. **2** a material made from woven glass fibers.

Fi·bo·nac·ci se·ries /ˌfēbəˈnäCHē ˈsi(ə)rēz/ ▸ n. Math a series of numbers in which each number (**Fibonacci number**) is the sum of the two preceding numbers (e.g., the series 1, 1, 2, 3, 5, 8, etc.).

fi·bril /ˈfībrəl, ˈfib-/ ▸ n. technical a small or slender fiber.

fi·brin /ˈfībrən/ ▸ n. an insoluble protein formed as a fibrous mesh during the clotting of blood.

fi·broid /ˈfīˌbroid/ ▸ adj. relating to fibers or fibrous tissue. ▸ n. a non-cancerous tumor of fibrous tissues, developing in the womb.

fi·bro·sis /fīˈbrōsəs/ ▸ n. Medicine the thickening and scarring of connective tissue, as a result of injury.

fib·u·la /ˈfibyələ/ ▸ n. (plural **fibulae** /-ˌlē, -ˌlī/ or **fibulas**) the outer of the two bones between the knee and the ankle.

fick·le /ˈfikəl/ ▸ adj. changeable in your loyalties.

> SYNONYMS **capricious**, flighty, giddy, changeable, volatile, mercurial, erratic, unpredictable, unreliable, unsteady. ANTONYMS constant.

fic·tion /ˈfiksHən/ ▸ n. **1** literature describing imaginary events and people. **2** something that is invented and not true.

> SYNONYMS **1 novels**, stories, literature, creative writing. **2 fabrication**, invention, lie, fib, tall tale, untruth, falsehood, fantasy, nonsense. ANTONYMS fact.

fic·tion·al /ˈfiksHənl/ ▸ adj. relating to fiction.

fic·tion·al·ize /ˈfiksHənəˌlīz/ ▸ v. (**fictionalizes**, **fictionalizing**, **fictionalized**) make into a fictional story.

fic·ti·tious /fikˈtisHəs/ ▸ adj. imaginary or invented; not real.

> SYNONYMS **false**, fake, fabricated, bogus, spurious, assumed, affected, adopted, invented, concocted, made up; informal pretend, phony. ANTONYMS genuine.

fid·dle /ˈfidl/ ▸ n. informal **1** a violin. **2** something done dishonestly in order to obtain money. ▸ v. (**fiddles**, **fiddling**, **fiddled**) **1** touch or move something restlessly or nervously. **2** informal change the details of something dishonestly: *everyone is fiddling their expenses*. **3** (**fiddle about** or **around**) pass time aimlessly without achieving anything.

> SYNONYMS ▸ v. **1 fidget**, play, toy, finger, handle. **2 adjust**, tinker, play (about/around),

fool about/around, meddle, interfere, tamper; informal tweak, mess about/around. **3 falsify**, manipulate, massage, rig, distort, misrepresent, doctor, tamper with, interfere with; informal fix, cook (the books).

□ **fit as a fiddle** in very good health. **play second fiddle** take a less important role.

fid·dler /ˈfidlər/ ▶ **n.** informal a person who plays the violin. □ **fiddler crab** a small amphibious crab, the males of which have one greatly enlarged claw.

fid·dle·sticks /ˈfidlˌstiks/ ▶ **exclam.** informal nonsense.

fi·del·i·ty /fəˈdelətē/ ▶ **n. 1** faithfulness to a person or belief. **2** the accuracy with which something is copied or reproduced.

SYNONYMS **1 faithfulness**, loyalty, constancy, allegiance, commitment, devotion. **2 accuracy**, exactness, precision, correctness, strictness, closeness, authenticity. ANTONYMS disloyalty.

fidg·et /ˈfijit/ ▶ **v.** (**fidgets**, **fidgeting**, **fidgeted**) make small movements because you are nervous or impatient. ▶ **n. 1** a person who fidgets. **2** (**fidgets**) restlessness.

SYNONYMS ▶ **v. 1 wriggle**, squirm, twitch, jiggle, shuffle, be agitated; informal be jittery. **2 play**, fuss, toy, twiddle, fool about/around; informal fiddle, mess about/around.

fidg·et·y /ˈfijitē/ ▶ **adj.** inclined to fidget; uneasy or restless.

SYNONYMS **restless**, restive, on edge, uneasy, nervous, nervy, keyed up, anxious, agitated; informal jittery, twitchy.

fief /fēf/ ▶ **n.** historical a piece of land held under the feudal system. ■ **fief·dom n.**

field /fēld/ ▶ **n. 1** an enclosed area of land for growing crops or keeping animals. **2** a piece of land used for a sport or game. **3** a subject of study or area of activity. **4** an area within that a force has an effect: *a magnetic field*. **5** (**the field**) all the people taking part in a contest or sport. ▶ **v. 1** Baseball & Cricket attempt to catch or stop the ball after it has been hit. **2** try to deal with something: *we frantically fielded phone calls*. **3** choose someone to play in a game or to stand in an election.

SYNONYMS ▶ **n. 1 meadow**, pasture, paddock, grassland; literary lea, mead, greensward. **2 playing field**, ground, sports field; ballpark, soccer field. **3 area**, sphere, discipline, province, department, domain, territory, branch, subject. **4 scope**, range, sweep, reach, extent. **5 competitors**, entrants, competition, applicants, candidates, runners. ▶ **v. 1 catch**, stop, retrieve, return, throw back. **2 deal with**, handle, cope with, answer, reply to, respond to.

□ **field day** a good opportunity to do something. **field goal 1** Football a goal scored by a kick. **2** Basketball a goal scored during regular play. **field marshal** the highest rank of officer in the British and other armies. **field mouse** a common dark brown mouse with a long tail and large eyes. **field sports** hunting, shooting, and fishing. **field test** (or **trial**) a test carried out in the environment in which a product is to be used. **field-test** subject to a field test. **in the field 1** (of troops) engaged in combat or maneuvers. **2** engaged in practical work in the natural environment. **play the field** informal have a series of casual romantic relationships.

field·er /ˈfēldər/ ▶ **n.** Baseball & Cricket a player who occupies a defensive position in the field while the other side is batting.

field·fare /ˈfēldˌfe(ə)r/ ▶ **n.** a large Eurasian thrush with a gray head.

field·work /ˈfēldˌwərk/ ▶ **n.** practical work conducted by a researcher in the field.

fiend /fēnd/ ▶ **n. 1** an evil spirit. **2** a very wicked or cruel person. **3** informal a person who is very enthusiastic about something: *an exercise fiend*.

fiend·ish /ˈfēndisʜ/ ▶ **adj. 1** very cruel or unpleasant. **2** informal very difficult.

SYNONYMS **1 wicked**, cruel, vicious, evil, malevolent, villainous, brutal, savage, barbaric, barbarous, inhuman, murderous, ruthless, merciless. **2 cunning**, clever, ingenious, crafty, canny, wily, devious. **3 difficult**, complex, challenging, complicated, intricate.

■ **fiend·ish·ly adv.**

fierce /fi(ə)rs/ ▶ **adj. 1** violent or aggressive. **2** strong or powerful: *fierce opposition*.

SYNONYMS **1 ferocious**, savage, vicious, aggressive. **2 aggressive**, cutthroat, keen, intense, strong, relentless, dog-eat-dog. **3 intense**, powerful, vehement, passionate, impassioned, fervent, ardent. **4 powerful**, strong, violent, forceful, stormy, howling, raging, tempestuous. ANTONYMS gentle, mild.

■ **fierce·ly adv.**

SPELLING

Write **i** before **e**, when the sound is *ee*, except after **c**: fierce.

fier·y /ˈfī(ə)rē/ ▶ **adj.** (**fierier**, **fieriest**) **1** consisting of or resembling fire. **2** quick-tempered or passionate.

SYNONYMS **1 burning**, blazing, on fire, flaming, ablaze. **2 bright**, brilliant, vivid, intense, rich. **3 passionate**, impassioned, excitable, spirited, quick-tempered, volatile, explosive, impetuous.

fi·es·ta /fēˈestə/ ▶ **n.** (in Spanish-speaking countries) a religious festival.

fife /fīf/ ▶ **n.** a small, high-pitched flute used especially with the drum in military bands.

fif·teen /fifˈtēn, ˈfifˌtēn/ ▶ **cardinal number** one more than fourteen; 15. (Roman numeral: **xv** or **XV**) ■ **fif·teenth ordinal number.**

fifth /fi(f)ᴛʜ/ ▶ **ordinal number 1** being number five in a sequence; 5th. **2** (**a fifth** or **one fifth**) each of five equal parts of something. □ **fifth column** a group within a country at war who are working for its enemies. **take** (or **plead**) **the Fifth** exercise the right guaranteed by the Fifth Amendment to the Constitution to refuse to answer questions in order to avoid incriminating yourself.

fif·ty /ˈfiftē/ ▶ **cardinal number** (plural **fifties**) ten less than sixty; 50. (Roman numeral: **l** or **L**) □ **fifty-fifty** with equal shares or chances. ■ **fif·ti·eth ordinal number.**

fig /fig/ ▶ **n.** a soft, sweet fruit with many small seeds. □ **not give** (or **care**) **a fig** not care at all.

fight /fīt/ ▶ **v.** (**fights**, **fighting**, **fought** /fôt/) **1** take part in a violent struggle involving physical force. **2** (**fight someone off**) defend yourself against an attacker. **3** struggle to overcome or prevent: *she fought racial discrimination*. ▶ **n.** a period of fighting.

SYNONYMS ▶ **v. 1 brawl**, exchange blows, scuffle, grapple, wrestle, tussle, spar; informal scrap, rough-house. **2 do battle**, serve your country, go to war, take up arms, engage, meet, clash, skirmish. **3 wage**, engage in, conduct, prosecute, undertake. **4 quarrel**, argue, bicker, squabble, fall out, feud, wrangle; informal scrap. **5 campaign**, strive, battle, struggle, crusade, agitate, lobby, push, press. **6 oppose**, contest, confront, challenge, appeal against, take a stand against, dispute, resist. **7 repress**, restrain, suppress, stifle, smother, hold back, fight back, keep in check, curb, choke back; informal keep the lid on. ▶ **n. 1 brawl**, scuffle, disturbance, fisticuffs, fracas, melee, skirmish, clash, tussle; informal scrap, free-for-all, dust-up; dated affray. **2 boxing match**, bout, match, contest. **3 battle**, engagement, conflict, struggle, war, campaign, crusade, action, hostilities. **4 argument**, quarrel, squabble, wrangle, disagreement, falling-out, dispute, feud; informal tiff, spat, scrap. **5 struggle**, battle, campaign, push, effort. **6 will**, resistance, spirit, pluck, grit, strength, backbone, determination, resolution, resolve.

□ **fighting chance** a possibility of succeeding if you make an effort. **fight your way** move forward with difficulty.

fight·er /ˈfītər/ ▶ **n. 1** a person or animal that fights. **2** a fast military aircraft designed for attacking other aircraft.

SYNONYMS **1 soldier**, fighting man/woman, warrior, combatant, serviceman, servicewoman; (**fighters**) troops, personnel, militia. **2 boxer**, pugilist, prizefighter, wrestler.

fig·ment /ˈfigmənt/ ▶ **n.** a thing that exists only in the imagination.

fig·ur·a·tive /ˈfigyərətiv/ ▶ **adj. 1** not using words in their literal sense; metaphorical. **2** (of art) representing things as they appear in real life.

SYNONYMS **metaphorical**, nonliteral, symbolic, allegorical, representative, emblematic. ANTONYMS literal.

■ **fig·ur·a·tive·ly adv.**

fig·ure /ˈfigyər/ ▶ **n. 1** a number or numerical symbol. **2** the shape of a person's body, especially that of a woman. **3** an important or distinctive person: *senior figures in politics*. **4** a shape defined by one or more lines. **5** a diagram or drawing. ▶ **v.** (**figures**, **figuring**, **figured**) **1** play a significant part: *nuclear policy figured prominently in the talks*. **2** (**figure something out**) informal understand something. **3** informal think; consider. **4** calculate by arithmetic.

SYNONYMS ▶ **n. 1 statistic**, number, quantity, amount, level, total, sum; (**figures**) data, statistics. **2 digit**, numeral, character, symbol. **3 price**, cost, amount, value, valuation. **4 shape**, outline, form, silhouette, proportions, physique, build, frame. **5 person**, personage, individual, character, personality, celebrity. **6 shape**, pattern, design, motif. **7 diagram**, illustration, drawing, picture, plate. ▶ **v.** *he figures in many myths* **feature**, appear, be featured, be mentioned, be referred to.

□ **figure of speech** a word or phrase used in a way different from its usual sense. **figure skating** ice skating in set patterns.

fig·ure·head /ˈfigyərˌhed/ ▶ **n. 1** a leader without real power. **2** a wooden statue of a person at the front of a sailing ship.

fig·ur·ine /ˌfigyəˈrēn/ ▶ **n.** a small statue of a human form.

Fi·ji·an /ˌfējēən, fiˈjēən/ ▶ **n.** a person from Fiji, a country in the South Pacific. ▶ **adj.** relating to Fiji.

fil·a·ment /ˈfiləmənt/ ▶ **n. 1** a long, thin threadlike piece of something. **2** a metal wire in a light bulb, which glows when an electric current is passed through it.

fil·bert /ˈfilbərt/ ▶ **n.** a type of hazelnut.

filch /filCH/ ▶ **v.** informal steal something.

file[1] /fīl/ ▶ **n. 1** a folder or box for keeping loose papers together. **2** a collection of computer data stored under a single name. **3** a line of people or things one behind another. ▶ **v.** (**files**, **filing**, **filed**) **1** place in a file. **2** officially present a legal document, application, etc., so that it can be dealt with. **3** walk one behind the other.

SYNONYMS ▶ **n. 1 folder**, portfolio, binder. **2 dossier**, document, record, report, data, information, documentation, archives. **3 line**, column, row, queue, string, chain, procession. ▶ **v. 1 categorize**, classify, organize, put in order, order, arrange, catalog, store, archive. **2 bring**, press, lodge. **3 walk in a line**, queue, march, parade, troop.

file[2] ▶ **n.** a tool with a roughened surface, used for smoothing or shaping. ▶ **v.** (**files**, **filing**, **filed**) smooth or shape with a file.

SYNONYMS ▶ **v. smooth**, buff, rub down, polish, shape, scrape, abrade, rasp, manicure.

fil·i·al /ˈfilēəl, ˈfilyəl/ ▶ **adj.** having to do with a son or daughter.

fil·i·bus·ter /ˈfiləˌbəstər/ ▶ **n.** (in Congress or another legislative body) a very long speech made to prevent the passing of a new law.

fil·i·gree /ˈfiləˌgrē/ ▶ **n.** delicate ornamental work of thin wire.

fil·ings /ˈfīliNGz/ ▶ **pl.n.** small particles rubbed off by a file.

Fil·i·pi·no /ˌfiləˈpēnō/ ▶ **n.** (plural **Filipinos**; feminine **Filipina**, plural **Filipinas**) **1** a person from the Philippines. **2** the national language of the Philippines. ▶ **adj.** relating to the Philippines or to Filipinos.

fill /fil/ ▶ **v. 1** make or become full. **2** block up a hole or gap. **3** appoint a person to a vacant post. **4** hold a particular position or role. ▶ **n.** (**your fill**) as much as you want or can bear.

SYNONYMS ▶ **v. 1 fill up**, top off, charge. **2 crowd into**, throng, pack (into), occupy, squeeze into, cram (into). **3 stock**, pack, load, supply, replenish. **4 block up**, stop (up), plug, seal, caulk. **5 pervade**, permeate, suffuse, penetrate, infuse. **6 occupy**, hold, take up. ANTONYMS empty, clear, leave.

□ **fill in** act as a substitute. **fill something in 1** complete a form. **2** make a hole completely full of material. **fill someone in** give someone information. **fill out** put on weight.

fill·er /ˈfilər/ ▶ **n.** something used to fill a hole or gap, or to increase bulk.

fil·let /ˈfilit/ ▶ **n. 1** (or **filet** /fiˈlā, ˈfilā/) a piece of meat without bones. **2** a piece of fish with the bones taken out. **3** a decorative band or ribbon worn around the head. ▶ **v.** (**fillets**, **filleting**, **filleted**) take the bones out of a piece of fish.

fill·ing /ˈfiliNG/ ▶ **n.** a quantity or piece of material used to fill something. ▶ **adj.** (of food) giving you a pleasantly full feeling.

SYNONYMS ▶ n. **stuffing**, padding, wadding, filler, contents. ▶ adj. **substantial**, hearty, ample, satisfying, square, heavy, stodgy.

▫ **filling station** a gas station.

fil·lip /ˈfiləp/ ▶ n. a stimulus or boost.

fil·ly /ˈfilē/ ▶ n. (plural **fillies**) **1** a young female horse. **2** dated, humorous a lively girl or young woman.

film /film/ ▶ n. **1** a thin flexible strip coated with light-sensitive material, used in a camera to make photographs or motion pictures. **2** a story or event recorded by a camera and shown in a movie theater or on television. **3** material in the form of a very thin flexible sheet. **4** a thin layer of something on a surface. ▶ v. make a movie of; record on film.

SYNONYMS ▶ n. **1 movie**, picture, feature film, motion picture, video, DVD. **2 movies**, cinema, pictures, films, the motion picture industry, the silver screen, the big screen. **3 layer**, coat, coating, covering, cover, skin, patina, tissue. ▶ v. **1 photograph**, record on film, shoot, capture on film, videotape. **2 cloud**, mist, haze, blur.

film·y /ˈfilmē/ ▶ adj. (**filmier**, **filmiest**) thin and almost transparent: *a filmy black dress.*

fil·ter /ˈfiltər/ ▶ n. **1** a device or substance that lets liquid or gas pass through but holds back solid particles. **2** a screen, plate, or layer that absorbs some of the light passing through it. ▶ v. (**filters**, **filtering**, **filtered**) **1** pass through a filter. **2** move gradually in or out of somewhere: *people filtered out of the concert.*

SYNONYMS ▶ n. **strainer**, sifter, sieve, gauze, mesh, net. ▶ v. **1 sieve**, strain, sift, clarify, purify, refine, treat. **2 seep**, percolate, leak, trickle, ooze, leach.

▫ **filter tip** a filter attached to a cigarette that traps impurities from the smoke.

filth /filTH/ ▶ n. **1** disgusting dirt. **2** obscene and offensive language or material.

SYNONYMS **dirt**, muck, grime, mud, sludge, slime, excrement, excreta, ordure, sewage, pollution.

filth·y /ˈfilTHē/ ▶ adj. (**filthier**, **filthiest**) **1** disgustingly dirty. **2** obscene and offensive.

SYNONYMS **1 dirty**, mucky, grimy, foul, squalid, sordid, soiled, stained, polluted, contaminated, unwashed. **2 obscene**, rude, vulgar, dirty, smutty, improper, coarse, bawdy, lewd; informal blue. ANTONYMS clean, pleasant.

fil·trate /ˈfilˌtrāt/ ▶ n. a liquid that has passed through a filter.

fil·tra·tion /filˈtrāSHən/ ▶ n. the action of passing something through a filter.

fin /fin/ ▶ n. **1** a flattened projection on the body of a fish or whale, used for swimming and balancing. **2** an underwater swimmer's flipper. **3** a projection on an aircraft, rocket, or automobile for making it more stable.

fi·nal /ˈfīnl/ ▶ adj. **1** coming at the end; last. **2** allowing no further doubt or dispute: *the decision of the judges is final.* ▶ n. **1** the last game in a tournament, which will decide the overall winner. **2** (**finals**) a series of exams at the end of a degree course.

SYNONYMS ▶ adj. **1 last**, closing, concluding, finishing, end, ultimate, eventual. **2 irrevocable**, unalterable, absolute, conclusive, irrefutable, incontrovertible, indisputable, unchallengeable, binding. ANTONYMS first, provisional.

fi·na·le /fəˈnalē, -ˈnälē/ ▶ n. the last part of a piece of music or entertainment.

SYNONYMS **climax**, culmination, end, ending, finish, close, conclusion, termination, denouement. ANTONYMS opening.

fi·nal·ist /ˈfīnl-ist/ ▶ n. a person or team competing in a final.

fi·nal·i·ty /fīˈnalətē, fi-/ ▶ n. the fact or quality of being final.

fi·nal·ize /ˈfīnlˌīz/ ▶ v. (**finalizes**, **finalizing**, **finalized**) complete or agree on the last part of a plan, agreement, etc.

fi·nal·ly /ˈfīn(ə)lē/ ▶ adv. **1** after a long time and much difficulty or delay. **2** as a final point in a series.

SYNONYMS **1 eventually**, ultimately, in the end, at (long) last, in the long run, in the fullness of time, when all is said and done. **2 lastly**, last, in conclusion. **3 conclusively**, irrevocably, decisively, definitively, for ever, for good, once and for all.

fi·nance /ˈfīnans, fəˈnans/ ▶ n. **1** the management of large amounts of money by governments or large companies. **2** money to support an enterprise. **3** (**finances**) the money held by a state, organization, or person. ▶ v. (**finances**, **financing**, **financed**) provide funding for.

SYNONYMS ▶ n. **1 financial affairs**, money matters, economics, commerce, business, investment. **2 funds**, money, capital, cash, resources, assets, reserves, funding. ▶ v. **fund**, pay for, back, capitalize, endow, subsidize, invest in, sponsor; informal bankroll.

fi·nan·cial /fəˈnanCHəl, fī-/ ▶ adj. relating to finance.

SYNONYMS **monetary**, money, economic, pecuniary, fiscal, banking, commercial, business, investment.

▪ **fi·nan·cial·ly** adv.

fin·an·cier /ˌfinənˈsi(ə)r, fəˈnanˌsi(ə)r/ ▶ n. a person who manages money for large organizations.

finch /finCH/ ▶ n. a small bird with a short, stubby bill.

find /fīnd/ ▶ v. (**finds**, **finding**, **found** /found/) **1** discover by chance or by searching. **2** discover that something is the case: *she found that all the rumors were true.* **3** work out or confirm by research or calculation. **4** (of a court of law) officially declare that a defendant is guilty or not guilty, or for one side or the other in a civil case: *he was found guilty of speeding.* ▶ n. a valuable or interesting discovery.

SYNONYMS ▶ v. **1 locate**, spot, pinpoint, unearth, obtain, search out, track down, root out, come across/upon, run across/into, chance on, happen on, stumble on, encounter; informal bump into. **2 discover**, invent, come up with, hit on. **3 realize**, become aware, discover, observe, notice, note, learn. **4 consider**, think, feel to be, look on as, view as, see as, judge, deem, regard as. **5 judge**, deem, rule, declare, pronounce. ANTONYMS lose. ▶ n. **1 discovery**, acquisition. **2 bargain**, godsend, boon, catch, asset; informal good buy.

□ **find someone/something out** **1** discover information. **2** discover that someone has lied or been dishonest.

find·er /ˈfīndər/ ▶ **n.** a person who finds someone or something. □ **finders keepers** (**losers weepers**) informal used to say that whoever finds something by chance is entitled to keep it.

find·ing /ˈfīndiNG/ ▶ **n.** a conclusion reached as a result of an inquiry or trial.

fine[1] /fīn/ ▶ **adj.** **1** of very high quality. **2** satisfactory. **3** in good health and feeling well. **4** (of the weather) bright and clear. **5** (of a thread, strand, or hair) thin. **6** consisting of small particles: *a very fine sand*. **7** delicate or complex. **8** difficult to distinguish or describe accurately: *the ear makes fine distinctions between different noises*. ▶ **adv.** informal in a satisfactory or pleasing manner. ▶ **v.** (**fines**, **fining**, **fined**) (**fine down**) make or become thinner.

> SYNONYMS ▶ **adj.** **1** *fine wines* **good**, choice, select, excellent, first-class, first-rate, great, exceptional, outstanding, splendid, magnificent, exquisite, superb, wonderful, superlative, prime, quality, special, superior, of distinction, premium, classic, vintage; informal A1, top-notch. **2** *a fine fellow* **worthy**, admirable, praiseworthy, laudable, upright, upstanding, respectable. **3** **all right**, acceptable, suitable, good (enough), passable, satisfactory, adequate, reasonable, tolerable; informal OK, okay. **4** **healthy**, well, good, all right, (fighting) fit, thriving, in good shape/condition; informal OK, okay, in fine fettle, in the pink. **5** **fair**, dry, bright, clear, sunny, cloudless, balmy. **6** **keen**, quick, alert, sharp, razor-sharp, acute, bright, brilliant, astute, clever, intelligent. **7** **elegant**, stylish, expensive, smart, chic, fashionable, fancy, sumptuous, lavish, opulent; informal flashy. **8** **flyaway**, wispy, delicate, thin, light. **9** **sheer**, light, lightweight, thin, flimsy, diaphanous, filmy, see-through. **10** **subtle**, ultra-fine, nice, hairsplitting.

□ **fine art** art such as painting or sculpture. **fine-tune** make small adjustments to. **have something down to a fine art** achieve a high level of skill in something through experience. **not to put too fine a point on it** to speak bluntly. **with a fine-tooth comb** (or **fine-toothed comb**) with a very thorough search or examination. ■ **fine·ly** **adv.** **fine·ness** **n.**

fine[2] ▶ **n.** a sum of money that has to be paid as a punishment. ▶ **v.** (**fines**, **fining**, **fined**) make a person, company, etc., pay a fine.

> SYNONYMS ▶ **n.** **penalty**, forfeit, damages, fee, excess charge.

fin·er·y /ˈfīnərē/ ▶ **n.** fancy, colorful clothes or decoration.

fi·nesse /fəˈnes/ ▶ **n.** **1** elegant or delicate skill: *his acting showed dignity and finesse*. **2** subtle skill in handling people or situations.

fin·ger /ˈfiNGgər/ ▶ **n.** **1** each of the four long, thin parts attached to either hand (or five, if the thumb is included). **2** an object shaped like a finger. **3** an amount of alcohol in a glass equivalent to the width of a finger. ▶ **v.** (**fingers**, **fingering**, **fingered**) touch or feel with the fingers.

> SYNONYMS ▶ **n.** **digit**. ▶ **v.** **touch**, feel, handle, stroke, rub, caress, fondle, toy with, play (about/around) with, fiddle with.

□ **burn your fingers** suffer unpleasant consequences as a result of your actions. **finger bowl** a small bowl holding water for rinsing the fingers at a meal. **have a finger in the pie** be involved in a matter. **lay a finger on** touch someone with the intention of harming them. **put your finger on** identify a problem or difference.

fin·ger·board /ˈfiNGgərˌbôrd/ ▶ **n.** a flat strip on the neck of a stringed instrument, against which you press the strings.

fin·ger·ing /ˈfiNGgəriNG/ ▶ **n.** a way of using the fingers to play a musical instrument.

fin·ger·nail /ˈfiNGgərˌnāl/ ▶ **n.** the nail on the upper surface of the tip of each finger.

fin·ger·print /ˈfiNGgərˌprint/ ▶ **n.** a mark made on a surface by a person's fingertip, which can be used to identify the person. ▶ **v.** record the fingerprints of.

fin·ger·tip /ˈfiNGgərˌtip/ ▶ **n.** the tip of a finger. ▶ **adj.** using or operated by the fingers: *fingertip controls*. □ **at your fingertips** (of information) readily available.

fin·i·al /ˈfinēəl/ ▶ **n.** a decorative part at the top of a roof, wall, or other structure or object.

fin·ick·y /ˈfinikē/ ▶ **adj.** **1** fussy and hard to please. **2** excessively detailed or elaborate.

fin·ish /ˈfinisH/ ▶ **v.** **1** bring or come to an end: *they were too exhausted to finish the job*. **2** (**finish with**) have nothing more to do with. **3** reach the end of a race or other competition: *she finished first in the long jump*. **4** (**finish someone off**) kill or completely defeat someone. **5** give an article an attractive surface appearance. ▶ **n.** **1** an end or final stage. **2** the place at which a race or competition ends. **3** the way in which a manufactured article is finished.

> SYNONYMS ▶ **v.** **1** **complete**, end, conclude, close, terminate, wind up, achieve, accomplish, fulfill; informal wrap up, sew up. **2** **consume**, eat, devour, drink, finish off, polish off, use (up), exhaust, empty, drain, get through; informal down. **3** **end**, come to an end, stop, conclude, come to a close, cease. ANTONYMS start. ▶ **n.** **1** **end**, ending, completion, conclusion, close, termination, finale, denouement. **2** **surface**, texture, coating, covering, lacquer, glaze, veneer, gloss, patina, sheen, luster. ANTONYMS start.

□ **finishing school** a college where girls are taught how to behave in fashionable society. **finishing touch** a detail that completes and improves a piece of work. ■ **fin·ish·er** **n.**

fi·nite /ˈfīnīt/ ▶ **adj.** limited in size or extent: *every computer has a finite amount of memory*.

> SYNONYMS **limited**, restricted, determinate, fixed. ANTONYMS infinite.

fink /fiNGk/ ▶ **n.** informal an unpleasant or contemptible person, especially one who acts as an informant.

Finn /fin/ ▶ **n.** a person from Finland.

Finn·ish /ˈfinisH/ ▶ **n.** the language of the Finns. ▶ **adj.** relating to Finland or the Finns.

fir /fər/ ▶ **n.** an evergreen coniferous tree with needle-shaped leaves.

fire /fīr/ ▶ **n.** **1** the light, heat, and smoke produced when something burns. **2** an occasion in which a building is damaged or destroyed by a fire. **3** wood or coal that is burning for heating or cooking. **4** passionate emotion or enthusiasm. **5** critical questioning. **6** the firing of guns: *a burst* *of machine-gun fire.* ▶ v. (**fires**, **firing**, **fired**) **1** send a bullet, shell, etc., from a gun or other weapon. **2** direct a rapid series of questions or statements toward someone. **3** informal dismiss an employee from a job. **4** supply a furnace or power station with fuel. **5** stimulate: *the idea fired his imagination.* **6** bake or dry pottery or bricks in a kiln. **7** old use set fire to.

SYNONYMS ▶ n. **1 blaze**, conflagration, inferno, flames, burning, combustion. **2 dynamism**, energy, vigor, animation, vitality, exuberance, zest, elan, passion, zeal, spirit, verve, vivacity, enthusiasm; informal go, get-up-and-go, oomph. **3 gunfire**, firing, shooting, bombardment, shelling, volley, salvo, hail. ▶ v. **1 launch**, shoot, discharge, let fly (with). **2 shoot**, discharge, let off, set off. **3 dismiss**, discharge, give someone their notice, lay off, let go; informal sack. **4 stimulate**, stir up, excite, awaken, rouse, inflame, animate, inspire, motivate.

□ **catch fire** begin to burn. **fire alarm** a device making a loud noise that gives warning of a fire. **fire away** informal go ahead. **on fire 1** burning. **2** very excited. **set fire to** (or **set on fire**) cause to burn. **fire department** a team of people employed or acting as volunteers to put out fires. **fire door** a strong door for preventing the spread of fire. **fire drill** a practice of the emergency procedures to be used in case of fire. **fire engine** a vehicle carrying firefighters and their equipment. **fire escape** a staircase or ladder for escaping from a burning building. **fire extinguisher** a device that sprays a jet of liquid, foam, or gas to put out a fire. **fire station** the headquarters of a fire department. **the firing line 1** the front line of troops in a battle. **2** a situation in which you are likely to be criticized. **firing squad** a group of soldiers ordered to shoot a condemned person. **set the world on fire** do something remarkable or sensational. **under fire 1** being shot at. **2** being strongly criticized.

fire·arm /ˈfī(ə)rˌärm/ ▶ n. a rifle, pistol, or other portable gun.

fire·ball /ˈfīrˌbôl/ ▶ n. **1** a ball of flames. **2** an energetic or hot-tempered person.

fire·bomb /ˈfīrˌbäm/ ▶ n. a bomb intended to cause a fire.

fire·brand /ˈfīrˌbrand/ ▶ n. a person who passionately supports a particular cause.

fire·break /ˈfīrˌbrāk/ ▶ n. a strip of open space cleared in a forest to stop a fire from spreading.

fire·crack·er /ˈfīrˌkrakər/ ▶ n. a firework that makes a loud bang.

fire·fight·er /ˈfīrˌfītər/ ▶ n. a person whose job is to put out fires.

fire·fly /ˈfīrˌflī/ ▶ n. (plural **fireflies**) a kind of beetle that glows in the dark.

fire·guard /ˈfī(ə)rˌgärd/ ▶ n. a protective screen or grid in front of an open fire.

fire·house /ˈfīrˌhous/ ▶ n. a fire station.

fire·man /ˈfīrmən/ ▶ n. (plural **firemen**) a male firefighter.

fire·place /ˈfīrˌplās/ ▶ n. a space at the base of a chimney for lighting a fire.

fire·pow·er /ˈfīrˌpou(-ə)r/ ▶ n. the destructive capacity of guns, missiles, or armed forces.

fire·proof /ˈfīrˌpro͞of/ ▶ adj. able to withstand fire or great heat.

fire·side /ˈfīrˌsīd/ ▶ n. the part of a room around a fireplace.

fire·storm /ˈfīrˌstôrm/ ▶ n. a very fierce fire fanned by strong currents of air.

fire·trap /ˈfīrˌtrap/ ▶ n. a building that is difficult to escape from if there is a fire.

fire·wall /ˈfīrˌwôl/ ▶ n. a part of a computer system that prevents people from seeing the information stored in it unless they are authorized to do so.

fire·wa·ter /ˈfīrˌwôtər, -ˌwätər/ ▶ n. informal strong alcoholic liquor.

fire·wood /ˈfīrˌwo͝od/ ▶ n. wood that is burned as fuel.

fire·work /ˈfīrˌwərk/ ▶ n. **1** a device consisting of a small container of chemicals that produces spectacular effects and explosions when it is lit. **2** (**fireworks**) a display of fireworks. **3** (**fireworks**) an outburst of anger or a display of skill.

firm¹ /fərm/ ▶ adj. **1** not giving way under pressure. **2** solidly in place and stable. **3** having steady power or strength: *a firm grip.* **4** showing determination and strength of character. **5** fixed or definite: *she had no firm plans for the next day.* ▶ v. make firm: *equipment to firm up the upper arms.*

SYNONYMS ▶ adj. **1 hard**, solid, unyielding, resistant, compacted, compressed, dense, stiff, rigid, set. **2 secure**, stable, steady, strong, fixed, fast, tight, immovable, rooted, stationary, motionless. **3 resolute**, determined, decided, resolved, steadfast, adamant, emphatic, insistent, single-minded, wholehearted, unfaltering, unwavering, unflinching, unswerving, unbending, committed. **4 close**, good, boon, intimate, inseparable, dear, special, constant, devoted, loving, faithful, long-standing, steady, steadfast. **5 definite**, fixed, settled, decided, cut-and-dried, established, confirmed, agreed. ANTONYMS soft, unstable.

■ **firm·ly** adv. **firm·ness** n.

firm² ▶ n. a business organization.

SYNONYMS **business**, company, concern, enterprise, organization, corporation, conglomerate, office, bureau, agency, consortium; informal outfit, operation.

fir·ma·ment /ˈfərməmənt/ ▶ n. literary the heavens; the sky.

firm·ware /ˈfərmˌwer/ ▶ n. Computing permanent software programmed into a read-only memory.

first /fərst/ ▶ ordinal number **1** coming before all others in time, order, or importance. **2** before doing something else: *Do you mind if I take a shower first?* **3** informal something that has never happened or been done before: *traveling by air was a first for us.*

SYNONYMS **1 earliest**, initial, opening, introductory. **2 fundamental**, basic, rudimentary, primary, key, cardinal, central, chief, vital, essential. **3 foremost**, principal, highest, greatest, paramount, top, main, overriding, central, core; informal number-one. **4 top**, best, prime, premier, winning, champion. **5 novelty**, innovation, departure, break with tradition. ANTONYMS last.

□ **at first** at the beginning. **first aid** emergency medical help given to a sick or injured person. **first base** Baseball the base that is the first destination of a runner. **get to first base** informal succeed in the first step of an undertaking. **first class 1** the best accommodations on an airplane, train, ship, etc. **2** very good. **first-degree 1** (of burns) causing only reddening of the skin. **2** Law (of crime, especially murder) in the most serious category. **first lady** the wife of the president of the United States. **first mate** the officer second in command to the master of a merchant ship. **first officer 1** the first mate on a merchant ship. **2** the second in command to the captain on an aircraft. **first name** a name given to someone when they are born or baptized. **first-rate** very good. **of the first order** excellent or considerable of its kind. ■ **first·ly** adv.

first·born /ˈfərstˌbôrn/ ▶ n. the first child to be born to someone.

first·hand /ˈfərstˈhand/ ▶ adj. & adv. from the original source or personal experience; direct: *neither of them had any firsthand knowledge of Andean culture*.

firth /fərTH/ ▶ n. a narrow channel of the sea that runs inland.

fis·cal /ˈfiskəl/ ▶ adj. relating to the income received by a government, especially from taxes. ■ **fis·cal·ly** adv.

fish /fiSH/ ▶ n. (plural **fish** or **fishes**) **1** a cold-blooded animal with a backbone, gills, and fins, living in water. **2** the flesh of fish as food. **3** informal a person: *he's an odd fish*. ▶ v. **1** try to catch fish. **2** (**fish something out**) take something out of water or a container. **3** (**fish for**) search or feel for something hidden. **4** (**fish for**) try to get something: *fishing for compliments*.

SYNONYMS ▶ v. **1 go fishing**, angle, trawl. **2 search**, delve, look, hunt, grope, fumble, ferret, rummage.

□ **a big fish** an important person. **fishing line** a long thread of silk or nylon attached to a baited hook and used for catching fish. **fishing rod** a long, tapering rod to which a fishing line is attached. **a fish out of water** a person who feels out of place in their surroundings. **have other fish to fry** have more important things to do.

USAGE

The normal plural of **fish** is **fish**, as in *he caught two huge fish*; however, the form **fishes** is used when referring to different kinds of fish: *freshwater fishes of the Rocky Mountain streams*.

fish·er /ˈfiSHər/ ▶ n. a large North American marten.

fish·er·man /ˈfiSHərmən/ ▶ n. (plural **fishermen**) a person who catches fish for a living or as a sport.

fish·er·y /ˈfiSHərē/ ▶ n. (plural **fisheries**) a place where fish are reared for food, or caught in large quantities.

fish·mon·ger /ˈfiSHˌməNGgər, -ˌmäNGgər/ ▶ n. a person or store that sells fish for food.

fish·net /ˈfiSHˌnet/ ▶ n. an open mesh fabric resembling a fishing net.

fish·stick /ˈfiSHˌstik/ ▶ n. a small oblong piece of flaked or chopped fish coated in batter or breadcrumbs.

fish·tail /ˈfiSHˌtāl/ ▶ n. an object that is forked like a fish's tail. ▶ v. (of the back of a motor vehicle) travel with an uncontrolled side-to-side motion: *he hit the brakes, sending the car into a fishtail that carried him across the highway*.

fish·wife /ˈfiSHˌwīf/ ▶ n. (plural **fishwives** /-ˌwīvz/) a woman with a loud, coarse voice.

fish·y /ˈfiSHē/ ▶ adj. (**fishier**, **fishiest**) **1** resembling fish. **2** informal causing feelings of doubt or suspicion.

fis·sile /ˈfisəl, ˈfisˌīl/ ▶ adj. **1** able to undergo nuclear fission. **2** (of rock) easily split.

fis·sion /ˈfiSHən, ˈfiZHən/ ▶ n. **1** the action of splitting into two or more parts. **2** a reaction in which an atomic nucleus splits in two, releasing a great deal of energy. **3** reproduction by means of a cell dividing into two or more new cells.

fis·sure /ˈfiSHər/ ▶ n. a long, narrow crack.

fist /fist/ ▶ n. a person's hand when the fingers are bent in toward the palm and held there tightly. ■ **fist·ful** n.

fist·i·cuffs /ˈfistiˌkəfs/ ▶ pl.n. fighting with the fists.

fit¹ /fit/ ▶ adj. (**fitter**, **fittest**) **1** of a suitable quality, standard, or type: *the meat is fit for human consumption*. **2** in good health. ▶ v. (**fits**, **fitting**, **fitted**) **1** be the right shape and size for. **2** be able to occupy a particular position or space: *we can all fit in her car*. **3** fix into place. **4** provide with a part or attachment; equip. **5** be in harmony with; match: *the punishment should fit the crime*. **6** (**fit in**) be well-suited. ▶ n. the way in which something fits.

SYNONYMS ▶ adj. **1 suitable**, appropriate, suited, apposite, fitting, good enough, apt. **2 competent**, able, capable, ready, prepared, equipped. **3 healthy**, well, in good health, in (good) shape, in trim, in good condition, fighting fit, athletic, muscular, strapping, strong, robust, hale and hearty. ANTONYMS unsuitable, incapable. ▶ v. **1 lay**, install, put in, position, place, fix, arrange. **2 equip**, provide, supply, fit out, furnish. **3 join**, connect, piece together, attach, unite, link. **4 be appropriate to**, suit, match, correspond to, tally with, go with, accord with. **5 qualify**, prepare, make ready, train.

□ **have** (or **throw**) **a fit** informal be very surprised or angry. **in fits** informal highly amused. **see fit** consider it correct or acceptable. ■ **fit·ter** n.

fit² ▶ n. **1** a sudden attack when a person makes violent, uncontrolled movements. **2** a sudden attack of coughing, fainting, etc. **3** a sudden burst of strong feeling. ▶ v. (**fits**, **fitting**, **fitted**) have a fit or convulsion.

SYNONYMS ▶ n. **1 convulsion**, spasm, paroxysm, seizure, attack. **2 outbreak**, outburst, attack, bout, spell. **3 tantrum**, frenzy.

□ **in fits and starts** with irregular bursts of activity.

fit·ful /ˈfitfəl/ ▶ adj. not steady or continuous: *a few hours' fitful sleep*. ■ **fit·ful·ly** adv.

fit·ness /ˈfitnis/ ▶ n. **1** the condition of being physically fit and healthy. **2** the quality of being suitable to fulfill a particular role or task.

SYNONYMS **1 good health**, strength, robustness, vigor, athleticism, toughness, stamina. **2 suitability**, capability, competence, ability, aptitude, readiness, preparedness.

fit·ted /ˈfitid/ ▶ adj. made to fill a space or to cover something closely.

fit·ting /ˈfitiNG/ ▶ n. **1** a small part attached to furniture or equipment. **2** (**fittings**) items that are fixed in a building but can be removed when the owner moves. **3** a time when someone tries on an item of clothing that is being made or altered. ▶ adj. appropriate.

SYNONYMS ▶n. **1 attachment**, part, piece, component, accessory, apparatus. **2 furnishings**, furniture, fixtures, fitments, equipment. ▶adj. **apt**, appropriate, suitable, apposite, fit, proper, right, seemly, correct. ANTONYMS unsuitable.

■ **fit·ting·ly** adv.

five /fīv/ ▶cardinal number one more than four; 5. (Roman numeral: **v** or **V**) ▶n. a five-dollar bill. □ **five o'clock shadow** a slight growth of beard visible on a man's chin several hours after he has shaved.

fix /fiks/ ▶v. **1** attach or position securely. **2** mend or repair: *you've forgotten to fix the shelf.* **3** decide or settle on. **4** make arrangements for. **5** make something unchanging or permanent: *the rate of interest is fixed for five years.* **6** informal dishonestly influence the outcome of: *the mob attempted to fix the fight.* ▶n. informal **1** a difficult or awkward situation. **2** a dose of an addictive drug. **3** an act of fixing something.

SYNONYMS ▶v. **1 fasten**, attach, affix, secure, connect, couple, link, install, stick, glue, pin, nail, screw, bolt, clamp, clip. **2 lodge**, stick, embed. **3 focus**, direct, level, point, train. **4 repair**, mend, put right, get working, restore. **5 arrange**, organize, contrive, manage, engineer; informal swing, wangle. **6 arrange**, put in order, adjust, style, groom, comb, brush; informal do. **7 prepare**, cook, make, get; informal rustle up. **8 decide on**, select, choose, settle, set, arrange, establish, allot, designate, name, appoint, specify. **9 rig**, tamper with, skew, influence; informal fiddle. ▶n. **predicament**, plight, difficulty, quandary, corner, tight spot, mess; informal pickle, jam, hole, scrape, bind.

□ **be fixed for** informal be provided with: *How are you fixed for money?* **fix someone up** informal provide someone with something. **fix something up** arrange or organize something. **get a fix on** find out the position, nature, or facts of. ■ **fix·er** n.

fix·ate /'fikˌsāt/ ▶v. (**fixates**, **fixating**, **fixated**) (**fixate on** or **be fixated on**) be obsessed with.

fix·a·tion /fik'sāsʜən/ ▶n. an obsessive interest in someone or something.

SYNONYMS **obsession**, preoccupation, mania, addiction, compulsion; informal thing, bee in your bonnet.

fix·a·tive /'fiksətiv/ ▶n. a substance used to fix or protect something.

fixed /fikst/ ▶adj. **1** fastened securely in position. **2** not changing or able to be changed. **3** (of contests) with the outcome dishonestly arranged in advance: *charges of fixed games on the front pages.* **4** (**fixed for**) informal situated in terms of: *how are you fixed for cash?*

SYNONYMS **predetermined**, set, established, arranged, specified, decided, agreed, determined, confirmed, prescribed, definite, defined, explicit, precise.

fix·ings /'fiksiɴɢz/ ▶pl.n. **1** apparatus or equipment for a particular purpose. **2** the ingredients necessary to make a dish or meal: *a turkey dinner with all the fixings.*

fix·i·ty /'fiksitē/ ▶n. the state of being unchanging or permanent.

fix·ture /'fiksʜər/ ▶n. **1** a piece of equipment or furniture that is fixed in position. **2** (**fixtures**) articles attached to a house that normally remain in place when the owner moves.

fizz /fiz/ ▶v. make a hissing sound, like gas escaping in bubbles from a liquid. ▶n. the sound of fizzing or the quality of being fizzy.

SYNONYMS ▶v. **bubble**, sparkle, effervesce, froth. ▶n. **1 bubbles**, sparkle, fizziness, effervescence, gassiness, froth. **2 crackle**, buzz, hiss, white noise.

fiz·zle /'fizəl/ ▶v. (**fizzles**, **fizzling**, **fizzled**) **1** make a weak hissing sound. **2** (**fizzle out**) end or fail in a weak or disappointing way.

fizz·y /'fizē/ ▶adj. (**fizzier**, **fizziest**) (of a drink) containing bubbles of gas.

SYNONYMS **sparkling**, effervescent, carbonated, gassy, bubbly, frothy. ANTONYMS still, flat.

fjord /fē'ôrd, fyôrd/ (or **fiord**) ▶n. a long, narrow inlet of the sea between high cliffs, especially in Norway.

fl. ▶abbr. fluid.

flab /flab/ ▶n. informal excess fat on a person's body.

flab·ber·gast·ed /'flabərˌgastid/ ▶adj. informal very surprised.

flab·by /'flabē/ ▶adj. (**flabbier**, **flabbiest**) (of a part of a person's body) fat and floppy. ■ **flab·bi·ness** n.

flac·cid /'fla(k)səd/ ▶adj. soft and limp. ■ **flac·cid·i·ty** /fla(k)'sidətē/ n.

flack /flak/ ▶n. a publicity agent. ▶v. publicize or promote something or someone.

flag[1] /flag/ ▶n. a piece of cloth that is attached to a pole or rope and used as a symbol of a country or organization or as a signal. ▶v. (**flags**, **flagging**, **flagged**) **1** mark something as needing attention. **2** (**flag someone down**) signal to a driver to stop.

SYNONYMS ▶n. **banner**, standard, ensign, pennant, streamer, colors. ▶v. **indicate**, identify, point out, mark, label, tag, highlight.

□ **Flag Day** June 14, the anniversary of the adoption of the Stars and Stripes as the official US flag in 1777.

flag[2] (or **flagstone** /'flagˌstōn/) ▶n. a flat stone slab used for paving.

flag[3] ▶v. (**flags**, **flagging**, **flagged**) become tired or less enthusiastic.

SYNONYMS **1 tire**, grow tired, wilt, weaken, grow weak, droop. **2 fade**, decline, wane, ebb, diminish, decrease, lessen, dwindle. ANTONYMS revive.

flag[4] ▶n. a plant of the iris family.

flag·el·late /'flajəˌlāt/ /'flajələt, -ˌlāt/ ▶v. whip someone. ■ **flag·el·la·tion** /ˌflajə'lāsʜən/ n.

fla·gel·lum /ˌflə'jeləm/ ▶n. (plural **flagella** /-lə/) Biology a long thin projection that enables many single-celled organisms to swim.

flag·on /'flagən/ ▶n. a large bottle or jug for wine, cider, or beer.

flag·pole /'flagˌpōl/ (or **flagstaff** /'flagˌstaf/) ▶n. a pole used for flying a flag.

fla·grant /'flāgrənt/ ▶adj. very obvious and unashamed: *a flagrant violation of the law.*

SYNONYMS **blatant**, glaring, obvious, conspicuous, barefaced, shameless, brazen, undisguised.

■ **fla·grant·ly** adv.

flag·ship /ˈflagˌsHip/ ▶ **n. 1** the ship in a fleet that carries the admiral in command. **2** the best or most important thing owned or produced by an organization.

flail /flāl/ ▶ **v. 1** swing something wildly. **2** (**flail around** or **about**) move around in an uncontrolled way. ▶ **n.** a tool or machine that is swung to separate grains of wheat from the husks.

flair /fler/ ▶ **n. 1** a natural ability or talent. **2** stylishness.

SYNONYMS **1 aptitude**, talent, gift, instinct, ability, facility, knack, skill. **2 style**, elegance, panache, dash, elan, poise, taste; informal class.

USAGE
Don't confuse **flair** with **flare**, which means 'burn' or 'gradually become wider.'

flak /flak/ (or **flack**) ▶ **n. 1** anti-aircraft fire. **2** strong criticism.

flake /flāk/ ▶ **n.** a small, flat, very thin piece of something. ▶ **v.** (**flakes**, **flaking**, **flaked**) **1** come away from a surface in flakes. **2** separate into flakes. **3** (**flake out**) informal fall asleep or drop from exhaustion.

SYNONYMS ▶ **n. sliver**, wafer, shaving, paring, chip, fragment, scrap, shred. ▶ **v. peel** (**off**), chip, blister, come off.

flak·y /ˈflākē/ ▶ **adj.** (**flakier**, **flakiest**) **1** breaking or separating easily into flakes. **2** informal unconventional, eccentric, or undependable.
■ **flak·i·ness n.**

flam·bé /flämˈbā/ ▶ **v.** (**flambés**, **flambéing**, **flambéed**) cover food with alcohol and set it on fire briefly.

flam·boy·ant /flamˈboiənt/ ▶ **adj. 1** very confident and lively. **2** brightly colored or highly decorated.

SYNONYMS **1 ostentatious**, exuberant, confident, lively, animated, vibrant, vivacious. **2 colorful**, bright, vibrant, vivid, dazzling, bold, showy, gaudy, garish, loud; informal jazzy, flashy. ANTONYMS restrained.

■ **flam·boy·ance n. flam·boy·ant·ly adv.**

flame /flām/ ▶ **n. 1** a glowing stream of burning gas produced by something on fire. **2** a brilliant orange-red color. ▶ **v.** (**flames**, **flaming**, **flamed**) **1** give off flames. **2** set on fire. **3** (of a strong emotion) appear suddenly and fiercely. **4** informal send insulting email messages to.

SYNONYMS ▶ **n. fire**, blaze, conflagration, inferno.

□ **flame-thrower** a weapon that sprays out burning fuel. **old flame** informal a former lover.

fla·men·co /fləˈmeNGkō/ ▶ **n.** a lively style of Spanish guitar music accompanied by singing and dancing.

flam·ing /ˈflāmiNG/ ▶ **adj. 1** sending out flames. **2** very hot. **3** (of an argument) passionate. **4** informal expressing annoyance: *that flaming idiot*.

fla·min·go /fləˈmiNGgō/ ▶ **n.** (plural **flamingos** or **flamingoes**) a wading bird with mainly pink or red feathers and a long neck and legs.

flam·ma·ble /ˈflaməbəl/ ▶ **adj.** easily set on fire.

flan /flan/ ▶ **n. 1** a baked dish consisting of an open pastry case with a savory or sweet filling. **2** a baked custard with a caramel sauce.

flange /flanj/ ▶ **n.** a projecting flat rim for strengthening an object or attaching it to something.

flank /flaNGk/ ▶ **n. 1** the side of the body between the ribs and the hip. **2** the side of something such as a mountain. **3** the left or right side of a group of people. ▶ **v.** be on the side of: *the hall was flanked by two towers*.

SYNONYMS ▶ **n. 1 side**, haunch, quarter, thigh. **2 side**, wing, sector, face, aspect. ▶ **v. edge**, bound, line, border, fringe.

flan·nel /ˈflanl/ ▶ **n. 1** a kind of soft woolen or cotton fabric. **2** (**flannels**) men's trousers made of woolen flannel.

flan·nel·ette /ˌflanlˈet/ ▶ **n.** a cotton fabric resembling flannel.

flap /flap/ ▶ **v.** (**flaps**, **flapping**, **flapped**) move up and down or from side to side. ▶ **n. 1** a flat piece of paper, cloth, or metal that is attached to one side of something and covers an opening. **2** a movable section of an aircraft wing, used to control upward movement. **3** a flapping movement. **4** informal a panic.

SYNONYMS ▶ **v. 1** *ducks flapped their wings* **beat**, flutter, agitate, vibrate, wag, thrash, flail. **2** *the flag flapped in the breeze* **flutter**, wave, fly, blow, swing, ripple, stir. ▶ **n. 1 beat**, stroke, flutter, movement. **2 panic**, fluster; informal state, stew, tizzy, twit.

flap·jack /ˈflapˌjak/ ▶ **n.** a pancake.

flap·per /ˈflapər/ ▶ **n.** informal a fashionable young woman of the 1920s.

flare /fle(ə)r/ ▶ **n. 1** a sudden brief burst of flame or light. **2** a device that produces a very bright flame as a signal or marker. ▶ **v.** (**flares**, **flaring**, **flared**) **1** burn or shine suddenly and strongly. **2** (usu. **flare up**) suddenly become intense or violent: *in 1943 the Middle East crisis flared up again*. **3** gradually become wider at one end.

SYNONYMS ▶ **n. 1 blaze**, flame, flash, burst, flicker. **2 signal**, beacon, rocket, light, torch. ▶ **v. 1 blaze**, flash, flare up, flame, burn, flicker. **2 spread**, splay, broaden, widen, dilate.

USAGE
Don't confuse **flare** with **flair**, which means 'a natural ability or talent.'

flash /flasH/ ▶ **v. 1** shine with a bright but brief or irregular light. **2** move quickly: *the scenery flashed by*. **3** display words or images briefly or repeatedly. **4** informal display something in an obvious way to impress people: *they flash their money about*. ▶ **n. 1** a sudden brief burst of bright light. **2** a camera attachment that produces a flash of light, for taking photographs in bad light. **3** a sudden or brief occurrence: *a flash of inspiration*. ▶ **adj.** informal stylish or expensive in a showy way.

SYNONYMS ▶ **v. 1 shine**, flare, blaze, gleam, glint, sparkle, burn, blink, wink, flicker, shimmer, twinkle, glimmer, glisten. **2 show off**, flaunt, flourish, display, parade. **3 zoom**, streak, tear, shoot, dash, dart, fly, whistle, hurtle, rush, bolt, race, speed, careen; informal belt, barrel. ▶ **n. flare**, blaze, burst, gleam, glint, sparkle, flicker, shimmer, twinkle, glimmer.

□ **flash drive** a small removable data storage device containing flash memory. **flash flood** a sudden local flood resulting from very heavy rainfall. **flash in the pan** a sudden but brief success. **flash memory** computer memory that retains data in the absence of a power supply. **in a flash** very quickly.

flash·back /ˈflasʜˌbak/ ▶ **n.** **1** a scene in a movie or novel set in a time earlier than the main story. **2** a sudden vivid memory of a past event.

flash·bulb /ˈflasʜˌbəlb/ ▶ **n.** a bulb for a flash attachment on a camera.

flash·ing /ˈflasʜiɴɢ/ ▶ **n.** a strip of metal used to seal the join of a roof with another surface.

flash·light /ˈflasʜˌlīt/ ▶ **n.** **1** a battery-operated portable light. **2** a flashing light used for signals and in lighthouses.

flash·point /ˈflasʜˌpoint/ ▶ **n.** a point or place at which anger or violence flares up.

flash·y /ˈflasʜē/ ▶ **adj.** (**flashier**, **flashiest**) attractive in a showy or cheap way.

> SYNONYMS **ostentatious**, flamboyant, showy, conspicuous, extravagant, expensive, vulgar, tasteless, brash, garish, loud, gaudy; informal snazzy, fancy, swanky, flash, glitzy. ANTONYMS understated.

flask /flask/ ▶ **n.** **1** a bottle with a narrow neck. **2** a portable metal container for storing a small amount of liquor. **3** ⇒ **VACUUM FLASK**.

flat /flat/ ▶ **adj.** (**flatter**, **flattest**) **1** having a level and even surface. **2** not sloping; horizontal. **3** with a level surface and little height or depth. **4** not lively or interesting: *a flat voice*. **5** (of a sparkling drink) no longer fizzy. **6** (of something inflated) having lost its air. **7** (of a charge or price) fixed. **8** definite and firm: *his statement was a flat denial*. **9** (of a musical sound) below the proper pitch. **10** (of a note or key) lower by a half step than a stated note or key: *E flat*. ▶ **adv.** informal completely; absolutely: *she turned him down flat*. ▶ **n.** **1** the flat part of something. **2** (**flats**) low level ground near water. **3** (**flats**) shoes with no heels or very low heels. **4** informal a flat tire. **5** a musical note that is a half step lower than the named note, shown by the sign ♭.

> SYNONYMS ▶ **adj.** **1 level**, horizontal, smooth, even, plane. **2 calm**, still, glassy, smooth, placid, like a millpond. **3 stretched out**, prone, spread-eagled, prostrate, supine, recumbent. **4 monotonous**, toneless, lifeless, droning, boring, dull, tedious, uninteresting, unexciting. **5 inactive**, slow, sluggish, slack, quiet, depressed. **6 deflated**, punctured, burst, blown. **7 fixed**, set, invariable, regular, constant. **8 outright**, direct, absolute, definite, positive, straight, plain, explicit, categorical. ANTONYMS sloping, rough, uneven. ▶ **adv.** **stretched out**, outstretched, spread-eagled, sprawling, prone, prostrate.

□ **fall flat** fail to produce the intended effect. **flat feet** feet with arches that are lower than usual. **flat-footed 1** having flat feet. **2** informal clumsy. **flat out** as fast or as hard as possible. **flat race** a horse race over a course with no jumps. ■ **flat·ly** **adv.** **flat·ness** **n.**

flat·bed /ˈflatˌbed/ ▶ **n.** **1** a vehicle with a flat load-carrying area. **2** Computing a scanner, plotter, or other device that keeps paper flat during use.

flat·fish /ˈflatˌfisʜ/ ▶ **n.** (plural **flatfish** or **flatfishes**) a sea fish, such as sole or flounder, that has both eyes on the upper side of its flattened body.

flat·i·ron /ˈflatˌīərn/ ▶ **n.** historical an iron heated on a hotplate or fire.

flat·ten /ˈflatn/ ▶ **v.** make or become flat or flatter.

> SYNONYMS **1 level**, even out, smooth out, make/become flat. **2 squash**, compress, press down, crush, compact, trample. **3 demolish**, raze (to the ground), tear down, knock down, destroy, wreck, devastate. ANTONYMS crumple.

flat·ter /ˈflatər/ ▶ **v.** (**flatters**, **flattering**, **flattered**) **1** compliment someone too much or in an insincere way. **2** (**be flattered**) feel honored and pleased. **3** make someone appear attractive: *a green dress that flattered her fair skin*.

> SYNONYMS **1 compliment**, praise, express admiration for, fawn on, humor, wheedle; informal sweet-talk, soft-soap, butter up, play up to. **2 honor**, gratify, please, delight; informal tickle pink. **3 suit**, become, look good on, go well with; informal do something for. ANTONYMS insult, offend.

flat·ter·ing /ˈflatəriɴɢ/ ▶ **adj.** **1** full of praise and compliments. **2** pleasing or gratifying. **3** enhancing someone's appearance.

> SYNONYMS **1 complimentary**, praising, favorable, admiring, appreciative, fulsome, honeyed, obsequious, ingratiating, sycophantic. **2 pleasing**, gratifying, an honor. **3 becoming**, enhancing. ANTONYMS unflattering.

flat·ter·y /ˈflatərē/ ▶ **n.** excessive or insincere praise.

> SYNONYMS **praise**, adulation, compliments, blandishments, honeyed words, fawning; informal sweet talk, soft soap, buttering up.

flat·u·lent /ˈflacʜələnt/ ▶ **adj.** suffering from a buildup of gas in the intestines or stomach. ■ **flat·u·lence** **n.**

flat·ware /ˈflatˌwe(ə)r/ ▶ **n.** eating utensils such as knives, forks, and spoons.

flat·worm /ˈflatˌwərm/ ▶ **n.** a type of worm with a simple flattened body.

flaunt /flônt, flänt/ ▶ **v.** display proudly or obviously.

> SYNONYMS **show off**, display, make a great show of, put on show/display, parade, draw attention to, brag about, crow about, vaunt; informal flash.

> **USAGE**
>
> Don't confuse **flaunt** with **flout**, which means 'ignore a rule.'

flau·tist /ˈflôtist, ˈflou-/ ▶ **n.** ⇒ **FLUTIST**.

fla·vor /ˈflāvər/ ▶ **n.** **1** the distinctive taste of a food or drink. **2** a particular quality: *balconies gave the building a Spanish flavor*. ▶ **v.** give flavor to.

> SYNONYMS ▶ **n.** **1 taste**, savor, tang. **2 flavoring**, seasoning, taste, tang, relish, bite, piquancy, spice. **3 character**, quality, feel, feeling, ambience, atmosphere, air, mood, tone, spirit. **4 impression**, suggestion, hint, taste. ▶ **v.** **season**, spice (up), add piquancy to, ginger up, enrich, infuse.

□ **flavor of the month** a person or thing that is currently popular. ■ **fla·vor·less** **adj.**

fla·vor·ing /ˈflāvəriNG/ ▸ **n.** a substance used to add to or alter the flavor of a food or drink.

flaw /flô/ ▸ **n. 1** a mark or fault that spoils something. **2** a weakness or mistake: *there were flaws in the design.*

> SYNONYMS **defect**, blemish, fault, imperfection, deficiency, weakness, weak spot/point, failing; Computing bug; informal glitch. ANTONYMS strength.

flawed /flôd/ ▸ **adj. 1** damaged or imperfect in some way. **2** containing a mistake, weakness, or fault.

> SYNONYMS **1 faulty**, defective, unsound, imperfect, blemished, broken, cracked, scratched. **2 unsound**, distorted, inaccurate, incorrect, erroneous, fallacious, wrong. ANTONYMS flawless.

flaw·less /ˈflôləs/ ▸ **adj.** without any imperfections or defects.

> SYNONYMS **perfect**, unblemished, unmarked, unimpaired, whole, intact, sound, unbroken, undamaged, mint, pristine, impeccable, immaculate, accurate, correct, faultless, error-free, exemplary, model, ideal, copybook. ANTONYMS flawed.

flax /flaks/ ▸ **n.** a blue-flowered plant that is grown for its seed (linseed) and for its stalks, from which thread is made.

flax·en /ˈflaksən/ ▸ **adj.** literary (of hair) pale yellow.

flay /flā/ ▸ **v. 1** strip the skin from a body. **2** whip or beat very harshly.

flea /flē/ ▸ **n.** a small wingless jumping insect that feeds on the blood of mammals and birds. □ **a flea in your ear** a sharp reprimand. **flea market** a street market selling secondhand goods.

fleck /flek/ ▸ **n. 1** a very small patch of color or light. **2** a very small piece of something. ▸ **v.** mark or dot with flecks: *the towers are flecked with gold leaf.*

fled /fled/ past and past participle of **FLEE**.

fledged /flejd/ ▸ **adj.** (of a young bird) having developed wing feathers that are large enough for it to fly.

fledg·ling /ˈflejliNG/ (or **fledgeling**) ▸ **n.** a young bird that has just learned to fly.

flee /flē/ ▸ **v.** (**flees**, **fleeing**, **fled** /fled/) run away.

> SYNONYMS **run away**, run off, run for it, make off, take off, take to your heels, make a break for it, bolt, beat a (hasty) retreat, make a quick exit, escape; informal beat it, clear out/off, skedaddle, scram.

fleece /flēs/ ▸ **n. 1** the wool coat of a sheep. **2** a soft, warm fabric with a pile, or a jacket made from this. ▸ **v.** (**fleeces**, **fleecing**, **fleeced**) informal swindle someone. ■ **fleec·y adj.**

fleet¹ /flēt/ ▸ **n. 1** a group of ships traveling together. **2** a group of vehicles or aircraft with the same owner.

> SYNONYMS **navy**, naval force, (naval) task force, armada, flotilla, squadron, convoy.

fleet² ▸ **adj.** literary fast in movement.

fleet·ing /ˈflētiNG/ ▸ **adj.** lasting for a very short time.

> SYNONYMS **brief**, short-lived, quick, momentary, cursory, transient, ephemeral, passing, transitory. ANTONYMS lasting.

■ **fleet·ing·ly adv.**

Flem·ing /ˈflemiNG/ ▸ **n. 1** a Flemish person. **2** a member of the Flemish-speaking people living in northern and western Belgium.

Flem·ish /ˈflemisн/ ▸ **n. 1** (**the Flemish**) the people of Flanders, a region divided between Belgium, France, and the Netherlands. **2** the Dutch language as spoken in Flanders. ▸ **adj.** relating to Flanders or the Flemish.

flesh /flesн/ ▸ **n. 1** the soft substance in the body consisting of muscle and fat. **2** the edible part of a fruit or vegetable. **3** (**the flesh**) the physical aspects and needs of the body. ▸ **v.** (**flesh something out**) make something more detailed.

> SYNONYMS ▸ **n. 1 tissue**, skin, muscle, fat, meat, body. **2 pulp**, marrow, meat. **3** *the pleasures of the flesh* **the body**, human nature, physicality, sensuality, sexuality.

□ **in the flesh** in person. **make someone's flesh crawl** make someone feel fear, horror, or disgust. **flesh wound** a wound that breaks the skin but does not damage bones or vital organs.

flesh·ly /ˈflesнlē/ ▸ **adj.** relating to the body and its needs.

flesh·pots /ˈflesн,päts/ ▸ **pl.n.** humorous places with a lot of nightlife and lively entertainment.

flesh·y /ˈflesнē/ ▸ **adj.** (**fleshier**, **fleshiest**) **1** plump. **2** soft and thick.

fleur-de-lis /ˌflər dlˈē, ˌflo͝or-/ (or **fleur-de-lys**) ▸ **n.** (plural **fleurs-de-lis**) a design showing a lily made up of three petals bound together at the bottom.

flew /flo͞o/ past of **FLY¹**.

flex /fleks/ ▸ **v. 1** bend a limb or joint. **2** tighten a muscle.

flex·i·bil·i·ty /ˌfleksəˈbilətē/ ▸ **n.** the quality of being flexible.

> SYNONYMS **1 pliability**, suppleness, elasticity, stretchiness, springiness, spring, resilience, bounce; informal give. **2 adaptability**, adjustability, versatility, open-endedness, freedom, latitude. **3 willingness to compromise**, give and take, amenability, cooperation, tolerance. ANTONYMS rigidity.

flex·i·ble /ˈfleksəbəl/ ▸ **adj. 1** able to bend easily without breaking. **2** able to adapt to different circumstances.

> SYNONYMS **1 bendy**, pliable, supple, pliant, plastic, elastic, stretchy, springy, resilient, bouncy. **2 adaptable**, adjustable, variable, versatile, open-ended, open. **3 accommodating**, amenable, willing to compromise, cooperative, tolerant. ANTONYMS rigid, inflexible.

■ **flex·i·bly adv.**

flex·ion /ˈfleksнən/ (also **flection**) ▸ **n.** the action of bending or the state of being bent.

flex·time /ˈfleks,tīm/ ▸ **n.** a system that lets you vary your working hours.

flib·ber·ti·gib·bet /ˈflibərtē,jibit/ ▸ **n.** a person who is fond of gossiping and is not interested in serious things.

flick /flik/ ▸ **v. 1** hit or remove with a quick light movement: *he flicked ash on the floor.* **2** make a sudden quick movement. **3** (**flick through**) look quickly through a book, magazine, etc. ▸ **n. 1** a sudden quick movement. **2** informal a movie.

> SYNONYMS ▸ **v. 1 click**, snap, flip, jerk, throw. **2 swish**, twitch, wave, wag, waggle, shake. ▸ **n. jerk**, snap, flip, whisk.

flick·er¹ /ˈflikər/ ▶ v. (**flickers**, **flickering**, **flickered**) **1** shine or burn unsteadily. **2** appear briefly: *amusement flickered in his eyes*. **3** make small, quick movements. ▶ n. **1** a flickering movement or light. **2** a brief occurrence of a feeling.

SYNONYMS ▶ v. **1 glimmer**, dance, twinkle, sparkle, wink, flash. **2 flutter**, quiver, tremble, shiver, shudder, jerk, twitch.

flick·er² ▶ n. a colorful North American woodpecker.

fli·er /ˈflīər/ (or **flyer**) ▶ n. **1** a person or thing that flies. **2** a small printed advertisement. **3** informal a fast-moving person or thing.

flight /flīt/ ▶ n. **1** the action of flying. **2** a journey made in an aircraft or in space. **3** the path of something through the air. **4** the action of running away: *the enemy were in flight*. **5** a group of birds or aircraft flying together. **6** a series of steps between floors or levels. **7** the tail of an arrow or dart.

SYNONYMS **1 aviation**, flying, air transport, aeronautics. **2 flock**, swarm, cloud, throng. **3 escape**, getaway, hasty departure, exit, exodus, breakout, bolt, disappearance.

□ **flight attendant** a person who looks after the passengers on an aircraft. **flight deck 1** the cockpit of a large aircraft. **2** the deck of an aircraft carrier. **flight of fancy** a very imaginative idea or story. **flight recorder** an electronic device in an aircraft that records technical details during a flight. **take flight 1** (of a bird) take off and fly. **2** run away.
■ **flight·less** adj.

flight·y /ˈflītē/ ▶ adj. unreliable and uninterested in serious things.

flim·sy /ˈflimzē/ ▶ adj. (**flimsier**, **flimsiest**) **1** weak and fragile. **2** (of clothing) light and thin. **3** unconvincing: *a flimsy excuse*.

SYNONYMS **1 insubstantial**, fragile, frail, rickety, ramshackle, makeshift, jerry-built, shoddy. **2 thin**, light, fine, filmy, floaty, diaphanous, sheer, delicate, gossamer, gauzy. **3 weak**, feeble, poor, inadequate, insufficient, thin, unsubstantial, unconvincing, implausible. ANTONYMS sturdy.

flinch /flinch/ ▶ v. **1** make a quick, nervous movement as a reaction to fear or pain. **2** (**flinch from**) avoid something because you are scared or anxious.

SYNONYMS **1 wince**, start, shudder, quiver, jerk. **2** *he never flinched from his duty* **shrink from**, recoil from, shy away from, dodge, evade, avoid, duck, balk at.

fling /fliNG/ ▶ v. (**flings**, **flinging**, **flung** /fləNG/) throw or move forcefully: *she flung the tray against the wall*. ▶ n. **1** a short period of enjoyment or wild behavior. **2** a short romantic relationship.

SYNONYMS ▶ v. **throw**, hurl, toss, sling, launch, pitch, lob; informal chuck, heave. ▶ n. **1 good time**, party, spree, fun and games; informal binge, bash, night on the town. **2 affair**, love affair, relationship, romance, liaison, entanglement, involvement.

flint /flint/ ▶ n. **1** a hard gray rock. **2** a piece of flint or a metal alloy, used to produce a spark in a cigarette lighter.

flint·lock /ˈflintˌläk/ ▶ n. an old-fashioned type of gun fired by a spark from a flint.

flip /flip/ ▶ v. (**flips**, **flipping**, **flipped**) **1** turn over with a quick, smooth movement. **2** move or throw with a sudden sharp movement: *he flipped a switch*. **3** (also **flip your lid**) informal suddenly become very angry or lose your self-control. ▶ n. a flipping action or movement. ▶ adj. not serious or respectful; flippant.

SYNONYMS ▶ v. **1 overturn**, turn over, tip over, roll (over), upturn, capsize, upend, invert, knock over, keel over, topple over, turn turtle. **2 flick**, click, throw, push, pull.

□ **flip-flop** a light sandal with a thong that passes between the big and second toes. **flip side 1** informal the reverse and less welcome aspect of a situation. **2** the less important side of a pop single.

flip·pant /ˈflipənt/ ▶ adj. not properly serious or respectful.

SYNONYMS **frivolous**, facetious, tongue-in-cheek, disrespectful, irreverent, cheeky; informal flip, saucy, sassy. ANTONYMS serious.

■ **flip·pan·cy** n. **flip·pant·ly** adv.

flip·per /ˈflipər/ ▶ n. **1** a broad, flat limb used for swimming by sea creatures such as turtles. **2** a flat rubber attachment worn on each foot for swimming underwater.

flirt /flərt/ ▶ v. **1** behave as if you are trying to attract someone romantically, but without serious intentions. **2** (**flirt with**) show a casual interest in: *he flirted briefly with the idea*. **3** (**flirt with**) deliberately risk danger or death. ▶ n. a person who likes to flirt.

SYNONYMS ▶ n. **tease**, coquette, heartbreaker.

■ **flir·ta·tion** /-ˈtāSHən/ n.

flir·ta·tious /ˌflərˈtāSHəs/ ▶ adj. liking to flirt.

flit /flit/ ▶ v. (**flits**, **flitting**, **flitted**) move quickly and lightly.

flit·ter /ˈflitər/ ▶ v. move quickly here and there.

float /flōt/ ▶ v. **1** rest on the surface of a liquid without sinking. **2** move or be held up in a liquid or the air: *clouds floated across the sky*. **3** put forward a suggestion. **4** (**floating**) not having fixed opinions. **5** (**floating**) not living in a fixed location. **6** provide for a short period of time: *can you float me a loan until payday?* **7** put shares in a company on sale for the first time. ▶ n. **1** a lightweight object designed to float on water. **2** a vehicle that carries a display in a procession.

SYNONYMS ▶ v. **1 stay afloat**, stay on the surface, be buoyant, be buoyed up. **2 hover**, levitate, be suspended, hang, defy gravity. **3 drift**, glide, sail, slip, slide, waft. **4** (**floating**) **uncommitted**, undecided, undeclared, wavering; informal sitting on the fence. **5** (**floating**) **unsettled**, transient, temporary, migrant, wandering, nomadic, migratory, itinerant. **6 launch**, offer, sell, introduce. ANTONYMS sink.

■ **float·y** adj.

floc·cu·lent /ˈfläkyələnt/ ▶ adj. looking like tufts of wool.

flock¹ /fläk/ ▶ n. **1** a number of birds, sheep, or goats together. **2** (**a flock** or **flocks**) a large number or crowd. **3** a Christian congregation. ▶ v. gather or move in a flock.

SYNONYMS ▶ n. **1 herd**, drove. **2 flight**, swarm, cloud, gaggle, skein. ▶ v. **1** *people flocked around her* **gather**, collect, congregate, assemble, converge, mass, crowd, throng, cluster, swarm. **2** *tourists flock to the place* **stream**, go in large numbers, swarm, crowd, troop.

flock² ▶ **n.** **1** a soft material for stuffing cushions and quilts. **2** powdered wool or cloth, used to give a raised pattern on wallpaper.

floe /flō/ ▶ **n.** a sheet of floating ice.

flog /fläg/ ▶ **v.** (**flogs**, **flogging**, **flogged**) beat with a whip or stick as a punishment.

SYNONYMS **whip**, thrash, lash, scourge, birch, cane, beat.

flood /fləd/ ▶ **n.** **1** an overflow of a large amount of water over dry land. **2** an overwhelming quantity or amount: *a flood of complaints*. **3** the rising of the tide. ▶ **v.** **1** cover with water in a flood. **2** (of a river) overflow its banks. **3** arrive in very large numbers.

SYNONYMS ▶ **n.** **1** **inundation**, deluge, torrent, overflow, flash flood. **2** **gush**, outpouring, torrent, rush, stream, surge, cascade. **3** **succession**, series, string, barrage, volley, battery, avalanche, torrent, stream, storm. ▶ **v.** **1** *the town was flooded* **inundate**, swamp, deluge, immerse, submerge, drown, engulf. **2** *the river could flood* **overflow**, burst its banks, brim over, run over. **3** **glut**, swamp, saturate, oversupply. **4** **pour**, stream, flow, surge, swarm, pile, crowd.

□ **flood tide** an incoming tide.

flood·gate /ˈfləd,gāt/ ▶ **n.** **1** a gate that can be opened or closed to control a flow of water. **2** (**floodgates**) controls that hold back something powerful: *success could open the floodgates for similar mergers*.

flood·light /ˈfləd,līt/ ▶ **n.** a large, powerful light used to light up a sports field, a stage, or the exterior of a building. ▶ **v.** (**floodlights**, **floodlighting**, **floodlit**) light up with floodlights.

flood·plain /ˈfləd,plān/ ▶ **n.** an area of low ground next to a river that is regularly flooded.

floor /flôr/ ▶ **n.** **1** the lower surface of a room. **2** a story of a building. **3** the bottom of the sea, a cave, etc. **4** (**the floor**) the part of Congress or a parliament or other lawmaking assembly in which members sit and from which they speak. ▶ **v.** informal **1** knock someone to the ground. **2** surprise or confuse someone.

SYNONYMS ▶ **n.** **1** **ground**, flooring. **2** **story**, level, deck, tier, stage. ▶ **v.** **1** **knock down**, knock over, fell; informal deck, lay out. **2** **baffle**, defeat, confound, perplex, puzzle, disconcert; informal throw, beat, stump.

□ **floor exercise** gymnastic exercises performed without apparatus. **floor show** an entertainment presented on the floor of a nightclub or restaurant.

floor·board /ˈflôr,bôrd/ ▶ **n.** a long plank making up part of a wooden floor.

floor·ing /ˈflôriNG/ ▶ **n.** the boards or other material of which a floor is made.

floo·zy /ˈflo͞ozē/ (or **floozie**) ▶ **n.** (plural **floozies**) informal a girl or woman who has many casual romantic partners.

flop /fläp/ ▶ **v.** (**flops**, **flopping**, **flopped**) **1** hang or swing loosely. **2** sit or lie down heavily. **3** informal fail totally. ▶ **n.** **1** a heavy and clumsy fall. **2** informal a total failure.

SYNONYMS ▶ **v.** **1** **hang (down)**, dangle, droop, sag. **2** **collapse**, slump, crumple, sink, drop. **3** **be unsuccessful**, fail, fall flat, founder; informal bomb, tank. ▶ **n.** **failure**, disaster, fiasco, debacle, catastrophe; informal washout, also-ran. ANTONYMS success.

flop·py /ˈfläpē/ ▶ **adj.** not firm or rigid.

SYNONYMS **limp**, flaccid, slack, flabby, relaxed, drooping, droopy, loose, flowing. ANTONYMS erect, stiff.

□ **floppy disk** a flexible disk used for storing computer data.

flo·ra /ˈflôrə/ ▶ **n.** the plants of a particular area or period.

flo·ral /ˈflôrəl/ ▶ **adj.** having to do with flowers.

Flor·en·tine /ˈflôrən,tēn, -tīn/ ▶ **adj.** relating to the city of Florence in Italy. ▶ **n.** a person from Florence.

flo·ret /ˈflôrət/ ▶ **n.** **1** each of the small flowers making up a flower head. **2** each of the flowering stems making up a head of cauliflower or broccoli.

flor·id /ˈflôrid, ˈflär-/ ▶ **adj.** **1** having a red or flushed complexion. **2** too elaborate: *florid prose*.

flo·rist /ˈflôrist/ ▶ **n.** a person who sells cut flowers.

flo·ru·it /ˈflôr(y)o͞oit/ ▶ **v.** used to indicate when a historical figure lived, worked, or was most active: *the painter William Craig (floruit 1788–1828)*.

floss /flôs, fläs/ ▶ **n.** **1** (also **dental floss**) soft thread used to clean between the teeth. **2** silk thread used in embroidery. ▶ **v.** clean between the teeth with dental floss.

flo·ta·tion /flōˈtāSHən/ (or **floatation**) ▶ **n.** **1** the action of floating. **2** the capacity to float; buoyancy. **3** the offering of a company's shares for sale for the first time.

flo·til·la /flōˈtilə/ ▶ **n.** a small fleet of ships or boats.

flot·sam /ˈflätsəm/ ▶ **n.** wreckage found floating on the sea. □ **flotsam and jetsam** useless or discarded objects.

flounce /flouns/ ▶ **v.** (**flounces**, **flouncing**, **flounced**) move in an angry or impatient way. ▶ **n.** **1** an exaggerated action expressing annoyance or impatience. **2** a wide strip of material sewn to a skirt or dress.

floun·der¹ /ˈfloundər/ ▶ **v.** (**flounders**, **floundering**, **floundered**) **1** stagger clumsily in mud or water. **2** have trouble doing or understanding something.

SYNONYMS **1** *floundering in the water* **struggle**, thrash, flail, twist and turn, splash, stagger, stumble, reel, lurch, blunder. **2** *she floundered, not knowing what to say* **struggle**, be out of your depth, be confused; informal scratch your head, be flummoxed, be fazed, be floored.

floun·der² ▶ **n.** a small flatfish.

flour /ˈflou(ə)r/ ▶ **n.** a powder produced by grinding grain, used to make bread, cakes, and pastry, and for other cooking. ■ **flour·y adj.**

flour·ish /ˈflərisH/ ▶ **v.** **1** grow or develop well; thrive. **2** be successful. **3** wave something about in a noticeable way. ▶ **n.** **1** a dramatic or exaggerated movement or gesture. **2** a decorative flowing curve in handwriting. **3** a fanfare played by brass instruments.

SYNONYMS ▶ **v.** **1** *ferns flourish in the shade* **grow**, thrive, prosper, do well, burgeon, increase, multiply, proliferate, run riot. **2** *the arts flourished* **thrive**, prosper, bloom, be in good health, be vigorous, be in its heyday, make progress, advance, expand; informal go places. **3** **brandish**, wave, shake, wield, swing, display, show off. ANTONYMS wither, decline.

flout /flout/ ▶ v. openly fail to follow a rule, law, or custom.

SYNONYMS **defy**, refuse to obey, disobey, break, violate, fail to comply with, fail to observe, contravene, infringe, breach, commit a breach of, transgress against, ignore, disregard. ANTONYMS observe.

USAGE
Don't confuse **flout** with **flaunt**, which means 'display proudly or obviously.'

flow /flō/ ▶ v. **1** move steadily and continuously in a current or stream. **2** (**flow from**) result from; be caused by. ▶ n. a steady, continuous stream.

SYNONYMS ▶ v. **1 pour**, run, course, circulate, stream, swirl, surge, sweep, gush, cascade, roll, rush, trickle, seep, ooze, dribble. **2 result**, proceed, arise, follow, ensue, stem, originate, emanate, spring. ▶ n. **movement**, motion, current, circulation, stream, swirl, surge, gush, rush, spate, tide, trickle, ooze.

□ **flow chart** a diagram that shows the sequence of stages making up a complex process. **go with the flow** informal be relaxed and accept a situation.

flow·er /ˈflou(-ə)r/ ▶ n. **1** the part of a plant from which the seed or fruit develops, usually having brightly colored petals. **2** (**the flower of**) the best of a group. ▶ v. (**flowers**, **flowering**, **flowered**) **1** produce flowers. **2** develop fully and well: *she flowered into a striking beauty*.

SYNONYMS **bloom**, blossom.

□ **flower head** a compact mass of flowers at the top of a stem.

flow·er·pot /ˈflou(-ə)rˌpät/ ▶ n. a container for growing plants in.

flow·er·y /ˈflou(-ə)rē/ ▶ adj. **1** full of or decorated with flowers. **2** (of speech or writing) elaborate.

flown /flōn/ /flōn/ past participle of **FLY**[1].

fl. oz. ▶ abbr. fluid ounce.

flu /flo͞o/ ▶ n. short for **INFLUENZA**.

flub /fləb/ informal ▶ v. (**flubs**, **flubbing**, **flubbed**) botch or bungle. ▶ n. a thing badly or clumsily done.

fluc·tu·ate /ˈfləkcho͞oˌāt/ ▶ v. (**fluctuates**, **fluctuating**, **fluctuated**) rise and fall irregularly in number or amount.

SYNONYMS **vary**, change, shift, alter, waver, swing, oscillate, alternate, rise and fall.

■ **fluc·tu·a·tion** /ˌfləkcho͞oˈāshən/ n.

flue /flo͞o/ ▶ n. a pipe that takes smoke and gases away from a chimney, heater, etc.

flu·ent /ˈflo͞oənt/ ▶ adj. **1** able to use a language in a clear and natural way. **2** smoothly graceful and easy: *a runner in fluent motion*.

SYNONYMS **articulate**, eloquent, silver-tongued, communicative, natural, effortless. ANTONYMS inarticulate.

■ **flu·en·cy** n. **flu·ent·ly** adv.

fluff /fləf/ ▶ n. **1** soft fibers gathered in small, light clumps. **2** the soft fur or feathers of a young animal or bird. **3** trivial entertainment or writing. ▶ v. **1** (**fluff something up**) make something fuller and softer by shaking or patting it. **2** informal fail to do something properly: *he fluffed his only line*.

fluff·y /ˈfləfē/ ▶ adj. (**fluffier**, **fluffiest**) **1** covered with fluff. **2** (of food) light in texture.

flu·gel·horn /ˈflo͞ogəlˌhôrn/ ▶ n. a brass musical instrument like a cornet but with a broader tone.

flu·id /ˈflo͞oid/ ▶ n. a liquid or gas. ▶ adj. **1** able to flow easily. **2** not fixed or stable: *a fluid political situation*. **3** graceful: *fluid movements*.

SYNONYMS ▶ n. **liquid**, solution, liquor, gas, vapor. ▶ adj. **1 free-flowing**, runny, liquid, liquefied, melted, molten, gaseous. **2 smooth**, fluent, flowing, effortless, easy, continuous, graceful, elegant. ANTONYMS solid.

□ **fluid ounce** one sixteenth of a pint (approximately 0.03 liter). ■ **flu·id·i·ty** /flo͞oˈidətē/ n. **flu·id·ly** adv.

fluke /flo͝ok/ ▶ n. something lucky that happens by chance. ■ **fluk·y** adj.

flume /flo͞om/ ▶ n. **1** an artificial channel for carrying water. **2** a water slide at a swimming pool or amusement park.

flum·mer·y /ˈfləmərē/ ▶ n. (plural **flummeries**) empty talk or compliments.

flum·mox /ˈfləməks/ ▶ v. informal baffle someone completely.

flung /fləng/ past and past participle of **FLING**.

flunk /fləngk/ ▶ v. informal fail an exam.

flun·ky /ˈfləngkē/ (or **flunkey**) ▶ n. (plural **flunkies** or **flunkeys**) **1** a uniformed male servant. **2** a person who does menial tasks for someone else.

fluo·resce /flo͝o(ə)ˈres, flôrˈes/ ▶ v. (**fluoresces**, **fluorescing**, **fluoresced**) shine or glow brightly.

fluo·res·cent /ˌflo͝o(ə)ˈresənt, flôrˈesənt/ ▶ adj. **1** giving off bright light when exposed to radiation such as ultraviolet light. **2** vividly colorful. ■ **fluo·res·cence** n.

SPELLING
Write **fluor-**, not **flour-**: **fluor**escent.

fluor·i·date /ˈflo͝orəˌdāt, ˈflôr-/ ▶ v. (**fluoridates**, **fluoridating**, **fluoridated**) add fluoride to a water supply. ■ **fluor·i·da·tion** /ˌflo͝orəˈdāshən, ˌflôr-/ n.

fluor·ide /ˈflo͝orˌīd, ˈflôr-/ ▶ n. a compound of fluorine that is added to water supplies or toothpaste to reduce tooth decay.

fluor·ine /ˈflo͝orˌēn, flôr-/ ▶ n. a poisonous pale yellow gas.

fluo·rite /ˈflo͝orˌīt, flôr-/ ▶ n. a mineral found in the form of crystals.

flur·ry /ˈflərē, ˈflə-rē/ ▶ n. (plural **flurries**) **1** a small swirling mass of snow, leaves, etc., moved by a gust of wind. **2** a sudden short period of activity or excitement. **3** a number of things arriving suddenly and at the same time.

SYNONYMS **1 swirl**, whirl, eddy, shower, gust. **2 burst**, outbreak, spurt, fit, spell, bout, rash, eruption.

flush[1] /fləsh/ ▶ v. **1** (of a person's skin or face) become red and hot. **2** (**be flushed with**) be very pleased by: *be flushed with success*. **3** clean something by passing large quantities of water through it. **4** force a person or animal out into the open. **5** glow with warm color or light. ▶ n. **1** a reddening of the face or skin. **2** a sudden rush of strong emotion. **3** a period of freshness and energy: *the first flush of youth*. **4** an act of flushing.

SYNONYMS ▶ v. 1 **blush**, redden, go pink, go red, go crimson, go scarlet, color (up). 2 (**flushed**) **elated**, thrilled, glowing, impassioned; informal tingly. 3 **rinse**, wash, sluice, swill, cleanse, clean. 4 **chase**, force, drive, dislodge, expel. ▶ n. **blush**, color, rosiness, pinkness, ruddiness, bloom. ANTONYMS pallor.

flush² ▶ adj. 1 completely level with another surface. 2 informal having plenty of money.

flush³ ▶ n. (in poker) a hand of cards all of the same suit.

flust·er /ˈfləstər/ ▶ n. an agitated and confused state.

flust·ered /ˈfləstərd/ ▶ adj. agitated and confused.

flute /flo͞ot/ ▶ n. 1 a high-pitched wind instrument that you hold sideways and play by blowing across a hole at one end. 2 a tall, narrow wine glass.

flut·ed /flo͞otid/ ▶ adj. decorated with a series of gently rounded grooves.

flut·ist /ˈflo͞otist/ ▶ n. a flute player.

flut·ter /ˈflətər/ ▶ v. (**flutters**, **fluttering**, **fluttered**) 1 fly unsteadily by flapping the wings quickly and lightly. 2 move or fall with a light trembling motion. 3 (of a pulse or heartbeat) beat feebly or irregularly. ▶ n. a state of nervous excitement.

SYNONYMS ▶ v. 1 *butterflies fluttered around* **flit**, hover, dance. 2 *a robin fluttered its wings* **flap**, beat, quiver, agitate, vibrate, ruffle. 3 *she fluttered her eyelashes* **flicker**, bat. 4 *flags fluttered* **flap**, wave, ripple, undulate, quiver, fly.

■ **flut·ter·y** adj.

flu·vi·al /ˈflo͞ovēəl/ ▶ adj. technical having to do with a river.

flux /fləks/ ▶ n. 1 continuous change. 2 a flow.

fly¹ /flī/ ▶ v. (**flies**, **flying**, **flew** /flo͞o/; past participle **flown** /flōn/) 1 (of a winged creature or aircraft) move through the air. 2 control the flight of an aircraft. 3 move quickly through the air. 4 go or move quickly. 5 (of a flag) be displayed on a flagpole. 6 (**fly at**) attack. 7 old use run away. ▶ n. (plural **flies**) 1 an opening at the crotch of a pair of pants, closed with a zipper or buttons. 2 a flap of material covering the opening of a tent. 3 (**the flies**) the space over the stage in a theater.

SYNONYMS ▶ v. 1 **wing**, glide, soar, wheel, take wing, take to the air, hover, swoop. 2 **pilot**, operate, control, maneuver, steer. 3 *the ship flew a French flag* **display**, show, exhibit, hoist, raise, wave. 4 **dash**, race, rush, bolt, zoom, dart, speed, hurry, careen, hurtle; informal tear.

□ **fly-by-night** unreliable or untrustworthy. **flying fish** a fish that can leap out of the water and glide for some distance using its fins like wings. **flying saucer** a disk-shaped flying spacecraft supposedly piloted by aliens. **flying start** a good beginning that gives an advantage over competitors. **fly in the face of** do the opposite of what is usual or expected. **fly off the handle** informal lose your temper. **with flying colors** with distinction.

fly² ▶ n. (plural **flies**) 1 a flying insect with transparent wings. 2 an artificial fly used as a fishing bait. □ **a fly in the ointment** a small irritation that spoils the enjoyment of something. **fly-fishing** the sport of fishing using a rod and an artificial fly as bait. **a fly on the wall** an unnoticed observer.

fly·a·way /ˈflīəˌwā/ ▶ adj. (of hair) fine and difficult to control.

fly·blown /ˈflīˌblōn/ ▶ adj. contaminated by contact with flies.

fly·catch·er /ˈflīˌkacнər, -ˌkecнər/ ▶ n. a small bird that catches flying insects.

fly·er /ˈflīər/ = FLIER.

fly·leaf /ˈflīˌlēf/ ▶ n. (plural **flyleaves** /-ˌlēvz/) a blank page at the beginning or end of a book.

fly·o·ver /ˈflīˌōvər/ ▶ n. a low flight by one or more aircraft over a specific location.

fly·pa·per /ˈflīˌpāpər/ ▶ n. strips of sticky paper that are hung up to catch and kill flies.

fly·sheet /ˈflīˌsнēt/ ▶ n. a tract or circular of two or four pages.

fly·weight /ˈflīˌwāt/ ▶ n. a weight in boxing below bantamweight.

fly·wheel /ˈflīˌ(h)wēl/ ▶ n. a heavy revolving wheel in a machine that helps it to work smoothly.

FM ▶ abbr. frequency modulation.

foal /fōl/ ▶ n. a young horse or related animal. ▶ v. give birth to a foal.

foam /fōm/ ▶ n. 1 a mass of small bubbles formed on the surface of liquid. 2 a liquid substance containing many small bubbles: *shaving foam*. 3 a lightweight form of rubber or plastic that is full of small holes. ▶ v. form or produce foam.

SYNONYMS ▶ n. **froth**, spume, surf, spray, fizz, effervescence, bubbles, head, lather, suds. ▶ v. **froth**, fizz, effervesce, bubble, lather, ferment, boil, seethe.

□ **foam at the mouth** informal be very angry.
■ **foam·y** adj.

fob¹ /fäb/ ▶ n. 1 a chain attached to a watch for carrying in a pocket. 2 a tab on a key ring.

fob² ▶ v. (**fobs**, **fobbing**, **fobbed**) 1 (**fob someone off**) try to deceive someone into accepting excuses or something inferior. 2 (**fob something off on**) give something inferior to.

fo·cac·cia /fōˈkäcн(ē)ə/ ▶ n. a type of flat Italian bread made with olive oil.

fo·cal /ˈfōkəl/ ▶ adj. relating to a focus. □ **focal point** 1 the point at which rays or waves of light, sound, etc., meet, or from which they seem to come. 2 the center of interest or activity.

fo'c'·s'le /ˈfōksəl/ = FORECASTLE.

fo·cus /ˈfōkəs/ ▶ n. (plural **focuses** or **foci** /ˈfōˌsī, -ˌkī/) 1 the center of interest or activity. 2 the state of having or producing a clear image: *his face is out of focus*. 3 the point at which an object must be situated for a lens or mirror to produce a clear image of it. 4 a focal point. ▶ v. (**focuses**, **focusing** or **focussing**, **focused** or **focussed**) 1 adapt to the amount of light available and become able to see clearly. 2 (**focus on**) pay particular attention to. 3 adjust the focus of a telescope, camera, etc. 4 (of rays or waves) meet at a single point.

SYNONYMS ▶ n. 1 **center**, focal point, central point, center of attention, hub, pivot, nucleus, heart, cornerstone, linchpin. 2 **subject**, theme, concern, subject matter, topic, point, essence, gist. ▶ v. **bring into focus**, aim, point, turn.

□ **focus group** a group of people brought together to give their opinions of a new product, political campaign, etc.

fod·der /ˈfädər/ ▶ **n. 1** food for cattle and other livestock. **2** a person or thing viewed only as material to satisfy a particular need: *young people ending up as factory fodder.*

foe /fō/ ▶ **n.** an enemy or opponent.

fog /fôg, fäg/ ▶ **n.** a thick cloud of water droplets that is difficult to see through. ▶ **v.** (**fogs, fogging, fogged**) **1** become covered with steam. **2** confuse: *the issue fogged her brain.*

> SYNONYMS ▶ **n. mist**, smog, murk, haze.

fog·bound /ˈfôg,bound, ˈfäg-/ ▶ **adj.** unable to travel or function because of fog.

fo·gey /ˈfōgē/ (or **fogy**) ▶ **n.** (plural **fogeys** or **fogies**) a very old-fashioned or conservative person.

fog·gy /ˈfôgē, ˈfägē/ ▶ **adj.** (**foggier, foggiest**) **1** full of fog. **2** confused or unclear.

> SYNONYMS **1 misty**, smoggy, hazy, murky. **2** *a foggy memory* **muddled**, confused, dim, hazy, shadowy, cloudy, blurred, obscure, vague, indistinct, unclear. ANTONYMS clear.

▫ **not have the foggiest idea** informal have no idea at all.

fog·horn /ˈfôg,hôrn, ˈfäg-/ ▶ **n.** a device that makes a loud, deep sound as a warning to ships in fog.

foi·ble /ˈfoibəl/ ▶ **n.** a slight peculiarity in a person's character or habits.

foil[1] /foil/ ▶ **v. 1** prevent something from happening. **2** stop someone from doing something.

> SYNONYMS **thwart**, frustrate, stop, defeat, block, prevent, obstruct, hinder, snooker, scotch. ANTONYMS assist.

foil[2] ▶ **n. 1** metal in the form of a thin flexible sheet. **2** a person or thing that contrasts with and so emphasizes the qualities of another.

> SYNONYMS **contrast**, complement, antithesis.

foil[3] ▶ **n.** a light, blunt-edged fencing sword.

foist /foist/ ▶ **v.** (**foist someone/thing on**) make someone accept an unwelcome person or thing.

fold[1] /fōld/ ▶ **v. 1** bend something over on itself so that one part of it covers another. **2** be able to be folded into a flatter shape. **3** clasp someone in your arms. **4** informal (of a company) stop trading as a result of financial problems. **5** (**fold something in** or **into**) mix one ingredient gently with another. ▶ **n. 1** a folded part. **2** a line or crease produced by folding.

> SYNONYMS ▶ **v. 1 double**, crease, turn, bend, tuck, pleat. **2 fail**, collapse, founder, go bankrupt, cease trading, be wound up, be shut (down); informal crash, go bust, go under, go to the wall, go belly up. ▶ **n. crease**, knife-edge, wrinkle, crinkle, pucker, furrow, pleat.

▫ **fold your arms** bring your arms together and cross them over your chest.

fold[2] ▶ **n. 1** a pen or enclosure for livestock. **2** (**the fold**) a group or community.

fold·er /ˈfōldər/ ▶ **n. 1** a folding cover or holder for storing loose papers. **2** an icon on a computer screen that can be used to access a directory containing related files or documents.

fo·li·age /ˈfōl(ē)ij/ ▶ **n.** the leaves of plants.

fo·li·ar /ˈfōlēər/ ▶ **adj.** having to do with leaves.
▫ **foliar feed** plant food that is fed through leaves.

fo·li·ate /ˈfōlēət, -,āt/ ▶ **v.** (**foliates, foliating, foliated**) decorate with leaves or a leaflike pattern.

fo·lic ac·id /ˈfōlik, ˈfä-/ ▶ **n.** a vitamin found especially in green vegetables, liver, and kidney.

fo·li·o /ˈfōlē,ō/ ▶ **n.** (plural **folios**) **1** a sheet of paper folded once to form four pages of a book. **2** a large-sized book made up of such sheets.

folk /fōk/ ▶ **pl.n. 1** (also **folks**) informal people in general. **2** (**your folks**) informal your family. **3** (also **folk music**) traditional music whose composer is unknown, passed on through performances.

> SYNONYMS **1 people**, individuals, [men, women, and children], (living) souls, citizenry, inhabitants, residents, populace, population. **2 relatives**, relations, family, people; informal peeps.

▫ **folk dance** a traditional dance of a particular place. **folk tale** a traditional story passed on by word of mouth.

folk·lore /ˈfōk,lôr/ ▶ **n.** the traditional stories and customs of a community.

folk·sy /ˈfōksē/ ▶ **adj.** traditional and unpretentious: *the shop's folksy, small-town image.*

fol·li·cle /ˈfälikəl/ ▶ **n.** one of the small holes in the skin that hair grows out of.

fol·low /ˈfälō/ ▶ **v. 1** go after or move along behind. **2** go along a route. **3** come after in time or order. **4** be a result or consequence. **5** act according to advice or an instruction. **6** understand or pay attention to. **7** (**follow something through**) continue an action or task to its end. **8** (**follow something up**) pursue something further. **9** practice or undertake a career or course of action.

> SYNONYMS **1 come behind**, come after, go behind, go after, walk behind. **2 accompany**, go along with, go around with, travel with, escort, attend; informal tag along with. **3 shadow**, trail, stalk, track; informal tail. **4 obey**, comply with, conform to, adhere to, stick to, keep to, act in accordance with, abide by, observe. **5 understand**, comprehend, take in, grasp, fathom, see; informal make heads or tails of, figure out. **6 be a fan of**, be a supporter of, support, watch, keep up with. ANTONYMS lead, flout.

▫ **follow-the-leader** a children's game in which the players must copy the actions and words of a person acting as leader. **follow-through** the continuing of an action or task to its end. **follow-up 1** an activity carried out to check or further develop earlier work. **2** a work that follows or builds on an earlier work. **follow your nose 1** trust to your instincts. **2** go straight ahead. **follow suit 1** do the same as someone else. **2** (in card games) play a card of the suit that has just been played.

fol·low·er /ˈfälō-ər/ ▶ **n. 1** a supporter, fan, or disciple. **2** a person who follows.

> SYNONYMS **1 disciple**, apostle, defender, champion, believer, worshiper. **2 fan**, enthusiast, admirer, devotee, lover, supporter, adherent. ANTONYMS leader, opponent.

fol·low·ing /ˈfälō-iNG/ ▶ **prep.** coming after or as a result of. ▶ **n.** a group of supporters. ▶ **adj. 1** next in time or order. **2** about to be mentioned: *the following information.*

> SYNONYMS ▶ **n. admirers**, supporters, backers, fans, adherents, devotees, public, audience. ANTONYMS opposition. ▶ **adj. next**, ensuing, succeeding, subsequent, successive. ANTONYMS preceding.

fol·ly /ˈfälē/ ▶ **n.** (plural **follies**) **1** foolishness. **2** a foolish act. **3** an ornamental building with no practical purpose.

> SYNONYMS **foolishness**, foolhardiness, stupidity, idiocy, lunacy, madness, rashness, recklessness, irresponsibility. ANTONYMS wisdom.

fo·ment /ˈfōˌment, fōˈment/ ▶ **v.** stir up revolution or conflict.

fond /fänd/ ▶ **adj. 1** (**fond of**) having a liking or affection for. **2** affectionate: *fond memories*. **3** (of a hope or belief) unlikely to be fulfilled; naive.

> SYNONYMS **1** *she was fond of dancing* **keen on**, partial to, enthusiastic about, attached to; informal into. **2 adoring**, devoted, doting, loving, caring, affectionate, indulgent. **3 unrealistic**, naive, foolish, overoptimistic, absurd, vain. ANTONYMS indifferent, uncaring.

■ **fond·ly adv. fond·ness n.**

fon·dant /ˈfändənt/ ▶ **n.** a thick paste made of sugar and water, used in making candy and icing cakes.

fon·dle /ˈfändl/ ▶ **v.** (**fondles**, **fondling**, **fondled**) stroke or caress lovingly.

> SYNONYMS **caress**, stroke, pat, pet, finger, tickle, play with.

fon·due /fänˈd(y)o͞o/ ▶ **n.** a dish in which you dip small pieces of food into melted cheese or a hot sauce, or into a hot cooking medium such as oil or broth.

font /fänt/ ▶ **n. 1** a large stone bowl in a church for the water used in baptizing people. **2** a set of printed letters of a particular size and design.

food /fo͞od/ ▶ **n.** any substance that people or animals eat to stay alive.

> SYNONYMS **nourishment**, sustenance, nutriment, fare, cooking, cuisine, foodstuffs, refreshments, meals, provisions, rations; informal eats, grub, chow, vittles, nosh; literary viands; dated victuals.

□ **food chain** a series of organisms in which each depends on the next as a source of food. **food court** an area, typically in a shopping mall, where fast food outlets and tables are located. **food for thought** something that makes you think carefully about an issue. **food poisoning** illness caused by food contaminated by bacteria. **food processor** an electric appliance used for chopping and mixing foods.

food·ie /ˈfo͞odē/ (also **foody**) ▶ **n.** (plural **foodies**) informal a person with a strong interest in food.

food·stuff /ˈfo͞odˌstəf/ ▶ **n.** a substance that can be eaten as food.

fool /fo͞ol/ ▶ **n. 1** a person who behaves in a silly or stupid way. **2** historical a jester or clown. ▶ **v. 1** trick or deceive. **2** (**fool around**) act in a joking or silly way.

> SYNONYMS ▶ **n. 1 idiot**, ass, halfwit, blockhead, dunce, simpleton; informal nincompoop, clod, dimwit, dummy, fathead, numbskull, nitwit, twit, dork, twerp, schmuck. **2** *she made a fool of me* **laughingstock**, dupe, gull; informal stooge, sap, sucker, fall guy. ▶ **v. 1 deceive**, trick, hoax, dupe, take in, mislead, delude, hoodwink, bluff, gull; informal bamboozle, take for a ride, sucker. **2 pretend**, make believe, put on an act, act, sham, fake, joke, jest; informal kid.

□ **fool's gold** a yellowish mineral that can be mistaken for gold. **fool's paradise** a happy state that is based on ignoring possible trouble.

fool·har·dy /ˈfo͞olˌhärdē/ ▶ **adj.** recklessly daring.

fool·ish /ˈfo͞olisʜ/ ▶ **adj.** silly or stupid.

> SYNONYMS **stupid**, idiotic, senseless, mindless, unintelligent, thoughtless, imprudent, unwise, ill-advised, rash, reckless, foolhardy; informal dumb, dim, dim-witted, half-witted, moronic, thick, harebrained, daft. ANTONYMS sensible, wise.

■ **fool·ish·ly adv. fool·ish·ness n.**

fool·proof /ˈfo͞olˌpro͞of/ ▶ **adj.** incapable of failing or being wrongly used.

> SYNONYMS **infallible**, dependable, reliable, trustworthy, certain, sure, guaranteed, safe, sound, tried and tested, watertight, airtight, flawless, perfect; informal surefire.

foot /fo͝ot/ ▶ **n.** (plural **feet** /fēt/) **1** the part of the leg below the ankle, on which a person walks. **2** the bottom of something vertical. **3** the end of a bed. **4** a unit of length equal to 12 inches (30.48 cm). **5** a group of syllables making up a basic unit of rhythm in poetry. ▶ **v.** informal pay a bill.

> SYNONYMS ▶ **n. 1 paw**, hoof, pad. **2 bottom**, base, lowest part, end, foundation.

□ **feet of clay** a flaw in a person who is greatly admired. **foot-and-mouth disease** a disease of cattle and sheep, causing ulcers on the hoofs and around the mouth. **fleet of foot** able to move swiftly. **get** (or **start**) **off on the right** (or **wrong**) **foot** make a good (or bad) start at something. **have** (or **keep**) **your feet on the ground** be (or remain) practical and sensible. **have** (or **get**) **a foot in the door** have (or gain) a first introduction to a profession or organization. **have one foot in the grave** humorous be very old or ill. **land** (or **fall**) **on your feet** have good luck or success. **on foot** walking. **put your best foot forward** begin with as much effort and determination as possible. **put your foot down** informal be firm when faced with opposition or disobedience. **put your foot in it** informal say or do something tactless. **under your feet** in your way.

foot·age /ˈfo͝otij/ ▶ **n.** a length of film made for a movie or television.

foot·ball /ˈfo͝otˌbôl/ ▶ **n. 1** a form of team game played with an oval ball on a field marked out as a gridiron. **2** an inflated oval ball used in such a game.

foot·brake /ˈfo͝otˌbrāk/ ▶ **n.** a foot-operated brake in a motor vehicle.

foot·bridge /ˈfo͝otˌbrij/ ▶ **n.** a bridge for pedestrians.

foot·er /ˈfo͝otər/ ▶ **n. 1** a person or thing of a specified number of feet in length or height: *a six-footer*. **2** a line of text appearing at the foot of each page of a book or document.

foot·fall /ˈfo͝otˌfôl/ ▶ **n.** the sound of a footstep or footsteps.

foot·hill /ˈfo͝otˌhil/ ▶ **n.** a low hill at the base of a mountain.

foot·hold /ˈfo͝otˌhōld/ ▶ **n. 1** a place where you can put a foot down securely while climbing. **2** a secure position from which to make further progress.

foot·ing /ˈfo͝otiNG/ ▶ **n. 1** a secure grip with the feet. **2** the basis on which something is established or operates.

SYNONYMS **1** *a solid financial footing* **basis**, base, foundation. **2** *on an equal footing* **standing**, status, position, condition, arrangement, basis, relationship, terms.

foot·lights /ˈfo͝otˌlīts/ ▶ **pl.n.** a row of spotlights along the front of a stage at the level of the actors' feet.

foot·loose /ˈfo͝otˌlo͞os/ ▶ **adj.** free to do as you please.

foot·man /ˈfo͝otmən/ ▶ **n.** (plural **footmen**) a servant who lets in visitors and serves food at the table.

foot·note /ˈfo͝otˌnōt/ ▶ **n.** an additional piece of information printed at the bottom of a page.

foot·path /ˈfo͝otˌpaTH/ ▶ **n.** a path for people to walk along.

foot·print /ˈfo͝otˌprint/ ▶ **n.** the mark left by a foot or shoe on the ground.

foot·sie /ˈfo͝otsē/ ▶ **n.** (**play footsie**) informal flirtatiously touch someone's feet with your own.

foot·sore /ˈfo͝otˌsôr/ ▶ **adj.** having sore feet from walking.

foot·step /ˈfo͝otˌstep/ ▶ **n.** a step taken in walking. □ **follow in someone's footsteps** do as another person did before.

foot·stool /ˈfo͝otˌsto͞ol/ ▶ **n.** a low stool for resting the feet on when sitting.

foot·wear /ˈfo͝otˌwer/ ▶ **n.** shoes, boots, and other coverings for the feet.

foot·work /ˈfo͝otˌwərk/ ▶ **n.** the way in which you move your feet in dancing and sports.

fop /fäp/ ▶ **n.** a man who is too concerned with his clothes and appearance. ■ **fop·pish adj.**

for /fôr, fər/ ▶ **prep. 1** affecting or relating to: *tickets for the show*. **2** in favor of. **3** on behalf of. **4** because of: *I could dance for joy*. **5** so as to get, have, or do: *shall we go for a walk?* **6** in place of. **7** in exchange for. **8** in the direction of. **9** over a distance or during a period. **10** so as to happen at. ▶ **conj.** literary because.

fo·ra /ˈfôrə/ plural of FORUM.

for·age /ˈfôrij, ˈfär-/ ▶ **v.** (**forages, foraging, foraged**) search for food. ▶ **n.** food for horses and cattle.

for·ay /ˈfôrˌā, ˈfärˌā/ ▶ **n. 1** a sudden attack or move into enemy territory. **2** a brief but spirited attempt to become involved in a new activity.

for·bear /fərˈber, fôr-/ ▶ **v.** (**forbears, forbearing, forbore** /fərˈbôr, fôr-/; past participle **forborne** /fərˈbôrn, fôr-/) stop yourself from doing something.

for·bear·ance /fôrˈberəns, fər-/ ▶ **n.** patient self-control.

for·bear·ing /fôrˈberiNG, fər-/ ▶ **adj.** patient and self-controlled.

for·bid /fərˈbid, fôr-/ ▶ **v.** (**forbids, forbidding, forbade** /fərˈbad, fôr-, -ˈbād/ or **forbad** /fərˈbad, fôr-/; past participle **forbidden**) **1** refuse to allow something. **2** order someone not to do something.

SYNONYMS **1 prohibit**, ban, outlaw, make illegal, veto, proscribe, embargo, bar, debar, rule out. **2** (**forbidden**) **prohibited**, verboten, taboo, illegal, illicit, against the law. ANTONYMS permit, permitted.

□ **forbidden fruit** a thing that you desire all the more because it is not allowed. **God** (or **Heaven**) **forbid** expressing a heartfelt wish that something does not happen.

for·bid·ding /fərˈbidiNG, fôr-/ ▶ **adj.** appearing unfriendly or threatening.

SYNONYMS **threatening**, ominous, menacing, sinister, daunting, off-putting.

■ **for·bid·ding·ly adv.**

force /fôrs/ ▶ **n. 1** physical strength or energy that makes something move. **2** violence used to obtain or achieve something. **3** effect or influence: *the force of popular opinion*. **4** a person or thing that has influence: *a force for peace*. **5** an organized group of soldiers, police, or workers. ▶ **v.** (**forces, forcing, forced**) **1** make someone do something against their will. **2** use physical strength to move something. **3** achieve something by making an effort: *he forced a smile*. **4** (**force something on**) impose something on.

SYNONYMS ▶ **n. 1 strength**, power, energy, might, effort. **2 coercion**, compulsion, constraint, duress, pressure, oppression, harassment, intimidation, violence; informal arm-twisting. **3 power**, potency, weight, effectiveness, persuasiveness, validity, strength, significance, influence, authority; informal punch. **4 body**, group, outfit, party, team, detachment, unit, squad. ▶ **v. 1 compel**, coerce, make, constrain, oblige, impel, drive, pressure, pressurize, press-gang, bully; informal lean on, twist someone's arm. **2 break open**, knock/smash/break down, kick in. **3 propel**, push, thrust, shove, drive, press, pump.

□ **force-feed** force someone to eat food. **force someone's hand** make someone do something. **force the issue** make sure a decision is made. **in force 1** in great strength or numbers. **2** (of a law or rule) in effect.

forced /fôrsd/ ▶ **adj. 1** obtained or imposed by coercion or physical power. **2** (of a gesture or expression) affected or unnatural.

SYNONYMS **1 enforced**, compulsory, obligatory, mandatory, involuntary, imposed, required. **2 strained**, unnatural, artificial, false, feigned, simulated, contrived, labored, affected, hollow; informal phony, pretend, put on. ANTONYMS voluntary, natural.

force·ful /ˈfôrsfəl/ ▶ **adj.** powerful and confident.

SYNONYMS **1 dynamic**, energetic, assertive, authoritative, vigorous, powerful, strong, pushy; informal in-your-face, go-ahead, feisty. **2 convincing**, cogent, compelling, strong, powerful, persuasive, coherent. ANTONYMS weak.

■ **force·ful·ly adv.**

force·meat /ˈfôrsˌmēt/ ▶ **n.** chopped meat or vegetables used as a stuffing.

for·ceps /ˈfôrsəps, -ˌseps/ ▶ **pl.n.** a pair of pincers used in surgery.

for·ci·ble /ˈfôrsəbəl/ ▶ **adj.** done by force. ■ **for·ci·bly adv.**

ford /fôrd/ ▶ **n.** a shallow place in a river or stream where it can be crossed. ▶ **v.** cross a river or stream at a ford.

fore /fôr/ ▶ **adj.** found or placed in front. ▶ **n.** the front part of something. ▶ **exclam.** called out as a warning to people in the path of a golf ball. □ **to the fore** in or to a noticeable or leading position. **fore and aft 1** backward and forward. **2** at the front and rear. **3** (of a sail or rigging) set parallel to the length of a ship or boat.

fore·arm¹ /ˈfôrˌärm/ ▶ **n.** the part of a person's arm from the elbow to the wrist or the fingertips.

fore·arm² /fôrˈärm/ ▶ **v.** (**be forearmed**) be prepared in advance for danger or attack.

fore·bear /ˈfôrˌber/ (or **forbear**) ▶ **n.** an ancestor.

fore·bode /fôrˈbōd/ ▶ **v.** (**forebodes**, **foreboding**, **foreboded**) old use be an advance warning of something bad.

fore·bod·ing /fôrˈbōdiNG/ ▶ **n.** a feeling that something bad will happen. ▶ **adj.** suggesting that something bad will happen: *a dark, foreboding voice.*

fore·cast /ˈfôrˌkast/ ▶ **v.** (**forecasts**, **forecasting**, **forecast** or **forecasted**) predict what will happen in the future. ▶ **n.** a prediction.

> SYNONYMS ▶ **v.** **predict**, prophesy, foretell, foresee. ▶ **n.** **prediction**, prophecy, prognostication, prognosis.

■ **fore·cast·er** **n.**

fore·cas·tle /ˈfōksəl, ˈfôrˌkasəl/ (or **fo'c's'le**) ▶ **n.** the front part of a ship below the deck.

fore·close /fôrˈklōz/ ▶ **v.** (**forecloses**, **foreclosing**, **foreclosed**) take possession of a property because the occupant has not kept up their mortgage payments. ■ **fore·clo·sure** /fôrˈklōZHər/ **n.**

fore·court /ˈfôrˌkôrt/ ▶ **n.** **1** an open area in front of a large building or gas station. **2** Tennis the part of the court between the service line and the net.

fore·fa·ther /ˈfôrˌfäT͟Hər/ ▶ **n.** an ancestor.

fore·fin·ger /ˈfôrˌfiNGgər/ ▶ **n.** the finger next to the thumb.

fore·foot /ˈfôrˌfo͝ot/ ▶ **n.** (plural **forefeet**) each of the two front feet of a four-footed animal.

fore·front /ˈfôrˌfrənt/ ▶ **n.** the leading position.

fore·go /fôrˈgō/ ▶ **v.** (**foregoes**, **foregoing**, **forewent** /fôrˈwent/; past participle **foregone** /ˈfôrˌgôn/) old use come before in place or time.

> SYNONYMS **do without**, go without, give up, waive, renounce, surrender, relinquish, part with, drop, sacrifice, abstain from, refrain from, eschew, cut out; informal swear off; formal forswear, abjure.

□ **foregone conclusion** a result that can be easily predicted.

fore·go·ing /fôrˈgōiNG/ ▶ **adj.** previously mentioned.

fore·ground /ˈfôrˌground/ ▶ **n.** **1** the part of a view or image nearest to the observer. **2** the most important position.

fore·hand /ˈfôrˌhand/ ▶ **n.** (in tennis and similar games) a stroke played with the palm of the hand facing in the direction of the stroke.

fore·head /ˈfôrəd, ˈfôrˌhed/ ▶ **n.** the part of the face above the eyebrows.

for·eign /ˈfôrən, ˈfär-/ ▶ **adj.** **1** having to do with a country or language other than your own. **2** coming from outside: *a foreign influence.* **3** (**foreign to**) not familiar to or typical of.

> SYNONYMS **alien**, overseas, non-native, imported, distant, external, far-off, exotic, strange. ANTONYMS domestic, native.

□ **foreign body** a small piece of material that has entered the body from outside. **foreign exchange** **1** the money of other countries. **2** an institution or system for dealing in such currency. **Foreign Legion** a military formation of the French army made up chiefly of those who are not Frenchmen.

> SPELLING
> Write **-eign**, not **-iegn**: for**eign**.

for·eign·er /ˈfôrənər, ˈfär-/ ▶ **n.** **1** a person from a foreign country. **2** informal a stranger.

> SYNONYMS **alien**, non-native, stranger, outsider, immigrant, settler, newcomer, incomer. ANTONYMS native, national.

fore·knowl·edge /fôrˈnäləj/ ▶ **n.** awareness of something before it happens.

fore·land /ˈfôrlənd/ ▶ **n.** **1** an area of land in front of a particular feature. **2** a piece of land that projects into the sea.

fore·leg /ˈfôrˌleg/ ▶ **n.** either of the front legs of a four-legged animal.

fore·lock /ˈfôrˌläk/ ▶ **n.** a lock of hair growing just above the forehead.

fore·man /ˈfôrmən/ ▶ **n.** (plural **foremen**) **1** a worker who supervises other workers. **2** (in a court of law) a person who is head of a jury.

fore·mast /ˈfôrˌmast, -məst/ ▶ **n.** the mast of a ship nearest the bow.

fore·most /ˈfôrˌmōst/ ▶ **adj.** highest in rank, importance, or position. ▶ **adv.** in the first place.

> SYNONYMS ▶ **adj.** **leading**, principal, premier, prime, top, greatest, best, supreme, preeminent, ranking, outstanding, most important, most notable; informal number-one. ANTONYMS minor.

fore·name /ˈfôrˌnām/ ▶ **n.** a person's first name.

fore·noon /ˈfôrˌno͞on/ ▶ **n.** Nautical the morning.

fo·ren·sic /fəˈrenzik, -sik/ ▶ **adj.** **1** having to do with the use of scientific methods in investigating crime. **2** having to do with courts of law. □ **forensic medicine** medical knowledge used in the investigation of crime.

fore·play /ˈfôrˌplā/ ▶ **n.** activities such as kissing and touching that people may engage in before having sex.

fore·run·ner /ˈfôrˌrənər/ ▶ **n.** a person or thing that exists before another comes or is developed.

fore·sail /ˈfôrˌsāl, -səl/ ▶ **n.** the main sail on a foremast.

fore·see /fôrˈsē/ ▶ **v.** (**foresees**, **foreseeing**, **foresaw** /fôrˈsô/; past participle **foreseen**) be aware of something before it happens; predict.

> SYNONYMS **anticipate**, expect, envisage, predict, forecast, foretell, prophesy.

■ **fore·see·a·ble** **adj.**

fore·shad·ow /fôrˈSHadō/ ▶ **v.** be a warning or indication of a future event.

fore·shore /ˈfôrˌSHôr/ ▶ **n.** the part of a shore between the highest and lowest levels reached by the sea.

fore·short·en /fôrˈSHôrtn/ ▶ **v.** **1** portray something as being closer or shallower than it really is. **2** end something before the usual or intended time.

fore·sight /ˈfôrˌsīt/ ▶ **n.** the ability to predict future events and needs.

> SYNONYMS **forethought**, planning, farsightedness, vision, anticipation, prudence, care, caution. ANTONYMS hindsight.

fore·skin /'fôr,skin/ ▶ **n.** the roll of skin covering the end of the penis.

for·est /'fôrəst, 'fär-/ ▶ **n. 1** a large area covered thickly with trees and plants. **2** a large number of tangled or upright objects: *a forest of flags.*
■ **for·est·ed adj.**

fore·stall /fôr'stôl/ ▶ **v.** prevent or delay something by taking action in advance.

for·est·ry /'fôrəstrē, 'fär-/ ▶ **n.** the science or practice of planting and taking care of forests.
■ **for·est·er n.**

fore·taste /'fôr,tāst/ ▶ **n.** a sample of something that is to come.

fore·tell /fôr'tel/ ▶ **v.** (**foretells**, **foretelling**, **foretold** /fôr'tōld/) predict.

> SYNONYMS **predict**, forecast, prophesy, foresee, anticipate, envisage, warn of.

fore·thought /'fôr,THôt/ ▶ **n.** careful consideration of what will be necessary or may happen in the future.

for·ev·er /fə'revər, fô-/ ▶ **adv. 1** (also **for ever**) for all future time. **2** a very long time. **3** continually: *she is forever complaining.*

> SYNONYMS **1 for always**, evermore, for ever and ever, for good, for all time, until the end of time, eternally, forevermore; informal until the cows come home. **2 always**, continually, constantly, perpetually, incessantly, endlessly, persistently, repeatedly, regularly; informal 24-7.

fore·warn /fôr'wôrn/ ▶ **v.** warn in advance.

fore·word /'fôr,wərd/ ▶ **n.** a short introduction to a book.

for·feit /'fôrfit/ ▶ **v.** (**forfeits**, **forfeiting**, **forfeited**) lose property or a right as a punishment for doing wrong. ▶ **n.** a punishment for doing wrong. ▶ **adj.** lost or given up as a forfeit.

> SYNONYMS ▶ **v. lose**, be deprived of, surrender, relinquish, sacrifice, give up, renounce, forgo. ▶ **n. penalty**, sanction, punishment, penance, fine, confiscation, loss, forfeiture, surrender.

forge[1] /fôrj/ ▶ **v.** (**forges**, **forging**, **forged**) **1** shape a metal object by heating and hammering it. **2** create something through effort: *forge a close relationship.* **3** produce a copy of a banknote, signature, etc., to deceive people. ▶ **n. 1** a blacksmith's workshop. **2** a furnace for melting or refining metal.

> SYNONYMS ▶ **v. 1 hammer out**, beat out, fashion. **2 build**, construct, form, create, establish, set up. **3 fake**, falsify, counterfeit, copy, imitate, pirate. **4** (**forged**) **fake**, false, counterfeit, imitation, copied, pirate, bogus; informal phony, dud.

■ **forg·er n.**

forge[2] ▶ **v.** (**forges**, **forging**, **forged**) **1** move forward gradually or steadily. **2** (**forge ahead**) make progress.

for·ger·y /'fôrjərē/ ▶ **n.** (plural **forgeries**) **1** the action of forging a banknote, work of art, etc. **2** a forged or copied item.

> SYNONYMS **fake**, counterfeit, fraud, imitation, replica, copy, pirate copy; informal phony.

for·get /fər'get/ ▶ **v.** (**forgets**, **forgetting**, **forgot** /fər'gät/; past participle **forgotten** /fər'gätn/ or **forgot**) **1** be unable to remember. **2** fail to remember to do something. **3** stop thinking of. **4** (**forget yourself**) behave in an inappropriate or unacceptable way.

> SYNONYMS **1 fail to remember**, be unable to remember. **2 leave behind**, fail to take/bring, leave home without. **3** *I forgot to close the door* **neglect**, fail, omit. ANTONYMS remember.

□ **forget-me-not** a plant with light blue flowers.
■ **for·get·ta·ble adj.**

for·get·ful /fər'getfəl/ ▶ **adj.** tending to forget things.

> SYNONYMS **1 absentminded**, amnesiac, vague, scatterbrained, disorganized, dreamy, abstracted, with a mind/memory like a sieve. **2** *forgetful of the time* **heedless**, careless, inattentive to, negligent about, oblivious to, unconcerned about, indifferent to.

■ **for·get·ful·ly adv.**

for·give /fər'giv/ ▶ **v.** (**forgives**, **forgiving**, **forgave** /fər'gāv/; past participle **forgiven**) **1** stop feeling angry or resentful toward a person who has done something hurtful or wrong. **2** excuse an offense or mistake.

> SYNONYMS **1 pardon**, excuse, exonerate, absolve. **2 excuse**, overlook, disregard, ignore, make allowances for, turn a blind eye to, condone, indulge, tolerate. ANTONYMS blame, resent.

■ **for·giv·a·ble adj.**

for·give·ness /fər'givnəs/ ▶ **n.** the action of forgiving, or the state of being forgiven.

> SYNONYMS **pardon**, absolution, exoneration, indulgence, clemency, mercy, reprieve, amnesty. ANTONYMS punishment.

for·giv·ing /fər'giviNG/ ▶ **adj. 1** ready and willing to forgive: *Taylor was in a forgiving mood.* **2** tolerant: *these flooring planks are more forgiving of heavy traffic than real wood.*

> SYNONYMS **merciful**, lenient, compassionate, magnanimous, humane, softhearted, forbearing, tolerant, indulgent, understanding. ANTONYMS merciless, vindictive.

for·go /fôr'gō/ (or **forego**) ▶ **v.** (**forgoes**, **forgoing**, **forwent** /fôr'went/; past participle **forgone** /'fôr,gôn/) go without something that you want.

> SYNONYMS **do without**, go without, give up, waive, renounce, surrender, relinquish, part with, drop, sacrifice, abstain from, refrain from, eschew, cut out; informal swear off; formal forswear, abjure.

fork /fôrk/ ▶ **n. 1** an object with two or more prongs used for lifting or holding food. **2** a similar-shaped farm or garden tool used for digging or lifting. **3** the point where a road, river, etc., divides into two parts. **4** either of two such parts: *we took the left fork to get back to our campsite.* ▶ **v. 1** divide into two parts. **2** take one route or the other at a fork. **3** dig or lift with a fork. **4** (**fork something out**) informal pay money.

> SYNONYMS ▶ **v. split**, branch, divide, separate, part, diverge, go in different directions, bifurcate.

forked /fôrkt/ ▶ **adj. 1** having a divided or fork-shaped end. **2** in the shape of a zigzag.

fork·lift /'fôrk,lift/ (or **forklift truck**) ▶ **n.** a vehicle with a device on the front for lifting and carrying heavy loads.

for·lorn /fər'lôrn, fôr-/ ▶ **adj.** **1** pitifully sad and lonely. **2** unlikely to succeed or be fulfilled: *a forlorn hope.*

SYNONYMS **1 unhappy**, sad, miserable, sorrowful, dejected, despondent, disconsolate, wretched, down, downcast, dispirited, downhearted, crestfallen, depressed, melancholy, gloomy, glum, mournful, despairing, doleful, woebegone; informal blue, down in the mouth, down in the dumps, fed up. **2 hopeless**, useless, futile, pointless, purposeless, vain, unavailing. ANTONYMS happy.

■ **for·lorn·ly** **adv.**

form /fôrm/ ▶ **n.** **1** the shape or arrangement of something. **2** a particular way in which a thing exists: *passages in the form of poems.* **3** a type: *a form of cancer.* **4** a printed document with blank spaces for information to be filled in. **5** the current standard of play of an athlete or team. **6** a person's mood and state of health: *she was in good form.* **7** the way something is usually done: *the assistant knew the form.* ▶ **v.** **1** create something by shaping material or bringing together parts. **2** go to make up. **3** establish or develop.

SYNONYMS ▶ **n.** **1 shape**, configuration, formation, structure, construction, arrangement, appearance, exterior, outline, format, layout, design. **2 body**, shape, figure, frame, physique, anatomy; informal vital statistics. **3 manifestation**, appearance, embodiment, incarnation, semblance, shape, guise. **4 kind**, sort, type, class, category, variety, genre, brand, style. **5 questionnaire**, document, coupon, slip. **6 class**, year, grade. **7 condition**, fettle, shape, health. ▶ **v.** **1 make**, construct, build, manufacture, fabricate, assemble, put together, create, fashion, shape. **2 formulate**, devise, conceive, work out, think up, lay, draw up, put together, produce, fashion, concoct, forge, hatch; informal dream up. **3 set up**, establish, found, launch, create, institute, start, inaugurate. **4 materialize**, come into being/existence, emerge, develop, take shape, gather, accumulate, collect, amass. **5 arrange**, draw up, line up, assemble, organize, sort, order. **6 comprise**, make, make up, constitute, compose, add up to. ANTONYMS dissolve, disappear.

■ **form·less** **adj.**

for·mal /'fôrməl/ ▶ **adj.** **1** suitable for or referring to official or important occasions. **2** (of a person or their manner) not relaxed or friendly. **3** officially recognized: *a formal complaint.* **4** arranged in a regular way, according to an exact plan: *a formal garden.*

SYNONYMS **1 ceremonial**, ritualistic, ritual, official, conventional, traditional, stately, solemn, ceremonious. **2 aloof**, reserved, remote, detached, unapproachable, stiff, stuffy, correct, proper; informal standoffish. **3 official**, legal, authorized, approved, certified, endorsed, sanctioned, licensed, recognized. ANTONYMS informal, casual, unofficial.

■ **for·mal·ly** **adv.**

form·al·de·hyde /fôr'maldə,hīd, fər-/ ▶ **n.** a strong-smelling gas mixed with water and used as a preservative and disinfectant.

for·ma·lin /'fôrməlin/ ▶ **n.** a solution of formaldehyde in water.

for·mal·i·ty /fôr'malətē/ ▶ **n.** (plural **formalities**) **1** a thing done to follow rules or usual customs. **2** correct and formal behavior. **3** (**a formality**) a thing done or happening as a matter of course.

SYNONYMS **1 ceremony**, ritual, protocol, decorum, solemnity. **2 aloofness**, reserve, remoteness, detachment, unapproachability, stiffness, stuffiness, correctness; informal standoffishness. ANTONYMS informality.

for·mal·ize /'fôrmə,līz/ ▶ **v.** (**formalizes**, **formalizing**, **formalized**) make an arrangement official.

for·mat /'fôr,mat/ ▶ **n.** **1** the way in which something is arranged or presented. **2** the shape, size, and presentation of a book, document, etc. ▶ **v.** (**formats**, **formatting**, **formatted**) give something a particular format.

SYNONYMS ▶ **n.** **design**, style, appearance, look, form, shape, size, arrangement, plan, structure, scheme, composition, configuration.

for·ma·tion /fôr'māsʜən/ ▶ **n.** **1** the action of forming. **2** something that has been formed: *a cloud formation.* **3** a particular structure or arrangement.

SYNONYMS **1** *the formation of the island* **emergence**, genesis, development, evolution, shaping, origin. **2** *the formation of a new government* **establishment**, setting up, institution, foundation, creation, inauguration. **3 configuration**, arrangement, grouping, pattern, array, alignment, order. ANTONYMS destruction, dissolution.

for·ma·tive /'fôrmətiv/ ▶ **adj.** having a strong influence in the way something is formed.

form·er[1] /'fôrmər/ ▶ **adj.** **1** having been previously: *her former boyfriend.* **2** in the past: *in former times.* **3** (**the former**) referring to the first of two things mentioned.

SYNONYMS **1 one-time**, erstwhile, sometime, ex-, previous, preceding, earlier, prior, last; formal quondam. **2 earlier**, old, past, bygone, olden, long ago, gone by, long past, of old. **3 first-mentioned**, first. ANTONYMS future, current, latter.

form·er[2] ▶ **n.** a person or thing that forms something.

for·mer·ly /'fôrmərlē/ ▶ **adv.** in the past.

SYNONYMS **previously**, earlier, before, until now/then, once, once upon a time, at one time, in the past.

For·mi·ca /fôr'mīkə, fər-/ ▶ **n.** trademark a hard plastic material used for countertops, cupboard doors, etc.

for·mic ac·id /'fôrmik/ ▶ **n.** an acid present in the fluid produced by some ants.

for·mi·da·ble /'fôrmədəbəl, fôr'midəbəl, fər'mid-/ ▶ **adj.** frightening or intimidating through being very large, powerful, or capable.

SYNONYMS **1 intimidating**, daunting, indomitable, forbidding, alarming, frightening, awesome, fearsome; humorous redoubtable. **2 accomplished**, masterly, virtuoso, expert, impressive, powerful, terrific, superb; informal tremendous, nifty, crack, ace, wizard, magic, mean, wicked, deadly.

■ **for·mi·da·bly** **adv.**

for·mu·la /'fôrmyələ/ ▶ **n.** (plural **formulas** or **formulae** /-,lē, -,lī/) **1** a mathematical relationship or rule expressed in symbols. **2** a set of chemical symbols showing what elements are present in a compound. **3** a method for achieving something. **4** a fixed form of words used in particular situations. **5** a list of ingredients with which something is made. **6** a powder-based milky drink for babies.

SYNONYMS **1 form of words**, set expression, rubric, phrase, saying. **2 recipe**, prescription, blueprint, plan, policy, method, procedure.

for·mu·la·ic /ˌfôrmyəˈlāik/ ▶ **adj. 1** containing a set form of words. **2** made by closely following a rule or style: *much romantic fiction is formulaic.*

for·mu·late /ˈfôrmyəˌlāt/ ▶ **v.** (**formulates**, **formulating**, **formulated**) **1** create or prepare something methodically. **2** express an idea clearly and briefly.

SYNONYMS **1 devise**, conceive, work out, think up, lay, draw up, form, concoct, contrive, forge, hatch, prepare, develop. **2 express**, phrase, word, define, specify, put into words, frame, couch, put, articulate, say.

■ **for·mu·la·tion** /ˌfôrmyəˈlāshən/ **n.**

for·ni·cate /ˈfôrniˌkāt/ ▶ **v.** (**fornicates**, **fornicating**, **fornicated**) formal have sex with someone you are not married to. ■ **for·ni·ca·tion** /ˌfôrniˈkāshən/ **n.** **for·ni·ca·tor n.**

for·sake /fərˈsāk, fôr-/ ▶ **v.** (**forsakes**, **forsaking**, **forsook** /-ˈso͝ok/; past participle **forsaken**) literary **1** abandon. **2** give up.

for·sooth /fərˈso͞oth/ ▶ **adv.** old use indeed.

for·swear /fôrˈswe(ə)r/ ▶ **v.** (**forswears**, **forswearing**, **forswore** /fôrˈswôr/; past participle **forsworn** /fôrˈswôrn/) formal **1** agree to give up or do without. **2** (**forswear yourself** or **be forsworn**) lie after swearing to tell the truth.

for·syth·i·a /fərˈsithēə/ ▶ **n.** a shrub with bright yellow flowers.

fort /fôrt/ ▶ **n.** a building constructed to defend a place against attack.

SYNONYMS **fortress**, castle, citadel, bunker, stronghold, fortification, bastion.

□ **hold (down) the fort** be responsible for something while a person is away.

for·te¹ /ˈfôrˌtā, fôrt/ ▶ **n.** a thing for which someone has a particular talent.

SYNONYMS **strength**, strong point, specialty, strong suit, talent, skill, gift; informal thing.

for·te² /ˈfôrˌtā/ ▶ **adv. & adj.** Music loud or loudly.

forth /fôrth/ ▶ **adv.** old use **1** forward or into view. **2** onward in time.

forth·com·ing /fôrthˈkəming, ˈfôrthˌkəming/ ▶ **adj. 1** about to happen or appear. **2** made available when required: *help was not forthcoming.* **3** willing to reveal information.

SYNONYMS **1 coming**, upcoming, approaching, imminent, impending, future. **2 communicative**, talkative, chatty, informative, expansive, expressive, frank, open, candid. ANTONYMS past, current, reticent.

forth·right /ˈfôrthˌrīt/ ▶ **adj.** direct and outspoken.

SYNONYMS **frank**, direct, straightforward, honest, candid, open, sincere, outspoken, straight, blunt, plain-spoken, no-nonsense, bluff, matter-of-fact, to the point; informal upfront. ANTONYMS secretive, evasive.

forth·with /fôrthˈwith/ ▶ **adv.** without delay.

for·ti·fi·ca·tion /ˌfôrtəfəˈkāshən/ ▶ **n. 1** a defensive wall or other structure built to strengthen a place against attack. **2** the action of fortifying something.

for·ti·fy /ˈfôrtəˌfī/ ▶ **v.** (**fortifies**, **fortifying**, **fortified**) **1** strengthen a place to protect it against attack. **2** give strength or energy to. **3** add alcohol or vitamins to food or drink: *fortified wine.*

SYNONYMS **1 strengthen**, secure, barricade, protect, buttress, shore up. **2 invigorate**, strengthen, energize, enliven, animate, vitalize, buoy up; informal pep up, buck up. ANTONYMS weaken.

for·tis·si·mo /fôrˈtisəˌmō/ ▶ **adv. & adj.** Music very loud or loudly.

for·ti·tude /ˈfôrtəˌto͞od/ ▶ **n.** courage and strength when facing pain or trouble.

SYNONYMS **courage**, bravery, endurance, resilience, mettle, strength of character, backbone, grit; informal guts.

fort·night /ˈfôrtˌnīt/ ▶ **n.** a period of two weeks.

fort·night·ly /ˈfôrtˌnītlē/ ▶ **adj. & adv.** happening or produced every two weeks.

for·tress /ˈfôrtrəs/ ▶ **n.** a building or town that has been strengthened against attack.

SYNONYMS **fort**, castle, citadel, bunker, stronghold, fortification.

for·tu·i·tous /fôrˈto͞oətəs/ ▶ **adj. 1** happening by chance. **2** lucky. ■ **for·tu·i·tous·ly adv.**

for·tu·nate /ˈfôrchənət/ ▶ **adj. 1** involving good luck. **2** advantageous or favorable: *a most fortunate match for our daughter.*

SYNONYMS **1 lucky**, favored, blessed, leading a charmed life, in luck; informal born with a silver spoon in your mouth. **2 favorable**, advantageous, happy. ANTONYMS unfavorable, unlucky.

for·tu·nate·ly /ˈfôrchənətlē/ ▶ **adv.** it is fortunate that.

SYNONYMS **luckily**, as luck would have it, happily, mercifully, thankfully.

for·tune /ˈfôrchən/ ▶ **n. 1** chance or luck as it affects human affairs. **2** (**fortunes**) the success or failure of a person or undertaking. **3** a large amount of money or property.

SYNONYMS **1 chance**, accident, coincidence, serendipity, destiny, providence, happenstance. **2 luck**, fate, destiny, predestination, the stars, karma, kismet, lot. **3** *an upswing in their fortunes* **circumstances**, state of affairs, condition, position, situation. **4 wealth**, money, riches, assets, resources, means, possessions, property, estate.

□ **fortune-teller** a person who predicts what will happen in people's futures. **a small fortune** informal a large amount of money. **tell someone's fortune** make predictions about a person's future.

for·ty /ˈfôrtē/ ▶ **cardinal number** (plural **forties**) ten less than fifty; 40. (Roman numeral: **xl** or **XL**) □ **forty winks** informal a short daytime sleep. ■ **for·ti·eth ordinal number.**

SPELLING

Write **for-**, not **four-**: **forty**.

fo·rum /ˈfôrəm/ ▶ **n.** (plural **forums**) **1** a meeting or opportunity for exchanging views. **2** (plural **fora** /-rə/) (in ancient Roman cities) a square or marketplace used for public business. **3** an Internet site where people can post and read messages, usually on a specific area of interest.

> SYNONYMS **meeting**, assembly, gathering, rally, conference, seminar, convention, symposium.

for·ward /ˈfôrwərd/ (or **forwards**) ▶ **adv. & adj.** **1** in the direction that you are facing or traveling. **2** toward a successful end. **3** ahead in time. **4** in or near the front of a ship or aircraft. ▶ **adj.** behaving in a way that is too confident or friendly. ▶ **n.** an attacking player in sports. ▶ **v.** send a letter, especially on to a further destination.

> SYNONYMS ▶ **adv. & adj. 1 ahead**, forwards, onward, onwards, on, further. **2 toward the front**, out, forth, into view, up. ANTONYMS backward, back. ▶ **adj. 1 onward**, advancing. **2 front**, advance, foremost, leading. **3 future**, forward-looking, for the future, anticipatory. **4 bold**, brazen, shameless, familiar, overfamiliar, presumptuous, cheeky; informal fresh. ANTONYMS backward, rear. ▶ **v.** **1 send on**, post on, redirect, readdress, pass on. **2 send**, dispatch, transmit, carry, convey, deliver, ship.

□ **forward-looking** open to new ideas and developments.

fos·sil /ˈfäsəl/ ▶ **n.** **1** the remains of a prehistoric plant or animal that have become hardened into rock. **2** humorous a very out-of-date person or thing. □ **fossil fuel** a fuel such as coal or gas that is formed from the remains of animals and plants.

fos·sil·ize /ˈfäsəˌlīz/ ▶ **v.** (**fossilizes**, **fossilizing**, **fossilized**) preserve an animal or plant so that it becomes a fossil. ■ **fos·sil·i·za·tion** /ˌfäsəliˈzāsʜən/ **n.**

fos·ter /ˈfôstər, ˈfäs-/ ▶ **v.** (**fosters**, **fostering**, **fostered**) **1** encourage the development of. **2** bring up a child that is not your own by birth.

> SYNONYMS **1 encourage**, promote, further, nurture, help, aid, assist, support, back. **2 bring up**, rear, raise, care for, take care of, look after, provide for.

fought /fôt/ past and past participle of **FIGHT**.

foul /foul/ ▶ **adj.** **1** having a disgusting smell or taste. **2** very unpleasant. **3** polluted. **4** wicked or obscene. ▶ **n.** (in sports) a piece of play that is not allowed by the rules. ▶ **v.** **1** make foul or dirty. **2** (in sports) commit a foul against. **3** (**foul something up**) make a mistake with something. **4** make a cable or anchor become entangled or jammed.

> SYNONYMS ▶ **adj. 1 disgusting**, revolting, repulsive, repugnant, abhorrent, loathsome, offensive, sickening, nauseating; informal ghastly, gruesome, gross. **2 contaminated**, polluted, infected, tainted, impure, filthy, dirty, unclean. **3 vulgar**, crude, coarse, filthy, dirty, obscene, indecent, naughty, offensive; informal blue. ANTONYMS pleasant. ▶ **v. 1 dirty**, pollute, contaminate, poison, taint, sully. **2 tangle up**, entangle, snarl, catch, entwine.

□ **foul ball** Baseball a ball struck so that it falls outside the lines extending from home plate past first and third bases. **foul-mouthed** using bad language. **foul play 1** unfair play in sports. **2** criminal or violent activity. ■ **foul·ly adv.**

found¹ /found/ past and past participle of **FIND**.

found² ▶ **v.** **1** establish an institution or organization. **2** (**be founded on**) be based on a particular concept.

> SYNONYMS **establish**, set up, start, begin, get going, institute, inaugurate, launch, create, originate.

□ **founding father** a founder. **Founding Father** a member of the group of men that drew up the constitution of the United States in 1787.

found³ ▶ **v.** melt and mold metal to make an object.

foun·da·tion /founˈdāsʜən/ ▶ **n.** **1** the lowest part of a building, which supports the weight. **2** an underlying basis or reason. **3** an institution or organization. **4** the action of founding something. **5** a cream or powder applied to the face as a base for other makeup.

> SYNONYMS **1 footing**, foot, base, substructure, underpinning. **2 justification**, grounds, evidence, basis. **3 institution**, establishment, charitable body, agency.

□ **foundation stone** a stone laid at a ceremony to celebrate the founding of a building.

found·er¹ /ˈfoundər/ ▶ **n.** a person who founds an institution or settlement.

> SYNONYMS **originator**, creator, (founding) father, architect, developer, pioneer, author, inventor, mastermind.

found·er² ▶ **v.** (**founders**, **foundering**, **foundered**) **1** (of a plan or undertaking) fail; come to nothing. **2** (of a ship) fill with water and sink.

> SYNONYMS **1 fail**, be unsuccessful, fall flat, fall through, collapse, backfire, meet with disaster, be a fiasco; informal flop, bomb. **2 sink**, go to the bottom, go down, be lost at sea. ANTONYMS succeed.

found·ling /ˈfoundlɪɴɢ/ ▶ **n.** a child that has been abandoned by its parents and is discovered and cared for by other people.

found·ry /ˈfoundrē/ ▶ **n.** (plural **foundries**) a workshop or factory for casting metal.

fount /fänt, fount/ ▶ **n.** **1** a source of a desirable quality. **2** literary a spring or fountain.

foun·tain /ˈfountn/ ▶ **n.** **1** a decorative structure in a pool or lake from which a jet of water is pumped into the air. **2** literary a natural spring of water.

> SYNONYMS **1 jet**, spray, spout, spurt, cascade, water feature. **2 source**, fount, well, reservoir, fund, mine.

□ **fountain pen** a pen with a container from which ink flows to the nib.

foun·tain·head /ˈfountnˌhed/ ▶ **n.** an original source of something.

four /fôr/ ▶ **cardinal number** one more than three; 4. (Roman numeral: **iv** or **IV**) □ **four-poster** a bed with a post at each corner holding up a canopy. **four-square** having a square shape and solid appearance. **four-stroke** (of an internal combustion engine) having a cycle of four strokes (intake, compression, combustion, and exhaust). **four-wheel drive** a system that provides power to all four wheels of a vehicle.

four·some /ˈfôrsəm/ ▶ **n.** a group of four people.

four·teen /ˌfôrˈtēn, ˈfôrˌtēn/ ▶ **cardinal number** one more than thirteen; 14. (Roman numeral: **xiv** or **XIV**) ■ **four·teenth ordinal number.**

fourth /fôrTH/ ▶ **ordinal number** **1** number four in a sequence; 4th. **2** (**a fourth** or **one fourth**) a quarter. ▫ **the fourth estate** the press. **Fourth of July** ⇒ INDEPENDENCE DAY. ■ **fourth·ly** adv.

fowl /foul/ ▶ n. (plural **fowl** or **fowls**) **1** a bird kept for its eggs or meat, such as a chicken or turkey. **2** birds as a group.

fox /fäks/ ▶ n. **1** an animal with a pointed muzzle, bushy tail, and a reddish coat. **2** informal a sly or crafty person. ▶ v. informal baffle or deceive. ▫ **fox hunting** the sport of hunting a fox across country with a pack of hounds.

fox·glove /'fäks,gləv/ ▶ n. a tall plant with spikes of flowers shaped like the fingers of gloves.

fox·hole /'fäks,hōl/ ▶ n. a hole in the ground used by troops as a shelter against the enemy or as a place to fire from.

fox·hound /'fäks,hound/ ▶ n. a breed of dog trained to hunt foxes in packs.

fox·trot /'fäks,trät/ ▶ n. a ballroom dance that involves switching between slow and quick steps. ▶ v. (**foxtrots**, **foxtrotting**, **foxtrotted**) dance the foxtrot.

fox·y /'fäksē/ ▶ adj. (**foxier**, **foxiest**) **1** like a fox. **2** crafty or sly.

foy·er /'foiər, 'foi,ā/ ▶ n. a large entrance hall in a hotel, theater, or home.

> SYNONYMS **entrance hall**, hallway, entry, entryway, porch, reception area, atrium, concourse, lobby, anteroom.

Fr. ▶ abbr. Father (as a title of priests).

fr. ▶ abbr. franc(s).

fra·cas /'frākəs, 'frak-/ ▶ n. (plural **fracas**) a noisy disturbance or quarrel.

> SYNONYMS **disturbance**, brawl, melee, rumpus, skirmish, struggle, scuffle, clash, fisticuffs, altercation; informal roughhouse, scrap, set-to, shindig, dust-up; Law, dated affray.

frac·tion /'frakSHən/ ▶ n. **1** a number that is not a whole number (e.g., $^1/_2$, 0.5). **2** a very small part or amount.

> SYNONYMS **1** *a fraction of the population* **tiny part**, fragment, snippet, smattering. **2** *he moved a fraction closer* **bit**, little, touch, soupçon, trifle, mite, shade, jot; informal smidgen, tad. ANTONYMS whole.

frac·tion·al /'frakSHənl/ ▶ adj. **1** having to do with a fraction. **2** very small in amount. ■ **frac·tion·al·ly** adv.

frac·tious /'frakSHəs/ ▶ adj. **1** bad-tempered. **2** difficult to control.

> SYNONYMS **grumpy**, bad-tempered, irascible, irritable, crotchety, grouchy, cantankerous, touchy, testy, ill-tempered, peevish, cross, pettish, waspish, crabby, crusty, cranky, ornery.

frac·ture /'frakCHər/ ▶ n. **1** a crack or break. **2** the cracking or breaking of a hard object or material, typically a bone or a rock stratum. ▶ v. (**fractures**, **fracturing**, **fractured**) **1** break. **2** (of a group) break up.

> SYNONYMS ▶ n. **break**, crack, split, rupture, fissure. ▶ v. **break**, crack, split, rupture, snap, shatter, fragment, splinter.

frag·ile /'frajəl, -jīl/ ▶ adj. **1** easily broken or damaged. **2** (of a person) delicate and vulnerable.

> SYNONYMS **1 breakable**, delicate, brittle, flimsy, dainty, fine. **2 tenuous**, shaky, insecure, vulnerable, flimsy. **3 weak**, delicate, frail, debilitated, ill, unwell, poorly, sickly. ANTONYMS sturdy, robust.

■ **fra·gil·i·ty** /frə'jilitē/ n.

frag·ment ▶ n. /'fragmənt/ a small part that has broken off or come from something larger. ▶ v. /'frag,ment, ,frag'ment/ break into fragments.

> SYNONYMS ▶ n. **1 piece**, bit, particle, speck, chip, shard, sliver, splinter, flake. **2 scrap**, snippet, shred, bit. ▶ v. **break up**, crack open, shatter, splinter, fracture, disintegrate, fall to pieces, fall apart.

■ **frag·men·tar·y** /'fragmən,terē/ adj. **frag·men·ta·tion** /,fragmən'tāSHən/ n.

fra·grance /'frāgrəns/ ▶ n. **1** a pleasant, sweet smell. **2** a perfume or aftershave.

> SYNONYMS **1 sweet smell**, scent, perfume, bouquet, aroma, nose. **2 perfume**, scent, eau de toilette.

fra·grant /'frāgrənt/ ▶ adj. having a pleasant, sweet smell.

> SYNONYMS **sweet-scented**, sweet-smelling, scented, perfumed, aromatic. ANTONYMS smelly.

frail /frāl/ ▶ adj. **1** weak and delicate. **2** easily damaged or broken.

> SYNONYMS **1** *a frail old lady* **weak**, delicate, feeble, infirm, ill, unwell, sickly, poorly. **2** *a frail structure* **fragile**, easily damaged, delicate, flimsy, insubstantial, unsteady, unstable, rickety. ANTONYMS strong, robust.

frail·ty /'frāltē/ ▶ n. (plural **frailties**) the condition of being frail; weakness: *human frailty*.

frame /frām/ ▶ n. **1** a rigid structure surrounding a picture, door, etc., or giving support to a building or vehicle. **2** the structure of a person's body: *her slim frame*. **3** a single picture in a series forming a movie or video. **4** a single game of snooker. ▶ v. (**frames**, **framing**, **framed**) **1** put a picture in a frame. **2** create or develop a plan or system. **3** informal produce false evidence against someone to make them appear guilty of a crime.

> SYNONYMS ▶ n. **1 framework**, structure, substructure, skeleton, casing, chassis, shell. **2 body**, figure, form, shape, physique, anatomy, build. ▶ v. **1 mount**, set in a frame. **2 formulate**, draw up, draft, shape, compose, put together, form, devise.

▫ **frame of mind** a particular mood. **frame of reference** a set of values against which you can make a judgment. **frame-up** informal a plot to make an innocent person appear guilty of a crime.

frame·work /'frām,wərk/ ▶ n. a supporting or underlying structure.

> SYNONYMS **1 frame**, structure, skeleton, chassis, support, scaffolding. **2 structure**, shape, fabric, order, scheme, system, organization, anatomy; informal makeup.

franc /fraNGk/ ▶ n. the basic unit of money of Switzerland and some other countries, and formerly also of France, Belgium, and Luxembourg.

fran·chise /'fran,CHīz/ ▶ n. **1** a license allowing a person or company to use or sell certain products.

2 a business that has been given a franchise. **3** the right to vote in elections.

Fran·cis·can /fran'siskən/ ▶ **n.** a monk or nun of a Christian religious order following the rule of St. Francis of Assisi (*c.*1181–1226). ▶ **adj.** having to do with St. Francis or the Franciscans.

fran·glais /ˌfränˈglā/ ▶ **n.** a blend of French and English.

Frank /fraNGk/ ▶ **n.** a member of a Germanic people that conquered Gaul in the 6th century. ■ **Frank·ish adj. & n.**

frank[1] /fraNGk/ ▶ **adj. 1** honest and direct. **2** open or undisguised: *frank admiration.*

> SYNONYMS **1 candid**, direct, forthright, plain, plain-spoken, straight, to the point, matter-of-fact, open, honest; informal upfront. **2 undisguised**, open, unconcealed, naked, unmistakable, clear, obvious, transparent, patent, evident. ANTONYMS evasive.

■ **frank·ness n.**

frank[2] ▶ **v.** stamp a mark on a letter or parcel to indicate that postage has been paid or does not need to be paid.

Frank·en·stein /'fraNGkənˌstīn/ (also **Frankenstein's monster**) ▶ **n.** a thing that becomes terrifying or destructive to its maker.

frank·furt·er /'fraNGkˌfərtər/ ▶ **n.** a seasoned smoked sausage, usually made of beef and pork.

frank·in·cense /'fraNGkənˌsens/ ▶ **n.** a kind of sweet-smelling gum that is burned as incense.

frank·ly /'fraNGklē/ ▶ **adv. 1** in an honest and direct way. **2** to be frank.

> SYNONYMS **1 to be frank**, to be honest, to tell the truth, in all honesty. **2 candidly**, directly, plainly, straightforwardly, forthrightly, openly, honestly, without beating about/around the bush, bluntly.

fran·tic /'frantik/ ▶ **adj. 1** agitated because of fear, anxiety, etc. **2** done in a hurried and chaotic way.

> SYNONYMS **panic-stricken**, panicky, beside yourself, at your wits' end, distraught, overwrought, worked up, frenzied, frenetic, fraught, feverish, desperate; informal in a state, tearing your hair out. ANTONYMS calm.

■ **fran·ti·cal·ly adv.**

frap·pé /fra'pā/ ▶ **adj.** (of a drink) iced or chilled.

fra·ter·nal /frə'tərnl/ ▶ **adj. 1** brotherly. **2** having to do with a fraternity.

fra·ter·ni·ty /frə'tərnətē/ ▶ **n.** (plural **fraternities**) **1** a group of people sharing a common profession or interests. **2** a male students' society in a university or college. **3** friendship and support within a group.

> SYNONYMS **1 society**, club, association, group. **2 brotherhood**, fellowship, kinship, friendship, mutual support, solidarity, community. **3 profession**, community, trade, set, circle.

frat·er·nize /'fratərˌnīz/ ▶ **v.** (**fraternizes, fraternizing, fraternized**) be on friendly terms. ■ **frat·er·ni·za·tion** /ˌfratərni'zāSHən/ **n.**

frat·ri·cide /'fratrəˌsīd/ ▶ **n. 1** the killing by someone of their brother or sister. **2** the accidental killing of your own forces in war.

Frau /frou/ ▶ **n.** (plural **Frauen**) a form of address for a married or widowed German woman.

fraud /frôd/ ▶ **n. 1** the crime of deceiving someone in order to get money or goods. **2** a person who deceives other people by claiming to be something they are not.

> SYNONYMS **1 deception**, cheating, swindling, trickery, embezzlement, deceit, double-dealing, chicanery. **2 swindle**, racket, deception, trick, cheat, hoax; informal scam, con, hustle, rip-off, sting, fiddle. **3 impostor**, fake, sham, charlatan, swindler, fraudster, confidence trickster; informal phony.

fraud·ster /'frôdˌstər/ ▶ **n.** a person who commits fraud.

fraud·u·lent /'frôjələnt/ ▶ **adj. 1** involving fraud. **2** deceitful or dishonest.

> SYNONYMS **dishonest**, cheating, swindling, corrupt, criminal, deceitful, double-dealing, duplicitous; informal crooked, shady, dirty. ANTONYMS honest.

■ **fraud·u·lent·ly adv.**

fraught /frôt/ ▶ **adj. 1** (**fraught with**) filled with something undesirable. **2** causing or feeling anxiety or stress.

> SYNONYMS **1** *a world fraught with danger* **full of**, filled with, rife with. **2 anxious**, worried, stressed, upset, distraught, overwrought, worked up, agitated, distressed, desperate, frantic, panic-stricken, panicky, beside yourself, at your wits' end, at the end of your rope.

Fräu·lein /'froiˌlīn/ ▶ **n.** a form of address for a young unmarried German woman.

fray[1] /frā/ ▶ **v. 1** (of a fabric or rope) unravel or become worn at the edge. **2** (of a person's nerves or temper) show the effects of strain.

> SYNONYMS **1** (**frayed**) **worn**, threadbare, tattered, ragged, the worse for wear; informal raggedy, tatty. **2** (**frayed**) **strained**, fraught, tense, edgy, stressed.

fray[2] ▶ **n.** (**the fray**) **1** a battle or fight. **2** a very competitive situation.

fraz·zle /'frazəl/ ▶ **n.** (**a frazzle**) informal **1** an exhausted state. **2** a charred or burned state. ■ **fraz·zled adj.**

freak /frēk/ ▶ **n. 1** informal a person who is obsessed with a particular interest: *a fitness freak.* **2** a very unusual and unexpected event. **3** a person, animal, or plant with a physical abnormality. ▶ **v.** (**freak out**) informal behave in a wild, excited, or shocked way.

> SYNONYMS ▶ **n. 1 enthusiast**, fan, devotee, lover, aficionado; informal nut, fanatic, addict, maniac. **2 anomaly**, aberration, rarity, oddity, fluke, twist of fate. **3** *a freak accident* **unusual**, anomalous, aberrant, atypical, unrepresentative, irregular, exceptional, isolated. **4 eccentric**, misfit, oddity; informal oddball, weirdo, nut, wacko, kook. **5 aberration**, abnormality, oddity, monster, monstrosity, mutant, chimera.

freak·ish /'frēkisH/ ▶ **adj. 1** bizarre or grotesque; abnormal. **2** very unusual or unpredictable: *freakish weather.*

freak·y /'frēkē/▶ **adj.** (**freakier, freakiest**) informal very odd, strange, or eccentric. ■ **freak·i·ly adv. freak·i·ness n.**

freck·le /'frekəl/ ▶ **n.** a small light brown spot on the skin. ■ **freck·led adj. freck·ly adj.**

free /frē/ ▶ **adj.** (**freer**, **freest**) **1** not under the control of someone else. **2** not confined, obstructed, or fixed. **3** not being used. **4** (**free of** or **from**) not affected by. **5** given or available without charge. **6** (**free with**) giving something generously. **7** unrestrained in speech or manner. ▶ **adv.** without cost or payment. ▶ **v.** (**frees**, **freeing**, **freed**) make free.

SYNONYMS ▶ **adj.** **1 independent**, self-governing, self-determining, sovereign, autonomous, democratic. **2 on the loose**, at liberty, at large, loose, unrestrained. **3** *you are free to leave* **able**, in a position, allowed, permitted. **4 unobstructed**, unimpeded, unrestricted, unhampered, clear, open. **5 unoccupied**, not busy, available, off duty, off work, on leave, at leisure, with time to spare. **6 vacant**, empty, available, unoccupied, not in use. **7** *free of any pressures* **without**, unencumbered by, unaffected by, clear of, rid of, exempt from, not liable to, safe from, immune to, excused of. **8 free of charge**, without charge, for nothing, complimentary, gratis; informal for free, on the house. **9** *she was free with her money* **generous**, liberal, open-handed, unstinting. ANTONYMS busy, occupied, confined. ▶ **v.** **1 release**, set free, let go, liberate, set loose, untie. **2 extricate**, release, get out, cut free, pull free, rescue. ANTONYMS confine, trap.

□ **free and easy** informal and relaxed. **free enterprise** a system in which private businesses compete with each other. **free fall** unrestricted downward movement under the force of gravity. **free-for-all** a disorganized situation in which everyone may take part. **free-form** not in a regular or formal structure. **a free hand** freedom to do exactly what you want. **free kick** (in soccer and rugby) an unopposed kick of the ball awarded when the opposition has broken the rules. **a free ride** a situation in which someone benefits without contributing fairly. **the free market** a system in which prices are determined by unrestricted competition between privately owned businesses. **free port 1** a port open to all traders. **2** a port area where goods being transported are exempt from customs duty. **free-range** referring to farming in which animals are kept in natural conditions where they can move around freely. **free speech** the right to express any opinions without censorship. **free trade** unrestricted international trade without taxes or regulations on imports and exports. **free verse** poetry that does not rhyme or have a regular rhythm. **free will** the power to act according to your own wishes. **the free world** the noncommunist countries of the world.

free·bie /ˈfrēbē/ ▶ **n.** informal a thing given free of charge.

free·board /ˈfrēˌbôrd/ ▶ **n.** the height of a ship's side between the waterline and the deck.

free·born /ˈfrēˌbôrn/ ▶ **adj.** not born in slavery.

free·dom /ˈfrēdəm/ ▶ **n.** **1** the right to act or speak freely. **2** the state of not being a prisoner or slave. **3** (**freedom from**) not being affected by something undesirable. **4** unrestricted use of something: *the dog had the freedom of the house.*

SYNONYMS **1 liberty**, liberation, release, deliverance. **2 independence**, self-government, self-determination, self-rule, home rule, sovereignty, autonomy, democracy. **3** *freedom from political accountability* **exemption**, immunity, dispensation, impunity. **4 right**, entitlement, privilege, prerogative, discretion, latitude, elbow room, license, free rein, a free hand, carte blanche. ANTONYMS captivity, obligation.

□ **freedom fighter** a person who takes part in a struggle to achieve political freedom.

free·hand /ˈfrēˌhand/ ▶ **adj. & adv.** drawn by hand without a ruler or other aid.

free·hold /ˈfrēˌhōld/ ▶ **n.** permanent ownership of land or property with the freedom to sell it whenever you want. ■ **free·hold·er n.**

free·lance /ˈfrēˌlans/ ▶ **adj.** self-employed and working for different companies on particular assignments. ▶ **n.** (also **freelancer**) a freelance worker. ▶ **v.** (**freelances**, **freelancing**, **freelanced**) work as a freelance.

free·load·er /ˈfrēˌlōdər/ ▶ **n.** informal a person who takes advantage of other people's generosity.

free·ly /ˈfrēlē/ ▶ **adv.** **1** not under the control of someone else. **2** without restriction or restraint: *a world where people cannot speak freely.* **3** in abundant amounts. **4** willingly and readily.

SYNONYMS **1 voluntarily**, willingly, readily, of your own accord, of your own free will, without being told to. **2 openly**, candidly, frankly, directly, without beating about/around the bush, without mincing your words.

Free·ma·son /ˈfrēˈmāsən/ ▶ **n.** a member of an organization whose members help each other and hold secret ceremonies. ■ **Free·ma·son·ry n.**

free·sia /ˈfrēzнə/ ▶ **n.** a plant with sweet-smelling, colorful flowers.

free·stand·ing /ˈfrēˈstandiɴɢ/ ▶ **adj.** not attached to or supported by another structure.

free·style /ˈfrēˌstīl/ ▶ **adj.** (of a contest or sport) having few restrictions on the technique that competitors use.

free·think·er /ˈfrēˈᴛʜɪɴɢkər/ ▶ **n.** a person who questions or rejects accepted opinions.

free·way /ˈfrēˌwā/ ▶ **n.** **1** an express highway, especially one with controlled access. **2** a toll-free highway.

free·wheel /ˈfrēˌ(h)wēl/ ▶ **v.** ride a bicycle without using the pedals.

freeze /frēz/ ▶ **v.** (**freezes**, **freezing**, **froze** /frōz/; past participle **frozen** /ˈfrōzən/) **1** (of a liquid) turn into a solid as a result of extreme cold. **2** become blocked or rigid with ice. **3** be very cold. **4** preserve something by storing it at a very low temperature. **5** suddenly become motionless with fear, shock, etc. **6** (of a computer screen) suddenly become locked. **7** keep or hold at a fixed level. **8** (**freeze out**) informal exclude someone by treating them in a cold or hostile way. ▶ **n.** **1** an act of freezing. **2** a period of very cold weather.

SYNONYMS ▶ **v.** **1 ice over**, ice up, solidify. **2 stand still**, stop dead in your tracks, go rigid, become motionless, become paralyzed. **3 fix**, hold, set, limit, restrict, cap. ANTONYMS thaw.

□ **freeze-dry** preserve something by rapidly freezing it and then drying it in a vacuum. **freeze-frame** the stopping of a movie or videotape to obtain a single still image.

freez·er /ˈfrēzər/ ▶ **n.** a refrigerated cabinet or room for preserving food at very low temperatures.

freez·ing /ˈfrēziɴɢ/ ▶ **adj.** **1** having a temperature below 32°F or 0°C. **2** very cold. ▶ **n.** the temperature at which water freezes (32°F or 0°C).

SYNONYMS ▶ adj. **1 icy**, bitter, chill, frosty, glacial, arctic, wintry, subzero, raw, biting. **2 frozen**, numb with cold, chilled to the bone/marrow. ANTONYMS balmy, hot.

freight /frāt/ ▶ n. goods transported by truck, train, ship, or aircraft. ▶ v. transport goods by truck, train, etc.

SYNONYMS ▶ n. **goods**, cargo, merchandise.

□ **freight car** a railroad car for carrying freight.

freight·er /ˈfrātər/ ▶ n. a large ship or aircraft designed to carry freight.

French /frenCH/ ▶ adj. having to do with France or its language. ▶ n. the language of France, also used in parts of Belgium, Switzerland, Canada, etc. □ **excuse** (or **pardon**) **my French** informal used to apologize for swearing. **French Canadian** 1 a Canadian whose native language is French. 2 having to do with French Canadians. **French dressing** 1 a salad dressing of vinegar, oil, and seasonings. 2 a sweet, creamy salad dressing commercially prepared from oil, tomato purée, and spices. **French fries** potatoes cut into strips and deep-fried. **French horn** a brass instrument with a coiled tube and a wide opening at the end. **French toast** bread coated in egg and milk and then fried. **French windows** each of a pair of casement windows extending to the floor in an outside wall.

French·man /ˈfrenCHmən/ (or **Frenchwoman** /ˌ-wo͝omən/) ▶ n. (plural **Frenchmen** or **Frenchwomen**) a person who is French by birth or descent.

fre·net·ic /frəˈnetik/ ▶ adj. fast and energetic in a rather wild and uncontrolled way. ■ **fre·net·i·cal·ly** adv.

fren·zied /ˈfrenzēd/ ▶ adj. wildly excited or uncontrolled: *a frenzied attack.*

SYNONYMS **frantic**, wild, frenetic, hectic, feverish, fevered, mad, crazed, manic, furious, uncontrolled. ANTONYMS calm.

■ **fren·zied·ly** adv.

fren·zy /ˈfrenzē/ ▶ n. (plural **frenzies**) a state of uncontrolled excitement or wild behavior.

SYNONYMS **hysteria**, madness, mania, delirium, wild excitement, fever, lather, passion, panic, fury, rage.

fre·quen·cy /ˈfrēkwənsē/ ▶ n. (plural **frequencies**) 1 the rate at which something happens. 2 the state of being frequent. 3 the number of cycles per second of a sound, light, or radio wave. 4 the particular waveband at which radio signals are transmitted. □ **frequency modulation** the varying of the frequency of a wave, used as a means of broadcasting an audio signal by radio.

fre·quent ▶ adj. /ˈfrēkwənt/ 1 happening or done many times at short intervals. 2 doing something often: *a frequent visitor.* ▶ v. /frēˈkwent/ visit a place often.

SYNONYMS ▶ adj. **recurrent**, recurring, repeated, periodic, continual, habitual, regular, successive, numerous, several. ANTONYMS occasional. ▶ v. **visit**, patronize, spend time in, visit regularly, haunt; informal hang out at. ANTONYMS avoid.

fre·quent·ly /ˈfrēkwəntlē/ ▶ adv. at frequent intervals.

SYNONYMS **often**, all the time, habitually, regularly, customarily, routinely, again and again, repeatedly, recurrently, continually; old use oftentimes.

fres·co /ˈfreskō/ ▶ n. (plural **frescoes** or **frescos**) a painting that is done on wet plaster on a wall or ceiling.

fresh /freSH/ ▶ adj. 1 new or different. 2 (of food) recently made or obtained. 3 recently created and not faded: *the memory was fresh in their minds.* 4 pleasantly clean and cool: *fresh air.* 5 (of the wind) cool and fairly strong. 6 (of water) not salty. 7 full of energy. 8 informal too familiar with someone.

SYNONYMS **1 new**, modern, original, novel, different, innovative. **2 recently made**, just picked, crisp, raw, natural, unprocessed. **3 refreshed**, rested, restored, energetic, vigorous, invigorated, lively, sprightly, bright, alert, bouncing, perky; informal full of beans, bright-eyed and bushy-tailed. **4 bracing**, brisk, strong, invigorating, chilly, cool; informal nippy. **5 cool**, crisp, refreshing, invigorating, pure, clean, clear. **6 impudent**, impertinent, insolent, presumptuous, forward, cheeky, disrespectful, rude; informal mouthy, saucy, lippy, sassy. ANTONYMS stale, old.

■ **fresh·ly** adv. **fresh·ness** n.

fresh·en /ˈfreSHən/ ▶ v. 1 make or become fresh. 2 (**freshen up**) wash and tidy yourself.

fresh·man /ˈfreSHmən/ ▶ n. (plural **freshmen**) a first-year student at a university, college, or high school.

fresh·wa·ter /ˈfreSHˈwôtər, -ˈwätər/ ▶ adj. of or found in fresh water.

fret[1] /fret/ ▶ v. (**frets**, **fretting**, **fretted**) be anxious and restless.

SYNONYMS **worry**, be anxious, distress yourself, upset yourself, concern yourself, agonize, lose sleep.

fret[2] ▶ n. each of the ridges on the neck of guitars and similar instruments.

fret[3] ▶ n. Art & Architecture an ornamental design of vertical and horizontal lines.

fret·ful /ˈfretfəl/ ▶ adj. anxious and restless. ■ **fret·ful·ly** adv.

fret·work /ˈfretˌwərk/ ▶ n. decorative designs cut into in wood.

Freud·i·an /ˈfroidēən/ ▶ adj. having to do with the Austrian psychotherapist Sigmund Freud (1856–1939) and his methods of psychoanalysis.

Fri. ▶ abbr. Friday.

fri·a·ble /ˈfrīəbəl/ ▶ adj. easily crumbled.

fri·ar /ˈfrīər/ ▶ n. a member of certain religious orders of men.

fri·ar·y /ˈfrīərē/ ▶ n. (plural **friaries**) a building or community occupied by friars.

fric·as·see /ˈfrikəˌsē, ˌfrikəˈsē/ ▶ n. a dish of stewed or fried pieces of meat served in a thick white sauce.

fric·tion /ˈfrikSHən/ ▶ n. 1 the resistance that one surface or object encounters when moving over another. 2 the action of one surface or object rubbing against another. 3 conflict or disagreement.

SYNONYMS **1 rubbing**, chafing, grating, rasping, scraping, resistance, drag, abrasion. **2 discord**, disagreement, dissension, dispute, conflict, hostility, animosity, antipathy, antagonism, resentment, acrimony, bitterness, bad feeling. ANTONYMS harmony.

Fri·day /ˈfrīdā, -dē/ ▶ **n.** the day of the week before Saturday and following Thursday.

fridge /frij/ ▶ **n.** an appliance in which food and drink are stored at a low temperature. Short for "refrigerator".

fried /frīd/ past and past participle of **FRY**[1].

friend /frend/ ▶ **n.** **1** a person that you know well and like. **2** a supporter of a cause or organization. **3** (**Friend**) a Quaker.

SYNONYMS **companion**, comrade, confidant, confidante, familiar, intimate, soulmate, playmate, ally, associate; informal pal, buddy, bud, chum, amigo, compadre, homeboy. ANTONYMS enemy.

■ **friend·less adj.**

SPELLING

Write **-ie-**, not **-ei-**: friend.

friend·ly /ˈfrendlē/ ▶ **adj.** (**friendlier**, **friendliest**) **1** treating someone as a friend; on good terms. **2** kind and pleasant. **3** not harmful to a particular thing: *environment-friendly*. **4** Military having to do with your own forces.

SYNONYMS **1** *a friendly woman* **amiable**, companionable, sociable, gregarious, comradely, neighborly, hospitable, easy to get along with, affable, genial, cordial, warm, affectionate, convivial; informal chummy. **2** *friendly conversation* **amicable**, cordial, pleasant, easy, relaxed, casual, informal, close, intimate, familiar. ANTONYMS hostile.

□ **friendly fire** Military weapon fire coming from your own side that causes accidental injury or death to your own forces. ■ **friend·li·ness n.**

friend·ship /ˈfrend,sHip/ ▶ **n.** **1** a relationship between friends. **2** the state of being friends.

SYNONYMS **1** *lasting friendships* **relationship**, attachment, association, bond, tie, link, union. **2** *ties of friendship* **friendliness**, affection, camaraderie, comradeship, companionship, fellowship, closeness, affinity, unity, intimacy. ANTONYMS hostility.

frieze /frēz/ ▶ **n.** a broad horizontal band of sculpted or painted decoration.

frig·ate /ˈfrigit/ ▶ **n.** a kind of fast warship.

fright /frīt/ ▶ **n.** **1** a sudden strong feeling of fear. **2** a shock.

SYNONYMS **1 fear**, terror, horror, alarm, panic, dread, trepidation, dismay, nervousness. **2 scare**, shock, surprise, turn, jolt, start.

□ **look a fright** informal look ridiculous or grotesque. **take fright** suddenly become frightened.

fright·en /ˈfrītn/ ▶ **v.** **1** make someone afraid. **2** (**frighten someone/thing off**) drive someone away by frightening them.

SYNONYMS **1 scare**, startle, alarm, terrify, petrify, shock, chill, panic, unnerve, intimidate; informal spook. **2** (**frightening**) **terrifying**, horrifying, alarming, startling, chilling, spine-chilling, hair-raising, blood-curdling, disturbing, unnerving, intimidating, daunting, eerie, sinister, fearsome, nightmarish, menacing; informal scary, spooky, creepy.

■ **fright·en·ing·ly adv.**

fright·ful /ˈfrītfəl/ ▶ **adj.** **1** very unpleasant, serious, or shocking. **2** informal terrible; awful.

SYNONYMS **horrible**, horrific, ghastly, horrendous, awful, dreadful, terrible, nasty; informal horrid.

■ **fright·ful·ly adv.**

frig·id /ˈfrijid/ ▶ **adj.** literary very cold.

SYNONYMS **1 very cold**, bitterly cold, bitter, freezing, frozen, frosty, icy, chilly, chill, wintry, subzero, arctic, Siberian, polar, glacial; informal nippy. **2 stiff**, formal, stony, wooden, unemotional, passionless, unfeeling, distant, aloof, remote, reserved, unapproachable; frosty, cold, icy, cool, unsmiling, forbidding, unfriendly, unwelcoming; informal standoffish. ANTONYMS hot, friendly.

■ **fri·gid·i·ty** /frəˈjidətē/ **n.**

frill /fril/ ▶ **n.** **1** a decorative strip of gathered or pleated cloth attached to the edge of clothing or material. **2** (**frills**) unnecessary extra features. ■ **frilled adj.** **frill·y adj.**

fringe /frinj/ ▶ **n.** **1** a decorative border of threads or tassels attached to the edge of clothing or material. **2** the outer part of an area, group, etc. ▶ **v.** (**fringes**, **fringing**, **fringed**) add a fringe to something.

SYNONYMS ▶ **n.** **1 edging**, border, trimming, frill, flounce, ruffle. **2 edge**, border, margin, extremity, perimeter, periphery, rim, limits, outskirts. **3** *a fringe meeting* **alternative**, avant-garde, experimental, innovative, left-field, radical. ANTONYMS middle, mainstream.

□ **fringe benefit** something extra given to someone as well as wages.

frip·per·y /ˈfripərē/ ▶ **n.** (plural **fripperies**) showy or unnecessary decoration.

Fris·bee /ˈfrizbē/ ▶ **n.** trademark a plastic disk that you skim through the air as an outdoor game.

frisk /frisk/ ▶ **v.** **1** pass your hands over someone in a search for hidden weapons or drugs. **2** skip or move playfully. ▶ **n.** a playful skip or leap.

frisk·y /ˈfriskē/ ▶ **adj.** (**friskier**, **friskiest**) playful and full of energy.

SYNONYMS **lively**, bouncy, bubbly, perky, active, energetic, animated, playful, coltish, skittish, spirited, high-spirited, in high spirits, exuberant; informal full of beans.

fris·son /frēˈsôN/ ▶ **n.** a sudden shiver of excitement.

frit·il·lar·y /ˈfritl,erē/ ▶ **n.** (plural **fritillaries**) **1** a plant with hanging bell-like flowers. **2** a butterfly with orange-brown wings.

frit·ter[1] /ˈfritər/ ▶ **v.** (**fritters**, **frittering**, **frittered**) (**fritter something away**) waste time or money on unimportant matters.

frit·ter[2] ▶ **n.** a piece of food that is coated in batter and deep-fried.

fritz /frits/ ▶ **n.** (in phrase **go** or **be on the fritz**) informal (of a machine) stop working properly.

friv·o·lous /ˈfrivələs/ ▶ **adj.** **1** not having any serious purpose or value. **2** (of a person) not treating things seriously.

SYNONYMS **flippant**, glib, facetious, joking, jokey, lighthearted, fatuous, inane; informal flip. ANTONYMS serious.

■ **fri·vol·i·ty** /friˈvälətē/ **n.** **friv·o·lous·ly adv.**

frizz /friz/ ▶ v. (of hair) form into a mass of tight curls. ▶ n. a mass of tightly curled hair.

friz·zy /'frizē/ ▶ adj. (**frizzier**, **frizziest**) formed of a mass of small, tight curls. ■ **friz·zi·ness** n.

fro /frō/ ⇒ TO AND FRO.

frock /fräk/ ▶ n. **1** a dress. **2** a loose outer garment, worn by priests. □ **frock coat** a man's long, double-breasted coat, worn on formal occasions.

frog /frôg, fräg/ ▶ n. an amphibian with a short body, very long hind legs for leaping, and no tail. □ **have a frog in your throat** informal be hoarse.

frog·man /'frôg,man, 'fräg-, -mən/ ▶ n. (plural **frogmen**) a diver equipped with a rubber suit, flippers, and breathing equipment.

frog·march /'frôg,märCH, 'fräg-/ ▶ v. force someone to walk forward by holding their arms from behind.

frol·ic /'frälik/ ▶ v. (**frolics**, **frolicking**, **frolicked**) play or move about in a cheerful and lively way. ▶ n. a playful action or movement.

frol·ic·some /'fräliksəm/ ▶ adj. lively and playful.

from /frəm/ ▶ prep. **1** indicating the point at which a journey, process, or action starts. **2** indicating the source of something. **3** indicating separation, removal, or prevention. **4** indicating a cause. **5** indicating a difference. □ **from time to time** occasionally.

frond /fränd/ ▶ n. the leaf of a palm, fern, or similar plant.

front /frənt/ ▶ n. **1** the part of an object that faces forward or that is normally seen first. **2** the position directly ahead. **3** the furthest position that an army has reached. **4** a particular situation or area of activity: *good news on the job front*. **5** (in weather forecasting) the forward edge of an advancing mass of air. **6** a false appearance or way of behaving. **7** a person or organization that is a cover for secret or illegal activities. **8** a very confident manner. ▶ adj. having to do with the front. ▶ v. **1** have the front facing toward. **2** be at the front of. **3** (**be fronted with**) have the front covered with. **4** be the leader or host of. **5** act as a cover for someone who is doing something illegal.

SYNONYMS ▶ n. **1 fore**, foremost part, forepart, nose, head, bow, prow, foreground. **2 frontage**, face, facing, facade. **3 head**, beginning, start, top, lead. **4 appearance**, air, face, manner, exterior, veneer, (outward) show, act, pretense. **5 cover**, blind, disguise, facade, mask, cloak, screen, smokescreen, camouflage. ANTONYMS back. ▶ adj. **leading**, lead, first, foremost. ANTONYMS back, last.

□ **front-end** having to do with the front. **the front line** the part of an army that is closest to the enemy. **front runner** the leader in a competition. **front-wheel drive** a system that provides power to the front wheels of a motor vehicle. **in front of** in the presence of. ■ **front·ward** adj. & adv. **front·wards** adv.

front·age /'frəntij/ ▶ n. **1** the front of a building. **2** a strip of land next to a street or waterway.

fron·tal /'frəntl/ ▶ adj. having to do with the front. ■ **fron·tal·ly** adv.

fron·tier /,frən'ti(ə)r/ ▶ n. **1** a border separating two countries. **2** the furthest part of land that has been settled. **3** the limit of what is known about a subject or area of activity.

SYNONYMS **border**, boundary, borderline, dividing line, perimeter, limit, edge.

fron·tiers·man /,frən'ti(ə)rzmən/ (or **frontierswoman** /-wo͝omən/) ▶ n. (plural **frontiersmen** or **frontierswomen**) a man (or woman) living in the region of a frontier.

fron·tis·piece /'frəntis,pēs/ ▶ n. an illustration facing the title page of a book.

front·man /'frənt,man, -mən/ ▶ n. (plural **frontmen**) a person who represents an illegal organization to make it seem respectable.

frost /frôst/ ▶ n. **1** white ice crystals that form on surfaces when the temperature falls below freezing. **2** a period of cold weather when frost forms.

frost·bite /'frôs(t),bīt/ ▶ n. injury to parts of the body caused by exposure to extreme cold. ■ **frost·bit·ten** /'frôs(t),bitn/ adj.

frost·ed /'frôstid/ ▶ adj. **1** covered with frost. **2** (of glass) having a semitransparent textured surface. **3** (of a cake) covered with icing.

frost·ing /'frôstiNG/ ▶ n. icing.

frost·y /'frôstē/ ▶ adj. (**frostier**, **frostiest**) **1** (of the weather) very cold with frost forming on surfaces. **2** cold and unfriendly.

SYNONYMS **1 cold**, freezing, frozen, icy, bitter, chill, wintry, arctic; informal nippy. **2 unfriendly**, cold, frigid, icy, glacial, inhospitable, unwelcoming, forbidding, hostile, stony. ANTONYMS warm, friendly.

■ **frost·i·ly** adv.

froth /frôTH/ ▶ n. **1** a mass of small bubbles in liquid. **2** appealing but trivial ideas or activities. ▶ v. produce or contain froth.

SYNONYMS ▶ n. **foam**, head, bubbles, frothiness, fizz, effervescence, lather, suds. ▶ v. **bubble**, fizz, effervesce, foam, lather, churn, seethe.

froth·y /'frôTHē, -T͟Hē/ ▶ adj. (**frothier**, **frothiest**) **1** full of or covered with a mass of small bubbles. **2** light and entertaining but of little substance: *lots of frothy interviews*. ■ **froth·i·ly** adv. **froth·i·ness** n.

frou-frou /'fro͞o,fro͞o/ ▶ n. **1** a rustling noise made by someone walking in a dress. **2** frills or other ornamentation, particularly of women's clothes.

frown /froun/ ▶ v. **1** make an angry or worried expression by bringing your eyebrows together so that lines appear on your forehead. **2** (**frown on**) disapprove of. ▶ n. a frowning expression.

SYNONYMS ▶ v. **scowl**, glower, glare, lower/lour, make a face, look daggers, give someone a black look, knit/furrow your brows; informal give someone a dirty look. ANTONYMS smile.

frowz·y /'frouzē/ (or **frowsy**) ▶ adj. scruffy and neglected in appearance.

froze /frōz/ past of FREEZE.

fro·zen /'frōzən/ past participle of FREEZE.

fruc·tose /'frək,tōs, 'fro͝ok-, -,tōz/ ▶ n. a kind of sugar found in honey and fruit.

fru·gal /'fro͞ogəl/ ▶ adj. **1** careful in the use of money or food. **2** (of a meal) plain and cheap.

SYNONYMS **1 thrifty**, economical, careful, cautious, prudent, provident, sparing, abstemious, austere, self-denying, ascetic, spartan. **2 meager**, scanty, scant, paltry, skimpy, plain, simple, spartan, inexpensive, cheap, economical. ANTONYMS extravagant, lavish.

■ **fru·gal·i·ty** /fro͞o'galətē/ n. **fru·gal·ly** adv.

fruit /fro͞ot/ ▶ n. **1** a fleshy part of a plant that contains seed and can be eaten as food. **2** Botany the part of a plant in which seeds develop, e.g., an acorn. **3** the result of work or activity. ▶ v. produce fruit. □ **bear fruit** have good results. **fruit bat** a large bat that feeds chiefly on fruit or nectar. **fruit fly** a small fly that feeds on fruit. **fruit salad** a mixture of different types of chopped fruit, often served in syrup or juice.

fruit·cake /'fro͞otˌkāk/ ▶ n. **1** a cake containing dried fruit and nuts. **2** informal an eccentric or crazy person.

fruit·er·er /'fro͞otərər/ ▶ n. a person who sells fruit.

fruit·ful /'fro͞otfəl/ ▶ adj. **1** producing a lot of fruit. **2** producing good results.

SYNONYMS **productive**, constructive, useful, worthwhile, helpful, beneficial, valuable, rewarding, profitable, advantageous. ANTONYMS barren, futile.

■ **fruit·ful·ly** adv. **fruit·ful·ness** n.

fru·i·tion /fro͞o'isHən/ ▶ n. the fulfillment of a plan or project.

SYNONYMS **fulfillment**, realization, actualization, materialization, achievement, attainment, accomplishment, success, completion, consummation, conclusion, close, finish, perfection, maturity.

fruit·less /'fro͞otləs/ ▶ adj. **1** failing to achieve the desired results. **2** not producing fruit.

SYNONYMS **futile**, vain, in vain, to no avail, to no effect, idle, pointless, useless, worthless, hollow, ineffectual, ineffective, unproductive, unrewarding, profitless, unsuccessful, unavailing, abortive. ANTONYMS fruitful, productive.

■ **fruit·less·ly** adv.

fruit·y /'fro͞otē/ ▶ adj. (**fruitier**, **fruitiest**) **1** having to do with fruit. **2** (of someone's voice) mellow, deep, and rich.

frump /frəmp/ ▶ n. an unattractive woman who wears unfashionable clothes. ■ **frump·y** adj.

frus·trate /'frəsˌtrāt/ ▶ v. (**frustrates**, **frustrating**, **frustrated**) **1** prevent a plan or action from succeeding. **2** prevent someone from doing or achieving something. **3** make someone feel dissatisfied or unfulfilled.

SYNONYMS **1 thwart**, defeat, foil, block, stop, obstruct, counter, spoil, check, forestall, derail, snooker; informal stymie. **2 exasperate**, infuriate, discourage, dishearten, disappoint. ANTONYMS further, satisfy.

■ **frus·trat·ing** adj. **frus·tra·tion** n.

frus·trat·ed /frə'strātid/ ▶ adj. **1** feeling distressed and annoyed because you are unable to achieve something. **2** unable to follow or be successful in a particular career: *a frustrated actor*. **3** prevented from progressing, succeeding, or being fulfilled.

fry[1] /frī/ ▶ v. (**fries**, **frying**, **fried**) cook in hot fat or oil. ▶ n. (**fries**) French fries. □ **frying pan** a shallow pan used for frying food. **out of the frying pan into the fire** from a bad situation to one that is worse.

fry[2] ▶ pl.n. young fish.

fry·er /'frīər/ ▶ n. **1** a large, deep container for frying food. **2** a small young chicken suitable for frying.

ft. ▶ abbr. foot or feet.

fuch·sia /'fyo͞osHə/ ▶ n. a shrub with drooping purplish-red flowers.

fud·dled /'fədld/ ▶ adj. not able to think clearly.

fud·dy-dud·dy /'fədē ˌdədē/ ▶ n. (plural **fuddy-duddies**) informal a person who is very old-fashioned and pompous.

fudge /fəj/ ▶ n. **1** a soft candy made from sugar, butter, and milk or cream. **2** rich chocolate, used especially as a filling for cakes or a sauce on ice cream. **3** an attempt to present an issue in a vague or deceptive way. ▶ v. (**fudges**, **fudging**, **fudged**) present something in a vague or deceptive way.

SYNONYMS ▶ v. **evade**, avoid, dodge, skirt, duck, gloss over, cloud, hedge, beat about the bush, equivocate.

fu·el /'fyo͞oəl/ ▶ n. **1** material such as coal, gas, or oil that is burned to produce heat or power. **2** something that stirs up argument or strong emotion. ▶ v. (**fuels**, **fueling**, **fueled**) **1** supply or power with fuel. **2** stir up strong feeling.

SYNONYMS ▶ v. **1 power**, fire, drive, run. **2 fan**, feed, stoke up, inflame, intensify, stimulate, encourage, provoke, incite, sustain.

□ **fuel injection** the direct introduction of fuel into the cylinders of an engine.

fu·gi·tive /'fyo͞ojətiv/ ▶ n. a person who has escaped from captivity or is in hiding.

SYNONYMS **escapee**, runaway, deserter, absconder, refugee.

fugue /fyo͞og/ ▶ n. a piece of music in which a short melody is introduced and then successively taken up by other instruments or voices.

füh·rer /'fyo͝orər/ (or **fuehrer**) ▶ n. the title that Adolf Hitler (1889-1945) held as leader of Germany.

ful·crum /'fo͝olkrəm, 'fəl-/ ▶ n. the point on which a lever turns or is supported.

ful·fill /fo͝ol'fil/ ▶ v. (**fulfills**, **fulfilling**, **fulfilled**) **1** do or achieve something that was desired, promised, or predicted. **2** meet a requirement. **3** (**fulfill yourself**) fully develop your abilities.

SYNONYMS **1 achieve**, attain, realize, make happen, succeed in, bring to completion, bring to fruition, satisfy. **2 carry out**, perform, accomplish, execute, do, discharge, conduct. **3 meet**, satisfy, comply with, conform to, fill, answer. **4** (**fulfilled**) **satisfied**, content, contented, happy, pleased, at peace.

■ **ful·fill·ment** n.

full /fo͝ol/ ▶ adj. **1** holding as much or as many as possible. **2** (**full of**) having a large number or quantity of. **3** (also **full up**) filled to capacity. **4** complete: *full details*. **5** plump or rounded. **6** (of flavor, sound, or color) strong or rich. ▶ adv. straight; directly.

SYNONYMS ▶ adj. **1 filled**, brimming, brimful, packed, loaded, crammed, crowded, bursting, overflowing, congested; informal jam-packed, wall-to-wall, chock-a-block, chock-full, awash. **2 replete**, full up, satisfied, sated, satiated; informal stuffed. **3 eventful**, interesting, exciting, lively, action-packed, busy, active. **4 comprehensive**, thorough, exhaustive, all-inclusive, all-encompassing, all-embracing, in-depth, complete, entire, whole, unabridged, uncut. **5 plump**, rounded, buxom, shapely, ample, curvaceous, voluptuous; informal busty, curvy, well-endowed, zaftig. **6 loose-fitting**, loose, baggy, voluminous, roomy, capacious, billowing. ANTONYMS empty.

□ **full-blooded** wholehearted and enthusiastic. **full-blown** fully developed. **full-bodied** rich and satisfying in flavor or sound. **full-fledged** completely developed or established. **full-frontal** fully exposing the front of the body. **full house** **1** a theater that is filled to capacity. **2** a poker hand with three of a kind and a pair. **3** a winning card at bingo. **full moon** the moon when its whole disk is illuminated. **full of yourself** too pleased with yourself. **full-scale** **1** (of a model or plan) of the same size as the thing represented. **2** complete and thorough: *a full-scale invasion.* **full speed** (or **steam**) **ahead** proceeding with as much speed or energy as possible. **full-time** working for the whole of the available time. **to the full** to the greatest possible extent. ■ **full·ness** n.

full·back /ˈfo͝olˌbak/ ▶ n. **1** Football an offensive player in the backfield. **2** (in a game such as soccer or field hockey) a player in a defensive position near the goal.

ful·ler /ˈfo͝olər/ ▶ n. historical a person whose job was treating cloth to make it thicker.

ful·ly /ˈfo͝olē/ ▶ adv. **1** completely. **2** no less or fewer than: *fully 65 percent.*

SYNONYMS **completely**, entirely, wholly, totally, perfectly, quite, altogether, thoroughly, in all respects, (up) to the hilt. ANTONYMS partly.

ful·mar /ˈfo͝olmər, -ˌmär/ ▶ n. a gray and white seabird.

ful·mi·nate /ˈfo͝olməˌnāt, ˈfəl-/ ▶ v. (**fulminates**, **fulminating**, **fulminated**) protest strongly. ■ **ful·mi·na·tion** /ˌfo͝olməˈnāshən, -fəl-/ n.

ful·some /ˈfo͝olsəm/ ▶ adj. **1** too flattering or complimentary. **2** of large size or quantity: *fulsome details.* ■ **ful·some·ly** adv.

fum·ble /ˈfəmbəl/ ▶ v. (**fumbles**, **fumbling**, **fumbled**) **1** use the hands clumsily while doing something. **2** deal with something clumsily. **3** fail to catch a ball cleanly. ▶ n. an act of fumbling.

SYNONYMS ▶ v. **grope**, fish, scrabble, feel.

fume /fyo͞om/ ▶ n. a gas or vapor that smells strongly or is dangerous to breathe in. ▶ v. (**fumes**, **fuming**, **fumed**) **1** send out fumes. **2** be very angry.

SYNONYMS ▶ n. **smoke**, vapor, gas, exhaust, pollution. ▶ v. **be furious**, seethe, be livid, be incensed, boil, be beside yourself, spit; informal foam at the mouth, see red.

fu·mi·gate /ˈfyo͞oməˌgāt/ ▶ v. (**fumigates**, **fumigating**, **fumigated**) disinfect an area using chemical fumes.

SYNONYMS **disinfect**, purify, sterilize, sanitize, decontaminate, cleanse, clean out.

■ **fu·mi·ga·tion** /ˌfyo͞oməˈgāshən/ n.

fun /fən/ ▶ n. **1** lighthearted pleasure, or something that provides it. **2** playfulness: *she's full of fun.* ▶ adj. (informal) enjoyable.

SYNONYMS ▶ n. **1 enjoyment**, entertainment, amusement, pleasure, jollification, merrymaking, recreation, leisure, relaxation, a good time; informal living it up, a ball. **2 merriment**, cheerfulness, jollity, joviality, high spirits, mirth, laughter, hilarity, lightheartedness, levity. **3** *he became a figure of fun* **ridicule**, derision, mockery, scorn, contempt. ANTONYMS boredom. ▶ adj. **enjoyable**, entertaining, amusing, pleasurable, pleasant, agreeable, convivial.

□ **make fun of** laugh at in a mocking way.

func·tion /ˈfəNGkSHən/ ▶ n. **1** a purpose or natural activity of a person or thing. **2** a large social event. **3** a basic task of a computer. **4** Math a quantity whose value depends on the varying values of others. ▶ v. **1** work or operate. **2** (**function as**) fulfill the purpose of.

SYNONYMS ▶ n. **1 purpose**, task, use, role. **2 responsibility**, duty, role, province, activity, assignment, task, job, mission. **3 social event**, party, social occasion, affair, gathering, reception, soirée; informal do, bash. ▶ v. **1 work**, go, run, be in working/running order, operate. **2 act**, serve, operate, perform, do duty.

func·tion·al /ˈfəNGkSHənl/ ▶ adj. **1** having to do with a function. **2** designed to be practical and useful. **3** working or operating.

SYNONYMS **1 practical**, useful, utilitarian, workaday, serviceable, no-frills. **2 working**, in working order, functioning, in service, in use, going, running, operative; informal up and running.

■ **func·tion·al·i·ty** /ˌfəNGkSHəˈnalətē/ n. **func·tion·al·ly** adv.

func·tion·ar·y /ˈfəNGkSHəˌnerē/ ▶ n. (plural **functionaries**) an official.

fund /fənd/ ▶ n. **1** a sum of money saved or made available for a purpose. **2** (**funds**) financial resources. **3** a large stock. ▶ v. provide money for.

SYNONYMS ▶ n. **1 collection**, kitty, reserve, pool, purse, savings, coffers. **2 money**, cash, wealth, means, assets, resources, savings, capital, reserves, the wherewithal. ▶ v. **finance**, pay for, back, capitalize, subsidize, endow, invest in, sponsor; informal bankroll.

□ **fund-raiser** **1** a person who raises money for an organization or cause. **2** an event held to raise money for an organization or cause. **fund-raising** the act of raising money for an organization or cause.

fun·da·men·tal /ˌfəndəˈmentl/ ▶ adj. of basic importance. ▶ n. a basic rule or principle: *the fundamentals of navigation.*

SYNONYMS ▶ adj. **basic**, underlying, core, rudimentary, root, primary, prime, cardinal, principal, chief, key, central, vital, essential. ANTONYMS secondary, incidental.

fun·da·men·tal·ism /ˌfəndəˈmentlˌizəm/ ▶ n. strict following of the basic teachings of a religion. ■ **fun·da·men·tal·ist** n. & adj.

fun·da·men·tal·ly /ˌfəndəˈment(ə)lē/ ▶ adv. in central or primary respects.

SYNONYMS **essentially**, in essence, basically, at heart, at bottom, deep down, profoundly, primarily, above all.

fu·ner·al /ˈfyo͞on(ə)rəl/ ▶ n. a ceremony in which a dead person is buried or cremated.

SYNONYMS **burial**, interment, entombment, committal, laying to rest, cremation.

□ **funeral director** an undertaker. **funeral home** (or **parlor**) a place where dead people are prepared for burial or cremation.

fu·ner·ar·y /ˈfyo͞onəˌrerē/ ▶ adj. having to do with a funeral or other rites in which dead people are remembered.

fu·ne·re·al /fyəˈni(ə)rēəl, fyo͞o-/ ▶ **adj.** solemn, in a way appropriate to a funeral.

fun·gi /ˈfənˌjī, -ˌgī/ plural of **FUNGUS**.

fun·gi·cide /ˈfənjəˌsīd, ˈfəNGgə-/ ▶ **n.** a chemical that destroys fungus.

fun·gus /ˈfəNGgəs/ ▶ **n.** (plural **fungi** /ˈfənˌjī, -ˌgī/) an organism, such as a mushroom, that has no leaves or flowers and grows on plants or decaying vegetable matter and reproduces by spores. ■ **fun·gal** **adj.**

fu·nic·u·lar /fyo͝oˈnikyələr/ (also **funicular railway** or **railroad**) ▶ **n.** a rail system on a steep slope that is operated by cable.

funk¹ /fo͝oNGk, fəNGk/ ▶ **n.** a style of popular dance music with a strong rhythm.

funk² ▶ **n.** informal a state of depression.

funk·y /ˈfəNGkē/ ▶ **adj.** (**funkier**, **funkiest**) informal **1** (of music) having a strong dance rhythm. **2** modern and stylish.

fun·nel /ˈfənl/ ▶ **n.** **1** an object that is wide at the top and narrow at the bottom, used for guiding liquid or powder into a small opening. **2** a chimney on a ship or steam engine. ▶ **v.** (**funnels**, **funneling**, **funneled**) guide through a funnel or narrow space.

fun·ny /ˈfənē/ ▶ **adj.** (**funnier**, **funniest**) **1** causing laughter or amusement. **2** strange; odd. **3** suspicious or illegal: *something funny is going on.* **4** informal slightly unwell.

SYNONYMS **1 amusing**, humorous, witty, comic, comical, hilarious, hysterical, riotous, uproarious, farcical; informal rib-tickling, priceless. **2 strange**, peculiar, odd, weird, bizarre, curious, freakish, quirky, unusual. **3 suspicious**, suspect, dubious, untrustworthy, questionable; informal fishy, dodgy. ANTONYMS serious.

□ **funny bone** informal the part of the elbow over which a very sensitive nerve passes. **funny farm** informal a psychiatric hospital. ■ **fun·ni·ly** **adv.**

fur /fər/ ▶ **n.** **1** the short, soft hair of certain animals. **2** the skin of an animal with fur on it, or a coat made from this. **3** a coating formed on someone's tongue when they are not well. □ **the fur will fly** informal there will be a dramatic argument. ■ **furred** **adj.**

fur·be·low /ˈfərbəˌlō/ ▶ **n.** **1** a strip of gathered or pleated material sewn on a skirt or petticoat. **2** (**furbelows**) showy decorations or ornaments.

fu·ri·ous /ˈfyo͝orēəs/ ▶ **adj.** **1** very angry. **2** with great energy or speed: *he drove at a furious speed.*

SYNONYMS **1 very angry**, enraged, infuriated, irate, incensed, fuming, ranting, raving, seething, beside yourself, outraged; informal hopping mad, wild, livid. **2 fierce**, heated, passionate, fiery, tumultuous, turbulent, tempestuous, violent, stormy, acrimonious. ANTONYMS pleased, calm.

■ **fu·ri·ous·ly** **adv.**

furl /fərl/ ▶ **v.** roll or fold up neatly.

fur·long /ˈfərˌlôNG, -ˌläNG/ ▶ **n.** an eighth of a mile, 220 yards.

fur·lough /ˈfərlō/ ▶ **n.** a time when you have permission to be away from your work or duties.

fur·nace /ˈfərnəs/ ▶ **n.** **1** an enclosed space for heating material to very high temperatures. **2** an appliance fired by gas or oil in which air or water is heated to be circulated throughout a building in a heating system. **3** a very hot place.

fur·nish /ˈfərnisH/ ▶ **v.** **1** provide a room or building with furniture and fittings. **2** supply or provide.

SYNONYMS **1 fit out**, provide with furniture, appoint, equip, outfit. **2** *they furnished us with boots* **supply**, provide, equip, issue; informal fix up.

fur·nish·ings /ˈfərnisHiNGz/ ▶ **n.** furniture and fittings in a room or building.

fur·ni·ture /ˈfərnicHər/ ▶ **n.** the movable articles that make a room or building suitable for living or working in. □ **a part of the furniture** informal a person or thing that has become so familiar as to be unnoticed.

fu·ror /ˈfyo͝orˌôr, -ər/ (or **furore** /ˌfyo͝oˈrôrē/) ▶ **n.** an outbreak of public anger or excitement.

SYNONYMS **commotion**, uproar, outcry, fuss, upset, brouhaha, stir; informal to-do, hoo-ha, hullabaloo.

fur·ri·er /ˈfərēər/ ▶ **n.** a person who deals in clothes made of fur.

fur·row /ˈfərō, ˈfə-rō/ ▶ **n.** **1** a long, narrow trench made in the ground by a plow. **2** a deep wrinkle on a person's face. ▶ **v.** make a furrow in.

fur·ry /ˈfərē/ ▶ **adj.** (**furrier**, **furriest**) covered with or like fur.

fur·ther /ˈfərT͟Hər/ ▶ **adv.** (also **farther** /ˈfärT͟Hər/) **1** at, to, or by a greater distance. **2** at or to a more advanced stage. **3** in addition. ▶ **adj.** **1** (also **farther**) more distant in space. **2** additional. ▶ **v.** (**furthers**, **furthering**, **furthered**) help the progress of.

SYNONYMS ▶ **adv.** see **FURTHERMORE**. ▶ **adj.** **additional**, more, extra, supplementary, new, fresh. ▶ **v.** **promote**, advance, forward, develop, facilitate, aid, assist, help, boost, encourage. ANTONYMS impede.

fur·ther·ance /ˈfərT͟Hərəns/ ▶ **n.** the process of helping something to develop or succeed.

fur·ther·more /ˈfərT͟HərˌmôR/ ▶ **adv.** in addition.

SYNONYMS **moreover**, further, what's more, also, additionally, in addition, besides, as well, too, on top of that, into the bargain.

fur·thest /ˈfərT͟Hist/ (or **farthest** /ˈfärT͟Hist/) ▶ **adv. & adj.** at or to the greatest distance.

SYNONYMS **most distant**, remotest, farthest, furthermost, farthermost, outer, outermost, extreme. ANTONYMS nearest.

fur·tive /ˈfərtiv/ ▶ **adj.** secretively trying to avoid being noticed.

SYNONYMS **surreptitious**, secretive, secret, clandestine, hidden, covert, conspiratorial, cloak-and-dagger, sneaky; informal shifty. ANTONYMS open.

■ **fur·tive·ly** **adv.**

fu·ry /ˈfyo͝orē/ ▶ **n.** (plural **furies**) **1** extreme anger. **2** extreme strength or violence: *the fury of a gathering storm.* **3** (**the Furies**) Greek Mythology three goddesses who punished people for their crimes.

SYNONYMS **1 rage**, anger, wrath, outrage; literary ire. **2 ferocity**, violence, turbulence, tempestuousness, savagery, severity, intensity, vehemence, force.

furze /fərz/ ▶ **n.** the shrub gorse.

fuse /fyo͞oz/ ▶ **v.** (**fuses**, **fusing**, **fused**) **1** join or combine to form a whole. **2** melt something so it joins with something else. **3** fit a circuit or electrical appliance with a fuse. ▶ **n.** **1** a safety device consisting of a strip of wire that melts and breaks an electric circuit if the current goes beyond a safe level. **2** a length of material that is lit to explode a bomb or firework. **3** a device in a bomb that controls the timing of the explosion. ▫ **fuse box** a box housing the fuses for electrical circuits in a building.

fu·se·lage /ˈfyo͞osəˌläzʜ, -zə-/ ▶ **n.** the main body of an aircraft.

fu·si·ble /ˈfyo͞ozəbəl/ ▶ **adj.** able to be melted easily.

fu·sil·lade /ˈfyo͞osəˌläd, -ˌlād/ ▶ **n.** a series of shots fired at the same time or quickly one after the other.

fu·sion /ˈfyo͞ozʜən/ ▶ **n.** **1** the joining of two or more things together to form a whole. **2** a reaction in which the nuclei of atoms fuse to form a heavier nucleus, releasing a great deal of energy.

fuss /fəs/ ▶ **n.** **1** unnecessary excitement or activity. **2** a protest or complaint. ▶ **v.** (usu. **fuss over**) show unnecessary concern about something.

SYNONYMS ▶ **n.** **1** **commotion**, excitement, stir, confusion, disturbance, brouhaha, uproar, furor, tempest in a teapot; informal hoo-ha, to-do, song and dance, dog and pony show. **2** **protest**, complaint, objection, argument. **3** **trouble**, bother, inconvenience, effort, exertion, labor; informal hassle. ▶ **v.** **worry**, fret, be agitated, be worked up, make a big thing out of, make a mountain out of a molehill; informal be in a tizzy.

fuss·pot /ˈfəsˌpät/ ▶ **n.** informal a fussy person.

fuss·y /ˈfəsē/ ▶ **adj.** (**fussier**, **fussiest**) **1** hard to please. **2** full of unnecessary detail.

SYNONYMS **1** **particular**, finicky, fastidious, hard to please; informal persnickety, choosy, picky. **2** **over-elaborate**, ornate, fancy, busy, cluttered.

■ **fuss·i·ly** **adv.** **fuss·i·ness** **n.**

fus·tian /ˈfəscʜən/ ▶ **n.** a thick, hard-wearing cloth.

fus·ty /ˈfəstē/ ▶ **adj.** (**fustier**, **fustiest**) **1** smelling stale or damp. **2** old-fashioned.

fu·tile /ˈfyo͞otl, -ˌtil/ ▶ **adj.** pointless.

SYNONYMS **fruitless**, vain, pointless, useless, ineffectual, forlorn, hopeless. ANTONYMS useful.

■ **fu·tile·ly** **adv.** **fu·til·i·ty** /ˈfyo͞oˈtilətē/ **n.**

fu·ton /ˈfo͞oˌtän/ ▶ **n.** a padded mattress that can be rolled up.

fu·ture /ˈfyo͞ocʜər/ ▶ **n.** **1** (**the future**) time that is still to come. **2** a prospect of success or happiness: *I might have a future as an artist.* ▶ **adj.** **1** existing or happening in the future. **2** Grammar (of a verb) expressing an event yet to happen.

SYNONYMS ▶ **n.** **1** *plans for the future* **time to come**, what lies ahead, the hereafter. **2** *her future lay in acting* **destiny**, fate, fortune, prospects, chances. ANTONYMS past. ▶ **adj.** **1** **later**, to come, following, forthcoming, ensuing, succeeding, subsequent, coming, impending, approaching. **2** *her future husband* **to be**, destined, intended, planned, prospective. ANTONYMS previous, past.

▫ **future perfect** a tense of verbs expressing an action that will be completed in the future, as in English *will have done.* **in future** from now onward.

Fu·tur·ism /ˈfyo͞ocʜəˌrizəm/ ▶ **n.** an early 20th-century artistic movement that strongly rejected traditional forms and embraced modern technology. ■ **Fu·tur·ist** **n. & adj.**

fu·tur·is·tic /ˌfyo͞ocʜəˈristik/ ▶ **adj.** **1** having very modern technology or design. **2** (of a movie or book) set in the future.

fu·tu·ri·ty /fyo͞oˈto͝orətē, -ˈcʜo͝orətē/ ▶ **n.** (plural **futurities**) the future time.

fuzz /fəz/ ▶ **n.** **1** a frizzy mass of hair or fiber. **2** (**the fuzz**) informal the police.

fuzz·y /ˈfəzē/ ▶ **adj.** (**fuzzier**, **fuzziest**) **1** having a frizzy texture or appearance. **2** blurred; not clear: *the picture is very fuzzy.*

SYNONYMS **1** **frizzy**, fluffy, woolly, downy. **2** **blurred**, indistinct, unclear, out of focus, misty. **3** **unclear**, imprecise, unfocused, nebulous, vague, hazy, loose, woolly. ANTONYMS smooth, sharp, clear.

FX ▶ **abbr.** visual or sound effects.

FYI ▶ **abbr.** for your information.

Gg

G (or **g**) ▶ **n.** (plural **Gs** or **G's**) the seventh letter of the alphabet. ▶ **abbr. 1** (**g**) gram(s). **2** (**G**) gravity. □ **G-string** a garment consisting of a narrow strip of cloth that covers the genitals and is attached to a waistband.

gab /gab/ ▶ **v.** (**gabs**, **gabbing**, **gabbed**) informal talk at length. □ **the gift of gab** the ability to speak in a fluent and persuasive way.

gab·ar·dine /ˈgabərˌdēn/ ▶ **n.** a smooth, hard-wearing cloth used for making raincoats.

gab·ble /ˈgabəl/ ▶ **v.** (**gabbles**, **gabbling**, **gabbled**) talk very quickly and in a way that is difficult to understand. ▶ **n.** talk that is fast and difficult to understand.

ga·ble /ˈgābəl/ ▶ **n.** the triangular upper part of a wall at the end of a roof.

gad /gad/ ▶ **v.** (**gads**, **gadding**, **gadded**) (**gad about**) informal enjoy yourself by visiting many different places.

gad·a·bout /ˈgadəˌbout/ ▶ **n.** informal a person who gads about.

gad·fly /ˈgadˌflī/ ▶ **n.** (plural **gadflies**) **1** a fly that bites cattle. **2** an annoying person, especially one who provokes others into action by criticism.

gadg·et /ˈgajit/ ▶ **n.** a small mechanical device.

> SYNONYMS **device**, appliance, apparatus, instrument, implement, tool, utensil, contrivance, contraption, machine, mechanism, invention; informal gizmo.

■ **gadg·et·ry n.**

Gael /gāl/ ▶ **n.** a Gaelic-speaking person.

Gael·ic /ˈgālik/ ▶ **n.** a language spoken in parts of Ireland and western Scotland.

gaff /gaf/ ▶ **n.** a stick with a hook for landing large fish.

gaffe /gaf/ ▶ **n.** an embarrassing mistake made in a social situation.

> SYNONYMS **blunder**, mistake, error, slip, faux pas, indiscretion, solecism; informal slip-up, blooper, boo-boo, howler.

gaf·fer /ˈgafər/ ▶ **n. 1** the chief electrician in a motion-picture or television production unit. **2** informal an old man.

gag¹ /gag/ ▶ **n.** a piece of cloth put over a person's mouth to stop them speaking. ▶ **v.** (**gags**, **gagging**, **gagged**) **1** put a gag on. **2** choke or retch.

> SYNONYMS ▶ **v. 1 silence**, muzzle, suppress, stifle, censor, curb, restrain. **2 retch**, heave.

gag² ▶ **n.** a joke or funny story.

> SYNONYMS **joke**, quip, jest, witticism; informal crack, wisecrack, one-liner.

ga·ga /ˈgäˌgä/ ▶ **adj.** informal rambling in speech or thought, especially as a result of old age.

gag·gle /ˈgagəl/ ▶ **n. 1** a flock of geese. **2** informal a noisy group of people.

gai·e·ty /ˈgāitē/ ▶ **n.** (plural **gaieties**) the state or quality of being lighthearted or cheerful.

gai·ly /ˈgālē/ ▶ **adv. 1** in a lighthearted and cheerful way. **2** without thinking of the effect of your actions. **3** with a bright appearance.

gain /gān/ ▶ **v. 1** obtain or secure something. **2** reach a place: *we gained the ridge.* **3** (**gain on**) get closer to a person or thing that you are chasing. **4** increase in weight or speed. **5** (**gain in**) improve or progress in some respect. **6** (of a clock or watch) become fast. ▶ **n. 1** a thing that is gained. **2** an increase in wealth or resources.

> SYNONYMS ▶ **v. 1 obtain**, get, secure, acquire, come by, procure, attain, achieve, earn, win, capture; informal land. **2** *they stood to gain from the deal* **profit**, make money, benefit, do well. **3** *she gained weight* **put on**, increase in, build up. **4** *they're gaining on us* **catch up to/with**, catch; reduce someone's lead, narrow the gap. ANTONYMS lose. ▶ **n. 1 profit**, earnings, income, yield, return, reward, advantage, benefit; informal take. **2 increase**, addition, rise, increment, advance. ANTONYMS loss.

gain·ful /ˈgānfəl/ ▶ **adj.** (of employment) paid; profitable.

> SYNONYMS **profitable**, paid, well-paid, remunerative, lucrative, moneymaking, rewarding, fruitful, worthwhile, useful, productive, constructive, beneficial, advantageous, valuable.

■ **gain·ful·ly adv.**

gain·say /ˌgānˈsā, ˈgānˌsā/ ▶ **v.** (**gainsays**, **gainsaying**, **gainsaid**) formal deny or contradict.

gait /gāt/ ▶ **n. 1** a way of walking. **2** the paces of a horse or dog.

> SYNONYMS **walk**, step, stride, pace, tread, way of walking, bearing, carriage, deportment.

gait·er /ˈgātər/ ▶ **n.** a covering of cloth or leather for the ankle and lower leg.

gal /gal/ ▶ **n.** informal a girl or young woman.

gal. ▶ **abbr.** gallon(s).

ga·la /ˈgālə, ˈgalə/ ▶ **n.** a social occasion with special entertainment.

> SYNONYMS **festival**, fair, fete, carnival, pageant, jubilee, jamboree, celebration.

ga·lac·tic /gəˈlaktik/ ▶ **adj.** relating to a galaxy.

gal·ax·y /ˈgaləksē/ ▶ **n.** (plural **galaxies**) **1** a large system of stars. **2** (**the Galaxy**) the system of stars that includes the sun and the earth; the Milky Way.

gale /gāl/ ▶ **n. 1** a very strong wind. **2** an outburst of laughter.

SYNONYMS **1 high wind**, blast, squall, storm, tempest, hurricane, tornado, cyclone, whirlwind, typhoon. **2 peal**, howl, hoot, shriek, roar, fit, paroxysm.

gall¹ /gôl/ ▶ **n.** disrespectful or rude behavior.

gall² ▶ **n.** **1** annoyance; irritation. **2** a sore on the skin made by rubbing. ▶ **v.** annoy; irritate. ■ **gall·ing** adj.

gall³ ▶ **n.** an abnormal growth formed in response to the presence of insect larvae, mites, or fungi on plants and trees.

gal·lant ▶ **adj.** **1** /ˈgalənt/ brave or heroic. **2** /gəˈlant, -ˈlänt/ (of a man) polite and charming to women. ▶ **n.** /gəˈlant, -ˈlänt/ a man who is polite and charming to women.

SYNONYMS ▶ **adj.** **1 brave**, courageous, valiant, bold, plucky, daring, fearless, intrepid, heroic, stouthearted; informal gutsy, spunky. **2 chivalrous**, gentlemanly, courteous, polite, attentive, respectful, gracious, considerate, thoughtful. ANTONYMS cowardly, discourteous.

■ **gal·lant·ly** adv.

gal·lant·ry /ˈgaləntrē/ ▶ **n.** (plural **gallantries**) **1** courageous behavior. **2** polite attention given by men to women.

gall·blad·der /ˈgôlˌbladər/ ▶ **n.** a small organ beneath the liver, in which bile is stored.

gal·le·on /ˈgalēən, ˈgalyən/ ▶ **n.** historical a large sailing ship with three or more decks and masts.

gal·ler·y /ˈgalərē/ ▶ **n.** (plural **galleries**) **1** a room or building in which works of art are displayed or sold. **2** a balcony at the back of a large hall. **3** the highest part of a theater. □ **play to the gallery** aim to attract popular attention.

gal·ley /ˈgalē/ ▶ **n.** (plural **galleys**) **1** historical a low, flat ship with one or more sails and up to three banks of oars. **2** a narrow kitchen in a ship or aircraft. **3** (also **galley proof**) a printer's proof in the form of long single-column strips, not in sheets or pages. ▶ **adj.** (of a kitchen) long and narrow.

Gal·lic /ˈgalik/ ▶ **adj.** having to do with France or the French.

gal·li·mau·fry /ˌgaləˈmôfrē/ ▶ **n.** a jumble or medley.

gal·li·vant /ˈgaləˌvant/ ▶ **v.** informal go from place to place enjoying yourself.

gal·lon /ˈgalən/ ▶ **n.** **1** a unit of liquid capacity equal to four quarts or eight pints (3.79 liters). **2** (**gallons**) informal large quantities.

gal·lop /ˈgaləp/ ▶ **n.** **1** the fastest speed a horse can run. **2** a ride on a horse at its fastest speed. ▶ **v.** (**gallops**, **galloping**, **galloped**) **1** go at the speed of a gallop. **2** proceed very quickly.

gal·lows /ˈgalōz/ ▶ **pl.n.** **1** a structure used for hanging a person. **2** (**the gallows**) execution by hanging: *he was saved from the gallows.* □ **gallows humor** grim humor in a desperate or hopeless situation.

gall·stone /ˈgôlˌstōn/ ▶ **n.** a hard mass of crystals formed in the gall bladder or bile ducts, causing pain and obstruction.

Gal·lup poll /ˈgaləp/ ▶ **n.** trademark an assessment of public opinion by the questioning of a representative sample.

ga·lore /gəˈlôr/ ▶ **adj.** in large numbers or amounts: *there were prizes galore.*

ga·losh·es /gəˈläsʜiz/ ▶ **pl.n.** rubber shoes worn over normal shoes in wet weather.

ga·lumph /gəˈləmf/ ▶ **v.** informal move in a clumsy or noisy way.

gal·van·ic /galˈvanik/ ▶ **adj.** relating to electric currents produced by chemical action.

gal·va·nize /ˈgalvəˌnīz/ ▶ **v.** (**galvanizes**, **galvanizing**, **galvanized**) **1** shock or excite someone into doing something. **2** (**galvanized**) (of iron or steel) coated with a protective layer of zinc.

gal·va·nom·e·ter /ˌgalvəˈnämitər/ ▶ **n.** an instrument for measuring small electric currents.

Gam·bi·an /ˈgambēən/ ▶ **n.** a person from Gambia. ▶ **adj.** relating to Gambia.

gam·bit /ˈgambit/ ▶ **n.** **1** something that somebody says or does that is meant to give them an advantage. **2** (in chess) an opening in which a player makes a sacrifice, typically of a pawn, for the sake of some compensating advantage.

gam·ble /ˈgambəl/ ▶ **v.** (**gambles**, **gambling**, **gambled**) **1** play games of chance for money. **2** bet a sum of money. **3** risk losing something in the hope that you will be successful. ▶ **n.** a risky action.

SYNONYMS ▶ **v.** **1 bet**, place a bet, wager, hazard. **2 take a chance**, take a risk; informal stick your neck out. ▶ **n.** *I took a gamble* **risk**, chance, shot/leap in the dark, speculation, lottery, potluck.

■ **gam·bler** n.

gam·bol /ˈgambəl/ ▶ **v.** (**gambols**, **gamboling**, **gamboled**) run or jump about playfully.

game /gām/ ▶ **n.** **1** an activity that you take part in for amusement. **2** a competitive activity or sport played according to rules. **3** a period of play, ending in a final result. **4** a section of a tennis match, forming a unit in scoring. **5** (**games**) a meeting for sporting competitions. **6** informal a type of activity or business regarded as a game. **7** wild animals or birds that people hunt for food or as a sport. ▶ **adj.** eager and willing to do something new or challenging: *they were game for anything.* ▶ **v.** (**games**, **gaming**, **gamed**) play at games of chance for money.

SYNONYMS ▶ **n.** **1 pastime**, diversion, entertainment, amusement, distraction, recreation, sport, activity. **2 match**, contest, fixture, meeting, tie, clash. ▶ **adj.** **willing**, prepared, ready, disposed, interested, eager, keen, enthusiastic.

□ **ahead of the game** ahead of your competitors or peers. **beat someone at their own game** use someone's own methods to outdo them. **game bird** **1** a bird shot for sport or food. **2** a bird of a large group that includes pheasants, grouse, quails, etc. **game plan** a planned strategy in sports, politics, or business. **game show** a program on television in which people compete to win money and prizes. ■ **game·ly** adv.

game·keep·er /ˈgāmˌkēpər/ ▶ **n.** a person employed to breed and protect game for a large country estate.

gam·er /ˈgāmər/ ▶ **n.** a participant in a computer or role-playing game.

games·man·ship /ˈgāmzmənˌsʜip/ ▶ **n.** the ability to win games by making your opponent feel less confident.

gam·ete /ˈgamēt, gəˈmēt/ ▶ **n.** Biology a cell that is able to unite with another of the opposite sex in sexual reproduction to form a zygote.

gam·ine /'gamēn/ ▶ **adj.** (of a girl) having a mischievous, boyish charm.

gam·ma /'gamə/ ▶ **n.** the third letter of the Greek alphabet (Γ, γ). ▫ **gamma rays** (or **gamma radiation**) electromagnetic radiation of shorter wavelength than X-rays.

gam·ut /'gamət/ ▶ **n. 1** the complete range or scope of something. **2** Music a complete scale of musical notes; the compass or range of a voice or instrument. ▫ **run the gamut** experience or perform the complete range of something.

gam·y /'gāmē/ (also **gamey**) ▶ **adj.** (**gamier**, **gamiest**) (of meat) having the strong flavor or smell of game, especially when it is slightly tainted.

gan·der /'gandər/ ▶ **n. 1** a male goose. **2** informal a look.

gang /gaNG/ ▶ **n. 1** an organized group of criminals or rowdy young people. **2** informal a group of people who regularly meet and do things together. **3** an organized group of people doing manual work. **4** a set of switches, sockets, or other devices grouped together. ▶ **v. 1** (**gang together**) form a group or gang. **2** (**gang up**) join together to oppose or intimidate someone.

SYNONYMS ▶ **n. band**, group, crowd, pack, horde, throng, mob, herd, swarm, troop; informal bunch, gaggle, load.

gang·bust·ers /'gaNG,bəstər/ ▶ **pl.n.**(**go** (or **like**) **gangbusters**) informal used to refer to great energy, speed, or success.

gang·ling /'gaNGgliNG/ (or **gangly** /'gaNGglē/) ▶ **adj.** (of a person) tall, thin, and awkward.

gan·gli·on /'gaNGglēən/ ▶ **n.** (plural **ganglia** /-glēə/ or **ganglions**) **1** a mass of nerve cells. **2** a swelling in a tendon.

gang·plank /'gaNG,plaNGk/ ▶ **n.** a movable plank used as a bridge between a boat and the shore.

gan·grene /'gaNGgrēn, gaNG'grēn/ ▶ **n.** the decay of tissue in a part of the body, caused by an obstructed blood supply or by infection. ▪ **gan·gre·nous** /'gaNGgrənəs/ **adj.**

gang·ster /'gaNGstər/ ▶ **n.** a member of an organized gang of violent criminals.

SYNONYMS **hoodlum**, racketeer, thug, villain, criminal, Mafioso; informal mobster, crook, hood, tough.

gang·way /'gaNG,wā/ ▶ **n.** a bridge placed between a ship and the shore. ▶ **exclam.** make way!

gan·net /'ganit/ ▶ **n.** a large seabird.

gan·try /'gantrē/ ▶ **n.** (plural **gantries**) a bridgelike structure used as a support.

gap /gap/ ▶ **n. 1** a hole in an object or between two objects. **2** an empty space or period of time; a break in something.

SYNONYMS **1 opening**, aperture, space, breach, chink, slit, crack, crevice, cleft, cavity, hole, interstice. **2 pause**, intermission, interval, interlude, break, recess, breathing space, breather, respite, hiatus, lull. **3 omission**, blank, lacuna. **4** *the gap between rich and poor* **chasm**, gulf, separation, contrast, difference, disparity, divergence, imbalance.

▫ **gap year** a period taken by a student as a break from education between leaving high school and starting at a university or college.

gape /gāp/ ▶ **v.** (**gapes**, **gaping**, **gaped**) **1** stare with your mouth open wide in amazement. **2** be or become wide open. ▶ **n. 1** an open-mouthed stare. **2** a wide opening. **3** a widely open mouth or beak.

SYNONYMS ▶ **v. 1 stare**, goggle, gaze, ogle; informal rubberneck. **2 open**, yawn, part, split. **3** (**gaping**) **wide**, broad, vast, yawning, cavernous.

ga·rage /gə'räzH, -'räj/ ▶ **n. 1** a building in which a car or other vehicle is kept. **2** a business that sells fuel or that repairs motor vehicles. **3** a type of music with elements of drum and bass, house, and soul. ▶ **v.** (**garages**, **garaging**, **garaged**) keep a vehicle in a garage.

garb /gärb/ ▶ **n.** unusual or distinctive clothes. ▶ **v.** (**be garbed in**) be dressed in distinctive clothes.

gar·bage /'gärbij/ ▶ **n. 1** wasted or spoiled food and other refuse, as from a kitchen or household. **2** something worthless or meaningless.

SYNONYMS **1 trash**, refuse, waste, rubbish, detritus, litter, junk, scrap, scraps, leftovers, remains. **2 nonsense**, rubbish, balderdash, claptrap, twaddle, dross; informal hogwash, baloney, tripe, bilge, bull, bunk, poppycock, rot, piffle.

▫ **garbage can** a plastic or metal container for household refuse.

gar·ban·zo /gär'bänzō/ ▶ **n.** (plural **garbanzos**) ⇒ CHICKPEA.

gar·ble /'gärbəl/ ▶ **v.** (**garbles**, **garbling**, **garbled**) confuse or distort a message or transmission.

SYNONYMS **mix up**, muddle, jumble, confuse, obscure, distort.

gar·den /'gärdn/ ▶ **n. 1** a piece of ground, often near a house, used for growing flowers, fruit, or vegetables. **2** (**gardens**) a public park. ▶ **v.** work in a garden.

SYNONYMS ▶ **n.** plot, bed, patch, flower garden, vegetable garden, herb garden.

▫ **garden apartment** a ground-floor apartment with a door opening onto a yard or garden. **garden party** a social event held on a lawn or in a garden. **garden-variety** of the usual or ordinary type.

gar·den·er /'gärdnər/ ▶ **n.** a person who cultivates a garden as a pastime or for a living. ▪ **gar·den·ing n.**

gar·de·nia /gär'dēnyə/ ▶ **n.** a tree or shrub of the bedstraw family, with large fragrant white or yellow flowers.

gar·gan·tu·an /gär'ganCHo͞oən/ ▶ **adj.** enormous.

gar·gle /'gärgəl/ ▶ **v.** (**gargles**, **gargling**, **gargled**) hold liquid in your mouth and throat while slowly breathing out through it. ▶ **n. 1** an act of gargling. **2** a liquid used for gargling.

gar·goyle /'gär,goil/ ▶ **n.** a spout in the form of a grotesque person or animal face that carries water away from the roof of a building.

gar·ish /'gariSH/ ▶ **adj.** unpleasantly bright and showy.

SYNONYMS **gaudy**, lurid, loud, harsh, showy, glittering, brash, tasteless, vulgar; informal flashy. ANTONYMS drab, tasteful.

▪ **gar·ish·ly adv.**

gar·land /'gärlənd/ ▶ **n.** a wreath of flowers and leaves. ▶ **v.** crown or decorate with a garland.

gar·lic /'gärlik/ ▶ **n.** a plant of the onion family with a strong taste and smell.

gar·ment /'gärmənt/ ▶ **n.** a piece of clothing.

SYNONYMS (**garments**) **clothes**, clothing, dress, garb, wardrobe, costume, attire; informal threads, gear, togs; formal apparel.

gar·ner /'gärnər/ ▶ v. (**garners**, **garnering**, **garnered**) gather or collect.

gar·net /'gärnit/ ▶ n. a red semiprecious stone.

gar·nish /'gärnish/ ▶ v. decorate food. ▶ n. a decoration for food.

SYNONYMS ▶ v. **decorate**, adorn, ornament, trim, dress, embellish. ▶ n. **decoration**, adornment, ornament, embellishment, enhancement, finishing touch.

gar·ret /'garit/ ▶ n. a top-floor or attic room, especially a small dismal one (traditionally inhabited by an artist).

gar·ri·son /'garəsən/ ▶ n. a group of troops stationed in a fortress or town to defend it, or the building such troops occupy. ▶ v. provide a place with a garrison.

SYNONYMS ▶ n. **1 troops**, forces, militia, soldiers, force, detachment, unit. **2 base**, camp, station, barracks, fort, command post. ▶ v. **station**, post, deploy, base, site, place, billet.

gar·rote /gə'rät, -'rōt/ ▶ v. (**garrotes**, **garroting**, **garroted**) strangle someone with a wire or cord. ▶ n. a wire or cord used for garroting.

gar·ru·lous /'gar(y)ələs/ ▶ adj. very talkative.

SYNONYMS **talkative**, loquacious, voluble, verbose, chatty, gossipy, effusive, expansive, forthcoming, conversational, communicative; informal mouthy, having the gift of the gab. ANTONYMS taciturn.

■ **gar·ru·li·ty** /gə'ro͞olitē/ n.

gar·ter /'gärtər/ ▶ n. a band worn around the leg to keep up a stocking or sock.

gas /gas/ ▶ n. (plural **gases** or **gasses**) **1** an airlike substance that expands to fill any available space. **2** a type of gas used as a fuel. **3** a type of gas that stops you feeling pain, used during a medical operation. **4** gasoline. ▶ v. (**gases**, **gassing**, **gassed**) **1** attack with, expose to, or kill with gas. **2** informal talk or chat at length. □ **gas chamber** an airtight room that can be filled with poisonous gas to kill people or animals. **gas guzzler** informal a car with high fuel consumption. **gas mask** a mask used as protection against poisonous gas. **gas pedal** ⇒ ACCELERATOR (sense 1). **gas station** a service station, especially one without repair facilities. **gas turbine** a turbine driven by expanding hot gases produced by burning fuel, as in a jet engine.

gas·bag /'gas,bag/ ▶ n. informal a person who talks idly and excessively.

gas·e·ous /'gasēəs, 'gashəs/ ▶ adj. relating to or like a gas.

gash /gash/ ▶ n. a long deep cut or wound. ▶ v. make a gash in.

SYNONYMS ▶ n. **cut**, laceration, slash, slit, split, wound, injury. ▶ v. **cut**, lacerate, slash, slit, split, wound, injure.

gas·ket /'gaskit/ ▶ n. a rubber seal at the junction between two surfaces in an engine.

gas·light /'gas,līt/ ▶ n. light from a gas lamp. ■ **gas·lit** adj.

gas·o·line /,gasə'lēn, 'gasəlēn/ ▶ n. a liquid obtained by refining petroleum, used as fuel in motor vehicles.

gas·om·e·ter /gas'ämitər/ ▶ n. a large tank for storing and measuring gas.

gasp /gasp/ ▶ v. **1** take a quick breath with your mouth open, because you are surprised or in pain. **2** (**gasp for**) struggle for air. ▶ n. a sudden quick breath.

SYNONYMS ▶ v. **1 catch your breath**, gulp, draw in your breath. **2 pant**, puff, huff and puff, wheeze, breathe hard/heavily, choke, fight for breath. ▶ n. **gulp**, pant, puff.

gas·sy /'gasē/ ▶ adj. (**gassier**, **gassiest**) **1** full of gas. **2** informal talkative.

gas·tric /'gastrik/ ▶ adj. having to do with the stomach. □ **gastric juice** an acidic secretion of the stomach glands that promotes digestion.

gas·tro·en·ter·i·tis /,gastrō,entə'rītis/ ▶ n. inflammation of the stomach and intestines.

gas·tron·o·my /ga'stränəmē/ ▶ n. the practice or art of cooking and eating good food. ■ **gas·tro·nom·ic** /,gastrə'nämik/ adj.

gas·tro·pod /'gastrə,päd/ ▶ n. Zoology any of a large class of mollusks including snails and slugs.

gas·works /'gas,wərks/ ▶ pl.n. a place where gas is processed.

gate /gāt/ ▶ n. **1** a hinged barrier used to close an opening in a wall, fence, or hedge. **2** an exit from an airport building to an aircraft. **3** a barrier that controls the flow of water on a river or canal. **4** the number of people who pay to attend a sports or entertainment event, or the money collected from them.

SYNONYMS **barrier**, turnstile, gateway, doorway, entrance, entryway, exit, door, portal.

gate·crash /'gāt,krash/ ▶ v. go to a party without an invitation or ticket. ■ **gate·crash·er** n.

gate·fold /'gāt,fōld/ ▶ n. an oversized page in a book or magazine, intended to be opened out for reading.

gate·house /'gāt,hous/ ▶ n. a house standing by the gateway to a country estate.

gate·keep·er /'gāt,kēpər/ ▶ n. an attendant at a gate.

gate·leg ta·ble /'gāt,leg/ ▶ n. a table with hinged legs that may be swung out from the center to support folding leaves.

gate·post /'gāt,pōst/ ▶ n. a post on which a gate is hinged or against which it shuts.

gate·way /'gāt,wā/ ▶ n. **1** an opening that can be closed by a gate. **2** (**gateway to**) a means of entering somewhere or achieving something. **3** a frame built around or over a gate.

gath·er /'gat͟hər/ ▶ v. (**gathers**, **gathering**, **gathered**) **1** come or bring together. **2** increase in force, speed, etc.: *the movement is gathering pace.* **3** understand something to be the case: *you're still with Anthea, I gather.* **4** collect plants or fruits for food. **5** harvest a crop. **6** draw together or toward yourself: *she gathered the child in her arms.* **7** pull fabric into folds by drawing thread through it. ▶ n. (**gathers**) a part of a piece of clothing that is gathered.

SYNONYMS ▶ v. **1 congregate**, assemble, meet, collect, get together, convene, muster, rally, converge. **2 summon**, call together, bring together, assemble, convene, rally, round up, muster, marshal. **3 understand**, believe, be led to believe, conclude, infer, assume, take it, surmise, hear, learn, discover. **4 harvest**, reap, crop, pick, pluck, collect. **5 pleat**, pucker, tuck, fold, ruffle. ANTONYMS disperse.

gath·er·ing /'gaTHəriNG/ ▶ **n.** a group of people who have come together for a purpose.

SYNONYMS **assembly**, meeting, convention, rally, council, congress, congregation, audience, crowd, group, throng, mass; informal get-together.

gauche /gōSH/ ▶ **adj.** awkward in social situations.

SYNONYMS **awkward**, gawky, inelegant, graceless, ungraceful, clumsy, ungainly, maladroit, inept, unsophisticated. ANTONYMS elegant, sophisticated.

gau·cho /'gouCHō/ ▶ **n.** (plural **gauchos**) a cowboy from the South American plains.

gaud·y /'gôdē/ ▶ **adj.** (**gaudier**, **gaudiest**) tastelessly bright and showy.

SYNONYMS **garish**, lurid, loud, glaring, harsh, showy, glittering, ostentatious, tasteless; informal flashy, tacky. ANTONYMS drab, tasteful.

■ **gaud·i·ly adv.**

gauge /gāj/ (or **gage**) ▶ **n. 1** an instrument for measuring the amount or level of something. **2** the thickness or size of a wire, tube, bullet, etc. **3** the distance between the rails of a railroad track. ▶ **v.** (**gages**, **gaging**, **gaged**) **1** judge a situation or mood. **2** estimate or measure something.

SYNONYMS ▶ **n. meter**, measure, indicator, dial, scale, display. ▶ **v. 1 measure**, calculate, compute, work out, determine, ascertain, count, weigh, quantify, put a figure on. **2 assess**, evaluate, determine, estimate, form an opinion of, appraise, weigh up, judge, guess; informal size up.

gaunt /gônt/ ▶ **adj.** (of a person) looking thin and exhausted.

SYNONYMS **haggard**, drawn, thin, lean, skinny, spindly, spare, bony, angular, rawboned, pinched, hollow-cheeked, scrawny, scraggy, as thin as a rail, cadaverous, skeletal, emaciated, skin and bone(s), wasted, withered; informal like a bag of bones. ANTONYMS plump.

gaunt·let /'gôntlit, 'gänt-/ ▶ **n. 1** a strong glove with a long loose wrist. **2** a glove worn as part of medieval armor. □ **run the gauntlet** have to face criticism or hostility from a large number of people. **throw down the gauntlet** set a challenge.

gauze /gôz/ ▶ **n. 1** a thin transparent fabric. **2** thin, loosely woven cloth used for dressing wounds. **3** a fine wire mesh. ■ **gauz·y adj.**

gave /gāv/ past of GIVE.

gav·el /'gavəl/ ▶ **n.** a small hammer with which a judge or auctioneer hits a surface in order to get people's attention. ▶ **v.** (**gavels**, **gaveling**, **gaveled**) bring to order by use of a gavel.

ga·votte /gə'vät/ ▶ **n.** a French dance, popular in the 18th century.

gawk /gôk/ ▶ **v.** stare in a stupid or rude way.

gawk·y /'gôkē/ ▶ **adj.** awkward and clumsy.

gay /gā/ ▶ **adj.** (**gayer**, **gayest**) **1** (especially of a man) homosexual. **2** relating to homosexuals. **3** dated lighthearted and carefree. **4** dated brightly colored. ▶ **n.** a homosexual person, especially a man.

USAGE

gay is the term preferred by homosexual men to describe themselves (**lesbian** is the standard term for homosexual women). The meanings 'light-hearted' and 'colorful' are now old-fashioned.

gaze /gāz/ ▶ **v.** (**gazes**, **gazing**, **gazed**) look steadily. ▶ **n.** a steady look.

SYNONYMS ▶ **v. stare**, gape, look fixedly, eye, scrutinize, ogle; informal rubberneck, eyeball. ▶ **n. stare**, gape, fixed look, regard, scrutiny.

ga·ze·bo /gə'zēbō/ ▶ **n.** (plural **gazebos**) a roofed structure that offers an open view of the surrounding area.

ga·zelle /gə'zel/ ▶ **n.** a small antelope.

ga·zette /gə'zet/ ▶ **n.** a journal or newspaper.

gaz·et·teer /ˌgazi'ti(ə)r/ ▶ **n.** a list of place names.

GB ▶ **abbr. 1** Great Britain. **2** (also **Gb**) Computing gigabytes.

GDP ▶ **abbr.** gross domestic product.

GDR ▶ **abbr.** historical German Democratic Republic.

gear /gi(ə)r/ ▶ **n. 1** (**gears**) a set of machinery that connects the engine to the wheels of a vehicle and controls its speed. **2** a particular position of gears in a vehicle: *fifth gear*. **3** informal equipment or clothing. ▶ **v. 1** adapt something for a particular purpose. **2** adjust the gears in a vehicle to a particular level. **3** (**gear up**) get prepared for something.

SYNONYMS ▶ **n. 1 equipment**, apparatus, paraphernalia, tools, utensils, implements, instruments, rig, tackle. **2 belongings**, possessions, effects, paraphernalia, bits and pieces; informal things, stuff. **3 clothes**, clothing, garments, outfits, attire, garb, wardrobe; informal togs, threads; formal apparel.

gear·box /'gi(ə)rˌbäks/ ▶ **n.** a set of gears with its casing.

gear·shift /'gi(ə)rˌSHift/ ▶ **n.** a device used to change gears in an automobile.

gear·wheel /'gi(ə)rˌ(h)wēl/ ▶ **n. 1** a toothed wheel in a set of gears. **2** (on a bicycle) a cogwheel driven directly by the chain.

geck·o /'gekō/ ▶ **n.** (plural **geckos** or **geckoes**) a lizard with sticky pads on the feet, active at night.

GED ▶ **abbr.** general equivalency degree (or diploma).

gee /jē/ ▶ **exclam. 1** (**gee up**) a command to a horse to go faster. **2** (also **gee whiz**) informal a mild expression of surprise, enthusiasm, or sympathy.

gee·gaw /'gēgô/ ▶ **n.** a showy object, especially one that is useless or worthless.

geek /gēk/ ▶ **n.** informal **1** an awkward or unfashionable person. **2** a person who is obsessed with something: *a computer geek*. ■ **geek·y adj.**

geese /gēs/ plural of GOOSE.

gee·zer /'gēzər/ ▶ **n.** informal an old man.

ge·fil·te fish /gə'filtə/ ▶ **n.** a dish of fishcakes boiled in broth and served chilled.

Gei·ger count·er /'gīgər/ ▶ **n.** a device for measuring radioactivity.

gei·sha /'gāSHə, 'gē-/ ▶ **n.** (plural **geisha** or **geishas**) a Japanese woman who is paid to accompany and entertain men.

gel[1] /jel/ ▶ **n.** a jellylike substance used on the hair or skin. ▶ **v.** (**gels**, **gelling**, **gelled**) smooth your hair with gel.

gel² ▶ v. (**gels**, **gelling**, **gelled**) **1** (of jelly or a similar substance) set or become firmer. **2** take definite form or begin to work well.

gel·a·tin /ˈjelətn/ (or dated **gelatine**) ▶ n. **1** a clear substance made from animal bones and used to make jelly, glue, and photographic film. **2** a high explosive consisting chiefly of a gel of nitroglycerine with added cellulose nitrate. ■ **ge·lat·i·nous** /jəˈlatn-əs/ adj.

ge·la·to /jəˈlätō/ ▶ n. an Italian-style ice cream.

geld /geld/ ▶ v. castrate a male animal.

geld·ing /ˈgeldiNG/ ▶ n. a castrated male horse.

gel·ig·nite /ˈjeligˌnīt/ ▶ n. a powerful explosive made from nitroglycerine.

gem /jem/ ▶ n. **1** a precious stone. **2** an outstanding person or thing.

> SYNONYMS **1 jewel**, precious stone, semiprecious stone; informal rock, sparkler. **2 masterpiece**, classic, treasure, prize, find; informal one in a million; old use the bee's knees.

Gem·i·ni /ˈjeməˌnī, -ˌnē/ ▶ n. a sign of the zodiac (the Twins), May 21–June 20.

gem·stone /ˈjemˌstōn/ ▶ n. a gem used in a piece of jewelry.

gen·darme /ˈZHändärm/ ▶ n. a member of the French police force.

gen·der /ˈjendər/ ▶ n. **1** Grammar each of the classes into which nouns and pronouns are divided in some languages, usually referred to as masculine, feminine, and neuter. **2** the state of being male or female (in terms of social or cultural differences rather than biological ones). **3** the members of one or other sex.

> USAGE
>
> The words **gender** and **sex** both have the sense 'the state of being male or female,' but they are used in slightly different ways: **sex** tends to refer to biological differences, while **gender** refers to cultural or social ones.

gene /jēn/ ▶ n. Biology a distinct sequence of DNA forming part of a chromosome, by which offspring inherit characteristics from a parent. □ **gene pool** the stock of different genes in an interbreeding population. **gene therapy** the introduction of normal genes into cells in order to correct genetic disorders.

ge·ne·al·o·gy /ˌjēnēˈäləjē, -ˈal-/ ▶ n. (plural **genealogies**) **1** a line of descent traced from an ancestor. **2** the study of lines of descent.

> SYNONYMS **lineage**, line (of descent), family tree, bloodline, pedigree, ancestry, heritage, parentage, family, stock, blood, roots.

■ **ge·ne·a·log·i·cal** /ˌjēnēəˈläjikəl/ adj. **ge·ne·al·o·gist** n.

gen·er·a /ˈjenərə/ plural of GENUS.

gen·er·al /ˈjenərəl/ ▶ adj. **1** affecting or concerning all or most people or things. **2** involving only the main features of something; not detailed. **3** chief or principal: *the general manager*. ▶ n. a commander of an army, or an army officer ranking above lieutenant general.

> SYNONYMS ▶ adj. **1** *suitable for general use* **widespread**, common, extensive, universal, wide, popular, public, mainstream. **2** *a general pay increase* **comprehensive**, overall, across the board, blanket, global, universal, mass, wholesale. **3 usual**, customary, habitual, traditional, normal, conventional, typical, standard, regular, accepted, prevailing, routine, established, everyday. **4** *a general description* **broad**, rough, loose, approximate, unspecific, vague, imprecise, inexact.
> ANTONYMS restricted, unusual, detailed.

□ **general anesthetic** an anesthetic that affects the whole body and causes a loss of consciousness. **general election** the election of representatives to a legislative body by all the people of a country. **general practice** a medical practice treating patients of either sex and of any age. **general practitioner** a doctor who is trained to provide primary health care to patients of either sex and any age. **general-purpose** having a range of potential uses or functions. **general staff** the staff assisting a military commander. **general store** a store, typically in a rural area, that carries a wide variety of merchandise but does not have departments. **general strike** a strike of workers in all or most industries. **in general 1** usually; mainly. **2** as a whole.

gen·er·al·ist /ˈjenərəlist/ ▶ n. a person competent in several different fields.

gen·er·al·i·ty /ˌjenəˈralitē/ ▶ n. (plural **generalities**) **1** a general statement rather than one that is specific or detailed. **2** the quality or state of being general. **3** (**the generality**) the majority.

gen·er·al·ize /ˈjenərəˌlīz/ ▶ v. (**generalizes**, **generalizing**, **generalized**) **1** make a general or broad statement. **2** make something more common or more widely applicable. **3** (**generalized**) Medicine (of a disease) affecting much or all of the body. ■ **gen·er·al·i·za·tion** /ˌjenərəliˈzāSHən/ n.

gen·er·al·ly /ˈjenərəlē/ ▶ adv. **1** in most cases. **2** without discussing the details of something. **3** widely: *it is generally believed that these stories are only myths.*

> SYNONYMS **1 normally**, in general, as a rule, by and large, mainly, mostly, for the most part, predominantly, on the whole, usually. **2 widely**, commonly, extensively, universally, popularly.

gen·er·ate /ˈjenəˌrāt/ ▶ v. (**generates**, **generating**, **generated**) **1** create or produce something. **2** produce energy.

> SYNONYMS **create**, make, produce, engender, spawn, precipitate, prompt, provoke, trigger, spark, stir up, induce.

■ **gen·er·a·tive** /ˈjenərətiv, -ˌrātiv/ adj.

gen·er·a·tion /ˌjenəˈrāSHən/ ▶ n. **1** all the people born and living at about the same time. **2** the average period in which a person grows up and has children of their own. **3** a single stage in the history of a family. **4** a stage in the development of a product. **5** the producing or creating of something.

> SYNONYMS **1 age**, age group, peer group. **2 crop**, batch, wave, range.

□ **generation gap** a difference in attitudes between people of different generations.

gen·er·a·tor /ˈjenəˌrātər/ ▶ n. **1** a person or thing that generates. **2** a machine for producing electricity.

ge·ner·ic /jəˈnerik/ ▶ adj. **1** referring to a class or group of things. **2** (of goods) having no brand name. **3** Biology relating to a genus. ■ **ge·ner·i·cal·ly** adv.

gen·er·os·i·ty /ˌjenəˈräsitē/ ▶ **n.** **1** the quality of being kind and generous. **2** the fact of being plentiful or large: *diners cannot complain about the generosity of portions.*

> SYNONYMS **liberality**, lavishness, magnanimity, bounty, munificence, open-handedness, largesse, unselfishness, altruism, charity. ANTONYMS meanness, selfishness.

gen·er·ous /ˈjenərəs/ ▶ **adj.** **1** freely giving more than is necessary or expected. **2** kind toward other people. **3** larger or more plentiful than is usual: *a generous sprinkle of pepper.*

> SYNONYMS **1 liberal**, lavish, magnanimous, giving, open-handed, bountiful, unselfish, ungrudging, free, unstinting, munificent; literary bounteous. **2 plentiful**, copious, ample, liberal, large, abundant, rich. ANTONYMS mean, selfish, meager.

gen·e·sis /ˈjenəsis/ ▶ **n.** **1** the origin or development of something. **2** (**Genesis**) the first book of the Bible.

> SYNONYMS **origin**, source, root, beginning, start.

ge·net·ic /jəˈnetik/ ▶ **adj.** **1** relating to genes. **2** relating to genetics. □ **genetically modified** (of an animal or plant) containing genetic material that has been altered in order to produce a desired characteristic. **genetic code** the means by which DNA and RNA molecules carry genetic information. **genetic engineering** the changing of the characteristics of an animal or plant by altering its genetic material. **genetic fingerprinting** (also **genetic profiling**) the analysis of genetic material in order to identify individual people. ■ **ge·net·i·cal·ly** adv.

ge·net·ics /jəˈnetiks/ ▶ **pl.n.** the study of the way characteristics are passed from one generation to another. ■ **ge·net·i·cist** n.

ge·ni·al /ˈjēnyəl, -nēəl/ ▶ **adj.** friendly and cheerful.

> SYNONYMS **friendly**, affable, cordial, amiable, warm, easygoing, approachable, sympathetic, good-natured, good-humored, cheerful, hospitable, companionable, sociable, convivial, outgoing, gregarious; informal chummy. ANTONYMS unfriendly.

■ **ge·ni·al·i·ty** /ˌjēnēˈalitē/ n. **gen·ial·ly** adv.

ge·nie /ˈjēnē/ ▶ **n.** (plural **genii** /ˈjēnēˌī/ or **genies**) (in Arabian folklore) a spirit.

gen·i·tal /ˈjenitl/ ▶ **adj.** referring to the external reproductive organs of a person or animal. ▶ **n.** (**genitals**) the external reproductive organs.

gen·i·ta·li·a /ˌjeniˈtālēə, -ˈtālyə/ ▶ **pl.n.** formal or technical the genitals.

gen·i·tive /ˈjenitiv/ ▶ **n.** Grammar the form of a noun, pronoun, or adjective used to show possession.

gen·ius /ˈjēnyəs/ ▶ **n.** (plural **geniuses**) **1** exceptional natural ability. **2** an exceptionally intelligent or able person. **3** (plural **genii** /ˈjēnēˌī/) a mythological spirit associated with a person or place.

> SYNONYMS **1 brilliance**, intelligence, intellect, ability, cleverness, brains. **2 talent**, gift, flair, aptitude, facility, knack, ability, expertise, capacity, faculty. **3 brilliant person**, mastermind, Einstein, intellectual, brain, prodigy; informal egghead, brainiac, whiz kid.

gen·o·cide /ˈjenəˌsīd/ ▶ **n.** the deliberate killing of a very large number of people from a particular ethnic group or nation. ■ **gen·o·cid·al** /ˌjenəˈsīdl/ adj.

ge·nome /ˈjēˌnōm/ ▶ **n.** Biology **1** the full set of the chromosomes of an organism. **2** the complete set of genetic material of an organism.

gen·re /ˈzhänrə/ ▶ **n.** a type or style of art or literature.

> SYNONYMS **category**, class, classification, group, set, type, sort, kind, variety.

gent /jent/ ▶ **n.** informal a gentleman.

gen·teel /jenˈtēl/ ▶ **adj.** polite and refined in an affected or exaggerated way.

> SYNONYMS **refined**, respectable, well-mannered, courteous, polite, proper, correct, seemly, well-bred, ladylike, gentlemanly, dignified, gracious. ANTONYMS uncouth.

■ **gen·til·i·ty** /jenˈtilitē/ n.

gen·tian /ˈjenchən/ ▶ **n.** a plant with violet or blue trumpet-shaped flowers.

Gen·tile /ˈjentīl/ ▶ **adj.** not Jewish. ▶ **n.** a person who is not Jewish.

gen·tle /ˈjentl/ ▶ **adj.** (**gentler**, **gentlest**) **1** (of a person) mild and kind. **2** moderate; not harsh or severe: *a gentle breeze.*

> SYNONYMS **1 kind**, tender, sympathetic, considerate, understanding, compassionate, humane, mild, placid, serene. **2 light**, soft, quiet, low. **3 gradual**, slight, easy, slow, imperceptible. ANTONYMS brutal, strong, loud, steep.

■ **gen·tle·ness** n. **gen·tly** adv.

gent·le·folk /ˈjentlˌfōk/ ▶ **pl.n.** old use people of noble birth or good social position.

gent·le·man /ˈjentlmən/ ▶ **n.** (plural **gentlemen**) **1** a polite or honorable man. **2** a man of good social position. **3** (in polite or formal use) a man. □ **gentleman's agreement** an arrangement based on trust rather than a legal contract.

gen·tri·fy /ˈjentrəˌfī/ ▶ **v.** (**gentrifies**, **gentrifying**, **gentrified**) renovate a house or district so that it conforms to middle-class taste. ■ **gen·tri·fi·ca·tion** /ˌjentrəfiˈkāshən/ n.

gen·try /ˈjentrē/ ▶ **n.** (**the gentry**) people of good social position.

gen·u·flect /ˈjenyəˌflekt/ ▶ **v.** lower your body as a sign of respect by bending one knee. ■ **gen·u·flec·tion** /ˌjenyəˈflekshən/ n.

gen·u·ine /ˈjenyo͞oin/ ▶ **adj.** **1** truly what it is said to be. **2** honest.

> SYNONYMS **1 authentic**, real, actual, original, bona fide, true; informal the real McCoy, the real thing, kosher. **2 sincere**, honest, truthful, straightforward, direct, frank, candid, open, natural; informal straight, upfront. ANTONYMS bogus, insincere.

■ **gen·u·ine·ly** adv.

ge·nus /ˈjēnəs/ ▶ **n.** (plural **genera** /ˈjenərə/) a category in the classification of animals and plants.

ge·ode /ˈjēōd/ ▶ **n.** **1** a small cavity in rock lined with crystals. **2** a rock containing such a cavity.

ge·o·des·ic /ˌjēəˈdesik, -ˈdē-/ ▶ **adj.** relating to a method of construction based on straight lines between points on a curved surface.

ge·od·e·sy /jēˈädəsē/ ▶ **n.** the branch of mathematics concerned with the shape and area of the earth.

ge·og·ra·phy /jēˈägrəfē/ ▶ **n.** **1** the study of the physical features of the earth and how people relate to them. **2** the way in which places and physical features are arranged: *the geography of your college.* ■ **ge·og·ra·pher** **n.** **ge·o·graph·i·cal** /ˌjēəˈgrafikəl/ **adj.**

ge·ol·o·gy /jēˈäləjē/ ▶ **n.** **1** the scientific study of the physical structure and substance of the earth. **2** the geological features of a particular area. ■ **ge·o·log·i·cal** /ˌjēəˈläjikəl/ **adj.** **ge·ol·o·gist** **n.**

ge·o·met·ric /ˌjēəˈmetrik/ ▶ **adj.** **1** relating to geometry. **2** (of a design) featuring regular lines and shapes. □ **geometric mean** the central number in a geometric progression (e.g., 9 in 3, 9, 27). **geometric progression** (or **series**) a sequence of numbers with a constant ratio between each number and the one before (e.g., each number is three times the value of the preceding number in the sequence 1, 3, 9, 27, 81). ■ **ge·o·met·ri·cal** **adj.** **ge·o·met·ri·cal·ly** **adv.**

ge·om·e·try /jēˈämətrē/ ▶ **n.** (plural **geometries**) **1** the branch of mathematics that deals with the properties and relationships of lines, angles, surfaces, and solids. **2** the shape and relationship of the parts of something.

ge·o·mor·phol·o·gy /ˌjēōˌmôrˈfäləjē/ ▶ **n.** the study of the physical features of the surface of the earth and their relation to the earth's geological structures.

ge·o·pol·i·tics /ˌjēōˈpäləˌtiks/ ▶ **pl.n.** politics, especially international relations, as influenced by geographical factors.

geor·gette /jôrˈjet/ ▶ **n.** a thin silk or crêpe dress material.

ge·o·ther·mal /ˌjēōˈᴛʜərməl/ ▶ **adj.** relating to or produced by the internal heat of the earth.

ge·ra·ni·um /jəˈrānēəm/ ▶ **n.** a houseplant, garden plant, or small shrub with red, pink, or white flowers.

ger·bil /ˈjərbəl/ ▶ **n.** a small rodent, often kept as a pet.

ger·i·at·ric /ˌjerēˈatrik/ ▶ **adj.** relating to old people. ▶ **n.** an old person, especially one receiving special care.

ger·i·at·rics /ˌjerēˈatriks/ ▶ **pl.n.** the branch of medicine concerned with the health and care of old people.

germ /jərm/ ▶ **n.** **1** a microorganism, especially one that causes disease. **2** a part of an organism that is able to develop into a new one. **3** an initial stage from which something may develop: *the germ of an idea.*

> SYNONYMS **1 microbe**, microorganism, bacillus, bacterium, virus; informal bug. **2** *the germ of an idea* **start**, beginnings, seed, embryo, bud, root, origin, source.

□ **germ warfare** the use of germs as a military weapon.

Ger·man /ˈjərmən/ ▶ **n.** **1** a person from Germany. **2** the language of Germany, Austria, and parts of Switzerland. ▶ **adj.** relating to Germany or German. □ **German measles** a disease with symptoms like mild measles; rubella. **German shepherd** a large breed of dog, often used as a guard dog or police dog.

ger·mane /jərˈmān/ ▶ **adj.** (**germane to**) relevant or appropriate to.

Ger·man·ic /jərˈmanik/ ▶ **adj.** **1** of the language family that includes English, German, Dutch, and the Scandinavian languages. **2** characteristic of Germans or Germany.

ger·mi·cide /ˈjərməˌsīd/ ▶ **n.** a substance that destroys germs. ■ **ger·mi·cid·al** /ˌjərməˈsīdl/ **adj.**

ger·mi·nal /ˈjərmənl/ ▶ **adj.** **1** relating to a gamete or embryo. **2** in the earliest stage of development. **3** providing material for future development.

ger·mi·nate /ˈjərməˌnāt/ ▶ **v.** (**germinates**, **germinating**, **germinated**) (of a seed) begin to grow. ■ **ger·mi·na·tion** /ˌjərməˈnāsʜən/ **n.**

ger·on·tol·o·gy /ˌjerənˈtäləjē/ ▶ **n.** the scientific study of old age and old people.

ger·ry·man·der /ˈjerēˌmandər/ ▶ **v.** (**gerrymanders**, **gerrymandering**, **gerrymandered**) change the boundaries of an electoral district so as to give an unfair advantage to one party in an election.

ger·und /ˈjerənd/ ▶ **n.** Grammar a verb form that functions as a noun (e.g., *swimming* in *my favorite activity at camp was swimming*).

ges·so /ˈjesō/ ▶ **n.** a hard compound of plaster of Paris or whiting in glue, used in sculpture.

Ge·sta·po /gəˈstäpō/ ▶ **n.** the German secret police under Nazi rule.

ges·ta·tion /jeˈstāsʜən/ ▶ **n.** **1** the growth of a baby inside its mother's body. **2** the development of a plan or idea over a period of time.

ges·tic·u·late /jeˈstikyəˌlāt/ ▶ **v.** (**gesticulates**, **gesticulating**, **gesticulated**) make gestures instead of speaking or in order to emphasize what you are saying. ■ **ges·tic·u·la·tion** /jeˌstikyəˈlāsʜən/ **n.**

ges·ture /ˈjescʜər/ ▶ **n.** **1** a movement of part of the body to express an idea or meaning. **2** an action performed to convey your feelings or intentions. **3** an action performed for show in the knowledge that it will have no effect. ▶ **v.** (**gestures**, **gesturing**, **gestured**) make a gesture.

> SYNONYMS ▶ **n.** **1 signal**, sign, motion, indication, gesticulation. **2 action**, act, deed, move. ▶ **v.** **signal**, motion, gesticulate, wave, indicate, give a sign.

get /get/ ▶ **v.** (**gets**, **getting**, **got** /gät/; past participle **got** or **gotten** /ˈgätn/) **1** come to have or hold; receive. **2** succeed in achieving or experiencing. **3** experience or suffer: *I got a sudden pain in my eye.* **4** fetch. **5** reach a particular state or condition: *it's getting late.* **6** move to or from a particular place: *I got to the airport.* **7** travel by or catch a form of transport. **8** begin to be or do something. **9** catch or thwart.

> SYNONYMS **1 obtain**, acquire, come by, receive, gain, earn, win, be given; informal get (a) hold of, score. **2 become**, grow, turn, go. **3 fetch**, collect, go/come for, call for, pick up, bring, deliver, convey. **4 capture**, catch, arrest, apprehend, seize; informal collar, grab, pick up. **5 contract**, develop, go down with, catch, fall ill with. **6 hear**, catch, make out, follow, take in. **7 understand**, comprehend, grasp, see, fathom, follow. **8 arrive**, reach, make it, turn up, appear, present yourself, come along; informal show up. **9 persuade**, induce, prevail on, influence, talk into. **10 prepare**, get ready, cook, make; informal fix, rustle up. ANTONYMS give.

□ **get something across** manage to communicate an idea clearly. **get around someone** persuade someone to do or allow something. **get around to** deal with a task in due course. **get at 1** reach. **2** informal mean: *I don't understand what you're* *getting at.* **get away** escape. **get away with** escape blame or punishment for. **get back at** take revenge on. **get by** manage to live or do something with the things that you have. **get down to** begin to do or give serious attention to. **get-go** informal the very beginning. **get off** informal escape a punishment. **get on 1** make progress with a task. **2** (**be getting on**) informal be old. **get out of** manage to avoid or escape. **get over** recover from an illness or an unpleasant experience. **get something over** manage to communicate an idea. **get something over with** deal with an unpleasant but necessary task promptly. **get-together** an informal social gathering. **get through to 1** make contact with someone by telephone. **2** make someone understand what you are saying.

USAGE

Although it is such a common word, **get** still has a rather informal feel. When writing, try to use another word, e.g., *receive, catch, experience, suffer*, etc.

get·a·way /'getə,wā/ ▶ **n.** an escape.

get·up /'getəp/ ▶ **n.** informal a style or arrangement of dress, especially an elaborate or unusual one: *she looks ridiculous in that getup.*

gey·ser /'gīzər/ ▶ **n.** a hot spring that sometimes sprays water and steam into the air.

Gha·na·ian /gə'nāən, gə'nīən/ ▶ **n.** a person from Ghana. ▶ **adj.** relating to Ghana.

ghast·ly /'gastlē/ ▶ **adj.** (**ghastlier**, **ghastliest**) **1** causing great horror or fear. **2** informal very unpleasant. **3** looking very pale and ill.

SYNONYMS **1 terrible**, frightful, horrible, grim, awful, horrifying, shocking, appalling, gruesome, horrendous, monstrous. **2 unpleasant**, objectionable, disagreeable, distasteful, awful, terrible, dreadful, frightful, detestable, vile; informal horrible, horrid. ANTONYMS pleasant.

■ **ghast·li·ness n.**

ghee /gē/ ▶ **n.** clarified butter used in Indian cooking.

gher·kin /'gərkin/ ▶ **n.** a small pickled cucumber.

ghet·to /'getō/ ▶ **n.** (plural **ghettos** or **ghettoes**) **1** a part of a city lived in by people of a particular race, nationality, or ethnic group. **2** historical the Jewish quarter in a city. □ **ghetto blaster** informal a large portable radio and cassette or CD player.

ghost /gōst/ ▶ **n. 1** a spirit of a dead person that is believed to appear to the living. **2** (**a** or **the ghost of**) a faint trace of: *the ghost of a smile.* ▶ **v.** act as ghostwriter of.

SYNONYMS ▶ **n. specter**, phantom, wraith, spirit, presence, apparition; informal spook.

□ **ghost town** a town in which no one lives any more.

ghost·ing /'gōstiNG/ ▶ **n.** the appearance of a secondary image on a television or other display screen.

ghost·ly /'gōstlē/ ▶ **adj.** (**ghostlier**, **ghostliest**) like a ghost; eerie.

SYNONYMS **supernatural**, unearthly, spectral, phantom, unnatural, eerie, weird, uncanny; informal spooky.

ghost·write /'gōst,rīt/ ▶ **v.** write something for someone else who is named as the author.

ghost·writ·er /'gōst,rītər/ ▶ **n.** a person who writes something for someone else who is named as the author.

ghoul /go͞ol/ ▶ **n. 1** an evil spirit or phantom. **2** a person who is too interested in death or disaster.

ghoul·ish /'go͞olisH/ ▶ **adj.** like or characteristic of a ghoul.

SYNONYMS **macabre**, grisly, gruesome, grotesque, ghastly; unhealthy, unwholesome.

GHQ ▶ **abbr.** General Headquarters.

GHz ▶ **abbr.** gigahertz.

GI ▶ **n.** (plural **GIs**) a private soldier in the US Army.

gi·ant /'jīənt/ ▶ **n. 1** (in stories) a person of superhuman size and strength. **2** an unusually large person, animal, or plant. ▶ **adj.** unusually large.

SYNONYMS ▶ **n. colossus**, mammoth, monster, leviathan, ogre. ANTONYMS dwarf. ▶ **adj. huge**, colossal, massive, enormous, gigantic, mammoth, vast, immense, monumental, mountainous, titanic, towering, gargantuan; informal mega, monster, whopping, ginormous. ANTONYMS miniature.

□ **giant-killer** a person or team that defeats a more powerful opponent.

gib·ber /'jibər/ ▶ **v.** speak quickly in a way that is difficult to understand. ■ **gib·ber·ing adj.**

gib·ber·ish /'jibərisH/ ▶ **n.** speech or writing that is impossible to understand; nonsense.

gib·bet /'jibit/ ▶ **n.** (in the past) a post and beam used for hanging people, or for displaying the bodies of those who had been executed.

gib·bon /'gibən/ ▶ **n.** a small ape with long, powerful arms, native to Southeast Asia.

gib·bous /'gibəs/ ▶ **adj.** (of the moon) having the illuminated part greater than a semicircle and less than a circle.

gibe /jīb/ (or **jibe**) ▶ **n.** an insulting or mocking remark. ▶ **v.** (**gibes**, **gibing**, **gibed**) make insulting remarks.

gib·lets /'jiblits/ ▶ **pl.n.** the liver, heart, gizzard, and neck of a chicken or other bird.

gid·dy /'gidē/ ▶ **adj.** (**giddier**, **giddiest**) **1** having the feeling that everything is moving and that you are going to fall. **2** excitable and silly. ▶ **v.** (**giddies**, **giddying**, **giddied**) make someone feel excited to the point of disorientation.

SYNONYMS ▶ **adj. 1 dizzy**, lightheaded, faint, unsteady, wobbly, reeling; informal woozy. **2 flighty**, silly, frivolous, skittish, irresponsible; informal dizzy.

■ **gid·di·ly adv. gid·di·ness n.**

gid·dy-up /,gidē 'əp/ ▶ **exclam.** said to make a horse start moving or go faster.

GIF /jif/ ▶ **n.** Computing **1** a format for image files, with built-in data compression. **2** (also **gif**) a file in this format.

gift /gift/ ▶ **n. 1** a thing that you give to someone; a present. **2** a natural ability or talent. ▶ **v. 1** give something as a gift. **2** (**gift with**) endow (someone) with (an ability or talent). **3** (**gifted**) having exceptional talent or ability.

SYNONYMS ▶ **n. 1 present**, handout, donation, offering, bonus, award, endowment. **2 talent**, flair, aptitude, facility, knack, bent, ability, skill, capacity, faculty. ▶ **v.** (**gifted**) **talented**, skilled, accomplished, expert, able, proficient, intelligent, clever, bright, brilliant, precocious; informal crack, ace. ANTONYMS inept.

□ **gift certificate** a voucher that can be exchanged for merchandise in a store, given as a gift. **gift wrap** decorative paper for wrapping gifts. **gift-wrap** wrap a gift in decorative paper.

gig[1] /gig/ ▶ **n.** (in the past) a light two-wheeled carriage pulled by one horse.

gig[2] ▶ **n.** informal a live performance by a musician.

gig·a·byte /ˈgigəˌbīt, ˈjig-/ ▶ **n.** Computing a unit of information equal to one billion (10^9) bytes.

gig·a·hertz /ˈgigəˌhərts, ˈjig-/ ▶ **n.** a unit of frequency equivalent to one billion hertz.

gi·gan·tic /jīˈgantik/ ▶ **adj.** of very great size or extent.

SYNONYMS **huge**, enormous, vast, giant, massive, colossal, mammoth, immense, monumental, mountainous, gargantuan; informal mega, monster, whopping, humongous, ginormous. ANTONYMS tiny.

gig·gle /ˈgigəl/ ▶ **v.** (**giggles**, **giggling**, **giggled**) laugh lightly in a nervous or silly way. ▶ **n.** a laugh of this kind.

SYNONYMS **titter**, chuckle, chortle, laugh.

■ **gig·gly** **adj.**

gig·o·lo /ˈjigəˌlō/ ▶ **n.** (plural **gigolos**) a young man paid to be the companion or lover of an older woman.

gild /gild/ ▶ **v. 1** cover thinly with gold. **2** (**gilded**) wealthy and privileged: *gilded youth.* ■ **gild·ing** **n.**

gill[1] /gil/ ▶ **n. 1** the breathing organ in fish and some amphibians. **2** the plates on the underside of mushrooms and many toadstools.

gill[2] /jil/ ▶ **n.** a unit for measuring liquids, equal to a quarter of a pint.

gilt /gilt/ ▶ **adj.** covered thinly with gold. ▶ **n.** a thin layer of gold on a surface. □ **gilt-edged** (of investments) safe and reliable.

gim·crack /ˈjimˌkrak/ ▶ **adj.** showy but flimsy or poorly made. ▶ **n.** a cheap and showy ornament.

gim·let /ˈgimlit/ ▶ **n. 1** a T-shaped tool with a screw-tip for boring holes. **2** a cocktail of gin (or sometimes vodka) and lime juice.

gim·mick /ˈgimik/ ▶ **n.** a trick or device intended to attract attention rather than fulfill a useful purpose. ■ **gim·mick·y** **adj.**

gin[1] /jin/ ▶ **n. 1** a strong, clear alcoholic drink flavored with juniper berries. **2** (also **gin rummy**) a form of the card game rummy.

gin[2] ▶ **n. 1** a machine for separating cotton from its seeds. **2** a trap for catching small wild animals or birds.

gin·ger /ˈjinjər/ ▶ **n. 1** a hot fragrant spice made from the stem of an Asian plant. **2** a light reddish-yellow color. □ **ginger ale** a carbonated soft drink flavored with ginger. **ginger beer** a carbonated beverage similar to ginger ale, but usually with more ginger and sometimes alcoholic.

gin·ger·bread /ˈjinjərˌbred/ ▶ **n.** cake made with molasses and flavored with ginger.

gin·ger·ly /ˈjinjərlē/ ▶ **adv.** in a careful or cautious way.

ging·ham /ˈgiNGəm/ ▶ **n.** lightweight cotton cloth, typically checked.

gin·gi·vi·tis /ˌjinjəˈvītis/ ▶ **n.** inflammation of the gums.

gink·go /ˈgiNGkō/ ▶ **n.** (plural **ginkgos** or **ginkgoes**) a deciduous Chinese tree with fan-shaped leaves and yellow flowers.

gi·nor·mous /jiˈnôrməs, jī-/ ▶ **adj.** informal very large.

gin·seng /ˈjinseNG/ ▶ **n.** the root of an east Asian and North American plant, used in some medicines.

gip·sy = **GYPSY**.

gi·raffe /jəˈraf/ ▶ **n.** (plural **giraffe** or **giraffes**) a large African animal with a very long neck and legs.

gird /gərd/ ▶ **v.** (**girds**, **girding**, **girded**; past participle **girded** or **girt**) literary encircle with a belt or band. □ **gird your loins** get ready to do something.

gird·er /ˈgərdər/ ▶ **n.** a large metal beam.

gir·dle /ˈgərdl/ ▶ **n. 1** a belt or cord worn around the waist. **2** a corset encircling the body from waist to thigh. ▶ **v.** (**girdles**, **girdling**, **girdled**) encircle with a girdle or belt.

girl /gərl/ ▶ **n. 1** a female child. **2** a young woman. **3** a person's girlfriend.

SYNONYMS **young woman**, young lady, miss; informal gal, chick, broad, dame, babe.

■ **girl·ish** **adj.**

girl·friend /ˈgərlˌfrend/ ▶ **n. 1** a person's regular female romantic partner. **2** a woman's female friend.

SYNONYMS **sweetheart**, lover, partner, significant other, girl, woman; informal steady, (main) squeeze.

girl·ie /ˈgərlē/ ▶ **n.** (also **girly**) (plural **girlies**) informal a girl or young woman. ▶ **adj.** (usu. **girly**) often disapproving like or characteristic of a girl.

girt /gərt/ past participle of **GIRD**.

girth /gərTH/ ▶ **n. 1** the measurement around the middle of something. **2** a strap attached to a saddle and fastened around a horse's belly.

gist /jist/ ▶ **n.** the main or general meaning of a speech or piece of writing.

give /giv/ ▶ **v.** (**gives**, **giving**, **gave** /gāv/; past participle **given** /ˈgivən/) **1** make someone have, get, or experience something. **2** carry out an action or make a sound. **3** show: *he gave no sign of life.* **4** state information. **5** (**give something off** or **out**) send out a smell, heat, etc. **6** bend under pressure. ▶ **n.** the ability of something to bend under pressure.

SYNONYMS ▶ **v. 1** **donate**, contribute, present, award, grant, bestow, hand (over), bequeath, leave. **2** **convey**, pass on, impart, communicate, transmit, send, deliver, relay. **3** **sacrifice**, give up, relinquish, devote, dedicate. **4** **organize**, arrange, lay on, throw, host, hold, have. **5** **perform**, execute, make, do. **6** **utter**, let out, emit, produce, make. ANTONYMS receive, take.

□ **give and take** willingness on both sides of a relationship to make allowances. **give something away** reveal something secret. **give in** stop opposing something. **give out** stop operating. **give rise to** make happen. **give up** stop making an effort and accept that you have failed. **give something up** stop doing, eating, or drinking something regularly.

give·a·way /ˈgivəˌwā/ ▶ **n.** informal **1** something given free, usually with something else that is for sale. **2** something that reveals a secret: *the shape of the parcel was a dead giveaway.*

giv·en /ˈgivən/ past participle of GIVE ▸ **adj.** **1** already named or stated. **2** (**given to**) inclined to. ▸ **prep.** taking into account. ◻ **given name** a person's first name.

giz·mo /ˈgizmō/ ▸ **n.** (plural **gizmos**) informal a gadget.

giz·zard /ˈgizərd/ ▸ **n.** a muscular part of a bird's stomach for grinding food.

gla·cé /glaˈsā/ ▸ **adj.** (of fruit) preserved in sugar.

gla·cial /ˈglāsHəl/ ▸ **adj.** **1** relating to ice and glaciers. **2** very cold.

gla·ci·a·tion /ˌglāsHēˈāsHən/ ▸ **n.** the formation of glaciers.

gla·cier /ˈglāsHər/ ▸ **n.** a slowly moving mass of ice formed by the accumulation of snow on mountains.

glad /glad/ ▸ **adj.** (**gladder**, **gladdest**) **1** pleased; delighted. **2** (often **glad of**) grateful. **3** giving pleasure: *glad tidings*.

> SYNONYMS **1 pleased**, happy, gratified, delighted, thrilled, overjoyed; informal over the moon. **2** *I'd be glad to help* **willing**, eager, happy, pleased, delighted, ready, prepared.
> ANTONYMS dismayed, reluctant.

◻ **glad rags** informal clothes for a party or special occasion.

glad·den /ˈgladn/ ▸ **v.** make glad.

glade /glād/ ▸ **n.** an open space in a forest.

glad·i·a·tor /ˈgladēˌātər/ ▸ **n.** (in ancient Rome) a man trained to fight other men or animals in a public arena. ■ **glad·i·a·to·ri·al** /ˌgladēəˈtôrēəl/ **adj.**

glad·i·o·lus /ˌgladēˈōləs/ ▸ **n.** (plural **gladioli** /-lī/) a plant of the iris family with tall stems and spikes of brightly colored flowers.

glad·ly /ˈgladlē/ ▸ **adv.** with pleasure: *we gladly accepted the senator's invitation.*

> SYNONYMS **with pleasure**, happily, cheerfully, willingly, readily, eagerly, freely, ungrudgingly.

glam /glam/ ▸ **adj.** informal glamorous.

glam·or·ize /ˈglaməˌrīz/ ▸ **v.** (**glamorizes**, **glamorizing**, **glamorized**) often disapproving make something seem attractive or desirable.

glam·or·ous /ˈglamərəs/ ▸ **adj.** excitingly attractive.

> SYNONYMS **1 beautiful**, elegant, chic, stylish, fashionable. **2 exciting**, glittering, glossy, colorful, exotic; informal glitzy, jet-setting.
> ANTONYMS dowdy, dull.

■ **glam·or·ous·ly** **adv.**

> SPELLING
> **Glamorous** drops the **u** of **glamour**: glamor**ous**.

glam·our /ˈglamər/ (also **glamor**) ▸ **n.** an attractive and exciting quality.

> SYNONYMS **1** *she had undeniable glamour* **beauty**, allure, elegance, chic, style, charisma, charm, magnetism. **2** *the glamour of TV* **allure**, attraction, fascination, charm, magic, romance, excitement, thrill; informal glitz, glam.

glance /glans/ ▸ **v.** (**glances**, **glancing**, **glanced**) **1** look briefly. **2** (**glance off**) hit something at an angle and bounce off. ▸ **n.** a brief or hurried look.

> SYNONYMS ▸ **v.** **1 look briefly**, look quickly, peek, peep, glimpse, catch a glimpse. **2** *I glanced through the report* **read quickly** (**through**), scan (through), skim (through), leaf through, flick through, flip through, thumb through, browse (through).

■ **glanc·ing** **adj.**

gland /gland/ ▸ **n.** an organ of the body that produces a particular chemical substance.

glan·du·lar /ˈglanjələr/ ▸ **adj.** relating to a gland or glands.

glare /gle(ə)r/ ▸ **v.** (**glares**, **glaring**, **glared**) **1** stare in an angry way. **2** shine with a dazzling light. **3** (**glaring**) very obvious: *a glaring omission*. ▸ **n.** **1** a fierce or angry stare. **2** strong and dazzling light.

> SYNONYMS ▸ **v.** **1 scowl**, glower, look daggers, frown, lower/lour; informal give someone a dirty look. **2** (**glaring**) **dazzling**, blinding, blazing, strong, harsh. **3** (**glaring**) **obvious**, conspicuous, unmistakable, inescapable, unmissable, striking, flagrant, blatant.

glass /glas/ ▸ **n.** **1** a hard transparent substance made by fusing sand with soda and lime. **2** a drinking container made of glass. **3** a mirror. ◻ **glass ceiling** a situation in which women or minorities find that professional advancement is blocked but not acknowledged.

glass·blow·ing /ˈglasˌblō-iNG/ ▸ **n.** the craft of making glassware by blowing air into semimolten glass through a long tube.

glass·es /ˈglasiz/ ▸ **pl.n.** a pair of lenses set in a frame that rests on the nose and ears, used to correct eyesight.

glass·ware /ˈglasˌwe(ə)r/ ▸ **n.** ornaments and articles made from glass.

glass·y /ˈglasē/ ▸ **adj.** (**glassier**, **glassiest**) **1** resembling glass. **2** (of a person's eyes or expression) showing no interest or liveliness. ■ **glass·i·ly** **adv.**

Glas·we·gian /glazˈwējən, -jēən, glas-/ ▸ **n.** a person from Glasgow. ▸ **adj.** relating to Glasgow.

glau·co·ma /glôˈkōmə/ ▸ **n.** a condition of increased pressure within the eyeball, causing gradual loss of sight.

glaze /glāz/ ▸ **v.** (**glazes**, **glazing**, **glazed**) **1** fit panes of glass into a window frame or similar structure. **2** enclose or cover with glass. **3** cover with a glaze. **4** (**glaze over**) (of a person's eyes) lose brightness and liveliness: *her eyes glazed over*. ▸ **n.** **1** a glasslike substance fused on to the surface of pottery to form a hard coating. **2** a liquid such as milk or beaten egg, used to form a shiny coating on food.

> SYNONYMS ▸ **v.** **cover**, coat, varnish, lacquer, polish; ice, frost. ▸ **n.** **coating**, topping, varnish, lacquer, polish; icing, frosting.

gla·zier /ˈglāzHər/ ▸ **n.** a person who fits glass into windows and doors.

GLBT ▸ **abbr.** gay, lesbian, bisexual, and transgendered.

gleam /glēm/ ▸ **v.** shine brightly, especially with reflected light. ▸ **n.** **1** a faint or brief light. **2** a brief or faint show of a quality or emotion: *a gleam of hope*.

> SYNONYMS ▸ **v.** **shine**, glint, glitter, shimmer, glimmer, sparkle, twinkle, flicker, wink, glisten, flash. ▸ **n.** **flash**, glimmer, glint, shimmer, twinkle, sparkle, flicker, beam, ray, shaft.

glean /glēn/ ▶ v. **1** collect information from various sources. **2** gather leftover grain after a harvest.

glee /glē/ ▶ n. great delight.

glee·ful /ˈglēfəl/ ▶ adj. very happy, usually in a smug or gloating way. ■ **glee·ful·ly** adv.

glen /glen/ ▶ n. a narrow valley.

glib /glib/ ▶ adj. (**glibber**, **glibbest**) using words easily but without much thought or sincerity.

SYNONYMS **slick**, smooth-talking, fast-talking, silver-tongued, smooth; disingenuous, insincere, facile, shallow, superficial, flippant; informal flip, sweet-talking. ANTONYMS sincere.

■ **glib·ly** adv.

glide /glīd/ ▶ v. (**glides**, **gliding**, **glided**) **1** move with a smooth, quiet, continuous motion. **2** fly without power or in a glider. ▶ n. an instance of gliding.

SYNONYMS ▶ v. **1** *a gondola glided past* **slide**, slip, sail, float, drift, flow. **2** *seagulls gliding over the waves* **soar**, wheel, plane, fly.

glid·er /ˈglīdər/ ▶ n. a light aircraft that flies without an engine.

glim·mer /ˈglimər/ ▶ v. (**glimmers**, **glimmering**, **glimmered**) shine faintly with a wavering light. ▶ n. **1** a faint or wavering light. **2** a faint sign of a feeling or quality: *a glimmer of hope*.

glimpse /glimps/ ▶ n. a brief look at something. ▶ v. (**glimpses**, **glimpsing**, **glimpsed**) see something briefly or partially.

SYNONYMS ▶ n. **glance**, brief/quick look, sight, sighting, peek, peep. ▶ v. **catch sight of**, sight, spot, notice, discern, spy, pick out, make out; formal espy.

glint /glint/ ▶ v. give off small flashes of light. ▶ n. a sudden flash of light.

glis·san·do /gliˈsändō/ ▶ n. (plural **glissandi** /-dē/ or **glissandos**) Music a slide upward or downward between two notes.

glis·ten /ˈglisən/ ▶ v. (of something wet) shine or sparkle. ▶ n. a sparkling light reflected from something wet.

glitch /glicʜ/ ▶ n. informal a sudden problem or fault.

glit·ter /ˈglitər/ ▶ v. **1** shine with a shimmering reflected light. **2** (**glittering**) impressively successful or glamorous: *a glittering career*. ▶ n. **1** shimmering reflected light. **2** tiny pieces of sparkling material used for decoration. **3** an attractive but superficial quality.

SYNONYMS ▶ v. **sparkle**, twinkle, glint, shimmer, glimmer, wink, flash, shine. ▶ n. **sparkle**, twinkle, glint, shimmer, glimmer, flicker, flash.

■ **glit·ter·y** adj.

glit·te·ra·ti /ˌglitəˈrätē/ ▶ pl.n. informal fashionable people involved in show business or other glamorous activity.

glitz /glits/ ▶ n. superficial glamour. ■ **glitz·y** adj.

gloam·ing /ˈglōmiɴɢ/ ▶ n. (**the gloaming**) literary twilight; dusk.

gloat /glōt/ ▶ v. be smug or pleased about your own success or another person's failure. ▶ n. an act of gloating. ■ **gloat·ing** adj. & n.

glob /gläb/ ▶ n. informal a lump of a semiliquid substance.

glob·al /ˈglōbəl/ ▶ adj. **1** relating to the whole world; worldwide. **2** relating to all the parts of something. **3** Computing operating or applying through the whole of a file or program.

SYNONYMS **1 worldwide**, international, world, intercontinental, universal. **2 comprehensive**, overall, general, all-inclusive, all-encompassing, universal, broad.

□ **global warming** a gradual increase in the temperature of the earth's atmosphere because of the increase of gases such as carbon dioxide. ■ **glob·al·ly** adv.

glob·al·i·za·tion /ˌglōbəliˈzāsʜən/ ▶ n. the process by which businesses start to operate on a global scale. ■ **glob·al·ize** /ˈglōbəˌlīz/ v.

globe /glōb/ ▶ n. **1** a spherical or rounded object. **2** (**the globe**) the earth. **3** a model of the earth with a map on its surface.

globe·trot·ter /ˈglōbˌträtər/ ▶ n. informal a person who travels widely. ■ **globe·trot·ting** n. & adj.

glob·u·lar /ˈgläbyələr/ ▶ adj. **1** shaped like a globe; spherical. **2** consisting of globules.

glob·ule /ˈgläbyo͞ol/ ▶ n. a small drop or ball of a substance.

glob·u·lin /ˈgläbyəlin/ ▶ n. Biochemistry any of a group of simple proteins found in blood serum.

glock·en·spiel /ˈgläkənˌspēl, -ˌsʜpēl/ ▶ n. a musical instrument made of metal bars that you hit with small hammers.

gloom /glo͞om/ ▶ n. **1** darkness. **2** a feeling of sadness and hopelessness.

SYNONYMS **1 darkness**, dark, murk, shadows, shade. **2 despondency**, depression, dejection, melancholy, unhappiness, sadness, misery, woe, despair. ANTONYMS light, happiness.

gloom·y /ˈglo͞omē/ ▶ adj. (**gloomier**, **gloomiest**) **1** dark or badly lit. **2** sad or depressed.

SYNONYMS **1 dark**, shadowy, murky, sunless, dim, dingy. **2 despondent**, depressed, downcast, downhearted, dejected, dispirited, disheartened, demoralized, crestfallen, glum, melancholy; informal down in the mouth, down in the dumps. **3 pessimistic**, depressing, downbeat, disheartening, disappointing, unfavorable, bleak, black. ANTONYMS bright, cheerful.

■ **gloom·i·ly** adv. **gloom·i·ness** n.

glop /gläp/ ▶ n. informal sloppy or sticky semifluid matter. ■ **glop·py** adj.

glo·ri·fy /ˈglôrəˌfī/ ▶ v. (**glorifies**, **glorifying**, **glorified**) **1** represent something as admirable. **2** (**glorified**) made to appear more important than in reality: *a glorified courier*. **3** praise and worship God.

glo·ri·ous /ˈglôrēəs/ ▶ adj. **1** having or bringing glory. **2** very beautiful or impressive: *a glorious autumn day*.

SYNONYMS **wonderful**, marvelous, magnificent, superb, sublime, spectacular, lovely, fine, delightful; informal stunning, fantastic, terrific, tremendous, sensational, heavenly, divine, gorgeous, fabulous, awesome. ANTONYMS undistinguished.

■ **glo·ri·ous·ly** adv.

glo·ry /ˈglôrē/ ▶ n. (plural **glories**) **1** fame and honor. **2** magnificence; great beauty. **3** a very beautiful or impressive thing: *the glories of Paris*. **4** worship and praise of God. ▶ v. (**glories**, **glorying**, **gloried**) (**glory in**) take great pride or pleasure in.

SYNONYMS ▶ n. 1 **honor**, distinction, prestige, fame, renown, kudos, eminence, acclaim, celebrity, praise, recognition. 2 **magnificence**, splendor, grandeur, majesty, greatness, nobility, opulence, beauty, elegance. ANTONYMS shame. ▶ v. *we gloried in our independence* **delight in**, take pleasure in, revel in, rejoice in, exult in, relish, savor, be proud of; informal get a kick out of, get a thrill out of.

gloss[1] /gläs, glôs/ ▶ n. 1 the shine on a smooth surface. 2 a type of paint that dries to a bright shiny surface. 3 an attractive appearance that hides something ordinary or less attractive. ▶ v. 1 give a glossy appearance to. 2 (**gloss over**) give only brief or misleading details about something.

SYNONYMS ▶ n. **shine**, sheen, luster, gleam, patina, polish, brilliance, shimmer.

gloss[2] ▶ n. a translation or explanation of a word, phrase, or passage. ▶ v. provide a gloss for.

glos·sa·ry /ˈgläsərē, ˈglô-/ ▶ n. (plural **glossaries**) a list of words and their meanings.

gloss·y /ˈgläsē, ˈglô-/ ▶ adj. (**glossier**, **glossiest**) 1 shiny and smooth. 2 appearing attractive and stylish.

SYNONYMS **shiny**, gleaming, lustrous, brilliant, glistening, glassy, polished, lacquered, glazed. ANTONYMS dull.

glot·tal /ˈglätl/ ▶ adj. having to do with the glottis. □ **glottal stop** a speech sound made by opening and closing the glottis, sometimes used instead of a properly sounded *t*.

glot·tis /ˈglätis/ ▶ n. the part of the larynx made up of the vocal cords and the narrow opening between them.

glove /gləv/ ▶ n. 1 a covering for the hand having separate parts for each finger. 2 a padded covering for the hand used in boxing and other sports. □ **glove compartment** (or **glove box**) a small storage compartment in the dashboard of a car.

glow /glō/ ▶ v. 1 give out a steady light. 2 have flushed skin, especially after exercising. 3 look very happy. ▶ n. 1 a steady light or heat. 2 a feeling or appearance of warmth. 3 a strong feeling of pleasure or happiness.

SYNONYMS ▶ v. 1 **shine**, gleam, glimmer, flicker, flare. 2 **smolder**, burn. ▶ n. **radiance**, light, gleam, glimmer.

glow·er /ˈglouər/ ▶ v. have an angry or sullen expression. ▶ n. an angry or sullen look.

glow·ing /ˈglōiNG/ ▶ adj. expressing great praise: *a glowing report*.

SYNONYMS 1 **bright**, radiant, incandescent, luminous, smoldering; literary lambent. 2 **rosy**, pink, red, ruddy, flushed, blushing, burning. 3 **vivid**, vibrant, bright, brilliant, rich, intense, radiant. 4 **complimentary**, favorable, enthusiastic, admiring, rapturous, fulsome.

glow·worm /ˈglōˌwərm/ ▶ n. a soft-bodied beetle that gives off light.

glox·in·i·a /gläkˈsinēə/ ▶ n. a tropical plant with large, bell-shaped flowers.

glu·cose /ˈglo͞okōs/ ▶ n. a type of sugar that is easily changed into energy by the body.

glue /glo͞o/ ▶ n. a sticky substance used for joining things together. ▶ v. (**glues**, **gluing** or **glueing**, **glued**) 1 join something with glue. 2 (**be glued to**) informal be paying very close attention to.

SYNONYMS ▶ n. **adhesive**, gum, paste, (rubber) cement, mucilage; informal stickum. ▶ v. **stick**, paste, fix, seal, cement.

□ **glue-sniffing** the practice of breathing in the fumes from some types of glue.

glug /gləg/ informal ▶ v. (**glugs**, **glugging**, **glugged**) pour or drink something with a gurgling sound. ▶ n. a gurgling sound.

glum /gləm/ ▶ adj. (**glummer**, **glummest**) sad or miserable.

SYNONYMS **gloomy**, downcast, dejected, despondent, crestfallen, disheartened, depressed, doleful, miserable, woebegone; informal fed up, down in the dumps, down in the mouth. ANTONYMS cheerful.

■ **glum·ly** adv.

glut /glət/ ▶ n. more of something than is needed. ▶ v. (**gluts**, **glutting**, **glutted**) supply or provide with too much of something.

glu·ta·mate /ˈglo͞otəˌmāt/ ▶ n. Biochemistry a salt or ester of an amino acid that is a constituent of many proteins.

glu·ten /ˈglo͞otn/ ▶ n. a substance containing protein, found in wheat and other cereal plants.

glu·ti·nous /ˈglo͞otn-əs/ ▶ adj. like glue in texture; sticky.

glut·ton /ˈglətn/ ▶ n. 1 a very greedy eater. 2 a person who is very eager for something difficult or challenging: *a glutton for punishment*.

glut·ton·y /ˈglətn-ē/ ▶ n. the habit of eating too much.

glyc·er·in /ˈglisərin/ (or **glycerine** /-rin, -ˌrēn, ˌglisəˈrēn/) ▶ n. a liquid made from fats and oils, used in medicines and cosmetics.

glyc·er·ol /ˈglisəˌrôl, -ˌräl/ ▶ n. a liquid formed as a byproduct in soap manufacture, used as a softening agent and laxative.

GM ▶ abbr. genetically modified.

gm. ▶ abbr. grams.

GMO ▶ abbr. genetically modified organism.

GMT ▶ abbr. Greenwich Mean Time.

gnarled /närld/ ▶ adj. knobbly or twisted.

gnarl·y /ˈnärlē/ ▶ adj. (**gnarlier**, **gnarliest**) gnarled.

gnash /naSH/ ▶ v. grind your teeth together, especially as a sign of anger.

gnat /nat/ ▶ n. a small two-winged fly.

gnaw /nô/ ▶ v. 1 bite at or nibble something persistently. 2 cause persistent anxiety or pain: *doubts continued to gnaw at me*.

gnoc·chi /ˈnäkē/ ▶ pl.n. (in Italian cooking) small dumplings.

gnome /nōm/ ▶ n. (in stories) a creature like a tiny man, who lives underground and guards treasure.

gno·mic /ˈnōmik/ ▶ adj. clever but hard to understand.

Gnos·ti·cism /ˈnästəˌsizəm/ ▶ n. (in the past) a Christian movement that went against the teachings of the Church. ■ **Gnos·tic** adj.

GNP ▶ abbr. gross national product.

gnu /n(y)o͞o/ ▶ n. a large African antelope with a long head and a mane.

go ▶ v. (**goes**, **going**, **went** /went/; past participle **gone** /gôn, gän/) 1 move to or from a place. 2 pass into or be in a particular state: *her mind went blank*. 3 lie or extend in a certain direction. 4 come to an end. **5** disappear or be used up. **6** (of time) pass. **7** take part in a particular activity: *let's go and have a drink*. **8** have a particular outcome: *it all went off smoothly*. **9** (**be going to be** or **do**) used to express a future tense. **10** function or operate: *my car won't go*. **11** be harmonious or matching: *the earrings and the scarf don't really go*. **12** be acceptable or allowed: *anything goes*. **13** fit into or be regularly kept in a particular place. **14** make a particular sound. ▶ **n.** (plural **goes**) informal **1** an attempt: *give it a go*. **2** a turn to do or use something. **3** spirit or energy.

> SYNONYMS ▶ **v. 1** *he's gone into town* **travel**, move, proceed, make your way, journey, advance, progress, pass. **2** *the road goes to Amherst* **lead**, stretch, reach, extend. **3 leave**, depart, go away, withdraw, absent yourself, exit, set off, start out, get under way, take yourself off, be on your way; informal make tracks. **4 be used up**, be spent, be exhausted, be consumed. **5 become**, get, turn, grow. **6 turn out**, work out, develop, progress, result, end (up); informal pan out. **7 match**, harmonize, blend, be complementary, coordinate, be compatible. **8 function**, work, run, operate. ▶ **n. 1** *here, have a go* **try**, attempt, effort, bid; informal shot, stab, crack. **2 turn**, opportunity, chance, stint, spell, time.

□ **go about** begin or carry on work at something. **the go-ahead** informal permission to proceed. **go along with** agree to. **go back on** fail to keep a promise. **go-between** a person who acts as a messenger or negotiator. **go-cart** (or **go-kart**) a small racing car with a lightweight body. **go down 1** be defeated in a contest. **2** obtain a particular reaction: *the show went down well*. **go for 1** decide on. **2** try to gain. **3** attack. **go-getter** informal an energetic and ambitious person. **go-go** referring to an unrestrained style of dancing to popular music. **go in for 1** enter a contest. **2** like or habitually take part in. **go into 1** investigate or inquire into. **2** (of a whole number) be capable of dividing another. **go off** (of a gun or bomb) explode or fire. **go on 1** continue. **2** take place. **go out 1** stop shining or burning. **2** have a regular romantic relationship with someone. **go over** examine or check the details of. **go around** be enough to supply everybody present. **go through 1** undergo a difficult experience. **2** examine carefully. **3** informal use up or spend. **go without** suffer lack or hardship. **have a go at 1** make an attempt at; try. **2** attack or criticize. **make a go of** informal be successful in. **on the go** informal very active or busy.

goad /gōd/ ▶ **v. 1** keep annoying or criticizing someone until they react. **2** urge on with a goad. ▶ **n. 1** a thing that makes someone do something. **2** a spiked stick used for driving cattle.

> SYNONYMS ▶ **v. provoke**, spur, prod, egg on, hound, badger, rouse, stir, move, stimulate, motivate, prompt, induce, encourage, urge, inspire; impel, pressure.

goal /gōl/ ▶ **n. 1** (in football, soccer, rugby, etc.) a pair of posts linked by a crossbar and often with a net attached behind it, into or over which the ball has to be sent to score. **2** an instance of sending the ball into or over a goal. **3** an aim or desired result.

> SYNONYMS **objective**, aim, end, target, intention, plan, purpose, ambition, aspiration.

□ **goal kick 1** Soccer a free kick taken by the defending side after attackers send the ball over the end line outside the goal. **2** Rugby an attempt to kick a goal. **goal line** a line across a football, soccer, or hockey field on which the goal is placed or which acts as the boundary beyond which a touchdown or try is scored. ■ **goal·less adj.**

goal·ie /ˈgōlē/ ▶ **n.** informal a goaltender.

goal·post /ˈgōlˌpōst/ ▶ **n.** either of the two upright posts of a goal.

goal·scor·er /ˈgōlˌskôrər/ ▶ **n.** a player who scores a goal in soccer, hockey, etc.

goal·tend·er /ˈgōlˌtendər/ (also **goalkeeper** /ˈgōlˌkēpər/) ▶ **n.** (in soccer, hockey, etc.) a player whose role is to stop the ball from entering the goal.

goat /gōt/ ▶ **n.** an animal with horns and a hairy coat, often kept for milk.

goat·ee /gōˈtē/ ▶ **n.** a small pointed beard like that of a goat.

goat·herd /ˈgōtˌhərd/ ▶ **n.** a person who looks after goats.

gob[1] /gäb/ ▶ **n.** a lump of a slimy or sticky substance: *they look like gobs of honey*.

gob[2] ▶ **n.** informal, dated an American sailor.

gob·ble /ˈgäbəl/ ▶ **v.** (**gobbles**, **gobbling**, **gobbled**) **1** eat hurriedly and noisily. **2** (of a turkey) make a swallowing sound in the throat. **3** use a large amount of something very quickly.

> SYNONYMS **guzzle**, bolt, gulp, devour, wolf down; informal put away, scarf (down/up), tuck into, demolish.

gob·ble·de·gook /ˈgäbəldēˌgo͝ok, -ˌgo͞ok/ (or **gobbledygook**) ▶ **n.** informal complicated language that is difficult to understand.

gob·let /ˈgäblit/ ▶ **n.** a drinking glass with a foot and a stem.

gob·lin /ˈgäblin/ ▶ **n.** (in stories) a small, ugly, mischievous creature.

go·by /ˈgōbē/ ▶ **n.** (plural **gobies**) a small sea fish.

God /gäd/ ▶ **n. 1** (in Christianity and some other religions) the creator and supreme ruler of the universe. **2** (**god**) a superhuman being or spirit: *a moon god*.

> SYNONYMS (**god**) **deity**, goddess, divine being, divinity, immortal.

□ **God-fearing** earnestly religious. ■ **god·like adj.**

god·child /ˈgädˌchīld/ ▶ **n.** (plural **godchildren** /-ˌchildrən/) a person in relation to a godparent.

god·damn /ˈgädˈdam/ (also **goddamned**) ▶ **adj., adv., & n.** informal used for emphasis, especially to express anger or frustration.

god·daugh·ter /ˈgädˌdôtər/ ▶ **n.** a female godchild.

god·dess /ˈgädis/ ▶ **n.** a female deity.

go·de·tia /gəˈdēshə/ ▶ **n.** a plant with showy lilac to red flowers.

god·fa·ther /ˈgädˌfät͟hər/ ▶ **n. 1** a male godparent. **2** the male leader of an illegal organization.

god·for·sak·en /ˈgädfərˌsākən/ ▶ **adj.** (of a place) remote, unattractive, or depressing.

god·head /ˈgädˌhed/ ▶ **n. 1** (**the Godhead**) God. **2** divine nature.

god·less /ˈgädlis/ ▶ **adj. 1** not believing in God or a god. **2** wicked.

god·ly /ˈgädlē/ ▶ **adj.** very religious.

god·moth·er /ˈgädˌmət͟hər/ ▶ **n.** a female godparent.

god·par·ent /ˈgädˌpe(ə)rənt, -ˌpar-/ ▶ **n.** a person who promises to be responsible for a child's religious education.

god·send /ˈgädˌsend/ ▶ **n.** something that is very helpful or welcome.

god·son /ˈgädˌsən/ ▶ **n.** a male godchild.

go·er /ˈgōər/ ▶ **n.** a person who regularly attends a specified place or event: *a theatergoer*.

goes /gōōz/ 3rd person singular present of **GO**.

go·fer /ˈgōfər/ (also **gopher**) ▶ **n.** informal a person who runs errands.

gog·gle /ˈgägəl/ ▶ **v.** (**goggles**, **goggling**, **goggled**) **1** look with wide open eyes. **2** (of the eyes) stick out or open wide. ▶ **n.** (**goggles**) close-fitting protective glasses.

go·ing /ˈgōiNG/ ▶ **n. 1** the condition of the ground in terms of its suitability for walking, driving, or horse racing. **2** conditions for an activity: *the going gets tough*. ▶ **adj. 1** existing or available: *any jobs going?* **2** (of a price) normal or current. □ **going concern** a thriving business. **going-over** informal **1** a thorough cleaning or inspection. **2** a beating. **goings-on** informal suspect or unusual activities.

goi·ter /ˈgoitər/ ▶ **n.** a swelling of the neck that is caused by enlargement of the thyroid gland.

gold /gōld/ ▶ **n. 1** a yellow precious metal. **2** a deep yellow or yellow-brown color. **3** things made of gold. □ **gold dust** fine particles of gold. **gold leaf** gold beaten into a very thin sheet. **gold medal** a medal awarded for first place in a race or competition. **gold mine 1** a place where gold is mined. **2** a source of great wealth or resources. **gold plate 1** a thin layer of gold applied as a coating to another metal. **2** plates, dishes, etc., made of gold. **gold rush** a rapid movement of people to a place where gold has been discovered. **gold standard** (in the past) the system in which the value of money is based on the value of gold.

gold·en /ˈgōldən/ ▶ **adj. 1** made of or resembling gold. **2** (of a period) very happy and prosperous. **3** excellent: *a golden opportunity*.

> SYNONYMS **blonde**, yellow, fair, flaxen. ANTONYMS dark.

□ **golden age 1** the period when something is very successful: *the golden age of movies*. **2** a very happy time in the past. **golden boy** (or **golden girl**) informal a popular or successful young man (or woman). **golden eagle** a large eagle with yellow-tipped head feathers. **golden goose** a continuing source of wealth or profit that may be exhausted if it is misused. **golden handshake** informal a payment given to someone who is laid off from work or retires early. **golden mean** the ideal middle position between two extremes. **golden retriever** a breed of retriever with a thick golden-colored coat. **golden rule** a principle that should always be followed. **golden wedding** (or **golden wedding anniversary**) the fiftieth anniversary of a wedding.

gold·en·rod /ˈgōldənˌräd/ ▶ **n.** a plant with tall spikes of bright yellow flowers.

gold·field /ˈgōldˌfēld/ ▶ **n.** an area where gold is found as a mineral in the ground.

gold·finch /ˈgōldˌfinCH/ ▶ **n.** a brightly colored finch with a yellow patch on each wing.

gold·fish /ˈgōldˌfiSH/ ▶ **n.** (plural **goldfish** or **goldfishes**) a small orange carp, often kept in ponds or aquariums. □ **goldfish bowl 1** a round glass container for goldfish. **2** a place or situation without privacy.

gold·i·locks /ˈgōldēˌläks/ ▶ **n.** informal a person with golden hair.

gold·smith /ˈgōldˌsmiTH/ ▶ **n.** a person who makes things out of gold.

golf /gälf, gôlf/ ▶ **n.** a game played on an outdoor course, the aim of which is to hit a small ball into a series of small holes using a set of special clubs. ■ **golf·er n.**

gol·li·wog /ˈgälēˌwäg/ ▶ **n.** a soft doll with a black face and fuzzy hair.

gol·ly /ˈgälē/ ▶ **exclam.** informal used to express surprise or delight.

go·nad /ˈgōnad/ ▶ **n.** an organ in the body that produces gametes; a testis or ovary.

gon·do·la /ˈgändələ, gänˈdōlə/ ▶ **n.** a light flat-bottomed boat used on canals in Venice, worked by one oar at the stern.

gon·do·lier /ˌgändlˈi(ə)r/ ▶ **n.** a person who propels a gondola.

gone /gôn, gän/ past participle of **GO** ▶ **adj.** no longer present or in existence.

> SYNONYMS **1 away**, absent, off, out, missing. **2 past**, over (and done with), no more, done, finished, ended, forgotten. **3 used up**, consumed, finished, spent, depleted.

gon·er /ˈgônər/ ▶ **n.** informal a person or thing that cannot be saved.

gong /gäNG, gôNG/ ▶ **n.** a metal disk that makes a deep ringing sound when struck.

gon·na /ˈgônə, ˈgənə/ ▶ **contr.** informal going to.

gon·or·rhe·a /ˌgänəˈrēə/ ▶ **n.** a disease caused by bacteria that are passed on during sex.

goo /gōō/ ▶ **n.** informal a soft, sticky substance.

good /good/ ▶ **adj. 1** having the right qualities; of a high standard. **2** behaving in a way that is right, polite, or obedient. **3** enjoyable or satisfying: *a good time*. **4** suitable or appropriate. **5** (**good for**) having a useful or helpful effect on. **6** thorough: *a really good cleaning*. ▶ **n. 1** behavior that is right or acceptable: *she used her wealth to do good*. **2** something beneficial: *it's for your own good*. **3** (**goods**) products or possessions: *luxury goods*.

> SYNONYMS ▶ **adj. 1 fine**, superior, excellent, superb, outstanding, magnificent, exceptional, marvelous, wonderful, first-rate, first-class, quality; informal great, ace, terrific, fantastic, fabulous, class, awesome, wicked. **2 virtuous**, righteous, upright, upstanding, moral, ethical, principled, law-abiding, blameless, honorable, decent, respectable, trustworthy; informal squeaky clean. **3 well-behaved**, obedient, dutiful, polite, courteous, respectful. **4 capable**, able, proficient, adept, adroit, accomplished, skillful, talented, masterly, expert; informal mean, wicked, nifty, crackerjack. **5 close**, intimate, dear, bosom, special, best, loyal. **6 enjoyable**, pleasant, agreeable, pleasurable, delightful, lovely, amusing. **7** *it was good of you to come* **kind**, generous, charitable, gracious, noble, altruistic, unselfish. **8 convenient**, suitable, appropriate, fitting, fit, opportune, timely, favorable. **9** *milk is good for you* **wholesome**, healthy, nourishing, nutritious, beneficial. **10 tasty**, appetizing, flavorsome, palatable, succulent; informal scrumptious, yummy. **11 valid**, genuine, authentic, legitimate, sound, bona fide, convincing, compelling. **12 fine**, fair, dry, bright, clear, sunny, cloudless, calm, warm, mild. ANTONYMS bad, wicked, naughty. ▶ **n. 1 virtue**, righteousness, goodness, morality, integrity, honesty, truth, honor. **2 benefit**,

advantage, profit, gain, interest, welfare, well-being. **3 merchandise**, wares, stock, commodities, produce, products, articles. ANTONYMS wickedness, disadvantage.

□ **as good as** very nearly. **do someone good** be beneficial to someone. **for good** forever. **the Good Book** the Bible. **good faith** honest or sincere intentions. **good-for-nothing 1** (of a person) worthless: *his good-for-nothing son.* **2** a worthless person. **Good Friday** the Friday before Easter Sunday, on which Christians commemorate the crucifixion of Jesus. **good-humored** friendly or cheerful. **good-looking** attractive. **good-natured** kind and unselfish. **goods and chattels** all kinds of personal possessions. **good-tempered** not easily angered. **a good word** words in favor of or defending a person. **good works** charitable acts. **in good time 1** with no risk of being late. **2** (also **all in good time**) in due course but without haste. **make something good** (or **make good on something**) **1** compensate for loss or damage. **2** fulfill a promise or claim.

good·bye /ˌgo͝od'bī/ ▶ **exclam.** used to express good wishes when parting or ending a conversation. ▶ **n.** (plural **goodbyes**) a parting.

SYNONYMS ▶ **exclam. farewell**, adieu, au revoir, ciao, adios; informal bye, bye-bye, so long, see you later, see you, later.

good·ies /'go͝odēz/ ▶ **pl.n.** informal tasty things to eat.

good·ish /'go͝odisʜ/ ▶ **adj. 1** fairly good. **2** fairly large: *a goodish portion.*

good·ly /'go͝odlē/ ▶ **adj.** (**goodlier**, **goodliest**) quite large in size or quantity.

good·ness /'go͝odnis/ ▶ **n. 1** the quality of being good. **2** the nutritious element of food.

SYNONYMS **1 virtue**, good, righteousness, morality, integrity, rectitude, honesty, honor, decency, respectability, nobility, worth, merit. **2 kindness**, humanity, benevolence, tenderness, warmth, affection, love, goodwill, sympathy, compassion, care, concern, understanding, generosity, charity.

good·will /ˌgo͝od'wil/ ▶ **n.** friendly or helpful feelings toward other people.

SYNONYMS **kindness**, compassion, goodness, benevolence, consideration, charity, decency, neighborliness. ANTONYMS hostility.

good·y-good·y /'go͝odē ˌgo͝odē/ informal ▶ **n.** a person who behaves well so as to impress other people. ▶ **adj.** virtuous in a smug or showy way.

goo·ey /'go͞oē/ ▶ **adj.** informal soft and sticky.

goof /go͞of/ informal ▶ **v. 1** make a mistake. **2** fool around. ▶ **n. 1** a mistake. **2** a silly or stupid person.

goof·ball /'go͞ofˌbôl/ ▶ **n.** informal a naive, silly, or stupid person.

goof·y /'go͞ofē/ ▶ **adj.** informal **1** foolish; harmlessly eccentric. **2** (in surfing and other board sports) with the right leg in front.

gook /go͝ok/ ▶ **n.** informal a sloppy wet or viscous substance.

goon /go͞on/ ▶ **n.** informal **1** a silly person. **2** a thug.

goop /go͞op/ ▶ **n.** informal sloppy or sticky matter. ■ **goop·y adj.**

goose /go͞os/ ▶ **n.** (plural **geese** /gēs/) **1** a large waterbird with a long neck and webbed feet. **2** a female goose. **3** informal a silly person. □ **goose pimples** (or **goose flesh** or **goose bumps**) little raised bumps on your skin, caused by feeling cold or frightened. **goose step** a way of marching in which the legs are kept straight.

goose·ber·ry /'go͞osˌberē/ ▶ **n.** (plural **gooseberries**) an edible yellowish-green berry with a hairy skin.

go·pher /'gōfər/ ▶ **n.** a burrowing rodent with fur-lined pouches on the outside of the cheeks, found in North and Central America.

Gor·di·an knot /'gôrdēən/ ▶ **n.** (in phr. **cut the Gordian knot**) solve a difficult problem by using force or taking other strong action.

gore¹ /gôr/ ▶ **n.** blood that has been shed.

gore² ▶ **v.** (**gores**, **goring**, **gored**) (of an animal such as a bull) pierce with a horn or tusk.

gore³ ▶ **n.** a triangular piece of material used in making a garment, sail, or umbrella.

gorge /gôrj/ ▶ **n. 1** a narrow valley or ravine. **2** old use the contents of the stomach. ▶ **v.** (**gorges**, **gorging**, **gorged**) eat a large amount greedily.

SYNONYMS ▶ **n. ravine**, canyon, gully, flume, chasm, gulch, coulee, gulf.

gor·geous /'gôrjəs/ ▶ **adj. 1** beautiful. **2** informal very pleasant: *we had a gorgeous time!*

SYNONYMS **1 good-looking**, attractive, beautiful, pretty, handsome, lovely, stunning; informal cute, foxy, fanciable, hot; old use comely. **2 spectacular**, splendid, superb, wonderful, grand, impressive, awe-inspiring, awesome, stunning, breathtaking; informal sensational, fabulous, fantastic. **3 resplendent**, magnificent, sumptuous, luxurious, elegant, dazzling, brilliant. ANTONYMS ugly, drab.

Gor·gon /'gôrgən/ ▶ **n.** Greek Mythology each of three sisters with snakes for hair, who had the power to turn anyone who looked at them to stone.

Gor·gon·zo·la /ˌgôrgən'zōlə/ ▶ **n.** a strong-flavored Italian cheese with bluish-green veins.

go·ril·la /gə'rilə/ ▶ **n.** a powerfully built ape of central Africa.

gorse /gôrs/ ▶ **n.** a yellow-flowered shrub with spiny leaves.

gor·y /'gôrē/ ▶ **adj.** (**gorier**, **goriest**) **1** involving violence and bloodshed. **2** covered in blood.

SYNONYMS **grisly**, gruesome, violent, bloody, brutal, savage; ghastly, frightful, horrid, fearful, hideous, macabre, horrible, horrific.

gosh /gäsʜ/ ▶ **exclam.** informal used to express surprise or give emphasis.

gos·hawk /'gäsˌhôk/ ▶ **n.** a short-winged hawk resembling a large sparrowhawk.

gos·ling /'gäzliɴɢ/ ▶ **n.** a young goose.

gos·pel /'gäspəl/ ▶ **n. 1** the teachings of Jesus. **2** (the **Gospel**) the record of Jesus's life and teaching in the first four books of the New Testament. **3** (**Gospel**) each of these books. **4** (also **gospel truth**) something absolutely true. **5** (also **gospel music**) a style of black American religious singing.

gos·sa·mer /'gäsəmər/ ▶ **n.** a fine substance consisting of cobwebs spun by small spiders. ▶ **adj.** very fine and flimsy.

gos·sip /'gäsəp/ ▶ **n. 1** casual conversation about other people. **2** disapproving a person who likes talking about other people. ▶ **v.** (**gossips**, **gossiping**, **gossiped**) talk about other people.

SYNONYMS ▶ **n. 1 news**, rumors, scandal, hearsay, tittle-tattle; informal dirt, buzz, scuttlebutt. **2 chat**, talk, conversation, chatter, heart-to-heart, tête-à-tête; informal gabfest, jaw, gas, chinwag. **3 gossipmonger**, busybody, scandalmonger, rumor-monger, muckraker. ▶ **v. 1 talk**, whisper, tell tales, spread rumors; informal dish, dish the dirt. **2** *people sat around gossiping* **chat**, talk, converse; informal shoot the breeze, gas, chew the fat, jaw, chinwag.

□ **gossip column** a section of a newspaper devoted to gossip about well-known people.

got /gät/ past and past participle of GET.

got·cha /ˈgächə/ ▶ **exclam.** informal I have got you (said to express satisfaction at having captured or defeated someone or uncovered their faults).

Goth /gäth/ ▶ **n. 1** a member of a people that invaded the Roman Empire between the 3rd and 5th centuries. **2** (**goth**) a style of rock music typically having mystical lyrics. **3** (**goth**) a member of a subculture favoring black clothing, white and black makeup, and goth music.

Goth·ic /ˈgäthik/ ▶ **adj. 1** of the style of architecture common in western Europe in the 12th to 16th centuries. **2** very gloomy or horrifying. ▶ **n. 1** the language of the Goths. **2** Gothic architecture.

got·ta /ˈgätə/ ▶ **contr.** informal have got to: *you gotta be careful.*

got·ten /ˈgätn/ past participle of GET.

gouache /gwäsh, gōōˈäsh/ ▶ **n. 1** a method of painting using watercolors thickened with glue. **2** paint used in this method.

gouge /gouj/ ▶ **v.** (**gouges, gouging, gouged**) **1** make a rough hole in a surface. **2** (**gouge something out**) cut something out roughly. ▶ **n. 1** a chisel with a concave blade. **2** a hole or groove made by gouging.

gou·lash /ˈgōō,läsh/ ▶ **n.** a rich Hungarian stew of meat and vegetables, flavored with paprika.

gourd /gôrd, gŏŏrd/ ▶ **n.** a fruit with a hard skin, usually used as a container rather than as food.

gour·mand /gŏŏrˈmänd/ ▶ **n.** a person who enjoys eating.

gour·met /,gôrˈmā, ,gŏŏr-/ ▶ **n.** a person who knows a lot about good food. ▶ **adj.** suitable for a gourmet: *a gourmet meal.*

SYNONYMS ▶ **n. gastronome**, epicure, epicurean, connoisseur; informal foodie.

gout /gout/ ▶ **n.** a disease causing the joints to swell and become painful.

gov·ern /ˈgəvərn/ ▶ **v. 1** control the laws and affairs of a state, organization, or community. **2** control or influence.

SYNONYMS **1 rule**, preside over, control, be in charge of, command, run, head, manage, oversee, supervise. **2 determine**, decide, control, constrain, regulate, direct, rule, dictate, shape, affect.

gov·ern·ance /ˈgəvərnəns/ ▶ **n.** the action or style of governing.

gov·ern·ess /ˈgəvərnis/ ▶ **n.** a woman employed to teach the children of a family in their home.

gov·ern·ment /ˈgəvər(n)mənt/ ▶ **n. 1** the group of people who govern a state. **2** the system by which a state, organization, or community is governed.

SYNONYMS **administration**, executive, regime, authority, council, powers that be, cabinet, ministry.

■ **gov·ern·men·tal** /,gəvər(n)ˈmentl/ **adj.**

SPELLING

Remember that **government** is spelled with an **n** before the **m**.

gov·er·nor /ˈgəvə(r)nər/ ▶ **n. 1** the elected executive head of a state of the United States. **2** an official appointed to govern a town or region.

SYNONYMS **leader**, ruler, chief, head, administrator, principal, director, chairman, chairwoman, chair, superintendent, commissioner, controller; informal boss.

□ **governor general** (plural **governors general**) the chief representative of the British king or queen in a Commonwealth country of which the king or queen is head of state.

gown /goun/ ▶ **n. 1** a long dress worn on formal occasions. **2** a protective garment worn in the hospital by surgeons or patients. **3** a loose cloak showing your profession or status, worn by a lawyer, academic, or university student.

SYNONYMS **dress**, evening gown, prom dress/gown, wedding gown; robe, dressing gown.

GP ▶ **abbr.** general practitioner.

GPA ▶ **abbr.** grade point average: an indication of a student's academic achievement arrived at by averaging grades.

GPS ▶ **abbr.** Global Positioning System.

gr. ▶ **abbr. 1** grains. **2** grams. **3** gross.

grab /grab/ ▶ **v.** (**grabs, grabbing, grabbed**) **1** seize someone or something suddenly and roughly. **2** informal take the opportunity to get something: *I'll grab another drink while there's still time.* **3** informal impress: *how does that grab you?* ▶ **n.** a sudden attempt to seize someone or something.

SYNONYMS ▶ **v. seize**, grasp, snatch, take hold of, grip, clasp, clutch, catch.

□ **up for grabs** informal available.

grace /grās/ ▶ **n. 1** attractive smoothness of movement. **2** polite respect: *she had the grace to look sheepish.* **3** (**graces**) attractive qualities or behavior: *a horrible character with no saving graces.* **4** (in Christian belief) the unearned favor of God. **5** the condition of being trusted and respected by someone. **6** a period officially allowed to do something: *three days' grace.* **7** a short prayer of thanks said at a meal. **8** (**His, Her, Your,** etc., **Grace**) used as a way of addressing a duke, duchess, or archbishop. ▶ **v.** (**graces, gracing, graced**) **1** bring honor to someone or something by your presence. **2** make something more attractive.

SYNONYMS ▶ **n. 1 elegance**, poise, finesse, polish, fluency, smoothness, suppleness. **2** *he had the grace to apologize* **courtesy**, decency, (good) manners, politeness, respect. **3** *he fell from grace* **favor**, approval, approbation, acceptance, esteem, regard, respect. ANTONYMS awkwardness. ▶ **v. adorn**, embellish, decorate, ornament, enhance.

□ **grace note** Music an extra note that is not needed for the harmony or melody. **with good** (or **bad**) **grace** in a willing (or reluctant) way.

grace·ful /ˈgrāsfəl/ ▶ **adj.** having or showing grace or elegance.

SYNONYMS **elegant**, fluid, fluent, easy, polished, supple.

■ **grace·ful·ly adv.**

grace·less /ˈgrāslis/ ▶ **adj.** without grace or charm.

gra·cious /ˈgrāsHəs/ ▶ **adj. 1** kind, pleasant, and polite. **2** showing the elegance associated with high social status or wealth. **3** (in Christian belief) showing divine grace.

SYNONYMS **courteous**, polite, civil, well-mannered, tactful, diplomatic, kind, considerate, thoughtful, obliging, accommodating, hospitable.

■ **gra·cious·ly adv.**

grad /grad/ ▶ **n.** informal a graduate.

gra·da·tion /grāˈdāsHən/ ▶ **n. 1** a scale of gradual change from one thing to another. **2** a stage in such a scale.

grade /grād/ ▶ **n. 1** a level of rank or ability. **2** a mark indicating the quality of a student's work. **3** a class of school students grouped according to age or ability. ▶ **v.** (**grades**, **grading**, **graded**) **1** arrange people or things in groups according to quality, ability, etc. **2** give a grade to a student or their work. **3** pass gradually from one level to another.

SYNONYMS ▶ **n. 1** *hotels within the same grade* **category**, class, classification, ranking, quality, grouping, group, bracket. **2** *his job is of the lowest grade* **rank**, level, standing, position, class, status, order, echelon. **3 mark**, score, assessment, evaluation, appraisal. **4 year**, class. ▶ **v. classify**, class, categorize, bracket, sort, group, arrange, pigeonhole, rank, evaluate, rate, value.

□ **grade crossing** a place where a railroad and road cross at the same level. **grade school** elementary school. **make the grade** informal succeed.

grad·er /ˈgrādər/ ▶ **n. 1** a person or thing that grades. **2** a wheeled machine for leveling the ground or making roads. **3** a student in a specified grade in school: *a fifth grader*.

gra·di·ent /ˈgrādēənt/ ▶ **n. 1** a sloping part of a road or railroad. **2** the degree to which something slopes.

SYNONYMS **slope**, incline, grade, hill, rise, ramp, bank.

grad·u·al /ˈgrajo͞oəl/ ▶ **adj. 1** taking place in stages over a long period of time. **2** (of a slope) not steep.

SYNONYMS **1 slow**, steady, measured, unhurried, cautious, piecemeal, step-by-step, bit-by-bit, progressive, continuous. **2 gentle**, moderate, slight, easy. ANTONYMS abrupt, steep.

grad·u·al·ly /ˈgrajo͞oəlē/ ▶ **adv.** in a gradual manner: *the icicles gradually got longer throughout the day | gradually add the flour mixture*.

SYNONYMS **slowly**, steadily, slowly but surely, cautiously, gently, gingerly, piecemeal, bit by bit, by degrees, progressively, systematically.

grad·u·ate ▶ **n.** /ˈgrajo͞oit/ a person who has been awarded a high school, college, or university degree. ▶ **v.** /ˈgrajo͞oˌāt/ (**graduates**, **graduating**, **graduated**) **1** successfully complete a degree or course. **2** (**graduate to**) move up to something more advanced. **3** change something gradually. □ **graduate school** a division of a university offering advanced programs beyond the bachelor's degree.

grad·u·a·tion /ˌgrajo͞oˈāsHən/ ▶ **n. 1** the receiving or conferring of an academic degree or diploma. **2** the ceremony at which degrees are conferred. **3** the action of dividing into degrees or other proportionate divisions on a graduated scale. **4** a mark on a container or instrument indicating a degree of quantity.

graf·fi·ti /grəˈfētē/ ▶ **n.** writing or drawings on a wall in a public place.

SPELLING

Double **f**, single **t**: gra**ff**i**t**i.

graft¹ /graft/ ▶ **n. 1** a shoot from one plant inserted into another to form a new growth. **2** a piece of body tissue that is transplanted from one part of the body to another part that has been damaged. ▶ **v. 1** insert or transplant as a graft. **2** add something to something else, especially in a way that seems inappropriate.

SYNONYMS ▶ **n. transplant**, implant. ▶ **v. 1 splice**, join, insert, fix. **2 transplant**, implant.

graft² ▶ **n.** informal bribery and other illegal methods used to gain advantage in politics or business.

gra·ham /gram, ˈgrāəm/ ▶ **adj.** referring to a type of coarsely ground whole-wheat flour.

Grail /grāl/ ▶ **n.** (in medieval legend) the cup or dish used by Jesus at the Last Supper.

grain /grān/ ▶ **n. 1** wheat or another cereal plant grown for food. **2** a single seed or fruit of a cereal plant. **3** a small, hard particle of a substance such as sand. **4** the smallest unit of weight in the troy and avoirdupois systems. **5** the smallest possible amount: *there wasn't a grain of truth in it*. **6** the arrangement of fibers in wood, fabric, etc.

SYNONYMS **1 kernel**, seed. **2 granule**, particle, speck, bit, scrap, crumb, fragment, morsel. **3 trace**, hint, tinge, suggestion, shadow, soupçon, ounce, iota, jot, scrap, shred; informal smidgen. **4 texture**, weave, pattern, nap.

□ **against the grain** conflicting with your nature or instinct. ■ **grain·y adj.**

gram¹ /gram/ ▶ **n.** a metric unit of mass equal to one thousandth of a kilogram.

gram² ▶ **n.** informal your grandmother.

gram·mar /ˈgramər/ ▶ **n. 1** the whole system and structure of a language. **2** knowledge and use of the rules of grammar: *bad grammar*. **3** a book on grammar. □ **grammar school** elementary school.

SPELLING

The word ends with **-ar**, not **-er**: gramm**ar**.

gram·mat·i·cal /grəˈmatikəl/ ▶ **adj. 1** having to do with grammar. **2** conforming to the rules of grammar. ■ **gram·mat·i·cal·ly adv.**

Gram·my /ˈgramē/ ▶ **n.** (plural **Grammys** or **Grammies**) an annual award given by the American National Academy of Recording Arts and Sciences for achievement in the record industry.

gram·o·phone /ˈgraməˌfōn/ ▶ **n.** dated a record player.

gram·pus /ˈgrampəs/ ▶ **n.** (plural **grampuses**) a killer whale or other animal of the dolphin family.

gra·na·ry /ˈgrānərē, ˈgran-/ ▶ **n.** (plural **granaries**) a storehouse for grain.

grand /grand/ ▶ **adj. 1** magnificent and impressive. **2** large or ambitious in scale. **3** of the highest importance or rank. **4** dignified, noble, or proud. **5** informal excellent. ▶ **n.** (plural **grand**) informal a thousand dollars or pounds.

SYNONYMS ▶ **adj. 1 magnificent**, imposing, impressive, awe-inspiring, splendid, resplendent, majestic, monumental, palatial, stately, upscale, upmarket; informal fancy, posh, swish. **2 ambitious**, bold, epic, big, extravagant. **3 august**, distinguished, illustrious, eminent, venerable, dignified, proud. **4 excellent**, marvelous, splendid, first-class, first-rate, wonderful, outstanding; informal superb, terrific, great, super. ANTONYMS humble, poor.

□ **grand jury** Law a jury selected to examine the validity of an accusation prior to trial. **grand master** a chess player of the highest class. **grand piano** a large piano that has the strings arranged horizontally. **grand slam 1** the winning of each of a group of major sports championships or matches in the same year. **2** in baseball, a home run hit when there is a runner on each of the three bases, thus scoring four runs. **grand total** the final amount after everything is added up. **grand tour** (in the past) a cultural tour of Europe made by rich young men as part of their education. ■ **grand·ly** **adv.**

grand·child /'gran(d),CHīld/ ▶ **n.** (plural **grandchildren** /'gran(d),CHildrən/) the child of a person's son or daughter.

grand·daugh·ter /'gran,dôtər/ ▶ **n.** the daughter of a person's son or daughter.

grande dame /'gran 'dam, 'grän 'däm/ ▶ **n.** a woman who is influential within a particular sphere.

gran·dee /gran'dē/ ▶ **n. 1** a Spanish or Portuguese nobleman of the highest rank. **2** a person of high status and social rank.

gran·deur /'granjər, 'gran,dyo͝or/ ▶ **n. 1** the quality of being grand and impressive. **2** high status and social rank.

SYNONYMS **splendor**, magnificence, glory, resplendence, majesty, greatness, stateliness, pomp, ceremony.

grand·fa·ther /'gran(d),fäT͟Hər/ ▶ **n.** the father of a person's father or mother. □ **grandfather clock** a large clock in a tall wooden case.

gran·dil·o·quent /gran'diləkwənt/ ▶ **adj.** pompous in style and using long and fancy words.

gran·di·ose /'grandē,ōs, ,grandē'ōs/ ▶ **adj.** (of a plan or building) very large and ambitious and intended to impress.

grand·ma /'gran(d),mä, 'gram-/ ▶ **n.** informal your grandmother.

grand mal /,gran(d) 'mäl, 'mal/ ▶ **n.** a serious form of epilepsy with prolonged loss of consciousness.

grand·moth·er /'gran(d),məT͟Hər/ ▶ **n.** the mother of a person's father or mother.

grand·pa /'gran(d),pä, 'gram-/ ▶ **n.** informal your grandfather.

grand·par·ent /'gran(d),pe(ə)rənt, -,par-/ ▶ **n.** a grandmother or grandfather.

Grand Prix /,gräN 'prē, ,gran/ ▶ **n.** (plural **Grands Prix**) a race forming part of an auto-racing or motorcycling world championship.

grand·son /'gran(d),sən/ ▶ **n.** the son of a person's son or daughter.

grand·stand /'gran(d),stand/ ▶ **n.** the main seating area, usually roofed, with the best view for spectators at a racetrack or sports stadium. ▶ **v.** disapproving seek to attract applause or favorable attention from spectators or the media. □ **grandstand finish** an exciting finish to a race or other competition.

Grange /grānj/ ▶ **n.** (**the Grange**) a US farmers' association organized in 1867. The Grange sponsors social activities, community service, and political lobbying.

gran·ite /'granit/ ▶ **n.** a hard gray rock.

gran·ny /'granē/ (or **grannie**) ▶ **n.** (plural **grannies**) informal your grandmother. □ **granny knot** a square knot with the ends crossed the wrong way and therefore liable to slip.

gra·no·la /grə'nōlə/ ▶ **n.** a breakfast cereal or snack consisting typically of rolled oats, honey, nuts, and dried fruits.

grant /grant/ ▶ **v. 1** agree to give something to someone or to allow them to do something. **2** give something formally or legally. **3** admit to someone that something is true. ▶ **n.** a sum of money given by a government or public body for a particular purpose.

SYNONYMS ▶ **v. 1** *he granted them leave of absence* **allow**, permit, agree to, accord, afford, vouchsafe. **2** *he granted them $20,000* **give**, award, bestow on, confer on, present with, endow with. **3 admit**, accept, concede, allow, appreciate, recognize, acknowledge, confess. ANTONYMS refuse, deny. ▶ **n. award**, bursary, endowment, scholarship, allowance, subsidy, contribution, handout, donation, gift.

grant·ed /'grantid/ ▶ **adv.** admittedly; it is true. ▶ **conj.** (**granted that**) even assuming that.

gran·u·lat·ed /'granyə,lātid/ ▶ **adj.** in the form of granules. ■ **gran·u·la·tion** /,granyə'lāSHən/ **n.**

gran·ule /'granyo͞ol/ ▶ **n.** a small compact particle of a substance. ■ **gran·u·lar** /'granyələr/ **adj.**

grape /grāp/ ▶ **n.** a green or purple-black berry growing in clusters on a vine, eaten as fruit and used in making wine.

grape·fruit /'grāp,fro͞ot/ ▶ **n.** (plural **grapefruit**) a large yellow citrus fruit with a slightly bitter taste.

grape·shot /'grāp,SHät/ ▶ **n.** (in the past) ammunition consisting of a number of small iron balls fired together from a cannon.

grape·vine /'grāp,vīn/ ▶ **n. 1** a vine that produces grapes. **2** (**the grapevine**) the spreading of information through talk or rumor.

graph /graf/ ▶ **n.** a diagram showing how two or more sets of numbers relate to each other. □ **graph paper** paper printed with small squares, used for graphs and diagrams.

graph·ic /'grafik/ ▶ **adj. 1** relating to visual art, especially involving drawing and the design of printed material. **2** giving vivid details: *a graphic description*. ▶ **n. 1** a pictorial image or symbol on a computer screen. **2** (**graphics**) the use of designs or pictures to illustrate books, magazines, etc.

SYNONYMS ▶ **adj. 1 visual**, pictorial, illustrative, diagrammatic. **2 vivid**, explicit, detailed, realistic, descriptive, powerful, colorful, lurid, shocking. ANTONYMS vague.

□ **graphic arts** visual arts based on the use of line and tone rather than three-dimensional work or the use of color. **graphic design** the design of books, posters, and other printed material. **graphic equalizer** a device for controlling the strength and quality of selected frequency bands. **graphic novel** a novel in comic-strip format. ■ **graph·i·cal·ly** **adv.**

graph·ite /'gra,fīt/ ▶ **n.** a gray form of carbon used as pencil lead and as a lubricant in machinery.

graph·ol·o·gy /gra'fäləjē/ ▶ n. the study of handwriting as a guide to personality. ■ **graph·ol·o·gist** n.

grap·nel /'grapnəl/ (or **grappling hook** /'grapliNG/) ▶ n. a device with iron claws, used for dragging or grasping things.

grap·ple /'grapəl/ ▶ v. (**grapples, grappling, grappled**) **1** struggle or fight physically with someone. **2** (**grapple with**) struggle to deal with or understand. ▶ n. an act of grappling.

> SYNONYMS ▶ v. **1 wrestle**, struggle, tussle, scuffle, battle. **2 deal**, cope, come to grips, tackle, confront, face.

grasp /grasp/ ▶ v. **1** seize and hold something firmly. **2** understand something. ▶ n. **1** a firm grip. **2** a person's ability to understand something.

> SYNONYMS ▶ v. **1 grip**, clutch, clasp, clench, squeeze, catch, seize, grab, snatch. **2 understand**, comprehend, take in, see, apprehend, assimilate, absorb; informal get. ▶ n. **1 grip**, hold, squeeze. **2 reach**, scope, power, range, sights. **3 understanding**, comprehension, awareness, grip, knowledge, mastery, command.

grasp·ing /'graspiNG/ ▶ adj. greedy.

> SYNONYMS **greedy**, acquisitive, avaricious, rapacious, mercenary, materialistic; informal tightfisted, tight, money-grubbing.

grass /gräs/ ▶ n. **1** plants with long narrow leaves and stalks. **2** ground covered with grass. **3** informal marijuana. ▶ v. cover an area with grass. □ **grass snake** a harmless gray-green snake with a yellowish band around the neck. **grass roots** the ordinary people in an organization or society, rather than the leaders. **grass skirt** a skirt made of long grass and leaves, worn by female dancers from some Pacific islands.

grass·hop·per /'gras,häpər/ ▶ n. an insect with long hind legs that it uses for jumping and for producing a chirping sound.

grass·y /'grasē/ ▶ adj. (**grassier, grassiest**) covered with or resembling grass.

grate¹ /grāt/ ▶ v. (**grates, grating, grated**) **1** shred food by rubbing it on a grater. **2** make an unpleasant rasping sound. **3** have an irritating effect: *he grated on her nerves.*

> SYNONYMS **1 shred**, pulverize, mince, grind, crush, crumble. **2 grind**, rub, rasp, scrape, jar, creak.

grate² ▶ n. a metal frame or basket in a fireplace in which the coal or wood is placed.

grate·ful /'grātfəl/ ▶ adj. feeling thankful and appreciative.

> SYNONYMS **thankful**, appreciative, indebted, obliged, in someone's debt, beholden.

■ **grate·ful·ly** adv.

> SPELLING
> This word is spelled **grateful**, not **greatful**.

grat·er /'grātər/ ▶ n. a device having a surface covered with sharp-edged holes, used for grating food.

grat·i·fy /'gratə,fī/ ▶ v. (**gratifies, gratifying, gratified**) **1** give someone pleasure or satisfaction. **2** indulge or satisfy a desire. ■ **grat·i·fi·ca·tion** /,gratəfi'kāSHən/ n.

grat·in /'grätn, 'gratn/ ▶ n. a dish with a browned crust of breadcrumbs or melted cheese: *potatoes au gratin.*

grat·ing¹ /'grātiNG/ ▶ adj. **1** sounding harsh and unpleasant. **2** irritating.

grat·ing² ▶ n. a grid of metal bars used as a barrier.

grat·is /'gratis/ ▶ adv. & adj. free of charge.

grat·i·tude /'gratə,t(y)o͞od/ ▶ n. the feeling of being grateful.

> SYNONYMS **thanks**, gratefulness, thankfulness, appreciation, indebtedness, recognition, acknowledgment.

gra·tu·i·tous /grə't(y)o͞oitəs/ ▶ adj. having no justifiable reason or purpose: *gratuitous violence.*

> SYNONYMS **unjustified**, uncalled for, unwarranted, unprovoked, undue; indefensible, unjustifiable; needless, unnecessary, inessential, unmerited, groundless, senseless, wanton, indiscriminate; excessive, immoderate, inordinate, inappropriate. ANTONYMS necessary, paid.

■ **gra·tu·i·tous·ly** adv.

gra·tu·i·ty /grə't(y)o͞oitē/ ▶ n. (plural **gratuities**) formal a sum of money given to someone who has provided a service; a tip.

gra·ve¹ /grāv/ ▶ n. **1** a hole dug in the ground for a coffin or dead body. **2** (**the grave**) death.

> SYNONYMS **tomb**, burial place, last resting place, vault, mausoleum, sepulcher.

□ **turn in their grave** (of a dead person) be likely to have been angry or distressed about something had they been alive.

gra·ve² ▶ adj. **1** giving cause for alarm or concern. **2** solemn.

> SYNONYMS **1 serious**, important, weighty, profound, significant, momentous, critical, urgent, pressing, dire, terrible, dreadful. **2 solemn**, serious, sober, unsmiling, grim, somber, dour. ANTONYMS trivial, lighthearted.

■ **grave·ly** adv.

grave ac·cent /gräv, grāv/ ▶ n. a mark (`) placed over a vowel in some languages to indicate a change in its sound quality.

grav·el /'gravəl/ ▶ n. a loose mixture of small stones used for paths and roads.

gra·vel·ly /'gravəlē/ ▶ adj. **1** resembling or containing gravel. **2** (of a voice) deep and rough.

grav·en im·age /'grāvən/ ▶ n. a carved figure used as an object of worship.

grave·stone /'grāv,stōn/ ▶ n. a stone slab marking a grave.

grave·yard /'grāv,yärd/ ▶ n. a burial ground.

> SYNONYMS **cemetery**, churchyard, burial ground, necropolis, memorial park; informal boneyard; historical potter's field; archaic God's acre.

grav·i·tas /'gravi,täs/ ▶ n. a serious and dignified manner.

grav·i·tate /'gravi,tāt/ ▶ v. (**gravitates, gravitating, gravitated**) (**gravitate to/toward**) be drawn toward.

grav·i·ta·tion /,gravi'tāSHən/ ▶ n. movement toward a center of gravity. ■ **grav·i·ta·tion·al** adj.

grav·i·ty /'gravitē/ ▶ **n.** **1** the force that attracts a body toward the center of the earth, or toward any other physical body having mass. **2** extreme importance or seriousness: *crimes of the utmost gravity.* **3** a solemn manner.

SYNONYMS **1 seriousness**, importance, significance, weight, consequence, magnitude, acuteness, urgency, dreadfulness. **2 solemnity**, seriousness, sobriety, severity, grimness, somberness, dourness.

gra·vy /'grāvē/ ▶ **n.** (plural **gravies**) a sauce made from the fat and juices that come out of meat during cooking. ◻ **gravy boat** a long, narrow jug used for serving gravy. **gravy train** informal a situation in which someone can easily make a lot of money.

gray /grā/ ▶ **adj.** **1** of a color between black and white, like that of ashes or lead. **2** (of hair) turning or having turned gray or white with age. **3** (of the weather) cloudy and dull. **4** dull and lacking distinctive character: *gray, faceless men.* ▶ **n.** a gray color. ▶ **v.** (of hair) become gray with age.

SYNONYMS ▶ **adj.** **1** silvery, gunmetal, slate, charcoal, smoky. **2 cloudy**, overcast, dull, dark, sunless, murky, gloomy, cheerless. **3 pale**, wan, ashen, pasty, pallid, colorless, waxen. **4 characterless**, colorless, nondescript, flat, bland, dull, boring, tedious, monotonous. **5** *a gray area* **ambiguous**, doubtful, unclear, uncertain, indefinite, debatable.

◻ **gray area** a subject or area of activity that does not easily fit into existing categories. **gray matter** informal the brain. **gray seal** a large North Atlantic seal with a spotted grayish coat. **gray squirrel** a tree squirrel with mainly gray fur.

gray·lag /'grā,lag/ ▶ **n.** a large goose with mainly gray plumage.

gray·ling /'grāliNG/ ▶ **n.** a silvery-gray freshwater fish.

graze[1] /grāz/ ▶ **v.** (**grazes**, **grazing**, **grazed**) (of cattle, sheep, etc.) eat grass.

SYNONYMS **feed**, eat, crop, nibble, browse.

graze[2] ▶ **v.** (**grazes**, **grazing**, **grazed**) **1** scrape the skin on a part of your body. **2** touch something lightly in passing. ▶ **n.** an area where the skin has been scraped.

SYNONYMS ▶ **v.** **1 scrape**, skin, scratch, chafe, scuff, rasp. **2 touch**, brush, shave, skim, kiss, scrape, clip, glance off. ▶ **n.** **scratch**, scrape, abrasion.

graz·ing /'grāziNG/ ▶ **n.** grassland suitable for use as pasture.

grease /grēs/ ▶ **n.** **1** a thick oily substance used as a lubricant. **2** animal fat used or produced in cooking. ▶ **v.** (**greases**, **greasing**, **greased**) smear or lubricate something with grease.

SYNONYMS ▶ **n.** **oil**, fat, lubricant.

◻ **grease monkey** informal a mechanic.

grease·paint /'grēs,pānt/ ▶ **n.** a waxy substance used as makeup by actors.

greas·y /'grēsē, -zē/ ▶ **adj.** (**greasier**, **greasiest**) **1** covered with or resembling grease. **2** polite in an unpleasantly insincere way.

SYNONYMS **oily**, fatty, buttery, oleaginous, slippery, slick, slimy, slithery; informal slippy.

◻ **greasy spoon** informal a cheap cafe or restaurant serving fried foods.

great /grāt/ ▶ **adj.** **1** considerably above average in extent, amount, or strength. **2** considerably above average in ability or quality. **3** informal excellent. **4** used to emphasize something: *he's a great hockey fan.*

SYNONYMS **1 considerable**, substantial, significant, serious, exceptional, extraordinary. **2 large**, big, extensive, expansive, broad, wide, vast, immense, huge, enormous, massive; informal humongous, whopping, ginormous. **3 prominent**, eminent, distinguished, illustrious, celebrated, acclaimed, admired, esteemed, renowned, notable, famous, well-known, leading, top, major. **4 magnificent**, imposing, impressive, awe-inspiring, grand, splendid, majestic. **5 expert**, skillful, skilled, adept, accomplished, talented, fine, masterly, master, brilliant, virtuoso, marvelous, outstanding, first-class, superb; informal crack, class. **6 keen**, eager, enthusiastic, devoted, ardent, fanatical, passionate, dedicated, committed. **7 enjoyable**, delightful, lovely, excellent, marvelous, wonderful, fine, splendid; informal terrific, fantastic, fabulous, super, cool. ANTONYMS little, small, minor, modest.

◻ **great ape** a large ape of a family closely related to humans, including the gorilla and chimpanzees. **great-aunt** (or **great-uncle**) an aunt (or uncle) of your mother or father. **Great Dane** a very large breed of dog with short hair. **Great War** World War I.

great·ly /'grātlē/ ▶ **adv.** very much.

SYNONYMS **very much**, extremely, considerably, substantially, significantly, markedly, seriously, materially, enormously, vastly, immensely, tremendously, mightily.

great·ness /'grātnis/ ▶ **n.** the quality of being great, distinguished, or eminent.

SYNONYMS **1 eminence**, distinction, celebrity, fame, prominence, renown, importance. **2 brilliance**, genius, prowess, talent, expertise, mastery, artistry, skill, proficiency, flair.

greave /grēv/ ▶ **n.** historical a piece of armor for the shin.

grebe /grēb/ ▶ **n.** a diving bird with a long neck.

Gre·cian /'grēsHən/ ▶ **adj.** relating to ancient Greece.

greed /grēd/ ▶ **n.** **1** a strong and selfish desire for possessions, wealth, or power. **2** a desire to eat more food than you need.

SYNONYMS **1 avarice**, acquisitiveness, covetousness, materialism, mercenariness; informal money-grubbing. **2 gluttony**, hunger, voracity, self-indulgence; informal piggishness. **3 desire**, appetite, hunger, thirst, craving, longing, yearning, hankering; informal itch. ANTONYMS generosity, temperance, indifference.

greed·y /'grēdē/ ▶ **adj.** (**greedier**, **greediest**) having or showing greed.

SYNONYMS **1 gluttonous**, ravenous, voracious; informal piggish, piggy. **2 avaricious**, acquisitive, covetous, grasping, materialistic, mercenary; informal money-grubbing.

▪ **greed·i·ly** **adv.**

Greek /grēk/ ▶ **n.** **1** a person from Greece. **2** the ancient or modern language of Greece. ▶ **adj.**

relating to Greece. ▫ **Greek cross** a cross of which all four arms are of equal length. **Greek Orthodox Church** the Eastern Orthodox Church that uses the Byzantine rite in Greek.

green /grēn/ ▶ **adj. 1** of a color between blue and yellow, like that of grass. **2** covered with grass or other plants. **3** (**Green**) concerned with or supporting protection of the environment. **4** inexperienced or naive: *a green recruit*. ▶ **n. 1** a green color. **2** a piece of grassy land for public use. **3** an area of smooth grass surrounding a hole on a golf course, or used for lawn bowling. **4** (**greens**) green leafy vegetables. **5** (**Green**) a supporter of a Green political party.

> SYNONYMS ▶ **adj. 1** olive green, pea green, emerald green, lime green, avocado, pistachio, jade. **2 verdant**, grassy, leafy. **3 environmental**, ecological, conservationist, eco-, eco-friendly. **4 inexperienced**, callow, raw, unseasoned, untried, naive, innocent, unworldly; informal wet behind the ears.

▫ **green belt** an area of open land around a city, on which building is restricted. **green card** a permit allowing a foreigner to live and work permanently in the United States. **green-eyed monster** humorous jealousy. **green thumb** a natural ability to grow plants. **green light 1** permission to go ahead with a project. **2** a green traffic light indicating that you can go. **green pepper** an unripe sweet pepper. **green room** a room in a theater or television studio in which performers can relax when they are not performing. **green tea** tea made from unfermented leaves. ■ **green·ness** n.

green·back /ˈgrēnˌbak/ ▶ **n.** informal a dollar.

green·er·y /ˈgrēnərē/ ▶ **n.** green leaves or plants; green vegetation.

green·field /ˈgrēnˌfēld/ ▶ **adj.** (of a site) previously undeveloped.

green·fly /ˈgrēnˌflī/ ▶ **n.** (plural **greenflies**) a green aphid.

green·gage /ˈgrēnˌgāj/ ▶ **n.** a sweet greenish fruit like a small plum.

green·gro·cer /ˈgrēnˌgrōsər/ ▶ **n.** a retailer of fruit and vegetables.

green·horn /ˈgrēnˌhôrn/ ▶ **n.** informal an inexperienced or naive person.

green·house /ˈgrēnˌhous/ ▶ **n.** a glass structure in which plants are kept to protect them from cold weather. ▫ **greenhouse effect** the tendency of atmospheric temperature to rise because certain gases absorb infrared radiation from the earth. **greenhouse gas** a gas that contributes to the greenhouse effect by absorbing infrared radiation.

Green·wich Mean Time /ˈgrinij, -icH, ˈgren-/ ▶ **n.** the time measured at the meridian of zero longitude that passes through Greenwich in London, used as the standard time in a zone that includes the British Isles.

Green·wich me·rid·i·an /ˈgrinij, -icH, ˈgren-/ ▶ **n.** the meridian of zero longitude, passing through Greenwich.

green·wood /ˈgrēnˌwo͝od/ ▶ **n.** old use a wood or forest in leaf.

greet /grēt/ ▶ **v. 1** give a word or sign of welcome when meeting someone. **2** acknowledge or react to someone or something in a particular way.

> SYNONYMS **1 say hello to**, address, salute, hail, welcome, meet, receive. **2** *the decision was greeted with outrage* **receive**, respond to, react to, take.

■ **greet·er** n.

greet·ing /ˈgrētiNG/ ▶ **n. 1** a word or sign of welcome when meeting someone. **2** (**greetings**) a formal expression of good wishes.

> SYNONYMS **1 hello**, salutation, welcome, reception. **2 best wishes**, good wishes, congratulations, compliments, regards, respects. ANTONYMS farewell.

▫ **greeting card** a decorative card sent to convey good wishes.

gre·gar·i·ous /griˈge(ə)rēəs/ ▶ **adj. 1** enjoying being with people; sociable. **2** (of animals) living in flocks or colonies.

> SYNONYMS **sociable**, convivial, companionable, outgoing. ANTONYMS unsociable.

Gre·go·ri·an chant /grəˈgôrēən/ ▶ **n.** medieval church music for voices.

grem·lin /ˈgremlin/ ▶ **n.** an imaginary mischievous creature regarded as responsible for unexplained mechanical or electrical faults.

gre·nade /grəˈnād/ ▶ **n.** a small bomb that is thrown by hand.

Gre·na·di·an /grəˈnādēən/ ▶ **n.** a person from Grenada. ▶ **adj.** relating to Grenada.

gren·a·dier /ˌgrenəˈdi(ə)r/ ▶ **n.** historical a soldier armed with grenades.

grew /gro͞o/ past of **GROW**.

grey·hound /ˈgrāˌhound/ ▶ **n.** a swift, slender breed of dog used in racing.

grid /grid/ ▶ **n. 1** a set of bars lying parallel to or crossing each other. **2** a network of lines that cross each other to form a series of squares or rectangles. **3** a network of cables or pipes for distributing power.

grid·dle /ˈgridl/ ▶ **n.** a heavy iron plate that is heated and used for cooking food.

grid·i·ron /ˈgridˌīərn/ ▶ **n. 1** a frame of metal bars used for grilling food over an open fire. **2** a field for football, marked with regularly spaced parallel lines.

grid·lock /ˈgridˌläk/ ▶ **n.** a traffic jam affecting a whole network of intersecting streets. ■ **grid·locked** adj.

grief /grēf/ ▶ **n. 1** great sorrow and sadness, especially caused by someone's death. **2** informal trouble or annoyance.

> SYNONYMS **sorrow**, misery, sadness, anguish, pain, distress, heartache, heartbreak, agony, woe, desolation. ANTONYMS joy.

griev·ance /ˈgrēvəns/ ▶ **n.** a cause for complaint.

> SYNONYMS **complaint**, objection, grumble, grouse, ill feeling, bad feeling, resentment; informal gripe.

grieve /grēv/ ▶ **v.** (**grieves**, **grieving**, **grieved**) **1** feel great sorrow and sadness. **2** cause someone distress.

> SYNONYMS **1 mourn**, sorrow, cry, sob, weep. **2 sadden**, upset, distress, pain, hurt, wound, break someone's heart. ANTONYMS rejoice.

griev·ous /ˈgrēvəs/ ▶ **adj.** formal (of something bad) very severe or serious: *his death was a grievous blow*. ■ **griev·ous·ly** adv.

grif·fin /ˈgrifin/ (or **gryphon** /ˈgrifən/ or **griffon** /ˈgrifən/) ▶ **n.** a mythical creature with the head and wings of an eagle and the body of a lion.

grif·fon /ˈgrifən/ ▶ n. **1** a small breed of dog. **2** a large vulture with pale brown plumage. **3** a griffin.

grift /grift/ ▶ v. engage in petty swindling. ▶ n. a petty swindle. ■ **grift·er** n.

grill¹ /gril/ ▶ n. **1** a frame of metal bars used for cooking food on an open fire. **2** a portable device for cooking outdoors, fueled by charcoal or gas. **3** a dish of food cooked using a grill. ▶ v. **1** cook food with a grill. **2** informal question someone in a relentless or aggressive way.

grill² ▶ n. a grille.

grille /gril/ (or **grill**) ▶ n. **1** a grating or screen of metal bars or wires, placed in front of something as protection or to allow ventilation or discreet observation. **2** a grating at the front of a motor vehicle allowing air to circulate to the radiator to cool it.

grim /grim/ ▶ adj. (**grimmer**, **grimmest**) **1** very serious and stern or forbidding. **2** horrifying or depressing.

SYNONYMS **1 stern**, forbidding, uninviting, unsmiling, dour, formidable. **2 dreadful**, ghastly, horrible, terrible, awful, appalling, frightful, shocking, grisly, gruesome, depressing, distressing, upsetting. **3 bleak**, dismal, dingy, wretched, miserable, squalid, depressing, cheerless, joyless, gloomy, uninviting. ANTONYMS amiable, pleasant.

■ **grim·ly** adv.

grim·ace /ˈgriməs, griˈmās/ ▶ n. a twisted expression on a person's face, showing disgust, pain, or wry amusement. ▶ v. (**grimaces**, **grimacing**, **grimaced**) make a grimace.

grime /grīm/ ▶ n. dirt ingrained on a surface.

grim·y /ˈgrīmē/ ▶ adj. (**grimier**, **grimiest**) covered with grime; very dirty.

grin /grin/ ▶ v. (**grins**, **grinning**, **grinned**) smile broadly. ▶ n. a broad smile.

SYNONYMS **smile**, beam, smirk.

grinch /grinCH/ ▶ n. informal a spoilsport or killjoy.

grind /grīnd/ ▶ v. (**grinds**, **grinding**, **ground** /ground/) **1** reduce something to small particles or powder by crushing it. **2** cut and mix meat into a coarse paste by machine. **3** make something sharp or smooth by rubbing it against a hard or abrasive tool or surface. **4** rub together or move gratingly. **5** (**grind someone down**) wear someone down with continuous harsh treatment. **6** (**grind something out**) produce something slowly and with effort. **7** (**grinding**) (of an unpleasant situation) seemingly endless: *grinding poverty*. ▶ n. **1** an act or process of grinding. **2** hard dull work: *the daily grind*.

SYNONYMS ▶ v. **1 crush**, pound, pulverize, mill, crumble. **2 rub**, grate, scrape. **3 sharpen**, whet, hone, put an edge on, mill, machine, polish, smooth. ▶ n. **drudgery**, toil, labor, exertion, chores.

grind·stone /ˈgrīndˌstōn/ ▶ n. **1** a revolving disk of abrasive material used for sharpening or polishing metal objects. **2** a millstone. □ **keep your nose to the grindstone** keep working hard.

grin·go /ˈgriNGgō/ ▶ n. (plural **gringos**) informal (in Latin America) a white English-speaking person.

grip /grip/ ▶ v. (**grips**, **gripping**, **gripped**) **1** hold something tightly. **2** deeply affect someone: *she was gripped by a feeling of excitement*. **3** hold someone's attention: *a gripping TV thriller*. ▶ n. **1** a firm hold on something. **2** understanding of something. **3** a part or attachment by which something is held. **4** a traveling bag.

SYNONYMS ▶ v. **1 grasp**, clutch, clasp, take hold of, clench, cling to, grab, seize, squeeze. **2 engross**, enthrall, absorb, rivet, spellbind, fascinate, mesmerize. ▶ n. **1 grasp**, hold. **2 traction**, purchase, friction, adhesion. **3 control**, power, hold, stranglehold, clutches, influence.

□ **come to grips with** begin to deal with or understand. **lose your grip** become unable to understand or control the situation you are in.

gripe /grīp/ ▶ v. (**gripes**, **griping**, **griped**) **1** informal grumble. **2** (**griping**) (of pain in the stomach or intestines) sudden and sharp. ▶ n. **1** informal a trivial complaint. **2** pain in the stomach or intestines.

grip·ping /ˈgripiNG/ ▶ adj. very interesting or exciting.

SYNONYMS **engrossing**, enthralling, absorbing, riveting, captivating, spellbinding, fascinating, compelling, thrilling, exciting, action-packed, dramatic. ANTONYMS boring.

gris·ly /ˈgrizlē/ ▶ adj. (**grislier**, **grisliest**) causing horror or disgust.

USAGE
Don't confuse **grisly** with **grizzly**, as in *grizzly bear*.

grist /grist/ ▶ n. corn that is ground to make flour. □ **grist for** (or **to**) **the mill** useful experience or knowledge.

gris·tle /ˈgrisəl/ ▶ n. tough inedible cartilage in meat. ■ **gris·tly** adj.

grit /grit/ ▶ n. **1** small loose particles of stone or sand. **2** (also **gritstone** /ˈgritˌstōn/) a coarse sandstone. **3** courage and determination: *the true grit of the navy pilot*. ▶ v. (**grits**, **gritting**, **gritted**) spread grit on an icy road. □ **grit your teeth** resolve to do something difficult.

grits /grits/ ▶ pl.n. a dish of coarsely ground corn kernels boiled with water or milk.

grit·ty /ˈgritē/ ▶ adj. (**grittier**, **grittiest**) **1** containing or covered with grit. **2** brave and determined: *a typically gritty performance*. **3** showing something unpleasant as it really is: *a gritty look at urban life*. ■ **grit·ti·ly** adv.

griz·zled /ˈgrizəld/ ▶ adj. having gray or gray-streaked hair.

griz·zly bear /ˈgrizlē/ ▶ n. a large brown bear, often with white-tipped fur.

groan /grōn/ ▶ v. make a deep sound of pain or despair. ▶ n. a groaning sound.

SYNONYMS ▶ v. **1 moan**, cry. **2 complain**, grumble, moan, mutter; informal grouse, bellyache, bitch, whinge. **3 creak**, grate, rasp. ▶ n. **1 moan**, cry. **2 complaint**, grumble, grievance, moan, muttering; informal grouse, gripe. **3 creaking**, creak, grating, grinding.

gro·cer /ˈgrōsər/ ▶ n. a person who sells food and small household goods.

gro·cer·y /ˈgrōs(ə)rē/ ▶ n. (plural **groceries**) **1** (or **grocery store**) a grocer's store or business. **2** (**groceries**) items of food sold in a grocer's store or supermarket.

grog /gräg/ ▶ n. spirits mixed with water.

grog·gy /ˈgrägē/ ▶ adj. (**groggier**, **groggiest**) dazed and unsteady. ■ **grog·gi·ly** adv.

groin¹ /groin/ ▶ **n.** the area between the abdomen and the thigh on either side of the body.

groin² ▶ **n.** a low wall built out into the sea from a beach to prevent the beach from shifting or being eroded.

grom·met /ˈgrämit/ ▶ **n. 1** a protective metal ring or eyelet. **2** a tube fitted in the eardrum to drain fluid from the middle ear.

groom /gro͞om, gro͝om/ ▶ **v. 1** brush and clean the coat of a horse or dog. **2** keep yourself neat and tidy in appearance. **3** train someone for a particular activity: *students who are groomed for higher things.* ▶ **n. 1** a person employed to take care of horses. **2** a bridegroom.

> SYNONYMS ▶ **v. 1 curry**, brush, clean, rub down. **2 brush**, comb, arrange, do; informal fix. **3 prepare**, prime, condition, coach, train, drill, teach, school.

groove /gro͞ov/ ▶ **n. 1** a long, narrow cut in a hard surface. **2** a spiral track cut in a music record. **3** a routine or habit. ▶ **v.** (**grooves**, **grooving**, **grooved**) **1** make a groove or grooves in. **2** informal listen or dance to jazz or pop music.

> SYNONYMS ▶ **n. furrow**, channel, trench, trough, rut, gutter, canal, hollow, indentation.

□ **in the groove** informal **1** performing confidently. **2** enjoying yourself, especially by dancing.

groov·y /ˈgro͞ovē/ ▶ **adj.** (**groovier**, **grooviest**) informal, dated fashionable and exciting.

grope /grōp/ ▶ **v.** (**gropes**, **groping**, **groped**) **1** feel about with your hands. **2** ease your way forward using your hands to guide you.

> SYNONYMS **fumble**, scrabble, fish, ferret, rummage, feel, search, hunt.

gros point /ˈgrō ˌpoint/ ▶ **n.** a type of needlepoint embroidery consisting of stitches crossing two or more threads of the canvas in each direction.

gross /grōs/ ▶ **adj. 1** unattractively large. **2** very obvious and unacceptable: *a gross exaggeration.* **3** informal very unpleasant. **4** rude or vulgar. **5** (of income, profit, or interest) before tax has been deducted. **6** (of weight) including contents or other variable items. ▶ **adv.** in total. ▶ **v.** earn a particular amount of money as gross profit or income. ▶ **n. 1** (plural **gross**) twelve dozen; 144. **2** (plural **grosses**) a gross profit or income.

> SYNONYMS ▶ **adj. 1 disgusting**, repulsive, revolting, foul, nasty, obnoxious, sickening, nauseating, stomach-churning. **2 thorough**, complete, utter, out and out, shameful, serious, unacceptable, flagrant, blatant, obvious, barefaced, shameless, brazen. **3 total**, full, overall, combined, before deductions, before tax. ANTONYMS pleasant, net. ▶ **v. earn**, make, bring in, take, get, receive; informal rake in.

□ **gross domestic product** the total value of goods produced and services provided within a country during one year. **gross national product** the total value of goods produced and services provided by a country during one year, equal to the gross domestic product plus the net income from foreign investments. ■ **gross·ly adv.**

gro·tesque /grōˈtesk/ ▶ **adj. 1** ugly or distorted in a way that is funny or frightening. **2** shocking. ▶ **n.** a grotesque figure or image.

> SYNONYMS ▶ **adj. 1 misshapen**, deformed, distorted, twisted, monstrous, hideous, freakish, unnatural, abnormal, strange; informal weird. **2 outrageous**, monstrous, shocking, appalling, preposterous, ridiculous, ludicrous, unbelievable, incredible.

■ **gro·tesque·ly adv.**

gro·tes·quer·ie /grōˈteskərē/ ▶ **n.** (plural **grotesqueries**) grotesque quality or things.

grot·to /ˈgrätō/ ▶ **n.** (plural **grottoes** or **grottos**) a small cave, especially an artificial one.

grouch /groucн/ ▶ **n.** informal **1** a grumpy person. **2** a complaint.

grouch·y /ˈgroucнē/ ▶ **adj.** (**grouchier**, **grouchiest**) irritable and bad-tempered; grumpy. ■ **grouch·i·ly adv.**

ground¹ /ground/ ▶ **n. 1** the solid surface of the earth. **2** land or soil of a particular kind: *marshy ground.* **3** an area of land or sea with a particular use: *fishing grounds.* **4** (**grounds**) an area of enclosed land surrounding a large house. **5** a wire that connects an electrical circuit to the ground and makes it safe. **6** (**grounds**) good reasons for doing or believing something: *there are some grounds for optimism.* **7** (**grounds**) small pieces of solid matter in a liquid that settle at the bottom. ▶ **v. 1** ban or prevent a pilot or aircraft from flying. **2** run a ship aground. **3** connect an electrical device to the ground. **4** (**be grounded in** or **on**) have as a foundation or basis. **5** (of a parent) refuse to let a child go out socially, as a punishment.

> SYNONYMS ▶ **n. 1 floor**, earth, terra firma. **2 earth**, soil, turf, land, terrain. **3 stadium**, field, arena, park, track. **4** *the mansion's grounds* **estate**, gardens, park, land, property, surroundings, territory. **5** *grounds for dismissal* **reason**, cause, basis, foundation, justification, rationale, argument, occasion, excuse, pretext. ▶ **v. 1 base**, found, establish, root, build, form. **2** *she was well-grounded in the classics* **teach**, instruct, coach, tutor, educate, school, train, drill.

□ **break new ground** achieve or create something new. **get off the ground** start happening or functioning successfully. **ground ball** Baseball a hit ball that travels along the ground. **ground control** the people who direct the flight and landing of aircraft or spacecraft. **ground floor** the floor of a building at ground level. **ground rules** basic rules controlling the way in which something is done. **ground squirrel** a burrowing squirrel of a large group including the chipmunks. **give** (or **lose**) **ground** fall back or lose your advantage. **hold** (or **stand**) **your ground** stay firm and keep your advantage.

ground² past and past participle of GRIND.
□ **ground glass 1** glass with a smooth ground surface that makes it nontransparent. **2** glass ground into an abrasive powder.

ground·break·ing /ˈgroundˌbrākiɴɢ/ ▶ **adj.** involving completely new methods or discoveries.

ground·hog /ˈgroundˌhäg, -ˌhôg/ ▶ **n.** a burrowing rodent with a heavy body and short legs; a woodchuck.

ground·ing /ˈgroundiɴɢ/ ▶ **n.** basic training or instruction in a subject.

ground·less /ˈground-lis/ ▶ **adj.** not based on any good reason.

ground·sel /ˈgroun(d)səl/ ▶ **n.** a plant with small yellow flowers.

ground·sheet /ˈgroun(d)ˌsнēt/ ▶ **n.** a waterproof sheet spread on the ground, typically under such camping gear as a tent or a sleeping bag.

grounds·keep·er /'groun(d)z,kēpər/ ▶ n. a person who maintains an athletic field, a park, or the grounds of a large building.

ground·swell /'groun(d),swel/ ▶ n. **1** a large swell in the sea. **2** a buildup of public opinion.

ground·wa·ter /'ground,wôtər, -,wätər/ ▶ n. water held underground in the soil or in rock.

ground·work /'ground,wərk/ ▶ n. preliminary or basic work.

group /gro͞op/ ▶ n. **1** a number of people or things placed or classed together. **2** a band of pop musicians. ▶ v. put into a group.

SYNONYMS ▶ n. **1 category**, class, classification, grouping, cluster, set, batch, type, sort, kind, variety, family. **2 crowd**, party, body, band, company, gathering, congregation, assembly, collection, cluster, clump, knot, flock, pack, troop, gang; informal bunch. **3 band**, ensemble, act; informal lineup, combo, outfit. ▶ v. **1 categorize**, classify, class, catalog, sort, bracket, pigeonhole. **2 assemble**, collect, organize, place, arrange, range, line up, lay out.

□ **group home** a home where people requiring support or supervision can live together. **group therapy** a form of psychiatric therapy in which patients meet to discuss their problems.

group·ie /'gro͞opē/ ▶ n. informal a fan who follows a pop group or celebrity around.

grouse¹ /grous/ ▶ n. (plural **grouse**) a game bird with a plump body.

grouse² ▶ v. (**grouses**, **grousing**, **groused**) complain; grumble. ▶ n. a grumble or complaint.

grout /grout/ ▶ n. a substance used for filling the gaps between tiles. ▶ v. fill between tiles with grout.

grove /grōv/ ▶ n. a small wood, orchard, or group of trees.

grov·el /'grävəl, 'grə-/ ▶ v. (**grovels**, **groveling**, **groveled**) **1** crouch or crawl on the ground. **2** act very humbly toward someone to make them forgive you or treat you favorably.

SYNONYMS **1 prostrate yourself**, lie, kneel, cringe. **2 be obsequious**, fawn on, kowtow, bow and scrape, toady, pander to, dance attendance on, ingratiate yourself with; informal crawl, creep, suck up to, lick someone's boots.

grow /grō/ ▶ v. (**grows**, **growing**, **grew** /gro͞o/; past participle **grown** /grōn/) **1** (of a living thing) develop and get bigger. **2** (**grow up**) become an adult. **3** become larger or greater over a period of time. **4** become gradually or increasingly: *we grew braver*. **5** (**grow on**) become gradually more appealing to.

SYNONYMS **1 enlarge**, get bigger, get larger, get taller, expand, increase in size, extend, spread, swell, multiply, snowball, mushroom, balloon, build up, mount up, pile up. **2 sprout**, germinate, spring up, develop, bud, bloom, flourish, thrive, run riot. **3 cultivate**, produce, propagate, raise, rear, farm. **4 become**, get, turn, begin to be. ANTONYMS shrink, decline.

□ **growing pains** pains occurring in the arms and legs of children who are growing fast. ■ **grow·er** n.

growl /groul/ ▶ v. **1** (of a dog) make a low hostile sound in the throat. **2** say something in a low grating voice. **3** make a low or harsh rumbling sound. ▶ n. a growling sound.

SYNONYMS ▶ v. **snarl**, bark, yap, bay.

grown /grōn/ past participle of GROW. □ **grown-up** **1** adult. **2** informal an adult.

growth /grōTH/ ▶ n. **1** the process of growing. **2** something that has grown or is growing. **3** a tumor.

SYNONYMS **1 enlargement**, increase in size, expansion, extension, swelling, multiplication, mushrooming, snowballing, rise, escalation, buildup, development. **2 tumour**, malignancy, cancer, lump, swelling.

□ **growth hormone** a hormone that promotes growth in animal or plant cells. **growth industry** an industry that is developing particularly quickly. **growth ring** a concentric layer of wood, shell, or bone developed during a regular period of growth.

grub /grəb/ ▶ n. **1** the larva of an insect. **2** informal food. ▶ v. (**grubs**, **grubbing**, **grubbed**) **1** dig or poke about in soil. **2** (**grub something up**) dig something up.

grub·by /'grəbē/ ▶ adj. (**grubbier**, **grubbiest**) **1** rather dirty. **2** dishonest or immoral.

SYNONYMS **dirty**, grimy, filthy, mucky, unwashed, stained, soiled; informal cruddy, grungy, yucky. ANTONYMS clean.

grudge /grəj/ ▶ n. a persistent feeling of anger or dislike resulting from a past insult or injury. ▶ v. (**grudges**, **grudging**, **grudged**) **1** be unwilling to give or allow something. **2** feel resentful that someone has achieved something.

SYNONYMS ▶ n. **grievance**, resentment, bitterness, rancor, ill will, animosity, antipathy, antagonism; informal a chip on your shoulder.

□ **bear someone a grudge** feel resentment against someone.

grudg·ing /'grəjiNG/ ▶ adj. reluctantly given or allowed: *a grudging apology*. ■ **grudg·ing·ly** adv.

gru·el /'gro͞oəl/ ▶ n. a thin liquid food of oatmeal boiled in milk or water.

gruel·ing /'gro͞oəliNG/ ▶ adj. very tiring and demanding.

SYNONYMS **exhausting**, tiring, taxing, draining, demanding, exacting, difficult, arduous, strenuous, back-breaking, punishing, crippling; informal murderous.

grue·some /'gro͞osəm/ ▶ adj. causing disgust or horror.

SYNONYMS **grisly**, ghastly, frightful, horrifying, hideous, grim, awful, dreadful, terrible, horrific, disgusting, revolting; informal sick, gross. ANTONYMS pleasant.

gruff /grəf/ ▶ adj. **1** (of a voice) rough and low. **2** abrupt in manner.

SYNONYMS **1** *a gruff reply* **abrupt**, brusque, curt, short, blunt; taciturn; surly, grumpy, crusty, ungracious; informal grouchy. **2** *a gruff voice* **rough**, guttural, throaty, gravelly, husky, croaking, rasping, hoarse, harsh; low. ANTONYMS friendly, soft.

■ **gruff·ly** adv.

grum·ble /'grəmbəl/ ▶ v. (**grumbles**, **grumbling**, **grumbled**) **1** complain in a quiet but bad-tempered way. **2** make a low rumbling sound. ▶ n. a complaint.

SYNONYMS ▶ v. **complain**, grouse, whine, mutter, carp, make a fuss; informal moan, bellyache, bitch, whinge. ▶ n. **complaint**, grouse, grievance, protest; informal grouch, moan, beef, gripe.

grump /grəmp/ ▶ n. informal a grumpy person.

grump·y /ˈgrəmpē/ ▶ adj. (**grumpier**, **grumpiest**) bad-tempered and sulky.

SYNONYMS **bad-tempered**, crabby, tetchy, touchy, irascible, cantankerous, curmudgeonly, surly, fractious; informal grouchy, cranky, ornery. ANTONYMS good-humored.

■ **grump·i·ly** adv.

grunge /grənj/ ▶ n. a style of rock music with a raucous guitar sound.

grun·gy /ˈgrənjē/ ▶ adj. **1** dirty or grimy; untidy. **2** of poor quality; unappealing or unpleasant.

grunt /grənt/ ▶ v. **1** (of an animal) make a short, low sound. **2** (of a person) make a low sound because of physical effort or to show agreement. ▶ n. a grunting sound.

Gru·yère /grōōˈyer, grē-/ ▶ n. a tangy Swiss cheese.

gryph·on /ˈgrifən/ = GRIFFIN.

GT ▶ n. a high-performance car.

gua·ca·mo·le /ˌgwäkəˈmōlē/ ▶ n. a dish of mashed avocado mixed with chopped onion, tomatoes, chili peppers, and seasoning.

gua·no /ˈgwänō/ ▶ n. the excrement of seabirds, used as fertilizer.

guar·an·tee /ˌgarənˈtē/ ▶ n. **1** a promise that certain things will be done. **2** a promise that a product will remain in working order for a particular length of time. **3** something that makes a particular outcome certain. **4** (or **guaranty** /ˈgarənˌtē/) an undertaking to pay or do something on behalf of someone if they fail to do it. ▶ v. (**guarantees**, **guaranteeing**, **guaranteed**) **1** provide a guarantee for something. **2** promise something with certainty. **3** provide financial security for.

SYNONYMS ▶ n. **1 promise**, assurance, word (of honor), pledge, vow, oath, commitment. **2 warranty**. **3 collateral**, security, surety, bond. ▶ v. **1 promise**, swear, pledge, vow, give your word, give an assurance, give an undertaking. **2 underwrite**, put up collateral for.

SPELLING

Write **gua-**, not **gau-**: **gua**rantee.

guar·an·tor /ˌgarənˈtôr, ˈgarəntər/ ▶ n. a person or organization that gives a guarantee.

guard /gärd/ ▶ v. **1** watch over in order to protect or control. **2** (**guard against**) take precautions against. ▶ n. **1** a person who guards or keeps watch. **2** a group of soldiers guarding a place or person. **3** a state of looking out for possible danger: *she was on guard*. **4** a device worn or fitted to prevent injury or damage: *a blade guard*. **5** a prison guard.

SYNONYMS ▶ v. **protect**, defend, shield, secure, cover, mind, stand guard over, watch, keep an eye on. ▶ n. **1 sentry**, sentinel, watchman, nightwatchman, protector, defender, guardian, lookout, watch. **2 warden**, warder, keeper, jailer; informal screw. **3 cover**, shield, screen, fender, bumper, buffer.

SPELLING

Spell this word **gua-**, not **gau-**: **gua**rd.

guard·ed /ˈgärdid/ ▶ adj. cautious: *a guarded welcome*.

SYNONYMS **cautious**, careful, circumspect, wary, chary, reluctant, noncommittal; informal cagey.

guard·house /ˈgärdˌhous/ (also **guardroom** /ˈgärdˌrōōm, -ˌrōōm/) ▶ n. a building used to house a military guard or to detain military prisoners.

guard·i·an /ˈgärdēən/ ▶ n. **1** a person who defends and protects something. **2** a person who is legally responsible for someone who cannot take care of their own affairs.

SYNONYMS **protector**, defender, preserver, custodian, warden, guard, keeper, curator, caretaker, steward, trustee.

□ **guardian angel** a spirit who is believed to watch over and protect you. ■ **guard·i·an·ship** n.

guards·man /ˈgärdzmən/ (or **guardswoman** /-wōōmən/) ▶ n. (plural **guardsmen** or **guardswomen**) a member of the National Guard.

Gua·te·ma·lan /ˌgwätəˈmälən/ ▶ n. a person from Guatemala. ▶ adj. relating to Guatemala.

gua·va /ˈgwävə/ ▶ n. a tropical fruit with pink juicy flesh.

gu·ber·na·to·ri·al /ˌgōōbərnəˈtôrēəl/ ▶ adj. having to do with a governor.

guck /gək/ ▶ n. informal a slimy, dirty, or otherwise unpleasant substance.

gudg·eon /ˈgəjən/ ▶ n. a small freshwater fish.

guel·der rose /ˈgeldər/ ▶ n. a shrub with creamy-white flowers followed by semitransparent red berries.

Guern·sey /ˈgərnzē/ ▶ n. (plural **Guernseys**) a breed of dairy cattle from Guernsey in the Channel Islands of Great Britain.

guer·ril·la /gəˈrilə/ (or **guerilla**) ▶ n. a member of a small independent group fighting against the government or regular forces.

SYNONYMS **rebel**, irregular, freedom fighter, radical, revolutionary, terrorist, member of the resistance.

guess /ges/ ▶ v. **1** estimate or suppose something without having the information you need to be sure. **2** correctly estimate or suppose. ▶ n. an attempt to guess something.

SYNONYMS ▶ v. **1 estimate**, reckon, judge, speculate, conjecture, hypothesize, surmise. **2 suppose**, think, imagine, expect, suspect, dare say; informal reckon. ▶ n. **hypothesis**, theory, conjecture, surmise, estimate, belief, opinion, supposition, speculation, suspicion, impression, feeling.

guess·ti·mate /ˈgestəmit/ (also **guestimate**) ▶ n. informal an estimate based on a mixture of guesswork and calculation.

guess·work /ˈgesˌwərk/ ▶ n. the process or results of guessing.

guest /gest/ ▶ n. **1** a person who is invited to someone's house or to a social occasion. **2** a person invited to take part in a broadcast or entertainment. **3** a person staying at a hotel.

SYNONYMS **1 visitor**, caller, company. **2 client**, customer, resident, boarder, lodger, patron, diner, vacationer, tourist. ANTONYMS host.

□ **guest house 1** a kind of small hotel. **2** a small house or cottage on the grounds of someone's residence, used by overnight guests. **guest worker** a person with temporary permission to work in another country.

guff /gəf/ ▶ **n.** informal trivial, worthless, or insolent talk or ideas.

guf·faw /gə'fô/ ▶ **n.** a loud, deep laugh. ▶ **v.** give a loud, deep laugh.

guid·ance /'gīdns/ ▶ **n.** advice and information given by an experienced or skilled person.

SYNONYMS **1 advice**, counsel, instruction, suggestions, tips, hints, pointers, guidelines. **2 direction**, control, leadership, management, supervision.

guide /gīd/ ▶ **n. 1** a person who advises or shows the way to other people. **2** a thing that helps you to form an opinion or make a decision. **3** a book providing information on a subject. **4** a structure or marking that directs the movement or positioning of something. ▶ **v.** (**guides**, **guiding**, **guided**) **1** show someone the way. **2** direct the movement or positioning of something. **3** (**guided**) directed by remote control or internal equipment: *a guided missile.*

SYNONYMS ▶ **n. 1 escort**, attendant, courier, leader, usher. **2 outline**, template, example, exemplar, model, pattern, guideline, yardstick, precedent. **3 guidebook**, travel guide, vade mecum, companion, handbook, manual, directory, A to Z, instructions, directions; informal bible. ▶ **v. 1 lead**, conduct, show, usher, shepherd, direct, steer, pilot, escort. **2 direct**, steer, manage, conduct, run, be in charge of, govern, preside over, supervise, oversee. **3 advise**, counsel, direct.

□ **guide dog** a dog trained to lead a blind person.

guide·book /'gīd,bo͝ok/ ▶ **n.** a book containing information about a place for visitors.

guide·line /'gīd,līn/ ▶ **n.** a general rule, principle, or piece of advice.

guild /gild/ ▶ **n. 1** a medieval association of craftsmen or merchants. **2** an association of people who do the same work or have the same interests.

SYNONYMS **association**, society, union, league, organization, company, fellowship, club, order, lodge.

guild·er /'gildər/ ▶ **n.** (plural **guilder** or **guilders**) the former basic unit of money in the Netherlands.

guile /gīl/ ▶ **n.** clever but dishonest or deceitful behavior.

SYNONYMS **cunning**, craftiness, craft, artfulness, artifice, wiliness, slyness, deviousness; deception, deceit, duplicity, underhandedness, double-dealing, trickery. ANTONYMS honesty.

guile·less /'gīllis/ ▶ **adj.** innocent and honest.

guil·le·mot /'gilə,mät/ ▶ **n.** a seabird with a narrow pointed bill.

guil·lo·tine /'gilə,tēn, 'gēə-/ ▶ **n. 1** a machine with a heavy blade, used for beheading people. **2** a piece of equipment with a descending or sliding blade used for cutting paper or sheet metal. ▶ **v.** (**guillotines**, **guillotining**, **guillotined**) behead someone with a guillotine.

guilt /gilt/ ▶ **n. 1** the fact of having committed an offense or crime. **2** a feeling of having done something wrong.

SYNONYMS **1 culpability**, blameworthiness, responsibility. **2 remorse**, shame, regret, contrition, self-reproach, a guilty conscience. ANTONYMS innocence.

□ **guilt trip** informal a feeling of guilt, especially when self-indulgent or unjustified. ■ **guilt·less adj.**

guilt·y /'giltē/ ▶ **adj.** (**guiltier**, **guiltiest**) **1** responsible for doing something wrong. **2** having or showing a feeling of guilt.

SYNONYMS **1 culpable**, to blame, at fault, in the wrong, responsible. **2 ashamed**, guilt-ridden, conscience-stricken, remorseful, sorry, contrite, repentant, penitent, regretful, rueful, shamefaced. ANTONYMS innocent.

■ **guilt·i·ly adv.**

guin·ea /'ginē/ ▶ **n.** a former British gold coin worth 21 shillings (£1.05). □ **guinea pig 1** a South American rodent without a tail. **2** a person or thing used as a subject for experiment.

gui·nea·fowl /'ginē,foul/ ▶ **n.** (plural **guineafowl**) a large African bird with gray, white-spotted feathers.

guise /gīz/ ▶ **n.** an outward form, appearance, or manner: *in the guise of an inspector.*

SYNONYMS **1** *in the guise of a swan* **likeness**, appearance, semblance, form, shape, image; disguise. **2** *payments made under the guise of consultancy fees* **pretense**, disguise, front, facade, cover, blind, screen, smokescreen.

gui·tar /gi'tär/ ▶ **n.** a stringed musical instrument that you play by plucking or strumming. ■ **gui·tar·ist n.**

Gu·ja·ra·ti /,go͞ojə'rätē/ ▶ **n.** (plural **Gujaratis**) **1** a person from the Indian state of Gujarat. **2** the language of the Gujaratis.

Gu·lag /'go͞oläg/ ▶ **n.** (**the Gulag**) a system of harsh labor camps maintained in the Soviet Union.

gulch /gəlCH/ ▶ **n.** a narrow ravine.

gulf /gəlf/ ▶ **n. 1** a deep inlet of the sea with a narrow mouth. **2** a deep ravine. **3** a large difference or division between two people or groups, or between viewpoints, concepts, or situations: *the story is about the gulf between reality and fantasy.*

SYNONYMS **1 bay**, inlet, cove, bight, fjord, estuary, sound. **2 gap**, divide, separation, difference, contrast.

□ **Gulf War syndrome** an unexplained medical condition affecting some veterans of the 1991 Gulf War.

gull[1] /gəl/ ▶ **n.** a white seabird with long wings and a gray or black back. □ **gull-wing** (of a door on a car or aircraft) opening upward.

gull[2] ▶ **v.** fool or deceive. ▶ **n.** a person who is deceived.

gul·let /'gəlit/ ▶ **n.** the passage by which food passes from the mouth to the stomach.

gul·li·ble /'gələbəl/ ▶ **adj.** easily believing what people tell you.

SYNONYMS **credulous**, naive, easily deceived, impressionable, unsuspecting, ingenuous, innocent, inexperienced, green; informal wet behind the ears. ANTONYMS suspicious.

■ **gul·li·bil·i·ty** /,gələ'bilitē/ **n.**

gul·ly /'gəlē/ (or **gulley**) ▶ **n.** (plural **gullies** or **gulleys**) **1** a ravine or channel formed by running water. **2** a gutter or drain.

gulp /gəlp/ ▶ **v. 1** swallow food or drink quickly or in large mouthfuls. **2** swallow with difficulty because you are upset or nervous: *she gulped back the tears.* ▶ **n. 1** an act of gulping. **2** a large mouthful of liquid hastily drunk.

> SYNONYMS ▶ **v. 1 swallow**, quaff, swill down; informal swig, down, knock back. **2 gobble**, guzzle, devour, bolt, wolf down. **3** *she gulped back her tears* **choke back**, fight/hold back, suppress, stifle, smother. ▶ **n. mouthful**, swallow, draft; informal swig.

gum[1] /gəm/ ▶ **n. 1** a sticky substance produced by some trees. **2** glue used for sticking paper or other light materials together. **3** chewing gum.

gum[2] ▶ **n.** the firm area of flesh around the roots of the teeth.

gum·bo /ˈgəmbō/ ▶ **n.** (plural **gumbos**) (in Cajun cooking) a spicy chicken or seafood soup thickened with okra, filé, rice, or roux.

gum·drop /ˈgəm,dräp/ ▶ **n.** a firm, jellylike candy.

gum·my[1] /ˈgəmē/ ▶ **adj.** sticky.

gum·my[2] ▶ **adj.** toothless: *a gummy grin.*

gump·tion /ˈgəmpsHən/ ▶ **n.** informal initiative and resourcefulness.

gum·shoe /ˈgəm,sHo͞o/ ▶ **n.** informal, dated a detective.

gun /gən/ ▶ **n. 1** a weapon with a metal tube from which bullets or shells are fired by means of a small explosion. **2** a device using pressure to send out a substance or object: *a glue gun.* ▶ **v.** (**guns**, **gunning**, **gunned**) (**gun someone down**) shoot someone with a gun.

> SYNONYMS ▶ **n. firearm**, sidearm, handgun, weapon; informal piece, rod, gat, heater.

□ **gun dog** a dog trained to collect birds or animals that have been shot. **jump the gun** act before the proper or right time. **stick to your guns** refuse to compromise. **under the gun** under great pressure.

gun·boat /ˈgən,bōt/ ▶ **n.** a small ship armed with guns. □ **gunboat diplomacy** foreign policy supported by the use or threat of military force.

gun·fire /ˈgən,fī(ə)r/ ▶ **n.** the repeated firing of a gun or guns.

gung-ho /ˈgəNG ˈhō/ ▶ **adj.** overly and unthinkingly enthusiastic about taking part in something, especially fighting or warfare.

gunk /gəNGk/ ▶ **n.** informal unpleasantly sticky or messy matter.

gun·man /ˈgənmən/ ▶ **n.** (plural **gunmen**) a man who uses a gun to commit a crime.

> SYNONYMS **armed criminal**, assassin, sniper, terrorist, gunfighter; informal hit man, gunslinger, shootist.

gun·met·al /ˈgən,metl/ ▶ **n. 1** a gray form of bronze containing zinc. **2** a dull bluish-gray color.

gun·nel /ˈgənl/ ▶ **n.** the upper edge or planking of the side of a boat; a gunwale.

gun·ner /ˈgənər/ ▶ **n. 1** a person who operates a gun. **2** a British artillery soldier.

gun·ner·y /ˈgənərē/ ▶ **n.** the design, manufacture, or firing of heavy guns.

gun·play /ˈgən,plā/ ▶ **n.** the use of guns.

gun·point /ˈgən,point/ ▶ **n.** (**at gunpoint**) while threatening someone or being threatened with a gun.

gun·pow·der /ˈgən,poudər/ ▶ **n.** an explosive consisting of a powdered mixture of saltpeter, sulfur, and charcoal.

gun·run·ner /ˈgən,rənər/ ▶ **n.** a person involved in the illegal sale or importing of firearms. ■ **gun·run·ning n.**

gun·ship /ˈgən,sHip/ ▶ **n.** a heavily armed helicopter.

gun·sight /ˈgən,sīt/ ▶ **n.** a device on a gun enabling it to be aimed accurately.

gun·sling·er /ˈgən,sliNGər/ ▶ **n.** informal a person who carries a gun.

gun·smith /ˈgən,smiTH/ ▶ **n.** a person who makes and sells small firearms.

gun·wale /ˈgənl/ (or **gunnel**) ▶ **n.** the upper edge or planking of the side of a boat.

gup·py /ˈgəpē/ ▶ **n.** (plural **guppies**) a small colorful fish.

gur·gle /ˈgərgəl/ ▶ **v.** (**gurgles**, **gurgling**, **gurgled**) make a hollow bubbling sound. ▶ **n.** a hollow bubbling sound.

Gur·kha /ˈgo͝orkə/ ▶ **n.** a member of a Nepalese regiment in the British army.

gur·ney /ˈgərnē/ ▶ **n.** (plural **gurneys**) a stretcher on wheels for transporting hospital patients.

gu·ru /ˈgo͞oro͞o, go͞oˈro͞o/ ▶ **n. 1** a Hindu spiritual teacher. **2** a person who is an expert on a subject and has a lot of followers: *a management guru.*

> SYNONYMS **1 spiritual teacher**, tutor, sage, mentor, spiritual leader, master. **2 expert**, authority, pundit, leading light, master, specialist. ANTONYMS disciple.

gush /gəsH/ ▶ **v. 1** flow in a strong, fast stream. **2** express approval very enthusiastically. ▶ **n.** a strong, fast stream.

> SYNONYMS ▶ **v. 1 surge**, stream, spout, spurt, jet, rush, pour, spill, cascade, flood. **2** (**gushing**) **effusive**, overenthusiastic, extravagant, fulsome, lavish, unrestrained; informal over the top. ▶ **n. surge**, stream, spout, spurt, jet, rush, outpouring, spill, outflow, cascade, flood, torrent.

gush·y /ˈgəsHē/ ▶ **adj.** unrestrained in expressing approval: *her gushy manner.*

gus·set /ˈgəsit/ ▶ **n.** a piece of material sewn into a garment to strengthen or enlarge a part of it.

gust /gəst/ ▶ **n. 1** a brief, strong rush of wind. **2** a burst of sound or emotion. ▶ **v.** blow in gusts.

> SYNONYMS ▶ **n. flurry**, blast, puff, blow, rush, squall.

■ **gust·y adj.**

gus·to /ˈgəstō/ ▶ **n.** enthusiasm and energy.

gut /gət/ ▶ **n. 1** the stomach or intestine. **2** (**guts**) internal organs that have been removed or exposed. **3** (**guts**) the inner or most important part of something. **4** (**guts**) informal courage and determination. ▶ **v.** (**guts**, **gutting**, **gutted**) **1** take out the internal organs of a fish or other animal before cooking. **2** remove or destroy the internal parts of something: *the fire gutted most of the factory.* ▶ **adj.** instinctive: *that's my gut reaction.*

> SYNONYMS ▶ **n. 1 stomach**, belly, abdomen, paunch, intestines, viscera; informal tummy, insides, innards. **2** *he has a lot of guts* **courage**, bravery, backbone, nerve, pluck, spirit, daring, grit, fearlessness, determination; informal moxie. ▶ **v. 1 clean (out)**, disembowel, draw; formal eviscerate. **2 strip**, empty, devastate, lay waste, ravage, ruin, wreck. ▶ **adj. instinctive**,

intuitive, deep-seated, involuntary, spontaneous, unthinking, knee-jerk.

□ **bust a gut** informal make a strenuous effort. **hate someone's guts** informal dislike someone intensely.

gut·less /'gətləs/ ▶ **adj.** informal not showing courage or determination.

guts·y /'gətsē/ ▶ **adj.** (**gutsier**, **gutsiest**) informal brave and determined.

gut·ter /'gətər/ ▶ **n.** **1** a shallow trough beneath the edge of a roof, or a channel at the side of a street, for carrying off rainwater. **2** (**the gutter**) a very poor or unpleasant environment. ▶ **v.** (**gutters**, **guttering**, **guttered**) (of a flame) flicker and burn unsteadily.

SYNONYMS ▶ **n.** **drain**, trough, trench, ditch, sluice, sewer, channel, conduit, pipe.

gut·ter·snipe /'gətər,snīp/ ▶ **n.** disapproving a scruffy, badly behaved child.

gut·tur·al /'gətərəl/ ▶ **adj.** (of a speech sound) produced in the throat.

SPELLING

Write **-tur-**, not **-ter-**: gutt**ur**al.

guy[1] /gī/ ▶ **n.** **1** informal a man. **2** (**guys**) informal people of either sex. ▶ **v.** make fun of someone.

SYNONYMS ▶ **n.** **man**, fellow; informal lad, dude.

guy[2] ▶ **n.** a rope or line fixed to the ground to secure a tent.

guz·zle /'gəzəl/ ▶ **v.** (**guzzles**, **guzzling**, **guzzled**) eat or drink greedily.

SYNONYMS **1** **gobble**, bolt, wolf, devour; informal scarf down, tuck into. **2** **gulp down**, quaff, swill; informal knock back, swig, slug.

gym /jim/ ▶ **n.** **1** a gymnasium. **2** a private club with equipment for improving physical fitness. **3** gymnastics.

gym·kha·na /jim'känə/ ▶ **n.** a horse-riding event consisting of a series of competitions.

gym·na·si·um /jim'nāzēəm/ ▶ **n.** (plural **gymnasiums** or **gymnasia** /-zēə/) a hall or building equipped for gymnastics and other sports.

gym·nast /'jimnist/ ▶ **n.** a person trained in gymnastics.

gym·nas·tic /jim'nastik/ ▶ **adj.** of gymnastics: *a gymnastic display*.

gym·nas·tics /jim'nastiks/ ▶ **pl.n.** exercises involving physical agility and coordination.

gym·no·sperm /'jimnə,spərm/ ▶ **n.** a plant of a large group that has seeds unprotected by an ovary or fruit.

gy·ne·col·o·gy /,gīnə'käləjē, ,jinə-/ ▶ **n.** the branch of medicine concerned with conditions and diseases experienced by women. ■ **gyn·e·co·log·i·cal** /-kə'läjikəl/ **adj.** **gy·ne·col·o·gist** **n.**

gyp /jip/ informal ▶ **v.** (**gyps**, **gypping**, **gypped**) cheat or swindle. ▶ **n.** a swindle.

gyp·sum /'jipsəm/ ▶ **n.** a soft white or gray mineral used to make plaster of Paris and in the building industry.

gyp·sy /'jipsē/ (also **gipsy**) ▶ **n.** (plural **gypsies**) **1** a member of a traveling people with dark skin and hair who speak the Romany language. **2** a person who moves from place to place or who leads an unconventional life. ▶ **adj.** (of a business or business person) nonunion or unlicensed: *gypsy trucking firms*. ■ **gyp·sy·ish** **adj.**

gy·rate /'jīrāt/ ▶ **v.** (**gyrates**, **gyrating**, **gyrated**) **1** move in a circle or spiral. **2** dance in a wild manner.

SYNONYMS **rotate**, revolve, wheel, turn, whirl, circle, pirouette, twirl, swirl, spin, swivel.

■ **gy·ra·tion** **n.**

gyr·fal·con /'jər,falkən, -,fôl-/ ▶ **n.** a large arctic falcon, with mainly gray or white plumage.

gy·ro /'jīrō/ /'yērō, 'zhirō/ ▶ **n.** a gyroscope or gyrocompass.

gy·ro·com·pass /'jīrō,kəmpəs/ ▶ **n.** a compass in which the direction of true north is maintained by a gyroscope rather than magnetism.

gy·ro·scope /'jīrə,skōp/ ▶ **n.** a device, used to provide stability or maintain a fixed direction, consisting of a wheel or disk spinning rapidly about an axis that is itself free to alter in direction.

Hh

H (or **h**) ▶ **n.** (plural **Hs** or **H's**) the eighth letter of the alphabet. ▶ **abbr.** (**h**) hour(s). ▫ **H-bomb** a hydrogen bomb.

ha[1] ▶ **abbr.** hectares.

ha[2] /hä/ (also **hah**) ▶ **exclam.** used to express surprise, suspicion, triumph, or some other emotion.

ha·be·as cor·pus /ˈhābēəs ˈkôrpəs/ ▶ **n.** Law a written order saying that a person must come before a judge or court.

hab·er·dash·er·y /ˈhabərˌdasHərē/ ▶ **n. 1** a store selling men's clothing and accessories. **2** the goods sold by such a store.

hab·it /ˈhabit/ ▶ **n. 1** a thing you do regularly and repeatedly. **2** informal an addiction to a drug. **3** a long, loose garment worn by a monk or nun.

SYNONYMS **1 custom**, practice, routine, way; formal wont. **2 addiction**, dependence, craving, fixation.

▫ **habit-forming** (of a drug) addictive.

hab·it·a·ble /ˈhabitəbəl/ ▶ **adj.** suitable to live in.

hab·i·tat /ˈhabiˌtat/ ▶ **n.** the natural home or environment of a plant or animal.

hab·i·ta·tion /ˌhabiˈtāsHən/ ▶ **n. 1** the fact of living somewhere. **2** formal a house or home.

ha·bit·u·al /həˈbicHo͞oəl/ ▶ **adj. 1** done constantly or as a habit. **2** regular; usual: *his habitual dress.*

SYNONYMS **1 constant**, persistent, continual, continuous, perpetual, nonstop, endless, never-ending; informal eternal. **2 inveterate**, confirmed, compulsive, incorrigible, hardened, ingrained, chronic, regular. **3 customary**, accustomed, regular, usual, normal, characteristic; literary wonted. ANTONYMS occasional.

▪ **ha·bit·u·al·ly** **adv.**

ha·bit·u·ate /həˈbicHo͞oˌāt/ ▶ **v.** (**habituates, habituating, habituated**) make or become accustomed to something.

ha·bit·u·é /həˈbicHo͞oˌā/ ▶ **n.** a frequent visitor to a place.

ha·ci·en·da /ˌhäsēˈendə/ ▶ **n.** (in Spanish-speaking countries) a large estate with a house.

hack[1] /hak/ ▶ **v. 1** cut or hit at something with rough or heavy blows. **2** use a computer to read or alter information in another computer system without permission. ▶ **n.** a rough cut or blow.

SYNONYMS ▶ **v. cut**, chop, hew, lop, slash.

▫ **hacking cough** a harsh, dry, frequent cough.
▪ **hack·er** **n.**

hack[2] ▶ **n. 1** a journalist producing dull, unoriginal work. **2** a horse for ordinary riding.

hack·les /ˈhakəlz/ ▶ **pl.n.** hairs along an animal's back that rise when it is angry or alarmed.

hack·ney /ˈhaknē/ ▶ **n.** (plural **hackneys**) (in the past) a horse-drawn vehicle kept for hire.

hack·neyed /ˈhaknēd/ ▶ **adj.** (especially of a phrase) not original or interesting.

SYNONYMS **overused**, overdone, overworked, worn out, timeworn, stale, tired, threadbare, trite, banal, clichéd. ANTONYMS original.

hack·saw /ˈhakˌsô/ ▶ **n.** a saw with a narrow blade set in a frame.

had /had/ past and past participle of **HAVE**.

had·dock /ˈhadək/ ▶ **n.** (plural **haddock**) a silvery-gray sea fish used for food.

Ha·des /ˈhādēz/ ▶ **n.** Greek Mythology the world of the dead, under the earth.

had·n't /ˈhadnt/ ▶ **contr.** had not.

hadst /hadst/ old 2nd person singular past of **HAVE**.

haft /haft/ ▶ **n.** the handle of a knife, ax, or spear.

hag /hag/ ▶ **n. 1** an ugly old woman. **2** a witch.

hag·gard /ˈhagərd/ ▶ **adj.** looking exhausted and ill.

SYNONYMS **drawn**, tired, exhausted, drained, careworn, gaunt, pinched, hollow-cheeked, hollow-eyed.

hag·gis /ˈhagis/ ▶ **n.** (plural **haggis**) a Scottish dish consisting of the internal organs of a sheep or calf mixed with suet and oatmeal.

hag·gle /ˈhagəl/ ▶ **v.** (**haggles, haggling, haggled**) argue or negotiate with someone about the price of something. ▶ **n.** a period of haggling.

SYNONYMS ▶ **v. barter**, bargain, negotiate, wrangle.

hag·i·og·ra·phy /ˌhagēˈägrəfē, ˌhāgē-/ ▶ **n. 1** writing that is about the lives of saints. **2** a biography that presents its subject as better than in reality.

ha-ha /ˈhä ˌhä, ˌhä ˈhä/ ▶ **n.** a trench that forms a boundary to a park or garden without interrupting the view.

hai·ku /ˈhīˌko͞o, ˌhīˈko͞o/ ▶ **n.** (plural **haiku** or **haikus**) a Japanese poem of three lines and seventeen syllables.

hail[1] /hāl/ ▶ **n. 1** pellets of frozen rain falling in showers. **2** a large number of things hurled forcefully through the air: *a hail of bullets.* ▶ **v.** (**it hails, it is hailing, it hailed**) hail falls.

SYNONYMS ▶ **n. barrage**, volley, shower, stream, salvo.

hail[2] ▶ **v. 1** call out to someone to attract their attention. **2** (**hail someone/thing as**) enthusiastically describe someone or something as: *he has been hailed as the new Johnny Depp.* **3** (**hail from**) have your home or origins in.

SYNONYMS **1 call out to**, shout to, address, greet, salute, say hello to. **2 flag down**, wave down. **3 acclaim**, praise, applaud. **4** ***he hails from** Australia* **come from**, be from, be a native of.

□ **Hail Mary** (plural **Hail Marys**) a prayer to the Virgin Mary used chiefly by Roman Catholics.

hail·stone /ˈhālˌstōn/ ▶ **n.** a pellet of hail.

hair /he(ə)r/ ▶ **n. 1** each of the threadlike strands growing from the skin of animals, or from plants. **2** strands of hair.

SYNONYMS **1 head of hair**, shock of hair, mane, mop, locks, tresses, curls. **2 hairstyle**, haircut; informal hairdo. **3 fur**, wool, coat, fleece, pelt, mane.

□ **a hair's breadth** a very small margin. **hair-raising** very alarming or frightening. **hair shirt** (in the past) a shirt made of very rough cloth worn as a way of punishing yourself. **hair trigger** a firearm trigger set for release at the slightest pressure. **let your hair down** informal behave wildly or in a very relaxed way. **split hairs** make small and unnecessary distinctions.

hair·ball /ˈhe(ə)rˌbôl/ ▶ **n.** a ball of hair that collects in the stomach of an animal as a result of the animal licking its coat.

hair·band /ˈhe(ə)rˌband/ ▶ **n.** a band worn on the head to keep the hair off the face.

hair·brush /ˈhe(ə)rˌbrəsʜ/ ▶ **n.** a brush for smoothing your hair.

hair·cut /ˈheərˌkət/ ▶ **n. 1** the style in which someone's hair is cut. **2** an act of cutting someone's hair.

hair·do /ˈhe(ə)rˌdo͞o/ ▶ **n.** (plural **hairdos**) informal the style of a person's hair.

hair·dress·er /ˈhe(ə)rˌdresər/ ▶ **n.** a person who cuts and styles hair.

SYNONYMS **hairstylist**, stylist, coiffeur, coiffeuse, barber.

■ **hair·dress·ing n.**

hair·dry·er /ˈhe(ə)rˌdrīər/ (or **hairdrier**) ▶ **n.** an electrical device for drying the hair with warm air.

hair·line /ˈhe(ə)rˌlīn/ ▶ **n.** the edge of a person's hair. ▶ **adj.** very thin or fine: *a hairline fracture.*

hair·net /ˈhe(ə)rˌnet/ ▶ **n.** a fine net for holding the hair in place.

hair·piece /ˈhe(ə)rˌpēs/ ▶ **n.** a piece of false hair worn with your own hair to make it look thicker.

hair·pin /ˈhe(ə)rˌpin/ ▶ **n.** a U-shaped pin for fastening the hair. □ **hairpin turn** a sharp U-shaped curve in a road.

hair·split·ting /ˈhe(ə)rˌsplitiɴɢ/ ▶ **n.** the making of overly fine distinctions.

hair·spray /ˈhe(ə)rˌsprā/ ▶ **n.** a solution sprayed on to hair to keep it in place.

hair·spring /ˈhe(ə)rˌspriɴɢ/ ▶ **n.** a flat coiled spring regulating the movement of the balance wheel in a watch.

hair·style /ˈhe(ə)rˌstīl/ ▶ **n.** a way in which a person's hair is cut or arranged.

hair·styl·ist /ˈhe(ə)rˌstīlist/ ▶ **n.** a person whose job is cutting and styling people's hair. ■ **hair·styl·ing n.**

hair·y /ˈhe(ə)rē/ ▶ **adj.** (**hairier, hairiest**) **1** covered with or like hair. **2** informal dangerous or frightening: *a hairy mountain road.*

SYNONYMS **1 shaggy**, bushy, long-haired, woolly, furry, fleecy. **2 bearded**, unshaven, stubbly, bristly; formal hirsute. **3 risky**, dangerous, perilous, hazardous, tricky; informal dicey.

Hai·tian /ˈhāsʜən/ ▶ **n.** a person from Haiti. ▶ **adj.** relating to Haiti.

hajj /haj/ (or **haj**) ▶ **n.** the pilgrimage to Mecca that all Muslims are expected to make at least once if they can afford to.

hake /hāk/ ▶ **n.** a long-bodied sea fish used for food.

ha·lal /həˈläl, həˈlal/ ▶ **adj.** (of meat) prepared according to Muslim law.

hal·berd /ˈhalbərd, ˈhôl-/ ▶ **n.** historical a combined spear and battle-ax.

hal·cy·on /ˈhalsēən/ ▶ **adj.** (of a past time) very happy and peaceful: *halcyon days.*

hale /hāl/ ▶ **adj.** (of an old person) strong and healthy.

half /haf/ ▶ **n.** (plural **halves** /havz, hävz/) either of two equal parts into which something is or can be divided. ▶ **pron.** an amount equal to a half: *half an hour.* ▶ **adv. 1** to the extent of half. **2** partly: *half-cooked.* □ **at half mast** (of a flag) flown halfway down its mast, as a mark of respect for a person who has died. **half-and-half 1** in equal parts. **2** a mixture of milk and cream, used especially in coffee. **half-baked** informal badly planned or considered. **half-brother** (or **half-sister**) a brother (or sister) with whom you have one parent in common. **half dollar** a US or Canadian coin worth 50 cents. **half-dozen** (or **half a dozen**) a group of six. **half-hardy** (of a plant) able to grow outdoors except in severe frost. **half hitch** a knot formed by passing the end of a rope around itself and then through the loop created. **half-hour** (or **half an hour**) a period of thirty minutes. **half-life** the time taken for the radioactivity of a substance to fall to half its original value. **half-light** dim light, as at dusk. **half measures** actions or policies that are not forceful or decisive enough. **half nelson** a hold in wrestling in which you pass one arm under your opponent's arm from behind while applying your other hand to their neck. **half note** Music a note having the time value of two quarter notes or half of a whole note. **half-truth** a statement that is only partly true. **half-volley** (in sports) a strike or kick of the ball immediately after it bounces. **not half** not nearly. **too ... by half** excessively ....

half·back /ˈhafˌbak/ ▶ **n. 1** Football an offensive back usually positioned behind the quarterback and to the side of the fullback. **2** a usually defensive player in a game such as soccer, rugby, or field hockey whose position is behind the forward line.

half·heart·ed /ˌhafˈhärtid/ ▶ **adj.** without enthusiasm or energy.

half·time /ˈhafˌtīm/ ▶ **n.** a short interval between two halves of a game or sports contest.

half·way /ˈhafˈwā/ ▶ **adv. & adj. 1** at or to a point equal in distance between two others. **2** to some extent: *halfway decent.*

SYNONYMS **1** *the halfway point* **midway**, middle, mid, central, center, intermediate. **2** *he stopped halfway* **midway**, in the middle, in the center, part of the way.

□ **halfway house 1** a center for helping former drug addicts, prisoners, psychiatric patients, or others to adjust to life in general society. **2** a point halfway through something. **3** a compromise.

half·wit /ˈhafˌwit/ ▸ n. informal a stupid person. ■ **half-wit·ted** adj.

hal·i·but /ˈhaləbət/ ▸ n. (plural **halibut**) a large flat sea fish used for food.

hal·ide /ˈhaˌlīd, ˈhā-/ ▸ n. Chemistry a compound of a halogen and another element or group: *silver halide.*

hal·i·to·sis /ˌhaliˈtōsəs/ ▸ n. bad-smelling breath.

hall /hôl/ ▸ n. **1** (also **hallway** /ˈhôlˌwā/) a room or space inside a front door, or between a number of rooms. **2** a large room for meetings, concerts, etc. **3** (also **residence hall**) a university building in which students live.

> SYNONYMS **1 entrance hall**, hallway, entry, entrance, lobby, foyer, vestibule, atrium. **2 assembly room**, meeting room, chamber, auditorium, theater, house.

□ **Hall of Fame 1** the group of people who have excelled in a particular sphere. **2** a memorial or museum dedicated to such a group of people: *the Baseball Hall of Fame in Cooperstown.*

hal·le·lu·jah /ˌhaləˈlo͞oyə/ (or **alleluia** /ˌaləˈlo͞oyə/) ▸ exclam. God be praised.

hall·mark /ˈhôlˌmärk/ ▸ n. **1** an official mark stamped on objects made of pure gold, silver, or platinum. **2** a distinctive feature: *the hallmark of fine champagnes.* ▸ v. stamp an object with a hallmark.

hal·lo /həˈlō/ = **HELLO**.

hal·loo /həˈlo͞o/ ▸ exclam. **1** used to attract someone's attention. **2** used to urge on hunting dogs. ▸ n. a cry of "halloo." ▸ v. (**halloos hallooing hallooed**) shout "halloo" to attract attention or to urge on hunting dogs.

hal·lowed /ˈhalōd/ ▸ adj. **1** made holy. **2** very honored and respected.

Hal·low·een /ˌhaləˈwēn, ˌhälə-, -ōˈēn/ (or **Hallowe'en**) ▸ n. the night of October 31, the evening before All Saints' Day.

hal·lu·ci·nate /həˈlo͞osənˌāt/ ▸ v. (**hallucinates, hallucinating, hallucinated**) see something that is not actually there. ■ **hal·lu·ci·na·to·ry** /həˈlo͞osənəˌtôrē/ adj.

hal·lu·ci·na·tion /həˌlo͞osənˈāsʜən/ ▸ n. an experience in which you seem to see something that is not really there: *he continued to suffer from horrific hallucinations.*

> SYNONYMS **delusion**, illusion, figment of the imagination, mirage, chimera, fantasy.

hal·lu·ci·no·gen /həˈlo͞osənəˌjən/ ▸ n. a drug causing hallucinations. ■ **hal·lu·ci·no·gen·ic** adj.

hall·way /ˈhôlˌwā/ ▸ n. a room or space inside a front door, or between a number of rooms; a hall.

ha·lo /ˈhālō/ ▸ n. (plural **haloes** or **halos**) **1** (in a painting) a circle of light surrounding the head of a holy person. **2** a circle of light around the sun or moon. ▸ v. (**haloes, haloing, haloed**) surround something with or as if with a halo.

hal·o·gen /ˈhaləjən/ ▸ n. any of a group of elements including fluorine, chlorine, bromine, and iodine.

halt¹ /hôlt/ ▸ v. come or bring to a sudden stop. ▸ n. a stopping of movement or activity.

> SYNONYMS ▸ v. **1** *halt at the barrier* **stop**, come to a halt, come to a stop, come to a standstill, pull up. **2** *a strike halted production* **stop**, bring to a stop, put a stop to, suspend, arrest, check, curb, stem, staunch, block, stall. ▸ n. **1 stop**, standstill. **2 stoppage**, break, pause, interval, interruption. ANTONYMS start.

□ **call a halt** order people to stop doing something.

halt² ▸ adj. old use lame.

halt·er /ˈhôltər/ ▸ n. a rope or strap placed around the head of an animal and used to lead it. □ **halter neck** a style of woman's top that is fastened behind the neck, leaving the shoulders, upper back, and arms bare.

halt·ing /ˈhôltiɴɢ/ ▸ adj. slow and hesitant.

> SYNONYMS **hesitant**, faltering, hesitating, stumbling, stammering, stuttering, broken, imperfect. ANTONYMS fluent.

halve /hav, häv/ ▸ v. (**halves** /havz, hävz/, **halving, halved**) **1** divide into two halves. **2** reduce or be reduced by half.

halves /havz, hävz/ plural of **HALF**.

hal·yard /ˈhalyərd/ ▸ n. a rope used for raising and lowering a sail, yard, or flag on a ship.

ham¹ /ham/ ▸ n. **1** meat from the upper part of a pig's leg that is salted and dried or smoked. **2** (**hams**) the back of the thighs. □ **ham-fisted** (or **ham-handed**) clumsy.

ham² ▸ n. **1** an actor who overacts. **2** (also **radio ham**) informal an amateur radio operator. ▸ v. (**hams, hamming, hammed**) informal overact. ■ **ham·my** adj.

ham·bone /ˈhamˌbōn/ ▸ n. informal an inferior actor or performer.

ham·burg·er /ˈhamˌbərgər/ ▸ n. a small patty of ground beef, fried or grilled and typically served on a bun or roll.

ham·let /ˈhamlit/ ▸ n. a small village.

ham·mer /ˈhamər/ ▸ n. **1** a tool with a heavy metal head and a wooden handle, for driving in nails. **2** an auctioneer's mallet, tapped to indicate a sale. **3** a part of a mechanism that hits another. **4** a heavy metal ball attached to a wire for throwing in an athletic contest. ▸ v. (**hammers, hammering, hammered**) **1** hit repeatedly with a hammer. **2** (**hammer away**) work hard and persistently. **3** (**hammer something in** or **into**) make something stick in someone's mind by constantly repeating it. **4** (**hammer something out**) work out the details of a plan or agreement.

> SYNONYMS ▸ v. **beat**, batter, bang, pummel, pound, knock, thump.

□ **hammer and sickle** the symbols of the industrial and the agricultural worker used on the flag of the former USSR. **hammer drill** a power drill that delivers a rapid succession of blows.

ham·mer·head /ˈhamərˌhed/ ▸ n. a shark with flattened extensions on either side of the head.

ham·mer·toe /ˈhamərˌtō/ ▸ n. a toe that is bent permanently downward.

ham·mock /ˈhamək/ ▸ n. a wide strip of canvas or rope mesh suspended at both ends, used as a bed.

ham·per¹ /ˈhampər/ ▸ n. **1** a large basket with a lid used for laundry. **2** a basket used for food and other items needed for a picnic.

ham·per² ▸ v. (**hampers, hampering, hampered**) slow down or prevent the movement or progress of.

> SYNONYMS **hinder**, obstruct, impede, inhibit, delay, slow down, hold up, interfere with, handicap, hamstring. ANTONYMS help.

ham·ster /ˈhamstər/ ▸ n. a burrowing rodent with a short tail and large cheek pouches.

SPELLING

No **p**: **ham**ster, not **hamp-**.

ham·string /'ham,striNG/ ▶ **n.** any of five tendons at the back of a person's knee. ▶ **v.** (**hamstrings**, **hamstringing**, past and past participle **hamstrung**) **1** cripple by cutting the hamstrings. **2** severely restrict.

hand /hand/ ▶ **n. 1** the end part of the arm beyond the wrist, with four fingers and a thumb. **2** a pointer on a clock or watch indicating the passing of time. **3** (**hands**) a person's power or control: *taking the law into their own hands.* **4** an active role: *he had a big hand in organizing the event.* **5** help in doing something. **6** a person who does physical work. **7** a round of applause. **8** the set of cards dealt to a player in a card game. **9** a unit of measurement of a horse's height, equal to 4 inches (10.16 cm). ▶ **v. 1** give or pass something to. **2** (**hand over**) officially pass something to someone else.

SYNONYMS ▶ **n. 1 fist**, palm; informal paw, mitt. **2 handwriting**, writing, script. **3 worker**, employee, workman, laborer, hired hand, operative, craftsman. ▶ **v. pass**, give, present, let someone have.

□ **at hand** (or **on** or **to hand**) near; easy to reach. **from hand to mouth** meeting only your immediate needs. **keep your hand in** remain practiced in something. **hand grenade** a grenade that is thrown by hand. **hand in glove** working very closely together. **hand-me-down** a piece of clothing that has been passed on from another person. **hand-pick** choose carefully. **hands-on** involving direct participation in something. **hand-to-hand** (of fighting) involving physical contact. **in hand 1** in progress. **2** (of money) ready for use if needed. **on hand** present and available. **on your hands** under your responsibility. **on the one** (or **the other**) **hand** used to present reasons for (and against). **out of hand 1** not under control. **2** without taking time to think: *it was rejected out of hand.* **to hand** within easy reach.

hand·bag /'han(d),bag/ ▶ **n.** a small bag used by a woman to carry everyday personal items.

hand·ball /'han(d),bôl/ ▶ **n. 1** a game in which the ball is hit with the hand in a walled court. **2** Soccer unlawful touching of the ball with the hand or arm.

hand·bill /'han(d),bil/ ▶ **n.** a small printed advertisement handed out in the street.

hand·book /'han(d),bo͝ok/ ▶ **n.** a book giving basic information or instructions.

SYNONYMS **manual**, instructions, ABC, A to Z, companion, guide, guidebook, vade mecum.

hand·brake /'han(d),brāk/ ▶ **n.** a brake operated by hand, used to hold an already stationary vehicle.

hand·craft·ed /'han(d),kraftid/ ▶ **adj.** made skillfully by hand.

hand·cuff /'han(d),kəf/ ▶ **n.** (**handcuffs**) a pair of lockable linked metal rings for securing a prisoner's wrists. ▶ **v.** put handcuffs on.

SYNONYMS ▶ **n.** (**handcuffs**) **manacles**, shackles, irons; informal cuffs, bracelets. ▶ **v. manacle**, shackle, clap/put someone in irons; informal cuff.

hand·ful /'han(d),fo͝ol/ ▶ **n. 1** a quantity that fills the hand. **2** a small number or amount. **3** informal a person who is difficult to deal with or control.

SYNONYMS **few**, small number, small amount, small quantity, sprinkling, smattering, one or two, some, not many. ANTONYMS lot.

hand·gun /'han(d),gən/ ▶ **n.** a gun designed for use with one hand.

hand·hold /'hand,hōld/ ▶ **n.** something for a hand to grip on.

hand·i·cap /'handē,kap/ ▶ **n. 1** a condition that limits a person's ability to function physically, mentally, or socially. **2** something that makes progress or success difficult. **3** a disadvantage given to a leading competitor in a sport in order to make the chances of winning more equal, such as the extra weight given to certain racehorses. **4** the number of strokes by which a golfer normally exceeds par for a course. ▶ **v.** (**handicaps**, **handicapping**, **handicapped**) make it difficult for someone to do something.

SYNONYMS ▶ **n. 1 disability**, infirmity, defect, impairment, affliction. **2 impediment**, hindrance, obstacle, barrier, constraint, disadvantage, stumbling block. ANTONYMS benefit, advantage. ▶ **v. hamper**, impede, hinder, impair, hamstring, restrict, constrain. ANTONYMS help.

hand·i·capped /'handē,kapt/ ▶ **adj.** having a handicap or disability.

USAGE

When used to refer to people with physical and mental disabilities, the word **handicapped** sounds old-fashioned and may cause offense; it is better to use **disabled**, or, when referring to mental disability, **having learning difficulties**.

hand·i·craft /'handē,kraft/ ▶ **n. 1** the skilled making of decorative objects by hand. **2** an object made in this way.

hand·i·work /'handē,wərk/ ▶ **n. 1** (**your handiwork**) something that you have made or done. **2** the making of things by hand.

hand·ker·chief /'haNGkərCHif, -CHēf/ ▶ **n.** (plural **handkerchiefs** or **handkerchieves** /'haNGkərCHivz, -CHēvz/) a square of material for wiping or blowing the nose on.

han·dle /'handl/ ▶ **v.** (**handles**, **handling**, **handled**) **1** feel or move something with the hands. **2** control an animal, vehicle, or tool. **3** deal with a situation. **4** control, manage, or deal in something commercially. **5** (**handle yourself**) behave. ▶ **n. 1** the part by which a thing is held, carried, or controlled. **2** a means of understanding or approaching a person or situation.

SYNONYMS ▶ **v. 1 hold**, pick up, grasp, grip, lift, finger. **2 control**, drive, steer, operate, maneuver. **3 deal with**, manage, tackle, take care of, look after, take charge of, attend to, see to, sort out. **4 trade in**, deal in, buy, sell, supply, peddle, traffic in. ▶ **n. grip**, haft, hilt, stock, shaft.

han·dle·bar /'handl,bär/ (or **handlebars**) ▶ **n.** the steering bar of a bicycle or motorcycle.

han·dler /'handlər/ ▶ **n. 1** a person who handles a particular type of article: *baggage handlers.* **2** a person who trains or has charge of an animal. **3** a person who trains or manages another person.

hand·made /'han(d)'mād/ ▶ **adj.** made by hand rather than machine.

hand·maid /ˈhandˌmād/ (or **handmaiden** /ˈhan(d)ˌmādn/) ▶ **n.** old use a female servant.

hand·out /ˈhandˌout/ ▶ **n.** **1** a parcel of food, clothes, or money given to a person in need. **2** a piece of printed information provided free of charge.

hand·o·ver /ˈhandˌōvər/ ▶ **n.** an act of handing something over.

hand·print /ˈhandˌprint/ ▶ **n.** the mark left by the impression of a hand.

hand·set /ˈhan(d)ˌset/ ▶ **n.** **1** the part of a telephone that you speak into and listen to. **2** a hand-held control device for a piece of electronic equipment.

hand·shake /ˈhan(d)ˌSHāk/ ▶ **n.** an act of shaking a person's hand.

hand·some /ˈhansəm/ ▶ **adj.** (**handsomer**, **handsomest**) **1** (of a man) good-looking. **2** (of a woman) striking and impressive rather than pretty. **3** (of a thing) impressive and of good quality. **4** (of an amount) large: *elected by a handsome majority*.

SYNONYMS **1 good-looking**, attractive, striking; informal hunky, cute. **2 substantial**, considerable, sizable, princely, generous, lavish, ample, bumper; informal tidy. ANTONYMS ugly.

■ **hand·some·ly** **adv.**

hand·spring /ˈhandˌspriNG/ ▶ **n.** a jump through the air on to your hands followed by another on to your feet.

hand·stand /ˈhandˌstand/ ▶ **n.** an act of balancing on your hands with your legs in the air.

hand·writ·ing /ˈhan(d)ˌrītiNG/ ▶ **n.** **1** writing with a pen or pencil rather than by typing or printing. **2** a person's particular style of writing.

hand·writ·ten /ˈhan(d)ˌritn/ ▶ **adj.** written with a pen or pencil.

hand·y /ˈhandē/ ▶ **adj.** (**handier**, **handiest**) **1** convenient to handle or use. **2** close by and ready for use. **3** skillful; able to make repairs.

SYNONYMS **1 useful**, convenient, practical, neat, easy to use, user-friendly, helpful, functional. **2 ready**, at/on hand, within reach, accessible, readily available, nearby, at the ready. **3 skillful**, skilled, dexterous, deft, adept, proficient.

■ **hand·i·ly** **adv.**

hand·y·man /ˈhandēˌman/ ▶ **n.** (plural **handymen**) a person employed to do general building repairs.

hang /haNG/ ▶ **v.** (**hangs**, **hanging**, past and past participle **hung** /həNG/ except in sense 2) **1** suspend or be suspended from above with the lower part dangling freely. **2** (past and past participle **hanged**) kill someone by suspending them from a rope tied around the neck. **3** (of a piece of clothing) fall or drape in a particular way.

SYNONYMS **1** *lights hung from the trees* **be suspended**, dangle, swing, sway, hover, float. **2** *hang the picture at eye level* **suspend**, put up, pin up, display. **3 decorate**, adorn, drape, festoon, deck out. **4 send to the gallows**, execute, lynch; informal string up.

□ **get the hang of** informal learn how to do something. **hang around** wait around. **hang-glider** a simple aircraft consisting of a framework from which a person is suspended while they glide through the air. **hang on 1** hold tightly. **2** informal wait for a short time. **hang out** informal spend time relaxing or enjoying yourself. **hang tough** informal be or remain inflexible or firmly resolved. **hang-up** informal an emotional problem. **hang up** end a telephone conversation by cutting the connection.

USAGE

hang has two past tense and past participle forms, **hanged** and **hung**: use **hung** in general situations, as in *they hung out the washing*, and **hanged** when talking about execution by hanging, as in *the prisoner was hanged*.

hang·ar /ˈhaNGər/ ▶ **n.** a large building in which aircraft are kept.

SPELLING

Write **-ar**, not **-er**: hang**ar**.

hang·dog /ˈhaNGˌdôg, -ˌdäg/ ▶ **adj.** having a sad or guilty appearance.

hang·er /ˈhaNGər/ ▶ **n.** **1** a person who hangs something. **2** (also **coat hanger**) a curved frame with a hook at the top, for hanging clothes from a rail. □ **hanger-on** (plural **hangers-on**) a person who tries to be friendly with someone of higher status.

hang·ing /ˈhaNGiNG/ ▶ **n.** a decorative piece of fabric hung on the wall of a room or around a bed.

hang·man /ˈhaNGmən, -ˌman/ ▶ **n.** (plural **hangmen**) an executioner who hangs condemned people.

hang·nail /ˈhaNGˌnāl/ ▶ **n.** a piece of torn skin at the root of a fingernail.

hang·out /ˈhaNGˌout/ ▶ **n.** informal a place where someone spends a great deal of time.

hang·o·ver /ˈhaNGˌōvər/ ▶ **n.** **1** a headache or other aftereffects caused by drinking too much alcohol. **2** a thing that has survived from the past: *a hangover from the Sixties*.

hank /haNGk/ ▶ **n.** a coil or length of wool, hair, or other material.

hank·er /ˈhaNGkər/ ▶ **v.** (**hanker after** or **for** or **to do**) feel a desire for or to do.

SYNONYMS **yearn**, long, wish, hunger, thirst, lust, ache; informal itch.

han·ky /ˈhaNGkē/ (or **hankie**) ▶ **n.** (plural **hankies**) informal a handkerchief.

han·ky-pan·ky /ˈpaNGkē/ ▶ **n.** informal naughty behavior.

Han·o·ve·ri·an /ˌhanəˈve(ə)rēən/ ▶ **adj.** relating to the royal house of Hanover, who ruled as monarchs in Britain from 1714 to 1901.

Han·sard /ˈhansərd/ ▶ **n.** the official record of debates in the British, Canadian, Australian, or New Zealand parliament.

han·som /ˈhansəm/ (or **hansom cab**) ▶ **n.** (in the past) a horse-drawn carriage with two wheels and a hood, for two passengers.

Ha·nuk·kah /ˈKHänəkə, ˈhänəkə/ (or **Chanukah**) ▶ **n.** a Jewish festival of lights held in December, commemorating the rededication of the Jewish Temple in Jerusalem.

hap·haz·ard /ˌhapˈhazərd/ ▶ **adj.** having no particular order or plan.

SYNONYMS **random**, disorderly, indiscriminate, chaotic, hit-and-miss, aimless, chance; informal higgledy-piggledy. ANTONYMS methodical.

■ **hap·haz·ard·ly** **adv.**

hap·less /ˈhaplis/ ▶ **adj.** unlucky.

SYNONYMS **unfortunate**, unlucky, unhappy, wretched, miserable. ANTONYMS lucky.

hap·loid /ˈhapˌloid/ ▶ **adj.** (of a cell or nucleus) having a single set of unpaired chromosomes.

hap·pen /ˈhapən/ ▶ **v.** **1** take place without being planned or as the result of something. **2** (**happen to do**) do by chance. **3** (**happen on**) come across by chance. **4** (**happen to**) be experienced by: *the same thing happened to me.* **5** (**happen to**) become of: *I don't care what happens to the money.*

SYNONYMS **1 occur**, take place, come about, arise, develop, result, transpire; informal go down; literary come to pass. **2** *I happened to be in Yuma* **chance**, have the good/bad luck.

hap·pen·ing /ˈhap(ə)niNG/ ▶ **n.** an event or occurrence. ▶ **adj.** informal fashionable.

SYNONYMS ▶ **n. occurrence**, event, incident, episode, affair.

hap·pen·stance /ˈhapənˌstans/ ▶ **n.** coincidence.

hap·pi·ly /ˈhapəlē/ ▶ **adv.** **1** in a happy way: *Eleanor giggled happily.* **2** it is fortunate that: *happily, today's situation is very different.*

SYNONYMS **1 cheerfully**, contentedly, cheerily, merrily, joyfully. **2 gladly**, willingly, readily, freely. **3 fortunately**, luckily, thankfully, mercifully, as luck would have it.

hap·pi·ness /ˈhapēnis/ ▶ **n.** the condition of being happy.

SYNONYMS **pleasure**, contentment, well-being, satisfaction, cheerfulness, good spirits, merriment, joy, joyfulness, delight, elation, jubilation. ANTONYMS sadness.

hap·py /ˈhapē/ ▶ **adj.** (**happier**, **happiest**) **1** feeling or showing pleasure. **2** willing to do something. **3** fortunate and convenient: *a happy coincidence.*

SYNONYMS **1 cheerful**, cheery, merry, joyful, jovial, jolly, carefree, in good spirits, in a good mood, pleased, contented, content, satisfied, gratified, delighted, sunny, radiant, elated, jubilant; literary blithe. **2 glad**, pleased, delighted, more than willing. **3 fortunate**, lucky, timely, convenient. ANTONYMS sad, unhappy, unfortunate.

□ **happy-go-lucky** cheerfully unconcerned about the future. **happy hour** a period of the day when drinks are sold at reduced prices in a bar.

ha·ra-ki·ri /ˌhärə ˈki(ə)rē, ˌharə-, ˌharē ˈkarē/ ▶ **n.** a Japanese method of ritual suicide in which a person cuts open their stomach with a sword.

ha·rangue /həˈraNG/ ▶ **v.** (**harangues**, **haranguing**, **harangued**) use loud and aggressive language in criticizing someone or trying to persuade them to do something. ▶ **n.** an act of haranguing.

ha·rass /həˈras, ˈharəs/ ▶ **v.** **1** torment someone by putting constant pressure on them or by being unpleasant. **2** (**harassed**) tired or tense as a result of having too many demands made on you. **3** make repeated small-scale attacks on an enemy in order to wear down resistance.

SYNONYMS **1 persecute**, intimidate, hound, pester, bother; informal hassle, bug, ride. **2** (**harassed**) **stressed**, hard-pressed, careworn, worried, troubled; informal hassled.

SPELLING

Only one **r**: harass.

ha·rass·ment /həˈrasmənt, ˈharəsmənt/ ▶ **n.** the action of harassing or the state of being harassed.

SYNONYMS **persecution**, intimidation, victimization, trouble, bother; informal hassle.

har·bin·ger /ˈhärbənjər/ ▶ **n.** a person or thing that announces or signals the approach of something: *the harbingers of spring.*

har·bor /ˈhärbər/ ▶ **n.** a sheltered area of coast, where ships can be moored. ▶ **v.** **1** keep a thought or feeling secretly in your mind. **2** give a refuge or shelter to. **3** carry the germs of a disease.

SYNONYMS ▶ **n. port**, dock, haven, marina, mooring, wharf, anchorage, waterfront. ▶ **v.** **1 bear**, hold, nurse, foster. **2 shelter**, conceal, hide, shield, protect, give asylum to.

hard /härd/ ▶ **adj.** **1** solid, firm, and rigid. **2** needing a lot of endurance or effort; difficult. **3** (of a person) not showing any signs of weakness. **4** (of information) precise and definitely true: *hard science.* **5** harsh or unpleasant to the senses. **6** done with a lot of force or strength: *a hard whack.* **7** (of drink) strongly alcoholic. **8** (of a drug) very addictive. ▶ **adv.** **1** with a lot of effort or force. **2** so as to be solid or firm.

SYNONYMS ▶ **adj.** **1 firm**, solid, rigid, stiff, unbreakable, unyielding, compacted, compressed, tough, strong. **2 arduous**, strenuous, tiring, exhausting, back-breaking, grueling, heavy, laborious, demanding, uphill. **3 industrious**, diligent, assiduous, conscientious, energetic, keen, enthusiastic, indefatigable. **4 difficult**, puzzling, complicated, complex, intricate, knotty, thorny, problematic. **5 harsh**, unpleasant, grim, austere, difficult, bad, bleak, tough. **6 forceful**, heavy, strong, sharp, violent, powerful. ANTONYMS soft, easy, gentle. ▶ **adv.** **1 forcefully**, roughly, heavily, sharply, violently. **2 diligently**, industriously, assiduously, conscientiously, energetically, doggedly; informal like mad, like crazy. **3 closely**, intently, critically, carefully, searchingly.

□ **hard and fast** (of a rule) fixed and definitive. **hard-boiled** **1** (of an egg) boiled until the yolk is firm. **2** (of a person) tough and cynical. **hard cash** coins and banknotes as opposed to other forms of payment. **hard copy** a printed version of data held in a computer. **hard core** **1** the most committed or uncompromising members of a group. **2** pop music that is loud and aggressive in style. **hard disk** (or **hard drive**) (in a computer) a rigid magnetic disk on which a large amount of data can be stored. **hard feelings** feelings of resentment. **hard going** difficult to understand or enjoy. **hard hat** a rigid protective hat for wearing in a factory or on a building site. **hard-headed** tough and realistic. **hard-hearted** unfeeling. **hard labor** heavy manual work as a punishment. **hard line** a strict policy or attitude. **hard-nosed** realistic and tough-minded. **hard palate** the bony front part of the roof of the mouth. **hard-pressed** having difficulties such as not enough money or too much work to do. **hard sell** a policy or technique of aggressive selling or advertising. **hard up** informal short of money. ■ **hard·ness** n.

hard·bit·ten /ˈhärdˌbitn/ ▶ **adj.** tough and cynical.

hard·board /ˈhärdˌbôrd/ ▶ **n.** stiff board made of compressed wood pulp.

hard·cov·er /ˈhärdˌkəvər/ (or **hardback** /ˈhärdˌbak/) ▶ **n.** a book bound in stiff covers.

hard·en /ˈhärdn/ ▶ **v. 1** make or become hard or harder. **2** (**hardened**) fixed in a bad habit or way of life: *hardened criminals.*

SYNONYMS **1 solidify**, set, stiffen, thicken, cake, congeal. **2 toughen**, desensitize, inure, season, train, numb. **3** (**hardened**) **inveterate**, seasoned, habitual, chronic, compulsive, confirmed, incorrigible. ANTONYMS soften.

hard·ly /ˈhärdlē/ ▶ **adv. 1** scarcely; barely. **2** only with great difficulty.

SYNONYMS **scarcely**, barely, only just, just.

USAGE

Don't use **hardly** in a negative sentence, such as *I can't hardly wait*; say *I can hardly wait* instead.

hard·scrab·ble /ˈhärd,skrabəl/ ▶ **adj.** returning little in exchange for great effort.

hard·ship /ˈhärd,sHip/ ▶ **n.** severe suffering.

SYNONYMS **difficulty**, privation, destitution, poverty, austerity, need, distress, suffering, adversity. ANTONYMS prosperity, ease.

hard·ware /ˈhärd,we(ə)r/ ▶ **n. 1** tools and other items used in the home and in activities such as gardening. **2** the machines, wiring, and other parts of a computer. **3** heavy military equipment such as tanks and missiles.

SYNONYMS **equipment**, apparatus, gear, paraphernalia, tackle, machinery.

hard·wood /ˈhärd,wo͝od/ ▶ **n.** the wood from a broadleaved tree as distinguished from that of conifers.

har·dy /ˈhärdē/ ▶ **adj.** (**hardier**, **hardiest**) capable of surviving difficult conditions.

SYNONYMS **robust**, healthy, fit, strong, sturdy, tough, rugged. ANTONYMS delicate.

■ **har·di·ness n.**

hare /he(ə)r/ ▶ **n.** a fast-running animal like a large rabbit, with long hind legs. ▶ **v.** (**hares**, **haring**, **hared**) run very fast.

hare·bell /ˈhe(ə)r,bel/ ▶ **n.** a plant with pale blue bell-shaped flowers.

hare·brained /ˈhe(ə)r,brānd/ ▶ **adj.** foolish and unlikely to succeed.

Ha·re Krish·na /,härē ˈkrisHnə, ,harē/ ▶ **n.** a member of a religious sect based on the worship of the Hindu god Krishna.

hare·lip /ˈhe(ə)r,lip/ ▶ **n.** offensive a cleft lip.

har·em /ˈhe(ə)rəm, ˈhar-/ ▶ **n. 1** the separate part of a Muslim household reserved for women. **2** the women living in a harem.

har·i·cot /ˈhari,kō/ ▶ **n.** a bean of a variety with small white seeds, especially the kidney bean.

hark /härk/ ▶ **v. 1** literary listen. **2** (**hark back to**) recall or remind you of something in the past.

hark·en /ˈhärkən/ (or **hearken**) ▶ **v.** (usu. **harken to**) old use listen.

har·le·quin /ˈhärlik(w)ən/ ▶ **n.** (**Harlequin**) (in traditional pantomime) a character who wears a mask and a diamond-patterned costume. ▶ **adj.** in varied colors.

harm /härm/ ▶ **n. 1** hurt or injury to a person. **2** damage done to a thing. **3** a bad effect on something. ▶ **v. 1** hurt or injure someone. **2** damage or have a bad effect on something.

SYNONYMS ▶ **n. injury**, damage, mischief, detriment, disservice. ANTONYMS good. ▶ **v. 1 hurt**, injure, wound, lay a finger on, mistreat, ill-treat, maltreat. **2 damage**, spoil, affect, undermine, ruin. ANTONYMS heal, help.

harm·ful /ˈhärmfəl/ ▶ **adj.** causing or likely to cause harm.

SYNONYMS **damaging**, injurious, detrimental, dangerous, unhealthy, unwholesome, hurtful, destructive, hazardous. ANTONYMS beneficial.

■ **harm·ful·ly adv.**

harm·less /ˈhärmlis/ ▶ **adj.** not able or likely to cause harm.

SYNONYMS **1 safe**, innocuous, gentle, mild, nontoxic. **2 inoffensive**, innocuous, innocent, blameless, gentle. ANTONYMS harmful, objectionable.

■ **harm·less·ly adv.**

har·mon·ic /härˈmänik/ ▶ **adj.** relating to harmony.

har·mon·i·ca /härˈmänikə/ ▶ **n.** a small rectangular wind instrument with a row of metal reeds that produce different notes.

har·mo·ni·ous /härˈmōnēəs/ ▶ **adj. 1** tuneful. **2** arranged in a pleasing way so that each part goes well with the others. **3** free from conflict: *harmonious relationships.*

SYNONYMS **1 melodious**, tuneful, musical, sweet-sounding, mellifluous, dulcet, euphonious. **2 friendly**, amicable, cordial, amiable, congenial, peaceful, in harmony, in tune. **3 balanced**, coordinated, pleasing, tasteful. ANTONYMS discordant, hostile.

■ **har·mo·ni·ous·ly adv.**

har·mo·ni·um /härˈmōnēəm/ ▶ **n.** a keyboard instrument in which the notes are produced by air driven through metal reeds by foot-operated bellows.

har·mo·nize /ˈhärmə,nīz/ ▶ **v.** (**harmonizes**, **harmonizing**, **harmonized**) **1** add notes to a melody to produce harmony. **2** make or be harmonious.

SYNONYMS **1 coordinate**, go together, match, blend, mix, balance, tone in, be compatible, be harmonious, suit each other, set each other off. **2 standardize**, coordinate, integrate, synchronize, make consistent, bring into line, systematize. ANTONYMS clash.

har·mo·ny /ˈhärmənē/ ▶ **n.** (plural **harmonies**) **1** the combination of musical notes sounded at the same time to produce chords with a pleasing effect. **2** a pleasing quality when things are arranged together well. **3** agreement.

SYNONYMS **1 tunefulness**, euphony, melodiousness, unison. **2 accord**, agreement, peace, friendship, fellowship, cooperation, understanding, rapport, unity. ANTONYMS dissonance, disagreement.

har·ness /ˈhärnis/ ▶ **n. 1** a set of straps by which a horse or other animal is fastened to a cart, plow, etc. **2** an arrangement of straps used for attaching a person's body to something. ▶ **v. 1** fit a person or animal with a harness. **2** control and make use of resources: *attempts to harness solar energy.*

harp /härp/ ▶ **n.** a musical instrument consisting of a frame supporting a series of strings of different lengths, played by plucking with the fingers. ▶ **v.** (**harp on**) keep talking about something in a boring way. ■ **harp·ist** n.

har·poon /ˌhär'po͞on/ ▶ n. a barbed spearlike missile used for catching whales and other large sea creatures. ▶ v. spear with a harpoon.

harp·si·chord /'härpsiˌkôrd/ ▶ n. a keyboard instrument with horizontal strings plucked by points operated by pressing the keys.

har·py /'härpē/ ▶ n. (plural **harpies**) **1** Greek & Roman Mythology a cruel creature with a woman's head and body and a bird's wings and claws. **2** an unpleasant woman.

har·que·bus /'(h)ärk(w)əbəs/ (also **arquebus**) ▶ n. historical an early type of portable gun.

har·ri·dan /'haridn/ ▶ n. a bossy or aggressive old woman.

har·ri·er /'harēər/ ▶ n. **1** a hound used for hunting hares. **2** a bird of prey.

har·row /'harō/ ▶ n. a piece of equipment consisting of a heavy frame set with teeth that is dragged over plowed land to break up or spread the soil. ▶ v. draw a harrow over.

har·row·ing /'harōiNG/ ▶ adj. very distressing.

> SYNONYMS **distressing**, traumatic, upsetting, shocking, disturbing, painful, agonizing.

har·rumph /hə'rəmf/ ▶ v. **1** clear the throat noisily. **2** grumpily express dissatisfaction.

har·ry /'harē/ ▶ v. (**harries**, **harrying**, **harried**) **1** carry out repeated attacks on an enemy. **2** pester continuously.

> SYNONYMS **harass**, hound, torment, pester, worry, badger, nag, plague; informal hassle, bug.

harsh /härSH/ ▶ adj. **1** unpleasantly rough or jarring to the senses. **2** cruel or severe. **3** (of climate or conditions) difficult to survive in; hostile.

> SYNONYMS **1 grating**, rasping, strident, raucous, discordant, jarring, dissonant. **2 garish**, loud, glaring, gaudy, lurid. **3 cruel**, savage, barbarous, merciless, inhumane, ruthless, brutal, hard-hearted, unfeeling, unrelenting. **4 severe**, stringent, firm, stiff, stern, rigorous, uncompromising, draconian. **5 rude**, discourteous, unfriendly, sharp, bitter, unkind, critical, disparaging. **6 austere**, grim, spartan, hard, inhospitable. **7 cold**, freezing, icy, bitter, hard, severe, bleak. ANTONYMS kind, mild, gentle.

■ **harsh·ly** adv. **harsh·ness** n.

hart /härt/ ▶ n. an adult male deer.

har·te·beest /'härt(ə)ˌbēst/ ▶ n. a large African antelope with a long head and sloping back.

har·um-scar·um /'he(ə)rəm 'ske(ə)rəm/ ▶ adj. reckless.

har·vest /'härvist/ ▶ n. **1** the process or period of gathering in crops. **2** the season's yield or crop. ▶ v. gather in a crop.

> SYNONYMS ▶ n. **crop**, yield, vintage, produce. ▶ v. **gather**, bring in, reap, pick, collect.

□ **harvest mouse** a small mouse with a tail that it can use for grasping. ■ **har·vest·er** n.

has /haz/ 3rd person singular present of **HAVE**. □ **has-been** informal a person who is no longer important or famous.

hash¹ /hasH/ ▶ n. **1** a dish of chopped cooked meat and chopped vegetables, often potatoes, cooked together. **2** a jumble. □ **make a hash of** informal make a mess of. **hash browns** a dish of chopped and fried cooked potatoes.

hash² ⇨ **HASHISH**.

hash·ish /'haˌsHēsH/ (or **hash** /hasH/) ▶ n. an extract of the cannabis plant.

has·n't /'haznt/ ▶ contr. has not.

hasp /hasp/ ▶ n. a hinged metal plate that is fitted over a metal loop and secured by a pin or padlock to fasten something.

has·sle /'hasəl/ informal ▶ n. **1** annoying inconvenience. **2** a situation involving argument or disagreement. ▶ v. (**hassles**, **hassling**, **hassled**) harass or pester someone.

> SYNONYMS ▶ n. **inconvenience**, bother, nuisance, trouble, annoyance, irritation, fuss; informal aggravation, headache, pain in the neck. ▶ v. **harass**, pester, badger, hound, bother, nag, torment, needle; informal bug.

has·sock /'hasək/ ▶ n. a thick, firmly padded footstool.

hast /hast/ old 2nd person singular present of **HAVE**.

haste /hāst/ ▶ n. speed or urgency of action.

> SYNONYMS **speed**, hurriedness, swiftness, rapidity, quickness, briskness, alacrity; old use celerity. ANTONYMS delay.

has·ten /'hāsən/ ▶ v. **1** move or act quickly. **2** make something happen sooner than expected.

> SYNONYMS **1 hurry**, rush, dash, race, fly, speed; informal zip, scoot, hotfoot it, hightail it. **2 speed up**, bring on, precipitate, advance. ANTONYMS dawdle, delay.

hast·y /'hāstē/ ▶ adj. (**hastier**, **hastiest**) hurried; rushed.

> SYNONYMS **hurried**, rash, impetuous, impulsive, reckless, precipitate, spur-of-the-moment. ANTONYMS considered.

■ **hast·i·ly** adv.

hat /hat/ ▶ n. a covering for the head. □ **hat-trick** three successes of the same kind, especially three successive scores by one player in a sport such as ice hockey. **keep something under your hat** keep something a secret. **take your hat off to** feel admiration for. **talk through your hat** informal talk foolishly or ignorantly.

hat·band /'hatˌband/ ▶ n. a decorative ribbon around a hat.

hatch¹ /hacH/ ▶ n. **1** a small opening in a floor, wall, or roof allowing access to an area. **2** a door in an aircraft, spacecraft, or submarine.

hatch² ▶ v. **1** (of a young bird, fish, or reptile) come out of its egg. **2** (of an egg) open and produce a young animal. **3** form a plot or plan.

hatch³ ▶ v. (in drawing) shade an area with closely drawn parallel lines.

hatch·back /'hacHˌbak/ ▶ n. a car with a door that opens upward across the full width at the back end.

hatch·et /'hacHit/ ▶ n. a small ax with a short handle. □ **bury the hatchet** end a quarrel. **hatchet-faced** informal sharp-featured and grim-looking. **hatchet job** informal a fierce spoken or written attack. **hatchet man** informal **1** a person employed to carry out disagreeable tasks. **2** a harsh critic.

hatch·ling /'hacHliNG/ ▶ n. a newly hatched young animal.

hatch·way /'hacHˌwā/ ▶ n. an opening or hatch, especially in a ship's deck.

hate /hāt/ ▶ v. (**hates**, **hating**, **hated**) feel very strong dislike for. ▶ n. **1** very strong dislike. **2** informal a disliked person or thing.

SYNONYMS ▶ v. **1 loathe**, detest, despise, dislike, abhor, shrink from, be unable to bear/stand; formal abominate. **2 be sorry**, be reluctant, be loath. ▶ n. **hatred**, loathing, abhorrence, abomination, aversion, disgust. ANTONYMS love.

hate·ful /ˈhātfəl/ ▶ adj. very unkind or unpleasant.

hath /hath/ old 3rd person singular present of **HAVE**.

ha·tred /ˈhātrid/ ▶ n. very strong dislike; hate.

SYNONYMS see **HATE** (noun).

hat·ter /ˈhatər/ ▶ n. a person who makes and sells hats.

haugh·ty /ˈhôtē/ ▶ adj. (**haughtier**, **haughtiest**) arrogant and superior toward other people. ■ **haugh·ti·ly** adv.

haul /hôl/ ▶ v. **1** pull or drag something with a lot of effort. **2** transport something in a truck or cart. ▶ n. **1** a quantity of something obtained, especially illegally. **2** a number of fish caught at one time.

SYNONYMS ▶ v. **drag**, pull, heave, lug, hump; informal schlep. ▶ n. **booty**, loot, plunder, spoils, stolen goods; informal swag.

haul·age /ˈhôlij/ ▶ n. the commercial transport of goods.

haul·er /ˈhôlər/ ▶ n. a person or company employed in the commercial transport of goods by road.

haunch /hônch, hänch/ ▶ n. **1** a person's or animal's buttock and thigh. **2** the leg and loin of an animal, as food: *Uncle Joe brought us a haunch of venison.*

haunt /hônt, hänt/ ▶ v. **1** (of a ghost) appear regularly in a place. **2** (of a person) visit a place frequently. **3** keep coming into someone's mind in a disturbing way. ▶ n. a place where a particular type of person frequently goes: *a favorite haunt of pickpockets.*

SYNONYMS ▶ v. **torment**, disturb, trouble, worry, plague, prey on. ▶ n. **meeting place**, stomping ground, stamping ground, spot, venue; informal hangout.

haunt·ed /ˈhôntid, ˈhän-/ ▶ adj. **1** visited by a ghost. **2** showing signs of mental suffering: *haunted eyes.*

SYNONYMS **1 possessed**, cursed, jinxed, eerie. **2 tormented**, anguished, tortured, obsessed, troubled, worried.

haunt·ing /ˈhôntiNG, ˈhän-/ ▶ adj. making someone feel sad or thoughtful.

SYNONYMS **evocative**, affecting, stirring, powerful, poignant, memorable.

■ **haunt·ing·ly** adv.

haute cou·ture /ˌōt ˌko͞oˈto͝or/ ▶ n. the designing and making of high-quality clothes by leading fashion houses.

haute cui·sine /ˌōt ˌkwəˈzēn/ ▶ n. high-quality cooking in the traditional French style.

hau·teur /hōˈtər/ ▶ n. proud haughtiness of manner.

have /hav/ ▶ v. (**has**, **having**, **had**) **1** possess or own. **2** experience: *have difficulty.* **3** be able to make use of: *how much time have I got?* **4** (**have to**) be obliged to; must. **5** perform an action: *he had a look around.* **6** show a personal characteristic: *he had little patience.* **7** suffer from an illness or disability. **8** cause something to be or be done: *I want to have everything ready.* **9** place, hold, or keep something in a particular position. **10** eat or drink something. **11** take or be the host of: *we're having the children for the weekend.* ▶ auxiliary v. used with a past participle to form the perfect, pluperfect, and future perfect tenses, and the conditional mood.

SYNONYMS **1 own**, be in possession of, be blessed with, boast, enjoy. **2 comprise**, consist of, contain, include, incorporate, be composed of, be made up of. **3 eat**, drink, take. **4 organize**, hold, give, throw, put on, lay on. **5** *I have to get up at six* **must**, be obliged to, be required to, be compelled to, be forced to, be bound to.

USAGE

Be careful not to write **of** when you mean **have** or **'ve**: *I could've told you that* not *I could of told you that.*

ha·ven /ˈhāvən/ ▶ n. **1** a place of safety. **2** a harbor or small port.

SYNONYMS **refuge**, retreat, shelter, sanctuary, asylum, oasis.

have·n't /ˈhavənt/ ▶ contr. have not.

hav·er·sack /ˈhavərˌsak/ ▶ n. a small, sturdy bag carried on the back or over the shoulder.

hav·oc /ˈhavək/ ▶ n. great destruction, confusion, or disorder.

SYNONYMS **chaos**, mayhem, bedlam, pandemonium, a shambles.

□ **play havoc with** completely disrupt.

haw /hô/ ▶ n. the red fruit of the hawthorn.

Ha·wai·ian /həˈwīən, -ˈwoi-ən/ ▶ n. **1** a person from Hawaii. **2** the language of Hawaii. ▶ adj. relating to Hawaii.

hawk¹ /hôk/ ▶ n. **1** a fast-flying bird of prey with a long tail. **2** a person in favor of aggressive policies in foreign affairs. The opposite of **DOVE¹**. ▶ v. hunt with a trained hawk. ■ **hawk·ish** adj.

hawk² ▶ v. offer goods for sale in the street. ■ **hawk·er** n.

hawk³ ▶ v. clear the throat noisily.

haw·ser /ˈhôzər/ ▶ n. a thick rope for mooring or towing a ship.

haw·thorn /ˈhôˌTHôrn/ ▶ n. a thorny shrub or tree with small dark red fruits called **haws**.

hay /hā/ ▶ n. grass that has been mown and dried for use as animal feed. □ **hay fever** an allergy to pollen or dust, causing sneezing and watery eyes. **make hay** (**while the sun shines**) make good use of an opportunity while it lasts.

hay·cock /ˈhāˌkäk/ ▶ n. a cone-shaped heap of hay left in the field to dry.

hay·loft /ˈhāˌlôft/ ▶ n. a loft over a stable used for storing hay or straw.

hay·stack /ˈhāˌstak/ (or **hayrick** /ˈhāˌrik/) ▶ n. a large packed pile of hay.

hay·wire /ˈhāˌwīr/ ▶ adj. informal out of control.

haz·ard /ˈhazərd/ ▶ n. **1** a danger. **2** an obstacle, such as a bunker, on a golf course. ▶ v. **1** dare to say. **2** put at risk.

SYNONYMS ▶ n. **danger**, risk, peril, menace, jeopardy, threat.

□ **hazard lights** flashing lights on a vehicle, used to warn that the vehicle is not moving or is unexpectedly slow.

haz·ard·ous /ˈhazərdəs/ ▶ **adj.** dangerous.

SYNONYMS **risky**, dangerous, unsafe, perilous, fraught with danger, high-risk; informal dicey. ANTONYMS safe.

haze /hāz/ ▶ **n. 1** a thin mist caused by fine particles of dust, water, etc. **2** a state of mental confusion: *through a haze caused by lack of sleep.*

SYNONYMS **mist**, fog, cloud, vapor.

ha·zel /ˈhāzəl/ ▶ **n. 1** a shrub or small tree that produces round nuts called **hazelnuts**. **2** a rich reddish-brown color.

ha·zy /ˈhāzē/ ▶ **adj.** (**hazier**, **haziest**) **1** covered by a haze. **2** vague or unclear: *hazy memories.*

SYNONYMS **1 misty**, foggy, smoggy, murky. **2 vague**, dim, nebulous, blurred, fuzzy.

■ **ha·zi·ly adv.**

he /hē/ ▶ **pron. 1** used to refer to a man, boy, or male animal previously mentioned or easily identified. **2** used to refer to a person or animal whose sex is not specified. □ **he-man** informal a very well-built, masculine man.

USAGE

Until recently, **he** was used to refer to any person, male or female (as in *every child needs to know that he is loved*), but many people now think that this is old-fashioned and sexist. One solution is to use **he or she**; another is to use **they**, as in *everyone needs to feel that they matter.*

head /hed/ ▶ **n. 1** the upper part of the body, containing the brain, mouth, and sense organs. **2** a person in charge. **3** the front, forward, or upper part of something: *she stood poised at the head of the stairs.* **4** a person considered as a unit: *fifty pounds per head.* **5** a particular number of cattle or sheep: *seventy head of cattle.* **6** a compact mass of leaves or flowers at the top of a stem. **7** a part of a computer or a tape or video recorder that transfers information to and from a tape or disk. **8** the source of a river or stream. **9** the foam on top of a glass of beer. **10** (**heads**) the side of a coin showing the image of a head. **11** pressure of water or steam in an enclosed space: *a good head of steam.* ▶ **adj.** chief. ▶ **v. 1** be the head of: *the mayor headed the procession.* **2** move in a particular direction. **3** (**head someone/thing off**) intercept someone or something and force them to change direction. **4** give a heading to. **5** Soccer hit the ball with the head.

SYNONYMS ▶ **n. 1 skull**, cranium; informal nut. **2 brain(s)**, brainpower, intellect, intelligence, gray matter; informal smarts. **3** *a head for business* **aptitude**, talent, gift, capacity. **4 leader**, chief, controller, governor, superintendent, commander, captain, director, manager, principal, president; informal boss. **5 front**, beginning, start, top. ▶ **adj. chief**, principal, leading, main, first, top, highest. ▶ **v. command**, control, lead, manage, direct, supervise, superintend, oversee, preside over.

□ **be banging your head against a brick wall** keep trying to do something impossible. **come to a head** reach a crisis. **go to someone's head** **1** (of alcohol) make someone slightly drunk. **2** (of success) make someone conceited. **a head for** a talent for or ability to cope with: *a head for heights.* **head first 1** with the head in front of the rest of the body: *a head-first slide into third base.* **2** without thinking sufficiently beforehand: *you run head first into situations that do not even concern you.* **head of state** the official leader of a country. **head-on 1** with the front of a vehicle. **2** involving direct confrontation. **head over heels** madly in love. **head start** an advantage gained at the beginning of something. **head-to-head** involving two parties confronting each other. **heads-up** an advance warning of something. **keep your head** remain calm. **keep your head above water** avoid falling into debt or difficulty. **lose your head** panic. **make head or tail of** understand at all. **off the top of your head** without careful thought. **over someone's head** **1** (also **above someone's head**) beyond someone's ability to understand. **2** higher up than your immediate supervisor. **turn someone's head** make someone conceited. ■ **head·less adj. head·ship n.**

head·ache /ˈhedˌāk/ ▶ **n. 1** a continuous pain in the head. **2** informal something that causes worry.

SYNONYMS **1 sore head**, migraine. **2 problem**, worry, hassle, pain in the neck, bind.

head·band /ˈhedˌband/ ▶ **n.** a band of fabric worn around the head.

head·bang·ing /ˈhedˌbaNGiNG/ ▶ **n.** violent shaking of the head to the beat of heavy metal music. ■ **head·bang·er n.** (informal).

head·board /ˈhedˌbôrd/ ▶ **n.** an upright panel at the head of a bed.

head·butt /ˈhedˌbət/ ▶ **v.** attack someone by hitting them with the head. ▶ **n.** an act of headbutting.

head·count /ˈhedˌkount/ ▶ **n.** a count of the number of people present.

head·dress /ˈhedˌdres/ ▶ **n.** a decorative covering for the head.

head·er /ˈhedər/ ▶ **n. 1** Soccer a shot or pass made with the head. **2** a line of writing at the top of each page of a book or document.

head·gear /ˈhedˌgi(ə)r/ ▶ **n.** items worn on the head.

head·hunt /ˈhedˌhənt/ ▶ **v.** approach someone already employed elsewhere to fill a vacant post.

head·ing /ˈhediNG/ ▶ **n. 1** a title at the head of a page or section of a book. **2** a direction or bearing.

SYNONYMS **title**, caption, legend, rubric, headline.

head·land /ˈhedlənd, ˈhedˌland/ ▶ **n.** a narrow piece of land that sticks out into the sea.

head·light /ˈhedˌlīt/ (or **headlamp** /ˈhedˌlamp/) ▶ **n.** a powerful light at the front of a motor vehicle.

head·line /ˈhedˌlīn/ ▶ **n. 1** a heading at the top of a newspaper or magazine article. **2** (**the headlines**) a summary of the most important items of news. ▶ **v.** (**headlines**, **headlining**, **headlined**) **1** give an article a headline. **2** appear as the star performer at a concert.

head·lin·er /ˈhedˌlīnər/ ▶ **n.** a performer or act that is promoted as the star attraction on a program or advertisement.

head·lock /ˈhedˌläk/ ▶ **n.** a method of restraining someone by holding an arm firmly around their head.

head·long /ˈhedˌlôNG, -ˌläNG/ ▶ **adv. & adj. 1** with the head first. **2** in a rush.

SYNONYMS **1 head first**, on your head. **2 without thinking**, precipitously, impetuously, rashly, recklessly, hastily. **3 breakneck**, whirlwind, reckless, precipitous. ANTONYMS cautiously.

head·man /ˈhedmən/ ▶ **n.** (plural **headmen**) the leader of a tribe.

head·mas·ter /ˈhed,mastər/ (or **headmistress**) ▶ **n.** (especially in private schools) a teacher in charge of a school.

head·phones /ˈhed,fōnz/ ▶ **pl.n.** a pair of earphones joined by a band placed over the head.

head·piece /ˈhed,pēs/ ▶ **n.** a device worn on the head.

head·quar·ters /ˈhed,kwôrtərz/ ▶ **n.** the place from which an organization or military operation is directed.

SYNONYMS **head office**, HQ, base, nerve center, mission control.

head·rest /ˈhed,rest/ ▶ **n.** a padded support for the head on the back of a seat.

head·room /ˈhed,ro͞om, -,ro͝om/ ▶ **n.** the space between the top of a vehicle or a person's head and the ceiling or other structure above.

head·scarf /ˈhed,skärf/ ▶ **n.** (plural **headscarves** /-,skärvz/) a square of fabric worn as a covering for the head.

head·set /ˈhed,set/ ▶ **n.** a set of headphones with a microphone attached.

head·shot /ˈhed,sʜät/ ▶ **n. 1** a photograph of a person's head. **2** a bullet or gunshot aimed at the head.

head·stone /ˈhed,stōn/ ▶ **n.** a stone slab set up at the head of a grave.

head·strong /ˈhed,strôɴɢ/ ▶ **adj.** very independent and determined to have your own way.

SYNONYMS **willful**, strong-willed, stubborn, obstinate, obdurate; contrary, perverse, wayward.

head·wa·ter /ˈhed,wôtər, -,wätər/ ▶ **n.** a stream of a river close to its source.

head·way /ˈhed,wā/ ▶ **n.** (**make headway**) make progress.

head·wind /ˈhed,wind/ ▶ **n.** a wind blowing from directly in front, toward someone or something.

head·word /ˈhed,wərd/ ▶ **n.** a word that begins a separate entry in a dictionary or encyclopedia.

head·y /ˈhedē/ ▶ **adj.** (**headier**, **headiest**) **1** having a strong or exciting effect: *a heady, exotic perfume.* **2** (of an alcoholic drink) strong.

SYNONYMS **1 potent**, intoxicating, strong. **2 exhilarating**, exciting, stimulating, thrilling, intoxicating.

heal /hēl/ ▶ **v. 1** make or become healthy again. **2** put right: *heal a rift.*

SYNONYMS **1 cure**, make better, restore to health, treat. **2 get better**, be cured, recover, recuperate, mend, be on the mend. **3 put right**, repair, resolve, reconcile, settle; informal patch up.

■ **heal·er n.**

health /helтн/ ▶ **n. 1** the state of being free from illness or injury. **2** a person's mental or physical condition.

SYNONYMS **1 well-being**, fitness, good condition, strength, robustness, vigor. **2** *her poor health forced her to retire* **condition**, state of health, physical shape, constitution. ANTONYMS illness.

□ **health center** an establishment housing local medical services or the practice of a group of doctors. **health club** a private club where exercise facilities and health and beauty treatments are available. **health food** natural food that is believed to be good for your health.

health·care /ˈhelтн,ke(ə)r/ ▶ **n.** the maintenance and improvement of physical and mental health.

health·ful /ˈhelтнfəl/ ▶ **adj.** good for the health.

health·y /ˈhelтнē/ ▶ **adj.** (**healthier**, **healthiest**) **1** in good health, or helping toward good health. **2** normal, sensible, or desirable: *a healthy balance.* **3** of a very satisfactory size or amount: *a healthy profit.*

SYNONYMS **1 well**, fit, in good shape, in fine fettle, in tip-top condition, strong, fighting fit; informal in the pink. **2 wholesome**, good for you, health-giving, nutritious, nourishing, invigorating, sanitary, hygienic.

■ **health·i·ly adv.**

heap /hēp/ ▶ **n. 1** a pile of a substance or of a number of objects. **2** informal a large amount or number: *heaps of room.* **3** informal an old vehicle in bad condition. ▶ **v. 1** put in or form a heap. **2** (**heap something with**) load something heavily with. **3** (**heap something on**) give a lot of praise, criticism, etc., to: *the press heaped abuse on him.*

SYNONYMS ▶ **n. pile**, stack, mound, mountain. ▶ **v. pile (up)**, stack (up), make a mound of.

hear /hi(ə)r/ ▶ **v.** (**hears**, **hearing**, **heard**) **1** be aware of a sound with the ears. **2** be told of. **3** (**have heard of**) be aware of the existence of. **4** (**hear from**) receive a letter, phone call, or email from. **5** listen to. **6** listen to and judge a case in a court of law.

SYNONYMS **1 make out**, catch, get, perceive, overhear. **2 learn**, find out, discover, gather, glean. **3 try**, judge, adjudicate on.

□ **hear! hear!** used to show agreement with something said in a speech. **will** (or **would**) **not hear of** will (or would) not allow or agree to.

■ **hear·er n.**

hear·ing /ˈhi(ə)rɪɴɢ/ ▶ **n. 1** the ability to hear sounds. **2** the range within that sounds can be heard. **3** an opportunity to state your case: *a fair hearing.* **4** an act of listening to evidence.

SYNONYMS **1 earshot**, hearing distance. **2 trial**, court case, inquiry, inquest, tribunal.

□ **hearing aid** a small device worn by a partially deaf person to make them hear better.

heark·en /ˈhärkən/ (or **harken**) ▶ **v.** (usu. **hearken to**) old use listen.

hear·say /ˈhi(ə)r,sā/ ▶ **n.** information received from other people that is possibly unreliable.

hearse /hərs/ ▶ **n.** a vehicle for carrying the coffin to a funeral.

heart /härt/ ▶ **n. 1** the organ in the chest that pumps the blood around the body. **2** the central or innermost part of something: *the heart of the city.* **3** a person's ability to feel love or compassion. **4** mood or feeling: *a change of heart.* **5** courage or enthusiasm. **6** (**hearts**) one of the four suits in a pack of playing cards, represented by a red figure similar in shape to a heart (the body organ).

SYNONYMS **1 emotions**, feelings, sentiments, soul, mind. **2 compassion**, sympathy, humanity, fellow feeling(s), empathy, understanding, soul, goodwill. **3 enthusiasm**, spirit, determination, resolve, nerve. **4 center**, middle, hub, core. **5 essence**, crux, core, nub, root, meat, substance, kernel; informal nitty-gritty.

□ **after your own heart** sharing your tastes. **at heart** in your real nature. **break someone's heart** make someone deeply sad. **by heart** from memory. **close** (or **dear**) **to your heart** very important to you. **from the** (or **the bottom of your**) **heart** with sincere feeling. **have a heart** be merciful. **have a heart of gold** have a very kind nature. **have your heart in your mouth** be greatly alarmed or anxious. **have your heart in the right place** be well-intentioned. **heart attack** a sudden failure of the heart to work properly. **heart failure** severe failure of the heart to function properly. **heart-rending** very sad or upsetting. **heart-searching** thorough examination of your feelings and motives. **heart-to-heart** (of a conversation) very intimate and personal. **your heart's desire** something that you greatly wish for. **in your heart of hearts** in your innermost feelings. **take to heart** be greatly affected by criticism. **tug** (or **pull**) **at the heartstrings** arouse deep compassion or love. **wear your heart on your sleeve** show your feelings openly.

heart·ache /ˈhärtˌāk/ ▶ **n.** emotional suffering or grief.

SYNONYMS **anguish**, suffering, distress, unhappiness, grief, misery, sorrow, sadness, heartbreak, pain, hurt, woe. ANTONYMS happiness.

heart·beat /ˈhärtˌbēt/ ▶ **n. 1** a pulsation of the heart. **2** a very brief moment of time: *I'd go there in a heartbeat.* □ **a heartbeat away** very close.

heart·break /ˈhärtˌbrāk/ ▶ **n.** overwhelming distress.

heart·break·ing /ˈhärtˌbrākiNG/ ▶ **adj.** causing overwhelming distress.

SYNONYMS **distressing**, upsetting, disturbing, heart-rending, tragic, painful, sad, agonizing, harrowing. ANTONYMS comforting.

heart·bro·ken /ˈhärtˌbrōkən/ ▶ **adj.** suffering from overwhelming distress.

SYNONYMS **anguished**, devastated, broken-hearted, heavy-hearted, grieving, grief-stricken, inconsolable, crushed, shattered, desolate, despairing; miserable, sorrowful, sad, despondent.

heart·burn /ˈhärtˌbərn/ ▶ **n.** a form of indigestion felt as a burning sensation in the chest.

heart·en /ˈhärtn/ ▶ **v.** make more cheerful or confident. ■ **heart·en·ing adj.**

heart·felt /ˈhärtˌfelt/ ▶ **adj.** deeply and strongly felt.

SYNONYMS **sincere**, genuine, from the heart, earnest, profound, deep, wholehearted, honest. ANTONYMS insincere.

hearth /härTH/ ▶ **n.** the floor or surround of a fireplace.

hearth·rug /ˈhärTHˌrəg/ ▶ **n.** a rug laid in front of a fireplace.

heart·i·ly /ˈhärtl-ē/ ▶ **adv. 1** in a hearty way. **2** very: *heartily sick of them.*

SYNONYMS **1 wholeheartedly**, warmly, profoundly, eagerly, enthusiastically. **2 thoroughly**, completely, absolutely, exceedingly, downright, quite; informal seriously, real, mighty.

heart·land /ˈhärtˌland/ ▶ **n.** the central or most important part of a country or area.

heart·less /ˈhärtlis/ ▶ **adj.** feeling no pity for other people.

SYNONYMS **unfeeling**, unsympathetic, unkind, uncaring, hard-hearted, cold, callous, cruel, merciless, pitiless, inhuman. ANTONYMS compassionate.

heart·throb /ˈhärtˌTHräb/ ▶ **n.** informal a good-looking man, typically a celebrity.

heart·warm·ing /ˈhärtˌwôrmiNG/ ▶ **adj.** emotionally rewarding or uplifting.

SYNONYMS **touching**, heartening, stirring, uplifting, cheering, gratifying. ANTONYMS distressing.

heart·wood /ˈhärtˌwo͝od/ ▶ **n.** the dense inner part of a tree trunk, where the hardest wood is to be found.

heart·y /ˈhärtē/ ▶ **adj.** (**heartier**, **heartiest**) **1** enthusiastic and friendly. **2** strong and healthy. **3** heartfelt: *hearty congratulations.* **4** (of a meal) large and filling.

SYNONYMS **1 exuberant**, jovial, ebullient, cheerful, lively, loud, animated, vivacious, energetic, spirited. **2 wholehearted**, heartfelt, sincere, genuine, real. **3 robust**, healthy, hardy, fit, vigorous, sturdy, strong. **4 substantial**, large, ample, satisfying, filling, generous.

heat /hēt/ ▶ **n. 1** the quality of being hot. **2** hot weather or high temperature. **3** strength of feeling. **4** (**the heat**) informal pressure to do or achieve something. **5** one of a series of races or contests held to decide who will take part in the next stage of a competition. ▶ **v. 1** make or become hot or warm. **2** (**heat up**) become more intense and exciting. **3** (**heated**) passionate: *a heated argument.*

SYNONYMS ▶ **n. 1 warmth**, hotness, high temperature. **2 passion**, intensity, vehemence, fervor, excitement, agitation, anger. ANTONYMS cold, apathy. ▶ **v. 1 warm** (**up**), reheat, cook, keep warm, microwave. **2 get hot**, get warm, warm up, nuke. **3** (**heated**) **vehement**, passionate, impassioned, animated, lively, acrimonious, angry, bitter, furious, fierce. **4** (**heated**) **excited**, animated, worked up, fired up, wound up, keyed up; informal het up. ANTONYMS cool.

□ **heat-seeking** (of a missile) able to detect and home in on heat sent out by a target. **heat wave** a period of abnormally hot weather. **in heat** (of a female mammal) ready for mating. **in the heat of the moment** while temporarily angry or excited and without stopping for thought. ■ **heat·ed·ly adv.**

heat·er /ˈhētər/ ▶ **n.** a device for heating something.

heath /hēTH/ ▶ **n.** (especially in Great Britain) an area of open uncultivated land covered with heather, gorse, and coarse grasses.

hea·then /ˈhēT͟Hən/ ▶ **n.** old use a person who does not belong to a widely held religion.

heath·er /ˈheT͟Hər/ ▶ **n.** a shrub with small purple flowers, found on moors and heaths.

heat·ing /ˈhētiNG/ ▶ **n.** equipment used to provide heat.

heat·stroke /ˈhētˌstrōk/ ▶ **n.** a feverish condition caused by being exposed to very high temperatures.

heave /hēv/ ▶ **v.** (**heaves**, **heaving**, **heaved** or chiefly Nautical **hove** /hōv/) **1** lift or move with great effort. **2** produce a sigh noisily. **3** rise and fall: *his shoulders heaved.* **4** try to vomit. **5** (**heave to**) Nautical come to a stop.

SYNONYMS **1 haul**, pull, drag, tug; informal yank. **2 throw**, fling, cast, hurl, lob, pitch; informal chuck, sling. **3 let out**, breathe, give, emit, utter. **4 rise and fall**, roll, swell, surge, churn, seethe. **5 retch**, vomit, cough up, be/get sick; informal throw up, puke, barf, upchuck, hurl, spew.

□ **heave in sight** (or **into view**) Nautical come into view. **the heave-ho** dismissal from a job.

heav·en /ˈhevən/ ▶ **n. 1** (in Christianity and some other religions) the place where God or the gods live and where good people go when they die. **2** (**the heavens**) literary the sky. **3** a place or state of great happiness.

SYNONYMS **1 paradise**, the hereafter, the next world, the afterworld, nirvana, Zion, Elysium, Valhalla. **2 bliss**, ecstasy, rapture, contentment, happiness, delight, joy, paradise. ANTONYMS hell.

□ **the heavens open** it suddenly starts to rain heavily. **heaven-sent** occurring at a very favorable time. **in seventh heaven** very happy. **move heaven and earth to do** make extraordinary efforts to do.

heav·en·ly /ˈhevənlē/ ▶ **adj. 1** having to do with heaven. **2** having to do with the sky. **3** informal wonderful.

SYNONYMS **1 divine**, angelic, holy, celestial. **2 celestial**, cosmic, stellar, sidereal. **3 delightful**, wonderful, glorious, sublime, exquisite, beautiful, lovely, gorgeous, enchanting; informal divine, super, fantastic, fabulous.

□ **heavenly body** a planet, star, etc. **heavenly host** a literary or biblical term for the angels.

heav·i·ly /ˈhevəlē/ ▶ **adv. 1** slowly and laboriously. **2** decisively. **3** to excess. **4** to a considerable degree. **5** densely.

SYNONYMS **1 laboriously**, slowly, ponderously, awkwardly, clumsily. **2 decisively**, conclusively, roundly, soundly, utterly, completely, thoroughly. **3 excessively**, immoderately, copiously, intemperately. **4 densely**, closely, thickly. **5 deeply**, extremely, greatly, exceedingly, tremendously, profoundly.

heav·y /ˈhevē/ ▶ **adj.** (**heavier**, **heaviest**) **1** of great weight. **2** thick or dense. **3** of more than the usual size, amount, or force. **4** hard or forceful: *a heavy blow.* **5** needing a lot of physical effort. **6** informal very important or serious. **7** (of music) having a strong bass part and a forceful rhythm. ▶ **n.** (plural **heavies**) informal **1** a large, strong man. **2** a villainous role or actor in a book, movie, etc. **3** an important person.

SYNONYMS ▶ **adj. 1 weighty**, hefty, substantial, ponderous, solid, dense, cumbersome, unwieldy. **2 forceful**, hard, strong, violent, powerful, mighty, sharp, severe. **3 strenuous**, hard, physical, difficult, arduous, demanding, back-breaking, grueling. **4 intense**, fierce, relentless, severe, serious. **5 substantial**, filling, stodgy, rich, big. ANTONYMS light.

□ **heavy-duty** designed to withstand a lot of use or wear. **heavy going** a person or situation that is difficult or boring to deal with. **heavy-handed** clumsy, insensitive, or overly forceful. **heavy industry** large-scale production of large, heavy articles and materials. **heavy metal** very loud, forceful rock music. ■ **heav·i·ness n.**

heav·y·weight /ˈhevēˌwāt/ ▶ **n. 1** the heaviest weight in boxing. **2** informal an influential person.

He·bra·ic /hēˈbrāik/ ▶ **adj.** having to do with the Hebrew language or people.

He·brew /ˈhēbro͞o/ ▶ **n. 1** a member of an ancient people living in what is now Israel and Palestine. **2** the language of the Hebrews, in its ancient or modern form.

heck /hek/ ▶ **exclam.** used for emphasis, or to express surprise, annoyance, etc.

heck·le /ˈhekəl/ ▶ **v.** (**heckles**, **heckling**, **heckled**) interrupt a public speaker with comments or abuse. ■ **heck·ler n.**

hec·tare /ˈhekˌte(ə)r/ ▶ **n.** a unit of area equal to 100 ares (2.471 acres or 10,000 square meters).

hec·tic /ˈhektik/ ▶ **adj.** full of frantic activity.

SYNONYMS **frantic**, frenetic, frenzied, feverish, manic, busy, active, fast and furious. ANTONYMS leisurely.

■ **hec·ti·cal·ly adv.**

hec·to·gram /ˈhektəˌgram/ ▶ **n.** a unit of mass equal to one hundred grams.

hec·tor /ˈhektər/ ▶ **v.** talk to someone in a bullying way.

he'd /hēd/ ▶ **contr. 1** he had. **2** he would.

hedge /hej/ ▶ **n.** a fence formed by bushes growing closely together. ▶ **v.** (**hedges**, **hedging**, **hedged**) **1** surround with a hedge. **2** avoid making a definite statement or decision. □ **hedge your bets** avoid committing yourself.

hedge·hog /ˈhejˌhôg, -ˌhäg/ ▶ **n.** a small animal with a spiny coat, which can roll itself into a ball for defense.

hedge·row /ˈhejˌrō/ ▶ **n.** a hedge of wild shrubs and trees bordering a field.

hedg·ing /ˈhejiNG/ ▶ **n. 1** the planting or trimming of hedges. **2** bushes and shrubs planted to form hedges.

he·don·ism /ˈhēdnˌizəm/ ▶ **n.** behavior based on the belief that pleasure is the most important thing in life. ■ **he·don·ist n. he·don·is·tic** /ˌhēdnˈistik/ **adj.**

hee·bie-jee·bies /ˈhēbē ˈjēbēz/ ▶ **pl.n.** (**the heebie-jeebies**) informal a state of nervous fear or anxiety.

heed /hēd/ ▶ **v.** pay attention to. ▶ **n.** attention.

SYNONYMS ▶ **v. pay attention to**, take notice of, take note of, listen to, consider, take to heart, take into account, obey, adhere to, abide by, observe. ANTONYMS disregard. ▶ **n. attention**, notice, note, regard, thought.

□ **pay** (or **take**) **heed** pay careful attention.

heed·less /ˈhēdlis/ ▶ **adj.** showing a reckless lack of care or attention.

hee-haw /ˈhē ˌhô/ ▶ **n.** the loud, harsh cry of a donkey or mule; bray.

heel¹ /hēl/ ▶ **n.** **1** the back part of the foot below the ankle. **2** the part of a shoe or boot supporting the heel. **3** informal an inconsiderate or untrustworthy person. ▶ **v.** renew the heel on a shoe. □ **bring someone to heel** bring someone under control. **cool your heels** be kept waiting. **take to your heels** run away. **turn** (**on your**) **heel** turn sharply.

heel² ▶ **v.** (of a ship) lean over to one side.

heft /heft/ ▶ **v.** lift or carry something heavy.

heft·y /'heftē/ ▶ **adj.** (**heftier**, **heftiest**) **1** large, heavy, and powerful. **2** (of a number or amount) considerable.

> SYNONYMS **1 burly**, sturdy, strapping, bulky, strong, muscular, big, solid, well-built; informal hulking, beefy. **2 powerful**, violent, hard, forceful, mighty. **3 substantial**, sizable, considerable, stiff, large, heavy; informal whopping. ANTONYMS light.

he·gem·o·ny /hə'jemənē, 'hejə,mōnē/ ▶ **n.** formal leadership or dominance.

He·gi·ra /hi'jīrə, 'hejərə/ (or **Hejira**) ▶ **n.** **1** Muhammad's departure from Mecca to Medina in AD 622, marking the consolidation of the first Muslim community. **2** the Muslim era reckoned from this date.

heif·er /'hefər/ ▶ **n.** a young cow.

heigh-ho /hī-hō, hā-hō/ ▶ **exclam.** informal expressing boredom, resignation, or cheerfulness.

height /hīt/ ▶ **n.** **1** measurement from head to foot or from base to top. **2** distance above sea level or the ground. **3** the quality of being tall or high. **4** a high place. **5** the most intense or extreme part: *the height of the attack*.

> SYNONYMS **1 tallness**, stature, elevation, altitude. **2** *mountain heights* **summit**, top, peak, crest, crown, tip, cap, pinnacle. **3** *the height of their fame* **highest point**, peak, zenith, pinnacle, climax. ANTONYMS width, nadir.

height·en /'hītn/ ▶ **v.** **1** make or become more intense. **2** make higher.

> SYNONYMS **intensify**, increase, enhance, add to, augment, boost, strengthen, deepen, magnify, reinforce. ANTONYMS reduce.

hei·nous /'hānəs/ ▶ **adj.** very wicked: *a heinous crime*.

> SYNONYMS **odious**, wicked, evil, atrocious, monstrous, abominable, detestable, despicable, horrific, terrible, awful, abhorrent, loathsome, hideous, unspeakable, execrable. ANTONYMS admirable.

heir /e(ə)r/ ▶ **n.** **1** a person who will inherit the property or rank of another when that person dies. **2** a person who continues someone else's work.

> SYNONYMS **successor**, next in line, inheritor, beneficiary, legatee.

□ **heir apparent** (plural **heirs apparent**) **1** an heir whose rights cannot be taken away by the birth of another heir. **2** someone who is most likely to take the job or role of another person. **heir presumptive** (plural **heirs presumptive**) an heir whose claim may be set aside by the birth of another heir.

heir·ess /'e(ə)ris/ ▶ **n.** a female heir.

> SYNONYMS **successor**, next in line, inheritor, beneficiary, legatee.

heir·loom /'e(ə)r,lo͞om/ ▶ **n.** a valuable object that has belonged to a family for several generations.

heist /hīst/ ▶ **n.** informal a robbery.

held /held/ past and past participle of **HOLD**.

hel·i·cal /'helikəl, 'hē-/ ▶ **adj.** in the shape of a helix.

hel·i·ces /'hēlə,sēz/ plural of **HELIX**.

hel·i·cop·ter /'heli,käptər/ ▶ **n.** a type of aircraft that is powered and lifted by horizontally revolving blades.

he·li·o·graph /'hēlēə,graf/ ▶ **n.** a device that reflects sunlight in flashes from a movable mirror, used to send signals.

hel·i·pad /'helə,pad/ ▶ **n.** a landing and takeoff area for helicopters.

hel·i·port /'helə,pôrt/ ▶ **n.** an airport or landing place for helicopters.

he·li·um /'hēlēəm/ ▶ **n.** a light colorless gas that does not burn.

he·lix /'hēliks/ ▶ **n.** (plural **helices** /'hēlə,sēz/) an object in the shape of a spiral.

hell /hel/ ▶ **n.** **1** (in Christianity and some other religions) a place of evil and suffering where wicked people are sent after death. **2** a state or place of great suffering.

> SYNONYMS **1 the underworld**, the netherworld, eternal damnation, perdition, hellfire, fire and brimstone, the Inferno, Hades. **2 misery**, torture, agony, purgatory, torment, a nightmare. ANTONYMS heaven, bliss.

□ **all hell breaks loose** informal suddenly there is chaos. **come hell or high water** whatever difficulties may occur. **for the hell of it** informal just for fun. **hell-bent** determined to achieve something. **hell** (or **hell-bent**) **for leather** as fast as possible. **like hell** informal very fast, much, hard, etc. **not a hope in hell** informal no chance at all. **raise hell** informal create havoc or cause damage. **there will be hell to pay** informal serious trouble will result. **until hell freezes over** forever.

he'll /hēl/ ▶ **contr.** **1** he shall. **2** he will.

Hel·len·ic /he'lenik/ ▶ **adj.** Greek.

Hel·len·ism /'helə,nizəm/ ▶ **n.** **1** the national character or culture of Greece. **2** the study or imitation of ancient Greek culture.

Hel·len·is·tic /,helə'nistik/ ▶ **adj.** having to do with Greek culture from the death of Alexander the Great (323 BC) to the defeat of Cleopatra and Mark Antony by Octavian in 31 BC.

hell·fire /'hel,fīr/ ▶ **n.** the fire regarded as existing in hell.

hell·hole /'hel,hōl/ ▶ **n.** a very unpleasant place.

hell·ish /'helisʜ/ ▶ **adj.** informal very difficult or unpleasant. ■ **hell·ish·ly** **adv.**

hel·lo /hə'lō, he'lō, 'helō/ ▶ **exclam.** **1** used as a greeting. **2** used to attract someone's attention.

hell·rais·er /'hel,rāzər/ ▶ **n.** a person who causes trouble by drunken or outrageous behavior.

helm /helm/ ▶ **n.** **1** a wheel or tiller for steering a ship or boat. **2** (**the helm**) the position of leader.

hel·met /'helmit/ ▶ **n.** a hard or padded protective hat.

helms·man /'helmzmən/ ▶ **n.** (plural **helmsmen**) a person who steers a boat.

hel·ot /'helət/ ▶ **n.** a member of a class in ancient Sparta, having a status in between slaves and citizens.

help /help/ ▶ **v.** **1** make it easier for someone to do something. **2** improve a situation or problem. **3** (**help yourself**) take something without asking for it first. **4** (**cannot help**) be unable to stop yourself doing. **5** (**help someone to**) serve someone with food or drink. ▶ **n.** a person or thing that helps someone.

> SYNONYMS ▶ **v.** **1** **assist**, aid, abet, lend a hand, give assistance, come to the aid of, be of service, do someone a favor, do someone a service, do someone a good turn, rally around, pitch in. **2** **support**, contribute to, give money to, donate to, promote, boost, back. **3** **relieve**, soothe, ease, alleviate, improve, lessen. **4** *he could not help laughing* **resist**, avoid, refrain from, keep from, stop. ANTONYMS hinder, impede. ▶ **n.** **1** **assistance**, aid, support, succor, benefit, use, advantage, service. **2** **relief**, alleviation, improvement, healing. ANTONYMS hindrance.

□ **so help me** (**God**) used to emphasize that you mean what you are saying.

help·er /'helpər/ ▶ **n.** a person who helps.

> SYNONYMS **assistant**, aide, deputy, auxiliary, supporter, second, mate, right-hand man/woman, man/girl Friday, attendant; informal gal Friday.

help·ful /'helpfəl/ ▶ **adj.** **1** ready to give help. **2** useful.

> SYNONYMS **1** **obliging**, of assistance, supportive, accommodating, cooperative, neighborly, eager to please. **2** **useful**, beneficial, valuable, constructive, informative, instructive. **3** **handy**, useful, convenient, practical, easy-to-use, serviceable; informal neat, nifty. ANTONYMS useless.

■ **help·ful·ly** **adv.**

help·ing /'helpiNG/ ▶ **n.** a portion of food served to one person at one time.

> SYNONYMS **portion**, serving, piece, slice, share, plateful; informal dollop.

help·less /'helplis/ ▶ **adj.** **1** unable to defend yourself or to act without help. **2** uncontrollable: *helpless laughter*.

> SYNONYMS **dependent**, incapable, powerless, paralyzed, defenseless, vulnerable, exposed, unprotected. ANTONYMS independent.

■ **help·less·ly** **adv.**

help·line /'help,līn/ ▶ **n.** a telephone service providing help with problems.

help·mate /'help,māt/ (or **helpmeet** /-,mēt/) ▶ **n.** a helpful companion.

hel·ter-skel·ter /'heltər 'skeltər/ ▶ **adj. & adv.** in a hasty and confused or disorganized way.

hem /hem/ ▶ **n.** the edge of a piece of cloth or clothing that has been turned under and sewn. ▶ **v.** (**hems**, **hemming**, **hemmed**) **1** give something a hem. **2** (**hem someone/thing in**) surround someone or something and restrict their movement.

he·ma·tite /'hēmə,tīt/ ▶ **n.** a reddish-black mineral consisting of ferric oxide.

he·ma·tol·o·gy /,hēmə'täləjē/ ▶ **n.** the branch of medicine concerned with the blood.

hem·i·sphere /'hemə,sfi(ə)r/ ▶ **n.** **1** a half of a sphere. **2** a half of the earth. ■ **hem·i·spher·i·cal** /,hemə'sfi(ə)rikəl, -'sferikəl/ **adj.**

hem·line /'hem,līn/ ▶ **n.** the level of the lower edge of a garment such as skirt or coat.

hem·lock /'hem,läk/ ▶ **n.** a poison made from a plant with small white flowers.

he·mo·glo·bin /'hēmə,glōbin/ ▶ **n.** a red protein in the blood that carries oxygen.

he·mo·phil·i·a /,hēmə'filēə/ ▶ **n.** a condition in which the ability of the blood to clot is reduced, causing severe bleeding from even a slight injury. ■ **he·mo·phil·i·ac** /,hēmə'filē,ak/ **n.**

hem·or·rhage /'hem(ə)rij/ ▶ **n.** an escape of blood from a burst blood vessel. ▶ **v.** (**hemorrhages**, **hemorrhaging**, **hemorrhaged**) have a hemorrhage.

hem·or·rhoid /'hem(ə),roid/ ▶ **n.** a swollen vein in the region of the anus.

hemp /hemp/ ▶ **n.** **1** the cannabis plant, the fiber of which is used to make rope, fabrics, etc. **2** the drug cannabis.

hen /hen/ ▶ **n.** a female bird, especially of a domestic fowl. □ **hen party** informal a social gathering of women.

hence /hens/ ▶ **adv.** **1** for this reason. **2** from now.

> SYNONYMS **consequently**, as a consequence, for this reason, therefore, so, accordingly, as a result, that being so.

hence·forth /'hens,fôrTH/ (or **henceforward**) ▶ **adv.** from this time on.

hench·man /'hencHmən/ ▶ **n.** (plural **henchmen**) chiefly disapproving a faithful follower or assistant, especially one prepared to engage in crime or dishonest practices by way of service.

henge /henj/ ▶ **n.** a prehistoric monument consisting of a circle of stone or wooden uprights.

hen·na /'henə/ ▶ **n.** a reddish-brown dye made from the powdered leaves of a tropical shrub. ■ **hen·naed** /'henəd/ **adj.**

hen·pecked /'hen,pekt/ ▶ **adj.** (of a man) continually nagged or criticized by his wife.

hen·ry /'henrē/ ▶ **n.** (plural **henries** or **henrys**) the basic unit of inductance.

he·pat·ic /hə'patik/ ▶ **adj.** having to do with the liver.

hep·a·ti·tis /,hepə'titis/ ▶ **n.** a serious disease of the liver, mainly transmitted by viruses.

hep·ta·gon /'heptə,gän/ ▶ **n.** a figure with seven straight sides and angles.

hep·tath·lon /hep'taTH,län/ ▶ **n.** an athletic contest that consists of seven separate events. ■ **hep·tath·lete** **n.**

her /hər/ ▶ **pron.** used as the object of a verb or preposition to refer to a female person or animal previously mentioned. ▶ **possessive determiner** belonging to or associated with a female person or animal previously mentioned.

her·ald /'herəld/ ▶ **n.** **1** (in the past) a person who carried official messages and supervised tournaments. **2** a sign that something is about to happen or arrive. ▶ **v.** **1** be a sign that something is about to happen or arrive. **2** describe in enthusiastic terms.

> SYNONYMS ▶ **n.** **harbinger**, sign, indicator, signal, portent, omen; literary foretoken. ▶ **v.** **1** *shouts heralded their approach* **proclaim**, announce, broadcast, publicize, declare, advertise. **2** *the speech heralded a policy change* **signal**, indicate, announce, usher in, pave the way for, be a harbinger of; literary foretoken, betoken.

he·ral·dic /hə'raldik/ ▶ **adj.** having to do with heraldry.

her·ald·ry /'herəldrē/ ▶ **n.** the system by which coats of arms are organized and controlled.

herb /(h)ərb/ ▶ **n. 1** a plant used for flavoring food or in medicine. **2** Botany a plant that dies down to the ground after flowering.

her·ba·ceous /(h)ər'bāsHəs/ ▶ **adj.** relating to herbs (in the botanical sense). □ **herbaceous border** a garden border containing plants that flower every year.

herb·age /'(h)ərbij/ ▶ **n.** herbaceous plants.

herb·al /'(h)ərbəl/ ▶ **adj.** relating to or made from herbs. ▶ **n.** a book that describes herbs and their culinary and medicinal properties.

her·bal·ism /'(h)ərbə,lizəm/ ▶ **n.** the use of plants in medicine and cooking. ■ **herb·al·ist n.**

her·bar·i·um /(h)ər'be(ə)rēəm/ ▶ **n.** (plural **herbariums** or **herbaria** /-rēə/) an ordered collection of dried plants.

herb·i·cide /'(h)ərbə,sīd/ ▶ **n.** a substance used to destroy unwanted plants.

her·biv·ore /'(h)ərbə,vôr/ ▶ **n.** an animal that feeds on plants. ■ **her·biv·o·rous** /(h)ər'biv(ə)rəs/ **adj.**

Her·cu·le·an /,hərkyə'lēən, hər'kyo͞olēən/ ▶ **adj.** needing great strength or effort: *a Herculean task.*

herd /hərd/ ▶ **n. 1** a large group of animals that live or are kept together. **2** disapproving a large group of people. ▶ **v.** make animals or people move in a large group.

SYNONYMS ▶ **n. drove**, flock, pack, fold, swarm, mass, crowd, horde.

herds·man /'hərdzmən/ ▶ **n.** (plural **herdsmen**) the owner or keeper of a herd of animals.

here /hi(ə)r/ ▶ **adv.** in, at, or to this place or position. □ **here and now** at the present time. **here and there** in various places. **here goes** said when you are about to start something difficult or exciting. **here's to** used to wish health or success before drinking. **neither here nor there** of no importance.

here·a·bouts /'hirə,bouts/ (or **hereabout**) ▶ **adv.** near this place.

here·af·ter /hi(ə)r'aftər/ ▶ **adv.** formal **1** from now on or at some time in the future. **2** after death. ▶ **n.** (**the hereafter**) life after death.

here·by /,hi(ə)r'bī, 'hi(ə)r,bī/ ▶ **adv.** formal as a result of this.

he·red·i·tar·y /hə'redi,terē/ ▶ **adj. 1** passed on by parents to their children or young. **2** having to do with inheritance.

SYNONYMS **1 genetic**, inborn, inherited, inbred, innate, in the family, in the blood, in the genes. **2 inherited**, bequeathed, handed down, passed down, family, ancestral.

he·red·i·ty /hə'reditē/ ▶ **n. 1** the passing on of characteristics from one generation to another. **2** the inheriting of a title, office, etc.

here·in /,hi(ə)r'in/ ▶ **adv.** formal in this document, book, or matter.

here·of /,hi(ə)r'əv/ ▶ **adv.** formal of this document.

her·e·sy /'herəsē/ ▶ **n.** (plural **heresies**) **1** belief that goes against traditional religious teachings. **2** opinion that is very different from what is generally accepted.

her·e·tic /'herətik/ ▶ **n.** a person who is guilty of heresy. ■ **he·ret·i·cal** /hə'retikəl/ **adj.**

here·to /,hi(ə)r'to͞o/ ▶ **adv.** formal to this matter or document.

here·to·fore /'hi(ə)rtə,fôr/ ▶ **adv.** formal before now.

here·up·on /,hi(ə)rə'pän/ ▶ **adv.** old use after or as a result of this.

here·with /,hir'wiTH, -'wiTH/ ▶ **adv.** formal with this.

her·it·a·ble /'heritəbəl/ ▶ **adj.** able to be inherited.

her·it·age /'heritij/ ▶ **n.** valued things such as historic buildings that have been passed down from previous generations.

SYNONYMS **1 tradition**, history, past, background, culture, customs. **2 ancestry**, lineage, descent, extraction, parentage, roots, heredity, birth.

her·maph·ro·dite /hər'mafrədīt/ ▶ **n.** a person, animal, or plant with both male and female sex organs or characteristics.

her·met·ic /hər'metik/ ▶ **adj.** (of a seal or closure) complete and airtight. ■ **her·met·i·cal·ly adv.**

her·mit /'hərmit/ ▶ **n.** a person who lives completely alone, especially for religious reasons.

SYNONYMS **recluse**, loner, ascetic; historical anchorite, anchoress; old use eremite.

her·mit·age /'hərmitij/ ▶ **n. 1** the home of a hermit. **2** (**the Hermitage**) a major art museum in St. Petersburg, Russia. **3** (**the Hermitage**) an estate, the home of Andrew Jackson, in central Tennessee.

her·ni·a /'hərnēə/ ▶ **n.** a condition in which part of an organ pushes through the wall of the cavity containing it.

he·ro /'hi(ə)rō/ ▶ **n.** (plural **heroes**) **1** a person who is admired for their courage or outstanding achievements. **2** the chief male character in a book, play, or movie. **3** a sandwich made of a long roll typically filled with meat, cheese, and vegetables.

SYNONYMS **1 champion**, man of courage, man of the hour, victor, conqueror, lion. **2 main character**, starring role, male protagonist, (male) lead, leading man; informal good guy. ANTONYMS villain.

□ **hero worship** extreme admiration for someone.

he·ro·ic /hə'rōik/ ▶ **adj. 1** very brave. **2** very grand or ambitious in scale: *pyramids on a heroic scale.* ▶ **n.** (**heroics**) brave or dramatic behavior or talk.

SYNONYMS ▶ **adj. brave**, courageous, valiant, intrepid, bold, fearless, daring; informal gutsy, spunky. ANTONYMS cowardly.

■ **he·ro·i·cal·ly adv.**

her·o·in /'herō-in/ ▶ **n.** a very addictive painkilling drug.

her·o·ine /'herō-in/ ▶ **n. 1** a woman admired for her courage or outstanding achievements. **2** the chief female character in a book, play, or movie.

SYNONYMS **1 champion**, woman of courage, woman of the hour, victor, conqueror. **2 main character**, female protagonist, lead, leading lady, prima donna, diva.

her·o·ism /'herō,izəm/ ▶ **n.** great bravery.

SYNONYMS **bravery**, courage, valor, daring, fearlessness, pluck; informal guts, spunk, moxie. ANTONYMS cowardice.

her·on /'herən/ ▶ **n.** a large fish-eating bird with long legs, a long neck, and a long pointed bill.

her·pes /ˈhərpēz/ ▶ **n.** an infectious disease that causes blisters on the skin.

Herr /he(ə)r/ ▶ **n.** (plural **Herren**) a form of address for a German-speaking man.

her·ring /ˈheriNG/ ▶ **n.** a silvery fish that is found in shoals and is used for food.

her·ring·bone /ˈheriNG,bōn/ ▶ **n.** a zigzag pattern consisting of columns of short slanting parallel lines.

hers /hərz/ ▶ **possessive pron.** used to refer to something belonging to or associated with a female person or animal previously mentioned.

SPELLING
No apostrophe: **hers**.

her·self /hərˈself/ ▶ **pron. 1** used as the object of a verb or preposition to refer to a female person or animal previously mentioned as the subject of the clause. **2** she or her personally.

hertz /hərts/ ▶ **n.** (plural **hertz**) the basic unit of frequency, equal to one cycle per second.

he's /hēz/ ▶ **contr. 1** he is. **2** he has.

hes·i·tant /ˈhezitənt/ ▶ **adj.** slow to act or speak through indecision or reluctance.

SYNONYMS **1 uncertain**, undecided, unsure, doubtful, dubious, ambivalent, of two minds, wavering, vacillating, irresolute, indecisive, hemming and hawing; informal iffy. **2 timid**, diffident, shy, bashful, insecure, nervous. ANTONYMS certain, decisive, confident.

■ **hes·i·tan·cy n. hes·i·tant·ly adv.**

hes·i·tate /ˈhezi,tāt/ ▶ **v.** (**hesitates**, **hesitating**, **hesitated**) **1** pause indecisively. **2** be reluctant to do something.

SYNONYMS **1 pause**, delay, wait, stall, be uncertain, be unsure, be doubtful, be indecisive, vacillate, waver, hem and haw; informal dilly-dally. **2** ***don't hesitate to ask*** **be reluctant to**, be unwilling to, be disinclined to, scruple to, have misgivings about, have qualms about, think twice about.

■ **hes·i·ta·tion** /,heziˈtāSHən/ **n.**

hes·sian /ˈheSHən/ ▶ **n.** a strong, coarse fabric.

het·er·o·dox /ˈhetərə,däks/ ▶ **adj.** not following traditional standards or beliefs. ■ **het·er·o·dox·y n.**

het·er·o·ge·ne·ous /,hetərəˈjēnēəs/ ▶ **adj.** varied: *a heterogeneous collection.* ■ **het·er·o·ge·ne·i·ty** /-jəˈnēətē/ **n.**

het·er·o·sex·u·al /,hetərōˈsekSHōōəl/ ▶ **adj.** sexually attracted to people of the opposite sex. ▶ **n.** a heterosexual person. ■ **het·er·o·sex·u·al·i·ty** /-,sekSHōōˈalitē/ **n.**

het up /,het ˈəp/ ▶ **adj.** informal angry and agitated.

heu·ris·tic /hyōōˈristik/ ▶ **adj.** allowing a person to discover or learn something for themselves.

hew /hyōō/ ▶ **v.** (**hews**, **hewing**, **hewed**; past participle **hewn** or **hewed**) chop wood, coal, etc., with an ax or other tool.

hex /heks/ ▶ **v.** cast a spell on. ▶ **n.** a magic spell.

hex·a·gon /ˈheksə,gän/ ▶ **n.** a figure with six straight sides and angles. ■ **hex·ag·o·nal** /hekˈsagənl/ **adj.**

hex·a·gram /ˈheksə,gram/ ▶ **n.** a six-pointed star formed by two intersecting equilateral triangles.

hex·am·e·ter /hekˈsamitər/ ▶ **n.** a line of verse made up of six groups of syllables.

hey /hā/ ▶ **exclam.** used to attract attention or to express surprise, interest, etc.

hey·day /ˈhā,dā/ ▶ **n.** (**your heyday**) the period when you are most successful or active.

HF ▶ **abbr.** Physics high frequency.

hi /hī/ ▶ **exclam.** informal used as a friendly greeting.

hi·a·tus /hīˈātəs/ ▶ **n.** (plural **hiatuses**) a pause or gap in a series or sequence.

SYNONYMS **pause**, break, gap, lacuna, interval, intermission, interlude, interruption.

hi·ber·nate /ˈhībər,nāt/ ▶ **v.** (**hibernates**, **hibernating**, **hibernated**) (of an animal) spend the winter in a state like deep sleep. ■ **hi·ber·na·tion** /,hībərˈnāSHən/ **n.**

Hi·ber·ni·an /hīˈbərnēən/ ▶ **adj.** Irish. ▶ **n.** an Irish person.

hi·bis·cus /hīˈbiskəs/ ▶ **n.** a plant of the mallow family with large brightly colored flowers.

hic·cup /ˈhikəp/ (or **hiccough**) ▶ **n. 1** a sudden gulping sound caused by an involuntary spasm of the diaphragm. **2** a minor setback. ▶ **v.** (**hiccups**, **hiccuping**, **hiccuped**) make the sound of a hiccup.

hick /hik/ ▶ **n.** informal an unsophisticated country person.

hick·o·ry /ˈhik(ə)rē/ ▶ **n.** a tree with edible nuts.

hid /hid/ past of **HIDE**[1].

hid·den /ˈhidn/ past participle of **HIDE**[1].

SYNONYMS **1 concealed**, secret, invisible, unseen, camouflaged. **2 obscure**, unclear, concealed, cryptic, arcane, mysterious, secret, covert, abstruse, deep. ANTONYMS visible, obvious.

hide[1] /hīd/ ▶ **v.** (**hides**, **hiding**, **hid** /hid/; past participle **hidden** /ˈhidn/) **1** put or keep something out of sight. **2** get into a place where you cannot be seen. **3** keep secret.

SYNONYMS **1 conceal**, secrete, put out of sight, cache; informal stash. **2 conceal yourself**, secrete yourself, take cover, lie low, go to ground; informal hole up. **3 obscure**, block out, blot out, obstruct, cloud, shroud, veil, eclipse, camouflage. **4 keep secret**, conceal, cover up, keep quiet about, hush up, suppress, disguise, mask; informal keep a/the lid on. ANTONYMS reveal.

□ **hidden agenda** a secret motive or plan. **hide-and-seek** a game in which one player hides and the others have to look for them. **hide your light under a bushel** keep quiet about your talents or accomplishments.

hide[2] ▶ **n.** the skin of an animal.

hide·a·way /ˈhīdə,wā/ ▶ **n.** a hiding place or retreat.

SYNONYMS **retreat**, refuge, hiding place, hideout, safe house, den.

hide·bound /ˈhīd,bound/ ▶ **adj.** unwilling to give up old-fashioned ideas in favor of new ways of thinking.

hid·e·ous /ˈhidēəs/ ▶ **adj. 1** very ugly. **2** very unpleasant.

SYNONYMS **1 ugly**, repulsive, repellent, unsightly, revolting, grotesque. **2 horrific**, terrible, appalling, awful, dreadful, frightful, horrible, horrendous, horrifying, shocking, sickening, gruesome, ghastly. ANTONYMS beautiful, pleasant.

■ **hid·e·ous·ly adv.**

hide·out /ˈhīdˌout/ ▶ **n.** a hiding place.

hid·ing /ˈhīdiNG/ ▶ **n. 1** a physical beating. **2** informal a severe defeat.

SYNONYMS **beating**, thrashing, whipping, drubbing; informal licking, belting, pasting, walloping.

hi·er·ar·chy /ˈhī(ə)ˌrärkē/ ▶ **n.** (plural **hierarchies**) **1** a system in which people are ranked one above the other according to status or authority. **2** a classification of things according to their relative importance.

SYNONYMS **ranking**, order, pecking order, grading, ladder, scale.

■ **hi·er·ar·chi·cal** /ˌhī(ə)ˈrärkikəl/ **adj.**

SPELLING

Write **-ie-**, not **-ei-**, and remember the second **r**: hierarchy.

hi·er·o·glyph /ˈhī(ə)rəˌglif/ ▶ **n.** a picture of an object representing a word, syllable, or sound, as found in ancient Egyptian and certain other writing systems.

hi·er·o·glyph·ics /ˌhī(ə)rəˈglifiks/ ▶ **pl.n.** writing in which a picture represents a word, syllable, or sound, as used in ancient Egypt.

hi-fi /ˈhī ˈfī/ ▶ **n.** (plural **hi-fis**) a set of equipment for reproducing high-fidelity sound. ▶ **adj.** having to do with high-fidelity sound.

hig·gle·dy-pig·gle·dy /ˈhigəldē ˈpigəldē/ ▶ **adv. & adj.** in confusion or disorder.

high /hī/ ▶ **adj. 1** extending far upwards: *a high mountain*. **2** of a particular height. **3** far above ground or sea level. **4** large in amount, size, or intensity: *a high temperature*. **5** (of a period or movement) at its peak: *high summer*. **6** great in status; important. **7** (of a sound or note) not deep or low. **8** informal under the influence of drugs or alcohol. **9** (of food) beginning to go bad. ▶ **n. 1** a high point, level, or figure. **2** an area of high atmospheric pressure. **3** informal a state of high spirits. ▶ **adv.** (of a sound) at a high pitch.

SYNONYMS ▶ **adj. 1 tall**, lofty, towering, giant, big, multistory, high-rise, elevated. **2 high-ranking**, ranking, leading, top, prominent, senior, influential, powerful, important, exalted. **3 inflated**, excessive, unreasonable, expensive, exorbitant, extortionate; informal steep, stiff. **4 high-pitched**, shrill, piercing, squeaky, penetrating, soprano, treble, falsetto. ANTONYMS low, deep. ▶ **adv. at a great height**, high up, way up, in the sky, aloft, overhead, to a great height. ANTONYMS low.

□ **from on high** from heaven or another high authority. **high and dry 1** stranded by the sea as it retreats. **2** in a difficult position. **high and low** in many different places. **high and mighty** informal arrogant. **high chair** a small chair with long legs for an infant, fitted with a tray and used at mealtimes. **high-class** of a high standard, quality, or social class. **high command** the commander-in-chief and senior staff of an army, navy, or air force. **high court** a supreme court of justice. **higher education** education beyond high school, especially as provided at colleges and universities. **highest common factor** the highest number that can be divided exactly into each of two or more numbers. **high explosive** powerful chemical explosive used in shells and bombs. **high fidelity** the reproduction of sound with little distortion. **high five** a gesture of celebration or greeting in which two people slap each other's palms with their arms raised. **high-flown** grand-sounding. **high-flier** (or **high-flyer**) a very successful person. **high frequency** (in radio) a frequency of 3–30 megahertz. **high gear** a gear that causes a vehicle to move quickly. **the high ground** a position of superiority. **high-handed** using authority without considering the feelings of other people. **high-impact 1** (of a material) able to withstand great impact without breaking. **2** referring to exercises that place a great deal of stress on the body. **high jinks** high-spirited fun. **high jump** an athletic event in which competitors try to jump over a bar. **high-level** of high importance. **high life** an extravagant social life as enjoyed by the wealthy. **high-minded** having strong moral principles. **high-octane 1** (of gas) having a high octane number and therefore allowing an engine to run smoothly. **2** powerful or dynamic: *high-octane charm*. **high-pitched** (of a sound) high in pitch. **high point** the most enjoyable or significant part of an experience or period of time. **high-powered** informal **1** (of a machine or device) having greater than normal strength or capabilities. **2** (of a person) dynamic and forceful. **high priest 1** a chief priest of a non-Christian religion. **2** (also **high priestess**) the leader of a cult or movement. **high-rise** (of a building) having many stories. **high road** a main road. **high roller** informal a person who gambles or spends large sums of money. **high school** a secondary school. **the high seas** the areas of the sea that are not under the control of any one country. **high spot** ⇒ HIGH POINT. **high-spirited** lively and cheerful. **high-strung** very nervous and easily upset. **high-tech** (also **hi-tech**) using advanced technology. **high technology** advanced technology. **high-tensile** (of metal) very strong under tension. **high tide** the time when the sea is closest to the land. **it is high time that …** it is past the time when something should have happened or been done. **high water** ⇒ HIGH TIDE. **high-water mark** the level reached by the sea at high tide. **high wire** a high tightrope. **on your high horse** informal behaving arrogantly or pompously. **run high** (of feelings) be intense.

high·ball /ˈhīˌbôl/ ▶ **n.** a drink consisting of liquor and a mixer such as soda, served with ice in a tall glass.

high·brow /ˈhīˌbrou/ ▶ **adj.** very intellectual or refined in taste.

SYNONYMS **intellectual**, scholarly, bookish, academic, educated, donnish, bluestocking; erudite, learned; informal brainy. ANTONYMS lowbrow.

high·fa·lu·tin /ˌhīfəˈlo͞otn/ ▶ **adj.** informal grand or self-important in a pretentious way.

high·land /ˈhīlənd/ (or **highlands**) ▶ **n. 1** an area of high or mountainous land. **2** (**the Highlands**) the mountainous northern part of Scotland. □ **Highland fling** a lively solo Scottish dance consisting of a series of complex steps.

■ **high·land·er n.**

high·light /ˈhīˌlīt/ ▶ **n. 1** an outstanding part of an event or period of time. **2** a bright area in a picture. **3** (**highlights**) bright tints in hair, created by bleaching or dyeing. ▶ **v. 1** draw attention to. **2** create highlights in hair.

SYNONYMS ▶ **n. high point**, climax, peak, pinnacle, height, zenith, summit, focus, feature. ▶ **v. spotlight**, call attention to, focus on, underline, show up, bring out, accentuate, accent, stress, emphasize. ANTONYMS play down.

high·light·er /ˈhīˌlītər/ ▶ **n.** **1** a broad felt-tip pen used to mark transparent fluorescent color on text. **2** a cosmetic that is lighter than the wearer's foundation or skin, used to emphasize features.

high·ly /ˈhīlē/ ▶ **adv.** **1** to a high degree or level. **2** favorably.

high·ness /ˈhīnis/ ▶ **n.** **1** the state of being high. **2** (**His**, **Her**, **Your**, etc., **Highness**) a title given to a person of royal rank: *I am most grateful, Your Highness.*

high·tail /ˈhīˌtāl/ ▶ **v.** informal move or travel fast.

high·way /ˈhīˌwā/ ▶ **n.** **1** a main road. **2** a public road.

high·way·man /ˈhīˌwāmən/ ▶ **n.** (plural **highwaymen**) (in the past) a man who held up and robbed travelers.

hi·jack /ˈhīˌjak/ ▶ **v.** **1** illegally seize control of an aircraft while it is traveling somewhere. **2** take over something and use it for a different purpose. ▶ **n.** an act of hijacking.

SYNONYMS ▶ **v.** **commandeer**, seize, take over, appropriate, expropriate.

■ **hi·jack·er** **n.**

hike /hīk/ ▶ **n.** **1** a long walk or walking tour. **2** a sharp increase. ▶ **v.** (**hikes**, **hiking**, **hiked**) **1** go on a hike. **2** pull or lift up clothing. **3** increase a price sharply.

SYNONYMS ▶ **n.** **1** **walk**, trek, tramp, trudge, slog, march, ramble. **2** **increase**, rise. ▶ **v.** **1** **walk**, trek, tramp, trudge, slog, march, ramble, backpack. **2** **increase**, raise, up, boost, push up; informal jack up, bump up.

□ **take a hike** informal go away. ■ **hik·er** **n.**

hi·lar·i·ous /həˈle(ə)rēəs/ ▶ **adj.** very amusing.

SYNONYMS **very funny**, hysterical, uproarious, rib-tickling; informal side-splitting, priceless, a scream, a hoot.

■ **hi·lar·i·ous·ly** **adv.** **hi·lar·i·ty** /həˈle(ə)ritē/ **n.**

hill /hil/ ▶ **n.** a naturally raised area of land, not as high as a mountain.

SYNONYMS **high ground**, hillock, hillside, rise, mound, knoll, hummock, fell, mountain.

□ **hill station** a town in the low mountains of the Indian subcontinent, popular as a holiday resort during the hot season. **over the hill** informal old and past your best.

hill·bil·ly /ˈhilˌbilē/ ▶ **n.** (plural **hillbillies**) informal, offensive an unsophisticated country person, associated originally with the remote regions of the Appalachians.

hill·ock /ˈhilək/ ▶ **n.** a small hill or mound.

hill·side /ˈhilˌsīd/ ▶ **n.** the sloping side of a hill.

hill·top /ˈhilˌtäp/ ▶ **n.** the summit of a hill.

hill·y /ˈhilē/ ▶ **adj.** (**hillier**, **hilliest**) having many hills.

hilt /hilt/ ▶ **n.** the handle of a sword, dagger, or knife. □ **to the hilt** completely.

him /him/ ▶ **pron.** used as the object of a verb or preposition to refer to a male person or animal previously mentioned.

Him·a·la·yan /ˌhiməˈlāən/ ▶ **adj.** having to do with the Himalayas, a mountain system in southern Asia.

him·self /himˈself/ ▶ **pron.** **1** used as the object of a verb or preposition to refer to a male person or animal previously mentioned as the subject of the clause. **2** he or him personally.

hind[1] /hīnd/ ▶ **adj.** situated at the back.

hind[2] ▶ **n.** a female deer.

hind·er /ˈhindər/ /ˈhīndər/ ▶ **v.** (**hinders**, **hindering**, **hindered**) delay or obstruct.

SYNONYMS **hamper**, impede, inhibit, thwart, foil, delay, interfere with, slow down, hold back, hold up, restrict, handicap, hamstring. ANTONYMS facilitate.

Hin·di /ˈhindē/ ▶ **n.** a language of northern India.

hind·most /ˈhīn(d)ˌmōst/ ▶ **adj.** furthest back.

hind·quar·ters /ˈhīn(d)ˌkwôrtərz/ ▶ **pl.n.** the rear part and hind legs of a four-legged animal.

hin·drance /ˈhindrəns/ ▶ **n.** a thing that hinders someone or something.

SYNONYMS **impediment**, obstacle, barrier, obstruction, handicap, hurdle, restraint, restriction, encumbrance, complication, delay, drawback, setback, difficulty, inconvenience, hitch, stumbling block, fly in the ointment, hiccup. ANTONYMS aid, help.

SPELLING

No e: hindrance, not hinder-.

hind·sight /ˈhīn(d)ˌsīt/ ▶ **n.** understanding of a situation or event after it has happened.

Hin·du /ˈhindo͞o/ ▶ **n.** (plural **Hindus**) a follower of Hinduism.

Hin·du·ism /ˈhindo͞oˌizəm/ ▶ **n.** a religion of the Indian subcontinent, with a large number of gods and goddesses.

Hin·du·sta·ni /ˌhindo͞oˈstänē/ ▶ **n.** a group of languages and dialects spoken in northern India that includes Hindi and Urdu. ▶ **adj.** relating to the culture of northwestern India.

hinge /hinj/ ▶ **v.** (**hinges**, **hinging**, **hinged**) **1** attach or join with a hinge. **2** (**hinge on**) depend entirely on.

hint /hint/ ▶ **n.** **1** a slight or indirect suggestion. **2** a very small trace of something. **3** a small piece of practical information. ▶ **v.** **1** suggest indirectly. **2** (**hint at**) be a slight suggestion of.

SYNONYMS ▶ **n.** **1** **clue**, inkling, suggestion, indication, sign, signal, intimation. **2** **tip**, suggestion, pointer, guideline, recommendation. **3** **trace**, touch, suspicion, suggestion, dash, soupçon; informal smidgen, tad. ▶ **v.** **imply**, insinuate, intimate, suggest, refer to, drive at, mean; informal get at.

hin·ter·land /ˈhintərˌland/ ▶ **n.** **1** the areas of a country away from the coast. **2** the area around or beyond a major town.

hip[1] /hip/ ▶ **n.** a projection formed by the pelvis and upper thigh bone on each side of the body. □ **hip flask** a small flask for alcohol, carried in a hip pocket.

hip[2] ▶ **n.** the fruit of a rose.

hip[3] ▶ **adj.** (**hipper**, **hippest**) informal fashionable. □ **hip-hop** a style of pop music featuring rap with an electronic backing. ■ **hip·ness** **n.**

hip·bone /ˈhipˌbōn/ ▶ **n.** a large bone forming the main part of the pelvis on each side of the body.

hip·pie /ˈhipē/ (or **hippy**) ▶ n. (plural **hippies**) (especially in the 1960s) a person who rejects traditional social values and dresses in an unconventional way.

hip·po /ˈhipō/ ▶ n. informal a hippopotamus.

Hip·po·crat·ic oath /ˈhipəˈkratik/ ▶ n. an oath (formerly taken by those beginning medical practice) to observe a code of professional behavior.

hip·po·drome /ˈhipəˌdrōm/ ▶ n. **1** a theater or concert hall. **2** (in ancient Greece or Rome) a course for chariot or horse races.

hip·po·pot·a·mus /ˌhipəˈpätəməs/ ▶ n. (plural **hippopotamuses** or **hippopotami** /-ˌmī, -ˌmē/) a large African animal with massive jaws, living partly on land and partly in water.

hip·ster /ˈhipstər/ ▶ n. informal a person who follows the latest fashions.

hire /hīr/ ▶ v. (**hires**, **hiring**, **hired**) **1** pay to be allowed to use something temporarily. **2** (**hire something out**) allow something to be used temporarily in return for payment. **3** pay someone to work for you. ▶ n. the action of hiring.

> SYNONYMS ▶ v. **1 rent**, lease, charter. **2 employ**, engage, recruit, appoint, take on, sign up. ANTONYMS dismiss.

□ **for hire** available to be hired.

hire·ling /ˈhīrliNG/ ▶ n. a person who is willing to do any kind of work as long as they are paid.

hir·sute /ˈhərˌso͞ot, hərˈso͞ot, ˈhi(ə)rˌso͞ot/ ▶ adj. hairy.

his /hiz/ ▶ possessive determiner & pron. belonging to or associated with a male person or animal previously mentioned.

His·pan·ic /hiˈspanik/ ▶ adj. having to do with Spain or other Spanish-speaking countries. ▶ n. a Spanish-speaking person living in the United States.

hiss /his/ ▶ v. **1** make a sharp sound like that made when pronouncing the letter *s*. **2** whisper something in an urgent or angry way. ▶ n. a hissing sound.

> SYNONYMS ▶ v. **1 fizz**, whistle, wheeze. **2 jeer**, catcall, whistle, hoot. ANTONYMS cheer. ▶ n. **1 fizz**, whistle, wheeze. **2 jeer**, catcall, whistle, abuse, derision. ANTONYMS cheer.

his·ta·mine /ˈhistəˌmēn, -ˌmin/ ▶ n. a substance that is released by cells in response to an injury or allergy.

his·to·ri·an /hiˈstôrēən/ ▶ n. an expert in history.

his·tor·ic /hiˈstôrik, -ˈstär-/ ▶ adj. famous or important in history, or likely to be seen as such in the future.

> SYNONYMS **significant**, notable, important, momentous, memorable, groundbreaking; informal earth-shattering.

his·tor·i·cal /hiˈstôrikəl, -ˈstär-/ ▶ adj. **1** having to do with history. **2** belonging to or set in the past.

> SYNONYMS **1 documented**, recorded, chronicled, authentic, factual, actual. **2 past**, bygone, ancient, old, former.

■ **his·tor·i·cal·ly** adv.

his·to·ri·og·ra·phy /hiˌstôrēˈägrəfē, -ˌstär-/ ▶ n. **1** the study of the writing of history. **2** the writing of history.

his·to·ry /ˈhist(ə)rē/ ▶ n. (plural **histories**) **1** the study of past events. **2** the past considered as a whole. **3** the past events connected with someone or something. **4** a continuous record of past events or trends.

> SYNONYMS **1 the past**, former times, the olden days, yesterday, antiquity. **2 chronicle**, archive, record, report, narrative, account, study. **3 background**, past, life story, experiences, record.

□ **be history** informal be about to dismissed or dead. **the rest is history** the events following those already related are so well-known that they need not be told again.

his·tri·on·ic /ˌhistrēˈänik/ ▶ adj. too theatrical or dramatic. ▶ n. (**histrionics**) exaggerated behavior intended to attract attention.

> SYNONYMS ▶ n. **dramatics**, theatrics, tantrums; affectation.

hit /hit/ ▶ v. (**hits**, **hitting**, **hit**) **1** bring your hand or a tool, weapon, bat, etc., against someone or something quickly and with force. **2** (of something moving) come into contact with someone or something quickly and forcefully. **3** reach a target. **4** cause harm or distress to. **5** be suddenly realized by. **6** (**hit out**) criticize or attack strongly. **7** informal reach. **8** (**hit on**) suddenly discover or think of. ▶ n. **1** an instance of hitting or being hit. **2** a successful movie, CD, etc. **3** an instance of a website being accessed or a word being found in an Internet search. **4** informal a murder carried out by a criminal organization. **5** informal a dose of an addictive drug.

> SYNONYMS ▶ v. **1 strike**, smack, slap, beat, punch, thump, thrash, batter, club, pummel, cuff, swat; informal whack, wallop, bash, clout, belt, slug, clobber. **2 crash into**, run into, smash into, knock into, bump into, plow into, collide with, meet head-on. **3 devastate**, affect badly, upset, shatter, crush, traumatize; informal knock sideways. ▶ n. **1 blow**, slap, smack, thump, punch, knock, bang; informal whack, wallop, bash, clout, slug, belt. **2 success**, sellout, winner, triumph, sensation, bestseller; informal smash hit, chart-topper, crowd-puller. ANTONYMS failure.

□ **hit-and-miss** not done in a careful, planned way; random. **hit-and-run** (of a road accident) in which the driver responsible leaves rapidly without helping the other people involved. **hit someone below the belt 1** Boxing give your opponent an unlawful low blow. **2** behave unfairly toward someone. **hit the ground running** informal start something new with speed and enthusiasm. **hit it off** informal get on well with someone. **hit list** a list of people to be killed for criminal or political reasons. **hit the nail on the head** be exactly right. **hit man** informal a person paid to kill someone. **hit-or-miss** not done in a careful, planned way; random. **hit parade** a weekly listing of the current best-selling pop records.

hitch /hiCH/ ▶ v. **1** move into a different position with a jerk. **2** fasten with a rope. **3** travel by hitchhiking. ▶ n. **1** a temporary difficulty. **2** a temporary knot.

> SYNONYMS ▶ v. **1 pull**, lift, raise; informal yank. **2 harness**, yoke, couple, fasten, connect, attach. ▶ n. **problem**, difficulty, snag, setback, obstacle, complication; informal glitch, hiccup.

□ **get hitched** informal get married. ■ **hitch·er** n.

hitch·hike /ˈhiCHˌhīk/ ▶ v. travel by getting free rides in passing vehicles. ■ **hitch·hik·er** n.

hith·er /ˈhiT͟Hər/ ▶ adv. old use to or toward this place. □ **hither and thither** (or **yon**) to and fro.

hith·er·to /ˈhiT͟Hərˌto͞o, ˌhiT͟Hərˈto͞o/ ▶ **adv.** until this time.

HIV ▶ **abbr.** human immunodeficiency virus (the virus causing AIDS). ▫ **HIV-positive** having had a positive result in a blood test for HIV.

hive /hīv/ ▶ **n.** **1** a beehive. **2** a place full of people working hard.

hives /hīvz/ ▶ **pl.n.** a rash of red, itchy marks on the skin, caused by an allergy.

HK ▶ **abbr.** Hong Kong.

hmm /(h)m/ ▶ **exclam. & n.** a sound made when coughing or clearing the throat to attract someone's attention or express hesitation.

HMS ▶ **abbr.** (used with names of ships in the British navy) Her or His Majesty's Ship.

hoard /hôrd/ ▶ **n.** a store of money, valued objects, or useful information. ▶ **v.** build up a store of something.

> SYNONYMS ▶ **n.** **cache**, stockpile, store, collection, supply, reserve; informal stash. ▶ **v.** **stockpile**, store up, put aside, put by, set aside, cache, save, squirrel away, collect, accumulate; informal salt away. ANTONYMS squander.

■ **hoard·er** **n.**

> USAGE
>
> Don't confuse **hoard** with **horde**: a **hoard** is a store of something valuable; a **horde** is a large group of people.

hoar·frost /ˈhôrˌfrôst, -ˌfräst/ ▶ **n.** a feathery grayish-white deposit of frost.

hoarse /hôrs/ ▶ **adj.** (of a voice) rough and harsh.

> SYNONYMS **rough**, harsh, croaky, throaty, gruff, husky, grating, rasping.

■ **hoarse·ly** **adv.**

hoar·y /ˈhôrē/ ▶ **adj.** (**hoarier**, **hoariest**) **1** grayish-white. **2** having gray hair. **3** old and unoriginal: *a hoary old adage.*

hoax /hōks/ ▶ **n.** a humorous or cruel trick. ▶ **v.** deceive with a hoax.

> SYNONYMS ▶ **n.** **practical joke**, prank, trick, deception, fraud; informal con, spoof, scam.

■ **hoax·er** **n.**

hob·ble /ˈhäbəl/ ▶ **v.** (**hobbles**, **hobbling**, **hobbled**) **1** walk awkwardly. **2** strap together the legs of a horse to stop it wandering away. ▶ **n.** **1** an awkward way of walking. **2** a rope or strap for hobbling a horse.

> SYNONYMS ▶ **v.** **limp**, shamble, totter, dodder, stagger, stumble.

hob·by /ˈhäbē/ ▶ **n.** (plural **hobbies**) an activity that you do regularly in your leisure time for pleasure.

> SYNONYMS **pastime**, leisure activity, sideline, diversion, relaxation, recreation, amusement.

▫ **hobby horse** **1** a child's toy consisting of a stick with a model of a horse's head at one end. **2** something that a person talks about very often.

hob·gob·lin /ˈhäbˌgäblən/ ▶ **n.** a mischievous imp.

hob·nail /ˈhäbˌnāl/ ▶ **n.** a short nail used to strengthen the soles of boots. ■ **hob·nailed** **adj.**

hob·nob /ˈhäbˌnäb/ ▶ **v.** (**hobnobs**, **hobnobbing**, **hobnobbed**) informal spend time with rich or important people.

> SYNONYMS **associate**, mix, fraternize, socialize, spend time, go around, mingle, consort, rub elbows; informal hang around/out.

ho·bo /ˈhōˌbō/ ▶ **n.** (plural **hoboes** or **hobos**) a homeless person; a tramp.

Hob·son's choice /ˈhäbsənz/ ▶ **n.** a choice of taking what is offered or nothing at all.

hock[1] /häk/ ▶ **n.** the middle joint in an animal's back leg.

hock[2] ▶ **v.** informal pawn an object. ▫ **in hock** in debt.

hock·ey /ˈhäkē/ ▶ **n.** **1** (also **ice hockey**) a team game played on an ice rink by players on skates using hooked sticks to drive a small rubber disk (the puck) toward a goal. **2** (usually **field hockey**) a team game played using hooked sticks to drive a small, hard ball toward a goal.

ho·cus-po·cus /ˌhōkəsˈpōkəs/ ▶ **n.** **1** meaningless talk or activity used to deceive people, usually by diverting their attention away from what is really happening. **2** a form of words used by a magician.

hod /häd/ ▶ **n.** **1** a builder's V-shaped open trough attached to a short pole, used for carrying bricks. **2** a metal container for storing coal.

hodge·podge /ˈhäjˌpäj/ ▶ **n.** a confused mixture.

> SYNONYMS **mixture**, mixed bag, assortment, jumble, ragbag, miscellany, medley, potpourri, melange, mishmash.

Hodg·kin's dis·ease /ˈhäjkinz/ ▶ **n.** a cancerous disease causing enlargement of the lymph nodes, liver, and spleen.

hoe /hō/ ▶ **n.** a long-handled gardening tool with a thin metal blade. ▶ **v.** (**hoes**, **hoeing**, **hoed**) break up soil or dig up weeds with a hoe.

hoe·down /ˈhōˌdoun/ ▶ **n.** **1** a social gathering at which lively folk dancing takes place. **2** a lively folk dance.

hog /hôg, häg/ ▶ **n.** **1** a castrated male pig reared for its meat. **2** informal a greedy person. ▶ **v.** (**hogs**, **hogging**, **hogged**) informal take or hoard selfishly.

> SYNONYMS ▶ **v.** **monopolize**, dominate, corner, control, take over.

▫ **go (the) whole hog** informal do something fully.

hogs·head /ˈhôgzˌhed, ˈhägz-/ ▶ **n.** a large cask.

hog·wash /ˈhôgˌwôsʜ, ˈhägˌwäsʜ/ ▶ **n.** informal nonsense.

hoi pol·loi /ˈhoi pəˌloi/ ▶ **pl.n.** disapproving the common people.

hoist /hoist/ ▶ **v.** **1** raise with ropes and pulleys. **2** haul or lift up. ▶ **n.** a piece of equipment for hoisting something.

> SYNONYMS ▶ **v.** **raise**, lift, haul up, heave up, winch up, pull up, elevate. ▶ **n.** **crane**, winch, pulley, windlass.

hoi·ty-toi·ty /ˈhoitē ˈtoitē/ ▶ **adj.** informal snobbish.

hok·ey-pok·ey /ˌhōkē-ˈpōkē/ ▶ **n.** a group song and dance performed in a circle, involving the shaking of each limb in turn.

ho·kum /ˈhōkəm/ ▶ **n.** informal **1** nonsense. **2** unoriginal or sentimental material in a movie, book, etc.

hold /hōld/ ▶ **v.** (**holds**, **holding**, **held** /held/) **1** grasp, carry, or support. **2** contain or be able to contain. **3** have, own, or occupy. **4** keep or detain someone. **5** stay or keep at a certain level. **6** (**hold someone to**) make someone keep a promise. **7** (**hold someone/something in**) have a particular attitude to someone or something. **8** refrain from adding or using. ▶ **n. 1** a grip. **2** a place to grip while climbing. **3** a degree of control. **4** a storage space in the lower part of a ship or aircraft.

SYNONYMS ▶ **v. 1 clasp**, clutch, grasp, grip, clench, cling to, hold on to, embrace, hug, squeeze. **2 detain**, imprison, lock up, keep behind bars, confine, intern, incarcerate. **3 take**, contain, accommodate, fit, have room for. **4 maintain**, consider, take the view, believe, think, feel, deem, be of the opinion, rule, decide; informal reckon. **5 convene**, call, summon, conduct, organize, run. ANTONYMS release. ▶ **n. 1 grip**, grasp, clasp, clutch. **2 influence**, power, control, grip, dominance, authority, sway.

□ **get hold of 1** grasp. **2** informal find or contact. **hold something against someone** continue to feel resentful toward someone for something bad they have done to you. **hold back** hesitate. **hold something down** informal succeed in keeping a job. **hold fast 1** remain tightly secured. **2** stick to a principle. **hold forth** talk at length. **hold good** (or **true**) remain valid. **hold it** informal wait or stop doing something. **hold off** (of bad weather) fail to happen. **hold someone/something off** resist an attacker. **hold on 1** wait. **2** keep going in difficult circumstances. **hold out 1** resist difficult circumstances. **2** continue to be enough; last. **hold out for** continue to demand. **hold something over 1** postpone something. **2** threaten someone with damaging information or other power to affect them. **hold someone/something up 1** delay someone or something. **2** rob someone using the threat of violence. **no holds barred** without restrictions. **on hold** waiting to be dealt with or connected by telephone. **take hold** start to have an effect.

hold·er /ˈhōldər/ ▶ **n. 1** a device or implement for holding something: *a cup holder*. **2** a person who holds something: *a US passport holder*. **3** the possessor of a trophy, championship, or record: *the record holder in the 100-yard dash*.

SYNONYMS **1 bearer**, owner, possessor, keeper. **2 container**, receptacle, case, cover, housing, sheath.

hold·ing /ˈhōldiNG/ ▶ **n. 1** an area of land held by lease. **2** (**holdings**) stocks and property owned by a person or organization.

hold·o·ver /ˈhōldˌōvər/ ▶ **n.** a person or thing surviving from an earlier time: *Bootsie and Twiggs are holdovers from the original series*.

hold·up /ˈhōldˌəp/ ▶ **n. 1** a cause of delay. **2** a robbery carried out with the threat of violence.

SYNONYMS **1 delay**, setback, hitch, snag, difficulty, problem, glitch, hiccup, traffic jam, tailback. **2 robbery**, raid, armed robbery, mugging; informal stickup, heist.

hole /hōl/ ▶ **n. 1** a hollow space or opening in a solid object or surface. **2** (in golf) a hollow in the ground that you try to hit the ball into. **3** informal an awkward or unpleasant place or situation. ▶ **v.** (**holes**, **holing**, **holed**) **1** make a hole or holes in. **2** (**hole up**) informal hide yourself.

SYNONYMS ▶ **n. 1 opening**, aperture, orifice, gap, space, interstice, fissure, vent, chink, breach, crack, rupture, puncture. **2 pit**, crater, depression, hollow, cavern, cave, chamber. **3 burrow**, lair, den, earth, sett/set.

□ **hole-in-one** (plural **holes-in-one**) Golf a shot that enters the hole straight from the tee. **hole-in-the-wall** a small dingy place, especially a bar or restaurant. **in the hole** in debt. **make a hole in** use a large amount of. ■ **hol·ey adj.**

hol·i·day /ˈhäləˌdā/ ▶ **n.** a day of festivity or recreation when most people do not have to work.

SYNONYMS **day of observance**, festival, feast day, fiesta, celebration, anniversary, jubilee, saint's day, feast day.

ho·li·ness /ˈhōlēnis/ ▶ **n. 1** the state of being holy. **2** (**His** or **Your Holiness**) the title of the pope and some other religious leaders.

ho·lis·tic /hōˈlistik/ ▶ **adj.** treating the whole person rather than just the symptoms of a disease. ■ **ho·lism n.**

hol·ler /ˈhälər/ informal ▶ **v.** (**hollers**, **hollering**, **hollered**) give a loud shout. ▶ **n.** a loud shout.

hol·low /ˈhälō/ ▶ **adj. 1** having empty space inside. **2** curving inward: *hollow cheeks*. **3** (of a sound) echoing. **4** worthless or not sincere: *a hollow promise*. ▶ **n. 1** a hole. **2** a small valley. ▶ **v.** (usu. **hollow something out**) form by making a hole.

SYNONYMS ▶ **adj. 1 empty**, hollowed out, void. **2 sunken**, deep-set, concave, depressed, recessed. **3 worthless**, meaningless, empty, profitless, fruitless, pointless, pyrrhic. **4 insincere**, false, deceitful, hypocritical, sham, untrue. ANTONYMS solid, convex. ▶ **n. 1 hole**, pit, cavity, crater, trough, depression, indentation, dip. **2 valley**, vale, dale, dell. ▶ **v. gouge**, scoop, dig, cut, excavate, channel.

hol·ly /ˈhälē/ ▶ **n.** an evergreen shrub with prickly dark green leaves and red berries.

hol·ly·hock /ˈhälēˌhäk/ ▶ **n.** a tall plant with large showy flowers.

hol·o·caust /ˈhäləˌkôst, ˈhōlə-/ ▶ **n. 1** destruction or killing on a very large scale. **2** (**the Holocaust**) the mass murder of Jews under the German Nazi regime in World War II.

Hol·o·cene /ˈhäləˌsēn, ˈhōlə-/ ▶ **adj.** Geology having to do with the present epoch (from about 10,000 years ago).

hol·o·gram /ˈhäləˌgram, ˈhōlə-/ ▶ **n.** a picture that looks three-dimensional when it is lit up. ■ **hol·o·graph·ic adj.**

hol·ster /ˈhōlstər/ ▶ **n.** a holder for carrying a handgun.

ho·ly /ˈhōlē/ ▶ **adj.** (**holier**, **holiest**) **1** dedicated to God or a religious purpose. **2** morally and spiritually good.

SYNONYMS **1 saintly**, godly, pious, religious, devout, God-fearing, spiritual. **2 sacred**, consecrated, hallowed, sanctified, venerated, revered. ANTONYMS sinful, irreligious.

□ **holier-than-thou** offensively certain that you are morally superior. **holy day** a religious festival. **Holy Father** the pope. **the holy of holies** a very sacred place. **Holy See** the office of or the court surrounding the pope. **Holy Spirit** (or **Holy Ghost**) (in Christianity) God as a spirit that is active in the world. **holy war** a war waged in support of a religious cause. **holy water** water blessed by a priest and used in religious ceremonies. **Holy Week** the week before Easter. **Holy Writ** sacred writings as a group.

hom·age /ˈ(h)ämij/ ▶ **n.** honor shown to someone in public.

SYNONYMS **respect**, honor, reverence, worship, admiration, esteem, adulation, tribute. ANTONYMS contempt.

hom·burg /'hämbərg/ ▶ n. a man's felt hat with a narrow curled brim.

home /hōm/ ▶ n. **1** the place where you live. **2** a place where people who need special care live. **3** a place where something flourishes or where it started. ▶ adj. **1** relating to your home. **2** relating to your own country. **3** (of a sports game or match) played at a team's own field, ground, or stadium. ▶ adv. **1** to or at your home. **2** to the intended position: *slide the bolt home*. ▶ v. (**homes**, **homing**, **homed**) **1** (of an animal) return by instinct to its territory. **2** (**home in on**) move or be aimed toward.

SYNONYMS ▶ n. **1 residence**, house, accommodations, property, quarters, lodgings, address, place; informal pad; formal abode, dwelling. **2 homeland**, native land, hometown, birthplace, roots, fatherland, mother country, motherland. **3 institution**, hospice, shelter, refuge, retreat, asylum, hostel. ▶ adj. **domestic**, internal, local, national. ANTONYMS foreign, international.

□ **at home 1** comfortable and at ease. **2** ready to receive visitors. **bring something home to** make someone aware of the significance of something. **close to home** (of a remark) uncomfortably accurate. **drive** (or **hammer**) **something home** stress something forcefully. **hit** (or **strike**) **home 1** (of words) have the intended effect. **2** (of the significance of a situation) be fully realized. **home brew** alcoholic drink brewed at home. **home economics** the study of cooking and household management. **home free** having successfully achieved your objective. **home-grown** grown in your own garden or country. **home movie** an amateur movie made in the home or in a domestic setting. **home page** the main page of an individual's or organization's Internet site. **home plate** Baseball a mat next to which a batter stands and over which the pitcher must throw the ball for a strike. **home rule** the government of a place by its own citizens. **home run** Baseball a hit that allows the batter to make a run around all the bases and score. **homestretch** the final stretch of a racetrack. ■ **home·ward** adj. & adv. **home·wards** adv.

home·bod·y /'hōm,bädē/ ▶ n. (plural **homebodies**) informal a person who likes to stay at home.

home·boy /'hōm,boi/ ▶ n. informal **1** a person from your own town or neighborhood. **2** a member of your peer group or gang.

home·com·ing /'hōm,kəmiNG/ ▶ n. an instance of returning home.

home·land /'hōm,land/ ▶ n. a person's native land.

home·less /'hōmlis/ ▶ adj. not having anywhere to live.

SYNONYMS **of no fixed abode**, without a roof over your head, on the streets, vagrant, destitute.

■ **home·less·ness** n.

home·ly /'hōmlē/ ▶ adj. (**homelier**, **homeliest**) **1** (of a person) unattractive. **2** simple but comfortable; like home. **3** unsophisticated.

SYNONYMS **unattractive**, plain, unprepossessing, ugly.

home·made /'hō(m)'mād/ ▶ adj. made at home.

home·mak·er /'hōm,mākər/ ▶ n. a person who manages a home.

ho·me·op·a·thy /,hōmē'äpəTHē/ ▶ n. a system of treating diseases by tiny doses of substances that would normally produce symptoms of the disease. ■ **ho·me·o·path** /'hōmēə,paTH/ n. **ho·me·o·path·ic** adj.

ho·me·o·sta·sis /,hōmēə'stāsis/ ▶ n. (plural **homeostases**) the tendency of the body to keep its own temperature, blood pressure, etc., at a constant level. ■ **ho·me·o·stat·ic** adj.

ho·mer /'hōmər/ Baseball, informal ▶ n. a home run. ▶ v. hit a home run.

Ho·mer·ic /hō'merik/ ▶ adj. having to do with the ancient Greek poet Homer (8th century BC) or the poems he is believed to have written.

home·room /'hōm,ro͞om, -,ro͝om/ ▶ n. a classroom in which fixed groups of students gather, usually daily, for school administrative purposes.

home·sick /'hōm,sik/ ▶ adj. feeling upset because you are missing your home.

home·spun /'hōm,spən/ ▶ adj. **1** simple and unsophisticated. **2** (of cloth or yarn) made or spun at home. ▶ n. a coarse handwoven fabric similar to tweed.

home·stead /'hōm,sted/ ▶ n. a farmhouse with surrounding land and outbuildings. ■ **home·stead·er** n. **home·stead·ing** n.

home stretch (also **homestretch**) ▶ n. the final stretch of a racetrack.

home·work /'hōm,wərk/ ▶ n. **1** school work that you are expected to do at home. **2** preparation for an event. **3** paid work done at home.

hom·ey /'hōmē/ ▶ adj. **1** comfortable and cozy. **2** unsophisticated.

hom·i·cide /'hämə,sīd, 'hōmə-/ ▶ n. the killing of another person.

SYNONYMS **murder**, manslaughter, killing, slaughter, butchery, assassination.

■ **hom·i·cid·al** /,hämə'sīdl, ,hōmə-/ adj.

hom·i·let·ic /,hämə'letik/ ▶ adj. having to do with or like a homily.

hom·i·ly /'hämәlē/ ▶ n. (plural **homilies**) **1** a talk on a religious subject. **2** a dull talk on a moral issue.

hom·ing /'hōmiNG/ ▶ adj. **1** (of an animal) able to return home from a great distance. **2** (of a weapon) able to find and hit a target electronically.

hom·i·nid /'hämə,nid/ ▶ n. Zoology a member of a family of primates that includes humans and their prehistoric ancestors.

hom·i·ny /'hämənē/ ▶ n. coarsely ground corn used to make grits.

ho·mo·ge·ne·ous /,hōmə'jēnēəs/ ▶ adj. **1** alike: *if all jobs and workers were homogeneous*. **2** made up of parts that are all of the same kind. ■ **ho·mo·ge·ne·i·ty** /,hōməjə'nēitē, ,hämə-/ n.

SPELLING

The ending is **-eous**, with an **e**, not **-ous**: homogen**eous**.

ho·mog·e·nize /hə'mäjə,nīz/ ▶ v. (**homogenizes**, **homogenizing**, **homogenized**) **1** treat milk so that the cream is mixed in. **2** make different things more alike.

hom·o·graph /'hämə,graf, 'hōmə-/ ▶ n. a word that is spelled the same as another but has a different meaning (e.g., *bat* "a flying animal" and *bat* "a piece of wood for hitting a ball").

ho·mol·o·gous /hō'mäləgəs, hə-/ ▶ **adj.** having a related or similar position or structure; corresponding. ■ **ho·mol·o·gy n.**

hom·o·nym /'hämə,nim, 'hōmə-/ ▶ **n.** a word that is spelled or pronounced the same as another but has a different meaning.

ho·mo·pho·bi·a /,hōmə'fōbēə/ ▶ **n.** extreme hatred or fear of homosexuality and homosexuals. ■ **ho·mo·pho·bic adj.**

ho·mo·phone /'hämə,fōn, 'hōmə-/ ▶ **n.** a word that is pronounced the same as another but has a different meaning or spelling (e.g., *new* and *knew*).

Ho·mo sa·pi·ens /'hōmō 'sāpēənz/ ▶ **n.** the species to which modern humans belong.

ho·mo·sex·u·al /,hōmə'sekshōōəl/ ▶ **adj.** sexually attracted to people of your own sex. ▶ **n.** a homosexual person. ■ **ho·mo·sex·u·al·i·ty** /-,sekshōō'alitē/ **n.**

Hon. ▶ **abbr.** Honorary or Honorable.

hon·cho /'hänchō/ ▶ **n.** (plural **honchos**) informal a leader.

Hon·du·ran /hän'd(y)ŏŏrən/ ▶ **n.** a person from Honduras. ▶ **adj.** relating to Honduras.

hone /hōn/ ▶ **v.** (**hones**, **honing**, **honed**) **1** make better or more efficient. **2** sharpen a tool with a stone.

hon·est /'änist/ ▶ **adj. 1** truthful and sincere. **2** fairly earned: *an honest living.* **3** simple and straightforward: *good, honest food.*

> SYNONYMS **1** *an honest man* **upright**, honorable, principled, virtuous, good, decent, law-abiding, trustworthy, scrupulous, ethical, upstanding, right-minded. **2** *I haven't been honest with you* **truthful**, sincere, candid, frank, open, forthright, straight; informal upfront. ANTONYMS dishonest.

□ **honest-to-God** informal **1** genuine. **2** genuinely. **honest-to-goodness** genuine and straightforward.

hon·est·ly /'änistlē/ ▶ **adv. 1** in an honest way. **2** really (used for emphasis).

> SYNONYMS **1 fairly**, lawfully, legally, legitimately, honorably, decently, ethically; informal on the level. **2 sincerely**, genuinely, truthfully, truly, wholeheartedly, to be honest, to be frank, in all honesty, in all sincerity.

hon·es·ty /'änistē/ ▶ **n.** the quality of being honest.

> SYNONYMS **1 integrity**, uprightness, honor, righteousness, virtue, goodness, probity, trustworthiness. **2 sincerity**, candor, frankness, directness, truthfulness, truth, openness, straightforwardness. ANTONYMS dishonesty, insincerity.

hon·ey /'hənē/ ▶ **n.** (plural **honeys**) a sweet, sticky yellowish-brown fluid made by bees from flower nectar.

hon·ey·bee /'hənē,bē/ ▶ **n.** the common bee.

hon·ey·comb /'hənē,kōm/ ▶ **n.** a structure of six-sided wax compartments made by bees to store honey and eggs.

hon·ey·dew /'hənē,d(y)ōō/ ▶ **n.** a sweet, sticky substance produced by small insects feeding on the sap of plants. □ **honeydew melon** a variety of melon with sweet green flesh.

hon·eyed /'hənēd/ ▶ **adj. 1** containing or coated with honey. **2** (of words) soothing and soft: *honeyed words.*

hon·ey·moon /'hənē,mōōn/ ▶ **n. 1** a vacation taken by a newly married couple. **2** an initial period of enthusiasm or goodwill. ▶ **v.** spend a honeymoon somewhere.

hon·ey·pot /'hənē,pät/ ▶ **n.** a place that many people are attracted to.

hon·ey·suck·le /'hənē,səkəl/ ▶ **n.** a climbing shrub with sweet-smelling flowers.

honk /hängk, hôngk/ ▶ **n. 1** the cry of a goose. **2** the sound of a car horn. ▶ **v.** make a honk.

hon·ky-tonk /'hängkē ,tängk, 'hôngkē ,tôngk/ ▶ **n.** informal **1** a bar, especially a cheap or disreputable bar where country music is played. **2** ragtime piano music.

hon·or /'änər/ ▶ **n. 1** great respect. **2** a privilege. **3** a clear sense of what is right. **4** a person or thing that brings credit. **5** an award or title given as a reward for achievement. **6** (**honors**) a high school, college, or university course of a higher level than an ordinary one. **7** (**His**, **Your**, etc., **Honor**) a title for a judge. ▶ **v. 1** regard or treat with great respect. **2** fulfill an obligation or keep an agreement.

> SYNONYMS ▶ **n. 1 integrity**, honesty, uprightness, morality, probity, principles, high-mindedness, decency, scrupulousness, fairness, justness. **2 distinction**, privilege, glory, kudos, cachet, prestige. **3 reputation**, good name, character, repute, image, standing, status. **4 privilege**, pleasure, compliment. ANTONYMS shame. ▶ **v. 1 respect**, esteem, admire, look up to, value, cherish, revere, venerate. **2 applaud**, acclaim, praise, salute, recognize, celebrate, pay tribute to. **3 fulfill**, observe, keep, obey, heed, follow, carry out, keep to, abide by, adhere to, comply with, conform to, be true to. ANTONYMS disobey, break.

□ **do the honors** informal serve food or drink or perform another social duty for others. **in honor of** as an expression of respect for.

hon·or·a·ble /'änərəbəl/ ▶ **adj. 1** deserving honor. **2** having high moral standards. **3** (**Honorable**) a title given to judges, members of a congress or parliament, nobles, etc.

> SYNONYMS **1 honest**, moral, principled, righteous, decent, respectable, virtuous, good, upstanding, upright, noble, fair, trustworthy, law-abiding. **2 illustrious**, distinguished, eminent, great, glorious, prestigious. ANTONYMS dishonorable.

□ **honorable mention** a statement of praise for a candidate in an examination or competition not awarded a prize. ■ **hon·or·a·bly adv.**

hon·o·rar·i·um /,änə're(ə)rēəm/ ▶ **n.** (plural **honorariums** or **honoraria** /-reə/) a voluntary payment for professional services that are offered without charge.

hon·or·ar·y /'änə,rerē/ ▶ **adj.** (of a title or position) given as an honor.

> SYNONYMS **titular**, nominal, in name only, unofficial, token.

hon·or·if·ic /,änə'rifik/ ▶ **adj.** given as a mark of respect. ▶ **n.** a title or word implying or expressing high status, politeness, or respect.

hooch /hōōch/ ▶ **n.** informal alcoholic drink.

hood[1] /hŏŏd/ ▶ **n. 1** a covering for the head and neck with an opening for the face. **2** a metal part covering the engine of a vehicle. **3** a protective canopy. ■ **hood·ed** adj.

hood² ▶ n. informal a gangster or violent criminal.

hood³ ▶ n. informal a neighborhood.

hood·ie /'ho͝odē/ (or **hoody**) ▶ n. (plural **hoodies**) a hooded sweatshirt or other top.

hood·lum /'ho͞odləm, 'ho͝od-/ ▶ n. a gangster or violent criminal.

> SYNONYMS **gangster**, mobster, heavy, hit man, thug, criminal; informal hood.

hoo·doo /'ho͞o,do͞o/ ▶ n. **1** a run or cause of bad luck. **2** voodoo.

hood·wink /'ho͝od,wiNGk/ ▶ v. deceive or trick.

hoo·ey /'ho͞oē/ ▶ n. informal nonsense.

hoof /ho͝of/ ▶ n. (plural **hoofs** or **hooves** /ho͞ovz/) the horny part of the foot of a horse, cow, etc. ▶ v. informal **1** kick a ball powerfully. **2** (**hoof it**) go on foot. ■ **hoofed** adj.

hoof·er /'ho͝ofər, 'ho͞ofər/ ▶ n. informal a professional dancer.

hoo-ha /'ho͞o ˌhä/ ▶ n. informal a commotion.

hook /ho͝ok/ ▶ n. **1** a curved object for catching hold of things or hanging things on. **2** a punch made with the elbow bent and rigid. **3** a catchy passage in a song. ▶ v. **1** catch or fasten with a hook. **2** (**hook someone/thing up**) link someone or something to electronic equipment. **3** (**be hooked**) informal be very interested or addicted. **4** (in sports) hit the ball in a curving path.

> SYNONYMS ▶ n. **1 peg**, nail. **2 fastener**, clasp, hasp, clip. ▶ v. **1 attach**, hitch, fasten, fix, secure, hang, clasp. **2 catch**, land, net, take, bag.

□ **by hook or by crook** by any possible means. **hook and eye** a small metal hook and loop used to fasten a garment. **hook, line, and sinker** completely. **off the hook 1** informal no longer in trouble. **2** (of a telephone receiver) not on its rest. **3** informal noteworthy, fresh, or exciting: *those lyrics are off the hook!*

hook·ah /'ho͝okə, 'ho͞okə/ ▶ n. a kind of tobacco pipe in which the smoke is drawn through water to cool it.

hooked /ho͝okt/ ▶ adj. **1** having or resembling a hook or hooks. **2** informal captivated or addicted.

> SYNONYMS **1 curved**, hook-shaped, aquiline, angular, bent. **2** (**hooked on**) **addicted to**, dependent on, obsessed with, fanatical about, enthusiastic about; informal mad about.

hook·er /'ho͝okər/ ▶ n. informal a prostitute.

hook·worm /'ho͝ok,wərm/ ▶ n. a worm that can infest the intestines.

hook·y /'ho͝okē/ ▶ n. (**play hooky**) informal stay away from school or work without permission or explanation.

hoo·li·gan /'ho͞oləgin/ ▶ n. a violent young troublemaker.

> SYNONYMS **lout**, thug, vandal, delinquent, ruffian, troublemaker, rowdy; informal tough, bruiser.

■ **hoo·li·gan·ism** n.

hoop /ho͞op/ ▶ n. **1** a rigid circular band. **2** a large ring used as a toy or for circus performers to jump through. **3** a rigid ring with a net attached to it through which a basketball must fall in order to score. **4** a metal arch through which you hit the balls in croquet.

> SYNONYMS **ring**, band, circle, wheel, circlet, loop.

■ **hooped** adj.

hoop·la /'ho͞o,plä, 'ho͝op,lä/ ▶ n. excitement seen as unnecessary fuss.

hoo·poe /'ho͞o,pō, -,po͞o/ ▶ n. a salmon-pink bird with a long downcurved bill, a large crest, and black and white wings and tail.

hoo·ray /hə'rā, ho͞o-/ (or **hurray** or **hurrah** /ho͝o'rä, hə-/) ▶ exclam. used to express joy or approval.

hoot /ho͞ot/ ▶ n. **1** a low sound made by owls, or a similar sound made by a horn, siren, etc. **2** a shout of scorn or disapproval. **3** an outburst of laughter. **4** (**a hoot**) informal an amusing person or thing. ▶ v. make a hoot. □ **not care** (or **give**) **a hoot** (or **two hoots**) informal not care at all. ■ **hoot·er** n.

hooves /ho͝ovz, ho͞ovz/ plural of HOOF.

hop /häp/ ▶ v. (**hops, hopping, hopped**) **1** move by jumping on one foot. **2** (of a bird or animal) move by jumping. **3** jump over or onto. ▶ n. **1** a hopping movement. **2** an informal dance. **3** a short journey or distance.

> SYNONYMS **jump**, bound, spring, bounce, skip, leap, prance, caper.

□ **hopping mad** informal extremely angry.

hope /hōp/ ▶ n. **1** a feeling that something you want may happen. **2** a cause for hope. **3** something that you wish for. ▶ v. (**hopes, hoping, hoped**) **1** expect and want something to happen. **2** intend if possible to do something.

> SYNONYMS ▶ n. **1 aspiration**, desire, wish, expectation, ambition, aim, plan, dream. **2 optimism**, expectation, confidence, faith, belief. ANTONYMS pessimism. ▶ v. **1 expect**, anticipate, look for, be hopeful of, dream of. **2** *we hope to move in on Monday* **aim**, intend, be looking, have the intention, have in mind, plan.

□ **hope against hope** cling to a mere possibility. **not a hope** informal no chance at all.

hope·ful /'hōpfəl/ ▶ adj. feeling or inspiring hope. ▶ n. a person likely or hoping to succeed.

> SYNONYMS ▶ adj. **1 optimistic**, full of hope, confident, sanguine, positive, buoyant, bullish, upbeat. **2 promising**, encouraging, heartening, reassuring, favorable, optimistic. ANTONYMS pessimistic, discouraging.

hope·ful·ly /'hōpfəlē/ ▶ adv. **1** in a hopeful way. **2** it is to be hoped that.

> SYNONYMS **1 optimistically**, full of hope, confidently, buoyantly, expectantly. **2 all being well**, if all goes well, God willing, with luck, knock (on) wood, fingers crossed.

> USAGE
> Although the meaning 'it is to be hoped that' (as in *hopefully we'll see you tomorrow*) is now the more common one, some people feel that it is wrong and so it is best avoided in formal writing.

hope·less /'hōplis/ ▶ adj. **1** feeling or causing despair. **2** not at all skillful.

> SYNONYMS **1 forlorn**, beyond hope, lost, irreparable, irreversible, incurable, impossible, futile. **2 bad**, poor, awful, terrible, dreadful, appalling, atrocious, incompetent; informal pathetic, useless, lousy, rotten, rubbish. ANTONYMS competent.

hope·less·ly /'hōplislē/ ▶ adv. utterly; desperately.

SYNONYMS **utterly**, completely, irretrievably, desperately, impossibly, extremely, totally.

hop·per /'häpər/ ▶ n. a container that tapers downward and empties its contents at the bottom.

hops /häps/ ▶ pl.n. the dried flowers of a climbing plant, used to give beer a bitter flavor.

hop·scotch /'häp,skäcH/ ▶ n. a children's game in which you hop over squares marked on the ground.

horde /hôrd/ ▶ n. chiefly disapproving a large group of people.

SYNONYMS **crowd**, mob, pack, gang, troop, army, swarm, mass, throng.

USAGE

Don't confuse **horde** with **hoard**: a **horde** is a large group of people, whereas a **hoard** is a store of something valuable.

ho·ri·zon /hə'rīzən/ ▶ n. **1** the line at which the earth's surface and the sky appear to meet. **2** (**horizons**) the limits of a person's understanding, experience, or interest. ▫ **on the horizon** soon to happen.

hor·i·zon·tal /,hôrə'zän(t)l/ ▶ adj. parallel to the horizon. ▶ n. a horizontal line or surface.

SYNONYMS ▶ adj. **level**, flat, parallel. ANTONYMS vertical.

■ **hor·i·zon·tal·ly** adv.

hor·mone /'hôr,mōn/ ▶ n. a substance produced in the body that controls the action of particular cells or tissues. ■ **hor·mo·nal** /hôr'mōnl/ adj.

horn /hôrn/ ▶ n. **1** a hard bony growth on the heads of cattle, sheep, and other animals. **2** the substance that horns are made of. **3** a wind instrument shaped like a cone or wound into a spiral. **4** an instrument sounding a signal. ▫ **draw** (or **pull**) **in your horns** become less forceful or ambitious. **horn of plenty** a symbol of a goat's horn overflowing with flowers, fruit, and corn. **horn-rimmed** (of glasses) having rims made of horn or a similar substance. **on the horns of a dilemma** faced with a decision involving equally unfavorable alternatives. ■ **horned** adj.

horn·beam /'hôrn,bēm/ ▶ n. a tree with hard pale wood.

horn·bill /'hôrn,bil/ ▶ n. a tropical bird with a hornlike structure on its large curved bill.

horn·blende /'hôrn,blend/ ▶ n. a dark brown, black, or green mineral.

hor·net /'hôrnit/ ▶ n. a kind of large wasp. ▫ **stir up a hornets' nest** cause difficulties or angry feelings to arise.

horn·pipe /'hôrn,pīp/ ▶ n. a lively solo dance traditionally performed by sailors.

horn·y /'hôrnē/ ▶ adj. (**hornier**, **horniest**) **1** made of or resembling horn. **2** hard and rough.

ho·rol·o·gy /hə'räləjē/ ▶ n. **1** the study and measurement of time. **2** the art of making clocks and watches.

hor·o·scope /'hôrə,skōp, 'härə-/ ▶ n. a forecast of a person's future based on the positions of the stars and planets at the time of their birth.

hor·ren·dous /hə'rendəs, hô-/ ▶ adj. very unpleasant or horrifying. ■ **hor·ren·dous·ly** adv.

hor·ri·ble /'hôrəbəl, 'här-/ ▶ adj. **1** causing horror. **2** very unpleasant.

SYNONYMS **1 dreadful**, awful, terrible, shocking, appalling, horrifying, horrific, horrendous, grisly, ghastly, gruesome, harrowing, unspeakable, abhorrent. **2 nasty**, horrid, disagreeable, obnoxious, disgusting, hateful, odious, objectionable, insufferable. ANTONYMS pleasant.

■ **hor·ri·bly** adv.

hor·rid /'hôrid, 'här-/ ▶ adj. horrible.

hor·ri·fic /hô'rifik, hə-/ ▶ adj. causing horror.

SYNONYMS **dreadful**, horrendous, horrible, terrible, atrocious, horrifying, shocking, appalling, harrowing, hideous, grisly, ghastly, sickening.

■ **hor·rif·i·cal·ly** adv.

hor·ri·fy /'hôrə,fī, 'här-/ ▶ v. (**horrifies**, **horrifying**, **horrified**) fill with horror.

SYNONYMS **shock**, appall, outrage, scandalize, offend, disgust, revolt, nauseate, sicken.

hor·ror /'hôrər, 'här-/ ▶ n. **1** a strong feeling of fear, shock, disgust, or dismay. **2** a thing causing such a feeling. **3** informal a badly behaved person.

SYNONYMS **1 terror**, fear, fright, alarm, panic. **2 dismay**, consternation, alarm, distress, disgust, shock. ANTONYMS delight, satisfaction.

hors d'oeuvre /ôr 'dərv, 'dœvrə/ ▶ n. (plural **hors d'oeuvre** or **hors d'oeuvres**) a small first course of a meal; an appetizer.

horse /hôrs/ ▶ n. **1** a large four-legged animal used for riding and for pulling loads. **2** cavalry. ▶ v. (**horses**, **horsing**, **horsed**) (**horse around**) informal fool around.

SYNONYMS ▶ n. **mount**, charger, nag, colt, stallion, mare, filly, bronco.

▫ **beat** (or **flog**) **a dead horse** waste energy on something that can never be successful. **from the horse's mouth** from a person directly concerned. **hold your horses** informal wait a moment. **horse chestnut 1** a large tree that produces nuts in a spiny case. **2** a conker. **horse latitudes** a belt of calm air and sea occurring in both the northern and southern hemispheres between the trade winds and the westerlies. **horse laugh** a loud, coarse laugh. **horse sense** common sense.

horse·back /'hôrs,bak/ ▶ n. (**on horseback**) mounted on a horse.

horse·flesh /'hôrs,flesH/ ▶ n. horses considered as a group.

horse·fly /'hôrs,flī/ ▶ n. (plural **horseflies**) a large fly that bites horses and other large animals.

horse·hair /'hôrs,he(ə)r/ ▶ n. hair from the mane or tail of a horse, used in furniture for padding.

horse·man /'hôrsmən/ (or **horsewoman** /-,wo͝omən/) ▶ n. (plural **horsemen** or **horsewomen**) a rider on horseback.

horse·play /'hôrs,plā/ ▶ n. rough, high-spirited play.

horse·pow·er /'hôrs,pou(-ə)r/ ▶ n. (plural **horsepower**) a unit measuring the power of an engine.

horse·rad·ish /'hôrs,radisH/ ▶ n. a plant with strong-tasting roots that are made into a sauce.

horse·shoe /'hôr(s),sHōō/ ▶ **n.** **1** a U-shaped iron band attached to the base of a horse's hoof. **2** (**horseshoes**) a game in which horseshoes are thrown at a stake in the ground.

horse·whip /'hôrs,(h)wip/ ▶ **n.** a long whip for controlling horses. ▶ **v.** (**horsewhips**, **horsewhipping**, **horsewhipped**) beat with a horsewhip.

hors·ey /'hôrsē/ (also **horsy**) ▶ **adj.** (**horsier**, **horsiest**) **1** relating to or resembling a horse. **2** very interested in horses or horse racing.

hor·ta·to·ry /'hôrtə,tôrē/ ▶ **adj.** formal strongly urging someone to do something.

hor·ti·cul·ture /'hôrti,kəlcHər/ ▶ **n.** the cultivation of gardens. ■ **hor·ti·cul·tur·al** /,hôrti'kəlcHərəl/ **adj.**

ho·san·na /hō'zanə, -'zä-/ ▶ **n.** an exclamation of praise or joy used in the Bible.

hose /hōz/ ▶ **n.** **1** a flexible tube that conveys water. **2** hosiery. **3** historical men's breeches. ▶ **v.** (**hoses**, **hosing**, **hosed**) spray with a hose.

> SYNONYMS ▶ **n.** **pipe**, tube, duct, outlet, pipeline, siphon.

ho·sier·y /'hōzHərē/ ▶ **n.** socks, tights, and stockings.

hos·pice /'häspis/ ▶ **n.** a home for people who are very ill or dying.

hos·pi·ta·ble /hä'spitəbəl, 'häspitəbəl/ ▶ **adj.** **1** friendly and welcoming to strangers or guests. **2** (of an environment) pleasant and favorable for living in.

> SYNONYMS **welcoming**, friendly, sociable, cordial, gracious, accommodating, warm.

■ **hos·pi·ta·bly** **adv.**

hos·pi·tal /'hä,spitl/ ▶ **n.** a place where sick or injured people are looked after.

> SYNONYMS **infirmary**, clinic, sanatorium, hospice; Military field hospital.

hos·pi·tal·i·ty /,häspi'talitē/ ▶ **n.** the friendly and generous treatment of guests or strangers.

> SYNONYMS **friendliness**, neighborliness, sociability, welcome, warmth, kindness, cordiality, generosity.

hos·pi·tal·ize /'häspitl,īz/ ▶ **v.** (**hospitalizes**, **hospitalizing**, **hospitalized**) admit someone to hospital. ■ **hos·pi·tal·i·za·tion** /,häspitl-li'zāsHən/ **n.**

Host /hōst/ ▶ **n.** (**the Host**) the bread used in the Christian ceremony of Holy Communion.

host¹ /hōst/ ▶ **n.** **1** a person who receives or entertains guests. **2** the moderator or emcee of a television or radio program. **3** the place that holds an event to which others are invited. **4** Biology an animal or plant on or in which a parasite lives. ▶ **v.** **1** act as host at. **2** store a website or other electronic data on a computer connected to the Internet: *the library hosts a business website*.

> SYNONYMS ▶ **n.** **presenter**, compère, anchor, anchorman, anchorwoman, announcer. ANTONYMS guest. ▶ **v.** **present**, introduce, compère, front, anchor.

host² ▶ **n.** (**a host** or **hosts of**) a large number of.

hos·tage /'hästij/ ▶ **n.** a person held prisoner in an attempt to make other people give in to a demand.

> SYNONYMS **captive**, prisoner, detainee, internee.

hos·tel /'hästl/ ▶ **n.** a place that provides cheap food and accommodations for a particular group of people.

host·ess /'hōstis/ ▶ **n.** **1** a female host. **2** a woman employed to welcome customers at a nightclub or bar.

hos·tile /'hästl, 'hä,stīl/ ▶ **adj.** **1** aggressively unfriendly. **2** having to do with a military enemy.

> SYNONYMS **1** **unfriendly**, unkind, unsympathetic, antagonistic, aggressive, confrontational, belligerent. **2** **unfavorable**, adverse, bad, harsh, grim, inhospitable, forbidding. **3** *they are hostile to the idea* **opposed**, averse, antagonistic, ill-disposed, unsympathetic, antipathetic, against; informal anti. ANTONYMS friendly, favorable.

hos·til·i·ty /hä'stilitē/ ▶ **n.** (plural **hostilities**) **1** hostile behavior. **2** (**hostilities**) acts of warfare.

> SYNONYMS **1** **antagonism**, unfriendliness, malevolence, venom, hatred, aggression, belligerence. **2** **opposition**, antagonism, animosity, antipathy. **3** *a cessation of hostilities* **fighting**, armed conflict, combat, warfare, war, bloodshed, violence.

host·ler /'häslər/ ▶ **n.** (in the past) a man employed at an inn to look after customers' horses.

hot /hät/ ▶ **adj.** (**hotter**, **hottest**) **1** having a high temperature. **2** feeling or producing an uncomfortable sensation of heat. **3** informal currently popular or interesting. **4** informal (of goods) stolen. **5** (**hot on**) informal knowing a lot about. **6** (**hot on**) informal strict about.

> SYNONYMS **1** *hot food* **heated**, sizzling, roasting, boiling, scorching, scalding, red-hot. **2** *a hot day* **very warm**, balmy, summery, tropical, scorching, searing, blistering, sweltering, torrid, sultry; informal boiling, baking, roasting. **3** **spicy**, peppery, fiery, strong, piquant, powerful. **4** **fierce**, intense, keen, competitive, cutthroat, ruthless, aggressive, violent. **5** *she's hot on local history* **knowledgeable**, well-informed, au fait, well up, well-versed; informal clued up. ANTONYMS cold, mild.

□ **hot air** informal empty or boastful talk. **hot-blooded** passionate. **hot dog** a hot sausage usually served in a long, soft roll. **hot flash** (or **flush**) a sudden feeling of heat in the skin or face. **hot plate** **1** a flat heated surface (or a set of these), typically portable, used for cooking food or keeping it hot. **2** a flat heated surface on an electric stove. **hot potato** informal a controversial issue. **hot rod** a car specially adapted to be fast. **the hot seat** informal the position of having full responsibility for something. **hot spot** a place where there is a lot of activity or danger. **hot stuff** informal a person or thing of outstanding talent or interest. **hot-tempered** easily angered. **hot ticket** informal a person or thing that is in great demand. **hot tub** a large tub filled with hot bubbling water. **hot-water bottle** a container filled with hot water and used for warmth. **hot-wire** informal start a vehicle without using the ignition switch. **hot under the collar** informal angry or annoyed. **in hot water** informal in trouble.

hot·bed /'hät,bed/ ▶ **n.** a place where a lot of a particular activity is happening.

hot·cake /'hät,kāk/ ▶ **n.** a pancake. □ **sell like hotcakes** informal be sold quickly and in large amounts.

ho·tel /hō'tel/ ▶ **n.** a place providing accommodations and meals for travelers.

ho·te·lier /ˌôtel'yā, hōtl'i(ə)r/ ▶ **n.** a person who owns or manages a hotel.

hot·foot /'hätˌfo͝ot/ ▶ **adv.** quickly and eagerly. ◻ **hotfoot it** hurry eagerly.

hot·head /'hätˌhed/ ▶ **n.** an impetuous or quick-tempered person.

hot·house /'hätˌhous/ ▶ **n. 1** a heated greenhouse. **2** an environment that encourages rapid growth.

hot·line /'hätˌlīn/ ▶ **n.** a direct telephone line set up for a specific purpose.

hot·ly /'hätlē/ ▶ **adv.** in a passionate, excited, or angry way: *the rumors were hotly denied.*

> SYNONYMS **vehemently**, vigorously, strenuously, fiercely, heatedly.

hot·shot /'hätˌSHät/ ▶ **n.** informal an important or very skilled person.

hot·tie /'hätē/ (also **hotty**)▶ **n.** (plural **hotties**) informal a very attractive person.

hound /hound/ ▶ **n. 1** a hunting dog. **2** a person who pursues something eagerly: *a publicity hound.* ▶ **v.** harass someone.

> SYNONYMS ▶ **v. pursue**, chase, stalk, harry, harass, pester, badger, torment.

hour /ou(ə)r/ ▶ **n. 1** a twenty-fourth part of a day and night; 60 minutes. **2** (**hours**) a period set aside for a particular purpose: *leisure hours.* **3** a particular point in time. **4** (**hours**) informal a very long time. ◻ **on the hour 1** at an exact hour, or on each hour, of the day or night. **2** after a period of one hour.

hour·glass /'ou(ə)rˌglas/ ▶ **n.** an object consisting of two connected glass bulbs containing sand that takes an hour to fall from the upper to the lower bulb.

hour·ly /'ou(ə)rlē/ ▶ **adv. & adj. 1** every hour. **2** by the hour.

house ▶ **n.** /hous/ **1** a building for people to live in. **2** a firm or institution: *a fashion house.* **3** a long-established and powerful family. **4** (also **house music**) a style of popular dance music. **5** (**the House**) the House of Representatives of the United States Congress. ▶ **v.** /houz/ (**houses**, **housing**, **housed**) **1** provide with accommodations. **2** provide space for. **3** enclose something.

> SYNONYMS ▶ **n. 1 residence**, home; informal pad; formal dwelling, abode, habitation, domicile. **2 family**, clan, tribe, dynasty, line, bloodline, lineage. **3 firm**, business, company, corporation, enterprise, establishment, institution, concern, organization, operation; informal outfit. **4 assembly**, legislative body, congress, senate, chamber, council, parliament. ▶ **v. 1 accommodate**, give someone a roof over their head, lodge, quarter, board, billet, take in, put up. **2 contain**, hold, store, cover, protect, enclose.

◻ **house arrest** the state of being kept as a prisoner in your own house. **house-hunting** the process of seeking a house to buy or rent. **house husband** a man whose main occupation is caring for his family and looking after the home. **house lights** the lights in the part of a theater where the audience sits. **house martin** a black and white bird that nests on buildings. **House of Commons** the chamber of the British Parliament whose members are elected. **House of Lords** the chamber of the British Parliament whose members are peers and bishops. **House of Representatives** the lower house of the United States Congress. **house-proud** very concerned with the appearance of your home. **on the house** at the management's expense.

house·boat /'housˌbōt/ ▶ **n.** a boat that people can live in.

house·bound /'housˌbound/ ▶ **adj.** unable to leave your house.

house·break /'housˌbrāk/ ▶ **v.** train a pet to urinate and defecate outside the house or only in a special place.

house·break·ing /'housˌbrākiNG/ ▶ **n. 1** the action of breaking into a building to commit a crime. **2** the process of teaching a dog to urinate and defecate outside of the house.

house·coat /'housˌkōt/ ▶ **n.** a robe worn casually around the house by women.

house·fly /'housˌflī/ ▶ **n.** a common fly often found in houses.

house·hold /'housˌ(h)ōld/ ▶ **n.** a house and all the people living in it.

> SYNONYMS **1 family**, house, occupants, clan, tribe; informal brood. **2** *household goods* **domestic**, family, everyday, workaday.

◻ **household name** a famous person or thing. ■ **house·hold·er n.**

house·keep·er /'housˌkēpər/ ▶ **n.** a person employed to shop, cook, and clean the house. ■ **house·keep·ing n.**

house·maid /'housˌmād/ ▶ **n.** a female servant in a house.

house·mas·ter /'housˌmastər/ (or **housemistress**) ▶ **n.** a teacher in charge of a dormitory at a boarding school.

house·mate /'housˌmāt/ ▶ **n.** a person with whom you share a house.

house·plant /'housˌplant/ ▶ **n.** a plant grown indoors.

house·warm·ing /'housˌwôrmiNG/ ▶ **n.** a party celebrating a move to a new home.

house·wife /'housˌwīf/ ▶ **n.** (plural **housewives** /-ˌwīvz/) a woman whose main occupation is looking after her family and the home.

house·work /'housˌwərk/ ▶ **n.** cleaning, cooking, etc., done in running a home.

hous·ing /'houziNG/ ▶ **n. 1** houses and apartments as a whole. **2** a hard cover for a piece of equipment.

> SYNONYMS **1 accommodations**, houses, homes, living quarters; formal dwellings. **2 casing**, covering, case, cover, holder, sleeve.

hove /hōv/ chiefly Nautical past tense of **HEAVE**.

hov·el /'həvəl, 'hävəl/ ▶ **n.** a small house that is dirty and run-down.

> SYNONYMS **shack**, shanty, hut, slum; informal dump, hole.

hov·er /'həvər/ ▶ **v.** (**hovers**, **hovering**, **hovered**) **1** remain in one place in the air. **2** wait about uncertainly. **3** remain near a particular level or between two states: *inflation will hover around the 4 percent mark.*

> SYNONYMS **1 hang**, be poised, be suspended, float, fly, drift. **2 wait**, linger, loiter.

hov·er·craft /'həvərˌkraft/ ▶ **n.** (plural **hovercraft**) a vehicle that travels over land or water on a cushion of air.

how /hou/ ▶ **adv. 1** in what way or by what means. **2** in what condition. **3** to what extent or degree. **4** the way in which: *she described how she had lived.* ◻ **and how!** informal very much so. **how about?** would you like? **how do you do?** said when you meet someone for the first time in a formal situation. **how many** what number. **how much** what amount or price.

how·dah /'houdə/ ▶ **n.** a seat for riding on the back of an elephant.

how·dy /'houdē/ ▶ **exclam.** a friendly greeting, particularly associated with the western states: *howdy, stranger.*

how·ev·er /hou'evər/ ▶ **adv. 1** used to begin a statement that contrasts with something that has just been said: *People tend to put on weight in middle age. However, gaining weight is not inevitable.* **2** in whatever way or to whatever extent.

> SYNONYMS **nevertheless**, nonetheless, even so, but, for all that, despite that, in spite of that.

how·itz·er /'houətsər/ ▶ **n.** a short gun for firing shells at a high angle.

howl /houl/ ▶ **n. 1** a long wailing cry made by an animal. **2** a loud cry of pain, amusement, etc. ▶ **v.** make a howl.

> SYNONYMS ▶ **n. 1 baying**, cry, bark, yelp, yowl. **2 wail**, cry, yell, yelp, bellow, roar, shout, shriek, scream, screech. ▶ **v. 1 bay**, cry, bark, yelp, yowl. **2 wail**, cry, yell, bawl, bellow, shriek, scream, screech, caterwaul, ululate; informal holler.

howl·er /'houlər/ ▶ **n.** informal a stupid mistake.

howl·ing /'houliNG/ ▶ **adj.** informal great: *the meal was a howling success.*

hoy·den /'hoidn/ ▶ **n.** dated a girl who behaves in a high-spirited or wild way.

h.p. (or **HP**) ▶ **abbr.** horsepower.

HQ ▶ **abbr.** headquarters.

hr ▶ **abbr.** hour.

HRH ▶ **abbr.** British Her (or His) Royal Highness.

HTML ▶ **abbr.** Computing Hypertext Markup Language.

HTTP ▶ **abbr.** Computing Hypertext Transport (or Transfer) Protocol.

hub /həb/ ▶ **n. 1** the central part of a wheel. **2** the center of an activity or region.

> SYNONYMS **center**, core, heart, focus, focal point, nucleus, kernel, nerve center. ANTONYMS periphery.

hub·bub /'həbəb/ ▶ **n.** a loud confused noise caused by a crowd.

> SYNONYMS **1 noise**, din, racket, commotion, clamor, cacophony, babel, rumpus. **2 confusion**, chaos, commotion, pandemonium, bedlam, mayhem, tumult, fracas, hurly-burly; informal hullabaloo.

hub·by /'həbē/ ▶ **n.** (plural **hubbies**) informal a husband.

hu·bris /'(h)yo͞obris/ ▶ **n.** excessive pride or self-confidence.

huck·ster /'həkstər/ ▶ **n. 1** a person who sells things forcefully. **2** a person who sells small items in the street. ■ **huck·ster·ism n.**

hud·dle /'hədl/ ▶ **v.** (**huddles**, **huddling**, **huddled**) **1** crowd together. **2** curl your body into a small space. ▶ **n.** a number of people or things crowded together.

> SYNONYMS ▶ **v. 1 crowd**, cluster, gather, bunch, throng, flock, collect, group, congregate. **2 curl up**, snuggle, nestle, hunch up. ANTONYMS disperse. ▶ **n. group**, cluster, bunch, collection; informal gaggle.

hue /(h)yo͞o/ ▶ **n. 1** a color or shade. **2** a particular aspect of something: *men of all political hues.*

> SYNONYMS **color**, shade, tone, tint, tinge.

◻ **hue and cry** a strong public outcry.

huff /həf/ ▶ **v.** (often **huff and puff**) breathe out noisily. ▶ **n.** a bad mood.

huff·y /'həfē/ ▶ **adj.** (**huffier**, **huffiest**) easily offended. ■ **huff·i·ly adv. huff·i·ness n.**

hug /həg/ ▶ **v.** (**hugs**, **hugging**, **hugged**) **1** hold tightly in your arms. **2** keep close to: *a few craft hugged the shore.* ▶ **n.** an act of hugging.

> SYNONYMS ▶ **v. embrace**, cuddle, squeeze, clasp, clutch, hold tight. ▶ **n. embrace**, cuddle, squeeze, bear hug.

huge /(h)yo͞oj/ ▶ **adj.** (**huger**, **hugest**) very large.

> SYNONYMS **enormous**, vast, immense, massive, colossal, prodigious, gigantic, gargantuan, mammoth, monumental, giant, towering, mountainous, tremendous, considerable, sizable, substantial, titanic, epic; informal mega, monster, astronomical, ginormous, humongous, hulking, whopping. ANTONYMS tiny.

■ **huge·ly adv. huge·ness n.**

Hu·gue·not /'hyo͞ogəˌnät/ ▶ **n.** a French Protestant of the 16th–17th centuries.

huh /hə/ ▶ **exclam.** used to express scorn or surprise, or in questions to invite agreement.

hu·la /'ho͞olə/ ▶ **n.** a Hawaiian dance performed by women, in which the dancers sway their hips and use a variety of hand motions. ◻ **hula hoop** (also trademark **Hula-Hoop**) a large hoop that you spin around your body by moving your hips.

hulk /həlk/ ▶ **n. 1** an old ship stripped of fittings and no longer used. **2** a large or clumsy person or thing.

hulk·ing /'həlkiNG/ ▶ **adj.** informal very large or clumsy.

hull[1] /həl/ ▶ **n.** the main body of a ship.

> SYNONYMS **framework**, body, shell, frame, skeleton, structure.

hull[2] ▶ **n. 1** the outer covering of a fruit or seed. **2** the cluster of leaves and stalk on a strawberry or raspberry. ▶ **v.** remove the hulls from.

hul·la·ba·loo /'hələbəˌlo͞o, ˌhələbə'lo͞o/ ▶ **n.** informal an uproar.

hul·lo /hə'lō/ = **HELLO**.

hum /həm/ ▶ **v.** (**hums**, **humming**, **hummed**) **1** make a low continuous sound like that of a bee. **2** sing a tune with closed lips. **3** informal be in a state of great activity. ▶ **n.** a low continuous sound.

> SYNONYMS ▶ **v. 1 purr**, drone, murmur, buzz, whirr, throb. **2 be busy**, be active, be lively, buzz, bustle, be a hive of activity, throb. ▶ **n. murmur**, drone, purr, buzz.

■ **hum·ma·ble adj.**

hu·man /'(h)yo͞omən/ ▶ **adj. 1** having to do with men, women, or children. **2** showing the better qualities of people. ▶ **n.** (also **human being**) a man, woman, or child.

SYNONYMS ▶ **adj.** **1 mortal**, flesh and blood, fallible, weak, frail, imperfect, vulnerable, physical, bodily, fleshly. **2 compassionate**, humane, kind, considerate, understanding, sympathetic. ▶ **n.** **person**, human being, Homo sapiens, man, woman, individual, mortal, (living) soul, earthling; (**humans**) the human race, humanity, humankind, mankind, people.

□ **human nature** the way most people think or behave. **human resources** the department of an organization that deals with the hiring and training of personnel. **human rights** basic rights that belong to all people, such as freedom.

hu·mane /(h)yo͞o'mān/ ▶ **adj.** showing concern and kindness toward other people.

SYNONYMS **compassionate**, kind, considerate, understanding, sympathetic, tolerant, forbearing, forgiving, merciful, humanitarian, charitable. ANTONYMS cruel.

■ **hu·mane·ly** **adv.**

hu·man·ism /'(h)yo͞omə,nizəm/ ▶ **n.** a system of thought that sees people as able to live their lives without the need for religious beliefs. ■ **hu·man·ist** **n. & adj.** **hu·man·is·tic** /,(h)yo͞omə'nistik/ **adj.**

hu·man·i·tar·i·an /(h)yo͞o,mani'te(ə)rēən/ ▶ **adj.** concerned with the welfare of people. ▶ **n.** a humanitarian person.

SYNONYMS ▶ **adj.** **1 compassionate**, humane, unselfish, altruistic, generous. **2 charitable**, philanthropic, public-spirited, socially concerned. ▶ **n.** **philanthropist**, altruist, benefactor, social reformer, good Samaritan, do-gooder.

hu·man·i·ty /(h)yo͞o'manitē/ ▶ **n.** **1** people as a whole. **2** the condition of being human. **3** sympathy and kindness toward other people. **4** (**humanities**) studies concerned with human culture, such as literature or history.

SYNONYMS **1 humankind**, mankind, man, people, the human race, Homo sapiens. **2 compassion**, brotherly love, fellow feeling, humaneness, kindness, consideration, understanding, sympathy, tolerance.

hu·man·ize /'(h)yo͞omə,nīz/ ▶ **v.** (**humanizes**, **humanizing**, **humanized**) make more pleasant or suitable for people.

hu·man·kind /'(h)yo͞omən,kīnd/ ▶ **n.** people as a whole.

hu·man·ly /'(h)yo͞omənlē/ ▶ **adv.** **1** from a human point of view. **2** by human means; within human ability: *we did all that was humanly possible.*

hu·man·oid /'(h)yo͞omə,noid/ ▶ **adj.** like a human in appearance. ▶ **n.** a humanoid being.

hum·ble /'həmbəl/ ▶ **adj.** (**humbler**, **humblest**) **1** having a modest or low opinion of your own importance. **2** of low rank. **3** not large or important: *humble brick bungalows.* ▶ **v.** (**humbles**, **humbling**, **humbled**) make someone seem less important.

SYNONYMS ▶ **adj.** **1 meek**, deferential, respectful, submissive, self-effacing, unassertive, modest, unassuming, self-deprecating. **2 lowly**, poor, undistinguished, mean, common, ordinary, simple, modest. ANTONYMS proud, arrogant. ▶ **v.** **humiliate**, demean, lower, degrade, debase, mortify, shame.

□ **eat humble pie** make a humble apology. ■ **hum·bly** **adv.**

hum·bug /'həm,bəg/ ▶ **n.** **1** false or misleading talk or behavior. **2** a person who is not sincere or honest.

hum·ding·er /'həm'diNGər/ ▶ **n.** informal an outstanding person or thing.

hum·drum /'həm,drəm/ ▶ **adj.** ordinary; dull.

SYNONYMS **mundane**, dull, dreary, boring, tedious, monotonous, prosaic, routine, ordinary, everyday, run-of-the-mill, workaday, pedestrian.

hu·mer·us /'(h)yo͞omərəs/ ▶ **n.** (plural **humeri** /-,rī/) the bone of the upper arm, between the shoulder and the elbow.

hu·mid /'(h)yo͞omid/ ▶ **adj.** (of the air or weather) damp and warm.

SYNONYMS **muggy**, close, sultry, sticky, steamy, clammy, heavy. ANTONYMS dry, fresh.

hu·mid·i·fy /(h)yo͞o'midə,fī/ ▶ **v.** (**humidifies**, **humidifying**, **humidified**) increase the level of moisture in air. ■ **hu·mid·i·fi·er** **n.**

hu·mid·i·ty /(h)yo͞o'miditē/ ▶ **n.** **1** the state or quality of being humid. **2** a measure of the amount of water vapor in the atmosphere or a gas.

hu·mil·i·ate /(h)yo͞o'milē,āt/ ▶ **v.** (**humiliates**, **humiliating**, **humiliated**) make someone feel ashamed or stupid.

SYNONYMS **1 embarrass**, mortify, humble, shame, disgrace, chasten, deflate, crush, squash, demean, take down a peg or two; informal show up, put down, cut down to size, make someone eat crow. **2** (**humiliating**) **embarrassing**, mortifying, humbling, ignominious, inglorious, shaming, undignified, chastening, demeaning, degrading, deflating. ANTONYMS dignify.

hu·mil·i·a·tion /(h)yo͞o,milē'āSHən/ ▶ **n.** **1** the feeling of being ashamed or stupid. **2** a situation in which you are made to feel embarrassed or lose prestige.

SYNONYMS **embarrassment**, mortification, shame, indignity, ignominy, disgrace, dishonor, degradation, discredit, loss of face, blow to your pride.

hu·mil·i·ty /(h)yo͞o'militē/ ▶ **n.** the quality of being humble.

SYNONYMS **modesty**, humbleness, meekness, respect, deference, diffidence. ANTONYMS pride.

hum·ming·bird /'həmiNG,bərd/ ▶ **n.** a small bird able to hover by beating its wings very fast.

hum·mock /'həmək/ ▶ **n.** a small hill or mound.

hum·mus /'ho͝oməs, 'həm-/ (or **houmous**) ▶ **n.** a Middle Eastern dip made from chickpeas, sesame seeds, etc.

SPELLING

Because there are several ways in which the original Arabic word is converted to the English alphabet, there are several different English spellings: **hummus**, **houmous**, **hoummos**, and **humous** are all commonly used, but **hummus** is more common than the others.

hu·mor /ˈ(h)yo͞omər/ ▶ **n. 1** the quality of being amusing. **2** a state of mind: *her good humor vanished.* ▶ **v.** do as someone wishes in order to keep them happy.

> SYNONYMS ▶ **n. 1 comedy**, funny side, hilarity, absurdity, ludicrousness, satire, irony. **2 jokes**, jests, quips, witticisms, funny remarks, wit, comedy; informal gags, wisecracks. **3 mood**, temper, disposition, spirits. ANTONYMS seriousness. ▶ **v. indulge**, accommodate, pander to, cater to, give in to, go along with, flatter, mollify, placate.

□ **out of humor** in a bad mood. ■ **hu·mor·less** adj.

hu·mor·ist /ˈ(h)yo͞omərist/ ▶ **n.** a writer or speaker who is known for being amusing.

hu·mor·ous /ˈ(h)yo͞omərəs/ ▶ **adj. 1** causing amusement. **2** showing a sense of humor.

> SYNONYMS **amusing**, funny, comic, comical, entertaining, diverting, witty, jocular, lighthearted, hilarious. ANTONYMS serious.

■ **hu·mor·ous·ly** adv.

hump /həmp/ ▶ **n. 1** a rounded mass of earth or land. **2** a round part projecting from the back of a camel or other animal, or as an abnormal feature on a person's back. ▶ **v.** informal lift or carry with difficulty.

> SYNONYMS ▶ **n. protuberance**, prominence, lump, bump, knob, protrusion, projection, bulge, swelling, growth, outgrowth.

■ **humped** adj.

hump·back /ˈhəmpˌbak/ ▶ **n. 1** (also **humpback whale**) a baleen whale that has a hump (instead of a dorsal fin) and long white flippers. **2** offensive a person with an abnormal hump on their back; hunchback. ■ **hump·backed** adj.

hu·mus /ˈ(h)yo͞oməs/ ▶ **n.** a substance found in soil, made from dead leaves and plants.

Hun /hən/ ▶ **n. 1** a member of a people from Asia who invaded Europe in the 4th–5th centuries. **2** informal, disapproving a German.

hunch /hənCH/ ▶ **v.** raise your shoulders and bend the top part of your body forward. ▶ **n.** an idea based on a feeling rather than evidence.

> SYNONYMS ▶ **n. feeling**, guess, suspicion, impression, inkling, idea, notion, fancy, intuition; informal gut feeling.

hunch·back /ˈhənCHˌbak/ ▶ **n.** offensive a person with an abnormal hump on their back.

hun·dred /ˈhəndrid/ ▶ **cardinal number 1** ten more than ninety; 100. (Roman numeral: **c** or **C**) **2** (**hundreds**) informal a large number. □ **a** (or **one**) **hundred percent 1** completely. **2** informal completely fit and healthy. ■ **hun·dredth** ordinal number.

hun·dred·weight /ˈhəndridˌwāt/ ▶ **n.** (plural **hundredweight** or **hundredweights**) **1** a unit of weight equal to 100 lb (about 45.4 kg). **2** British a unit of weight equal to 112 lb (about 50.8 kg).

hung /həNG/ past and past participle of **HANG** ▶ **adj. 1** (of a jury) unable to agree on a verdict. **2** (**hung up**) informal emotionally confused or disturbed. **3** having no political party with an overall majority: *a hung parliament.*

Hun·gar·i·an /həNGˈge(ə)rēən/ ▶ **n. 1** a person from Hungary. **2** the language of Hungary. ▶ **adj.** relating to Hungary.

hun·ger /ˈhəNGgər/ ▶ **n. 1** a feeling of discomfort caused by a lack of food. **2** a strong desire: *her hunger for knowledge.* ▶ **v.** (**hungers**, **hungering**, **hungered**) (**hunger after** or **for**) have a strong desire for.

> SYNONYMS ▶ **n. 1 lack of food**, starvation, malnutrition, undernourishment. **2 desire**, craving, longing, yearning, hankering, appetite, thirst; informal itch.

□ **hunger strike** a refusal to eat for a long period, carried out as a protest about something.

hung·o·ver /ˈhəNGgˈōvər/ ▶ **adj.** suffering from a hangover.

hun·gry /ˈhəNGgrē/ ▶ **adj.** (**hungrier**, **hungriest**) **1** feeling that you want to eat something. **2** having a strong desire for something: *a party hungry for power.*

> SYNONYMS **1 ravenous**, famished, starving, starved, malnourished, undernourished, underfed; informal peckish. **2** *they are hungry for success* **eager**, keen, avid, longing, yearning, aching, greedy, craving, desirous of, hankering after; informal itching, dying. ANTONYMS full.

■ **hun·gri·ly** adv.

hunk /həNGk/ ▶ **n. 1** a large piece cut or broken from something larger. **2** informal a good-looking man.

> SYNONYMS **chunk**, wedge, block, slab, lump, square, gobbet.

hunk·er /ˈhəNGkər/ ▶ **v.** (**hunkers**, **hunkering**, **hunkered**) squat or crouch down low.

hunk·y /ˈhəNGkē/ ▶ **adj.** (of a man) large and physically attractive. □ **hunky-dory** informal fine; satisfactory.

hunt /hənt/ ▶ **v. 1** chase and kill a wild animal for food or as a sport. **2** search for something: *the market is a good place to hunt for antiques.* **3** (**hunt someone down**) chase and capture someone. **4** (**hunted**) looking worried and as if you are being chased. ▶ **n. 1** an act of hunting. **2** a group of people who meet regularly to hunt animals as a sport.

> SYNONYMS ▶ **v. 1 chase**, stalk, pursue, course, track, trail. **2 search**, seek, look high and low, scour the area. ▶ **n. 1 chase**, pursuit. **2 search**, quest.

hunt·er /ˈhən(t)ər/ ▶ **n. 1** a person or animal that hunts. **2** a breed of horse developed for stamina in fox hunting. ■ **hunt·ress** n.

hunts·man /ˈhəntsmən/ ▶ **n.** (plural **huntsmen**) a person who hunts.

hur·dle /ˈhərdl/ ▶ **n. 1** each of a series of upright frames that an athlete jumps over in a race. **2** a frame used as a temporary fence. **3** an obstacle or difficulty. ▶ **v.** (**hurdles**, **hurdling**, **hurdled**) jump over an obstacle while running.

> SYNONYMS ▶ **n. obstacle**, difficulty, problem, barrier, bar, snag, stumbling block, impediment, obstruction, complication, hindrance.

■ **hur·dler** n.

hur·dy-gur·dy /ˈhərdē ˌgərdē/ ▶ **n.** (plural **hurdy-gurdies**) a musical instrument played by turning a handle.

hurl /hərl/ ▶ **v. 1** throw something with great force. **2** shout insults.

> SYNONYMS **throw**, toss, fling, launch, pitch, cast, lob; informal chuck, sling.

hurl·y-burl·y /ˈhərlē ˈbərlē/ ▶ **n.** busy and noisy activity.

hur·rah /hŏŏ'rä, hə-/ (or **hooray** /hə'rā, hŏŏ-/ or **hurray**) ▶ **exclam.** used to express joy or approval.

hur·ri·cane /'hərˌkān, 'hə-ri-/ ▶ **n.** a severe storm with a violent wind.

SYNONYMS **typhoon**, storm, windstorm, whirlwind, gale, tempest.

□ **hurricane lamp** an oil lamp in which the flame is protected from the wind by a glass tube.

hur·ry /'hərē, 'hə-rē/ ▶ **v.** (**hurries**, **hurrying**, **hurried**) **1** move or act quickly. **2** do something quickly or too quickly: *guided tours tend to be hurried.* ▶ **n.** great haste.

SYNONYMS ▶ **v. 1 be quick**, hurry up, hasten, speed up, run, dash, rush, race, scurry, scramble, scuttle, sprint; informal get a move on, step on it, hightail it, hotfoot it. **2 hustle**, hasten, push, urge. **3** (**hurried**) **quick**, fast, swift, rapid, speedy, brisk, cursory, perfunctory, brief, short, fleeting. **4** (**hurried**) **hasty**, rushed, precipitate, spur-of-the-moment. ANTONYMS dawdle, delay. ▶ **n. rush**, haste, speed, urgency, hustle and bustle.

□ **in a hurry 1** hurrying; in a rushed way. **2** informal easily: *you won't forget that in a hurry.*
■ **hur·ried·ly adv.**

hurt /hərt/ ▶ **v.** (**hurts**, **hurting**, **hurt**) **1** make someone feel physical pain. **2** feel pain. **3** upset someone. ▶ **n. 1** injury or pain. **2** unhappiness or distress. ▶ **adj. 1** injured. **2** feeling or showing distress.

SYNONYMS ▶ **v. 1 be painful**, ache, be sore, be tender, smart, sting, burn, throb; informal be agony. **2 injure**, wound, damage, disable, bruise, cut, gash, graze, scrape, scratch. **3 distress**, pain, wound, sting, upset, sadden, devastate, grieve, mortify. ▶ **n. distress**, pain, suffering, grief, misery, anguish, upset, sadness, sorrow. ▶ **adj. 1 injured**, wounded, bruised, grazed, cut, gashed, sore, painful, aching. **2 pained**, aggrieved, offended, distressed, upset, sad, mortified; informal miffed.

hurt·ful /'hərtfəl/ ▶ **adj.** upsetting; unkind.

SYNONYMS **upsetting**, distressing, wounding, unkind, cruel, nasty, mean, malicious, spiteful.

■ **hurt·ful·ly adv.**

hur·tle /'hərtl/ ▶ **v.** (**hurtles**, **hurtling**, **hurtled**) move very fast.

SYNONYMS **speed**, rush, run, race, careen, whiz, zoom, charge, shoot, streak, gallop, fly, go like the wind; informal belt, pelt, tear, barrel, go like a bat out of hell.

hus·band /'həzbənd/ ▶ **n.** the man that a woman is married to. ▶ **v.** use something carefully without wasting it.

hus·band·ry /'həzbəndrē/ ▶ **n. 1** farming. **2** careful management of resources.

hush /həsн/ ▶ **v. 1** make or become quiet. **2** (**hush something up**) stop something from becoming known. ▶ **n.** a silence.

SYNONYMS ▶ **v. silence**, quiet (down), shush, gag, muzzle; informal shut up. ▶ **n. silence**, quiet, stillness, peace, calm, tranquility. ANTONYMS noise.

□ **hush-hush** informal highly secret. **hush money** informal money paid to someone to prevent them from revealing information.

husk /həsk/ ▶ **n.** the dry outer covering of some fruits or seeds. ▶ **v.** remove the husk from.

SYNONYMS ▶ **n. shell**, hull, pod, case, covering, integument; Botany pericarp.

husk·y¹ /'həskē/ ▶ **adj.** (**huskier**, **huskiest**) **1** (of a voice) deep and rough. **2** big and strong.

SYNONYMS *a husky voice* **throaty**, gruff, gravelly, hoarse, croaky, rough, guttural, harsh, rasping, raspy. ANTONYMS shrill, soft.

■ **husk·i·ly adv.**

husk·y² ▶ **n.** (plural **huskies**) a powerful dog used for pulling sleds.

hus·sar /hə'zär/ ▶ **n.** historical a soldier in a light cavalry regiment.

hus·sy /'həsē, 'həzē/ ▶ **n.** (plural **hussies**) a girl or woman who behaves in an immoral or impudent way.

hust·ings /'həstiNGz/ ▶ **n.** the political meetings and speeches that take place before an election.

hus·tle /'həsəl/ ▶ **v.** (**hustles**, **hustling**, **hustled**) **1** push or move roughly. **2** informal obtain something dishonestly. ▶ **n.** busy movement and activity.

SYNONYMS ▶ **v. 1 push**, shove, thrust, manhandle, frogmarch. **2** *I was hustled into joining their church* **coerce**, force, compel, pressure, badger, hound, harass, nag, urge, goad, browbeat. **3** *we got hustled by a guy selling expired tickets* **swindle**, cheat, trick, bamboozle, hoodwink; informal con, fleece, rip off.

■ **hus·tler n.**

hut /hət/ ▶ **n.** a small, simple house or shelter.

SYNONYMS **shack**, shanty, cabin, cabana, shelter, shed, lean-to, hovel.

hutch /həcн/ ▶ **n.** a box with a front made of wire, used for keeping rabbits.

huz·zah /hə'zä/ (also **huzza**) old use ▶ **exclam.** used to express approval or delight; hurrah. ▶ **v.** cry "huzzah.".

hy·a·cinth /'hīəˌsinтн/ ▶ **n.** a plant with bell-shaped flowers.

hy·brid /'hīˌbrid/ ▶ **n. 1** the offspring of two plants or animals of different species or varieties. **2** something made by combining two different things. **3** a motor vehicle that runs on both gasoline and an electric battery.

SYNONYMS **1 cross**, crossbreed, mixture, blend, combination, composite, fusion, amalgam. **2** *hybrid roses* **composite**, crossbred, interbred, mixed, blended, compound.

hy·brid·ize /'hībriˌdīz/ ▶ **v.** (**hybridizes**, **hybridizing**, **hybridized**) breed individuals of two different species or varieties to produce hybrids.

hy·dra /'hīdrə/ ▶ **n.** a minute freshwater invertebrate animal with a tubular body and tentacles around the mouth.

hy·dran·gea /hī'drānjə/ ▶ **n.** a shrub with white, blue, or pink clusters of flowers.

hy·drant /'hīdrənt/ ▶ **n.** a water pipe with a nozzle for attaching a fire hose.

hy·drate /ˌhī'drāt/ ▶ **v.** (**hydrates**, **hydrating**, **hydrated**) make something absorb or combine with water. ■ **hy·dra·tion n.**

hy·drau·lic /hī'drôlik/ ▶ **adj.** operated by a liquid moving through pipes under pressure. ▶ **n.**

(**hydraulics**) the branch of science concerned with the use of liquids moving under pressure to provide mechanical force. ■ **hy·drau·li·cal·ly** adv.

hy·dro·car·bon /ˈhīdrəˌkärbən/ ▶ n. any of the compounds of hydrogen and carbon.

hy·dro·ceph·a·lus /ˌhīdrōˈsefələs/ ▶ n. a condition in which fluid collects in the brain.

hy·dro·chlo·ric ac·id /ˌhīdrəˈklôrik/ ▶ n. an acid containing hydrogen and chlorine.

hy·dro·dy·nam·ics /ˌhīdrōdīˈnamiks/ ▶ n. the branch of science concerned with the forces acting on or generated by liquids. ■ **hy·dro·dy·nam·ic** adj.

hy·dro·e·lec·tric /ˌhīdrōəˈlektrik/ ▶ adj. having to do with the use of flowing water to generate electricity.

hy·dro·foil /ˈhīdrəˌfoil/ ▶ n. **1** a boat designed to rise above the water when it is traveling fast. **2** each of the foils of such a craft.

hy·dro·gen /ˈhīdrəjən/ ▶ n. a highly flammable gas that is the lightest of the chemical elements. □ **hydrogen bomb** a very powerful nuclear bomb. **hydrogen sulfide** a poisonous gas with a smell of bad eggs. **hydrogen peroxide** a liquid used in some disinfectants and bleaches.

hy·dro·gen·a·ted /ˈhīdrəjəˌnātid, hīˈdräjənātid/ ▶ adj. combined with hydrogen. ■ **hy·dro·gen·a·tion** /ˌhīdrəjəˈnāshən, hīˌdräjə-/ n.

hy·drog·ra·phy /hīˈdrägrəfē/ ▶ n. the science of charting seas, lakes, and rivers. ■ **hy·drog·ra·pher** n. **hy·dro·graph·ic** /ˌhīdrəˈgrafik/ adj.

hy·drol·o·gy /hīˈdräləjē/ ▶ n. the branch of science concerned with the properties and distribution of water on the earth's surface. ■ **hy·dro·log·i·cal** /ˌhīdrəˈläjikəl/ adj. **hy·drol·o·gist** n.

hy·drol·y·sis /hīˈdräləsis/ ▶ n. the chemical breakdown of a compound due to reaction with water.

hy·dro·lyze /ˈhīdrəˌlīz/ ▶ v. (**hydrolyzes**, **hydrolyzing**, **hydrolyzed**) break down a compound by chemical reaction with water.

hy·drom·e·ter /hīˈdrämitər/ ▶ n. an instrument for measuring the density of liquids.

hy·drop·a·thy /hīˈdräpəthē/ ▶ n. the treatment of illness through the use of water, either internally or by external means such as steam baths. ■ **hy·dro·path·ic** /ˌhīdrəˈpathik/ adj.

hy·dro·phil·ic /ˌhīdrəˈfilik/ ▶ adj. having a tendency to mix with or dissolve in water.

hy·dro·pho·bi·a /ˌhīdrəˈfōbēə/ ▶ n. **1** extreme fear of water, especially as a symptom of rabies. **2** rabies. ■ **hy·dro·pho·bic** adj.

hy·dro·plane /ˈhīdrəˌplān/ ▶ n. **1** a light, fast motorboat designed to skim over the surface of water. **2** an airplane that can take off and land in water. ▶ v. **1** (of a vehicle) slide uncontrollably on a wet surface. **2** (of a boat) skim over the surface of water with its hull lifted.

hy·dro·pon·ics /ˌhīdrəˈpäniks/ ▶ n. the growing of plants in sand, gravel, or liquid, with added nutrients but without soil. ■ **hy·dro·pon·ic** adj.

hy·dro·sphere /ˈhīdrəˌsfir/ ▶ n. the seas, lakes, and other waters of the earth's surface.

hy·dro·stat·ic /ˌhīdrəˈstatik/ ▶ adj. relating to the pressure and other characteristics of liquid at rest.

hy·dro·ther·a·py /ˌhīdrəˈtherəpē/ ▶ n. the use of exercises in a pool to treat conditions such as arthritis.

hy·dro·ther·mal /ˌhīdrəˈthərməl/ ▶ adj. relating to the action of heated water in the earth's crust.

hy·drous /ˈhīdrəs/ ▶ adj. containing water.

hy·drox·ide /hīˈdräkˌsīd/ ▶ n. a compound containing oxygen and hydrogen together with a metallic element.

hy·e·na /hīˈēnə/ ▶ n. a doglike African animal.

hy·giene /ˈhīˌjēn/ ▶ n. the practice of keeping yourself and your surroundings clean in order to prevent illness and disease.

> SYNONYMS **cleanliness**, sanitation, sterility, purity, disinfection.

hy·gi·en·ic /hīˈjenik, -ˈjē-/ ▶ adj. clean and not likely to spread disease.

> SYNONYMS **sanitary**, clean, germ-free, disinfected, sterilized, sterile, antiseptic, aseptic. ANTONYMS insanitary.

■ **hy·gi·en·i·cal·ly** adv.

> **SPELLING**
>
> Remember, **i** before **e**, when the sound is *ee*, except after **c**: hyg**ie**nic.

hy·gien·ist /hīˈjenəst, -jē-/ ▶ n. a dental worker who specializes in oral hygiene.

hy·grom·e·ter /hīˈgrämitər/ ▶ n. an instrument for measuring humidity.

hy·gro·scop·ic /ˌhīgrəˈskäpik/ ▶ adj. (of a substance) tending to absorb moisture from the air.

hy·men /ˈhīmən/ ▶ n. a membrane at the opening of the vagina, usually broken when a female first has sex.

hy·me·nop·ter·ous /ˌhīməˈnäptərəs/ ▶ adj. (of an insect) belonging to a large group that includes the bees, wasps, and ants, having four transparent wings.

hymn /him/ ▶ n. a religious song of praise, especially a Christian one. ▶ v. praise or celebrate.

hym·nal /ˈhimnəl/ ▶ n. a book of hymns.

hym·no·dy /ˈhimnədē/ ▶ n. the singing or composition of hymns.

hype /hīp/ informal ▶ n. extravagant publicity given to a product. ▶ v. (**hypes**, **hyping**, **hyped**) **1** publicize a product in an extravagant way. **2** (**be hyped up**) be very excited or tense.

hy·per /ˈhīpər/ ▶ adj. informal having a lot of nervous energy.

hy·per·ac·tive /ˌhīpərˈaktiv/ ▶ adj. very active; unable to keep still.

hy·per·bo·la /hīˈpərbələ/ ▶ n. (plural **hyperbolas** or **hyperbolae** /-lē/) a symmetrical curve formed when a cone is cut by a plane nearly parallel to the cone's axis.

hy·per·bo·le /hīˈpərbəlē/ ▶ n. a way of speaking or writing that exaggerates things and is not meant to be understood literally.

> SYNONYMS **exaggeration**, overstatement, magnification, embroidery, embellishment, excess, overkill. ANTONYMS understatement.

hy·per·bol·ic /ˌhīpərˈbälik/ ▶ adj. **1** deliberately exaggerated. **2** relating to a hyperbola.

hy·per·crit·i·cal /ˌhīpərˈkritikəl/ ▶ adj. excessively critical.

hy·per·in·fla·tion /hīpərinˈflāshən/ ▶ n. inflation of prices or wages occurring at a very high rate.

hy·per·link /ˈhīpərˌlingk/ ▶ n. Computing a link from a hypertext document to another location.

hy·per·me·di·a /ˌhīpər'mēdēə/ ▶ **n.** Computing an extension to hypertext that provides facilities such as sound and video.

hy·per·sen·si·tive /ˌhīpər'sensitiv/ ▶ **adj.** too sensitive.

hy·per·son·ic /ˌhīpər'sänik/ ▶ **adj. 1** relating to speeds of more than five times the speed of sound. **2** relating to sound frequencies above about a billion hertz.

hy·per·space /'hīpərˌspās/ ▶ **n. 1** space of more than three dimensions. **2** (in science fiction) a notional space-time continuum in which it is possible to travel faster than light.

hy·per·ten·sion /ˌhīpər'tenSHən/ ▶ **n.** abnormally high blood pressure.

hy·per·text /'hīpərˌtekst/ ▶ **n.** Computing a system that lets you move quickly between documents or sections of data.

hy·per·tro·phy /hī'pərtrəfē/ ▶ **n.** abnormal enlargement of an organ or tissue resulting from an increase in size of its cells. ■ **hy·per·troph·ied adj.**

hy·per·ven·ti·late /ˌhīpər'ventlˌāt/ ▶ **v.** (**hyperventilates**, **hyperventilating**, **hyperventilated**) breathe at an abnormally rapid rate. ■ **hy·per·ven·ti·la·tion** /-ˌventl'āSHən/ **n.**

hy·pha /'hīfə/ ▶ **n.** (plural **hyphae** /-fē/) each of the branching strands that make up the mycelium (vegetative part) of a fungus.

hy·phen /'hīfən/ ▶ **n.** a sign (-) used to join words together or to divide a word into parts between one line and the next.

hy·phen·ate /'hīfəˌnāt/ ▶ **v.** (**hyphenates**, **hyphenating**, **hyphenated**) join or divide words with a hyphen. ■ **hy·phen·a·tion** /ˌhīfə'nāSHən/ **n.**

hyp·no·sis /hip'nōsis/ ▶ **n.** the practice of causing a person to enter a state in which they respond very readily to suggestions or commands.

hyp·no·ther·a·py /ˌhipnō'THerəpē/ ▶ **n.** the use of hypnosis to treat physical or mental problems.

hyp·not·ic /hip'nätik/ ▶ **adj. 1** having to do with hypnosis. **2** making you feel very relaxed or sleepy: *her voice had a hypnotic quality.* ■ **hyp·not·i·cal·ly adv.**

hyp·no·tism /'hipnəˌtizəm/ ▶ **n.** the study or practice of hypnosis. ■ **hyp·no·tist n.**

hyp·no·tize /'hipnəˌtīz/ ▶ **v.** (**hypnotizes**, **hypnotizing**, **hypnotized**) put someone into a state of hypnosis.

SYNONYMS **entrance**, spellbind, enthrall, transfix, captivate, bewitch, enrapture, grip, rivet, absorb.

hy·po·al·ler·gen·ic /ˌhīpōˌalər'jenik/ ▶ **adj.** unlikely to cause an allergic reaction.

hy·po·chon·dri·a /ˌhīpə'kändrēə/ ▶ **n.** extreme anxiety about your health.

hy·po·chon·dri·ac /ˌhīpə'kändrēˌak/ ▶ **n.** a person who is too anxious about their health.

hy·poc·ri·sy /hi'päkrisē/ ▶ **n.** behavior in which a person pretends to have higher standards than they really have.

hyp·o·crite /'hipəˌkrit/ ▶ **n.** a person who pretends to have higher standards than they really have.

SPELLING

Write **hypo-**, not **hyper-**: **hypo**crite.

hyp·o·crit·i·cal /ˌhipə'kritikəl/ ▶ **adj.** exhibiting hypocrisy.

SYNONYMS **sanctimonious**, pious, self-righteous, holier-than-thou, superior, insincere, two-faced.

hy·po·der·mic /ˌhīpə'dərmik/ ▶ **adj.** (of a needle or syringe) used to inject a drug or other substance beneath the skin. ▶ **n.** a hypodermic syringe or injection.

hy·po·ten·sion /ˌhīpə'tenSHən/ ▶ **n.** abnormally low blood pressure.

hy·pot·e·nuse /hī'pätnˌ(y)o͞os/ ▶ **n.** the longest side of a right triangle, opposite the right angle.

hy·po·ther·mi·a /ˌhīpə'THərmēə/ ▶ **n.** the condition of having an abnormally low body temperature.

hy·poth·e·sis /hī'päTHəsis/ ▶ **n.** (plural **hypotheses**) an idea that has not yet been proved to be true or correct.

hy·poth·e·size /hī'päTHəˌsīz/ ▶ **v.** (**hypothesizes**, **hypothesizing**, **hypothesized**) put forward as a hypothesis.

hy·po·thet·i·cal /ˌhīpə'THetikəl/ ▶ **adj.** based on a situation that is imagined rather than true: *the hypothetical benefits of joining their association.*

SYNONYMS **theoretical**, speculative, conjectured, notional, supposed, assumed; academic, imaginary. ANTONYMS actual.

■ **hy·po·thet·i·cal·ly adv.**

hy·rax /'hīˌraks/ ▶ **n.** a small plant-eating mammal with a short tail, found in Africa and Arabia.

hys·sop /'hisəp/ ▶ **n.** a bushy plant whose bitter minty leaves are used in cooking and herbal medicine.

hys·ter·ec·to·my /ˌhistə'rektəmē/ ▶ **n.** (plural **hysterectomies**) a surgical operation to remove all or part of the womb.

hys·te·ri·a /hi'sterēə, -'sti(ə)rēə/ ▶ **n. 1** wild or uncontrollable emotion: *election hysteria.* **2** dated a medical condition in which a person loses control of their emotions.

SYNONYMS **frenzy**, feverishness, hysterics, agitation, mania, panic, alarm, distress. ANTONYMS calm.

hys·ter·i·cal /hi'sterikəl/ ▶ **adj. 1** affected by wild or uncontrolled emotion. **2** informal very funny. **3** having to do with hysteria.

SYNONYMS **1 overwrought**, overemotional, out of control, frenzied, frantic, wild, beside yourself, manic, delirious; informal in a state. **2 very funny**, hilarious, uproarious, rib-tickling; informal side-splitting, priceless, a scream, a hoot. ANTONYMS calm.

■ **hys·ter·i·cal·ly adv.**

hys·ter·ics /hi'steriks/ ▶ **pl.n. 1** wildly emotional behavior. **2** informal uncontrollable laughter.

Hz ▶ **abbr.** hertz.

I[1] (or **i**) ▶ **n.** (plural **Is** or **I's**) **1** the ninth letter of the alphabet. **2** the Roman numeral for one.

I[2] ▶ **pron.** used by a speaker to refer to himself or herself.

I. ▶ **abbr.** Island(s) or Isle(s).

i·amb /ˈīamb/ ▶ **n.** Poetry a unit of rhythm consisting of one short or unstressed syllable followed by one long or stressed syllable.

i·am·bic /īˈambik/ ▶ **adj.** (of rhythm in poetry) having one unstressed syllable followed by one stressed syllable.

I·be·ri·an /īˈbi(ə)rēən/ ▶ **adj.** relating to Iberia (the peninsula that consists of modern Spain and Portugal). ▶ **n.** a person from Iberia.

i·bex /ˈīˌbeks/ ▶ **n.** (plural **ibexes**) a wild mountain goat with long horns.

ib·id. /ˈibid/ ▶ **adv.** in the same book as the one that has just been mentioned.

i·bis /ˈībis/ ▶ **n.** (plural **ibises**) a large wading bird with a long curved bill.

i·bu·pro·fen /ˌībyo͞oˈprōfən/ ▶ **n.** a medicine used to relieve pain and reduce inflammation.

IC ▶ **abbr.** integrated circuit.

ICBM ▶ **abbr.** intercontinental ballistic missile.

ice /īs/ ▶ **n.** water that has frozen and become solid. ▶ **v.** (**ices**, **icing**, **iced**) **1** decorate a cake with icing. **2** (**ice up** or **over**) become covered with ice.

> SYNONYMS ▶ **n. 1** icicles, black ice, frost, permafrost, hoar (frost); literary rime. **2 sorbet**, water ice, sherbet, gelato, ice cream. **3 coldness**, coolness, frostiness, iciness, hostility, unfriendliness.

□ **break the ice** say something to start a conversation when people meet for the first time. **ice age** a period of time when ice covered much of the earth's surface. **ice-breaker** a ship designed for breaking a channel through ice. **ice cap** a large area that is permanently covered with ice, especially at the North and South Poles. **ice cream** a frozen dessert made with sweetened milk fat. **ice field** a large permanent expanse of ice at the North and South Poles. **ice hockey** ⇨ HOCKEY. **ice pack** a bag filled with ice and held against part of the body to reduce swelling or lower temperature. **ice pick 1** a small pick used by climbers. **2** a small pick used to break ice into pieces for drinks. **ice skate** a boot with a blade attached to the sole, used for skating on ice. **on ice** (of a plan or proposal) waiting to be dealt with at a later time. **on thin ice** in a risky situation.

ice·berg /ˈīsˌbərg/ ▶ **n.** a large mass of ice floating in the sea. □ **iceberg lettuce** a kind of lettuce having a closely packed round head of crisp leaves. **the tip of the iceberg** the small visible part of a much larger problem that remains hidden.

ice·box /ˈīsˌbäks/ ▶ **n. 1** a chilled box or cupboard. **2** dated refrigerator.

iced /īsd/ ▶ **adj. 1** cooled or mixed with ice: *iced water*. **2** decorated with icing.

Ice·land·er /ˈīsləndər/ ▶ **n.** a person from Iceland.

Ice·lan·dic /īsˈlandik/ ▶ **n.** the language of Iceland. ▶ **adj.** relating to Iceland.

ich·thy·ol·o·gy /ˌikᴛʜēˈäləjē/ ▶ **n.** the branch of zoology concerned with fish. ■ **ich·thy·ol·o·gist n.**

ich·thy·o·saur /ˈikᴛʜēəˌsôr/ (also **ichthyosaurus** /-ˈsôrəs/) ▶ **n.** a fossil reptile that lived in the sea, having a long pointed head, four flippers, and a vertical tail.

i·ci·cle /ˈīsikəl/ ▶ **n.** a hanging piece of ice formed when dripping water freezes.

ic·ing /ˈīsɪɴɢ/ ▶ **n.** a mixture of sugar and water or fat, used to cover cakes. □ **the icing on the cake** an extra thing that makes something good even better.

i·con /ˈīˌkän/ ▶ **n. 1** (also **ikon**) (in the Orthodox Church) a painting of a holy person that is also regarded as holy. **2** a person or thing that is seen as a symbol of something: *he's an iron-jawed icon of American manhood*. **3** Computing a symbol on a computer screen that represents a program. ■ **i·con·ic** /īˈkänik/ **adj.**

i·con·o·clast /īˈkänəˌklast/ ▶ **n.** a person who attacks established customs and values. ■ **i·con·o·clasm n.** **i·con·o·clas·tic** /īˌkänəˈklastik/ **adj.**

i·co·nog·ra·phy /ˌīkəˈnägrəfē/ ▶ **n. 1** the use or study of pictures or symbols in visual arts. **2** the pictures or symbols associated with a person or movement. ■ **i·con·o·graph·ic** /īˌkänəˈgrafik/ **adj.**

i·co·sa·he·dron /īˌkōsəˈhēdrən, īˌkäsə-/ ▶ **n.** (plural **icosahedrons** or **icosahedra** /-drə/) a three-dimensional shape with twenty plane faces.

ICT ▶ **abbr.** information and computing technology.

i·cy /ˈīsē/ ▶ **adj.** (**icier**, **iciest**) **1** covered with ice. **2** very cold. **3** very unfriendly; hostile.

> SYNONYMS **1 iced (over)**, frozen, frosty, slippery, treacherous; literary rimy. **2 freezing**, chill, biting, bitter, raw, arctic. **3 unfriendly**, hostile, forbidding, cold, chilly, frosty, stern.

■ **i·ci·ly adv.**

ID ▶ **abbr.** identification or identity.

id /id/ ▶ **n.** the part of the mind that consists of a person's unconscious instincts and feelings.

I'd /īd/ ▶ **contr. 1** I had. **2** I should or I would.

i·de·a /īˈdēə/ ▶ **n. 1** a thought or suggestion about a possible course of action. **2** a mental picture or impression: *the campus tour gives an idea of the life of a student*. **3** a belief. **4** (**the idea**) the aim or purpose.

> SYNONYMS **1 concept**, notion, conception, thought. **2 plan**, scheme, design, proposal, proposition, suggestion, aim, intention, objective, goal. **3 thought**, theory, view,

opinion, feeling, belief. **4 sense**, feeling, suspicion, fancy, inkling, hunch, notion. **5 estimate**, approximation, guess, conjecture; informal guesstimate.

i·de·al /īˈdē(ə)l/ ▶ **adj. 1** most suitable; perfect. **2** existing only in the imagination: *in an ideal world, we might have made a different decision.* ▶ **n. 1** a person or thing regarded as perfect. **2** a principle or standard that is worth trying to achieve: *tolerance and freedom, the liberal ideals.*

SYNONYMS ▶ **adj. perfect**, faultless, exemplary, classic, archetypal, quintessential, model, ultimate, utopian, fairy-tale. ▶ **n. 1** *an ideal to aim at* **model**, pattern, archetype, exemplar, example, perfection, epitome, last word. **2** *liberal ideals* **principle**, standard, value, belief, conviction, ethos.

■ **i·de·al·ly** adv.

i·de·al·ism /īˈdē(ə)ˌlizəm/ ▶ **n. 1** the belief that ideals can be achieved. **2** the representation of things as better than they really are. ■ **i·de·al·ist** n.

i·de·al·is·tic /īˌdē(ə)ˈlistik/ ▶ **adj.** believing that ideals can be achieved, even when this is unrealistic: *some say I'm drawing a wildly idealistic portrait of what the Church can become.*

SYNONYMS **Utopian**, visionary, romantic, quixotic, unrealistic, impractical.

i·de·al·ize /īˈdē(ə)ˌlīz/ ▶ **v.** (**idealizes**, **idealizing**, **idealized**) represent someone or something as better than they really are. ■ **i·de·al·i·za·tion** /īˌdē(ə)liˈzāsʜən/ n.

i·dée fixe /ēˌdā ˈfēks/ ▶ **n.** (plural **idées fixes**) an obsession.

i·den·ti·cal /īˈdentikəl/ ▶ **adj. 1** exactly alike. **2** the same. **3** (of twins) very similar in appearance.

SYNONYMS **(exactly) the same**, twin, duplicate, indistinguishable, interchangeable, alike, carbon-copy, matching. ANTONYMS different.

■ **i·den·ti·cal·ly** adv.

i·den·ti·fi·ca·tion /īˌdentəfiˈkāsʜən/ ▶ **n. 1** the action of identifying. **2** an official document or other proof of your identity.

SYNONYMS **1 recognition**, singling out, pinpointing, naming. **2 determination**, establishing, ascertainment, discovery, diagnosis. **3 ID**, papers, documents, credentials, card, pass, badge.

i·den·ti·fy /īˈdentəˌfī/ ▶ **v.** (**identifies**, **identifying**, **identified**) **1** prove or recognize that someone or something is a specified person or thing: *he couldn't identify his attackers*. **2** recognize as being worthy of attention: *I identified four problem areas*. **3** (**identify with**) feel that you understand or share the feelings of. **4** (**identify someone/thing with**) associate someone or something closely with.

SYNONYMS **1 recognize**, pick out, spot, point out, pinpoint, put your finger on, name. **2 determine**, establish, ascertain, make out, discern, distinguish. **3** *we identify sport with glamour* **associate**, link, connect, relate. **4** *he identified with the team captain* **empathize with**, sympathize with, understand, relate to, feel for.

■ **i·den·ti·fi·a·ble** adj.

i·den·ti·ty /īˈdentitē/ ▶ **n.** (plural **identities**) **1** the fact of being who or what a person or thing is: *she knows the identity of the thief*. **2** a close similarity or feeling of understanding.

SYNONYMS **individuality**, self, personality, character, originality, distinctiveness, uniqueness.

□ **identity theft** the fraudulent use of another person's name and other personal information in order to obtain money or goods.

id·e·o·gram /ˈidēəˌgram, ˈīdēə-/ (also **ideograph** /ˈidēəˌgraf, ˈīdēə-/) ▶ **n.** a symbol used in a writing system to represent the idea of a thing rather than the sounds of a word (e.g., a numeral or a Chinese character).

i·de·o·logue /ˈīdēəˌlôg, -ˌläg, ˈidēə-/ ▶ **n.** a person who follows an ideology in a strict and inflexible way.

i·de·ol·o·gy /ˌīdēˈäləjē, ˌidē-/ ▶ **n.** (plural **ideologies**) **1** a system of ideas that an economic or political theory is based on. **2** the set of beliefs held by a particular group.

SYNONYMS **belief**; doctrine, creed, theory.

■ **i·de·o·log·i·cal** /-əˈläjikəl/ adj. **i·de·o·log·i·cal·ly** /-əˈläjik(ə)lē/ adv.

ides /īdz/ ▶ **pl.n.** (in the ancient Roman calendar) a day falling roughly in the middle of each month, from which other dates were calculated.

id·i·o·cy /ˈidēəsē/ ▶ **n.** (plural **idiocies**) very stupid behavior.

id·i·om /ˈidēəm/ ▶ **n. 1** a group of words whose overall meaning is different from the meanings of the individual words (e.g., *raining cats and dogs*). **2** a form of language used by a particular group of people. **3** a style of music or art: *they were working in an Impressionist idiom.*

id·i·o·mat·ic /ˌidēəˈmatik/ ▶ **adj.** using expressions that are natural to a native speaker of a language.

SYNONYMS **colloquial**, everyday, conversational, vernacular, natural.

id·i·o·syn·cra·sy /ˌidēəˈsiɴɢkrəsē/ ▶ **n.** (plural **idiosyncrasies**) **1** a person's particular way of behaving or thinking. **2** a distinctive or peculiar feature.

SYNONYMS **peculiarity**, oddity, eccentricity, mannerism, quirk, characteristic.

■ **id·i·o·syn·crat·ic** /ˌidēəsiɴɢˈkratik, ˌidē-ō-/ adj.

SPELLING

The ending is **-asy**, not **-acy**: idiosyncr**asy**.

id·i·ot /ˈidēət/ ▶ **n.** a stupid person.

SYNONYMS **fool**, ass, halfwit, blockhead, dunce, simpleton; informal nincompoop, clod, dimwit, dummy, fathead, numbskull; informal nitwit, twit, dork, twerp, moron, schmuck. ANTONYMS genius.

■ **id·i·ot·ic** /ˌidēˈätik/ adj. **id·i·ot·i·cal·ly** adv.

i·dle /ˈīdl/ ▶ **adj.** (**idler**, **idlest**) **1** avoiding work; lazy. **2** not working or in use. **3** having no purpose or effect: *she did not make idle threats*. ▶ **v.** (**idles**, **idling**, **idled**) **1** spend time doing nothing. **2** (of an engine) run slowly while out of gear.

SYNONYMS ▶ **adj. 1 lazy**, indolent, slothful, shiftless, work-shy. **2 unemployed**, jobless, out of work, unoccupied; informal on the dole. **3 unoccupied**, spare, empty, unfilled. **4 frivolous**, trivial, trifling, minor, insignificant, unimportant, empty, meaningless, vain. ANTONYMS industrious, busy.

■ **i·dle·ness** n. **i·dler** n. **i·dly** adv.

i·dol /ˈīdl/ ▶ **n.** **1** a statue or picture of a god that is worshiped. **2** a person who is very much admired: *a movie idol.*

SYNONYMS **1 icon**, effigy, statue, figurine, totem. **2 hero**, heroine, star, superstar, icon, celebrity, darling; informal pinup, heartthrob.

i·dol·a·try /īˈdälətrē/ ▶ **n.** worship of idols.

i·dol·ize /ˈīdlˌīz/ ▶ **v.** (**idolizes**, **idolizing**, **idolized**) admire or love someone very much.

SYNONYMS **hero-worship**, worship, revere, venerate, look up to, exalt; informal put on a pedestal.

i·dyll /ˈīdl/ ▶ **n.** **1** a very happy or peaceful time or situation. **2** a short piece of writing describing a peaceful scene of country life.

i·dyl·lic /īˈdilik/ ▶ **adj.** very happy, peaceful, or beautiful.

SYNONYMS **perfect**, wonderful, blissful, halcyon, happy; literary Arcadian.

■ **i·dyl·li·cal·ly adv.**

i.e. ▶ **abbr.** that is to say.

if /if/ ▶ **conj.** **1** on the condition or in the event that: *if you have a complaint, write to the manager.* **2** despite the possibility that: *if it takes me seven years, I shall do it.* **3** whether. **4** whenever.

SYNONYMS **provided**, providing, on condition that, presuming, supposing, assuming, as long as, in the event that.

USAGE

if and **whether** can both be used in sentences like *I'll see if he left an address* and *I'll see whether he left an address*, although **whether** is more formal and more suitable for written use.

if·fy /ˈifē/ ▶ **adj.** (**iffier**, **iffiest**) informal **1** uncertain. **2** of doubtful quality or legality.

ig·loo /ˈiglo͞o/ ▶ **n.** a dome-shaped Eskimo house built from blocks of solid snow.

ig·ne·ous /ˈignēəs/ ▶ **adj.** (of rock) formed when molten rock has solidified.

ig·nite /igˈnīt/ ▶ **v.** (**ignites**, **igniting**, **ignited**) **1** catch fire, or set on fire. **2** provoke or stir up.

SYNONYMS **1 catch fire**, burst into flames, explode. **2 light**, set fire to, set alight, kindle. ANTONYMS extinguish.

ig·ni·tion /igˈnisʜən/ ▶ **n.** **1** the action of igniting. **2** the mechanism in a vehicle that ignites the fuel to start the engine.

ig·no·ble /igˈnōbəl/ ▶ **adj.** not good or honest; dishonorable.

ig·no·min·i·ous /ˌignəˈminēəs/ ▶ **adj.** deserving or causing disgrace or shame: *no other party risked ignominious defeat.* ■ **ig·no·min·i·ous·ly adv.**

ig·no·min·y /ˈignəˌminē, igˈnäminē/ ▶ **n.** public shame or disgrace.

ig·no·ra·mus /ˌignəˈrāməs, -ˈraməs/ ▶ **n.** (plural **ignoramuses**) an ignorant or stupid person.

ig·no·rance /ˈignərəns/ ▶ **n.** lack of knowledge or information.

SYNONYMS **1 lack of knowledge**, lack of education, unenlightenment. **2 unfamiliarity**, incomprehension, inexperience, innocence. ANTONYMS education, knowledge.

ig·no·rant /ˈignərənt/ ▶ **adj.** **1** lacking knowledge or information. **2** informal not polite; rude.

SYNONYMS **1 uneducated**, unschooled, illiterate, uninformed, unenlightened, inexperienced, unsophisticated. **2 unaware**, unconscious, unfamiliar, unacquainted, uninformed; informal in the dark. ANTONYMS educated, knowledgeable.

ig·nore /igˈnôr/ ▶ **v.** (**ignores**, **ignoring**, **ignored**) **1** deliberately take no notice of. **2** fail to consider something important.

SYNONYMS **1 snub**, look right through, cold-shoulder, take no notice of, pay no attention to; informal blank. **2 disregard**, take no account of, fail to observe, disobey, defy, overlook, brush aside, turn a blind eye to. ANTONYMS acknowledge, obey.

i·gua·na /iˈgwänə/ ▶ **n.** a large tropical American lizard with a spiny crest along the back.

i·kon = ICON.

il·e·um /ˈilēəm/ ▶ **n.** (plural **ilea** /ˈilēə/) the third and lowest part of the small intestine.

il·i·ac /ˈilēˌak/ ▶ **adj.** relating to the ilium or the nearby regions of the lower body.

il·i·um /ˈilēəm/ ▶ **n.** (plural **ilia** /ˈilēə/) the large broad bone forming the upper part of each half of the pelvis.

ilk /ilk/ ▶ **n.** a type: *musicians, artists, and others of that ilk.*

ill /il/ ▶ **adj.** **1** not in good health; unwell. **2** bad or harmful. ▶ **adv.** **1** badly or wrongly: *ill-chosen.* **2** only with difficulty: *she could ill afford the cost.* ▶ **n.** **1** a problem or misfortune. **2** evil or harm.

SYNONYMS ▶ **adj.** **1 unwell**, sick, poorly, peaked, indisposed, nauseous, queasy; informal under the weather. **2** *ill effects* **harmful**, damaging, detrimental, deleterious, adverse, injurious, destructive, dangerous. ANTONYMS well, beneficial. ▶ **adv.** **1 barely**, scarcely, hardly, only just. **2 inadequately**, insufficiently, poorly, badly. ▶ **n. problem**, trouble, difficulty, misfortune, trial, tribulation; informal headache, hassle.

□ **ill-advised** not sensible or well-thought-out. **ill at ease** uncomfortable or embarrassed. **ill-bred** badly brought up or rude. **ill-disposed** unfriendly or unsympathetic. **ill-fated** destined to fail or be unlucky. **ill-gotten** obtained by illegal or unfair means. **ill-starred** unlucky. **ill-tempered** irritable or surly. **ill-treat** treat in a cruel or unkind way. **ill will** hostility.

I'll /īl/ ▶ **contr.** **1** I shall. **2** I will.

il·le·gal /i(l)ˈlēgəl/ ▶ **adj.** against the law.

SYNONYMS **unlawful**, illicit, illegitimate, criminal, fraudulent, corrupt, dishonest, outlawed, banned, forbidden, prohibited, proscribed, unlicensed, unauthorized; informal crooked, shady. ANTONYMS legal.

■ **il·le·gal·i·ty** /ˌi(l)liˈgalitē/ **n.** **il·le·gal·ly adv.**

il·leg·i·ble /i(l)ˈlejəbəl/ ▶ **adj.** not clear enough to be read.

SYNONYMS **unreadable**, indecipherable, unintelligible.

■ **il·leg·i·bil·i·ty** /i(l)ˌlejəˈbilitē/ **n.**

il·le·git·i·mate /ˌi(l)ləˈjitəmit/ ▶ **adj.** **1** not allowed by law or rules. **2** (of a child) born to parents who are not married to each other.

SYNONYMS **illegal**, unlawful, illicit, criminal, felonious, fraudulent, corrupt, dishonest; informal crooked, shady. ANTONYMS legal, legitimate.

■ **il·le·git·i·ma·cy** n.

il·lib·er·al /i(l)'lib(ə)rəl/ ▶ adj. not allowing freedom of thought or behavior.

il·lic·it /i(l)'lisit/ ▶ adj. forbidden by law, rules, or standards.

SYNONYMS **illegal**, unlawful, criminal, outlawed, banned, forbidden, prohibited, proscribed, unlicensed, unauthorized, improper, disapproved of. ANTONYMS legal.

■ **il·lic·it·ly** adv.

il·lit·er·ate /i(l)'litərit/ ▶ adj. **1** unable to read or write. **2** not knowing very much about a particular subject: *politically illiterate*. ■ **il·lit·er·a·cy** n.

ill·ness /'ilnis/ ▶ n. a disease, or a period of being ill.

SYNONYMS **sickness**, poor health, disease, ailment, disorder, complaint, indisposition, malady, affliction, infection; informal bug, virus. ANTONYMS health.

il·log·i·cal /i(l)'läjikəl/ ▶ adj. not sensible or based on sound reasoning: *an illogical fear of the dark*.

SYNONYMS **irrational**, unreasonable, erroneous, invalid, spurious, fallacious, specious.

■ **il·log·i·cal·i·ty** /i(l),läji'kalitē/ n. **il·log·i·cal·ly** adv.

il·lu·mi·nate /i'lo͞omə,nāt/ ▶ v. (**illuminates**, **illuminating**, **illuminated**) **1** light something up. **2** help to explain something: *he illuminates science for the interested reader*. **3** decorate a manuscript with colored designs, especially as was common during the medieval period.

SYNONYMS (**illuminating**) **informative**, enlightening, revealing, explanatory, instructive, helpful, educational. ANTONYMS confusing.

il·lu·mi·na·tion /i,lo͞omə'nāsʜən/ ▶ n. **1** lighting or light. **2** (**illuminations**) lights used in decorating a building for a special occasion. **3** understanding.

SYNONYMS **light**, lighting, radiance, gleam, glow, glare.

il·lu·mine /i'lo͞omən/ ▶ v. literary light up; illuminate.

il·lu·sion /i'lo͞ozʜən/ ▶ n. **1** a false idea or belief: *he had no illusions about his playing*. **2** a thing that seems to be something that it is not.

SYNONYMS **1 delusion**, misapprehension, misconception, false impression, mistaken impression, fantasy, dream, fancy. **2 appearance**, impression, semblance. **3 mirage**, hallucination, apparition, figment of the imagination, trick of the light.

il·lu·sion·ist /i'lo͞ozʜənist/ ▶ n. a magician or conjuror.

il·lu·so·ry /i'lo͞osərē, -zərē/ (or **illusive** /i'lo͞osiv/) ▶ adj. not real, although seeming to be.

SYNONYMS **false**, imagined, imaginary, fanciful, unreal, sham, fallacious. ANTONYMS genuine.

il·lus·trate /'ilə,strāt/ ▶ v. (**illustrates**, **illustrating**, **illustrated**) **1** provide a book or magazine with pictures. **2** make something clear by using examples, charts, etc. **3** act as an example of.

SYNONYMS **1 decorate**, ornament, accompany, support. **2 explain**, elucidate, clarify, demonstrate, show, point up; informal get across/over.

■ **il·lus·tra·tive** /i'ləstrətiv, 'ilə,strātiv/ adj. **il·lus·tra·tor** n.

il·lus·tra·tion /,ilə'strāsʜən/ ▶ n. **1** a picture illustrating a book or magazine. **2** the action of illustrating. **3** an example that helps to explain something.

SYNONYMS **1 picture**, drawing, sketch, figure, plate, image, print. **2 example**, sample, case, instance, exemplification, demonstration.

il·lus·tri·ous /i'ləstrēəs/ ▶ adj. famous and admired for what you have achieved.

IM ▶ abbr. Computing **1** instant message. **2** instant messaging.

I'm /īm/ ▶ contr. I am.

im·age /'imij/ ▶ n. **1** a picture or statue of someone or something. **2** a picture seen on a television or computer screen, through a lens, or reflected in a mirror. **3** a picture in the mind. **4** the impression that a person or group gives to the public: *she tries to project an image of youth*. **5** (**the image of**) a person or thing that looks very similar to another. **6** a word or phrase describing something in an imaginative way; a simile or metaphor. ▶ v. (**images**, **imaging**, **imaged**) make or form an image of.

SYNONYMS ▶ n. **1 likeness**, depiction, portrayal, representation, painting, picture, portrait, drawing, photograph. **2 conception**, impression, perception, notion, idea. **3 persona**, profile, face.

im·ag·er /'imijər/ ▶ n. an electronic device that records images.

im·age·ry /'imij(ə)rē/ ▶ n. **1** language that produces images in the mind. **2** pictures as a whole.

im·ag·i·nar·y /i'majə,nerē/ ▶ adj. **1** existing only in the imagination. **2** Math (of a number or quantity) expressed in terms of the square root of −1 (represented by *i* or *j*).

SYNONYMS **unreal**, nonexistent, fictional, pretend, make-believe, invented, made-up, illusory. ANTONYMS real.

SPELLING

The ending is **-ary** not **-ery**: imagin**ary**.

im·ag·i·na·tion /i,majə'nāsʜən/ ▶ n. **1** the part of the mind that imagines things. **2** the ability to be creative or solve problems.

SYNONYMS **1 mind's eye**, fancy. **2 creativity**, vision, inventiveness, resourcefulness, ingenuity, originality.

im·ag·i·na·tive /i'maj(ə)nətiv/ ▶ adj. using the imagination in a creative or inventive way.

SYNONYMS **creative**, visionary, inventive, resourceful, ingenious, original, innovative.

■ **i·mag·i·na·tive·ly** adv.

im·ag·ine /i'majən/ ▶ v. (**imagines**, **imagining**, **imagined**) **1** form a mental picture of. **2** think that something is probable: *I imagine that he was at home*. **3** believe that something unreal exists.

SYNONYMS **1 visualize**, envisage, picture, see in your mind's eye, dream up, think up/of, conceive. **2 assume**, presume, expect, reckon, suppose, deem.

■ **im·ag·i·na·ble** adj.

im·ag·in·ings /iˈmajəniNGz/ ▶ **pl.n.** thoughts or fantasies.

i·ma·go /iˈmāgō, iˈmä-/ ▶ **n.** (plural **imagos** or **imagines** /iˈmāgəˌnēz/) the final and fully developed adult stage of an insect.

i·mam /iˈmäm/ ▶ **n.** the person who leads prayers in a mosque.

im·bal·ance /imˈbaləns/ ▶ **n.** a lack of proportion or balance.

im·be·cile /ˈimbəsəl, -ˌsil/ ▶ **n.** informal a stupid person. ■ **im·be·cil·ic** /ˌimbəˈsilik/ **adj.** **im·be·cil·i·ty** /ˌimbəˈsilitē/ **n.**

im·bed = EMBED.

im·bibe /imˈbīb/ ▶ **v.** (**imbibes**, **imbibing**, **imbibed**) **1** formal drink alcohol. **2** absorb ideas or knowledge.

im·bro·glio /imˈbrōlyō/ ▶ **n.** (plural **imbroglios**) a very confused or complicated situation.

im·bue /imˈbyoo/ ▶ **v.** (**imbues**, **imbuing**, **imbued**) fill with a feeling or quality: *we were imbued with a sense of purpose.*

> SYNONYMS **permeate**, saturate, suffuse, inject, inculcate, fill.

IMF ▶ **abbr.** International Monetary Fund.

im·i·tate /ˈimiˌtāt/ ▶ **v.** (**imitates**, **imitating**, **imitated**) **1** follow as a model; copy: *his style was imitated by other writers.* **2** copy the way that a person speaks or behaves in order to amuse people.

> SYNONYMS **1 copy**, emulate, follow, echo, ape, parrot; informal rip off. **2 mimic**, do an impression of, impersonate, parody, caricature; informal take off, send up.

■ **im·i·ta·tor** **n.**

im·i·ta·tion /ˌimiˈtāSHən/ ▶ **n.** **1** a copy. **2** the action of imitating.

> SYNONYMS **1 copy**, simulation, reproduction, replica, forgery. **2 emulation**, copying. **3 impersonation**, impression, parody, caricature; informal takeoff, sendup, spoof. **4** *an imitation pearl necklace* **artificial**, synthetic, mock, fake, simulated, man-made, manufactured, substitute, ersatz. ANTONYMS real.

im·i·ta·tive /ˈimiˌtātiv/ ▶ **adj.** imitating or copying something.

im·mac·u·late /iˈmakyəlit/ ▶ **adj.** **1** completely clean or tidy. **2** free from mistakes; perfect.

> SYNONYMS **1 clean**, spotless, shining, shiny, gleaming, perfect, pristine, mint, flawless, faultless, unblemished; informal tip-top, A1. **2** *his immaculate record* **impeccable**, unsullied, spotless, unblemished, untarnished; informal squeaky clean. ANTONYMS dirty, damaged.

□ **Immaculate Conception** (in the Roman Catholic Church) the doctrine the Virgin Mary was free from original sin from the moment she was conceived by her mother. ■ **im·mac·u·late·ly** **adv.**

im·ma·nent /ˈimənənt/ ▶ **adj.** **1** present within or throughout something: *love is a force immanent in the world.* **2** (of God) permanently present throughout the universe. ■ **im·ma·nence** **n.**

im·ma·te·ri·al /ˌi(m)məˈti(ə)rēəl/ ▶ **adj.** **1** unimportant under the circumstances. **2** spiritual rather than physical.

im·ma·ture /ˌiməˈCHoor, -ˈt(y)oor/ ▶ **adj.** **1** not fully developed. **2** behaving in a way that is typical of someone younger: *his immature sense of humor.*

> SYNONYMS **childish**, babyish, infantile, juvenile, puerile, callow.

■ **im·ma·tu·ri·ty** **n.**

im·meas·ur·a·ble /iˈmeZHərəbəl/ ▶ **adj.** too large or extreme to measure. ■ **im·meas·ur·a·bly** **adv.**

im·me·di·ate /iˈmēdē-it/ ▶ **adj.** **1** happening or done at once. **2** nearest in time, space, or relationship. **3** most urgent; current: *his immediate priority was to deal with the rebels.* **4** without anything coming between; direct: *an ice storm was the immediate cause of the car accident.*

> SYNONYMS **1 instant**, instantaneous, prompt, swift, speedy, rapid, quick. **2 current**, present, urgent, pressing. **3 nearest**, close, next-door, adjacent, adjoining. ANTONYMS delayed.

■ **im·me·di·a·cy** **n.**

im·me·di·ate·ly /iˈmēdē-itlē/ ▶ **adv.** **1** at once. **2** very close in time, space, or relationship.

> SYNONYMS **1 straightaway**, at once, right away, instantly, (right) now, directly, forthwith, here and now, there and then; informal pronto. **2 directly**, right, exactly, precisely, squarely, just, dead; informal smack dab. ANTONYMS later.

> **SPELLING**
> Write **-tely**, not **-tly**: immedia**tely**.

im·me·mo·ri·al /ˌi(m)məˈmôrēəl/ ▶ **adj.** existing for longer than people can remember: *the family had lived in the highlands from time immemorial.*

im·mense /iˈmens/ ▶ **adj.** very large or great.

> SYNONYMS **huge**, massive, vast, enormous, gigantic, colossal, monumental, towering, giant, mammoth; informal monster, whopping, ginormous. ANTONYMS tiny.

■ **im·men·si·ty** **n.**

im·mense·ly /iˈmenslē/ ▶ **adv.** to a great extent; extremely.

im·merse /iˈmərs/ ▶ **v.** (**immerses**, **immersing**, **immersed**) **1** dip or cover completely in a liquid. **2** (**immerse yourself in**) involve yourself deeply in an activity.

> SYNONYMS **1 dip**, submerge, dunk, duck, sink. **2 absorb**, engross, occupy, engage, involve, bury, preoccupy; informal lose.

im·mer·sion /iˈmərZHən, -SHən/ ▶ **n.** **1** the action of immersing. **2** deep involvement in an activity: *his total immersion in football.*

im·mi·grant /ˈimigrənt/ ▶ **n.** a person who comes to live permanently in a foreign country.

> SYNONYMS **newcomer**, settler, incomer, migrant, non-native, foreigner, alien, expatriate. ANTONYMS native.

im·mi·gra·tion /ˌimiˈgrāSHən/ ▶ **n.** the action of coming to live permanently in a foreign country. ■ **im·mi·grate** /ˈimiˌgrāt/ **v.**

im·mi·nent /ˈimənənt/ ▶ **adj.** about to happen.

> SYNONYMS **near**, close (at hand), impending, approaching, coming, forthcoming, on the way, expected, looming. ANTONYMS distant.

■ **im·mi·nence** **n.** **im·mi·nent·ly** **adv.**

im·mis·ci·ble /i(m)ˈmisəbəl/ ▶ **adj.** (of liquids) not able to be mixed together.

im·mo·bile /i(m)ˈmōbəl, -bēl, -bīl/ ▶ **adj.** not moving or able to move.

SYNONYMS **motionless**, still, stock-still, static, stationary, rooted to the spot, rigid, frozen, transfixed, paralyzed.

■ **im·mo·bil·i·ty** /ˌi(m)mōˈbilitē/ n.

im·mo·bi·lize /i(m)ˈmōbəˌlīz/ ▶ v. (**immobilizes**, **immobilizing**, **immobilized**) prevent from moving or operating normally. ■ **im·mo·bi·li·za·tion** /-ˌmōbəliˈzāsʜən/ n.

im·mod·er·ate /i(m)ˈmädərit/ ▶ adj. not sensible or controlled; excessive.

im·mod·est /i(m)ˈmädist/ ▶ adj. **1** conceited or boastful. **2** showing too much of the body.

SYNONYMS **indecorous**, improper, indecent, indelicate, immoral, forward, bold, brazen, shameless.

im·mo·late /ˈiməˌlāt/ ▶ v. kill or sacrifice by burning. ■ **im·mo·la·tion** /ˌiməˈlāsʜən/ n.

im·mor·al /i(m)ˈmôrəl, -ˈmärəl/ ▶ adj. not following accepted standards of morality.

SYNONYMS **wicked**, bad, wrong, unethical, unprincipled, unscrupulous, dishonest, corrupt, sinful, impure. ANTONYMS moral, ethical.

■ **im·mor·al·i·ty** /ˌiməˈralitē, ˌimô-/ n.

im·mor·tal /i(m)ˈmôrtl/ ▶ adj. **1** living forever. **2** deserving to be remembered forever. ▶ n. **1** an immortal god. **2** a person who will be famous for a very long time.

SYNONYMS ▶ adj. **1 undying**, deathless, eternal, everlasting, imperishable, indestructible. **2 timeless**, perennial, classic, time-honored, enduring, evergreen. ANTONYMS mortal, ephemeral.

■ **im·mor·tal·i·ty** /ˌi(m)ˌmôrˈtalitē/ n.

im·mor·tal·ize /i(m)ˈmôrtlˌīz/ ▶ v. (**immortalizes**, **immortalizing**, **immortalized**) prevent someone or something from being forgotten for a very long time.

im·mov·a·ble /i(m)ˈmo͞ovəbəl/ ▶ adj. **1** not able to be moved. **2** unable to be changed or persuaded: *an immovable truth.*

SYNONYMS **1 fixed**, secure, set firm, set fast, stuck, jammed, stiff. **2 motionless**, unmoving, stationary, still, stock-still, rooted to the spot, transfixed, paralyzed, frozen. ANTONYMS mobile.

im·mune /iˈmyo͞on/ ▶ adj. **1** having a natural ability to resist a particular infection. **2** not affected by something: *no one is immune to his charm.* **3** exempt or protected from something: *they are immune from legal action.*

SYNONYMS **resistant**, not subject, not liable, not vulnerable, protected from, safe from, secure against. ANTONYMS susceptible, liable.

im·mu·ni·ty /iˈmyo͞onitē/ ▶ n. (plural **immunities**) **1** the body's ability to resist a particular infection. **2** freedom from a duty or punishment.

SYNONYMS **1 resistance**, protection, defense. **2 exemption**, exception, freedom, indemnity, privilege, prerogative, license, impunity, protection. ANTONYMS susceptibility, liability.

im·mu·nize /ˈimyəˌnīz/ ▶ v. (**immunizes**, **immunizing**, **immunized**) make immune to infection.

SYNONYMS **vaccinate**, inoculate, inject.

■ **im·mu·ni·za·tion** /ˌimyəniˈzāsʜən/ n.

im·mu·no·de·fi·cien·cy /ˌimyənōdəˈfisʜənsē, iˌmyo͞o-/ ▶ n. failure of the body's ability to resist infection.

im·mu·nol·o·gy /ˌimyəˈnäləjē/ ▶ n. the branch of medicine and biology concerned with immunity to infection. ■ **im·mu·no·log·i·cal** /ˌimyənəˈläjikəl, iˌmyo͞o-/ adj. **im·mu·nol·o·gist** n.

im·mu·no·ther·a·py /ˌimyənōˈᴛʜerəpē, iˌmyo͞o-/ ▶ n. the prevention or treatment of disease with substances that stimulate the body's immune system.

im·mure /iˈmyo͝or/ ▶ v. (**immures**, **immuring**, **immured**) literary shut someone up in a place.

im·mu·ta·ble /iˈmyo͞otəbəl/ ▶ adj. not changing or able to be changed.

imp /imp/ ▶ n. **1** (in stories) a small, mischievous devil. **2** a mischievous child.

im·pact ▶ n. /ˈimˌpakt/ **1** an instance of one object hitting another. **2** a noticeable effect or influence: *man's impact on the environment.* ▶ v. /imˈpakt/ **1** hit another object with force. **2** (**impact on**) have a strong effect on: *the staff cuts impacted on the service the company provided.* **3** (**impacted**) (of a tooth) wedged between another tooth and the jaw.

SYNONYMS ▶ n. **1 collision**, crash, smash, bump, knock. **2 effect**, influence, consequences, repercussions, ramifications. ▶ v. **1 crash into**, smash into, collide with, hit, strike, smack into, bang into. **2** ***interest rates impacted on spending*** **affect**, influence, hit, have an effect, make an impression.

im·pair /imˈpe(ə)r/ ▶ v. weaken or damage.

SYNONYMS **weaken**, damage, harm, undermine, diminish, reduce, lessen, decrease. ANTONYMS improve, enhance.

■ **im·pair·ment** n.

im·pal·a /imˈpalə, -ˈpälə/ ▶ n. (plural same) an antelope of southern and East Africa, with lyre-shaped horns.

im·pale /imˈpāl/ ▶ v. (**impales**, **impaling**, **impaled**) pierce with a sharp instrument.

im·pal·pa·ble /imˈpalpəbəl/ ▶ adj. **1** unable to be felt by touch. **2** not easily understood.

im·part /imˈpärt/ ▶ v. **1** communicate information. **2** give a particular quality to: *the trees impart a certain grandeur to the scene.*

SYNONYMS **communicate**, pass on, convey, transmit, relay, relate, tell, make known, report, announce.

im·par·tial /imˈpärsʜəl/ ▶ adj. not favoring one person or thing more than another.

SYNONYMS **unbiased**, unprejudiced, neutral, nonpartisan, disinterested, detached, dispassionate, objective. ANTONYMS biased, partisan.

■ **im·par·ti·al·i·ty** /-ˌpärsʜēˈalitē/ n. **im·par·tial·ly** adv.

im·pass·a·ble /imˈpasəbəl/ ▶ adj. impossible to travel along or over.

im·passe /ˈimˌpas, imˈpas/ ▶ n. a situation in which no progress is possible.

SYNONYMS **deadlock**, dead end, stalemate, standoff, standstill.

im·pas·sioned /imˈpasʜənd/ ▶ adj. filled with or showing great emotion.

im·pas·sive /im'pasiv/ ▶ **adj.** not feeling or showing emotion. ■ **im·pas·sive·ly adv.**

im·pas·to /im'pastō, -'pästō/ ▶ **n.** the technique of laying on paint thickly so that it stands out from the surface of a painting.

im·pa·tient /im'pāsнənt/ ▶ **adj. 1** not having much patience or tolerance. **2** restlessly eager: *they are impatient for change.*

> SYNONYMS **1 irritated**, annoyed, angry, touchy, snappy, cross, curt, brusque. **2 restless**, agitated, nervous, anxious. **3 anxious**, eager, keen; informal itching, dying. ANTONYMS patient.

■ **im·pa·tience n. im·pa·tient·ly adv.**

im·peach /im'pēcн/ ▶ **v. 1** call into question the integrity or validity of a practice. **2** charge a person who holds an important public office with a serious crime. ■ **im·peach·ment n.**

im·pec·ca·ble /im'pekəbəl/ ▶ **adj.** without faults or mistakes.

> SYNONYMS **flawless**, faultless, unblemished, spotless, stainless, perfect, exemplary, irreproachable; informal squeaky clean. ANTONYMS imperfect.

■ **im·pec·ca·bly adv.**

im·pe·cu·ni·ous /ˌimpə'kyo͞onēəs/ ▶ **adj.** having little or no money.

im·ped·ance /im'pēdns/ ▶ **n.** the total resistance of an electric circuit to the flow of alternating current.

im·pede /im'pēd/ ▶ **v.** (**impedes**, **impeding**, **impeded**) delay or block the progress of: *an injury that could impede her gymnastics ability.*

> SYNONYMS **hinder**, obstruct, hamper, hold back/up, delay, interfere with, disrupt, retard, slow (down). ANTONYMS facilitate.

im·ped·i·ment /im'pedəmənt/ ▶ **n. 1** something that delays or blocks progress. **2** (also **speech impediment**) a defect in a person's speech, such as a stammer.

> SYNONYMS **1 hindrance**, obstruction, obstacle, barrier, bar, block, check, curb, restriction. **2 defect**, impairment, stammer, stutter, lisp.

im·pel /im'pel/ ▶ **v.** (**impels**, **impelling**, **impelled**) **1** drive, force, or urge someone to do something. **2** drive forward.

im·pend·ing /im'pendiɴɢ/ ▶ **adj.** be about to happen: *awareness of his impending death.*

> SYNONYMS **imminent**, close (at hand), near, approaching, coming, brewing, looming, threatening.

im·pen·e·tra·ble /im'penətrəbəl/ ▶ **adj. 1** impossible to get through or into. **2** impossible to understand.

> SYNONYMS **1 unbreakable**, indestructible, solid, thick, unyielding. **2 impassable**, dense, thick, overgrown. **3 incomprehensible**, unfathomable, unintelligible, baffling, bewildering, confusing, opaque.

im·pen·i·tent /im'penitnt/ ▶ **adj.** not feeling shame or regret.

im·per·a·tive /im'perətiv/ ▶ **adj. 1** of vital importance. **2** giving a command. **3** Grammar (of a verb) expressing a command, as in *come here!* ▶ **n.** an essential or urgent thing.

> SYNONYMS ▶ **adj. vital**, crucial, critical, essential, pressing, urgent.

im·per·cep·ti·ble /ˌimpər'septəbəl/ ▶ **adj.** too slight or gradual to be seen or felt.

> SYNONYMS **unnoticeable**, undetectable, indiscernible, invisible, inaudible, impalpable, slight, small, subtle, faint.

■ **im·per·cep·ti·bly adv.**

im·per·fect /im'pərfikt/ ▶ **adj. 1** faulty or incomplete. **2** Grammar (of a verb) referring to a past action that is not yet completed.

> SYNONYMS **faulty**, flawed, defective, inferior, second-rate, shoddy, substandard, damaged, blemished, torn, broken, cracked, scratched.

■ **im·per·fect·ly adv.**

im·per·fec·tion /ˌimpər'feksнən/ ▶ **n. 1** a fault, blemish, or undesirable feature. **2** the state of being faulty or incomplete.

im·pe·ri·al /im'pi(ə)rēəl/ ▶ **adj. 1** relating to an empire or an emperor. **2** (of weights and measures) in a nonmetric system formerly used in the UK for all measures, and still used for some.

im·pe·ri·al·ism /im'pi(ə)rēəˌlizəm/ ▶ **n.** a system in which one country extends its power and influence by defeating other countries in war, forming colonies, etc. ■ **im·pe·ri·al·ist n. & adj.**

im·per·il /im'perəl/ ▶ **v.** (**imperils**, **imperiling**, **imperiled**) put into danger.

im·pe·ri·ous /im'pi(ə)rēəs/ ▶ **adj.** expecting to be obeyed.

> SYNONYMS **peremptory**, high-handed, overbearing, domineering, authoritarian, dictatorial, authoritative, bossy, arrogant; informal pushy, high and mighty.

■ **im·pe·ri·ous·ly adv.**

im·per·ma·nent /im'pərmənənt/ ▶ **adj.** not permanent. ■ **im·per·ma·nence n.**

im·per·me·a·ble /im'pərmēəbəl/ ▶ **adj.** not allowing a liquid or gas to pass through.

im·per·son·al /im'pərsənl/ ▶ **adj. 1** not influenced by or involving personal feelings. **2** lacking human feelings or atmosphere: *an impersonal condo complex.* **3** Grammar (of a verb) used only with *it* as a subject (as in *it is snowing*).

> SYNONYMS **aloof**, distant, remote, detached, unemotional, unsentimental, cold, cool, indifferent, unconcerned, formal, stiff, businesslike, matter-of-fact; informal standoffish.

■ **im·per·son·al·i·ty** /-ˌpərsə'nalitē/ **n. im·per·son·al·ly adv.**

im·per·son·ate /im'pərsəˌnāt/ ▶ **v.** (**impersonates**, **impersonating**, **impersonated**) pretend to be another person in order to entertain or deceive people.

> SYNONYMS **imitate**, mimic, do an impression of, ape, parody, caricature, satirize, lampoon, masquerade as, pose as, pass yourself off as; informal take off on.

■ **im·per·son·a·tion** /-ˌpərsə'nāsнən/ **n. im·per·son·a·tor n.**

im·per·ti·nent /im'pərtn-ənt/ ▶ **adj.** not showing proper respect.

> SYNONYMS **rude**, insolent, impolite, ill-mannered, disrespectful, impudent, cheeky, presumptuous, forward. ANTONYMS polite, respectful.

■ **im·per·ti·nence n.**

im·per·turb·a·ble /ˌimpərˈtərbəbəl/ ▶ **adj.** not easily upset or excited.

im·per·vi·ous /imˈpərvēəs/ ▶ **adj.** **1** not allowing a liquid or a gas to pass through. **2** (**impervious to**) unable to be affected by.

im·pe·ti·go /ˌimpiˈtīgō, -tē-/ ▶ **n.** a contagious skin infection forming spots and yellow crusty sores.

im·pet·u·ous /imˈpechōōəs/ ▶ **adj.** acting quickly and without thinking or being careful.

SYNONYMS **impulsive**, rash, hasty, reckless, foolhardy, imprudent, ill-considered, spontaneous, impromptu, spur-of-the-moment.

■ **im·pet·u·ous·ly** **adv.**

im·pe·tus /ˈimpitəs/ ▶ **n.** **1** the force or energy with which something moves. **2** the force that makes something happen: *war conditions added to the impetus for change.*

SYNONYMS **1 momentum**, drive, thrust, energy, force, power, push. **2 motivation**, stimulus, incentive, inspiration, driving force.

im·pinge /imˈpinj/ ▶ **v.** (**impinges**, **impinging**, **impinged**) (**impinge on**) have an effect or impact on: *parents impinge on our lives.*

im·pi·ous /ˈimpēəs, imˈpī-/ ▶ **adj.** not showing respect or reverence.

im·plac·a·ble /imˈplakəbəl/ ▶ **adj.** **1** unwilling to stop being hostile toward someone or something: *an implacable enemy.* **2** (of strong negative feelings) unable to be changed. ■ **im·plac·a·bly** **adv.**

im·plant ▶ **v.** /imˈplant/ **1** put tissue or an artificial object into someone's body by means of a surgical operation. **2** fix an idea firmly in someone's mind. ▶ **n.** /ˈimˌplant/ a thing that is implanted.

SYNONYMS ▶ **v. 1 insert**, embed, bury, inject, transplant, graft. **2 instill**, inculcate, introduce, plant, sow.

■ **im·plan·ta·tion** /ˌimplanˈtāshən/ **n.**

im·plau·si·ble /imˈplôzəbəl/ ▶ **adj.** not seeming reasonable or probable.

SYNONYMS **unlikely**, improbable, questionable, doubtful, debatable, unconvincing, far-fetched. ANTONYMS convincing.

■ **im·plau·si·bil·i·ty** /-ˌplôzəˈbilitē/ **n.** **im·plau·si·bly** **adv.**

im·ple·ment ▶ **n.** /ˈimpləmənt/ a tool that is used for a particular purpose. ▶ **v.** /ˈimpləˌmənt/ put something into effect.

SYNONYMS ▶ **n. tool**, utensil, instrument, device, apparatus, gadget, contraption, appliance; informal gizmo. ▶ **v. execute**, apply, put into effect, put into practice, carry out/through, perform, enact, fulfill. ANTONYMS abolish, cancel.

■ **im·ple·men·ta·tion** /ˌimpləmənˈtāshən/ **n.**

im·pli·cate /ˈimpliˌkāt/ ▶ **v.** (**implicates**, **implicating**, **implicated**) **1** show that someone is involved in a crime. **2** (**be implicated in**) be partly responsible for: *he is heavily implicated in the bombing.*

SYNONYMS **incriminate**, involve, connect, embroil, enmesh.

im·pli·ca·tion /ˌimpliˈkāshən/ ▶ **n.** **1** a conclusion that can be drawn from something. **2** a possible effect. **3** involvement in something.

SYNONYMS **1 suggestion**, inference, insinuation, innuendo, intimation, imputation. **2 consequence**, result, ramification, repercussion, reverberation, effect. **3 incrimination**, involvement, connection, entanglement, association.

im·plic·it /imˈplisit/ ▶ **adj.** **1** suggested without being directly expressed: *his comments were seen as implicit criticism of the policy.* **2** (**implicit in**) forming part of something. **3** not doubted or questioned: *an implicit faith in God.*

SYNONYMS **1 implied**, inferred, understood, hinted at, suggested, unspoken, unstated, tacit, taken for granted. **2 inherent**, latent, underlying, inbuilt, incorporated. **3 absolute**, complete, total, wholehearted, utter, unqualified, unconditional, unshakable, unquestioning, firm. ANTONYMS explicit.

■ **im·plic·it·ly** **adv.**

im·plode /imˈplōd/ ▶ **v.** (**implodes**, **imploding**, **imploded**) collapse violently inward.
■ **im·plo·sion** **n.**

im·plore /imˈplôr/ ▶ **v.** (**implores**, **imploring**, **implored**) beg earnestly or desperately.

SYNONYMS **plead with**, beg, entreat, appeal to, ask, request, call on, exhort, urge.

im·ply /imˈplī/ ▶ **v.** (**implies**, **implying**, **implied**) **1** suggest rather than state directly. **2** suggest as a possible effect: *the forecast traffic increase implied more pollution.*

SYNONYMS **1 insinuate**, suggest, infer, hint, intimate, give someone to understand, make out. **2 involve**, entail, mean, point to, signify, indicate, presuppose.

USAGE

Don't confuse the words **imply** and **infer**. They can describe the same situation, but from different points of view. If you **imply** something, as in *he implied that the General was a traitor*, it means that you are suggesting something though not saying it directly. If you **infer** something from what has been said, as in *we inferred from his words that the General was a traitor*, you come to the conclusion that this is what the speaker really means, although they are not saying it directly.

im·po·lite /ˌimpəˈlīt/ ▶ **adj.** not having good manners.

SYNONYMS **rude**, bad-mannered, ill-mannered, discourteous, uncivil, disrespectful, insolent, impudent, impertinent, cheeky; informal lippy.

im·pol·i·tic /imˈpäliˌtik/ ▶ **adj.** unwise.

im·pon·der·a·ble /imˈpändərəbəl/ ▶ **n.** something that is difficult or impossible to assess. ▶ **adj.** difficult or impossible to assess.

im·port /imˈpôrt/ ▶ **v.** **1** bring goods into a country from abroad. **2** transfer computer data into a file. ▶ **n.** **1** an imported article. **2** the action of importing. **3** importance. **4** the implied meaning of something.

SYNONYMS ▶ **v. bring in**, buy in, ship in. ANTONYMS export. ▶ **n. 1 importance**, significance, consequence, momentousness, magnitude, substance, weight, note, gravity, seriousness. **2 meaning**, sense, essence, gist, drift, message, thrust, substance, implication. ANTONYMS insignificance.

■ **im·por·ta·tion** /ˌimpôrˈtāshən/ **n.** **im·port·er** **n.**

im·por·tance /im'pôrtns/ ▶ **n.** the state or fact of being important.

SYNONYMS **1 significance**, momentousness, moment, import, consequence, note, weight, seriousness, gravity. **2 status**, eminence, prestige, worth, influence, power, authority. ANTONYMS insignificance.

im·por·tant /im'pôrtnt/ ▶ **adj. 1** having a great effect or value: *important meetings*. **2** (of a person) having great authority or influence.

SYNONYMS **1 significant**, consequential, momentous, of great import, major, valuable, necessary, crucial, vital, essential, pivotal, decisive, far-reaching, historic. **2 powerful**, influential, well-connected, high-ranking, prominent, eminent, notable, distinguished, esteemed, respected, great, prestigious. ANTONYMS insignificant.

■ **im·por·tant·ly adv.**

im·por·tu·nate /im'pôrCHənit/ ▶ **adj.** very persistent.

im·por·tune /ˌimpôr't(y)o͞on, im'pôrCHən/ ▶ **v.** (**importunes**, **importuning**, **importuned**) ask someone persistently for something.

im·pose /im'pōz/ ▶ **v.** (**imposes**, **imposing**, **imposed**) **1** force something to be accepted. **2** introduce something that must be obeyed, paid, or done. **3** (often **impose on**) take unfair advantage of someone.

SYNONYMS **1** *he imposed his ideas on everyone* **foist**, force, inflict, press. **2 levy**, charge, apply, enforce, set, establish, institute, introduce, bring into effect. ANTONYMS abolish.

im·pos·ing /im'pōziNG/ ▶ **adj.** grand and impressive.

SYNONYMS **impressive**, spectacular, striking, dramatic, commanding, arresting, awesome, formidable, splendid, grand, majestic. ANTONYMS modest.

im·po·si·tion /ˌimpə'ziSHən/ ▶ **n. 1** the action of imposing something. **2** an unreasonable thing that you are asked or expected to do or accept.

SYNONYMS **1 imposing**, foisting, forcing, inflicting. **2 levying**, charging, application, enforcement, enforcing, setting, establishment, introduction. **3 burden**, encumbrance, liberty, bother, worry; informal hassle.

im·pos·si·ble /im'päsəbəl/ ▶ **adj. 1** not able to exist or be done. **2** very difficult to deal with: *an impossible situation*.

SYNONYMS **1 out of the question**, impracticable, nonviable, unworkable. **2 unattainable**, unachievable, unobtainable, hopeless, impracticable, unworkable. **3 unbearable**, intolerable, unendurable. **4 unreasonable**, difficult, awkward, intolerable, unbearable, exasperating, maddening, infuriating. ANTONYMS possible.

■ **im·pos·si·bil·i·ty** /imˌpäsə'bilitē/ **n. im·pos·si·bly adv.**

im·pos·tor /im'pästər/ (or **imposter**) ▶ **n.** a person who pretends to be someone else in order to deceive other people.

SYNONYMS **impersonator**, deceiver, hoaxer, fraudster, fake, fraud; informal phony.

im·pos·ture /im'päsCHər/ ▶ **n.** an act of pretending to be someone else in order to deceive.

im·po·tent /'impətnt/ ▶ **adj.** helpless or powerless.

SYNONYMS **powerless**, ineffective, ineffectual, useless, feeble, paralyzed, incapacitated. ANTONYMS powerful, effective.

■ **im·po·tence n.**

im·pound /im'pound/ ▶ **v. 1** officially seize something. **2** shut up domestic animals in an enclosure.

SYNONYMS **confiscate**, appropriate, take possession of, seize, commandeer, expropriate, requisition, take over.

im·pov·er·ish /im'päv(ə)riSH/ ▶ **v. 1** make someone poor. **2** make something worse in quality: *grazing impoverished the land*. ■ **im·pov·er·ish·ment n.**

im·prac·ti·ca·ble /im'praktikəbəl/ ▶ **adj.** not able to be done: *it was impracticable to widen the road here*.

SYNONYMS **unworkable**, unfeasible, nonviable, unachievable, unattainable, impractical. ANTONYMS practicable.

im·prac·ti·cal /im'praktikəl/ ▶ **adj.** not sensible or realistic: *impractical high heels*.

SYNONYMS **1 unrealistic**, unworkable, unfeasible, nonviable, ill-thought-out, absurd, idealistic, fanciful, romantic, starry-eyed, pie-in-the-sky; informal cockeyed, crackpot, crazy. **2 unsuitable**, not sensible, inappropriate, unserviceable. ANTONYMS realistic, practical.

im·pre·ca·tion /ˌimpri'kāSHən/ ▶ **n.** formal a spoken curse.

im·pre·cise /ˌimpri'sīs/ ▶ **adj.** not exact.

SYNONYMS **1 vague**, loose, indistinct, inaccurate, nonspecific, sweeping, broad, general, hazy, fuzzy, woolly, nebulous, ambiguous, equivocal, uncertain. **2 inexact**, approximate, rough; informal ballpark. ANTONYMS exact.

■ **im·pre·ci·sion n.**

im·preg·na·ble /im'preg-nəbəl/ ▶ **adj. 1** (of a building) unable to be captured or broken into. **2** unable to be defeated: *an impregnable halftime lead*.

im·preg·nate /im'pregˌnāt/ ▶ **v.** (**impregnates**, **impregnating**, **impregnated**) **1** soak with a substance. **2** fill with a feeling or quality: *an atmosphere impregnated with tension*. **3** make pregnant. ■ **im·preg·na·tion** /ˌimpreg'nāSHən/ **n.**

im·pre·sa·ri·o /ˌimprə'särēˌō, -'se(ə)r-/ ▶ **n.** (plural **impresarios**) a person who organizes plays, concerts, or operas.

SPELLING

Unlike **impress**, this word has just one **s**: impre**s**ario.

im·press ▶ **v.** /im'pres/ **1** make someone feel admiration and respect. **2** (**impress something on**) make someone aware of something important. **3** make a mark or design using a stamp or seal. ▶ **n.** /'imˌpres/ **1** an act of impressing a mark. **2** a mark or impression: *he wanted to put his own impress on the movies he made*.

SYNONYMS ▶ **v. make an impression on**, have an impact on, influence, affect, move, stir, rouse, excite, inspire, dazzle, awe. ANTONYMS disappoint.

im·pres·sion /im'preSHən/ ▶ **n. 1** an idea, feeling, or opinion: *his first impressions of London were* *positive.* **2** the effect that something has on someone: *her courtesy made a good impression.* **3** an imitation of the way that a person speaks or behaves done in order to entertain people. **4** a mark made by pressing on a surface.

> SYNONYMS **1 feeling**, sense, fancy, (sneaking) suspicion, inkling, intuition, hunch, notion, idea. **2 opinion**, view, image, picture, perception, reaction, judgment, verdict, estimation. **3 impact**, effect, influence. **4 impersonation**, imitation, caricature; informal takeoff. **5 indentation**, dent, mark, outline, imprint.

im·pres·sion·a·ble /im'presн(ə)nəbəl/ ▶ **adj.** easily influenced.

> SYNONYMS **easily influenced**, suggestible, susceptible, persuadable, pliable, malleable, pliant, ingenuous, trusting, naive, gullible.

Im·pres·sion·ism /im'presнə,nizəm/ ▶ **n.** a style of painting concerned with showing the visual impression of a particular moment.
■ **Im·pres·sion·ist** **n. & adj.**

im·pres·sion·ist /im'presнənist/ ▶ **n.** an entertainer who impersonates famous people.

im·pres·sion·is·tic /im,presнə'nistik/ ▶ **adj.** **1** based on personal ideas or feelings. **2** (**Impressionistic**) in the style of Impressionism.

im·pres·sive /im'presiv/ ▶ **adj.** arousing admiration through size, quality, or skill.

> SYNONYMS **magnificent**, majestic, imposing, splendid, spectacular, grand, awe-inspiring, stunning, breathtaking.

■ **im·pres·sive·ly** **adv.**

im·pri·ma·tur /,imprə'mätər, -'mātər/ ▶ **n.** the authority or approval of someone.

im·print /im'print/ ▶ **v.** /im'print/ make a mark on an object by pressing something on to it. ▶ **n.** /'imprint/ **1** a mark made by pressing something on to an object. **2** a publisher's name and other details printed in a book.

> SYNONYMS ▶ **v. stamp**, print, impress, mark, emboss. ▶ **n. impression**, print, mark, stamp, indentation.

im·pris·on /im'prizən/ ▶ **v.** put or keep in prison.

> SYNONYMS **incarcerate**, send to prison, jail, lock up, put away, intern, detain, hold prisoner, hold captive; informal send up/down, send up the river.

im·pris·on·ment /im'prizənmənt/ ▶ **n.** the state of being imprisoned.

> SYNONYMS **custody**, incarceration, internment, confinement, detention, captivity; informal time.

im·prob·a·ble /im'präbəbəl/ ▶ **adj.** not likely to be true or to happen.

> SYNONYMS **1 unlikely**, doubtful, dubious, debatable, questionable, uncertain. **2 unconvincing**, unbelievable, implausible, unlikely.

■ **im·prob·a·bil·i·ty** /-,präbə'bilitē/ **n.** **im·prob·a·bly** **adv.**

im·promp·tu /im'präm(p),t(y)o͞o/ ▶ **adj. & adv.** done without being planned or rehearsed.

> SYNONYMS **unrehearsed**, unprepared, unscripted, extempore, extemporized, improvised, spontaneous, unplanned; informal off-the-cuff.

im·prop·er /im'präpər/ ▶ **adj.** **1** not fitting in with accepted standards of behavior. **2** not modest or decent.

> SYNONYMS **1 unacceptable**, unprofessional, irregular, unethical, dishonest. **2 unseemly**, unfitting, unbecoming, unladylike, ungentlemanly, inappropriate, indelicate, indecent, immodest, indecorous, immoral. **3 indecent**, risqué, suggestive, naughty, dirty, filthy, vulgar, crude, rude, obscene, lewd; informal blue, raunchy, steamy. ANTONYMS proper, seemly.

□ **improper fraction** a fraction in which the numerator is greater than the denominator, such as $^5/_4$.

im·pro·pri·e·ty /,imprə'prī-itē/ ▶ **n.** (plural **improprieties**) improper behavior.

im·prove /im'pro͞ov/ ▶ **v.** (**improves**, **improving**, **improved**) **1** make or become better. **2** (**improve on**) produce something better than.

> SYNONYMS **1 make better**, ameliorate, upgrade, refine, enhance, boost, build on, raise. **2 get better**, advance, progress, develop, make headway, make progress, pick up, look up, move forward. **3 recover**, get better, recuperate, rally, revive, be on the mend. ANTONYMS worsen, deteriorate.

im·prove·ment /im'pro͞ovmənt/ ▶ **n.** **1** the action of making or becoming better. **2** a thing that improves something or is better than something else: *home improvements.*

> SYNONYMS **advance**, development, upgrade, refinement, enhancement, betterment, amelioration, boost, augmentation, rally, recovery, upswing.

im·prov·i·dent /im'prävidənt/ ▶ **adj.** not thinking about or preparing for the future.

im·pro·vise /'imprə,vīz/ ▶ **v.** (**improvises**, **improvising**, **improvised**) **1** invent and perform music or drama without planning it in advance. **2** make something from whatever is available.

> SYNONYMS **1 extemporize**, ad-lib; informal speak off the cuff, play (it) by ear, wing it. **2 contrive**, devise, throw together, cobble together, rig up; informal whip up, rustle up.

■ **im·prov·i·sa·tion** /im,prävi'zāsнən/ **n.**

im·pru·dent /im'pro͞odnt/ ▶ **adj.** not sensible or careful.

im·pu·dent /'impyəd(ə)nt/ ▶ **adj.** not showing respect for another person.

> SYNONYMS **impertinent**, insolent, cheeky, cocky, brazen; presumptuous, forward, disrespectful, insubordinate; rude, impolite, ill-mannered, discourteous; informal saucy, sassy, lippy. ANTONYMS polite.

■ **im·pu·dence** **n.** **im·pu·dent·ly** **adv.**

im·pugn /im'pyo͞on/ ▶ **v.** formal express doubts about whether something is true or honest.

im·pulse /'im,pəls/ ▶ **n.** **1** a sudden urge to do something. **2** a force that makes something happen: *the impulse for the book came from personal experience.* **3** a pulse of electrical energy.

> SYNONYMS **1 urge**, instinct, drive, compulsion, itch, whim, desire, fancy, notion. **2 spontaneity**, impetuosity, recklessness, rashness.

im·pul·sion /im'pəlsʜən/ ▸ **n.** **1** an urge to do something. **2** a driving force.

im·pul·sive /im'pəlsiv/ ▸ **adj.** acting without thinking ahead.

SYNONYMS **1 hasty**, sudden, quick, precipitate, impetuous, impromptu, spontaneous, snap, unplanned, unpremeditated, thoughtless, rash, reckless. **2 impetuous**, instinctive, passionate, intuitive, emotional, devil-may-care. ANTONYMS cautious, premeditated.

■ **im·pul·sive·ly** **adv.**

im·pu·ni·ty /im'pyo͞onitē/ ▸ **n.** freedom from being punished or hurt: *rebels were crossing the border with impunity.*

im·pure /im'pyo͝or/ ▸ **adj.** **1** mixed with unwanted substances: *impure coal.* **2** morally wrong.

im·pu·ri·ty /im'pyo͝oritē/ ▸ **n.** (plural **impurities**) **1** the state of being impure. **2** a thing that makes something less pure.

SYNONYMS **1** *the impurity of the air* **contamination**, pollution; dirtiness, filthiness, foulness, unwholesomeness. **2** *the impurities in beer* **contaminant**, pollutant, foreign body; dross, dirt, filth. **3** *sin and impurity* **immorality**, sin, sinfulness, wickedness; lustfulness, lechery, lewdness, lasciviousness, obscenity, crudeness, indecency, impropriety, vulgarity, coarseness.

im·pute /im'pyo͞ot/ ▸ **v.** (**imputes**, **imputing**, **imputed**) (**impute something to**) believe that something has been done or caused by: *depression among the troops was imputed to shell shock.*
■ **im·pu·ta·tion** /ˌimpyə'tāsʜən/ **n.**

in /in/ ▸ **prep.** **1** expressing the position of something that is enclosed or surrounded: *he got in his car.* **2** expressing movement that results in something being enclosed or surrounded. **3** expressing a period of time before or during which something happens. **4** expressing a state or quality: *he's in love.* **5** indicating that something is included or involved: *acting in a movie.* **6** indicating the language or material used by someone: *say it in French.* **7** used to express a value as a proportion of a whole.
▸ **adv.** **1** expressing the state of being enclosed or surrounded. **2** expressing movement that results in being enclosed or surrounded. **3** present at your home or office. **4** having arrived at a destination. **5** (of the tide) rising or at its highest level. ▸ **adj.** informal fashionable. □ **be in for** have good reason to expect: *we're in for a storm.* **be in on** know about. **in-depth** thorough and detailed. **in-house** within an organization. **in-law** a relative by marriage. **in-joke** a joke shared only by a small group. **in that** for the reason that. **the ins and outs** informal all the details.

in. ▸ **abbr.** inches.

in·a·bil·i·ty /ˌinə'bilitē/ ▸ **n.** the state of being unable to do something.

in ab·sen·tia /ˌin əb'sensʜ(ē)ə/ ▸ **adv.** while not present: *the suspects will be tried in absentia.*

in·ac·ces·si·ble /ˌinak'sesəbəl/ ▸ **adj.** **1** unable to be reached or used. **2** difficult to understand.

in·ac·cu·rate /ˌin'akyərit/ ▸ **adj.** not accurate.

SYNONYMS **inexact**, imprecise, incorrect, wrong, erroneous, faulty, imperfect, defective, unreliable, false, mistaken, untrue.

■ **in·ac·cu·ra·cy** **n.** (plural **inaccuracies**)
in·ac·cu·rate·ly **adv.**

in·ac·tive /in'aktiv/ ▸ **adj.** not active or working.
■ **in·ac·tion** **n.**

in·ac·tiv·i·ty /ˌinak'tivitē/ ▸ **n.** the state of being inactive.

SYNONYMS **inaction**, inertia, idleness, nonintervention, negligence, apathy, indolence, laziness, slothfulness. ANTONYMS action.

in·ad·e·quate /ˌin'adikwit/ ▸ **adj.** **1** not enough or not good enough: *inadequate funding.* **2** unable to deal with a situation.

SYNONYMS **1 insufficient**, deficient, poor, scant, scarce, sparse, in short supply, paltry, meager. **2 incapable**, incompetent, ineffective, inefficient, inept, unfit; informal not up to snuff/scratch.

■ **in·ad·e·qua·cy** **n.** (plural **inadequacies**)
in·ad·e·quate·ly **adv.**

in·ad·mis·si·ble /ˌinəd'misəbəl/ ▸ **adj.** (of evidence in court) not accepted as valid.

in·ad·vert·ent /ˌinəd'vərtnt/ ▸ **adj.** not deliberate or intentional.

SPELLING

Write **-ent**, not **-ant**: inadvert**ent**.

in·ad·vert·ent·ly /ˌinəd'vərtntlē/ ▸ **adv.** unintentionally: *his name had been inadvertently omitted from the list.*

SYNONYMS **accidentally**, by accident, unintentionally, by mistake, mistakenly, unwittingly. ANTONYMS intentionally.

in·ad·vis·a·ble /ˌinəd'vīzəbəl/ ▸ **adj.** likely to have unfortunate results.

in·al·ien·a·ble /in'ālēənəbəl/ ▸ **adj.** unable to be taken away or given away: *inalienable rights.*

in·ane /i'nān/ ▸ **adj.** silly or stupid. ■ **in·ane·ly** **adv.** **in·an·i·ty** **n.**

in·an·i·mate /in'anəmit/ ▸ **adj.** **1** not alive. **2** showing no sign of life.

in·ap·pli·ca·ble /in'aplikəbəl, ˌinə'plik-/ ▸ **adj.** not relevant or appropriate.

in·ap·pro·pri·ate /ˌinə'prōprē-it/ ▸ **adj.** not suitable or appropriate.

SYNONYMS **unsuitable**, unfitting, unseemly, unbecoming, improper, out of place/keeping, inapposite; informal out of line.

■ **in·ap·pro·pri·ate·ly** **adv.**

in·ar·tic·u·late /ˌinär'tikyəlit/ ▸ **adj.** **1** unable to express your ideas clearly. **2** not expressed in words: *inarticulate longing.*

in·as·much /ˌinəz'məcʜ/ ▸ **adv.** (**inasmuch as**) **1** to the extent that. **2** considering that; since.

in·at·ten·tive /ˌinə'tentiv/ ▸ **adj.** not paying attention. ■ **in·at·ten·tion** **n.**

in·au·di·ble /ˌin'ôdəbəl/ ▸ **adj.** unable to be heard.

SYNONYMS **unclear**, indistinct, faint, muted, soft, low, muffled, whispered, muttered, murmured, mumbled.

■ **in·au·di·bly** **adv.**

in·au·gu·ral /in'ôg(y)ərəl/ ▸ **adj.** marking the start of something important.

in·au·gu·rate /in'ôg(y)əˌrāt/ ▸ **v.** (**inaugurates**, **inaugurating**, **inaugurated**) **1** begin or introduce a system or project. **2** admit someone formally to public office. **3** mark the beginning of an organization or the opening of a building with a ceremony.

SYNONYMS **1 initiate**, begin, start, institute, launch, get going, get under way, establish, bring in, usher in; informal kick off. **2 install**, instate, swear in, invest, ordain, crown.

■ **in·au·gu·ra·tion** /-ôg(y)ə'rāsʜən/ **n.**

in·aus·pi·cious /ˌinô'spisʜəs/ ▶ **adj.** not likely to lead to success; ill-omened.

in·au·then·tic /ˌinô'ᴛʜentik/ ▶ **n.** not genuine or sincere.

in·board /'inˌbôrd/ ▶ **adv. & adj.** within or toward the center of a ship, aircraft, or vehicle.

in·born /'in'bôrn/ ▶ **adj.** existing from birth.

in·bound /'inˌbound/ ▶ **adj. & adv.** traveling back to an original point of departure.

in·bred /'inˌbred/ ▶ **adj. 1** produced by breeding from closely related people or animals. **2** existing from birth; inborn.

in·breed·ing /'inˌbrēdiɴɢ/ ▶ **n.** breeding from closely related people or animals.

in·built /'inˌbilt/ ▶ **adj.** existing as an original or important part.

Inc. /iɴɢk/ ▶ **abbr.** Incorporated.

In·ca /'iɴɢkə/ ▶ **n.** a member of a South American Indian people living in the central Andes before the Spanish conquest in the early 1530s.

in·cal·cu·la·ble /in'kalkyələbəl, iɴɢ-/ ▶ **adj. 1** too great to be calculated or estimated: *an archive of incalculable value.* **2** not able to be calculated or estimated.

in·can·des·cent /ˌinkən'desənt/ ▶ **adj. 1** glowing as a result of being heated. **2** (of an electric light) containing a filament that glows white-hot when heated by an electric current. ■ **in·can·des·cence n.**

in·can·ta·tion /ˌinkan'tāsʜən/ ▶ **n.** a magic spell or charm. ■ **in·can·ta·to·ry** /in'kantəˌtôrē/ **adj.**

in·ca·pa·ble /ˌin'kāpəbəl/ ▶ **adj. 1** (**incapable of**) not able to do something. **2** not able to look after yourself.

SYNONYMS **incompetent**, inept, inadequate, ineffective, ineffectual, unfit, unqualified; informal not up to it. ANTONYMS competent.

in·ca·pac·i·tate /ˌinkə'pasiˌtāt/ ▶ **v.** (**incapacitates, incapacitating, incapacitated**) prevent from working in a normal way. ■ **in·ca·pac·i·ta·tion** /-ˌpasi'tāsʜən/ **n.**

in·ca·pac·i·ty /ˌinkə'pasitē/ ▶ **n.** (plural **incapacities**) inability to do something.

in·car·cer·ate /in'kärsəˌrāt/ ▶ **v.** (**incarcerates, incarcerating, incarcerated**) imprison. ■ **in·car·cer·a·tion** /-ˌkärsə'rāsʜən/ **n.**

in·car·nate ▶ **adj.** /in'kärnit, -ˌnāt/ **1** in human form. **2** in physical form: *she was beauty incarnate.* ▶ **v.** /'inkärˌnāt/ be the living embodiment of a quality.

in·car·na·tion /ˌinkär'nāsʜən/ ▶ **n. 1** a god, spirit, or quality in human form. **2** (**the Incarnation**) (in Christian belief) God taking human form as Jesus.

in·cau·tious /in'kôsʜəs/ ▶ **adj.** not concerned about possible problems.

in·cen·di·ar·y /in'sendēˌerē/ ▶ **adj. 1** (of a bomb) designed to cause fires. **2** tending to cause strong feelings. ▶ **n.** (plural **incendiaries**) an incendiary bomb.

in·cense¹ /'inˌsens/ ▶ **n.** a substance that produces a sweet smell when you burn it.

in·cense² /in'sens/ ▶ **v.** (**incenses, incensing, incensed**) make very angry.

SYNONYMS **1 enrage**, infuriate, anger, madden, outrage, exasperate, antagonize, provoke; informal make someone see red. **2** (**incensed**) **enraged**, furious, infuriated, irate, raging, incandescent, fuming, seething, beside yourself, outraged; informal mad, hopping mad, wild, livid. ANTONYMS placate.

in·cen·tive /in'sentiv/ ▶ **n.** something that influences or encourages you to do something.

SYNONYMS **inducement**, motivation, motive, reason, stimulus, spur, impetus, encouragement, carrot; informal sweetener. ANTONYMS deterrent.

in·cep·tion /in'sepsʜən/ ▶ **n.** the beginning of an organization or activity.

in·ces·sant /in'sesənt/ ▶ **adj.** never stopping. ■ **in·ces·sant·ly adv.**

in·cest /'inˌsest/ ▶ **n.** sex between people who are very closely related in a family.

in·ces·tu·ous /in'sesᴄʜo͞oəs/ ▶ **adj. 1** involving incest. **2** involving a group of people who are very close and do not want to include others.

inch /iɴᴄʜ/ ▶ **n. 1** a unit of length equal to one twelfth of a foot (2.54 cm). **2** a very small amount or distance: *don't move an inch.* ▶ **v.** move along slowly and carefully. □ **every inch** very much so. **(to) within an inch of your life** almost to the point of death.

in·cho·ate /in'kō-it, -āt/ ▶ **adj.** just begun and so not fully formed or developed.

in·ci·dence /'insidəns/ ▶ **n. 1** the extent to which something happens: *an increased incidence of cancer.* **2** Physics the meeting of a line or ray with a surface.

in·ci·dent /'insidənt/ ▶ **n. 1** something that happens. **2** a violent event. **3** the occurrence of dangerous or exciting events: *the plane landed without incident.* ▶ **adj. 1** (**incident to**) resulting from. **2** (of light or other radiation) falling on a surface.

SYNONYMS ▶ **n. 1 event**, occurrence, episode, happening, affair, business, adventure, exploit, escapade. **2 disturbance**, commotion, clash, confrontation, scene, accident, fracas, contretemps. **3** *the journey was not without incident* **excitement**, adventure, drama, crisis, danger.

in·ci·den·tal /ˌinsi'dentl/ ▶ **adj. 1** occurring in connection with something else: *a sensor that detects incidental damage.* **2** relatively unimportant: *incidental expenses.*

SYNONYMS **1 secondary**, subsidiary, minor, peripheral, background, by-the-by, unimportant, insignificant, tangential. **2 chance**, accidental, random, fluky, fortuitous, serendipitous, coincidental, unlooked-for. ANTONYMS essential.

□ **incidental music** background music in a movie or play.

in·ci·den·tal·ly /ˌinsi'dent(ə)lē/ ▶ **adv. 1** by the way. **2** in an incidental way.

SYNONYMS **1 by the way**, by the by, in passing, speaking of which; informal as it happens. **2 by chance**, by accident, accidentally, fortuitously, by a fluke, by happenstance.

in·cin·er·ate /in'sinəˌrāt/ ▶ **v.** (**incinerates, incinerating, incinerated**) destroy by burning.

■ **in·cin·er·a·tion** /-ˌsinəˈrāsʜən/ **n.**

in·cin·er·a·tor /inˈsinəˌrātər/ ▶ **n.** a device for burning waste material.

in·cip·i·ent /inˈsipēənt/ ▶ **adj.** beginning to happen or develop.

in·cise /inˈsīz/ ▶ **v.** (**incises**, **incising**, **incised**) **1** mark a surface by cutting into it. **2** make a cut or cuts in a surface.

in·ci·sion /inˈsizʜən/ ▶ **n. 1** a cut made as part of a surgical operation. **2** the action of cutting into something.

in·ci·sive /inˈsīsiv/ ▶ **adj.** showing clear thought and good understanding: *incisive criticism.*

SYNONYMS **penetrating**, acute, sharp, razor-sharp, keen, astute, trenchant, shrewd, piercing, perceptive, insightful, perspicacious; concise, succinct, pithy, to the point, crisp, clear. ANTONYMS rambling, vague.

in·ci·sor /inˈsīzər/ ▶ **n.** a narrow-edged tooth at the front of the mouth.

in·cite /inˈsīt/ ▶ **v.** (**incites**, **inciting**, **incited**) encourage someone to do something violent or unlawful.

SYNONYMS **1 stir up**, whip up, encourage, stoke up, fuel, kindle, inflame, instigate, provoke, excite, trigger, spark off. **2 provoke**, encourage, urge, goad, spur on, egg on, drive, prod, prompt; informal put up to. ANTONYMS discourage, deter.

■ **in·cite·ment n.**

in·ci·vil·i·ty /ˌinsəˈvilətē/ ▶ **n.** rude speech or behavior.

in·clem·ent /inˈklemənt/ ▶ **adj.** (of the weather) unpleasantly cold or wet. ■ **in·clem·en·cy n.**

in·cli·na·tion /ˌinkləˈnāsʜən, ˌiɴɢklə-/ ▶ **n. 1** a tendency to do things in a particular way: *his inclination was to take the slower route home.* **2** (**inclination for** or **to do**) an interest in or liking for. **3** a slope or slant.

SYNONYMS **tendency**, propensity, leaning, predisposition, predilection, impulse, bent, liking, taste, penchant, preference. ANTONYMS aversion.

in·cline ▶ **v.** /inˈklīn/ (**inclines**, **inclining**, **inclined**) **1** (**incline to** or **be inclined to**) tend to do or think in a particular way: *he was inclined to accept the offer.* **2** lean or bend. **3** bend your head forward and downward. ▶ **n.** /ˈinˌklīn/ a slope.

SYNONYMS ▶ **v. 1 predispose**, lead, make, dispose, prejudice, prompt, induce. **2** (**inclined**) **disposed**, minded, of a mind. **3** *I incline to the opposite view* **tend to/toward**, lean to/toward, swing to/toward, veer to/toward, gravitate to/toward, be drawn to/toward, prefer, favor, go for. **4** (**inclined**) **prone**, given, in the habit of, liable, apt. **5 bend**, bow, nod, bob, lower, dip. ▶ **n. slope**, gradient, grade, pitch, ramp, bank, ascent, rise, hill, dip, descent.

□ **inclined plane** a plane inclined at an angle to the horizontal, used as a means of reducing the force needed to raise a load.

in·clude /inˈklo͞od/ ▶ **v.** (**includes**, **including**, **included**) **1** have something as part of a whole: *the price includes bed and breakfast.* **2** make part of a whole.

SYNONYMS **1 incorporate**, comprise, encompass, cover, embrace, take in, number, contain. **2 allow for**, count, take into account, take into consideration. **3 add**, insert, put in, append, enter. ANTONYMS exclude, leave out.

in·clud·ing /inˈklo͞odiɴɢ/ ▶ **prep.** having as part of a whole.

in·clu·sion /inˈklo͞ozʜən/ ▶ **n. 1** the act of including. **2** a person or thing that is included.

in·clu·sive /inˈklo͞osiv/ ▶ **adj. 1** including everything expected or required. **2** between the limits stated: *the ages of 55 to 59 inclusive.*

SYNONYMS **all-in**, comprehensive, overall, full, all-around, umbrella, catch-all, blanket. ANTONYMS exclusive, limited.

in·cog·ni·to /ˌinkägˈnētō, inˈkägniˌtō/ ▶ **adj. & adv.** having your true identity concealed.

in·co·her·ent /ˌinkōˈhi(ə)rənt, ˌiɴɢ-, -ˈher-/ ▶ **adj. 1** hard to understand; not clear. **2** not logical or well-organized. ■ **in·co·her·ence n. in·co·her·ent·ly adv.**

in·com·bus·ti·ble /ˌinkəmˈbəstəbəl/ ▶ **adj.** (of a material) that does not burn.

in·come /ˈinˌkəm, ˈiɴɢ-/ ▶ **n.** money received for work or from investments.

SYNONYMS **earnings**, salary, wages, pay, remuneration, revenue, receipts, take, profits, proceeds, yield, dividend. ANTONYMS expenditure, outgoings.

□ **income tax** tax that must be paid on personal income.

in·com·ing /ˈinˌkəmiɴɢ/ ▶ **adj. 1** coming in or arriving. **2** (of a public official) having just been chosen to replace someone.

SYNONYMS **1 arriving**, approaching, inbound, inward, returning, homeward. **2 new**, next, future, elect, designate. ANTONYMS outward, outgoing.

in·com·men·su·ra·ble /ˌinkəˈmensərəbəl, -sʜər-/ ▶ **adj.** not able to be compared.

in·com·men·su·rate /ˌinkəˈmensərit, -sʜə-/ ▶ **adj.** (**incommensurate with**) out of proportion with.

in·com·mode /ˌinkəˈmōd/ ▶ **v.** (**incommodes**, **incommoding**, **incommoded**) formal cause someone difficulties or problems.

in·com·mu·ni·ca·do /ˌinkəˌmyo͞oniˈkädō/ ▶ **adj. & adv.** not able or not willing to communicate with other people.

in·com·pa·ra·ble /inˈkämp(ə)rəbəl/ ▶ **adj.** so good that nothing can be compared to it: *the incomparable beauty of Venice.* ■ **in·com·pa·ra·bly adv.**

in·com·pat·i·ble /ˌinkəmˈpatəbəl, ˌiɴɢ-/ ▶ **adj. 1** (of two things) not able to exist or be used together. **2** (of two people) unable to live or work together without disagreeing.

SYNONYMS **mismatched**, unsuited, poles apart, irreconcilable, inconsistent, conflicting, opposed, opposite, contradictory, at odds, at variance. ANTONYMS harmonious, consistent.

■ **in·com·pat·i·bil·i·ty** /-ˌpatəˈbilitē/ **n.**

in·com·pe·tent /inˈkämpətənt, iɴɢ-/ ▶ **adj.** not having the skill to do something well.

SYNONYMS **inept**, unskilled, inexpert, amateurish, unprofessional, bungling, blundering, clumsy; informal useless, not up to it.

■ **in·com·pe·tence n. in·com·pe·tent·ly adv.**

in·com·plete /ˌinkəmˈplēt, ˌiɴɢ-/ ▶ **adj.** not complete.

SYNONYMS **1 unfinished**, uncompleted, partial, half-finished. **2 deficient**, insufficient, partial, sketchy, fragmentary. ANTONYMS completed, full.

■ **in·com·plete·ly** adv.

in·com·pre·hen·si·ble /ˌinkämprəˈhensəbəl, inˌkäm-/ ▶ adj. not able to be understood.

SYNONYMS **unintelligible**, impenetrable, unclear, indecipherable, unfathomable, abstruse, difficult, involved. ANTONYMS intelligible, clear.

■ **in·com·pre·hen·sion** n.

in·con·ceiv·a·ble /ˌinkənˈsēvəbəl/ ▶ adj. not able to be imagined or believed. ■ **in·con·ceiv·a·bly** adv.

in·con·clu·sive /ˌinkənˈklo͞osiv, ˌiNG-/ ▶ adj. not leading to a firm conclusion. ■ **in·con·clu·sive·ly** adv.

in·con·gru·ous /inˈkäNGgro͞oəs/ ▶ adj. out of place. ■ **in·con·gru·i·ty** /ˌinkənˈgro͞o-itē, ˌiNG-, -käNG-/ n. (plural **incongruities**) **in·con·gru·ous·ly** adv.

in·con·se·quen·tial /ˌinkänsəˈkwenCHəl/ ▶ adj. not important. ■ **in·con·se·quen·tial·ly** adv.

in·con·sid·er·a·ble /ˌinkənˈsidərəbəl/ ▶ adj. small in size or amount: *a not inconsiderable number*.

in·con·sid·er·ate /ˌinkənˈsidərit/ ▶ adj. not thinking about other people's feelings.

SYNONYMS **thoughtless**, unthinking, insensitive, selfish, self-centered, impolite, discourteous, rude; tactless, undiplomatic; informal ignorant. ANTONYMS thoughtful.

in·con·sist·ent /ˌinkənˈsistənt/ ▶ adj. **1** having parts that contradict each other. **2** (**inconsistent with**) not in keeping with.

SYNONYMS **1 erratic**, changeable, unpredictable, variable, unstable, fickle, unreliable, volatile; informal up and down. **2 incompatible**, conflicting, at odds, at variance, irreconcilable, out of keeping, contrary.

■ **in·con·sist·en·cy** n. (plural **inconsistencies**).

in·con·sol·a·ble /ˌinkənˈsōləbəl/ ▶ adj. not able to be comforted.

in·con·spic·u·ous /ˌinkənˈspikyo͞oəs/ ▶ adj. not noticeable. ■ **in·con·spic·u·ous·ly** adv.

in·con·stant /inˈkänstənt/ ▶ adj. **1** formal not faithful or dependable. **2** frequently changing.

in·con·test·a·ble /ˌinkənˈtestəbəl/ ▶ adj. not able to be disputed.

in·con·ti·nent /inˈkäntənənt, -ˈkäntn-ənt/ ▶ adj. **1** unable to control your bladder or bowels. **2** lacking self-control. ■ **in·con·ti·nence** n.

in·con·tro·vert·i·ble /inˌkäntrəˈvərtəbəl/ ▶ adj. not able to be denied or disputed. ■ **in·con·tro·vert·i·bly** adv.

in·con·ven·ience /ˌinkənˈvēn-yəns/ ▶ n. slight trouble or difficulty. ▶ v. (**inconveniences**, **inconveniencing**, **inconvenienced**) cause someone inconvenience.

SYNONYMS ▶ n. **trouble**, nuisance, bother, problem, disruption, difficulty, disturbance; informal aggravation, hassle, headache, pain, pain in the neck. ▶ v. **trouble**, bother, put out, put to any trouble, disturb, impose on.

in·con·ven·ient /ˌinkənˈvēn-yənt/ ▶ adj. causing trouble, difficulties, or discomfort.

SYNONYMS **awkward**, difficult, inopportune, badly timed, unsuitable, inappropriate, unfortunate.

■ **in·con·ven·ient·ly** adv.

in·cor·po·rate /inˈkôrpəˌrāt/ ▶ v. (**incorporates**, **incorporating**, **incorporated**) include something as part of a whole.

SYNONYMS **1 absorb**, include, subsume, assimilate, integrate, swallow up. **2 include**, contain, embrace, build in, offer, boast. **3 blend**, mix, combine, fold in, stir in.

■ **in·cor·po·ra·tion** /-ˌkôrpəˈrāSHən/ n.

in·cor·po·rat·ed /inˈkôrpəˌrātid/ ▶ adj. (of a company) formed into a legal corporation.

in·cor·po·re·al /ˌinkôrˈpôrēəl/ ▶ adj. without a body or form.

in·cor·rect /ˌinkəˈrekt/ ▶ adj. **1** not true or accurate. **2** not following accepted standards.

SYNONYMS **1 wrong**, erroneous, mistaken, untrue, false, fallacious, flawed; informal wide of the mark. **2 inappropriate**, unsuitable, unacceptable, improper, unseemly; informal out of line.

■ **in·cor·rect·ly** adv.

in·cor·ri·gi·ble /inˈkôrijəbəl, -ˈkär-/ ▶ adj. having bad habits that cannot be changed: *an incorrigible liar*.

in·cor·rupt·i·ble /ˌinkəˈrəptəbəl/ ▶ adj. **1** too honest to be corrupted by taking bribes. **2** not prone to death or decay.

in·crease ▶ v. /inˈkrēs/ (**increases**, **increasing**, **increased**) make or become greater in size, amount, or strength: *milk prices have increased by 20%*. ▶ n. /ˈinˌkrēs/ a rise in amount, size, or strength.

SYNONYMS ▶ v. **1 grow**, get bigger, get larger, enlarge, expand, swell, rise, climb, mount, intensify, strengthen, extend, spread, widen. **2 add to**, make larger, make bigger, augment, supplement, top off, build up, extend, raise, swell, inflate, intensify, heighten; informal up, bump up. ▶ n. **growth**, rise, enlargement, expansion, extension, increment, gain, addition, augmentation, surge; informal hike. ANTONYMS decrease.

in·creas·ing·ly /inˈkrēsiNGlē/ ▶ adv. more and more.

in·cred·i·ble /inˈkredəbəl/ ▶ adj. **1** impossible or hard to believe. **2** informal very good.

SYNONYMS **1 unbelievable**, unconvincing, far-fetched, implausible, improbable, inconceivable, unimaginable. **2 wonderful**, marvelous, spectacular, remarkable, phenomenal, prodigious, breathtaking; informal fantastic, terrific.

■ **in·cred·i·bly** adv.

USAGE

Don't confuse **incredible** with **incredulous**, which means 'unwilling or unable to believe something.'

in·cre·du·li·ty /ˌinkrəˈd(y)o͞olitē/ ▶ n. unwillingness or inability to believe something.

in·cred·u·lous /inˈkrejələs/ ▶ adj. unwilling or unable to believe something. ■ **in·cred·u·lous·ly** adv.

in·cre·ment /ˈiNGkrəmənt, ˈin-/ ▶ n. an increase in a number or amount: *salary increments*. ■ **in·cre·men·tal** /ˌiNGkrəˈmentl, ˌin-/ adj.

in·crim·i·nate /inˈkriməˌnāt/ ▶ v. (**incriminates**, **incriminating**, **incriminated**) make it look as though someone has done something wrong or illegal. ■ **in·crim·i·na·tion** /-ˌkriməˈnāsʜən/ **n.**

in·cu·bate /ˈinkyəˌbāt, ˈɪɴɢ-/ ▶ **v.** (**incubates, incubating, incubated**) **1** (of a bird) sit on eggs to keep them warm so that they hatch. **2** keep bacteria and cells at a suitable temperature so that they develop. **3** (of an infectious disease) develop slowly without obvious signs. ■ **in·cu·ba·tion** /ˌinkyəˈbāsʜən, ˌɪɴɢ-/ **n.** **in·cu·ba·tor n.**

in·cu·bus /ˈɪɴɢkyəbəs, ˈin-/ ▶ **n.** (plural **incubi** /-ˌbī/) a male demon believed to have sexual intercourse with sleeping women.

in·cul·cate /inˈkəlˌkāt, ˈinkəl-/ ▶ **v.** (**inculcates, inculcating, inculcated**) fix ideas in someone's mind by repeating them. ■ **in·cul·ca·tion** /ˌinkəlˈkāsʜən/ **n.**

in·cum·ben·cy /inˈkəmbənsē/ ▶ **n.** (plural **incumbencies**) the period during which an official position is held.

in·cum·bent /inˈkəmbənt/ ▶ **adj. 1** (**incumbent on**) necessary for someone as a duty. **2** currently holding an official position: *the incumbent president.* ▶ **n.** the holder of an official position.

in·cur /inˈkər, ɪɴɢ-/ ▶ **v.** (**incurs, incurring, incurred**) make something unwelcome happen.

> SYNONYMS **bring on yourself**, expose yourself to, lay yourself open to, run up, earn, sustain, experience.

in·cur·a·ble /ˌinˈkyo͝orəbəl/ ▶ **adj.** not able to be cured.

> SYNONYMS **1 untreatable**, inoperable, irremediable; terminal, fatal; chronic. **2** *an incurable romantic* **inveterate**, dyed-in-the-wool, confirmed, established, absolute, complete, utter, thoroughgoing, out-and-out; incorrigible, hopeless, hard-core.

■ **in·cur·a·bly adv.**

in·cu·ri·ous /inˈkyo͝orēəs/ ▶ **adj.** not curious.

in·cur·sion /inˈkərzʜən/ ▶ **n.** a sudden invasion or attack.

in·debt·ed /inˈdetid/ ▶ **adj. 1** feeling grateful to someone. **2** owing money.

in·de·cent /inˈdēsənt/ ▶ **adj. 1** immodest or offending against accepted morals. **2** not appropriate: *they leaped on the suggestion with indecent haste.*

> SYNONYMS **1 obscene**, dirty, filthy, rude, naughty, vulgar, smutty, pornographic; informal blue; euphemistic adult. **2 unseemly**, improper, unbecoming, inappropriate.

□ **indecent exposure** the crime of deliberately showing your genitals in public. ■ **in·de·cen·cy n.** **in·de·cent·ly adv.**

in·de·ci·pher·a·ble /ˌindiˈsīfərəbəl/ ▶ **adj.** not able to be read or understood.

in·de·ci·sive /ˌindiˈsīsiv/ ▶ **adj. 1** not able to make decisions quickly. **2** not settling an issue: *an indecisive battle.*

> SYNONYMS **1** *an indecisive result* **inconclusive**, proving nothing, open, indeterminate, unclear, ambiguous. **2** *an indecisive leader* **irresolute**, hesitant, tentative, weak; vacillating, dithering, wavering; blowing hot and cold, unsure, uncertain; undecided.

■ **in·de·ci·sion n.** **in·de·ci·sive·ly adv.** **in·de·ci·sive·ness n.**

in·deed /inˈdēd/ ▶ **adv. 1** used to emphasize a statement: *this is praise indeed.* **2** used to introduce a further and stronger point.

in·de·fat·i·ga·ble /ˌindəˈfatigəbəl/ ▶ **adj.** never tiring.

in·de·fen·si·ble /ˌindəˈfensəbəl/ ▶ **adj.** not able to be justified or defended: *apartheid was morally indefensible.*

in·de·fin·a·ble /ˌindəˈfīnəbəl/ ▶ **adj.** not able to be defined or described exactly.

in·def·i·nite /inˈdefənit/ ▶ **adj. 1** not clearly stated, seen, or heard; vague. **2** lasting for an unknown length of time. □ **indefinite article** Grammar the word *a* or *an*. ■ **in·def·i·nite·ly adv.**

in·del·i·ble /inˈdeləbəl/ ▶ **adj. 1** (of ink or a mark) unable to be removed. **2** unable to be forgotten. ■ **in·del·i·bly adv.**

in·del·i·cate /inˈdelikit/ ▶ **adj.** likely to be thought indecent or embarrassing.

in·dem·ni·fy /inˈdemnəˌfī/ ▶ **v.** (**indemnifies, indemnifying, indemnified**) **1** pay money to someone to compensate for harm or loss. **2** insure someone against legal responsibility for their actions.

in·dem·ni·ty /inˈdemnitē/ ▶ **n.** (plural **indemnities**) **1** insurance against legal responsibility for your actions. **2** a sum of money paid to compensate for damage or loss.

in·dent ▶ **v.** /inˈdent/ **1** form hollows or notches in. **2** begin a line of writing further from the margin than the other lines. ▶ **n.** /inˈdent, ˈinˌdent/ a hollow or notch.

in·den·ta·tion /ˌindenˈtāsʜən/ ▶ **n. 1** a deep recess or notch on an edge or surface. **2** the action of indenting something, especially a line of writing.

in·den·ture /inˈdencʜər/ ▶ **n.** a formal agreement or contract.

in·de·pend·ence /ˌindəˈpendəns/ ▶ **n.** the fact or state of being independent.

> SYNONYMS **1 self-government**, self-rule, home rule, self-determination, sovereignty, autonomy. **2 impartiality**, neutrality, disinterestedness, detachment, objectivity.

□ **Independence Day** a national holiday on July 4 celebrating the adoption of the Declaration of Independence in 1776.

in·de·pend·ent /ˌindəˈpendənt/ ▶ **adj. 1** free from the control or influence of others: *you should take independent advice.* **2** (of a country) self-governing. **3** having or earning enough money to support yourself. **4** not connected with another; separate. ▶ **n.** an independent person or body.

> SYNONYMS ▶ **adj. 1 self-governing**, self-ruling, self-determining, sovereign, autonomous, nonaligned, free. **2 separate**, different, unconnected, unrelated, discrete. **3 private**, private-sector, fee-paying, privatized, deregulated, denationalized. **4 impartial**, unbiased, unprejudiced, neutral, disinterested, uninvolved, detached, dispassionate, objective, nonpartisan. ANTONYMS related, biased.

> **SPELLING**
> Write **-ent**, not **-ant**: independ**ent**.

in·de·pend·ent·ly /ˌindəˈpendəntlē/ ▶ **adv.** on your own: *I prefer to work independently.*

SYNONYMS **alone**, on your own, separately, individually, unaccompanied, solo, unaided, unassisted, without help, by your own efforts, under your own steam, single-handedly.

in·de·scrib·a·ble /ˌindiˈskrībəbəl/ ▶ **adj.** too extreme or unusual to be described. ■ **in·de·scrib·a·bly adv.**

in·de·struct·i·ble /ˌindiˈstrəktəbəl/ ▶ **adj.** not able to be destroyed.

SYNONYMS **unbreakable**, shatterproof, vandal-proof, durable; lasting, enduring, everlasting, undying, immortal, imperishable; literary adamantine. ANTONYMS fragile.

in·de·ter·mi·nate /ˌindiˈtərmənit/ ▶ **adj.** not certain; vague: *a woman of indeterminate age.*

in·dex /ˈinˌdeks/ ▶ **n.** (plural **indexes** or **indices** /ˈindiˌsēz/) **1** a list of names or subjects referred to in a book, arranged in alphabetical order. **2** an alphabetical list or catalog of books or documents. **3** a sign or measure of something: *test results serve as an index of the teacher's effectiveness.* **4** Math an exponent. ▶ **v. 1** record in or provide with an index. **2** link the value of prices, wages, etc. automatically to the value of a price index.

SYNONYMS ▶ **n. list**, listing, inventory, catalog, register, directory, database.

□ **index finger** the forefinger.

In·di·an /ˈindēən/ ▶ **n. 1** a person from India. **2** an American Indian. ▶ **adj. 1** relating to India. **2** relating to American Indians. □ **Indian summer** a period of dry, warm weather in late autumn.

in·di·cate /ˈindiˌkāt/ ▶ **v.** (**indicates, indicating, indicated**) **1** point something out. **2** be a sign of. **3** mention briefly. **4** (**be indicated**) formal be necessary or recommended: *in certain cases, surgery may be indicated.*

SYNONYMS **1 point to**, be a sign of, be evidence of, demonstrate, show, testify to, be symptomatic of, denote, mark, signal, reflect, signify, suggest, imply. **2 state**, declare, make known, communicate, announce, put on record. **3 specify**, designate, stipulate, show.

in·di·ca·tion /ˌindiˈkāsHən/ ▶ **n. 1** a sign or piece of information that indicates something: *early indications of success.* **2** a reading given by a gauge or meter. **3** a symptom that suggests certain medical treatment is necessary: *stomach pain is a common indication for gallbladder removal.*

SYNONYMS **sign**, signal, indicator, symptom, mark, demonstration, pointer, guide, hint, clue, omen, warning.

in·dic·a·tive /inˈdikətiv/ ▶ **adj. 1** acting as a sign. **2** Grammar (of a verb) expressing a simple statement of fact (e.g., *she left*).

in·di·ca·tor /ˈindiˌkātər/ ▶ **n. 1** a thing that shows the state or level of something. **2** a chemical compound that changes color at a specific pH value or in the presence of a particular substance. **3** a light on a vehicle that flashes to show that it is about to turn left or right; a blinker.

SYNONYMS **measure**, gauge, meter, barometer, guide, index, mark, sign, signal.

in·di·ces /ˈindiˌsēz/ plural of **INDEX**.

in·dict /inˈdīt/ ▶ **v.** formally accuse someone of a serious crime. ■ **in·dict·a·ble** /inˈdītəbəl/ **adj.**

in·dict·ment /inˈdītmənt/ ▶ **n. 1** a formal accusation that someone has committed a serious crime. **2** an indication that something is bad and deserves to be condemned: *rising crime is an indictment of our society.*

SYNONYMS **charge**, accusation, impeachment, arraignment, prosecution, citation, summons.

in·dif·fer·ence /inˈdif(ə)rəns/ ▶ **n.** lack of interest, concern, or sympathy: *his apparent indifference infuriated her.*

SYNONYMS **detachment**, lack of concern, disinterest, lack of interest, nonchalance, boredom, unresponsiveness, impassivity, coolness. ANTONYMS concern.

in·dif·fer·ent /inˈdif(ə)rənt/ ▶ **adj. 1** not interested in or caring about something. **2** not very good; mediocre.

SYNONYMS **1 detached**, unconcerned, uninterested, uncaring, casual, nonchalant, offhand, unenthusiastic, unimpressed, unmoved, impassive, cool. **2 mediocre**, ordinary, average, middle-of-the-road, uninspired, undistinguished, unexceptional, pedestrian, forgettable, amateurish; informal no great shakes, nothing to write home about. ANTONYMS enthusiastic, brilliant.

■ **in·dif·fer·ent·ly adv.**

in·dig·e·nous /inˈdijənəs/ ▶ **adj.** belonging to a place; native.

in·di·gent /ˈindijənt/ ▶ **adj.** poor; needy.

in·di·gest·i·ble /ˌindiˈjestəbəl/ ▶ **adj.** difficult or impossible to digest.

in·di·ges·tion /ˌindiˈjescHən, -dī-/ ▶ **n.** pain or discomfort caused by difficulty in digesting food.

in·dig·nant /inˈdignənt/ ▶ **adj.** feeling or showing indignation.

SYNONYMS **aggrieved**, affronted, displeased, resentful, angry, annoyed, offended, exasperated; informal peeved, irked, sore, put out.

■ **in·dig·nant·ly adv.**

in·dig·na·tion /ˌindigˈnāsHən/ ▶ **n.** anger caused by something that you consider to be unfair.

in·dig·ni·ty /inˈdignitē/ ▶ **n.** (plural **indignities**) a thing that causes you to feel ashamed or embarrassed.

in·di·go /ˈindiˌgō/ ▶ **n.** a dark blue color or dye.

in·di·rect /ˌindəˈrekt/ ▶ **adj. 1** not going in a straight line. **2** not saying something in a straightforward way. **3** happening as a secondary effect or consequence.

SYNONYMS **1 roundabout**, circuitous, meandering, winding, tortuous. **2 oblique**, implicit, implied. **3 incidental**, secondary, subordinate, ancillary, collateral, concomitant, contingent.

□ **indirect object** Grammar a person or thing that is affected by the action of a verb but is not the main object (e.g., *him* in *give him the book*). **indirect question** a question in reported speech (e.g., *they asked who I was*). **indirect speech** reported speech. ■ **in·di·rect·ly adv.**

in·dis·ci·pline /inˈdisəplin/ ▶ **n.** lack of discipline.

in·dis·creet /ˌindiˈskrēt/ ▶ **adj.** too ready to reveal things that should remain secret or private.

SYNONYMS **imprudent**, unwise, impolitic, injudicious, incautious, irresponsible, ill-judged, careless, rash; undiplomatic, indelicate, tactless.

■ **in·dis·creet·ly** adv.

in·dis·cre·tion /ˌindiˈskresʜən/ ▶ n. **1** indiscreet behavior. **2** an indiscreet act or remark.

in·dis·crim·i·nate /ˌindiˈskrimənit/ ▶ adj. done or acting without careful judgment. ■ **in·dis·crim·i·nate·ly** adv.

in·dis·pen·sa·ble /ˌindiˈspensəbəl/ ▶ adj. absolutely necessary.

SPELLING

Write -**able**, not -**ible**: indispens**able**.

in·dis·posed /ˌindiˈspōzd/ ▶ adj. **1** slightly unwell. **2** unwilling.

in·dis·po·si·tion /ˌindispəˈzisʜən/ ▶ n. **1** a slight illness. **2** unwillingness.

in·dis·put·a·ble /ˌindisˈpyo͞otəbəl/ ▶ adj. unable to be challenged or denied. ■ **in·dis·put·a·bly** adv.

in·dis·sol·u·ble /ˌindiˈsälyəbəl/ ▶ adj. unable to be destroyed; lasting.

in·dis·tinct /ˌindisˈtiɴɢkt/ ▶ adj. not clear or sharply defined. ■ **in·dis·tinct·ly** adv.

in·dis·tin·guish·a·ble /indisˈtiɴɢgwisʜəbəl/ ▶ adj. not able to be distinguished. ■ **in·dis·tin·guish·a·bly** adv.

in·di·um /ˈindēəm/ ▶ n. a soft, silvery-white metallic chemical element, used in some alloys and semiconductor devices.

in·di·vid·u·al /ˌindəˈvijəwəl/ ▶ adj. **1** considered separately; single. **2** having to do with one particular person: *the individual needs of the children*. **3** striking or unusual; original. ▶ n. **1** a single person or item as distinct from a group. **2** a distinctive or original person.

SYNONYMS ▶ adj. **1 single**, separate, discrete, independent, lone. **2 unique**, characteristic, distinctive, distinct, particular, idiosyncratic, peculiar, personal, special. **3 original**, exclusive, different, unusual, novel, unorthodox, out of the ordinary. ANTONYMS multiple, shared, ordinary. ▶ n. **person**, human being, soul, creature, character; informal type, sort, customer.

in·di·vid·u·al·ism /ˌindəˈvijo͞oəˌlizəm/ ▶ n. **1** the quality of doing things in your own way; independence. **2** the belief that individual people should have freedom of action. ■ **in·di·vid·u·al·ist** n. & adj. **in·di·vid·u·al·is·tic** /-ˌvijo͞oəˈlistik/ adj.

in·di·vid·u·al·i·ty /ˌindəˌvijəˈwalitē/ ▶ n. the quality or character of a person or thing that makes them different from other people or things.

in·di·vid·u·al·ize /ˌindəˈvijo͞oəˌlīz/ ▶ v. (**individualizes**, **individualizing**, **individualized**) give something an individual character.

in·di·vid·u·al·ly /ˌindəˈvijəwəlē/ ▶ adv. **1** one by one; singly; separately: *individually wrapped cheese slices*. **2** in a distinctive manner. **3** personally; in an individual capacity.

SYNONYMS **separately**, singly, one by one, one at a time, independently.

in·di·vis·i·ble /ˌindiˈvizəbəl/ ▶ adj. unable to be divided or separated.

in·doc·tri·nate /inˈdäktrəˌnāt/ ▶ v. (**indoctrinates**, **indoctrinating**, **indoctrinated**) force someone to accept a set of beliefs. ■ **in·doc·tri·na·tion** /-ˌdäktrəˈnāsʜən/ n.

In·do-Eu·ro·pe·an /ˌindō-/ ▶ n. the family of languages spoken over most of Europe and Asia as far as northern India. ▶ adj. relating to Indo-European.

in·do·lent /ˈindələnt/ ▶ adj. lazy. ■ **in·do·lence** n.

in·dom·i·ta·ble /inˈdämitəbəl/ ▶ adj. impossible to defeat or subdue.

In·do·ne·sian /ˌindəˈnēzʜən/ ▶ n. **1** a person from Indonesia. **2** the group of languages spoken in Indonesia. ▶ adj. relating to Indonesia.

in·door /ˈinˌdôr/ ▶ adj. situated, done, or used inside a building. ▶ adv. (**indoors**) into or inside a building.

in·du·bi·ta·ble /inˈd(y)o͞obitəbəl/ ▶ adj. impossible to doubt; certain. ■ **in·du·bi·ta·bly** adv.

in·duce /inˈd(y)o͞os/ ▶ v. (**induces**, **inducing**, **induced**) **1** persuade or influence someone to do something. **2** bring about or cause: *herbs to induce sleep*. **3** make a woman begin to give birth to her baby by means of special drugs.

SYNONYMS **1 persuade**, convince, prevail on, get, make, prompt, encourage, cajole into, talk into. **2 bring about**, cause, produce, create, give rise to, generate, engender. ANTONYMS dissuade.

in·duce·ment /inˈd(y)o͞osmənt/ ▶ n. a thing that persuades someone to do something.

in·duct /inˈdəkt/ ▶ v. formally admit someone to an organization or establish them in a position of authority.

in·duc·tance /inˈdəktəns/ ▶ n. a process by which a change in the current of an electric circuit produces an electromotive force.

in·duc·tion /inˈdəksʜən/ ▶ n. **1** introduction to a post or organization. **2** the action of inducing. **3** a method of reasoning in which a general rule or conclusion is drawn from particular facts or examples. **4** the passing of electricity or magnetism from one object to another without their touching. **5** the drawing of the fuel mixture into the cylinders of an internal combustion engine. ■ **in·duc·tive** adj.

in·dulge /inˈdəlj/ ▶ v. (**indulges**, **indulging**, **indulged**) **1** (**indulge in**) allow yourself to do something that you enjoy. **2** satisfy a desire or interest. **3** allow someone to do or have whatever they wish.

SYNONYMS **1 satisfy**, gratify, fulfill, feed, yield to, give in to, go along with. **2 pamper**, spoil, overindulge, coddle, mollycoddle, cosset, pander to, wait on hand and foot.

in·dul·gence /inˈdəljəns/ ▶ n. **1** the action of indulging in something. **2** a thing that is indulged in; a luxury. **3** willingness to tolerate someone's faults. **4** chiefly historical (in the Roman Catholic Church) the pope's setting aside of the punishment still due for sins after formal forgiveness.

SYNONYMS **1 satisfaction**, gratification, fulfilment. **2 self-gratification**, self-indulgence, overindulgence, intemperance, excess, extravagance, hedonism. **3 extravagance**, luxury, treat, nonessential, extra, frill. **4 pampering**, coddling, mollycoddling, cosseting. **5 tolerance**, forbearance, understanding, compassion, sympathy, leniency. ANTONYMS asceticism, intolerance.

in·dul·gent /in'dəljənt/ ▶ **adj.** allowing someone to do or have whatever they want or overlooking their faults.

SYNONYMS **generous**, permissive, easygoing, liberal, tolerant, forgiving, forbearing, lenient, kind, kindly, softhearted. ANTONYMS strict.

■ **in·dul·gent·ly adv.**

in·dus·tri·al /in'dəstrēəl/ ▶ **adj.** having to do with industry. ■ **in·dus·tri·al·ly adv.**

in·dus·tri·al·ism /in'dəstrēə,lizəm/ ▶ **n.** a social system in which industry forms the basis of the economy.

in·dus·tri·al·ist /in'dəstrēəlist/ ▶ **n.** a person who owns or controls a large factory or manufacturing business.

SYNONYMS **manufacturer**, factory owner, captain of industry, magnate, tycoon.

in·dus·tri·al·ize /in'dəstrēə,līz/ ▶ **v.** (**industrializes, industrializing, industrialized**) develop industries in a country or region on a wide scale. ■ **in·dus·tri·al·i·za·tion** /in,dəstrēəli'zāsʜən/ **n.**

in·dus·tri·ous /in'dəstrēəs/ ▶ **adj.** hard-working.

SYNONYMS **hard-working**, diligent, assiduous, dedicated, conscientious, studious; busy, active, bustling, energetic, productive; with your shoulder to the wheel, with your nose to the grindstone. ANTONYMS indolent.

■ **in·dus·tri·ous·ly adv.**

in·dus·try /'indəstrē/ ▶ **n.** (plural **industries**) **1** the manufacture of goods in factories. **2** a branch of economic or commercial activity: *the tourist industry*. **3** hard work.

SYNONYMS **1 manufacturing**, production, construction, trade, commerce. **2 business**, trade, field, line of business, profession. **3 activity**, energy, effort, endeavor, hard work, industriousness, diligence, application.

in·e·bri·at·ed /i'nēbrē,ātid/ ▶ **adj.** drunk. ■ **in·e·bri·a·tion** /i,nēbrē'āsʜən/ **n.**

in·ed·i·ble /,in'edəbəl/ ▶ **adj.** not fit for eating.

in·ed·u·ca·ble /,in'ejə,kəbəl/ ▶ **adj.** considered incapable of being educated.

in·ef·fa·ble /in'efəbəl/ ▶ **adj.** too great or extreme to be expressed in words: *the ineffable beauty of the Everglades*.

in·ef·fec·tive /,ini'fektiv/ ▶ **adj.** not having any effect or achieving what you want.

SYNONYMS **1 unsuccessful**, unproductive, unprofitable, ineffectual, unavailing, to no avail, fruitless, futile. **2 ineffectual**, inefficient, inadequate, incompetent, incapable, unfit, inept; informal useless, hopeless. ANTONYMS effective.

■ **in·ef·fec·tive·ly adv.**

in·ef·fec·tu·al /,ini'fekcʜo͞oəl/ ▶ **adj. 1** ineffective. **2** not forceful enough to do something well. ■ **in·ef·fec·tu·al·ly adv.**

in·ef·fi·cient /,ini'fisʜənt/ ▶ **adj.** failing to make the best use of time or resources.

SYNONYMS **1 ineffective**, ineffectual, incompetent, inept, disorganized. **2 uneconomical**, wasteful, unproductive, unprofitable, slow, unsystematic.

■ **in·ef·fi·cien·cy n. in·ef·fi·cient·ly adv.**

in·el·e·gant /in'eligənt/ ▶ **adj.** not elegant or graceful.

in·el·i·gi·ble /,in'eləjəbəl/ ▶ **adj.** not qualified to have or do something.

in·e·luc·ta·ble /,ini'ləktəbəl/ ▶ **adj.** rare unable to be resisted or avoided.

in·ept /i'nept/ ▶ **adj.** lacking skill.

SYNONYMS **incompetent**, unskillful, unskilled, inexpert, amateurish; clumsy, awkward, maladroit, bungling, blundering. ANTONYMS competent.

■ **in·ept·i·tude** /-ti,t(y)o͞od/ **n. in·ept·ly adv.**

in·e·qual·i·ty /,ini'kwälitē/ ▶ **n.** (plural **inequalities**) lack of equality.

SYNONYMS **imbalance**, inequity, inconsistency, disparity, discrepancy, dissimilarity, difference, bias, prejudice, discrimination, unfairness.

in·eq·ui·ta·ble /in'ekwitəbəl/ ▶ **adj.** unfair; unjust.

in·eq·ui·ty /in'ekwitē/ ▶ **n.** (plural **inequities**) lack of fairness or justice.

in·e·rad·i·ca·ble /,inə'radikəbəl/ ▶ **adj.** unable to be rooted out or destroyed.

in·ert /i'nərt/ ▶ **adj. 1** lacking the ability or strength to move or act. **2** without active chemical properties: *an inert gas*.

in·er·tia /i'nərsʜə/ ▶ **n. 1** a tendency to do nothing or to remain unchanged. **2** Physics a property by which matter remains still or continues moving unless acted on by an external force.

in·es·cap·a·ble /,ini'skāpəbəl/ ▶ **adj.** unable to be avoided or denied.

in·es·sen·tial /,ini'sencʜəl/ ▶ **adj.** not absolutely necessary.

in·es·ti·ma·ble /in'estəməbəl/ ▶ **adj.** too great to be measured.

in·ev·i·ta·ble /in'evitəbəl/ ▶ **adj.** certain to happen; unavoidable.

SYNONYMS **unavoidable**, inescapable, inexorable, assured, certain, sure. ANTONYMS avoidable.

■ **in·ev·i·ta·bil·i·ty** /-,evitə'bilitē/ **n.**

in·ev·i·ta·bly /in'evitəblē/ ▶ **adv.** unavoidably.

SYNONYMS **unavoidably**, necessarily, automatically, naturally, as a matter of course, of necessity, inescapably, certainly, surely; informal like it or not.

in·ex·act /,inig'zakt/ ▶ **adj.** not quite accurate.

in·ex·cus·a·ble /,inik'skyo͞ozəbəl/ ▶ **adj.** too bad to be justified or tolerated.

in·ex·haust·i·ble /,inig'zôstəbəl/ ▶ **adj.** (of a supply) never ending because available in unlimited quantities.

in·ex·o·ra·ble /in'eksərəbəl/ ▶ **adj. 1** impossible to stop or prevent. **2** unable to be persuaded. ■ **in·ex·o·ra·bly adv.**

in·ex·pen·sive /,inik'spensiv/ ▶ **adj.** not costing a lot of money.

SYNONYMS **cheap**, affordable, low-cost, economical, competitive, reasonable, budget, economy, bargain, cut-rate, reduced.

in·ex·pe·ri·ence /,inik'spi(ə)rēəns/ ▶ **n.** lack of experience.

in·ex·pe·ri·enced /,inik'spi(ə)rēənst/ ▶ **adj.** lacking experience: *she's inexperienced, but we expect her to become an excellent teacher*.

SYNONYMS **inexpert**, untrained, unqualified, unskilled, unseasoned, naive, new, callow, immature; informal wet behind the ears, wide-eyed.

in·ex·pert /in'ekspərt/ ▶ **adj.** lacking skill or knowledge in a particular field.

in·ex·pli·ca·ble /ˌinek'splikəbəl, in'eksplikəbəl/ ▶ **adj.** unable to be explained. ■ **in·ex·pli·ca·bly adv.**

in·ex·pres·sive /ˌinik'spresiv/ ▶ **adj.** showing no feelings.

in ex·tre·mis /ˌin ek'strāmēs, ik'strēmis/ ▶ **adv.** **1** in a very difficult situation. **2** at the point of death.

in·ex·tri·ca·ble /ˌinik'strikəbəl, in'ekstri-/ ▶ **adj.** impossible to untangle or separate: *the past and the present are inextricable.* ■ **in·ex·tri·ca·bly adv.**

in·fal·li·ble /in'faləbəl/ ▶ **adj.** incapable of making mistakes or being wrong. ■ **in·fal·li·bil·i·ty** /inˌfalə'bilitē/ **n.** **in·fal·li·bly adv.**

in·fa·mous /'infəməs/ ▶ **adj.** **1** well-known for some bad quality or act. **2** morally bad.

SYNONYMS **notorious**, disreputable, scandalous. ANTONYMS reputable.

■ **in·fa·mous·ly adv.**

in·fa·my /'infəmē/ ▶ **n.** (plural **infamies**) **1** the state of being known for something bad. **2** a wicked act.

in·fan·cy /'infənsē/ ▶ **n.** **1** the state or period of early childhood or babyhood. **2** an early stage of development.

SYNONYMS **beginnings**, early days, early stages, emergence, dawn, outset, birth, inception. ANTONYMS end.

in·fant /'infənt/ ▶ **n.** a very young child or baby.

SYNONYMS **baby**, newborn, young child, tiny tot, little one; Medicine neonate.

in·fan·ta /in'fantə/ ▶ **n.** historical a daughter of the king or queen of Spain or Portugal.

in·fan·ti·cide /in'fantiˌsīd/ ▶ **n.** the killing of a child.

in·fan·tile /'infənˌtīl, 'infənt-il/ ▶ **adj.** **1** relating to infants. **2** disapproving childish.

in·fan·try /'infəntrē/ ▶ **n.** soldiers who fight on foot.

in·farc·tion /in'färksʜən/ ▶ **n.** formation of dead tissue because of failure of the blood supply.

in·fat·u·ate /in'facʜo͞oˌāt/ ▶ **v.** (**be infatuated with**) have a strong but short-lived feeling of love for. ■ **in·fat·u·a·tion** /-ˌfacʜo͞o'āsʜən/ **n.**

in·fect /in'fekt/ ▶ **v.** **1** pass a germ that causes disease to a person, animal, or plant. **2** contaminate with something harmful. **3** make someone share a particular feeling.

SYNONYMS **contaminate**, pollute, taint, foul, poison, blight.

in·fec·tion /in'feksʜən/ ▶ **n.** **1** the process of infecting. **2** an infectious disease.

SYNONYMS **1 disease**, virus, illness, ailment, disorder, sickness; informal bug. **2 contamination**, poison, bacteria, germs; Medicine sepsis.

in·fec·tious /in'feksʜəs/ ▶ **adj.** **1** (of a disease or germ) able to be passed on through the environment. **2** liable to spread infection. **3** likely to spread to or influence other people.

SYNONYMS **communicable**, contagious, transmittable, transmissible, transferable; informal catching.

■ **in·fec·tious·ly adv.**

in·fer /in'fər/ ▶ **v.** (**infers**, **inferring**, **inferred**) work something out from the information you have available.

SYNONYMS **deduce**, conclude, surmise, reason; gather, understand, presume, assume, figure, take it, read between the lines.

USAGE

On the difference between the words **infer** and **imply**, see the note at **IMPLY**.

in·fer·ence /'inf(ə)rəns/ ▶ **n.** **1** a conclusion drawn from the information available to you. **2** the process of inferring.

in·fe·ri·or /in'fi(ə)rēər/ ▶ **adj.** lower in quality or status. ▶ **n.** a person who is lower in status or less good at doing something.

SYNONYMS ▶ **adj. 1 second-class**, lower-ranking, subordinate, junior, minor, lowly, humble, menial, beneath someone. **2 second-rate**, mediocre, substandard, low-grade, unsatisfactory, shoddy, poor; informal crummy, lousy. ANTONYMS superior. ▶ **n. subordinate**, junior, underling, minion.

■ **in·fe·ri·or·i·ty** /inˌfi(ə)rē'ôritē, -'äritē/ **n.**

in·fer·nal /in'fərnl/ ▶ **adj.** **1** having to do with hell or the underworld. **2** informal very annoying: *an infernal nuisance.*

in·fer·no /in'fərnō/ ▶ **n.** (plural **infernos**) a large uncontrollable fire.

in·fer·tile /in'fərtl/ ▶ **adj.** **1** unable to have babies or other young. **2** (of land) unable to produce crops or plants.

SYNONYMS **1 sterile**, barren, childless. **2 barren**, unfruitful, unproductive, sterile, arid, impoverished.

■ **in·fer·til·i·ty** /ˌinfər'tilitē/ **n.**

in·fest /in'fest/ ▶ **v.** (especially of insects or rats) be present in large numbers so as to cause damage or disease.

SYNONYMS (**infested**) **overrun**, swarming, teeming, crawling, alive, plagued.

■ **in·fes·ta·tion** /ˌinfe'stāsʜən/ **n.**

in·fi·del /'infədl, -ˌdel/ ▶ **n.** old use a person who has no religion or whose religion is not that of the majority.

in·fi·del·i·ty /ˌinfi'delitē/ ▶ **n.** (plural **infidelities**) the action or state of not being faithful to your romantic partner.

in·field /'inˌfēld/ ▶ **n.** Baseball the area within and near the four bases. ▶ **adv.** into or toward the infield. ■ **in·field·er n.**

in·fight·ing /'inˌfītiɴɢ/ ▶ **n.** conflict within a group or organization.

in·fil·trate /'infilˌtrāt, in'fil-/ ▶ **v.** enter or gain access to an organization or place secretly and gradually.

SYNONYMS **penetrate**, insinuate yourself into, worm your way into, sneak into, slip into, creep into, invade.

■ **in·fil·tra·tion** /ˌinfil'trāsʜən/ **n.**

in·fil·tra·tor /'infilˌtrātər, in'fil-/ ▶ **n.** a person who infiltrates.

SYNONYMS **spy**, secret agent, plant, intruder, interloper, subversive, informer, mole, fifth columnist.

in·fi·nite /'infənit/ ▶ **adj.** **1** having no limits and impossible to measure. **2** very great in amount or degree: *with infinite care.*

SYNONYMS **boundless**, unbounded, unlimited, limitless, never-ending, incalculable, untold, countless, uncountable, innumerable, numberless, immeasurable. ANTONYMS limited.

■ **in·fi·nite·ly** **adv.**

in·fin·i·tes·i·mal /ˌinfini'tes(ə)məl/ ▶ **adj.** very small. ■ **in·fin·i·tes·i·mal·ly** **adv.**

in·fin·i·tive /in'finitiv/ ▶ **n.** the basic form of a verb, normally occurring in English with the word *to* (as in *to see, to ask*).

in·fin·i·ty /in'finitē/ ▶ **n.** (plural **infinities**) **1** the state or quality of being infinite. **2** a very great number or amount. **3** Math a number greater than any quantity or countable number (symbol ∞).

in·firm /in'fərm/ ▶ **adj.** physically weak.

in·fir·ma·ry /in'fərm(ə)rē/ ▶ **n.** (plural **infirmaries**) a place where sick people are cared for.

in·fir·mi·ty /in'fərmitē/ ▶ **n.** (plural **infirmities**) physical or mental weakness.

in fla·gran·te de·lic·to /ˌin flə'gräntā də'liktō, flə'grantē/ ▶ **adv.** in the very act of wrongdoing.

in·flame /in'flām/ ▶ **v.** (**inflames**, **inflaming**, **inflamed**) **1** make someone feel something passionately. **2** make a difficult situation worse. **3** (**inflamed**) (of a part of the body) red, swollen, and hot as a result of infection or injury.

SYNONYMS **1 enrage**, incense, anger, madden, infuriate, exasperate, provoke, antagonize; informal make someone see red. **2 aggravate**, exacerbate, intensify, worsen, compound. **3** (**inflamed**) **swollen**, red, hot, burning, itchy, sore, painful, tender, infected. ANTONYMS placate.

in·flam·ma·ble /in'flaməbəl/ ▶ **adj.** easily set on fire.

USAGE

inflammable and **flammable** both mean 'easily set on fire.' It's safer to use **flammable**, however, because **inflammable** is sometimes thought to mean 'non-flammable.'

in·flam·ma·tion /ˌinflə'māsʜən/ ▶ **n.** a condition in which an area of the skin is red, swollen, and hot.

in·flam·ma·to·ry /in'flaməˌtôrē/ ▶ **adj.** **1** making people feel angry. **2** relating to or causing inflammation.

in·flat·a·ble /in'flātəbəl/ ▶ **adj.** capable of being inflated. ▶ **n.** **1** an inflatable plastic or rubber boat. **2** an object that is inflated so that it will float.

in·flate /in'flāt/ ▶ **v.** (**inflates**, **inflating**, **inflated**) **1** expand something by filling it with air or gas. **2** increase the cost or price of something by a large amount. **3** (**inflated**) exaggerated: *you have a very inflated opinion of your worth.* **4** bring about inflation of a currency.

SYNONYMS **1 blow up**, pump up, fill, puff up/out, dilate, distend, swell, bloat. **2 increase**, raise, boost, escalate, put up; informal hike up, jack up. **3** (**inflated**) **high**, sky-high, excessive, unreasonable, outrageous, exorbitant, extortionate; informal steep. **4** (**inflated**) **exaggerated**, immoderate, overblown, overstated. ANTONYMS deflate, lower.

in·fla·tion /in'flāsʜən/ ▶ **n.** **1** the action of inflating. **2** a general increase in prices and fall in the value of money. ■ **in·fla·tion·ar·y** **adj.**

in·flect /in'flekt/ ▶ **v.** **1** Grammar (of a word) be changed by inflection. **2** vary the tone or pitch of your voice.

in·flec·tion /in'fleksʜən/ ▶ **n.** **1** Grammar a change in the form of a word to show its grammatical function, number, or gender. **2** a variation in the tone or pitch of a voice. **3** chiefly Math a change of curvature from convex to concave.

in·flex·i·ble /in'fleksəbəl/ ▶ **adj.** **1** not able to be altered or adapted. **2** unwilling to change or compromise. **3** not able to be bent. ■ **in·flex·i·bil·i·ty** /-ˌfleksə'bilitē/ **n.**

in·flict /in'flikt/ ▶ **v.** (**inflict something on**) make someone experience something unpleasant or painful.

SYNONYMS **1 give**, administer, deal out, mete out, exact, wreak. **2 impose**, force, thrust, foist.

■ **in·flic·tion** **n.**

in·flo·res·cence /ˌinflô'resəns, -flə-/ ▶ **n.** Botany **1** the complete flowerhead of a plant. **2** the process of flowering.

in·flu·ence /'inflo͞oəns/ ▶ **n.** **1** the power or ability to affect someone's beliefs or actions. **2** a person or thing with such ability or power. **3** the power arising out of status, contacts, or wealth. ▶ **v.** (**influences**, **influencing**, **influenced**) have an influence on.

SYNONYMS ▶ **n.** **1 effect**, impact, control, spell, hold. **2** *a good* ***influence on*** *on her* **example to**, role model for, inspiration to. **3 power**, authority, sway, leverage, weight, pull; informal clout. ▶ **v.** **1 affect**, have an impact on, determine, guide, control, shape, govern, decide, change, alter. **2 sway**, bias, prejudice, manipulate, persuade, induce.

in·flu·en·tial /ˌinflo͞o'encʜəl/ ▶ **adj.** having great influence.

SYNONYMS **powerful**, controlling, important, authoritative, leading, significant, instrumental, guiding.

in·flu·en·za /ˌinflo͞o'enzə/ ▶ **n.** a disease spread by a virus and causing fever, aching, and mucus buildup.

in·flux /'inˌfləks/ ▶ **n.** the arrival or entry of large numbers of people or things.

in·form /in'fôrm/ ▶ **v.** **1** give facts or information to. **2** (**inform on**) give information about someone's involvement in a crime to the police.

SYNONYMS **1 tell**, notify, apprise, advise, impart to, communicate to, let someone know, brief, enlighten, send word to. **2** *he* ***informed on*** *two colleagues* **betray**, give away, denounce, incriminate, report on; informal rat on/out, squeal on, snitch on, tell on, blow the whistle on, finger.

in·for·mal /in'fôrməl/ ▶ **adj.** **1** relaxed and friendly, and not following strict rules of behavior. **2** (of clothes) suitable for wearing when relaxing. **3** (of language) used in everyday speech and writing, rather than official contexts.

SYNONYMS **1 unofficial**, casual, relaxed, easygoing, low-key. **2 casual**, relaxed, comfortable, everyday; informal comfy. **3 colloquial**, vernacular, idiomatic, popular, familiar, everyday; informal slangy, chatty. ANTONYMS formal.

■ **in·for·mal·i·ty** /ˌinfôrˈmalitē/ n. **in·for·mal·ly** adv.

in·form·ant /inˈfôrmənt/ ▶ n. a person who gives information to another.

in·for·ma·tion /ˌinfərˈmāsʜən/ ▶ n. facts or details supplied to or learned by someone.

SYNONYMS **facts**, particulars, details, figures, statistics, data, knowledge, intelligence; informal info, the 411.

□ **information superhighway** an extensive electronic network such as the Internet, used for the rapid transfer of information in digital form. **information technology** the use of computers and telecommunications for storing, retrieving, and sending information.

in·for·ma·tive /inˈfôrmətiv/ ▶ adj. providing useful information.

SYNONYMS **instructive**, illuminating, enlightening, revealing, explanatory, factual, educational, edifying.

in·formed /inˈfôrmd/ ▶ adj. **1** having or showing knowledge. **2** (of a judgment) based on a sound understanding of the facts.

SYNONYMS **knowledgeable**, enlightened, educated, briefed, up to date, up to speed, in the picture, in the know, au fait; informal clued in. ANTONYMS ignorant.

in·form·er /inˈfôrmər/ ▶ n. a person who informs on another person to the police.

SYNONYMS **informant**, betrayer, traitor, Judas, collaborator, stool pigeon, fifth columnist, spy, Benedict Arnold, double agent, infiltrator, plant, tattletale; informal rat, squealer, whistle-blower, snitch, fink, stoolie.

in·frac·tion /inˈfraksʜən/ ▶ n. a breaking of a law, rule, or agreement.

in·fra dig /ˌinfrə ˈdig/ ▶ adj. informal beneath your dignity.

in·fra·red /ˌinfrəˈred/ ▶ adj. (of electromagnetic radiation) having a wavelength just greater than that of red light.

in·fra·struc·ture /ˈinfrəˌstrəkcʜər/ ▶ n. the basic things (e.g., buildings, roads, power supplies) needed for the operation of a society or enterprise.

in·fre·quent /inˈfrēkwənt/ ▶ adj. not happening often. ■ **in·fre·quen·cy** n. **in·fre·quent·ly** adv.

in·fringe /inˈfrinj/ ▶ v. **1** break a law, rule, or agreement. **2** restrict a right or privilege. ■ **in·fringe·ment** n.

in·fu·ri·ate /inˈfyo͝orēˌāt/ ▶ v. (**infuriates**, **infuriating**, **infuriated**) make someone angry.

SYNONYMS **enrage**, incense, provoke, anger, madden, exasperate; informal make someone see red. ANTONYMS please.

■ **in·fu·ri·at·ing** adj.

in·fuse /inˈfyo͞oz/ ▶ v. (**infuses**, **infusing**, **infused**) **1** spread throughout something. **2** soak tea or herbs to extract the flavor or healing properties.

in·fu·sion /inˈfyo͞ozʜən/ ▶ n. **1** a drink prepared by soaking tea or herbs. **2** the action of infusing.

in·gen·ious /inˈjēnyəs/ ▶ adj. clever, original, and inventive.

SYNONYMS **inventive**, creative, imaginative, original, innovative, pioneering, resourceful, enterprising, inspired, clever. ANTONYMS unimaginative.

■ **in·gen·ious·ly** adv.

in·gé·nue /ˈanjəˌno͞o, ˈänzʜ-/ ▶ n. **1** a naive young woman. **2** a part for a naive young woman in a play or movie. **3** an actress who plays such a part.

in·ge·nu·i·ty /ˌinjəˈn(y)o͞oitē/ ▶ n. the quality of being clever, original, or inventive.

in·gen·u·ous /inˈjenyo͞oəs/ ▶ adj. innocent and unsuspecting.

SYNONYMS **naive**, innocent, simple, childlike, trusting, trustful, wide-eyed, inexperienced, artless, guileless. ANTONYMS artful.

in·gest /inˈjest/ ▶ v. take food or drink into the body by swallowing it. ■ **in·ges·tion** n.

in·glo·ri·ous /inˈglôrēəs/ ▶ adj. not making you feel proud; rather shameful.

in·go·ing /ˈinˌgōiɴɢ/ ▶ adj. going toward or into.

in·got /ˈiɴɢgət/ ▶ n. a rectangular block of steel, gold, or other metal.

in·grain /inˈgrān/ (or **engrain** /enˈgrān/) ▶ v. firmly fix or establish a habit or belief in someone.

in·grained /inˈgrānd/ (or **engrained** /enˈgrānd/) ▶ adj. **1** (of a habit or belief) firmly established. **2** (of dirt) deeply embedded.

in·grate /ˈinˌgrāt/ ▶ n. formal or literary an ungrateful person.

in·gra·ti·ate /inˈgrāsʜēˌāt/ ▶ v. (**ingratiates**, **ingratiating**, **ingratiated**) (**ingratiate yourself**) do things in order to make someone like you.

in·grat·i·tude /inˈgratiˌt(y)o͞od/ ▶ n. a lack of appropriate gratitude.

in·gre·di·ent /inˈgrēdēənt, iɴɢ-/ ▶ n. **1** any of the substances that are combined to make a particular dish. **2** a component part or element.

SYNONYMS **constituent**, component, element, item, part, strand, unit, feature, aspect, attribute.

in·gress /ˈinˌgres/ ▶ n. **1** the action of entering or coming in. **2** a place or means of access.

in·grown /ˈinˌgrōn/ (or **ingrowing** /ˈinˌgrōiɴɢ/) ▶ adj. (of a toenail) having grown into the flesh.

in·hab·it /inˈhabit/ ▶ v. (**inhabits**, **inhabiting**, **inhabited**) live in or occupy.

SYNONYMS **live in**, occupy, settle, people, populate, colonize.

■ **in·hab·it·a·ble** adj.

in·hab·it·ant /inˈhabitnt/ ▶ n. a person or animal that lives in or occupies a place.

SYNONYMS **resident**, occupant, occupier, settler, local, native; (**inhabitants**) population, populace, people, public, community, citizenry, townsfolk, townspeople.

in·hal·ant /inˈhālənt/ ▶ n. a medical preparation for inhaling.

in·hale /inˈhāl/ ▶ v. (**inhales**, **inhaling**, **inhaled**) breathe in air, smoke, etc.

SYNONYMS **breathe in**, draw in, suck in, sniff (in), drink in, gasp. ANTONYMS exhale.

■ **in·ha·la·tion** /ˌinhəˈlāsʜən/ n.

in·hal·er /inˈhālər/ ▶ n. a portable device used for inhaling a drug.

in·her·ent /inˈhi(ə)rənt, -ˈher-/ ▶ adj. existing in something as a permanent or essential quality. ■ **in·her·ent·ly** adv.

in·her·it /in'herit/ ▶ v. (**inherits**, **inheriting**, **inherited**) **1** receive money or property from someone when they die. **2** have a quality or characteristic passed on to you from your parents or ancestors. **3** be left with something previously belonging to someone else: *commitments inherited from previous administrations.*

SYNONYMS **be bequeathed**, be left, be willed, come into, succeed to, assume, take over.

in·her·it·ance /in'heritəns/ ▶ n. **1** a thing that is inherited. **2** the action of inheriting.

SYNONYMS **legacy**, bequest, endowment, birthright, heritage, patrimony.

□ **inheritance** (or **death**) **tax** tax on property or money that you have inherited.

in·hib·it /in'hibit/ ▶ v. (**inhibits**, **inhibiting**, **inhibited**) **1** prevent or slow down a process. **2** make someone unable to act in a relaxed and natural way.

SYNONYMS **1 impede**, hinder, hamper, hold back, discourage, interfere with, obstruct, slow down, retard. **2** (**inhibited**) **reserved**, reticent, guarded, self-conscious, insecure, withdrawn, repressed, undemonstrative, shy, diffident, bashful; informal uptight. ANTONYMS assist, allow.

in·hi·bi·tion /ˌin(h)i'bisʜən/ ▶ n. a feeling that makes you unable to act in a relaxed and natural way.

in·hos·pi·ta·ble /ˌinhä'spitəbəl, in'häs-/ ▶ adj. **1** (of an environment) harsh and difficult to live in. **2** unwelcoming.

in·hu·man /in'(h)yo͞omən/ ▶ adj. **1** lacking positive human qualities; cruel and barbaric. **2** not human in nature or character.

SYNONYMS **1** *inhuman treatment* **cruel**, harsh, inhumane, brutal, callous, sadistic, savage, vicious, barbaric. **2** *inhuman shapes* **monstrous**, devilish, ghostly, demonic, animal, bestial; unearthly. ANTONYMS humane.

in·hu·mane /ˌin(h)yo͞o'mān/ ▶ adj. without pity; cruel.

in·hu·man·i·ty /ˌin(h)yo͞o'manitē/ ▶ n. (plural **inhumanities**) cruel and brutal behavior.

in·im·i·cal /i'nimikəl/ ▶ adj. having a harmful effect on something; not helpful.

in·im·i·ta·ble /i'nimitəbəl/ ▶ adj. impossible to imitate; unique. ■ **in·im·i·ta·bly** adv.

in·iq·ui·ty /i'nikwitē/ ▶ n. (plural **iniquities**) great injustice or immorality. ■ **in·iq·ui·tous** adj.

in·i·tial /i'nisʜəl/ ▶ adj. existing or occurring at the beginning. ▶ n. the first letter of a name or word. ▶ v. (**initials**, **initialing**, **initialed**) mark something with your initials as a sign of approval or agreement.

SYNONYMS ▶ adj. **beginning**, opening, commencing, starting, first, earliest, primary, preliminary, preparatory, introductory, inaugural. ANTONYMS final.

in·i·tial·ly /i'nisʜəlē/ ▶ adv. at first: *initially, we thought it might be pilot error.*

SYNONYMS **at first**, at the start, at the outset, in/at the beginning, to begin with, to start with, originally.

in·i·ti·ate ▶ v. /i'nisʜēˌāt/ (**initiates**, **initiating**, **initiated**) **1** make a process or action start. **2** admit someone into a society or group with a formal ceremony. **3** introduce someone to a new activity.

SYNONYMS **1 begin**, start (off), commence, institute, inaugurate, launch, instigate, establish, set up. **2** *initiated into the club* **introduce**, admit, induct, install, swear in, ordain, invest. ANTONYMS end, expel.

■ **in·i·ti·a·tion** /iˌnisʜē'āsʜən/ n.

in·i·ti·a·tive /i'nisʜ(ē)ətiv/ ▶ n. **1** the ability to act independently and with a fresh approach. **2** the power or opportunity to act before other people do: *we have lost the initiative.* **3** a new development or approach to a problem.

SYNONYMS **1 enterprise**, resourcefulness, inventiveness, imagination, ingenuity, originality, creativity. **2 advantage**, upper hand, edge, lead, start. **3 scheme**, plan, strategy, measure, proposal, step, action.

in·ject /in'jekt/ ▶ v. **1** put a drug or other substance into the body with a syringe. **2** add a new or different quality: *she tried to inject scorn into her tone.*

SYNONYMS **1 administer**, take; informal shoot (up), mainline, fix. **2 inoculate**, vaccinate. **3 insert**, introduce, feed, push, force, shoot. **4 introduce**, instill, infuse, imbue, breathe.

in·jec·tion /in'jeksʜən/ ▶ n. **1** an act of giving a person or animal a drug using a syringe. **2** a substance that is injected. **3** a large sum of additional money used to help a situation, business, etc.

SYNONYMS **1 inoculation**, vaccination, immunization, booster; informal jab, shot. **2 addition**, introduction, investment, dose, infusion, insertion.

in·ju·di·cious /ˌinjo͞o'disʜəs/ ▶ adj. unwise.

in·junc·tion /in'jənɢ(k)sʜən/ ▶ n. **1** Law an order saying that someone must or must not carry out a certain action. **2** a strong warning.

SYNONYMS **order**, ruling, direction, directive, command, instruction, mandate.

in·jure /'injər/ ▶ v. (**injures**, **injuring**, **injured**) **1** do physical harm to; wound. **2** have a bad effect on; damage.

SYNONYMS **1 hurt**, wound, damage, harm, disable, break; Medicine traumatize. **2 damage**, mar, spoil, weaken, ruin, blight, blemish, tarnish, blacken.

in·jured /'injərd/ ▶ adj. **1** harmed or wounded. **2** offended. **3** having had an offense committed against you.

SYNONYMS **1 hurt**, wounded, damaged, sore, bruised, broken, fractured; Medicine traumatized. **2 upset**, hurt, wounded, offended, reproachful, pained, aggrieved. ANTONYMS healthy.

in·ju·ri·ous /in'jo͝orēəs/ ▶ adj. causing or likely to cause injury.

in·ju·ry /'injərē/ ▶ n. (plural **injuries**) **1** harm done to the body. **2** hurt feelings.

SYNONYMS **1 wound**, bruise, cut, gash, scratch, graze; Medicine trauma, lesion. **2 harm**, hurt, damage, pain, suffering. **3 offense**, abuse, injustice, disservice, affront, insult.

in·jus·tice /in'jəstis/ ▶ n. **1** lack of justice. **2** an unjust act.

SYNONYMS **1 unfairness**, one-sidedness, inequity, bias, prejudice, discrimination, intolerance, exploitation, corruption. **2 wrong**, offense, crime, sin, outrage, scandal, disgrace, affront.

ink /iNGk/ ▶ **n. 1** a colored fluid used for writing, drawing, or printing. **2** a black liquid produced by a cuttlefish, octopus, or squid. ▶ **v.** cover with ink before printing.

ink·jet print·er /ˈiNGkˌjet/ ▶ **n.** a printer in which the characters are formed by tiny jets of ink.

ink·ling /ˈiNGkliNG/ ▶ **n.** a slight suspicion; a hint.

ink·stand /ˈiNGkˌstand/ ▶ **n.** a stand for ink bottles, pens, and other stationery items.

ink·well /ˈiNGkˌwel/ ▶ **n.** a container for ink, normally housed in a hole in a desk.

ink·y /ˈiNGkē/ ▶ **adj.** (**inkier**, **inkiest**) **1** as dark as ink. **2** stained with ink.

in·laid /ˈinˌlād/ past and past participle of **INLAY**.

in·land /ˈinˌland, -lənd/ ▶ **adj. & adv.** in or into the interior of a country. ▶ **n.** the interior of a country or region.

SYNONYMS ▶ **adj. & adv. interior**, inshore, internal, upcountry. ANTONYMS coastal.

in·lay ▶ **v.** (**inlays**, **inlaying**, **inlaid**) /ˌinˈlā/ fix pieces of a different material into a surface as a form of decoration: *mahogany paneling inlaid with rosewood.* ▶ **n.** /ˈinˌlā/ decoration of this type.

in·let /ˈinˌlet, -lit/ ▶ **n. 1** a small arm of the sea, a lake, or a river. **2** a place or means of entry.

SYNONYMS **1 cove**, bay, bight, creek, estuary, fjord, sound. **2 vent**, flue, shaft, duct, channel, pipe.

in·line skate /ˈinlīn/ ▶ **n.** a type of roller skate in which the wheels are fixed in a single line along the sole.

in lo·co pa·ren·tis /in ˌlōkō pəˈrentis/ ▶ **adv.** having the same responsibility for a child or young person as a parent has.

in·ly·ing /ˈinˌlīiNG/ ▶ **adj.** within or near a center.

in·mate /ˈinˌmāt/ ▶ **n.** a person living in an institution such as a prison or hospital.

SYNONYMS **1 prisoner**, convict, captive, detainee, internee. **2 patient**, mental patient, resident.

in me·di·as res /in ˈmēdēəs ˈres, ˈmādēˌäs/ ▶ **adv.** into the middle of things.

in me·mo·ri·am /ˌin məˈmôrēəm/ ▶ **prep.** in memory of someone who has died.

inn /in/ ▶ **n. 1** an establishment providing accommodations, food, and drink, especially for travelers. **2** a restaurant or bar, especially in the country.

in·nards /ˈinərdz/ ▶ **pl.n.** informal **1** internal organs. **2** the internal workings of a machine.

in·nate /iˈnāt/ ▶ **adj.** natural or inborn. ■ **in·nate·ly adv.**

in·ner /ˈinər/ ▶ **adj. 1** situated inside or close to the center. **2** private; not expressed. **3** mental or spiritual: *inner strength.*

SYNONYMS **1 central**, innermost. **2 internal**, interior, inside, innermost. **3 hidden**, secret, deep, underlying, veiled. ANTONYMS outer.

□ **inner city** an area in or near the center of a large city. **inner tube** a separate inflatable tube inside a tire.

in·ner·most /ˈinərˌmōst/ ▶ **adj. 1** furthest in; closest to the center. **2** (of thoughts) most private.

in·ning /ˈiniNG/ ▶ **n.** Baseball each division of a game during which both sides have a turn at batting.

in·nings /ˈiniNGz/ ▶ **n.** (plural **innings**) Cricket each of the divisions of a game during which one side has a turn at batting.

inn·keep·er /ˈinˌkēpər/ ▶ **n.** chiefly old use a person who runs an inn.

in·no·cence /ˈinəsəns/ ▶ **n.** the state, quality, or fact of being innocent.

SYNONYMS **1 guiltlessness**, blamelessness. **2 naivety**, credulity, inexperience, gullibility, ingenuousness.

in·no·cent /ˈinəsənt/ ▶ **adj. 1** not guilty of a crime or offense. **2** having little experience of life. **3** not intended to cause offense: *an innocent mistake.* ▶ **n.** an innocent person.

SYNONYMS ▶ **adj. 1 guiltless**, blameless, clean, irreproachable, above reproach, honest, upright, law-abiding. **2 naive**, ingenuous, trusting, credulous, impressionable, easily led, inexperienced, unsophisticated, artless. **3 harmless**, innocuous, safe, inoffensive, unobjectionable. ANTONYMS guilty.

■ **in·no·cent·ly adv.**

in·noc·u·ous /iˈnäkyo͞oəs/ ▶ **adj.** not harmful or offensive.

SYNONYMS **1 harmless**, safe, nontoxic, edible. **2** *an innocuous comment* **inoffensive**, unobjectionable, unexceptionable, harmless, anodyne. ANTONYMS harmful, offensive.

in·no·vate /ˈinəˌvāt/ ▶ **v.** (**innovates**, **innovating**, **innovated**) introduce new ideas or products. ■ **in·no·va·tor n.**

in·no·va·tion /ˌinəˈvāsHən/ ▶ **n. 1** the introduction of new ideas or products. **2** a new idea or product.

SYNONYMS **change**, alteration, upheaval, reorganization, restructuring, novelty, departure.

in·no·va·tive /ˈinəˌvātiv/ ▶ **adj. 1** featuring new ideas or methods; advanced and original: *innovative designs.* **2** (of a person) original and creative in their thinking.

SYNONYMS **original**, new, novel, fresh, unusual, experimental, inventive, ingenious, pioneering, groundbreaking, revolutionary, radical.

in·nu·en·do /ˌinyo͞oˈendō/ ▶ **n.** (plural **innuendoes** or **innuendos**) a remark that makes a vague and indirect reference to something.

SYNONYMS **insinuation**, suggestion, intimation, implication; aspersion, slur.

in·nu·mer·a·ble /iˈn(y)o͞omərəbəl/ ▶ **adj.** too many to be counted.

in·nu·mer·ate /iˈn(y)o͞omərit/ ▶ **adj.** without a basic knowledge of mathematics and arithmetic.

in·oc·u·late /iˈnäkyəˌlāt/ ▶ **v.** treat someone with a vaccine to stop them getting a disease. ■ **in·oc·u·la·tion** /iˌnäkyəˈlāsHən/ **n.**

SPELLING

One **n**, one **c**: inoculate.

in·of·fen·sive /ˌinəˈfensiv/ ▶ **adj.** causing no offense or harm.

in·op·er·a·ble /in'äp(ə)rəbəl/ ▶ **adj.** **1** (of an illness) not able to be cured by an operation. **2** not able to be used or operated.

in·op·er·a·tive /in'äp(ə)rətiv/ ▶ **adj.** not working or taking effect.

in·op·por·tune /ˌinˌäpər't(y)o͞on/ ▶ **adj.** happening at an inconvenient time.

in·or·di·nate /i'nôrdn-it/ ▶ **adj.** much greater than is usual or expected; excessive. ■ **in·or·di·nate·ly adv.**

in·or·gan·ic /ˌinôr'ganik/ ▶ **adj.** **1** not consisting of or coming from living matter. **2** (of a chemical compound) not containing carbon.

in·pa·tient /'inˌpāsHənt/ ▶ **n.** a patient who is staying day and night in a hospital.

in·put /'inˌpo͝ot/ ▶ **n.** **1** what is put or taken into a system or process. **2** the putting or feeding in of something. **3** a person's contribution: *he likes her input on issues.* ▶ **v.** (**inputs**, **inputting**, **input** or **inputted**) put data into a computer.

in·quest /'inˌkwest, 'iNG-/ ▶ **n.** a legal inquiry to gather the facts relating to an incident, such as a death.

SYNONYMS **inquiry**, investigation, probe, examination, review, hearing.

in·quire /in'kwīr/ (or **enquire** /en'kwīr/) ▶ **v.** (**inquires, inquiring, inquired**) **1** ask for information. **2** (**inquire after**) ask how someone is. **3** (**inquire into**) investigate.

SYNONYMS **1 ask**, query, question. **2** *we are inquiring into the incident* **investigate**, probe, look into, make inquiries of/about, research, examine, explore, delve into; informal check out.

in·quir·y /in'kwī(ə)rē, 'inˌkwī(ə)rē, 'inkwərē/ (or **enquiry** /en'kwī(ə)rē, 'enkwərē/) ▶ **n.** (plural **inquiries**) **1** an act of asking for information. **2** an official investigation.

SYNONYMS **1 question**, query. **2 investigation**, probe, examination, exploration, inquest, hearing.

in·qui·si·tion /ˌinkwi'zisHən, ˌiNG-/ ▶ **n.** **1** a long period of questioning or investigation. **2** (**the Inquisition**) an ecclesiastical tribunal established by the Catholic church for the suppression of heresy and to combat Protestantism, chiefly in France, Italy, and Spain, notorious for its use of torture.

in·quis·i·tive /in'kwizitiv, iNG-/ ▶ **adj.** **1** eager to find things out. **2** prying. ■ **in·quis·i·tive·ly adv.**

in·quis·i·tor /in'kwizitər/ ▶ **n.** a person conducting an inquisition.

in·road /'inˌrōd/ ▶ **n.** a gradual entry into or effect on a place or situation: *the company is beginning to make inroads into the US market.*

in·rush /'inˌrəsH/ ▶ **n.** a sudden inward rush or flow.

in·sa·lu·bri·ous /ˌinsə'lo͞obrēəs/ ▶ **adj.** (especially of a climate or locality) unhealthy; unpleasant because not clean or well-kept.

in·sane /in'sān/ ▶ **adj.** **1** seriously mentally ill. **2** very foolish.

SYNONYMS **1 mad**, of unsound mind, certifiable, psychotic, schizophrenic, unhinged; informal crazy, nuts, raving mad, bonkers, loony. **2 stupid**, idiotic, nonsensical, absurd, ridiculous, ludicrous, preposterous; informal crazy, mad, daft. ANTONYMS sane.

■ **in·sane·ly adv. in·san·i·ty n.**

in·sa·tia·ble /in'sāsHəbəl/ ▶ **adj.** always wanting more and not able to be satisfied. ■ **in·sa·tia·bly adv.**

in·scribe /in'skrīb/ ▶ **v.** (**inscribes**, **inscribing**, **inscribed**) **1** write or carve something on a surface. **2** write a dedication to someone in a book.

in·scrip·tion /in'skripsHən/ ▶ **n.** words or symbols written or carved on a surface or in a book.

in·scru·ta·ble /in'skro͞otəbəl/ ▶ **adj.** impossible to understand or interpret. ■ **in·scru·ta·bly adv.**

in·sect /'inˌsekt/ ▶ **n.** a small arthropod animal with six legs and no backbone.

SYNONYMS **bug**; informal creepy-crawly.

in·sec·ti·cide /in'sektiˌsīd/ ▶ **n.** a substance used for killing insects.

in·sec·ti·vore /in'sektəˌvôr/ ▶ **n.** an animal that eats insects. ■ **in·sec·tiv·o·rous** /ˌinˌsek'tivərəs/ **adj.**

in·se·cure /ˌinsi'kyo͝or/ ▶ **adj.** **1** not confident or assured. **2** not firm or firmly fixed.

SYNONYMS **1 unconfident**, uncertain, unsure, doubtful, diffident, hesitant, self-conscious, anxious, fearful. **2 unprotected**, unguarded, vulnerable, unsecured. **3 unstable**, rickety, wobbly, shaky, unsteady, precarious. ANTONYMS confident, stable.

in·se·cu·ri·ty /ˌinsi'kyo͝orətē/ ▶ **n.** the state of feeling insecure.

SYNONYMS **lack of confidence**, uncertainty, self-doubt, diffidence, hesitancy, nervousness, self-consciousness, anxiety, worry, unease.

in·sem·i·nate /in'seməˌnāt/ ▶ **v.** (**inseminates**, **inseminating**, **inseminated**) introduce semen into a woman or a female animal. ■ **in·sem·i·na·tion** /-ˌsemə'nāsHən/ **n.**

in·sen·sate /in'senˌsāt, -sit/ ▶ **adj.** **1** lacking physical sensation. **2** lacking sympathy for other people. **3** lacking good sense.

in·sen·si·ble /in'sensəbəl/ ▶ **adj.** **1** unconscious. **2** numb; without feeling.

in·sen·si·tive /in'sensitiv/ ▶ **adj.** **1** showing or feeling no concern for the feelings of other people. **2** not sensitive to physical sensation. **3** not aware of or able to respond to something.

SYNONYMS **1 heartless**, unfeeling, inconsiderate, thoughtless, thick-skinned; hard-hearted, uncaring, unsympathetic, unkind. **2** *he was insensitive to her feelings* **impervious to**, oblivious to, unaware of, unresponsive to, indifferent to. ANTONYMS compassionate.

■ **in·sen·si·tive·ly adv. in·sen·si·tiv·i·ty** /-ˌsensi'tivitē/ **n.**

in·sep·a·ra·ble /in'sep(ə)rəbəl/ ▶ **adj.** unable to be separated or treated separately. ■ **in·sep·a·ra·bly adv.**

in·sert ▶ **v.** /in'sərt/ place, fit, or incorporate something into something else. ▶ **n.** /'inˌsərt/ a loose page or section in a magazine.

SYNONYMS ▶ **v. put**, place, push, thrust, slide, slip, load, fit, slot, install; informal pop, stick. ANTONYMS extract, remove.

■ **in·ser·tion n.**

in·set ▶ **n.** /'inˌset/ **1** a thing inserted. **2** a small picture or map inserted within the border of a larger one. ▶ **v.** /in'set/ (**insets**, **insetting**, **inset** or **insetted**) insert.

in·shore /'in'sHôr/ ▶ **adj. & adv.** **1** at sea but close to the shore. **2** toward the shore.

in·side ▶ n. /ˈinˈsīd/ **1** the inner side or surface of a thing. **2** the inner part; the interior. **3** (**insides**) informal a person's stomach and bowels. ▶ adj. /ˌinˈsīd, ˈinˌsīd/ **1** situated on or in the inside. **2** (of information) only available to people in an organization. ▶ prep. & adv. /ˌinˈsīd/ **1** situated or moving within. **2** informal in prison. **3** within a particular time.

SYNONYMS ▶ n. **1 interior**, center, core, middle, heart. **2** (**insides**) **stomach**, gut, bowels, intestines; informal tummy, belly, guts. ▶ adj. **1 inner**, interior, internal, innermost. **2 confidential**, classified, restricted, privileged, private, secret, exclusive; informal hush-hush. ANTONYMS outside.

□ **inside job** informal a crime committed by or with the assistance of a person associated with the place where it occurred. **inside out** with the inner surface turned outward.

in·sid·er /inˈsīdər/ ▶ n. a person working within an organization. □ **insider trading** (or **dealing**) the illegal practice of trading on the stock exchange to your own advantage through having access to confidential information.

in·sid·i·ous /inˈsidēəs/ ▶ adj. proceeding in a gradual, subtle way, but with harmful effects. ■ **in·sid·i·ous·ly** adv.

in·sight /ˈinˌsīt/ ▶ n. **1** the ability to understand the truth about people and situations. **2** understanding of this kind.

SYNONYMS **intuition**, perception, vision, understanding, comprehension, appreciation, judgment, discernment, imagination, wisdom.

■ **in·sight·ful** /inˈsītfəl/ adj.

in·sig·ni·a /inˈsignēə/ ▶ n. (plural **insignia**) a badge or symbol showing someone's rank, position, or membership of an organization.

in·sig·nif·i·cant /ˌinsigˈnifikənt/ ▶ adj. having very little importance or value.

SYNONYMS **unimportant**, trivial, trifling, negligible, inconsequential, of no account, paltry, petty, insubstantial; informal piddling.

■ **in·sig·nif·i·cance** n. **in·sig·nif·i·cant·ly** adv.

in·sin·cere /ˌinsinˈsi(ə)r/ ▶ adj. saying or doing things that you do not mean.

SYNONYMS **false**, fake, hollow, artificial, feigned, pretended, put-on, disingenuous, hypocritical, cynical; informal phony, pretend.

■ **in·sin·cere·ly** adv. **in·sin·cer·i·ty** /-ˈseritē/ n.

in·sin·u·ate /inˈsinyəˌwāt/ ▶ v. (**insinuates**, **insinuating**, **insinuated**) **1** suggest or hint at something bad in an indirect way. **2** (**insinuate yourself into**) move yourself gradually into a favorable position.

in·sin·u·a·tion /inˌsinyo͞oˈāsʜən/ ▶ n. an unpleasant hint or suggestion.

in·sip·id /inˈsipid/ ▶ adj. **1** having almost no flavor. **2** not interesting or lively.

in·sist /inˈsist/ ▶ v. **1** demand forcefully that something is done. **2** firmly state that something is the case, without letting anyone disagree. **3** (**insist on**) persist in doing something.

SYNONYMS **1 demand**, command, order, require. **2 maintain**, assert, protest, swear, declare, repeat. **3 stand firm**, stand your ground, be resolute, be determined, hold out, persist, be emphatic, lay down the law, not take no for an answer; informal stick to your guns, put your foot down.

in·sist·ent /inˈsistənt/ ▶ adj. **1** insisting that someone does something or that something is the case. **2** continuing for a long time and demanding attention.

SYNONYMS **persistent**, determined, tenacious, unyielding, dogged, unrelenting, importunate, relentless, inexorable.

■ **in·sist·ence** n. **in·sis·tent·ly** adv.

SPELLING

Write **-ent**, not **-ant**: insis**tent**.

in si·tu /ˌin ˈsīto͞o, ˈsē-/ ▶ adv. & adj. in the natural or original place.

in·sole /ˈinˌsōl/ ▶ n. the inner sole of a boot or shoe.

in·so·lent /ˈinsələnt/ ▶ adj. rude and disrespectful.

SYNONYMS **impertinent**, impudent, cheeky, ill-mannered, bad mannered, rude, impolite, discourteous, disrespectful, insubordinate; cocky; informal fresh, lippy, sassy, saucy. ANTONYMS polite.

■ **in·so·lence** n. **in·so·lent·ly** adv.

in·sol·u·ble /inˈsälyəbəl/ ▶ adj. **1** impossible to solve. **2** (of a substance) incapable of being dissolved.

in·sol·vent /inˈsälvənt/ ▶ adj. not having enough money to pay your debts. ■ **in·sol·ven·cy** n.

in·som·ni·a /inˈsämnēə/ ▶ n. inability to sleep. ■ **in·som·ni·ac** /-nēˌak/ n. & adj.

in·so·much /ˌinsōˈməcʜ/ ▶ adv. (**insomuch that** or **as**) to the extent that.

in·sou·ci·ant /inˈso͞osēənt, ˌaɴso͞oˈsyäɴ/ ▶ adj. carefree and unconcerned. ■ **in·sou·ci·ance** n.

in·spect /inˈspekt/ ▶ v. **1** look at something closely. **2** make an official visit to a school, factory, etc., to check on standards.

SYNONYMS **examine**, check, scrutinize, investigate, vet, test, monitor, survey, study, look over; informal check out, give something a/the once-over.

in·spec·tion /inˈspeksʜən/ ▶ n. an examination or investigation: *on further inspection, we detected a slight crack in the pipe.*

SYNONYMS **examination**, checkup, survey, scrutiny, exploration, investigation; informal once-over, going-over.

in·spec·tor /inˈspektər/ ▶ n. **1** an official who makes sure that regulations are obeyed. **2** a police officer ranking below a superintendent or police chief.

SYNONYMS **examiner**, scrutineer, investigator, surveyor, assessor, supervisor, monitor, watchdog, ombudsman, auditor.

in·spi·ra·tion /ˌinspəˈrāsʜən/ ▶ n. **1** the process of being inspired. **2** a person or thing that inspires. **3** a sudden clever idea.

SYNONYMS **1 creativity**, invention, innovation, ingenuity, imagination, originality, insight, vision. **2 stimulus**, motivation, encouragement, influence, spur, fillip; informal shot in the arm. **3 bright idea**, revelation; informal brainstorm, brainwave.

■ **in·spi·ra·tion·al** adj.

in·spire /inˈspīr/ ▶ v. (**inspires**, **inspiring**, **inspired**) **1** fill someone with the urge or ability to do something. **2** create a feeling in a person. **3** give rise to: *the movie was successful enough to inspire a sequel.*

SYNONYMS **1 stimulate**, motivate, encourage, influence, move, spur, energize, galvanize. **2** (**inspiring**) **inspirational**, encouraging, heartening, uplifting, stirring, rousing, electrifying, moving. **3 give rise to**, lead to, bring about, prompt, spawn, engender. **4 arouse**, awaken, prompt, induce, ignite, trigger, kindle, produce, bring out.

in·spired /in'spīrd/ ▶ **adj.** showing great creativity or imagination.

SYNONYMS **outstanding**, wonderful, marvelous, excellent, magnificent, exceptional, first-class, virtuoso, superlative; informal tremendous, superb, awesome, out of this world.

in·sta·bil·i·ty /ˌinstə'bilitē/ ▶ **n.** (plural **instabilities**) lack of stability.

SYNONYMS **unreliability**, uncertainty, unpredictability, insecurity, volatility, capriciousness, changeability, variability, inconsistency, mutability. ANTONYMS stability.

in·stall /in'stôl/ ▶ **v.** (**installs**, **installing**, **installed**) **1** place or fix equipment in position ready for use. **2** establish someone in a new place or role.

SYNONYMS **1 put**, place, station, site, insert. **2 swear in**, induct, inaugurate, invest, appoint, ordain, consecrate, anoint, enthrone, crown. **3 ensconce**, position, settle, seat, plant, sit (down); informal plonk, park. ANTONYMS remove.

in·stal·la·tion /ˌinstə'lāsʜən/ ▶ **n. 1** the installing of something. **2** a large piece of equipment installed for use. **3** a military or industrial establishment. **4** a large piece of art constructed within a gallery.

in·stall·ment /in'stôlmənt/ ▶ **n. 1** each of several payments made over a period of time. **2** each of several parts of something published or broadcast at intervals.

SYNONYMS **1 payment**, repayment, tranche, portion. **2 part**, episode, chapter, issue, program, section, segment, volume.

in·stance /'instəns/ ▶ **n.** a particular example or occurrence of something. ▶ **v.** (**instances**, **instancing**, **instanced**) mention something as an example.

SYNONYMS ▶ **n. example**, occasion, occurrence, case, illustration, sample.

□ **for instance** as an example.

in·stant /'instənt/ ▶ **adj. 1** happening immediately. **2** (of food) processed so that it can be prepared very quickly. ▶ **n. 1** a precise moment of time. **2** a very short time.

SYNONYMS ▶ **adj. 1 immediate**, instantaneous, on-the-spot, prompt, swift, speedy, rapid, quick; informal snappy. **2 prepared**, precooked, microwaveable. ANTONYMS delayed. ▶ **n. moment**, minute, second, split second, trice, twinkling of an eye, flash; informal jiffy.

□ **instant messaging** the exchange of typed messages between computer users in real time via the Internet. **instant replay 1** a playback of part of a television broadcast, especially one in slow motion showing an action in a sports event. **2** the use of such a playback to uphold or overturn an official's call during a game such as football, tennis, etc.

in·stan·ta·ne·ous /ˌinstən'tānēəs/ ▶ **adj.** happening or done immediately or at the same time.
▪ **in·stan·ta·ne·ous·ly adv.**

in·stant·ly /'instəntlē/ ▶ **adv. 1** at once; immediately: *she fell asleep almost instantly.* **2** old use urgently or persistently.

SYNONYMS **immediately**, at once, straightaway, right away, instantaneously, forthwith, there and then, here and now, this/that minute, this/that second.

in·stead /in'sted/ ▶ **adv. 1** as an alternative. **2** (**instead of**) in place of.

SYNONYMS **as an alternative**, in lieu, alternatively, alternately, rather, on second thought.

in·step /'inˌstep/ ▶ **n.** the part of a person's foot between the ball and the ankle.

in·sti·gate /'instiˌgāt/ ▶ **v.** (**instigates**, **instigating**, **instigated**) make something happen or come about. ▪ **in·sti·ga·tion** /ˌinsti'gāsʜən/ **n.** **in·sti·ga·tor n.**

in·still /in'stil/ ▶ **v.** (**instills**, **instilling**, **instilled**) gradually but firmly establish an idea or attitude in someone's mind.

in·stinct /'inˌstiɴɢkt/ ▶ **n. 1** an inborn tendency to behave in a certain way. **2** a natural ability or skill.

SYNONYMS **1 inclination**, urge, drive, compulsion, intuition, feeling, sixth sense, nose. **2 talent**, gift, ability, aptitude, skill, flair, feel, knack.

▪ **in·stinc·tu·al** /ins'tiɴɢkcʜo͞oəl/ **adj.**

in·stinc·tive /in'stiɴɢ(k)tiv/ ▶ **adj.** based on instinct rather than thought or training.

SYNONYMS **intuitive**, natural, instinctual, innate, inborn, inherent, unconscious, subconscious, automatic, reflex, knee-jerk; informal gut.

▪ **in·stinc·tive·ly adv.**

in·sti·tute /'instiˌt(y)o͞ot/ ▶ **n.** an organization for the promotion of science, education, or a profession. ▶ **v.** (**institutes**, **instituting**, **instituted**) set up or establish.

SYNONYMS ▶ **n. organization**, establishment, institution, foundation, center, academy, school, college, university, society, association, federation, body. ▶ **v. set up**, inaugurate, found, establish, organize, initiate, set in motion, get under way, get off the ground, start, launch. ANTONYMS abolish, end.

in·sti·tu·tion /ˌinsti't(y)o͞osʜən/ ▶ **n. 1** an important organization or public body. **2** an organization providing residential care for people who have special needs. **3** an established law or custom.

SYNONYMS **1 establishment**, organization, institute, foundation, center, academy, school, college, university, society, association, body. **2** (**residential**) **home**, hospital, asylum, prison. **3** *the institution of marriage* **practice**, custom, convention, tradition.

in·sti·tu·tion·al /ˌinsti't(y)o͞osʜənl/ ▶ **adj. 1** relating to an institution. **2** typical of an institution, especially in being impersonal or unimaginative.

SYNONYMS **organized**, established, bureaucratic, conventional, procedural, formal, formalized, systematic, systematized, structured, regulated.

■ **in·sti·tu·tion·al·ism** n. **in·sti·tu·tion·al·ly** adv.

in·sti·tu·tion·al·ize /ˌinstiˈt(y)o͞osʜənlˌīz/ ▶ v. (**institutionalizes**, **institutionalizing**, **institutionalized**) **1** establish something as a feature of an organization or culture: *claims that discrimination is institutionalized in education.* **2** place someone in a residential institution. **3** (**become institutionalized**) lose your individuality as a result of staying for a long time in a residential institution.

in·struct /inˈstrəkt/ ▶ v. **1** tell or order someone to do something. **2** teach. **3** inform someone of a fact or situation.

SYNONYMS **1 order**, direct, command, tell, mandate; old use bid. **2 teach**, coach, train, educate, tutor, guide, school, show.

in·struc·tion /inˈstrəksʜən/ ▶ n. **1** an order. **2** a piece of information about how something should be done. **3** teaching or education.

SYNONYMS **1 order**, command, directive, direction, decree, injunction, mandate, commandment; old use bidding. **2** (**instructions**) **directions**, handbook, manual, guide, advice, guidance. **3 teaching**, coaching, schooling, lessons, classes, lectures, training, drill, guidance.

■ **in·struc·tion·al** adj.

in·struc·tive /inˈstrəktiv/ ▶ adj. useful and informative.

in·struc·tor /inˈstrəktər/ ▶ n. a teacher.

SYNONYMS **trainer**, coach, teacher, tutor, adviser, counselor, guide.

in·stru·ment /ˈinstrəmənt/ ▶ n. **1** a tool or piece of equipment used for delicate or scientific work. **2** a measuring device. **3** (also **musical instrument**) a device for producing musical sounds. **4** a means of achieving something.

SYNONYMS **1 implement**, tool, utensil, device, apparatus, gadget. **2 gauge**, meter, indicator, dial, display. **3 agent**, cause, agency, channel, medium, means, vehicle.

in·stru·men·tal /ˌinstrəˈmentl/ ▶ adj. **1** important in making something happen. **2** (of music) performed on instruments. ▶ n. a piece of music performed by instruments, with no vocals.

SYNONYMS ▶ adj. (**be instrumental in**) **play a part in**, contribute to, be a factor in, have a hand in, promote, advance, further.

in·stru·men·tal·ist /ˌinstrəˈmentl-ist/ ▶ n. a player of a musical instrument.

in·stru·men·ta·tion /ˌinstrəmənˈtāsʜən, -men-/ ▶ n. **1** the instruments used in a piece of music. **2** the arrangement of a piece of music for particular instruments.

in·sub·or·di·nate /ˌinsəˈbôrdn-it/ ▶ adj. disobedient. ■ **in·sub·or·di·na·tion** /-ˌbôrdnˈāsʜən/ n.

in·sub·stan·tial /ˌinsəbˈstancʜəl/ ▶ adj. not strong or solid.

in·suf·fer·a·ble /inˈsəf(ə)rəbəl/ ▶ adj. **1** unbearable. **2** unbearably arrogant or conceited. ■ **in·suf·fer·a·bly** adv.

in·suf·fi·cient /ˌinsəˈfisʜənt/ ▶ adj. not enough.

SYNONYMS **inadequate**, deficient, poor, scant, scanty, not enough, too little, too few.

■ **in·suf·fi·cien·cy** n. **in·suf·fi·cient·ly** adv.

in·su·lar /ˈins(y)ələr/ ▶ adj. **1** narrow-minded through being isolated from outside influences. **2** relating to an island. ■ **in·su·lar·i·ty** /ˌins(y)əˈlaritē/ n.

in·su·late /ˈins(y)əˌlāt/ ▶ v. (**insulates**, **insulating**, **insulated**) **1** place material between one thing and another to prevent loss of heat or intrusion of sound. **2** cover something with nonconducting material to prevent the passage of electricity. **3** protect from something unpleasant: *insulated from outside pressures.*

SYNONYMS **1 wrap**, sheathe, cover, encase, enclose, lag, soundproof. **2 protect**, save, shield, shelter, screen, cushion, cocoon.

■ **in·su·la·tor** n.

in·su·la·tion /ˌins(y)əˈlāsʜən/ ▶ n. **1** material used to insulate something. **2** the action of insulating or state of being insulated: *his comparative insulation from the world.*

in·su·lin /ˈinsələn/ ▶ n. a hormone that regulates glucose levels in the blood.

in·sult ▶ v. /inˈsəlt/ say or do hurtful or disrespectful things to someone. ▶ n. /ˈinˌsəlt/ an insulting remark or action.

SYNONYMS ▶ v. **1 abuse**, be rude to, call someone names, slight, disparage, discredit, malign, defame, denigrate, offend, hurt, humiliate; informal bad-mouth. **2** (**insulting**) **abusive**, rude, offensive, disparaging, belittling, derogatory, deprecating, disrespectful, uncomplimentary; informal bitchy, catty. ANTONYMS compliment. ▶ n. **jibe**, affront, slight, slur, barb, indignity, abuse, aspersions; informal dig, put-down.

in·su·per·a·ble /inˈso͞op(ə)rəbəl/ ▶ adj. impossible to overcome.

in·sup·port·a·ble /ˌinsəˈpôrtəbəl/ ▶ adj. **1** unable to be justified. **2** unbearable: *the heat was insupportable.*

in·sur·ance /inˈsʜo͝orəns/ ▶ n. **1** an arrangement by which you make regular payments to a company that will pay an agreed amount if something is lost or damaged or someone is hurt or killed. **2** money paid by or to an insurance company. **3** a thing that provides protection in case anything bad happens.

SYNONYMS **indemnity**, assurance, protection, security, cover, safeguard, warranty.

in·sure /inˈsʜo͝or/ ▶ v. (**insures**, **insuring**, **insured**) **1** pay money in order to receive financial compensation if something is lost or damaged or someone is hurt or killed. **2** (**insure against**) provide protection in case anything bad happens. **3** make certain that something will turn out a particular way.

SYNONYMS **provide insurance for**, indemnify, cover, assure, protect, underwrite, warrant.

in·sur·gent /inˈsərjənt/ ▶ n. a rebel or revolutionary. ▶ adj. fighting against a system or authority. ■ **in·sur·gen·cy** n.

in·sur·mount·a·ble /ˌinsərˈmountəbəl/ ▶ adj. too great to be overcome.

in·sur·rec·tion /ˌinsəˈreksʜən/ ▶ n. a violent uprising against authority.

in·tact /inˈtakt/ ▶ adj. not damaged.

SYNONYMS **whole**, entire, complete, unbroken, undamaged, unscathed, unblemished, unmarked, in one piece. ANTONYMS damaged.

in·ta·glio /in'talyō, -'täl-/ ▶ **n.** (plural **intaglios**) **1** an incised or engraved design. **2** a gem with an incised design.

in·take /'in,tāk/ ▶ **n. 1** an amount or quantity of something that is taken in. **2** an opening through which fluid or air is taken in. **3** an act of taking something in.

in·tan·gi·ble /in'tanjəbəl/ ▶ **adj. 1** not solid or real. **2** vague and abstract. ▶ **n.** an intangible thing. ■ **in·tan·gi·bly adv.**

in·te·ger /'intijər/ ▶ **n.** a whole number.

in·te·gral /'intigrəl, in'teg-/ ▶ **adj. 1** necessary to make a whole complete; fundamental. **2** included as part of a whole.

> SYNONYMS **1 essential**, fundamental, component, basic, intrinsic, inherent, vital, necessary. **2 built-in**, inbuilt, integrated, inboard, fitted. **3 unified**, integrated, comprehensive, holistic, all-embracing. ANTONYMS peripheral, supplementary.

□ **integral calculus** Math the part of calculus concerned with the integrals of functions.

in·te·grate /'inti,grāt/ ▶ **v.** (**integrates**, **integrating**, **integrated**) **1** combine with something to form a whole. **2** bring into equal participation in or membership of society or an institution or body.

> SYNONYMS **combine**, amalgamate, merge, unite, fuse, blend, consolidate, meld, mix, incorporate, assimilate, homogenize, desegregate. ANTONYMS separate.

□ **integrated circuit** an electronic circuit on a small piece of semiconducting material, performing the same function as a larger circuit of separate components. ■ **in·te·gra·tion** /,inti'grāsʜən/ **n.**

in·teg·ri·ty /in'tegritē/ ▶ **n. 1** the quality of being honest, fair, and good. **2** the state of being whole or unified. **3** soundness of construction.

> SYNONYMS **1 honesty**, probity, rectitude, uprightness, fairness, honor, sincerity, truthfulness, trustworthiness. **2 unity**, coherence, cohesion, solidity. **3 soundness**, strength, sturdiness, solidity, durability, stability, rigidity. ANTONYMS dishonesty.

in·teg·u·ment /in'tegyəmənt/ ▶ **n.** a tough outer protective layer, especially of an animal or plant.

in·tel·lect /'intl,ekt/ ▶ **n.** the power of using your mind to think logically and understand things.

> SYNONYMS **mind**, brain(s), intelligence, reason, judgment, gray matter, brain cells.

in·tel·lec·tu·al /,intl'ekcʜo͞oəl/ ▶ **adj. 1** relating or appealing to the intellect. **2** having a highly developed intellect. ▶ **n.** a person with a highly developed intellect.

> SYNONYMS ▶ **adj. 1 mental**, cerebral, rational, conceptual, theoretical, analytical, logical, cognitive. **2 learned**, academic, erudite, bookish, highbrow, scholarly, donnish.

■ **in·tel·lec·tu·al·ly adv.**

in·tel·lec·tu·al·ize /,intl'ekcʜo͞oə,līz/ ▶ **v.** (**intellectualizes**, **intellectualizing**, **intellectualized**) talk or write in an intellectual way.

in·tel·li·gence /in'telijəns/ ▶ **n. 1** the ability to gain and apply knowledge and skills. **2** the secret gathering of information about an enemy or opponent. **3** information of this sort.

> SYNONYMS **1 intellect**, cleverness, brainpower, judgment, reasoning, acumen, wit, insight, perception. **2 information**, facts, details, particulars, data, knowledge.

in·tel·li·gent /in'telijənt/ ▶ **adj.** good at learning, understanding, and thinking.

> SYNONYMS **clever**, bright, quick-witted, smart, astute, sharp, insightful, perceptive, penetrating, educated, knowledgeable, enlightened; informal brainy.

□ **intelligent design** a theory that the universe cannot have arisen by chance and was created by some intelligent entity. ■ **in·tel·li·gent·ly adv.**

in·tel·li·gent·si·a /in,teli'jentsēə/ ▶ **n.** intellectuals or highly educated people.

in·tel·li·gi·ble /in'telijəbəl/ ▶ **adj.** able to be understood.

> SYNONYMS **comprehensible**, understandable, accessible, digestible, user-friendly, clear, coherent, plain, unambiguous.

■ **in·tel·li·gi·bly adv.**

in·tem·per·ate /in'temp(ə)rit/ ▶ **adj.** lacking self-control. ■ **in·tem·per·ance n.**

in·tend /in'tend/ ▶ **v. 1** have something as your aim or plan. **2** plan that something should be, do, or mean something: *the book was intended as a satire.* **3** (**intend something for** or **to do**) design or plan something for a particular purpose.

> SYNONYMS **plan**, mean, have in mind, aim, propose, hope, expect, envisage.

in·tend·ed /in'tendid/ ▶ **adj.** planned or meant. ▶ **n.** informal the person you are engaged to be married to.

in·tense /in'tens/ ▶ **adj.** (**intenser**, **intensest**) **1** of great force or strength. **2** very earnest or serious.

> SYNONYMS **1 extreme**, great, acute, fierce, severe, high, exceptional, extraordinary, harsh, strong, powerful, violent; informal serious. **2 passionate**, impassioned, zealous, vehement, fervent, earnest, eager, committed. ANTONYMS mild, apathetic.

■ **in·tense·ly adv.**

in·ten·si·fy /in'tensə,fī/ ▶ **v.** (**intensifies**, **intensifying**, **intensified**) make or become more intense.

> SYNONYMS **escalate**, increase, step up, raise, strengthen, reinforce, pick up, build up, heighten, deepen, extend, expand, amplify, magnify, aggravate, exacerbate, worsen, inflame, compound. ANTONYMS abate.

in·ten·si·ty /in'tensitē/ ▶ **n.** (plural **intensities**) **1** the quality of being great in force, degree, or strength: *the pain grew in intensity.* **2** chiefly Physics the measurable amount of a property, such as force or brightness.

> SYNONYMS **1 strength**, power, force, severity, ferocity, fierceness, harshness, violence. **2 passion**, ardor, fervor, vehemence, fire, emotion, eagerness.

in·ten·sive /in'tensiv/ ▶ **adj. 1** involving a lot of effort over a short time. **2** (of agriculture) aiming to produce the highest possible yields.

> SYNONYMS **thorough**, thoroughgoing, in-depth, rigorous, exhaustive, vigorous, detailed, minute, meticulous, painstaking, methodical, extensive. ANTONYMS cursory.

□ **intensive care** special medical treatment given to a dangerously ill patient. ■ **in·ten·sive·ly** adv.

in·tent /in'tent/ ▶ n. intention or purpose. ▶ adj. 1 (**intent on**) determined to do. 2 (**intent on**) giving all your attention to. 3 showing great interest and attention.

SYNONYMS ▶ n. **aim**, intention, purpose, objective, goal. ▶ adj. 1 *he was* ***intent on*** *proving his point* **bent on**, set on, determined to (be), insistent on, resolved to (be), hell-bent on, keen on, committed to, determined to (be). 2 **attentive**, absorbed, engrossed, fascinated, enthralled, rapt, focused, concentrating, preoccupied. ANTONYMS distracted.

□ **to all intents and purposes** in all important respects. ■ **in·tent·ly** adv.

in·ten·tion /in'tenCHən/ ▶ n. 1 an aim or plan. 2 the fact of intending something. 3 (**intentions**) a man's plans about getting married.

SYNONYMS **aim**, purpose, intent, objective, goal.

in·ten·tion·al /in'tenCHənl/ ▶ adj. deliberate.

SYNONYMS **deliberate**, done on purpose, willful, calculated, conscious, intended, planned, meant, knowing.

■ **in·ten·tion·al·ly** adv.

in·ter /in'tər/ ▶ v. (**inters**, **interring**, **interred**) place a dead body in a grave or tomb.

SYNONYMS **bury**, lay to rest, consign to the grave, entomb. ANTONYMS exhume.

in·ter·act /ˌintər'akt/ ▶ v. (of two people or things) do things that have an effect on each other. ■ **in·ter·ac·tion** n.

in·ter·ac·tive /ˌintər'aktiv/ ▶ adj. 1 influencing each other. 2 (of a computer or other electronic device) allowing a two-way flow of information between it and a user.

in·ter a·li·a /'intər 'ālēə, 'älēə/ ▶ adv. among other things.

in·ter·breed /ˌintər'brēd/ ▶ v. (**interbreeds**, **interbreeding**, **interbred**) breed with an animal of a different species.

in·ter·cede /ˌintər'sēd/ ▶ v. intervene on behalf of someone else.

in·ter·cept /ˌintər'sept/ ▶ v. stop someone or something and prevent them from continuing to a destination.

SYNONYMS **stop**, head off, cut off, catch, seize, block, interrupt.

■ **in·ter·cep·tion** n.

in·ter·cep·tor /ˌintər'septər/ ▶ n. 1 a person or thing that stops or catches someone or something. 2 a fast aircraft for stopping or repelling enemy aircraft.

in·ter·ces·sion /ˌintər'sesHən/ ▶ n. 1 the action of interceding. 2 the saying of a prayer on behalf of another person.

in·ter·change ▶ v. /ˌintər'CHānj/ (**interchanges**, **interchanging**, **interchanged**) 1 (of two people) exchange things with each other. 2 put each of two things in the place of the other. ▶ n. /'intərˌCHānj/ 1 the action of interchanging things. 2 an exchange of words. 3 a road junction built on several levels. ■ **in·ter·change·a·ble** /ˌintər'CHānjəbəl/ adj. **in·ter·change·a·bly** adv.

in·ter·cit·y /'intərˌsitē/ ▶ adj. existing or traveling between cities.

in·ter·com /'intərˌkäm/ ▶ n. a system of communication by telephone or radio inside a building or group of buildings.

in·ter·con·nect /ˌintərkə'nekt/ ▶ v. (of two things) connect with each other.

in·ter·con·ti·nen·tal /ˌintərˌkäntn'entl/ ▶ adj. relating to or traveling between continents.

in·ter·course /'intərˌkôrs/ ▶ n. communication or dealings between people.

SYNONYMS 1 **dealings**, relations, relationships, contact, interchange, communication, networking. 2 **sexual intercourse**, sex, sexual relations, mating, copulation, fornication; technical coitus.

in·ter·cut /ˌintər'kət/ ▶ v. (**intercuts**, **intercutting**, **intercut**) alternate scenes with contrasting scenes in a movie.

in·ter·de·nom·i·na·tion·al /ˌintərdiˌnämə'nāsHənl/ ▶ adj. relating to more than one religious denomination.

in·ter·de·part·men·tal /ˌintərdiˌpärt'mentl, -ˌdēpärt-/ ▶ adj. relating to more than one department.

in·ter·de·pend·ent /ˌintərdi'pendənt/ ▶ adj. (of two or more people or things) dependent on each other.

in·ter·dict /ˌintər'dikt/ ▶ v. prohibit or forbid something. ■ **in·ter·dic·tion** n.

in·ter·dis·ci·pli·nar·y /ˌintər'disəpliˌnerē/ ▶ adj. relating to more than one branch of knowledge.

in·ter·est /'int(ə)rist/ ▶ n. 1 the state of wanting to know about something or someone. 2 the quality of making someone curious or holding their attention. 3 a subject about which you are concerned or enthusiastic. 4 money that is paid for the use of money lent. 5 a person's advantage or benefit: *it is in his own interest*. 6 a share, right, or stake in property or a financial undertaking. ▶ v. 1 make someone curious or attentive. 2 (**interested**) not impartial: *interested parties*. 3 (**interest in**) persuade someone to do or buy something.

SYNONYMS ▶ n. 1 **attentiveness**, attention, regard, notice, curiosity, enjoyment, delight. 2 *this will be of interest* **concern**, consequence, importance, import, significance, note, relevance, value. 3 **hobby**, pastime, leisure pursuit, amusement, recreation, diversion, passion. 4 **stake**, share, claim, investment, involvement, concern. ANTONYMS boredom. ▶ v. 1 **appeal to**, be of interest to, attract, intrigue, amuse, divert, entertain, arouse someone's curiosity, whet someone's appetite; informal tickle someone's fancy. 2 (**interested**) **attentive**, fascinated, riveted, gripped, captivated, agog, intrigued, curious, keen, eager. 3 (**interested**) **concerned**, involved, affected.

in·ter·est·ing /'int(ə)ristiNG, 'intəˌrestiNG/ ▶ adj. arousing curiosity or interest.

SYNONYMS **absorbing**, engrossing, fascinating, riveting, gripping, compelling, captivating, engaging, enthralling, appealing, entertaining, stimulating, diverting, intriguing.

■ **in·ter·est·ing·ly** adv.

in·ter·face /'intərˌfās/ ▶ n. 1 a point where two things meet and interact. 2 a device or program enabling a user to communicate with a computer, or for connecting two items of hardware or software. ▶ v. (**interfaces**, **interfacing**, **interfaced**) (**interface with**) **1** connect with another computer by an interface. **2** interact with.

in·ter·faith /ˈintərˈfāTH/ ▶ **adj.** relating to or between different religions.

in·ter·fere /ˌintərˈfi(ə)r/ ▶ **v.** (**interferes, interfering, interfered**) **1** (**interfere with**) prevent something from continuing or being carried out properly. **2** (**interfere with**) handle or adjust something without permission. **3** become involved in something without being asked.

> SYNONYMS **butt in**, barge in, intrude, meddle, tamper, encroach; informal poke your nose in, stick your oar in.

■ **in·ter·fer·ing adj.**

in·ter·fer·ence /ˌintərˈfi(ə)rəns/ ▶ **n. 1** the action of interfering. **2** disturbance to radio signals caused by unwanted signals from other sources.

> SYNONYMS **1 intrusion**, intervention, involvement, meddling, prying. **2 disruption**, disturbance, static, noise.

in·ter·fer·on /ˌintərˈfi(ə)rˌän/ ▶ **n.** a protein released by animal cells that prevents a virus from reproducing itself.

in·ter·ga·lac·tic /ˌintərgəˈlaktik/ ▶ **adj.** relating to or situated between galaxies.

in·ter·gov·ern·men·tal /ˌintərˌgəvər(n)ˈmentl/ ▶ **adj.** relating to or conducted between governments.

in·ter·im /ˈintərəm/ ▶ **n.** (**the interim**) the time between two events. ▶ **adj.** lasting for a short time, until a replacement is found.

in·te·ri·or /inˈti(ə)rēər/ ▶ **adj. 1** situated within or inside; inner. **2** remote from the coast or frontier; inland. **3** existing or occurring in the mind or soul: *driven by interior forces.* **4** relating to a country's internal affairs. ▶ **n. 1** the interior part. **2** the internal affairs of a country.

> SYNONYMS ▶ **adj. 1 inside**, inner, internal, inland, upcountry, central. **2 internal**, home, domestic, national, state, civil, local. **3 inner**, mental, spiritual, psychological, private, personal, secret. ▶ **n. 1 inside**, depths, recesses, bowels, belly, heart. **2 center**, heartland. ANTONYMS exterior.

□ **interior design** the design, decoration, and furnishing of the interior of a room or building.

in·ter·ject /ˌintərˈjekt/ ▶ **v.** say something suddenly as an interruption.

in·ter·jec·tion /ˌintərˈjekSHən/ ▶ **n.** an exclamation (e.g., *ah!*).

in·ter·lace /ˌintərˈlās/ ▶ **v.** (**interlaces, interlacing, interlaced**) **1** weave together. **2** (**interlace with**) mingle something with.

in·ter·leave /ˌintərˈlēv/ ▶ **v. 1** insert between the pages of a book. **2** place between the layers of something else.

in·ter·link /ˌintərˈliNGk/ ▶ **v.** (of two things) join or connect together.

in·ter·lock /ˌintərˈläk/ ▶ **v.** (of two parts, fibers, etc.) engage with each other by overlapping or fitting together.

in·ter·loc·u·tor /ˌintərˈläkyətər/ ▶ **n.** formal a person who takes part in a conversation.

in·ter·lop·er /ˈintərˌlōpər, ˌintərˈlōpər/ ▶ **n.** a person who is in a place or situation where they are not wanted or do not belong.

in·ter·lude /ˈintərˌlo͞od/ ▶ **n. 1** a period of time that contrasts with what goes before and after: *a romantic interlude.* **2** a pause between the acts of a play or the parts of a long movie. **3** a piece of music played between other pieces.

in·ter·mar·ry /ˌintərˈmarē/ ▶ **v.** (**intermarries, intermarrying, intermarried**) (of people of different races or religions) marry each other. ■ **in·ter·mar·riage n.**

in·ter·me·di·ar·y /ˌintərˈmēdēˌerē/ ▶ **n.** (plural **intermediaries**) a person who tries to settle a dispute between other people. ▶ **adj.** in the role of an intermediary.

> SYNONYMS ▶ **n. mediator**, go-between, negotiator, arbitrator, peacemaker, middleman, broker.

in·ter·me·di·ate /ˌintərˈmēdē-it/ ▶ **adj. 1** coming between two things in time, place, character, etc. **2** having more than basic knowledge or skills but not yet advanced. ▶ **n.** an intermediate person or thing.

> SYNONYMS ▶ **adj. halfway**, in-between, middle, mid, midway, intervening, transitional.

in·ter·ment /inˈtərmənt/ ▶ **n.** the burial of a dead body.

in·ter·mez·zo /ˌintərˈmetsō/ ▶ **n.** (plural **intermezzi** /-ˈmetsē/ or **intermezzos**) a short piece of music connecting parts of an opera or other work.

in·ter·mi·na·ble /inˈtərmənəbəl/ ▶ **adj.** lasting a very long time and therefore boring: *interminable discussions.* ■ **in·ter·mi·na·bly adv.**

in·ter·min·gle /ˌintərˈmiNGgəl/ ▶ **v.** (**intermingles, intermingling, intermingled**) mix or mingle together.

in·ter·mis·sion /ˌintərˈmiSHən/ ▶ **n. 1** a pause or break. **2** an interval between parts of a play or movie.

in·ter·mit·tent /ˌintərˈmitnt/ ▶ **adj.** stopping and starting at irregular intervals.

> SYNONYMS **sporadic**, irregular, fitful, spasmodic, discontinuous, isolated, random, patchy, scattered, occasional, periodic. ANTONYMS continuous.

■ **in·ter·mit·tent·ly adv.**

in·ter·mix /ˌintərˈmiks/ ▶ **v.** mix together.

in·tern ▶ **v.** /inˈtərn/ confine someone as a prisoner. ▶ **n.** /ˈinˌtərn/ **1** a recent medical graduate receiving supervised training in a hospital. **2** a student or trainee doing a job to gain work experience. ■ **in·tern·ment** /inˈtərnmənt/ **n. in·tern·ship n.**

in·ter·nal /inˈtərnl/ ▶ **adj. 1** relating to or situated on the inside. **2** inside the body. **3** relating to affairs and activities within a country. **4** existing or used within an organization. **5** within the mind: *internal feelings.*

> SYNONYMS **1 inner**, interior, inside, central. **2 domestic**, home, interior, civil, local, national, state. ANTONYMS external, foreign.

□ **internal combustion engine** an engine in which power is generated by the expansion of hot gases from the burning of fuel with air inside the engine. ■ **in·ter·nal·ly adv.**

in·ter·nal·ize /inˈtərnlˌīz/ ▶ **v.** (**internalizes, internalizing, internalized**) make a feeling or belief part of the way you think.

in·ter·na·tion·al /ˌintərˈnaSHənl/ ▶ **adj. 1** existing or happening between nations. **2** agreed on or used by all or many nations.

> SYNONYMS **global**, worldwide, world, intercontinental, universal, cosmopolitan, multiracial, multinational. ANTONYMS national, local.

□ **International Date Line** an imaginary North–South line, to the east of which the date is a day earlier than it is to the west. **international law** a body of rules recognized by nations as binding in their relations with one another. ■ **in·ter·na·tion·al·ly** adv.

in·ter·na·tion·al·ism /ˌintərˈnasʜənlˌizəm/ ▶ n. belief in the value of cooperation between nations.

in·ter·na·tion·al·ize /ˌintərˈnasʜənlˌīz/ ▶ v. (**internationalizes**, **internationalizing**, **internationalized**) make something international.

in·ter·ne·cine /ˌintərˈnesēn, -ˈnēsēn, -sin/ ▶ adj. (of fighting) taking place between members of the same country or group: *internecine rivalries*.

in·tern·ee /ˌintərˈnē/ ▶ n. a prisoner.

In·ter·net /ˈintərˌnet/ ▶ n. a very large international computer network.

in·ter·per·son·al /ˌintərˈpərsənəl/ ▶ adj. having to do with relationships or communication between people.

in·ter·plan·e·tar·y /ˌintərˈplaniˌterē/ ▶ adj. situated or traveling between planets.

in·ter·play /ˈintərˌplā/ ▶ n. the way in which things interact.

In·ter·pol /ˈintərˌpōl/ ▶ n. an international organization that coordinates investigations made by the police forces of member countries into crimes committed at an international level.

in·ter·po·late /inˈtərpəˌlāt/ ▶ v. (**interpolates**, **interpolating**, **interpolated**) **1** add a remark to a conversation. **2** add something to a piece of writing. ■ **in·ter·po·la·tion** /-ˌtərpəˈlāsʜən/ n.

in·ter·pose /ˌintərˈpōz/ ▶ v. (**interposes**, **interposing**, **interposed**) **1** place something between two other things. **2** say something as an interruption. **3** intervene between parties.

in·ter·pret /inˈtərprit/ ▶ v. (**interprets**, **interpreting**, **interpreted**) **1** explain the meaning of. **2** translate aloud the words of a person speaking a different language. **3** understand something as having a particular meaning.

> SYNONYMS **1 explain**, elucidate, expound, clarify. **2 understand**, construe, take (to mean), see, regard. **3 decipher**, decode, translate, understand.

■ **in·ter·pret·er** n.

in·ter·pre·ta·tion /inˌtərpriˈtāsʜən/ ▶ n. **1** the action of explaining the meaning of something. **2** an explanation. **3** the way in which a performer expresses a creative work.

> SYNONYMS **1 explanation**, elucidation, exposition, clarification, analysis. **2 meaning**, understanding, explanation, inference. **3 rendition**, execution, presentation, performance, reading, playing, singing.

■ **in·ter·pre·ta·tion·al** adj.

in·ter·ra·cial /ˌintərˈrāsʜəl/ ▶ adj. existing between or involving different races.

in·ter·reg·num /ˌintərˈregnəm/ ▶ n. (plural **interregnums**) a period between regimes when normal government is suspended.

in·ter·re·late /ˌintərəˈlāt/ ▶ v. (**interrelates**, **interrelating**, **interrelated**) (of two people or things) relate or connect to one other. ■ **in·ter·re·la·tion** n.

in·ter·ro·gate /inˈterəˌgāt/ ▶ v. (**interrogates**, **interrogating**, **interrogated**) ask someone a lot of questions, often in an aggressive way. ■ **in·ter·ro·ga·tion** /inˌterəˈgāsʜən/ n. **in·ter·ro·ga·tor** n.

in·ter·rog·a·tive /ˌintəˈrägətiv/ ▶ adj. in the form of or used in a question. ▶ n. a word used in questions, e.g., *how* or *what*.

in·ter·rog·a·to·ry /ˌintəˈrägəˌtôrē/ ▶ adj. questioning. ▶ n. Law a written question that is formally put to one party in a case by another party and that must be answered.

in·ter·rupt /ˌintəˈrəpt/ ▶ v. **1** stop the continuous progress of. **2** stop a person who is speaking by saying or doing something. **3** break the continuity of a line, surface, or view.

> SYNONYMS **1 suspend**, discontinue, adjourn, break off, stop, halt; informal put on ice. **2 cut in (on)**, break in (on), barge in (on), intrude, intervene; informal butt in (on), chime in (on).

> SPELLING
> Double **r** in the middle: inte**rr**upt.

in·ter·rup·tion /ˌintəˈrəpsʜən/ ▶ n. **1** an act, remark, or period that stops the progress of something. **2** the action of interrupting someone or something.

> SYNONYMS **1 suspension**, breaking off, discontinuance, stopping. **2 cutting in**, barging in, interference, intervention, intrusion, disturbance; informal butting in.

in·ter·sect /ˌintərˈsekt/ ▶ v. **1** divide something by passing or lying across it. **2** (of lines, roads, etc.) cross or cut each other.

in·ter·sec·tion /ˌintərˈseksʜən/ ▶ n. **1** a point or line where lines or surfaces intersect. **2** a point where roads intersect.

in·ter·sperse /ˌintərˈspərs/ ▶ v. (**intersperses**, **interspersing**, **interspersed**) place or scatter among or between other things.

in·ter·state /ˈintərˌstāt/ ▶ adj. existing or carried on between states.

in·ter·stel·lar /ˌintərˈstelər/ ▶ adj. occurring or situated between stars.

in·ter·stice /inˈtərstis/ ▶ n. a small crack or space in something.

in·ter·twine /ˌintərˈtwīn/ ▶ v. (**intertwines**, **intertwining**, **intertwined**) twist or twine together.

in·ter·val /ˈintərvəl/ ▶ n. **1** a period of time between two events. **2** a pause or break. **3** the difference in pitch between two sounds.

> SYNONYMS **intermission**, interlude, break, recess, time out.

in·ter·vene /ˌintərˈvēn/ ▶ v. (**intervenes**, **intervening**, **intervened**) **1** become involved in a situation in order to improve or control it. **2** happen in the time or space between other things.

> SYNONYMS **intercede**, involve yourself, get involved, step in, interfere, intrude.

in·ter·ven·tion /ˌintərˈvensʜən/ ▶ n. action taken to improve or control a situation.

in·ter·ven·tion·ist /ˌintərˈvensHənist/ ▶ **adj.** favoring intervention. ▶ **n.** an interventionist person.

in·ter·view /ˈintərˌvyo͞o/ ▶ **n. 1** a meeting at which a journalist asks someone questions about their work or their opinions. **2** a formal meeting at which someone is asked questions to judge whether they are suitable for a job, college place, etc. ▶ **v.** ask someone questions in an interview.

SYNONYMS ▶ **n. meeting**, discussion, interrogation, cross-examination, debriefing, audience, talk, chat; informal grilling. ▶ **v. talk to**, question, quiz, interrogate, cross-examine, debrief, poll, canvass, sound out; informal grill, pump, work over.

■ **in·ter·view·ee** /ˌintərˌvyo͞oˈē/ **n.**

in·ter·view·er /ˈintərˌvyo͞oər/ ▶ **n.** a person who conducts an interview.

SYNONYMS **questioner**, interrogator, examiner, assessor, journalist, reporter, inquisitor.

in·ter·war /ˌintərˈwôr/ ▶ **adj.** existing in the period between two wars, especially the two world wars.

in·ter·weave /ˌintərˈwēv/ ▶ **v.** (**interweaves**, **interweaving**, **interwove** /ˌintərˈwōv/; past participle **interwoven** /ˌintərˈwōvən/) weave two or more fibers or strands together.

in·tes·tate /inˈtestāt, -tit/ ▶ **adj.** (of someone who has died) not having made a will.

in·tes·tine /inˈtestən/ (or **intestines**) ▶ **n.** the long tube leading from the stomach to the anus. ■ **in·tes·ti·nal adj.**

in·ti·ma·cy /ˈintəməsē/ ▶ **n.** (plural **intimacies**) **1** close familiarity or friendship. **2** an intimate act or remark.

SYNONYMS **closeness**, togetherness, rapport, attachment, familiarity, friendliness, affection, warmth. ANTONYMS formality.

in·ti·mate¹ /ˈintəmit/ ▶ **adj. 1** familiar: *intimate friends*. **2** private and personal: *intimate details*. **3** involving very close connection: *an intimate involvement*. **4** (of knowledge) detailed. **5** having a friendly, informal atmosphere. ▶ **n.** a very close friend.

SYNONYMS ▶ **adj. 1 close**, bosom, dear, cherished, fast, firm. **2 friendly**, warm, welcoming, hospitable, relaxed, informal, cozy, comfortable. **3 personal**, private, confidential, secret, inward. **4 detailed**, thorough, exhaustive, deep, in-depth, profound. ANTONYMS distant, formal, cold.

■ **in·ti·mate·ly adv.**

in·ti·mate² /ˈintəˌmāt/ ▶ **v.** (**intimates**, **intimating**, **intimated**) say or suggest that something is the case.

SYNONYMS **1 announce**, state, make known, disclose, reveal, divulge, let it be known. **2 imply**, suggest, hint at, indicate, insinuate.

■ **in·ti·ma·tion** /ˌintəˈmāsHən/ **n.**

in·tim·i·date /inˈtimiˌdāt/ ▶ **v.** (**intimidates**, **intimidating**, **intimidated**) frighten or threaten someone, especially to force them to do something.

SYNONYMS **frighten**, menace, scare, terrorize, threaten, browbeat, bully, harass, hound; informal lean on.

■ **in·tim·i·da·tion** /-ˌtimiˈdāsHən/ **n.**

in·to /ˈinto͞o/ ▶ **prep. 1** expressing motion or direction to a point on or within. **2** expressing a change of state or the result of an action. **3** indicating the direction toward that something is turned. **4** indicating an object of interest: *an inquiry into the squad's practices*. **5** expressing division: *three into twelve*.

in·tol·er·a·ble /inˈtälərəbəl/ ▶ **adj.** unable to be endured.

SYNONYMS **unbearable**, insufferable, insupportable, unendurable, more than flesh and blood can stand, too much to bear. ANTONYMS bearable.

■ **in·tol·er·a·bly adv.**

in·tol·er·ant /inˈtälərənt/ ▶ **adj. 1** not willing to accept ideas or ways of behaving that are different from your own. **2** unable to take a medicine or eat a food without bad effects.

SYNONYMS **1 bigoted**, narrow-minded, prejudiced, illiberal. **2 allergic**, sensitive, hypersensitive.

■ **in·tol·er·ance n.**

in·to·na·tion /ˌintəˈnāsHən, -tō-/ ▶ **n.** the rise and fall of the voice in speaking.

in·tone /inˈtōn/ ▶ **v.** (**intones**, **intoning**, **intoned**) say or recite something with your voice hardly rising or falling.

in·tox·i·cate /inˈtäksiˌkāt/ ▶ **v.** (**intoxicates**, **intoxicating**, **intoxicated**) **1** (of an alcoholic drink or a drug) make someone lose control of themselves. **2** (**be intoxicated**) be excited or exhilarated by something: *he was intoxicated by music*.

SYNONYMS **1** (**intoxicating**) *intoxicating drink* **alcoholic**, strong, hard. **2** (**intoxicating**) *an intoxicating sense of freedom* **heady**, exhilarating, thrilling, stirring, stimulating, invigorating, powerful, potent, electrifying; informal mind-blowing. ANTONYMS nonalcoholic.

■ **in·tox·i·ca·tion** /inˌtäksiˈkāsHən/ **n.**

in·trac·ta·ble /inˈtraktəbəl/ ▶ **adj. 1** hard to solve or deal with. **2** stubborn.

in·tra·mu·ral /ˌintrəˈmyo͝orəl/ ▶ **adj. 1** situated or done within a building. **2** forming part of normal university or college studies.

in·tra·net /ˈintrəˌnet/ ▶ **n.** a computer network for use within an organization.

in·tran·si·gent /inˈtransijənt, -zi-/ ▶ **adj.** refusing to change your views or behavior.

SYNONYMS **uncompromising**, inflexible, unbending, unyielding, unwavering, stubborn, obstinate, pigheaded. ANTONYMS compliant.

■ **in·tran·si·gence n.**

in·tran·si·tive /inˈtransitiv, -zi-/ ▶ **adj.** (of a verb) not taking a direct object, e.g., *look* in *look at the sky*.

in·tra·u·ter·ine /ˌintrəˈyo͞otərin, -rīn/ ▶ **adj.** within the womb.

in·tra·ve·nous /ˌintrəˈvēnəs/ ▶ **adj.** within or into a vein.

in·trep·id /inˈtrepid/ ▶ **adj.** not afraid of danger or difficulties.

SYNONYMS **fearless**, unflinching, bold, daring, heroic, dynamic, brave, valiant, courageous, indomitable. ANTONYMS fearful.

■ **in·trep·id·ly adv.**

in·tri·ca·cy /ˈintrikəsē/ ▶ **n.** (plural **intricacies**) **1** the quality of being intricate. **2** (**intricacies**) details.

in·tri·cate /ˈintrikit/ ▶ adj. very complicated or detailed.

SYNONYMS **complex**, complicated, convoluted, tangled, elaborate, ornate, detailed. ANTONYMS simple.

■ **in·tri·cate·ly** adv.

in·trigue ▶ v. /inˈtrēg/ (**intrigues, intriguing, intrigued**) **1** arouse great curiosity in someone. **2** plot something illegal or harmful. ▶ n. /ˈinˌtrēg/ **1** the plotting of something illegal or harmful. **2** a secret plan or relationship.

SYNONYMS ▶ v. **interest**, fascinate, arouse someone's curiosity, attract, engage. ▶ n. **plotting**, conniving, scheming, machination, double-dealing, subterfuge.

■ **in·tri·guing** adj. **in·tri·guing·ly** adv.

in·trin·sic /inˈtrinzik, -sik/ ▶ adj. forming part of the fundamental nature of something.

SYNONYMS **inherent**, innate, inborn, inbred, congenital, natural; integral, basic, fundamental, essential.

■ **in·trin·si·cal·ly** adv.

in·tro /ˈintrō/ ▶ n. introduction.

in·tro·duce /ˌintrəˈd(y)o͞os/ ▶ v. (**introduces, introducing, introduced**) **1** bring something into use or operation for the first time. **2** present someone by name. **3** (**introduce something to**) bring a subject to someone's attention for the first time. **4** insert or bring something into: *a device that introduces chlorine into the pool.* **5** happen at the start of. **6** provide an opening announcement for.

SYNONYMS **1 institute**, initiate, launch, inaugurate, establish, found, bring in, set in motion, start, begin, get going. **2 present**, make known, acquaint with. **3 insert**, inject, put, force, shoot, feed. **4 instill**, infuse, inject, add. ANTONYMS end, remove.

in·tro·duc·tion /ˌintrəˈdəksHən/ ▶ n. **1** the action of introducing or being introduced. **2** a thing that introduces another, such as a section at the beginning of a book. **3** a thing newly brought in. **4** a book or course intended to introduce a newcomer to a subject of study. **5** a person's first experience of a subject or activity: *my introduction to drama.*

SYNONYMS **1 institution**, establishment, initiation, launch, inauguration, foundation. **2 presentation**, meeting, audience. **3 foreword**, preface, preamble, prologue, prelude; informal intro. ANTONYMS ending, epilogue.

in·tro·duc·to·ry /ˌintrəˈdəktərē/ ▶ adj. forming an introduction; basic.

SYNONYMS **1 opening**, initial, starting, initiatory, first, preliminary. **2 elementary**, basic, rudimentary, entry-level. ANTONYMS final, advanced.

in·tro·spec·tion /ˌintrəˈspeksHən/ ▶ n. concentration on your own thoughts or feelings.

in·tro·spec·tive /ˌintrəˈspektiv/ ▶ adj. given to examining your own thoughts or feelings: *an introspective poet.*

SYNONYMS **inward-looking**, self-analyzing, introverted, introvert, contemplative, thoughtful, reflective; informal navel-gazing.

in·tro·vert /ˈintrəˌvərt/ ▶ n. a shy, quiet person who is focused on their own thoughts and feelings. ▶ adj. (also **introverted**) characteristic of an introvert.

SYNONYMS ▶ adj. **shy**, reserved, withdrawn, reticent, diffident, retiring, quiet; introspective, introvert, inward-looking; pensive. ANTONYMS extrovert.

in·trude /inˈtro͞od/ ▶ v. (**intrudes, intruding, intruded**) come into a place or situation where you are unwelcome or uninvited.

SYNONYMS **encroach**, impinge, trespass, infringe, invade, violate, disturb, disrupt.

in·trud·er /inˈtro͞odər/ ▶ n. **1** a person who intrudes. **2** a person who goes into a building or an area illegally.

SYNONYMS **trespasser**, interloper, invader, infiltrator, burglar, housebreaker; informal gatecrasher.

in·tru·sion /inˈtro͞ozHən/ ▶ n. **1** the action of intruding. **2** a thing that has intruded.

in·tru·sive /inˈtro͞osiv/ ▶ adj. having a disturbing and unwelcome effect.

SYNONYMS **1** *intrusive neighbors* **intruding**, invasive, inquisitive, prying; informal nosy. **2** *intrusive questions* **personal**, prying, impertinent.

in·tu·it /inˈt(y)o͞o-it/ ▶ v. understand or work something out by intuition.

in·tu·i·tion /ˌint(y)o͞oˈisHən/ ▶ n. the ability to understand or know something without conscious reasoning.

SYNONYMS **1 instinct**, feeling, insight, sixth sense. **2 hunch**, feeling in your bones, inkling, sneaking suspicion, premonition; informal gut feeling.

in·tu·i·tive /inˈt(y)o͞oitiv/ ▶ adj. able to understand or know something without conscious reasoning.

SYNONYMS **instinctive**, innate, inborn, inherent, natural, unconscious, subconscious; informal gut.

■ **in·tu·i·tive·ly** adv.

In·u·it /ˈin(y)o͞o-it/ ▶ n. (plural **Inuit** or **Inuits**) **1** a member of a people of northern Canada and parts of Greenland and Alaska; an Eskimo. **2** the language of the Inuit.

USAGE

Inuit is the official term in Canada, and many of the peoples traditionally called **Eskimos** prefer it.

in·un·date /ˈinənˌdāt/ ▶ v. (**inundates, inundating, inundated**) **1** give or send someone so many things that they cannot deal with them all. **2** flood a place. ■ **in·un·da·tion** /ˌinənˈdāsHən/ n.

in·ure /iˈn(y)o͝or/ ▶ v. (**be inured to**) make someone used to something unpleasant: *these children have been inured to violence.*

in·vade /inˈvād/ ▶ v. (**invades, invading, invaded**) **1** enter a country so as to conquer or occupy it. **2** enter a place in large numbers: *demonstrators invaded the presidential palace.* **3** intrude on: *his privacy was being invaded.* **4** (of a parasite or disease) spread into.

SYNONYMS **1 occupy**, conquer, capture, seize, take (over), annex, overrun, storm. **2 intrude**

on, violate, encroach on, infringe on, trespass on, disturb, disrupt. ANTONYMS leave, liberate.

in·vad·er /in'vādər/ ▶ **n.** a person who invades.

SYNONYMS **attacker**, conqueror, raider, marauder, occupier, intruder, trespasser.

in·va·lid¹ /'invəlid/ ▶ **n.** a person suffering from an illness or injury. ▶ **v.** (**be invalided**) be removed from active military service because of injury or illness.

SYNONYMS ▶ **v. disable**, incapacitate, hospitalize, put out of action, lay up.

in·va·lid² /in'valid/ ▶ **adj. 1** not legally or officially recognized. **2** not correct because based on a mistake.

SYNONYMS **1 void**, null and void, not binding, illegitimate, inapplicable. **2 false**, fallacious, spurious, unsound, wrong, untenable.

■ **in·va·lid·i·ty** /ˌinvə'liditē/ **n.**

in·val·i·date /in'valiˌdāt/ ▶ **v.** (**invalidates**, **invalidating**, **invalidated**) make something invalid.

in·val·u·a·ble /in'valyo͞oəbəl/ ▶ **adj.** very useful; indispensable.

SYNONYMS **indispensable**, irreplaceable, all-important, crucial, vital, worth its weight in gold. ANTONYMS dispensable.

in·var·i·a·ble /in've(ə)rēəbəl/ ▶ **adj. 1** never changing. **2** Math (of a quantity) constant.

in·var·i·a·bly /in've(ə)rēəblē/ ▶ **adv.** always.

SYNONYMS **always**, at all times, without fail, without exception, consistently, habitually, unfailingly.

in·va·sion /in'vāzʜən/ ▶ **n. 1** an act of invading a country. **2** the arrival of a large number of unwelcome people or things.

SYNONYMS **1 occupation**, conquering, capture, seizure, annexation, takeover. **2 violation**, infringement, interruption, encroachment, disturbance, disruption, breach. ANTONYMS withdrawal.

in·va·sive /in'vāsiv/ ▶ **adj. 1** tending to invade or intrude: *invasive grasses*. **2** (of medical procedures) involving the introduction of instruments or other objects into the body.

in·vec·tive /in'vektiv/ ▶ **n.** strongly abusive or critical language.

in·veigh /in'vā/ ▶ **v.** (**inveigh against**) speak or write about someone or something with great hostility.

in·vei·gle /in'vāgəl/ ▶ **v.** (**inveigles**, **inveigling**, **inveigled**) **1** (**inveigle someone into**) cleverly persuade someone to do something. **2** (**inveigle yourself into**) gain entry into a place or situation by persuasion or trickery.

in·vent /in'vent/ ▶ **v. 1** create or design a new device or process. **2** make up a false story, name, etc.

SYNONYMS **1 originate**, create, design, devise, develop. **2 make up**, fabricate, concoct, hatch, contrive, dream up; informal cook up.

in·ven·tion /in'vensʜən/ ▶ **n. 1** the action of inventing. **2** a thing that has been invented. **3** creative ability: *his powers of invention*. **4** a false story.

SYNONYMS **1 origination**, creation, development, design, discovery. **2 innovation**, contraption, contrivance, device, gadget. **3 fabrication**, concoction, (piece of) fiction, story, tale, lie, untruth, falsehood, fib.

in·ven·tive /in'ventiv/ ▶ **adj.** having or showing creativity or original thought.

SYNONYMS **creative**, original, innovative, imaginative, resourceful, unusual, fresh, novel, new, groundbreaking, unorthodox, unconventional. ANTONYMS unimaginative.

■ **in·ven·tive·ly adv.**

in·ven·tor ▶ **n.** a person who creates or designs a new device or process.

SYNONYMS **originator**, creator, designer, deviser, developer, author, architect, father.

in·ven·to·ry /'invənˌtôrē/ ▶ **n.** (plural **inventories**) **1** a complete list of items. **2** a quantity of goods in stock.

SYNONYMS **list**, listing, catalog, database, record, register, checklist, log, archive.

in·verse /'invərs, in'vərs/ ▶ **adj.** opposite in position, direction, order, or effect. ▶ **n. 1** a thing that is the opposite or reverse of another. **2** Math a reciprocal quantity. □ **inverse proportion** (or **ratio**) a relation between two quantities such that one increases in proportion as the other decreases.
■ **in·ver·sion** /in'vərzʜən/ **n.**

in·vert /in'vərt/ ▶ **v.** put something upside down or in the opposite position, order, or arrangement.

in·ver·te·brate /in'vərtəbrit, -ˌbrāt/ ▶ **n.** an animal that has no backbone. ▶ **adj.** relating to such animals.

in·vest /in'vest/ ▶ **v. 1** put money into financial schemes, shares, or property in the hope of making a profit. **2** put time or energy into something in the hope of worthwhile results. **3** (**invest in**) buy something expensive. **4** (**invest something with**) give something a particular quality. **5** give someone a rank, honor, official title, etc., in a special ceremony.

SYNONYMS **put in**, put up, advance, expend, spend; informal lay out.

■ **in·ves·tor n.**

in·ves·ti·gate /in'vestiˌgāt/ ▶ **v. 1** carry out a systematic inquiry so as to establish the truth of something. **2** carry out research into a subject.

SYNONYMS **inquire into**, look into, go into, probe, explore, scrutinize, analyze, study, examine; informal check out.

in·ves·ti·ga·tion /inˌvesti'gāsʜən/ ▶ **n. 1** the action of investigating something or someone. **2** a formal inquiry or systematic study.

SYNONYMS **examination**, inquiry, study, inspection, exploration, analysis, research, scrutiny, probe, review.

in·ves·ti·ga·tive /in'vestiˌgātiv/ ▶ **adj. 1** relating to investigation or research. **2** (of journalism or a journalist) investigating and seeking to expose dishonesty or injustice.

in·ves·ti·ga·tor /in'vestiˌgātər/ ▶ **n.** a person who investigates.

SYNONYMS **researcher**, examiner, analyst, inspector, scrutineer, detective.

in·ves·ti·ture /in'vestichər, -ˌchoŏr/ ▶ **n.** **1** the action of formally giving a person a rank, honor, or special title. **2** a ceremony at which this takes place.

in·vest·ment /in'ves(t)mənt/ ▶ **n.** **1** the process of investing in something. **2** a thing worth buying because it may be profitable or useful in the future.

> SYNONYMS **1 investing**, speculation, outlay, funding, backing, financing, underwriting. **2 stake**, payment, outlay, venture, proposition.

in·vet·er·ate /in'vetərit/ ▶ **adj.** **1** having done a particular thing so often that you are now unlikely to stop doing it: *an inveterate gambler*. **2** (of a feeling or habit) firmly established.

> SYNONYMS **1** *an inveterate gambler* **confirmed**, hardened, incorrigible, addicted, compulsive, obsessive; informal pathological, chronic. **2** *an inveterate Democrat* **staunch**, steadfast, committed, devoted, dedicated, dyed-in-the-wool, diehard.

in·vid·i·ous /in'vidēəs/ ▶ **adj.** unfair and likely to arouse resentment or anger in other people.

> SYNONYMS **1 unpleasant**, awkward, difficult, undesirable, unenviable. **2 unfair**, unjust, unwarranted.

in·vig·or·ate /in'vigəˌrāt/ ▶ **v.** (**invigorates**, **invigorating**, **invigorated**) give strength or energy to.

> SYNONYMS **revitalize**, energize, refresh, revive, enliven, liven up, perk up, wake up, animate, galvanize, fortify, rouse, exhilarate; informal buck up, pep up. ANTONYMS tire.

in·vin·ci·ble /in'vinsəbəl/ ▶ **adj.** too powerful to be defeated or overcome.

> SYNONYMS **invulnerable**, indestructible, unconquerable, unbeatable, indomitable, unassailable, impregnable. ANTONYMS vulnerable.

in·vi·o·la·ble /in'vīələbəl/ ▶ **adj.** that must be respected; never to be broken or attacked.

in·vi·o·late /in'vīəlit/ ▶ **adj.** free from injury or violation.

in·vis·i·ble /in'vizəbəl/ ▶ **adj.** **1** not able to be seen. **2** ignored.

> SYNONYMS **unseen**, imperceptible, undetectable, inconspicuous, unnoticed, unobserved, hidden, out of sight. ANTONYMS visible.

■ **in·vis·i·bil·i·ty** /-ˌvizə'bilitē/ **n.** **in·vis·i·bly** **adv.**

in·vi·ta·tion /ˌinvi'tāshən/ ▶ **n.** **1** a request that someone should join you in going somewhere or doing something. **2** the action of inviting. **3** a situation or action that is likely to provoke a particular outcome or response: *his tactics were an invitation to disaster*.

> SYNONYMS **request**, call, summons; informal invite.

in·vite ▶ **v.** /in'vīt/ (**invites**, **inviting**, **invited**) **1** ask someone to join you in going somewhere or doing something. **2** ask formally or politely for a response to something. **3** tend to provoke a particular outcome or response. ▶ **n.** /'inˌvīt/ informal an invitation.

> SYNONYMS ▶ **v.** **1 ask**, summon. **2 ask for**, request, call for, appeal for, solicit, seek. **3 cause**, induce, provoke, ask for, encourage, lead to, bring on yourself, arouse.

in·vit·ing /in'vīting/ ▶ **adj.** tempting or attractive.

> SYNONYMS **tempting**, enticing, alluring, attractive, appealing, appetizing, mouthwatering, intriguing, seductive. ANTONYMS repellent.

■ **in·vit·ing·ly** **adv.**

in vi·tro /in 'vēˌtrō/ ▶ **adj. & adv.** taking place in a test tube, culture dish, or elsewhere outside a living animal or plant.

in·vo·ca·tion /ˌinvə'kāshən/ ▶ **n.** **1** the action of invoking. **2** an appeal to a god or supernatural being. **3** (in the Christian church) a form of words such as "in the name of the Father" introducing a prayer, sermon, etc.

in·voice /'inˌvois/ ▶ **n.** a list of goods or services provided, with a statement of the payment that is due. ▶ **v.** (**invoices**, **invoicing**, **invoiced**) send an invoice to someone.

in·voke /in'vōk/ ▶ **v.** (**invokes**, **invoking**, **invoked**) **1** appeal to someone or something as an authority or in support of an argument. **2** call on a god or supernatural being. **3** call earnestly for.

> SYNONYMS **1 cite**, refer to, resort to, have recourse to, turn to. **2 pray to**, call on, appeal to. **3 bring forth**, bring out, elicit, conjure up, generate.

in·vol·un·tar·y /in'välənˌterē/ ▶ **adj.** **1** done without conscious control. **2** (especially of muscles or nerves) unable to be consciously controlled. **3** done against someone's will.

> SYNONYMS **1 reflex**, automatic, instinctive, unintentional, uncontrollable. **2 compulsory**, obligatory, mandatory, forced, prescribed. ANTONYMS deliberate, optional.

■ **in·vol·un·tar·i·ly** /inˌvälən'te(ə)rəlē, -'välənˌter-/ **adv.**

in·volve /in'välv/ ▶ **v.** (**involves**, **involving**, **involved**) **1** (of a situation or event) include something as a necessary part or result. **2** make someone experience or take part in something.

> SYNONYMS **1 entail**, require, necessitate, demand, call for. **2 include**, take in, incorporate, encompass, comprise, cover. ANTONYMS preclude, exclude.

in·volved /in'välvd/ ▶ **adj.** **1** connected with someone or something on an emotional or personal level: *she was involved with someone else*. **2** complicated.

> SYNONYMS **1** *social workers* ***involved in*** *the case* **associated with**, connected with/to, concerned with. **2** *he had been involved in burglaries* **implicated**, caught up, mixed up. **3 complicated**, intricate, complex, elaborate, convoluted, confusing. **4 engrossed**, absorbed, immersed, caught up, preoccupied, intent.

in·volve·ment /in'välvmənt/ ▶ **n.** **1** the fact or condition of being involved with or participating in something. **2** emotional or personal association with someone.

> SYNONYMS **1 participation**, collaboration, collusion, complicity, association, connection, entanglement. **2 attachment**, friendship, intimacy, commitment.

in·vul·ner·a·ble /in'vəlnərəbəl/ ▶ **adj.** impossible to harm or damage.

SYNONYMS **impervious**, immune; indestructible, impregnable, unassailable, invincible, secure.

in·ward /'inwərd/ (or **inwards** /'inwərdz/) ▶ **adv.** **1** toward the inside. **2** into or toward the mind, spirit, or soul.

SYNONYMS **inside**, toward the inside, into the interior, within, inwards.

■ **in·ward·ly adv.**

i·o·dide /'īə,dīd/ ▶ **n.** a compound of iodine with another element or group.

i·o·dine /'īə,dīn/ ▶ **n.** **1** a black, nonmetallic chemical element. **2** a solution of iodine in alcohol used as an antiseptic.

i·on /'īən, 'ī,än/ ▶ **n.** an atom or molecule with a net electric charge through loss or gain of electrons. ■ **i·on·ic** /ī'änik/ **adj.**

i·on·ize /'īə,nīz/ ▶ **v.** convert an atom, molecule, or substance into an ion or ions. ■ **i·on·i·za·tion** /,īəni'zāsʜən/ **n.**

i·on·iz·er /'īə,nīzər/ ▶ **n.** a device that produces ions, used to improve the quality of the air in a room.

i·on·o·sphere /ī'änə,sfi(ə)r/ ▶ **n.** the layer of the atmosphere above the mesosphere.

i·o·ta /ī'ōtə/ ▶ **n.** **1** a very small amount: *it won't make an iota of difference.* **2** the ninth letter of the Greek alphabet (Ι, ι).

SYNONYMS (**little**) **bit**, mite, speck, scrap, shred, ounce, jot.

IOU ▶ **n.** a signed document acknowledging a debt.

iPod /'ī,päd/ ▶ **n.** trademark a type of personal digital audio player.

ip·so fac·to /'ipsō 'faktō/ ▶ **adv.** by that very fact or act.

IQ ▶ **abbr.** intelligence quotient, a number representing a person's ability to reason, calculated from the results of special tests.

IRA /'īrə/ ▶ **abbr.** **1** Individual Retirement Account. **2** Irish Republican Army.

I·ra·ni·an /i'rānēən, i'rä-/ ▶ **n.** a person from Iran. ▶ **adj.** relating to Iran.

I·ra·qi /i'räkē, i'rakē/ ▶ **n.** (plural **Iraqis**) a person from Iraq. ▶ **adj.** relating to Iraq.

i·ras·ci·ble /i'rasəbəl/ ▶ **adj.** hot-tempered; irritable.

i·rate /ī'rāt/ ▶ **adj.** very angry.

ire /ī(ə)r/ ▶ **n.** literary anger.

i·ren·ic /ī'renik, ī'rē-/ (also **eirenic**) ▶ **adj.** formal aiming or aimed at peace.

ir·i·des·cent /,iri'desənt/ ▶ **adj.** showing bright colors that seem to change when seen from different angles. ■ **ir·i·des·cence n.**

SPELLING

Just one r: iridescent.

i·ris /'īris/ ▶ **n.** **1** the round colored part of the eye, with the pupil in the center. **2** a plant with sword-shaped leaves and purple, yellow, or white flowers.

I·rish /'īrisʜ/ ▶ **n.** (also **Irish Gaelic**) the language of Ireland. ▶ **adj.** relating to Ireland, its people, or Irish. □ **Irish coffee** coffee mixed with a dash of Irish whiskey. **Irish wolfhound** a large, grayish hound with a rough coat.

irk /ərk/ ▶ **v.** irritate; annoy.

irk·some /'ərksəm/ ▶ **adj.** irritating; annoying.

i·ron /'īərn/ ▶ **n.** **1** a strong magnetic silvery-gray metal. **2** a tool made of iron. **3** a hand-held piece of equipment with a heated steel base, used to smooth clothes. **4** a golf club used for hitting the ball at a high angle. **5** (**irons**) handcuffs or chains used as a restraint. ▶ **v.** **1** smooth clothes with an iron. **2** (**iron something out**) settle a difficulty or problem. □ **Iron Age** an ancient period when weapons and tools were made of iron. **Iron Curtain** an imaginary barrier separating the communist countries of the former Soviet bloc and western Europe. **iron lung** (in the past) a large iron tube inside which a person lay, used with a mechanical pump to give prolonged artificial respiration.

i·ron·ic /ī'ränik/ ▶ **adj.** **1** using irony. **2** happening in the opposite way to what is expected.

SYNONYMS **1 sarcastic**, sardonic, satirical, dry, wry, double-edged, mocking, derisive, scornful. **2 paradoxical**, funny, strange.

■ **i·ron·i·cal·ly adv.**

i·ron·ing /'īərniɴɢ/ ▶ **n.** clothes and linen that need to be or have just been ironed. □ **ironing board** a long narrow board on a stand, on which things are ironed.

i·ron·works /'īərn,wərks/ ▶ **n.** a place where iron is smelted or iron goods are made.

i·ro·ny /'īrənē, 'iərnē/ ▶ **n.** (plural **ironies**) **1** the use of words that say the opposite of what you really mean in order to be funny or to make a point. **2** aspects of a situation that are opposite to what are expected.

SYNONYMS **1 sarcasm**, mockery, ridicule, derision, scorn. **2 paradox**.

ir·ra·di·ate /i'rādē,āt/ ▶ **v.** (**irradiates**, **irradiating**, **irradiated**) **1** expose to radiation. **2** shine light on. ■ **ir·ra·di·a·tion** /i,rādē'āsʜən/ **n.**

ir·ra·tion·al /i'rasʜənl/ ▶ **adj.** not logical or reasonable.

SYNONYMS **unreasonable**, illogical, groundless, baseless, unfounded, unjustifiable.
ANTONYMS rational, logical.

■ **ir·ra·tion·al·i·ty** /i,rasʜə'nalitē/ **n.** **ir·ra·tion·al·ly adv.**

ir·rec·on·cil·a·ble /i,rekən'sīləbəl, i'rekən,sī-/ ▶ **adj.** **1** incompatible: *the two points of view were irreconcilable.* **2** (of differences) not able to be settled.

ir·re·cov·er·a·ble /,iri'kəvərəbəl/ ▶ **adj.** not able to be recovered.

ir·re·deem·a·ble /,iri'dēməbəl/ ▶ **adj.** not able to be saved, improved, or corrected.

ir·re·den·tist /,iri'dentist/ ▶ **n.** a person who argues for the restoration to their country of any territory formerly belonging to it.

ir·re·duc·i·ble /,iri'd(y)ōōsəbəl/ ▶ **adj.** not able to be reduced or simplified.

ir·ref·u·ta·ble /,irə'fyōōtəbəl, i'refyə-/ ▶ **adj.** impossible to deny or disprove.

SYNONYMS **indisputable**, undeniable, unquestionable, incontrovertible, incontestable, beyond question, beyond doubt, conclusive, definite, definitive, decisive.

ir·reg·u·lar /i'regyələr/ ▶ **adj.** **1** not regular in shape, arrangement, or occurrence. **2** against a rule, standard, or convention. **3** not belonging to regular army units. 4 Grammar (of a word) having inflections that do not conform to the usual rules.

SYNONYMS 1 **uneven**, crooked, misshapen, lopsided, asymmetrical, twisted. 2 **rough**, bumpy, uneven, pitted, rutted, lumpy, knobbly, gnarled. 3 **inconsistent**, unsteady, uneven, fitful, patchy, variable, varying, changeable, inconstant, erratic, unstable, spasmodic, intermittent. 4 **improper**, illegitimate, unethical, unprofessional; informal shady, dodgy. 5 **guerrilla**, underground, paramilitary, partisan, mercenary, terrorist.

■ **ir·reg·u·lar·i·ty** /iˌregyəˈlaritē/ n. (plural **irregularities**).

ir·rel·e·vant /iˈreləvənt/ ▶ adj. not relevant.

SYNONYMS **beside the point**, immaterial, unconnected, unrelated, peripheral, extraneous.

■ **ir·rel·e·vance** n. **ir·rel·e·vant·ly** adv.

SPELLING
Write -**ant**, not -**ent**: irrelev**ant**.

ir·re·li·gious /ˌiriˈlijəs/ ▶ adj. indifferent or hostile to religion.

ir·re·me·di·a·ble /ˌiriˈmēdēəbəl/ ▶ adj. impossible to cure or put right.

ir·re·mov·a·ble /ˌiriˈmo͞ovəbəl/ ▶ adj. incapable of being removed.

ir·rep·a·ra·ble /iˈrep(ə)rəbəl/ ▶ adj. impossible to put right or repair.

SYNONYMS **irreversible**, irrevocable, irrecoverable, unrepairable, beyond repair.

■ **ir·rep·a·ra·bly** adv.

ir·re·place·a·ble /iriˈplāsəbəl/ ▶ adj. impossible to replace if lost or damaged.

ir·re·press·i·ble /ˌiriˈpresəbəl/ ▶ adj. not able to be restrained.

SYNONYMS **ebullient**, exuberant, buoyant, breezy, jaunty, high-spirited, vivacious, animated, full of life, lively; informal bubbly, bouncy, peppy, chipper, chirpy, full of beans.

ir·re·proach·a·ble /ˌiriˈprōcнəbəl/ ▶ adj. very good and unable to be criticized.

ir·re·sist·i·ble /ˌiriˈzistəbəl/ ▶ adj. too tempting or powerful to be resisted.

SYNONYMS 1 **captivating**, enticing, alluring, enchanting, fascinating, seductive. 2 **uncontrollable**, overwhelming, overpowering, ungovernable, compelling.

■ **ir·re·sist·i·bly** adv.

SPELLING
Write -**ible**, not -**able**: irresist**ible**.

ir·res·o·lute /i(r)ˈrezəˌlo͞ot/ ▶ adj. uncertain.

ir·re·spec·tive /ˌiriˈspektiv/ ▶ adj. (**irrespective of**) regardless of.

ir·re·spon·si·ble /ˌiriˈspänsəbəl/ ▶ adj. not showing a proper sense of responsibility.

SYNONYMS **reckless**, rash, careless, unwise, imprudent, ill-advised, injudicious, hasty, impetuous, foolhardy, foolish, unreliable, undependable, untrustworthy.

■ **ir·re·spon·si·bil·i·ty** /-ˌspänsəˈbilitē/ n. **ir·re·spon·si·bly** adv.

ir·re·triev·a·ble /ˌiriˈtrēvəbəl/ ▶ adj. not able to be brought back or made right. ■ **ir·re·triev·a·bly** adv.

ir·rev·er·ent /iˈrev(ə)rənt/ ▶ adj. disrespectful.

SYNONYMS **disrespectful**, impertinent, cheeky, flippant, rude, discourteous. ANTONYMS respectful.

■ **ir·rev·er·ence** n. **ir·rev·er·ent·ly** adv.

ir·re·vers·i·ble /ˌiriˈvərsəbəl/ ▶ adj. impossible to be reversed or altered. ■ **ir·re·vers·i·bly** adv.

ir·rev·o·ca·ble /ˌiˈrevəkəbəl/ ▶ adj. not able to be changed or reversed.

SYNONYMS **irreversible**, unalterable, unchangeable, immutable, final, binding, permanent, set in stone.

■ **ir·rev·o·ca·bly** adv.

ir·ri·gate /ˈirigāt/ ▶ v. (**irrigates**, **irrigating**, **irrigated**) supply water to land or crops through channels. ■ **ir·ri·ga·tion** /ˌiriˈgāsнən/ n.

ir·ri·ta·ble /ˈiritəbəl/ ▶ adj. 1 easily annoyed or angered. 2 Medicine unusually sensitive.

SYNONYMS **bad-tempered**, short-tempered, irascible, touchy, testy, grumpy, grouchy, crotchety, cantankerous, fractious, curmudgeonly. ANTONYMS good-humored.

■ **ir·ri·ta·bil·i·ty** /ˌiritəˈbilitē/ n. **ir·ri·ta·bly** adv.

ir·ri·tant /ˈiritənt/ ▶ n. 1 a substance that irritates the skin or a part of the body. 2 a source of continual annoyance.

SYNONYMS **annoyance**, (source of) irritation, thorn in someone's side/flesh, nuisance; informal pain (in the neck), headache, burr in/under someone's saddle.

ir·ri·tate /ˈiriˌtāt/ ▶ v. (**irritates**, **irritating**, **irritated**) 1 make someone annoyed or angry. 2 cause soreness, itching, or inflammation.

SYNONYMS 1 **annoy**, bother, vex, make cross, exasperate, infuriate, anger, madden, rub the wrong way; informal aggravate, peeve, rile, needle, get (to), bug, tee off, tick off. 2 **inflame**, hurt, chafe, scratch, scrape, rub. ANTONYMS delight, soothe.

■ **ir·ri·tat·ing·ly** adv.

ir·ri·ta·tion /ˌiriˈtāsнən/ ▶ n. the state of feeling annoyed or angry.

SYNONYMS **annoyance**, exasperation, vexation, indignation, anger, displeasure, chagrin. ANTONYMS delight.

ir·rupt /iˈrəpt/ ▶ v. enter forcibly or suddenly. ■ **ir·rup·tion** n.

IRS ▶ abbr. Internal Revenue Service.

is /iz/ 3rd person singular present of **BE**.

ISA ▶ abbr. Computing industry standard architecture, a standard for connecting computers and their peripherals.

ISBN ▶ abbr. international standard book number.

Is·lam /isˈläm, iz-/ ▶ n. 1 the religion of the Muslims, revealed through Muhammad as the Prophet of Allah. 2 the Muslim world. ■ **Is·lam·ic** adj.

is·land /ˈīlənd/ ▶ n. 1 a piece of land surrounded by water. 2 a thing that is isolated, detached, or surrounded.

SYNONYMS **isle**, islet, atoll; (**islands**) archipelago.

■ **is·land·er** n.

isle /īl/ ▶ n. literary an island.

is·let /'īlət/ ▶ n. a small island. □ **islets of Langerhans** groups of cells in the pancreas that produce insulin.

is·n't /'izənt/ ▶ contr. is not.

ISO ▶ abbr. International Organization for Standardization.

i·so·bar /'īsə,bär/ ▶ n. a line on a map connecting points having the same atmospheric pressure.

i·so·late /'īsə,lāt/ ▶ v. (**isolates**, **isolating**, **isolated**) **1** place something or someone apart from others and on their own. **2** extract a substance in a pure form.

SYNONYMS **separate**, segregate, detach, cut off, shut away, alienate, distance, cloister, seclude, cordon off, seal off, close off, fence off. ANTONYMS integrate.

i·so·lat·ed /'īsə,lātid/ ▶ adj. **1** (of a place) remote. **2** (of a person) cut off from other people; lonely. **3** single; exceptional: *isolated incidents*.

SYNONYMS **1 remote**, out of the way, outlying, off the beaten track, in the back of beyond, godforsaken, inaccessible, cut-off; informal in the middle of nowhere, in the sticks, jerkwater. **2 solitary**, lonely, secluded, lonesome, reclusive, hermitlike. **3 unique**, lone, solitary, unusual, exceptional, untypical, freak. ANTONYMS accessible.

i·so·la·tion /,īsə'lāsHən/ ▶ n. the process of isolating someone or something or the fact of being isolated.

SYNONYMS **1 solitariness**, loneliness, friendlessness. **2 remoteness**, inaccessibility. ANTONYMS contact.

i·so·la·tion·ism /,īsə'lāsHə,nizəm/ ▶ n. a policy of remaining apart from the political affairs of other countries.

i·so·mer /'īsəmər/ ▶ n. Chemistry each of two or more compounds with the same formula but a different arrangement of atoms.

i·so·met·ric /,īsə'metrik/ ▶ adj. having equal dimensions.

i·so·mor·phic /,īsə'môrfik/ ▶ adj. corresponding in form and relations. ■ **i·so·mor·phism** n. **i·so·morph·ous** adj.

i·sos·ce·les /ī'säsə,lēz/ ▶ adj. (of a triangle) having two sides of equal length.

i·so·therm /'īsə,THərm/ ▶ n. a line on a map or diagram connecting points having the same temperature. ■ **i·so·ther·mal** /,īsə'THərməl/ adj. & n.

i·so·tope /'īsə,tōp/ ▶ n. each of two or more forms of the same element that contain equal numbers of protons but different numbers of neutrons in their nuclei.

ISP ▶ abbr. Internet service provider.

Is·rae·li /iz'rālē/ ▶ n. (plural **Israelis**) a person from Israel. ▶ adj. relating to the modern country of Israel.

Is·ra·el·ite /'izrēə,līt/ ▶ n. a member of the people of ancient Israel.

is·sue /'isHo͞o/ ▶ n. **1** an important topic to be discussed or settled. **2** a problem or difficulty. **3** each of a regular series of publications. **4** the action of supplying something. ▶ v. (**issues**, **issuing**, **issued**) **1** supply or give out. **2** formally send out or make known: *issue a statement*. **3** (**issue from**) come, go, or flow out from.

SYNONYMS ▶ n. **1 matter**, question, point at issue, affair, case, subject, topic, problem, situation. **2 edition**, number, installment, copy, impression. **3 issuing**, release, publication, distribution. ▶ v. **1 release**, put out, deliver, publish, broadcast, circulate, distribute. **2 supply**, provide, furnish, arm, equip, fit out, rig out; informal fix up.

□ **at issue** under discussion. **make an issue of** treat something too seriously or as a problem. **take issue with** challenge someone.

isth·mus /'isməs/ ▶ n. (plural **isthmuses**) a narrow strip of land with sea on either side, linking two larger areas of land.

IT ▶ abbr. information technology.

it /it/ ▶ pron. **1** used to refer to a thing previously mentioned or easily identified. **2** referring to an animal or child whose sex is not specified. **3** used in the normal subject position in statements about time, distance, or weather: *it is raining*. **4** the situation or circumstances: *if it's convenient*.

I·tal·ian /i'talyən/ ▶ n. **1** a person from Italy. **2** the language of Italy. ▶ adj. relating to Italy or Italian.

i·tal·ic /i'talik, ī'tal-/ ▶ adj. (of a typeface) sloping to the right, used especially for emphasis and for foreign words. ▶ n. (also **italics**) an italic typeface or letter. ■ **i·tal·i·cize** v.

itch /icH/ ▶ n. **1** an uncomfortable sensation that makes you want to scratch your skin. **2** informal an impatient desire. ▶ v. **1** experience an itch. **2** informal feel an impatient desire to do something: *we itch to explore*.

SYNONYMS ▶ n. **1 tingling**, irritation, itchiness, prickle. **2 longing**, yearning, craving, ache, hunger, thirst, urge, hankering; informal yen. ▶ v. **1 tingle**, be irritated, be itchy, sting, hurt, be sore. **2 long**, yearn, ache, burn, crave, hanker for/after, hunger, thirst, be eager, be desperate; informal be dying to/for.

itch·y /'icHē/ ▶ adj. (**itchier**, **itchiest**) having or causing an itch. □ **have itchy feet** informal have a strong urge to travel. ■ **itch·i·ness** n.

it'd /'itid/ ▶ contr. **1** it had. **2** it would.

i·tem /'ītəm/ ▶ n. an individual article or unit.

SYNONYMS **1 thing**, article, object, piece, element, constituent, component, ingredient. **2 issue**, matter, affair, case, subject, topic, question, point. **3 report**, story, article, piece, write-up, bulletin, feature, review.

i·tem·ize /'ītə,mīz/ ▶ v. (**itemizes**, **itemizing**, **itemized**) present a quantity as a list of individual items or parts.

i·tin·er·ant /ī'tinərənt, i'tin-/ ▶ adj. traveling from place to place. ▶ n. an itinerant person.

i·tin·er·ar·y /ī'tinə,rerē, i'tin-/ ▶ n. (plural **itineraries**) a planned route or journey.

SYNONYMS **route**, plan, schedule, timetable, program.

SPELLING

Write itin**erary**, not -**ery**.

it'll /'itl/ ▶ contr. **1** it shall. **2** it will.

its /its/ ▶ possessive determiner **1** belonging to or associated with a thing previously mentioned or easily identified. **2** belonging to or associated with a child or animal whose sex is not specified: *a baby in its mother's womb.*

USAGE

Don't confuse the possessive **its** (as in *turn the camera on its side*) with the form **it's** (short for either **it is** or **it has**, as in *it's my fault* or *it's been a hot day*).

it's /its/ ▶ **contr.** **1** it is. **2** it has.

it·self /it'self/ ▶ **pron.** **1** used to refer to something previously mentioned as the subject of the clause: *his horse hurt itself.* **2** used to emphasize a particular thing mentioned.

IUD ▶ **abbr.** intrauterine device.

IV ▶ **abbr.** intravenous. ▶ **n.** an intravenous drip feed: *they put an IV in me.*

I've /īv/ ▶ **contr.** I have.

IVF ▶ **abbr.** in vitro fertilization.

i·vo·ry /'īvərē/ ▶ **n.** (plural **ivories**) **1** the hard creamy-white substance that elephants' tusks are made of. **2** the creamy-white color of ivory. **3** (**the ivories**) informal the keys of a piano. □ **ivory tower** a situation in which someone leads a privileged life and does not have to face normal difficulties.

i·vy /'īvē/ ▶ **n.** an evergreen climbing plant. □ **Ivy League** a group of long-established universities in the eastern United States, with high academic and social prestige. The group includes Harvard, Yale, Princeton, Columbia, Dartmouth, Cornell, Brown, and the University of Pennsylvania.

Jj

J (or **j**) ▶ n. (plural **Js** or **J's**) the tenth letter of the alphabet. ▶ abbr. (**J**) joule(s).

jab /jab/ ▶ v. (**jabs, jabbing, jabbed**) poke someone with something sharp or pointed. ▶ n. a quick, sharp poke or blow.

SYNONYMS **poke**, prod, dig, elbow, nudge, thrust, stab, push.

jab·ber /ˈjabər/ ▶ v. (**jabbers, jabbering, jabbered**) talk quickly and excitedly but without making much sense.

ja·bot /zhaˈbō, ja-/ ▶ n. a ruffle on the front of a shirt or blouse.

jac·a·ran·da /ˌjakəˈrandə/ ▶ n. a tropical American tree that has blue trumpet-shaped flowers and fragrant wood.

jack /jak/ ▶ n. **1** a device for lifting a vehicle off the ground so that a wheel can be changed or the underside examined. **2** a playing card ranking next below a queen. **3** a connection between two pieces of electrical equipment. **4** (in lawn bowling) a small white ball at which players aim the balls they are bowling. ▶ v. (**jack something up**) **1** raise something with a jack. **2** informal increase something by a large amount. □ **Jack Frost** a figure representing frost. **jack-in-the-box** a toy consisting of a box containing a figure on a spring, which pops up when the lid is opened.

jack·al /ˈjakəl/ ▶ n. a wild dog that often hunts or scavenges in packs.

jack·ass /ˈjakˌas/ ▶ n. **1** a stupid person. **2** a male ass or donkey.

jack·boot /ˈjakˌbo͞ot/ ▶ n. a leather military boot reaching to the knee.

jack·daw /ˈjakˌdô/ ▶ n. a small crow with a gray head.

jack·et /ˈjakit/ ▶ n. **1** an outer garment reaching to the waist or hips, with sleeves. **2** a covering placed around something for protection or insulation. **3** the dust jacket of a book. **4** the skin of a potato.

jack·ham·mer /ˈjakˌhamər/ ▶ n. a portable pneumatic hammer or drill.

jack·knife /ˈjakˌnīf/ ▶ n. (plural **jackknives**) **1** a large knife with a folding blade. **2** a dive in which the body is bent at the waist and then straightened. ▶ v. (**jackknifes, jackknifing, jackknifed**) **1** (of a tractor-trailer) bend into a V-shape in an uncontrolled skidding movement. **2** move your body into a bent or doubled-up position.

jack-o'-lan·tern /ˈjak ə ˌlantərn/ ▶ n. a lantern made from a hollowed-out pumpkin in which holes are cut to represent features of the face, typically made at Halloween.

jack·pot /ˈjakˌpät/ ▶ n. a large cash prize in a game or lottery. □ **hit the jackpot** have great or unexpected success.

jack·rab·bit /ˈjakˌrabət/ ▶ n. a hare found in open country in western North America.

Jack Rus·sell /ˈrəsəl/ (also **Jack Russell terrier**) ▶ n. a small breed of terrier with short legs.

Jac·o·be·an /ˌjakəˈbēən/ ▶ adj. having to do with the reign of James I of England (1603–1625). ▶ n. a person who lived in the Jacobean period.

Jac·o·bin /ˈjakəbən/ ▶ n. **1** historical a member of a radical democratic club formed in Paris in 1789. **2** an extreme political radical. ■ **Jac·o·bin·ism** n.

jac·quard /ˈjaˌkärd, jəˈkärd/ ▶ n. **1** a fabric with a woven pattern. **2** a loom used for weaving patterned and brocaded fabrics.

Ja·cuz·zi /jəˈko͞ozē/ ▶ n. (plural **Jacuzzis**) trademark a large, wide bath with jets of water to massage the body.

jade /jād/ ▶ n. a hard bluish-green precious stone.

jad·ed /ˈjādid/ ▶ adj. tired out or lacking enthusiasm after having had too much of something.

jag /jag/ ▶ v. (**jags, jagging, jagged** /ˈjagid/) stab, pierce, or prick. ▶ n. a sharp projection.

jag·ged /ˈjagid/ ▶ adj. with rough, sharp points or edges sticking out.

SYNONYMS **spiky**, barbed, ragged, rough, uneven, irregular, serrated. ANTONYMS smooth.

jag·uar /ˈjagˌwär/ ▶ n. a large cat with a spotted coat, found in Central and South America.

jail /jāl/ ▶ n. a place for holding people who are accused or convicted of a crime. ▶ v. put someone in jail.

SYNONYMS ▶ n. **prison**, lockup, jailhouse, detention center, penitentiary; informal clink, cooler, slammer, inside, can, pen, pokey, big house. ▶ v. **imprison**, incarcerate, lock up, put away, detain; informal send down/up, send up the river, put behind bars, put inside. ANTONYMS acquit, release.

■ **jail·er** n.

jail·bird /ˈjālˌbərd/ ▶ n. informal a person who is or has repeatedly been in prison.

jail·break /ˈjālˌbrāk/ ▶ n. an escape from jail.

jail·house /ˈjālˌhous/ ▶ n. a prison.

Jain·ism /ˈjāˌnizəm/ ▶ n. an Indian religion founded in the 6th century BC, featuring nonviolence and self-discipline. ■ **Jain** n.

ja·lop·y /jəˈläpē/ ▶ n. (plural **jalopies**) informal an old car.

jal·ou·sie /ˈjaləˌsē/ ▶ n. a blind or shutter made of a row of angled slats.

jam[1] /jam/ ▶ v. (**jams, jamming, jammed**) **1** squeeze or pack tightly into a space. **2** push something roughly and forcibly into a position. **3** block something through crowding. **4** make or become unable to function because a part is stuck. **5** (**jam something on**) apply a brake suddenly and with force: *he jammed on the brakes.* **6** interrupt a radio transmission by causing interference. **7** informal improvise with other musicians. ▶ **n. 1** an instance of something being jammed. **2** informal a difficult situation: *I'm in a jam.* **3** informal an improvised performance by a group of musicians.

SYNONYMS ▶ **v. 1 stuff**, shove, force, ram, thrust, press, push, wedge, stick, cram. **2 crowd**, pack, pile, press, squeeze, sandwich, cram, throng, mob, fill, block, clog, congest. **3 stick**, become stuck, catch, seize (up). ▶ **n. 1 bottleneck**, holdup, traffic jam, congestion, gridlock; informal snarl-up. **2 predicament**, difficulty, problem, dilemma, trouble, quandary; informal fix, hole, scrape, box, corner, hot water.

□ **jam-packed** informal extremely crowded or full to capacity.

jam² ▶ **n.** a spread or preserve made from fruit and sugar.

Ja·mai·can /jəˈmākən/ ▶ **n.** a person from Jamaica. ▶ **adj.** relating to Jamaica.

jamb /jam/ ▶ **n.** a side post of a doorway, window, or fireplace.

jam·bo·ree /ˌjambəˈrē/ ▶ **n.** a large celebration or party.

Jane Doe /ˈjān ˈdō/ ▶ **n.** an anonymous female party in a legal action or an unidentified woman.

jan·gle /ˈjaNGgəl/ ▶ **v.** (**jangles**, **jangling**, **jangled**) **1** make a ringing metallic sound. **2** (of your nerves) be set on edge. ▶ **n.** a ringing metallic sound. ■ **jan·gly adj.**

jan·i·tor /ˈjanitər/ ▶ **n.** a caretaker of a building.

Jan·u·ar·y /ˈjanyo͞oˌerē/ ▶ **n.** (plural **Januaries**) the first month of the year.

ja·pan /jəˈpan/ ▶ **n.** a black glossy varnish of a type originating in Japan. ▶ **v.** (**japans**, **japanning**, **japanned**) cover with japan.

Jap·a·nese /ˌjapəˈnēz, -ˈnēs/ ▶ **n.** (plural **Japanese**) **1** a person from Japan. **2** the language of Japan. ▶ **adj.** relating to Japan.

jape /jāp/ ▶ **n.** a practical joke.

ja·pon·i·ca /jəˈpänikə/ ▶ **n.** a flowering shrub with bright red flowers and edible fruits.

jar¹ /jär/ ▶ **n.** a cylindrical container made of glass or pottery.

SYNONYMS **pot**, container, crock.

jar² ▶ **v.** (**jars**, **jarring**, **jarred**) **1** send a painful shock through a part of the body. **2** hit something with an unpleasant vibration or jolt. **3** have an unpleasant or strange effect. ▶ **n.** an instance of jarring.

SYNONYMS ▶ **v. 1 jolt**, jerk, shake, vibrate. **2 grate**, set someone's teeth on edge, irritate, annoy, get on someone's nerves. **3 clash**, conflict, contrast, be incompatible, be at variance, be at odds.

■ **jar·ring adj.**

jar·di·nière /ˌjärdnˈi(ə)r, ˌZHärdnˈye(ə)r/ ▶ **n.** an ornamental pot or stand for displaying plants.

jar·gon /ˈjärgən/ ▶ **n.** words or phrases used by a particular group that are difficult for other people to understand.

SYNONYMS **slang**, idiom, terminology, vocabulary, patois, cant, argot, gobbledegook; informal lingo, -speak, -ese.

jas·mine /ˈjazmən/ ▶ **n.** a shrub or climbing plant with sweet-smelling flowers.

jas·per /ˈjaspər/ ▶ **n.** a reddish-brown variety of quartz.

jaun·dice /ˈjôndis/ ▶ **n. 1** a condition in which the skin takes on a yellow color. **2** bitterness or resentment. ■ **jaun·diced adj.**

jaunt /jônt/ ▶ **n.** a short trip or journey taken for pleasure.

SYNONYMS **trip**, outing, excursion, tour, drive, ride, run; informal spin, junket.

jaun·ty /ˈjôntē/ ▶ **adj.** (**jauntier**, **jauntiest**) lively and self-confident. ■ **jaun·ti·ly adv.**

jave·lin /ˈjav(ə)lən/ ▶ **n.** a long spear thrown in a competitive sport or as a weapon.

jaw /jô/ ▶ **n.** each of the upper and lower bony structures forming the framework of the mouth and containing the teeth. ▶ **v.** informal talk at length.

SYNONYMS ▶ **n.** (**jaws**) **mouth**, maw, muzzle, mandibles; informal chops.

□ **jaw-dropping** informal amazing.

jaw·bone /ˈjôˌbōn/ ▶ **n.** the lower jaw, or the lower part of the face.

jay /jā/ ▶ **n.** a noisy bird of the crow family with brightly colored feathers.

jay·walk /ˈjāˌwôk/ ▶ **v.** walk in or across a road unlawfully or without paying proper attention to the traffic. ■ **jay·walk·er n.**

jazz /jaz/ ▶ **n.** a type of music of black American origin that is mainly instrumental, in which the players often improvise. ▶ **v.** (**jazz something up**) make something more lively.

jazz·y /ˈjazē/ ▶ **adj.** (**jazzier**, **jazziest**) **1** in the style of jazz. **2** bright, colorful, and showy.

jeal·ous /ˈjeləs/ ▶ **adj. 1** envious of someone else's achievements or advantages. **2** resentful of someone who you think is a romantic rival. **3** very protective of your rights or possessions: *they kept a jealous eye on their interests.*

SYNONYMS **1 envious**, covetous, resentful, grudging, green with envy. **2 suspicious**, distrustful, possessive, proprietorial, overprotective. **3 protective**, vigilant, watchful, mindful, careful. ANTONYMS trusting.

■ **jeal·ous·ly adv.**

jeal·ous·y /ˈjeləsē/ ▶ **n.** (plural **jealousies**) the state or feeling of being jealous.

SYNONYMS **envy**, resentment, bitterness; humorous the green-eyed monster.

jeans /jēnz/ ▶ **n.** casual trousers made of denim.

Jeep /jēp/ ▶ **n.** trademark a sturdy motor vehicle with four-wheel drive.

jeer /ji(ə)r/ ▶ **v.** (**jeers**, **jeering**, **jeered**) shout rude and mocking remarks at someone. ▶ **n.** a rude and mocking remark.

SYNONYMS ▶ **v. taunt**, mock, ridicule, deride, insult, abuse, heckle, catcall (at), boo (at), whistle at, scoff at, sneer at. ANTONYMS applaud, cheer. ▶ **n. taunt**, sneer, insult, shout, jibe, boo, catcall, derision, teasing, scoffing, abuse, scorn, heckling, catcalling. ANTONYMS applause, cheer.

jeez /jēz/ ▶ **exclam.** a mild expression used to show surprise or annoyance.

Je·ho·vah /jə'hōvə/ ▶ n. a form of the Hebrew name of God used in some translations of the Bible. ▫ **Jehovah's Witness** a member of a Christian sect that denies many traditional Christian doctrines and preaches the Second Coming.

je·june /ji'jo͞on/ ▶ adj. **1** naive and simplistic. **2** dry and uninteresting.

Jek·yll /'jekəl/ ▶ n. (in phrase **a Jekyll and Hyde**) a person displaying alternately good and evil personalities.

jell /jel/ ▶ v. **1** (of jelly or a similar substance) set or become firmer. **2** (of a project or idea) take a definite shape; begin to work well. **3** (of people) relate well to one another.

jell·o /'jelō/ (also trademark **Jell-O**) ▶ n. a fruit-flavored gelatin dessert made from a powder.

jel·ly /'jelē/ ▶ n. (plural **jellies**) **1** a sweet, clear, semisolid spread or preserve made from boiling fruit juice and sugar to a thick consistency. **2** a substance with a similar semisolid consistency. ■ **jel·lied** adj.

jel·ly·fish /'jelē,fisн/ ▶ n. (plural **jellyfish** or **jellyfishes**) a sea creature with a soft jellylike body that has stinging tentacles around the edge.

jen·ny /'jenē/ ▶ n. (plural **jennies**) a female donkey or ass.

jeop·ard·ize /'jepər,dīz/ ▶ v. (**jeopardizes, jeopardizing, jeopardized**) risk harming or destroying something.

> SYNONYMS **threaten**, endanger, imperil, risk, compromise, prejudice. ANTONYMS safeguard.

jeop·ard·y /'jepərdē/ ▶ n. danger of loss, harm, or failure.

> SYNONYMS **danger**, peril, risk.

jer·bo·a /jər'bōə/ ▶ n. a desert rodent with very long hind legs.

jer·e·mi·ad /,jerə'mīəd, -,ad/ ▶ n. a long, mournful complaint; a list of troubles.

jerk /jərk/ ▶ n. **1** a quick, sharp, sudden movement. **2** informal a stupid or obnoxious person. ▶ v. move or raise with a jerk.

> SYNONYMS ▶ n. **1 yank**, tug, pull, wrench. **2 jolt**, lurch, bump, jump, bounce, jounce, shake. ▶ v. **1 yank**, tug, pull, wrench, wrest, drag, snatch. **2 jolt**, lurch, bump, bounce, jounce.

jer·kin /'jərkin/ ▶ n. a sleeveless jacket.

jerk·y[1] /'jərkē/ ▶ adj. (**jerkier, jerkiest**) moving in sudden stops and starts.

> SYNONYMS **convulsive**, spasmodic, fitful, twitchy, shaky. ANTONYMS smooth.

■ **jerk·i·ly** adv.

jerk·y[2] ▶ n. meat that has been cured by being cut into long, thin strips and dried: *beef jerky*.

jer·ry-built /'jerē,bilt/ ▶ adj. badly or quickly built, using cheap materials.

jer·sey /'jərzē/ ▶ n. (plural **jerseys**) **1** a knitted garment with long sleeves. **2** a distinctive shirt worn by people who play certain sports. **3** a soft knitted fabric. **4** (**Jersey**) a breed of light brown dairy cattle.

Je·ru·sa·lem ar·ti·choke /jə'ro͞os(ə)ləm, -'ro͞oz-/ ▶ n. a knobbly root vegetable with white flesh.

jest /jest/ ▶ n. a joke. ▶ v. speak or behave in a joking way.

jest·er /'jestər/ ▶ n. a man who entertained people in a medieval court.

Jes·u·it /'jezнo͞oit, 'jez(y)o͞o-/ ▶ n. a member of the Society of Jesus, a Roman Catholic order. ■ **Jes·u·it·i·cal** /,jezнo͞o'itikəl, ,jez(y)o͞o-/ adj.

jet[1] /jet/ ▶ n. **1** a rapid stream of liquid or gas forced out of a small opening. **2** an aircraft powered by jet engines. ▶ v. (**jets, jetting, jetted**) **1** spurt out in a jet. **2** travel by jet aircraft.

> SYNONYMS ▶ n. **1 stream**, spurt, spray, fountain, rush, spout, gush, surge, burst. **2 nozzle**, head, spout.

▫ **jet engine** an aircraft engine that gives propulsion by sending out a high-speed jet of gas obtained by burning fuel. **jet lag** extreme tiredness felt after a long flight across different time zones. **the jet set** informal wealthy people who frequently travel abroad for pleasure. **Jet Ski** trademark a small vehicle that skims across the surface of water. **jet stream** a narrow band of very strong mainly westerly air currents encircling the earth several miles up.

jet[2] ▶ n. **1** a hard black semiprecious mineral. **2** (also **jet black**) a glossy black color.

je·té /zнə'tā/ ▶ n. Ballet a spring from one foot to the other, with the following leg extended backward while in the air.

jet·sam /'jetsəm/ ▶ n. unwanted material thrown overboard from a ship and washed ashore.

jet·ti·son /'jetisən, -zən/ ▶ v. **1** throw or drop something from an aircraft or ship. **2** abandon or get rid of something.

> SYNONYMS **dump**, drop, ditch, throw out, get rid of, discard, dispose of, scrap.

jet·ty /'jetē/ ▶ n. (plural **jetties**) a landing stage or small pier where boats can be moored.

> SYNONYMS **pier**, landing (stage), quay, wharf, dock, levee, breakwater, mole.

Jew /jo͞o/ ▶ n. a member of the people whose religion is Judaism and who trace their origins to the Hebrew people of ancient Israel. ▫ **Jew's harp** a small musical instrument like a U-shaped harp, held between the teeth and struck with a finger.

jew·el /'jo͞oəl/ ▶ n. **1** a precious stone. **2** (**jewels**) pieces of jewelry. **3** a highly valued person or thing.

> SYNONYMS **1 gem**, gemstone, (precious) stone; informal sparkler, rock. **2 showpiece**, pride (and joy), cream, crème de la crème, jewel in the crown, prize, pick.

▫ **the jewel in the crown** the most valuable part of something. ■ **jew·eled** adj.

jew·el·er /'jo͞o(ə)lər/ ▶ n. a person who makes or sells jewelry.

jew·el·ry /'jo͞o(ə)lrē/ ▶ n. objects such as necklaces, rings, or bracelets worn on the body for decoration.

Jew·ish /'jo͞o-isн/ ▶ adj. having to do with Jews or Judaism. ■ **Jew·ish·ness** n.

Jew·ry /'jo͞orē/ ▶ n. Jews as a group.

Je·ze·bel /'jezə,bel, -bəl/ ▶ n. an immoral woman.

jib /jib/ ▶ n. **1** Sailing a triangular sail in front of the mast. **2** the projecting arm of a crane.

jibe[1] /jīb/ ▶ v. change course by swinging a sail across a following wind.

jibe² ▶ **v.** informal be in accord; agree: *the verdict does not jibe with the medical evidence.*

jif·fy /'jifē/ (or **jiff**) ▶ **n.** informal a moment.

jig /jig/ ▶ **n. 1** a lively dance. **2** a device that holds something in position and guides the tools working on it. ▶ **v.** (**jigs, jigging, jigged**) **1** move up and down with a quick, jerky motion. **2** dance a jig. □ **the jig is up** the deception or crime is revealed or foiled.

jig·ger /'jigər/ ▶ **n. 1** a machine or vehicle with a part that rocks or moves to and fro. **2** a person who dances a jig. **3** a small sail set at the stern of a ship. **4** a measure of alcohol or wine. ▶ **v.** (**jiggers, jiggering, jiggered**) informal **1** tamper with. **2** (**jiggered**) broken or exhausted.

jig·gle /'jigəl/ ▶ **v.** (**jiggles, jiggling, jiggled**) move lightly and quickly from side to side or up and down. ▶ **n.** a quick, light shake. ■ **jig·gly adj.**

jig·saw /'jig,sô/ ▶ **n. 1** (or **jigsaw puzzle**) a picture printed on cardboard or wood and cut into many interlocking shapes that have to be fitted together. **2** a machine saw with a fine blade allowing it to cut curved lines in a sheet of wood, metal, etc.

ji·had /ji'häd/ ▶ **n.** (among Muslims) a war or struggle against unbelievers.

jilt /jilt/ ▶ **v.** abruptly break off a relationship with a lover.

> SYNONYMS **leave**, walk out on, throw over, finish with, break up with, stand up, leave at the altar; informal ditch, dump, drop, run out on, give someone the brush off.

Jim Crow /'jim 'krō/ ▶ **n.** the former practice of segregating black people in the US. ■ **Jim Crow·ism n.**

jim·my /'jimē/ ▶ **n.** (plural **jimmies**) a short crowbar used by a burglar to force open a window or door. ▶ **v.** (**jimmies, jimmying, jimmied**) force open a window or door with a jimmy.

jin·gle /'jiNGgəl/ ▶ **n. 1** a light ringing sound. **2** a short easily remembered slogan, verse, or tune. ▶ **v.** (**jingles, jingling, jingled**) make a jingle.

> SYNONYMS **clink**, chink, tinkle, jangle, ring.

■ **jin·gly adj.**

jin·go·ism /'jiNGgō,izəm/ ▶ **n.** too much pride in your country. ■ **jin·go·is·tic** /,jiNGgō'istik/ **adj.**

jink /jiNGk/ ▶ **v.** change direction suddenly and nimbly. ▶ **n.** a sudden quick change of direction.

jinx /jiNGks/ ▶ **n.** a person or thing that brings bad luck. ▶ **v.** bring bad luck to.

> SYNONYMS ▶ **n. curse**, spell, the evil eye, hex, black magic, voodoo, bad luck. ▶ **v. curse**, cast a spell on, hex.

jit·ter·bug /'jitər,bəg/ ▶ **n.** a fast dance performed to swing music, popular in the 1940s.

jit·ters /'jitərz/ ▶ **n.** informal a feeling of being very nervous. ■ **jit·ter·y adj.**

jive /jīv/ ▶ **n. 1** a style of lively dance popular in the 1940s and 1950s, performed to swing music or rock and roll. **2** (or **jive talk**) a form of slang associated with black jazz musicians. **3** (or **jive talk**) a thing, especially talk, that is deceptive or worthless. ▶ **v.** (**jives, jiving, jived**) **1** dance the jive. **2** talk nonsense.

job /jōb/ ▶ **n. 1** a paid position of regular employment. **2** a task. **3** informal a crime. **4** informal a procedure to improve the appearance of something: *a nose job.* ▶ **v.** (**jobs, jobbing, jobbed**) do casual or occasional work.

> SYNONYMS ▶ **n. 1 position**, post, situation, appointment, occupation, profession, trade, career, work, vocation, calling, métier. **2 task**, piece of work, assignment, mission, project, undertaking, operation, duty, chore, errand, responsibility, charge, role, function; informal department.

□ **job lot** a batch of articles sold or bought at one time. **job-share** (of two part-time employees) share a single full-time job. **on the job** at work.

job·less /'jābləs/ ▶ **adj.** without a paid job.

> SYNONYMS **unemployed**, out of work, without work, laid off. ANTONYMS employed.

■ **job·less·ness n.**

jock /jäk/ ▶ **n.** informal **1** an athlete. **2** short for JOCKSTRAP.

jock·ey /'jäkē/ ▶ **n.** (plural **jockeys**) a professional rider in horse races. ▶ **v.** (**jockeys, jockeying, jockeyed**) struggle to gain or achieve something: *two men will be jockeying for the top job.*

jock·strap /'jäk,strap/ ▶ **n.** a support or protection for the male genitals.

jo·cose /jō'kōs/ ▶ **adj.** formal playful or humorous.

joc·u·lar /'jäkyələr/ ▶ **adj.** humorous. ■ **joc·u·lar·i·ty** /,jäkyə'laritē/ **n. joc·u·lar·ly adv.**

joc·und /'jäkənd, 'jō-/ ▶ **adj.** formal cheerful and lighthearted.

jodh·purs /'jädpərz/ ▶ **pl.n.** trousers worn for horse riding that are close-fitting below the knee.

Joe Blow /jō/ ▶ **n.** informal a name for a hypothetical average man.

jog /jäg/ ▶ **v.** (**jogs, jogging, jogged**) **1** run at a steady, gentle pace. **2** knock or nudge slightly. **3** (of a horse) move at a slow trot. ▶ **n. 1** a period of jogging. **2** a gentle running pace. **3** a slight knock or nudge.

> SYNONYMS ▶ **v. 1 run**, trot, lope. **2 nudge**, prod, poke, push, bump, jar.

□ **jog someone's memory** make someone remember something. ■ **jog·ger n.**

jog·gle /'jägəl/ ▶ **v.** (**joggles, joggling, joggled**) move with repeated small jerks.

john /jän/ ▶ **n.** informal a toilet.

John Bull ▶ **n.** a character representing England or the typical Englishman.

John Doe ▶ **n.** an anonymous male party in a legal action or an unidentified man.

john·ny-come-late·ly ▶ **n.** informal a newcomer or late starter.

joie de vi·vre /,zHwä də 'vēvrə/ ▶ **n.** lively and cheerful enjoyment of life.

join /join/ ▶ **v. 1** connect things together, or become connected. **2** come together to form a whole. **3** become a member or employee of. **4** (also **join in**) take part in an activity. **5** (**join up**) become a member of the armed forces. **6** do something or go somewhere with someone else. ▶ **n.** a place where two or more things are joined.

> SYNONYMS ▶ **v. 1** *the two parts are joined with clay* **connect**, unite, couple, fix, affix, attach, fasten, stick, glue, fuse, weld, amalgamate, bond, link, yoke, merge, secure, make fast, tie, bind. **2** *the path joins a major road* **meet**, touch, reach. **3 help in**, participate in, get involved in, contribute to, enlist in, join up, sign up, band together, get together, team up. ANTONYMS separate, leave.

□ **join forces** combine efforts.

join·er /ˈjoinər/ ▶ **n.** **1** a person who puts together the wooden parts of a building. **2** informal a person who readily joins groups.

join·er·y /ˈjoinərē/ ▶ **n.** **1** the wooden parts of a building. **2** the work of a joiner.

joint /joint/ ▶ **n.** **1** a point at which parts are joined. **2** a structure in a body that joins two bones. **3** the part of a plant stem from which a leaf or branch grows. **4** informal a particular kind of place: *a burger joint.* ▶ **adj.** **1** shared, held, or made by two or more people. **2** sharing in an achievement or activity: *a joint winner.* ▶ **v.** cut the body of an animal into joints.

SYNONYMS ▶ **n.** **join**, junction, intersection, link, connection, weld, seam, coupling. ▶ **adj.** **common**, shared, communal, collective, mutual, cooperative, collaborative, concerted, combined, united, allied. ANTONYMS separate.

□ **out of joint** **1** (of a joint of the body) out of position. **2** in a state of disorder. ■ **joint·ed** **adj.**

joint·ly /ˈjointlē/ ▶ **adv.** together; in collaboration: *the two companies will jointly develop business software.*

SYNONYMS **together**, in partnership, in cooperation, cooperatively, in conjunction, in combination, mutually, in league.

joist /joist/ ▶ **n.** a length of timber or steel supporting the floor or ceiling of a building.

jo·jo·ba /hōˈhōbə/ ▶ **n.** an oil extracted from the seeds of a shrub native to the southwestern US.

joke /jōk/ ▶ **n.** **1** a thing that someone says to cause amusement or laughter. **2** a trick played for fun. **3** informal a person or thing that is ridiculously inadequate: *public transport is a joke.* ▶ **v.** (**jokes**, **joking**, **joked**) make jokes.

SYNONYMS ▶ **n.** **1** **witticism**, jest, quip, pun; informal gag, wisecrack, crack, funny, one-liner. **2** **trick**, prank, stunt, hoax, jape; informal leg-pulling, spoof. **3** **laughingstock**, object of ridicule, butt (of someone's joke), stooge. **4** **farce**, travesty. ▶ **v.** **tell jokes**, jest, banter, quip; informal wisecrack, josh.

■ **jok·ey** (or **joky**) **adj.**

jok·er /ˈjōkər/ ▶ **n.** **1** a person who likes making or playing jokes. **2** a playing card with the figure of a jester, used as a wild card. **3** informal a foolish or incompetent person.

SYNONYMS **comedian**, comedienne, comic, humorist, wit, jester, prankster, practical joker, clown.

□ **the joker in the deck** an unpredictable person or factor.

jol·li·fi·ca·tion /ˌjäləfiˈkāsʜən/ ▶ **n.** time spent having fun.

jol·li·ty /ˈjälitē/ ▶ **n.** **1** lively and cheerful activity. **2** the quality of being cheerful.

jol·ly /ˈjälē/ ▶ **adj.** (**jollier**, **jolliest**) **1** happy and cheerful. **2** lively and entertaining. ▶ **v.** (**jollies**, **jollying**, **jollied**) (**jolly someone along**) informal encourage someone in a friendly way: *he jollied her along.*

SYNONYMS ▶ **adj.** **cheerful**, happy, cheery, good-humored, jovial, merry, sunny, joyful, lighthearted, in high spirits, buoyant, bubbly, genial; informal chipper, chirpy, perky; literary blithe. ANTONYMS miserable.

□ **Jolly Roger** a pirate's flag with a white skull and crossbones on a black background.

jolt /jōlt/ ▶ **v.** **1** push or shake abruptly and roughly. **2** shock someone into taking action. ▶ **n.** **1** an act of jolting. **2** a shock.

SYNONYMS ▶ **v.** **1** **push**, jar, bump, knock, bang, shake, jog. **2** **bump**, bounce, jerk, rattle, lurch, shudder, jounce. **3** **startle**, surprise, shock, stun, shake; informal rock, knock sideways. ▶ **n.** **bump**, bounce, shake, jerk, lurch, jounce.

josh /jäsʜ/ ▶ **v.** informal tease playfully.

jos·tle /ˈjäsəl/ ▶ **v.** (**jostles**, **jostling**, **jostled**) **1** push or bump against someone roughly. **2** (**jostle for**) struggle for.

SYNONYMS **1** **push**, shove, elbow, barge into, bang into, bump against, knock against. **2** *photographers jostled for position* **struggle**, vie, jockey, scramble, fight.

jot /jät/ ▶ **v.** (**jots**, **jotting**, **jotted**) write something quickly. ▶ **n.** a very small amount: *it made not a jot of difference.*

jot·ting /ˈjätiɴɢ/ ▶ **n.** a brief note.

joule /jo͞ol/ ▶ **n.** a unit of work or energy.

jounce /jouns/ ▶ **v.** (**jounces**, **jouncing**, **jounced**) jolt or bounce.

jour·nal /ˈjərnl/ ▶ **n.** **1** a newspaper or magazine dealing with a particular subject. **2** a diary or daily record.

SYNONYMS **1** **periodical**, magazine, gazette, review, newsletter, news-sheet, bulletin, newspaper, paper, daily, weekly, monthly, quarterly. **2** **diary**, log, logbook, daybook, weblog, blog, chronicle, history, yearbook.

jour·nal·ese /ˌjərnlˈēz/ ▶ **n.** informal a bad writing style thought to be typical of that used in newspapers.

jour·nal·ism /ˈjərnlˌizəm/ ▶ **n.** the activity or profession of being a journalist.

jour·nal·ist /ˈjərnl-ist/ ▶ **n.** a person who writes for newspapers or magazines or prepares news to be broadcast.

SYNONYMS **reporter**, correspondent, columnist, newsman, newswoman; informal news hound, hack, stringer.

■ **jour·nal·is·tic** /ˌjərnlˈistik/ **adj.**

jour·ney /ˈjərnē/ ▶ **n.** (plural **journeys**) an act of traveling from one place to another. ▶ **v.** (**journeys**, **journeying**, **journeyed**) travel.

SYNONYMS ▶ **n.** **trip**, expedition, tour, trek, travels, voyage, cruise, ride, drive, crossing, passage, flight, odyssey, pilgrimage, safari, globetrotting; old use peregrinations. ▶ **v.** **travel**, go, voyage, sail, cruise, fly, hike, trek, ride, drive, make your way.

jour·ney·man /ˈjərnēmən/ ▶ **n.** (plural **journeymen**) **1** a trained worker who is employed by another. **2** a worker who is reliable but not outstanding.

joust /joust/ ▶ **v.** **1** (of medieval knights) fight each other with lances while on horseback. **2** compete for superiority. ▶ **n.** a jousting contest.

Jove /jōv/ ▶ **n.** (in phrase **by Jove**) dated used for emphasis or to indicate surprise.

jo·vi·al /ˈjōvēəl/ ▶ **adj.** cheerful and friendly.

SYNONYMS **cheerful**, jolly, happy, cheery, jocular, good-humored, convivial, genial, good-natured, affable, outgoing, smiling, merry, sunny; informal blithe. ANTONYMS miserable.

■ **jo·vi·al·i·ty** /ˌjōvēˈalitē/ n. **jo·vi·al·ly** adv.

jowl /joul/ ▶ n. the lower part of a person's or animal's cheek. ■ **jowl·y** adj.

joy /joi/ ▶ n. **1** great pleasure and happiness. **2** something that brings joy.

SYNONYMS **delight**, pleasure, jubilation, triumph, exultation, rejoicing, happiness, elation, euphoria, bliss, ecstasy, rapture. ANTONYMS misery.

■ **joy·less** adj.

joy·ful /ˈjoifəl/ ▶ adj. feeling or causing joy.

SYNONYMS **1 cheerful**, happy, jolly, merry, sunny, joyous, cheery, smiling, jovial, mirthful, gleeful, pleased, delighted, thrilled, jubilant, elated, ecstatic; informal over the moon, on cloud nine. **2** *joyful news* **pleasing**, happy, good, cheering, gladdening, welcome, gratifying, heartwarming. ANTONYMS sad.

■ **joy·ful·ly** adv.

joy·ous /ˈjoiəs/ ▶ adj. full of happiness and joy. ■ **joy·ous·ly** adv.

joy·rid·ing /ˈjoiˌrīdiNG/ ▶ n. informal the crime of stealing a vehicle and driving it in a fast and dangerous way. ■ **joy·ride** n. **joy·rid·er** n.

joy·stick /ˈjoiˌstik/ ▶ n. informal **1** the rod used for controlling an aircraft. **2** a lever for controlling the movement of an image on a computer screen, used especially for playing games.

JP ▶ abbr. Justice of the Peace.

JPEG /ˈjāˌpeg/ ▶ n. Computing a format for compressing images.

Jr. ▶ abbr. junior (in names): *George Smith, Jr.*

ju·bi·lant /ˈjo͞obələnt/ ▶ adj. happy and triumphant.

SYNONYMS **overjoyed**, exultant, triumphant, joyful, elated, thrilled, gleeful, euphoric, ecstatic; informal over the moon, on cloud nine. ANTONYMS despondent.

■ **ju·bi·lant·ly** adv.

ju·bi·la·tion /ˌjo͞obəˈlāSHən/ ▶ n. a feeling of great happiness and triumph.

ju·bi·lee /ˈjo͞obəˌlē, jo͞obəˈlē/ ▶ n. a special anniversary, especially one celebrating twenty-five or fifty years of a reign or activity: *celebrating the diamond jubilee of her reign.*

SYNONYMS **anniversary**, commemoration, celebration, festival.

Ju·da·ism /ˈjo͞odēˌizəm, -dā-/ ▶ n. **1** the religion of the Jews, based on the Old Testament and the Talmud. **2** Jews as a group. ■ **Ju·da·ic** /jo͞oˈdāik/ adj.

Ju·das /ˈjo͞odəs/ ▶ n. a person who betrays a friend.

judge /jəj/ ▶ n. **1** a public official who has the authority to decide cases in a court of law. **2** a person who decides the results of a competition. **3** a person who is qualified to give an opinion. ▶ v. (**judges**, **judging**, **judged**) **1** form an opinion about something. **2** give a verdict on a case or person in a court of law. **3** decide the results of a competition.

SYNONYMS ▶ n. **1 justice**, jurist, justice of the peace, magistrate, sheriff. **2 adjudicator**, referee, umpire, arbiter, assessor, examiner, moderator, scrutineer; informal ref, ump. ▶ v. **1 conclude**, decide, consider, believe, think, deduce, infer, gauge, estimate, guess, surmise, conjecture, regard as, rate as; informal reckon, figure. **2** *she was judged innocent* **pronounce**, decree, rule, find. **3 adjudicate**, arbitrate, moderate, referee, umpire. **4 assess**, evaluate, appraise, examine, review.

judg·ment /ˈjəjmənt/ (or **judgement**) ▶ n. **1** the ability to make good decisions or form sensible opinions. **2** an opinion or conclusion. **3** a decision of a court of law or judge.

SYNONYMS **1 sense**, discernment, perception, discrimination, understanding, powers of reasoning, reason, logic. **2 opinion**, view, estimate, appraisal, conclusion, diagnosis, assessment, impression, conviction, perception, thinking. **3** *a court judgment* **verdict**, decision, adjudication, ruling, pronouncement, decree, finding, sentence.

□ **against your better judgment** in conflict with what you feel to be wise. **Judgment Day** the time of the Last Judgment.

judg·men·tal /jəjˈmentl/ (or **judgemental**) ▶ adj. **1** having to do with the use of judgment. **2** too critical of other people.

SYNONYMS **critical**, censorious, disapproving, disparaging, deprecating, negative, overcritical.

ju·di·ca·ture /ˈjo͞odikəˌCHo͝or, -ˌkāCHər/ ▶ n. **1** the organization and putting into practice of justice. **2** (**the judicature**) judges as a group.

ju·di·cial /jo͞oˈdiSHəl/ ▶ adj. having to do with a court of law or judge. ■ **ju·di·cial·ly** adv.

ju·di·ci·ar·y /jo͞oˈdiSHēˌerē, -ˈdiSHərē/ ▶ n. (plural **judiciaries**) (**the judiciary**) judges as a group.

ju·di·cious /jo͞oˈdiSHəs/ ▶ adj. having or done with good judgment.

SYNONYMS **wise**, sensible, prudent, shrewd, astute, canny, discerning, sagacious, strategic, politic, expedient. ANTONYMS ill-advised.

■ **ju·di·cious·ly** adv.

ju·do /ˈjo͞odō/ ▶ n. a kind of unarmed combat performed as a sport.

jug /jəg/ ▶ n. a cylindrical container with a handle and a lip, for holding and pouring liquids.

jug·ger·naut /ˈjəgərˌnôt/ ▶ n. a huge, powerful, and overwhelming force or institution.

jug·gle /ˈjəgəl/ ▶ v. (**juggles**, **juggling**, **juggled**) **1** continuously toss and catch a number of objects so as to keep at least one in the air at any time. **2** do several things at the same time. **3** present facts or figures in a way that makes them seem good. ▶ n. an act of juggling. ■ **jug·gler** n.

jug·u·lar /ˈjəgyələr/ (or **jugular vein**) ▶ n. any of several large veins in the neck, carrying blood from the head.

juice /jo͞os/ ▶ n. **1** the liquid present in fruit and vegetables. **2** a drink made from this liquid. **3** (**juices**) fluid produced by the stomach. **4** (**juices**) liquid coming from food during cooking. **5** informal electrical energy. **6** informal gas. **7** (**juices**) informal creative abilities. ▶ v. (**juices**, **juicing**, **juiced**) extract the juice from.

SYNONYMS ▶ n. **liquid**, fluid, sap, extract, concentrate, essence.

juic·er /ˈjo͞osər/ ▶ n. an appliance for extracting juice from fruit and vegetables.

juic·y /ˈjo͞osē/ ▸ **adj.** (**juicier**, **juiciest**) **1** full of juice. **2** informal (of gossip) very interesting: *juicy details.* **3** informal profitable.

SYNONYMS **1 succulent**, tender, moist, ripe. **2 sensational**, fascinating, intriguing, exciting, graphic, lurid. ANTONYMS dry.

ju·jit·su /jo͞oˈjitso͞o/ (or **ju-jitsu**) ▸ **n.** a Japanese system of unarmed combat.

juke·box /ˈjo͞okˌbäks/ ▸ **n.** a machine that plays a selected musical recording when a coin is inserted.

ju·lep /ˈjo͞oləp/ ▸ **n. 1** a sweet drink made from sugar syrup. **2** (or **mint julep**) a drink consisting of bourbon, crushed ice, sugar, and fresh mint.

ju·li·enne /ˌjo͞olēˈen/ ▸ **n.** a portion of food cut into short, thin strips.

Ju·ly /jo͝oˈlī/ ▸ **n.** (plural **Julys**) the seventh month of the year.

jum·ble /ˈjəmbəl/ ▸ **n.** an untidy collection of things. ▸ **v.** (**jumbles**, **jumbling**, **jumbled**) mix things up in a confused way.

SYNONYMS ▸ **n. heap**, muddle, mess, tangle, confusion, disarray, chaos, hodgepodge; informal shambles. ▸ **v. mix up**, muddle (up), disorganize, disorder, tangle, confuse.

jum·bo /ˈjəmbō/ informal ▸ **n.** (plural **jumbos**) **1** a very large person or thing. **2** (also **jumbo jet**) a very large airliner. ▸ **adj.** very large.

jump /jəmp/ ▸ **v. 1** push yourself off the ground using the muscles in your legs and feet. **2** move over something by jumping. **3** (of prices or figures) rise suddenly and by a large amount. **4** make a sudden involuntary movement in surprise. **5** (**jump at** or **on**) accept something eagerly. **6** (often **jump on**) informal attack someone suddenly. **7** pass abruptly from one subject or state to another. **8** (**be jumping**) informal (of a place) be very lively. ▸ **n. 1** an act of jumping. **2** a large or sudden increase. **3** an obstacle to be jumped by a horse.

SYNONYMS ▸ **v. 1 leap**, spring, bound, vault, hop, skip, caper, dance, prance. **2** *pretax profits jumped* **rise**, go up, shoot up, soar, surge, climb, increase; informal skyrocket. **3** *the noise made her jump* **start**, jolt, flinch, recoil, shudder. ▸ **n. 1 leap**, spring, bound, hop, skip. **2 rise**, leap, increase, upsurge, upswing; informal hike. **3 start**, jerk, spasm, shudder.

□ **get** (or **have**) **the jump on someone** informal get (or have) an advantage over someone as a result of your prompt action. **jump down someone's throat** informal respond in a sudden and angry way. **jump out of your skin** informal be startled. **jump jet** a jet aircraft that can take off and land without a runway. **jump rope** a length of rope used for jumping that is swung over the head and under the feet. **jump ship** (of a sailor) leave a ship without permission. **jump shot** Basketball a shot made while jumping. **jump-start** start a car with jumper cables or by a sudden release of the clutch while it is being pushed. **jump through hoops** be made to go through a complicated procedure. **one jump ahead** one stage ahead of a rival.

jump·er[1] /ˈjəmpər/ ▸ **n.** a collarless, sleeveless dress, typically worn over a blouse.

jump·er[2] ▸ **n. 1** a person or animal that jumps. **2** Basketball a jump shot. □ **jumper cables** a pair of cables used to recharge a battery in a vehicle by connecting it to the battery of a vehicle whose engine is running.

jump·suit /ˈjəm(p)ˌso͞ot/ ▸ **n.** a one-piece garment incorporating trousers and a sleeved top.

jump·y /ˈjəmpē/ ▸ **adj.** (**jumpier**, **jumpiest**) informal **1** anxious and uneasy. **2** stopping and starting abruptly.

SYNONYMS **nervous**, on edge, edgy, tense, anxious, restless, fidgety, keyed up, overwrought; informal jittery, uptight, spooked, hyper, antsy. ANTONYMS calm.

junc·tion /ˈjəNGkSHən/ ▸ **n. 1** a point where things meet or are joined. **2** a place where roads or railroad lines meet.

SYNONYMS **crossroads**, intersection, interchange, turn, turnoff, cloverleaf, exit.

junc·ture /ˈjəNGkCHər/ ▸ **n. 1** a particular point in time. **2** a place where things join.

June /jo͞on/ ▸ **n.** the sixth month of the year.

jun·gle /ˈjəNGgəl/ ▸ **n. 1** an area of land with thick forest and tangled vegetation. **2** a very bewildering or competitive situation. **3** a style of dance music with very fast electronic drum tracks.

jun·ior /ˈjo͞onyər/ ▸ **adj. 1** having to do with young or younger people. **2** (after a name) referring to the younger of two with the same name in a family. **3** low or lower in status. **4** having to do with a student in the third year of high school or college. ▸ **n. 1** a person who is a stated number of years younger than someone else: *he's five years her junior.* **2** a student in the third year of high school or college. **3** a person with low status.

SYNONYMS ▸ **adj. younger**, minor, subordinate, lower, lesser, low-ranking, inferior, secondary. ANTONYMS senior, older.

□ **junior college** a two-year college. **junior high school** a school in between an elementary school and a high school.

ju·ni·per /ˈjo͞onəpər/ ▸ **n.** an evergreen shrub with sweet-smelling berries.

junk[1] /jəNGk/ ▸ **n.** informal useless or worthless articles. ▸ **v.** get rid of something unwanted.

SYNONYMS ▸ **n. rubbish**, clutter, odds and ends, bric-a-brac, refuse, trash, litter, scrap, waste, debris. ▸ **v. throw away/out**, discard, get rid of, dispose of, scrap, jettison; informal chuck, dump, ditch, trash, deep-six.

□ **junk food** unhealthy food. **junk mail** unwanted advertising material sent to you in the mail.

junk[2] ▸ **n.** a flat-bottomed sailboat used in China and the East Indies.

jun·ket /ˈjəNGkit/ ▸ **n. 1** informal a trip or excursion made by government officials and paid for using public funds. **2** a dish of sweetened curds of milk.

junk·ie /ˈjəNGkē/ (or **junky**) ▸ **n.** informal a drug addict.

junk·yard /ˈjəNGkˌyärd/ ▸ **n.** a place where scrap is collected before being discarded, reused, or recycled.

jun·ta /ˈho͝ontə, ˈjəntə/ ▸ **n.** a group ruling a country after taking power by force.

Ju·pi·ter /ˈjo͞opitər/ ▸ **n.** the largest planet in the solar system.

Ju·ras·sic /jəˈrasik/ ▸ **adj.** Geology having to do with the second period of the Mesozoic era (about 208 to 146 million years ago), a time when large reptiles flourished and the first birds appeared.

ju·ris·dic·tion /ˌjo͝orisˈdikSHən/ ▸ **n. 1** the official power to make legal decisions. **2** the area over which the legal authority of a court, police force, or other institution extends.

ju·ris·pru·dence /jo͝oris'pro͞odns/ ▶ **n.** the study of law.

ju·rist /'jo͝orist/ ▶ **n.** an expert in law.

ju·ror /'jo͝orər, -ôr/ ▶ **n.** a member of a jury.

ju·ry /'jo͝orē/ ▶ **n.** (plural **juries**) **1** a group of people who are required to attend a legal case and come to a verdict based on the evidence given in court. **2** a group of people judging a competition. □ **the jury is out** a decision has not yet been reached. **jury-rigged** (of a ship) having makeshift rigging.

just /jəst/ ▶ **adj. 1** right and fair. **2** deserved: *we all get our just deserts.* **3** (of an opinion) based on good evidence or reasons. ▶ **adv. 1** exactly. **2** exactly or nearly at that moment. **3** very recently. **4** barely. **5** only.

> SYNONYMS ▶ **adj. 1** *a just society* **fair**, fair-minded, equitable, evenhanded, impartial, unbiased, objective, neutral, disinterested, unprejudiced, honorable, upright, decent, principled. **2** *a just reward* **deserved**, well-deserved, well-earned, merited, rightful, due, proper, fitting, appropriate, defensible, justified, justifiable. ANTONYMS unfair. ▶ **adv. 1 exactly**, precisely, absolutely, completely, totally, entirely, perfectly, utterly, thoroughly; informal dead. **2 narrowly**, only just, by a hair's breadth, by the skin of your teeth, barely, scarcely, hardly; informal by a whisker.

□ **just in case** as a precaution. **just so 1** arranged or done very carefully. **2** formal expressing agreement. ■ **just·ly adv.**

jus·tice /'jəstis/ ▶ **n. 1** just behavior or treatment. **2** the quality of being fair and reasonable. **3** a judge or magistrate.

> SYNONYMS **1 fairness**, justness, fair play, fair-mindedness, equity, right, rightness, even-handedness, honesty, morality. **2** *the justice of his case* **validity**, justification, soundness, well-foundedness, legitimacy. **3 judge**, jurist, magistrate, justice of the peace, sheriff.

□ **do yourself justice** perform as well as you are able. **do someone/something justice** treat someone or something with due fairness. **justice of the peace** a magistrate appointed to hear minor cases, perform marriages, etc., in a town or district.

jus·ti·fi·a·ble /'jəstə,fīəbəl, ,jəstə'fī-/ ▶ **adj.** able to be shown to be right or reasonable.

> SYNONYMS **valid**, legitimate, warranted, well-founded, justified, just, reasonable, tenable, defensible, sound, warrantable. ANTONYMS unjustifiable, unwarranted.

■ **jus·ti·fi·a·bly adv.**

jus·ti·fi·ca·tion /,jəstəfi'kāshən/ ▶ **n. 1** the action of justifying something. **2** good reason for something that exists or has been done: *there's no justification for the job losses.*

> SYNONYMS **grounds**, reason, basis, rationale, premise, vindication, explanation, defense, argument, case.

jus·ti·fy /'jəstə,fī/ ▶ **v.** (**justifies**, **justifying**, **justified**) **1** prove something to be right or reasonable. **2** be a good reason for. **3** adjust lines of type so that they form straight edges at both sides.

> SYNONYMS **1 give grounds for**, give reasons for, explain, account for, defend, vindicate, excuse, exonerate. **2 warrant**, be good reason for.

jut /jət/ ▶ **v.** (**juts**, **jutting**, **jutted**) extend out beyond the main body or line of something.

> SYNONYMS **stick out**, project, protrude, bulge out, overhang, beetle.

jute /jo͞ot/ ▶ **n.** rough fiber made from the stems of a tropical plant, used for making rope or woven into sacking.

ju·ve·nile /'jo͞ovə,nīl, -vənl/ ▶ **adj. 1** having to do with young people, birds, or animals. **2** childish. ▶ **n. 1** a young person, bird, or animal. **2** Law a person below the age at which they have adult status in law (18 in most countries).

> SYNONYMS ▶ **adj. 1 young**, teenage, adolescent, junior. **2 childish**, immature, puerile, infantile, babyish. ANTONYMS adult, mature. ▶ **n. child**, youngster, teenager, adolescent, minor, junior; informal kid. ANTONYMS adult.

□ **juvenile delinquent** a young person who regularly commits crimes.

ju·ve·nil·i·a /,jo͞ovə'nilēə/ ▶ **pl.n.** works produced by an author or artist when they were young.

jux·ta·pose /'jəkstə,pōz, ,jəkstə'pōz/ ▶ **v.** (**juxtaposes**, **juxtaposing**, **juxtaposed**) place two things close together. ■ **jux·ta·po·si·tion** /,jəkstəpə'zishən/ **n.**

Reference Section

1.
US Presidents

	Name	Life dates	Party	Term in office
1.	George Washington	1732–1799	Federalist	1789–1797
2.	John Adams	1735–1826	Federalist	1797–1801
3.	Thomas Jefferson	1743–1826	Democratic-Republican	1801–1809
4.	James Madison	1751–1836	Democratic-Republican	1809–1817
5.	James Monroe	1758–1831	Democratic-Republican	1817–1825
6.	John Quincy Adams	1767–1848	Democratic-Republican	1825–1829
7.	Andrew Jackson	1767–1845	Democrat	1829–1837
8.	Martin Van Buren	1782–1862	Democrat	1837–1841
9.	William Henry Harrison	1773–1841	Whig	1841
10.	John Tyler	1790–1862	Whig	1841–1845
11.	James Knox Polk	1795–1849	Democrat	1845–1849
12.	Zachary Taylor	1784–1850	Whig	1849–1850
13.	Millard Fillmore	1800–1874	Whig	1850–1853
14.	Franklin Pierce	1804–1869	Democrat	1853–1857
15.	James Buchanan	1791–1868	Democrat	1857–1861
16.	Abraham Lincoln	1809–1865	Republican	1861–1865
17.	Andrew Johnson	1808–1875	Democrat	1865–1869
18.	Ulysses Simpson Grant	1822–1885	Republican	1869–1877
19.	Rutherford Birchard Hayes	1822–1893	Republican	1877–1881
20.	James Abram Garfield	1831–1881	Republican	1881
21.	Chester Alan Arthur	1830–1886	Republican	1881–1885
22.	(Stephen) Grover Cleveland	1837–1908	Democrat	1885–1889
23.	Benjamin Harrison	1833–1901	Republican	1889–1893
24.	(Stephen) Grover Cleveland	1837–1908	Democrat	1893–1897
25.	William McKinley	1843–1901	Republican	1897–1901
26.	Theodore Roosevelt	1858–1919	Republican	1901–1909
27.	William Howard Taft	1857–1930	Republican	1909–1913
28.	(Thomas) Woodrow Wilson	1856–1924	Democrat	1913–1921
29.	Warren Gamaliel Harding	1865–1923	Republican	1921–1923
30.	(John) Calvin Coolidge	1872–1933	Republican	1923–1929
31.	Herbert Clark Hoover	1874–1964	Republican	1929–1933
32.	Franklin Delano Roosevelt	1882–1945	Democrat	1933–1945
33.	Harry S Truman	1884–1972	Democrat	1945–1953
34.	Dwight David Eisenhower	1890–1969	Republican	1953–1961
35.	John Fitzgerald Kennedy	1917–1963	Democrat	1961–1963
36.	Lyndon Baines Johnson	1908–1973	Democrat	1963–1969
37.	Richard Milhous Nixon	1913–1994	Republican	1969–1974

	Name	Life dates	Party	Term in office
38.	Gerald Rudolph Ford	1913–2006	Republican	1974–1977
39.	James Earl Carter, Jr.	1924–	Democrat	1977–1981
40.	Ronald Wilson Reagan	1911–2004	Republican	1981–1989
41.	George Herbert Walker Bush	1924–	Republican	1989–1993
42.	William Jefferson Clinton	1946–	Democrat	1993–2001
43.	George Walker Bush	1946–	Republican	2001–2009
44.	Barack Hussein Obama	1961–	Democrat	2009–

2.
US States

State	Abbreviations		Capital
	traditional	postal	
Alabama	Ala.	AL	Montgomery
Alaska	Alas.	AK	Juneau
Arizona	Ariz.	AZ	Phoenix
Arkansas	Ark.	AR	Little Rock
California	Calif.	CA	Sacramento
Colorado	Colo.	CO	Denver
Connecticut	Conn.	CT	Hartford
Delaware	Del.	DE	Dover
Florida	Fla.	FL	Tallahassee
Georgia	Ga.	GA	Atlanta
Hawaii	—	HI	Honolulu
Idaho	Ida.	ID	Boise
Illinois	Ill.	IL	Springfield
Indiana	Ind.	IN	Indianapolis
Iowa	Ia.	IA	Des Moines
Kansas	Kan.	KS	Topeka
Kentucky	Ky.	KY	Frankfort
Louisiana	La.	LA	Baton Rouge
Maine	Me.	ME	Augusta
Maryland	Md.	MD	Annapolis
Massachusetts	Mass.	MA	Boston
Michigan	Mich.	MI	Lansing
Minnesota	Minn.	MN	St. Paul
Mississippi	Miss.	MS	Jackson
Missouri	Mo.	MO	Jefferson City
Montana	Mont.	MT	Helena
Nebraska	Nebr.	NE	Lincoln
Nevada	Nev.	NV	Carson City
New Hampshire	N.H.	NH	Concord
New Jersey	N.J.	NJ	Trenton
New Mexico	N. Mex.	NM	Santa Fe
New York	N.Y.	NY	Albany
North Carolina	N.C.	NC	Raleigh
North Dakota	N. Dak.	ND	Bismarck
Ohio	—	OH	Columbus
Oklahoma	Okla.	OK	Oklahoma City

State	Abbreviations		Capital
	traditional	postal	
Oregon	Ore.	OR	Salem
Pennsylvania	Pa.	PA	Harrisburg
Rhode Island	R.I.	RI	Providence
South Carolina	S.C.	SC	Columbia
South Dakota	S. Dak.	SD	Pierre
Tennessee	Tenn.	TN	Nashville
Texas	Tex.	TX	Austin
Utah	—	UT	Salt Lake City
Vermont	Vt.	VT	Montpelier
Virginia	Va.	VA	Richmond
Washington	Wash.	WA	Olympia
West Virginia	W. Va.	WV	Charleston
Wisconsin	Wis.	WI	Madison
Wyoming	Wyo.	WY	Cheyenne

3. Countries of the World

Country	Capital	Continent/Area	Nationality
Afghanistan	Kabul	Asia	Afghan
Albania	Tirana	Europe	Albanian
Algeria	Algiers	Africa	Algerian
Andorra	Andorra la Vella	Europe	Andorran
Angola	Luanda	Africa	Angolan
Antigua and Barbuda	St. John's	North America	Antiguan, Barbudan
Argentina	Buenos Aires	South America	Argentinian, Argentine
Armenia	Yerevan	Europe	Armenian
Australia	Canberra	Australia	Australian
Austria	Vienna	Europe	Austrian
Azerbaijan	Baku	Europe	Azerbaijani
Bahamas,The	Nassau	North America	Bahamian
Bahrain	Manama	Asia	Bahraini
Bangladesh	Dhaka	Asia	Bangladeshi
Barbados	Bridgetown	North America	Barbadian
Belarus	Minsk	Europe	Belorussian, Belarussian, *or* Belarusian
Belgium	Brussels	Europe	Belgian
Belize	Belmopan	North America	Belizean
Benin	Porto Novo	Africa	Beninese
Bhutan	Thimphu	Asia	Bhutanese
Bolivia	La Paz; Sucre	South America	Bolivian
Bosnia and Herzegovina	Sarajevo	Europe	Bosnian, Herzegovinian
Botswana	Gaborone	Africa	Motswana, *sing.*, Batswana, *pl.*
Brazil	Brasilia	South America	Brazilian
Brunei	Bandar Seri Begawan	Asia	Bruneian
Bulgaria	Sofia	Europe	Bulgarian
Burkina Faso	Ouagadougou	Africa	Burkinese
Burma (Myanmar)	Rangoon (Yangon); Nay Pyi Taw	Asia	Burmese
Burundi	Bujumbura	Africa	Burundian, *n.*; Burundi, *adj.*

Country	Capital	Continent/Area	Nationality
Cambodia	Phnom Penh	Asia	Cambodian
Cameroon	Yaoundé	Africa	Cameroonian
Canada	Ottawa	North America	Canadian
Cape Verde	Praia	Africa	Cape Verdean
Central African Republic	Bangui	Africa	Central African
Chad	N'Djamena	Africa	Chadian
Chile	Santiago	South America	Chilean
China	Beijing	Asia	Chinese
Colombia	Bogotá	South America	Colombian
Comoros	Moroni	Africa	Comoran
Congo, Democratic Republic of the (*formerly* Zaire)	Kinshasa	Africa	Congolese
Congo, Republic of the	Brazzaville	Africa	Congolese, *n.*; Congolese *or* Congo, *adj.*
Costa Rica	San José	North America	Costa Rican
Côte d'Ivoire	Yamoussoukro	Africa	Ivorian
Croatia	Zagreb	Europe	Croat, *n.*; Croatian, *adj.*
Cuba	Havana	North America	Cuban
Cyprus	Nicosia	Europe	Cypriot
Czech Republic	Prague	Europe	Czech
Denmark	Copenhagen	Europe	Dane, *n.*; Danish, *adj.*
Djibouti	Djibouti	Africa	Djiboutian
Dominica	Roseau	North America	Dominican
Dominican Republic	Santo Domingo	North America	Dominican
Ecuador	Quito	South America	Ecuadorean
Egypt	Cairo	Africa	Egyptian
El Salvador	San Salvador	North America	Salvadoran
Equatorial Guinea	Malabo	Africa	Equatorial Guinean *or* Equatoguinean
Eritrea	Asmara	Africa	Eritrean
Estonia	Tallinn	Europe	Estonian
Ethiopia	Addis Ababa	Africa	Ethiopian
Fiji	Suva	Oceania	Fijian
Finland	Helsinki	Europe	Finn, *n.*; Finnish, *adj.*
France	Paris	Europe	French
Gabon	Libreville	Africa	Gabonese
Gambia	Banjul	Africa	Gambian
Georgia	Tbilisi	Europe	Georgian
Germany	Berlin	Europe	German
Ghana	Accra	Africa	Ghanaian
Greece	Athens	Europe	Greek

Country	Capital	Continent/Area	Nationality
Grenada	St. George's	North America	Grenadian
Guatemala	Guatemala City	North America	Guatemalan
Guinea	Conakry	Africa	Guinean
Guinea-Bissau	Bissau	Africa	Guinea-Bissauan
Guyana	Georgetown	South America	Guyanese
Haiti	Port-au-Prince	North America	Haitian
Holy See	Vatican City	Europe	
Honduras	Tegucigalpa	North America	Honduran
Hungary	Budapest	Europe	Hungarian
Iceland	Reykjavik	Europe	Icelander, *n.*; Icelandic, *adj.*
India	New Delhi	Asia	Indian
Indonesia	Djakarta	Asia	Indonesian
Iran	Tehran	Asia	Iranian
Iraq	Baghdad	Asia	Iraqi
Ireland, Republic of	Dublin	Europe	Irish
Israel	Jerusalem	Asia	Israeli
Italy	Rome	Europe	Italian
Jamaica	Kingston	North America	Jamaican
Japan	Tokyo	Asia	Japanese
Jordan	Amman	Asia	Jordanian
Kazakhstan	Astana	Asia	Kazakhstani
Kenya	Nairobi	Africa	Kenyan
Kiribati	Tarawa	Oceania	I-Kiribati
Korea, North (*see* North Korea)			
Korea, South (*see* South Korea)			
Kuwait	Kuwait City	Asia	Kuwaiti
Kyrgyzstan	Bishkek	Asia	Kyrgyz
Laos	Vientiane	Asia	Lao *or* Laotian
Latvia	Riga	Europe	Latvian
Lebanon	Beirut	Asia	Lebanese
Lesotho	Maseru	Africa	Mosotho, *sing.*; Basotho, *pl.*; Basotho, *adj.*
Liberia	Monrovia	Africa	Liberian
Libya	Tripoli	Africa	Libyan
Liechtenstein	Vaduz	Europe	Liechtensteiner, *n.*; Liechtenstein, *adj.*
Lithuania	Vilnius	Europe	Lithuanian
Luxembourg	Luxembourg	Europe	Luxembourger, *n.*; Luxembourg, *adj.*
Macedonia	Skopje	Europe	Macedonian
Madagascar	Antananarivo	Africa	Malagasy

Country	Capital	Continent/Area	Nationality
Malawi	Lilongwe	Africa	Malawian
Malaysia	Kuala Lumpur	Asia	Malaysian
Maldives	Male	Asia	Maldivian
Mali	Bamako	Africa	Malian
Malta	Valletta	Europe	Maltese
Marshall Islands	Majuro	Oceania	Marshallese
Mauritania	Nouakchott	Africa	Mauritanian
Mauritius	Port Louis	Africa	Mauritian
Mexico	Mexico City	North America	Mexican
Micronesia	Kolonia	Oceania	Micronesian
Moldova	Chişinău	Europe	Moldovan
Monaco	Monaco	Europe	Monacan *or* Monegasque
Mongolia	Ulaanbaatar	Asia	Mongolian
Montenegro	Podgorica	Europe	Montenegrin
Morocco	Rabat	Africa	Moroccan
Mozambique	Maputo	Africa	Mozambican
Myanmar (*see* Burma)			
Namibia	Windhoek	Africa	Namibian
Nauru	Yaren District	Oceania	Nauruan
Nepal	Kathmandu	Asia	Nepalese
Netherlands	Amsterdam; The Hague	Europe	Dutchman *or* Dutchwoman, *n.*; Dutch, *adj.*
New Zealand	Wellington	Oceania	New Zealander, *n.*; New Zealand, *adj.*
Nicaragua	Managua	North America	Nicaraguan
Niger	Niamey	Africa	Nigerien
Nigeria	Abuja	Africa	Nigerian
North Korea	Pyongyang	Asia	North Korean
Norway	Oslo	Europe	Norwegian
Oman	Muscat	Asia	Omani
Pakistan	Islamabad	Asia	Pakistani
Palau	Koror	Oceania	Palauan
Panama	Panama City	North America	Panamanian
Papua New Guinea	Port Moresby	Oceania	Papua New Guinean
Paraguay	Asunción	South America	Paraguayan
Peru	Lima	South America	Peruvian
Philippines	Manila	Asia	Filipino, *n.*; Philippine, *adj.*
Poland	Warsaw	Europe	Pole, *n.*; Polish, *adj.*
Portugal	Lisbon	Europe	Portuguese
Qatar	Doha	Asia	Qatari
Romania	Bucharest	Europe	Romanian
Russia	Moscow	Europe & Asia	Russian

Country	Capital	Continent/Area	Nationality
Rwanda	Kigali	Africa	Rwandan, Rwandese
Saint Kitts and Nevis	Basseterre	North America	Kittsian; Nevisian
Saint Lucia	Castries	North America	St. Lucian
Saint Vincent and the Grenadines	Kingstown	North America	St. Vincentian *or* Vincentian
Samoa (*formerly* Western Samoa)	Apia	Oceania	Samoan
San Marino	San Marino	Europe	Sammarinese
São Tomé and Príncipe	São Tomé	Africa	Sao Tomean
Saudi Arabia	Riyadh	Asia	Saudi *or* Saudi Arabian
Senegal	Dakar	Africa	Senegalese
Serbia	Belgrade	Europe	Serbian
Seychelles	Victoria	Indian Ocean	Seychellois, *n.*; Seychelles, *adj.*
Sierra Leone	Freetown	Africa	Sierra Leonean
Singapore	Singapore	Asia	Singaporean, *n.*; Singapore, *adj.*
Slovakia	Bratislava	Europe	Slovak
Slovenia	Ljubljana	Europe	Slovene, *n.*; Slovenian, *adj.*
Solomon Islands	Honiara	Oceania	Solomon Islander
Somalia	Mogadishu	Africa	Somali
South Africa	Pretoria; Cape Town	Africa	South African
South Korea	Seoul	Asia	South Korean
Spain	Madrid	Europe	Spanish
Sri Lanka	Colombo	Asia	Sri Lankan
Sudan	Khartoum	Africa	Sudanese
Suriname	Paramaribo	South America	Surinamer, *n.*; Surinamese, *adj.*
Swaziland	Mbabane	Africa	Swazi
Sweden	Stockholm	Europe	Swede, *n.*; Swedish, *adj.*
Switzerland	Berne	Europe	Swiss
Syria	Damascus	Asia	Syrian
Taiwan	Taipei	Asia	Taiwanese
Tajikistan	Dushanbe	Asia	Tajik
Tanzania	Dodoma	Africa	Tanzanian
Thailand	Bangkok	Asia	Thai
Timor-Leste	Dili	Asia	Timor-Lestean
Togo	Lomé	Africa	Togolese
Tonga	Nuku'alofa	Oceania	Tongan
Trinidad and Tobago	Port-of-Spain	South America	Trinidadian; Tobagonian
Tunisia	Tunis	Africa	Tunisian
Turkey	Ankara	Asia & Europe	Turk, *n.*; Turkish, *adj.*
Turkmenistan	Ashgabat	Asia	Turkmen

Country	Capital	Continent/Area	Nationality
Tuvalu	Funafuti	Oceania	Tuvaluan
Uganda	Kampala	Africa	Ugandan
Ukraine	Kiev	Europe	Ukrainian
United Arab Emirates	Abu Dhabi	Africa	Emirati *or* Emirian
United Kingdom	London	Europe	Briton, *n.*; British, *collective pl. & adj.*
United States of America	Washington, DC	North America	American
Uruguay	Montevideo	South America	Uruguayan
Uzbekistan	Tashkent	Asia	Uzbek
Vanuatu	Vila	Oceania	Ni-Vanuatu
Venezuela	Caracas	South America	Venezuelan
Vietnam	Hanoi	Asia	Vietnamese
Western Samoa (*see* Samoa)			
Yemen	Sana'a	Asia	Yemeni
Zaire (*see* Congo)			
Zambia	Lusaka	Africa	Zambian
Zimbabwe	Harare	Africa	Zimbabwean

4. Standard Weights and Measures with Metric Equivalents and Conversions

Equivalents

Length

1 inch	= 2.54 centimeters
1 foot = 12 inches	= 0.3048 meter
1 yard = 3 feet = 36 inches	= 0.9144 meter
1 (statute) mile = 1,760 yards = 5,280 feet	= 1.609 kilometers

Area

1 sq. inch	= 6.45 sq. centimeters
1 sq. foot = 144 sq. inches	= 9.29 sq. decimeters
1 sq. yard = 9 sq. feet	= 0.836 sq. meter
1 acre = 4,840 sq. yards	= 0.405 hectare
1 sq. mile = 640 acres	= 259 hectares

Volume

CUBIC	
1 cu. inch	= 16.4 cu. centimeters
1 cu. foot = 1,728 cu. inches	= 0.0283 cu. meter
1 cu. yard = 27 cu. feet	= 0.765 cu. meter
DRY	
1 pint = 33.60 cu. inches	= 0.550 liter
1 quart = 2 pints	= 1.101 liters
1 peck = 8 quarts	= 8.81 liters
1 bushel = 4 pecks	= 35.3 liters
LIQUID	
1 fluid ounce	= 29.573 milliliters
1 gill = 4 fluid ounces	= 118.294 milliliters
1 pint = 16 fluid ounces = 28.88 cu. inches	= 0.473 liter
1 quart = 2 pints	= 0.946 liter
1 gallon = 4 quarts	= 3.785 liters

Avoirdupois Weight

1 grain	= 0.065 gram
1 dram	= 1.772 grams
1 ounce = 16 drams	= 28.35 grams
1 pound = 16 ounces = 7,000 grains	= 0.4536 kilogram (0.45359237 exactly)
1 stone (British) = 14 pounds	= 6.35 kilograms
1 ton = 2,000 pounds	
1 hundredweight (US) = 100 pounds	
20 hundredweight (US) = 2,000 pounds	

Conversions

Standard	Multiply by	To get metric
LENGTH		
inches	2.5	centimeters
feet	30	centimeters
yards	0.9	meters
miles	1.6	kilometers
AREA		
square inches	6.5	square centimeters
square feet	0.09	square meters
square yards	0.8	square meters
square miles	2.6	square kilometers
acres	0.4	hectares
VOLUME		
cubic feet	0.03	cubic meters
cubic yards	0.76	cubic meters
teaspoons	5	milliliters
tablespoons	15	milliliters
cubic inches	16	milliliters
fluid ounces	30	milliliters
cups	0.24	liters
pints	0.47	liters
quarts	0.95	liters
gallons	3.8	liters
WEIGHT		
ounces	28	grams
pounds	0.45	kilograms
short tons	0.9	metric tons
TEMPERATURE		
degrees Fahrenheit	subtract 32, then multiply by 5/9	degrees Celsius

5. Metric Weights and Measures with Standard Equivalents and Conversions

Equivalents

Length

1 millimeter (mm)	= 0.039 inch
1 centimeter (cm) = 10 millimeters	= 0.394 inch
1 decimeter (dm) = 10 centimeters	= 3.94 inches
1 meter (m) = 10 decimeters	= 1.094 yards
1 decameter = 10 meters	= 10.94 yards
1 hectometer = 100 meters	= 109.4 yards
1 kilometer (km) = 1,000 meters	= 0.6214 mile

Area

1 sq. centimeter	= 0.155 sq. inch
1 sq. meter = 10,000 sq. centimeters	= 1.196 sq. yards
1 are = 100 sq. meters	= 119.6 sq. yards
1 hectare = 100 ares	= 2.471 acres
1 sq. kilometer = 100 hectares	= 0.386 sq. mile

Volume

CUBIC

1 cu. centimeter	= 0.061 cu. inch
1 cu. meter = 1,000,000 cu. centimeters	= 1.308 cu. yards

CAPACITY

1 milliliter (ml)	= 0.034 fluid ounce
1 centiliter (cl) = 10 milliliters	= 0.34 fluid ounce
1 deciliter (dl) = 10 centiliters	= 3.38 fluid ounces
1 liter (l) = 10 deciliters	= 1.06 quarts
1 decaliter = 10 liters	= 2.64 gallons
1 hectoliter = 100 liters	= 2.75 bushels

Weight	
1 milligram (mg)	= 0.015 grain
1 centigram = 10 milligrams	= 0.154 grain
1 decigram (dg) = 10 centigrams	= 1.543 grains
1 gram (g) = 10 decigrams	= 15.43 grains
1 decagram = 10 grams	= 5.64 drams
1 hectogram = 100 grams	= 3.527 ounces
1 kilogram (kg) = 1,000 grams	= 2.205 pounds
1 ton (metric ton) = 1,000 kilograms	= 0.984 (long) ton

Conversions

Metric	Multiply by	To get standard
LENGTH		
millimeters	0.04	inches
centimeters	0.4	inches
meters	3.3	feet
meters	1.1	yards
kilometers	0.6	miles
AREA		
square centimeters	0.16	square inches
square meters	1.2	square yards
square kilometers	0.4	square miles
hectares	2.5	acres
VOLUME		
cubic meters	35	cubic feet
cubic meters	1.3	cubic yards
milliliters	0.03	fluid ounces
milliliters	0.06	cubic inches
liters	2.1	pints
liters	1.06	quarts
liters	0.26	gallons
WEIGHT		
grams	0.035	ounces
kilograms	2.2	pounds
metric tons	1.1	short tons
TEMPERATURE		
degrees Celsius	9/5, then add 32	degrees Fahrenheit

6. Chemical Elements

Element	Symbol	Atomic Number
actinium	Ac	89
aluminum	Al	13
americium	Am	95
antimony	Sb	51
argon	Ar	18
arsenic	As	33
astatine	At	85
barium	Ba	56
berkelium	Bk	97
beryllium	Be	4
bismuth	Bi	83
bohrium	Bh	107
boron	B	5
bromine	Br	35
cadmium	Cd	48
calcium	Ca	20
californium	Cf	98
carbon	C	6
cerium	Ce	58
cesium	Cs	55
chlorine	Cl	17
chromium	Cr	24
cobalt	Co	27
copper	Cu	29
curium	Cm	96
darmstadtium	Ds	110
dubnium	Db	105
dysprosium	Dy	66
einsteinium	Es	99
erbium	Er	68
europium	Eu	63
fermium	Fm	100
fluorine	F	9
francium	Fr	87
gadolinium	Gd	64
gallium	Ga	31

Element	Symbol	Atomic Number
germanium	Ge	32
gold	Au	79
hafnium	Hf	72
hassium	Hs	108
helium	He	2
holmium	Ho	67
hydrogen	H	1
indium	In	49
iodine	I	53
iridium	Ir	77
iron	Fe	26
krypton	Kr	36
lanthanum	La	57
lawrencium	Lr	103
lead	Pb	82
lithium	Li	3
lutetium	Lu	71
magnesium	Mg	12
manganese	Mn	25
meitnerium	Mt	109
mendelevium	Md	101
mercury	Hg	80
molybdenum	Mo	42
neodymium	Nd	60
neon	Ne	10
neptunium	Np	93
nickel	Ni	28
niobium	Nb	41
nitrogen	N	7
nobelium	No	102
osmium	Os	76
oxygen	O	8
palladium	Pd	46
phosphorus	P	15
platinum	Pt	78
plutonium	Pu	94

Element	Symbol	Atomic Number
polonium	Po	84
potassium	K	19
praseodymium	Pr	59
promethium	Pm	61
protactinium	Pa	91
radium	Ra	88
radon	Rn	86
rhenium	Re	75
rhodium	Rh	45
rubidium	Rb	37
ruthenium	Ru	44
rutherfordium	Rf	104
samarium	Sm	62
scandium	Sc	21
seaborgium	Sg	106
selenium	Se	34
silicon	Si	14
silver	Ag	47
sodium	Na	11
strontium	Sr	38

Element	Symbol	Atomic Number
sulfur	S	16
tantalum	Ta	73
technetium	Tc	43
tellurium	Te	52
terbium	Tb	65
thallium	Tl	81
thorium	Th	90
thulium	Tm	69
tin	Sn	50
titanium	Ti	22
tungsten (or wolfram)	W	74
uranium	U	92
vanadium	V	23
xenon	Xe	54
ytterbium	Yb	70
yttrium	Y	39
zinc	Zn	30
zirconium	Zr	40

7. Punctuation

Punctuation is an essential element of good writing because it makes the author's meaning clear to the reader. Although precise punctuation styles may vary somewhat among published sources, there are a number of fundamental principles worthy of consideration.

Comma

The comma is the most used punctuation mark in the English language. It signals to the reader a pause, which generally clarifies the author's meaning and establishes a sensible order to the elements of written language. Among the most typical functions of the comma are the following:

1. It can separate the clauses of a compound sentence when there are two independent clauses joined by a conjunction, especially when the clauses are not very short:

   It never occurred to me to look there, and I'm sure it didn't occur to Rachel either.

   The Nelsons wanted to see the Grand Canyon at sunrise, but they overslept.

2. It can separate the clauses of a compound sentence when there is a series of independent clauses, the last two of which are joined by a conjunction:

   The bus ride to the campsite was very uncomfortable, the cabins were not ready for us, the cook had forgotten to start dinner, and the rain was torrential.

3. It is used to precede or set off, and therefore indicate, a nonrestrictive dependent clause (a clause that could be omitted without changing the meaning of the main clause):

   I read her autobiography, which was published last July.

   They showed up at midnight, after most of the guests had gone home.

   The coffee, which is freshly brewed, is in the kitchen.

4. It can follow an introductory phrase:

   Having enjoyed the movie so much, he agreed to see it again.

   Born and raised in Paris, she had never lost her French accent.

   In the beginning, they had very little money to invest.

5. It can set off words used in direct address:

   Listen, people, you have no choice in the matter.

   Yes, Mrs. Greene, I will be happy to feed your cat.

6. It can separate two or more coordinate adjectives (adjectives that could otherwise be joined with *and*) that modify one noun:

   The cruise turned out to be the most entertaining, fun, and relaxing vacation ever.

   The horse was tall, lean, and sleek.

Note that cumulative adjectives (those not able to be joined with *and*) are not separated by a comma:

She wore bright yellow rubber boots.

7. It is used to separate three or more items in a series or list:

   Charlie, Melissa, Stan, and Mark will be this year's soloists in the spring concert.

   We need furniture, toys, clothes, books, tools, housewares, and other useful merchandise for the benefit auction.

   Note that the comma between the last two items in a series is sometimes omitted in less precise style:

   The most popular foods served in the cafeteria are pizza, hamburgers and nachos.

8. It is used to separate and set off the elements in an address or other geographical designation:

   My new house is at 1657 Nighthawk Circle, South Kingsbury, Michigan.

   We arrived in Pamplona, Spain, on Thursday.

9. It is used to set off direct quotations (note the placement or absence of commas with other punctuation):

   "Kim forgot her gloves," he said, "but we have a pair she can borrow."

   There was a long silence before Jack blurted out, "This must be the world's ugliest painting."

   "What are you talking about?" she asked in a puzzled manner.

   "Happy New Year!" everyone shouted.

10. It is used to set off titles after a person's name:

    Katherine Bentley, M.D.

    Martin Luther King, Jr., delivered the sermon.

Semicolon

The semicolon has two basic functions:

1. It can separate two main clauses, particularly when these clauses are of equal importance:

   The crowds gathered outside the museum hours before the doors were opened; this was one exhibit no one wanted to miss.

   She always complained when her relatives stayed for the weekend; even so, she usually was a little sad when they left.

2. It can be used as a comma is used to separate such elements as clauses or items in a series or list, particularly when one or more of the elements already includes a comma:

   The path took us through the deep, dark woods; across a small meadow into a cold, wet cave; and up a hillside overlooking the lake.

   Listed for sale in the ad were two bicycles; a battery-powered, leaf-mulching lawn mower; and a maple bookcase.

Colon

The colon has five basic functions:

1. It can introduce something, especially a list of items:
   In the basket were three pieces of mail: a postcard, a catalog, and a wedding invitation.
   Students should have the following items: backpack, loose-leaf notebook, pens and pencils, pencil sharpener, and ruler.
2. It can separate two clauses in a sentence when the second clause is being used to explain or illustrate the first clause:
   We finally understood why she would never go sailing with us: she had a deep fear of the water.
   Most of the dogs in our neighborhood are quite large: two of them are St. Bernards.
3. It can introduce a statement or a quotation:
   His parents say the most important rule is this: Always tell the truth.
   We repeated the final words of his poem: "And such is the plight of fools like me."
4. It can be used to follow the greeting in a formal or business letter:
   Dear Ms. Daniels:
   Dear Sir or Madam:
   Gentlemen:
5. It is used in the United States to separate minutes from hours, and seconds from minutes, in showing time of day and measured length of time:
   Please be at the restaurant before 6:45.
   Her best running time so far has been 00:12:35.

Period

The period has two basic functions:

1. It is used to mark the end of a sentence:
   It was reported that there is a shortage of nurses at the hospital. Several of the patients have expressed concern about this problem.
2. It is often used at the end of an abbreviation:
   On Fri., Sept. 12, Dr. Brophy noted that the patient's weight was 168 lb. and that his height was 6 ft. 2 in.
   (Note that another period is not added to the end of the sentence when the last word is an abbreviation.)

Question Mark and Exclamation Point

The only sentences that do not end in a period are those that end in either a question mark or an exclamation point.

Question marks are used to mark the end of a sentence that asks a direct question (generally, a question that expects an answer):

Is there any reason for us to bring more than a few dollars?
Who is your science teacher?

Exclamation points are used to mark the end of a sentence that expresses a strong feeling, typically surprise, joy, or anger:

I want you to leave and never come back!

What a beautiful view this is!

Apostrophe

The apostrophe has two basic functions:

1. It is used to show where a letter or letters are missing in a contraction.
   The directions are cont'd [continued] *on the next page.*
   We've [we have] *decided that if she can't* [cannot] *go, then we aren't* [are not] *going either.*

2. It can be used to show possession:
   The possessive of a singular noun or an irregular plural noun is created by adding an apostrophe and an *s*:
   the pilot's uniform
   Mrs. Mendoza's house
   a tomato's bright red color
   the oxen's yoke

   The possessive of a regular plural noun is created by adding just an apostrophe:
   the pilots' uniforms [referring to more than one pilot]
   the Mendozas' house [referring to the Mendoza family]
   the tomatoes' bright red color [referring to more than one tomato]

Quotation Marks

Quotation marks have two basic functions:

1. They are used to set off direct quotations (an exact rendering of someone's spoken or written words):
   "I think the new library is wonderful," she remarked to David.
   We were somewhat lost, so we asked, "Are we anywhere near the gallery?"
   In his letter he had written, "The nights here are quiet and starry. It seems like a hundred years since I've been wakened by the noise of city traffic."
   Note that indirect quotes (which often are preceded by that, if, or whether) are not set off by quotation marks:
   He told me that he went to school in Boston.
   We asked if we could still get tickets to the game.

2. They can be used to set off words or phrases that have specific technical usage, or to set off meanings of words, or to indicate words that are being used in a special way in a sentence:
   The part of the flower that bears the pollen is the "stamen."
   When I said "plain," I meant "flat land," not "ordinary."
   In the theater, the statement "break a leg" is meant as an expression of good luck.
   What you call "hoagies," we call "grinders" or "submarine sandwiches."
   He will never be a responsible adult until he outgrows his "Peter Pan" behavior.

Note that sometimes single quotation marks, rather than double quotation marks, may be used to set off words or phrases:

The part of the flower that bears the pollen is the 'stamen.'

What is most important is to be consistent in such usage. Single quotation marks are also used to set off words or phrases within material already in double quotation marks, as:

"I want the sign to say 'Ellen's Bed and Breakfast' in large gold letters," she explained.

Parentheses

Parentheses are used, in pairs, to enclose information that gives extra detail or explanation to the regular text. They are used in two basic ways:

1. They can separate a word or words in a sentence from the rest of the sentence:

   On our way to school, we walk past the Turner Farm (the oldest dairy farm in town) and watch the cows being fed.

   The stores were filled with holiday shoppers (even more so than last year).

   Note that the period goes outside the parentheses, because the words in the parentheses are only part of the sentence.

2. They can form a separate complete sentence:

   Please bring a dessert to the dinner party. (It can be something very simple.) I look forward to seeing you there.

   Note that the period goes inside the parentheses, because the words in the parentheses are a complete and independent sentence.

Dash

A dash is used most commonly to replace the usage of parentheses within sentences. If the information being set off is in the middle of the sentence, a pair of long (or "em") dashes is used; if it is at the end of the sentence, just one long dash is used:

On our way to school, we walk past the Turner Farm—the oldest dairy farm in town—and watch the cows being fed.

The stores were filled with holiday shoppers—even more so than last year.

Hyphen

A hyphen has three basic functions:

1. It can join two or more words to make a compound, especially when doing so makes the meaning more clear to the reader:

   We met to discuss long-range planning.

   There were six four-month-old piglets at the fair.

   That old stove was quite a coal-burner.

2. It can replace the word "to" when a span or range of data is given. This kind of hyphen is sometimes keyed as a short (or "en") dash:

   John Adams was president of the United States 1797–1801.

   Today we will look for proper nouns in the L–N section of the dictionary.

   The ideal weight for that breed of dog would be 75–85 pounds.

3. It can be used to break a word at the end of a line.

Kk

K (or **k**) ▶ **n.** (plural **Ks** or **K's**) the eleventh letter of the alphabet. ▶ **abbr.** informal a thousand.

k ▶ **abbr.** kilo-.

Kab·ba·lah /ˈkabələ, kəˈbä-/ (also **Kabbala**, **Cabbala**, or **Cabala**) ▶ **n.** the ancient Jewish tradition of mystical interpretation of the Bible. ■ **Kab·ba·lism** /ˈkabəˌlizəm/ **n.** **Kab·ba·list** /-list/ **n.**

ka·bob = KEBAB.

Kaf·ka·esque /ˌkäfkəˈesk/ ▶ **adj.** having a perplexing and nightmarish quality.

kaf·tan /ˈkaftən, -ˌtan/ (or **caftan**) ▶ **n. 1** a woman's long, loose dress or top. **2** a man's long tunic, worn in the countries of the Near East. **3** a loose shirt or top.

kai·ser /ˈkīzər/ ▶ **n.** historical the German or Austrian Emperor.

kale /kāl/ ▶ **n.** a type of cabbage with large curly leaves.

ka·lei·do·scope /kəˈlīdəˌskōp/ ▶ **n. 1** a tube containing mirrors and pieces of colored glass or paper, whose reflections produce changing patterns when the tube is turned. **2** a constantly changing pattern: *a kaleidoscope of color.* ■ **ka·lei·do·scop·ic** /-ˌlīdəˈskäpik/ **adj.**

ka·mi·ka·ze /ˌkämiˈkäzē/ ▶ **n.** (in World War II) a Japanese aircraft loaded with explosives and deliberately crashed on to an enemy target in a suicide mission. ▶ **adj.** potentially causing death or harm to yourself.

kan·ga·roo /ˌkaNGgəˈro͞o/ ▶ **n.** a large Australian animal with a long powerful tail and strong hind legs that enable it to travel by leaping. □ **kangaroo court** a court set up unofficially with the aim of finding someone guilty.

ka·o·lin /ˈkāəlin/ ▶ **n.** a fine soft white clay, used for making china and in medicine.

ka·pok /ˈkāˌpäk/ ▶ **n.** a substance resembling absorbent cotton that grows around the seeds of a tropical tree, used as padding.

ka·put /kəˈpo͝ot, kä-/ ▶ **adj.** informal broken and useless.

kar·a·o·ke /ˌkarēˈōkē/ ▶ **n.** a form of entertainment in which people sing popular songs over prerecorded backing tracks.

kar·at /ˈkarət/ (or **carat**) ▶ **n.** a measure of the purity of gold.

ka·ra·te /kəˈrätē/ ▶ **n.** a Japanese system of fighting using the hands and feet rather than weapons.

kar·ma /ˈkärmə/ ▶ **n.** (in Hinduism and Buddhism) a person's actions in this and previous lives, seen as affecting their future fate.

karst /kärst/ ▶ **n.** a limestone region with underground streams and many cavities in the rock.

kart /kärt/ ▶ **n.** a small racing car with no suspension and having the engine at the back.

kas·bah /ˈkasˌbä, ˈkaz-/ (or **casbah**) ▶ **n.** a fortress in the old part of a North African city, and the narrow streets that surround it.

kay·ak /ˈkīˌak/ ▶ **n.** a canoe made of a light frame with a watertight covering. ▶ **v.** (**kayaks**, **kayaking**, **kayaked**) travel in a kayak.

kay·o /ˈkāˈō/ informal ▶ **n.** (plural **kayos**) a knockout. ▶ **v.** (**kayoes**, **kayoing**, **kayoed**) knock someone out.

ka·zoo /kəˈzo͞o/ ▶ **n.** a simple musical instrument consisting of a pipe that produces a buzzing sound when you hum into it.

KB (or **Kb**) ▶ **abbr.** kilobyte(s).

kcal ▶ **abbr.** kilocalorie(s).

ke·a /ˈkēə/ ▶ **n.** a New Zealand mountain parrot with a long, narrow bill and olive-green plumage.

ke·bab /kəˈbäb/ (or **kabob**) ▶ **n.** a dish of pieces of meat, fish, or vegetables roasted or grilled on a skewer or spit.

kedge /kej/ ▶ **v.** (**kedges**, **kedging**, **kedged**) move a boat by hauling in a rope attached at a distance to an anchor. ▶ **n.** a small anchor used for such a purpose.

keel /kēl/ ▶ **n.** a structure running along the length of the base of a ship. ▶ **v.** (**keel over**) **1** (of a boat or ship) turn over on its side. **2** fall over, especially because of fainting.

> SYNONYMS ▶ **v. 1 capsize**, turn turtle, turn upside down, founder, overturn, turn over, tip over. **2 collapse**, faint, pass out, black out, swoon.

keel·boat /ˈkēlˌbōt/ ▶ **n. 1** a large, flat boat used on rivers for transporting goods in bulk. **2** a yacht built with a permanent keel rather than a centerboard.

keel·haul /ˈkēlˌhôl/ ▶ **v.** (in the past) punish someone by dragging them through the water from one side of a boat to the other.

keel·son /ˈkēlsən/ (also **kelson** /ˈkelsən/) ▶ **n.** a structure running the length of a ship that fastens the timbers of the floor to the keel.

keen[1] /kēn/ ▶ **adj. 1** eager and enthusiastic. **2** (of a blade) sharp. **3** quick to understand. **4** (of a sense) highly developed.

> SYNONYMS **1** *I'm keen to help* **eager**, anxious, intent, impatient, determined; informal raring, itching, dying. **2** *a keen birdwatcher* **enthusiastic**, avid, ardent, fervent, conscientious, committed, dedicated. **3** *a girl he was keen on* **attracted to**, interested in, fond of, infatuated with, taken with, smitten with, enamored of; informal stuck on. **4** *a keen mind* **acute**, penetrating, astute, incisive, sharp,

perceptive, piercing, razor-sharp, shrewd, discerning, clever, intelligent, brilliant, bright, smart, wise, insightful. **5** *a keen sense of duty* **intense**, acute, fierce, passionate, burning, fervent, strong, powerful. ANTONYMS reluctant, unenthusiastic.

■ **keen·ly** adv. **keen·ness** n.

keen² ▶ v. **1** wail in grief for a person who has died. **2** make an eerie wailing sound.

keep /kēp/ ▶ v. (**keeps**, **keeping**, **kept**) **1** continue to have something. **2** save something for use in the future. **3** store something in a regular place. **4** continue in a particular condition, position, or activity: *she kept quiet*. **5** do something that you have promised or agreed to do. **6** (of food) remain in good condition. **7** make a note about something. **8** provide accommodations and food for someone. ▶ n. **1** food, clothes, and other essentials for living. **2** the strongest or central tower of a castle.

SYNONYMS ▶ v. **1** *I kept the forms* **retain**, hold on to, save, store, put aside, set aside; informal hang on to. **2** *keep calm* **remain**, stay. **3** *he keeps going on about it* **persist in**, keep on, carry on, continue, insist on. **4** *keep the law* **comply with**, obey, observe, conform to, abide by, adhere to, stick to, heed, follow, carry out, act on, make good (on), honor, keep to, stand by. **5** *keeping the old traditions* **preserve**, keep alive/up, carry on, perpetuate, maintain, uphold. **6** *he stole to keep his family* **provide for**, support, feed, maintain, sustain, take care of, look after. **7** *she keeps rabbits* **breed**, rear, raise, tend, farm, own. ▶ n. **maintenance**, upkeep, sustenance, board, room and board, food, livelihood.

□ **for keeps** informal permanently. **keep from** avoid doing something. **keep someone from** prevent someone from doing something. **keep something from** cause something to remain a secret from someone. **keep on** continue to do, use, or employ something. **keep to 1** avoid leaving a path, road, or place. **2** stick to a schedule or point. **3** observe a promise. **keep up** move at the same rate as someone or something else. **keep something up** continue a course of action. **keep up with 1** be aware of current events or developments. **2** continue to be in contact with someone. **keep up with the Joneses** strive not to be outdone by your neighbors or peers.

keep·er /ˈkēpər/ ▶ n. **1** a person who manages or looks after something or someone. **2** informal a thing worth keeping. **3** a goalkeeper. **4** an object that protects another or keeps it in place.

SYNONYMS **curator**, custodian, guardian, conservator, administrator, overseer, steward, caretaker, attendant, concierge.

keep·ing /ˈkēpiNG/ ▶ n. (**in** (or **out of**) **keeping with**) in (or not in) harmony or agreement with.

SYNONYMS **care**, custody, charge, guardianship, possession, trust, protection.

keep·sake /ˈkēpˌsāk/ ▶ n. a small item kept in memory of the person who gave it or originally owned it.

keg /keg/ ▶ n. a small barrel.

keis·ter /ˈkēstər/ ▶ n. informal a person's buttocks.

kelp /kelp/ ▶ n. a very large brown seaweed.

kel·pie /ˈkelpē/ ▶ n. a water spirit of Scottish folklore, usually taking the form of a horse.

kel·vin /ˈkelvən/ ▶ n. a unit of temperature, equal to one degree Celsius.

Kel·vin scale ▶ n. the scale of temperature with absolute zero as zero and the freezing point of water as 273.15 kelvins.

ken /ken/ ▶ n. (**your ken**) the range of your knowledge and experience. ▶ v. (**kens**, **kenning**, **kenned** or **kent**) Scottish & Northern English know or recognize.

ken·do /ˈkenˌdō/ ▶ n. a Japanese form of fencing with two-handed bamboo swords.

ken·nel /ˈkenl/ ▶ n. **1** a small shelter for a dog. **2** (**kennels**) a place where dogs are looked after or bred.

Ken·yan /ˈkenyən, ˈkēnyən/ ▶ n. a person from Kenya. ▶ adj. relating to Kenya.

kept /kept/ past and past participle of **KEEP**.

ker·a·tin /ˈkerətin/ ▶ n. a protein forming the basis of hair, feathers, hoofs, claws, and horns.

ker·chief /ˈkərCHəf, -ˌCHēf/ ▶ n. **1** a piece of fabric used to cover the head. **2** dated a handkerchief.

ker·nel /ˈkərnl/ ▶ n. **1** the softer part inside the shell of a nut, seed, or fruit stone. **2** the seed and hard husk of a cereal. **3** the central part of something.

SPELLING

The word ends with **-el**, not **-al**: kern**el**.

ker·o·sene /ˈkerəˌsēn, ˈkar-, ˌkerəˈsēn, ˌkar-/ ▶ n. a light fuel oil obtained by distilling petroleum.

kes·trel /ˈkestrəl/ ▶ n. a small falcon that hovers in the air with rapidly beating wings.

ketch /keCH/ ▶ n. a small sailboat with two masts.

ketch·up /ˈkeCHəp/ (or **catsup** /ˈkeCHəp, ˈkaCHəp, ˈkatsəp/) ▶ n. a spicy sauce made from tomatoes and vinegar.

ke·tone /ˈkēˌtōn/ ▶ n. Chemistry any of a class of organic compounds including acetone.

ket·tle /ˈketl/ ▶ n. a container with a spout and handle, used for boiling water. □ **the pot calling the kettle black** used to suggest that a person is aiming at someone criticisms that could equally well apply to themselves. **a fine** (or **pretty**) **kettle of fish** informal an awkward state of affairs.

ket·tle·drum /ˈketlˌdrəm/ ▶ n. a large drum shaped like a bowl.

key /kē/ ▶ n. (plural **keys**) **1** a small piece of shaped metal that is inserted into a lock and turned to open or close it. **2** a lever pressed down by the finger in playing an instrument such as the organ, piano, or flute. **3** each of several buttons on a panel for operating a computer or typewriter. **4** a list explaining the symbols used in a map or table. **5** a word or system for solving a code. **6** Music a group of notes making up a scale. **7** an instrument for turning a screw, peg, or nut. ▶ adj. of great importance: *a key figure*. ▶ v. (**keys**, **keying**, **keyed**) **1** enter data using a computer keyboard. **2** (**be keyed up**) be nervous, tense, or excited. **3** (**key into** or **in with**) be connected or in harmony with.

SYNONYMS ▶ n. **1** *the key to the mystery* **answer**, clue, solution, explanation, basis, foundation. **2** *the key to success* **means**, way, route, path, passport, secret, formula. ▶ adj. **crucial**, central, essential, indispensable, pivotal, critical, vital, principal, prime, major, leading, main, important.

□ **key grip** the person in a movie crew who is

in charge of the camera equipment. **key ring** a metal ring for holding keys together in a bunch. **key signature** Music a combination of sharps or flats after the clef at the beginning of each stave, indicating the key of a composition.

key·board /ˈkēˌbôrd/ ▶ **n.** **1** a panel of keys for use with a computer or typewriter. **2** a set of keys on a musical instrument. **3** an electronic musical instrument with keys arranged as on a piano. ▶ **v.** enter data by means of a keyboard. ■ **key·board·er** **n.**

key·hole /ˈkēˌhōl/ ▶ **n.** a hole in a lock into which the key is inserted.

key·note /ˈkēˌnōt/ ▶ **n.** **1** a central theme of a book, speech, etc. **2** Music the note on which a key is based. ▶ **adj.** (of a speech) setting out the theme of a conference.

key·pad /ˈkēˌpad/ ▶ **n.** a small keyboard or set of buttons for operating a portable electronic device or telephone.

key·punch /ˈkēˌpənch/ ▶ **n.** a device for transferring data by means of punched holes on a series of cards or paper tape.

key·stone /ˈkēˌstōn/ ▶ **n.** **1** the most important part of a policy or system. **2** a central stone at the top of an arch.

key·stroke /ˈkēˌstrōk/ ▶ **n.** a single act of pressing a key on a keyboard.

key·word /ˈkēˌwərd/ ▶ **n.** **1** a significant word mentioned in an index. **2** a word used in a computer system to indicate the content of a document.

kg ▶ **abbr.** kilograms.

khak·i /ˈkakē/ ▶ **n.** (plural **khakis**) **1** a dull greenish- or yellowish-brown color. **2** a cotton or wool fabric of this color. **3** (**khakis**) clothing, especially pants, of this fabric and color.

khan /kän/ ▶ **n.** a title given to rulers and officials in central Asia, Afghanistan, and certain other Muslim countries.

kHz ▶ **abbr.** kilohertz.

kib·butz /kiˈbo͝ots/ ▶ **n.** a farming settlement in Israel in which work is shared between all of its members.

ki·bosh /kəˈbäsh, ˈkīˌbäsh/ ▶ **n.** (**put the kibosh on**) informal firmly put an end to.

kick /kik/ ▶ **v.** **1** hit or propel something forcibly with the foot. **2** hit out with the foot or feet. **3** informal succeed in giving up a habit. **4** (**kick off**) (of a football game, soccer match, etc.) start or restart with a kick of the ball from the center. **5** (**kick someone out**) informal force someone to leave. **6** (of a gun) spring back when fired. **7** (**kick against**) disagree or be frustrated with. ▶ **n.** **1** an instance of kicking. **2** informal a thrill of excitement. **3** informal the strong effect of alcohol or a drug.

> SYNONYMS ▶ **v.** **boot**, punt. ▶ **n.** *I get a kick out of driving* **thrill**, excitement, stimulation, tingle, frisson; informal charge, buzz, high.

□ **kick around** (or **about**) **1** lie unwanted or unused. **2** treat someone roughly or without respect. **3** discuss an idea casually. **kick-boxing** a form of martial art that combines boxing with kicking with bare feet. **kick-start** **1** start a motorcycle engine with a downward thrust of a lever. **2** take action to make something start or develop more quickly: *kick-start the economy.* **kick the bucket** informal die. **a kick in the teeth** informal a serious setback or disappointment. **kick yourself** be annoyed with yourself. ■ **kick·er** **n.**

kick·back /ˈkikˌbak/ ▶ **n.** **1** informal an underhand payment to someone who has helped in a business deal. **2** an instance of a gun springing back when fired.

kick·off /ˈkikˌôf/ ▶ **n.** **1** the start or resumption of a football game, in which a player kicks the ball from the center of the field: *we had to be in our seats to see the kickoff.* **2** informal a start of an event or activity.

kick·stand /ˈkikˌstand/ ▶ **n.** a metal rod attached to a bicycle or motorcycle that may be kicked into a upright position to support the vehicle when it is not being ridden.

kid[1] /kid/ ▶ **n.** **1** informal a child or young person. **2** a young goat.

> SYNONYMS **child**, youngster, baby, toddler, tot, infant, boy, girl, minor, juvenile, adolescent, teenager, youth, stripling; informal kiddie, rug rat, (little) nipper; disapproving brat.

□ **handle** (or **treat**) **someone/something with kid gloves** deal with very carefully. **kid brother** (or **sister**) informal a younger brother (or sister).

kid[2] ▶ **v.** (**kids**, **kidding**, **kidded**) informal **1** fool someone into believing something. **2** tease.

kid·die /ˈkidē/ (also **kiddy**) ▶ **n.** (plural **kiddies**) informal a young child.

kid·nap /ˈkidˌnap/ ▶ **v.** (**kidnaps**, **kidnaping**, **kidnaped**) take someone by force and hold them captive. ▶ **n.** an instance of kidnapping someone.

> SYNONYMS ▶ **v.** **abduct**, carry off, capture, seize, snatch, take hostage.

■ **kid·nap·per** **n.**

kid·ney /ˈkidnē/ ▶ **n.** (plural **kidneys**) **1** each of a pair of organs that remove waste products from the blood and produce urine. **2** the kidney of a sheep, ox, or pig as food. □ **kidney bean** an edible dark red bean shaped like a kidney. **kidney machine** a device that performs the functions of a kidney, used if a person has a damaged kidney. **kidney stone** a hard mass formed in the kidneys.

ki·lim /kəˈlēm, kēˈlēm, ˈkiləm/ (or **kelim** /kəˈlēm, kēˈlēm/) ▶ **n.** a carpet or rug of a kind made in Turkey and neighboring areas.

kill /kil/ ▶ **v.** **1** cause the death of. **2** put an end to. **3** informal cause someone pain. **4** pass time. **5** informal overwhelm someone with an emotion: *the suspense is killing me.* ▶ **n.** **1** an act of killing. **2** an animal or animals killed by a hunter or another animal.

> SYNONYMS ▶ **v.** **murder**, assassinate, eliminate, terminate, dispatch, execute, slaughter, exterminate, butcher, massacre; informal bump off, do away with, do in, take out, blow away, rub out, whack, waste; literary slay.

□ **be in at the kill** be present at or benefit from the successful conclusion of an undertaking. **kill with kindness** spoil someone with overindulgence.

kill·er /ˈkilər/ ▶ **n.** **1** a person or thing that kills. **2** informal something that is very difficult or very impressive.

> SYNONYMS **murderer**, assassin, butcher, gunman, terminator, executioner; informal hit man.

□ **killer whale** ⇨ **ORCA**.

kill·ing /ˈkiliNG/ ▶ **n.** an act of causing death. ▶ **adj.** informal exhausting.

> SYNONYMS ▶ **n.** **murder**, assassination, homicide, manslaughter, execution, slaughter, massacre, butchery, bloodshed, carnage, extermination, genocide.

▫ **killing fields** a place where many people have been killed in war or genocide. **make a killing** make a lot of money out of something.

kill·joy /ˈkilˌjoi/ ▶ **n.** a person who spoils the enjoyment of other people.

kiln /kiln, kil/ ▶ **n.** a furnace for baking or drying things, especially used for firing pottery.

ki·lo /ˈkēlō/ ▶ **n.** (plural **kilos**) a kilogram.

kil·o·byte /ˈkiləˌbīt/ ▶ **n.** Computing a unit of memory or data equal to 1,024 bytes.

kil·o·cal·o·rie /ˈkiləˌkalərē/ ▶ **n.** a unit of energy of one thousand calories (equal to one large calorie).

kil·o·gram /ˈkiləˌgram/ ▶ **n.** a unit of mass, equal to 1,000 grams (approximately 2.205 lb).

kil·o·hertz /ˈkiləˌhərts/ ▶ **n.** a measure of frequency equivalent to 1,000 cycles per second.

kil·o·joule /ˈkiləˌjo͞ol, ˈkiləˌjoul/ ▶ **n.** 1,000 joules.

kil·o·li·ter /ˈkiləˌlētər/ ▶ **n.** 1,000 liters (equivalent to 220 imperial gallons).

kil·o·me·ter /kiˈlämitər, ˈkiləˌmētər/ ▶ **n.** a metric unit of measurement equal to 1,000 meters (0.62 miles).

kil·o·ton /ˈkiləˌtən/ ▶ **n.** a unit of explosive power equivalent to 1,000 tons of TNT.

kil·o·volt /ˈkiləˌvōlt/ ▶ **n.** 1,000 volts.

kil·o·watt /ˈkiləˌwät/ ▶ **n.** 1,000 watts. ▫ **kilowatt-hour** a measure of electrical energy equivalent to one kilowatt operating for one hour.

kilt /kilt/ ▶ **n.** a skirt of pleated tartan cloth, traditionally worn by men as part of Scottish Highland dress.

kil·ter /ˈkiltər/ ▶ **n.** (**out of** (or **off**) **kilter**) out of balance.

ki·mo·no /kəˈmōnō, -nə/ ▶ **n.** (plural **kimonos**) a long, loose Japanese robe with wide sleeves, tied with a sash.

kin /kin/ ▶ **pl.n.** your family and relations.

SYNONYMS **relatives**, relations, family, kith and kin, kindred, kinsfolk, kinsmen, kinswomen, people; informal folks.

kind¹ /kīnd/ ▶ **n.** a class or type of similar people or things.

SYNONYMS **sort**, type, variety, style, form, class, category, genre, genus, species.

▫ **in kind 1** in the same way. **2** (of payment) in goods or services instead of money. **kind of** informal rather. **of a kind** only partly deserving the name. **one of a kind** unique. **two** (or **three, four**, etc.) **of a kind 1** the same or very similar. **2** (of cards) having the same face value but of a different suit.

USAGE

Use **this kind of** to refer to a singular noun (e.g., *this kind of behavior is not acceptable*), and **these kinds of** to refer to a plural noun (e.g., *these kinds of questions are not relevant*).

kind² ▶ **adj.** considerate and generous.

SYNONYMS **kindly**, good-natured, kindhearted, warmhearted, caring, affectionate, loving, warm, considerate, obliging, compassionate, sympathetic, understanding, benevolent, benign, altruistic, unselfish, generous, charitable, philanthropic, helpful, thoughtful, humane; informal decent. ANTONYMS unkind.

kin·der·gar·ten /ˈkindərˌgärtn, -ˌgärdn/ ▶ **n.** a school or class that prepares children for first grade. ▪ **kin·der·gart·ner** (also **kin·der·gar·ten·er**) **n.**

kin·dle /ˈkindl/ ▶ **v.** (**kindles, kindling, kindled**) **1** light a flame; make a fire start burning. **2** arouse an emotion.

SYNONYMS **1 light**, ignite, set light to, set fire to; informal torch. **2 rouse**, arouse, wake, awaken, stimulate, inspire, stir (up), excite, fire, trigger, activate, spark. ANTONYMS extinguish.

kin·dling /ˈkindliNG/ ▶ **n.** small sticks used for lighting fires.

kind·ly /ˈkīn(d)lē/ ▶ **adv. 1** in a kind way. **2** please (used in a polite request). ▶ **adj.** (**kindlier, kindliest**) kind.

SYNONYMS ▶ **adj. benevolent**, kind, kindhearted, warmhearted, generous, good-natured, gentle, warm, compassionate, caring, loving, benign, well-meaning, considerate. ANTONYMS unkind, cruel.

▫ **not take kindly to** not be pleased by. ▪ **kind·li·ness n.**

kind·ness /ˈkīn(d)nis/ ▶ **n. 1** the quality of being kind. **2** a kind act.

SYNONYMS **kindliness**, affection, warmth, gentleness, concern, care, consideration, altruism, unselfishness, compassion, sympathy, benevolence, generosity. ANTONYMS unkindness.

kin·dred /ˈkindrid/ ▶ **pl.n.** your family and relations. ▶ **adj.** having similar qualities. ▫ **kindred spirit** a person whose interests or attitudes are similar to your own.

kin·e·mat·ics /ˌkinəˈmatiks/ ▶ **pl.n.** the branch of mechanics concerned with the motion of objects. ▪ **kin·e·mat·ic adj.**

ki·ne·sis /kəˈnēsis/ ▶ **n.** (plural **kineses**) technical movement.

ki·net·ic /kəˈnetik/ ▶ **adj.** relating to or resulting from motion. ▫ **kinetic energy** Physics energy that a body possesses as a result of being in motion. ▪ **ki·net·i·cal·ly adv.**

ki·net·ics /kəˈnetiks/ ▶ **n. 1** the branch of chemistry concerned with the rates of chemical reactions. **2** Physics the study of the forces involved in movement.

kin·folk /ˈkinˌfōk/ (or **kinsfolk** /ˈkinzˌfōk/) ▶ **pl.n. 1** (in anthropological or formal use) a person's blood relations, regarded collectively. **2** a group of people related by blood.

king /kiNG/ ▶ **n. 1** the male ruler of an independent state. **2** the best or most important person or thing of their kind. **3** a playing card ranking next below an ace. **4** the most important chess piece, which the opponent has to checkmate in order to win.

SYNONYMS **ruler**, sovereign, monarch, Crown, His Majesty, emperor, prince, potentate.

▫ **King Charles spaniel** a small breed of spaniel with a white, black, and tan coat. **king of beasts** the lion. **King of Kings** (in the Christian Church) God or Jesus Christ. **king-sized** (or **king-size**) of a larger than normal size. ▪ **king·ly adj. king·ship n.**

king·dom /ˈkiNGdəm/ ▶ **n. 1** a country, state, or territory ruled by a king or queen. **2** each of the three divisions (animal, vegetable, and mineral) in which natural objects are classified.

SYNONYMS **realm**, domain, dominion, country, empire, land, territory, nation, (sovereign) state, province.

□ **to kingdom come** informal to death or destruction.

king·fish·er /ˈkiNG,fiSHər/ ▶ **n.** a colorful bird with a long sharp beak that dives to catch fish in streams and ponds.

king·mak·er /ˈkiNG,mākər/ ▶ **n.** a person who brings leaders to power by using their political influence.

king·pin /ˈkiNG,pin/ ▶ **n.** **1** a person or thing that is essential to the success of an organization or operation. **2** a large bolt in a central position. **3** a vertical bolt used as a pivot.

kink /kiNGk/ ▶ **n.** **1** a sharp twist in something long and narrow. **2** a flaw or difficulty. **3** a peculiar habit or characteristic. ▶ **v.** form a kink.

kink·y /ˈkiNGkē/ ▶ **adj.** (**kinkier**, **kinkiest**) having kinks or twists.

kin·ship /ˈkin,SHip/ ▶ **n.** **1** the relationship between members of the same family. **2** a state of having similar characteristics or origins: *they felt a kinship with architects*.

kins·man /ˈkinzmən/ (or **kinswoman**) ▶ **n.** (plural **kinsmen** or **kinswomen**) one of your relations.

ki·osk /ˈkē,äsk/ ▶ **n.** a small open-fronted booth from which newspapers, refreshments, or tickets are sold.

kip·per /ˈkipər/ ▶ **n.** a herring that has been split open, salted, and dried or smoked.

kirk /kərk/ ▶ **n.** Scottish & Northern English a church.

kis·met /ˈkizmit, -,met/ ▶ **n.** fate.

kiss /kis/ ▶ **v.** touch someone or something with the lips as a sign of love, affection, or greeting. ▶ **n.** an act of kissing.

SYNONYMS ▶ **v.** informal peck, smooch, canoodle, neck, buss, make out, lock lips; formal osculate. ▶ **n.** French kiss; informal peck, smooch, smack, buss, X.

□ **kiss of death** an action that makes certain the failure of an enterprise. **the kiss of life** mouth-to-mouth resuscitation.

kiss·er /ˈkisər/ ▶ **n.** **1** a person who kisses someone. **2** informal a person's mouth.

kit /kit/ ▶ **n.** **1** a set of equipment or clothes for a specific purpose. **2** a set of drums, cymbals, and other percussion instruments. ▶ **v.** (**kits**, **kitting**, **kitted**) (**kit someone out**) provide someone with the clothes or equipment needed for a particular activity.

SYNONYMS ▶ **n.** **1 equipment**, tools, implements, instruments, gadgets, utensils, appliances, gear, tackle, hardware, paraphernalia; informal things, stuff; Military accoutrements. **2** *a tool kit* **set**, selection, collection, pack.

kit·bag /ˈkit,bag/ ▶ **n.** a long canvas bag for carrying a soldier's possessions.

kitch·en /ˈkiCHən/ ▶ **n.** **1** a room where food is prepared and cooked. **2** a set of fittings and units installed in a kitchen. □ **everything but the kitchen sink** everything imaginable. **kitchen cabinet** a group of unofficial advisers thought to be unduly influential.

kitch·en·ette /,kiCHəˈnet/ ▶ **n.** a small kitchen or cooking area.

kitch·en·ware /ˈkiCHən,we(ə)r/ ▶ **n.** kitchen utensils.

kite /kīt/ ▶ **n.** **1** a toy consisting of a light frame with thin material stretched over it, flown in the wind at the end of a long string. **2** a long-winged bird of prey with a forked tail. **3** Geometry a four-sided figure having two pairs of equal sides next to each other.

kith /kiTH/ ▶ **n.** (**kith and kin**) your family and relations.

kitsch /kiCH/ ▶ **n.** art, objects, or design that are thought to be inartistic or show poor taste. ■ **kitsch·y adj.**

kit·ten /ˈkitn/ ▶ **n.** **1** a young cat. **2** the young of certain other animals, such as the rabbit and beaver. □ **have kittens** informal be very nervous or upset.

kit·ten·ish /ˈkitn-iSH/ ▶ **adj.** playful, lively, or flirtatious.

kit·ti·wake /ˈkitē,wāk/ ▶ **n.** a small gull that nests on sea cliffs, with a loud call that resembles its name.

kit·ty¹ /ˈkitē/ ▶ **n.** (plural **kitties**) **1** a fund of money for use by a number of people. **2** a pool of money in some card games.

kit·ty² ▶ **n.** (plural **kitties**) informal a cat.

ki·wi /ˈkēwē/ ▶ **n.** (plural **kiwis**) **1** a bird from New Zealand that cannot fly. **2** (**Kiwi**) informal a person from New Zealand. □ **kiwi fruit** the fruit of an Asian plant, with green flesh and black seeds.

kJ ▶ **abbr.** kilojoule(s).

KKK ▶ **abbr.** Ku Klux Klan.

kl ▶ **abbr.** kiloliter(s).

Klans·man /ˈklanzmən/ (or **Klanswoman** /-wo͝omən/) ▶ **n.** (plural **Klansmen** or **Klanswomen**) a member of the Ku Klux Klan.

Klax·on /ˈklaksən/ ▶ **n.** trademark a vehicle horn or similar loud warning device.

Kleen·ex /ˈklē,neks/ ▶ **n.** (plural **Kleenex** or **Kleenexes**) trademark a paper facial tissue.

klep·to·ma·ni·a /,kleptəˈmānēə, -ˈmānyə/ ▶ **n.** a compulsive urge to steal. ■ **klep·to·ma·ni·ac n. & adj.**

kludge /klo͞oj/ ▶ **n.** informal something hastily or badly put together, especially in computing.

klutz /kləts/ ▶ **n.** informal a clumsy, awkward, or foolish person. ■ **klutz·y adj.**

km ▶ **abbr.** kilometers.

knack /nak/ ▶ **n.** **1** a skill at performing a task. **2** a habit of doing something.

SYNONYMS **1 gift**, talent, flair, instinct, genius, ability, capability, capacity, aptitude, bent, facility, trick; informal the hang of something. **2 tendency**, habit, liability, propensity.

knap·sack /ˈnap,sak/ ▶ **n.** a bag with shoulder straps, carried on the back.

knave /nāv/ ▶ **n.** **1** old use a dishonest man. **2** (in cards) a jack. ■ **knav·ish adj.**

knead /nēd/ ▶ **v.** **1** work dough or clay with the hands. **2** massage something as if kneading it.

knee /nē/ ▶ **n.** **1** the joint between the thigh and the lower leg. **2** the upper surface of your thigh when you are in a sitting position. ▶ **v.** (**knees**, **kneeing**, **kneed**) hit someone with your knee. □ **at your mother's knee** at an early age. **bring someone to their knees** reduce someone to a state of weakness or submissiveness. **knee-high** so high as to reach the knees. **knee-high to a grasshopper** informal very small or young. **knee-jerk** done automatically and without thinking.

knee·cap /ˈnēˌkap/ ▶ **n.** the bone in front of the knee joint. ▶ **v.** (**kneecaps**, **kneecapping**, **kneecapped**) shoot someone in the knee.

kneel /nēl/ ▶ **v.** (**kneels**, **kneeling**, **knelt** or **kneeled**) be in a position in which you rest your weight on your knees.

kneel·er /ˈnēlər/ ▶ **n.** a cushion or bench for kneeling on.

knell /nel/ ▶ **n.** literary the sound of a bell ringing to mark a person's death. ▶ **v.** (of a bell) ring solemnly.

knelt /nelt/ past and past participle of KNEEL.

knew /n(y)o͞o/ past of KNOW.

knick·ers /ˈnikərz/ (or **knickerbockers** /ˈnikərˌbäkərz/) ▶ **pl.n.** loose-fitting pants gathered at the knee or calf.

knick-knack /ˈnikˌnak/ ▶ **n.** a small worthless decorative object.

knife /nīf/ ▶ **n.** (plural **knives** /nīvz/) a cutting tool consisting of a blade fixed into a handle. ▶ **v.** (**knifes**, **knifing**, **knifed**) **1** stab someone with a knife. **2** cut through or into something like a knife.

SYNONYMS ▶ **v.** **stab**, hack, gash, slash, lacerate, cut, bayonet, wound.

□ **that you could cut with a knife** (of an accent or atmosphere) very obvious. **under the knife** informal undergoing surgery.

knight /nīt/ ▶ **n.** **1** (in the Middle Ages) a man of noble rank with a duty to fight for his king. **2** (in the UK) a man awarded a title by the king or queen and entitled to use "Sir" in front of his name. **3** a chess piece that moves by jumping to the opposite corner of a rectangle two squares by three. ▶ **v.** give a man the title of knight. □ **knight errant** a medieval knight who wandered in search of adventure. **knight in shining armor** a man who comes to the rescue of a woman in a difficult situation. ■ **knight·hood** /ˈnītˌho͝od/ **n.**

knit /nit/ ▶ **v.** (**knits**, **knitting**, **knitted** or **knit**) **1** make a garment by looping yarn together with knitting needles or on a machine. **2** make a plain stitch in knitting. **3** join together. **4** tighten your eyebrows in a frown. ▶ **n.** (**knits**) knitted clothes.

SYNONYMS ▶ **v.** **unite**, unify, bond, fuse, coalesce, merge, meld, blend, join, link.

□ **knitting needle** a long thin pointed rod used as part of a pair in knitting by hand. ■ **knit·ter** **n.** **knit·ting** **n.**

knit·wear /ˈnitˌwe(ə)r/ ▶ **n.** knitted clothes.

knives /nīvz/ plural of KNIFE.

knob /näb/ ▶ **n.** **1** a rounded lump at the end or on the surface of something. **2** a ball-shaped handle. **3** a round button on a machine. **4** a small lump of something.

SYNONYMS **lump**, bump, protrusion, protuberance, bulge, swelling, knot, nodule, boss.

■ **knob·by** **adj.**

knock /näk/ ▶ **v.** **1** hit a surface noisily to attract attention. **2** collide with. **3** hit someone or something so that they move or fall. **4** make a hole, dent, etc., in something by hitting it. **5** informal criticize. **6** (of a motor) make a thumping or rattling noise. ▶ **n.** **1** a sound of knocking. **2** a blow or collision. **3** a setback.

SYNONYMS ▶ **v.** **1** **bang**, tap, rap, thump, pound, hammer, beat, strike, hit; informal bash. **2** **collide with**, bump into, run into, crash into, smash into, plow into, impact. ▶ **n.** **tap**, rap, rat-a-tat, knocking, bang, banging, pounding, hammering, thump, thud.

□ **knock around** (or **about**) informal travel or spend time aimlessly. **knock something back** informal consume a drink quickly. **knock something down** informal reduce the price of an article. **knock it off** informal stop doing something. **knock-kneed** having legs that curve inward at the knee. **knock off** informal stop work. **knock something off** informal produce a piece of work quickly and easily. **knock-on effect** an effect or result that causes a series of other things to happen. **knock someone out** **1** make someone unconscious. **2** informal astonish or greatly impress. **the school of hard knocks** difficult but useful life experiences.

knock·a·bout /ˈnäkəˌbout/ ▶ **adj.** (of comedy) lively and involving deliberately clumsy or rough actions.

knock·er /ˈnäkər/ ▶ **n.** a hinged object fixed to a door and rapped by visitors to attract attention.

knock·off /ˈnäkˌôf/ ▶ **n.** informal a copy or imitation.

knock·out /ˈnäkˌout/ ▶ **n.** **1** an act of knocking someone out. **2** informal a very impressive person or thing.

knoll /nōl/ ▶ **n.** a small hill or mound.

knot /nät/ ▶ **n.** **1** a fastening made by looping a piece of string or rope and tightening it. **2** a tangled mass in hair, wool, etc. **3** a hard mass in wood at the point where the trunk and a branch join. **4** a hard lump of muscle tissue. **5** a small group of people. **6** a unit of speed of a ship, aircraft, or the wind, equivalent to one nautical mile per hour. ▶ **v.** (**knots**, **knotting**, **knotted**) **1** fasten with a knot. **2** tangle. **3** make a muscle tense and hard. **4** (of the stomach) tighten as a result of tension.

SYNONYMS ▶ **n.** *a knot of people* **cluster**, group, band, huddle, bunch, circle, ring. ▶ **v.** **1** **tie**, fasten, secure, bind, do up. **2** (**knotted**) **tangled**, matted, snarled, unkempt, tousled; informal mussed up.

□ **tie (up) in knots** informal confuse completely. **tie the knot** informal get married.

knot·hole /ˈnätˌhōl/ ▶ **n.** a hole in a piece of wood where a knot has fallen out.

knot·ty /ˈnätē/ ▶ **adj.** (**knottier**, **knottiest**) **1** full of knots. **2** very complex: *a knotty problem.*

know /nō/ ▶ **v.** (**knows**, **knowing**, **knew** /n(y)o͞o/; past participle **known**) **1** be aware of something as a result of observing, asking, or being told. **2** be absolutely sure of something. **3** be familiar with. **4** have a good grasp of a subject or language. **5** have personal experience of. **6** (**be known as**) be thought of as having a particular quality or title: *she was known as a tough negotiator.*

SYNONYMS **1** *she doesn't know I'm here* **be aware**, realize, be conscious, be cognizant. **2** *I know the rules* **be familiar with**, be conversant with, be acquainted with, be versed in, have a grasp of, understand, comprehend; informal be clued in on. **3** *do you know her?* **be acquainted with**, have met, be familiar with.

□ **be in the know** informal be aware of something known only to a few people. **know-it-all** informal a person who behaves as if they know everything.

know-how practical knowledge or skill. **God** (or **goodness** or **heaven**) **knows** I have no idea. **know better than** be wise enough to avoid doing something. **know no bounds** have no limits. **know-nothing** an ignorant person. **know your own mind** be decisive and certain. **know the ropes** have experience of the right way of doing something. **know what's what** informal be experienced and competent in a particular area. ■ **know·a·ble** **adj.**

know·ing /'nōiNG/ ▶ **adj.** **1** suggesting that you know something that is meant to be secret: *a knowing smile.* **2** experienced or cunning.

SYNONYMS **significant**, meaningful, expressive, suggestive, eloquent, superior.

□ **there is no knowing** no one can tell. ■ **know·ing·ly** **adv.**

knowl·edge /'nälij/ ▶ **n.** **1** information and awareness gained through experience or education. **2** the state of knowing about something.

SYNONYMS **1 understanding**, comprehension, grasp, command, mastery, familiarity, acquaintance; informal know-how. **2 learning**, erudition, education, scholarship, schooling, wisdom. **3 awareness**, consciousness, realization, cognition, apprehension, perception, appreciation, cognizance. ANTONYMS ignorance.

□ **to (the best of) my knowledge** **1** so far as I know. **2** as I know for certain.

SPELLING

Remember the **d**: knowle**d**ge.

knowl·edge·a·ble /'nälijəbəl/ (or **knowledgable**) ▶ **adj.** intelligent and well-informed.

SYNONYMS **1 well-informed**, learned, well-read, (well-)educated, erudite, scholarly, cultured, cultivated, enlightened. **2** *he's knowledgeable about art* **conversant with**, familiar with, well-acquainted with, au fait with, up on, up to date with, abreast of; informal clued in on. ANTONYMS ignorant.

■ **know·ledge·a·bly** **adv.**

known /nōn/ past participle of **KNOW** ▶ **adj.** **1** identified as being: *a known criminal.* **2** Math (of a quantity or variable) having a value that can be stated. **3** recognized, familiar, or within the scope of knowledge.

SYNONYMS **recognized**, well-known, widely known, noted, celebrated, notable, notorious, acknowledged.

knuck·le /'nəkəl/ ▶ **n.** **1** each of the joints of a finger. **2** a knee joint of a four-legged animal, or the part joining the leg to the foot. ▶ **v.** (**knuckles**, **knuckling**, **knuckled**) **1** (**knuckle down**) apply yourself seriously to a task. **2** (**knuckle under**) accept someone's authority. □ **knuckle sandwich** informal a punch in the mouth.

knuck·le·dust·er /'nəkəl,dəstər/ ▶ **n.** a metal fitting worn over the knuckles in fighting to increase the effect of blows.

knuck·le·head /'nəkəl,hed/ ▶ **n.** informal a stupid person.

knurl /nərl/ ▶ **n.** a small projecting knob or ridge. ■ **knurled** **adj.**

KO /,kā'ō/ ▶ **n.** a knockout in a boxing match. ▶ **v.** (**KO's**, **KO'ing**, **KO'd**) knock out in a boxing match.

ko·a·la /kō'älə/ ▶ **n.** a bearlike Australian animal that lives in trees.

kohl /kōl/ ▶ **n.** a black powder used as eye makeup.

kohl·ra·bi /kōl'räbē/ ▶ **n.** a variety of cabbage with an edible thick, round stem.

koi /koi/ ▶ **n.** (plural **koi**) a large common Japanese carp.

kook /ko͞ok/ ▶ **n.** informal a crazy or unconventional person. ■ **kook·y** **adj.**

kook·a·bur·ra /'ko͝okə,bərə/ ▶ **n.** a very large, noisy kingfisher found in Australia and New Zealand.

ko·pek /'kōpek/ (or **copeck** or **kopeck**) ▶ **n.** a unit of money in Russia.

Ko·ran /kə'rän, kô-, 'kōrän/ (**Qur'an** /kə'rän, -'ran/) ▶ **n.** the sacred book of Islam, believed to be the word of God as told to Muhammad and written down in Arabic.

Ko·re·an /kə'rēən, kô-/ ▶ **n.** **1** a person from Korea. **2** the language of Korea. ▶ **adj.** relating to Korea.

kor·ma /'kôrmə/ ▶ **n.** a mild Indian curry of meat or fish marinated in yogurt or curds.

ko·sher /'kōSHər/ ▶ **adj.** **1** (of food) prepared according to the requirements of Jewish law. **2** informal genuine and legitimate.

Ko·so·var /'kôsə,vär, 'käs-/ ▶ **n.** a person from Kosovo, a province of Serbia whose population is largely of Albanian descent. ■ **Ko·so·van** **n. & adj.**

kow·tow /'kou,tou, ,kou'tou/ ▶ **v.** **1** be too meek and obedient toward someone. **2** (in the past, as part of Chinese custom) kneel and touch the ground with the forehead, in worship or as a sign of respect.

KP (or **KP duty**) ▶ **abbr.** (in the US military) kitchen police, or kitchen patrol: *I've been on KP since August.*

kraal /kräl/ ▶ **n.** South African **1** a traditional African village of huts. **2** an enclosure for sheep and cattle.

kraft /kraft/ (also **kraft paper**) ▶ **n.** a kind of strong, smooth brown wrapping paper.

kra·ken /'kräkən/ ▶ **n.** an enormous mythical sea monster said to appear off the coast of Norway.

Krem·lin /'kremlin/ ▶ **n.** the fortified complex of buildings in Moscow that used to house the Russian government.

krill /kril/ ▶ **pl.n.** small shrimplike crustaceans that are the main food of baleen whales.

kro·na /'krōnə/ ▶ **n.** **1** (plural **kronor**) the basic unit of money of Sweden. **2** (plural **kronur**) the unit of money of Iceland.

kro·ne /'krōnə/ ▶ **n.** (plural **kroner**) the basic unit of money of Denmark and Norway.

kru·ger·rand /'kro͞ogə,rand/ (also **Kruger** /'kro͞ogər/) ▶ **n.** a South African gold coin with a portrait of President Kruger on it.

kryp·ton /'krip,tän/ ▶ **n.** a gaseous chemical element used in some kinds of electric light.

Kshat·ri·ya /k(ə)'SHätrēə/ ▶ **n.** a member of the second-highest Hindu caste, that of the military.

kt ▶ **abbr.** knot(s).

ku·dos /'k(y)o͞o,dōs, -,dōz, -,däs/ ▶ **n.** praise and honor.

SYNONYMS **prestige**, cachet, glory, honor, status, standing, distinction, admiration, respect, esteem.

USAGE

kudos is a singular word and it is generally considered wrong to use it as if it were a plural; for example, it is better to say *he received much kudos for his work* than *he received many kudos for his work*.

ku·du /ˈko͞odo͞o/ ▶ **n.** (plural **kudu** or **kudus**) a striped African antelope, the male of which has long spirally curved horns.

Ku Klux Klan /ˈko͞o ˌkləks ˈklan/ ▶ **n.** a secret organization of white people in the United States who terrorize black people.

kum·quat /ˈkəmˌkwät/ ▶ **n.** a very small orangelike fruit.

kung fu /ˈkəNG ˈfo͞o, ˈko͝oNG/ ▶ **n.** a Chinese martial art resembling karate.

Kurd /kərd/ ▶ **n.** a member of a mainly Islamic people living in Kurdistan, a region in the Middle East.

Ku·wai·ti /kəˈwātē, ko͞o-/ ▶ **n.** a person from Kuwait. ▶ **adj.** relating to Kuwait.

kV ▶ **abbr.** kilovolts.

kvetch /k(ə)veCH, kfeCH/ informal ▶ **n. 1** a person who complains a great deal. **2** a complaint. ▶ **v.** complain.

kW ▶ **abbr.** kilowatts.

kWh ▶ **abbr.** kilowatt-hour(s).

Ll

L (or **l**) ▶ **n.** (plural **Ls** or **L's**) **1** the twelfth letter of the alphabet. **2** the Roman numeral for 50. ▶ **abbr.** (**l**) liter(s).

la /lä/ ▶ **n.** Music the sixth note of a major scale, coming after "sol" and before "ti."

lab /lab/ ▶ **n.** informal a laboratory.

la·bel /'lābəl/ ▶ **n. 1** a small piece of paper, fabric, etc., attached to an object and giving information about it. **2** the name or trademark of a fashion company. **3** a company that produces recorded music. **4** a classifying name given to a person or thing. ▶ **v.** (**labels**, **labeling**, **labeled**) **1** attach a label to. **2** put someone or something in a category.

SYNONYMS ▶ **n. 1 tag**, ticket, tab, sticker, marker, docket. **2 description**, designation, name, epithet, nickname, sobriquet, title. ▶ **v. 1 tag**, ticket, mark, stamp. **2 categorize**, classify, class, describe, designate, identify, mark, stamp, brand, call, name, term, dub.

SPELLING

The word ends with **-el**, not **-le**: label.

la·bor /'lābər/ ▶ **n. 1** work. **2** workers as a group. **3** the process of giving birth. ▶ **v. 1** do hard physical work. **2** have difficulty doing something in spite of working hard. **3** move with difficulty and effort. **4** (**labor under**) believe something that is not true.

SYNONYMS ▶ **n. 1 work**, toil, exertion, effort, industry, drudgery; informal slog, grind; old use travail. **2 workers**, employees, laborers, workforce, staff. **3 childbirth**, birth, delivery; technical parturition. ▶ **v. work (hard)**, toil, slave (away), struggle, strive, exert yourself, endeavor, try hard; informal slog away, plug away.

□ **a labor of love** a task done for pleasure, not reward. **labor camp** a prison camp where prisoners have to do hard physical work. **Labor Day** a public holiday held in honor of working people on the first Monday in September (in the United States and Canada), or in some countries on May 1. **labor force** the members of a population who are able to work. **labor-intensive** needing a lot of work. **labor the point** repeat something that has already been said and understood. **labor-saving** designed to reduce the amount of work needed to do something. **labor union** an association of workers formed to protect and further their rights and interests.

lab·o·ra·to·ry /'labrəˌtôrē/ ▶ **n.** (plural **laboratories**) a room or building for scientific research or teaching, or for the making of drugs or chemicals.

la·bored /'lābərd/ ▶ **adj. 1** done with great difficulty. **2** not spontaneous or natural: *a labored joke.*

SYNONYMS **1** *labored breathing* **strained**, difficult, forced, laborious. **2** *a labored metaphor* **contrived**, forced, unconvincing, unnatural, artificial, overdone. ANTONYMS natural, easy.

la·bor·er /'lāb(ə)rər/ ▶ **n.** a person who does hard physical work that does not need any special skill or training.

SYNONYMS **workman**, worker, manual worker, blue-collar worker, (hired) hand, roustabout, drudge, menial.

la·bo·ri·ous /lə'bôrēəs/ ▶ **adj. 1** needing a lot of time and effort. **2** showing obvious signs of effort: *a slow, laborious speech.*

SYNONYMS **1 arduous**, hard, heavy, difficult, strenuous, grueling, punishing, exacting, tough, onerous, challenging, painstaking, time-consuming. **2 labored**, strained, forced, stiff, stilted, unnatural, artificial, ponderous. ANTONYMS easy, effortless.

■ **la·bo·ri·ous·ly** **adv.**

La·bour Par·ty ▶ **n.** a British political party formed to represent the interests of ordinary working people.

Lab·ra·dor /'labrəˌdôr/ ▶ **n.** a breed of dog with a black or yellow coat, used as a retriever and as a guide dog.

la·bur·num /lə'bərnəm/ ▶ **n.** a small tree with hanging clusters of yellow flowers.

lab·y·rinth /'lab(ə)ˌrinTH/ ▶ **n.** a complicated network of passages or paths in which it is difficult to find your way; a maze.

lab·y·rin·thine /ˌlabə'rinˌTHēn, -'rinTHin, -'rinˌTHīn/ ▶ **adj. 1** resembling a labyrinth. **2** complicated and confusing.

SYNONYMS **1 mazelike**, winding, twisting, serpentine, meandering. **2 complicated**, intricate, complex, involved, tortuous, convoluted, elaborate, confusing, puzzling, mystifying, bewildering, baffling.

lac /lak/ ▶ **n.** a substance secreted by an Asian insect, used to make varnish, shellac, etc.

lace /lās/ ▶ **n. 1** a delicate open fabric made by looping, twisting, or knitting thread in patterns. **2** a cord used to fasten a shoe or garment. ▶ **v.** (**laces**, **lacing**, **laced**) **1** fasten something with a lace or laces. **2** add an ingredient to a drink or dish to make it stronger or improve the flavor.

SYNONYMS ▶ **v. 1 fasten**, do up, tie up, secure, knot. **2 flavor**, mix, blend, fortify, strengthen, season, spice (up), liven up, doctor, adulterate; informal spike.

lac·er·ate /'lasəˌrāt/ ▶ **v.** (**lacerates**, **lacerating**, **lacerated**) tear or deeply cut the flesh or skin.

lac·er·a·tion /ˌlasə'rāSHən/ ▶ **n.** a cut or wound.

SYNONYMS **gash**, cut, wound, injury, tear, slash, scratch, scrape, abrasion, graze.

lach·ry·mal /'lakrəməl/ (or **lacrimal**) ▶ **adj.** connected with weeping or tears.

lach·ry·mose /'lakrə,mōs, -,mōz/ ▶ **adj.** literary tearful.

lac·ing /'lāsiNG/ ▶ **n. 1** a laced fastening of a shoe or garment. **2** a dash of liquor added to a drink.

lack /lak/ ▶ **n.** the state of being without or not having enough of something. ▶ **v.** (also **lack for**) be without or without enough of.

SYNONYMS ▶ **n. absence**, want, need, deficiency, dearth, shortage, shortfall, scarcity, paucity. ANTONYMS abundance. ▶ **v. be without**, be in need of, be short of, be deficient in, be low on, be pressed for, need; informal be strapped for.

lack·a·dai·si·cal /,lakə'dāzikəl/ ▶ **adj.** not showing enthusiasm or thoroughness.

lack·ey /'lakē/ ▶ **n.** (plural **lackeys**) **1** a servant. **2** a person who is too willing to serve or obey other people.

lack·ing /'lakiNG/ ▶ **adj.** missing or not having enough of.

lack·lus·ter /'lak,ləstər/ ▶ **adj. 1** not exciting or interesting: *the team's lackluster performance.* **2** (of the hair or eyes) not shining.

SYNONYMS **uninspired**, uninspiring, unimaginative, dull, humdrum, colorless, bland, insipid, flat, dry, lifeless, tame, prosaic, boring, dreary, tedious. ANTONYMS inspired.

la·con·ic /lə'känik/ ▶ **adj.** using very few words. ■ **la·con·i·cal·ly adv.**

lac·quer /'lakər/ ▶ **n. 1** a liquid applied to wood or metal to give it a hard, glossy surface. **2** decorative wooden goods coated with lacquer. **3** hairspray. ■ **lac·quered adj.**

lac·ri·mal = LACHRYMAL.

la·crosse /lə'krôs, -'kräs/ ▶ **n.** a team game in which a ball is thrown, caught, and carried with a long-handled stick that has a net at one end.

lac·ry·mal = LACHRYMAL.

lac·tate /,lak'tāt/ ▶ **v.** (**lactates**, **lactating**, **lactated**) (of a woman or female animal) produce milk in the breasts or mammary glands, for feeding babies or young. ■ **lac·ta·tion** /lak'tāsHən/ **n.**

lac·tic /'laktik/ ▶ **adj.** relating to or obtained from milk. □ **lactic acid** an acid present in sour milk, and produced in the muscles during strenuous exercise.

lac·tose /'lak,tōs, -,tōz/ ▶ **n.** a sugar present in milk.

lac·to·veg·e·tar·i·an /,laktō,veji'te(ə)rēən/ ▶ **n.** a person who does not eat meat or eggs, but who eats dairy products and vegetables.

la·cu·na /lə'k(y)o͞onə/ ▶ **n.** (plural **lacunae** /-nī, -nē/ or **lacunas**) a gap or missing part.

lac·y /'lāsē/ ▶ **adj.** (**lacier**, **laciest**) made of, resembling, or trimmed with lace.

lad /lad/ ▶ **n.** informal a boy or young man.

SYNONYMS **1 boy**, schoolboy, youth, youngster, juvenile, stripling; informal kid, (little) nipper, (little) shaver; disapproving brat. **2 (young) man**, fellow; informal guy, dude.

lad·der /'ladər/ ▶ **n. 1** a structure consisting of a series of bars or steps between two uprights, used for climbing up or down. **2** a series of stages by which progress can be made: *the career ladder.* □ **ladder-back** an upright chair with a back resembling a ladder.

lad·en /'lādn/ ▶ **adj.** heavily loaded or weighed down.

SYNONYMS **loaded**, burdened, weighed down, overloaded, encumbered, piled high, full, packed, stuffed, crammed; informal chock-full, chock-a-block.

la-di-da /,lä dē 'dä/ (or **lah-di-dah**) ▶ **adj.** informal affected or snobbish.

la·dle /'lādl/ ▶ **n.** a large spoon with a cup-shaped bowl and a long handle, for serving soup, stew, etc. ▶ **v.** (**ladles**, **ladling**, **ladled**) **1** serve or transfer soup, stew, etc., with a ladle. **2** (**ladle out**) give out in large amounts. ■ **la·dle·ful n.**

la·dy /'lādē/ ▶ **n.** (plural **ladies**) **1** (in polite or formal use) a woman. **2** a well-mannered woman, or a woman of high social position. **3** (**Lady**) a title used by peeresses, female relatives of peers, and the wives and widows of knights.

SYNONYMS **1 woman**, female, girl; informal dame, broad. **2 noblewoman**, aristocrat, duchess, countess, peeress, viscountess, baroness.

□ **ladies' man** (or **lady's man**) a man who enjoys spending time and flirting with women. **ladies' room** a restroom for women in a public or institutional building. **Lady chapel** a chapel dedicated to the Virgin Mary in a church or cathedral. **Lady Day** the feast of the Annunciation, March 25. **lady-in-waiting** (plural **ladies-in-waiting**) a woman who accompanies and looks after a queen or princess. **lady's maid** chiefly historical a maid who attended to the personal needs of her mistress.

la·dy·bug /'lādē,bəg/ (or **ladybird** /'lādē,bərd/) ▶ **n.** a small beetle that has a red back with black spots.

la·dy·kill·er /'lādē,kilər/ ▶ **n.** informal a man who is successful in seducing women.

la·dy·like /'lādē,līk/ ▶ **adj.** typical of a well-mannered woman or girl.

SYNONYMS **genteel**, polite, refined, well-bred, cultivated, polished, decorous, proper, respectable, well-mannered, cultured, sophisticated, elegant.

La·dy·ship /'lādē,sHip/ ▶ **n.** (**Her**/**Your Ladyship**) a respectful way of referring to or addressing a Lady.

lag[1] /lag/ ▶ **v.** (**lags**, **lagging**, **lagged**) fall behind. ▶ **n.** (also **time lag**) a period of time between two events.

SYNONYMS ▶ **v. fall behind**, trail, bring up the rear, dawdle, hang back, delay, loiter, linger, dally, straggle.

lag[2] ▶ **v.** (**lags**, **lagging**, **lagged**) cover a water tank or pipes with material designed to prevent heat loss.

la·ger /'lägər/ ▶ **n.** a light fizzy beer.

lag·gard /'lagərd/ ▶ **n.** a person who falls behind other people.

lag·ging /'lagiNG/ ▶ **n.** material wrapped around a water tank and pipes to prevent heat loss.

la·goon /lə'go͞on/ ▶ **n.** a stretch of salt water separated from the sea by a low sandbank or coral reef.

lah-di-dah = LA-DI-DA.

laid /lād/ past and past participle of LAY[1]. ▫ **laid-back** informal relaxed and easygoing.

lain /lān/ past participle of LIE[1].

lair /le(ə)r/ ▶ n. **1** a wild animal's resting place. **2** a person's secret den.

laird /le(ə)rd/ ▶ n. (in Scotland) a person who owns a large estate.

lais·sez-faire /ˌlesā ˈfe(ə)r, ˌlezā/ ▶ n. a policy of leaving things to take their own course, without interfering.

la·i·ty /ˈlāətē/ ▶ n. (**the laity**) people who are not priests or ministers of the church; ordinary people.

lake /lāk/ ▶ n. a large area of water surrounded by land.

> SYNONYMS **pool**, pond, tarn, reservoir, lagoon, waterhole, watering hole, bayou (lake).

▫ **Lake District** a region of lakes and mountains in Cumbria in England.

lam[1] /lam/ ▶ v. (**lams, lamming, lammed**) informal hit someone hard.

lam[2] ▶ n. (**on the lam**) in flight, especially from the police: *he went on the lam and is living under a false name.*

la·ma /ˈlämə/ ▶ n. **1** a title given to a spiritual leader in Tibetan Buddhism. **2** a Tibetan or Mongolian Buddhist monk.

lamb /lam/ ▶ n. **1** a young sheep. **2** a gentle or innocent person. ▶ v. **1** (of a female sheep) give birth to lambs. **2** look after ewes at lambing time. ▪ **lamb·ing** n.

lam·ba·da /lamˈbädə/ ▶ n. a fast Brazilian dance.

lam·baste /lamˈbāst, -ˈbast/ (or **lambast**) ▶ v. (**lambastes** or **lambasts, lambasting, lambasted**) criticize someone harshly.

lam·bent /ˈlambənt/ ▶ adj. literary lit up or flickering with a soft glow.

lame /lām/ ▶ adj. **1** walking with difficulty because of an injury or illness affecting the leg or foot. **2** (of an explanation or excuse) unconvincing and feeble. **3** (of something meant to be entertaining) dull. ▶ v. (**lames, laming, lamed**) make a person or animal lame.

> SYNONYMS ▶ adj. **1 limping**, hobbling, crippled, disabled, incapacitated; old use game. **2 feeble**, weak, thin, flimsy, poor, unconvincing, implausible, unlikely.

▫ **lame duck 1** an official (especially the president) in the final period of office, after the election of a successor. **2** an ineffectual or unsuccessful person or thing. ▪ **lame·ly** adv. **lame·ness** n.

la·mé /laˈmā, lä-/ ▶ n. fabric with interwoven gold or silver threads.

la·ment /ləˈment/ ▶ n. **1** a passionate expression of grief. **2** a song or poem expressing grief or regret. ▶ v. **1** mourn a person's death. **2** express regret or disappointment about.

> SYNONYMS ▶ v. **1 mourn**, grieve, sorrow, weep, cry, wail, keen. **2 complain about**, bewail, bemoan, deplore. ANTONYMS celebrate, welcome.

▪ **lam·en·ta·tion** /ˌlamənˈtāsʜən/ n.

lam·en·ta·ble /ˈlaməntəbəl, ləˈmentəbəl/ ▶ adj. very bad or disappointing.

> SYNONYMS **deplorable**, regrettable, terrible, awful, wretched, woeful, dire, disastrous, desperate, grave, appalling, dreadful, pitiful, shameful, unfortunate; formal egregious. ANTONYMS wonderful.

▪ **la·men·ta·bly** adv.

lam·i·na /ˈlamənə/ ▶ n. (plural **laminae** /-ˌnē, -ˌnī/) technical a thin layer, plate, or scale of rock, tissue, or other material. ▪ **lam·i·nar** adj.

lam·i·nate ▶ v. /ˈlaməˌnāt/ (**laminates, laminating, laminated**) **1** cover a flat surface with a layer of protective material. **2** make something by sticking layers of material together. **3** split into layers or leaves. **4** beat or roll metal into thin plates. ▶ n. /-nit, -ˌnāt/ a laminated product or material. ▪ **lam·i·na·tion** /ˌlaməˈnāsʜən/ n.

lamp /lamp/ ▶ n. a device using electricity, oil, or gas to give light.

lamp·black /ˈlampˌblak/ ▶ n. a black pigment made from soot.

lam·poon /lamˈpo͞on/ ▶ v. mock or ridicule. ▶ n. a mocking attack.

lam·prey /ˈlamprē/ ▶ n. (plural **lampreys**) a fish like an eel, having a round sucking mouth with horny teeth.

LAN /lan/ ▶ abbr. local area network.

lance /lans/ ▶ n. (in the past) a weapon with a long shaft and a pointed steel head, used by people on horseback. ▶ v. (**lances, lancing, lanced**) Medicine prick or cut open a boil or wound with a sharp instrument. ▫ **lance corporal** a rank of an enlisted officer in the US Marine Corps, above private first class and below corporal.

lan·ce·o·late /ˈlansēəlit, -ˌlāt/ ▶ adj. technical of a narrow oval shape tapering to a point at each end.

lanc·er /ˈlansər/ ▶ n. (in the past) a soldier armed with a lance.

lan·cet /ˈlansit/ ▶ n. a small two-edged knife with a sharp point, used in surgery.

land /land/ ▶ n. **1** the part of the earth's surface that is not covered by water. **2** an area of ground: *waste land.* **3** (**the land**) ground or soil used for farming. **4** a country or state. ▶ v. **1** put or go ashore. **2** come or bring something down to the ground. **3** bring a fish out of the water with a net or rod. **4** informal succeed in obtaining or achieving something. **5** (**land up**) reach a particular place or destination. **6** (**land someone in**) informal put someone in a difficult situation. **7** (**land someone with**) inflict something unwelcome on someone. **8** informal inflict a blow on someone. **9** (**land up with**) end up with an unwelcome situation.

> SYNONYMS ▶ n. **1 dry land**, terra firma, coast, coastline, shore. **2 grounds**, fields, property, acres, acreage, estate, real estate. **3 country**, nation, state, realm, kingdom, province, region, territory, area, domain. ▶ v. **1 disembark**, go ashore, debark, alight, light, get off, berth, dock, moor, (drop) anchor, tie up, put in, touch down, come to rest. **2 get**, obtain, acquire, secure, gain, net, win, achieve, attain, bag, carry off. ANTONYMS embark, take off.

▫ **how the land lies** what the state of affairs is. **in the land of the living** humorous alive or awake. **the land of Nod** humorous a state of sleep.

lan·dau /ˈlanˌdou/ ▶ n. an enclosed horse-drawn carriage.

land·ed /ˈlandid/ ▶ adj. owning a lot of land.

land·fall /ˈlan(d)ˌfôl/ ▶ n. arrival on land after a sea journey.

land·fill /ˈlan(d)ˌfil/ ▶ n. **1** the disposal of garbage by burying it. **2** buried garbage.

land·form /ˈlan(d)ˌfôrm/ ▶ **n.** a natural feature of the earth's surface.

land·hold·er /ˈlandˌhōldər/ ▶ **n.** a landowner.

land·ing /ˈlandiNG/ ▶ **n.** **1** a level area at the top of a staircase. **2** a place where people and goods can be landed from a boat. ▫ **landing craft** a boat for putting troops and equipment ashore on a beach. **landing gear** the undercarriage of an aircraft. **landing stage** a platform on to which passengers or cargo can be landed from a boat.

land·less /ˈlandlis/ ▶ **adj.** owning no land.

land·line /ˈlan(d)ˌlīn/ ▶ **n.** a conventional telecommunications connection by cable laid across land.

land·locked /ˈlan(d)ˌläkt/ ▶ **adj.** (of a place) surrounded by land.

land·lord /ˈlan(d)ˌlôrd/ (or **landlady** /ˈlan(d)ˌlādē/) ▶ **n.** a person who rents out property or land.

> SYNONYMS (**property**) **owner**, proprietor, lessor, householder, landowner; slumlord. ANTONYMS tenant.

land·lub·ber /ˈlan(d)ˌləbər/ ▶ **n.** informal a person who is not familiar with the sea or sailing.

land·mark /ˈlan(d)ˌmärk/ ▶ **n.** **1** an object or feature that is easily seen from a distance. **2** an important stage or turning point: *a landmark of research.*

> SYNONYMS **1 feature**, sight, monument, building. **2** *a landmark in Indian history* **turning point**, milestone, watershed.

land·mass /ˈlan(d)ˌmas/ ▶ **n.** a continent or other large body of land.

land·mine /ˈlan(d)ˌmīn/ ▶ **n.** an explosive mine laid on or just under the surface of the ground.

land·own·er /ˈlanˌdōnər/ ▶ **n.** a person who owns land.

land·scape /ˈlan(d)ˌskāp/ ▶ **n.** **1** all the visible features of an area of land. **2** a picture of an area of countryside. ▶ **v.** (**landscapes**, **landscaping**, **landscaped**) improve the appearance of land by changing its contours, planting trees and shrubs, etc.

> SYNONYMS ▶ **n. scenery**, country, countryside, topography, terrain, view, panorama.

▫ **landscape gardening** the art and practice of laying out grounds.

land·slide /ˈlan(d)ˌslīd/ ▶ **n.** **1** a mass of earth or rock that slides down a mountain or cliff. **2** an overwhelming majority of votes for one party in an election.

> SYNONYMS **1 avalanche**, rockfall, mudslide, rockslide. **2 decisive victory**, runaway victory, overwhelming majority; informal whitewash.

lane /lān/ ▶ **n.** **1** a narrow road. **2** a division of a road for a single line of traffic. **3** a strip of track or water for each of the competitors in a race. **4** a course followed by ships or aircraft.

> SYNONYMS **road**, street, track, trail, alley, alleyway, passage, path.

lan·guage /ˈlaNGgwij/ ▶ **n.** **1** human communication through the use of spoken or written words. **2** a particular system or style of spoken or written communication. **3** a system of symbols and rules for writing computer programs.

> SYNONYMS **1 speech**, speaking, talk, discourse, communication, words, vocabulary. **2 tongue**, mother tongue, native tongue, dialect, patois; informal lingo. **3 wording**, phrasing, phraseology, style, vocabulary, terminology, expressions, turn of phrase, parlance.

> SPELLING
> Write **-guage**, not **-gage**: lan**guage**.

lan·guid /ˈlaNGgwid/ ▶ **adj.** **1** relaxed and not inclined to be physically active. **2** weak or faint.

> SYNONYMS **1 relaxed**, unhurried, languorous, slow; listless, lethargic, sluggish, lazy, apathetic; informal laid-back. **2 sickly**, weak, faint, feeble, frail, delicate; tired, weary, fatigued. ANTONYMS energetic.

▪ **lan·guid·ly** **adv.**

lan·guish /ˈlaNGgwiSH/ ▶ **v.** **1** become weak or faint. **2** be kept in an unpleasant place or situation: *he was languishing in jail.*

> SYNONYMS **1 deteriorate**, decline, go downhill, wither, droop, wilt, fade. **2 waste away**, rot, be abandoned, be neglected, be forgotten, suffer. ANTONYMS thrive.

lan·guor /ˈlaNG(g)ər/ ▶ **n.** a pleasant feeling of being tired or without energy.

> SYNONYMS **lassitude**, lethargy, listlessness, torpor, fatigue, weariness, sleepiness, drowsiness; laziness, idleness, indolence, inertia, sluggishness, apathy. ANTONYMS vigor.

▪ **lan·guor·ous** **adj.**

lank /laNGk/ ▶ **adj.** (of hair) long, limp, and straight.

lank·y /ˈlaNGkē/ ▶ **adj.** (**lankier**, **lankiest**) tall, thin, and moving in an awkward or ungraceful way.

> SYNONYMS **tall**, **thin**, slender, slim, lean, lank, skinny, spindly, spare, gangling, gangly, gawky, rangy. ANTONYMS stocky.

lan·o·lin /ˈlanl-in/ ▶ **n.** a fatty substance from sheep's wool, used in skin cream.

lan·tern /ˈlantərn/ ▶ **n.** a lamp enclosed in a metal frame with glass panels. ▫ **lantern-jawed** having a long, thin jaw.

lan·tha·nide /ˈlanTHəˌnīd/ ▶ **n.** any of the series of fifteen rare-earth elements from lanthanum to lutetium in the periodic table.

lan·tha·num /ˈlanTHənəm/ ▶ **n.** a silvery-white metallic element.

lan·yard /ˈlanyərd/ ▶ **n.** **1** a rope used on a ship. **2** a cord around the neck or shoulder for holding a whistle or similar object.

lap¹ /lap/ ▶ **n.** the flat area between the waist and knees of a seated person.

> SYNONYMS **circuit**, leg, circle, round, stretch.

▫ **in the lap of luxury** in conditions of great comfort and wealth.

lap² ▶ **n.** **1** one circuit of a track or racetrack. **2** an overlapping part. ▶ **v.** (**laps**, **lapping**, **lapped**) overtake a competitor in a race to become a lap ahead.

> SYNONYMS ▶ **n. circuit**, leg, circle, round, stretch.

lap³ ▶ **v.** (**laps**, **lapping**, **lapped**) **1** (of an animal) take up liquid with the tongue. **2** (**lap something up**) accept something with obvious pleasure. **3** (of water) wash against something with a gentle rippling sound.

SYNONYMS **1 drink**, lick up, sup, swallow, slurp, gulp. **2 splash**, wash, swish, slosh, break, plash; literary purl.

lap·dog /ˈlapˌdôg, -ˌdäg/ ▸ **n. 1** a small pampered pet dog. **2** a person who is completely under the influence of someone else.

la·pel /ləˈpel/ ▸ **n.** the part that is folded back at the front opening of a jacket or coat.

lap·i·dar·y /ˈlapəˌderē/ ▸ **adj. 1** relating to the engraving, cutting, or polishing of stone or gems. **2** (of language) elegant and concise.

lap·is laz·u·li /ˈlapis ˈlazyəˌlī, ˈlazHəˌlī, ˈlazyəlē/ ▸ **n.** a bright blue stone used in jewelry.

Lapp /lap/ ▸ **n.** a member of a people of the extreme north of Scandinavia.

USAGE
The people themselves prefer to be called **Sami**.

lap·pet /ˈlapit/ ▸ **n. 1** a fold or hanging piece of flesh in some animals. **2** a loose or overlapping part of a garment.

lapse /laps/ ▸ **n. 1** a brief failure of concentration, memory, or judgment. **2** a decline from previously high standards. **3** an interval of time. ▸ **v.** (**lapses**, **lapsing**, **lapsed**) **1** (of a right, agreement, etc.) become invalid because it is not used or renewed. **2** stop following a religion or doctrine. **3** (**lapse into**) pass gradually into a different state.

SYNONYMS ▸ **n. 1 failure**, slip, error, mistake, blunder, fault, omission; informal slip-up. **2 decline**, fall, deterioration, degeneration, backsliding, regression. **3 interval**, gap, pause, interlude, lull, hiatus, break. ▸ **v. 1 expire**, run out, (come to an) end, cease, stop, terminate. **2 revert**, relapse, drift, slide, slip, sink.

lap·top /ˈlapˌtäp/ ▸ **n.** a portable computer.

lap·wing /ˈlapˌwiNG/ ▸ **n.** a black and white bird with a crest on the head.

lar·board /ˈlärˌbôrd, -bərd/ ⇒ PORT[3].

lar·ce·ny /ˈlärs(ə)nē/ ▸ **n.** (plural **larcenies**) theft of personal property. ▫ **grand larceny** larceny having a value above a legally specified amount.

larch /lärCH/ ▸ **n.** a coniferous tree with needles that fall in winter.

lard /lärd/ ▸ **n.** fat from a pig, used in cooking. ▸ **v. 1** insert strips of fat or bacon in meat before cooking. **2** add technical or obscure expressions to talk or writing.

lard·er /ˈlärdər/ ▸ **n.** a room or large cupboard for storing food.

large /lärj/ ▸ **adj. 1** of relatively great size, extent, or capacity. **2** of wide range or scope.

SYNONYMS **big**, great, sizable, substantial, considerable, huge, extensive, voluminous, vast, prodigious, massive, immense, enormous, colossal, king-size(d), heavy, mammoth, gigantic, giant, fat, stout, strapping, bulky, burly; informal jumbo, mega, whopping. ANTONYMS small.

▫ **at large 1** escaped or not yet captured. **2** as a whole. **large intestine** Anatomy the cecum, colon, and rectum collectively. **large-scale** extensive.

large·ly /ˈlärjlē/ ▸ **adv.** on the whole; mostly.

SYNONYMS **mostly**, mainly, to a large/great extent, chiefly, predominantly, primarily, principally, for the most part, in the main, on the whole.

lar·gesse /lärˈZHes, -ˈjes/ (or **largess**) ▸ **n. 1** generosity. **2** money or gifts given generously.

SYNONYMS **generosity**, liberality, munificence, bountifulness, beneficence, charity, philanthropy, magnanimity, benevolence, charitableness. ANTONYMS meanness.

lar·go /ˈlärˌgō/ ▸ **adv. & adj.** Music in a slow tempo and dignified style.

lar·i·at /ˈlarēət/ ▸ **n.** a rope used as a lasso or for tying an animal to a post.

lark[1] /lärk/ ▸ **n.** a brown bird that sings while flying.

lark[2] informal ▸ **n.** something done for fun or as a joke. ▸ **v.** (**lark about** or **around**) behave in a playful and mischievous way.

lark·spur /ˈlärkˌspər/ ▸ **n.** a plant of the buttercup family with spikes of spurred flowers.

lar·va /ˈlärvə/ ▸ **n.** (plural **larvae** /-vē, -ˌvī/) an immature form of an insect that looks very different from the adult creature, e.g., a caterpillar.

lar·yn·gi·tis /ˌlarənˈjītis/ ▸ **n.** inflammation of the larynx.

lar·ynx /ˈlariNGks, ˈler-/ ▸ **n.** (plural **larynxes** or **larynges** /ləˈrinˌjēz/) the area at the top of the throat forming an air passage to the lungs and containing the vocal cords.

la·sa·gna /ləˈzänyə/ (also **lasagne**) ▸ **n.** pasta in the form of sheets, baked in layers with meat or vegetables and a cheese sauce.

las·civ·i·ous /ləˈsivēəs/ ▸ **adj.** showing strong or inappropriate sexual desire.

SYNONYMS **lecherous**, lewd, lustful, licentious, libidinous, salacious, lubricious, prurient, dirty, smutty, naughty, suggestive, indecent; formal concupiscent.

▪ **las·civ·i·ous·ly** adv. **las·civ·i·ous·ness** n.

la·ser /ˈlāzər/ ▸ **n.** a device that produces an intense narrow beam of light. ▫ **laser printer** a computer printer in which a laser is used to form a pattern on a light-sensitive drum, which attracts toner that is then transferred to the paper.

la·ser·disc /ˈlāzərˌdisk/ ▸ **n.** a disc resembling a large compact disc, used for high-quality video and multimedia.

lash /laSH/ ▸ **v. 1** beat with a whip or stick. **2** beat strongly against: *waves lashed the coast*. **3** (**lash out**) attack someone verbally or physically. **4** (of an animal) move its tail quickly and violently. **5** fasten securely with a cord or rope. ▸ **n. 1** an eyelash. **2** a sharp blow with a whip or stick. **3** the flexible part of a whip.

SYNONYMS ▸ **v. 1 beat against**, dash against, pound, batter, hammer against, strike, hit, drum. **2 fasten**, bind, tie (up), tether, hitch, knot, rope.

lash·ing /ˈlaSHiNG/ ▸ **n. 1** a whipping or beating. **2** a cord used to fasten something securely.

lass /las/ (or **lassie**) ▸ **n.** Scottish & Northern English a girl or young woman.

Las·sa fe·ver /ˈläsə, ˈlasə/ ▸ **n.** an often fatal disease transmitted by a virus and occurring chiefly in West Africa.

las·si·tude /ˈlasəˌt(y)o͞od/ ▸ **n.** lack of energy.

las·so /ˈlasō, ˈlaso͞o, laˈso͞o/ ▸ **n.** (plural **lassos** or **lassoes**) a rope with a noose at one end, used for catching cattle. ▸ **v.** (**lassoes**, **lassoing**, **lassoed**) catch with a lasso.

last[1] /last/ ▶ **adj.** **1** coming after all others in time or order. **2** most recent in time. **3** lowest in importance or rank. **4** (**the last**) the least likely or suitable. **5** only remaining. ▶ **adv.** on the last occasion before the present: *a woman last heard of in Cleveland.* ▶ **n.** (plural **last**) **1** the last person or thing. **2** (**the last of**) the only remaining part of.

> SYNONYMS ▶ **adj.** **1** **final**, closing, concluding, end, ultimate, terminal, later, latter. **2** **rearmost**, hindmost, endmost, furthest (back). **3** **previous**, preceding, prior, former, latest, most recent. ANTONYMS first, next.

□ **at last** in the end; after much delay. **last-ditch** referring to a final desperate attempt to achieve something. **last-gasp** informal at the last possible moment. **Last Judgment** (in some religions) the judgment of humankind expected to take place at the end of the world. **last minute** (or **moment**) the latest possible time before an event. **last name** your surname. **last rites** a Christian religious ceremony performed for a person who is about to die. **Last Supper** the supper eaten by Jesus and his disciples on the night before the Crucifixion. **the last word** the most modern or advanced example of something: *the last word in luxury.* **on your last legs** about to die or stop functioning. ■ **last·ly** **adv.**

last[2] ▶ **v.** **1** continue for a particular period of time. **2** remain operating for a considerable or particular length of time: *the car is built to last.* **3** be enough for someone to use for a particular length of time: *enough food to last him for three months.*

> SYNONYMS **1** *the hearing lasted for six days* **continue**, go on, carry on, keep on/going, take. **2** *he won't last long as manager* **survive**, endure, hold on/out, keep going, persevere, persist, stay, remain; informal stick it out, hang on, go the distance. ANTONYMS end.

last[3] ▶ **n.** a block used by a shoemaker for shaping or repairing shoes.

last·ing /ˈlastiNG/ ▶ **adj.** enduring or able to endure for a long time: *a lasting impression.*

> SYNONYMS **enduring**, long-lasting, long-lived, abiding, continuing, long-term, permanent, durable, stable, secure, long-standing, eternal, undying, everlasting, unending, never-ending. ANTONYMS passing, ephemeral.

lat. ▶ **abbr.** latitude.

latch /laCH/ ▶ **n.** **1** a bar with a catch and lever used for fastening a door or gate. **2** a type of door lock that can be opened from the outside only with a key. ▶ **v.** **1** fasten a door or gate with a latch. **2** (**latch on to**) associate yourself enthusiastically with. □ **on the latch** (of a door or gate) closed but not locked.

latch·key /ˈlaCH,kē/ ▶ **n.** (plural **latchkeys**) a key to an outer door of a house.

late /lāt/ ▶ **adj.** **1** acting, arriving, or happening after the proper or usual time. **2** far on in a period. **3** far on in the day or night. **4** (of a person) recently dead: *her late husband.* **5** (**latest**) of most recent date or origin. ▶ **adv.** **1** after the proper or usual time. **2** toward the end of a period. **3** far on in the day or night. **4** (**later**) afterward or in the near future.

> SYNONYMS ▶ **adj.** **1** **behind schedule**, tardy, overdue, delayed, belated, behindhand. **2** (**later**) **subsequent**, following, succeeding, future, upcoming, to come, ensuing, next. **3** **dead**, departed, lamented, passed on/away; formal deceased. **4** (**latest**) **most recent**, newest, up to the minute, current, state-of-the-art, cutting-edge; informal in, with it, trendy, hip, hot, happening, cool. ANTONYMS punctual, early, dead, passé. ▶ **adv.** **1** **behind schedule**, behind time, tardily, belatedly, behindhand, at the last minute. **2** (**later**) **subsequently**, eventually, then, next, later on, afterward, at a later date, in the future, in due course, by and by, in a while, in time; formal thereafter.

□ **of late** recently. ■ **late·ness** **n.**

late·com·er /ˈlāt,kəmər/ ▶ **n.** a person who arrives late.

la·teen sail /ləˈtēn, la-/ ▶ **n.** a triangular sail set at an angle of 45° to the mast.

late·ly /ˈlātlē/ ▶ **adv.** recently; not long ago.

> SYNONYMS **recently**, not long ago, of late, latterly, in recent times.

la·tent /ˈlātnt/ ▶ **adj.** existing but not yet developed, showing, or active: *her latent talent.*

> SYNONYMS **dormant**, untapped, undiscovered, hidden, concealed, undeveloped, unrealized, unfulfilled, potential.

■ **la·ten·cy** **n.**

lat·er·al /ˈlatərəl, ˈlatrəl/ ▶ **adj.** of, at, toward, or from the side or sides. □ **lateral pass** Football a pass thrown either sideways or backward from the position of the passer. ■ **lat·er·al·ly** **adv.**

la·tex /ˈlā,teks/ ▶ **n.** **1** a milky fluid in some plants that thickens when exposed to the air. **2** a synthetic product resembling this, used to make paints, coatings, gloves, and other articles.

lath /laTH/ ▶ **n.** (plural **laths**) a thin, flat strip of wood.

lathe /lāT͟H/ ▶ **n.** a machine that shapes pieces of wood or metal by turning them against a cutting tool.

lath·er /ˈlaT͟Hər/ ▶ **n.** **1** a frothy mass of bubbles produced by soap when mixed with water. **2** heavy sweat visible on a horse's coat as a white foam. ▶ **v.** (**lathers**, **lathering**, **lathered**) **1** cover with or form a lather. **2** cover or spread generously with a substance.

Lat·in /ˈlatn/ ▶ **n.** the language of ancient Rome and its empire. ▶ **adj.** relating to the Latin language. □ **Latin American** **1** a person from Latin America, the parts of the American continent where Spanish or Portuguese is spoken. **2** relating to Latin America.

Lat·in·ate /ˈlatn,āt/ ▶ **adj.** (of language) having the character of Latin.

La·ti·no /ləˈtēnō, la-/ ▶ **n.** (plural **Latinos**; feminine **Latina**, plural **Latinas**) (in the United States) a person of Latin American origin.

lat·i·tude /ˈlatə,t(y)o͞od/ ▶ **n.** **1** the distance of a place north or south of the equator. **2** (**latitudes**) regions at a particular distance from the equator: *northern latitudes.* **3** scope for freedom of action or thought.

> SYNONYMS **freedom**, scope, leeway, (breathing) space, flexibility, liberty, independence, free rein, license. ANTONYMS restriction.

la·trine /ləˈtrēn/ ▶ **n.** a communal toilet, especially a temporary one in a camp or barracks.

lat·te /ˈlä,tā/ ▶ **n.** a drink of frothy steamed milk to which a shot of espresso coffee is added.

lat·ter /ˈlatər/ ▶ **adj.** **1** nearer to the end than to the beginning. **2** recent: *in latter years.* **3** (**the latter**) referring to the second-mentioned of two people or things.

SYNONYMS **1 later**, closing, end, concluding, final. **2 last-mentioned**, second, last, final. ANTONYMS earlier, former.

□ **latter-day** modern or contemporary. **Latter-Day Saints** the Mormons' name for themselves. ■ **lat·ter·ly** adv.

lat·tice /'latis/ ▶ n. a structure or pattern of strips crossing each other with square or diamond-shaped spaces left between.

lat·tice·work /'latis,wərk/ ▶ n. strips of wood, metal, or other material forming a lattice.

Lat·vi·an /'latvēən/ ▶ n. **1** a person from Latvia. **2** the Baltic language of Latvia. ▶ adj. relating to Latvia.

laud /lôd/ ▶ v. formal praise highly.

laud·a·ble /'lôdəbəl/ ▶ adj. deserving praise.

SYNONYMS **praiseworthy**, commendable, admirable, worthy, deserving, creditable, estimable, exemplary. ANTONYMS shameful.

lau·da·num /'lôdn-əm, 'lôdnəm/ ▶ n. a liquid containing opium, formerly used as a sedative.

laud·a·to·ry /'lôdə,tôrē/ ▶ adj. formal expressing praise.

laugh /laf/ ▶ v. **1** make sounds and movements that express amusement. **2** (**laugh at**) make fun of. **3** (**laugh something off**) dismiss something by treating it lightheartedly. ▶ n. **1** an act of laughing. **2** (**a laugh**) informal someone or something that makes people laugh.

SYNONYMS ▶ v. **chuckle**, chortle, guffaw, giggle, titter, snigger, roar, split your sides; informal be in stitches, be rolling in the aisles, crack up. ▶ n. **1 chuckle**, chortle, guffaw, giggle, titter, snigger, roar, shriek. **2 joke**, prank, jest; informal lark, hoot, scream.

□ **have the last laugh** be successful eventually. **laughing gas** nitrous oxide, used as an anesthetic.

laugh·a·ble /'lafəbəl/ ▶ adj. ridiculous or absurd; deserving to be laughed at. ■ **laugh·a·bly** adv.

laugh·ing·stock /'lafiNG,stäk/ ▶ n. a person who is ridiculed by everyone.

laugh·ter /'laftər/ ▶ n. the action or sound of laughing.

SYNONYMS **1 laughing**, chuckling, chortling, guffawing, giggling, tittering, sniggering. **2 amusement**, entertainment, humor, mirth, merriment, gaiety, hilarity, jollity, fun.

launch[1] /lônCH, länCH/ ▶ v. **1** move a boat or ship from land into the water. **2** send a rocket or missile on its course. **3** begin an enterprise or introduce a new product. **4** (**launch into**) begin something energetically and enthusiastically. ▶ n. an act of launching something.

SYNONYMS ▶ v. **1 propel**, fire, shoot, throw, hurl, fling, pitch, lob, let fly; informal chuck, heave, sling. **2 start**, begin, initiate, put in place, set up, inaugurate, introduce; informal kick off.

■ **launch·er** n.

launch[2] ▶ n. a large motorboat.

laun·der /'lôndər, 'län-/ ▶ v. (**launders, laundering, laundered**) **1** wash and iron clothes, sheets, etc. **2** informal pass illegally obtained money through a bank or business to conceal its origins.

laun·dress /'lôndrəs, 'län-/ ▶ n. a woman employed to launder clothes and linen.

Laun·dro·mat /'lôndrə,mat, 'län-/ ▶ n. trademark an establishment with coin-operated washing machines and dryers for public use.

laun·dry /,lôndrē, 'län-/ ▶ n. (plural **laundries**) **1** clothes, sheets, etc., that need to be washed or that have been newly washed. **2** a room or building where clothes, sheets, etc., are washed.

lau·re·ate /'lôrē-it, 'lär-/ ▶ n. **1** a person given an award for outstanding creative or intellectual achievement. **2** a poet laureate.

lau·rel /'lôrəl, 'lär-/ ▶ n. **1** an evergreen shrub or small tree with dark green glossy leaves. **2** (**laurels**) a crown of bay leaves awarded as a mark of honor in classical times. **3** (**laurels**) honor or praise. □ **rest on your laurels** be so satisfied with what you have achieved that you make no more effort.

la·va /'lävə, 'lavə/ ▶ n. hot molten rock that erupts from a volcano, or solid rock formed when this cools.

lav·a·to·ry /'lavə,tôrē/ ▶ n. (plural **lavatories**) a room or compartment with a toilet and washbasin.

SYNONYMS see **BATHROOM**.

lav·en·der /'lavəndər/ ▶ n. **1** a strong-smelling shrub with bluish-purple flowers. **2** a pale bluish-purple color. □ **lavender water** a perfume made from distilled lavender.

la·ver /'lāvər/ (also **purple laver**) ▶ n. an edible seaweed with thin reddish-purple and green fronds.

lav·ish /'laviSH/ ▶ adj. **1** very rich, elaborate, or luxurious. **2** giving or given in large amounts. ▶ v. give something in large or generous quantities.

SYNONYMS ▶ adj. **1 sumptuous**, luxurious, gorgeous, costly, expensive, opulent, grand, splendid, rich, fancy; informal posh, bling-bling. **2 generous**, liberal, bountiful, unstinting, unsparing, free, munificent, extravagant, abundant, copious, plentiful, prolific, excessive, wasteful, prodigal; literary plenteous. ANTONYMS meager, frugal. ▶ v. **shower**, heap, pour, deluge, throw at, squander, dissipate. ANTONYMS begrudge, stint.

■ **lav·ish·ly** adv.

law /lô/ ▶ n. **1** a rule or system of rules that regulates the actions of the people in a country or community. **2** a rule laying down the correct procedure or behavior in a sport. **3** a statement of fact to the effect that a particular phenomenon always occurs if certain conditions are present: *the second law of thermodynamics*.

SYNONYMS **1 regulation**, statute, ordinance, act, bill, decree, edict, rule, ruling, dictum, command, order, directive, dictate, diktat, fiat, bylaw; (**laws**) legislation, constitution, code. **2 principle**, rule, precept, commandment, belief, creed, credo, maxim, tenet, doctrine, canon.

□ **be a law unto yourself** behave in an unconventional or unpredictable manner. **law-abiding** obeying the laws of society. **law court** a court of law. **law of averages** the supposed principle that future events are likely to balance out past events. **lay down the law** give instructions in an authoritative way. **take the law into your own hands** illegally or violently punish someone according to your own ideas of justice.

law·break·er /'lô,brākər/ ▶ n. a person who breaks the law.

law·ful /'lôfəl/ ▶ adj. allowed by or obeying law or rules.

SYNONYMS **legitimate**, legal, licit, permissible, permitted, allowable, allowed, rightful, sanctioned, authorized, warranted; informal legit. ANTONYMS illegal.

■ **law·ful·ly** adv.

law·less /ˈlôləs/ ▶ adj. not governed by or obeying laws. ■ **law·less·ness** n.

law·mak·er /ˈlôˌmākər/ ▶ n. a legislator.

law·man /ˈlôˌmən, -man/ ▶ n. (plural **lawmen**) a law-enforcement officer, especially a sheriff.

lawn /lôn/ ▶ n. **1** an area of mown grass in a yard, garden, or park. **2** a fine linen or cotton fabric. □ **lawn tennis** dated or formal the standard form of tennis, played with a soft ball on an open court.

lawn·mow·er /ˈlônˌmōər/ ▶ n. a machine for cutting the grass on a lawn.

law·suit /ˈlôˌso͞ot/ ▶ n. a claim brought to a court of law to be decided.

law·yer /ˈloi-ər, ˈlôyər/ ▶ n. a person who practices or studies law.

SYNONYMS **attorney**, attorney-at-law, counsel, counselor, legal practitioner, member of the bar, litigator, advocate; informal mouthpiece, legal eagle; informal, disapproving ambulance chaser, shyster.

lax /laks/ ▶ adj. **1** not strict, severe, or careful enough. **2** (of limbs or muscles) relaxed.

SYNONYMS **slack**, slipshod, negligent, remiss, careless, sloppy, slapdash, offhand, casual. ANTONYMS strict.

■ **lax·i·ty** n.

lax·a·tive /ˈlaksətiv/ ▶ adj. tending to make someone empty their bowels. ▶ n. a laxative drug or medicine.

lay[1] /lā/ ▶ v. (**lays**, **laying**, past and past participle **laid**) **1** put something down gently or carefully. **2** put something down in position for use: *have your carpet laid by a professional.* **3** assign or place: *lay the blame.* **4** (of a female bird, reptile, etc.) produce an egg from inside the body. **5** stake an amount of money in a bet.

SYNONYMS **1 put (down)**, place, set (down), deposit, rest, position, shove; informal stick, dump, park, plonk. **2** *we laid plans for the voyage* **devise**, arrange, prepare, work out, hatch, design, plan, scheme, plot, conceive, put together, draw up, produce, develop, formulate; informal cook up. **3** *I'd lay money on it* **bet**, wager, gamble, stake.

□ **lay off** informal stop doing something. **lay someone off** dismiss a worker because of a shortage of work. **lay of the land 1** the features of an area. **2** the current situation. **lay something on** provide food or entertainment. **lay something out** arrange something according to a plan. **lay someone up** put someone out of action through illness or injury.

USAGE

Don't confuse **lay** and **lie**. You *lay* something, as in *they are going to lay the carpet*, but you *lie* down on a bed or other flat surface. The past tense and past participle of **lay** is **laid**, as in *they laid the groundwork*; the past tense of **lie** is **lay** (*he lay on the floor*) and the past participle is **lain** (*she had lain on the bed for hours*).

lay[2] ▶ adj. **1** not having an official position in the church. **2** not having professional qualifications or expert knowledge.

SYNONYMS **1** *a lay preacher* **nonordained**, nonclerical, secular. **2** *science books for a lay audience* **nonexpert**, nonprofessional, nonspecialist, nontechnical, amateur, unqualified, untrained.

lay[3] ▶ n. a short poem intended to be sung.

lay[4] past of LIE[1].

lay·a·bout /ˈlāəˌbout/ ▶ n. disapproving a person who does little or no work.

lay·er /ˈlāər/ ▶ n. a sheet or thickness of material covering a surface. ▶ v. arrange or cut in a layer or layers: *layered clothes*.

SYNONYMS ▶ n. **sheet**, stratum, level, tier, seam, coat, coating, film, covering, blanket, skin.

lay·man /ˈlāmən/ (or **laywoman** /ˈlāˌwo͝omən/) ▶ n. (plural **laymen** or **laywomen**) **1** a member of a church who is not a priest or minister. **2** a person without professional or specialized knowledge.

lay·off /ˈlāˌôf, -ˌäf/ ▶ n. **1** an instance of dismissing workers because of a shortage of work. **2** a temporary break from an activity.

lay·out /ˈlāˌout/ ▶ n. the way in which something is laid out.

SYNONYMS **arrangement**, design, plan, formation, format, configuration, composition, organization, geography, structure.

lay·o·ver /ˈlāˌōvər/ ▶ n. a rest or wait before a further stage in a trip.

laze /lāz/ ▶ v. (**lazes**, **lazing**, **lazed**) spend time relaxing or doing very little.

SYNONYMS **relax**, unwind, lounge about/around, loaf (about/around), loll about/around, lie around/about, take it easy, idle; informal hang around, chill (out), veg (out).

la·zy /ˈlāzē/ ▶ adj. (**lazier**, **laziest**) **1** unwilling to work or use energy. **2** showing a lack of effort or care.

SYNONYMS **1 idle**, indolent, slothful, bone idle, work-shy, shiftless. **2 slow**, slow-moving, languid, leisurely, lethargic, sluggish, torpid. ANTONYMS industrious.

□ **lazy eye** an eye with poor vision due to lack of use. ■ **la·zi·ly** adv. **la·zi·ness** n.

la·zy·bones /ˈlāzēˌbōnz/ ▶ n. informal a lazy person.

lb. ▶ abbr. pounds (in weight).

LCD ▶ abbr. **1** Electronics & Computing liquid crystal display. **2** Math lowest (or least) common denominator.

LCM ▶ abbr. Math lowest (or least) common multiple.

lea /lē/ ▶ n. literary an area of grassy land.

leach /lēcʜ/ ▶ v. (of chemicals or minerals) be removed from soil by water passing through it.

lead[1] /lēd/ ▶ v. (**leads**, **leading**, **led**) **1** cause a person or animal to go with you. **2** be a route or means of access: *the street led into the square.* **3** (**lead to**) result in. **4** cause someone to do or believe something: *that may lead them to reconsider.* **5** be in charge of. **6** have the advantage in a race or game. **7** have a particular way of life. **8** (**lead up to**) come before or result in. **9** (**lead someone on**) deceive someone into believing that you are attracted to them. ▶ n. **1** an example for other people to copy: *others followed our lead.* **2** a position of advantage in a contest. **3** the chief part in a play or movie. **4** a clue to follow when trying to solve a problem. **5** a strap or cord for controlling and guiding a dog. **6** a wire conveying electric current.

SYNONYMS ▶ v. **1 guide**, conduct, show (the way), usher, escort, steer, shepherd, accompany, see, take. **2** *what led you to believe him?* **cause**, induce, prompt, move, persuade, drive, make. **3 control**, preside over, head, command, govern, run, manage, rule, be in charge of; informal head up. **4 be ahead**, be winning, be in front, be in the lead, be first, outrun, outstrip, outpace, leave behind, outdo, outclass, beat. **5** *I want to lead a normal life* **live**, have, spend, follow, pass, enjoy. ANTONYMS follow. ▶ n. **1 example**, model, pattern, standard, guidance, direction, role model. **2** *a 3–0 lead* **margin**, advantage, gap, edge. **3 first place**, winning position, vanguard. **4 leading role**, starring role, title role, principal role. **5 clue**, pointer, hint, tip, tip-off, suggestion, indication. **6 leash**, tether, rope, chain.

□ **lead someone astray** make someone behave foolishly or wrongly. **leading man** (or **lady**) the actor playing the main part in a play, movie, or television show. **lead-up** an event or sequence that leads up to something else.

lead² /led/ ▶ n. **1** a heavy bluish-gray metal. **2** the part of a pencil that makes a mark.

lead·ed /ˈledid/ ▶ adj. **1** framed or covered with lead. **2** (of gas) containing lead.

lead·en /ˈledn/ ▶ adj. **1** dull, heavy, or slow. **2** dull gray in color: *a leaden sky.*

lead·er /ˈlēdər/ ▶ n. **1** a person or thing that leads. **2** the most successful or advanced person or thing in a particular area. **3** the main player in a music group. **4** a newspaper article giving the editor's opinion.

SYNONYMS **chief**, head, principal, commander, captain, controller, superior, chairman, chair, director, manager, superintendent, supervisor, overseer, master, mistress, prime minister, president, premier, governor, ruler, monarch, sovereign; informal boss, skipper, numero uno, (head) honcho, boss man/lady. ANTONYMS follower, supporter.

lead·er·ship /ˈlēdərˌsʜip/ ▶ n. **1** the action of leading a group or organization. **2** the state or position of being a leader: *the leadership of the party*. **3** the leaders of an organization, country, etc.: *a change of leadership had become desirable.* **4** the ability to lead skillfully.

SYNONYMS **1** *the leadership of the party* **control**, rule, command, dominion, headship, directorship, premiership, chairmanship, governorship, captaincy. **2** *firm leadership* **guidance**, direction, authority, management, supervision, government.

lead·ing /ˈlēdiɴɢ/ ▶ adj. most important, or in first place: *leading politicians.*

SYNONYMS **main**, chief, top, front, major, prime, principal, foremost, key, central, dominant, greatest, preeminent, star. ANTONYMS subordinate, minor.

□ **leading light** a prominent or influential person. **leading question** a question that encourages someone to give the answer that you want.

leaf /lēf/ ▶ n. (plural **leaves** /lēvz/) **1** a flat green part of a plant that is attached to a stem. **2** a single sheet of paper in a book. **3** gold or silver in the form of a very thin sheet. **4** a hinged or detachable part of a tabletop. **5** the state of having leaves: *the trees were in leaf.* ▶ v. (**leaf through**) turn over pages or papers, reading quickly or casually.

SYNONYMS ▶ n. **1** (**leaves**) **foliage**, greenery. **2 page**, sheet, folio. ▶ v. ***I leafed through a magazine*** **flip through**, flick through, thumb through, skim through/over, browse through, glance through/over, riffle through, scan, run your eye over, peruse.

□ **turn over a new leaf** start to behave in a better way. **leaf peeper** a person who views autumn foliage, especially in New England.

leaf·let /ˈlēflit/ ▶ n. **1** a printed sheet of paper, sometimes folded, containing information or advertising. **2** a small leaf. ▶ v. (**leaflets**, **leafleting**, **leafleted**) distribute leaflets to.

SYNONYMS ▶ n. **pamphlet**, booklet, brochure, handbill, circular, flyer, handout.

leaf·y /ˈlēfē/ ▶ adj. (**leafier**, **leafiest**) **1** having many leaves. **2** full of trees and shrubs: *a leafy avenue.* ■ **leaf·i·ness** n.

league¹ /lēg/ ▶ n. **1** a collection of people, countries, or groups that combine to help or protect each other. **2** a group of sports teams that play each other over a period for a championship. **3** a class of quality or excellence: *the two men were not in the same league.*

SYNONYMS **1 alliance**, confederation, confederacy, federation, union, association, coalition, consortium, affiliation, cooperative, partnership, fellowship, syndicate. **2 class**, group, category, level, standard.

□ **in league** (of two or more people) making secret plans.

league² ▶ n. old use a measure of distance, of about three miles.

lea·guer /ˈlēgər/ ▶ n. a member of a particular league, especially in sport: *minor leaguers in spring training.*

leak /lēk/ ▶ v. **1** accidentally allow contents to escape or enter through a hole or crack. **2** (of liquid, gas, etc.) escape or enter accidentally through a hole or crack. **3** deliberately give out secret information. ▶ n. **1** a hole or crack through which contents leak. **2** an instance of leaking.

SYNONYMS ▶ v. **1 seep**, escape, ooze, drip, dribble, drain, run. **2 disclose**, divulge, reveal, make public, bring into the open, tell, expose, release, let slip. ▶ n. **1 hole**, opening, puncture, perforation, gash, slit, break, crack, chink, fissure, rupture, tear. **2 escape**, leakage, discharge, seepage. **3 disclosure**, revelation, exposé.

■ **leak·age** n.

leak·y /lēkē/ ▶ adj. (**leakier**, **leakiest**) having a leak or leaks: *a leaky roof.*

lean¹ /lēn/ ▶ v. (**leans**, **leaning**, past and past participle **leaned** or **leant** /lent/) **1** be in a sloping position. **2** (**lean against** or **on**) rest against. **3** (**lean on**) rely on for support. **4** (**lean to** or **toward**) favor a particular point of view.

SYNONYMS **1 rest**, recline, be propped. **2 slant**, incline, bend, tilt, slope, tip, list. **3** (**lean on**) **depend on**, rely on, count on, bank on, trust in, have faith in. **4** (**lean toward**) **tend toward**, incline toward, gravitate toward, favor, prefer, have a preference for, have an affinity with.

□ **lean-to** (plural **lean-tos**) a small building sharing a wall with a larger building.

lean² ▶ adj. **1** (of a person) having little fat; thin. **2** (of meat) containing little fat. **3** (of a period of time) unproductive: *the lean years.*

> SYNONYMS **1 thin**, slim, slender, skinny, spare, angular, spindly, wiry, lanky. **2 meager**, sparse, poor, mean, inadequate, insufficient, paltry. ANTONYMS fat, abundant.

lean·ing /ˈlēniNG/ ▶ n. a tendency or preference: *communist leanings.*

> SYNONYMS **inclination**, tendency, bent, propensity, penchant, preference, predisposition, predilection, proclivity.

leap /lēp/ ▶ v. (**leaps**, **leaping**, past and past participle **leaped** /lēpt/ or **leapt** /lept/) **1** jump high or a long way. **2** move quickly and suddenly: *Polly leaped to her feet.* **3** (**leap at**) accept something eagerly. **4** increase dramatically. **5** jump across. ▶ n. an act of leaping.

> SYNONYMS ▶ v. **1 jump**, vault, spring, bound, hop, clear. **2 rise**, soar, rocket, skyrocket, shoot up, escalate. ▶ n. **rise**, surge, upsurge, escalation, upswing, upturn.

□ **leap year** a year with 366 days, occurring every four years.

leap·frog /ˈlēpˌfrôg, -ˌfräg/ ▶ n. a game in which players in turn jump over others who are bending down. ▶ v. (**leapfrogs**, **leapfrogging**, **leapfrogged**) **1** jump over someone in leapfrog. **2** overtake others to move into a leading position.

learn /lərn/ ▶ v. (**learns**, **learning**, past and past participle **learned** or **learnt** /lərnt/) **1** gain knowledge or skill through study or experience. **2** become aware of something through observing or hearing about it. **3** memorize.

> SYNONYMS **1 master**, grasp, take in, absorb, assimilate, digest, familiarize yourself with; informal get the hang of. **2 memorize**, learn by heart, learn by rote, get down pat. **3 discover**, find out, become aware, be informed, hear, understand, gather; informal get wind of.

□ **learning disability** difficulty in gaining knowledge and skills to the level expected of your age. **learning disabled** having a learning disability.

learn·ed /ˈlərnid/ ▶ adj. having gained a lot of knowledge by studying.

> SYNONYMS **scholarly**, erudite, knowledgeable, widely read, cultured, intellectual, academic, literary, bookish, highbrow; informal brainy. ANTONYMS ignorant.

learn·er /ˈlərnər/ ▶ n. a person who is learning a subject or skill.

> SYNONYMS **beginner**, novice, starter, trainee, apprentice, student, pupil, fledgling, neophyte, tyro; informal rookie, greenhorn. ANTONYMS expert, veteran.

learn·ing /ˈlərniNG/ ▶ n. knowledge or skills gained by studying.

> SYNONYMS **study**, knowledge, education, schooling, tuition, teaching, scholarship, erudition, understanding, wisdom. ANTONYMS ignorance.

□ **learning curve** the rate of a person's progress in gaining experience or new skills.

lease /lēs/ ▶ n. an agreement by which one person uses land, property, etc., which belongs to another person for a stated time in return for payment. ▶ v. (**leases**, **leasing**, **leased**) let out or rent land, property, etc., by a lease.

> SYNONYMS ▶ v. **rent** (**out**), hire (out), charter, let (out), sublet.

lease·hold /ˈlēsˌhōld/ ▶ n. the holding of property by a lease.

leash /lēsH/ ▶ n. a dog's lead.

least /lēst/ ▶ determiner & pron. (usu. **the least**) smallest in amount, extent, or significance. ▶ adv. to the smallest extent or degree. □ **at least 1** not less than. **2** if nothing else. **3** anyway. **at the least** (or **very least**) **1** not less than. **2** taking the most unfavorable view. **not least** in particular. **to say the least** to put it mildly.

least·ways /ˈlēstˌwāz/ ▶ adv. dialect or informal at least.

leath·er /ˈleT͟Hər/ ▶ n. a material made from the skin of an animal by tanning or a similar process.

leath·er·y /ˈleT͟H(ə)rē/ ▶ adj. tough and hard like leather.

leave¹ /lēv/ ▶ v. (**leaves**, **leaving**, **left**) **1** go away from. **2** stop attending or working for. **3** go away without taking someone or something. **4** (**be left**) remain to be used or dealt with. **5** let someone do something without interfering. **6** put something somewhere to be collected or dealt with. **7** give something to someone in a will. **8** (**leave someone/something out**) fail to include someone or something.

> SYNONYMS **1 go away**, depart, withdraw, retire, take your leave, pull out, quit, decamp, flee, escape, abandon, desert, vacate; informal vamoose, push off, shove off, clear out/off, split, make tracks. **2 set off**, set sail, get going. **3 abandon**, desert, jilt, leave in the lurch, leave high and dry, throw over; informal dump, ditch, walk/run out on. **4 resign**, retire, step down, give up, drop out; informal quit. **5 leave behind**, forget, lose, mislay. **6 entrust**, hand over, pass on, refer, delegate. **7 bequeath**, will, endow, hand down. ANTONYMS arrive.

□ **leave someone/something be** informal avoid disturbing or interfering with someone or someone. ■ **leav·er** n.

leave² ▶ n. **1** (also **leave of absence**) time when you have permission to be absent from work or duty. **2** formal permission: *seeking leave to appeal.*

> SYNONYMS **1 permission**, consent, authorization, sanction, dispensation, approval, clearance, blessing, agreement, assent; informal the go-ahead, the green light. **2 vacation**, break, furlough, sabbatical, leave of absence, holiday.

□ **leave-taking** an act of saying goodbye. **take your leave** formal say goodbye.

leav·en /ˈlevən/ ▶ n. a substance added to dough to make it ferment and rise. ▶ v. make something less serious or dull by adding something: *leavened by humor.*

leaves /lēvz/ plural of LEAF.

leav·ings /ˈlēviNGz/ ▶ pl.n. things that have been left as worthless.

Leb·a·nese /ˌlebəˈnēz, -ˈnēs/ ▶ n. (plural **Lebanese**) a person from Lebanon. ▶ adj. relating to Lebanon.

lech /lecH/ informal, disapproving ▶ n. a lecher. ▶ v. act in a lecherous manner.

lech·er /'lecHər/ ▶ n. a lecherous man.

SYNONYMS **womanizer**, libertine, debauchee, rake, roué; Don Juan, Casanova, Lothario, Romeo; informal lech, dirty old man; formal fornicator.

■ **lech·er·y** n.

lech·er·ous /'lecH(ə)rəs/ ▶ adj. (of a man) showing sexual desire in an offensive way.

SYNONYMS **lustful**, licentious, lascivious, libidinous, lewd, salacious, prurient; formal concupiscent.

lec·tern /'lektərn/ ▶ n. a tall stand with a sloping top from which a speaker can read while standing up.

lec·ture /'lekCHər/ ▶ n. **1** an educational talk to an audience. **2** a long reprimand or critical talk. ▶ v. (**lectures**, **lecturing**, **lectured**) **1** give a lecture, or a series of lectures. **2** give someone a long reprimand.

SYNONYMS ▶ n. **1 speech**, talk, address, discourse, presentation, oration. **2 reprimand**, scolding, rebuke, reproach; informal dressing-down, telling-off, talking-to, tongue-lashing. ▶ v. **1 talk**, speak, discourse, hold forth, teach; informal spout, sound off. **2 reprimand**, scold, rebuke, reproach, take to task, berate, upbraid, remonstrate with, castigate; informal tell off, bawl out.

lec·tur·er /'lekCHərər/ ▶ n. a person who gives lectures, such as a teacher at a college or university.

LED ▶ abbr. light-emitting diode, a semiconductor diode that glows when a voltage is applied.

led /led/ past and past participle of **LEAD**[1].

ledge /lej/ ▶ n. a narrow horizontal surface sticking out from a wall, cliff, etc.

ledg·er /'lejər/ ▶ n. a book in which financial accounts are kept. □ **ledger line** Music a short line added for notes above or below the range of a stave.

lee /lē/ ▶ n. the side of something that provides shelter from wind or weather.

leech /lēcH/ ▶ n. **1** a worm that sucks the blood of animals or people. **2** a person who lives off other people.

leek /lēk/ ▶ n. a plant with a long cylindrical bulb that is eaten as a vegetable.

leer /li(ə)r/ ▶ v. look or smile at someone in a suggestive or unpleasant way. ▶ n. a suggestive or unpleasant look or smile.

leer·y /'li(ə)rē/ ▶ adj. informal wary.

SYNONYMS **wary**, cautious, careful, guarded, chary, suspicious, distrustful; worried, anxious, apprehensive.

lees /lēz/ ▶ pl.n. the sediment left in the bottom of a bottle or barrel of wine.

lee·ward /'lēwərd, 'lo͞oərd/ ▶ adj. & adv. on or toward the side that is sheltered from the wind.

lee·way /'lē,wā/ ▶ n. the amount of freedom to move or act that is available: *we have a lot of leeway in how we do our jobs.*

SYNONYMS **freedom**, scope, latitude, space, room, liberty, flexibility, license, free hand, free rein.

left[1] /left/ ▶ adj. **1** on or toward the side of a person or thing that is to the west when the person or thing is facing north. **2** left-wing. ▶ adv. on or to the left side. ▶ n. **1** (**the left**) the left-hand part, side, or direction. **2** a left turn. **3** (often **the Left**) a left-wing group or party.

SYNONYMS ▶ adj. **left-hand**, sinistral; Nautical port; Heraldry sinister. ANTONYMS right.

□ **have two left feet** be clumsy or awkward. **left field 1** Baseball the part of the outfield to the left of center field from the perspective of home plate. **2** a position or opinion that is unconventional or surprising. **left hand 1** the hand of a person's left side. **2** the region or direction on the left side. **3** on or toward the left side. **4** done with or using the left hand. **left-handed 1** using or done with the left hand. **2** turning to the left; toward the left. **left-hander 1** a left-handed person. **2** a blow struck with a person's left hand. **left, right, and center** on all sides. **left-wing** socialist, or supporting political or social change. ■ **left·ward** (also **leftwards**) adj. & adv.

left[2] past and past participle of **LEAVE**[1].

left·o·vers /'left,ōvərz/ ▶ pl.n. food remaining after the rest has been eaten. ▶ adj. (**leftover**) remaining after the rest of something has been used.

left·y /'leftē/ (or **leftie**) ▶ n. (plural **lefties**) informal a left-wing person.

leg /leg/ ▶ n. **1** each of the limbs on which a person or animal moves and stands. **2** each of the parts of a table, chair, etc., that rest on the floor and support its weight. **3** a section of a journey, race, etc. **4** (in sports) each of two or more games making up a round of a competition. ▶ v. (**legs**, **legging**, **legged**) (**leg it**) informal **1** run away. **2** travel by foot.

SYNONYMS ▶ n. **1 limb**, member, shank; informal pin, peg. **2 part**, stage, section, phase, stretch, lap.

□ **leg iron** a metal band or chain placed around a prisoner's ankle as a restraint. **leg warmers** a pair of knitted garments covering the legs from ankle to knee or thigh. **not have a leg to stand on** be unable to justify your arguments or actions.

leg·a·cy /'legəsē/ ▶ n. (plural **legacies**) **1** an amount of money or property left to someone in a will. **2** something handed down by a predecessor.

SYNONYMS **bequest**, inheritance, endowment, gift, birthright, estate, heirloom.

le·gal /'lēgəl/ ▶ adj. **1** having to do with the law. **2** permitted by law.

SYNONYMS **1 lawful**, legitimate, legalized, valid, permissible, permitted, sanctioned, authorized, licensed, allowed, allowable, aboveboard, acceptable, constitutional; informal legit. **2** *the legal system* **judicial**, juridical, forensic. ANTONYMS illegal.

□ **legal aid** payment for legal advice given from public funds to people who cannot afford to pay for a lawyer. **legal tender** accepted methods of payment such as coins or banknotes. ■ **le·gal·i·ty** /lə'galətē/ n. **le·gal·ly** adv.

le·gal·ese /,lēgə'lēz, -'lēs/ ▶ n. informal the formal and technical language of legal documents.

le·gal·ize /'lēgə,līz/ ▶ v. (**legalizes**, **legalizing**, **legalized**) make something legal. ■ **le·gal·i·za·tion** /,lēgələ'zāsHən, -,lī'zā-/ n.

leg·ate /'legit/ ▶ n. a representative of the pope.

le·ga·tion /li'gāsHən/ ▶ n. **1** a diplomat below the rank of ambassador, and their staff. **2** the official residence of a diplomat.

le·ga·to /li'gäto/ ▶ adv. & adj. Music in a smooth, flowing way.

leg·end /ˈlejənd/ ▶ **n.** **1** a traditional story from long ago that is not definitely true. **2** a very famous person: *a screen legend.* **3** an inscription, caption, or list explaining the symbols used in a map or table.

> SYNONYMS **1 myth**, saga, epic, folk tale, folk story, fable; (**legends**) lore, folklore, mythology. **2 celebrity**, star, superstar, icon, phenomenon, luminary, giant, hero; informal celeb, megastar. **3 caption**, inscription, dedication, slogan, heading, title.

leg·end·ar·y /ˈlejənˌderē/ ▶ **adj.** **1** described in legends. **2** remarkable enough to be famous.

> SYNONYMS **1 fabled**, mythical, traditional, fairy-tale, storybook, mythological, fictional, fictitious. **2 famous**, celebrated, famed, renowned, acclaimed, illustrious, esteemed, honored, exalted, venerable, eminent, distinguished, great.

leg·er·de·main /ˌlejərdəˈmān, ˈlejərdəˌmān/ ▶ **n.** **1** skillful use of the hands when performing conjuring tricks. **2** deception; trickery.

leg·gings /ˈlegiNGz/ ▶ **pl.n.** **1** women's tight-fitting stretchy trousers. **2** strong protective coverings for the legs, worn over trousers.

leg·gy /ˈlegē/ ▶ **adj.** (**leggier**, **leggiest**) long-legged.

leg·i·ble /ˈlejəbəl/ ▶ **adj.** (of handwriting or print) clear enough to read. ■ **leg·i·bil·i·ty** /ˌlejəˈbilətē/ **n.** **leg·i·bly** **adv.**

le·gion /ˈlējən/ ▶ **n.** **1** a division of 3,000 to 6,000 men in the army of ancient Rome. **2** (**a legion** or **legions of**) a vast number of. ▶ **adj.** literary great in number: *her fans are legion.*

> SYNONYMS ▶ **n. horde**, throng, multitude, crowd, mass, mob, gang, swarm, flock, herd, army.

le·gion·naire /ˌlējəˈner/ ▶ **n.** a member of a legion. □ **legionnaires' disease** a form of pneumonia.

> SPELLING
> **Legionnaire** comes from French and has a double **n**: legionnaire.

leg·is·late /ˈlejəˌslāt/ ▶ **v.** (**legislates**, **legislating**, **legislated**) **1** make laws. **2** (**legislate for** or **against**) prepare for or try to prevent a situation. ■ **leg·is·la·tor** **n.**

leg·is·la·tion /ˌlejəˈslāSHən/ ▶ **n.** laws.

> SYNONYMS **law**, rules, rulings, regulations, acts, bills, statutes, ordinances.

leg·is·la·tive /ˈlejəˌslātiv/ ▶ **adj.** **1** having the power to make laws. **2** relating to laws.

leg·is·la·ture /ˈlejəˌslāCHər/ ▶ **n.** the group of people who make a country's laws.

> SYNONYMS **parliament**, senate, congress, council, chamber, house.

le·git·i·mate ▶ **adj.** /liˈjitəmit/ **1** allowed by the law or rules. **2** able to be defended; reasonable: *a legitimate excuse.* **3** (of a child) born to parents who are married to each other. ▶ **v.** /-ˌmāt/ (**legitimates**, **legitimating**, **legitimated**) make something legitimate.

> SYNONYMS ▶ **adj. 1** *the legitimate use of such weapons* **legal**, lawful, authorized, permitted, sanctioned, approved, licensed; informal legit. **2** *the legitimate heir* **rightful**, lawful, genuine, authentic, real, true, proper; informal kosher. **3** *a legitimate excuse* **valid**, sound, admissible, acceptable, well-founded, justifiable, reasonable, sensible, just, fair, bona fide. ANTONYMS illegal, invalid.

■ **le·git·i·ma·cy** /-məsē/ **n.** **le·git·i·mate·ly** /-mitlē/ **adv.**

> SPELLING
> Write **leg-**, not **lig-**: **leg**itimate.

le·git·i·mize /liˈjitəˌmīz/ ▶ **v.** (**legitimizes**, **legitimizing**, **legitimized**) make something legitimate.

leg·room /ˈlegˌro͞om, -ˌro͝om/ ▶ **n.** space in which a seated person can put their legs.

leg·ume /ˈlegˌyo͞om, ləˈgyo͞om/ ▶ **n.** a plant with seeds in pods, such as the pea. ■ **le·gu·mi·nous** /liˈgyo͞omənəs/ **adj.**

leg·work /ˈlegˌwərk/ ▶ **n.** work that involves tiring or tedious movement from place to place.

lei /lā/ ▶ **n.** a Polynesian garland of flowers.

lei·sure /ˈlēZHər, ˈlezHər/ ▶ **n.** time for relaxation or enjoyment.

> SYNONYMS **free time**, spare time, time off, rest, recreation, relaxation, R & R. ANTONYMS work.

□ **at leisure** **1** not occupied; free. **2** in an unhurried way.

lei·sure·ly /ˈlēZHərlē, ˈlezHər-/ ▶ **adj.** relaxed and unhurried. ▶ **adv.** without hurry.

> SYNONYMS ▶ **adj. unhurried**, relaxed, easy, gentle, sedate, comfortable, restful, undemanding, slow. ANTONYMS hurried.

lei·sure·wear /ˈlēZHərˌwe(ə)r, ˈlezHər-/ ▶ **n.** casual clothes worn for leisure activities.

leit·mo·tif /ˈlītmōˌtēf/ (also **leitmotiv**) ▶ **n.** a frequently repeated theme in a musical or literary composition.

lem·ming /ˈlemiNG/ ▶ **n.** **1** a small Arctic rodent, some kinds of which periodically migrate in large numbers (they are popularly believed to run headlong into the sea and drown). **2** a person who unthinkingly joins a mass movement.

lem·on /ˈlemən/ ▶ **n.** **1** a pale yellow citrus fruit with thick skin and acidic juice. **2** a pale yellow color.

lem·on·ade /ˌleməˈnād, ˈleməˌnād/ ▶ **n.** a sweet drink made with lemon juice or flavoring.

le·mur /ˈlēmər/ ▶ **n.** an animal resembling a monkey, found only in Madagascar.

lend /lend/ ▶ **v.** (**lends**, **lending**, **lent**) **1** allow someone to use something on the understanding that they will return it. **2** give someone money on condition that they will pay it back later. **3** add or contribute a particular quality. **4** (**lend itself to**) be suitable for.

> SYNONYMS **1 loan**, advance. **2 add**, impart, give, bestow, confer, provide, supply, furnish, contribute. ANTONYMS borrow.

□ **lending library** a public library from which you may borrow books. ■ **lend·er** **n.**

length /leNG(k)TH, lenth/ ▶ **n.** **1** the measurement or extent of something from end to end. **2** the amount of time that something lasts. **3** the quality of being long. **4** a stretch or piece of something. **5** the extent to which someone does something: *going to great lengths.*

> SYNONYMS **1 extent**, distance, span, reach, area, expanse, range. **2 period**, duration, stretch, span, term. **3** *a length of silk* **piece**, strip, section, swatch.

□ **at length 1** in detail; fully. **2** after a long time.

length·en /ˈleNG(k)THən, ˈlenTHən/ ▶ **v.** make or become longer.

> SYNONYMS **extend**, elongate, increase, prolong, draw out, protract, spin out. ANTONYMS shorten.

length·wise /ˈleNG(k)TH,wīz, ˈlenTH-/ (or **lengthways** /ˈleNG(k)TH,wāz, ˈlenTH-/) ▶ **adv.** in a direction parallel with a thing's length.

length·y /ˈleNG(k)THē, ˈlenTHē/ ▶ **adj.** (**lengthier**, **lengthiest**) lasting a long time.

> SYNONYMS (**very**) **long**, long-lasting, protracted, extended, long-drawn-out, prolonged, interminable, time-consuming, long-winded. ANTONYMS short.

■ **length·i·ly adv.**

le·ni·ent /ˈlēnēənt, ˈlēnyənt/ ▶ **adj.** not strict; merciful or tolerant.

> SYNONYMS **merciful**, forgiving, forbearing, tolerant, charitable, humane, indulgent, magnanimous, clement. ANTONYMS severe.

■ **le·ni·en·cy n. le·ni·ent·ly adv.**

lens /lenz/ ▶ **n. 1** a piece of transparent curved material that concentrates or spreads out light rays, used in cameras, glasses, etc. **2** the transparent part of the eye that focuses light on to the retina.

Lent /lent/ ▶ **n.** (in the Christian church) the period immediately before Easter.

lent /lent/ past and past participle of **LEND**.

len·til /ˈlent(ə)l/ ▶ **n.** an edible seed with one flat and one curved side.

len·to /ˈlentō/ ▶ **adv. & adj.** Music slow or slowly.

Le·o /ˈlēō/ ▶ **n.** a sign of the zodiac (the Lion), July 23–August 22.

le·o·nine /ˈlēə,nīn/ ▶ **adj.** relating to or like a lion or lions.

leop·ard /ˈlepərd/ ▶ **n.** (feminine **leopardess**) a large cat with a spotted coat, found in Africa and southern Asia.

le·o·tard /ˈlēə,tärd/ ▶ **n.** a close-fitting, stretchy one-piece garment covering the body to the top of the thighs, worn for dance, exercise, etc.

lep·er /ˈlepər/ ▶ **n. 1** a person who has leprosy. **2** someone who is rejected or avoided by other people: *a social leper*.

Lep·i·dop·ter·a /,lepəˈdäptərə/ ▶ **pl.n.** an order of insects comprising the butterflies and moths.

lep·re·chaun /ˈleprə,kän, -,kôn/ ▶ **n.** (in Irish folklore) a mischievous elf.

lep·ro·sy /ˈleprəsē/ ▶ **n.** a contagious disease that affects the skin and can cause deformities.
■ **lep·rous adj.**

les·bi·an /ˈlezbēən/ ▶ **n.** a woman who is sexually attracted to other women. ▶ **adj.** relating to lesbians. ■ **les·bi·an·ism n.**

le·sion /ˈlēZHən/ ▶ **n.** an area of skin or part of the body that has been damaged.

less /les/ ▶ **determiner & pron. 1** a smaller amount of; not as much. **2** fewer in number. ▶ **adv.** to a smaller extent; not so much. ▶ **prep.** minus.

> USAGE
>
> Make sure you distinguish between **less** and **fewer**. Use **fewer** with plural nouns, as in *there are fewer tourists this year*; use **less** with nouns referring to things that cannot be counted, as in *there is less time left to finish the project*. Using **less** with a plural noun (*less tourists*) may be considered wrong.

les·see /leˈsē/ ▶ **n.** a person who holds the lease of a property.

less·en /ˈlesən/ ▶ **v.** make or become less.

> SYNONYMS **1 reduce**, decrease, minimize, moderate, diminish, allay, assuage, alleviate, dull, deaden, take the edge off. **2 decrease**, decline, subside, slacken, abate, fade, die down, let up, ease off, tail off, drop (off/away), dwindle, ebb, wane, recede. ANTONYMS increase.

less·er /ˈlesər/ ▶ **adj.** not so great, large, or important as the other or the rest.

> SYNONYMS **1 less important**, minor, secondary, subsidiary, peripheral. **2 subordinate**, inferior, second-class, subservient, lowly, humble. ANTONYMS greater, superior.

les·son /ˈlesən/ ▶ **n. 1** a period of learning or teaching. **2** a thing that has been learned. **3** a thing that acts as a warning or encouragement. **4** a passage from the Bible read aloud during a church service.

> SYNONYMS **1 class**, session, seminar, tutorial, lecture, period. **2 warning**, deterrent, caution, example, message, moral.

les·sor /ˈles,ôr, leˈsôr/ ▶ **n.** a person who leases or lets a property to someone else.

lest /lest/ ▶ **conj.** formal **1** with the intention of preventing; to avoid the risk of. **2** because of the possibility of.

let /let/ ▶ **v.** (**lets**, **letting**, **let**) **1** allow. **2** used to express an intention, suggestion, or order: *let's have a drink*. **3** allow someone to use a room or property in return for payment. ▶ **n.** (in racket sports) a situation in which a point is not counted and is played for again.

> SYNONYMS ▶ **v. 1 allow**, permit, give permission to, give leave to, authorize, license, empower, enable, entitle; informal give the go-ahead to, OK. **2 rent** (**out**), lease, hire (out), sublet. ANTONYMS prevent, prohibit.

□ **let alone** not to mention. **let someone down** fail to support or help someone. **let someone/something go** release someone or something. **let yourself go 1** act in a relaxed way. **2** become careless in your habits or appearance. **let someone off 1** choose not to punish someone. **2** excuse someone from a task. **let up** informal become less strong or severe. **to let** available for rent.

let·down /ˈlet,doun/ ▶ **n.** a disappointment.

> SYNONYMS **disappointment**, anticlimax, comedown, nonevent, fiasco; informal washout.

le·thal /ˈlēTHəl/ ▶ **adj. 1** able to cause death. **2** very harmful or destructive.

> SYNONYMS **fatal**, deadly, mortal, terminal, life-threatening, murderous, poisonous, toxic, noxious, venomous, dangerous. ANTONYMS harmless, safe.

■ **le·thal·ly adv.**

le·thar·gic /ləˈTHärjik/ ▶ **adj.** lacking energy or enthusiasm.

> SYNONYMS **sluggish**, inert, inactive, slow, lifeless, languid, listless, apathetic, weary, tired, fatigued, enervated. ANTONYMS energetic.

■ **le·thar·gi·cal·ly adv.**

leth·ar·gy /ˈleTHərjē/ ▶ **n.** a lack of energy and enthusiasm.

let's /lets/ ▶ **contr.** let us.

let·ter /ˈletər/ ▶ **n. 1** any of the symbols of an alphabet. **2** a written communication, usually sent by post. **3** (**letters**) old use knowledge of literature. ▶ **v.** (**letters**, **lettering**, **lettered**) **1** write something with letters. **2** (**lettered**) old use able to read and write.

SYNONYMS ▶ **n. 1 character**, sign, symbol, figure. **2 message**, note, line, missive, dispatch, communication; formal epistle; (**letters**) correspondence, mail, post.

□ **letter bomb** an explosive device hidden in a small package, which explodes when the package is opened. **the letter of the law** the precise terms of a law or rule.

let·ter·head /ˈletərˌhed/ ▶ **n.** a printed heading on stationery.

let·ter·ing /ˈletəriNG/ ▶ **n. 1** the process of marking letters on something. **2** letters marked on something, especially decorative ones.

let·tuce /ˈletis/ ▶ **n.** a plant whose leaves are eaten in salads.

let·up /ˈletəp/ ▶ **n.** informal a pause or lowering of the intensity of something dangerous, difficult, or tiring.

leu·ke·mi·a /lo͞oˈkēmēə/ ▶ **n.** a serious disease in which too many white blood cells are produced.

leu·ko·cyte /ˈlo͞okəˌsīt/ (or **leucocyte**) ▶ **n.** technical a white blood cell.

lev·ee /ˈlevē/ ▶ **n.** an embankment built to stop a river overflowing.

lev·el /ˈlevəl/ ▶ **n. 1** a position on a scale. **2** the amount of something that is present. **3** a horizontal line or surface. **4** a glass tube partially filled with a liquid, containing an air bubble whose position reveals whether a surface is perfectly level. **5** height in relation to the ground. **6** a particular floor in a building. ▶ **adj. 1** having a flat horizontal surface. **2** having the same relative height or position as someone or something else. ▶ **v.** (**levels**, **leveling**, **leveled**) **1** make or become level. **2** aim or direct a weapon, criticism, or accusation. **3** (**level with**) informal be honest with.

SYNONYMS ▶ **n. 1 rank**, position, degree, grade, stage, standard, class, group, set, classification. **2** *a high level of employment* **quantity**, amount, extent, measure, degree, volume. ▶ **adj. 1** *a level surface* **flat**, smooth, even, uniform, plane, flush, horizontal. **2** *a level voice* **steady**, even, uniform, regular, constant, unchanging. **3** *the scores were level* **equal**, even, drawn, tied, all square, neck and neck, on a par, evenly matched; informal even-steven, nip and tuck. ANTONYMS uneven, unequal. ▶ **v. 1 even off**, even out, flatten, smooth (out). **2 raze** (**to the ground**), demolish, flatten, bulldoze, destroy. **3 equalize**, equal, even (up), make level. **4 aim**, point, direct, train, focus, turn.

□ **level playing field** a situation in which everyone has an equal chance of succeeding.

lev·el·head·ed /ˈlevəlˈhedid/ ▶ **adj.** calm and sensible.

SYNONYMS **sensible**, practical, realistic, prudent, pragmatic, reasonable, rational, mature, sound, sober, businesslike, no-nonsense, having your feet on the ground; informal unflappable, together. ANTONYMS excitable.

■ **lev·el·head·ed·ly adv. lev·el·head·ed·ness n.**

lev·er /ˈlevər, ˈlēvər/ ▶ **n. 1** a bar used to move a load with one end when pressure is applied to the other. **2** an arm or handle that is moved to operate a mechanism. ▶ **v.** (**levers**, **levering**, **levered**) lift or move with a lever.

SYNONYMS ▶ **n. handle**, arm, switch, crowbar, bar, jimmy. ▶ **v. pry**, prize, force, wrench; informal jimmy.

lev·er·age /ˈlev(ə)rij, ˈlēv(ə)rij/ ▶ **n. 1** the application of force by means of a lever. **2** the power to influence other people: *political leverage*.

SYNONYMS **1 force**, purchase, grip, hold, anchorage. **2** *more leverage in negotiations* **influence**, power, authority, weight, sway, pull, control, say, advantage, pressure; informal clout, muscle, teeth.

lev·er·et /ˈlev(ə)rit/ ▶ **n.** a young hare.

le·vi·a·than /ləˈvīəTHən/ ▶ **n. 1** (in the Bible) a sea monster. **2** a very large or powerful thing.

lev·i·tate /ˈlevəˌtāt/ ▶ **v.** (**levitates**, **levitating**, **levitated**) rise and hover in the air. ■ **lev·i·ta·tion** /ˌlevəˈtāSHən/ **n.**

lev·i·ty /ˈlevətē/ ▶ **n.** the treatment of a serious matter with humor or lack of respect.

SYNONYMS **lightheartedness**, high spirits, cheerfulness, humor, gaiety, hilarity, frivolity, amusement, mirth, laughter, merriment, glee, jollity. ANTONYMS seriousness.

le·vy /ˈlevē/ ▶ **v.** (**levies**, **levying**, **levied**) **1** make a person, organization, etc., pay a tax or fine. **2** old use enlist someone for military service. ▶ **n.** (plural **levies**) **1** a sum of money paid as a tax. **2** old use a group of enlisted troops.

SYNONYMS ▶ **v. impose**, charge, exact, raise, collect. ▶ **n. tax**, tariff, toll, excise, duty.

lewd /lo͞od/ ▶ **adj.** referring to sex in a crude and offensive way.

lex·i·cal /ˈleksikəl/ ▶ **adj. 1** relating to the words of a language. **2** relating to a dictionary.

lex·i·cog·ra·phy /ˌleksəˈkägrəfē/ ▶ **n.** the writing of dictionaries. ■ **lex·i·cog·ra·pher n.**

lex·i·con /ˈleksiˌkän, -kən/ ▶ **n. 1** the vocabulary of a person, language, or branch of knowledge. **2** a dictionary.

LF ▶ **abbr.** low frequency.

li·a·bil·i·ty /ˌlīəˈbilətē/ ▶ **n.** (plural **liabilities**) **1** the state of being liable. **2** an amount of money that a person or company owes. **3** a person or thing likely to cause you embarrassment or trouble.

SYNONYMS **1 responsibility**, accountability. **2** (**liabilities**) **obligations**, debts, arrears, dues, commitments. **3** *he became a liability on and off the field* **hindrance**, handicap, nuisance, inconvenience, embarrassment, impediment, disadvantage, millstone, encumbrance, burden. ANTONYMS asset.

li·a·ble /ˈlī(ə)bəl/ ▶ **adj. 1** responsible by law. **2** (**liable to**) able to be punished by law for something. **3** (**liable to do**) likely to do or to be affected by.

SYNONYMS **1 responsible**, accountable, answerable, blameworthy, at fault. **2 likely**, inclined, tending, apt, prone, given, subject, susceptible, vulnerable, exposed, in danger of, at risk of.

li·aise /lēˈāz/ ▶ v. (**liaises, liaising, liaised**) **1** (of two or more people or groups) cooperate with each other and share information. **2** (**liaise between**) act as a link between two or more people or groups.

SYNONYMS **cooperate**, collaborate, communicate, network, interface, link up; informal hook up.

SPELLING

Remember the second **i** in **liaise** and **liaison**.

li·ai·son /ˈlēəˌzän, lēˈā-/ ▶ n. communication or cooperation between people or organizations.

SYNONYMS **1 cooperation**, contact, association, connection, collaboration, communication, alliance, partnership. **2 love affair**, relationship, romance, attachment, fling.

li·a·na /lēˈänə, -ˈanə/ ▶ n. a tropical climbing plant that hangs from trees.

li·ar /ˈlīər/ ▶ n. a person who tells lies.

SYNONYMS **fibber**, deceiver, perjurer, dissembler, faker, hoaxer, impostor.

lib /lib/ ▶ n. informal (in the names of political movements) the liberation of a specified group: *women's lib.* ■ **lib·ber** n.

li·ba·tion /līˈbāsHən/ ▶ n. **1** (in the past) a drink poured as an offering to a god. **2** humorous a drink: *would you like a little light libation?*

li·bel /ˈlībəl/ ▶ n. the crime of publishing something false that is damaging to a person's reputation. ▶ v. (**libels, libeling, libeled**) publish something false about.

SYNONYMS ▶ n. **defamation (of character)**, character assassination, calumny, misrepresentation, scandalmongering, slur, smear; informal mud-slinging. ▶ v. **defame**, malign, blacken someone's name, sully someone's reputation, smear, cast aspersions on, drag someone's name through the mud/mire, denigrate, traduce, slur.

li·bel·ous /ˈlībələs/ ▶ adj. containing or constituting a libel: *a libelous newspaper story.*

SYNONYMS **defamatory**, denigratory, disparaging, derogatory, false, untrue, insulting, scurrilous.

lib·er·al /ˈlib(ə)rəl/ ▶ adj. **1** willing to respect and accept behavior or opinions different from your own. **2** (in politics) supporting the freedom of individuals and in favor of political and social reform. **3** generous in applying or adding something. **4** not strictly literal or exact. ▶ n. a person with liberal views.

SYNONYMS ▶ adj. **1 tolerant**, unprejudiced, broad-minded, open-minded, enlightened, permissive, free (and easy), easygoing, libertarian, indulgent, lenient. **2** *a liberal social agenda* **progressive**, advanced, modern, forward-looking, forward-thinking, enlightened, reformist, radical; informal go-ahead. **3** *a liberal interpretation of the law* **flexible**, broad, loose, rough, free, nonliteral. **4 abundant**, copious, ample, plentiful, lavish, generous, open-handed, unsparing, unstinting, free, munificent. ANTONYMS reactionary, strict.

□ **liberal arts** literature, philosophy, mathematics, and social and physical sciences as distinct from professional and technical subjects. ■ **lib·er·al·ism** n. **lib·er·al·i·ty** /ˌlibəˈralətē/ n. **lib·er·al·ly** adv.

lib·er·al·ize /ˈlib(ə)rəˌlīz/ ▶ v. (**liberalizes, liberalizing, liberalized**) remove or loosen restrictions on. ■ **lib·er·al·i·za·tion** /ˌlib(ə)rələˈzāsHən, -ˌlīˈzā-/ n.

lib·er·ate /ˈlibəˌrāt/ ▶ v. (**liberates, liberating, liberated**) **1** set free. **2** (**liberated**) free from traditional ideas about social behavior.

SYNONYMS (**set**) **free**, release, let out, let go, set loose, save, rescue, emancipate; historical enfranchise. ANTONYMS imprison, enslave.

■ **lib·er·a·tion** /ˌlibəˈrāsHən/ n. **lib·er·a·tor** n.

lib·er·tar·i·an /ˌlibərˈte(ə)rēən/ ▶ n. **1** a person who believes in libertarianism. **2** a person who argues for civil liberty.

lib·er·tar·i·an·ism /ˌlibərˈte(ə)rēəˌnizəm/ ▶ n. a political philosophy arguing for very limited state intervention in the lives of citizens.

lib·er·tine /ˈlibərˌtēn/ ▶ n. a man who is immoral and indulges too much in pleasure.

lib·er·ty /ˈlibərtē/ ▶ n. (plural **liberties**) **1** the state of being free. **2** a right or privilege. **3** the ability to act as you please. **4** informal a rude remark or disrespectful act.

SYNONYMS **freedom**, independence, immunity, self-determination, autonomy, emancipation, sovereignty, self-government, self-rule, self-determination, civil liberties, human rights. ANTONYMS slavery.

□ **take liberties** behave in a disrespectful or overfamiliar way. **take the liberty** do something without first asking permission.

li·bid·i·nous /ləˈbidn-əs/ ▶ adj. having a strong sexual drive.

li·bi·do /ləˈbēdō/ ▶ n. (plural **libidos**) sexual desire.

Li·bra /ˈlēbrə, ˈlī-/ ▶ n. a sign of the zodiac (the Scales or Balance), September 23–October 22.

li·brar·i·an /līˈbre(ə)rēən/ ▶ n. a person who works in a library.

li·brar·y /ˈlīˌbrerē, -brərē/ ▶ n. (plural **libraries**) **1** a building or room containing a collection of books that people can read or borrow. **2** a private collection of books.

li·bret·to /ləˈbretō/ ▶ n. (plural **libretti** /-tē/ or **librettos**) the words of an opera or musical. ■ **li·bret·tist** n.

lice /līs/ plural of LOUSE.

li·cense /ˈlīsəns/ ▶ n. **1** an official permit to own, use, or do something. **2** the freedom to do or say what you want. ▶ v. (**licenses, licensing, licensed**) **1** grant a license to. **2** authorize or permit.

SYNONYMS ▶ n. **1 permit**, certificate, document, documentation, authorization, warrant, credentials, pass, papers. **2 franchise**, consent, sanction, warrant, charter, concession. **3 freedom**, liberty, free rein, latitude, independence, scope, carte blanche; informal a blank check. ▶ v. **permit**, allow, authorize, give authority to, give permission to, certify, accredit, empower, entitle, enable, sanction. ANTONYMS ban.

□ **license number** the series of letters or numbers on a license plate. **license plate** a sign affixed to a vehicle displaying a series of letters or numbers or a combination of these, indicating that the vehicle has been registered with the state.

li·cen·see /ˌlīsən'sē/ ▶ **n.** a person who holds a license, especially a license to sell alcoholic drinks.

li·cen·ti·ate /lī'sensʜ(ē)it/ ▶ **n.** the holder of a certificate of competence to practice a particular profession.

li·cen·tious /lī'sensʜəs/ ▶ **adj.** behaving in a sexually immoral way.

li·chen /'līkən/ ▶ **n.** a plant resembling moss that grows on rocks, walls, and trees.

lick /lik/ ▶ **v. 1** pass the tongue over something. **2** move lightly and quickly: *the flames licked around the wood.* **3** informal totally defeat. ▶ **n. 1** an act of licking. **2** informal a small amount or quick application of something: *a lick of paint.*

lick·spit·tle /'likˌspitl/ ▶ **n.** a person who behaves with excessive obedience to those in power.

lic·o·rice /'lik(ə)risʜ, -ris/ ▶ **n.** a black substance made from the juice of a root and used as a candy and in medicine.

lid /lid/ ▶ **n. 1** a removable or hinged cover for the top of a container. **2** an eyelid.

SYNONYMS **cover**, top, cap, covering, stopper.

li·do /'lēdō/ ▶ **n.** (plural **lidos**) a public open-air swimming pool or beach used for swimming.

lie[1] /lī/ ▶ **v.** (**lies**, **lying**, **lay** /lā/; past participle **lain** /lān/) **1** be in a horizontal position on a supporting surface. **2** be in a particular state: *the abbey lies in ruins.* **3** be situated or found.

SYNONYMS **1** *he was lying on the bed* **recline**, lie down, be recumbent, be prostrate, be supine, be prone, be stretched out, sprawl, rest, repose, lounge, loll. **2** *her bag lay on the chair* **be**, be situated, be positioned, be located, be placed, be found, be sited, be arranged, rest. ANTONYMS stand.

□ **let something lie** take no action on a sensitive matter. **lie low** keep out of sight.

lie[2] ▶ **n.** a false statement made deliberately by someone who knows it is not true. ▶ **v.** (**lies**, **lying**, **lied**) tell a lie or lies.

SYNONYMS ▶ **n. untruth**, falsehood, fib, fabrication, deception, invention, (piece of) fiction, falsification, white lie; **dishonesty**, fibbing, perjury, untruthfulness, mendacity, misrepresentation, deceit, duplicity; informal tall story, whopper. ANTONYMS truth. ▶ **v. 1 tell a lie**, fib, dissemble, perjure yourself. **2** *he was a sleazy, lying cheat* **dishonest**, untruthful, false, mendacious, deceitful, duplicitous, double-dealing, two-faced.

□ **lie detector** an instrument for determining whether a person is telling the truth by testing for physiological changes considered to be associated with lying.

lied /lēd, lēt/ ▶ **n.** (plural **lieder** /'lēdər/) a type of German song, typically for solo voice with piano accompaniment.

liege /lēj, lēzʜ/ ▶ **n.** historical **1** (also **liege lord**) a lord under the feudal system. **2** a person who served a feudal lord.

lieu /lo͞o/ ▶ **n.** (**in lieu of**) instead of.

lieu·ten·ant /lo͞o'tenənt/ ▶ **n. 1** a deputy or substitute acting for a superior. **2** a rank of officer in the army and navy.

life /līf/ ▶ **n.** (plural **lives** /līvz/) **1** the condition of being alive. **2** the existence of an individual human being or animal. **3** a particular type or aspect of existence: *school life.* **4** living things and their activity. **5** vitality or energy. **6** informal a sentence of imprisonment for life.

SYNONYMS **1 existence**, being, living, animation, sentience, creation, viability. **2 living creatures**, fauna, flora, the ecosystem, the biosphere, the ecosphere. **3 way of life**, lifestyle, situation, fate, lot. **4 lifetime**, lifespan, days, time (on earth), existence. **5 vitality**, animation, liveliness, vivacity, verve, high spirits, exuberance, zest, enthusiasm, energy, vigor, dynamism, elan, gusto, bounce, spirit, fire. **6 biography**, autobiography, history, chronicle, account, memoirs, diary. ANTONYMS death.

□ **for the life of me** informal however hard I try. **life cycle** the series of changes in the life of a living thing. **life expectancy** the average period that a person may expect to live. **life force** the force that gives something its life, vitality, or strength. **life form** any living thing. **life insurance** insurance that pays out money either when the insured person dies or after a set period. **life jacket** a jacket for keeping a person afloat in water. **the life of Riley** informal a luxurious or carefree existence. **life raft** an inflatable raft used in an emergency at sea. **life sciences** the sciences concerned with the study of living organisms, including biology, botany, and zoology. **life sentence** a punishment of life imprisonment. **life support** Medicine maintenance of vital functions following disablement or in an unfavorable environment. **life-threatening** potentially fatal. **take your life in your hands** risk being killed.

life·belt /'līfˌbelt/ ▶ **n.** a ring used to help a person who has fallen into water to stay afloat.

life·blood /'līfˌbləd/ ▶ **n.** a vital factor or force: *the lifeblood of American railroads.*

life·boat /'līfˌbōt/ ▶ **n.** a boat that is launched from land to rescue people at sea, or that is kept on a ship for use in an emergency.

life·guard /'līfˌgärd/ ▶ **n.** a person employed to rescue people who get into difficulty at a beach or swimming pool.

life·less /'līflis/ ▶ **adj. 1** dead or apparently dead. **2** not containing living things. **3** lacking energy or excitement.

SYNONYMS **1 dead**, stiff, cold, inert, inanimate; formal deceased. **2 barren**, sterile, bare, desolate, stark, bleak, arid, infertile, uninhabited. **3 lackluster**, apathetic, lethargic, uninspired, dull, colorless, characterless, wooden. ANTONYMS alive, lively.

life·like /'līfˌlīk/ ▶ **adj.** accurate in its representation of a living person or thing.

SYNONYMS **realistic**, true to life, faithful, detailed, vivid, graphic, natural, naturalistic, representational.

life·line /'līfˌlīn/ ▶ **n. 1** a thing on which someone or something depends. **2** a rope thrown to rescue someone in difficulties in water.

life·long /'līfˌlôɴɢ, -ˌläɴɢ/ ▶ **adj.** lasting or remaining throughout a person's life.

life·sav·er /'līfˌsāvər/ ▶ **n.** informal a thing that saves someone from serious difficulty.

life·span /'līfˌspan/ ▶ **n.** the length of time that a person or animal is likely to live.

life·style /'līfˌstīl/ ▶ **n.** the way in which a person lives.

SYNONYMS **way of life**, life, situation, conduct, behavior, ways, habits, mores.

life·time /ˈlīfˌtīm/ ▶ **n.** the length of time that a person lives or a thing functions.

SYNONYMS **lifespan**, life, days, time (on earth), existence, career.

lift /lift/ ▶ **v. 1** raise to a higher position. **2** pick up and move to a different position. **3** formally end a restriction. **4** (**lift off**) (of an aircraft, spacecraft, etc.) take off. ▶ **n. 1** a free ride in another person's vehicle. **2** (or **ski lift**) a device for carrying people up or down a mountain. **3** upward force exerted by the air on an aircraft wing or similar structure.

SYNONYMS ▶ **v. 1 raise**, hoist, heave, haul up, heft, elevate, hold high, pick up, grab, take up, winch up, jack up. **2** *the fog had lifted* **clear**, rise, disperse, dissipate, disappear, vanish, dissolve. **3** *the ban has been lifted* **cancel**, remove, withdraw, revoke, rescind, end, stop, terminate. ▶ **n.** *the goal will give his confidence a lift* **boost**, fillip, impetus, encouragement, spur, push; informal shot in the arm.

□ **lift a finger** make the slightest effort: *he wouldn't lift a finger to help.*

lift·off /ˈliftˌôf, -ˌäf/ ▶ **n.** the vertical takeoff of a spacecraft, rocket, etc.

lig·a·ment /ˈligəmənt/ ▶ **n.** a band of tissue that connects two bones or holds together a joint.

li·ga·ture /ˈligəchər, -ˌchŏŏr/ ▶ **n.** a thing used for tying something tightly, especially a cord used to stop the flow of blood from a bleeding artery.

light[1] /līt/ ▶ **n. 1** the natural energy that makes things visible. **2** a device that uses electricity, oil, or gas to give light. **3** a match or cigarette lighter. **4** understanding or enlightenment: *she saw light dawn on the woman's face.* **5** an expression in someone's eyes. ▶ **v.** (**lights**, **lighting**, **lit**; past participle **lit** or **lighted**) **1** provide an area or object with light. **2** make something start burning. **3** (**light up**) become lively or happy. **4** (**light on**) discover by chance. ▶ **adj. 1** having a lot of light. **2** pale in color.

SYNONYMS ▶ **n. 1 illumination**, brightness, shining, gleam, brilliance, radiance, luminosity, luminescence, incandescence, blaze, glare, glow, luster; literary refulgence, effulgence. **2 lamp**, lantern, flashlight, bulb, beacon, candle, torch. **3 daylight**, daytime, day, sunlight. ANTONYMS darkness. ▶ **v. 1 illuminate**, irradiate, floodlight; literary illumine. **2 set fire to**, ignite, kindle. ▶ **adj. 1 bright**, well-lit, sunny. **2 pale**, pastel, delicate, subtle, faded, bleached. ANTONYMS dark.

□ **bring** (or **come**) **to light** make (or become) widely known. **in (the) light of** taking something into consideration. **light at the end of the tunnel** an indication that a period of difficulty is ending. **light bulb** a glass ball containing wire or a coiled fluorescent tube, which provides light when an electric current is passed through it. **light meter** an instrument measuring the intensity of light. **light pen 1** Computing a hand-held penlike device used for passing information to a computer. **2** a hand-held device for reading bar codes. **light pollution** excessive brightening of the night sky by street lights and other man-made sources. **light year** the distance that light travels in one year, nearly 6 trillion miles. **see the light 1** understand or realize something. **2** undergo religious conversion.

light[2] ▶ **adj. 1** of little weight; not heavy. **2** not heavy enough. **3** not strongly or heavily built. **4** relatively low in density, amount, or strength. **5** gentle or delicate. **6** not profound or serious.

SYNONYMS **1 lightweight**, portable, underweight. **2 flimsy**, thin, lightweight, floaty, gauzy, diaphanous, filmy. **3** *a light dinner* **small**, modest, simple, insubstantial, frugal. **4** *light duties* **easy**, simple, undemanding, untaxing; informal cushy. **5** *a light touch* **gentle**, delicate, dainty, soft, faint, careful, sensitive, subtle. **6** *light entertainment* **undemanding**, middle-of-the-road, mainstream, lightweight, lowbrow, mass-market, superficial, frivolous, trivial. ANTONYMS heavy.

□ **light-fingered** informal tending to steal things. **light heavyweight** a weight in boxing intermediate between middleweight and heavyweight. **light industry** the manufacture of small or light articles. **make light of** treat as unimportant. ■ **light·ness n.**

light·en /ˈlītn/ ▶ **v. 1** make or become lighter in weight. **2** make or become brighter.

SYNONYMS **1 reduce**, lessen, decrease, diminish, ease, alleviate, relieve. **2 bleach**, whiten, blanch. **3 brighten**, light up, illuminate, irradiate; literary illumine. **4 cheer** (**up**), brighten, gladden, lift, boost, buoy (up), revive, restore, revitalize. ANTONYMS darken, increase.

light·er[1] /ˈlītər/ ▶ **n.** a device producing a small flame, used to light cigarettes.

light·er[2] ▶ **n.** a barge used to transfer goods to and from ships in harbor.

light·head·ed /ˈlītˌhedid/ ▶ **adj.** dizzy and slightly faint.

SYNONYMS **dizzy**, giddy, faint; informal woozy.

light·heart·ed /ˈlītˌhärtid/ ▶ **adj. 1** amusing and entertaining. **2** cheerful and carefree.

SYNONYMS **carefree**, cheerful, cheery, happy, merry, glad, playful, blithe, bright, entertaining, amusing, diverting; informal upbeat; dated gay. ANTONYMS miserable.

light·house /ˈlītˌhous/ ▶ **n.** a tower containing a powerful light to guide ships at sea.

light·ing /ˈlītiNG/ ▶ **n. 1** equipment for producing light. **2** the arrangement or effect of lights.

light·ly /ˈlītlē/ ▶ **adv. 1** with little force; gently. **2** to a slight extent or amount. **3** without sufficient care or thought.

SYNONYMS **1 softly**, gently, faintly, delicately. **2 sparingly**, sparsely, moderately, slightly, subtly. **3 carelessly**, airily, readily, heedlessly, uncaringly, unthinkingly, thoughtlessly, flippantly.

light·ning /ˈlītniNG/ ▶ **n.** a flow of high-voltage electricity between a cloud and the ground or within a cloud, accompanied by a bright flash. ▶ **adj.** very quick: *lightning speed.* □ **lightning rod** a rod or wire fixed to a high place to divert lightning into the ground.

SPELLING

There is no **e** is **lightning**. **Lightening** is a form of the verb to **lighten**.

light·weight /ˈlītˌwāt/ ▶ **n. 1** a weight in boxing between featherweight and welterweight. **2** informal a person who is not very important: *a political* *lightweight*. ▶ **adj.** **1** of thin material or build. **2** lacking seriousness or importance.

SYNONYMS ▶ **adj.** **1 thin**, light, filmy, flimsy, insubstantial, summery. **2 trivial**, insubstantial, superficial, shallow, undemanding, frivolous. ANTONYMS heavy, serious.

lig·ne·ous /'lignēəs/ ▶ **adj.** consisting of, or resembling, wood.

lig·nin /'lignin/ ▶ **n.** Botany an organic substance deposited in the cell walls of many plants, making them rigid and woody.

lig·nite /'lig,nīt/ ▶ **n.** soft brownish coal.

lik·a·ble /'līkəbəl/ (or **likeable**) ▶ **adj.** pleasant; easy to like.

SYNONYMS **pleasant**, friendly, agreeable, affable, amiable, genial, personable, nice, good-natured, engaging, appealing, endearing, convivial, congenial. ANTONYMS unpleasant.

like[1] /līk/ ▶ **prep.** **1** similar to. **2** in a similar way to. **3** in a way appropriate to. **4** such as. ▶ **conj.** informal **1** in the same way that. **2** as though. ▶ **n.** (**the like**) things of the same kind. ▶ **adj.** having similar characteristics to someone or something else.

SYNONYMS ▶ **prep.** **1 similar to**, the same as, identical to, akin to, resembling. **2 in the manner of**, in the same way/manner as, in a similar way to. **3 such as**, for example, for instance, namely, in particular, viz. **4 characteristic of**, typical of, in character with. ANTONYMS unlike.

□ **and the like** et cetera. **like-minded** having similar tastes or opinions. **like so** informal in this manner.

USAGE

Don't use **like** to mean 'as if,' as in *he's behaving like he owns the place*. Use **as if** or **as though** instead.

like[2] ▶ **v.** (**likes, liking, liked**) **1** find pleasant or satisfactory. **2** wish for; want. ▶ **n.** (**likes**) the things that you like.

SYNONYMS ▶ **v.** **1 be fond of**, have a soft spot for, care about, think well/highly of, admire, respect; be attracted to, fancy, be keen on, be taken with; informal rate. **2 enjoy**, have a taste for, care for, be partial to, take pleasure in, be keen on, appreciate, love, adore, relish; informal have a thing about, be into, be mad about, be hooked on. **3** *feel free to say what you like* **choose**, please, wish, want, see/think fit, care to, will. ANTONYMS hate.

like·li·hood /'līklē,ho͝od/ ▶ **n.** the state of being likely; probability.

SYNONYMS **probability**, chance, prospect, possibility, odds, risk, threat, danger, hope, promise.

like·ly /'līklē/ ▶ **adj.** (**likelier, likeliest**) **1** probable. **2** promising: *a likely-looking spot*. ▶ **adv.** probably.

SYNONYMS ▶ **adj.** **1 probable**, possible, odds-on, expected, anticipated; informal in the cards. **2 plausible**, reasonable, feasible, acceptable, believable, credible, tenable. **3 suitable**, promising, appropriate. ANTONYMS unlikely, implausible.

□ **a likely story!** used to express disbelief.

lik·en /'līkən/ ▶ **v.** (**liken someone/thing to**) point out the resemblance of someone or something to.

SYNONYMS **compare**, equate, set beside. ANTONYMS contrast.

like·ness /'līknis/ ▶ **n.** **1** resemblance. **2** outward appearance: *humans are made in God's likeness*. **3** a portrait or representation.

SYNONYMS **1 resemblance**, similarity, similitude, correspondence. **2 representation**, image, depiction, portrayal, picture, drawing, sketch, painting, portrait, photograph, study. ANTONYMS dissimilarity.

like·wise /'līk,wīz/ ▶ **adv.** **1** also; moreover. **2** similarly.

SYNONYMS **1 also**, equally, in addition, too, as well, to boot, besides, moreover, furthermore. **2 the same**, similarly, correspondingly.

lik·ing /'līkiNG/ ▶ **n.** **1** a fondness for someone or something. **2** (**your liking**) your taste: *the coffee was just to her liking*.

SYNONYMS **fondness**, love, affection, penchant, soft spot, attachment, taste, passion, preference, partiality, predilection, weakness. ANTONYMS dislike.

li·lac /'lī,läk, -,lak, -lək/ ▶ **n.** **1** a shrub or small tree with sweet-smelling violet, pink, or white blossom. **2** a pale pinkish-violet color.

lilt /lilt/ ▶ **n.** **1** a rising and falling of the voice when speaking. **2** a gentle rhythm in a tune. ■ **lilt·ing** adj.

lil·y /'lilē/ ▶ **n.** (plural **lilies**) a plant with large trumpet-shaped flowers on a tall, slender stem. □ **lily pad** a leaf of a water lily. **lily-livered** cowardly. **lily of the valley** a plant with broad leaves and white bell-shaped flowers. **lily-white** **1** pure white. **2** totally innocent or pure.

li·ma bean /'līmə/ ▶ **n.** an edible flat whitish bean.

limb /lim/ ▶ **n.** **1** an arm, leg, or wing. **2** a large branch of a tree.

SYNONYMS **1 arm, leg**, wing, appendage; old use member. **2 branch**, bough.

□ **out on a limb** not supported by other people.

lim·ber /'limbər/ ▶ **v.** (**limbers, limbering, limbered**) (**limber up**) warm up in preparation for exercise or activity. ▶ **adj.** supple; flexible.

lim·bo[1] /'limbō/ ▶ **n.** an uncertain period of waiting.

lim·bo[2] ▶ **n.** (plural **limbos**) a West Indian dance in which you bend backward to pass under a horizontal bar.

Lim·bur·ger /'limbərgər/ ▶ **n.** a soft white cheese with a strong smell.

lime[1] /līm/ ▶ **n.** a white alkaline substance used as a building material or fertilizer.

lime[2] ▶ **n.** **1** a green citrus fruit similar to a lemon. **2** a bright light green color.

lime[3] (or **lime tree**) ▶ **n.** a European linden.

lime·ade /,līm'ād, 'līm,ād/ ▶ **n.** a drink made from lime juice sweetened with sugar.

lime·kiln /'līm,kil(n)/ ▶ **n.** a kiln in which quicklime is produced.

lime·light /'līm,līt/ ▶ **n.** (**the limelight**) the focus of public attention.

SYNONYMS **attention**, interest, scrutiny, the public eye, publicity, prominence, the spotlight, fame, celebrity. ANTONYMS obscurity.

lim·er·ick /ˈlim(ə)rik/ ▶ **n.** a humorous five-line poem with a rhyme scheme *aabba.*

lime·stone /ˈlīmˌstōn/ ▶ **n.** a hard rock composed mainly of calcium carbonate.

lim·it /ˈlimit/ ▶ **n. 1** a point beyond which something does not or may not pass. **2** a restriction on the size or amount of something. ▶ **v.** (**limits, limiting, limited**) put a limit on.

SYNONYMS ▶ **n. 1 boundary** (**line**), border, frontier, bound, edge, perimeter, margin. **2 maximum**, ceiling, cap, cutoff point. ▶ **v. restrict**, curb, cap, (hold in) check, restrain, circumscribe, regulate, control, govern, ration.

□ **off limits** out of bounds. ■ **lim·it·less** adj.

lim·i·ta·tion /ˌliməˈtāsʜən/ ▶ **n. 1** a restriction. **2** a fault or failing.

SYNONYMS **1 restriction**, curb, restraint, control, check. **2 imperfection**, flaw, defect, failing, shortcoming, weak point, deficiency, frailty, weakness. ANTONYMS strength.

lim·it·ed /ˈlimitid/ ▶ **adj.** restricted in size, amount, extent, or ability.

SYNONYMS **restricted**, circumscribed, finite, small, tight, slight, in short supply, short, meager, scanty, sparse, inadequate, insufficient, paltry, poor, minimal. ANTONYMS limitless, ample.

□ **limited liability company** a company whose owners have only a limited responsibility for its debts.

limn /lim/ ▶ **v.** literary depict or describe in painting or words.

lim·o /ˈlimō/ ▶ **n.** (plural **limos**) informal a limousine.

lim·ou·sine /ˈliməˌzēn, ˌliməˈzēn/ ▶ **n.** a large, luxurious car, usually driven by a chauffeur.

limp[1] /limp/ ▶ **v. 1** walk with difficulty because of an injured leg or foot. **2** (of a damaged ship or aircraft) proceed with difficulty. ▶ **n.** a limping walk.

SYNONYMS ▶ **v. hobble**, hop, lurch, stagger, shuffle, totter, shamble.

limp[2] ▶ **adj. 1** not stiff or firm. **2** without energy or strength.

SYNONYMS **soft**, flaccid, loose, slack, lax, floppy, drooping, droopy, sagging. ANTONYMS firm.

■ **limp·ly** adv.

lim·pet /ˈlimpit/ ▶ **n.** a shellfish with a muscular foot for clinging tightly to rocks.

lim·pid /ˈlimpid/ ▶ **adj.** (of a liquid or the eyes) clear.

SYNONYMS **1** *a limpid pool* **clear**, transparent, glassy, crystal clear, translucent, unclouded. **2** *his limpid prose style* **lucid**, clear, transparent, plain, unambiguous, simple; accessible. ANTONYMS opaque.

linch·pin /ˈlincʜˌpin/ (or **lynchpin**) ▶ **n. 1** a pin through the end of an axle keeping a wheel in position. **2** a very important person or thing.

lin·den /ˈlindən/ ▶ **n.** a deciduous tree with heart-shaped leaves and fragrant yellowish blossoms.

line[1] /līn/ ▶ **n. 1** a long, narrow mark or band. **2** a length of cord, wire, etc. **3** a row or series of people or things. **4** a row of written or printed words. **5** a direction, course, or channel: *lines of communication.* **6** a telephone connection. **7** a railroad track or route. **8** a series of military defenses facing an enemy force. **9** a wrinkle in the skin. **10** a range of commercial products. **11** an area of activity: *their line of work.* **12** (**lines**) a way of doing or thinking about something: *thinking along the same lines.* **13** (**lines**) the words of an actor's part. ▶ **v.** (**lines, lining, lined**) **1** be positioned at intervals along a route. **2** (**line someone/thing up**) arrange people or things in a row. **3** (**line something up**) have something prepared. **4** (**lined**) marked or covered with lines.

SYNONYMS ▶ **n. 1 stroke**, dash, score, underline, underscore, slash, stripe, strip, band, belt. **2 wrinkle**, furrow, crease, crinkle, crow's foot. **3** *the Bentley's classic lines* **contour**, outline, configuration, shape, design, profile, silhouette. **4** *the county line* **boundary**, limit, border, frontier, touchline, margin, perimeter. **5 cord**, rope, cable, wire, thread, string. **6 file**, rank, column, string, train, procession, row, queue. **7 course**, direction, route, track, path, trajectory. ▶ **v. 1 furrow**, wrinkle, crease, score. **2 border**, edge, fringe, bound. **3** (**lined**) **ruled**, feint, striped, banded. **4** (**lined**) **wrinkled**, wrinkly, furrowed, wizened.

□ **in line** under control. **in line for** likely to receive. **line dancing** country and western dancing in which a line of dancers follow a set pattern of steps. **line drawing** a drawing based on the use of line rather than shading. **on the line** at serious risk. **out of line** informal behaving badly or wrongly.

line[2] ▶ **v.** (**lines, lining, lined**) cover the inner surface of something with different material.

lin·e·age /ˈlinē-ij/ ▶ **n.** ancestry or pedigree.

SYNONYMS **ancestry**, family, parentage, birth, descent, extraction, genealogy, roots, origins.

lin·e·al /ˈlinēəl/ ▶ **adj. 1** in a direct line of descent or ancestry. **2** linear.

lin·e·a·ment /ˈlin(ē)əmənt/ ▶ **n.** literary a distinctive feature, especially of the face.

lin·e·ar /ˈlinēər/ ▶ **adj. 1** arranged in or extending along a straight line. **2** consisting of lines or outlines. **3** involving one dimension only. **4** progressing from one stage to another in a series of steps: *linear narrative.* ■ **lin·e·ar·i·ty** /ˌlinēˈaritē/ n.

line·back·er /ˈlīnˌbakər/ ▶ **n.** Football a defensive player normally positioned behind the line of scrimmage.

line·man /ˈlīnmən/ ▶ **n.** (plural **linemen**) **1** a person employed to lay and maintain railroad tracks. **2** a person employed to repair and maintain telephone or power lines. **3** Football a player normally positioned on the line of scrimmage.

lin·en /ˈlinin/ ▶ **n. 1** cloth woven from flax. **2** articles such as sheets, pillowcases, and duvet covers.

lin·er[1] /ˈlīnər/ ▶ **n. 1** a large passenger ship. **2** a cosmetic for outlining or emphasizing a facial feature.

lin·er[2] ▶ **n.** a lining of a garment, container, etc.

lines·man /ˈlīnzmən/ ▶ **n.** (plural **linesmen**) (in sports) an official who decides or who helps the referee or umpire to decide whether the ball is out of play.

line·up /ˈlīnˌəp/ ▶ **n. 1** a group of people or things brought together in a particular context: *a talented batting lineup.* **2** the schedule of television programs for a particular period. **3** a group of people assembled so that an eyewitness may identify someone suspected of a crime from among them.

SYNONYMS **1 roster**, team, squad, side, configuration. **2 cast**, bill, program.

lin·ger /'lingər/ ▶ v. **1** be slow or reluctant to leave. **2** (**linger over**) spend a long time over. **3** be slow to fade, disappear, or die.

SYNONYMS **1 wait (around)**, stand (around), remain, loiter; informal stick around, hang around. **2 persist**, continue, remain, stay, endure, carry on, last.

lin·ge·rie /ˌlänzhəˈrā, -jə-/ ▶ n. women's underwear and nightclothes.

lin·go /'linggō/ ▶ n. (plural **lingos** or **lingoes**) informal **1** a foreign language. **2** the jargon of a particular subject or group.

lin·gua fran·ca /'linggwə 'frangkə/ ▶ n. (plural **lingua francas**) a language used as a common language between speakers whose native languages are different.

lin·gui·ne /ling'gwēnē/ ▶ pl.n. long slender ribbons of pasta.

lin·guist /'linggwist/ ▶ n. **1** a person who is good at foreign languages. **2** a person who studies linguistics.

lin·guis·tic /ling'gwistik/ ▶ adj. relating to language or linguistics.

lin·guis·tics /ling'gwistiks/ ▶ pl.n. the scientific study of language.

lin·i·ment /'linəmənt/ ▶ n. an ointment rubbed on the body to relieve pain or bruising.

lin·ing /'līning/ ▶ n. a layer of material covering or attached to the inside of something.

SYNONYMS **backing**, facing, padding, insulation.

link /lingk/ ▶ n. **1** a relationship or connection between people or things. **2** something that lets people communicate. **3** a means of contact or transport between two places: *a satellite link*. **4** a code or instruction that connects one website or one part of a computer program to another, or a button that activates it. **5** a loop in a chain. ▶ v. connect or join.

SYNONYMS ▶ n. **connection**, relationship, association, linkage, tie-up, tie, bond, attachment, affiliation. ▶ v. **1 join**, connect, fasten, attach, bind, secure, fix, tie, couple, yoke. **2** *the evidence linking him with the body* **associate**, connect, relate, bracket. ANTONYMS separate.

link·age /'lingkij/ ▶ n. **1** the action of linking or the state of being linked. **2** a system of links.

links /lingks/ ▶ pl.n. a golf course, especially one near the sea.

link·up /'lingkˌəp/ ▶ n. **1** an instance of two or more people or things linking. **2** a connection enabling people or machines to communicate with each other.

lin·net /'linit/ ▶ n. a type of finch (songbird).

li·no·le·um /lə'nōlēəm/ ▶ n. a floor covering made from a mixture of linseed oil and powdered cork.

lin·seed /'linˌsēd/ ▶ n. the seeds of the flax plant, which are crushed to make an oil. ▫ **linseed oil** oil extracted from linseed, used especially in paint and varnish.

lint /lint/ ▶ n. **1** short, fine fibers that separate from cloth when it is being made. **2** a fabric used for dressing wounds.

lin·tel /'lintl/ ▶ n. a horizontal support across the top of a door or window.

li·on /'līən/ ▶ n. (feminine **lioness**) a large cat of Africa and northwestern India, the male of which has a shaggy mane. ▫ **the lion's share** the largest part of something.

li·on·heart·ed /'līənˌhärtid/ ▶ adj. brave and determined.

li·on·ize /'līəˌnīz/ ▶ v. (**lionizes**, **lionizing**, **lionized**) treat as a celebrity.

lip /lip/ ▶ n. **1** either of the two fleshy parts forming the edges of the mouth opening. **2** the edge of a hollow container or an opening. **3** informal impudent talk.

SYNONYMS **edge**, rim, brim, border, verge, brink.

▫ **bite your lip** stifle laughter or a reply. **lip-read** understand speech from watching a speaker's lip movements. **lip-sync** (or **lip-synch**) (**lip-syncs**, **lip-syncing**, **lip-synced**) move your lips in time with prerecorded music or speech.

li·pase /'lipˌās, 'līˌpās/ ▶ n. Biochemistry an enzyme produced by the pancreas that promotes the breakdown of fats.

lip·gloss /'lipˌgläs, -ˌglôs/ (or **lip gloss**) ▶ n. a glossy cosmetic applied to the lips.

lip·id /'lipid/ ▶ n. Chemistry any of a class of fats that are insoluble in water.

lip·o·suc·tion /'lipōˌsəkshən, 'lī-/ ▶ n. a technique in cosmetic surgery for sucking out excess fat from under the skin.

lip·py /'lipē/ ▶ adj. informal impudent.

lip·stick /'lipˌstik/ ▶ n. colored cosmetic applied to the lips from a small solid stick.

liq·ue·fy /'likwəˌfī/ (or **liquify**) ▶ v. (**liquefies**, **liquefying**, **liquefied**) make or become liquid. ■ **liq·ue·fac·tion** /ˌlikwə'fakshən/ n.

li·queur /li'kər, -'k(y)o͝or/ ▶ n. a strong, sweet alcoholic liquor, usually drunk after a meal.

liq·uid /'likwid/ ▶ n. a substance such as water or oil that flows freely. ▶ adj. **1** in the form of a liquid. **2** clear, like water. **3** (of assets) held in cash, or easily converted into cash. **4** (of a sound) pure and flowing.

SYNONYMS ▶ n. **fluid**, moisture, solution, liquor, juice, sap. ▶ adj. **fluid**, liquefied, melted, molten, thawed, dissolved, runny. ANTONYMS solid.

▫ **liquid crystal display** an electronic visual display in which the application of an electric current to a liquid crystal layer makes it no longer transparent. **liquid measure** a unit for measuring the volume of liquids.

liq·ui·date /'likwəˌdāt/ ▶ v. (**liquidates**, **liquidating**, **liquidated**) **1** close a business and sell what it owns so as to pay its debts. **2** convert assets into cash. **3** pay off a debt. **4** informal kill. ■ **liq·ui·da·tion** /ˌlikwə'dāshən/ n.

liq·uid·i·ty /li'kwidətē/ ▶ n. **1** the state of owning assets that are held in or easily converted to cash. **2** liquid assets.

liq·uor /'likər/ ▶ n. **1** alcoholic drink, especially distilled spirits. **2** liquid that has been produced in cooking.

SYNONYMS **1 alcohol**, spirits, drink; informal booze, the hard stuff, hooch, moonshine. **2 stock**, broth, bouillon, juice, liquid.

li·ra /ˈli(ə)rə/ ▶ **n.** (plural **lire** /ˈli(ə)rā, -rə/) the basic unit of money of Turkey and formerly also of Italy.

lisp /lisp/ ▶ **n.** a speech defect in which the sound *s* is pronounced like *th.* ▶ **v.** speak with a lisp.

lis·some /ˈlisəm/ ▶ **adj.** slim, supple, and graceful.

list¹ /list/ ▶ **n.** a number of connected items or names written one after the other. ▶ **v. 1** make a list of. **2** include in a list.

SYNONYMS ▶ **n. catalog**, inventory, record, register, roll, file, index, directory, checklist. ▶ **v. record**, register, enter, itemize, enumerate, catalog, file, log, minute, categorize, inventory, classify, group, sort, rank, index.

□ **list price** the price of an article as stated by the manufacturer.

list² ▶ **v.** (of a ship) lean over to one side.

SYNONYMS **lean (over)**, tilt, tip, heel (over), pitch, incline, slant, slope, bank, careen, cant.

lis·ten /ˈlisən/ ▶ **v. 1** give your attention to a sound. **2** make an effort to hear something. **3** pay attention to advice or a request: *she wouldn't listen.* ▶ **n.** an act of listening.

SYNONYMS ▶ **v. 1 pay attention**, be attentive, attend, concentrate, keep your ears open, prick up your ears; informal be all ears. **2 heed**, take heed of, take notice/note of, bear in mind, take into consideration/account.

■ **lis·ten·er** n.

lis·te·ri·a /liˈstirēə/ ▶ **n.** a type of bacterium that infects humans and animals through contaminated food.

list·ing /ˈlistiNG/ ▶ **n. 1** a list or catalog. **2** an entry in a list.

list·less /ˈlis(t)lis/ ▶ **adj.** lacking energy or enthusiasm.

SYNONYMS **lethargic**, lifeless, enervated, languid, inactive, inert, sluggish, apathetic, passive, supine, indifferent, uninterested, impassive. ANTONYMS energetic.

■ **list·less·ly** adv.

lit /lit/ past and past participle of LIGHT¹.

lit·a·ny /ˈlitn-ē/ ▶ **n.** (plural **litanies**) **1** a series of prayers to God used in church services. **2** a long, boring list of complaints, reasons, etc.

lite /līt/ ▶ **adj.** relating to low-fat or low-sugar versions of food or drink products.

li·ter /ˈlētər/ ▶ **n.** a metric unit of capacity equal to 1,000 cubic centimeters (about 1.75 pints).

lit·er·a·cy /ˈlit(ə)rəsē/ ▶ **n.** the ability to read and write.

lit·er·al /ˈlit(ə)rəl/ ▶ **adj. 1** using or interpreting words in their usual or most basic sense. **2** (of a translation) representing the exact words of the original piece of writing. **3** not exaggerated or distorted.

SYNONYMS **1 strict**, technical, original, true. **2 word for word**, verbatim, exact, accurate, faithful. ANTONYMS figurative.

lit·er·al·ly /ˈlit(ə)rəlē/ ▶ **adv. 1** in a literal way. **2** informal used to emphasize what you are saying: *we were literally killing ourselves laughing.*

lit·er·ar·y /ˈlitəˌrerē/ ▶ **adj. 1** having to do with literature. **2** (of language) characteristic of literature or formal writing.

SYNONYMS **1 artistic**, poetic, dramatic. **2 scholarly**, intellectual, academic, bookish, erudite, well-read, cultured.

□ **literary criticism** the art or practice of judging the qualities and character of literary works.

lit·er·ate /ˈlitərit/ ▶ **adj. 1** able to read and write. **2** knowledgeable in a particular field: *computer-literate.*

SYNONYMS **(well-)educated**, well-read, widely read, scholarly, learned, knowledgeable, cultured, cultivated. ANTONYMS ignorant.

lit·e·ra·ti /ˌlitəˈrätē/ ▶ **pl.n.** educated people who are interested in literature.

lit·er·a·ture /ˈlit(ə)rəCHər, -ˌCHo͝or, -ˌt(y)o͝or/ ▶ **n. 1** written works that are regarded as having artistic merit. **2** books and printed information on a particular subject.

SYNONYMS **1 writing**, poetry, drama, plays, prose. **2 publications**, reports, studies, material, documentation, leaflets, pamphlets, brochures, handouts, publicity, advertising.

lithe /līT͟H/ ▶ **adj.** slim, supple, and graceful.

SYNONYMS **agile**, graceful, supple, flexible, lissome, loose-limbed, nimble. ANTONYMS clumsy.

lith·i·um /ˈliTHēəm/ ▶ **n.** a silver-white metallic element.

lith·o·graph /ˈliTHəˌgraf/ ▶ **n.** a print made by lithography.

li·thog·ra·phy /liˈTHägrəfē/ ▶ **n.** printing from a flat metal surface that has been prepared so that ink sticks only where it is required.

Lith·u·a·ni·an /ˌliTHəˈwānēən/ ▶ **n. 1** a person from Lithuania. **2** the Baltic language of Lithuania. ▶ **adj.** relating to Lithuania.

lit·i·ga·tion /ˌlitəˈgāSHən/ ▶ **n.** the process of taking a dispute to a court of law.

SYNONYMS **legal proceedings**, legal action, case, lawsuit, suit, prosecution, indictment.

li·ti·gious /ləˈtijəs/ ▶ **adj.** frequently choosing to go to a court of law to settle a dispute.

lit·mus /ˈlitməs/ ▶ **n.** a dye that is red under acid conditions and blue under alkaline conditions. □ **litmus paper** paper stained with litmus, used as a test for acids or alkalis. **litmus test** a reliable test of the quality or truth of something.

li·to·tes /ˈlītəˌtēz, ˈlit-, līˈtōtēz/ ▶ **n.** understatement in which something is expressed by the negative of its opposite (e.g., *you won't be sorry* for *you will be glad*).

lit·ter /ˈlitər/ ▶ **n. 1** trash left in an open or public place. **2** an untidy collection of things. **3** a number of young born to an animal at one time. **4** (also **cat litter**) absorbent material that is put into a tray for a cat to use as a toilet indoors. **5** straw or other material used as bedding for animals. **6** (also **leaf litter**) decomposing leaves forming a layer on top of soil. **7** (in the past) an enclosed chair or bed carried by men or animals. ▶ **v.** (**litters**, **littering**, **littered**) make a place untidy by dropping litter.

SYNONYMS ▶ **n. trash**, rubbish, garbage, refuse, junk, waste, debris, detritus. ▶ **v. clutter up**, mess up, be scattered about/around, be strewn about/around.

lit·ter·bug /ˈlitərˌbəg/ ▶ **n.** informal a person who carelessly drops trash on the ground.

lit·tle /ˈlitl/ ▶ **adj. 1** small in size, amount, or degree. **2** (of a person) young or younger. **3** (of distance or time) short. ▶ **determiner & pron.** not much. ▶ **adv.** hardly, or not at all.

SYNONYMS ▶ **adj.** **1 small**, compact, miniature, tiny, minute, minuscule, toy, baby, undersized, dwarf, midget; informal teeny-weeny, teensy-weensy, vest-pocket. **2 short**, small, slight, petite, diminutive, tiny, elfin; informal pint-sized. **3 young**, younger, baby. **4 brief**, short, quick, hasty, cursory. **5 minor**, unimportant, insignificant, trivial, trifling, petty, paltry, inconsequential, negligible. ANTONYMS big, large, elder, major. ▶ **adv.** **1 hardly**, barely, scarcely, not much, only slightly. **2 rarely**, seldom, infrequently, hardly (ever), scarcely ever, not much. ANTONYMS well, often.

□ **a little 1** a small amount of. **2** a short time or distance. **3** to a limited extent. **little finger** the smallest finger, at the outer side of the hand. **Little League** youth baseball or softball for children up to age 12. **Little Leaguer** a player of Little League. **little or nothing** hardly anything. **little people 1** the ordinary people of a country or organization. **2** fairies or leprechauns.

lit·to·ral /ˈlitərəl/ ▶ **adj.** relating to the shore of the sea or a lake.

lit·ur·gy /ˈlitərjē/ ▶ **n.** (plural **liturgies**) a set form of public worship used in the Christian church. ■ **li·tur·gi·cal** /liˈtərjikəl/ **adj.**

liv·a·ble /ˈlivəbəl/ (or **liveable**) ▶ **adj. 1** worth living: *fatherhood makes life more livable.* **2** (of an environment or climate) fit to live in.

live¹ /liv/ ▶ **v.** (**lives, living, lived**) **1** remain alive. **2** be alive at a particular time. **3** spend your life in a particular way: *they are living in fear.* **4** have your home in a particular place. **5** obtain the things necessary for staying alive: *they live by hunting and fishing.*

SYNONYMS **1 exist**, be alive, be, have life, breathe, draw breath, walk the earth. **2 reside**, have your home, lodge, inhabit, occupy; formal dwell; old use abide, bide. **3** *she had lived a difficult life* **experience**, spend, pass, lead, have, go through, undergo. **4** *he lived by scavenging* **survive**, make a living, eke out a living, subsist, support yourself, sustain yourself, make ends meet, keep body and soul together. ANTONYMS die.

□ **lived-in** (of a room or building) showing comforting signs of wear and use. **live something down** manage to make other people forget something embarrassing. **live-in 1** (of a domestic employee) resident in an employer's house. **2** living with another in a romantic relationship. **live off** (or **on**) **1** depend on a source of income or support. **2** eat a particular food as the main part of your diet. **live rough** live outdoors with no home.

live² /līv/ ▶ **adj. 1** living. **2** (of music) played in front of an audience; not recorded. **3** (of a broadcast) transmitted at the time it happens, rather than recorded. **4** (of a wire or device) connected to a source of electric current. **5** containing explosive that can be detonated. ▶ **adv.** as a live performance: *the game will be televised live.*

SYNONYMS ▶ **adj. 1 living**, alive, conscious, animate, vital. **2** *a live rail* **electrified**, charged, powered up, active, switched on. **3** *a live grenade* **unexploded**, explosive, active, primed. **4** *a live issue* **topical**, current, controversial, hot, burning, pressing, important, relevant. ANTONYMS dead, inanimate.

□ **live action** action in movies involving real people or animals, as contrasted with animation or computer-generated effects. **live wire** informal an energetic and lively person.

live·li·hood /ˈlīvlēˌho͝od/ ▶ **n.** a way of earning enough money to live on.

SYNONYMS **(source of) income**, living, subsistence, bread and butter, job, work, employment, occupation.

live·long /ˈlivˌlôNG, -ˌläNG/ ▶ **adj.** literary (of a period of time) entire.

live·ly /ˈlīvlē/ ▶ **adj.** (**livelier, liveliest**) **1** full of life and energy. **2** (of a place) full of activity.

SYNONYMS **1 energetic**, active, animated, dynamic, full of life, outgoing, spirited, sprightly, high-spirited, vivacious, enthusiastic, vibrant, buoyant, exuberant, boisterous, effervescent, cheerful; informal chipper, chirpy, full of beans. **2 busy**, crowded, bustling, hectic, buzzing, vibrant, colorful. **3** *a lively debate* **stimulating**, interesting, vigorous, animated, spirited, heated. ANTONYMS quiet, dull.

■ **live·li·ness n.**

liv·en /ˈlīvən/ ▶ **v.** (**liven someone/thing up** or **liven up**) make or become more lively or interesting.

liv·er /ˈlivər/ ▶ **n. 1** a large organ in the abdomen that produces bile. **2** the liver of some animals used as food.

liv·er·wort /ˈlivərˌwərt, -ˌwôrt/ ▶ **n.** a small flowerless green plant with leaflike stems or lobed leaves.

liv·er·y /ˈliv(ə)rē/ ▶ **n.** (plural **liveries**) **1** a special uniform worn by a servant or official. **2** a distinctive design and color scheme used on the vehicles or products of a company. ■ **liv·er·ied adj.**

lives /līvz/ plural of LIFE.

live·stock /ˈlīvˌstäk/ ▶ **n.** farm animals.

liv·id /ˈlivid/ ▶ **adj. 1** furiously angry. **2** dark bluish gray in color.

SYNONYMS **furious**, enraged, very angry, infuriated, irate, incensed, fuming, ranting, raving, seething, beside yourself, outraged; informal hopping mad, wild.

liv·ing /ˈliviNG/ ▶ **n. 1** being alive. **2** an income that is enough to live on. ▶ **adj.** alive.

SYNONYMS ▶ **n. 1 livelihood**, (source of) income, subsistence, keep, daily bread, bread and butter, job, work, employment, occupation. **2 way of life**, lifestyle, life, conduct, behavior, activities, habits. ▶ **adj. 1 alive**, live, animate, sentient, breathing, existing. **2** *a living language* **current**, contemporary. ANTONYMS dead, extinct.

□ **living room** a room in a house used for relaxing in. **living wage** a wage that is high enough to maintain a normal standard of living. **living will** a written statement of a person's desires regarding their medical treatment in circumstances in which they are no longer able to give consent.

liz·ard /ˈlizərd/ ▶ **n.** a small four-legged reptile with a long body and tail.

lla·ma /ˈlämə/ ▶ **n.** a South American domestic pack animal related to the camel.

lo /lō/ ▶ **exclam.** old use used to draw attention to something.

loach /lōCH/ ▶ **n.** a small freshwater fish.

load /lōd/ ▶ **n. 1** a heavy or bulky thing that is being carried. **2** a weight or source of pressure. **3** the total number or amount carried in a vehicle or container. **4** (**a load** or **loads of**) informal a lot of.

▶ v. **1** put a load on or in. **2** put ammunition into a gun. **3** put something into a device so that it will operate: *load the cassette into the camcorder.*

SYNONYMS ▶ n. **1 cargo**, freight, consignment, delivery, shipment, goods, pack, bundle, parcel. **2** *a heavy teaching load* **commitment**, responsibility, duty, obligation, burden, onus. ▶ v. **1 fill (up)**, pack, stock, stack, stow, store, bundle, place, put, deposit, pile, stuff, cram; old use lade. **2 burden**, weigh down, saddle, oppress, charge, overburden, overwhelm, encumber, tax, strain, trouble, worry. **3** *he loaded the gun* **prime**, charge, set up, prepare. **4** *load the cassette into the camcorder* **insert**, put, place, slot, slide.

load·ed /ˈlōdid/ ▶ adj. **1** carrying or supporting a load. **2** biased toward a particular outcome. **3** having an underlying meaning: *a loaded question.* **4** informal wealthy.

SYNONYMS **1 full**, filled, laden, packed, stuffed, crammed, brimming, stacked; informal chock-full, chock-a-block. **2** *a politically loaded word* **charged**, emotive, sensitive, delicate.

loaf[1] /lōf/ ▶ n. (plural **loaves** /lōvz/) a quantity of bread that is shaped and baked in one piece.

loaf[2] ▶ v. spend your time in a lazy or aimless way.

SYNONYMS **laze**, lounge, loll, idle; informal hang around, bum around.

loaf·er /ˈlōfər/ ▶ n. **1** a person who spends their time in a lazy or aimless way. **2** a casual leather shoe with a flat heel.

loam /lōm/ ▶ n. a fertile soil of clay and sand containing humus.

loan /lōn/ ▶ n. **1** a sum of money that is lent to someone. **2** the action of lending something. ▶ v. give something as a loan.

SYNONYMS ▶ n. **credit**, advance, mortgage, overdraft. ▶ v. **lend**, advance.

□ **loan shark** informal a moneylender who charges very high rates of interest. **on loan** being borrowed.

loath /lōTH, lō<u>TH</u>/ (or **loth**) ▶ adj. (**loath to do**) reluctant or unwilling to do: *I was loath to leave.*

SYNONYMS **reluctant**, unwilling, disinclined, averse, opposed, resistant. ANTONYMS eager, willing.

USAGE

Don't confuse **loath** with **loathe**, which means 'feel hatred for.'

loathe /lō<u>TH</u>/ ▶ v. (**loathes**, **loathing**, **loathed**) feel hatred or disgust for.

SYNONYMS **hate**, detest, abhor, despise, abominate, not be able to bear/stand, execrate. ANTONYMS love.

loath·ing /ˈlō<u>TH</u>iNG/ ▶ n. hatred or disgust.

SYNONYMS **hatred**, hate, detestation, abhorrence, abomination, antipathy, aversion, dislike, disgust, repugnance.

loath·some /ˈlōTHsəm, ˈlō<u>TH</u>-/ ▶ adj. causing hatred or disgust.

SYNONYMS **hateful**, detestable, abhorrent, repulsive, odious, repugnant, repellent, disgusting, revolting, sickening, nauseating, abominable, despicable, contemptible, reprehensible, vile, horrible, nasty, obnoxious, gross, foul, execrable; informal horrid; literary noisome.

loaves /lōvz/ plural of LOAF[1].

lob /läb/ ▶ v. (**lobs**, **lobbing**, **lobbed**) throw or hit something in a high arc. ▶ n. (in soccer or tennis) a ball lobbed over an opponent.

lob·by /ˈläbē/ ▶ n. (plural **lobbies**) **1** an open area inside the entrance of a public building. **2** a group of people who try to influence politicians on a particular issue. ▶ v. (**lobbies**, **lobbying**, **lobbied**) try to influence a politician on an issue.

SYNONYMS ▶ n. **1 entrance (hall)**, hallway, hall, vestibule, foyer, reception. **2** *the anti-hunt lobby* **pressure group**, interest group, movement, campaign, crusade, faction, camp. ▶ v. **1 approach**, contact, petition, appeal to, pressurize, importune. **2 campaign**, crusade, press, push, ask, call, demand, promote, advocate, champion.

■ **lob·by·ist** n.

lobe /lōb/ ▶ n. **1** a roundish and flattish part that projects from or divides something. **2** the rounded fleshy part at the lower edge of the ear. **3** each of the sections of the main part of the brain.

lo·bel·ia /lōˈbēlēə, -ˈbēlyə/ ▶ n. a garden plant of the bellflower family with blue or red flowers.

lo·bot·o·my /ləˈbätəmē/ ▶ n. (plural **lobotomies**) an operation that involves cutting into part of the brain, formerly used to treat mental illness.

lob·ster /ˈläbstər/ ▶ n. a large edible shellfish with large pincers. □ **lobster pot** a basketlike trap in which lobsters are caught.

lo·cal /ˈlōkəl/ ▶ adj. having to do with a particular area, or with the place where you live: *the local post office.* ▶ n. a person who lives in a particular place.

SYNONYMS ▶ adj. **1** *the local council* **district**, regional, town, municipal, provincial, parish. **2** *a local restaurant* **neighborhood**, nearby, near, at hand, close by, handy, convenient. **3** *a local infection* **confined**, restricted, contained, localized. ANTONYMS national, widespread. ▶ n. **resident**, native, inhabitant, parishioner. ANTONYMS outsider.

□ **local anesthetic** an anesthetic that causes a loss of feeling in a particular part of the body. **local area network** a computer network that links devices within a building or group of buildings. **local government** the administration of a particular county or district, with representatives elected by those who live there. **local time** time as reckoned in a particular region or time zone. ■ **lo·cal·ly** adv.

lo·cale /lōˈkal/ ▶ n. a place where something happens: *the bay has become the locale for tuna fishing.*

lo·cal·i·ty /lōˈkalətē/ ▶ n. (plural **localities**) **1** an area or neighborhood. **2** the position or site of something.

lo·cal·ize /ˈlōkəˌlīz/ ▶ v. (**localizes**, **localizing**, **localized**) restrict to a particular place. ■ **lo·cal·i·za·tion** /ˌlōkələˈzāSHən/ n.

lo·cate /ˈlōˌkāt, lōˈkāt/ ▶ v. (**locates**, **locating**, **located**) **1** discover the exact place or position of. **2** (**be located**) be situated in a particular place.

SYNONYMS **1 find**, pinpoint, track down, unearth, sniff out, smoke out, search out, uncover, run to earth. **2 situate**, site, position, place, base, put, build, establish, station.

lo·ca·tion /lō'kāsʜən/ ▶ **n.** **1** a place where something is located. **2** the action of locating someone or something. **3** an actual place in which a movie or broadcast is made, as distinct from a studio.

SYNONYMS **position**, place, situation, site, locality, locale, spot, whereabouts, scene, setting, area, environment, venue, address; technical locus.

loc. cit. /'läk 'sit/ ▶ **abbr.** in the passage already mentioned.

loch /läk, läᴋʜ/ ▶ **n.** Scottish a lake, or a narrow strip of sea that is almost surrounded by land.

lo·ci /'lō,sī, -,sē, -,kē, -,kī/ plural of LOCUS.

lock[1] /läk/ ▶ **n.** **1** a mechanism for keeping a door or container fastened, operated by a key. **2** a similar device used to prevent a vehicle or other machine from operating. **3** a short section of a canal or river with gates at each end that can be opened or closed to change the water level, used for raising and lowering boats. **4** a hold in wrestling that prevents an opponent from moving a limb. **5** the maximum extent that the front wheels of a vehicle can be turned. ▶ **v.** **1** fasten with a lock. **2** shut in or imprison by locking a door. **3** become fixed in one position.

SYNONYMS ▶ **n.** **bolt**, catch, fastener, clasp, hasp, latch, padlock. ▶ **v.** **1** **bolt**, fasten, secure, padlock, latch, chain. **2** **join**, interlock, link, engage, combine, connect, couple. **3** **become stuck**, stick, jam, seize. **4** **clasp**, clench, grasp, embrace, hug, squeeze. ANTONYMS unlock, open.

□ **lock horns** be involved in a conflict or dispute. **lock, stock, and barrel** including everything.
■ **lock·a·ble** **adj.**

lock[2] ▶ **n.** **1** a coil or hanging piece of a person's hair. **2** (**locks**) literary a person's hair.

SYNONYMS **strand**, tress, curl, ringlet, hank, tuft, wisp, coil, tendril.

lock·er /'läkər/ ▶ **n.** a small cupboard or compartment that can be locked, typically one of a number placed together for public or general use.

lock·et /'läkit/ ▶ **n.** a piece of jewelry in the form of a small case on a chain, worn around a person's neck and used to hold a tiny photograph, a lock of hair, etc.

lock·jaw /'läk,jô/ ▶ **n.** a form of the disease tetanus in which the jaws become stiff and tightly closed.

lock·out /'läk,out/ ▶ **n.** a situation in which an employer refuses to allow employees to enter their place of work until they agree to certain conditions.

lock·smith /'läk,smiᴛʜ/ ▶ **n.** a person who makes and repairs locks.

lock·up /'läk,əp/ ▶ **n.** **1** a jail, especially a temporary one. **2** the locking up of premises for the night or the time of doing this. **3** the action of becoming fixed or immovable: *anti-lock braking helps prevent wheel lockup.*

lo·co /,lōkō/ ▶ **adj.** informal crazy.

lo·co·mo·tion /,lōkə'mōsʜən/ ▶ **n.** movement from one place to another.

lo·co·mo·tive /,lōkə'mōtiv/ ▶ **n.** a powered railroad vehicle used for pulling trains. ▶ **adj.** relating to locomotion.

lo·co·weed /'lōkō,wēd/ ▶ **n.** a plant of the pea family that, if eaten by livestock, can cause a brain disorder marked by unpredictable behavior and loss of coordination.

lo·cus /'lōkəs/ ▶ **n.** (plural **loci** /'lō,sī, -,sē, -,kē, -,kī/) technical a particular position, point, or place.

lo·cust /'lōkəst/ ▶ **n.** a large tropical grasshopper that migrates in vast swarms.

lo·cu·tion /lō'kyo͞osʜən/ ▶ **n.** **1** a word or phrase. **2** a person's particular way of speaking.

lode /lōd/ ▶ **n.** a vein of metal ore in the earth.

lode·stone /'lōd,stōn/ ▶ **n.** a piece of magnetic iron ore used as a magnet.

lodge /läj/ ▶ **n.** **1** a small country house where people stay while hunting and shooting. **2** a beaver's den. **3** a branch of an organization such as the Freemasons. **4** a small house at the gates of a large house with grounds. **5** a room for a porter at the entrance of a large building. ▶ **v.** (**lodges**, **lodging**, **lodged**) **1** formally present a complaint, appeal, etc. **2** firmly fix something in a place. **3** rent accommodations in another person's house. **4** leave something valuable in a safe place or with someone reliable.

SYNONYMS ▶ **n.** **1** *a hunting lodge* **house**, chalet, cottage, cabin. **2** *a Masonic lodge* **section**, branch, chapter, wing, group. ▶ **v.** **1** **submit**, register, enter, put forward, advance, lay, present, tender, proffer, put on record, record, table, file. **2** *the bullet lodged in his back* **become embedded**, get stuck, stick, catch, get caught, wedge. **3** **reside**, board, stay, room, live; literary sojourn. **4** **deposit**, put, bank, stash, store, stow, put away.

lodg·er /'läjər/ ▶ **n.** a person who pays rent to live in a house or apartment with the owner.

lodg·ing /'läjiɴɢ/ ▶ **n.** **1** temporary accommodations. **2** (usu. **lodgings**) a rented room or rooms, usually in the same house as the owner.

SYNONYMS **accommodations**, rooms, chambers, living quarters, a roof over your head, housing, shelter; informal digs, crib; formal residence, dwelling, abode.

lo·ess /les, ləs, 'lō,es/ ▶ **n.** a loose, fine soil, originally deposited by the wind.

lo-fi /'lō 'fī/ (also **low-fi**) ▶ **adj.** having to do with sound reproduction of a lower quality than hi-fi.

loft /lôft, läft/ ▶ **n.** **1** a room or storage space directly under the roof of a house. **2** a large, open apartment in a converted warehouse or factory. **3** a gallery in a church or hall. **4** the thickness of insulating matter in an object such as a comforter, sleeping bag, or padded coat. ▶ **v.** kick, hit, or throw a ball or missile high into the air.

loft·y /'lôftē, 'läf-/ ▶ **adj.** (**loftier**, **loftiest**) **1** tall and impressive. **2** morally good; noble: *lofty ideals.* **3** proud and superior.

SYNONYMS **1** **tall**, high, towering. **2** *lofty ideals* **noble**, exalted, high, high-minded, worthy, grand, fine, elevated. **3** *lofty disdain* **haughty**, arrogant, disdainful, supercilious, condescending, patronizing, scornful, contemptuous, self-important, conceited, snobbish; informal stuck-up, snooty. ANTONYMS low, short.

■ **loft·i·ly** **adv.**

log[1] /lôg, läg/ ▶ **n.** **1** a part of the trunk or a large branch of a tree that has fallen or been cut off. **2** an official record of the voyage of a ship or aircraft. **3** a device for measuring the speed of a ship. ▶ **v.** (**logs**, **logging**, **logged**) **1** record facts in a log. **2** achieve a certain distance, speed, or time. **3** (**log in**/**on** or **log out**/**off**) begin or finish using a computer system. **4** cut down an area of forest to use the wood commercially.

SYNONYMS ▶ **n. record**, register, logbook, journal, diary, minutes, ledger, account, tally. ▶ **v. 1 register**, record, note, write down, put in writing, enter, file. **2** *the pilot had logged 95 hours* **attain**, achieve, chalk up, make, do, go, cover, clock.

■ **log·ger n.**

log² ▶ **n.** a logarithm.

lo·gan·ber·ry /'lōgən,berē/ ▶ **n.** (plural **loganberries**) an edible red soft fruit, similar to a raspberry.

log·a·rithm /'lôgə,riTHəm, 'lägə-/ ▶ **n.** each of a series of numbers that allow you to do calculations by adding and subtracting rather than multiplying and dividing. ■ **log·a·rith·mic** /,lôgə'riTHmik, ,lägə-/ **adj.**

log·book /'lôg,bo͝ok, 'läg-/ ▶ **n.** a log of a ship or aircraft.

log·ger·heads /'lôgər,hedz, 'lägər-/ ▶ **pl.n.** (**at loggerheads**) in strong disagreement.

log·gia /'lōj(ē)ə, 'lô-/ ▶ **n.** a long room with one or more open sides.

log·ic /'läjik/ ▶ **n. 1** the science of reasoning. **2** clear, sound reasoning: *the strategy has a certain logic to it.* **3** a set of principles used in preparing a computer or electronic device to perform a task.

SYNONYMS **1 reason**, judgment, rationality, wisdom, sense, good sense, common sense, sanity. **2** *the logic of their argument* **reasoning**, rationale, argument.

■ **lo·gi·cian** /lə'jisHən, lō-/ **n.**

log·i·cal /'läjikəl/ ▶ **adj. 1** following the rules of logic. **2** using clear, sound reasoning: *the information is displayed in a logical fashion.* **3** expected or reasonable under the circumstances: *a bridge is the logical choice.*

SYNONYMS **1 reasoned**, rational, sound, cogent, valid, coherent, clear, systematic, orderly, methodical, analytical, consistent. **2** *the logical outcome* **natural**, reasonable, sensible, understandable, predictable, unsurprising, likely. ANTONYMS illogical.

■ **log·i·cal·ly adv.**

lo·gis·tics /lə'jistiks, lō-/ ▶ **n.** the detailed organization of a large and complex project or event. ▶ **adj.** relating to logistics. ■ **lo·gis·tic adj. lo·gis·ti·cal adj.**

log·jam /'lôg,jam, 'läg-/ ▶ **n.** a situation in which progress is difficult or impossible.

lo·go /'lō,gō/ ▶ **n.** (plural **logos**) a design or symbol used by an organization to identify its products.

SYNONYMS **design**, symbol, emblem, trademark, motif, monogram.

log·roll·ing /'lôg,rōliNG, 'läg-/ ▶ **n.** informal the practice of exchanging favors, especially in politics.

loin /loin/ ▶ **n. 1** the part of the body between the ribs and the hip bones. **2** a joint of meat from this part of an animal.

loin·cloth /'loin,klôTH, -,kläTH/ ▶ **n.** a piece of cloth wrapped around the hips, worn by men in some hot countries.

loi·ter /'loitər/ ▶ **v.** (**loiters**, **loitering**, **loitered**) stand around without any obvious purpose.

SYNONYMS **linger**, wait, skulk, loaf, lounge, idle; informal hang about/around.

loll /läl/ ▶ **v. 1** sit, lie, or stand in a lazy, relaxed way. **2** hang loosely: *he let his head loll back.*

lol·la·pa·loo·za /,läləpə'lo͞ozə/ ▶ **n.** informal a very impressive or attractive person or thing.

lol·li·pop /'lälē,päp/ ▶ **n.** a large, flat, rounded boiled candy on the end of a stick.

lol·ly·gag /'lälē,gag/ ▶ **v.** (**lollygags**, **lollygagging**, **lollygagged**) informal spend time in an aimless way.

lone /lōn/ ▶ **adj. 1** having no companions. **2** not having the support of other people: *I am certainly not a lone voice.*

SYNONYMS **1 solitary**, single, solo, unaccompanied, sole, isolated. **2** *a lone parent* **single**, unmarried, separated, divorced, widowed.

□ **lone wolf** a person who prefers to be alone.

lone·li·ness /'lōnlēnis/ ▶ **n.** the state or quality of being lonely.

SYNONYMS **1 isolation**, friendlessness, lonesomeness, abandonment, rejection. **2 solitariness**, solitude, aloneness, separation, seclusion.

lone·ly /'lōnlē/ ▶ **adj.** (**lonelier**, **loneliest**) **1** sad because of having no friends or company. **2** (of time) spent alone: *lonely days.* **3** (of a place) remote.

SYNONYMS **1 isolated**, alone, friendless, lonesome, with no one to turn to, abandoned, rejected, unloved, unwanted. **2 deserted**, uninhabited, desolate, solitary, isolated, remote, out of the way, off the beaten track, secluded, in the back of beyond, godforsaken; informal in the middle of nowhere.

lon·er /'lōnər/ ▶ **n.** a person who prefers to be alone.

SYNONYMS **recluse**, introvert, lone wolf, hermit, misanthrope, outsider; historical anchorite.

lone·some /'lōnsəm/ ▶ **adj.** lonely.

long¹ /lôNG, läNG/ ▶ **adj.** (**longer**, **longest**) **1** of great length in space or time. **2** having or lasting a particular length, distance, or time: *the ship will be 150 feet long.* **3** (of odds in betting) reflecting a low level of probability. **4** (of a drink) large and refreshing. **5** (**long on**) informal well-supplied with. ▶ **adv.** (**longer**, **longest**) **1** for a long time. **2** at a distant time: *long ago.* **3** throughout a stated period of time: *all day long.*

SYNONYMS ▶ **adj. lengthy**, extended, prolonged, protracted, long-lasting, drawn-out, endless, lingering, interminable. ANTONYMS short, brief.

□ **as** (or **so**) **long as** provided that. **in the long run** (or **term**) eventually. **the long and the short of it** in brief; essentially: *the long and the short of it is that he got mugged.* **long-distance 1** traveling or operating between distant places. **2** between distant places. **long division** a way of dividing one number by another in which you write down all the calculations. **long face** an unhappy or disappointed expression. **long haul 1** a long distance in terms of travel or transport of goods. **2** a long period of time. **long in the tooth** rather old. **long johns** informal underpants with close-fitting legs extending to the ankles. **long jump** a sports event in which competitors jump as far as possible. **long-lived** living or lasting a long time. **long-range 1** able to be travel long distances. **2** relating to a period of time far into the future: *a long-range forecast*. **long shot** a scheme or guess that has only the slightest chance of succeeding. **long-standing** having existed for a long time. **long-suffering** patiently putting up with problems or annoying behavior. **long wave** a radio wave of a wavelength above one kilometer (and a frequency below 300 kilohertz). **long-winded** long and boring.

long² ▶ **v.** (**long for** or **to do**) have a strong wish to do or have something.

SYNONYMS *I **longed for** the holidays* **yearn for**, pine for, ache for, hanker for/after, hunger for, thirst for, itch for, be eager for, be desperate for, crave, dream of, set your heart on; informal be dying for.

long. ▶ **abbr.** longitude.

long·boat /'lông,bōt, 'läng-/ ▶ **n.** historical **1** the largest boat carried by a sailing ship. **2** a longship.

long·bow /'lông,bō, 'läng-/ ▶ **n.** a large bow used for shooting arrows; formerly used by the English armies before the introduction of firearms.

lon·gev·i·ty /lôn'jevətē, län-/ ▶ **n.** long life.

long·hand /'lông,hand, 'läng-/ ▶ **n.** ordinary handwriting (as opposed to shorthand, typing, or printing).

long·house /'lông,hous, 'läng-/ ▶ **n. 1** the traditional dwelling of the Iroquois and other North American Indians. **2** a large communal house in parts of Malaysia and Indonesia.

long·ing /'lôngiŋg/ ▶ **n.** a strong wish to do or have something. ▶ **adj.** strongly wishing for something.

SYNONYMS ▶ **n. yearning**, craving, ache, burning, hunger, thirst, hankering, desire, wish, hope, aspiration; informal yen, itch.

■ **long·ing·ly adv.**

lon·gi·tude /'länji,t(y)o͞od, 'lôn-/ ▶ **n.** the distance of a place east or west of the Greenwich (England) meridian, measured in degrees.

lon·gi·tu·di·nal /,länjə't(y)o͞odn-əl, ,lôn-/ ▶ **adj. 1** extending lengthwise. **2** relating to longitude. ■ **lon·gi·tu·di·nal·ly adv.**

long·ship /'lông,ship, 'läng-/ ▶ **n.** a long, narrow warship with oars and a sail, used by the Vikings.

long·shore /'lông,shôr, 'läng-/ ▶ **adj.** relating to or moving along the seashore.

loo·fah /'lo͞ofə/ ▶ **n.** a long, rough object used to wash yourself with in the bath, consisting of the dried inner parts of a tropical fruit.

look /lo͝ok/ ▶ **v. 1** direct your eyes in a particular direction. **2** have the appearance of being; seem: *her father looked unhappy*. **3** face in a particular direction: *the rooms look out over the harbor*. ▶ **n. 1** an act of looking. **2** appearance: *he has the look of a professor*. **3** (**looks**) a person's facial appearance. **4** a style or fashion.

SYNONYMS ▶ **v. 1 glance**, gaze, stare, gape, peer, peep, peek, watch, observe, view, regard, examine, inspect, eye, scan, scrutinize, survey, study, contemplate, take in, ogle, leer at; informal take a gander, rubberneck, get a load of, eyeball. **2 seem (to be)**, appear (to be), come across/over as. ▶ **n. 1 glance**, examination, study, inspection, scrutiny, peep, peek, glimpse; informal eyeful, once-over, squint. **2 expression**, mien, countenance. **3 appearance**, air, style, effect, ambience, impression, aspect, manner, demeanor.

□ **look after** take care of. **look at 1** think of in a specified way. **2** examine (a matter) and consider what action to take. **look down on** think that you are better than. **look for** try to find. **looking glass** a mirror. **look into** investigate. **look lively** (or **sharp**) informal be quick; get moving. **look on** watch without getting involved. **look out** be alert for possible trouble. **look to 1** rely on someone to do something. **2** hope or expect to do. **look up** improve. **look someone/something up 1** search for information in a reference book. **2** informal visit or contact a friend. **look up to** have a lot of respect for.

look·a·like /'lo͝okə,līk/ ▶ **n.** a person who looks very similar to another.

SYNONYMS **double**, twin, clone, living image, doppelgänger, replica; informal spitting image, dead ringer.

look·er /'lo͝okər/ ▶ **n.** informal a person with a specified appearance: *she's not a bad looker*.

look·out /'lo͝ok,out/ ▶ **n. 1** a place from which you can keep watch or view landscape. **2** a person who keeps watch for danger or trouble.

SYNONYMS **watchman**, watch, guard, sentry, sentinel, observer.

□ **be on the lookout** (or **keep a lookout**) **for 1** be alert to. **2** keep searching for.

loom¹ /lo͞om/ ▶ **n.** a machine for weaving cloth.

loom² ▶ **v. 1** appear as a vague and threatening shape: *vehicles loomed out of the darkness*. **2** (of something bad) seem about to happen.

SYNONYMS **1 emerge**, appear, materialize, take shape. **2 be imminent**, be on the horizon, impend, threaten, brew, be just around the corner.

loon·y /'lo͞onē/ informal ▶ **n.** (plural **loonies**) a crazy or silly person. ▶ **adj.** crazy or silly.

loop /lo͞op/ ▶ **n. 1** a shape produced by a curve that bends around and crosses itself. **2** a strip of tape or film with the ends joined, allowing sounds or images to be continuously repeated. **3** a complete circuit for an electric current. ▶ **v.** form into or have the shape of a loop: *she looped her arms around his neck*.

SYNONYMS ▶ **n. coil**, ring, circle, noose, spiral, curl, bend, curve, arc, twirl, whorl, twist, helix. ▶ **v. 1 coil**, wind, twist, snake, spiral, curve, bend, turn. **2 fasten**, tie, join, connect, knot, bind.

□ **loop the loop** (of an aircraft) fly in a vertical circle.

loop·hole /'lo͞op,(h)ōl/ ▶ **n.** a mistake or piece of vague wording that lets someone avoid obeying a law or keeping to a contract.

SYNONYMS **ambiguity**, means of evasion, discrepancy, inconsistency, omission, excuse, escape clause.

loop·y /'lo͞opē/ ▶ **adj.** informal crazy or silly.

loose /lo͞os/ ▶ **adj. 1** not firmly or tightly fixed in place. **2** not fastened or packaged together. **3** not tied up or shut in: *the horses broke loose*. **4** (of a garment) not fitting tightly. **5** not exact: *a loose translation*. **6** careless and indiscreet: *loose talk*. **7** dated immoral. **8** not tightly packed together. ▶ **v.** (**looses, loosing, loosed**) **1** unfasten or set free. **2** (**loose something off**) fire a shot, bullet, etc.

SYNONYMS ▶ **adj. 1 not secure**, unsecured, unattached, untied, detached, wobbly, unsteady, dangling, free. **2 free**, at large, at liberty, on the loose. **3 baggy**, roomy, oversized, voluminous, shapeless, sloppy. **4** *a loose interpretation* **vague**, imprecise, approximate, broad, general, rough, liberal. ANTONYMS secure, tight. ▶ **v. 1 free**, let loose, release, untie, unchain, unfasten, unleash, relax. **2 relax**, slacken, loosen. ANTONYMS confine, tighten.

□ **at loose ends** uncertain; disorganized. **loose cannon** a person who behaves in an unpredictable and potentially harmful way. **loose-leaf** (of a notebook) having sheets of paper that can be added or removed. **on the loose** having escaped from being shut in or tied up. ■ **loose·ly adv. loose·ness n.**

USAGE
Don't confuse **loose** with **lose**, which means 'no longer have' or 'become unable to find.'

loos·en /'lo͞osən/ ▶ **v. 1** make or become loose. **2** (**loosen up**) warm up in preparation for an activity.

SYNONYMS **1 undo**, slacken, unfasten, detach, release, disconnect. **2 weaken**, relax, slacken, loose, let go. ANTONYMS tighten.

□ **loosen someone's tongue** make someone talk freely.

loot /lo͞ot/ ▶ **v.** steal goods from empty buildings during a war, riot, etc. ▶ **n. 1** goods stolen from empty buildings during a war, riot, etc. **2** goods stolen by a thief. **3** informal money.

SYNONYMS ▶ **v. plunder**, pillage, ransack, sack, rifle, rob, strip, gut. ▶ **n. booty**, spoils, plunder, haul; informal swag, boodle.

■ **loot·er n.**

lop /läp/ ▶ **v.** (**lops, lopping, lopped**) **1** cut off a branch or limb from a tree or body. **2** informal reduce by a particular amount: *the seller lopped a hundred off the price of the car.* □ **lop-eared** (of an animal) having drooping ears.

lope /lōp/ ▶ **v.** (**lopes, loping, loped**) run with long, relaxed strides. ▶ **n.** a long bounding stride.

lop·sid·ed /'läp,sīdid/ ▶ **adj.** with one side lower or smaller than the other.

SYNONYMS **crooked**, askew, awry, off-centrer, uneven, out of true, asymmetrical, tilted, at an angle, slanting; informal cockeyed. ANTONYMS even, level.

lo·qua·cious /lō'kwāsʜəs/ ▶ **adj.** formal talkative.

SYNONYMS **talkative**, voluble, garrulous, chatty, gossipy; informal gabby, gassy. ANTONYMS reticent, taciturn.

■ **lo·quac·i·ty** /lō'kwasətē/ **n.**

lord /lôrd/ ▶ **n. 1** a master or ruler. **2** (**Lord**) a name for God or Jesus. **3** a nobleman. **4** (**Lord**) a title given to certain British peers or high officials: *Lord Derby.* **5** (**the Lords**) ⇨ **House of Lords**.

SYNONYMS **1 noble**, nobleman, peer, aristocrat. **2 master**, ruler, leader, chief, superior, monarch, sovereign, king, emperor, prince, governor, commander.

□ **lord it over** act in an arrogant and bullying way toward someone. **the Lord's Prayer** the prayer taught by Christ to his disciples.

lord·ly /'lôrdlē/ ▶ **adj.** (**lordlier, lordliest**) proud or superior.

lord·ship /'lôrd,sʜip/ ▶ **n. 1** supreme power or rule. **2** (**His, Your**, etc., **Lordship**) (in the UK) a respectful form of reference or address to a judge, a bishop, or a man with a title.

lore /lôr/ ▶ **n.** all the traditions and knowledge relating to a particular subject: *farming lore.*

lor·gnette /lôrn'yet/ (or **lorgnettes**) ▶ **n.** a pair of glasses held by a long handle at one side.

lose /lo͞oz/ ▶ **v.** (**loses, losing, lost** /lôst, läst/) **1** have something or someone taken away from you; no longer have: *she lost her job in a hotel.* **2** become unable to find. **3** fail to win a game or contest. **4** earn less money than you are spending. **5** waste an opportunity. **6** (**be lost**) be destroyed or killed. **7** escape from: *he came after me, but I lost him.* **8** (**lose yourself in** or **be lost in**) be or become deeply involved in. **9** (of a clock or watch) become slow.

SYNONYMS **1 mislay**, misplace, be unable to find, lose track of. **2 escape from**, evade, elude, dodge, avoid, give someone the slip, shake off, throw off, leave behind, outdistance, outrun. **3 waste**, squander, let pass, miss; informal pass up, blow. **4 be defeated**, be beaten; informal come a cropper, go down. ANTONYMS find, seize, win.

□ **lose heart** become discouraged. **lose out** not get a fair chance or share. **lose your** (or **the**) **way** become lost. **losing battle** a struggle in which failure seems certain.

USAGE
Don't confuse **lose** with **loose**, which means 'not fixed in place or tied up.'

los·er /'lo͞ozər/ ▶ **n. 1** the person who loses a contest. **2** informal a person who is generally unsuccessful in life.

SYNONYMS **failure**, underachiever, dead loss, write-off, has-been; informal also-ran.

loss /lôs, läs/ ▶ **n. 1** the losing of something or someone. **2** a person or thing that is lost. **3** the feeling of sadness after losing a valued person or thing.

SYNONYMS **1 mislaying**, deprivation, forfeiture, erosion, reduction, depletion. **2 death**, demise, passing away, bereavement. **3 casualty**, fatality, victim, death toll. **4 deficit**, debit, debt. ANTONYMS recovery, profit.

□ **at a loss 1** uncertain or puzzled. **2** losing more money than is being made. **loss-leader** a product sold at a very low price to attract customers.

lost /lôst, läst/ past and past participle of **lose**. ▶ **adj. 1** unable to find your way. **2** not knowing where you are. **3** no longer in existence.

SYNONYMS ▶ **adj. 1 missing**, mislaid, misplaced, gone astray. **2 stray**, off course, going around in circles, adrift, at sea. **3** *a lost opportunity* **missed**, wasted, squandered, gone by the board(s); informal down the drain. **4** *lost traditions* **bygone**, past, former, old, vanished, forgotten, dead. **5** *lost species and habitats* **extinct**, died out, defunct, vanished, gone, destroyed, wiped out, exterminated. **6** *lost in thought* **engrossed**, absorbed, rapt, immersed, deep, intent, engaged, wrapped up.

□ **be lost for words** be so surprised or upset

that you cannot think what to say. **be lost on** not be noticed or understood by: *the irony is lost on him*. **lost cause** something that has no chance of success. **get lost!** informal go away!

lot /lät/ ▶ **pron. & adv.** (**a lot** or informal **lots**) a large number or amount. ▶ **n. 1** an item or set of items for sale at an auction. **2** informal a particular group of people: *you lot think you're clever*. **3** (**the lot**) informal the whole number or quantity. **4** a method of deciding something by chance in which one piece is chosen from a number of marked pieces of paper. **5** a person's luck or situation in life: *plans to improve the lot of the poor*. **6** a plot of land.

> SYNONYMS ▶ **pron. & adv. 1 a large amount**, a good/great deal, an abundance, a wealth, a profusion, plenty, many, a great many, a large number, a considerable number; informal hundreds, loads, masses, heaps, piles, stacks, tons, oodles. **2 a great deal**, a good deal, much, often, frequently, regularly. ▶ **n. 1 group**, crowd, circle, crew; informal bunch, gang, mob. **2** *an auction lot* **item**, article, batch, group, bundle, parcel. **3** *his lot in life* **fate**, destiny, fortune, situation, circumstances, plight, predicament.

▫ **draw** (or **cast**) **lots** decide by lot. **throw in your lot with** decide to join a person or group and share their successes and failures.

> SPELLING
>
> **A lot** is a two-word phrase; don't spell it as one word.

loth = LOATH.

Lo·thar·i·o /lōˈᴛʜe(ə)rēˌō, -ˈᴛʜär-/ ▶ **n.** (plural **Lotharios**) a man who has many casual romantic relationships with women.

lo·tion /ˈlōsʜən/ ▶ **n.** a creamy liquid put on the skin as a medicine or cosmetic.

> SYNONYMS **ointment**, cream, balm, rub, moisturizer, lubricant, embrocation, liniment, salve, unguent.

lot·ter·y /ˈlätərē/ ▶ **n.** (plural **lotteries**) **1** a way of raising money by selling numbered tickets and giving prizes to the holders of numbers drawn at random. **2** something whose success is controlled by luck.

> SYNONYMS **raffle**, drawing, sweepstakes, lotto, pool.

lo·tus /ˈlōtəs/ ▶ **n.** a kind of large water lily. ▫ **lotus position** a cross-legged position with the feet resting on the thighs, used in meditation.

louche /lo͞osʜ/ ▶ **adj.** having a bad reputation but still attractive: *his louche, creepy charm*.

loud /loud/ ▶ **adj. 1** producing a lot of noise. **2** expressed forcefully: *loud protests*. **3** very brightly colored and in bad taste: *a loud checked suit*.

> SYNONYMS **1 noisy**, blaring, booming, roaring, thunderous, resounding, sonorous, powerful, stentorian, deafening, ear-splitting, piercing, shrill, raucous; Music forte, fortissimo. **2 vociferous**, clamorous, insistent, vehement, emphatic. **3 garish**, gaudy, lurid, showy, flamboyant, ostentatious, vulgar, tasteless; informal flashy. ANTONYMS quiet.

▫ **out loud** aloud. ▪ **loud·ness n.**

loud·ly /ˈloudlē/ ▶ **adv.** in a loud way.

> SYNONYMS **at the top of your voice**, noisily, stridently, vociferously, shrilly.

loud·mouth /ˈloudˌmouᴛʜ/ ▶ **n.** informal a person who talks too much or who makes offensive remarks.

loud·speak·er /ˈloudˌspēkər/ ▶ **n.** a device that converts electrical impulses into sound.

lounge /lounj/ ▶ **v.** (**lounges**, **lounging**, **lounged**) lie, sit, or stand in a relaxed way. ▶ **n. 1** a room in a hotel, airport, etc., in which people can relax or wait. **2** a couch or sofa, especially a backless one having a headrest at one end.

> SYNONYMS ▶ **v. laze**, lie, loll, recline, relax, rest, take it easy, sprawl, slump, slouch, loaf, idle. ▶ **n. 1 waiting room**, waiting area, reception area, parlor. **2 bar**, tavern, pub, taproom, club, barroom.

loung·er /ˈlounjər/ ▶ **n.** an outdoor chair that you can lie back in.

lour /ˈlou(ə)r/ (or **lower**) ▶ **v. 1** (of the sky) look dark and threatening. **2** scowl.

louse /lous/ ▶ **n. 1** (plural **lice** /līs/) a small insect that lives as a parasite on animals or plants. **2** (plural **louses**) informal an unpleasant person. ▶ **v.** (**louses**, **lousing**, **loused**) (**louse up**) informal spoil something.

lous·y /ˈlouzē/ ▶ **adj.** (**lousier**, **lousiest**) informal very bad.

lout /lout/ ▶ **n.** a rude or aggressive man or boy.

> SYNONYMS **hooligan**, ruffian, thug, boor, oaf, rowdy; informal tough, bruiser.

▪ **lout·ish adj.**

lou·ver /ˈlo͞ovər/ ▶ **n.** each of a set of slanting slats fixed at intervals in a door, shutter, etc., to allow air or light through.

lov·a·ble /ˈləvəbəl/ (or **loveable**) ▶ **adj.** easy to love or feel affection for.

> SYNONYMS **adorable**, dear, sweet, cute, charming, lovely, likeable, engaging, endearing, winning, winsome. ANTONYMS hateful, loathsome.

lov·age /ˈləvij/ ▶ **n.** an herb used in cooking.

love /ləv/ ▶ **n. 1** a very strong feeling of affection. **2** a strong feeling of affection linked with physical attraction. **3** a great interest and pleasure in something. **4** a person or thing that you love. **5** (in tennis, squash, etc.) a score of zero. ▶ **v.** (**loves**, **loving**, **loved**) **1** feel love for. **2** like very much.

> SYNONYMS ▶ **n. 1 adoration**, devotion, affection, fondness, tenderness, attachment, warmth, passion, desire, lust, yearning, infatuation, besottedness. **2 liking**, taste, zeal, zest, enthusiasm, keenness, fondness, weakness, partiality, predilection, penchant. **3 compassion**, care, regard, concern, altruism, unselfishness, philanthropy, benevolence, humanity. **4 beloved**, loved one, dearest, darling, sweetheart, sweet, angel, honey. ANTONYMS hatred. ▶ **v. 1 be in love with**, adore, be devoted to, be infatuated with, be smitten with, be besotted with, idolize, worship, think the world of, dote on, care for, hold dear, cherish; informal be mad/crazy about, carry a torch for. **2 like**, delight in, relish, enjoy, have a soft spot for, have a weakness for, be addicted to, be taken with; informal have a thing about, be hooked on, get a kick out of. ANTONYMS hate.

▫ **love affair** a romantic or physical relationship between two people who are not married to each other. **love child** a child born to parents who are not married to each other. ■ **love·less** adj.

love·bird /ˈləvˌbərd/ ▶ n. **1** a kind of small parrot. **2** (**lovebirds**) informal an affectionate couple.

love·lorn /ˈləvˌlôrn/ ▶ adj. unhappy because you love someone who does not feel the same way about you.

love·ly /ˈləvlē/ ▶ adj. (**lovelier**, **loveliest**) **1** very beautiful. **2** very pleasant.

SYNONYMS **1 beautiful**, pretty, attractive, good-looking, handsome, adorable, charming, engaging, enchanting, gorgeous, alluring, ravishing, glamorous; informal cute, foxy, drop-dead gorgeous; old use comely. **2 delightful**, marvelous, magnificent, stunning, splendid, wonderful, superb, pleasant, enjoyable; informal terrific, fabulous, heavenly, divine, amazing, glorious. ANTONYMS ugly, horrible.

■ **love·li·ness** n.

lov·er /ˈləvər/ ▶ n. **1** a person having a romantic relationship with someone. **2** a person who enjoys a particular thing: *a music lover.*

SYNONYMS **1 boyfriend**, **girlfriend**, beloved, sweetheart, inamorato/inamorata, mistress, partner, gigolo; dated beau; literary swain; old use paramour. **2 devotee**, admirer, fan, enthusiast, aficionado; informal buff, nut.

love·sick /ˈləvˌsik/ ▶ adj. unable to think clearly or act normally as a result of being in love.

love·y-dove·y /ˈləvē ˈdəvē/ ▶ adj. informal very affectionate or romantic.

lov·ing /ˈləviNG/ ▶ adj. feeling or showing love: *a kind and loving father.* ▶ n. the feeling or showing of love.

SYNONYMS ▶ adj. **affectionate**, fond, devoted, adoring, doting, caring, tender, warm, close, amorous, passionate. ANTONYMS cold, cruel.

■ **lov·ing·ly** adv.

low¹ /lō/ ▶ adj. **1** not high or tall or far above the ground. **2** below average in amount, extent, or strength: *cook over a low heat.* **3** not good or important. **4** (of a sound) deep or quiet. **5** depressed or without energy. **6** not honest or moral: *low cunning.* **7** unfavorable: *a low opinion.* ▶ n. **1** a low point or level. **2** an area of low atmospheric pressure. ▶ adv. (of a sound) at a low pitch.

SYNONYMS ▶ adj. **1 short**, small, little, squat, stubby, stunted. **2 cheap**, economical, moderate, reasonable, affordable, modest, bargain, bargain-basement, rock-bottom. **3 scarce**, scant, meager, sparse, few, little, reduced, depleted, diminished. **4 inferior**, substandard, poor, low-grade, unsatisfactory, inadequate, second-rate. **5 quiet**, soft, faint, gentle, muted, subdued, muffled, hushed. **6 bass**, low-pitched, deep, rumbling, booming, sonorous. **7 depressed**, dejected, despondent, downhearted, downcast, down, miserable, dispirited, gloomy, glum, flat; informal fed up, down in the dumps, blue. ANTONYMS high, expensive, loud.

□ **Low Church** the section of the Church of England that places little emphasis on ritual and the authority of bishops and priests. **low-cost** cheap. **lowest common denominator** Math the lowest number that the bottom number of a group of fractions can be divided into exactly. **lowest common multiple** Math the lowest quantity that is a multiple of two or more given quantities. **low frequency** (in radio) 30–300 kilohertz. **low gear** a gear that causes a vehicle to move slowly. **low-key** not elaborate or showy. **low-level** Computing (of a programming language) similar to machine code in form. **low-lying** (of land) not far above sea level. **low-rise** (of a building) having few stories. **low spirits** sadness and depression. **low tide** the time when the sea is furthest out. **low water** ⇒ LOW TIDE. **low-water mark** the level reached by the sea at low tide.

low² ▶ v. (of a cow) moo.

low·ball /ˈlōˌbôl/ ▶ v. informal offer someone a deceptively or unrealistically low estimate or bid.

low·brow /ˈlōˌbrou/ ▶ adj. not intellectual or interested in culture.

low·down /ˈlōˌdoun/ informal ▶ adj. unfair or dishonest. ▶ n. (**the lowdown**) the true or most important facts about something.

low·er¹ /ˈlōər/ ▶ adj. **1** less high. **2** (in place names) situated on less high land, nearer the sea, or to the south. ▶ v. (**lowers**, **lowering**, **lowered**) **1** make or become lower. **2** move downward. **3** (**lower yourself**) behave in a way that makes other people lose respect for you.

SYNONYMS ▶ adj. **1 subordinate**, inferior, lesser, junior, minor, secondary, subsidiary, subservient. **2** *her lower lip* **bottom**, nether, bottommost, under. ANTONYMS upper. ▶ v. **1 let down**, take down, drop, let fall. **2 soften**, modulate, quieten, hush, tone down, muffle, turn down, mute. **3 reduce**, decrease, lessen, bring down, cut, slash. ANTONYMS raise, increase.

□ **lower class** the working class. **lower house** the larger body of a bicameral legislature or parliament, e.g., the House of Representatives of the US Congress.

low·er² /ˈlou(ə)r/ = LOUR.

low·er·case /ˈlōərˌkās/ ▶ n. small letters as opposed to capitals.

low·er·most /ˈlōərˌmōst/ ▶ adj. farthest down; lowest.

low·land /ˈlōlənd, -ˌland/ (or **lowlands**) ▶ n. **1** low-lying country. **2** (**the Lowlands**) the part of Scotland lying south and east of the Highlands. ■ **low·land·er** n.

low·life /ˈlōˌlīf/ ▶ n. (plural **lowlifes**) **1** dishonest or immoral people or activities. **2** informal a dishonest or immoral person.

low·light /ˈlōˌlīt/ ▶ n. **1** (**lowlights**) darker dyed streaks in the hair. **2** informal a disappointing or dull event.

low·ly /ˈlōlē/ ▶ adj. (**lowlier**, **lowliest**) low in status or importance: *she started as a lowly administrative assistant.*

SYNONYMS **humble**, low, low-ranking, common, ordinary, plain, modest, simple, obscure. ANTONYMS aristocratic, exalted.

■ **low·li·ness** n.

loy·al /ˈloiəl/ ▶ adj. firm and faithful in your support for a person, organization, etc.

SYNONYMS **faithful**, true, true-blue, devoted, constant, steadfast, staunch, dependable, reliable, trustworthy, trusty, patriotic, unswerving. ANTONYMS disloyal, treacherous.

■ **loy·al·ly** adv.

loy·al·ist /ˈloiəlist/ ▶ n. **1** a person who remains loyal to the established ruler or government. **2** (**Loyalist**) a colonist of the American revolutionary period who supported the British cause. **3** (**Loyalist**) a person who believes that Northern Ireland should remain part of Great Britain. ■ **loy·al·ism** n.

loy·al·ty /ˈloiəltē/ ▶ n. (plural **loyalties**) **1** the state of being loyal. **2** a strong feeling of support.

SYNONYMS **allegiance**, faithfulness, fidelity, obedience, adherence, devotion, steadfastness, staunchness, dedication, commitment, patriotism; old use fealty. ANTONYMS disloyalty, treachery.

loz·enge /ˈläzənj/ ▶ n. **1** a tablet of medicine that is sucked to soothe a sore throat. **2** a diamond-shaped figure.

LP ▶ abbr. long-playing (record).

LPN ▶ abbr. Licensed Practical Nurse.

LSD ▶ n. lysergic acid diethylamide, a drug that causes hallucinations.

Lt. ▶ abbr. Lieutenant.

lube /lo͞ob/ informal ▶ n. **1** a lubricant. **2** lubrication. ▶ v. lubricate something.

lu·bri·cant /ˈlo͞obrəkənt/ ▶ n. a substance, e.g., oil, for lubricating part of a machine.

lu·bri·cate /ˈlo͞obrəˌkāt/ ▶ v. (**lubricates**, **lubricating**, **lubricated**) apply oil or grease to machinery so that it moves easily. ■ **lu·bri·ca·tion** /ˌlo͞obrəˈkāsʜən/ n.

lu·cent /ˈlo͞osənt/ ▶ adj. literary shining.

lu·cid /ˈlo͞osid/ ▶ adj. **1** easy to understand; clear. **2** able to think clearly.

SYNONYMS **1 clear**, crystal-clear, intelligible, comprehensible, cogent, coherent, articulate. **2 rational**, sane, in possession of your faculties, compos mentis, clear-headed, sober; informal all there. ANTONYMS confused.

■ **lu·cid·i·ty** /lo͞oˈsidətē/ n. **lu·cid·ly** adv.

Lu·ci·fer /ˈlo͞osəfər/ ▶ n. the Devil.

luck /lək/ ▶ n. **1** good things that happen by chance: *it was luck that the first kick went in.* **2** chance considered as a force that causes good or bad things to happen.

SYNONYMS **1 good fortune**, good luck, stroke of luck, fluke; informal lucky break. **2 fortune**, fate, serendipity, chance, accident, a twist of fate. ANTONYMS bad luck, misfortune.

□ **no such luck** unfortunately not. **try your luck** attempt something risky.

luck·i·ly /ˈləkəlē/ ▶ adv. it is fortunate that.

SYNONYMS **fortunately**, happily, providentially, by good fortune, as luck would have it, mercifully, thankfully.

luck·less /ˈləkləs/ ▶ adj. unlucky.

luck·y /ˈləkē/ ▶ adj. (**luckier**, **luckiest**) having, bringing, or resulting from good luck: *he had a lucky escape.*

SYNONYMS **1 fortunate**, in luck, favored, charmed, successful. **2 providential**, fortunate, timely, opportune, serendipitous, chance, fortuitous, accidental. ANTONYMS unlucky.

lu·cra·tive /ˈlo͞okrətiv/ ▶ adj. making a large profit.

SYNONYMS **profitable**, gainful, remunerative, moneymaking, well-paid, rewarding, worthwhile. ANTONYMS unprofitable.

lu·cre /ˈlo͞okər/ ▶ n. literary money.

Lud·dite /ˈlədˌīt/ ▶ n. a person who is opposed to new technology.

lu·di·crous /ˈlo͞odəkrəs/ ▶ adj. absurd; ridiculous.

SYNONYMS **absurd**, ridiculous, farcical, laughable, risible, preposterous, mad, insane, idiotic, stupid, asinine, nonsensical; informal crazy. ANTONYMS sensible.

■ **lu·di·crous·ly** adv.

luff /ləf/ ▶ v. steer a sailing ship nearer the wind.

lug[1] /ləg/ ▶ v. (**lugs**, **lugging**, **lugged**) carry or drag with great effort.

lug[2] ▶ n. **1** informal an ear. **2** a projection on an object for carrying it or fixing it in place.

luge /lo͞ozʜ/ ▶ n. a light toboggan ridden in supine position.

lug·gage /ˈləgij/ ▶ n. suitcases or other bags for a traveler's belongings.

SYNONYMS **baggage**, bags, suitcases, cases.

lug·ger /ˈləgər/ ▶ n. a small ship with two or three masts and a four-sided sail on each.

lu·gu·bri·ous /ləˈg(y)o͞obrēəs/ ▶ adj. sad and gloomy.

SYNONYMS **mournful**, gloomy, sad, unhappy, melancholy, doleful, woeful, miserable, forlorn, somber, solemn, sorrowful, morose, dour, cheerless, joyless, dismal; funereal; literary dolorous. ANTONYMS cheerful.

lug·worm /ˈləgˌwərm/ ▶ n. a worm living in muddy sand by the sea, used as fishing bait.

luke·warm /ˈlo͝okˈwôrm/ ▶ adj. **1** only slightly warm. **2** unenthusiastic.

SYNONYMS *a lukewarm response* **indifferent**, cool, halfhearted, apathetic, tepid, unenthusiastic, uninterested, noncommittal. ANTONYMS warm.

lull /ləl/ ▶ v. **1** make someone relaxed or calm. **2** make someone feel safe or confident, even if they are at risk of something bad: *slick advertising may lull you into an unwise buy.* ▶ n. a quiet period between times of activity.

SYNONYMS ▶ v. **soothe**, calm, quiet, still, assuage, allay, ease, quell. ▶ n. **1 pause**, respite, interval, break, suspension, breathing space, hiatus; informal letup, breather. **2** *the lull before the storm* **calm**, stillness, quiet, tranquility, peace, silence, hush.

lull·a·by /ˈləlәˌbī/ ▶ n. (plural **lullabies**) a soothing song sung to send a child to sleep.

lu·lu /ˈlo͞oˌlo͞o/ ▶ n. informal an outstanding example of a particular type of person or thing.

lum·ba·go /ˌləmˈbāgō/ ▶ n. pain in the lower back.

lum·bar /ˈləmbər, -ˌbär/ ▶ adj. relating to the lower back.

lum·ber /ˈləmbər/ ▶ n. timber sawn into rough planks. ▶ v. (**lumbers**, **lumbering**, **lumbered**) **1** move in a heavy, awkward way. **2** (**lumbering**) slow and clumsy: *he was a lumbering bear of a man.*

SYNONYMS ▶ v. **1 trundle**, stump, clump, plod, stumble, shamble, shuffle, trudge. **2** (**lumbering**) **clumsy**, awkward, slow, blundering, bumbling, ponderous, ungainly; informal clodhopping. ANTONYMS nimble, agile.

lum·ber·jack /ˈləmbərˌjak/ ▶ n. a person who cuts down trees and saws them into logs.

lu·men /ˈlo͞omən/ ▶ **n.** Physics the SI unit of luminous flux.

lu·mi·nar·y /ˈlo͞oməˌnerē/ ▶ **n.** (plural **luminaries**) an important or influential person: *sports luminaries*.

lu·mi·nes·cence /ˌlo͞oməˈnesəns/ ▶ **n.** light given off by a substance that has not been heated, e.g., fluorescent light. ■ **lu·mi·nes·cent adj.**

lu·mi·nous /ˈlo͞omənəs/ ▶ **adj.** bright or shining, especially in the dark.

> SYNONYMS **shining**, bright, brilliant, radiant, dazzling, glowing, luminescent, phosphorescent, fluorescent, incandescent. ANTONYMS dark.

■ **lu·mi·nos·i·ty** /ˌlo͞oməˈnäsətē/ **n. lu·mi·nous·ly adv.**

lum·mox /ˈləməks/ ▶ **n.** informal a clumsy, stupid person.

lump /ləmp/ ▶ **n. 1** an irregularly shaped piece of something hard or solid. **2** a swelling under the skin. ▶ **v.** (**lump together**) casually group different people or things together: *for analysis, all data were lumped together*.

> SYNONYMS ▶ **n. 1 chunk**, hunk, piece, block, wedge, slab, ball, knob, pat, clod, clump, nugget, gobbet. **2 swelling**, bump, bulge, protuberance, protrusion, growth, nodule, tumor. ▶ **v. combine**, put, group, bunch, throw.

□ **a lump in the throat** a feeling of tightness in the throat caused by strong emotion. **lump sum** a single payment as opposed to a number of smaller payments.

lum·pen /ˈləmpən, ˈlo͞om-/ ▶ **adj. 1** lumpy and misshapen. **2** stupid or loutish.

lump·ish /ˈləmpisʜ/ ▶ **adj. 1** roughly or clumsily shaped. **2** stupid and lethargic.

lump·y /ˈləmpē/ ▶ **adj.** (**lumpier**, **lumpiest**) full of or covered with lumps. ■ **lump·i·ly adv. lump·i·ness n.**

lu·na·cy /ˈlo͞onəsē/ ▶ **n. 1** insanity; mental illness. **2** great stupidity: *such a policy would be sheer lunacy*.

lu·nar /ˈlo͞onər/ ▶ **adj.** having to do with the moon: *a lunar landscape*. □ **lunar eclipse** an eclipse in which the moon is hidden by the earth's shadow. **lunar month 1** a month measured between one new moon and the next. **2** a period of four weeks.

lu·na·tic /ˈlo͞onəˌtik/ ▶ **n. 1** a person who is mentally ill. **2** a very foolish person. ▶ **adj.** very foolish.

> SYNONYMS ▶ **n. maniac**, psychopath, madman, madwoman, idiot; informal loony, screwball, nutcase, headcase, psycho. ▶ **adj. stupid**, foolish, idiotic, insane, absurd, ridiculous, ludicrous, preposterous, asinine; informal crazy, mad, daft.

□ **lunatic fringe** a small section of a political group with extreme or eccentric views.

lunch /lənʜ/ ▶ **n.** a meal eaten in the middle of the day. ▶ **v.** eat lunch. □ **out to lunch** informal crazy or stupid.

lunch·eon /ˈlənʜən/ ▶ **n.** formal lunch.

lunch·meat /ˈlənʜˌmēt/ ▶ **n.** meat sold in slices for sandwiches; cold cuts.

lunch·time /ˈlənʜˌtīm/ ▶ **n.** the time when lunch is eaten.

lung /ləɴɢ/ ▶ **n.** each of a pair of organs in the chest into which humans and animals draw air when breathing. ■ **lung·ful n.**

lunge /lənj/ ▶ **n.** a sudden forward movement of the body. ▶ **v.** (**lunges**, **lunging** or **lungeing**, **lunged**) make a sudden forward movement.

> SYNONYMS ▶ **n.** *Darren made a lunge at his attacker* **thrust**, dive, rush, charge, grab. ▶ **v.** *he lunged at her with a knife* **thrust**, dive, spring, launch yourself, rush.

lunk /ləɴɢk/ (or **lunk·head**) ▶ **n.** informal a slow-witted person.

lu·pine[1] /ˈlo͞opin/ (or **lupin**) ▶ **n.** a plant of the pea family with spikes of tall flowers.

lu·pine[2] /ˈlo͞oˌpīn/ ▶ **adj.** resembling a wolf.

lurch /lərʜ/ ▶ **v.** make a sudden, unsteady movement. ▶ **n.** a sudden, unsteady movement.

> SYNONYMS ▶ **v. 1 stagger**, stumble, sway, reel, roll, totter. **2 swing**, list, roll, pitch, veer, swerve.

□ **leave someone in the lurch** leave someone in a difficult situation without help or support.

lure /lo͝or/ ▶ **v.** (**lures**, **luring**, **lured**) tempt someone to do something by offering a reward. ▶ **n. 1** the attractive and tempting qualities of something: *the lure of the city*. **2** a type of bait used in fishing or hunting.

> SYNONYMS ▶ **v. tempt**, entice, attract, induce, coax, persuade, inveigle, seduce, beguile, draw. ANTONYMS deter, put off. ▶ **n. temptation**, attraction, pull, draw, appeal, inducement, allure, fascination, interest, glamour.

Lur·ex /ˈlo͝orˌeks/ ▶ **n.** trademark yarn or fabric containing a glittering metallic thread.

lu·rid /ˈlo͝orid/ ▶ **adj. 1** unpleasantly bright in color. **2** (of a description) deliberately containing many shocking details.

> SYNONYMS **1 bright**, vivid, glaring, fluorescent, gaudy, loud. **2** *lurid details* **sensational**, colorful, salacious, graphic, explicit, prurient, shocking, gruesome, gory, grisly; informal juicy.

■ **lu·rid·ly adv.**

lurk /lərk/ ▶ **v. 1** wait in hiding to attack someone. **2** read communications on the Internet without making your presence known.

> SYNONYMS **skulk**, loiter, lie in wait, hide.

lus·cious /ˈləsʜəs/ ▶ **adj. 1** having a pleasantly rich, sweet taste. **2** (of a woman) very attractive.

> SYNONYMS **1** *luscious fruit* **delicious**, succulent, juicy, mouthwatering, sweet, tasty, appetizing; informal scrumptious, yummy. **2** *a luscious woman* **gorgeous**, nubile, ravishing, alluring, sultry, beautiful, stunning; informal foxy, cute. ANTONYMS unappetizing, plain, scrawny.

lush /ləsʜ/ ▶ **adj. 1** (of plants) growing thickly and strongly. **2** rich or luxurious: *lush growth*. ▶ **n.** a drunkard.

> SYNONYMS ▶ **adj. 1 profuse**, abundant, luxuriant, flourishing, rich, riotous, vigorous, dense, thick, rampant. **2 luxurious**, sumptuous, palatial, opulent, lavish, elaborate, extravagant, fancy; informal plush, posh, swanky, swank, swish, bling-bling. ANTONYMS sparse, austere.

■ **lush·ly adv. lush·ness n.**

lust /ləst/ ▶ **n.** a passionate desire for something. ▶ **v.** feel lust.

> SYNONYMS ▶ **n. 1 desire**, longing, passion, libido, sex drive, sexuality, lecherousness, lasciviousness. **2 greed**, desire, craving, eagerness, longing, yearning, hunger, thirst, appetite, hankering.

■ **lust·ful** adj.

lus·ter /'ləstər/ ▶ n. **1** a soft glow or shine. **2** prestige or honor: *a celebrity player added luster to the lineup.*

lus·trous /'ləstrəs/ ▶ adj. having a soft glow or sheen.

SYNONYMS **shiny**, shining, satiny, silky, glossy, gleaming, burnished, polished; bright, brilliant, luminous. ANTONYMS dull, dark.

lust·y /'ləstē/ ▶ adj. (**lustier**, **lustiest**) healthy and strong. ■ **lust·i·ly** adv.

lute /lo͞ot/ ▶ n. a stringed instrument with a long neck and a rounded body, which you play by plucking.

lu·te·nist /'lo͞otn-ist, 'lo͞otnist/ ▶ n. a lute player.

Lu·ther·an /'lo͞oTH(ə)rən/ ▶ n. **1** a follower of the German Protestant theologian Martin Luther (1483–1546). **2** a member of the Lutheran Church, the Protestant Church based on his beliefs. ▶ adj. relating to the teachings of Martin Luther or to the Lutheran Church.

lux /ləks/ ▶ n. (plural **lux**) the SI unit of illumination.

luxe /ləks, lo͝oks/ ▶ n. luxury.

lux·u·ri·ant /ˌləg'ZHo͝orēənt, ˌlək'SHo͝or-/ ▶ adj. growing thickly and strongly. ■ **lux·u·ri·ance** n. **lux·u·ri·ant·ly** adv.

lux·u·ri·ate /ˌləg'ZHo͝orēˌāt, ˌlək'SHo͝or-/ ▶ v. (**luxuriates**, **luxuriating**, **luxuriated**) (**luxuriate in**) relax and enjoy something very pleasant.

lux·u·ri·ous /ˌləg'ZHo͝orēəs, ˌlək'SHo͝or-/ ▶ adj. very comfortable or elegant and expensive.

SYNONYMS **opulent**, sumptuous, grand, palatial, magnificent, extravagant, fancy, deluxe, expensive, uptown, upmarket, upscale; informal plush, posh, classy, swanky, swank, swish, bling-bling. ANTONYMS plain, basic.

■ **lux·u·ri·ous·ly** adv.

lux·u·ry /'ləksH(ə)rē, 'ləgzH(ə)-/ ▶ n. (plural **luxuries**) **1** comfortable and expensive living or surroundings: *he lived a life of luxury.* **2** something that is expensive and enjoyable but not essential.

SYNONYMS **1 opulence**, sumptuousness, grandeur, magnificence, splendor, luxuriousness, affluence. **2 indulgence**, extravagance, treat, extra, frill. ANTONYMS simplicity, necessity.

ly·chee /'lēCHē, 'lī-/ ▶ n. a small, sweet fruit with thin, rough skin.

lych·gate /'licHˌgāt/ ▶ n. a roofed gateway to a churchyard.

Ly·cra /'līkrə/ ▶ n. trademark an elastic fabric used for close-fitting clothing.

lye /lī/ ▶ n. an alkaline solution used for washing or cleaning.

ly·ing /'lī-iNG/ present participle of **LIE**[1], **LIE**[2].

lymph /limf/ ▶ n. a colorless fluid in the body that contains white blood cells. □ **lymph node** (or **lymph gland**) each of a number of small swellings where lymph is filtered. ■ **lym·phat·ic** /lim'fatik/ adj.

lym·phat·ic sys·tem /lim'fatik/ ▶ n. the network of vessels through which lymph drains from the tissues into the blood.

lym·pho·cyte /'limfəˌsīt/ ▶ n. a type of small white blood cell with a single round nucleus.

lym·pho·ma /lim'fōmə/ ▶ n. cancer of the lymph nodes.

lynch /linCH/ ▶ v. (of a group) kill someone, especially by hanging, for an alleged offense, with or without a legal trial.

lynch·pin /'linCHˌpin/ = **LINCHPIN**.

lynx /liNGks/ ▶ n. a wild cat with a short tail and tufted ears.

lyre /līr/ ▶ n. a stringed instrument like a small harp, used in ancient Greece.

lyr·ic /'lirik/ ▶ n. **1** (also **lyrics**) the words of a song. **2** a poem that expresses the writer's thoughts and emotions. ▶ adj. (of poetry) expressing the writer's thoughts and emotions.

lyr·i·cal /'lirikəl/ ▶ adj. **1** (of writing or music) expressing the writer's emotions in an imaginative and beautiful way. **2** relating to the words of a popular song.

SYNONYMS **1 expressive**, emotional, deeply felt, personal. **2 enthusiastic**, effusive, rapturous, ecstatic, euphoric, passionate, impassioned. ANTONYMS unenthusiastic.

□ **wax lyrical** talk about something in a very enthusiastic way. ■ **lyr·i·cal·ly** adv.

lyr·i·cism /'lirəˌsizəm/ ▶ n. expression of emotion in writing or music in an imaginative and beautiful way.

lyr·i·cist /'lirəsist/ ▶ n. a person who writes the words to popular songs.

Mm

M (or **m**) ▶ **n.** (plural **Ms** or **M's**) **1** the thirteenth letter of the alphabet. **2** the Roman numeral for 1,000. ▶ **abbr. 1** (**M**) Monsieur. **2** meter(s). **3** mile(s). **4** million(s).

MA ▶ **abbr.** Master of Arts.

ma /mä/ ▶ **n.** informal your mother.

ma'am /mam/ ▶ **n.** madam.

ma·ca·bre /mə'käbrə, -'käb/ ▶ **adj.** disturbing and horrifying because concerned with death and injury.

mac·ad·am /mə'kadəm/ ▶ **n.** broken stone used for surfacing roads and paths.

mac·a·da·mi·a /ˌmakə'dāmēə/ ▶ **n.** the round edible nut of an Australian tree.

ma·caque /mə'käk, -'kak/ ▶ **n.** a medium-sized monkey with a long face and cheek pouches for holding food.

mac·a·ro·ni /ˌmakə'rōnē/ ▶ **n.** pasta in the form of narrow tubes.

mac·a·roon /ˌmakə'ro͞on/ ▶ **n.** a light cookie made with egg white, sugar, and usually ground almonds or coconut.

ma·caw /mə'kô/ ▶ **n.** a brightly colored parrot found in Central and South America.

mace¹ /mās/ ▶ **n. 1** a decorated stick carried by an official such as a mayor. **2** (in the past) a heavy club with a spiked metal head.

mace² ▶ **n.** a spice made from the dried outer covering of nutmeg.

mac·er·ate /'masəˌrāt/ ▶ **v.** (**macerates, macerating, macerated**) soften food by soaking it in a liquid. ■ **mac·er·a·tion** /ˌmasə'rāsʜən/ **n.**

Mach /mäk, mäkʜ/ ▶ **n.** (**Mach 1**, **Mach 2**, etc.) the speed of sound, twice the speed of sound, etc.

ma·chet·e /mə'sʜetē, mə'cʜetē/ ▶ **n.** a broad, heavy knife used as a tool or weapon.

Mach·i·a·vel·li·an /ˌmakēə'velēən, ˌmäk-/ ▶ **adj.** using cunning and underhand methods to get what you want.

mach·i·na·tions /ˌmakə'nāsʜənz, ˌmasʜə-/ ▶ **pl.n.** plots and scheming.

ma·chine /mə'sʜēn/ ▶ **n. 1** a mechanical device for performing a particular task. **2** an efficient group of influential people: *the city council's publicity machine.* ▶ **v.** (**machines, machining, machined**) make or work on something with a machine.

> SYNONYMS ▶ **n. 1 device**, appliance, apparatus, engine, gadget, mechanism, tool, instrument, contraption. **2** *an efficient publicity machine* **organization**, system, structure, machinery; informal setup.

□ **machine code** (or **language**) a computer programming language consisting of instructions that a computer can respond to directly. **machine gun** a gun that fires many bullets in rapid succession. **machine-readable** in a form that a computer can process. **machine tool** a fixed powered tool for cutting or shaping metal, wood, etc.

ma·chin·er·y /mə'sʜēn(ə)rē/ ▶ **n. 1** machines as a whole, or the parts of a machine. **2** an organized system or structure: *the machinery of the state.*

> SYNONYMS **1 equipment**, apparatus, plant, hardware, gear, gadgetry, technology. **2** *the machinery of local government* **workings**, organization, system, structure; informal setup.

ma·chin·ist /mə'sʜēnist/ ▶ **n.** a person who operates a machine or makes machinery.

ma·chis·mo /mä'cʜēzmō, mə-'kēz-/ ▶ **n.** strong or aggressive male pride.

ma·cho /'mäcʜō, 'macʜō/ ▶ **adj.** showing aggressive pride in being male.

> SYNONYMS **manly**, male, masculine, virile, red-blooded; informal butch.

mack·er·el /'mak(ə)rəl/ ▶ **n.** an edible migratory surface-dwelling sea fish.

mack·in·tosh /'makənˌtäsʜ/ (or **macintosh**) ▶ **n.** a full-length waterproof coat.

mac·ra·mé /'makrəˌmā/ ▶ **n.** the craft of knotting cord to make decorative articles.

mac·ro /'makrō/ ▶ **n.** (plural **macros**) Computing a single instruction that expands automatically into a set of instructions to perform a particular task.

mac·ro·bi·ot·ic /ˌmakrōbī'ätik/ ▶ **adj.** (of diet) consisting of foods grown or produced without the use of chemicals.

mac·ro·cosm /'makrəˌkäzəm/ ▶ **n.** the whole of a complex structure, contrasted with a small or representative part of it (a microcosm).

mac·ro·ec·o·nom·ics /'makrōˌekə'nämiks, -ˌēkə-/ ▶ **n.** economics concerned with general economic factors, such as interest rates.

mac·ro·mol·e·cule /ˌmakrō'mäləˌkyo͞ol/ ▶ **n.** Chemistry a molecule containing a very large number of atoms, such as a protein.

ma·cron /'māˌkrän, 'mak-, 'mākrən/ ▶ **n.** a written or printed mark (¯) used to indicate a long vowel in some languages, or a stressed vowel in verse.

mac·ro·scop·ic /ˌmakrə'skäpik/ ▶ **adj. 1** large enough to be seen without a microscope. **2** relating to general analysis.

mad /mad/ ▶ **adj.** (**madder, maddest**) **1** seriously mentally ill. **2** very foolish. **3** done without thought or control: *it was a mad dash to get ready.* **4** informal very enthusiastic about something. **5** informal very angry.

> SYNONYMS **1 insane**, crazy, out of your mind, deranged, demented, crazed, lunatic, unbalanced, unhinged, psychotic, non compos

mentis; informal mental, nuts, nutty, off your rocker, bonkers, loony, loopy, batty, cuckoo. **2 angry**, furious, infuriated, enraged, fuming, incensed, beside yourself; informal livid, sore. **3** *a mad scheme* **foolish**, insane, stupid, lunatic, idiotic, foolhardy, absurd, ludicrous, silly, asinine, wild, crackbrained, senseless, preposterous; informal crazy, crackpot, daft. **4** *he's mad about her* **passionate about**, fanatical about, ardent about, fervent about, devoted to, infatuated with; informal crazy about, gaga over/about, nuts about, wild about, hooked on. **5** *a mad dash to get ready* **frenzied**, frantic, frenetic, feverish, hysterical, wild, hectic, manic. ANTONYMS sane, sensible.

□ **mad cow disease** BSE, bovine spongiform encephalopathy, a usually fatal disease of cattle. ■ **mad·ly** adv.

mad·am /'madəm/ ▶ **n. 1** a polite form of address for a woman. **2** a woman who runs a brothel.

Mad·ame /mə'däm, -'dam/ ▶ **n.** (plural **Mesdames** /mā'däm/) a form of address for a French woman.

mad·cap /'mad,kap/ ▶ **adj.** acting without thought; reckless.

SYNONYMS **1** *a madcap scheme* **reckless**, rash, foolhardy, foolish, harebrained, wild; informal crazy, crackpot. **2** *a madcap comedy* **zany**, eccentric; informal wacky.

mad·den /'madn/ ▶ **v.** make someone mad or very annoyed.

SYNONYMS **infuriate**, exasperate, irritate, incense, anger, enrage, provoke, make someone see red, inflame; informal aggravate, tee off, tick off, make someone's blood boil. ANTONYMS calm.

mad·der /'madər/ ▶ **n.** a red dye obtained from the roots of a plant.

made /mād/ past and past participle of **MAKE**.

Ma·dei·ra /mə'di(ə)rə, mə'de(ə)rə/ ▶ **n.** a strong, sweet, dull-red wine from the island of Madeira.

Mad·e·moi·selle /,mad(ə)m(w)ə'zel, mam'zel/ ▶ **n.** (plural **Mesdemoiselles** /'mādəm(w)ə,zel, 'mād,mwä,zel/) a form of address for an unmarried French woman.

mad·house /'mad,hous/ ▶ **n. 1** historical a mental home or hospital. **2** informal a scene of great confusion or uproar.

mad·man /'mad,man, -mən/ (or **madwoman**) ▶ **n.** (plural **madmen** or **madwomen**) **1** a person who is mentally ill. **2** a foolish or reckless person.

SYNONYMS **lunatic**, maniac, psychotic, psychopath; informal loony, nut, nutcase, headcase, screwball, psycho.

mad·ness /'madnəs/ ▶ **n. 1** the state of being mentally ill. **2** extremely foolish behavior. **3** frenzied or chaotic activity.

SYNONYMS **1 insanity**, mental illness, dementia, derangement, lunacy, mania, psychosis. **2 folly**, foolishness, idiocy, stupidity, foolhardiness. **3 bedlam**, mayhem, chaos, pandemonium, uproar, turmoil. ANTONYMS sanity.

Ma·don·na /mə'dänə/ ▶ **n.** (**the Madonna**) the Virgin Mary.

mad·ras /'madrəs, mə'dras, mə'dräs/ ▶ **n.** a colorful striped or checked cotton fabric.

mad·ri·gal /'madrigəl/ ▶ **n.** a 16th- or 17th-century song for several voices without instrumental accompaniment.

mael·strom /'māl,sträm, -strəm/ ▶ **n. 1** a situation of confusion or upheaval. **2** a powerful whirlpool.

mae·nad /'mē,nad/ ▶ **n.** (in ancient Greece) a female follower of the god Bacchus.

maes·tro /'mīstrō/ ▶ **n.** (plural **maestros**) a famous and talented man, especially a classical musician.

Ma·fi·a /'mäfēə/ ▶ **n. 1** (**the Mafia**) an international criminal organization originating in Sicily. **2** (**mafia**) a powerful group who secretly influence matters: *the top tennis mafia*.

Ma·fi·o·so /,mäfē'ōsō, -zō/ ▶ **n.** (plural **Mafiosi** /-sē, -zē/) a member of the Mafia.

mag·a·zine /'magə,zēn, ,magə'zēn/ ▶ **n. 1** a weekly or monthly publication that contains articles and pictures. **2** the part of a gun that holds bullets before they are fired. **3** a store for weapons, ammunition, and explosives.

SYNONYMS **journal**, periodical, supplement, fanzine; informal glossy, mag.

ma·gen·ta /mə'jentə/ ▶ **n.** a light crimson.

mag·got /'magət/ ▶ **n.** the soft-bodied larva of a fly or other insect.

mag·ic /'majik/ ▶ **n. 1** the supposed use of mysterious or supernatural forces to influence events. **2** conjuring tricks performed to entertain people. **3** a mysterious or wonderful quality: *the magic of the theater*. ▶ **adj. 1** having supernatural powers. **2** informal wonderful. ▶ **v.** (**magics**, **magicking**, **magicked**) use magic to make something happen.

SYNONYMS ▶ **n. 1 sorcery**, witchcraft, wizardry, necromancy, enchantment, the supernatural, occultism, the occult, black magic, the black arts, voodoo, hoodoo. **2 illusion**, conjuring (tricks), sleight of hand, legerdemain; formal prestidigitation. **3 allure**, excitement, fascination, charm, glamour.

□ **magic lantern** an early form of projector for showing photographic slides.

mag·i·cal /'majikəl/ ▶ **adj. 1** relating to or using magic. **2** wonderful; very enjoyable.

SYNONYMS **1 supernatural**, magic, mystical, otherworldly. **2 enchanting**, entrancing, spellbinding, bewitching, fascinating, captivating, alluring, enthralling, charming, lovely, delightful, beautiful, amazing; informal heavenly, gorgeous.

■ **mag·i·cal·ly** adv.

ma·gi·cian /mə'jisʜən/ ▶ **n. 1** a person with magic powers. **2** a conjuror.

SYNONYMS **1 sorcerer**, sorceress, witch, wizard, warlock, enchanter, enchantress, necromancer; formal thaumaturge. **2 illusionist**, conjuror; formal prestidigitator.

mag·is·te·ri·al /,majə'sti(ə)rēəl/ ▶ **adj. 1** having or showing great authority: *a magisterial pronouncement*. **2** relating to a magistrate.

mag·is·trate /'majə,strāt/ ▶ **n.** an official who judges minor cases and holds preliminary hearings for more serious ones. ■ **mag·is·tra·cy** **n.** (plural **magistracies**).

mag·ma /'magmə/ ▶ **n.** very hot fluid or semifluid rock under the earth's crust.

mag·nan·i·mous /mag'nanəməs/ ▶ **adj.** generous or forgiving toward a rival or enemy.

SYNONYMS **generous**, charitable, benevolent, beneficent, big-hearted, open-handed, munificent, philanthropic, noble, unselfish, altruistic. ANTONYMS mean.

■ **mag·na·nim·i·ty** /ˌmagnəˈnimətē/ **n.**

mag·nate /ˈmagˌnāt, ˈmagnət/ ▶ **n.** a wealthy and influential person, especially in business.

mag·ne·sia /magˈnēzнə, -ˈnēsнə/ ▶ **n.** a compound of magnesium used to reduce stomach acid.

mag·ne·si·um /magˈnēzēəm, -zнəm/ ▶ **n.** a silvery-white substance that burns with a brilliant white flame.

mag·net /ˈmagnət/ ▶ **n. 1** a piece of iron that attracts objects containing iron and that points north and south when suspended. **2** a person, place, etc., that someone or something is strongly attracted to: *the beach is a magnet for sun-worshippers.*

mag·net·ic /magˈnetik/ ▶ **adj. 1** having the property of magnetism. **2** very attractive: *a magnetic smile.*

SYNONYMS **attractive**, irresistible, seductive, charismatic, hypnotic, alluring, fascinating, captivating.

□ **magnetic field** a region around a magnet within which the force of magnetism acts. **magnetic north** the direction in which the north end of a compass needle will point in response to the earth's magnetic field. **magnetic pole** each of the points near the geographical North and South Poles, which the needle of a compass points to. **magnetic storm** a disturbance of the magnetic field of the earth. **magnetic tape** tape used in recording sound, pictures, or computer data.
■ **mag·net·i·cal·ly** **adv.**

mag·net·ism /ˈmagnəˌtizəm/ ▶ **n. 1** the property displayed by magnets of attracting or pushing away metal objects. **2** the ability to attract and charm people.

mag·net·ize /ˈmagnəˌtīz/ ▶ **v.** (**magnetizes**, **magnetizing**, **magnetized**) make magnetic.

mag·ne·to /magˈnētō/ ▶ **n.** (plural **magnetos**) a small generator that uses a magnet to produce pulses of electricity.

Mag·nif·i·cat /magˈnifiˌkät, mänˈyifi-/ ▶ **n.** the hymn of the Virgin Mary, beginning "my soul magnifies the Lord," sung as a regular part of a Christian service.

mag·ni·fi·ca·tion /ˌmagnəfiˈkāsнən/ ▶ **n. 1** the action of magnifying something. **2** the degree to which something is magnified: *the particles cannot be seen at this magnification.*

mag·nif·i·cent /magˈnifəsənt/ ▶ **adj. 1** very attractive and impressive; splendid. **2** very good.

SYNONYMS **1 splendid**, spectacular, impressive, striking, glorious, superb, majestic, awe-inspiring, breathtaking, sublime, resplendent, sumptuous, grand, imposing, monumental, palatial, opulent, luxurious, lavish, rich, dazzling, beautiful. **2 excellent**, outstanding, marvelous, brilliant, wonderful, virtuoso, fine, superb. ANTONYMS uninspiring, ordinary.

■ **mag·nif·i·cence** **n.** **mag·nif·i·cent·ly** **adv.**

mag·ni·fy /ˈmagnəˌfī/ ▶ **v.** (**magnifies**, **magnifying**, **magnified**) **1** make something appear larger than it is with a lens or microscope. **2** make larger or stronger: *the tin roof magnified the tropical heat.* **3** old use praise.

SYNONYMS **enlarge**, increase, augment, extend, expand, boost, enhance, maximize, amplify, intensify; informal blow up. ANTONYMS reduce, minimize.

□ **magnifying glass** a lens used to help you see something very small by magnifying it.

mag·ni·tude /ˈmagnəˌto͞od/ ▶ **n. 1** great size or importance: *they were discouraged by the magnitude of the task.* **2** size.

SYNONYMS **1 size**, extent, immensity, vastness, hugeness, enormity. **2 importance**, import, significance, consequence.

mag·no·lia /magˈnōlyə/ ▶ **n.** a tree or shrub with large white or pale pink flowers.

mag·num /ˈmagnəm/ ▶ **n.** (plural **magnums**) a wine bottle of twice the standard size, normally $1^1/_2$ liters.

mag·num o·pus /ˈmagnəm ˈōpəs/ ▶ **n.** (plural **magnum opuses** or **magna opera** /ˌmagnə ˈōpərə, ˈäpərə/) a work of art, music, or literature that is the most important that a person has produced.

mag·pie /ˈmagˌpī/ ▶ **n. 1** a long-tailed crow with boldly marked (or green) plumage and a raucous voice. **2** a person who collects things of little use or value.

ma·gus /ˈmāgəs/ ▶ **n.** (plural **magi** /ˈmāˌjī/) **1** a priest of ancient Persia. **2** a sorcerer. **3** (**the Magi**) the three wise men from the East who brought gifts to the infant Jesus.

Mag·yar /ˈmagˌyär/ ▶ **n. 1** a member of the predominant people in Hungary. **2** the Hungarian language.

ma·ha·ra·ja /ˌmähəˈräjə, -ˈräzнə/ (or **maharajah**) ▶ **n.** an Indian prince.

ma·ha·ra·ni /ˌmähəˈränē/ ▶ **n.** a maharaja's wife or widow.

Ma·ha·ri·shi /ˌmähəˈrēsнē/ ▶ **n.** a great Hindu wise man or spiritual leader.

ma·hat·ma /məˈhätmə, -ˈhatmə/ ▶ **n.** a wise or holy Hindu leader.

mah-jongg /mä ˈzнäng, ˈzнông, ˈjäng, ˈjông/ (or **mah-jong**) ▶ **n.** a Chinese game played with 136 or 144 small rectangular tiles.

ma·hog·a·ny /məˈhägənē/ ▶ **n. 1** hard reddish-brown wood from a tropical tree. **2** a rich reddish-brown color.

ma·hout /məˈhout/ ▶ **n.** (in the Indian subcontinent and southeast Asia) a person who works with elephants.

maid /mād/ ▶ **n. 1** a female servant. **2** old use a girl or young unmarried woman. □ **maid of honor 1** the chief bridesmaid at a wedding. **2** an unmarried noblewoman who waits on a queen or princess.

maid·en /ˈmādn/ ▶ **n.** old use a girl or young unmarried woman. ▶ **adj.** first of its kind: *a maiden voyage.* □ **maiden name** the surname of a married woman before her marriage.

maid·en·hair fern /ˈmādnˌhe(ə)r/ ▶ **n.** a fern with fine stems and delicate foliage.

maid·serv·ant /ˈmādˌsərvənt/ ▶ **n.** dated a female servant.

mail¹ /māl/ ▶ **n. 1** letters and packages sent by the postal system. **2** the postal system. **3** email. ▶ **v. 1** send by the postal system. **2** send a letter or package or email to.

SYNONYMS ▶ n. **post**, letters, correspondence, email. ▶ v. **send**, post, dispatch, forward, ship, email.

□ **mail carrier** a person whose job is to deliver and collect letters and packages. **mailing list** a list of people to whom advertising matter or information may be mailed regularly. **mail order** the buying or selling of goods by mail.

mail² ▶ n. (in the past) armor made of metal rings or plates.

mail·ing /'māliNG/ ▶ n. an item of advertising mailed to a large number of people.

mail·man /'māl,man/ ▶ n. (plural **mailmen**) a person who is employed to deliver and collect letters and packages; a mail carrier.

maim /mām/ ▶ v. inflict a permanent injury on.

SYNONYMS **injure**, wound, cripple, disable, incapacitate, mutilate, disfigure, mangle.

main /mān/ ▶ adj. greatest or most important; principal: *a main road.* ▶ n. a principal pipe carrying water or gas to buildings, or taking sewage from them.

SYNONYMS ▶ adj. **principal**, chief, head, leading, foremost, most important, major, dominant, central, focal, key, prime, primary, first, fundamental, predominant, preeminent, paramount. ANTONYMS subsidiary, minor.

□ **in the main** on the whole. **main drag** informal the main street of a town. **main line** a chief railroad line.

main·frame /'mān,frām/ ▶ n. a large high-speed computer supporting a network of workstations.

main·land /'mānlənd, -,land/ ▶ n. the main area of land of a country, not including islands and separate territories.

main·ly /'mānlē/ ▶ adv. for the most part; chiefly.

SYNONYMS **mostly**, for the most part, in the main, on the whole, largely, by and large, to a large extent, predominantly, chiefly, principally, primarily.

main·mast /'mān,mast/ ▶ n. the principal mast of a ship.

main·spring /'mān,spriNG/ ▶ n. the most important or influential part of something: *faith was the mainspring of her life.*

main·stay /'mān,stā/ ▶ n. a thing on which something depends or is based: *cotton is the mainstay of the country's economy.*

main·stream /'mān,strēm/ ▶ n. the ideas, attitudes, or activities that are shared by most people.

main·tain /mān'tān/ ▶ v. **1** keep something in the same state or at the same level: *he maintained close links with the United States.* **2** regularly check and repair a building, machine, etc. **3** provide someone with financial support. **4** strongly state that something is the case.

SYNONYMS **1 preserve**, conserve, keep, retain, keep going, prolong, perpetuate, sustain, carry on, continue. **2 look after**, service, care for, take care of, support, provide for, keep. **3 insist**, declare, assert, protest, affirm, profess, avow, claim, contend, argue; formal aver. ANTONYMS discontinue.

main·te·nance /'mānt(ə)nəns, 'māntn-əns/ ▶ n. **1** the action of maintaining something. **2** financial support that someone gives to their former husband or wife after divorce.

SYNONYMS **1 preservation**, conservation, prolongation, continuation. **2 servicing**, service, repair, running repairs, care. **3 support**, upkeep, alimony, allowance.

SPELLING

Write **-ten-**, not **-tain-**: mainte**n**ance.

maî·tre d'hô·tel /,mātrə dō'tel, ,metrə/ ▶ n. (plural **maîtres d'hôtel**) the head waiter of a restaurant.

maize /māz/ ▶ n. ⇒ CORN¹.

ma·jes·tic /mə'jestik/ ▶ adj. impressively grand or beautiful.

SYNONYMS **stately**, dignified, distinguished, magnificent, grand, splendid, glorious, impressive, regal, noble, awe-inspiring, monumental, palatial, imposing. ANTONYMS modest.

■ **ma·jes·ti·cal·ly** adv.

maj·es·ty /'majəstē/ ▶ n. (plural **majesties**) **1** impressive beauty or grandeur: *the majesty of Mount McKinley.* **2** (**His**, **Your**, etc., **Majesty**) a title given to a king or queen or their wife or widow.

SYNONYMS **stateliness**, dignity, magnificence, pomp, grandeur, splendor, glory, impressiveness, nobility.

ma·jor /'mājər/ ▶ adj. **1** important or serious. **2** greater or more important; main. **3** Music (of a scale) having an interval of a semitone between the third and fourth degrees and seventh and eighth degrees. ▶ n. **1** the rank of army officer above captain. **2** a student specializing in a particular subject. ▶ v. (**major in**) specialize in a particular subject at college or university.

SYNONYMS ▶ adj. **1 greatest**, best, finest, most important, chief, main, prime, principal, leading, foremost, outstanding, preeminent. **2 crucial**, vital, important, big, significant, considerable, weighty, serious, key, utmost, great, paramount, prime. ANTONYMS minor, trivial.

□ **major-domo** (plural **major-domos**) a person employed to manage a large household. **major general** the rank of army officer above brigadier. **major league** a main league in a professional sport, especially baseball.

ma·jor·i·ty /mə'jôrətē, -'jär-/ ▶ n. (plural **majorities**) **1** the greater number. **2** the age when a person is legally an adult, usually 18 or 21.

SYNONYMS **1 most**, bulk, mass, best part, lion's share, (main) body, preponderance, predominance. **2 coming of age**, age of consent, adulthood, seniority. ANTONYMS minority.

□ **majority rule** the principle that the greater number of people should exercise greater power.

USAGE

Strictly speaking, **majority** should be used with plural nouns to mean 'the greater number,' as in *the majority of cases*. Use with nouns that do not take a plural to mean 'the greatest part,' as in *she ate the majority of the meal*, is not considered good English.

make /māk/ ▶ v. (**makes**, **making**, **made** /mād/) **1** form something by putting parts together or mixing substances. **2** cause something to happen or come into existence: *the drips had made a pool on* *the floor*. **3** force someone to do something. **4** add up to. **5** be suitable as: *this fern makes a good house plant*. **6** estimate as or decide on. **7** earn money or profit. **8** arrive at or achieve. **9** prepare to go in a particular direction or to do something: *he made toward the car*. ▶ **n.** the manufacturer or trade name of a product.

SYNONYMS ▶ **v.** **1 construct**, build, erect, assemble, put together, manufacture, produce, fabricate, create, form, forge, fashion, model, improvise. **2 force**, compel, coerce, press, drive, dragoon, pressurize, oblige, require; informal railroad, steamroller. **3 cause**, create, bring about, produce, generate, give rise to, effect. **4** *they made him chairman* **appoint**, designate, name, nominate, select, elect, vote in. **5** *he's made a lot of money* **acquire**, obtain, gain, get, secure, win, earn. **6** *he made the tea* **prepare**, concoct, cook, whip up, brew; informal fix. ANTONYMS destroy. ▶ **n.** **brand**, marque, label, type, sort, kind, variety.

□ **have (got) it made** informal be sure of success. **made-up 1** wearing makeup. **2** invented; untrue. **make-believe** fantasy or pretense. **make do** manage with something that is not satisfactory. **make for 1** move toward. **2** tend to result in: *the rock formations make for a remarkable sight*. **3** (**be made for**) be very suitable for. **make it** become successful. **make something of 1** give attention or importance to. **2** understand the meaning of. **make off** leave hurriedly. **make off with** steal. **make or break** be the factor that decides whether something will succeed or fail. **make out** claim or pretend to be. **make something out 1** manage with difficulty to see, hear, or understand something. **2** draw up a list or document. **3** informal make progress. **make something over 1** transfer the ownership of. **2** give a new image to. **make time** find time to do something. **make up** be friendly again after a quarrel. **make someone up** apply cosmetics to someone. **make something up 1** put something together from parts or ingredients. **2** invent a story. **make up for** compensate for. **make up your mind** make a decision. **on the make** informal trying to make money or gain an advantage.

make·o·ver /ˈmākˌōvər/ ▶ **n.** a transformation of someone's appearance with cosmetics, hairstyling, and clothes.

mak·er /ˈmākər/ ▶ **n.** **1** a person or thing that makes something. **2** (**our**, **the**, etc., **Maker**) God.

SYNONYMS **creator**, manufacturer, constructor, builder, producer.

□ **meet your Maker** chiefly humorous die.

make·shift /ˈmākˌsHift/ ▶ **adj.** temporary and improvised: *chairs formed a makeshift bed*.

SYNONYMS **temporary**, provisional, stopgap, standby, rough and ready, improvised, ad hoc.

make·up /ˈmākˌəp/ ▶ **n.** **1** cosmetics applied to the face. **2** the way in which something is formed or put together: *the makeup of the rock*. **3** the arrangement of written matter, illustrations, etc., on a printed page.

SYNONYMS **1 cosmetics**, greasepaint; informal warpaint. **2 composition**, constitution, structure, configuration, arrangement. **3 character**, nature, temperament, personality, mentality, persona.

make·weight /ˈmākˌwāt/ ▶ **n.** an unimportant person or thing that is only added or included to make up the correct number, amount, etc.

mak·ings /ˈmākiNGz/ ▶ **pl.n.** the necessary ingredients or qualities.

SYNONYMS **qualities**, characteristics, ingredients, potential, capacity, capability, stuff.

mal·a·chite /ˈmaləˌkīt/ ▶ **n.** a bright green mineral.

mal·ad·just·ed /ˌmaləˈjəstid/ ▶ **adj.** not able to cope well with normal life.

SYNONYMS **disturbed**, unstable, neurotic, dysfunctional; informal mixed up, screwed up.

mal·a·droit /ˌmaləˈdroit/ ▶ **adj.** clumsy.

mal·a·dy /ˈmalədē/ ▶ **n.** (plural **maladies**) literary a disease or illness.

SYNONYMS **illness**, sickness, disease, infection, ailment, disorder, complaint, affliction, infirmity; informal bug, virus.

ma·laise /məˈlāz, -ˈlez/ ▶ **n.** **1** a general feeling of illness or low spirits. **2** a long-standing problem that is difficult to identify.

mal·a·prop·ism /ˈmaləˌpräpizəm/ ▶ **n.** the mistaken use of a word in place of a similar-sounding one.

ma·lar·i·a /məˈle(ə)rēə/ ▶ **n.** a disease that causes fever and is transmitted by the bite of some mosquitoes. ■ **ma·lar·i·al** **adj.**

ma·lar·key /məˈlärkē/ ▶ **n.** informal nonsense.

Ma·lay /məˈlā, ˈmāˌlā/ ▶ **n.** **1** a member of a people inhabiting Malaysia and Indonesia. **2** the language of the Malays.

Ma·lay·an /məˈlāən/ ⇒ **MALAY** ▶ **adj.** relating to Malays or Malaya (now part of Malaysia).

Ma·lay·sian /məˈlāzHən/ ▶ **n.** a person from Malaysia. ▶ **adj.** relating to Malaysia.

mal·con·tent /ˌmalkənˈtent, ˈmalkənˌtent/ ▶ **n.** a person who is dissatisfied and rebellious.

male /māl/ ▶ **adj.** **1** of the sex that can fertilize or inseminate the female. **2** having to do with men: *a deep male voice*. **3** (of a plant or flower) having stamens but not a pistil. **4** (of parts of machinery, fittings, etc.) made to fit inside a corresponding part. ▶ **n.** a male person, animal, or plant.

SYNONYMS ▶ **adj.** **masculine**, manly, virile, macho. ANTONYMS female.

mal·e·dic·tion /ˌmaləˈdiksHən/ ▶ **n.** formal a curse.

mal·e·fac·tor /ˈmaləˌfaktər/ ▶ **n.** formal a criminal or wrongdoer.

ma·lev·o·lent /məˈlevələnt/ ▶ **adj.** wishing to harm other people. ■ **ma·lev·o·lence** **n.**

mal·for·ma·tion /ˌmalfôrˈmāsHən, -fər-/ ▶ **n.** the state of being abnormally shaped or formed. ■ **mal·formed** /malˈfôrmd/ **adj.**

mal·func·tion /malˈfəNGksHən/ ▶ **v.** (of equipment or machinery) fail to function normally. ▶ **n.** a failure to function normally.

SYNONYMS ▶ **v.** **break down**, fail, stop working, crash, go down; informal conk out, go kaput.

mal·ice /ˈmaləs/ ▶ **n.** the desire to harm someone.

SYNONYMS **spite**, malevolence, ill will, vindictiveness, vengefulness, malignity, animus, enmity, rancor. ANTONYMS benevolence.

ma·li·cious /məˈlisHəs/ ▶ **adj.** meaning to harm other people.

SYNONYMS **spiteful**, malevolent, vindictive, vengeful, resentful, malign, nasty, hurtful, cruel, catty, venomous, poisonous, barbed; informal bitchy. ANTONYMS benevolent.

■ **ma·li·cious·ly** adv.

ma·lign /mə'līn/ ▶ adj. harmful or evil. ▶ v. say unpleasant things about.

SYNONYMS ▶ v. **defame**, slander, libel, blacken someone's name/character, smear, vilify, cast aspersions on, run down, denigrate, disparage, slur, abuse; informal bad-mouth, knock. ANTONYMS praise.

■ **ma·lig·ni·ty** /-'lignətē/ n.

ma·lig·nan·cy /mə'lignənsē/ ▶ n. (plural **malignancies**) **1** a cancerous growth. **2** the quality of being harmful or evil.

ma·lig·nant /mə'lignənt/ ▶ adj. **1** (of a tumor) cancerous. **2** having or showing a desire to harm other people.

ma·lin·ger /mə'liNGgər/ ▶ v. (**malingers**, **malingering**, **malingered**) pretend to be ill in order to avoid work. ■ **ma·lin·ger·er** n.

mall /môl/ ▶ n. **1** a large enclosed shopping area. **2** a sheltered walk.

mal·lard /'malərd/ ▶ n. a kind of duck, the male of which has a dark green head.

mal·le·a·ble /'malyəbəl, 'malēə-/ ▶ adj. **1** able to be hammered or pressed into shape. **2** easily influenced: *a malleable youth*.

mal·let /'malət/ ▶ n. **1** a hammer with a large wooden head. **2** a wooden stick with a head like a hammer, for hitting a croquet or polo ball.

mal·low /'malō/ ▶ n. a herbaceous plant with pink or purple flowers.

malm·sey /'mä(l)mzē/ ▶ n. a very sweet Madeira wine.

mal·nour·ished /mal'nərisHt, -'nə-risHt/ ▶ adj. suffering from malnutrition.

mal·nu·tri·tion /ˌmalno͞o'trisHən/ ▶ n. bad health caused by not having enough food, or not enough of the right food.

mal·o·dor·ous /mal'ōdərəs/ ▶ adj. smelling very unpleasant.

mal·prac·tice /mal'praktəs/ ▶ n. illegal, corrupt, or careless behavior by a professional person.

malt /môlt/ ▶ n. barley or other grain that has been soaked in water and then dried. □ **malt whiskey** whiskey made only from malted barley. ■ **malt·ed** adj.

Mal·tese /môl'tēz/ ▶ n. **1** (plural **Maltese**) a person from Malta. **2** the language of Malta. ▶ adj. relating to Malta.

Mal·thu·sian /mal'tHə(y)o͞ozHən, môl-/ ▶ adj. relating to the theory of the English economist Thomas Malthus (1766–1834) that, if unchecked, the population tends to increase at a greater rate than its food supplies.

malt·ose /'môlˌtōs, -ˌtōz/ ▶ n. a sugar produced by the breakdown of starch, for example by enzymes found in malt and saliva.

mal·treat /mal'trēt/ ▶ v. treat badly or cruelly.

SYNONYMS **ill-treat**, mistreat, abuse, ill-use, mishandle, misuse, persecute, harm, hurt, injure.

■ **mal·treat·ment** n.

ma·ma /'mämə/ (or **mamma**) ▶ n. your mother.

mam·ba /'mämbə/ ▶ n. a large, highly poisonous African snake.

mam·bo /'mämbō/ ▶ n. (plural **mambos**) a Latin American dance similar to the rumba.

mam·mal /'maməl/ ▶ n. a warm-blooded animal that has hair or fur, produces milk, and gives birth to live young. ■ **mam·ma·li·an** /mə'mālēən/ adj.

mam·ma·ry /'mamərē/ ▶ adj. relating to the breasts or the milk-producing organs of other mammals.

mam·mo·gram /'maməˌgram/ ▶ n. an image obtained by mammography.

mam·mog·ra·phy /ma'mägrəfē/ ▶ n. a technique using X-rays to examine the breasts for tumors.

Mam·mon /'mamən/ ▶ n. money thought of as being worshiped like a god.

mam·moth /'maməTH/ ▶ n. a large extinct form of elephant with a hairy coat and long curved tusks. ▶ adj. huge.

man /man/ ▶ n. (plural **men** /men/) **1** an adult human male. **2** a person. **3** human beings in general: *places untouched by man*. **4** a figure or token used in a board game. ▶ v. (**mans**, **manning**, **manned**) **1** provide a place with people to defend it. **2** provide people to operate a machine.

SYNONYMS ▶ n. **1 male**, gentleman, fellow, youth; informal guy, dude, hombre, gent, geezer. **2 human being**, human, person, mortal, individual, soul. **3 the human race**, Homo sapiens, humankind, humanity, human beings, humans, people, mankind. ▶ v. **1 staff**, crew, occupy. **2 operate**, work, use.

□ **man-at-arms** old use a soldier. **man Friday** a man who does a variety of low-grade tasks. **the man in the street** the average man. **man-made** made or caused by human beings. **man of the cloth** a clergyman. **man of letters** a male scholar or author. **man-of-war** historical an armed sailing ship. **to a man** with no exceptions.

man·a·cle /'manikəl/ ▶ n. a metal band fastened around a person's hands or ankles to restrict their movement. ▶ v. (**manacles**, **manacling**, **manacled**) restrict someone with manacles.

man·age /'manij/ ▶ v. (**manages**, **managing**, **managed**) **1** be in charge of people or an organization. **2** succeed in doing: *she finally managed to call a cab*. **3** be able to cope despite difficulties. **4** control the use of money or other resources.

SYNONYMS **1 be in charge of**, run, head, direct, control, preside over, lead, govern, rule, command, supervise, oversee, administer; informal head up. **2 accomplish**, achieve, carry out, perform, undertake, deal with, cope with. **3 cope**, get along/on, make do, survive, get by, muddle through/along, make ends meet; informal make out, hack it.

man·age·a·ble /'manijəbəl/ ▶ adj. able to be dealt with or controlled without difficulty.

SYNONYMS **1 achievable**, doable, practicable, feasible, reasonable, attainable, viable. **2 compliant**, tractable, pliant, biddable, docile, amenable, accommodating, acquiescent.

man·age·ment /'manijmənt/ ▶ n. **1** the action of managing. **2** the managers of an organization.

SYNONYMS **1 administration**, running, managing, organization, direction, leadership, control, governance, rule, command, supervision, guidance, operation. **2 managers**, employers, directors, board, directorate, executive, administration; informal bosses, top brass. ANTONYMS employees.

man·ag·er /'manijər/ ▶ **n.** **1** a person who manages staff, an organization, or a sports team. **2** a person in charge of the business affairs of a performer, group of musicians, etc.

SYNONYMS **executive**, head, supervisor, principal, director, superintendent, foreman, forewoman, overseer, organizer, administrator; informal boss, chief.

■ **man·a·ge·ri·al** /ˌmanə'ji(ə)rēəl/ **adj.**

ma·ña·na /mən'yänə/ ▶ **adv.** tomorrow, or at some time in the future.

man·a·tee /'manəˌtē/ ▶ **n.** a large plant-eating animal that lives in tropical seas.

man·da·la /'mandələ, 'mən-/ ▶ **n.** a circular design symbolizing the universe in Hinduism and Buddhism.

man·da·rin /'mandərən/ ▶ **n.** **1** (**Mandarin**) the official form of the Chinese language. **2** (in the past) a high-ranking Chinese official. **3** a powerful official. **4** a small citrus fruit with a loose yellow-orange skin.

man·date /'manˌdāt/ ▶ **n.** **1** an official order or permission to do something. **2** the authority to carry out a policy that is given by voters to the winner of an election: *he made way for a government with a popular mandate.* ▶ **v.** (**mandates**, **mandating**, **mandated**) give someone authority to do something.

SYNONYMS ▶ **n.** **1** **authority**, approval, ratification, endorsement, sanction, authorization. **2** **instruction**, directive, decree, command, order, injunction.

man·da·to·ry /'mandəˌtôrē/ ▶ **adj.** required by law or rules; compulsory.

SYNONYMS **obligatory**, compulsory, binding, required, requisite, necessary. ANTONYMS optional.

man·di·ble /'mandəbəl/ ▶ **n.** **1** the lower jawbone in mammals or fish. **2** either of the upper and lower parts of a bird's beak. **3** either of the parts of an insect's mouth that crush its food.

man·do·lin /ˌmandə'lin, 'mandələn/ ▶ **n.** a musical instrument with a rounded back and metal strings.

man·drake /'manˌdrāk/ ▶ **n.** a plant whose root is used in herbal medicine and magic.

man·drel /'mandrəl/ ▶ **n.** **1** a shaft or spindle in a lathe to which work is fixed while being turned. **2** a cylindrical rod around which metal or other material is forged or shaped.

man·drill /'mandrəl/ ▶ **n.** a large West African baboon with a red and blue face.

mane /mān/ ▶ **n.** **1** a growth of long hair on the neck of a horse, lion, etc. **2** a person's long hair.

ma·neu·ver /mə'n(y)o͞ovər/ ▶ **n.** **1** a movement or series of moves needing skill and care. **2** a carefully planned scheme. **3** (**maneuvers**) a large-scale military exercise. ▶ **v.** (**maneuvers**, **maneuvering**, **maneuvred**) **1** make a movement or series of moves skillfully and carefully. **2** cleverly influence someone or something in order to achieve an aim: *she had been maneuvered into seeming a weak female.*

SYNONYMS ▶ **n.** **1** **operation**, exercise, move, movement, action. **2** **stratagem**, tactic, gambit, ploy, trick, dodge, ruse, scheme, device, plot, machination, artifice, subterfuge, intrigue. ▶ **v.** **1** **steer**, guide, drive, negotiate, jockey, navigate, pilot, direct, move, work. **2** **manipulate**, contrive, manage, engineer, fix, organize, arrange, orchestrate, choreograph, stage-manage; informal wangle, pull strings.

■ **ma·neu·ver·a·ble** **adj.**

man·ful /'manfəl/ ▶ **adj.** brave and determined.
■ **man·ful·ly** **adv.**

man·ga /'mäNGˌga/ ▶ **n.** Japanese comic books and cartoon movies with a science-fiction or fantasy theme.

man·ga·nese /'maNGgəˌnēz, -ˌnēs/ ▶ **n.** a hard gray metallic element.

ma·nge /mānj/ ▶ **n.** a skin disease of some animals that causes itching and hair loss.

man·gel /'maNGgəl/ (or **mangel-wurzel** /'wərzəl/) ▶ **n.** a variety of beet grown as feed for farm animals.

man·ger /'mānjər/ ▶ **n.** a long trough from which horses or cattle eat.

man·gle /'maNGgəl/ ▶ **v.** (**mangles**, **mangling**, **mangled**) destroy or severely damage by crushing or twisting. ▶ **n.** a machine with rollers for squeezing wet laundry to remove the water.

man·go /'maNGgō/ ▶ **n.** (plural **mangoes** or **mangos**) a tropical fruit with yellow flesh.

man·gold /'maNGgōld/ ▶ **n.** a variety of beet grown as feed for farm animals.

man·go·steen /'maNGgəˌstēn/ ▶ **n.** a tropical fruit with juicy white flesh inside a reddish-brown rind.

man·grove /'manˌgrōv, 'maNG-/ ▶ **n.** a tropical tree or shrub found in coastal swamps, typically having numerous tangled roots above ground.

man·gy /'mānjē/ ▶ **adj.** **1** (of an animal) having mange. **2** in bad condition; shabby.

man·han·dle /'manˌhandl/ ▶ **v.** (**manhandles**, **manhandling**, **manhandled**) **1** move a heavy object with effort. **2** push or drag someone roughly.

man·hole /'manˌhōl/ ▶ **n.** a covered opening giving access to a sewer or other underground structure.

man·hood /'manˌho͝od/ ▶ **n.** **1** the state or period of being a man. **2** the men of a country or society. **3** the qualities traditionally associated with men, such as strength and potency.

ma·ni·a /'mānēə/ ▶ **n.** **1** mental illness in which a person imagines things and has periods of wild excitement. **2** an extreme enthusiasm: *he had a mania for cars.*

SYNONYMS **obsession**, compulsion, fixation, fetish, fascination, preoccupation, passion, enthusiasm, desire, urge, craving, craze, fad, rage; informal thing.

ma·ni·ac /'mānēˌak/ ▶ **n.** **1** a person who behaves in a very wild or violent way. **2** informal a person who is very enthusiastic about something.

SYNONYMS **lunatic**, madman, madwoman, psychopath; informal loony, nutcase, nut, headcase, screwball, psycho, sicko.

■ **ma·ni·a·cal** /mə'nīəkəl/ **adj.**

man·ic /'manik/ ▶ **adj.** **1** having to do with mania. **2** showing wild excitement and energy.

SYNONYMS **1** **mad**, insane, deranged, demented, maniacal, wild, crazed, demonic, hysterical, raving, unhinged; informal crazy. **2** *manic activity*

frenzied, feverish, frenetic, hectic, intense. ANTONYMS sane, calm.

□ **manic depression** ⇒ BIPOLAR DISORDER. ■ **man·i·cal·ly** adv.

man·i·cure /ˈmaniˌkyo͝or/ ▶ n. treatment to improve the appearance of the hands and nails. ■ **man·i·cured** adj. **man·i·cur·ist** n.

man·i·fest /ˈmanəˌfest/ ▶ adj. clear and obvious. ▶ v. **1** show or display: *Laura manifested signs of depression.* **2** appear; become apparent. ▶ n. a document listing the cargo, crew, and passengers of a ship or aircraft.

SYNONYMS ▶ adj. **obvious**, clear, plain, apparent, evident, patent, distinct, definite, blatant, overt, glaring, transparent, conspicuous, undisguised. ▶ v. **display**, show, exhibit, demonstrate, betray, present, reveal; formal evince. ANTONYMS hide.

■ **man·i·fest·ly** adv.

man·i·fes·ta·tion /ˌmanəfəˈstāsʜən, -ˌfesˈtāsʜən/ ▶ n. **1** a sign or evidence of something. **2** an appearance of a ghost or spirit.

SYNONYMS **1 display**, demonstration, show, exhibition, presentation. **2 sign**, indication, evidence, symptom, testimony, proof, mark, reflection, example, instance.

man·i·fes·to /ˌmanəˈfestō/ ▶ n. (plural **manifestos**) a public declaration of the policy and aims of a political party or an artist.

man·i·fold /ˈmanəˌfōld/ ▶ adj. of many kinds: *the buildings have led to manifold problems.* ▶ n. a pipe with several openings, especially in a car engine.

man·i·kin /ˈmanikən/ ▶ n. a very small person.

ma·nil·a /məˈnilə/ ▶ n. strong brown paper.

man·i·oc /ˈmanēˌäk/ ⇒ CASSAVA.

ma·nip·u·late /məˈnipyəˌlāt/ ▶ v. (**manipulates**, **manipulating**, **manipulated**) **1** handle skillfully. **2** control or influence in a clever or underhand way.

SYNONYMS **1 operate**, work, handle, turn, pull, push, twist, slide. **2 control**, influence, use to your advantage, exploit, twist.

■ **ma·nip·u·la·tion** /məˌnipyəˈlāsʜən/ n. **ma·nip·u·la·tor** n.

ma·nip·u·la·tive /məˈnipyələtiv, -ˌlātiv/ ▶ adj. manipulating other people in a clever or underhand way.

man·kind /ˌmanˈkīnd, ˈmanˌkīnd/ ▶ n. human beings as a whole.

SYNONYMS **the human race**, humankind, humanity, human beings, humans, Homo sapiens, people, man, men and women.

man·li·ness /ˈmanlēnis/ ▶ n. good qualities associated with men, such as courage and strength.

man·ly /ˈmanlē/ ▶ adj. (**manlier**, **manliest**) **1** having good qualities associated with men, such as courage and strength. **2** suitable for a man.

SYNONYMS **virile**, masculine, strong, all-male, red-blooded, muscular, muscly, strapping, well built, rugged, tough, powerful, brawny; informal hunky. ANTONYMS effeminate.

man·na /ˈmanə/ ▶ n. **1** (in the Bible) the substance supplied by God as food to the Israelites in the wilderness. **2** something unexpected and beneficial.

manned /mand/ ▶ adj. having a human crew.

man·ne·quin /ˈmanikən/ ▶ n. a dummy used to display clothes in a store window.

man·ner /ˈmanər/ ▶ n. **1** a way in which something is done or happens: *he was dancing in a peculiar manner.* **2** a person's outward behavior: *her shy manner.* **3** (**manners**) polite social behavior. **4** literary a kind or sort.

SYNONYMS **1 way**, fashion, mode, means, method, methodology, system, style, approach, technique, procedure, process. **2** *her unfriendly manner* **behavior**, attitude, demeanor, air, aspect, mien, bearing, conduct. **3** (**manners**) **social graces**, politeness, Ps and Qs, etiquette, protocol, decorum, propriety, civility.

□ **all manner of** many different kinds of. **in a manner of speaking** in a way. **to the manner born** naturally at ease in a particular job or situation.

man·nered /ˈmanərd/ ▶ adj. **1** behaving in a particular way: *a well-mannered girl.* **2** artificial and exaggerated.

man·ner·ism /ˈmanəˌrizəm/ ▶ n. a distinctive gesture or way of speaking.

SYNONYMS **idiosyncrasy**, quirk, oddity, foible, trait, peculiarity, habit, characteristic.

man·ner·ly /ˈmanərlē/ ▶ adj. well-mannered; polite.

man·nish /ˈmanisʜ/ ▶ adj. (of a woman) like a man in appearance or behavior.

ma·nom·e·ter /məˈnämətər/ ▶ n. an instrument for measuring the pressure of fluids.

man·or /ˈmanər/ ▶ n. a large country house with lands. ■ **ma·no·ri·al** /məˈnôrēəl/ adj.

man·pow·er /ˈmanˌpouər/ ▶ n. the number of people working or available for work.

man·qué /mänɢˈkā/ ▶ adj. (of a person) having never become what they might have become: *an actor manqué.*

man·sard /ˈmanˌsärd, -sərd/ ▶ n. a roof with four sides, each of which becomes steeper halfway down.

manse /mans/ ▶ n. the house provided for a minister of certain Christian Churches.

man·serv·ant /ˈmanˌsərvənt/ ▶ n. a male servant.

man·sion /ˈmansʜən/ ▶ n. a large, impressive house.

SYNONYMS **estate**, stately home, hall, manor (house). ANTONYMS hovel.

man·slaugh·ter /ˈmanˌslôtər/ ▶ n. the crime of killing a person without meaning to do so.

man·tel /ˈmantl/ ▶ n. a mantelpiece or mantelshelf.

man·tel·piece /ˈmantlˌpēs/ ▶ n. **1** a structure surrounding a fireplace. **2** (also **mantelshelf** /ˈmantlˌsʜelf/) a shelf forming the top of a mantelpiece.

man·til·la /manˈtē(y)ə, -ˈtilə/ ▶ n. a lace or silk scarf worn by Spanish women over the hair and shoulders.

man·tis /ˈmantis/ (or **praying mantis**) ▶ n. (plural **mantis** or **mantises**) a large insect that waits for its prey with its forelegs folded like hands in prayer.

man·tle /ˈmantl/ ▶ n. **1** a woman's loose sleeveless cloak. **2** a close covering, e.g., of snow. **3** a cover around a gas jet that produces a glowing light when heated. **4** a role or responsibility that passes from one person to another. **5** the region of very hot, dense rock between the earth's crust and its core.

man·tra /'mäntrə, 'man-/ ▶ n. a word or sound repeated to aid concentration when meditating.

man·u·al /'manyə(wə)l/ ▶ adj. 1 having to do with the hands. 2 operated by or using the hands: *a manual worker*. ▶ n. a book giving instructions or information.

> SYNONYMS ▶ adj. **physical**, laboring, blue-collar, hand. ▶ n. **handbook**, instructions, guide, companion, ABC, guidebook, vade mecum; informal bible.

■ **man·u·al·ly** adv.

man·u·fac·ture /,manyə'fakCHər/ ▶ v. (**manufactures**, **manufacturing**, **manufactured**) 1 make something on a large scale using machinery. 2 invent evidence or a story. ▶ n. the manufacturing of things.

> SYNONYMS ▶ v. 1 **make**, produce, mass-produce, build, construct, assemble, put together, turn out, process. 2 **make up**, invent, fabricate, concoct, hatch, dream up, think up, contrive; informal cook up. ▶ n. **production**, making, manufacturing, mass production, construction, building, assembly.

man·u·fac·tur·er /,manyə'fakCHərər/ ▶ n. a person or organization that manufactures something: *local manufacturers are important sources of tax revenue*.

> SYNONYMS **maker**, producer, builder, constructor, industrialist.

ma·nure /mə'n(y)o͝or/ ▶ n. animal dung used for fertilizing land.

man·u·script /'manyə,skript/ ▶ n. 1 a handwritten book, document, etc. 2 an author's handwritten or typed work, before printing and publication.

Manx /maNGks/ ▶ adj. relating to the Isle of Man. □ **Manx cat** a breed of cat that has no tail.

man·y /'menē/ ▶ determiner, pron., & adj. a large number of. ▶ n. (**the many**) the majority of people.

> SYNONYMS ▶ determiner, pron., & adj. **numerous**, a lot of, plenty of, countless, innumerable, scores of, untold, copious, abundant; informal lots of, umpteen, loads of, masses of, stacks of, heaps of, oodles of, a slew of; literary myriad. ANTONYMS few.

Mao·ism /'mou,izəm/ ▶ n. the communist policies and theories of the former Chinese head of state Mao Zedong (1893–1976). ■ **Mao·ist** n. & adj.

Ma·o·ri /'mourē/ ▶ n. (plural **Maori** or **Maoris**) a member of the aboriginal people of New Zealand.

map /map/ ▶ n. a flat diagram of an area showing physical features, cities, roads, etc. ▶ v. (**maps**, **mapping**, **mapped**) 1 show something on a map. 2 (**map something out**) plan something in detail.

> SYNONYMS ▶ n. **plan**, chart, A to Z, atlas. ▶ v. **chart**, plot, draw, record.

□ **put something on the map** make a place famous.

ma·ple /'māpəl/ ▶ n. a tree with five-pointed leaves and a sap from which syrup is made. □ **maple syrup** sugary syrup produced from the sap of a maple tree.

mar /mär/ ▶ v. (**mars**, **marring**, **marred**) spoil the appearance or quality of.

> SYNONYMS **spoil**, impair, detract from, disfigure, blemish, scar, deface, ruin, damage, wreck, taint, tarnish. ANTONYMS enhance.

mar·a·bou /'marə,bo͞o/ ▶ n. 1 an African stork with a large neck pouch. 2 down feathers from marabou used as trimming for hats or clothing.

ma·rac·a /mə'räkə/ ▶ n. a container filled with small beans or stones, shaken as a musical instrument.

mar·a·schi·no cher·ry /,marə'SHē,nō, -'skē-/ ▶ n. a cherry preserved in maraschino, a liqueur made from cherries.

mar·a·thon /'marə,THän/ ▶ n. 1 a long-distance running race, strictly one of 26 miles 385 yards (42.195 km). 2 a long-lasting and difficult task.

ma·raud /mə'rôd/ ▶ v. go about a place in search of things to steal or people to attack. ■ **ma·raud·er** n.

mar·ble /'märbəl/ ▶ n. 1 a hard stone, usually white with colored streaks, which can be polished and used in sculpture and building. 2 a small ball of colored glass used as a toy. 3 (**your marbles**) informal your mental powers.

mar·bled /'märbəld/ ▶ adj. 1 patterned with colored streaks. 2 (of steak) containing streaks of fat.

mar·ca·site /'märkə,sīt/ ▶ n. a semiprecious stone consisting of iron pyrites.

March /märCH/ ▶ n. the third month of the year.

march /märCH/ ▶ v. 1 walk in time and with regular paces, like a soldier. 2 walk quickly and with determination. 3 force someone to walk quickly. 4 take part in an organized procession to make a protest. ▶ n. 1 an act of marching. 2 a procession organized as a protest.

> SYNONYMS ▶ v. 1 **stride**, walk, troop, step, pace, tread, slog, tramp, hike, trudge, parade, file. 2 **strut**, storm, stomp, sweep. ▶ n. 1 **walk**, trek, hike. 2 **parade**, procession, cortège, demonstration; informal demo.

□ **marching orders** 1 instructions for troops to depart. 2 informal a dismissal. **on the march** 1 marching. 2 making progress. ■ **march·er** n.

mar·chion·ess /'märSH(ə)nəs/ ▶ n. 1 the wife or widow of a marquess. 2 a woman who holds the rank of marquess.

Mar·di Gras /'märdē ,grä/ ▶ n. a carnival held in some countries on Shrove Tuesday, the day before Ash Wednesday.

ma·re /me(ə)r/ ▶ n. the female of a horse or related animal. □ **mare's nest** 1 a muddle. 2 a discovery that turns out to be worthless.

mar·ga·rine /'märjərən/ ▶ n. a butter substitute made from vegetable oils or animal fats.

mar·gin /'märjən/ ▶ n. 1 an edge or border. 2 the blank border on each side of the print on a page. 3 an amount by which something is won: *they won by a 17-point margin*.

> SYNONYMS 1 **edge**, side, verge, border, perimeter, brink, brim, rim, fringe, boundary, periphery, extremity. 2 **leeway**, latitude, scope, room, space, allowance.

□ **margin of** (or **for**) **error** a small amount allowed for or included so as to be sure of success or safety.

mar·gin·al /'märjənl/ ▶ adj. 1 in a margin. 2 slight, or of minor importance.

> SYNONYMS **slight**, small, tiny, minute, insignificant, minimal, negligible. ANTONYMS considerable.

■ **mar·gin·al·i·ty** /ˌmärjəˈnalətē/ **n.** **mar·gin·al·ly** **adv.**

mar·gi·na·li·a /ˌmärjəˈnālēə/ ▶ **pl.n.** notes written or printed in the margin of a book or manuscript.

mar·gin·al·ize /ˈmärjənəˌlīz/ ▶ **v.** (**marginalizes, marginalizing, marginalized**) reduce the power or importance of. ■ **mar·gin·al·i·za·tion** /ˌmärjənələˈzāSHən/ **n.**

mar·gue·rite /ˌmärg(y)əˈrēt/ ▶ **n.** an oxeye daisy.

mar·i·gold /ˈmariˌgōld/ ▶ **n.** a plant of the daisy family with yellow or orange flowers.

ma·ri·jua·na /ˌmarəˈ(h)wänə/ ▶ **n.** cannabis.

ma·ri·na /məˈrēnə/ ▶ **n.** a purpose-built harbor with moorings for yachts and small boats.

mar·i·nade /ˌmarəˈnād, ˈmarəˌnād/ ▶ **n.** a mixture of ingredients in which food is soaked before cooking to flavor or soften it. ▶ **v.** (**marinades, marinading, marinaded**) marinate food before cooking.

mar·i·nate /ˈmarəˌnāt/ ▶ **v.** (**marinates, marinating, marinated**) soak food in a marinade.

ma·rine /məˈrēn/ ▶ **adj.** **1** relating to the sea. **2** relating to shipping or matters concerning a navy. ▶ **n.** a soldier trained to serve on land or sea.

> SYNONYMS ▶ **adj.** **1 seawater**, sea, saltwater, aquatic. **2 maritime**, nautical, naval, seafaring, seagoing, ocean-going.

mar·i·ner /ˈmarənər/ ▶ **n.** literary a sailor.

> SYNONYMS **sailor**, seaman, seafarer; informal sea dog, old salt; dated tar.

mar·i·on·ette /ˌmarēəˈnet/ ▶ **n.** a puppet worked by strings.

mar·i·tal /ˈmaritl/ ▶ **adj.** having to do with marriage.

> SYNONYMS **matrimonial**, conjugal, married, wedded, nuptial.

mar·i·time /ˈmariˌtīm/ ▶ **adj.** **1** relating to shipping or other activity taking place at sea. **2** living or found in or near the sea. **3** (of a climate) moist and having a mild temperature because of the influence of the sea.

> SYNONYMS **naval**, marine, nautical, seafaring, seagoing, sea, ocean-going, oceanic, coastal.

mar·jo·ram /ˈmärjərəm/ ▶ **n.** a sweet-smelling plant of the mint family, used as an herb in cooking.

mark[1] /märk/ ▶ **n.** **1** a small area on a surface having a different color from its surroundings. **2** something that indicates position or acts as a pointer. **3** a line, figure, or symbol made to identify or record something. **4** a sign of a quality or feeling: *a mark of respect.* **5** a characteristic feature of something. **6** a point awarded for a correct answer or for a piece of work. **7** a particular model of a vehicle or machine. ▶ **v.** **1** make a mark on. **2** write a word or symbol on an object in order to identify it. **3** indicate the position of. **4** (**mark someone/thing out**) show someone or something to be different or special. **5** do something to celebrate or remember a significant event. **6** (**mark something up** or **down**) increase or reduce the price of an item. **7** assess and give a mark to a piece of work. **8** pay careful attention to.

> SYNONYMS ▶ **n.** **1 blemish**, streak, spot, fleck, blot, stain, smear, speck, smudge, blotch, bruise, scratch, scar, dent, chip, nick. **2 sign**, token, symbol, emblem, badge, indication, characteristic, feature, trait, attribute, quality, hallmark, indicator, symptom, proof. **3 grade**, grading, rating, score, percentage. ▶ **v.** **1 discolor**, stain, smear, smudge, streak, dirty, scratch, scar, dent. **2 label**, identify, flag, tag, initial, highlight, name, brand. **3 celebrate**, observe, recognize, acknowledge, keep, honor, commemorate, remember, solemnize. **4 represent**, signify, indicate, herald. **5 characterize**, distinguish, identify, typify. **6 assess**, evaluate, appraise, grade, correct.

□ **make a** (or **your** or **its**) **mark** have a notable effect. **mark time 1** fill in time with routine activities. **2** (of troops) march on the spot without moving forward. **near** (or **close**) **to the mark** almost accurate. **off** (or **wide of**) **the mark** incorrect or inaccurate. **on your mark(s)** be ready to start (used to instruct competitors in a race). **up to the mark** up to the required standard.

mark[2] ▶ **n.** the former basic unit of money in Germany.

marked /märkt/ ▶ **adj.** **1** having an identifying mark. **2** clearly noticeable. **3** singled out as a target for attack: *a marked man.*

> SYNONYMS **noticeable**, pronounced, decided, distinct, striking, clear, unmistakable, obvious, conspicuous, notable. ANTONYMS imperceptible.

■ **mark·ed·ly** /ˈmärkədlē/ **adv.**

mark·er /ˈmärkər/ ▶ **n.** **1** an object used to indicate a position, place, or route. **2** a felt-tip pen with a broad tip. **3** (in team games) a player who marks an opponent. **4** a person who marks a test or exam.

mar·ket /ˈmärkit/ ▶ **n.** **1** a regular gathering for the buying and selling of food, livestock, or other goods. **2** an outdoor space or large hall where traders offer their goods for sale. **3** a particular area of trade or competitive activity. **4** demand for a particular product or service. ▶ **v.** (**markets, marketing, marketed**) advertise or promote a product.

> SYNONYMS ▶ **n.** **grocery store**, supermarket, store, convenience store, mart. ▶ **v.** **sell**, retail, merchandise, trade, advertise, promote.

□ **market research** the gathering of information about what people choose to buy. **market value** the amount for which something can be sold. **on the market** available for sale. ■ **mar·ket·a·ble** **adj.**

mar·ket·eer /ˌmärkəˈti(ə)r/ ▶ **n.** a person who sells goods or services in a market.

mar·ket·ing /ˈmärkitiNG/ ▶ **n.** the promoting and selling of products or services.

mar·ket·place /ˈmärkətˌplās/ ▶ **n.** **1** an open space where a market is held. **2** the world of trade and commerce: *the global marketplace.*

mark·ing /ˈmärkiNG/ ▶ **n.** **1** an identification mark. **2** (also **markings**) a pattern of marks on an animal's fur, feathers, or skin.

marks·man /ˈmärksmən/ ▶ **n.** (plural **marksmen**) a person skilled in shooting. ■ **marks·man·ship** **n.**

mark·up /ˈmärˌkəp/ ▶ **n.** the difference between the basic cost of producing something and the amount it is sold for.

marl[1] /märl/ ▶ **n.** a rock or soil consisting of clay and lime.

marl[2] ▶ **n.** a type of yarn or fabric with differently colored threads.

mar·lin /ˈmärlən/ ▶ **n.** a large edible fish of warm seas, with a pointed snout.

mar·lin·spike /ˈmärlən,spīk/ (or **marlinespike**) ▶ **n.** a pointed metal tool used by sailors to separate strands of rope or wire.

mar·ma·lade /ˈmärmə,lād/ ▶ **n.** a thick spread like jam made from oranges.

mar·mo·re·al /märˈmôrēəl/ ▶ **adj.** literary made of or resembling marble.

mar·mo·set /ˈmärmə,set, -,zet/ ▶ **n.** a small tropical American monkey with a long tail.

mar·mot /ˈmärmət/ ▶ **n.** a heavily built burrowing rodent.

ma·roon¹ /məˈro͞on/ ▶ **n.** a dark brownish-red color.

ma·roon² ▶ **v.** (**be marooned**) be abandoned or isolated in a place that cannot be reached.

SYNONYMS **strand**, cast away, cast ashore, abandon, desert, leave behind, leave.

marque /märk/ ▶ **n.** a make of car, as distinct from a specific model.

mar·quee /märˈkē/ ▶ **n.** a rooflike canopy over the entrance to a building.

mar·quess /ˈmärkwəs/ ▶ **n.** a British nobleman ranking above an earl and below a duke.

mar·que·try /ˈmärkətrē/ ▶ **n.** patterns or pictures made from small pieces of colored wood inlaid into a surface, used to decorate furniture.

mar·quis /märˈkē, ˈmärkwəs/ ▶ **n.** (in some European countries) a nobleman ranking above a count and below a duke.

mar·quise /märˈkēz/ ▶ **n.** **1** the wife or widow of a marquis, or a woman holding the rank of marquis in her own right. **2** a finger ring set with a pointed oval gem.

mar·riage /ˈmarij/ ▶ **n.** **1** the formal union of a man and woman, by which they become husband and wife. **2** the relationship between a husband and wife.

SYNONYMS **1 matrimony**, wedlock, wedding, nuptials, union, match. **2** *a marriage of jazz, pop, and gospel* **union**, fusion, mixture, mix, blend, amalgamation, combination, hybrid. ANTONYMS divorce, separation.

□ **marriage of convenience** a marriage concluded primarily to achieve a practical purpose. ■ **mar·riage·a·ble** **adj.**

mar·ried /ˈmarēd/ ▶ **adj.** joined in marriage. ▶ **n.** (**marrieds**) married people.

mar·row /ˈmarō/ ▶ **n.** (also **bone marrow**) a soft fatty substance inside bones, in which blood cells are produced. □ **to the marrow** to your innermost being.

mar·row·bone /ˈmarō,bōn/ ▶ **n.** a bone containing edible bone marrow.

mar·ry /ˈmarē/ ▶ **v.** (**marries**, **marrying**, **married**) **1** become the husband or wife of. **2** join two people in marriage. **3** join two things together. **4** (**marry into**) become a member of a family by marriage.

SYNONYMS **1 get married**, wed, become husband and wife; informal tie the knot, walk down the aisle, get hitched. **2** *the show marries poetry with art* **join**, unite, combine, fuse, mix, blend, merge, amalgamate. ANTONYMS divorce, separate.

Mars /märz/ ▶ **n.** the fourth planet from the sun in the solar system and the nearest to the earth.

marsh /märsʜ/ ▶ **n.** an area of low-lying land that usually remains waterlogged.

SYNONYMS **swamp**, marshland, bog, morass, mire, quagmire, slough, fen.

□ **marsh mallow** a tall pink-flowered plant growing in marshes, whose roots were formerly used to make marshmallow. ■ **marsh·y** **adj.**

mar·shal /ˈmärsʜəl/ ▶ **n.** **1** an officer of the highest rank in the armed forces of some countries. **2** a federal or municipal law enforcement officer, including the head of a police or fire department. **3** an official responsible for supervising public events, such as a parade or sports event. ▶ **v.** (**marshals**, **marshaling**, **marshaled**) **1** assemble a group of people in order. **2** bring facts together in an organized way.

SYNONYMS ▶ **v. assemble**, gather (together), collect, muster, call together, draw up, line up, array, organize, group, arrange, deploy, position, summon, round up.

marsh·mal·low /ˈmärsʜ,melō, -,malō/ ▶ **n.** a spongy candy made from sugar, egg white, and gelatin.

mar·su·pi·al /märˈso͞opēəl/ ▶ **n.** a mammal whose young are carried and suckled in a pouch on the mother's belly.

mart /märt/ ▶ **n.** **1** a store. **2** a trade center or market.

mar·ten /ˈmärtn/ ▶ **n.** a forest animal resembling a weasel.

mar·tial /ˈmärsʜəl/ ▶ **adj.** having to do with war.

SYNONYMS **military**, soldierly, warlike, fighting, militaristic; informal gung-ho.

□ **martial arts** sports that started as forms of self-defense or attack, such as judo and karate. **martial law** government by the military forces of a country.

Mar·tian /ˈmärsʜən/ ▶ **n.** a supposed inhabitant of the planet Mars. ▶ **adj.** relating to Mars.

mar·tin /ˈmärtn/ ▶ **n.** a small short-tailed swallow.

mar·ti·net /,märtnˈet/ ▶ **n.** a person who is very strict and insists on being obeyed.

mar·tyr /ˈmärtər/ ▶ **n.** **1** a person who is killed because of their beliefs. **2** a person who exaggerates their difficulties in order to obtain sympathy or admiration. ▶ **v.** make a martyr of. ■ **mar·tyr·dom** **n.**

mar·vel /ˈmärvəl/ ▶ **v.** (**marvels**, **marveling**, **marveled**) be filled with wonder. ▶ **n.** a person or thing that causes a feeling of wonder.

SYNONYMS ▶ **v. be amazed**, be astonished, be in awe, wonder. ▶ **n. wonder**, miracle, sensation, spectacle, phenomenon, prodigy.

mar·vel·ous /ˈmärv(ə)ləs/ ▶ **adj.** wonderful; very good.

SYNONYMS **excellent**, splendid, wonderful, magnificent, superb, sensational, glorious, sublime, lovely, delightful; informal super, great, amazing, fantastic, terrific, tremendous, fabulous, cracking, awesome, divine, ace, wicked. ANTONYMS commonplace, awful.

■ **mar·vel·ous·ly** **adv.**

Marx·ism /ˈmärk,sizəm/ ▶ **n.** the political and economic theories of Karl Marx and Friedrich Engels, which formed the basis for communism. ■ **Marx·ist** **n. & adj.**

mar·zi·pan /ˈmärzə,pan, ˈmärtsə-/ ▶ **n.** a sweet paste of ground almonds, sugar, and egg whites.

mas·car·a /ma'skarə/ ▶ n. a cosmetic for darkening the eyelashes.

mas·cot /'mas,kät, -kət/ ▶ n. a person, animal, or object that is supposed to bring good luck or that is used to symbolize a particular event, organization, or team.

mas·cu·line /'maskyələn/ ▶ adj. **1** relating to men. **2** having the qualities or appearance traditionally associated with men. **3** Grammar referring to a gender of nouns and adjectives including most males.

SYNONYMS **1 virile**, macho, manly, male, muscular, muscly, strong, strapping, well built, rugged, robust, brawny, powerful, red-blooded, vigorous; informal hunky, laddish. **2 mannish**, unfeminine, unladylike; informal butch. ANTONYMS feminine, effeminate.

mas·cu·lin·i·ty /,maskyə'linitē/ ▶ n. **1** the quality or condition of being male. **2** the qualities or appearance traditionally associated with men.

mash /mash/ ▶ v. crush or beat something into a soft mass. ▶ n. **1** a soft mass made by crushing a substance. **2** bran mixed with hot water given as a warm food to horses or other animals.

SYNONYMS ▶ v. **pulp**, crush, purée, cream, pound, beat.

mask /mask/ ▶ n. **1** a covering for all or part of the face, worn for protection, as a disguise, or for theatrical effect. **2** a likeness of a person's face molded in clay or wax. ▶ v. **1** (**masked**) wearing a mask. **2** conceal or disguise.

SYNONYMS ▶ n. **pretense**, semblance, veil, screen, front, facade, veneer, disguise, cover, cloak, camouflage. ▶ v. **hide**, conceal, disguise, cover up, obscure, screen, cloak, camouflage.

mas·och·ism /'masə,kizəm, 'maz-/ ▶ n. enjoyment felt in being hurt or humiliated by someone. ■ **mas·och·ist** n. **mas·och·is·tic** /,masə'kistik, ,maz-/ adj.

ma·son /'māsən/ ▶ n. **1** a person who works with stone. **2** (**Mason**) a Freemason.

Ma·son·ic /mə'sänik/ ▶ adj. relating to Freemasons.

ma·son·ry /'māsənrē/ ▶ n. the parts of a building that are made of stone.

masque /mask/ ▶ n. (in the past) a form of entertainment consisting of dancing and acting performed by masked players.

mas·quer·ade /,maskə'rād/ ▶ n. **1** a pretense. **2** a ball at which people wear masks. ▶ v. (**masquerades**, **masquerading**, **masqueraded**) pretend to be someone or something else.

Mass /mas/ ▶ n. **1** the Christian service of the Eucharist or Holy Communion. **2** a musical setting of parts of this service.

mass /mas/ ▶ n. **1** an amount of matter with no definite shape. **2** a large number of people or objects gathered together. **3** (**the masses**) the ordinary people. **4** (**a mass of**) a large amount of. **5** Physics the quantity of matter that something contains. ▶ v. gather together in a mass.

SYNONYMS ▶ n. **1** *a mass of fallen leaves* **pile**, heap, accumulation, aggregation, mat, tangle. **2** *a mass of cyclists* **crowd**, horde, throng, host, troop, army, herd, flock, swarm, mob, pack, flood, multitude. **3** *the mass of the population* **majority**, most, preponderance, greater part, best/better part, bulk, body. **4** *a mass movement* **widespread**, general, extensive, large-scale, wholesale, universal, indiscriminate. ▶ v. **assemble**, gather together, collect, rally.

□ **mass-market** (of goods) produced in large quantities and appealing to a large number of people. **mass-produce** produce goods in large quantities in a factory.

mas·sa·cre /'masikər/ ▶ n. a brutal killing of a large number of people. ▶ v. (**massacres**, **massacring**, **massacred**) brutally kill a large number of people.

SYNONYMS ▶ n. **slaughter**, mass murder, mass execution, ethnic cleansing, genocide, holocaust, annihilation, liquidation, extermination, carnage, butchery, bloodbath, bloodletting. ▶ v. **slaughter**, butcher, murder, kill, annihilate, exterminate, execute, liquidate, eliminate, mow down.

mas·sage /mə'säzн, -'säj/ ▶ n. the rubbing and kneading of parts of the body with the hands to relieve tension or pain. ▶ v. (**massages**, **massaging**, **massaged**) **1** give a massage to. **2** alter facts or figures to make them seem better than they really are.

SYNONYMS ▶ n. **rub**, rubdown, kneading. ▶ v. **1 rub**, knead, manipulate, pummel, work. **2 alter**, tamper with, manipulate, doctor, falsify, juggle, fiddle with, tinker with, distort, rig; informal cook, fiddle.

□ **massage parlor 1** a place where massage is provided. **2** a brothel.

mas·seur /ma'sər, mə-/ ▶ n. (feminine **masseuse** /ma'so͞os, mə-, ma'sœz/) a person who gives massages professionally.

mas·sif /ma'sēf/ ▶ n. a compact group of mountains.

mas·sive /'masiv/ ▶ adj. **1** large and heavy or solid. **2** very large, powerful, or severe.

SYNONYMS **huge**, enormous, vast, immense, mighty, great, colossal, tremendous, gigantic, mammoth, monumental, giant, mountainous; informal monster, whopping, astronomical, ginormous, mega. ANTONYMS tiny.

■ **mas·sive·ly** adv.

mast¹ /mast/ ▶ n. **1** a tall upright post on a boat carrying a sail or sails. **2** any tall upright post or structure.

mast² ▶ n. nuts and other fruit that have fallen from trees.

mas·tec·to·my /ma'stektəmē/ ▶ n. (plural **mastectomies**) an operation to remove a breast.

mas·ter /'mastər/ ▶ n. **1** a man in a position of authority, control, or ownership. **2** a person skilled in a particular art or activity. **3** the head of a college or school. **4** a person who holds a second or further degree from a university or other academic institution. **5** an original movie, recording, or document from which copies can be made. ▶ v. (**masters**, **mastering**, **mastered**) **1** gain great knowledge of or skill in. **2** gain control of.

SYNONYMS ▶ n. **1 lord**, overlord, lord and master, liege, ruler, sovereign, monarch. **2 expert**, genius, maestro, virtuoso, authority; informal ace, wizard, whiz, hotshot, pro, maven, crackerjack. **3 guru**, teacher, leader, guide, mentor. **4** *a master carpenter* **expert**, adept, proficient, skilled, skillful, deft, dexterous, adroit, practiced, experienced, masterly, accomplished; informal crack, ace, crackerjack. ANTONYMS servant, student, amateur. ▶ v. **1 overcome**, conquer, beat, quell, suppress, control, triumph over, subdue, vanquish, subjugate, curb, check, defeat, get the better of; informal lick. **2** *he'd mastered the technique* **learn**, become proficient in, pick up, grasp, understand; informal get the hang of.

□ **master key** a key that opens several locks, each of which has its own key. **master of ceremonies** a person in charge of proceedings at a special event.

mas·ter·class /ˈmastərˌklas/ ▶ **n.** a class given to students by a leading musician.

mas·ter·ful /ˈmastərfəl/ ▶ **adj. 1** powerful and able to control other people. **2** performed or performing very skillfully.

SYNONYMS **commanding**, powerful, imposing, magisterial, authoritative. ANTONYMS weak.

■ **mas·ter·ful·ly** adv.

mas·ter·ly /ˈmastərlē/ ▶ **adj.** performed or performing very skillfully.

SYNONYMS **expert**, adept, skillful, skilled, adroit, proficient, deft, dexterous, accomplished, polished, consummate. ANTONYMS inept.

mas·ter·mind /ˈmastərˌmīnd/ ▶ **n.** a person who plans and directs a complex scheme or project. ▶ **v.** plan and direct a complex scheme or project.

SYNONYMS ▶ **n. genius**, intellect; informal brain(s). ▶ **v. plan**, control, direct, be in charge of, run, conduct, organize, arrange, preside over, orchestrate, stage-manage, engineer, manage, coordinate.

mas·ter·piece /ˈmastərˌpēs/ ▶ **n.** a work of outstanding skill.

SYNONYMS **magnum opus**, pièce de résistance, chef-d'œuvre, masterwork, tour de force, classic.

mas·ter·y /ˈmast(ə)rē/ ▶ **n. 1** complete knowledge or command of a subject or skill. **2** control or superiority.

SYNONYMS **1 proficiency**, ability, capability, knowledge, understanding, comprehension, command, grasp. **2 control**, domination, command, supremacy, superiority, power, authority, jurisdiction, dominion, sovereignty.

mast·head /ˈmastˌhed/ ▶ **n. 1** the highest part of a ship's mast. **2** the name of a newspaper or magazine printed at the top of the first page. **3** the details of a newspaper's or magazine's owner, advertising rates, etc.

mas·tic /ˈmastik/ ▶ **n. 1** a gum from the bark of a Mediterranean tree, used in making varnish and chewing gum. **2** a waterproof substance like putty, used in building.

mas·ti·cate /ˈmastiˌkāt/ ▶ **v.** (**masticates, masticating, masticated**) chew food. ■ **mas·ti·ca·tion** /ˌmastiˈkāsʜən/ **n.**

mas·tiff /ˈmastif/ ▶ **n.** a dog of a large, strong breed with drooping ears and lips.

mas·to·don /ˈmastəˌdän/ ▶ **n.** a large extinct elephantlike mammal.

mas·toid /ˈmasˌtoid/ ▶ **n.** a part of the bone behind the ear, which has air spaces linked to the middle ear.

mat /mat/ ▶ **n. 1** a thick piece of material placed on the floor, used for decoration or to protect the floor. **2** a piece of springy material for landing on in gymnastics or similar sports. **3** a small piece of material placed on a surface to protect it. **4** a thick layer of hairy or woolly material.

SYNONYMS **rug**, carpet, doormat, runner.

mat·a·dor /ˈmatəˌdôr/ ▶ **n.** a bullfighter.

match¹ /macʜ/ ▶ **n. 1** an event at which two people or teams compete against each other. **2** a person or thing that can compete with another as an equal in quality or strength. **3** an exact equivalent. **4** a pair of things that correspond or are very similar. ▶ **v. 1** correspond or fit with something. **2** be equal to. **3** place a person or team in competition with another.

SYNONYMS ▶ **n. 1 contest**, competition, game, tournament, meet, derby, bout, fight. **2** *an exact match* **lookalike**, double, twin, duplicate, mate, companion, counterpart, pair, replica, copy, doppelgänger; informal spitting image, dead ringer. ▶ **v. 1 go with**, coordinate with, complement, suit, set off. **2** (**matching**) **corresponding**, equivalent, parallel, analogous, complementary, paired, twin, identical, alike. **3 correspond**, tally, agree, coincide, square. **4 equal**, compare with, be in the same league as, touch, rival, compete with; informal hold a candle to.

□ **match point** (in sports) a point that if won by one of the players will also win them the match.

match² ▶ **n.** a short, thin stick tipped with a substance that ignites when rubbed against a rough surface.

match·box /ˈmacʜˌbäks/ ▶ **n.** a small box in which matches are sold.

match·less /ˈmacʜləs/ ▶ **adj.** so good that nothing is an equal.

match·mak·er /ˈmacʜˌmākər/ ▶ **n.** a person who tries to bring about marriages or relationships between other people.

match·stick /ˈmacʜˌstik/ ▶ **n.** the stem of a match.

mate /māt/ ▶ **n. 1** each of a pair of birds or other animals. **2** informal a person's husband or wife. **3** an assistant to a skilled worker. ▶ **v.** (**mates, mating, mated**) (of animals or birds) come together for breeding.

SYNONYMS ▶ **n. 1 partner**, husband, wife, spouse, consort, lover; informal better half, other half. **2 assistant**, helper, apprentice. ▶ **v. breed**, couple, copulate, pair.

ma·te·ri·al /məˈti(ə)rēəl/ ▶ **n. 1** the matter from which something is or can be made. **2** items needed for doing or creating something. **3** cloth. ▶ **adj. 1** having to do with physical things rather than the mind or spirit. **2** essential or relevant.

SYNONYMS ▶ **n. 1 matter**, substance, stuff, constituents. **2 fabric**, cloth, textiles. **3 information**, data, facts, facts and figures, statistics, evidence, details, particulars, background; informal info. ▶ **adj. 1 physical**, corporeal, fleshly, bodily, tangible, mundane, worldly, earthly, secular, temporal, concrete, real. **2** *information material to the inquiry* **relevant**, pertinent, applicable, germane, vital, essential, key. ANTONYMS spiritual.

■ **ma·te·ri·al·ly** adv.

ma·te·ri·al·ism /məˈti(ə)rēəˌlizəm/ ▶ **n.** a strong interest in possessions and physical comfort rather than spiritual values. ■ **ma·te·ri·al·ist** adj. & n. **ma·te·ri·al·is·tic** /məˌti(ə)rēəˈlistik/ adj.

ma·te·ri·al·ize /məˈti(ə)rēəˌlīz/ ▶ **v.** (**materialize, materializing, materialized**) **1** happen. **2** appear suddenly.

SYNONYMS **1 happen**, occur, come about, take place, transpire; informal come off; literary come to pass. **2 appear**, turn up, arrive, emerge, surface, pop up; informal show up.

ma·ter·nal /mə'tərnl/ ▶ **adj. 1** having to do with a mother. **2** related through the mother's side of the family.

SYNONYMS **motherly**, protective, caring, nurturing, maternalistic.

■ **ma·ter·nal·ly adv.**

ma·ter·ni·ty /mə'tərnətē/ ▶ **n.** motherhood.

math /maTH/ ▶ **n.** mathematics.

math·e·mat·ics /maTH(ə)'matiks/ ▶ **n.** the branch of science concerned with numbers, quantities, and space. ■ **math·e·mat·i·cal** /ˌmaTH(ə)'matikəl/ **adj. math·e·mat·i·cal·ly adv. math·e·ma·ti·cian** /ˌmaTH(ə)mə'tisHən/ **n.**

mat·i·nee /ˌmatn'ā/ ▶ **n.** an afternoon performance in a live or movie theater.

mat·ins /'matnz/ ▶ **n.** a Christian service of morning prayer.

ma·tri·arch /'mātrēˌärk/ ▶ **n.** a woman who is the head of a family or tribe.

ma·tri·ar·chy /'mātrēˌärkē/ ▶ **n.** a society led or controlled by women. ■ **ma·tri·ar·chal** /ˌmātrē'ärkəl/ **adj.**

mat·ri·cide /'matrəˌsīd, 'mā-/ ▶ **n. 1** the killing by someone of their own mother. **2** a person who kills their mother.

ma·tric·u·late /mə'trikyəˌlāt/ ▶ **v.** (**matriculates**, **matriculating**, **matriculated**) enroll or be enrolled at a college or university. ■ **ma·tric·u·la·tion** /məˌtrikyə'lāsHən/ **n.**

mat·ri·mo·ni·al /ˌmatrə'mōnēəl/ ▶ **adj.** of or relating to marriage or married people.

SYNONYMS **marital**, conjugal, married, wedded, nuptial; literary connubial.

mat·ri·mo·ny /'matrəˌmōnē/ ▶ **n.** the state of being married.

ma·trix /'mātriks/ ▶ **n.** (plural **matrices** /'mātrisēz/ or **matrixes**) **1** an environment or material in which something develops. **2** a mold in which something is cast or shaped. **3** a gridlike arrangement of elements.

ma·tron /'mātrən/ ▶ **n. 1** an older married woman. **2** a woman in charge of medical and living arrangements at a boarding school. **3** a female prison officer. □ **matron of honor** a married woman attending the bride at a wedding. ■ **ma·tron·ly adj.**

matte /mat/ (or **matt**) ▶ **adj.** (of a color, paint, or surface) not shiny.

mat·ted /'matid/ ▶ **adj.** (of hair or fur) tangled into a thick mass.

SYNONYMS **tangled**, knotted, tousled, disheveled, uncombed, unkempt, ratty.

mat·ter /'matər/ ▶ **n. 1** physical substance or material. **2** a subject or situation to be considered or dealt with. **3** (**the matter**) the reason for a problem. ▶ **v.** (**matters**, **mattering**, **mattered**) be important.

SYNONYMS ▶ **n. 1 material**, stuff, substance. **2 affair**, business, situation, concern, incident, episode, subject, topic, issue, question, point at issue, case. ▶ **v. be important**, make any difference, be of consequence, be relevant, count, signify.

□ **for that matter** and indeed also. **in the matter of** as regards. **a matter of 1** no more than (a specified period). **2** a question of. **a matter of course** the natural or expected thing. **matter-of-fact** unemotional and practical.

mat·tock /'matək/ ▶ **n.** a farming tool similar to a pickax.

mat·tress /'matrəs/ ▶ **n.** a fabric case filled with soft or firm material and sometimes incorporating springs, used for sleeping on.

ma·ture /mə'CHŏŏr, -'t(y)ŏŏr/ ▶ **adj. 1** fully grown. **2** like a sensible adult. **3** (of certain foods or drinks) developed over a long period in order to achieve a full flavor. ▶ **v.** (**matures**, **maturing**, **matured**) **1** become mature. **2** (of an insurance policy) reach the end of its term and so become payable.

SYNONYMS ▶ **adj. 1 adult**, of age, fully grown, in your prime. **2 grown-up**, sensible, responsible, adult. **3 ripe**, ripened, mellow, seasoned, ready. ANTONYMS immature. ▶ **v. 1 grow up**, come of age, reach adulthood. **2 ripen**, mellow, age. **3 develop**, grow, bloom, blossom, evolve.

■ **mat·u·ra·tion** /ˌmacHə'rāsHən/ **n. ma·ture·ly adv.**

ma·tu·ri·ty /mə'CHŏŏritē, mə't(y)ŏŏr-/ ▶ **n. 1** the state or period of being mature. **2** the time when an insurance policy matures.

SYNONYMS **1 adulthood**, coming of age, manhood, womanhood. **2 responsibility**, sense, wisdom.

mat·zo /'mätsə/ (also **matzoh**) ▶ **n.** (plural **matzos**) a cracker of unleavened bread, traditionally eaten by Jews during Passover.

maud·lin /'môdlin/ ▶ **adj.** sentimental in a self-pitying way.

maul /môl/ ▶ **v. 1** wound by scratching and tearing. **2** treat roughly.

SYNONYMS **savage**, attack, claw, scratch, lacerate, mangle, tear.

maun·der /'môndər/ ▶ **v.** (**maunders**, **maundering**, **maundered**) move, talk, or act in a rambling way.

mau·so·le·um /ˌmôzə'lēəm, ˌmôsə-/ ▶ **n.** (plural **mausolea** /-'lēə/ or **mausoleums**) a building containing a tomb or tombs.

mauve /mōv, môv/ ▶ **n.** a pale or reddish-purple color.

ma·ven /'māvən/ ▶ **n.** informal an expert or connoisseur.

mav·er·ick /'mav(ə)rik/ ▶ **n.** an unconventional and independent-minded person.

SYNONYMS **individualist**, nonconformist, free spirit, original, eccentric, rebel, dissenter, dissident. ANTONYMS conformist.

maw /mô/ ▶ **n.** the jaws or throat.

mawk·ish /'môkisH/ ▶ **adj.** foolishly sentimental.

max. /maks/ ▶ **abbr.** maximum.

max·im /'maksim/ ▶ **n.** a short statement expressing a general truth or rule of behavior.

SYNONYMS **saying**, adage, aphorism, proverb, motto, saw, axiom, dictum, precept, epigram.

max·i·mize /'maksəˌmīz/ ▶ **v.** (**maximizes**, **maximizing**, **maximized**) **1** make something as large or great as possible. **2** make the best use of.

max·i·mum /'maksəməm/ ▶ **n.** (plural **maxima** /-mə/or **maximums**) the greatest amount, size, or strength that is possible or that has been gained. ▶ **adj.** greatest in amount, size, or strength.

> SYNONYMS ▶ **n.** **upper limit**, utmost, greatest, most, peak, pinnacle, height, ceiling, top. ANTONYMS minimum. ▶ **adj.** **greatest**, highest, biggest, largest, top, most, utmost, supreme.

■ **max·i·mal** **adj.**

May /mā/ ▶ **n.** **1** the fifth month of the year. **2** (**may**) the hawthorn or its blossom.

may /mā/ ▶ **modal v.** (3rd singular present **may**; past **might** /mīt/) **1** expressing possibility. **2** expressing permission. **3** expressing a wish or hope.

Ma·ya /ˈmīə/ ▶ **n.** (plural **Maya** or **Mayas**) a member of a Central American people whose civilization collapsed *c.* 900 AD. ■ **Ma·yan** **adj. & n.**

may·be /ˈmābē/ ▶ **adv.** perhaps.

> SYNONYMS **perhaps**, possibly, for all you know; literary perchance.

May·day /ˈmāˌdā/ ▶ **n.** an international distress signal used by ships and aircraft.

may·fly /ˈmāˌflī/ ▶ **n.** (plural **mayflies**) an insect that lives as an adult for only a very short time.

may·hem /ˈmāˌhem/ ▶ **n.** violent disorder.

> SYNONYMS **chaos**, havoc, bedlam, pandemonium, uproar, turmoil, a riot, anarchy; informal a madhouse.

may·n't /ˈmā(ə)nt/ ▶ **contr.** may not.

may·on·naise /ˈmāəˌnāz, ˌmāəˈnāz/ ▶ **n.** a creamy dressing made from egg yolks, oil, and vinegar.

may·or /ˈmāər/ ▶ **n.** the elected head of a city, town, or other municipality. ■ **may·or·al** /māˈôrəl, ˈmāərəl/ **adj.**

may·or·al·ty /ˈmāərəltē/ ▶ **n.** (plural **mayoralties**) the period of office of a mayor.

may·or·ess /ˈmāərəs/ ▶ **n.** **1** the wife of a mayor. **2** a woman elected as mayor.

may·pole /ˈmāˌpōl/ ▶ **n.** a decorated pole with long ribbons attached to the top, traditionally used for dancing around on the first day of May.

maze /māz/ ▶ **n.** a complicated network of paths and walls or hedges designed as a challenge to find a way through.

> SYNONYMS **labyrinth**, network, warren, web, tangle, confusion, jungle.

ma·zur·ka /məˈzərkə, -ˈzo͝or-/ ▶ **n.** a lively Polish dance.

MBA ▶ **abbr.** Master of Business Administration.

MC ▶ **abbr.** **1** master of ceremonies. **2** member of Congress. **3** Military Cross.

Mc·Car·thy·ism /məˈkärᴛʜēˌizəm/ ▶ **n.** a campaign against suspected communists in US public life carried out under Senator Joseph McCarthy from 1950 to 1954. ■ **Mc·Car·thy·ite** **adj. & n.**

MD ▶ **abbr.** Doctor of Medicine.

MDT ▶ **abbr.** Mountain Daylight Time.

me /mē/ ▶ **pron.** used as the object of a verb or preposition or after "than," "as," or the verb "to be," to refer to the speaker himself or herself.

> USAGE
>
> It is wrong to use **me** as the subject of a verb, as in *John and me went to the shops*; use **I** instead.

mead /mēd/ ▶ **n.** an alcoholic drink made from fermented honey and water.

mead·ow /ˈmedō/ ▶ **n.** an area of grassland.

> SYNONYMS **field**, paddock, pasture; literary lea, mead.

mea·ger /ˈmēgər/ ▶ **adj.** small in quantity and of bad quality.

> SYNONYMS **inadequate**, scant, paltry, limited, restricted, sparse, negligible, skimpy, slender, pitiful, miserly, niggardly; informal measly, stingy. ANTONYMS abundant.

■ **mea·ger·ness** **n.**

meal¹ /mēl/ ▶ **n.** **1** a regular daily occasion when food is eaten. **2** the food eaten on such an occasion.

> SYNONYMS dinner, lunch, breakfast, brunch, snack, feast, banquet; informal spread; formal repast.

□ **meal ticket** a person or thing that is exploited as a source of money.

meal² ▶ **n.** the edible part of any grain or pulse ground to powder.

meal·time /ˈmēlˌtīm/ ▶ **n.** the time at which you eat a meal.

meal·y /ˈmēlē/ ▶ **adj.** (**mealier**, **mealiest**) **1** relating to or containing ground grain or seeds. **2** pale in color. □ **mealy-mouthed** not wanting to speak honestly or frankly.

mean¹ /mēn/ ▶ **v.** (**means**, **meaning**, **meant** /ment/) **1** intend to say or show something. **2** (of a word) have as its explanation in the same language or its equivalent in another language. **3** intend something to happen or be the case. **4** have something as a result. **5** intend something for a particular purpose. **6** have a particular level of importance: *animals mean more to him than people*.

> SYNONYMS **1 signify**, denote, indicate, convey, designate, show, express, spell out, stand for, represent, symbolize, imply, suggest, intimate, portend. **2 intend**, aim, plan, have in mind, set out, want. **3** *this will mean war* **entail**, involve, necessitate, lead to, result in, give rise to, bring about, cause, engender, produce.

mean² ▶ **adj.** **1** unwilling to give or share things. **2** unkind or unfair. **3** vicious or aggressive. **4** (of a place) poor and dirty in appearance.

> SYNONYMS **1 miserly**, niggardly, parsimonious, penny-pinching, cheese-paring; informal tightfisted, stingy, tight, cheap. **2 unkind**, nasty, unpleasant, spiteful, malicious, unfair, shabby, horrible, despicable, contemptible, obnoxious, vile, loathsome, base, low; informal rotten. ANTONYMS generous, kind.

■ **mean·ly** **adv.** **mean·ness** **n.**

mean³ ▶ **n.** **1** the average value of a set of quantities. **2** something in the middle of two extremes. ▶ **adj.** **1** calculated as a mean. **2** equally far from two extremes.

me·an·der /mēˈandər/ ▶ **v.** (**meanders**, **meandering**, **meandered**) **1** follow a winding course. **2** wander in a leisurely way. ▶ **n.** a winding bend of a river or road.

mean·ing /ˈmēniɴɢ/ ▶ **n.** **1** the thing or idea that a word, signal, or action represents. **2** a sense of purpose.

> SYNONYMS **1 significance**, sense, signification, import, gist, thrust, drift, implication, message. **2 definition**, sense, explanation, interpretation, connotation.

mean·ing·ful /ˈmēniNGfəl/ ▶ **adj.** **1** having meaning. **2** worthwhile. **3** expressive.

SYNONYMS **1 significant**, relevant, important, telling, expressive, eloquent, pointed, pregnant, revealing, suggestive. **2 sincere**, deep, serious, earnest, significant, important.

■ **mean·ing·ful·ly** **adv.**

mean·ing·less /ˈmēniNGlis/ ▶ **adj.** having no meaning or significance.

SYNONYMS **unintelligible**, incomprehensible, incoherent, senseless, pointless.

■ **mean·ing·less·ly** **adv.**

means /mēnz/ ▶ **n.** **1** a thing or method used to achieve a result. **2** money or wealth.

SYNONYMS **1 method**, way, manner, course, agency, channel, avenue, procedure, process, methodology, expedient. **2 money**, resources, capital, income, finance, funds, cash, the wherewithal, assets, wealth, riches, affluence, fortune.

□ **by all means** of course. **by no means** certainly not. **means test** an official investigation into how much money or income a person has, to find out whether they qualify for welfare benefits.

meant /ment/ past and past participle of **MEAN**[1].

mean·time /ˈmēnˌtīm/ ▶ **adv.** (**in the meantime**) meanwhile.

SYNONYMS **1 for now**, for the moment, for the present, for the time being, in the meanwhile, in the meantime, in the interim. **2 at the same time**, simultaneously, concurrently.

mean·while /ˈmēnˌ(h)wīl/ ▶ **adv.** **1** in the period of time between two events. **2** at the same time.

SYNONYMS **1 for now**, for the moment, for the present, for the time being, in the meanwhile, in the meantime, in the interim. **2 at the same time**, simultaneously, concurrently.

mea·sles /ˈmēzəlz/ ▶ **n.** an infectious disease causing fever and a red rash.

mea·sly /ˈmēzlē, ˈmēzl-ē/ ▶ **adj.** informal ridiculously small or few.

meas·ure /ˈmezHər/ ▶ **v.** (**measures**, **measuring**, **measured**) **1** find out what the size, amount, or degree of something is in standard units. **2** be of a particular size, amount, or degree. **3** (**measure something out**) take an exact quantity of. **4** (**measure up**) reach the required standard. ▶ **n.** **1** a course of action taken to achieve a purpose. **2** a proposal for a new law. **3** a standard unit used to express size, amount, or degree. **4** a measuring device marked with such units. **5** (**a measure of**) an indication of the extent or quality of.

SYNONYMS ▶ **v. quantify**, gauge, size, count, weigh, evaluate, assess, determine, calculate, compute. ▶ **n. 1 action**, act, course of action, deed, procedure, step, expedient, initiative, program. **2 statute**, act, bill, law. **3 ruler**, tape measure, gauge, meter, scale. **4** *sales are a measure of their success* **yardstick**, test, standard, barometer, touchstone, benchmark.

□ **for good measure** as an amount or item that is additional to what is strictly necessary. **have the measure of** understand the character of. ■ **meas·ur·a·ble** **adj.** **meas·ur·a·bly** **adv.**

meas·ured /ˈmezHərd/ ▶ **adj.** **1** slow and regular in rhythm. **2** carefully considered.

SYNONYMS **1 regular**, steady, even, rhythmic, unfaltering, slow, dignified, stately, sedate, leisurely, unhurried. **2 careful**, thoughtful, considered, reasoned, calculated.

meas·ure·ment /ˈmezHərmənt/ ▶ **n.** **1** the action of measuring. **2** an amount, size, or extent found by measuring.

SYNONYMS **1 quantification**, evaluation, assessment, calculation, computation, mensuration. **2 size**, dimension, proportions, value, amount, quantity.

meat /mēt/ ▶ **n.** the flesh of an animal used as food.

SYNONYMS **flesh**.

meat·ball /ˈmētˌbôl/ ▶ **n.** a ball of ground or chopped meat.

meat·loaf /ˈmētˌlōf/ ▶ **n.** ground or chopped meat baked in the shape of a loaf.

meat·y /ˈmētē/ ▶ **adj.** (**meatier**, **meatiest**) **1** full of meat. **2** fleshy or muscular. **3** substantial or challenging.

mecca /ˈmekə/ ▶ **n.** a place that attracts many people.

me·chan·ic /məˈkanik/ ▶ **n.** a skilled worker who repairs and maintains machinery.

me·chan·i·cal /məˈkanikəl/ ▶ **adj.** **1** relating to or operated by a machine or machinery. **2** done without thought. **3** relating to physical forces or movement.

SYNONYMS **1 mechanized**, machine-driven, automated, automatic. **2 automatic**, knee-jerk, unthinking, instinctive, habitual, routine, unemotional, unfeeling. ANTONYMS manual.

■ **me·chan·i·cal·ly** **adv.**

me·chan·ics /məˈkaniks/ ▶ **n.** **1** the branch of study concerned with the forces producing movement. **2** machinery or working parts. **3** the practical aspects of something.

mech·an·ism /ˈmekəˌnizəm/ ▶ **n.** **1** a piece of machinery. **2** the way in which something works or is made to happen.

SYNONYMS **1 apparatus**, machine, machinery, appliance, device, instrument, tool, contraption, gadget; informal gizmo. **2** *a complaints mechanism* **procedure**, process, system, method, means, medium, channel.

mech·a·nize /ˈmekəˌnīz/ ▶ **v.** (**mechanizes**, **mechanizing**, **mechanized**) equip with machines or automatic devices. ■ **mech·a·ni·za·tion** /ˌmekənəˈzāsHən/ **n.**

med /med/ informal ▶ **adj.** medical. ▶ **n.** (usu. **meds**) a medication.

med·al /ˈmedl/ ▶ **n.** a metal disk with an inscription or design on it, awarded to someone for a special achievement.

SYNONYMS **decoration**, ribbon, star, badge, award, commendation, honor.

□ **Medal of Honor** the highest US military decoration, awarded by Congress for bravery in combat above and beyond the call of duty.

med·al·ist /ˈmedl-ist/ ▶ **n.** a person who has been awarded a medal.

me·dal·lion /məˈdalyən/ ▶ **n.** **1** a piece of jewelry in the shape of a medal, worn as a pendant. **2** a decorative oval or circular painting, panel, or design.

med·dle /ˈmedl/ ▶ v. (**meddles**, **meddling**, **meddled**) interfere in something that is not your concern.

SYNONYMS **1 interfere**, intrude, intervene, pry; informal poke your nose in. **2 fiddle**, interfere, tamper, mess (around).

■ **med·dler** n.

med·dle·some /ˈmedlsəm/ ▶ adj. fond of interfering in other people's affairs.

me·di·a /ˈmēdēə/ ▶ n. **1** television, radio, and newspapers as providers of information. **2** plural of MEDIUM.

USAGE

The word **media** comes from the Latin plural of **medium**. In its normal sense, 'television, radio, and newspapers,' it can be used with either a singular or a plural verb.

me·di·ae·val = MEDIEVAL.

me·di·an /ˈmēdēən/ ▶ adj. technical situated in the middle. ▶ n. **1** a median value. **2** Geometry a straight line drawn from one of the angles of a triangle to the middle of the opposite side.

me·di·ate /ˈmēdēˌāt/ ▶ v. (**mediates**, **mediating**, **mediated**) try to settle a dispute between other people or groups.

SYNONYMS **arbitrate**, conciliate, moderate, make peace, intervene, intercede, act as (an) intermediary, negotiate, liaise, referee.

me·di·a·tion /ˌmēdēˈāsʜən/ ▶ n. the action of trying to settle a dispute.

SYNONYMS **arbitration**, conciliation, reconciliation, intervention, intercession, negotiation, shuttle diplomacy.

me·di·a·tor /ˈmēdēˌātər/ ▶ n. a person who tries to settle a dispute.

SYNONYMS **arbitrator**, arbiter, negotiator, conciliator, peacemaker, go-between, middleman, intermediary, moderator, honest broker, liaison officer, umpire, referee, adjudicator, judge.

med·ic /ˈmedik/ ▶ n. informal **1** a medical corpsman in the military. **2** a doctor or medical student.

Med·i·caid /ˈmediˌkād/ ▶ n. a federal system of health insurance for people requiring financial assistance.

med·i·cal /ˈmedikəl/ ▶ adj. relating to the science or practice of medicine. ▶ n. an examination to see how healthy someone is. ■ **med·i·cal·ly** adv.

me·dic·a·ment /məˈdikəmənt, ˈmedikəˌment/ ▶ n. a medicine.

Med·i·care /ˈmediˌke(ə)r/ ▶ n. a federal system of health insurance for people over 65 years of age and for certain younger people with disabilities.

med·i·cate /ˈmediˌkāt/ ▶ v. (**medicates**, **medicating**, **medicated**) **1** give medicine or a drug to. **2** (**medicated**) containing a substance that has healing properties.

med·i·ca·tion /ˌmedəˈkāsʜən/ ▶ n. **1** a medicine or drug. **2** treatment with medicines.

me·dic·i·nal /məˈdisənl/ ▶ adj. **1** having healing properties. **2** relating to medicines.

SYNONYMS **curative**, healing, remedial, therapeutic, restorative, health-giving.

■ **me·dic·i·nal·ly** adv.

med·i·cine /ˈmedisən/ ▶ n. **1** the science or practice of the treatment and prevention of disease. **2** a substance taken by mouth in order to treat or prevent disease.

SYNONYMS **medication**, drug, prescription, treatment, remedy, cure, nostrum, panacea, cure-all.

□ **medicine man** a person believed to have supernatural healing powers.

me·di·e·val /ˌmed(ē)ˈēvəl, ˌmēd-, ˌmid-/ (or **mediaeval**) ▶ adj. relating to the Middle Ages, the period between about 1000 and 1450.

me·di·e·val·ist /ˌmed(ē)ˈēvəlist, ˌmēd-/ (or **mediaevalist**) ▶ n. a person who studies medieval history or literature.

me·di·o·cre /ˌmēdēˈōkər/ ▶ adj. of only average or fairly low quality.

SYNONYMS **average**, ordinary, undistinguished, uninspired, indifferent, unexceptional, unexciting, unremarkable, run-of-the-mill, pedestrian, prosaic, lackluster, forgettable, amateurish; informal so-so. ANTONYMS excellent.

me·di·oc·ri·ty /ˌmēdēˈäkrətē/ ▶ n. (plural **mediocrities**) **1** the state of being average in quality. **2** a person of average ability and lacking originality.

med·i·tate /ˈmedəˌtāt/ ▶ v. (**meditates**, **meditating**, **meditated**) **1** focus your mind and free it of uncontrolled thoughts, as a spiritual exercise or for relaxation. **2** (**meditate on** or **about**) think carefully about.

SYNONYMS **contemplate**, think, consider, ponder, muse, reflect, deliberate, ruminate, brood, mull over.

■ **med·i·ta·tion** /ˌmedəˈtāsʜən/ n.

med·i·ta·tive /ˈmedəˌtātiv/ ▶ adj. involving or absorbed in focused thought or deep reflection. ■ **med·i·ta·tive·ly** adv.

Med·i·ter·ra·ne·an /ˌmedətəˈrānēən/ ▶ adj. relating to the Mediterranean Sea or the countries around it.

SPELLING

One **d**, one **t**, double **r**: Mediter**r**anean.

me·di·um /ˈmēdēəm/ ▶ n. (plural **media** /ˈmēdēə/ or **mediums**) **1** a means by which something is communicated or achieved. **2** a substance that something lives or exists in, or through which it travels. **3** the type of material used by an artist. **4** (plural **mediums**) a person who claims to be able to communicate with the spirits of dead people. **5** the middle state between two extremes. ▶ adj. between two extremes.

SYNONYMS ▶ n. *a medium of expression* **means**, method, avenue, channel, vehicle, organ, instrument, mechanism. ▶ adj. **average**, middling, medium-sized, middle-sized, moderate, normal, standard.

med·lar /ˈmedlər/ ▶ n. a fruit resembling a small brown apple.

med·ley /ˈmedlē/ ▶ n. (plural **medleys**) a varied mixture.

meek /mēk/ ▶ adj. quiet, gentle, and obedient.

SYNONYMS **submissive**, obedient, compliant, tame, biddable, acquiescent, timid, quiet, mild, gentle, docile, shy, diffident, unassuming, self-effacing. ANTONYMS assertive.

■ **meek·ly** adv.

meer·kat /ˈmi(ə)rˌkat/ ▶ n. a small southern African mongoose.

meet /mēt/ ▶ v. (**meets**, **meeting**, **met**) **1** come together with someone at the same place and time. **2** be introduced to or come across someone for the first time. **3** touch or join. **4** come across a situation. **5** (**meet with**) receive a particular reaction. **6** fulfill or satisfy a requirement. ▶ n. a gathering or meeting, especially of athletes for a contest or competition.

SYNONYMS ▶ v. **1 encounter**, come face to face with, run into, run across, come across/upon, chance on, happen on, stumble across; informal bump into. **2 get to know**, be introduced to, make the acquaintance of. **3 assemble**, gather, congregate, convene; formal foregather. **4 converge**, connect, touch, link up, intersect, cross, join.

meet·ing /ˈmētiNG/ ▶ n. **1** an occasion when people meet to discuss or decide something. **2** a situation in which people come together.

SYNONYMS **1 gathering**, assembly, conference, congregation, convention, forum, summit, rally, consultation, audience, interview, conclave; informal get-together. **2 encounter**, contact, appointment, assignation, rendezvous; literary tryst. **3** *the meeting of land and sea* **convergence**, confluence, conjunction, union, intersection, crossing.

meet·ing·house /ˈmētiNGˌhous/ ▶ n. a Quaker place of worship.

meg·a /ˈmegə/ ▶ adj. informal **1** very large. **2** excellent.

meg·a·bucks /ˈmegəˌbəks/ ▶ pl.n. informal a huge sum of money.

meg·a·byte /ˈmegəˌbīt/ ▶ n. Computing a unit of information equal to one million bytes.

meg·a·hertz /ˈmegəˌhərts/ ▶ n. (plural **megahertz**) a unit of frequency equal to one million hertz.

meg·a·lith /ˈmegəˌliTH/ ▶ n. a large stone that forms a prehistoric monument or part of one. ■ **meg·a·lith·ic** /ˌmegəˈliTHik/ adj.

meg·a·lo·ma·ni·a /ˌmegəlōˈmānēə/ ▶ n. **1** the false belief that you are very powerful and important. **2** a strong desire for power. ■ **meg·a·lo·ma·ni·ac** n. & adj.

meg·a·phone /ˈmegəˌfōn/ ▶ n. a cone-shaped device for making the voice sound louder.

meg·a·pix·el /ˈmegəˌpiksəl/ ▶ n. a unit for measuring the resolution of a digital image, equal to one million pixels.

meg·a·ton /ˈmegəˌtən/ ▶ n. a unit for measuring the power of an explosive, equivalent to one million tons of TNT.

meg·a·watt /ˈmegəˌwät/ ▶ n. a unit of power equal to one million watts.

mel·a·mine /ˈmeləˌmēn/ ▶ n. a hard plastic used to coat the surfaces of tables or countertops.

mel·an·cho·li·a /ˌmelənˈkōlēə/ ▶ n. great sadness or depression.

mel·an·chol·y /ˈmelənˌkälē/ ▶ n. deep and long-lasting sadness. ▶ adj. sad or depressed.

SYNONYMS ▶ n. **sadness**, sorrow, unhappiness, depression, despondency, dejection, gloom, misery; informal the blues. ANTONYMS happiness. ▶ adj. **sad**, sorrowful, unhappy, gloomy, despondent, dejected, disconsolate, downcast, downhearted, woebegone, glum, miserable, morose, depressed, dispirited, mournful, doleful, lugubrious; informal down in the dumps, blue. ANTONYMS cheerful.

■ **mel·an·chol·ic** /ˌmelənˈkälik/ adj.

mel·a·nin /ˈmelənin/ ▶ n. a dark pigment in the hair and skin, responsible for the tanning of skin exposed to sunlight.

mel·a·no·ma /ˌmeləˈnōmə/ ▶ n. a form of skin cancer.

meld /meld/ ▶ v. blend.

me·lee /ˈmāˌlā, māˈlā/ ▶ n. **1** a confused fight or scuffle. **2** a disorderly crowd of people.

mel·lif·lu·ous /məˈliflo͞oəs/ ▶ adj. pleasingly smooth and musical to hear.

mel·low /ˈmelō/ ▶ adj. **1** pleasantly smooth or soft in sound, taste, or color. **2** relaxed and good-humored. ▶ v. make or become mellow.

SYNONYMS ▶ adj. **1 sweet-sounding**, dulcet, melodious, mellifluous, soft, smooth, rich. **2 genial**, affable, amiable, good-humored, good-natured, pleasant, relaxed, easygoing. ANTONYMS harsh, rough.

me·lod·ic /məˈlädik/ ▶ adj. **1** relating to melody. **2** sounding pleasant. ■ **me·lod·i·cal·ly** adv.

me·lo·di·ous /məˈlōdēəs/ ▶ adj. tuneful.

SYNONYMS **tuneful**, melodic, musical, mellifluous, dulcet, sweet-sounding, harmonious, euphonious, lyrical. ANTONYMS discordant.

mel·o·dra·ma /ˈmeləˌdrämə/ ▶ n. **1** a play full of exciting events, in which the characters seem too exaggerated to be realistic. **2** behavior or events that are very dramatic.

mel·o·dra·mat·ic /ˌmelədrəˈmatik/ ▶ adj. too dramatic and exaggerated.

SYNONYMS **exaggerated**, histrionic, extravagant, overdramatic, overdone, sensationalized, overemotional, theatrical, stagy; informal hammy.

■ **mel·o·dra·mat·i·cal·ly** adv.

mel·o·dy /ˈmelədē/ ▶ n. (plural **melodies**) **1** a piece of music with a clear or simple tune. **2** the main tune in a piece of music.

SYNONYMS **tune**, air, strain, theme, song, refrain.

mel·on /ˈmelən/ ▶ n. a large round fruit with sweet pulpy flesh.

melt /melt/ ▶ v. **1** make or become liquid by heating. **2** (**melt away**) gradually disappear. **3** become more tender or loving.

SYNONYMS **1 liquefy**, thaw, defrost, soften, dissolve; technical deliquesce. **2 vanish**, disappear, fade, evaporate. ANTONYMS freeze, solidify.

□ **melting pot** a place where different peoples, ideas, or styles are mixed together.

melt·down /ˈmeltˌdoun/ ▶ n. an accident in a nuclear reactor in which the fuel overheats and melts the reactor core.

mem·ber /ˈmembər/ ▶ n. **1** a person or organization belonging to a group or society. **2** old use a part of the body.

SYNONYMS **subscriber**, associate, fellow, representative.

mem·ber·ship /ˈmembərˌship/ ▶ **n. 1** the fact of being a member of a group. **2** the members or the number of members in a group.

mem·brane /ˈmemˌbrān/ ▶ **n. 1** a skinlike tissue that connects, covers, or lines cells or parts of the body. **2** a layer of thin, skinlike material. ■ **mem·bra·nous** /ˈmembrənəs, memˈbrānəs/ **adj.**

me·men·to /məˈmenˌtō/ ▶ **n.** (plural **mementos** or **mementoes**) an object kept as a reminder.

SYNONYMS **souvenir**, keepsake, reminder, remembrance, token, memorial.

mem·o /ˈmemō/ ▶ **n.** (plural **memos**) a written note sent from one person to another within an organization.

mem·oir /ˈmemˌwär, -ˌwôr/ ▶ **n. 1** a historical account or biography written from personal knowledge. **2** (**memoirs**) an account written by a public figure of their life and experiences.

SYNONYMS **1 account**, history, record, chronicle, narrative, story, portrayal, depiction, portrait, profile. **2** (**memoirs**) **autobiography**, life story, journal, diary.

mem·o·ra·bil·i·a /ˌmem(ə)rəˈbilēə/ ▶ **pl.n.** objects kept or collected because of their associations with people or events.

mem·o·ra·ble /ˈmem(ə)rəbəl/ ▶ **adj.** worth remembering or easily remembered.

SYNONYMS **unforgettable**, momentous, significant, historic, remarkable, notable, noteworthy, important, outstanding, arresting, indelible, catchy, haunting.

■ **mem·o·ra·bly adv.**

mem·o·ran·dum /ˌmeməˈrandəm/ ▶ **n.** (plural **memoranda** /-də/ or **memorandums**) **1** formal a memo. **2** a note recording something for future use.

me·mo·ri·al /məˈmôrēəl/ ▶ **n.** a column or other structure made or built in memory of a person or event. ▶ **adj.** created or done in memory of someone.

SYNONYMS ▶ **n. 1 monument**, cenotaph, mausoleum, statue, plaque, cairn, shrine, tombstone. **2 tribute**, testimonial, remembrance, memento.

□ **Memorial Day** a day on which people who died in military service are remembered, observed in the US on the last Monday in May.

mem·o·rize /ˈmeməˌrīz/ ▶ **v.** (**memorizes**, **memorizing**, **memorized**) learn and remember exactly.

SYNONYMS **commit to memory**, remember, learn (by heart), become word-perfect in, get down pat.

mem·o·ry /ˈmem(ə)rē/ ▶ **n.** (plural **memories**) **1** the power that the mind has to store and remember information. **2** a thing remembered. **3** the length of time over which you can remember things. **4** a computer's equipment or capacity for storing data.

SYNONYMS **1 recollection**, remembrance, reminiscence, recall. **2 commemoration**, remembrance, honor, tribute, recognition, respect.

□ **Memory Stick** trademark (or **memory card**) a small removable data storage device used especially in digital cameras and cell phones.

men /men/ plural of **MAN**.

men·ace /ˈmenəs/ ▶ **n. 1** a dangerous or troublesome person or thing. **2** a threatening quality. ▶ **v.** (**menaces**, **menacing**, **menaced**) threaten.

SYNONYMS ▶ **n. 1 threat**, intimidation, malevolence, oppression. **2 danger**, peril, risk, hazard, threat. **3 nuisance**, pest, troublemaker, mischief-maker. ▶ **v. 1 threaten**, endanger, put at risk, jeopardize, imperil. **2 intimidate**, threaten, terrorize, frighten, scare, terrify. **3** (**menacing**) **threatening**, ominous, intimidating, frightening, forbidding, hostile, sinister, baleful.

me·nag·er·ie /məˈnajərē, -ˈnazh-/ ▶ **n.** a small zoo.

mend /mend/ ▶ **v. 1** restore something so that it is no longer broken, torn, or out of action. **2** improve an unpleasant situation. ▶ **n.** a repair.

SYNONYMS ▶ **v. repair**, fix, restore, sew (up), stitch, darn, patch, renew, renovate; informal patch up. ANTONYMS break.

men·da·cious /menˈdāshəs/ ▶ **adj.** untruthful; lying. ■ **men·dac·i·ty n.**

men·di·cant /ˈmendikənt/ ▶ **adj. 1** living by begging. **2** (of a religious order) originally dependent on charitable donations. ▶ **n. 1** a beggar. **2** a member of a mendicant religious order.

men·hir /ˈmenˌhi(ə)r/ ▶ **n.** a tall upright prehistoric stone erected as a monument.

me·ni·al /ˈmēnēəl/ ▶ **adj.** (of work) needing little skill and lacking status. ▶ **n.** a person with a menial job.

SYNONYMS ▶ **adj. unskilled**, lowly, humble, low-grade, low-status, humdrum, routine, boring, dull.

men·in·gi·tis /ˌmenənˈjītis/ ▶ **n.** an infectious disease in which the membranes enclosing the brain and spinal cord become inflamed.

me·nis·cus /məˈniskəs/ ▶ **n.** (plural **menisci** /-kē, -kī/) **1** the curved upper surface of a liquid in a tube. **2** a thin lens curving outward on one side and inward on the other.

men·o·pause /ˈmenəˌpôz/ ▶ **n.** the time when a woman gradually stops having menstrual periods, on average around the age of 50. ■ **men·o·pau·sal** /ˌmenəˈpôzəl/ **adj.**

me·nor·ah /məˈnôrə/ ▶ **n.** a large candlestick with several branches, used in Jewish worship.

men·stru·al /ˈmenstr(o͞o)əl/ ▶ **adj.** having to do with menstruation.

men·stru·ate /ˈmenstrəˌwāt, ˈmenˌstrāt/ ▶ **v.** (**menstruates**, **menstruating**, **menstruated**) (of a woman) have a flow of blood from the lining of the womb each month. ■ **men·stru·a·tion** /ˌmenstro͞oˈāshən, menˈstrā-/ **n.**

men·tal /ˈmentl/ ▶ **adj. 1** having to do with the mind. **2** relating to disorders of the mind. **3** informal crazy.

SYNONYMS **1 intellectual**, cerebral, cognitive, rational. **2 psychiatric**, psychological, behavioral. ANTONYMS physical.

men·tal·i·ty /menˈtalitē/ ▶ **n.** (plural **mentalities**) a characteristic way of thinking.

SYNONYMS **way of thinking**, mindset, mind, psychology, attitude, outlook, makeup, disposition, character.

men·tal·ly /ˈmentlē/ ▶ **adv.** in your mind: *mentally, I was prepared to deal with the situation.*

SYNONYMS **psychologically**, intellectually, in your mind, in your head, inwardly, internally.

men·thol /ˈmen,THôl, -,THäl/ ▶ **n.** a substance found in peppermint oil, used in medicines and as a flavoring. ■ **men·tho·lat·ed** /ˈmenTHə,lātid/ **adj.**

men·tion /ˈmenCHən/ ▶ **v.** refer to something or someone briefly. ▶ **n. 1** a brief reference to someone or something. **2** a formal acknowledgment that someone has done something well.

SYNONYMS ▶ **v. 1 allude to**, refer to, touch on, bring up, raise, broach. **2 state**, say, observe, remark, indicate, disclose, divulge, reveal. ▶ **n. reference**, allusion, comment, citation; informal namecheck, name-drop, plug.

men·tor /ˈmen,tôr, -tər/ ▶ **n.** an experienced person who advises you over a period of time.

SYNONYMS **adviser**, counselor, guide, guru, consultant, confidant(e), trainer, teacher, tutor, instructor.

men·u /ˈmenyo͞o/ ▶ **n. 1** a list of dishes available in a restaurant. **2** the food to be served in a restaurant or at a meal. **3** Computing a list of commands or facilities displayed on screen.

SYNONYMS **bill of fare**, carte du jour, table d'hôte, wine list.

me·ow /mēˈou/ ▶ **n.** the cry of a cat. ▶ **v.** make a meow.

mer·can·tile /ˈmərkən,tēl, -,tīl/ ▶ **adj.** relating to trade or commerce.

mer·ce·nar·y /ˈmərsə,nerē/ ▶ **adj.** wanting to do only things that make you money. ▶ **n.** (plural **mercenaries**) a professional soldier who is hired to serve in a foreign army.

SYNONYMS ▶ **adj. grasping**, greedy, acquisitive, avaricious, materialistic, venal; informal money-grubbing.

mer·chan·dise /ˈmərCHən,dīz, -,dīs/ ▶ **n.** goods for sale.

SYNONYMS **goods**, wares, stock, commodities, produce, products.

mer·chant /ˈmərCHənt/ ▶ **n.** a trader who sells goods in large quantities. ▶ **adj.** (of ships, sailors, or shipping activity) involved with commerce.

SYNONYMS ▶ **n. trader**, tradesman, dealer, wholesaler, broker, agent, seller, retailer, supplier, buyer, vendor, distributor.

□ **merchant bank** a bank whose customers are large businesses. **merchant navy** a country's commercial shipping.

mer·chant·a·ble /ˈmərCHəntəbəl/ ▶ **adj.** suitable for sale.

mer·ci·ful /ˈmərsifəl/ ▶ **adj. 1** showing mercy. **2** giving relief from suffering.

SYNONYMS **forgiving**, compassionate, pitying, forbearing, lenient, humane, mild, kind, softhearted, tenderhearted, sympathetic, humanitarian, liberal, generous, magnanimous. ANTONYMS cruel.

mer·ci·ful·ly /ˈmərsif(ə)lē/ ▶ **adv. 1** in a merciful way. **2** to your great relief; fortunately.

mer·ci·less /ˈmərsiləs/ ▶ **adj.** showing no mercy.

SYNONYMS **ruthless**, remorseless, pitiless, unforgiving, implacable, inexorable, relentless, inhumane, inhuman, unfeeling, severe, cold-blooded, hard-hearted, stony-hearted, heartless, harsh, callous, cruel, brutal. ANTONYMS compassionate.

■ **mer·ci·less·ly adv.**

mer·cu·ri·al /mər,kyo͝orēəl/ ▶ **adj. 1** tending to change mood suddenly. **2** having to do with the element mercury.

SYNONYMS **volatile**, capricious, temperamental, excitable, fickle, changeable, unpredictable, variable, mutable, erratic, inconstant, inconsistent, unstable, unsteady, fluctuating, ever-changing, moody, flighty, wayward, impulsive; technical labile. ANTONYMS stable.

mer·cu·ry /ˈmərkyərē/ ▶ **n. 1** a heavy silvery-white liquid metallic element used in some thermometers and barometers. **2** (**Mercury**) the planet closest to the sun in the solar system.

mer·cy /ˈmərsē/ ▶ **n.** (plural **mercies**) **1** kindness or forgiveness shown toward someone who is in your power. **2** something to be grateful for.

SYNONYMS **pity**, compassion, leniency, clemency, charity, forgiveness, forbearance, kindness, sympathy, indulgence, tolerance, generosity, magnanimity. ANTONYMS ruthlessness, cruelty.

□ **at the mercy of** in the power of.

mere /mi(ə)r/ ▶ **adj. 1** being no more than what is stated or described. **2** (**the merest**) the smallest or slightest.

mere·ly /ˈmi(ə)rlē/ ▶ **adv.** only.

SYNONYMS **only**, purely, solely, simply, just, but.

mer·e·tri·cious /merəˈtrisHəs/ ▶ **adj.** superficially attractive but having no real value.

merge /mərj/ ▶ **v.** (**merges**, **merging**, **merged**) **1** combine or be combined into a whole. **2** blend gradually into something else.

SYNONYMS **1 join (together)**, join forces, unite, affiliate, team up. **2 amalgamate**, bring together, join, consolidate, conflate, unite, unify, combine, incorporate, integrate. **3 mingle**, blend, fuse, mix, intermix, intermingle, coalesce. ANTONYMS separate.

merg·er /ˈmərjər/ ▶ **n.** a merging of two organizations into one.

SYNONYMS **amalgamation**, combination, union, fusion, coalition, affiliation, unification, incorporation, consolidation, linkup, alliance. ANTONYMS split.

me·rid·i·an /məˈridēən/ ▶ **n.** a circle passing at the same longitude through a given place on the earth's surface and the two poles.

me·ringue /məˈraNG/ ▶ **n.** beaten egg whites and sugar baked until crisp.

me·ri·no /məˈrēnō/ ▶ **n.** (plural **merinos**) a soft wool obtained from a breed of sheep with a long fleece.

mer·it /ˈmerit/ ▶ **n. 1** the quality of being good and deserving praise. **2** a good point or feature. ▶ **v.** (**merits**, **meriting**, **merited**) deserve.

SYNONYMS ▶ **n. 1 excellence**, quality, caliber, worth, value, distinction, eminence. **2 good point**, strong point, advantage, benefit, value, asset, plus. ANTONYMS fault, disadvantage.

▶ v. **deserve**, warrant, justify, earn, rate, be worthy of, be entitled to, have a right to, have a claim to.

mer·i·toc·ra·cy /ˌmeri'täkrəsē/ ▶ n. (plural **meritocracies**) a society in which power is held by those people who have the greatest ability. ■ **mer·i·to·crat·ic** /ˌmeritə'kratik/ adj.

mer·i·to·ri·ous /'meriˌtôrēəs/ ▶ adj. deserving reward or praise.

mer·maid /'mərˌmād/ ▶ n. a mythical sea creature with a woman's head and body and a fish's tail instead of legs.

mer·ri·ment /'merēmənt/ ▶ n. fun.

mer·ry /'merē/ ▶ adj. (**merrier**, **merriest**) cheerful and lively.

SYNONYMS **cheerful**, cheery, in high spirits, sunny, smiling, lighthearted, lively, carefree, joyful, joyous, jolly, convivial, festive, gleeful, happy, laughing; informal chirpy. ANTONYMS miserable.

□ **merry-go-round** a revolving platform fitted with model horses or other animals, on which people ride for fun. ■ **mer·ri·ly** adv.

mer·ry·mak·ing /'merēˌmākiNG/ ▶ n. lively celebration and fun.

Mes·dames /mā'däm/ plural of **MADAME**.

Mes·de·moi·selles /'mādəm(w)əˌzel, 'mādˌmwäˌzel/ plural of **MADEMOISELLE**.

mesh /mesH/ ▶ n. **1** material made of a network of wire or thread. **2** the spacing of the strands of a net. ▶ v. **1** fit together or be in harmony. **2** (of a gearwheel) lock together with another.

SYNONYMS ▶ n. **netting**, net, grille, screen, lattice, gauze. ▶ v. **1 engage**, connect, lock, interlock. **2 harmonize**, fit together, match, dovetail, connect, interconnect.

mes·mer·ic /mez'merik/ ▶ adj. hypnotic.

mes·mer·ism /'mezməˌrizəm/ ▶ n. hypnotism.

mes·mer·ize /'mezməˌrīz/ ▶ v. (**mesmerizes**, **mesmerizing**, **mesmerized**) capture someone's attention so that they are completely enthralled.

mes·quite /mə'skēt, mes-/ ▶ n. a spiny tree of the southwestern US and Mexico, yielding wood, medicinal products, and edible pods.

mess /mes/ ▶ n. **1** a dirty or untidy state. **2** a state of confusion or difficulty. **3** a portion of semisolid food. **4** a dog or cat's excrement. **5** a place where members of the armed forces eat and relax. ▶ v. **1** make something untidy or dirty. **2** (**mess about** or **around**) behave in a silly or playful way. **3** (**mess with**) informal meddle with.

SYNONYMS ▶ n. **1 untidiness**, disorder, disarray, clutter, muddle, jumble, chaos; informal shambles. **2 plight**, predicament, tight spot, tight corner, difficulty, trouble, quandary, dilemma, problem, muddle, mix-up; informal jam, fix, pickle, hole.

mes·sage /'mesij/ ▶ n. **1** a spoken, written, or electronic communication. **2** a significant point or central theme. ▶ v. (**messages**, **messaging**, **messaged**) send a message to.

SYNONYMS ▶ n. **1 communication**, news, note, memo, email, letter, missive, report, bulletin, communiqué, dispatch. **2** *the message of his teaching* **meaning**, sense, import, idea, point, thrust, moral, gist, essence, implication.

mes·sen·ger /'mesənjər/ ▶ n. a person who carries a message.

SYNONYMS **courier**, postman, runner, dispatch rider, envoy, emissary, agent, go-between.

mes·si·ah /mə'sīə/ ▶ n. **1** (**the Messiah**) (in Judaism) the person who will be sent by God as the savior of the Jewish people. **2** (**the Messiah**) (in Christianity) Jesus, regarded as this savior. **3** a great leader seen as the savior of a country, group, etc.

mes·si·an·ic /ˌmesē'anik/ ▶ adj. relating to a messiah.

Mes·sieurs /məs'yœ(r)(z), mās-, mə'si(ə)r(z)/ plural of **MONSIEUR**.

Mes·srs. /'mesərz/ plural of **MR.**

mess·y /'mesē/ ▶ adj. (**messier**, **messiest**) **1** untidy or dirty. **2** confused and difficult to deal with.

SYNONYMS **1 dirty**, filthy, grubby, soiled, grimy, mucky, muddy, stained, smeared, smudged, disheveled, scruffy, unkempt, rumpled, matted, tousled. **2 untidy**, disordered, in a muddle, chaotic, confused, disorganized, in disarray, cluttered; informal like a bomb's hit it. **3** *a messy legal battle* **complex**, tangled, confused, convoluted, unpleasant, nasty, bitter, acrimonious. ANTONYMS clean, tidy.

■ **mess·i·ly** adv. **mess·i·ness** n.

mes·ti·zo /me'stēzō/ (**mestiza** /me'stēzə/) ▶ n. (plural **mestizos** or **mestizas**) a Latin American of mixed race, especially one of Spanish and American Indian parentage.

met /met/ past and past participle of **MEET**.

me·tab·o·lism /mə'tabəˌlizəm/ ▶ n. the process by which food is used for the growth of tissue or the production of energy. ■ **met·a·bol·ic** /ˌmetə'bälik/ adj.

me·tab·o·lize /mə'tabəˌlīz/ ▶ v. (**metabolizes**, **metabolizing**, **metabolized**) process by metabolism.

met·al /'metl/ ▶ n. a hard, solid, shiny material that conducts electricity and heat.

me·tal·lic /mə'talik/ ▶ adj. **1** having to do with metal. **2** (of sound) sharp and ringing.

met·al·lur·gy /'metlˌərjē/ ▶ n. the scientific study of metals. ■ **met·al·lur·gi·cal** adj. **met·al·lur·gist** n.

met·al·work /'metlˌwərk/ ▶ n. **1** the art of making things from metal. **2** metal objects as a group.

met·a·mor·phic /ˌmetə'môrfik/ ▶ adj. (of rock) having been changed by heat and pressure.

met·a·mor·pho·sis /ˌmetə'môrfəsəs/ ▶ n. (plural **metamorphoses**) **1** the transformation of an insect or amphibian from an immature form or larva to an adult form. **2** a change in form or nature. ■ **met·a·mor·phose** /ˌmetə'môrˌfōz, -ˌfōs/ v.

met·a·phor /'metəˌfôr, -fər/ ▶ n. a word or phrase used in an imaginative way to represent or stand for something else (e.g., *the long arm of the law*).

SYNONYMS **figure of speech**, image, trope, analogy, comparison, symbol.

met·a·phor·i·cal /ˌmetə'fôrikəl/ ▶ adj. having to do with metaphor. ■ **met·a·phor·i·cal·ly** adv.

met·a·phys·i·cal /ˌmetə'fizikəl/ ▶ adj. **1** relating to metaphysics. **2** beyond physical matter. ■ **met·a·phys·i·cal·ly** adv.

met·a·phys·ics /ˌmetə'fiziks/ ▶ n. the branch of philosophy dealing with the nature of existence, truth, and knowledge.

mete /mēt/ ▶ v. (**metes, meting, meted**) (**mete something out**) give someone a punishment, or subject them to harsh treatment.

me·te·or /ˈmētēər, -ēˌôr/ ▶ n. a small body of matter from space that glows as a result of friction with the earth's atmosphere, and appears as a shooting star.

me·te·or·ic /ˌmētēˈôrik/ ▶ adj. **1** relating to meteors or meteorites. **2** rapid in achieving success or promotion.

me·te·or·ite /ˈmētēəˌrīt/ ▶ n. a piece of rock or metal that has fallen to the earth from space.

me·te·or·ol·o·gy /ˌmētēəˈräləjē/ ▶ n. the study of conditions in the atmosphere, especially for weather forecasting. ■ **me·te·or·o·log·i·cal** /-rəˈläjikəl/ adj. **me·te·or·ol·o·gist** n.

me·ter¹ /ˈmētər/ ▶ n. the basic unit of length in the metric system, equal to 100 centimeters (approximately 39.37 inches).

me·ter² ▶ n. a device that measures and records the quantity, degree, or rate of something. ▶ v. (**meters, metering, metered**) measure something with a meter.

me·ter³ ▶ n. the regular rhythm of a piece of poetry.

meth·a·done /ˈmeTHəˌdōn/ ▶ n. a powerful painkiller, used as a substitute for morphine and heroin in treating people addicted to these drugs.

meth·ane /ˈmeTHˌān/ ▶ n. a flammable gas that is the main constituent of natural gas.

meth·a·nol /ˈmeTHəˌnôl, -ˌnōl/ ▶ n. a poisonous flammable alcohol, used to make methylated spirit.

me·thinks /miˈTHiNGks/ ▶ v. (past **methought** /miˈTHôt/) old use it seems to me.

meth·od /ˈmeTHəd/ ▶ n. **1** a way of doing something. **2** the quality of being well planned and organized.

> SYNONYMS **1 procedure**, technique, system, practice, routine, modus operandi, process, strategy, tactic, approach, way, manner, mode. **2** *there's no method in his approach* **order**, organization, structure, form, system, logic, planning, design, consistency. ANTONYMS disorder.

me·thod·i·cal /məˈTHädikəl/ ▶ adj. done or doing something in a well-organized and systematic way.

> SYNONYMS **orderly**, well ordered, well organized, well planned, efficient, businesslike, systematic, structured, logical, disciplined, consistent, scientific.

■ **me·thod·i·cal·ly** adv.

Meth·od·ist /ˈmeTHədəst/ ▶ n. a member of a Christian Protestant group that separated from the Church of England in the 18th century. ▶ adj. relating to Methodists or their beliefs. ■ **Meth·od·ism** n.

meth·od·ol·o·gy /ˌmeTHəˈdäləjē/ ▶ n. (plural **methodologies**) a particular system of methods. ■ **meth·od·o·log·i·cal** /-dəˈläjikəl/ adj.

me·tic·u·lous /məˈtikyələs/ ▶ adj. very careful and precise.

> SYNONYMS **careful**, conscientious, diligent, scrupulous, punctilious, painstaking, thorough, studious, rigorous, detailed, perfectionist, fastidious. ANTONYMS careless.

■ **me·tic·u·lous·ly** adv.

mé·tier /meˈtyā, ˈmeˌtyā/ ▶ n. a person's trade, profession, or special ability.

met·ric /ˈmetrik/ ▶ adj. relating to or using the metric system. □ **metric system** the decimal measuring system based on the meter, liter, and gram. **metric ton** (or **metric tonne**) a unit of weight equal to 1,000 kilograms (2,205 lb).

met·ri·cal /ˈmetrikəl/ ▶ adj. having to do with poetic meter. ■ **met·ri·cal·ly** adv.

met·ro /ˈmetrō/ ▶ n. (plural **metros**) an underground railroad system in a city.

met·ro·nome /ˈmetrəˌnōm/ ▶ n. a device that marks time at a selected rate by giving a regular tick, used by musicians. ■ **met·ro·nom·ic** /ˌmetrəˈnämik/ adj.

me·trop·o·lis /məˈträp(ə)ləs/ ▶ n. the main city of a country or region.

met·ro·pol·i·tan /ˌmetrəˈpälitn/ ▶ adj. relating to the main city of a country or region.

met·tle /ˈmetl/ ▶ n. spirit and strength of character.

mew /myo͞o/ ▶ v. (of a cat or gull) make a soft, high-pitched sound like a cry.

mewl /myo͞ol/ ▶ v. **1** cry feebly. **2** mew.

Mex·i·can /ˈmeksəkən/ ▶ n. a person from Mexico. ▶ adj. relating to Mexico.

me·zu·zah /məˈzo͝ozə/ ▶ n. a parchment inscribed with religious texts and attached in a case to the door frame of a Jewish house as a sign of faith.

mez·za·nine /ˈmezəˌnēn, ˌmezəˈnēn/ ▶ n. a floor extending over only part of the full area of a building, built between two full floors.

mez·zo /ˈmetsō, ˈmedzō/ (or **mezzo-soprano**) ▶ n. (plural **mezzos**) a female singer with a voice pitched between soprano and contralto.

mg ▶ abbr. milligrams.

MHz ▶ abbr. megahertz.

mi /mē/ ▶ n. Music the third note of a major scale.

MIA ▶ abbr. missing in action.

mi·as·ma /mīˈazmə, mē-/ ▶ n. an unpleasant or unhealthy atmosphere.

mic /mīk/ ▶ n. informal a microphone.

mi·ca /ˈmīkə/ ▶ n. a mineral found as tiny shiny scales in rocks.

mice /mīs/ plural of **MOUSE**.

mick·ey /ˈmikē/ ▶ n. informal (short for **Mickey Finn**) a drugged or doctored drink given to someone without their realizing it to make them drunk or insensible.

mi·cro /ˈmīkrō/ ▶ n. (plural **micros**) a microcomputer or microprocessor. ▶ adj. extremely small.

mi·crobe /ˈmīˌkrōb/ ▶ n. a bacterium; a germ. ■ **mi·cro·bi·al** /mīˈkrōbēəl/ adj.

mi·cro·bi·ol·o·gy /ˌmīkrōˌbīˈäləjē/ ▶ n. the scientific study of living creatures that are so tiny that they can only be seen using a microscope.

mi·cro·chip /ˈmīkrōˌCHip/ ▶ n. a miniature electronic circuit made from a tiny wafer of silicon.

mi·cro·cli·mate /ˈmīkrōˌklīmət/ ▶ n. the climate of a very small or restricted area.

mi·cro·com·pu·ter /ˈmīkrōkəmˌpyo͞otər/ ▶ n. a small computer with a microprocessor as its central processor.

mi·cro·cosm /ˈmīkrəˌkäzəm/ ▶ n. a thing that has the features and qualities of something much larger.

mi·cro·fi·ber /ˈmīkrōˌfībər/ ▶ **n.** a very fine synthetic yarn.

mi·cro·fiche /ˈmīkrəˌfēsʜ/ (or **microfilm** /ˈmīkrəˌfilm/) ▶ **n.** a piece of film containing very small-sized photographs of the pages of a newspaper, book, etc.

mi·cro·man·age /ˌmīkrōˈmanij/ ▶ **v.** control every part, however small, of an enterprise or activity. ■ **mi·cro·man·age·ment** **n.**

mi·crom·e·ter¹ /mīˈkrämətər/ ▶ **n.** one millionth of a meter.

mi·crom·e·ter² ▶ **n.** an instrument that measures small distances or thicknesses.

mi·cro·or·gan·ism /ˌmīkrōˈôrgəˌnizəm/ ▶ **n.** an organism that is so small that it can only be seen using a microscope.

mi·cro·phone /ˈmīkrəˌfōn/ ▶ **n.** an instrument for changing sound waves into electrical energy that is then amplified and transmitted or recorded.

mi·cro·proc·es·sor /ˌmīkrōˈpräsesər, -ˈprōˌsesər/ ▶ **n.** an integrated circuit that can function as the main part of a computer.

mi·cro·scope /ˈmīkrəˌskōp/ ▶ **n.** an instrument for magnifying very small objects.

mi·cro·scop·ic /ˌmīkrəˈskäpik/ ▶ **adj.** so small as to be visible only with a microscope. ■ **mi·cro·scop·i·cal·ly** **adv.**

mi·cros·co·py /mīˈkräskəpē/ ▶ **n.** the use of a microscope.

mi·cro·sur·ger·y /ˌmīkrōˈsərjərē/ ▶ **n.** surgery performed using very small instruments and a microscope.

mi·cro·wave /ˈmīkrəˌwāv/ ▶ **n.** **1** an electromagnetic wave with a wavelength in the range 0.001–0.3 m. **2** (also **microwave oven**) an oven that uses microwaves to cook or heat food. ▶ **v.** (**microwaves**, **microwaving**, **microwaved**) cook food in a microwave oven.

mid /mid/ ▶ **adj.** having to do with the middle position of a range. ▶ **prep.** literary amid; in the middle of.

mid·air /ˈmidˈe(ə)r/ ▶ **n.** a part or section of the air above ground level or above another surface.

Mi·das touch /ˈmīdəs/ ▶ **n.** the ability to make a lot of money out of anything you do.

mid·day /ˈmidˈdā/ ▶ **n.** twelve o'clock in the day; noon.

> SYNONYMS **noon**, twelve noon, high noon, noonday. ANTONYMS midnight.

mid·den /ˈmidn/ ▶ **n.** a heap of dung or refuse.

mid·dle /ˈmidl/ ▶ **adj.** **1** positioned at an equal distance from the edges or ends of something. **2** medium in rank, quality, or ability. ▶ **n.** **1** a middle point or position. **2** informal a person's waist and stomach.

> SYNONYMS ▶ **adj.** **central**, mid, mean, medium, median, midway, halfway, equidistant. ▶ **n.** **1** **center**, midpoint, halfway point, dead center, hub, eye, heart, core, kernel. **2** **midriff**, waist, belly, stomach; informal tummy. ANTONYMS edge.

□ **middle age** the period when a person is between about 45 and 60 in age. **Middle Ages** the period of European history between about 1000 and 1450. **Middle America** middle-class Americans, thought of as fairly conservative. **middle class** the social group between the upper and the working class. **middle ear** the air-filled central cavity of the ear, behind the eardrum. **Middle East** an area of southwestern Asia and northern Africa, stretching from the Mediterranean to Pakistan. **middle-of-the-road** **1** (of views) not extreme. **2** (of music) generally popular but rather unadventurous. **middle school** a school for children in the sixth, seventh, and eighth grades.

mid·dle·man /ˈmidlˌman/ ▶ **n.** (plural **middlemen**) **1** a person who buys goods from the company who makes them and sells them on to stores or consumers. **2** a person who arranges business or political deals between other people.

mid·dling /ˈmidlɪɴɢ, ˈmidlin/ ▶ **adj.** average in size, amount, or rank.

mid·field /ˈmidˌfēld, midˈfēld/ ▶ **n.** the central part of a sports field. ■ **mid·field·er** **n.**

midge /mij/ ▶ **n.** a small fly that breeds near water.

mid·get /ˈmijit/ ▶ **n.** a very small person. ▶ **adj.** very small.

mid·land /ˈmidlənd/ ▶ **n.** **1** the middle part of a country. **2** (**the Midlands**) the inland counties of central England.

mid·night /ˈmidˌnīt/ ▶ **n.** twelve o'clock at night.

mid·riff /ˈmidˌrif/ ▶ **n.** the front of the body between the chest and the waist.

mid·ship /ˈmidˌsʜip/ ▶ **n.** the middle part of a ship or boat.

mid·ship·man /ˈmidˌsʜipmən, midˈsʜip-/ ▶ **n.** (plural **midshipmen**) a naval cadet in the US Navy.

mid·ships /ˈmidˌsʜips/ ⇒ AMIDSHIPS.

midst /midst, mitst/ old use ▶ **prep.** in the middle of. ▶ **n.** the middle point or part.

mid·stream /ˈmidˈstrēm/ ▶ **n.** the middle of a stream or river.

mid·sum·mer /ˈmidˈsəmər/ ▶ **n.** **1** the middle part of summer. **2** the summer solstice.

mid·term /ˈmidˌtərm/ ▶ **n.** the middle of a period of office, an academic term, or a pregnancy.

mid·way /ˈmidˌwā, -ˈwā/ ▶ **adv. & adj.** in or toward the middle. ▶ **n.** an area of sideshows, games of chance or skill, or other amusements at a fair or exhibition.

mid·week /ˈmidˌwēk/ ▶ **n.** the middle of the week. ▶ **adj. & adv.** in the middle of the week.

Mid·west /ˈmidˈwest/ ▶ **n.** the region of northern states of the US from Ohio west to the Rocky Mountains. ■ **Mid·west·ern** **adj.** **Mid·west·ern·er** **n.**

mid·wife /ˈmidˌwīf/ ▶ **n.** (plural **midwives** / ˈmidˌwīvz/) a nurse who is trained to help women during childbirth. ■ **mid·wife·ry** /midˈwif(ə)rē, -ˈwīf(ə)rē/ **n.**

mid·win·ter /ˈmidˈwintər/ ▶ **n.** **1** the middle part of winter. **2** the winter solstice.

mien /mēn/ ▶ **n.** a person's look or manner.

miffed /mifd/ ▶ **adj.** informal slightly angry or upset.

might¹ /mīt/ ▶ **modal v.** (3rd singular present **might**) **1** past of MAY. **2** used to express possibility or make a suggestion. **3** used politely in questions and requests.

might² ▶ **n.** great power or strength.

> SYNONYMS **strength**, force, forcefulness, power, vigor, energy, brawn.

might·n't /ˈmītnt/ ▶ **contr.** might not.

might·y /ˈmītē/ ▶ **adj.** (**mightier**, **mightiest**) very strong or powerful. ▶ **adv.** informal very.

SYNONYMS ▶ adj. **powerful**, forceful, strong, hard, heavy, violent, vigorous, hefty. ANTONYMS feeble.

■ **might·i·ly** adv.

mi·graine /ˈmīˌgrān/ ▶ n. a severe headache that is accompanied by symptoms such as nausea and disturbed vision.

mi·grant /ˈmīgrənt/ ▶ n. **1** a worker who moves from one place to another to find work. **2** an animal that migrates. ▶ adj. tending to migrate or having migrated.

SYNONYMS ▶ n. **immigrant**, **emigrant**, nomad, itinerant, traveler, transient, wanderer, drifter. ▶ adj. **traveling**, wandering, drifting, nomadic, itinerant, transient.

mi·grate /ˈmīˌgrāt/ ▶ v. (**migrates**, **migrating**, **migrated**) **1** (of an animal) move to warmer regions in the winter and back to colder regions in the summer. **2** move to settle in a new area in order to find work. ■ **mi·gra·tion** /mīˈgrāsʜən/ n. **mi·gra·to·ry** /ˈmīgrəˌtôrē/ adj.

mike /mīk/ ▶ n. informal a microphone.

mi·la·dy /məˈlādē, mī-/ ▶ n. historical or humorous used to address or refer to an English noblewoman.

milch /milk, milcʜ/ ▶ adj. (of an animal) giving or kept for milk.

mild /mīld/ ▶ adj. **1** not severe or harsh. **2** (of weather) fairly warm. **3** not sharp or strong in flavor. **4** (of a person or their behavior) calm and gentle.

SYNONYMS **1** **gentle**, tender, soft, sympathetic, peaceable, good-natured, quiet, placid, docile, meek. **2** *a mild punishment* **lenient**, light. **3** **warm**, balmy, temperate, clement. **4** **bland**, tasteless, insipid. ANTONYMS harsh, strong, severe.

■ **mild·ly** adv. **mild·ness** n.

mil·dew /ˈmilˌd(y)o͞o/ ▶ n. a coating of tiny fungi on plants or damp material such as paper or leather. ■ **mil·dewed** adj.

mile /mīl/ ▶ n. **1** a unit of length equal to 1,760 yards (approximately 1.609 kilometers). **2** (**miles**) informal a very long way.

mile·age /ˈmīlij/ ▶ n. **1** a number of miles covered. **2** informal advantage.

mile·stone /ˈmīlˌstōn/ ▶ n. **1** a stone set up beside a road, marking the distance in miles to a place further along the road. **2** an event marking a significant new development or stage.

mi·lieu /milˈyo͞o, -ˈyə(r)/ ▶ n. (plural **milieux** or **milieus**) the social environment that you live or work in.

mil·i·tant /ˈmilətənt/ ▶ adj. supporting a cause in a forceful and aggressive way. ▶ n. a militant person.

SYNONYMS ▶ adj. **hard-line**, extreme, extremist, committed, zealous, fanatical, radical. ▶ n. **activist**, extremist, partisan, radical, zealot.

■ **mil·i·tan·cy** n. **mil·i·tant·ly** adv.

mil·i·ta·rism /ˈmilətəˌrizəm/ ▶ n. a belief in the value of military strength. ■ **mil·i·ta·rist** n. & adj. **mil·i·ta·ris·tic** /ˌmilətəˈristik/ adj.

mil·i·tar·ized /ˈmilətəˌrīzd/ ▶ adj. supplied with soldiers and military equipment.

mil·i·tar·y /ˈmiləˌterē/ ▶ adj. having to do with soldiers or armed forces. ▶ n. (**the military**) the armed forces of a country.

SYNONYMS ▶ adj. **fighting**, service, army, armed, defense, martial. ANTONYMS civilian. ▶ n. (**armed**) **forces**, services, militia, army, navy, air force, marines.

■ **mil·i·tar·i·ly** /ˌmiləˈte(ə)rəlē/ adv.

mil·i·tate /ˈmiləˌtāt/ ▶ v. (**militates**, **militating**, **militated**) (**militate against**) make it very difficult for something to happen or exist.

SYNONYMS **work against**, hinder, discourage, be prejudicial to, be detrimental to.

USAGE

Don't confuse **militate** with **mitigate**, which means 'make something bad less severe.'

mi·li·tia /məˈlisʜə/ ▶ n. **1** a group of people who are not professional soldiers but who act as an army. **2** a rebel force opposing a regular army. ■ **mi·li·tia·man** n.

milk /milk/ ▶ n. **1** a white fluid produced by female mammals to feed their young. **2** the milk of cows as a food and drink for humans. **3** the milklike juice of certain plants. ▶ v. **1** draw milk from an animal. **2** take money from someone dishonestly and over a period of time. **3** take full advantage of a situation.

SYNONYMS ▶ v. **exploit**, take advantage of; informal bleed (dry), squeeze, fleece.

□ **milk chocolate** solid chocolate made with milk. **milk tooth** a temporary tooth in a child or young mammal.

milk·maid /ˈmilkˌmād/ ▶ n. old use a girl or woman who worked in a dairy.

milk·man /ˈmilkmən, -ˌman/ ▶ n. (plural **milkmen**) a man who delivers milk to houses.

milk·shake /ˈmilkˌsʜāk/ ▶ n. a cold drink made from milk whisked with ice cream or a flavoring.

milk·sop /ˈmilkˌsäp/ ▶ n. a timid person.

milk·y /ˈmilkē/ ▶ adj. **1** containing milk. **2** having a soft white color or clouded appearance. □ **Milky Way** the galaxy of which our solar system is a part, visible at night as a faint band of light crossing the sky. ■ **milk·i·ly** adv. **milk·i·ness** n.

mill /mil/ ▶ n. **1** a building equipped with machinery for grinding grain into flour. **2** a device for grinding coffee beans, peppercorns, etc. **3** a building fitted with machinery for a manufacturing process. ▶ v. **1** grind something in a mill. **2** cut or shape metal with a rotating tool. **3** (**milled**) (of a coin) having ribbed markings on the edge. **4** (**mill about** or **around**) move around in a confused mass.

SYNONYMS ▶ n. **factory**, plant, works, workshop, shop, foundry. ▶ v. **grind**, pulverize, powder, granulate, pound, crush, press.

□ **mill wheel** a wheel used to drive a watermill.

mil·len·ni·um /məˈlenēəm/ ▶ n. (plural **millennia** /-nēə/ or **millenniums**) **1** a period of a thousand years. **2** (**the millennium**) the point at which one period of a thousand years ends and another begins. **3** an anniversary of a thousand years. ■ **mil·len·ni·al** adj.

SPELLING

Double **l**, double **n**: millennium.

mill·er /ˈmilər/ ▶ n. a person who owns or works in a grain mill.

mil·let /'milit/ ▶ **n.** a cereal plant used to make flour or alcoholic drinks.

mil·li·bar /'milə,bär/ ▶ **n.** a unit for measuring the pressure of the atmosphere.

mil·li·gram /'milə,gram/ ▶ **n.** one thousandth of a gram.

mil·li·li·ter /'milə,lētər/ ▶ **n.** one thousandth of a liter.

mil·li·me·ter /'milə,mētər/ ▶ **n.** one thousandth of a meter.

mil·li·ner /'milənər/ ▶ **n.** a person who makes or sells women's hats. ■ **mil·li·ner·y** **n.**

mil·lion /'milyən/ ▶ **cardinal number** (plural **millions** or (with another word or number) **million**) **1** a thousand times a thousand; 1,000,000. **2** (also **millions**) informal a very large number or amount. ■ **mil·lionth** **ordinal number.**

mil·lion·aire /,milyə'ne(ə)r, 'milyə,ne(ə)r/ ▶ **n.** a person whose money and property are worth one million dollars or pounds or more.

SPELLING
Just one n: millionaire.

mil·li·pede /'milə,pēd/ ▶ **n.** an insectlike creature with a long body and a lot of legs.

mil·li·sec·ond /'milə,sekənd/ ▶ **n.** one thousandth of a second.

mill·pond /'mil,pänd/ ▶ **n.** **1** a pool created to provide the water that turns the wheel of a watermill. **2** a very still and calm stretch of water.

mill·stone /'mil,stōn/ ▶ **n.** **1** each of a pair of circular stones used for grinding grain. **2** a heavy responsibility that you cannot escape from.

mime /mīm/ ▶ **n.** the use of silent gestures and facial expressions to tell a story or show feelings. ▶ **v.** (**mimes**, **miming**, **mimed**) **1** use mime to tell a story or show feelings. **2** pretend to sing or play an instrument as a recording is being played.

mim·e·o·graph /'mimēə,graf/ ▶ **n.** a machine that produces copies from a stencil, now superseded by the photocopier.

mim·ic /'mimik/ ▶ **v.** (**mimics**, **mimicking**, **mimicked**) **1** imitate the voice or actions of someone else. **2** (of an animal or plant) take on the appearance of another in order to hide or for protection. ▶ **n.** a person skilled in mimicking others.

SYNONYMS ▶ **v.** **imitate**, copy, impersonate, do an impression of, ape, caricature, parody. ▶ **n.** **impersonator**, impressionist; informal copycat.

■ **mim·ic·ry** **n.**

mi·mo·sa /mi'mōsə, mī-, -zə/ ▶ **n.** **1** an acacia tree with delicate leaves and yellow flowers. **2** champagne mixed with orange juice.

min. ▶ **abbr.** **1** minute (of time). **2** minimum.

min·a·ret /,minə'ret/ ▶ **n.** a slender tower of a mosque, with a balcony from which Muslims are called to prayer.

min·a·to·ry /'minə,tôrē, 'mī-/ ▶ **adj.** formal threatening.

mince /mins/ ▶ **v.** **1** cut and mix meat into a coarse paste by machine. **2** walk with short, quick steps and swinging hips.

SYNONYMS **grind**, chop up, cut up, dice, crumble, hash.

□ **not mince your words** speak plainly.

mince·meat /'mins,mēt/ ▶ **n.** a mixture of dried fruit, candied peel, sugar, spices, and suet.

mind /mīnd/ ▶ **n.** **1** the faculty of consciousness and thought. **2** a person's intellect or memory. **3** a person's attention or will. ▶ **v.** **1** be upset or annoyed by. **2** remember or take care to do. **3** watch out for. **4** temporarily take care of. **5** (**be minded**) be inclined to do.

SYNONYMS ▶ **n.** **1** **brain**, intelligence, intellect, brains, brainpower, wits, understanding, reasoning, judgment, sense, head; informal gray matter, smarts. **2** **attention**, thoughts, concentration. **3** **sanity**, mental faculties, senses, wits, reason, reasoning, judgment. **4** **intellect**, thinker, brain, scholar, genius. ▶ **v.** **1** **object**, care, be bothered, be annoyed, be upset, take offense, disapprove, look askance; informal give/care a damn. **2** **be careful of**, watch out for, look out for, beware of. **3** **look after**, take care of, keep an eye on, watch, attend to, care for.

□ **bear something in mind** remember and take something into account. **be of one mind** share the same opinion. **give someone a piece of your mind** rebuke someone. **have a** (or **a good** or **half a**) **mind to do** be inclined to do. **have something in mind** **1** be thinking of something. **2** intend to do something. **in your mind's eye** in your imagination. **mind-numbing** **1** so powerful as to prevent normal thought. **2** tediously dull. **mind your Ps & Qs** be careful to be polite and avoid giving offense. **mind you** used to add something to what you have just said, to soften or change it slightly. **out of your mind** not thinking sensibly; crazy. **to my mind** in my opinion.

mind·ed /'mīndid/ ▶ **adj.** inclined to think in a particular way.

mind·er /'mīndər/ ▶ **n.** a person whose job is to take care of or protect someone or something.

mind·ful /'mīndfəl/ ▶ **adj.** (**mindful of** or **that**) aware of or recognizing that.

mind·less /'mīn(d)lis/ ▶ **adj.** **1** acting or done without good reason and with no concern for the consequences. **2** (of an activity) simple and repetitive.

SYNONYMS **1** **stupid**, idiotic, brainless, asinine, witless, empty-headed; informal dumb, dopey, dim, halfwitted, fatheaded, boneheaded. **2** **unthinking**, thoughtless, senseless, gratuitous, wanton, indiscriminate. **3** **mechanical**, routine, tedious, boring, monotonous, mind-numbing.

■ **mind·less·ly** **adv.**

mind·set /'mīnd,set/ ▶ **n.** a person's particular way of thinking and set of beliefs.

mine¹ /mīn/ ▶ **possessive pron.** referring to a thing or things belonging to or associated with the person speaking. ▶ **possessive determiner** old use my.

mine² ▶ **n.** **1** a hole or channel dug in the earth for extracting coal or other minerals. **2** an abundant source. **3** a type of bomb placed on or in the ground or water, which explodes on contact. ▶ **v.** (**mines**, **mining**, **mined**) **1** obtain coal or other minerals from a mine. **2** lay explosive mines on or in.

SYNONYMS ▶ **n.** **1** **pit**, colliery, excavation, quarry. **2** *a mine of information* **store**, storehouse, reservoir, repository, gold mine, treasure house, treasury. ▶ **v.** **quarry**, excavate, dig, extract.

mine·field /ˈmīnˌfēld/ ▶ **n.** **1** an area planted with explosive mines. **2** a subject or situation presenting unseen dangers.

min·er /ˈmīnər/ ▶ **n.** a person who works in a mine.

min·er·al /ˈmin(ə)rəl/ ▶ **n.** **1** a solid substance occurring naturally, such as copper and silicon. **2** an inorganic substance needed by the human body for good health, such as calcium and iron. ▫ **mineral water** water from a natural spring, containing dissolved mineral salts.

min·er·al·o·gy /ˌminəˈräləjē, -ˈral-/ ▶ **n.** the scientific study of minerals. ■ **min·er·al·og·i·cal** /ˌmin(ə)rəˈläjikəl/ **adj.** **min·er·al·o·gist** **n.**

mine·shaft /ˈmīnˌsʜaft/ ▶ **n.** a deep, narrow shaft that gives access to a mine.

min·e·stro·ne /ˌminəˈstrōnē/ ▶ **n.** an Italian soup containing vegetables and pasta.

mine·sweep·er /ˈmīnˌswēpər/ ▶ **n.** a warship equipped for detecting and removing or destroying explosive mines.

min·gle /ˈmiɴɢgəl/ ▶ **v.** (**mingles**, **mingling**, **mingled**) mix together.

> SYNONYMS **1 mix**, blend, intermingle, intermix, interweave, interlace, combine, merge, fuse, unite, join, amalgamate. **2 socialize**, circulate, associate, fraternize, get together; informal hobnob. ANTONYMS separate.

min·i /ˈminē/ ▶ **adj.** very small of its kind. ▶ **n.** (plural **minis**) a very short skirt.

min·i·a·ture /ˈmin(ē)əcʜər, -ˌcʜo͝or/ ▶ **adj.** of a much smaller size than normal. ▶ **n.** **1** a thing that is much smaller than normal. **2** a tiny, detailed portrait or picture.

> SYNONYMS ▶ **adj.** **small**, mini, little, small-scale, baby, toy, pocket, diminutive, vest-pocket; informal pint-sized. ANTONYMS giant.

> **SPELLING**
>
> Don't forget the **a** in the middle: miniature.

min·i·a·tur·ist /ˈmin(ē)əˌcʜo͝orist, -cʜərist/ ▶ **n.** an artist who paints miniatures.

min·i·a·tur·ize /ˈmin(ē)əcʜəˌrīz/ ▶ **v.** (**miniaturizes**, **miniaturizing**, **miniaturized**) make a smaller version of.

min·i·bar /ˈminēˌbär/ ▶ **n.** a small refrigerator in a hotel room containing a selection of drinks and sometimes snacks.

min·i·bus /ˈminēˌbəs/ ▶ **n.** a small bus for about ten to fifteen passengers.

min·i·disc /ˈminēˌdisk/ ▶ **n.** a disc similar to a small CD but able to record sound or data as well as play it back.

min·i·mal /ˈminəməl/ ▶ **adj.** of a minimum amount, quantity, or degree.

> SYNONYMS **very little**, very small, minimum, the least (possible), nominal, token, negligible. ANTONYMS maximum.

■ **min·i·mal·ly** **adv.**

min·i·mal·ist /ˈminəməlist/ ▶ **adj.** **1** (of art) using simple forms and structures. **2** deliberately simple or basic in design. ▶ **n.** an artist who uses simple forms and structures. ■ **min·i·mal·ism** **n.**

min·i·mize /ˈminəˌmīz/ ▶ **v.** (**minimizes**, **minimizing**, **minimized**) **1** make something as small as possible. **2** represent something as less important or significant than it really is.

> SYNONYMS **1 keep down**, keep to a minimum, reduce, decrease, cut (down), lessen, curtail, prune; informal slash. **2 belittle**, make light of, play down, underrate, downplay, undervalue. ANTONYMS maximize, exaggerate.

min·i·mum /ˈminəməm/ ▶ **n.** (plural **minima** /-mə/ or **minimums**) the smallest amount, extent, or strength possible. ▶ **adj.** smallest in amount, extent, or strength.

> SYNONYMS ▶ **n.** **lowest level**, lower limit, rock bottom, least, lowest. ▶ **adj.** **minimal**, least, smallest, least possible, slightest, lowest. ANTONYMS maximum.

min·ion /ˈminyən/ ▶ **n.** a worker or assistant who has a low or unimportant status.

min·i·se·ries /ˈminēˌsi(ə)rēz/ ▶ **n.** a television drama shown in a small number of episodes.

min·i·skirt /ˈminēˌskərt/ ▶ **n.** a very short skirt.

min·is·ter /ˈminəstər/ ▶ **n.** **1** a person who carries out religious duties in the Christian church. **2** (in some countries) a head of a government department. **3** a person who represents their government in a foreign country. ▶ **v.** (**ministers**, **ministering**, **ministered**) (**minister to**) attend to the needs of.

> SYNONYMS ▶ **n.** **1 member of the government**, member of the cabinet, secretary. **2 clergyman**, clergywoman, cleric, pastor, rector, priest, parson, vicar, curate; informal reverend, padre. ▶ **v.** *doctors **ministered to** the injured* **tend to**, care for, take care of, look after, nurse, treat, attend to, see to, help.

■ **min·is·te·ri·al** /ˌminəˈsti(ə)rēəl/ **adj.**

min·is·tra·tions /ˌminəˈstrāsʜənz/ ▶ **pl.n.** the providing of help or care.

min·is·try /ˈminəstrē/ ▶ **n.** (plural **ministries**) **1** the work of a minister in the Christian church. **2** (in some countries) a government department headed by a minister.

> SYNONYMS **1 department**, bureau, agency, office. **2 the priesthood**, holy orders, the church.

min·i·van /ˈminēˌvan/ ▶ **n.** a small van fitted with seats for passengers.

mink /miɴɢk/ ▶ **n.** a small stoatlike animal that is farmed for its fur.

min·now /ˈminō/ ▶ **n.** a small freshwater fish.

mi·nor /ˈmīnər/ ▶ **adj.** **1** not important or serious. **2** Music (of a scale) having intervals of a semitone between the second and third, fifth and sixth, and seventh and eighth notes. ▶ **n.** a person under the age of full legal responsibility.

> SYNONYMS ▶ **adj.** **1 slight**, small, unimportant, insignificant, inconsequential, negligible, trivial, trifling, paltry, petty, nickel-and-dime; informal piffling. **2** *a minor poet* **little known**, unknown, lesser, unimportant, obscure, minor-league; informal small-time, two-bit. ANTONYMS major, important. ▶ **n.** **child**, infant, youth, adolescent, teenager, boy, girl; informal kid. ANTONYMS adult.

▫ **minor league** a league below the level of a major league in a professional sport, especially baseball.

mi·nor·i·ty /məˈnôrətē/ ▶ **n.** (plural **minorities**) **1** the smaller number or part. **2** a relatively small group of people differing from the majority in race, religion, etc.

min·strel /ˈminstrəl/ ▶ **n.** a medieval singer or musician.

mint¹ /mint/ ▶ **n. 1** a sweet-smelling plant, used as an herb in cooking. **2** the flavor of mint. **3** a peppermint candy. ■ **mint·y adj.**

mint² ▶ **n. 1** a place where money is made. **2** (**a mint**) informal a large sum of money. ▶ **v.** make a coin by stamping metal.

> SYNONYMS ▶ **v. coin**, stamp, strike, cast, make, manufacture.

□ **in mint condition** new, or as good as new.

min·u·et /ˌminyo͞oˈet/ ▶ **n.** a ballroom dance popular in the 18th century.

mi·nus /ˈmīnəs/ ▶ **prep. 1** with the subtraction of. **2** (of temperature) falling below zero by. **3** informal lacking. ▶ **adj. 1** (before a number) below zero. **2** (after a grade) slightly below. **3** having a negative electric charge. ▶ **n. 1** (also **minus sign**) the symbol –, indicating subtraction or a negative value. **2** informal a disadvantage.

mi·nus·cule /ˈminəˌskyo͞ol, minˈəsˌkyo͞ol/ ▶ **adj.** very tiny.

> SPELLING
>
> Write -u-, not -i-, in the middle: minuscule.

mi·nute¹ /ˈminit/ ▶ **n. 1** a period of time equal to sixty seconds or a sixtieth of an hour. **2** (**a minute**) informal a very short time. **3** a measurement of an angle equal to one sixtieth of a degree.

> SYNONYMS **moment**, short time, little while, second, instant; informal sec, jiffy.

mi·nute² /mīˈn(y)o͞ot, mə-/ ▶ **adj.** (**minutest**) **1** very small. **2** precise and careful.

> SYNONYMS **1 tiny**, minuscule, microscopic, miniature; informal teeny, teensy, teeny-weeny, teensy-weensy. **2** *minute detail* **exhaustive**, painstaking, meticulous, rigorous, thorough. ANTONYMS huge.

■ **mi·nute·ly adv.**

mi·nute³ /ˈminit/ ▶ **n. 1** (**minutes**) a written summary of the points discussed at a meeting. **2** an official written message. ▶ **v.** (**minutes, minuting, minuted**) record the points discussed at a meeting.

> SYNONYMS ▶ **n.** (**minutes**) **record**(**s**), proceedings, log, notes, transcript, summary.

min·ute·man /ˈminətˌman/ ▶ **n.** (plural **minutemen**) (during the American Revolution) an American militiaman who volunteered to be ready for service at a minute's notice.

mi·nu·ti·ae /məˈn(y)o͞osнēˌē, -sнēˌī/ ▶ **pl.n.** small or precise details.

minx /mingks/ ▶ **n.** a impudent, cunning, or flirtatious girl or young woman.

mir·a·cle /ˈmirikəl/ ▶ **n. 1** a welcome event that is so extraordinary that it is thought to be the work of God or a saint. **2** an outstanding example or achievement.

> SYNONYMS **wonder**, marvel, sensation, phenomenon.

□ **miracle play** a medieval play based on stories from the Bible.

mi·rac·u·lous /məˈrakyələs/ ▶ **adj.** like a miracle; very surprising and welcome.

> SYNONYMS **amazing**, astounding, remarkable, extraordinary, incredible, unbelievable, sensational, phenomenal, inexplicable.

■ **mi·rac·u·lous·ly adv.**

mi·rage /məˈräzн/ ▶ **n. 1** an effect caused by hot air, in which a sheet of water seems to appear in a desert or on a hot road. **2** something that appears real or possible but is not in fact so.

Mi·ran·da rights /məˈrandə/ ▶ **pl.n.** the rights to have an attorney and to remain silent under questioning, explained to someone being taken into police custody.

mire /mīr/ ▶ **n. 1** a stretch of swampy or boggy ground. **2** a difficult situation from which it is hard to escape. ▶ **v.** (**be mired**) **1** become stuck in mud. **2** be in a difficult situation.

mir·ror /ˈmirər/ ▶ **n. 1** a surface that reflects a clear image. **2** something that accurately represents something else. ▶ **v.** reflect.

> SYNONYMS ▶ **v. reflect**, match, reproduce, imitate, copy, mimic, echo, parallel.

□ **mirror image** an image that is identical in form to another but is reversed, as if seen in a mirror.

mirth /mərтн/ ▶ **n.** laughter. ■ **mirth·ful adj.**

mis·ad·ven·ture /ˌmisədˈvencнər/ ▶ **n. 1** (also **death by misadventure**) Law death caused accidentally and not involving crime. **2** a mishap.

mis·al·li·ance /ˌmisəˈlīəns/ ▶ **n.** an unsuitable or unhappy relationship or marriage.

mis·an·thrope /ˈmisənˌтнrōp, ˈmiz-/ (or **misanthropist**) ▶ **n.** a person who dislikes and avoids other people. ■ **mis·an·throp·ic** /ˌmisənˈтнräpik/ **adj.** **mis·an·thro·py** /misˈanтнrəpē/ **n.**

mis·ap·pre·hen·sion /ˌmisˌapriˈhensнən/ ▶ **n.** a mistaken belief.

mis·ap·pro·pri·ate /ˌmisəˈprōprēˌāt/ ▶ **v.** (**misappropriates, misappropriating, misappropriated**) dishonestly take something for your own use.

> SYNONYMS **embezzle**, expropriate, steal, thieve, pilfer, pocket, help yourself to; informal swipe, rip off.

■ **mis·ap·pro·pri·a·tion** /-ˌprōprēˈāsнən/ **n.**

mis·be·got·ten /ˌmisbəˈgätn/ ▶ **adj.** badly thought out or planned.

mis·be·have /ˌmisbiˈhāv/ ▶ **v.** (**misbehaves, misbehaving, misbehaved**) behave badly.

> SYNONYMS **behave badly**, be naughty, be disobedient, get up to mischief, get up to no good, be rude; informal carry on, act up.

■ **mis·be·hav·ior n.**

mis·cal·cu·late /misˈkalkyəˌlāt/ ▶ **v.** (**miscalculates, miscalculating, miscalculated**) calculate or assess wrongly. ■ **mis·cal·cu·la·tion** /ˌmisˌkalkyəˈlāsнən/ **n.**

mis·car·riage /misˈkarij, ˈmisˌkarij/ ▶ **n.** the birth of a baby or fetus before it is able to survive outside the mother's uterus. □ **miscarriage of justice** a situation in which a court of law fails to achieve justice.

mis·car·ry /misˈkarē, ˈmisˌkarē/ ▶ **v.** (**miscarries, miscarrying, miscarried**) **1** (of a pregnant woman) have a miscarriage. **2** (of a plan) fail.

mis·cast /misˈkast/ ▶ **v.** (**be miscast**) (of an actor) be given an unsuitable role.

mis·cel·la·ne·ous /ˌmisəˈlānēəs/ ▶ **adj.** consisting of many different kinds.

SYNONYMS **various**, varied, different, assorted, mixed, sundry, diverse, disparate, heterogeneous.

mis·cel·la·ny /ˈmisəˌlānē/ ▶ **n.** (plural **miscellanies**) a collection of different things.

mis·chance /misˈcʜans/ ▶ **n.** bad luck.

mis·chief /ˈmiscʜif/ ▶ **n. 1** playful bad behavior that does not cause serious damage or harm. **2** harm caused by someone or something.

SYNONYMS **naughtiness**, bad behavior, misbehavior, misconduct, disobedience, wrongdoing; informal monkey business, shenanigans.

mis·chie·vous /ˈmiscʜivəs/ ▶ **adj. 1** causing mischief. **2** intended to cause trouble.

SYNONYMS **1 naughty**, bad, badly behaved, troublesome, disobedient, rascally. **2 playful**, wicked, impish, roguish. ANTONYMS well behaved.

■ **mis·chie·vous·ly adv.**

SPELLING

The ending is **-ous**, not **-ious**: mischiev**ous**.

mis·ci·ble /ˈmisəbəl/ ▶ **adj.** (of liquids) able to be mixed together.

mis·con·ceived /ˌmiskənˈsēvd/ ▶ **adj.** badly judged or planned.

mis·con·cep·tion /ˌmiskənˈsepsʜən/ ▶ **n.** a failure to understand something correctly.

SYNONYMS **misapprehension**, misunderstanding, mistake, error, misinterpretation, misconstruction, misreading, misjudgment, misbelief, miscalculation, false impression, illusion, fallacy, delusion.

mis·con·duct /misˈkänˌdəkt/ ▶ **n.** bad behavior.

SYNONYMS **1 wrongdoing**, criminality, unprofessionalism, malpractice, negligence, impropriety; formal maladministration. **2 misbehavior**, bad behavior, mischief, misdeeds, naughtiness.

mis·con·struc·tion /ˌmiskənˈstrəksʜən/ ▶ **n.** a failure to interpret something correctly.

mis·con·strue /ˌmiskənˈstro͞o/ ▶ **v.** (**misconstrues**, **misconstruing**, **misconstrued**) interpret something wrongly.

mis·cre·ant /ˈmiskrēənt/ ▶ **n.** a person who behaves badly or unlawfully.

mis·deed /misˈdēd/ ▶ **n.** a bad or evil act.

mis·de·mean·or /ˈmisdiˌmēnər/ ▶ **n.** an action that is bad or unacceptable, but does not amount to a serious crime.

SYNONYMS **wrongdoing**, crime, felony; misdeed, misconduct, offense, error, peccadillo, transgression, sin; old use trespass.

mis·di·ag·nose /misˈdī-igˌnōs, -ˌnōz/ ▶ **v.** (**misdiagnoses**, **misdiagnosing**, **misdiagnosed**) diagnose something incorrectly. ■ **mis·di·ag·no·sis** /ˌmisˌdī-igˈnōsəs/ **n.**

mis·di·rect /ˌmisdəˈrekt, -dī-/ ▶ **v.** direct or instruct wrongly. ■ **mis·di·rec·tion n.**

mi·ser /ˈmīzər/ ▶ **n.** a person who hoards wealth and spends as little as possible.

SYNONYMS **penny-pincher**, Scrooge; informal skinflint, cheapskate, tightwad. ANTONYMS spendthrift.

mis·er·a·ble /ˈmiz(ə)rəbəl/ ▶ **adj. 1** very unhappy or depressed. **2** causing unhappiness or discomfort. **3** (of a person) gloomy and humorless. **4** very small or inadequate.

SYNONYMS **1 unhappy**, sad, sorrowful, melancholy, dejected, depressed, downhearted, downcast, despondent, disconsolate, wretched, glum, gloomy, forlorn, woebegone, mournful; informal blue, down in the dumps. **2** *their miserable surroundings* **dreary**, dismal, gloomy, drab, wretched, depressing, grim, cheerless, bleak, desolate. ANTONYMS cheerful, lovely.

■ **mis·er·a·bly adv.**

mis·er·i·cord /məˈzeriˌkôrd/ ▶ **n.** a ledge projecting from the underside of a hinged seat in the choir of a church, giving support to someone standing when the seat is folded up.

mi·ser·ly /ˈmīzərlē/ ▶ **adj. 1** not willing to spend money. **2** (of a quantity) too small.

SYNONYMS **mean**, parsimonious, close-fisted, penny-pinching, grasping, niggardly, cheese-paring; informal stingy, tight, tightfisted, cheap. ANTONYMS generous.

■ **mi·ser·li·ness n.**

mis·er·y /ˈmiz(ə)rē/ ▶ **n.** (plural **miseries**) **1** great unhappiness. **2** a cause of this.

SYNONYMS **unhappiness**, distress, wretchedness, suffering, angst, anguish, anxiety, torment, pain, grief, heartache, heartbreak, despair, despondency, dejection, depression, gloom, sorrow; informal the blues. ANTONYMS contentment, pleasure.

mis·fire /misˈfīr/ ▶ **v.** (**misfires**, **misfiring**, **misfired**) **1** (of a gun) fail to fire properly. **2** (of an internal combustion engine) fail to ignite the fuel correctly. **3** fail to produce the intended result.

mis·fit /ˈmisˌfit/ ▶ **n.** a person whose attitudes and actions set them apart from other people.

mis·for·tune /misˈfôrcʜən/ ▶ **n. 1** bad luck. **2** an unfortunate event.

SYNONYMS **problem**, difficulty, setback, trouble, adversity, (stroke of) bad luck, misadventure, mishap, blow, failure, accident, disaster, trial, tribulation.

mis·giv·ings /misˈgiviNGz/ ▶ **pl.n.** feelings of doubt or worry.

SYNONYMS **qualms**, doubts, reservations; suspicions, second thoughts; trepidation, skepticism, unease, anxiety, apprehension, disquiet.

mis·guid·ed /misˈgīdid/ ▶ **adj.** badly judged.

SYNONYMS **unwise**, foolish, ill-advised, ill-judged, ill-considered, injudicious, imprudent, unsound, mistaken, misplaced. ANTONYMS wise.

mis·han·dle /misˈhandəl/ ▶ **v.** (**mishandles**, **mishandling**, **mishandled**) handle a situation badly or wrongly.

mis·hap /ˈmisˌhap/ ▶ **n.** an unlucky accident.

SYNONYMS **accident**, trouble, problem, difficulty, setback, adversity, misfortune, blow, disaster, tragedy, catastrophe, calamity.

mis·hear /mis'hi(ə)r/ ▶ **v.** (**mishears**, **mishearing**, **misheard**) hear incorrectly.

mis·hit /ˌmis'hit/ ▶ **v.** (**mishits**, **mishitting**, **mishit**) hit or kick a ball badly.

mish·mash /'misʜˌmasʜ, -ˌmäsʜ/ ▶ **n.** a confused mixture.

mis·in·form /ˌmisin'fôrm/ ▶ **v.** give someone false or inaccurate information. ■ **mis·in·for·ma·tion** /ˌmisinfər'māsʜən/ **n.**

mis·in·ter·pret /ˌmisin'tərprət/ ▶ **v.** (**misinterprets**, **misinterpreting**, **misinterpreted**) interpret something wrongly. ■ **mis·in·ter·pre·ta·tion** /-inˌtərprə'tāsʜən/ **n.**

mis·judge /ˌmis'jəj/ ▶ **v.** (**misjudges**, **misjudging**, **misjudged**) **1** form a wrong opinion about. **2** estimate wrongly. ■ **mis·judg·ment** (or **misjudgement**) **n.**

mis·lay /mis'lā/ ▶ **v.** (**mislays**, **mislaying**, **mislaid**) lose something because you have forgotten where you put it.

SYNONYMS **lose**, misplace, be unable to find. ANTONYMS find.

mis·lead /mis'lēd/ ▶ **v.** (**misleads**, **misleading**, **misled** /mis'led/) give someone a wrong impression or wrong information.

SYNONYMS **1 deceive**, delude, take in, lie to, fool, hoodwink, misinform; informal lead up the garden path, take for a ride, give someone a bum steer. **2** (**misleading**) **deceptive**, confusing, deceiving, equivocal, false.

mis·man·age /mis'manij/ ▶ **v.** (**mismanages**, **mismanaging**, **mismanaged**) manage something badly or wrongly. ■ **mis·man·age·ment n.**

mis·match /'misˌmacʜ/ ▶ **n.** a combination of things or people that do not go together well. ▶ **v.** match people or things unsuitably or incorrectly.

mis·no·mer /mis'nōmər/ ▶ **n. 1** a name or term that is wrong or inaccurate. **2** the wrong use of a name or term.

mi·sog·y·nist /mə'säjənist/ ▶ **n.** a man who hates women. ■ **mi·sog·y·nis·tic** /məˌsäjə'nistik/ **adj.** **mi·sog·y·ny n.**

mis·place /mis'plās/ ▶ **v.** (**misplaces**, **misplacing**, **misplaced**) put in the wrong place.

mis·placed /mis'plāst/ ▶ **adj. 1** wrongly placed. **2** unwise or inappropriate.

mis·print /'misˌprint/ ▶ **n.** a mistake in printed material.

mis·pro·nounce /ˌmisprə'nouns/ ▶ **v.** (**mispronounces**, **mispronouncing**, **mispronounced**) pronounce wrongly. ■ **mis·pro·nun·ci·a·tion** /-prəˌnənsē'āsʜən/ **n.**

mis·quote /mis'kwōt/ ▶ **v.** (**misquotes**, **misquoting**, **misquoted**) quote inaccurately.

mis·read /mis'rēd/ ▶ **v.** (**misreads**, **misreading**, **misread** /mis'red/) read or interpret wrongly.

mis·rep·re·sent /ˌmisˌrepri'zent/ ▶ **v.** give a false or misleading account of. ■ **mis·rep·re·sen·ta·tion** /misˌreprəzən'tāsʜən/ **n.**

mis·rule /mis'ro͞ol/ ▶ **n. 1** bad government. **2** disorder.

miss¹ /mis/ ▶ **v. 1** fail to hit, reach, or come into contact with. **2** be too late for. **3** fail to notice, hear, or understand. **4** fail to be present at. **5** avoid something unpleasant. **6** fail to include someone or something. **7** feel sad because of the absence of. ▶ **n.** a failure to hit, catch, or reach something.

SYNONYMS ▶ **v. 1 go wide of**, fall short of, pass, overshoot. **2 avoid**, beat, evade, escape, dodge, sidestep, elude, circumvent, bypass. **3 pine for**, yearn for, ache for, long for. **4 fail to attend**, be absent from, cut, skip, omit. ANTONYMS hit, catch.

miss² ▶ **n. 1** (**Miss**) a title coming before the name of an unmarried woman or girl. **2** a girl or young woman.

SYNONYMS **young woman**, young lady, girl, schoolgirl; literary maiden, maid, damsel.

mis·sal /'misəl/ ▶ **n.** a book containing the prayers and responses used in the Catholic Mass.

mis·shap·en /mis'sʜāpən/ ▶ **adj.** not having the normal or natural shape.

mis·sile /'misəl/ ▶ **n. 1** an object or weapon that is thrown or fired at a target. **2** a self-propelled weapon carrying explosive.

miss·ing /'misiɴɢ/ ▶ **adj. 1** absent and unable to be found. **2** not present when expected to be.

SYNONYMS **1 lost**, mislaid, misplaced, absent, gone (astray), unaccounted for. **2 absent**, lacking, wanting. ANTONYMS present.

mis·sion /'misʜən/ ▶ **n. 1** an important assignment, typically involving travel abroad. **2** an organization involved in a long-term assignment abroad. **3** a military or scientific expedition. **4** the work of teaching people about Christianity. **5** a strongly felt aim or calling.

SYNONYMS **1 assignment**, commission, expedition, journey, trip, undertaking, operation, project. **2** *her mission in life* **vocation**, calling, goal, aim, quest, purpose, function, task, job, labor, work, duty.

mis·sion·ar·y /'misʜəˌnerē/ ▶ **n.** (plural **missionaries**) a person sent on a religious mission. ▶ **adj.** having to do with a religious mission.

SYNONYMS ▶ **n. evangelist**, apostle, proselytizer, preacher.

mis·sive /'misiv/ ▶ **n.** formal a letter.

mis·spell /mis'spel/ ▶ **v.** (**misspells**, **misspelling**, past and past participle **misspelled** or **misspelt**) spell wrongly.

mis·spend /mis'spend/ ▶ **v.** (**misspends**, **misspending**, **misspent**) spend time or money foolishly.

mis·sus /'misəz, -əs/ (or **missis**) ▶ **n.** informal a person's wife.

miss·y /'misē/ ▶ **n.** (plural **missies**) an affectionate or contemptuous form of address to a young girl.

mist /mist/ ▶ **n.** a thin cloud of tiny water droplets that makes it difficult to see. ▶ **v.** cover or become covered with mist.

SYNONYMS ▶ **n. haze**, fog, smog, murk, cloud, vapor, steam, spray, condensation.

mis·take /mə'stāk/ ▶ **n. 1** a thing that is incorrect. **2** an error of judgment. ▶ **v.** (**mistakes**, **mistaking**, **mistook** /mə'sto͝ok/; past participle **mistaken**) **1** be wrong about. **2** (**mistake someone/thing for**) confuse someone or something with.

SYNONYMS ▶ **n. error**, fault, inaccuracy, omission, slip, blunder, miscalculation, misunderstanding, oversight, misinterpretation, gaffe, faux pas, solecism; informal slip-up, boo-boo, goof, boner.

mis·tak·en /mə'stākən/ ▶ **adj.** **1** wrong in your opinion or judgment. **2** based on a misunderstanding.

SYNONYMS **1 inaccurate**, wrong, erroneous, incorrect, off the beam, false, fallacious, unfounded, misguided. **2 misinformed**, wrong, in error, under a misapprehension, barking up the wrong tree. ANTONYMS correct.

■ **mis·tak·en·ly** adv.

mis·ter /'mistər/ ▶ **n.** **1** (**Mister**) ⇨ **Mr.** **2** informal a form of address to a man.

mis·time /mis'tīm/ ▶ **v.** (**mistimes**, **mistiming**, **mistimed**) choose an inappropriate moment to do or say something.

SYNONYMS (**mistimed**) **ill-timed**, badly timed, inopportune, inappropriate, untimely.

mis·tle·toe /'misəl,tō/ ▶ **n.** a plant that grows as a parasite on trees, producing white berries in winter.

mis·treat /mis'trēt/ ▶ **v.** treat badly or unfairly.

SYNONYMS **ill-treat**, maltreat, abuse, knock about/around, hit, beat, molest, injure, harm, hurt, misuse.

■ **mis·treat·ment** n.

mis·tress /'mistris/ ▶ **n.** **1** a woman in a position of authority. **2** a woman who is very skilled in something. **3** a woman having an intimate relationship with a man who is married to someone else.

mis·tri·al /'mis,trī(ə)l/ ▶ **n.** a trial that is not considered valid because of a mistake in proceedings.

mis·trust /mis'trəst/ ▶ **v.** have no trust in. ▶ **n.** lack of trust.

SYNONYMS ▶ **v.** **be suspicious of**, be skeptical of, be wary of, be chary of, distrust, have doubts about, have misgivings about, have reservations about, suspect.

mist·y /'mistē/ ▶ **adj.** (**mistier**, **mistiest**) **1** covered with mist. **2** having an outline that is not clear.

SYNONYMS **hazy**, foggy, cloudy, blurred, vague, indistinct. ANTONYMS clear.

mis·un·der·stand /,mis,əndər'stand/ ▶ **v.** (**misunderstands**, **misunderstanding**, **misunderstood** /-,əndər'stood/) fail to understand correctly.

SYNONYMS **misapprehend**, misinterpret, misconstrue, misconceive, mistake, misread, be mistaken, get the wrong idea.

mis·un·der·stand·ing /,mis,əndər'standiNG/ ▶ **n.** **1** a failure to understand something correctly. **2** a disagreement with someone.

SYNONYMS **1 misinterpretation**, misreading, misapprehension, misconception, false impression. **2 disagreement**, difference (of opinion), dispute, falling-out, quarrel, argument, clash.

mis·use ▶ **v.** (**misuses**, **misusing**, **misused**) /mis'yo͞oz, 'mis,yo͞oz/ **1** use wrongly. **2** treat badly or unfairly. ▶ **n.** /,mis'yo͞os, 'mis,yo͞os/ the action of misusing.

SYNONYMS ▶ **v.** **put to wrong use**, misapply, misemploy, abuse, squander, waste, dissipate, misappropriate, embezzle.

mite /mīt/ ▶ **n.** **1** a tiny insectlike creature. **2** a small child or animal. **3** a very small amount.

mi·ter /'mītər/ ▶ **n.** **1** a tall headdress that tapers to a point at the front and back, worn by bishops. **2** a joint made between two pieces of wood cut at an angle in order to form a corner of 90°.

mit·i·gate /'mitə,gāt/ ▶ **v.** (**mitigates**, **mitigating**, **mitigated**) make something bad less severe or serious. ■ **mit·i·ga·tion** /,mitə'gāsHən/ **n.**

USAGE

Don't confuse **mitigate** with **militate**: **militate against** means 'make it very difficult for something to happen or exist.'

mitt /mit/ ▶ **n.** **1** a mitten. **2** informal a person's hand.

mit·ten /'mitn/ ▶ **n.** a glove having a single section for all four fingers, with a separate section for the thumb.

mix /miks/ ▶ **v.** **1** combine or be combined to form a whole. **2** make by mixing ingredients. **3** combine different recordings to form one piece of music. **4** (**mix something up**) spoil the arrangement of something. **5** (**mix someone/thing up**) confuse one person or thing with another. **6** meet different people socially. ▶ **n.** **1** a mixture. **2** the proportion of different people or things making up a mixture. **3** a version of a piece of music mixed in a different way from the original.

SYNONYMS ▶ **v.** **1 blend**, mingle, combine, jumble, fuse, unite, join, amalgamate, incorporate, meld, homogenize; technical admix; literary commingle. **2 associate**, socialize, keep company, consort, mingle, circulate, rub elbows; informal hang out/around, hobnob. ANTONYMS separate. ▶ **n.** **mixture**, blend, combination, compound, fusion, union, amalgamation, medley, selection, assortment, variety.

□ **mix-up** informal a misunderstanding or mistake.

mixed /mikst/ ▶ **adj.** **1** made up of different qualities or things. **2** having to do with males and females.

SYNONYMS **1 assorted**, varied, variegated, miscellaneous, disparate, diverse, diversified, motley, sundry, jumbled, heterogeneous. **2** *mixed reactions* **ambivalent**, equivocal, contradictory, conflicting, confused, muddled. ANTONYMS homogeneous.

□ **mixed bag** an assortment of people or things of very different types. **mixed metaphor** a combination of metaphors that don't make sense when combined (e.g., *this tower of strength will forge ahead*).

mix·er /'miksər/ ▶ **n.** **1** a machine or device for mixing things. **2** a soft drink that can be mixed with alcohol. **3** a social gathering where people can make new acquaintances.

mix·ture /'miksCHər/ ▶ **n.** **1** a substance made by mixing other substances together. **2** (**a mixture of**) a combination of different things in which each thing is distinct.

SYNONYMS **1 blend**, mix, brew, combination, concoction, composition, compound, alloy, amalgam. **2 assortment**, miscellany, medley, blend, variety, mixed bag, mix, diversity, collection, selection, hodgepodge, ragbag.

miz·zen /'mizən/ (or **mizzenmast** /'mizən,mast/) ▶ **n.** the mast behind a ship's mainmast.

ml ▶ **abbr.** **1** miles. **2** milliliters.

mm ▶ **abbr.** millimeters.

mne·mon·ic /nə'mänik/ ▶ **n.** a pattern of letters or words used to help remember something. ▶ **adj.** designed to help remember something.

moan /mōn/ ▶ **n.** **1** a low mournful sound, usually expressing suffering. **2** informal a complaint. ▶ **v.** **1** make a moan. **2** complain; grumble.

SYNONYMS ▶ **v.** **1** **groan**, wail, whimper, sob, cry. **2** **complain**, grouse, grumble, whine, carp; informal gripe, grouch, bellyache, bitch, beef.

moat /mōt/ ▶ **n.** a wide defensive ditch surrounding a castle or town.

mob /mäb/ ▶ **n.** **1** a disorderly crowd of people. **2** (**the Mob**) the Mafia. **3** (**the mob**) disapproving the ordinary people. ▶ **v.** (**mobs**, **mobbing**, **mobbed**) (of a large group of people) crowd around someone.

SYNONYMS ▶ **n.** **crowd**, horde, multitude, rabble, mass, throng, gathering, assembly. ▶ **v.** **surround**, crowd round, besiege, jostle.

mo·bile ▶ **adj.** /'mōbəl, 'mō,bēl/ **1** able to move or be moved freely or easily. **2** (of a store, library, etc.) set up inside a vehicle and able to travel around. **3** able to change your occupation, social class, or where you live. **4** (of a person's face) easily changing expression. ▶ **n.** /'mō,bēl/ a decoration that is hung so as to turn freely in the air.

SYNONYMS ▶ **adj.** **1** **able to move**, able to walk, walking; informal up and about. **2** *a mobile library* **traveling**, transportable, portable, movable, itinerant, peripatetic. ANTONYMS immobile, stationary.

□ **mobile home** a large trailer used as permanent living accommodations.

mo·bil·i·ty /mō'bilətē/ ▶ **n.** the quality of being mobile.

mo·bi·lize /'mōbə,līz/ ▶ **v.** (**mobilizes**, **mobilizing**, **mobilized**) **1** organize troops for active service. **2** organize people or resources for a particular task.

SYNONYMS **1** *mobilize the troops* **marshal**, deploy, muster, rally, call up, assemble, mass, organize, prepare. **2** *mobilizing support for the party* **generate**, arouse, awaken, excite, stimulate, stir up, encourage, inspire, whip up.

■ **mo·bi·li·za·tion** /,mōbələ'zāsHən/ **n.**

mob·ster /'mäbstər/ ▶ **n.** informal a gangster.

moc·ca·sin /'mäkəsən/ ▶ **n.** a soft leather shoe with the sole turned up and sewn to the upper, originally worn by North American Indians.

mo·cha /'mōkə/ ▶ **n.** **1** a type of fine-quality coffee. **2** a drink made with coffee and chocolate.

mock /mäk/ ▶ **v.** tease or imitate someone in an unkind way. ▶ **adj.** **1** not genuine or real. **2** (of an exam, battle, etc.) arranged for training or practice.

SYNONYMS ▶ **v.** **1** **ridicule**, jeer at, sneer at, deride, make fun of, laugh at, scoff at, tease, taunt; informal goof on, rag on. **2** (**mocking**) **sneering**, derisive, contemptuous, scornful, sardonic, ironic, sarcastic, satirical. ▶ **adj.** **imitation**, artificial, man-made, simulated, synthetic, ersatz, fake, reproduction, pseudo, false, spurious; informal pretend. ANTONYMS genuine.

□ **mock-up** a model of a machine or structure that is used for teaching or testing.

mock·er·y /'mäk(ə)rē/ ▶ **n.** (plural **mockeries**) **1** unkind teasing; ridicule. **2** (**a mockery of**) an absurd or worthless version of something. □ **make a mockery of** make something seem ridiculous or useless.

mock·ing·bird /'mäkiNG,bərd/ ▶ **n.** a long-tailed songbird, noted for copying the calls of other birds.

mod·al verb /'mōdl/ ▶ **n.** Grammar an auxiliary verb expressing necessity or possibility, e.g., *must*, *shall*, *will*.

mode /mōd/ ▶ **n.** **1** a way in which something occurs or is done. **2** a style in clothes, art, etc. **3** Statistics the value that occurs most frequently in a given set of data.

SYNONYMS **1** **manner**, way, means, method, system, style, approach. **2** *the camera is in manual mode* **function**, position, operation, setting, option.

mod·el /'mädl/ ▶ **n.** **1** a three-dimensional representation of something. **2** something used as an example. **3** a person or thing seen as an excellent example of a quality: *he was a model of self-control.* **4** a person whose job is to display clothes by wearing them. **5** a person who poses for an artist or photographer. **6** a particular design or version of a product. **7** a simplified mathematical description of a system or process. ▶ **v.** (**models**, **modeling**, **modeled**) **1** make a figure in clay, wax, etc. **2** (**model something on**) design or plan something using another thing as an example. **3** work as a fashion model. **4** devise a mathematical model of.

SYNONYMS ▶ **n.** **1** **replica**, copy, representation, mock-up, dummy, imitation, duplicate, reproduction, facsimile. **2** **prototype**, archetype, type, paradigm, version, mold, template, framework, pattern, design, blueprint. **3** *a model teacher* **ideal**, perfect, exemplary, classic, flawless, faultless, nonpareil. **4** **fashion model**, supermodel, mannequin; informal clothes horse.

□ **model home** a new house that is furnished and decorated to be shown to possible buyers.

mo·dem /'mōdəm, 'mō,dem/ ▶ **n.** a device that connects a computer to a telephone line.

mod·er·ate ▶ **adj.** /'mäd(ə)rət/ **1** average in amount, strength, or degree. **2** (of a political position) not extreme. ▶ **n.** /'mäd(ə)rət/ a person with moderate views. ▶ **v.** /'mädə,rāt/ (**moderates**, **moderating**, **moderated**) **1** make or become less extreme or strong. **2** preside over; act as a moderator.

SYNONYMS ▶ **adj.** **1** **average**, modest, medium, middling, tolerable, passable, adequate, fair; informal OK, so-so, bog-standard, fair-to-middling. **2** *moderate prices* **reasonable**, within reason, acceptable, affordable, inexpensive, fair, modest. **3** *moderate views* **middle-of-the-road**, nonextremist, liberal, pragmatic. ANTONYMS immoderate, extreme. ▶ **v.** **1** **die down**, abate, let up, calm down, lessen, decrease, diminish, recede, weaken, subside. **2** **curb**, control, check, temper, restrain, subdue, tame, lessen, decrease, lower, reduce, diminish, alleviate, allay, appease, ease, soothe, calm, tone down. ANTONYMS increase.

mod·er·ate·ly /ˈmäd(ə)rətlē/ ▶ **adv.** to a certain extent.

SYNONYMS **somewhat**, quite, fairly, reasonably, comparatively, relatively, to some extent, tolerably, adequately; informal pretty.

mod·er·a·tion /ˌmädəˈrāsʜən/ ▶ **n. 1** the avoidance of extremes in your actions or opinions. **2** the process of moderating.

mod·er·a·tor /ˈmädəˌrātər/ ▶ **n. 1** a person who helps others to solve a dispute. **2** a chairman of a debate.

mod·ern /ˈmädərn/ ▶ **adj. 1** relating to the present or to recent times. **2** using the most up-to-date techniques or equipment. **3** (of art, architecture, music, etc.) new and intended to be different from traditional styles.

SYNONYMS **1 present-day**, contemporary, present, current, twenty-first-century, latter-day, recent. **2 fashionable**, up to date, trendsetting, stylish, chic, à la mode, the latest, new, newest, newfangled, advanced; informal trendy, cool, in, funky. ANTONYMS past, old-fashioned.

■ **mo·der·ni·ty** /mäˈdərnitē, mə-, -ˈder-/ **n.**

mod·ern·ism /ˈmädərˌnizəm/ ▶ **n. 1** modern ideas, methods, or styles. **2** a movement in the arts or religion that aims to break with traditional forms or ideas. ■ **mod·ern·ist n. & adj.**

mod·ern·ize /ˈmädərˌnīz/ ▶ **v.** (**modernizes**, **modernizing**, **modernized**) bring up to date with modern equipment, techniques, etc.

SYNONYMS **update**, bring up to date, streamline, rationalize, overhaul, renovate, remodel, refashion, revamp.

■ **mod·ern·i·za·tion** /ˌmädərnəˈzāsʜən/ **n.**

mod·est /ˈmädəst/ ▶ **adj. 1** not boasting about your abilities or achievements. **2** relatively moderate, limited, or small. **3** not showing off the body; decent.

SYNONYMS **1 humble**, self-deprecating, self-effacing, unassuming, shy, diffident, reserved, bashful. **2** *modest success* **moderate**, fair, limited, tolerable, passable, adequate, satisfactory, acceptable, unexceptional. **3** *a modest house* **small**, ordinary, simple, plain, humble, inexpensive, unostentatious, unpretentious. **4** *her modest dress* **demure**, decent, seemly, decorous, proper. ANTONYMS conceited, grand, indecent.

■ **mod·est·ly adv.**

mod·es·ty /ˈmädəstē/ ▶ **n.** the quality or state of being humble, decent, or moderate.

SYNONYMS **humility**, self-effacement, shyness, bashfulness, self-consciousness, reserve.

mod·i·cum /ˈmädikəm, ˈmōd-/ ▶ **n.** a small quantity of something.

mod·i·fi·ca·tion /ˌmädəfəˈkāsʜən/ ▶ **n. 1** the action of modifying something. **2** a change made.

SYNONYMS **change**, adjustment, alteration, adaptation, refinement, revision, amendment; informal tweak.

mod·i·fi·er /ˈmädəˌfīər/ ▶ **n. 1** a person or thing that modifies. **2** Grammar a word that qualifies the sense of a noun (e.g., *family* in *a family house*).

mod·i·fy /ˈmädəˌfī/ ▶ **v.** (**modifies**, **modifying**, **modified**) make partial changes to.

SYNONYMS **1 change**, alter, adjust, adapt, amend, revise, refine; informal tweak. **2 moderate**, temper, soften, tone down, qualify.

mod·ish /ˈmōdisʜ/ ▶ **adj.** fashionable.

mod·u·lar /ˈmäjələr/ ▶ **adj.** made up of separate units.

mod·u·late /ˈmäjəˌlāt/ ▶ **v.** (**modulates**, **modulating**, **modulated**) **1** adjust, change, or control something. **2** vary the strength, tone, or pitch of your voice. **3** Music change from one key to another. ■ **mod·u·la·tion** /ˌmäjəˈlāsʜən/ **n.**

mod·ule /ˈmäjo͞ol/ ▶ **n. 1** each of a set of parts or units that can be used to create a more complex structure. **2** a unit forming part of a course of study. **3** an independent unit of a spacecraft.

mo·gul /ˈmōgəl/ ▶ **n.** informal an important or powerful person.

SYNONYMS **magnate**, tycoon, VIP, notable, personage, baron, captain, king, lord; informal bigwig, big shot, big noise, top dog, top banana, big enchilada.

mo·hair /ˈmōˌhe(ə)r/ ▶ **n.** a yarn or fabric made from the hair of the angora goat.

Mo·hawk /ˈmōˌhôk/ ▶ **n. 1** a member of an American Indian people originally inhabiting parts of eastern New York. **2** a hairstyle in which the sides of the head are shaved and a central strip of hair is made to stand up.

moi·e·ty /ˈmoiətē/ ▶ **n.** (plural **moieties**) formal a half.

moist /moist/ ▶ **adj.** slightly wet; damp.

SYNONYMS **1 damp**, steamy, humid, muggy, clammy, dank, wet, soggy, sweaty, sticky. **2 succulent**, juicy, soft, tender. ANTONYMS dry.

mois·ten /ˈmoisən/ ▶ **v.** make or become slightly wet.

SYNONYMS **dampen**, wet, damp, water, humidify.

mois·ture /ˈmoiscʜər/ ▶ **n.** tiny droplets of water making something damp.

SYNONYMS **wetness**, wet, water, liquid, condensation, steam, vapor, dampness, damp, humidity.

mois·tur·ize /ˈmoiscʜəˌrīz/ ▶ **v.** (**moisturizes**, **moisturizing**, **moisturized**) make something, especially the skin, less dry.

mois·tur·iz·er /ˈmoiscʜəˌrīzər/ ▶ **n.** a lotion or cream used to prevent dryness in the skin.

mo·jo /ˈmōˌjō/ ▶ **n.** (plural **mojos**) **1** a magic charm, talisman, or spell. **2** magic power.

mo·lar /ˈmōlər/ ▶ **n.** a grinding tooth at the back of the mouth.

mo·las·ses /məˈlasəz/ ▶ **n.** a thick brown liquid obtained from raw sugar.

mold[1] /mōld/ ▶ **n. 1** a container into which you pour hot liquid in order to produce a solid object of a desired shape when it cools. **2** a distinctive style or character. ▶ **v. 1** form an object of a particular shape out of a soft substance. **2** influence the development of something.

SYNONYMS ▶ n. **1 cast**, die, matrix, form, shape, template, pattern, frame. **2** *an actress in the Hollywood mold* **pattern**, form, type, style, tradition, school. ▶ v. **1 shape**, form, fashion, model, work, construct, make, create, sculpt, cast. **2 determine**, direct, control, guide, influence, shape, form, fashion, make.

mold[2] ▶ n. a furry growth of tiny fungi that occurs typically in moist warm conditions. ■ **mold·y** adj.

mold·board /ˈmōldˌbôrd/ ▶ n. the blade or plate in a plow that turns the earth over.

mold·er /ˈmōldər/ ▶ v. (**molders**, **moldering**, **moldered**) slowly decay.

mold·ing /ˈmōldiNG/ ▶ n. a carved or molded strip of wood, stone, or plaster as a decorative feature on a building.

mole[1] /mōl/ ▶ n. **1** a small burrowing mammal with dark fur, a long muzzle, and very small eyes. **2** someone within an organization who secretly passes confidential information to another organization or country.

mole[2] ▶ n. a dark brown mark on the skin.

mole[3] ▶ n. **1** a pier, breakwater, or causeway. **2** a harbor formed by a mole.

mole[4] ▶ n. Chemistry the amount of a particular substance that contains as many atoms or molecules as there are atoms in a standard amount of carbon.

mol·e·cule /ˈmäləˌkyo͞ol/ ▶ n. a group of atoms forming the smallest unit into which a substance can be divided. ■ **mo·lec·u·lar** /məˈlekyələr/ adj.

mole·hill /ˈmōlˌhil/ ▶ n. a small mound of earth thrown up by a burrowing mole.

mole·skin /ˈmōlˌskin/ ▶ n. **1** the skin of a mole used as fur. **2** a thick cotton fabric with a soft surface.

mo·lest /məˈlest/ ▶ v. **1** assault or abuse someone sexually. **2** dated pester or harass someone in a hostile way.

SYNONYMS **1 harass**, harry, pester, persecute, torment. **2 (sexually) abuse**, (sexually) assault, interfere with, rape, violate; informal grope, paw; literary ravish.

moll /mäl/ ▶ n. informal a gangster's girlfriend.

mol·li·fy /ˈmäləˌfī/ ▶ v. (**mollifies**, **mollifying**, **mollified**) make someone feel less angry.

mol·lusk /ˈmäləsk/ ▶ n. an animal of a group with a soft unsegmented body and often an external shell, such as slugs and snails.

mol·ly·cod·dle /ˈmälēˌkädl/ ▶ v. (**mollycoddles**, **mollycoddling**, **mollycoddled**) treat someone too indulgently or protectively.

molt /mōlt/ ▶ v. shed old feathers, hair, or skin. ▶ n. a period of molting.

mol·ten /ˈmōltn/ ▶ adj. (especially of metal and glass) made liquid by heat.

mol·to /ˈmōlˌtō, ˈmôl-/ ▶ adv. Music very.

mo·lyb·de·num /məˈlibdənəm/ ▶ n. a brittle silver-gray metallic element.

mom /mäm/ ▶ n. informal your mother.

mo·ment /ˈmōmənt/ ▶ n. **1** a brief period of time. **2** an exact point in time. **3** formal importance.

SYNONYMS **1 little while**, short time, bit, minute, instant, (split) second; informal sec, jiffy. **2 point (in time)**, stage, juncture, instant, time, hour, second, minute, day.

mo·men·tar·i·ly /ˌmōmənˈte(ə)rəlē/ ▶ adv. **1** for a very short time. **2** very soon.

SYNONYMS **1** *he paused momentarily* **briefly**, fleetingly, for a moment, for a second, for an instant. **2** *my husband will be here momentarily* **in a moment**, very soon, in a minute, in a second, shortly.

mo·men·tar·y /ˈmōmənˌterē/ ▶ adj. very brief or short-lived.

SYNONYMS **brief**, short, short-lived, fleeting, passing, transitory, transient, ephemeral. ANTONYMS lengthy.

mo·men·tous /mōˈmen(t)əs, məˈ-/ ▶ adj. of great importance or significance.

SYNONYMS **important**, significant, historic, critical, crucial, decisive, pivotal, consequential, far-reaching; informal earth-shattering. ANTONYMS insignificant.

mo·men·tum /mōˈmentəm, mə-/ ▶ n. (plural **momenta** /-tə/) **1** the force gained by a moving object. **2** the force caused by the development of something.

SYNONYMS **impetus**, energy, force, driving force, power, strength, thrust, speed, velocity.

mom·my /ˈmämē/ ▶ n. informal your mother.

mon·arch /ˈmänərk, ˈmänˌärk/ ▶ n. a king, queen, or emperor.

SYNONYMS **sovereign**, ruler, Crown, crowned head, potentate, king, queen, emperor, empress, prince, princess.

■ **mo·nar·chi·cal** /məˈnärkikəl/ adj.

mon·ar·chist /ˈmänərkist/ ▶ n. someone who believes a country should be ruled by a king or queen. ■ **mon·ar·chism** n.

mon·ar·chy /ˈmänərkē, ˈmänˌär-/ ▶ n. (plural **monarchies**) **1** government by a monarch. **2** a state with a monarch.

mon·as·ter·y /ˈmänəˌsterē/ ▶ n. (plural **monasteries**) a community of monks living under religious vows.

SYNONYMS friary, abbey, priory, cloister.

mo·nas·tic /məˈnastik/ ▶ adj. **1** relating to monks or nuns. **2** resembling monks or their way of life.

Mon·day /ˈməndā, -dē/ ▶ n. the day of the week before Tuesday and following Sunday.

mon·e·ta·rism /ˈmänitəˌrizəm, ˈmən-/ ▶ n. the theory that inflation is best controlled by limiting the supply of money. ■ **mon·e·ta·rist** n. & adj.

mon·e·tar·y /ˈmänəˌterē, ˈmən-/ ▶ adj. having to do with money.

SYNONYMS **financial**, fiscal, pecuniary, money, cash, capital, economic, budgetary.

mon·ey /ˈmənē/ ▶ n. **1** a means of paying for things in the form of coins and banknotes. **2** wealth. **3** payment or financial gain. **4** (**moneys** or **monies**) formal sums of money.

SYNONYMS **cash**, hard cash, means, wherewithal, funds, capital, finances, notes, coins, change, currency, specie; informal dough, bread, loot, dinero.

□ **money order** a printed order for payment of a specified sum, issued by a bank or post office. **put your money where your mouth is** informal take action to support your statements.

mon·eyed /ˈmənēd/ (or **monied**) ▶ **adj.** having a lot of money.

Mon·gol /ˈmäNGgəl, -gōl/ ▶ **n. 1** a person from Mongolia. **2** (**mongol**) offensive a person with Down syndrome. ■ **Mon·go·li·an** /mänˈgōlēən, mäNG-/ **n. & adj.**

mon·goose /ˈmän,go͞os, ˈmäNG-/ ▶ **n.** (plural **mongooses**) a small meat-eating animal with a long body and tail, native to Africa and Asia.

mon·grel /ˈmäNGgrəl, ˈməNG-/ ▶ **n.** a dog of no definite breed.

mon·i·ker /ˈmänikər/ ▶ **n.** informal a name.

mon·i·tor /ˈmänətər/ ▶ **n. 1** a person or device that monitors something. **2** a television used to view a picture from a particular camera or a display from a computer. **3** a school student with special duties. **4** (also **monitor lizard**) a large tropical lizard. ▶ **v.** keep under observation.

SYNONYMS ▶ **n. 1 detector**, scanner, recorder, sensor, security camera, CCTV. **2** *UN monitors* **observer**, watchdog, overseer, supervisor, scrutineer. **3** *a computer monitor* **screen**, display, VDU. ▶ **v. observe**, watch, track, keep an eye on, keep under surveillance, record, note, oversee; informal keep tabs on.

monk /məNGk/ ▶ **n.** a man belonging to a religious community typically living under vows of poverty, chastity, and obedience.

mon·key /ˈməNGkē/ ▶ **n.** (plural **monkeys**) a primate typically having a long tail and living in trees in tropical countries. ▶ **v.** (**monkeys**, **monkeying**, **monkeyed**) **1** (**monkey around**) behave in a silly or playful way. **2** (**monkey with**) tamper with.

SYNONYMS ▶ **n. simian**, primate, ape.

□ **monkey puzzle** a coniferous tree with branches covered in spirals of tough spiny leaves. **monkey wrench** a wrench with large adjustable jaws.

mon·o /ˈmänō/ ▶ **n.** sound reproduction that uses only one transmission channel.

mon·o·chrome /ˈmänə,krōm/ ▶ **adj.** (of a photograph or picture) produced in black and white or in varying tones of one color. ■ **mon·o·chro·mat·ic** /,mänəkrōˈmatik/ **adj.**

mon·o·cle /ˈmänikəl/ ▶ **n.** a single lens worn at one eye.

mo·nog·a·my /məˈnägəmē/ ▶ **n.** the practice of having only one wife or husband at any one time. ■ **mo·nog·a·mous adj.**

mon·o·gram /ˈmänə,gram/ ▶ **n.** a motif of two or more interwoven letters, typically a person's initials. ■ **mon·o·grammed adj.**

mon·o·graph /ˈmänə,graf/ ▶ **n.** a book or academic paper written on a single subject.

mon·o·lin·gual /,mänəˈliNGg(yə)wəl/ ▶ **adj.** speaking or expressed in only one language.

mon·o·lith /ˈmänə,liTH/ ▶ **n.** a large single upright block of stone.

mon·o·lith·ic /,mänəˈliTHik/ ▶ **adj. 1** formed of a single large block of stone. **2** very large and impersonal.

mon·o·logue /ˈmänə,lôg, -,läg/ ▶ **n. 1** a long speech by one actor in a play or movie. **2** a long, boring speech by one person.

mon·o·ma·ni·a /,mänəˈmānēə/ ▶ **n.** an obsession with one thing. ■ **mon·o·ma·ni·ac n.**

mon·o·mer /ˈmänəmər/ ▶ **n.** Chemistry a molecule that can be linked to other identical molecules to form a polymer.

mon·o·phon·ic /,mänəˈfänik/ ▶ **adj.** (of sound reproduction) using only one channel. Compare with.

mon·o·plane /ˈmänə,plān/ ▶ **n.** an aircraft with one pair of wings.

mo·nop·o·lize /məˈnäpə,līz/ ▶ **v.** (**monopolizes**, **monopolizing**, **monopolized**) dominate or take control of.

mo·nop·o·ly /məˈnäpəlē/ ▶ **n.** (plural **monopolies**) the complete control of the supply of a product or service by one person or organization.

mon·o·rail /ˈmänə,rāl/ ▶ **n.** a railroad in which the track consists of a single rail.

mon·o·syl·lab·ic /,mänəsəˈlabik/ ▶ **adj. 1** (of a word) having one syllable. **2** (of a person) saying very little.

mon·o·syl·la·ble /,mänəˈsiləbəl, ˈmänə,sil-/ ▶ **n.** a word of one syllable.

mon·o·the·ism /ˈmänə,THē,izəm/ ▶ **n.** the belief that there is only one god. ■ **mon·o·the·is·tic** /,mänəTHēˈistik/ **adj.**

mon·o·tone /ˈmänə,tōn/ ▶ **n.** a continuing sound that does not change pitch.

mo·not·o·nous /məˈnätn-əs/ ▶ **adj.** boring and unchanging.

SYNONYMS **tedious**, boring, uninteresting, unexciting, dull, repetitive, repetitious, unvarying, unchanging, mechanical, mind-numbing, soul-destroying; informal deadly. ANTONYMS interesting.

■ **mo·not·o·nous·ly adv. mo·not·o·ny n.**

mon·ox·ide /məˈnäk,sīd/ ▶ **n.** Chemistry an oxide containing one atom of oxygen.

Mon·roe Doc·trine /mənˈrō/ ▶ **n.** the policy, originated by President Monroe in 1823, that the US opposed any intervention by European powers in the politics of the Americas.

Mon·sieur /məˈsyœ(r), məˈsyər/ ▶ **n.** (plural **Messieurs** /məsˈyœ(r)(z), mās-, məˈsi(ə)r(z)/) a title for a French man, corresponding to *Mr.* or *sir.*

Mon·si·gnor /mänˈsēnyər, mən-/ ▶ **n.** (plural **Monsignori** /-rē/) the title of a senior Roman Catholic priest.

mon·soon /mänˈso͞on, ˈmän,so͞on/ ▶ **n. 1** a seasonal wind in the Indian subcontinent and southeastern Asia. **2** the rainy season accompanying the monsoon.

mon·ster /ˈmänstər/ ▶ **n. 1** a frightening imaginary creature. **2** a cruel or wicked person. **3** something that is very large: *a monster of a book.*

SYNONYMS **1 giant**, mammoth, demon, dragon, colossus, leviathan. **2 fiend**, animal, beast, devil, demon, barbarian, savage, brute; informal swine.

mon·stros·i·ty /mänˈsträsətē/ ▶ **n.** (plural **monstrosities**) something that is very large and ugly.

mon·strous /ˈmänstrəs/ ▶ **adj. 1** very large, ugly, or frightening. **2** shocking and morally wrong.

SYNONYMS **1 grotesque**, hideous, ugly, ghastly, gruesome, horrible, horrific, horrifying, grisly, disgusting, repulsive, dreadful, frightening, terrible, terrifying. **2 appalling**, wicked, abominable, terrible, horrible, dreadful, vile, outrageous, unspeakable, despicable, vicious, savage, barbaric, inhuman. ANTONYMS beautiful, humane.

■ **mon·strous·ly** adv.

mon·tage /män'täzh, mōn-, mōN-/ ▶ n. **1** a picture or movie made by putting together pieces from other pictures or movies. **2** a movie sequence consisting of a rapid succession of images.

month /mənTH/ ▶ n. **1** each of the twelve periods of time into which a year is divided. **2** a period of time between a date in one month and the same date in the next month. **3** a period of 28 days or four weeks.

month·ly /'mənTHlē/ ▶ adj. & adv. happening or produced once a month.

mon·u·ment /'mänyəmənt/ ▶ n. **1** a statue or structure built in memory of a person or event. **2** a site of historical importance. **3** a lasting example of something: *a monument to good taste.*

SYNONYMS **memorial**, statue, pillar, cairn, column, obelisk, cross, cenotaph, tomb, mausoleum, shrine.

mon·u·men·tal /ˌmänyə'mentl/ ▶ adj. **1** very large or impressive. **2** forming a monument.

SYNONYMS **1 huge**, enormous, gigantic, massive, colossal, mammoth, immense, tremendous, mighty, stupendous. **2 significant**, important, majestic, memorable, remarkable, noteworthy, momentous, grand, awe-inspiring, heroic, epic. ANTONYMS tiny.

■ **mon·u·men·tal·ly** adv.

moo /mōō/ ▶ v. (**moos, mooing, mooed**) (of a cow) make a long, deep sound.

mooch /mōōCH/ ▶ v. **1** ask for or obtain something without paying for it. **2** stand or walk around in a bored way.

mood /mōōd/ ▶ n. **1** the way you feel at a particular time. **2** a period of being bad-tempered. **3** the atmosphere of a work of art. **4** Grammar a form of a verb expressing fact, command, question, wish, or a condition.

SYNONYMS **1 frame of mind**, state of mind, humor, temper. **2 bad mood**, temper, bad temper, sulk, low spirits, the doldrums, the blues. **3 atmosphere**, feeling, spirit, ambience, aura, character, flavor, feel, tone.

mood·y /'mōōdē/ ▶ adj. (**moodier, moodiest**) **1** having moods that change quickly. **2** gloomy or bad-tempered.

SYNONYMS **temperamental**, emotional, volatile, capricious, erratic, bad-tempered, petulant, sulky, sullen, morose. ANTONYMS cheerful.

moo·lah /'mōōˌlä/ ▶ n. informal money.

moon /mōōn/ ▶ n. **1** (also **Moon**) the natural satellite of the earth. **2** a natural satellite of any planet. **3** literary a month. ▶ v. **1** (**moon around**) behave or walk about in a dreamy way. **2** informal expose your buttocks to someone as an insult or joke.

SYNONYMS ▶ v. **daydream**, loaf, idle, brood, mope, pine.

□ **moon-faced** having a round face. **over the moon** informal delighted.

moon·light /'mōōnˌlīt/ ▶ n. the light of the moon. ▶ v. (**moonlights, moonlighting, moonlighted**) informal do a second job without declaring it for tax purposes. ■ **moon·lit** adj.

moon·scape /'mōōnˌskāp/ ▶ n. a landscape that is rocky and barren like the moon.

moon·shine /'mōōnˌSHīn/ ▶ n. informal **1** foolish talk or ideas. **2** alcohol that is made and sold illegally.

SYNONYMS **alcohol**, corn liquor, corn mash; informal white lightning, hooch, booze, homebrew, mountain dew, firewater.

moon·stone /'mōōnˌstōn/ ▶ n. a white semiprecious mineral.

moon·y /'mōōnē/ ▶ adj. dreamy as a result of being in love.

Moor /mŏŏr/ ▶ n. a member of a northwestern African Muslim people. ■ **Moor·ish** adj.

moor¹ /mŏŏr/ ▶ n. a high open area of land that is not cultivated.

moor² ▶ v. fasten a boat to the shore or to an anchor.

SYNONYMS **tie (up)**, secure, make fast, berth, dock.

moor·hen /'mŏŏrˌhen/ ▶ n. a waterbird with black feathers.

moor·ing /'mŏŏriNG/ (or **moorings**) ▶ n. a place where a boat is moored, or the ropes used to moor it.

moose /mōōs/ ▶ n. a large deer with antlers, a sloping back, and a growth of skin hanging from the neck.

moot /mōōt/ ▶ adj. uncertain or undecided: *a moot point.* ▶ v. put forward a topic for discussion.

mop /mäp/ ▶ n. **1** a bundle of thick strings or a sponge attached to a handle, used for wiping floors. **2** a thick mass of hair. ▶ v. (**mops, mopping, mopped**) **1** clean or soak up by wiping. **2** (**mop something up**) complete something by dealing with the things that remain.

SYNONYMS ▶ n. *a tousled mop of hair* **shock**, mane, tangle, mass.

mope /mōp/ ▶ v. (**mopes, moping, moped**) be listless and gloomy.

SYNONYMS **brood**, sulk, be miserable, be despondent, pine, eat your heart out, fret, grieve; informal be down in the dumps.

mo·ped /'mōˌped/ ▶ n. a motorcycle with a small engine.

mo·raine /mə'rān/ ▶ n. rocks and stones deposited by a glacier.

mor·al /'môrəl, 'mär-/ ▶ adj. **1** concerned with the principles of right and wrong behavior. **2** conforming to accepted standards of behavior. ▶ n. **1** a lesson about right or wrong that you learn from a story or experience. **2** (**morals**) standards of good behavior.

SYNONYMS ▶ adj. **1 ethical**, good, virtuous, righteous, upright, upstanding, high-minded, principled, honorable, honest, just, noble. **2** *moral support* **psychological**, emotional, mental. ANTONYMS immoral, unethical. ▶ n. **1 lesson**, message, meaning, significance, import, point, teaching. **2** (**morals**) **moral code**, code of ethics, values, principles, standards, (sense of) morality, scruples.

■ **mor·al·ly** adv.

mo·rale /mə'ral/ ▶ n. a feeling of confidence and satisfaction.

SYNONYMS **confidence**, self-confidence, self-esteem, spirit(s), team spirit, esprit de corps, motivation.

mor·al·ist /ˈmôrəlist/ ▶ **n.** a person with strict views about morals. ■ **mor·al·is·tic** /ˌmôrəˈlistik/ **adj.**

mo·ral·i·ty /məˈralətē, mô-/ ▶ **n.** (plural **moralities**) **1** principles concerning the difference between right and wrong or good and bad behavior. **2** moral behavior. **3** the extent to which an action is right or wrong.

> SYNONYMS **1 ethics**, rights and wrongs, whys and wherefores. **2 virtue**, good behavior, righteousness, uprightness, morals, standards, principles, honesty, integrity, propriety, honor, decency.

mor·al·ize /ˈmôrəˌlīz, ˈmär-/ ▶ **v.** (**moralizes**, **moralizing**, **moralized**) comment on moral issues, usually in a disapproving way.

mo·rass /məˈras, mô-/ ▶ **n. 1** an area of muddy or boggy ground. **2** a complicated or confused situation.

mor·a·to·ri·um /ˌmôrəˈtôrēəm, ˌmär-/ ▶ **n.** (plural **moratoriums** or **moratoria** /-rēə/) a temporary ban on an activity.

mo·ray /ˈmôrˌā, məˈrā/ (also **moray eel**) ▶ **n.** a fish like an eel of warm seas.

mor·bid /ˈmôrbəd/ ▶ **adj. 1** having a strong interest in unpleasant subjects, especially death and disease. **2** Medicine having to do with disease.

> SYNONYMS **ghoulish**, macabre, unhealthy, gruesome, unwholesome; informal sick. ANTONYMS wholesome.

■ **mor·bid·i·ty** /môrˈbidətē/ **n. mor·bid·ly adv.**

mor·dant /ˈmôrdnt/ ▶ **adj.** (of humor) sharply sarcastic.

more /môr/ ▶ **determiner & pron.** a greater or additional amount or degree. ▶ **adv. 1** forming the comparative of adjectives and adverbs. **2** to a greater extent. **3** again. **4** (**more than**) very.

> SYNONYMS ▶ **determiner & pron. extra**, further, added, additional, supplementary, increased, new. ANTONYMS less, fewer.

mo·rel·lo /məˈrelō/ ▶ **n.** (plural **morellos**) a kind of sour dark cherry.

more·o·ver /môrˈōvər/ ▶ **adv.** in addition to what has been said already.

> SYNONYMS **besides**, furthermore, what's more, in addition, also, as well, too, to boot, additionally, on top of that, into the bargain.

mo·res /ˈmôrˌāz/ ▶ **pl.n.** the customs of a community.

morgue /môrg/ ▶ **n.** a mortuary.

mor·i·bund /ˈmôrəˌbənd, ˈmär-/ ▶ **adj. 1** at the point of death. **2** about to come to an end.

Mor·mon /ˈmôrmən/ ▶ **n.** a member of the Church of Jesus Christ of Latter-Day Saints. ■ **Mor·mon·ism n.**

morn /môrn/ ▶ **n.** literary morning.

morn·ing /ˈmôrniNG/ ▶ **n. 1** the period of time between midnight and noon, especially from sunrise to noon. **2** sunrise.

> SYNONYMS **1 before lunch**, a.m., forenoon; literary morn. **2 dawn**, daybreak, sunrise, sunup, first light.

□ **morning sickness** nausea felt by a woman when she is pregnant.

Mo·roc·can /məˈräkən/ ▶ **n.** a person from Morocco. ▶ **adj.** relating to Morocco.

mo·ron /ˈmôrˌän/ ▶ **n.** informal a stupid person. ■ **mo·ron·ic** /məˈränik, mô-/ **adj.**

mo·rose /məˈrōs, mô-/ ▶ **adj.** unhappy and bad-tempered. ■ **mo·rose·ly adv.**

morph /môrf/ ▶ **v.** (in computer animation) change smoothly and gradually from one image to another.

mor·phine /ˈmôrˌfēn/ ▶ **n.** a drug made from opium and used to relieve pain.

mor·ris danc·ing /ˈmôris, ˈmär-/ ▶ **n.** traditional English folk dancing.

mor·row /ˈmôrō, ˈmärō/ ▶ **n.** (**the morrow**) old use the next day.

Morse code /ˈmôrs/ ▶ **n.** a code in which letters are represented by combinations of long and short sounds or flashes of light.

mor·sel /ˈmôrsəl/ ▶ **n.** a small piece of food.

mor·tal /ˈmôrtl/ ▶ **adj. 1** having to die at some time. **2** causing death. **3** (of a battle or enemy) lasting until death. ▶ **n.** a human being.

> SYNONYMS ▶ **adj. 1** *all men are mortal* **perishable**, physical, bodily, corporeal, human, fleshly, earthly, impermanent, transient, ephemeral. **2** *a mortal blow* **fatal**, lethal, deadly, death-dealing, murderous, terminal. **3** *mortal enemies* **deadly**, sworn, irreconcilable, bitter, implacable, unrelenting, remorseless. ANTONYMS eternal. ▶ **n. human** (**being**), person, man, woman, earthling.

□ **mortal sin** (in Christian belief) a sin so serious as to result in damnation. ■ **mor·tal·ly adv.**

mor·tal·i·ty /môrˈtalətē/ ▶ **n. 1** the state of being mortal. **2** death. **3** (also **mortality rate**) the number of deaths in a particular area or period of time.

mor·tar /ˈmôrtər/ ▶ **n. 1** a mixture of lime with cement, sand, and water, used to stick bricks or stones together. **2** a cup-shaped container in which substances are crushed with a pestle. **3** a short cannon for firing shells at high angles.

mor·tar·board /ˈmôrtərˌbôrd/ ▶ **n. 1** an academic cap with a flat square top and a tassel. **2** a flat square board for holding mortar.

mort·gage /ˈmôrgij/ ▶ **n. 1** a legal agreement by which a bank lends you money, using your house as security. **2** an amount of money borrowed or lent under such an agreement. ▶ **v.** (**mortgages**, **mortgaging**, **mortgaged**) give a bank the right to hold your house as security for the money they agree to lend you.

mor·ti·cian /môrˈtiSHən/ ▶ **n.** an undertaker.

mor·ti·fy /ˈmôrtəˌfī/ ▶ **v.** (**mortifies**, **mortifying**, **mortified**) make someone feel embarrassed or ashamed. ■ **mor·ti·fi·ca·tion** /ˌmôrtəfəˈkāSHən/ **n.**

mor·tise /ˈmôrtis/ (or **mortice**) ▶ **n.** a slot cut in a piece of wood in order to hold the end of another piece of wood. □ **mortise lock** a lock fitted into a hole in a door.

mor·tu·ar·y /ˈmôrCHo͞oˌerē/ ▶ **n.** (plural **mortuaries**) a room or building in which dead bodies are kept until they are buried or cremated.

> SYNONYMS **morgue**, funeral parlor/home.

mo·sa·ic /mōˈzā-ik/ ▶ **n.** a picture or pattern made by fitting together small colored pieces of stone, tile, or glass.

mo·sey /ˈmōzē/ ▶ **v.** (**moseys**, **moseying**, **moseyed**) informal walk in a leisurely way.

Mos·lem /ˈmäzləm, ˈmäs-/ = **MUSLIM**.

mosque /mäsk/ ▶ **n.** a Muslim place of worship.

mos·qui·to /mə'skētō/ ▶ **n.** (plural **mosquitoes**) a small long-legged fly, some kinds of which transmit diseases through their bite.

moss /môs/ ▶ **n.** a very small green spreading plant that grows in damp places.

moss·y /'môsē, 'mäsē/ ▶ **adj. 1** covered in or resembling moss: *mossy tree trunks.* **2** informal old-fashioned or extremely conservative.

most /mōst/ ▶ **determiner & pron. 1** greatest in amount or degree. **2** the majority of. ▶ **adv. 1** to the greatest extent. **2** forming the superlative of adjectives and adverbs. **3** very.

most·ly /'mōstlē/ ▶ **adv. 1** on the whole; mainly. **2** usually.

SYNONYMS **1 mainly**, for the most part, on the whole, in the main, largely, chiefly, predominantly, principally, primarily. **2 usually**, generally, in general, as a rule, ordinarily, normally, customarily, typically, most of the time, almost always.

mote /mōt/ ▶ **n.** a speck.

mo·tel /mō'tel/ ▶ **n.** a roadside hotel designed for motorists.

mo·tet /mō'tet/ ▶ **n.** a short piece of choral music.

moth /môTH/ ▶ **n.** an insect like a butterfly, which is active at night. □ **moth-eaten 1** eaten by the larvae of moths. **2** shabby and worn.

moth·ball /'môTH,bôl/ ▶ **n.** a small ball of camphor, placed among stored clothes to deter moths.

moth·er /'məT͟Hər/ ▶ **n. 1** a female parent. **2** (**Mother**) (especially as a title or form of address) the head of a convent. ▶ **v.** look after somebody protectively.

SYNONYMS ▶ **n.** matriarch, materfamilias; informal mom, mommy, mama, ma. ▶ **v. look after**, care for, take care of, nurse, protect, tend, raise, rear, pamper, coddle, cosset, fuss over.

□ **mother-in-law** (plural **mothers-in-law**) the mother of a person's husband or wife. **mother-of-pearl** a smooth pearly substance lining the shells of oysters. **Mother's Day** the second Sunday in May, a day on which mothers are honored with greeting cards and gifts. **mother tongue** a person's native language. ■ **moth·er·hood n.**

moth·er·land /'məT͟Hər,land/ ▶ **n.** your native country.

moth·er·ly /'məT͟Hərlē/ ▶ **adj.** relating to or like a mother, especially in being caring, protective, and kind.

SYNONYMS **maternal**, maternalistic, protective, caring, loving, affectionate, nurturing.

mo·tif /mō'tēf/ ▶ **n. 1** a pattern or design. **2** a theme that is repeated in a work of literature or piece of music.

SYNONYMS **1 design**, pattern, decoration, figure, shape, device, emblem. **2 theme**, idea, concept, subject, topic, leitmotif.

mo·tion /'mōSHən/ ▶ **n. 1** the action of moving. **2** a movement or gesture. **3** a formal proposal that is discussed at a meeting. ▶ **v.** direct someone with a gesture.

SYNONYMS ▶ **n. 1 movement**, locomotion, progress, passage, transit, course, travel, orbit. **2 gesture**, movement, signal, sign, indication, wave, nod, gesticulation. **3 proposal**, proposition, recommendation. ▶ **v. gesture**, signal, direct, indicate, wave, beckon, nod.

□ **motion picture** a movie. ■ **mo·tion·less adj.**

mo·ti·vate /'mōtə,vāt/ ▶ **v.** (**motivates, motivating, motivated**) **1** provide someone with a motive for doing something. **2** make someone want to do something.

SYNONYMS **prompt**, drive, move, inspire, stimulate, influence, activate, impel, propel, push, spur (on), encourage, incentivize.

■ **mo·ti·va·tor n.**

mo·ti·va·tion /,mōtə'vāSHən/ ▶ **n. 1** the reason for your actions or behavior. **2** enthusiasm.

SYNONYMS **motive**, motivating force, incentive, stimulus, stimulation, inspiration, inducement, incitement, spur.

■ **mo·ti·va·tion·al adj.**

mo·tive /'mōtiv/ ▶ **n.** something that makes someone act in a particular way. ▶ **adj.** causing motion.

SYNONYMS ▶ **n. reason**, motivation, motivating force, rationale, grounds, cause, basis.

mot·ley /'mätlē/ ▶ **adj.** made up of a variety of different things or people.

mo·to·cross /'mōtō,krôs, -,kräs/ ▶ **n.** cross-country racing on motorcycles.

mo·tor /'mōtər/ ▶ **n.** a device that produces power and movement for a vehicle or machine. ▶ **adj.** giving or producing motion. ▶ **v.** travel in a car. □ **motor home** a motor vehicle equipped like a trailer for living in during vacations. **motor vehicle** a road vehicle powered by an engine. ■ **mo·tor·ized adj.**

mo·tor·bike /'mōtər,bīk/ ▶ **n.** a motorcycle.

mo·tor·boat /'mōtər,bōt/ ▶ **n.** a boat powered by a motor.

mo·tor·cade /'mōtər,kād/ ▶ **n.** a procession of motor vehicles.

mo·tor·cy·cle /'mōtər,sīkəl/ ▶ **n.** a two-wheeled vehicle powered by a motor. ■ **mo·tor·cy·cling n. mo·tor·cy·clist n.**

mo·tor·ist /'mōtərist/ ▶ **n.** the driver of a car.

mo·tor·man /'mōtər,mən/ ▶ **n.** (plural **motormen**) the driver of a subway train or streetcar.

mot·tled /'mätld/ ▶ **adj.** marked with patches of a different color.

mot·to /'mätō/ ▶ **n.** (plural **mottoes** or **mottos**) a short sentence or phrase that expresses a belief or aim.

SYNONYMS **slogan**, maxim, saying, proverb, aphorism, adage, saw, axiom, formula, catchphrase.

mound /mound/ ▶ **n. 1** a raised mass of earth or other material. **2** a small hill. **3** a heap or pile. ▶ **v.** heap up into a mound.

SYNONYMS ▶ **n. 1 heap**, pile, stack, mountain. **2 hillock**, hill, knoll, rise, hummock, hump.

mount[1] /mount/ ▶ **v. 1** climb up or on to. **2** get up on an animal or bicycle to ride it. **3** increase in size, number, or strength. **4** organize a campaign, bid, etc. **5** put or fix something in place. ▶ **n. 1** (also **mounting**) something on which an object is mounted for support or display. **2** a horse used for riding.

SYNONYMS ▶ **v.** **1 go up**, ascend, climb (up), scale. **2** *mount a horse* **get on to**, bestride, climb on to, leap on to, hop on to. **3** *mount an exhibition* **put on**, present, install, organize, stage, set up, prepare, launch, set in motion. **4 increase**, grow, rise, escalate, soar, spiral, shoot up, rocket, climb, accumulate, build up, multiply. ANTONYMS descend, dismount, fall. ▶ **n.** **setting**, backing, support, mounting, frame, stand.

mount² ▶ **n.** old use a mountain or hill.

moun·tain /'mountn/ ▶ **n.** **1** a very high and steep hill. **2** a large pile or quantity.

SYNONYMS **1 peak**, summit; (**mountains**) range, massif, sierra. **2 lot**; informal heap, pile, stack, slew, lots, loads, tons, masses.

□ **mountain lion** ⇒ COUGAR. **Mountain time** the standard time in a zone including the Rocky Mountain areas of the US and Canada.

moun·tain·eer·ing /,mountn'i(ə)riNG/ ▶ **n.** the sport or activity of climbing mountains. ■ **moun·tain·eer** **n.**

moun·tain·ous /'mountn-əs/ ▶ **adj.** **1** having many mountains. **2** huge.

moun·te·bank /'mounti,baNGk/ ▶ **n.** a person who tricks people in order to get money from them.

Moun·tie /'mountē/ ▶ **n.** informal a member of the Royal Canadian Mounted Police.

mourn /môrn/ ▶ **v.** feel deep sorrow following the death or loss of.

SYNONYMS **1 grieve for**, sorrow over, lament for, weep for. **2 deplore**, bewail, bemoan, rue, regret.

mourn·er /'môrnər/ ▶ **n.** a person who attends a funeral.

mourn·ful /'môrnfəl/ ▶ **adj.** very sad or depressing. ■ **mourn·ful·ly** **adv.**

mourn·ing /'môrniNG/ ▶ **n.** **1** the expression of deep sorrow for someone who has died. **2** black clothes worn in a period of mourning.

SYNONYMS **grief**, grieving, sorrowing, lamentation.

mouse /mous/ ▶ **n.** (plural **mice** /mīs/) **1** a small rodent with a pointed snout and a long thin tail. **2** a timid and quiet person. **3** Computing a small hand-held device that controls the cursor on a computer screen. □ **mouse pad** a piece of rigid or slightly spongy material on which a computer mouse is moved.

mous·sa·ka /mōō'säkə, ,mōōsə'kä/ ▶ **n.** a Greek dish of ground lamb layered with eggplant and tomatoes and topped with a cheese sauce.

mousse /mōōs/ ▶ **n.** **1** a dish made from whipped cream and egg whites. **2** a light substance used to style hair.

mous·tache = MUSTACHE.

mous·y /'mousē, -zē/ (or **mousey**) ▶ **adj.** **1** (of hair) of a light brown color. **2** timid and shy.

SYNONYMS **timid**, quiet, timorous, shy, self-effacing, diffident.

mouth /mouTH/ ▶ **n.** **1** the opening in the body through which food is taken and sounds are made. **2** an opening or entrance to something. **3** the place where a river enters the sea. ▶ **v.** **1** move your lips as if you were saying something. **2** say something in a pompous way.

SYNONYMS ▶ **n.** **1 lips**, jaws, muzzle; informal trap, chops, kisser, puss. **2 entrance**, opening. **3 estuary**, delta, firth, outlet, outfall.

□ **mouth organ** a harmonica. **mouth-to-mouth (resuscitation)** a method of artificial respiration in which a person breathes into someone's lungs through their mouth.

mouth·ful /'mouTH,fōōl/ ▶ **n.** **1** an amount of food or drink that fills your mouth. **2** a long or complicated word or phrase.

mouth·piece /'mouTH,pēs/ ▶ **n.** a part of a musical instrument, telephone, etc., that is put in or against the mouth.

mouth·wash /'mouTH,wôsH, -,wäsH/ ▶ **n.** an antiseptic liquid for rinsing the mouth or gargling.

mouth·wa·ter·ing /'mouTH,wôtəriNG, -,wätəriNG/ ▶ **adj.** smelling or looking delicious.

mouth·y /'mouT͟Hē, 'mouTHē/ ▶ **adj.** informal inclined to talk a lot.

move /mōōv/ ▶ **v.** (**moves**, **moving**, **moved**) **1** go or make something go in a particular direction or way. **2** change or make something change position. **3** change the place where you live. **4** change from one state or activity to another. **5** take action. **6** make progress. **7** provoke a strong feeling in someone. ▶ **n.** **1** an instance of moving. **2** an action taken toward achieving a purpose. **3** a player's turn during a board game.

SYNONYMS ▶ **v.** **1 go**, walk, step, proceed, progress, advance, budge, stir, shift, change position. **2 carry**, transfer, shift, push, pull, lift, slide. **3 progress**, advance, develop, evolve, change, happen. **4 act**, take steps, do something, take measures; informal get moving. **5 relocate**, move house, move away/out, change address, go (away), decamp. **6 affect**, touch, impress, shake, upset, disturb. **7 inspire**, prompt, stimulate, motivate, provoke, influence, rouse, induce, incite. **8 propose**, submit, suggest, advocate, recommend, urge. ▶ **n.** **1 movement**, motion, action, gesture. **2 relocation**, change of house/address, transfer, posting. **3 initiative**, step, action, measure, maneuver, tactic, stratagem. **4 turn**, go.

■ **mov·a·ble** (or **moveable**) **adj.**

move·ment /'mōōvmənt/ ▶ **n.** **1** an act of moving. **2** the process of moving. **3** a group of people who share the same aims. **4** a trend or development. **5** (**movements**) a person's activities during a particular period of time. **6** a main division of a piece of music.

SYNONYMS **1 motion**, move, gesture, sign, signal, action. **2 transportation**, shifting, conveyance, moving, transfer. **3 group**, party, faction, wing, lobby, camp. **4 campaign**, crusade, drive, push, initiative.

mov·ie /'mōōvē/ ▶ **n.** a story or event recorded by a camera as a set of moving images and shown in a theater or on television.

SYNONYMS **film**, picture, motion picture, feature film; informal flick.

mov·ie·go·er /'mōōvē,gōər/ ▶ **n.** a person who goes to the movies, especially regularly. ■ **mov·ie·go·ing** **n.** & **adj.**

mov·ing /'mōōviNG/ ▶ **adj.** **1** in motion. **2** arousing strong emotion.

SYNONYMS **1 in motion**, operating, operational, working, on the move, active, movable, mobile. **2 touching**, poignant, heartwarming, heart-rending, affecting, emotional, inspiring, inspirational, stimulating, stirring. ANTONYMS stationary, fixed.

■ **mov·ing·ly** adv.

mow /mō/ ▶ v. (**mows**, **mowing**, **mowed**; past participle **mowed** or **mown**) **1** cut down or trim grass, hay, etc. **2** (**mow someone down**) kill someone with a gun or by knocking them down with a vehicle.

SYNONYMS **cut**, trim, crop, clip, shear.

mow·er /ˈmōər/ ▶ n. a machine that cuts down or trims grass, hay, etc.

mox·ie /ˈmäksē/ ▶ n. informal force of character, determination, or nerve.

moz·za·rel·la /ˌmätsəˈrelə/ ▶ n. a firm white Italian cheese made from buffalo's or cow's milk.

MP ▶ abbr. **1** military police. **2** (in the UK and Canada) Member of Parliament.

MP3 ▶ n. a means of compressing a sound sequence into a very small file, used as a way of downloading audio files from the Internet.

Mr. /ˈmistər/ ▶ n. a title used before a man's surname or full name.

MRI ▶ abbr. magnetic resonance imaging.

Mrs. /ˈmisəz, ˈmiz-, -əs/ ▶ n. a title used before a married woman's surname or full name.

MS ▶ abbr. **1** manuscript. **2** multiple sclerosis.

Ms. /miz/ ▶ n. a title used before a married or unmarried woman's surname or full name.

MSc ▶ abbr. Master of Science.

MST ▶ abbr. Mountain Standard Time.

Mt. ▶ abbr. Mount.

much /məCH/ ▶ determiner & pron. a large amount. ▶ adv. **1** to a great extent. **2** often.

SYNONYMS ▶ determiner & pron. **1** *is there much time available?* **a lot of**, a great/good deal of, a great/large amount of, plenty of, ample, abundant, plentiful; informal lots of, loads of, heaps of, masses of, tons of, stacks of. **2** *there was much to do* **a lot**, a great/good deal, plenty; informal lots, loads, heaps, masses, tons. ANTONYMS little. ▶ adv. **1 greatly**, a great deal, a lot, considerably, appreciably. **2 often**, frequently, many times, regularly, habitually, routinely, usually, normally, commonly.

muck /mək/ ▶ n. **1** dirt or rubbish. **2** manure. ▶ v. **1** (**muck something up**) informal bungle a job; spoil something. **2** (**muck something out**) remove manure and dirt from a stable.

SYNONYMS ▶ n. **1 dirt**, grime, filth, mud, mess. **2 dung**, manure, excrement, droppings, ordure.

■ **muck·y** adj. (**muckier**, **muckiest**).

mu·cous /ˈmyo͞okəs/ ▶ adj. having to do with mucus. □ **mucous membrane** a tissue that produces mucus, lining the nose, mouth, and other organs.

mu·cus /ˈmyo͞okəs/ ▶ n. a slimy substance produced by the mucous membranes.

mud /məd/ ▶ n. soft, wet, sticky earth.

SYNONYMS **dirt**, sludge, ooze, silt, clay, mire, soil.

mud·dle /ˈmədl/ ▶ v. (**muddles**, **muddling**, **muddled**) **1** put things in the wrong order or mix them up. **2** confuse someone. **3** (**muddle something up**) confuse two or more things with each other. **4** (**muddle along** or **through**) manage to cope in spite of a lack of skill, knowledge, etc. ▶ n. a muddled state.

SYNONYMS ▶ v. **1 confuse**, mix up, jumble (up), disarrange, disorganize, disorder, mess up. **2 bewilder**, confuse, bemuse, perplex, puzzle, baffle, mystify. ▶ n. **mess**, confusion, jumble, tangle, chaos, disorder, disarray, disorganization.

mud·dy /ˈmədē/ ▶ adj. (**muddier**, **muddiest**) **1** covered in mud. **2** not bright or clear. ▶ v. (**muddies**, **muddying**, **muddied**) make something muddy.

SYNONYMS ▶ adj. **1 marshy**, boggy, swampy, waterlogged, squelchy, squishy, mucky, slimy, wet, soft. **2 dirty**, filthy, mucky, grimy, soiled. **3 murky**, cloudy, turbid. ANTONYMS clean, clear.

mud·flap /ˈmədflap/ ▶ n. a flap hung behind the wheel of a vehicle to protect against mud and stones thrown up from the road.

mud·flat /ˈmədˌflat/ ▶ n. a stretch of muddy land left uncovered at low tide.

mud·guard /ˈmədˌgärd/ ▶ n. a curved strip fitted over a wheel of a bicycle or motorcycle to protect against water and dirt thrown up from the road.

mues·li /ˈm(y)o͞oslē, ˈm(y)o͞ozlē/ ▶ n. (plural **mueslis**) a mixture of oats, dried fruit, and nuts, eaten with milk.

mu·ez·zin /m(y)o͞oˈezən, ˈmo͞oəzən/ ▶ n. a man who calls Muslims to prayer.

muff[1] /məf/ ▶ n. a short tube made of fur or other warm material into which you place your hands for warmth.

muff[2] ▶ v. informal handle something clumsily or badly.

muf·fin /ˈməfən/ ▶ n. a type of small cake.

muf·fle /ˈməfəl/ ▶ v. (**muffles**, **muffling**, **muffled**) **1** wrap or cover for warmth. **2** make a sound quieter.

SYNONYMS **1 wrap** (**up**), swathe, enfold, envelop, cloak. **2 deaden**, dull, dampen, mute, soften, quiet, mask, stifle, smother.

muf·fler /ˈməf(ə)lər/ ▶ n. **1** a scarf. **2** a part of a motor vehicle's exhaust system, serving to muffle the sound of the vehicle.

muf·ti /ˈməftē/ ▶ n. (plural **muftis**) **1** a Muslim legal expert allowed to give rulings on religious matters. **2** civilian clothes when worn by military or police staff.

mug /məg/ ▶ n. **1** a cylindrical cup drinking with a handle. **2** informal a person's face. **3** informal a hoodlum or thug. ▶ v. (**mugs**, **mugging**, **mugged**) attack and rob someone in a public place.

mug·ger /ˈməgər/ ▶ n. a person who attacks and robs someone in a public place.

mug·gy /ˈməgē/ ▶ adj. (of the weather) unpleasantly warm and humid.

SYNONYMS **humid**, close, sultry, sticky, oppressive, airless, stifling, suffocating, stuffy. ANTONYMS fresh.

mug·shot /ˈməɡˌSHät/ ▶ **n.** informal a photograph of a person's face made for an official purpose, especially police records.

muk·luk /ˈməkˌlək/ ▶ **n.** a high, soft sealskin boot worn in the American Arctic.

mu·lat·to /m(y)o͝oˈlätō, -ˈlatō/ ▶ **n.** (plural **mulattoes** or **mulattos**) offensive a person with one white and one black parent.

mul·ber·ry /ˈməlˌberē/ ▶ **n.** (plural **mulberries**) **1** a dark red or white fruit resembling the loganberry. **2** a dark red or purple color.

mulch /məlCH/ ▶ **n.** a mass of leaves or compost, used to protect the base of a plant or to enrich the soil. ▶ **v.** cover with mulch.

mule /myo͞ol/ ▶ **n.** the offspring of a male donkey and a female horse.

mul·ish /ˈmyo͞olisH/ ▶ **adj.** stubborn.

mull¹ /məl/ ▶ **v.** (**mull something over**) think about something at length.

> SYNONYMS **ponder**, consider, think over/about, reflect on, contemplate, chew over; formal cogitate on.

mull² ▶ **v.** warm wine or beer and add sugar and spices to it.

mul·lah /ˈmələ, ˈmo͝olə, ˈmo͞olə/ ▶ **n.** a Muslim who is an expert in Islamic theology and sacred law.

mul·let /ˈmələt/ ▶ **n.** a sea fish that is caught for food.

mul·li·ga·taw·ny /ˌməligəˈtônē, -ˈtänē/ ▶ **n.** a spicy meat soup originally made in India.

mul·lion /ˈməlyən/ ▶ **n.** a vertical bar between the panes of glass in a window. ■ **mul·lioned adj.**

mul·ti·col·ored /ˌməltiˈkələrd, ˌməltī-/ (or **multicolor**) ▶ **adj.** having many colors.

> SYNONYMS **kaleidoscopic**, psychedelic, colorful, many-hued, jazzy, variegated. ANTONYMS monochrome.

mul·ti·cul·tur·al /ˌməltēˈkəlCH(ə)rəl, ˌməltī-/ ▶ **adj.** relating to or made up of several cultural or ethnic groups. ■ **mul·ti·cul·tur·al·ism n.**

mul·ti·fac·et·ed /ˌməltiˈfasətəd, ˌməltī-/ ▶ **adj.** having many sides or aspects.

mul·ti·far·i·ous /ˌməlt(ə)ˈfe(ə)rēəs/ ▶ **adj.** having great variety.

mul·ti·lat·er·al /ˌməltiˈlatərəl, ˌməltī/ ▶ **adj.** involving three or more participants.

mul·ti·lin·gual /ˌməltēˈliNGɡ(yə)wəl, ˌməltī-/ ▶ **adj.** in or using several languages.

mul·ti·me·di·a /ˌməltiˈmēdēə, ˌməltī-/ ▶ **n.** the use of sound and pictures as well as text on a computer screen.

mul·ti·na·tion·al /ˌməltiˈnasHənl, ˌməltī-/ ▶ **adj.** involving several countries. ▶ **n.** a company operating in several countries.

mul·ti·ple /ˈməltəpəl/ ▶ **adj.** **1** having or involving several parts or elements. **2** (of a disease or injury) affecting several parts of the body. ▶ **n.** a number that may be divided by another number without a remainder.

> SYNONYMS ▶ **adj.** **numerous**, many, various, different, diverse, several, manifold. ANTONYMS single.

□ **multiple-choice** (of a question in an exam) giving several possible answers, from which you must choose one. **multiple sclerosis** a serious disease of the nervous system that can cause partial paralysis.

mul·ti·plex /ˈməltəˌpleks/ ▶ **n.** a movie theater with several separate screens.

mul·ti·pli·ca·tion /ˌməltəpləˈkāsHən/ ▶ **n.** the process of multiplying. □ **multiplication sign** the symbol ×, indicating that one number is to be multiplied by another.

mul·ti·plic·i·ty /ˌməltəˈplisətē/ ▶ **n.** (plural **multiplicities**) a large number or variety of something.

mul·ti·ply /ˈməltəˌplī/ ▶ **v.** (**multiplies**, **multiplying**, **multiplied**) **1** add a number to itself a stated number of times. **2** increase in number or quantity. **3** increase in number by reproducing.

> SYNONYMS **increase**, grow, accumulate, proliferate, mount up, mushroom, snowball. ANTONYMS decrease.

■ **mul·ti·pli·er n.**

mul·ti·ra·cial /ˌməltiˈrāsHəl, ˌməltī-/ ▶ **adj.** having to do with people of many races.

mul·ti·sto·ry /ˈməltiˌstôrē, ˈməltī-/ ▶ **adj.** (of a building) having several stories.

mul·ti·task /ˈməltiˌtask, ˈməltī-/ ▶ **v.** **1** Computing operate more than one program at the same time. **2** do several things at the same time.

mul·ti·tude /ˈməltəˌt(y)o͞od/ ▶ **n.** **1** a large number of people or things. **2** (**the multitude**) the mass of ordinary people.

mul·ti·tu·di·nous /ˌməltəˈt(y)o͞odn-əs/ ▶ **adj.** very numerous.

mum¹ /məm/ ▶ **n.** short for **CHRYSANTHEMUM**.

mum² ▶ **adj.** (**keep mum**) informal stay silent so as not to reveal a secret. □ **mum's the word** it's a secret.

mum·ble /ˈməmbəl/ ▶ **v.** (**mumbles**, **mumbling**, **mumbled**) say something in a quiet voice that is difficult to hear or understand. ▶ **n.** quiet speech that is difficult to hear or understand.

> SYNONYMS ▶ **v.** **mutter**, murmur, talk under your breath.

mum·bo-jum·bo /ˈməmbō ˈjəmbō/ ▶ **n.** informal language that sounds mysterious but has no real meaning.

mum·mi·fy /ˈməməˌfī/ ▶ **v.** (**mummifies**, **mummifying**, **mummified**) preserve a body as a mummy. ■ **mum·mi·fi·ca·tion** /ˌməməfiˈkāsHən/ **n.**

mum·my /ˈməmē/ ▶ **n.** (plural **mummies**) (especially in ancient Egypt) a body that has been embalmed and wrapped in bandages in order to preserve it.

mumps /məmps/ ▶ **pl.n.** a disease causing swelling of the glands at the sides of the face.

munch /mənCH/ ▶ **v.** eat something steadily and often noisily.

munch·kin /ˈmənCHkin/ ▶ **n.** informal a child.

mun·dane /ˌmənˈdān/ ▶ **adj.** lacking interest or excitement.

> SYNONYMS **humdrum**, dull, boring, tedious, monotonous, tiresome, unexciting, uninteresting, uneventful, unremarkable, routine, ordinary. ANTONYMS extraordinary.

mu·nic·i·pal /myo͝oˈnisəpəl, myə-/ ▶ **adj.** relating to a municipality.

> SYNONYMS **civic**, civil, metropolitan, urban, city, town, borough, council.

mu·nic·i·pal·i·ty /myo͝oˌnisəˈpalətē, myə-/ ▶ **n.** (plural **municipalities**) a town or district with its own local government.

mu·nif·i·cent /myo͞o'nifəsənt, myə-/ ▶ **adj.** very generous. ■ **mu·nif·i·cence** **n.**

mu·ni·tions /myo͞o'nisнənz, myə-/ ▶ **pl.n.** military weapons, ammunition, and equipment.

mu·ral /'myo͝orəl/ ▶ **n.** a painting done directly on a wall.

mur·der /'mərdər/ ▶ **n.** the unlawful planned killing of one person by another. ▶ **v.** (**murders**, **murdering**, **murdered**) kill someone unlawfully, having planned to in advance.

> SYNONYMS ▶ **n.** **killing**, homicide, assassination, extermination, execution, slaughter, butchery, massacre, manslaughter; literary slaying. ▶ **v.** **kill**, put to death, assassinate, execute, butcher, slaughter, massacre, wipe out; informal bump off, ice, waste; literary slay.

mur·der·er /'mərdərər/ (or **murderess**) ▶ **n.** a person who commits murder.

> SYNONYMS **killer**, assassin, serial killer, butcher; informal hit man, hired gun.

mur·der·ous /'mərdərəs/ ▶ **adj.** capable of murdering someone or being very violent.

> SYNONYMS **homicidal**, brutal, violent, savage, ferocious, fierce, vicious, bloodthirsty, barbarous, barbaric, fatal, lethal, deadly.

murk /mərk/ ▶ **n.** darkness or fog.

murk·y /'mərkē/ ▶ **adj.** (**murkier**, **murkiest**) **1** dark and gloomy. **2** (of water) dirty or cloudy. **3** suspicious and kept hidden.

> SYNONYMS **1** **dark**, gloomy, gray, leaden, dull, dim, overcast, cloudy, clouded, sunless, dismal, dreary, bleak. **2** **dirty**, muddy, cloudy, turbid. ANTONYMS bright, clear.

mur·mur /'mərmər/ ▶ **v.** **1** say something quietly. **2** make a low continuous sound. ▶ **n.** **1** the sound made by a person speaking quietly. **2** a low continuous background noise. **3** Medicine a recurring sound heard in the heart through a stethoscope and usually indicating disease or damage.

> SYNONYMS ▶ **v.** **mutter**, mumble, whisper, talk under your breath, talk sotto voce. ▶ **n.** **1** **whisper**, mutter, mumble, undertone. **2** **hum**, buzz, drone.

mus·cle /'məsəl/ ▶ **n.** **1** a band of body tissue that can be tightened or relaxed in order to move a part of the body. **2** power or strength. ▶ **v.** (**muscle in**) informal force your way into something to gain an advantage.

> SYNONYMS ▶ **n.** **1** **strength**, power, brawn; informal beef, beefiness. **2** *financial muscle* **influence**, power, strength, might, force, forcefulness, weight; informal clout.

□ **muscle-bound** having overdeveloped muscles. ■ **mus·cly** **adj.**

mus·cu·lar /'məskyələr/ ▶ **adj.** **1** having to do with the muscles. **2** having well-developed muscles.

> SYNONYMS **strong**, brawny, muscly, well built, burly, strapping, sturdy, powerful, athletic; informal hunky, beefy.

□ **muscular dystrophy** an inherited condition in which the muscles gradually become weaker.

mus·cu·la·ture /'məskyələcнər, -ˌcнo͝or/ ▶ **n.** the arrangement of muscles in a body.

muse¹ /myo͞oz/ ▶ **n.** **1** (**Muse**) (in Greek and Roman mythology) each of nine goddesses representing or associated with a particular art or science. **2** a woman who is the inspiration for a creative artist.

muse² ▶ **v.** (**muses**, **musing**, **mused**) **1** be absorbed in thought. **2** say something to yourself in a thoughtful way.

> SYNONYMS **ponder**, consider, think over/about, mull over, reflect on, contemplate, turn over in your mind, chew over.

mu·se·um /myo͞o'zēəm/ ▶ **n.** a building in which objects of interest are kept and shown to the public.

mush /məsн/ ▶ **n.** **1** a soft, wet, pulpy mass. **2** something that is too sentimental.

mush·room /'məsн,ro͞om, -ˌro͝om/ ▶ **n.** a fungus in the form of a domed cap on a short stalk, many kinds of which are edible. ▶ **v.** increase or develop quickly. □ **mush·room cloud** a mushroom-shaped cloud of dust formed after a nuclear explosion.

mush·y /'məsнē/ ▶ **adj.** (**mushier**, **mushiest**) **1** soft and pulpy. **2** excessively sentimental. ■ **mush·i·ness** **n.**

mu·sic /'myo͞ozik/ ▶ **n.** **1** the sounds of voices or instruments arranged in a pleasing way. **2** the art of writing or playing music. **3** the written or printed signs representing a piece of music. □ **music hall** **1** (in the past) a popular form of entertainment involving singing, dancing, and comedy. **2** a theater where such entertainment took place.

mu·si·cal /'myo͞ozikəl/ ▶ **adj.** **1** relating to or accompanied by music. **2** fond of or skilled in music. **3** having a pleasant sound. ▶ **n.** a play or movie that involves singing or dancing.

> SYNONYMS ▶ **adj.** **tuneful**, melodic, melodious, harmonious, sweet-sounding, dulcet, euphonious, mellifluous. ANTONYMS discordant.

■ **mu·si·cal·ly** **adv.**

mu·si·cian /myo͞o'zisнən/ ▶ **n.** a person who plays a musical instrument or writes music. ■ **mu·si·cian·ship** **n.**

mu·si·col·o·gy /ˌmyo͞ozi'käləjē/ ▶ **n.** the study of the history and theory of music.

musk /məsk/ ▶ **n.** a strong-smelling substance produced by the male of a small breed of deer, used as an ingredient in perfume. ■ **musk·y** **adj.**

mus·keg /'məs,keg/ ▶ **n.** a swamp or bog formed by an accumulation of decayed vegetation and sphagnum moss.

mus·ket /'məskit/ ▶ **n.** (in the past) a light gun with a long barrel.

mus·ket·eer /ˌməskə'ti(ə)r/ ▶ **n.** (in the past) a soldier armed with a musket.

musk·rat /'məˌskrat/ ▶ **n.** a large rodent with a musky smell.

Mus·lim /'məzləm, 'mo͝oz-/ (or **Moslem** /'mäzləm/) ▶ **n.** a follower of Islam. ▶ **adj.** relating to Muslims or Islam.

mus·lin /'məzlən/ ▶ **n.** lightweight cotton cloth in a plain weave.

muss /məs/ ▶ **v.** informal make untidy or messy.

mus·sel /'məsəl/ ▶ **n.** a small shellfish with a dark brown or purplish-black shell.

must¹ /məst/ ▶ **modal v.** (past **had to** or in reported speech **must**) **1** be obliged to; should. **2** used to insist on something. **3** used to say that something is very likely: *you must be tired.* ▶ **n.** informal something that should not be missed.

SYNONYMS ▶ modal v. **ought to**, should, have (got) to, need to, be obliged to, be required to, be compelled to.

must² ▶ n. grape juice before it is fermented.

mus·tache /'məs,tash, mə'stash/ (or **moustache**) ▶ n. a strip of hair above a man's upper lip.

mus·tang /'məs,tang/ ▶ n. a small wild horse of the southwestern United States.

mus·tard /'məstərd/ ▶ n. **1** a hot-tasting yellow or brown paste made from the crushed seeds of a plant. **2** a brownish-yellow color. □ **mus·tard gas** a liquid whose vapor causes severe irritation and blistering of the skin, used in chemical weapons.

mus·ter /'məstər/ ▶ v. (**musters**, **mustering**, **mustered**) **1** summon up a feeling or attitude. **2** bring troops together in preparation for battle. **3** (of people) gather together. ▶ n. an instance of mustering troops.

SYNONYMS ▶ v. **1 assemble**, mobilize, rally, raise, summon, gather, call up, call to arms, recruit, draft, conscript. **2 congregate**, assemble, gather (together), come together, collect, convene, mass, rally. **3** *she mustered her courage* **summon (up)**, screw up, call up, rally.

□ **pass muster** be accepted as satisfactory.

must·n't /'məsənt/ ▶ contr. must not.

mus·ty /'məstē/ ▶ adj. having a stale or moldy smell.

SYNONYMS **moldy**, stale, fusty, damp, dank, mildewy, smelly, stuffy, airless, unventilated. ANTONYMS fresh.

■ **mus·ti·ness** n.

mu·ta·ble /'myo͞otəbəl/ ▶ adj. able or tending to change. ■ **mu·ta·bil·i·ty** /,myo͞otə'bilətē/ n.

mu·tant /'myo͞otnt/ ▶ adj. resulting from or showing the effect of mutation. ▶ n. a mutant form.

mu·tate /'myo͞o,tāt/ ▶ v. (**mutates**, **mutating**, **mutated**) undergo mutation.

mu·ta·tion /myo͞o'tāshən/ ▶ n. **1** the process of changing. **2** a change in genetic structure that may be passed on to subsequent generations. **3** a distinct form resulting from such a change.

SYNONYMS **1 alteration**, change, transformation, metamorphosis, transmutation. **2 mutant**, freak (of nature), deviant, monstrosity, monster.

mute /myo͞ot/ ▶ adj. **1** not speaking. **2** unable to speak. **3** (of a letter) not pronounced. ▶ n. **1** dated a person who is unable to speak. **2** a device used to make the sound of a musical instrument quieter or softer. ▶ v. (**mutes**, **muting**, **muted**) **1** make the sound of something quieter or softer. **2** reduce the strength or intensity of. **3** (**muted**) (of a sound or voice) quiet and soft. **4** (**muted**) (of color or lighting) not bright; subdued.

SYNONYMS ▶ adj. **1 silent**, speechless, dumb, unspeaking, tight-lipped, taciturn; informal mum. **2 wordless**, silent, dumb, unspoken. ANTONYMS voluble, spoken. ▶ v. (**muted**) **1 muffled**, faint, indistinct, quiet, soft, low, distant, faraway. **2 subdued**, pastel, delicate, subtle, understated, restrained.

■ **mute·ly** adv.

mu·ti·late /'myo͞otl,āt/ ▶ v. (**mutilates**, **mutilating**, **mutilated**) severely injure or damage.

SYNONYMS **1 disfigure**, maim, mangle, dismember, slash, hack up. **2 vandalize**, damage, slash, deface, violate, desecrate.

■ **mu·ti·la·tion** /,myo͞otl'āshən/ n.

mu·ti·neer /,myo͞otn'i(ə)r/ ▶ n. a person who takes part in a mutiny.

mu·ti·nous /'myo͞otn-əs/ ▶ adj. rebellious.

SYNONYMS **rebellious**, insubordinate, subversive, seditious, insurgent, insurrectionary, disobedient, restive.

mu·ti·ny /'myo͞otn-ē/ ▶ n. (plural **mutinies**) an open rebellion against authority, especially by soldiers or sailors against their officers. ▶ v. (**mutinies**, **mutinying**, **mutinied**) take part in a mutiny; rebel.

SYNONYMS ▶ n. **insurrection**, rebellion, revolt, riot, uprising, insurgence, insubordination. ▶ v. **rise up**, rebel, revolt, riot, strike.

mutt /mət/ ▶ n. informal a mongrel dog.

mut·ter /'mətər/ ▶ v. (**mutters**, **muttering**, **muttered**) **1** say something in a voice that can barely be heard. **2** talk or grumble in private. ▶ n. speech that can barely be heard.

SYNONYMS ▶ v. **1 murmur**, talk under your breath, talk sotto voce, mumble, whisper. **2 grumble**, complain, grouse, carp, whine; informal moan, whinge.

mut·ton /'mətn/ ▶ n. the flesh of a fully grown sheep used as food.

mu·tu·al /'myo͞ochəo͞oəl/ ▶ adj. **1** experienced by two or more people equally. **2** shared by two or more people: *a mutual friend.*

SYNONYMS **reciprocal**, reciprocated, requited, returned, common, joint, shared.

■ **mu·tu·al·i·ty** /,myo͞ocho͞o'alitē/ n. **mu·tu·al·ly** adv.

muz·zle /'məzəl/ ▶ n. **1** the nose and mouth of an animal. **2** a guard fitted over an animal's muzzle to stop it biting. **3** the open end of the barrel of a gun. ▶ v. (**muzzles**, **muzzling**, **muzzled**) **1** put a muzzle on an animal. **2** prevent someone speaking freely.

muz·zy /'məzē/ ▶ adj. **1** dazed or confused. **2** blurred or indistinct.

MVP ▶ abbr. Sports most valuable player.

my /mī/ ▶ possessive determiner belonging to or associated with the speaker.

my·al·gi·a /mī'alj(ē)ə/ ▶ n. pain in a muscle.

my·col·o·gy /mī'käləjē/ ▶ n. the scientific study of fungi.

my·nah /'mīnə/ (or **myna** or **mynah bird**) ▶ n. an Asian or Australasian bird, some kinds of which can mimic human speech.

my·o·pi·a /mī'ōpēə/ ▶ n. nearsightedness. ■ **my·op·ic** /mī'äpik/ adj.

myr·i·ad /'mirēəd/ ▶ n. (also **myriads**) a countless or very great number. ▶ adj. countless.

myrrh /mər/ ▶ n. a sweet-smelling substance obtained from certain trees, used in perfumes and incense.

myr·tle /'mərtl/ ▶ n. an evergreen shrub with white flowers and purple-black berries.

my·self /mī'self, mə-/ ▶ pron. **1** used by a speaker to refer to himself or herself as the object of a verb or preposition when he or she is the subject of the clause. **2** I or me personally.

mys·te·ri·ous /mi'sti(ə)rēəs/ ▶ adj. difficult or impossible to understand or explain.

SYNONYMS **1 puzzling**, strange, peculiar, curious, funny, odd, weird, queer, bizarre, mystifying, inexplicable, baffling, perplexing, arcane, esoteric, cryptic, obscure. **2 secretive**, inscrutable, impenetrable, enigmatic, reticent, evasive.

■ **mys·te·ri·ous·ly** adv.

mys·ter·y /ˈmist(ə)rē/ ▶ n. (plural **mysteries**) **1** something that is difficult or impossible to understand or explain. **2** secrecy. **3** a novel, movie, etc., dealing with a puzzling crime.

SYNONYMS **1 puzzle**, enigma, conundrum, riddle, secret, paradox, question mark, closed book. **2 secrecy**, obscurity, uncertainty.

□ **mystery play** a medieval play based on biblical stories or the lives of the saints.

mys·tic /ˈmistik/ ▶ n. a person who seeks to know God through prayer and contemplation. ▶ adj. mystical.

SYNONYMS ▶ adj. **spiritual**, religious, transcendental, paranormal, other-worldly, supernatural, occult, metaphysical.

mys·ti·cal /ˈmistikəl/ ▶ adj. **1** relating to mystics or mysticism. **2** having a spiritual significance that goes beyond human understanding. **3** inspiring a sense of spiritual mystery and awe.

SYNONYMS **spiritual**, religious, transcendental, paranormal, otherworldly, supernatural, occult, metaphysical.

mys·ti·cism /ˈmistəˌsizəm/ ▶ n. **1** the belief that knowledge of God can be found through prayer and contemplation. **2** vague or ill-defined religious or spiritual belief.

mys·ti·fy /ˈmistəˌfī/ ▶ v. (**mystifies, mystifying, mystified**) **1** completely bewilder someone. **2** make something uncertain or mysterious.

SYNONYMS **bewilder**, puzzle, perplex, baffle, confuse, confound, bemuse, throw; informal flummox, stump, bamboozle.

■ **mys·ti·fi·ca·tion** /ˌmistəfiˈkāsʜən/ n.

mys·tique /misˈtēk/ ▶ n. a quality of mystery, glamour, or power that makes someone or something seem impressive or attractive.

myth /miтʜ/ ▶ n. **1** a traditional story that describes the early history of a people or explains a natural event. **2** a widely held but false belief. **3** an imaginary person or thing.

SYNONYMS **1 folk tale**, folk story, legend, fable, saga, lore, folklore. **2 misconception**, fallacy, old wives' tale, fairy story, fiction; informal cock and bull story.

myth·i·cal /ˈmiтʜikəl/ ▶ adj. **1** found in or characteristic of myths or folk tales. **2** imaginary or not real.

my·thol·o·gy /miˈтʜäləjē/ ▶ n. (plural **mythologies**) **1** a collection of myths. **2** a set of widely held but exaggerated or false beliefs. ■ **myth·o·log·i·cal** /ˌmiтʜəˈläjikəl/ adj.

myx·o·ma·to·sis /mikˌsōməˈtōsəs/ ▶ n. a highly infectious and usually fatal disease of rabbits.

Nn

N (or **n**) ▶ **n.** (plural **Ns** or **N's**) the fourteenth letter of the alphabet. ▶ **abbr.** (**N**) North or Northern.

n/a ▶ **abbr.** not applicable.

nab /nab/ ▶ **v.** (**nabs**, **nabbing**, **nabbed**) informal catch a wrongdoer.

na·cho /ˈnächō/ ▶ **n.** (plural **nachos**) a small piece of tortilla topped with melted cheese, peppers, etc.

na·da /ˈnädə/ ▶ **pron.** informal nothing.

na·dir /ˈnādər, ˈnādi(ə)r/ ▶ **n. 1** the lowest or most unsuccessful point. **2** the point in space directly opposite the zenith and below an observer.

SYNONYMS **low point**, all-time low, bottom, rock bottom; informal the pits. ANTONYMS zenith.

nag¹ /nag/ ▶ **v.** (**nags**, **nagging**, **nagged**) **1** constantly tell someone they should be doing something. **2** be constantly worrying or painful. ▶ **n. 1** a person who nags. **2** a persistent feeling of anxiety.

SYNONYMS ▶ **v. 1 harass**, keep on at, badger, hound, plague, criticize, find fault with, grumble at, henpeck; informal hassle, ride. **2 trouble**, worry, bother, torment, niggle, prey on your mind; informal bug.

nag² ▶ **n.** informal an old horse.

nai·ad /ˈnāad, -əd, nī-/ ▶ **n.** (in classical mythology) a water nymph.

nail /nāl/ ▶ **n. 1** a small metal spike with a flat head, used for joining pieces of wood together. **2** a thin hard layer covering the upper part of the tip of the finger and toe. ▶ **v. 1** fasten with a nail or nails. **2** informal catch a criminal.

SYNONYMS ▶ **n. tack**, pin, brad, hobnail, spike, staple, rivet. ▶ **v. fasten**, fix, attach, secure, affix, pin, tack, hammer.

□ **nail-biting** making you feel great anxiety or tension.

na·ive /nīˈēv/ (or **naïve**) ▶ **adj.** lacking experience or judgment.

SYNONYMS **innocent**, unsophisticated, artless, inexperienced, unworldly, trusting, gullible, credulous, immature, callow, raw, green; informal wet behind the ears. ANTONYMS worldly.

■ **na·ive·ly** adv.

na·ive·té /ˌnīˌēv(ə)ˈtā, nīˈēv(ə)ˌtā/ (or **na·ïve·té**) ▶ **n.** lack of experience, wisdom, or judgment.

na·ked /ˈnākid/ ▶ **adj. 1** without clothes. **2** (of an object) without the usual covering or protection. **3** (of feelings) not hidden; open. **4** vulnerable.

SYNONYMS **nude**, bare, in the nude, stark naked, stripped, unclothed, undressed; informal without a stitch on, in your birthday suit, in the raw/buff, in the altogether, buck naked. ANTONYMS dressed.

□ **the naked eye** the normal power of the eyes, without using a telescope, microscope, etc.
■ **na·ked·ly** adv. **na·ked·ness** n.

nam·by-pam·by /ˈnambē ˈpambē/ ▶ **adj.** lacking strength or courage; feeble.

name /nām/ ▶ **n. 1** a word or words by which someone or something is known. **2** a famous person. **3** a reputation: *he made a name for himself.* ▶ **v.** (**names**, **naming**, **named**) **1** give a name to. **2** identify or mention by name. **3** specify a sum of money, time, or place.

SYNONYMS ▶ **n. title**, designation, tag, nickname, sobriquet, epithet, label, honorific; informal moniker, handle; formal appellation, denomination, cognomen. ▶ **v. 1 call**, dub, label, style, term, title, baptize, christen. **2 nominate**, designate, select, pick, decide on, choose.

□ **name-dropping** mentioning the names of famous people as if you know them, in order to impress other people.

name·less /ˈnāmlis/ ▶ **adj. 1** having no name. **2** having a name that is kept secret.

name·ly /ˈnāmlē/ ▶ **adv.** that is to say.

SYNONYMS **that is (to say)**, to be specific, specifically, viz., to wit, in other words.

name·sake /ˈnāmˌsāk/ ▶ **n.** a person or thing with the same name as another.

nan·ny /ˈnanē/ ▶ **n.** (plural **nannies**) **1** a woman employed to look after a child in its own home. **2** (also **nanny goat**) a female goat.

nan·o·sec·ond /ˈnanəˌsekənd/ ▶ **n.** one billionth of a second.

nan·o·tech·nol·o·gy /ˌnanəˌtekˈnäləjē, ˌnanō-/ ▶ **n.** technology on a very tiny (atomic or molecular) scale.

nap¹ /nap/ ▶ **n.** a short sleep. ▶ **v.** (**naps**, **napping**, **napped**) have a nap.

SYNONYMS ▶ **n. sleep**, catnap, siesta, doze, lie-down, rest; informal snooze, forty winks, shut-eye.

nap² ▶ **n.** short raised fibers on the surface of certain fabrics.

na·palm /ˈnāˌpä(l)m/ ▶ **n.** a highly flammable thickened form of gasoline, used in firebombs.

nape /nāp/ ▶ **n.** the back of the neck.

naph·tha /ˈnafTHə, ˈnap-/ ▶ **n.** a flammable oil extracted from coal and petroleum.

nap·kin /ˈnapkin/ ▶ **n.** a piece of cloth or paper used at a meal to wipe the fingers or lips and to protect clothes.

narc /närk/ (or **nark**) ▶ **n. 1** informal a federal agent or police officer who enforces the laws regarding illicit sale or use of drugs and narcotics. **2** informal a police informer.

nar·cis·sism /ˈnärsəˌsizəm/ ▶ **n.** too much interest in yourself and your appearance. ■ **nar·cis·sist n. nar·cis·sis·tic** /ˌnärsəˈsistik/ **adj.**

nar·cis·sus /närˈsisəs/ ▶ **n.** (plural **narcissi** /-ˈsisī, -sē/ or **narcissuses**) a daffodil with a flower that has pale outer petals and an orange or yellow center.

nar·cot·ic /närˈkätik/ ▶ **n. 1** an addictive drug that affects mood or behavior. **2** a drug that causes drowsiness or unconsciousness, or relieves pain. ▶ **adj.** relating to narcotics.

SYNONYMS ▶ **n. drug**, sedative, opiate, painkiller, analgesic, palliative. ▶ **adj. soporific**, sedative, calming, painkilling, pain-relieving, analgesic, anodyne.

nar·rate /ˈnarˌāt/ ▶ **v.** (**narrates**, **narrating**, **narrated**) **1** give an account of something. **2** provide a commentary for a movie, television program, etc.

SYNONYMS **tell**, relate, recount, recite, describe, chronicle, report, present.

■ **nar·ra·tion** /naˈrāsʜən/ **n.**

nar·ra·tive /ˈnarətiv/ ▶ **n.** an account of connected events; a story. ▶ **adj.** having to do with stories or the telling of stories.

SYNONYMS ▶ **n. account**, chronicle, history, description, record, report, story, tale.

nar·ra·tor /ˈnaˌrātər/ ▶ **n.** a person who narrates something, especially a character who recounts the events of a novel.

SYNONYMS **storyteller**, chronicler, commentator, presenter, author. ANTONYMS listener, audience.

nar·row /ˈnarō/ ▶ **adj.** (**narrower**, **narrowest**) **1** of small width in comparison to length. **2** limited in extent, amount, or scope. **3** only just achieved: *a narrow escape.* ▶ **v. 1** become or make narrower. **2** (**narrow something down**) reduce the number of possibilities of something. ▶ **n.** (**narrows**) a narrow channel connecting two larger areas of water.

SYNONYMS ▶ **adj. 1 slender**, slim, small, slight, attenuated, tapering, thin, tiny. **2 confined**, cramped, tight, restricted, limited, constricted, small, tiny, inadequate, insufficient. ANTONYMS wide, broad. ▶ **v. reduce**, restrict, limit, decrease, diminish, taper, contract, shrink, constrict. ANTONYMS widen.

□ **narrow-minded** unwilling to listen to or accept the views of other people. ■ **nar·row·ness n.**

nar·row·ly /ˈnarōlē/ ▶ **adv.** by only a small margin: *one bullet narrowly missed him.*

SYNONYMS (**only**) **just**, barely, scarcely, hardly, by a hair's breadth; informal by a whisker.

nar·whal /ˈnärwəl/ ▶ **n.** a small Arctic whale, the male of which has a long spirally twisted tusk.

NASA /ˈnasə/ ▶ **abbr.** National Aeronautics and Space Administration.

na·sal /ˈnāzəl/ ▶ **adj.** relating to the nose. ■ **na·sal·ly adv.**

nas·cent /ˈnāsənt, ˈnasənt/ ▶ **adj.** just coming into existence and beginning to develop.

nas·tur·tium /naˈstərsʜəm, nə-/ ▶ **n.** a trailing garden plant with bright orange, yellow, or red flowers.

nas·ty /ˈnastē/ ▶ **adj.** (**nastier**, **nastiest**) **1** unpleasant or disgusting. **2** spiteful, violent, or bad-tempered. **3** painful or harmful: *a nasty bang on the head.*

SYNONYMS **1 unpleasant**, disagreeable, disgusting, vile, foul, abominable, revolting, repulsive, repellent, horrible, obnoxious, unsavory, loathsome, noxious, foul-smelling, smelly, stinking, rank, fetid, malodorous; informal ghastly, horrid, yucky, lousy; literary noisome. **2 unkind**, unpleasant, unfriendly, disagreeable, rude, spiteful, malicious, mean, vicious, malevolent, hurtful. **3** *a nasty accident* **serious**, dangerous, bad, awful, dreadful, terrible, severe, painful. ANTONYMS nice, pleasant.

■ **nas·ti·ly adv. nas·ti·ness n.**

na·tal /ˈnātl/ ▶ **adj.** relating to the place or time of your birth.

na·tion /ˈnāsʜən/ ▶ **n.** a large group of people sharing the same language, culture, or history and inhabiting a particular territory.

SYNONYMS **country**, state, land, realm, kingdom, republic, people, race, tribe.

na·tion·al /ˈnasʜənəl/ ▶ **adj. 1** having to do with a nation. **2** owned, controlled, or financially supported by a country's government. ▶ **n.** a citizen of a particular country.

SYNONYMS ▶ **adj. 1** *national politics* **federal**, public, governmental, state. **2** *a national strike* **nationwide**, countrywide, general, widespread. ANTONYMS local, international. ▶ **n. citizen**, subject, native, resident, inhabitant, voter.

□ **national debt** the total amount of money that a country's government has borrowed. **National Guard** the main reserve military force partly maintained by each state of the US but also available for federal use. **national park** an area of countryside that is protected by the national government. ■ **na·tion·al·ly adv.**

na·tion·al·ism /ˈnasʜənəˌlizəm/ ▶ **n. 1** very strong feelings of support for and pride in your own country. **2** belief in independence for a particular country.

SYNONYMS **patriotism**, allegiance, xenophobia, chauvinism, jingoism, flag-waving.

■ **na·tion·al·ist n. & adj. na·tion·al·is·tic** /ˌnasʜənəˈlistik/ **adj.**

na·tion·al·i·ty /ˌnasʜəˈnalitē/ ▶ **n.** (plural **nationalities**) **1** the status of belonging to a particular nation. **2** an ethnic group.

na·tion·al·ize /ˈnasʜənəˌlīz/ ▶ **v.** (**nationalizes**, **nationalizing**, **nationalized**) put an industry or business under the control of the government. ■ **na·tion·al·i·za·tion** /ˌnasʜənəliˈzāsʜən/ **n.**

na·tion·wide /ˌnāsʜənˈwīd/ ▶ **adj. & adv.** throughout the whole nation.

SYNONYMS **national**, countrywide, state, general, widespread, extensive. ANTONYMS local.

na·tive /ˈnātiv/ ▶ **n. 1** a person born in a particular place. **2** a local inhabitant. **3** an animal or plant that lives or grows naturally in a particular area. **4** dated, offensive a nonwhite person living in a country before the arrival of white colonists or settlers. ▶ **adj. 1** associated with the place where you were born. **2** (of a plant or animal) living or growing naturally in a place. **3** having to do with the original inhabitants of a place. **4** in a person's character: *his native wit.*

SYNONYMS ▶ n. **inhabitant**, resident, local, citizen, national, countryman. ANTONYMS foreigner. ▶ adj. **1** *native species* **indigenous**, original, local, domestic. **2** *native wit* **innate**, inborn, natural, inherent, intrinsic.

□ **native speaker** a person who has spoken a particular language from earliest childhood. **Native American** a member of any of the original peoples of North and South America.

na·tiv·i·ty /nə'tivitē, nā-/ ▶ n. (plural **nativities**) **1** (**the Nativity**) the birth of Jesus. **2** formal a person's birth.

NATO /'nātō/ ▶ abbr. North Atlantic Treaty Organization.

nat·ter /'natər/ informal ▶ v. (**natters**, **nattering**, **nattered**) chat for a long time. ▶ n. a long chat.

nat·ty /'natē/ ▶ adj. (**nattier**, **nattiest**) informal neat and fashionable in appearance. ■ **nat·ti·ly** adv.

nat·u·ral /'nacHərəl/ ▶ adj. **1** existing in or obtained from nature; not made or caused by people. **2** as you would expect; normal. **3** born with a particular skill or quality: *a natural leader*. **4** having a relaxed, easy manner. **5** (of a parent or child) related by blood. **6** Music (of a note) not sharp or flat. ▶ n. **1** a person with a particular gift or talent. **2** Music a natural note or a sign (♮) denoting one.

SYNONYMS ▶ adj. **1 unprocessed**, organic, pure, unrefined, additive-free, green. **2** *a natural occurrence* **normal**, ordinary, everyday, usual, regular, common, commonplace, typical, routine, standard, logical, understandable, (only) to be expected, predictable. **3** *a natural leader* **born**, instinctive, congenital, pathological. **4** *his natural instincts* **innate**, inborn, inherent, native, inherited, hereditary. **5** *she seemed very natural* **unaffected**, spontaneous, uninhibited, relaxed, unselfconscious, genuine, open, artless, guileless, unpretentious, unstudied. ANTONYMS abnormal, artificial, affected.

□ **natural gas** gas that is found underground and used as fuel. **natural history** the scientific study of animals or plants. **natural selection** the evolutionary process by which creatures better adapted to their environment tend to survive and produce more offspring.

nat·u·ral·ism /'nacHərə,lizəm/ ▶ n. a style in art or literature that shows things how they are in everyday life.

nat·u·ral·ist /'nacHərəlist/ ▶ n. a person who studies animals or plants.

nat·u·ral·is·tic /,nacHərə'listik/ ▶ adj. **1** having to do with real life or nature. **2** based on the theory of naturalism.

nat·u·ral·ize /'nacHərə,līz/ ▶ v. (**naturalizes**, **naturalizing**, **naturalized**) **1** make a foreigner a citizen of a country. **2** introduce a plant or animal into a region where it is not native.

nat·u·ral·ly /'nacHərəlē/ ▶ adv. **1** in a natural way. **2** of course.

SYNONYMS **of course**, as might be expected, needless to say, obviously, clearly, it goes without saying.

na·ture /'nācHər/ ▶ n. **1** the physical world, including plants, animals, and all things that are not made by people. **2** the typical qualities or character of a person, animal, or thing. **3** a type or kind of something.

SYNONYMS **1 the natural world**, the environment, Mother Nature, Mother Earth, the universe, the cosmos, wildlife, the countryside, the land. **2 character**, personality, disposition, temperament, makeup, psyche. **3 kind**, sort, type, variety, category, class, genre, order, quality, complexion, stripe.

na·tur·ism /'nācHə,rizəm/ ▶ n. nudism. ■ **na·tur·ist** n. & adj.

naught /nôt/ ▶ n. the digit 0; zero. ▶ pron. old use nothing.

SYNONYMS ▶ pron. **nil**, zero, nothing; Tennis love; informal zilch, zip, nada.

naugh·ty /'nôtē, nä-/ ▶ adj. (**naughtier**, **naughtiest**) **1** (of a child) disobedient; badly behaved. **2** informal mildly indecent.

SYNONYMS **1 badly behaved**, disobedient, bad, wayward, defiant, unruly, insubordinate, willful, delinquent, undisciplined, refractory, disruptive, mischievous, impish. **2 indecent**, risqué, rude, racy, vulgar, dirty, filthy, smutty, crude, coarse. ANTONYMS well behaved, clean.

■ **naugh·ti·ly** adv. **naugh·ti·ness** n.

nau·se·a /'nôzēə, -zHə/ ▶ n. a feeling of sickness and wanting to vomit.

SYNONYMS **sickness**, biliousness, queasiness, vomiting, retching.

nau·se·ate /'nôzē,āt, - zHē,āt/ ▶ v. (**nauseates**, **nauseating**, **nauseated**) make someone feel sick or disgusted.

nau·seous /'nôsHəs, -zHəs, -zēəs/ ▶ adj. **1** suffering from nausea. **2** causing nausea.

nau·ti·cal /'nôtikəl/ ▶ adj. having to do with sailors or navigation.

SYNONYMS **maritime**, marine, naval, seafaring, seagoing, sailing.

□ **nautical mile** a unit used to measure distances at sea, equal to approximately 2,025 yards (1,852 meters).

nau·ti·lus /'nôtl-əs/ ▶ n. (plural **nautiluses** or **nautili** /'nôtl-ī/) a swimming mollusk with a spiral shell and numerous short tentacles around the mouth.

na·val /'nāvəl/ ▶ adj. having to do with a navy or navies.

nave /nāv/ ▶ n. the central part of a church.

na·vel /'nāvəl/ ▶ n. the small hollow in the center of a person's belly where the umbilical cord was cut at birth.

nav·i·ga·ble /'navigəbəl/ ▶ adj. able to be used by boats and ships.

nav·i·gate /'navi,gāt/ ▶ v. (**navigates**, **navigating**, **navigated**) **1** plan and direct the route of a ship, aircraft, etc. **2** guide a boat or vehicle over a particular route.

SYNONYMS **steer**, pilot, guide, direct, captain; informal skipper.

nav·i·ga·tion /,navi'gāsHən/ ▶ n. **1** the activity of navigating. **2** the movement of ships. ■ **nav·i·ga·tion·al** adj.

nav·i·ga·tor /'navi,gātər/ ▶ n. **1** a person who navigates a ship, aircraft, etc. **2** historical a person who explored by sea. **3** a browser program for accessing data on the World Wide Web or another information system.

na·vy /ˈnāvē/ ▶ **n.** (plural **navies**) **1** the branch of a country's armed forces that fights at sea. **2** (also **navy blue**) a dark blue color.

SYNONYMS **fleet**, flotilla, armada.

nay /nā/ ▶ **adv.** old use or dialect no.

Na·zi /ˈnätsē, ˈnat-/ ▶ **n.** (plural **Nazis**) historical a member of the far-right National Socialist German Workers' Party. ■ **Na·zism n.**

NB ▶ **abbr.** nota bene; take special note (used to precede a written note).

NE ▶ **abbr.** northeast or northeastern.

Ne·an·der·thal /nēˈandərTHôl/ ▶ **n.** an extinct human living in Europe between about 120,000 and 35,000 years ago.

neap tide /nēp/ ▶ **n.** the tide when there is least difference between high and low water.

near /ni(ə)r/ ▶ **adv. 1** at or to a short distance in space or time. **2** almost. ▶ **prep.** (also **near to**) **1** at or to a short distance in space or time from. **2** close to. ▶ **adj. 1** at a short distance away. **2** close to being. ▶ **v.** approach.

SYNONYMS ▶ **adj. 1 close**, nearby, (close/near) at hand, a stone's throw away, neighboring, within reach, accessible, handy, convenient; informal within spitting distance. **2 imminent**, in the offing, on its way, coming, impending, looming. ANTONYMS far, distant.

□ **Near East** the countries of southwestern Asia between the Mediterranean and India (including the Middle East). ■ **near·ness n.**

near·by /ˌni(ə)rˈbī/ ▶ **adj. & adv.** not far away.

SYNONYMS **not far away**, not far off, close at hand, close by, near, within reach, neighboring, local, accessible, convenient, handy. ANTONYMS distant.

near·ly /ˈni(ə)rlē/ ▶ **adv.** very close to; almost.

SYNONYMS **almost**, just about, more or less, practically, virtually, all but, as good as, not far off, to all intents and purposes, not quite; informal pretty well.

near·sight·ed /ˈni(ə)rˌsītəd/ ▶ **adj.** unable to see things clearly unless they are relatively close to the eyes.

neat /nēt/ ▶ **adj. 1** tidy or carefully arranged. **2** clever but simple: *a neat solution to the labor shortage*. **3** (of a drink of liquor) not diluted. **4** excellent.

SYNONYMS **1 tidy**, orderly, well-ordered, in (good) order, spick-and-span, uncluttered, shipshape, straight, trim. **2 smart**, spruce, dapper, trim, well-groomed, well turned out; informal natty. **3** *his neat footwork* **skillful**, deft, dexterous, adroit, adept, expert, nimble, elegant, graceful, accurate; informal nifty. **4** *a neat solution* **clever**, ingenious, inventive, imaginative. **5** *neat gin* **undiluted**, straight, pure. ANTONYMS untidy.

■ **neat·ly adv.**

neat·en /ˈnētn/ ▶ **v.** make something neat.

neb·u·la /ˈnebyələ/ ▶ **n.** (plural **nebulae** /-lē/ or **nebulas**) a cloud of gas or dust in outer space.

neb·u·liz·er /ˈnebyəˌlīzər/ ▶ **n.** a device for producing a fine spray of liquid, used for example for inhaling a medicinal drug.

neb·u·lous /ˈnebyələs/ ▶ **adj.** not clearly defined; vague.

nec·es·sar·i·ly /ˌnesəˈse(ə)rəlē/ ▶ **adv.** as a necessary result; unable to be avoided.

SYNONYMS **as a consequence**, as a result, automatically, as a matter of course, certainly, incontrovertibly, inevitably, unavoidably, inescapably, of necessity.

nec·es·sar·y /ˈnesəˌserē/ ▶ **adj. 1** needing to be present, or to be done or achieved. **2** unavoidable.

SYNONYMS **1 obligatory**, required, requisite, compulsory, mandatory, imperative, needed, essential, vital, indispensable, de rigueur; formal needful. **2** *a necessary consequence* **inevitable**, unavoidable, inescapable, inexorable.

SPELLING

One **c**, double **s**: necessary.

ne·ces·si·tate /nəˈsesəˌtāt/ ▶ **v.** (**necessitates**, **necessitating**, **necessitated**) make something necessary.

ne·ces·si·ty /nəˈsesətē/ ▶ **n.** (plural **necessities**) **1** the fact of being necessary. **2** a thing that it is essential to have.

SYNONYMS **1 essential**, prerequisite, requisite, sine qua non; informal must-have. **2** *political necessity forced him to resign* **force of circumstance**, obligation, need, call, exigency, force majeure.

neck /nek/ ▶ **n. 1** the part connecting the head to the rest of the body. **2** the part of a bottle near the mouth. **3** the part of a violin, guitar, etc., to which the fingerboard is fixed. ▶ **v.** informal kiss and caress. □ **neck and neck** level in a race or other competition. **up to your neck in** informal heavily or busily involved in.

neck·er·chief /ˈnekərˌCHif, -ˌCHēf/ ▶ **n.** a square of cloth worn around the neck.

neck·lace /ˈneklis/ ▶ **n.** a piece of jewelry consisting of a chain, string of beads, etc., worn around the neck.

neck·line /ˈnekˌlīn/ ▶ **n.** the edge of a dress or top at or below the neck.

neck·tie /ˈnekˌtī/ ▶ **n.** a tie worn around the neck.

nec·ro·man·cy /ˈnekrəˌmansē/ ▶ **n. 1** attempted communication with dead people in order to predict the future. **2** witchcraft or black magic. ■ **nec·ro·man·cer n.**

ne·crop·o·lis /neˈkräpəlis/ ▶ **n.** a cemetery.

ne·cro·sis /neˈkrōsis/ ▶ **n.** the death of cells in an organ or tissue.

nec·tar /ˈnektər/ ▶ **n. 1** a fluid produced by flowers and made into honey by bees. **2** (in Greek and Roman mythology) the drink of the gods.

nec·tar·ine /ˌnektəˈrēn/ ▶ **n.** a variety of peach with smooth skin.

née /nā/ ▶ **adj.** born (used in giving a married woman's maiden name).

need /nēd/ ▶ **v. 1** require something because it is essential or very important. **2** used to express what should or must be done. ▶ **n. 1** a situation in which something is necessary or must be done. **2** a thing that is needed. **3** the state of being very poor.

SYNONYMS ▶ **v. 1 require**, be in need of, want, be crying out for, demand, call for, necessitate, entail, involve, lack, be without, be short of. **2** (**needed**) **necessary**, required, called for, wanted, desired, lacking. ▶ **n. 1** *there's no* *need to apologize* **necessity**, requirement, call, demand. **2** *basic human needs* **requirement**, necessity, want, requisite, prerequisite, desideratum. **3** *my hour of need* **difficulty**, trouble, distress, crisis, emergency, urgency, extremity.

need·ful /'nēdfəl/ ▶ **adj.** formal necessary.

nee·dle /'nēdl/ ▶ **n.** **1** a very thin pointed piece of metal with a hole or eye for thread at the blunter end, used in sewing. **2** a long, thin rod used in knitting. **3** the pointed hollow end of a hypodermic syringe. **4** a stylus used to play records. **5** a thin pointer on a dial, compass, etc. **6** the thin, stiff leaf of a fir or pine tree. ▶ **v.** (**needles**, **needling**, **needled**) informal deliberately annoy someone.

nee·dle·point /'nēdl,point/ ▶ **n.** closely stitched embroidery done on canvas.

need·less /'nēdlis/ ▶ **adj.** unnecessary; avoidable.

SYNONYMS **unnecessary**, unneeded, uncalled for, gratuitous, pointless, superfluous, redundant, excessive. ANTONYMS necessary.

■ **need·less·ly** **adv.**

nee·dle·work /'nēdl,wərk/ ▶ **n.** sewing or embroidery.

need·n't /'nēdnt/ ▶ **contr.** need not.

need·y /'nēdē/ ▶ **adj.** (**needier**, **neediest**) very poor.

SYNONYMS **poor**, deprived, disadvantaged, underprivileged, in need, hard up, poverty-stricken, impoverished, destitute, penniless, dirt poor; informal broke, strapped (for cash); dated needful. ANTONYMS wealthy.

ne'er /ne(ə)r/ ▶ **contr.** old use or dialect never. □ **ne'er-do-well** a useless or lazy person.

ne·far·i·ous /ni'fe(ə)rēəs/ ▶ **adj.** bad or illegal.

ne·gate /nə'gāt/ ▶ **v.** (**negates**, **negating**, **negated**) **1** stop or undo the effect of. **2** say that something does not exist. ■ **ne·ga·tion** **n.**

neg·a·tive /'negətiv/ ▶ **adj.** **1** showing the absence rather than the presence of something. **2** expressing denial, disagreement, or refusal. **3** not hopeful or favorable. **4** (of a quantity) less than zero. **5** having to do with the kind of electric charge carried by electrons. **6** (of a photograph) showing light and shade or colors reversed from those of the original. ▶ **n.** **1** a negative word or statement. **2** a negative photograph, from which positive prints may be made.

SYNONYMS ▶ **adj.** **1** **pessimistic**, defeatist, gloomy, critical, cynical, fatalistic, dismissive, unenthusiastic, apathetic, unresponsive. **2** **harmful**, bad, adverse, damaging, detrimental, unfavorable, disadvantageous. ANTONYMS positive, optimistic, favorable.

■ **neg·a·tive·ly** **adv.** **neg·a·tiv·i·ty** /,negə'tivitē/ **n.**

ne·glect /ni'glekt/ ▶ **v.** **1** fail to give enough care or attention to. **2** fail to do. ▶ **n.** the action of neglecting.

SYNONYMS ▶ **v.** **1** **fail to look after**, fail to care for, leave alone, abandon, ignore, pay no attention to, let slide, not attend to, be remiss about, be lax about, shirk; mistreat, maltreat. **2** (**neglected**) *a neglected cottage* **derelict**, dilapidated, tumbledown, ramshackle, untended, uncared for. **3** (**neglected**) *a neglected masterpiece* **disregarded**, forgotten, overlooked, ignored, unrecognized, unnoticed, unsung, underrated. **4** **fail**, omit, forget. ANTONYMS cherish, remember. ▶ **n.** **1** **disrepair**, dilapidation, shabbiness, abandonment, disuse. **2** **negligence**, dereliction (of duty), carelessness, laxity, slackness, irresponsibility. ANTONYMS care.

ne·glect·ful /ni'glektfəl/ ▶ **adj.** failing to give enough care or attention.

neg·li·gee /'neglə,zʜā/ ▶ **n.** a woman's robe made of a very light, thin fabric.

neg·li·gence /'negləjəns/ ▶ **n.** a failure to give someone or something enough care or attention.

neg·li·gent /'negləjənt/ ▶ **adj.** failing to take proper care in doing something: *a negligent safety inspector.*

SYNONYMS **neglectful**, remiss, careless, lax, irresponsible, inattentive, thoughtless, uncaring, unmindful, forgetful, slack, sloppy, derelict. ANTONYMS dutiful.

neg·li·gi·ble /'neglijəbəl/ ▶ **adj.** so small or unimportant as to be not worth considering.

SYNONYMS **trivial**, trifling, insignificant, unimportant, of no account, minor, inconsequential, minimal, small, slight, infinitesimal, minuscule. ANTONYMS significant.

ne·go·ti·ate /nə'gōsʜē,āt/ ▶ **v.** (**negotiates**, **negotiating**, **negotiated**) **1** reach an agreement by discussion. **2** bring something about by discussion. **3** find a way through a difficult path or route.

SYNONYMS **1** **discuss** (**terms**), talk, consult, confer, debate, compromise, bargain, haggle. **2** **arrange**, broker, work out, thrash out, complete, close, conclude, agree on. **3** **get around**, get past, get over, clear, cross, surmount, overcome, deal with, cope with.

■ **ne·go·ti·a·ble** **adj.**

SPELLING

Write **-tiate**, not **-ciate**: **negotiate**.

ne·go·ti·a·tion /nə,gōsʜē'āsʜən/ (also **negotiations**) ▶ **n.** discussion aimed at reaching an agreement or compromise.

SYNONYMS **1** **discussion**(**s**), talks, conference, debate, dialogue, consultation. **2** **arrangement**, brokering, settlement, conclusion, completion.

ne·go·ti·a·tor /nə'gōsʜē,ātər/ ▶ **n.** a person who negotiates: *they brought in an impartial negotiator to help settle the dispute.*

SYNONYMS **mediator**, arbitrator, moderator, go-between, middleman, intermediary, representative, spokesperson, broker.

Ne·gro /'nēgrō/ ▶ **n.** (plural **Negroes**) a black person.

USAGE

The term **Negro** is now regarded as old-fashioned or even offensive.

neigh /nā/ ▶ **n.** a high-pitched cry made by a horse. ▶ **v.** make this cry.

neigh·bor /'nābər/ ▶ **n.** a person who lives next door to you, or very close by.

neigh·bor·hood /'nābər,ho͝od/ ▶ **n.** **1** a district within a town or city. **2** the area surrounding a place, person, or object.

SYNONYMS **1 district**, area, locality, locale, quarter, community; informal neck of the woods, hood. **2 vicinity**, environs.

neigh·bor·ing /ˈnābəriNG/ ▶ **adj.** situated next to or very near something.

SYNONYMS **adjacent**, adjoining, bordering, connecting, next-door, nearby, in the vicinity. ANTONYMS remote.

neigh·bor·ly /ˈnābərlē/ ▶ **adj.** characteristic of a good neighbor: *most of the tenants here are pretty neighborly.*

SYNONYMS **obliging**, helpful, friendly, kind, considerate, amicable, sociable, hospitable, companionable, civil, cordial. ANTONYMS unfriendly.

nei·ther /ˈnēT͟Hər, ˈnī-/ ▶ **determiner & pron.** not either. ▶ **adv.** used to show that a negative statement is true of two things, or also true of something else.

SPELLING
Neither is spelled with the **e** before the **i**.

nem·a·tode /ˈnēməˌtōd/ ▶ **n.** a worm of a group with slender, cylindrical, unsegmented bodies.

nem·e·sis /ˈneməsis/ ▶ **n.** (plural **nemeses** /-ˌsēz/) **1** something that brings about someone's deserved and unavoidable downfall. **2** a person's rival or archenemy.

ne·o·clas·si·cal /ˌnēōˈklasikəl/ ▶ **adj.** relating to the revival of a classical style in the arts. ■ **ne·o·clas·si·cism n.**

ne·o·con /ˈnēōˌkän/ ▶ **adj.** neoconservative, especially in advocating democratic capitalism. ▶ **n.** a neoconservative.

ne·o·con·serv·a·tive /ˌnēōkənˈsərvətiv/ ▶ **adj.** relating to an approach to politics, economics, etc., that represents a return to a traditional conservative viewpoint. ▶ **n.** a person with neoconservative views.

Ne·o·lith·ic /ˌnēəˈliTHik/ ▶ **adj.** relating to the later part of the Stone Age.

ne·ol·o·gism /nēˈäləˌjizəm/ ▶ **n.** a new word or expression.

ne·on /ˈnēän/ ▶ **n.** a gas that glows when electricity is passed through it, used in fluorescent lighting.

ne·o·na·tal /ˌnēōˈnātl/ ▶ **adj.** relating to birth and newborn children.

ne·o·phyte /ˈnēəˌfīt/ ▶ **n. 1** a person who is new to a subject, skill, or belief. **2** a novice in a religious order, or a newly ordained priest.

neph·ew /ˈnefyo͞o/ ▶ **n.** a son of your brother or sister.

ne·phri·tis /nəˈfrītis/ ▶ **n.** inflammation of the kidneys.

nep·o·tism /ˈnepəˌtizəm/ ▶ **n.** favoritism shown to relatives or friends, especially in giving them jobs.

Nep·tune /ˈnept(y)o͞on/ ▶ **n.** the eighth planet from the sun in the solar system.

nerd /nərd/ ▶ **n.** informal **1** an unfashionable person who is obsessed with a particular subject or interest. **2** an intelligent, single-minded expert in a particular discipline or profession.

nerve /nərv/ ▶ **n. 1** a fiber or bundle of fibers in the body along which impulses of sensation pass. **2** steadiness and courage in a difficult situation. **3** (**nerves**) nervousness. **4** informal impudently disrespectful or inappropriate behavior. ▶ **v.** (**nerves**, **nerving**, **nerved**) (**nerve yourself**) brace yourself for a difficult situation.

SYNONYMS ▶ **n. 1 confidence**, assurance, courage, bravery, determination, will power, spirit, grit; informal guts, moxie. **2** (**nerves**) **anxiety**, tension, nervousness, stress, worry, cold feet, apprehension; informal butterflies (in your stomach), collywobbles, jitters, the heebie-jeebies. **3 audacity**, cheek, effrontery, gall, temerity, presumption, impudence, impertinence, arrogance; informal face, front, brass, chutzpah.

□ **get on someone's nerves** informal irritate someone. **nerve cell** a neuron. **nerve gas** a poisonous gas that affects the nervous system. **nerve-racking** (or **nerve-wracking**) causing nervousness or fear.

nerve·less /ˈnərvlis/ ▶ **adj. 1** lacking strength or feeling. **2** confident.

nerv·ous /ˈnərvəs/ ▶ **adj. 1** easily frightened or worried. **2** anxious. **3** having to do with the nerves.

SYNONYMS **anxious**, worried, apprehensive, on edge, edgy, tense, stressed, agitated, uneasy, restless, worked up, keyed up, overwrought, jumpy, on tenterhooks, highly strung, nervy, excitable, neurotic; informal jittery, twitchy, in a state, uptight, wired, trepidatious, squirrelly. ANTONYMS relaxed, calm.

□ **nervous breakdown** a period of mental illness resulting from severe depression or stress. **nervous system** the network of nerves that transmits nerve impulses between parts of the body. ■ **ner·vous·ly adv. ner·vous·ness n.**

nerv·y /ˈnərvē/ ▶ **adj.** (**nervier**, **nerviest**) bold or impudent.

nest /nest/ ▶ **n. 1** a structure made by a bird in which it lays eggs and shelters its young. **2** a place where an animal or insect breeds or shelters. **3** a set of similar objects that are designed to fit inside each other. ▶ **v. 1** use or build a nest. **2** fit an object inside a larger one. □ **nest egg** a sum of money saved for the future.

nes·tle /ˈnesəl/ ▶ **v.** (**nestles**, **nestling**, **nestled**) **1** settle comfortably within or against something. **2** (of a place) lie in a sheltered position.

SYNONYMS **snuggle**, cuddle, huddle, nuzzle, settle, burrow.

nest·ling /ˈnes(t)liNG/ ▶ **n.** a bird that is too young to leave the nest.

net[1] /net/ ▶ **n. 1** a material made of strands of cord or string that are knotted together to form small open squares. **2** a piece or structure of net for catching fish or insects, surrounding a goal, etc. **3** a thin fabric with a very open weave. **4** (**the Net**) the Internet. ▶ **v.** (**nets**, **netting**, **netted**) **1** catch something in a net. **2** earn or obtain something.

SYNONYMS ▶ **n. netting**, mesh, tulle, fishnet, lace, openwork. ▶ **v. 1 catch**, capture, trap, snare; informal nab, bag, collar, bust. **2 earn**, make, clear, take home, bring in, pocket, realize.

net[2] ▶ **adj. 1** (of a sum of money) remaining after tax or expenses have been deducted. **2** (of a weight) not including the packaging. **3** (of an effect or result) overall. ▶ **v.** (**nets**, **netting**, **netted**) gain a sum of money as clear profit.

SYNONYMS ▶ **adj. after tax**, after deductions, take-home, final. ANTONYMS gross.

netbook /ˈnetˌbo͝ok/ ▶ **n.** a portable computer smaller than a notebook, designed mainly for using the Internet.

neth·er /ˈneT͟Hər/ ▶ **adj.** lower in position.

net·tle /ˈnetl/ ▶ **n.** a plant with leaves that are covered with stinging hairs. ▶ **v.** (**nettles**, **nettling**, **nettled**) annoy.

net·work /ˈnetˌwərk/ ▶ **n. 1** an arrangement of intersecting horizontal and vertical lines. **2** a complex system of railways, roads, etc., that cross or connect with each other. **3** a group of radio or television stations that connect to broadcast a program at the same time. **4** a number of interconnected computers, operations, etc. **5** a group of people who keep in contact with each other to exchange information. ▶ **v.** keep in contact with other people to exchange information.

> SYNONYMS ▶ **n.** **web**, lattice, net, matrix, mesh, criss-cross, grid, maze, labyrinth, warren, tangle.

■ **net·work·er** **n.**

neu·ral /ˈn(y)o͝orəl/ ▶ **adj.** relating to a nerve or the nervous system.

neu·ral·gia /n(y)o͝oˈraljə/ ▶ **n.** severe pain along a nerve in the head or face. ■ **neu·ral·gic** **adj.**

neu·rol·o·gy /n(y)o͝oˈräləjē/ ▶ **n.** the branch of medicine concerned with the nervous system. ■ **neu·ro·log·i·cal** /-rəˈläjikəl/ **adj.** **neu·rol·o·gist** **n.**

neu·ron /ˈn(y)o͝orän/ (or **neurone** /-rōn/) ▶ **n.** a cell that transmits nerve impulses.

neu·ro·sis /n(y)o͝oˈrōsis/ ▶ **n.** (plural **neuroses** /-ˌsēz/) a mild mental illness in which a person feels depressed or anxious, or behaves in an obsessive way.

neu·rot·ic /n(y)o͝oˈrätik/ ▶ **adj. 1** having to do with neurosis. **2** informal obsessive, or too sensitive or anxious.

> SYNONYMS **highly strung**, oversensitive, nervous, tense, paranoid, obsessive, fixated, hysterical, overwrought, irrational. ANTONYMS stable, calm.

neu·ro·trans·mit·ter /ˌn(y)o͝orōˈtranzmitər, -ˈtrans-/ ▶ **n.** a chemical substance released from a nerve fiber and bringing about the transfer of an impulse to another nerve, muscle, etc.

neu·ter /ˈn(y)o͞otər/ ▶ **adj. 1** (of a noun) neither masculine nor feminine. **2** having no sexual or reproductive organs. ▶ **v.** (**neuters**, **neutering**, **neutered**) operate on an animal so that it cannot produce young.

neu·tral /ˈn(y)o͞otrəl/ ▶ **adj. 1** not supporting either side in a dispute or war. **2** lacking noticeable or strong qualities. **3** Chemistry neither acid nor alkaline; having a pH of about 7. ▶ **n.** a position of a gear mechanism in which the engine is disconnected from the driven parts.

> SYNONYMS ▶ **adj. 1 impartial**, unbiased, unprejudiced, objective, open-minded, nonpartisan, evenhanded, disinterested, dispassionate, detached, nonaligned, unaffiliated, uninvolved. **2 inoffensive**, bland, unobjectionable, unexceptionable, anodyne, uncontroversial, safe, harmless, innocuous. **3 pale**, light, colorless, indeterminate, drab, insipid, nondescript, dull. ANTONYMS biased, provocative.

■ **neu·tral·i·ty** /n(y)o͞oˈtralitē/ **n.** **neu·tral·ly** **adv.**

neu·tral·ize /ˈn(y)o͞otrəˌlīz/ ▶ **v.** (**neutralizes**, **neutralizing**, **neutralized**) **1** stop something from having an effect. **2** make neutral.

> SYNONYMS **counteract**, offset, counterbalance, balance, cancel out, nullify, negate.

■ **neu·tral·i·za·tion** /ˌn(y)o͞otrəliˈzāSHən/ **n.**

neu·tri·no /n(y)o͞oˈtrēnō/ ▶ **n.** (plural **neutrinos**) a subatomic particle with a mass close to zero and no electric charge.

neu·tron /ˈn(y)o͞oträn/ ▶ **n.** a subatomic particle of about the same mass as a proton but without an electric charge.

nev·er /ˈnevər/ ▶ **adv. 1** not ever. **2** not at all. □ **nev·er-end·ing** (especially of something unpleasant) having or seeming to have no end.

nev·er·more /ˌnevərˈmôr/ ▶ **adv.** never again.

nev·er·the·less /ˌnevərT͟Həˈles/ ▶ **adv.** in spite of that.

> SYNONYMS **nonetheless**, even so, however, still, yet, in spite of that, despite that, be that as it may, notwithstanding.

new /n(y)o͞o/ ▶ **adj. 1** made, introduced, discovered, or experienced recently. **2** not previously used or owned. **3** (**new to**) not experienced in. **4** different from a recent previous one. **5** better than before; renewed or reformed. ▶ **adv.** newly.

> SYNONYMS ▶ **adj. 1 recent**, up to date, the latest, current, state-of-the-art, contemporary, advanced, cutting-edge, modern, avant-garde. **2 unused**, brand new, pristine, fresh. **3 different**, another, alternative, additional, extra, supplementary, further, unfamiliar, unknown, strange. **4 reinvigorated**, restored, revived, improved, refreshed, regenerated. ANTONYMS old, secondhand.

□ **New Age** an alternative movement concerned with spirituality, care for the environment, etc. **new math** a system of teaching mathematics to children, with emphasis on investigation by them and on set theory. **new moon** the phase of the moon when it first appears as a thin crescent. **New Testament** the second part of the Christian Bible, recording the life and teachings of Jesus. **New World** North and South America. **new year** the calendar year that has just begun or is about to begin, following December 31. **New Year's Eve** (or **New Year's**) December 31.

new·bie /ˈn(y)o͞obē/ ▶ **n.** (plural **newbies**) an inexperienced newcomer.

new·born /ˈn(y)o͞oˌbôrn/ ▶ **adj.** recently born.

new·com·er /ˈn(y)o͞oˌkəmər/ ▶ **n. 1** a person who has recently arrived. **2** a person who is new to an activity or situation.

> SYNONYMS **1 (new) arrival**, immigrant, settler, stranger, outsider, foreigner, alien; informal new kid on the block, johnny-come-lately. **2 beginner**, novice, learner, trainee, apprentice, probationer; informal rookie, newbie, tenderfoot.

new·el /ˈn(y)o͞owəl/ ▶ **n.** the post at the top or bottom of a stair rail.

new·fan·gled /ˈn(y)o͞oˈfaNGgəld, -ˌfaNG-/ ▶ **adj.** disapproving newly developed and unfamiliar.

New·found·land /ˌn(y)o͞ofəndˈland, ˈn(y)o͞ofəndlənd, -ˌland/ ▶ **n.** a dog of a very large breed with a thick coarse coat.

new·ly /ˈn(y)o͞olē/ ▶ **adv.** recently.

> SYNONYMS **recently**, only just, lately, freshly, not long ago.

new·ly·wed /ˈn(y)o͞olēˌwed/ ▶ **n.** a person who has recently been married.

news /n(y)o͞oz/ ▶ **n. 1** new information about recent events. **2** (**the news**) a broadcast or published news report.

SYNONYMS **report**, story, account, announcement, press release, communication, communiqué, bulletin, intelligence, information, word, revelation, disclosure, exposé; informal scoop; literary tidings.

news·cast /ˈn(y)o͞ozˌkast/ ▶ **n.** a broadcast news report. ■ **news·cast·er n.**

news·flash /ˈn(y)o͞ozˌflasн/ ▶ **n.** a brief item of important news, interrupting other radio or television programs.

news·group /ˈn(y)o͞ozˌgro͞op/ ▶ **n.** a group of Internet users who exchange information about a particular subject online.

news·let·ter /ˈn(y)o͞ozˌletər/ ▶ **n.** a bulletin issued on a regular basis to the members of a society or organization.

news·pa·per /ˈn(y)o͞ozˌpāpər/ ▶ **n.** a daily or weekly publication containing news and articles on current affairs.

SYNONYMS **paper**, journal, gazette, tabloid, broadsheet, periodical; informal rag.

new·speak /ˈn(y)o͞oˌspēk/ ▶ **n.** deliberately misleading and indirect language, used by politicians.

news·print /ˈn(y)o͞ozˌprint/ ▶ **n.** cheap, low-quality paper used for newspapers.

news·read·er /ˈn(y)o͞ozˌrēdər/ ▶ **n.** Computing a computer program for reading e-mail messages posted to newsgroups.

news·reel /ˈn(y)o͞ozˌrēl/ ▶ **n.** a short movie showing news and current affairs.

news·room /ˈn(y)o͞ozˌro͞om, -ˌro͝om/ ▶ **n.** the area in a newspaper or broadcasting office where news is processed.

news·stand /ˈn(y)o͞ozˌstand/ ▶ **n.** a stand for the sale of newspapers.

news·wor·thy /ˈn(y)o͞ozˌwərт͟нē/ ▶ **adj.** important enough to be mentioned as news.

newt /n(y)o͞ot/ ▶ **n.** a small animal with a slender body and a long tail, that can live in water or on land.

new·ton /ˈn(y)o͞otn/ ▶ **n.** Physics a unit of force.

next /nekst/ ▶ **adj. 1** coming immediately after the present one in time, space, or order. **2** (of a day of the week) nearest (or the nearest but one) after the present. ▶ **adv.** immediately afterward.

SYNONYMS ▶ **adj. 1 following**, succeeding, subsequent, ensuing, upcoming, to come. **2 neighboring**, adjacent, adjoining, next-door, bordering, connected, closest, nearest; formal contiguous, proximate. ANTONYMS previous. ▶ **adv. afterward**, after, then, later, subsequently; formal thereafter.

□ **next door** in or to the next house or room. **next of kin** a person's closest living relative or relatives. **the next world** (in some religious beliefs) the place where you go after death.

nex·us /ˈneksəs/ ▶ **n.** (plural **nexus** or **nexuses**) a connection or series of connections.

NFC ▶ **abbr.** National Football Conference.

NFL ▶ **abbr.** National Football League.

ni·a·cin /ˈnīəsin/ ▶ **n.** vitamin B_3, found in milk, liver, and yeast.

nib /nib/ ▶ **n.** the pointed end part of a pen.

nib·ble /ˈnibəl/ ▶ **v.** (**nibbles, nibbling, nibbled**) **1** take small bites out of. **2** bite gently. ▶ **n. 1** a small piece of food bitten off. **2** (**nibbles**) informal small savory snacks.

Nic·a·ra·guan /nikəˈrägwən/ ▶ **n.** a person from Nicaragua. ▶ **adj.** relating to Nicaragua.

nice /nīs/ ▶ **adj. 1** enjoyable or attractive; pleasant. **2** good-natured; kind. **3** involving a very small detail or difference.

SYNONYMS **1** *have a nice time* **enjoyable**, pleasant, agreeable, good, pleasurable, satisfying, entertaining, amusing; informal lovely, great. **2** *nice people* **pleasant**, likable, agreeable, personable, good-natured, congenial, amiable, affable, genial, friendly, charming, delightful, engaging, sympathetic, polite, courteous, well-mannered, civil, kind, obliging, helpful. **3** *nice weather* **fine**, dry, sunny, warm, mild, clement. **4** *a nice distinction* **subtle**, fine, slight, delicate, precise. ANTONYMS unpleasant, nasty.

■ **nice·ly adv. nice·ness n.**

ni·ce·ty /ˈnīsitē/ ▶ **n.** (plural **niceties**) **1** a very small detail or difference. **2** accuracy.

niche /nicн, nēsн/ ▶ **n. 1** a small hollow in a wall. **2** (**your niche**) a role or job that suits you.

SYNONYMS **1 recess**, alcove, nook, cranny, hollow, bay, cavity, pigeonhole. **2 position**, slot, place, vocation, calling, métier, station, job, level.

nick /nik/ ▶ **n.** a small cut. ▶ **v.** make a nick or nicks in.

SYNONYMS ▶ **n. cut**, scratch, incision, notch, chip, dent, indentation. ▶ **v. cut**, scratch, graze, chip, dent.

□ **in the nick of time** only just in time.

nick·el /ˈnikəl/ ▶ **n. 1** a silvery-white metallic element. **2** a five-cent coin.

nick·el·o·de·on /ˌnikəˈlōdēən/ ▶ **n. 1** informal, dated a jukebox, originally one operated by inserting a nickel coin. **2** dated a movie theater with an admission fee of one nickel.

nick·name /ˈnikˌnām/ ▶ **n.** an informal or unofficial name by which someone is known. ▶ **v.** (**nicknames, nicknaming, nicknamed**) give a nickname to.

SYNONYMS ▶ **n. pet name**, diminutive, endearment, tag, label, sobriquet, epithet; informal handle, moniker.

nic·o·tine /ˈnikəˌtēn/ ▶ **n.** a poisonous oily liquid found in tobacco.

niece /nēs/ ▶ **n.** a daughter of your brother or sister.

SPELLING

Write **i** before **e**, when the sound is *ee*, except after **c**: niece.

nif·ty /ˈniftē/ ▶ **adj.** (**niftier, niftiest**) informal very skillful, effective, or useful.

Ni·ge·ri·an /nīˈji(ə)rēən/ ▶ **n.** a person from Nigeria. ▶ **adj.** relating to Nigeria.

nig·gard·ly /ˈnigərdlē/ ▶ **adj.** not generous; stingy.

nig·ger /ˈnigər/ ▶ **n.** offensive a black person.

nig·gle /ˈnigəl/ ▶ **v.** (**niggles, niggling, niggled**) slightly worry or annoy. ▶ **n.** a minor worry or criticism.

nigh /nī/ ▶ „ **adv. prep. & adj.** old use near.

night /nīt/ ▶ **n.** **1** the time from sunset to sunrise. **2** an evening.

> SYNONYMS **nighttime**, (hours of) darkness, dark. ANTONYMS day.

night·cap /ˈnīt,kap/ ▶ **n.** **1** a hot or alcoholic drink taken at bedtime. **2** (in the past) a soft hat worn in bed.

night·club /ˈnīt,kləb/ ▶ **n.** a club that is open at night, with a bar and music.

night·fall /ˈnīt,fôl/ ▶ **n.** dusk.

> SYNONYMS **sunset**, sundown, dusk, twilight, evening, dark; literary eventide. ANTONYMS dawn.

night·gown /ˈnīt,goun/ (or **nightdress** /ˈnīt,dres/) ▶ **n.** a light, loose garment worn by a woman or girl in bed.

night·ie /ˈnītē/ ▶ **n.** informal a nightdress.

night·in·gale /ˈnītn,gāl, ˈnītiNG-/ ▶ **n.** a small bird with a tuneful song, often heard at night.

night·life /ˈnīt,līf/ ▶ **n.** social activities or entertainment available at night.

night·ly /ˈnītlē/ ▶ **adj. & adv.** happening or done every night.

night·mare /ˈnīt,me(ə)r/ ▶ **n.** **1** a frightening or unpleasant dream. **2** a very unpleasant experience.

> SYNONYMS **ordeal**, trial, hell, misery, agony, torture, murder, purgatory, disaster; informal the pits.

■ **night·mar·ish** **adj.**

night·shade /ˈnīt,SHād/ ▶ **n.** a plant related to the potato, typically having poisonous black or red berries.

night·shirt /ˈnīt,SHərt/ ▶ **n.** a long shirt worn in bed.

night·spot /ˈnīt,spät/ ▶ **n.** informal a nightclub.

ni·hil·ism /ˈnīə,lizəm, ˈnē-/ ▶ **n.** the belief that nothing has any value. ■ **ni·hil·ist** **n.** **ni·hil·is·tic** /,nīəˈlistik, ,nēə-/ **adj.**

nil /nil/ ▶ **n.** nothing; zero.

> SYNONYMS **nothing**, none, naught, zero; Tennis love.

nim·ble /ˈnimbəl/ ▶ **adj.** (**nimbler**, **nimblest**) **1** quick and light in movement. **2** able to think and understand quickly.

> SYNONYMS **1 agile**, light, quick, lithe, skillful, deft, dexterous, adroit, sprightly, spry; informal zippy. **2** *a nimble mind* **quick**, alert, lively, astute, perceptive, penetrating, discerning, shrewd, sharp, intelligent, bright, smart, clever, brilliant; informal quick on the uptake. ANTONYMS clumsy, dim.

■ **nim·bly** **adv.**

nim·bus /ˈnimbəs/ ▶ **n.** (plural **nimbi** /-,bī, -bē/ or **nimbuses**) a large gray rain cloud.

nin·com·poop /ˈninkəm,po͞op, ˈniNG-/ ▶ **n.** a stupid person.

nine /nīn/ ▶ **cardinal number** one less than ten; 9. (Roman numeral: **ix** or **IX**)

nine·teen /nīnˈtēn, ˈnīn,tēn/ ▶ **cardinal number** one more than eighteen; 19. (Roman numeral: **xix** or **XIX**) ■ **nine·teenth** **ordinal number.**

nine·ty /ˈnīntē/ ▶ **cardinal number** (plural **nineties**) ten less than one hundred; 90. (Roman numeral: **xc** or **XC**) ■ **nine·ti·eth** **ordinal number.**

nin·ja /ˈninjə/ ▶ **n.** a person skilled in ninjutsu (the Japanese technique of espionage).

nin·ny /ˈninē/ ▶ **n.** (plural **ninnies**) informal a silly person.

ninth /nīnTH/ ▶ **ordinal number** **1** at number nine in a sequence; 9th. **2** (**a ninth** or **one ninth**) each of nine equal parts into which something is divided.

ni·o·bi·um /nīˈōbēəm/ ▶ **n.** a silver-grey metallic element.

nip[1] /nip/ ▶ **v.** (**nips**, **nipping**, **nipped**) pinch, squeeze, or bite sharply. ▶ **n.** **1** a sharp bite or pinch. **2** a sharp feeling of coldness.

> SYNONYMS **bite**, nibble, peck, pinch, tweak.

nip[2] ▶ **n.** a small quantity or sip of liquor.

nip·per /ˈnipər/ ▶ **n.** informal a child.

nip·ple /ˈnipəl/ ▶ **n.** a small projection in the center of each breast, from which (in a woman who has recently had a baby) a baby is able to suck milk.

nip·py /ˈnipē/ ▶ **adj.** (**nippier**, **nippiest**) informal **1** able to move quickly. **2** chilly.

nir·va·na /nərˈvänə, nir-/ ▶ **n.** **1** the ultimate goal of Buddhism, a state in which there is no suffering or desire. **2** a state of perfect happiness.

nit /nit/ ▶ **n.** informal the egg of a louse or other parasitic insect.

nit·pick·ing /ˈnit,pikiNG/ ▶ **n.** fault-finding over small or unimportant errors or faults, especially in order to criticize unnecessarily.

ni·trate /ˈnītrāt/ ▶ **n.** a salt or ester of nitric acid.

ni·tric ac·id /ˈnītrik/ ▶ **n.** a very corrosive acid.

ni·trite /ˈnītrīt/ ▶ **n.** a salt or ester of nitrous acid.

ni·tro·gen /ˈnītrəjən/ ▶ **n.** a gas forming about 78 percent of the earth's atmosphere.

ni·tro·gly·ce·rin /,nītrōˈglisərin/ (or **nitroglycerine** /,nītrōˈglisərēn/) ▶ **n.** an explosive liquid used in dynamite.

ni·trous /ˈnītrəs/ ▶ **adj.** of or containing nitrogen.

ni·trous ox·ide ▶ **n.** a colorless gas used as an anesthetic.

nit·ty-grit·ty /ˈnitē ˈgritē/ ▶ **n.** informal the most important details.

nit·wit /ˈnit,wit/ ▶ **n.** informal a stupid person.

nix /niks/ ▶ **pron.** informal nothing.

no /nō/ ▶ **determiner** not any. ▶ **exclam.** used to refuse or disagree with something. ▶ **adv.** not at all. ▶ **n.** (plural **noes**) a decision or vote against something.

> SYNONYMS ▶ **adv.** **absolutely not**, of course not, under no circumstances, not at all, never; informal nope, no way, not a chance, not on your life; old use nay. ANTONYMS yes.

□ **no-brainer** informal something that requires little or no effort. **no-hitter** Baseball a complete game in which the pitcher yields no hits to the opposing team. **no-no** (plural **no-nos**) informal a thing that is not possible or acceptable. **no-nonsense** simple and straightforward; sensible. **no one** no person. **no two ways about it** no possible doubt about something. **no way** informal not at all; certainly not.

no. ▶ **abbr.** number.

No·bel Prize /,nōˈbel/ ▶ **n.** six international prizes awarded annually for outstanding work in physics, chemistry, physiology or medicine, literature, economics, and the promotion of peace.

no·bil·i·ty /nōˈbilitē/ ▶ **n.** **1** the quality of being noble. **2** the aristocracy.

no·ble /ˈnōbəl/ ▶ **adj.** (**nobler**, **noblest**) **1** belonging to the aristocracy. **2** having personal qualities that people admire, such as courage and honesty. **3** magnificent; impressive. ▶ **n.** a nobleman or noblewoman.

SYNONYMS ▶ **adj.** **1** **aristocratic**, blue-blooded, patrician, high-born, titled. **2** **worthy**, righteous, good, honorable, virtuous, upright. **3** **magnificent**, splendid, grand, impressive, stately, imposing, dignified, proud, striking, majestic. ANTONYMS humble, lowly. ▶ **n.** **aristocrat**, nobleman, noblewoman, lord, lady, peer (of the realm), peeress, patrician; informal aristo. ANTONYMS commoner.

■ **no·bly** **adv.**

no·ble·man /ˈnōbəlmən/ (or **noblewoman** /ˈnōbəlˌwo͝omən/) ▶ **n.** (plural **noblemen** or **noblewomen**) a member of the aristocracy.

no·bod·y /ˈnōˌbädē, -bədē/ ▶ **pron.** no person. ▶ **n.** (plural **nobodies**) a person who is not considered important.

noc·tur·nal /näkˈtərnl/ ▶ **adj.** done or active at night. ■ **noc·tur·nal·ly** **adv.**

noc·turne /ˈnäkˌtərn/ ▶ **n.** a short piece of music in a dreamy, romantic style.

nod /näd/ ▶ **v.** (**nods**, **nodding**, **nodded**) **1** lower and raise your head briefly to show agreement or as a greeting or signal. **2** let your head fall forward when you are drowsy or asleep. **3** (**nod off**) informal fall asleep. ▶ **n.** an act of nodding.

SYNONYMS ▶ **v.** **1** **incline**, bob, bow, dip. **2** **signal**, gesture, gesticulate, motion, sign, indicate.

node /nōd/ ▶ **n.** technical **1** a point in a network at which lines cross or branch. **2** the part of a plant stem from which one or more leaves grow. **3** a small mass of tissue in the body.

nod·ule /ˈnäjo͞ol/ ▶ **n.** a small swelling or lump. ■ **nod·u·lar** **adj.**

No·el /nōˈel/ ▶ **n.** Christmas.

nog·gin /ˈnägin/ ▶ **n.** informal **1** a person's head. **2** a small quantity of liquor.

Noh /nō/ ▶ **n.** a type of traditional Japanese theater with dance and song.

noise /noiz/ ▶ **n.** **1** a sound or series of sounds, especially an unpleasant one. **2** disturbances that accompany and interfere with an electrical signal.

SYNONYMS **sound**, din, hubbub, clamor, racket, uproar, tumult, commotion, pandemonium; informal hullabaloo. ANTONYMS silence.

noise·less /ˈnoizlis/ ▶ **adj.** silent or very quiet.

noi·some /ˈnoisəm/ ▶ **adj.** literary having a very unpleasant smell.

nois·y /ˈnoizē/ ▶ **adj.** (**noisier**, **noisiest**) full of or making a lot of noise.

SYNONYMS **1** **raucous**, rowdy, strident, clamorous, vociferous, boisterous. **2** **loud**, blaring, booming, deafening, thunderous, ear-splitting, piercing, cacophonous, tumultuous. ANTONYMS quiet, soft.

■ **nois·i·ly** **adv.**

no·mad /ˈnōˌmad/ ▶ **n.** a member of a people that travels from place to place to find fresh pasture for its animals.

no·mad·ic /nōˈmadik/ ▶ **adj.** having the life of a nomad; wandering.

nom de plume /ˌnäm də ˈplo͞om/ ▶ **n.** (plural **noms de plume** same pronunciation) a name used by a writer instead of their real name; a pen name.

no·men·cla·ture /ˈnōmənˌklāCHər/ ▶ **n.** a system of names used in a particular subject.

nom·i·nal /ˈnäminəl/ ▶ **adj.** **1** in name but not in reality. **2** (of a sum of money) very small.

SYNONYMS **1** **in name only**, titular, formal, official, theoretical, supposed, ostensible, so-called, self-styled. **2** **token**, symbolic, minimal. ANTONYMS real, considerable.

■ **nom·i·nal·ly** **adv.**

nom·i·nate /ˈnäməˌnāt/ ▶ **v.** (**nominates**, **nominating**, **nominated**) **1** put someone forward as a candidate for a job or award. **2** arrange a time, date, or place.

SYNONYMS **1** **propose**, put forward, put up, submit, present, recommend, suggest, name. **2** **appoint**, name, choose, decide on, select, designate, assign.

■ **nom·i·nee** /ˌnäməˈnē/ **n.**

nom·i·na·tion /ˌnäməˈnāSHən/ ▶ **n.** **1** the action of nominating or state of being nominated: *the movie received five nominations.* **2** a person or thing that is nominated.

nom·i·na·tive /ˈnämənətiv/ ▶ **n.** Grammar the case used for the subject of a verb.

non·a·ge·nar·i·an /ˌnänəjəˈne(ə)rēən, ˌnōnə-/ ▶ **n.** a person from 90 to 99 years old.

non·cha·lant /ˌnänSHəˈlänt/ ▶ **adj.** relaxed and unconcerned.

SYNONYMS **calm**, composed, unconcerned, cool, imperturbable, casual, blasé, offhand, insouciant; informal laid-back. ANTONYMS anxious.

■ **non·cha·lance** **n.** **non·cha·lant·ly** **adv.**

non·com·mis·sioned /ˌnankəˈmiSHənd/ ▶ **adj.** (of a military officer) appointed from the lower ranks.

non·com·mit·tal /ˌnänkəˈmitl/ ▶ **adj.** not showing what you think or which side you are on.

SYNONYMS **evasive**, equivocal, guarded, circumspect, reserved; informal cagey.

■ **non·com·mit·tal·ly** **adv.**

non com·pos men·tis /ˌnän ˈkämpəs ˈmentis/ ▶ **adj.** not in your right mind; distracted or crazy.

non·con·form·ist /ˌnänkənˈfôrmist/ ▶ **n.** **1** a person who does not follow accepted ideas or behavior. **2** (**Nonconformist**) a member of a Protestant church that does not follow the beliefs of the established Church of England.

SYNONYMS **dissenter**, protester, rebel, freethinker, individualist, free spirit, maverick, renegade, schismatic, apostate, heretic.

■ **non·con·form·i·ty** **n.**

non·de·script /ˌnändəˈskript/ ▶ **adj.** having no interesting or special features.

SYNONYMS **undistinguished**, unremarkable, featureless, unmemorable, ordinary, average, run-of-the-mill, mundane, uninteresting, uninspiring, colorless, bland. ANTONYMS distinctive.

none /nən/ ▶ **pron.** **1** not any. **2** no one. ▶ **adv.** (**none the**) not at all.

non·en·ti·ty /nänˈentitē/ ▶ **n.** (plural **nonentities**) an unimportant person or thing.

none·the·less /ˌnənT͟Hə'les/ ▶ **adv.** in spite of that; nevertheless.

non·e·vent /ˌnäni'vent/ ▶ **n.** a very disappointing or uninteresting event.

non·ex·ist·ent /ˌnänig'zistənt/ ▶ **adj.** not real or present.

> SYNONYMS **imaginary**, imagined, unreal, fictional, fictitious, made up, invented, fanciful, mythical, illusory. ANTONYMS real.

non·pa·reil /ˌnänpə'rel/ ▶ **adj.** having no match or equal. ▶ **n. 1** a person or thing having no match or equal. **2** a small piece of sugared chocolate.

non·plussed /nän'pləst/ ▶ **adj.** surprised and confused.

non·prof·it /'nän'präfit/ ▶ **adj.** not intended to make a profit. ▶ **n.** a nonprofit organization.

non·pro·lif·er·a·tion /ˌnänprəˌlifə'rāsHən/ ▶ **n.** the prevention of an increase in the number of nuclear weapons that are produced.

non·sense /'nänˌsens/ ▶ **n. 1** words or statements that make no sense. **2** silly behavior.

> SYNONYMS **1 rubbish**, gibberish, claptrap, balderdash, garbage; informal baloney, bosh, tripe, drivel, gobbledegook, mumbo-jumbo, poppycock, twaddle, guff, bilge, hogwash, piffle. **2 mischief**, misbehavior; informal tomfoolery, monkey business, shenanigans, malarkey. ANTONYMS sense.

non·sen·si·cal /nän'sensikəl/ ▶ **adj.** making no sense; ridiculous.

non se·qui·tur /ˌnän 'sekwitər/ ▶ **n.** a statement that does not follow logically from what has just been said.

non·start·er /'nän'stärtər/ ▶ **n.** informal something that has no chance of succeeding.

non·stick /'nän'stik/ ▶ **adj.** (of a pan) covered with a substance that prevents food sticking to it during cooking.

non·stop /'nän'stäp/ ▶ **adj. & adv. 1** continuing without stopping. **2** having no stops on the way to a destination.

> SYNONYMS **1 continuous**, constant, continual, incessant, ceaseless, uninterrupted, unbroken, never-ending, perpetual, round/around-the-clock, persistent, steady, unremitting, relentless, interminable. **2 continuously**, continually, incessantly, ceaselessly, all the time, constantly, perpetually, persistently, steadily, relentlessly, interminably; informal 24/7. ANTONYMS intermittent(ly), occasional(ly).

noo·dle /'no͞odl/ ▶ **n.** informal **1** a stupid or silly person. **2** a person's head.

noo·dles /'no͞odlz/ ▶ **pl.n.** strips, rings, or tubes of pasta.

nook /no͝ok/ ▶ **n.** a place that is sheltered or hidden.

noon /no͞on/ ▶ **n.** twelve o'clock in the day; midday.

> SYNONYMS **midday**, twelve o'clock, high noon, noonday, twelve hundred hours.

noon·day /'no͞onˌdā/ ▶ **adj.** taking place or appearing in the middle of the day.

noose /no͞os/ ▶ **n.** a loop with a knot that tightens as the rope or wire is pulled, used to hang people or trap animals.

nor /nôr/ ▶ **conj. & adv.** and not; and not either.

Nor·dic /'nôrdik/ ▶ **adj.** relating to Scandinavia, Finland, and Iceland.

norm /nôrm/ ▶ **n. 1** (**the norm**) the usual or standard thing. **2** a standard that is required or acceptable.

> SYNONYMS **standard**, convention, criterion, yardstick, benchmark, touchstone, rule, formula, pattern.

nor·mal /'nôrməl/ ▶ **adj.** usual and typical; what you would expect. ▶ **n.** the normal state or condition.

> SYNONYMS ▶ **adj. 1 usual**, standard, ordinary, customary, conventional, habitual, accustomed, typical, common, regular, routine, traditional, commonplace, everyday. **2 ordinary**, average, run-of-the-mill, middle-of-the-road, conventional, mainstream, garden-variety. **3 sane**, in your right mind, right in the head, of sound mind, compos mentis; informal all there. ANTONYMS unusual, insane.

■ **nor·mal·i·ty** /nôr'malitē/ **n.**

nor·mal·ize /'nôrməˌlīz/ ▶ **v.** (**normalizes**, **normalizing**, **normalized**) make or become normal. ■ **nor·mal·i·za·tion** /ˌnôrmələ'zāsHən/ **n.**

nor·mal·ly /'nôrməlē/ ▶ **adv. 1** under normal or usual conditions; as a rule. **2** in a normal manner; in the usual way.

> SYNONYMS **1 naturally**, conventionally, properly, like everyone else. **2 usually**, ordinarily, as a rule, generally, in general, mostly, on the whole, typically, habitually.

Nor·man /'nôrmən/ ▶ **n.** a member of a people from Normandy in northern France who conquered England in 1066. ▶ **adj.** relating to the Normans or Normandy.

nor·ma·tive /'nôrmətiv/ ▶ **adj.** relating to or setting a standard or norm.

Norse /nôrs/ ▶ **n.** ancient or medieval Norwegian or another Scandinavian language. ▶ **adj.** relating to ancient or medieval Norway or Scandinavia.

north /nôrTH/ ▶ **n. 1** the direction that is on your left-hand side when you are facing east. **2** the northern part of a place. ▶ **adj. 1** lying toward or facing the north. **2** (of a wind) blowing from the north. ▶ **adv.** to or toward the north. □ **North American 1** a person from North America, especially a citizen of the US or Canada. **2** relating to North America. ■ **north·ward adj. & adv. north·wards adv.**

north·east /ˌnôrTH'ēst/ ▶ **n.** the direction or region halfway between north and east. ▶ **adj. & adv. 1** toward or facing the northeast. **2** (of a wind) blowing from the northeast. ■ **north·east·ern adj.**

north·east·er·ly /ˌnôrTH'ēstərlē/ ▶ **adj. & adv. 1** facing or moving toward the northeast. **2** (of a wind) blowing from the northeast.

north·er·ly /'nôrT͟Hərlē/ ▶ **adj. & adv. 1** facing or moving toward the north. **2** (of a wind) blowing from the north.

north·ern /'nôrT͟Hərn/ ▶ **adj. 1** situated in or facing the north. **2** coming from or characteristic of the north. □ **Northern Lights** the aurora borealis.

north·ern·er /'nôrT͟Hərnər/ ▶ **n.** a person from the north of a region.

north·west /ˌnôrTH'west/ ▶ **n.** the direction or region halfway between north and west. ▶ **adj. & adv. 1** toward or facing the northwest. **2** (of a wind) blowing from the northwest. ■ **north·west·ern adj.**

north·west·er·ly /ˌnôrTHˈwestərlē/ ▶ **adj. & adv.** **1** facing or moving toward the northwest. **2** (of a wind) blowing from the northwest.

Nor·we·gian /nôrˈwējən/ ▶ **n. 1** a person from Norway. **2** the language spoken in Norway. ▶ **adj.** relating to Norway.

nose /nōz/ ▶ **n. 1** the part of the face containing the nostrils and used in breathing and smelling. **2** the front end of an aircraft, car, or other vehicle. **3** a talent for finding something. **4** the characteristic smell of a wine. ▶ **v.** (**noses**, **nosing**, **nosed**) **1** make your way slowly forward. **2** look around or pry into something. **3** (of an animal) push its nose against or into.

SYNONYMS ▶ **n. snout**, muzzle, proboscis, trunk; informal beak, conk, schnozz, hooter. ▶ **v. 1 pry**, inquire, poke around/about, interfere (in), meddle (in), stick/poke your nose in; informal snoop. **2 ease**, inch, edge, move, maneuver, steer, guide.

nose·bag /ˈnōzˌbag/ ▶ **n.** a bag containing fodder, hung from a horse's head.

nose·bleed /ˈnōzˌblēd/ ▶ **n.** an instance of bleeding from the nose.

nose·dive /ˈnōzˌdīv/ ▶ **n. 1** a sudden dramatic decline. **2** a steep downward plunge by an aircraft. ▶ **v.** (**nosedives**, **nosediving**, **nosedived**) **1** fall or decline suddenly. **2** (of an aircraft) make a nosedive.

nose·gay /ˈnōzˌgā/ ▶ **n.** a small bunch of flowers.

nosh /näsH/ informal ▶ **n. 1** food. **2** a snack. ▶ **v.** eat a snack.

nos·tal·gia /näˈstaljə, nə-/ ▶ **n.** longing for a happier or better time in the past.

nos·tal·gic /näˈstaljik, nə-/ ▶ **adj.** featuring or exhibiting feelings of nostalgia.

SYNONYMS **wistful**, sentimental, emotional, homesick, regretful, dewy-eyed, maudlin.

■ **nos·tal·gi·cal·ly adv.**

nos·tril /ˈnästrəl/ ▶ **n.** either of the two openings of the nose through which air passes to the lungs.

nos·trum /ˈnästrəm/ ▶ **n. 1** a favorite method for improving something. **2** an ineffective medicine.

nos·y /ˈnōzē/ (or **nosey**) ▶ **adj.** (**nosier**, **nosiest**) informal too inquisitive about other people's affairs.

SYNONYMS **prying**, inquisitive, curious, spying, eavesdropping, intrusive; informal snooping.

not /nät/ ▶ **adv. 1** used to express a negative. **2** less than.

no·ta·ble /ˈnōtəbəl/ ▶ **adj.** deserving to be noticed or given attention. ▶ **n.** a famous or important person.

SYNONYMS ▶ **adj. 1 noteworthy**, remarkable, outstanding, important, significant, memorable, marked, striking, impressive, momentous, uncommon. **2 prominent**, well-known, famous, famed, noted, of note. ANTONYMS unremarkable, unknown. ▶ **n. celebrity**, VIP, dignitary, luminary, star, big name, personage; informal celeb, bigwig.

no·ta·bly /ˈnōtəblē/ ▶ **adv. 1** in particular. **2** in a way that is noticeable or remarkable.

SYNONYMS **1 in particular**, particularly, especially, primarily, principally, chiefly. **2 remarkably**, especially, exceptionally, singularly, particularly, peculiarly, distinctly, significantly, unusually, uncommonly, conspicuously.

no·ta·ry /ˈnōtərē/ (in full **notary public**) ▶ **n.** (plural **notaries**) a person who is authorized to perform certain legal formalities, such as witnessing signatures.

no·ta·tion /nōˈtāsHən/ ▶ **n.** a system of symbols used in music, mathematics, etc.

notch /näcH/ ▶ **n. 1** a V-shaped cut on an edge or surface. **2** a point or level on a scale. ▶ **v. 1** make notches in. **2** (**notch something up**) score or achieve something.

SYNONYMS ▶ **n. nick**, cut, incision, score, scratch, slit, slot, groove.

note /nōt/ ▶ **n. 1** a brief written record of something. **2** a short written message. **3** a single sound of a particular pitch and length made by a musical instrument or voice, or a symbol representing this. ▶ **v.** (**notes**, **noting**, **noted**) **1** pay attention to. **2** record something in writing.

SYNONYMS ▶ **n. 1 record**, entry, reminder, comment, jotting. **2 message**, letter, line, missive; informal memo; formal memorandum, epistle. **3 annotation**, footnote, marginalia. **4** *the note of hopelessness in her voice* **tone**, hint, indication, sign, element, suggestion, sense. ▶ **v. 1 bear in mind**, be mindful of, consider, take notice of, register, be aware, take in, notice, observe, see, perceive. **2 write down**, put down, jot down, take down, scribble, enter, mark, record, register, pencil in.

□ **of note** important. **take note** pay attention.

note·book /ˈnōtˌbo͝ok/ ▶ **n. 1** a small book for writing notes in. **2** a portable computer smaller than a laptop.

SYNONYMS **notepad**, register, logbook, log, diary, journal, record; trademark Filofax.

not·ed /ˈnōtid/ ▶ **adj.** well-known.

SYNONYMS **famous**, famed, well-known, renowned, prominent, notable, important, eminent, great, acclaimed, celebrated, distinguished. ANTONYMS unknown.

note·pad /ˈnōtˌpad/ ▶ **n. 1** a pad of paper for writing notes on. **2** a pocket-sized personal computer.

note·pa·per /ˈnōtˌpāpər/ ▶ **n.** paper for writing letters on.

note·wor·thy /ˈnōtˌwərTHē/ ▶ **adj.** interesting or important.

SYNONYMS **notable**, interesting, significant, important, remarkable, striking, memorable, unique, special, unusual. ANTONYMS unexceptional.

noth·ing /ˈnəTHiNG/ ▶ **pron. 1** not anything. **2** something that is not important or interesting. **3** naught. ▶ **adv.** not at all.

SYNONYMS ▶ **pron. 1 not a thing**, zero; informal zilch, zip, nada, diddly-squat. **2 zero**, naught, nil, o; Tennis love.

noth·ing·ness /ˈnəTHiNGnis/ ▶ **n.** a state of not existing, or in which nothing exists.

no·tice /ˈnōtis/ ▶ **n. 1** the fact of being aware of or paying attention to something. **2** warning that something is going to happen. **3** a formal statement that you are going to leave a job or end an agreement. **4** a sheet of paper displaying information. **5** a small published announcement or advertisement in a newspaper. **6** a short published review of a new movie, play, or book. ▶ v. (**notices**, **noticing**, **noticed**) become aware of.

> SYNONYMS ▶ n. 1 **sign**, announcement, advertisement, poster, placard, bill, handbill, flyer. 2 **attention**, observation, awareness, consciousness, perception, regard, consideration, scrutiny; formal cognizance. 3 *advance notice of the price increase* **notification**, warning, information, news, word. ▶ v. **observe**, note, see, discern, detect, spot, perceive, make out. ANTONYMS overlook.

no·tice·a·ble /ˈnōtisəbəl/ ▶ adj. easily seen or noticed.

> SYNONYMS **obvious**, evident, apparent, manifest, plain, clear, conspicuous, perceptible, discernible, detectable, observable, visible, appreciable, unmistakable, patent. ANTONYMS imperceptible.

■ **no·tice·a·bly** adv.

> SPELLING
> Remember the **e** in the middle: noticeable.

no·ti·fi·a·ble /ˌnōtəˈfīəbəl/ ▶ adj. (of an infectious disease) that must be reported to the health authorities.

no·ti·fy /ˈnōtəˌfī/ ▶ v. (**notifies**, **notifying**, **notified**) formally tell someone about something.

> SYNONYMS **inform**, tell, let someone know, advise, apprise, alert, warn.

■ **no·ti·fi·ca·tion** /ˌnōtəfiˈkāsHən/ n.

no·tion /ˈnōsHən/ ▶ n. 1 an idea or belief. 2 an understanding. 3 (**notions**) items used in sewing, such as buttons and pins.

> SYNONYMS **idea**, impression, belief, opinion, view, concept, conception, understanding, feeling, suspicion, intuition, inkling.

no·tion·al /ˈnōsHənəl/ ▶ adj. based on an idea rather than reality. ■ **no·tion·al·ly** adv.

no·to·ri·e·ty /ˌnōtəˈrīətē/ ▶ n. the state of being notorious.

no·to·ri·ous /nəˈtôrēəs, nō-/ ▶ adj. famous for something bad.

> SYNONYMS **infamous**, scandalous, disreputable, of ill repute.

■ **no·to·ri·ous·ly** adv.

not·with·stand·ing /ˌnätwiTHˈstandiNG, -wiT͟H-/ ▶ prep. in spite of. ▶ adv. nevertheless.

nou·gat /ˈno͞ogit/ ▶ n. a candy made from sugar or honey, nuts, and egg white.

nought /nôt/ ▶ n. = NAUGHT.

noun /noun/ ▶ n. a word (other than a pronoun) that refers to a person, place, or thing.

nour·ish /ˈnərisH, ˈnə-risH/ ▶ v. 1 give a person, animal, or plant the food and other substances they need in order to grow and be healthy. 2 (**nourishing**) (of food) containing substances necessary for growth and health: *a simple but nourishing meal.* 3 keep a feeling or belief in your mind for a long time.

> SYNONYMS 1 **feed**, sustain, provide for, care for, nurture. 2 (**nourishing**) **nutritious**, wholesome, good for you, nutritive, healthy, health-giving, beneficial.

nour·ish·ment /ˈnərisHmənt, ˈnə-risH-/ ▶ n. the food and other substances necessary for life, growth, and good health.

> SYNONYMS **food**, nutriment, nutrients, nutrition, sustenance.

nou·veau riche /ˈno͞ovō ˈrēsH/ ▶ n. people who have recently become rich and who display their wealth in an obvious or tasteless way.

nou·velle /no͞oˈvel kwiˈzēn/ ▶ adj. referring to nouvelle cuisine, a modern style of cooking that avoids rich, heavy foods and emphasizes the presentation of dishes.

no·va /ˈnōvə/ ▶ n. (plural **novae** /-vē, -ˌvī/ or **novas**) a star that suddenly becomes very bright for a short period.

nov·el¹ /ˈnävəl/ ▶ n. a story of book length about imaginary people and events.

> SYNONYMS **story**, tale, narrative, romance, novella.

nov·el² ▶ adj. new in an interesting or unusual way.

> SYNONYMS **new**, original, unusual, unconventional, unorthodox, different, fresh, imaginative, innovative, unfamiliar, surprising. ANTONYMS traditional.

nov·el·ist /ˈnävəlist/ ▶ n. a person who writes novels.

no·vel·la /nōˈvelə/ ▶ n. a short novel or long short story.

nov·el·ty /ˈnävəltē/ ▶ n. (plural **novelties**) 1 the quality of being new and unusual. 2 a new or unfamiliar thing. 3 a small toy or ornament.

> SYNONYMS 1 **originality**, newness, freshness, unconventionality, innovation, unfamiliarity. 2 **knick-knack**, trinket, bauble, toy, trifle, kickshaw, ornament.

No·vem·ber /nōˈvembər, nə-/ ▶ n. the eleventh month of the year.

nov·ice /ˈnävəs/ ▶ n. 1 a person who is new to and lacks experience in a job or situation. 2 a person who has entered a religious community but has not yet taken their vows.

> SYNONYMS **beginner**, learner, newcomer, fledgling, trainee, probationer, student, pupil, apprentice, tyro, neophyte; informal rookie, newbie, tenderfoot, greenhorn. ANTONYMS expert, veteran.

no·vi·ti·ate /nōˈvisH(ē)ət, nə-/ (or **noviciate**) ▶ n. a period of being a novice in a religious community.

NOW ▶ abbr. National Organization for Women.

now /nou/ ▶ adv. 1 at the present time. 2 immediately. ▶ conj. as a result of the fact.

> SYNONYMS ▶ adv. 1 **at the moment**, at present, presently, at this moment in time, currently, nowadays, these days, today, in this day and age. 2 **at once**, straightaway, right away, (right) this minute, this instant, immediately, instantly, directly; informal pronto, asap.

now·a·days /ˈnouəˌdāz/ ▶ adv. at the present time, in contrast with the past.

no·where /ˈnōˌ(h)we(ə)r/ ▶ adv. not anywhere. ▶ pron. no place.

nox·ious /ˈnäksHəs/ ▶ adj. harmful or very unpleasant.

> SYNONYMS **poisonous**, toxic, deadly, harmful, dangerous, unhealthy, unpleasant. ANTONYMS innocuous.

noz·zle /ˈnäzəl/ ▶ n. a spout used to control a stream of liquid or gas.

NRA ▶ abbr. National Rifle Association.

nu·ance /ˈn(y)o͞oˌäns/ ▶ n. a very slight difference in meaning, expression, sound, etc.

SYNONYMS **distinction**, shade, gradation, refinement, degree, subtlety, nicety.

nub /nəb/ ▶ n. **1** (**the nub**) the central point of a matter. **2** a small lump. ■ **nub·by** adj.

nu·bile /ˈn(y)o͞oˌbīl, -bəl/ ▶ adj. (of a girl or young woman) sexually attractive.

nu·cle·ar /ˈn(y)o͞oklēər, -kli(ə)r/ ▶ adj. **1** relating to the nucleus of an atom or cell. **2** using energy released in the fission (splitting) or fusion of atomic nuclei. **3** possessing or involving nuclear weapons. □ **nuclear family** a couple and their children. **nuclear physics** the science of atomic nuclei and the way they interact.

nu·cle·ic ac·id /n(y)o͞oˈklē-ik/ ▶ n. either of two substances, DNA and RNA, that are present in all living cells.

nu·cle·us /ˈn(y)o͞oklēəs/ ▶ n. (plural **nuclei** /-klēˌī/) **1** the central and most important part of an object or group. **2** Physics the positively charged central core of an atom. **3** Biology a structure present in most cells, containing the genetic material.

SYNONYMS **core**, center, heart, kernel, nub, hub, middle, focus.

nude /n(y)o͞od/ ▶ adj. wearing no clothes. ▶ n. a painting or sculpture of a naked human figure.

SYNONYMS ▶ adj. **naked**, stark naked, bare, unclothed, undressed, stripped; informal without a stitch on, in your birthday suit, in the raw/buff, in the altogether, buck naked. ANTONYMS dressed.

■ **nu·di·ty** n.

nudge /nəj/ ▶ v. (**nudges**, **nudging**, **nudged**) **1** prod someone with your elbow to attract their attention. **2** touch or push something gently. ▶ n. a light prod or push.

SYNONYMS ▶ v. **prod**, elbow, dig, poke, jab, jog, push, touch. ▶ n. **prod**, dig (in the ribs), poke, jab, push.

nud·ist /ˈn(y)o͞odist/ ▶ n. a person who prefers to wear no clothes. ■ **nud·ism** n.

nu·ga·to·ry /ˈn(y)o͞ogəˌtôrē/ ▶ adj. formal having no purpose or value.

nug·get /ˈnəgət/ ▶ n. a small lump of precious metal found in the earth.

nui·sance /ˈn(y)o͞osəns/ ▶ n. a person or thing that causes annoyance or difficulty.

SYNONYMS **annoyance**, inconvenience, bore, bother, irritation, trial, burden, pest; informal pain (in the neck), hassle, bind, drag, headache.

nuke /n(y)o͞ok/ informal ▶ n. a nuclear weapon. ▶ v. (**nukes**, **nuking**, **nuked**) attack with nuclear weapons.

null /nəl/ ▶ adj. (**null and void**) having no legal force; invalid.

nul·li·fy /ˈnələˌfī/ ▶ v. (**nullifies**, **nullifying**, **nullified**) **1** make something legally invalid. **2** cancel out the effect of.

SYNONYMS **annul**, render null and void, invalidate, repeal, reverse, rescind, revoke, cancel, neutralize, negate, counteract.

■ **nul·li·fi·ca·tion** /ˌnələfəˈkāsнən/ n.

nul·li·ty /ˈnəlitē/ ▶ n. the state of being legally invalid.

numb /nəm/ ▶ adj. **1** (of a part of the body) having no sensation. **2** lacking the power to feel, think, or react. ▶ v. make something numb.

SYNONYMS ▶ adj. **1 without feeling**, without sensation, dead, numbed, desensitized, frozen, anesthetized, insensible, insensate. **2 dazed**, stunned, stupefied, paralyzed, immobilized. ▶ v. **1 deaden**, desensitize, anesthetize, immobilize, freeze. **2 daze**, stun, stupefy, paralyze, immobilize.

■ **numb·ly** adv. **numb·ness** n.

num·ber /ˈnəmbər/ ▶ n. **1** a quantity or value expressed by a word or symbol. **2** a quantity or amount. **3** (**a number of**) several. **4** a single issue of a magazine. **5** a song, dance, or piece of music. **6** a grammatical classification of words depending on whether one or more people or things are being referred to. ▶ v. (**numbers**, **numbering**, **numbered**) **1** amount to. **2** give a number to each thing in a series. **3** count. **4** include as a member of a group.

SYNONYMS ▶ n. **1 numeral**, integer, figure, digit, character. **2 quantity**, total, aggregate, tally, quota. **3 song**, piece, tune, track, dance. ▶ v. **1 add up to**, amount to, total, come to. **2 include**, count, reckon, deem.

□ **someone's number is up** informal someone is finished or doomed to die.

num·ber·less /ˈnəmbərləs/ ▶ adj. too many to be counted.

numb·skull /ˈnəmˌskəl/ (or **numskull**) ▶ n. informal a stupid person.

nu·mer·al /ˈn(y)o͞om(ə)rəl/ ▶ n. a symbol or word representing a number.

nu·mer·ate /ˈn(y)o͞om(ə)rət/ ▶ adj. having a good basic knowledge of arithmetic. ■ **nu·mer·a·cy** n.

nu·mer·a·tion /ˌn(y)o͞oməˈrāsнən/ ▶ n. the action of numbering or calculating.

nu·mer·a·tor /ˈn(y)o͞oməˌrātər/ ▶ n. Math the number above the line in a fraction.

nu·mer·i·cal /n(y)o͞oˈmerikəl/ ▶ adj. having to do with numbers. ■ **nu·mer·i·cal·ly** adv.

nu·mer·ous /ˈn(y)o͞om(ə)rəs/ ▶ adj. **1** many. **2** consisting of many members.

SYNONYMS **many**, a number of, a lot of, lots of, several, plenty of, countless, copious, an abundance of, frequent; informal umpteen. ANTONYMS few.

nu·mi·nous /ˈn(y)o͞omənəs/ ▶ adj. having a strong religious or spiritual quality.

nu·mis·mat·ic /ˌn(y)o͞oməzˈmatik, -məs-/ ▶ adj. having to do with coins or medals. ▶ n. (**numismatics**) the study or collection of coins, banknotes, and medals. ■ **nu·mis·ma·tist** /n(y)o͞oˈmizmətist, -ˈmis-/ n.

num·skull = NUMBSKULL.

nun /nən/ ▶ n. a member of a female religious community who has taken vows of chastity and obedience.

nun·ci·o /ˈnənsēˌō, ˈno͝on-/ ▶ n. (plural **nuncios**) a person who represents the pope in a foreign country.

nun·ner·y /ˈnən(ə)rē/ ▶ n. (plural **nunneries**) a convent.

nup·tial /ˈnəpsHəl, -cHəl/ ▶ **adj.** having to do with marriage or weddings. ▶ **n.** (**nuptials**) a wedding.

nurse /nərs/ ▶ **n. 1** a person who is trained to care for sick or injured people. **2** dated a person employed to look after young children. ▶ **v.** (**nurses**, **nursing**, **nursed**) **1** look after a sick person. **2** treat or hold carefully or protectively. **3** feed a baby from the breast. **4** hold on to a belief or feeling for a long time.

> SYNONYMS ▶ **v. 1 care for**, take care of, look after, tend, minister to. **2** *they nursed old grievances* **harbor**, foster, bear, have, hold (on to), retain.

□ **nursing home** a place providing accommodations and healthcare for old people. **nurse practitioner** a nurse qualified to treat certain medical conditions without the direct supervision of a doctor.

nurse·maid /ˈnərs,mād/ ▶ **n.** dated a woman or girl employed to look after a young child.

nurs·er·y /ˈnərs(ə)rē/ ▶ **n.** (plural **nurseries**) **1** a room in a house where young children sleep or play. **2** a nursery school. **3** a place where young plants and trees are grown for sale or for planting elsewhere. □ **nursery rhyme** a simple traditional song or poem for children. **nursery school** a school for young children between the ages of three and five.

nur·ture /ˈnərcHər/ ▶ **v.** (**nurtures**, **nurturing**, **nurtured**) **1** care for and protect a child or young plant while they are growing and developing. **2** have a feeling or belief for a long time. ▶ **n.** the state of being nurtured.

> SYNONYMS ▶ **v. 1 bring up**, care for, take care of, look after, tend, rear, raise. **2** *he nurtured my love of art* **encourage**, promote, stimulate, develop, foster, cultivate, boost, strengthen, fuel. ANTONYMS neglect.

nut /nət/ ▶ **n. 1** a fruit consisting of a hard shell around an edible kernel. **2** the kernel of such a fruit. **3** a small flat piece of metal with a hole through the center, for screwing on to a bolt. **4** (also **nutcase** /ˈnət,kās/) informal a crazy person. **5** (**nuts**) informal crazy. **6** informal a person's head.

> SYNONYMS **1 maniac**, lunatic, madman, madwoman; informal loony, nutcase, head case, screwball. **2 enthusiast**, fan, devotee, aficionado; informal freak, fanatic, addict, buff.

□ **in a nutshell** in the fewest possible words. **nuts and bolts** informal basic facts or practical details.

nut·crack·er /ˈnət,krakər/ ▶ **pl.n.** a device for cracking nuts.

nut·meg /ˈnət,meg/ ▶ **n.** a spice made from the seed of a tropical tree.

nu·tri·ent /ˈn(y)o͞otrēənt/ ▶ **n.** a substance that provides nourishment.

nu·tri·ment /ˈn(y)o͞otrəmənt/ ▶ **n.** nourishment.

nu·tri·tion /n(y)o͞oˈtrisHən/ ▶ **n.** the process of eating or taking nourishment. ■ **nu·tri·tion·al** **adj.** **nu·tri·tion·ist** **n.**

nu·tri·tious /n(y)o͞oˈtrisHəs/ ▶ **adj.** full of nourishing things; good for you.

> SYNONYMS **nourishing**, nutritive, wholesome, good for you, healthy, health-giving, beneficial.

nu·tri·tive /ˈn(y)o͞otrətiv/ ▶ **adj. 1** having to do with nutrition. **2** nutritious.

nut·ty /ˈnətē/ ▶ **adj.** (**nuttier**, **nuttiest**) **1** tasting like nuts. **2** containing a lot of nuts. **3** informal peculiar or mad. □ **be nutty about** informal like very much: *he is nutty about boats*. (**as**) **nutty as a fruitcake** informal completely insane. ■ **nut·ti·ness** **n.**

nuz·zle /ˈnəzəl/ ▶ **v.** (**nuzzles**, **nuzzling**, **nuzzled**) gently rub or push against someone or something with the nose.

NW ▶ **abbr.** northwest or northwestern.

ny·lon /ˈnī,län/ ▶ **n. 1** a strong, lightweight synthetic material. **2** (**nylons**) nylon stockings or tights.

nymph /nimf/ ▶ **n. 1** (in Greek and Roman mythology) a spirit in the form of a beautiful young woman. **2** an immature form of an insect such as a dragonfly.

nymph·et /nimˈfet, ˈnimfit/ ▶ **n.** an attractive and physically mature young girl.

O (or **o**) ▶ **n.** (plural **Os** or **O's**) **1** the fifteenth letter of the alphabet. **2** zero.

oaf /ōf/ ▶ **n.** a stupid, rude, or clumsy man. ■ **oaf·ish adj.**

oak /ōk/ ▶ **n.** a large tree that produces acorns and a hard wood used in building and for furniture.

oak·en /'ōkən/ ▶ **adj.** literary made of oak.

oar /ôr/ ▶ **n.** a pole with a flat blade, used for rowing a boat.

oar·lock /'ôr,läk/ ▶ **n.** a fitting on the side of a boat for holding an oar.

oars·man /'ôrzmən/ (or **oarswoman**) ▶ **n.** (plural **oarsmen** or **oarswomen**) a rower.

o·a·sis /ō'āsis/ ▶ **n.** (plural **oases**) a fertile place in a desert where water rises to ground level.

oat /ōt/ ▶ **n. 1** a cereal plant grown in cool climates. **2** (**oats**) the grain of this plant.

oath /ōTH/ ▶ **n.** (plural **oaths**) **1** a solemn promise to do something or that something is true. **2** a swear word.

SYNONYMS **1 vow**, pledge, promise, affirmation, word (of honor), guarantee. **2 swear word**, expletive, profanity, four-letter word, dirty word, obscenity, curse; formal imprecation.

oat·meal /'ōt,mēl/ ▶ **n.** ground oats, used in making breakfast cereals or other food.

ob·du·rate /'äbd(y)ərit/ ▶ **adj.** refusing to change your mind; stubborn. ■ **ob·du·ra·cy n.**

o·be·di·ence /ō'bēdēəns/ ▶ **n. 1** the quality of being obedient or of doing what you are told. **2** submission to a law or rule. □ **in obedience to** in accordance with.

o·be·di·ent /ō'bēdēənt/ ▶ **adj.** willingly doing what you are told.

SYNONYMS **compliant**, biddable, acquiescent, good, law-abiding, deferential, governable, docile, submissive. ANTONYMS rebellious.

■ **o·be·di·ent·ly adv.**

o·bei·sance /ō'bāsəns, ō'bē-/ ▶ **n. 1** respect for someone and willingness to obey them. **2** a gesture expressing this, such as a bow.

ob·e·lisk /'äbə,lisk/ ▶ **n.** a stone pillar that tapers to a point, set up as a monument.

o·bese /ō'bēs/ ▶ **adj.** very fat.

SYNONYMS **fat**, overweight, corpulent, gross, stout, fleshy, heavy, portly, potbellied, bloated, flabby; informal porky, roly-poly, blubbery. ANTONYMS thin.

■ **o·be·si·ty n.**

o·bey /ō'bā/ ▶ **v.** do what a person or a rule tells you to do.

SYNONYMS **1 do as you are told**, defer to, submit to, bow to. **2** *he refused to obey the order* **carry out**, perform, act on, execute, discharge, implement. **3** *rules have to be obeyed* **comply with**, adhere to, observe, abide by, act in accordance with, conform to, respect, follow, keep to, stick to. ANTONYMS defy, ignore.

ob·fus·cate /'äbfə,skāt/ ▶ **v.** (**obfuscates, obfuscating, obfuscated**) make something unclear or hard to understand. ■ **ob·fus·ca·tion** /,äbfə'skāSHən/ **n.**

o·bit·u·ar·y /ō'biCHōō,erē/ ▶ **n.** (plural **obituaries**) a short piece of writing about a person and their life that is published in a newspaper when they die.

ob·ject ▶ **n.** /'äbjəkt/ **1** a thing that you can see and touch. **2** a person or thing to which an action or feeling is directed. **3** a purpose. **4** Grammar a noun acted on by a transitive verb or by a preposition. ▶ **v.** /əb'jekt/ say that you disagree with or disapprove of something.

SYNONYMS ▶ **n. 1 thing**, article, item, entity, device, gadget. **2 target**, butt, focus, recipient, victim. **3 objective**, aim, goal, target, purpose, end, plan, point, ambition, intention, idea. ▶ **v.** *they objected to the scheme* **protest about**, oppose, take exception to, take issue with, take a stand against, argue against, quarrel with, condemn, draw the line at, demur at, mind, complain about. ANTONYMS approve of, accept.

■ **ob·jec·tor** /əb'jektər/ **n.**

ob·jec·ti·fy /əb'jektə,fī/ ▶ **v.** (**objectifies, objectifying, objectified**) **1** refer to something abstract as if it has a physical form. **2** treat someone as an object rather than a person. ■ **ob·jec·ti·fi·ca·tion** /əb,jektəfi'kāSHən/ **n.**

ob·jec·tion /əb'jekSHən/ ▶ **n.** a statement of disagreement or disapproval.

SYNONYMS **protest**, protestation, complaint, opposition, demurral, counterargument, disagreement, disapproval, dissent.

ob·jec·tion·a·ble /əb'jekSHənəbəl/ ▶ **adj.** unpleasant or offensive.

ob·jec·tive /əb'jektiv/ ▶ **adj. 1** considering the facts about something without being influenced by personal feelings or opinions. **2** having actual existence outside the mind. ▶ **n.** a goal or aim.

SYNONYMS ▶ **adj. 1 impartial**, unbiased, unprejudiced, nonpartisan, disinterested, neutral, uninvolved, evenhanded, fair, dispassionate, detached. **2 factual**, actual, real, empirical, verifiable. ANTONYMS subjective, emotional. ▶ **n. aim**, intention, purpose, target, goal, object, end, idea, plan, ambition.

■ **ob·jec·tiv·i·ty** /,äbjek'tivitē/ **n.**

ob·jec·tive·ly /əb'jektivlē/ ▶ **adv.** in an objective way.

SYNONYMS **impartially**, without bias/prejudice, even-handedly, fairly, dispassionately, with an open mind, without fear or favor.

ob·jet d'art /ˌôbzHä 'där/ ▶ **n.** (plural **objets d'art**) a small decorative object or piece of art.

ob·la·tion /ə'blāsHən/ ▶ **n.** a thing presented or offered to a god.

ob·li·gate /'äbliˌgāt/ ▶ **v.** (**be obligated**) having a moral or legal duty to do something.

ob·li·ga·tion /ˌäbli'gāsHən/ ▶ **n.** **1** something you must do in order to keep to an agreement or fulfill a duty. **2** the state of having to do something of this kind.

SYNONYMS **1 commitment**, duty, responsibility, function, task, job, charge, onus, liability, requirement, debt. **2** *a sense of obligation* **duty**, compulsion, indebtedness, necessity, pressure, constraint.

o·blig·a·to·ry /ə'bligəˌtôrē/ ▶ **adj.** required by a law, rule, or custom; compulsory.

SYNONYMS **compulsory**, mandatory, prescribed, required, statutory, enforced, binding, requisite, necessary, imperative, de rigueur. ANTONYMS optional.

o·blige /ə'blīj/ ▶ **v.** (**obliges**, **obliging**, **obliged**) **1** make someone do something because it is a law, a necessity, or their duty. **2** do something to help someone. **3** (**be obliged**) be grateful.

SYNONYMS **1 compel**, force, require, make, bind, constrain. **2 do someone a favor**, accommodate, help, assist, indulge, humor. **3** (**obliged**) **thankful**, grateful, appreciative, beholden, indebted, in someone's debt.

o·blig·ing /ə'blījiNG/ ▶ **adj.** willing to help.

SYNONYMS **helpful**, accommodating, cooperative, agreeable, amenable, generous, kind, decent.

■ **o·blig·ing·ly** **adv.**

o·blique /ə'blēk, ō'blēk/ ▶ **adj.** **1** at an angle; slanting. **2** not done in a direct way.

SYNONYMS **1** *an oblique line* **slanting**, slanted, sloping, at an angle, angled, diagonal, askew, squint. **2** *an oblique reference* **indirect**, roundabout, circuitous, implicit, implied, elliptical, evasive. ANTONYMS straight, direct.

■ **o·blique·ly** **adv.**

ob·lit·er·ate /ə'blitəˌrāt/ ▶ **v.** (**obliterates**, **obliterating**, **obliterated**) destroy or remove all signs of something.

SYNONYMS **1 destroy**, wipe out, annihilate, demolish; informal zap. **2 hide**, obscure, blot out, block, cover, screen.

■ **ob·lit·er·a·tion** /əˌblitə'rāsHən/ **n.**

ob·liv·i·on /ə'blivēən/ ▶ **n.** **1** the state of being unaware of what is happening around you. **2** the state of being forgotten or destroyed.

ob·liv·i·ous /ə'blivēəs/ ▶ **adj.** not aware of what is happening around you.

SYNONYMS **unaware**, unconscious, heedless, unmindful, insensible, ignorant, blind, deaf, impervious. ANTONYMS conscious.

ob·long /'äbˌlôNG, -ˌläNG/ ▶ **adj.** rectangular in shape. ▶ **n.** an oblong shape.

ob·lo·quy /'äbləkwē/ ▶ **n.** **1** strong public criticism. **2** disgrace.

ob·nox·ious /əb'näksHəs/ ▶ **adj.** very unpleasant and offensive.

SYNONYMS **unpleasant**, disagreeable, nasty, offensive, objectionable, unsavory, revolting, repulsive, repellent, repugnant, disgusting, odious, vile, foul, loathsome, nauseating, sickening, hateful, insufferable, intolerable; informal horrible, horrid, ghastly, gross, yucky, God-awful. ANTONYMS delightful.

o·boe /'ōbō/ ▶ **n.** a woodwind instrument that you play by blowing through a double-reed mouthpiece. ■ **o·bo·ist** **n.**

ob·scene /əb'sēn/ ▶ **adj.** **1** dealing with sex in an offensive way. **2** (of a payment, pay raise, etc.) unacceptably large.

SYNONYMS **1 pornographic**, indecent, smutty, dirty, filthy, X-rated, explicit, lewd, rude, vulgar, coarse, scatological; informal blue; euphemistic adult. **2 scandalous**, shocking, outrageous, immoral.

■ **ob·scene·ly** **adv.**

ob·scen·i·ty /əb'senitē/ ▶ **n.** (plural **obscenities**) obscene language or behavior, or an obscene action or word.

ob·scure /əb'skyo͝or/ ▶ **adj.** **1** not discovered or known about. **2** hard to understand or see. ▶ **v.** (**obscures**, **obscuring**, **obscured**) make something difficult to see, hear, or understand.

SYNONYMS ▶ **adj.** **1 unclear**, uncertain, unknown, mysterious, hazy, vague, indeterminate. **2 abstruse**, oblique, opaque, cryptic, arcane, enigmatic, puzzling, perplexing, baffling, incomprehensible, impenetrable, elliptical. **3 little known**, unknown, unheard of, unsung, minor, unrecognized, forgotten. ANTONYMS clear, plain, famous. ▶ **v.** **1 hide**, conceal, cover, veil, shroud, screen, mask, cloak, block, obliterate, eclipse. **2 confuse**, complicate, obfuscate, cloud, blur, muddy. ANTONYMS reveal, clarify.

■ **ob·scure·ly** **adv.**

ob·scu·ri·ty /əb'skyo͝oritē/ ▶ **n.** (plural **obscurities**) **1** the state of being unknown or forgotten. **2** the quality of being hard to understand.

ob·se·quies /'äbsəkwēz/ ▶ **pl.n.** funeral ceremonies.

ob·se·qui·ous /əb'sēkwēəs/ ▶ **adj.** too attentive and respectful toward someone. ■ **ob·se·qui·ous·ly** **adv.** **ob·se·qui·ous·ness** **n.**

ob·serv·ance /əb'zərvəns/ ▶ **n.** **1** the obeying of a rule or following of a custom. **2** (**observances**) acts performed for religious or ceremonial reasons.

ob·serv·ant /əb'zərvənt/ ▶ **adj.** quick to notice things.

SYNONYMS **alert**, sharp-eyed, eagle-eyed, attentive, watchful; informal beady-eyed, on the ball. ANTONYMS inattentive.

ob·ser·va·tion /ˌäbzər'vāsHən/ ▶ **n.** **1** the close watching of someone or something. **2** the ability to notice important details. **3** a comment.

SYNONYMS **1 monitoring**, watching, scrutiny, survey, surveillance, attention, study. **2 remark**, comment, opinion, impression, thought, reflection.

■ **ob·ser·va·tion·al** **adj.**

ob·serv·a·to·ry /əb'zərvə,tôrē/ ▶ **n.** (plural **observatories**) a building containing a telescope for looking at the stars and planets.

ob·serve /əb'zərv/ ▶ **v.** (**observes**, **observing**, **observed**) **1** notice. **2** watch something carefully. **3** make a remark. **4** obey a rule. **5** celebrate or take part in a particular festival.

SYNONYMS **1 notice**, see, note, perceive, discern, spot. **2 watch**, look at, contemplate, view, survey, regard, keep an eye on, scrutinize, keep under surveillance, monitor; informal keep tabs on. **3 remark**, comment, say, mention, declare, announce, state; formal opine. **4 comply with**, abide by, keep, obey, adhere to, heed, honor, fulfill, respect, follow, consent to, accept.

■ **ob·serv·a·ble adj.**

ob·serv·er /əb'zərvər/ ▶ **n. 1** a person who watches or notices something. **2** an official sent to an area to monitor political or military events.

SYNONYMS **spectator**, onlooker, watcher, fly on the wall, viewer, witness, eyewitness.

ob·sess /əb'ses/ ▶ **v.** preoccupy someone to a disturbing extent.

SYNONYMS (**obsessed**) **fixated**, possessed, haunted, consumed, infatuated, besotted; informal smitten, hung up.

ob·ses·sion /əb'sesʜən/ ▶ **n. 1** the state of being obsessed. **2** something that you cannot stop thinking about.

SYNONYMS **fixation**, passion, mania, compulsion, fetish, preoccupation, infatuation, phobia, complex, neurosis; informal bee in your bonnet, hang-up, thing.

■ **ob·ses·sion·al adj.**

ob·ses·sive /əb'sesiv/ ▶ **adj.** unable to stop thinking about someone or something.

SYNONYMS **consuming**, all-consuming, compulsive, controlling, fanatical, neurotic, excessive; informal pathological.

■ **ob·ses·sive·ly adv. ob·ses·sive·ness n.**

ob·sid·i·an /əb'sidēən, äb-/ ▶ **n.** a dark glasslike volcanic rock.

ob·so·les·cent /,äbsə'lesənt/ ▶ **adj.** becoming obsolete. ■ **ob·so·les·cence n.**

ob·so·lete /,äbsə'lēt/ ▶ **adj.** no longer produced or used; out of date.

SYNONYMS **out of date**, outdated, outmoded, old-fashioned, passé, antiquated, antediluvian, anachronistic, superannuated, archaic, ancient, fossilized, extinct, defunct. ANTONYMS current, modern.

ob·sta·cle /'äbstəkəl/ ▶ **n.** a thing that blocks the way or makes it difficult to do something.

SYNONYMS **barrier**, hurdle, stumbling block, obstruction, bar, block, impediment, hindrance, snag, catch, drawback, hitch, fly in the ointment, handicap, difficulty, problem, disadvantage. ANTONYMS advantage, aid.

ob·ste·tri·cian /,äbstə'trisʜən/ ▶ **n.** a doctor who is trained in obstetrics.

ob·stet·rics /əb'stetriks, äb-/ ▶ **n.** the branch of medicine concerned with childbirth. ■ **ob·stet·ric adj.**

ob·sti·nate /'äbstənit/ ▶ **adj. 1** refusing to change your mind or stop what you are doing. **2** hard to deal with.

SYNONYMS **stubborn**, pigheaded, mulish, self-willed, unyielding, inflexible, unbending, intransigent, intractable; old use contumacious. ANTONYMS compliant.

■ **ob·sti·na·cy n. ob·sti·nate·ly adv.**

ob·strep·er·ous /əb'strepərəs, äb-/ ▶ **adj.** noisy and difficult to control.

ob·struct /əb'strəkt, äb-/ ▶ **v.** be in the way or stop the progress of.

SYNONYMS **1 block (up)**, clog (up), cut off, choke, dam up; technical occlude. **2 impede**, hinder, interfere with, hamper, block, interrupt, hold up, stand in the way of, frustrate, slow down, delay, bring to a standstill, stop, halt. ANTONYMS clear, facilitate.

ob·struc·tion /əb'strəksʜən, äb-/ ▶ **n. 1** a thing that is in the way; an obstacle or blockage. **2** the obstructing of someone or something.

SYNONYMS **obstacle**, barrier, stumbling block, impediment, hindrance, difficulty, check, restriction, blockage, stoppage, congestion, bottleneck, holdup.

ob·struc·tive /əb'strəktiv, äb-/ ▶ **adj.** deliberately causing a delay or difficulty.

ob·tain /əb'tān, äb-/ ▶ **v. 1** get possession of. **2** formal be established or usual.

SYNONYMS **get**, acquire, come by, secure, procure, pick up, gain, earn, achieve, attain; informal get (a) hold of, lay your hands on, land.

ob·tain·a·ble /əb'tānəbəl, äb-/ ▶ **adj.** able to be obtained.

SYNONYMS **available**, to be had, in circulation, on the market, on offer, in season, at your disposal, accessible; informal up for grabs, on tap.

ob·trude /əb'tro͞od/ ▶ **v.** (**obtrudes**, **obtruding**, **obtruded**) become noticeable in an unpleasant or unwelcome way.

ob·tru·sive /əb'tro͞osiv, äb-/ ▶ **adj.** noticeable in an unwelcome way.

ob·tuse /əb't(y)o͞os, äb-/ ▶ **adj. 1** annoyingly slow to understand. **2** (of an angle) more than 90° and less than 180°. **3** not sharp or pointed; blunt.

SYNONYMS **stupid**, foolish, slow-witted, slow, unintelligent, simple-minded; informal dim, dimwitted, dense, dumb, slow on the uptake, halfwitted, brain-dead, moronic, cretinous, thick. ANTONYMS clever.

ob·verse /'äb,vərs/ ▶ **n. 1** the side of a coin or medal showing the head or main design. **2** the opposite of something.

ob·vi·ate /'äbvē,āt/ ▶ **v.** (**obviates**, **obviating**, **obviated**) remove or prevent a need or difficulty.

ob·vi·ous /'äbvēəs/ ▶ **adj.** easily seen or understood; clear.

SYNONYMS **clear**, plain, evident, apparent, patent, manifest, conspicuous, pronounced, prominent, distinct, noticeable, unmistakable, perceptible, visible, palpable; informal sticking out like a sore thumb. ANTONYMS imperceptible.

■ **ob·vi·ous·ly adv.**

oc·a·ri·na /,äkə'rēnə/ ▶ **n.** a small egg-shaped wind instrument with holes for the fingers.

oc·ca·sion /ə'kāzʜən/ ▶ **n. 1** a particular event, or the time at which it happens. **2** a special event or celebration. **3** a suitable time for something. **4** formal reason or cause. ▶ **v.** formal cause.

SYNONYMS ▶ **n. 1 time**, instance, juncture, point, moment, experience, case. **2 event**, affair, function, celebration, party, get-together, gathering; informal do, bash. ▶ **v. cause**, give rise to, bring about, result in, lead to, prompt, create, engender.

SPELLING

Two **c**s and one **s**: occasion.

oc·ca·sion·al /ə'kāzʜənl/ ▶ **adj.** happening or done from time to time.

SYNONYMS **infrequent**, intermittent, irregular, periodic, sometime, sporadic, odd. ANTONYMS regular, frequent.

oc·ca·sion·al·ly /ə'kāzʜənlē/ ▶ **adv.** once in a while: *I occasionally have wine with dinner.*

SYNONYMS **sometimes**, from time to time, (every) now and then, (every) now and again, at times, every so often, (every) once in a while, on occasion, periodically. ANTONYMS often.

oc·ci·den·tal /,äksə'dentl/ ▶ **adj.** relating to the countries of the West.

oc·clude /ə'klo͞od/ ▶ **v.** (**occludes**, **occluding**, **occluded**) technical close up; block.

oc·cult /ə'kəlt/ ▶ **n.** (**the occult**) the world of magic and supernatural beliefs and practices. ▶ **adj.** relating to the occult.

SYNONYMS ▶ **adj. supernatural**, magic, magical, satanic, mystical, unearthly, esoteric, psychic.

■ **oc·cult·ism n. oc·cult·ist n.**

oc·cu·pan·cy /'äkyəpənsē/ ▶ **n. 1** the action of occupying a place. **2** the proportion of accommodations that is occupied.

oc·cu·pant /'äkyəpənt/ ▶ **n.** a person who occupies a place.

SYNONYMS **resident**, inhabitant, owner, householder, tenant, leaseholder, lessee.

oc·cu·pa·tion /,äkyə'pāsʜən/ ▶ **n. 1** a job or profession. **2** a way of spending time. **3** the occupying of a place.

SYNONYMS **1 job**, profession, work, line of work, trade, employment, business, career, métier, calling. **2 pastime**, activity, hobby, pursuit, interest, entertainment, recreation. **3 conquest**, capture, invasion, seizure, annexation, colonization, subjugation.

oc·cu·pa·tion·al /,äkyə'pāsʜənl/ ▶ **adj.** having to do with a job or profession. □ **occupational therapy** the use of certain activities and crafts to help someone recover from an illness.

oc·cu·py /'äkyə,pī/ ▶ **v.** (**occupies**, **occupying**, **occupied**) **1** live or work in a building. **2** fill or take up a space, time, or position. **3** (**occupied**) in use; not available. **4** keep someone busy. **5** enter and take control of a place.

SYNONYMS **1 live in**, inhabit, lodge in, move into, people, populate, settle, tenant. **2** (**occupied**) **in use**, full, engaged, taken. **3 engage**, busy, distract, absorb, engross, hold, interest, involve, entertain. **4** (**occupied**) **busy**, working, at work, active; informal tied up, hard at it, on the go. **5** *the region was occupied by Japan* **capture**, seize, conquer, invade, colonize, annex, subjugate.

■ **oc·cu·pi·er n.**

oc·cur /ə'kər/ ▶ **v.** (**occurs**, **occurring**, **occurred**) **1** happen. **2** be found or present. **3** (**occur to**) come into someone's mind.

SYNONYMS **1 happen**, take place, come about, transpire; informal go down. **2 be found**, be present, exist, appear, develop, manifest itself. **3** (**occur to**) **enter your head**, cross your mind, come/spring to mind, strike, dawn on, suggest itself.

SPELLING

Double **c**, and there is a double **r** in **occurred**, **occurring**, and **occurrence**.

oc·cur·rence /ə'kərəns/ ▶ **n. 1** a thing that happens or exists. **2** the fact of something happening or existing.

SYNONYMS **1 event**, incident, happening, phenomenon, circumstance, episode. **2 existence**, instance, appearance, frequency, incidence, prevalence, rate; Statistics distribution.

o·cean /'ōsʜən/ ▶ **n.** a very large area of sea.

o·cean·front /'ōsʜən,frənt/ ▶ **n.** the land that borders an ocean.

o·cean·go·ing /'ōsʜən,gō-iɴɢ/ ▶ **adj.** (of a ship) designed to cross oceans.

o·ce·an·ic /,ōsʜē'anik/ ▶ **adj.** relating to the ocean.

o·cea·nog·ra·phy /,ōsʜə'nägrəfē/ ▶ **n.** the study of the sea. ■ **o·cea·nog·ra·pher n.**

oc·e·lot /'äsə,lät, 'ōsə-/ ▶ **n.** a medium-sized striped and spotted wild cat, found in South and Central America.

o·cher /'ōkər/ ▶ **n.** a type of light yellow or reddish earth, used as a pigment.

o'·clock /ə'kläk/ ▶ **adv.** used to say which hour it is when telling the time.

oc·ta·gon /'äktə,gän, -gən/ ▶ **n.** a figure with eight straight sides and eight angles. ■ **oc·tag·o·nal** /äk'tagənl/ **adj.**

oc·ta·he·dron /,äktə'hēdrən/ ▶ **n.** (plural **octahedrons** or **octahedra** /-drə/) a three-dimensional shape with eight flat faces.

oc·tane /'äktān/ ▶ **n.** a liquid hydrocarbon present in petroleum.

oc·tave /'äktəv, 'äk,tāv/ ▶ **n. 1** a series of eight musical notes occupying the interval between (and including) two notes. **2** the interval between two such notes.

oc·ta·vo /äk'tävō, -'tā-/ ▶ **n.** (plural **octavos**) a size of book page that results from folding each printed sheet into eight leaves (sixteen pages).

oc·tet /äk'tet/ ▶ **n. 1** a group of eight musicians. **2** a piece of music for an octet.

Oc·to·ber /äk'tōbər/ ▶ **n.** the tenth month of the year.

oc·to·ge·nar·i·an /,äktəjə'ne(ə)rēən/ ▶ **n.** a person who is from 80 to 89 years old.

oc·to·pus /'äktəpəs/ ▶ **n.** (plural **octopuses**) a sea creature with a soft body and eight long tentacles.

oc·u·lar /'äkyələr/ ▶ **adj.** having to do with the eyes.

OD ▶ **v.** (**OD's**, **OD'ing**, **OD'd**) informal take an overdose of a drug.

odd /äd/ ▶ **adj.** **1** unusual or unexpected; strange. **2** (of whole numbers such as 3 and 5) having one left over as a remainder when divided by two. **3** occasional. **4** spare; available. **5** separated from a pair or set. **6** in the region of.

SYNONYMS **1 strange**, peculiar, queer, funny, bizarre, eccentric, unconventional, outlandish, unusual, weird, curious, abnormal, puzzling, mystifying, baffling, unaccountable; informal wacky. **2** *odd jobs* **occasional**, casual, irregular, isolated, sporadic, periodic, miscellaneous, various, varied, sundry. **3** *an odd shoe* **mismatched**, unmatched, unpaired, single, lone, solitary, extra, leftover, spare. ANTONYMS normal, ordinary, regular.

□ **odd man out** a person or thing differing from others in a group.
■ **odd·ly** **adv.** **odd·ness** **n.**

odd·ball /ˈädˌbôl/ ▶ **n.** informal a strange or eccentric person.

odd·i·ty /ˈäditē/ ▶ **n.** (plural **oddities**) **1** the quality of being strange. **2** a strange person or thing.

odd·ment /ˈädmənt/ ▶ **n.** an item or piece left over from a larger piece or set.

odds /ädz/ ▶ **pl.n.** **1** the ratio between the amount placed as a bet and the money that would be received if the bet was won. **2** (**the odds**) the chances of something happening. **3** (**the odds**) the advantage thought to be possessed by one person or side compared to another.

SYNONYMS **likelihood**, probability, chances.

□ **at odds** in conflict or disagreement. **odds and ends** miscellaneous articles or remnants. **odds-on 1** (of a horse) with betting odds in favor of winning. **2** very likely to happen or succeed.

ode /ōd/ ▶ **n.** a poem addressed to a person or thing or celebrating an event.

o·di·ous /ˈōdēəs/ ▶ **adj.** very unpleasant.

SYNONYMS **revolting**, repulsive, repellent, repugnant, disgusting, offensive, objectionable, vile, foul, abhorrent, loathsome, nauseating, sickening, hateful, detestable, abominable, monstrous, appalling, insufferable, intolerable, despicable, contemptible, unspeakable, atrocious, awful, terrible, dreadful, frightful, obnoxious, unpleasant, disagreeable, nasty; informal ghastly, horrible, horrid, God-awful. ANTONYMS delightful.

o·di·um /ˈōdēəm/ ▶ **n.** widespread hatred or disgust.

o·dom·e·ter /ōˈdämitər/ ▶ **n.** an instrument on a vehicle for recording the number of miles traveled.

o·dor /ˈōdər/ ▶ **n.** a smell.

SYNONYMS **smell**, stench, stink, reek, aroma, bouquet, scent, perfume, fragrance; literary redolence.

■ **o·dor·ous** **adj.** **o·dor·less** **adj.**

o·dor·if·er·ous /ˌōdəˈrifərəs/ ▶ **adj.** smelly.

od·ys·sey /ˈädəsē/ ▶ **n.** (plural **odysseys**) a long, eventful journey.

SYNONYMS **journey**, voyage, trip, trek, travels, quest, crusade, pilgrimage.

oeu·vre /ˈœvrə/ ▶ **n.** all the works of a particular artist, composer, or author.

of /əv/ ▶ **prep.** **1** expressing the relationship between a part and a whole. **2** belonging to; coming from. **3** used in expressions of measurement, value, or age. **4** made from. **5** used to show position. **6** used to show that something belongs to a category.

USAGE

It's wrong to say or write **of** instead of **have** in sentences such as *I could have told you* (don't say or write *I could of told you*).

off /ôf, äf/ ▶ **adv.** **1** away from a place. **2** so as to be removed or separated. **3** starting a journey or race. **4** so as to finish or be discontinued. **5** (of an electrical appliance or power supply) not working or connected. **6** having a particular level of wealth. ▶ **prep.** **1** away from. **2** situated or leading in a direction away from. **3** so as to be removed or separated from. **4** having a temporary dislike of. ▶ **adj.** (of food) no longer fresh.

SYNONYMS ▶ **adj.** **1 away**, absent, off duty, on leave, on vacation. **2 canceled**, postponed, called off. **3 rotten**, bad, stale, moldy, sour, rancid, turned, spoiled.

□ **off-center 1** not quite in the center. **2** strange or eccentric. **off-color** slightly indecent or obscene. **off-key 1** not in tune. **2** inappropriate. **off-limits** out of bounds. **off-peak** at a time when demand is less. **off-putting** unpleasant or unsettling. **off-ramp** an exit road from a main highway. **off white** a white color with a gray or yellowish tinge.

of·fal /ˈôfəl, ˈäfəl/ ▶ **n.** the internal organs of an animal used as food.

off·beat /ˈôfˌbēt, ˈäf-/ ▶ **adj.** unconventional; unusual.

SYNONYMS **unconventional**, unorthodox, unusual, eccentric, idiosyncratic, strange, bizarre, weird, peculiar, odd, freakish, outlandish, out of the ordinary, Bohemian, alternative, left-field, zany, quirky; informal wacky, freaky, way-out, off the wall, kooky, oddball. ANTONYMS conventional.

of·fend /əˈfend/ ▶ **v.** **1** make someone feel upset, insulted, or annoyed. **2** seem unpleasant to. **3** do something illegal.

SYNONYMS **1 upset**, give offense to, affront, hurt someone's feelings, insult, hurt, wound, slight. **2 break the law**, commit a crime, do wrong.

of·fend·er /əˈfendər/ ▶ **n.** a person who commits an illegal act.

SYNONYMS **wrongdoer**, criminal, lawbreaker, crook, villain, miscreant, felon, delinquent, malefactor, culprit, guilty party.

of·fense /əˈfens/ ▶ **n.** **1** an act that breaks a law or rule. **2** a feeling of hurt or annoyance.

SYNONYMS **1 crime**, illegal act, misdemeanor, felony, infringement, violation, wrongdoing, sin. **2 annoyance**, resentment, indignation, displeasure, bad feeling, animosity.

of·fen·sive /əˈfensiv/ ▶ **adj.** **1** causing someone to feel upset, insulted, or annoyed. **2** used in attack. ▶ **n.** a campaign to attack or achieve something.

SYNONYMS ▶ **adj.** **1 insulting**, rude, derogatory, disrespectful, personal, hurtful, upsetting, wounding, abusive. **2 unpleasant**, disagreeable, nasty, distasteful, objectionable, off-putting, dreadful, frightful, obnoxious, abominable, disgusting, repulsive, repellent, vile, foul, horrible, sickening, nauseating; informal ghastly, horrid, gross. **3 hostile**, attacking, aggressive, invading, incursive, combative, threatening, martial, warlike, belligerent, bellicose. ANTONYMS complimentary, pleasant, defensive. ▶ **n. attack**, assault, onslaught, invasion, push, thrust, charge, raid, incursion, blitz, campaign.

■ **of·fen·sive·ly** adv.

of·fer /ˈôfər, ˈäfər/ ▶ v. (**offers**, **offering**, **offered**) **1** present something for a person to accept or reject as they wish. **2** say you are willing to do something for someone. **3** provide. ▶ **n. 1** an expression of readiness to do or give something. **2** an amount of money that someone is willing to pay for something. **3** a specially reduced price.

SYNONYMS ▶ **v. 1 put forward**, proffer, give, present, come up with, suggest, propose, advance, submit, tender. **2 volunteer**, step/come forward. **3 bid**, tender, put in a bid/offer of. ANTONYMS withdraw, refuse. ▶ **n. 1 proposal**, proposition, suggestion, submission, approach, overture. **2 bid**, tender, bidding price.

□ **on offer 1** available. **2** for sale at a reduced price.

of·fer·ing /ˈôf(ə)riNG, äf-/ ▶ **n.** something that is offered; a gift or contribution.

SYNONYMS **contribution**, donation, gift, present, sacrifice, tribute.

of·fer·to·ry /ˈôfərˌtôrē, ˈäfər-/ ▶ **n.** (plural **offertories**) **1** the offering of the bread and wine at the Christian service of Holy Communion. **2** a collection of money made at a Christian church service.

off·hand /ˈôfˈhand, ˈäf-/ ▶ **adj.** rudely casual or cool in manner. ▶ **adv.** without previous thought.

SYNONYMS ▶ **adj. casual**, careless, uninterested, indifferent, cool, nonchalant, blasé, insouciant, cavalier, glib, perfunctory, cursory, dismissive.

of·fice /ˈôfis, ˈäf-/ ▶ **n. 1** a room, set of rooms, or building where people work at desks. **2** a position of authority. **3** (**offices**) formal things done for other people.

SYNONYMS **1 place of work**, workplace, workroom. **2** *the company's Paris office* **branch**, division, section, bureau, department. **3** *the office of president* **post**, position, appointment, job, occupation, role, situation, function.

of·fi·cer /ˈôfisər, ˈäf-/ ▶ **n. 1** a person holding a position of authority, especially in the armed forces. **2** a policeman or policewoman.

SYNONYMS **official**, functionary, executive.

of·fi·cial /əˈfisHəl/ ▶ **adj. 1** relating to an authority or public organization. **2** agreed or done by a person or group in a position of authority. ▶ **n.** a person holding public office or having official duties.

SYNONYMS ▶ **adj. 1 authorized**, approved, validated, authenticated, certified, accredited, endorsed, sanctioned, licensed, recognized, legitimate, legal, lawful, valid, bona fide, proper; informal kosher. **2 ceremonial**, formal, solemn, bureaucratic. ANTONYMS unauthorized, informal. ▶ **n. officer**, executive, functionary, administrator, bureaucrat, mandarin, representative, agent; disapproving apparatchik.

■ **of·fi·cial·dom** n. **of·fi·cial·ly** adv.

of·fi·ci·ate /əˈfisHēˌāt/ ▶ **v.** (**officiates**, **officiating**, **officiated**) **1** act as an official in charge of something. **2** perform a religious service or ceremony.

SYNONYMS **be in charge of**, take charge of, preside over; oversee, superintend, supervise, conduct, run.

of·fi·cious /əˈfisHəs/ ▶ **adj.** using your authority or interfering in a bossy way.

SYNONYMS **self-important**, bumptious, self-assertive, overbearing, interfering, intrusive, meddlesome, meddling; informal bossy.

off·ing /ˈôfiNG, ˈäf-/ ▶ **n.** (**in the offing**) likely to happen or appear soon.

off·line /ˈôfˈlīn, ˈäf-/ ▶ **adj.** not connected to a computer or external network.

off·load /ˈôfˌlōd, ˈäf-/ ▶ **v. 1** unload a cargo. **2** get rid of.

off·set /ˈôfˌset, ˈäf-/ ▶ **v.** (**offsets**, **offsetting**, **offset**) cancel out something with an equal and opposite force or effect.

SYNONYMS **counteract**, balance (out), even out/up, counterbalance, compensate for, make up for, neutralize, cancel (out).

off·shoot /ˈôfˌsHo͞ot, ˈäf-/ ▶ **n.** a thing that develops from something else.

off·shore /ˈôfˈsHôr, ˈäf-/ ▶ **adj. & adv. 1** at sea some distance from the shore. **2** (of the wind) blowing toward the sea from the land. **3** situated or registered abroad.

off·side /ˈôfˈsīd, ˈäf-/ ▶ **adj. & adv.** (of a player in certain sports) occupying a position on the field where playing the ball is not allowed.

off·spring /ˈôfˌspriNG, ˈäf-/ ▶ **n.** (plural **offspring**) a person's child or children.

SYNONYMS **children**, family, progeny, young, brood, descendants, heirs, successors; informal kids.

off·stage /ˈôfˈstāj, ˈäf-/ ▶ **adj. & adv.** (in a theater) not on the stage.

of·ten /ˈôf(t)ən, ˈäf-/ ▶ **adv. 1** frequently. **2** in many instances.

SYNONYMS **frequently**, oftentimes, many times, a lot, repeatedly, again and again, time after time, regularly, commonly, generally, ordinarily. ANTONYMS seldom.

o·gle /ˈōgəl, ä-/ ▶ **v.** (**ogles**, **ogling**, **ogled**) stare at someone in a way that shows obvious amorous interest.

o·gre /ˈōgər/ ▶ **n. 1** (in stories) a man-eating giant. **2** a cruel or terrifying person.

ohm /ōm/ ▶ **n.** the basic unit of electrical resistance.

oil /oil/ ▶ **n. 1** a thick, sticky liquid obtained from petroleum. **2** a thick liquid that cannot be dissolved in water and is obtained from plants. **3** (also **oils**) oil paint. ▶ **v.** treat or coat with oil.
□ **oil paint** artist's paint made from powder mixed with linseed or other oil. **oil well** a shaft dug in the ground for extracting oil.

oil·can /ˈoilˌkan/ ▶ **n.** a can with a long nozzle used for applying oil to machinery.

oil·field /ˈoilˌfēld/ ▶ **n.** an area where oil is found beneath the ground or seabed.

oil·skin /'oil,skin/ ▶ n. **1** heavy cotton cloth waterproofed with oil. **2** (**oilskins**) a set of clothes made of oilskin.

oil·y /'oilē/ ▶ adj. (**oilier**, **oiliest**) **1** containing, covered with, or like oil. **2** (of a person) insincerely polite and flattering.

SYNONYMS **greasy**, fatty, buttery, rich, oleaginous.

■ **oil·i·ness** n.

oink /oiNGk/ ▶ n. the grunting sound made by a pig. ▶ v. make such a sound.

oint·ment /'ointmənt/ ▶ n. a smooth substance that is rubbed on the skin to heal a wound or sore place.

SYNONYMS **lotion**, cream, salve, liniment, embrocation, rub, gel, balm, emollient, unguent.

OK /'ō'kā/ (or **okay**) informal ▶ exclam. said to express agreement or acceptance. ▶ adj. **1** satisfactory, but not especially good. **2** allowed. ▶ adv. in a satisfactory way. ▶ n. permission to do something. ▶ v. (**OK's**, **OK'ing**, **OK'd**) approve or authorize.

SYNONYMS ▶ adj. **1 satisfactory**, all right, acceptable, competent, adequate, tolerable, passable, reasonable, decent, fair, not bad, average, middling, moderate, unremarkable, unexceptional; informal so-so, fair-to-middling. **2 permissible**, allowable, acceptable, all right, in order, permitted, fitting, suitable, appropriate. ANTONYMS unsatisfactory. ▶ n. **authorization**, (seal of) approval, agreement, consent, assent, permission, endorsement, ratification, sanction, blessing, leave; informal the go-ahead, the green light, the thumbs up, say-so.

o·ka·pi /ō'käpē/ ▶ n. (plural **okapi** or **okapis**) a large plant-eating African animal with stripes on the hindquarters and upper legs.

o·kra /'ōkrə/ ▶ n. the long seed pods of a tropical plant, eaten as a vegetable.

old /ōld/ ▶ adj. (**older**, **oldest**) **1** having lived for a long time. **2** made, built, or originating long ago. **3** owned or used for a long time. **4** former. **5** of a stated age.

SYNONYMS **1** *old people* **elderly**, aged, older, senior, venerable, in your dotage, past your prime, long in the tooth, grizzled, ancient, decrepit, senescent, senile; informal getting on, over the hill. **2** *old clothes* **worn**, shabby, threadbare, frayed, patched, tattered, moth-eaten, ragged; informal tatty. **3** *the old days* **bygone**, olden, past, prehistoric, primitive. **4** *old cars* **antique**, veteran, vintage, classic. **5** *an old girlfriend* **former**, previous, earlier, past, ex-, one-time, sometime, erstwhile; formal quondam. ANTONYMS young, new, modern, current.

□ **of the old school** of the traditional form or type. **old age** the later part of normal life. **Old English** the language spoken in England until about 1150. **old-fashioned** no longer current or modern. **the old guard** the long-standing members of a group, who are often unwilling to accept change. **old hand** a very experienced person. **old hat** informal boringly familiar or out of date. **old maid** disapproving a single woman thought of as too old for marriage. **old master** a great painter of former times. **Old Nick** the Devil. **Old Testament** the first part of the Christian Bible. **old-time** pleasingly traditional or old-fashioned. **old-timer** informal a very experienced or long-serving person. **old wives' tale** a widely held traditional belief that is incorrect. **Old World** Europe, Asia, and Africa.

old·en /'ōldən/ ▶ adj. of a former age.

old·ster /'ōl(d)stər/ ▶ n. informal an older person.

o·le·ag·i·nous /,ōlē'ajənəs/ ▶ adj. **1** oily. **2** insincerely flattering.

o·le·an·der /'ōlē,andər/ ▶ n. a poisonous evergreen shrub with clusters of white, pink, or red flowers.

ol·fac·to·ry /äl'fakt(ə)rē, ōl-/ ▶ adj. relating to the sense of smell.

ol·i·garch /'äli,gärk, 'ōl-/ ▶ n. a ruler in an oligarchy.

ol·i·gar·chy /'äli,gärkē, 'ōli-/ ▶ n. (plural **oligarchies**) **1** a small group of people having control of a state. **2** a state governed by a small group of people. ■ **ol·i·gar·chic** /,äli'gärkik, ,ōli-/ adj.

ol·ive /'äliv/ ▶ n. **1** a small oval fruit with a hard stone and bitter flesh. **2** (also **olive green**) a grayish-green color like that of an unripe olive. ▶ adj. (of a person's complexion) yellowish brown. □ **olive branch** an offer to restore friendly relations. **olive oil** oil obtained from olives, used in cooking and salad dressing.

O·lym·pi·ad /ō'limpē,ad, ə'lim-/ ▶ n. a staging of the Olympic Games.

O·lym·pi·an /ə'limpēən, ō'lim-/ ▶ adj. **1** relating to the Olympic Games. **2** having to do with Mount Olympus, traditional home of the Greek gods. ▶ n. **1** a competitor in the Olympic Games. **2** any of the twelve main Greek gods.

O·lym·pic /ə'limpik, ō'lim-/ ▶ adj. relating to the Olympic Games. ▶ n. (**the Olympics** or **the Olympic Games**) a sports competition held every four years, or the ancient Greek festival of athletic, literary, and musical competitions that it was based on.

om·buds·man /'ämbədzmən, -,bo͝odz-/ ▶ n. (plural **ombudsmen**) an official who investigates people's complaints against companies or the government.

o·me·ga /ō'māgə, ō'mē-/ ▶ n. the last letter of the Greek alphabet (Ω, ω).

om·e·let /'äm(ə)lit/ (or **omelette**) ▶ n. a dish of beaten eggs cooked in a frying pan, usually with a savory filling.

o·men /'ōmən/ ▶ n. an event seen as a sign of future good or bad luck.

SYNONYMS **portent**, sign, signal, token, forewarning, warning, harbinger, presage, indication; literary foretoken.

om·i·nous /'ämənəs/ ▶ adj. giving the worrying impression that something bad is going to happen.

SYNONYMS **threatening**, menacing, baleful, forbidding, foreboding, fateful, sinister, black, dark, gloomy. ANTONYMS promising.

■ **om·i·nous·ly** adv.

o·mis·sion /ō'misHən/ ▶ n. **1** the action of leaving something out. **2** a failure to do something. **3** something that has been left out or not done.

SYNONYMS **1 exclusion**, leaving out, deletion, elimination. **2 negligence**, neglect, dereliction, oversight, lapse, failure.

o·mit /ō'mit/ ▶ v. (**omits**, **omitting**, **omitted**) **1** leave out or exclude. **2** fail to do.

SYNONYMS **1 leave out**, exclude, miss out, miss, cut, drop, skip. **2 forget**, neglect, overlook, fail. ANTONYMS include, remember.

SPELLING

Just one **m**: omit.

om·ni·bus /ˈämnəˌbəs/ ▶ **n. 1** a volume containing several works previously published separately. **2** dated a bus.

om·nip·o·tent /ämˈnipətənt/ ▶ **adj.** having unlimited or very great power.

SYNONYMS **all-powerful**, almighty, supreme, preeminent; invincible.

■ **om·nip·o·tence n.**

om·ni·pres·ent /ˌämnəˈpreznt/ ▶ **adj. 1** (of God) present everywhere at the same time. **2** widespread. ■ **om·ni·pres·ence n.**

om·nis·cient /ämˈnisʜənt/ ▶ **adj.** knowing everything.

SYNONYMS **all-knowing**, all-wise, all-seeing.

■ **om·nis·cience n.**

om·ni·vore /ˈämnəˌvôr/ ▶ **n.** an animal that eats both plants and meat.

om·niv·o·rous /ämˈniv(ə)rəs/ ▶ **adj.** eating both plants and meat.

on /än, ôn/ ▶ **prep. & adv.** in contact with and supported by a surface. ▶ **prep. 1** (also **on to**) into contact with a surface, or aboard a vehicle. **2** about; concerning. **3** as a member of. **4** stored in or broadcast by. **5** in the course of. **6** indicating a day or date when something takes place. **7** engaged in. **8** regularly taking a drug or medicine. **9** informal paid for by. ▶ **adv. 1** with continued movement or action. **2** (of clothing) being worn. **3** taking place or being presented. **4** (of an electrical appliance or power supply) functioning. □ **be on to** informal **1** be close to discovering that (someone) has done something wrong. **2** (**be on to something**) have an idea that is likely to lead to an important discovery. **on-ramp** a lane for traffic entering a highway.

once /wəns/ ▶ **adv. 1** on one occasion or for one time only. **2** formerly. **3** multiplied by one. ▶ **conj.** as soon as.

SYNONYMS ▶ **adv. 1 on one occasion**, one time. **2 formerly**, previously, in the past, once upon a time, in days/times gone by, in the (good) old days, long ago. ▶ **conj. as soon as**, the moment, when, after.

□ **at once 1** immediately. **2** at the same time. **once** (or **every once**) **in a while** occasionally. **once-over** informal a quick inspection, or act of cleaning something.

on·com·ing /ˈänˌkəmiɴɢ, ˈôn-/ ▶ **adj.** moving toward you.

one /wən/ ▶ **cardinal number 1** the lowest cardinal number; 1. (Roman numeral: **i** or **I**) **2** single, or a single person or thing. **3** (before a person's name) a certain. **4** the same. ▶ **pron. 1** used to refer to a person or thing previously mentioned or easily identified. **2** used to refer to the speaker, or to represent people in general. □ **one after another** (or **the other**) following one another in quick succession. **one and all** everyone. **one and only** unique. **one another** each other. **one-armed bandit** informal a slot machine operated by pulling a long handle at the side. **one day** at some time in the past or future. **one-dimensional** lacking depth or complexity. **one-liner** informal a short joke or witty remark. **one-sided 1** giving only one point of view; biased. **2** (of a contest or conflict) not involving participants of equal ability. **one-two** a pair of punches in quick succession with alternate hands. **one-upmanship** informal the technique of gaining an advantage over someone else. **one-way** moving or allowing movement in one direction only.

one·ness /ˈwən(n)is/ ▶ **n.** the state of being whole or in agreement.

on·er·ous /ˈōnərəs, ˈänərəs/ ▶ **adj.** involving a lot of effort and difficulty.

one·self /wənˈself/ ▶ **pron. 1** used as the object of a verb or preposition when this is the same as the subject of the clause and the subject is "one." **2** used to emphasize that you is doing something individually or without help. **3** in your normal state of body or mind.

on·go·ing /ˈänˌgōiɴɢ, ˈôn-/ ▶ **adj.** still in progress.

SYNONYMS **in progress**, under way, going on, continuing, proceeding.

on·ion /ˈənyən/ ▶ **n.** a vegetable consisting of a round bulb with a strong taste and smell.

on·line /ˌänˈlīn, ˌôn-/ ▶ **adj. & adv. 1** controlled by or connected to a computer. **2** available on or carried out via the Internet.

on·look·er /ˈänˌlo͝okər, ˈôn-/ ▶ **n.** a spectator.

SYNONYMS **eyewitness**, witness, observer, spectator, bystander; informal rubberneck.

on·ly /ˈōnlē/ ▶ **adv. 1** and no one or nothing more besides. **2** no longer ago than. **3** not until. **4** with the negative result that. ▶ **adj. 1** single or solitary. **2** alone deserving consideration. ▶ **conj.** informal except that.

SYNONYMS ▶ **adv. 1 at most**, at best, just, no more than, hardly, barely, scarcely. **2 exclusively**, solely, purely. ▶ **adj. sole**, single, one (and only), solitary, lone, unique, exclusive.

on·o·mat·o·poe·ia /ˌänəˌmatəˈpēə, -ˌmätə-/ ▶ **n.** the use of words that sound like the thing they refer to (e.g., *sizzle*). ■ **on·o·mat·o·poe·ic adj.**

on·rush /ˈänˌrəsʜ, ˈôn-/ ▶ **n.** a surging rush forward. ■ **on·rush·ing adj.**

on·set /ˈänˌset, ˈôn-/ ▶ **n.** the beginning of something.

SYNONYMS **start**, beginning, commencement, arrival, appearance, inception, day one, outbreak; informal kickoff. ANTONYMS end.

on·shore /ˈänˈsʜôr, ˈôn-/ ▶ **adj. & adv. 1** situated on land. **2** (of the wind) blowing from the sea toward the land.

on·side /ˈänˈsīd, ˈôn-/ ▶ **adj. & adv.** (in sports) not offside.

on·slaught /ˈänˌslôt, ˈôn-/ ▶ **n. 1** a fierce or destructive attack. **2** an overwhelmingly large quantity of people or things.

SYNONYMS **attack**, assault, offensive, advance, charge, blitz, bombardment, barrage.

on·stage /ˈänˈstāj, ˈôn-/ ▶ **adj. & adv.** (in a theater) on the stage.

on·to /ˈänˌto͞o, ˈôn-/ ▶ **prep.** moving to a place on: *they went up onto the ridge.* □ **be onto** informal **1** be close to discovering that someone has done something wrong. **2** have an idea that is likely to lead to an important discovery.

USAGE

It is important to maintain a distinction between the preposition **onto** or **on to** and the use of the adverb **on** followed by the preposition **to**: *she climbed onto* (sometimes *on to*) *the roof,* but *let's go on to* (never onto) *the next chapter.*

on·tol·o·gy /än'täləjē/ ▶ **n.** philosophy concerned with the nature of being. ■ **on·to·log·i·cal** /ˌäntə'läjikəl/ **adj.**

o·nus /'ōnəs/ ▶ **n.** a duty or responsibility.

SYNONYMS **burden**, responsibility, obligation, duty, weight, load.

on·ward /'änwərd, 'ôn-/ ▶ **adj. & adv.** in a forward direction. ■ **on·wards adv.**

on·yx /'äniks/ ▶ **n.** a semiprecious stone with layers of different colors.

oo·dles /'o͞odlz/ ▶ **pl.n.** informal a very great number or amount.

oomph /o͝omf, o͞omf/ ▶ **n.** informal excitement or energy.

oops /o͝ops, o͞ops/ ▶ **exclam.** informal used to show awareness of a mistake or minor accident.

ooze /o͞oz/ ▶ **v.** (**oozes**, **oozing**, **oozed**) slowly seep out. ▶ **n.** the very slow flow of a liquid.

SYNONYMS ▶ **v. seep**, discharge, flow, exude, trickle, drip, dribble, drain, leak.

■ **ooz·y adj.**

o·pac·i·ty /ō'pasitē/ ▶ **n.** the condition of being opaque.

o·pal /'ōpəl/ ▶ **n.** a semitransparent gemstone in which small points of shifting color can be seen.

o·pal·es·cent /ˌōpə'lesənt/ ▶ **adj.** having small points of shifting color.

o·paque /ō'pāk/ ▶ **adj. 1** not able to be seen through. **2** difficult or impossible to understand.

SYNONYMS **1 nontransparent**, cloudy, filmy, blurred, smeared, misty. **2 obscure**, unclear, unfathomable, incomprehensible, unintelligible, impenetrable; informal as clear as mud. ANTONYMS transparent, clear.

op. cit. /ˌäp 'sit/ ▶ **adv.** in the work already cited.

o·pen /'ōpən/ ▶ **adj. 1** not closed, fastened, or restricted. **2** not covered or protected. **3** (**open to**) likely to suffer from or be affected by. **4** spread out, expanded, or unfolded. **5** accessible or available. **6** not hiding thoughts and feelings. **7** not disguised or hidden. **8** not finally settled. ▶ **v. 1** make or become open. **2** formally begin or establish. **3** (**open on to** or **into**) give access to. **4** (**open up**) begin to talk freely. ▶ **n.** (**the open**) fresh air or open countryside.

SYNONYMS ▶ **adj. 1 unlocked**, unlatched, off the latch, ajar, gaping, yawning. **2** *open country* | *open spaces* **unenclosed**, rolling, sweeping, wide open, exposed, spacious, uncrowded, uncluttered, undeveloped. **3** *the position is still open* **available**, free, vacant, unfilled; informal up for grabs. **4** *open to abuse* **vulnerable**, subject, susceptible, liable, exposed, an easy target for. **5** *she was very open* **frank**, candid, honest, forthcoming, communicative, forthright, direct, unreserved, plain-spoken, outspoken, blunt; informal upfront. **6** *open hostility* **overt**, manifest, conspicuous, plain, undisguised, unconcealed, clear, naked, blatant, flagrant, barefaced, brazen. ANTONYMS shut, closed. ▶ **v. 1 unfasten**, unlock, unbolt, throw wide. **2 unwrap**, undo, untie. **3 spread out**, unfold, unfurl, unroll, straighten out. **4 begin**, start, commence, initiate, set in motion, get going, get under way, get off the ground; informal kick off. ANTONYMS close, shut.

□ **in** (or **into**) **the open** not secret. **the open air** an unenclosed space outdoors. **open-air** positioned or taking place out of doors. **open-and-shut** straightforward. **open-ended** having no limit decided in advance. **open-heart surgery** surgery in which the heart is exposed. **open house** a place or situation in which all visitors are welcome. **open letter** a letter addressed to a particular person but intended to be published. **open market** a situation in which companies can trade without restrictions. **open-minded** willing to consider new ideas. **open-pit** (of mining) in which coal or ore is extracted from a level near the earth's surface, rather than from shafts. **open-plan** having large rooms with few or no dividing walls. **open secret** a supposed secret that is in fact known to many people. ■ **o·pen·er n. o·pen·ness n.**

o·pen·ing /'ōp(ə)niNG/ ▶ **n. 1** a gap. **2** the beginning of something. **3** a ceremony at which a building, show, etc., is declared to be open. **4** an opportunity to achieve something. **5** an available job or position. ▶ **adj.** coming at the beginning.

SYNONYMS ▶ **n. 1 hole**, gap, aperture, space, orifice, vent, crack, slit, chink, fissure, cleft, crevice, interstice. **2 beginning**, start, commencement, outset; informal kickoff. **3 vacancy**, position, post, job, opportunity. ▶ **adj. first**, initial, introductory, preliminary, maiden, inaugural. ANTONYMS final, closing.

o·pen·ly /'ōpənlē/ ▶ **adv.** in a frank, honest, or public way.

SYNONYMS **1 publicly**, blatantly, flagrantly, overtly. **2 frankly**, candidly, explicitly, honestly, sincerely, forthrightly, freely.

o·pe·ra[1] /'äp(ə)rə/ ▶ **n.** a dramatic work that is set to music for singers and musicians. □ **opera glasses** small binoculars used at the opera or theater.

o·pe·ra[2] plural of **OPUS**.

op·er·a·ble /'äp(ə)rəbəl/ ▶ **adj. 1** able to be used. **2** able to be treated by a surgical operation.

op·er·ate /'äpəˌrāt/ ▶ **v.** (**operates**, **operating**, **operated**) **1** function or work. **2** use or control a machine. **3** (of an organization or armed force) carry out activities. **4** be in effect. **5** carry out a surgical operation.

SYNONYMS **1 work**, run, use, handle, control, manage, drive, steer, maneuver, function, go, perform. **2 direct**, control, manage, run, handle, be in control/charge of.

op·er·at·ic /ˌäpə'ratik/ ▶ **adj. 1** having to do with opera. **2** overly dramatic.

op·er·a·tion /ˌäpə'rāSHən/ ▶ **n. 1** the action of operating. **2** an act of cutting into a patient's body to remove or repair a damaged part. **3** an organized action involving a number of people. **4** a business organization.

SYNONYMS **1 functioning**, working, running, performance, action. **2** *a military operation* **action**, exercise, undertaking, enterprise, maneuver, campaign. **3 business**, enterprise, company, firm.

op·er·a·tion·al /ˌäpəˈrāsHənl/ ▶ **adj. 1** ready for use, or being used. **2** relating to the functioning of an organization.

SYNONYMS **running**, up and running, working, functioning, operative, in operation, in use, in action, in working order, serviceable, functional.

■ **op·er·a·tion·al·ly adv.**

op·er·a·tive /ˈäp(ə)rətiv, ˈäpəˌrātiv/ ▶ **adj. 1** working or functioning. **2** (of a word) having the most significance in a phrase. **3** relating to surgery. ▶ **n. 1** a worker, especially a skilled one in a manufacturing industry. **2** a private detective or secret agent.

SYNONYMS ▶ **adj. running**, up and running, working, functioning, operational, in operation, in use, in action, in effect. ▶ **n. 1 machinist**, operator, mechanic, engineer, worker, workman, (factory) hand. **2 agent**, secret/undercover agent, spy, mole, plant.

op·er·a·tor /ˈäpəˌrātər/ ▶ **n. 1** a person who operates equipment or a machine. **2** a person who works at the switchboard of a telephone exchange. **3** a person or company that runs a business or enterprise. **4** informal a person who acts in a particular way: *a smooth operator*.

op·er·et·ta /ˌäpəˈretə/ ▶ **n.** a short opera on a light or humorous theme.

oph·thal·mic /äfˈTHalmik, äp-/ ▶ **adj.** relating to the eye and its diseases.

oph·thal·mol·o·gy /ˌäfTHə(l)ˈmäləjē, ˌäp-/ ▶ **n.** the study and treatment of disorders and diseases of the eye. ■ **oph·thal·mol·o·gist n.**

o·pi·ate /ˈōpēət, -ˌāt/ ▶ **n.** a drug containing opium.

o·pine /ōˈpīn/ ▶ **v.** (**opines**, **opining**, **opined**) formal say something as your opinion.

o·pin·ion /əˈpinyən/ ▶ **n. 1** a personal view not necessarily based on fact or knowledge. **2** the views of people in general. **3** a formal statement of advice by an expert.

SYNONYMS **belief**, thought(s), idea, way of thinking, feeling, mind, view, point of view, viewpoint, standpoint, assessment, estimation, judgment, conviction.

□ **opinion poll** the questioning of a selection of people in order to assess the views of people in general.

o·pin·ion·at·ed /əˈpinyəˌnātid/ ▶ **adj.** having strong opinions that you are not willing to change.

o·pi·um /ˈōpēəm/ ▶ **n.** an addictive drug made from the juice of a poppy.

o·pos·sum /(ə)ˈpäsəm/ ▶ **n.** an American animal (a marsupial) with a tail that it can use for grasping.

op·po·nent /əˈpōnənt/ ▶ **n. 1** a person who competes with another in a contest or argument. **2** a person who disagrees with a proposal or practice.

SYNONYMS **1 rival**, adversary, competitor, enemy, antagonist, combatant, contender, challenger; literary foe. **2 critic**, objector, dissenter. ANTONYMS ally, supporter.

op·por·tune /ˌäpərˈt(y)o͞on/ ▶ **adj.** happening at a good or convenient time.

op·por·tun·ist /ˌäpərˈt(y)o͞onist/ ▶ **n.** a person who takes advantage of opportunities without worrying about whether or not they are right to do so. ▶ **adj.** (also **opportunistic** /ˌäpərt(y)o͞oˈnistik/) taking advantage of opportunities when they come up. ■ **op·por·tun·ism n.**

op·por·tu·ni·ty /ˌäpərˈt(y)o͞onitē/ ▶ **n.** (plural **opportunities**) **1** a good time or set of circumstances for doing something. **2** a chance for employment or promotion.

SYNONYMS **chance**, time, occasion, moment, opening, option, window, possibility, scope, freedom; informal shot, break.

SPELLING

Two **p**s: op**p**ortunity.

op·pose /əˈpōz/ ▶ **v.** (**opposes**, **opposing**, **opposed**) **1** (also **be opposed to**) disapprove of and try to prevent or resist. **2** compete with or fight. **3** (**opposed**) (of two or more things) contrasting or conflicting. **4** (**opposing**) opposite.

SYNONYMS **1 be against**, object to, be hostile to, disagree with, disapprove of, resist, take a stand against, put up a fight against, fight, counter, challenge, take issue with. **2** (**opposed to**) **against**, dead set against, averse to, hostile to, antagonistic to, antipathetic to; informal anti. **3** (**opposing**) **conflicting**, contrasting, opposite, incompatible, irreconcilable, contradictory, clashing, at variance, at odds, opposed. **4** (**opposing**) **rival**, opposite, enemy, competing. ANTONYMS support, similar, allied.

op·po·site /ˈäpəzit/ ▶ **adj. 1** facing. **2** completely different. **3** being the other of a contrasted pair: *the opposite sex*. ▶ **n.** an opposite person or thing. ▶ **adv.** in an opposite position. ▶ **prep.** in a position opposite to.

SYNONYMS ▶ **adj. 1 facing**, face to face with, across from. **2 conflicting**, contrasting, incompatible, irreconcilable, contradictory, at variance, at odds, differing. **3 rival**, opposing, competing, enemy. ▶ **n. reverse**, converse, antithesis, contrary, polar opposite. ANTONYMS same.

■ **op·po·site·ly adv.**

op·po·si·tion /ˌäpəˈzisHən/ ▶ **n. 1** resistance or disagreement. **2** a group of opponents. **3** a contrast or direct opposite.

SYNONYMS **1 resistance**, hostility, antagonism, antipathy, objection, dissent, disapproval. **2 opponent**(s), opposing side, competition, rival(s), adversary. ANTONYMS agreement.

■ **op·po·si·tion·al adj.**

op·press /əˈpres/ ▶ **v. 1** treat in a harsh and unfair way. **2** make someone feel distressed or anxious.

SYNONYMS **persecute**, tyrannize, crush, repress, subjugate, subdue, keep down, rule with a rod of iron, rule with an iron fist.

■ **op·pres·sor n.**

SPELLING

Double **p**, double **s**: o**pp**re**ss**.

op·pres·sion /əˈpresHən/ ▶ **n. 1** cruel or unjust treatment or control. **2** mental pressure or distress.

SYNONYMS **persecution**, abuse, ill-treatment, tyranny, repression, suppression, subjugation, cruelty, brutality, injustice. ANTONYMS freedom.

op·pres·sive /ə'presiv/ ▶ **adj.** **1** harsh and unfair. **2** causing depression or anxiety. **3** (of weather) hot and airless.

SYNONYMS **1 harsh**, cruel, brutal, repressive, tyrannical, despotic, draconian, ruthless, merciless, pitiless. **2 muggy**, close, heavy, hot, humid, sticky, airless, stuffy, stifling, sultry. ANTONYMS lenient, fresh.

■ **op·pres·sive·ly** adv.

op·pro·bri·ous /ə'prōbrēəs/ ▶ **adj.** formal very critical or scornful.

op·pro·bri·um /ə'prōbrēəm/ ▶ **n.** formal **1** harsh criticism or scorn. **2** public disgrace as a result of bad behavior.

opt /äpt/ ▶ **v.** make a choice.

SYNONYMS **choose**, select, pick, decide, elect; (**opt for**) go for, settle on.

□ **opt out** choose not to take part.

op·tic /'äptik/ ▶ **adj.** relating to the eye or vision.

op·ti·cal /'äptikəl/ ▶ **adj.** relating to vision, light, or optics. □ **optical fiber** a thin glass fiber through which light can be transmitted. **optical illusion** something that deceives the eye by appearing to be different from what it really is. ■ **op·ti·cal·ly** adv.

op·ti·cian /äp'tisHən/ ▶ **n.** a person qualified to examine people's eyes and to prescribe glasses and contact lenses.

op·tics /'äptiks/ ▶ **n.** the study of vision and the behavior of light.

op·ti·mal /'äptəməl/ ▶ **adj.** best or most favorable. ■ **op·ti·mal·ly** adv.

op·ti·mism /'äptə͵mizəm/ ▶ **n.** hopefulness and confidence about the future or success of something. ■ **op·ti·mist** n.

op·ti·mis·tic /͵äptə'mistik/ ▶ **adj.** hopeful and confident about the future.

SYNONYMS **1 positive**, confident, hopeful, sanguine, bullish, buoyant, upbeat. **2 encouraging**, promising, reassuring, favorable. ANTONYMS pessimistic, depressing.

■ **op·ti·mis·ti·cal·ly** adv.

op·ti·mize /'äptə͵mīz/ ▶ **v.** (**optimizes**, **optimizing**, **optimized**) make the best use of.

op·ti·mum /'äptəməm/ ▶ **adj.** most likely to lead to a favorable outcome. ▶ **n.** (plural **optima** /-mə/ or **optimums**) the most favorable conditions for growth or success.

SYNONYMS ▶ **adj. best**, most favorable, most advantageous, ideal, perfect, prime, optimal.

op·tion /'äpsHən/ ▶ **n.** **1** a thing that you may choose. **2** the freedom or right to choose. **3** a right to buy or sell something at a stated price within a set time.

SYNONYMS **choice**, preference, alternative, selection, possibility.

op·tion·al /'äpsHənl/ ▶ **adj.** available to be chosen, but not compulsory.

SYNONYMS **voluntary**, noncompulsory, elective, discretionary. ANTONYMS compulsory.

■ **op·tion·al·ly** adv.

op·tom·e·trist /äp'tämitrist/ ▶ **n.** a person who practices optometry.

op·tom·e·try /äp'tämitrē/ ▶ **n.** the occupation of measuring people's eyesight, prescribing lenses, and detecting eye disease.

op·u·lent /'äpyələnt/ ▶ **adj.** expensive and luxurious.

SYNONYMS **luxurious**, sumptuous, palatial, lavishly appointed, rich, splendid, magnificent, grand, fancy; informal plush, swank, swish. ANTONYMS spartan.

■ **op·u·lence** n. **op·u·lent·ly** adv.

o·pus /'ōpəs/ ▶ **n.** (plural **opuses** or **opera** /'äp(ə)rə/) **1** a musical work or set of works. **2** a literary work.

or /ôr/ ▶ **conj.** **1** used to link alternatives. **2** introducing a word that means the same as a preceding word or phrase, or that explains it. **3** otherwise.

or·a·cle /'ôrəkəl/ ▶ **n.** (in ancient Greece or Rome) a priest or priestess through whom the gods were believed to give prophecies about the future.

o·rac·u·lar /ô'rakyələr/ ▶ **adj.** having to do with an oracle.

o·ral /'ôrəl/ ▶ **adj.** **1** spoken rather than written. **2** relating to the mouth. **3** done or taken by the mouth. ▶ **n.** a spoken exam.

SYNONYMS ▶ **adj. spoken**, verbal, unwritten, vocal, uttered. ANTONYMS written.

■ **o·ral·ly** adv.

or·ange /ô'rinzH, 'är-/ ▶ **n.** **1** a large round citrus fruit with a tough reddish-yellow rind. **2** a bright reddish-yellow color.

or·ange·ade /'ôrənj͵ād, 'är-/ ▶ **n.** a drink made with orange juice, sweetener, and water, sometimes carbonated.

o·rang·u·tan /ə'raNG(g)ə͵tan/ (or **orangutang** /ō'raNG(g)ə͵taNG/) ▶ **n.** a large ape with long reddish hair.

o·ra·tion /ô'rāsHən/ ▶ **n.** a formal speech.

or·a·tor /'ôrətər, 'är-/ ▶ **n.** a person who is good at public speaking.

or·a·to·ri·o /͵ôrə'tôrē͵ō, ͵är-/ ▶ **n.** (plural **oratorios**) a large-scale musical work on a religious theme for orchestra and voices.

or·a·to·ry[1] /'ôrə͵tôrē, 'är-/ ▶ **n.** (plural **oratories**) a small chapel.

or·a·to·ry[2] ▶ **n.** **1** formal public speaking. **2** exciting and inspiring speech. ■ **or·a·tor·i·cal** /͵ôrə'tôrikəl/ adj.

orb /ôrb/ ▶ **n.** **1** an object shaped like a ball. **2** a golden globe with a cross on top, carried by a king or queen.

or·bit /'ôrbit/ ▶ **n.** **1** the regularly repeated course of a moon, spacecraft, etc., around a star or planet. **2** a particular area of activity or influence. ▶ **v.** (**orbits**, **orbiting**, **orbited**) move in orbit around a star or planet.

SYNONYMS ▶ **n. circuit**, course, path, track, trajectory, rotation, revolution. ▶ **v. circle**, go around/round, revolve around, travel around, circumnavigate.

or·bit·al /'ôrbitl/ ▶ **adj.** relating to an orbit or orbits.

or·ca /'ôrkə/ ▶ **n.** a large whale with teeth and black and white markings.

or·chard /'ôrcHərd/ ▶ **n.** a piece of enclosed land planted with fruit trees.

or·ches·tra /'ôrkistrə, -͵kestrə/ ▶ **n.** **1** a large group of musicians with string, woodwind, brass, and percussion sections. **2** (also **orchestra pit**) the part of a theater where the orchestra plays.

SYNONYMS **ensemble**, group; informal band, combo.

■ **or·ches·tral** /ôrˈkestrəl/ **adj.**

or·ches·trate /ˈôrkiˌstrāt/ ▶ **v.** (**orchestrates, orchestrating, orchestrated**) **1** arrange music to be performed by an orchestra. **2** organize a situation to produce a particular effect.

SYNONYMS **organize**, arrange, plan, set up, mobilize, mount, stage, mastermind, coordinate, direct.

■ **or·ches·tra·tion** /ˌôrkəˈstrāsʜən/ **n.**

or·chid /ˈôrkid/ ▶ **n.** a plant with showy, unusually shaped flowers.

or·dain /ôrˈdān/ ▶ **v.** **1** make someone a priest or minister. **2** order officially.

SYNONYMS **1 confer holy orders on**, admit to the priesthood, appoint, anoint, consecrate. **2 determine**, predestine, preordain, predetermine, prescribe, designate.

or·deal /ôrˈdēl/ ▶ **n.** a prolonged painful or horrific experience.

SYNONYMS **trial**, hardship, suffering, nightmare, trauma, hell, torture, torment, agony.

or·der /ˈôrdər/ ▶ **n.** **1** the arrangement of people or things according to a particular sequence or method. **2** a situation in which everything is in its correct place. **3** a situation in which the law is being obeyed and no one is behaving badly. **4** a statement telling someone to do something. **5** a request for something to be made, supplied, or served. **6** the procedure followed in a meeting, court, or religious service. **7** quality or class. **8** a social class or system. **9** a classifying category of plants and animals. **10** (**orders** or **holy orders**) the rank of an ordained Christian minister. **11** a group of people living in a religious community. **12** an institution founded by a ruler to honor people: *the Order of the Garter*. ▶ **v.** (**orders, ordering, ordered**) **1** tell someone to do something. **2** request that something be made, supplied, or served. **3** organize or arrange.

SYNONYMS ▶ **n.** **1** *alphabetical order* **sequence**, arrangement, organization, codification, classification, system, series, succession. **2** *some semblance of order* **tidiness**, neatness, orderliness, method, symmetry, uniformity, regularity, routine. **3** *the police managed to keep order* **peace**, control, law and order, calm. **4** *in good order* **condition**, state, repair, shape, situation. **5** *I had to obey orders* **command**, instruction, directive, direction, decree, edict, injunction, dictate. **6** *the lower orders of society* **class**, level, rank, grade, caste. **7** *a religious order* **community**, brotherhood, sisterhood. **8** *the Benevolent and Protective Order of Elks* **organization**, association, society, fellowship, fraternity, lodge, guild, league, union, club. ANTONYMS chaos. ▶ **v.** **1 instruct**, tell, command, direct, charge, require, enjoin, ordain, decree, rule. **2 request**, apply for, book, reserve, requisition. **3 organize**, arrange, sort out, lay out, group, classify, categorize, catalog.

□ **in order for** (or **that**) so that. **in order to** so as to. **of** (or **in**) **the order of** approximately. **the order of the day 1** the current state of affairs. **2** the day's business to be considered in a meeting, legislature, or parliament. **out of order** not functioning.

or·der·ly /ˈôrdərlē/ ▶ **adj.** **1** arranged in a neat, organized way. **2** well-behaved. ▶ **n.** (plural **orderlies**) **1** a hospital attendant responsible for various nonmedical tasks. **2** a soldier who carries orders or performs minor tasks.

SYNONYMS ▶ **adj.** **1 neat**, tidy, well-ordered, in order, trim, in apple-pie order, shipshape. **2 organized**, efficient, methodical, systematic, coherent, structured, logical. **3 well-behaved**, law-abiding, disciplined, peaceful, peaceable. ANTONYMS untidy, unruly.

■ **or·der·li·ness** **n.**

or·di·nal /ˈôrdn-əl/ ▶ **adj.** relating to order in a series. □ **ordinal number** a number defining a thing's position in a series, such as *first* or *second*.

or·di·nance /ˈôrdn-əns/ ▶ **n.** formal **1** an official order. **2** a religious rite.

or·di·nar·y /ˈôrdnˌerē/ ▶ **adj.** **1** normal or usual. **2** not interesting or exceptional.

SYNONYMS **1 usual**, normal, standard, typical, common, customary, habitual, everyday, regular, routine, day-to-day, quotidian. **2 average**, run-of-the-mill, typical, middle-of-the-road, conventional, humdrum, unremarkable, unexceptional, pedestrian, prosaic, workaday; informal garden-variety. ANTONYMS unusual.

□ **out of the ordinary** unusual. ■ **or·di·nar·i·ly** **adv.** **or·di·nar·i·ness** **n.**

or·di·na·tion /ˌôrdnˈāsʜən/ ▶ **n.** the ordaining of someone as a priest or minister.

ord·nance /ˈôrdnəns/ ▶ **n.** **1** mounted guns. **2** military equipment and stores.

or·dure /ˈôrjər/ ▶ **n.** formal dung; excrement.

ore /ôr/ ▶ **n.** a naturally occurring material from which a metal or mineral can be extracted.

o·reg·a·no /əˈregəˌnō/ ▶ **n.** a sweet-smelling plant used in cooking.

or·gan /ˈôrgən/ ▶ **n.** **1** a part of the body that has a particular function, e.g., the heart or kidneys. **2** a musical keyboard instrument with rows of pipes supplied with air from bellows, or one that produces similar sounds electronically. **3** a periodical that puts forward particular views.

SYNONYMS **newspaper**, paper, journal, periodical, magazine, voice, mouthpiece.

■ **or·gan·ist** **n.**

or·gan·ic /ôrˈganik/ ▶ **adj.** **1** having to do with living matter. **2** produced without the aid of artificial chemicals such as fertilizers. **3** (of chemical compounds) containing carbon. **4** having to do with an organ of the body. **5** (of development or change) continuous or natural.

SYNONYMS **1** *organic matter* **living**, live, animate, biological. **2** *organic vegetables* **natural**, chemical-free, pesticide-free, bio-. **3** *an organic whole* **structured**, organized, coherent, integrated, coordinated, ordered, harmonious.

■ **or·gan·i·cal·ly** **adv.**

or·gan·ism /ˈôrgəˌnizəm/ ▶ **n.** **1** an individual animal, plant, or life form. **2** a whole made up of parts that are dependent on each other.

SYNONYMS **living thing**, being, creature, animal, plant, life form.

or·gan·i·za·tion /ˌôrgəniˈzāsʜən/ ▶ **n.** **1** an organized group of people, e.g., a business. **2** the action of organizing. **3** a systematic arrangement or approach.

SYNONYMS **1 planning**, arrangement, coordination, organizing, running, management. **2 structure**, arrangement, plan, pattern, order, form, format, framework, composition. **3 institution**, body, group, company, concern, firm, business, corporation, conglomerate, consortium, syndicate, agency, association, society; informal outfit.

■ **or·gan·i·za·tion·al** **adj.**

or·gan·ize /ˈôrgəˌnīz/ ▶ **v.** (**organizes**, **organizing**, **organized**) **1** arrange in a particular order or structure. **2** make arrangements for an event or activity.

SYNONYMS **1 order**, arrange, sort, assemble, marshal, put straight, group, classify, collate, categorize, catalog, codify. **2 arrange**, coordinate, sort out, put together, fix up, set up, lay on, orchestrate, see to, mobilize.

or·gan·iz·er /ˈôrgəˌnīzər/ ▶ **n.** **1** a person who organizes. **2** a thing used for organizing.

or·gan·za /ôrˈganzə/ ▶ **n.** a thin, stiff, transparent fabric.

o·ri·el /ˈôrēəl/ ▶ **n.** a projecting part of an upper story with a window.

o·ri·ent /ˈôrēˌənt/ ▶ **n.** (**the Orient**) literary the countries of the East. ▶ **v.** (also **orientate**) **1** position something in relation to the points of a compass or other points. **2** (**orient yourself**) find your position in relation to your surroundings. **3** adapt something to meet particular needs.

SYNONYMS ▶ **v.** **1** *you need time to orient yourself* **acclimatize**, familiarize, adjust, accustom, find your feet, get your bearings. **2 aim**, direct, pitch, design, intend. **3 align**, place, position, arrange.

o·ri·en·tal /ˌôrēˈentl/ (or **Oriental**) ▶ **adj.** having to do with the Far East. ▶ **n.** dated or offensive a person of Far Eastern descent.

o·ri·en·ta·tion /ˌôrēənˈtāsʜən/ ▶ **n.** **1** the action of orienting. **2** a position in relation to something else. **3** a person's attitude or natural tendency.

o·ri·en·teer·ing /ˌôriənˈti(ə)riɴɢ/ ▶ **n.** the sport of finding your way across country using a map and compass.

or·i·fice /ˈôrəfis/ ▶ **n.** an opening.

o·ri·ga·mi /ˌôrəˈgämē/ ▶ **n.** the Japanese art of folding paper into decorative shapes.

or·i·gin /ˈôrəjən/ ▶ **n.** **1** the point where something begins. **2** a person's background or ancestry.

SYNONYMS **1 beginning**, start, genesis, birth, dawning, dawn, emergence, creation, source, basis, cause, root(s), derivation, provenance. **2 descent**, ancestry, parentage, pedigree, lineage, line (of descent), heritage, birth, extraction, family, roots.

o·rig·i·nal /əˈrijənl/ ▶ **adj.** **1** existing from the beginning. **2** not a copy. **3** new in an interesting or unusual way. ▶ **n.** the earliest form of something, from which copies can be made.

SYNONYMS ▶ **adj.** **1 indigenous**, aboriginal, native, first, earliest, early, ur-. **2 authentic**, genuine, actual, true, bona fide. **3 innovative**, creative, imaginative, inventive, new, novel, fresh, unusual, unconventional, unorthodox, groundbreaking, pioneering, unique, distinctive. ▶ **n.** **prototype**, source, master.

□ **original sin** (in Christian belief) the tendency to be sinful that is thought to be present in all people. ■ **o·rig·i·nal·i·ty** /əˌrijəˈnalitē/ **n.**

o·rig·i·nal·ly /əˈrijənlē/ ▶ **adv.** in the beginning; at first: *the conference was originally scheduled for November.*

SYNONYMS **at first**, in the beginning, to begin with, initially, in the first place, at the outset.

o·rig·i·nate /əˈrijəˌnāt/ ▶ **v.** (**originates**, **originating**, **originated**) **1** begin in a particular place or situation. **2** create.

SYNONYMS **1 arise**, have its origin, begin, start, stem, spring, emerge, emanate. **2 invent**, create, devise, think up, dream up, conceive, formulate, form, develop, produce, mastermind, pioneer.

■ **o·rig·i·na·tion** /əˌrijəˈnāsʜən/ **n.** **o·rig·i·na·tor** **n.**

or·mo·lu /ˈôrməˌlo͞o/ ▶ **n.** a gold-colored alloy of copper, zinc, and tin.

or·na·ment /ˈôrnəmənt/ ▶ **n.** **1** an object used as a decoration. **2** decorative items considered together.

SYNONYMS **1 knick-knack**, trinket, bauble, gewgaw; informal kickshaw. **2 decoration**, adornment, embellishment, ornamentation, trimming, accessories, frills.

■ **or·na·men·ta·tion** /ˌôrnəmenˈtāsʜən/ **n.**

or·na·men·tal /ˌôrnəˈmentl/ ▶ **adj.** acting or intended as an ornament; decorative.

SYNONYMS **decorative**, fancy, ornate, ornamented, attractive.

or·nate /ôrˈnāt/ ▶ **adj.** elaborately decorated.

SYNONYMS **elaborate**, decorated, embellished, adorned, ornamented, rococo, fancy, fussy, ostentatious, showy; informal flashy. ANTONYMS plain.

■ **or·nate·ly** **adv.**

or·ner·y /ˈôrn(ə)rē/ ▶ **adj.** informal bad-tempered.

or·ni·thol·o·gy /ˌôrnəˈᴛʜäləjē/ ▶ **n.** the scientific study of birds. ■ **or·ni·tho·log·i·cal** /ˌôrniᴛʜəˈläjikəl/ **adj.** **or·ni·thol·o·gist** **n.**

or·phan /ˈôrfən/ ▶ **n.** a child whose parents are dead. ▶ **v.** (**be orphaned**) (of a child) be made an orphan.

or·phan·age /ˈôrfənij/ ▶ **n.** a place where orphans are looked after.

or·tho·don·tist /ˌôrᴛʜəˈdäntist/ ▶ **n.** a dentist who treats irregularities in the position of the teeth and jaws.

or·tho·dox /ˈôrᴛʜəˌdäks/ ▶ **adj.** **1** in keeping with generally accepted beliefs. **2** normal. **3** (**Orthodox**) relating to the Orthodox Church.

SYNONYMS **1 conventional**, mainstream, conformist, established, traditional, traditionalist, prevalent, popular, conservative, received. **2** *an orthodox Muslim* **observant**, devout, strict. ANTONYMS unconventional.

□ **Orthodox Church** a branch of the Christian Church mainly in Greece and eastern Europe.

or·tho·dox·y /ˈôrᴛʜəˌdäksē/ ▶ **n.** (plural **orthodoxies**) **1** the traditional beliefs or practices of a religion. **2** a generally accepted idea.

or·thog·ra·phy /ôr'THägrəfē/ ▶ **n.** (plural **orthographies**) the spelling system of a language. ■ **or·tho·graph·ic** /ˌôrTHə'grafik/ **adj.**

or·tho·pe·dics /ˌôrTHə'pēdiks/ ▶ **n.** the branch of medicine concerned with bones and muscles.

Os·car /'äskər/ ▶ **n.** a gold statuette given annually for achievement in various categories of filmmaking; an Academy Award.

os·cil·late /'äsəˌlāt/ ▶ **v.** (**oscillates**, **oscillating**, **oscillated**) **1** move back and forth in a regular rhythm. **2** waver in your opinions or emotions.

> SYNONYMS **1 swing to and fro**, swing back and forth, sway. **2 waver**, swing, fluctuate, alternate, seesaw, yo-yo, vacillate.

■ **os·cil·la·tion** /ˌäsə'lāSHən/ **n.**

os·cil·la·tor /'äsəˌlātər/ ▶ **n.** a device for generating electric currents or voltages.

o·sier /'ōZHər/ ▶ **n.** **1** a type of willow tree with long, flexible shoots that are used for making baskets. **2** a rod made from one of these shoots.

os·mi·um /'äzmēəm/ ▶ **n.** a hard, dense silvery-white metallic element.

os·mo·sis /äz'mōsis, äs-/ ▶ **n.** **1** a process by which molecules pass through a membrane from a less concentrated solution into a more concentrated one. **2** the gradual absorbing of ideas. ■ **os·mot·ic** /-mätik/ **adj.**

os·prey /'äsprā, -prē/ ▶ **n.** (plural **ospreys**) a large fish-eating bird of prey.

os·se·ous /'äsēəs/ ▶ **adj.** consisting of bone.

os·si·fy /'äsəˌfī/ ▶ **v.** (**ossifies**, **ossifying**, **ossified**) **1** turn into bone or bony tissue. **2** stop developing or progressing. ■ **os·si·fi·ca·tion** /ˌäsəfi'kāSHən/ **n.**

os·ten·si·ble /ä'stensəbəl, ə'sten-/ ▶ **adj.** apparently true, but not necessarily so. ■ **os·ten·si·bly adv.**

os·ten·ta·tion /ˌästən'tāSHən/ ▶ **n.** a showy display of wealth, knowledge, etc., that is intended to impress.

os·ten·ta·tious /ˌästən'tāSHəs/ ▶ **adj.** expensive or showy in a way that is designed to impress.

> SYNONYMS **showy**, conspicuous, flamboyant, gaudy, brash, vulgar, loud, extravagant, fancy, ornate, rococo; informal flash, flashy, bling-bling, over the top, OTT, glitzy. ANTONYMS restrained.

■ **os·ten·ta·tious·ly adv.**

os·te·o·ar·thri·tis /ˌästēōär'THrītis/ ▶ **n.** a disease that causes pain and stiffness in the joints of the body.

os·te·op·a·thy /ˌästē'äpəTHē/ ▶ **n.** a system of complementary medicine involving manipulation of the bones and muscles. ■ **os·te·o·path** /'ästēəˌpaTH/ **n.**

os·te·o·po·ro·sis /ˌästēōpə'rōsis/ ▶ **n.** a medical condition in which the bones become brittle.

os·ti·na·to /ˌästi'nätō/ ▶ **n.** (plural **ostinatos** or **ostinati** /-tē/) a continually repeated musical phrase or rhythm.

os·tler /'äslər/ ▶ **n.** ⇒ **HOSTLER.**

os·tra·cize /'ästrəˌsīz/ ▶ **v.** (**ostracizes**, **ostracizing**, **ostracized**) exclude someone from a society or group.

> SYNONYMS **exclude**, shun, spurn, cold-shoulder, reject, ignore, snub, blackball, blacklist; informal freeze out.

■ **os·tra·cism n.**

os·trich /'ästricH/ ▶ **n.** a large African bird with a long neck and long legs that is unable to fly.

oth·er /'əTHər/ ▶ **adj. & pron.** **1** used to refer to a person or thing that is different from one already mentioned or known. **2** additional. **3** the alternative of two. **4** those not already mentioned.

> SYNONYMS **1 alternative**, different, distinct, separate, various. **2 more**, further, additional, extra, fresh, new, added, supplementary.

oth·er·ness /'əTHərnis/ ▶ **n.** the quality of being different or unusual.

oth·er·wise /'əTHərˌwīz/ ▶ **adv.** **1** in different circumstances. **2** in other respects. **3** in a different way. **4** alternatively.

oth·er·world·ly /ˌəTHər'wərldlē/ ▶ **adj.** **1** of or relating to an imaginary or spiritual world. **2** not aware of the realities of life.

o·ti·ose /'ōSHēˌōs, 'ōtēˌōs/ ▶ **adj.** serving no practical purpose.

ot·ter /'ätər/ ▶ **n.** a fish-eating animal with a long body, living partly in water and partly on land.

ot·to·man /'ätəmən/ ▶ **n.** (plural **ottomans**) a low padded seat without a back or arms.

ou·bli·ette /ˌo͞oblē'et/ ▶ **n.** a secret dungeon with access only through a trapdoor in its ceiling.

ought /ôt/ ▶ **modal v.** (3rd singular present and past **ought**) **1** used to indicate duty or correctness. **2** used to indicate something that is probable. **3** used to indicate a desirable or expected state. **4** used to give or ask advice.

> USAGE
>
> When using **ought** in a negative sentence, you should say, for example, *he ought not to have gone* rather than *he didn't/hadn't ought to have gone*.

ought·n't /'ôtnt/ ▶ **contr.** ought not.

Oui·ja board /'wējə, -jē/ ▶ **n.** trademark a board marked with letters and numbers, used at a seance supposedly to receive messages from dead people.

ounce /ouns/ ▶ **n.** **1** a unit of weight of one sixteenth of a pound (approximately 28 grams). **2** a very small amount.

our /ou(ə)r, är/ ▶ **possessive determiner 1** belonging to or associated with the speaker and one or more other people. **2** belonging to or associated with people in general.

ours /'ou(ə)rz, ärz/ ▶ **possessive pron.** used to refer to something belonging to or associated with the speaker and one or more other people.

> SPELLING
>
> No apostrophe: **ours**.

our·selves /ou(ə)r'selvz, är-/ ▶ **pron.** **1** used as the object of a verb or preposition when this is the same as the subject of the clause and the subject is the speaker and one or more other people. **2** we or us personally.

oust /oust/ ▶ **v.** force someone out from a job or position.

> SYNONYMS **expel**, drive out, force out, eject, get rid of, depose, topple, unseat, overthrow, bring down, overturn, dismiss, dislodge.

oust·er /'oustər/ ▶ **n.** dismissal or expulsion from a position.

out /out/ ▶ **adv.** **1** away from a place. **2** away from your home or office. **3** outdoors. **4** so as to be revealed, heard, or known. **5** to an end. **6** not possible or worth considering. **7** (of the tide) falling or at its lowest level. **8** (of the ball in tennis, squash, etc.) not in the playing area. **9** (in baseball, cricket, etc.) removed from play by the defense. ▫ **out for** intent on having. **out-and-out** absolute or complete. **out of 1** from. **2** not having a supply of something. **out of date 1** old-fashioned. **2** no longer valid. **out to do** keenly striving to do.

out·back /ˈoutˌbak/ ▶ **n.** (**the outback**) the part of Australia that is remote and has few inhabitants.

out·bid /ˌoutˈbid/ ▶ **v.** (**outbids**, **outbidding**, **outbid**) bid more than.

out·board /ˈoutˌbô(ə)rd/ ▶ **adj. & adv.** on, toward, or near the outside of a ship or aircraft. ▶ **n. 1** an outboard motor. **2** a boat with an outboard motor. ▫ **outboard motor** a motor attached to the outside of a boat.

out·break /ˈoutˌbrāk/ ▶ **n.** a sudden occurrence of war, disease, etc.

> SYNONYMS **1 eruption**, flare-up, upsurge, rash, wave, spate, burst, flurry. **2 start**, beginning, commencement, onset.

out·build·ing /ˈoutˌbildiNG/ ▶ **n.** a smaller building on the same property as a main building.

out·burst /ˈoutˌbərst/ ▶ **n. 1** a sudden release of strong emotion. **2** a sudden or violent occurrence of something.

> SYNONYMS **eruption**, explosion, flare-up, storm, outpouring, burst, surge, fit, paroxysm, spasm.

out·cast /ˈoutˌkast/ ▶ **n.** a person who is rejected by their social group.

> SYNONYMS **pariah**, persona non grata, reject, outsider.

out·class /ˌoutˈklas/ ▶ **v.** be far better than.

out·come /ˈoutˌkəm/ ▶ **n.** a result or effect.

> SYNONYMS **result**, end result, net result, consequence, upshot, conclusion, end product; informal payoff.

out·crop /ˈoutˌkräp/ ▶ **n.** a part of a rock formation that is visible on the surface.

out·cry /ˈoutˌkrī/ ▶ **n.** (plural **outcries**) a strong expression of public disapproval.

> SYNONYMS **protest**, protestation, complaints, objections, furor, hue and cry, fuss, uproar, opposition, dissent; informal hullabaloo, ruction(s), stink.

out·dat·ed /ˌoutˈdātid/ ▶ **adj.** no longer used or fashionable.

> SYNONYMS **old-fashioned**, out of date, outmoded, out of fashion, unfashionable, dated, passé, old, behind the times, antiquated; informal old hat, square. ANTONYMS modern.

out·dis·tance /ˌoutˈdistəns/ ▶ **v.** (**outdistances**, **outdistancing**, **outdistanced**) leave a competitor or pursuer far behind.

out·do /ˌoutˈdo͞o/ ▶ **v.** (**outdoes** /ˌoutˈdəz/, **outdoing**, **outdid** /ˌoutˈdid/; past participle **outdone** /ˌoutˈdən/) do better than someone else.

> SYNONYMS **surpass**, outshine, overshadow, eclipse, outclass, outmaneuver, put in the shade, upstage, exceed, transcend, top, cap, beat, better; informal be a cut above.

out·door /ˈoutˈdôr/ ▶ **adj.** done, situated, or used outdoors.

> SYNONYMS **open-air**, out-of-doors, outside, alfresco. ANTONYMS indoor.

out·doors /ˌoutˈdôrz/ ▶ **adv.** in or into the open air. ▶ **n.** any area outside buildings or shelter.

out·er /ˈoutər/ ▶ **adj. 1** outside. **2** further from the center or the inside.

> SYNONYMS **1 outside**, outermost, outward, exterior, external, surface. **2 outlying**, distant, remote, faraway, far-flung, furthest. ANTONYMS inner.

▫ **outer space** the universe beyond the earth's atmosphere.

out·er·most /ˈoutərˌmōst/ ▶ **adj.** furthest from the center.

out·fall /ˈoutˌfôl/ ▶ **n.** the place where a river or drain empties into the sea, a river, or a lake.

out·field /ˈoutˌfēld/ ▶ **n.** the outer part of a baseball field.

out·fit /ˈoutˌfit/ ▶ **n. 1** a set of clothes worn together. **2** informal a group of people working together as a business, team, etc. ▶ **v.** (**outfits**, **outfitting**, **outfitted**) provide someone with an outfit of clothes.

> SYNONYMS ▶ **n. 1 costume**, suit, uniform, ensemble, clothes, clothing, dress, garb; informal getup, gear. **2 organization**, enterprise, company, firm, business, group, body, team; informal setup.

■ **out·fit·ter** /ˈoutˌfitər/ **n.**

out·flank /ˌoutˈflaNGk/ ▶ **v. 1** surround in order to attack. **2** defeat.

out·go·ing /ˈoutˌgōiNG/ ▶ **adj. 1** friendly and confident. **2** leaving an office or position. **3** going out or away from a place.

> SYNONYMS **1 extrovert**, uninhibited, unreserved, demonstrative, affectionate, warm, sociable, gregarious, convivial, lively, expansive. **2 departing**, retiring, leaving. ANTONYMS introverted, incoming.

out·grow /ˌoutˈgrō/ ▶ **v.** (**outgrows**, **outgrowing**, **outgrew** /ˌoutˈgro͞o/; past participle **outgrown**) **1** grow too big for. **2** stop doing something as you grow older.

out·house /ˈoutˌhous/ ▶ **n. 1** a smaller building attached or close to a house. **2** an outbuilding containing a toilet, typically with no plumbing.

out·ing /ˈoutiNG/ ▶ **n.** a short trip made for pleasure.

> SYNONYMS **trip**, excursion, jaunt, expedition, day out, tour, drive, ride, run; informal spin, junket.

out·land·ish /outˈlandisH/ ▶ **adj.** bizarre or unfamiliar.

> SYNONYMS **weird**, queer, far out, eccentric, unconventional, unorthodox, funny, bizarre, unusual, strange, peculiar, odd, curious; informal offbeat, off the wall, way-out, wacky, freaky, kinky, oddball. ANTONYMS ordinary.

out·last /ˌoutˈlast/ ▶ **v.** last longer than.

out·law /ˈoutˌlô/ ▶ **n.** a person who has broken the law and remains at large. ▶ **v.** make something illegal.

SYNONYMS ▶ **n. fugitive**, bandit, robber. ▶ **v. ban**, bar, prohibit, forbid, make illegal, proscribe. ANTONYMS permit.

out·lay /'out,lā/ ▶ **n.** an amount of money spent.

out·let /'out,let/ ▶ **n. 1** a pipe or hole through which water or gas may escape. **2** a point from which goods are sold or distributed. **3** a way of expressing your talents, energy, or emotions.

SYNONYMS **1 vent**, way out, outfall, opening, channel, conduit, duct. **2 market**, shop, store.

out·line /'out,līn/ ▶ **n. 1** a sketch or diagram showing the shape of an object. **2** the outer edges of an object. **3** a general description of something, with no detail. ▶ **v.** (**outlines**, **outlining**, **outlined**) **1** draw the outer edge or shape of. **2** give a summary of.

SYNONYMS ▶ **n. 1 silhouette**, profile, shape, contour(s), form, lines. **2 rough idea**, thumbnail sketch, rundown, summary, synopsis, résumé, précis, gist, bare bones. ▶ **v. rough out**, sketch out, draft, summarize, précis.

out·live /,out'liv/ ▶ **v.** live or last longer than.

out·look /'out,lo͝ok/ ▶ **n. 1** a person's attitude to life. **2** a view. **3** what is likely to happen in the future.

SYNONYMS **1 point of view**, viewpoint, way of thinking, perspective, attitude, standpoint, stance, frame of mind. **2 view**, vista, prospect, panorama. **3 prospects**, future, expectations, prognosis.

out·ly·ing /'out,lī-iNG/ ▶ **adj.** situated far from a center.

out·ma·neu·ver /,outmə'no͞ovər/ ▶ **v.** (**outmaneuvers**, **outmaneuvering**, **outmaneuvered**) gain an advantage over an opponent by using skill and cunning.

out·mod·ed /,out'mōdid/ ▶ **adj.** old-fashioned.

out·num·ber /,out'nəmbər/ ▶ **v.** (**outnumbers**, **outnumbering**, **outnumbered**) be more numerous than.

out·pace /,out'pās/ ▶ **v.** (**outpaces**, **outpacing**, **outpaced**) go faster than.

out·pa·tient /'out,pāsHənt/ ▶ **n.** a patient being treated in a hospital without staying overnight.

out·per·form /,outpər'fôrm/ ▶ **v.** perform better than.

out·play /,out'plā/ ▶ **v.** play better than.

out·post /'out,pōst/ ▶ **n. 1** a small military camp at a distance from the main army. **2** a remote part of a country or empire.

out·pour·ing /'out,pôriNG/ ▶ **n. 1** something that streams out rapidly. **2** an outburst of strong emotion.

out·put /'out,po͝ot/ ▶ **n. 1** the amount of something produced. **2** the process of producing something. **3** the power, energy, etc., supplied by a device or system. **4** a place where power, information, etc., leaves a system.

SYNONYMS **production**, yield, product, productivity, work, result.

out·rage /'out,rāj/ ▶ **n. 1** a very strong reaction of anger or annoyance. **2** a very immoral or shocking act. ▶ **v.** (**outrages**, **outraging**, **outraged**) make someone feel outrage.

SYNONYMS ▶ **n. 1 indignation**, fury, anger, rage, wrath, annoyance; literary ire. **2 scandal**, offense, insult, affront, disgrace, atrocity. ▶ **v. enrage**, infuriate, incense, anger, scandalize, offend, affront, shock.

out·ra·geous /out'rājəs/ ▶ **adj. 1** shockingly bad or unacceptable. **2** very unusual and slightly shocking.

SYNONYMS **1 shocking**, disgraceful, scandalous, atrocious, appalling, dreadful, insufferable, intolerable. **2 exaggerated**, improbable, preposterous, ridiculous, unwarranted.

■ **out·ra·geous·ly adv.**

out·ran /,out'ran/ past of **OUTRUN**.

out·rank /,out'raNGk/ ▶ **v.** have a higher rank than.

ou·tré /o͞o'trā/ ▶ **adj.** unusual and rather shocking.

out·reach /'out,rēcH/ ▶ **n.** an organization's involvement with the community.

out·rid·er /'out,rīdər/ ▶ **n.** a person in a vehicle or on horseback who escorts another vehicle.

out·rig·ger /'out,rigər/ ▶ **n.** a structure fixed to a boat's side to help keep it stable.

out·right /'out,rīt/ ▶ **adv. 1** altogether. **2** openly. **3** immediately. ▶ **adj. 1** open and direct. **2** complete.

SYNONYMS ▶ **adv. 1 completely**, entirely, wholly, totally, categorically, absolutely, utterly, flatly, unreservedly, out of hand. **2 explicitly**, directly, frankly, candidly, bluntly, plainly, to someone's face, straight up. **3 instantly**, instantaneously, immediately, at once, straightaway, then and there, on the spot. ▶ **adj. 1 complete**, absolute, out-and-out, downright, utter, sheer, categorical. **2 definite**, unequivocal, unmistakable, clear.

out·run /,out'rən/ ▶ **v.** (**outruns**, **outrunning**, **outran** /,out'ran/; past participle **outrun**) run or travel faster or further than.

out·sell /,out'sel/ ▶ **v.** (**outsells**, **outselling**, **outsold**) be sold in greater quantities than.

out·set /'out,set/ ▶ **n.** the beginning.

SYNONYMS **start**, starting point, beginning, inception; informal the word go. ANTONYMS end.

out·shine /,out'sHīn/ ▶ **v.** (**outshines**, **outshining**, **outshone** /,out'sHōn/) **1** shine more brightly than. **2** be much better than.

out·side /'out'sīd/ ▶ **n. 1** the external side or surface of something. **2** the external appearance of someone or something. **3** the side of a curve where the edge is longer. ▶ **adj. 1** situated on or near the outside. **2** not belonging to a particular group. ▶ **prep. & adv. 1** situated or moving beyond the boundaries of. **2** beyond the limits of. **3** not being a member of.

SYNONYMS ▶ **n. exterior**, case, skin, shell, covering, facade. ▶ **adj. 1 exterior**, external, outer, outdoor, out-of-doors. **2 independent**, freelance, consultant, external. ▶ **prep. & adv. outdoors**, out of doors, alfresco. ANTONYMS inside.

out·sid·er /,out'sīdər/ ▶ **n. 1** a person who does not belong to a particular group. **2** a competitor thought to have little chance of success.

SYNONYMS **stranger**, visitor, foreigner, alien, interloper, immigrant, incomer, newcomer.

out·size /,out'sīz/ (or **outsized**) ▶ **adj.** very large.

out·skirts /'out,skərts/ ▶ **pl.n.** the outer parts of a town or city.

SYNONYMS **edges**, fringes, margins, suburbs, suburbia, environs, borders, periphery.

out·smart /ˌout'smärt/ ▶ **v.** defeat someone by being cleverer than them.

SYNONYMS **outwit**, outmaneuver, trick, get the better of; informal pull a fast one on, put one over on.

out·sold /ˌout'sōld/ past and past participle of **OUTSELL**.

out·spo·ken /ˌout'spōkən/ ▶ **adj.** stating your opinions in an open and direct way.

SYNONYMS **forthright**, direct, candid, frank, straightforward, open, straight from the shoulder, plain-spoken, blunt.

out·stand·ing /ˌout'standiNG, 'out-/ ▶ **adj.** **1** exceptionally good. **2** clearly noticeable. **3** not yet dealt with or paid.

SYNONYMS **1 excellent**, marvelous, fine, magnificent, superb, wonderful, superlative, exceptional, preeminent, renowned, celebrated; informal great, terrific, tremendous, super. **2 to be done**, undone, unfinished, incomplete, remaining, pending. **3 unpaid**, unsettled, owing, owed, to be paid, payable, due, overdue, delinquent.

■ **out·stand·ing·ly** **adv.**

out·stay /ˌout'stā/ ▶ **v.** stay for longer than the expected or allowed time.

out·strip /ˌout'strip/ ▶ **v.** (**outstrips**, **outstripping**, **outstripped**) **1** move faster than. **2** surpass.

out·ta /'outə/ ▶ **contr.** informal out of: *let's get outta here!*

out·vote /ˌout'vōt/ ▶ **v.** (**outvotes**, **outvoting**, **outvoted**) defeat by gaining more votes.

out·ward /'outwərd/ ▶ **adj. & adv.** **1** on or from the outside. **2** out or away from a place.

SYNONYMS **external**, surface, superficial, seeming, apparent, ostensible. ANTONYMS inward.

■ **out·ward·ly** **adv.** **out·wards** **adv.**

out·weigh /ˌout'wā/ ▶ **v.** be more significant than.

SYNONYMS **be greater than**, exceed, be superior to, prevail over, override, supersede, offset, cancel out, outbalance, compensate for.

out·wit /ˌout'wit/ ▶ **v.** (**outwits**, **outwitting**, **outwitted**) deceive someone through being cleverer than them.

SYNONYMS **outsmart**, outmaneuver, trick, get the better of; informal pull a fast one on, put one over on.

ou·zo /'o͞ozō/ ▶ **n.** an anise-flavored Greek liqueur.

o·va /'ōvə/ plural of **OVUM**.

o·val /'ōvəl/ ▶ **adj.** having a rounded and slightly elongated outline. ▶ **n.** an oval object or design.

o·va·ry /'ōv(ə)rē/ ▶ **n.** (plural **ovaries**) **1** a female reproductive organ in which eggs are produced. **2** the base of the reproductive organ of a flower.
■ **o·var·i·an** /ō've(ə)rēən/ **adj.**

o·va·tion /ō'vāSHən/ ▶ **n.** a long, enthusiastic round of applause.

SYNONYMS **applause**, round of applause, cheers, bravos, acclaim, standing ovation; informal (big) hand.

ov·en /'əvən/ ▶ **n.** **1** an enclosed compartment in which food is cooked or heated. **2** a small furnace or kiln.

ov·en·proof /'əvənˌpro͞of/ ▶ **adj.** suitable for use in an oven.

o·ver /'ōvər/ ▶ **prep. & adv.** **1** expressing movement across an area. **2** beyond and falling or hanging from a point. ▶ **prep.** **1** extending upward from or above. **2** above so as to cover or protect. **3** expressing length of time. **4** higher or more than. **5** expressing authority or control. ▶ **adv.** **1** in or to the place indicated. **2** expressing action and result. **3** finished. **4** expressing repetition of a process.

SYNONYMS ▶ **prep.** **1 above**, on top of, atop, covering. **2 more than**, above, in excess of, upwards of. ANTONYMS under.
▶ **adv.** **1 overhead**, post, by. **2 at an end**, finished, ended, no more, a thing of the past; informal finito.

o·ver·a·chiev·er /ˌōvərə'CHēvər/ ▶ **n.** a person who does better than expected.

o·ver·act /ˌōvər'akt/ ▶ **v.** act a role in an exaggerated way.

o·ver·ac·tive /ˌōvər'aktiv/ ▶ **adj.** more active than is normal or desirable.

o·ver·all /'ōvərˌäl/ ▶ **adj. & adv.** including everything; taken as a whole. ▶ **n.** (**overalls**) a garment consisting of trousers with a front flap over the chest held up by straps over the shoulders, made of sturdy material and worn especially as casual or working clothes.

SYNONYMS ▶ **adj. & adv.** **1 total**, all-inclusive, gross, final, inclusive, complete, entire, blanket. **2 generally** (**speaking**), in general, altogether, all in all, on balance, on average, for the most part, in the main, on the whole, by and large.

o·ver·arch·ing /ˌōvər'ärCHiNG/ ▶ **adj.** covering or dealing with everything.

o·ver·arm /'ōvərˌärm/ ▶ **adj. & adv.** done with the hand brought forward and down from above shoulder level.

o·ver·awe /ˌōvər'ô/ ▶ **v.** (**overawes**, **overawing**, **overawed**) impress someone so much that they are nervous or silent.

o·ver·bal·ance /ˌōvər'baləns/ ▶ **v.** (**overbalances**, **overbalancing**, **overbalanced**) fall due to loss of balance.

o·ver·bear·ing /ˌōvər'be(ə)riNG/ ▶ **adj.** trying to control other people; domineering.

SYNONYMS **domineering**, dominating, autocratic, tyrannical, despotic, high-handed; informal bossy.

o·ver·bite /'ōvərˌbīt/ ▶ **n.** the overlapping of the lower teeth by the upper.

o·ver·blown /ˌōvər'blōn/ ▶ **adj.** made to seem more important or impressive than it really is.

SYNONYMS **florid**, grandiose, pompous, flowery, pretentious, high-flown; informal highfalutin.

o·ver·board /'ōvərˌbôrd/ ▶ **adv.** from a ship into the water. □ **go overboard** be very enthusiastic.

o·ver·cast /'ōvərˌkast, ˌōvər'kast/ ▶ **adj.** cloudy.

SYNONYMS **cloudy**, sunless, dark, gray, black, leaden, heavy, dull, murky. ANTONYMS bright.

o·ver·charge /ˌōvər'CHärj/ ▶ **v.** (**overcharges**, **overcharging**, **overcharged**) charge too high a price.

o·ver·coat /ˈōvərˌkōt/ ▶ **n.** **1** a long, warm coat. **2** a top layer of paint or varnish.

o·ver·come /ˌōvərˈkəm/ ▶ **v.** (**overcomes**, **overcoming**, **overcame** /ˌōvərˈkām/; past participle **overcome**) **1** succeed in dealing with a problem. **2** defeat; overpower.

> SYNONYMS **1 conquer**, defeat, beat, prevail over, control, get/bring under control, master, get the better of; informal lick, best. **2** *she was overcome with excitement* **overwhelm**, move, affect, render speechless.

o·ver·com·pen·sate /ˌōvərˈkämpənˌsāt/ ▶ **v.** (**overcompensates**, **overcompensating**, **overcompensated**) do too much when trying to correct a problem.

o·ver·con·fi·dent /ˌōvərˈkänfidənt/ ▶ **adj.** excessively confident. ■ **o·ver·con·fi·dence** **n.**

o·ver·crowd·ed /ˌōvərˈkroudid/ ▶ **adj.** filled beyond what is usual or comfortable.

o·ver·do /ˌōvərˈdo͞o/ ▶ **v.** (**overdoes** /ˌōvərˈdəz/, **overdoing**, **overdid** /ˌōvərˈdid/; past participle **overdone** /ˌōvərˈdən/) ç do something excessively or in an exaggerated way. **2** (**overdone**) cooked too much.

o·ver·dose /ˈōvərˌdōs/ ▶ **n.** an excessive and dangerous dose of a drug. ▶ **v.** (**overdoses**, **overdosing**, **overdosed**) take an overdose.

o·ver·draft /ˈōvərˌdraft/ ▶ **n.** an arrangement with a bank that lets you take out more money than your account holds.

o·ver·drawn /ˌōvərˈdrôn/ ▶ **adj.** having taken out more money than there is in your bank account.

o·ver·dressed /ˌōvərˈdrest/ ▶ **adj.** dressed too elaborately or formally.

o·ver·drive /ˈōvərˌdrīv/ ▶ **n.** **1** a mechanism in a motor vehicle providing an extra gear above the usual top gear. **2** a state of high activity.

o·ver·due /ˌōvərˈd(y)o͞o/ ▶ **adj.** not having arrived, happened, or been done at the expected or required time.

> SYNONYMS **1 late**, behind schedule, behind time, delayed, tardy. **2 unpaid**, unsettled, owing, owed, payable, due, outstanding, delinquent, undischarged. ANTONYMS early, punctual.

o·ver·ea·ger /ˌōvərˈēgər/ ▶ **adj.** excessively eager.

o·ver·es·ti·mate /ˌōvərˈestəˌmāt/ ▶ **v.** (**overestimates**, **overestimating**, **overestimated**) estimate that something is larger or better than it really is. ▶ **n.** /-mit/ an estimate that is too high.

o·ver·ex·pose /ˌōvərikˈspōz/ ▶ **v.** (**overexposes**, **overexposing**, **overexposed**) **1** subject photographic film to too much light. **2** (**overexposed**) seen too much on television, in the newspapers, etc.

o·ver·flow /ˌōvərˈflō/ ▶ **v.** **1** flow over the edge of a container. **2** be too full or crowded. **3** (**overflow with**) be very full of an emotion. ▶ **n.** **1** the number of people or things that do not fit into a particular space. **2** an outlet for excess water.

> SYNONYMS ▶ **v. spill over**, flow over, brim over, well over, flood. ▶ **n. surplus**, excess, extra, remainder, overspill.

o·ver·ground /ˈōvərˌground/ ▶ **adv. & adj.** on or above the ground.

o·ver·grown /ˌōvərˈgrōn/ ▶ **adj.** **1** covered with plants that have grown wild. **2** having grown too large.

o·ver·hang ▶ **v.** /ˌōvərˈhang/ (**overhangs**, **overhanging**, **overhung** /ˌōvərˈhəng/) project outward over. ▶ **n.** /ˈōvərˌhang/ an overhanging part.

o·ver·haul ▶ **v.** /ˌōvərˈhôl/ examine and repair or improve something. ▶ **n.** /ˈōvərˌhôl/ an act of overhauling something.

> SYNONYMS ▶ **v. service**, maintain, repair, mend, fix up, rebuild, renovate, recondition, refit, refurbish.

o·ver·head /ˌōvərˈhed/ ▶ **adv. & adj.** above your head. ▶ **n.** /ˈōvərˌhed/ (**overheads**) regular expenses involved in running a business or organization.

> SYNONYMS ▶ **adv. & adj.** **1** *the sky overhead* **above**, high up, in the sky, on high, above your head. ANTONYMS below. **2** *overhead lines* **aerial**, elevated, raised, suspended, overhanging. ANTONYMS surface, underground. ▶ **n. running costs**, operating costs, fixed costs, expenses.

o·ver·hear /ˌōvərˈhi(ə)r/ ▶ **v.** (**overhears**, **overhearing**, **overheard** /ˌōvərˈhərd/) hear something accidentally.

o·ver·heat /ˌōvərˈhēt/ ▶ **v.** make or become too hot.

o·ver·in·dulge /ˌōvərinˈdəlj/ ▶ **v.** (**overindulges**, **overindulging**, **overindulged**) **1** have too much of something enjoyable. **2** give in to the wishes of someone too easily. ■ **o·ver·in·dul·gence** **n.**

o·ver·joyed /ˌōvərˈjoid/ ▶ **adj.** very happy.

> SYNONYMS **ecstatic**, euphoric, thrilled, elated, delighted, on cloud nine, in seventh heaven, jubilant, rapturous, jumping for joy, delirious, blissful, in raptures; informal over the moon, on top of the world, tickled pink, as happy as a clam. ANTONYMS unhappy.

o·ver·kill /ˈōvərˌkil/ ▶ **n.** too much of something.

o·ver·land /ˈōvərˌland/ ▶ **adj. & adv.** by land.

o·ver·lap ▶ **v.** /ˌōvərˈlap/ (**overlaps**, **overlapping**, **overlapped**) **1** extend over something so as to cover it partially. **2** (of two events) happen at the same time for part of their duration. ▶ **n.** /ˈōvərˌlap/ an overlapping part or amount.

o·ver·lay ▶ **v.** /ˌōvərˈlā/ (**overlays**, **overlaying**, **overlaid**) **1** coat the surface of. **2** add a quality, feeling, etc., to. ▶ **n.** /ˈōvərˌlā/ a covering.

o·ver·leaf /ˈōvərˌlēf/ ▶ **adv.** on the other side of the page.

o·ver·load ▶ **v.** /ˌōvərˈlōd/ **1** load too heavily. **2** put too great a demand on. ▶ **n.** /ˈōvərˌlōd/ too much of something.

> SYNONYMS ▶ **v. strain**, overtax, overwork, overuse, swamp, overwhelm.

o·ver·look /ˌōvərˈlo͝ok/ ▶ **v.** **1** fail to notice. **2** ignore or disregard. **3** have a view of something from above.

> SYNONYMS **1 fail to notice**, fail to spot, miss. **2 disregard**, neglect, ignore, pass over, forget, take no notice of, make allowances for, turn a blind eye to, excuse, pardon, forgive. **3 look over/across**, look on to, look out on.

o·ver·lord /ˈōvərˌlôrd/ ▶ **n.** a ruler.

o·ver·ly /ˈōvərlē/ ▶ **adv.** excessively.

o·ver·much /ˈōvərˈməch/ ▶ **adv. & pron.** too much.

o·ver·night ▶ **adv.** /ˌōvərˈnīt/ & **adj.** /ˈōvərˌnīt/ **1** during or for a night. **2** happening suddenly or very quickly.

o·ver·pass /ˈōvərˌpas/ ▶ **n.** a bridge by which a road or railroad line passes over another.

o·ver·play /ˌōvərˈplā/ ▶ **v.** give too much importance to.

o·ver·pow·er /ˌōvərˈpou(-ə)r/ ▶ **v.** (**overpowers**, **overpowering**, **overpowered**) **1** defeat through having greater strength. **2** overwhelm. **3** (**overpowering**) extremely strong.

SYNONYMS **1 overwhelm**, get the better of, overthrow, subdue, suppress, subjugate, repress. **2** (**overpowering**) **overwhelming**, oppressive, unbearable, unendurable, intolerable, shattering.

o·ver·priced /ˌōvərˈprīst/ ▶ **adj.** too expensive.

o·ver·pro·tec·tive /ˌōvərprəˈtektiv/ ▶ **adj.** excessively protective.

o·ver·qual·i·fied /ˌōvərˈkwäləˌfīd/ ▶ **adj.** too highly qualified.

o·ver·rat·ed /ˌōvərˈrātid/ ▶ **adj.** rated more highly than is deserved.

o·ver·reach /ˌōvərˈrēCH/ ▶ **v.** (**overreach yourself**) fail through being too ambitious or trying too hard.

o·ver·re·act /ˌōvər-rēˈakt/ ▶ **v.** react more strongly than is justified. ■ **o·ver·re·ac·tion** **n.**

o·ver·ride ▶ **v.** /ˌōvərˈrīd/ (**overrides**, **overriding**, **overrode** /ˌōvərˈrōd/; past participle **overridden** /ˌōvərˈridn/) **1** use your authority to reject someone else's decision or order. **2** be more important than. **3** interrupt the action of an automatic device. **4** (**overriding**) more important than any other considerations. ▶ **n.** /ˈōvərˌrīd/ a device on a machine for overriding an automatic process.

SYNONYMS ▶ **v. 1 disallow**, overrule, countermand, veto, quash, overturn, overthrow, cancel, reverse, rescind, revoke, repeal. **2 outweigh**, supersede, take precedence over, take priority over, cancel out, outbalance. **3** (**overriding**) **most important**, top, first (and foremost), predominant, principal, primary, paramount, chief, main, major, foremost, central, key.

o·ver·rule /ˌōvərˈro͞ol/ ▶ **v.** (**overrules**, **overruling**, **overruled**) use your authority to reject someone else's decision or order.

SYNONYMS **countermand**, cancel, reverse, rescind, repeal, revoke, disallow, override, veto, quash, overturn, overthrow.

o·ver·run ▶ **v.** /ˌōvərˈrən/ (**overruns**, **overrunning**, **overran** /ˌōvərˈran/; past participle **overrun**) **1** occupy a place in large numbers. **2** use more time or money than expected. ▶ **n.** /ˈōvərˌrən/ an instance of using more time or money than expected.

SYNONYMS **invade**, storm, occupy, swarm into, surge into, inundate, overwhelm.

o·ver·seas /ˈōvərˈsēz/ ▶ **adv. & adj.** in or to a foreign country.

o·ver·see /ˌōvərˈsē/ ▶ **v.** (**oversees**, **overseeing**, **oversaw** /ˌōvərˈsô/; past participle **overseen**) supervise.

SYNONYMS **supervise**, superintend, be in charge/control of, be responsible for, look after, keep an eye on, inspect, administer, organize, manage, direct, preside over.

■ **o·ver·se·er** /ˈōvərˌsi(ə)r, -ˌsēər/ **n.**

o·ver·shad·ow /ˌōvərˈSHadō/ ▶ **v. 1** appear more important or successful than. **2** make something sad or less enjoyable.

SYNONYMS **outshine**, eclipse, surpass, exceed, outclass, outstrip, outdo, upstage; informal be head and shoulders above.

o·ver·shoot /ˌōvərˈSHo͞ot/ ▶ **v.** (**overshoots**, **overshooting**, **overshot**) go past the place you intended to stop at.

o·ver·sight /ˈōvərˌsīt/ ▶ **n.** an unintentional failure to notice or do something.

SYNONYMS **1 mistake**, error, omission, lapse, slip, blunder; informal slip-up, boo-boo, goof. **2** *the omission was due to oversight* **carelessness**, inattention, negligence, forgetfulness.

o·ver·sim·pli·fy /ˌōvərˈsimpləˌfī/ ▶ **v.** (**oversimplifies**, **oversimplifying**, **oversimplified**) simplify something so much that an inaccurate impression of it is given.

o·ver·sized /ˌōvərˈsīzd/ (or **oversize**) ▶ **adj.** bigger than the usual size.

o·ver·sleep /ˌōvərˈslēp/ ▶ **v.** (**oversleeps**, **oversleeping**, **overslept**) sleep later than you intended to.

o·ver·spend /ˌōvərˈspend/ ▶ **v.** (**overspends**, **overspending**, **overspent**) spend too much.

o·ver·state /ˌōvərˈstāt/ ▶ **v.** (**overstates**, **overstating**, **overstated**) state too strongly; exaggerate.

o·ver·state·ment /ˌōvərˈstātmənt/ ▶ **n.** an exaggeration.

o·ver·stay /ˌōvərˈstā/ ▶ **v.** stay longer than is allowed by.

o·ver·step /ˌōvərˈstep/ ▶ **v.** (**oversteps**, **overstepping**, **overstepped**) go beyond a limit.

o·ver·stretch /ˌōvərˈstreCH/ ▶ **v.** make too many demands on a resource.

o·ver·sub·scribed /ˌōvərsəbˈskrībd/ ▶ **adj.** offering too few places to satisfy demand.

o·vert /ōˈvərt, ˈōvərt/ ▶ **adj.** done or shown openly.

SYNONYMS **undisguised**, unconcealed, plain (to see), clear, conspicuous, obvious, noticeable, manifest, patent, open, blatant. ANTONYMS covert.

■ **o·vert·ly** **adv.**

o·ver·take /ˌōvərˈtāk/ ▶ **v.** (**overtakes**, **overtaking**, **overtook** /ˌōvərˈto͝ok/; past participle **overtaken**) **1** pass while traveling in the same direction. **2** suddenly affect.

SYNONYMS **1 pass**, go past, pull ahead of. **2 outstrip**, surpass, overshadow, eclipse, outshine, outclass, exceed, top, cap. **3 befall**, happen to, come upon, hit, strike, overwhelm, overcome.

o·ver·throw ▶ **v.** /ˌōvərˈTHrō/ (**overthrows**, **overthrowing**, **overthrew** /ˌōvərˈTHro͞o/; past participle **overthrown**) remove from power by force. ▶ **n.** /ˈōvərˌTHrō/ a removal from power.

SYNONYMS ▶ **v. oust**, remove, bring down, topple, depose, displace, unseat, defeat, conquer. ▶ **n. removal**, ousting, defeat, fall, collapse, demise.

o·ver·time /ˈōvərˌtīm/ ▶ **n.** time worked in addition to normal working hours.

o·ver·tone /ˈōvərˌtōn/ ▶ **n.** a subtle or secondary quality or implication.

SYNONYMS **connotation**, hidden meaning, implication, association, undercurrent, undertone, echo, vibrations, hint, suggestion, insinuation, intimation, suspicion, feeling, nuance.

o·ver·ture /ˈōvərCHər, -ˌCHŏŏr/ ▶ **n.** **1** an orchestral piece at the beginning of a musical work. **2** an orchestral composition in one movement. **3** (**overtures**) approaches made with the aim of opening negotiations or establishing a relationship.

SYNONYMS **1 preliminary**, prelude, introduction, lead-in, precursor, start, beginning. **2 opening move**, approach, advances, feeler, signal.

o·ver·turn /ˌōvərˈtərn/ ▶ **v.** **1** turn over and come to rest upside down. **2** abolish or reverse a decision, system, etc.

SYNONYMS **1 capsize**, turn turtle, keel over, tip over, topple over, upset, turn over, knock over, upend. **2 cancel**, reverse, rescind, repeal, revoke, countermand, disallow, override, overrule, veto, quash, overthrow.

o·ver·use ▶ **v.** /ˌōvərˈyo͞oz/ (**overuses**, **overusing**, **overused**) use too much. ▶ **n.** /ˈōvərˈyo͞os/ excessive use.

o·ver·view /ˈōvərˌvyo͞o/ ▶ **n.** a general review or summary.

o·ver·ween·ing /ˌōvərˈwēniNG/ ▶ **adj.** showing too much confidence or pride.

o·ver·weight /ˌōvərˈwāt/ ▶ **adj.** heavier or fatter than is usual or desirable.

SYNONYMS **fat**, obese, stout, plump, portly, chubby, potbellied, flabby; informal tubby.

o·ver·whelm /ˌōvərˈ(h)welm/ ▶ **v.** **1** have a strong emotional effect on. **2** overpower. **3** bury or drown beneath a huge mass.

SYNONYMS **1 trounce**, rout, beat hollow, conquer, crush; informal thrash, lick, wipe the floor with. **2 overcome**, move, stir, affect, touch, strike, dumbfound, shake, leave speechless; informal bowl over, knock sideways.

o·ver·whelm·ing /ˌōvərˈ(h)welmiNG/ ▶ **adj.** **1** very great in amount: *he was elected president by an overwhelming majority*. **2** (especially of an emotion) very strong.

SYNONYMS **1 very large**, enormous, immense, inordinate, massive, huge. **2 very strong**, powerful, uncontrollable, irrepressible, irresistible, overpowering, compelling.

■ **o·ver·whelm·ing·ly** **adv.**

o·ver·work /ˌōvərˈwərk/ ▶ **v.** **1** work too hard. **2** use a word or idea too much. ▶ **n.** too much work.

o·ver·write /ˌōvərˈrīt/ ▶ **v.** (**overwrites**, **overwriting**, **overwrote** /ˌōvərˈrōt/; past participle **overwritten** /ˌōvərˈritn/) **1** destroy computer data by entering new data in its place. **2** write too elaborately or ornately.

o·ver·wrought /ˌōvəˈrôt/ ▶ **adj.** **1** in a state of nervous excitement or anxiety. **2** too elaborate or complicated.

SYNONYMS **tense**, agitated, nervous, on edge, edgy, keyed up, worked up, highly strung, neurotic, overexcited, beside yourself, distracted, distraught, frantic, hysterical; informal in a state, in a tizzy, uptight, wound up.
ANTONYMS calm.

o·ver·zeal·ous /ˌōvərˈzeləs/ ▶ **adj.** overly enthusiastic or energetic.

ov·u·late /ˈōvyəˌlāt, ˈäv-/ ▶ **v.** (**ovulates**, **ovulating**, **ovulated**) (of a woman or female animal) release ova (reproductive cells) from the ovary.
■ **ov·u·la·tion** /ˌōvyəˈlāSHən, ˌäv-/ **n.**

o·vum /ˈōvəm/ ▶ **n.** (plural **ova** /ˈōvə/) a female reproductive cell, which can develop into an embryo if fertilized by a male cell.

owe /ō/ ▶ **v.** (**owes**, **owing**, **owed**) **1** be required to give money or goods to someone in return for something received. **2** be obliged to show someone gratitude, respect, etc. **3** (**owe something to**) have something because of.

SYNONYMS **be in debt** (**to**), be indebted (to), be in arrears (to), be under an obligation (to).

ow·ing /ˈō-iNG/ ▶ **adj.** yet to be paid or supplied.

SYNONYMS **unpaid**, to be paid, payable, due, overdue, undischarged, owed, outstanding, in arrears, delinquent.

□ **owing to** because of.

owl /oul/ ▶ **n.** a bird of prey with large eyes, which is active at night.

owl·ish /ˈouliSH/ ▶ **adj.** resembling an owl.

own /ōn/ ▶ **adj. & pron.** belonging to or done by the person specified. ▶ **v.** **1** have something as your property. **2** take or acknowledge responsibility for something: *you can own those feelings and deal with them*. **3** formal admit that something is the case. **4** (**own up**) admit that you have done something wrong or embarrassing.

SYNONYMS ▶ **adj. & pron.** **personal**, individual, particular, private, personalized, unique. ▶ **v.** **possess**, keep, hold, be the owner of, have to/in your name.

□ **come into your own** become fully effective. **hold your own** remain in a strong position.

own·er /ˈōnər/ ▶ **n.** a person who owns something.

SYNONYMS **possessor**, holder, proprietor, homeowner, freeholder, landlord, landlady.

own·er·ship /ˈōnərˌSHip/ ▶ **n.** the act, state, or right of possessing something.

SYNONYMS **possession**, freehold, proprietorship, title.

ox /äks/ ▶ **n.** (plural **oxen**) **1** a cow or bull. **2** a castrated bull.

ox·eye dai·sy /ˈäksˌī/ ▶ **n.** a daisy that has large white flowers with yellow centers.

ox·ford /ˈäksfərd/ ▶ **n.** a type of lace-up shoe with a low heel.

ox·i·da·tion /ˌäksiˈdāSHən/ ▶ **n.** the process of oxidizing, or the result of being oxidized.

ox·ide /ˈäkˌsīd/ ▶ **n.** a compound of oxygen with another substance.

ox·i·dize /ˈäksiˌdīz/ ▶ **v.** (**oxidizes**, **oxidizing**, **oxidized**) cause to combine with oxygen.
■ **ox·i·di·za·tion** /ˌäksidiˈzāSHən/ **n.**

ox·tail /ˈäksˌtāl/ ▶ **n.** the tail of an ox, used in making soup.

ox·y·gen /ˈäksəjən/ ▶ **n.** a colorless, odorless gas that forms about 20 percent of the earth's atmosphere.

ox·y·gen·ate /ˈäksəjəˌnāt/ ▶ **v.** (**oxygenates**, **oxygenating**, **oxygenated**) supply or treat with oxygen.

ox·y·mo·ron /ˌäksēˈmôrˌän/ ▶ **n.** a figure of speech in which apparently contradictory terms appear together (e.g., *bittersweet*).

oys·ter /ˈoistər/ ▶ **n. 1** a shellfish with two hinged shells, some kinds of which are edible. **2** a shade of grayish white.

oz. ▶ **abbr.** ounces.

o·zone /ˈōˌzōn/ ▶ **n. 1** a strong-smelling, poisonous form of oxygen. **2** informal fresh air blowing from the sea. □ **ozone layer** a layer in the stratosphere containing a lot of ozone, which protects the earth from the sun's ultraviolet radiation.

Pp

P (or **p**) ▶ **n.** (plural **Ps** or **P's**) the sixteenth letter of the alphabet. ▶ **abbr.** page.

PA ▶ **abbr. 1** personal assistant. **2** public address.

pa /pä/ ▶ **n.** informal father.

p.a. ▶ **abbr.** per annum (year).

pab·lum /'pabləm/ ▶ **n.** literary bland intellectual matter or entertainment.

pa·ce /pās/ ▶ **n. 1** a single step taken when walking or running. **2** the rate at which something happens or develops. ▶ **v.** (**paces**, **pacing**, **paced**) **1** walk to and fro in a small area. **2** measure a distance by counting the number of steps taken to cover it. **3** (**pace yourself**) do something at a controlled and steady rate.

SYNONYMS ▶ **n. 1** **step**, stride. **2** **gait**, walk, march, tread. **3** **speed**, rate, velocity, tempo. ▶ **v.** **walk**, step, stride, march, pound.

□ **keep pace with** progress at the same speed as. **put someone through their paces** make someone demonstrate their abilities.

pace·mak·er /'pās,mākər/ ▶ **n.** a device for stimulating and regulating the heart muscle.

pach·y·derm /'pakə,dərm/ ▶ **n.** an elephant or other very large mammal with thick skin.

pa·cif·ic /pə'sifik/ ▶ **adj. 1** formal peaceful. **2** (**Pacific**) having to do with the Pacific Ocean. □ **Pacific time** the standard time in a zone including the Pacific coastal region of the US and Canada.

pac·i·fi·er /'pasə,fīər/ ▶ **n. 1** a person or thing that pacifies. **2** a rubber or plastic nipple for a baby to suck on.

pac·i·fism /'pasə,fizəm/ ▶ **n.** the belief that disputes should be settled by peaceful means and that violence should never be used. ■ **pac·i·fist n. & adj.**

pac·i·fy /'pasə,fī/ ▶ **v.** (**pacifies**, **pacifying**, **pacified**) **1** make someone less angry or upset. **2** make a country peaceful, especially by the use or threat of force.

SYNONYMS **placate**, appease, calm (down), conciliate, propitiate, assuage, mollify, soothe. ANTONYMS enrage.

■ **pa·cif·i·ca·tion** /,pasifi'kāshən/ **n.**

pack /pak/ ▶ **n. 1** a cardboard or paper container and the items inside it. **2** a group of animals that live and hunt together. **3** chiefly disapproving a group of similar things or people. **4** (**the pack**) the main group of competitors following the leader in a race. **5** Rugby a team's forwards. **6** an organized group of Cub Scouts or Brownies. **7** a knapsack. **8** a hot or cold pad, often of absorbent material, used for treating an injury. ▶ **v. 1** fill a suitcase or bag with items needed for travel. **2** put something in a container for transport or storage. **3** cram a large number of things into. **4** (**packed**) crowded. **5** cover, surround, or fill.

SYNONYMS ▶ **n. 1** **packet**, container, package, box, carton, parcel. **2** **group**, herd, troop, crowd, mob, band, party, set, gang, rabble, horde, throng, huddle, mass, assembly, gathering, host; informal crew, bunch. ▶ **v. 1** **fill**, load, stow, store, bundle, stuff, cram. **2** **wrap** (**up**), package, parcel, swathe, swaddle, encase, envelop, bundle. **3** **throng**, crowd, fill, cram, jam, squash into, squeeze into. **4** (**packed**) **crowded**, full, filled (to capacity), crammed, jammed, solid, teeming, seething, swarming; informal jam-packed, chock-full, chock-a-block, full to the gunwales, bursting at the seams.

□ **pack ice** a mass of ice floating in the sea. **pack something in** informal give up an activity or job. **pack someone off** informal send someone somewhere without much notice. **send someone packing** informal dismiss someone abruptly.

pack·age /'pakij/ ▶ **n. 1** an object or group of objects wrapped in paper or packed in a box. **2** a paper or cardboard container or parcel. **3** a set of proposals or terms as a whole. ▶ **v.** (**packages**, **packaging**, **packaged**) **1** put into a box or wrapping. **2** present in an attractive way.

SYNONYMS ▶ **n. 1** **parcel**, packet, box, carton. **2** **collection**, bundle, combination, range, complement, raft, platform. ▶ **v.** **wrap**, gift-wrap, pack, box, seal.

pack·ag·ing /'pakijiNG/ ▶ **n.** materials used to wrap or protect goods.

pack·et /'pakit/ ▶ **n.** a package or parcel.

SYNONYMS **pack**, carton, container, case, package.

pack·horse /'pak,hôrs/ ▶ **n.** a horse that is used to carry loads.

pact /pakt/ ▶ **n.** a formal agreement between two or more people, groups, or countries.

SYNONYMS **agreement**, treaty, entente, protocol, deal, settlement, armistice, truce.

pad /pad/ ▶ **n. 1** a thick piece of soft or absorbent material. **2** a number of sheets of blank paper fastened together at one edge. **3** the fleshy underpart of an animal's foot or of a human finger. **4** a protective guard worn by an athlete. **5** a structure or area used for helicopter takeoff and landing or for launching rockets. **6** informal a person's home. ▶ **v.** (**pads**, **padding**, **padded**) **1** fill or cover with padding. **2** (**pad something out**) add unnecessary material to a speech, article, or book to make it longer. **3** walk with quiet, steady steps.

SYNONYMS ▶ **n. 1** **dressing**, pack, wad. **2** **notebook**, notepad, writing pad, scratch pad. ▶ **v. 1** (**padded**) **cushioned**, insulated, lined, quilted, stuffed. **2** **creep**, sneak, steal, tiptoe, pussyfoot.

pad·ding /'padiNG/ ▶ **n.** **1** soft material used to pad or stuff something. **2** unnecessary material added to make a speech, article, or book longer.

SYNONYMS **1 cushioning**, stuffing, packing, filling, lining. **2 verbiage**, wordiness.

pad·dle /'padl/ ▶ **n.** **1** a short pole with a broad end, used to propel a small boat. **2** a paddle-shaped tool for stirring or mixing. **3** a short-handled bat used in table tennis or other games. **4** a paddle-shaped instrument used for corporal punishment. ▶ **v.** (**paddles**, **paddling**, **paddled**) **1** walk with bare feet in shallow water. **2** propel a boat with a paddle or paddles. **3** (of a bird or other animal, or a human imitating this motion) swim with short fast strokes. **4** punish someone with a paddle.

SYNONYMS ▶ **n. oar**, scull. ▶ **v. 1 splash (around/ about)**, dabble, wade. **2 row**, pull, scull.

□ **paddle steamer** a boat powered by steam and propelled by large wheels that move the water as they turn.

pad·dle·boat /'padl,bōt/ ▶ **n.** a small pedal-operated pleasure boat.

pad·dock /'padək/ ▶ **n.** **1** a small field or enclosure for horses. **2** an enclosure where horses or cars are displayed before a race.

pad·dy /'padē/ ▶ **n.** (plural **paddies**) a field where rice is grown.

pad·lock /'pad,läk/ ▶ **n.** a detachable lock that is attached by a hinged hook. ▶ **v.** secure with a padlock.

pae·an /'pēən/ ▶ **n.** formal a song of praise or triumph.

pa·el·la /pä'āyä, pə'elə/ ▶ **n.** a Spanish dish of rice, chicken, seafood, etc.

pa·gan /'pāgən/ ▶ **n.** a person who holds religious beliefs other than those of the main world religions. ▶ **adj.** relating to pagans or their beliefs.

SYNONYMS **heathen**, infidel, non-Christian.

■ **pa·gan·ism** **n.**

page¹ /pāj/ ▶ **n.** **1** one side of a sheet of paper in a book, magazine, etc. **2** both sides of such a sheet of paper considered as a single unit. **3** a section of data displayed on a computer screen. ▶ **v.** (**pages**, **paging**, **paged**) (**page through**) turn the pages of a book, magazine, etc.

SYNONYMS ▶ **n. folio**, sheet, side, leaf.

page² ▶ **n.** **1** a boy or young man employed in a hotel to run errands, open doors, etc. **2** a young boy who attends a bride at a wedding. **3** historical a boy in training for knighthood. ▶ **v.** (**pages**, **paging**, **paged**) summon or call someone over a public address system or with a pager.

SYNONYMS ▶ **n. 1 errand boy/girl**, messenger (boy/girl), bellboy, bellhop, bellman, runner. **2 attendant**, pageboy, train-bearer. ▶ **v. call (for)**, summon, send for.

pag·eant /'pajənt/ ▶ **n.** an entertainment performed by people in elaborate or historical costumes.

SYNONYMS **parade**, procession, cavalcade, tableau, spectacle, extravaganza, show.

pag·eant·ry /'pajəntrē/ ▶ **n.** elaborate display or ceremonial events.

SYNONYMS **spectacle**, display, ceremony, magnificence, pomp, splendor, grandeur, show; informal razzle-dazzle, razzmatazz.

page·boy /'pāj,boi/ ▶ **n.** **1** a woman's hairstyle consisting of a shoulder-length bob with the ends rolled under. **2** a page in a hotel or attending a bride at a wedding.

pag·er /'pājər/ ▶ **n.** a small device that beeps or vibrates to inform you that it has received a message; a beeper.

pag·i·nate /'pajə,nāt/ ▶ **v.** (**paginates**, **paginating**, **paginated**) give numbers to the pages of a book, magazine, etc. ■ **pag·i·na·tion** /,pajə'nāSHən/ **n.**

pa·go·da /pə'gōdə/ ▶ **n.** a Hindu or Buddhist temple or other sacred building.

paid /pād/ past and past participle of **PAY**.

pail /pāl/ ▶ **n.** a bucket.

pain /pān/ ▶ **n.** **1** a strongly unpleasant physical sensation caused by illness or injury. **2** mental suffering. **3** (**pains**) great care or trouble. **4** informal an annoying or boring person or thing. ▶ **v.** **1** cause pain to. **2** (**pained**) showing that you are annoyed or upset.

SYNONYMS ▶ **n. 1 suffering**, agony, torture, torment. **2 ache**, aching, soreness, throbbing, sting, twinge, stab, pang, discomfort, irritation. **3 sorrow**, grief, heartache, heartbreak, sadness, unhappiness, distress, misery, despair, agony, torment, torture. **4** (**pains**) *he took pains to hide his feelings* **care**, effort, bother, trouble. ▶ **v. sadden**, grieve, distress, trouble, perturb, cause anguish to.

□ **on** (or **under**) **pain of** with the threat of being punished by.

pain·ful /'pānfəl/ ▶ **adj.** suffering or causing pain.

SYNONYMS **1 sore**, hurting, tender, aching, throbbing. **2 disagreeable**, unpleasant, nasty, distressing, upsetting, sad, traumatic, miserable, heartbreaking, agonizing.

pain·ful·ly /'pānfəlē/ ▶ **adv.** in a painful way.

SYNONYMS **distressingly**, disturbingly, uncomfortably, unpleasantly, dreadfully.

pain·kil·ler /'pān,kilər/ ▶ **n.** a medicine for relieving pain.

pain·less /'pānləs/ ▶ **adj.** **1** not causing pain. **2** involving little effort or stress.

SYNONYMS **1 pain-free**, without pain. **2 easy**, trouble-free, straightforward, simple, uncomplicated; informal child's play. ANTONYMS painful, difficult.

■ **pain·less·ly** **adv.**

pains·tak·ing /'pānz,tākiNG, 'pān,stākiNG/ ▶ **adj.** very careful and thorough.

SYNONYMS **careful**, meticulous, thorough, assiduous, attentive, conscientious, punctilious, scrupulous, rigorous. ANTONYMS slapdash.

■ **pains·tak·ing·ly** **adv.**

paint /pānt/ ▶ **n.** a colored substance that is spread over a surface to give a thin decorative or protective coating. ▶ **v.** **1** put paint on something. **2** produce a picture with paint. **3** describe.

SYNONYMS ▶ **n. coloring**, color, tint, dye, stain, pigment, emulsion, gloss. ▶ **v. 1 color**, decorate, whitewash, airbrush, daub, smear. **2 portray**, picture, paint a picture/portrait of, depict, represent.

paint·ball /ˈpāntˌbôl/ ▶ n. a combat game in which participants shoot capsules of paint at each other with air guns.

paint·brush /ˈpāntˌbrəsʜ/ ▶ n. a brush for applying paint.

paint·er¹ /ˈpāntər/ ▶ n. **1** an artist who paints pictures. **2** a person who paints buildings.

paint·er² ▶ n. a rope attached to the bow of a boat for tying it to a dock, quay, etc.

paint·ing /ˈpāntiɴɢ/ ▶ n. **1** the action of painting. **2** a painted picture.

> SYNONYMS **picture**, illustration, portrayal, depiction, representation, image, portrait, landscape, artwork, canvas, oil, watercolor.

paint·work /ˈpāntˌwərk/ ▶ n. painted surfaces in a building or on a vehicle.

pair /pe(ə)r/ ▶ n. **1** a set of two things used together or seen as a unit. **2** an article consisting of two joined or corresponding parts. **3** two people or animals related in some way or considered together. ▶ v. **1** join or connect to form a pair. **2** (**pair off** or **up**) form a couple.

> SYNONYMS ▶ n. **set**, brace, couple, duo, two, twosome, team, yoke. ▶ v. **match**, put together, couple, combine, yoke.

pais·ley /ˈpāzlē/ ▶ n. an intricate pattern of curved feather-shaped figures.

pa·ja·mas /pəˈjäməz, -jaməz/ ▶ pl.n. a loose top and pants for sleeping in.

Pak·i·sta·ni /ˌpakəˈstanē, ˌpäkiˈstänē/ ▶ n. a person from Pakistan. ▶ adj. relating to Pakistan.

pal /pal/ informal ▶ n. a friend. ▶ v. (**pals**, **palling**, **palled**) (**pal up**) form a friendship.

pal·ace /ˈpalis/ ▶ n. a large building where a king, queen, president, etc. lives.

> SYNONYMS **castle**, château, mansion, stately home, royal estate.

pal·at·a·ble /ˈpalətəbəl/ ▶ adj. **1** pleasant to taste. **2** acceptable.

> SYNONYMS **1 edible**, tasty, appetizing, delicious, mouthwatering, toothsome, succulent; informal scrumptious, yummy. **2 pleasant**, acceptable, agreeable, to your liking. ANTONYMS disagreeable.

pal·ate /ˈpalit/ ▶ n. **1** the roof of the mouth. **2** a person's ability to distinguish between different flavors.

pa·la·tial /pəˈlāsʜəl/ ▶ adj. large and impressive, like a palace.

> SYNONYMS **luxurious**, magnificent, sumptuous, splendid, grand, opulent, lavish, stately, fancy, upscale, upmarket; informal plush, swanky, posh, ritzy, swish. ANTONYMS modest.

pa·lav·er /pəˈlavər, -ˈläv-/ ▶ n. informal a lot of fuss about something.

pale¹ /pāl/ ▶ adj. **1** of a light shade or color. **2** (of a person's face) having little color, especially as a result of illness or shock. ▶ v. (**pales**, **paling**, **paled**) **1** become pale in your face. **2** seem or become less important.

> SYNONYMS ▶ adj. **1 white**, pallid, pasty, wan, colorless, anemic, washed out, peaked, ashen, sickly; informal like death warmed over. **2 light**, pastel, muted, subtle, soft, faded, bleached, washed out. **3 dim**, faint, weak, feeble. ANTONYMS ruddy, dark. ▶ v. **turn white**, turn pale, blanch, lose color.

pale² ▶ n. **1** a wooden stake used with others to form a fence. **2** a boundary. ◻ **beyond the pale** (of behavior) considered by most people to be unacceptable.

pa·le·on·tol·o·gy /ˌpālēˌänˈtäləjē/ ▶ n. the study of fossil animals and plants. ■ **pa·le·on·tol·o·gist** n.

Pal·es·tin·i·an /ˌpaləˈstinēən/ ▶ adj. relating to Palestine. ▶ n. a member of the native Arab population of Palestine.

pal·ette /ˈpalit/ ▶ n. **1** a thin board on which an artist lays and mixes paints. **2** the range of colors used by an artist. ◻ **palette knife** a blunt knife with a flexible blade, for applying or removing paint.

pal·imp·sest /ˈpalimpˌsest/ ▶ n. an ancient sheet of parchment from which the original writing has been removed to make room for new writing.

pal·in·drome /ˈpalinˌdrōm/ ▶ n. a word or phrase that reads the same backward as forward, e.g., *madam*.

pal·ing /ˈpāliɴɢ/ ▶ n. **1** a fence made from stakes. **2** a stake used in such a fence.

pal·i·sade /ˌpaləˈsād/ ▶ n. **1** a fence of stakes or iron railings. **2** (**palisades**) a line of high cliffs.

pall¹ /pôl/ ▶ n. **1** a cloth spread over a coffin, hearse, or tomb. **2** a dark cloud of smoke or dust. **3** a general atmosphere of gloom or fear.

> SYNONYMS **cloud**, covering, cloak, shroud, layer, blanket.

pall² ▶ v. become less appealing through being too familiar.

pal·la·di·um /pəˈlādēəm/ ▶ n. a rare silvery-white metallic element.

pall·bear·er /ˈpôlˌbe(ə)rər/ ▶ n. a person helping to carry a coffin at a funeral.

pal·let /ˈpalit/ ▶ n. **1** a portable platform on which goods can be moved, stacked, and stored. **2** a straw mattress.

pal·li·ate /ˈpalēˌāt/ ▶ v. (**palliates**, **palliating**, **palliated**) **1** reduce the pain or bad effects of a disease, though not curing it. **2** make something bad easier to cope with. ■ **pal·li·a·tive** /ˈpalēˌātiv, ˈpalēətiv/ adj.

pal·lid /ˈpalid/ ▶ adj. **1** pale, especially because of bad health. **2** (of colors or light) not strong or bright.

> SYNONYMS **1 pale**, white, pasty, wan, colorless, anemic, washed out, peaked, ashen, gray, drained, sickly, sallow; informal like death warmed over. **2 insipid**, uninspired, colorless, uninteresting, unexciting, unimaginative, lifeless, sterile, bland.

pal·lor /ˈpalər/ ▶ n. an unhealthy pale appearance.

pal·ly /ˈpalē/ ▶ adj. informal having a close, friendly relationship.

palm¹ /pä(l)m/ ▶ n. an evergreen tree of warm regions, with a crown of large feathered or fan-shaped leaves.

palm² ▶ n. the inner surface of the hand between the wrist and fingers. ▶ v. informal **1** (**palm something off**) sell or dispose of something in a way that is dishonest or unfair. **2** (**palm someone off with**) persuade someone to accept something that is unwanted or has no value.

pal·met·to /pä(l)'metō, pal-/ ▶ **n.** (plural **palmettos**) an American palm with large fan-shaped leaves.

palm·is·try /'pä(l)məstrē/ ▶ **n.** the activity of interpreting a person's character or predicting their future by examining the palm of their hand. ■ **palm·ist** **n.**

palm·top /'pä(l)m,täp/ ▶ **n.** a computer small and light enough to be held in one hand.

palm·y /'pä(l)mē/ ▶ **adj.** (especially of a previous period of time) comfortable and prosperous.

pal·o·mi·no /,palə'mēnō/ ▶ **n.** (plural **palominos**) a tan-colored horse with a white mane and tail.

pal·pa·ble /'palpəbəl/ ▶ **adj.** **1** able to be touched or felt. **2** (of a feeling or quality) very strong or obvious.

> SYNONYMS **1 tangible**, touchable. **2 perceptible**, visible, noticeable, discernible, detectable, observable, unmistakable, transparent, obvious, clear, plain (to see), evident, apparent, manifest, staring you in the face, written all over someone. ANTONYMS imperceptible.

■ **pal·pa·bly** **adv.**

pal·pate /'pal,pāt/ ▶ **v.** (**palpates**, **palpating**, **palpated**) (of a doctor or nurse) examine a part of the body by touching it.

pal·pi·tate /'palpi,tāt/ ▶ **v.** (**palpitates**, **palpitating**, **palpitated**) **1** (of the heart) beat fast or irregularly. **2** shake; tremble.

pal·pi·ta·tions /,palpi'tāsʜənz/ ▶ **pl.n.** a noticeably fast, strong, or irregular heartbeat.

pal·sy /'pôlzē/ ▶ **n.** (plural **palsies**) dated paralysis. ■ **palsied** **adj.**

pal·try /'pôltrē/ ▶ **adj.** (**paltrier**, **paltriest**) (of an amount) very small.

> SYNONYMS **small**, meager, trifling, insignificant, negligible, inadequate, insufficient, derisory, pitiful, pathetic, miserable, niggardly, beggarly; informal measly, piddling. ANTONYMS considerable.

pam·pas /'pampəz, 'päm-, -pəs/ ▶ **n.** large treeless plains in South America.

pam·per /'pampər/ ▶ **v.** (**pampers**, **pampering**, **pampered**) give someone a great deal of care and attention.

> SYNONYMS **spoil**, indulge, overindulge, cosset, mollycoddle, coddle, baby, wait on someone hand and foot.

pam·phlet /'pamflit/ ▶ **n.** a small booklet or leaflet.

> SYNONYMS **brochure**, leaflet, booklet, circular, mailer, folder.

pan[1] /pan/ ▶ **n.** **1** a metal container for cooking food in. **2** a bowl fitted at either end of a pair of scales. **3** a hollow in the ground in which water collects. ▶ **v.** (**pans**, **panning**, **panned**) **1** informal criticize harshly. **2** (**pan out**) informal end up or conclude. **3** (**pan out**) informal turn out well. **4** wash gravel in a pan to separate out gold.

> SYNONYMS ▶ **n. saucepan**, pot, frying pan, skillet, roasting pan, roaster, baking sheet.

pan[2] ▶ **v.** (**pans**, **panning**, **panned**) swing a video or movie camera to give a wide view or follow a subject.

> SYNONYMS **swing (around)**, sweep, move, turn.

pan·a·ce·a /,panə'sēə/ ▶ **n.** something that will cure all diseases or solve all difficulties.

pa·nache /pə'nasʜ, -'näsʜ/ ▶ **n.** impressive skill and confidence.

> SYNONYMS **flamboyance**, confidence, self-assurance, style, flair, elan, dash, verve, zest, spirit, brio, vivacity, gusto, liveliness, vitality, energy; informal pizzazz, oomph, zip, zing.

pan·a·ma /'panə,mä, -,mô/ ▶ **n.** a man's wide-brimmed hat made of strawlike material.

pan·cake /'pan,kāk/ ▶ **n.** a thin, flat cake of batter, cooked in a skillet or on a griddle.

pan·cre·as /'paɴɢkrēəs, 'pankrēəs/ ▶ **n.** (plural **pancreases**) a large gland behind the stomach that produces insulin and a liquid used in digestion. ■ **pan·cre·at·ic** /-krē'atik/ **adj.**

pan·da /'pandə/ ▶ **n.** **1** (also **giant panda**) a large black and white bearlike animal native to bamboo forests in China. **2** (also **red panda**) a Himalayan animal like a raccoon, with thick reddish-brown fur and a bushy tail.

pan·dem·ic /pan'demik/ ▶ **adj.** (of a disease) widespread over a whole country or large part of the world. ▶ **n.** an outbreak of such a disease.

pan·de·mo·ni·um /,pandə'mōnēəm/ ▶ **n.** a state of uproar and confusion.

pan·der /'pandər/ ▶ **v.** (**panders**, **pandering**, **pandered**) (**pander to**) indulge someone in an unreasonable desire or bad habit.

pane /pān/ ▶ **n.** a single sheet of glass in a window or door.

pan·e·gyr·ic /,panə'jirik/ ▶ **n.** a speech or piece of writing praising someone or something.

pan·el /'panl/ ▶ **n.** **1** a section in a door, vehicle, garment, etc. **2** a flat board on which instruments or controls are fixed. **3** a small group of people brought together to investigate a matter, or to take part in a broadcast quiz or game.

> SYNONYMS **1 console**, dashboard, instruments, controls, dials. **2 group**, team, body, committee, board.

□ **panel truck** a small, enclosed delivery truck. ■ **pan·eled** **adj.** **pan·el·ist** **n.**

pan·el·ing /'panəliɴɢ/ ▶ **n.** wooden panels used as a decorative covering for a wall.

pang /paɴɢ/ ▶ **n.** a sudden sharp pain or painful emotion.

pan·han·dle /'pan,handl/ ▶ **n.** a narrow strip of territory projecting from the main territory of one state into another. ▶ **v.** informal beg in the street. ■ **pan·han·dler** **n.**

pan·ic /'panik/ ▶ **n.** **1** sudden uncontrollable fear or anxiety. **2** frenzied hurry to do something. ▶ **v.** (**panics**, **panicking**, **panicked**) feel sudden uncontrollable fear or anxiety.

> SYNONYMS ▶ **n. alarm**, anxiety, fear, fright, trepidation, dread, terror, hysteria, apprehension; informal flap, fluster, cold sweat. ANTONYMS calm. ▶ **v. 1 be alarmed**, be scared, be afraid, be hysterical, lose your nerve, get worked up; informal run around like a chicken with its head cut off. **2 frighten**, alarm, scare, unnerve.

■ **pan·ick·y** **adj.**

pan·nier /'panyər, 'panēər/ ▶ **n.** each of a pair of bags, boxes, or baskets fitted on either side of a bicycle or motorcycle, or carried by a horse or donkey.

pan·o·ply /ˈpanəplē/ ▶ **n.** a large and impressive collection or number of things.

pan·o·ram·a /ˌpanəˈramə, -ˈrämə/ ▶ **n. 1** a broad view of a surrounding region. **2** a complete survey of a subject or sequence of events.

SYNONYMS **view**, vista, prospect, scenery, landscape, seascape, cityscape, skyline.

pan·o·ram·ic /ˌpanəˈramik/ ▶ **adj.** with an unbroken view.

SYNONYMS **sweeping**, wide, extensive, scenic, commanding.

pan·pipes /ˈpanˌpīps/ ▶ **pl.n.** a musical instrument made from a row of short pipes fixed together.

pan·sy /ˈpanzē/ ▶ **n.** a garden plant with brightly colored flowers.

pant /pant/ ▶ **v.** breathe with short, quick breaths. ▶ **n.** a short, quick breath.

SYNONYMS ▶ **v. breathe heavily**, breathe hard, huff and puff, gasp, heave, wheeze.

pan·ta·loons /ˌpantəˈlo͞onz/ ▶ **pl.n. 1** women's baggy trousers gathered at the ankles. **2** (in the past) men's close-fitting trousers fastened below the calf or at the foot.

pan·the·ism /ˈpanᴛʜēˌizəm/ ▶ **n.** the belief that God is all around us and is present in all things. ■ **pan·the·ist n. pan·the·is·tic** /ˌpanᴛʜēˈistik/ **adj.**

pan·the·on /ˈpanᴛʜēˌän, -ᴛʜēən/ ▶ **n. 1** all the gods of a people or religion. **2** an ancient temple dedicated to all the gods. **3** a group of particularly famous or important people.

pan·ther /ˈpanᴛʜər/ ▶ **n. 1** a black leopard. **2** ⇨ **COUGAR.**

pant·ies /ˈpantēz/ ▶ **pl.n.** legless underpants worn by women and girls.

pan·tile /ˈpanˌtīl/ ▶ **n.** a curved roof tile, fitted to overlap its neighbor.

pan·to·mime /ˈpantəˌmīm/ ▶ **n.** the use of gestures and facial expressions to convey meaning without speech, especially in drama and dance. ▶ **v.** convey meaning without speech using only gestures.

pan·try /ˈpantrē/ ▶ **n.** (plural **pantries**) a small room or cupboard for storing food.

pants /pants/ ▶ **pl.n.** an outer garment that covers the body from the waist down and has a separate part for each leg.

SYNONYMS **trousers**, slacks, jeans, khakis, leggings, shorts, clamdiggers; informal cords.

pant·suit /ˈpantˌso͞ot/ ▶ **n.** a pair of pants and a matching jacket worn by women.

pant·y·hose /ˈpantēˌhōz/ ▶ **pl.n.** women's thin nylon tights.

pap /pap/ ▶ **n. 1** bland soft or semiliquid food suitable for babies or invalids. **2** trivial books, television programs, etc.

pa·pa /ˈpäpə/ ▶ **n.** your father.

pa·pa·cy /ˈpāpəsē/ ▶ **n.** (plural **papacies**) the position or role of the pope.

pa·pal /ˈpāpəl/ ▶ **adj.** relating to the pope or the papacy.

pa·pa·raz·zo /ˌpäpəˈrätsō/ ▶ **n.** (plural **paparazzi** /-tsē/) a photographer who follows celebrities to get photographs of them.

pa·pa·ya /pəˈpīə/ ▶ **n.** a tropical fruit like a long melon, with orange flesh and small black seeds.

pa·per /ˈpāpər/ ▶ **n. 1** material manufactured in thin sheets from the pulp of wood, used for writing or printing on or as wrapping material. **2** (**papers**) sheets of paper covered with writing or printing. **3** a newspaper. **4** a government report or policy document. **5** an essay or thesis, especially one read at a conference or published in a journal. ▶ **v.** (**papers**, **papering**, **papered**) **1** cover a wall with wallpaper. **2** (**paper something over**) conceal or disguise an awkward problem instead of resolving it.

SYNONYMS ▶ **n. 1 newspaper**, journal, gazette, periodical, tabloid, broadsheet, daily, weekly; informal rag. **2 essay**, article, monograph, theme, thesis, work, dissertation, treatise, study, report, analysis. **3 document**, certificate, letter, file, deed, record, archive; (**papers**) paperwork, documentation. **4** (**papers**) **identification**, identity card, ID, credentials.

□ **on paper 1** in writing. **2** in theory rather than in reality. **paper clip** a piece of bent wire or plastic used for holding sheets of paper together. **paper tiger** a person or thing that appears threatening but is actually weak. ■ **pa·per·y adj.**

pa·per·back /ˈpāpərˌbak/ ▶ **n.** a book bound in stiff paper or thin cardboard.

pa·per·weight /ˈpāpərˌwāt/ ▶ **n.** a small, heavy object for keeping loose papers in place.

pa·per·work /ˈpāpərˌwərk/ ▶ **n.** routine work involving written documents.

pa·pier mâ·ché /ˌpāpər məˈsʜā, päˈp(y)ā/ ▶ **n.** a mixture of paper and glue that becomes hard when dry.

pa·pist /ˈpāpist/ ▶ **n.** disapproving a Roman Catholic.

pap·pa·dam /ˈpäpäˌdəm/ ▶ **n.** (in Indian cooking) a thin circular piece of bread fried until crisp.

pap·ri·ka /pəˈprēkə, pa-/ ▶ **n.** a powdered spice made from sweet red peppers.

Pap smear /pap/ (also **Pap test**) ▶ **n.** a test to detect signs of cervical cancer.

pa·py·rus /pəˈpīrəs/ ▶ **n.** (plural **papyri** /-ˈpīrī/ or **papyruses**) a material made in ancient Egypt from the stem of a water plant, used for writing or painting on.

par /pär/ ▶ **n.** Golf the number of strokes a first-class player normally requires for a particular hole or course. □ **above** (or **below** or **under**) **par** above (or below) the usual or expected level or amount. **on a par with** equal to.

par·a·ble /ˈparəbəl/ ▶ **n.** a simple story that teaches a moral or spiritual lesson.

SYNONYMS **allegory**, moral tale, fable.

pa·rab·o·la /pəˈrabələ/ ▶ **n.** (plural **parabolas** or **parabolae** /-lē/) a curve of the kind formed by the intersection of a cone with a plane parallel to its side. ■ **par·a·bol·ic** /ˌparəˈbälik/ **adj.**

par·a·chute /ˈparəˌsʜo͞ot/ ▶ **n.** a cloth canopy that allows a person or heavy object attached to it to descend slowly when dropped from a high position. ▶ **v.** (**parachutes**, **parachuting**, **parachuted**) drop by parachute. ■ **par·a·chut·ist n.**

pa·rade /pəˈrād/ ▶ **n. 1** a public procession. **2** a formal occasion when soldiers march or stand in line in order to be inspected or for display. **3** a series or succession. ▶ **v.** (**parades**, **parading**, **paraded**) **1** walk, march, or display in a parade. **2** display something publicly in order to impress people or attract attention.

SYNONYMS ▶ **n. 1 procession**, march, cavalcade, motorcade, spectacle, display, pageant, review, tattoo. **2 promenade**, walkway, esplanade, boardwalk, mall. ▶ v. **1 march**, process, file, troop. **2 strut**, swagger, stride, sashay. **3 display**, exhibit, make a show of, flaunt, show (off), demonstrate.

par·a·digm /ˈparəˌdīm/ ▶ n. a typical example, pattern, or model of something. ▪ **par·a·dig·mat·ic** /ˌparədigˈmatik/ adj.

par·a·dise /ˈparəˌdīs/ ▶ n. **1** (in some religions) heaven. **2** the Garden of Eden. **3** an ideal place or state.

SYNONYMS **1 heaven**, the promised land, the Elysian Fields. **2 Utopia**, Shangri-La, Eden, idyll. **3 bliss**, heaven (on earth), ecstasy, delight, joy, happiness. ANTONYMS hell.

par·a·dox /ˈparəˌdäks/ ▶ n. **1** a statement that sounds absurd or seems to contradict itself, but is in fact true. **2** a person or thing that combines two contradictory features or qualities.

SYNONYMS **contradiction**, self-contradiction, inconsistency, incongruity, conflict, enigma, puzzle, conundrum.

▪ **par·a·dox·i·cal** /ˌparəˈdäksikəl/ adj. **par·a·dox·i·cal·ly** adv.

par·af·fin /ˈparəfin/ ▶ n. a waxy substance obtained from petroleum, used for sealing and waterproofing and in candles.

par·a·glid·ing /ˈparəˌglīdiNG/ ▶ n. a sport in which a person glides through the air attached to a wide parachute after jumping from a high place.

par·a·gon /ˈparəˌgän, -gən/ ▶ n. a model of excellence or of a particular quality.

par·a·graph /ˈparəˌgraf/ ▶ n. a distinct section of a piece of writing, beginning on a new line.

SYNONYMS **section**, division, part, portion, segment, passage, clause.

Par·a·guay·an /ˌparəˈgwīən, -ˈgwā-/ ▶ n. a person from Paraguay. ▶ adj. relating to Paraguay.

par·a·keet /ˈparəˌkēt/ ▶ n. a small parrot with green feathers and a long tail.

par·a·le·gal /ˌparəˈlēgəl/ ▶ n. a person trained in some legal matters but not fully qualified as a lawyer.

par·al·lax /ˈparəˌlaks/ ▶ n. the apparent difference in the position of an object when viewed from different positions.

par·al·lel /ˈparəˌlel, -ˌləl/ ▶ adj. **1** (of lines or surfaces) side by side and having the same distance continuously between them. **2** happening or existing at the same time or in a similar way; corresponding. ▶ n. **1** a person or thing that is similar to or can be compared to another. **2** a similarity or comparison. **3** each of the imaginary parallel circles of latitude on the earth's surface. ▶ v. (**parallels**, **paralleling**, **paralleled**) correspond to or happen at the same time as.

SYNONYMS ▶ adj. **1 aligned**, side by side, equidistant. **2 similar**, analogous, comparable, corresponding, like, equivalent, matching. ANTONYMS divergent, different. ▶ n. **1 counterpart**, analog, equivalent, match, twin, duplicate, mirror. **2 similarity**, likeness, resemblance, analogy, correspondence, comparison, equivalence, symmetry. ANTONYMS divergence, difference.

SPELLING
Double **l** in the middle: parallel.

par·al·lel·o·gram /ˌparəˈleləˌgram/ ▶ n. a figure with four straight sides and opposite sides parallel.

pa·ral·y·sis /pəˈraləsis/ ▶ n. (plural **paralyses**) **1** the loss of the ability to move part of the body. **2** inability to do things or function normally.

SYNONYMS **1 immobility**, powerlessness, incapacity; Medicine paraplegia, quadriplegia. **2 shutdown**, immobilization, stoppage, gridlock, standstill, blockage.

par·a·lyt·ic /ˌparəˈlitik/ ▶ adj. relating to paralysis.

par·a·lyze /ˈparəˌlīz/ ▶ v. (**paralyzes**, **paralyzing**, **paralyzed**) **1** make someone unable to move a part of their body. **2** prevent something from functioning normally.

SYNONYMS **1 disable**, cripple, immobilize, incapacitate; (**paralyzed**) Medicine paraplegic, quadriplegic. **2 bring to a standstill**, immobilize, bring to a halt, freeze, cripple, disable.

par·a·med·ic /ˌparəˈmedik/ ▶ n. a person who is trained to do medical work, especially emergency first aid, but is not a fully qualified doctor.

pa·ram·e·ter /pəˈramitər/ ▶ n. a thing that decides or limits the way in which something can be done.

SYNONYMS **framework**, variable, limit, boundary, limitation, restriction, criterion, guideline.

par·a·mil·i·tar·y /ˌparəˈmiliˌterē/ ▶ adj. organized on similar lines as a military force. ▶ n. (plural **paramilitaries**) a member of a paramilitary organization.

par·a·mount /ˈparəˌmount/ ▶ adj. **1** more important than anything else. **2** having the highest position or the greatest power.

SYNONYMS **most important**, supreme, chief, overriding, predominant, foremost, prime, primary, principal, main, key, central; informal number-one.

par·a·mour /ˈparəˌmo͝or/ ▶ n. old use a person's lover.

par·a·noi·a /ˌparəˈnoiə/ ▶ n. a mental condition in which someone wrongly believes that other people want to harm them, or that they are very important.

par·a·noid /ˈparəˌnoid/ ▶ adj. **1** wrongly believing that other people want to harm you. **2** having to do with paranoia.

SYNONYMS **suspicious**, mistrustful, anxious, fearful, insecure, obsessive.

par·a·nor·mal /ˌparəˈnôrməl/ ▶ adj. beyond the scope of scientific knowledge.

par·a·pet /ˈparəpit/ ▶ n. a low wall along the edge of a roof, bridge, or balcony.

par·a·pher·na·lia /ˌparəfə(r)ˈnālyə/ ▶ n. the objects needed for a particular activity.

SYNONYMS **equipment**, stuff, things, apparatus, kit, implements, tools, utensils, material(s), appliances, accoutrements, appurtenances, odds and ends, bits and pieces; informal gear.

par·a·phrase /ˈparəˌfrāz/ ▶ v. (**paraphrases**, **paraphrasing**, **paraphrased**) express the meaning of something using different words. ▶ n. a rewording of something written or spoken.

SYNONYMS ▶ v. **reword**, rephrase, express differently, rewrite, gloss.

par·a·ple·gi·a /ˌparəˈplēj(ē)ə/ ▶ **n.** paralysis of the legs and lower body. ■ **par·a·ple·gic adj. & n.**

par·a·quat /ˈparəˌkwät/ ▶ **n.** a powerful weedkiller.

par·a·site /ˈparəˌsīt/ ▶ **n. 1** an animal or plant that lives on or inside another, and gets its food from it. **2** a person who relies on or benefits from someone else but gives nothing in return.

SYNONYMS **hanger-on**, leech, passenger; informal freeloader, sponger, scrounger, mooch.

■ **par·a·sit·ic** /ˌparəˈsitik/ **adj. par·a·sit·ism** /ˈparəsiˌtizəm, -ˌsī-/ **n.**

par·a·sol /ˈparəˌsôl, -ˌsäl/ ▶ **n.** a light umbrella used to give shade from the sun.

par·a·troops /ˈparəˌtro͞ops/ ▶ **pl.n.** troops trained to be dropped by parachute from aircraft. ■ **par·a·troop·er n.**

par·boil /ˈpärˌboil/ ▶ **v.** boil something until it is partly cooked.

par·cel /ˈpärsəl/ ▶ **n.** an object or collection of objects wrapped in paper in order to be carried or sent by mail. ▶ **v.** (**parcels, parceling, parceled**) **1** (**parcel something up**) make something into a parcel. **2** (**parcel something out**) divide something between several people.

SYNONYMS ▶ **n. package**, packet, pack, bundle, box, case, bale. ▶ **v. pack (up)**, package, wrap (up), gift-wrap, tie up, bundle up.

parch /pärch/ ▶ **v. 1** make something dry through strong heat. **2** (**parched**) informal very thirsty.

SYNONYMS **1** (**parched**) (**bone**) **dry**, dried up/out, arid, desiccated, dehydrated, baked, burned, scorched, withered, shriveled. **2** (**parched**) **dehydrated**, dry; informal gasping.

parch·ment /ˈpärchmənt/ ▶ **n. 1** (in the past) a stiff material made from the skin of a sheep or goat and used for writing on. **2** thick paper resembling parchment.

par·don /ˈpärdn/ ▶ **n. 1** forgiveness for a mistake, sin, or crime. **2** a cancelation of the punishment for a crime. ▶ **v. 1** forgive or excuse a person, mistake, sin, or crime. **2** give an offender a pardon. ▶ **exclam.** used to ask a speaker to repeat something because you did not hear or understand it.

SYNONYMS ▶ **n. 1 forgiveness**, absolution. **2 reprieve**, amnesty, exoneration, release, acquittal, discharge. ▶ **v. 1 forgive**, absolve. **2 exonerate**, acquit, reprieve; informal let off. ANTONYMS blame, punish.

■ **par·don·a·ble adj.**

pare /pe(ə)r/ ▶ **v.** (**pares, paring, pared**) **1** trim something by cutting away the outer edges. **2** (**pare something away** or **down**) gradually reduce the amount of something.

par·ent /ˈpe(ə)rənt, ˈpar-/ ▶ **n. 1** a father or mother. **2** an animal or plant from which young or new ones are produced. **3** an organization or company that owns or controls a number of smaller organizations or companies. ▶ **v.** be or act as a parent to. ■ **pa·ren·tal** /pəˈrentl/ **adj. par·ent·hood n.**

par·ent·age /ˈpe(ə)rəntij, ˈpar-/ ▶ **n.** the identity and origins of your parents.

SYNONYMS **origins**, extraction, birth, family, ancestry, lineage, heritage, pedigree, descent, blood, stock, roots.

pa·ren·the·sis /pəˈrenthəsis/ ▶ **n.** (plural **parentheses**) **1** a word or phrase added as an explanation or afterthought, indicated in writing by brackets, dashes, or commas. **2** (**parentheses**) a pair of rounded brackets () surrounding a word or phrase. ■ **par·en·thet·ic·al** /ˌparənˈthetikəl/ **adj.**

par ex·cel·lence /ˌpär ˌeksəˈläns/ ▶ **adj.** better or more than all others of the same kind: *a designer par excellence.*

pa·ri·ah /pəˈrīə/ ▶ **n.** a person who is rejected by other people; an outcast.

par·ings /ˈpe(ə)ringz/ ▶ **pl.n.** thin strips pared off from something.

par·ish /ˈparish/ ▶ **n. 1** (in the Christian church) a district with its own church and church ministers. **2** (in Louisiana) a territorial division corresponding to a county in other states.

SYNONYMS **1 district**, community. **2 parishioners**, churchgoers, congregation, fold, flock, community.

par·ish·ion·er /pəˈrishənər/ ▶ **n.** a person who lives in a particular church parish.

Pa·ri·sian /pəˈrizhən, -ˈrē-, -ˈrizē-/ ▶ **n.** a person from Paris. ▶ **adj.** relating to Paris.

par·i·ty /ˈparitē/ ▶ **n.** the quality of being equal with or equivalent to something.

park /pärk/ ▶ **n. 1** a large public garden in a town. **2** a stadium or enclosed area used for sports. **3** a large area of land attached to a country house. **4** an area used for a particular purpose: *a wildlife park.* ▶ **v.** leave a vehicle somewhere for a time.

SYNONYMS ▶ **n. 1** public garden, recreation ground, playground. **2 parkland**, wilderness area, protected area, nature preserve/reserve, game preserve/reserve. ▶ **v. 1 leave**, position, stop, pull up, pull over. **2 put (down)**, place, deposit, leave, stick, dump; informal plonk.

□ **parking garage** a multilevel building in which vehicles are parked. **parking lot** an area where vehicles are parked.

par·ka /ˈpärkə/ ▶ **n.** a hooded winter jacket.

Par·kin·son's dis·ease /ˈpärkinsənz/ ▶ **n.** a disease of the brain and nervous system marked by trembling, stiffness in the muscles, and slowness of movement.

park·way /ˈpärkˌwā/ ▶ **n.** a highway or main road with trees, grass, etc., planted alongside.

par·lance /ˈpärləns/ ▶ **n.** a way of speaking.

par·lay /ˈpärˌlā, -lē/ ▶ **v. 1** (**parlay something into**) turn an initial stake or winnings from a previous bet into a greater amount by gambling. **2** informal transform into something greater or more valuable.

par·ley /ˈpärlē/ ▶ **n.** (plural **parleys**) a meeting between enemies to discuss terms for a truce. ▶ **v.** (**parleys, parleying, parleyed**) hold a parley.

par·lia·ment /ˈpärləmənt/ ▶ **n. 1** (**Parliament**) (in the UK) the assembly that makes laws, consisting of the king or queen, the House of Lords, and the House of Commons. **2** a similar assembly in other countries.

SYNONYMS **legislature**, assembly, chamber, house, congress, senate, diet.

SPELLING

Write **-lia-** in the middle, not **-la-**: par**lia**ment.

par·lia·men·tar·i·an /ˌpärləmenˈte(ə)rēən/ ▶ **n.** a member of a parliament.

par·lia·men·ta·ry /ˌpärləˈmentərē/ ▶ **adj.** relating to, enacted by, or suitable for a parliament.

SYNONYMS **legislative**, lawmaking, governmental, congressional, democratic, elected.

par·lor /ˈpärlər/ ▶ **n.** **1** dated a sitting room. **2** a store providing particular goods or services: *an ice-cream parlor.*

par·lous /ˈpärləs/ ▶ **adj.** old use dangerously uncertain; precarious.

Par·me·san /ˈpärməˌzän/ ▶ **n.** a hard, dry Italian cheese.

pa·ro·chi·al /pəˈrōkēəl/ ▶ **adj.** **1** relating to a parish. **2** having a narrow outlook.

SYNONYMS **narrow-minded**, small-minded, provincial, small-town, conservative; informal jerkwater. ANTONYMS broad-minded.

□ **parochial school** a school supported or run by a church. ■ **pa·ro·chi·al·ism** **n.**

par·o·dy /ˈparədē/ ▶ **n.** (plural **parodies**) a piece of writing, art, or music that deliberately copies the style of someone or something, in order to be funny. ▶ **v.** (**parodies**, **parodying**, **parodied**) produce a parody of.

SYNONYMS ▶ **n.** **1 satire**, burlesque, lampoon, pastiche, caricature, imitation; informal spoof, takoff, sendup. **2 distortion**, travesty, misrepresentation, perversion, corruption.

pa·role /pəˈrōl/ ▶ **n.** the temporary or permanent release of a prisoner before the end of their sentence, on the condition that they behave well. ▶ **v.** (**paroles**, **paroling**, **paroled**) release a prisoner on parole.

par·ox·ysm /ˈparəkˌsizəm, pəˈräk-/ ▶ **n.** a sudden attack of pain, coughing, etc., or a sudden feeling of overwhelming emotion.

par·quet /pärˈkā/ ▶ **n.** flooring consisting of wooden blocks arranged in a geometric pattern.

par·ra·keet = PARAKEET.

par·ri·cide /ˈparəˌsīd/ ▶ **n.** the killing by someone of their own parent or other close relative.

par·rot /ˈparət/ ▶ **n.** a tropical bird with brightly colored feathers and a hooked bill, some kinds of which can copy human speech. ▶ **v.** (**parrots**, **parroting**, **parroted**) repeat something without thought or understanding.

par·ry /ˈparē/ ▶ **v.** (**parries**, **parrying**, **parried**) **1** ward off a weapon or attack. **2** say something in order to avoid answering a question directly.

SYNONYMS **1** *he parried the blow* **ward off**, fend off, deflect, block. **2** *I parried her questions* **evade**, sidestep, avoid, dodge, field.

parse /pärs/ ▶ **v.** analyze a sentence in terms of grammar.

par·sec /ˈpärˌsek/ ▶ **n.** a unit of distance in astronomy, equal to about 3.25 light years.

par·si·mo·ny /ˈpärsəˌmōnē/ ▶ **n.** the fact of being very unwilling to spend money. ■ **par·si·mo·ni·ous** /ˌpärsəˈmōnēəs/ **adj.**

pars·ley /ˈpärslē/ ▶ **n.** an herb with crinkly or flat leaves, used in cooking.

pars·nip /ˈpärsnip/ ▶ **n.** a long tapering cream-colored root vegetable.

par·son /ˈpärsən/ ▶ **n.** **1** a rector or a vicar. **2** informal any member of the clergy, especially a Protestant one.

SYNONYMS **priest**, minister, clergyman, vicar, rector, cleric, chaplain, pastor, curate; informal reverend, padre.

par·son·age /ˈpärsənij/ ▶ **n.** a house provided by a church for a parson.

part /pärt/ ▶ **n.** **1** a piece or section that is combined with others to make up a whole. **2** some but not all of something. **3** a role played by an actor or actress. **4** a line of scalp seen in a person's hair by combing the hair in opposite directions on either side. **5** a person's contribution to an action or situation. **6** (**parts**) informal a region. ▶ **v.** **1** move apart or divide to leave a central space. **2** (of two or more people) leave each other. **3** (**part with**) give up possession of; hand over. ▶ **adv.** partly.

SYNONYMS ▶ **n.** **1 piece**, amount, portion, proportion, percentage, fraction; informal slice, chunk. **2 component**, bit, constituent, element, module, unit. **3 organ**, limb, member. **4 section**, division, volume, chapter, act, scene, installment. **5 district**, neighborhood, quarter, section, area, region. **6 role**, character. **7 involvement**, role, function, hand, responsibility, capacity, participation, contribution; informal bit. ANTONYMS whole. ▶ **v.** **1 separate**, divide, split, move apart. **2 leave each other**, part company, say goodbye/farewell, say your goodbyes/farewells, go your separate ways, take your leave. ANTONYMS join, meet.

□ **part company** go in different directions. **part of speech** a category in which a word is placed according to its function in grammar, e.g., noun, adjective, and verb. **part song** a song with three or more voice parts and no musical accompaniment. **part-time** for only part of the usual working day or week. **take part** join in or be involved in an activity.

par·take /pärˈtāk/ ▶ **v.** (**partakes**, **partaking**, **partook** /pärˈto͝ok/; past participle **partaken**) formal **1** (**partake of**) eat or drink. **2** (**partake in**) participate in.

par·tial /ˈpärsHəl/ ▶ **adj.** **1** not complete or whole. **2** favoring one side in a dispute. **3** (**partial to**) liking something.

SYNONYMS **1 incomplete**, limited, qualified, imperfect, fragmentary, unfinished. **2 biased**, prejudiced, partisan, one-sided, slanted, skewed, colored, unbalanced. ANTONYMS complete, unbiased.

■ **par·ti·al·i·ty** /ˌpärsHēˈalitē/ **n.**

par·tial·ly /ˈpärsHəlē/ ▶ **adv.** in part; to some extent: *the plan was only partially successful.*

SYNONYMS **somewhat**, to a limited extent, to a certain extent, partly, in part, up to a point, slightly. ANTONYMS wholly.

par·tic·i·pant /pärˈtisəpənt/ ▶ **n.** a person who takes part in something.

SYNONYMS **participator**, contributor, party, member, entrant, competitor, player, contestant, candidate.

par·tic·i·pate /pärˈtisəˌpāt/ ▶ **v.** (**participates**, **participating**, **participated**) join in something; take part.

SYNONYMS **take part**, join, engage, get involved, share, play a part, play a role, contribute, partake, have a hand in.

■ **par·tic·i·pa·to·ry** /-pəˌtôrē/ **adj.**

par·tic·i·pa·tion /pär,tisə'pāsʜən/ ▶ **n.** the action of taking part in an activity or event: *your participation is appreciated.*

SYNONYMS **involvement**, part, contribution, association.

par·ti·ci·ple /'pärtə,sipəl/ ▶ **n.** Grammar a word such as *going* or *burned* that is formed from a verb and used as an adjective or noun (as in *burned toast* or *the going was good*), or to make compound verb forms (as in *was going*).

par·ti·cle /'pärtikəl/ ▶ **n. 1** a tiny portion of matter. **2** a minute piece of matter smaller than an atom, e.g., an electron.

SYNONYMS **(tiny) bit**, (tiny) piece, speck, spot, fragment, sliver, splinter, iota.

par·ti·cle·board /'pärtikəl,bôrd/ ▶ **n.** a material made from compressed wood chips and resin, used in furniture and building.

par·tic·u·lar /pə(r)'tikyələr/ ▶ **adj. 1** relating to an individual member of a group or class. **2** more than is usual: *particular care.* **3** very careful or concerned about something. ▶ **n.** a detail.

SYNONYMS ▶ **adj. 1 specific**, individual, certain, distinct, separate, definite, precise. **2 special**, exceptional, unusual, uncommon, notable, noteworthy, remarkable, unique. **3 fussy**, fastidious, finicky, discriminating, selective; informal persnickety, choosy, picky. ANTONYMS general, indiscriminate. ▶ **n. detail**, item, point, element, fact, circumstance, feature.

□ **in particular** especially.

par·tic·u·lar·ly /pə(r)'tikyələrlē/ ▶ **adv. 1** more than is usual. **2** in particular; especially.

SYNONYMS **1 especially**, specially, exceptionally, unusually, remarkably, outstandingly, uncommonly, uniquely. **2 specifically**, explicitly, expressly, in particular, especially, specially.

SPELLING

Particular**ly**, not **-culy**.

parting /'pärtiɴɢ/ ▶ **n.** an act of leaving someone and going away.

SYNONYMS **farewell**, leave-taking, goodbye, adieu, departure.

□ **parting shot** a cutting remark made by someone as they leave.

par·ti·san /'pärtəzən/ ▶ **n. 1** a committed supporter of a cause, group, or person. **2** a member of an armed group fighting secretly against an occupying force. ▶ **adj.** prejudiced.

SYNONYMS ▶ **n. guerrilla**, freedom fighter, resistance fighter, underground fighter, irregular. ▶ **adj. biased**, prejudiced, one-sided, discriminatory, partial, sectarian, factional. ANTONYMS neutral.

par·ti·tion /pär'tisʜən, pər-/ ▶ **n. 1** a structure that divides a space into separate areas. **2** division into parts. ▶ **v. 1** divide into parts. **2** divide a room with a partition.

SYNONYMS ▶ **n. 1 division**, partitioning, separation, break-up. **2 screen**, divider, dividing wall, barrier, panel. ▶ **v. 1 divide**, separate, split up, break up. **2 subdivide**, divide (up), separate, section off, screen off.

part·ly /'pärtlē/ ▶ **adv.** not completely but to some extent.

SYNONYMS **in part**, partially, somewhat, a little, up to a point, in some measure, slightly, to some extent. ANTONYMS wholly.

part·ner /'pärtnər/ ▶ **n. 1** each of two people doing something as a pair. **2** the person you are having a romantic relationship with. **3** each of two or more people who are involved in a project or undertaking or who own a business. ▶ **v.** (**partners**, **partnering**, **partnered**) be the partner of.

SYNONYMS ▶ **n. 1 colleague**, associate, coworker, fellow worker, collaborator, comrade, teammate. **2 accomplice**, confederate, accessory, collaborator, fellow conspirator, helper; informal sidekick. **3 spouse**, husband, wife, life partner, lover, girlfriend, boyfriend, fiancé, fiancée, significant other, live-in lover, mate; informal better half, other half.

part·ner·ship /'pärtnər,sʜip/ ▶ **n. 1** the state of being a partner or partners. **2** an association of two or more people as partners.

SYNONYMS **1 cooperation**, association, collaboration, coalition, alliance, union, affiliation, connection. **2 company**, association, consortium, syndicate, firm, business, organization.

par·took /pär'to͝ok/ past of **PARTAKE**.

par·tridge /'pärtrij/ ▶ **n.** (plural **partridge** or **partridges**) a game bird with brown feathers and a short tail.

par·tu·ri·ent /pär't(y)o͝orēənt/ ▶ **adj.** technical about to give birth; in labor.

par·tu·ri·tion /,pärcʜo͝o'risʜən/ ▶ **n.** formal or technical the action of giving birth.

par·ty /'pärtē/ ▶ **n.** (plural **parties**) **1** a social event with food and drink and sometimes dancing. **2** an organized political group that puts forward candidates for election to government. **3** a group of people taking part in an activity or trip. **4** a person or group forming one side in an agreement or dispute. ▶ **v.** (**parties**, **partying**, **partied**) informal enjoy yourself at a party.

SYNONYMS ▶ **n. 1 social gathering**, function, get-together, celebration, reunion, festivity, reception, soirée, social; informal bash, do. **2 group**, company, body, gang, band, crowd, pack, contingent; informal bunch, crew, load. **3 faction**, group, bloc, camp, caucus, alliance.

□ **be party** (or **a party**) **to** be involved in. **party line** a policy officially adopted by a political party. **party pooper** informal a person who spoils other people's fun.

par·ty·go·er /'pärtē,gōər/ ▶ **n.** a person who goes to a party.

par·ve·nu /'pärvə,n(y)o͞o/ ▶ **n.** disapproving a person of obscure origin who has recently gained wealth or celebrity.

pas·cal /pä'skäl/ ▶ **n.** a unit of pressure.

pass[1] /pas/ ▶ **v. 1** move or go onward, past, through, or across. **2** change from one state or condition to another. **3** transfer something to someone. **4** kick, hit, or throw the ball to a teammate. **5** (of time) go by. **6** spend time. **7** be done or said. **8** come to an end. **9** be successful in an exam or test. **10** declare something to be satisfactory. **11** approve a proposal or law by voting. **12** express an opinion or judgment. ▶ n. **1** an act of passing. **2** a success in an exam. **3** an official document that allows you to go somewhere or use something. **4** a particular situation.

> SYNONYMS ▶ v. **1** **go**, proceed, move, progress, make your way, travel. **2** **overtake**, go past/by, pull ahead of, leave behind. **3** **elapse**, go by, advance, wear on, roll by, tick by. **4** *he passed the time reading* **occupy**, spend, fill, use (up), employ, while away. **5** **hand**, let someone have, give. **6** *her estate passed to her grandson* **be transferred**, go, be left, be bequeathed, be handed down/on, be passed on; Law devolve. **7** **happen**, occur, take place. **8** **come to an end**, fade (away), blow over, run its course, die out/down, finish, end, cease. **9** **be successful in**, succeed in, get through; informal sail through, scrape through. **10** **approve**, vote for, accept, ratify, adopt, agree to, authorize, endorse, legalize, enact; informal OK. ANTONYMS fail, reject. ▶ n. **permit**, warrant, authorization, license.

□ **pass away** die. **pass something off as** pretend that something is something else. **pass out** become unconscious. **pass something up** choose not to take up an opportunity.

pass² ▶ n. a route over or through mountains.

pass·a·ble /ˈpasəbəl/ ▶ adj. **1** acceptable, but not outstanding. **2** able to be traveled along or on.

> SYNONYMS **1** **adequate**, all right, acceptable, satisfactory, not (too) bad, average, tolerable, fair, mediocre, middling, ordinary, indifferent, unremarkable, unexceptional; informal OK, so-so. **2** **navigable**, traversable, negotiable, open, clear.

■ **pass·a·bly** adv.

pas·sage /ˈpasij/ ▶ n. **1** the passing of someone or something. **2** a way through or across something. **3** a journey by sea or air. **4** the right to pass through a place. **5** a short section from a book, document, or musical work.

> SYNONYMS **1** **journey**, voyage, crossing, transit, trip. **2** **passing**, progress, advance, course, march, flow. **3** **corridor**, hall, hallway. **4** **alley**, alleyway, passageway, lane, path, footpath, track, thoroughfare. **5** **extract**, excerpt, quotation, quote.

pas·sage·way /ˈpasijˌwā/ ▶ n. a corridor or other narrow passage between buildings or rooms.

pas·sé /paˈsā/ ▶ adj. no longer fashionable.

pas·sen·ger /ˈpasinjər/ ▶ n. a person traveling in a car, bus, train, ship, or aircraft, other than the driver, pilot, or crew.

> SYNONYMS **traveler**, commuter, rider, fare.

pass·er·by /ˈpasərˌbī/ ▶ n. (plural **passersby**) a person who happens to be walking past something or someone.

pas·sim /ˈpasim/ ▶ adv. used to show that a reference appears at various places throughout a document.

pass·ing /ˈpasiNG/ ▶ adj. **1** done quickly and casually. **2** (of a similarity) slight. ▶ n. **1** the ending of something. **2** a person's death.

> SYNONYMS ▶ adj. **1** **fleeting**, transient, transitory, ephemeral, brief, short-lived, temporary, momentary. **2** **hasty**, rapid, hurried, brief, quick, cursory, superficial, casual, perfunctory, desultory. ▶ n. **1** **passage**, course, progress, advance. **2** **death**, demise, passing away, end, loss.

pas·sion /ˈpasHən/ ▶ n. **1** very strong emotion. **2** a strong enthusiasm for something. **3** (**the Passion**) Jesus's suffering and death on the cross.

> SYNONYMS **1** **intensity**, enthusiasm, fervor, eagerness, zeal, vigor, fire, energy, spirit, fanaticism. **2** **love**, desire, ardor, lust, lasciviousness, lustfulness. **3** **fascination**, love, mania, obsession, preoccupation, fanaticism, fixation, compulsion, appetite, addiction; informal thing. ANTONYMS apathy.

□ **passion fruit** the edible fruit of some species of passion flower. **Passion play** a play about Jesus's crucifixion.

pas·sion·ate /ˈpasHənit/ ▶ adj. showing or caused by passion.

> SYNONYMS **1** **intense**, impassioned, ardent, fervent, vehement, fiery, heated, emotional, heartfelt, excited. **2** **very keen**, very enthusiastic, addicted; informal mad, crazy, hooked. **3** **amorous**, ardent, hot-blooded, loving, sexy, sensual, erotic, lustful; informal steamy, hot, turned on. ANTONYMS apathetic, cool.

■ **pas·sion·ate·ly** adv.

pas·sion·flow·er /ˈpasHənˌflou(-ə)r/ ▶ n. a climbing plant with large and showy flowers.

pas·sive /ˈpasiv/ ▶ adj. **1** accepting what happens without resisting or trying to change anything. **2** Grammar (of a verb) having the form used when the subject is affected by the action of the verb (e.g., *they were killed* as opposed to the active form *he killed them*).

> SYNONYMS **1** **inactive**, nonactive, nonparticipative, uninvolved. **2** **submissive**, acquiescent, unresisting, compliant, docile. ANTONYMS active, resistant.

□ **passive smoking** the inhaling of smoke from other people's cigarettes. ■ **pas·sive·ly** adv. **pas·siv·i·ty** /paˈsivitē/ n.

Pass·o·ver /ˈpasˌōvər/ ▶ n. the major Jewish spring festival, commemorating the liberation of the Israelites from slavery in Egypt.

pass·port /ˈpasˌpôrt/ ▶ n. an official document that identifies you as a citizen of a particular country and is required in order to enter and leave other countries.

pass·word /ˈpasˌwərd/ ▶ n. a secret word or phrase used to enter a place or use a computer.

past /past/ ▶ adj. **1** gone by in time and no longer existing. **2** (of time) that has gone by. **3** Grammar (of a tense of a verb) expressing a past action or state. ▶ n. **1** a past period or the events in it. **2** a person's or thing's history or earlier life. ▶ prep. **1** beyond in time or space. **2** in front of or from one side to the other of. **3** beyond the scope or power of. ▶ adv. **1** so as to pass from one side to the other. **2** used to indicate the passage of time.

> SYNONYMS ▶ adj. **1** **gone by**, bygone, former, previous, old, of old, olden, long-ago. **2** **last**, recent, preceding. **3** **previous**, former, foregoing, erstwhile, one-time, sometime, ex-. ANTONYMS present, future. ▶ n. **history**, background, past life, life story.

□ **past master** an expert in a particular activity. **past participle** Grammar the form of a verb that is used in perfect tenses (e.g., *have you looked?*), to form passive sentences (e.g., *it was broken*), and sometimes as an adjective (e.g., *lost property*).

pas·ta /ˈpästə/ ▶ **n.** a type of food made from flour and water, formed into various shapes and cooked in boiling water.

paste /pāst/ ▶ **n. 1** a soft, moist substance. **2** a glue made from water and starch. **3** a hard substance used in making imitation gems. ▶ **v.** (**pastes, pasting, pasted**) **1** coat or stick with paste. **2** (in computing) insert a section of text into a document.

SYNONYMS ▶ **n. 1 purée**, pulp, mush, spread, pâté. **2 adhesive**, glue, mucilage. ▶ **v. stick**, glue, fix, affix.

pas·tel /paˈstel/ ▶ **n. 1** a soft colored chalk or crayon used for drawing. **2** a pale shade of a color. ▶ **adj.** (of a color) pale.

SYNONYMS ▶ **adj. pale**, soft, light, delicate, muted. ANTONYMS dark, bright.

pas·teur·ize /ˈpascHəˌrīz/ ▶ **v.** (**pasteurizes, pasteurizing, pasteurized**) destroy the germs in milk by a process of heating and cooling. ■ **pas·teur·i·za·tion** /ˌpascHəriˈzāsHən/ **n.**

pas·tiche /paˈstēsH, pä-/ ▶ **n.** a piece of writing or work of art produced in a style that imitates that of another work, artist, or period.

pas·tille /paˈstēl/ ▶ **n.** a small candy or throat lozenge.

pas·time /ˈpasˌtīm/ ▶ **n.** an activity done regularly for enjoyment.

SYNONYMS **hobby**, leisure activity, leisure pursuit, recreation, game, amusement, diversion, entertainment, interest.

pas·tor /ˈpastər/ ▶ **n.** a minister in charge of a Christian church or group.

SYNONYMS **priest**, minister, parson, clergyman, cleric, chaplain, vicar, rector, curate; informal reverend, padre.

pas·to·ral /ˈpastərəl, pasˈtôrəl/ ▶ **adj. 1** relating to or portraying country life. **2** relating to the farming or grazing of sheep or cattle. **3** relating to the work of a Christian minister in giving personal and spiritual guidance. ▶ **n.** a pastoral poem, picture, or piece of music.

SYNONYMS ▶ **adj. 1 rural**, country, rustic, agricultural, bucolic; literary Arcadian. **2 priestly**, clerical, ecclesiastical, ministerial. ANTONYMS urban, lay.

pas·tra·mi /pəˈsträmē/ ▶ **n.** highly seasoned smoked beef.

pas·try /ˈpāstrē/ ▶ **n.** (plural **pastries**) **1** dough made from flour, fat, and water, used in baked dishes such as pies. **2** a cake consisting of sweet pastry with a filling.

pas·ture /ˈpascHər/ ▶ **n.** land covered with grass, suitable for grazing cattle or sheep. ▶ **v.** (**pastures, pasturing, pastured**) put animals to graze in a pasture.

SYNONYMS ▶ **n. grassland**, grass, grazing, meadow, field; literary lea.

■ **pas·tur·age** **n.**

past·y /ˈpāstē/ ▶ **adj.** (**pastier, pastiest**) (of a person's skin) unhealthily pale.

pat[1] /pat/ ▶ **v.** (**pats, patting, patted**) tap quickly and gently with the flat of your hand. ▶ **n. 1** an act of patting. **2** a compact mass of a soft substance.

SYNONYMS **tap**, touch, stroke, caress.

pat[2] ▶ **adj.** (of something said) too quick or easy; not convincing. □ **have something down pat** know facts or words perfectly so that you can repeat them without hesitation.

patch /pacH/ ▶ **n. 1** a small area differing in color or texture from its surroundings. **2** a piece of material used to mend a hole or strengthen a weak point. **3** a cover worn over an injured eye. **4** a small plot of land. ▶ **v. 1** mend, strengthen, or protect with a patch. **2** (**patch something up**) treat injuries or repair damage quickly or temporarily.

SYNONYMS ▶ **n. 1 blotch**, mark, spot, smudge, smear, stain, streak, blemish. **2 plot**, area, lot, piece, strip, tract, parcel, bed. ▶ **v. mend**, repair, sew up, stitch up, cover, reinforce.

patch·work /ˈpacHˌwərk/ ▶ **n.** needlework in which small pieces of cloth of different colors are sewn edge to edge.

patch·y /ˈpacHē/ ▶ **adj.** (**patchier, patchiest**) **1** existing or happening in small, isolated areas. **2** uneven in quality; inconsistent.

pate /pāt/ ▶ **n.** old use a person's head.

pâ·té /päˈtā/ ▶ **n.** a rich savory paste made from meat, fish, etc.

pa·tel·la /pəˈtelə/ ▶ **n.** (plural **patellae** /-lē/) the kneecap.

pat·ent ▶ **n.** /ˈpatnt/ a government license giving someone the sole right to make, use, or sell their invention for a set period. ▶ **v.** /ˈpatnt/ obtain a patent for. ▶ **adj.** /ˈpātnt, ˈpat-/ **1** easily recognizable; obvious. **2** /ˈpatnt/ made and marketed under a patent.

SYNONYMS ▶ **adj. 1 obvious**, clear, plain, evident, manifest, conspicuous, blatant, barefaced, flagrant. **2 proprietary**, patented, licensed, branded.

□ **patent leather** shiny varnished leather. ■ **pat·ent·ly** **adv.**

pa·ter·fa·mil·i·as /ˌpātərfəˈmilēəs, ˌpä-/ ▶ **n.** the man who is the head of a family or household.

pa·ter·nal /pəˈtərnl/ ▶ **adj. 1** having to do with or like a father. **2** related through the father. ■ **pa·ter·nal·ly** **adv.**

pa·ter·nal·ism /pəˈtərnlˌizəm/ ▶ **n.** the policy of protecting the people you have control over but also of restricting their freedom. ■ **pa·ter·nal·ist** **n.** & **adj.** **pa·ter·nal·is·tic** /pəˌtərnlˈistik/ **adj.**

pa·ter·ni·ty /pəˈternitē/ ▶ **n. 1** the state of being a father. **2** descent from a father.

pa·ter·nos·ter /ˈpätərˌnästər, ˈpatər-/ ▶ **n.** (in the Roman Catholic Church) the Lord's Prayer.

path /paTH/ ▶ **n. 1** a way or track laid down for walking or made by repeated treading. **2** the direction in which a person or thing moves. **3** a course of action.

SYNONYMS **1 footpath**, pathway, track, trail, bridle path, lane, towpath. **2 route**, way, course, direction, orbit, trajectory. **3 course of action**, route, road, avenue, line, approach, tack.

pa·thet·ic /pəˈTHetik/ ▶ **adj. 1** arousing pity or sadness. **2** informal weak or inadequate.

SYNONYMS **1 pitiful**, piteous, moving, touching, poignant, plaintive, wretched, heart-rending, sad. **2 feeble**, woeful, sorry, poor, weak, pitiful, lamentable, deplorable, contemptible.

■ **pa·thet·i·cal·ly** **adv.**

path·o·log·i·cal /ˌpaTHəˈläjikəl/ ▶ **adj.** **1** relating to or caused by a disease. **2** informal unable to stop yourself doing something; compulsive.

> SYNONYMS **1 morbid**, diseased. **2 compulsive**, obsessive, inveterate, habitual, persistent, chronic, hardened, confirmed.

■ **path·o·log·i·cal·ly** **adv.**

pa·thol·o·gy /pəˈTHäləjē/ ▶ **n.** **1** the study of the causes and effects of diseases. **2** the typical behavior of a disease. ■ **pa·thol·o·gist** **n.**

pa·thos /ˈpāˌTHäs, -ˌTHôs/ ▶ **n.** a quality that arouses pity or sadness.

path·way /ˈpaTHˌwā/ ▶ **n.** a path or route.

pa·tience /ˈpāSHəns/ ▶ **n.** the ability to accept delay, trouble, or suffering without becoming angry or upset.

> SYNONYMS **1 forbearance**, tolerance, restraint, equanimity, understanding, indulgence. **2 perseverance**, persistence, endurance, tenacity, application, doggedness, staying power.

pa·tient /ˈpāSHənt/ ▶ **adj.** having or showing patience. ▶ **n.** a person receiving or registered to receive medical treatment.

> SYNONYMS ▶ **adj.** **1 forbearing**, uncomplaining, long-suffering, resigned, stoical, calm, imperturbable, tolerant, accommodating, indulgent. **2 persevering**, persistent, tenacious, dogged, determined. ANTONYMS impatient.

■ **pa·tient·ly** **adv.**

pat·i·na /pəˈtēnə, ˈpatinə/ ▶ **n.** **1** a green or brown film on the surface of old bronze. **2** a soft glow on wooden furniture produced by age and polishing.

pat·i·o /ˈpatēˌō/ ▶ **n.** (plural **patios**) a paved outdoor area adjoining a house.

pa·tis·se·rie /pəˈtisərē/ ▶ **n.** a store where pastries and cakes are sold.

pat·ois /ˈpaˌtwä, ˈpä-, paˈtwä/ ▶ **n.** (plural **patois**) the dialect of a region.

pa·tri·arch /ˈpātrēˌärk/ ▶ **n.** **1** a man who is the head of a family or tribe. **2** a biblical figure regarded as a father of the human race. **3** a respected older man.

pa·tri·arch·y /ˈpātrēˌärkē/ ▶ **n.** (plural **patriarchies**) a society led or controlled by men. ■ **pa·tri·ar·chal** /ˌpātrēˈärkəl/ **adj.**

pa·tri·cian /pəˈtriSHən/ ▶ **n.** an aristocrat. ▶ **adj.** relating to or characteristic of aristocrats.

pat·ri·cide /ˈpatrəˌsīd/ ▶ **n.** **1** the killing by someone of their own father. **2** a person who kills their father.

pat·ri·mo·ny /ˈpatrəˌmōnē/ ▶ **n.** (plural **patrimonies**) property inherited from your father or male ancestor.

pa·tri·ot /ˈpātrēət/ ▶ **n.** a person who strongly supports their country and is prepared to defend it. ■ **pa·tri·ot·ism** **n.**

pa·tri·ot·ic /ˌpātrēˈätik/ ▶ **adj.** devoted to and vigorously supporting your country.

> SYNONYMS **nationalistic**, loyalist, loyal, chauvinistic, jingoistic, flag-waving. ANTONYMS traitorous.

pa·trol /pəˈtrōl/ ▶ **n.** **1** a person or group sent to keep watch over an area. **2** the action of patrolling an area. ▶ **v.** (**patrols**, **patrolling**, **patrolled**) keep watch over an area by regularly walking or traveling around it.

> SYNONYMS ▶ **n.** **1 squad**, detachment, party, force. **2** *ships on patrol in the straits* **guard**, watch, vigil. ▶ **v.** **guard**, keep watch on, police, make the rounds (of), stand guard (over), defend, safeguard.

pa·trol·man /pəˈtrōlmən/ ▶ **n.** (plural **patrolmen**) a patrolling police officer.

pa·tron /ˈpātrən/ ▶ **n.** **1** a person who gives financial support to a person or organization. **2** a regular customer of a restaurant, hotel, etc.

> SYNONYMS **1 sponsor**, backer, benefactor, contributor, subscriber, donor, philanthropist, promoter, friend, supporter; informal angel. **2 customer**, client, consumer, user, visitor, guest; informal regular.

□ **patron saint** a saint who is believed to protect a particular place or group of people.

pa·tron·age /ˈpatrənij, ˈpā-/ ▶ **n.** **1** support given by a patron. **2** custom attracted by a restaurant, hotel, etc.

> SYNONYMS **1 sponsorship**, backing, funding, financing, assistance, support. **2 custom**, trade, business.

pa·tron·ize /ˈpātrəˌnīz, ˈpa-/ ▶ **v.** (**patronizes**, **patronizing**, **patronized**) **1** treat someone as if they lack experience or are not very intelligent. **2** go regularly to a restaurant, hotel, etc.

> SYNONYMS **1 talk down to**, look down on, condescend to, treat like a child. **2** (**patronizing**) **condescending**, supercilious, superior, imperious, scornful; informal uppity, high and mighty. **3 use**, buy from, shop at, be a customer/client of, deal with, frequent, support.

pat·sy /ˈpatsē/ ▶ **n.** (plural **patsies**) a person who is deceived, taken advantage of, etc.

pat·ter[1] /ˈpatər/ ▶ **v.** (**patters**, **pattering**, **pattered**) make a repeated light tapping sound. ▶ **n.** a repeated light tapping sound.

pat·ter[2] ▶ **n.** fast continuous talk.

pat·tern /ˈpatərn/ ▶ **n.** **1** a repeated decorative design. **2** (**patterned**) decorated with a pattern. **3** a regular form or order in which a series of things happen. **4** a model, design, or set of instructions for making something. **5** an example for other people to follow.

> SYNONYMS **1 design**, decoration, motif, device, marking. **2 system**, order, arrangement, form, method, structure, scheme, plan, format. **3 model**, example, blueprint, criterion, standard, norm, yardstick, touchstone, benchmark.

pat·ty /ˈpatē/ ▶ **n.** (plural **patties**) **1** a small flat cake of ground or finely chopped food, especially meat. **2** a small, round, flat chocolate-covered peppermint candy.

pau·ci·ty /ˈpôsitē/ ▶ **n.** a very small or inadequate amount of something.

paunch /pônCH, pänCH/ ▶ **n.** an abdomen or stomach that is large and sticks out. ■ **paunch·y** **adj.**

pau·per /ˈpôpər/ ▶ **n.** a very poor person.

pause /pôz/ ▶ **v.** (**pauses**, **pausing**, **paused**) stop talking or doing something for a short time before continuing again. ▶ **n.** a temporary stop.

> SYNONYMS ▶ **v.** **stop**, break off, take a break, adjourn, rest, wait, hesitate; informal take a breather. ▶ **n.** **break**, interruption, lull, respite,

breathing space, gap, interlude, adjournment, rest, wait, hesitation; informal letup, breather.

pave /pāv/ ▶ v. (**paves**, **paving**, **paved**) cover a piece of ground with flat stones. ■ **pav·ing** n.

pave·ment /ˈpāvmənt/ ▶ n. **1** any paved area or surface. **2** the hard surface of a road or street. **3** British a sidewalk.

pa·vil·ion /pəˈvilyən/ ▶ n. **1** a summer house in a park or large garden. **2** a temporary display stand at a trade exhibition. **3** a usually highly decorated projecting subdivision of a building.

paw /pô/ ▶ n. an animal's foot that has claws and pads. ▶ v. **1** feel or scrape something with a paw or hoof. **2** informal touch someone in a way that is clumsy or unwanted.

pawn[1] /pôn/ ▶ n. **1** a chess piece of the smallest size and value. **2** a person used by more powerful people for their own purposes.

pawn[2] ▶ v. leave an object with a pawnbroker in exchange for money.

pawn·brok·er /ˈpônˌbrōkər/ ▶ n. a person who is licensed to lend money in exchange for an object that is left with them, and that they can sell if the borrower fails to pay the money back.

pawn·shop /ˈpônˌshäp/ ▶ n. a pawnbroker's shop.

paw·paw /ˈpôpô/ ▶ n. **1** a tree with purple flowers and edible oblong yellow fruit. **2** a papaya.

pay /pā/ ▶ v. (**pays**, **paying**, **paid**) **1** give someone money for work or goods. **2** give a sum of money that is owed. **3** be profitable, or result in an advantage. **4** suffer something as a result of an action. **5** give someone attention, respect, or a compliment. **6** make a visit or a call to. ▶ n. money that you get for work that you have done.

SYNONYMS ▶ v. **1 reward**, reimburse, recompense, remunerate. **2 spend**, pay out; informal lay out, shell out, fork out/over, cough up, ante up, pony up. **3 discharge**, settle, pay off, clear. **4 be profitable**, make money, make a profit. **5 be advantageous to**, benefit, be of advantage to, be beneficial to. **6** *he will pay for his mistakes* **suffer**, be punished, atone, pay the penalty/price. ▶ n. **salary**, wages, payment, earnings, remuneration, fee, reimbursement, income, revenue, stipend, emolument.

□ **pay someone back** take revenge on someone. **pay dirt** informal profit or reward.

pay·a·ble /ˈpāəbəl/ ▶ adj. **1** that must be paid. **2** able to be paid.

SYNONYMS **due**, owed, owing, outstanding, unpaid, overdue, delinquent.

pay·back /ˈpāˌbak/ ▶ n. **1** financial return or reward. **2** an act of revenge or retaliation: *the drive-by shootings are mainly paybacks.*

pay·check /ˈpāˌchek/ ▶ n. a check for salary or wages made out to an employee.

pay·ee /pāˈē/ ▶ n. a person to whom money is paid.

pay·load /ˈpāˌlōd/ ▶ n. **1** the part of a vehicle's load that earns revenue; passengers and cargo. **2** an explosive warhead carried by an aircraft or missile.

pay·mas·ter /ˈpāˌmastər/ ▶ n. an official who pays troops or workers.

pay·ment /ˈpāmənt/ ▶ n. **1** the process of paying someone or of being paid. **2** an amount that is paid.

SYNONYMS **1 remittance**, settlement, discharge, clearance. **2 installment**, premium. **3 salary**, wages, pay, earnings, fees, remuneration, reimbursement, income, stipend, emolument.

pay·off /ˈpāˌôf/ ▶ n. informal **1** a payment made to someone, especially as a bribe or reward. **2** the return on an investment or a bet. **3** a final outcome; a conclusion.

pay·o·la /pāˈōlə/ ▶ n. the illegal payment of money to someone in return for their promoting a product in the media.

pay·roll /ˈpāˌrōl/ ▶ n. a list of a company's employees and the amount of money they are to be paid.

PC ▶ abbr. **1** personal computer. **2** politically correct, or political correctness.

PDF ▶ n. Computing a kind of electronic file that can be sent by any system and displayed on any computer.

PE ▶ abbr. physical education.

pea /pē/ ▶ n. an edible round green seed growing in pods on a climbing plant.

peace /pēs/ ▶ n. **1** freedom from disturbance, noise, or anxiety. **2** freedom from war, or the ending of war.

SYNONYMS **1 quiet**, silence, peace and quiet, hush, stillness, still. **2 serenity**, peacefulness, tranquility, calm, calmness, composure, ease, contentment, rest, repose. **3 treaty**, truce, ceasefire, armistice. ANTONYMS noise, war.

□ **Peace Corps** an organization that enables Americans to work as volunteers in developing countries. **peace pipe** a tobacco pipe smoked as a token of peace among North American Indians.

peace·a·ble /ˈpēsəbəl/ ▶ adj. **1** wanting to avoid war. **2** free from conflict; peaceful. ■ **peace·a·bly** adv.

peace·ful /ˈpēsfəl/ ▶ adj. **1** free from disturbance or noise. **2** not involving war or violence. **3** wanting to avoid conflict.

SYNONYMS **1 tranquil**, calm, restful, quiet, still, relaxing, serene, composed, placid, at ease, untroubled, unworried. **2 harmonious**, on good terms, amicable, friendly, cordial, nonviolent. ANTONYMS noisy.

■ **peace·ful·ly** adv.

peace·mak·er /ˈpēsˌmākər/ ▶ n. a person who brings about peace.

SYNONYMS **arbitrator**, arbiter, mediator, negotiator, conciliator, go-between, intermediary.

peach /pēch/ ▶ n. **1** a round fruit with yellow and red skin and juicy yellow flesh, with a rough stone inside. **2** a pinkish-orange color.

pea·cock /ˈpēˌkäk/ ▶ n. a large, colorful bird with very long tail feathers that can be fanned out in display.

pea·hen /ˈpēˌhen/ ▶ n. the female of the peacock.

peak /pēk/ ▶ n. **1** the pointed top of a mountain, or a mountain with a pointed top. **2** the point of highest strength, activity, or achievement. ▶ v. reach a maximum or the highest point. ▶ adj. **1** greatest; maximum. **2** involving the greatest number of people; busiest.

SYNONYMS ▶ n. **1 summit**, top, crest, pinnacle, cap. **2 mountain**, hill, height. **3 height**, high point, pinnacle, summit, top, climax, culmination, apex, zenith, acme. ▶ v. **reach its height**, climax, culminate. ▶ adj. **maximum**, greatest, busiest, highest.

peak·ed /'pē,kid/ ▶ **adj.** pale from illness or tiredness.

peal /pēl/ ▶ **n. 1** the loud ringing sound of a bell or bells. **2** a loud sound of thunder or laughter. **3** a set of bells. ▶ **v.** ring or sound loudly.

pea·nut /'pēnət/ ▶ **n. 1** an oval edible seed that develops in a pod underground. **2** (**peanuts**) informal a very small sum of money. □ **peanut butter** a spread made from ground roasted peanuts.

pear /pe(ə)r/ ▶ **n.** a green edible fruit that has a narrow top and rounded base.

pearl /pərl/ ▶ **n. 1** a small hard, shiny white ball that sometimes forms inside the shell of an oyster and has great value as a gem. **2** a thing that is highly valued. □ **pearl barley** barley that is reduced to small round grains by grinding. ■ **pearl·y adj.**

pearl·es·cent /pər'lesənt/ ▶ **adj.** seeming to shine with many soft colors, like mother-of-pearl.

peas·ant /'pezənt/ ▶ **n.** (in the past, or in poor countries) an agricultural worker. ■ **peas·ant·ry n.**

peat /pēt/ ▶ **n.** a soft brown or black substance formed in damp areas from decayed plants. ■ **peat·y adj.**

peb·ble /'pebəl/ ▶ **n.** a small, smooth round stone. ■ **peb·bly adj.**

pe·can /pə'kän, 'pē,kan/ ▶ **n.** the smooth edible nut of a hickory tree of the southern United States.

pec·ca·dil·lo /,pekə'dilō/ ▶ **n.** (plural **peccadilloes** or **peccadillos**) a small sin or fault.

peck[1] /pek/ ▶ **v. 1** (of a bird) hit or bite something with its beak. **2** kiss someone lightly or casually. ▶ **n. 1** an act of pecking. **2** a light or casual kiss. □ **pecking order** the order of importance that people or animals give each other within a group.

peck[2] ▶ **n.** a measure of dry goods, equal to a quarter of a bushel.

peck·ish /'pekisʜ/ ▶ **adj.** informal hungry.

pec·tin /'pektin/ ▶ **n.** a substance present in ripe fruits, used as a setting agent in jams and jellies.

pec·to·ral /'pektərəl/ ▶ **adj.** relating to the breast or chest. ▶ **n.** each of four large paired muscles that cover the front of the ribcage.

pe·cu·liar /pə'kyo͞olyər/ ▶ **adj. 1** strange or odd. **2** (**peculiar to**) belonging only to.

> SYNONYMS **1 strange**, unusual, odd, funny, curious, bizarre, weird, eccentric, queer, abnormal, unconventional, outlandish, anomalous, out of the ordinary, unexpected, offbeat. **2** *customs peculiar to the area* **distinctive**, exclusive, unique, characteristic, distinct, individual, typical, special. ANTONYMS ordinary.

■ **pe·cu·liar·ly adv.**

> SPELLING
> Write **-ar**, not **-er**: peculi**ar**.

pe·cu·li·ar·i·ty /pə,kyo͞olē'aritē/ ▶ **n.** (plural **peculiarities**) **1** a feature or habit that is strange or unusual, or that belongs only to a particular person, thing, or place. **2** the state of being peculiar.

pe·cu·ni·ar·y /pi'kyo͞onē,erē/ ▶ **adj.** formal relating to money.

ped·a·gogue /'pedə,gäg/ ▶ **n.** formal a teacher. ■ **ped·a·go·gy** /'pedə,gäjē, -,gōjē/ **n.**

ped·al /'pedl/ ▶ **n. 1** each of a pair of levers that you press with your foot to make a bicycle move along. **2** a lever that you press with your foot to operate an accelerator, brake, or clutch in a motor vehicle. **3** a similar lever on a piano or organ used to sustain or soften the tone. ▶ **v.** (**pedals**, **pedaling**, **pedaled**) work the pedals of a bicycle to move along.

> USAGE
> Don't confuse **pedal** with **peddle**, which means 'sell goods.'

ped·ant /'pednt/ ▶ **n.** a person who cares too much about small details or rules.

> SYNONYMS **dogmatist**, purist, literalist, formalist, quibbler, hair-splitter; informal nit-picker.

■ **ped·ant·ry n.**

pe·dan·tic /pə'dantik/ ▶ **adj.** caring too much about small details or rules.

> SYNONYMS **finicky**, fussy, fastidious, dogmatic, purist, hair-splitting, quibbling; informal nitpicking, pernickety.

ped·dle /'pedl/ ▶ **v.** (**peddles**, **peddling**, **peddled**) **1** sell goods by going from house to house. **2** sell an illegal drug or stolen item. **3** disapproving spread an idea or view widely or persistently.

> SYNONYMS **sell**, hawk, tout, trade, deal in, traffic in.

> USAGE
> Don't confuse **peddle** with **pedal**, which means 'a foot lever' or 'to make a biycle work.'

ped·dler /'pedlər, 'pedl-ər/ (or **pedlar**) ▶ **n. 1** a person who goes from place to place selling small goods. **2** a person who sells illegal drugs or stolen goods. **3** a person who promotes an idea or view persistently or widely.

ped·er·ast /'pedə,rast/ ▶ **n.** a man who has sexual intercourse with a boy. ■ **ped·er·as·ty n.**

ped·es·tal /'pedəstl/ ▶ **n. 1** the base or support on which a statue or column is mounted. **2** the supporting column of a washbasin or toilet.

> SYNONYMS **plinth**, base, support, mount, stand, pillar, column.

pe·des·tri·an /pə'destrēən/ ▶ **n.** a person who is walking rather than traveling in a vehicle. ▶ **adj.** dull.

> SYNONYMS ▶ **n. walker**, person on foot. ▶ **adj. dull**, boring, tedious, monotonous, unremarkable, uninspired, unimaginative, unexciting, routine, commonplace, ordinary, everyday, run-of-the-mill, mundane, humdrum. ANTONYMS exciting.

pe·di·at·rics /,pēdē'atriks/ ▶ **n.** the branch of medicine concerned with children and their diseases. ■ **pe·di·at·ric adj. pe·di·a·tri·cian** /,pēdēə'trisʜən/ **n.**

ped·i·cure /'pedi,kyo͝or/ ▶ **n.** treatment to improve the appearance of the feet and toenails.

ped·i·gree /'pedə,grē/ ▶ **n. 1** the record of an animal's origins, showing that all the animals from which it is descended are of the same breed. **2** a person's family history and background.

> SYNONYMS **1 ancestry**, lineage, line, descent, genealogy, extraction, parentage, bloodline,

family tree. **2** *a pedigree horse* **purebred**, full-blooded, thoroughbred.

ped·i·ment /ˈpedəmənt/ ▶ **n.** the triangular upper part of the front of a classical building, above the columns.

pe·dom·e·ter /pəˈdämitər/ ▶ **n.** an instrument for estimating how far you are walking by recording the number of steps you take.

pe·do·phile /ˈpedəˌfīl, ˌpēdə-/ ▶ **n.** a person who is sexually attracted to children. ■ **pe·do·phil·i·a** /ˌpedəˈfilēə, ˌpēdə-/ **n.**

pee /pē/ informal ▶ **v.** (**pees**, **peeing**, **peed**) urinate. ▶ **n. 1** an act of urinating. **2** urine.

peek /pēk/ ▶ **v. 1** look quickly or secretly. **2** be just visible. ▶ **n.** a quick look.

SYNONYMS ▶ **v. 1 peep**, look; informal take a gander, have a squint. **2 appear**, show, peep (out). ▶ **n. look**, peep, glance, glimpse.

peek·a·boo /ˈpēkəˌbo͞o/ ▶ **n.** a game played with a young child, which involves hiding and suddenly reappearing, saying "peekaboo."

peel /pēl/ ▶ **v. 1** remove the skin or rind from a fruit or vegetable. **2** remove a thin covering or layer from. **3** (of a surface) come off in small pieces. ▶ **n.** the outer covering or rind of a fruit or vegetable.

SYNONYMS ▶ **v. 1 pare**, skin, hull, shell, shuck. **2 flake** (**off**), come off, fall off, strip off. ▶ **n. rind**, skin, covering, zest.

peep[1] /pēp/ ▶ **v. 1** look quickly and secretly. **2** (**peep out**) be just visible. ▶ **n. 1** a quick or secret look. **2** a momentary or partial view of something.

SYNONYMS ▶ **v. peek**, look, sneak a peek/look, glance; informal squint. ▶ **n. peek**, look, glance; informal squint.

□ **peep show** a series of pictures in a box that you look at through a small opening.

peep[2] ▶ **n.** a short, high-pitched sound. ▶ **v.** make a short, high-pitched sound.

peep·hole /ˈpēpˌhōl/ ▶ **n.** a small hole in a door or wall that you can look through.

peer[1] /pi(ə)r/ ▶ **v.** (**peers**, **peering**, **peered**) **1** look at something with difficulty or concentration. **2** be just visible.

SYNONYMS **look closely**, squint, gaze, stare.

peer[2] ▶ **n. 1** a person who is the same age or has the same social status as you. **2** a member of the nobility in Britain or Ireland.

SYNONYMS **1 aristocrat**, lord, lady, noble, nobleman, noblewoman. **2 equal**, fellow, contemporary.

□ **peer group** a group of people of approximately the same age, status, and interests.

peer·age /ˈpi(ə)rij/ ▶ **n. 1** the title and rank of peer or peeress. **2** (**the peerage**) all the peers in Britain or Ireland.

peer·ess /ˈpi(ə)ris/ ▶ **n. 1** a woman holding the rank of a peer in her own right. **2** the wife or widow of a peer.

peer·less /ˈpi(ə)rlis/ ▶ **adj.** better than all others.

peeve /pēv/ ▶ **v.** annoy or irritate someone: *he was peeved at being left out.*

SYNONYMS **irritate**, annoy, vex, anger, irk, gall, pique, put out, nettle; informal aggravate, rile, tee off, tick off, needle, get to, bug, get someone's goat, get/put someone's back up.

peeved /pēvd/ ▶ **adj.** informal annoyed; irritated.

peev·ish /ˈpēvisн/ ▶ **adj.** irritable.

peg /peg/ ▶ **n. 1** a pin or bolt used for hanging things on, securing something in place, or marking a position. **2** a clip for holding things together or hanging up clothes. ▶ **v.** (**pegs**, **pegging**, **pegged**) **1** fix, attach, or mark something with a peg or pegs. **2** fix a price, rate, etc., at a particular level.

SYNONYMS ▶ **n. pin**, nail, dowel. ▶ **v. 1 fix**, pin, attach, fasten, secure. **2 set**, hold, fix, limit, freeze, keep down, hold down.

peign·oir /ˌpānˈwär/ ▶ **n.** a woman's light robe or negligee.

pe·jo·ra·tive /pəˈjôrətiv, ˈpejəˌrātiv/ ▶ **adj.** expressing contempt or disapproval. ■ **pe·jo·ra·tive·ly adv.**

Pe·kin·ese /ˈpēkəˌnēz, -ˌnēs/ ▶ **n.** (plural **Pekinese**) a small dog with long hair and a snub nose.

pel·i·can /ˈpelikən/ ▶ **n.** a large waterbird with a bag of skin hanging from a long bill.

pel·la·gra /pəˈlagrə, -ˈlāgrə, -ˈlägrə/ ▶ **n.** a disease caused by an inadequate diet, whose symptoms include inflamed skin and diarrhea.

pel·let /ˈpelit/ ▶ **n. 1** a small compressed mass of a substance. **2** a lightweight bullet or piece of small shot.

pell-mell /ˈpel ˈmel/ ▶ **adj. & adv.** in a confused or rushed way.

pel·lu·cid /pəˈlo͞osid/ ▶ **adj.** translucent or transparent; clear.

pelt[1] /pelt/ ▶ **v. 1** hurl missiles at. **2** (**pelt down**) fall very heavily. □ (**at**) **full pelt** as fast as possible.

pelt[2] ▶ **n.** the skin of an animal with the fur, wool, or hair still on it.

pel·vis /ˈpelvis/ ▶ **n.** the large bony frame at the base of the spine to which the legs are attached. ■ **pel·vic adj.**

pen[1] /pen/ ▶ **n.** an instrument for writing or drawing with ink. ▶ **v.** (**pens**, **penning**, **penned**) write or compose.

SYNONYMS ▶ **v. write**, compose, draft, dash off, scribble.

□ **pen name** a name used by a writer that is not their real name.

pen[2] ▶ **n.** a small enclosure for farm animals. ▶ **v.** (**pens**, **penning**, **penned**) **1** put or keep animals in a pen. **2** (**pen someone/thing up** or **in**) shut a person or animal up in a small space.

SYNONYMS ▶ **n. enclosure**, fold, pound, compound, stockade, sty, coop, corral. ▶ **v. confine**, coop, cage, shut, box, lock, trap, imprison, incarcerate.

pe·nal /ˈpēnəl/ ▶ **adj. 1** relating to the use of punishment as part of the legal system. **2** very severe.

pe·nal·ize /ˈpenəlˌīz, ˈpē-/ ▶ **v.** (**penalizes**, **penalizing**, **penalized**) **1** give someone a penalty or punishment. **2** put in an unfavorable position.

SYNONYMS **1 punish**, discipline. **2 handicap**, disadvantage, discriminate against.
ANTONYMS reward.

pen·al·ty /ˈpenltē/ ▶ **n.** (plural **penalties**) **1** a punishment given to someone for breaking a law, rule, or contract. **2** something unpleasant suffered as a result of an action or circumstance. **3** (also **penalty kick**) Soccer a free shot at the goal awarded to the attacking team after a foul within the area around the goal (the **penalty area**).

SYNONYMS **punishment**, sanction, fine, forfeit, sentence. ANTONYMS reward.

pen·ance /ˈpenəns/ ▶ **n. 1** something that you yourself do or that a priest gives you to do as punishment for having done wrong. **2** a religious act in which someone confesses their sins to a priest and is given penance or formal forgiveness.

SYNONYMS **atonement**, expiation, amends, punishment, penalty.

pen·chant /ˈpencʜənt/ ▶ **n.** a strong liking for something.

SYNONYMS **liking**, fondness, preference, taste, appetite, partiality, love, passion, weakness, inclination, bent, proclivity, predilection, predisposition.

pen·cil /ˈpensəl/ ▶ **n.** an instrument for writing or drawing, consisting of a thin stick of graphite enclosed in a wooden case. ▶ **v.** (**pencils**, **penciling**, **penciled**) **1** write or draw something with a pencil. **2** (**pencil something in**) enter a time or date in your diary on the understanding that it might have to be changed later. □ **pencil-pusher** a person who does repetitive and tedious work in an office.

pend·ant /ˈpendənt/ ▶ **n. 1** a piece of jewelry worn hanging from a chain around the neck. **2** a light designed to hang from the ceiling. ▶ **adj.** (also **pendent**) hanging downward.

pend·ing /ˈpendiɴɢ/ ▶ **adj. 1** waiting to be decided or settled. **2** about to happen. ▶ **prep.** awaiting the outcome of.

SYNONYMS ▶ **adj. 1 unresolved**, undecided, unsettled, up in the air, ongoing, outstanding; informal on the back burner. **2 imminent**, impending, about to happen, forthcoming, on the way, coming, approaching, looming, near, on the horizon, in the offing.

pen·du·lous /ˈpenjələs, ˈpendyə-/ ▶ **adj.** hanging down; drooping.

pen·du·lum /ˈpenjələm, ˈpendyə-/ ▶ **n.** a weight hung from a fixed point so that it can swing freely, used in regulating the mechanism of a clock.

pen·e·trate /ˈpeniˌtrāt/ ▶ **v.** (**penetrates**, **penetrating**, **penetrated**) **1** force a way into or through. **2** gain access to an enemy organization or a competitor's market. **3** understand something. **4** (**penetrating**) (of a sound) clearly heard through or above other sounds.

SYNONYMS **1 pierce**, puncture, enter, perforate, stab, gore. **2 permeate**, pervade, fill, imbue, suffuse, seep through, saturate. **3** (**penetrating**) **perceptive**, insightful, keen, sharp, intelligent, clever, smart, incisive, trenchant, astute. **4** (**penetrating**) **cold**, cutting, biting, keen, sharp, harsh, raw, freezing, chill, bitter.

■ **pen·e·tra·tion** /ˌpeniˈtrāsʜən/ **n.** **pen·e·tra·tive** /ˈpeniˌtrātiv/ **adj.**

pen·guin /ˈpeɴɢgwin, ˈpengwin/ ▶ **n.** a black and white seabird living in the Antarctic and unable to fly.

pen·i·cil·lin /ˌpenəˈsilən/ ▶ **n.** a type of antibiotic.

pen·in·su·la /pəˈninsələ/ ▶ **n.** a long, narrow piece of land projecting into the sea. ■ **pen·in·su·lar adj.**

pe·nis /ˈpēnis/ ▶ **n.** the male organ used for urinating and having sex.

pen·i·tent /ˈpenitnt/ ▶ **adj.** feeling sorrow and regret for having done wrong. ▶ **n.** a person who is doing penance. ■ **pen·i·tence n.** **pen·i·ten·tial** /ˌpenəˈtensʜəl/ **adj.**

pen·i·ten·tia·ry /ˌpenəˈtensʜərē/ ▶ **n.** (plural **penitentiaries**) a prison for people convicted of serious crimes.

pen·knife /ˈpenˌnīf/ ▶ **n.** a small knife with a blade that folds into the handle.

pen·light /ˈpenˌlīt/ ▶ **n.** a small electric flashlight shaped like a pen.

pen·nant /ˈpenənt/ ▶ **n.** a long, narrow pointed flag.

pen·ne /ˈpenā/ ▶ **pl.n.** pasta in the form of short wide tubes.

pen·ni·less /ˈpenēlis/ ▶ **adj.** having no money.

pen·ny /ˈpenē/ ▶ **n.** (plural **pennies** (for separate coins); British **pence** /pens/ (for a sum of money)) **1** a one-cent coin equal to one hundredth of a dollar. **2** a British bronze coin worth one hundredth of a pound. **3** (in the past) a British coin worth one twelfth of a shilling and one 240th of a pound. □ **penny ante 1** poker played for very small stakes. **2** informal petty; contemptible. **penny-pinching** unwilling to spend money. **penny wise and pound foolish** careful and economical in small matters while being wasteful or extravagant in large ones.

pen·pal /ˈpenˌpal/ ▶ **n.** a person with whom you form a friendship through exchanging letters.

pen·sion¹ /ˈpensʜən/ ▶ **n.** a regular payment made to retired people, widows, etc., either by the state or from an investment fund. ▶ **v.** (**pension someone off**) dismiss someone from employment and pay them a pension.

SYNONYMS ▶ **n. retirement** (**benefits**), superannuation, Social Security, allowance, benefit, support, welfare.

■ **pen·sion·a·ble adj.** **pen·sion·er n.**

pen·sion² /pänsēˈōn/ ▶ **n.** a small hotel in France and other European countries.

pen·sive /ˈpensiv/ ▶ **adj.** thinking deeply about something.

SYNONYMS **thoughtful**, reflective, contemplative, meditative, introspective, ruminative, absorbed, preoccupied, deep/lost in thought, brooding.

■ **pen·sive·ly adv.**

pen·ta·cle /ˈpentəkəl/ ▶ **n.** a pentagram.

pen·ta·gon /ˈpentəˌgän/ ▶ **n. 1** a figure with five straight sides and five angles. **2** (**the Pentagon**) the headquarters of the United States Department of Defense.

pen·ta·gram /ˈpentəˌgram/ ▶ **n.** a five-pointed star used as a magical symbol.

pen·tam·e·ter /penˈtamitər/ ▶ **n.** a line of poetry with five stressed syllables.

Pen·ta·teuch /ˈpentəˌt(y)o͞ok/ ▶ **n.** the first five books of the Old Testament and Hebrew Scriptures.

pen·tath·lon /penˈtaᴛʜ(ə)ˌlän/ ▶ **n.** an athletic event consisting of five different activities. ■ **pen·tath·lete** /penˈtaᴛʜlēt/ **n.**

Pen·te·cost /ˈpentəˌkôst, -ˌkäst/ ▶ **n. 1** the Christian festival celebrating the coming of the Holy Spirit to the disciples of Jesus after his Ascension. **2** a Jewish festival that takes place fifty days after the second day of Passover.

Pen·te·cos·tal /ˌpentəˈkôstl, -ˈkästl/ ▶ **adj.** having to do with a Christian movement that emphasizes the gifts of the Holy Spirit, e.g., the healing of the sick.

pent·house /ˈpentˌhous/ ▶ **n.** an apartment on the top floor of a tall building.

pent-up /pent/ ▶ **adj.** not expressed or released.

pe·nul·ti·mate /peˈnəltəmit/ ▶ **adj.** last but one.

pe·num·bra /peˈnəmbrə/ ▶ **n.** the partially shaded outer part of a shadow.

pe·nu·ri·ous /pəˈn(y)o͝orēəs/ ▶ **adj.** formal very poor.

pen·u·ry /ˈpenyərē/ ▶ **n.** extreme poverty.

pe·on /ˈpēˌän, ˈpēən/ ▶ **n.** **1** an unskilled Spanish-American worker. **2** a person who does menial work; a drudge.

pe·o·ny /ˈpēənē/ ▶ **n.** a plant with large red, pink, or white flowers.

peo·ple /ˈpēpəl/ ▶ **pl.n.** **1** human beings in general. **2** (**the people**) all those living in a country or society. **3** (plural **peoples**) the members of a particular nation, community, or ethnic group. ▶ **v.** (**peoples**, **peopling**, **peopled**) live in a place or fill it with people.

> SYNONYMS ▶ **pl.n.** **1 human beings**, persons, individuals, humans, mortals, living souls, personages, [men, women, and children]; informal folk. **2 citizens**, subjects, electors, voters, taxpayers, residents, inhabitants, public, citizenry, nation, population, populace. **3 the common people**, the proletariat, the masses, the populace, the rank and file; disapproving the hoi polloi, the great unwashed; informal, disapproving the proles, the plebs. **4 family**, parents, relatives, relations, folk, kinfolk, kinsfolk, flesh and blood, nearest and dearest; informal folks. **5 race**, ethnic group, tribe, clan, nation. ▶ **v.** **populate**, settle (in), colonize, inhabit, live in, occupy.

pep /pep/ informal ▶ **v.** (**peps**, **pepping**, **pepped**) (**pep someone/thing up**) make someone or something more lively. ▶ **n.** liveliness. □ **pep talk** a talk given to someone to make them feel braver or more enthusiastic.

pep·per /ˈpepər/ ▶ **n.** **1** a hot-tasting powder made from peppercorns, used to flavor food. **2** the fruit of a tropical American plant, of which sweet peppers and chili peppers are varieties. ▶ **v.** (**peppers**, **peppering**, **peppered**) **1** season food with pepper. **2** (**pepper something with**) scatter large amounts of something over an area. **3** hit a place repeatedly with small missiles or gunshot.

> SYNONYMS ▶ **v.** **1 sprinkle**, fleck, dot, spot, stipple. **2 bombard**, pelt, shower, rain down on, strafe, rake, blitz.

■ **pep·per·y** **adj.**

pep·per·corn /ˈpepərˌkôrn/ ▶ **n.** the dried berry of a climbing vine, used whole as a spice or crushed to make pepper.

pep·per·mint /ˈpepərˌmint/ ▶ **n.** **1** a plant of the mint family whose leaves and oil are used as a flavoring in food. **2** a candy flavored with peppermint oil.

pep·per·o·ni /ˌpepəˈrōnē/ ▶ **n.** a dried sausage made from beef and pork and seasoned with pepper.

pep·tic /ˈpeptik/ ▶ **adj.** relating to digestion. □ **peptic ulcer** an ulcer in the lining of the stomach or small intestine.

per /pər/ ▶ **prep.** **1** for each. **2** by means of. **3** (**as per**) according to.

per·am·bu·late /pəˈrambyəˌlāt/ ▶ **v.** (**perambulates**, **perambulating**, **perambulated**) formal walk or travel from place to place. ■ **per·am·bu·la·tion** /pəˌrambyəˈlāsʜən/ **n.** **per·am·bu·la·tor** **n.**

per an·num /pər ˈanəm/ ▶ **adv.** for each year.

per cap·i·ta /pər ˈkapitə/ ▶ **adv. & adj.** for each person.

per·ceive /pərˈsēv/ ▶ **v.** (**perceives**, **perceiving**, **perceived**) **1** become aware of something through starting to see, smell, or hear it. **2** (**perceive something as**) understand or interpret something in a particular way.

> SYNONYMS **1 see**, discern, detect, catch sight of, spot, observe, notice; literary espy. **2 regard**, look on, view, consider, think of, judge, deem.

■ **per·ceiv·a·ble** **adj.**

> SPELLING
>
> Remember, **i** before **e**, when the sound is *ee*, except after **c**: perceive.

per·cent /pərˈsent/ ▶ **adv.** by a stated amount in or for every hundred. ▶ **n.** one part in every hundred.

per·cent·age /pərˈsentij/ ▶ **n.** **1** a rate, number, or amount in each hundred. **2** a proportion or share of a whole.

per·cen·tile /pərˈsenˌtīl/ ▶ **n.** Statistics each of 100 equal groups into which a population can be divided.

per·cep·ti·ble /pərˈseptəbəl/ ▶ **adj.** able to be noticed or felt. ■ **per·cep·ti·bly** **adv.**

per·cep·tion /pərˈsepsʜən/ ▶ **n.** **1** the ability to see, hear, or become aware of something. **2** a particular understanding of something. **3** the process of perceiving.

> SYNONYMS **1 impression**, idea, conception, notion, thought, belief. **2 insight**, perceptiveness, understanding, intelligence, intuition, incisiveness.

per·cep·tive /pərˈseptiv/ ▶ **adj.** having a good understanding of people and situations.

> SYNONYMS **insightful**, discerning, sensitive, intuitive, observant, penetrating, intelligent, clever, canny, keen, sharp, astute, shrewd, quick, smart, acute; informal on the ball.
> ANTONYMS obtuse.

■ **per·cep·tive·ly** **adv.**

per·cep·tu·al /pərˈsepcʜo͞oəl/ ▶ **adj.** relating to the ability to perceive.

perch[1] /pərcʜ/ ▶ **n.** **1** a branch, bar, or ledge on which a bird rests or roosts. **2** a high or narrow seat or resting place. ▶ **v.** **1** sit or rest somewhere. **2** place or balance something somewhere.

> SYNONYMS ▶ **v.** **1 sit**, rest, alight, settle, land, roost. **2 put**, place, set, rest, balance.

perch[2] ▶ **n.** (plural **perch** or **perches**) a freshwater fish with a spiny fin on its back.

per·chance /pərˈcʜans/ ▶ **adv.** old use perhaps.

per·cip·i·ent /pərˈsipēənt/ ▶ **adj.** having good insight or understanding.

per·co·late /ˈpərkəˌlāt/ ▶ **v.** (**percolates**, **percolating**, **percolated**) **1** filter through a porous surface or substance. **2** (of information or ideas) spread gradually through a group of people. **3** prepare coffee in a percolator. ■ **per·co·la·tion** /ˌpərkəˈlāsʜən/ **n.**

per·co·la·tor /ˈpərkəˌlātər/ ▶ **n.** a machine for making coffee, consisting of a pot in which boiling water is circulated through a small chamber that holds the ground beans.

per·cus·sion /pərˈkəsʜən/ ▶ **n.** musical instruments that you play by hitting or shaking them. ■ **per·cus·sion·ist n.**

per·di·tion /pərˈdisʜən/ ▶ **n.** (in Christian thinking) a state of eternal damnation into which people who have sinned and not repented pass when they die.

pe·re·gri·na·tions /ˌperigrəˈnāsʜənz/ ▶ **pl.n.** old use journeys or wanderings from place to place.

per·e·grine /ˈperəgrin/ ▶ **n.** a powerful falcon with a bluish-gray back and wings.

per·emp·to·ry /pəˈremptərē/ ▶ **adj.** insisting on immediate attention or obedience. ■ **per·emp·to·ri·ly adv.**

per·en·ni·al /pəˈrenēəl/ ▶ **adj. 1** lasting or doing something for a very long time. **2** (of a plant) living for several years. ▶ **n.** a perennial plant.

> SYNONYMS ▶ **adj. lasting**, enduring, abiding, long-lasting, long-lived, perpetual, continuing, continual, recurring. ANTONYMS ephemeral.

■ **per·en·ni·al·ly adv.**

pe·re·stroi·ka /ˌperəˈstroikə/ ▶ **n.** (in the former Soviet Union) the economic and political reforms introduced during the 1980s.

per·fect ▶ **adj.** /ˈpərfikt/ **1** having all the parts and qualities that are needed or wanted, and no flaws or weaknesses. **2** total; complete: *it made perfect sense*. **3** Grammar (of a verb) referring to a completed action or to a state in the past. ▶ **v.** /pərˈfekt/ make something perfect.

> SYNONYMS ▶ **adj. 1 ideal**, model, faultless, flawless, consummate, exemplary, best, ultimate, textbook. **2 flawless**, mint, as good as new, pristine, immaculate, optimum, prime, peak; informal tip-top, A1. **3 exact**, precise, accurate, faithful, true, on the money, spot on. **4 absolute**, complete, total, real, out-and-out, thorough, downright, utter. ▶ **v. improve**, polish (up), hone, refine, brush up, fine-tune.

per·fec·tion /pərˈfeksʜən/ ▶ **n.** the process of perfecting, or the state of being perfect.

> SYNONYMS **the ideal**, a paragon, the last word, the ultimate; informal the tops.

per·fec·tion·ism /pərˈfeksʜəˌnizəm/ ▶ **n.** the refusal to be satisfied with something unless it is done perfectly.

per·fec·tion·ist /pərˈfeksʜəˌnist/ ▶ **n.** a person who refuses to be satisfied with something unless it is perfect.

per·fect·ly /ˈpərfik(t)lē/ ▶ **adv. 1** in a perfect way. **2** completely; absolutely (used for emphasis).

per·fid·i·ous /pərˈfidēəs/ ▶ **adj.** deceitful and disloyal.

per·fi·dy /ˈpərfidē/ ▶ **n.** literary deceit; disloyalty.

per·fo·rate /ˈpərfəˌrāt/ ▶ **v.** (**perforates, perforating, perforated**) pierce and make a hole or holes in. ■ **per·fo·ra·tion** /ˌpərfəˈrāsʜən/ **n.**

per·force /pərˈfôrs/ ▶ **adv.** formal necessarily; inevitably.

per·form /pərˈfôrm/ ▶ **v. 1** carry out an action, task, or function. **2** work, function, or do something to a particular standard. **3** entertain an audience by playing a piece of music, acting in a play, etc.

> SYNONYMS **1 carry out**, do, execute, discharge, conduct, implement; informal pull off. **2 function**, work, operate, run, go, respond, behave, act. **3 stage**, put on, present, mount, act, produce. **4 play**, sing, appear.

per·for·mance /pərˈfôrməns/ ▶ **n. 1** an act of performing a play, piece of music, etc. **2** the process of performing. **3** informal a fuss. **4** the capabilities of a machine or product.

> SYNONYMS **1 show**, production, showing, presentation, staging, concert, recital; informal gig. **2 rendition**, interpretation, playing, acting. **3 carrying out**, execution, discharge, completion, fulfillment. **4 functioning**, working, operation, running, behavior, response.

□ **performance art** an art form that combines visual art with drama.

per·form·er /pərˈfôrmər/ ▶ **n.** a person who performs.

> SYNONYMS **actor, actress**, artiste, artist, entertainer, trouper, player, musician, singer, dancer, comic, comedian, comedienne.

per·fume /ˈpərˌfyo͞om, ˌpərˈfyo͞om/ ▶ **n. 1** a sweet-smelling liquid put on the body. **2** a pleasant smell. ▶ **v.** (**perfumes, perfuming, perfumed**) **1** give a pleasant smell to. **2** put perfume on or in.

> SYNONYMS ▶ **n. 1 scent**, fragrance, eau de toilette, toilet water, cologne, eau de cologne. **2 smell**, scent, fragrance, aroma, bouquet, nose.

■ **per·fum·er·y** /pərˈfyo͞omərē/ **n.**

per·func·to·ry /pərˈfəɴɢktərē/ ▶ **adj.** carried out without much care or effort. ■ **per·func·to·ri·ly adv.**

per·go·la /ˈpərgələ/ ▶ **n.** an arched structure forming a framework for climbing plants.

per·haps /pərˈ(h)aps/ ▶ **adv.** possibly; maybe.

> SYNONYMS **maybe**, for all you know, it could be, it may be, it's possible, possibly, conceivably.

per·il /ˈperəl/ ▶ **n.** a situation of serious and immediate danger.

> SYNONYMS **danger**, jeopardy, risk, hazard, menace, threat. ANTONYMS safety.

per·il·ous /ˈperələs/ ▶ **adj.** full of danger or risk. ■ **per·il·ous·ly adv.**

pe·rim·e·ter /pəˈrimitər/ ▶ **n.** the boundary or outside edge of something.

> SYNONYMS **boundary**, border, limits, bounds, edge, margin, fringe(s), periphery. ANTONYMS center.

pe·ri·od /ˈpi(ə)rēəd/ ▶ **n. 1** a length or portion of time. **2** one of the set divisions into which a day's lessons are divided in school. **3** a dot used as a punctuation mark at the end of a sentence or in an abbreviation. **4** (also **menstrual period**) a flow of blood each month from the lining of a woman's uterus. ▶ **adj.** belonging to or characteristic of a past historical time.

> SYNONYMS ▶ **n. 1 time**, spell, interval, stretch, term, span, phase, bout; informal patch. **2 era**, age, epoch, eon, time, days, years.

□ **period piece** an object made or a book or play set in an earlier period.

pe·ri·od·ic /ˌpi(ə)rēˈädik/ ▶ **adj.** appearing or happening at intervals.

SYNONYMS **regular**, at fixed intervals, recurrent, recurring, repeated, cyclical, seasonal, occasional, intermittent, sporadic, odd.

□ **periodic table** a table of all the chemical elements.

pe·ri·od·i·cal /ˌpi(ə)rēˈädikəl/ ▶ **adj. 1** happening or appearing at intervals. **2** (of a magazine or newspaper) published at regular intervals. ▶ **n.** a periodical magazine or newspaper.

SYNONYMS ▶ **n. journal**, magazine, newspaper, paper, review, newsletter, digest, gazette, organ; informal mag.

■ **pe·ri·od·i·cal·ly adv.**

per·i·pa·tet·ic /ˌperipəˈtetik/ ▶ **adj.** traveling from place to place.

pe·riph·er·al /pəˈrifərəl/ ▶ **adj. 1** relating to or situated on an edge or boundary. **2** outside the most important part of something; marginal. **3** (of a device) able to be attached to and used with a computer, although not an integral part of it.

SYNONYMS **secondary**, subsidiary, incidental, tangential, marginal, minor, unimportant, ancillary. ANTONYMS central.

■ **pe·riph·er·al·ly adv.**

pe·riph·er·y /pəˈrifərē/ ▶ **n.** (plural **peripheries**) **1** the outside edge or boundary of something. **2** an area of activity that is outside the most important part of something.

per·i·scope /ˈperəˌskōp/ ▶ **n.** a device consisting of a tube attached to a set of mirrors, through which you can see things that are above or behind something else.

per·ish /ˈperisн/ ▶ **v. 1** die. **2** be completely ruined or destroyed. **3** (of rubber or a similar material) become weak or rot.

SYNONYMS **1 die**, lose your life, be killed, fall, be lost; informal buy it. **2 go bad**, spoil, rot, decay, decompose.

□ **perish the thought** informal let that not happen or be true.

per·ish·a·ble /ˈperisнəbəl/ ▶ **adj.** (of food) not able to be kept beyond a certain time because it will rot or decay.

per·i·stal·sis /ˌperəˈstôlsis, -ˈstal-/ ▶ **n.** the contraction and relaxation of muscles in the digestive system and intestines, creating wavelike movements that push food through the body.

per·i·to·ne·um /ˌperitnˈēəm/ ▶ **n.** (plural **peritoneums** or **peritonea** /-ˈnēə/) a membrane lining the inside of the abdomen. ■ **per·i·to·ne·al adj.**

per·i·to·ni·tis /ˌperitnˈītis/ ▶ **n.** inflammation of the peritoneum.

per·i·win·kle /ˈperiˌwiNGkəl/ ▶ **n.** a plant with purple flowers and glossy leaves.

per·jure /ˈpərjər/ ▶ **v.** (**perjures**, **perjuring**, **perjured**) (**perjure yourself**) tell a lie in court after swearing to tell the truth.

per·ju·ry /ˈpərjərē/ ▶ **n.** the offense of deliberately telling a lie in court after swearing to tell the truth.

perk[1] /pərk/ ▶ **v.** (**perk up**) become more cheerful or lively.

perk[2] ▶ **n.** informal an extra benefit given to an employee in addition to their wages.

SYNONYMS **fringe benefit**, advantage, bonus, extra, plus; informal freebie.

perk·y /ˈpərkē/ ▶ **adj.** (**perkier**, **perkiest**) cheerful and lively.

SYNONYMS **cheerful**, lively, vivacious, bubbly, effervescent, bouncy, spirited, cheery, merry, buoyant, exuberant, jaunty, frisky, sprightly, spry, bright, sunny, jolly; informal full of beans, bright-eyed and bushy-tailed, chirpy, chipper, peppy.

perm /pərm/ ▶ **n.** (also **permanent wave**) a method of setting the hair in waves or curls and treating it with chemicals so that the style lasts for several months. ▶ **v.** treat hair in such a way.

per·ma·frost /ˈpərməˌfrôst, -ˌfräst/ ▶ **n.** a layer of soil beneath the surface that remains below freezing point throughout the year.

per·ma·nent /ˈpərmənənt/ ▶ **adj.** lasting for a long time or forever.

SYNONYMS **lasting**, enduring, indefinite, continuing, constant, perpetual, indelible, irreparable, irreversible, lifelong, perennial, established, standing, long-term, stable, secure. ANTONYMS temporary.

■ **per·ma·nence n.**

SPELLING

Permane**nt**, not -ant.

per·ma·nent·ly /ˈpərmənəntlē/ ▶ **adv. 1** forever. **2** continually; always.

SYNONYMS **1 forever**, for all time, for good, irreversibly, incurably, irreparably, indelibly; informal for keeps. **2 continually**, constantly, perpetually, always.

per·me·a·ble /ˈpərmēəbəl/ ▶ **adj.** allowing liquids or gases to pass through.

per·me·ate /ˈpərmēˌāt/ ▶ **v.** (**permeates**, **permeating**, **permeated**) spread throughout.

per·mis·si·ble /pərˈmisəbəl/ ▶ **adj.** permitted.

per·mis·sion /pərˈmisнən/ ▶ **n.** the act of allowing someone to do something.

SYNONYMS **authorization**, consent, leave, authority, sanction, license, dispensation, assent, agreement, approval, blessing, clearance; informal the go-ahead, the green light, say-so. ANTONYMS ban.

per·mis·sive /pərˈmisiv/ ▶ **adj.** allowing someone a lot of freedom of behavior. ■ **per·mis·sive·ness n.**

per·mit ▶ **v.** /pərˈmit/ (**permits**, **permitting**, **permitted**) **1** say that someone is allowed to do something. **2** make something possible. ▶ **n.** /ˈpərmit/ an official document saying that someone is allowed to do something or go somewhere.

SYNONYMS ▶ **v. allow**, let, authorize, give permission, sanction, grant, license, consent to, assent to, agree to; informal give the go-ahead to, give the green light to. ANTONYMS forbid. ▶ **n. authorization**, license, pass, ticket, warrant, passport, visa.

per·mu·ta·tion /ˌpərmyo͝oˈtāsнən/ ▶ **n.** each of several possible ways in which a number of things can be ordered or arranged.

per·ni·cious /pərˈnisнəs/ ▶ **adj.** having a harmful effect.

per·o·ra·tion /ˌperəˈrāsнən/ ▶ **n.** the concluding part of a speech.

per·ox·ide /pəˈräksīd/ ▶ **n.** (also **hydrogen peroxide**) a chemical that is used as a bleach or disinfectant.

per·pen·dic·u·lar /ˌpərpənˈdikyələr/ ▶ **adj.** at an angle of 90° to the ground, or to another line or surface. ▶ **n.** a perpendicular line.

per·pe·trate /ˈpərpəˌtrāt/ ▶ **v.** (**perpetrates, perpetrating, perpetrated**) carry out a bad or illegal action. ■ **per·pe·tra·tion** /ˌpərpəˈtrāsнən/ **n.** **per·pe·tra·tor n.**

per·pet·u·al /pərˈpecнo͞oəl/ ▶ **adj.** **1** never ending or changing. **2** so frequent as to seem continual.

> SYNONYMS **1 constant**, permanent, uninterrupted, continuous, unremitting, unending, everlasting, eternal, unceasing, without end, persistent, lasting, abiding. **2 interminable**, incessant, ceaseless, endless, relentless, unrelenting, persistent, continual, continuous, nonstop, never-ending, repeated, unremitting, around-the-clock, unabating; informal eternal. ANTONYMS temporary, intermittent.

■ **per·pet·u·al·ly adv.**

per·pet·u·ate /pərˈpecнo͞oˌāt/ ▶ **v.** (**perpetuates, perpetuating, perpetuated**) cause something to continue indefinitely.

> SYNONYMS **keep alive**, keep going, preserve, conserve, sustain, maintain, continue, extend.

■ **per·pet·u·a·tion** /pərˌpecнo͞oˈāsнən/ **n.**

per·pe·tu·i·ty /ˌpərpiˈt(y)o͞oitē/ ▶ **n.** (plural **perpetuities**) the state of lasting forever.

per·plex /pərˈpleks/ ▶ **v.** puzzle someone very much.

> SYNONYMS **puzzle**, baffle, mystify, bemuse, bewilder, confound, confuse, nonplus, disconcert; informal flummox.

per·plex·i·ty /pərˈpleksitē/ ▶ **n.** (plural **perplexities**) **1** the state of being puzzled. **2** a puzzling situation or thing.

per·qui·site /ˈpərkwəzit/ ▶ **n.** formal a special right or privilege.

per se /pər ˈsā/ ▶ **adv.** in itself.

per·se·cute /ˈpərsəˌkyo͞ot/ ▶ **v.** (**persecutes, persecuting, persecuted**) **1** treat badly over a long period. **2** harass.

> SYNONYMS **1 oppress**, abuse, victimize, ill-treat, mistreat, maltreat, torment, torture. **2 harass**, hound, plague, badger, harry, intimidate, pick on, pester; informal hassle.

■ **per·se·cu·tor n.**

per·se·cu·tion /ˌpərsəˈkyo͞osнən/ ▶ **n.** **1** cruel or unfair treatment. **2** persistent harassment.

> SYNONYMS **1 oppression**, victimization, ill-treatment, mistreatment, abuse, discrimination. **2 harassment**, hounding, intimidation, bullying.

per·se·vere /ˌpərsəˈvi(ə)r/ ▶ **v.** continue doing something in spite of difficulty or lack of success.

> SYNONYMS **persist**, continue, carry on, go on, keep on, keep going, struggle on, hammer away, be persistent, keep at it, not take no for an answer, be tenacious, plod on, plow on; informal soldier on, hang on, plug away, stick to your guns, stick it out, hang in there. ANTONYMS give up.

■ **per·se·ver·ance n.**

Per·sian /ˈpərzнən/ ▶ **n.** **1** a person from Persia (now Iran). **2** the language of ancient Persia or modern Iran. **3** a breed of cat with long hair. ▶ **adj.** relating to Persia or Iran.

per·sim·mon /pərˈsimən/ ▶ **n.** a fruit that looks like a large tomato but is very sweet.

per·sist /pərˈsist/ ▶ **v.** **1** continue doing something in spite of difficulty or opposition. **2** continue to exist.

> SYNONYMS **1** *he persisted with his questioning* **persevere**, continue, carry on, go on, keep on, keep going, hammer away, keep at it; informal soldier on, plug away. **2** *the dry weather persists* **continue**, hold, carry on, last, keep on, remain, linger, stay, endure. ANTONYMS give up, stop.

per·sist·ence /pərˈsistəns/ ▶ **n.** **1** the quality of continuing to do something in spite of difficulty or opposition. **2** the continued or prolonged existence of something: *the persistence of huge environmental problems*.

> SYNONYMS **perseverance**, tenacity, determination, staying power, endurance, doggedness, stamina; informal stickability; formal pertinacity.

per·sist·ent /pərˈsistənt/ ▶ **adj.** **1** continuing to do something in spite of difficulty or opposition. **2** continuing or recurring over a long period.

> SYNONYMS **1 tenacious**, determined, resolute, dogged, tireless, indefatigable, insistent, unrelenting; formal pertinacious. **2 constant**, continuous, continuing, continual, nonstop, never-ending, steady, uninterrupted, unbroken, interminable, incessant, endless, unending, unrelenting. **3** *a persistent cough* **chronic**, nagging, frequent, repeated, habitual. ANTONYMS irresolute, intermittent.

■ **per·sist·ent·ly adv.**

> SPELLING
> **Persistent**, not **-ant**.

per·snick·et·y /pərˈsnikitē/ ▶ **adj.** fussy.

per·son /ˈpərsən/ ▶ **n.** (plural **people** /ˈpēpəl/ or **persons**) **1** an individual human being. **2** a person's body. **3** Grammar a category used in classifying pronouns and verb forms according to whether they indicate the speaker (**first person**), the person spoken to (**second person**), or a third party (**third person**).

> SYNONYMS **human being**, individual, man, woman, human, being, living soul, mortal, creature; informal type, sort.

□ **in person** physically present.

per·so·na /pərˈsōnə/ ▶ **n.** (plural **personas** or **personae** /-ˈsōnē/) the part of a person's character that is revealed to other people.

per·son·a·ble /ˈpərsənəbəl/ ▶ **adj.** having a pleasant appearance and manner.

per·son·age /ˈpərsənij/ ▶ **n.** a person of importance or high status.

per·son·al /ˈpərsənəl/ ▶ **adj.** **1** having to do with or belonging to a particular person. **2** done by a particular person themselves, rather than someone acting for them. **3** concerning a person's private rather than professional or public life. **4** referring to someone's character or appearance in a way that is offensive. **5** relating to a person's body.

SYNONYMS **1 distinctive**, characteristic, unique, individual, idiosyncratic. **2 in person**, in the flesh, actual, live, physical. **3 private**, intimate. **4 derogatory**, disparaging, belittling, insulting, rude, disrespectful, offensive, pejorative.

□ **personal pronoun** Grammar each of the pronouns that show person, gender, number, and case (such as *I*, *you*, *he*, *she*, etc.).

per·son·al·i·ty /ˌpərsəˈnalitē/ ▶ **n.** (plural **personalities**) **1** the qualities that form a person's character. **2** qualities that make someone interesting or popular. **3** a celebrity.

SYNONYMS **1 character**, nature, disposition, temperament, makeup, psyche. **2 charisma**, magnetism, character, charm, presence. **3 celebrity**, VIP, star, superstar, big name, somebody, leading light, luminary, notable; informal celeb.

per·son·al·ize /ˈpərsənəlˌīz/ ▶ **v.** (**personalizes, personalizing, personalized**) **1** design or produce something to meet someone's individual requirements. **2** cause an issue or argument to become concerned with personalities or feelings.

per·son·al·ly /ˈpərsənəlē/ ▶ **adv.** **1** in person. **2** from your own viewpoint.

SYNONYMS **1 in person**, yourself. **2 for my part**, for myself, as far as I am concerned, from my own point of view, subjectively.

□ **take something personally** think that a remark or action is directed against yourself and be upset by it.

per·so·na non gra·ta /pərˈsōnə nän ˈgrätə/ ▶ **n.** a person who is not welcome in a place.

per·son·i·fi·ca·tion /pərˌsänəfiˈkāsʜən/ ▶ **n.** a person who represents or embodies a quality or concept: *he is the personification of heroism.*

SYNONYMS **embodiment**, incarnation, epitome, quintessence, essence, type, symbol, soul, model, exemplification, exemplar, image, representation.

per·son·i·fy /pərˈsänəˌfī/ ▶ **v.** (**personifies, personifying, personified**) **1** give human characteristics to something that is not human. **2** be an example of a quality or characteristic.

per·son·nel /ˌpərsəˈnel/ ▶ **pl.n.** people employed in an organization.

SYNONYMS **staff**, employees, workforce, workers, labor force, manpower, human resources.

per·spec·tive /pərˈspektiv/ ▶ **n.** **1** the art of representing things in a picture so that they seem to have height, width, depth, and relative distance. **2** a way of seeing something. **3** understanding of how important things are in relation to others.

SYNONYMS **outlook**, view, viewpoint, point of view, standpoint, position, stand, stance, angle, slant, attitude.

per·spi·ca·cious /ˌpərspiˈkāsʜəs/ ▶ **adj.** quickly gaining insight into things. ■ **per·spi·cac·i·ty n.**

per·spic·u·ous /pərˈspikyo͞owəs/ ▶ **adj.** **1** clearly expressed and easily understood. **2** (of a person) expressing things clearly.

per·spi·ra·tion /ˌpərspəˈrāsʜən/ ▶ **n.** **1** sweat. **2** the process of sweating.

per·spire /pərˈspīr/ ▶ **v.** (**perspires, perspiring, perspired**) produce sweat through the pores of your skin.

per·suade /pərˈswād/ ▶ **v.** (**persuades, persuading, persuaded**) use reasoning or argument to make someone do or believe something.

SYNONYMS **1 prevail on**, talk into, coax, convince, get, induce, win over, bring around, influence, sway; informal sweet-talk. **2 cause**, lead, move, dispose, incline. ANTONYMS dissuade, deter.

per·sua·sion /pərˈswāzʜən/ ▶ **n.** **1** the process of persuading or of being persuaded. **2** a belief or set of beliefs.

SYNONYMS **1 coaxing**, urging, inducement, encouragement; informal sweet-talking. **2 group**, grouping, sect, denomination, party, camp, side, faction, school of thought, belief, creed, faith.

per·sua·sive /pərˈswāsiv, -ziv/ ▶ **adj.** **1** good at persuading someone to do or believe something. **2** providing evidence or reasoning that makes you believe something.

SYNONYMS **convincing**, compelling, effective, telling, forceful, powerful, eloquent, impressive, sound, cogent, valid, strong, plausible, credible. ANTONYMS unconvincing.

■ **per·sua·sive·ly adv.**

pert /pərt/ ▶ **adj.** **1** attractively lively or impudent. **2** (of a bodily feature) attractively small and firm.

per·tain /pərˈtān/ ▶ **v.** (**pertain to**) be appropriate, related, or relevant to.

SYNONYMS **1** *developments pertaining to the economy* **concern**, relate to, connected with, relevant to, apply to, refer to, have a bearing on, affect, involve, touch on. **2 exist**, be the case, prevail.

per·ti·na·cious /ˌpərtnˈāsʜəs/ ▶ **adj.** formal persistent. ■ **per·ti·nac·i·ty n.**

per·ti·nent /ˈpərtn-ənt/ ▶ **adj.** relevant or appropriate.

SYNONYMS **relevant**, to the point, apposite, appropriate, suitable, applicable, material, germane. ANTONYMS irrelevant.

■ **per·ti·nence n. per·ti·nent·ly adv.**

per·turb /pərˈtərb/ ▶ **v.** make someone worried or anxious.

SYNONYMS **worry**, upset, disturb, unsettle, concern, trouble, disquiet, disconcert, discomfit, unnerve, alarm, bother; informal rattle. ANTONYMS reassure.

■ **per·tur·ba·tion** /ˌpərtərˈbāsʜən/ **n.**

pe·ruse /pəˈro͞oz/ ▶ **v.** (**peruses, perusing, perused**) formal read or examine thoroughly or carefully. ■ **pe·rus·al n.**

Pe·ru·vi·an /pəˈro͞ovēən/ ▶ **n.** a person from Peru. ▶ **adj.** relating to Peru.

per·vade /pərˈvād/ ▶ **v.** (**pervades, pervading, pervaded**) spread or be present throughout.

SYNONYMS **permeate**, spread through, fill, suffuse, imbue, penetrate, filter through, infuse, inform.

per·va·sive /pərˈvāsiv/ ▶ **adj.** spreading widely through something.

SYNONYMS **prevalent**, pervading, extensive, ubiquitous, omnipresent, universal, widespread, general.

■ **per·va·sive·ly** adv. **per·va·sive·ness** n.

per·verse /pər'vərs/ ▶ adj. **1** deliberately choosing to behave in a way that other people find unacceptable. **2** contrary to what is accepted or expected.

SYNONYMS **1 awkward**, contrary, difficult, unreasonable, uncooperative, unhelpful, obstructive, stubborn, obstinate. **2 illogical**, irrational, wrongheaded.

■ **per·verse·ly** adv. **per·ver·si·ty** n.

per·ver·sion /pər'vərzHən/ ▶ n. the action of perverting.

SYNONYMS **1 distortion**, misrepresentation, travesty, twisting, corruption, misuse. **2 deviance**, abnormality, depravity.

per·vert ▶ v. /pər'vərt/ **1** change the form or meaning of something in a way that distorts it. **2** make someone perverted. ▶ n. /'pər,vərt/ a person whose sexual behavior is abnormal and unacceptable.

SYNONYMS ▶ v. **distort**, warp, corrupt, subvert, twist, bend, abuse, divert. ▶ n. **deviant**, degenerate; informal perv, dirty old man, sicko.

per·vert·ed /pər'vərtid/ ▶ adj. sexually abnormal or unacceptable.

SYNONYMS **unnatural**, deviant, warped, twisted, abnormal, unhealthy, depraved, perverse, aberrant, debased, degenerate; informal sick, kinky.

per·vi·ous /'pərvēəs/ ▶ adj. allowing water to pass through.

pe·se·ta /pə'sātə/ ▶ n. the former basic unit of money in Spain.

pes·ky /'peskē/ ▶ adj. informal annoying.

pe·so /'pāsō/ ▶ n. (plural **pesos**) the basic unit of money of several Latin American countries and of the Philippines.

pes·si·mist /'pesə,mist/ ▶ n. a person who tends to expect the worst to happen.

SYNONYMS **defeatist**, fatalist, prophet of doom, alarmist, cynic, skeptic, misery, killjoy, Cassandra; informal doom (and gloom) merchant, wet blanket. ANTONYMS optimist.

pes·si·mis·tic /,pesə'mistik/ ▶ adj. expecting the worst to happen.

SYNONYMS **gloomy**, negative, cynical, defeatist, downbeat, bleak, fatalistic, depressed. ANTONYMS optimistic.

■ **pes·si·mism** /'pesə,mizəm/ adv. **pes·si·mis·ti·cal·ly** adv.

pest /pest/ ▶ n. **1** a destructive insect or other animal that attacks plants, crops, or livestock. **2** informal an annoying person or thing.

SYNONYMS **nuisance**, annoyance, irritant, thorn in your flesh/side, trial, menace, trouble, problem, worry, bother; informal pain in the neck, headache.

pes·ter /'pestər/ ▶ v. (**pesters**, **pestering**, **pestered**) annoy someone with repeated questions or requests.

SYNONYMS **badger**, hound, harass, plague, annoy, bother, harry, worry; informal hassle, bug.

pes·ti·cide /'pestə,sīd/ ▶ n. a substance for destroying insects or other pests.

pes·ti·lence /'pestələns/ ▶ n. old use a disease that spreads widely and causes many deaths.
■ **pes·ti·lent** adj.

pes·ti·len·tial /,pestə'lencHəl/ ▶ adj. **1** old use relating to or causing a pestilence. **2** informal annoying.

pes·tle /'pestl, 'pesəl/ ▶ n. a small, heavy tool with a rounded end, used for grinding substances in a mortar.

pes·to /'pestō/ ▶ n. a sauce of crushed basil leaves, pine nuts, garlic, Parmesan cheese, and olive oil, served with pasta.

pet /pet/ ▶ n. **1** an animal or bird that you keep for pleasure. **2** a person treated with special favor. ▶ adj. favorite. ▶ v. (**pets**, **petting**, **petted**) stroke or pat an animal.

SYNONYMS ▶ adj. **1 tame**, domesticated, housebroken, companion. **2 favorite**, favored, cherished, particular, special, personal. ▶ v. **1 stroke**, caress, fondle, pat, tickle. **2 cuddle**, embrace, caress, kiss; informal neck, make out, smooch, canoodle.

□ **pet name** a name used to express fondness or familiarity.

pet·al /'petl/ ▶ n. each of the segments forming the outer part of a flower.

pe·ter /'pētər/ ▶ v. (**peters**, **petering**, **petered**) (**peter out**) gradually come to an end.

SYNONYMS **fizzle out**, fade (away), die away/out, dwindle, diminish, taper off, tail off, trail away/off, wane, ebb, melt away, evaporate, disappear.

pe·tite /pə'tēt/ ▶ adj. (of a woman) small and dainty.

pe·tit four /'petē 'fôr/ ▶ n. (plural **petits fours**) a very small fancy cake, cookie, or candy.

pe·ti·tion /pə'tisHən/ ▶ n. **1** an appeal or request, especially a written one signed by a large number of people and presented formally to someone in authority. **2** Law an application to a court for a writ, legal action, etc. ▶ v. make or present a petition to.

SYNONYMS ▶ n. **appeal**, round robin, letter, request, entreaty, application, plea. ▶ v. **appeal to**, request, ask, call on, entreat, beg, implore, plead with, apply to, press, urge.

pet·rel /'petrəl/ ▶ n. a seabird that flies far from land.

pe·tri dish /'pētrē/ ▶ n. a shallow transparent dish with a flat lid, used in laboratories.

pet·ri·fy /'petrə,fī/ ▶ v. (**petrifies**, **petrifying**, **petrified**) **1** make someone so frightened that they cannot move. **2** change organic matter into stone.

SYNONYMS (**petrified**) **1 terrified**, horrified, scared/frightened out of your wits, scared/frightened to death. **2 ossified**, fossilized, calcified.

pet·ro·chem·i·cal /,petrō'kemikəl/ ▶ adj. relating to petroleum and natural gas. ▶ n. a chemical obtained from petroleum and natural gas.

pe·tro·le·um /pə'trōlēəm/ ▶ n. an oil that is refined to produce fuels, including gas, paraffin, and diesel oil.

pet·ti·coat /ˈpetē,kōt/ ▶ **n.** a woman's light undergarment in the form of a skirt or dress.

pet·ti·fog·ging /ˈpetē,fôgiNG, -,fäg-/ ▶ **adj.** petty; trivial.

pet·tish /ˈpetisH/ ▶ **adj.** childishly sulky. ■ **pet·tish·ly adv.**

pet·ty /ˈpetē/ ▶ **adj.** (**pettier**, **pettiest**) **1** of little importance. **2** too concerned with unimportant things. **3** minor.

> SYNONYMS **1 trivial**, trifling, minor, insignificant, paltry, unimportant, inconsequential, footling, negligible; informal piffling. **2 small-minded**, mean, shabby, spiteful. ANTONYMS important, magnanimous.

□ **petty cash** a store of money that is available for spending on small items. **petty officer** a noncommissioned officer in a navy, in particular one in the US Navy or Coast Guard ranking above seaman and below chief petty officer. ■ **pet·ti·ness n.**

pet·u·lant /ˈpecHələnt/ ▶ **adj.** childishly sulky or bad-tempered.

> SYNONYMS **peevish**, bad-tempered, querulous, pettish, fretful, irritable, sulky, tetchy, crotchety, testy, fractious; informal grouchy, cranky. ANTONYMS good-humored.

■ **pet·u·lance n. pet·u·lant·ly adv.**

pe·tu·nia /pəˈt(y)o͞onyə/ ▶ **n.** a plant of the nightshade family with white, purple, or red funnel-shaped flowers.

pew /pyo͞o/ ▶ **n.** a long wooden bench with a back, arranged with others in rows to provide seating in a church.

pew·ter /ˈpyo͞otər/ ▶ **n.** a metal made by mixing tin with copper and antimony.

pfen·nig /ˈfenig/ ▶ **n.** a former unit of money in Germany, equal to one hundredth of a mark.

PG ▶ **abbr.** (in movie classification) parental guidance.

pH ▶ **n.** a figure expressing how acid or alkaline a substance is.

pha·lanx /ˈfālaNGks, ˈfal-/ ▶ **n.** (plural **phalanxes**) a group of people standing or moving forward closely together.

phan·tasm /ˈfantazəm/ ▶ **n.** literary a thing that exists only in the imagination.

phan·tas·ma·go·ri·a /fan,tazməˈgôrēə/ ▶ **n.** a sequence of real or imaginary images like that seen in a dream.

phan·tom /ˈfantəm/ ▶ **n. 1** a ghost. **2** a thing that exists only in the imagination. ▶ **adj.** not really existing.

> SYNONYMS ▶ **n. ghost**, apparition, spirit, specter, wraith; informal spook.

phar·aoh /ˈfar,ō, ˈfe(ə)r,ō, ˈfā,rō/ ▶ **n.** a ruler in ancient Egypt.

> SPELLING
> Remember, **-aoh**, not **-oah**: phar**aoh**.

Phar·i·see /ˈfarəsē/ ▶ **n.** a member of an ancient Jewish sect who followed religious laws very strictly.

phar·ma·ceu·ti·cal /,färməˈso͞otikəl/ ▶ **adj.** relating to medicinal drugs. ▶ **n.** a medicinal drug.

phar·ma·cist /ˈfärməsist/ ▶ **n.** a person who is qualified to prepare and dispense medicinal drugs.

phar·ma·col·o·gy /,färməˈkäləjē/ ▶ **n.** the branch of medicine concerned with drugs. ■ **phar·ma·co·log·i·cal** /-ˈläjikəl/ **adj. phar·ma·col·o·gist n.**

phar·ma·cy /ˈfärməsē/ ▶ **n.** (plural **pharmacies**) **1** a place where medicinal drugs are prepared or sold. **2** the science or practice of preparing and dispensing medicinal drugs.

phar·ynx /ˈfariNGks/ ▶ **n.** (plural **pharynges** /fəˈrinjēz/) the cavity connecting the nose and mouth to the throat.

phase /fāz/ ▶ **n.** a distinct period or stage in a process of change or development. ▶ **v.** (**phases**, **phasing**, **phased**) **1** carry something out in gradual stages. **2** (**phase something in** or **out**) gradually introduce or withdraw something.

> SYNONYMS ▶ **n. stage**, period, chapter, episode, part, step.

PhD ▶ **abbr.** Doctor of Philosophy.

pheas·ant /ˈfezənt/ ▶ **n.** a large long-tailed game bird.

phe·nom·e·nal /fəˈnämənəl/ ▶ **adj.** remarkable or outstanding.

> SYNONYMS **remarkable**, exceptional, extraordinary, marvelous, miraculous, wonderful, outstanding, unprecedented; informal fantastic, terrific, tremendous, stupendous.

■ **phe·nom·e·nal·ly adv.**

phe·nom·e·non /fəˈnämə,nän, -nən/ ▶ **n.** (plural **phenomena** /-nə/) **1** a fact or situation that is known to exist or happen. **2** a remarkable person or thing.

> SYNONYMS **1 occurrence**, event, happening, fact, situation, circumstance, experience, case, incident, episode. **2 marvel**, sensation, wonder, prodigy.

> USAGE
> The word **phenomenon** comes from Greek, and its plural form is **phenomena**. Don't use **phenomena** as a singular form: say *this is a strange phenomenon*, not *this is a strange phenomena*.

pher·o·mone /ˈferə,mōn/ ▶ **n.** a chemical substance released by an animal and causing a response in others of its species.

phi·al /ˈfīəl/ ▶ **n.** a small cylindrical glass bottle.

phi·lan·der·er /fəˈlandərər/ ▶ **n.** a man who has many casual sexual relationships with women.

> SYNONYMS **womanizer**, Casanova, Don Juan, Lothario, flirt, ladies' man, playboy; informal stud, ladykiller.

phil·an·throp·ic /,filənˈTHräpik/ ▶ **adj.** helping other people in need, especially by giving money to good causes.

> SYNONYMS **charitable**, generous, benevolent, humanitarian, public-spirited, altruistic, magnanimous, unselfish, kind. ANTONYMS selfish, mean.

■ **phi·lan·thro·pist** /fəˈlanTHrəpist/ **n. phi·lan·thro·py** /fəˈlanTHrəpē/ **n.**

phi·lat·e·ly /fəˈlatl-ē/ ▶ **n.** the hobby of collecting postage stamps. ■ **phi·lat·e·list n.**

phil·har·mon·ic /,filərˈmänik, ,filhär-/ ▶ **adj.** devoted to music (used in the names of orchestras).

phi·lip·pic /fə'lipik/ ▶ **n.** a verbal attack.

Phil·is·tine /'filəˌstēn, -ˌstīn/ ▶ **n. 1** a member of a people of ancient Palestine who fought with the Israelites. **2** (**philistine**) a person who is not interested in culture and the arts. ▶ **adj.** (**philistine**) not interested in culture and the arts.

> SYNONYMS ▶ **n. barbarian**, boor, yahoo, materialist. ▶ **adj. uncultured**, lowbrow, uncultivated, uncivilized, uneducated, unenlightened, commercial, materialist, bourgeois, ignorant, crass, boorish, barbarian.

■ **phil·is·tin·ism** /'filəstēˌnizəm, fə'listə-/ **n.**

Phil·lips /'filəps/ ▶ **adj.** trademark referring to a screw with a cross-shaped slot for turning, or a corresponding screwdriver.

phi·lol·o·gy /fə'läləjē/ ▶ **n.** the study of the structure and development of language and the relationships between languages. ■ **phil·o·log·i·cal** /ˌfilə'läjikəl/ **adj. phi·lol·o·gist n.**

phi·los·o·pher /fə'läsəfər/ ▶ **n. 1** a person who is engaged in philosophy. **2** a person who thinks deeply about things.

> SYNONYMS **thinker**, theorist, theoretician, scholar, intellectual, sage.

phil·o·soph·i·cal /ˌfilə'säfikəl/ ▶ **adj. 1** relating to the study of philosophy. **2** having a calm attitude when things are difficult.

> SYNONYMS **1 theoretical**, metaphysical. **2 thoughtful**, reflective, pensive, meditative, contemplative, introspective. **3 stoical**, self-possessed, serene, dispassionate, phlegmatic, long-suffering, resigned.

■ **phil·o·soph·i·cal·ly adv.**

phi·los·o·phize /fə'läsəˌfīz/ ▶ **v.** (**philosophizes**, **philosophizing**, **philosophized**) talk about serious issues, especially in a boring way.

phi·los·o·phy /fə'läsəfē/ ▶ **n.** (plural **philosophies**) **1** the study of the fundamental nature of knowledge, reality, and existence. **2** a set or system of beliefs.

> SYNONYMS **1 thinking**, thought, reasoning, logic. **2 beliefs**, credo, ideology, ideas, thinking, theories, doctrine, principles, views, outlook.

phish·ing /'fisʜiɴɢ/ ▶ **n.** a type of Internet fraud in which a person impersonates a legitimate company in order to persuade people to reveal personal information, such as credit card numbers.

phlegm /flem/ ▶ **n.** mucus in the nose and throat.

phleg·mat·ic /fleg'matik/ ▶ **adj.** calm and reasonable, and tending not to get upset.

phlo·em /'flōˌem/ ▶ **n.** Botany the tissue in plants that carries food materials downward from the leaves.

pho·bi·a /'fōbēə/ ▶ **n.** a strong irrational fear of something.

> SYNONYMS **fear**, dread, horror, terror, aversion, antipathy, revulsion; informal hang-up.

■ **pho·bic adj.**

Phoe·ni·cian /fə'nēsʜən/ ▶ **n.** a person from ancient Phoenicia in the eastern Mediterranean. ▶ **adj.** relating to Phoenicia.

phoe·nix /'fēniks/ ▶ **n.** (in classical mythology) a bird that lived for hundreds of years before burning itself to death and being born again from its ashes.

> SPELLING
> Write **-oe-**, not **-eo-**: phoenix.

phone /fōn/ ▶ **n.** a telephone. ▶ **v.** (**phones**, **phoning**, **phoned**) make a telephone call to someone.

> SYNONYMS ▶ **n. telephone**, cell phone, cellular phone, mobile phone, cordless phone; informal horn, blower. ▶ **v. call**, telephone, ring (up); informal call up, give someone a ring/buzz.

□ **phone card** a card allowing the user to make telephone calls. **phone-in** a radio or television program in which listeners or viewers participate over the telephone.

pho·net·ic /fə'netik/ ▶ **adj. 1** having to do with speech sounds. **2** (of a system of writing) using symbols that represent sounds. ▶ **n.** (**phonetics**) the study of speech sounds. ■ **pho·net·i·cal·ly adv.**

phon·ic /'fänik/ ▶ **adj.** relating to speech sounds. ▶ **n.** (**phonics**) a way of teaching people to read based on the sounds that letters represent.

pho·no·graph /'fōnəˌgraf/ ▶ **n.** a record player.

pho·ny /'fōnē/ (also **pho·ney**) informal ▶ **adj.** (**phonier**, **phoniest**) not genuine. ▶ **n.** (plural **phonies**) a person or thing that is not genuine.

> SYNONYMS ▶ **adj. bogus**, false, fake, fraudulent, counterfeit, forged, imitation, affected, insincere; informal pretend. ANTONYMS authentic. ▶ **n. 1 impostor**, sham, fake, fraud, charlatan; informal con artist. **2 fake**, imitation, counterfeit, forgery.

phoo·ey /'fo͞oē/ informal ▶ **exclam.** used to express disdain or disbelief. ▶ **n.** nonsense: *those excuses are a lot of phooey.*

phos·phate /'fäsfāt/ ▶ **n.** a salt or ester of phosphoric acid.

phos·pho·res·cence /ˌfäsfə'resəns/ ▶ **n.** a faint light that is given out by a substance with little or no heat. ■ **phos·pho·res·cent adj.**

phos·pho·rus /'fäsfərəs/ ▶ **n.** a yellowish waxy solid that can ignite spontaneously and that glows in the dark. ■ **phos·pho·rous adj.**

pho·to /'fōtō/ ▶ **n.** (plural **photos**) a photograph. □ **photo finish** a close finish of a race in which the winner can be identified only from a photograph of competitors crossing the line.

pho·to·cop·y /'fōtəˌkäpē/ ▶ **n.** (plural **photocopies**) a photographic copy of something produced by a process involving the action of light on a specially prepared surface. ▶ **v.** (**photocopies**, **photocopying**, **photocopied**) make a photocopy of.

> SYNONYMS ▶ **n. copy**, duplicate, reproduction, facsimile; trademark Xerox, photostat. ▶ **v. copy**, duplicate, xerox, photostat, reproduce.

■ **pho·to·cop·i·er** /'fōtəˌkäpēər/ **n.**

pho·to·e·lec·tric /ˌfōtōi'lektrik/ ▶ **adj.** involving the production of electrons as a result of the action of light on a surface.

pho·to·gen·ic /ˌfōtə'jenik/ ▶ **adj.** looking attractive in photographs.

pho·to·graph /'fōtəˌgraf/ ▶ **n.** a picture made with a camera. ▶ **v.** take a photograph of.

> SYNONYMS ▶ **n. picture**, photo, snap, snapshot, shot, print, still, transparency.

■ **pho·tog·ra·pher** /fə'tägrəfər/ **n.**

pho·to·graph·ic /ˌfōtəˈgrafik/ ▶ **adj. 1** relating to photographs or photography. **2** extremely detailed and accurate.

SYNONYMS **1 pictorial**, graphic, in photographs. **2 detailed**, exact, precise, accurate, vivid.

pho·tog·ra·phy /fəˈtägrəfē/ ▶ **n.** the taking and processing of photographs.

pho·to·jour·nal·ist /ˌfōtōˈjərnəlist/ ▶ **n.** a person who uses photographs to tell a news story.

pho·tom·e·ter /fōˈtämitər/ ▶ **n.** an instrument measuring the strength of light.

pho·ton /ˈfōtän/ ▶ **n.** a particle representing a quantum of light or other electromagnetic radiation.

pho·to·sen·si·tive /ˌfōtəˈsensitiv/ ▶ **adj.** responding to light.

pho·to·shop /ˈfōtōˌshäp/ ▶ **v.** (**photoshops**, **photoshopping**, **photoshopped**) alter a photograph digitally using computer software.

Pho·to·stat /ˈfōtōˌstat/ ▶ **n.** trademark **1** a type of machine for making photocopies on special paper. **2** a copy made by a photostat. ▶ **v.** (**photostats**, **photostatting**, **photostatted**) copy something with a photostat.

pho·to·syn·the·sis /ˌfōtōˈsinthəsis/ ▶ **n.** the process by which green plants use sunlight to form nutrients from carbon dioxide and water.

phrase /frāz/ ▶ **n. 1** a group of words forming a unit within a sentence. **2** Music a group of notes forming a unit within a longer passage. ▶ **v.** (**phrases**, **phrasing**, **phrased**) put an idea into a particular form of words.

SYNONYMS ▶ **n. expression**, construction, term, turn of phrase, idiom, saying. ▶ **v. express**, put into words, put, word, formulate, couch, frame.

□ **phrase book** a book listing and translating useful phrases in a foreign language. ■ **phras·al adj.**

phra·se·ol·o·gy /ˌfrāzēˈäləjē/ ▶ **n.** (plural **phraseologies**) a form of words used to express an idea.

phre·nol·o·gy /freˈnäləjē/ ▶ **n.** (mainly in the past) the study of the shape and size of the skull in the belief that this can indicate someone's character.

phyl·lo /ˈfēlō/ (or **filo**) ▶ **n.** a kind of dough that can be stretched into thin sheets and used in layers to make pastries, especially in eastern Mediterranean cooking.

phy·lum /ˈfīləm/ ▶ **n.** (plural **phyla** /-lə/) a category used in the classification of animals.

phys·i·cal /ˈfizikəl/ ▶ **adj. 1** relating to the body rather than the mind. **2** relating to things that you can see, hear, or feel. **3** involving bodily contact or activity. **4** relating to physics and natural forces such as heat, light, sound, etc. ▶ **n.** a medical examination to find out the state of someone's health.

SYNONYMS ▶ **adj. 1 bodily**, corporeal, corporal, carnal, fleshly, nonspiritual. **2 manual**, laboring, blue-collar. **3 material**, concrete, tangible, palpable, solid, substantial, real, actual, visible. ANTONYMS mental, spiritual.

□ **physical education** instruction in physical exercise, sports, and games. **physical therapy** the treatment of disease and injury by physical methods such as massage, heat treatment, and exercise. ■ **phys·i·cal·i·ty** /ˌfiziˈkalitē/ **n.** **phys·i·cal·ly adv.**

phy·si·cian /fiˈzishən/ ▶ **n.** a person qualified to practice medicine.

SYNONYMS **doctor**, medical practitioner, general practitioner, GP, clinician, specialist, consultant; informal doc, medic, quack.

phys·ics /ˈfiziks/ ▶ **n.** the branch of science concerned with the nature and properties of matter and energy. ■ **phys·i·cist n.**

phys·i·og·no·my /ˌfizēˈä(g)nəmē/ ▶ **n.** (plural **physiognomies**) a person's face or facial expression.

phys·i·ol·o·gy /ˌfizēˈäləjē/ ▶ **n.** the scientific study of the way in which living things function. ■ **phys·i·o·log·i·cal** /ˌfizēəˈläjikəl/ **adj.** **phys·i·ol·o·gist n.**

phy·sique /fiˈzēk/ ▶ **n.** the shape and size of a person's body.

SYNONYMS **body**, build, figure, frame, anatomy, shape, form, proportions; muscles, musculature; informal vital statistics, bod.

pi /pī/ ▶ **n.** the numerical value of the ratio of the circumference of a circle to its diameter (approximately 3.14159).

pi·a·nis·si·mo /ˌpēəˈnisiˌmō/ ▶ **adv. & adj.** Music very soft or softly.

pi·an·o[1] /pēˈanō/ ▶ **n.** (plural **pianos**) a musical instrument that you play by pressing black or white keys on a large keyboard, the sound being produced by small hammers hitting metal strings. ■ **pi·an·ist** /ˈpēənist, pēˈanist/ **n.**

pi·an·o[2] /pēˈänō, pēˈanō/ ▶ **adv. & adj.** Music soft or softly.

pi·an·o·forte /pēˌanōˈfôrtā, pēˈanōˌfôrt/ ▶ **n.** formal a piano.

pi·az·za /pēˈätsə, pēˈazə/ ▶ **n.** a public square or marketplace.

pic /pik/ ▶ **n.** informal a picture, photograph, or movie.

pi·ca·dor /ˈpikəˌdôr/ ▶ **n.** (in bullfighting) a person on horseback who goads the bull with a lance.

pic·a·resque /ˌpikəˈresk/ ▶ **adj.** (of fiction) dealing with the adventures of a dishonest but appealing hero.

pic·ca·lil·li /ˈpikəˌlilē/ ▶ **n.** a pickle of chopped vegetables, mustard, and hot spices.

pic·co·lo /ˈpikəˌlō/ ▶ **n.** (plural **piccolos**) a small flute sounding an octave higher than the ordinary flute.

pick[1] /pik/ ▶ **v. 1** choose from a number of alternatives. **2** (often **pick something up**) take hold of something and lift or move it. **3** remove a flower or fruit from where it is growing. ▶ **n. 1** an act of choosing something. **2** (**the pick of**) the best person or thing in a particular group.

SYNONYMS ▶ **v. 1 harvest**, gather (in), collect, pluck. **2 choose**, select, single out, opt for, elect, decide on, settle on, fix on, name, nominate, identify. **3** *pick a fight* **provoke**, start, cause, incite, instigate, prompt. ▶ **n. best**, finest, choice, choicest, cream, flower, crème de la crème, elite.

□ **pick at 1** repeatedly pull at something with your fingers. **2** eat food in small amounts. **pick a fight** provoke an argument or fight. **pick holes in** criticize. **pick a lock** open a lock with something other than the proper key. **pick-me-up** informal a thing that makes someone feel more energetic or cheerful. **pick on** single someone out for unfair treatment. **pick someone's pockets** steal something from a person's pocket. **pick up** improve or increase. **pick someone/something up 1** go to collect someone. **2** informal flirtatiously start talking to a stranger with the aim of having a casual romantic relationship with them. **3** detect or receive a signal or sound. **4** obtain or learn something.

pick² ▶ **n. 1** (also **pickax**) a tool consisting of a curved iron bar with pointed ends and a wooden handle, used for breaking up hard ground or rock. **2** a plectrum.

pick·er /ˈpikər/ ▶ **n. 1** a person or machine that gathers or collects something: *a tomato picker*. **2** a person who plays an instrument such as a guitar, banjo, or mandolin.

pick·et /ˈpikit/ ▶ **n. 1** a group of people standing outside a workplace and trying to persuade others not to work during a strike. **2** a pointed wooden stake driven into the ground. ▶ **v.** (**pickets, picketing, picketed**) act as a picket outside a workplace.

> SYNONYMS ▶ **n. 1 demonstrator**, striker, protester. **2 demonstration**, picket line, blockade, boycott, strike.

pick·ings /ˈpikiNGz/ ▶ **pl.n. 1** profits or gains. **2** scraps or leftovers.

pick·le /ˈpikəl/ ▶ **n. 1** a small cucumber preserved in vinegar, salt water, or a similar solution. **2** any preserve of vegetables or fruit in vinegar or salt water, used as a relish. **3** (**a pickle**) informal a difficult situation. ▶ **v.** (**pickles, pickling, pickled**) preserve food in vinegar or salt water.

pick·pock·et /ˈpikˌpäkət/ ▶ **n.** a person who steals from people's pockets.

pick·up /ˈpikˌəp/ ▶ **n. 1** a small truck with low sides. **2** the part of a record player that holds the stylus. **3** a device on an electric guitar that converts sound vibration into electrical signals for amplification.

> SYNONYMS **improvement**, recovery, revival, upturn, upswing, rally, resurgence, renewal, turnaround.

pick·y /ˈpikē/ ▶ **adj.** informal fussy.

pic·nic /ˈpikˌnik/ ▶ **n.** a meal that is eaten outdoors and away from home. ▶ **v.** (**picnics, picnicking, picnicked**) have a picnic. ■ **pic·nick·er n.**

Pict /pikt/ ▶ **n.** a member of an ancient people inhabiting northern Scotland in Roman times.

pic·to·graph /ˈpiktəˌgraf/ (or **pictogram** /-ˌgram/) ▶ **n.** a small image or picture representing a word or phrase.

pic·to·ri·al /pikˈtôrēəl/ ▶ **adj.** having to do with or expressed in pictures.

pic·ture /ˈpikCHər/ ▶ **n. 1** a painting, drawing, or photograph. **2** an image on a television screen. **3** a movie. **4** (**the pictures**) the movies. **5** an image formed in the mind. ▶ **v.** (**pictures, picturing, pictured**) **1** represent in a picture. **2** form an image of something in your mind.

> SYNONYMS ▶ **n. 1 painting, drawing**, sketch, watercolor, print, canvas, portrait, illustration, depiction, likeness, representation, image. **2 photograph**, photo, snap, snapshot, shot, frame, exposure, still, print. **3 concept**, idea, impression, image, vision, visualization, notion. **4 personification**, embodiment, epitome, essence, quintessence, soul, model. ▶ **v. 1 depict**, portray, show, represent, draw, sketch, photograph, paint. **2 visualize**, see (in your mind's eye), imagine, remember.

□ **picture window** a large window consisting of a single pane of glass.

pic·tur·esque /ˌpikCHəˈresk/ ▶ **adj.** (of a place) very pleasant to look at.

> SYNONYMS **attractive**, pretty, beautiful, lovely, scenic, charming, quaint, pleasing, delightful. ANTONYMS ugly.

pid·dle /ˈpidl/ ▶ **v.** (**piddles, piddling, piddled**) informal **1** urinate. **2** (**piddling**) very unimportant or trivial.

> SYNONYMS (**piddling**) **trivial**, trifling, petty, meager, inadequate, insufficient, paltry, derisory, pitiful, miserable, puny, niggardly, mere, tiny, insignificant, unimportant, inconsequential; informal measly, pathetic, piffling, nickel-and-dime, mingy.

pidg·in /ˈpijən/ ▶ **n.** a simple form of a language with elements taken from local languages.

pie /pī/ ▶ **n.** a baked dish of meat, vegetables, fruit, etc., inside a pastry case. □ **pie chart** a diagram in which a circle is divided into segments to show the size of particular amounts in relation to the whole.

pie·bald /ˈpīˌbôld/ ▶ **adj.** (of a horse) having irregular patches of two colors.

piece /pēs/ ▶ **n. 1** a portion that is separated or seen separately from the whole. **2** an item used in building something or forming part of a set. **3** a musical or written work. **4** a token used to make moves in a board game. **5** a coin of a particular value. ▶ **v.** (**pieces, piecing, pieced**) (**piece something together**) assemble something from individual parts.

> SYNONYMS ▶ **n. 1 bit**, slice, chunk, segment, section, lump, hunk, wedge, slab, block, cake, bar, stick, length. **2 component**, part, bit, constituent, element, section, unit, module. **3 item**, article, specimen. **4 share**, portion, slice, quota, part, percentage, amount, quantity, ration, fraction. **5 work** (**of art**), artwork, artifact, composition, opus. **6 article**, item, story, report, essay, feature, review, column.

pièce de ré·sis·tance /pēˈes də ˌrəziˈstäns, -rāziˈstäNs/ ▶ **n.** the most important or impressive part of something.

piece·meal /ˈpēsˌmēl/ ▶ **adj. & adv.** done in stages over a period of time.

piece·work /ˈpēsˌwərk/ ▶ **n.** work that is paid for by the amount done and not the hours worked.

pied /pīd/ ▶ **adj.** having two or more different colors.

pied-à-terre /pēˌyād ə ˈter/ ▶ **n.** (plural **pieds-à-terre**) a small apartment or house kept for occasional use.

pier /pi(ə)r/ ▶ **n. 1** a structure leading out to sea or into a lake, used as a landing stage for boats. **2** a pillar supporting an arch or bridge.

> SYNONYMS **jetty**, quay, wharf, dock, landing stage.

pierce /pi(ə)rs/ ▶ **v.** (**pierces, piercing, pierced**) **1** make a hole in something with a sharp object. **2** force or cut a way through. **3** (**piercing**) very sharp, cold, or high-pitched. **4** (**piercing**) (of eyes or a look) appearing to see through someone; searching. **5** (**piercing**) (of the wind) very cold.

> SYNONYMS **1 penetrate**, puncture, perforate, prick, spike, stab, drill, bore. **2** (**piercing**) **shrill**, ear-splitting, high-pitched, penetrating,

strident. **3** (**piercing**) **searching**, probing, penetrating, sharp, keen, shrewd.

pi·e·ty /ˈpī-itē/ ▸ n. (plural **pieties**) the quality of being religious in a respectful and serious way.

SYNONYMS **devoutness**, devotion, piousness, holiness, godliness, reverence, faith, spirituality.

pif·fle /ˈpifəl/ ▸ n. informal nonsense.

pig /pig/ ▸ n. **1** an animal with a short, curly tail and a flat snout. **2** informal a greedy, dirty, or unpleasant person. ▸ v. (**pigs**, **pigging**, **pigged**) informal eat too much food.

SYNONYMS ▸ n. **hog**, boar, sow, porker, swine, piglet.

□ **a pig in a poke** something that is bought or accepted without first being seen. **pig iron** iron when it is first taken out of a smelting furnace. ■ **pig·gish** adj.

pi·geon /ˈpijən/ ▸ n. a plump gray and white bird with a cooing voice. □ **pigeon-toed** having the toes and feet turned inward.

SPELLING

Note that there is no **d**: pi**g**eon.

pi·geon·hole /ˈpijənˌhōl/ ▸ n. **1** a small hole in a wall leading into a place where pigeons nest. **2** each of a set of small compartments in a workplace, college, etc., where letters or messages may be left for individuals. **3** a category in which someone or something is put. ▸ v. (**pigeonholes**, **pigeonholing**, **pigeonholed**) put into a particular category.

pig·ger·y /ˈpigərē/ ▸ n. (plural **piggeries**) a place where pigs are kept.

pig·gy /ˈpigē/ ▸ n. (plural **piggies**) a child's word for a pig or piglet. ▸ adj. like a pig. □ **piggy bank** a money box shaped like a pig.

pig·gy·back /ˈpigēˌbak/ ▸ n. a ride on someone's back and shoulders. ▸ adv. on the back and shoulders of another person.

pig·head·ed /ˈpigˌhedid/ ▸ adj. stupidly stubborn.

pig·let /ˈpiglit/ ▸ n. a young pig.

pig·ment /ˈpigmənt/ ▸ n. **1** the substance that gives natural coloring to animal or plant tissue. **2** a colored powder mixed with a liquid to make paints, crayons, etc.

SYNONYMS **coloring**, color, tint, dye, stain.

■ **pig·men·ta·tion** /ˌpigmənˈtāsʜən/ n. **pig·ment·ed** /ˈpigməntid, ˌpigˈməntid/ adj.

pig·my = PYGMY.

pig·skin /ˈpigˌskin/ ▸ n. **1** leather made from the hide of a pig. **2** informal a football.

pig·sty /ˈpigˌstī/ ▸ n. (plural **pigsties**) (or **pigpen** /ˈpigˌpen/) **1** an enclosure for a pig or pigs. **2** a very dirty or untidy place.

pig·tail /ˈpigˌtāl/ ▸ n. a length of hair worn in a braid at the back or on each side of the head.

pike¹ /pīk/ ▸ n. (plural **pike**) a freshwater fish with a long body and sharp teeth.

pike² ▸ n. (in the past) a weapon with a pointed metal head on a long wooden shaft.

pi·las·ter /pəˈlastər/ ▸ n. a column that projects from a wall.

Pi·la·tes /piˈlätēz/ ▸ n. a system of exercises designed to improve physical strength, flexibility, and posture.

pil·chard /ˈpilcʜərd/ ▸ n. a small fish of the herring family.

pile¹ /pīl/ ▸ n. **1** a heap of things lying one on top of another. **2** informal a large amount. **3** a large and impressive building. ▸ v. (**piles**, **piling**, **piled**) **1** place things one on top of the other. **2** (**pile up**) form a pile or very large quantity. **3** (**pile into** or **out of**) get into or out of a vehicle in a disorganized way.

SYNONYMS ▸ n. **1 heap**, stack, mound, pyramid, mass, collection, accumulation, assemblage, stockpile, hoard. **2 lot**, mountain, reams, abundance; informal load, heap, mass, slew, stack, ton, oodles. ▸ v. **1 heap**, stack, load, fill, charge. **2 crowd**, clamber, pack, squeeze, scramble, struggle.

pile² ▸ n. the soft surface of a carpet or a fabric, consisting of the cut ends of many small threads.

SYNONYMS **nap**, fibers, threads.

pile³ ▸ n. a heavy post driven into the ground to support foundations.

pile·driv·er /ˈpīlˌdrīvər/ ▸ n. a machine for driving piles into the ground.

piles /pīlz/ ▸ pl.n. hemorrhoids.

pile·up /ˈpīlˌəp/ ▸ n. informal a crash involving several vehicles.

SYNONYMS **crash**, collision, accident, wreck, smash.

pil·fer /ˈpilfər/ ▸ v. (**pilfers**, **pilfering**, **pilfered**) steal small items of little value.

pil·grim /ˈpilgrəm/ ▸ n. **1** a person who travels to a sacred place for religious reasons. **2** (**Pilgrim**) a member of a group of English Puritans fleeing religious persecution who sailed in the *Mayflower* and founded the colony of Plymouth, Massachusetts, in 1620.

SYNONYMS **traveler**, wayfarer, haji, worshiper, devotee, believer.

pil·grim·age /ˈpilgrəmij/ ▸ n. a pilgrim's journey.

SYNONYMS **journey**, expedition, mission, hajj, visit, trek, trip, odyssey.

pill /pil/ ▸ n. a small round mass of solid medicine for swallowing whole.

SYNONYMS **tablet**, capsule, pellet, lozenge, pastille.

pil·lage /ˈpilij/ ▸ v. (**pillages**, **pillaging**, **pillaged**) steal from a place in a rough and violent way. ▸ n. the action of pillaging.

SYNONYMS ▸ v. **1** *the abbey was pillaged* **ransack**, rob, plunder, raid, sack, devastate, lay waste, ravage, loot. **2** *columns pillaged from an ancient tomb* **steal**, pilfer, take, purloin, loot; informal swipe, rob, nab, rip off, heist, lift, liberate, borrow, filch.

pil·lar /ˈpilər/ ▸ n. **1** a tall upright structure used as a support for a building. **2** a source of help and support.

SYNONYMS **1 column**, post, support, upright, pier, pile, prop, stanchion, obelisk. **2 stalwart**, mainstay, bastion, leading light, worthy, backbone, supporter, upholder, champion.

□ **from pillar to post** from one place to another without achieving anything.

pill·box /ˈpilˌbäks/ ▶ **n.** **1** a small round hat with a flat top and no brim. **2** a small concrete fort.

pil·lion /ˈpilyən/ ▶ **n.** a seat for a passenger behind a motorcyclist.

pil·lo·ry /ˈpilərē/ ▶ **n.** (plural **pillories**) (in the past) a wooden framework with holes for the head and hands, in which people were locked and left on display as a punishment. ▶ **v.** (**pillories**, **pillorying**, **pilloried**) criticize or ridicule someone publicly.

pil·low /ˈpilō/ ▶ **n.** a soft pad used to support the head when you lie down in bed.

pil·low·case /ˈpilōˌkās/ ▶ **n.** a removable cloth cover for a pillow.

pi·lot /ˈpīlət/ ▶ **n.** **1** a person who flies an aircraft. **2** a person qualified to take charge of a ship entering or leaving a harbor. **3** something done or produced as a test before being introduced more widely. ▶ **v.** (**pilots**, **piloting**, **piloted**) **1** act as a pilot of an aircraft or ship. **2** test a plan, project, etc., before introducing it more widely.

> SYNONYMS ▶ **n.** **1 airman**, **airwoman**, flyer, aviator, captain; informal skipper; dated aviatrix. **2 navigator**, helmsman, steersman, coxswain. **3 trial**, sample, experiment, test. **4** *a pilot study* **trial**, sample, experimental, exploratory, test, preliminary. ▶ **v.** **navigate**, guide, maneuver, steer, control, direct, captain, fly, drive, sail; informal skipper.

□ **pilot light** a small gas burner that is kept alight permanently, used to light a larger burner when necessary, especially on a stove or water heater.

pi·men·to /pəˈmentō/ (or **pimiento** /pəˈmyentō/) ▶ **n.** (plural **pimentos**) a sweet red pepper.

pim·ple /ˈpimpəl/ ▶ **n.** a small inflamed lump on the skin. ■ **pim·ply adj.**

PIN /pin/ (or **PIN number**) ▶ **abbr.** personal identification number.

pin /pin/ ▶ **n.** **1** a very thin pointed piece of metal with a round head, used to hold pieces of fabric together or as a fastener. **2** a metal projection from an electric plug or an integrated circuit that makes an electrical connection with a socket or another part of a circuit. **3** a small brooch. **4** a steel rod used to join the ends of broken bones while they heal. **5** a metal peg in a hand grenade that prevents it exploding. **6** (in bowling) one of a set of bottle-shaped wooden pieces that are arranged in an upright position at the end of a lane in order to be toppled by a rolling ball. **7** (**pins**) informal legs. ▶ **v.** (**pins**, **pinning**, **pinned**) **1** attach or fasten with a pin or pins. **2** hold someone firmly so they are unable to move. **3** (**pin someone down**) force someone to be specific about their plans. **4** (**pin someone down**) trap an enemy by firing at them. **5** (**pin something on**) fix blame or responsibility on.

> SYNONYMS ▶ **n.** **1 tack**, safety pin, nail, staple, fastener. **2 bolt**, peg, rod, rivet, dowel. **3 badge**, brooch. ▶ **v.** **1 attach**, fasten, affix, fix, join, secure, clip, nail. **2 hold**, press, pinion.

□ **pin money** a small sum of money for spending on everyday items. **pins and needles** a tingling sensation in a part of the body that is recovering from numbness. **pin your hopes** (or **faith**) **on** rely heavily on.

pin·a·fore /ˈpinəˌfôr/ ▶ **n.** **1** a sleeveless apronlike garment worn over a child's dress. **2** a collarless, sleeveless dress worn over a blouse or sweater.

pin·ball /ˈpinˌbôl/ ▶ **n.** a game in which balls are shot across a sloping board to score points by hitting targets.

pince-nez /ˈpansˌnā, ˈpins-/ ▶ **n.** a pair of glasses kept in place with a nose clip instead of parts that rest on the ears.

pin·cer /ˈpinsər/ ▶ **n.** **1** (**pincers**) a metal tool with blunt inward-curving jaws for gripping and pulling things. **2** a front claw of a lobster or similar shellfish.

pinch /pinCH/ ▶ **v.** **1** grip flesh tightly between your finger and thumb. **2** (of a shoe) hurt a foot by being too tight. **3** informal steal. ▶ **n.** **1** an act of pinching. **2** an amount of an ingredient that can be held between your fingers and thumb.

> SYNONYMS ▶ **v.** **nip**, tweak, squeeze, grasp, compress. ▶ **n.** **1 nip**, tweak, squeeze. **2 bit**, touch, dash, spot, trace, soupçon, speck, taste; informal smidgen, tad.

□ **in a pinch** if absolutely necessary. **feel the pinch** experience financial hardship. **pinch-hit 1** Baseball bat in place of another player, typically at a critical point in the game. **2** informal act as a substitute for someone, especially in an emergency.

pinched /pinCHt/ ▶ **adj.** (of a person's face) tight with cold or suffering.

pin·cush·ion /ˈpinˌko͝oSHən/ ▶ **n.** a small pad into which you stick pins to store them.

pine¹ /pīn/ ▶ **n.** an evergreen tree that produces cones and has clusters of long needle-shaped leaves. □ **pine nut** the edible seed of various pines. **pine marten** an arboreal weasel.

pine² ▶ **v.** (**pines**, **pining**, **pined**) **1** become very sad or weak because you miss someone so much. **2** (**pine for**) miss or long for.

> SYNONYMS **fade**, waste away, weaken, decline, languish, wilt, sicken.

pine·ap·ple /ˈpīˌnapəl/ ▶ **n.** a large juicy tropical fruit consisting of yellow flesh surrounded by a tough skin.

ping /piNG/ ▶ **n.** a short high-pitched ringing sound. ▶ **v.** make such a sound. □ **ping-pong** (also trademark **Ping-Pong**) informal table tennis.

pin·ion¹ /ˈpinyən/ ▶ **v.** tie or hold someone's arms or legs so that they cannot move. ▶ **n.** the outer part of a bird's wing.

pin·ion² ▶ **n.** a small cogwheel or spindle that engages with a large cogwheel.

pink¹ /piNGk/ ▶ **adj.** of a color midway between red and white. ▶ **n.** a pink color.

> SYNONYMS ▶ **adj.** **rose**, rosy, rosé, pale red, salmon, coral, flushed, blushing.

□ **in the pink** informal in the best condition. **pink slip** informal a notice of dismissal from employment.

pink² ▶ **n.** a herbaceous plant with sweet-smelling pink or white flowers.

pink·ing shears /ˈpiNGkiNG/ ▶ **pl.n.** scissors with a thick serrated blade, used for cutting a zigzag edge on fabric to prevent it fraying.

pink·o /ˈpiNGkō/ ▶ **n.** (plural **pinkos** or **pinkoes**) informal, disapproving a left-wing or liberal person.

pink·y /ˈpiNGkē/ (or **pinkie**) ▶ **n.** informal the little finger.

pin·na·cle /ˈpinəkəl/ ▶ **n.** **1** the most successful point. **2** a high pointed piece of rock. **3** a small pointed turret on a roof.

> SYNONYMS **1 height**, peak, high point, top, apex, zenith, acme. **2 peak**, needle, crag, tor. ANTONYMS nadir.

pi·ñon /ˈpinyən, ˌpinˈyōn/ (also **pi·nyon**) ▶ **n. 1** a small pine tree with edible seeds, native to Mexico and the southwestern US. **2** a pine nut from this tree.

pin·point /ˈpinˌpoint/ ▶ **v.** locate or identify something precisely. ▶ **adj.** absolutely precise. ▶ **n.** a tiny dot.

> SYNONYMS ▶ **v. identify**, determine, distinguish, discover, find, locate, detect, track down, spot, diagnose, recognize, pin down, home in on. ▶ **adj.** *pinpoint accuracy* **precise**, exact, strict, absolute, complete, scientific.

pin·prick /ˈpinˌprik/ ▶ **n.** a very small dot or amount.

pin·stripe /ˈpinˌstrīp/ ▶ **n.** a very narrow stripe woven into fabric of a contrasting color.
■ **pin·striped adj.**

pint /pīnt/ ▶ **n.** a unit of liquid capacity equal to one half of a quart. □ **pint-sized** (or **pint-size**) informal very small.

pin·to /ˈpintō/ ▶ **n.** (plural **pintos**) a piebald horse. □ **pinto bean** a medium-sized speckled variety of kidney bean.

pin·up /ˈpinˌəp/ ▶ **n. 1** a poster of an attractive person. **2** the person shown on such a poster.

pin·wale /ˈpinˌwāl/ ▶ **n.** a lightweight corduroy fabric with narrow ridges.

pin·wheel /ˈpinˌ(h)wēl/ ▶ **n. 1** a child's toy consisting of a stick with colored vanes that twirl in the wind. **2** a fireworks device that whirls and emits colored fire.

pi·o·neer /ˌpīəˈni(ə)r/ ▶ **n. 1** a person who explores or settles in a new region. **2** a developer of new ideas or techniques. ▶ **v.** (**pioneers**, **pioneering**, **pioneered**) be a pioneer of a new idea or technique.

> SYNONYMS ▶ **n. 1 settler**, colonist, colonizer, frontiersman, explorer. **2 developer**, innovator, trailblazer, groundbreaker, founding father, architect, creator. ▶ **v. introduce**, develop, launch, instigate, initiate, spearhead, institute, establish, found.

pi·ous /ˈpīəs/ ▶ **adj. 1** religious in a very respectful and serious way. **2** pretending to be moral and good in order to impress other people. **3** (of a hope) very much wanted, but unlikely to be achieved.

> SYNONYMS **religious**, devout, God-fearing, churchgoing, holy, godly, saintly, reverent, righteous. ANTONYMS irreligious.

■ **pi·ous·ly adv.**

pip¹ /pip/ ▶ **n. 1** a small hard seed in a fruit. **2** informal an excellent or very attractive person or thing.

pip² ▶ **n.** any of the spots on a playing card, dice, or domino.

pipe /pīp/ ▶ **n. 1** a tube through which water, gas, oil, etc., can flow. **2** a device for smoking tobacco, consisting of a narrow tube that opens into a small bowl in which the tobacco is burned. **3** a wind instrument consisting of a single tube with holes along its length that you cover with your fingers to produce different notes. **4** each of the tubes by which notes are produced in an organ. **5** (**pipes**) bagpipes. ▶ **v.** (**pipes**, **piping**, **piped**) **1** send a liquid through a pipe. **2** transmit music, a program, a signal, etc., by wire or cable. **3** play a tune on a pipe. **4** sing or say something in a high voice. **5** decorate something with piping.

> SYNONYMS ▶ **n. tube**, conduit, hose, main, duct, line, channel, pipeline, drain. ▶ **v. feed**, siphon, channel, run, convey.

□ **piped-in music** prerecorded background music played through loudspeakers. **pipe dream** a hope or plan that is impossible to achieve. **pipe down** informal be less noisy. **pipe up** informal say something suddenly.

pipe·line /ˈpīpˌlīn/ ▶ **n.** a long pipe for carrying oil, gas, etc., over a distance. □ **in the pipeline** in the process of being developed.

pip·er /ˈpīpər/ ▶ **n.** a person who plays a pipe or bagpipes.

pi·pette /pīˈpet/ ▶ **n.** a thin tube used in a laboratory for transferring small quantities of liquid.

pip·ing /ˈpīpiNG/ ▶ **n. 1** lengths of pipe. **2** lines of icing or cream used to decorate cakes and desserts. **3** thin cord covered in fabric and used for decorating a garment or the fabric covering a piece of furniture. □ **piping hot** (of food or water) very hot.

pip·i·strelle /ˌpipəˈstrel, ˈpipəˌstrel/ ▶ **n.** a small insect-eating bat.

pip·it /ˈpipit/ ▶ **n.** a bird that lives on the ground in open country.

pip·pin /ˈpipin/ ▶ **n.** a sweet red and yellow apple.

pip·squeak /ˈpipˌskwēk/ ▶ **n.** informal a person considered unimportant, especially because they are small or young.

pi·quant /ˈpēkənt, -känt/ ▶ **adj.** having a pleasantly strong and sharp taste.

> SYNONYMS **1** *a piquant sauce* **spicy**, tangy, peppery, hot, tasty, flavorsome, savory, pungent, sharp, tart, zesty, strong, salty. **2** *a piquant story* **intriguing**, stimulating, interesting, fascinating, colorful, exciting, lively, spicy, provocative, racy; informal juicy. ANTONYMS bland, dull.

■ **pi·quan·cy** /ˈpēkənsē/ **n. pi·quant·ly adv.**

pique /pēk/ ▶ **n.** a feeling of irritation mixed with hurt pride. ▶ **v.** (**piques**, **piquing**, **piqued**) **1** (**be piqued**) feel both irritated and hurt. **2** stimulate someone's interest.

> SYNONYMS ▶ **n. irritation**, annoyance, resentment, anger, displeasure, indignation, petulance, ill humor, vexation, exasperation, disgruntlement, discontent. ▶ **v. 1** *his curiosity was piqued* **stimulate**, arouse, rouse, provoke, whet, awaken, excite, kindle, stir, galvanize. **2** *she was piqued by his neglect* **irritate**, annoy, bother, vex, displease, upset, offend, affront, anger, gall, irk, nettle; informal peeve, aggravate, miff, rile, tick off, tee off, bug, needle, get someone's back up, get someone's goat.

pi·ra·cy /ˈpīrəsē/ ▶ **n. 1** the attacking and robbing of ships at sea. **2** the reproduction of a movie or recording without permission and so as to make a profit.

pi·ra·nha /pəˈränə/ ▶ **n.** a freshwater fish with very sharp teeth.

pi·rate /ˈpīrət/ ▶ **n.** a person who attacks and robs ships at sea. ▶ **adj. 1** (of a movie or recording) having been reproduced and used for profit without permission. **2** (of an organization) broadcasting without permission. ▶ **v.** (**pirates**, **pirating**, **pirated**) reproduce a movie or recording for profit without permission.

SYNONYMS ▶ **n.** **raider**, hijacker, freebooter, marauder; historical privateer, buccaneer; old use corsair. ▶ **v.** **steal**, copy, plagiarize, poach, appropriate, bootleg; informal crib, lift, rip off.

pir·ou·ette /ˌpiro͞oˈet/ ▶ **n.** a movement in ballet involving spinning on one foot. ▶ **v.** (**pirouettes**, **pirouetting**, **pirouetted**) perform a pirouette.

pis·ca·to·ri·al /ˌpiskəˈtôrēəl/ ▶ **adj.** having to do with fish.

Pis·ces /ˈpīsēz, ˈpisēz/ ▶ **n.** a sign of the zodiac (the Fish or Fishes), February 21–March 19.

pis·tach·i·o /pəˈstasHēˌō/ ▶ **n.** (plural **pistachios**) a small pale green nut.

piste /pēst/ ▶ **n.** a course or run for skiing.

pis·til /ˈpistl/ ▶ **n.** Botany the female organs of a flower (the stigma, style, and ovary).

pis·tol /ˈpistl/ ▶ **n.** a small gun designed to be held in one hand.

SYNONYMS **handgun**, gun, revolver, sidearm; six-shooter; informal piece, gat, rod, shooting iron, derringer, Saturday night special.

pis·ton /ˈpistn/ ▶ **n.** a sliding disk or cylinder fitting closely inside a tube in which it moves up and down as part of an engine or pump.

pit¹ /pit/ ▶ **n.** **1** a large hole in the ground. **2** a mine for coal, chalk, etc. **3** a hollow in a surface. **4** a sunken area in a workshop floor where people can work on the underside of vehicles. **5** an area at the side of a track where racing cars are serviced and refueled. **6** a part of a theater where the orchestra plays. **7** (**the pits**) informal a very bad place or situation. ▶ **v.** (**pits**, **pitting**, **pitted**) **1** (**pit someone/thing against**) test someone or something in a contest with. **2** make a hollow in the surface of something.

SYNONYMS ▶ **n.** **1** **hole**, trough, hollow, excavation, cavity, crater, pothole. **2** **coal mine**, colliery, quarry, shaft. ▶ **v.** **mark**, pockmark, pock, scar, dent, indent.

□ **pit bull (terrier)** a fierce breed of bull terrier. **the pit of the stomach** an area low down in the stomach.

pit² ▶ **n.** the stone of a fruit. ▶ **v.** (**pits**, **pitting**, **pitted**) remove the pit from a fruit.

pi·ta /ˈpētə/ ▶ **n.** a type of flat bread that can be split to form a pocket and then filled.

pitch¹ /picH/ ▶ **n.** **1** the action of throwing something. **2** Baseball the throw made by a pitcher to a batter. **3** the degree of highness or lowness in a sound or tone. **4** a particular level of intensity. **5** a form of words used when trying to sell something: *a sales pitch*. **6** the steepness of a roof. ▶ **v.** **1** throw heavily or roughly. **2** throw a baseball to a batter. **3** set your voice, a sound, or a piece of music at a particular pitch. **4** aim something at a particular level, target, or audience. **5** set up a tent or camp. **6** (**pitch in**) informal join in enthusiastically with an activity. **7** (of a moving ship, aircraft, or vehicle) rock up and down. **8** (**pitched**) (of a roof) sloping.

SYNONYMS ▶ **n.** **1** **tone**, key, modulation, frequency. **2** **gradient**, grade, slope, slant, angle, tilt, incline. **3** **level**, intensity, point, degree, height, extent. **4** **patter**, talk; informal spiel, line. ▶ **v.** **1** **throw**, toss, fling, hurl, cast, lob, flip; informal chuck, sling, heave. **2** **fall**, tumble, topple, plunge, plummet. **3** **put up**, set up, erect, raise. **4** **lurch**, toss, plunge, roll, reel, sway, rock, list.

□ **pitched battle** a battle in which the time and place are decided beforehand.

pitch² ▶ **n.** a sticky black substance made from tar or turpentine and used for waterproofing. □ **pitch-black** (or **pitch-dark**) completely dark. **pitch pine** a pine tree that yields pitch or turpentine.

pitch·er¹ /ˈpicHər/ ▶ **n.** a large jug.

pitch·er² ▶ **n.** Baseball the player who throws the ball to the batter.

pitch·fork /ˈpicHˌfôrk/ ▶ **n.** a farm tool with a long handle and two sharp metal prongs, used for lifting hay.

pit·e·ous /ˈpitēəs/ ▶ **adj.** deserving or arousing pity. ■ **pit·e·ous·ly** **adv.**

pit·fall /ˈpitˌfôl/ ▶ **n.** a hidden danger or difficulty.

SYNONYMS **hazard**, danger, risk, peril, difficulty, catch, snag, stumbling block, drawback.

pith /piTH/ ▶ **n.** **1** spongy white tissue lining the rind of citrus fruits. **2** spongy tissue in the stems of many plants. **3** the most important part of something. □ **pith helmet** a lightweight hat made from the dried pith of a plant, used for protection from the sun.

pith·y /ˈpiTHē/ ▶ **adj.** (**pithier**, **pithiest**) (of language) concise and clear.

SYNONYMS **succinct**, terse, concise, compact, short (and sweet), brief, condensed, to the point, epigrammatic, crisp, significant, meaningful, telling. ANTONYMS verbose.

pit·i·a·ble /ˈpitēəbəl/ ▶ **adj.** **1** deserving or arousing pity. **2** deserving contempt.

pit·i·ful /ˈpitifəl/ ▶ **adj.** **1** deserving or arousing pity. **2** very small or inadequate.

SYNONYMS **1** **distressing**, sad, piteous, pitiable, pathetic, heart-rending, moving, touching, tear-jerking, plaintive, poignant, forlorn, poor, sorry, wretched, miserable. **2** **paltry**, miserable, meager, trifling, negligible, pitiable, derisory; informal pathetic, measly. **3** **dreadful**, awful, terrible, appalling, lamentable, hopeless, feeble, pitiable, woeful, inadequate, deplorable, laughable; informal pathetic, useless, lousy, abysmal, dire.

■ **pit·i·ful·ly** **adv.**

pit·i·less /ˈpitēlis/ ▶ **adj.** showing no pity.

SYNONYMS **merciless**, unmerciful, ruthless, cruel, heartless, remorseless, hard-hearted, cold-hearted, harsh, callous, severe, unsparing, unforgiving, unfeeling, uncaring, unsympathetic, uncharitable. ANTONYMS merciful.

pi·ton /ˈpētän/ ▶ **n.** (in rock climbing) a peg or spike driven into a crack to support a climber or hold a rope.

pit·tance /ˈpitns/ ▶ **n.** a very small or inadequate amount of money.

pit·ter-pat·ter /ˈpitər ˈpatər/ ▶ **n.** the sound of quick light steps or taps.

pi·tu·i·tar·y gland /pəˈt(y)o͞oəˌterē/ ▶ **n.** a gland at the base of the brain that controls growth and development.

pit·y /ˈpitē/ ▶ **n.** (plural **pities**) **1** a feeling of sympathy and sadness caused by the suffering of other people. **2** a cause for regret or disappointment. ▶ **v.** (**pities**, **pitying**, **pitied**) feel pity for.

SYNONYMS ▶ n. 1 **compassion**, commiseration, condolence, sympathy, fellow feeling, understanding. 2 *it's a pity you can't go* **shame**, misfortune. ANTONYMS indifference. ▶ v. **feel sorry for**, feel for, sympathize with, empathize with, commiserate with, take pity on, be moved by, bleed for.

piv·ot /ˈpivət/ ▶ n. the central point, pin, or shaft on which a mechanism turns or is balanced. ▶ v. (**pivots**, **pivoting**, **pivoted**) 1 turn on or as if on a pivot. 2 (**pivot on**) depend on.

SYNONYMS ▶ n. **fulcrum**, axis, axle, swivel, pin, shaft, hub, spindle, hinge, kingpin. ▶ v. 1 **rotate**, turn, swivel, revolve, spin. 2 *it all* **pivoted on** *his response* **depend on**, hinge on, turn on, center on, hang on, rely on, rest on, revolve around.

piv·ot·al /ˈpivətl/ ▶ adj. of central importance.

SYNONYMS **central**, crucial, vital, critical, focal, essential, key, decisive.

pix·el /ˈpiksəl/ ▶ n. any of the tiny areas of light on a computer screen that make up an image.

pix·ie /ˈpiksē/ (or **pixy**) ▶ n. (plural **pixies**) an imaginary being portrayed as a tiny person with pointed ears.

SYNONYMS **elf**, fairy, sprite, imp, brownie, puck, leprechaun.

piz·za /ˈpētsə/ ▶ n. a flat, round base of dough baked with a topping of tomatoes, cheese, and other ingredients.

piz·zazz /pəˈzaz/ (also **pizazz** or **pzazz**) ▶ n. informal a combination of liveliness and style.

piz·ze·ri·a /ˌpētsəˈrēə/ ▶ n. a pizza restaurant.

piz·zi·ca·to /ˌpitsiˈkätō/ ▶ adv. & adj. plucking the strings of a stringed instrument such as a violin with your finger.

PJ's ▶ abbr. informal pajamas.

plac·ard /ˈplakärd, -ərd/ ▶ n. a large written sign fixed to a wall or carried during a demonstration.

pla·cate /ˈplākāt/ ▶ v. (**placates**, **placating**, **placated**) make someone less angry or upset.

SYNONYMS **pacify**, calm, appease, mollify, soothe, win over, conciliate, propitiate, make peace with, humor. ANTONYMS provoke.

■ **pla·ca·to·ry** /-kəˌtôrē, ˈplakə-/ adj.

place /plās/ ▶ n. 1 a particular position or location. 2 an opportunity to study at a particular school or be a member of a team. 3 a position in a sequence. 4 (in place names) a square or short street. ▶ v. (**places**, **placing**, **placed**) 1 put something in a particular position or situation. 2 find an appropriate place or role for. 3 remember where you have seen someone before. 4 make a reservation or order.

SYNONYMS ▶ n. 1 **location**, site, spot, setting, position, situation, area, region, locale, venue. 2 **country**, state, area, region, town, city. 3 **home**, house, flat, apartment, pied-à-terre, accommodations, property, rooms, quarters; informal pad; formal residence, abode, dwelling. 4 **situation**, position, circumstances. 5 **seat**, chair, space. 6 **job**, position, post, appointment, situation, employment. 7 **status**, position, standing, rank, niche. 8 **responsibility**, duty, job, task, role, function, concern, affair, charge. ▶ v. 1 **put (down)**, set (down), lay, deposit, position, plant, rest, stand, station, situate, leave; informal stick, dump, park, plonk, plunk, plop. 2 **rank**, order, grade, class, classify, put. 3 **identify**, recognize, remember, put a name to, pin down, locate, pinpoint.

□ **in place of** instead of. **take place** happen.

pla·ce·bo /pləˈsēbō/ ▶ n. (plural **placebos**) 1 a medicine given to a patient to make them feel happier or more confident rather than for any physical effect. 2 a substance with no healing effect, given to some participants in a drug trial for comparison.

place·ment /ˈplāsmənt/ ▶ n. 1 the action of placing. 2 the action of finding a home, job, or school for someone.

pla·cen·ta /pləˈsentə/ ▶ n. (plural **placentae** /-tē/ or **placentas**) an organ formed in the uterus during pregnancy that supplies blood and nourishment to the fetus through the umbilical cord.

plac·id /ˈplasid/ ▶ adj. not easily upset or excited.

SYNONYMS 1 **even-tempered**, calm, tranquil, equable, unexcitable, serene, mild, composed, self-possessed, poised, easygoing, levelheaded, steady, unruffled, unperturbed, phlegmatic; informal unflappable. 2 **quiet**, calm, tranquil, still, peaceful, undisturbed, restful, sleepy. ANTONYMS excitable.

■ **pla·cid·i·ty** /pləˈsiditē/ n. **plac·id·ly** adv.

plack·et /ˈplakit/ ▶ n. an opening in a garment, covering fastenings or giving access to a pocket.

pla·gia·rize /ˈplājəˌrīz/ ▶ v. (**plagiarizes**, **plagiarizing**, **plagiarized**) copy another person's words or ideas and pretend that they are your own.

SYNONYMS **copy**, pirate, steal, poach, appropriate; informal rip off, crib.

■ **pla·gia·rism** n. **pla·gia·rist** n.

plague /plāg/ ▶ n. 1 an infectious disease causing fever and delirium. 2 an unusually and unpleasantly large number of insects or animals. ▶ v. (**plagues**, **plaguing**, **plagued**) 1 cause continual trouble to. 2 pester someone.

SYNONYMS ▶ n. 1 **pandemic**, epidemic, disease, sickness; dated contagion; old use pestilence. 2 **infestation**, invasion, swarm. ▶ v. 1 **afflict**, trouble, torment, beset, dog, curse, bedevil. 2 **pester**, harass, badger, bother, torment, harry, hound, trouble, nag, molest; informal hassle, bug.

plaice /plās/ ▶ n. (plural **plaice**) a flat brown fish with orange spots, used for food.

plaid /plad/ ▶ n. fabric woven in a checkered or tartan design.

plain /plān/ ▶ adj. 1 simple or ordinary. 2 without a pattern. 3 unmarked. 4 easy to understand; clear. 5 (of a woman or girl) not attractive. ▶ n. a large area of flat land with few trees.

SYNONYMS ▶ adj. 1 **obvious**, clear, evident, apparent, manifest, unmistakable. 2 **intelligible**, comprehensible, understandable, clear, lucid, simple, straightforward, user-friendly. 3 **candid**, frank, outspoken, forthright, direct, honest, truthful, blunt, bald, unequivocal; informal upfront. 4 **simple**, ordinary, unadorned, homely, basic, modest, unsophisticated, restrained. 5 **unattractive**, unprepossessing, ugly, homely, ordinary. 6 **sheer**, pure, downright, out-and-out. ANTONYMS obscure, fancy, attractive. ▶ n. **grassland**, flatland, prairie, savannah, steppe, tundra, pampas, veld, plateau.

■ **plain·ly** adv. **plain·ness** n.

plain·clothes /ˈplānˌklōTHz/ ▶ pl.n. ordinary clothes rather than a uniform, especially when worn by police officers.

plain·song /ˈplānˌsôNG, -säNG/ (or **plainchant**) ▶ n. a kind of medieval church music that was sung by a number of voices without any accompanying instruments.

plain·tiff /ˈplāntif/ ▶ n. a person who brings a case against someone in a court of law.

plain·tive /ˈplāntiv/ ▶ adj. sounding sad and mournful.

SYNONYMS **mournful**, sad, pathetic, pitiful, melancholy, sorrowful, unhappy, wretched, woeful, forlorn.

■ **plain·tive·ly** adv.

plait /plāt, plat/ ▶ n. a braid. ▶ v. form into a braid or braids.

plan /plan/ ▶ n. **1** a detailed proposal for doing or achieving something. **2** an intention. **3** a map or diagram. **4** a scheme for making regular payments toward a pension, insurance policy, etc. ▶ v. (**plans**, **planning**, **planned**) **1** decide on and arrange something in advance. **2** intend to do something. **3** (**plan for**) make preparations for. **4** make a plan of a building, town, garden, etc.

SYNONYMS ▶ n. **1 scheme**, idea, proposal, proposition, project, program, system, method, strategy, stratagem, formula, recipe. **2 intention**, aim, idea, objective, object, goal, target, ambition. **3 map**, diagram, chart, blueprint, plat, drawing, sketch, impression. ▶ v. **1 organize**, arrange, work out, outline, map out, prepare, formulate, frame, develop, devise. **2 intend**, aim, propose, mean, hope. **3 design**, draw up a plan for, sketch out, plat, map out.

plane¹ /plān/ ▶ n. **1** a completely flat surface. **2** a level of existence or thought. ▶ adj. **1** completely flat. **2** relating to two-dimensional surfaces or sizes. ▶ v. (**planes**, **planing**, **planed**) **1** (of a bird) soar without moving its wings. **2** skim over the surface of water.

SYNONYMS ▶ n. **level**, degree, standard, stratum, dimension. ▶ v. **skim**, glide.

plane² ▶ n. an airplane.

SYNONYMS **airplane**, aircraft, airliner, jet, flying machine, ship.

plane³ (or **planer**) ▶ n. a tool used to smooth a wooden surface by cutting thin shavings from it. ▶ v. (**planes**, **planing**, **planed**) smooth a surface with a plane.

plane⁴ ▶ n. a tall tree with broad leaves and peeling bark.

plan·et /ˈplanit/ ▶ n. a large round mass in space that orbits a star. ■ **plan·e·tar·y** adj.

plan·e·tar·i·um /ˌplaniˈte(ə)rēəm/ ▶ n. (plural **planetariums** or **planetaria** /-rēə/) a building in which images of stars, planets, and constellations are projected on to a domed ceiling.

plan·gent /ˈplanjənt/ ▶ adj. (of a sound) loud and melancholy.

plank /plaNGk/ ▶ n. a long, flat piece of timber.

plank·ing /ˈplaNGkiNG/ ▶ n. planks used as a building material.

plank·ton /ˈplaNGktən/ ▶ n. tiny creatures living in the sea or fresh water.

plan·ner /ˈplanər/ ▶ n. **1** a person who controls or plans urban development: *city planners*. **2** a list or chart with information that is an aid to planning: *my day planner*.

plant /plant/ ▶ n. **1** a living thing that absorbs substances through its roots and makes nutrients in its leaves by photosynthesis. **2** a place where a manufacturing process takes place. **3** machinery used in a manufacturing process. **4** a person placed in a group as a spy. ▶ v. **1** place a seed, bulb, or plant in the ground so that it can grow. **2** place in a particular position. **3** secretly place a bomb. **4** hide something among someone's belongings to make them appear guilty of something. **5** send someone to join a group to act as a spy. **6** fix an idea in someone's mind.

SYNONYMS ▶ n. **1 flower**, vegetable, herb, shrub, bush, weed; (**plants**) vegetation, greenery, flora. **2 spy**, informant, informer, secret agent, mole, infiltrator, operative; informal spook. **3 factory**, works, facility, refinery, mill. **4 machinery**, machines, equipment, apparatus, appliances, gear. ▶ v. **1 sow**, scatter. **2 place**, put, set, position, situate, settle; informal plonk. **3 instill**, implant, put, place, introduce, fix, establish, lodge.

Plan·tag·e·net /planˈtajənit/ ▶ n. a member of the English royal house that ruled 1154–1485.

plan·tain /ˈplantən/ ▶ n. **1** a type of banana eaten as a vegetable. **2** a wild plant with small green flowers and broad leaves that spread out near the ground.

plan·ta·tion /planˈtāSHən/ ▶ n. **1** a large estate on which crops such as coffee, sugar, and tobacco are grown. **2** an area in which trees have been planted.

plant·er /ˈplantər/ ▶ n. **1** a manager or owner of a plantation. **2** a decorative container in which plants are grown.

plaque /plak/ ▶ n. **1** an ornamental tablet fixed to a wall in memory of a person or event. **2** a sticky deposit that forms on teeth and in which bacteria grow quickly.

plas·ma /ˈplazmə/ ▶ n. **1** the clear fluid part of blood in which blood cells are suspended. **2** a gas of positive ions and free electrons with little or no overall electric charge. □ **plasma screen** a flat television screen that uses cells containing a gas plasma to produce different colors in each cell.

plas·ter /ˈplastər/ ▶ n. **1** a soft mixture of lime with sand or cement and water for spreading on walls and ceilings to form a smooth, hard surface when dried. **2** (also **plaster of Paris**) a hard white substance made by adding water to powdered gypsum, used for setting broken bones and making sculptures and casts. **3** a sticky strip of material for covering cuts and wounds. ▶ v. (**plasters**, **plastering**, **plastered**) **1** apply plaster to. **2** coat something thickly. **3** make hair lie flat by applying liquid to it. **4** (**plastered**) informal drunk.

SYNONYMS ▶ v. **1 spread**, smother, smear, cake, coat, bedaub. **2 flatten** (**down**), smooth down, slick down.

■ **plas·ter·er** n.

plas·ter·board /ˈplastərˌbôrd/ ▶ n. board made of plaster set between two sheets of paper, used to line interior walls and ceilings.

plas·tic /ˈplastik/ ▶ n. a chemically produced material that can be molded into shape while soft and then set into a hard or slightly flexible form. ▶ adj. **1** made of plastic. **2** easily shaped.

SYNONYMS ▶ adj. 1 **soft**, pliable, pliant, flexible, malleable, workable, moldable; informal bendy. 2 **artificial**, false, fake, bogus, insincere; informal phony, pretend.

□ **plastic surgery** surgery performed to repair or reconstruct parts of the body. ■ **plas·tic·i·ty** /pla'stisitē/ n. **plas·tick·y** adj.

Plas·ti·cine /'plastə,sēn/ ▶ n. trademark a soft modeling material.

plate /plāt/ ▶ n. 1 a flat dish for holding food. 2 bowls, cups, and other utensils made of gold or silver. 3 a thin, flat piece of metal, plastic, etc. 4 a small, flat piece of metal with writing on it, fixed to a wall or door. 5 a printed photograph or illustration in a book. 6 each of the several rigid pieces that together make up the earth's surface. ▶ v. (**plates**, **plating**, **plated**) cover a metal object with a thin coating of a different metal.

SYNONYMS ▶ n. 1 **dish**, platter, salver; historical trencher; old use charger. 2 **plateful**, helping, portion, serving. 3 **panel**, sheet, slab. 4 **plaque**, sign, tablet. 5 **picture**, print, illustration, photograph, photo. ▶ v. **cover**, coat, overlay, laminate, gild.

□ **on your plate** occupying your time or energy. **plate glass** thick glass used for store windows and doors.

pla·teau /pla'tō/ ▶ n. (plural **plateaux** or **plateaus**) 1 an area of fairly level high ground. 2 a state of little or no change after a period of activity or progress. ▶ v. (**plateaus**, **plateauing**, **plateaued**) reach a plateau.

SYNONYMS ▶ n. **upland**, mesa, highland, tableland.

plate·let /'plāt-lit/ ▶ n. a disk-shaped cell fragment found in large numbers in blood and involved in clotting.

plat·en /'platn/ ▶ n. a cylindrical roller in a typewriter against which the paper is held.

plat·form /'platfôrm/ ▶ n. 1 a raised level surface on which people or things can stand. 2 a raised structure along the side of a railroad track where passengers get on and off trains. 3 a raised structure standing in the sea from which oil or gas wells can be drilled. 4 the stated policy of a political party or group. 5 an opportunity for the expression or exchange of views. 6 a very thick sole on a shoe.

SYNONYMS 1 **stage**, dais, rostrum, podium, stand. 2 **program**, manifesto, policies, principles, party line.

plat·i·num /'platn-əm/ ▶ n. a precious silvery-white metallic element.

plat·i·tude /'plati,t(y)o͞od/ ▶ n. a remark that has been used too often to be interesting.

SYNONYMS **cliché**, truism, commonplace, old chestnut, banality.

■ **plat·i·tu·di·nous** /,plati't(y)o͞odn-əs/ adj.

pla·ton·ic /plə'tänik/ ▶ adj. 1 (of love or friendship) intimate and affectionate but not sexual. 2 (**Platonic**) having to do with the ideas of Plato, a philosopher of ancient Greece.

pla·toon /plə'to͞on/ ▶ n. a subdivision of a company of soldiers.

plat·ter /'platər/ ▶ n. a large flat serving dish.

SYNONYMS **plate**, dish, salver, tray; old use charger.

plat·y·pus /'platəpəs, -,po͝os/ (or **duck-billed platypus**) ▶ n. (plural **platypuses**) an animal with a ducklike bill and webbed feet, which lays eggs.

plau·dits /'plôdits/ ▶ pl.n. praise.

SYNONYMS **praise**, acclaim, commendation, congratulations, accolades, compliments, cheers, applause, tributes. ANTONYMS criticism.

plau·si·ble /'plôzəbəl/ ▶ adj. 1 seeming reasonable or probable. 2 skilled at making people believe something.

SYNONYMS **credible**, believable, reasonable, likely, possible, conceivable, imaginable, convincing, persuasive. ANTONYMS unlikely.

■ **plau·si·bil·i·ty** /,plôzə'bilitē/ n. **plau·si·bly** adv.

play /plā/ ▶ v. 1 take part in games for enjoyment. 2 take part in a sport or contest. 3 compete against another player or team. 4 act the role of a character in a play or movie. 5 perform on a musical instrument. 6 perform a piece of music. 7 make a CD or record produce sounds. 8 move a piece or display a playing card when it is your turn in a game. 9 move or flicker over a surface. ▶ n. 1 a piece of writing performed by actors. 2 games that people take part in for enjoyment. 3 the performing of a sports match. 4 a move in a sport or game. 5 freedom of movement. 6 constantly changing movement.

SYNONYMS ▶ v. 1 **amuse yourself**, entertain yourself, enjoy yourself, have fun, relax, occupy yourself, frolic, romp, cavort; informal mess around. 2 **take part in**, participate in, be involved in, compete in, do. 3 **compete against**, take on, meet. 4 **act the part of**, take the role of, appear as, portray, perform. ▶ n. 1 **amusement**, relaxation, recreation, diversion, leisure, enjoyment, pleasure, fun. 2 **drama**, theatrical work, piece, comedy, tragedy, production, performance.

□ **into play** into an active or effective state. **make great play of** draw attention to something in an exaggerated way. **make a play for** informal attempt to attract or gain. **play along** pretend to cooperate with someone. **play something by ear** 1 perform music without having seen a score. 2 (**play it by ear**) informal proceed without having formed a plan. **play something down** disguise the importance of something. **playing card** each of a set of rectangular pieces of card with numbers and symbols on one side, used in various games. **play on** take advantage of someone's weak point. **play up** 1 emphasize the extent or importance of. 2 (**play up to**) humor or flatter. **play with fire** take foolish risks.

play·boy /'plā,boi/ ▶ n. a wealthy man who spends his time enjoying himself.

SYNONYMS **socialite**, man about town, ladies' man, womanizer, philanderer, rake, roué, pleasure-seeker; informal ladykiller.

play·er /'plāər/ ▶ n. 1 a person taking part in a sport or game. 2 a person who plays a musical instrument. 3 a device for playing CDs, cassettes, etc. 4 a person who has influence in a particular area. 5 an actor.

SYNONYMS 1 **participant**, contestant, competitor, contender, sportsman, sportswoman. 2 **musician**, performer, artist, virtuoso, instrumentalist. 3 **actor**, **actress**, performer, thespian, entertainer, artiste, trouper.

play·ful /ˈplāfəl/ ▶ **adj. 1** fond of games and amusement. **2** lighthearted.

SYNONYMS **1 frisky**, lively, full of fun, frolicsome, high-spirited, exuberant, mischievous, impish; informal full of beans. **2 lighthearted**, humorous, jocular, teasing, jokey, facetious, frivolous, flippant. ANTONYMS serious.

■ **play·ful·ly** adv.

play·ground /ˈplāˌground/ ▶ **n.** an outdoor area provided for children to play in.

play·house /ˈplāˌhous/ ▶ **n. 1** a theater. **2** a toy house for children to play in.

play·list /ˈplāˌlist/ ▶ **n.** a list of songs or pieces of music chosen to be broadcast on a radio station or played by an individual's CD player, MP3 player, etc.

play·mak·er /ˈplāˌmākər/ ▶ **n.** a player in a team game who leads attacks or brings teammates into attacking positions.

play·mate /ˈplāˌmāt/ ▶ **n.** a friend with whom a child plays.

play·off /ˈplāˌôf/ ▶ **n. 1** an additional game or period of play that decides the outcome of a tied contest. **2** (**playoffs**) a series of contests played to determine the winner of a championship, as between the leading teams in different divisions or leagues.

play·pen /ˈplāˌpen/ ▶ **n.** a small portable enclosure in which a baby or small child can play safely.

play·thing /ˈplāˌTHiNG/ ▶ **n. 1** a person who is treated as amusing but unimportant. **2** a toy.

play·time /ˈplāˌtīm/ ▶ **n.** time for play or recreation.

play·wright /ˈplāˌrīt/ ▶ **n.** a person who writes plays.

pla·za /ˈplazə, ˈpläzə/ ▶ **n. 1** an open public space in a built-up area. **2** a shopping center.

plea /plē/ ▶ **n. 1** a request made in an urgent and emotional way. **2** a formal statement made by or on behalf of a person charged with an offense in a court of law.

SYNONYMS **appeal**, entreaty, supplication, petition, request, call.

plead /plēd/ ▶ **v.** (**pleads**, **pleading**, **pleaded** or **pled** /pled/) **1** make an emotional appeal. **2** argue in support of something. **3** state formally in court whether you are guilty or not guilty of the offense with which you are charged. **4** present something as an excuse for doing or not doing something.

SYNONYMS **claim**, use as an excuse, assert, allege, argue.

■ **plead·ing·ly** adv.

pleas·ant /ˈplezənt/ ▶ **adj. 1** satisfactory and enjoyable. **2** friendly and likable.

SYNONYMS **1 enjoyable**, pleasurable, nice, agreeable, entertaining, amusing, delightful, charming; informal lovely, great. **2 friendly**, charming, agreeable, amiable, nice, delightful, sweet, genial, cordial, good-natured, personable, hospitable, polite.

■ **pleas·ant·ly** adv.

pleas·ant·ry /ˈplezntrē/ ▶ **n.** (plural **pleasantries**) **1** an unimportant remark made as part of a polite conversation. **2** a mildly amusing joke.

please /plēz/ ▶ **v.** (**pleases**, **pleasing**, **pleased**) **1** make someone feel happy and satisfied. **2** wish or choose to do something. **3** (**please yourself**) consider only your own wishes. ▶ **adv.** used in polite requests or questions, or to accept an offer.

SYNONYMS ▶ **v. 1 make happy**, give pleasure to, delight, charm, amuse, entertain, divert, satisfy, gratify, humor. **2** (**pleasing**) **good**, agreeable, pleasant, pleasurable, satisfying, gratifying, great. **3** (**pleasing**) **friendly**, amiable, pleasant, agreeable, affable, nice, genial, likable, charming, engaging, delightful; informal lovely. **4 like**, want, wish, desire, see fit, think fit, choose, will, prefer. ANTONYMS annoy.

pleased /plēzd/ ▶ **adj.** feeling or showing pleasure and satisfaction.

SYNONYMS **happy**, glad, delighted, gratified, grateful, thankful, content, contented, satisfied, thrilled; informal over the moon, on cloud nine. ANTONYMS unhappy.

pleas·ur·a·ble /ˈpleZHərəbəl/ ▶ **adj.** enjoyable.
■ **pleas·ur·a·bly** adv.

pleas·ure /ˈpleZHər/ ▶ **n. 1** a feeling of happy satisfaction and enjoyment. **2** an event or activity that you enjoy. ▶ **v.** (**pleasures**, **pleasuring**, **pleasured**) give pleasure to.

SYNONYMS ▶ **n. happiness**, delight, joy, gladness, glee, satisfaction, gratification, contentment, enjoyment, amusement, fun, entertainment, relaxation, recreation, diversion.

pleat /plēt/ ▶ **n.** a fold in fabric, held by stitching at the top or side. ▶ **v.** fold or form into pleats.

pleb /pleb/ ▶ **n.** informal, disapproving a member of the lower social classes.

ple·be·ian /pliˈbēən/ ▶ **adj.** ordinary or unsophisticated. ▶ **n.** a member of the ordinary people or the lower classes.

pleb·i·scite /ˈplebəˌsīt/ ▶ **n.** a vote made by everyone entitled to do so on an important public question.

plec·trum /ˈplektrəm/ ▶ **n.** (plural **plectrums** or **plectra** /-trə/) a thin flat piece of plastic used to pluck the strings of a guitar.

pled /pled/ past participle of **PLEAD**.

pledge /plej/ ▶ **n. 1** a solemn promise or undertaking. **2** something valuable promised as a guarantee that a debt will be paid or a promise kept. **3** a thing given as a token of love or loyalty. ▶ **v.** (**pledges**, **pledging**, **pledged**) **1** solemnly undertake to do or give something. **2** promise something as a pledge.

SYNONYMS ▶ **n. promise**, vow, undertaking, word, commitment, assurance, oath, guarantee. ▶ **v. promise**, vow, undertake, swear, commit yourself, declare, affirm.

ple·na·ry /ˈplenərē/ ▶ **adj. 1** (of a meeting at a conference or assembly) to be attended by all participants. **2** full; complete.

plen·i·po·ten·ti·ar·y /ˌplenəpəˈtensHēˌerē, -ˈtensHərē/ ▶ **n.** (plural **plenipotentiaries**) a person given full power by a government to act on its behalf. ▶ **adj.** having full power to take independent action.

plen·i·tude /ˈpleniˌt(y)o͞od/ ▶ **n.** formal a large amount of something.

plen·te·ous /ˈplentēəs/ ▶ **adj.** literary plentiful.

plen·ti·ful /ˈplentəfəl/ ▶ **adj.** existing in or producing great quantities.

> SYNONYMS **abundant**, copious, ample, profuse, rich, lavish, generous, bountiful, bumper, prolific; informal galore. ANTONYMS scarce.

■ **plen·ti·ful·ly** adv.

plen·ty /ˈplentē/ ▶ pron. as much as is wanted or needed; quite enough. ▶ n. a situation in which food and other necessities are available in large enough quantities.

> SYNONYMS ▶ pron. *we've got* **plenty of** *games* **a lot of**, many, a great deal of, a plethora of, enough and to spare, no lack of, a wealth of; informal loads of, heaps of, stacks of, masses of, oodles of. ▶ n. **prosperity**, affluence, wealth, opulence, comfort, luxury, abundance.

ple·num /ˈplenəm, ˈplēnəm/ ▶ n. an assembly of all the members of a group or committee.

pleth·o·ra /ˈpleTHərə/ ▶ n. an excessive amount or number of something.

> SYNONYMS **excess**, abundance, superabundance, surplus, glut, surfeit, profusion, enough and to spare. ANTONYMS dearth.

pleu·ri·sy /ˈplo͝orəsē/ ▶ n. inflammation of the membranes around the lungs, causing pain during breathing.

Plex·i·glas /ˈpleksiˌglas/ ▶ n. trademark a tough transparent plastic used as a substitute for glass.

plex·us /ˈpleksəs/ ▶ n. (plural **plexus** or **plexuses**) a complex network or weblike structure.

pli·a·ble /ˈplīəbəl/ ▶ adj. **1** easily bent. **2** easily influenced or persuaded.

> SYNONYMS **1 flexible**, pliant, bendable, supple, workable, plastic; informal bendy. **2 malleable**, impressionable, flexible, adaptable, biddable, pliant, tractable, suggestible, persuadable. ANTONYMS rigid.

■ **pli·a·bil·i·ty** /ˌplīəˈbilitē/ n.

pli·ant /ˈplīənt/ ▶ adj. pliable.

pli·ers /ˈplīərz/ ▶ pl.n. pincers having jaws with flat surfaces, used for gripping small objects and bending or cutting wire.

plight¹ /plīt/ ▶ n. a dangerous or difficult situation.

> SYNONYMS **predicament**, difficult situation, dire straits, trouble, difficulty, bind; informal tight corner, tight spot, hole, pickle, jam, fix.

plight² ▶ v. (**plight your troth**) old use promise to marry.

plink /pliNGk/ ▶ v. make a short, metallic ringing sound. ▶ n. a plinking sound.

plinth /plinTH/ ▶ n. a heavy block or slab supporting a statue or forming the base of a column.

PLO ▶ abbr. Palestine Liberation Organization.

plod /pläd/ ▶ v. (**plods**, **plodding**, **plodded**) **1** walk slowly with heavy steps. **2** work slowly and steadily at a dull task. ▶ n. a slow, heavy walk.

> SYNONYMS ▶ v. **trudge**, walk heavily, clump, stomp, tramp, lumber, slog.

plonk /pläNGk/ ▶ v. informal put something down heavily or carelessly.

plop /päp/ ▶ n. a sound like that of a small, solid object dropping into water without a splash. ▶ v. (**plops**, **plopping**, **plopped**) fall or drop with a plop.

plot /plät/ ▶ n. **1** a secret plan to do something illegal or harmful. **2** the main sequence of events in a play, novel, or movie. **3** a small piece of ground marked out for building, gardening, etc. ▶ v. (**plots**, **plotting**, **plotted**) **1** secretly make plans to carry out something illegal or harmful. **2** mark a route or position on a chart or graph.

> SYNONYMS ▶ n. **1 conspiracy**, intrigue, stratagem, plan, machinations. **2 storyline**, story, scenario, action, thread, narrative. **3 piece of ground**, patch, area, tract, lot, acreage, plat. ▶ v. **1 plan**, scheme, arrange, organize, contrive. **2 conspire**, scheme, intrigue, connive. **3 mark**, chart, map.

■ **plot·ter** n.

plov·er /ˈpləvər, ˈplō-/ ▶ n. a wading bird with a short bill.

plow /plou/ ▶ n. a piece of farming equipment with one or more blades fixed in a frame, used to turn over soil. ▶ v. **1** turn earth with a plow. **2** move forward with difficulty or force. **3** (of a ship or boat) travel through an area of water.

> SYNONYMS ▶ v. **1 till**, furrow, harrow, cultivate, work. **2 crash**, smash, career, plunge, bulldoze, hurtle, cannon.

ploy /ploi/ ▶ n. a cunning act performed to gain an advantage.

> SYNONYMS **ruse**, tactic, move, device, stratagem, scheme, trick, gambit, plan, maneuver, dodge, subterfuge.

pluck /plək/ ▶ v. **1** take hold of something and quickly remove it from its place. **2** pull out a hair or feather. **3** pull the feathers from a bird's carcass to prepare it for cooking. **4** pull at. **5** sound a stringed instrument with your fingers or a plectrum. ▶ n. courage.

> SYNONYMS ▶ v. **1 remove**, pick, pull, extract. **2 pull**, tug, clutch, snatch, grab, catch, tweak, jerk; informal yank. **3 strum**, pick, thrum, twang. ▶ n. **courage**, bravery, nerve, daring, spirit, grit; informal guts, moxie.

□ **pluck up courage** summon up enough courage to do something frightening.

pluck·y /ˈpləkē/ ▶ adj. (**pluckier**, **pluckiest**) having a lot of courage and determination. ■ **pluck·i·ly** adv.

plug /pləg/ ▶ n. **1** a piece of solid material that tightly blocks a hole. **2** a device with metal pins that fit into holes in a socket to make an electrical connection. **3** an electrical socket. **4** informal a piece of publicity promoting a product or event. ▶ v. (**plugs**, **plugging**, **plugged**) **1** block a hole. **2** (**plug something in**) connect an appliance to an electric circuit. **3** informal promote a product or event by mentioning it publicly. **4** (**plug away**) informal proceed steadily with a task.

> SYNONYMS ▶ n. **1 stopper**, bung, cork. **2 advertisement**, promotion, commercial, recommendation, mention, good word; informal hype, push. ▶ v. **1 stop**, seal, close, block, fill. **2 publicize**, promote, advertise, mention, bang the drum for, draw attention to; informal hype, push.

plum /pləm/ ▶ n. **1** an oval fruit that is purple, reddish, or yellow when ripe. **2** a reddish-purple color. ▶ adj. informal highly desirable: *a plum job*.

plum·age /ˈplo͞omij/ ▶ n. a bird's feathers.

plumb¹ /pləm/ ▶ v. **1** explore or experience something fully. **2** measure the depth of water. **3** test an upright surface to find out if it is vertical. ▶ n. a heavy object attached to a plumb line. ▶ adv.

informal exactly: *plumb in the center*. ▶ **adj.** vertical.

SYNONYMS ▶ **v. explore**, probe, delve into, search, examine, investigate, fathom, penetrate, understand. ▶ **adv. right**, exactly, precisely, directly, dead, straight; informal (slam) bang.

□ **plumb line** a line with a heavy object attached to it, used for measuring the depth of water or checking that a wall, post, etc., is vertical.

plumb² ▶ **v.** (**plumb something in**) install a bathtub, washing machine, etc., and connect it to water and drainage pipes.

plumb·er /ˈpləmər/ ▶ **n.** a person who fits and repairs the pipes and fittings used in the supply of water and heating in a building.

plumb·ing /ˈpləmiNG/ ▶ **n.** the system of pipes and fittings required for the water supply and heating in a building.

plume /plo͞om/ ▶ **n. 1** a long, soft feather or group of feathers. **2** a long spreading cloud of smoke or vapor. ■ **plumed adj.**

plum·met /ˈpləmit/ ▶ **v.** (**plummets**, **plummeting**, **plummeted**) **1** fall straight down very quickly. **2** decrease rapidly in value or amount. ▶ **n.** a steep and rapid fall or drop.

SYNONYMS ▶ **v. plunge**, dive, drop, fall, hurtle, nosedive, tumble. ANTONYMS soar.

plump¹ /pləmp/ ▶ **adj. 1** rather fat. **2** full and rounded in shape. ▶ **v.** (**plump something up**) make something more full and rounded.

SYNONYMS ▶ **adj. fat**, chubby, rotund, ample, round, stout, portly, overweight; informal tubby, roly-poly, pudgy, zaftig, corn-fed. ANTONYMS thin.

plump² ▶ **v. 1** set or sit down heavily. **2** (**plump for**) decide in favor of one of two or more possibilities.

plun·der /ˈpləndər/ ▶ **v.** (**plunders**, **plundering**, **plundered**) force your way into a place and steal everything of value. ▶ **n. 1** goods obtained by plundering. **2** the action of plundering.

SYNONYMS ▶ **v. 1 pillage**, loot, rob, raid, ransack, rifle, strip, sack. **2 steal**, seize, thieve, pilfer, embezzle. ▶ **n. booty**, loot, stolen goods, spoils, ill-gotten gains; informal swag.

plunge /plənj/ ▶ **v.** (**plunges**, **plunging**, **plunged**) **1** fall or move suddenly and uncontrollably. **2** jump or dive quickly. **3** push or thrust something quickly. **4** (**plunge in**) begin a course of action without thought or care. **5** (**be plunged into**) be suddenly brought into a particular state. ▶ **n.** an act of plunging.

SYNONYMS ▶ **v. 1 dive**, jump, throw yourself, immerse yourself. **2 plummet**, nosedive, drop, fall, tumble, descend. **3 charge**, hurtle, career, plough, tear; informal barrel. **4 thrust**, stab, sink, stick, ram, drive, push, shove, force.

□ **take the plunge** informal finally decide to do something difficult or challenging.

plung·er /ˈplənjər/ ▶ **n. 1** a part of a device that works with a plunging or thrusting movement. **2** a rubber cup on a long handle, used to clear blocked pipes by means of suction.

plu·per·fect /ˌplo͞oˈpərfikt/ ▶ **adj.** Grammar (of a tense) referring to an action completed earlier than some past point of time, formed by *had* and the past participle (as in *he had gone by then*).

plu·ral /ˈplo͝orəl/ ▶ **adj. 1** more than one in number. **2** Grammar (of a word or form) referring to more than one. ▶ **n.** Grammar a plural word or form.

plu·ral·ism /ˈplo͝orəˌlizəm/ ▶ **n. 1** a system in which power is shared among a number of political parties. **2** the acceptance within a society of a number of groups with different beliefs or ethnic backgrounds. ■ **plu·ral·ist n. & adj.**

plu·ral·i·ty /plo͝oˈralitē/ ▶ **n.** (plural **pluralities**) **1** the fact or state of being plural. **2** a large number of people or things.

plus /pləs/ ▶ **prep. 1** with the addition of. **2** together with; as well as. ▶ **adj. 1** (after a number or amount) at least. **2** (after a grade) better than. **3** (before a number) above zero. **4** having a positive electric charge. ▶ **n. 1** (also **plus sign**) the symbol +, indicating addition or a positive value. **2** informal an advantage. ▶ **conj.** informal also.

SYNONYMS ▶ **prep. as well as**, together with, along with, in addition to, and, added to, not to mention. ANTONYMS minus. ▶ **n. advantage**, good point, asset, pro, benefit, bonus, attraction; informal perk. ANTONYMS disadvantage.

□ **plus-size** (of women's clothing) of a larger size than normal.

plush /pləsн/ ▶ **n.** a fabric with a thick, velvety surface. ▶ **adj.** informal luxurious.

SYNONYMS ▶ **adj. luxurious**, luxury, deluxe, sumptuous, opulent, magnificent, rich, expensive, fancy, upmarket, upscale; informal posh, classy, swish, swank. ANTONYMS austere.

Plu·to /ˈplo͞otō/ ▶ **n.** a dwarf planet of our solar system in the Kuiper belt beyond Neptune.

plu·toc·ra·cy /plo͞oˈtäkrəsē/ ▶ **n.** (plural **plutocracies**) **1** government by the richest people in a country. **2** a society governed by the richest people in it.

plu·to·crat /ˈplo͞otəˌkrat/ ▶ **n.** a person who is powerful because of their wealth.

plu·to·ni·um /plo͞oˈtōnēəm/ ▶ **n.** a radioactive metallic element used as a fuel in nuclear reactors and as an explosive in atomic weapons.

ply¹ /plī/ ▶ **n.** (plural **plies**) a thickness or layer of a material.

SYNONYMS **layer**, thickness, strand, sheet, leaf.

ply² ▶ **v.** (**plies**, **plying**, **plied**) **1** (**ply someone with**) keep presenting someone with food or drink, or asking them questions. **2** (of a ship or vehicle) travel regularly over a route. **3** work steadily with a tool.

SYNONYMS **1 engage in**, carry on, pursue, conduct, practice. **2 travel**, shuttle, go back and forth. **3** *she plied me with fresh pastries* **provide**, supply, shower. **4** *he plied her with questions* **bombard**, assail, pester, plague, harass; informal hassle.

□ **ply your trade** do your job or business.

ply·wood /ˈplīˌwo͝od/ ▶ **n.** board consisting of layers of wood glued together.

PM ▶ **abbr.** Prime Minister.

p.m. ▶ **abbr.** after noon.

pneu·mat·ic /n(y)o͞oˈmatik/ ▶ **adj.** containing or operated by air or gas under pressure.

pneu·mo·nia /n(y)o͞oˈmōnēə, -ˈmōnyə/ ▶ **n.** an infection causing inflammation in the lungs.

poach¹ /'pōCH/ ▶ v. cook something by simmering it in a small amount of liquid.

poach² ▶ v. **1** hunt game or catch fish illegally from private or protected areas. **2** unfairly entice customers, workers, etc., away from someone else.

poach·er¹ /'pōCHər/ ▶ n. a pan for cooking eggs or other food by poaching.

poach·er² ▶ n. a person who hunts or catches game or fish illegally.

pocked /päkt/ ▶ adj. having pockmarks.

pock·et /'päkət/ ▶ n. **1** a small bag sewn into or on clothing, used for carrying small articles. **2** a small area or group that is different from its surroundings. **3** informal the money that you have available: *gifts to suit every pocket.* **4** an opening at the corner or on the side of a billiard table into which balls are struck. ▶ v. (**pockets**, **pocketing**, **pocketed**) **1** put something into your pocket. **2** take something that is not yours.

SYNONYMS ▶ n. **1 pouch**, compartment. **2 area**, patch, region, cluster. **3** *a pocket calculator* **small**, little, miniature, mini, compact, concise, abridged, portable. ▶ v. **1 acquire**, obtain, gain, get, secure, win, make, earn. **2 steal**, appropriate, purloin, misappropriate, embezzle.

□ **in someone's pocket** dependent on and influenced by someone. **line your pocket** make money dishonestly. **pocket money** a small amount of money for minor expenses.

pock·et·book /'päkət,bo͝ok/ ▶ n. a wallet, purse, or handbag.

pock·mark /'päk,märk/ ▶ n. **1** a hollow scar or mark on the skin left by a pustule or pimple. **2** a mark or hollow area on a surface. ■ **pock·marked** adj.

pod¹ /päd/ ▶ n. a long seed case of a pea, bean, etc. ▶ v. (**pods**, **podding**, **podded**) remove peas or beans from their pods before cooking.

SYNONYMS ▶ n. **shell**, husk, hull, case, shuck.

pod² ▶ n. a small herd of whales or similar sea mammals.

pod·cast /'päd,kast/ ▶ n. a digital recording of a radio broadcast made available on the Internet for downloading to a personal audio player.

po·di·a·try /pə'dīətrē/ ▶ n. the treatment of the feet and their ailments. ■ **po·di·a·trist** n.

po·di·um /'pōdēəm/ ▶ n. (plural **podiums** or **podia** /-dēə/) a small platform on which a person stands to conduct an orchestra or give a speech.

SYNONYMS **platform**, stage, dais, rostrum, stand.

po·em /'pōəm, 'pōim, pōm/ ▶ n. a piece of imaginative writing in verse.

SYNONYMS **verse**, rhyme, lyric, piece of poetry.

po·e·sy /'pōəzē, -sē/ ▶ n. old use poetry.

po·et /'pōət, 'pōit/ ▶ n. a person who writes poems. □ **poet laureate** (plural **poets laureate**) a poet appointed by a government, sometimes responsible for writing poems for official occasions. ■ **po·et·ess** n.

po·et·ic /pō'etik/ (or **poetical** /pō'etikəl/) ▶ adj. **1** having to do with poetry. **2** expressed in a sensitive and imaginative way.

SYNONYMS **expressive**, figurative, symbolic, flowery, artistic, imaginative, creative.

□ **poetic justice** a situation in which something bad happens to someone who has done something wrong. **poetic license** freedom to change facts or the normal rules of language to achieve a special effect in writing. ■ **po·et·i·cal·ly** adv.

po·et·ry /'pōətrē, 'pōitrē/ ▶ n. **1** poems as a whole or as a form of literature. **2** a quality of beauty and sensitivity.

SYNONYMS **poems**, verse, versification, rhyme.

po·go stick /'pōgō/ ▶ n. a toy for bouncing around on, consisting of a pole on a spring, with a bar to stand on and a handle at the top.

po·grom /'pōgrəm, pə'gräm/ ▶ n. an organized massacre of an ethnic group, originally that of Jews in Russia or eastern Europe.

poign·ant /'poinyənt/ ▶ adj. making you feel sadness or regret.

SYNONYMS **touching**, moving, sad, affecting, pitiful, pathetic, plaintive.

■ **poign·an·cy** n. **poign·ant·ly** adv.

point /point/ ▶ n. **1** the tapered, sharp end of a tool, weapon, or other object. **2** a particular place or moment. **3** an item, detail, or idea. **4** (**the point**) the most important part of what is being discussed. **5** the advantage or purpose of something. **6** a unit of scoring, value, or measurement. **7** a small dot used as punctuation or in decimal numbers; a period. **8** each of thirty-two directions marked at equal distances around a compass. **9** a narrow piece of land jutting out into the sea. **10** (**points**) a set of electrical contacts in the distributor of a motor vehicle. ▶ v. **1** direct someone's attention by extending your finger. **2** aim, indicate, or face in a particular direction. **3** (**point something out**) make someone aware of something. **4** (**point to**) indicate that something is likely to happen. **5** fill in the joints of brickwork or tiling with mortar or cement.

SYNONYMS ▶ n. **1 tip**, (sharp) end, extremity, prong, spike, tine, nib, barb. **2 pinpoint**, dot, spot, speck. **3 place**, position, location, site, spot. **4 time**, stage, juncture, period, phase. **5 level**, degree, stage, pitch, extent. **6 detail**, item, fact, thing, argument, consideration, factor, element, subject, issue, topic, question, matter. **7 heart of the matter**, essence, nub, core, crux; informal nitty-gritty. **8 purpose**, aim, object, objective, goal, intention, use, sense, value, advantage. **9 attribute**, characteristic, feature, trait, quality, property, aspect, side. ▶ v. **aim**, direct, level, train, focus.

□ **point of view** a particular attitude or opinion.

point·ed /'pointid/ ▶ adj. **1** having a sharpened or tapered tip or end. **2** (of a remark or look) directed toward a particular person and expressing a clear message.

SYNONYMS **1 sharp**, spiky, spiked, tapering, barbed. **2 cutting**, biting, incisive, trenchant, acerbic, caustic, scathing, venomous, sarcastic.

point·er /'pointər/ ▶ n. **1** a long, thin piece of metal on a scale or dial that moves to give a reading. **2** a hint or tip. **3** a breed of dog that, when it scents game, stands rigid and looks toward it.

SYNONYMS **1 indicator**, needle, arrow, hand. **2 indication**, indicator, clue, hint, sign, signal, evidence. **3 tip**, hint, suggestion, guideline, recommendation.

point·less /'pointlis/ ▶ adj. having little or no sense or purpose.

SYNONYMS **senseless**, futile, useless, hopeless, unavailing, unproductive, aimless, idle, worthless, valueless. ANTONYMS valuable.

■ **point·less·ly** adv.

point·y /'pointē/ ▶ adj. (**pointier**, **pointiest**) informal having a pointed tip or end.

poise /poiz/ ▶ n. **1** a graceful way of holding your body. **2** a calm and confident manner. ▶ v. **1** cause to be balanced or suspended. **2** (**be poised to do**) be ready to do. **3** (**poised**) calm and confident.

SYNONYMS ▶ n. **1 grace**, gracefulness, elegance, balance, control. **2 composure**, equanimity, self-possession, aplomb, self-assurance, self-control, sangfroid, dignity, presence of mind; informal cool. ▶ v. **1** (**poised**) **balanced**, suspended, motionless, hanging, hovering. **2** (**poised**) **prepared**, ready, braced, geared up, all set, standing by.

poi·son /'poizən/ ▶ n. **1** a substance that causes death or injury to a person or animal that swallows or absorbs it. **2** a harmful influence. ▶ v. **1** harm or kill a person or animal with poison. **2** put poison on or in. **3** have a harmful effect on.

SYNONYMS ▶ n. **toxin**, venom. ▶ v. **pollute**, contaminate, infect, taint, spoil.

■ **poi·son·er** n.

poi·son·ous /'poiz(ə)nəs/ ▶ adj. **1** (of an animal) producing poison. **2** (of a plant or substance) causing or capable of causing death or illness if taken into the body. **3** very unpleasant or spiteful.

SYNONYMS **1 venomous**, deadly. **2 toxic**, noxious, deadly, fatal, lethal, mortal. **3 malicious**, malevolent, hostile, spiteful, bitter, venomous, malign. ANTONYMS harmless.

poke /pōk/ ▶ v. (**pokes**, **poking**, **poked**) **1** prod with a finger or a sharp object. **2** (**poke around**) look or search around. **3** push or stick out in a particular direction. ▶ n. an act of poking.

SYNONYMS ▶ v. **1 prod**, jab, dig, elbow, nudge, shove, jolt, stab, stick. **2** *leave the cable* **poking out stick out**, jut out, protrude, project, extend. ▶ n. **prod**, jab, dig, elbow, nudge.

pok·er¹ /'pōkər/ ▶ n. a metal rod used for prodding an open fire.

pok·er² ▶ n. a card game in which the players bet on the value of the hands dealt to them. □ **poker face** a blank expression that hides your true feelings.

pok·y /'pōkē/ (or **pokey**) ▶ adj. (**pokier**, **pokiest**) **1** annoyingly slow or dull. **2** (of a room or building) uncomfortably small and cramped.

SYNONYMS **1 slow**, plodding, dawdling, sluggish, sluggardly. **2 small**, little, tiny, cramped, confined, restricted, boxy. ANTONYMS lively, roomy.

po·lar /'pōlər/ ▶ adj. **1** relating to the North or South Poles or the regions around them. **2** having an electrical or magnetic field. **3** completely opposite.

SYNONYMS **opposite**, opposed, dichotomous, extreme, contrary, contradictory, antithetical.

□ **polar bear** a large white bear from the Arctic.

po·lar·i·ty /pō'laritē, pə-/ ▶ n. (plural **polarities**) **1** the state of having poles or opposites. **2** the direction of a magnetic or electric field.

po·lar·ize /'pōlə,rīz/ ▶ v. (**polarizes**, **polarizing**, **polarized**) **1** divide people into two sharply contrasting groups with different opinions. **2** Physics restrict the vibrations of a wave of light to one direction. **3** give magnetic or electric polarity to. ■ **po·lar·i·za·tion** /,pōlərə'zāsʜən/ n.

Po·lar·oid /'pōlə,roid/ ▶ n. trademark **1** a material that polarizes the light passing through it, used in sunglasses. **2** a camera that produces a finished print rapidly after each exposure.

Pole /pōl/ ▶ n. a person from Poland.

pole¹ /pōl/ ▶ n. a long, thin rounded piece of wood or metal, used as a support.

SYNONYMS **post**, pillar, stanchion, stake, support, prop, stick, paling, staff.

□ **pole position** the most favorable position at the start of a motor race. **pole vault** an athletic event in which competitors vault over a high bar with the aid of a long pole.

pole² ▶ n. **1** either of the two points (**North Pole** or **South Pole**) at opposite ends of the earth's axis. **2** each of the two opposite points of a magnet at which magnetic forces are strongest. **3** the positive or negative terminal of an electric cell or battery. □ **be poles apart** have nothing in common.

pole·ax /'pōl,aks/ (or **poleaxe**) ▶ v. (**poleaxes**, **poleaxing**, **poleaxed**) **1** kill or knock down with a heavy blow. **2** shock someone very much.

pole·cat /'pōl,kat/ ▶ n. **1** a dark brown weasellike animal with an unpleasant smell. **2** a skunk.

po·lem·ic /pə'lemik/ ▶ n. **1** a speech or piece of writing that argues strongly for or against something. **2** (also **polemics**) the practice of using fierce argument or discussion. ▶ adj. (also **polemical**) having to do with fierce argument or discussion. ■ **po·lem·i·cist** n.

po·lice /pə'lēs/ ▶ n. an official body of people employed by a state to prevent and solve crime and keep public order. ▶ v. (**polices**, **policing**, **policed**) **1** keep law and order in an area. **2** make sure that a particular set of rules is obeyed.

SYNONYMS ▶ n. **police force**, police officers, policemen, policewomen; informal the cops, the boys in blue, [city's] finest, the fuzz, the heat, the law. ▶ v. **1 guard**, watch over, protect, defend, patrol. **2 enforce**, regulate, oversee, supervise, monitor, observe, check.

□ **police officer** a policeman or policewoman. **police state** a state in which the government requires the police to watch people secretly and control their activities.

po·lice·man /pə'lēsmən/ (or **policewoman** /pə'lēs,wo͝omən/) ▶ n. (plural **policemen** or **policewomen**) a member of a police force.

SYNONYMS **police officer**, patrolman, (state) trooper; informal cop, uniform.

pol·i·cy /'päləsē/ ▶ n. (plural **policies**) **1** a plan of action adopted by an organization or person. **2** a contract of insurance.

SYNONYMS **plans**, approach, code, system, guidelines, theory, line, position, stance.

po·li·o /'pōlē,ō/ (or **poliomyelitis** /,pōlēō,mīə'lītis/) ▶ n. a disease that can cause temporary or permanent paralysis.

Pol·ish /'pōlisʜ/ ▶ n. the language of Poland. ▶ adj. relating to Poland.

pol·ish /'pälisʜ/ ▶ v. **1** make something smooth and shiny by rubbing. **2** (**polish something up**) improve a skill. **3** (**polished**) accomplished and skillful. **4** (**polish something off**) finish eating or doing something quickly. ▶ **n. 1** a substance used to polish something. **2** an act of polishing. **3** a shiny appearance produced by polishing. **4** refinement or elegance.

> SYNONYMS ▶ **v. 1 shine**, wax, buff, rub up/down, gloss, burnish. **2** (**polished**) **shiny**, glossy, gleaming, lustrous, glassy, waxed, buffed, burnished. **3 polish up** *your essay* **perfect**, refine, improve, hone, enhance, brush up, revise, edit, correct, rewrite, go over, touch up. **4** (**polished**) **expert**, accomplished, masterly, skillful, adept, adroit, dexterous, consummate, superlative, superb. ▶ **n. sophistication**, refinement, urbanity, suaveness, elegance, style, grace, finesse; informal class.

■ **pol·ish·er n.**

po·lite /pə'līt/ ▶ **adj.** (**politer**, **politest**) **1** respectful and considerate toward other people; courteous. **2** civilized or refined.

> SYNONYMS **1 well-mannered**, civil, courteous, respectful, well-behaved, well-bred, gentlemanly, ladylike, genteel, gracious, tactful, diplomatic. **2 civilized**, refined, cultured, sophisticated, urbane. ANTONYMS rude.

■ **po·lite·ly adv. po·lite·ness n.**

pol·i·tic /'pälə,tik/ ▶ **adj.** (of an action) sensible and wise in the circumstances.

> SYNONYMS **wise**, prudent, sensible, shrewd, astute, judicious, expedient, advantageous, beneficial, profitable. ANTONYMS unwise.

po·lit·i·cal /pə'litikəl/ ▶ **adj. 1** relating to the government or public affairs of a country. **2** related to or interested in politics.

> SYNONYMS **governmental**, government, constitutional, ministerial, parliamentary, diplomatic, legislative, administrative.

□ **political correctness** the avoidance of language or behavior that could offend certain groups of people. **political prisoner** a person who is imprisoned for their beliefs rather than because they have committed a crime. ■ **po·lit·i·cal·ly adv.**

pol·i·ti·cian /,pälə'tisHən/ ▶ **n.** a person who holds an elected position within the government.

> SYNONYMS **legislator**, representative, senator, congressman, congresswoman, statesman, stateswoman, member of Parliament, MP, minister; informal politico, pol.

po·lit·i·cize /pə'litə,sīz/ ▶ **v.** (**politicizes**, **politicizing**, **politicized**) **1** make someone interested in politics. **2** make something a political issue. ■ **po·lit·i·ci·za·tion** /pə,litəsi'zāsHən/ **n.**

pol·i·tics /'pälə,tiks/ ▶ **n. 1** the activities concerned with governing a country or area. **2** a particular set of political beliefs. **3** activities concerned with gaining or using power within an organization or group: *office politics*.

pol·i·ty /'pälətē/ ▶ **n.** (plural **polities**) **1** a form of government. **2** a society as a politically organized state.

pol·ka /'pō(l)kə/ ▶ **n.** a lively dance for couples. □ **polka dot** each of a number of dots that are evenly spaced to form a pattern.

poll /pōl/ ▶ **n. 1** the process of voting in an election. **2** a record of the number of votes cast. ▶ **v. 1** record the opinion or vote of. **2** (of a candidate in an election) receive a particular number of votes.

> SYNONYMS ▶ **n. 1 vote**, ballot, show of hands, referendum, plebiscite, election. **2 survey**, opinion poll, market research, census. ▶ **v. 1 canvass**, survey, ask, question, interview, ballot. **2 get**, gain, register, record, return.

□ **poll tax** a tax paid at the same rate by every adult.

pol·lard /'pälərd/ ▶ **v.** cut off the top and side branches of a tree to encourage new growth.

pol·len /'pälən/ ▶ **n.** a powder produced by the male part of a flower, which is carried by bees, the wind, etc., and can fertilize other flowers. □ **pollen count** a measure of the amount of pollen in the air.

pol·li·nate /'pälə,nāt/ ▶ **v.** (**pollinates**, **pollinating**, **pollinated**) carry pollen to and fertilize a flower or plant. ■ **pol·li·na·tion** /,pälə'nāsHən/ **n.**

poll·ster /'pōlstər/ ▶ **n.** a person who carries out opinion polls.

pol·lu·tant /pə'lo͞otnt/ ▶ **n.** a substance that causes pollution.

pol·lute /pə'lo͞ot/ ▶ **v.** (**pollutes**, **polluting**, **polluted**) make something dirty or poisonous with unwanted or harmful substances.

> SYNONYMS **contaminate**, taint, poison, foul, dirty, soil, infect. ANTONYMS purify.

■ **pol·lut·er n.**

pol·lu·tion /pə'lo͞osHən/ ▶ **n.** the presence in the air, soil, or water of a substance with unpleasant or harmful effects.

> SYNONYMS **contamination**, impurity, dirt, filth, infection.

po·lo /'pōlō/ ▶ **n.** a game similar to hockey, played on horseback with a long-handled mallet. □ **polo shirt** a casual short-sleeved shirt with a collar and two or three buttons at the neck.

pol·ter·geist /'pōltər,gīst/ ▶ **n.** a kind of ghost that is said to make loud noises and throw objects around.

pol·y·chrome /'päli,krōm/ ▶ **adj.** consisting of several colors. ■ **pol·y·chro·mat·ic** /,pälikrō'matik/ **adj.**

pol·y·es·ter /'pälē,estər/ ▶ **n.** a synthetic fiber used to make fabric for clothes.

pol·y·eth·yl·ene /,pälē'eTHəlēn/ ▶ **n.** a tough, light, flexible plastic.

po·lyg·a·my /pə'ligəmē/ ▶ **n.** the practice of having more than one wife or husband at the same time. ■ **po·lyg·a·mist n. po·lyg·a·mous adj.**

pol·y·glot /'päli,glät/ ▶ **adj.** knowing or using several languages.

pol·y·gon /'päli,gän/ ▶ **n.** a figure with three or more straight sides and angles.

pol·y·graph /'päli,graf/ ▶ **n.** a lie detector.

pol·y·he·dron /,päli'hēdrən/ ▶ **n.** (plural **polyhedrons** or **polyhedra** /-drə/) a solid figure with many sides.

pol·y·math /'päli,maTH/ ▶ **n.** a person with a wide knowledge of many subjects.

pol·y·mer /'päləmər/ ▶ **n.** a substance with a molecular structure formed from many identical small molecules bonded together.

pol·y·mor·phic /,päli'môrfik/ (or **polymorphous** /-'môrfəs/) ▶ **adj.** having several different forms.

pol·yp /'päləp/ ▶ **n. 1** a simple sea creature that remains fixed in the same place, such as coral.

2 Medicine a small lump sticking out from a mucous membrane.

po·lyph·o·ny /pə'lifənē/ ▶ **n.** the combination of a number of musical parts, each forming an individual melody and harmonizing with each other. ■ **pol·y·phon·ic** /ˌpäli'fänik/ **adj.**

pol·y·sty·rene /ˌpäli'stīrēn/ ▶ **n.** a light synthetic material.

pol·y·syl·lab·ic /ˌpälisə'labik/ ▶ **adj.** having more than one syllable.

pol·y·tech·nic /ˌpäli'teknik/ ▶ **n.** an institution of higher education offering courses in many subjects, especially vocational or technical subjects.

pol·y·the·ism /'päliᴛʜēˌizəm/ ▶ **n.** the worship of more than one god. ■ **pol·y·the·is·tic** /ˌpäliᴛʜē'istik/ **adj.**

pol·y·un·sat·u·rat·ed /ˌpälēən'sacʜəˌrātid/ ▶ **adj.** (of a fat) having a chemical structure that is thought not to lead to the formation of cholesterol in the blood.

pol·y·u·re·thane /ˌpäli'yŏŏrəˌᴛʜān/ ▶ **n.** a synthetic material used in paints and varnishes.

po·made /pō'mād, -'mäd/ ▶ **n.** a scented oil or cream for making the hair glossy and smooth.

po·man·der /pō'mandər, 'pōˌmandər/ ▶ **n.** a ball or container of sweet-smelling substances used to perfume a room or cupboard.

pome·gran·ate /'päm(ə)ˌgranit, 'pəm-/ ▶ **n.** a round tropical fruit with a tough orange outer skin and red flesh containing many seeds.

pom·mel /'päməl, 'pəməl/ ▶ **n. 1** the curving or projecting front part of a saddle. **2** a rounded knob on the handle of a sword.

pomp /pämp/ ▶ **n.** the special clothes, music, and customs that are part of a grand public ceremony.

> SYNONYMS **ceremony**, solemnity, ritual, display, spectacle, pageantry, show, ostentation, splendor, grandeur, magnificence, majesty, stateliness, glory; informal razzmatazz.

pom-pom /'pämˌpäm/ (or **pompon**) ▶ **n. 1** a small woolen ball attached to a garment, especially a hat, for decoration. **2** a cluster of brightly colored strands of yarn or plastic, waved in pairs by cheerleaders. **3** a dahlia, chrysanthemum, or other flower with small tightly clustered petals.

pomp·ous /'pämpəs/ ▶ **adj.** showing in a rather solemn or arrogant way that you have a high opinion of yourself and your own views.

> SYNONYMS **self-important**, overbearing, sententious, grandiose, affected, pretentious, puffed up, haughty, proud, conceited, supercilious, condescending, patronizing.

■ **pom·pos·i·ty** /päm'päsətē/ **n. pomp·ous·ly adv.**

pon·cho /'päncʜō/ ▶ **n.** (plural **ponchos**) a garment made of a thick piece of cloth with a slit in the middle for the head.

pond /pänd/ ▶ **n.** a small area of still water.

pon·der /'pändər/ ▶ **v.** (**ponders**, **pondering**, **pondered**) consider something carefully.

> SYNONYMS **think about**, contemplate, consider, review, reflect on, mull over, meditate on, muse on, dwell on.

pon·der·ous /'pändərəs/ ▶ **adj. 1** moving slowly and heavily. **2** boringly solemn or long-winded.

> SYNONYMS **1** *a ponderous procession* **slow**, awkward, lumbering, cumbersome, ungainly, graceless. **2** *a ponderous speech* **labored**, laborious, lifeless, plodding, pedestrian, boring, dull, tedious, monotonous. ANTONYMS light, lively.

■ **pon·der·ous·ly adv.**

pond·weed /'pändˌwēd/ ▶ **n.** a plant that grows in still or running water.

pon·tiff /'päntəf/ ▶ **n.** the pope.

pon·tif·i·cal /pän'tifikəl/ ▶ **adj.** having to do with a pope; papal.

pon·tif·i·cate ▶ **v.** /pän'tifiˌkāt/ (**pontificates**, **pontificating**, **pontificated**) express your opinions in a pompous and overbearing way. ▶ **n.** /-kət/ (**the Pontificate**) the official position of a pope or bishop.

> SYNONYMS ▶ **v. hold forth**, expound, declaim, preach, lay down the law, sound off, lecture; informal mouth off.

pon·toon /ˌpän'tōōn/ ▶ **n. 1** a flat-bottomed boat or hollow cylinder used with others to support a temporary bridge or floating landing stage. **2** a bridge or landing stage supported by pontoons.

po·ny /'pōnē/ ▶ **n.** (plural **ponies**) a small breed of horse, especially one of less than 15 hands.

po·ny·tail /'pōnēˌtāl/ ▶ **n.** a hairstyle in which the hair is drawn back and tied at the back of the head.

pooch /pōōcʜ/ ▶ **n.** informal a dog.

poo·dle /'pōōdl/ ▶ **n.** a breed of dog with a curly coat that is usually clipped.

pooh-pooh /'pōō ˌpōō, pōō 'pōō/ ▶ **v.** informal dismiss an idea as being silly or impractical.

pool¹ /pōōl/ ▶ **n. 1** a small area of still water. **2** (also **swimming pool**) an artificial pool for swimming in. **3** a small, shallow patch of liquid on a surface.

> SYNONYMS **puddle**, pond, lake; literary mere.

pool² ▶ **n. 1** a supply of vehicles, goods, money, etc., that is shared between a number of people and available for use when needed. **2** a game played on a billiard table using sixteen balls. ▶ **v.** put something into a common fund to be used by a number of people.

> SYNONYMS ▶ **n. 1 supply**, reserve(s), reservoir, fund, store, bank, stock, cache. **2 fund**, reserve, kitty, pot, bank, purse. ▶ **v. combine**, group, join, unite, merge, share.

poop¹ /pōōp/ (or **poop deck**) ▶ **n.** a raised deck at the back of a ship.

poop² ▶ **v.** informal exhaust someone.

poor /pŏŏr, pôr/ ▶ **adj. 1** having very little money. **2** of a low standard or quality. **3** (**poor in**) not having enough of something. **4** deserving pity or sympathy.

> SYNONYMS **1 poverty-stricken**, penniless, impoverished, impecunious, needy, destitute, dirt poor; informal hard up, strapped; formal penurious. **2 substandard**, bad, deficient, defective, faulty, imperfect, inferior, unsatisfactory, shoddy, crude, inadequate, unacceptable; informal crummy, rotten. **3 meager**, scanty, scant, paltry, reduced, modest, sparse, spare, deficient, insubstantial, skimpy, lean; informal measly, stingy. **4 unfortunate**, unlucky, unhappy, hapless, wretched, luckless, ill-fated, ill-starred. ANTONYMS rich.

poor·house /ˈpo͝orˌhous, ˈpôr-/ ▶ **n.** historical an institution where very poor people were maintained with public funds.

poor·ly /ˈpo͝orlē, ˈpôr-/ ▶ **adv.** badly. ▶ **adj.** unwell.

> SYNONYMS ▶ **adv. badly**, imperfectly, incompetently, crudely, shoddily, inadequately. ▶ **adj. ill**, unwell, not very well, ailing, indisposed, out of sorts, under par, peaked; informal under the weather.

pop¹ /päp/ ▶ **v.** (**pops**, **popping**, **popped**) **1** make a sudden short explosive sound. **2** go or come quickly or unexpectedly. **3** put something somewhere quickly or for a short time. **4** (of a person's eyes) open wide and appear to bulge. ▶ **n.** **1** a sudden short explosive sound. **2** informal a soda.

> SYNONYMS ▶ **v. 1 go bang**, go off, crack, snap, burst, explode. **2 put**, place, slip, throw, slide, stick, set, lay, position. ▶ **n. bang**, crack, snap, explosion, report.

pop² ▶ **n.** (also **pop music**) modern popular music, usually with a strong melody and beat. ▶ **adj.** **1** relating to pop music. **2** often disapproving made easy for the general public to understand; popularized: *pop psychology*. □ **pop art** a style of art that uses images taken from popular culture, such as advertisements or movies.

pop³ ▶ **n.** informal father.

pop·corn /ˈpäpˌkôrn/ ▶ **n.** a snack consisting of corn kernels that are heated until they burst open.

pope /pōp/ ▶ **n.** the Bishop of Rome as head of the Roman Catholic Church.

pop·er·y /ˈpōpərē/ ▶ **n.** disapproving Roman Catholicism. ■ **pop·ish** **adj.**

pop·in·jay /ˈpäpənˌjā/ ▶ **n.** old use a person who is vain and dresses in a showy way.

pop·lar /ˈpäplər/ ▶ **n.** a tall, slender tree with soft wood.

pop·lin /ˈpäplən/ ▶ **n.** a cotton fabric with a finely ribbed surface.

pop·py /ˈpäpē/ ▶ **n.** a plant with bright flowers and small black seeds.

pop·py·cock /ˈpäpēˌkäk/ ▶ **n.** informal nonsense.

Pop·si·cle /ˈpäpˌsikəl/ ▶ **n.** trademark a piece of flavored ice on a stick.

pop·u·lace /ˈpäpyələs/ ▶ **n.** the general public.

> SYNONYMS **population**, inhabitants, residents, natives, community, country, (general) public, people, nation, common people, masses, multitude, rank and file; informal John Q. Public; disapproving hoi polloi, rabble, riffraff.

pop·u·lar /ˈpäpyələr/ ▶ **adj.** **1** liked or admired by many people. **2** suited to the tastes of the general public. **3** connected with or carried out by ordinary people.

> SYNONYMS **1 well-liked**, sought-after, in demand, commercial, marketable, fashionable, in vogue, all the rage, hot; informal in, cool, big. **2 nonspecialist**, nontechnical, amateur, lay person's, general, middle-of-the-road, accessible, simplified, understandable, mass-market. **3 widespread**, general, common, current, prevailing, standard, ordinary, conventional.

■ **pop·u·lar·ly** **adv.**

pop·u·lar·i·ty /ˌpäpyəˈlaritē/ ▶ **n.** the state of being liked or supported by many people.

pop·u·lar·ize /ˈpäpyələˌrīz/ ▶ **v.** (**popularizes**, **popularizing**, **popularized**) **1** make something popular. **2** make something understandable or interesting to the general public. ■ **pop·u·lar·i·za·tion** /ˌpäpyələrəˈzāsʜən/ **n.**

pop·u·late /ˈpäpyəˌlāt/ ▶ **v.** (**populates**, **populating**, **populated**) **1** live in an area and form its population. **2** cause people to settle in an area.

> SYNONYMS **inhabit**, occupy, people, settle, colonize.

pop·u·la·tion /ˌpäpyəˈlāsʜən/ ▶ **n.** **1** all the people living in an area. **2** the number of people living in an area.

> SYNONYMS **inhabitants**, residents, people, citizens, public, community, populace, society, natives, occupants.

pop·u·list /ˈpäpyələst/ ▶ **adj.** aiming to appeal to ordinary people, especially in politics. ▶ **n.** a populist politician. ■ **pop·u·lism** **n.**

pop·u·lous /ˈpäpyələs/ ▶ **adj.** having a large population.

> SYNONYMS **densely populated**, congested, crowded, packed, teeming. ANTONYMS deserted.

por·bea·gle /ˈpôrˌbēgəl/ ▶ **n.** a large shark of the North Atlantic and Mediterranean.

por·ce·lain /ˈpôrs(ə)lən/ ▶ **n.** a type of delicate china.

porch /pôrcʜ/ ▶ **n.** **1** a covered shelter at the entrance to a building. **2** a veranda.

por·cine /ˈpôrˌsīn/ ▶ **adj.** relating to pigs, or like a pig.

por·cu·pine /ˈpôrkyəˌpīn/ ▶ **n.** an animal with long protective spines on the body and tail.

pore¹ /pôr/ ▶ **n.** each of many tiny openings in the skin or another surface.

pore² ▶ **v.** (**pores**, **poring**, **pored**) (**pore over** or **through**) study or read something with close attention.

> USAGE
> Don't confuse **pore** and **pour**: you **pore over** a book, you do not **pour over** it.

pork /pôrk/ ▶ **n.** the flesh of a pig used as food. □ **pork barrel** informal referring to the use of government funds for projects designed to win votes.

pork·er /ˈpôrkər/ ▶ **n.** a young pig raised and fattened for food.

por·no·graph·ic /ˌpôrnəˈgrafik/ ▶ **adj.** designed to cause sexual excitement.

> SYNONYMS **obscene**, indecent, dirty, smutty, filthy, erotic, titillating, sexy, risqué, X-rated, adult.

por·nog·ra·phy /pôrˈnägrəfē/ ▶ **n.** photographs, writing, movies, etc., intended to cause sexual excitement. ■ **por·nog·ra·pher** **n.**

po·rous /ˈpôrəs/ ▶ **adj.** having tiny spaces through which liquid or air can pass.

> SYNONYMS **permeable**, penetrable, absorbent, spongy. ANTONYMS impermeable.

■ **po·ros·i·ty** /pəˈräsətē, pôrˈäs-/ **n.**

por·poise /ˈpôrpəs/ ▶ **n.** a type of small whale with a rounded snout.

por·ridge /ˈpôrij/ ▶ **n.** a dish consisting of oats or oatmeal boiled with water or milk.

port¹ /pôrt/ ▶ **n. 1** a town or city with a harbor. **2** a harbor.

SYNONYMS **harbor**, docks, marina, haven, seaport.

□ **port of call** a place where a ship or person stops on a journey.

port² ▶ **n.** a strong, sweet dark red wine from Portugal.

port³ ▶ **n.** the side of a ship or aircraft that is on the left when you are facing forward.

port⁴ ▶ **n. 1** an opening in the side of a ship for boarding or loading. **2** an opening in an aircraft or vehicle through which a gun can be fired. **3** a socket in a computer network into which a device can be plugged.

port·a·ble /ˈpôrtəbəl/ ▶ **adj.** able to be carried or moved easily.

SYNONYMS **transportable**, movable, mobile, wireless, lightweight, compact, handy, convenient.

■ **port·a·bil·i·ty** /ˌpôrtəˈbilətē/ **n.**

por·tal /ˈpôrtl/ ▶ **n.** a large and impressive doorway or gate.

port·cul·lis /pôrtˈkələs/ ▶ **n.** a strong, heavy grating that can be lowered to block a gateway to a castle.

por·tend /pôrˈtend/ ▶ **v.** be a sign or warning that something important or unpleasant is likely to happen.

SYNONYMS **presage**, augur, foreshadow, foretell, prophesy, be a sign, warn, be an omen, indicate, herald, signal, bode, promise, threaten, signify, spell, denote.

por·tent /ˈpôrˌtent/ ▶ **n.** a sign or warning that something important or unpleasant is likely to happen.

por·ten·tous /pôrˈtentəs/ ▶ **adj. 1** warning or showing that something important is likely to happen. **2** very serious or solemn.
■ **por·ten·tous·ly** **adv.**

por·ter /ˈpôrtər/ ▶ **n. 1** a person employed to carry luggage and other loads. **2** a hospital employee who moves equipment or patients. **3** dark brown bitter beer.

SYNONYMS **carrier**, bearer, redcap, skycap.

por·ter·house steak /ˈpôrtərˌhous/ ▶ **n.** a choice steak cut from the thick end of a sirloin.

port·fo·li·o /pôrtˈfōlēˌō/ ▶ **n.** (plural **portfolios**) **1** a thin, flat case for carrying drawings, maps, etc. **2** a set of pieces of creative work collected together to show someone's ability. **3** a range of investments held by a person or organization. **4** the position and duties of a government minister.

port·hole /ˈpôrtˌhōl/ ▶ **n.** a small window in the side of a ship or aircraft.

por·ti·co /ˈpôrtiˌkō/ ▶ **n.** (plural **porticoes** or **porticos**) a roof supported by columns, built over the entrance to a building.

por·tion /ˈpôrsʜən/ ▶ **n. 1** a part or share of something. **2** an amount of food for one person. ▶ **v.** share something out in portions.

SYNONYMS ▶ **n. 1 part**, piece, bit, section, segment. **2 share**, quota, ration, allocation, tranche. **3 helping**, serving, plateful, slice, piece.

port·ly /ˈpôrtlē/ ▶ **adj.** rather fat.

SYNONYMS **stout**, plump, fat, overweight, heavy, corpulent, fleshy, potbellied, well-padded, rotund, stocky, bulky; informal tubby, roly-poly, beefy, porky, corn-fed. ANTONYMS slim.

port·man·teau /pôrtˈmantō/ ▶ **n.** (plural **portmanteaus** or **portmanteaux** /-tōz/) a large traveling bag that opens into two parts.

por·trait /ˈpôrtrət, -ˌtrāt/ ▶ **n. 1** a painting, drawing, or photograph of a particular person. **2** a piece of writing or a movie about a particular person.

SYNONYMS **1 picture**, likeness, painting, drawing, photograph, image. **2 description**, portrayal, representation, depiction, impression, account, profile.

por·trai·ture /ˈpôrtricʜər, -ˌcʜo͝or/ ▶ **n.** the art of making portraits.

por·tray /pôrˈtrā/ ▶ **v. 1** show or describe in a work of art or literature. **2** describe in a particular way.

SYNONYMS **1 paint**, draw, sketch, picture, depict, represent, illustrate, render, show. **2 describe**, depict, characterize, delineate, put into words. **3 play**, act the part of, take the role of, represent, appear as.

por·tray·al /pôrˈtrā(ə)l/ ▶ **n.** a dramatic representation of a person or character in a book, play, movie, etc.

SYNONYMS **description**, representation, characterization, depiction, delineation, evocation, interpretation.

Por·tu·guese /ˈpôrcʜəˌgēz/ ▶ **n.** (plural **Portuguese**) **1** a person from Portugal. **2** the language of Portugal and Brazil. ▶ **adj.** relating to Portugal.

SPELLING
Write **-guese**, not **-gese**: Portu**guese**.

pose /pōz/ ▶ **v.** (**poses**, **posing**, **posed**) **1** present a problem, question, etc. **2** sit or stand in a particular position in order to be photographed, painted, or drawn. **3** (**pose as**) pretend to be. **4** behave in a way that is intended to impress people. ▶ **n. 1** a position adopted in order to be painted, drawn, or photographed. **2** a way of behaving that is intended to impress people.

SYNONYMS ▶ **v. 1 constitute**, present, offer. **2 raise**, ask, put, submit, advance, propose. **3 posture**, attitudinize, put on airs; informal show off. ▶ **n. 1 posture**, position, stance, attitude. **2 act**, affectation, show, display, front, airs.

pos·er /ˈpōzər/ ▶ **n. 1** a person who behaves in a way intended to impress other people. **2** a puzzling question or problem.

SYNONYMS **1 exhibitionist**, poseur, posturer, fake; informal show-off. **2 difficult question**, problem, puzzle, mystery, riddle, conundrum; informal dilemma.

po·seur /pōˈzər/ ▶ **n.** a person who poses in order to impress; a poser.

posh /päsʜ/ ▶ **adj.** informal very elegant or luxurious; stylish.

SYNONYMS **smart**, stylish, fancy, high-class, fashionable, chic, upmarket, upscale, luxurious, luxury, exclusive; informal classy, plush, flash, swish, swank, tony.

pos·it /ˈpäzit/ ▶ **v.** (**posits**, **positing**, **posited**) present something as a fact or as a basis for argument.

po·si·tion /pəˈzisHən/ ▶ **n.** **1** a place where something is situated. **2** a way in which someone or something is placed or arranged. **3** a situation or set of circumstances. **4** a job. **5** a person's place or importance in relation to others. **6** a point of view. ▶ **v.** put or arrange in a particular position.

SYNONYMS ▶ **n.** **1** **location**, place, situation, spot, site, locality, setting, area, whereabouts, bearings. **2** **posture**, stance, attitude, pose. **3** **situation**, state, condition, circumstances, predicament, plight. **4** **status**, place, level, rank, standing, stature, prestige, reputation. **5** **job**, post, situation, appointment, opening, vacancy, placement. **6** **viewpoint**, opinion, outlook, attitude, stand, standpoint, stance, perspective, thinking, policy, feelings. ▶ **v.** **put**, place, locate, situate, set, site, stand, station, plant, stick; informal plonk, plunk, park.

■ **po·si·tion·al** **adj.**

pos·i·tive /ˈpäzətiv/ ▶ **adj.** **1** indicating agreement with or support for something. **2** hopeful, favorable, or confident. **3** with no possibility of doubt; certain. **4** (of the results of a test or experiment) showing the presence of something. **5** (of a quantity) greater than zero. **6** having to do with the kind of electric charge opposite to that carried by electrons. **7** (of an adjective or adverb) expressing the basic degree of a quality (e.g., *brave*). ▶ **n.** a positive quality.

SYNONYMS ▶ **adj.** **1** **affirmative**, favorable, good, enthusiastic, supportive, constructive, useful, productive, helpful, worthwhile, beneficial. **2** **optimistic**, hopeful, confident, cheerful, sanguine, buoyant; informal upbeat. **3** *positive economic signs* **good**, promising, favorable, encouraging, heartening, propitious, auspicious. **4** **definite**, certain, reliable, concrete, tangible, clear-cut, explicit, firm, decisive, real, actual. **5** **convinced**, sure, confident, satisfied. ANTONYMS negative, pessimistic.

■ **pos·i·tiv·i·ty** /ˌpäzəˈtivətē/ **n.**

pos·i·tive·ly /ˈpäzətivlē/ ▶ **adv.** **1** with certainty. **2** extremely.

SYNONYMS **1** **confidently**, definitely, firmly, categorically, with certainty, conclusively. **2** **absolutely**, utterly, downright, simply, virtually; informal plain.

pos·i·tiv·ism /ˈpäzətivˌizəm, ˈpäztiv-/ ▶ **n.** a system of philosophy that recognizes only things that can be scientifically or logically proved. ■ **pos·i·tiv·ist** **n. & adj.**

pos·i·tron /ˈpäzəˌträn/ ▶ **n.** a subatomic particle with the same mass as an electron and an equal but positive charge.

pos·se /ˈpäsē/ ▶ **n.** **1** (in the past) a group of men summoned by a sheriff to enforce the law. **2** informal a group of people.

pos·sess /pəˈzes/ ▶ **v.** **1** have or own something. **2** (also **be possessed of**) have a particular ability or quality. **3** dominate or have complete power over someone.

SYNONYMS **1** **own**, have (to your name), be in possession of. **2** **have**, be blessed with, be endowed with, enjoy, boast. **3** **take control of**, take over, bewitch, enchant, enslave.

■ **pos·ses·sor** **n.**

SPELLING

Double **s** in the middle as well as at the end: possess.

pos·ses·sion /pəˈzesHən/ ▶ **n.** **1** the state of having or owning something. **2** a thing owned.

SYNONYMS **1** **ownership**, control, hands, keeping, care, custody, charge. **2** *she packed her possessions* **belongings**, things, property, worldly goods, goods and chattels, personal effects, stuff, bits and pieces; informal gear, junk.

pos·ses·sive /pəˈzesiv/ ▶ **adj.** **1** demanding someone's total attention and love. **2** unwilling to share your possessions. **3** Grammar (of a pronoun or determiner) showing that someone owns something.

SYNONYMS **proprietorial**, overprotective, controlling, dominating, jealous, clingy.

■ **pos·ses·sive·ly** **adv.**

pos·si·bil·i·ty /ˌpäsəˈbilətē/ ▶ **n.** (plural **possibilities**) **1** a thing that is possible. **2** the state of being possible. **3** (**possibilities**) qualities suggesting that something might be good or could be improved.

SYNONYMS **1** **chance**, likelihood, probability, potentiality, hope, risk, hazard, danger, fear. **2** **option**, alternative, choice, course of action, solution. **3** **potential**, promise, prospects.

pos·si·ble /ˈpäsəbəl/ ▶ **adj.** **1** capable of existing, happening, or being done. **2** that may be so. ▶ **n.** a person or thing that may be chosen.

SYNONYMS ▶ **adj.** **1** **feasible**, practicable, viable, attainable, achievable, workable, within reach; informal on, doable. **2** **likely**, plausible, imaginable, believable, potential, probable, credible, tenable. ANTONYMS impossible, unlikely.

pos·si·bly /ˈpäsəblē/ ▶ **adv.** **1** perhaps. **2** in accordance with what is possible.

SYNONYMS **1** **perhaps**, maybe, it is possible, for all you know. **2** **conceivably**, under any circumstances, by any means.

pos·sum /ˈpäsəm/ ▶ **n.** **1** informal an American opossum, a marsupial with a tail that it can use for grasping. **2** Australian/New Zealand a marsupial that lives in trees. □ **play possum** pretend to be unconscious, dead, or unaware of something.

post¹ /pōst/ ▶ **n.** **1** a strong, upright piece of timber or metal used as a support or a marker. **2** (**the post**) a post marking the start or finish of a race. ▶ **v.** **1** display a notice in a public place. **2** send a message to a blog, Internet bulletin board, or newsgroup.

SYNONYMS ▶ **n.** **pole**, stake, upright, shaft, prop, support, picket, strut, pillar, stanchion, baluster. ▶ **v.** **1** **affix**, attach, fasten, display, pin up, put up, stick up. **2** **announce**, report, make known, publish.

post² ▶ **n.** **1** postal service. **2** letters and packages delivered. ▶ **v.** send something via the postal system. □ **keep someone posted** keep someone up to date with the latest news about something.

post office 1 the organization responsible for postal services. **2** a building where postal business is carried out.

post³ ▶ **n. 1** a place where someone is on duty or where an activity is carried out. **2** a job. ▶ **v. 1** put a soldier, police officer, etc., in a particular place. **2** send someone to a place to take up a job.

SYNONYMS ▶ **n. 1 assigned position**, station, place, base. **2 job**, position, appointment, situation, place, vacancy, opening. ▶ **v. 1 put on duty**, mount, station. **2 send**, assign, dispatch, consign.

post·age /ˈpōstij/ ▶ **n. 1** the sending of letters and packages by mail. **2** the charge for sending something by mail.

post·al /ˈpōstəl/ ▶ **adj.** relating to or carried out by the post office or mail.

post·card /ˈpōstˌkärd/ ▶ **n.** a card for sending a message by mail without an envelope.

post·date /pōstˈdāt/ ▶ **v.** (**postdates, postdating, postdated**) **1** put a date later than the actual one on a check or document. **2** happen, exist, or be found later than.

post·er /ˈpōstər/ ▶ **n.** a large picture or notice used for decoration or advertisement.

SYNONYMS **notice**, placard, bill, sign, advertisement, playbill.

pos·te·ri·or /päˈsti(ə)rēər, pō-/ ▶ **adj.** at or near the rear. ▶ **n.** humorous a person's buttocks.

pos·ter·i·ty /päˈsteritē/ ▶ **n.** all future generations of people.

post·grad·u·ate /pōstˈgrajo͞oit/ ▶ **adj.** relating to study done after completing a first degree. ▶ **n.** a person taking a course of postgraduate study.

post·haste /ˈpōstˈhāst/ ▶ **adv.** very fast.

post·hu·mous /ˈpäschəməs, pästˈ(h)yo͞oməs/ ▶ **adj.** happening or appearing after the person involved has died. ■ **post·hu·mous·ly adv.**

post·ing¹ /ˈpōstiNG/ ▶ **n.** an appointment to a job, especially one abroad or in the armed forces.

post·ing² ▶ **n.** a message sent to a blog, Internet bulletin board, or newsgroup.

post·man /ˈpōstmən/ ▶ **n.** (plural **postmen**) a mail carrier.

post·mark /ˈpōstˌmärk/ ▶ **n.** an official mark stamped on a letter or package, giving the date of mailing and canceling the postage stamp. ▶ **v.** stamp a letter or package with a postmark.

post·mas·ter /ˈpōstˌmastər/ (or **postmistress** /ˈpōstˌmistris/) ▶ **n.** a person in charge of a post office.

post·mod·ern·ism /pōstˈmädərˌnizəm/ ▶ **n.** a late 20th-century movement in the arts. ■ **post·mod·ern adj. post·mod·ern·ist n. & adj.**

post·mor·tem /pōstˈmôrtəm/ ▶ **n.** an examination of a dead body to find out the cause of death.

post·na·tal /pōstˈnātl/ ▶ **adj.** having to do with the period after childbirth.

post·pone /pōstˈpōn/ ▶ **v.** (**postpones, postponing, postponed**) arrange for something to take place at a time later than that first planned.

SYNONYMS **put off**, put back, delay, defer, hold over, reschedule, adjourn, shelve; informal put on ice, put on the back burner.

■ **post·pone·ment n.**

post·script /ˈpōs(t)ˌskript/ ▶ **n.** a remark added at the end of a letter.

pos·tu·lant /ˈpäschələnt/ ▶ **n.** a person who has recently entered a religious order.

pos·tu·late /ˈpäschəˌlāt/ ▶ **v.** (**postulates, postulating, postulated**) assume that something is true, as a basis for a theory or discussion. ■ **pos·tu·la·tion** /ˌpäschəˈlāsHən/ **n.**

pos·ture /ˈpäschər/ ▶ **n. 1** a particular position of the body. **2** the usual way in which a person holds their body. **3** an approach or attitude toward something. ▶ **v.** (**postures, posturing, postured**) behave in a way that is meant to impress or mislead other people.

SYNONYMS ▶ **n. 1 position**, pose, attitude, stance, carriage, bearing, deportment, comportment. **2 attitude**, standpoint, point of view, viewpoint, opinion, position, stance. ▶ **v. pose**, strike an attitude, attitudinize, strut; informal show off.

■ **pos·tur·al adj.**

post·war /ˈpōstˈwôr/ ▶ **adj.** after a war, especially World War II.

po·sy /ˈpōzē/ ▶ **n.** (plural **posies**) a small bunch of flowers.

pot¹ /pät/ ▶ **n. 1** a rounded container used for storage or cooking. **2** (**the pot**) the total sum of bets made on a round in poker and other card games. ▶ **v.** (**pots, potting, potted**) **1** plant a young plant in a flowerpot. **2** informal hit or kill by shooting. □ **go to pot** informal be ruined through neglect. **pot belly** a large stomach that sticks out. **pot pie** a meat and vegetable pie baked in a deep dish. **pot roast** a piece of meat cooked slowly in a covered dish. **potting shed** a shed used for potting plants and storing garden tools.

pot² ▶ **n.** informal marijuana.

po·ta·ble /ˈpōtəbəl/ ▶ **adj.** formal (of water) safe to drink.

pot·ash /ˈpätˌasH/ ▶ **n.** a substance obtained from potassium, used in making soap and fertilizers.

po·tas·si·um /pəˈtasēəm/ ▶ **n.** a soft silvery-white metallic element.

po·ta·to /pəˈtātō/ ▶ **n.** (plural **potatoes**) an oval vegetable with starchy white or yellow flesh and a brown skin, that grows underground as a tuber.

SPELLING

The singular has no **e** on the end: potato.

po·tent /ˈpōtnt/ ▶ **adj.** very powerful.

SYNONYMS **1 powerful**, strong, mighty, formidable, influential, dominant. **2 forceful**, convincing, cogent, compelling, persuasive, powerful, strong. ANTONYMS weak.

■ **po·ten·cy n.**

po·ten·tate /ˈpōtnˌtāt/ ▶ **n.** a monarch or ruler.

po·ten·tial /pəˈtencHəl/ ▶ **adj.** capable of becoming or developing into something. ▶ **n. 1** qualities or abilities that may be developed and lead to future success. **2** the possibility of something happening.

SYNONYMS ▶ **adj. possible**, likely, prospective, future, probable. ▶ **n. possibilities**, potentiality, prospects, promise, capability, capacity.

■ **po·ten·ti·al·i·ty** /pəˌtencHēˈalətē/ **n. po·ten·tial·ly adv.**

pot·hole /ˈpätˌhōl/ ▶ n. **1** a hole in the surface of a road. **2** a deep underground cave. ■ **pot·holed** adj.

po·tion /ˈpōsʜən/ ▶ n. a drink with healing, magical, or poisonous powers.

> SYNONYMS **concoction**, mixture, brew, elixir, drink, medicine, tonic, philter.

pot·latch /ˈpätˌlacʜ/ ▶ n. (among some North American Indian peoples) a ceremonial feast at which possessions are given away or destroyed as an indication of wealth.

pot·luck /ˈpätˈlək/ ▶ n. **1** a situation in which you must take a chance that whatever is available will prove to be good or acceptable: *he could take potluck in a town not noted for its hotels.* **2** a meal or party to which each of the guests contributes a dish.

pot·pour·ri /ˌpōpəˈrē, ˌpōpo͝oˈrē/ ▶ n. (plural **potpourris**) a mixture of dried petals and spices used to perfume a room.

pot·shot /ˈpätˌsʜät/ ▶ n. a shot aimed unexpectedly or at random.

pot·tage /ˈpätij/ ▶ n. old use soup or stew.

pot·ted /ˈpätid/ ▶ adj. **1** (of a plant) planted or grown in a flowerpot. **2** informal intoxicated by drink or drugs.

pot·ter /ˈpätər/ ▶ n. a person who makes pottery.

pot·ter·y /ˈpätərē/ ▶ n. (plural **potteries**) **1** articles made of fired clay. **2** the craft of making such articles. **3** a place where pottery is made.

> SYNONYMS **ceramics**, crockery, earthenware, terracotta, stoneware, china, porcelain.

pot·ty /ˈpätē/ ▶ n. (plural **potties**) a bowl for a child to sit on and use as a toilet. □ **go potty** informal use a toilet.

pouch /poucʜ/ ▶ n. **1** a small flexible bag. **2** a pocket of skin in an animal's body, especially that in which animals such as kangaroos carry their young.

> SYNONYMS **bag**, purse, sack, sac, pocket.

pouffe /po͞of/ (or **pouf**) ▶ n. a large, firm cushion used as a seat or for resting your feet on.

poul·tice /ˈpōltəs/ ▶ n. a soft, moist mass of flour or plant material that is put on the skin to reduce inflammation.

poul·try /ˈpōltrē/ ▶ n. chickens, turkeys, ducks, and geese.

pounce /pouns/ ▶ v. (**pounces**, **pouncing**, **pounced**) **1** suddenly spring to seize or attack something. **2** (**pounce on**) quickly notice and criticize something that someone has said or done. ▶ n. an act of pouncing.

> SYNONYMS ▶ v. **jump**, spring, leap, dive, lunge, swoop, attack.

pound¹ /pound/ ▶ n. **1** a unit of weight equal to 16 ounces avoirdupois (0.4536 kilograms). **2** (also **pound sterling**) the basic unit of money of the UK, equal to 100 pence. □ **pound sign** the sign #, representing a pound as a unit of weight or mass or indicating a function key on a telephone.

pound² ▶ v. **1** hit something heavily again and again. **2** walk or run with heavy steps. **3** beat or throb with a strong regular rhythm. **4** crush or grind something into a powder or paste.

> SYNONYMS **1 beat**, strike, hit, batter, thump, pummel, punch, rain blows on, belabor, hammer; informal bash, clobber, wallop. **2 beat against**, crash against, batter, dash against, lash, buffet. **3 bombard**, bomb, shell. **4 crush**, grind, pulverize, mash, pulp. **5 stomp**, stamp, clomp, clump, tramp, lumber. **6 throb**, thump, thud, hammer, pulse, race.

pound³ ▶ n. a place where stray dogs or illegally parked vehicles are officially taken and kept until claimed.

> SYNONYMS **enclosure**, compound, pen, yard, corral.

pour /pôr/ ▶ v. **1** flow or cause to flow in a steady stream. **2** (of rain) fall heavily. **3** prepare and serve a drink. **4** come or go in large numbers. **5** (**pour something out**) express your feelings freely.

> SYNONYMS **1 stream**, flow, run, gush, course, jet, spurt, surge, spill. **2 tip**, splash, spill, decant; informal slosh, slop. **3 rain hard**, teem down, pelt down, rain cats and dogs. **4 crowd**, throng, swarm, stream, flood.

> USAGE
>
> Don't confuse **pour** and **pore**: you **pore over** a book, you do not **pour over** it.

pout /pout/ ▶ v. push your lips forward as a sign of sulking or to make yourself look attractive. ▶ n. a pouting expression. ■ **pout·y** adj.

pov·er·ty /ˈpävərtē/ ▶ n. **1** the state of being very poor. **2** the state of being inferior in quality or insufficient in amount.

> SYNONYMS **1 destitution**, pennilessness, penury, impoverishment, neediness, hardship, impecuniousness, indigence. **2 scarcity**, deficiency, dearth, shortage, paucity, absence, lack, inadequacy. ANTONYMS wealth, abundance.

pow·der /ˈpoudər/ ▶ n. **1** a mass of fine dry particles. **2** a cosmetic in this form applied to a person's face. ▶ v. (**powders**, **powdering**, **powdered**) **1** sprinkle powder over. **2** make something into a powder. □ **powder room** a women's toilet in a public building.

pow·der·y /ˈpoudərē/ ▶ adj. consisting of or resembling powder.

> SYNONYMS **fine**, dry, fine-grained, powderlike, dusty, chalky, floury, sandy, crumbly, friable.

pow·er /ˈpou(-ə)r/ ▶ n. **1** the ability to do something: *the power of speech.* **2** the ability to influence people or events. **3** the right or authority to do something. **4** political authority or control. **5** a country seen as having international influence and military strength: *a world power.* **6** strength, force, or energy. **7** capacity or performance of an engine or other device. **8** energy that is produced by mechanical, electrical, or other means. **9** Physics the rate of doing work, measured in watts or horsepower. **10** Math the product obtained when a number is multiplied by itself a certain number of times. ▶ v. (**powers**, **powering**, **powered**) **1** supply with power. **2** move with speed or force.

> SYNONYMS ▶ n. **1 ability**, capacity, capability, potential, potentiality, faculty. **2 control**, command, authority, dominance, supremacy, ascendancy, mastery, influence, sway, leverage; informal clout, teeth. **3 authority**, right, authorization. **4 state**, country, nation. **5 strength**, might, force, vigor, energy. **6 forcefulness**, powerfulness, strength, force,

cogency, persuasiveness. **7 driving force**, horsepower, acceleration, torque; informal oomph. **8 energy**, electricity. ANTONYMS weakness.

□ **do someone a power of good** informal be very good for someone. **power cut** a temporary interruption in an electricity supply. **power of attorney** the authority to act for another person in particular legal or financial matters. **power station** a building where electrical power is generated. **power steering** steering aided by power from a vehicle's engine. **the powers that be** the authorities.

pow·er·boat /ˈpou(-ə)rˌbōt/ ▶ **n.** a fast motorboat.

pow·er·ful /ˈpou(-ə)rfəl/ ▶ **adj.** having power.

SYNONYMS **1 strong**, muscular, muscly, sturdy, strapping, robust, brawny, burly, athletic, manly, well-built, solid; informal beefy. **2 intoxicating**, hard, strong, stiff, potent. **3 violent**, forceful, hard, mighty. **4 intense**, keen, fierce, strong, irresistible, overpowering, overwhelming. **5 influential**, strong, important, dominant, commanding, formidable. **6 cogent**, compelling, convincing, persuasive, forceful, potent. ANTONYMS weak, gentle.

■ **pow·er·ful·ly adv.**

pow·er·house /ˈpou(-ə)rˌhous/ ▶ **n.** a person or thing having great energy or power.

pow·er·less /ˈpou(-ə)rləs/ ▶ **adj.** without the power to take action.

SYNONYMS **impotent**, helpless, ineffectual, ineffective, useless, defenseless, vulnerable.

pow·wow /ˈpouˌwou/ ▶ **n. 1** informal a meeting for discussion. **2** a North American Indian ceremony involving feasting and dancing.

pox /päks/ ▶ **n.** any disease that produces a rash of pus-filled pimples that leave pockmarks on healing.

pp (or **p.p.**) ▶ **abbr.** used when signing a letter on someone else's behalf.

PR ▶ **abbr. 1** proportional representation. **2** public relations.

prac·ti·ca·ble /ˈpraktikəbəl/ ▶ **adj.** able to be done successfully.

SYNONYMS **realistic**, feasible, possible, viable, reasonable, sensible, workable, achievable; informal doable.

■ **prac·ti·ca·bil·i·ty** /ˌpraktikəˈbilətē/ **n.**

prac·ti·cal /ˈpraktikəl/ ▶ **adj. 1** relating to the actual doing or use of something rather than theory. **2** likely to be successful or useful. **3** skilled at making or doing things.

SYNONYMS **1 empirical**, hands-on, actual. **2 feasible**, practicable, realistic, viable, workable, possible, reasonable, sensible; informal doable. **3 functional**, sensible, utilitarian. **4 realistic**, sensible, down-to-earth, businesslike, commonsensical, hardheaded, no-nonsense; informal hard-nosed. ANTONYMS theoretical.

□ **practical joke** a trick played on someone to make them look silly. **practical nurse** a nurse who has completed a training course of a lower standard than a registered nurse.

prac·ti·cal·i·ty /ˌpraktiˈkalətē/ ▶ **n.** (plural **practicalities**) **1** the state of being practical. **2** (**practicalities**) the real facts or aspects of a situation.

prac·ti·cal·ly /ˈpraktik(ə)lē/ ▶ **adv. 1** almost; virtually. **2** in a practical way.

SYNONYMS **1 almost**, very nearly, virtually, just about, all but, more or less, as good as, to all intents and purposes; informal pretty well. **2 realistically**, sensibly, reasonably, rationally, matter-of-factly.

prac·tice /ˈpraktəs/ ▶ **v.** (**practices**, **practicing**, **practiced**) **1** do something repeatedly to improve your skill. **2** do something regularly as part of your normal behavior. **3** be working in a particular profession. **4** (**practiced**) skillful as a result of experience. **5** follow the teaching and rules of a religion. ▶ **n. 1** the actual doing of something rather than the theories about it. **2** the usual way of doing something. **3** the work, business, or place of work of a doctor, dentist, or lawyer. **4** the doing of something repeatedly to improve your skill.

SYNONYMS ▶ **v. 1 rehearse**, run through, go over/through, work on/at, polish, perfect, refine. **2 train**, rehearse, prepare, go through your paces. **3 carry out**, perform, observe, follow. **4 work in**, pursue a career in, engage in. **5** (**practiced**) **expert**, experienced, seasoned, skilled, skillful, accomplished, proficient, talented, able, adept. ▶ **n. 1 application**, exercise, use, operation, implementation, execution. **2 custom**, procedure, policy, convention, tradition. **3 training**, rehearsal, repetition, preparation, dummy run, run-through; informal dry run. **4 profession**, career, business, work. **5 business**, firm, office, company; informal outfit.

prac·ti·tion·er /prakˈtisHənər/ ▶ **n.** a person who practices a profession or activity.

prag·mat·ic /pragˈmatik/ ▶ **adj.** dealing with things in a sensible and realistic way.

SYNONYMS **practical**, matter-of-fact, sensible, down-to-earth, commonsensical, businesslike, hardheaded, no-nonsense; informal hard-nosed. ANTONYMS impractical.

■ **prag·mat·i·cal·ly adv.**

prag·ma·tism /ˈpragməˌtizəm/ ▶ **n.** a realistic and sensible attitude or approach to something. ■ **prag·ma·tist n.**

prai·rie /ˈpre(ə)rē/ ▶ **n.** (in North America) a large open area of grassland. □ **prairie dog** a type of rodent that lives in burrows in the prairies of North America.

praise /prāz/ ▶ **v.** (**praises**, **praising**, **praised**) **1** show approval of or admiration for. **2** express thanks to or respect for God. ▶ **n.** words that show approval or admiration.

SYNONYMS ▶ **v. commend**, applaud, pay tribute to, speak highly of, compliment, congratulate, sing the praises of, rave about. ANTONYMS criticize. ▶ **n. approval**, acclaim, admiration, approbation, plaudits, congratulations, commendation, accolade, compliment, a pat on the back, eulogy. ANTONYMS criticism.

praise·wor·thy /ˈprāzˌwərT͟Hē/ ▶ **adj.** deserving praise.

SYNONYMS **commendable**, admirable, laudable, worthy (of admiration), meritorious, estimable, excellent, exemplary.

pra·line /'prä,lēn, 'prā-/ ▶ **n.** a sweet substance made from nuts boiled in sugar.

prance /prans/ ▶ **v.** (**prances**, **prancing**, **pranced**) walk with exaggerated steps.

SYNONYMS **cavort**, dance, jig, trip, caper, jump, leap, spring, bound, skip, hop, frisk, romp, frolic.

prank /praNGk/ ▶ **n.** a practical joke or mischievous act.

SYNONYMS **(practical) joke**, trick, escapade, stunt, caper, jape, game, hoax; informal lark, leg-pull.

prank·ster /'praNGkstər/ ▶ **n.** a person who is fond of playing pranks.

prate /prāt/ ▶ **v.** (**prates**, **prating**, **prated**) talk too much in a silly or boring way.

prat·tle /'pratl/ ▶ **v.** (**prattles**, **prattling**, **prattled**) talk too much in a silly or trivial way. ▶ **n.** foolish or silly talk.

prawn /prôn/ ▶ **n.** an edible shellfish like a large shrimp.

pray /prā/ ▶ **v.** **1** say a prayer. **2** hope strongly for something. ▶ **adv.** formal or old use please. □ **praying mantis** ⇨ MANTIS.

prayer /pre(ə)r/ ▶ **n.** **1** a request for help or expression of thanks made to God or a god. **2** (**prayers**) a religious service at which people gather to pray together. **3** an earnest hope or wish.

PRC ▶ **abbr.** People's Republic of China.

preach /prēCH/ ▶ **v.** **1** give a religious talk to a group of people. **2** recommend a particular way of thinking or behaving. **3** (**preach at**) tell someone how they should think or behave in a way that is boring or annoying.

SYNONYMS **1 give a sermon**, sermonize, evangelize, spread the gospel. **2 proclaim**, teach, spread, propagate, expound. **3 advocate**, recommend, advise, urge, teach, counsel.

■ **preach·er n.**

pre·am·ble /'prē,ambəl/ ▶ **n.** an opening statement; an introduction.

pre·ar·range /,prēə'rānj/ ▶ **v.** (**prearranges**, **prearranging**, **prearranged**) arrange something in advance.

pre·car·i·ous /pri'ke(ə)rēəs/ ▶ **adj.** **1** likely to tip over or fall. **2** (of a situation) not safe or certain.

SYNONYMS **insecure**, uncertain, unpredictable, risky, hazardous, dangerous, unsafe, unstable, unsteady, shaky; informal dicey, iffy; old use parlous. ANTONYMS safe.

■ **pre·car·i·ous·ly adv.**

pre·cau·tion /pri'kôSHən/ ▶ **n.** something done to avoid problems or danger.

SYNONYMS **safeguard**, preventive measure, safety measure, insurance; informal backstop.

■ **pre·cau·tion·ar·y adj.**

pre·cede /pri'sēd/ ▶ **v.** (**precedes**, **preceding**, **preceded**) **1** happen before something in time or order. **2** go somewhere in front of someone.

SYNONYMS **1 go before**, come before, lead up to, pave the way for, herald, introduce, usher in. **2 go ahead of**, go in front of, lead the way. ANTONYMS follow.

prec·e·dence /'presədəns, pri'sēdns/ ▶ **n.** the state of coming before others in order or importance.

SYNONYMS **seniority**, superiority, ascendancy, supremacy.

prec·e·dent /'presid(ə)nt/ ▶ **n.** an earlier event, action, or legal case that is taken as an example to be followed in similar situations.

SYNONYMS **model**, exemplar, example, pattern, paradigm, criterion, yardstick, standard.

pre·cept /'prē,sept/ ▶ **n.** a general rule about how to behave.

pre·cinct /'prē,siNGkt/ ▶ **n.** **1** an enclosed area around a place or building. **2** each of the districts into which a city or town is divided for elections or policing.

SYNONYMS **district**, zone, sector, quarter, area.

pre·cious /'preSHəs/ ▶ **adj.** **1** rare and worth a lot of money. **2** greatly loved or valued. **3** sophisticated in a way that is artificial and exaggerated.

SYNONYMS **1 valuable**, costly, expensive, invaluable, priceless. **2 valued**, cherished, treasured, prized, favorite, dear, beloved, special. **3 affected**, pretentious; informal la-di-da.

□ **precious little** (or **few**) informal very little (or few). **precious metal** a valuable metal such as gold, silver, or platinum. **precious stone** an attractive and valuable piece of mineral, used in jewelry.

prec·i·pice /'presəpəs/ ▶ **n.** a tall and very steep rock face or cliff.

SYNONYMS **cliff (face)**, rock face, sheer drop, crag, bluff, escarpment.

pre·cip·i·tate ▶ **v.** /pri'sipə,tāt/ (**precipitates**, **precipitating**, **precipitated**) **1** make something bad happen suddenly or sooner than it should. **2** make something move or happen suddenly and with force. **3** Chemistry cause a substance to be deposited in solid form from a solution. **4** cause moisture in the air to condense and fall as rain, snow, etc. ▶ **adj.** /pri'sipətət/ done or happening suddenly or without careful thought. ▶ **n.** /pri'sipətət, -ə,tāt/ Chemistry a substance precipitated from a solution.

SYNONYMS ▶ **v.** **bring about**, bring on, cause, lead to, give rise to, instigate, trigger, spark, touch off, provoke, hasten, speed up, accelerate. ▶ **adj.** **hasty**, overhasty, rash, hurried, rushed, impetuous, impulsive, precipitous, incautious, imprudent, injudicious, ill-advised, reckless.

pre·cip·i·ta·tion /pri,sipə'tāSHən/ ▶ **n.** **1** rain, snow, sleet, or hail. **2** Chemistry the action of precipitating a substance from a solution.

pre·cip·i·tous /pri'sipətəs/ ▶ **adj.** dangerously high or steep.

SYNONYMS **1 steep**, sheer, perpendicular, abrupt, sharp, vertical. **2 sudden**, rapid, swift, abrupt, headlong, speedy, quick, fast.

pré·cis /prā'sē, 'prāsē/ ▶ **n.** (plural **précis**) a short summary.

pre·cise /pri'sīs/ ▶ **adj.** **1** presented in a detailed and accurate way. **2** taking care to be exact and accurate. **3** particular.

SYNONYMS **1 exact**, accurate, correct, specific, detailed, explicit, careful, meticulous, strict, rigorous. **2** *at that precise moment* **exact**, particular, actual, specific, distinct. ANTONYMS inaccurate.

pre·cise·ly /pri'sīslē/ ▶ **adv.** **1** in exact terms; without vagueness. **2** exactly. **3** said to show that you agree very much with a statement.

SYNONYMS **1 exactly**, sharp, on the dot, promptly; informal on the button, on the nose, bang (on). **2 just**, exactly, in all respects; informal to a T.

pre·ci·sion /pri'sizHən/ ▶ **n.** the quality of being exact, accurate, and careful.

SYNONYMS **exactness**, accuracy, exactitude, correctness, care, meticulousness, scrupulousness, punctiliousness, rigor.

pre·clude /pri'klo͞od/ ▶ **v.** (**precludes**, **precluding**, **precluded**) prevent something from happening.

SYNONYMS **prevent**, make it impossible for, rule out, stop, prohibit, debar, bar, hinder, impede, inhibit, exclude.

pre·co·cious /pri'kōsHəs/ ▶ **adj.** having developed certain abilities or tendencies at an earlier age than usual. ■ **pre·coc·i·ty** /pri'käsətē/ **n.**

pre·cog·ni·tion /ˌprēkäg'nisHən/ ▶ **n.** knowledge of an event before it happens.

pre·con·ceived /ˌprēkən'sēvd/ ▶ **adj.** (of an idea or opinion) formed before full knowledge or evidence is available.

pre·con·cep·tion /ˌprēkən'sepsHən/ ▶ **n.** a preconceived idea or opinion.

SYNONYMS **preconceived idea**, presupposition, assumption, presumption, prejudgment, prejudice.

pre·con·di·tion /ˌprēkən'disHən/ ▶ **n.** something that must exist or happen before other things can happen or be done.

pre·cur·sor /'prēˌkərsər, pri'kər-/ ▶ **n.** a person or thing that comes before another of the same kind.

pre·date /prē'dāt/ ▶ **v.** happen, exist, or be found earlier than.

pred·a·tor /'predətər/ ▶ **n.** an animal that hunts and kills others for food.

pred·a·to·ry /'predəˌtôrē/ ▶ **adj.** **1** (of an animal) killing other animals for food. **2** taking advantage of weaker people.

SYNONYMS **1 predacious**, carnivorous, hunting. **2 exploitative**, wolfish, rapacious, manipulative.

pre·de·cease /ˌprēdi'sēs/ ▶ **v.** (**predeceases**, **predeceasing**, **predeceased**) formal die before another person.

pred·e·ces·sor /'predəˌsesər, 'prē-/ ▶ **n.** **1** a person who held a job or office before the current holder. **2** a thing that has been followed or replaced by another.

SYNONYMS **1 forerunner**, precursor, antecedent. **2 ancestor**, forefather, forebear, antecedent. ANTONYMS successor, descendant.

pre·des·ti·na·tion /prēˌdestə'nāsHən/ ▶ **n.** the belief that everything that happens has been decided in advance by God or fate.

pre·des·tined /prē'destind/ ▶ **adj.** already decided by God or fate.

pre·de·ter·mine /ˌprēdi'tərmən/ ▶ **v.** (**predetermines**, **predetermining**, **predetermined**) establish or decide in advance.

pre·dic·a·ment /pri'dikəmənt/ ▶ **n.** a difficult situation.

SYNONYMS **difficulty**, mess, plight, quandary, muddle, dilemma; informal hole, fix, jam, pickle.

pred·i·cate ▶ **n.** /'predikət/ Grammar the part of a sentence or clause containing a verb and stating something about the subject (e.g., *went home* in *she went home*). ▶ **v.** /'predəˌkāt/ (**predicates**, **predicating**, **predicated**) (**predicate something on**) base something on.

pred·i·ca·tive /'predəˌkātiv, -ikətiv/ ▶ **adj.** Grammar (of an adjective) coming after a verb, as *old* in *the dog is old.*

pre·dict /pri'dikt/ ▶ **v.** state that an event will happen in the future.

SYNONYMS **forecast**, foretell, prophesy; old use augur.

■ **pre·dic·tive** **adj.** **pre·dic·tor** **n.**

pre·dict·a·ble /pri'diktəbəl/ ▶ **adj.** **1** able to be predicted. **2** always behaving or happening in the way that you would expect.

SYNONYMS **foreseeable**, to be expected, anticipated, likely, foreseen, unsurprising, reliable; informal inevitable.

■ **pre·dict·a·bil·i·ty** /-ˌdiktə'bilətē/ **n.** **pre·dict·a·bly** **adv.**

pre·dic·tion /pri'diksHən/ ▶ **n.** **1** a statement saying that something will happen; a forecast. **2** the action of predicting.

SYNONYMS **forecast**, prophecy, prognosis, prognostication.

pre·di·lec·tion /ˌpredl'eksHən, ˌprēdl-/ ▶ **n.** a preference or special liking for something.

pre·dis·pose /ˌprēdi'spōz/ ▶ **v.** (**predisposes**, **predisposing**, **predisposed**) make someone likely to be, do, or think something.

pre·dis·po·si·tion /ˌprēˌdispə'zisHən/ ▶ **n.** a liability or tendency to do, be, or think something.

SYNONYMS **1 susceptibility**, proneness, tendency, liability, inclination, vulnerability. **2 preference**, predilection, inclination, leaning, bent.

pre·dom·i·nant /pri'dämənənt/ ▶ **adj.** **1** present as the main part of something. **2** having the greatest power. ■ **pre·dom·i·nance** **n.**

pre·dom·i·nant·ly /pri'dämənəntlē/ ▶ **adv.** mainly; for the most part.

SYNONYMS **mainly**, mostly, for the most part, chiefly, principally, primarily, in the main, on the whole, largely, by and large, typically, generally, usually.

pre·dom·i·nate /pri'däməˌnāt/ ▶ **v.** (**predominates**, **predominating**, **predominated**) **1** be the main part of something. **2** have control or power.

pre·em·i·nent /prē'emənənt/ ▶ **adj.** better than all others. ■ **pre·em·i·nence** **n.**

pre·empt /prē'empt/ ▶ **v.** **1** take action so as to prevent something happening. **2** stop someone from saying something by speaking first. ■ **pre·emp·tion** **n.** **pre·emp·tive** **adj.**

preen /prēn/ ▶ **v.** **1** (of a bird) tidy and clean its feathers with its beak. **2** attend to and admire your appearance. **3** (**preen yourself**) feel very pleased with yourself.

pre·e·xist·ing /ˌprē-igˈzistiNG/ ▶ **adj.** existing from an earlier time.

pre·fab /prēˈfab, ˈprēˌfab/ ▶ **n.** informal a prefabricated building.

pre·fab·ri·cat·ed /prēˈfabriˌkātid/ ▶ **adj.** (of a building) made in previously constructed sections that can be easily put together on site.

pref·ace /ˈprefəs/ ▶ **n.** an introduction to a book. ▶ **v.** (**prefaces**, **prefacing**, **prefaced**) (**preface something with** or **by**) say or do something to introduce a book, speech, or event.

> SYNONYMS ▶ **n.** **introduction**, foreword, preamble, prologue, prelude, front matter; informal intro. ▶ **v.** **precede**, introduce, begin, open, start.

pre·fect /ˈprēˌfekt/ ▶ **n.** a chief officer, magistrate, or regional governor in certain countries.

pre·fec·ture /ˈprēˌfekCHər/ ▶ **n.** (in certain countries) a district administered by a prefect.

pre·fer /priˈfər/ ▶ **v.** (**prefers**, **preferring**, **preferred**) like one person or thing better than another.

> SYNONYMS **like better**, would rather (have), would sooner (have), favor, be more partial to, choose, select, pick, opt for, go for.

> SPELLING
> Double the **r** in prefe**rr**ing and prefe**rr**ed.

pref·er·a·ble /ˈpref(ə)rəbəl/ ▶ **adj.** more desirable or suitable.

> SYNONYMS **better**, best, more desirable, more suitable, advantageous, superior, preferred, recommended.

pref·er·a·bly /ˈpref(ə)rəblē/ ▶ **adv.** ideally; if possible.

> SYNONYMS **ideally**, if possible, for preference, from choice.

pref·er·ence /ˈpref(ə)rəns/ ▶ **n.** **1** a greater liking for one person or thing than another. **2** a thing preferred. **3** favor shown to one person over another.

> SYNONYMS **1 liking**, partiality, fondness, taste, inclination, leaning, bent, penchant, predisposition. **2 priority**, favor, precedence, preferential treatment.

pref·er·en·tial /ˌprefəˈrenCHəl/ ▶ **adj.** favoring a particular person or group. ■ **pref·er·en·tial·ly** **adv.**

pre·fer·ment /priˈfərmənt/ ▶ **n.** formal promotion to a job or position.

pre·fig·ure /prēˈfigyər/ ▶ **v.** (**prefigures**, **prefiguring**, **prefigured**) be an early sign or version of.

pre·fix /ˈprēˌfiks/ ▶ **n.** **1** a letter or group of letters placed at the beginning of a word to alter its meaning (e.g., *non-*). **2** a word, letter, or number placed before another. ▶ **v.** add a prefix to.

preg·nan·cy /ˈpregnənsē/ ▶ **n.** (plural **pregnancies**) the state or period of being pregnant.

preg·nant /ˈpregnənt/ ▶ **adj.** **1** (of a woman) having a baby developing inside her uterus. **2** full of meaning.

> SYNONYMS **1 expecting**, expectant, carrying a child, with child; informal in the family way. **2 meaningful**, significant, suggestive, expressive, charged.

pre·hen·sile /prēˈhensəl, -ˌsīl/ ▶ **adj.** (of an animal's limb or tail) capable of grasping things.

pre·his·tor·ic /ˌprē(h)iˈstôrik/ ▶ **adj.** relating to the period before written records of events were made.

pre·his·to·ry /prēˈhist(ə)rē/ ▶ **n.** **1** the period of time before written records were made. **2** the early stages in the development of something.

pre·in·dus·tri·al /ˌprē-inˈdəstrēəl/ ▶ **adj.** before the development of industries.

pre·judge /prēˈjəj/ ▶ **v.** (**prejudges**, **prejudging**, **prejudged**) make a judgment before you have all the necessary information.

prej·u·dice /ˈprejədəs/ ▶ **n.** **1** an opinion that is not based on reason or experience. **2** unfair reactions or behavior based on such opinions. ▶ **v.** (**prejudices**, **prejudicing**, **prejudiced**) **1** influence someone so that they form an opinion that is not based on reason or experience. **2** (**prejudiced**) having or showing a dislike or distrust that is derived from prejudice. **3** cause harm to.

> SYNONYMS ▶ **n.** **1 preconceived idea**, preconception. **2 bigotry**, bias, partiality, intolerance, discrimination, unfairness, inequality. ▶ **v.** **1 bias**, influence, sway, predispose, make partial, color. **2** (**prejudiced**) **biased**, bigoted, discriminatory, partisan, intolerant, narrow-minded, unfair, unjust, inequitable. **3 damage**, be detrimental to, be prejudicial to, injure, harm, hurt, spoil, impair, undermine, compromise.

prej·u·di·cial /ˌprejəˈdiSHəl/ ▶ **adj.** **1** harmful to someone or something. **2** causing premature judgment.

prel·ate /ˈprelət/ ▶ **n.** a bishop or other high-ranking minister in the Christian Church.

pre·lim·i·nar·y /priˈliməˌnerē/ ▶ **adj.** taking place before a main action or event. ▶ **n.** (plural **preliminaries**) a preliminary action or event.

> SYNONYMS ▶ **adj.** **preparatory**, introductory, initial, opening, early, exploratory. ANTONYMS final. ▶ **n.** **introduction**, preamble, preface, opening remarks, formalities.

prel·ude /ˈprelˌ(y)o͞od, ˈprāˌl(y)o͞od/ ▶ **n.** **1** an action or event acting as an introduction to something more important. **2** a piece of music introducing a longer piece.

> SYNONYMS **preliminary**, overture, opening, preparation, introduction, lead-in, precursor.

pre·mar·i·tal /prēˈmaritl/ ▶ **adj.** happening before marriage.

pre·ma·ture /ˌprēməˈCHo͝or, -ˈt(y)o͝or/ ▶ **adj.** **1** happening or done before the proper time. **2** (of a baby) born before the normal length of pregnancy is completed.

> SYNONYMS **1 untimely**, too early, before time, unseasonable. **2 rash**, overhasty, hasty, precipitate, impulsive, impetuous; informal previous. ANTONYMS overdue.

■ **pre·ma·ture·ly** **adv.**

pre·med·i·tat·ed /priˈmedəˌtātid, prē-/ ▶ **adj.** (of a crime or other bad action) planned in advance.

> SYNONYMS **planned**, intentional, deliberate, preplanned, calculated, cold-blooded, conscious, prearranged. ANTONYMS spontaneous.

■ **pre·med·i·ta·tion** /-ˌmedəˈtāSHən/ **n.**

pre·men·stru·al /prē'menstr(o͞o)əl/ ▶ **adj.** happening or experienced in the days of the month before menstruation.

pre·mier /prē'm(y)i(ə)r, 'prēmēər, 'prē,mi(ə)r/ ▶ **adj.** first in importance, order, or position. ▶ **n.** a prime minister or other head of government.

> SYNONYMS ▶ **adj. leading**, foremost, chief, principal, head, ranking, top-ranking, top, prime, primary, first, highest, preeminent, senior, outstanding. ▶ **n. head of government**, prime minister, PM, president, chancellor.

■ **pre·mier·ship** **n.**

pre·miere /prē'myer, -'mi(ə)r/ ▶ **n.** the first performance or showing of a play, movie, ballet, etc.

> SYNONYMS **first performance**, first night, opening night, debut.

prem·ise /'premis/ ▶ **n.** a statement or idea that forms the basis for a theory or argument.

> SYNONYMS **proposition**, assumption, hypothesis, thesis, presupposition, supposition, presumption, assertion.

prem·is·es /'preməsəz/ ▶ **pl.n.** the building and land occupied by a business.

> SYNONYMS **building(s)**, property, site, office, establishment.

pre·mi·um /'prēmēəm/ ▶ **n.** (plural **premiums**) **1** an amount paid for an insurance policy. **2** an extra sum added to a basic price. ▶ **adj.** of high quality and more expensive.

> SYNONYMS ▶ **n. 1 (regular) payment**, installment. **2 surcharge**, additional payment, extra.

□ **at a premium 1** scarce and in demand. **2** above the usual price.

pre·mo·ni·tion /,prēmə'nisʜən, ,prem-/ ▶ **n.** a strong feeling that something is going to happen.

> SYNONYMS **foreboding**, presentiment, intuition, (funny) feeling, hunch, suspicion, feeling in your bones.

■ **pre·mon·i·to·ry** /prē'mänə,tôrē/ **adj.**

pre·na·tal /prē'nātl/ ▶ **adj.** before birth.

pre·oc·cu·pa·tion /,prē,äkyə'pāsʜən/ ▶ **n. 1** the state of being preoccupied. **2** a matter that preoccupies someone.

> SYNONYMS **obsession**, fixation, concern, passion, enthusiasm, hobbyhorse; informal bee in your bonnet.

pre·oc·cu·py /prē'äkyə,pī/ ▶ **v.** (**preoccupies**, **preoccupying**, **preoccupied**) completely fill someone's mind.

> SYNONYMS (**preoccupied**) **lost in thought**, deep in thought, oblivious, pensive, distracted, absorbed, engrossed, involved, wrapped up, concerned.

pre·or·dained /,prēôr'dānd/ ▶ **adj.** decided or determined beforehand.

prep /prep/ ▶ **n.** preparation (especially of a patient before surgery). ▶ **v.** prepare a person for surgery, an examination, etc. □ **prep school** a preparatory school.

pre·paid /prē'pād/ ▶ **adj.** paid for in advance.

prep·a·ra·tion /,prepə'rāsʜən/ ▶ **n. 1** the process of getting ready for something. **2** something that is done to get ready for something. **3** a substance prepared for use as a medicine, cosmetic, etc.

> SYNONYMS **1 preparations** *for the party* **arrangements**, planning, plans, groundwork, spadework, provision. **2 devising**, drawing up, construction, composition, development. **3 mixture**, compound, concoction, solution, medicine, potion.

pre·par·a·to·ry /pri'pe(ə)rə,tôrē, -'parə-, 'prep(ə)rə-/ ▶ **adj.** done in order to prepare for something. □ **preparatory school** a private school that prepares students for college.

pre·pare /pri'pe(ə)r/ ▶ **v.** (**prepares**, **preparing**, **prepared**) **1** make something ready for use. **2** get ready to do or deal with something. **3** (**be prepared to do**) be willing to do.

> SYNONYMS **1 get ready**, put together, draw up, produce, arrange, assemble, construct, compose, formulate. **2** (**prepared**) **ready**, (all) set, equipped, primed, waiting, poised. **3 cook**, make, get, concoct; informal fix, rustle up. **4 get ready**, make preparations, arrange things, make provision. **5 train**, get into shape, practice, get ready, warm up, limber up. **6** *prepare yourself for a shock* **brace**, ready, tense, steel, steady. **7** (**prepared**) **willing**, ready, disposed, (favorably) inclined, of a mind, minded.

pre·par·ed·ness /prə'pe(ə)r(ə)dnis/ ▶ **n.** readiness.

pre·pon·der·ance /pri'pändərəns/ ▶ **n.** a greater number or incidence of something.

pre·pon·der·ant /pri'pändərənt/ ▶ **adj.** greater in number or happening more often.

prep·o·si·tion /,prepə'zisʜən/ ▶ **n.** Grammar a word used with a noun or pronoun to show place, time, or method. ■ **prep·o·si·tion·al** **adj.**

pre·pos·sess·ing /,prēpə'zesiɴɢ/ ▶ **adj.** attractive or appealing in appearance.

pre·pos·ter·ous /pri'päst(ə)rəs/ ▶ **adj.** completely ridiculous or outrageous.

> SYNONYMS **absurd**, ridiculous, foolish, stupid, ludicrous, outrageous, farcical, laughable, comical, risible, nonsensical, senseless, insane; informal crazy. ANTONYMS sensible.

■ **pre·pos·ter·ous·ly** **adv.**

pre·pu·bes·cent /,prēpyo͞o'besənt/ ▶ **adj.** having to do with the period before puberty.

pre·re·cord·ed /,prēri'kôrdid/ ▶ **adj.** (of sound or film) recorded in advance.

pre·req·ui·site /prē'rekwəzət/ ▶ **n.** a thing that must exist or happen before something else can exist or happen.

> SYNONYMS **1 (necessary) condition**, precondition, essential, requirement, requisite, necessity, sine qua non; informal must. **2** *the prerequisite number* **necessary**, required, called for, essential, requisite, obligatory, compulsory.

pre·rog·a·tive /pri'rägətiv, pə'räg-/ ▶ **n.** a right or privilege belonging to a particular person or group.

> SYNONYMS **entitlement**, right, privilege, advantage, due, birthright.

pres·age /'presij, pri'sāj/ ▶ **v.** (**presages**, **presaging**, **presaged**) be a sign or warning of. ▶ **n.** an omen.

Pres·by·te·ri·an /,prezbə'tirēən, ,pres-/ ▶ **adj.** relating to a Protestant church governed by elders who are all of equal rank. ▶ n. a member of a Presbyterian Church. ■ **Pres·by·te·ri·an·ism** n.

pres·by·ter·y /ˈprezbəˌterē, ˈpres-, -bətrē/ ▶ n. (plural **presbyteries**) **1** an administrative body in a Presbyterian Church. **2** the house of a Roman Catholic parish priest. **3** the eastern part of a church near the altar.

pre·school /ˈprēˈsko͞ol/ ▶ adj. **1** of to the time before a child is old enough to go to elementary school. **2** (of a child) too young to go to school. ▶ n. a nursery school. ■ **pre·school·er** n.

pre·scient /ˈpresʜ(ē)ənt, ˈprē-, -s(ē)ənt/ ▶ adj. knowing about things before they happen. ■ **pre·science** n.

pre·scribe /priˈskrīb/ ▶ v. (**prescribes**, **prescribing**, **prescribed**) **1** (of a doctor) state officially that someone should take a particular medicine or have a particular treatment. **2** state officially that something should be done.

> SYNONYMS **1 advise**, recommend, advocate, suggest. **2 stipulate**, lay down, dictate, order, direct, specify, determine.

pre·scrip·tion /priˈskripsʜən/ ▶ n. **1** a piece of paper on which a doctor states that a patient may be supplied with a medicine or treatment. **2** the action of prescribing a medicine or treatment.

pre·scrip·tive /priˈskriptiv/ ▶ adj. stating what should be done.

pres·ence /ˈprezəns/ ▶ n. **1** the state of being in a particular place. **2** a person's impressive manner or appearance. **3** a person or thing that seems to be present but is not seen.

> SYNONYMS **1 existence**, being. **2 attendance**, appearance. **3 aura**, charisma, personality, magnetism. ANTONYMS absence.

□ **presence of mind** the ability to remain calm and act sensibly in a difficult situation.

pres·ent¹ /ˈprezənt/ ▶ adj. **1** being or existing in a particular place. **2** existing or happening now. **3** Grammar (of a tense of a verb) expressing an action or state happening or existing now. ▶ n. the period of time happening now.

> SYNONYMS ▶ adj. **1 in attendance**, here, there, near, nearby, at hand, available. **2 in existence**, detectable, occurring, existing, extant, current. ANTONYMS absent. ▶ n. **now**, today, the present time, the here and now, modern times. ANTONYMS past, future.

□ **for the present** for now; temporarily. **present participle** Grammar the form of a verb, ending in *-ing*, that is used in forming tenses describing continuous action (e.g., *I'm thinking*), as a noun (e.g., *good thinking*), and as an adjective (e.g., *running water*).

pres·ent² ▶ v. /priˈzent/ **1** formally give someone something. **2** offer something for consideration or payment. **3** formally introduce someone to someone else. **4** produce a show, broadcast, etc., for the public. **5** introduce and take part in a television or radio show. **6** be the cause of a problem. **7** give a particular impression to other people: *we must present a united front*. **8** (**present yourself**) appear at or attend a formal or official occasion. ▶ n. /ˈprezənt/ a thing given to someone as a gift.

> SYNONYMS ▶ v. **1 hand over**, give (out), confer, bestow, award, grant, accord. **2 submit**, set forth, put forward, offer, tender, table. **3 introduce**, make known, acquaint someone with. **4 host**, introduce, compère; informal emcee, MC. **5 represent**, describe, portray, depict. ▶ n. **gift**, donation, offering, contribution, gratuity, tip, handout.

■ **pre·sent·er** /priˈzentər/ n.

pre·sent·a·ble /priˈzentəbəl/ ▶ adj. in good enough condition to be seen in public.

pres·en·ta·tion /ˌprēˌzenˈtāsʜən, ˌprezən-, ˌprēzən-/ ▶ n. the action of presenting something, or the way in which it is presented.

> SYNONYMS **1 awarding**, presenting, bestowal, granting. **2 appearance**, arrangement, packaging, layout. **3 demonstration**, talk, lecture, address, speech, show, exhibition, display, introduction, launch, unveiling.

■ **pres·en·ta·tion·al** adj.

pre·sen·ti·ment /priˈzentəmənt/ ▶ n. a feeling that something unpleasant is going to happen.

pres·ent·ly /ˈprezəntlē/ ▶ adv. **1** soon. **2** now.

> SYNONYMS **1 soon**, shortly, momentarily, quite soon, in a short time, in a little while, at any moment/minute/second, before long; informal in a sec. **2 at present**, currently, at the/this moment.

pres·er·va·tion /ˌprezərˈvāsʜən/ ▶ n. **1** the action of preserving something. **2** the degree to which something has been preserved: *the chapel is in a poor state of preservation*.

> SYNONYMS **1 conservation**, protection, care. **2 continuation**, conservation, maintenance, upholding, sustaining, perpetuation.

pre·serv·a·tive /priˈzərvətiv/ ▶ n. a substance used to prevent food or wood from decaying.

pre·serve /priˈzərv/ ▶ v. (**preserves**, **preserving**, **preserved**) **1** keep something in its original state or in good condition. **2** keep someone safe from harm. **3** treat food to prevent it from decaying. ▶ n. **1** a food preserved in sugar, salt, vinegar, or alcohol, such as jam or pickles. **2** something reserved for a particular person or group. **3** a place where game is protected and kept for private hunting.

> SYNONYMS ▶ v. **1 conserve**, protect, maintain, care for, look after. **2 continue** (**with**), conserve, keep going, maintain, uphold, sustain, perpetuate, prolong. **3 guard**, protect, keep, defend, safeguard, shelter, shield. ANTONYMS attack, abandon. ▶ n. **1** *jobs that are no longer the preserve of men* **domain**, area, field, sphere, orbit, realm, province, territory; informal turf, bailiwick. **2 sanctuary**, (game) reserve, reservation.

■ **pre·serv·er** n.

pre·set /prēˈset/ ▶ v. (**presets**, **presetting**, **preset**) set the controls of an electrical device before it is used.

pre·side /priˈzīd/ ▶ v. (**presides**, **presiding**, **presided**) lead or be in charge of a meeting or event.

> SYNONYMS (**preside over**) **be in charge of**, be responsible for, head, manage, administer, control, direct, chair, conduct, officiate at, lead, govern, rule, command, supervise, oversee; informal head up.

pres·i·den·cy /ˈprez(ə)dənsē, ˈprezəˌdensē/ ▶ n. (plural **presidencies**) the job of president, or the period of time it is held.

pres·i·dent /ˈprez(ə)dənt, ˈprezəˌdent/ ▶ n. **1** the elected head of a republic. **2** the head of an organization. ■ **pres·i·den·tial** /ˌprezəˈdencнəl/ **adj.**

pre·sid·i·um /priˈsidēəm, -ˈzid-/ ▶ **n.** a permanent decision-making committee within a political organization, especially a communist one.

press¹ /pres/ ▶ **v. 1** (**press against** or **to**) move into contact with something by using steady force. **2** push something that operates a device. **3** apply pressure to something to flatten or shape it. **4** move by pushing. **5** (**press on** or **ahead**) continue in what you are doing. **6** express or repeat an opinion or claim in a forceful way. **7** make strong efforts to persuade someone to do something. **8** (**be pressed for**) have too little of. **9** (**be pressed to do**) have difficulty doing. ▶ **n. 1** a device for crushing, flattening, or shaping something. **2** a printing press. **3** (**the press**) newspapers or journalists as a whole.

SYNONYMS ▶ **v. 1 push** (**down**), depress, hold down, force, thrust, squeeze, compress. **2 iron**, smooth out, flatten. **3 clasp**, hold close, hug, cuddle, squeeze, clutch, grasp, embrace. **4 cluster**, gather, converge, congregate, flock, swarm, crowd. **5 plead**, urge, advance, present, submit, put forward. **6 urge**, put pressure on, pressurize, force, push, coerce, dragoon, steamroller, browbeat; informal lean on, put the screws on, twist someone's arm, railroad, bulldoze. **7** *they pressed for a ban* **call**, ask, clamor, push, campaign, demand. ▶ **n. the media**, the newspapers, journalism, reporters, the fourth estate.

□ **press conference** a meeting with journalists in order to make an announcement or answer questions. **press release** a statement or piece of publicity issued to journalists.

press² ▶ **v.** (in the past) force someone to serve in the army or navy. □ **press gang** (in the past) a group of men employed to force men to serve in the army or navy. **press-gang** force someone into doing something. **press someone/something into service** use someone or something for a particular purpose as a temporary or emergency measure.

press·ing /ˈpresiNG/ ▶ **adj. 1** needing urgent action. **2** strongly expressed and difficult to refuse or ignore. ▶ **n.** an object made by pressing.

SYNONYMS ▶ **adj. 1 urgent**, critical, crucial, acute, desperate, serious, grave, life-and-death. **2 important**, high-priority, critical, crucial, unavoidable.

pres·sure /ˈpresHər/ ▶ **n. 1** steady force applied to an object by something that is in contact with it. **2** the use of persuasion or threats to make someone do something. **3** a feeling of stress caused by the need to do something. **4** the force per unit area applied by a fluid against a surface. ▶ **v.** (**pressures**, **pressuring**, **pressured**) persuade or force someone into doing something.

SYNONYMS ▶ **n. 1 force**, load, stress, thrust, compression, weight. **2 persuasion**, intimidation, coercion, compulsion, duress, harassment, nagging, badgering. **3 strain**, stress, tension, trouble, difficulty, burden; informal hassle. ▶ **v. coerce**, pressurize, push, persuade, force, bulldoze, hound, nag, badger, browbeat, bully, intimidate, dragoon, twist someone's arm; informal railroad, lean on, hustle.

□ **pressure cooker** a large airtight saucepan in which food is cooked quickly in steam held under pressure. **pressure group** a group that tries to influence the government or public opinion in order to help a cause.

pres·sur·ize /ˈpresHəˌrīz/ ▶ **v.** (**pressurizes**, **pressurizing**, **pressurized**) **1** persuade or force someone into doing something. **2** keep the air pressure in an aircraft cabin the same as it is at ground level.

pres·tige /presˈtēzн, -ˈtēj/ ▶ **n.** respect and admiration resulting from achievements or high quality.

SYNONYMS **status**, standing, kudos, cachet, stature, reputation, repute, renown, honor, esteem, importance, prominence, distinction.

pres·tig·ious /preˈstijəs, -ˈstē-/ ▶ **adj.** having or bringing prestige.

SYNONYMS **reputable**, distinguished, respected, high-status, esteemed, eminent, highly regarded, renowned, influential. ANTONYMS disreputable, obscure.

pres·to /ˈprestō/ ▶ **adv. & adj.** Music in a quick tempo.

pre·stressed /prēˈstrest/ ▶ **adj.** (of concrete) strengthened by means of rods inserted under tension before setting.

pre·sum·a·bly /priˈzo͞oməblē/ ▶ **adv.** as may be supposed.

pre·sume /priˈzo͞om/ ▶ **v.** (**presumes**, **presuming**, **presumed**) **1** suppose that something is probably true. **2** show a lack of respect by doing something that you do not have authority or permission to do. **3** (**presume on**) take advantage of someone's kindness, friendship, etc.

SYNONYMS **1 assume**, suppose, surmise, imagine, take it, expect. **2 dare**, venture, have the effrontery, be so bold as, go so far as, take the liberty of.

pre·sump·tion /priˈzəmpsнən/ ▶ **n. 1** something that is thought to be true or probable. **2** an act of presuming. **3** behavior that is too confident.

pre·sump·tu·ous /priˈzəmpcн(o͞o)əs/ ▶ **adj.** behaving too confidently.

SYNONYMS **brazen**, audacious, forward, familiar, impertinent, insolent, impudent, rude.

■ **pre·sump·tu·ous·ly adv.**

SPELLING

Write **-uous**, not **-ious**: presumpt**uous**.

pre·sup·pose /ˌprēsəˈpōz/ ▶ **v.** (**presupposes**, **presupposing**, **presupposed**) **1** need something to have happened in order to exist or be true. **2** assume, without knowing for sure, that something exists or is true and act on that basis. ■ **pre·sup·po·si·tion** /ˌprēˌsəpəˈzisнən/ **n.**

pre·tend /priˈtend/ ▶ **v. 1** make it seem that something is the case when in fact it is not. **2** give the appearance of feeling or having an emotion or quality. **3** (**pretend to**) claim to have a skill, quality, or title.

SYNONYMS **1 put on an act**, act, play-act, put it on, dissemble, sham, feign, fake, dissimulate, make believe, put on a false front, posture, go through the motions, make as if. **2** *a pretend gun* **mock**, fake, sham, simulated, artificial, false, pseudo; informal phony.

pre·tend·er /priˈtendər/ ▶ **n.** a person who claims a right to a title or position.

pre·tense /ˈprēˌtens, priˈtens/ ▶ **n. 1** an act of pretending. **2** a claim to have or be something.

SYNONYMS **1 make-believe**, acting, faking, play-acting, posturing, deception, trickery. **2 show**, semblance, affectation, appearance, outward appearance, impression, guise, facade. ANTONYMS honesty.

pre·ten·sion /pri'tencHən/ ▶ **n. 1** the act of trying to appear more important or better than you actually are. **2** (also **pretensions**) a claim to have or be something.

pre·ten·tious /pri'tencHəs/ ▶ **adj.** trying to appear more important or better than you actually are so as to impress other people.

SYNONYMS **affected**, ostentatious, showy, pompous, overblown, high-sounding, flowery, grandiose; informal pseudo.

■ **pre·ten·tious·ness n.**

pre·ter·nat·u·ral /ˌprētər'nacH(ə)rəl/ ▶ **adj.** beyond what is normal or natural. ■ **pre·ter·nat·u·ral·ly adv.**

pre·text /'prēˌtekst/ ▶ **n.** a false reason used to justify an action.

pret·ti·fy /'pritəˌfī/ ▶ **v.** (**prettifies, prettifying, prettified**) try to make something look pretty.

pret·ty /'pritē/ ▶ **adj.** (**prettier, prettiest**) **1** (of a woman or girl) having an attractive face. **2** pleasant to look at. ▶ **adv.** informal to a certain extent; fairly.

SYNONYMS ▶ **adj. attractive**, good-looking, nice-looking, personable, fetching, prepossessing, appealing, charming, delightful, cute; old use fair, comely. ANTONYMS plain, ugly. ▶ **adv. quite**, rather, somewhat, fairly.

■ **pret·ti·ly adv. pret·ti·ness n.**

pret·zel /'pretsəl/ ▶ **n.** a crisp salty biscuit in the shape of a knot or stick.

pre·vail /pri'vāl/ ▶ **v. 1** be widespread or current. **2** (**prevailing**) most common or frequent. **3** (**prevail against** or **over**) be more powerful than. **4** (**prevail on**) persuade someone to do something.

SYNONYMS **1** (**prevailing**) **current**, existing, prevalent, usual, common, general, widespread. **2 win**, triumph, be victorious, carry the day, come out on top, succeed, rule, reign. **3 exist**, be present, be the case, occur, be prevalent, be in force.

prev·a·lent /'prevələnt/ ▶ **adj.** widespread; common.

SYNONYMS **widespread**, frequent, usual, common, current, popular, general. ANTONYMS rare.

■ **prev·a·lence n.**

pre·var·i·cate /pri'variˌkāt/ ▶ **v.** (**prevaricates, prevaricating, prevaricated**) avoid giving a direct answer to a question. ■ **pre·var·i·ca·tion** /priˌvari'kāsHən/ **n.**

pre·vent /pri'vent/ ▶ **v. 1** keep something from happening. **2** stop someone from doing something.

SYNONYMS **stop**, avert, nip in the bud, foil, inhibit, thwart, prohibit, forbid. ANTONYMS allow.

■ **pre·vent·a·ble adj. pre·ven·tion n.**

pre·ven·tive /pri'ventiv/ (or **preventative**) ▶ **adj.** designed to prevent something from happening.

pre·view /'prēˌvyo͞o/ ▶ **n. 1** a viewing or showing of something before it becomes generally available. **2** a review of a forthcoming movie, book, or performance.

pre·vi·ous /'prēvēəs/ ▶ **adj. 1** coming before something else in time or order. **2** (**previous to**) before.

SYNONYMS **1 preceding**, foregoing, prior, past, last. **2 former**, preceding, old, earlier, ex-, past, last, sometime, one-time, erstwhile; formal quondam. ANTONYMS next.

pre·vi·ous·ly /'prēvēəslē/ ▶ **adv.** at an earlier time.

SYNONYMS **formerly**, earlier (on), before, hitherto, at one time, in the past.

pre·war /prē'wôr/ ▶ **adj.** before a war, especially World War II.

prey /prā/ ▶ **n. 1** an animal that is hunted and killed by another for food. **2** a person who is harmed or deceived by someone or something. ▶ **v.** (**prey on**) **1** hunt and kill another animal for food. **2** take advantage of or cause distress to someone.

SYNONYMS ▶ **n. 1 quarry**, kill. **2 victim**, target, dupe; informal sucker. ANTONYMS predator.

price /prīs/ ▶ **n. 1** the amount of money for which something is bought or sold. **2** something unwelcome that must be done in order to achieve something. **3** the odds in betting. ▶ **v.** (**prices, pricing, priced**) decide the price of.

SYNONYMS ▶ **n. 1 cost**, charge, fee, fare, amount, sum; informal damage. **2 consequence**, result, cost, penalty, toll, sacrifice, downside, drawback, disadvantage, minus.

price·less /'prīsləs/ ▶ **adj. 1** very valuable. **2** informal very amusing.

SYNONYMS **invaluable**, beyond price, irreplaceable, expensive, costly. ANTONYMS worthless, cheap.

pric·ey /'prīsē/ ▶ **adj.** (**pricier, priciest**) informal expensive.

prick /prik/ ▶ **v. 1** make a small hole in something with a sharp point. **2** cause someone to feel a small, sharp pain. ▶ **n.** a mark, hole, or pain caused by pricking.

SYNONYMS ▶ **v. pierce**, puncture, stab, perforate, spike, penetrate, jab. ▶ **n. jab**, sting, pinprick, stab, pinhole, wound.

□ **prick up your ears 1** (of a horse or dog) raise the ears when alert. **2** suddenly begin to pay attention.

prick·le /'prikəl/ ▶ **n. 1** a small thorn on a plant or a pointed spine on an animal. **2** a tingling feeling on the skin. ▶ **v.** (**prickles, prickling, prickled**) have a tingling feeling on the skin.

prick·ly /'prik(ə)lē/ ▶ **adj. 1** having prickles. **2** causing a prickling feeling. **3** easily offended or annoyed.

SYNONYMS **spiky**, spiked, thorny, barbed, spiny, bristly.

□ **prickly pear** a cactus that produces prickly, pear-shaped fruits.

pride /prīd/ ▶ **n. 1** deep pleasure or satisfaction felt if you or people close to you have done something well. **2** a source of pride: *the team is the pride of the town*. **3** self-respect. **4** the feeling that you are better than other people. **5** a group of lions. ▶ **v.**

(**prides, priding, prided**) (**pride yourself on**) be especially proud of a quality or skill.

SYNONYMS ▶ n. 1 **self-esteem**, dignity, honor, self-respect. 2 **pleasure**, joy, delight, gratification, fulfillment, satisfaction, sense of achievement. 3 **arrogance**, vanity, self-importance, hubris, conceitedness, egotism, snobbery. ANTONYMS shame, humility.

□ **pride of place** the most noticeable or important position.

priest /prēst/ ▶ n. 1 a person who is qualified to perform religious ceremonies in the Christian Church. 2 (also **priestess** /ˈprēstis/) a person who performs ceremonies in a non-Christian religion.

SYNONYMS **clergyman**, clergywoman, minister, cleric, pastor, vicar, rector, parson, churchman, churchwoman, father, curate; informal reverend, padre.

■ **priest·hood** n. **priest·ly** adj.

prig /prig/ ▶ n. a person who behaves as if they are morally superior to other people. ■ **prig·gish** adj.

prim /prim/ ▶ adj. very formal and correct and disapproving of anything improper.

SYNONYMS **demure**, formal, stuffy, strait-laced, prudish, prissy, mimsy, priggish, puritanical; informal starchy.

■ **prim·ly** adv.

pri·ma bal·le·ri·na /ˈprēmə/ ▶ n. the chief female dancer in a ballet company.

pri·ma·cy /ˈprīməsē/ ▶ n. the fact of being most important.

pri·ma don·na /ˌprimə ˈdänə, ˌprēmə/ ▶ n. 1 the chief female singer in an opera. 2 a very temperamental and self-important person.

pri·ma fa·ci·e /ˌprīmə ˈfāsнə, ˈfāsнē, ˈfāsнēˌē/ ▶ adj. & adv. Law accepted as correct until proved otherwise.

pri·mal /ˈprīməl/ ▶ adj. having to do with early human life; primeval.

pri·ma·ri·ly /prīˈme(ə)rəlē/ ▶ adv. for the most part; mainly.

SYNONYMS 1 **first and foremost**, firstly, essentially, in essence, fundamentally, principally, predominantly. 2 **mostly**, for the most part, chiefly, mainly, in the main, on the whole, largely, principally, predominantly.

pri·ma·ry /ˈprīˌmerē, ˈprīm(ə)rē/ ▶ adj. 1 of chief importance. 2 earliest in time or order. 3 (of education) for children between the ages of about five and eleven. ▶ n. (plural **primaries**) a preliminary election to appoint delegates to a party conference or to choose candidates for an election.

SYNONYMS ▶ adj. **main**, chief, key, prime, central, principal, foremost, first, most important, predominant, paramount; informal number-one. ANTONYMS secondary.

□ **primary color** each of the colors blue, red, and yellow, from which all other colors can be obtained by mixing.

pri·mate /ˈprīˌmāt, ˈprīmət/ ▶ n. 1 an animal belonging to the group that includes monkeys, apes, and humans. 2 (in the Christian Church) an archbishop.

prime¹ /prīm/ ▶ adj. 1 of chief importance. 2 of the highest quality; excellent. 3 (of a number) that can be divided only by itself and one (e.g., 2, 3, 5). ▶ n. the time in a person's life when they are the strongest and most successful.

SYNONYMS ▶ adj. 1 **main**, chief, key, primary, central, principal, foremost, first, most important, paramount, major; informal number-one. 2 **top-quality**, top, best, first-class, superior, choice, select, finest; informal tip-top, A1. ANTONYMS secondary, inferior. ▶ n. **heyday**, peak, pinnacle, high point/spot, zenith, flower, bloom, flush.

□ **prime minister** the head of a government. **prime time** the time at which a radio or television audience is greatest.

prime² ▶ v. (**primes, priming, primed**) 1 prepare someone for a situation by giving them information. 2 make something ready for use or action. 3 cover a surface with primer.

SYNONYMS **brief**, fill in, prepare, advise, instruct, coach, drill, train.

prim·er /ˈprīmər/ ▶ n. 1 a substance painted on a surface as a base coat. 2 a book for teaching children to read or giving a basic introduction to a subject.

pri·me·val /prīˈmēvəl/ ▶ adj. relating to the earliest times in history.

prim·i·tive /ˈprimətiv/ ▶ adj. 1 relating to the earliest times in history or stages in development. 2 offering a very basic level of comfort. 3 (of behavior or emotion) not based on reason; instinctive.

SYNONYMS 1 **ancient**, earliest, first, prehistoric, primordial, primeval. 2 **crude**, simple, rough (and ready), basic, rudimentary, makeshift. ANTONYMS modern, sophisticated.

■ **prim·i·tive·ly** adv.

pri·mor·di·al /prīˈmôrdēəl/ ▶ adj. existing at the beginning of time.

primp /primp/ ▶ v. make small adjustments to your appearance.

prim·rose /ˈprimˌrōz/ ▶ n. a plant of woods and hedges with pale yellow flowers.

prim·u·la /ˈprimyələ/ ▶ n. a plant of a group that includes primroses and cowslips.

prince /prins/ ▶ n. a son or other close male relative of a king or queen.

SYNONYMS **ruler**, sovereign, monarch, crowned head.

□ **prince consort** the husband of a reigning queen who is himself a prince.

prince·ling /ˈprinslɪɴɢ/ ▶ n. 1 the ruler of a small country. 2 a young prince.

prince·ly /ˈprinslē/ ▶ adj. 1 relating to or suitable for a prince. 2 (of a sum of money) generous.

prin·cess /ˈprinsəs, ˈprinˌses, prinˈses/ ▶ n. 1 a daughter or other close female relative of a king or queen. 2 the wife or widow of a prince.

prin·ci·pal /ˈprinsəpəl/ ▶ adj. most important; main. ▶ n. 1 the most important person in an organization or group. 2 the head of a school or college. 3 a sum of money lent or invested, on which interest is paid.

SYNONYMS ▶ adj. **main**, chief, primary, leading, foremost, first, most important, predominant, dominant, preeminent, highest, top; informal number-one. ANTONYMS minor.

USAGE

Don't confuse the words **principal** and **principle**. **Principal** is usually an adjective meaning 'main or most important,' whereas **principle** is a noun meaning 'a law, rule, or theory on which something is based.'

prin·ci·pal·i·ty /ˌprinsəˈpalətē/ ▶ **n.** (plural **principalities**) a state ruled by a prince.

prin·ci·pal·ly /ˈprinsəp(ə)lē/ ▶ **adv.** for the most part; chiefly.

SYNONYMS **mainly**, mostly, chiefly, for the most part, in the main, on the whole, largely, predominantly, primarily.

prin·ci·ple /ˈprinsəpəl/ ▶ **n.** **1** a law, rule, or theory on which something is based. **2** (**principles**) rules or beliefs that govern the way you behave. **3** a scientific theorem or natural law that explains why something happens or how it works.

SYNONYMS **1 truth**, concept, idea, theory, fundamental, essential, precept, rule, law. **2 doctrine**, belief, creed, credo, code, ethic. **3 morals**, morality, ethics, ideals, standards, integrity, virtue, probity, honor, decency, conscience, scruples.

□ **in principle** in theory. **on principle** because of your moral principles.

prin·ci·pled /ˈprinsəpəld/ ▶ **adj.** acting according to strong moral principles.

SYNONYMS **moral**, ethical, virtuous, righteous, upright, upstanding, honorable, honest.

print /print/ ▶ **v.** **1** produce a book, newspaper, etc., by a process involving the transfer of words or pictures to paper. **2** produce a photographic print from a negative. **3** write words clearly without joining the letters. **4** mark fabric with a colored design. ▶ **n.** **1** printed words in a book, newspaper, etc. **2** a mark where something has pressed or touched a surface. **3** a printed picture or design.

SYNONYMS ▶ **v.** **1 publish**, issue, release, circulate, run off, copy, reproduce. **2 imprint**, impress, stamp, mark. ▶ **n.** **1 type**, printing, letters, lettering, characters, typeface, font. **2 impression**, handprint, fingerprint, footprint. **3 picture**, engraving, etching, lithograph, woodcut. **4 photograph**, photo, snap, snapshot, picture, still, enlargement, reproduction, copy.

□ **in** (or **out of**) **print** (of a book) available (or no longer available) from the publisher.

print·er /ˈprintər/ ▶ **n.** **1** a person or business involved in printing. **2** a machine for printing, especially one linked to a computer.

print·ing /ˈprintiNG/ ▶ **n.** **1** the transfer of words or pictures to paper in the production of books, newspapers, etc. **2** handwriting in which the letters are written separately. □ **printing press** a machine for printing books, newspapers, etc., by pressing an ink-covered surface on to paper.

print·out /ˈprintˌout/ ▶ **n.** a page of printed material from a computer's printer.

pri·on /ˈprēˌän/ ▶ **n.** a protein particle believed to be the cause of brain diseases such as BSE and CJD.

pri·or[1] /ˈprīər/ ▶ **adj.** **1** coming before in time, order, or importance. **2** (**prior to**) before.

SYNONYMS **earlier**, previous, preceding, advance, preexisting. ANTONYMS subsequent.

pri·or[2] ▶ **n.** (feminine **prioress**) **1** (in an abbey) the person next in rank below an abbot or abbess. **2** the head of a house of friars or nuns.

pri·or·i·tize /prīˈôrəˌtīz, ˈprīərə-/ ▶ **v.** (**prioritizes, prioritizing, prioritized**) **1** decide the order of importance of a number of tasks. **2** treat something as being more important than other things.

pri·or·i·ty /prīˈôrətē/ ▶ **n.** (plural **priorities**) **1** the condition of being more important than other things. **2** a thing seen as more important than others.

SYNONYMS **1 prime concern**, main consideration, most important thing. **2 precedence**, preference, preeminence, predominance, primacy.

pri·o·ry /ˈprīərē/ ▶ **n.** (plural **priories**) a monastery or nunnery governed by a prior or prioress.

prise /prīz/ = **PRIZE**[2].

prism /ˈprizəm/ ▶ **n.** **1** a piece of glass or other transparent material with facets, used to separate white light into a spectrum of colors. **2** a solid geometric figure whose two ends are parallel and of the same size and shape, and whose sides are parallelograms. ■ **pris·mat·ic** /prizˈmatik/ **adj.**

pris·on /ˈprizən/ ▶ **n.** a building where criminals are kept as a punishment.

SYNONYMS **1** *they're being transferred to a prison upstate* **jail**, jailhouse, penitentiary, correctional facility, penal institution. **2** *you're lucky they didn't send you to prison* **jail**; informal the clink, the slammer, the can, the pen, the hoosegow, the big house, the joint, stir, the pokey, the cooler.

pris·on·er /ˈpriz(ə)nər/ ▶ **n.** **1** a person who has been found guilty of a crime and sent to prison. **2** a person who has been captured by someone and kept confined.

SYNONYMS **1 convict**, detainee, inmate; informal jailbird, con, yardbird. **2 prisoner of war**, POW, internee, captive, hostage.

□ **prisoner of war** a person captured and imprisoned by the enemy in war.

pris·sy /ˈprisē/ ▶ **adj.** too concerned with behaving in a correct and respectable way.

pris·tine /ˈprisˌtēn, priˈstēn/ ▶ **adj.** **1** in its original condition. **2** clean and fresh as if new.

SYNONYMS **immaculate**, perfect, in mint condition, as new, spotless, unspoiled. ANTONYMS dirty, spoiled.

pri·va·cy /ˈprīvəsē/ ▶ **n.** a state in which you are not watched or disturbed by other people.

SYNONYMS **seclusion**, solitude, isolation.

pri·vate /ˈprīvit/ ▶ **adj.** **1** intended for or involving a particular person or group. **2** (of thoughts, feelings, etc.) that you do not tell other people about. **3** not sharing thoughts and feelings with other people. **4** where you will not be disturbed; secluded. **5** (of a service or industry) provided by an individual or commercial company rather than the state. **6** not connected with a person's work or official role. ▶ **n.** (also **private soldier**) a soldier of the lowest rank in the army.

SYNONYMS ▶ **adj.** **1 personal**, own, special, exclusive. **2 confidential**, secret, classified, privileged, unofficial, off the record; informal hush-hush. **3 intimate**, personal, secret, innermost, undisclosed, unspoken, unvoiced. **4 reserved**, introverted, self-contained, reticent, retiring, unsociable, withdrawn, solitary, reclusive, secretive. **5 secluded**, undisturbed, out of the way, remote, isolated. **6 independent**, nongovernmental, privatized, commercial, private-enterprise. ANTONYMS public, open, official. ▶ n. **soldier**, GI, trooper.

□ **private enterprise** business or industry managed by independent companies rather than the state. **private eye** informal a private investigator. **private investigator** (or **private detective**) a detective who is not a police officer and who carries out investigations for clients. **private practice** the work of a doctor, lawyer, etc., who is self-employed. **private school** a school supported by a private organization or private individuals rather than by the government. **private secretary** **1** a secretary who deals with the personal matters of their employer. **2** a civil servant acting as an assistant to a senior government official. **private sector** the part of the national economy not under direct state control. ■ **pri·vate·ly** adv.

pri·va·teer /ˌprīvəˈtir/ ▶ n. (in the past) an armed but privately owned ship, authorized by a government for use in war.

pri·va·tion /prīˈvāsʜən/ ▶ n. a state in which you do not have the basic things you need, such as food and warmth.

pri·va·tize /ˈprīvəˌtīz/ ▶ v. (**privatizes**, **privatizing**, **privatized**) transfer a business or industry from ownership by the state to private ownership. ■ **pri·va·ti·za·tion** /ˌprīvətəˈzāsʜən/ n.

priv·et /ˈprivit/ ▶ n. a shrub with small white flowers.

priv·i·lege /ˈpriv(ə)lij/ ▶ n. **1** a special right or advantage for a particular person or group. **2** an opportunity to do something regarded as a special honor. **3** the advantages available to people who are rich and powerful.

SYNONYMS **1 advantage**, benefit, prerogative, entitlement, right, concession, freedom, liberty. **2 honor**, pleasure.

SPELLING

Write **-il-**, not **-el-**, and no **d**: privi**le**ge.

priv·i·leged /ˈpriv(ə)lijd/ ▶ adj. **1** having a privilege or privileges. **2** (of information) protected from being made public.

SYNONYMS **1 wealthy**, rich, affluent, prosperous, elite, advantaged. **2 confidential**, private, secret, restricted, classified, not for publication, off the record, inside; informal hush-hush. ANTONYMS underprivileged, disadvantaged.

priv·y /ˈprivē/ ▶ adj. (**privy to**) sharing in the knowledge of something secret. ▶ n. (plural **privies**) a toilet in a small shed outside a house.

SYNONYMS ▶ adj. **in the know about**, acquainted with, in on, apprised of; formal cognizant of.

prize¹ /prīz/ ▶ n. **1** a thing given to someone who wins a competition or race or to mark an outstanding achievement. **2** something that is worth struggling to achieve. ▶ adj. **1** having been awarded a prize. **2** outstanding. **3** (**prized**) highly valued. ▶ v. (**prizes**, **prizing**, **prized**) value highly.

SYNONYMS ▶ n. **award**, reward, trophy, medal, cup, winnings, purse, honor. ▶ adj. **1 champion**, prize-winning, award-winning, top, best. **2 utter**, complete, total, absolute, real, perfect. **3** (**prized**) **treasured**, precious, cherished, much loved, beloved, valued, esteemed, highly regarded.

prize² (or **prise**) ▶ v. (**prizes**, **prizing**, **prized**) pry or force something open or apart.

pro¹ /prō/ informal ▶ n. (plural **pros**) a professional, especially in sports. ▶ adj. professional.

pro² ▶ n. (plural **pros**) (usually in **pros and cons**) an advantage of or argument in favor of something.

pro·ac·tive /prōˈaktiv/ ▶ adj. creating or controlling a situation rather than just responding to it. ■ **pro·ac·tive·ly** adv.

prob·a·bil·i·ty /ˌpräbəˈbilətē/ ▶ n. (plural **probabilities**) **1** the extent to which something is probable. **2** an event that is likely to happen.

SYNONYMS **likelihood**, prospect, expectation, chance(s), odds, possibility.

prob·a·ble /ˈpräbəbəl/ ▶ adj. likely to happen or be the case.

SYNONYMS **likely**, odds-on, expected, anticipated, predictable; informal in the cards, a safe bet. ANTONYMS unlikely.

prob·a·bly /ˈpräbəblē, ˈpräblē/ ▶ adv. almost certainly.

SYNONYMS **in all likelihood**, in all probability, as likely as not, ten to one, the chances are, doubtless.

pro·bate /ˈprōˌbāt/ ▶ n. the official process of proving that a will is valid.

pro·ba·tion /prōˈbāsʜən/ ▶ n. **1** a system in which a person who has committed a crime does not have to go to prison if they behave well and report regularly to an official. **2** a period of training and testing when you start a new job.

SYNONYMS **trial**, trial period, apprenticeship, training.

■ **pro·ba·tion·ar·y** adj. **pro·ba·tion·er** n.

probe /prōb/ ▶ n. **1** an investigation. **2** a surgical instrument used to examine the body. **3** a small device for measuring or testing something. **4** (also **space probe**) an unmanned spacecraft used for exploration. ▶ v. (**probes**, **probing**, **probed**) **1** physically explore or examine something with the hands or an instrument. **2** investigate something closely.

SYNONYMS ▶ n. **investigation**, inquiry, examination, inquest, study. ▶ v. **1 prod**, poke, dig into, delve into, explore, feel around in, examine. **2 investigate**, inquire into, look into, go into, study, examine, explore.

■ **prob·ing** adj.

pro·bi·ty /ˈprōbitē/ ▶ n. formal the quality of being honest and having high moral standards.

SYNONYMS **integrity**, honesty, uprightness, decency, morality, rectitude, goodness, virtue. ANTONYMS untrustworthiness.

prob·lem /ˈpräbləm/ ▶ n. a thing that is difficult to deal with or understand.

SYNONYMS **1 difficulty**, worry, complication, snag, hitch, drawback, stumbling block, obstacle, hiccup, setback, catch, dilemma, quandary; informal headache, fly in the ointment. **2 nuisance**, bother; informal drag, pain, hassle. **3 puzzle**, question, poser, riddle, conundrum; informal brain-teaser.

prob·lem·at·ic /ˌpräbləˈmatik/ (or **problematical**) ▶ **adj.** difficult to deal with or understand.

SYNONYMS **difficult**, troublesome, tricky, awkward, controversial, ticklish, complicated, complex, knotty. ANTONYMS easy, straightforward.

pro·bos·cis /prəˈbäsəs, -ˈbäskəs/ ▶ **n.** (plural **probosces** /-ˈbäsēz/ or **proboscises**) **1** a mammal's long, flexible snout, e.g., an elephant's trunk. **2** the long, thin mouth of some insects.

pro·ce·dure /prəˈsējər/ ▶ **n. 1** an established or official way of doing something. **2** a series of actions done in a certain way.

SYNONYMS **course of action**, method, system, strategy, way, approach, formula, mechanism, technique, routine, drill, practice.

■ **pro·ce·dur·al adj.**

pro·ceed /prəˈsēd, prō-/ ▶ **v. 1** begin a course of action. **2** go on to do something. **3** carry on or continue.

SYNONYMS **1 begin**, make a start, get going, move. **2 go**, make your way, advance, move, progress, carry on, continue, press on, push on. ANTONYMS stop.

pro·ceed·ings /prəˈsēdiNGz, prō-/ ▶ **pl.n. 1** an event or a series of actions. **2** action taken in a court of law to settle a dispute.

SYNONYMS **1 events**, activities, action, happenings, goings-on. **2 report**, transactions, minutes, account, story, record(s). **3 legal action**, litigation, suit, lawsuit, case, prosecution.

pro·ceeds /ˈprōˌsēdz/ ▶ **pl.n.** money obtained from an event or activity.

SYNONYMS **profits**, earnings, receipts, returns, take, income, revenue, profit, yield; Sports gate.

proc·ess¹ /ˈpräˌses, ˈpräsəs, ˈprō-/ ▶ **n. 1** a series of actions that are done to achieve a particular end. **2** a natural series of changes: *the aging process*. ▶ **v. 1** perform a series of actions on something to change or preserve it. **2** deal with someone or something using an established procedure.

SYNONYMS ▶ **n. 1 procedure**, operation, action, activity, exercise, business, job, task, undertaking. **2** *a new manufacturing process* **method**, system, technique, means. ▶ **v. deal with**, attend to, see to, sort out, handle, take care of.

■ **proc·es·sor n.**

proc·ess² /prəˈses/ ▶ **v.** walk in procession.

pro·ces·sion /prəˈsesHən/ ▶ **n. 1** a number of people or vehicles moving forward in an orderly way. **2** a large number of people or things that come one after another.

SYNONYMS **parade**, march, cavalcade, motorcade, cortège, column, file.

pro·claim /prəˈklām, prō-/ ▶ **v. 1** announce officially or publicly. **2** show something clearly.

SYNONYMS **declare**, announce, pronounce, state, make known, give out, advertise, publish, broadcast, trumpet.

proc·la·ma·tion /ˌprākləˈmāsHən/ ▶ **n.** a public or official announcement: *the Church issued a proclamation denouncing the movie*.

SYNONYMS **declaration**, announcement, pronouncement, statement, notification, broadcast, assertion, profession, protestation, decree, order, edict, ruling.

pro·cliv·i·ty /prōˈklivətē, prə-/ ▶ **n.** (plural **proclivities**) a tendency to do something regularly.

SYNONYMS **inclination**, tendency, leaning, disposition, proneness, propensity, bent, bias, penchant, predisposition, predilection, partiality, liking, preference, taste, fondness.

pro·cras·ti·nate /prəˈkrastəˌnāt, prō-/ ▶ **v.** (**procrastinates**, **procrastinating**, **procrastinated**) delay or postpone action.

SYNONYMS **delay**, put off doing something, postpone action, defer action, play for time, dawdle; informal dilly-dally.

■ **pro·cras·ti·na·tion** /prəˌkrastəˈnāsHən, prō-/ **n.**

pro·cre·ate /ˈprōkrēˌāt/ ▶ **v.** (**procreates**, **procreating**, **procreated**) produce a baby or young animal. ■ **pro·cre·a·tion** /ˌprōkrēˈāsHən/ **n.**

proc·tor /ˈpräktər/ ▶ **n.** a person who monitors students during an examination. ▶ **v.** serve as a proctor.

pro·cure /prəˈkyo͝or, prō-/ ▶ **v.** (**procures**, **procuring**, **procured**) obtain. ■ **pro·cure·ment n.**

prod /präd/ ▶ **v.** (**prods**, **prodding**, **prodded**) **1** push someone or something with a finger or pointed object. **2** prompt or remind someone to do something. ▶ **n. 1** an act of prodding. **2** a prompt or reminder. **3** a pointed object like a stick.

SYNONYMS ▶ **v. 1 poke**, jab, stab, dig, nudge, elbow. **2 spur**, stimulate, prompt, push, galvanize, persuade, urge, remind.

prod·i·gal /ˈprädigəl/ ▶ **adj. 1** using time, money, etc., in a wasteful way. **2** lavish. ▶ **n.** (also **prodigal son**) a person who leaves home and leads a wasteful life but is later sorry for their actions and returns.

SYNONYMS ▶ **adj. wasteful**, extravagant, spendthrift. ANTONYMS thrifty.

■ **prod·i·gal·i·ty** /ˌprädəˈgalətē/ **n.**

pro·di·gious /prəˈdijəs/ ▶ **adj.** impressively large. ■ **pro·di·gious·ly adv.**

prod·i·gy /ˈprädəjē/ ▶ **n.** (plural **prodigies**) a young person with exceptional abilities.

SYNONYMS **genius**, mastermind, virtuoso, wunderkind; informal whiz kid, whiz.

pro·duce ▶ **v.** /prəˈd(y)o͞os, prō-/ (**produces**, **producing**, **produced**) **1** make, manufacture, or create. **2** make something happen or exist. **3** show or provide something for consideration. **4** be in charge of the financial aspects of a movie or the staging of a play. **5** supervise the making of a musical recording. ▶ **n.** /ˈpräd(y)o͞os, ˈprō-/ things that have been produced or grown.

SYNONYMS ▶ **v. 1 manufacture**, make, construct, build, fabricate, put together, assemble, turn out, create, mass-produce. **2 yield**, grow, give, supply, provide, furnish, bear. **3 give birth to**, bear, deliver, bring forth, bring into the world. **4 create**, fashion, turn out, compose, write, pen, paint. **5 pull out**, extract, fish out, present, offer, proffer, show. **6 cause**, bring about, give rise to, occasion, generate, lead to, result in, provoke, precipitate, spark, trigger. **7 stage**, put on, mount, present, exhibit. ▶ **n. food**, foodstuff(s), products, crops, harvest.

pro·duc·er /prə'd(y)o͞osər, prō-/ ▶ **n. 1** a person or thing that makes, causes, or supplies something: *an oil producer*. **2** a person who supervises the making of a movie and is responsible for its financial aspects. **3** a person who supervises the making of a musical recording.

SYNONYMS **1 manufacturer**, maker, builder, constructor. **2 grower**, farmer. **3 impresario**, manager, administrator, promoter, director.

prod·uct /'prädəkt/ ▶ **n. 1** an article or substance manufactured for sale. **2** a result of an action or process. **3** a substance produced during a natural, chemical, or manufacturing process. **4** Math a quantity obtained by multiplying one number by another.

SYNONYMS **1 commodity**, artifact; (**products**) goods, wares, -ware, merchandise, produce. **2 result**, consequence, outcome, effect, upshot.

pro·duc·tion /prə'dəksʜən, prō-/ ▶ **n. 1** the action of producing something. **2** the amount of something produced.

SYNONYMS **1 manufacture**, making, construction, building, fabrication, assembly, creation, mass production. **2 creation**, origination, fashioning, composition, writing. **3 output**, yield, productivity. **4 performance**, staging, presentation, show, piece, play.

□ **production line** an assembly line.

pro·duc·tive /prə'dəktiv, prō-/ ▶ **adj. 1** producing large amounts of goods or crops. **2** doing or achieving a lot.

SYNONYMS **1 prolific**, inventive, creative. **2 useful**, constructive, profitable, fruitful, valuable, effective, worthwhile, helpful. **3 fertile**, fruitful, rich, fecund.

■ **pro·duc·tive·ly** adv.

pro·duc·tiv·i·ty /ˌprōˌdək'tivətē, ˌprädək-, prəˌdək-/ ▶ **n. 1** the quality of being productive. **2** the efficiency with which things are produced.

SYNONYMS **efficiency**, work rate, output, yield, production.

pro·fane /prə'fān, prō-/ ▶ **adj. 1** not religious; secular. **2** not having respect for God or holy things. ▶ **v.** (**profanes**, **profaning**, **profaned**) treat something holy with a lack of respect.

SYNONYMS ▶ **adj.** *profane language* **obscene**, blasphemous, indecent, foul, vulgar, crude, filthy, dirty, coarse, rude, offensive. ANTONYMS decorous. ▶ **v.** *invaders profaned our temples* **desecrate**, violate, defile.

pro·fan·i·ty /prə'fanətē, prō-/ ▶ **n.** (plural **profanities**) **1** language or behavior that shows a lack of respect for God or holy things. **2** a swear word.

SYNONYMS **1 swear word**, oath, expletive, curse, obscenity, four-letter word, dirty word, blasphemy, swearing, foul language, bad language, cursing. **2** *acts of profanity* **sacrilege**, blasphemy, ungodliness, impiety, irreverence, disrespect.

pro·fess /prə'fes, prō-/ ▶ **v. 1** claim that something is true. **2** (**professed**) (of a quality or feeling) claimed openly but often falsely. **3** (**professed**) openly declared to be: *a professed liberal*. **4** declare your faith in a religion.

SYNONYMS **1 declare**, announce, proclaim, assert, state, affirm, maintain, protest, avow. **2 claim**, pretend, purport, affect, make out. **3** (**professed**) **claimed**, supposed, ostensible, self-styled, apparent, pretended, purported. **4** (**professed**) **declared**, sworn, confirmed, self-confessed.

pro·fes·sion /prə'fesʜən/ ▶ **n. 1** a job that needs special training and a formal qualification. **2** all the people working in a particular profession. **3** a claim. **4** a declaration of belief in a religion.

SYNONYMS **career**, occupation, calling, vocation, métier, line of work, job, business, trade, craft.

pro·fes·sion·al /prə'fesʜənl/ ▶ **adj. 1** relating to or belonging to a profession. **2** doing something as a job rather than as a hobby. **3** having the skills or qualities of a professional person. ▶ **n. 1** a professional person. **2** a person who is very skilled in a particular activity.

SYNONYMS ▶ **adj. 1 white-collar**, nonmanual, graduate, qualified, chartered. **2 paid**, salaried. **3 expert**, accomplished, skillful, masterly, fine, polished, skilled, proficient, competent, able, businesslike, deft. **4** *he always behaved in a professional way* **appropriate**, fitting, proper, honorable, ethical. ANTONYMS amateur, amateurish. ▶ **n. expert**, virtuoso, old hand, master, maestro, past master; informal pro, ace.

■ **pro·fes·sion·al·ly** adv.

SPELLING

Only one f: professional.

pro·fes·sion·al·ism /prə'fesʜənlˌizəm/ ▶ **n.** the ability or skill that you expect from a professional person.

pro·fes·sor /prə'fesər/ ▶ **n. 1** a university teacher of the highest rank. **2** an associate professor or an assistant professor. ■ **pro·fes·so·ri·al** /ˌpräfə'sôrēəl/ **adj. pro·fes·sor·ship n.**

prof·fer /'präfər/ ▶ **v.** (**proffers**, **proffering**, **proffered**) offer something for someone to accept.

pro·fi·cient /prə'fisʜənt/ ▶ **adj.** competent; skilled.

SYNONYMS **skilled**, skillful, expert, accomplished, competent, masterly, adept, adroit, deft, dexterous, able, professional; informal crack, ace, mean. ANTONYMS incompetent.

■ **pro·fi·cien·cy n.**

pro·file /'prōˌfīl/ ▶ **n. 1** an outline of someone's face, seen from the side. **2** a short article that describes someone or something. **3** the extent to which someone attracts attention: *her high profile*. ▶ **v.** (**profiles**, **profiling**, **profiled**) describe in a short article.

SYNONYMS ▶ **n. 1 outline**, silhouette, side view, contour, shape, form, lines. **2 description**, account, study, portrait, rundown, sketch, outline.

□ **keep a low profile** try not to attract attention.

prof·it /'präfit/ ▶ **n. 1** a financial gain. **2** advantage or benefit. ▶ **v.** (**profits**, **profiting**, **profited**) benefit someone.

SYNONYMS ▶ n. **1 financial gain**, return(s), yield, proceeds, earnings, winnings, surplus; informal pay dirt, bottom line. **2 advantage**, benefit, value, use, good; informal mileage. ANTONYMS loss, disadvantage. ▶ v. **1 make money**, earn; informal rake it in, clean up, make a fast buck, make a killing. **2 benefit**, be advantageous to, be of use to, do someone good, help, be of service to, serve. ANTONYMS lose.

□ **profit margin** the difference between the cost of producing something and the price at which it is sold.

prof·it·a·ble /ˈpräfitəbəl/ ▶ adj. **1** (of a business or activity) making a profit. **2** useful.

SYNONYMS **1 moneymaking**, profit-making, paying, lucrative, commercial, successful, gainful. **2 beneficial**, useful, advantageous, valuable, productive, worthwhile, rewarding, fruitful, illuminating, informative, well-spent.

■ **prof·it·a·bil·i·ty** /ˌpräfitəˈbilətē/ n. **prof·it·a·bly** adv.

prof·it·eer·ing /ˌpräfəˈti(ə)riNG/ ▶ n. the making of a large profit in an unfair way. ■ **prof·it·eer** n.

pro·fit·er·ole /prəˈfitəˌrōl/ ▶ n. a small ball of choux pastry filled with cream and covered with chocolate.

prof·li·gate /ˈpräfligət, -ləˌgāt/ ▶ adj. **1** using time or money in a wasteful or extravagant way. **2** indulging too much in physical pleasures. ▶ n. a profligate person. ■ **prof·li·ga·cy** n.

pro·found /prəˈfound, prō-/ ▶ adj. (**profounder**, **profoundest**) **1** very great. **2** showing great knowledge or understanding. **3** needing a lot of study or thought.

SYNONYMS **1 heartfelt**, intense, keen, extreme, acute, severe, sincere, earnest, deep, deep-seated, overpowering, overwhelming. **2 far-reaching**, radical, extensive, sweeping, exhaustive, thoroughgoing. **3 wise**, learned, intelligent, scholarly, discerning, penetrating, perceptive, astute, thoughtful, insightful. ANTONYMS superficial.

■ **pro·found·ly** adv. **pro·fun·di·ty** /prəˈfəndətē/ n.

pro·fuse /prəˈfyo͞os, prō-/ ▶ adj. produced or appearing in large quantities.

SYNONYMS **1** *profuse apologies* **copious**, prolific, abundant, liberal, unstinting, fulsome, effusive, extravagant, lavish, gushing. **2** *profuse blooms* **luxuriant**, plentiful, copious, abundant, lush, rich, exuberant, riotous, teeming, rank, rampant. ANTONYMS meager, sparse.

■ **pro·fuse·ly** adv.

pro·fu·sion /prəˈfyo͞ozHən, prō-/ ▶ n. a very large quantity of something.

pro·gen·i·tor /prəˈjenətər, prō-/ ▶ n. **1** an ancestor or parent. **2** the person who started an artistic, political, or intellectual movement.

prog·e·ny /ˈpräjənē/ ▶ n. offspring.

pro·ges·ter·one /prōˈjestəˌrōn, prə-/ ▶ n. a hormone that stimulates the uterus to prepare for pregnancy.

prog·no·sis /prägˈnōsəs/ ▶ n. (plural **prognoses**) **1** an opinion about how an illness is likely to develop. **2** the likely course of a situation. ■ **prog·nos·tic** /prägˈnästik/ adj.

pro·gram /ˈprōˌgram, -grəm/ ▶ n. **1** a plan of future events or things to be done. **2** a radio or television broadcast. **3** a sheet or booklet giving details about a play, concert, etc. **4** a series of software instructions to control the operation of a computer. ▶ v. (**programs**, **programming**, **programmed** or **programing**, **programed**) **1** provide a computer with a program. **2** make something behave in a particular way. **3** arrange something according to a plan.

SYNONYMS ▶ n. **1 schedule**, agenda, calendar, timetable, order (of the day), lineup. **2 scheme**, plan, package, strategy, initiative, proposal. **3 broadcast**, production, show, presentation, transmission, performance. **4 course**, syllabus, curriculum. ▶ v. **arrange**, organize, schedule, slate, plan, map out, timetable, line up.

■ **pro·gram·ma·ble** /ˈprōˌgraməbəl, prōˈgraməbəl/ adj. **pro·gram·mer** n.

pro·gram·mat·ic /ˌprōgrəˈmatik/ ▶ adj. having to do with or following a program.

prog·ress ▶ n. /ˈprägrəs, ˈprägˌres, ˈprōˌgres/ **1** forward movement toward a place. **2** the process of improving or developing. ▶ v. /prəˈgres/ **1** move forward. **2** improve or develop.

SYNONYMS ▶ n. **1 (forward) movement**, advance, going, headway, passage. **2 development**, advance, advancement, headway, step forward, improvement, growth. ▶ v. **1 go**, make your way, move, proceed, advance, go on, continue, make headway, work your way. **2 develop**, make progress, advance, make headway, move on, get on, gain ground, improve, get better, come on, come along, make strides. ANTONYMS regress.

pro·gres·sion /prəˈgresHən/ ▶ n. **1** a gradual movement from one place or state to another. **2** a number of things coming one after another.

SYNONYMS **1 progress**, advancement, movement, passage, development, evolution, growth. **2 succession**, series, sequence, string, stream, chain, train, row, cycle.

pro·gres·sive /prəˈgresiv/ ▶ adj. **1** proceeding gradually or in stages. **2** favoring new ideas or social reform. ▶ n. a person who is in favor of social reform.

SYNONYMS ▶ adj. **1 continuing**, continuous, ongoing, gradual, step-by-step, cumulative. **2 modern**, liberal, advanced, forward-thinking, enlightened, pioneering, reforming, reformist, radical; informal go-ahead. ANTONYMS conservative.

■ **pro·gres·sive·ly** adv.

pro·hib·it /prəˈhibit, prō-/ ▶ v. (**prohibits**, **prohibiting**, **prohibited**) **1** formally forbid something by law. **2** prevent something from happening.

SYNONYMS **1 forbid**, ban, bar, proscribe, make illegal, outlaw, disallow, veto. **2 prevent**, stop, rule out, preclude, make impossible. ANTONYMS allow.

pro·hi·bi·tion /ˌprō(h)əˈbisHən/ ▶ n. **1** the action of prohibiting. **2** an order that forbids something. **3** (**Prohibition**) the prevention by law of the manufacture and sale of alcohol in the United States from 1920 to 1933.

SYNONYMS **ban**, bar, veto, embargo, boycott, injunction, moratorium, interdict.

pro·hib·i·tive /prə'hibitiv, prō-/ ▶ **adj.** **1** forbidding or restricting something. **2** (of a price) too high. ■ **pro·hib·i·tive·ly adv.**

proj·ect ▶ **n.** /'präj,ekt, 'präj,ikt/ **1** a piece of work that is carefully planned to achieve a particular aim. **2** a piece of work by a school or college student in which they carry out their own research. ▶ **v.** /prə'jekt, prō'jekt/ **1** estimate or predict something based on what is happening now. **2** (**be projected**) be planned. **3** stick out beyond something else. **4** make light or an image fall on a surface or screen. **5** present yourself to other people in a particular way.

SYNONYMS ▶ **n. 1 scheme**, plan, program, enterprise, undertaking, venture, proposal, idea, concept. **2 assignment**, piece of work, task. ▶ **v. 1 forecast**, predict, expect, estimate, calculate, reckon. **2 stick out**, jut (out), protrude, extend, stand out, bulge out. **3 cast**, throw, send, shed, shine.

pro·jec·tile /prə'jektl, -,tīl/ ▶ **n.** an object that is fired or thrown at a target.

pro·jec·tion /prə'jeksHən/ ▶ **n. 1** a prediction about something based on what is happening now. **2** the projecting of an image, sound, etc. **3** a thing that sticks out from something else.

SYNONYMS **1 forecast**, prediction, prognosis, expectation, estimate. **2 outcrop**, outgrowth, overhang, ledge, shelf, prominence, protrusion, protuberance.

■ **pro·jec·tion·ist n.**

pro·jec·tor /prə'jektər/ ▶ **n.** a device for projecting slides or film on to a screen.

pro·lapse /prō'laps, 'prō,laps/ ▶ **n.** a condition in which an organ of the body has slipped forward or down from its normal position.

pro·le·tar·i·an /,prōli'te(ə)rēən/ ▶ **adj.** relating to the proletariat. ▶ **n.** a member of the proletariat.

pro·le·tar·i·at /,prōli'te(ə)rēət/ ▶ **n.** workers or working-class people.

pro·lif·er·ate /prə'lifə,rāt/ ▶ **v.** (**proliferates**, **proliferating**, **proliferated**) reproduce rapidly; increase rapidly in number.

SYNONYMS **increase**, grow, multiply, rocket, mushroom, snowball, burgeon, spread, expand, run riot. ANTONYMS decrease, dwindle.

■ **pro·lif·er·a·tion** /prə,lifə'rāsHən/ **n.**

pro·lif·ic /prə'lifik/ ▶ **adj. 1** (of a plant or animal) producing a lot of fruit, leaves, or young. **2** (of an artist, author, etc.) producing many works.

SYNONYMS **1 plentiful**, abundant, bountiful, profuse, copious, luxuriant, rich, lush, fruitful. **2 productive**, fertile, creative, inventive. ANTONYMS meager.

■ **pro·lif·i·cal·ly adv.**

pro·lix /prō'liks/ ▶ **adj.** (of speech or writing) long and boring. ■ **pro·lix·i·ty n.**

pro·logue /'prō,lôg, -,läg/ ▶ **n. 1** a separate introductory part of a play, book, or piece of music. **2** an event that leads to another.

pro·long /prə'lôNG, -'läNG/ ▶ **v.** make something last longer.

SYNONYMS **lengthen**, extend, drag out, draw out, protract, spin out, carry on, continue, keep up, perpetuate. ANTONYMS shorten.

■ **pro·lon·ga·tion** /prō,lôNG'gāsHən, prə-/ **n.**

pro·longed /prə'lôNGd, -'läNGd/ ▶ **adj.** continuing for a long time.

prom /präm/ ▶ **n.** informal a formal dance at a high school or college.

prom·e·nade /,prämə'nād, -'näd/ ▶ **n. 1** a paved walkway along a seafront. **2** a leisurely walk. ▶ **v.** (**promenades**, **promenading**, **promenaded**) go for a leisurely walk.

prom·i·nence /'prämənəns/ ▶ **n.** the state of being prominent.

SYNONYMS **1 fame**, celebrity, eminence, importance, distinction, greatness, prestige, stature, standing. **2** *the press gave prominence to the reports* **wide coverage**, importance, precedence, weight, a high profile, top billing.

prom·i·nent /'prämənənt/ ▶ **adj. 1** important; famous. **2** sticking out. **3** particularly noticeable.

SYNONYMS **1 important**, well-known, leading, eminent, distinguished, notable, noteworthy, noted, illustrious, celebrated, famous, renowned, major-league. **2 jutting** (**out**), protruding, projecting, protuberant, standing out, sticking out, proud, bulging. **3 conspicuous**, noticeable, obvious, unmistakable, eye-catching, pronounced, salient, striking, dominant, obtrusive. ANTONYMS unimportant, inconspicuous.

■ **prom·i·nent·ly adv.**

prom·ise /'präməs/ ▶ **n. 1** an assurance that you will do something or that something will happen. **2** qualities or abilities that may lead to future success. ▶ **v.** (**promises**, **promising**, **promised**) **1** make a promise. **2** give good grounds for expecting something.

SYNONYMS ▶ **n. 1 word** (**of honor**), assurance, pledge, vow, guarantee, oath, bond, undertaking, agreement, commitment, contract. **2 potential**, ability, talent, aptitude, possibility. ▶ **v. 1 give your word**, swear, pledge, vow, undertake, give an undertaking, guarantee, warrant, contract, give an assurance, commit yourself. **2 indicate**, lead someone to expect, point to, be a sign of, betoken, give hope of, augur, herald, portend, presage.

prom·is·ing /'präməsiNG/ ▶ **adj.** showing signs of future success.

SYNONYMS **1 good**, encouraging, favorable, hopeful, auspicious, propitious, bright, rosy, heartening. **2 talented**, gifted, budding, up-and-coming, rising, coming, in the making. ANTONYMS unfavorable.

■ **prom·is·ing·ly adv.**

prom·is·so·ry note /'prämə,sôrē/ ▶ **n.** a signed document containing a written promise to pay a stated amount of money.

pro·mo /'prōmō/ ▶ **n.** (plural **promos**) informal a promotional movie, video, etc.

prom·on·to·ry /'prämən,tôrē/ ▶ **n.** (plural **promontories**) a point of high land jutting out into the sea.

pro·mote /prə'mōt/ ▶ **v.** (**promotes**, **promoting**, **promoted**) **1** help something to happen. **2** give publicity to a product, event, etc., in order to increase sales or make people aware of it. **3** raise someone to a higher position or rank.

SYNONYMS 1 **upgrade**, give promotion to, elevate, advance, move up. 2 **encourage**, further, advance, foster, develop, contribute to, boost, stimulate. 3 **advertise**, publicize, give publicity to, beat/bang the drum for, market, merchandise; informal push, plug, hype. ANTONYMS demote, obstruct.

pro·mot·er /prəˈmōtər/ ▶ **n.** 1 the organizer of a sports event or theatrical production. 2 a supporter of a cause or aim.

pro·mo·tion /prəˈmōshən/ ▶ **n.** 1 activity that supports or encourages a cause or aim. 2 the action of promoting a product, event, etc. 3 movement to a higher position or rank.

SYNONYMS 1 **upgrading**, preferment, elevation, advancement, step up (the ladder). 2 **encouragement**, furtherance, furthering, advancement, contribution to, fostering, boosting, stimulation. 3 **advertising**, marketing, publicity, propaganda; informal hard sell, plug, hype.

pro·mo·tion·al /prəˈmōshənəl/ ▶ **adj.** intended to publicize a product or organization.

prompt /prämpt/ ▶ **v.** 1 make something happen. 2 (**prompt someone to**) make someone take a course of action. 3 encourage someone to speak. 4 tell an actor a word that they have forgotten. ▶ **n.** 1 a word or phrase used to prompt an actor. 2 a symbol on a computer screen to show that more input is needed. ▶ **adj.** done without delay.

SYNONYMS ▶ **v.** 1 **induce**, make, move, motivate, lead, dispose, persuade, incline, encourage, stimulate, prod, impel, spur on, inspire. 2 **give rise to**, bring about, cause, occasion, result in, lead to, elicit, produce, precipitate, trigger, spark, provoke. 3 **remind**, cue, feed, help out, jog someone's memory. ANTONYMS deter. ▶ **adj. quick**, swift, rapid, speedy, fast, expeditious, direct, immediate, instant, early, punctual, in good time, on time. ANTONYMS slow, late.

■ **prompt·er** **n.**

prompt·ly /ˈprämptlē/ ▶ **adv.** 1 punctually: *William arrived promptly at 7:30.* 2 without delay: *I expect the matter to be dealt with promptly.*

SYNONYMS 1 **punctually**, on time; informal on the button, on the nose, on the dot, bang on. 2 **without delay**, straightaway, right away, at once, immediately, now, as soon as possible, quickly, swiftly, rapidly, speedily, fast; informal pronto, ASAP. ANTONYMS late.

prom·ul·gate /ˈprämәlˌgāt, prōˈməl-/ ▶ **v.** (**promulgates**, **promulgating**, **promulgated**) 1 make an idea widely known. 2 announce the official beginning of a new law. ■ **prom·ul·ga·tion** /ˌprämәlˈgāshən, ˌprōməl-/ **n.**

prone /prōn/ ▶ **adj.** 1 (**prone to** or **to do**) likely to suffer from, do, or experience something unfortunate. 2 lying flat, especially face downward.

SYNONYMS 1 **susceptible**, vulnerable, subject, open, liable, given, predisposed, likely, disposed, inclined, apt. 2 **lying face down**, on your stomach/front, lying flat, lying down, horizontal, prostrate.

prong /prôNG/ ▶ **n.** 1 each of two or more long pointed parts on a fork. 2 each of the separate parts of an attack. ■ **pronged** **adj.**

pro·noun /ˈprōˌnoun/ ▶ **n.** a word used instead of a noun to indicate someone or something already mentioned or known, e.g., *I*, *this*.

pro·nounce /prəˈnouns/ ▶ **v.** (**pronounces**, **pronouncing**, **pronounced**) 1 make the sound of a word or part of a word. 2 declare or announce. 3 (**pronounce on**) pass judgment or make a decision on.

SYNONYMS 1 **say**, enunciate, articulate, utter, voice, sound, vocalize, get your tongue around. 2 **declare**, proclaim, judge, rule, decree, ordain.

pro·nounced /prəˈnounst/ ▶ **adj.** very noticeable.

SYNONYMS **noticeable**, marked, strong, conspicuous, striking, distinct, prominent, unmistakable, obvious. ANTONYMS slight.

pro·nounce·ment /prəˈnounsmənt/ ▶ **n.** a formal public statement.

pron·to /ˈpräntō/ ▶ **adv.** informal promptly.

pro·nun·ci·a·tion /prəˌnənsēˈāshən/ ▶ **n.** the way in which a word is pronounced.

SPELLING

Pronunciation has no **o** in the middle: it is not like **pronounce**.

proof /pro͞of/ ▶ **n.** 1 evidence that shows that something is true. 2 the process of finding out whether something is true. 3 a series of stages in the solving of a mathematical problem. 4 a copy of printed material used for making corrections before final printing. 5 a standard used to measure the strength of alcohol. ▶ **adj.** resistant to: *waterproof.*

SYNONYMS ▶ **n. evidence**, verification, corroboration, demonstration, authentication, confirmation, certification, documentation. ▶ **adj. resistant**, immune, unaffected, impervious.

proof·read /ˈpro͞ofˌrēd/ ▶ **v.** read written or printed material and mark any mistakes. ■ **proof·read·er** **n.**

prop[1] /präp/ ▶ **n.** 1 a pole or beam used as a temporary support. 2 a source of support or assistance. 3 (also **prop forward**) Rugby a forward at either end of the front row of a scrum. ▶ **v.** (**props**, **propping**, **propped**) 1 support with a prop. 2 lean something against something else. 3 (**prop something up**) help something that is in difficulty.

SYNONYMS ▶ **n.** 1 **pole**, post, support, upright, brace, buttress, stay, strut. 2 **mainstay**, pillar, anchor, support, cornerstone. ▶ **v. lean**, rest, stand, balance.

prop[2] ▶ **n.** a portable object used by actors during a play or movie.

prop·a·gan·da /ˌpräpəˈgandə/ ▶ **n.** false or exaggerated information, used to win support for a political cause or point of view.

SYNONYMS **information**, promotion, advertising, publicity, disinformation; informal hype.

■ **prop·a·gan·dist** **n.**

SPELLING

Write **propa-**, not **propo-**: **propa**ganda.

prop·a·gate /ˈpräpəˌgāt/ ▶ v. (**propagates**, **propagating**, **propagated**) **1** grow a new plant from a parent plant. **2** spread an idea or information widely. ■ **prop·a·ga·tion** /ˌpräpəˈgāshən/ n.

pro·pane /ˈprōˌpān/ ▶ n. a flammable gas present in natural gas and used as fuel.

pro·pel /prəˈpel/ ▶ v. (**propels**, **propelling**, **propelled**) drive or push forwards.

> SYNONYMS **1 move**, power, push, drive. **2 throw**, thrust, toss, fling, hurl, pitch, send, shoot.

pro·pel·lant /prəˈpelənt/ ▶ n. a gas that forces out the contents of an aerosol.

pro·pel·ler /prəˈpelər/ ▶ n. a device that uses two or more angled blades to propel a ship or aircraft.

pro·pen·si·ty /prəˈpensətē/ ▶ n. (plural **propensities**) a tendency to behave in a particular way.

prop·er /ˈpräpər/ ▶ adj. **1** truly what it is said to be; real. **2** in its true form: *the World Cup proper*. **3** appropriate or correct. **4** (**proper to**) belonging exclusively to.

> SYNONYMS **1 real**, genuine, actual, true, bona fide; informal kosher. **2 right**, correct, accepted, conventional, established, official, regular, acceptable, appropriate, suitable, apt. **3 formal**, conventional, correct, orthodox, polite, respectable, seemly. ANTONYMS wrong, improper.

□ **proper fraction** a fraction that is less than one. **proper noun** (or **proper name**) a name of a person, place, or organization, written with a capital letter.

prop·er·ly /ˈpräpərlē/ ▶ adv. **1** in a proper way. **2** in the precise sense.

prop·er·ty /ˈpräpərtē/ ▶ n. (plural **properties**) **1** a thing or things belonging to someone. **2** a building and the land belonging to it. **3** a characteristic or quality.

> SYNONYMS **1 possessions**, belongings, things, effects, stuff, goods; informal gear. **2 real estate**, building(s), premises, house(s), land, holdings. **3 quality**, attribute, characteristic, feature, power, trait, hallmark.

proph·e·cy /ˈpräfəsē/ ▶ n. (plural **prophecies**) **1** a prediction about what will happen in the future. **2** the ability to predict the future.

> SYNONYMS **prediction**, forecast, prognostication, prognosis, divination.

proph·e·sy /ˈpräfəˌsī/ ▶ v. (**prophesies**, **prophesying**, **prophesied**) predict that a particular thing will happen in the future.

> SYNONYMS **predict**, foretell, forecast, foresee, prognosticate.

proph·et /ˈpräfit/ ▶ n. **1** a person regarded as being sent by God to teach people. **2** (**the Prophet**) (in Islam) Muhammad. **3** a person who predicts the future.

> SYNONYMS **forecaster**, seer, soothsayer, fortune teller, clairvoyant, oracle.

pro·phet·ic /prəˈfetik/ ▶ adj. **1** accurately predicting the future. **2** having to do with a prophet or prophecy.

pro·phy·lac·tic /ˌprōfəˈlaktik/ ▶ adj. intended to prevent disease. ▶ n. a medicine intended to prevent disease.

pro·pin·qui·ty /prəˈpiNGkwətē/ ▶ n. nearness in time or space.

pro·pi·ti·ate /prəˈpisHēˌāt/ ▶ v. (**propitiates**, **propitiating**, **propitiated**) win or regain the favor of. ■ **pro·pi·ti·a·tion** /prəˌpisHēˈāsHən/ n. **pro·pi·ti·a·to·ry** /-ˈpisHēəˌtôrē/ adj.

pro·pi·tious /prəˈpisHəs/ ▶ adj. indicating a good chance of success; favorable.

pro·po·nent /prəˈpōnənt/ ▶ n. a person who proposes a theory or plan.

> SYNONYMS **advocate**, champion, supporter, booster, promoter, protagonist, campaigner.

pro·por·tion /prəˈpôrsHən/ ▶ n. **1** a part or share of a whole. **2** the relationship of one thing to another in terms of quantity or size. **3** the correct relationship between one thing and another. **4** (**proportions**) the size and shape of something.

> SYNONYMS **1 part**, portion, amount, quantity, bit, piece, percentage, fraction, section, segment, share. **2 ratio**, distribution, relative amount/number, relationship. **3 balance**, symmetry, harmony, correspondence, correlation, agreement. **4** *men of huge* **proportions size**, dimensions, magnitude, measurements, mass, volume, bulk, expanse, extent.

pro·por·tion·al /prəˈpôrsHənl/ (or **proportionate** /prəˈpôrsHənət/) ▶ adj. corresponding in size or amount to something else.

> SYNONYMS **corresponding**, comparable, in proportion, pro rata, commensurate, equivalent, consistent. ANTONYMS disproportionate.

□ **proportional representation** an electoral system in which parties gain seats in proportion to the number of votes cast for them. ■ **pro·por·tion·al·ly** adv.

pro·pos·al /prəˈpōzəl/ ▶ n. **1** a plan or suggestion. **2** the action of proposing something. **3** an offer of marriage.

> SYNONYMS **scheme**, plan, idea, project, program, motion, proposition, suggestion, submission.

pro·pose /prəˈpōz/ ▶ v. (**proposes**, **proposing**, **proposed**) **1** put forward an idea or plan for consideration by other people. **2** nominate someone for an official position. **3** plan or intend to do something. **4** make an offer of marriage to someone.

> SYNONYMS **1 put forward**, suggest, submit, advance, offer, present, move, come up with, nominate, recommend. **2 intend**, mean, plan, have in mind, aim.

prop·o·si·tion /ˌpräpəˈzisHən/ ▶ n. **1** a statement that expresses an opinion. **2** a plan of action. **3** a problem to be dealt with.

> SYNONYMS **1 proposal**, scheme, plan, project, idea, program. **2 task**, job, undertaking, venture, activity, affair.

pro·pound /prəˈpound/ ▶ v. put forward an idea or theory for consideration.

pro·pri·e·tar·y /p(r)əˈprī-iˌterē/ ▶ adj. **1** having to do with an owner or ownership. **2** (of a product) marketed under a registered trademark. □ **proprietary name** a name of a product or service registered as a trademark.

pro·pri·e·tor /p(r)əˈprīətər/ ▶ n. the owner of a business.

SYNONYMS **owner**, possessor, holder, householder, master, mistress, landowner, landlord, landlady, store owner, shopkeeper.

pro·pri·e·to·ri·al /p(r)əˌprīəˈtôrēəl/ ▶ adj. behaving as if you owned something; possessive.

pro·pri·e·ty /p(r)əˈprīətē/ ▶ n. (plural **proprieties**) **1** correctness of behavior or morals. **2** the condition of being right or appropriate.

SYNONYMS **decorum**, respectability, decency, correctness, good manners, courtesy, politeness, rectitude. ANTONYMS indecorum.

pro·pul·sion /prəˈpəlsʜən/ ▶ n. the action of propelling or driving something forward.
■ **pro·pul·sive** adj.

pro ra·ta /prō ˈrātə, ˈrätə, ˈratə/ ▶ adj. proportional. ▶ adv. proportionally.

pro·sa·ic /prōˈzāik/ ▶ adj. ordinary or unimaginative; dull.

SYNONYMS **ordinary**, everyday, commonplace, conventional, straightforward, routine, run-of-the-mill; **unimaginative**, uninspired, uninspiring, matter-of-fact, dull, dreary, humdrum, mundane, pedestrian, tame, plodding. ANTONYMS interesting, imaginative, inspired.

■ **pro·sa·i·cal·ly** adv.

pro·sce·ni·um /prəˈsēnēəm, prō-/ ▶ n. (plural **prosceniums** or **proscenia** /-nēə/) **1** the part of a stage in front of the curtain. **2** (also **proscenium arch**) an arch framing the opening between the stage and the part of the theater in which the audience sits.

pro·scribe /prōˈskrīb/ ▶ v. (**proscribes**, **proscribing**, **proscribed**) **1** forbid. **2** criticize or condemn.

prose /prōz/ ▶ n. ordinary written or spoken language.

pros·e·cute /ˈpräsiˌkyo͞ot/ ▶ v. (**prosecutes**, **prosecuting**, **prosecuted**) **1** take legal proceedings against someone. **2** continue doing or taking part in something.

SYNONYMS **charge**, take to court, take legal action against, sue, try, bring to trial, put on trial, put in the dock, impeach, indict. ANTONYMS defend.

■ **pros·e·cu·tor** n.

pros·e·cu·tion /ˌpräsiˈkyo͞osʜən/ ▶ n. **1** the action of prosecuting. **2** (**the prosecution**) the party prosecuting someone in a lawsuit.

pros·e·lyte /ˈpräsəˌlīt/ ▶ n. a person who has converted from one religion or belief to another.

pros·e·lyt·ize /ˈpräsələˌtīz/ ▶ v. (**proselytizes**, **proselytizing**, **proselytized**) convert someone from one religion or belief to another.

pros·o·dy /ˈpräsədē, ˈpräzədē/ ▶ n. **1** the patterns of rhythm and sound used in poetry. **2** the study of these patterns.

pros·pect /ˈpräsˌpekt/ ▶ n. **1** a possibility of something happening. **2** an idea about what will happen in the future. **3** (**prospects**) chances of being successful. **4** a person who is likely to be successful. ▶ v. search for mineral deposits.

SYNONYMS ▶ n. **likelihood**, hope, expectation, chance, odds, probability, possibility, promise, outlook, lookout. ▶ v. **search**, look, explore, survey, scout, hunt, dowse.

■ **pros·pec·tor** n.

pro·spec·tive /prəˈspektiv/ ▶ adj. expected or likely to happen or be something in the future.

SYNONYMS **potential**, possible, probable, likely, future, eventual, -to-be, soon-to-be, in the making, intending, aspiring, would-be.

■ **pro·spec·tive·ly** adv.

pro·spec·tus /prəˈspektəs/ ▶ n. (plural **prospectuses**) a printed booklet advertising a school, university, or business.

SYNONYMS **brochure**, syllabus, curriculum, catalog, program, list, schedule.

pros·per /ˈpräspər/ ▶ v. (**prospers**, **prospering**, **prospered**) be successful, especially in making money.

SYNONYMS **flourish**, thrive, do well, bloom, blossom, burgeon, progress, do all right for yourself, get ahead, get on (in the world), be successful; informal go places. ANTONYMS fail.

pros·per·i·ty /präˈsperitē/ ▶ n. the state of being rich and successful.

SYNONYMS **success**, affluence, wealth, ease, plenty. ANTONYMS hardship, failure.

pros·per·ous /ˈpräspərəs/ ▶ adj. rich and successful.

SYNONYMS **1 thriving**, flourishing, successful, strong, vigorous, profitable, lucrative, expanding, booming, burgeoning. **2 affluent**, wealthy, rich, moneyed, well off, well-to-do; informal in the money. ANTONYMS ailing, poor.

pros·tate /ˈpräsˌtāt/ ▶ n. a gland in men and male mammals that produces the fluid part of semen.

pros·thet·ic /präsˈᴛʜetik/ ▶ adj. (of a body part) artificial.

pros·ti·tute /ˈprästəˌt(y)o͞ot/ ▶ n. a person who has sex with people for money. ▶ v. (often **prostitute oneself**) **1** do something unworthy or corrupt for the sake of money or personal advantage: *he decided that he would no longer prostitute his talent to win popularity*. **2** offer someone or work as a prostitute.

SYNONYMS ▶ n. whore, call girl, courtesan; informal hooker, hustler, lady of the night/evening, working girl. ▶ v. **betray**, sacrifice, sell, sell out, debase, degrade, demean, devalue, cheapen, lower, shame, misuse.

■ **pros·ti·tu·tion** /ˌprästəˈt(y)o͞osʜən/ n.

pros·trate /ˈpräsˌtrāt/ ▶ adj. **1** lying stretched out on the ground with the face downward. **2** completely overcome or helpless. ▶ v. (**prostrates**, **prostrating**, **prostrated**) **1** (**prostrate yourself**) throw yourself flat on the ground. **2** (**be prostrated**) be completely overcome with stress or exhaustion.

SYNONYMS ▶ adj. **1 prone**, lying flat, lying down, stretched out, spread-eagle, sprawling, horizontal, recumbent. **2** *prostrate with grief* **overwhelmed**, overcome, overpowered, stunned, dazed; speechless, helpless. ANTONYMS upright.

■ **pros·tra·tion** /präˈstrāsʜən/ n.

pro·tag·o·nist /prōˈtagənist, prə-/ ▶ n. **1** the leading character in a drama, movie, or novel. **2** an important person in a real event.

pro·te·an /ˈprōtēən, prōˈtēən/ ▶ adj. tending or able to change or adapt.

pro·tect /prə'tekt/ ▶ v. keep someone or something safe from harm or injury.

SYNONYMS **keep safe**, keep from harm, guard, defend, shield, save, safeguard, preserve, cushion, insulate, shelter, screen, keep, look after. ANTONYMS expose, harm.

pro·tec·tion /prə'teksʜən/ ▶ n. **1** the action of protecting. **2** a person or thing that protects. **3** the payment of money to criminals so that they will not attack your property.

SYNONYMS **1 defense**, security, safeguard, safety, sanctuary, shelter, refuge, immunity, indemnity. **2 safekeeping**, care, charge, guardianship, support, aegis, patronage. **3 barrier**, buffer, shield, screen, cushion, bulwark, armor, insulation.

pro·tec·tion·ism /prə'teksʜə,nizəm/ ▶ n. the practice of protecting a country's industries from foreign competition by taxing imported goods. ■ **pro·tec·tion·ist** n. & adj.

pro·tec·tive /prə'tektiv/ ▶ adj. **1** protecting someone or something. **2** having a strong wish to protect someone.

SYNONYMS **1 protecting**, covering, insulated, impermeable, -proof, -resistant. **2 solicitous**, careful, caring, defensive, paternal, maternal, overprotective, possessive.

■ **pro·tec·tive·ly** adv.

pro·tec·tor /prə'tektər/ ▶ n. **1** a person or thing that protects someone or something. **2** (**Protector**) historical a regent in charge of a kingdom when the monarch is away, ill, or too young to reign.

SYNONYMS **1 defender**, preserver, guardian, champion, patron, custodian. **2 guard**, shield, buffer, cushion, pad, screen.

■ **pro·tect·ress** /'prōtektres/ n.

pro·tec·tor·ate /prə'tektərət/ ▶ n. a state that is controlled and protected by another.

pro·té·gé /'prōtə,zʜā, ,prōtə'zʜā/ ▶ n. (feminine **protégée**) a person who is guided and supported by an older and more experienced person.

pro·tein /'prō,tē(ə)n/ ▶ n. a substance that forms part of body tissues and is an important part of the human diet.

SPELLING

Protein is an exception to the usual rule of **i** before **e**, when the sound is *ee*, except after **c**.

pro·test ▶ n. /'prō,test/ a statement or action expressing disapproval or objection to something. ▶ v. /prə'test, prō'test, 'prō,test/ **1** express an objection to what someone has said or done. **2** take part in a public protest. **3** state something strongly in response to an accusation: *she protested her innocence*.

SYNONYMS ▶ n. **1 objection**, complaint, challenge, dissent, demurral, remonstration, fuss, outcry. **2 demonstration**, rally, vigil, sit-in, occupation, stoppage, strike, walkout, mutiny, picket, boycott; informal demo. ▶ v. **1 object**, express opposition, dissent, take issue, take a stand, put up a fight, take exception, complain, express disapproval, disagree, make a fuss, speak out; informal kick up a fuss. **2 insist on**, maintain, assert, affirm, announce, proclaim, declare, profess, avow.

■ **pro·test·er** /'prō,testər, prə'tes-/ (or **protestor**) n.

Prot·es·tant /'prätəstənt/ ▶ n. a member or follower of any of the western Christian churches that are separate from the Roman Catholic Church. ▶ adj. relating to or belonging to any of the Protestant churches. ■ **Prot·es·tant·ism** n.

prot·es·ta·tion /,prätə'stāsʜən, ,prō,tes'tā-/ ▶ n. **1** a firm declaration that something is or is not the case. **2** an objection or protest.

pro·to·col /'prōtə,kôl, -,käl/ ▶ n. **1** the system of rules governing formal occasions. **2** the accepted way to behave in a particular situation.

SYNONYMS **etiquette**, convention, formalities, custom, the rules, procedure, ritual, decorum, the done thing.

pro·ton /'prō,tän/ ▶ n. a subatomic particle with a positive electric charge.

pro·to·type /'prōtə,tīp/ ▶ n. a first form of something from which other forms are copied or developed.

SYNONYMS **original**, master, template, pattern, sample.

pro·to·zo·an /,prōtə'zōən/ ▶ n. a microscopic animal that is made up of a single cell.

pro·tract /prə'trakt, prō-/ ▶ v. (often **protracted**) make something longer than expected or normal: *a protracted length of time*.

SYNONYMS **prolong**, lengthen, extend, draw out, drag out, spin out, stretch out, string out. ANTONYMS curtail, shorten.

pro·trac·tor /'prō,traktər/ ▶ n. an instrument for measuring angles, in the form of a flat semicircle marked with degrees.

pro·trude /prə'trōōd, prō-/ ▶ v. (**protrudes**, **protruding**, **protruded**) stick out from a surface.

SYNONYMS **stick out**, jut (out), project, extend, stand out, bulge out, poke out.

■ **pro·tru·sion** n.

pro·tu·ber·ance /prə't(y)ōōb(ə)rəns, prō-/ ▶ n. a thing that sticks out from a surface. ■ **pro·tu·ber·ant** adj.

SPELLING

Pro**tu**berance has no **r** immediately after the **t**, unlike a word with a similar meaning, pro**tru**sion.

proud /proud/ ▶ adj. **1** feeling pleased or satisfied by your own or another's achievements. **2** having too high an opinion of yourself. **3** having respect for yourself. **4** slightly sticking out from a surface.

SYNONYMS **1 pleased**, glad, happy, delighted, thrilled, satisfied, gratified. **2** *a proud moment* **pleasing**, gratifying, satisfying, cheering, heartwarming, happy, glorious. **3 arrogant**, conceited, vain, self-important, full of yourself, overbearing, bumptious, presumptuous, overweening, haughty, high and mighty; informal bigheaded, too big for your britches, stuck-up. ANTONYMS ashamed, humble.

■ **proud·ly** adv.

prove /prōōv/ ▶ v. (**proves**, **proving**, **proved**; past participle **proved** or **proven**) **1** use evidence to show that something is true or exists. **2** be found to be. **3** (**prove yourself**) show your abilities or courage. **4** (**proven**) found through experience to be effective or true.

SYNONYMS **show (to be true)**, demonstrate, substantiate, corroborate, verify, validate, authenticate, confirm. ANTONYMS disprove.

■ **prov·a·ble** adj.

prov·e·nance /ˈprävənəns/ ▶ n. the place where something originally comes from.

prov·en·der /ˈprävəndər/ ▶ n. old use food or animal fodder.

pro·verb /ˈpräˌvərb/ ▶ n. a short saying that gives advice or states something that is generally true.

SYNONYMS **saying**, adage, saw, maxim, axiom, motto, aphorism, epigram.

pro·ver·bi·al /prəˈvərbēəl/ ▶ adj. **1** referred to in a proverb. **2** well-known. ■ **pro·ver·bi·al·ly** adv.

pro·vide /prəˈvīd/ ▶ v. (**provides**, **providing**, **provided**) **1** make something available for someone to use. **2** (**provide for**) make enough preparation for a possible event.

SYNONYMS **1 supply**, give, come up with, produce, deliver, donate, contribute; informal fork out, lay out. **2** *he was* **provided with** *tools* **equip with**, furnish with, issue, supply with, fit out with, rig out with, arm with, provision with; informal fix up with. **3 offer**, present, afford, give, add, bring, yield, impart, lend.

pro·vid·ed /prəˈvīdid/ (or **providing** /prəˈvīdiNG/) ▶ conj. on the condition that.

SYNONYMS **if**, on condition that, provided that, presuming (that), assuming (that), as long as, with/on the understanding that.

prov·i·dence /ˈprävəˌdens, -dəns/ ▶ n. **1** the protective care of God or of nature. **2** careful preparation for the future.

prov·i·dent /ˈprävədənt, -ˌdent/ ▶ adj. careful in preparing for the future.

prov·i·den·tial /ˌprävəˈdenCHəl/ ▶ adj. happening at a favorable time.

pro·vid·er /prəˈvīdər/ ▶ n. a person or thing that provides something.

SYNONYMS **supplier**, donor, giver, contributor, source.

prov·ince /ˈprävins/ ▶ n. **1** a main administrative division of a country or empire. **2** (**the provinces**) the whole of a country outside the capital city. **3** your particular area of knowledge, interest, or responsibility.

SYNONYMS **1 territory**, region, state, department, canton, area, district, sector, zone, division. **2** (**the provinces**) **the regions**, the rest of the country, rural areas/districts, the countryside; informal the sticks, the boondocks, the boonies, the middle of nowhere. **3 domain**, area, department, responsibility, sphere, world, realm, field, discipline, territory; informal bailiwick.

pro·vin·cial /prəˈvinSHəl/ ▶ adj. **1** relating to a province or the provinces. **2** unsophisticated or narrow-minded. ▶ n. a person who lives in a province.

SYNONYMS ▶ adj. **1 local**, small-town, rural, country, outlying, backwoods; informal one-horse. **2 unsophisticated**, parochial, insular, narrow-minded, inward-looking, suburban, small-town; informal corn-fed. ANTONYMS cosmopolitan, sophisticated.

■ **pro·vin·cial·ism** n.

pro·vi·sion /prəˈviZHən/ ▶ n. **1** the action of providing. **2** something supplied or provided. **3** (**provision for** or **against**) arrangements for possible future events or needs. **4** (**provisions**) supplies of food, drink, or equipment. **5** a condition or requirement in a legal document. ▶ v. supply with provisions.

SYNONYMS ▶ n. **1** *limited provision for young children* **facilities**, services, amenities, resource(s), arrangements. **2** (**provisions**) **supplies**, food and drink, stores, groceries, foodstuff(s), rations. **3 term**, requirement, specification, stipulation.

pro·vi·sion·al /prəˈviZHənl/ ▶ adj. arranged for the present time only, possibly to be changed later.

SYNONYMS **interim**, temporary, transitional, changeover, stopgap, short-term, fill-in, acting, working. ANTONYMS permanent, definite.

■ **pro·vi·sion·al·ly** adv.

pro·vi·so /prəˈvīzō/ ▶ n. (plural **provisos**) a condition attached to an agreement.

SYNONYMS **condition**, stipulation, provision, clause, rider, qualification, restriction, caveat.

prov·o·ca·tion /ˌprävəˈkāSHən/ ▶ n. action or speech that makes someone angry or causes a strong reaction.

SYNONYMS **goading**, prodding, incitement, harassment, pressure, teasing, taunting, torment; informal hassle, aggravation.

pro·voc·a·tive /prəˈväkətiv/ ▶ adj. intended to make someone annoyed or angry.

SYNONYMS **annoying**, irritating, maddening, galling, insulting, offensive, inflammatory, incendiary; informal aggravating.

■ **pro·voc·a·tive·ly** adv.

pro·voke /prəˈvōk/ ▶ v. (**provokes**, **provoking**, **provoked**) **1** cause a strong reaction. **2** deliberately make someone feel angry. **3** stir someone up to do something.

SYNONYMS **1 arouse**, produce, evoke, cause, give rise to, excite, spark, touch off, kindle, generate, engender, instigate, result in, lead to, bring on, precipitate, prompt, trigger. **2 goad**, spur, prick, sting, prod, incite, rouse, stimulate. **3 annoy**, anger, enrage, irritate, rub the wrong way, madden, nettle; informal aggravate, rile, needle, get/put someone's back up. ANTONYMS allay, appease.

pro·vost /ˈprōˌvōst, -vō/ ▶ n. **1** a senior administrative officer in certain colleges and universities. **2** (in full **provost marshal**) the head of military police in camp or on active service.

prow /prou/ ▶ n. the pointed front part of a ship.

prow·ess /ˈprou-əs, ˈprōəs/ ▶ n. skill or expertise.

SYNONYMS **skill**, expertise, mastery, ability, capability, capacity, talent, aptitude, dexterity, proficiency, finesse; informal know-how. ANTONYMS inability, ineptitude.

prowl /proul/ ▶ v. move about stealthily or restlessly.

SYNONYMS **steal**, slink, skulk, sneak, stalk, creep; informal snoop.

□ **on the prowl** moving about in a stealthy way.

prowl·er /ˈproulər/ ▶ n. a person who walks or drives around a place with a view to committing a crime, especially burglary.

prox·im·i·ty /präk'simətē/ ▶ n. nearness or closeness. ■ **prox·i·mate** /'präksəmit/ adj.

prox·y /'präksē/ ▶ n. (plural **proxies**) **1** the authority to represent someone else. **2** a person authorized to act on behalf of another.

> SYNONYMS **deputy**, representative, substitute, delegate, agent, surrogate, stand-in, go-between.

prude /pro͞od/ ▶ n. a person who is easily shocked by matters relating to sex.

> SYNONYMS **puritan**, prig, killjoy, moralist; informal goody-goody, bluenose.

pru·dent /'pro͞odnt/ ▶ adj. acting in a cautious and sensible way.

> SYNONYMS **1 wise**, well-judged, sensible, politic, judicious, shrewd, sage, sagacious, farsighted, canny. **2 cautious**, careful, provident, circumspect, thrifty, economical. ANTONYMS unwise, extravagant.

■ **pru·dence** n. **pru·dent·ly** adv.

pru·den·tial /pro͞o'denchəl/ ▶ adj. prudent.

prud·ish /'pro͞odish/ ▶ adj. easily shocked by matters relating to sex or nudity.

> SYNONYMS **puritanical**, priggish, prim, moralistic, censorious, strait-laced, Victorian, stuffy; informal goody-goody. ANTONYMS permissive.

prune¹ /pro͞on/ ▶ n. a dried plum.

prune² ▶ v. (**prunes, pruning, pruned**) **1** trim a tree or bush by cutting away dead or overgrown branches. **2** remove unwanted parts from. ▶ n. an instance of pruning.

> SYNONYMS ▶ v. **1 cut back**, trim, clip, shear, shorten, thin, shape. **2 reduce**, cut (back/down), pare (down), slim down, trim, downsize, ax, shrink; informal slash. ANTONYMS increase.

pru·ri·ent /'pro͝orēənt/ ▶ adj. having too much interest in sexual matters.

> SYNONYMS **salacious**, licentious, voyeuristic, lascivious, lecherous, lustful, lewd, libidinous.

■ **pru·ri·ence** n.

pry¹ /prī/ ▶ v. (**pries, prying, pried**) ask someone unwelcome questions about their private life.

> SYNONYMS **be inquisitive**, poke about/around, ferret about/around, spy, be a busybody; informal stick/poke your nose in/into, be nosy, snoop.

■ **pry·ing** adj.

pry² ▶ v. force something apart or open.

PS ▶ abbr. postscript.

psalm /sä(l)m/ ▶ n. a song or poem that praises God.

psal·ter /'sôltər/ ▶ n. a copy of the Book of Psalms in the Bible.

pseu·do /'so͞odō/ ▶ adj. informal not genuine; false.

pseu·do·nym /'so͞odn-im/ ▶ n. a false name, especially one used by an author.

> SYNONYMS **pen name**, nom de plume, assumed name, alias, sobriquet, stage name, nom de guerre.

pso·ri·a·sis /sə'rīəsəs/ ▶ n. a condition in which patches of skin become red and itchy.

psych /sīk/ ▶ v. **1** (**psych yourself up**) informal prepare yourself mentally for a difficult task. **2** (**psych someone out**) intimidate an opponent by appearing very confident or aggressive.

psy·che /'sīkē/ ▶ n. the human soul, mind, or spirit.

psych·e·de·lia /,sīkə'dēlyə/ ▶ n. music or art based on the experiences produced by taking psychedelic drugs.

psy·che·del·ic /,sīkə'delik/ ▶ adj. **1** (of drugs) producing hallucinations. **2** having a strong, vivid color or a swirling abstract pattern.

psy·chi·a·trist /sə'kīətrist, sī-/ ▶ n. a doctor specializing in the diagnosis and treatment of mental illness.

> SYNONYMS **psychotherapist**, psychoanalyst, analyst; informal shrink.

psy·chi·a·try /sə'kīətrē, sī-/ ▶ n. the branch of medicine concerned with mental illness. ■ **psy·chi·at·ric** /,sīkē'atrik/ adj.

psy·chic /'sīkik/ ▶ adj. **1** relating to or possessing abilities that cannot be explained by science, e.g., telepathy or clairvoyance. **2** relating to the mind. ▶ n. a person considered or claiming to have psychic powers.

> SYNONYMS ▶ adj. **1 supernatural**, paranormal, otherworldly, metaphysical, extrasensory, magic(al), mystic(al), occult. **2 clairvoyant**, telepathic. ▶ n. **clairvoyant**, fortune teller, medium, spiritualist, telepath, mind-reader.

■ **psy·chi·cal·ly** adv.

psy·cho /'sīkō/ ▶ n. (plural **psychos**) informal a psychopath.

psy·cho·a·nal·y·sis /,sīkōə'naləsəs/ ▶ n. a method of treating mental disorders by investigating the unconscious elements of the mind. ■ **psy·cho·an·a·lyst** /,sīkō'anl-əst/ n. **psy·cho·an·a·lyt·ic** /,sīkō,anl'itik/ adj.

psy·cho·an·a·lyze /,sīkō'anl,īz/ ▶ v. (**psychoanalyzes, psychoanalyzing, psychoanalyzed**) treat someone using psychoanalysis.

psy·cho·log·i·cal /,sīkə'läjəkəl/ ▶ adj. **1** having to do with the mind. **2** relating to psychology.

> SYNONYMS **1 mental**, emotional, inner, cognitive. **2 (all) in the mind**, psychosomatic, emotional, subjective, subconscious, unconscious. ANTONYMS physical.

■ **psy·cho·log·i·cal·ly** adv.

psy·chol·o·gy /sī'käləjē/ ▶ n. **1** the scientific study of the human mind. **2** the way in which someone thinks or behaves.

> SYNONYMS **mind**, mindset, thought processes, way of thinking, mentality, psyche, attitude(s), make-up, character, temperament; informal what makes someone tick.

■ **psy·chol·o·gist** n.

psy·cho·path /'sīkə,path/ ▶ n. a person suffering from a serious mental illness that makes them behave violently. ■ **psy·cho·path·ic** /,sīkə'pathik/ adj.

psy·cho·sis /sī'kōsəs/ ▶ n. (plural **psychoses**) a serious mental illness in which a person loses contact with external reality.

psy·cho·so·mat·ic /,sīkōsə'matik/ ▶ adj. (of a physical illness) caused or made worse by a mental factor such as stress.

psy·cho·ther·a·py /,sīkō'therəpē/ ▶ n. the treatment of mental disorders by psychological rather than medical means. ■ **psy·cho·ther·a·pist** n.

psy·chot·ic /sī'kätik/ ▶ **adj.** relating to or suffering from a psychosis.

PT ▶ **abbr.** physical training.

Pt ▶ **abbr.** **1** Part. **2** (**pt.**) pint. **3** (in scoring) point.

PTA ▶ **abbr.** parent–teacher association.

ptar·mi·gan /'tärməgən/ ▶ **n.** a grouse with gray and black feathers that change to white in winter.

pter·o·dac·tyl /ˌterə'daktəl/ ▶ **n.** a fossil flying reptile with a long, slender head and neck.

PTO ▶ **abbr.** **1** please turn over. **2** parent-teacher organization.

pub /pəb/ ▶ **n.** **1** chiefly British a tavern or bar. **2** Australian a hotel.

> SYNONYMS **bar**, tavern, lounge; informal watering hole; historical saloon.

pu·ber·ty /'pyo͞obərtē/ ▶ **n.** the period during which adolescents reach sexual maturity.

> SYNONYMS **adolescence**, pubescence, youth, teenage years, teens.

pu·bes /'pyo͞obēz, pyo͞obz/ ▶ **n.** the lower front part of the abdomen.

pu·bes·cence /pyo͞o'besəns/ ▶ **n.** the time when puberty begins. ■ **pu·bes·cent** **adj. & n.**

pu·bic /'pyo͞obik/ ▶ **adj.** relating to the pubes or pubis.

pu·bis /'pyo͞obəs/ ▶ **n.** (plural **pubes**) either of a pair of bones forming the two sides of the pelvis.

pub·lic /'pəblik/ ▶ **adj.** **1** having to do with the people as a whole. **2** involved in the affairs of the community: *a public figure*. **3** intended to be seen or heard by people in general. **4** provided by the government rather than an independent company. ▶ **n.** **1** (**the public**) ordinary people in general. **2** a group of people with a particular interest: *the reading public*.

> SYNONYMS ▶ **adj.** **1 state**, national, constitutional, civic, civil, official, social, municipal, nationalized. **2 popular**, general, common, communal, collective, shared, joint, universal, widespread. **3 prominent**, well-known, important, leading, eminent, distinguished, celebrated, household, famous. **4 open** (**to the public**), communal, available, free, unrestricted. ANTONYMS private, secret. ▶ **n.** **1 people**, citizens, subjects, electors, electorate, voters, taxpayers, residents, inhabitants, citizenry, population, populace, community, society, country, nation. **2 audience**, spectators, followers, following, fans, devotees, admirers.

□ **in public** when other people are present. **public address system** a system of microphones and loudspeakers used to amplify speech or music. **public relations** the business of creating a good public image for an organization or famous person. **public school** **1** a school supported by public funds. **2** (in the UK) a private boarding school. **public sector** the part of an economy that is controlled by the state. **public transportation** buses, trains, and other forms of transport that are available to the public and run on fixed routes. ■ **pub·lic·ly** **adv.**

pub·li·ca·tion /ˌpəbli'kāsʜən/ ▶ **n.** **1** the action of publishing something. **2** a book or journal that is published.

> SYNONYMS **1 book**, volume, title, opus, tome, newspaper, paper, magazine, periodical, newsletter, bulletin, journal, report. **2 issuing**, publishing, printing, distribution.

pub·li·cist /'pəbləsist/ ▶ **n.** a person responsible for publicizing a product or celebrity.

pub·lic·i·ty /pə'blisətē/ ▶ **n.** **1** attention given to someone or something by television, newspapers, etc. **2** information used for advertising or promoting a product, person, event, etc.

> SYNONYMS **1 public attention**, media attention, exposure, glare, limelight, spotlight. **2 promotion**, advertising, propaganda, boost, push; informal hype, ballyhoo, buildup, plug.

pub·li·cize /'pəbləˌsīz/ ▶ **v.** (**publicizes**, **publicizing**, **publicized**) **1** make something widely known. **2** give out information about a product, person, event, etc., in order to advertise or promote them.

> SYNONYMS **1 make known**, make public, announce, broadcast, spread, promulgate, disseminate, circulate, air. **2 advertise**, promote, build up, talk up, push, beat the drum for, boost; informal hype, plug. ANTONYMS conceal, suppress.

pub·lish /'pəblisʜ/ ▶ **v.** **1** produce a book, newspaper, etc., for public sale. **2** print something in a book or newspaper.

> SYNONYMS **1 issue**, bring out, produce, print. **2 make known**, make public, publicize, announce, broadcast, issue, put out, distribute, spread, promulgate, disseminate, circulate, air.

■ **pub·lish·er** **n.**

puce /pyo͞os/ ▶ **n.** a dark red or purple-brown color.

puck /pək/ ▶ **n.** a black disk made of hard rubber, used in ice hockey.

puck·er /'pəkər/ ▶ **v.** (**puckers**, **puckering**, **puckered**) tightly gather into wrinkles or small folds. ▶ **n.** a wrinkle or small fold.

> SYNONYMS ▶ **v.** **wrinkle**, crinkle, crease, furrow, crumple, rumple, ruck up, scrunch up, ruffle, screw up, shrivel. ▶ **n.** **wrinkle**, crinkle, crumple, furrow, line, fold.

pud·ding /'po͝odiNG/ ▶ **n.** **1** a dessert with a creamy consistency. **2** a savory steamed dish made with suet and flour.

pud·dle /'pədl/ ▶ **n.** a small pool of liquid, especially of rain on the ground.

pudg·y /'pəjē/ ▶ **adj.** (**pudgier**, **pudgiest**) informal rather fat.

pueb·lo /'pweblō/ ▶ **n.** (plural **pueblos**) a town or village in Spain, Latin America, or the southwestern US, especially an American Indian settlement.

pu·er·ile /'pyo͝o(ə)rəl, 'pyo͝orˌīl/ ▶ **adj.** childishly silly.

> SYNONYMS **childish**, immature, infantile, juvenile, babyish, silly, inane, fatuous, foolish. ANTONYMS mature.

Puer·to Ri·can /ˌpôrtə 'rēkən, ˌpwertə/ ▶ **n.** a person from Puerto Rico. ▶ **adj.** relating to Puerto Rico.

puff /pəf/ ▶ **n.** **1** a small amount of air or smoke that is blown out from somewhere. **2** an act of breathing in smoke from a pipe, cigarette, or cigar. **3** a hollow piece of light pastry that is filled with cream or jam. ▶ **v.** **1** breathe in repeated short gasps. **2** move with short, noisy puffs of air or steam. **3** smoke a pipe, cigarette, or cigar. **4** (**be

puffed or **puffed out**) informal be out of breath. **5** (**puff out** or **up**) swell.

SYNONYMS ▶ **n. 1 gust**, blast, flurry, rush, draft, waft, breeze, breath. **2 pull**; informal drag, toke. ▶ **v. 1 breathe heavily**, pant, blow, gasp. **2 smoke**, draw on, drag on, inhale.

□ **puff pastry** light flaky pastry.

puff·ball /ˈpəfˌbôl/ ▶ **n.** a fungus with a round head that bursts to release its seeds.

puf·fin /ˈpəfən/ ▶ **n.** a seabird with a large brightly colored triangular bill.

puff·y /ˈpəfē/ ▶ **adj.** (**puffier**, **puffiest**) **1** (of a part of the body) swollen and soft. **2** softly rounded: *puffy clouds.*

SYNONYMS **swollen**, puffed up, distended, enlarged, inflated, dilated, bloated, engorged, bulging.

pug /pəg/ ▶ **n.** a very small breed of dog with a broad flat nose and a wrinkled face.

pu·gi·list /ˈpyo͞ojəlist/ ▶ **n.** chiefly humorous a boxer. ■ **pu·gi·lis·tic** /ˌpyo͞ojəˈlistik/ **adj.**

pug·na·cious /pəgˈnāsʜəs/ ▶ **adj.** eager or quick to argue or fight.

SYNONYMS **combative**, aggressive, antagonistic, belligerent, quarrelsome, argumentative, hostile, truculent. ANTONYMS peaceable.

■ **pug·nac·i·ty** /ˌpəgˈnasətē/ **n.**

puke /pyo͞ok/ informal ▶ **v.** (**pukes**, **puking**, **puked**) vomit. ▶ **n.** vomit.

puk·ka /ˈpəkə/ ▶ **adj.** informal **1** genuine. **2** socially acceptable. **3** excellent.

pul·chri·tude /ˈpəlkrəˌt(y)o͞od/ ▶ **n.** literary beauty.

pull /po͝ol/ ▶ **v. 1** apply force to something so as to move it toward yourself. **2** remove from a place by pulling. **3** move steadily: *the bus pulled away.* **4** strain a muscle. **5** attract someone as a customer. **6** informal bring out a weapon for use. ▶ **n. 1** an act of pulling. **2** a force, influence, or attraction. **3** a deep drink of something or a deep breath of smoke from a cigarette, pipe, etc.

SYNONYMS ▶ **v. 1 tug**, haul, drag, draw, tow, heave, jerk, wrench; informal yank. **2 strain**, sprain, wrench, tear. **3 attract**, draw, bring in, pull in, lure, seduce, entice, tempt. ANTONYMS push. ▶ **n. 1 tug**, jerk, heave; informal yank. **2 gulp**, draft, drink, swallow, mouthful, slug; informal swig. **3 puff**; informal drag, toke. **4 attraction**, draw, lure, magnetism, fascination, appeal, allure.

□ **pull back** retreat. **pull someone's leg** deceive someone for a joke. **pull something off** informal succeed in doing something difficult. **pull out** withdraw. **pull strings** use your influence to gain an advantage. **pull yourself together** regain your self-control. **pull your weight** do your fair share of work.

pul·let /ˈpo͝olət/ ▶ **n.** a young hen.

pul·ley /ˈpo͝olē/ ▶ **n.** (plural **pulleys**) a wheel around which a rope or chain passes, used to raise heavy objects.

pull·o·ver /ˈpo͝olˌōvər/ ▶ **n.** a garment, especially a sweater or jacket, put on over the head and covering the top half of the body.

pul·mo·nar·y /ˈpo͝olməˌnerē, ˈpəl-/ ▶ **adj.** relating to the lungs.

pulp /pəlp/ ▶ **n. 1** a soft, wet mass of crushed material. **2** the soft fleshy part of a fruit. ▶ **v.** crush into a pulp. ▶ **adj.** (of writing) popular and undemanding or sensational: *pulp fiction.*

SYNONYMS ▶ **n. 1 mush**, mash, paste, purée, slop, slush, mulch. **2 flesh**, marrow, meat. ▶ **v. mash**, purée, cream, crush, press, liquidize.

■ **pulp·y adj.**

pul·pit /ˈpo͝olˌpit, ˈpəl-, -pət/ ▶ **n.** a raised platform in a church from which the preacher gives a sermon.

pul·sar /ˈpəlˌsär/ ▶ **n.** a star that gives off regular rapid pulses of radio waves.

pul·sate /ˈpəlˌsāt/ ▶ **v.** (**pulsates**, **pulsating**, **pulsated**) **1** expand and contract with strong regular movements. **2** produce a regular throbbing sensation or sound. ■ **pul·sa·tion** /ˌpəlˈsāsʜən/ **n.**

pulse¹ /pəls/ ▶ **n. 1** the regular beat of the blood as it is pumped around the body. **2** a single vibration or short burst of sound, electric current, light, etc. **3** a regular musical rhythm. ▶ **v.** (**pulses**, **pulsing**, **pulsed**) pulsate.

SYNONYMS ▶ **n. 1 heartbeat**, heart rate. **2 rhythm**, beat, tempo, pounding, throb, throbbing, thudding, drumming. ▶ **v. throb**, pulsate, vibrate, beat, pound, thud, thump, drum, reverberate, echo.

pulse² ▶ **n.** the edible seeds of various plants, such as lentils or beans.

pul·ver·ize /ˈpəlvəˌrīz/ ▶ **v.** (**pulverizes**, **pulverizing**, **pulverized**) **1** crush into fine particles. **2** informal completely defeat.

SYNONYMS **1 grind**, crush, pound, powder, mill, press, pulp, mash; technical comminute. **2** see **DEFEAT** (sense 1 of the verb).

pu·ma /ˈp(y)o͞omə/ ▶ **n.** ⇨ **COUGAR.**

pum·ice /ˈpəməs/ ▶ **n.** a very light rock formed from lava.

pum·mel /ˈpəməl/ ▶ **v.** (**pummels**, **pummeling**, **pummeled**) hit repeatedly with the fists.

SYNONYMS **batter**, pound, belabor, beat, punch, strike, hit, thump; informal clobber, wallop, bash, whack, beat the living daylights out of, belt, lay into.

pump¹ /pəmp/ ▶ **n.** a device used to move liquids and gases or to force air into inflatable objects. ▶ **v. 1** move with a pump, or with something that works like a pump. **2** fill something with liquid, gas, etc. **3** move something up and down energetically. **4** informal try to get information from someone.

SYNONYMS ▶ **v. 1 force**, drive, push, inject, suck, draw. **2 inflate**, blow up, fill up, swell, enlarge, distend, expand, dilate, puff up. **3 spurt**, spout, squirt, jet, surge, spew, gush, stream, flow, pour, spill, well, cascade.

□ **pump iron** informal exercise with weights.

pump² ▶ **n. 1** a woman's plain, lightweight shoe that has a low-cut upper, no fastening, and typically a medium heel. **2** a man's slip-on patent leather shoe for formal wear.

pump·kin /ˈpəm(p)kən, ˈpəɴɢkən/ ▶ **n.** a large round fruit with a thick orange skin and edible flesh.

pun /pən/ ▶ **n.** a joke that uses a word or words with more than one meaning. ▶ **v.** (**puns**, **punning**, **punned**) make a pun.

punch¹ /pənʧ/ ▶ **v. 1** hit with the fist. **2** press a button or key on a machine. ▶ **n. 1** a blow with the fist. **2** informal the power to impress someone.

SYNONYMS ▶v. **hit**, strike, thump, jab, smash; informal sock, slug, bop, boff. ▶n. **blow**, hit, knock, thump, box, jab, clip; informal sock, slug, bop, boff.

□ **punch-drunk 1** dazed by a series of punches. **2** very confused or shocked. **punching bag** a heavy bag hung on a rope, used for punching as exercise or training.

punch² ▶n. a device for cutting holes in paper, metal, leather, etc. ▶v. pierce a hole in something.

SYNONYMS ▶v. **perforate**, puncture, pierce, prick, hole, spike, skewer.

punch³ ▶n. a drink made from fruit juices, soda, spices, and sometimes liquor.

punch·line /ˈpənCHˌlīn/ ▶n. the final part of a joke that makes it funny.

punch·y /ˈpənCHē/ ▶adj. (**punchier**, **punchiest**) **1** effective; forceful. **2** = PUNCH-DRUNK.

punc·til·i·ous /ˌpəNGkˈtilēəs/ ▶adj. showing great attention to detail or correct behavior.

punc·tu·al /ˈpəNGkCHo͞oəl/ ▶adj. happening or doing something at the agreed or proper time.

SYNONYMS **on time**, prompt, on schedule, in (good) time; informal on the dot. ANTONYMS late.

■ **punc·tu·al·i·ty** /ˌpəNGkCHo͞oˈalitē/ n. **punc·tu·al·ly** adv.

punc·tu·ate /ˈpəNGkCHo͞oˌāt/ ▶v. (**punctuates**, **punctuating**, **punctuated**) **1** interrupt something at intervals. **2** add punctuation marks to a piece of writing.

SYNONYMS **break up**, interrupt, intersperse, pepper, sprinkle, scatter.

punc·tu·a·tion /ˌpəNGkCHo͞oˈāSHən/ ▶n. the marks, such as period, comma, and brackets, used in writing to separate sentences and make meaning clear.

punc·ture /ˈpəNGkCHər/ ▶n. a small hole caused by a sharp object. ▶v. (**punctures**, **puncturing**, **punctured**) make a puncture in.

SYNONYMS ▶n. **1 hole**, perforation, rupture, cut, gash, slit, leak. **2 flat tire**; informal flat. ▶v. **prick**, pierce, stab, rupture, perforate, cut, slit, deflate.

pun·dit /ˈpəndit/ ▶n. a person who frequently gives opinions about a subject in public.

SYNONYMS **expert**, authority, specialist, doyen/doyenne, master, guru, sage, savant; informal buff, whiz.

pun·gent /ˈpənjənt/ ▶adj. **1** having a sharply strong taste or smell. **2** (of remarks or humor) having a strong effect.

SYNONYMS **strong**, powerful, pervasive, penetrating, sharp, acid, sour, biting, bitter, tart, vinegary, tangy, aromatic, spicy, piquant, peppery, hot, garlicky. ANTONYMS bland, mild.

■ **pun·gen·cy** n.

pun·ish /ˈpəniSH/ ▶v. **1** make someone experience something unpleasant because they have done something criminal or wrong. **2** (**punishing**) arduous and demanding: *a punishing schedule.* **3** treat harshly or unfairly.

SYNONYMS **1 discipline**, penalize, correct, sentence, teach someone a lesson; informal come down on (like a ton of bricks); dated chastise. **2** (**punishing**) **arduous**, demanding, taxing, strenuous, rigorous, stressful, trying, heavy, difficult, tough, exhausting, tiring, grueling.

pun·ish·a·ble /ˈpəniSHəbəl/ ▶adj. for which you can be punished: *a punishable offense.*

pun·ish·ment /ˈpəniSHmənt/ ▶n. **1** an unpleasant experience imposed on someone because they have done something criminal or wrong. **2** the action of punishing. **3** harsh or rough treatment.

SYNONYMS **penalty**, sanction, penance, discipline, forfeit, sentence.

pu·ni·tive /ˈpyo͞onətiv/ ▶adj. intended as punishment.

SYNONYMS **penal**, disciplinary, corrective.

Pun·ja·bi /ˌpənˈjäbē, po͝on-/ ▶n. (plural **Punjabis**) **1** a person from Punjab, a region of northwestern India and Pakistan. **2** the language of Punjab.

punk /pəNGk/ ▶n. **1** (also **punk rock**) a loud and aggressive form of rock music. **2** (also **punk rocker**) a person who likes or plays punk music. **3** informal a worthless person.

punt¹ /pənt/ ▶v. (in football) kick a ball after it has dropped from the hands and before it reaches the ground. ▶n. a kick of this kind.

punt² ▶n. a long, narrow boat with a flat bottom, moved forward with a long pole. ▶v. travel in a punt.

pu·ny /ˈpyo͞onē/ ▶adj. (**punier**, **puniest**) **1** small and weak. **2** not very impressive.

SYNONYMS **1 small**, weak, feeble, slight, undersized, stunted, underdeveloped; informal weedy. **2 pitiful**, pitiable, miserable, sorry, meager, paltry; informal pathetic, measly. ANTONYMS sturdy.

pup /pəp/ ▶n. **1** a young dog. **2** a young wolf, seal, rat, or other animal.

pu·pa /ˈpyo͞opə/ ▶n. (plural **pupae** /-ˌpē, -ˌpī/) an insect in the form between larva and adult.

■ **pu·pal** adj.

pu·pate /ˈpyo͞oˌpāt/ ▶v. (**pupates**, **pupating**, **pupated**) become a pupa.

pu·pil¹ /ˈpyo͞opəl/ ▶n. a person who is being taught; a student.

SYNONYMS **1 student**, scholar, schoolchild, schoolboy, schoolgirl. **2 disciple**, follower, student, protégé, apprentice, trainee, novice. ANTONYMS teacher.

pu·pil² ▶n. the dark circular opening in the center of the iris of the eye.

pup·pet /ˈpəpət/ ▶n. **1** a model of a person or animal that can be moved either by strings or by a hand inside it. **2** a person under the control of someone else.

SYNONYMS **1 marionette**, sock puppet, finger puppet. **2 pawn**, tool, instrument, cat's paw, poodle, mouthpiece, stooge.

■ **pup·pet·ry** n.

pup·pet·eer /ˌpəpəˈtir/ ▶n. a person who works puppets.

pup·py /ˈpəpē/ ▶n. (plural **puppies**) a young dog. □ **puppy love** strong but short-lived love.

pur·blind /ˈpərˌblīnd/ ▶adj. literary **1** partially sighted. **2** lacking awareness or understanding.

pur·chase /ˈpərCHəs/ ▶ **v.** (**purchases**, **purchasing**, **purchased**) buy. ▶ **n. 1** the action of buying. **2** a thing bought. **3** firm contact or grip.

SYNONYMS ▶ **v. buy**, acquire, obtain, pick up, procure, pay for, invest in; informal get (a) hold of, score. ANTONYMS sell. ▶ **n. 1 acquisition**, buy, investment, order. **2 grip**, grasp, hold, foothold, toehold, anchorage, support, traction, leverage. ANTONYMS sale.

■ **pur·chas·er n.**

pur·dah /ˈpərdə/ ▶ **n.** the practice in certain Muslim and Hindu societies of screening women from men or strangers.

pure /pyo͝or/ ▶ **adj. 1** not mixed with any other substance or material: *pure wool.* **2** not containing any harmful or polluting substances. **3** innocent or morally good. **4** sheer; nothing but: *a shout of pure anger.* **5** theoretical rather than practical: *pure mathematics.* **6** (of a sound) perfectly in tune and with a clear tone.

SYNONYMS **1 unadulterated**, undiluted, sterling, solid, unalloyed. **2 clean**, clear, fresh, sparkling, unpolluted, uncontaminated, untainted. **3 virtuous**, moral, good, righteous, honorable, reputable, wholesome, clean, honest, upright, upstanding, exemplary, innocent, chaste, unsullied, undefiled; informal squeaky clean. **4 sheer**, utter, absolute, out-and-out, complete, total, perfect. ANTONYMS impure, polluted.

pu·rée /pyo͝oˈrā, -ˈrē/ ▶ **n.** a mass of crushed fruit or vegetables. ▶ **v.** (**purées**, **puréeing**, **puréed**) make a purée of.

pure·ly /ˈpyo͝orlē/ ▶ **adv.** entirely; exclusively: *the purpose of the meeting was purely to give information.*

SYNONYMS **entirely**, wholly, exclusively, solely, only, just, merely.

pur·ga·tive /ˈpərgətiv/ ▶ **adj.** having a strong laxative effect. ▶ **n.** a laxative.

pur·ga·to·ry /ˈpərgəˌtôrē/ ▶ **n.** (plural **purgatories**) (in Roman Catholic belief) a place inhabited by the souls of sinners who are making up for their sins before going to heaven.

SYNONYMS **torment**, torture, misery, suffering, affliction, anguish, agony, woe, an ordeal, a nightmare, hell. ANTONYMS paradise.

■ **pur·ga·to·ri·al** /ˌpərgəˈtôrēəl/ **adj.**

purge /pərj/ ▶ **v.** (**purges**, **purging**, **purged**) rid someone or something of undesirable or harmful people or things. ▶ **n.** an act of purging.

SYNONYMS ▶ **v. 1 cleanse**, clear, purify, rid, empty, strip, scour. **2 remove**, get rid of, eliminate, clear out, sweep out, expel, eject, evict, dismiss, sack, oust, ax, depose, root out, weed out. ▶ **n. removal**, elimination, expulsion, ejection, exclusion, eviction, dismissal.

pu·ri·fy /ˈpyo͝orəˌfī/ ▶ **v.** (**purifies**, **purifying**, **purified**) make something pure.

SYNONYMS **clean**, cleanse, refine, decontaminate, filter, clear, freshen, deodorize, sanitize, disinfect, sterilize.

■ **pu·ri·fi·ca·tion** /ˌpyo͝orəfiˈkāSHən/ **n.**

SPELLING

Write this word with an **i** not an **e**: purify.

Pu·rim /ˈpo͝orim, po͝oˈrēm/ ▶ **n.** a Jewish festival held in spring to commemorate the defeat of a plot by Haman (a Persian minister) to massacre the Jews.

pur·ist /ˈpyo͝orist/ ▶ **n.** a person who insists on following traditional rules, especially in language or style. ■ **pur·ism n.**

pu·ri·tan /ˈpyo͝oritn/ ▶ **n. 1** (**Puritan**) a member of a group of English Protestants in the 16th and 17th centuries who tried to simplify forms of worship. **2** a person with strong moral beliefs who is critical of the behavior of other people.

pu·ri·tan·i·cal /ˌpyo͝oriˈtanikəl/ ▶ **adj.** having a very strict or critical attitude toward self-indulgent behavior.

SYNONYMS **moralistic**, puritan, strait-laced, stuffy, prudish, prim, priggish, narrow-minded, censorious, austere, severe, ascetic, abstemious; informal goody-goody, starchy. ANTONYMS permissive.

pu·ri·ty /ˈpyo͝oritē/ ▶ **n.** the state of being pure.

SYNONYMS **1 cleanness**, freshness, cleanliness. **2 virtue**, morality, goodness, righteousness, piety, honor, honesty, integrity, innocence.

purl /pərl/ ▶ **adj.** (of a knitting stitch) made by putting the needle through the front of the stitch from right to left. ▶ **v.** knit with a purl stitch.

pur·loin /pərˈloin/ ▶ **v.** formal steal.

pur·ple /ˈpərpəl/ ▶ **adj.** of a color between red and blue. ▶ **n.** a purple color. □ **Purple Heart** a US military decoration for members of the armed forces wounded or killed in action. **purple prose** prose that is too elaborate.

pur·port ▶ **v.** /pərˈpôrt/ appear or claim to be or do. ▶ **n.** /ˈpərˌpôrt/ the meaning or purpose of something.

pur·pose /ˈpərpəs/ ▶ **n. 1** the reason for which something is done or for which something exists. **2** strong determination.

SYNONYMS **1 motive**, motivation, grounds, occasion, reason, point, basis, justification. **2 intention**, aim, object, objective, goal, plan, ambition, aspiration. **3 function**, role, use. **4 determination**, resolution, resolve, steadfastness, single-mindedness, enthusiasm, ambition, motivation, commitment, conviction, dedication.

□ **on purpose** intentionally.

pur·pose·ful /ˈpərpəsfəl/ ▶ **adj. 1** having or showing determination. **2** having a purpose.

SYNONYMS **determined**, resolute, steadfast, single-minded, committed. ANTONYMS aimless.

■ **pur·pose·ful·ly adv.**

pur·pose·ly /ˈpərpəslē/ ▶ **adv.** on purpose.

SYNONYMS **deliberately**, intentionally, on purpose, willfully, knowingly, consciously.

pur·pos·ive /ˈpərpəsiv, pərˈpō-/ ▶ **adj.** having or done with a purpose.

purr /pər/ ▶ **v. 1** (of a cat) make a low continuous sound taken to indicate contentment. **2** (of an engine) run smoothly while making a similar sound. ▶ **n.** a purring sound.

purse /pərs/ ▶ **n. 1** a handbag. **2** a small pouch for carrying money. **3** money for spending. **4** a sum of money given as a prize. ▶ **v.** (**purses**, **pursing**, **pursed**) form the lips into a tight round shape.

SYNONYMS ▶ n. 1 **wallet**, change purse, billfold. 2 **handbag**, pocketbook, shoulder bag, clutch (purse/bag). 3 **prize**, reward, winnings, stake(s). ▶ v. **press together**, compress, tighten, pucker, pout.

purs·er /'pərsər/ ▶ n. a ship's officer who keeps the accounts.

pur·su·ance /pər'so͞oəns/ ▶ n. formal the carrying out of a plan or action.

pur·su·ant /pər'so͞oənt/ ▶ adv. (**pursuant to**) formal in accordance with.

pur·sue /pər'so͞o/ ▶ v. (**pursues**, **pursuing**, **pursued**) 1 follow someone or something in order to catch or attack them. 2 try to achieve a goal. 3 follow a course of action. 4 continue to investigate or discuss a topic.

SYNONYMS 1 **follow**, run after, chase, hunt, stalk, track, trail, hound. 2 **strive for**, work toward, seek, search for, aim at/for, aspire to. 3 **engage in**, be occupied in, practice, follow, conduct, ply, take up, undertake, carry on with, continue, proceed with, apply yourself to.

■ **pur·su·er** n.

SPELLING

Write **pur-**, not **per-**: **pursue**.

pur·suit /pər'so͞ot/ ▶ n. 1 the action of pursuing someone or something. 2 a recreational or athletic activity.

SYNONYMS *a range of leisure pursuits* **activity**, hobby, pastime, diversion, recreation, amusement, occupation.

pu·ru·lent /'pyo͝or(y)ələnt/ ▶ adj. made up of or giving out pus.

pur·vey /pər'vā/ ▶ v. 1 formal provide or supply food or drink as a business. 2 spread or promote an idea, view, etc. ■ **pur·vey·or** n.

pur·view /'pərˌvyo͞o/ ▶ n. formal the range of something's influence or concerns.

pus /pəs/ ▶ n. a thick yellowish or greenish liquid produced in infected body tissue.

push /po͝osн/ ▶ v. 1 apply force to something so as to move it away from yourself. 2 move part of your body into a particular position. 3 move by using force. 4 encourage someone to work hard. 5 (**push for**) repeatedly demand something. 6 informal promote the use, sale, or acceptance of. 7 informal sell an illegal drug. ▶ n. 1 an act of pushing. 2 a great effort: *one last push*.

SYNONYMS ▶ v. 1 **shove**, thrust, propel, send, drive, force, prod, poke, nudge, elbow, shoulder, ram, squeeze, jostle. 2 **press**, depress, hold down, squeeze, operate, activate. 3 **urge**, press, pressure, pressurize, force, coerce, dragoon, browbeat; informal lean on, twist someone's arm. ANTONYMS pull. ▶ n. 1 **shove**, thrust, nudge, bump, jolt, prod, poke. 2 *the army's eastward push* **advance**, drive, thrust, charge, attack, assault, onslaught, onrush, offensive.

□ **push-up** 1 an exercise in which you lie facing the floor and, keeping your back straight, raise your body by pressing down on your hands. 2 denoting a bra that gives uplift to the breasts. ■ **push·er** n.

push·o·ver /'po͝osнˌōvər/ ▶ n. informal 1 a person who is easy to influence or defeat. 2 a thing that is easily done.

push·y /'po͝osнē/ ▶ adj. (**pushier**, **pushiest**) too assertive or ambitious.

SYNONYMS **assertive**, overbearing, domineering, aggressive, forceful, forward, thrusting, ambitious, overconfident, cocky; informal bossy.

pu·sil·lan·i·mous /ˌpyo͞osə'lanəməs/ ▶ adj. weak or cowardly. ■ **pu·sil·la·nim·i·ty** /-lə'nimətē/ n.

pus·sy /'po͝osē/ (or **puss** /po͝os/) ▶ n. (plural **pussies** or **pusses**) (also **pussycat** /'po͝osēˌkat/) informal a cat. □ **pussy willow** a willow with soft, fluffy catkins that appear before the leaves.

pus·sy·foot /'po͝osēˌfo͝ot/ ▶ v. (**pussyfoots**, **pussyfooting**, **pussyfooted**) act very cautiously.

pus·tule /'pəst(y)o͞ol/ ▶ n. a small blister on the skin containing pus. ■ **pus·tu·lar** adj.

put /po͝ot/ ▶ v. (**puts**, **putting**, **put**) 1 move something into a particular position. 2 bring into a particular state or condition: *she tried to put me at ease*. 3 (**put something on** or **on to**) make a person or thing subject to something. 4 give a value, figure, or limit to. 5 express something in a particular way. 6 (of a ship) go in a particular direction: *the boat put out to sea*. 7 throw a shot or weight as a sport.

SYNONYMS 1 **place**, set, lay, deposit, position, leave, plant, locate, situate, settle, install; informal stick, dump, park, plunk, plonk, pop. 2 **express**, word, phrase, frame, formulate, render, convey, state.

□ **put someone/something down** 1 end a riot by using force. 2 kill a sick, old, or injured animal. 3 pay a sum as a deposit. 4 informal criticize someone in public. **put someone/thing off** 1 postpone something. 2 make someone feel dislike or lose enthusiasm. 3 distract someone. **put something on** 1 organize an event. 2 gain weight. 3 adopt an expression, accent, etc. **put someone out** 1 cause someone trouble or inconvenience. 2 Baseball cause a batter or runner to be out. **put someone/something up** 1 present, provide, or offer something. 2 give someone a place to stay. **put someone up to** informal encourage someone to do something wrong. **put up with** tolerate.

pu·ta·tive /'pyo͞otətiv/ ▶ adj. formal generally considered to be.

pu·tre·fy /'pyo͞otrəˌfī/ ▶ v. (**putrefies**, **putrefying**, **putrefied**) decay or rot and produce a very unpleasant smell. ■ **pu·tre·fac·tion** /ˌpyo͞otrə'faksнən/ n.

pu·trid /'pyo͞otrid/ ▶ adj. 1 decaying or rotting and producing a very unpleasant smell. 2 informal very unpleasant.

SYNONYMS **decomposing**, decaying, rotting, rotten, bad, foul, fetid, rank, putrefied, putrescent, rancid, moldy.

putsch /po͝ocн/ ▶ n. a violent attempt to overthrow a government.

putt /pət/ ▶ v. (**putts**, **putting**, **putted**) hit a golf ball gently so that it rolls into or near a hole. ▶ n. a stroke of this kind. □ **putting green** a smooth area of short grass surrounding a hole on a golf course.

put·ter¹ /'pətər/ ▶ n. a golf club designed for putting.

put·ter² ▶ n. the rapid irregular sound of a small gas engine. ▶ v. (**putters**, **puttering**, **puttered**) move with this sound.

put·ter³ ▶ v. (**putters**, **puttering**, **puttered**) 1 spend your time doing small tasks in a relaxed way. 2 move in an unhurried way.

put·ty /'pətē/ ▶ n. a soft paste that hardens as it dries, used for sealing glass in window frames.

puz·zle /'pəzəl/ ▶ v. (**puzzles**, **puzzling**, **puzzled**) **1** make someone feel confused because they cannot understand something. **2** think hard about something difficult to understand. ▶ n. **1** a game, toy, or problem designed to test mental skills or knowledge. **2** a person or thing that is difficult to understand.

SYNONYMS ▶ v. **1 baffle**, perplex, bewilder, confuse, bemuse, mystify, nonplus; informal flummox, stump, beat. **2** (**puzzling**) **baffling**, perplexing, bewildering, confusing, complicated, unclear, mysterious, enigmatic. ▶ n. **enigma**, mystery, paradox, conundrum, poser, riddle, problem.

■ **puz·zle·ment** n. **puz·zler** n.

PVC ▶ abbr. polyvinyl chloride, a kind of plastic.

Pvt. ▶ abbr. (in the US Army and in company names) private.

PX ▶ abbr. post exchange (a store on an army base).

pyg·my /'pigmē/ (or **pigmy**) ▶ n. (plural **pygmies**) **1** (**Pygmy**) a member of a race of very short people living in parts of Africa. **2** a very small person or thing. ▶ adj. very small.

py·lon /'pī,län, -lən/ ▶ n. **1** a tall towerlike structure for carrying electricity cables. **2** a post marking a lane for traffic.

pyr·a·mid /'pirə,mid/ ▶ n. a very large stone structure with a square or triangular base and sloping sides that meet in a point at the top. ■ **py·ram·i·dal** /pi'ramidl/ adj.

pyre /pīr/ ▶ n. a large pile of wood for the ritual burning of a dead body.

py·ri·tes /pə'rītēz, pī-/ (or **pyrite** /'pī,rīt/) ▶ n. a shiny yellow mineral that is a compound of iron and sulfur.

py·ro·ma·ni·a /,pīrō'mānēə/ ▶ n. a strong urge to set fire to things. ■ **py·ro·ma·ni·ac** n.

py·ro·tech·nics /,pīrə'tekniks/ ▶ pl.n. **1** a fireworks display. **2** the art of making fireworks or staging fireworks displays. ■ **py·ro·tech·nic** adj.

pyr·rhic /'pirik/ ▶ adj. (of a victory) won at too great a cost to have been worthwhile.

py·thon /'pī,THän, 'pīTHən/ ▶ n. a large snake that crushes its prey.

Qq

Q (or **q**) ▶ **n.** (plural **Qs** or **Q's**) the seventeenth letter of the alphabet. ▶ **abbr.** question.

QED ▶ **abbr.** used to say that something proves the truth of your claim.

qt. ▶ **abbr.** quarts.

qua /kwä, kwā/ ▶ **conj.** formal in the role or capacity of.

quack¹ /kwak/ ▶ **n.** the harsh sound made by a duck. ▶ **v.** make this sound.

quack² ▶ **n.** an unqualified person who claims to have medical knowledge.

quad /kwäd/ ▶ **n. 1** a quadrangle. **2** a quadruplet.

quad·ran·gle /ˈkwäˌdraNGgəl/ ▶ **n. 1** a square or rectangular courtyard enclosed by buildings. **2** a four-sided geometrical figure. ■ **quad·ran·gu·lar** /kwäˈdraNGgyələr/ **adj.**

quad·rant /ˈkwädrənt/ ▶ **n. 1** a quarter of a circle or of a circle's circumference. **2** historical an instrument for measuring angles in astronomy and navigation.

quad·ra·phon·ic /ˌkwädrəˈfänik/ (or **quadrophonic**) ▶ **adj.** (of sound reproduction) using four channels.

quad·rat·ic /kwäˈdratik/ ▶ **adj.** Math involving the second and no higher power of an unknown quantity.

quad·ri·ceps /ˈkwädrəˌseps/ ▶ **n.** (plural **quadriceps**) a large muscle at the front of the thigh.

quad·ri·lat·er·al /ˌkwädrəˈlatərəl/ ▶ **n.** a four-sided figure. ▶ **adj.** having four straight sides.

quad·rille /kwäˈdril, k(w)ə-/ ▶ **n.** a square dance performed by four couples.

quad·ri·ple·gi·a /ˌkwädrəˈplēj(ē)ə/ ▶ **n.** paralysis of all four limbs. ■ **quad·ri·ple·gic adj. & n.**

quad·ru·ped /ˈkwädrəˌped/ ▶ **n.** an animal that has four feet.

quad·ru·ple /kwäˈdro͞opəl/ ▶ **adj. 1** consisting of four parts. **2** four times as much or as many. ▶ **v.** (**quadruples**, **quadrupling**, **quadrupled**) multiply by four.

quad·ru·plet /kwäˈdro͞oplit/ ▶ **n.** each of four children born at one birth.

quaff /kwäf/ ▶ **v.** drink a large amount of something quickly.

quag·mire /ˈkwagˌmīr/ ▶ **n.** a soft, wet area of land.

quail¹ /kwāl/ ▶ **n.** (plural **quail** or **quails**) a small short-tailed game bird.

quail² ▶ **v.** feel or show fear.

quaint /kwānt/ ▶ **adj.** attractively unusual or old-fashioned.

> SYNONYMS **1 picturesque**, charming, sweet, attractive, old-fashioned, old-world. **2 unusual**, curious, eccentric, quirky, bizarre, whimsical, unconventional; informal offbeat.
> ANTONYMS ugly.

■ **quaint·ly adv.**

quake /kwāk/ ▶ **v.** (**quakes**, **quaking**, **quaked**) **1** (especially of the earth) shake or tremble. **2** shudder with fear. ▶ **n.** informal an earthquake.

> SYNONYMS ▶ **v. shake**, tremble, quiver, shudder, sway, rock, wobble, move, heave, convulse.

Quak·er /ˈkwākər/ ▶ **n.** a member of the Religious Society of Friends, a Christian movement devoted to peaceful principles and rejecting set forms of worship. ■ **Quak·er·ism n.**

qual·i·fi·ca·tion /ˌkwäləfəˈkāsʜən/ ▶ **n. 1** the action of qualifying. **2** a pass of an exam or an official completion of a course. **3** a quality that makes someone suitable for a job or activity. **4** a statement that limits the meaning of another statement.

> SYNONYMS **1 certificate**, diploma, degree, license, document, warrant. **2 modification**, limitation, reservation, stipulation, alteration, amendment, revision, moderation, mitigation, condition, proviso, caveat.

qual·i·fy /ˈkwäləˌfī/ ▶ **v.** (**qualifies**, **qualifying**, **qualified**) **1** meet the necessary standard or conditions to be able to do or receive something. **2** become officially recognized as able to do a particular job. **3** add something to a statement to limit its meaning. **4** Grammar (of a word or phrase) give a quality to another word.

> SYNONYMS **1 be eligible**, meet the requirements, be entitled, be permitted. **2 be certified**, be licensed, pass, graduate, succeed. **3 authorize**, empower, allow, permit, license, charter, certify, certificate. **4 modify**, limit, restrict, make conditional, moderate, temper, modulate, mitigate. **5** (**qualified**) *a qualified success* **limited**, conditional, restricted, contingent, circumscribed, guarded, equivocal, modified, adapted, amended, adjusted, moderated, reduced.

■ **qual·i·fi·er n.**

qual·i·ta·tive /ˈkwäləˌtātiv/ ▶ **adj.** relating to or measured by quality. ■ **qual·i·ta·tive·ly adv.**

qual·i·ty /ˈkwälətē/ ▶ **n.** (plural **qualities**) **1** the standard of something as measured against other similar things; how good or bad something is. **2** general excellence. **3** a distinctive characteristic.

> SYNONYMS **1 standard**, grade, class, caliber, condition, character, nature, form, rank, value, level. **2 excellence**, superiority, merit, worth, value, virtue, caliber, distinction. **3 feature**, trait, attribute, characteristic, point, aspect, facet, side, property.

qualm /kwä(l)m, kwô(l)m/ ▶ **n.** a feeling of doubt about what you are doing.

quan·da·ry /ˈkwänd(ə)rē/ ▶ **n.** (plural **quandaries**) a state of uncertainty.

quan·ti·fy /ˈkwäntəˌfī/ ▶ v. (**quantifies**, **quantifying**, **quantified**) express or measure the quantity of. ■ **quan·ti·fi·a·ble** adj.

quan·ti·ta·tive /ˈkwäntəˌtātiv/ ▶ adj. relating to or measured by quantity. ■ **quan·ti·ta·tive·ly** adv.

quan·ti·ty /ˈkwäntətē/ ▶ n. (plural **quantities**) **1** a certain amount or number. **2** the property of something that can be measured in number, amount, size, or weight. **3** a large number or amount.

> SYNONYMS **amount**, total, aggregate, sum, quota, mass, weight, volume, bulk.

quan·tum /ˈkwäntəm/ ▶ n. (plural **quanta** /-tə/) Physics a distinct quantity of energy corresponding to that involved in the absorption or emission of energy by an atom. □ **quantum leap** a sudden large increase or advance. **quantum mechanics** the branch of physics concerned with describing the behavior of subatomic particles in terms of quanta.

quar·an·tine /ˈkwôrənˌtēn/ ▶ n. a period of time when an animal or person that may have a disease is kept in isolation. ▶ v. (**quarantines**, **quarantining**, **quarantined**) put in quarantine.

quark /kwärk, kwôrk/ ▶ n. any of a group of subatomic particles that carry a very small electric charge and are believed to form protons, neutrons, and other particles.

quar·rel /ˈkwôrəl, ˈkwä-/ ▶ n. **1** an angry argument or disagreement. **2** a reason for disagreement. ▶ v. (**quarrels**, **quarreling**, **quarreled**) **1** have a quarrel. **2** (**quarrel with**) disagree with.

> SYNONYMS ▶ n. **argument**, disagreement, squabble, fight, dispute, wrangle, clash, altercation, feud, vendetta; informal tiff, run-in, spat. ANTONYMS agreement. ▶ v. **argue**, fight, disagree, fall out, differ, be at odds, bicker, squabble, cross swords. ANTONYMS agree.

quar·rel·some /ˈkwôrəlsəm, ˈkwä-/ ▶ adj. tending to quarrel with people.

> SYNONYMS **argumentative**, disputatious, confrontational, captious, pugnacious, combative, antagonistic, bellicose, belligerent, cantankerous, choleric. ANTONYMS peaceable.

quar·ry[1] /ˈkwôrē, ˈkwä-/ ▶ n. (plural **quarries**) a place where stone or other materials are dug out of the earth. ▶ v. (**quarries**, **quarrying**, **quarried**) dig out stone or other materials from a quarry.

quar·ry[2] ▶ n. (plural **quarries**) an animal or person that is being hunted or chased.

> SYNONYMS **prey**, victim, object, goal, target, kill, game, prize.

quart /kwôrt/ ▶ n. a unit of liquid capacity equal to a quarter of a gallon or two pints (0.94 liter).

quar·ter /ˈkwôrtər/ ▶ n. **1** each of four equal parts of something. **2** a period of three months. **3** a quarter of an hour; fifteen minutes. **4** one fourth of a pound weight, equal to 4 ounces. **5** a part of a town. **6** a US or Canadian coin worth 25 cents. **7** one fourth of a hundredweight, equal to 25 pounds. **8** (**quarters**) rooms to live in. **9** a person or area seen as the source of something: *help from an unexpected quarter*. **10** mercy shown to an opponent. ▶ v. (**quarters**, **quartering**, **quartered**) **1** divide into quarters. **2** (**be quartered**) be provided with rooms to live in. **3** historical cut the body of an executed person into four parts.

> SYNONYMS ▶ n. **1 district**, area, region, part, side, neighborhood, precinct, locality, sector, zone, ghetto, community, enclave. **2 source**, direction, place, location. **3** *the servants' quarters* **accommodations**, rooms, chambers, home, lodgings; informal pad, digs; formal abode, residence, domicile. **4** *riot squads gave no quarter* **mercy**, leniency, clemency, compassion, pity, charity, sympathy, tolerance. ▶ v. **accommodate**, house, board, lodge, put up, take in, install, shelter; Military billet.

□ **quarter note** Music a note having the time value of half a half note.

quar·ter·back /ˈkwôrtərˌbak/ ▶ n. Football a player who directs a team's attacking play.

quar·ter·deck /ˈkwôrtərˌdek/ ▶ n. the part of a ship's upper deck near the stern.

quar·ter·fi·nal /ˈkwôrtərˌfīnl/ ▶ n. a match or round of a tournament that precedes the semifinal.

quar·ter·ly /ˈkwôrtərlē/ ▶ adj. & adv. produced or happening once every quarter of a year. ▶ n. (plural **quarterlies**) a publication produced four times a year.

quar·ter·mas·ter /ˈkwôrtərˌmastər/ ▶ n. an army officer in charge of accommodations and supplies.

quar·tet /kwôrˈtet/ ▶ n. **1** a group of four people playing music or singing together. **2** a piece of music for a quartet. **3** a set of four.

quar·to /ˈkwôrtō/ ▶ n. (plural **quartos**) a size of page for a book, resulting from folding a sheet into four leaves.

quartz /kwôrts/ ▶ n. a hard mineral consisting of silica.

qua·sar /ˈkwāˌzär/ ▶ n. (in astronomy) a kind of galaxy that gives off enormous amounts of energy.

quash /kwôsн, kwäsн/ ▶ v. **1** officially declare that a legal decision is no longer valid. **2** put an end to.

> SYNONYMS **1 cancel**, reverse, rescind, repeal, revoke, retract, countermand, withdraw, overturn, overrule. **2 stop**, put an end to, stamp out, crush, put down, check, curb, nip in the bud, squash, suppress, stifle.

quat·rain /ˈkwäˌtrān, kwäˈtrān/ ▶ n. a poem or verse of four lines.

qua·ver /ˈkwāvər/ ▶ v. (**quavers**, **quavering**, **quavered**) (of a voice) tremble. ▶ n. a tremble in a voice. ■ **qua·ver·y** adj.

quay /kē, k(w)ā/ ▶ n. a platform in a harbor for loading and unloading ships.

quay·side /ˈkēˌsīd, ˈk(w)ā-/ ▶ n. a quay and the area around it.

quea·sy /ˈkwēzē/ ▶ adj. (**queasier**, **queasiest**) feeling sick.

> SYNONYMS **nauseous**, bilious, sick, ill, unwell, poorly, green around the gills.

■ **quea·si·ness** n.

queen /kwēn/ ▶ n. **1** the female ruler of an independent state. **2** (also **queen consort**) a king's wife. **3** the best or most important woman or thing in a particular group. **4** a playing card ranking next below a king. **5** the most powerful chess piece, able to move in any direction. **6** a female that lays eggs for a colony of ants, bees, wasps, or termites.

> SYNONYMS **monarch**, sovereign, ruler, head of state, Crown, Her Majesty.

□ **queen mother** the widow of a king who is also mother of the current king or queen. ■ **queen·ly** adj.

Queens·ber·ry Rules /ˈkwēnzˌberē/ ▶ **pl.n.** the standard rules of boxing.

queer /kwi(ə)r/ ▶ **adj. 1** strange; odd. **2** informal, chiefly disapproving homosexual.

SYNONYMS **odd**, strange, unusual, funny, peculiar, curious, bizarre, weird, uncanny, freakish, eerie, unnatural, abnormal, anomalous; informal spooky. ANTONYMS normal.

quell /kwel/ ▶ **v. 1** put an end to a rebellion by force. **2** suppress a feeling.

SYNONYMS **1 put an end to**, put a stop to, stop, crush, put down, check, crack down on, curb, nip in the bud, squash, quash, subdue, suppress, overcome. **2 calm**, soothe, pacify, settle, quieten, silence, allay, assuage, mitigate, moderate.

quench /kwenCH/ ▶ **v. 1** satisfy thirst by drinking. **2** put out a fire. **3** suppress a feeling.

quer·u·lous /ˈkwer(y)ələs/ ▶ **adj.** complaining in an irritable way. ■ **quer·u·lous·ly adv.**

que·ry /ˈkwi(ə)rē/ ▶ **n.** (plural **queries**) a question, especially one expressing a doubt about something. ▶ **v.** (**queries**, **querying**, **queried**) ask a question expressing doubt about something.

SYNONYMS ▶ **n. 1 question**, inquiry. **2 doubt**, uncertainty, question (mark), reservation. ▶ **v. 1 ask**, inquire, question. **2 challenge**, question, dispute, doubt, have suspicions about, distrust. ANTONYMS accept.

quest /kwest/ ▶ **n.** a long or difficult search. ▶ **v.** search for something.

SYNONYMS ▶ **n. 1 search**, hunt, pursuance. **2 expedition**, journey, voyage, trek, travels, odyssey, adventure, exploration, search, crusade, mission, pilgrimage.

ques·tion /ˈkwesCHən/ ▶ **n. 1** a sentence worded so as to obtain information. **2** doubt, or the raising of a doubt about something. **3** a problem needing to be solved. **4** a matter depending on stated conditions: *it's only a question of time*. ▶ **v. 1** ask someone questions. **2** express doubt about something.

SYNONYMS ▶ **n. 1 inquiry**, query, interrogation. **2 doubt**, dispute, argument, debate, uncertainty, reservation. **3 issue**, matter, topic, business, problem, concern, debate, argument, dispute, controversy. ANTONYMS answer, certainty. ▶ **v. 1 interrogate**, cross-examine, cross-question, quiz, interview, debrief, examine; informal grill, pump. **2 query**, challenge, dispute, cast aspersions on, doubt, suspect.

□ **out of the question** not possible. **question mark** a punctuation mark (?) indicating a question. ■ **ques·tion·er n.**

ques·tion·a·ble /ˈkwesCHənəbəl/ ▶ **adj. 1** doubtful as regards truth or quality. **2** not clearly honest, honorable, or wise.

SYNONYMS **suspicious**, suspect, dubious, irregular, odd, strange, murky, dark, unsavory, disreputable; informal funny, fishy, shady, iffy.

ques·tion·naire /ˌkwesCHəˈne(ə)r/ ▶ **n.** a set of questions written for a survey.

SPELLING

There are two **n**s: question*nn*aire.

queue /kyo͞o/ ▶ **n. 1** a line of people or vehicles waiting their turn for something. **2** Computing a list of data items, commands, etc., stored for retrieval in a specified order. ▶ **v.** (**queues**, **queuing** or **queueing**, **queued**) **1** wait in a queue. **2** Computing arrange in a queue.

SYNONYMS ▶ **n. row**, line, column, file, chain, string, procession.

quib·ble /ˈkwibəl/ ▶ **n.** a minor objection. ▶ **v.** (**quibbles**, **quibbling**, **quibbled**) raise a minor objection.

SYNONYMS ▶ **v.** *no one **quibbled** with the title* **object to**, find fault with, complain about, cavil at, split hairs over, criticize, fault, poke holes in; informal nitpick (over/about).

quiche /kēSH/ ▶ **n.** a baked dish consisting of a bottom crust with a savory filling thickened with eggs.

quick /kwik/ ▶ **adj. 1** moving fast. **2** lasting or taking a short time. **3** with little or no delay. **4** intelligent. **5** (of temper) easily roused. ▶ **n.** (**the quick**) the tender flesh below the growing part of a fingernail or toenail.

SYNONYMS ▶ **adj. 1 fast**, swift, rapid, speedy, brisk, smart, lightning, whirlwind, whistle-stop, breakneck; informal zippy; literary fleet. **2 hasty**, hurried, cursory, perfunctory, desultory, superficial, brief. **3 sudden**, instantaneous, instant, immediate, abrupt, precipitate. **4 intelligent**, bright, clever, gifted, able, astute, sharp-witted, smart, alert, sharp, perceptive; informal brainy, on the ball. ANTONYMS slow, long.

□ **cut someone to the quick** upset someone very much. **quick-tempered** easily angered. **quick-witted** able to think or respond quickly.

quick·en /ˈkwikən/ ▶ **v. 1** make or become quicker. **2** make or become active or alive.

SYNONYMS **1 speed up**, accelerate, step up, hasten, hurry (up). **2 stimulate**, excite, arouse, rouse, stir up, activate, whet, inspire, kindle.

quick·lime /ˈkwikˌlīm/ ▶ **n.** a white alkaline substance consisting of calcium oxide, obtained by heating limestone.

quick·ly /ˈkwiklē/ ▶ **adv. 1** with haste or speed: *he walked quickly*. **2** immediately: *you'd better leave quickly*. **3** briefly; without care or attention: *he quickly inspected it*.

SYNONYMS **1 fast**, swiftly, briskly, rapidly, speedily, at full tilt, at a gallop, on the double, posthaste, hotfoot; informal like (greased) lightning, hell-bent for leather, like blazes, like the wind, lickety-split. **2 immediately**, directly, at once, straightaway, right away, instantly, forthwith, momentarily; informal like a shot, ASAP, PDQ, pronto. **3 briefly**, fleetingly, briskly, hastily, hurriedly, cursorily, perfunctorily.

quick·sand /ˈkwikˌsand/ (or **quicksands**) ▶ **n.** loose wet sand that sucks in anything resting on it.

quick·sil·ver /ˈkwikˌsilvər/ ▶ **n.** mercury. ▶ **adj.** moving or changing rapidly.

quick·step /ˈkwikˌstep/ ▶ **n.** a fast foxtrot.

quid pro quo /ˈkwid ˌprō ˈkwō/ ▶ **n.** (plural **quid pro quos**) a favor given in return for something.

qui·es·cent /kwēˈesnt, kwī-/ ▶ **adj.** not active. ■ **qui·es·cence n.**

qui·et /ˈkwīət/ ▶ **adj.** (**quieter**, **quietest**) **1** making little or no noise. **2** free from activity or excitement. **3** without being disturbed: *a quiet drink*. **4** discreet: *a quiet word*. **5** (of a person) shy and not tending to talk very much. ▶ **n.** absence of noise or disturbance. ▶ **v.** make or become quiet.

> SYNONYMS ▶ **adj.** **1** **silent**, still, hushed, noiseless, soundless, mute, dumb, speechless. **2** **soft**, low, muted, muffled, faint, hushed, whispered, suppressed. **3** **peaceful**, sleepy, tranquil, calm, still, restful. ANTONYMS loud, busy. ▶ **n.** **silence**, still, hush, restfulness, calm, tranquility, serenity, peace.

qui·et·ly /ˈkwīətlē/ ▶ **adv.** **1** with little or no noise: *she quietly entered the room*. **2** with low volume: *he spoke quietly*.

> SYNONYMS **1** **silently**, noiselessly, soundlessly, inaudibly. **2** **softly**, faintly, in a low voice, in a whisper, in a murmur, under your breath, in an undertone, sotto voce.

qui·e·tude /ˈkwīəˌt(y)o͞od/ ▶ **n.** a state of calmness and quiet.

quill /kwil/ ▶ **n.** **1** a main wing or tail feather of a bird. **2** the hollow shaft of a feather. **3** a pen made from a quill. **4** a spine of a porcupine or hedgehog.

quilt /kwilt/ ▶ **n.** a warm bed covering made of padding enclosed between layers of fabric.

> SYNONYMS **comforter**, cover(s), coverlet, duvet.

■ **quilt·er** **n.** **quilt·ing** **n.**

quilt·ed /ˈkwiltid/ ▶ **adj.** made of two layers of cloth filled with padding.

quince /kwins/ ▶ **n.** a hard yellow pear-shaped fruit.

qui·nine /ˈkwīˌnīn/ ▶ **n.** a bitter drug made from the bark of a South American tree.

quin·tes·sence /kwinˈtesəns/ ▶ **n.** **1** a perfect example of something. **2** the central and most important part or quality of something.

quin·tes·sen·tial /ˌkwintəˈsenᴄʜəl/ ▶ **adj.** representing the most perfect example.

> SYNONYMS **typical**, prototypical, stereotypical, archetypal, classic, model, standard, stock, representative, conventional; ideal, consummate, exemplary, best, ultimate.

■ **quin·tes·sen·tial·ly** **adv.**

quin·tet /kwinˈtet/ ▶ **n.** **1** a group of five people playing music or singing together. **2** a piece of music for a quintet. **3** a set of five.

quin·tu·ple /kwinˈt(y)o͞opəl, -ˈtəpəl/ ▶ **adj.** **1** consisting of five parts or elements. **2** five times as much or as many.

quin·tu·plet /kwinˈtəplət, -ˈt(y)o͞oplət/ ▶ **n.** each of five children born at one birth.

quip /kwip/ ▶ **n.** a witty remark. ▶ **v.** (**quips**, **quipping**, **quipped**) make a witty remark.

> SYNONYMS ▶ **n.** **joke**, witticism, jest, pun, pleasantry, bon mot; informal one-liner, gag, wisecrack, funny.

quire /kwīr/ ▶ **n.** **1** four sheets of paper folded to form eight leaves. **2** 25 sheets of paper.

quirk /kwərk/ ▶ **n.** **1** a peculiar habit. **2** a strange thing that happens by chance.

> SYNONYMS **1** **idiosyncrasy**, peculiarity, oddity, eccentricity, foible, whim, vagary, habit, characteristic, trait, fad. **2** **chance**, fluke, freak, anomaly, twist.

quirk·y /ˈkwərkē/ ▶ **adj.** (**quirkier**, **quirkiest**) having peculiar or unexpected habits or qualities.

> SYNONYMS **eccentric**, idiosyncratic, unconventional, unorthodox, unusual, strange, bizarre, peculiar, zany; informal wacky, way-out, offbeat. ANTONYMS conventional.

quis·ling /ˈkwizlinɢ/ ▶ **n.** a traitor who collaborates with an enemy force that has occupied their country.

quit /kwit/ ▶ **v.** (**quits**, **quitting**, **quitted** or **quit**) **1** leave a place. **2** resign from a job. **3** informal stop doing something.

> SYNONYMS **1** **leave**, vacate, exit, depart from. **2** **resign from**, leave, give up, hand in your notice; informal pack (it) in. **3** **give up**, stop, discontinue, drop, abandon, abstain from; informal pack in, leave off.

quite /kwīt/ ▶ **adv.** **1** to a certain extent; fairly. **2** to the greatest degree; completely. ▶ **exclam.** expressing agreement.

> SYNONYMS ▶ **adv.** **1** **completely**, entirely, totally, wholly, absolutely, utterly, thoroughly, altogether. **2** **fairly**, rather, somewhat, relatively, comparatively, moderately, reasonably; informal pretty.

quits /kwits/ ▶ **adj.** on equal terms because a debt or score has been settled.

quit·ter /ˈkwitər/ ▶ **n.** informal a person who gives up easily.

quiv·er[1] /ˈkwivər/ ▶ **v.** (**quivers**, **quivering**, **quivered**) shake or vibrate slightly. ▶ **n.** a quivering movement.

> SYNONYMS ▶ **v.** **1** **tremble**, shake, shiver, quaver, quake, shudder. **2** **flutter**, flap, beat, agitate, vibrate.

quiv·er[2] ▶ **n.** a case for carrying arrows.

quix·ot·ic /kwikˈsätik/ ▶ **adj.** idealistic but impractical.

> SYNONYMS **idealistic**, romantic, visionary, Utopian, extravagant, starry-eyed, unrealistic, unworldly; impracticable, unworkable, impossible.

quiz /kwiz/ ▶ **n.** (plural **quizzes**) **1** a competition in which people answer questions that test their knowledge. **2** a short test given to students. ▶ **v.** (**quizzes**, **quizzing**, **quizzed**) question someone.

> SYNONYMS ▶ **n.** **test**, exam, pop quiz, questionnaire. ▶ **v.** **question**, interrogate, cross-examine, cross-question, interview; informal grill, pump.

quiz·mas·ter /ˈkwizˌmastər/ ▶ **n.** a person who asks the questions in a television or radio quiz program.

quiz·zi·cal /ˈkwizəkəl/ ▶ **adj.** showing mild or amused puzzlement.

> SYNONYMS **inquiring**, questioning, curious; puzzled, perplexed, baffled, mystified; amused, mocking, teasing.

■ **quiz·zi·cal·ly** **adv.**

quoin /k(w)oin/ ▶ **n.** **1** an external angle of a wall or building. **2** a cornerstone.

quoit /k(w)oit/ ▶ **n.** a ring that you throw over an upright peg in the game of **quoits**.

Quon·set /ˈkwänsət/ (usu. **Quonset hut**) ▶ **n.** trademark a prefabricated building with a semicylindrical corrugated roof.

quo·rum /ˈkwôrəm/ ▶ **n.** (plural **quorums**) the minimum number of people that must be present at a meeting to make its business valid.

quo·ta /ˈkwōtə/ ▶ **n. 1** a limited quantity of people or things that is officially allowed. **2** a share of something that you have to contribute.

SYNONYMS **share**, allocation, allowance, ration, portion, slice, percentage.

quo·ta·tion /ˌkwōˈtāsʜən/ ▶ **n. 1** a passage or remark repeated by someone other than the person who originally said or wrote it. **2** a formal statement of the estimated cost of a job or service.

SYNONYMS **1 extract**, quote, citation, excerpt, passage. **2 estimate**, quote, price, tender, bid, costing.

□ **quotation marks** a pair of punctuation marks, (' ') or (" "), used to mark the beginning and end of a quotation or passage of speech.

quote /kwōt/ ▶ **v.** (**quotes**, **quoting**, **quoted**) **1** repeat a passage or remark by another person. **2** (**quote something as**) mention something as an example to support a point. **3** give someone an estimated price. **4** give a company a listing on a stock exchange. ▶ **n. 1** a quotation. **2** (**quotes**) quotation marks.

SYNONYMS ▶ **v. 1 recite**, repeat, reproduce, retell, echo. **2 mention**, cite, refer to, name, instance, allude to, point out. ▶ **n.** see **QUOTATION** (senses 1 & 2).

■ **quot·a·ble** **adj.**

quoth /kwōᴛʜ/ ▶ **v.** old use said.

quo·tid·i·an /kwōˈtidēən/ ▶ **adj.** formal **1** daily. **2** ordinary or everyday.

quo·tient /ˈkwōsʜənt/ ▶ **n.** Math a result obtained by dividing one quantity by another.

q.v. ▶ **abbr.** used to direct a reader to another part of a book for further information.

R (or **r**) ▶ **n.** (plural **Rs** or **R's**) the eighteenth letter of the alphabet.

R & B ▶ **abbr.** rhythm and blues. ▶ **n.** a kind of pop music with soulful vocals.

R & D ▶ **abbr.** research and development.

rab·bet /'rabit/ ▶ **n.** a step-shaped recess cut into wood, to which the edge or tongue of another piece may be joined. ▶ **v.** (**rabbets**, **rabbeting**, **rabbeted**) **1** make a rabbet in. **2** join with a rabbet.

rab·bi /'rab,ī/ ▶ **n.** (plural **rabbis**) a Jewish religious leader or teacher of Jewish law. ■ **rab·bin·ic** /rə'binik, ra-/ (or **rabbinical** /rə'binikəl, ra-/) **adj.**

rab·bit /'rabit/ ▶ **n.** a burrowing animal with long ears and a short tail.

rab·ble /'rabəl/ ▶ **n. 1** a disorderly crowd of people. **2** (**the rabble**) disapproving ordinary people. □ **rabble-rouser** a person who makes speeches intended to make people angry or excited, usually for political reasons.

rab·id /'rabəd, 'rā-/ ▶ **adj. 1** having extreme opinions; fanatical. **2** having rabies. ■ **rab·id·ly adv.**

ra·bies /'rābēz/ ▶ **n.** a dangerous disease of dogs and other animals, which can be transmitted through saliva to humans.

rac·coon /ra'ko͞on, rə-/ (or **racoon**) ▶ **n.** a grayish-brown American animal with a black face and striped tail.

race¹ /rās/ ▶ **n. 1** a competition to see who or which is fastest over a set course. **2** a strong current flowing through a narrow channel. ▶ **v.** (**races**, **racing**, **raced**) **1** compete against someone or something in a race. **2** move or progress rapidly. **3** (of an engine) operate at too high a speed.

> SYNONYMS ▶ **n. 1 contest**, competition, event, heat, trial(s). **2** *the race for naval domination* **rivalry**, competition, contention, quest. ▶ **v. 1 compete**, contend, run, be pitted against. **2 hurry**, dash, rush, run, sprint, bolt, charge, career, shoot, hurtle, fly, speed, zoom; informal tear, belt.

race² ▶ **n. 1** each of the major divisions of humankind. **2** a group of people or things with a common feature. **3** a subdivision of a species.

> SYNONYMS **1 ethnic group**, origin, bloodline, stock. **2 people**, nation.

□ **race relations** relations between members of different races within a country.

race·course /'rās,kôrs/ ▶ **n.** a ground or track for horse or dog racing.

race·horse /'rās,hôrs/ ▶ **n.** a horse bred and trained for racing.

ra·ceme /rā'sēm, rə-/ ▶ **n.** a flower cluster with separate flowers along a central stem.

race·track /'rās,trak/ ▶ **n. 1** a ground or track for horse or dog racing. **2** a track for motor racing.

ra·cial /'rāsʜəl/ ▶ **adj. 1** having to do with race. **2** relating to relations or differences between races.

> SYNONYMS **ethnic**, ethnological, race-related, cultural, national, tribal, genetic.

■ **ra·cial·ly adv.**

ra·cial·ism /'rāsʜə,lizəm/ ▶ **n.** racism. ■ **ra·cial·ist n. & adj.**

rac·ism /'rā,sizəm/ ▶ **n. 1** the belief that certain races are better than others. **2** discrimination against, or hostility toward, other races. ■ **rac·ist n. & adj.**

rack /rak/ ▶ **n. 1** a framework for holding or storing things. **2** (**the rack**) (in the past) a frame on which people were tortured by being stretched. **3** a cut of meat that includes the front ribs. ▶ **v. 1** (also **wrack**) cause great pain to. **2** (**rack something up**) achieve a score or amount.

> SYNONYMS ▶ **n. frame**, framework, stand, holder, trestle, support, shelf. ▶ **v. torment**, afflict, torture, agonize, harrow, plague, persecute, trouble, worry.

□ **go to rack and ruin** fall into a bad condition. **rack** (or **wrack**) **your brains** think very hard.

rack·et¹ /'rakit/ (or **racquet** same pronunciation) ▶ **n. 1** a bat with a round or oval frame, used in tennis, badminton, and squash. **2** (**rackets**) a ball game played with rackets in a four-walled court.

rack·et² ▶ **n. 1** a loud, unpleasant noise. **2** informal a dishonest scheme for making money.

> SYNONYMS **1 noise**, din, hubbub, clamor, uproar, tumult, commotion, rumpus, pandemonium; informal hullabaloo. **2 fraud**, swindle; informal scam, rip-off, con job.

■ **rack·et·y adj.**

rack·et·eer /,raki'ti(ə)r/ ▶ **n.** a person who makes money through dishonest activities. ■ **rack·et·eer·ing n.**

rac·on·teur /,rak,än'tər, -ən-/ ▶ **n.** a person who tells stories in an interesting and amusing way.

ra·coon = RACCOON.

rac·quet·ball /'rakit,bôl/ ▶ **n.** a game played with a rubber ball and a short-handled racket in a four-walled court.

rac·y /'rāsē/ ▶ **adj.** lively and exciting.

> SYNONYMS **risqué**, suggestive, naughty, sexy, spicy, ribald; indecorous, indecent, immodest, off-color, dirty, rude, smutty, crude, salacious; informal raunchy, blue; euphemistic adult. ANTONYMS prim.

ra·dar /'rā,där/ ▶ **n.** a system for detecting aircraft, ships, etc., by sending out radio waves that are reflected back off the object.

ra·di·al /'rādēəl/ ▶ **adj.** **1** arranged in lines coming out from a central point to the edge of a circle. **2** (of a tire) in which the layers of fabric run at right angles to the circumference of the tire.
■ **ra·di·al·ly** adv.

ra·di·an /'rādēən/ ▶ **n.** an angle of 57.3 degrees, equal to the angle at the center of a circle formed by an arc equal in length to the radius.

ra·di·ant /'rādēənt/ ▶ **adj.** **1** shining or glowing brightly. **2** glowing with joy, love, or health. **3** transmitted by radiation.

> SYNONYMS **1 shining**, bright, illuminated, brilliant, gleaming, glowing, ablaze, luminous, lustrous, incandescent, dazzling, shimmering. **2 joyful**, elated, thrilled, overjoyed, jubilant, rapturous, ecstatic, euphoric, in seventh heaven, on cloud nine, delighted, very happy; informal on top of the world, over the moon.
> ANTONYMS dark, gloomy.

■ **ra·di·ance** n. **ra·di·ant·ly** adv.

ra·di·ate /'rādē,āt/ ▶ **v.** (**radiates**, **radiating**, **radiated**) **1** (of light, heat, or other energy) be sent out in rays or waves. **2** show a strong feeling or quality. **3** spread out from a central point.

> SYNONYMS **1 emit**, give off, discharge, diffuse, scatter, shed, cast. **2 shine**, beam, emanate, pour. **3 fan out**, spread out, branch out/off, extend, issue.

ra·di·a·tion /,rādē'āsʜən/ ▶ **n.** energy sent out as electromagnetic waves or subatomic particles.

ra·di·a·tor /'rādē,ātər/ ▶ **n.** **1** a metal device for heating a room, usually filled with hot water pumped in through pipes. **2** a cooling device in a vehicle or aircraft engine.

rad·i·cal /'radikəl/ ▶ **adj.** **1** having to do with the basic nature of something; fundamental: *a radical overhaul of the regulations*. **2** supporting complete political or social reform. **3** departing from tradition; new: *a radical approach to music*. **4** Math relating to the root of a number or quantity. ▶ **n.** **1** a supporter of radical reform. **2** Chemistry a group of atoms behaving as a unit in a compound.

> SYNONYMS ▶ **adj. 1 thorough**, complete, total, comprehensive, exhaustive, sweeping, far-reaching, wide-ranging, extensive, profound, major. **2 fundamental**, basic, deep-seated, essential, structural. **3 revolutionary**, progressive, reformist, revisionist, progressivist, extreme, fanatical, militant.
> ANTONYMS superficial, minor, conservative.

■ **rad·i·cal·ism** n. **rad·i·cal·ly** adv.

ra·di·i /'rādē,ī/ plural of RADIUS.

ra·di·o /'rādē,ō/ ▶ **n.** (plural **radios**) **1** the sending and receiving of electromagnetic waves carrying sound messages. **2** the activity or medium of broadcasting in sound. **3** a device for receiving radio programs, or for sending and receiving radio messages. ▶ **v.** (**radioes**, **radioing**, **radioed**) send a message to someone by radio.

ra·di·o·ac·tive /,rādēō'aktiv/ ▶ **adj.** giving out harmful radiation or particles.

ra·di·o·ac·tiv·i·ty /,rādēōak'tivətē/ ▶ **n.** harmful radiation or particles sent out when atomic nuclei break up.

ra·di·o·car·bon /,rādēō'kärbən/ ▶ **n.** a radioactive isotope of carbon used in carbon dating.

ra·di·og·ra·phy /,rādē'ägrəfē/ ▶ **n.** the production of images by X-rays or other radiation.
■ **ra·di·og·ra·pher** n.

ra·di·o·i·so·tope /,rādēō'īsə,tōp/ ▶ **n.** a radioactive isotope.

ra·di·ol·o·gy /,rādē'äləjē/ ▶ **n.** the science of X-rays and similar radiation, especially as used in medicine. ■ **ra·di·ol·o·gist** n.

ra·di·o·ther·a·py /,rādēō'ᴛʜerəpē/ ▶ **n.** the treatment of disease using X-rays or similar radiation.

rad·ish /'radisʜ/ ▶ **n.** a crisp, hot-tasting root vegetable, eaten raw in salads.

ra·di·um /'rādēəm/ ▶ **n.** a radioactive metallic element.

ra·di·us /'rādēəs/ ▶ **n.** (plural **radii** /'rādē,ī/ or **radiuses**) **1** a straight line from the center to the edge of a circle or sphere. **2** a stated distance from a center in all directions. **3** the thicker and shorter of the two bones in the human forearm.

ra·don /'rā,dän/ ▶ **n.** a rare radioactive gas.

RAF ▶ **abbr.** (in the UK) Royal Air Force.

raf·fi·a /'rafēə/ ▶ **n.** fiber from the leaves of a tropical palm tree.

raff·ish /'rafisʜ/ ▶ **adj.** slightly disreputable, but in an attractive way.

raf·fle /'rafəl/ ▶ **n.** a lottery with goods as prizes. ▶ **v.** (**raffles**, **raffling**, **raffled**) offer something as a prize in a raffle.

> SYNONYMS ▶ **n. lottery**, (prize) drawing, lotto, sweepstakes.

raft /raft/ ▶ **n.** **1** a flat structure used as a boat or floating platform. **2** a small inflatable boat. **3** a large amount.

raft·er /'raftər/ ▶ **n.** a beam forming part of the internal framework of a roof.

rag /rag/ ▶ **n.** **1** a piece of old cloth. **2** (**rags**) old or tattered clothes. **3** informal a low-quality newspaper. **4** a piece of ragtime music.

rag·a·muf·fin /'ragə,məfən/ ▶ **n.** a person in ragged, dirty clothes.

rag·bag /'rag,bag/ ▶ **n.** a collection of widely different things.

rage /rāj/ ▶ **n.** violent, uncontrollable anger. ▶ **v.** (**rages**, **raging**, **raged**) **1** feel or express rage. **2** continue with great force.

> SYNONYMS ▶ **n. 1 fury**, anger, wrath, outrage, indignation, temper, spleen; formal ire. **2 craze**, passion, fashion, taste, trend, vogue, fad, mania; informal thing. ▶ **v. be angry**, be furious, be enraged, be incensed, seethe, be beside yourself, rave, storm, fume, spit; informal be livid, be wild, be steamed up.

□ **all the rage** temporarily very popular or fashionable.

rag·ged /'ragid/ ▶ **adj.** **1** (of cloth or clothes) old and torn. **2** rough or irregular. **3** not smooth or steady.

> SYNONYMS **1 tattered**, torn, ripped, frayed, worn (out), threadbare, scruffy, shabby; informal tatty. **2 jagged**, craggy, rugged, uneven, rough, irregular, indented.

■ **rag·ged·ly** adv.

ra·gout /ra'go͞o/ ▶ **n.** a spicy stew of meat and vegetables.

rag·tag /'rag,tag/ ▶ **adj.** disorganized and made up of a mixture of different types of people.

rag·time /ˈragˌtīm/ ▶ **n.** an early form of jazz played especially on the piano.

rag·wort /ˈragˌwərt, -ˌwôrt/ ▶ **n.** a plant of the daisy family with yellow flowers and ragged leaves.

raid /rād/ ▶ **n. 1** a sudden attack on an enemy, or on a building to commit a crime. **2** a surprise visit by police to arrest suspects or seize illegal goods. ▶ **v.** make a raid on.

> SYNONYMS ▶ **n. 1 attack**, assault, descent, blitz, incursion, sortie, onslaught, storming. **2 robbery**, burglary, holdup, break-in; informal stickup, heist. ▶ **v. 1 attack**, assault, set upon, descend on, swoop on, storm, rush. **2 rob**, hold up, break into, plunder, steal from, pillage, loot, ransack; informal stick up.

raid·er /ˈrādər/ ▶ **n.** a person who attacks an enemy or a building to commit a crime.

> SYNONYMS **robber**, burglar, thief, housebreaker, plunderer, pillager, looter, marauder, attacker, assailant, invader.

rail /rāl/ ▶ **n. 1** a fixed bar forming part of a fence or barrier or used to hang things on. **2** each of the two metal bars laid on the ground to form a railroad track. **3** railroads as a means of transport. ▶ **v. 1** enclose with a rail or rails. **2** (**rail against** or **at**) complain strongly about. ◻ **go off the rails** informal behave in an uncontrolled way.

railcar /ˈrālˌkär/ ▶ **n.** a railroad car.

rail·ing /ˈrāliNG/ ▶ **n.** a fence or barrier made of rails.

> SYNONYMS **fence**, fencing, rail(s), palisade, balustrade, banister.

rail·ler·y /ˈrālərē/ ▶ **n.** good-humored teasing.

rail·road /ˈrālˌrōd/ ▶ **n. 1** a track or set of tracks made of steel rails along which passenger and freight trains run. **2** a system of such tracks with the trains, organization, and personnel required for its working. ▶ **v.** informal rush or force someone into doing something.

rai·ment /ˈrāmənt/ ▶ **n.** old use or literary clothing.

rain /rān/ ▶ **n. 1** condensed moisture from the atmosphere falling in separate drops. **2** (**rains**) falls of rain. **3** a large quantity of things falling together. ▶ **v. 1** (**it rains, it is raining, it rained**) rain falls. **2** (**be rained out**) (of an event) be prevented by rain from continuing or taking place. **3** fall in large quantities.

> SYNONYMS ▶ **n. 1 rainfall**, precipitation, raindrops, drizzle, shower, rainstorm, cloudburst, torrent, downpour, deluge, storm. **2** *a rain of hot ash* **shower**, deluge, flood, torrent, avalanche, flurry, storm, hail. ▶ **v. 1 pour (down)**, pelt down, teem down, beat down, drizzle. **2** *bombs rained on the city* **fall**, hail, drop, shower.

◻ **rain date** an alternative date for an event in case of bad weather. **take a rain check** refuse an offer but imply that you may take it up later.

rain·bow /ˈrānˌbō/ ▶ **n.** an arch of colors in the sky, caused by the sun shining through water droplets in the atmosphere.

rain·coat /ˈrānˌkōt/ ▶ **n.** a coat made from water-resistant fabric.

rain·fall /ˈrānˌfôl/ ▶ **n.** the amount of rain falling.

rain·for·est /ˈrānˌfôrəst/ ▶ **n.** a dense forest found in tropical areas with consistently heavy rainfall.

rain·y /ˈrānē/ ▶ **adj.** (**rainier, rainiest**) having a lot of rain.

> SYNONYMS **wet**, showery, drizzly, damp, inclement. ANTONYMS dry, fine.

◻ **a rainy day** a time in the future when money may be needed.

raise /rāz/ ▶ **v.** (**raises, raising, raised**) **1** lift or move upward or into an upright position. **2** increase the amount, level, or strength of. **3** express doubts, objections, etc.: *doubts have been raised.* **4** collect money. **5** bring up a child. **6** breed or grow animals or plants. **7** (**raise something to**) Math multiply a quantity to a particular power. **8** establish contact with someone by telephone or radio. ▶ **n.** an increase in salary.

> SYNONYMS ▶ **v. 1 lift (up)**, hold aloft, elevate, uplift, hoist, haul up, hitch up. **2 increase**, put up, push up, up, mark up, inflate; informal hike (up), jack up, bump up. **3 amplify**, louden, magnify, intensify, boost, lift, increase. **4 get**, obtain, acquire, accumulate, amass, collect, fetch, net, make. **5 bring up**, air, present, table, propose, submit, advance, suggest, put forward. **6 give rise to**, occasion, cause, produce, engender, elicit, create, result in, lead to, prompt. **7 bring up**, rear, nurture, educate. ANTONYMS lower, reduce.

◻ **raise the roof** cheer very loudly.

rai·sin /ˈrāzən/ ▶ **n.** a partially dried grape.

rai·son d'ê·tre /rāˈzôN ˈdetr(ə)/ ▶ **n.** (plural **raisons d'être** /rāˈzôn(z)/) the most important reason for someone or something's existence.

ra·jah /ˈräjə, ˈräZHə/ (or **raja**) ▶ **n.** historical an Indian king or prince.

rake[1] /rāk/ ▶ **n.** a pole with metal or plastic prongs at the end, used for drawing together leaves, smoothing soil, etc. ▶ **v.** (**rakes, raking, raked**) **1** draw together or smooth with a rake. **2** scratch or sweep with a long broad movement. **3** search through.

> SYNONYMS ▶ **v. 1 scrape**, collect, gather. **2 smooth (out)**, level, even out, flatten, comb. **3 rummage**, search, hunt, sift, rifle.

◻ **rake it in** informal make a lot of money. **rake something up** bring up something that is best forgotten.

rake[2] ▶ **n.** a fashionable, rich, but immoral man.

rake[3] ▶ **v.** (**rakes, raking, raked**) set something at a sloping angle. ▶ **n.** the angle at which something slopes.

rak·ish /ˈrākiSH/ ▶ **adj.** having a dashing, jaunty, or slightly disreputable appearance.

ral·ly /ˈralē/ ▶ **n.** (plural **rallies**) **1** a mass meeting held as a protest or in support of a cause. **2** a long-distance competition for motor vehicles over roads or rough ground. **3** a quick or strong recovery. **4** (in tennis and similar games) a long exchange of strokes between players. ▶ **v.** (**rallies, rallying, rallied**) **1** (of troops) come together again to continue fighting. **2** come together to support a person or cause. **3** recover health or strength. **4** (of shares or currency) increase in value after a fall. **5** (**rallying**) the sport of taking part in a motor rally.

> SYNONYMS ▶ **n. 1 (mass) meeting**, gathering, assembly, demonstration, march; informal demo. **2 recovery**, upturn, improvement, comeback, resurgence. ▶ **v. 1 regroup**, reassemble, re-form, reunite, convene, mobilize. **2 recover**,

improve, get better, pick up, revive, bounce back, perk up, look up, turn a corner.

ram /ram/ ▶ n. **1** an adult male sheep. **2** a long, heavy object swung against a door to break it down. **3** a striking or plunging device in a machine. ▶ v. (**rams**, **ramming**, **rammed**) **1** hit with force. **2** roughly force into place.

SYNONYMS ▶ v. **1 force**, thrust, plunge, stab, push, sink, dig, stick, cram, jam, stuff. **2 hit**, strike, crash into, collide with, impact, smash into, butt.

Ram·a·dan /ˈrämə,dän, ˈramə,dan/ ▶ n. the ninth month of the Muslim year, during which Muslims do not eat from dawn to sunset.

ram·ble /ˈrambəl/ ▶ v. (**rambles**, **rambling**, **rambled**) **1** walk for pleasure in the countryside. **2** talk or write in a confused way. **3** (**rambling**) (of writing or speech) straying from one subject to another. ▶ n. a country walk taken for pleasure.

SYNONYMS ▶ v. **1 walk**, hike, tramp, trek, backpack. **2 chatter**, babble, prattle, blather, gabble, jabber, twitter, rattle. **3** (**rambling**) **long-winded**, verbose, wordy, prolix, disjointed, disconnected.

■ **ram·bler** n.

ram·e·kin /ˈramikən/ ▶ n. a small dish for baking and serving an individual portion of food.

ram·i·fi·ca·tions /,raməfəˈkāshənz/ ▶ pl.n. complex results of an action or event.

SYNONYMS **consequence**(s), result(s), aftermath, outcome(s), effect(s), upshot, development, implication(s).

ramp /ramp/ ▶ n. **1** a sloping surface joining two different levels. **2** a set of steps for entering or leaving an aircraft.

SYNONYMS **slope**, bank, incline, gradient, rise, drop.

ram·page ▶ v. /,ramˈpāj, ˈram,pāj/ (**rampages**, **rampaging**, **rampaged**) rush around in a wild and violent way. ▶ n. /ˈram,pāj/ a period of wild and violent behavior.

SYNONYMS ▶ v. **riot**, run amok, go berserk, storm, charge, tear.

ramp·ant /ˈrampənt/ ▶ adj. **1** flourishing or spreading in an uncontrolled way. **2** Heraldry (of an animal) shown standing on its left hind foot with its forefeet in the air.

SYNONYMS **uncontrolled**, unrestrained, unchecked, unbridled, out of control, out of hand, widespread, rife, spreading. ANTONYMS controlled.

ram·part /ˈram,pärt/ ▶ n. a wall defending a castle or town, having a broad top with a walkway.

ram·rod /ˈram,räd/ ▶ n. a rod formerly used to ram down the charge of a firearm.

ram·shack·le /ˈram,shakəl/ ▶ adj. in a very bad condition.

ran /ran/ past of RUN.

ranch /ranch/ ▶ n. **1** a large farm where cattle or other animals are bred. **2** (or **ranch house**) a single-story house. □ **ranch dressing** a thick white salad dressing made with buttermilk. ■ **ranch·er** n.

ran·che·ro /ranˈcherō/ ▶ n. (plural **rancheros**) a person who farms or works on a ranch, especially in the southwestern US and Mexico.

ran·cid /ˈransid/ ▶ adj. (of fatty or oily food) stale and smelling or tasting unpleasant.

SYNONYMS **putrid**, turned, rank, sour, foul, rotten, bad; gamy, fetid. ANTONYMS fresh.

ran·cor /ˈrangkər/ ▶ n. bitter feeling or resentment. ■ **ran·cor·ous** adj.

rand /rand, ränd, ränt/ ▶ n. the basic unit of money of South Africa.

ran·dom /ˈrandəm/ ▶ adj. done or happening without any plan, purpose, or regular pattern.

SYNONYMS **unsystematic**, unmethodical, arbitrary, unplanned, chance, casual, indiscriminate, nonspecific, haphazard, stray, erratic, hit-or-miss. ANTONYMS systematic.

□ **at random** without thinking or planning in advance. ■ **ran·dom·ly** adv. **ran·dom·ness** n.

rang /rang/ past of RING².

range /rānj/ ▶ n. **1** the limits between which something varies. **2** a set of different things of the same general type. **3** the distance over which a sound, missile, etc., can travel. **4** a line of mountains or hills. **5** a large area of open land for grazing or hunting. **6** an area for testing military equipment or practicing shooting. **7** a large stove with several burners or hotplates. ▶ v. (**ranges**, **ranging**, **ranged**) **1** vary between particular limits. **2** arrange things in a particular way. **3** (**be ranged against**) be in opposition to. **4** travel over a wide area.

SYNONYMS ▶ n. **1 extent**, limit, reach, span, scope, compass, sweep, area, field, orbit, ambit, horizon, latitude. **2 row**, chain, sierra, ridge, massif. **3 assortment**, variety, diversity, mixture, collection, array, selection, choice. ▶ v. **1 vary**, fluctuate, differ, extend, stretch, reach, go, run, cover. **2 roam**, wander, travel, journey, rove, traverse, walk, hike, trek.

rang·er /ˈrānjər/ ▶ n. a keeper of a park, forest, or area of countryside.

rang·y /ˈrānjē/ ▶ adj. (of a person) tall and slim with long limbs.

SYNONYMS **long-legged**, long-limbed, leggy, tall; slender, slim, lean, thin, gangly, lanky, spindly, skinny, spare. ANTONYMS squat.

rank¹ /rangk/ ▶ n. **1** a position within the armed forces or an organization. **2** a row of people or things. **3** high social position. **4** (**the ranks**) (in the armed forces) those who are not commissioned officers. ▶ v. **1** give a rank to. **2** hold a particular rank. **3** arrange in a row or rows.

SYNONYMS ▶ n. **1 position**, level, grade, echelon, class, status, standing. **2 high standing**, blue blood, high birth, nobility, aristocracy. **3 row**, line, file, column, string, train, procession. ▶ v. **1 classify**, class, categorize, rate, grade, bracket, group, designate, list. **2 line up**, align, order, arrange, dispose, set out, array, range.

□ **close ranks** unite to defend shared interests. **pull rank** use your higher rank to take advantage of someone. **rank and file** the ordinary members of an organization.

rank² ▶ adj. **1** having a very unpleasant smell. **2** complete: *a rank amateur*. **3** (of plants) growing too thickly.

SYNONYMS **1 abundant**, lush, luxuriant, dense, profuse, vigorous, overgrown; informal jungly.

2 offensive, nasty, revolting, sickening, obnoxious, foul, fetid, rancid, putrid. **3** *rank stupidity* **downright**, utter, out-and-out, absolute, complete, sheer, blatant, thorough, unqualified; dated arrant.

ran·kle /'raNGkəl/ ▶ v. (**rankles**, **rankling**, **rankled**) cause continuing annoyance or resentment.

SYNONYMS **annoy**, upset, anger, irritate, offend, affront, displease, provoke, irk, vex, pique, nettle, gall; informal rile, miff, peeve, aggravate, tick off.

ran·sack /'ran͵sak, ran'sak/ ▶ v. go hurriedly through a place stealing or searching for things.

SYNONYMS **1 plunder**, pillage, raid, rob, loot, sack, strip, despoil, ravage, devastate. **2** scour, rifle through, comb, search, turn upside down.

ran·som /'ransəm/ ▶ n. a sum of money demanded for the release of someone who is held captive. ▶ v. cause someone to be released by paying a ransom.

SYNONYMS ▶ n. **payoff**, payment, sum, price.

□ **hold someone to ransom 1** hold someone captive and demand payment for their release. **2** force someone to do something by threatening them.

rant /rant/ ▶ v. speak in a loud, angry, and forceful way.

SYNONYMS **shout**, sound off, hold forth, go on, fulminate, spout, bluster; informal mouth off.

rap /rap/ ▶ v. (**raps**, **rapping**, **rapped**) **1** hit a hard surface several times. **2** hit sharply. **3** informal criticize sharply. **4** say sharply or suddenly. ▶ n. **1** a quick, sharp knock or blow. **2** a type of popular music in which words are spoken rhythmically over an instrumental backing.

SYNONYMS ▶ v. **hit**, knock, strike, smack, bang; informal whack, thwack, bash, wallop.

□ **bum rap** informal a false charge or unfair criticism. **take the rap** informal be punished or blamed for something. ■ **rap·per** n.

ra·pa·cious /rə'pāsHəs/ ▶ adj. very greedy.

ra·pac·i·ty /rə'pasətē/ ▶ n. greed.

rape[1] /rāp/ ▶ v. (**rapes**, **raping**, **raped**) **1** (of a man) force someone to have sex with him against their will. **2** spoil or destroy a place. ▶ n. an act of raping.

rape[2] ▶ n. a plant with bright yellow flowers, grown for its oil-rich seed.

rap·id /'rapid/ ▶ adj. very fast. ▶ n. (**rapids**) a part of a river where the water flows very fast.

SYNONYMS ▶ adj. **quick**, fast, swift, speedy, express, expeditious, brisk, lightning, meteoric, whirlwind, sudden, instantaneous, instant, immediate. ANTONYMS slow.

■ **ra·pid·i·ty** /rə'pidətē/ n. **rap·id·ly** adv.

ra·pi·er /'rāpēər/ ▶ n. a thin, light sword.

rap·ist /'rāpist/ ▶ n. a man who commits rape.

rap·pel /rə'pel/ ▶ v. climb down a rock face using a rope wrapped around the body and fixed at a higher point.

rap·port /ra'pôr, rə-/ ▶ n. a close relationship in which people understand each other and communicate well.

SYNONYMS **affinity**, close relationship, (mutual) understanding, bond, empathy, sympathy, accord.

rap·proche·ment /͵rap͵rōsH'mäN, -͵rôsH-/ ▶ n. a renewal of friendly relations between two countries or groups.

rap·scal·lion /rap'skalyən/ ▶ n. old use a rascal.

rapt /rapt/ ▶ adj. completely fascinated or absorbed.

SYNONYMS **fascinated**, enthralled, spellbound, captivated, riveted, gripped, mesmerized, enchanted, entranced, bewitched; transported, enraptured, thrilled, ecstatic. ANTONYMS inattentive.

rap·ture /'rapCHər/ ▶ n. **1** great pleasure or joy. **2** (**raptures**) the expression of great pleasure or enthusiasm.

SYNONYMS **ecstasy**, bliss, exaltation, euphoria, elation, joy, enchantment, delight, happiness, pleasure.

rap·tur·ous /'rapCHərəs/ ▶ adj. very pleased or enthusiastic. ■ **rap·tur·ous·ly** adv.

rare /re(ə)r/ ▶ adj. (**rarer**, **rarest**) **1** not happening or found very often. **2** unusually good. **3** (of red meat) lightly cooked, so that the inside is still red.

SYNONYMS **1 infrequent**, scarce, sparse, few and far between, occasional, limited, isolated, odd, unaccustomed. **2 unusual**, recherché, uncommon, thin on the ground, unfamiliar, atypical. **3 exceptional**, outstanding, unparalleled, peerless, matchless, unique, unrivaled, beyond compare. ANTONYMS common, commonplace.

rare·bit /'re(ə)rbit/ ⇒ **WELSH RAREBIT**.

rar·e·fied /'rerə͵fīd/ ▶ adj. **1** (of air) of lower pressure than usual; thin. **2** understood by only a limited group of people.

SPELLING

Write **-ref-**, not **-rif-**: rarefied.

rare·ly /'re(ə)rlē/ ▶ adv. not often; seldom.

SYNONYMS **seldom**, infrequently, hardly (ever), scarcely. ANTONYMS often.

rar·ing /'re(ə)riNG/ ▶ adj. (**raring to do**) informal very eager to do something.

SYNONYMS **eager**, keen, enthusiastic, impatient, longing, desperate; informal dying, itching.

rar·i·ty /'re(ə)ritē/ ▶ n. (plural **rarities**) **1** the state of being rare. **2** a rare thing.

SYNONYMS **1 infrequency**, scarcity. **2 curiosity**, oddity, collector's item, rare bird, wonder, nonpareil, one of a kind.

ras·cal /'raskəl/ ▶ n. **1** a mischievous or impudent person. **2** a dishonest man.

SYNONYMS **scallywag**, imp, monkey, mischief-maker; informal scamp, tyke, horror, monster.

■ **ras·cal·ly** adj.

rash[1] /rasH/ ▶ adj. acting or done without careful consideration of the possible results.

SYNONYMS **reckless**, impulsive, impetuous, hotheaded, daredevil, madcap, hasty, foolhardy, incautious, precipitate, careless, heedless, thoughtless, unthinking, imprudent, foolish. ANTONYMS prudent.

■ **rash·ly** adv.

rash² ▶ **n.** **1** an area of red spots or patches on a person's skin. **2** a series of unpleasant things happening within a short time.

SYNONYMS **1 spots**, eruption, hives. **2** *a rash of articles in the press* **series**, succession, spate, wave, flood, deluge, torrent, outbreak, epidemic, flurry.

rash·er /'rasHər/ ▶ **n.** a thin slice of bacon.

rasp /rasp/ ▶ **n.** **1** a harsh, grating noise. **2** a tool with a rough edge, used for smoothing surfaces. ▶ **v.** **1** make a harsh, grating noise. **2** scrape roughly. **3** file with a rasp.

rasp·ber·ry /'raz,berē, -b(ə)rē/ ▶ **n.** (plural **raspberries**) **1** a reddish-pink soft fruit. **2** informal a sound made with the tongue and lips to express derision or contempt.

Ras·ta /'rastə, 'rästə/ ▶ **n.** informal a Rastafarian.

Ras·ta·far·i·an /,rastə'fe(ə)rēən, 'räs-, -'färēən/ ▶ **n.** a member of a Jamaican religious movement that worships Haile Selassie, the former Emperor of Ethiopia. ■ **Ras·ta·far·i·an·ism n.**

rat /rat/ ▶ **n.** **1** a rodent resembling a large mouse. **2** informal an unpleasant person. ▶ **v.** (**rats**, **ratting**, **ratted**) (**rat on**) informal **1** inform on someone. **2** break an agreement or promise. □ **the rat race** informal a way of life that is a fiercely competitive struggle for money or power.

ra·ta·touille /,ratə'to͞o-ē, ,rä,tä-/ ▶ **n.** a vegetable dish of stewed onions, eggplant, tomatoes, etc.

ratch·et /'racHit/ ▶ **n.** a device with a set of angled teeth in which a cog, tooth, or bar fits, allowing movement in one direction only.

rate /rāt/ ▶ **n.** **1** a measure, quantity, or frequency measured against another. **2** the speed of something. **3** a fixed price paid or charged for something. ▶ **v.** (**rates**, **rating**, **rated**) **1** give something a standard or value according to a particular scale. **2** consider to be of a certain quality or standard. **3** be worthy of; deserve. **4** informal have a high opinion of.

SYNONYMS ▶ **n.** **1 percentage**, ratio, proportion, scale, standard. **2 charge**, price, cost, tariff, fare, fee, remuneration, payment. **3 speed**, pace, tempo, velocity. ▶ **v.** **1 assess**, evaluate, appraise, judge, weigh up, estimate, gauge. **2 merit**, deserve, warrant, be worthy of.

■ **rate·a·ble** (or **ratable**) **adj.**

rath·er /'raTHər/ ▶ **adv.** **1** (**would rather**) would prefer. **2** to some extent; fairly. **3** used to correct something you have said or to be more precise. **4** instead of.

SYNONYMS **1 sooner**, by preference, by choice, more readily. **2 quite**, a bit, a little, fairly, slightly, somewhat, relatively, comparatively; informal pretty.

rat·i·fy /'ratə,fī/ ▶ **v.** (**ratifies**, **ratifying**, **ratified**) make a treaty, contract, etc., valid by signing or agreeing to it.

SYNONYMS **confirm**, approve, sanction, endorse, agree to, accept, uphold, authorize, formalize, sign.

■ **rat·i·fi·ca·tion** /,ratəfə'kāsHən/ **n.**

rat·ing /'rātiNG/ ▶ **n.** **1** a classification based on quality, standard, or performance. **2** (**ratings**) the estimated audience size of a television or radio program.

SYNONYMS **grade**, classification, ranking, position, category, assessment, evaluation, mark, score.

ra·tio /'rāsHō, 'rāsHē,ō/ ▶ **n.** (plural **ratios**) an indication of the relationship between two amounts, showing the number of times one contains the other.

SYNONYMS **proportion**, relationship, rate, percentage, fraction, correlation.

ra·ti·oc·i·na·tion /,ratē,ōsə'nāsHən, ,rasHē-/ ▶ **n.** formal the process of thinking in a logical way; reasoning.

ra·tion /'rasHən, 'rā-/ ▶ **n.** **1** a fixed amount of food, fuel, etc., officially allowed to each person. **2** (**rations**) a regular allowance of food supplied to members of the armed forces. ▶ **v.** limit the supply of food, fuel, etc.

SYNONYMS ▶ **n.** **1 allowance**, allocation, quota, share, portion, helping. **2** *the garrison ran out of rations* **supplies**, provisions, food, stores. ▶ **v. control**, limit, restrict, conserve.

ra·tion·al /'rasHənl, 'rasHnəl/ ▶ **adj.** **1** based on reason or logic. **2** able to think sensibly or logically.

SYNONYMS **logical**, reasoned, sensible, reasonable, realistic, cogent, intelligent, shrewd, common-sense, sane, sound.

■ **ra·tion·al·i·ty** /,rasHə'nalətē/ **n.** **ra·tion·al·ly adv.**

ra·tion·ale /,rasHə'nal/ ▶ **n.** the reasons for doing or believing something.

SYNONYMS **reason(s)**, thinking, logic, grounds, sense.

ra·tion·al·ism /'rasHənl,izəm, 'rasHnə,lizəm/ ▶ **n.** the belief that opinions and actions should be based on reason rather than on religious belief or emotions. ■ **ra·tion·al·ist n.**

ra·tion·al·ize /'rasHənl,īz, 'rasHnə,līz/ ▶ **v.** (**rationalizes**, **rationalizing**, **rationalized**) **1** try to find a logical reason for an action or attitude. **2** reorganize a business, system, etc., to make it more efficient.

SYNONYMS **1 justify**, explain (away), account for, defend, vindicate, excuse. **2 streamline**, reorganize, modernize, update, trim, hone, simplify, downsize, prune.

■ **ra·tion·al·i·za·tion** /,rasHənl-ə'zāsHən, ,rasHnələ-/ **n.**

rat·tan /ra'tan, rə-/ ▶ **n.** the thin stems of a tropical palm, used to make furniture.

rat·tle /'ratl/ ▶ **v.** (**rattles**, **rattling**, **rattled**) **1** make a rapid series of short, sharp sounds. **2** informal make someone nervous or irritated. **3** (**rattle something off**) say or do something quickly and easily. ▶ **n.** **1** a rattling sound. **2** a toy that makes a rattling sound.

SYNONYMS ▶ **v.** **1 clatter**, clank, knock, clunk, clink, jangle, tinkle. **2 unnerve**, disconcert, disturb, fluster, shake, perturb, throw, discomfit; informal faze.

rat·tle·snake /'ratl,snāk/ ▶ **n.** a viper with horny rings on the tail that produce a rattling sound.

rat·ty /'ratē/ ▶ **adj.** (**rattier**, **rattiest**) shabby; seedy.

rau·cous /'rôkəs/ ▶ **adj.** sounding loud and harsh.

SYNONYMS **1 harsh**, strident, screeching, piercing, shrill, grating, discordant, dissonant, noisy, loud, cacophonous. **2 rowdy**, noisy, boisterous, roisterous, wild. ANTONYMS soft, quiet.

■ **rau·cous·ly adv.**

rav·age /ˈravij/ ▶ **v.** (**ravages**, **ravaging**, **ravaged**) cause great damage to. ▶ **n.** (**ravages**) the destruction caused by something.

> SYNONYMS ▶ **v.** **lay waste**, devastate, ruin, destroy, wreak havoc on.

rave /rāv/ ▶ **v.** (**raves**, **raving**, **raved**) **1** talk angrily or without making sense. **2** speak or write about someone or something with great enthusiasm. ▶ **n.** a large event with dancing to loud, fast electronic music.

> SYNONYMS ▶ **v.** **1 rant**, rage, lose your temper, storm, fume, shout; informal fly off the handle, hit the roof, flip your wig. **2 enthuse**, go into raptures, wax lyrical, rhapsodize, sing the praises of, acclaim, eulogize, extol; informal ballyhoo. ANTONYMS criticize.

ra·ven /ˈrāvən/ ▶ **n.** a large black crow. ▶ **adj.** (of hair) of a glossy black color.

rav·en·ing /ˈravəniNG/ ▶ **adj.** literary very fierce and hungry.

rav·en·ous /ˈravənəs/ ▶ **adj.** very hungry. ■ **rav·en·ous·ly adv.**

rav·er /ˈrāvər/ ▶ **n.** informal a person who has an exciting or wild social life.

ra·vine /rəˈvēn/ ▶ **n.** a deep, narrow gorge.

rav·ing /ˈrāviNG/ ▶ **n.** (**ravings**) wild talk that makes no sense. ▶ **adj. & adv.** informal used for emphasis: *raving mad.*

ra·vi·o·li /ˌravēˈōlē/ ▶ **pl.n.** small pasta cases containing ground meat, cheese, or vegetables.

rav·ish /ˈravisH/ ▶ **v.** **1** dated rape. **2** (**ravishing**) very beautiful.

raw /rô/ ▶ **adj.** **1** (of food) not cooked. **2** (of a material) in its natural state. **3** (of the skin) red and painful from being rubbed or scraped. **4** (of an emotion or quality) strong and undisguised. **5** (of the weather) cold and damp. **6** new to an activity and lacking experience.

> SYNONYMS **1 uncooked**, fresh, natural. **2 unprocessed**, untreated, unrefined, crude, natural. **3 inexperienced**, new, untrained, untried, untested, callow, green; informal wet behind the ears. **4 sore**, red, painful, tender, chafed. ANTONYMS cooked, processed.

□ **a raw deal** unfair treatment. ■ **raw·ness n.**

ray¹ /rā/ ▶ **n.** **1** a narrow line or beam of light or radiation. **2** a trace of something good: *a ray of hope.*

> SYNONYMS **beam**, shaft, stream, streak, flash, glimmer, flicker, spark.

ray² ▶ **n.** a broad flat fish with a long, thin tail.

ray·on /ˈrāˌän/ ▶ **n.** a synthetic fabric made from viscose.

raze /rāz/ ▶ **v.** (**razes**, **razing**, **razed**) completely destroy a building, town, etc.

> SYNONYMS **destroy**, demolish, tear down, pull down, knock down, level, flatten, bulldoze, wipe out, lay waste.

ra·zor /ˈrāzər/ ▶ **n.** an instrument used to shave hair.

razz /raz/ ▶ **v.** informal tease someone playfully.

raz·zle-daz·zle /ˌrazəl ˈdazəl/ ▶ **n.** informal noisy and exciting activity designed to attract attention.

RC ▶ **abbr.** Roman Catholic.

re¹ /rā, rē/ ▶ **prep.** with reference to.

re² /rā/ ▶ **n.** Music the second note of a major scale.

reach /rēcH/ ▶ **v.** **1** stretch out an arm to touch or grasp something. **2** be able to touch something with an outstretched arm or leg. **3** arrive at; get as far as. **4** come to a particular level or point. **5** make contact with. ▶ **n.** **1** the distance to which someone can stretch out their arm or arms to touch something. **2** a continuous stretch of river between two bends.

> SYNONYMS ▶ **v.** **1 extend**, stretch, outstretch, thrust, stick, hold. **2 arrive at**, get to, come to, end up at. **3** *the temperature reached 75°* **attain**, get to, rise to, fall to, sink to, drop to; informal hit. **4** *the senators reached an agreement* **achieve**, work out, draw up, put together, negotiate, thrash out, hammer out. **5 contact**, get in touch with, get through to, get, speak to; informal get (a) hold of. ▶ **n.** **1 grasp**, range, stretch, capabilities, capacity. **2 jurisdiction**, authority, influence, power, scope, range, compass, ambit.

re·act /rēˈakt/ ▶ **v.** **1** respond to something in a particular way. **2** interact and undergo a chemical or physical change.

> SYNONYMS **respond**, act in response, reply, answer, behave.

■ **re·ac·tive adj.**

re·ac·tion /rēˈaksHən/ ▶ **n.** **1** something done or experienced as a result of an event. **2** (**reactions**) a person's ability to respond to an event. **3** a bad response by the body to a drug or substance. **4** a process in which substances interact causing chemical or physical change. **5** a force exerted in opposition to an applied force.

> SYNONYMS **1 response**, answer, reply, rejoinder, retort, riposte; informal comeback. **2 backlash**, counteraction.

re·ac·tion·ar·y /rēˈaksHəˌnerē/ ▶ **adj.** opposing political or social progress or reform. ▶ **n.** (plural **reactionaries**) a person holding reactionary views.

> SYNONYMS ▶ **adj.** **right-wing**, conservative, traditionalist, conventional, diehard. ANTONYMS radical, progressive.

re·ac·ti·vate /rēˈaktivāt/ ▶ **v.** (**reactivates**, **reactivating**, **reactivated**) bring something back into action. ■ **re·ac·ti·va·tion** /rēˌaktiˈvāsHən/ **n.**

re·ac·tor /rēˈaktər/ ▶ **n.** an apparatus in which material is made to undergo a controlled nuclear reaction that releases energy.

read /rēd/ ▶ **v.** (**reads**, **reading**, **read** /red/) **1** understand the meaning of written or printed words or symbols. **2** speak written or printed words aloud. **3** have a particular wording. **4** understand the nature or meaning of. **5** (**read something into**) think that something has a meaning that it may not possess. **6** (of an instrument) show a measurement or figure. ▶ **n.** informal a book considered in terms of its readability: *the book is a thoroughly entertaining read.*

> SYNONYMS ▶ **v.** **1 peruse**, study, scrutinize, look through, pore over, run your eye over, cast an eye over, leaf through, scan. **2 understand**, make out, make sense of, decipher, interpret, construe. **3 register**, record, display, show, indicate.

read·a·ble /ˈrēdəbəl/ ▶ **adj.** **1** able to be read or deciphered. **2** easy or enjoyable to read.

SYNONYMS **1 legible**, decipherable, clear, intelligible, comprehensible. **2 enjoyable**, entertaining, interesting, absorbing, gripping, enthralling, engrossing; informal unputdownable. ANTONYMS illegible.

read·er /'rēdər/ ▶ **n. 1** a person who reads. **2** a person who assesses the quality of manuscripts submitted for publication. **3** a device that produces a readable image from microfiche or microfilm on a screen. ■ **read·er·ly adj.**

read·er·ship /'rēdər,sHip/ ▶ **n.** the readers of a publication regarded as a group.

read·i·ly /'redl-ē/ ▶ **adv. 1** willingly. **2** easily.

SYNONYMS **1 willingly**, unhesitatingly, ungrudgingly, gladly, happily, eagerly. **2 easily**, without difficulty.

read·i·ness /'redēnis/ ▶ **n. 1** willingness to do something: *their readiness to accept change*. **2** the state of being fully prepared for something.

SYNONYMS **willingness**, eagerness, keenness, enthusiasm, alacrity.

read·ing /'rēdiNG/ ▶ **n. 1** the action of reading. **2** something that is read. **3** knowledge gained by reading. **4** a figure recorded on a measuring instrument. **5** an interpretation.

SYNONYMS **1 perusal**, study, scanning. **2 learning**, scholarship, education, erudition. **3 recital**, recitation, performance. **4 lesson**, passage, excerpt. **5 interpretation**, understanding, explanation, analysis, construction.

re·ad·just /,rēə'jəst/ ▶ **v. 1** adjust again. **2** adapt to a changed situation. ■ **re·ad·just·ment n.**

read·y /'redē/ ▶ **adj.** (**readier**, **readiest**) **1** prepared for an activity or situation. **2** made available for immediate use. **3** easily available or obtained. **4** (**ready to do**) willing or eager to do. **5** immediate or quick. ▶ **v.** (**readies**, **readying**, **readied**) prepare.

SYNONYMS ▶ **adj. 1 prepared**, equipped, all set, organized, primed; informal fit, psyched (up), geared up. **2 completed**, finished, prepared, organized, done, arranged, fixed. **3** *he's always ready to help* **willing**, prepared, pleased, inclined, disposed, eager, keen, happy, glad; informal game. **4** *a ready supply of food* (**easily**) **available**, accessible, handy, close/near at hand, on hand, convenient, within reach, near, at your fingertips; informal on tap. **5** *a ready answer* **prompt**, quick, swift, speedy, fast, immediate, unhesitating. ▶ **v. prepare**, organize, gear up; informal psych up.

re·a·gent /rē'ājənt/ ▶ **n.** a substance that produces a chemical reaction, used to detect the presence of another substance.

re·al /'rē(ə)l/ ▶ **adj. 1** actually existing or happening. **2** not artificial; genuine. **3** worthy of the description; proper. ▶ **adv.** informal really; very.

SYNONYMS ▶ **adj. 1 actual**, true, factual, nonfictional, historical, material, physical, tangible, concrete. **2 genuine**, authentic, bona fide, proper, true; informal kosher. **3 sincere**, genuine, true, unfeigned, heartfelt. **4 complete**, utter, thorough, absolute, total, prize, perfect. ANTONYMS imaginary, false.

□ **real estate** land or housing. **real estate agent** a person who sells or rents out houses or apartments, or who helps clients find a house or apartment. **the real McCoy** informal the real thing. **real property** Law property consisting of land or buildings.

re·a·lign /,rēə'līn/ ▶ **v.** change something to a different position or state. ■ **re·a·lign·ment n.**

re·al·ism /'rēə,lizəm/ ▶ **n. 1** the acceptance of a situation as it is. **2** the presentation of things in a way that is accurate and true to life.

SYNONYMS **1 pragmatism**, practicality, common sense, levelheadedness. **2 authenticity**, accuracy, fidelity, truthfulness, verisimilitude.

■ **re·al·ist n.**

re·al·is·tic /,rēə'listik/ ▶ **adj. 1** having a sensible and practical idea of what can be achieved. **2** showing things in a way that is accurate and true to life.

SYNONYMS **1 practical**, pragmatic, matter-of-fact, down-to-earth, sensible, commonsensical, rational, levelheaded; informal no-nonsense. **2 achievable**, attainable, feasible, practicable, reasonable, sensible, workable; informal doable. **3 authentic**, accurate, true to life, lifelike, truthful, faithful, natural, naturalistic. ANTONYMS unrealistic.

■ **re·al·is·ti·cal·ly adv.**

re·al·i·ty /rē'alətē/ ▶ **n.** (plural **realities**) **1** the state of things as they actually exist. **2** a thing that is real. **3** the state of being real.

SYNONYMS **1 the real world**, real life, actuality, corporeality. **2 fact**, actuality, truth. **3 authenticity**, verisimilitude, fidelity, truthfulness, accuracy. ANTONYMS fantasy.

□ **reality TV** television programs based on real people or situations, presented as entertainment.

re·al·i·za·tion /,rē(ə)lə'zāsHən/ ▶ **n. 1** the act of becoming fully aware of something: *realization dawned suddenly*. **2** the achievement of something that you have worked for. **3** the conversion of an asset into cash. **4** a sale of goods.

SYNONYMS **1 awareness**, understanding, comprehension, consciousness, appreciation, recognition, discernment. **2 fulfillment**, achievement, accomplishment, attainment.

re·al·ize /'rē(ə),līz/ ▶ **v.** (**realizes**, **realizing**, **realized**) **1** become fully aware of a fact. **2** achieve or fulfill a wish or plan. **3** be sold for a particular amount. **4** convert property, shares, etc., into money by selling them.

SYNONYMS **1 register**, perceive, understand, grasp, comprehend, see, recognize, take in. **2 fulfill**, achieve, accomplish, make happen, bring to fruition, bring about/off, actualize. **3 make**, clear, gain, earn, return, produce. **4 be sold for**, fetch, go for, make, net.

re·al·ly /'rē(ə)lē/ ▶ **adv. 1** in actual fact. **2** very; thoroughly. ▶ **exclam.** expressing interest, surprise, doubt, etc.

SYNONYMS ▶ **adv. 1 in (actual) fact**, actually, in reality, in truth. **2 genuinely**, truly, certainly, honestly, undoubtedly, unquestionably.

realm /relm/ ▶ **n. 1** chiefly literary a kingdom. **2** an area of activity or interest.

SYNONYMS **1 kingdom**, country, land, state, nation, territory, dominion, empire, monarchy, principality. **2** *the realm of academia* **domain**, sphere, area, field, world, province.

Re·al·tor /ˈrē(ə)ltər, -ˌtôr, ˈrē(ə)lətər/ ▶ **n.** trademark a person who acts as an agent for the sale and purchase of buildings and land; a real estate agent.

re·al·ty /ˈrē(ə)ltē/ ▶ **n.** Law a person's real property.

ream /rēm/ ▶ **n.** **1** 500 sheets of paper. **2** (**reams**) a large quantity.

reap /rēp/ ▶ **v.** **1** gather in a crop or harvest. **2** receive a reward or benefit as a result of your actions.

> SYNONYMS **1 harvest**, cut, pick, gather, garner. **2 receive**, obtain, get, derive, acquire, secure, realize.

reap·er /ˈrēpər/ ▶ **n.** a person or machine that harvests a crop. □ **the Grim Reaper** death, shown as a cloaked skeleton holding a scythe.

re·ap·pear /ˌrēəˈpi(ə)r/ ▶ **v.** appear again. ■ **re·ap·pear·ance n.**

rear¹ /ri(ə)r/ ▶ **n.** the back part of something. ▶ **adj.** at the back.

> SYNONYMS ▶ **n. back (part)**, hind part, end, tail (end), back (end); Nautical stern. ▶ **adj. back**, end, rearmost, hind, last. ANTONYMS front.

□ **rear admiral** the US Navy and Coast Guard rank above commodore. ■ **rear·most adj. rear·ward adj. & adv. rear·wards adv.**

rear² ▶ **v.** **1** bring up offspring. **2** breed animals. **3** (of an animal) raise itself upright on its hind legs. **4** extend to a great height.

> SYNONYMS **1 bring up**, raise, care for, look after, nurture, parent. **2 breed**, raise, keep, grow, cultivate.

rear·guard /ˈri(ə)rˌgärd/ ▶ **n.** a group of soldiers protecting the rear of the main force.

re·arm /rēˈärm/ ▶ **v.** provide with or obtain a new supply of weapons. ■ **re·ar·ma·ment** /rēˈärməmənt/ **n.**

re·ar·range /ˌrēəˈrānj/ ▶ **v.** (**rearranges**, **rearranging**, **rearranged**) arrange again in a different way. ■ **re·ar·range·ment n.**

rea·son /ˈrēzən/ ▶ **n.** **1** a cause or explanation. **2** good or obvious cause to do something. **3** the power to think and draw conclusions logically. **4** (**your reason**) your sanity. **5** what is right, practical, or possible. ▶ **v.** **1** think and draw conclusions logically. **2** (**reason with**) persuade someone by using logical arguments.

> SYNONYMS ▶ **n. 1 cause**, ground(s), basis, rationale, motive, explanation, justification, defense, vindication, excuse, apologia. **2 rationality**, logic, cognition, reasoning, intellect, thought, understanding; formal ratiocination. **3 sanity**, mind, mental faculties, senses, wits; informal marbles. ▶ **v. calculate**, conclude, reckon, think, judge, deduce, infer, surmise; informal figure.

□ **stand to reason** be logical.

rea·son·a·ble /ˈrēz(ə)nəbəl/ ▶ **adj.** **1** fair and sensible. **2** appropriate in a particular situation. **3** fairly good. **4** not too expensive.

> SYNONYMS **1 sensible**, rational, logical, fair, just, equitable, intelligent, wise, levelheaded, practical, realistic, sound, valid, commonsensical, tenable, plausible, credible, believable. **2 practicable**, sensible, appropriate, suitable. **3 fairly good**, acceptable, satisfactory, average, adequate, fair, tolerable, passable; informal OK. **4 inexpensive**, affordable, moderate, low, cheap, within your means.

■ **rea·son·a·bly adv.**

re·as·sign /ˌrēəˈsīn/ ▶ **v.** assign again or differently. ■ **re·as·sign·ment n.**

re·as·sure /ˌrēəˈsho͝or/ ▶ **v.** (**reassures**, **reassuring**, **reassured**) make someone feel less worried or afraid.

> SYNONYMS **put someone's mind at rest**, encourage, hearten, buoy up, cheer up, comfort, soothe. ANTONYMS alarm.

■ **re·as·sur·ance n.**

re·bar·ba·tive /rəˈbärbətiv/ ▶ **adj.** unpleasant.

re·bate /ˈrēˌbāt/ ▶ **n.** **1** a partial refund to someone who has paid too much for tax, rent, etc. **2** a discount on a sum that is due.

> SYNONYMS **partial refund**, partial repayment, discount, deduction, reduction.

reb·el ▶ **v.** /riˈbel/ (**rebels**, **rebelling**, **rebelled**) **1** refuse to obey the government or ruler. **2** oppose authority, or refuse to behave conventionally. ▶ **n.** /ˈrebəl/ a person who rebels.

> SYNONYMS ▶ **v. revolt**, mutiny, riot, rise up, take up arms. ▶ **n. 1 revolutionary**, insurgent, insurrectionist, mutineer, guerrilla, terrorist, freedom fighter. **2** *rebel forces* **rebellious**, insurgent, revolutionary, mutinous. **3 nonconformist**, dissenter, dissident, maverick. **4** *a rebel faction of the party* **defiant**, disobedient, insubordinate, subversive, rebellious, nonconformist, maverick. ANTONYMS loyalist, loyal, conformist, obedient.

re·bel·lion /riˈbelyən/ ▶ **n.** **1** an act of rebelling. **2** opposition to authority or control.

> SYNONYMS **1 revolt**, uprising, insurrection, mutiny, revolution, insurgence. **2 defiance**, disobedience, insubordination, subversion, resistance. ANTONYMS compliance.

re·bel·lious /riˈbelyəs/ ▶ **adj.** choosing to rebel.

> SYNONYMS **1 rebel**, insurgent, mutinous, revolutionary. **2 defiant**, disobedient, insubordinate, unruly, mutinous, obstreperous, recalcitrant, intractable. ANTONYMS loyal, obedient.

■ **re·bel·lious·ly adv.**

re·birth /rēˈbərTH, ˈrēˌbərTH/ ▶ **n.** a return to life or activity.

re·born /rēˈbôrn/ ▶ **adj.** brought back to life or activity.

re·bound ▶ **v.** /riˈbound, ˈrēˌbound/ **1** bounce back after hitting a hard surface. **2** increase again. **3** Basketball gain possession of a missed shot after it bounces off the backboard or basket rim. **4** (**rebound on**) have an unexpected and unpleasant effect on. ▶ **n.** /ˈrēˌbound/ a ball or shot that rebounds.

> SYNONYMS ▶ **v. 1 bounce (back)**, spring back, ricochet, boomerang. **2 backfire**, misfire, come back on.

□ **on the rebound** while still upset after the ending of a romantic relationship.

re·buff /riˈbəf/ ▶ **v.** reject in an abrupt or unkind way. ▶ **n.** an abrupt or unkind rejection.

> SYNONYMS ▶ **v. reject**, turn down, spurn, refuse, decline, snub, slight, dismiss, brush off.

ANTONYMS accept. ▶ n. **rejection**, snub, slight, refusal, spurning; informal brush-off, kick in the teeth, slap in the face.

re·build /rē'bild/ ▶ v. (**rebuilds**, **rebuilding**, **rebuilt**) build again.

re·buke /ri'byo͞ok/ ▶ v. (**rebukes**, **rebuking**, **rebuked**) sharply criticize or tell off. ▶ n. a sharp criticism.

SYNONYMS ▶ v. **reprimand**, reproach, scold, admonish, reprove, chastise, upbraid, berate, take to task; informal tell off, chew out; formal castigate. ▶ n. **reprimand**, reproach, scolding, admonition; informal telling-off, chewing-out, dressing-down. ANTONYMS praise.

re·bus /'rēbəs/ ▶ n. (plural **rebuses**) a puzzle in which words are represented by combinations of pictures and letters.

re·but /ri'bət/ ▶ v. (**rebuts**, **rebutting**, **rebutted**) claim or prove that something is false.

re·but·tal /ri'bətl/ ▶ n. an act of rebutting evidence or an accusation.

SYNONYMS **refutation**, denial, countering, invalidation, negation, contradiction.

re·cal·ci·trant /ri'kalsətrənt/ ▶ adj. unwilling to cooperate; disobedient.

SYNONYMS **uncooperative**, intractable, insubordinate, defiant, rebellious, willful, wayward, headstrong, self-willed, contrary, perverse, difficult, awkward; formal refractory. ANTONYMS amenable.

■ **re·cal·ci·trance** n.

re·call ▶ v. /ri'kôl/ **1** remember. **2** make someone think of; bring to mind. **3** officially order someone to return. **4** (of a manufacturer) ask for faulty products to be returned. ▶ n. /'rēˌkôl, ri'kôl, rē'kôl/ **1** the action of remembering. **2** an official order for someone to return.

SYNONYMS ▶ v. **1 remember**, recollect, call to mind, think back on/to, reminisce about. **2 remind someone of**, bring to mind, call up, conjure up, evoke. **3 call back**, order home, withdraw. ANTONYMS forget. ▶ n. **recollection**, remembrance, memory.

re·cant /ri'kant/ ▶ v. withdraw a former opinion or belief.

re·cap /rē'kap/ ▶ v. (**recaps**, **recapping**, **recapped**) recapitulate.

re·ca·pit·u·late /ˌrēkə'picнəˌlāt/ ▶ v. (**recapitulates**, **recapitulating**, **recapitulated**) give a summary of.
■ **re·ca·pit·u·la·tion** /ˌrēkəˌpicнə'lāsнən/ n.

re·cap·ture /rē'kapcнər/ ▶ v. (**recaptures**, **recapturing**, **recaptured**) **1** capture a person or animal that has escaped. **2** recover something taken or lost. **3** bring back or experience again a past time or feeling. ▶ n. an act of recapturing.

re·cast /rē'kast/ ▶ v. (**recasts**, **recasting**, **recast**) present something in a different form.

re·cede /ri'sēd/ ▶ v. (**recedes**, **receding**, **receded**) **1** move back or further away. **2** gradually become weaker or smaller. **3** (**receding**) (of part of the face) sloping backward. **4** (**receding**) (of a man's hair) cease to grow at the temples and above the forehead.

SYNONYMS **1 retreat**, go back/down/away, withdraw, ebb, subside. **2 diminish**, lessen, dwindle, fade, abate, subside. ANTONYMS advance, grow.

re·ceipt /ri'sēt/ ▶ n. **1** a written statement confirming that something has been paid for or received. **2** the action of receiving something. **3** (**receipts**) the amount of money received over a period by a business.

re·ceive /ri'sēv/ ▶ v. (**receives**, **receiving**, **received**) **1** be given or paid. **2** accept something sent or offered. **3** experience or meet with. **4** form an idea or impression from an experience. **5** entertain someone as a guest. **6** detect or pick up broadcast signals. **7** (**received**) widely accepted as true.

SYNONYMS **1 be given**, be presented with, be awarded, be sent, be in receipt of, get, obtain, gain, acquire, be paid. **2 hear**, listen to, respond to, react to. **3 experience**, sustain, undergo, meet with, suffer, bear. ANTONYMS give, send.

SPELLING

Remember, the rule is **i** before **e**, when the sound is *ee*, except after **c**: rec**ei**ve.

re·ceiv·er /ri'sēvər/ ▶ n. **1** a radio or television apparatus that converts broadcast signals into sound or images. **2** the part of a telephone that converts electrical signals into sounds. **3** (also **official receiver**) a person appointed to manage the financial affairs of a bankrupt business.
■ **re·ceiv·er·ship** n.

re·cent /'rēsənt/ ▶ adj. having happened or been done shortly before the present.

SYNONYMS **new**, the latest, current, fresh, modern, late, contemporary, up to date, up to the minute. ANTONYMS old.

re·cent·ly /'rēsəntlē/ ▶ adv. in the recent past: *they recently installed a new flagpole.*

SYNONYMS **not long ago**, a little while back, just now, newly, freshly, of late, lately, latterly.

re·cep·ta·cle /ri'septikəl/ ▶ n. an object used to contain something.

re·cep·tion /ri'sepsнən/ ▶ n. **1** the action of receiving. **2** the way in which people react to something. **3** a formal social occasion held to welcome someone or celebrate an event. **4** the area in a hotel, office, etc., where visitors are greeted. **5** the quality with which broadcast signals are received.

SYNONYMS **1 response**, reaction, treatment. **2 party**, function, social occasion, celebration, get-together, gathering, soirée; informal do.

re·cep·tion·ist /ri'sepsнənist/ ▶ n. a person who greets and deals with visitors to an office, hotel, etc.

re·cep·tive /ri'septiv/ ▶ adj. **1** able or willing to receive something. **2** willing to consider new ideas.

SYNONYMS **open-minded**, responsive, amenable, well-disposed, flexible, approachable, accessible. ANTONYMS unresponsive.

■ **re·cep·tiv·i·ty** /ˌrēˌsep'tivətē/ n.

re·cep·tor /ri'septər/ ▶ n. a nerve ending in the body that responds to a stimulus such as light.

re·cess /'rēˌses, ri'ses/ ▶ n. **1** a small space set back in a wall or in a surface. **2** a break between sessions of the US Congress, a parliament, court of law, etc. **3** a break between school classes. **4** (**recesses**) remote or hidden places. ▶ v. fit something so that it is set back into a surface.

SYNONYMS ▶ n. **1 alcove**, bay, niche, nook, corner. **2 break**, adjournment, interlude, interval, rest, holiday, vacation.

re·ces·sion /ri'seshən/ ▶ n. a period during which trade and industrial activity in a country are reduced.

SYNONYMS **downturn**, depression, slump, slowdown. ANTONYMS boom.

re·ces·sive /ri'sesiv/ ▶ adj. (of a gene) appearing in offspring only if a contrary gene is not also inherited.

re·charge /rē'chärj/ ▶ v. (**recharges**, **recharging**, **recharged**) charge a battery or device again. ■ **re·charge·a·ble** adj. **re·charg·er** n.

re·cher·ché /rə,sher'shā, rə'sher,shā/ ▶ adj. unusual and not easily understood.

re·cid·i·vist /ri'sidəvist/ ▶ n. a person who repeatedly commits crimes. ■ **re·cid·i·vism** n.

rec·i·pe /'resə,pē/ ▶ n. **1** a list of ingredients and instructions for preparing a dish. **2** something likely to lead to a particular outcome: *a recipe for disaster*.

SYNONYMS *a recipe for success* **formula**, prescription, blueprint.

re·cip·i·ent /ri'sipēənt/ ▶ n. a person who receives something.

re·cip·ro·cal /ri'siprəkəl/ ▶ adj. **1** given or done in return. **2** affecting two parties equally.

SYNONYMS **mutual**, common, shared, give-and-take, joint, corresponding, complementary.

■ **re·cip·ro·cal·ly** adv.

re·cip·ro·cate /ri'siprə,kāt/ ▶ v. (**reciprocates**, **reciprocating**, **reciprocated**) respond to an action or emotion with a similar one.

SYNONYMS **requite**, return, give back.

rec·i·proc·i·ty /,resə'präsətē/ ▶ n. a situation in which two parties provide the same help to each other.

re·cit·al /ri'sītl/ ▶ n. **1** the performance of a program of music by a soloist or small group. **2** a long account of a series of facts or events.

SYNONYMS **1 performance**, concert, recitation, reading. **2 report**, account, listing, catalog, litany.

rec·i·ta·tion /,resi'tāshən/ ▶ n. **1** the repetition of a passage aloud from memory. **2** a statement of a series of facts or events.

re·cite /ri'sīt/ ▶ v. (**recites**, **reciting**, **recited**) **1** repeat a passage aloud from memory. **2** state facts, events, etc., in order.

SYNONYMS **1 quote**, say, speak, read aloud, declaim, deliver, render. **2 recount**, list, detail, reel off, relate, enumerate.

reck·less /'rekləs/ ▶ adj. without thought or care for the results of an action.

SYNONYMS **rash**, careless, thoughtless, heedless, precipitate, impetuous, impulsive, irresponsible, foolhardy, devil-may-care. ANTONYMS cautious.

■ **reck·less·ly** adv. **reck·less·ness** n.

reck·on /'rekən/ ▶ v. **1** have an opinion about something; think. **2** (**reckon on**) rely on or expect. **3** calculate. **4** (**reckon with** or **without**) take (or fail to take) something into account.

SYNONYMS **1 calculate**, compute, work out, figure, count (up), add up, total, tally. **2 include**, count, regard as, look on as, consider, judge, think of as, deem, rate. **3 think**, believe, be of the opinion, suppose, assume.

□ **to be reckoned with** to be treated as important.

reck·on·ing /'rekəniNG/ ▶ n. **1** the action of calculating or estimating something. **2** punishment for past actions.

SYNONYMS **calculation**, estimation, computation, working out, addition, count.

re·claim /ri'klām/ ▶ v. **1** get possession of something again. **2** make land usable.

SYNONYMS **1 get back**, claim back, recover, retrieve, recoup. **2 save**, rescue, redeem, salvage.

■ **rec·la·ma·tion** /,reklə'māshən/ n.

re·cline /ri'klīn/ ▶ v. (**reclines**, **reclining**, **reclined**) lie back in a relaxed position.

SYNONYMS **lie**, lie down/back, lean back, relax, loll, lounge, sprawl, stretch out.

re·clin·er /ri'klīnər/ ▶ n. an upholstered armchair that can be tilted backward, especially one with a footrest.

rec·luse /'rek,lo͞os, ri'klo͞os, 'rek,lo͞oz/ ▶ n. a person who avoids other people and lives alone.

SYNONYMS **hermit**, ascetic, eremite, loner, lone wolf; historical anchorite.

■ **re·clu·sive** /ri'klo͞osiv, -ziv/ adj.

rec·og·ni·tion /,rekig'nishən/ ▶ n. **1** the action of recognizing. **2** appreciation or acknowledgment.

SYNONYMS **1 identification**, recollection, remembrance. **2 acknowledgment**, acceptance, admission, confession. **3 appreciation**, gratitude, thanks, congratulations, credit, commendation, acclaim, acknowledgment.

rec·og·nize /'rekig,nīz, 'rekə(g),nīz/ ▶ v. (**recognizes**, **recognizing**, **recognized**) **1** know someone or something from having come across them before. **2** accept something as genuine, legal, or valid. **3** show official appreciation of.

SYNONYMS **1 identify**, place, know, put a name to, remember, recall, recollect. **2 acknowledge**, accept, admit, concede, confess, realize. **3 pay tribute to**, appreciate, be grateful for, acclaim, commend.

re·coil /ri'koil/ ▶ v. **1** suddenly move back in fear, horror, or disgust. **2** (of a gun) suddenly move backward as a reaction on being fired. **3** (**recoil on**) have an unpleasant effect on. ▶ n. the action of recoiling.

SYNONYMS ▶ v. **1 draw back**, jump back, pull back, flinch, shy away, shrink (back), blench. **2 feel revulsion**, feel disgust, shrink from, wince at.

rec·ol·lect /,rekə'lekt/ ▶ v. remember.

SYNONYMS **remember**, recall, call to mind, think of, think back to, reminisce about. ANTONYMS forget.

rec·ol·lec·tion /,rekə'lekshən/ ▶ n. **1** the action of remembering, or the ability to remember. **2** a memory.

SYNONYMS **memory**, recall, remembrance, impression, reminiscence.

rec·om·mend /ˌrekəˈmend/ ▶ **v. 1** say that someone or something is suitable for a particular purpose or role. **2** make something seem appealing or desirable.

SYNONYMS **1 advocate**, endorse, commend, suggest, put forward, propose, nominate, put up, speak favorably of, put in a good word for, vouch for; informal plug. **2 advise**, counsel, urge, exhort, enjoin, prescribe, argue for, back, support.

SPELLING

One **c** and two **ms**: recommend.

rec·om·men·da·tion /ˌrekəmənˈdāsʜən, -ˌmen-/ ▶ **n. 1** a suggestion or proposal as to the best course of action. **2** the action of recommending.

SYNONYMS **1 advice**, counsel, guidance, suggestion, proposal. **2 commendation**, endorsement, good word, testimonial, tip; informal plug.

rec·om·pense /ˈrekəmˌpens/ ▶ **v.** (**recompenses**, **recompensing**, **recompensed**) **1** compensate someone for loss or harm suffered. **2** pay or reward someone for effort or work. ▶ **n.** compensation or reward.

rec·on·cile /ˈrekənˌsīl/ ▶ **v.** (**reconciles**, **reconciling**, **reconciled**) **1** make two people or groups friendly again. **2** find a satisfactory way of dealing with opposing facts, ideas, etc. **3** (**reconcile someone to**) make someone accept something unwelcome.

SYNONYMS **1 reunite**, bring (back) together, pacify, appease, placate, mollify; formal conciliate. **2** *reconciling his religious beliefs with his career* **make compatible**, harmonize, square, make congruent, balance. **3 settle**, resolve, sort out, smooth over, iron out, mend, remedy, heal, rectify; informal patch up. **4** *they had to reconcile themselves to drastic losses* **accept**, resign yourself to, come to terms with, learn to live with, get used to, make the best of.

rec·on·cil·i·a·tion /ˌrekənˌsilēˈāsʜən/ ▶ **n. 1** the end of a disagreement and the return to friendly relations. **2** the action of reconciling opposing ideas, facts, etc.

rec·on·dite /ˈrekənˌdīt, riˈkän-/ ▶ **adj.** not known about or understood by many people.

re·con·di·tion /ˌrēkənˈdisʜən/ ▶ **v.** bring back to a good condition; renovate.

re·con·nais·sance /riˈkänəzəns, -səns/ ▶ **n.** military observation of an area to gain information.

re·con·noi·ter /ˌrēkəˈnoitər, ˌrek-/ ▶ **v.** (**reconnoiters**, **reconnoitering**, **reconnoitered**) make a military observation of an area.

SYNONYMS **survey**, explore, scout (out), find out the lay of the land, investigate, examine, scrutinize, inspect, observe, take a look at, patrol; informal check out.

re·con·sid·er /ˌrēkənˈsidər/ ▶ **v.** (**reconsiders**, **reconsidering**, **reconsidered**) consider again, with the possibility of changing a decision.

SYNONYMS **rethink**, review, revise, re-evaluate, reassess, have second thoughts, change your mind.

■ **re·con·sid·er·a·tion** /ˌrēkənˌsidəˈrāsʜən/ **n.**

re·con·sti·tute /rēˈkänstəˌt(y)o͞ot/ ▶ **v.** (**reconstitutes**, **reconstituting**, **reconstituted**) **1** change the form of an organization. **2** restore dried food to its original state by adding water. ■ **re·con·sti·tu·tion** /ˌrēˌkänstəˈt(y)o͞osʜən/ **n.**

re·con·struct /ˌrēkənˈstrəkt/ ▶ **v. 1** construct again. **2** show how a past event happened by using the evidence that has been gathered.

SYNONYMS **rebuild**, remake, recreate, restore, reassemble, remodel, revamp, renovate.

■ **re·con·struc·tion** **n.**

re·con·vene /ˌrēkənˈvēn/ ▶ **v.** (**reconvenes**, **reconvening**, **reconvened**) meet again after a break.

rec·ord ▶ **n.** /ˈrekərd/ **1** a permanent account of something, kept for evidence or information. **2** the previous behavior or performance of a person or thing. **3** (also **criminal record**) a list of a person's previous criminal convictions. **4** the best performance of its kind that has been officially recognized. **5** a thin plastic disk carrying recorded sound in grooves on each surface. ▶ **v.** /riˈkôrd/ **1** make a record of. **2** convert sound or vision into a permanent form so that it can be reproduced later.

SYNONYMS ▶ **n. 1 account**, document, data, file, dossier, evidence, report, annals, archive, chronicle, minutes, transactions, proceedings, transcript, certificate, deed, register, log. **2** recording, album, LP, single. ▶ **v. 1 write down**, take down, note, jot down, put down on paper, document, enter, log, register. **2 indicate**, register, show, display. **3 film**, photograph, tape, tape-record, video-record, videotape.

□ **on record** officially measured and noted. **off the record** not made as an official statement or for publication. **record player** a device for playing records. ■ **re·cord·ing** **n.**

re·cord·er /riˈkôrdər/ ▶ **n. 1** a device for recording sound, pictures, etc. **2** a person who keeps records. **3** a musical instrument that you play by blowing through a mouthpiece and putting your fingers over holes.

re·count¹ /riˈkount/ ▶ **v.** describe something to someone.

SYNONYMS **tell**, relate, narrate, describe, report, relay, convey, communicate, impart.

re·count² ▶ **v.** /rēˈkount, ˈrē-/ count again. ▶ **n.** /ˈrēkount/ an act of counting something again.

re·coup /riˈko͞op/ ▶ **v.** recover an amount of money that has been lost or spent.

re·course /ˈrēˌkôrs, riˈkôrs/ ▶ **n. 1** a source of help in a difficult situation. **2** (**recourse to**) the use of a particular source of help.

SYNONYMS **option**, possibility, alternative, resort, way out, hope, remedy, choice, expedient.

re·cov·er /riˈkəvər/ ▶ **v.** (**recovers**, **recovering**, **recovered**) **1** return to a normal state of health or strength. **2** regain possession or control of. **3** regain an amount of money that has been spent or lent.

SYNONYMS **1 get better**, improve, rally, recuperate, convalesce, revive, be on the mend, get back on your feet, pick up, heal, bounce back, pull through. **2 retrieve**, regain, get back, recoup, reclaim, repossess, recapture.

3 **salvage**, save, rescue, retrieve. ANTONYMS deteriorate.

■ **re·cov·er·a·ble** adj.

re·cov·er·y /ri'kəvərē/ ▶ n. (plural **recoveries**) the action or an act of recovering.

SYNONYMS **1 improvement**, recuperation, convalescence, rally, revival. **2 retrieval**, repossession, reclamation, recapture. ANTONYMS relapse.

re-cre·ate /ˌrēkrē'āt/ ▶ v. (**recreates**, **recreating**, **recreated**) make or do again.

rec·re·a·tion[1] /ˌrekrē'āsʜən/ ▶ n. enjoyable leisure activity.

SYNONYMS **1 pleasure**, leisure, relaxation, fun, enjoyment, entertainment, amusement, diversion. **2 pastime**, hobby, leisure activity. ANTONYMS work.

■ **rec·re·a·tion·al** adj.

re·cre·a·tion[2] /ˌrēkrē'āsʜən/ ▶ n. the action of recreating something.

re·crim·i·na·tion /riˌkrimə'nāsʜən/ ▶ n. an accusation made in response to one from someone else.

re·cru·des·cence /ˌrēkro͞o'desns/ ▶ n. formal a recurrence.

re·cruit /ri'kro͞ot/ ▶ v. take on someone to serve in the armed forces or work for an organization. ▶ n. a newly recruited person.

SYNONYMS ▶ v. **1 enlist**, draft, call up, conscript. **2 muster**, form, raise, mobilize. **3 hire**, employ, take on, enroll, sign up, engage. ANTONYMS demobilize. ▶ n. **1 conscript**, draftee; informal yardbird. **2 newcomer**, trainee, initiate, joiner, beginner, novice; informal rookie, newbie.

re·cruit·ment /ri'kro͞otmənt/ ▶ n. the action of finding new people to serve in the armed forces or work for an organization.

rec·tal /'rektəl/ ▶ adj. relating to or affecting the rectum.

rec·tan·gle /'rekˌtaɴɢgəl/ ▶ n. a flat shape with four right angles and four straight sides, two of which are longer than the others.

rec·tan·gu·lar /rek'taɴɢgyələr/ ▶ adj. **1** shaped like a rectangle. **2** (of a solid) having a base, section, or side shaped like a rectangle: *a rectangular prism*. **3** having parts placed at right angles.

rec·ti·fy /'rektəˌfī/ ▶ v. (**rectifies**, **rectifying**, **rectified**) **1** put right; correct. **2** convert alternating current to direct current.

SYNONYMS **correct**, (put) right, sort out, deal with, amend, remedy, repair, fix, make good, resolve, settle; informal patch up.

■ **rec·ti·fi·ca·tion** /ˌrektəfi'kāsʜən/ n. **rec·ti·fi·er** n.

rec·ti·lin·e·ar /ˌrektə'linēər/ ▶ adj. having or moving in a straight line or lines.

rec·ti·tude /'rektəˌt(y)o͞od/ ▶ n. morally correct behavior.

rec·to /'rektō/ ▶ n. (plural **rectos**) a right-hand page of an open book, or the front of a loose document.

rec·tor /'rektər/ ▶ n. **1** a Christian priest in charge of a parish. **2** the head of certain universities, colleges, and schools.

rec·to·ry /'rektərē/ ▶ n. (plural **rectories**) the house of a rector.

rec·tum /'rektəm/ ▶ n. the final section of the large intestine, ending at the anus.

re·cum·bent /ri'kəmbənt/ ▶ adj. lying down.

re·cu·per·ate /ri'ko͞opəˌrāt/ ▶ v. (**recuperates**, **recuperating**, **recuperated**) **1** recover from illness or tiredness. **2** get back something that has been lost or spent.

SYNONYMS **get better**, recover, convalesce, get well, regain your strength/health, get over something.

■ **re·cu·per·a·tion** /riˌko͞opə'rāsʜən/ n.

re·cur /ri'kər/ ▶ v. (**recurs**, **recurring**, **recurred**) happen again or repeatedly.

SYNONYMS **happen again**, reoccur, repeat (itself), come back, return, reappear.

■ **re·cur·rence** n.

re·cur·rent /ri'kərənt, -'kə-rənt/ ▶ adj. happening often or repeatedly.

re·cy·cle /rē'sīkəl/ ▶ v. (**recycles**, **recycling**, **recycled**) **1** convert waste into a form in which it can be reused. **2** use something again.

SYNONYMS **reuse**, reprocess, reclaim, recover, salvage.

red /red/ ▶ adj. (**redder**, **reddest**) **1** of the color of blood or rubies. **2** (of hair or fur) of a reddish-brown color. ▶ n. **1** red color. **2** informal, chiefly disapproving a communist or socialist.

SYNONYMS ▶ adj. **1 scarlet**, vermilion, ruby, cherry, cerise, cardinal, carmine, crimson, maroon, magenta, burgundy, claret. **2 flushed**, blushing, pink, rosy, florid, ruddy. **3** auburn, Titian, chestnut, carroty, ginger.

□ **in the red** having spent more than is in your bank account. **red blood cell** a blood cell that contains hemoglobin and carries oxygen to the tissues. **red-blooded** energetic and healthy. **red card** (in soccer) a red card shown by the referee to a player being sent off the field. **red-handed** in the act of doing something wrong. **red herring** a thing that takes people's attention away from something important. **red-hot 1** so hot that it glows red. **2** very exciting. **red-letter day** an important or memorable day. **red pepper** a ripe sweet pepper. **red tape** complicated official rules that cause irritation because they take up your time. **see red** informal suddenly become very angry. ■ **red·dish** adj.

red·den /'redn/ ▶ v. make or become red.

re·deem /ri'dēm/ ▶ v. **1** make up for the faults of. **2** save someone from sin or evil. **3** fulfill a promise. **4** pay a debt. **5** exchange a coupon for goods or money. **6** regain possession of something in exchange for payment.

SYNONYMS **1 save**, deliver from sin, absolve. **2 retrieve**, regain, recover, get back, reclaim, repossess, buy back. **3 exchange**, convert, trade in, cash in.

■ **re·deem·er** n.

re·demp·tion /ri'dempsʜən/ ▶ n. the action of redeeming.

re·de·ploy /ˌrēdə'ploi/ ▶ v. move troops, resources, etc., to a new place or task. ■ **re·de·ploy·ment** n.

re·de·sign /ˌrēdi'zīn/ ▶ v. design again or differently. ▶ n. the action or process of redesigning.

red·head /'redˌhed/ ▶ n. a person with red hair.

re·di·rect /ˌrēdə'rekt, -ˌdī-/ ▶ v. direct to a different place or purpose.

re·dis·cov·er /ˌrēdis'kəvər/ ▶ v. (**rediscovers**, **rediscovering**, **rediscovered**) discover something forgotten or ignored again. ■ **re·dis·cov·er·y** n.

re·dis·tri·bute /ˌrēdəˈstribˌyo͞ot/ ▶ v. (**redistributes**, **redistributing**, **redistributed**) distribute again or differently. ■ **re·dis·tri·bu·tion** /ˌrēˌdistrəˈbyo͞osʜən/ n.

red·neck /ˈredˌnek/ ▶ n. informal, disapproving, and often offensive a conservative working-class white person, usually living in a rural area.

re·do /rēˈdo͞o/ ▶ v. (**redoes** /rēˈdəz/, **redoing**, **redid** /rēˈdid/; past participle **redone** /rēˈdən/) do again or differently.

red·o·lent /ˈredl-ənt/ ▶ adj. (**redolent of** or **with**) **1** making you think of a particular thing. **2** literary smelling of.

SYNONYMS **evocative**, suggestive, reminiscent.

■ **red·o·lence** n.

re·dou·ble /rēˈdəbəl/ ▶ v. (**redoubles**, **redoubling**, **redoubled**) make or become greater or stronger.

re·doubt /riˈdout/ ▶ n. a small or temporary structure from which soldiers can defend a place under attack.

re·doubt·a·ble /riˈdoutəbəl/ ▶ adj. worthy of respect or fear; formidable.

re·dound /riˈdound/ ▶ v. (**redound to**) formal be to someone's credit.

re·dress /riˈdres/ ▶ v. put right something that is unfair or wrong. ▶ n. , /riˈdres, ˈrēˌdres/ payment or action to make amends for a wrong.

SYNONYMS ▶ v. **rectify**, correct, right, compensate for, make amends for, remedy, make good. ▶ n. **compensation**, reparation, restitution, recompense, repayment, amends.

red·skin /ˈredˌskin/ ▶ n. dated or offensive an American Indian.

re·duce /riˈd(y)o͞os/ ▶ v. (**reduces**, **reducing**, **reduced**) **1** make or become less. **2** (**reduce something to**) change something to a simpler form. **3** (**reduce someone to**) bring someone to a particular state or condition. **4** boil a liquid so that it becomes thicker.

SYNONYMS **1 lessen**, make smaller, lower, decrease, diminish, minimize, shrink, narrow, cut, curtail, contract, shorten, downsize; informal chop. **2 bring down**, make cheaper, lower, mark down, slash, discount. **3** *he reduced her to tears* **bring to**, bring to the point of, drive to. ANTONYMS increase.

□ **reduced circumstances** a state in which you have become poorer than you were before. ■ **re·duc·i·ble** adj.

re·duc·tion /riˈdəksʜən/ ▶ n. **1** the action of reducing. **2** the amount by which something is reduced.

SYNONYMS **1 lessening**, lowering, decrease, diminution, cut, cutback, downsizing. **2 discount**, deduction, cut.

re·duc·tive /riˈdəktiv/ ▶ adj. presenting something in an oversimplified form.

re·dun·dant /riˈdəndənt/ ▶ adj. **1** no longer needed or useful. **2** repeating the same sense with different words.

SYNONYMS **unnecessary**, not required, unneeded, superfluous.

■ **re·dun·dan·cy** n. (plural **redundancies**).

red·wood /ˈredˌwo͝od/ ▶ n. a giant coniferous tree with reddish wood.

reed /rēd/ ▶ n. **1** a tall, slender plant that grows in water or on marshy ground. **2** a piece of thin cane or metal in musical instruments such as the clarinet, which vibrates when air is blown over it and produces sound.

reed·y /ˈrēdē/ ▶ adj. **1** (of a sound or voice) high and thin in tone. **2** full of reeds.

reef /rēf/ ▶ n. **1** a ridge of jagged rock or coral just above or below the surface of the sea. **2** each of several strips across a sail that can be taken in when the wind is strong. ▶ v. make a sail smaller by taking in a reef.

reek /rēk/ ▶ v. have a very unpleasant smell. ▶ n. a very unpleasant smell.

reel /rēl/ ▶ n. **1** a cylinder on which film, thread, etc., can be wound. **2** a device for winding and unwinding a line as required, in particular a fishing reel. **3** a lively Scottish or Irish folk dance. ▶ v. **1** (**reel something in**) bring something toward you by turning a reel. **2** (**reel something off**) recite something quickly and with ease. **3** stagger. **4** feel giddy, shocked, or bewildered.

SYNONYMS ▶ v. **1 stagger**, lurch, sway, rock, stumble, totter, wobble, teeter. **2 go round** (**and around**/**round**), whirl, spin, revolve, swirl, twirl, turn, swim.

re-en·try /rē ˈentrē/ ▶ n. (plural **re-entries**) **1** the action of entering again. **2** the return of a spacecraft or missile into the earth's atmosphere.

re-es·tab·lish /ˌrēiˈstablisʜ/ ▶ v. establish something again. ■ **re-es·tab·lish·ment** n.

ref /ref/ ▶ n. informal (in sports) a referee.

re·fec·to·ry /riˈfekt(ə)rē/ ▶ n. (plural **refectories**) a room used for meals in an educational or religious institution.

re·fer /riˈfər/ ▶ v. (**refers**, **referring**, **referred**) (**refer to**) **1** write or say something about; mention. **2** (of a word or phrase) describe. **3** turn to a person, book, etc., for information. **4** (**refer someone**/**thing to**) pass a person or matter on to someone else for help or a decision.

SYNONYMS **pass**, direct, hand on/over, send on, transfer, entrust, assign.

ref·er·ee /ˌrefəˈrē/ ▶ n. **1** an official who supervises a game to ensure that players keep to the rules. **2** a person consulted in a dispute, etc. ▶ v. (**referees**, **refereeing**, **refereed**) be a referee of.

SYNONYMS ▶ n. **umpire**, judge, adjudicator, arbitrator; informal ref.

ref·er·ence /ˈref(ə)rəns/ ▶ n. **1** the action of referring to something. **2** a mention of a source of information in a book or article. **3** a letter giving information about how suitable someone is for a new job.

SYNONYMS **1 mention**, allusion, quotation, comment, remark. **2 source**, citation, authority, credit. **3 testimonial**, recommendation, character reference, credentials.

SPELLING

One **r** in the middle, not two: reference.

ref·er·en·dum /ˌrefəˈrendəm/ ▶ n. (plural **referendums** or **referenda** /-də/) a vote by the people of a country or state on a single political issue.

SYNONYMS (**popular**) **vote**, ballot, poll, plebiscite.

re·fer·ral /ri'fərəl/ ▶ n. the action of referring someone or something to a specialist or higher authority.

re·fill ▶ v. /rē'fil/ fill again. ▶ n. /'rē,fil/ an act of refilling something. ■ **re·fill·a·ble** adj.

re·fine /ri'fīn/ ▶ v. (**refines**, **refining**, **refined**) **1** make something pure by removing unwanted substances. **2** improve something by making minor changes. **3** (**refined**) well-educated, elegant, and having good taste.

SYNONYMS **1 purify**, filter, distill, process, treat. **2 improve**, perfect, polish (up), hone, fine-tune. **3** (**refined**) **cultivated**, cultured, polished, elegant, sophisticated, urbane, polite, gracious, well bred. **4** (**refined**) **discriminating**, discerning, fastidious, exquisite, impeccable, fine.

re·fine·ment /ri'fīnmənt/ ▶ n. **1** the process of refining. **2** an improvement. **3** the quality of being well-educated, elegant, and having good taste.

re·fin·er·y /ri'fīnərē/ ▶ n. (plural **refineries**) a factory where a substance such as oil is refined.

re·fit /rē'fit/ ▶ v. (**refits**, **refitting**, **refitted**) replace or repair equipment and fittings in a ship, building, etc. ▶ n. an act of refitting.

re·flect /ri'flekt/ ▶ v. **1** throw back heat, light, or sound from a surface. **2** (of a mirror) show an image of. **3** show in a realistic or appropriate way. **4** (**reflect well** or **badly on**) give a good or bad impression of. **5** (**reflect on**) think seriously about.

SYNONYMS **1 mirror**, send back, throw back, echo. **2 indicate**, show, display, demonstrate, be evidence of, evince, reveal, betray. **3 think**, consider, review, mull over, ponder, contemplate, deliberate, ruminate, meditate, muse, brood; formal cogitate.

re·flec·tion /ri'flekshən/ ▶ n. **1** the process of reflecting. **2** a reflected image. **3** a sign of something's true nature. **4** something that brings discredit. **5** serious thought.

SYNONYMS **1 image**, likeness. **2 indication**, display, demonstration, manifestation, expression, evidence. **3 thought**, consideration, contemplation, deliberation, pondering, rumination, meditation, musing; formal cogitation.

re·flec·tive /ri'flektiv/ ▶ adj. **1** providing a reflection. **2** thoughtful. ■ **re·flec·tive·ly** adv.

re·flec·tor /ri'flektər/ ▶ n. a piece of glass or plastic on the back of a vehicle for reflecting light.

re·flex /'rē,fleks/ ▶ n. an action done without conscious thought as a response to something. ▶ adj. **1** done as a reflex. **2** (of an angle) more than 180°.

re·flex·ive /ri'fleksiv/ ▶ adj. Grammar referring back to the subject of a clause or verb, e.g., *myself* in *I hurt myself*.

re·flex·ol·o·gy /,rē,flek'säləjē/ ▶ n. a system of massage used to relieve tension and treat illness. ■ **re·flex·ol·o·gist** n.

re·fo·cus /rē'fōkəs/ ▶ v. (**refocuses**, **refocusing** or **refocussing**, **refocused** or **refocussed**) **1** adjust the focus of a lens or your eyes. **2** focus attention on something new or different.

re·form /ri'fôrm/ ▶ v. **1** change something to improve it. **2** make someone improve their behavior. ▶ n. an act of reforming.

SYNONYMS ▶ v. **1 improve**, better, ameliorate, correct, rectify, restore, revise, refine, adapt, revamp, redesign, reconstruct, reorganize. **2 mend your ways**, change for the better, turn over a new leaf. ▶ n. **improvement**, amelioration, refinement, rectification, restoration, adaptation, revision, redesign, revamp, reconstruction, reorganization.

■ **re·form·er** n.

ref·or·ma·tion /,refər'māshən/ ▶ n. **1** the action of reforming. **2** (**the Reformation**) a 16th-century movement for reforming the Roman Catholic Church, leading to the establishment of the Protestant churches.

re·form·ist /ri'fôrmist/ ▶ adj. supporting political or social reform. ▶ n. a supporter of such reform. ■ **re·form·ism** n.

re·fract /ri'frakt/ ▶ v. (of water, air, or glass) make a ray of light change direction when it enters at an angle. ■ **re·frac·tive** adj.

re·frac·tion /ri'frakshən/ ▶ n. the fact or phenomenon of light changing direction when it enters water, air, or glass at an angle.

re·frac·to·ry /ri'fraktərē/ ▶ adj. **1** stubborn or difficult to control. **2** (of an illness) not responding to treatment.

re·frain[1] /ri'frān/ ▶ v. (**refrain from**) stop yourself from doing something.

SYNONYMS **abstain**, desist, hold back, stop yourself, forbear, avoid; informal swear off.

re·frain[2] ▶ n. a part of a song that is repeated at the end of each verse.

re·fresh /ri'fresh/ ▶ v. make someone feel less tired or hot.

SYNONYMS **1 reinvigorate**, revitalize, revive, rejuvenate, restore, energize, enliven, perk up, brace, freshen, wake up, breathe new life into; informal buck up. **2** *refresh your memory* **jog**, stimulate, prompt, prod.

re·fresh·er /ri'freshər/ ▶ n. a course intended to improve or update your skills or knowledge.

re·fresh·ing /ri'freshing/ ▶ adj. **1** making you feel less tired or hot. **2** pleasingly new or different.

SYNONYMS **1 invigorating**, revitalizing, reviving, bracing, fortifying, enlivening, stimulating, exhilarating, energizing. **2** *a refreshing change of direction* **welcome**, stimulating, fresh, new, imaginative, innovative.

■ **re·fresh·ing·ly** adv.

re·fresh·ment /ri'freshmənt/ ▶ n. **1** a snack or drink. **2** the giving of fresh energy.

SYNONYMS (**refreshments**) **food and drink**, snacks, tidbits; informal nosh, goodies, nibbles.

re·frig·er·ate /ri'frijə,rāt/ ▶ v. (**refrigerates**, **refrigerating**, **refrigerated**) make food or drink cold to keep it fresh. ■ **re·frig·er·a·tion** /ri,frijə'rāshən/ n.

re·frig·er·a·tor /ri'frijə,rātər/ ▶ n. an appliance or compartment that is artificially kept cool and used to store food and drink to keep it fresh.

SPELLING

No **d** in the middle: ref**rig**erator, not **-ridg-**.

re·fu·el /rē'fyo͞o(ə)l/ ▶ **v.** (**refuels**, **refueling**, **refueled**) supply with more fuel.

ref·uge /'ref,yo͞oj, -,yo͞ozн/ ▶ **n.** **1** shelter from danger or trouble. **2** a safe place.

SYNONYMS **1 shelter**, protection, safety, security, asylum, sanctuary. **2 place of safety**, shelter, haven, sanctuary, sanctum, retreat, hideout, den, hiding place.

ref·u·gee /,refyo͝o'jē, 'refyo͝o,jē/ ▶ **n.** a person who has been forced to leave their country because of a war or because they are being persecuted.

SYNONYMS **asylum seeker**, fugitive, displaced person, exile, émigré.

re·fund ▶ **v.** /ri'fənd, 'rē,fənd/ pay back money to. ▶ **n.** /'rē,fənd/ a repayment of a sum of money.

SYNONYMS ▶ **v. repay**, give back, return, pay back, reimburse, compensate, recompense. ▶ **n. repayment**, reimbursement, compensation, rebate.

re·fur·bish /ri'fərbisн/ ▶ **v.** redecorate and improve a building or room.

SYNONYMS **renovate**, recondition, rehabilitate, revamp, overhaul, restore, redecorate, upgrade, refit; informal do up.

■ **re·fur·bish·ment** **n.**

re·fus·al /ri'fyo͞ozəl/ ▶ **n.** **1** an act of refusing to do something. **2** an expression of unwillingness to accept or grant an offer or request.

SYNONYMS **nonacceptance**, no, rejection, rebuff; informal thumbs down.

ref·use[1] /ri'fyo͞oz/ ▶ **v.** (**refuses**, **refusing**, **refused**) say that you are unwilling to do or accept something.

SYNONYMS **1 decline**, turn down, say no to, reject, spurn, rebuff; informal pass up. **2 withhold**, deny. ANTONYMS accept.

ref·use[2] /'ref,yo͞os, -,yo͞oz/ ▶ **n.** things thrown away; rubbish.

SYNONYMS **trash**, garbage, rubbish, waste, litter; informal dreck, junk.

re·fute /ri'fyo͞ot/ ▶ **v.** (**refutes**, **refuting**, **refuted**) prove a statement or person to be wrong.

SYNONYMS **1 disprove**, prove wrong, rebut, explode, debunk, discredit, invalidate; informal shoot full of holes. **2 deny**, reject, repudiate, rebut, contradict.

■ **ref·u·ta·tion** /,refyo͝o'tāsнən/ **n.**

re·gain /ri'gān/ ▶ **v.** **1** get something back after losing possession of it. **2** get back to a place.

SYNONYMS **recover**, get back, win back, recoup, retrieve, repossess, take back, retake, recapture, reconquer.

re·gal /'rēgəl/ ▶ **adj.** having to do with a king or queen, especially in being magnificent or dignified.

SYNONYMS **royal**, kingly, queenly, princely, majestic.

■ **re·gal·ly** **adv.**

re·gale /ri'gāl/ ▶ **v.** (**regales**, **regaling**, **regaled**) **1** entertain someone with anecdotes or stories. **2** supply someone generously with food or drink.

re·ga·li·a /ri'gālyə/ ▶ **n.** **1** objects such as the crown and scepter used at coronations or other state occasions. **2** the distinctive clothes and items worn or carried on official occasions by important people.

re·gard /ri'gärd/ ▶ **v.** **1** think of in a particular way. **2** look steadily at. ▶ **n.** **1** concern or care. **2** high opinion; respect. **3** (**regards**) best wishes.

SYNONYMS ▶ **v. 1 consider**, look on, view, see, think of, judge, deem, estimate, assess, reckon, rate. **2 look at**, contemplate, eye, gaze at, stare at, observe, view, study, scrutinize. ▶ **n. 1 consideration**, care, concern, thought, notice, heed, attention. **2** *doctors are held in high regard* **esteem**, respect, admiration, approval, honor, estimation. **3** (**fixed**) **look**, gaze, stare, observation, contemplation, study, scrutiny. **4** *he sends his regards* **best wishes**, greetings, respects, compliments.

□ **as regards** (or **with regard to**) concerning.

re·gard·ing /ri'gärdiNG/ ▶ **prep.** about; concerning.

SYNONYMS **concerning**, as regards, with/in regard to, with respect to, with reference to, relating to, respecting, re, about, apropos, on the subject of, in connection with, vis-à-vis.

re·gard·less /ri'gärdləs/ ▶ **adv.** **1** (**regardless of**) without concern for. **2** despite what is happening.

SYNONYMS **anyway**, anyhow, in any case, nevertheless, nonetheless, despite everything, even so, all the same, in any event, come what may.

re·gat·ta /ri'gätə, ri'gatə/ ▶ **n.** a sports event consisting of a series of boat or yacht races.

re·gen·cy /'rējənsē/ ▶ **n.** (plural **regencies**) **1** a period of government by a regent. **2** (**the Regency**) the period when George, Prince of Wales, acted as regent in Britain (1811–20).

re·gen·er·ate /ri'jenə,rāt/ ▶ **v.** (**regenerates**, **regenerating**, **regenerated**) **1** bring new life or strength to. **2** grow new tissue. ■ **re·gen·er·a·tion** /ri,jenə'rāsнən, ,rē-/ **n.**

re·gent /'rējənt/ ▶ **n.** a person appointed to rule a state because the king or queen is too young or ill to rule, or is absent.

reg·gae /'regā, 'rāgā/ ▶ **n.** a style of popular music originating in Jamaica.

reg·i·cide /'rejə,sīd/ ▶ **n.** **1** the killing of a king. **2** a person who kills a king.

re·gime /ri'zнēm, rā-/ ▶ **n.** **1** a government, especially one that strictly controls a state. **2** an ordered way of doing something; a system.

SYNONYMS **1 government**, administration, leadership, rule, authority, control, command. **2 system**, arrangement, scheme, policy, method, course, plan, program.

reg·i·men /'rejəmən, 'rezн-/ ▶ **n.** a course of medical treatment, diet, or exercise.

reg·i·ment /'rejəmənt/ ▶ **n.** **1** a permanent unit of an army. **2** a large number of people. ■ **reg·i·men·tal** /,rejə'mentl/ **adj.**

re·gi·ment·ed /'rejəmantid/ ▶ **adj.** organized according to a strict system.

re·gion /'rējən/ ▶ **n.** **1** an area of a country or the world. **2** an administrative district of a city or country. **3** a part of the body.

SYNONYMS **district**, province, territory, division, area, section, sector, zone, belt, quarter.

□ **in the region of** approximately.

re·gion·al /'rējənl/ ▶ **adj.** relating to or typical of a region.

SYNONYMS **1 geographical**, territorial. **2 local**, provincial, district, parochial, zonal. ANTONYMS national.

■ **re·gion·al·ize** v. **re·gion·al·ly** adv.

reg·is·ter /ˈrejəstər/ ▶ n. **1** an official list or record. **2** a particular part of the range of a musical instrument or voice. **3** the level and style of a piece of writing or speech (e.g., informal, formal). ▶ v. (**registers**, **registering**, **registered**) **1** enter in a register. **2** put your name on a register. **3** express an opinion or emotion. **4** become aware of. **5** (of a measuring instrument) show a reading.

SYNONYMS ▶ n. **1 list**, roll, roster, index, directory, catalog, inventory. **2 record**, chronicle, log, ledger, archive, annals, files. ▶ v. **1 record**, enter, file, lodge, write down, submit, report, note, minute, log. **2 enroll**, put your name down, enlist, sign on/up, apply. **3 indicate**, read, record, show. **4 display**, show, express, exhibit, betray, reveal.

□ **registered nurse** a nurse who has graduated from a college or school of nursing.

reg·is·trar /ˈrejəˌsträr/ ▶ n. an official responsible for keeping official records.

reg·is·tra·tion /ˌrejəˈstrāsʜən/ ▶ n. **1** the action of registering or being registered. **2** a certificate that attests to the registering of a person, a car, etc.

reg·is·try /ˈrejəstrē/ ▶ n. (plural **registries**) **1** a place where registers are kept. **2** registration.

re·gress /riˈgres/ ▶ v. return to an earlier or less advanced state.

SYNONYMS **revert**, retrogress, relapse, lapse, backslide, slip back; deteriorate, decline, worsen, degenerate; informal go downhill. ANTONYMS progress.

■ **re·gres·sion** n.

re·gres·sive /riˈgresiv/ ▶ adj. **1** returning to a less advanced state. **2** (of a tax) taking a proportionally greater amount from those on lower incomes.

re·gret /riˈgret/ ▶ v. (**regrets**, **regretting**, **regretted**) feel sorry or disappointed about something you have done or should have done. ▶ n. a feeling of regretting something.

SYNONYMS ▶ v. **1 be sorry about**, feel contrite about, feel remorse for, rue, repent of. **2 mourn**, grieve for/over, weep over, sigh over, lament, bemoan. ANTONYMS welcome. ▶ n. **1 remorse**, contrition, repentance, compunction, ruefulness, self-reproach, pangs of conscience. **2 sadness**, sorrow, disappointment, unhappiness, grief.

re·gret·ful /riˈgretfəl/ ▶ adj. feeling or showing regret.

re·gret·ful·ly /riˈgretfəlē/ ▶ adv. **1** in a regretful way. **2** it is regrettable or undesirable that.

USAGE

The main sense of **regretfully** is 'in a regretful way' (*he sighed regretfully*). However, it is now also used to mean 'it is regrettable or undesirable that' (*regretfully, mounting costs forced the branch to close*), although some people object to this use.

re·gret·ta·ble /riˈgretəbəl/ ▶ adj. causing regret.

SYNONYMS **unfortunate**, unwelcome, sorry, woeful, disappointing, reprehensible, deplorable, disgraceful.

■ **re·gret·ta·bly** adv.

reg·u·lar /ˈregyələr, ˈreg(ə)lər/ ▶ adj. **1** following or arranged in an evenly spaced pattern or sequence. **2** done or happening frequently. **3** doing the same thing often. **4** following an accepted standard. **5** usual. **6** (in surfing and other board sports) with the left leg in front. **7** Grammar (of a word) following the normal pattern of inflection. **8** belonging to the permanent professional armed forces of a country. **9** (of a geometrical figure) having all sides and angles equal. ▶ n. a regular customer, member of a team, etc.

SYNONYMS ▶ adj. **1 uniform**, even, consistent, constant, unchanging, unvarying, fixed. **2 frequent**, repeated, continual, recurrent, periodic, constant, perpetual, numerous. **3 usual**, normal, customary, habitual, routine, typical, accustomed, established. ANTONYMS erratic, occasional, unusual.

■ **reg·u·lar·i·ty** /ˌregyəˈlaritē/ n. **reg·u·lar·ly** adv.

reg·u·lar·ize /ˈregyələˌrīz/ ▶ v. (**regularizes**, **regularizing**, **regularized**) **1** make regular. **2** make a temporary situation legal or official.

reg·u·late /ˈregyəˌlāt/ ▶ v. (**regulates**, **regulating**, **regulated**) **1** control the rate or speed of a machine or process. **2** control or supervise by means of rules.

SYNONYMS **1 control**, adjust, balance, set, synchronize. **2 police**, supervise, monitor, be responsible for, control, manage, direct, govern.

■ **reg·u·la·tor** n. **reg·u·la·to·ry** /ˈregyələˌtôrē/ adj.

reg·u·la·tion /ˌreg(y)əˈlāsʜən/ ▶ n. **1** a rule made by an authority. **2** the action of regulating. ▶ adj. informal of a familiar or expected type: *regulation blonde hair*.

SYNONYMS ▶ n. **1 rule**, order, directive, act, law, bylaw, statute, dictate, decree. **2 control**, policing, supervision, superintendence, monitoring, governance, management, administration, responsibility.

re·gur·gi·tate /riˈgərjəˌtāt/ ▶ v. (**regurgitates**, **regurgitating**, **regurgitated**) **1** bring swallowed food up again to the mouth. **2** repeat information without understanding it. ■ **re·gur·gi·ta·tion** /riˌgərjəˈtāsʜən/ n.

re·ha·bil·i·tate /ˌrē(h)əˈbiləˌtāt/ ▶ v. (**rehabilitates**, **rehabilitating**, **rehabilitated**) **1** help someone who has been ill or in prison to return to normal life. **2** restore the reputation of someone previously out of favor.

SYNONYMS **1 reintegrate**, readapt; informal rehab. **2 reinstate**, restore, bring back, pardon, absolve, exonerate, forgive; formal exculpate. **3 recondition**, restore, renovate, refurbish, revamp, overhaul, redevelop, rebuild, reconstruct.

■ **re·ha·bil·i·ta·tion** /-ˌbiləˈtāsʜən/ n.

re·hash /rēˈhasʜ/ ▶ v. reuse old ideas or material. ▶ n. a reuse of old ideas or material.

re·hears·al /riˈhərsəl/ ▶ n. a trial performance of a play or other work for later public performance.

SYNONYMS **practice**, trial performance, read-through, run-through, drill, training, coaching; informal dry run.

re·hearse /riˈhərs/ ▶ v. (**rehearses**, **rehearsing**, **rehearsed**) **1** practice a play, piece of music, etc., for later public performance. **2** state points that have been made many times before.

SYNONYMS **1 prepare**, practice, read through, run through/over, go over. **2 train**, drill, prepare, coach. **3 list**, enumerate, itemize, detail, spell out, catalog, recite, repeat, go over, run through, recap.

re·hy·drate /rē'hī͵drāt/ ▶ **v.** (**rehydrates**, **rehydrating**, **rehydrated**) add moisture to something dehydrated. ■ **re·hy·dra·tion** /͵rēhī'drāsʜən/ **n.**

Reich /rīk, rīʜ/ ▶ **n.** the former German state, in particular the **Third Reich** (the Nazi regime, 1933–45).

reign /rān/ ▶ **v. 1** rule as king or queen. **2** be the main quality or aspect: *confusion reigned.* **3** (**reigning**) currently holding a particular title in sports. ▶ **n.** the period of rule of a king or queen.

SYNONYMS ▶ **v. 1 be king/queen**, sit on the throne, wear the crown, be supreme, rule. **2** *chaos reigned* **prevail**, exist, be present, be the case, occur, be rife, be rampant, be the order of the day. ▶ **n. rule**, sovereignty, monarchy, dominion, control.

re·im·burse /͵rē-im'bərs/ ▶ **v.** (**reimburses**, **reimbursing**, **reimbursed**) repay money to. ■ **re·im·burse·ment n.**

rein /rān/ ▶ **n.** (**reins**) **1** long, narrow straps attached to a horse's bit, used to control the horse. **2** the power to direct and control something. ▶ **v. 1** control a horse by pulling on its reins. **2** (**rein someone/thing in** or **back**) restrain someone or something.

SYNONYMS ▶ **v. restrain**, check, curb, constrain, hold back/in, keep under control, regulate, restrict, control, curtail, limit.

□ **free rein** freedom of action.

re·in·car·nate /͵rē-in'kär͵nāt/ ▶ **v.** (**be reincarnated**) be born again in another body. ■ **re·in·car·na·tion** /͵rē-inkär'nāsʜən/ **n.**

rein·deer /'rān͵di(ə)r/ ▶ **n.** (plural **reindeer** or **reindeers**) a deer with large antlers, found in cold northern regions.

re·in·force /͵rē-in'fôrs/ ▶ **v.** (**reinforces**, **reinforcing**, **reinforced**) **1** make something stronger. **2** strengthen a military force with additional personnel.

SYNONYMS **1 strengthen**, fortify, bolster up, shore up, buttress, prop up, underpin, brace, support, boost. **2 augment**, increase, add to, supplement, boost, top off.

re·in·force·ment /͵rē-in'fôrsmənt/ ▶ **n. 1** the action of reinforcing. **2** (**reinforcements**) extra personnel sent to strengthen a military force.

SYNONYMS **1 strengthening**, fortification, bolstering, shoring up, buttressing. **2** *we need reinforcements* **additional troops**, auxiliaries, reserves, support, backup, help.

re·in·state /͵rē-in'stāt/ ▶ **v.** (**reinstates**, **reinstating**, **reinstated**) restore to a former position.

SYNONYMS **restore**, put back, bring back, reinstitute, reinstall, re-establish.

■ **re·in·state·ment n.**

re·it·er·ate /rē'itə͵rāt/ ▶ **v.** (**reiterates**, **reiterating**, **reiterated**) say something again or repeatedly.

SYNONYMS **repeat**, restate, recapitulate, recap, go over, rehearse.

■ **re·it·er·a·tion** /rē͵itə'rāsʜən/ **n.**

re·ject ▶ **v.** /ri'jekt/ **1** refuse to accept or agree to. **2** fail to show proper affection or concern for. **3** (of the body) react against a transplanted organ or tissue. ▶ **n.** /'rē͵jekt/ a rejected person or thing.

SYNONYMS ▶ **v. 1 turn down**, refuse, decline, say no to, spurn; informal pass up, give the thumbs down to. **2 rebuff**, spurn, shun, snub, cast off/aside, discard, abandon, desert, turn your back on, cold-shoulder; informal give someone the brush-off. ANTONYMS accept, welcome. ▶ **n. second**, discard, misshape, faulty item, castoff.

re·joice /ri'jois/ ▶ **v.** (**rejoices**, **rejoicing**, **rejoiced**) feel or show great joy.

SYNONYMS **be happy**, be glad, be delighted, celebrate, make merry; informal be over the moon. ANTONYMS mourn.

re·join[1] /rē'join, 'rē-/ ▶ **v.** join again.

SYNONYMS **return to**, be reunited with, join again, reach again, regain.

re·join[2] /ri'join/ ▶ **v.** formal say in reply; retort.

re·join·der /ri'joindər/ ▶ **n.** a quick reply.

re·ju·ve·nate /ri'jo͞ovə͵nāt/ ▶ **v.** (**rejuvenates**, **rejuvenating**, **rejuvenated**) make more lively or youthful.

SYNONYMS **revive**, revitalize, regenerate, breathe new life into, revivify, reanimate, resuscitate, refresh, reawaken; informal give a shot in the arm to, pep up, buck up.

re·kin·dle /rē'kindəl/ ▶ **v.** (**rekindles**, **rekindling**, **rekindled**) **1** revive a past feeling, relationship, etc. **2** relight a fire.

re·lapse ▶ **v.** /ri'laps, 'rē͵laps/ (**relapses**, **relapsing**, **relapsed**) **1** become ill again after a period of improvement. **2** (**relapse into**) return to a worse state. ▶ **n.** /'rē͵laps/ a return to bad health after a temporary improvement.

SYNONYMS ▶ **v. deteriorate**, degenerate, lapse, slip back, slide back, regress, revert, retrogress. ANTONYMS improve.

re·late /ri'lāt/ ▶ **v.** (**relates**, **relating**, **related**) **1** make or show a connection between. **2** (**be related**) be connected by blood or marriage. **3** (**relate to**) have to do with; concern. **4** (**relate to**) feel sympathy with. **5** give a spoken or written account of.

SYNONYMS **1** (**related**) **connected**, interconnected, associated, linked, allied, corresponding, analogous, parallel, comparable, equivalent. **2 tell**, recount, narrate, report, describe, recite, rehearse.

re·la·tion /ri'lāsʜən/ ▶ **n. 1** the way in which people or things are connected or related. **2** (**relations**) the way in which people or groups behave toward each other. **3** a relative.

SYNONYMS **1 connection**, relationship, association, link, tie-in, correlation, correspondence, parallel. **2 relative**, family member, kinsman, kinswoman; (**relations**) family, kin, kith and kin, kindred. **3** *our relations with Europe* **dealings**, communication, relationship, connections, contact, interaction.

re·la·tion·ship /ri'lāsʜən,sʜip/ ▶ **n. 1** the way in which people or things are connected or related. **2** the way in which people or groups behave toward each other. **3** an emotional and romantic association between two people.

SYNONYMS **1 connection**, relation, association, link, correlation, correspondence, parallel. **2 family ties**, kinship, affinity, common ancestry. **3 romance**, affair, love affair, liaison, amour, fling.

rel·a·tive /'relətiv/ ▶ **adj. 1** considered in relation or in proportion to something else. **2** existing or possessing a quality only in comparison to something else. **3** Grammar referring to an earlier noun, sentence, or clause. ▶ **n.** a person connected to another by blood or marriage.

SYNONYMS ▶ **adj. 1 comparative**, respective, comparable. **2 proportionate**, in proportion, commensurate, corresponding. ANTONYMS disproportionate. ▶ **n. relation**, member of the family, kinsman, kinswoman; (**relatives**) family, kin, kith and kin, kindred.

rel·a·tive·ly /'relətivlē/ ▶ **adv. 1** in comparison or proportion to something else. **2** quite.

rel·a·tiv·ism /'relətə,vizəm/ ▶ **n.** the idea that truth, morality, etc., exist only in relation to other things and are not absolute. ■ **rel·a·tiv·ist n.**

rel·a·tiv·i·ty /,relə'tivətē/ ▶ **n. 1** the state of being relative; ability to be judged only in comparison with something else. **2** Physics a description of matter, energy, space, and time according to Albert Einstein's theories.

re·lax /ri'laks/ ▶ **v. 1** become less tense, anxious, or rigid. **2** rest from work; do something recreational. **3** make a rule or restriction less strict.

SYNONYMS **1 rest**, loosen up, ease up/off, slow down, de-stress, unbend, unwind, put your feet up, take it easy; informal chill (out), hang loose, decompress. **2 loosen**, slacken, unclench, weaken, lessen. **3 moderate**, temper, ease, loosen, lighten, dilute, weaken, reduce, decrease; informal let up on. ANTONYMS tense, tighten.

re·lax·a·tion /ri,lak'sāsʜən, rē-/ ▶ **n. 1** the state of being free from tension and worry. **2** the action of making something less strict.

SYNONYMS **recreation**, enjoyment, amusement, entertainment, fun, pleasure, leisure.

re·lay ▶ **n.** /'rē,lā/ **1** a group of people or animals carrying out a task for a time and then replaced by a similar group. **2** a race between teams of runners, each team member in turn covering part of the total distance. **3** an electrical device that opens or closes a circuit in response to a current in another circuit. **4** a device that receives, strengthens, and transmits a signal again. ▶ **v.** /ri'lā, 'rē,lā/ **1** receive and pass on information. **2** broadcast something by means of a relay.

SYNONYMS ▶ **n. broadcast**, transmission, showing, feed. ▶ **v. pass on**, hand on, transfer, repeat, communicate, send, transmit, circulate.

re·lease /ri'lēs/ ▶ **v.** (**releases**, **releasing**, **released**) **1** set someone free from a place where they have been kept or trapped. **2** free someone from a duty, responsibility, etc. **3** allow to move freely. **4** allow information to be made available. **5** make a movie or recording available to the public. ▶ **n. 1** the action of releasing. **2** a movie or recording made available to the public.

SYNONYMS ▶ **v. 1 free**, set free, turn loose, let go/out, liberate, discharge. **2 untie**, undo, unfasten, loose, let go, unleash. **3 make public**, make known, issue, put out, publish, broadcast, circulate, launch, distribute. ANTONYMS imprison.

rel·e·gate /'relə,gāt/ ▶ **v.** (**relegates**, **relegating**, **relegated**) place in a lower rank or position.

SYNONYMS **downgrade**, demote, lower, put down, move down. ANTONYMS upgrade, promote.

■ **rel·e·ga·tion** /,relə'gāsʜən/ **n.**

re·lent /ri'lent/ ▶ **v. 1** finally agree to something after first refusing it. **2** become less severe or intense.

SYNONYMS **1 change your mind**, do a U-turn, back-pedal, back down, give way/in, capitulate, do an about-face; informal do a one-eighty. **2 ease**, slacken, let up, abate, drop, die down, lessen, decrease, subside, weaken, tail off.

re·lent·less /ri'lentləs/ ▶ **adj. 1** never stopping or ending. **2** harsh or inflexible.

SYNONYMS **1 persistent**, unfaltering, unremitting, unflagging, untiring, unwavering, dogged, single-minded, tireless, indefatigable. **2 harsh**, cruel, remorseless, unrelenting, merciless, pitiless, implacable, inexorable, unforgiving, unbending, unyielding.

■ **re·lent·less·ly adv.**

rel·e·vant /'reləvənt/ ▶ **adj.** closely connected or appropriate to the current subject.

SYNONYMS **pertinent**, applicable, apposite, material, apropos, to the point, germane.

■ **rel·e·vance n.**

SPELLING

Write **-ant**, not **-ent**: relev**ant**.

re·li·a·ble /ri'līəbəl/ ▶ **adj.** able to be depended on or trusted.

SYNONYMS **dependable**, trustworthy, good, safe, authentic, faithful, genuine, sound, true, loyal, unfailing; humorous trusty. ANTONYMS unreliable.

■ **re·li·a·bil·i·ty** /ri,līə'bilətē/ **n. re·li·a·bly adv.**

re·li·ance /ri'līəns/ ▶ **n.** dependence on or trust in someone or something.

SYNONYMS **1 dependence**, need. **2 trust**, confidence, faith, belief, conviction.

■ **re·li·ant adj.**

rel·ic /'relik/ ▶ **n. 1** an object or custom that survives from an earlier time. **2** a part of a holy person's body or belongings kept after their death.

SYNONYMS **artifact**, historical object, antiquity, remnant, vestige, remains.

re·lief /ri'lēf/ ▶ **n. 1** a feeling of reassurance and relaxation after anxiety or stress. **2** a cause of relief. **3** the action of relieving. **4** (also **light relief**) a temporary break in a tense or boring situation. **5** help given to people in need or difficulty. **6** a person or group replacing others who have been on duty. **7** a way of carving in which the design stands out from the surface.

SYNONYMS **1 respite**, remission, interruption, variation, diversion; informal letup. **2 alleviation**, relieving, palliation, soothing, easing, lessening, mitigation. **3 help**, aid, assistance, charity, succor. **4 replacement**, substitute, deputy, reserve, cover, stand-in, supply, locum, understudy.

□ **relief map** a map that indicates hills and valleys by shading. **relief pitcher** Baseball a pitcher who enters the game in place of the previous pitcher.

re·lieve /ri'lēv/ ▶ v. (**relieves**, **relieving**, **relieved**) **1** lessen or remove pain, difficulty, etc. **2** (**be relieved**) stop feeling anxious or stressed. **3** replace someone who is on duty. **4** (**relieve someone of**) take a responsibility from someone. **5** bring military support for a place that is surrounded by the enemy. **6** make something less boring. **7** (**relieve yourself**) go to the bathroom.

SYNONYMS **1 alleviate**, mitigate, ease, counteract, dull, reduce. **2** (**relieved**) **glad**, thankful, grateful, pleased, happy, reassured. **3 replace**, take over from, stand in for, fill in for, substitute for, deputize for, cover for. **4 free**, release, exempt, excuse, absolve, let off. ANTONYMS aggravate.

SPELLING

Remember, **i** before **e**, when the sound is *ee*, except after **c**: rel**ie**ve.

re·liev·er /ri'lēvər/ ▶ n. **1** a person or thing that relieves. **2** ⇨ RELIEF PITCHER.

re·li·gion /ri'lijən/ ▶ n. **1** belief in and worship of a God or gods. **2** a particular system of faith and worship.

SYNONYMS **faith**, belief, worship, creed, church, sect, denomination, cult.

re·li·gious /ri'lijəs/ ▶ adj. **1** concerned with or believing in a religion. **2** very careful and regular.

SYNONYMS **1 devout**, pious, reverent, godly, God-fearing, churchgoing. **2 spiritual**, theological, scriptural, doctrinal, ecclesiastical, church, holy, divine, sacred. **3 scrupulous**, conscientious, meticulous, punctilious, strict, rigorous. ANTONYMS atheistic, secular.

■ **re·li·gious·ly** adv.

SPELLING

Remember the second **i**: rel**i**g**i**ous, not -**gous**.

re·lin·quish /ri'linGkwisH/ ▶ v. give up something, especially unwillingly.

SYNONYMS **1 renounce**, resign, give up/away, hand over, let go of. **2 leave**, resign from, stand down from, bow out of, give up; informal quit. ANTONYMS retain.

rel·i·quar·y /'relə,kwerē/ ▶ n. (plural **reliquaries**) a container for holy relics.

rel·ish /'relisH/ ▶ n. **1** great enjoyment or anticipation. **2** a strongly flavored sauce or pickle. ▶ v. enjoy or look forward to.

SYNONYMS ▶ n. **1 enjoyment**, gusto, delight, pleasure, glee, appreciation, enthusiasm. **2 condiment**, sauce, dressing. ANTONYMS distaste. ▶ v. **enjoy**, delight in, love, adore, take pleasure in, rejoice in, appreciate, savor, revel in, luxuriate in, glory in. ANTONYMS dislike.

re·live /rē'liv, 'rē-/ ▶ v. (**relives**, **reliving**, **relived**) live through an experience or feeling again in your mind.

re·load /rē'lōd/ ▶ v. load something, especially a gun, again.

re·lo·cate /rē'lō,kāt, ,rēlō'kāt/ ▶ v. (**relocates**, **relocating**, **relocated**) move your home or business to a new place. ■ **re·lo·ca·tion** /,rēlō'kāsHən/ n.

re·luc·tance /ri'ləktəns/ ▶ n. unwillingness to do something.

SYNONYMS **unwillingness**, disinclination, hesitation, wavering, vacillation, doubts, second thoughts, misgivings.

re·luc·tant /ri'ləktənt/ ▶ adj. unwilling and hesitant.

SYNONYMS **unwilling**, disinclined, unenthusiastic, resistant, opposed, hesitant, loath. ANTONYMS willing, eager.

■ **re·luc·tant·ly** adv.

re·ly /ri'lī/ ▶ v. (**relies**, **relying**, **relied**) (**rely on**) **1** need or be dependent on. **2** have faith in; trust.

SYNONYMS **depend on**, count on, bank on, be confident of, be sure of, have faith in, trust in; informal swear by, figure on.

re·main /ri'mān/ ▶ v. **1** still be in the same place or condition. **2** continue to be. **3** be left over.

SYNONYMS **1 continue**, endure, last, abide, carry on, persist, stay around, survive, live on. **2 stay**, stay behind, stay put, wait behind, be left, hang on; informal hang around. **3** *he remained calm* **continue to be**, stay, keep.

re·main·der /ri'māndər/ ▶ n. **1** a part, number, or amount that is left over. **2** a part that is still to come. **3** the number left over when one quantity does not exactly divide another.

SYNONYMS **rest**, balance, residue, others, remnant(s), leftovers, surplus, extra, excess.

re·mains /ri'mānz/ ▶ pl.n. **1** things that remain or are left. **2** historical or archaeological relics. **3** a person's body after death.

SYNONYMS **1 remainder**, residue, rest, remnant(s), leftovers, scraps, debris, detritus. **2 antiquities**, relics, artifacts. **3 corpse**, body, carcass, bones; Medicine cadaver.

re·make ▶ v. /rē'māk, 'rē-/ (**remakes**, **remaking**, past and past participle **remade**) make again or differently. ▶ n. /'rē,māk/ a movie or piece of music that has been filmed or recorded again and re-released.

re·mand /ri'mand/ ▶ v. send a defendant to wait for their trial, either on bail or in jail. □ **on remand** in jail before being tried.

re·mark /ri'märk/ ▶ v. **1** say as a comment. **2** notice. ▶ n. a comment.

SYNONYMS ▶ v. **comment**, say, observe, mention, reflect; formal opine. ▶ n. **comment**, statement, utterance, observation, reflection.

re·mark·a·ble /ri'märkəbəl/ ▶ adj. extraordinary or striking.

SYNONYMS **extraordinary**, exceptional, outstanding, notable, striking, memorable, unusual, conspicuous, momentous. ANTONYMS ordinary.

■ **re·mark·a·bly** adv.

re·match /ˈrēˌmacн/ ▶ **n.** a second match between two teams or players.

re·me·di·al /riˈmēdēəl/ ▶ **adj.** **1** intended as a remedy. **2** provided for children with learning difficulties.

rem·e·dy /ˈremədē/ ▶ **n.** (plural **remedies**) **1** a medicine or treatment for a disease or injury. **2** a means of dealing with something undesirable. ▶ **v.** (**remedies**, **remedying**, **remedied**) put right an undesirable situation.

SYNONYMS ▶ **n.** **1 treatment**, cure, medicine, medication, medicament, drug. **2 solution**, answer, cure, fix, antidote, panacea. ▶ **v.** **put right**, set right, rectify, solve, sort out, straighten out, resolve, correct, repair, mend, fix.

re·mem·ber /riˈmembər/ ▶ **v.** (**remembers**, **remembering**, **remembered**) **1** have in your mind someone or something from the past. **2** not forget to do something necessary or important. **3** (**remember someone to**) pass on greetings from one person to another.

SYNONYMS **1 recall**, call to mind, recollect, think of, reminisce about, look back on. **2 memorize**, retain, learn by heart, get down pat. **3 bear in mind**, be mindful of, take into account. **4 commemorate**, pay tribute to, honor, salute, pay homage to. ANTONYMS forget.

re·mem·brance /riˈmembrəns/ ▶ **n.** **1** the action of remembering. **2** a memory. **3** a thing acting as a reminder of someone.

SYNONYMS **1 recollection**, reminiscence, recall. **2 commemoration**, memory, recognition.

re·mind /riˈmīnd/ ▶ **v.** **1** help someone to remember something. **2** (**remind someone of**) make someone think of someone or something because of a resemblance.

SYNONYMS **jog someone's memory**, prompt.

re·mind·er /riˈmīndər/ ▶ **n.** a thing that makes someone remember something.

rem·i·nisce /ˌreməˈnis/ ▶ **v.** (**reminisces**, **reminiscing**, **reminisced**) think or talk about the past.

rem·i·nis·cence /ˌreməˈnisəns/ ▶ **n.** **1** an account of something that you remember. **2** the enjoyable remembering of past events.

rem·i·nis·cent /ˌreməˈnisənt/ ▶ **adj.** **1** (**reminiscent of**) tending to remind you of something. **2** absorbed in memories.

SYNONYMS *the painting is* ***reminiscent of*** *an early Picasso* **similar to**, comparable with, evocative of, suggestive of, redolent of.

re·miss /riˈmis/ ▶ **adj.** not giving something proper attention or care.

SYNONYMS **negligent**, neglectful, irresponsible, careless, thoughtless, heedless, derelict, lax, slack, slipshod, lackadaisical; informal sloppy. ANTONYMS careful.

re·mis·sion /riˈmisнən/ ▶ **n.** **1** a temporary period during which a serious illness becomes less severe. **2** the cancelation of a debt, penalty, etc.

re·mit ▶ **n.** /riˈmit, ˈrēˌmit/ the task or area of activity officially given to a person or organization. ▶ **v.** /riˈmit/ (**remits**, **remitting**, **remitted**) **1** send money in payment. **2** cancel a debt or punishment. **3** refer a matter to an authority for a decision.

SYNONYMS ▶ **v.** **1 send**, dispatch, forward, hand over, pay. **2 pardon**, forgive, excuse.

re·mit·tance /riˈmitns/ ▶ **n.** **1** a sum of money sent as payment. **2** the action of remitting money.

re·mix ▶ **v.** /rēˈmiks, ˈrē-/ produce a different version of a musical recording by altering the balance of the separate parts. ▶ **n.** /ˈrēˌmiks/ a remixed recording.

rem·nant /ˈremnənt/ ▶ **n.** a small remaining quantity of something.

SYNONYMS **remains**, remainder, leftovers, residue, rest.

re·mon·strate /riˈmänˌstrāt, ˈremən-/ ▶ **v.** (**remonstrates**, **remonstrating**, **remonstrated**) complain or protest strongly.

SYNONYMS **protest**, complain, object, take issue, argue, expostulate.

■ **re·mon·stra·tion** /riˌmänˈstrāsнən, ˌremən-/ **n.**

re·morse /riˈmôrs/ ▶ **n.** deep regret or guilt for something wrong that you have done.

SYNONYMS **regret**, guilt, contrition, repentance, shame.

re·morse·ful /riˈmôrsfəl/ ▶ **adj.** filled with deep regret or guilt.

SYNONYMS **sorry**, regretful, contrite, repentant, penitent, guilt-ridden, conscience-stricken, chastened, self-reproachful. ANTONYMS unrepentant.

■ **re·morse·ful·ly adv.**

re·morse·less /riˈmôrsləs/ ▶ **adj.** **1** (of something unpleasant) never ending or improving. **2** without remorse. ■ **re·morse·less·ly adv.**

re·mote /riˈmōt/ ▶ **adj.** (**remoter**, **remotest**) **1** far away in space or time. **2** situated far from the main centers of population. **3** having very little connection. **4** (of a chance or possibility) unlikely to happen. **5** unfriendly and distant in manner. **6** operating or operated by means of radio or infrared signals.

SYNONYMS **1 isolated**, far-off, faraway, distant, out of the way, off the beaten track, secluded, lonely, inaccessible, in the backwoods; informal in the middle of nowhere. **2** *a remote possibility* **unlikely**, improbable, doubtful, dubious, faint, slight, slim, small, slender. **3 aloof**, distant, detached, withdrawn, unforthcoming, unapproachable, unresponsive, unfriendly, unsociable, introspective, introverted; informal standoffish. ANTONYMS close.

□ **remote control 1** control of a machine from a distance by means of signals transmitted from a radio or electronic device. **2** a device that controls a machine in this way. ■ **re·mote·ly adv.** **re·mote·ness n.**

re·mov·al /riˈmo͞ovəl/ ▶ **n.** **1** the act of removing something, especially something unwanted. **2** the dismissal of someone from a job or office.

SYNONYMS **1 taking away**, withdrawal, abolition. **2 dismissal**, ejection, expulsion, ousting, deposition; informal sacking, firing. **3 move**, transfer, relocation.

re·move /riˈmo͞ov/ ▶ **v.** (**removes**, **removing**, **removed**) **1** take something away from the position it occupies. **2** abolish or get rid of. **3** dismiss from a post. **4** (**be removed**) be very different from. **5** (**removed**) separated by a particular number of steps of descent: *a second cousin once removed.* ▶ **n.** the amount by which things are separated.

> SYNONYMS ▶ **v. 1 take off**, take away, move, take out, pull out, withdraw, detach, undo, unfasten, disconnect. **2 dismiss**, discharge, get rid of, eject, expel, oust, depose, unseat; informal sack, fire, kick out. **3 abolish**, withdraw, eliminate, get rid of, do away with, stop, cut; informal ax. ANTONYMS attach, insert.

■ **re·mov·a·ble adj.**

re·mu·ner·ate /ri'myo͞onə,rāt/ ▶ **v.** (**remunerates**, **remunerating**, **remunerated**) formal pay someone for work they have done. ■ **re·mu·ner·a·tion** /ri,myo͞onə'rāsʜən/ **n.**

re·mu·ner·a·tive /-rətiv, -,rātiv/ ▶ **adj.** formal paying a lot of money.

Ren·ais·sance /'renə,säns, -,zäns/ ▶ **n. 1** the revival of classical styles in art and literature in the 14th–16th centuries. **2** (**renaissance**) a period of renewed interest in something.

> SYNONYMS (**renaissance**) **revival**, renewal, resurrection, reawakening, re-emergence, rebirth, reappearance, resurgence.

re·nal /'rēnl/ ▶ **adj.** technical to do with the kidneys.

re·name /rē'nām, 'rē-/ ▶ **v.** (**renames**, **renaming**, **renamed**) give a new name to.

re·nas·cence /ri'nasəns, ri'nāsəns/ ▶ **n.** formal a revival or rebirth. ■ **re·nas·cent adj.**

rend /rend/ ▶ **v.** (**rends**, **rending**, **rent**) literary tear something to pieces.

rend·er /'rendər/ ▶ **v.** (**renders**, **rendering**, **rendered**) **1** provide or give a service, help, etc. **2** hand over for inspection, consideration, or payment. **3** cause to be or become: *he was rendered speechless*. **4** perform a piece of music or drama. **5** melt down fat to separate out its impurities. **6** cover a wall with a coat of plaster.

> SYNONYMS **1 make**, cause to be/become, turn, leave. **2 give**, provide, supply, contribute, furnish. **3 act**, perform, play, depict, portray, interpret, represent, draw, paint, execute.

ren·dez·vous /'rändi,vo͞o, -dā-/ ▶ **n.** (plural **rendezvous** /-,vo͞oz/) **1** a meeting at an agreed time and place. **2** a meeting place. ▶ **v.** (**rendezvouses** /-,vo͞oz/ , **rendezvousing** /-,vo͞oiɴɢ/ , **rendezvoused** /-,vo͞od/) meet at an agreed time and place.

> SYNONYMS ▶ **n. meeting**, appointment, assignation; informal date; literary tryst. ▶ **v. meet**, come together, gather, assemble.

ren·di·tion /ren'disʜən/ ▶ **n. 1** a performance or version of a piece of music or drama. **2** (also **extraordinary rendition**) sending a prisoner to be interrogated in a country where they may be tortured.

ren·e·gade /'reni,gād/ ▶ **n. 1** a person who deserts and betrays an organization, country, or set of principles. **2** a person who behaves in a rebelliously unconventional manner.

> SYNONYMS **1 traitor**, defector, deserter, turncoat, rebel, mutineer. **2** *a renegade militia commander* **treacherous**, traitorous, disloyal, treasonous, rebel, mutinous. **3** *a renegade cleric* **apostate**, heretic, heretical, dissident.

re·nege /ri'neg, -'nig/ ▶ **v.** (**reneges**, **reneging**, **reneged**) go back on an agreement or promise.

> SYNONYMS **default on**, fail to honor, go back on, break, back out of, withdraw from, retreat from, backtrack on, break your word/promise. ANTONYMS honor.

re·new /ri'n(y)o͞o/ ▶ **v. 1** start doing something again after an interruption. **2** give fresh life or strength to. **3** make a license, subscription, etc., valid for a further period. **4** replace something broken or worn out.

> SYNONYMS **1 resume**, return to, take up again, come back to, begin again, restart, recommence, continue (with), carry on (with). **2 reaffirm**, repeat, reiterate, restate. **3 revive**, regenerate, revitalize, reinvigorate, restore, resuscitate. **4 renovate**, restore, refurbish, revamp, remodel, modernize; informal do up.

■ **re·new·a·ble adj. re·new·al n.**

ren·net /'renit/ ▶ **n.** a substance used to curdle milk in order to make cheese.

re·nounce /ri'nouns/ ▶ **v.** (**renounces**, **renouncing**, **renounced**) **1** formally give up a title or possession. **2** state that you no longer have a particular belief or allegiance. **3** abandon a cause, habit, etc.

> SYNONYMS **1 give up**, relinquish, abandon, surrender, waive, forego, desist from, keep off; informal say goodbye to. **2 reject**, repudiate, deny, abandon, wash your hands of, turn your back on, disown, spurn, shun.

ren·o·vate /'renə,vāt/ ▶ **v.** (**renovates**, **renovating**, **renovated**) restore something old to a good state; repair.

> SYNONYMS **modernize**, restore, refurbish, revamp, recondition, rehabilitate, update, upgrade, refit; informal do up.

■ **ren·o·va·tion** /,renə'vāsʜən/ **n.**

re·nown /ri'noun/ ▶ **n.** the state of being famous.

> SYNONYMS **fame**, distinction, eminence, illustriousness, prominence, repute, reputation, prestige, acclaim, celebrity, notability.

re·nowned /ri'nound/ ▶ **adj.** known or talked about by many people; famous.

> SYNONYMS **famous**, well-known, celebrated, famed, eminent, distinguished, acclaimed, illustrious, prominent, great, esteemed. ANTONYMS unknown.

rent¹ /rent/ ▶ **n.** a regular payment made for the use of property or land. ▶ **v. 1** regularly pay money to someone for the use of property or land. **2** let someone use property or land in return for payment.

> SYNONYMS ▶ **n. rental**, (rental) fee, (rental) payment. ▶ **v. 1 hire**, lease, charter. **2 let (out)**, lease (out), hire (out), charter (out).

rent² past and past participle of **REND** ▶ **n.** a large tear in a piece of fabric.

ren·tal /'rentl/ ▶ **n. 1** an amount paid as rent. **2** the action of renting.

re·nun·ci·a·tion /ri,nənsē'āsʜən/ ▶ **n.** the action of renouncing or giving up something.

re·or·gan·ize /rē'ôrgə,nīz/ ▶ **v.** (**reorganizes**, **reorganizing**, **reorganized**) change the organization of. ■ **re·or·gan·i·za·tion** /,rē,ôrgənə'zāsʜən/ **n.**

rep /rep/ ▶ **n.** informal **1** a representative. **2** repertory.

Rep. ▶ abbr. **1** (in a legislature) Representative. **2** a Republican.

re·paid /rē'pād/ past and past participle of **REPAY**.

re·pair¹ /ri'pe(ə)r/ ▶ v. restore something damaged or worn to a good condition. ▶ n. **1** an act of repairing something. **2** the condition of an object: *in good repair*.

SYNONYMS ▶ v. **1 mend**, fix (up), put/set right, restore (to working order), overhaul, renovate; informal patch up. **2 rectify**, make good, (put) right, correct, make up for, make amends for, compensate for, redress. ▶ n. **1 restoration**, mending, overhaul, renovation. **2 mend**, darn, patch. **3** *in good repair* **condition**, working order, state, shape, fettle.

■ **re·pair·er** n.

re·pair² ▶ v. (**repair to**) go to a place.

rep·a·ra·ble /'rep(ə)rəbəl/ ▶ adj. able to be repaired.

rep·a·ra·tion /ˌrepə'rāsʜən/ ▶ n. **1** something done to make up for a wrong. **2** (**reparations**) compensation for war damage paid by a defeated country.

rep·ar·tee /ˌrepər'tē, ˌrepˌär'tē, -'tā/ ▶ n. quick, witty comments or conversation.

re·past /ri'past, 'rēˌpast/ ▶ n. formal a meal.

re·pa·tri·ate /rē'pātrēˌāt, rē'pa-/ ▶ v. (**repatriates**, **repatriating**, **repatriated**) send someone back to their own country. ■ **re·pa·tri·a·tion** /ˌrēˌpātrē'āsʜən, ˌrēˌpa-/ n.

re·pay /rē'pā/ ▶ v. (**repays**, **repaying**, **repaid**) **1** pay back money owed to someone. **2** do something as a reward for a favor or kindness. **3** be worthy of investigation, attention, etc.

SYNONYMS **1 reimburse**, refund, pay back, recompense, compensate, remunerate, settle up with. **2** *he repaid her kindness* **reciprocate**, return, requite, reward.

■ **re·pay·ment** n.

re·peal /ri'pēl/ ▶ v. make a law no longer valid. ▶ n. the action of repealing.

SYNONYMS ▶ v. **cancel**, abolish, reverse, rescind, revoke, annul, quash. ANTONYMS enact. ▶ n. **cancellation**, abolition, reversal, rescinding, annulment.

re·peat /ri'pēt/ ▶ v. **1** say or do again. **2** (**repeat yourself**) say the same thing again. **3** (**repeat itself**) happen again in the same way or form. ▶ n. **1** something that happens or is done again. **2** a repeated broadcast of a television or radio program.

SYNONYMS ▶ v. **1 say again**, restate, reiterate, go/run through again, recapitulate, recap. **2 recite**, quote, parrot, regurgitate, echo. **3 do again**, redo, replicate, duplicate. **4** (**repeated**) **recurrent**, frequent, persistent, continual, incessant, constant, regular, periodic, numerous, (very) many. ▶ n. **repetition**, replication, duplicate.

re·peat·ed·ly /ri'pētidlē/ ▶ adv. more than once; frequently: *he tried repeatedly to hit that low note*.

SYNONYMS **frequently**, often, again and again, over and over (again), time and (time) again, many times, persistently, recurrently, constantly, continually, regularly, oftentimes.

re·pel /ri'pel/ ▶ v. (**repels**, **repelling**, **repelled**) **1** drive back or away. **2** make someone feel disgust. **3** force away something with a similar magnetic charge.

SYNONYMS **1 fight off**, repulse, drive back, force back, beat back, hold off, ward off, fend off, keep at bay. **2 revolt**, disgust, repulse, sicken, nauseate, turn someone's stomach; informal turn off, gross out. ANTONYMS attract.

re·pel·lent /ri'pelənt/ ▶ adj. **1** causing disgust or distaste. **2** able to keep a particular substance out: *water-repellent nylon*. ▶ n. **1** a substance that keeps insects away. **2** a substance used to treat something so that water cannot pass through it.

SYNONYMS ▶ adj. **1 revolting**, repulsive, disgusting, repugnant, sickening, nauseating, stomach-turning, vile, nasty, foul, awful, horrible, dreadful, terrible, obnoxious, loathsome, offensive, objectionable, abhorrent, despicable, reprehensible, contemptible, odious, hateful; informal ghastly, horrid, gross; literary noisome. **2 impermeable**, impervious, resistant, -proof.

re·pent /ri'pent/ ▶ v. feel sorry for something bad that you have done.

SYNONYMS **feel remorse**, regret, be sorry, rue, reproach yourself, be ashamed, feel contrite, be penitent, be remorseful.

re·pent·ant /ri'pentənt/ ▶ adj. feeling or expressing sincere regret or remorse about something bad or wrong that one has done.

SYNONYMS **penitent**, contrite, regretful, rueful, remorseful, apologetic, chastened, ashamed, shamefaced. ANTONYMS impenitent.

■ **re·pent·ance** n.

re·per·cus·sions /ˌrēpər'kəsʜənz, ˌrep-/ ▶ pl.n. the consequences of an event or action.

SYNONYMS **consequence(s)**, result(s), effect(s), outcome(s), reverberation(s), backlash, aftermath, fallout.

rep·er·toire /'repə(r)ˌtwär/ ▶ n. the material known or regularly performed by a performer or company.

SYNONYMS **collection**, range, repertory, list, store, stock, repository, supply.

rep·er·to·ry /'repə(r)ˌtôrē/ ▶ n. (plural **repertories**) **1** the performance by a company of various plays, operas, etc., at regular intervals. **2** a repertoire.

rep·e·ti·tion /ˌrepə'tisʜən/ ▶ n. **1** the action of repeating. **2** a repeat of something.

SYNONYMS **1 reiteration**, restatement, retelling. **2 repetitiousness**, repetitiveness, tautology.

rep·e·ti·tious /ˌrepə'tisʜəs/ ▶ adj. having too much repetition; repetitive.

SYNONYMS **recurring**, recurrent, repeated, unvaried, unchanging, routine, mechanical, automatic, monotonous, boring. ANTONYMS varied.

re·pet·i·tive /ri'petətiv/ ▶ adj. involving repetition; repeated many or too many times.

SYNONYMS **recurring**, recurrent, repeated, unvaried, unchanging, routine, mechanical, automatic, monotonous, boring. ANTONYMS varied.

■ **re·pet·i·tive·ly** adv.

re·phrase /rē'frāz/ ▶ v. (**rephrases**, **rephrasing**, **rephrased**) express something in an alternative way.

re·pine /ri'pīn/ ▶ v. (**repines**, **repining**, **repined**) literary be unhappy or anxious.

re·place /ri'plās/ ▶ v. (**replaces**, **replacing**, **replaced**) **1** take the place of. **2** provide a substitute for. **3** put something back in its previous position.

SYNONYMS **1 put back**, return, restore. **2 take the place of**, succeed, take over from, supersede, stand in for, substitute for, deputize for; informal step into someone's shoes/boots. **3 substitute**, exchange, change, swap.

■ **re·place·a·ble** adj.

re·place·ment /ri'plāsmənt/ ▶ n. **1** the action of replacing. **2** a person or thing that takes the place of another.

SYNONYMS **substitute**, stand-in, fill-in, locum, understudy, relief, cover, proxy, surrogate.

re·play /'rē,plā/ ▶ n. **1** a match or contest that is played again because the previous game was a draw. **2** an act of playing a recording again, especially so as to be able to watch an incident or sports play more closely. ▶ v. /rē'plā, 'rē,plā/ **1** play back a recording. **2** play a match or game again.

re·plen·ish /ri'plenisн/ ▶ v. fill up a supply again after using some of it.

SYNONYMS **1 refill**, top off, fill up, recharge, freshen. **2 stock up**, restock, restore, replace. ANTONYMS empty.

■ **re·plen·ish·ment** n.

re·plete /ri'plēt/ ▶ adj. **1** (**replete with**) filled or well-supplied with. **2** very full with food.
■ **re·ple·tion** n.

rep·li·ca /'replikə/ ▶ n. an exact copy or model of something.

SYNONYMS **copy**, model, duplicate, reproduction, dummy, imitation, facsimile.

rep·li·cate /'repli,kāt/ ▶ v. (**replicates**, **replicating**, **replicated**) make an exact copy of. ■ **rep·li·ca·tion** /,repli'kāsнən/ n.

re·ply /ri'plī/ ▶ v. (**replies**, **replying**, **replied**) **1** say or write a response to something said or written. **2** respond with a similar action. ▶ n. (plural **replies**) a spoken or written response.

SYNONYMS ▶ v. **respond**, answer, write back, rejoin, retort, riposte, counter, come back. ▶ n. **answer**, response, rejoinder, retort, riposte; informal comeback.

re·port /ri'pôrt/ ▶ v. **1** give a spoken or written account of something. **2** (**be reported**) be said or rumored. **3** make a formal complaint about. **4** tell someone in authority that you have arrived or are ready to do something. **5** (**report to**) be responsible to a manager. ▶ n. **1** a spoken or written account of something. **2** the sound of an explosion or a gun being fired.

SYNONYMS ▶ v. **1 communicate**, announce, divulge, disclose, reveal, relay, describe, narrate, delineate, detail, document, give an account of, make public, publish, broadcast, proclaim, publicize. **2** *his son reported him to the police* **inform on**; informal tell on, squeal on, rat on. **3** *I reported for duty* **present yourself**, arrive, turn up, clock in; informal show up. ▶ n. **1 account**, record, minutes, proceedings, transcript. **2 news**, information, word, intelligence. **3 story**, account, article, piece, item, column, feature, bulletin, dispatch, communiqué. **4 rumor**, whisper; informal buzz. **5 bang**, crack, explosion, boom.

□ **report card** a teacher's written assessment of a student's progress. **reported speech** a speaker's words reported with the required changes of person and tense (e.g., *he said that he would go*, based on *I will go*).

re·port·age /rə'pôrtij, ,repôr'täzн/ ▶ n. the reporting of news by the press and the broadcasting media.

re·port·er /ri'pôrtər/ ▶ n. a person who reports news for a newspaper or broadcasting company.

SYNONYMS **journalist**, correspondent, newsman, newswoman, columnist; informal hack, stringer.

re·pose /ri'pōz/ ▶ n. a state of restfulness, peace, or calm. ▶ v. (**reposes**, **reposing**, **reposed**) lie or be kept in a particular place.

re·pos·i·to·ry /ri'päzə,tôrē/ ▶ n. (plural **repositories**) **1** a place or container for storage. **2** a place where a lot of something is found.

re·pos·sess /,rēpə'zes/ ▶ v. take possession of something when a buyer fails to make the required payments. ■ **re·pos·ses·sion** n.

rep·re·hen·si·ble /,repri'hensəbəl/ ▶ adj. deserving condemnation; bad.

SYNONYMS **deplorable**, disgraceful, discreditable, despicable, blameworthy, culpable, wrong, bad, shameful, dishonorable, inexcusable, unforgivable, indefensible, unjustifiable. ANTONYMS praiseworthy.

rep·re·sent /,repri'zent/ ▶ v. **1** act and speak on behalf of. **2** amount to. **3** be a specimen or example of. **4** show or describe in a particular way. **5** depict in a work of art. **6** signify or symbolize.

SYNONYMS **1 stand for**, symbolize, personify, epitomize, typify, embody, illustrate, exemplify. **2 depict**, portray, render, picture, delineate, show, illustrate. **3 appear for**, act for, speak on behalf of.

rep·re·sen·ta·tion /,repri,zen'tāsнən, -zən-/ ▶ n. **1** the action of representing. **2** an image, model, etc., of something. **3** (**representations**) statements made to an authority.

SYNONYMS **1 portrayal**, depiction, delineation, presentation, rendition. **2 likeness**, painting, drawing, picture, illustration, sketch, image, model, figure, statue.

rep·re·sen·ta·tion·al /,repri,zen'tāsнənl/ ▶ adj. **1** relating to representation. **2** (of art) not abstract.

rep·re·sen·ta·tive /,repri'zentətiv/ ▶ adj. **1** typical of a class or group. **2** consisting of people chosen to act and speak on behalf of a wider group. **3** portraying or symbolizing something. ▶ n. **1** a person chosen to act and speak for another or others. **2** a person who travels around trying to sell their company's products. **3** an example of a class or group.

SYNONYMS ▶ adj. **1 typical**, archetypal, characteristic, illustrative, indicative. **2 symbolic**, emblematic. ANTONYMS atypical. ▶ n. **1 spokesperson**, spokesman, spokeswoman, agent, official, mouthpiece. **2 salesman**, commercial traveler, agent, negotiator; informal rep. **3 deputy**, substitute, stand-in, proxy, delegate, ambassador, emissary.

re·press /ri'pres/ ▶ v. **1** bring under control by force. **2** try not to have or show a thought or feeling. **3** (**repressed**) tending to keep your feelings or desires hidden.

SYNONYMS **1 suppress**, quell, quash, subdue, put down, crush, extinguish, stamp out, defeat, contain. **2 oppress**, subjugate, keep down, tyrannize. **3 restrain**, hold back/in, suppress, keep in check, control, curb, stifle, bottle up; informal button up, keep the lid on. ANTONYMS express.

re·pres·sion /ri'presHən/ ▶ n. the action of repressing, or the state of being repressed.

SYNONYMS **1 suppression**, quashing, subduing, crushing, stamping out. **2 oppression**, subjugation, suppression, tyranny, authoritarianism, despotism. **3 restraint**, suppression, control, curbing, stifling.

re·pres·sive /ri'presiv/ ▶ adj. restricting personal freedom.

SYNONYMS **oppressive**, authoritarian, despotic, tyrannical, dictatorial, fascist, autocratic, totalitarian, undemocratic.

re·prieve /ri'prēv/ ▶ n. **1** the cancelation or postponement of a punishment, especially the death penalty. **2** a brief delay before something undesirable happens. ▶ v. (**reprieves**, **reprieving**, **reprieved**) give someone a reprieve.

SYNONYMS ▶ n. **pardon**, stay of execution, amnesty. ▶ v. **pardon**, spare, give/grant amnesty to; informal let off (the hook).

rep·ri·mand /'reprə,mand/ ▶ v. speak severely to someone because they have done something wrong. ▶ n. an act of reprimanding someone.

SYNONYMS ▶ v. **rebuke**, reproach, scold, admonish, reprove, chastise, upbraid, berate, take to task, castigate; informal tell off, chew out. ANTONYMS praise. ▶ n. **rebuke**, reproach, scolding, admonition; informal telling-off, chewing-out, dressing-down.

re·print ▶ v. /rē'print, 'rē-/ print again. ▶ n. /'rē,print/ **1** an act of reprinting. **2** a copy of a book that has been reprinted.

re·pris·al /ri'prīzəl/ ▶ n. an act of retaliation.

SYNONYMS **retaliation**, counterattack, comeback, revenge, vengeance, retribution, requital; informal a taste of your own medicine.

re·prise /ri'prēz, -'prīz/ ▶ n. **1** a repeated passage in music. **2** a further performance of something. ▶ v. (**reprises**, **reprising**, **reprised**) repeat a piece of music or a performance.

re·proach /ri'prōcH/ ▶ v. express disapproval of or disappointment with. ▶ n. an expression of disapproval or disappointment.

re·proach·ful /ri'prōcHfəl/ ▶ adj. expressing disapproval or disappointment.

SYNONYMS **disapproving**, reproving, critical, censorious, disparaging, withering, accusatory, admonitory. ANTONYMS approving.

■ **re·proach·ful·ly** adv.

rep·ro·bate /'reprə,bāt/ ▶ n. a person who behaves in an immoral way.

re·pro·duce /,rēprə'd(y)o͞os/ ▶ v. (**reproduces**, **reproducing**, **reproduced**) **1** produce a copy or representation of. **2** recreate in a different medium or context. **3** produce young or offspring.

SYNONYMS **1 copy**, duplicate, replicate, photocopy, xerox, photostat, print. **2 repeat**, replicate, recreate, redo, simulate, imitate, emulate, mimic. **3 breed**, procreate, propagate, multiply, proliferate.

re·pro·duc·tion /,rēprə'dəksHən/ ▶ n. **1** the process of reproducing. **2** a copy of a work of art.

SYNONYMS **1 print**, copy, reprint, duplicate, facsimile, photocopy; trademark Xerox. **2 breeding**, procreation, propagation, proliferation.

■ **re·pro·duc·tive** adj.

re·proof /ri'pro͞of/ ▶ n. a reprimand.

re·prove /ri'pro͞ov/ ▶ v. (**reproves**, **reproving**, **reproved**) reprimand; tell off.

rep·tile /'reptəl, 'rep,tīl/ ▶ n. a cold-blooded animal of a class that includes snakes, lizards, crocodiles, and tortoises. ■ **rep·til·i·an** /rep'tilēən, -'tilyən/ adj.

re·pub·lic /ri'pəblik/ ▶ n. a state in which power is held by the people and their representatives, and which has a president rather than a king or queen.

re·pub·li·can /ri'pəblikən/ ▶ adj. **1** belonging to or characteristic of a republic. **2** in favor of republican government. **3** (**Republican**) (in the United States) relating to or supporting the Republican Party. ▶ n. **1** a person in favor of republican government. **2** (**Republican**) (in the United States) a member or supporter of the Republican Party. **3** (**Republican**) a person who wants Ireland to be one country.

■ **re·pub·li·can·ism** n.

re·pu·di·ate /ri'pyo͞odē,āt/ ▶ v. (**repudiates**, **repudiating**, **repudiated**) **1** refuse to accept or support. **2** deny that something is true or valid.

SYNONYMS **1 reject**, renounce, disown, abandon, give up, turn your back on, cast off, lay aside, wash your hands of of; formal forswear; literary forsake. **2 deny**, refute, contradict, controvert, rebut, dispute, dismiss, brush aside; formal gainsay. ANTONYMS embrace.

■ **re·pu·di·a·tion** /ri,pyo͞odē'āsHən/ n.

re·pug·nance /ri'pəgnəns/ ▶ n. great disgust.

re·pug·nant /ri'pəgnənt/ ▶ adj. very unpleasant.

SYNONYMS **abhorrent**, revolting, repulsive, repellent, disgusting, offensive, objectionable, vile, foul, nasty, loathsome, sickening, nauseating, hateful, detestable, execrable, abominable, monstrous, appalling, unsavory, unpalatable. ANTONYMS pleasant.

re·pulse /ri'pəls/ ▶ v. (**repulses**, **repulsing**, **repulsed**) **1** drive back by force. **2** reject or refuse to accept. **3** give someone a feeling of strong disgust. ▶ n. the action of repulsing.

re·pul·sion /ri'pəlsHən/ ▶ n. **1** a feeling of strong disgust. **2** a force by which objects tend to push each other away.

re·pul·sive /ri'pəlsiv/ ▶ adj. arousing a feeling of strong disgust.

SYNONYMS **disgusting**, revolting, foul, nasty, obnoxious, sickening, nauseating, stomach-churning, vile; informal ghastly, gross, horrible; literary noisome. ANTONYMS attractive.

rep·u·ta·ble /'repyətəbəl/ ▶ adj. having a good reputation.

SYNONYMS **well thought of**, highly regarded, respected, respectable, of (good) repute, prestigious, established, reliable, dependable, trustworthy. ANTONYMS untrustworthy.

rep·u·ta·tion /ˌrepyəˈtāSHən/ ▶ **n.** the beliefs or opinions that people generally hold about someone or something.

SYNONYMS **name**, good name, character, repute, standing, stature, position, renown, esteem, prestige.

re·pute /riˈpyo͞ot/ ▶ **n. 1** the opinion that people have of someone or something. **2** good reputation. ▶ **v. 1** (**be reputed**) have a particular reputation. **2** (**reputed**) believed to exist.

SYNONYMS ▶ **v.** (**reputed**) **1** *they are reputed to be very rich* **thought**, said, reported, rumored, believed, held, considered, deemed, alleged. **2** *a reputed physicist* **well thought of**, (well-) respected, highly regarded. **3** *his reputed father* **supposed**, putative.

■ **re·put·ed·ly** adv.

re·quest /riˈkwest/ ▶ **n. 1** an act of asking politely or formally for something. **2** something that is asked for in this way. ▶ **v.** politely or formally ask for something, or ask someone to do something.

SYNONYMS ▶ **n. 1 appeal**, entreaty, plea, petition, application, demand, call, solicitation. **2 requirement**, wish, desire, choice. ▶ **v. ask for**, appeal for, call for, seek, solicit, plead for, beg for, apply for, put in for, demand, petition for, sue for, implore, entreat; literary beseech.

req·ui·em /ˈrekwēəm, ˈrā-/ ▶ **n. 1** a Christian mass for the souls of dead people. **2** a musical work based on such a mass.

re·quire /riˈkwīr/ ▶ **v.** (**requires**, **requiring**, **required**) **1** need or want something for a purpose. **2** instruct or expect someone to do something. **3** regard a particular thing as necessary or compulsory.

SYNONYMS **1 need**, have need of, be short of, want, desire, lack, miss. **2 necessitate**, demand, call for, involve, entail, take. **3 demand**, insist on, call for, ask for, expect. **4 order**, instruct, command, enjoin, oblige, compel, force.

re·quire·ment /riˈkwīrmənt/ ▶ **n. 1** something that you need or want. **2** something that is compulsory.

SYNONYMS **need**, necessity, prerequisite, stipulation, demand, want, essential.

req·ui·site /ˈrekwəzət/ ▶ **adj.** necessary because of circumstances or regulations. ▶ **n.** a thing that is needed for a particular purpose.

req·ui·si·tion /ˌrekwəˈzisHən/ ▶ **n. 1** an official order allowing property or materials to be taken or used. **2** the taking of goods for military or public use. ▶ **v.** officially take possession of something, especially during a war.

SYNONYMS ▶ **n. 1 order**, request, call, application, claim, demand. **2 appropriation**, commandeering, seizure, confiscation, expropriation. ▶ **v. 1 commandeer**, appropriate, take over, take possession of, occupy, seize, confiscate, expropriate. **2 request**, order, call for, demand.

re·run ▶ **v.** /rēˈrən/ (**reruns**, **rerunning**, **reran**; past participle **rerun**) show, stage, or perform again. ▶ **n.** /ˈrēˌrən/ a rerun event, competition, or program.

re·sched·ule /rēˈskejo͞o(ə)l/ ▶ **v.** (**reschedules**, **rescheduling**, **rescheduled**) change the timing of.

re·scind /riˈsind/ ▶ **v.** cancel or repeal a law, order, etc.

SYNONYMS **revoke**, repeal, cancel, reverse, overturn, overrule, annul, nullify, void, invalidate, quash, abolish; formal abrogate. ANTONYMS enforce.

res·cue /ˈreskyo͞o/ ▶ **v.** (**rescues**, **rescuing**, **rescued**) save from danger or distress. ▶ **n.** an act of rescuing or being rescued.

SYNONYMS ▶ **v. 1 save**, free, set free, release, liberate, deliver. **2 retrieve**, recover, salvage. ▶ **n. saving**, rescuing, release, freeing, liberation, deliverance.

re·search /ˈrēˌsərCH, riˈsərCH/ ▶ **n.** the study of materials and sources in order to establish facts and reach new conclusions. ▶ **v.** carry out research into a subject, or for a book, program, etc.

SYNONYMS ▶ **n. investigation**, experimentation, testing, analysis, fact-finding, examination, scrutiny. ▶ **v. investigate**, study, inquire into, look into, probe, explore, analyze, examine, scrutinize.

□ **research and development** work directed toward new ideas and improvement of products and processes. ■ **re·search·er** n.

re·sem·blance /riˈzembləns/ ▶ **n. 1** the state of resembling. **2** a way in which things resemble each other.

SYNONYMS **similarity**, likeness, similitude, correspondence, congruence, conformity, comparability, parallel. ANTONYMS dissimilarity.

re·sem·ble /riˈzembəl/ ▶ **v.** (**resembles**, **resembling**, **resembled**) look or be like.

SYNONYMS **look like**, be similar to, remind someone of, take after, approximate to, smack of, correspond to, echo, mirror, parallel. ANTONYMS differ from.

re·sent /riˈzent/ ▶ **v.** feel bitter toward.

SYNONYMS **begrudge**, feel aggrieved at/about, feel bitter about, grudge, be resentful of, take exception to, object to, take amiss, take offense at. ANTONYMS welcome.

re·sent·ful /riˈzentfəl/ ▶ **adj.** bitter about something you think is unfair.

SYNONYMS **aggrieved**, indignant, irritated, piqued, put out, in high dudgeon, dissatisfied, disgruntled, discontented, offended, bitter, jaundiced, envious, jealous; informal miffed, peeved, sore.

■ **re·sent·ful·ly** adv.

re·sent·ment /riˈzentmənt/ ▶ **n.** a feeling of bitterness about something unfair.

SYNONYMS **bitterness**, indignation, irritation, pique, dissatisfaction, disgruntlement, discontentment, acrimony, rancor.

res·er·va·tion /ˌrezərˈvāSHən/ ▶ **n. 1** the action of reserving. **2** an arrangement for something to be reserved. **3** an area of land set aside for a native people. **4** an expression of doubt about a statement.

SYNONYMS **1 doubt**, qualm, scruple; (**reservations**) misgivings, skepticism, unease, hesitation, objection. **2 reserve**, enclave, sanctuary, territory, homeland.

re·serve /ri'zərv/ ▶ v. (**reserves, reserving, reserved**) **1** keep something to be used in the future. **2** arrange for a seat, ticket, etc., to be kept for a particular person. **3** have or keep a right or power. ▶ n. **1** a supply of something available for use if required. **2** money kept available by a bank, company, etc. **3** a military force kept to reinforce others or for use in an emergency. **4** an extra player in a team, who can be called on to play if necessary. **5** (**the reserves**) the second-choice team. **6** an area of land set aside for wildlife or for a native people. **7** a lack of warmth or openness.

> SYNONYMS ▶ v. **1 put aside**, set aside, keep (back), save, hold back, keep in reserve, earmark, retain. **2 book**, order, arrange for, secure, engage, hire. ▶ n. **1 stock**, store, supply, stockpile, pool, hoard, cache, fund. **2 reinforcements**, extras, auxiliaries. **3** *a reserve outfielder* **substitute**, stand-in, relief, replacement, fallback, spare, extra. **4 national park**, sanctuary, preserve, reservation. **5 shyness**, diffidence, timidity, taciturnity, inhibition, reticence, detachment, aloofness, distance, remoteness. **6** *she trusted him without reserve* **reservation**, qualification, condition, limitation, hesitation, doubt.

□ **reserve bank** a regional bank operating under and implementing the policies of the Federal Reserve.

re·served /ri'zərvd/ ▶ adj. slow to reveal emotion or opinions.

> SYNONYMS **1 uncommunicative**, reticent, unforthcoming, aloof, cool, undemonstrative, unsociable, unfriendly, quiet, silent, taciturn, withdrawn, secretive, shy, retiring, diffident, timid, introverted; informal standoffish. **2 booked**, taken, spoken for, prearranged.
> ANTONYMS outgoing.

re·serv·ist /ri'zərvist/ ▶ n. a member of a military reserve force.

res·er·voir /'rezə(r),vwär, -,v(w)ôr/ ▶ n. **1** a large lake used as a source of water supply. **2** a place where fluid collects. **3** a supply or source of something.

> SYNONYMS **1 lake**, pool, pond, basin. **2 receptacle**, container, holder, tank. **3 stock**, store, stockpile, reserve(s), supply, bank, pool.

re·set /rē'set/ ▶ v. (**resets, resetting**; past and past participle **reset**) **1** set again or differently. **2** set a counter, clock, etc. to zero.

re·shuf·fle /rē'sHəfəl/ ▶ v. (**reshuffles, reshuffling, reshuffled**) **1** shuffle cards again. **2** change the roles or positions of government appointees, members of a team, etc. **3** rearrange. ▶ n. an act of reshuffling.

re·side /ri'zīd/ ▶ v. (**resides, residing, resided**) formal **1** live in a particular place. **2** (**reside in** or **with**) (of a right or power) belong to a person or group. **3** (**reside in**) (of a quality) be naturally present in.

> SYNONYMS **1 live**, lodge, stay, occupy, inhabit; formal dwell, be domiciled. **2** *power resides with the president* **be vested in**, be bestowed on, be conferred on, be in the hands of.

res·i·dence /'rez(ə)dəns, 'rezə,dens/ ▶ n. **1** the fact of living somewhere. **2** the place where a person lives.

> SYNONYMS **home**, house, address, quarters, lodgings; informal pad; formal dwelling, abode, domicile.

res·i·den·cy /'rez(ə)dənsē, 'rezə,densē/ ▶ n. (plural **residencies**) the fact of living in a place.

res·i·dent /'rez(ə)dənt, 'rezə,dent/ ▶ n. a person who lives somewhere on a long-term basis. ▶ adj. living somewhere on a long-term basis.

> SYNONYMS ▶ n. **inhabitant**, local, citizen, native, householder, homeowner, occupier, tenant; humorous denizen.

res·i·den·tial /,rezə'dencHəl/ ▶ adj. **1** involving residence. **2** providing accommodations. **3** occupied by private houses.

re·sid·u·al /ri'zijo͞oəl/ ▶ adj. remaining after the greater part has gone or been taken away.

res·i·due /'rezə,d(y)o͞o/ ▶ n. a small amount of something that remains after the main part has gone or been taken.

> SYNONYMS **remainder**, rest, remnant(s), surplus, extra, excess, remains, leftovers.

re·sign /ri'zīn/ ▶ v. **1** voluntarily leave a job or position or office. **2** (**be resigned**) accept that something bad cannot be avoided.

> SYNONYMS **1 leave**, give notice, stand down, step down; informal quit, pack (it) in. **2 give up**, leave, vacate, renounce, relinquish, surrender. **3** (**resigned**) **patient**, long-suffering, uncomplaining, forbearing, stoical, philosophical, fatalistic.

res·ig·na·tion /,rezig'nāsHən/ ▶ n. **1** an act of resigning. **2** a document stating that you intend to resign. **3** acceptance of something bad but inevitable.

> SYNONYMS *he accepted his fate with resignation* **patience**, forbearance, stoicism, fortitude, fatalism, acceptance.

re·sil·ient /ri'zilyənt/ ▶ adj. **1** able to spring back into shape after bending, stretching, or being compressed. **2** able to withstand or recover quickly from difficult conditions.

> SYNONYMS **1 flexible**, pliable, supple, durable, hard-wearing, stout, strong, sturdy, tough. **2 strong**, tough, hardy, quick to recover, buoyant, irrepressible.

■ **re·sil·ience** n.

res·in /'rezən/ ▶ n. **1** a sticky substance produced by some trees. **2** a synthetic substance used as the basis of plastics, adhesives, etc.

re·sist /ri'zist/ ▶ v. **1** withstand the action or effect of. **2** try to prevent or fight against. **3** stop yourself having or doing something tempting.

> SYNONYMS **1 withstand**, be proof against, combat, weather, endure, be resistant to, keep out. **2 oppose**, fight against, object to, defy, kick against, obstruct. **3 refrain from**, abstain from, forbear from, desist from, not give in to, restrain yourself from.

re·sist·ance /ri'zistəns/ ▶ n. **1** the action of resisting. **2** a secret organization that fights against an occupying enemy. **3** the ability not to be affected by something. **4** the degree to which a material or device resists the passage of an electric current.

> SYNONYMS **1 opposition**, hostility, struggle, fight, battle, stand, defiance. **2 immunity**, defenses.

re·sist·ant /ri'zistənt/ ▶ adj. resisting something or someone.

SYNONYMS **1 impervious**, immune, invulnerable, proof, unaffected. **2 opposed**, averse, hostile, inimical, against; informal anti. ANTONYMS vulnerable.

re·sis·tor /ri'zistər/ ▶ n. a device that resists the passage of an electric current.

res·o·lute /'rezə,lo͞ot, -lət/ ▶ adj. determined.

SYNONYMS **determined**, purposeful, resolved, adamant, single-minded, firm, unswerving, unwavering, steadfast, staunch, stalwart, unfaltering, indefatigable, tenacious, strong-willed, unshakable. ANTONYMS halfhearted.

■ **res·o·lute·ly** adv.

res·o·lu·tion /,rezə'lo͞osʜən/ ▶ n. **1** a firm decision. **2** a formal statement of opinion or intention by a legislative body, committee, or other formal meeting. **3** determination. **4** the resolving of a problem or dispute. **5** the degree to which detail is visible in a photograph or an image on a computer or television screen.

SYNONYMS **1 intention**, decision, intent, aim, plan, commitment, pledge, promise. **2 motion**, proposal, proposition. **3 determination**, purpose, purposefulness, resolve, single-mindedness, firmness, willpower, strength of character. **4 solution**, answer, end, settlement, conclusion.

re·solve /ri'zälv, -'zôlv/ ▶ v. (**resolves**, **resolving**, **resolved**) **1** find a solution to. **2** decide firmly on a course of action. **3** take a decision by a formal vote. **4** (**resolve into**) separate into different parts. ▶ n. determination.

SYNONYMS ▶ v. **1 settle**, sort out, solve, fix, straighten out, deal with, put right, rectify; informal hammer out, thrash out. **2 determine**, decide, make up your mind. **3 vote**, rule, decide formally, agree. ▶ n. **determination**, purpose, resolution, single-mindedness; informal guts.

res·o·nant /'rezənənt/ ▶ adj. **1** (of sound) deep, clear, and ringing. **2** having the power to bring images, memories, or feelings into your mind.
■ **res·o·nance** n.

res·o·nate /'rezn,āt/ ▶ v. (**resonates**, **resonating**, **resonated**) make a deep, clear, ringing sound.

re·sort /ri'zôrt/ ▶ n. **1** a place visited for holidays. **2** a strategy or course of action. ▶ v. (**resort to**) turn to a strategy or course of action so as to resolve a difficult situation.

SYNONYMS ▶ n. **option**, alternative, choice, possibility, hope, measure, step, recourse, expedient.

re·sound /ri'zound/ ▶ v. **1** make a ringing, booming, or echoing sound. **2** (**resounding**) definite; unmistakable.

SYNONYMS **1 echo**, reverberate, ring, boom, thunder, rumble, resonate. **2** (**resounding**) **reverberating**, resonating, echoing, ringing, sonorous, deep, rich. **3** (**resounding**) *a resounding success* **enormous**, huge, very great, tremendous, terrific, colossal, emphatic, outstanding, remarkable, phenomenal.

re·source /'rē,sôrs, 'rē'zôrs, ri'sôrs, ri'zôrs/ ▶ n. **1** (**resources**) a stock or supply of materials or assets. **2** something that can be used to help achieve an aim. **3** (**resources**) personal qualities that help you to cope with difficult circumstances. ▶ v. (**be resourced**) be provided with resources.

SYNONYMS ▶ n. **1 facility**, amenity, aid, help, support. **2 initiative**, resourcefulness, enterprise, ingenuity, inventiveness. **3** *we lack resources* **assets**, funds, wealth, money, capital, supplies, materials, stores, stocks, reserves.

re·source·ful /ri'sôrsfəl, -'zôrs-/ ▶ adj. able to find quick and clever ways to overcome difficulties.

SYNONYMS **ingenious**, enterprising, inventive, creative, clever, talented, able, capable.

■ **re·source·ful·ly** adv. **re·source·ful·ness** n.

re·spect /ri'spekt/ ▶ n. **1** a feeling of admiration for someone because of their qualities or achievements. **2** consideration for the feelings or rights of other people. **3** (**respects**) polite greetings. **4** a particular aspect, point, or detail. ▶ v. **1** have respect for. **2** avoid harming or interfering with. **3** agree to observe a law, principle, etc.

SYNONYMS ▶ n. **1 esteem**, regard, high opinion, admiration, reverence, deference, honor. **2** (**respects**) **regards**, compliments, greetings, best/good wishes. **3** *the report was accurate in every respect* **aspect**, regard, feature, way, sense, particular, point, detail. ANTONYMS contempt. ▶ v. **1 esteem**, admire, think highly of, have a high opinion of, look up to, revere, honor. **2 show consideration for**, have regard for, observe, be mindful of, be heedful of. **3 abide by**, comply with, follow, adhere to, conform to, act in accordance with, obey, observe, keep (to). ANTONYMS despise, disobey.

re·spect·a·bil·i·ty /ri,spektə'bilətē/ ▶ n. **1** the state or quality of being proper, correct, and socially acceptable. **2** the state or quality of being adequate or acceptable.

re·spect·a·ble /ri'spektəbəl/ ▶ adj. **1** regarded by society as being correct or proper. **2** adequate or acceptable.

SYNONYMS **1 reputable**, upright, honest, honorable, trustworthy, decent, good, well-bred, clean-living. **2 fairly good**, decent, fair-sized, reasonable, moderately good, large, sizable, considerable. ANTONYMS disreputable.

■ **re·spect·a·bly** adv.

re·spect·ful /ri'spektfəl/ ▶ adj. feeling or showing respect.

SYNONYMS **deferential**, reverent, dutiful, polite, well-mannered, civil, courteous, gracious. ANTONYMS rude.

■ **re·spect·ful·ly** adv.

re·spect·ing /ri'spektiɴɢ/ ▶ prep. with reference to.

re·spec·tive /ri'spektiv/ ▶ adj. belonging or relating separately to each of two or more people or things.

SYNONYMS **separate**, personal, own, particular, individual, specific, special.

re·spec·tive·ly /ri'spektivlē/ ▶ adv. individually and in the order already mentioned.

res·pi·ra·tion /,respə'rāsʜən/ ▶ n. the action of breathing.

res·pi·ra·tor /'respə,rātər/ ▶ n. **1** a device worn over the face to prevent your breathing in dust, smoke, etc. **2** a device that enables someone to breathe when they cannot do so naturally.

res·pi·ra·to·ry /'respərə,tôrē, ri'spīrə-/ ▶ adj. relating to breathing.

re·spire /ri'spī(ə)r/ ▶ v. (**respires**, **respiring**, **respired**) technical breathe.

res·pite /'respət, ri'spīt/ ▶ n. a short period of rest or relief from something difficult or unpleasant.

SYNONYMS **rest**, break, breathing space, interval, lull, pause, time out, relief; informal breather, letup.

re·splend·ent /ri'splendənt/ ▶ adj. attractive and impressive.

re·spond /ri'spänd/ ▶ v. say or do something in reply or as a reaction.

SYNONYMS **1 answer**, reply, write back, come back, rejoin, retort, riposte, counter. **2 react**, reciprocate, retaliate.

re·spond·ent /ri'spändənt/ ▶ n. **1** Law a person against whom a petition is filed, especially one in a divorce case. **2** a person who responds to a questionnaire or advertisement.

re·sponse /ri'späns/ ▶ n. an answer or reaction.

SYNONYMS **1 answer**, reply, rejoinder, retort, riposte; informal comeback. **2 reaction**, reply, retaliation; informal comeback. ANTONYMS question.

re·spon·si·bil·i·ty /ri,spänsə'bilətē/ ▶ n. (plural **responsibilities**) **1** the state of being responsible. **2** the opportunity to act independently. **3** a thing that you are required to do or look after as part of a job, role, or obligation.

SYNONYMS **1 duty**, task, function, job, role, onus. **2 blame**, fault, guilt, culpability, liability, accountability, answerability. **3 trustworthiness**, (common) sense, maturity, reliability, dependability. **4** *managerial responsibility* **authority**, control, power, leadership.

re·spon·si·ble /ri'spänsəbəl/ ▶ adj. **1** obliged to do something or look after someone. **2** being the cause of something and so able to be blamed or credited for it. **3** able to be trusted. **4** (of a job) involving important duties or decisions. **5** (**responsible to**) having to report to a senior person.

SYNONYMS **1 in charge of**, in control of, at the helm of, accountable for, liable for. **2 accountable**, answerable, liable, to blame, guilty, culpable, blameworthy, at fault, in the wrong. **3 trustworthy**, sensible, mature, reliable, dependable, levelheaded, stable. ANTONYMS irresponsible.

■ **re·spon·si·bly** adv.

SPELLING

Respons**ible**, not -able.

re·spon·sive /ri'spänsiv/ ▶ adj. responding readily and positively.

SYNONYMS **reactive**, receptive, open to suggestions, amenable, flexible, forthcoming.

rest[1] /rest/ ▶ v. **1** stop working or moving in order to relax or recover your strength. **2** place something so that it stays in a particular position. **3** remain or be left in a particular condition: *rest assured*. **4** (**rest on**) depend or be based on. **5** (**rest with**) (of power, responsibility, etc.) belong to. ▶ n. **1** a period of resting. **2** a motionless state. **3** an object that is used to hold or support something. **4** a brief interval of silence in a piece of music.

SYNONYMS ▶ v. **1 relax**, ease up/off, let up, slow down, take a break, unbend, unwind, take it easy, put your feet up; informal take five, have/take a breather, chill out. **2** *her hands rested on the rail* **lie**, be laid, repose, be placed, be positioned, be supported by. **3 support**, prop (up), lean, lay, set, stand, position, place, put. ▶ n. **1 relaxation**, repose, leisure, time off. **2 break**, breathing space, interval, interlude, intermission, time off/out, respite, lull, pause; informal breather. **3 stand**, base, holder, support, rack, frame, shelf.

□ **lay someone to rest** bury someone's body in a grave.

rest[2] ▶ n. the remaining part, people, or things.

SYNONYMS **remainder**, residue, balance, others, remnant(s), surplus, excess.

res·tau·rant /'rest(ə)rənt, 'restə,ränt, 'res,tränt/ ▶ n. a place where people pay to sit and eat meals that are cooked on the premises.

res·tau·ra·teur /,restərə'tər/ ▶ n. a person who owns and manages a restaurant.

SPELLING

Note that there is no **n**: restaur**ateur**.

rest·ful /'restfəl/ ▶ adj. having a quiet and soothing quality.

SYNONYMS **relaxing**, quiet, calm, tranquil, soothing, peaceful, leisurely, undisturbed, untroubled. ANTONYMS exciting.

res·ti·tu·tion /,restə't(y)o͞osнən/ ▶ n. **1** the restoration of something lost or stolen to its proper owner. **2** payment for injury or loss that has been suffered.

SYNONYMS **1** *restitution of the land seized* **return**, restoration, handing back, surrender. **2** *restitution for the damage caused* **compensation**, recompense, reparation, damages, indemnification, reimbursement, repayment, remuneration, redress.

res·tive /'restiv/ ▶ adj. unable to keep still or silent; restless.

rest·less /'restləs/ ▶ adj. unable to rest or relax.

SYNONYMS **1 uneasy**, ill at ease, fidgety, edgy, tense, worked up, nervous, nervy, agitated, anxious; informal jumpy, jittery, twitchy, uptight. **2** *a restless night* **sleepless**, wakeful, fitful, broken, disturbed, troubled, unsettled.

■ **rest·less·ly** adv.

res·to·ra·tion /,restə'rāsнən/ ▶ n. **1** the action of returning something to a former condition, place, or owner. **2** the process of repairing or renovating a building, work of art, etc. **3** the reinstatement of a previous practice, right, or situation. **4** the return of a monarch to a throne, a head of state to government, or a regime to power. **5** (**the Restoration**) the setting up of Charles II as King of England in 1660, or the period following this.

SYNONYMS **1 reinstatement**, reinstitution, re-establishment, reimposition, return. **2 repair**, renovation, mending, refurbishment, reconditioning, rehabilitation, rebuilding, reconstruction; informal rehab.

re·stor·a·tive /ri'stôrətiv/ ▶ adj. able to restore health or strength.

re·store /ri'stôr/ ▶ v. (**restores**, **restoring**, **restored**) **1** bring back a previous practice, situation, etc. **2** return someone or something to a previous condition, place, position, etc. **3** repair or renovate a building, work of art, etc.

> SYNONYMS **1 reinstate**, bring back, reinstitute, reimpose, reinstall, re-establish. **2** *he restored it to its rightful owner* **return**, give back, hand back. **3 repair**, fix, mend, refurbish, recondition, rehabilitate, renovate, revamp, rebuild. **4 reinvigorate**, revitalize, revive, refresh, energize, freshen.

■ **re·stor·er** n.

re·strain /ri'strān/ ▶ v. **1** keep under control or within limits. **2** stop someone moving or acting freely.

> SYNONYMS **control**, check, hold in check, curb, suppress, repress, contain, rein back/in, smother, stifle, bottle up; informal keep the lid on.

re·strained /ri'strānd/ ▶ adj. **1** reserved or unemotional. **2** not richly decorated or brightly colored; subtle.

> SYNONYMS **1 self-controlled**, sober, steady, unemotional, undemonstrative. **2 muted**, soft, discreet, subtle, quiet, unobtrusive, unostentatious, understated, tasteful. ANTONYMS impetuous, brash.

re·straint /ri'strānt/ ▶ n. **1** the action of keeping someone or something under control. **2** a device that limits or prevents freedom of movement. **3** self-controlled behavior.

> SYNONYMS **1 constraint**, check, control, restriction, limitation, curtailment, rein, brake, deterrent. **2 self-control**, self-restraint, self-discipline, control, moderation, judiciousness.

re·strict /ri'strikt/ ▶ v. **1** put a limit on. **2** stop someone moving or acting freely.

> SYNONYMS **1 limit**, keep within bounds, regulate, control, moderate, cut down, curtail. **2 hinder**, interfere with, impede, hamper, obstruct, block, check, curb.

re·strict·ed /ri'striktid/ ▶ adj. **1** limited in extent, number, or scope. **2** not open to the public; secret.

> SYNONYMS **1 cramped**, confined, constricted, small, narrow, tight. **2 limited**, controlled, regulated, reduced.

re·stric·tion /ri'strikshən/ ▶ n. **1** a rule, law, etc., that prevents free movement or action. **2** the action of restricting.

> SYNONYMS **limitation**, constraint, control, regulation, check, curb, reduction, diminution, curtailment.

re·stric·tive /ri'striktiv/ ▶ adj. preventing freedom of action or movement.

rest·room /'rest,ro͞om, -,ro͝om/ ▶ n. a bathroom in a public building.

re·sult /ri'zəlt/ ▶ n. **1** a thing that is caused or produced by something else. **2** a piece of information obtained by experiment or calculation. **3** a final score or mark in an exam or sports event. **4** a satisfactory or favorable outcome. ▶ v. **1** happen because of something else. **2** (**result in**) have a particular outcome.

> SYNONYMS ▶ n. **consequence**, outcome, upshot, sequel, effect, reaction, repercussion. ANTONYMS cause. ▶ v. **follow**, ensue, develop, stem, spring, arise, derive, proceed; (**result from**) be caused by, be brought about by, be produced by, originate in.

re·sult·ant /ri'zəltnt/ ▶ adj. happening or produced as a result.

re·sume /ri'zo͞om/ ▶ v. (**resumes**, **resuming**, **resumed**) begin again or continue after a pause.

> SYNONYMS **restart**, recommence, begin again, start again, reopen, renew, return to, continue with, carry on with. ANTONYMS suspend, abandon.

ré·su·mé /'rezə,mā, ,rezə'mā/ ▶ n. **1** a summary. **2** a brief account of a person's education, qualifications, and previous occupations, typically sent with a job application.

> SYNONYMS **1 summary**, précis, synopsis, abstract, outline, abridgment, overview. **2** curriculum vitae.

re·sump·tion /ri'zəmpshən/ ▶ n. the action of beginning something again after an interruption.

> SYNONYMS **restart**, recommencement, reopening, continuation, renewal, return, revival.

re·sur·gence /ri'sərjəns/ ▶ n. a case of becoming stronger or more popular again.

> SYNONYMS **renewal**, revival, renaissance, recovery, comeback, reawakening, resurrection, reappearance, re-emergence.

■ **re·sur·gent** adj.

res·ur·rect /,rezə'rekt/ ▶ v. **1** restore to life. **2** start using or doing again.

> SYNONYMS **revive**, restore, regenerate, revitalize, breathe new life into, reinvigorate, resuscitate, rejuvenate, re-establish, relaunch.

res·ur·rec·tion /,rezə'rekshən/ ▶ n. **1** the action of resurrecting. **2** (**the Resurrection**) (in Christian belief) the time when Jesus rose from the dead.

re·sus·ci·tate /ri'səsə,tāt/ ▶ v. (**resuscitates**, **resuscitating**, **resuscitated**) make someone conscious again after they nearly died. ■ **re·sus·ci·ta·tion** /ri,səsə'tāshən/ n.

> **SPELLING**
>
> Note that it is **-susc-**, not **-suss-**: resu**sc**itate.

re·tail /'rē,tāl/ ▶ n. the sale of goods to the public. ▶ v. **1** sell goods to the public. **2** (**retail at** or **for**) be sold for a particular price. ■ **re·tail·er** n.

re·tain /ri'tān/ ▶ v. **1** continue to have; keep possession of. **2** absorb and continue to hold a substance. **3** (**retaining**) keeping something in place.

> SYNONYMS **keep** (**possession of**), keep (a) hold of, hang on to, maintain, preserve, conserve.

re·tain·er /ri'tānər/ ▶ n. **1** a fee paid in advance to someone, especially a lawyer, to secure their services. **2** a servant who has worked for a family for a long time.

re·take /rē'tāk, 'rē-/ ▶ v. (**retakes**, **retaking**, **retook** /rē'to͝ok/; past participle **retaken**) **1** take a test or exam again. **2** regain possession of. ▶ n. a test or exam that is retaken.

re·tal·i·ate /ri'talē,āt/ ▶ **v.** (**retaliates**, **retaliating**, **retaliated**) make an attack in return for a similar attack.

> SYNONYMS **fight back**, hit back, respond, react, reply, reciprocate, counterattack, get back at someone, pay someone back; informal get your own back.

■ **re·tal·i·a·to·ry** /ri'talēə,tôrē/ **adj.**

re·tal·i·a·tion /ri,talē'āsHən/ ▶ **n.** an act of retaliating.

> SYNONYMS **revenge**, vengeance, reprisal, retribution, repayment, response, reaction, reply, counterattack.

re·tard /ri'tärd/ ▶ **v.** stop from developing or progressing.

> SYNONYMS **delay**, slow down/up, hold back/up, postpone, detain, decelerate, hinder, impede, check. ANTONYMS accelerate.

■ **re·tar·da·tion** /,rē,tär'dāsHən, ri-/ **n.**

re·tard·ed /ri'tärdid/ ▶ **adj.** offensive less developed mentally than is usual at a particular age.

retch /recH/ ▶ **v.** make the sound and movements of vomiting.

re·tell /rē'tel/ ▶ **v.** (past and past participle **retold** /rē'tōld/) tell a story again or differently.

re·ten·tion /ri'tencHən/ ▶ **n.** the action of retaining, or the state of being retained.

re·ten·tive /ri'tentiv/ ▶ **adj.** (of a person's memory) effective in retaining facts and impressions.

re·think /rē'THiNGk/ ▶ **v.** (**rethinks**, **rethinking**, **rethought**) consider a policy or course of action again. ▶ **n.** an instance of rethinking.

ret·i·cent /'retəsənt/ ▶ **adj.** not revealing your thoughts or feelings readily.

> SYNONYMS **uncommunicative**, unforthcoming, unresponsive, tight-lipped, quiet, taciturn, silent, reserved. ANTONYMS expansive.

■ **ret·i·cence** **n.**

ret·i·na /'retn-ə/ ▶ **n.** (plural **retinas** or **retinae** /'retn,ē, 'retn,ī/) a layer at the back of the eyeball that is sensitive to light and sends impulses to the brain.

ret·i·nue /'retn,(y)o͞o/ ▶ **n.** a group of assistants accompanying an important person.

re·tire /ri'tīr/ ▶ **v.** (**retires**, **retiring**, **retired**) **1** leave your job and stop working, especially because you have reached a particular age. **2** withdraw from a race or match because of accident or injury. **3** formal leave a place. **4** (of a jury) leave the courtroom to decide the verdict of a trial. **5** go to bed.

> SYNONYMS **1 give up work**, stop work, stop working, pack it in, call it quits. **2 withdraw**, go away, exit, leave, take yourself off, absent yourself. **3 go to bed**, call it a day; informal turn in, hit the hay/sack.

re·tired /ri'tīrd/ ▶ **adj.** having left your job and stopped working.

re·tire·ment /ri'tīrmənt/ ▶ **n.** **1** the action of retiring. **2** the period of life after retiring from work.

re·tir·ing /ri'tīriNG/ ▶ **adj.** tending to avoid company; shy.

> SYNONYMS **1 departing**, outgoing. **2 shy**, diffident, self-effacing, unassuming, unassertive, reserved, reticent, quiet, timid, modest. ANTONYMS incoming, outgoing.

re·took /rē'to͝ok/ past of RETAKE.

re·tort¹ /ri'tôrt/ ▶ **v.** say something sharp or witty in answer to a remark or accusation. ▶ **n.** a sharp or witty reply.

> SYNONYMS ▶ **v. answer**, reply, respond, return, counter, riposte, retaliate. ▶ **n. answer**, reply, response, counter, rejoinder, riposte, retaliation; informal comeback.

re·tort² ▶ **n.** a glass container with a long neck, used for distilling liquids and heating chemicals.

re·touch /rē'təcH/ ▶ **v.** make slight improvements to a painting, photograph, etc.

re·trace /rē'trās/ ▶ **v.** (**retraces**, **retracing**, **retraced**) **1** go back over the route that you have just taken. **2** follow a route taken by someone else. **3** trace something back to its source.

re·tract /ri'trakt/ ▶ **v.** **1** draw something back. **2** withdraw a statement or accusation. **3** go back on an undertaking.

> SYNONYMS **1 pull in**, pull back, draw in. **2 take back**, withdraw, recant, disavow, disclaim, repudiate, renounce, reverse, revoke, rescind, go back on, backtrack on; formal abjure.

■ **re·tract·a·ble** **adj.** **re·trac·tion** **n.**

re·treat /ri'trēt/ ▶ **v.** **1** (of an army) withdraw from confrontation with enemy forces. **2** move back from a difficult situation. **3** withdraw to a quiet or secluded place. ▶ **n.** **1** an act of retreating. **2** a quiet or secluded place. **3** a quiet place where people go for a time to pray and meditate.

> SYNONYMS ▶ **v. withdraw**, retire, draw back, pull back/out, fall back, give way, give ground. ANTONYMS advance. ▶ **n. 1 withdrawal**, retirement, pullback, flight. **2 refuge**, haven, sanctuary, hideaway, hideout, hiding place.

re·trench /ri'trencH/ ▶ **v.** reduce costs or spending in times of economic difficulty. ■ **re·trench·ment** **n.**

re·tri·al /rē'trīəl, 'rē,trīəl/ ▶ **n.** a second or further trial.

ret·ri·bu·tion /,retrə'byo͞osHən/ ▶ **n.** severe punishment inflicted as revenge.

> SYNONYMS **punishment**, penalty, your just deserts, revenge, reprisal, requital, retaliation, vengeance, an eye for an eye (and a tooth for a tooth), tit for tat, nemesis.

re·triev·al /ri'trēvəl/ ▶ **n.** **1** the process of getting something back from somewhere. **2** the obtaining or consulting of material stored in a computer system.

re·trieve /ri'trēv/ ▶ **v.** (**retrieves**, **retrieving**, **retrieved**) **1** get or bring back. **2** find or extract information stored in a computer. **3** improve a bad situation.

> SYNONYMS **get back**, bring back, recover, recapture, regain, recoup, salvage, rescue.

re·triev·er /ri'trēvər/ ▶ **n.** a breed of dog used for finding and bringing back game that has been shot.

ret·ro /'retrō/ ▶ **adj.** imitative of a style from the recent past.

ret·ro·ac·tive /,retrō'aktiv/ ▶ **adj.** taking effect from a date in the past.

ret·ro·grade /'retrə,grād/ ▶ **adj.** directed or moving backward or to a worse state.

> SYNONYMS **for the worse**, regressive, retrogressive, negative, downhill, backward(s), unwelcome.

ret·ro·gres·sive /retrō'gresiv/ ▶ **adj.** going back to an earlier and inferior state. ■ **ret·ro·gres·sion n.**

ret·ro·rock·et /'retrō,räkit/ ▶ **n.** a small rocket on a spacecraft or missile, fired in the direction of travel to slow it down.

ret·ro·spect /'retrə,spekt/ ▶ **n.** (**in retrospect**) when looking back on a past event.

> SYNONYMS **looking back**, on reflection, in hindsight.

ret·ro·spec·tive /,retrə'spektiv/ ▶ **adj. 1** looking back on or dealing with past events or situations. **2** taking effect from a date in the past. ▶ **n.** an exhibition showing the development of an artist's work over a period of time. ■ **ret·ro·spec·tive·ly adv.**

ret·rous·sé /rə,troo͞'sā, ,retroo͞-/ ▶ **adj.** (of a person's nose) turned up at the tip.

ret·si·na /ret'sēnə/ ▶ **n.** a Greek white wine flavored with resin.

re·turn /ri'tərn/ ▶ **v. 1** come or go back to a place. **2** (**return to**) go back to a particular state or activity. **3** give, send, or put back. **4** feel, say, or do the same thing in response. **5** (in tennis) hit the ball back to an opponent. **6** (of a judge or jury) give a verdict. **7** produce a profit. **8** elect someone to a political office. ▶ **n. 1** an act of returning. **2** a profit from an investment.

> SYNONYMS ▶ **v. 1 go back**, come back, arrive back, come home. **2 recur**, reoccur, repeat itself, reappear. **3 give back**, hand back, pay back, repay, restore, put back, replace, reinstall, reinstate. ANTONYMS leave. ▶ **n. 1 recurrence**, reoccurrence, repeat, reappearance. **2 replacement**, restoration, reinstatement, restitution. **3 yield**, profit, gain, revenue, interest, dividend.

re·u·ni·fy /rē'yoo͞nə,fī/ ▶ **v.** (**reunifies**, **reunifying**, **reunified**) make a place a united country again. ■ **re·u·ni·fi·ca·tion** /,rē,yoo͞nəfi'kāsʜən/ **n.**

re·un·ion /rē'yoo͞nyən/ ▶ **n. 1** the process of reuniting. **2** a gathering of people who have not seen each other for some time.

re·u·nite /,rēyoo͝'nīt/ ▶ **v.** (**reunites**, **reuniting**, **reunited**) bring two or more people or things together again.

re·use /rē'yoo͞z/ ▶ **v.** (**reuses**, **reusing**, **reused**) use something again. ■ **re·us·a·ble adj.**

rev /rev/ informal ▶ **n.** (**revs**) the number of revolutions of an engine per minute. ▶ **v.** (**revs**, **revving**, **revved**) make an engine run quickly by pressing the accelerator.

Rev. (or **Revd**) ▶ **abbr.** Reverend.

re·vamp ▶ **v.** /rē'vamp/ alter something so as to improve it. ▶ **n.** /'rē,vamp/ a new and improved version of something.

> SYNONYMS ▶ **v. renovate**, redecorate, refurbish, remodel, refashion, redesign, restyle; informal do up, give something a facelift, give something a makeover.

re·veal /ri'vēl/ ▶ **v. 1** make previously unknown or secret information known. **2** allow something hidden to be seen.

> SYNONYMS **1 disclose**, make known, make public, broadcast, publicize, circulate, divulge, tell, let slip/drop, give away/out, blurt out, release, leak, bring to light, lay bare, unveil; informal let on. **2 show**, display, exhibit, unveil, uncover. ANTONYMS conceal, hide.

re·veal·ing /ri'vēlɪɴɢ/ ▶ **adj. 1** giving out interesting or significant information. **2** (of a garment) allowing a lot of your body to be seen.

rev·eil·le /'revəlē/ ▶ **n.** a signal sounded on a bugle, drum, etc., to wake up soldiers in the morning.

rev·el /'revəl/ ▶ **v.** (**revels**, **reveling**, **reveled**) **1** spend time enjoying yourself in a lively, noisy way. **2** (**revel in**) get great pleasure from. ▶ **n.** (**revels**) lively, noisy celebrations.

> SYNONYMS ▶ **v. celebrate**, make merry; informal party, live it up, whoop it up, paint the town red. ▶ **n. celebration**, festivity, jollification, merrymaking, party; informal rave, shindig, blast, bash, wingding.

■ **rev·el·er n.**

rev·e·la·tion /,revə'lāsʜən/ ▶ **n. 1** the revealing of something previously unknown. **2** a surprising or remarkable thing.

> SYNONYMS **disclosure**, announcement, report, admission, confession, divulging, giving away/out, leak, betrayal, publicizing.

re·vel·a·to·ry /'revələ,tôrē, ri'vel-/ ▶ **adj.** revealing something previously unknown.

rev·el·ry /'revəlrē/ ▶ **n.** (plural **revelries**) lively and noisy celebrations.

> SYNONYMS **celebration(s)**, parties, festivity, jollification, merrymaking, carousal, roistering, fun and games; informal partying.

re·venge /ri'venj/ ▶ **n.** something harmful done to someone in return for something bad that they did to you. ▶ **v.** (**revenges**, **revenging**, **revenged**) (**revenge yourself** or **be revenged**) harm someone in return for something bad that they did to you.

> SYNONYMS ▶ **n. retaliation**, retribution, vengeance, reprisal, recrimination, an eye for an eye (and a tooth for a tooth), redress. ANTONYMS forgiveness. ▶ **v. avenge**, exact retribution for, take reprisals for, get redress for, make someone pay for; informal get your own back for.

rev·e·nue /'revə,n(y)oo͞/ ▶ **n.** the income received by an organization, or by a government from taxes.

> SYNONYMS **income**, takings, receipts, proceeds, earnings, profit(s), gain, yield, take, gate. ANTONYMS expenditure.

re·ver·ber·ate /ri'vərbə,rāt/ ▶ **v.** (**reverberates**, **reverberating**, **reverberated**) **1** (of a loud noise) be repeated as an echo. **2** have continuing serious effects.

> SYNONYMS **resound**, echo, resonate, ring, boom, rumble.

■ **re·ver·ber·a·tion** /ri,vərbə'rāsʜən/ **n.**

re·vere /ri'vi(ə)r/ ▶ **v.** (**reveres**, **revering**, **revered**) respect or admire deeply.

> SYNONYMS **respect**, admire, think highly of, esteem, venerate, look up to, be in awe of. ANTONYMS despise.

rev·er·ence /'rev(ə)rəns/ ▶ **n.** deep respect.

> SYNONYMS **high esteem**, high regard, great respect, honor, veneration, homage, admiration, appreciation, deference. ANTONYMS scorn.

rev·er·end /'rev(ə)rənd, 'revərnd/ ▶ **adj.** a title given to Christian ministers.

rev·er·ent /ˈrev(ə)rənt, ˈrevərnt/ ▶ **adj.** showing reverence; deeply respectful.

SYNONYMS **reverential**, respectful, admiring, devoted, devout, awed, deferential.

■ **rev·er·en·tial** /ˌrevəˈrencʜəl/ **adj.** **rev·er·ent·ly** **adv.**

rev·er·ie /ˈrevərē/ ▶ **n.** a daydream.

re·ver·sal /riˈvərsəl/ ▶ **n.** **1** a change to an opposite direction, position, or course of action. **2** a harmful change of fortune.

SYNONYMS **1 turnaround**, turnabout, about-face, volte-face, change of heart, U-turn, backtracking. **2 swap**, exchange, change, interchange, switch. **3 alteration**, overturning, overthrow, disallowing, overriding, overruling, veto, revocation. **4 setback**, upset, failure, misfortune, mishap, disaster, blow, disappointment, adversity, hardship, affliction, vicissitude, defeat.

re·verse /riˈvərs/ ▶ **v.** (**reverses**, **reversing**, **reversed**) **1** move backward. **2** make something the opposite of what it was. **3** turn something the other way around. **4** cancel a judgment by a lower court. ▶ **adj.** **1** going in or turned toward the opposite direction. **2** opposite of the usual way. ▶ **n.** **1** a complete change of direction or action. **2** (**the reverse**) the opposite or contrary. **3** a setback or defeat. **4** the opposite side of something to the observer.

SYNONYMS ▶ **v.** **1 back**, move back/backward(s). **2 turn upside down**, turn over, upend, invert, turn back to front. **3 swap**, change (around), exchange, switch (around), transpose. **4 alter**, change, overturn, overthrow, disallow, override, overrule, veto, revoke. ▶ **adj.** **backward**(s), inverted, transposed, opposite. ▶ **n.** **1 opposite**, contrary, converse, inverse, antithesis. **2 setback**, reversal, upset, failure, misfortune, mishap, disaster, blow, disappointment, adversity, hardship, affliction, vicissitude, defeat. **3 other side**, back, underside, flip side. ANTONYMS front.

■ **re·vers·i·ble** **adj.**

re·ver·sion /riˈvərzʜən/ ▶ **n.** a return to a previous state, practice, etc.

re·vert /riˈvərt/ ▶ **v.** (**revert to**) return to a previous state, practice, etc.

SYNONYMS **return**, go back, change back, default, relapse.

re·view /riˈvyo͞o/ ▶ **n.** **1** an examination of something to decide whether changes are necessary. **2** a critical assessment of a book, play, etc. **3** a report of an event that has already happened. **4** a ceremonial display of military forces. ▶ **v.** **1** examine or consider something again. **2** write a review of.

SYNONYMS ▶ **n.** **1 analysis**, evaluation, assessment, appraisal, examination, investigation, inquiry, probe, inspection, study. **2 reconsideration**, reassessment, re-evaluation, reappraisal. **3 criticism**, critique, write-up, assessment, commentary. ▶ **v.** **1 survey**, study, research, consider, analyze, examine, scrutinize, explore, look into, probe, investigate, inspect, assess, evaluate, appraise, weigh up; informal size up. **2 reconsider**, re-examine, reassess, re-evaluate, reappraise, rethink.

re·view·er /riˈvyo͞oər/ ▶ **n.** a person who writes critical appraisals of books, plays, etc.

SYNONYMS **critic**, commentator, judge.

re·vile /riˈvīl/ ▶ **v.** (**reviles**, **reviling**, **reviled**) criticize in a rude or scornful way.

SYNONYMS **criticize**, censure, condemn, attack, inveigh against, rail against, lambaste, denounce; slander, libel, malign, vilify, besmirch, abuse; informal knock, slam, pan, crucify, roast, bad-mouth, pummel; formal excoriate. ANTONYMS praise.

re·vise /riˈvīz/ ▶ **v.** (**revises**, **revising**, **revised**) **1** examine and alter a piece of writing. **2** reconsider and change an opinion.

SYNONYMS **1 reconsider**, review, re-examine, reassess, re-evaluate, reappraise, rethink, change, alter, modify. **2 amend**, correct, edit, rewrite, redraft, rephrase, rework.

re·vi·sion /riˈvizʜən/ ▶ **n.** **1** the action of revising something. **2** a revised edition or form of something.

SYNONYMS **1 alteration**, adaptation, editing, rewriting, redrafting, correction, updating. **2 reconsideration**, review, re-examination, reassessment, re-evaluation, reappraisal, rethink, change, modification.

re·vi·sion·ism /riˈvizʜəˌnizəm/ ▶ **n.** disapproving the changing of accepted theories or principles. ■ **re·vi·sion·ist** **n. & adj.**

re·vi·tal·ize /rēˈvītlˌīz/ ▶ **v.** (**revitalizes**, **revitalizing**, **revitalized**) give new life and vitality to.

SYNONYMS **reinvigorate**, re-energize, boost, regenerate, revive, revivify, rejuvenate, reanimate, resuscitate, refresh, stimulate, breathe new life into; informal give a shot in the arm to, pep up, buck up.

■ **re·vi·tal·i·za·tion** /rēˌvītl-əˈzāsʜən/ **n.**

re·viv·al /riˈvīvəl/ ▶ **n.** **1** an improvement in the condition, strength, or popularity of something. **2** a new production of an old play.

SYNONYMS **1 improvement**, rallying, turn for the better, upturn, upswing, resurgence. **2 comeback**, re-establishment, reintroduction, restoration, reappearance, resurrection, rebirth. ANTONYMS downturn.

re·viv·al·ism /riˈvīvəˌlizəm/ ▶ **n.** **1** the process of trying to reawaken interest in a particular religious faith. **2** the practice of returning to former customs, fashions, etc. ■ **re·viv·al·ist** **n. & adj.**

re·vive /riˈvīv/ ▶ **v.** (**revives**, **reviving**, **revived**) **1** make conscious, healthy, or strong again. **2** start doing, using, or performing something again.

SYNONYMS **1 resuscitate**, bring around, bring back to consciousness, administer CPR to; informal give the kiss of life to. **2 reinvigorate**, revitalize, refresh, energize, reanimate. **3** *reviving old traditions* **reintroduce**, re-establish, restore, resurrect, bring back.

re·viv·i·fy /rēˈvivəˌfī/ ▶ **v.** (**revivifies**, **revivifying**, **revivified**) formal revive.

re·voke /riˈvōk/ ▶ **v.** (**revokes**, **revoking**, **revoked**) make a decree, law, etc., no longer valid.

SYNONYMS **cancel**, repeal, rescind, reverse, annul, nullify, void, invalidate, countermand, retract, withdraw, overrule, override; formal abrogate.

■ **rev·o·ca·tion** /ˌrevəˈkāsʜən, riˌvō-/ **n.**

re·volt /riˈvōlt/ ▶ **n.** an act of rebellion or defiance. ▶ **v. 1** rebel against an authority. **2** make someone feel disgust.

SYNONYMS ▶ **n. rebellion**, revolution, insurrection, mutiny, uprising, riot, insurgence, coup (d'état). ▶ **v. 1 rebel**, rise up, take to the streets, riot, mutiny. **2 disgust**, sicken, nauseate, turn someone's stomach, put off, offend; informal turn off, gross out.

re·volt·ing /riˈvōltiɴɢ/ ▶ **adj.** very unpleasant; disgusting.

SYNONYMS **disgusting**, sickening, nauseating, stomach-turning, repulsive, repugnant, hideous, nasty, foul, offensive; informal ghastly, horrid, gross. ANTONYMS attractive, pleasant.

rev·o·lu·tion /ˌrevəˈlo͞osʜən/ ▶ **n. 1** the overthrow of a government by force in favor of a new system. **2** a dramatic and far-reaching change. **3** a single circular movement around a central point.

SYNONYMS **1 rebellion**, revolt, insurrection, mutiny, uprising, rising, riot, insurgence, coup (d'état). **2 dramatic change**, sea change, metamorphosis, transformation, innovation, reorganization, restructuring; informal shake-up, shakedown. **3 turn**, rotation, circle, spin, orbit, circuit, lap.

rev·o·lu·tion·ar·y /ˌrevəˈlo͞osʜəˌnerē/ ▶ **adj. 1** involving or causing dramatic change. **2** taking part in, or relating to, political revolution. ▶ **n.** (plural **revolutionaries**) a person who starts or supports a political revolution.

SYNONYMS ▶ **adj. 1 rebellious**, rebel, insurgent, rioting, mutinous, renegade. **2 new**, novel, original, unusual, unconventional, unorthodox, newfangled, innovatory, modern, state-of-the-art, futuristic, pioneering. ▶ **n. rebel**, insurgent, mutineer, insurrectionist, agitator.

rev·o·lu·tion·ize /ˌrevəˈlo͞osʜəˌnīz/ ▶ **v.** (**revolutionizes**, **revolutionizing**, **revolutionized**) change something completely or fundamentally.

SYNONYMS **transform**, shake up, turn upside down, restructure, reorganize, transmute, metamorphose; humorous transmogrify.

re·volve /riˈvälv, riˈvôlv/ ▶ **v.** (**revolves**, **revolving**, **revolved**) **1** move in a circle around a central point. **2** (**revolve around**) treat as the most important element.

SYNONYMS **1 go around/round**, turn around/round, rotate, spin. **2 circle**, travel, orbit.

re·volv·er /riˈvälvər, -ˈvôl-/ ▶ **n.** a pistol with revolving chambers that allow several shots to be fired without reloading.

re·vue /riˈvyo͞o/ ▶ **n.** a theatrical show with short sketches, songs, and dances.

re·vul·sion /riˈvəlsʜən/ ▶ **n.** a sense of disgust and loathing.

SYNONYMS **disgust**, repulsion, abhorrence, repugnance, nausea, horror, aversion, abomination, distaste. ANTONYMS delight.

re·ward /riˈwôrd/ ▶ **n.** something given in recognition of service, effort, or achievement. ▶ **v. 1** give a reward to. **2** show appreciation of an action or quality by giving a reward.

SYNONYMS ▶ **n. award**, honor, decoration, bonus, premium, bounty, present, gift, payment, recompense, prize; informal payoff. ▶ **v. recompense**, pay, remunerate. ANTONYMS punish.

re·ward·ing /riˈwôrdiɴɢ/ ▶ **adj.** providing satisfaction.

SYNONYMS **satisfying**, gratifying, pleasing, fulfilling, enriching, illuminating, worthwhile, productive, fruitful.

re·wind /rēˈwīnd/ ▶ **v.** (**rewinds**, **rewinding**, **rewound** /rēˈwound/) wind a movie or tape back to the beginning.

re·wire /rēˈwīr/ ▶ **v.** (**rewires**, **rewiring**, **rewired**) provide with new wiring.

re·work /rēˈwərk/ ▶ **v.** alter something in order to improve or update it.

re·write /rēˈrīt/ ▶ **v.** (**rewrites**, **rewriting**, **rewrote** /rēˈrōt/; past participle **rewritten** /rēˈritn/) write again in an altered or improved form. ▶ **n.** an instance of rewriting.

rhap·so·dize /ˈrapsəˌdīz/ ▶ **v.** (**rhapsodizes**, **rhapsodizing**, **rhapsodized**) express great enthusiasm about someone or something.

rhap·so·dy /ˈrapsədē/ ▶ **n.** (plural **rhapsodies**) **1** an expression of great enthusiasm. **2** a piece of music in one extended movement. ■ **rhap·sod·ic** /rapˈsädik/ **adj.**

rhe·o·stat /ˈrēəˌstat/ ▶ **n.** a device for varying the amount of resistance in an electrical circuit.

rhe·sus fac·tor /ˈrēsəs/ ▶ **n.** a substance found in the red blood cells of many humans.

rhe·sus mon·key /ˈrēsəs/ ▶ **n.** a small monkey found in southern Asia.

rhet·o·ric /ˈretərik/ ▶ **n. 1** effective or persuasive public speaking. **2** persuasive but insincere language.

SYNONYMS **1 oratory**, eloquence, command of language, way with words. **2 wordiness**, verbosity, grandiloquence, bombast, pomposity, extravagant language, purple prose, turgidity; informal hot air.

rhe·tor·i·cal /rəˈtôrikəl/ ▶ **adj. 1** relating to rhetoric. **2** intended to persuade or impress. **3** (of a question) asked for effect or to make a statement rather than to obtain an answer.

SYNONYMS **1** *a rhetorical device* **stylistic**, oratorical, linguistic, verbal. **2 extravagant**, grandiloquent, high-flown, bombastic, grandiose, pompous, pretentious, overblown, turgid, flowery; informal highfalutin.

■ **rhe·tor·i·cal·ly** **adv.**

rheu·ma·tism /ˈro͞oməˌtizəm/ ▶ **n.** a disease with inflammation and pain in the joints and muscles. ■ **rheu·mat·ic** /ro͝oˈmatik/ **adj.**

rheum·y /ˈro͞omē/ ▶ **adj.** (of a person's eyes) watery.

rhine·stone /ˈrīnˌstōn/ ▶ **n.** an imitation diamond.

rhi·no /ˈrīnō/ ▶ **n.** (plural **rhino** or **rhinos**) informal a rhinoceros.

rhi·noc·er·os /rīˈnäs(ə)rəs/ ▶ **n.** (plural **rhinoceros** or **rhinoceroses**) a large plant-eating animal with one or two horns on the nose and thick skin, found in Africa and Asia.

rhi·zome /ˈrīˌzōm/ ▶ **n.** a horizontal underground plant stem producing both roots and shoots.

Rhodes schol·ar /rōdz/ ▶ **n.** a student who holds one of the number of scholarships awarded annually for study at Oxford University.

rho·do·den·dron /ˌrōdəˈdendrən/ ▶ **n.** a shrub with large clusters of bright flowers.

rhom·bus /ˈrämbəs/ ▶ **n.** (plural **rhombuses** or **rhombi** /-ˌbī, -ˌbē/) a flat shape with four straight sides of equal length.

rhu·barb /ˈro͞oˌbärb/ ▶ **n.** the thick leaf stalks of a plant, cooked and eaten as fruit.

rhum·ba = RUMBA.

rhyme /rīm/ ▶ **n. 1** a word that has the same sound or ends with the same sound as another. **2** similarity of sound between words or the endings of words. **3** a short poem with rhyming lines. ▶ **v.** (**rhymes**, **rhyming**, **rhymed**) have or end with the same sound as another word or line.

> SYNONYMS ▶ **n. poem**, verse, ode; (**rhymes**) poetry, doggerel.

□ **rhyme or reason** logical explanation.

> SPELLING
>
> Remember the first **h**, following the **r**, in rhyme and rhythm.

rhy·thm /ˈriTHəm/ ▶ **n. 1** a strong, regular repeated pattern of sound or movement. **2** a regularly recurring sequence of events or actions.

> SYNONYMS **1 beat**, cadence, tempo, time, pulse. **2 meter**, measure, pattern.

□ **rhythm and blues** a type of music that is a combination of blues and jazz.

rhyth·mic /ˈriTHmik/ ▶ **adj. 1** having or relating to rhythm. **2** happening regularly. ■ **rhyth·mi·cal·ly adv.**

rib /rib/ ▶ **n. 1** each of a series of bones that are attached to the spine and curve around the chest. **2** a curved structure supporting an arched roof or forming part of a boat's framework. ▶ **v.** (**ribs**, **ribbing**, **ribbed**) informal tease someone good-naturedly.

ribbed /ribd/ ▶ **adj.** having a pattern of raised bands.

rib·bon /ˈribən/ ▶ **n. 1** a long, narrow strip of fabric, used for tying something or for decoration. **2** a long, narrow strip. **3** a narrow band of inked material used to produce the characters in some typewriters.

rib·cage /ˈribˌkāj/ ▶ **n.** the bony frame formed by the ribs.

ri·bo·fla·vin /ˌrībəˈflāvin, ˈrībəˌflā-/ ▶ **n.** vitamin B_2.

rice /rīs/ ▶ **n.** grains of a cereal plant that is grown for food on wet land in warm countries. □ **rice paper** thin edible paper made from a type of plant, used in oriental painting and in baking cookies and cakes.

rich /riCH/ ▶ **adj. 1** having a lot of money, assets, or resources. **2** made of expensive materials. **3** plentiful. **4** having or producing something in large amounts. **5** (of food) containing a lot of fat, sugar, etc. **6** (of a color, sound, or smell) pleasantly deep and strong. **7** (of soil or land) fertile.

> SYNONYMS **1 wealthy**, affluent, moneyed, well off, well-to-do, prosperous; informal loaded, well-heeled, made of money. **2 sumptuous**, opulent, luxurious, lavish, gorgeous, splendid, magnificent, costly, expensive, fancy, palatial; informal plush, swish, swank. **3** *a garden rich in flowers* **well-stocked**, well-provided, abounding, crammed, packed, teeming, bursting. **4** *a rich supply* **plentiful**, abundant, copious, ample, profuse, lavish, liberal, generous. **5 fertile**, productive, fruitful, fecund. **6 creamy**, fatty, heavy, full-flavored. **7** *rich colors* **strong**, deep, full, intense, vivid, brilliant. ANTONYMS poor, plain.

■ **rich·ness n.**

rich·es /ˈriCHiz/ ▶ **pl.n. 1** large amounts of money or valuable possessions. **2** valuable natural resources.

> SYNONYMS **money**, wealth, funds, cash, means, assets, capital, resources; informal bread, loot, (big) bucks.

rich·ly /ˈriCHlē/ ▶ **adv. 1** in a rich way. **2** fully; thoroughly.

> SYNONYMS **1 sumptuously**, opulently, luxuriously, lavishly, gorgeously, splendidly, magnificently. **2** *the reward she richly deserves* **fully**, amply, well, thoroughly, completely, wholly, totally, entirely, absolutely, utterly.

Rich·ter scale /ˈriktər/ ▶ **n.** a scale for measuring the severity of an earthquake.

rick[1] /rik/ ▶ **n.** a stack of hay, corn, or straw.

rick[2] ▶ **n.** a slight sprain or strain, especially in your neck or back. ▶ **v.** strain part of your body slightly.

rick·ets /ˈrikits/ ▶ **n.** a disease of children, caused by vitamin D deficiency, in which the bones are softened and distorted.

rick·et·y /ˈrikitē/ ▶ **adj.** badly made and likely to collapse.

> SYNONYMS **shaky**, unsteady, unsound, unsafe, tumbledown, broken-down, dilapidated, ramshackle.

rick·shaw /ˈrikˌSHô/ ▶ **n.** a light two-wheeled vehicle pulled by a person walking or riding a bicycle.

ric·o·chet /ˈrikəˌSHā, -ˌSHet/ ▶ **v.** (**ricochets**, **ricocheting**, **ricocheted**) (of a bullet or other fast-moving object) rebound off a surface. ▶ **n.** a shot or hit that ricochets.

ri·cot·ta /riˈkätə/ ▶ **n.** a soft white Italian cheese.

ric·tus /ˈriktəs/ ▶ **n.** a fixed grimace or grin.

rid /rid/ ▶ **v.** (**rids**, **ridding**, **rid**) **1** (**rid someone/thing of**) free a person or place of something unwanted. **2** (**be** or **get rid of**) be or make yourself free of.

> SYNONYMS **clear**, free, purge, empty, strip.

rid·dance /ˈridns/ ▶ **n.** (**good riddance**) said when expressing relief at getting rid of someone or something.

rid·den /ˈridn/ past participle of **RIDE** ▶ **adj.** full of a particular unpleasant thing;: *disease-ridden*.

rid·dle[1] /ˈridl/ ▶ **n. 1** a cleverly worded question that is asked as a game. **2** a puzzling person or thing.

> SYNONYMS **puzzle**, conundrum, brain-teaser, problem, question, poser, enigma, mystery.

rid·dle[2] ▶ **v.** (usu. **be riddled with**) **1** make a lot of holes in. **2** fill with something bad or unpleasant. ▶ **n.** a type of large sieve.

ride /rīd/ ▶ **v.** (**rides**, **riding**, **rode** /rōd/; past participle **ridden** /ˈridn/) **1** sit on and control the movement of a horse, bicycle, or motorcycle. **2** travel in a vehicle. **3** be carried or supported by. **4** (**ride up**) (of clothing) gradually move upward out of its proper position. **5** (**ride on**) depend on. ▶ **n.** **1** an act of riding. **2** a roller coaster, merry-go-round, etc., ridden at a fair or amusement park. **3** a path for horse riding.

SYNONYMS ▶ **v.** **1** **sit on**, mount, control, manage, handle. **2** **travel**, move, proceed, drive, cycle, trot, canter, gallop. ▶ **n.** **trip**, journey, drive, run, excursion, outing, jaunt, lift; informal spin.

□ **take someone for a ride** informal deceive someone.

rid·er /ˈrīdər/ ▶ **n.** **1** a person who rides a horse, bicycle, etc. **2** an added condition on an official document.

ridge /rij/ ▶ **n.** **1** a long, narrow hilltop or mountain range. **2** a narrow raised band on a surface. **3** the edge formed where the two sloping sides of a roof meet at the top. ■ **ridged adj.**

rid·i·cule /ˈridiˌkyo͞ol/ ▶ **n.** making fun of someone in an unkind way; mockery. ▶ **v.** (**ridicules**, **ridiculing**, **ridiculed**) make fun of.

SYNONYMS ▶ **n.** **mockery**, derision, laughter, scorn, scoffing, jeering. ANTONYMS respect. ▶ **v.** **mock**, deride, laugh at, heap scorn on, jeer at, make fun of, scoff at, satirize, caricature, parody.

ri·dic·u·lous /riˈdikyələs/ ▶ **adj.** very silly or unreasonable; absurd.

SYNONYMS **laughable**, absurd, ludicrous, risible, comical, funny, hilarious, amusing, farcical, silly, stupid, idiotic, preposterous. ANTONYMS sensible.

■ **ri·dic·u·lous·ly adv.**

rid·ing /ˈrīdiNG/ ▶ **n.** the activity or sport of riding a horse, bicycle, etc.

rife /rīf/ ▶ **adj.** **1** (of something bad or unpleasant) widespread. **2** (**rife with**) full of something bad or unpleasant.

SYNONYMS **widespread**, general, common, universal, extensive, ubiquitous, endemic, inescapable.

riff /rif/ ▶ **n.** a short repeated phrase in pop music or jazz.

rif·fle /ˈrifəl/ ▶ **v.** (**riffles**, **riffling**, **riffled**) (**riffle through**) turn over the pages of a book quickly and casually.

riff·raff /ˈrifˌraf/ ▶ **n.** people who are considered socially undesirable.

SYNONYMS **rabble**, good-for-nothings, undesirables, the lowest of the low, scum; informal peasants. ANTONYMS elite.

ri·fle /ˈrīfəl/ ▶ **n.** a gun with a long barrel. ▶ **v.** (**rifles**, **rifling**, **rifled**) **1** search through something hurriedly to find or steal something. **2** hit, throw, or kick a ball hard and straight.

SYNONYMS ▶ **v.** **1** **rummage**, search, hunt, forage. **2** **ransack**, plunder, loot, raid, rob, steal from, burgle, burglarize.

rift /rift/ ▶ **n.** **1** a crack, split, or break. **2** a serious break in friendly relations.

SYNONYMS **1** **crack**, split, breach, fissure, fracture, cleft, crevice, opening. **2** **disagreement**, estrangement, breach, split, schism, quarrel, falling-out, conflict, feud.

rig /rig/ ▶ **v.** (**rigs**, **rigging**, **rigged**) **1** secretly arrange something in order to gain an advantage. **2** fit sails and rigging on a boat. **3** (often **rig something up**) set up a device or structure: *he will rig up a shelter*. ▶ **n.** **1** a piece of equipment for a particular purpose: *a lighting rig*. **2** a large piece of equipment for extracting oil or gas from the ground.

SYNONYMS ▶ **v.** **1** **manipulate**, engineer, distort, misrepresent, pervert, tamper with, falsify, fake; informal fix. **2** **equip**, fit out, supply, furnish, provide, arm. **3** **set up**, erect, assemble, put together, whip up, improvise, contrive; informal knock together.

rig·ging /ˈrigiNG/ ▶ **n.** the system of ropes or chains supporting a ship's masts.

right /rīt/ ▶ **adj.** **1** on or toward the side of a person or thing that is to the east when the person or thing is facing north. **2** justified or morally good. **3** factually correct. **4** most appropriate. **5** satisfactory, sound, or normal. **6** right-wing. ▶ **adv.** **1** on or to the right side. **2** completely; totally. **3** exactly; directly. **4** correctly or satisfactorily. ▶ **n.** **1** what is morally right. **2** an entitlement to have or do something. **3** (**rights**) the authority to perform, publish, or film a work or event. **4** (**the right**) the right-hand part, side, or direction. **5** a right turn. **6** (often **the Right**) a right-wing group or party. ▶ **v.** **1** put something back in a normal or upright position. **2** correct or make up for a wrong.

SYNONYMS ▶ **adj.** **1** **just**, fair, equitable, proper, good, upright, righteous, virtuous, moral, ethical, principled, honorable, honest, lawful, legal. **2** **correct**, unerring, accurate, exact, precise, valid. **3** **suitable**, appropriate, fitting, apposite, apt, correct, proper, desirable, preferable, ideal. **4** **opportune**, advantageous, favorable, convenient, good, lucky, fortunate. **5** **right-hand**; Nautical starboard; Heraldry dexter. ANTONYMS wrong, left. ▶ **adv.** **1** **completely**, fully, totally, absolutely, utterly, thoroughly, quite. **2** **exactly**, precisely, directly, immediately, just, squarely, dead; informal (slam) bang, smack, plumb. **3** **correctly**, accurately, perfectly. ANTONYMS wrong, badly. ▶ **n.** **1** **goodness**, righteousness, virtue, integrity, propriety, probity, morality, truth, honesty, honor, justice, fairness, equity. **2** **entitlement**, prerogative, privilege, liberty, authority, power, license, permission, dispensation, leave, due. ANTONYMS wrong. ▶ **v.** **remedy**, rectify, retrieve, fix, resolve, sort out, settle, square, straighten out, correct, repair, mend, redress.

□ **by rights** if things were fair or correct. **in your own right** as a result of your own qualifications or efforts. **right angle** an angle of 90°, as in a corner of a square. **right field** Baseball the part of the outfield to the right of center field from the perspective of home plate. **right of way** **1** the legal right to go through someone's property along a specific route. **2** a public path through someone's property. **3** the right to proceed before another vehicle. **right-wing** conservative or opposed to political or social change. ■ **right·ward** (also **rightwards**) **adj. & adv.**

right·eous /ˈrīCHəs/ ▶ **adj.** morally right.

SYNONYMS **good**, virtuous, upright, upstanding, decent, ethical, principled, moral, honest, honorable, blameless. ANTONYMS wicked.

■ **right·eous·ly adv.**

right·ful /'rītfəl/ ▶ **adj.** **1** having a clear right to something. **2** proper; fitting.

SYNONYMS **1 legal**, lawful, legitimate, real, true, proper, correct, recognized, genuine, authentic, acknowledged, approved, valid, bona fide; informal legit, kosher. **2 deserved**, merited, due, just, right, fair, proper, fitting, appropriate, suitable. ANTONYMS wrongful.

■ **right·ful·ly** adv.

right·ly /'rītlē/ ▶ **adv.** **1** in accordance with what is true, morally right, or just. **2** with good reason.

rig·id /'rijid/ ▶ **adj.** **1** unable to bend or be put out of shape. **2** (of a person) stiff and unmoving. **3** not able to be changed or adapted.

SYNONYMS **1 stiff**, hard, taut, firm, inflexible, unbendable, unyielding, inelastic. **2** *a rigid routine* **fixed**, set, firm, inflexible, invariable, hard and fast, cast-iron, strict, stringent, rigorous, uncompromising, intransigent. ANTONYMS flexible.

■ **ri·gid·i·ty** /rə'jidətē/ **n.** **rig·id·ly** adv.

rig·ma·role /'rig(ə)mə,rōl/ ▶ **n.** a lengthy and complicated procedure.

rig·or /'rigər/ ▶ **n.** **1** the quality of being rigorous. **2** (**rigors**) difficult or extreme conditions.

rig·or mor·tis /,rigər 'môrtəs/ ▶ **n.** stiffening of the joints and muscles that happens a few hours after death.

rig·or·ous /'rigərəs/ ▶ **adj.** **1** very thorough or accurate. **2** (of a rule, system, etc.) strictly applied or followed. **3** harsh or severe.

SYNONYMS **1 meticulous**, conscientious, punctilious, careful, scrupulous, painstaking, exact, precise, accurate, particular, strict. **2 strict**, stringent, rigid, inflexible, draconian, intransigent, uncompromising. **3** *rigorous conditions* **harsh**, severe, bleak, extreme, demanding. ANTONYMS slapdash, lax.

■ **rig·or·ous·ly** adv.

rile /rīl/ ▶ **v.** (**riles**, **riling**, **riled**) informal annoy or irritate.

rill /ril/ ▶ **n.** literary a small stream.

rim /rim/ ▶ **n.** **1** the upper or outer edge of something circular. **2** a limit or boundary. ▶ **v.** (**rims**, **rimming**, **rimmed**) provide with a rim.

SYNONYMS ▶ **n. edge**, brim, lip, border, side, margin, brink, boundary, perimeter, circumference, limits, periphery.

rime /rīm/ ▶ **n.** literary hoarfrost.

rind /rīnd/ ▶ **n.** a tough outer layer or covering of fruit, cheese, bacon, etc.

SYNONYMS **skin**, peel, zest, integument.

ring[1] /riNG/ ▶ **n.** **1** a small circular metal band worn on a finger. **2** a circular band, object, or mark. **3** an enclosed space in which a sport, performance, or show takes place. **4** a group of people with a shared interest or goal. ▶ **v.** **1** surround. **2** draw a circle around.

SYNONYMS ▶ **n.** **1 circle**, band, halo, disk/disc. **2 arena**, enclosure, amphitheater, bowl. **3 gang**, syndicate, cartel, mob, band, circle, organization, association, society, alliance, league. ▶ **v. surround**, circle, encircle, enclose, hem in, confine, seal off.

□ **ring binder** a binder with ring-shaped clasps.

ring[2] ▶ **v.** (**rings**, **ringing**, **rang** /raNG/; past participle **rung** /rəNG/) **1** make a clear and repeated or long-lasting sound. **2** (**ring with**) echo with such a sound. **3** call for attention by sounding a bell. **4** (of the ears) be filled with a buzzing or humming sound. **5** (**ring something up**) record an amount on a cash register. ▶ **n.** **1** an act of ringing. **2** a loud, clear sound or tone. **3** a quality or feeling conveyed by words: *a ring of truth*.

SYNONYMS ▶ **v.** **1 chime**, sound, peal, toll, clang, bong; literary knell. **2 resound**, reverberate, resonate, echo. **3 telephone**, phone (up), call (up); informal give someone a buzz/ring.

□ **give someone a ring** informal telephone someone.

ring·er /'riNGər/ ▶ **n.** **1** a person or device that rings. **2** informal ⇒ **DEAD RINGER**. **3** informal an athlete or horse that is dishonestly substituted for another in a competition.

ring·ing /'riNGiNG/ ▶ **adj.** **1** having a clear, resonant sound. **2** forceful and clear.

ring·lead·er /'riNG,lēdər/ ▶ **n.** a person who leads others in committing a crime or causing trouble.

ring·let /'riNGlit/ ▶ **n.** a corkscrew-shaped curl of hair.

ring·mas·ter /'riNG,mastər/ ▶ **n.** the person who directs a circus performance.

ring·tone /'riNG,tōn/ ▶ **n.** a sound made by a cell phone when an incoming call is received.

ring·worm /'riNG,wərm/ ▶ **n.** a skin disease that causes small, itchy circular patches.

rink /riNGk/ ▶ **n.** **1** (also **ice rink**) an enclosed area of ice for skating, ice hockey, or curling. **2** the strip of a bowling green used for a match.

rinse /rins/ ▶ **v.** (**rinses**, **rinsing**, **rinsed**) **1** wash with clean water to remove soap or dirt. **2** remove soap or dirt by rinsing. ▶ **n.** **1** an act of rinsing. **2** an antiseptic solution for cleaning the mouth. **3** a liquid for conditioning or coloring the hair.

SYNONYMS ▶ **v. wash (out)**, clean, cleanse, bathe, dip, drench, splash, swill, sluice.

ri·ot /'rīət/ ▶ **n.** **1** a violent disturbance caused by an angry crowd. **2** a confused combination or display: *a riot of color*. **3** (**a riot**) informal a very entertaining person or thing. ▶ **v.** take part in a riot.

SYNONYMS ▶ **n. disorder**, disturbance, lawlessness, upheaval, uproar, commotion, free-for-all, uprising, insurrection. ▶ **v.** (**go on the**) **rampage**, run wild, run amok, run riot, go berserk; informal raise hell.

□ **run riot** behave in an uncontrolled way.
■ **ri·ot·er** n.

ri·ot·ous /'rīətəs/ ▶ **adj.** **1** wild and uncontrolled. **2** involving public disorder.

SYNONYMS **1 unruly**, rowdy, disorderly, uncontrollable, unmanageable, undisciplined, uproarious, tumultuous, violent, wild, lawless, anarchic. **2 boisterous**, lively, loud, noisy, unrestrained, uninhibited, uproarious; informal rambunctious. ANTONYMS peaceful.

RIP ▶ **abbr.** rest in peace.

rip /rip/ ▶ **v.** (**rips**, **ripping**, **ripped**) **1** suddenly tear or become torn. **2** pull forcibly away. ▶ **n.** a long tear.

SYNONYMS ▶ **v. tear**, pull, wrench, snatch, drag, pluck; informal yank.

□ **let rip** informal move or act without restraint. **rip someone off** informal cheat someone. **rip something**

off informal steal something. **rip-off** informal an article or service that is greatly overpriced. **rip-roaring** very energetic and exciting. **rip tide** a stretch of fast-flowing rough water caused by currents meeting.

ri·par·i·an /ri'pe(ə)rēən, rī-/ ▶ **adj.** technical relating to or on the banks of a river.

rip·cord /'ripˌkôrd/ ▶ **n.** a cord that you pull to open a parachute.

ripe /rīp/ ▶ **adj. 1** ready for harvesting and eating. **2** (of a cheese or wine) fully matured. **3** (**ripe for**) having reached the right time for. **4** (of a person's age) advanced.

SYNONYMS **1 mature**, full grown, fully developed. **2** *ripe for development* **ready**, fit, suitable, right. **3** *the time is ripe* **opportune**, advantageous, favorable, auspicious, good, right. ANTONYMS immature.

■ **ripe·ly** **adv.** **ripe·ness** **n.**

rip·en /'rīpən/ ▶ **v.** become or make ripe.

SYNONYMS **mature**, mellow, develop.

ri·poste /ri'pōst/ ▶ **n.** a quick reply.

SYNONYMS **retort**, counter, rejoinder, sally, return, answer, reply, response; informal comeback.

rip·ple /'ripəl/ ▶ **n. 1** a small wave or series of waves. **2** a feeling, effect, or sound that spreads through someone or something. **3** ice cream with wavy lines of syrup running through it. ▶ **v.** (**ripples**, **rippling**, **rippled**) **1** form ripples. **2** (of a sound, feeling, etc.) spread through a person or place.

rise /rīz/ ▶ **v.** (**rises**, **rising**, **rose** /rōz/; past participle **risen** /'rizən/) **1** come or go up. **2** get up after lying, sitting, or kneeling. **3** increase in number, size, strength, etc. **4** (of land) slope upward. **5** (of the sun, moon, or stars) appear above the horizon. **6** (**rise above**) manage not to be restricted by. **7** (**rise to**) respond well to a difficult situation. **8** (**rise up**) rebel. **9** (of a river) have its source. ▶ **n. 1** an act of rising. **2** an upward slope or hill.

SYNONYMS ▶ **v. 1 climb**, come up, arise, ascend, mount, soar. **2 loom**, tower, soar. **3 go up**, increase, soar, shoot up, surge, leap, jump, rocket, escalate, spiral. **4 get higher**, grow, increase, become louder, swell, intensify. **5 stand up**, get to your feet, get up, jump up, leap up, stir, bestir yourself. ANTONYMS fall, descend, drop. ▶ **n. 1 increase**, hike, leap, upsurge, upswing, climb. **2 raise**, increase, increment. **3 slope**, incline, hill, elevation, acclivity.

ris·er /'rīzər/ ▶ **n. 1** a person who gets up at a particular time. **2** a vertical section between the treads of a staircase.

ris·i·ble /'rizəbəl/ ▶ **adj.** causing laughter. ■ **ris·i·bly** **adv.**

ris·ing /'rīziNG/ ▶ **n.** a rebellion or revolt; uprising. ▶ **adj. 1** increasing. **2** advancing to maturity or high standing.

risk /risk/ ▶ **n. 1** a situation that involves being exposed to danger. **2** the possibility that something bad will happen. **3** a person or thing that causes a risk. ▶ **v. 1** expose to danger or loss. **2** act in such a way that there is a chance of something bad happening.

SYNONYMS ▶ **n. 1 chance**, uncertainty, unpredictability, instability, insecurity. **2 possibility**, chance, probability, likelihood, danger, peril, threat, menace, prospect. ▶ **v. endanger**, jeopardize, imperil, hazard, gamble (with), chance, put at risk, put on the line.

risk·y /'riskē/ ▶ **adj.** (**riskier**, **riskiest**) involving the possibility of danger or a bad outcome.

SYNONYMS **dangerous**, hazardous, perilous, unsafe, insecure, precarious, touch-and-go, treacherous, uncertain, unpredictable; informal dicey.

■ **risk·i·ly** **adv.** **risk·i·ness** **n.**

ri·sot·to /ri'zôtō, -'sôtō/ ▶ **n.** (plural **risottos**) a dish of rice cooked in stock and with other ingredients such as meat, seafood, vegetables, etc.

SPELLING

Only one **s**: risotto.

ris·qué /ri'skā/ ▶ **adj.** slightly indecent.

SYNONYMS **ribald**, rude, bawdy, racy, earthy, indecent, vulgar, dirty, smutty, crude, coarse, obscene, lewd, X-rated, suggestive, improper, naughty, locker-room; informal **blue**, **off color**, raunchy; euphemistic **adult**.

ris·sole /ri'sōl, 'risˌōl/ ▶ **n.** a small flat mass of chopped meat that is coated in breadcrumbs and fried.

rite /rīt/ ▶ **n.** a religious ceremony, or other solemn procedure.

SYNONYMS **ceremony**, ritual, ceremonial, custom, service, observance, liturgy, worship, office.

□ **rite of passage** a ceremony or event that marks an important stage in someone's life.

rit·u·al /'ricHo͞oəl/ ▶ **n. 1** a ceremony that involves a series of actions performed in a set order. **2** something that is habitually done in the same way. ▶ **adj.** done as a ritual.

SYNONYMS ▶ **n. ceremony**, rite, act, practice, custom, tradition, convention, formality, protocol. ▶ **adj. ceremonial**, prescribed, set, conventional, traditional, formal.

■ **rit·u·al·ly** **adv.**

ritz·y /'ritsē/ ▶ **adj.** (**ritzier**, **ritziest**) informal expensively stylish.

ri·val /'rīvəl/ ▶ **n. 1** a person or thing competing with another for the same thing. **2** a person or thing equal to another in quality. ▶ **v.** (**rivals**, **rivaling**, **rivaled**) be comparable to.

SYNONYMS ▶ **n. 1 opponent**, opposition, challenger, competitor, contender, adversary, antagonist, enemy; literary foe. **2** *rival candidates* **competing**, opposing, in competition. ANTONYMS ally, allied. ▶ **v. match**, compare with, compete with, vie with, equal, emulate, measure up to, touch; informal hold a candle to.

ri·val·ry /'rīvəlrē/ ▶ **n.** (plural **rivalries**) a situation in which two people or groups are competing for the same thing.

SYNONYMS **competition**, contention, opposition, conflict, feuding; informal keeping up with the Joneses.

riven /'rivən/ ▶ **adj.** literary torn apart; split.

riv·er /'rivər/ ▶ **n. 1** a large natural flow of water moving in a channel to the sea or another river. **2** a large quantity of a flowing substance.

SYNONYMS **1 stream**, brook, creek, watercourse, rivulet, tributary. **2** *a river of molten lava* **stream**, torrent, flood, deluge, cascade.

riv·er·bank /ˈrivərˌbaNGk/ ▶ **n.** the bank of a river.

riv·er·boat /ˈrivərˌbōt/ ▶ **n.** a boat designed for use on rivers.

riv·er·side /ˈrivərˌsīd/ ▶ **n.** the ground along a riverbank.

riv·et /ˈrivit/ ▶ **n.** a short metal pin or bolt for holding together two metal plates. ▶ **v.** (**rivets, riveting, riveted**) **1** fasten with a rivet or rivets. **2** (**be riveted**) be completely fascinated by something.

riv·i·er·a /ˌrivēˈe(ə)rə, riˈvye(ə)rə/ ▶ **n.** a coastal area of a warm country, especially in southern France and northern Italy.

riv·u·let /ˈriv(y)ələt/ ▶ **n.** a small stream.

RN ▶ **abbr.** registered nurse.

RNA ▶ **n.** a substance in living cells that carries instructions from DNA.

roach[1] /rōCH/ ▶ **n.** (plural **roach**) a common freshwater fish of the carp family.

roach[2] ▶ **n.** informal a cockroach.

road /rōd/ ▶ **n. 1** a wide track with a hard surface for vehicles to travel on. **2** a way to achieving a particular outcome.

SYNONYMS **1 street**, thoroughfare, roadway, avenue, boulevard, highway, lane. **2** *the road to recovery* **way**, path, route, course.

□ **road rage** informal violent anger caused by conflict with the driver of another vehicle. **road test** a test of the performance of a vehicle or of other equipment.

road·block /ˈrōdˌbläk/ ▶ **n.** a barrier put across a road by the police or army to stop and examine traffic.

road·hold·ing /ˈrōdˌhōldiNG/ ▶ **n.** the ability of a moving vehicle to remain stable.

road·house /ˈrōdˌhous/ ▶ **n.** a tavern, restaurant, etc., on a country road.

road·ie /ˈrōdē/ ▶ **n.** informal a person who sets up equipment for a rock group, usually at different stops on a road tour.

road·run·ner /ˈrōdˌrənər/ ▶ **n.** a fast-running long-tailed bird found from the southern US to Central America.

road·show /ˈrōdˌSHō/ ▶ **n. 1** a show broadcast from a different place each day. **2** a touring political or promotional campaign.

road·ster /ˈrōdstər/ ▶ **n.** an open-top sports car.

road·way /ˈrōdˌwā/ ▶ **n. 1** a road. **2** the part of a road intended for vehicles.

road·wor·thy /ˈrōdˌwərTHē/ ▶ **adj.** (of a vehicle) fit to be used on the road.

roam /rōm/ ▶ **v.** travel aimlessly over a wide area.

SYNONYMS **wander**, rove, ramble, drift, walk, traipse, range, travel, tramp, trek; informal cruise.

roam·ing /ˈrōmiNG/ ▶ **n.** the use of a cell phone on another operator's network, often while abroad.

roan /rōn/ ▶ **adj.** (of a horse) having a bay, chestnut, or black coat mixed with hairs of another color.

roar /rôr/ ▶ **n.** a loud, deep sound made by a lion, engine, etc., or by a person who is angry, amused, or in pain. ▶ **v. 1** make a roar. **2** (**roaring**) burning strongly. **3** laugh loudly. **4** (**roaring**) informal complete: *a roaring success*. **5** move very fast.

SYNONYMS ▶ **v. 1 bellow**, yell, shout, thunder, bawl, howl, scream, cry, bay; informal holler. **2** (**roaring**) *a roaring fire* **blazing**, burning, flaming.

roast /rōst/ ▶ **v. 1** cook food in an oven or over a fire. **2** make or become very warm. ▶ **adj.** (of food) having been roasted. ▶ **n.** a cut of meat that has been roasted.

roast·ing /ˈrōstiNG/ informal ▶ **adj.** very hot and dry. ▶ **n.** a severe reprimand.

rob /räb/ ▶ **v.** (**robs, robbing, robbed**) **1** steal property from a person or place by using force or threatening violence. **2** deprive someone of something.

SYNONYMS **1 steal from**, burglarize, burgle, hold up, break into, raid, loot, plunder, pillage; informal mug. **2 cheat**, swindle, defraud; informal do out of, con out of.

rob·ber /ˈräbər/ ▶ **n.** a person who commits robbery.

SYNONYMS **burglar**, thief, housebreaker, mugger, shoplifter, raider, looter.

rob·ber·y /ˈräb(ə)rē/ ▶ **n.** (plural **robberies**) the action of robbing a person or place.

SYNONYMS **burglary**, theft, stealing, housebreaking, shoplifting, embezzlement, fraud, holdup, raid; informal mugging, stickup, heist.

robe /rōb/ ▶ **n. 1** a loose garment reaching to the ankles, worn on formal or ceremonial occasions. **2** a bathrobe. ▶ **v.** (**robes, robing, robed**) clothe someone in a robe.

SYNONYMS ▶ **n. 1 cloak**, kaftan, wrap, wrapper, mantle, cape. **2** *ceremonial robes* **garb**, vestments, regalia, finery.

rob·in /ˈräbən/ ▶ **n.** a small bird with a red breast and brown back and wings.

ro·bot /ˈrōˌbät, ˈrōbət/ ▶ **n.** a machine capable of carrying out a complex series of actions automatically.

SYNONYMS **machine**, automaton, android; informal bot, droid.

ro·bot·ic /rōˈbätik/ ▶ **adj. 1** relating to robots. **2** mechanical, stiff, or unemotional.

ro·bot·ics /rōˈbätiks/ ▶ **pl.n.** the science of constructing and using robots.

ro·bust /rōˈbəst, ˈrōˌbəst/ ▶ **adj. 1** sturdy or able to withstand difficult conditions. **2** strong and healthy. **3** determined and forceful.

SYNONYMS **1 strong**, vigorous, sturdy, tough, powerful, solid, rugged, hardy, strapping, healthy, (fighting) fit, hale and hearty. **2 durable**, resilient, tough, hard-wearing, long-lasting, sturdy, strong. ANTONYMS frail, fragile.

■ **ro·bust·ly** **adv.**

rock[1] /räk/ ▶ **n. 1** the hard material that makes up the earth's crust. **2** a projecting mass of rock. **3** a boulder. **4** informal a diamond or other precious stone.

SYNONYMS **boulder**, stone, pebble.

□ **on the rocks** informal **1** in difficulties and likely to fail. **2** (of a drink) served undiluted and with ice cubes. **rock bottom** the lowest possible level.

rock candy sugar crystallized in large masses onto a string or stick, eaten as candy. **rock salt** salt occurring naturally as a mineral.

rock² ▶ **v. 1** move gently to and fro or from side to side. **2** shake violently. **3** shock or distress very much. ▶ **n. 1** (also **rock music**) a type of loud popular music with a heavy beat. **2** a rocking movement.

SYNONYMS ▶ **v. 1 move to and fro**, sway, seesaw, roll, pitch, plunge, toss, lurch. **2 stun**, shock, stagger, astonish, startle, surprise, shake, take aback, throw, unnerve, disconcert.

□ **rock and roll** a type of popular music with simple melodies, originating in the 1950s. **rocking chair** a chair mounted on curved bars. **rocking horse** a model horse mounted on curved bars for a child to ride on.

rock·a·bil·ly /ˈräkəˌbilē/ ▶ **n.** music that combines rock and roll and country music.

rock·er /ˈräkər/ ▶ **n. 1** a curved piece of wood on the bottom of a rocking chair. **2** a person who performs or likes rock music. □ **off your rocker** informal crazy.

rock·et /ˈräkit/ ▶ **n. 1** a tube-shaped missile or spacecraft propelled by a stream of burning gases. **2** a firework that shoots high in the air and explodes. **3** ⇒ ARUGULA. ▶ **v.** (**rockets**, **rocketing**, **rocketed**) move or increase very quickly and suddenly.

rock·y /ˈräkē/ ▶ **adj.** (**rockier**, **rockiest**) **1** consisting or formed of rock. **2** full of rocks. **3** unsteady or unstable.

SYNONYMS **1 stony**, pebbly, shingly, rough, bumpy, craggy, mountainous. **2 unsteady**, shaky, unstable, wobbly, tottery, rickety.
ANTONYMS steady, stable.

ro·co·co /rəˈkōkō, ˌrōkəˈkō/ ▶ **adj.** (of furniture or architecture) in a highly decorated style popular in the 18th century.

rod /räd/ ▶ **n. 1** a thin straight bar of wood, metal, etc. **2** ⇒ FISHING ROD.

SYNONYMS **bar**, stick, pole, baton, staff, shaft, strut, rail, spoke.

rode /rōd/ past of RIDE.

ro·dent /ˈrōdnt/ ▶ **n.** a mammal of a large group including rats, mice, and squirrels, with large front teeth.

ro·de·o /ˈrōdēˌō, rəˈdāō/ ▶ **n.** (plural **rodeos**) a contest or entertainment in which cowboys show their horse-riding and lassoing skills.

roe /rō/ ▶ **n.** the eggs or sperm of a fish, used as food. □ **roe deer** a small deer with a coat that is reddish in summer.

roe·buck /ˈrōˌbək/ ▶ **n.** a male roe deer.

roent·gen /ˈrentgən, ˈrənt-, -jən/ (or **röntgen**) ▶ **n.** a unit of radiation.

rog·er /ˈräjər/ ▶ **exclam.** your message has been received (used in radio communication).

rogue /rōg/ ▶ **n. 1** a dishonest or immoral man. **2** a mischievous but likable person. **3** an elephant that is living apart from the herd.

SYNONYMS **scoundrel**, rascal, good-for-nothing, wretch, villain, criminal, lawbreaker; informal crook.

ro·guish /ˈrōgisʜ/ ▶ **adj.** mischievous.

roist·er /ˈroistər/ ▶ **v.** (**roisters**, **roistering**, **roistered**) old use enjoy yourself in a lively, noisy way.

role /rōl/ ▶ **n. 1** an actor's part in a play, movie, etc. **2** a person's or thing's function in a particular situation.

SYNONYMS **1 part**, character. **2 capacity**, position, function, job, post, office, duty, responsibility.

□ **role model** a person that others look up to as an example to be imitated. **role-playing** the acting out of a role or situation.

USAGE

Don't confuse **role** with **roll**, which mainly means 'move by turning over and over' or 'a rolling movement.'

roll /rōl/ ▶ **v. 1** move by turning over and over. **2** move forward on wheels or with a smooth motion. **3** (of a moving ship, aircraft, etc.) sway from side to side. **4** (of a machine or device) begin operating. **5** (often **roll something up**) turn something flexible over and over on itself. **6** (**roll up**) curl up tightly. **7** (**roll something out**) officially launch a new product. **8** flatten with a roller. **9** (of a loud, deep sound) reverberate. **10** (**roll up**) informal arrive. ▶ **n. 1** a cylinder formed by rolling flexible material. **2** a rolling movement. **3** a long, deep, reverberating sound. **4** a very small loaf of bread. **5** an official list or register of names.

SYNONYMS ▶ **v. 1 turn over and over**, spin, rotate, revolve, wheel, trundle, bowl. **2 flow**, run, course, stream, pour, trickle. **3 wind**, coil, fold, curl, twist. **4 rock**, sway, reel, list, pitch, plunge, lurch, toss. ▶ **n. 1 cylinder**, tube, scroll, reel, spool, bobbin. **2 turn**, rotation, revolution, spin, whirl. **3 list**, register, directory, record, file, index, catalog, inventory. **4** *a roll of thunder* **rumble**, reverberation, echo, boom, clap, crack.

□ **roll call** an occasion when a list of names is read out to discover who is present. **rolling pin** a cylinder for rolling out dough. **rolling stock** locomotives, railroad cars, and other vehicles used on a railroad. **roll-on** applied by means of a rotating ball.

USAGE

Don't confuse **roll** with **role**, which means 'an actor's part in a play or movie.'

roll·er /ˈrōlər/ ▶ **n. 1** a rotating cylinder used to move, flatten, or spread something. **2** a small cylinder on which you roll your hair to make it curly. **3** a long wave moving toward the shore. □ **roller coaster** a fairground attraction in which you ride in an open carriage on a steep, twisting track. **roller skate** a boot with wheels on which you can glide across a hard surface.

Roll·er·blade /ˈrōlərˌblād/ ▶ **n.** trademark a roller skate with wheels in a single line along the sole. ■ **roll·er·blad·ing n.**

rol·lick·ing /ˈrälikiɴɢ/ ▶ **adj.** cheerfully lively and amusing.

ro·ly-po·ly /ˈrōlē ˈpōlē/ ▶ **adj.** informal round and plump.

Ro·man /ˈrōmən/ ▶ **adj. 1** relating to Rome or its ancient empire. **2** referring to the alphabet used for writing Latin, English, and most European languages. **3** (**roman**) (of a typeface) plain and upright, used in ordinary print. ▶ **n. 1** an inhabitant of Rome. **2** (**roman**) roman type. □ **Roman Catholic 1** of the Christian church that has the pope as its head. **2** a member of the Roman Catholic Church. ▫ **Roman numeral** each of the letters, I, V, X, L, C, D, and M, used in ancient Rome to represent numbers.

ro·mance /rō'mans, 'rō,mans/ ▶ **n. 1** a pleasurable feeling of excitement associated with love. **2** a love affair. **3** a book or movie that deals with love in a sentimental or idealized way. **4** a feeling of mystery, excitement, and remoteness from everyday life. **5** (**Romance**) French, Spanish, Italian, and other languages descended from Latin. ▶ **v.** (**romances**, **romancing**, **romanced**) try to win the love of someone.

SYNONYMS ▶ **n. 1 love affair**, relationship, liaison, courtship, attachment, amour. **2 story**, tale, legend, fairy tale. **3 mystery**, glamour, excitement, exoticism, mystique, appeal, allure, charm.

Ro·man·esque /,rōmə'nesk/ ▶ **adj.** relating to a style of architecture common in Europe *c.*900–1200.

Ro·ma·ni·an /rō'mānēən, ro͝o-/ (or **Rumanian** /ro͝o'mānēən/) ▶ **n. 1** a person from Romania. **2** the language of Romania. ▶ **adj.** relating to Romania.

ro·man·tic /rō'mantik, rə-/ ▶ **adj. 1** having to do with love or romance. **2** thinking about or showing life in an idealized rather than realistic way. **3** (**Romantic**) relating to the artistic and literary movement of Romanticism. ▶ **n. 1** a person with romantic beliefs or attitudes. **2** (**Romantic**) an artist or writer of the Romantic movement.

SYNONYMS ▶ **adj. 1 loving**, amorous, passionate, tender, affectionate; informal lovey-dovey. **2 sentimental**, hearts-and-flowers; informal sappy, slushy, schmaltzy. **3 idyllic**, picturesque, fairy-tale, beautiful, lovely, charming, pretty. **4 idealistic**, unrealistic, fanciful, impractical, head-in-the-clouds, starry-eyed, utopian, rose-tinted. ANTONYMS unsentimental, realistic. ▶ **n. idealist**, sentimentalist, dreamer, fantasist. ANTONYMS realist.

▪ **ro·man·ti·cal·ly adv.**

Ro·man·ti·cism /rō'mantə,sizəm, rə-/ ▶ **n.** a literary and artistic movement that emphasized creative inspiration and individual feeling.

ro·man·ti·cize /rō'mantə,sīz, rə-/ ▶ **v.** (**romanticizes**, **romanticizing**, **romanticized**) make something seem more attractive and inspiring than it really is.

Rom·a·ny /'rämənē, 'rō-/ ▶ **n.** (plural **Romanies**) **1** the language of the Gypsies. **2** a Gypsy.

Ro·me·o /'rōmē,ō/ ▶ **n.** (plural **Romeos**) an attractive, passionate male lover.

romp /rämp, rômp/ ▶ **v. 1** play about roughly and energetically. **2** informal proceed without effort to achieve something. ▶ **n. 1** a spell of rough, energetic play. **2** a lighthearted movie or other work. **3** informal an easy victory.

SYNONYMS ▶ **v. play**, frolic, frisk, gambol, skip, prance, caper, cavort.

romp·ers /'rämpər, 'rôm-/ ▶ **pl.n.** a young child's one-piece garment.

ron·do /'rändō, rän'dō/ ▶ **n.** (plural **rondos**) a piece of music with a recurring leading theme.

rönt·gen = ROENTGEN.

rood screen /ro͞od/ ▶ **n.** a screen of wood or stone separating the nave from the chancel of a church.

roof /ro͞of, ro͝of/ ▶ **n.** (plural **roofs**) **1** the upper covering of a building or vehicle. **2** the top inner surface of a covered space. ▶ **v.** put a roof over. ▫ **hit** (or **go through**) **the roof** informal suddenly become very angry. **roof rack** a framework for carrying luggage or other items on the roof of a vehicle.

roof·er /'ro͞ofər/ ▶ **n.** a person who builds or repairs roofs.

roof·top /'ro͞of,täp, 'ro͝of-/ ▶ **n.** the outer surface of a building's roof.

rook[1] /ro͝ok/ ▶ **n.** a crow that nests in colonies in treetops.

rook[2] ▶ **n.** a chess piece that can move in any direction except diagonally.

rook·er·y /'ro͝okərē/ ▶ **n.** (plural **rookeries**) **1** a collection of rooks' nests high in a clump of trees. **2** a breeding place of seabirds, seals, or turtles.

rook·ie /'ro͝okē/ ▶ **n.** informal **1** a new recruit. **2** a sports player in their first season.

room /ro͞om, ro͝om/ ▶ **n. 1** a part of a building enclosed by walls, a floor, and a ceiling. **2** (**rooms**) a set of rooms rented out to a lodger. **3** empty space in which you can do or put things. ▶ **v.** share a rented room or apartment.

SYNONYMS ▶ **n. 1 space**, headroom, legroom, area, expanse, extent. **2** *there's very little room for maneuver* **scope**, opportunity, capacity, leeway, latitude, freedom.

▫ **rooming house** a private house providing rented accommodations.

room·ie /'ro͞omē, 'ro͝omē/ ▶ **n.** informal a roommate.

room·mate /'ro͞om,māt, 'ro͝om-/ ▶ **n.** a person occupying the same room, apartment, or house as another.

room·y /'ro͞omē, 'ro͝omē/ ▶ **adj.** (**roomier**, **roomiest**) having plenty of space.

SYNONYMS **spacious**, capacious, sizable, generous, big, large, extensive, voluminous, ample; formal commodious. ANTONYMS cramped.

roost /ro͞ost/ ▶ **n.** a place where birds regularly settle to rest. ▶ **v.** (of a bird or birds) settle or gather for rest.

roost·er /'ro͞ostər, 'ro͝ostər/ ▶ **n.** a male chicken.

root[1] /ro͞ot/ ▶ **n. 1** the part of a plant that is normally below ground, which acts as a support and collects water and nourishment. **2** the part of a hair, tooth, nail, etc., that is fixed in the body tissue. **3** the basic cause or origin of something: *money is the root of all evil.* **4** (**roots**) your family or origins. **5** Math a number that when multiplied by itself one or more times gives a particular number. ▶ **v. 1** (of a plant or cutting) grow roots. **2** (**be rooted**) be firmly established. **3** (**root something out**) find and get rid of something. **4** (**be rooted in**) have something as an origin or cause.

SYNONYMS ▶ **n. 1 source**, origin, cause, reason, basis, foundation, bottom, seat. **2** *his Irish roots* **origins**, beginnings, family, birth, heritage. ▶ **v.** (**rooted**) **1** *Neil was rooted to the spot* **frozen**, riveted, paralyzed, glued, fixed. **2** *views rooted in Indian culture* **embedded**, fixed, established, entrenched, ingrained.

▫ **put down roots** begin to have a settled life in a place. **root beer** a carbonated drink made from an extract of the roots and bark of certain plants. **root vegetable** a vegetable that grows as the root of a plant. **take root** become established.

root² ▶ v. **1** (of an animal) turn up the ground with its snout in search of food. **2** rummage. **3** (**root for**) informal support someone enthusiastically.

SYNONYMS **rummage**, hunt, search, rifle, delve, forage, dig, poke.

root·less /'ro͞otlis/ ▶ adj. having nowhere where you feel settled and at home.

root·stock /'ro͞ot,stäk, 'ro͞ot-/ ▶ n. **1** a rhizome. **2** a plant on to which another variety is grafted.

rope /rōp/ ▶ n. **1** a length of thick cord made by twisting together thinner strands of fiber. **2** a number of objects strung together. **3** (**the ropes**) the ropes enclosing a boxing or wrestling ring. **4** (**the ropes**) informal the established way of doing something. ▶ v. (**ropes**, **roping**, **roped**) **1** secure something with rope. **2** (**rope someone in** or **into**) informal persuade someone to take part in something.

SYNONYMS ▶ n. **cord**, cable, line, hawser, string.

Roque·fort /'rōkfərt/ ▶ n. trademark a soft blue cheese made from sheep's milk.

ro·sa·ry /'rōzərē/ ▶ n. (plural **rosaries**) a string of beads used by some Roman Catholics for keeping count of how many prayers they have said.

rose¹ /rōz/ ▶ n. **1** a sweet-smelling flower that grows on a prickly bush. **2** a cap with holes in it attached to a spout, hose, shower, etc., to produce a spray. **3** a soft pink color. ▫ **rose hip** the fruit of a rose.

rose² past of **RISE**.

ro·sé /rō'zā/ ▶ n. light pink wine made from red grapes, colored by only brief contact with the skins.

rose·mar·y /'rōz,me(ə)rē/ ▶ n. an evergreen shrub with sweet-smelling leaves that are used as an herb in cooking.

ro·sette /rō'zet/ ▶ n. **1** a rose-shaped decoration made of ribbon, worn by supporters of a sports team or political party or awarded as a prize. **2** a piece of decoration in the shape of a rose.

rose·wood /'rōz,wo͝od/ ▶ n. the wood of a tropical tree, used for making furniture and musical instruments.

Rosh Ha·sha·nah /,rōsн (h)ə'sнōnə, ,räsн, -'sнänə/ (or **Rosh Hashana**) ▶ n. the Jewish New Year festival.

ros·in /'räzən/ ▶ n. a kind of resin that is rubbed on the bows of stringed instruments.

ros·ter /'rästər, 'rô-/ ▶ n. **1** a list of people's names and the jobs they have to do at a particular time. **2** a list of sports players available for team selection. ▶ v. (**rosters**, **rostering**, **rostered**) put a person's name on a roster.

SYNONYMS ▶ n. **schedule**, list, lineup, register, agenda, calendar.

ros·trum /'rästrəm, 'rô-/ ▶ n. (plural **rostra** /-trə/or **rostrums**) a platform on which a person stands to make a speech, receive a prize, or conduct an orchestra.

ros·y /'rōzē/ ▶ adj. (**rosier**, **rosiest**) **1** of a soft pink color. **2** promising: *a rosy future*.

SYNONYMS **1 pink**, roseate, reddish, glowing, healthy, fresh, radiant, blooming, blushing, flushed, ruddy. **2 promising**, optimistic, auspicious, hopeful, encouraging, favorable, bright, golden. ANTONYMS pale, bleak.

rot /rät/ ▶ v. (**rots**, **rotting**, **rotted**) gradually decay. ▶ n. **1** the process of decaying. **2** informal nonsense.

SYNONYMS ▶ v. **1 decay**, decompose, disintegrate, crumble, perish. **2 go bad**, spoil, molder, putrefy, fester. **3 deteriorate**, degenerate, decline, decay, go to seed, go downhill; informal go to pot, go to the dogs. ▶ n. **decay**, decomposition, putrefaction, mold, mildew, blight, canker.

ro·ta·ry /'rōtərē/ ▶ adj. **1** revolving around a center or axis. **2** having a rotating part or parts.

ro·tate /'rō,tāt/ ▶ v. (**rotates**, **rotating**, **rotated**) **1** move in a circle around an axis. **2** (of a job) pass on a regular basis to each member of a group in turn. **3** grow different crops one after the other on a piece of land.

SYNONYMS **1 revolve**, go around/round, turn (around/round), spin, gyrate, whirl, twirl, swivel, circle, pivot. **2 alternate**, take turns, change, switch, interchange, exchange, swap.

▪ **ro·ta·tor** n. **ro·ta·to·ry** /'rōtə,tôrē/ adj.

ro·ta·tion /rō'tāsнən/ ▶ n. **1** the action of rotating around a central point. **2** the action or system of changing people or things in a repeated sequence: *crop rotation*. **3** a complete circular movement around a central point.

SYNONYMS **1 revolving**, turning, spinning, gyration, circling. **2 turn**, revolution, orbit, spin. **3 sequence**, succession, alternation, cycle.

rote /rōt/ ▶ n. regular repetition of something to be learned.

ro·tis·ser·ie /rō'tisərē/ ▶ n. a rotating spit for roasting meat.

ro·tor /'rōtər/ ▶ n. **1** the rotating part of a turbine, electric motor, or other device. **2** a hub with a number of blades spreading out from it that is rotated to provide the lift for a helicopter.

rot·ten /'rätn/ ▶ adj. **1** decayed. **2** corrupt. **3** informal very bad.

SYNONYMS **1 decaying**, moldy, bad, decomposing, spoiled, putrid, rancid, festering, fetid. **2 corrupt**, unprincipled, dishonest, dishonorable, unscrupulous, untrustworthy, immoral; informal crooked. ANTONYMS fresh.

Rott·wei·ler /'rät,wīlər, 'rôt,vīlər/ ▶ n. a large, powerful breed of dog.

ro·tund /rō'tənd, 'rō,tənd/ ▶ adj. rounded and plump.

ro·tun·da /rō'təndə/ ▶ n. a round building or room.

rou·ble /'ro͞obəl/ = **RUBLE**.

rou·é /ro͞o'ā/ ▶ n. a man who leads an immoral life.

rouge /ro͞ozн/ ▶ n. a red powder or cream used for coloring the cheeks.

rough /rəf/ ▶ adj. **1** not smooth or level. **2** not gentle. **3** (of weather or the sea) wild and stormy. **4** plain and basic. **5** not worked out in every detail. **6** harsh in sound or taste. **7** unsophisticated. **8** informal difficult and unpleasant. ▶ n. **1** a basic draft of a design, piece of writing, etc. **2** (on a golf course) the area of longer grass around the fairway and the green. ▶ v. **1** (**rough something out**) make a draft or first version of something. **2** (**rough it**) informal live with only very basic necessities. **3** (**rough someone up**) informal beat someone up.

SYNONYMS ▶ **adj.** 1 **uneven**, irregular, bumpy, stony, rocky, rugged, rutted, pitted. 2 **coarse**, bristly, scratchy, prickly, shaggy, hairy, bushy. 3 **dry**, leathery, weather-beaten, chapped, calloused, scaly. 4 **gruff**, hoarse, harsh, rasping, husky, throaty, gravelly. 5 **violent**, aggressive, belligerent, pugnacious, boisterous, rowdy, disorderly, unruly, riotous. 6 **boorish**, loutish, oafish, brutish, coarse, crude, uncouth, vulgar, unrefined, unladylike, ungentlemanly, uncultured. 7 **turbulent**, stormy, squally, tempestuous, violent, heavy, choppy. 8 **preliminary**, hasty, quick, sketchy, cursory, basic, crude, rudimentary, raw, unpolished, incomplete, unfinished. 9 **approximate**, inexact, imprecise, vague, estimated; informal ballpark. ANTONYMS smooth, gentle, calm, exact. ▶ **n. sketch**, draft, outline, mock-up.

□ **diamond in the rough** a person who lacks good manners and education but has a good character. **rough and ready** basic but effective. **rough edges** small flaws in something that is otherwise satisfactory. ■ **rough·ness** **n.**

rough·age /ˈrəfij/ ▶ **n.** material in cereals, fruit, and vegetables that cannot be digested.

rough·en /ˈrəfən/ ▶ **v.** make or become rough.

rough·ly /ˈrəflē/ ▶ **adv.** 1 in a rough way. 2 approximately.

rough·neck /ˈrəfˌnek/ ▶ **n.** informal 1 a rough, rude person. 2 a person who works on an oil rig.

rough·shod /ˈrəfˌsHäd/ ▶ **adj.** (**ride roughshod over**) fail to consider someone's needs or wishes.

rou·lette /ro͞oˈlet/ ▶ **n.** a gambling game in which a ball is dropped on to a revolving wheel.

round /round/ ▶ **adj.** 1 shaped like a circle, sphere, or cylinder. 2 having a curved surface with no sharp projections. 3 (of a person's shoulders) bent forward. 4 (of a sound) rich and smooth. 5 (of a number) expressed in convenient units rather than exactly. ▶ **n.** 1 a circular shape or piece. 2 a route by which you visit a number of people or places in turn. 3 a sequence of things that you do regularly. 4 each of a sequence of stages in a process. 5 a single division of a boxing or wrestling match. 6 a song for three or more voices or parts, each singing the same theme but starting one after another. 7 the amount of ammunition needed to fire one shot. 8 a set of drinks bought for all the members of a group. ▶ **adv.** 1 so as to rotate or cause rotation. 2 so as to cover the whole area surrounding a particular center. 3 so as to turn and face in the opposite direction. 4 used in describing the position of something: *the wrong way round.* 5 so as to surround someone or something. 6 so as to reach a new place or position. ▶ **prep.** 1 on every side of. 2 so as to encircle. 3 from or on the other side of. 4 so as to cover the whole area of. ▶ **v.** 1 pass and go around. 2 (**round something up** or **down**) make a figure less exact but easier to use in calculations. 3 make or become round in shape.

SYNONYMS ▶ **adj. circular**, spherical, globular, cylindrical. ▶ **n.** 1 **ball**, sphere, globe, orb, circle, disk/disc, ring, hoop. 2 *a policeman on his rounds* **circuit**, beat, route, tour. 3 **stage**, level, heat, game, bout, contest. 4 **succession**, sequence, series, cycle. ▶ **v. go around/round**, travel around/round, skirt, circumnavigate, orbit.

□ **round something off** complete in a suitable or satisfying way. **round robin** 1 a tournament in which every player or team plays against every other player or team. 2 a petition. **round trip** a journey to a place and back again. **round someone/something up** collect a number of people or animals together.

round·a·bout /ˈroundəˌbout/ ▶ **adj.** not following a direct route.

SYNONYMS **circuitous**, indirect, meandering, serpentine, tortuous, oblique, circumlocutory. ANTONYMS direct.

round·ed /ˈroundid/ ▶ **adj.** 1 round or curved. 2 complete and balanced.

roun·del /ˈroundl/ ▶ **n.** a small disk or circular design.

Round·head /ˈroundˌhed/ ▶ **n.** a supporter of the Parliamentary party in the English Civil War.

round·ly /ˈroundlē/ ▶ **adv.** in a firm or thorough way.

SYNONYMS 1 **vehemently**, emphatically, fiercely, forcefully, severely, plainly, frankly, candidly. 2 **utterly**, completely, thoroughly, decisively, conclusively, heavily, soundly.

round·up /ˈroundˌəp/ ▶ **n.** 1 a gathering together of people or things. 2 a summary of facts or events: *a news roundup.*

round·worm /ˈroundˌwərm/ ▶ **n.** a parasitic worm found in the intestines of animals.

rouse /rouz/ ▶ **v.** (**rouses**, **rousing**, **roused**) 1 wake someone up. 2 make someone move or take an interest in something.

SYNONYMS 1 **wake** (**up**), awaken, arouse. 2 **wake up**, awake, come to, get up, rise, bestir yourself. 3 **stir up**, excite, galvanize, electrify, stimulate, inspire, move, inflame, agitate, goad, provoke, prompt, whip up.

rous·ing /ˈrouziNG/ ▶ **adj.** stirring: *a rousing speech.*

SYNONYMS **stirring**, inspiring, exciting, stimulating, moving, electrifying, invigorating, energizing, exhilarating.

roust /roust/ ▶ **v.** make someone get up or start moving.

rout /rout/ ▶ **n.** 1 a disorderly retreat of defeated troops. 2 a decisive defeat. ▶ **v.** defeat troops decisively and force them to retreat.

SYNONYMS ▶ **n. defeat**, beating, retreat, flight; informal licking, hammering, thrashing, pasting, drubbing. ANTONYMS victory. ▶ **v. defeat**, beat, conquer, vanquish, crush, put to flight, drive off, scatter; informal lick, hammer, clobber, thrash.

route /ro͞ot, rout/ ▶ **n.** a way taken in getting from a starting point to a destination. ▶ **v.** (**routes**, **routeing** or **routing**, **routed**) send along a particular route.

SYNONYMS ▶ **n. way**, course, road, path, direction.

rout·er[1] /ˈroutər/ ▶ **n.** a power tool with a shaped cutter, used in carpentry.

rout·er[2] /ˈro͞otər, ˈroutər/ ▶ **n.** a device that forwards data packets to the appropriate parts of a computer network.

rou·tine /ro͞oˈtēn/ ▶ **n.** 1 the order and way in which you regularly do things. 2 a set sequence in a stage performance. ▶ **adj.** 1 performed as part of a regular procedure. 2 without variety.

SYNONYMS ▶ n. 1 **procedure**, practice, pattern, drill, regime, program, schedule, plan. 2 **act**, performance, number, turn, piece; informal spiel, patter. ▶ adj. 1 **standard**, regular, customary, normal, usual, ordinary, typical, everyday. 2 **boring**, tedious, monotonous, humdrum, run-of-the-mill, pedestrian, predictable, hackneyed, unimaginative, unoriginal, banal, trite. ANTONYMS unusual.

■ **rou·tine·ly** adv.

roux /ro͞o/ ▶ n. (plural **roux**) a mixture of butter and flour used in making sauces.

rove /rōv/ ▶ v. (**roves**, **roving**, **roved**) 1 travel from place to place without a fixed destination. 2 (of eyes) look around in all directions. ■ **rov·er** n.

row¹ /rō/ ▶ n. a number of people or things in a more or less straight line.

SYNONYMS 1 **line**, column, file, queue, procession, chain, string, succession. 2 **tier**, line, rank, bank.

□ **row house** any of a row of houses joined by side walls.

row² ▶ v. move a boat through water with oars.

row³ /rou/ ▶ n. a noisy quarrel. ▶ v. have a quarrel.

row·an /ˈrōən/ ▶ n. a small tree with white flowers and red berries.

row·boat /ˈrōˌbōt/ ▶ n. a small boat propelled by oars.

row·dy /ˈroudē/ ▶ adj. (**rowdier**, **rowdiest**) noisy and disorderly. ▶ n. (plural **rowdies**) a rowdy person.

SYNONYMS ▶ adj. **unruly**, disorderly, riotous, undisciplined, uncontrollable, ungovernable, disruptive, obstreperous, out of control, rough, wild, boisterous, uproarious, noisy, loud; informal rambunctious. ANTONYMS peaceful.

■ **row·di·ly** adv. **row·di·ness** n.

roy·al /ˈroiəl/ ▶ adj. 1 having the status of a king or queen or a member of their family. 2 having to do with a king or queen. 3 of a quality or size suitable for a king or queen. ▶ n. informal a member of a royal family.

SYNONYMS ▶ adj. **regal**, kingly, queenly, princely, sovereign.

□ **royal blue** a deep, vivid blue. **royal jelly** a substance produced by worker bees and fed by them to larvae raised to be queen bees. ■ **roy·al·ly** adv.

roy·al·ist /ˈroiəlist/ ▶ n. a person who supports the principle of having a king or queen.

roy·al·ty /ˈroiəltē/ ▶ n. (plural **royalties**) 1 the members of a royal family. 2 the status or power of a king or queen. 3 a sum of money paid for the use of a patent, to an author for each copy of a book sold, or to a composer for each performance of a work.

rpm ▶ abbr. revolutions per minute.

RR ▶ abbr. 1 railroad. 2 rural route.

RSVP ▶ abbr. please reply.

rub /rəb/ ▶ v. (**rubs**, **rubbing**, **rubbed**) 1 move your hand, a cloth, etc., over the surface while pressing down firmly. 2 apply a substance with a rubbing action. 3 (**rub off**) come off a surface through being rubbed. 4 (**rub something out**) erase pencil marks with an eraser. 5 (**rub something down**) dry, smooth, or clean something by rubbing. 6 (**rub it in**) informal keep reminding someone of an embarrassing fact they would rather forget. ▶ n. 1 an act of rubbing. 2 a substance for rubbing on the skin.

SYNONYMS ▶ v. 1 **massage**, knead, stroke, pat. 2 **apply**, smear, spread, work in. 3 **chafe**, scrape, pinch.

rub·ber¹ /ˈrəbər/ ▶ n. 1 a tough stretchy waterproof substance obtained from a tropical plant or from chemicals. 2 informal a condom. □ **rubber band** a stretchy loop of rubber for holding things together. **rubber plant** an evergreen plant with large shiny leaves. **rubber-stamp** approve something automatically without proper consideration. ■ **rub·ber·y** adj.

rub·ber² ▶ n. a unit of play in the card game bridge.

rub·ber·neck /ˈrəbərˌnek/ ▶ v. informal turn to look at something as you pass it.

rub·bing /ˈrəbiNG/ ▶ n. 1 the action of rubbing. 2 an impression of a design on brass or stone, made by placing paper over it and rubbing it with chalk or pencil.

rub·bish /ˈrəbisH/ ▶ n. 1 waste material and discarded items. 2 something that has no value or makes no sense.

SYNONYMS 1 **refuse**, trash, garbage, waste, litter, scrap, detritus, debris, dross; informal dreck, junk. 2 **nonsense**, gibberish, claptrap, garbage; informal baloney, tripe, drivel, bilge, bunk, piffle, twaddle, poppycock, gobbledygook.

rub·ble /ˈrəbəl/ ▶ n. rough fragments of stone, brick, or concrete.

SYNONYMS **debris**, remains, ruins, wreckage.

ru·bel·la /ro͞oˈbelə/ ▶ n. German measles, a disease with symptoms like mild measles.

ru·bi·cund /ˈro͞obəˌkənd/ ▶ adj. having a red complexion.

ru·ble /ˈro͞obəl/ (or **rouble**) ▶ n. the basic unit of money in Russia.

ru·bric /ˈro͞obrik/ ▶ n. 1 a heading on a document. 2 a set of instructions.

ru·by /ˈro͞obē/ ▶ n. (plural **rubies**) 1 a deep red precious stone. 2 a deep red color.

ruche /ro͞osH/ ▶ n. a frill or pleat of fabric. ■ **ruched** adj.

ruck·sack /ˈrəkˌsak, ˈro͝ok-/ ▶ n. a backpack.

ruck·us /ˈrəkəs/ ▶ n. a row or commotion.

rud·der /ˈrədər/ ▶ n. a flat piece hinged in an upright position at the back of a boat, used for steering.

rud·dy /ˈrədē/ ▶ adj. (**ruddier**, **ruddiest**) 1 (of a person's face) having a healthy red color. 2 reddish.

SYNONYMS **rosy**, red, pink, roseate, rubicund, healthy, glowing, fresh, flushed, blushing, florid. ANTONYMS pale.

rude /ro͞od/ ▶ adj. 1 saying impolite things that offend and hurt someone. 2 very abrupt.

SYNONYMS 1 **ill-mannered**, bad-mannered, impolite, discourteous, uncivil, impertinent, insolent, impudent, disparaging, abusive, curt, brusque, offhand. 2 **vulgar**, coarse, smutty, dirty, filthy, crude, lewd, obscene, risqué; informal blue. ANTONYMS polite.

■ **rude·ly** adv.

rude·ness /ˈro͞odnis/ ▶ n. 1 the quality of saying impolite things that offend and hurt others.

2 abruptness.

ru·di·men·ta·ry /ˌro͞odəˈment(ə)rē/ ▶ **adj.** **1** involving only basic matters or facts. **2** undeveloped.

> SYNONYMS **1 basic**, elementary, fundamental, essential. **2 primitive**, crude, simple, unsophisticated, rough (and ready), makeshift. **3 vestigial**, undeveloped, incomplete.

ru·di·ments /ˈro͞odəmənts/ ▶ **pl.n.** **1** the essential matters or facts relating to a subject. **2** a basic form of something.

> SYNONYMS **basics**, fundamentals, essentials, foundations; informal nuts and bolts, ABCs.

rue /ro͞o/ ▶ **v.** (**rues**, **rueing** or **ruing**, **rued**) bitterly regret a past event or action.

> SYNONYMS **regret**, be sorry about, feel remorseful about, repent of, reproach yourself for, deplore, lament, bemoan, bewail.

rue·ful /ˈro͞ofəl/ ▶ **adj.** expressing regret.

> SYNONYMS **regretful**, apologetic, sorry, remorseful, shamefaced, sheepish, hangdog, contrite, repentant, penitent, conscience-stricken, self-reproachful, sorrowful, sad.

■ **rue·ful·ly adv.**

ruff /rəf/ ▶ **n.** **1** a frill worn around the neck. **2** a ring of feathers or hair around the neck of a bird or mammal.

ruf·fi·an /ˈrəfēən/ ▶ **n.** a rough person.

> SYNONYMS **thug**, lout, hooligan, hoodlum, vandal, delinquent, rowdy, scoundrel, villain, rogue, bully, brute; informal tough (guy), bruiser.

ruf·fle /ˈrəfəl/ ▶ **v.** (**ruffles**, **ruffling**, **ruffled**) **1** disturb the smooth surface of. **2** upset or worry. **3** (**ruffled**) gathered into a frill. ▶ **n.** a gathered frill on a garment.

> SYNONYMS ▶ **v. 1 disarrange**, tousle, dishevel, rumple, mess up; informal muss up. **2 disconcert**, unnerve, fluster, agitate, upset, disturb, discomfit, put off, perturb, unsettle; informal faze, throw, get to. ANTONYMS smooth.

ru·fous /ˈro͞ofəs/ ▶ **adj.** reddish brown in color.

rug /rəg/ ▶ **n.** a small carpet. □ **pull the rug out from under** abruptly withdraw support from.

rug·by /ˈrəgbē/ (or **rugby football**) ▶ **n.** a team game played with an oval ball that may be kicked, carried, and passed by hand.

rug·ged /ˈrəgid/ ▶ **adj.** **1** having a rocky surface. **2** tough and determined. **3** (of a man) having attractively masculine features.

> SYNONYMS **1 rough**, uneven, bumpy, rocky, stony, pitted. **2 robust**, durable, sturdy, strong, tough, resilient. **3 well-built**, burly, strong, muscular, muscly, brawny, strapping, tough, hardy, robust, sturdy, solid; informal hunky. **4** *his rugged features* **strong**, craggy, rough-hewn, manly, masculine. ANTONYMS smooth, delicate.

■ **rug·ged·ly adv. rug·ged·ness n.**

ru·in /ˈro͞oin/ ▶ **v.** **1** completely spoil or destroy something. **2** make someone bankrupt or very poor. ▶ **n.** **1** the destruction or collapse of something. **2** (also **ruins**) a building that has been badly damaged or allowed to deteriorate. **3** the complete loss of a person's money and property.

> SYNONYMS ▶ **v. 1 spoil**, wreck, blight, shatter, dash, mess up, sabotage; informal screw up. **2** (**ruined**) **derelict**, dilapidated, tumbledown, ramshackle, decrepit, falling to pieces, crumbling, decaying, disintegrating, in ruins. **3 bankrupt**, make insolvent, impoverish, pauperize, wipe out, break, cripple, bring someone to their knees. **4 destroy**, devastate, lay waste, ravage, raze, demolish, wreck, wipe out, flatten. ▶ **n. 1 disintegration**, decay, disrepair, dilapidation, destruction, demolition, devastation. **2** *the ruins of a church* **remains**, remnants, fragments, rubble, debris, wreckage. **3 downfall**, collapse, defeat, undoing, failure. **4 bankruptcy**, insolvency, penury, destitution, poverty.

ru·in·a·tion /ˌro͞oəˈnāsʜən/ ▶ **n.** the process of ruining something.

ru·in·ous /ˈro͞oənəs/ ▶ **adj.** **1** disastrous or destructive. **2** in ruins.

> SYNONYMS **1 disastrous**, devastating, catastrophic, calamitous, crippling, crushing, damaging, destructive, harmful, costly. **2 extortionate**, exorbitant, excessive, sky-high, outrageous, inflated; informal steep.

rule /ro͞ol/ ▶ **n.** **1** a statement saying what you must or must not do. **2** authority and control over a people or country. **3** (**the rule**) the normal state of things. **4** a ruler (for measuring or drawing). ▶ **v.** (**rules**, **ruling**, **ruled**) **1** have authority and control over a people or country. **2** control or influence. **3** state with legal authority that something is the case. **4** (**rule something out**) say that something is not possible. **5** (**ruled**) (of paper) marked with thin horizontal lines.

> SYNONYMS ▶ **n. 1 regulation**, ruling, directive, order, law, statute, ordinance. **2 procedure**, practice, protocol, convention, norm, routine, custom, habit. **3 principle**, precept, standard, axiom, truth, maxim. **4 government**, jurisdiction, command, power, dominion, control, administration, sovereignty, leadership. ▶ **v. 1 govern**, preside over, control, lead, dominate, run, head, administer. **2 reign**, be on the throne, be in power, govern. **3 decree**, order, pronounce, judge, adjudge, ordain, decide, determine, find.

□ **rule of thumb** a rough guide.

rul·er /ˈro͞olər/ ▶ **n.** **1** a person who has authority and control over a people or country. **2** a strip of rigid material marked with inches or centimeters, used to measure short distances or draw straight lines.

> SYNONYMS **leader**, sovereign, monarch, potentate, king, queen, emperor, empress, prince, princess, crowned head, head of state, president, premier, governor. ANTONYMS subject.

rul·ing /ˈro͞oliɴɢ/ ▶ **n.** a decision or statement made by an authority. ▶ **adj.** governing; in control.

> SYNONYMS ▶ **n. judgment**, decision, adjudication, finding, verdict, pronouncement, resolution, decree, injunction. ▶ **adj. 1 governing**, controlling, commanding, supreme. **2 main**, chief, principal, major, dominating, consuming; informal number-one.

rum /rəm/ ▶ **n.** a strong alcoholic drink made from sugarcane.

Ru·ma·ni·an /ro͝o'mānēən/ = **Romanian**.

rum·ba /'rəmbə, 'ro͝om-, 'ro͞om-/ (or **rhumba**) ▶ **n.** a rhythmic dance with Spanish and African elements.

rum·ble /'rəmbəl/ ▶ **v.** (**rumbles**, **rumbling**, **rumbled**) **1** make a continuous deep sound, like distant thunder. **2** (**rumble on**) (of a dispute) continue in a low-key way. ▶ **n.** a continuous deep sound like that of distant thunder.

ru·mi·nant /'ro͞omənənt/ ▶ **n.** an animal that chews the cud, such as a cow or sheep.

ru·mi·nate /'ro͞omə,nāt/ ▶ **v.** (**ruminates**, **ruminating**, **ruminated**) **1** think deeply about something. **2** (of an animal) chew the cud.

rum·mage /'rəmij/ ▶ **v.** (**rummages**, **rummaging**, **rummaged**) search for something by turning things over or moving them around in an untidy way. ▶ **n.** an act of rummaging.

SYNONYMS ▶ **v.** **search**, hunt, root about/around, ferret about/around, fish about/around, dig, delve, go through, explore, sift through, rifle through.

□ **rummage sale** a sale of various secondhand goods, especially for charity.

rum·my /'rəmē/ ▶ **n.** a card game in which the players try to form sets and sequences of cards.

ru·mor /'ro͞omər/ ▶ **n.** a piece of information spread among a number of people that is not confirmed and may be false. ▶ **v.** (**be rumored**) be spread as a rumor.

SYNONYMS ▶ **n.** **gossip**, hearsay, talk, tittle-tattle, speculation, word, report, story, whisper; informal the grapevine, the word on the street, the buzz.

ru·mor·mon·ger /'ro͞omər,məNGər, -mäNGgər/ ▶ **n.** disapproving a person who spreads rumors.

rump /rəmp/ ▶ **n.** **1** the hind part of the body of a mammal. **2** a piece left over from something larger.

rum·ple /'rəmpəl/ ▶ **v.** (**rumples**, **rumpling**, **rumpled**) make something less smooth and neat.

rum·pus /'rəmpəs/ ▶ **n.** (plural **rumpuses**) a noisy disturbance.

run /rən/ ▶ **v.** (**runs**, **running**, **ran**; past participle **run**) **1** move at a speed faster than a walk, never having both feet on the ground at the same time. **2** be in charge of people or an organization. **3** continue, operate, or proceed. **4** function or cause to function. **5** pass into or reach a particular state or level. **6** (of a liquid) flow. **7** (**run in**) (of a quality) be common or lasting in. **8** (of dye or color) dissolve and spread when wet. **9** stand as a candidate in an election. **10** compete in a race. **11** (of a bus or train) make a regular journey on a particular route. **12** take someone somewhere in a car. **13** publish a story in a newspaper or magazine. **14** smuggle goods. ▶ **n.** **1** an act or period of running. **2** a journey or route. **3** a course that is regularly used: *a ski run*. **4** a continuous period or sequence. **5** an enclosed area in which chickens or animals can run around. **6** (**the run of**) unrestricted use of or access to a place. **7** a point scored in baseball or cricket. **8** a line of unraveled stitches in stockings or tights.

SYNONYMS ▶ **v.** **1** **sprint**, race, dart, rush, dash, hasten, hurry, scurry, scamper, gallop, jog, trot. **2** **flee**, take flight, make off, take off, take to your heels, bolt, make your getaway, escape; informal beat it, clear off/out, scram, leg it. **3** **extend**, stretch, reach, continue. **4** **flow**, pour, stream, gush, flood, cascade, roll, course, glide, spill, trickle, drip, dribble, leak. **5** **be in charge of**, manage, direct, control, head, govern, supervise, superintend, oversee, organize, coordinate. **6** *it's expensive to run a car* **maintain**, keep, own, possess, have, use, operate. **7** *I left the engine running* **operate**, function, work, go. ▶ **n.** **1** **jog**, sprint, dash, gallop, trot. **2** **route**, journey, circuit, round, beat. **3** **drive**, ride, turn, trip, excursion, outing, jaunt; informal spin, tootle. **4** **series**, succession, sequence, string, streak, spate. **5** **enclosure**, pen, coop. **6** *a ski run* **slope**, trail, track, piste.

□ **a** (**good**) **run for your money** **1** challenging competition. **2** reward or enjoyment in return for your efforts. **on the run** **1** escaping from arrest. **2** while moving. **run across** meet or find by chance. **run away with** **1** escape the control of. **2** win (a competition or prize) easily. **run before you can walk** attempt something difficult before you have grasped the basic skills. **run something by** (or **past**) tell someone about something to find out their opinion. **run down** **1** gradually lose power. **2** in a bad or neglected state. **3** tired and rather unwell. **run someone down** **1** knock someone down with a vehicle. **2** criticize someone unfairly or unkindly. **run-in** informal a disagreement or fight. **run into** **1** collide with. **2** meet someone by chance. **run-of-the-mill** ordinary. **run on** continue without stopping. **run out** **1** be used up. **2** be no longer valid. **run someone over** knock someone down with a vehicle. **run through** (or **over**) go over something as a quick rehearsal or reminder. **run-through** **1** a rehearsal. **2** a brief summary. **run something up** **1** allow a bill to build up. **2** make something quickly.

run·a·bout /'rənə,bout/ ▶ **n.** a small car or motorboat.

run·a·round /'rənə,round/ ▶ **n.** informal (**give someone the runaround**) give someone irrelevant or misleading information in order to delay or confuse them.

run·a·way /'rənə,wā/ ▶ **n.** a person who has run away from home or an institution. ▶ **adj.** **1** (of an animal or vehicle) running out of control. **2** happening or done quickly or uncontrollably.

SYNONYMS ▶ **n.** **fugitive**, refugee, truant, absconder, deserter.

run·down /'rən,doun/ ▶ **n.** **1** a brief summary. **2** Baseball an attempt by two or more fielders to tag out a base runner who is trapped between two bases.

SYNONYMS **summary**, synopsis, précis, run-through, recap, review, overview, briefing, sketch, outline; informal lowdown.

rune /ro͞on/ ▶ **n.** **1** a letter of an ancient Germanic alphabet. **2** a symbol with mysterious or magical significance. ■ **ru·nic adj.**

rung[1] /rəNG/ ▶ **n.** **1** a horizontal support on a ladder for the foot. **2** a level or rank.

rung[2] past participle of **ring**[2].

run·nel /'rənl/ ▶ **n.** a stream.

run·ner /'rənər/ ▶ **n.** **1** a person who runs in a race or for exercise. **2** a messenger. **3** a rod, groove, or blade on which something slides. **4** a shoot that grows along the ground and can take root at points along its length. **5** a long, narrow rug.

SYNONYMS **1 athlete**, sprinter, hurdler, racer, jogger. **2 messenger**, courier, errand boy/girl; informal gofer.

□ **runner bean** a climbing bean plant with long edible pods. **runner-up** (plural **runners-up**) a competitor who comes second.

run·ning /ˈrəniNG/ ▶ **n. 1** the activity or movement of a runner. **2** the action of managing or operating something. ▶ **adj. 1** (of water) flowing naturally or supplied through pipes and taps. **2** producing liquid or pus. **3** continuous or recurring. **4** done while running. **5** in succession: *the third week running.*

SYNONYMS ▶ **n. 1 administration**, management, organization, coordination, orchestration, handling, direction, control, supervision. **2 operation**, working, function, performance. ▶ **adj. 1 flowing**, gushing, rushing, moving. **2 in succession**, in a row, in sequence, consecutively, straight, together.

□ **in** (or **out of**) **the running** in (or no longer in) with a chance of success. **running board** a board acting as a step that extends along the side of a vehicle. **running commentary** a description of events given as they happen.

run·ny /ˈrənē/ ▶ **adj.** (**runnier**, **runniest**) **1** more liquid than is usual. **2** (of a person's nose) producing mucus.

SYNONYMS **liquid**, liquefied, fluid, melted, molten, watery, thin. ANTONYMS solid, thick.

runt /rənt/ ▶ **n.** the smallest animal in a litter.

run·way /ˈrənˌwā/ ▶ **n.** a strip of hard ground where aircraft take off and land.

ru·pee /ro͞oˈpē, ˈro͞oˌpē/ ▶ **n.** the basic unit of money of India and Pakistan.

rup·ture /ˈrəpCHər/ ▶ **v.** (**ruptures**, **rupturing**, **ruptured**) **1** break or burst suddenly. **2** (**be ruptured** or **rupture yourself**) develop a hernia in the abdomen. ▶ **n. 1** an instance of rupturing. **2** a hernia in the abdomen.

SYNONYMS **break**, fracture, crack, burst, split, fissure, breach.

ru·ral /ˈro͝orəl/ ▶ **adj.** having to do with the countryside.

SYNONYMS **country**, rustic, bucolic, pastoral, agricultural, agrarian. ANTONYMS urban.

■ **ru·ral·ly** **adv.**

ruse /ro͞oz, ro͞os/ ▶ **n.** something done to deceive or trick someone.

SYNONYMS **ploy**, stratagem, tactic, scheme, trick, gambit, dodge, subterfuge, machination, wile.

rush¹ /rəSH/ ▶ **v. 1** move or act very quickly, often too quickly. **2** produce, deal with, or transport very quickly. **3** (of air or a liquid) flow strongly. **4** dash toward a person or place as a form of attack. ▶ **n. 1** a sudden quick movement toward something. **2** a sudden period of hasty activity. **3** a sudden strong demand for a product. **4** a sudden strong feeling. **5** informal a sudden thrill experienced after taking certain drugs. **6** (**rushes**) the first prints made of a movie after a period of shooting.

SYNONYMS ▶ **v. 1 hurry**, dash, run, race, sprint, bolt, dart, gallop, career, charge, shoot, hurtle, fly, speed, zoom, scurry, scuttle, scamper, hasten; informal tear, belt, pelt, scoot, zip, whip, hotfoot it. **2** (**rushed**) *a rushed job* **hasty**, fast, speedy, quick, swift, rapid, hurried. **3 gush**, pour, surge, stream, course, cascade. **4 attack**, charge, storm. ▶ **n. 1 dash**, run, sprint, dart, bolt, charge, scramble. **2 hustle and bustle**, commotion, hubbub, hurly-burly, stir; informal hullabaloo. **3 charge**, onslaught, attack, assault.

□ **rush hour** a time at the start and end of the working day when traffic is at its heaviest.

rush² ▶ **n.** a water plant used in making mats, baskets, etc.

rusk /rəsk/ ▶ **n.** a dry biscuit or piece of baked bread.

rus·set /ˈrəsət/ ▶ **adj.** reddish brown. ▶ **n. 1** a kind of apple with a greenish-brown skin. **2** a long potato suitable for baking.

Rus·sian /ˈrəSHən/ ▶ **n. 1** a person from Russia. **2** the language of Russia. ▶ **adj.** relating to Russia. □ **Russian roulette** a dangerous game of chance in which a person loads one bullet into a revolver, spins the cylinder, and then pulls the trigger while pointing the gun at their own head.

rust /rəst/ ▶ **n.** a reddish-brown flaky coating that forms on iron or steel when it is wet. ▶ **v.** be affected by rust.

SYNONYMS ▶ **v. corrode**, oxidize, tarnish.

□ **rust belt** a region where heavy industry is in decline, especially in the northeastern US.

rus·tic /ˈrəstik/ ▶ **adj. 1** having to do with life in the country. **2** simple and charming in a way seen as typical of the countryside. ▶ **n.** an unsophisticated country person.

SYNONYMS ▶ **adj. 1 rural**, country, pastoral, bucolic, agricultural, agrarian; literary Arcadian. **2 plain**, simple, homey, unpretentious, unsophisticated, rough, crude. ANTONYMS urban. ▶ **n. peasant**, countryman, countrywoman, bumpkin, yokel, country cousin; informal hillbilly, hayseed, hick.

■ **rus·tic·i·ty** /rəˈstisətē/ **n.**

rus·tle /ˈrəsəl/ ▶ **v. 1** make a soft crackling sound. **2** round up and steal cattle, horses, or sheep. **3** (**rustle something up**) informal produce food or a drink quickly. ▶ **n.** a rustling sound.

SYNONYMS ▶ **v. 1 swish**, whoosh, whisper, sigh. **2 steal**, thieve, take, abduct, kidnap.

rus·tler /ˈrəslər/ ▶ **n.** a person who rounds up and steals cattle, horses, or sheep.

rust·y /ˈrəstē/ ▶ **adj. 1** affected by rust. **2** of the color of rust; reddish-brown. **3** (of knowledge or a skill) less good than it used to be because of a lack of recent practice.

SYNONYMS **1** *rusty wire* **rusted**, rust-covered, corroded, oxidized, tarnished, discolored. **2** *a rusty color* **reddish-brown**, chestnut, auburn, tawny, russet, coppery, Titian, red. **3** *my French is a little rusty* **out of practice**, below par, deficient, weak, unpracticed.

rut¹ /rət/ ▶ **n. 1** a long deep track made by the wheels of vehicles. **2** a way of living or working that has become routine and dull but is hard to change.

SYNONYMS **1 furrow**, groove, trough, ditch, hollow, pothole, crater. **2 boring routine**, humdrum existence, groove, dead end.

rut² ▶ **n.** an annual period of sexual activity in deer and some other animals, during which the males fight each other for access to the females.

▶ v. (**ruts**, **rutting**, **rutted**) be in such a period of activity.

ruth·less /ˈro͞oᴛʜləs/ ▶ adj. hard, determined, and showing no sympathy.

SYNONYMS **merciless**, pitiless, cruel, heartless, hard-hearted, cold-hearted, cold-blooded, harsh, callous. ANTONYMS merciful.

■ **ruth·less·ly** adv. **ruth·less·ness** n.

RV ▶ abbr. recreational vehicle.

rye /rī/ ▶ n. **1** a type of cereal plant. **2** whiskey made from rye.

rye·grass /ˈrīˌgras/ ▶ n. a grass used for lawns and as food for farm animals.

Ss

S (or **s**) ▶ n. (plural **Ss** or **S's**) the nineteenth letter of the alphabet. ▶ abbr. (**S**) South or Southern.

sab·bath /'sabəTH/ ▶ n. (often **the Sabbath**) a day for rest and religious worship.

sab·bat·i·cal /sə'batikəl/ ▶ n. a period of paid leave for study or travel.

sa·ber /'sābər/ ▶ n. **1** a heavy sword with a curved blade. **2** a light fencing sword with a thin blade.

sa·ber·tooth ti·ger /'sābər,to͞oTH/ (or **saber-toothed tiger**) ▶ n. a large extinct member of the cat family with massive curved upper canine teeth.

sa·ble /'sābəl/ ▶ n. a marten native to Japan and Siberia, hunted for its dark brown fur.

sab·o·tage /'sabə,täZH/ ▶ v. (**sabotages, sabotaging, sabotaged**) deliberately damage or destroy. ▶ n. the action of sabotaging.

> SYNONYMS ▶ v. **vandalize**, wreck, damage, destroy, incapacitate, obstruct, disrupt, spoil, ruin, undermine; informal throw a monkey wrench in the works. ▶ n. **vandalism**, wrecking, destruction, damage, obstruction, disruption; informal a monkey wrench in the works.

sab·o·teur /,sabə'tər/ ▶ n. a person who sabotages something.

sac /sak/ ▶ n. a hollow, flexible structure resembling a bag or pouch.

sac·cha·rin /'sak(ə)rən/ ▶ n. a sweet-tasting substance used as a low-calorie substitute for sugar.

sac·cha·rine /'sak(ə)rin, -rēn, -rīn/ ▶ adj. too sweet or sentimental.

sac·er·do·tal /,sasər'dōtl, ,sakər-/ ▶ adj. relating to priests.

sa·chet /sa'SHā/ ▶ n. a small perfumed bag used to scent clothes.

sack¹ /sak/ ▶ n. **1** a large bag made of rough material or thick paper, used for storing and carrying goods. **2** (**the sack**) informal dismissal from employment. **3** (**the sack**) informal bed. ▶ v. informal dismiss someone from employment.

> SYNONYMS ▶ n. **bag**, pouch, pocket, pack. ▶ v. **dismiss**, discharge, lay off, make redundant, let go, throw out; informal fire, give someone the sack, give someone their walking papers.

■ **sack·a·ble** adj.

sack² ▶ v. violently attack, steal from, and destroy a town or city (used when talking about the past). ▶ n. the sacking of a town or city.

sack·cloth /'sak,klôTH, -,kläTH/ ▶ n. a rough fabric woven from flax or hemp.

sa·cra /'sakrə, 'sā-/ plural of SACRUM.

sac·ra·ment /'sakrəmənt/ ▶ n. **1** (in the Christian church) an important religious ceremony in which the people taking part are believed to receive the grace of God. **2** (also **the Blessed Sacrament** or **the Holy Sacrament**) (in Catholic use) the bread and wine used in the Mass. ■ **sac·ra·men·tal** /,sakrə'mentl/ adj.

sa·cred /'sākrid/ ▶ adj. **1** connected with God or a god or goddess, and treated as holy. **2** (of a piece of writing) containing the teachings of a religion. **3** religious.

> SYNONYMS **1 holy**, hallowed, blessed, consecrated, sanctified. **2 religious**, spiritual, devotional, church, ecclesiastical. ANTONYMS secular, profane.

□ **sacred cow** a thing that people believe must not be criticized.

sac·ri·fice /'sakrə,fīs/ ▶ n. **1** the killing of an animal or person or giving up of a possession as an offering to a god or goddess. **2** an animal, person, or object offered in this way. **3** an act of giving up something you value for the sake of something that is more important. ▶ v. (**sacrifices, sacrificing, sacrificed**) offer as a sacrifice.

> SYNONYMS ▶ n. **1 offering**, gift, oblation. **2 surrender**, giving up, abandonment, renunciation, forfeiture. ▶ v. **1 offer up**, immolate. **2 give up**, forgo, abandon, renounce, relinquish, cede, surrender, forfeit.

■ **sac·ri·fi·cial** /,sakrə'fiSHəl/ adj.

sac·ri·lege /'sakrəlij/ ▶ n. an act of treating a sacred or highly valued thing without respect.

> SYNONYMS **desecration**, profanity, blasphemy, irreverence, disrespect.

■ **sac·ri·le·gious** /,sakrə'lijəs/ adj.

> SPELLING
> Sac**rilege**, not -relige or -rilige.

sac·ris·tan /'sakristən/ ▶ n. a person in charge of a sacristy.

sac·ris·ty /'sakristē/ ▶ n. (plural **sacristies**) a room in a church where a priest prepares for a service.

sac·ro·sanct /'sakrō,saNG(k)t/ ▶ adj. too important or valuable to be changed.

sac·rum /'sakrəm, 'sā-/ ▶ n. (plural **sacra** /-krə/ or **sacrums**) a triangular bone in the lower back between the two hip bones.

sad /sad/ ▶ adj. (**sadder, saddest**) **1** unhappy. **2** causing sorrow. **3** informal very inadequate or unfashionable.

> SYNONYMS **1 unhappy**, sorrowful, depressed, downcast, miserable, down, despondent, wretched, glum, gloomy, doleful, melancholy, mournful, woebegone, forlorn, heartbroken; informal blue, down in the mouth, down in the dumps. **2 tragic**, unhappy, miserable,

wretched, sorry, pitiful, pathetic, heartbreaking, heart-rending. **3 unfortunate**, regrettable, sorry, deplorable, lamentable, pitiful, shameful, disgraceful. ANTONYMS happy, cheerful.

sad·den /'sadn/ ▶ v. make someone unhappy.

SYNONYMS **depress**, dispirit, deject, dishearten, grieve, discourage, upset, get down.

sad·dle /'sadl/ ▶ n. **1** a seat with a raised ridge at the front and back, fastened on the back of a horse for riding. **2** a seat on a bicycle or motorcycle. **3** a piece of meat from the back of an animal. ▶ v. (**saddles**, **saddling**, **saddled**) **1** put a saddle on a horse. **2** (**saddle someone with**) give someone an unpleasant responsibility or task.

SYNONYMS ▶ v. **burden**, encumber, land, impose something on.

sad·dle·bag /'sadl,bag/ ▶ n. a bag attached to a saddle.

sad·dler /'sadlər/ ▶ n. a person who makes, sells, and repairs saddles and other equipment for horses. ■ **sad·dler·y** /'sadlərē, -əlrē/ (plural **saddleries**).

sa·dism /'sā,dizəm/ ▶ n. enjoyment felt in hurting or humiliating other people. ■ **sa·dist** n. **sa·dis·tic** /sə'distik/ adj.

sad·ly /'sadlē/ ▶ adv. **1** showing or feeling sadness. **2** it is a sad or regrettable fact that; unfortunately: *sadly, the rainforests are now under threat*. **3** to a regrettable extent; regrettably.

sad·ness /'sadnis/ ▶ n. the state of being sad.

SYNONYMS **unhappiness**, sorrow, dejection, depression, misery, despondency, wretchedness, gloom, gloominess, melancholy.

sa·do·mas·o·chism /,sādō'masə,kizəm, ,sadō-/ ▶ n. enjoyment felt in hurting or being hurt by someone else. ■ **sa·do·mas·o·chist** n. **sa·do·mas·o·chis·tic** /',sādō,masə'kistik, ,sadō-/ adj.

sa·fa·ri /sə'färē/ ▶ n. (plural **safaris**) an expedition to observe or hunt animals in their natural environment. □ **safari park** an area of parkland where wild animals are kept in the open and may be observed by visitors.

safe /sāf/ ▶ adj. **1** protected from danger or risk. **2** not leading to harm or injury; not risky. **3** (of a place) giving security or protection. **4** based on good reasons and not likely to be proved wrong. ▶ n. a strong fireproof cabinet with a complex lock, used for storing valuable items.

SYNONYMS ▶ adj. **1 secure**, protected, sheltered, guarded, out of harm's way. **2 unharmed**, unhurt, uninjured, unscathed, all right, fine, well, in one piece, out of danger, safe and sound. **3 cautious**, circumspect, prudent, careful, unadventurous, conservative. **4 harmless**, innocuous, nontoxic, nonpoisonous. ANTONYMS dangerous, harmful.

□ **safe house** a house in a secret location, used by people in hiding. ■ **safe·ly** adv.

safe·guard /'sāf,gärd/ ▶ n. a thing done in order to protect or prevent something. ▶ v. protect with a safeguard.

SYNONYMS ▶ n. **protection**, defense, buffer, provision, security, cover, insurance. ▶ v. **protect**, preserve, conserve, save, secure, shield, guard, keep safe. ANTONYMS jeopardize.

safe·keep·ing /'sāf'kēpiNG/ ▶ n. the keeping of something in a safe place.

safe·ty /'sāftē/ ▶ n. (plural **safeties**) the condition of being safe.

SYNONYMS **1 welfare**, well-being, protection, security. **2 shelter**, sanctuary, refuge.

□ **safety belt** a belt that secures a person to their seat in a vehicle or aircraft. **safety net 1** a net placed to catch an acrobat should they fall. **2** something arranged as a safeguard. **safety pin** a pin with a point that is bent back to the head and held in a guard when closed.

saf·fron /'safrən/ ▶ n. a yellow spice made from the dried stigmas of a crocus.

sag /sag/ ▶ v. (**sags**, **sagging**, **sagged**) **1** sink downward gradually under weight or pressure or through weakness. **2** hang down loosely or unevenly. ▶ n. an instance of sagging.

SYNONYMS ▶ v. **1 sink**, slump, loll, flop, crumple. **2 dip**, droop, bulge, bag.

■ **sag·gy** adj.

sa·ga /'sägə/ ▶ n. **1** a long traditional story describing brave acts. **2** a story covering a long period of time. **3** a long and complicated series of incidents.

SYNONYMS **1 epic**, legend, (folk) tale, romance, narrative, myth. **2 story**, tale, yarn.

sa·ga·cious /sə'gāsHəs/ ▶ adj. having good judgment; wise. ■ **sa·gac·i·ty** /sə'gasitē/ n.

sage[1] /sāj/ ▶ n. a sweet-smelling Mediterranean plant with grayish-green leaves, used as an herb in cooking.

sage[2] ▶ n. a very wise man. ▶ adj. wise.

SYNONYMS ▶ n. **wise man**, philosopher, scholar, guru, prophet, mystic.

■ **sage·ly** adv.

Sag·it·tar·i·us /,saji'te(ə)rēəs/ ▶ n. a sign of the zodiac (the Archer), November 22–December 20.

sa·go /'sāgō/ ▶ n. a pudding made with starchy granules obtained from a palm tree, cooked with milk.

sa·hib /'sä(h)ib/ ▶ n. Indian a polite form of address for a man.

said /sed/ past and past participle of **SAY** ▶ adj. referring to someone or something already mentioned.

sail /sāl/ ▶ n. **1** a piece of material spread on a mast to catch the wind and propel a boat or ship. **2** a trip in a sailboat or ship. **3** a flat board attached to the arm of a windmill. ▶ v. **1** travel in a sailboat as a sport or pastime. **2** travel in a ship or boat using sails or engine power. **3** begin a voyage. **4** direct or control a boat or ship. **5** move smoothly or confidently. **6** (**sail through**) informal succeed easily at.

SYNONYMS ▶ v. **1 voyage**, travel, navigate, cruise. **2 set sail**, put to sea, leave, weigh anchor. **3 steer**, pilot, captain; informal skipper. **4 glide**, drift, float, flow, sweep, skim, coast, flit, scud.

□ **sail close to the wind** take risks.

sail·board /'sāl,bôrd/ ▶ n. a board with a mast and a sail, used in windsurfing. ■ **sail·board·er** n. **sail·board·ing** n.

sail·boat /'sāl,bōt/ ▶ n. a boat propelled by sails.

sail·cloth /ˈsāl,klôTH, -ˌkläTH/ ▶ **n.** strong fabric used for making sails.

sail·or /ˈsālər/ ▶ **n. 1** a member of the crew of a ship or boat. **2** a person who sails as a sport or pastime. **3** (**a good** or **bad sailor**) a person who rarely (or often) becomes seasick.

> SYNONYMS **seaman**, seafarer, mariner, yachtsman, yachtswoman, hand; informal old salt, tar.

saint /sānt/ ▶ **n. 1** a good person who, in Christian belief, will go to heaven when they die. **2** a person of great goodness who after their death is formally declared by the church to be a saint, and to whom people offer prayers. **3** informal a very good or kind person. □ **saint's day** a day on which a saint is particularly remembered in the Christian Church. ■ **saint·hood n.**

St. Ber·nard /bərˈnärd/ ▶ **n.** a breed of very large dog originally kept in the Alps for rescue.

saint·ed /ˈsāntid/ ▶ **adj.** dated very good or kind, like a saint.

St. John's wort /wərt, wôrt/ ▶ **n.** a herbaceous plant with yellow flowers, used in medicinal preparations.

saint·ly /ˈsāntlē/ ▶ **adj.** very holy or good.

> SYNONYMS **holy**, godly, pious, religious, devout, spiritual, virtuous, righteous, good, pure. ANTONYMS ungodly.

■ **saint·li·ness n.**

sa·ke[1] /sāk/ ▶ **n. 1** (**for the sake of**) in the interest of. **2** (**for the sake of**) out of consideration for. **3** (**for old times' sake**) in memory of former times.

> SYNONYMS **1** *for the sake of clarity* **purpose**(s), reason(s). **2** *for her son's sake* **benefit**, advantage, good, well-being, welfare.

sa·ke[2] /ˈsäkē/ ▶ **n.** a Japanese alcoholic drink made from rice.

sa·laam /səˈläm/ ▶ **n.** a low bow with the hand touching the forehead, used by Muslims as a gesture of respect. ▶ **v.** make a salaam.

sa·la·cious /səˈlāSHəs/ ▶ **adj.** containing a great deal of sexual detail.

sal·ad /ˈsaləd/ ▶ **n.** a cold dish of raw vegetables. □ **your salad days** the time when you are young and inexperienced.

sal·a·man·der /ˈsalə,mandər/ ▶ **n. 1** an animal like a newt that can live in water or on land. **2** a mythical creature resembling a lizard, said to be able to stay alive in fire.

sa·la·mi /səˈlämē/ ▶ **n.** (plural **salami** or **salamis**) a type of spicy preserved sausage.

sal·a·ry /ˈsalərē/ ▶ **n.** (plural **salaries**) a fixed payment made every month to an employee.

> SYNONYMS **pay**, wages, earnings, payment, remuneration, fee(s), stipend, income.

■ **sal·a·ried adj.**

sale /sāl/ ▶ **n. 1** the exchange of something for money. **2** (**sales**) the activity or profession of selling. **3** a period in which goods in a store are sold at reduced prices. **4** a public event at which goods are sold or auctioned.

> SYNONYMS **1 selling**, dealing, trading. **2 deal**, transaction, bargain. ANTONYMS purchase.

□ **sales tax** a tax on sales or on the receipts from sales. ■ **sal·a·ble** (or **saleable**) **adj.**

sales·clerk /ˈsālz,klərk/ ▶ **n.** an assistant in a store.

sales·man /ˈsālzmən/ (or **saleswoman** /ˈsālz,wo͝omən/) ▶ **n.** (plural **salesmen** or **saleswomen**) a person whose job involves selling goods. ■ **sales·man·ship n.**

sales·per·son /ˈsālz,pərsən/ ▶ **n.** a salesman or saleswoman.

sales·room /ˈsālz,ro͞om, -ˌro͝om/ ▶ **n.** a room in which auctions are held or cars are sold.

sa·li·ent /ˈsālyənt, -lēənt/ ▶ **adj.** most noticeable or important. ■ **sa·li·ence n.**

sa·line /ˈsā,lēn, -ˌlīn/ ▶ **adj.** containing salt. ■ **sa·lin·i·ty** /səˈlinitē/ **n.**

sa·li·va /səˈlīvə/ ▶ **n.** a watery liquid in the mouth produced by glands, that helps chewing, swallowing, and digestion. ■ **sal·i·var·y** /ˈsalə,verē/ **adj.**

sal·i·vate /ˈsalə,vāt/ ▶ **v.** (**salivates**, **salivating**, **salivated**) have a lot of saliva in the mouth. ■ **sal·i·va·tion** /ˌsaləˈvāSHən/ **n.**

sal·low /ˈsalō/ ▶ **adj.** (of a person's skin) yellowish or pale brown in color.

sal·ly /ˈsalē/ ▶ **n.** (plural **sallies**) **1** a sudden charge out of a place surrounded by an enemy. **2** a witty or lively reply. ▶ **v.** (**sallies**, **sallying**, **sallied**) (**sally forth**) set out.

salm·on /ˈsamən/ ▶ **n.** (plural **salmon** or **salmons**) a large fish with pink flesh, which matures in the sea and moves to freshwater streams to release eggs.

sal·mo·nel·la /ˌsalməˈnelə/ ▶ **n.** a germ that can cause food poisoning.

sa·lon /səˈlän, saˈlôN/ ▶ **n. 1** a place where a hairdresser, beautician, or clothes designer works. **2** a reception room in a large house. **3** (in the past) a regular gathering of writers and artists held in someone's house.

sa·loon /səˈlo͞on/ ▶ **n.** old use a bar or tavern.

sal·sa /ˈsälsə/ ▶ **n. 1** a spicy sauce made with tomatoes, onions, and chili peppers. **2** a Latin American dance performed to music that combines jazz and rock.

salt /sôlt/ ▶ **n. 1** sodium chloride, a white substance in the form of crystals, used for flavoring or preserving food. **2** Chemistry any compound formed by the reaction of an acid with a base. ▶ **v. 1** season or preserve food with salt. **2** sprinkle a road or path with salt in order to melt snow or ice. □ **the salt of the earth** a person who is very kind, reliable, or honest. **take something with a grain of salt** recognize that something may be exaggerated or untrue.

salt·cel·lar /ˈsôlt,selər/ ▶ **n.** a shaker or small dish for salt.

salt·pe·ter /sôltˈpētər/ ▶ **n.** a white powder (potassium nitrate) used to make gunpowder and preserve meat.

salt·wa·ter /ˈsôlt,wôtər, -ˌwätər/ ▶ **adj.** having to do with or found in salt water.

salt·y /ˈsôltē/ ▶ **adj.** (**saltier**, **saltiest**) **1** containing or tasting of salt. **2** (of language or humor) rather improper.

> SYNONYMS **salt**, salted, saline, briny, brackish.

■ **salt·i·ness n.**

sa·lu·bri·ous /səˈlo͞obrēəs/ ▶ **adj. 1** good for your health. **2** (of a place) well-maintained and pleasant to be in.

SYNONYMS **pleasant**, agreeable, nice, select, high-class, upscale, upmarket; informal posh, classy, swish.

sal·u·tar·y /ˈsalyəˌterē/ ▶ **adj.** (with reference to something unpleasant) producing a good effect because it teaches you something.

sal·u·ta·tion /ˌsalyəˈtāsʜən/ ▶ **n.** a greeting.

sa·lute /səˈlo͞ot/ ▶ **n. 1** a raising of a hand to the head, made as a formal gesture of respect by a member of a military force. **2** a gesture of admiration or respect. **3** the shooting of a gun or guns as a formal sign of respect or celebration. ▶ **v.** (**salutes**, **saluting**, **saluted**) **1** make a formal salute to. **2** greet. **3** express admiration and respect for.

SYNONYMS ▶ **n. tribute**, testimonial, homage, honor, celebration (of), acknowledgment (of). ▶ **v. pay tribute to**, pay homage to, honor, celebrate, acknowledge, take your hat off to.

sal·vage /ˈsalvij/ ▶ **v.** (**salvages**, **salvaging**, **salvaged**) **1** rescue something that is in danger of being lost or destroyed. **2** rescue a ship or its contents from being lost at sea. ▶ **n. 1** the action of salvaging. **2** contents rescued from a wrecked ship.

SYNONYMS ▶ **v. rescue**, save, recover, retrieve, reclaim.

sal·va·tion /salˈvāsʜən/ ▶ **n. 1** the saving of a person from sin and its consequences, believed by Christians to be brought about by faith in Jesus. **2** the protecting or saving of someone or something from harm or loss.

SYNONYMS **1 redemption**, deliverance. **2 lifeline**, means of escape, savior. ANTONYMS damnation, ruin.

salve /sav, säv/ ▶ **n. 1** an ointment that soothes the skin. **2** something that makes you feel less guilty. ▶ **v.** (**salves**, **salving**, **salved**) reduce feelings of guilt.

sal·ver /ˈsalvər/ ▶ **n.** a tray.

sal·vo /ˈsalˌvō/ ▶ **n.** (plural **salvos** or **salvoes**) **1** a shooting of a number of guns at the same time. **2** a sudden series of aggressive statements or acts.

Sa·mar·i·tan /səˈmaritn, -ˈme(ə)r-/ ▶ **n. 1** (**good Samaritan**) a helpful person. **2** a member of a people living in Samaria, an ancient city and region of Palestine.

sam·ba /ˈsambə, ˈsäm-/ ▶ **n.** a Brazilian dance of African origin.

same /sām/ ▶ **adj. 1** (**the same**) exactly alike. **2** (**this** or **that same**) referring to a person or thing just mentioned. ▶ **pron. 1** (**the same**) the same thing as previously mentioned. **2** (**the same**) identical people or things. ▶ **adv.** in the same way.

SYNONYMS ▶ **adj. 1 identical**, selfsame, very same. **2 matching**, identical, alike, carbon-copy, twin, indistinguishable, interchangeable, corresponding, equivalent, parallel, like, comparable, similar, homogeneous. ANTONYMS another, different.

■ **same·ness n.**

sam·o·var /ˈsaməˌvär/ ▶ **n.** a highly decorated Russian tea urn.

sam·ple /ˈsampəl/ ▶ **n. 1** a small part or quantity of something intended to show what the whole is like. **2** a specimen taken for scientific testing. ▶ **v.** (**samples**, **sampling**, **sampled**) **1** take a sample of. **2** try out. **3** take a short extract from one musical recording and reuse it as part of another recording.

SYNONYMS ▶ **n. 1 specimen**, example, snippet, swatch, taste. **2 cross section**, sampling, selection. ▶ **v. try (out)**, taste, test, put to the test, appraise, evaluate; informal check out.

sam·pler /ˈsamplər/ ▶ **n. 1** a piece of fabric decorated with a number of different embroidery stitches. **2** a device for sampling music.

sam·u·rai /ˈsaməˌrī/ ▶ **n.** (plural **samurai**) (in the past) a member of a powerful Japanese military class.

san·a·to·ri·um /ˌsanəˈtôrēəm/ ▶ **n.** (plural **sanatoriums** or **sanatoria** /-rēə/) a place like a hospital where people who have a long-term illness or who are recovering from an illness are treated.

sanc·ti·fy /ˈsaɴɢ(k)təˌfī/ ▶ **v.** (**sanctifies**, **sanctifying**, **sanctified**) **1** make something holy. **2** make something legal or right. ■ **sanc·ti·fi·ca·tion** /-fiˈkāsʜən/ **n.**

sanc·ti·mo·ni·ous /ˌsaɴɢ(k)təˈmōnēəs/ ▶ **adj.** disapproving making a show of being morally superior to other people.

SYNONYMS **self-righteous**, holier-than-thou, pious, moralizing, smug, superior, priggish, hypocritical, insincere; informal goody-goody.

sanc·tion /ˈsaɴɢ(k)sʜən/ ▶ **n. 1** (**sanctions**) measures taken by a state to try to force another state to behave well. **2** a penalty for disobeying a law or rule. **3** official permission or approval. ▶ **v.** give official permission for.

SYNONYMS ▶ **n. 1 penalty**, punishment, deterrent, restriction, embargo, ban, prohibition, boycott. **2 authorization**, consent, leave, permission, authority, dispensation, assent, acquiescence, agreement, approval, endorsement, blessing; informal the thumbs up, the OK, the green light. ANTONYMS prohibition. ▶ **v. authorize**, permit, allow, endorse, approve, accept, back, support; informal OK. ANTONYMS prohibit.

sanc·ti·ty /ˈsaɴɢ(k)titē/ ▶ **n.** (plural **sanctities**) **1** the state of being holy. **2** the state of being very important.

sanc·tu·ar·y /ˈsaɴɢ(k)ᴄʜo͞oˌerē/ ▶ **n.** (plural **sanctuaries**) **1** a place of safety. **2** a nature reserve. **3** a place where injured or unwanted animals are cared for. **4** a holy place. **5** the part of the chancel of a church containing the high altar.

SYNONYMS **1 refuge**, haven, oasis, shelter, retreat, hideaway. **2 safety**, protection, shelter, immunity, asylum. **3 reserve**, wildlife reserve, park.

sanc·tum /ˈsaɴɢ(k)təm/ ▶ **n. 1** a sacred place. **2** a private place.

sand /sand/ ▶ **n. 1** a substance consisting of very fine particles resulting from the wearing down of rocks, found in beaches and deserts and on the seabed. **2** (**sands**) a wide area of sand. ▶ **v.** smooth a surface with sandpaper or a sander.

san·dal /ˈsandl/ ▶ **n.** a shoe with a partly open upper part or straps attaching the sole to the foot.

san·dal·wood /ˈsandlˌwo͝od/ ▶ **n.** the sweet-smelling wood of an Asian tree.

sand·bag /ˈsan(d)ˌbag/ ▶ **n.** a bag of sand, used to protect or strengthen a structure or as a weight.

sand·bank /ˈsan(d)ˌbaɴɢk/ ▶ **n.** a deposit of sand forming a shallow area in the sea or a river.

sand·bar /ˈsan(d)ˌbär/ ▶ n. a long, narrow sandbank.

sand·blast /ˈsan(d)ˌblast/ ▶ v. roughen or clean a surface with a jet of sand.

sand·box /ˈsan(d)ˌbäks/ ▶ n. a shallow box or hollow containing sand, for children to play in.

sand·cas·tle /ˈsan(d)ˌkasəl/ ▶ n. a model of a castle built out of sand.

sand·er /ˈsandər/ ▶ n. a power tool used for smoothing a surface.

sand·pa·per /ˈsan(d)ˌpāpər/ ▶ n. paper coated with sand or another rough substance, used for smoothing surfaces. ▶ v. smooth with sandpaper.

sand·pi·per /ˈsan(d)ˌpīpər/ ▶ n. a wading bird with a long bill and long legs, found in coastal areas.

sand·stone /ˈsan(d)ˌstōn/ ▶ n. rock formed from compressed sand.

sand·storm /ˈsan(d)ˌstôrm/ ▶ n. a strong wind in a desert carrying clouds of sand.

sand·wich /ˈsan(d)wicʜ/ ▶ n. two pieces of bread with a filling between them. ▶ v. (**sandwich someone/thing between**) squeeze someone or something between two people or things. □ **sandwich board** a pair of boards hung in front of and behind a person's body as they walk around, used especially to advertise something.

sand·y /ˈsandē/ ▶ adj. (**sandier**, **sandiest**) **1** covered in or consisting of sand. **2** light yellowish brown.

sane /sān/ ▶ adj. **1** not mad. **2** sensible.

> SYNONYMS **1 of sound mind**, in your right mind, compos mentis, lucid, rational, balanced, normal; informal all there. **2 sensible**, practical, realistic, prudent, reasonable, rational, levelheaded, commonsensical. ANTONYMS mad, foolish.

sang /saɴɢ/ past of **SING**.

sang·froid /säɴɢˈfrwä/ ▶ n. the ability to stay calm in difficult circumstances.

san·gri·a /saɴɢˈgrēə/ ▶ n. a drink of red wine, lemonade, fruit, and spices.

san·gui·nar·y /ˈsaɴɢgwəˌnerē/ ▶ adj. old use involving a lot of bloodshed.

san·guine /ˈsaɴɢgwin/ ▶ adj. cheerful and confident about things that are going to happen.

> SYNONYMS **optimistic**, hopeful, buoyant, positive, confident, cheerful, bullish; informal upbeat. ANTONYMS gloomy.

san·i·tar·i·um /ˌsaniˈte(ə)rēəm/ ▶ n. (plural **sanitariums** or **sanitaria** /-rēə/) a place for treating people who are recovering from illness or have a chronic illness.

san·i·tar·y /ˈsaniˌterē/ ▶ adj. **1** relating to sanitation. **2** hygienic.

san·i·ta·tion /ˌsaniˈtāsʜən/ ▶ n. arrangements to protect public health, such as the provision of clean drinking water and the disposal of sewage.

san·i·tize /ˈsaniˌtīz/ ▶ v. (**sanitizes**, **sanitizing**, **sanitized**) **1** make something hygienic. **2** make something unpleasant seem more acceptable.

san·i·ty /ˈsanitē/ ▶ n. **1** the condition of being sane. **2** reasonable behavior.

> SYNONYMS **1 mental health**, reason, rationality, stability, lucidity, sense, wits, mind. **2 sense**, good sense, common sense, wisdom, prudence, rationality.

sank /saɴɢk/ past of **SINK**.

San·skrit /ˈsanˌskrit/ ▶ n. an ancient language of India.

San·ta Claus /ˈsantə ˌklôz/ (or informal **Santa**) ▶ n. an imaginary figure said to bring presents for children on Christmas.

sap /sap/ ▶ n. the liquid that circulates in plants, carrying food to all parts. ▶ v. (**saps**, **sapping**, **sapped**) gradually weaken a person's strength.

> SYNONYMS ▶ n. **juice**, secretion, fluid, liquid. ▶ v. **erode**, wear away/down, deplete, reduce, lessen, undermine, drain, bleed.

sa·pi·ent /ˈsāpēənt/ ▶ adj. wise.

sap·ling /ˈsaplɪɴɢ/ ▶ n. a young tree.

sap·phire /ˈsafˌī(ə)r/ ▶ n. **1** a transparent blue precious stone. **2** a bright blue color.

sap·py /ˈsapē/ ▶ adj. (**sappier**, **sappiest**) informal oversentimental.

sap·ro·phyte /ˈsaprəˌfīt/ ▶ n. a plant or fungus that lives on decaying matter. ■ **sap·ro·phyt·ic** /ˌsaprəˈfitik/ adj.

Sar·a·cen /ˈsarəsən/ ▶ n. an Arab or Muslim at the time of the Crusades.

sar·casm /ˈsärˌkazəm/ ▶ n. the use of words that say the opposite of what you mean, as a way of hurting or mocking someone.

> SYNONYMS **irony**, derision, mockery, ridicule, scorn.

sar·cas·tic /särˈkastik/ ▶ adj. using sarcasm.

> SYNONYMS **ironic**, sardonic, derisive, scornful, contemptuous, mocking, caustic, scathing, trenchant, acerbic.

■ **sar·cas·ti·cal·ly** adv.

sar·co·ma /särˈkōmə/ ▶ n. (plural **sarcomas** or **sarcomata** /-mətə/) Medicine a cancerous tumor found chiefly in connective tissue.

sar·coph·a·gus /särˈkäfəgəs/ ▶ n. (plural **sarcophagi** /-jī/) a stone coffin.

sar·dine /särˈdēn/ ▶ n. a small edible sea fish.

sar·don·ic /särˈdänik/ ▶ adj. mocking.

> SYNONYMS **mocking**, cynical, scornful, derisive, sneering, scathing, caustic, trenchant, cutting, acerbic.

■ **sar·don·i·cal·ly** adv.

sa·ri /ˈsärē/ (or **saree**) ▶ n. (plural **saris** or **sarees**) a length of fabric draped around the body, worn by women from the Indian subcontinent.

sa·rong /səˈrôɴɢ, -ˈräɴɢ/ ▶ n. a long piece of cloth wrapped around the body and tucked at the waist or under the armpits.

sar·sa·pa·ril·la /ˌsärs(ə)pəˈrilə, ˌsaspə-/ ▶ n. **1** the dried roots of various plants, used as a flavoring. **2** a carbonated soft drink flavored with this.

sar·to·ri·al /särˈtôrēəl/ ▶ adj. having to do with the way a person dresses. ■ **sar·to·ri·al·ly** adv.

sash[1] /sasʜ/ ▶ n. a strip of fabric worn over one shoulder or around the waist.

sash[2] ▶ n. a frame holding the glass in a window. □ **sash window** a window with two sashes that can be slid up and down to open it.

sa·shay /saˈsʜā/ ▶ v. informal swing the hips from side to side when walking.

Sas·quatch /ˈsaskwäcʜ, -kwacʜ/ ▶ n. ⇒ **BIGFOOT**.

sas·sa·fras /ˈsasəˌfras/ ▶ n. a tree whose bark and sweet-smelling leaves were formerly used in medicinal preparations.

Sas·se·nach /ˈsasəˌnak/ Scottish & Irish disapproving ▶ **n.** an English person. ▶ **adj.** English.

sas·sy /ˈsasē/ ▶ **adj.** (**sassier**, **sassiest**) informal confident, spirited, and impudent.

SAT ▶ **n.** trademark a US college entrance test.

sat /sat/ past and past participle of SIT.

Sa·tan /ˈsātn/ ▶ **n.** the devil.

sa·tan·ic /səˈtanik, sā-/ ▶ **adj.** having to do with Satan or the worship of Satan.

SYNONYMS **diabolical**, fiendish, devilish, demonic, ungodly, hellish, infernal, wicked, evil, sinful. ANTONYMS godly.

sa·tan·ism /ˈsātnˌizəm/ ▶ **n.** the worship of Satan. ■ **sa·tan·ist n. & adj.**

satch·el /ˈsaCHəl/ ▶ **n.** a bag with a long strap worn over one shoulder.

sat·ed /ˈsātid/ ▶ **adj.** having had at least as much of something as you want.

sa·teen /saˈtēn/ ▶ **n.** a cotton fabric woven like satin with a glossy surface.

sat·el·lite /ˈsatlˌīt/ ▶ **n.** **1** a man-made device placed in orbit around the earth or another planet to collect information or for communication. **2** a celestial body that moves in orbit around a planet. **3** a thing that is separate from but controlled by something else. □ **satellite television** television in which the signals are broadcast via satellite.

sa·ti·ate /ˈsāSHēˌāt/ ▶ **v.** give someone at least as much of something as they want. ■ **sa·ti·a·tion** /ˌsāSHēˈāSHən/ **n.**

sa·ti·e·ty /səˈtīətē/ ▶ **n.** the state of being fully satisfied or of having had too much of something.

sat·in /ˈsatn/ ▶ **n.** a smooth, glossy fabric. ■ **sat·in·y adj.**

sat·ire /ˈsaˌtīr/ ▶ **n.** **1** the use of humor, irony, exaggeration, or ridicule to reveal and criticize people's bad points. **2** a play or other piece of writing that uses satire.

SYNONYMS **parody**, burlesque, caricature, irony, lampoon, skit; informal spoof, takeoff, sendup.

■ **sat·i·rist** /ˈsatərist/ **n.**

sa·tir·i·cal /səˈti(ə)rikəl/ (or **satiric** /-ˈti(ə)rik/) ▶ **adj.** using satire.

SYNONYMS **mocking**, ironic, sardonic, critical, irreverent, disparaging, disrespectful.

■ **sa·tir·i·cal·ly adv.**

sat·i·rize /ˈsatəˌrīz/ ▶ **v.** (**satirizes**, **satirizing**, **satirized**) mock or criticize using satire.

SYNONYMS **mock**, ridicule, deride, make fun of, parody, lampoon, caricature, take off, criticize.

sat·is·fac·tion /ˌsatisˈfakSHən/ ▶ **n.** the feeling of pleasure that arises when you have the things you need or want or when the things you want to happen have happened.

SYNONYMS **contentment**, content, pleasure, gratification, fulfillment, enjoyment, happiness, pride.

sat·is·fac·to·ry /ˌsatisˈfakt(ə)rē/ ▶ **adj.** acceptable.

SYNONYMS **adequate**, all right, acceptable, good enough, sufficient, reasonable, competent, fair, decent, average, passable, fine, in order, up to scratch, up to the mark.

■ **sat·is·fac·to·ri·ly adv.**

sat·is·fy /ˈsatisˌfī/ ▶ **v.** (**satisfies**, **satisfying**, **satisfied**) **1** give someone the things they need or want or bring about the things they want to happen. **2** meet a particular demand, desire, or need.

SYNONYMS **1 fulfill**, gratify, meet, fill, indulge, appease, assuage, quench, slake, satiate. **2 convince**, assure, reassure, put someone's mind at rest. **3 comply with**, meet, fulfill, answer, conform to, measure up to, come up to. ANTONYMS frustrate.

sat·su·ma /satˈso͞omə, ˈsatsəˌmä/ ▶ **n.** a kind of tangerine with a loose skin.

sat·u·rate /ˈsaCHəˌrāt/ ▶ **v.** (**saturates**, **saturating**, **saturated**) **1** soak thoroughly with a liquid. **2** make a substance combine with, dissolve, or hold the greatest possible quantity of another substance. **3** put more than is needed of a particular product into the market.

SYNONYMS **1 soak**, drench, wet through. **2 flood**, glut, oversupply, overfill, overload.

■ **sat·u·ra·tion** /ˌsaCHəˈrāSHən/ **n.**

sat·u·rat·ed /ˈsaCHəˌrātid/ ▶ **adj.** Chemistry (of fats) having only single bonds between carbon atoms in their molecules and therefore being less easily processed by the body.

SYNONYMS **1 soaked**, soaking (wet), wet through, sopping (wet), sodden, dripping, wringing wet, drenched, soaked to the skin. **2 waterlogged**, flooded, boggy, awash. ANTONYMS dry.

Sat·ur·day /ˈsatərˌdā, -dē/ ▶ **n.** the day of the week before Sunday and following Friday.

Sat·urn /ˈsatərn/ ▶ **n.** the sixth planet from the sun in the solar system, circled by broad flat rings.

sat·ur·nine /ˈsatərˌnīn/ ▶ **adj.** **1** (of a person or their manner) gloomy. **2** (of looks) dark and brooding.

sa·tyr /ˈsatər, ˈsātər/ ▶ **n.** (in Greek mythology) a lecherous woodland god, with a man's face and body and a horse's or goat's ears, tail, and legs.

sauce /sôs/ ▶ **n.** **1** a thick liquid served with food to add moistness and flavor. **2** informal impudent talk or behavior.

SYNONYMS **gravy**, jus, dressing, dip, condiment, ketchup.

sauce·boat /ˈsôsˌbōt/ ▶ **n.** a a boat-shaped container for serving sauce or gravy.

sauce·pan /ˈsôsˌpan/ ▶ **n.** a deep cooking pan, with one long handle and a lid.

sau·cer /ˈsôsər/ ▶ **n.** a small shallow dish on which a cup stands.

sau·cy /ˈsôsē/ ▶ **adj.** (**saucier**, **sauciest**) informal **1** impudent; flippant. **2** bold and lively; smart-looking. ■ **sau·ci·ly adv.**

Sau·di /ˈsoudē, ˈsô-/ ▶ **n.** (plural **Saudis**) a person from Saudi Arabia. ▶ **adj.** relating to Saudi Arabia.

sau·er·kraut /ˈsou(ə)rˌkrout/ ▶ **n.** a German dish of pickled cabbage.

sau·na /ˈsônə, ˈsou-/ ▶ **n.** **1** a small room used as a hot-air or steam bath for cleaning and refreshing the body. **2** a session in a sauna.

saun·ter /ˈsôntər/ ▶ **v.** (**saunters**, **sauntering**, **sauntered**) walk in a slow, relaxed way. ▶ **n.** a leisurely stroll.

SYNONYMS ▶ **v. stroll**, amble, wander, meander, walk; informal mosey, tootle; formal promenade.

sau·sage /ˈsôsij/ ▶ **n. 1** a short tube of raw ground meat encased in a skin and grilled or fried before eating. **2** a tube of seasoned ground meat that is cooked or preserved and eaten cold in slices.

sau·té /sôˈtā, sō-/ ▶ **adj.** fried quickly in shallow fat or oil. ▶ **v.** (**sautés**, **sautéing**, **sautéed** or **sautéd**) cook in such a way.

sav·age /ˈsavij/ ▶ **adj. 1** fierce and violent. **2** cruel and vicious. **3** primitive and uncivilized. ▶ **n. 1** a member of a people seen as primitive and uncivilized. **2** a brutal person. ▶ **v.** (**savages**, **savaging**, **savaged**) **1** attack ferociously; maul. **2** criticize severely.

SYNONYMS ▶ **adj. 1 vicious**, brutal, cruel, sadistic, ferocious, fierce, violent, barbaric, bloodthirsty, merciless, pitiless. **2 untamed**, wild, feral, undomesticated. **3** *a savage attack on the government* **fierce**, blistering, scathing, searing, stinging, devastating, withering, virulent, vitriolic. ANTONYMS mild, tame. ▶ **n. brute**, beast, monster, barbarian, sadist, animal. ▶ **v. maul**, attack, lacerate, claw, bite, tear to pieces.

■ **sav·age·ly adv. sav·age·ry** /-rē/ **n.**

sa·van·na /səˈvanə/ (or **savannah**) ▶ **n.** a grassy plain in hot regions.

sa·vant /saˈvänt, sə-/ (or **savante**) ▶ **n.** a wise and knowledgeable person.

save¹ /sāv/ ▶ **v.** (**saves**, **saving**, **saved**) **1** rescue or protect someone or something from harm or danger. **2** prevent someone from dying. **3** store or keep for future use. **4** (in computing) store data. **5** avoid, lessen, or guard against. **6** prevent an opponent from scoring a goal. **7** (in Christian use) prevent a soul from being damned. ▶ **n.** an act of preventing an opponent's goal.

SYNONYMS ▶ **v. 1 rescue**, set free, free, liberate, deliver, redeem. **2 preserve**, keep, protect, safeguard, salvage, retrieve, reclaim, rescue. **3 put aside**, set aside, put by, keep, conserve, retain, store, hoard, stockpile; informal squirrel away. **4 prevent**, avoid, forestall, spare, stop, obviate, avert.

save² ▶ **prep. & conj.** formal except.

sav·er /ˈsāvər/ ▶ **n. 1** a person who regularly saves money through a bank or recognized plan. **2** something that prevents a resource from being used up: *a space-saver*.

sav·ing /ˈsāviNG/ ▶ **n. 1** a reduction in money, time, or some other resource. **2** (**savings**) money saved. ▶ **prep.** except.

SYNONYMS ▶ **n. 1 reduction**, cut, decrease, economy. **2** (**savings**) **nest egg**, capital, assets, funds, resources, reserves.

□ **saving grace** a good quality that makes up for someone or something's faults. **savings and loan (association)** an institution that pays interest on deposits and lends money to savers chiefly for home mortgages. **savings bank** a bank that pays interest on deposits.

sav·ior /ˈsāvyər/ ▶ **n. 1** a person who saves someone or something from danger or harm. **2** (**Savior**) (in Christianity) God or Jesus.

SYNONYMS **rescuer**, liberator, deliverer, champion, protector, redeemer.

sav·oir faire /ˌsavwär ˈfe(ə)r/ ▶ **n.** the ability to act appropriately in social situations.

sa·vor /ˈsāvər/ ▶ **v. 1** eat or drink something slowly while enjoying its full flavor. **2** enjoy a feeling or experience thoroughly. ▶ **n.** a characteristic flavor or smell.

SYNONYMS ▶ **v. relish**, enjoy, appreciate, delight in, revel in, luxuriate in. ▶ **n. smell**, aroma, fragrance, scent, perfume, bouquet; **taste**, flavor, tang.

sa·vor·y /ˈsāv(ə)rē/ ▶ **adj. 1** (of food) salty or spicy rather than sweet. **2** morally acceptable or respectable.

SYNONYMS **salty**, spicy, tangy, piquant. ANTONYMS sweet.

sav·vy /ˈsavē/ informal ▶ **n.** intelligence and good judgment. ▶ **adj.** having intelligence and good judgment.

saw¹ /sô/ ▶ **n.** a tool with a long, thin jagged blade, used with a backward and forward movement to cut wood and other hard materials. ▶ **v.** (**saws**, **sawing**, **sawed**; past participle **sawed** or **sawn**) cut through or cut off with a saw.

saw² past of SEE¹.

saw³ ▶ **n.** a proverb or wise saying.

saw·dust /ˈsôˌdəst/ ▶ **n.** powdery particles of wood produced by sawing.

saw·horse /ˈsôˌhôrs/ ▶ **n.** a frame or trestle that supports wood for sawing.

saw·mill /ˈsôˌmil/ ▶ **n.** a place where logs are sawed by machine.

saw·tooth /ˈsôˌto͞oTH/ (or **sawtoothed**) ▶ **adj.** shaped like the jagged teeth of a saw.

saw·yer /ˈsôyər/ ▶ **n.** a person who saws timber.

sax /saks/ ▶ **n.** informal a saxophone.

Sax·on /ˈsaksən/ ▶ **n.** a member of a people from Germany that settled in southern England in the 5th and 6th centuries.

sax·o·phone /ˈsaksəˌfōn/ ▶ **n.** a metal wind instrument with a reed in the mouthpiece. ■ **sax·o·phon·ist** /-ˌfōnist/ **n.**

say /sā/ ▶ **v.** (**says** /sez/, **saying**, **said** /sed/) **1** speak words to communicate something. **2** (of a piece of writing or a symbol) convey information or instructions. **3** (of a clock or watch) indicate a time. **4** (**be said**) be reported. **5** assume something in order to work out what its consequences would be. ▶ **n.** an opportunity to state your opinion.

SYNONYMS ▶ **v. 1 speak**, utter, voice, pronounce. **2 declare**, state, announce, remark, observe, mention, comment, note, add. **3 recite**, repeat, utter, deliver, perform. **4 indicate**, show, read. ▶ **n. influence**, sway, weight, voice, input.

□ **say-so** informal the power to decide or allow something.

say·ing /ˈsāiNG/ ▶ **n.** a well-known statement expressing a general truth.

SYNONYMS **proverb**, maxim, aphorism, axiom, expression, phrase, formula, slogan, catchphrase.

scab /skab/ ▶ **n. 1** a crust that forms over a wound as it heals. **2** informal, disapproving a person who refuses to take part in a strike.

scab·bard /ˈskabərd/ ▶ **n.** a cover for the blade of a sword or dagger.

scab·by /ˈskabē/ ▶ **adj.** (**scabbier**, **scabbiest**) **1** covered in scabs. **2** informal loathsome; despicable.

sca·bies /ˈskābēz/ ▶ **n.** a skin disease that causes itching and small red spots.

scab·rous /ˈskabrəs/ ▶ **adj. 1** rough and covered with scabs. **2** indecent or sordid.

scads /skadz/ ▶ **pl.n.** informal a large number or quantity.

scaf·fold /ˈskafəld, -ˌfōld/ ▶ **n. 1** (in the past) a raised wooden platform on which people stood when they were to be executed. **2** a structure made using scaffolding.

scaf·fold·ing /ˈskafəldiNG, -ˌfōl-/ ▶ **n. 1** a structure made of wooden planks and metal poles, for people to stand on when building or repairing a building. **2** the planks and poles used in such a structure.

scal·a·wag /ˈskaləˌwag/ (or **scallywag** /ˈskalēˌwag/) ▶ **n.** informal a mischievous person.

scald /skôld/ ▶ **v. 1** burn with very hot liquid or steam. **2** heat a liquid to near its boiling point. **3** dip something briefly in boiling water. ▶ **n.** an injury caused by hot liquid or steam.

scale[1] /skāl/ ▶ **n. 1** each of the small overlapping plates protecting the skin of fish and reptiles. **2** a dry flake of skin. **3** a white deposit that is left in a kettle, water pipe, etc., when water containing lime is heated. **4** a hard deposit that forms on teeth. ▶ **v.** (**scales**, **scaling**, **scaled**) **1** remove the scales from. **2** form or flake off in scales.

scale[2] ▶ **n. 1** (usu. **scales**) an instrument for weighing. **2** either of the dishes on a simple set of scales.

scale[3] ▶ **n. 1** a range of values forming a system for measuring or grading something. **2** a measuring instrument based on such a system. **3** relative size or extent. **4** a ratio of size in a map, model, drawing, or plan. **5** Music an arrangement of notes in order of pitch. ▶ **v.** (**scales**, **scaling**, **scaled**) **1** climb up or over something high and steep. **2** (**scale something down** or **up**) reduce (or increase) something in size, number, or extent. **3** represent something in a size that is larger or smaller than the original but exactly in proportion to it.

> SYNONYMS ▶ **n. 1 hierarchy**, ladder, ranking, pecking order, order, spectrum. **2 ratio**, proportion. **3 extent**, size, scope, magnitude, dimensions, range, breadth, degree. ▶ **v. climb**, ascend, clamber up, scramble up, shinny (up), mount.

□ **to scale** reduced or enlarged in proportion to something.

scal·lion /ˈskalyən/ ▶ **n.** a spring onion.

scal·lop /ˈskäləp, ˈskal-/ ▶ **n. 1** an edible shellfish with two hinged fan-shaped shells. **2** each of a series of small curves like the edge of a scallop shell, forming a decorative edging.

scal·lop·ed /ˈskäləpt, ˈskal-/ ▶ **adj.** (of the edge of something) decorated with a series of small curves.

scalp /skalp/ ▶ **n. 1** the skin covering the top and back of the head. **2** (in the past, among American Indians) the scalp and hair cut away from an enemy's head as a battle trophy. ▶ **v.** historical take the scalp of an enemy.

scal·pel /ˈskalpəl/ ▶ **n.** a knife with a small sharp blade, used by a surgeon.

scal·y /ˈskālē/ ▶ **adj.** (**scalier**, **scaliest**) **1** covered in scales. **2** (of skin) dry and flaking.

> SYNONYMS **dry**, flaky, scurfy, rough, scabrous.

scam /skam/ ▶ **n.** informal a dishonest scheme for making money.

scamp /skamp/ ▶ **n.** informal a mischievous person.

scamp·er /ˈskampər/ ▶ **v.** (**scampers**, **scampering**, **scampered**) run with quick light steps.

scam·pi /ˈskampē/ ▶ **pl.n.** the tails of large shrimp or prawns, covered in breadcrumbs or batter and fried in garlic and butter.

scan /skan/ ▶ **v.** (**scans**, **scanning**, **scanned**) **1** look at something quickly in order to find the parts that are most relevant or important. **2** move a detector or beam across. **3** convert a document or picture into digital form for storing or processing on a computer. **4** analyze the meter of a line of verse. **5** (of poetry) follow metrical rules. ▶ **n. 1** an act of scanning. **2** a medical examination using a scanner. **3** an image obtained by scanning.

> SYNONYMS ▶ **v. 1 study**, examine, scrutinize, inspect, survey, search, scour, sweep, watch. **2 glance through**, look through, have a look at, run/cast your eye over, flick through, browse through, leaf through, thumb through.

scan·dal /ˈskandl/ ▶ **n. 1** an action or event that causes public outrage. **2** outrage or gossip arising from such an action or event. **3** an action or situation that you find shocking and unacceptable.

> SYNONYMS **1 gossip**, rumor(s), slander, libel, aspersions, muckraking; informal dirt. **2** *it's a scandal that the hospital has closed* **disgrace**, outrage, sin, (crying) shame.

scan·dal·ize /ˈskandlˌīz/ ▶ **v.** (**scandalizes**, **scandalizing**, **scandalized**) shock other people by acting in way that is considered shameful or immoral.

scan·dal·ous /ˈskandl-əs/ ▶ **adj. 1** causing public outrage. **2** shocking and unacceptable.

> SYNONYMS **1 disgraceful**, shocking, outrageous, monstrous, criminal, wicked, shameful, appalling, deplorable, inexcusable, intolerable, unforgivable, unpardonable. **2 discreditable**, disreputable, dishonorable, improper, unseemly, sordid. **3 scurrilous**, malicious, slanderous, libelous, defamatory.

■ **scan·dal·ous·ly** adv.

Scan·di·na·vi·an /ˌskandəˈnāvēən/ ▶ **adj.** relating to the countries of Scandinavia, especially Norway, Sweden, and Denmark. ▶ **n.** a person from Scandinavia.

scan·ner /ˈskanər/ ▶ **n. 1** a machine that uses X-rays or ultrasound to record images, used by doctors to examine the inside of someone's body. **2** a device that scans documents or pictures and converts them into digital data.

scan·sion /ˈskanSHən/ ▶ **n. 1** the action of scanning a line of verse to find out its rhythm. **2** the rhythm of a line of verse.

scant /skant/ ▶ **adj.** barely reaching the amount specified or needed.

> SYNONYMS **little**, little or no, minimal, limited, negligible, meager, insufficient, inadequate.
> ANTONYMS abundant, ample.

scant·y /ˈskantē/ ▶ **adj.** (**scantier**, **scantiest**) too little in size or amount for what is needed.

> SYNONYMS **1 meager**, scant, minimal, limited, modest, restricted, sparse, tiny, small, paltry, negligible, scarce, in short supply, few and far between; informal measly, piddling, mingy,

pathetic. **2 skimpy**, revealing, short, brief, low-cut. ANTONYMS ample, plentiful.

■ **scant·i·ly** adv.

scape·goat /ˈskāpˌgōt/ ▶ n. a person who is blamed for the things other people do wrong. ▶ v. make a scapegoat of.

SYNONYMS ▶ n. **whipping boy**; informal fall guy, patsy.

scap·u·la /ˈskapyələ/ ▶ n. the shoulder blade.

scar /skär/ ▶ n. **1** a mark left on the skin or in body tissue after the healing of a wound. **2** a lasting effect left after an unpleasant experience. **3** a mark left at the point where a leaf or other part separates from a plant. ▶ v. (**scars**, **scarring**, **scarred**) mark or be marked with a scar.

SYNONYMS ▶ n. **1 mark**, blemish, disfigurement, discoloration, pockmark, pit, lesion, cicatrix. **2** *psychological scars* **trauma**, damage, injury. ▶ v. **disfigure**, mark, blemish, discolor, mar, spoil.

scar·ab /ˈskarəb/ ▶ n. **1** a kind of large beetle, seen as sacred in ancient Egypt. **2** an ancient Egyptian gem in the form of a scarab beetle.

scarce /ske(ə)rs/ ▶ adj. **1** (of a resource) only available in small quantities that do not meet a demand. **2** rarely found.

SYNONYMS **in short supply**, scant, scanty, inadequate, lacking, meager, sparse, hard to come by, at a premium, few and far between, rare. ANTONYMS plentiful.

scarce·ly /ˈske(ə)rslē/ ▶ adv. **1** only just. **2** just moments before. **3** definitely or very probably not.

SYNONYMS **1 hardly**, barely, only just. **2 rarely**, seldom, infrequently, not often, hardly ever; informal once in a blue moon.

scar·ci·ty /ˈskersitē/ ▶ n. insufficiency of supply: *the scarcity of affordable housing.*

SYNONYMS **shortage**, dearth, lack, undersupply, insufficiency, paucity, poverty, deficiency, inadequacy, unavailability, absence.

scare /ske(ə)r/ ▶ v. (**scares**, **scaring**, **scared**) **1** frighten or become frightened. **2** (**scare someone away** or **off**) drive or keep someone away by frightening them. ▶ n. **1** a sudden attack of fright. **2** a period of general alarm.

SYNONYMS ▶ v. **1 frighten**, startle, alarm, terrify, unnerve, worry, intimidate, terrorize, cow; informal freak out, spook. **2** (**scared**) **frightened**, afraid, fearful, nervous, panicky, terrified; informal in a cold sweat, spooked. ▶ n. **fright**, shock, start, turn, jump.

scare·crow /ˈske(ə)rˌkrō/ ▶ n. an object made to look like a person, set up to scare birds away from crops.

scarf¹ /skärf/ ▶ n. (plural **scarves** /skärvz/ or **scarfs**) a length or square of fabric worn around the neck or head.

scarf² ▶ v. informal eat or drink hungrily or enthusiastically.

scar·i·fy /ˈskarəˌfī/ ▶ v. (**scarifies**, **scarifying**, **scarified**) **1** rake out unwanted material from a lawn. **2** break up the surface of soil. **3** make shallow cuts in the skin.

scar·let /ˈskärlit/ ▶ n. a bright red color. □ **scarlet fever** an infectious disease that affects children, causing fever and a scarlet rash.

scarp /skärp/ ▶ n. a very steep slope.

scarves /skärvz/ plural of **SCARF¹**.

scar·y /ˈske(ə)rē/ ▶ adj. (**scarier**, **scariest**) informal frightening.

SYNONYMS **frightening**, terrifying, hair-raising, spine-chilling, blood-curdling, eerie, sinister; informal creepy, spine-tingling, spooky.

■ **scar·i·ly** adv.

scath·ing /ˈskāTHiNG/ ▶ adj. severely critical.

SYNONYMS **withering**, blistering, searing, devastating, fierce, ferocious, savage, severe, stinging, biting, cutting, virulent, vitriolic, scornful, bitter, harsh. ANTONYMS mild.

■ **scath·ing·ly** adv.

scat·o·log·i·cal /ˌskatlˈäjikəl/ ▶ adj. obsessed with excrement and excretion. ■ **sca·tol·o·gy** /skəˈtäləjē/ n.

scat·ter /ˈskatər/ ▶ v. (**scatters**, **scattering**, **scattered**) **1** throw in various random directions. **2** separate and move off in different directions. **3** (**be scattered**) be found at various places.

SYNONYMS **1 spread**, sprinkle, distribute, strew, disseminate, sow, throw, toss, fling. **2 disperse**, break up, disband, separate, dissolve. ANTONYMS gather, assemble.

scat·ter·brained /ˈskatərˌbrānd/ ▶ adj. informal disorganized and rather silly.

scav·enge /ˈskavənj/ ▶ v. (**scavenges**, **scavenging**, **scavenged**) **1** search through waste for anything that can be used again. **2** (of an animal) search for and eat dead animals.

SYNONYMS **search**, hunt, look, forage, rummage, root about/around, grub about/around.

scav·eng·er /ˈskavənjər/ ▶ n. **1** an animal that feeds on dead animals or waste material. **2** a person who searches for and collects usable items from trash.

sce·nar·i·o /səˈne(ə)rēˌō, -ˈnär-/ ▶ n. (plural **scenarios**) **1** a possible sequence of events in the future. **2** a written outline of a movie, play, or novel.

SYNONYMS **1 plot**, outline, storyline, framework, screenplay, script. **2 situation**, chain of events, course of events.

scene /sēn/ ▶ n. **1** the place where an incident happens. **2** a view or landscape as seen by a spectator. **3** an incident: *scenes of violence.* **4** a sequence of continuous action in a play, movie, etc. **5** an area of activity or interest: *the literary scene.* **6** a public display of emotion or anger.

SYNONYMS **1 location**, site, place, position, spot, locale. **2 background**, setting, context, milieu, backdrop. **3 incident**, event, episode, happening, proceeding. **4 view**, vista, outlook, panorama, landscape, scenery. **5** *she made a scene* **fuss**, exhibition of yourself, performance, tantrum, commotion, disturbance, row; informal to-do. **6** *the political scene* **arena**, stage, sphere, world, milieu, realm. **7 clip**, section, segment, part, sequence, extract.

□ **behind the scenes** out of public view.

scen·er·y /ˈsēn(ə)rē/ ▶ n. **1** a landscape considered in terms of its appearance. **2** the background used to represent a place on a stage or movie set.

SYNONYMS **1 landscape**, countryside, country, terrain, setting, surroundings, environment. **2 set**, setting, backdrop.

sce·nic /ˈsēnik/ ▶ **adj.** having beautiful natural scenery.

SYNONYMS **picturesque**, pretty, attractive, beautiful, charming, impressive, striking, spectacular, breathtaking, panoramic.

■ **sce·ni·cal·ly adv.**

scent /sent/ ▶ **n. 1** a distinctive smell, especially a pleasant one. **2** pleasant-smelling liquid worn on the skin; perfume. **3** a trail left by an animal, indicated by its smell. ▶ **v. 1** give a pleasant scent to. **2** find or recognize something by using the sense of smell. **3** sense that something is about to happen.

SYNONYMS ▶ **n. 1 smell**, fragrance, aroma, perfume, savor, odor. **2 perfume**, fragrance, cologne, eau de cologne, eau de toilette, toilet water, body spray. **3 spoor**, trail, track. ▶ **v. smell**, nose out, detect, pick up, sense.

scent·ed /ˈsentid/ ▶ **adj.** having a distinctive smell, especially a pleasant one.

SYNONYMS **perfumed**, fragranced, fragrant, sweet-smelling, aromatic.

scep·ter /ˈseptər/ ▶ **n.** a decorated rod carried by a king or queen on ceremonial occasions.

sched·ule /ˈskejo͞ol, -jəl/ ▶ **n. 1** a plan for doing something, with a list of intended events and times. **2** a timetable. ▶ **v.** (**schedules**, **scheduling**, **scheduled**) **1** plan for something to happen at a particular time. **2** (**scheduled**) (of a flight) forming part of a regular service rather than specially chartered.

SYNONYMS ▶ **n. plan**, program, timetable, scheme, agenda, diary, calendar, itinerary. ▶ **v. arrange**, organize, plan, program, slate, set up, line up.

sche·ma /ˈskēmə/ ▶ **n.** (plural **schemata** /-mətə/ or **schemas**) technical an outline of a plan or theory.

sche·mat·ic /skəˈmatik, skē-/ ▶ **adj. 1** (of a diagram) simplified and using symbols. **2** presented according to a plan. ■ **sche·mat·i·cal·ly adv.**

scheme /skēm/ ▶ **n. 1** a careful plan for achieving something. **2** a secret or devious plan; a plot. **3** a system or pattern. ▶ **v.** (**schemes**, **scheming**, **schemed**) make secret plans; plot.

SYNONYMS ▶ **n. 1 plan**, project, program, strategy, stratagem, tactic. **2 plot**, intrigue, conspiracy, ruse, ploy, stratagem, maneuver, subterfuge, machinations; informal racket, scam. ▶ **v. 1 plot**, conspire, intrigue, connive, maneuver, plan. **2** (**scheming**) **cunning**, crafty, calculating, devious, conniving, wily, sly, tricky, artful.

■ **schem·er n.**

scher·zo /ˈskertsō/ ▶ **n.** (plural **scherzos** or **scherzi** /-tsē/) a short, lively piece of music.

schism /ˈs(k)izəm/ ▶ **n.** a disagreement or division between two groups or within an organization.

SYNONYMS **division**, split, rift, breach, rupture, break, separation, severance, chasm, gulf, disagreement.

■ **schis·mat·ic** /s(k)izˈmatik/ **adj.**

schist /sʜist/ ▶ **n.** a metamorphic rock that consists of layers of different minerals.

schiz·oid /ˈskitˌsoid/ ▶ **adj.** having a mental condition similar to schizophrenia.

schiz·o·phre·ni·a /ˌskitsəˈfrēnēə, -ˈfrenēə/ ▶ **n.** a mental disorder whose symptoms include a withdrawal from reality into fantasy.

schiz·o·phren·ic /ˌskitsəˈfrenik/ ▶ **adj. 1** suffering from schizophrenia. **2** having contradictory elements. ▶ **n.** a schizophrenic person.

schle·miel /sʜləˈmēl/ (also **shle·miel**) ▶ **n.** informal an ineffectual, awkward, or unlucky person.

schlep /sʜlep/ (also **shlep**) informal ▶ **v.** (**schleps**, **schlepping**, **schlepped**) **1** drag or carry with difficulty. **2** go or move reluctantly or with effort. ▶ **n.** a tedious or difficult journey.

schlock /sʜläk/ (also **shlock**) ▶ **n.** informal cheap or poor quality goods. ■ **schlock·y adj.**

schmaltz /sʜmälts, sʜmôlts/ ▶ **n.** informal the quality of being too sentimental. ■ **schmaltz·y adj.**

schmooze /sʜmo͞oz/ informal ▶ **v.** (**schmoozes**, **schmoozing**, **schmoozed**) **1** chat. **2** chat to someone in order to gain an advantage. ▶ **n.** an intimate conversation.

schnapps /sʜnäps, sʜnaps/ ▶ **n.** a strong alcoholic drink resembling gin and often flavored with fruit.

schol·ar /ˈskälər/ ▶ **n. 1** a person who is studying at an advanced level. **2** a student who has a scholarship.

SYNONYMS **academic**, intellectual, learned person, man/woman of letters, authority, expert; informal egghead.

schol·ar·ly /ˈskälərlē/ ▶ **adj. 1** relating to serious academic study. **2** very knowledgeable and keen on studying.

SYNONYMS **learned**, educated, erudite, academic, well-read, intellectual, literary, highbrow. ANTONYMS uneducated, illiterate.

schol·ar·ship /ˈskälərˌsʜip/ ▶ **n. 1** academic work. **2** an amount of money given to a student to help pay for their education.

SYNONYMS **1 learning**, knowledge, erudition, education, academic study. **2 grant**, award, endowment.

scho·las·tic /skəˈlastik/ ▶ **adj.** having to do with schools and education.

school /sko͞ol/ ▶ **n. 1** a place where children are educated. **2** a place where instruction is given in a particular subject. **3** a college or university. **4** a group of artists, philosophers, etc., sharing similar ideas. **5** a large group of fish or sea mammals. ▶ **v. 1** educate. **2** train in a particular skill or activity.

SYNONYMS ▶ **n. 1 college**, academy, alma mater. **2 department**, faculty, division. **3 tradition**, approach, style, way of thinking, persuasion, creed, credo, doctrine, belief, opinion, point of view. ▶ **v. train**, teach, tutor, coach, instruct, drill.

□ **school of thought** a particular way of thinking.

school·er /ˈsko͞olər/ ▶ **n.** a student who goes to a school of the specified kind: *a high-schooler*.

school·house /ˈsko͞olˌhous/ ▶ **n.** a building used as a school, especially in a rural community.

school·ing /ˈsko͞oliɴɢ/ ▶ **n.** education received at school.

school·marm /ˈsko͞olˌmä(r)m/ ▶ **n.** a female teacher, especially one regarded as prim and strict.

school·mas·ter /ˈsko͞olˌmastər/ ▶ **n.** a male teacher in a school.

school·teach·er /ˈsko͞olˌtēCHər/ ▶ **n.** a person who teaches in a school.

schoon·er /ˈsko͞onər/ ▶ **n. 1** a sailing ship with two or more masts. **2** a tall beer glass.

sci·at·ic /sīˈatik/ ▶ **adj.** having to do with the hip or with the nerve that goes down the back of the thigh (the **sciatic nerve**).

sci·at·i·ca /sīˈatikə/ ▶ **n.** pain affecting the back, hip, and leg, caused by pressure on the sciatic nerve.

sci·ence /ˈsīəns/ ▶ **n. 1** study or knowledge of the physical and natural world, based on observation and experiment. **2** a particular branch of science. **3** a body of knowledge on any subject.

SYNONYMS *the science of physics* **subject**, discipline, field, branch of knowledge, body of knowledge, area of study.

□ **science fiction** fiction set in the future and dealing with imagined scientific advances. **science park** an area where a number of science-based companies are located.

sci·en·tif·ic /ˌsīənˈtifik/ ▶ **adj. 1** relating to or based on science. **2** systematic; methodical.

SYNONYMS **1 technological**, technical, evidence-based, empirical. **2 systematic**, methodical, organized, ordered, rigorous, exact, precise, accurate, mathematical.

■ **sci·en·tif·i·cal·ly adv.**

sci·en·tist /ˈsīəntist/ ▶ **n.** a person who studies or is an expert in science.

sci-fi /ˈsī ˈfī/ ▶ **n.** science fiction.

scim·i·tar /ˈsimətər, -ˌtär/ ▶ **n.** a short sword with a curved blade.

scin·til·lat·ing /ˈsin(t)lˌātiNG/ ▶ **adj.** very skillful and exciting.

SYNONYMS **brilliant**, dazzling, exciting, exhilarating, stimulating, sparkling, lively, vivacious, vibrant, animated, effervescent, witty, clever. ANTONYMS dull, boring.

sci·on /ˈsīən/ ▶ **n. 1** a young shoot or twig of a plant. **2** literary a descendant of a notable family.

scis·sors /ˈsizərz/ ▶ **pl.n.** a device for cutting cloth, paper, and other materials, consisting of two crossing blades pivoted in the middle.

scle·ro·sis /skləˈrōsis/ ▶ **n. 1** abnormal hardening of body tissue. **2** (also **multiple sclerosis**) a serious disease of the nervous system that can cause partial paralysis.

scoff[1] /skôf, skäf/ ▶ **v.** speak about something in a scornful way.

SYNONYMS **sneer**, jeer, laugh; (**scoff at**) mock, deride, ridicule, dismiss, belittle; informal pooh-pooh.

scoff[2] ▶ **v.** informal eat something quickly and greedily.

scold /skōld/ ▶ **v.** angrily criticize or tell off.

SYNONYMS **rebuke**, reprimand, reproach, reprove, admonish, chastise, chide, upbraid, berate, haul over the coals; informal tell off, dress down, give someone an earful, bawl out, give someone hell, chew out; formal castigate. ANTONYMS praise.

sconce /skäns/ ▶ **n.** a candle holder attached to a wall.

scone /skōn, skän/ ▶ **n.** a small plain cake, usually eaten with butter.

scooch /sko͞oCH/ (also **scootch**) ▶ **v. 1** crouch or squat. **2** move in or pass through a tight or narrow space.

scoop /sko͞op/ ▶ **n. 1** an implement like a spoon, with a short handle and a deep bowl. **2** the bowl-shaped part of a digging machine. **3** informal a piece of news printed by one newspaper before its rivals. ▶ **v. 1** pick something up with a scoop. **2** create a hollow or hole in something. **3** pick someone or something up in a quick, smooth movement. **4** informal be quicker than other newspapers to print a piece of news.

SYNONYMS ▶ **n. spoon**, ladle, dipper.

scoot /sko͞ot/ ▶ **v.** informal move or go quickly.

scoot·er /ˈsko͞otər/ ▶ **n. 1** (also **motor scooter**) a light motorcycle. **2** a child's vehicle with two wheels and a long steering handle, which you move by pushing one foot against the ground.

scope /skōp/ ▶ **n. 1** the opportunity or possibility for doing something. **2** the extent of the area or subject matter that something deals with.

SYNONYMS **1 extent**, range, breadth, reach, sweep, span, area, sphere, realm, compass, orbit, ambit, terms of reference, remit. **2 opportunity**, freedom, latitude, leeway, capacity, room (to maneuver).

scorch /skôrCH/ ▶ **v. 1** burn something on the surface or edges. **2** (**scorched**) dried out and withered as a result of extreme heat. (**scorching**) very hot.

SYNONYMS **1 burn**, sear, singe, char, blacken, discolor. **2 dry up**, parch, wither, shrivel, desiccate. **3** (**scorching**) **hot**, red-hot, blazing, flaming, fiery, burning, blistering, searing; informal boiling, baking, sizzling.

scorch·er /ˈskôrCHər/ ▶ **n.** informal a very hot day.

score /skôr/ ▶ **n. 1** the number of points, goals, etc., achieved by a person or team in a game. **2** (plural **score**) a group or set of twenty. **3** (**scores of**) a lot of. **4** the written music for a composition. ▶ **v.** (**scores**, **scoring**, **scored**) **1** win a point, goal, etc., in a game. **2** record the score during a game. **3** cut or scratch a mark on a surface. **4** (**score something out**) cross out a word or words. **5** arrange a piece of music.

SYNONYMS ▶ **n. 1 result**, outcome, total, tally, count. **2 rating**, grade, mark, percentage. ▶ **v. 1 get**, gain, chalk up, achieve, make, record, rack up, notch up; informal bag. **2 arrange**, set, adapt, orchestrate, write, compose. **3 scratch**, cut, notch, incise, scrape, nick, gouge.

score·board /ˈskôrˌbôrd/ ▶ **n.** a large board on which the score in a game or match is displayed.

score·card /ˈskôrˌkärd/ ▶ **n. 1** (also **scoresheet** /ˈskôrˌSHēt/ or **scorebook** /ˈskôrˌbo͝ok/) a card, sheet, or book in which scores are entered. **2** a card listing the names and positions of players in a team.

scorn /skôrn/ ▶ **n.** a strong feeling that someone or something is worthless; contempt. ▶ **v. 1** express scorn for. **2** reject in a contemptuous way.

SYNONYMS ▶ **n. contempt**, derision, disdain, mockery, sneering. ANTONYMS admiration, respect. ▶ **v. 1 deride**, treat with contempt, mock, scoff at, sneer at, jeer at, laugh at. **2 spurn**, rebuff, reject, ignore, shun, snub. ANTONYMS admire, respect.

scorn·ful /ˈskôrnfəl/ ▶ **adj.** showing or feeling scorn.

SYNONYMS **contemptuous**, derisive, withering, mocking, sneering, jeering, scathing, snide, disparaging, supercilious, disdainful. ANTONYMS admiring.

▪ **scorn·ful·ly** **adv.**

Scor·pi·o /ˈskôrpēˌō/ ▶ **n.** a sign of the zodiac (the Scorpion), October 23–November 21.

scor·pi·on /ˈskôrpēən/ ▶ **n.** a small creature with six legs, pincers, and a poisonous sting at the end of its tail.

Scot /skät/ ▶ **n.** a person from Scotland.

Scotch /skäch/ ▶ **n.** (also **Scotch whisky**) whiskey distilled in Scotland. ▶ **adj.** dated Scottish.

USAGE

Use **Scots** or **Scottish** rather than **Scotch** to refer to people or things from Scotland.

scotch /skäch/ ▶ **v.** decisively put an end to.

scot-free ▶ **adv.** without suffering any punishment or injury.

Scots /skäts/ ▶ **adj.** Scottish. ▶ **n.** the form of English used in Scotland.

Scots·man /ˈskätsmən/ (or **Scotswoman** /ˈskätsˌwo͝omən/) ▶ **n.** (plural **Scotsmen** or **Scotswomen**) a person from Scotland.

Scot·tish /ˈskätish/ ▶ **adj.** relating to Scotland or its people.

scoun·drel /ˈskoundrəl/ ▶ **n.** old use a dishonest or immoral person.

SYNONYMS **rogue**, rascal, miscreant, good-for-nothing, reprobate; cheat, swindler, fraudster, trickster, charlatan; informal villain, rat, louse, swine, dog, skunk, heel, wretch, scumbag, rat fink; dated cad; old use blackguard, knave.

scour /skou(ə)r/ ▶ **v.** **1** clean by rubbing with rough material. **2** search a place thoroughly.

SYNONYMS **1 scrub**, rub, clean, polish, buff, shine, burnish, grind, abrade. **2 search**, comb, hunt through, rummage through, look high and low in, ransack, turn upside-down.

scourge /skərj/ ▶ **n.** **1** a cause of great suffering. **2** old use a whip. ▶ **v.** (**scourges**, **scourging**, **scourged**) **1** cause great suffering to. **2** old use whip someone.

SYNONYMS ▶ **n.** **affliction**, bane, curse, plague, menace, evil, misfortune, burden, blight, cancer, canker.

scout /skout/ ▶ **n.** **1** a person who is sent ahead to gather information about the enemy. **2** (also **Scout**) a member of the Boy Scouts or Girl Scouts, organizations for young people. **3** (also **talent scout**) a person whose job is searching for talented performers. ▶ **v.** **1** search a place to find something or gather information. **2** act as a scout.

SYNONYMS ▶ **n.** **1 lookout**, spy. **2 reconnaissance**, reconnoiter, survey, exploration, search; informal recce. ▶ **v.** **1** *I scouted around for some logs* **search**, look, hunt, ferret around, root around. **2** *a patrol was sent to scout out the area* **reconnoiter**, explore, inspect, investigate, spy out, survey, scan, study; informal check out, case.

scow /skou/ ▶ **n.** a flat-bottomed sailing dinghy.

scowl /skoul/ ▶ **n.** a bad-tempered expression. ▶ **v.** frown in an angry or bad-tempered way.

SYNONYMS ▶ **v.** **glower**, frown, glare, grimace, lour, look daggers. ANTONYMS smile.

scrab·ble /ˈskrabəl/ ▶ **v.** (**scrabbles**, **scrabbling**, **scrabbled**) **1** grope around with your fingers to find or hold on to something. **2** move quickly and awkwardly; scramble.

scrag·gly /ˈskrag(ə)lē/ (or **scraggy** /ˈskragē/) ▶ **adj.** thin and bony.

scraggy /ˈskragē/ ▶ **adj.** thin and bony.

SYNONYMS **scrawny**, thin, skinny, skin-and-bones, gaunt, bony, angular, gawky, rawboned. ANTONYMS fat.

scram /skram/ ▶ **v.** (**scrams**, **scramming**, **scrammed**) informal leave quickly.

scram·ble /ˈskrambəl/ ▶ **v.** (**scrambles**, **scrambling**, **scrambled**) **1** move quickly and awkwardly, using hands as well as feet. **2** muddle. **3** put a transmission into a form that can only be understood by using a decoding device. **4** cook beaten eggs in a pan. **5** (of fighter aircraft) take off immediately in an emergency. ▶ **n.** an act of scrambling.

SYNONYMS ▶ **v.** **1 clamber**, climb, shinny, crawl, claw your way, scrabble, struggle. **2 muddle**, confuse, mix up, jumble (up), disarrange, disorganize, disorder, disturb, mess up. ▶ **n.** **1 clamber**, climb. **2** *the scramble for a seat* **struggle**, jostle, scrimmage, scuffle, tussle, free-for-all, jockeying, competition, race.

scrap[1] /skrap/ ▶ **n.** **1** a small piece or amount of something. **2** (**scraps**) bits of uneaten food left after a meal. **3** unwanted material, especially some that can be used again. ▶ **v.** (**scraps**, **scrapping**, **scrapped**) **1** abolish or cancel a plan, policy, etc. **2** remove from use.

SYNONYMS ▶ **n.** **1 fragment**, piece, bit, snippet, oddment, remnant, morsel, sliver. **2** *not a scrap of evidence* **bit**, shred, speck, iota, particle, ounce, jot. **3 waste**, garbage, trash, rubbish, refuse, debris; informal junk. ▶ **v.** **1 abandon**, drop, abolish, withdraw, do away with, put an end to, cancel, ax; informal ditch, dump, junk. **2 throw away**, throw out, dispose of, get rid of, discard, dispense with, bin, decommission, break up, demolish; informal trash, chuck, ditch, dump, junk. ANTONYMS keep.

scrap[2] ▶ **n.** a short fight or quarrel. ▶ **v.** (**scraps**, **scrapping**, **scrapped**) be involved in a scrap.

scrap·book /ˈskrapˌbo͝ok/ ▶ **n.** a book for sticking cuttings or pictures in.

scrape /skrāp/ ▶ **v.** (**scrapes**, **scraping**, **scraped**) **1** drag something hard or sharp across a surface to remove dirt or waste matter. **2** rub against a rough or hard surface. **3** just manage to achieve, succeed, or pass. ▶ **n.** **1** an act or sound of scraping. **2** an injury or mark caused by scraping. **3** informal an awkward or difficult situation.

SYNONYMS ▶ **v.** **1 rub**, scratch, scour, grind, sand, sandpaper, abrade, file. **2 grate**, creak, rasp, scratch. **3 graze**, scratch, scuff, rasp, skin, cut, lacerate, bark, chafe. ▶ **n.** **1 grating**, creaking, rasp, scratch. **2 graze**, scratch, abrasion, cut, laceration, wound.

scrap·py /ˈskrapē/ ▶ **adj.** disorganized, untidy, or incomplete.

scrap·yard /ˈskrapˌyärd/ ▶ **n.** a place where scrap metal is collected.

scratch /skraCH/ ▶ **v. 1** make a long mark or wound on a surface with something sharp or pointed. **2** rub part of the body with your fingernails to relieve itching. **3** (**scratch something out**) cross out a word or words. **4** withdraw from a competition. **5** cancel or abandon a plan, project, etc. ▶ **n. 1** a mark or wound made by scratching. **2** informal a slight injury. ▶ **adj.** put together from whatever is available: *a scratch squad.*

SYNONYMS ▶ **v. scrape**, abrade, graze, score, scuff, skin, cut, lacerate, bark, chafe. ▶ **n. abrasion**, graze, scrape, cut, laceration, wound, mark, line.

▫ **from scratch 1** from the very beginning. **2** (of food) homemade, without the use of prepackaged mixes, etc. **up to scratch** up to the required standard.

scratch·y /ˈskraCHē/ ▶ **adj.** (**scratchier**, **scratchiest**) **1** rough in texture and causing scratching. **2** (of a voice or sound) rough; grating.

scrawl /skrôl/ ▶ **v.** write in a hurried, careless way. ▶ **n.** scrawled handwriting.

scrawn·y /ˈskrônē/ ▶ **adj.** (**scrawnier**, **scrawniest**) thin and bony.

SYNONYMS **skinny**, thin, as thin as a rail, skin-and-bones, gaunt, bony, angular, gawky, scraggy. ANTONYMS fat.

scream /skrēm/ ▶ **v.** make a loud, piercing cry or sound. ▶ **n. 1** a loud, piercing cry or sound. **2** (**a scream**) informal a very funny person or thing.

SYNONYMS **shriek**, screech, yell, howl, bawl, yelp, squeal, wail, squawk.

scree /skrē/ ▶ **n.** a mass of small loose stones on a mountain slope.

screech /skrēCH/ ▶ **n.** a loud, harsh cry or sound. ▶ **v.** make a screech.

SYNONYMS **squeal**, shriek, squawk, scream, yell.

screed /skrēd/ ▶ **n. 1** a long speech or piece of writing. **2** a layer of material applied to make a floor level.

screen /skrēn/ ▶ **n. 1** an upright partition used to divide a room or conceal something. **2** the front part of a television or computer monitor, on which images and data are displayed. **3** a blank surface on which movies are projected. **4** (**the screen**) movies or television. ▶ **v. 1** conceal or protect with a screen. **2** test a group of people for the presence of a disease. **3** show or broadcast a movie or television program.

SYNONYMS ▶ **n. 1 partition**, divider, windbreak. **2 display**, monitor, visual display unit. **3 mesh**, net, netting. **4 buffer**, protection, shield, shelter, guard. ▶ **v. 1 partition**, divide, separate, curtain. **2 conceal**, hide, veil, shield, shelter, shade, protect. **3** *all blood is screened for the virus* **check**, test, examine, investigate, vet; informal check out. **4 show**, broadcast, transmit, televise, put on, air.

▫ **screen printing** a process in which ink is forced through a screen of fine material to create a picture or pattern. **screen test** a filmed audition for a movie part.

screen·play /ˈskrēnˌplā/ ▶ **n.** the script of a movie, including acting instructions.

screen·writ·er /ˈskrēnˌrītər/ ▶ **n.** a person who writes a screenplay.

screw /skrōō/ ▶ **n. 1** a metal pin with a spiral thread running around it, which is turned and pressed into a surface to join things together. **2** a ship's or aircraft's propeller. **3** informal a prison guard. ▶ **v. 1** fasten or tighten with a screw or screws. **2** rotate something to attach or remove it. **3** informal cheat or swindle.

SYNONYMS ▶ **n. 1 bolt**, fastener. **2 screw propeller**, propeller, rotor. ▶ **v. 1 tighten**, turn, twist, wind. **2 fasten**, secure, fix, attach. **3 extort**, force, extract, wrest, wring, squeeze; informal bleed.

▫ **screw someone/something up 1** crush something into a tight mass. **2** informal make something fail or go wrong. **3** informal make someone emotionally disturbed.

screw·driv·er /ˈskrōōˌdrīvər/ ▶ **n.** a tool with a tip that fits into the head of a screw to turn it.

screw·y /ˈskrōōē/ ▶ **adj.** informal rather odd or eccentric.

scrib·ble /ˈskribəl/ ▶ **v.** (**scribbles**, **scribbling**, **scribbled**) write or draw carelessly or hurriedly. ▶ **n.** a scribbled picture or piece of writing.

SYNONYMS ▶ **v. scrawl**, scratch, dash off, jot (down), doodle, sketch. ▶ **n. scrawl**, squiggle(s), jottings, doodle, doodlings.

scribe /skrīb/ ▶ **n.** (in the past) a person who copied out documents.

scrim·mage /ˈskrimij/ ▶ **n. 1** a confused struggle or fight. **2** Football offensive play begun with the ball on the ground between the offensive and defensive lines.

scrimp /skrimp/ ▶ **v.** be very careful with money; economize.

SYNONYMS **economize**, skimp, save; be thrifty, be frugal, tighten your belt, cut back, watch your pennies, pinch pennies.

script /skript/ ▶ **n. 1** the written text of a play, movie, or broadcast. **2** handwriting as distinct from print. ▶ **v.** write a script for.

SYNONYMS ▶ **n. 1 handwriting**, writing, hand. **2 text**, screenplay, libretto, score, lines, dialogue, words.

scrip·ture /ˈskripCHər/ (or **scriptures**) ▶ **n. 1** the sacred writings of Christianity contained in the Bible. **2** the sacred writings of another religion. ■ **scrip·tur·al adj.**

scrof·u·la /ˈskrôfyələ, ˈskräf-/ ▶ **n.** (in the past) the name for a form of tuberculosis. ■ **scrof·u·lous adj.**

scroll /skrōl/ ▶ **n.** a roll of parchment or paper for writing or painting on. ▶ **v.** move data on a computer screen in order to view different parts of it.

Scrooge /skrōōj/ ▶ **n.** a person who is miserly with money.

scro·tum /ˈskrōtəm/ ▶ **n.** (plural **scrota** /-tə/ or **scrotums**) the pouch of skin containing the testicles.

scrounge /skrounj/ ▶ **v.** (**scrounges**, **scrounging**, **scrounged**) informal try to get something from someone without having to pay or work for it.

SYNONYMS **beg**, borrow; informal cadge, sponge, bum, touch someone for, mooch.

scroung·er /ˈskrounjər/ ▶ **n.** informal a person who scrounges.

SYNONYMS **beggar**, borrower, parasite; informal sponger, freeloader, mooch, moocher, bottom feeder.

scrub[1] /skrəb/ ▶ v. (**scrubs, scrubbing, scrubbed**) rub something hard to clean it. ▶ n. an act of scrubbing.

SYNONYMS ▶ v. **1 brush**, scour, rub, clean, cleanse, wash. **2 abandon**, scrap, drop, cancel, call off, ax; informal ditch, dump, junk.

scrub[2] ▶ n. **1** vegetation consisting mainly of bushes and small trees. **2** land covered with such vegetation.

scrub·ber /'skrəbər/ ▶ n. **1** a person or thing that scrubs. **2** an apparatus used for purifying gases or vapors.

scrub·by /'skrəbē/ ▶ adj. (of land) covered with bushes and small trees.

scruff /skrəf/ ▶ n. the back of a person's or animal's neck.

scruff·y /'skrəfē/ ▶ adj. (**scruffier, scruffiest**) shabby and untidy or dirty.

SYNONYMS **shabby**, worn, down at the heels, ragged, tattered, mangy, dirty, untidy, unkempt, bedraggled, messy, disheveled, ill-groomed; informal tatty. ANTONYMS smart.

■ **scruff·i·ness** n.

scrum /skrəm/ ▶ n. (also **scrummage** /'skrəmij/) Rugby a formation in which players push against each other with heads down and try to gain possession of the ball when it is thrown in between them.

scrump·tious /'skrəm(p)sHəs/ ▶ adj. informal delicious.

scrunch /skrəncH/ ▶ v. crush or squeeze into a tight mass.

scru·ple /'skro͞opəl/ ▶ n. a feeling of doubt as to whether an action is morally right. ▶ v. (**not scruple to do**) formal not hesitate to do something, even if it may be wrong.

SYNONYMS ▶ n. (**scruples**) **qualms**, compunction, hesitation, reservations, second thoughts, doubt(s), misgivings, uneasiness, reluctance.

scru·pu·lous /'skro͞opyələs/ ▶ adj. **1** very careful and thorough. **2** very concerned to avoid doing wrong.

SYNONYMS **careful**, meticulous, painstaking, thorough, assiduous, sedulous, attentive, conscientious, punctilious, searching, close, rigorous, strict. ANTONYMS careless.

■ **scru·pu·lous·ly** adv.

scru·ti·nize /'skro͞otn,īz/ ▶ v. (**scrutinizes, scrutinizing, scrutinized**) examine thoroughly.

SYNONYMS **examine**, inspect, survey, study, look at, peruse, investigate, explore, probe, inquire into, go into, check.

scru·ti·ny /'skro͞otn-ē/ ▶ n. (plural **scrutinies**) close and critical examination.

scu·ba /'sko͞obə/ ▶ n. self-contained underwater breathing apparatus; a portable breathing apparatus for divers, consisting of cylinders of compressed air attached to a mouthpiece or mask.

scu·ba div·ing ▶ n. swimming underwater using an aqualung.

scud /skəd/ ▶ v. (**scuds, scudding, scudded**) move quickly, driven by the wind.

scuff /skəf/ ▶ v. **1** make a mark on the surface of something by scraping it against something rough. **2** drag your feet when walking. ▶ n. a mark made by scuffing.

scuf·fle /'skəfəl/ ▶ n. a short, confused fight or struggle. ▶ v. (**scuffles, scuffling, scuffled**) take part in a scuffle.

scull /skəl/ ▶ n. **1** each of a pair of small oars used by a single rower. **2** an oar used over the stern of a boat to propel it. **3** a light, narrow boat propelled with one or two sculls. ▶ v. propel a boat with sculls.

scul·ler·y /'skəl(ə)rē/ ▶ n. (plural **sculleries**) a small room in an old house, used for washing dishes and laundry.

sculpt /skəlpt/ ▶ v. carve or shape.

sculp·tor /'skəlptər/ ▶ n. (feminine **sculptress**) an artist who makes sculptures.

sculp·ture /'skəlpcHər/ ▶ n. **1** the art of making three-dimensional figures and shapes by carving or shaping wood, stone, metal, etc. **2** a work of such a kind. ▶ v. (**sculptures, sculpturing, sculptured**) **1** make or represent by sculpture. **2** (**sculptured**) pleasingly shaped, with strong, smooth lines.

SYNONYMS ▶ n. **carving**, statue, statuette, figure, figurine, effigy, bust, head, model.

■ **sculp·tur·al** adj.

scum /skəm/ ▶ n. **1** a layer of dirt or froth on the surface of a liquid. **2** informal a worthless person or group of people.

SYNONYMS **film**, layer, covering, froth, dross.

■ **scum·my** adj.

scup·per /'skəpər/ ▶ n. a hole at the edge of a ship's deck to allow water to run off.

scurf /skərf/ ▶ n. flakes of skin.

scur·ril·ous /'skərələs/ ▶ adj. rude and insulting; slanderous.

SYNONYMS **defamatory**, slanderous, libelous, scandalous, insulting, offensive, abusive, malicious; informal bitchy.

scur·ry /'skərē/ ▶ v. (**scurries, scurrying, scurried**) move hurriedly with short, quick steps.

scur·vy /'skərvē/ ▶ n. a disease caused by a lack of vitamin C.

scut·tle[1] /'skətl/ ▶ n. a metal container used to store coal for a domestic fire.

scut·tle[2] ▶ v. (**scuttles, scuttling, scuttled**) run hurriedly or secretively with short, quick steps.

scut·tle[3] ▶ v. (**scuttles, scuttling, scuttled**) **1** cause a plan to fail. **2** sink your own ship deliberately.

scythe /sīTH/ ▶ n. a tool with a long curved blade for cutting grass or corn. ▶ v. (**scythes, scything, scythed**) cut with a scythe.

SE ▶ abbr. southeast or southeastern.

sea /sē/ ▶ n. **1** the salt water that surrounds the land masses of the earth. **2** a particular area of sea. **3** a vast expanse or quantity.

SYNONYMS **1 ocean**, waves; informal the drink; literary the (briny) deep. **2** *a sea of roofs* **expanse**, stretch, area, tract, sweep, carpet, mass. **3** *sea creatures* **marine**, ocean, oceanic, maritime, naval, nautical.

□ **at sea** very confused and uncertain. **sea anemone** a sea creature with stinging tentacles that make it resemble a flower. **sea change** a great or remarkable change in a situation. **sea cow** a manatee or other large plant-eating sea animal.

sea level the average level of the sea's surface, used in calculating the height of land. **sea lion** a large seal with a mane on the neck and shoulders. **sea urchin** a small sea creature with a shell covered in spines.

sea·bird /ˈsēˌbərd/ ▶ **n.** a bird that lives near the sea.

sea·board /ˈsēˌbôrd/ ▶ **n.** a region bordering the sea; the coastline.

sea·far·er /ˈsēˌfe(ə)rər/ ▶ **n.** a person who travels by sea, especially someone who does this for a living; a sailor.

sea·far·ing /ˈsēˌfe(ə)riNG/ ▶ **adj. & n.** traveling by sea.

sea·food /ˈsēˌfo͞od/ ▶ **n.** shellfish and sea fish as food.

sea·go·ing /ˈsēˌgōiNG/ ▶ **adj.** traveling on the sea.

sea·gull /ˈsēˌgəl/ ▶ **n.** a gull.

sea·horse /ˈsēˌhôrs/ ▶ **n.** a small sea fish with a head and neck resembling a horse's.

SEAL /sēl/ ▶ **n.** a member of an elite US Navy force specializing in guerrilla warfare and counterinsurgency.

seal[1] /sēl/ ▶ **n. 1** a device or substance used to join two things together or to stop fluid getting in. **2** a piece of wax with a design stamped into it, attached to letters and documents to guarantee they are genuine. **3** a confirmation or guarantee: *a seal of approval.* ▶ **v. 1** fasten or close securely. **2** (**seal something off**) stop people entering and leaving an area. **3** coat a surface to stop fluid passing through it. **4** conclude; make definite.

> SYNONYMS ▶ **n. 1 sealant**, adhesive, mastic. **2 emblem**, symbol, insignia, badge, crest. ▶ **v. 1 stop up**, seal up, cork, stopper, plug, make watertight. **2 clinch**, secure, settle, conclude, complete, finalize, confirm.

■ **seal·er n.**

seal[2] ▶ **n.** a sea mammal with flippers and a streamlined body.

seal·ant /ˈsēlənt/ ▶ **n.** material used to make something airtight or watertight.

seam /sēm/ ▶ **n. 1** a line where two pieces of fabric are sewn together. **2** an underground layer of a mineral.

> SYNONYMS **1 join**, stitching, joint. **2 layer**, stratum, vein, lode.

■ **seamed adj.**

sea·man /ˈsēmən/ ▶ **n.** (plural **seamen**) a sailor, especially one below the rank of officer.

> SYNONYMS **sailor**, seafarer, mariner, boatman, hand, merchant seaman. ANTONYMS landlubber.

seam·less /ˈsēmlis/ ▶ **adj.** smooth and without seams or obvious joins. ■ **seam·less·ly adv.**

seam·stress /ˈsēmstris/ ▶ **n.** a woman who sews, especially as a job.

seam·y /ˈsēmē/ ▶ **adj.** (**seamier**, **seamiest**) immoral and unpleasant.

se·ance /ˈsāˌäns/ ▶ **n.** a meeting at which people attempt to make contact with the dead.

sea·plane /ˈsēˌplān/ ▶ **n.** an aircraft designed to land on and take off from water.

sear /si(ə)r/ ▶ **v. 1** scorch with a sudden intense heat. **2** (of pain) be experienced as a burning sensation.

> SYNONYMS **1 scorch**, burn, singe, char, dry up, wither. **2 flash-fry**, seal, brown.

search /sərCH/ ▶ **v. 1** try to find something by looking carefully and thoroughly. **2** examine something thoroughly in order to find something or someone. **3** look for information on the Internet by using a search engine. **4** (**searching**) investigating very deeply. ▶ **n.** an act of searching.

> SYNONYMS ▶ **v. 1 hunt**, look, seek, forage, look high and low, ferret about, root about, rummage. **2** *he searched the house* **look through**, scour, go through, sift through, comb, turn upside down, ransack, rifle through. **3 examine**, inspect, check, frisk. **4** (**searching**) **penetrating**, piercing, probing, keen, shrewd, sharp, intent. ▶ **n. hunt**, look, quest, examination, exploration.

□ **search engine** a computer program that searches the Internet for web pages containing a specified word or words. **search warrant** a document authorizing a police officer to enter and search a place. ■ **search·er n. search·ing·ly adv.**

search·light /ˈsərCHˌlīt/ ▶ **n.** a powerful electric light with a concentrated beam that can be turned in any direction.

sea·scape /ˈsēˌskāp/ ▶ **n.** a view or picture of the sea.

sea·shell /ˈsēˌSHel/ ▶ **n.** the shell of a marine shellfish.

sea·shore /ˈsēˌSHôr/ ▶ **n.** an area of sandy, stony, or rocky land next to the sea.

sea·sick /ˈsēˌsik/ ▶ **adj.** suffering from nausea caused by the motion of a ship at sea. ■ **sea·sick·ness n.**

sea·side /ˈsēˌsīd/ ▶ **n.** a place by the sea, especially a beach area or holiday resort.

> SYNONYMS **coast**, shore, seashore, beach, sand, sands.

sea·son /ˈsēzən/ ▶ **n. 1** each of the four divisions of the year (spring, summer, autumn, and winter). **2** a part of the year with particular weather, or when a particular sport is played. ▶ **v. 1** add salt or spices to food. **2** dry wood for use as timber. **3** (**seasoned**) experienced.

> SYNONYMS ▶ **n. period**, time, time of year, spell, term. ▶ **v. 1 flavor**, add salt and pepper to, salt, spice. **2** (**seasoned**) **experienced**, practiced, well-versed, knowledgeable, established, veteran, hardened.

□ **in season 1** (of food) available and ready to eat. **2** (of a female mammal) ready to mate. **season ticket** a ticket that lets you travel within a particular period or gain admission to a series of events.

sea·son·a·ble /ˈsēzənəbəl/ ▶ **adj.** usual or appropriate for a particular season of the year.

sea·son·al /ˈsēzənəl/ ▶ **adj. 1** relating to or characteristic of a particular season of the year. **2** changing according to the season. ■ **sea·son·al·ly adv.**

sea·son·ing /ˈsēzəniNG/ ▶ **n.** salt or spices added to food to improve the flavor.

> SYNONYMS **flavoring**, salt and pepper, herbs, spice(s), condiments.

seat /sēt/ ▶ **n. 1** a thing made or used for sitting on. **2** the part of a chair designed for sitting on. **3** a place for a person to sit in a vehicle, theater, etc. **4** a person's buttocks. **5** a place in an elected legislature, parliament, or council. **6** a site or location. ▶ **v. 1** arrange for someone to sit somewhere. **2** (**seat yourself** or **be seated**) formal sit down. **3** (of a place) have enough seats for.

SYNONYMS ▶n. **1 chair**, bench, stool; (**seats**) seating. **2 headquarters**, base, center, nerve center, hub, heart, location, site. **3 residence**, ancestral home, mansion. ▶v. **1 position**, put, place, ensconce, install, settle. **2 have room for**, contain, take, sit, hold, accommodate.

□ **seat belt** a belt used to secure someone in the seat of a motor vehicle or aircraft.

sea·weed /'sē,wēd/ ▶n. plants growing in the sea or on rocks below the high-water mark.

sea·wor·thy /'sē,wərTHē/ ▶adj. (of a boat) in a good enough condition to sail on the sea.

se·ba·ceous /sə'bāsHəs/ ▶adj. technical producing oil or fat.

sec. ▶abbr. second (of time).

se·cede /si'sēd/ ▶v. (**secedes**, **seceding**, **seceded**) withdraw formally from an alliance, federation, or union of states.

se·ces·sion /sə'sesHən/ ▶n. the action of seceding.

se·clud·ed /si'klo͞odid/ ▶adj. (of a place) sheltered and private.

SYNONYMS **sheltered**, private, concealed, hidden, unfrequented, sequestered, tucked away, remote, isolated, off the beaten track.

se·clu·sion /si'klo͞ozHən/ ▶n. the state of being private and away from other people.

sec·ond[1] /'sekənd/ ▶ordinal number **1** that is number two in a sequence; 2nd. **2** lower in position, rank, or importance. **3** (**seconds**) goods that are not of perfect quality. **4** a person who helps someone fighting in a duel or boxing match. ▶v. **1** formally support a nomination or resolution before voting or discussion. **2** express agreement with.

SYNONYMS ▶ordinal number **1 next**, following, subsequent. **2 additional**, extra, alternative, another, spare, backup, alternate. **3 secondary**, subordinate, subsidiary, lesser, inferior. ANTONYMS first. ▶v. **support**, vote for, back, approve, endorse.

□ **second best** not quite as good as the best. **second class 1** the second-best accommodations in a train, ship, etc. **2** of a lower standard or quality than the best. **second-degree** (of burns) causing blistering but not permanent scars. **second-guess** predict someone's actions or thoughts by guesswork. **second nature** a habit that has become instinctive. **second-rate** of bad quality. **second sight** the supposed ability to know what will happen in the future. **second thoughts** a change of opinion after reconsidering something. **second wind** fresh energy gained during exercise after having been out of breath.

sec·ond[2] ▶n. **1** a unit of time equal to one sixtieth of a minute. **2** (**a second**) informal a very short time. **3** a measurement of an angle equal to one sixtieth of a minute.

SYNONYMS **moment**, bit, little while, instant, flash; informal sec, jiffy.

sec·ond·ar·y /'sekən,derē/ ▶adj. **1** coming after, or less important than, something else. **2** (of education) for children from the age of eleven to sixteen or eighteen.

SYNONYMS **1 less important**, subordinate, lesser, minor, peripheral, incidental, subsidiary, ancillary. **2 accompanying**, attendant, concomitant, consequential, resulting, resultant. ANTONYMS primary, main.

■ **sec·ond·ar·i·ly** adv.

sec·ond·hand /'sekən(d)'hand/ ▶adj. **1** (of goods) having had a previous owner; not new. **2** (of information or experience) accepted on another's authority and not from original investigation. ▶adv. not from the original source: *I heard the news secondhand.*

SYNONYMS ▶adj. **used**, old, worn, pre-owned, nearly new, handed-down, hand-me-down, castoff. ANTONYMS new, direct. ▶adv. **indirectly**; informal through the grapevine. ANTONYMS directly.

sec·ond·ly /'sekən(d)lē/ ▶adv. in the second place; second.

SYNONYMS **furthermore**, also, moreover, second, in the second place, next.

se·cre·cy /'sēkrəsē/ ▶n. the action of keeping something secret or the state of being kept secret.

SYNONYMS **confidentiality**, privacy, mystery, concealment, stealth.

se·cret /'sēkrit/ ▶adj. **1** hidden from, or not known by, other people. **2** secretive. ▶n. **1** something that other people do not know about. **2** a method of achieving something that is not generally known.

SYNONYMS ▶adj. **1 confidential**, top secret, classified, undisclosed, unknown, private, under wraps; informal hush-hush. **2 hidden**, concealed, disguised, camouflaged. **3 clandestine**, covert, undercover, underground, surreptitious, stealthy, cloak-and-dagger, furtive, conspiratorial. ANTONYMS public, open.

□ **secret agent** a spy. **secret police** a police force working in secret against a government's political opponents. **secret service 1** a government department concerned with spying. **2** (**Secret Service**) a branch of the Treasury Department dealing with counterfeiting and providing protection for the president.

sec·re·tar·i·at /,sekri'te(ə)rēət/ ▶n. a government office or department.

sec·re·tar·y /'sekri,terē/ ▶n. (plural **secretaries**) **1** a person employed to type letters, keep records, etc. **2** an official of a society or other organization. □ **secretary general** (plural **secretaries general**) the principal administrator of some organizations. **secretary of state** (in the US) the head of the State Department, responsible for foreign affairs. ■ **sec·re·tar·i·al** /-'te(ə)rēəl/ adj.

SPELLING

Secret**ary** ends with **-ary**, not **-ery**.

se·crete /si'krēt/ ▶v. (**secretes**, **secreting**, **secreted**) **1** (of a cell, gland, or organ) produce a liquid substance. **2** hide an object. ■ **se·cre·tion** n.

se·cre·tive /'sēkritiv/ ▶adj. inclined to hide your feelings or not give out information.

SYNONYMS **uncommunicative**, secret, unforthcoming, playing your cards close to your chest, reticent, tight-lipped. ANTONYMS open, communicative.

■ **se·cre·tive·ly** adv.

se·cret·ly /'sēkritlē/ ▶adv. in secret.

SYNONYMS **in secret**, in private, privately, behind closed doors, under cover, furtively, stealthily, on the QT, covertly.

sect /sekt/ ▶ n. a small religious or political group with different beliefs from those of the larger group that they belong to.

SYNONYMS **group**, cult, denomination, order, splinter group, faction, camp.

sec·tar·i·an /sek'te(ə)rēən/ ▶ adj. having to do with a sect or group.

SYNONYMS **factional**, separatist, partisan, doctrinaire, dogmatic, illiberal, intolerant, bigoted, narrow-minded.

■ **sec·tar·i·an·ism** n.

sec·tion /'seksHən/ ▶ n. **1** any of the parts into which something is divided. **2** a distinct group within a larger body of people or things. **3** the shape that results from cutting through something. ▶ v. divide into sections.

SYNONYMS ▶ n. **1 part**, bit, portion, segment, compartment, module, element, unit. **2 passage**, subsection, chapter, subdivision, clause. **3 department**, area, division.

sec·tor /'sektər/ ▶ n. **1** a distinct area or part. **2** a part of a circle between two lines drawn from its center to its circumference.

SYNONYMS **1 part**, branch, arm, division, area, department, field, sphere. **2 district**, quarter, section, zone, region, area, belt.

sec·u·lar /'sekyələr/ ▶ adj. not religious or spiritual.

SYNONYMS **nonreligious**, lay, temporal, civil, worldly, earthly, profane. ANTONYMS sacred, religious.

■ **sec·u·lar·ism** n.

se·cure /si'kyo͝or/ ▶ adj. **1** certain to remain safe. **2** fixed or fastened so as not to give way or become loose. **3** free from fear or anxiety. ▶ v. (**secures, securing, secured**) **1** protect against danger or threat. **2** firmly fix or fasten. **3** succeed in obtaining.

SYNONYMS ▶ adj. **1 fastened**, fixed, secured, done up, closed, shut, locked. **2 safe**, protected, safe and sound, out of harm's way, in safe hands, invulnerable, undamaged, unharmed. **3** *his position as leader was secure* **certain**, assured, settled, stable, not at risk. **4 unworried**, at ease, relaxed, happy, confident. ANTONYMS loose, insecure. ▶ v. **1 fasten**, close, shut, lock, bolt, chain, seal. **2 obtain**, acquire, gain, get, get (a) hold of, come by; informal land.

■ **se·cure·ly** adv.

se·cu·ri·ty /si'kyo͝oritē/ ▶ n. (plural **securities**) **1** the state of being or feeling secure. **2** the safety of a state or organization. **3** a valuable item offered as a guarantee that you will repay a loan.

SYNONYMS **1 safety**, protection. **2 safety measures**, safeguards, surveillance, defense, policing. **3 guarantee**, collateral, surety, pledge, bond.

se·dan /si'dan/ ▶ n. **1** a car for four or more people. **2** an enclosed chair carried between two horizontal poles.

se·date /si'dāt/ ▶ adj. **1** calm and unhurried. **2** respectable and rather dull. ▶ v. (**sedates, sedating, sedated**) give someone a sedative drug.

SYNONYMS ▶ adj. **1 slow**, steady, dignified, unhurried, relaxed, measured, leisurely, slow-moving, easy, gentle. **2 calm**, placid, tranquil, quiet, uneventful, staid, boring, dull. ANTONYMS fast, exciting. ▶ v. **tranquilize**, put under sedation, drug.

■ **se·date·ly** adv.

se·da·tion /si'dāsHən/ ▶ n. the action of sedating someone.

sed·a·tive /'sedətiv/ ▶ adj. having the effect of making someone calm or sleepy. ▶ n. a sedative drug.

sed·en·tar·y /'sedn,terē/ ▶ adj. **1** involving a lot of sitting and not much exercise. **2** sitting down a lot; getting little exercise.

SYNONYMS **sitting**, seated, desk-bound; inactive. ANTONYMS active.

sedge /sej/ ▶ n. a grasslike plant that grows in wet ground.

sed·i·ment /'sedəmənt/ ▶ n. **1** matter that settles to the bottom of a liquid. **2** material carried by water or wind and deposited on land.

SYNONYMS **dregs**, grounds, lees, residue, deposit, silt.

■ **sed·i·men·ta·ry** /,sedə'mentərē/ adj.

se·di·tion /si'disHən/ ▶ n. things done or said to stir up rebellion against a ruler or government.

SYNONYMS **rabble-rousing**, subversion, troublemaking, provocation; rebellion, insurrection, mutiny, insurgence, civil disorder.

se·di·tious /si'disHəs/ ▶ adj. inciting or causing people to rebel against the authority of a government or ruler: *a seditious speech*.

SYNONYMS **rabble-rousing**, provocative, inflammatory, subversive, troublemaking; rebellious, mutinous, insurgent.

se·duce /si'd(y)o͞os/ ▶ v. (**seduces, seducing, seduced**) persuade someone to do something unwise.

SYNONYMS **1 attract**, allure, lure, tempt, entice, beguile, inveigle, manipulate. **2 have your way with**, take advantage of.

■ **se·duc·tion** /si'dəksHən/ n.

se·duc·tive /si'dəktiv/ ▶ adj. tempting and attractive.

SYNONYMS **tempting**, inviting, enticing, alluring, beguiling, attractive.

■ **se·duc·tive·ly** adv.

sed·u·lous /'sejələs/ ▶ adj. showing great care or effort; diligent.

see[1] /sē/ ▶ v. (**sees, seeing, saw** /sô/; past participle **seen**) **1** become aware of with the eyes. **2** experience or witness. **3** realize something after thinking or getting information. **4** think of in a particular way. **5** meet someone socially or by chance. **6** meet someone regularly as a boyfriend or girlfriend. **7** consult a specialist or professional. **8** guide or lead someone somewhere.

SYNONYMS **1 discern**, detect, perceive, spot, notice, catch sight of, glimpse, make out, pick out, distinguish, spy; literary behold, espy, descry. **2 watch**, look at, view, catch. **3 inspect**, view, look around, tour, survey, examine, scrutinize. **4 understand**, grasp, comprehend, follow, realize, appreciate, recognize, work out, fathom; informal get, latch on to, figure out. **5** *see what he's up to* **find out**, discover, learn, ascertain, determine, establish. **6** *see that no harm comes to him* **ensure**, make sure/certain, see to it, take care, mind. **7** *I see trouble ahead* **foresee**, predict, forecast, prophesy, anticipate, envisage. **8 consult**, confer with, talk to, have recourse to, call in, turn to. **9 go out with**, date, take out, be involved with; informal go steady with; dated court.

□ **see someone off** accompany and say goodbye to a person as they leave on a journey. **see something through** carry on with a project until it is completed. **see-through** transparent or semitransparent. **see to** deal with.

see² ▶ **n.** the district or position of a bishop or archbishop.

seed /sēd/ ▶ **n. 1** a small, hard object produced by a plant, from which a new plant may grow. **2** the beginning of a feeling, process, etc. **3** any of the stronger competitors in a sports tournament who are kept from playing each other in the early rounds. ▶ **v. 1** sow land with seeds. **2** remove the seeds from. **3** (**be seeded**) be made a seed in a sports tournament.

SYNONYMS ▶ **n. pip**, stone, kernel.

seed·ling /ˈsēdliNG/ ▶ **n.** a young plant raised from seed.

seed·y /ˈsēdē/ ▶ **adj.** (**seedier**, **seediest**) unpleasant because dirty or immoral.

SYNONYMS **1** *the seedy world of prostitution* **sordid**, disreputable, seamy, sleazy, squalid, unsavory. **2** *a seedy part of town* **dilapidated**, tumbledown, ramshackle, decrepit, run-down, shabby, dingy, slummy, insalubrious, squalid; informal crummy. ANTONYMS high-class.

■ **seed·i·ness n.**

see·ing /ˈsē-iNG/ ▶ **conj.** because; since.

seek /sēk/ ▶ **v.** (**seeks**, **seeking**, **sought** /sôt/) **1** try to find or get. **2** ask for. **3** (**seek to do**) try or want to do. **4** (**seek someone/thing out**) search for and find someone or something.

SYNONYMS **1 search for**, try to find, look for, be after, hunt for. **2 ask for**, request, solicit, call for, appeal for, apply for. **3 try**, attempt, endeavor, strive, work, do your best.

■ **seek·er n.**

seem /sēm/ ▶ **v. 1** give the impression of being. **2** (**cannot seem to do**) be unable to do, despite having tried.

SYNONYMS **appear (to be)**, have the appearance/air of being, give the impression of being, look, sound, come across as, strike someone as.

seem·ing /ˈsēmiNG/ ▶ **adj.** appearing to be real or true. ■ **seem·ing·ly adv.**

seem·ly /ˈsēmlē/ ▶ **adj.** respectable or in good taste.

seen /sēn/ past participle of SEE¹.

seep /sēp/ ▶ **v.** (of a liquid) flow or leak slowly through a substance.

SYNONYMS **ooze**, trickle, exude, drip, dribble, flow, leak, drain, bleed, filter, percolate, soak.

■ **seep·age n.**

seer /ˈsēər, si(ə)r/ ▶ **n.** a person supposedly able to see visions of the future.

seer·suck·er /ˈsi(ə)rˌsəkər/ ▶ **n.** a fabric with a crinkled surface.

see·saw /ˈsēˌsô/ ▶ **n.** a long plank supported in the middle, on each end of which children sit and move up and down by pushing the ground with their feet. ▶ **v.** repeatedly change between two states or positions.

seethe /sēTH/ ▶ **v.** (**seethes**, **seething**, **seethed**) **1** be very angry but try not to show it. **2** be filled with a crowd that is moving about. **3** (of a liquid) boil or churn.

SYNONYMS **1 teem**, swarm, boil, swirl, churn, surge, bubble, heave. **2 be angry**, be furious, be enraged, rage, be incensed, be beside yourself, boil, rant, fume; informal be livid, foam at the mouth.

seg·ment ▶ **n.** /ˈsegmənt/ each of the parts into which something is divided. ▶ **v.** /ˈsegˌment, segˈment/ divide into segments.

SYNONYMS ▶ **n. piece**, bit, section, part, portion, division, slice, wedge.

seg·re·gate /ˈsegriˌgāt/ ▶ **v.** (**segregates**, **segregating**, **segregated**) **1** keep separate from the rest or from each other. **2** keep people of different races, sexes, or religions separate.

SYNONYMS **separate**, set apart, keep apart, isolate, quarantine, partition, divide, discriminate against. ANTONYMS integrate.

■ **seg·re·ga·tion** /ˌsegriˈgāSHən/ **n.**

se·gue /ˈsegwā, ˈsā-/ ▶ **v.** (**segues**, **segueing** or **seguing**, **segued**) move without interruption from one song or movie scene to another.

seine /sān, sen/ ▶ **n.** a fishing net that hangs vertically in the water, with floats at the top.

seis·mic /ˈsīzmik/ ▶ **adj. 1** having to do with earthquakes. **2** enormous in size or effect.

seis·mol·o·gy /sīzˈmäləjē/ ▶ **n.** the study of earthquakes. ■ **seis·mol·o·gist n.**

seize /sēz/ ▶ **v.** (**seized**, **seizing**, **seized**) **1** take hold of suddenly and forcibly. **2** (of the police or government authorities) officially take possession of. **3** take an opportunity eagerly and decisively. **4** (**seize on**) take advantage of eagerly. **5** (often **seize up**) (of a machine) become jammed.

SYNONYMS **1 grab**, grasp, snatch, take (a) hold of, clutch, grip. **2 capture**, take, overrun, occupy, conquer, take over. **3 confiscate**, impound, commandeer, requisition, appropriate, expropriate, sequestrate. **4 kidnap**, abduct, take captive, take prisoner, take hostage, hijack; informal snatch. ANTONYMS release.

SPELLING

Seize is an exception to the usual rule of **i** before **e**, when the sound is *ee*, except after **c**.

sei·zure /ˈsēZHər/ ▶ **n. 1** the action of seizing. **2** a sudden attack of illness, especially a stroke or an epileptic fit.

SYNONYMS **1 capture**, takeover, annexation, invasion, occupation. **2 confiscation**, appropriation, expropriation, sequestration. **3 kidnap/kidnapping**, abduction, hijack/hijacking. **4 convulsion**, fit, spasm, paroxysm.

sel·dom /ˈseldəm/ ▶ **adv.** not often.

SYNONYMS **rarely**, infrequently, hardly (ever), scarcely (ever); informal once in a blue moon. ANTONYMS often.

se·lect /sə'lekt/ ▶ v. carefully choose from a group. ▶ adj. **1** carefully chosen as being among the best. **2** used by, or made up of, wealthy people.

SYNONYMS ▶ v. **choose**, pick (out), single out, opt for, decide on, settle on, sort out, take, adopt. ▶ adj. **1 choice**, prime, hand-picked, top-quality, first-class; informal top-flight. **2 exclusive**, elite, privileged, wealthy; informal posh. ANTONYMS inferior.

□ **select committee** a small legislative committee appointed for a special purpose. ■ **se·lec·tor** n.

se·lec·tion /sə'leksHən/ ▶ n. **1** the action of selecting. **2** a number of selected things. **3** a range of things from which you can choose.

SYNONYMS **1 choice**, pick, option, preference. **2 range**, array, diversity, variety, assortment, mixture. **3 anthology**, assortment, collection, assemblage, miscellany, medley.

se·lec·tive /sə'lektiv/ ▶ adj. **1** involving selection. **2** choosing carefully. **3** affecting some things and not others.

SYNONYMS **discerning**, discriminating, exacting, demanding, particular; informal choosy, picky. ANTONYMS indiscriminate.

■ **se·lec·tive·ly** adv. **se·lec·tiv·i·ty** /səlek'tivitē/ n.

se·le·ni·um /sə'lēnēəm/ ▶ n. a gray crystalline chemical element.

self /self/ ▶ n. (plural **selves** /selvz/) **1** a person's essential being that distinguishes them from other people. **2** a person's particular nature or personality.

self-ab·sorbed ▶ adj. obsessed with your own emotions or interests.

self-ad·dressed ▶ adj. (of an envelope) addressed to yourself.

self-ad·he·sive ▶ adj. sticking without needing to be moistened.

self-ap·point·ed ▶ adj. having taken up a position or role without the approval of other people.

self-as·sess·ment ▶ n. assessment of your own performance.

self-as·sur·ance ▶ n. confidence in your own abilities or character. ■ **self-as·sured** adj.

self-a·ware ▶ adj. knowledgeable about your own character, feelings, motives, etc. ■ **self-a·ware·ness** n.

self-cen·tered ▶ adj. obsessed with yourself and your affairs.

SYNONYMS **egocentric**, egotistic, self-absorbed, self-obsessed, self-seeking, self-serving, narcissistic, vain, inconsiderate, thoughtless; informal looking after number one.

self-con·fessed ▶ adj. admitting to having certain characteristics.

self-con·fi·dence ▶ n. a feeling of trust in your abilities and judgment.

SYNONYMS **self-assurance**, assurance, confidence, composure, aplomb, poise, sangfroid.

■ **self-con·fi·dent** adj.

self-con·scious ▶ adj. nervous or awkward through being worried about what other people think of you.

SYNONYMS **embarrassed**, uncomfortable, uneasy, ill at ease, nervous, awkward, shy, diffident, timid. ANTONYMS confident.

self-con·tained ▶ adj. **1** complete in itself. **2** not depending on or influenced by other people.

self-con·trol ▶ n. the ability to control your emotions or behavior. ■ **self-con·trolled** adj.

self-de·feat·ing ▶ adj. making things worse rather than achieving the desired aim.

self-de·fense ▶ n. defense of yourself.

self-de·ni·al ▶ n. not allowing yourself to have things that you want.

self-dep·re·cat·ing ▶ adj. modest about yourself. ■ **self-dep·re·ca·tion** n.

self-de·struct ▶ v. explode or disintegrate automatically.

self-de·struc·tive ▶ adj. causing harm to yourself.

self-de·ter·mi·na·tion ▶ n. the right or ability of a country or person to manage their own affairs.

self-dis·ci·pline ▶ n. the ability to control your feelings and actions. ■ **self-dis·ci·plined** adj.

self-doubt ▶ n. lack of confidence in yourself and your abilities.

self-ef·fac·ing ▶ adj. not wanting to attract attention.

self-em·ployed ▶ adj. working for yourself rather than for an employer. ■ **self-em·ploy·ment** n.

self-es·teem ▶ n. confidence in your own worth or abilities.

SYNONYMS **self-respect**, pride, dignity, self-regard, faith in yourself; morale, self-confidence, confidence, self-assurance.

self-ev·i·dent ▶ adj. obvious.

self-ex·plan·a·to·ry ▶ adj. not needing explanation; clearly understood.

self-ex·pres·sion ▶ n. the expression of your feelings or thoughts.

self-ful·fill·ing ▶ adj. (of a prediction) bound to come true because people behave in a way that makes it happen.

self-help ▶ n. reliance on your own efforts and resources to achieve things.

self-im·por·tance ▶ n. an exaggerated sense of your own value or importance. ■ **self-im·por·tant** adj.

self-in·dul·gent ▶ adj. allowing yourself to have or do things that you like, especially to an excessive extent. ■ **self-in·dul·gence** n.

self-in·ter·est ▶ n. your personal interest or advantage.

self·ish /'selfisH/ ▶ adj. concerned mainly with your own needs and wishes.

SYNONYMS **egocentric**, egotistic, self-centered, self-absorbed, self-obsessed, self-seeking, wrapped up in oneself, mean, greedy; informal looking after number one. ANTONYMS unselfish, altruistic.

■ **self·ish·ly** adv. **self·ish·ness** n.

self·less /'selfləs/ ▶ adj. concerned more with the needs and wishes of other people than with your own.

SYNONYMS **unselfish**, altruistic, considerate, compassionate, kind, noble, generous, magnanimous, ungrudging. ANTONYMS selfish, inconsiderate.

self-made ▶ adj. having become successful by your own efforts.

self-pit·y ▶ n. too much sorrow and concern for yourself and your own problems. ■ **self-pit·y·ing** adj.

self-por·trait ▶ n. a portrait by an artist of himself or herself.

self-pos·sessed ▶ adj. calm, confident, and in control of your feelings. ■ **self-pos·ses·sion** n.

self-pro·claimed ▶ adj. proclaimed to be such by yourself, without the approval of others.

self-re·li·ance ▶ n. reliance on your own powers and resources. ■ **self-re·li·ant** adj.

self-re·spect ▶ n. pride and confidence in yourself.

self-right·eous ▶ adj. certain that you are right or morally superior.

> SYNONYMS **sanctimonious**, holier-than-thou, pious, self-satisfied, smug, priggish, complacent, moralizing, superior, hypocritical; informal goody-goody. ANTONYMS humble.

self-ris·ing flour ▶ n. flour that has baking powder already added.

self-sac·ri·fice ▶ n. the giving up of your own needs or wishes to help other people. ■ **self-sac·ri·fic·ing** adj.

self·same /ˈselfˌsām/ ▶ adj. (**the selfsame**) the very same.

self-sat·is·fied ▶ adj. smugly pleased with yourself. ■ **self-sat·is·fac·tion** n.

self-seek·ing (or **self-serving**) ▶ adj. concerned only with your own welfare and interests.

self-serv·ice ▶ adj. (of a store or restaurant) where customers choose goods for themselves and pay at a checkout.

self-styled ▶ adj. using a description or title that you have given yourself: *self-styled experts*.

self-suf·fi·cient ▶ adj. able to satisfy your basic needs without outside help. ■ **self-suf·fi·cien·cy** n.

self-worth ▶ n. self-esteem.

sell /sel/ ▶ v. (**sells**, **selling**, **sold** /sōld/) **1** hand over something in exchange for money. **2** (of goods) be bought. **3** persuade someone that something is good.

> SYNONYMS **put up for sale**, put on the market, auction (off), trade in, deal in, retail, market, traffic in, peddle, hawk. ANTONYMS buy.

□ **sell out 1** sell all your stock of something. **2** (of tickets for an event) be all sold. **3** abandon your principles for reasons of convenience.

sell·er /ˈselər/ ▶ n. **1** a person who sells something. **2** a product that sells in a particular way.

> SYNONYMS **vendor**, dealer, retailer, trader, merchant, agent, hawker, peddler, purveyor, supplier. ANTONYMS buyer.

sell·out /ˈselˌout/ ▶ n. **1** the selling of an entire stock of something, especially tickets for an entertainment or sports event. **2** an event for which all tickets are sold: *the game is sure to be a sellout*. **3** a betrayal of your principles.

selt·zer /ˈseltsər/ ▶ n. carbonated mineral water.

selv·edge /ˈselvij/ ▶ n. an edge on woven fabric that prevents it from fraying or unraveling.

selves /selvz/ plural of **SELF**.

se·man·tic /səˈmantik/ ▶ adj. having to do with meaning. ■ **se·man·ti·cal·ly** adv.

se·man·tics /səˈmantiks/ ▶ pl.n. **1** the study of the meaning of words and phrases. **2** the meaning of words, phrases, etc.

sem·a·phore /ˈseməˌfôr/ ▶ n. a system of sending messages by holding the arms or two flags in positions that represent letters of the alphabet.

sem·blance /ˈsembləns/ ▶ n. the way that something looks or seems.

> SYNONYMS **(outward) appearance**, air, show, facade, front, veneer, guise, pretense.

se·men /ˈsēmən/ ▶ n. a fluid containing sperm that is produced by men and male animals.

se·mes·ter /səˈmestər/ ▶ n. a half-year term in a school or university.

sem·i /ˈsemī/ ▶ n. (plural **semis**) informal **1** a tractor-trailer. **2** a semifinal.

sem·i·au·to·mat·ic /ˌsemēˌôtəˈmatik, ˌsemˌī-/ ▶ adj. (of a gun) able to load bullets automatically but not fire continuously.

sem·i·cir·cle /ˈsemēˌsərkəl, ˈsemˌī-/ ▶ n. a half of a circle. ■ **sem·i·cir·cu·lar** /ˌsemēˈsərkyələr, ˌsemīˈsərkyələr/ adj.

sem·i·co·lon /ˈsemiˌkōlən, ˈsemˌī-/ ▶ n. a punctuation mark (;) indicating a bigger pause than that indicated by a comma.

sem·i·con·duc·tor /ˈsemēkənˌdəktər, ˈsemˌī-/ ▶ n. a solid that conducts electricity, but to a smaller extent than a metal.

sem·i·de·tached /ˌsemēdiˈtacht, ˌsemˌī-/ ▶ adj. (of a house) joined to another house on one side by a common wall.

sem·i·fi·nal /ˌsemēˈfīnl, ˌsemˌī-/ ▶ n. (in sports) a match or round coming immediately before the final. ■ **sem·i·fi·nal·ist** n.

sem·i·nal /ˈsemənl/ ▶ adj. **1** strongly influencing later developments. **2** referring to semen.

sem·i·nar /ˈseməˌnär/ ▶ n. **1** a meeting for discussion or training. **2** a university class for discussion of topics with a teacher.

> SYNONYMS **1 conference**, symposium, meeting, convention, forum, summit. **2 study group**, workshop, tutorial, class.

sem·i·nar·y /ˈseməˌnerē/ ▶ n. (plural **seminaries**) a training college for priests or rabbis.

se·mi·ot·ics /ˌsēmēˈätiks, ˌsemē-, ˌsemˌī-/ ▶ pl.n. the study of signs and symbols. ■ **se·mi·ot·ic** adj.

sem·i·pre·cious /ˌsemēˈpreshəs, ˌsemˌī-/ ▶ adj. (of minerals) used as gems but less valuable than precious stones.

sem·i·tone /ˈsemēˌtōn, ˈsemˌī-/ ▶ n. a musical interval equal to half a tone or a twelfth of an octave; a half step.

sem·o·li·na /ˌseməˈlēnə/ ▶ n. the hard grains left after flour has been milled, used to make puddings and pasta.

Sen. ▶ abbr. **1** Senate. **2** Senator.

sen·ate /ˈsenit/ ▶ n. **1** the smaller but higher lawmaking assembly in the United States, France, etc. **2** the governing body of a university or college. **3** the state council of ancient Rome.

sen·a·tor /ˈsenətər/ ▶ n. a member of a senate. ■ **sen·a·to·ri·al** /ˌsenəˈtôrēəl/ adj.

send /send/ ▶ v. (**sends**, **sending**, **sent**) **1** cause to go or be taken to a destination. **2** cause to move sharply or quickly.

SYNONYMS **1 dispatch**, post, mail, email, consign, forward, transmit, convey, communicate, broadcast, radio. **2 propel**, project, eject, deliver, discharge, spout, fire, shoot, release, throw, fling, cast, hurl. ANTONYMS receive.

□ **send-off** a gathering to say goodbye to someone who is leaving. **send-up** informal an exaggerated imitation of someone or something. **send someone up** informal **1** sentence someone to imprisonment. **2** make fun of someone by imitating them.

se·nile /'sē,nīl, 'sen-/ ▶ **adj.** suffering a loss of mental faculties because of old age.

SYNONYMS **doddering**, decrepit, senescent, infirm, feeble; (mentally) confused, having Alzheimer's (disease), having senile dementia; informal gaga.

■ **se·nil·i·ty** /si'nilitē/ **n.**

sen·ior /'sēnyər/ ▶ **adj. 1** having to do with older people. **2** of the final year at a college or high school. **3** (after a name) referring to the elder of two with the same name in a family. **4** high or higher in status. ▶ **n. 1** a person who is a stated number of years older than someone else: *she was two years his senior*. **2** a student in their senior year of high school or college. **3** (in sports) a competitor of above a certain age or of the highest status.

SYNONYMS ▶ **adj. 1 older**, elder. **2 superior**, higher-ranking, more important, ranking. ANTONYMS junior, subordinate.

□ **senior citizen** an elderly person, especially one who is retired and living on a pension.

sen·ior·i·ty /sēn'yôritē, -'yär-/ ▶ **n.** a high or higher status, especially because of being older or having been in an office or service longer.

sen·na /'senə/ ▶ **n.** a laxative prepared from the dried pods of a tree.

sen·sa·tion /sen'sāsʜən/ ▶ **n. 1** a feeling resulting from something that happens to or comes into contact with the body. **2** the ability to have such feelings. **3** a vague awareness or impression. **4** a widespread reaction of interest and excitement, or a person or thing that causes it.

SYNONYMS **1 feeling**, sense, perception, impression. **2 commotion**, stir, uproar, furor, scandal, impact; informal splash, to-do.

sen·sa·tion·al /sen'sāsʜənl/ ▶ **adj. 1** causing or trying to cause great public interest and excitement. **2** informal very impressive or attractive.

SYNONYMS **1 shocking**, scandalous, fascinating, exciting, thrilling, interesting, dramatic, momentous, historic, newsworthy. **2 overdramatized**, melodramatic, exaggerated, sensationalist, graphic, explicit, lurid; informal juicy. **3 gorgeous**, stunning, wonderful, superb, excellent, first-class; informal great, terrific, tremendous, fantastic, fabulous, out of this world, smashing. ANTONYMS dull, unremarkable.

■ **sen·sa·tion·al·ism n. sen·sa·tion·al·ist n. & adj. sen·sa·tion·al·ly adv.**

sen·sa·tion·al·ize /sen'sāsʜənl,īz/ ▶ **v.** (**sensationalizes**, **sensationalizing**, **sensationalized**) present information in an exaggerated way to make it seem more interesting.

sense /sens/ ▶ **n. 1** any of the powers of sight, smell, hearing, taste, and touch, which allow the body to perceive things. **2** a feeling that something is the case. **3** (**sense of**) awareness of or sensitivity to. **4** a sensible and practical attitude or behavior. **5** a meaning of a word or expression. ▶ **v.** (**senses**, **sensing**, **sensed**) **1** perceive by a sense or senses. **2** be vaguely aware of.

SYNONYMS ▶ **n. 1 feeling**, faculty, awareness, sensation, recognition, perception. **2 appreciation**, awareness, understanding, comprehension. **3 wisdom**, common sense, wit, reason, intelligence, judgment, brain(s), sagacity; informal gumption, horse sense, savvy, smarts. **4 purpose**, point, use, value, advantage, benefit. **5 meaning**, definition, denotation, nuance, drift, gist, thrust, tenor, message. ANTONYMS stupidity. ▶ **v. detect**, feel, observe, notice, recognize, pick up, be aware of, distinguish, make out, perceive, discern, divine, intuit; informal catch on to.

□ **make sense** be understandable or sensible.

sense·less /'sensləs/ ▶ **adj. 1** lacking meaning, purpose, or common sense. **2** unconscious.

SYNONYMS **pointless**, futile, useless, needless, meaningless, absurd, foolish, insane, stupid, idiotic, mindless, illogical. ANTONYMS wise.

sen·si·bil·i·ty /,sensə'bilitē/ ▶ **n.** (plural **sensibilities**) **1** the ability to experience and understand emotion or art; sensitivity. **2** (**sensibilities**) the degree to which a person can be offended or shocked.

sen·si·ble /'sensəbəl/ ▶ **adj. 1** having or showing common sense. **2** practical rather than decorative.

SYNONYMS **practical**, realistic, responsible, reasonable, commonsensical, rational, logical, sound, no-nonsense, levelheaded, down-to-earth, wise. ANTONYMS foolish.

■ **sen·si·bly adv.**

sen·si·tive /'sensitiv/ ▶ **adj. 1** quick to detect or be affected by slight changes. **2** appreciating the feelings of other people. **3** easily offended or upset. **4** secret or controversial.

SYNONYMS **1** *she's sensitive to changes in temperature* **responsive to**, reactive to, sensitized to, aware of, conscious of, susceptible to, affected by, vulnerable to. **2 delicate**, fragile, tender, sore. **3 tactful**, careful, thoughtful, diplomatic, delicate, subtle, kid-glove. **4 touchy**, oversensitive, hypersensitive, easily offended, thin-skinned, defensive, paranoid, neurotic. **5 difficult**, delicate, tricky, awkward, problematic, ticklish, controversial, emotive. ANTONYMS insensitive, resilient.

■ **sen·si·tive·ly adv.**

sen·si·tiv·i·ty /,sensi'tivitē/ ▶ **n.** (plural **sensitivities**) **1** the quality of being sensitive. **2** (**sensitivities**) a person's feelings that might be offended or hurt.

SYNONYMS **1 responsiveness**, sensitiveness, reactivity, susceptibility. **2 tact**, diplomacy, delicacy, subtlety, understanding. **3 touchiness**, oversensitivity, hypersensitivity, defensiveness. **4 delicacy**, trickiness, awkwardness, ticklishness.

sen·si·tize /'sensi,tīz/ ▶ **v.** (**sensitizes**, **sensitizing**, **sensitized**) make sensitive or aware.

sen·sor /'sensər/ ▶ **n.** a device that detects or measures a light, heat, pressure, etc.

sen·so·ry /'sensərē/ ▶ **adj.** relating to sensation or the senses.

sen·su·al /'sensHōōəl/ ▶ **adj.** relating to the physical senses as a source of pleasure.

SYNONYMS **1 physical**, carnal, bodily, fleshly, animal. **2 passionate**, sexual, physical, tactile, hedonistic. ANTONYMS spiritual.

■ **sen·su·al·i·ty** /ˌsensHōō'alitē/ **n.** **sen·su·al·ly adv.**

sen·su·ous /'sensHōōəs/ ▶ **adj.** **1** relating to or affecting the senses rather than the intellect. **2** attractive or pleasing physically.

SYNONYMS **1 rich**, sumptuous, luxurious. **2 voluptuous**, sexy, seductive, luscious, lush, ripe.

■ **sen·su·ous·ly adv.**

sent /sent/ past and past participle of **SEND**.

sen·tence /'sentns/ ▶ **n.** **1** a set of words that is complete in itself, conveying a statement, question, exclamation, or command. **2** the punishment given to someone found guilty by a court. ▶ **v.** (**sentences**, **sentencing**, **sentenced**) say officially in a court of law that an offender is to receive a particular punishment.

SYNONYMS ▶ **n.** **1 judgment**, ruling, decision, verdict. **2** *a long sentence* **punishment**, prison term; informal time, stretch. ▶ **v.** **condemn**, doom, punish, convict.

sen·ten·tious /sen'tencHəs/ ▶ **adj.** given to making pompous comments on moral issues.

sen·tient /'sencH(ē)ənt/ ▶ **adj.** able to perceive or feel things.

sen·ti·ment /'sen(t)əmənt/ ▶ **n.** **1** an opinion or feeling. **2** exaggerated feelings of tenderness, sadness, or nostalgia.

SYNONYMS **1 view**, feeling, attitude, thought, opinion, belief. **2 sentimentality**, emotion, tenderness, softness; informal schmaltz.

sen·ti·men·tal /ˌsen(t)ə'men(t)l/ ▶ **adj.** having or causing exaggerated feelings of tenderness, sadness, or nostalgia.

SYNONYMS **1 nostalgic**, emotional, affectionate, loving, tender. **2 mawkish**, overemotional, romantic, hearts-and-flowers; informal schmaltzy, sappy, corny.

■ **sen·ti·men·tal·i·ty** /ˌsen(t)əmen'talitē, -mən-/ **n.** **sen·ti·men·tal·ly adv.**

sen·ti·nel /'sentn-əl/ ▶ **n.** a guard whose job is to stand and keep watch.

sen·try /'sentrē/ ▶ **n.** (plural **sentries**) a soldier whose job is to guard or control access to a place.

se·pal /'sēpəl/ ▶ **n.** each of the leaflike parts of a flower that surround the petals.

sep·a·ra·ble /'sep(ə)rəbəl/ ▶ **adj.** able to be separated or treated separately.

sep·a·rate ▶ **adj.** /'sep(ə)rit/ **1** forming a unit by itself. **2** different; distinct. ▶ **v.** /'sepəˌrāt/ (**separates**, **separating**, **separated**) **1** move or come apart. **2** stop living together as a couple. **3** divide into distinct parts. **4** form a distinction or boundary between.

SYNONYMS ▶ **adj.** **1 unconnected**, unrelated, different, distinct, discrete, detached, divorced, disconnected, independent. **2 set apart**, detached, cut off, segregated, isolated, freestanding, self-contained. ▶ **v.** **1 disconnect**, detach, disengage, uncouple, split, sunder, sever. **2 partition**, divide, stand between, come between, keep apart, isolate, section off. **3 part** (**company**), go their separate ways, split up, disperse, scatter. **4 split up**, break up, part, become estranged, divorce. ANTONYMS unite, join.

SPELLING

The middle is **-par-**, not **-per-**: sep**a**rate.

sep·a·rate·ly /'sep(ə)ritlē/ ▶ **adv.** individually; without others: *I'll have to interview you all separately.*

SYNONYMS **individually**, one by one, one at a time, singly, severally, apart, independently, alone, by yourself, on your own.

sep·a·ra·tion /ˌsepə'rāsHən/ ▶ **n.** **1** the action of separating. **2** the state in which a husband and wife remain married but live apart.

SYNONYMS **1 disconnection**, splitting, division, breaking-up. **2 break-up**, split, estrangement, divorce.

sep·a·ra·tism /'sep(ə)rəˌtizəm/ ▶ **n.** separation of a group of people from a larger group.
■ **sep·a·ra·tist n. & adj.**

Se·phar·di /sə'färdē/ ▶ **n.** (plural **Sephardim** /-'färdim/) a Jew of Spanish or Portuguese descent.
■ **Se·phar·dic adj.**

se·pi·a /'sēpēə/ ▶ **n.** a reddish-brown color.

sep·sis /'sepsis/ ▶ **n.** the infection of body tissues with harmful bacteria.

Sep·tem·ber /sep'tembər/ ▶ **n.** the ninth month of the year.

sep·tet /sep'tet/ ▶ **n.** a group of seven people playing music or singing together.

sep·tic /'septik/ ▶ **adj.** (of a wound or a part of the body) infected with bacteria.

SYNONYMS **infected**, festering, suppurating, putrid, putrefying, poisoned; Medicine purulent.

□ **septic tank** an underground tank in which sewage is allowed to decompose before draining slowly into the soil.

sep·ti·ce·mi·a /ˌsepti'sēmēə/ ▶ **n.** blood poisoning caused by bacteria.

sep·tu·a·ge·nar·i·an /ˌsepˌtōōəjə'ne(ə)rēən/ ▶ **n.** a person who is from 70 to 79 years old.

sep·tum /'septəm/ ▶ **n.** (plural **septa** /-tə/) a partition separating two hollow areas in the body, such as that between the nostrils.

sep·ul·cher /'sepəlkər/ ▶ **n.** a stone tomb.

se·pul·chral /sə'pəlkrəl/ ▶ **adj.** **1** having to do with a tomb or burial. **2** gloomy.

se·quel /'sēkwəl/ ▶ **n.** **1** a book, movie, or program that continues the story of an earlier one. **2** something that takes place after or as a result of an earlier event.

SYNONYMS **continuation**, further episode, follow-up.

se·quence /'sēkwəns/ ▶ **n.** **1** a particular order in which things follow each other. **2** a set of things that follow each other in a particular order. ▶ **v.** (**sequences**, **sequencing**, **sequenced**) arrange in a sequence.

SYNONYMS ▶ **n.** **1 succession**, order, course, series, chain, train, progression, chronology, pattern, flow. **2 excerpt**, clip, extract, section.

se·quen·tial /si'kwenCHəl/ ▶ **adj.** following in a logical order or sequence. ■ **se·quen·tial·ly adv.**

se·ques·ter /sə'kwestər/ ▶ **v.** (**sequesters, sequestering, sequestered**) **1** isolate or hide away. **2** sequestrate.

se·ques·trate /'sēkwi,strāt, 'sek-, sə'kwes,trāt/ ▶ **v.** (**sequestrates, sequestrating, sequestrated**) take legal possession of assets until a debt has been paid. ■ **se·ques·tra·tion** /,sēkwi'strāSHən, ,sek-/ **n.**

se·quin /'sēkwin/ ▶ **n.** a small, shiny disk sewn on to clothing for decoration. ■ **se·quined** (or **sequinned**) **adj.**

se·quoi·a /sə'k(w)oi-ə/ ▶ **n.** a redwood tree.

se·ragl·io /sə'rälyō/ ▶ **n.** (plural **seraglios**) **1** the women's apartments in a Muslim palace. **2** a harem.

ser·aph /'serəf/ ▶ **n.** (plural **seraphim** /'serə,fim/ or **seraphs**) an angelic being associated with light and purity. ■ **se·raph·ic** /sə'rafik/ **adj.**

Ser·bi·an /'sərbēən/ ▶ **n.** **1** the language of the Serbs. **2** (also **Serb**) a person from Serbia. ▶ **adj.** relating to Serbia.

ser·e·nade /,serə'nād/ ▶ **n.** a piece of music sung or played by a man for a woman he loves, outdoors and at night. ▶ **v.** (**serenades, serenading, serenaded**) perform a serenade for.

ser·en·dip·i·ty /,serən'dipitē/ ▶ **n.** the occurrence of something by chance in a fortunate way. ■ **ser·en·dip·i·tous** /-'dipitəs/ **adj.**

se·rene /sə'rēn/ ▶ **adj.** calm and peaceful.

> SYNONYMS **calm**, composed, tranquil, peaceful, placid, untroubled, relaxed, at ease, unperturbed, unruffled, unworried, centered; informal together, unflappable. ANTONYMS agitated.

■ **se·rene·ly adv. se·ren·i·ty** /sə'renitē/ **n.**

serf /sərf/ ▶ **n.** (in the feudal system) an agricultural laborer who had to work on a particular estate and was not allowed to leave. ■ **serf·dom n.**

serge /sərj/ ▶ **n.** a durable woolen fabric.

ser·geant /'särjənt/ ▶ **n.** **1** the rank of officer in the armed forces, in particular an officer in the US Army or Marine Corps ranking above corporal, or in the US Air Force an officer ranking above airman. **2** a police officer ranking below a lieutenant. □ **sergeant major** a noncommissioned officer in the US Army or Marine Corps of the highest rank, above master sergeant.

se·ri·al /'si(ə)rēəl/ ▶ **adj.** **1** arranged in a series. **2** repeatedly committing the same offense or doing the same thing. ▶ **n.** a story published or broadcast in regular installments. □ **serial number** an identification number given to a manufactured item.

se·ri·al·ize /'si(ə)rēə,līz/ ▶ **v.** (**serializes, serializing, serialized**) **1** publish or broadcast a story in regular installments. **2** arrange in a series. ■ **se·ri·al·i·za·tion** /,si(ə)rēələ'zāSHən/ **n.**

se·ries /'si(ə)rēz/ ▶ **n.** (plural **series**) **1** a number of related things coming one after another. **2** a sequence of related television or radio programs.

> SYNONYMS **succession**, sequence, string, chain, run, round, spate, wave, rash, course, cycle, row.

se·ri·ous /'si(ə)rēəs/ ▶ **adj.** **1** dangerous or very bad: *serious injury*. **2** needing careful consideration or action. **3** solemn or thoughtful. **4** sincere and in earnest.

> SYNONYMS **1 solemn**, earnest, grave, somber, unsmiling, stern, grim, humorless, stony, dour, poker-faced, long-faced. **2 important**, significant, momentous, weighty, far-reaching, consequential. **3 intellectual**, highbrow, heavyweight, deep, profound, literary, learned, scholarly; informal heavy. **4** *a serious injury* **severe**, grave, bad, critical, acute, terrible, dire, dangerous, grievous. **5 sincere**, earnest, genuine, wholehearted, committed, resolute, determined. ANTONYMS lighthearted, trivial, minor.

■ **se·ri·ous·ly adv. se·ri·ous·ness n.**

ser·mon /'sərmən/ ▶ **n.** a talk on a religious or moral subject, especially one given during a church service.

> SYNONYMS **address**, homily, talk, speech, lecture.

ser·pent /'sərpənt/ ▶ **n.** literary a large snake.

ser·pen·tine /'sərpən,tēn, -,tīn/ ▶ **adj.** winding or twisting like a snake.

ser·rat·ed /'ser,ātid, sə'rātid/ ▶ **adj.** having a jagged edge like the teeth of a saw.

ser·ra·tion /se'rāSHən/ ▶ **n.** a tooth or point of a serrated edge.

ser·ried /'serēd/ ▶ **adj.** (of rows of people or things) standing close together.

se·rum /'si(ə)rəm/ ▶ **n.** (plural **sera** /-rə/ or **serums**) a thin liquid that separates out when blood solidifies.

serv·ant /'sərvənt/ ▶ **n.** a person employed to perform domestic duties in a household or for a person.

> SYNONYMS **attendant**, domestic, maid, housemaid, retainer, flunky, minion, slave, lackey, drudge.

serve /sərv/ ▶ **v.** (**serves, serving, served**) **1** perform duties or services for. **2** be employed as a member of the armed forces. **3** spend a period in a job or in prison. **4** present food or drink to. **5** (of food or drink) be enough for. **6** attend to a customer in a store. **7** fulfill a purpose. **8** treat in a particular way. **9** (in tennis, volleyball, badminton, etc.) hit the ball or shuttlecock to begin play for each point of a game. ▶ **n.** an act of serving in tennis, volleyball, badminton, etc.

> SYNONYMS ▶ **v. 1 work for**, obey, do the bidding of. **2** *this job serves the community* **benefit**, help, assist, aid, make a contribution to. **3** *he served a six-month apprenticeship* **carry out**, perform, do, fulfill, complete, discharge, spend. **4 present**, give out, distribute, dish up, provide, supply. **5 attend to**, deal with, see to, assist, help, look after. **6** *a saucer serving as an ashtray* **act as**, function as, do duty.

□ **serve someone right** be someone's deserved punishment.

serv·er /'sərvər/ ▶ **n.** **1** a person or thing that serves. **2** a computer or program that controls or supplies information to a network of computers.

serv·ice /'sərvis/ ▶ **n.** **1** the action of serving. **2** a period of employment with an organization. **3** an act of assistance. **4** a ceremony of religious worship. **5** a system supplying a public need such as water or electricity. **6** a department or organization run by the state. **7** (**the services**) the armed forces. **8** a set of matching dishes. **9** (in tennis, volleyball, badminton, etc.) a serve. **10** a routine inspection and maintenance of a vehicle or machine. **11** (**service area**) a roadside area with a gas station, restaurant, bathrooms, etc., for motorists. ▶ v. (**services**, **servicing**, **serviced**) **1** perform routine maintenance or repair work on. **2** provide a service or services for someone. **3** pay interest on a debt.

SYNONYMS ▶ n. **1 work**, employment, labor. **2** *he has done us a service* **favor**, kindness, good turn, helping hand. **3 ceremony**, ritual, rite, sacrament. **4 overhaul**, check, maintenance, servicing, repair. **5** *a range of local services* **amenity**, facility, resource, utility. **6** (**armed**) **forces**, military, army, navy, air force. ▶ v. **overhaul**, check, go over, maintain, repair.

□ **service industry** a business that provides a service rather than manufacturing things. **service station** a garage selling gas, oil, etc., and usually providing automobile repair and maintenance.

serv·ice·a·ble /ˈsərvəsəbəl/ ▶ adj. **1** in working order. **2** useful and durable.

SYNONYMS **1 in working order**, working, functioning, operational, usable, workable, viable. **2 functional**, utilitarian, sensible, practical, hard-wearing, durable, tough, robust.

serv·ice·man /ˈsərvəsˌmən, -ˌman/ (or **servicewoman** /ˈsərvəsˌwo͝omən/) ▶ n. (plural **servicemen** or **servicewomen**) a member of the armed forces.

ser·vile /ˈsərvəl, -ˌvīl/ ▶ adj. **1** too willing to serve or please other people. **2** of a slave or slaves. ■ **ser·vil·i·ty** /sərˈvilitē/ n.

serv·ing /ˈsərviNG/ ▶ n. a quantity of food for one person.

ser·vi·tude /ˈsərviˌt(y)o͞od/ ▶ n. the state of being a slave, or of being under the complete control of someone more powerful.

servo /ˈsərvō/ ▶ n. a device in a vehicle that converts a force into a larger force.

ses·a·me /ˈsesəmē/ ▶ n. a tropical plant grown for its oil-rich seeds.

ses·sion /ˈseSHən/ ▶ n. **1** a period devoted to a particular activity. **2** a meeting of a council, court, etc., or the period when such meetings are held.

SYNONYMS **1 meeting**, sitting, assembly, caucus, conclave. **2 period**, time, term.

set /set/ ▶ v. (**sets**, **setting**, **set**) **1** put in a particular place or position. **2** bring into a particular state. **3** give someone a task. **4** decide on or fix a time or limit. **5** establish as an example or record. **6** adjust a device as required. **7** prepare a table for a meal. **8** harden into a solid, semisolid, or fixed state. **9** arrange damp hair into the required style. **10** put a broken or dislocated bone into the right position for healing. **11** (of the sun, moon, etc.) appear to move toward and below the earth's horizon. ▶ n. **1** a number of things or people grouped together. **2** the way in which something is set. **3** a radio or television receiver. **4** (in tennis and similar games) a group of games counting as a unit toward a match. **5** a collection of scenery, furniture, etc., used for a scene in a play or movie. ▶ adj. **1** fixed or arranged in advance. **2** firmly fixed and unchanging. **3** having a conventional or fixed wording. **4** ready, prepared, or likely to do something.

SYNONYMS ▶ v. **1 put** (**down**), place, lay, deposit, position, settle, leave, stand, plant; informal stick, dump, park, plonk, pop. **2 fix**, embed, insert, mount. **3** *set the table* **lay**, prepare, arrange. **4** *he set us some work* **assign**, allocate, give, allot. **5 arrange**, schedule, fix (on), decide on, settle on, choose, agree on, determine, designate, appoint, name, specify, stipulate. **6 adjust**, regulate, synchronize, calibrate, put right, correct. **7 solidify**, harden, stiffen, thicken, gel, cake, congeal, coagulate, clot. ▶ n. **1 series**, collection, group, batch, arrangement, array, assortment, selection. **2 group**, circle, crowd, crew, band, fraternity, company, ring, camp, school, clique, faction; informal gang, bunch. ▶ adj. **1 fixed**, established, scheduled, specified, appointed, arranged, settled, decided, agreed, predetermined, hard and fast, unvarying, unchanging, invariable, rigid, inflexible. **2 ready**, prepared, organized, equipped, primed; informal geared up, psyched up. ANTONYMS variable, unprepared.

□ **set about** start doing. **set something aside** **1** temporarily stop using land for growing crops. **2** declare that a legal decision is no longer valid. **set off** begin a journey. **set something off** make a bomb or alarm go off. **set on** attack violently. **set out 1** begin a journey. **2** aim or intend to do something. **set piece** a formal or elaborate arrangement in a novel, movie, etc. **set square** a flat triangular piece of plastic or metal with a right angle, for drawing lines and angles. **set-top box** a device that converts a digital television signal into a form that can be viewed on an ordinary television. **set something up** establish a business or other organization.

set·back /ˈsetˌbak/ ▶ n. a difficulty or problem that holds back progress.

SYNONYMS **problem**, difficulty, hitch, complication, upset, blow; informal glitch, hiccup. ANTONYMS breakthrough.

set·tee /seˈtē/ ▶ n. a long padded seat for more than one person, usually with a back and arms.

set·ter /ˈsetər/ ▶ n. a breed of dog trained to stand rigid when it scents game.

set·ting /ˈsetiNG/ ▶ n. **1** the way or place in which something is set. **2** the metal in which a precious stone or gem is fixed to form a piece of jewelry. **3** a piece of music composed for particular words. **4** (also **place setting**) a complete set of dishes and cutlery for one person at a meal.

SYNONYMS **surroundings**, position, situation, environment, background, backdrop, spot, place, location, locale, site, scene.

set·tle /ˈsetl/ ▶ v. (**settles**, **settling**, **settled**) **1** resolve a dispute or difficulty. **2** decide or arrange something finally. **3** make your home in a new place. **4** (often **settle down**) start to live in a more steady or secure way. **5** make or become calmer. **6** sit or rest comfortably or securely. **7** (often **settle in**) begin to feel comfortable in a new situation. **8** pay a debt. **9** (**settle for**) accept after negotiation.

SYNONYMS **1 resolve**, sort out, clear up, end, fix, work out, iron out, set right, reconcile; informal patch up. **2 put in order**, sort out, tidy up, arrange, organize, order, clear up, straighten out. **3 decide on**, set, fix, agree on, name, establish, arrange, choose, pick. **4** *I've settled the bill* **pay**, square, clear. **5 make your home**, set up home, take up residence, put down roots, establish yourself, live, move to. **6** *a drink will settle your nerves* **calm**, quiet, soothe, relax. **7 land**, come to rest, alight, perch.

set·tle·ment /'setlmənt/ ▶ n. **1** the process of settling. **2** an agreement that is intended to settle a dispute. **3** a place where people establish a community.

SYNONYMS **1 agreement**, deal, arrangement, conclusion, resolution, understanding, pact. **2 community**, colony, outpost, encampment, post, village.

set·tler /'setl-ər, 'setlər/ ▶ n. a person who establishes a community in a new area.

SYNONYMS **colonist**, frontiersman, pioneer, immigrant, newcomer, incomer.

set·up /'set,əp/ ▶ n. informal **1** the way in which something is organized. **2** an organization. **3** a scheme intended to trick someone or make it appear that they have done something wrong.

sev·en /'sevən/ ▶ cardinal number one more than six; 7. (Roman numeral: **vii** or **VII**)

sev·en·teen /,sevən'tēn, 'sevən,tēn/ ▶ cardinal number one more than sixteen; 17. (Roman numeral: **xvii** or **XVII**) ■ **sev·en·teenth** ordinal number.

sev·enth /'sevənTH/ ▶ ordinal number **1** at number seven in a sequence; 7th. **2** (**a seventh** or **one seventh**) each of seven equal parts of something.

sev·en·ty /'sevəntē/ ▶ cardinal number (plural **seventies**) ten less than eighty; 70. (Roman numeral: **lxx** or **LXX**) ■ **sev·en·ti·eth** ordinal number.

sev·er /'sevər/ ▶ v. (**severs**, **severing**, **severed**) **1** cut off, or cut into two pieces. **2** put an end to a connection or relationship.

SYNONYMS **1 cut off**, chop off, detach, separate, amputate. **2 cut** (**through**), rupture, split, pierce. **3 break off**, discontinue, suspend, end, cease, dissolve. ANTONYMS join.

sev·er·al /'sev(ə)rəl/ ▶ determiner & pron. more than two but not many. ▶ adj. separate or respective.

SYNONYMS ▶ adj. **some**, a number of, a few, various, assorted.

■ **sev·er·al·ly** adv.

sev·er·ance /'sev(ə)rəns/ ▶ n. **1** the ending of a connection, relationship, or period of employment. **2** the state of being separated or cut off.

se·vere /sə'vi(ə)r/ ▶ adj. **1** (of something bad or difficult) very great. **2** strict or harsh. **3** very plain in style or appearance.

SYNONYMS **1 acute**, very bad, serious, grave, critical, dire, dangerous, life-threatening. **2** *severe storms* **fierce**, violent, strong, powerful, intense, forceful. **3 cold**, freezing, icy, arctic, harsh, bitter. **4** *severe criticism* **harsh**, scathing, sharp, strong, fierce, savage, devastating, withering. **5** *a severe expression* **stern**, dour, grim, forbidding, disapproving, unsmiling, unfriendly, somber, stony, cold, frosty. **6 plain**, simple, austere, spartan, unadorned, stark, clinical, uncluttered, minimalist, functional. ANTONYMS minor, gentle, mild.

■ **se·vere·ly** adv. **se·ver·i·ty** /-'veritē/ n.

sew /sō/ ▶ v. (**sews**, **sewing**, **sewed**; past participle **sewed** or **sewn**) join or repair by making stitches with a needle and thread or a machine.

SYNONYMS **stitch**, tack, seam, hem, embroider.

sew·age /'so͞oij/ ▶ n. human waste and water carried away in sewers.

sew·er /'so͞oər/ ▶ n. an underground channel for carrying away human waste and water. ■ **sew·er·age** n.

sex /seks/ ▶ n. **1** either of the two main categories (male and female) into which humans and most other living things are divided. **2** the fact of being male or female. **3** the group of all members of either sex.

SYNONYMS **1 sexual intercourse**, lovemaking, making love, sexual relations, mating, copulation; formal fornication, coitus. **2 gender**.

□ **sex something up** informal present something in a more interesting way.

sex·a·ge·nar·i·an /,seksəjə'ne(ə)rēən/ ▶ n. a person from 60 to 69 years old.

sex·ism /'sek,sizəm/ ▶ n. prejudice or discrimination on the basis of a person's sex. ■ **sex·ist** adj. & n.

sex·less /'sekslǝs/ ▶ adj. neither male nor female.

sex·tant /'sekstənt/ ▶ n. an instrument for measuring angles and distances, used in navigation and surveying.

sex·tet /sek'stet/ ▶ n. **1** a group of six musicians. **2** a piece of music for a sextet.

sex·ton /'sekstən/ ▶ n. a person who looks after a church and churchyard.

sex·tu·ple /sek'st(y)o͞opəl, -'təpəl/ ▶ adj. **1** made up of six parts or elements. **2** six times as much or as many.

sex·tu·plet /sek'stəplit, -'st(y)o͞oplət/ ▶ n. each of six children born at one birth.

sex·u·al /'sekSHo͞oəl/ ▶ adj. **1** relating to sex, or to physical attraction or contact between individuals. **2** connected with the state of being male or female. **3** (of reproduction) involving the fusion of male and female cells. ■ **sex·u·al·ly** adv.

sex·u·al·i·ty /,sekSHo͞o'alitē/ ▶ n. (plural **sexualities**) **1** capacity for sexual feelings. **2** a person's sexual preference.

SYNONYMS **1 sensuality**, sexiness, seductiveness, eroticism, physicality, sexual appetite, passion, desire, lust. **2 sexual orientation**, sexual preference, leaning, persuasion.

sex·y /'seksē/ ▶ adj. (**sexier**, **sexiest**) **1** sexually attractive or exciting. **2** sexually aroused. **3** informal exciting and interesting.

SYNONYMS **1 sexually attractive**, seductive, desirable, alluring; informal foxy, hot. **2 erotic**, sexually explicit, titillating, naughty, X-rated, rude, pornographic, crude; informal raunchy, steamy; euphemistic adult.

■ **sex·i·ly** adv. **sex·i·ness** n.

shab·by /'SHabē/ ▶ adj. (**shabbier**, **shabbiest**) **1** worn out or scruffy. **2** mean and unfair.

SYNONYMS **1 run-down**, scruffy, dilapidated, in disrepair, ramshackle, tumbledown, dingy. **2 scruffy**, old, worn out, threadbare, ragged, frayed, tattered, battered, faded, moth-eaten, the worse for wear; informal tatty, raggedy. **3 mean**, unkind, unfair, shameful, shoddy, unworthy, contemptible, despicable, discreditable, ignoble; informal rotten. ANTONYMS smart.

■ **shab·bi·ly** adv. **shab·bi·ness** n.

shack /SHak/ ▶ n. a roughly built hut or cabin.

SYNONYMS **hut**, cabin, shanty, lean-to, shed, hovel.

shack·le /'sʜakəl/ ▶ n. (**shackles**) **1** rings connected by a chain, used to fasten a prisoner's wrists or ankles together. **2** restraints or restrictions. ▶ v. (**shackles**, **shackling**, **shackled**) **1** chain with shackles. **2** restrain; limit.

SYNONYMS ▶ n. (**shackles**) **chains**, fetters, irons, leg irons, manacles, handcuffs. ▶ v. **1 chain**, fetter, manacle, secure, tie (up), bind, tether, hobble, put in chains, clap in irons, handcuff. **2 restrain**, restrict, limit, constrain, handicap, hamstring, hamper, hinder, impede, obstruct, inhibit.

shade /sʜād/ ▶ n. **1** relative darkness and coolness caused by shelter from direct sunlight. **2** a color, especially in terms of how light or dark it is. **3** a variety. **4** a slight amount. **5** (**shades**) informal sunglasses. **6** literary a ghost. ▶ v. (**shades**, **shading**, **shaded**) **1** screen from direct light. **2** cover or lessen the light of. **3** represent a darker area with pencil or a block of color. **4** change gradually into something else.

SYNONYMS ▶ n. **1 shadow**, shadiness, shelter, cover. **2 color**, hue, tone, tint, tinge. **3 nuance**, gradation, degree, difference, variation, variety, nicety, subtlety, undertone, overtone. **4 little**, bit, trace, touch, modicum, tinge; informal tad, smidgen. **5 blind**, curtain, screen, cover, covering, awning, canopy. ANTONYMS light. ▶ v. **cast a shadow over**, shadow, shelter, cover, screen.

shad·ow /'sʜadō/ ▶ n. **1** a dark area or shape produced by an object coming between light rays and a surface. **2** partial or complete darkness. **3** sadness or gloom. **4** the slightest trace. **5** a weak or less good version. **6** a person who constantly accompanies or secretly follows another. ▶ v. **1** cast a shadow over. **2** follow and observe secretly.

SYNONYMS ▶ n. **1 silhouette**, outline, shape, contour, profile. **2 shade**, darkness, twilight, gloom. ▶ v. **follow**, trail, track, stalk, pursue; informal tail, keep tabs on.

shad·ow·box·ing /'sʜadōˌbäksiɴɢ/ ▶ n. sparring with an imaginary opponent as a form of training.

shad·ow·y /'sʜadōē/ ▶ adj. (**shadowier**, **shadowiest**) **1** full of shadows. **2** not well known; full of mystery: *the shadowy world of computer hacking*. ■ **shad·ow·i·ness** n.

shad·y /'sʜādē/ ▶ adj. (**shadier**, **shadiest**) **1** giving, or situated in, shade. **2** informal seeming to be dishonest or illegal.

SYNONYMS **1 shaded**, shadowy, dim, dark, sheltered, leafy. **2 suspicious**, suspect, questionable, dubious, irregular, underhanded/underhand; informal fishy, murky. ANTONYMS bright, honest.

shaft /sʜaft/ ▶ n. **1** the long, narrow handle of a tool or club, body of a spear or arrow, etc. **2** a ray of light or bolt of lightning. **3** a narrow vertical passage giving access to a mine, housing an elevator, etc. **4** each of the pair of poles between which a horse is harnessed to a vehicle. **5** a rotating rod for transmitting mechanical power in a machine.

SYNONYMS **1 pole**, stick, rod, staff, shank, handle, stem. **2** *a shaft of light* **ray**, beam, gleam, streak, pencil. **3 tunnel**, passage, hole, bore, duct, well, flue, vent.

shag¹ /sʜag/ ▶ n. coarse tobacco. ▶ adj. (of pile on a carpet) long and rough.

shag² ▶ n. a cormorant (seabird) with greenish-black feathers.

shag·gy /'sʜagē/ ▶ adj. (**shaggier**, **shaggiest**) **1** (of hair or fur) long, thick, and untidy. **2** having shaggy hair or fur.

SYNONYMS **hairy**, bushy, thick, woolly; tangled, tousled, unkempt, disheveled, untidy; formal hirsute. ANTONYMS sleek.

shah /sʜä/ ▶ n. (in the past) the title of the king of Iran.

shake /sʜāk/ ▶ v. (**shakes**, **shaking**, **shook** /sʜŏŏk/; past participle **shaken**) **1** move quickly and jerkily up and down or to and fro. **2** tremble. **3** shock or upset. **4** get rid of or put an end to. ▶ n. **1** an act of shaking. **2** informal a milkshake.

SYNONYMS ▶ v. **1 vibrate**, tremble, quiver, quake, shiver, shudder, wobble, rock, sway, convulse. **2 jiggle**, joggle, jerk, agitate; informal wiggle, waggle. **3 brandish**, wave, flourish, swing, wield. **4 upset**, distress, disturb, unsettle, disconcert, discompose, unnerve, throw off balance, agitate, fluster, shock, alarm, scare, worry; informal rattle. ▶ n. **tremor**, trembling, quivering, quake, shiver, shudder, wobble.

□ **no great shakes** informal not very good. **shake hands** (**with someone**) clasp someone's right hand in your own when meeting or leaving them, to congratulate them, or as a sign of agreement. **shake someone/something up 1** stir someone into action. **2** make major changes to an institution or system. ■ **shak·er** n.

Shake·spear·e·an /sʜāk'spi(ə)rēən/ (or **Shakespearian**) ▶ adj. having to do with the English dramatist William Shakespeare or his works.

shak·y /'sʜākē/ ▶ adj. (**shakier**, **shakiest**) **1** shaking; unsteady. **2** not safe or certain.

SYNONYMS **1 unsteady**, unstable, rickety, wobbly. **2 faint**, dizzy, lightheaded, giddy, weak, wobbly, in shock. **3 unreliable**, untrustworthy, questionable, dubious, doubtful, tenuous, suspect, flimsy, weak; informal iffy. ANTONYMS steady, stable.

■ **shak·i·ly** adv.

shale /sʜāl/ ▶ n. soft rock formed from compressed mud or clay.

shall /sʜal/ ▶ modal v. (3rd singular present **shall**) **1** used with *I* and *we* to express the future tense. **2** expressing a strong statement, intention, or order. **3** used in questions to make offers or suggestions: *shall we go?*

USAGE

The traditional rule is that you should use **shall** when forming the future tense with **I** and **we** (*I shall be late*) and **will** with **you**, **he**, **she**, **it**, and **they** (*he will not be there*). Nowadays, people do not follow this rule so strictly and are more likely to use the shortened forms **I'll**, **she'll**, etc.

shal·lot /sʜə'lät, 'sʜalət/ ▶ n. a vegetable like a small onion.

shal·low /'sʜalō/ ▶ adj. **1** having a short distance between the top and the bottom; not deep. **2** not thinking or thought out seriously. ▶ n. (**shallows**) a shallow area of water.

SYNONYMS ▶ **adj.** **superficial**, trivial, facile, insubstantial, lightweight, empty, trifling, surface, skin-deep, frivolous, foolish, silly. ANTONYMS profound.

■ **shal·low·ly** adv.

sham /sHam/ ▶ **n.** **1** a thing that is not what it appears to be or is not as good as it seems. **2** a person who pretends to be something they are not. ▶ **adj.** not genuine; false. ▶ **v.** (**shams**, **shamming**, **shammed**) pretend.

SYNONYMS ▶ **n.** **pretense**, fake, act, simulation, fraud, lie, counterfeit, humbug. ▶ **adj.** **fake**, pretended, feigned, simulated, false, artificial, bogus, insincere, affected, make-believe; informal pretend, put-on, phony. ANTONYMS genuine. ▶ **v.** **pretend**, fake, malinger; informal put it on.

sha·man /'sHämən, 'sHā-/ ▶ **n.** (plural **shamans**) (in some societies) a person believed to be able to contact good and evil spirits. ■ **sha·man·ic** /sHə'manik/ **adj.** **sha·man·ism** **n.**

sham·ble /'sHambəl/ ▶ **v.** (**shambles**, **shambling**, **shambled**) walk in a slow, shuffling, awkward way.

sham·bles /'sHambəlz/ ▶ **n.** informal a state of complete disorder.

SYNONYMS **1** **chaos**, muddle, jumble, confusion, disorder, havoc. **2** **mess**, pigsty; informal disaster zone.

shame /sHām/ ▶ **n.** **1** the feeling you have of embarrassment or distress when you know you have done something wrong or foolish. **2** loss of respect; dishonor. **3** a cause of shame. **4** a cause for regret or disappointment. ▶ **v.** (**shames**, **shaming**, **shamed**) make someone feel shame.

SYNONYMS ▶ **n.** **1** **guilt**, remorse, contrition. **2** **humiliation**, embarrassment, indignity, loss of face, mortification, disgrace, dishonor, discredit, ignominy, disrepute, infamy, scandal. **3** *it's a shame she never married* **pity**, sad thing, bad luck; informal crime, sin. ANTONYMS pride, honor. ▶ **v.** **1** **disgrace**, dishonor, discredit, blacken, drag through the mud. **2** **humiliate**, embarrass, humble, take down a peg or two, cut down to size; informal show up. ANTONYMS honor.

□ **put someone/something to shame** be much better than someone or something.

shame·faced /'sHām,fāst/ ▶ **adj.** showing shame.

SYNONYMS **ashamed**, abashed, sheepish, guilty, contrite, sorry, remorseful, repentant, penitent, regretful, rueful, apologetic; informal with your tail between your legs. ANTONYMS unrepentant.

shame·ful /'sHāmfəl/ ▶ **adj.** causing a feeling of shame.

SYNONYMS **1** **disgraceful**, deplorable, despicable, contemptible, discreditable, unworthy, reprehensible, shabby, shocking, scandalous, outrageous, abominable, atrocious, appalling, inexcusable, unforgivable. **2** **embarrassing**, mortifying, humiliating, ignominious. ANTONYMS admirable.

■ **shame·ful·ly** adv.

shame·less /'sHāmlis/ ▶ **adj.** showing no shame.

SYNONYMS **flagrant**, blatant, barefaced, overt, brazen, undisguised, unconcealed, unabashed, unashamed, unblushing, unrepentant.

■ **shame·less·ly** adv.

sham·my /'sHamē/ ▶ **n.** (plural **shammies**) informal chamois leather.

sham·poo /sHam'po͞o/ ▶ **n.** **1** a liquid soap for washing the hair. **2** a similar substance for cleaning a carpet, car, etc. **3** an act of washing with shampoo. ▶ **v.** (**shampoos**, **shampooing**, **shampooed**) wash or clean with shampoo.

sham·rock /'sHam,räk/ ▶ **n.** a cloverlike plant with three leaves on each stem, the national emblem of Ireland.

shang·hai /'sHaNG'hī/ ▶ **v.** (**shanghais**, **shanghaiing**, **shanghaied**) informal force or trick into doing something.

shank /sHaNGk/ ▶ **n.** **1** the lower part of the leg. **2** the shaft of a tool.

shan't /sHant/ ▶ **contr.** shall not.

shan·tung /sHan'təNG/ ▶ **n.** a type of silk fabric with a rough surface.

shant·y[1] /'sHantē/ ▶ **n.** (plural **shanties**) a small roughly built hut.

shant·y[2] ▶ **n.** (plural **shanties**) a song with alternating solo and chorus, sung by sailors when working.

shan·ty·town /'sHantē,toun/ ▶ **n.** a settlement in or near a city where poor people live in makeshift houses or shacks.

shape /sHāp/ ▶ **n.** **1** the form of something produced by its outline. **2** a piece of material, paper, etc., cut in a particular form. **3** a particular condition or state. **4** well-defined structure or arrangement. ▶ **v.** (**shapes**, **shaping**, **shaped**) **1** give a shape to. **2** have a big influence on.

SYNONYMS ▶ **n.** **1** **form**, appearance, configuration, structure, contours, lines, outline, silhouette, profile. **2** **guise**, likeness, semblance, form, appearance, image. **3** **condition**, health, trim, fettle, order. ▶ **v.** **1** **form**, fashion, make, mold, model. **2** *events that shaped the course of her life* **determine**, form, influence, affect.

□ **out of shape** **1** not having its usual or original shape. **2** in poor physical condition. **shape up** **1** develop in a particular way. **2** improve your fitness, behavior, etc.

shape·less /'sHāplis/ ▶ **adj.** lacking a definite or attractive shape.

SYNONYMS **1** **formless**, amorphous, unformed, indefinite. **2** **baggy**, saggy, ill-fitting, oversized, unstructured, badly cut.

shape·ly /'sHāplē/ ▶ **adj.** having an attractive shape.

SYNONYMS **well-proportioned**, curvaceous, voluptuous, full-figured, attractive, sexy; informal curvy.

shard /sHärd/ ▶ **n.** a sharp piece of broken pottery, glass, etc.

share /sHe(ə)r/ ▶ **n.** **1** a part of a larger amount that is divided among or contributed to by a number of people. **2** any of the equal parts into which a company's wealth is divided, which can be bought by people in return for a proportion of the profits. **3** an amount thought to be normal or acceptable. ▶ **v.** (**shares**, **sharing**, **shared**) **1** have or give a share of. **2** have, use, or experience jointly with others. **3** tell someone about.

SYNONYMS ▶ **n.** **portion**, part, division, quota, allowance, ration, allocation; informal cut, slice. ▶ **v.** **1 split**, divide, go halves on; informal go fifty-fifty on. **2 apportion**, divide up, allocate, portion out, measure out, carve up; informal divvy up. **3 participate**, take part, play a part, be involved, have a hand.

■ **shar·er n.**

share·crop·per /ˈsHe(ə)rˌkräpər/ ▶ **n.** a tenant farmer who gives a part of each crop as rent.

share·hold·er /ˈsHe(ə)rˌhōldər/ ▶ **n.** an owner of shares in a company.

shark¹ /sHärk/ ▶ **n.** a large and sometimes aggressive sea fish with a triangular fin on its back.

shark² ▶ **n.** informal a person who dishonestly obtains money from other people.

sharp /sHärp/ ▶ **adj. 1** having a cutting or piercing edge or point. **2** tapering to a point or edge. **3** sudden and noticeable. **4** clear and definite. **5** producing a sudden, piercing feeling. **6** quick to understand, notice, or respond. **7** (of a taste or smell) strong and slightly bitter. **8** (of a note or key) higher by a half step than a stated note or key. **9** (of musical sound) above true or normal pitch. ▶ **adv. 1** precisely. **2** suddenly or abruptly. ▶ **n.** a musical note raised a semitone above natural pitch, shown by the sign ♯.

SYNONYMS ▶ **adj. 1 keen**, razor-edged, sharpened, well-honed. **2 intense**, acute, severe, agonizing, excruciating, stabbing, shooting, searing. **3 tangy**, piquant, acidic, acid, sour, tart, pungent, vinegary. **4 cold**, chilly, icy, bitter, biting, brisk, keen, penetrating. **5 harsh**, bitter, cutting, caustic, scathing, barbed, spiteful, hurtful, unkind, cruel, malicious. **6** *a sharp increase* **sudden**, abrupt, unexpected, rapid, steep. **7 astute**, intelligent, bright, incisive, keen, quick-witted, shrewd, canny, perceptive, smart, quick; informal on the ball, quick on the uptake, heads-up. ANTONYMS blunt, mild. ▶ **adv. precisely**, exactly, prompt, promptly, punctually; informal on the dot, on the nose, on the button.

□ **sharp practice** dishonest business dealings. **sharp-witted** intelligent and shrewd. ■ **sharp·ly adv. sharp·ness n.**

sharp·en /ˈsHärpən/ ▶ **v.** make or become sharp.

SYNONYMS **hone**, whet, strop, grind, file.

■ **shar·pen·er n.**

sharp·shoot·er /ˈsHärpˌsHo͞otər/ ▶ **n.** a person skilled in shooting.

shat·ter /ˈsHatər/ ▶ **v.** (**shatters**, **shattering**, **shattered**) **1** break suddenly and violently into pieces. **2** damage or destroy. **3** upset someone greatly.

SYNONYMS **1 smash**, break, splinter, crack, fracture, fragment, disintegrate. **2 destroy**, wreck, ruin, dash, crush, devastate, demolish, torpedo, scotch.

shave /sHāv/ ▶ **v.** (**shaves**, **shaving**, **shaved**) **1** remove hair by cutting it off close to the skin with a razor. **2** cut a thin slice or slices from something. **3** reduce something by a small amount. ▶ **n.** an act of shaving.

SYNONYMS ▶ **v. 1 cut off**, crop, trim, barber. **2 plane**, pare, whittle, scrape, shear.

shav·en /ˈsHāvən/ ▶ **adj.** shaved.

shav·er /ˈsHāvər/ ▶ **n.** an electric razor.

shav·ing /ˈsHāviNG/ ▶ **n.** a thin strip cut off a surface.

shawl /sHôl/ ▶ **n.** a large piece of fabric worn by women over the shoulders or head or wrapped around a baby.

she /sHē/ ▶ **pron. 1** used to refer to a female person or animal previously mentioned or easily identified. **2** used to refer to a ship, country, or other thing thought of as female.

sheaf /sHēf/ ▶ **n.** (plural **sheaves** /sHēvz/) **1** a bundle of papers. **2** a bundle of grain stalks tied together after reaping.

shear /sHi(ə)r/ ▶ **v.** (**shears**, **shearing**, **sheared**; past participle **sheared** or **shorn** /sHôrn/) **1** cut the wool off a sheep. **2** cut off something such as wool or grass with shears. **3** (**be shorn of**) have something taken away from you. **4** (**shear off**) tear or break off under pressure. ■ **shear·er n.**

USAGE

Don't confuse **shear** with **sheer**, which is a verb meaning 'change course quickly' and also an adjective meaning 'nothing but; absolute.'

shears /sHi(ə)rz/ ▶ **pl.n.** a cutting tool like very large scissors.

sheath /sHēTH/ ▶ **n.** (plural **sheaths** /sHēT͟Hz, sHēTHs/) **1** a cover for the blade of a knife or sword. **2** a close-fitting covering.

SYNONYMS **covering**, cover, case, casing, sleeve, scabbard.

sheathe /sHēT͟H/ ▶ **v.** (**sheathes**, **sheathing**, **sheathed**) **1** put a knife or sword into a sheath. **2** encase something in a close-fitting or protective covering.

she·bang /sHəˈbaNG/ ▶ **n.** (**the whole shebang**) informal the whole thing.

shed¹ /sHed/ ▶ **n.** a simple building used for storage.

SYNONYMS **hut**, lean-to, outhouse, outbuilding, cabin, shack, woodshed, toolshed.

shed² ▶ **v.** (**sheds**, **shedding**, **shed**) **1** allow leaves, hair, skin, etc., to fall off naturally. **2** get rid of. **3** take off clothes. **4** give off light. **5** be able not to absorb water, etc.

SYNONYMS **1 drop**, scatter, spill. **2 throw off**, cast off, discard, slough off, molt. **3 take off**, remove, discard, climb out of, slip out of; informal peel off. **4** *the moon shed a faint light* **cast**, radiate, emit, give out.

□ **shed tears** cry.

she'd /sHēd/ ▶ **contr.** she had or she would.

sheen /sHēn/ ▶ **n.** a soft shine on a surface.

SYNONYMS **shine**, luster, gloss, patina, burnish, polish, shimmer.

sheep /sHēp/ ▶ **n.** (plural **sheep**) an animal with a thick woolly coat, kept in flocks for its wool or meat. □ **sheep dip** a liquid in which sheep are dipped to clean and disinfect their wool.

sheep·dog /ˈsHēpˌdôg, -ˌdäg/ ▶ **n.** a breed of dog trained to guard and herd sheep.

sheep·ish /ˈsHēpisH/ ▶ **adj.** feeling embarrassed from shame or shyness.

SYNONYMS **embarrassed**, uncomfortable, hangdog, self-conscious; shamefaced, ashamed, abashed, mortified, chastened, remorseful, contrite, apologetic, penitent, repentant.

■ **sheep·ish·ly** adv.

sheep·skin /ˈSHēpˌskin/ ▶ n. a sheep's skin with the wool on.

sheer¹ /SHi(ə)r/ ▶ adj. **1** nothing but; absolute. **2** (of a cliff or wall) vertical or almost vertical. **3** (of fabric) very thin.

SYNONYMS **1 utter**, complete, absolute, total, thorough, pure, downright, out-and-out, unqualified, unmitigated, unalloyed. **2 steep**, abrupt, sharp, precipitous, vertical. **3 thin**, fine, gauzy, diaphanous, transparent, see-through, flimsy, filmy, translucent.

USAGE

Don't confuse **sheer** with **shear**, which is a verb meaning 'cut.'

sheer² ▶ v. (**sheers, sheering, sheered**) **1** (especially of a boat) change course quickly. **2** move away from an unpleasant topic.

sheet¹ /SHēt/ ▶ n. **1** a large rectangular piece of cotton or other fabric, used on a bed to lie on or under. **2** a broad flat piece of metal or glass. **3** a rectangular piece of paper. **4** a wide expanse or moving mass of water, flames, etc.

SYNONYMS **1 layer**, covering, blanket, coat, film, veneer, crust, skin, surface, stratum. **2 pane**, panel, slab, plate, piece. **3 page**, leaf, folio. **4** *a sheet of water* **expanse**, area, stretch, sweep.

□ **sheet music** music printed on loose sheets of paper.

sheet² ▶ n. a rope attached to the lower corner of a sail.

sheikh /SHēk, SHāk/ (or **sheik**) ▶ n. a Muslim or Arab leader.

shei·la /SHēlə/ ▶ n. Australian/New Zealand informal a girl or woman.

shek·el /ˈSHekəl/ ▶ n. the basic unit of money of modern Israel.

shelf /SHelf/ ▶ n. (plural **shelves** /SHelvz/) **1** a flat length of wood or other rigid material, fixed horizontally and used to display or store things. **2** a ledge of rock. □ **off the shelf** taken from existing supplies, not made to order. **shelf life** the length of time for which an item to be sold can be stored.

shell /SHel/ ▶ n. **1** the hard protective outer case of an animal such as a shellfish or turtle. **2** the outer covering of an egg, nut kernel, or seed. **3** a metal case filled with explosive, to be fired from a large gun. **4** a hollow case. **5** an outer structure or framework. ▶ v. **1** fire explosive shells at. **2** remove the shell or pod from. **3** (**shell something out**) informal pay an amount of money.

SYNONYMS ▶ n. **1 pod**, hull, husk. **2 body**, case, casing, framework, hull, fuselage, hulk. ▶ v. **1 pod**, hull, husk, shuck. **2 bombard**, fire on, attack, bomb, blitz.

□ **shell shock** a mental condition resembling a state of shock that can affect soldiers who have been in battle for a long time.

she'll /SHēl/ ▶ contr. she shall or she will.

shell·fish /ˈSHelˌfiSH/ ▶ n. a water animal that has a shell and that can be eaten, such as a crab or oyster.

shel·ter /ˈSHeltər/ ▶ n. **1** a place giving protection from bad weather or danger. **2** a place providing food and accommodations for the homeless. **3** protection from danger or bad weather. ▶ v. (**shelters, sheltering, sheltered**) **1** provide with shelter. **2** find protection or take cover. **3** (**sheltered**) protected from the more unpleasant aspects of life.

SYNONYMS ▶ n. **1 protection**, cover, shade, safety, security, refuge. **2 sanctuary**, refuge, home, haven, safe house. ANTONYMS exposure. ▶ v. **1 protect**, shield, screen, cover, shade, defend, cushion, guard, insulate, cocoon. **2** (**sheltered**) **shady**, shaded, protected, still, tranquil. **3 take shelter**, take refuge, take cover; informal hole up. **4** (**sheltered**) **protected**, cloistered, isolated, secluded, cocooned, insulated, secure, safe, quiet. ANTONYMS expose.

shelve /SHelv/ ▶ v. (**shelves, shelving, shelved**) **1** decide not to continue with a plan for the time being. **2** place something on a shelf. **3** (of ground) slope downward.

SYNONYMS **postpone**, put off, delay, defer, put back, reschedule, hold over/off, put to one side, table, suspend, stay, mothball; informal put on ice, put on the back burner.

shelves /SHelvz/ plural of **SHELF**.

she·nan·i·gans /SHəˈnanəgənz/ ▶ pl.n. informal mischievous behavior.

shep·herd /ˈSHepərd/ ▶ n. a person who looks after sheep. ▶ v. guide or direct someone.

SYNONYMS ▶ v. **usher**, steer, herd, lead, take, escort, guide, conduct, marshal, walk.

□ **shepherd's pie** a dish of ground meat under a layer of mashed potato and often corn or peas.
■ **shep·herd·ess** n.

sher·bet /ˈSHərbit/ ▶ n. **1** a frozen dessert made with fruit juice added to milk or cream, egg white, or gelatin. **2** a frozen fruit juice and sugar mixture served as a dessert or between courses of a meal to cleanse the palate.

sher·iff /ˈSHerif/ ▶ n. **1** (in the United States) an elected officer in a county, responsible for keeping the peace. **2** (also **high sheriff**) (in England and Wales) the chief executive officer in a county, working on behalf of a king or queen. **3** (in Scotland) a judge.

Sher·pa /ˈSHərpə/ ▶ n. (plural **Sherpa** or **Sherpas**) a member of a Himalayan people living on the borders of Nepal and Tibet, known for their skill in mountaineering.

sher·ry /ˈSHerē/ ▶ n. (plural **sherries**) a strong wine from southern Spain.

she's /SHēz/ ▶ contr. she is or she has.

Shet·land po·ny /ˈSHetlənd/ ▶ n. a small breed of pony with a rough coat.

Shi·a /ˈSHēˌä/ ▶ n. (plural **Shia** or **Shias**) **1** one of the two main branches of Islam. The other is **SUNNI**. **2** a Muslim who follows the Shia branch of Islam.

shi·at·su /SHēˈätso͞o/ ▶ n. a medical treatment from Japan in which pressure is applied with the hands to points on the body.

shib·bo·leth /ˈSHibəliTH, -ˌleTH/ ▶ n. a long-standing belief or principle held by a group of people.

shied /SHīd/ past and past participle of **SHY²**.

shield /SHēld/ ▶ n. **1** a broad piece of armor held for protection against blows or missiles. **2** a person or thing that acts as a protective barrier or screen. **3** a sports trophy consisting of an engraved metal plate mounted on a piece of wood. **4** a drawing or model of a shield used for displaying a coat of arms. ▶ **v.** protect or hide.

SYNONYMS ▶ **n. protection**, guard, defense, cover, screen, shelter. ▶ **v. protect**, guard, defend, cover, screen, shade, shelter. ANTONYMS expose.

shift /SHift/ ▶ **v. 1** move or change from one position to another. **2** transfer blame or responsibility to someone else. ▶ **n. 1** a slight change in position or direction. **2** a period of time worked by someone who starts work as another finishes. **3** a straight dress without a fitted waist. **4** a key used to switch between two sets of characters or functions on a keyboard.

SYNONYMS ▶ **v. 1 move**, transfer, transport, switch, relocate, reposition, rearrange. **2** *the wind shifted* **veer**, alter, change, turn. ▶ **n. 1 change**, alteration, adjustment, variation, modification, revision, reversal, U-turn. **2 stint**, stretch, spell.

shift·less /ˈSHiftlis/ ▶ **adj.** lazy and lacking ambition.

SYNONYMS **lazy**, idle, indolent, slothful, lethargic, feckless, good-for-nothing, worthless.

shift·y /ˈSHiftē/ ▶ **adj.** informal seeming dishonest or untrustworthy.

SYNONYMS **devious**, evasive, slippery, duplicitous, deceitful, untrustworthy. ANTONYMS honest.

Shi·ite /ˈSHēˌīt/ ▶ **n.** a follower of the Shia branch of Islam.

shil·ling /ˈSHiliNG/ ▶ **n.** a former British coin worth one twentieth of a pound or twelve old pence (equivalent to 5p).

shil·ly-shal·ly /ˈSHilē ˌSHalē/ ▶ **v.** (**shilly-shallies**, **shilly-shallying**, **shilly-shallied**) be unable to make up your mind.

shim·mer /ˈSHimər/ ▶ **v.** (**shimmers**, **shimmering**, **shimmered**) shine with a soft wavering light. ▶ **n.** a soft wavering light or shine.

SYNONYMS ▶ **v. glint**, glisten, twinkle, sparkle, flash, gleam, glow, glimmer, wink. ▶ **n. glint**, twinkle, sparkle, flash, gleam, glow, glimmer, luster, glitter.

■ **shim·mer·y** adj.

shim·my /ˈSHimē/ ▶ **v.** (**shimmies**, **shimmying**, **shimmied**) move quickly and smoothly.

shin /SHin/ ▶ **n.** the front of the leg below the knee. ▶ **v.** (**shins**, **shinning**, **shinned**) (**shin up** or **down**) climb quickly up or down by gripping with your arms and legs.

shin·dig /ˈSHinˌdig/ ▶ **n.** informal a lively party.

shine /SHīn/ ▶ **v.** (**shines**, **shining**, past and past participle **shone** /SHän/ or **shined**) **1** give out or reflect light. **2** direct a flashlight or other light somewhere. **3** (of a person's eyes) be bright with an emotion. **4** be very good at something. **5** (past and past participle **shined**) polish. ▶ **n.** a quality of brightness.

SYNONYMS ▶ **v. 1 beam**, gleam, radiate, glow, glint, glimmer, sparkle, twinkle, glitter, glisten, shimmer, flash. **2 polish**, burnish, buff, rub up, brush, clean. **3 excel**, stand out. ▶ **n. polish**, gleam, gloss, luster, sheen, patina.

□ **take a shine to** informal develop a liking for.

shin·er /ˈSHīnər/ ▶ **n.** informal a black eye.

shin·gle[1] /ˈSHiNGgəl/ ▶ **n.** a mass of small rounded pebbles on a seashore.

shin·gle[2] ▶ **n.** a wooden tile used on walls or roofs. ■ **shin·gled** adj.

shin·gles /ˈSHiNGgəlz/ ▶ **n.** a disease in which painful blisters form along the path of a nerve.

shin·y /ˈSHīnē/ ▶ **adj.** (**shinier**, **shiniest**) reflecting light.

SYNONYMS **glossy**, bright, glassy, polished, gleaming, satiny, lustrous. ANTONYMS matte.

ship /SHip/ ▶ **n.** a large boat for transporting people or goods by sea. ▶ **v.** (**ships**, **shipping**, **shipped**) **1** transport goods on a ship or by other means. **2** (of a boat) take in water over the side.

SYNONYMS ▶ **n. boat**, vessel, craft. ▶ **v. deliver**, send, dispatch, transport, carry, distribute.

ship·build·er /ˈSHipˌbildər/ ▶ **n.** a person or company that designs and builds ships. ■ **ship·build·ing** n.

ship·mate /ˈSHipˌmāt/ ▶ **n.** a fellow member of a ship's crew.

ship·ment /ˈSHipmənt/ ▶ **n. 1** the action of transporting goods. **2** an amount of goods shipped.

ship·ping /ˈSHipiNG/ ▶ **n. 1** ships as a whole. **2** the transport of goods.

ship·shape /ˈSHipˌSHāp/ ▶ **adj.** orderly and neat.

ship·wreck /ˈSHipˌrek/ ▶ **n. 1** the sinking or breaking up of a ship at sea. **2** a ship that has been lost or destroyed at sea. ▶ **v.** (**be shipwrecked**) suffer a shipwreck.

ship·yard /ˈSHipˌyärd/ ▶ **n.** a place where ships are built and repaired.

shire /SHī(ə)r/ ▶ **n.** a county, especially in England.

shirk /SHərk/ ▶ **v.** avoid work or a duty.

SYNONYMS **evade**, dodge, avoid, get out of, sidestep, shrink from, shun, skip, neglect; informal duck (out of), book (out of), cop out of, cut.

■ **shirk·er** n.

shirred /SHərd/ ▶ **adj.** (of fabric) gathered by means of threads in parallel rows.

shirt /SHərt/ ▶ **n.** a garment for the upper body, with a collar and sleeves and buttons down the front.

shirt·sleeves /ˈSHərtˌslēvz/ ▶ **pl.n.** (**in your shirtsleeves**) wearing a shirt without a jacket.

shirt·waist /ˈSHərtˌwāst/ ▶ **n. 1** a woman's blouse that resembles a shirt. **2** a shirt dress with a seam at the waist.

shish ke·bab /ˈSHiSH kəˌbäb/ ▶ **n.** a dish of pieces of meat and vegetables cooked and served on skewers.

shiv·er /ˈSHivər/ ▶ **v.** (**shivers**, **shivering**, **shivered**) shake slightly from fear, cold, or excitement. ▶ **n.** a trembling movement.

SYNONYMS ▶ **v. tremble**, quiver, shake, shudder, quake. ▶ **n. shudder**, twitch, start.

■ **shiv·er·y** adj.

shoal[1] /SHōl/ ▶ **n.** a large number of fish swimming together.

shoal[2] ▶ **n. 1** an area of shallow water. **2** a submerged sandbank that can be seen at low tide.

shock[1] /SHäk/ ▶ **n. 1** a sudden upsetting or surprising event or experience. **2** an unpleasant feeling of sudden surprise and distress. **3** a serious medical condition associated with a fall in blood pressure, caused by loss of blood, severe burns, etc. **4** a violent shaking movement caused by an impact, explosion, or earthquake. **5** an electric shock. ▶ **v. 1** greatly surprise and upset someone. **2** make someone feel outraged or disgusted.

SYNONYMS ▶ **n. 1 blow**, upset, surprise, revelation, bolt from the blue, rude awakening, eye-opener. **2 fright**, scare, start; informal turn. **3 trauma**, collapse, breakdown, post-traumatic stress disorder. **4 vibration**, reverberation, shake, jolt, impact, blow. ▶ **v. appall**, horrify, outrage, scandalize, disgust, traumatize, distress, upset, disturb, stun, rock, shake. ANTONYMS delight.

□ **shock absorber** a device for absorbing jolts and vibrations on a vehicle. **shocking pink** a very bright shade of pink. **shock troops** troops trained to carry out sudden attacks. **shock wave** a moving wave of very high pressure caused by an explosion or by something traveling faster than sound. ■ **shock·er n.**

shock² ▶ **n.** an untidy or thick mass of hair.

SYNONYMS **mass**, mane, mop, thatch, head, bush, tangle, cascade.

shock·ing /ˈshäkiNG/ ▶ **adj.** causing shock or disgust.

SYNONYMS **appalling**, horrifying, horrific, dreadful, awful, terrible, scandalous, outrageous, disgraceful, abominable, atrocious, disgusting, distressing, upsetting, disturbing, startling.

■ **shock·ing·ly adv.**

shod·dy /ˈshädē/ ▶ **adj.** (**shoddier**, **shoddiest**) **1** badly made or done. **2** dishonest or unfair.

SYNONYMS **poor-quality**, inferior, second-rate, tawdry, jerry-built, cheapjack, gimcrack; informal tatty.

■ **shod·di·ly adv.**

shoe /SHo͞o/ ▶ **n. 1** a covering for the foot with a stiff sole. **2** a horseshoe. ▶ **v.** (**shoes**, **shoeing**, **shod** /SHäd/) **1** fit a horse with a shoe or shoes. **2** (**be shod**) be wearing shoes of a particular kind. □ **shoe tree** a shaped block put into a shoe when it is not being worn, to keep it in shape.

shoe·horn /ˈSHo͞oˌhôrn/ ▶ **n.** a curved piece of metal or plastic, used for easing your heel into a shoe. ▶ **v.** force into a tight space.

shoe·lace /ˈSHo͞oˌlās/ ▶ **n.** a cord passed through holes or hooks on opposite sides of the opening in a shoe to fasten it.

shoe·mak·er /ˈSHo͞oˌmākər/ ▶ **n.** a person who makes footwear as a profession.

shoe·shine /ˈSHo͞oˌSHīn/ ▶ **n.** an act of polishing someone's shoes.

shoe·string /ˈSHo͞oˌstriNG/ ▶ **n.** (**on a shoestring**) informal with only a very small amount of money.

sho·gun /ˈSHōgən/ ▶ **n.** (in the past, in Japan) a hereditary leader of the army.

shone /SHän/ past and past participle of **SHINE**.

shoo-in /SHo͞o/ ▶ **n.** informal a person or thing that is certain to succeed or win.

shook /SHo͝ok/ past of **SHAKE**

shoot /SHo͞ot/ ▶ **v.** (**shoots**, **shooting**, **shot** /SHät/) **1** kill or wound someone with a bullet, arrow, etc. **2** fire a gun. **3** move suddenly and rapidly. **4** direct a glance, question, or remark at someone. **5** (in sports) kick, hit, or throw the ball or puck in an attempt to score a goal. **6** photograph or film a scene or movie. **7** (**shooting**) (of a pain) sudden and piercing. **8** (of a boat) travel quickly down rapids. **9** move a bolt to fasten a door. **10** send out buds or shoots. **11** (**shoot up**) informal inject yourself with an illegal drug. ▶ **n. 1** a new part growing from a plant. **2** an occasion of taking photographs or making a movie. **3** an occasion when a group of people hunt and shoot animals or birds.

SYNONYMS ▶ **v. 1 gun down**, mow down, pick off, hit, wound, injure, kill. **2 fire**, open fire, snipe, let fly, bombard, shell, discharge, launch. **3 race**, speed, flash, dash, rush, hurtle, streak, whiz, zoom, career, fly; informal belt, tear, zip, whip, hightail it, barrel. **4 film**, photograph, record. ▶ **n. sprout**, bud, runner, tendril, offshoot, cutting.

□ **shoot the breeze** informal have a casual conversation. **shoot your mouth off** informal talk boastfully or too freely. **the whole shooting match** informal everything. **shooting star** a small rapidly moving meteor that burns up on entering the earth's atmosphere.

shoot·er /ˈSHo͞otər/ ▶ **n. 1** a person who uses a gun. **2** informal a gun. **3** a member of a team in games such as basketball whose role is to attempt to score goals. **4** a marble used to shoot at other marbles. **5** informal a small alcoholic drink, especially of distilled liquor.

shop /SHäp/ ▶ **n. 1** a building or part of a building where goods are sold. **2** a place where things are manufactured or repaired; a workshop. ▶ **v.** (**shops**, **shopping**, **shopped**) **1** go to a store or stores to buy goods. **2** (**shop around**) look for the best available price or rate for something.

SYNONYMS ▶ **n. 1 store**, retail outlet, mart, boutique, emporium. **2 factory**, plant, workshop, workroom, works, mill.

□ **shop floor** the area in a factory where things are made or put together by the workers. **shop steward** a person elected by workers in a factory to represent them in dealings with the management. **talk shop** discuss work matters with a colleague when you are not at work.

shop·keep·er /ˈSHäpˌkēpər/ ▶ **n.** the owner and manager of a shop.

shop·lift·ing /ˈSHäpˌliftiNG/ ▶ **n.** the stealing of goods from a store. ■ **shop·lift·er n.**

shop·per /ˈSHäpər/ ▶ **n.** a person who is shopping.

shop·ping /ˈSHäpiNG/ ▶ **n. 1** the buying of goods from stores. **2** goods bought from stores. □ **shopping center** a group of stores situated together.

shop·worn /ˈSHäpˌwôrn/ ▶ **n.** (of an article) dirty or damaged from being displayed or handled in a shop.

shore¹ /SHôr/ ▶ **n. 1** the land along the edge of a sea or other stretch of water. **2** (**shores**) literary a foreign country or region.

SYNONYMS **seashore**, beach, sand(s), shoreline, coast; literary littoral.

□ **on shore** on land.

shore² ▶ **v.** (**shores**, **shoring**, **shored**) (**shore something up**) **1** support or strengthen something. **2** hold something up with a prop or beam.

shore·line /ˈSHôrˌlīn/ ▶ **n.** the line along which a sea or other stretch of water meets the land.

shorn /SHôrn/ past participle of **SHEAR**.

short /SHôrt/ ▶ **adj.** **1** of a small length in space or time. **2** small in height. **3** smaller than is usual or expected. **4** (**short of** or **on**) not having enough of. **5** not available in large enough quantities; scarce. **6** rude and abrupt. **7** (of odds in betting) reflecting a high level of probability. **8** (of pastry) containing a high proportion of fat to flour and therefore crumbly. ▶ **adv.** not as far as expected or required. ▶ **v.** have a short circuit.

> SYNONYMS ▶ **adj.** **1 small**, little, petite, tiny, diminutive, elfin; informal pint-sized, knee-high to a grasshopper. **2 concise**, brief, succinct, to the point, compact, pithy, abridged, abbreviated, condensed. **3 brief**, fleeting, short-lived, momentary, passing, lightning, quick, rapid, cursory. **4 scarce**, scant, meager, sparse, insufficient, deficient, inadequate, lacking. **5 curt**, sharp, abrupt, blunt, brusque, terse, offhand. ANTONYMS tall, long, plentiful. ▶ **adv.** *she stopped short* **abruptly**, suddenly, sharply, all of a sudden, unexpectedly, without warning.

□ **in short** to sum up; briefly. **in the short run** (or **term**) in the near future. **in short supply** (of a product) scarce. **make short work of** do, eat, or drink quickly. **run short** not have enough of something. **short for** an abbreviation or nickname for. **short of 1** less than or not reaching as far as. **2** without going so far as (some extreme action). **short circuit** a faulty connection in an electrical circuit in which the current flows along a shorter route than it should do. **short-circuit** cause a short circuit in. **short-handed** (or **short-staffed**) having fewer staff than you need or than is usual. **short-lived** lasting only a short time. **short shrift** abrupt and unsympathetic treatment. **short-sleeved** having sleeves that do not reach below the elbow. **short-tempered** losing your temper quickly. **stop short** suddenly stop. ■ **short·ness** **n.**

short·age /'SHôrtij/ ▶ **n.** a lack of something needed.

> SYNONYMS **scarcity**, dearth, poverty, insufficiency, deficiency, inadequacy, famine, lack, deficit, shortfall. ANTONYMS abundance.

short·bread /'SHôrt,bred/ (or **shortcake** /'SHôrt,kāk/) ▶ **n.** a rich, crumbly type of cookie made with butter, flour, and sugar.

short·change /'SHôrt'CHānj/ ▶ **v.** cheat someone by giving them less than the correct change.

short·com·ing /'SHôrt,kəmiNG/ ▶ **n.** a fault in someone's character or in a system.

> SYNONYMS **fault**, defect, flaw, imperfection, deficiency, limitation, failing, drawback, weakness, weak point. ANTONYMS strength.

short·cut /'SHôrt,kət/ ▶ **n.** **1** a way of going somewhere or doing something that is quicker than usual. **2** Computing a record of the address of a file or other data that lets you access it quickly.

short·en /'SHôrtn/ ▶ **v.** make or become shorter.

> SYNONYMS **abbreviate**, abridge, condense, contract, compress, reduce, shrink, diminish, cut (down), trim, pare (down), prune, curtail, truncate. ANTONYMS lengthen.

short·en·ing /'SHôrtniNG, 'SHôrtn-iNG/ ▶ **n.** butter or other fat used for making pastry or bread.

short·fall /'SHôrt,fôl/ ▶ **n.** a situation in which something amounts to less than is required.

short·hand /'SHôrt,hand/ ▶ **n.** a way of writing very quickly when recording what someone is saying by using abbreviations and symbols.

short·list /'SHôrt,list/ ▶ **n.** a list of selected candidates from which a final choice is made. ▶ **v.** put on a shortlist.

short·ly /'SHôrtlē/ ▶ **adv.** **1** in a short time; soon. **2** abruptly or sharply.

> SYNONYMS **soon**, presently, momentarily, in a little while, at any moment, in a minute, in next to no time, before long, by and by; informal anon, any time now, in a sec, in a jiffy.

shorts /SHôrts/ ▶ **pl.n.** **1** short pants that reach to the thighs or knees. **2** underpants.

short·sight·ed /'SHôrt'sītid/ ▶ **adj.** lacking imagination or foresight.

short·stop /'SHôrt,stäp/ ▶ **n.** Baseball a fielder positioned between second and third base.

shot¹ /SHät/ ▶ **n.** **1** the firing of a gun, arrow, etc. **2** (in sports) a hit, stroke, throw, or kick of the ball as an attempt to score. **3** informal an attempt. **4** a photograph. **5** a movie sequence photographed continuously by one camera. **6** a person with a particular level of ability in shooting. **7** (also **lead shot**) tiny lead pellets used in a shotgun. **8** a heavy ball thrown in the sport of shot put. **9** the launch of a rocket. **10** informal a small drink of liquor. **11** informal an injection of a drug or vaccine.

> SYNONYMS **1 report**, crack, bang, blast; (**shots**) gunfire, firing. **2** *the winning shot* **stroke**, hit, strike, kick, throw. **3 marksman**, markswoman, shooter. **4 photograph**, photo, snap, snapshot, picture, print, slide, still.

□ **like a shot** informal without hesitation. **shot put** an athletic contest in which a very heavy ball is pushed through the air as far as possible.

shot² past and past participle of **SHOOT** ▶ **adj.** woven with a warp and weft of different colors, giving a contrasting effect.

shot·gun /'SHät,gən/ ▶ **n.** a gun for firing small pellets at short range.

should /SHŏŏd/ ▶ **modal v.** (3rd singular **should**) **1** used to indicate what is right or ought to be done. **2** used to indicate what is probable. **3** formal used to state what would happen if something else was the case: *if you should change your mind, I'll be at the hotel.* **4** used with *I* and *we* to express a polite request, opinion, or hope.

shoul·der /'SHōldər/ ▶ **n.** the joint between the upper arm and the main part of the body. ▶ **v.** (**shoulders**, **shouldering**, **shouldered**) **1** take on a responsibility. **2** push aside with your shoulder. **3** carry on your shoulder.

> SYNONYMS ▶ **v.** **1 take on (yourself)**, undertake, accept, assume, bear, carry. **2 push**, shove, thrust, jostle, force, bulldoze, bundle.

□ **shoulder arms** hold a rifle against the right side of the body, barrel upward. **shoulder blade** either of the triangular bones at the top of the back.

should·n't /'SHŏŏdnt/ ▶ **contr.** should not.

shout /SHout/ ▶ **v.** **1** speak or call out very loudly. **2** (**shout someone down**) prevent someone from being heard by shouting. ▶ **n.** a loud cry or call.

> SYNONYMS ▶ **v.** **yell**, cry (out), call (out), roar, howl, bellow, bawl, raise your voice; informal holler. ANTONYMS whisper. ▶ **n.** **yell**, cry, call, roar, howl, bellow, bawl; informal holler.

shove /SHəv/ ▶ v. (**shoves**, **shoving**, **shoved**) **1** push roughly. **2** place carelessly or roughly. **3** (**shove off**) informal go away. ▶ n. a strong push.

SYNONYMS ▶ v. **push**, thrust, propel, drive, force, ram, knock, elbow, shoulder, jostle.

shov·el /ˈSHəvəl/ ▶ n. a tool resembling a spade with a broad blade and upturned sides, used for moving dirt, snow, etc. ▶ v. (**shovels**, **shoveling**, **shoveled**) move dirt, snow, etc., with a shovel.

show /SHō/ ▶ v. (**shows**, **showing**, **showed**; past participle **shown** or **showed**) **1** be or make visible. **2** offer for inspection or viewing. **3** present an image of. **4** lead or guide. **5** behave in a particular way toward someone. **6** be evidence of; prove. **7** make someone understand something by explaining it or doing it yourself. **8** (also **show up**) informal arrive for an appointment. ▶ n. **1** a stage performance involving singing and dancing. **2** an entertainment program on television or radio. **3** an event or competition in which animals, plants, or products are displayed. **4** an impressive or pleasing sight. **5** a display of a quality or feeling. **6** a display intended to give a false impression.

SYNONYMS ▶ v. **1 be visible**, be seen, be in view, be obvious. **2 display**, exhibit, put on show, put on display, put on view. **3** *he showed his frustration* **manifest**, exhibit, reveal, convey, communicate, make known, express, make plain, make obvious, disclose, evince, betray. **4 demonstrate**, explain, describe, illustrate, teach, instruct. **5 prove**, demonstrate, confirm, substantiate, corroborate, verify, bear out. **6** *she showed them to their seats* **escort**, accompany, take, conduct, lead, usher, guide, direct. ANTONYMS conceal. ▶ n. **1 display**, array, sight, spectacle. **2 exhibition**, exhibit, display, fair, exposition, festival, parade. **3 program**, broadcast, presentation, production. **4 appearance**, outward appearance, image, pretense, (false) front, guise, pose, affectation, semblance.

□ **show someone around** point out interesting features in a place to someone. **show business** the world of theater, movies, television, and pop music as a profession or industry. **show someone the door** tell someone to leave or make them leave. **show your hand** reveal your plans. **show jumping** the competitive sport of riding horses over a course of obstacles in an arena. **show off** try to impress other people by talking about your abilities or possessions. **show something off** display something that you are proud of. **show-off** a person who tries to impress other people by showing off. **show trial** a public trial held to influence or please people, rather than to ensure that justice is done. **show someone/something up 1** reveal someone or something to be bad or at fault. **2** informal humiliate someone.

showbiz /ˈSHōˌbiz/ ▶ n. informal show business.

show·boat /ˈSHōˌbōt/ ▶ n. **1** a river steamboat on which theatrical performances are given. **2** informal a show-off; an exhibitionist. ▶ v. informal show off.

show·case /ˈSHōˌkās/ ▶ n. **1** an occasion for presenting someone or something to their best advantage. **2** a glass case used for displaying articles.

show·down /ˈSHōˌdoun/ ▶ n. a final argument, fight, or test, to settle a dispute.

SYNONYMS **confrontation**, clash, face-off.

show·er /ˈSHou(-ə)r/ ▶ n. **1** a short period of rain or snow. **2** a large number of things that fall or arrive together. **3** a device that creates a spray of water under which you stand to wash yourself. **4** an act of washing yourself in a shower. ▶ v. (**showers**, **showering**, **showered**) **1** fall or make things fall in a shower. **2** (**shower someone with**) give large quantities of something to someone. **3** wash yourself in a shower.

SYNONYMS ▶ n. **1 fall**, drizzle, sprinkling, flurry. **2 volley**, hail, salvo, barrage. ▶ v. **1 rain**, fall, hail. **2 deluge**, flood, inundate, swamp, overwhelm, snow under.

■ **show·er·y** adj.

show·girl /ˈSHōˌgərl/ ▶ n. an actress who sings and dances in a musical or variety show.

show·man·ship /ˈSHōmənˌSHip/ ▶ n. skill at entertaining people or getting attention.

shown /SHōn/ past participle of **SHOW**.

show·piece /ˈSHōˌpēs/ ▶ n. an outstanding example of something.

show·room /ˈSHōˌro͞om, -ˌro͝om/ ▶ n. a room used to display cars, furniture, or other goods for sale.

show·y /ˈSHō-ē/ ▶ adj. (**showier**, **showiest**) very bright or colorful and attracting a lot of attention.

SYNONYMS **ostentatious**, flamboyant, gaudy, garish, brash, vulgar, loud, fancy, ornate; informal flash, flashy. ANTONYMS restrained.

shrank /SHraNGk/ past of **SHRINK**.

shrap·nel /ˈSHrapnəl/ ▶ n. small metal fragments from an exploding shell or bomb.

shred /SHred/ ▶ n. **1** a strip of material that has been torn, cut, or scraped from something. **2** a very small amount. ▶ v. (**shreds**, **shredding**, **shredded**) tear or cut into shreds.

SYNONYMS ▶ n. **1 tatter**, ribbon, rag, fragment, sliver, snippet, remnant. **2 scrap**, bit, speck, particle, ounce, jot, crumb, fragment, grain, drop, trace. ▶ v. **grate**, cut up, tear up.

shred·der /ˈSHredər/ ▶ n. **1** a machine or other device for shredding something, especially documents. **2** informal a snowboarder.

shrew /SHro͞o/ ▶ n. **1** a small mouselike animal with a long, pointed snout. **2** a bad-tempered woman.

shrewd /SHro͞od/ ▶ adj. having or showing good judgment.

SYNONYMS **astute**, sharp, smart, intelligent, clever, canny, perceptive; informal on the ball. ANTONYMS stupid.

■ **shrewd·ly** adv. **shrewd·ness** n.

shrew·ish /ˈSHro͞oiSH/ ▶ adj. (of a woman) bad-tempered or nagging.

shriek /SHrēk/ ▶ v. make a piercing cry. ▶ n. a piercing cry.

SYNONYMS **scream**, screech, squeal, squawk, roar, howl, shout, yell, yelp; informal holler.

shrike /SHrīk/ ▶ n. a songbird with a strong hooked bill.

shrill /SHril/ ▶ adj. high-pitched and piercing. ▶ v. make a shrill noise.

SYNONYMS ▶ adj. **high-pitched**, piercing, high, sharp, ear-piercing, ear-splitting, penetrating.

■ **shril·ly** adv.

shrimp /SHrimp/ ▶ n. (plural **shrimp** or **shrimps**) a small edible shellfish.

shrine /SHrīn/ ▶ **n.** **1** a place connected with a holy person or event, where people go to pray. **2** a place containing a religious statue or object.

shrink /SHriNGk/ ▶ **v.** (**shrinks**, **shrinking**, **shrank** /SHraNGk/; past participle **shrunk** /SHrəNGk/ or (especially as adjective) **shrunken** /'SHrəNGkən/) **1** become or make smaller. **2** move back or away in fear or disgust. **3** (**shrink from**) be unwilling to do. ▶ **n.** informal a psychiatrist.

SYNONYMS ▶ **v.** **1** **get smaller**, contract, diminish, lessen, reduce, decrease, dwindle, decline, fall off. **2** **recoil**, shy away, flinch, be averse, be afraid, hesitate. ANTONYMS expand, increase.

□ **shrinking violet** informal a very shy person. **shrink-wrap** wrap in clinging plastic film.
■ **shrink·age** **n.**

shriv·el /'SHrivəl/ ▶ **v.** (**shrivels**, **shriveling**, **shriveled**) wrinkle and shrink through loss of moisture.

SYNONYMS **wither**, shrink, wilt, dry up, dehydrate, parch, frazzle.

shroud /SHroud/ ▶ **n.** **1** a length of cloth in which a dead person is wrapped for burial. **2** a thing that closely surrounds or hides something. **3** (**shrouds**) a set of ropes supporting the mast of a sailboat. ▶ **v.** **1** wrap in a shroud. **2** cover or hide.

SYNONYMS ▶ **n.** **covering**, cover, cloak, mantle, blanket, layer, cloud, veil, winding sheet. ▶ **v.** **cover**, envelop, veil, cloak, blanket, screen, conceal, hide, mask, obscure.

shrub /SHrəb/ ▶ **n.** a woody plant that is smaller than a tree and divided into separate stems from near the ground. ■ **shrub·by** **adj.**

shrub·ber·y /'SHrəb(ə)rē/ ▶ **n.** (plural **shrubberies**) an area planted with shrubs.

shrug /SHrəg/ ▶ **v.** (**shrugs**, **shrugging**, **shrugged**) **1** raise your shoulders slightly and briefly as a sign that you do not know or care about something. **2** (**shrug something off**) treat something as unimportant. ▶ **n.** an act of shrugging your shoulders.

shuck /SHək/ ▶ **v.** **1** remove the husks or shells from corn or shellfish. **2** informal get rid of something. ▶ **n.** **1** the husk of an ear of corn. **2** the shell of an oyster, scallop, or clam.

shucks /SHəks/ ▶ **exclam.** informal used to express surprise, regret, etc.

shud·der /'SHədər/ ▶ **v.** (**shudders**, **shuddering**, **shuddered**) tremble or shake violently. ▶ **n.** an act of shuddering.

SYNONYMS ▶ **v.** **shake**, shiver, tremble, quiver. ▶ **n.** **shake**, shiver, tremor, trembling, quivering, vibration.

shuf·fle /'SHəfəl/ ▶ **v.** (**shuffles**, **shuffling**, **shuffled**) **1** walk without lifting your feet completely from the ground. **2** move about restlessly while sitting or standing. **3** rearrange a deck of cards by sliding them over and under each other quickly. **4** rearrange people or things. ▶ **n.** an act of shuffling.

SYNONYMS ▶ **v.** **1** **shamble**, hobble, limp, drag your feet. **2** **mix** (**up**), rearrange, jumble (up), reorganize.

shun /SHən/ ▶ **v.** (**shuns**, **shunning**, **shunned**) avoid or reject.

SYNONYMS **avoid**, steer clear of, give a wide berth to, have nothing to do with; informal freeze out, give the cold shoulder to. ANTONYMS welcome.

shunt /SHənt/ ▶ **v.** **1** push or pull a railroad vehicle from one set of tracks to another. **2** move something around or along. **3** move someone to a less important position. ■ **shunt·er** **n.**

shut /SHət/ ▶ **v.** (**shuts**, **shutting**, **shut**) **1** move something into position to block an opening. **2** (**shut someone/thing in** or **out**) keep a person or animal in or out by closing a door, gate, etc. **3** prevent access to a place or along a route. **4** (with reference to a store or other business) stop operating for business. **5** close a book, curtains, etc.

SYNONYMS **close**, pull to, push to, slam, fasten, put the lid on, lock, secure. ANTONYMS open.

□ **shut down** stop opening for business, or stop operating. **shut-eye** informal sleep. **shut up** informal stop talking.

shut·ter /'SHətər/ ▶ **n.** **1** each of a pair of hinged panels inside or outside a window that can be closed for security or to keep out the light. **2** a device that opens and closes to expose the film in a camera. ▶ **v.** (**shutters**, **shuttering**, **shuttered**) close the shutters of a window or building.

shut·tle /'SHətl/ ▶ **n.** **1** a form of transport that travels regularly between two places. **2** (in weaving) a bobbin for carrying the weft thread across the warp. ▶ **v.** (**shuttles**, **shuttling**, **shuttled**) **1** travel regularly between places. **2** transport in a shuttle.

SYNONYMS ▶ **v.** **commute**, run, ply, go/travel back and forth, ferry.

shut·tle·cock /'SHətlˌkäk/ ▶ **n.** a light cone-shaped object that is struck with rackets in the game of badminton.

shy¹ /SHī/ ▶ **adj.** (**shyer**, **shyest**) nervous about meeting or talking to other people. ▶ **v.** (**shies**, **shying**, **shied**) **1** (of a horse) turn aside in fright. **2** (**shy away from**) avoid doing something through lack of confidence.

SYNONYMS ▶ **adj.** **bashful**, diffident, timid, reserved, introverted, retiring, self-effacing, withdrawn. ANTONYMS confident.

■ **shy·ly** **adv.**

shy² ▶ **v.** (**shies**, **shying**, **shied**) throw something at a target.

shy·ster /'SHīstər/ ▶ **n.** informal a dishonest person, especially a lawyer.

SI ▶ **abbr.** Système International, the international system of units of measurement.

Si·a·mese /ˌsīə'mēz/ ▶ **adj.** relating to Siam (the old name for Thailand). □ **Siamese cat** a breed of cat that has short pale fur with darker face, ears, feet, and tail. **Siamese twins** twins whose bodies are joined at birth.

sib·i·lant /'sibələnt/ ▶ **adj.** making a hissing sound. ■ **sib·i·lance** **n.**

sib·ling /'sibliNG/ ▶ **n.** a brother or sister.

sib·yl /'sibəl/ ▶ **n.** (in ancient Greece and Rome) a woman supposedly able to pass on messages from a god. ■ **sib·yl·line** /'sibəˌlīn, -ˌlēn/ **adj.**

sic /sik/ ▶ **adv.** (after a copied word that seems odd or wrong) written exactly as it stands in the original.

sick /sik/ ▶ **adj.** **1** physically or mentally ill. **2** wanting to vomit. **3** (**sick of**) bored by or annoyed about. **4** informal behaving in an abnormal or cruel way. **5** informal (of humor) dealing with unpleasant subjects in a way that is offensive.

SYNONYMS **1 ill**, unwell, poorly, ailing, indisposed, out of sorts; informal under the weather, laid up. **2 nauseous**, queasy, bilious, green around the gills. **3** *I'm sick of this music* **fed up with**, bored with, tired of, weary of. **4 macabre**, tasteless, ghoulish, morbid, black, gruesome, perverted, cruel. ANTONYMS well.

□ **be sick 1** be ill. **2** vomit.

sick·bay /'sik,bā/ ▶ **n.** a room set aside for sick people, especially within a military base or on board a ship.

sick·bed /'sik,bed/ ▶ **n.** the bed of a person who is ill.

sick·en /'sikən/ ▶ **v. 1** disgust or shock. **2** start to develop an illness.

SYNONYMS **1 nauseate**, make sick, turn someone's stomach, disgust, revolt, repel, appall; informal gross out. **2** (**sickening**) **nauseating**, stomach-turning, repulsive, revolting, disgusting, offensive, off-putting, distasteful, obscene, gruesome, grisly; informal gross. **3 fall ill**, become infected, be stricken.

sick·le /'sikəl/ ▶ **n.** a tool for cutting grain, with a semicircular blade and a short handle.

sick·ly /'siklē/ ▶ **adj.** (**sicklier**, **sickliest**) **1** often ill. **2** looking or seeming unhealthy. **3** (of flavor, color, etc.) so bright or sweet as to cause sickness.

SYNONYMS **1 unhealthy**, in poor health, delicate, frail, weak. **2 pale**, wan, pasty, sallow, pallid, ashen, anemic. **3 sentimental**, mawkish, cloying, sugary, syrupy, saccharine; informal sappy, schmaltzy, cheesy, corny. ANTONYMS healthy.

sick·ness /'siknis/ ▶ **n. 1** the state of being ill. **2** a particular type of illness or disease. **3** nausea or vomiting.

SYNONYMS **1 illness**, disease, ailment, infection, malady, infirmity; informal bug, virus. **2 nausea**, biliousness, queasiness, vomiting, retching; informal throwing up, puking.

sick·o /'sikō/ ▶ **n.** (plural **sickos**) informal a perverted or disturbed person.

side /sīd/ ▶ **n. 1** a position to the left or right of an object, place, or central point. **2** either of the two halves into which something can be divided. **3** an upright or sloping surface of something that is not the top, bottom, front, or back. **4** each of the flat surfaces of a solid object, or either of the two surfaces of something flat and thin, e.g., paper. **5** either of the two surfaces of a record or the corresponding parts of a cassette tape. **6** a part near the edge of something. **7** a person or group opposing another in a dispute or contest. **8** a sports team. **9** a particular aspect. **10** Geometry each of the lines forming the boundary of a plane figure. ▶ **adj.** additional or less important. ▶ **v.** (**sides**, **siding**, **sided**) (**side with** or **against**) support or oppose in a conflict or dispute.

SYNONYMS ▶ **n. 1 edge**, border, verge, boundary, margin, rim, fringe(s), flank, bank, perimeter, extremity, periphery, limit(s). **2 district**, quarter, area, region, part, neighborhood, sector, zone. **3 surface**, face. **4 point of view**, viewpoint, perspective, opinion, standpoint, position, outlook, slant, angle, aspect, facet. **5 faction**, camp, bloc, party, wing. **6 team**, squad, lineup. ANTONYMS center, end. ▶ **adj. 1 lateral**, wing, flanking. **2 subordinate**, secondary, minor, peripheral, incidental, subsidiary. ANTONYMS front, central.

□ **side effect** a secondary effect of a drug. **side** (or **side-view**) **mirror** a mirror projecting from the side of a vehicle, giving the driver a view of the road behind. **side road** (or **street**) a minor road. **take sides** support one person or cause against another.

side·board /'sīd,bôrd/ ▶ **n.** a piece of furniture with cupboards and drawers, used for storing dishes, glasses, etc.

side·burns /'sīd,bərnz/ ▶ **pl.n.** a strip of hair growing down each side of a man's face in front of his ears.

side·car /'sīd,kär/ ▶ **n.** a small, low vehicle attached to the side of a motorcycle for carrying passengers.

side·kick /'sīd,kik/ ▶ **n.** informal a person's assistant.

side·line /'sīd,līn/ ▶ **n. 1** something you do in addition to your main job. **2** either of the two lines along the longer sides of a sports field or court. **3** (**the sidelines**) a position of watching a situation rather than being directly involved in it. ▶ **v.** (**sidelines**, **sidelining**, **sidelined**) remove from a team, game, or influential position.

side·long /'sīd,lôNG/ ▶ **adj. & adv.** to or from one side; sideways.

si·de·re·al /sī'di(ə)rēəl/ ▶ **adj.** relating to the distant stars or their apparent positions in the sky.

side·sad·dle /'sīd,sadl/ ▶ **n.** a saddle in which the rider has both feet on the same side of the horse. It is typically used by a woman rider wearing a skirt. ▶ **adv.** (of a rider) sitting with both feet on the same side of the horse.

side·show /'sīd,SHō/ ▶ **n.** a small show or stall at an exhibition, fair, or circus.

side·step /'sīd,step/ ▶ **v.** (**sidesteps**, **sidestepping**, **sidestepped**) **1** avoid dealing with a difficult issue. **2** avoid someone or something by stepping sideways.

side·swipe /'sīd,swīp/ ▶ **n. 1** a glancing blow from or on the side of something, especially a motor vehicle. **2** a critical or harsh remark made while discussing another matter.

side·track /'sīd,trak/ ▶ **v.** distract someone from the main issues of what they are discussing or doing.

SYNONYMS **distract**, divert, deflect, draw away.

side·walk /'sīd,wôk/ ▶ **n.** a raised paved or asphalted path for pedestrians at the side of a road.

side·ways /'sīd,wāz/ ▶ **adv. & adj.** to, toward, or from the side.

SYNONYMS **1 to the side**, laterally. **2 edgewise**, edgeways, side first, end on. **3 lateral**, sideward, on the side, side to side. **4 indirect**, oblique, sidelong, surreptitious, furtive, covert, sly.

sid·ing /'sīdiNG/ ▶ **n.** a short track beside a main railroad line, where trains are left.

si·dle /'sīdl/ ▶ **v.** (**sidles**, **sidling**, **sidled**) walk in a secretive or timid way.

siege /sēj/ ▶ n. **1** a military operation in which forces surround a town and cut off its supplies. **2** a similar operation by a police team to force an armed person to surrender.

SPELLING

Remember, **i** before **e** in both **siege** and **sieve**.

si·en·na /sē'enə/ ▶ n. a kind of earth used as a brown coloring in painting.

si·es·ta /sē'estə/ ▶ n. an afternoon rest or nap.

sieve /siv/ ▶ n. a piece of mesh held in a frame, used for straining solids from liquids or separating coarser from finer particles. ▶ v. (**sieves, sieving, sieved**) put a substance through a sieve.

sift /sift/ ▶ v. **1** put a substance through a sieve. **2** examine something thoroughly to sort out what is important or useful.

SYNONYMS **1 sieve**, strain, screen, filter. **2** *we sift out unsuitable applications* **separate out**, filter out, sort out, weed out, get rid of, remove. **3** *sifting through the data* **search**, look, examine, inspect, scrutinize.

sigh /sī/ ▶ v. let out a long, deep breath expressing sadness, relief, etc. ▶ n. such a breath.

SYNONYMS ▶ v. **1 breathe (out)**, exhale, groan, moan. **2 rustle**, whisper, murmur.

sight /sīt/ ▶ n. **1** the ability to see. **2** the act of seeing something. **3** the area or distance within that you can see something. **4** a thing that you see. **5** (**sights**) places of interest to tourists. **6** (**a sight**) informal a person or thing that looks ridiculous or unattractive. **7** (also **sights**) a device that you look through to aim a gun or see with a telescope. ▶ v. see or glimpse.

SYNONYMS ▶ n. **1 eyesight**, vision, eyes. **2 view**, glimpse, glance, look. **3 landmark**, place of interest, monument, spectacle, marvel, wonder. ▶ v. **glimpse**, catch sight of, see, spot, spy, make out, pick out, notice, observe.

□ **catch sight of** glimpse. **in** (or **out of**) **sight** able (or not able) to be seen. **in** (or **within**) **sight of 1** so as to see or be seen from. **2** close to gaining. **lose sight of 1** be no longer able to see. **2** fail to consider or be aware of. **on** (or **at**) **sight** as soon as someone or something has been seen. **raise** (or **lower**) **your sights** increase (or lower) your expectations. **set your sights on** have something as an ambition. **sight-read** read a musical score and play it without preparation.

USAGE

Don't confuse **sight** with **site**, which means 'a place where something is located or happens.'

sight·ed /'sītid/ ▶ adj. **1** having the ability to see; not blind. **2** having a particular kind of sight.

sight·less /'sītlis/ ▶ adj. blind.

sight·see·ing /'sīt,sēiNG/ ▶ n. the activity of visiting places of interest. ■ **sight·se·er** n.

sign /sīn/ ▶ n. **1** an indication that something exists, is happening, or may happen. **2** a signal, gesture, or notice giving information or an instruction. **3** a symbol used to represent something in algebra, music, or other subjects. **4** each of the twelve divisions of the zodiac. ▶ v. **1** write your name on something to show that you have written it, or to authorize it. **2** recruit an athlete, musician, etc., by signing a contract. **3** use gestures to give information or instructions.

SYNONYMS ▶ n. **1 indication**, signal, symptom, pointer, suggestion, intimation, mark, manifestation, demonstration, token. **2 warning**, omen, portent, threat, promise. **3 notice**, board, placard, signpost. **4 symbol**, figure, emblem, device, logo, character. ▶ v. **1 write your name on/to**, autograph, initial, countersign. **2 endorse**, validate, agree to, approve, ratify, adopt. **3 write**, inscribe, pen.

□ **sign language** a system of hand movements and facial expressions used to communicate with people who are deaf. **sign off** end a letter, broadcast, or other message. **sign on** commit yourself to a job. **sign someone on** employ someone. **sign up** commit yourself to a course, job, etc. ■ **sign·er** n.

sig·nal /'signəl/ ▶ n. **1** a gesture, action, or sound giving information or an instruction. **2** a sign indicating a particular situation. **3** a device that uses lights or a movable arm to tell drivers to stop or beware on a road or railroad. **4** an electrical impulse or radio wave that is sent or received. ▶ v. (**signals, signaling, signaled**) give a signal. ▶ adj. noteworthy.

SYNONYMS ▶ n. **1 gesture**, gesticulation, sign, wave, cue, indication, warning, prompt, reminder. **2 indication**, sign, symptom, hint, pointer, clue, demonstration, evidence, proof. ▶ v. **1 gesture**, gesticulate, sign, indicate, motion, wave, beckon, nod. **2** *his death signals the end of an era* **mark**, signify, mean, indicate, be a sign of, be evidence of.

sig·na·to·ry /'signə,tôrē/ ▶ n. (plural **signatories**) a person who has signed an agreement.

sig·na·ture /'signəCHər, -,CHo͝or/ ▶ n. **1** a person's name written in a distinctive way, used in signing something. **2** a distinctive product or quality by which someone or something can be recognized. □ **signature tune** a tune announcing a particular television or radio program.

sig·net /'signit/ ▶ n. (in the past) a small seal used to authorize an official document. □ **signet ring** a ring with letters or a design set into it.

sig·nif·i·cance /sig'nifikəns/ ▶ n. **1** importance. **2** the meaning of something.

SYNONYMS **importance**, import, consequence, seriousness, gravity, weight, magnitude.

sig·nif·i·cant /sig'nifikənt/ ▶ adj. **1** important or large enough to have an effect or be noticed. **2** having a particular or secret meaning.

SYNONYMS **1 notable**, noteworthy, remarkable, important, of consequence, momentous. **2 large**, considerable, sizable, appreciable, conspicuous, obvious, sudden. **3 meaningful**, expressive, eloquent, suggestive, knowing, telling.

■ **sig·nif·i·cant·ly** adv.

sig·ni·fy /'signə,fī/ ▶ v. (**signifies, signifying, signified**) **1** be a sign of; mean. **2** make a feeling or intention known.

SYNONYMS **mean**, denote, designate, represent, symbolize, stand for.

■ **sig·ni·fi·ca·tion** /,signəfi'kāSHən/ n.

sign·ing /'sīniNG/ ▶ n. **1** an event at which an author signs copies of their book. **2** the use of sign language.

sign·post /ˈsīnˌpōst/ ▶ n. a sign on a post, giving information such as the direction and distance to a nearby place.

Sikh /sēk/ ▶ n. a follower of a religion that developed from Hinduism. ■ **Sikh·ism** n.

si·lage /ˈsīlij/ ▶ n. grass or other green crops that are stored in a silo without being dried, used as animal feed in the winter.

si·lence /ˈsīləns/ ▶ n. **1** complete lack of sound. **2** a situation in which someone is unwilling to speak or discuss something. ▶ v. (**silences, silencing, silenced**) **1** stop someone from speaking. **2** make something silent.

> SYNONYMS ▶ n. **1 quietness**, quiet, still, stillness, hush, tranquillity, peace, peacefulness. **2 failure to speak**, dumbness, muteness, reticence, taciturnity. ANTONYMS noise, loquacity. ▶ v. **1 quiet**, hush, still, muffle, quieten. **2 gag**, muzzle, censor.

si·lenc·er /ˈsīlənsər/ ▶ n. a device for reducing the noise made by a gun or exhaust system.

si·lent /ˈsīlənt/ ▶ adj. **1** without any sound. **2** not speaking or not spoken aloud.

> SYNONYMS **1 quiet**, still, hushed, noiseless, soundless, inaudible. **2 speechless**, quiet, unspeaking, dumb, mute, taciturn, uncommunicative, tight-lipped. **3 unspoken**, wordless, tacit, unvoiced, unexpressed, implied, implicit, understood. ANTONYMS audible, loquacious.

■ **si·lent·ly** adv.

sil·hou·ette /ˌsilo͞oˈet/ ▶ n. a dark shape and outline seen against a lighter background. ▶ v. (**silhouettes, silhouetting, silhouetted**) show as a silhouette.

> SYNONYMS ▶ n. **outline**, contour(s), profile, form, shape. ▶ v. **outline**, define.

sil·i·ca /ˈsilikə/ ▶ n. a hard substance formed from silicon and oxygen that occurs as quartz and is found in sandstone and other rocks.

sil·i·con /ˈsiləˌkän, -kən/ ▶ n. a chemical element that is a semiconductor and is used to make electronic circuits. □ **silicon chip** a microchip.

sil·i·cone /ˈsiləˌkōn/ ▶ n. a synthetic substance made from silicon.

silk /silk/ ▶ n. a fine, soft shiny fiber produced by silkworms, made into thread or fabric.

silk·en /ˈsilkən/ ▶ adj. **1** smooth and shiny like silk. **2** made of silk.

silk·worm /ˈsilkˌwərm/ ▶ n. a caterpillar that spins a silk cocoon from which silk fiber is obtained.

silk·y /ˈsilkē/ ▶ adj. (**silkier, silkiest**) smooth and shiny like silk.

sill /sil/ ▶ n. a shelf or slab at the foot of a window or doorway.

sil·ly /ˈsilē/ ▶ adj. (**sillier, silliest**) showing a lack of good judgment or common sense.

> SYNONYMS **1 foolish**, stupid, inane, featherbrained, birdbrained, frivolous, immature, childish, empty-headed, scatterbrained; informal dotty, scatty. **2 unwise**, imprudent, thoughtless, foolish, stupid, unintelligent, rash, reckless, foolhardy, irresponsible, harebrained; informal crazy, balmy, daft. **3** *he brooded about silly things* **trivial**, trifling, petty, small, insignificant, unimportant. ANTONYMS sensible.

■ **sil·li·ness** n.

si·lo /ˈsīlō/ ▶ n. (plural **silos**) **1** a tower used to store grain. **2** a pit or airtight structure for storing silage. **3** an underground chamber in which a guided missile is kept ready for firing.

silt /silt/ ▶ n. fine sand or clay carried by running water and deposited as a sediment. ▶ v. (**silt up**) fill or block with silt. ■ **silt·y** adj.

sil·ver /ˈsilvər/ ▶ n. **1** a shiny grayish-white precious metal. **2** a shiny grayish-white color. **3** coins made from silver or a metal that looks like silver. **4** silver dishes, containers, or cutlery. ▶ v. (**silvers, silvering, silvered**) cover or plate with silver. □ **silver birch** a birch tree with silver-gray bark. **silver jubilee** the twenty-fifth anniversary of an important event. **silver medal** a medal awarded for second place in a race or competition. **silver plate 1** a thin layer of silver applied as a coating to another metal. **2** plates, dishes, etc., made of or plated with silver. **silver wedding** (or **silver wedding anniversary**) the twenty-fifth anniversary of a wedding.

sil·ver·fish /ˈsilvərˌfisH/ ▶ n. (plural **silverfish**) a small silvery wingless insect that lives in buildings.

sil·ver·smith /ˈsilvərˌsmiTH/ ▶ n. a person who makes silver articles.

sil·ver·ware /ˈsilvərˌwer/ ▶ n. **1** dishes, containers, or cutlery made of or coated with silver. **2** eating and serving utensils made of any material.

sil·ver·y /ˈsilvərē/ ▶ adj. **1** like silver in color or appearance. **2** (of a sound) gentle, clear, and melodious: *a little silvery laugh.* ■ **sil·ver·i·ness** n.

SIM card /sim/ ▶ n. a small card inside a cell phone that stores information such as details of calls made and received.

sim·i·an /ˈsimēən/ ▶ adj. relating to or like apes or monkeys. ▶ n. an ape or monkey.

sim·i·lar /ˈsimələr/ ▶ adj. like something but not exactly the same.

> SYNONYMS **alike**, like, much the same, comparable, corresponding, equivalent, parallel, analogous, kindred. ANTONYMS different, dissimilar.

sim·i·lar·i·ty /ˌsiməˈlaritē/ ▶ n. (plural **similarities**) **1** the state or fact of being similar. **2** (usu. **similarities**) a similar feature or aspect.

> SYNONYMS **resemblance**, likeness, comparability, correspondence, parallel, equivalence, uniformity.

sim·i·lar·ly /ˈsimələrlē/ ▶ adv. in a similar way: *the two vases are similarly flawed at the base.*

> SYNONYMS **likewise**, comparably, correspondingly, in the same way, by the same token.

sim·i·le /ˈsiməlē/ ▶ n. a word or phrase that compares one thing to another of a different kind (e.g., *the family was as solid as a rock*).

sim·mer /ˈsimər/ ▶ v. (**simmers, simmering, simmered**) **1** stay or cause to stay just below boiling point. **2** be in a state of anger or excitement that you only just keep under control. **3** (**simmer down**) become calmer and quieter.

> SYNONYMS **1 boil gently**, cook gently, bubble, stew, poach. **2 seethe**, fume, smolder.

sim·per /ˈsimpər/ ▶ v. (**simpers, simpering, simpered**) smile in a coy and silly way. ▶ n. a coy and silly smile.

sim·ple /'simpəl/ ▶ **adj.** (**simpler**, **simplest**) **1** easily understood or done. **2** plain and basic. **3** composed of a single element; not compound. **4** of very low intelligence.

> SYNONYMS **1 straightforward**, easy, uncomplicated, uninvolved, undemanding, elementary; informal child's play, a cinch, a piece of cake, like falling off a log. **2 clear**, plain, lucid, straightforward, unambiguous, understandable, comprehensible, accessible; informal user-friendly. **3 plain**, unadorned, basic, unsophisticated, no-frills, classic, understated, uncluttered, restrained. **4 unpretentious**, unsophisticated, ordinary, unaffected, unassuming, natural, straightforward. ANTONYMS difficult, complex, ornate.

□ **simple fracture** a fracture of a bone without any breaking of the skin.

sim·ple·ton /'simpəltən/ ▶ **n.** a foolish or unintelligent person.

sim·plic·i·ty /sim'plisitē/ ▶ **n.** the quality of being simple.

> SYNONYMS **1 straightforwardness**, ease. **2 clarity**, plainness, lucidity, intelligibility, comprehensibility, accessibility. **3 austerity**, plainness, spareness, clean lines. **4 plainness**, modesty, naturalness. ANTONYMS complexity.

sim·pli·fy /'simplə,fī/ ▶ **v.** (**simplifies**, **simplifying**, **simplified**) make easier to do or understand.

> SYNONYMS **make simpler**, clarify, put into words of one syllable, streamline; informal dumb down. ANTONYMS complicate.

■ **sim·pli·fi·ca·tion** /,simpləfi'kāsHən/ **n.**

sim·plis·tic /sim'plistik/ ▶ **adj.** treating complex issues as more simple than they really are. ■ **sim·plis·ti·cal·ly adv.**

sim·ply /'simplē/ ▶ **adv.** **1** in a simple way. **2** just; merely. **3** absolutely.

> SYNONYMS **1 straightforwardly**, directly, clearly, plainly, intelligibly, lucidly, unambiguously. **2 plainly**, soberly, unfussily, without clutter, classically. **3 merely**, just, purely, solely, only.

sim·u·la·crum /,simyə'lākrəm, -'lak-/ ▶ **n.** (plural **simulacra** /-krə/ or **simulacrums**) something that is similar to something else.

sim·u·late /'simyə,lāt/ ▶ **v.** (**simulates**, **simulating**, **simulated**) **1** imitate the appearance or nature of. **2** use a computer to create a model of something or conditions that are like those in real life. **3** pretend to have or feel a particular emotion.

> SYNONYMS **1 feign**, pretend, fake, affect, put on. **2 replicate**, reproduce, imitate, mimic.

■ **sim·u·la·tion** /,simyə'lāsHən/ **n.** **sim·u·la·tor n.**

si·mul·ta·ne·ous /,sīməl'tānēəs/ ▶ **adj.** happening or done at the same time.

> SYNONYMS **concurrent**, happening at the same time, contemporaneous, coinciding, coincident, synchronized. ANTONYMS separate.

■ **si·mul·ta·ne·i·ty** /,sīməltə'nēitē/ **n.**

> SPELLING
> The ending is **-eous**, not **-ious**: simultan**eous**.

si·mul·ta·ne·ous·ly /,sīməl'tānēəslē/ ▶ **adv.** at the same time: *Alison and Frank spoke simultaneously.*

> SYNONYMS **at the same time**, at one and the same time, at once, concurrently, (all) together, in unison, in concert, in chorus.

sin /sin/ ▶ **n.** **1** an act that breaks a religious or moral law. **2** an act that causes strong disapproval. ▶ **v.** (**sins**, **sinning**, **sinned**) commit a sin.

> SYNONYMS ▶ **n.** **1 wrong**, act of wickedness, transgression, crime, offense, misdeed; old use trespass. **2 wickedness**, wrongdoing, evil, immorality, iniquity, vice, crime. ANTONYMS virtue. ▶ **v.** **transgress**, do wrong, misbehave, err, go astray; old use trespass.

since /sins/ ▶ **prep.** in the period between a time in the past and the present. ▶ **conj.** **1** during or in the time after. **2** because. ▶ **adv.** **1** from the time mentioned until the present. **2** ago.

sin·cere /sin'si(ə)r/ ▶ **adj.** (**sincerer**, **sincerest**) not pretending anything or deceiving anyone; genuine and honest.

> SYNONYMS **1 heartfelt**, wholehearted, profound, deep, true, honest, earnest, fervent. **2 honest**, genuine, truthful, direct, frank, candid; informal straight, on the level, upfront, on the up and up.

sin·cere·ly /sin'si(ə)rlē/ ▶ **adv.** **1** in a sincere or genuine way. **2** (also **sincerely yours** or **yours sincerely**) a way of ending a formal letter.

> SYNONYMS **genuinely**, honestly, really, truly, truthfully, wholeheartedly, earnestly.

sin·cer·i·ty /sin'seritē/ ▶ **n.** the quality of being genuine and truthful: *there's no reason to doubt her sincerity.*

> SYNONYMS **genuineness**, honesty, truthfulness, integrity, directness, openness, candor.

sine /sīn/ ▶ **n.** Math (in a right triangle) the ratio of the side opposite a particular acute angle to the hypotenuse.

si·ne·cure /'sīnə,kyo͝or, 'si-/ ▶ **n.** a job for which you are paid but which requires little or no work.

si·ne qua non /,sini ,kwä 'nōn, ,sini ,kwä 'nän/ ▶ **n.** a thing that is absolutely necessary.

sin·ew /'sinyo͞o/ ▶ **n.** a band of strong tissue that joins a muscle to a bone. ■ **sin·ew·y adj.**

sin·ful /'sinfəl/ ▶ **adj.** **1** wicked. **2** disgraceful.

> SYNONYMS **immoral**, wicked, (morally) wrong, evil, bad, iniquitous, ungodly, irreligious, sacrilegious. ANTONYMS virtuous.

■ **sin·ful·ly adv.** **sin·ful·ness n.**

sing /siNG/ ▶ **v.** (**sings**, **singing**, **sang** /saNG/; past participle **sung** /səNG/) **1** make musical sounds with your voice; perform a song. **2** make a whistling sound.

> SYNONYMS **1 chant**, trill, intone, croon, chorus. **2 trill**, warble, chirp, cheep.

sing·a·long /'siNGə,lôNG, 'siNGə,läNG/ ▶ **n.** an informal occasion when people sing together.

singe /sinj/ ▶ **v.** (**singes**, **singeing**, **singed**) burn the surface of something slightly. ▶ **n.** a slight burn.

> SYNONYMS ▶ **v.** **scorch**, burn, sear, char.

sing·er /'siNGgər/ ▶ **n.** a person who sings, especially professionally.

> SYNONYMS **vocalist**, songster, songstress, soloist, chorister, cantor.

sin·gle /ˈsiNGgəl/ ▶ **adj. 1** one only. **2** designed for one person. **3** consisting of one part. **4** taken separately from others. **5** not involved in a romantic relationship. ▶ **n. 1** a single person or thing. **2** a short record or CD, typically featuring only one song. **3** (**singles**) a game or competition for individual players. ▶ **v.** (**singles, singling, singled**) (**single someone/thing out**) choose someone or something from a group for special treatment.

SYNONYMS ▶ **adj. 1 sole**, one, lone, solitary, unaccompanied, alone. **2 individual**, separate, particular, distinct. **3 unmarried**, unwed, unattached, free. ANTONYMS double, multiple.

□ **single-breasted** (of a jacket or coat) fastened by one row of buttons at the center of the front. **single file** a line of people moving one behind another. **single-handed** done without help from other people. **single-minded** determined to concentrate on one particular aim. **single parent** a person bringing up a child or children without a partner.

sin·gle·ton /ˈsiNGgəltən/ ▶ **n.** a single person or thing.

sin·gly /ˈsiNGglē/ ▶ **adv.** one by one: *people, please enter singly into the hallway.*

SYNONYMS **one by one**, one at a time, one after the other, individually, separately. ANTONYMS together.

sing·song /ˈsiNG,sôNG/ ▶ **adj.** (of a person's voice) having a repeated rising and falling rhythm. ▶ **n.** a singsong way of speaking. ▶ **v.** (**singsongs, singsonging, singsonged**) speak or recite something in a singsong manner.

sin·gu·lar /ˈsiNGgyələr/ ▶ **adj. 1** Grammar (of a word or form) referring to just one person or thing. **2** very good or interesting; remarkable. ▶ **n.** Grammar the singular form of a word.

SYNONYMS ▶ **adj. remarkable**, extraordinary, exceptional, outstanding, signal, notable, noteworthy.

■ **sin·gu·lar·i·ty** /,siNGgyəˈlaritē/ **n. sin·gu·lar·ly adv.**

sin·is·ter /ˈsinistər/ ▶ **adj.** seeming evil or dangerous.

SYNONYMS **1 menacing**, threatening, forbidding, baleful, frightening, alarming, disturbing, ominous. **2 evil**, wicked, criminal, nefarious, villainous; informal shady. ANTONYMS innocent.

sink /siNGk/ ▶ **v.** (**sinks, sinking, sank** /saNGk/; past participle **sunk** /səNGk/) **1** go down below the surface of liquid. **2** go or cause to go to the bottom of the sea. **3** move slowly downward. **4** gradually decrease in amount or strength. **5** (**sink something into**) force something sharp through a surface. **6** (**sink in**) become fully understood. **7** pass into a particular state. **8** (**sink something into**) put money or resources into. ▶ **n.** a fixed basin with a water supply and a drainage pipe.

SYNONYMS ▶ **v. 1 submerge**, founder, capsize, go down, be engulfed. **2 scuttle**. **3 fall**, drop, descend, plunge, plummet, slump. **4 embed**, insert, drive, plant. ANTONYMS float, rise.

sink·er /ˈsiNGkər/ ▶ **n.** a weight used to keep a fishing line beneath the water.

sin·ner /ˈsinər/ ▶ **n.** a person who sins.

SYNONYMS **wrongdoer**, evildoer, transgressor, miscreant, offender, criminal; old use trespasser.

sin·u·ous /ˈsinyo͞oəs/ ▶ **adj. 1** having many curves and turns. **2** moving in a graceful, swaying way.

SYNONYMS **1** *a sinuous river* **winding**, windy, serpentine, curving, twisting, meandering, snaking, zigzag, curling, coiling. **2** *sinuous grace* **lithe**, supple, graceful, loose-limbed, lissome. ANTONYMS straight, awkward.

■ **sin·u·ous·ly adv.**

si·nus /ˈsīnəs/ ▶ **n.** a hollow space within the bones of the face that connects with the nostrils.

si·nus·i·tis /,sīn(y)əˈsītis/ ▶ **n.** inflammation of a sinus.

Sioux /so͞o/ ▶ **n.** (plural **Sioux**) a member of a North American Indian people living in the northern Mississippi valley area.

sip /sip/ ▶ **v.** (**sips, sipping, sipped**) drink something in small mouthfuls. ▶ **n.** a small mouthful of liquid.

SYNONYMS ▶ **v. drink**, taste, sample, nip. ▶ **n. mouthful**, swallow, drink, drop, dram, nip; informal swig.

si·phon /ˈsīfən/ (or **syphon**) ▶ **n.** a tube used to move liquid from one container to another, using air pressure to maintain the flow. ▶ **v. 1** draw off or move liquid by means of a siphon. **2** (**siphon something off**) take small amounts of money over a period of time.

sir /sər/ ▶ **n. 1** a polite form of address to a man. **2** used as a title for a knight or baronet.

sire /sīr/ ▶ **n. 1** the male parent of an animal. **2** literary a father. **3** old use a respectful form of address to a king. ▶ **v.** (**sires, siring, sired**) be the male parent of.

si·ren /ˈsīrən/ ▶ **n. 1** a device that makes a loud prolonged warning sound. **2** Greek Mythology each of a group of creatures who were part woman, part bird, whose singing lured sailors on to rocks. **3** a woman whose attractiveness is regarded as dangerous to men.

sir·loin /ˈsərloin/ ▶ **n.** the best part of a loin of beef.

si·sal /ˈsisəl, ˈsī-/ ▶ **n.** fiber made from the leaves of a tropical Mexican plant, used for ropes or matting.

sis·sy /ˈsisē/ ▶ **n.** (plural **sissies**) informal a weak or cowardly person.

sis·ter /ˈsistər/ ▶ **n. 1** a woman or girl in relation to other children of her parents. **2** a female friend or colleague. **3** a member of a religious order of women. □ **sister-in-law** (plural **sisters-in-law**) **1** the sister of a person's wife or husband. **2** the wife of a person's brother or brother-in-law. ■ **sis·ter·ly adj.**

sis·ter·hood /ˈsistər,ho͝od/ ▶ **n. 1** the relationship between sisters. **2** a bond of friendship and understanding between women. **3** a group of women linked by a shared interest.

sit /sit/ ▶ **v.** (**sits, sitting, sat**) **1** rest your weight on your bottom with your back upright. **2** be in a particular position or state. **3** serve as a member of a council, jury, or other official body. **4** (of a legislature, parliament, committee, or court of law) be carrying on its business. **5** (**sit for**) pose for an artist or photographer.

SYNONYMS **1 take a seat**, sit down, be seated, perch, ensconce yourself, flop; informal take a load off (your feet). **2 be placed**, be positioned, be situated, be set, rest, stand, perch. **3 be in session**, meet, be convened. **4** *she sits on the* *tribunal* **serve on**, have a seat on, be a member of. ANTONYMS stand.

□ **sit-in** the occupation of a college or workplace as a form of protest. **sit on** informal fail to deal with. **sit out** not take part in. **sit tight** informal hold back from taking action or changing your mind. **sit-up** an exercise designed to strengthen the abdominal muscles, in which a person sits up from a horizontal position without using their arms.

si·tar /si'tär/ ▶ n. an Indian lute with a long neck.

sit·com /'sit,käm/ ▶ n. a situation comedy.

site /sīt/ ▶ n. **1** a place where something is located or happens. **2** a website. ▶ v. (**sites**, **siting**, **sited**) build or establish something in a particular place.

SYNONYMS ▶ n. **location**, place, position, situation, locality, whereabouts. ▶ v. **place**, put, position, situate, locate.

USAGE

Don't confuse **site** with **sight**, which means 'the ability to see.'

Sit·ka /'sitkə/ ▶ n. a fast-growing spruce tree, grown for its strong lightweight wood.

sit·rep /'sit,rep/ ▶ n. informal a report on the current military situation in a particular area.

sit·ter /'sitər/ ▶ n. **1** a person who sits for a portrait. **2** a person who looks after children, pets, or a house while the parents or owners are away.

sit·ting /'sitiNG/ ▶ n. **1** a period of time when a group of people are served a meal. **2** a period of posing for a portrait. **3** a period of time during which a committee or legislature is carrying on its business. □ **sitting duck** informal a person or thing that is easy to attack. **sitting room** a room for sitting and relaxing in.

sit·u·ate /'sicHo͞o,āt/ ▶ v. (**situates**, **situating**, **situated**) **1** put in a particular place. **2** (**be situated**) be in a particular set of circumstances.

sit·u·a·tion /,sicHo͞o'āsHən/ ▶ n. **1** a set of circumstances. **2** the location and surroundings of a place. **3** a job.

SYNONYMS **1 circumstances**, state of affairs, condition, case, predicament, plight. **2 location**, position, spot, site, environment, setting. **3 post**, position, job, employment.

□ **situation comedy** a comedy series in which the same characters are involved in various amusing situations. ■ **sit·u·a·tion·al** adj.

six /siks/ ▶ cardinal number one more than five; 6. (Roman numeral: **vi** or **VI**) □ **at sixes and sevens** in a state of confusion.

six·teen /sik'stēn, 'sik,stēn/ ▶ cardinal number one more than fifteen; 16. (Roman numeral: **xvi** or **XVI**) ■ **six·teenth** ordinal number.

sixth /siksTH/ ▶ ordinal number **1** being number six in a sequence; 6th. **2** (**a sixth** or **one sixth**) each of six equal parts of something. □ **sixth sense** a supposed ability to know things by intuition rather than using your sight, hearing, etc.

six·ty /'sikstē/ ▶ cardinal number (plural **sixties**) ten more than fifty; 60. (Roman numeral: **lx** or **LX**) ■ **six·ti·eth** /-iTH/ ordinal number.

siz·a·ble /'sīzəbəl/ (or **sizeable**) ▶ adj. fairly large.

SYNONYMS **large**, substantial, considerable, respectable, significant, goodly. ANTONYMS small.

size[1] /sīz/ ▶ n. **1** the overall measurements or extent of something. **2** each of the series of standard measurements in which clothes, shoes, and other goods are made. ▶ v. (**sizes**, **sizing**, **sized**) **1** group things according to size. **2** (**size someone/thing up**) informal form a judgment of a person or thing.

SYNONYMS ▶ n. **dimensions**, measurements, proportions, magnitude, largeness, area, expanse, breadth, width, length, height, depth. ▶ v. **sort**, categorize, classify.

□ **size zero** a very small size of women's clothing.

size[2] ▶ n. a sticky solution used to glaze paper, stiffen textiles, and prepare plastered walls for decoration. ▶ v. (**sizes**, **sizing**, **sized**) treat with size.

siz·zle /'sizəl/ ▶ v. (**sizzles**, **sizzling**, **sizzled**) **1** (of food) make a hissing sound when being fried. **2** (**sizzling**) informal very hot or exciting.

SYNONYMS **crackle**, fizzle, sputter, hiss, spit.

skate[1] /skāt/ ▶ n. an ice skate or roller skate. ▶ v. (**skates**, **skating**, **skated**) **1** move on skates. **2** (**skate over** or **around**) pass over or refer only briefly to. ■ **skat·er** n.

skate[2] ▶ n. (plural **skate** or **skates**) an edible sea fish with a diamond-shaped body.

skate·board /'skāt,bôrd/ ▶ n. a short narrow board fitted with two small wheels at each end, on which a person can ride. ■ **skate·board·er** n. **skate·board·ing** n.

skate·park /'skāt,pärk/ ▶ n. an area designed for skateboarding.

ske·dad·dle /ski'dadl/ ▶ v. (**skedaddles**, **skedaddling**, **skedaddled**) informal leave quickly.

skeet /skēt/ (also **skeet shooting**) ▶ n. a shooting sport in which a clay target is launched from a trap.

skein /skān/ ▶ n. a length of yarn held in a loose coil or knot.

skel·e·tal /'skelətl/ ▶ adj. **1** having to do with a skeleton. **2** very thin.

skel·e·ton /'skelitn/ ▶ n. **1** a framework of bone or cartilage supporting or containing the body of an animal. **2** a supporting framework or structure. ▶ adj. referring to an essential or minimum number of people: *a skeleton staff*. □ **skeleton in the closet** a shocking or embarrassing fact that someone wishes to keep secret. **skeleton key** a key designed to fit a number of locks.

skep·tic /'skeptik/ ▶ n. a person who questions accepted opinions.

SYNONYMS **cynic**, doubter, unbeliever, doubting Thomas.

skep·ti·cal /'skeptikəl/ ▶ adj. not easily convinced; having doubts.

SYNONYMS **dubious**, doubtful, doubting, cynical, distrustful, mistrustful, suspicious, disbelieving, unconvinced. ANTONYMS certain, convinced.

■ **skep·ti·cal·ly** adv.

skep·ti·cism /'skeptə,sizəm/ ▶ n. doubt about the truth of something.

SYNONYMS **doubt**, disbelief, cynicism, distrust, suspicion, incredulity.

sketch /skecH/ ▶ n. **1** a rough drawing or painting. **2** a short humorous scene in a comedy show. **3** a brief written or spoken account. ▶ v. **1** make a sketch of. **2** give a brief account of.

SYNONYMS ▶ n. **drawing**, outline, draft, diagram, design, plan; informal rough. ▶ v. **draw**, make a drawing of, pencil, rough out, outline.

sketch·book /'skecʜ,bo͝ok/ ▶ n. a pad of drawing paper for sketching on.

sketch·y /'skecʜē/ ▶ adj. (**sketchier**, **sketchiest**) not thorough or detailed; rough.

SYNONYMS **incomplete**, patchy, fragmentary, scrappy, cursory, perfunctory, scanty, vague, inadequate, insufficient. ANTONYMS detailed.

■ **sketch·i·ly** adv.

skew /skyo͞o/ ▶ v. **1** suddenly change direction or move at an angle. **2** make something biased or distorted. ▶ n. a bias toward one particular group or subject.

skew·bald /'skyo͞o,bôld/ ▶ adj. (of a horse) having patches of white and brown.

skew·er /'skyo͞oər/ ▶ n. a long piece of metal or wood used for holding pieces of food together during cooking. ▶ v. (**skewers**, **skewering**, **skewered**) hold or pierce with a pin or skewer.

ski /skē/ ▶ n. (plural **skis**) each of a pair of long, narrow pieces of wood, metal, or plastic, attached to boots for traveling over snow. ▶ v. (**skis**, **skiing**, **skied**) travel on skis. □ **ski jump** a steep slope leveling off before a sharp drop to allow a skier to leap through the air. **ski lift** a system of moving seats attached to an overhead cable, used for taking skiers to the top of a run. ■ **ski·er** n.

SPELLING

The plural of the noun is **skis**, without an **e**.

skid /skid/ ▶ v. (**skids**, **skidding**, **skidded**) **1** (of a vehicle) slide sideways in an uncontrolled way. **2** slip; slide. ▶ n. **1** an act of skidding. **2** a runner attached to the underside of a helicopter and some other aircraft. □ **skid row** informal a run-down part of a town or city where homeless people and alcoholics live.

skiff /skif/ ▶ n. a light rowboat.

skill /skil/ ▶ n. **1** the ability to do something well. **2** a particular ability.

SYNONYMS **expertise**, accomplishment, skillfulness, mastery, talent, deftness, dexterity, prowess, competence, artistry. ANTONYMS incompetence.

skilled /skild/ ▶ adj. **1** having or showing skill. **2** (of work) needing special abilities or training.

SYNONYMS **experienced**, trained, qualified, proficient, practiced, accomplished, expert, skillful, adept, adroit, deft, dexterous, able, good, competent; informal crack, crackerjack. ANTONYMS inexperienced.

skil·let /'skilit/ ▶ n. a frying pan.

skill·ful /'skilfəl/ ▶ adj. having or showing skill. ■ **skill·ful·ly** adv.

skim /skim/ ▶ v. (**skims**, **skimming**, **skimmed**) **1** remove a substance from the surface of a liquid. **2** move quickly and lightly over a surface or through the air. **3** read through quickly. **4** (**skim over**) deal with briefly.

SYNONYMS **1** *skim off the fat* **remove**, scoop off, separate. **2 glide**, move lightly, slide, sail, skate. **3** *she **skimmed** through the paper* **glance through**, flick through, flip through, leaf through, thumb through, read quickly, scan, run your eye over.

□ **skim milk** milk from which the cream has been removed.

skimp /skimp/ ▶ v. spend less money or use less of something than is really needed in an attempt to economize.

skimp·y /'skimpē/ ▶ adj. (**skimpier**, **skimpiest**) **1** not large enough in amount or size. **2** (of clothes) short and revealing.

skin /skin/ ▶ n. **1** the thin layer of tissue forming the outer covering of the body. **2** the skin of a dead animal used for clothing or other items. **3** the peel or outer layer of a fruit or vegetable. ▶ v. (**skins**, **skinning**, **skinned**) **1** remove the skin from. **2** graze a part of your body.

SYNONYMS ▶ n. **1 hide**, pelt, fleece. **2 peel**, rind. **3 film**, layer, membrane, crust, covering, coating. ▶ v. **1 peel**, pare. **2 graze**, scrape, abrade, bark, rub raw, chafe.

□ **by the skin of your teeth** only just. **have a thick skin** be unaffected by criticism or insults. **skin-deep** not deep or lasting; superficial. **skin-diving** swimming underwater without a diving suit, using an aqualung and flippers.

skin·flint /'skin,flint/ ▶ n. informal a very miserly person.

skin·head /'skin,hed/ ▶ n. a young person of a social group with very short shaved hair.

skin·ny /'skinē/ ▶ adj. (**skinnier**, **skinniest**) **1** (of a person) very thin. **2** (of a garment) tight-fitting.

SYNONYMS **thin**, underweight, scrawny, bony, gaunt, emaciated, skeletal, wasted, pinched, spindly, gangly; informal anorexic.

skin·tight /'skin'tīt/ ▶ adj. (of a garment) very tight-fitting.

skip /skip/ ▶ v. (**skips**, **skipping**, **skipped**) **1** move along lightly, stepping from one foot to the other with a little jump. **2** jump repeatedly over a rope turned over the head and under the feet. **3** leave out or move quickly over. **4** fail to attend or deal with. ▶ n. a skipping movement.

SYNONYMS ▶ v. **1 caper**, prance, trip, dance, bound, bounce, gambol. **2 omit**, leave out, miss out, dispense with, pass over, skim over, disregard; informal give something a miss.

skip·per /'skipər/ informal ▶ n. **1** the captain of a ship, boat, or aircraft. **2** the captain of a sports team. ▶ v. (**skippers**, **skippering**, **skippered**) be captain of.

skirl /skərl/ ▶ n. a shrill sound made by bagpipes. ▶ v. make such a sound.

skir·mish /'skərmisʜ/ ▶ n. a short period of fighting. ▶ v. take part in a skirmish.

skirt /skərt/ ▶ n. a woman's garment that hangs from the waist and surrounds the lower body and legs. ▶ v. **1** go around or past the edge of. **2** (also **skirt around**) avoid dealing with.

SYNONYMS ▶ v. **1 go around**, walk around, circle. **2 border**, edge, flank, line. **3** *he skirted the subject* **avoid**, evade, sidestep, dodge, pass over, gloss over; informal duck.

skirt·ing /'skərtiɴɢ/ (or **skirting board**) ▶ n. a baseboard.

skit /skit/ ▶ n. a short comedy sketch that makes fun of something by imitating it.

skit·ter /'skitər/ ▶ v. (**skitters**, **skittering**, **skittered**) move lightly and quickly.

skit·tish /'skitisн/ ▶ **adj.** **1** (of a horse) nervous and tending to shy. **2** lively or changeable. ■ **skit·tish·ly adv.**

skiv·vies /'skivēz/ ▶ **pl.n.** informal men's underwear, especially a T-shirt paired with shorts.

sku·a /'skyo͞oə/ ▶ **n.** a large seabird like a gull.

skul·dug·ger·y /skəl'dəgərē/ (or **skullduggery**) ▶ **n.** underhanded behavior.

skulk /skəlk/ ▶ **v.** hide or move around in a secretive way.

skull /skəl/ ▶ **n.** the bony framework that surrounds and protects the brain.

SYNONYMS cranium.

□ **skull and crossbones** a picture of a skull with two thigh bones crossed below it, used in the past by pirates and now as a sign of danger.

skull·cap /'skəl,kap/ ▶ **n.** a small close-fitting cap without a bill.

skunk /skəɴɢk/ ▶ **n.** an animal with black and white stripes that can spray foul-smelling liquid at attackers.

sky /skī/ ▶ **n.** (plural **skies**) the region of the atmosphere and space seen from the earth.

SYNONYMS literary the heavens, the firmament, the ether, the (wild) blue yonder.

□ **sky-high** very high.

sky·cap /'skī,kap/ ▶ **n.** a porter at an airport.

sky·div·ing /'skī,dīviɴɢ/ ▶ **n.** the sport of jumping from an aircraft and performing movements in the air before landing by parachute. ■ **sky·div·er n.**

sky·lark /'skī,lärk/ ▶ **n.** a lark that sings while flying. ▶ **v.** behave in a playful and mischievous way.

sky·light /'skī,līt/ ▶ **n.** a window set in a roof.

sky·line /'skī,līn/ ▶ **n.** an outline of land and buildings seen against the sky.

sky·rock·et /'skī,räkit/ ▶ **v.** (**skyrockets, skyrocketing, skyrocketed**) informal (of a price or amount) increase rapidly.

sky·scrap·er /'skī,skrāpər/ ▶ **n.** a very tall building.

sky·ward /'skīwərd/ ▶ **adv.** (also **skywards**) toward the sky. ▶ **adj.** moving or directed toward the sky.

sky·way /'skī,wā/ ▶ **n.** **1** a route used by aircraft. **2** (also **sky·walk** /'skī,wôk/) a covered overhead walkway between buildings.

sky·writ·ing /'skī,rītiɴɢ/ ▶ **n.** words in the form of smoke trails made by an airplane.

slab /slab/ ▶ **n.** **1** a large, thick, flat piece of stone or concrete. **2** a thick slice of cake, bread, etc.

SYNONYMS **piece**, block, hunk, chunk, lump, cake, tablet, brick, panel, plate, sheet.

slack /slak/ ▶ **adj.** **1** not taut or held tightly. **2** (of business or trade) quiet. **3** careless or lazy. **4** (of a tide) between the ebb and the flow. ▶ **n.** **1** the part of a rope or line that is not held taut. **2** (**slacks**) casual trousers. ▶ **v.** (**slack off** or **up**) become slower or less intense.

SYNONYMS ▶ **adj.** **1 limp**, loose. **2 sagging**, flabby, flaccid, loose, saggy. **3 sluggish**, slow, quiet, slow-moving, flat, depressed, stagnant. **4 lax**, negligent, careless, slapdash, slipshod; informal sloppy. ANTONYMS taut, firm. ▶ **v. idle**, shirk, be lazy, be indolent, waste time, lounge about; informal goof off.

■ **slack·er n. slack·ly adv. slack·ness n.**

slack·en /'slakən/ ▶ **v.** **1** make or become less active or intense. **2** make or become less tight.

slag /slag/ ▶ **n.** stony waste matter left when metal has been separated from ore by smelting or refining. □ **slag heap** a mound of waste material from a mine.

slain /slān/ past participle of **SLAY**.

slake /slāk/ ▶ **v.** (**slakes, slaking, slaked**) satisfy a desire, thirst, etc.

sla·lom /'släləm/ ▶ **n.** a skiing or canoeing race following a winding course marked out by poles.

slam /slam/ ▶ **v.** (**slams, slamming, slammed**) **1** shut forcefully and loudly. **2** put down with great force. **3** hit a ball with great force. **4** informal criticize severely. ▶ **n.** **1** a loud bang caused when a door is slammed. **2** Baseball ⇒ **GRAND SLAM.** ▶ **adv.** (also **slam bang**) informal suddenly and with great force.

SYNONYMS ▶ **v.** *the car slammed into a post* **crash into**, smash into, collide with, plow into, run into, bump into, hit, strike, ram, impact.

□ **slam dunk 1** Basketball a shot thrust down through the basket. **2** informal a foregone conclusion or certainty.

slam·mer /'slamər/ ▶ **n.** informal prison.

slan·der /'slandər/ ▶ **n.** the crime of saying something untrue that harms a person's reputation. ▶ **v.** (**slanders, slandering, slandered**) say something untrue and damaging about.

slan·der·ous /'slandərəs/ ▶ **adj.** untrue and damaging to a person's reputation.

SYNONYMS **defamatory**, denigratory, disparaging, libelous, pejorative, false, misrepresentative, scurrilous, scandalous, malicious.

slang /slaɴɢ/ ▶ **n.** very informal words and phrases that are more common in speech than in writing and are used by a particular group of people. ■ **slang·y adj.**

slant /slant/ ▶ **v.** **1** slope or lean. **2** present information from a particular point of view. ▶ **n.** **1** a sloping position. **2** a point of view.

SYNONYMS ▶ **v.** **1 slope**, tilt, incline, be at an angle, tip, lean, dip, pitch, shelve, list, bank. **2 bias**, distort, twist, skew, weight. ▶ **n.** **1 slope**, incline, tilt, gradient, grade, pitch, angle, camber. **2 point of view**, viewpoint, standpoint, stance, angle, perspective, approach, view, attitude, position, bias, spin.

slap /slap/ ▶ **v.** (**slaps, slapping, slapped**) **1** hit with the palm of your hand or a flat object. **2** hit against a surface with a slapping sound. **3** (**slap something on**) put something on a surface quickly or carelessly. ▶ **n.** an act or sound of slapping.

SYNONYMS ▶ **v. smack**, strike, hit, cuff, clip, spank; informal whack. ▶ **n. smack**, blow, cuff, clip, spank; informal whack.

□ **slap in the face** an unexpected rejection.

slap·dash /'slap,dasн/ ▶ **adj.** done too hurriedly and carelessly.

slap·stick /'slap,stik/ ▶ **n.** comedy consisting of deliberately clumsy actions and embarrassing situations.

slash /slasн/ ▶ **v.** **1** cut with a violent sweeping movement. **2** informal greatly reduce a price or quantity. ▶ **n.** **1** a cut made with a wide sweeping stroke. **2** a slanting stroke (/) used between alternatives, in fractions and ratios, and as a part of some web addresses.

SYNONYMS ▶ v. **1 cut**, gash, slit, lacerate, knife. **2 reduce**, cut, lower, bring down, mark down. ▶ n. **cut**, gash, slit, laceration, incision, wound.

slat /slat/ ▶ n. each of a series of thin, narrow pieces of wood or other material, arranged so as to overlap or fit into each other. ■ **slat·ted** adj.

slate /slāt/ ▶ n. **1** a dark gray or bluish-gray rock that is easily split into smooth, flat plates, used in building and in the past for writing on. **2** the color of slate. **3** a list of nominees for office, etc. ▶ v. (**slates**, **slating**, **slated**) nominate for office, etc. ▶ adj. made of slate.

slath·er /'slaTHər/ ▶ v. (**slathers**, **slathering**, **slathered**) informal spread or smear thickly over.

slat·tern /'slatərn/ ▶ n. old use a dirty, untidy woman. ■ **slat·tern·ly** adj.

slaugh·ter /'slôtər/ ▶ n. **1** the killing of farm animals for food. **2** the killing of a large number of people in a cruel or violent way. ▶ v. (**slaughters**, **slaughtering**, **slaughtered**) **1** kill animals for food. **2** kill a number of people in a cruel or violent way.

SYNONYMS ▶ n. **massacre**, (mass) murder, (mass) killing, (mass) execution, extermination, carnage, bloodshed, bloodletting, bloodbath; literary slaying. ▶ v. **1 kill**, butcher, cull, put down. **2 massacre**, murder, butcher, kill, exterminate, wipe out, put to death, execute; literary slay.

slaugh·ter·house /'slôtər,hous/ ▶ n. a place where animals are killed for food.

Slav /släv/ ▶ n. a member of a group of peoples in central and eastern Europe. ■ **Slav·ic** adj.

slave /slāv/ ▶ n. **1** (in the past) a person who was the legal property of another and was forced to obey them. **2** a person who is strongly influenced or controlled by something: *a slave to fashion*. ▶ v. (**slaves**, **slaving**, **slaved**) work very hard.

SYNONYMS ▶ n. **servant**, lackey, drudge; historical serf, vassal. ANTONYMS master. ▶ v. **toil**, labor, sweat, work like a Trojan/dog, work your fingers to the bone; informal sweat blood.

□ **slave-driver** informal a person who makes other people work very hard. **slave labor** very demanding work that is very badly paid. **slave trade** (in the past) the buying and selling of human beings as slaves.

slav·er /'slavər/ ▶ v. (**slavers**, **slavering**, **slavered**) let saliva run from the mouth. ▶ n. saliva running from the mouth.

slav·er·y /'slāvərē/ ▶ n. **1** the state of being a slave. **2** the practice or system of owning slaves.

SYNONYMS **enslavement**, servitude, serfdom, bondage, captivity. ANTONYMS freedom.

slav·ish /'slāvisH/ ▶ adj. showing no attempt to be original. ■ **slav·ish·ly** adv.

slay /slā/ ▶ v. (**slays**, **slaying**, **slew** /slo͞o/; past participle **slain** /slān/) violently kill. ■ **slay·er** n.

sleaze /slēz/ ▶ n. informal immoral or dishonest behavior.

slea·zy /'slēzē/ ▶ adj. (**sleazier**, **sleaziest**) **1** immoral or dishonest. **2** (of a place) dirty and seedy.

SYNONYMS **1 corrupt**, immoral, ignoble, dishonorable. **2 squalid**, seedy, seamy, sordid, insalubrious.

sled /sled/ ▶ n. **1** a vehicle on runners for traveling over snow or ice, sometimes pulled by dogs. **2** a toboggan. ▶ v. (**sleds**, **sledding**, **sledded**) ride or carry on a sled.

sledge /slej/ ▶ n. & v. (**sledges**, **sledging**, **sledged**) ⇒ SLED.

sledge·ham·mer /'slej,hamər/ ▶ n. a large, heavy hammer.

sleek /slēk/ ▶ adj. **1** smooth and glossy. **2** having a wealthy and well-groomed appearance. **3** elegant and streamlined.

SYNONYMS **1 smooth**, glossy, shiny, shining, lustrous, silken, silky. **2 streamlined**, elegant, graceful. ANTONYMS scruffy.

■ **sleek·ly** adv.

sleep /slēp/ ▶ n. a condition of rest in which the eyes are closed, the muscles are relaxed, and the mind is unconscious. ▶ v. (**sleeps**, **sleeping**, **slept** /slept/) **1** be asleep. **2** (**sleep in**) remain asleep or in bed later than usual in the morning. **3** provide a particular number of people with beds.

SYNONYMS ▶ n. **nap**, doze, siesta, catnap; informal snooze, forty winks, shut-eye; literary slumber. ▶ v. **be asleep**, doze, take a nap, take a siesta, catnap; informal snooze, get some shut-eye; literary slumber. ANTONYMS wake up.

□ **put to sleep** kill an animal painlessly. **sleeping bag** a warm padded bag for sleeping in when camping or traveling. **sleeping car** a railroad car fitted with beds or berths. **sleeping pill** a tablet taken to help you fall asleep.

sleep·er /'slēpər/ ▶ n. a train carrying cars with berths for sleeping.

sleep·less /'slēplis/ ▶ adj. **1** not sleeping; unable to sleep. **2** literary continually active or moving: *the sleepless river*. ■ **sleep·less·ness** n.

sleep·o·ver /'slēp,ōvər/ ▶ n. a night spent by children at another person's house.

sleep·walk /'slēp,wôk/ ▶ v. walk around while asleep. ■ **sleep·walk·er** n.

sleep·y /'slēpē/ ▶ adj. (**sleepier**, **sleepiest**) **1** ready for, or needing, sleep. **2** (of a place) without much activity.

SYNONYMS **1 drowsy**, tired, somnolent, heavy-eyed; informal dopey. **2 quiet**, peaceful, tranquil, placid, slow-moving, dull, boring. ANTONYMS awake, alert.

■ **sleep·i·ly** adv. **sleep·i·ness** n.

sleet /slēt/ ▶ n. rain containing some ice, or snow melting as it falls. ▶ v. (**it sleets**, **it is sleeting**, **it sleeted**) sleet falls.

sleeve /slēv/ ▶ n. **1** the part of a garment covering a person's arm. **2** a protective cover for a record. **3** a tube fitting over a rod or smaller tube. □ **up your sleeve** kept secret and ready for use when needed. ■ **sleeve·less** adj.

sleigh /slā/ ▶ n. a sled pulled by horses or reindeer.

sleight /slīt/ ▶ n. (**sleight of hand**) **1** skillful use of the hands when performing magic tricks. **2** skillful deception.

slen·der /'slendər/ ▶ adj. (**slenderer**, **slenderest**) **1** gracefully thin. **2** barely enough.

SYNONYMS **1 slim**, lean, willowy, svelte, lissome, graceful, slight, thin, skinny. **2 faint**, remote, tenuous, fragile, slim, small, slight. ANTONYMS plump, strong.

slept /slept/ past and past participle of SLEEP.

sleuth /slo͞oTH/ ▶ **n.** informal a detective. ■ **sleuth·ing n.**

slew¹ /slo͞o/ ▶ **v.** turn or slide violently or uncontrollably.

slew² past of SLAY.

slice /slīs/ ▶ **n. 1** a thin, broad piece of food cut from a larger portion. **2** a portion or share. **3** a kitchen implement with a broad, flat blade for lifting cake, fish, etc. **4** (in sports) a sliced stroke or shot. ▶ **v.** (**slices**, **slicing**, **sliced**) **1** cut into slices. **2** cut with something sharp. **3** (in sports) hit the ball so that it spins or curves away to the side.

> SYNONYMS ▶ **n. 1 piece**, portion, slab, wedge, sliver, wafer. **2 share**, part, portion, percentage, proportion, allocation; informal cut. ▶ **v. cut**, carve, divide.

slick /slik/ ▶ **adj. 1** impressively smooth and efficient. **2** self-confident but insincere. **3** (of a surface) smooth, glossy, or slippery. ▶ **n.** a smooth patch of oil. ▶ **v.** make hair smooth and glossy with water, oil, or cream.

> SYNONYMS ▶ **adj. 1 efficient**, smooth, smooth-running, polished, well-organized, well-run, streamlined. **2 glib**, polished, assured, self-assured, smooth-talking, plausible; informal smarmy. ▶ **v. smooth**, plaster, sleek, grease, oil, gel.

■ **slick·ly adv.**

slide /slīd/ ▶ **v.** (**slides**, **sliding**, **slid**) **1** move along a smooth surface while remaining in contact with it. **2** move smoothly, quickly, or without being noticed. **3** become gradually lower or worse. ▶ **n. 1** a structure with a smooth sloping surface for children to slide down. **2** an act of sliding. **3** a piece of glass that you place an object on to look at it through a microscope. **4** a small piece of photographic film that you view using a projector.

> SYNONYMS ▶ **v. glide**, slip, slither, skim, skate, skid, slew.

□ **slide rule** a ruler with a sliding central strip, used for making calculations quickly. **sliding scale** a scale of fees, wages, etc., that varies according to some other factor.

slight /slīt/ ▶ **adj. 1** small in degree. **2** not sturdy or strongly built. **3** lacking depth; trivial. ▶ **v.** insult someone by treating them without proper respect or attention. ▶ **n.** an insult.

> SYNONYMS ▶ **adj. 1 small**, tiny, minute, negligible, insignificant, minimal, remote, slim, faint. **2 slim**, slender, delicate, dainty, fragile. ANTONYMS large, plump. ▶ **v. insult**, snub, rebuff, spurn, give someone the cold shoulder, take no notice of, scorn, ignore. ▶ **n. insult**, affront, snub, rebuff; informal put-down, slap in the face.

slight·ly /slītlē/ ▶ **adv. 1** to a small degree; inconsiderably. **2** (with reference to a person's build) in a slender way: *a slightly built girl*.

> SYNONYMS **a little**, a bit, somewhat, faintly, vaguely, a shade. ANTONYMS very.

slim /slim/ ▶ **adj.** (**slimmer**, **slimmest**) **1** gracefully thin. **2** small in width and long and narrow in shape. **3** very small: *a slim chance*. ▶ **v.** (**slims**, **slimming**, **slimmed**) make or become thinner.

> SYNONYMS ▶ **adj. 1 slender**, lean, thin, willowy, sylphlike, svelte, lissome, slight, trim. **2** *a slim chance* **slight**, small, slender, faint, remote. ANTONYMS fat. ▶ **v. lose weight**, diet, go on a diet, slenderize.

■ **slim·mer n.**

slime /slīm/ ▶ **n.** an unpleasantly moist, soft, and slippery substance.

slim·y /ˈslīmē/ ▶ **adj.** (**slimier**, **slimiest**) **1** like or covered by slime. **2** informal polite and flattering in a way that is not sincere.

> SYNONYMS **slippery**, slithery, greasy, sticky, viscous; informal slippy.

sling /sliNG/ ▶ **n. 1** a loop of fabric used to support or raise a hanging weight. **2** a strap or loop used to hurl small missiles. ▶ **v.** (**slings**, **slinging**, **slung** /sləNG/) **1** hang or carry with a sling or strap. **2** informal throw.

> SYNONYMS ▶ **v. 1 hang**, suspend, string, swing. **2 throw**, toss, fling, hurl, cast, pitch, lob, flip; informal chuck, heave.

sling·back /ˈsliNG,bak/ ▶ **n.** a shoe held in place by a strap around the ankle.

sling·shot /ˈsliNG,SHät/ ▶ **n.** a forked stick with elastic fastened to the two prongs, used for shooting small stones.

slink /sliNGk/ ▶ **v.** (**slinks**, **slinking**, **slunk** /sləNGk/) move quietly in a secretive way.

slink·y /ˈsliNGkē/ ▶ **adj.** (**slinkier**, **slinkiest**) informal (of a woman's garment) close-fitting and sexy.

slip¹ /slip/ ▶ **v.** (**slips**, **slipping**, **slipped**) **1** lose your balance and slide for a short distance. **2** accidentally slide out of position or from someone's grasp. **3** fail to grip a surface. **4** get gradually worse. **5** (usually **slip up**) make a careless mistake. **6** move or place quietly, quickly, or secretly. **7** get free from. ▶ **n. 1** an act of slipping. **2** a minor or careless mistake. **3** a loose-fitting short petticoat.

> SYNONYMS ▶ **v. 1 slide**, skid, slither, fall (over), lose your balance, lose your footing, tumble. **2 creep**, steal, sneak, slide, sidle, slope, slink, tiptoe. ▶ **n. 1 false step**, slide, skid, fall, tumble. **2 mistake**, error, blunder, gaffe, oversight, miscalculation, omission, lapse; informal slip-up, boo-boo, goof, blooper, howler.

□ **let something slip** reveal something accidentally in conversation. **slip knot** a knot that can be undone by a pull, or that can slide along the rope on which it is tied. **slip-on** (of shoes or clothes) having no fastenings. **slipped disk** a displaced disk in the spine that presses on nearby nerves and causes pain. ■ **slip·page n.**

slip² ▶ **n. 1** a small piece of paper. **2** a cutting from a plant.

slip·cov·er /ˈslip,kəvər/ ▶ **n. 1** a detachable fitted cover for a chair or sofa. **2** a jacket for a book.

slip·per /ˈslipər/ ▶ **n.** a comfortable slip-on shoe worn indoors.

slip·per·y /ˈslipərē/ ▶ **adj. 1** difficult to hold firmly or stand on through being smooth, wet, or slimy. **2** (of a person) difficult to pin down.

> SYNONYMS **1 slithery**, greasy, oily, icy, glassy, smooth, slimy, wet; informal slippy. **2 sneaky**, sly, devious, crafty, cunning, tricky, evasive, scheming, unreliable, untrustworthy; informal shady, shifty.

■ **slip·per·i·ness n.**

slip·shod /ˈslip,SHäd/ ▶ **adj.** careless, thoughtless, or disorganized.

SYNONYMS **careless**, lackadaisical, slapdash, disorganized, haphazard, hit-or-miss, untidy, messy, unsystematic, casual, negligent, neglectful, lax, slack; informal sloppy, slaphappy. ANTONYMS meticulous.

slip·stream /ˈslipˌstrēm/ ▶ **n. 1** a current of air or water driven back by a propeller or jet engine. **2** the partial vacuum created in the wake of a moving vehicle.

slip·way /ˈslipˌwā/ ▶ **n.** a slope leading into water, used for launching and landing boats and ships.

slit /slit/ ▶ **n.** a long, narrow cut or opening. ▶ **v.** (**slits**, **slitting**, **slit**) make a slit in.

SYNONYMS ▶ **n. 1 cut**, incision, split, slash, gash. **2 opening**, gap, chink, crack, aperture, slot. ▶ **v. cut**, slash, split open, slice open.

slith·er /ˈsli<u>TH</u>ər/ ▶ **v.** (**slithers**, **slithering**, **slithered**) **1** move smoothly over a surface with a twisting motion. **2** slide unsteadily on a loose or slippery surface. ▶ **n.** a slithering movement.

SYNONYMS ▶ **v. slide**, slip, glide, wriggle, crawl, skid.

■ **slith·er·y adj.**

sliv·er /ˈslivər/ ▶ **n.** a small, narrow, sharp piece cut or split off a larger piece.

SYNONYMS **splinter**, shard, chip, flake, shred, scrap, shaving, paring, piece, fragment.

slob /släb/ informal ▶ **n.** a lazy, untidy person. ▶ **v.** (**slobs**, **slobbing**, **slobbed**) behave in a lazy, untidy way.

SYNONYMS ▶ **n. layabout**, good-for-nothing, sluggard, laggard; informal slacker, couch potato.

slob·ber /ˈsläbər/ ▶ **v.** (**slobbers**, **slobbering**, **slobbered**) have saliva dripping from the mouth. ▶ **n.** saliva dripping from the mouth.

SYNONYMS ▶ **v. drool**, slaver, dribble, salivate.

■ **slob·ber·y adj.**

sloe /slō/ ▶ **n.** the small bluish-black fruit of the blackthorn.

slog /släg/ ▶ **v.** (**slogs**, **slogging**, **slogged**) **1** work hard over a period of time. **2** move with difficulty or effort. **3** hit forcefully. **4** (**slog it out**) fight or compete fiercely. ▶ **n.** a period of difficult, tiring work or traveling.

slo·gan /ˈslōgən/ ▶ **n.** a short, memorable phrase used in advertising or associated with a political group.

SYNONYMS **catchphrase**, catchline, sound bite, motto, jingle; informal tag line.

sloop /slo͞op/ ▶ **n.** a type of sailboat with one mast.

slop /släp/ ▶ **v.** (**slops**, **slopping**, **slopped**) (of a liquid) spill over the edge of a container. ▶ **n.** (**slops**) **1** waste liquid that has to be emptied by hand. **2** unappetizing semiliquid food.

slope /slōp/ ▶ **n. 1** a surface with one end at a higher level than another. **2** a part of the side of a hill or mountain. ▶ **v.** (**slopes**, **sloping**, **sloped**) **1** slant up or down. **2** (**slope off**) informal leave without attracting attention.

SYNONYMS ▶ **n. tilt**, pitch, slant, angle, gradient, grade, incline, inclination, fall, camber. ▶ **v. 1 tilt**, slant, incline, lean, drop/fall away, descend, shelve, camber, rise, ascend, climb. **2** (**sloping**) **slanting**, leaning, inclined, angled, cambered, tilted.

slop·py /ˈsläpē/ ▶ **adj.** (**sloppier**, **sloppiest**) **1** careless and disorganized. **2** containing too much liquid. **3** too sentimental.

SYNONYMS **1 runny**, watery, liquid, mushy; informal gloppy. **2 careless**, slapdash, slipshod, disorganized, untidy, slack, slovenly; informal slaphappy.

■ **slop·pi·ly adv. slop·pi·ness n.**

slosh /släsн/ ▶ **v. 1** (of liquid in a container) move around with a splashing sound. **2** move through liquid with a splashing sound. **3** pour liquid clumsily.

sloshed /släsнt/ ▶ **adj.** informal drunk.

slot /slät/ ▶ **n. 1** a long, narrow opening into which something may be inserted. **2** a place in an arrangement or plan. ▶ **v.** (**slots**, **slotting**, **slotted**) **1** place into a slot. **2** (**slot in** or **into**) fit easily into a new role or situation.

SYNONYMS ▶ **n. 1 aperture**, slit, crack, hole, opening. **2 time**, spot, period, niche, space; informal window. ▶ **v. insert**, slide, fit, put, place.

□ **slot machine** a machine worked by inserting a coin, especially a gaming machine.

sloth /slôтн, släтн, slōтн/ ▶ **n. 1** laziness. **2** a slow-moving animal that hangs upside down.

SYNONYMS **laziness**, idleness, indolence, slothfulness, inactivity, inertia, sluggishness, shiftlessness, apathy, listlessness, lassitude, lethargy, languor. ANTONYMS industriousness.

■ **sloth·ful adj.**

slouch /slouсн/ ▶ **v.** stand, move, or sit in a lazy, drooping way. ▶ **n.** a lazy, drooping posture. □ **be no slouch** informal be fast or good at something.

slough¹ /slou, slo͞o/ ▶ **n. 1** a swamp. **2** a situation without progress or activity.

slough² /sləf/ ▶ **v.** (of an animal) cast off an old skin.

Slo·va·ki·an /slōˈväkēən/ (also **Slovak** /ˈslōväk, -vak/) ▶ **n.** a person from Slovakia. ▶ **adj.** relating to Slovakia.

Slo·vene /ˈslōvēn/ ▶ **n. 1** a person from Slovenia. **2** the language of Slovenia. ■ **Slo·ve·ni·an** /slōˈvēnēən/ **n. & adj.**

slov·en·ly /ˈsləvənlē, ˈslä-/ ▶ **adj. 1** untidy and dirty. **2** careless.

SYNONYMS **1 scruffy**, untidy, messy, unkempt, ill-groomed, disheveled, bedraggled, rumpled, frowzy. **2 careless**, slapdash, slipshod, haphazard, hit-or-miss, untidy, messy, negligent, lax, lackadaisical, slack; informal sloppy, slaphappy. ANTONYMS tidy, careful.

■ **slov·en·li·ness n.**

slow /slō/ ▶ **adj. 1** moving or capable of moving only at a low speed. **2** taking a long time. **3** (of a clock or watch) showing a time earlier than the correct time. **4** not quick to understand, think, or learn. ▶ **v.** (often **slow down** or **up**) **1** reduce speed. **2** be less busy or active.

SYNONYMS ▶ **adj. 1 unhurried**, leisurely, steady, sedate, measured, ponderous, sluggish, plodding. **2 lengthy**, time-consuming, long-drawn-out, protracted, prolonged, gradual. **3 stupid**, unintelligent, obtuse; informal dense, dim, thick, slow on the uptake, dumb, dopey. ANTONYMS fast, quick. ▶ **v. 1 reduce speed**, go slower, decelerate, brake. **2 hold back**, hold up, delay, retard, set back, check, curb. ANTONYMS accelerate.

□ **slow motion** the showing of a movie or video more slowly than it was made or recorded. **slow-worm** a small snakelike lizard. ■ **slow·ness** n.

slow·ly /ˈslōlē/ ▶ adv. at a slow speed; not quickly: *they moved forward slowly.*

SYNONYMS **1 unhurriedly**, without hurrying, steadily, at a leisurely pace, at a snail's pace. **2 gradually**, bit by bit, little by little, slowly but surely, step by step. ANTONYMS quickly.

□ **slowly but surely** achieving the desired results gradually and reliably rather than quickly and spectacularly: *the new church began, slowly but surely, to grow.*

slow·poke /ˈslō,pōk/ ▶ n. informal a person who acts or moves slowly, especially in an annoying or inconvenient way.

sludge /sləj/ ▶ n. thick, soft, wet mud or a similar mixture. ■ **sludg·y** adj.

slug¹ /sləg/ ▶ n. **1** a small creature like a snail without a shell. **2** informal a small amount of an alcoholic drink. **3** informal a bullet. ▶ v. (**slugs**, **slugging**, **slugged**) informal gulp a drink.

slug² ▶ v. (**slugs**, **slugging**, **slugged**) informal **1** hit with a hard blow. **2** (**slug it out**) settle a dispute by fighting or competing fiercely.

slug·gard /ˈsləgərd/ ▶ n. a lazy, inactive person.

slug·gish /ˈsləgisн/ ▶ adj. **1** slow-moving or inactive. **2** not energetic or alert.

SYNONYMS **lethargic**, listless, lacking in energy, lifeless, inactive, slow, torpid, enervated. ANTONYMS vigorous.

■ **slug·gish·ly** adv.

sluice /slo͞os/ ▶ n. **1** (also **sluice gate**) a sliding device for controlling the flow of water. **2** a channel for carrying off surplus water. ▶ v. (**sluices**, **sluicing**, **sluiced**) wash or rinse with water.

slum /sləm/ ▶ n. **1** a rundown area of a city or town inhabited by very poor people. **2** a house or building unfit to be lived in. ▶ v. (**slums**, **slumming**, **slummed**) (**slum it**) informal choose to spend time in uncomfortable conditions or at a low social level.

SYNONYMS ▶ n. **hovel**; (**slums**) ghetto, shanty town.

slum·ber /ˈsləmbər/ ▶ v. (**slumbers**, **slumbering**, **slumbered**) sleep. ▶ n. a sleep.

slump /sləmp/ ▶ v. **1** sit, lean, or fall heavily and limply. **2** fall in price, value, number, etc., suddenly and by a large amount. ▶ n. an instance of slumping.

SYNONYMS ▶ v. **1 sit heavily**, flop, collapse, sink. **2 fall**, plummet, tumble, collapse, drop; informal crash, nosedive. ▶ n. **1 fall**, drop, tumble, downturn, downswing, slide, decline, decrease; informal nosedive. **2 recession**, decline, depression, slowdown. ANTONYMS rise, boom.

slung /sləNG/ past and past participle of SLING.

slunk /sləNGk/ past and past participle of SLINK.

slur /slər/ ▶ v. (**slurs**, **slurring**, **slurred**) **1** speak in a way that is difficult to understand. **2** perform a group of musical notes in a smooth, flowing way. ▶ n. **1** an insult or accusation intended to damage someone's reputation. **2** a curved line indicating that musical notes are to be slurred.

SYNONYMS ▶ v. **mumble**, speak unclearly, garble. ▶ n. **insult**, slight, slander, smear, allegation, imputation.

slurp /slərp/ ▶ v. eat or drink with a loud sucking sound. ▶ n. a slurping sound.

slur·ry /ˈslərē/ ▶ n. (plural **slurries**) a semiliquid mixture of water and manure, cement, or coal.

slush /sləsн/ ▶ n. **1** partially melted snow or ice. **2** informal very sentimental talk or writing. □ **slush fund** a reserve of money used for something illegal.

slush·y /ˈsləsнē/ ▶ adj. (**slushier**, **slushiest**) **1** resembling, consisting of, or covered with slush. **2** informal too sentimental.

sly /slī/ ▶ adj. (**slyer**, **slyest**) **1** cunning and deceitful. **2** (of a remark, glance, or expression) suggesting secret knowledge.

SYNONYMS **1 cunning**, crafty, clever, wily, artful, tricky, scheming, devious, underhanded/underhand, sneaky. **2 roguish**, mischievous, impish, playful, wicked, arch, knowing. **3 surreptitious**, furtive, stealthy, covert. ANTONYMS open, straightforward.

■ **sly·ly** adv.

smack¹ /smak/ ▶ n. **1** a sharp blow with the palm of the hand. **2** a loud, sharp sound. **3** a loud kiss. ▶ v. **1** give someone a smack. **2** smash or drive into. **3** part your lips noisily. ▶ adv. informal exactly or directly.

SYNONYMS ▶ n. **slap**, blow, cuff, clip, spank; informal whack. ▶ v. **slap**, strike, hit, cuff, clip, spank; informal whack. ▶ adv. **exactly**, precisely, straight, right, directly, squarely, dead, plumb; informal slam bang, smack dab.

smack² ▶ v. (**smack of**) **1** seem to contain or involve something wrong or unpleasant. **2** smell or taste of.

smack³ ▶ n. a fishing boat, often one equipped with a well for keeping the caught fish alive.

smack⁴ ▶ n. informal heroin.

smack·er /ˈsmakər/ ▶ n. informal **1** a loud kiss. **2** a dollar bill.

small /smôl/ ▶ adj. **1** of less than normal size. **2** not great in amount, number, strength, or power. **3** young.

SYNONYMS **1 little**, tiny, short, petite, diminutive, elfin, miniature, mini, minute, toy, baby, undersized, poky, cramped; informal teeny, teensy, teeny-weeny, teensy-weensy, tiddly, pint-sized. **2 slight**, minor, unimportant, trifling, trivial, insignificant, inconsequential, negligible, inappreciable; informal piffling. ANTONYMS big, large.

□ **small arms** guns that can be carried in the hands. **small fry** young or unimportant people or things. **the small hours** the early hours of the morning after midnight. **the small of the back** the lower part of a person's back where the spine curves in. **small print** details printed so small that they are not easily noticed in an agreement or contract. **small talk** polite conversation about unimportant things. ■ **small·ness** n.

small·pox /ˈsmôl,päks/ ▶ n. a serious disease that causes blisters that usually leave permanent scars.

smarm·y /ˈsmärmē/ ▶ adj. informal friendly or flattering in an unpleasant and insincere way.

SYNONYMS **unctuous**, ingratiating, slick, oily, greasy, obsequious, sycophantic, fawning; informal slimy.

smart /smärt/ ▶ **adj.** **1** clean, tidy, and stylish. **2** bright and fresh in appearance. **3** (of a place) fashionable and upmarket. **4** informal quick-witted. **5** impertinently clever. **6** quick. ▶ **v.** **1** give a sharp, stinging pain. **2** feel upset and annoyed.

SYNONYMS ▶ **adj.** **1** **well-dressed**, well turned out, stylish, chic, fashionable, modish, elegant, dapper; informal natty, snappy. **2** *a smart restaurant* **fashionable**, stylish, high-class, exclusive, chic, fancy, upscale, upmarket, high-toned; informal trendy, classy, swanky, swank, swish. **3** **clever**, bright, intelligent, quick-witted, shrewd, astute, perceptive; informal brainy, quick on the uptake. **4** *a smart pace* **brisk**, quick, fast, rapid, lively, energetic, vigorous; informal cracking. ANTONYMS scruffy, stupid. ▶ **v.** **1** **sting**, burn, tingle, prickle, hurt. **2** *she smarted at the accusation* **feel hurt**, feel upset, take offense, feel aggrieved, feel indignant, be put out.

□ **smart card** a plastic card on which information is stored in electronic form. ■ **smart·ly** **adv.** **smart·ness** **n.**

smart·en /ˈsmärtn/ ▶ **v.** (**smarten up**) make or become smarter.

smash /smash/ ▶ **v.** **1** break violently into pieces. **2** hit or collide forcefully. **3** (in sports) hit the ball hard. **4** completely defeat or destroy. ▶ **n.** **1** an act or sound of smashing. **2** (also **smash hit**) informal a very successful song, movie, or show.

SYNONYMS ▶ **v.** **1** **break**, shatter, splinter, crack; informal bust. **2** *he smashed into a wall* **crash into**, smack into, slam into, plow into, run into, bump into, hit, strike, ram, collide with, impact. ▶ **n.** **crash**, collision, accident, wreck; informal pile-up.

smat·ter·ing /ˈsmatəriNG/ ▶ **n.** **1** a small amount. **2** a slight knowledge of a language.

SYNONYMS **bit**, little, modicum, touch, soupçon, rudiments, basics; informal smidgen, smidge, tad.

smear /smi(ə)r/ ▶ **v.** **1** coat or mark with a greasy or sticky substance. **2** blur or smudge. **3** make false accusations about someone so as to damage their reputation. ▶ **n.** **1** a greasy or sticky mark. **2** a false accusation.

SYNONYMS ▶ **v.** **1** **spread**, rub, daub, slap, cover, coat, smother, plaster. **2** **smudge**, streak, mark. **3** **sully**, tarnish, blacken, drag through the mud, damage, defame, malign, slur, slander, libel. ▶ **n.** **1** **streak**, smudge, daub, dab, spot, patch, blotch, mark; informal splotch. **2** **accusation**, lie, untruth, slur, slander, libel, defamation.

smell /smel/ ▶ **n.** **1** the ability to sense different things by means of the organs in the nose. **2** something sensed by the organs in the nose; an odor. **3** an act of smelling. ▶ **v.** (**smells**, **smelling**, **smelled** or **smelt**) **1** sense by means of the organs in the nose. **2** sniff at something to find out its smell. **3** send out a smell. **4** have a strong or unpleasant smell. **5** sense or detect.

SYNONYMS ▶ **n.** **1** **odor**, aroma, fragrance, scent, perfume, bouquet, nose. **2** **stink**, stench, reek. ▶ **v.** **1** **scent**, sniff, get a sniff/whiff of, detect. **2** **stink**, reek.

□ **smell a rat** informal suspect a trick. **smelling salts** a strong-smelling liquid formerly sniffed by people who felt faint.

smell·y /ˈsmelē/ ▶ **adj.** (**smellier**, **smelliest**) having a strong or unpleasant smell.

SYNONYMS **foul-smelling**, stinking, reeking, rank, fetid, malodorous, pungent; literary noisome.

smelt[1] /smelt/ ▶ **v.** extract metal from its ore by heating and melting it.

smelt[2] past and past participle of SMELL.

smelt[3] ▶ **n.** (plural **smelt** or **smelts**) a small silvery fish.

smid·gen /ˈsmijin/ (or **smidgeon**) ▶ **n.** informal a tiny amount.

smile /smīl/ ▶ **v.** (**smiles**, **smiling**, **smiled**) form your features into a pleased, friendly, or amused expression, with the corners of the mouth turned up. ▶ **n.** an act of smiling.

SYNONYMS ▶ **v.** **beam**, grin (from ear to ear), smirk, simper, leer. ANTONYMS frown. ▶ **n.** **beam**, grin, smirk, simper, leer.

smil·ey /ˈsmīlē/ ▶ **adj.** informal smiling; cheerful. ▶ **n.** (plural **smileys**) a symbol that represents a smiling face, formed by the characters :-) and used in emails and similar electronic communications.

smirk /smərk/ ▶ **v.** smile in a smug or silly way. ▶ **n.** a smug or silly smile.

SYNONYMS ▶ **v.** **sneer**, simper, snigger, leer, grin.

smite /smīt/ ▶ **v.** (**smites**, **smiting**, **smote** /smōt/; past participle **smitten** /ˈsmitn/) **1** old use hit with a hard blow. **2** (**be smitten**) be strongly attracted to someone. **3** (**be smitten**) be severely affected by a disease.

SYNONYMS (**smitten**) **1** **infatuated**, besotted, in love, obsessed, head over heels, enamored, captivated, enchanted, under someone's spell; informal bowled over, swept off your feet. **2** **struck down**, laid low, suffering, affected, afflicted.

smith /smiTH/ ▶ **n.** **1** a person who works in metal. **2** a blacksmith.

smith·er·eens /ˌsmiT͟Həˈrēnz/ ▶ **pl.n.** informal small pieces.

smith·y /ˈsmiTHē/ ▶ **n.** (plural **smithies**) a blacksmith's workshop.

smock /smäk/ ▶ **n.** **1** a loose dress or blouse with the upper part gathered into decorative stitched pleats. **2** a loose overall worn to protect your clothes.

smog/ smäg/ ▶ **n.** fog or haze made worse by pollution in the atmosphere.

smoke /smōk/ ▶ **n.** **1** a visible vapor in the air produced by a burning substance. **2** an act of smoking tobacco. **3** informal a cigarette or cigar. ▶ **v.** (**smokes**, **smoking**, **smoked**) **1** give out smoke. **2** breathe smoke from a cigarette, pipe, etc., in and out again. **3** preserve meat or fish by exposing it to smoke. **4** (**smoke someone/thing out**) drive someone or something out of a place by using smoke. **5** (**smoked**) (of glass) darkened.

SYNONYMS ▶ **n.** **fumes**, exhaust, gas, vapor, smog. ▶ **v.** **1** **smolder**; old use reek. **2** **puff on**, draw on, pull on, inhale; informal drag on.

■ **smoke·less** **adj.** **smok·er** **n.**

smoke·screen /ˈsmōkˌskrēn/ ▶ **n. 1** something designed to disguise your real intentions or activities. **2** a cloud of smoke created to conceal military operations.

smoke·stack /ˈsmōkˌstak/ ▶ **n.** a chimney or funnel that takes away smoke produced by a locomotive, ship, factory, etc.

smok·y /ˈsmōkē/ ▶ **adj.** (**smokier**, **smokiest**) producing, filled with, or like smoke.

> SYNONYMS **smoke-filled**, sooty, smoggy, hazy, foggy, murky, thick.

smol·der /ˈsmōldər/ ▶ **v.** (**smolders**, **smoldering**, **smoldered**) **1** burn slowly with smoke but no flame. **2** feel strong and barely hidden anger, hatred, lust, etc.

smooch /smo͞oCH/ ▶ **v.** informal kiss.

smooth /smo͞oTH/ ▶ **adj. 1** having an even and regular surface. **2** (of a liquid) without lumps. **3** (of movement) without jerks. **4** without difficulties. **5** charming in a very confident or flattering way. **6** (of a flavor) not harsh or bitter. ▶ **v.** (also **smoothe**) (**smooths** or **smoothes**, **smoothing**, **smoothed**) **1** make something smooth. **2** (**smooth something over**) deal successfully with a problem.

> SYNONYMS ▶ **adj. 1 even**, level, flat, plane, unwrinkled, glassy, glossy, silky, polished. **2 creamy**, fine, velvety. **3 calm**, still, tranquil, undisturbed, unruffled, even, flat, like a millpond. **4 steady**, regular, uninterrupted, unbroken, easy, effortless, trouble-free. **5 suave**, urbane, sophisticated, polished, debonair, courteous, gracious, persuasive, glib, slick, smooth-tongued; informal smarmy. ANTONYMS uneven, rough. ▶ **v. 1 flatten**, level (out/off), even out/off, press, roll, iron, plane. **2 ease**, facilitate, expedite, help, assist, aid, pave the way for. ANTONYMS roughen, hinder.

□ **smooth-talking** informal using very persuasive or flattering language. ■ **smooth·ly** adv. **smooth·ness** n.

smooth·ie /ˈsmo͞oTHē/ ▶ **n. 1** a thick, smooth drink of fresh fruit with milk, yogurt, or ice cream. **2** informal a man with a charming, confident manner.

smor·gas·bord /ˈsmôrgəsˌbôrd/ ▶ **n.** a buffet offering a variety of hot and cold meats, salads, hors d'oeuvres, etc.

smote /smōt/ past of SMITE.

smoth·er /ˈsməTHər/ ▶ **v.** (**smothers**, **smothering**, **smothered**) **1** suffocate someone by covering their nose and mouth. **2** (**smother someone/thing in** or **with**) cover someone or something thickly with. **3** be oppressively protective or loving toward someone.

> SYNONYMS **1 suffocate**, asphyxiate, stifle, choke. **2 extinguish**, put out, snuff out, douse, stamp out. **3 smear**, daub, spread, cover, plaster. **4** *she smothered a giggle* **stifle**, muffle, strangle, suppress, hold back, fight back, swallow, conceal.

SMS ▶ **abbr.** Short Message (or Messaging) Service, a system for sending and receiving text messages. ▶ **n.** a message sent by SMS.

smudge /sməj/ ▶ **v.** (**smudges**, **smudging**, **smudged**) make or become blurred or smeared. ▶ **n.** a smudged mark or image.

> SYNONYMS ▶ **v. streak**, mark, dirty, soil, blotch, blacken, smear, blot, daub, stain; informal splotch. ▶ **n. streak**, smear, mark, stain, blotch, blob, dab; informal splotch.

■ **smudg·y** adj.

smug /sməg/ ▶ **adj.** (**smugger**, **smuggest**) irritatingly pleased with yourself.

> SYNONYMS **self-satisfied**, conceited, complacent, superior, pleased with yourself.

■ **smug·ly** adv. **smug·ness** n.

smug·gle /ˈsməgəl/ ▶ **v.** (**smuggles**, **smuggling**, **smuggled**) **1** move goods illegally into or out of a country. **2** secretly convey. ■ **smug·gler** n.

smut /smət/ ▶ **n. 1** a small flake of soot or dirt. **2** indecent talk, writing, or pictures. ■ **smut·ty** adj.

snack /snak/ ▶ **n.** a small quantity of food eaten between meals or in place of a meal. ▶ **v.** eat a snack.

> SYNONYMS ▶ **n. light meal**, sandwich, refreshments, nibbles, tidbit(s); informal bite (to eat).

sna·fu /snaˈfo͞o/ ▶ **n.** informal a situation that is confused, disorganized, or that has gone wrong.

snag /snag/ ▶ **n. 1** an unexpected difficulty. **2** a sharp or jagged projection. **3** a small tear. ▶ **v.** (**snags**, **snagging**, **snagged**) catch or tear on a snag.

> SYNONYMS ▶ **n. complication**, difficulty, catch, hitch, obstacle, pitfall, problem, setback, disadvantage, drawback. ▶ **v. catch**, hook, tear.

snail /snāl/ ▶ **n.** a small, slow-moving creature with a spiral shell into which it can withdraw its whole body.

snake /snāk/ ▶ **n.** a reptile with no legs and a long slender body. ▶ **v.** (**snakes**, **snaking**, **snaked**) move with the twisting motion of a snake.

> SYNONYMS ▶ **n.** serpent. ▶ **v.** *the road snakes inland* **twist**, wind, meander, zigzag, curve.

□ **snake in the grass** a person who pretends to be someone's friend but is secretly working against them.

snak·y /ˈsnākē/ (also **snakey**) ▶ **adj.** (**snakier**, **snakiest**) **1** long and winding. **2** cold and cunning.

snap /snap/ ▶ **v.** (**snaps**, **snapping**, **snapped**) **1** break with a sharp cracking sound. **2** open or close with a brisk movement or sharp sound. **3** (of an animal) make a sudden bite. **4** say something quickly and irritably. **5** suddenly lose self-control. **6** take a snapshot of. ▶ **n. 1** an act or sound of snapping. **2** a snapshot. ▶ **adj.** done on the spur of the moment: *a snap decision*.

> SYNONYMS ▶ **v. 1 break**, fracture, splinter, split, crack; informal bust. **2 bark**, snarl, growl, retort; informal jump down someone's throat. ▶ **n. photograph**, picture, photo, shot, snapshot, print, slide.

□ **snap something up** quickly buy something that is in short supply. **snap out of** informal get out of a bad mood by a sudden effort.

snap·drag·on /ˈsnapˌdragən/ ▶ **n.** a plant with brightly colored flowers that have a mouthlike opening.

snap·per /ˈsnapər/ ▶ **n.** a sea fish noted for snapping its jaws.

snap·pish /ˈsnapisH/ ▶ **adj. 1** (of a dog) irritable and likely to bite. **2** (of a person) irritable.

snap·py /ˈsnapē/ ▶ **adj.** (**snappier**, **snappiest**) informal **1** short and clever or amusing: *snappy slogans*. **2** neat and stylish. **3** irritable; speaking sharply. □ **make it snappy** do it quickly.

snap·shot /ˈsnap,sHät/ ▶ **n.** an informal photograph, taken quickly.

snare /sne(ə)r/ ▶ **n. 1** a trap for catching animals, consisting of a loop of wire that pulls tight. **2** a thing likely to lure someone into trouble. **3** (also **snare drum**) a drum with a length of wire stretched across the head to produce a rattling sound. ▶ **v.** (**snares**, **snaring**, **snared**) catch in a snare or trap.

> SYNONYMS ▶ **n. trap**, gin, wire, net, noose. ▶ **v. trap**, catch, net, bag, ensnare, hook.

snarl /snärl/ ▶ **v. 1** growl with bared teeth. **2** say something aggressively. **3** (**snarl something up**) make something tangled. ▶ **n.** an act of snarling.

snatch /snacH/ ▶ **v. 1** seize quickly in a rude or eager way. **2** informal steal or kidnap. **3** quickly take the chance to have. ▶ **n. 1** an act of snatching. **2** a fragment of music or talk.

> SYNONYMS ▶ **v. 1 grab**, seize, take hold of, take, pluck, grasp at, clutch at. **2 steal**, take, thieve, make off with; informal swipe, nab, lift. **3 kidnap**, abduct, take as hostage.

snaz·zy /ˈsnazē/ ▶ **adj.** (**snazzier**, **snazziest**) informal neat and stylish in appearance.

sneak /snēk/ ▶ **v.** (**sneaks**, **sneaking**, **sneaked** or informal **snuck** /snək/) move or take in a secretive way. ▶ **n.** informal a mean-spirited, underhanded person. ▶ **adj.** secret or unofficial: *a sneak preview*.

> SYNONYMS ▶ **v. creep**, slink, steal, slip, slide, sidle, tiptoe, pad.

sneak·er /ˈsnēkər/ ▶ **n.** a soft shoe worn for sports or casual occasions.

sneak·ing /ˈsnēkiNG/ ▶ **adj. 1** (of a feeling) persisting in your mind but not fully recognized; nagging. **2** informal furtive and contemptible.

> SYNONYMS **1 secret**, private, hidden, concealed, unvoiced, unexpressed. **2** *a sneaking suspicion* **niggling**, nagging, insidious, lingering, persistent.

sneak·y /ˈsnēkē/ ▶ **adj.** (**sneakier**, **sneakiest**) secretive in a sly or dishonest way.

> SYNONYMS **sly**, crafty, cunning, wily, scheming, devious, deceitful, underhanded/underhand.

■ **sneak·i·ly adv.**

sneer /sni(ə)r/ ▶ **n.** a scornful or mocking smile or remark. ▶ **v.** (**sneers**, **sneering**, **sneered**) smile or speak in a scornful or mocking way.

> SYNONYMS ▶ **n. 1 smirk**, snigger. **2 jeer**, jibe, insult; informal dig. ▶ **v. 1 smirk**, snigger, curl your lip. **2 scoff**, laugh, scorn, disdain, be contemptuous, mock, ridicule, deride, jeer, jibe.

sneeze /snēz/ ▶ **v.** (**sneezes**, **sneezing**, **sneezed**) suddenly expel air from the nose and mouth because of irritation of the nostrils. ▶ **n.** an act of sneezing. □ **not to be sneezed at** informal worth having or considering. ■ **sneez·y adj.**

snick·er /ˈsnikər/ ▶ **v.** (**snickers**, **snickering**, **snickered**) **1** snigger. **2** (of a horse) make a gentle high-pitched neigh. ▶ **n.** a sound of snickering.

snide /snīd/ ▶ **adj.** disrespectful or mocking in an indirect way.

> SYNONYMS **disparaging**, derogatory, deprecating, insulting, mocking, taunting, sneering, scornful, derisive, sarcastic, spiteful, nasty, mean, contemptuous.

sniff /snif/ ▶ **v. 1** draw in air audibly through the nose. **2** (**sniff around**) informal investigate secretly. **3** (**sniff something out**) informal discover something by investigation. ▶ **n.** an act of sniffing.

> SYNONYMS ▶ **v. 1 inhale**, snuffle. **2 smell**, scent, get a whiff of. ▶ **n. 1 snuffle**, snort. **2 smell**, scent, whiff, lungful.

□ **not to be sniffed at** informal worth having or considering. **sniffer dog** a dog trained to find drugs or explosives by smell. ■ **sniff·er n. snif·fy adj.**

snif·fle /ˈsnifəl/ ▶ **v.** (**sniffles**, **sniffling**, **sniffled**) sniff slightly or repeatedly. ▶ **n. 1** an act of sniffling. **2** a slight cold. ■ **snif·fly adj.**

snif·ter /ˈsniftər/ ▶ **n. 1** a footed glass that is wide at the bottom and tapers to the top, used for brandy and other drinks. **2** informal a small quantity of an alcoholic drink.

snig·ger /ˈsnigər/ ▶ **v.** (**sniggers**, **sniggering**, **sniggered**) give a half-suppressed laugh. ▶ **n.** a half-suppressed laugh.

> SYNONYMS **giggle**, titter, snicker, chortle, laugh, sneer, smirk.

snip /snip/ ▶ **v.** (**snips**, **snipping**, **snipped**) cut with small, quick strokes. ▶ **n.** an act of snipping.

> SYNONYMS ▶ **v. 1** *she snipped my bangs* **cut**, clip, trim. **2** *snip off the faded flowers* **cut off**, trim (off), clip, prune, chop off, sever, detach, remove, take off. ▶ **n. 1** *make snips along the edge* **cut**, slit, snick, nick, notch, incision. **2** *snips of wallpaper* **scrap**, snippet, cutting, shred, remnant, fragment, sliver, bit, piece.

snipe /snīp/ ▶ **v.** (**snipes**, **sniping**, **sniped**) **1** shoot at someone from a hiding place at long range. **2** criticize someone in an unpleasant or petty way. ▶ **n.** (plural **snipe** or **snipes**) a wading bird with brown feathers and a long straight bill. ■ **snip·er n.**

snip·pet /ˈsnipit/ ▶ **n.** a small piece or brief extract.

> SYNONYMS **piece**, bit, scrap, fragment, particle, shred, excerpt, extract.

snitch /snicH/ informal ▶ **v. 1** steal. **2** inform on someone. ▶ **n.** an informer.

sniv·el /ˈsnivəl/ ▶ **v.** (**snivels**, **sniveling**, **sniveled**) cry or complain in a whining way.

> SYNONYMS **sniffle**, snuffle, whimper, whine, weep, cry; informal blubber.

snob /snäb/ ▶ **n. 1** a person who has great respect for people with social status or wealth and looks down on lower-class people. **2** a person who believes that they have superior taste in a particular area: *a wine snob*. ■ **snob·ber·y n.**

snob·bish /ˈsnäbisH/ (or **snobby** /ˈsnäbē/) ▶ **adj.** relating to or typical of a snob: *his snobbish contempt for the lower classes*.

> SYNONYMS **elitist**, superior, supercilious, arrogant, condescending, pretentious, affected; informal snooty, high and mighty, la-di-da, stuck-up.

snood /snoo͞d/ ▶ **n.** a hairnet worn at the back of a woman's head.

snook·er /ˈsno͝okər/ ▶ **n. 1** a game played with cues on a billiard table. **2** a position in a game of snooker or pool in which a player cannot make a direct shot at any permitted ball. ▶ **v.** (**snookers**, **snookering**, **snookered**) (**be snookered**) informal be placed in an impossible position.

snoop /sno͞op/ informal ▶ **v.** look around or investigate secretly in order to find out something. ▶ **n.** an act of snooping.

SYNONYMS ▶ **v. pry**, spy, be a busybody, poke your nose into, root about, ferret about; informal be nosy.

■ **snoop·er n.**

snoot·y /ˈsno͞otē/ ▶ **adj.** (**snootier, snootiest**) informal behaving as if you are better or more important than other people. ■ **snoot·i·ly adv.**

snooze /sno͞oz/ informal ▶ **n.** a short, light sleep. ▶ **v.** (**snoozes, snoozing, snoozed**) take a snooze.

snore /snôr/ ▶ **n.** a snorting or rumbling sound in a person's breathing while they are asleep. ▶ **v.** (**snores, snoring, snored**) make a snorting or rumbling sound while asleep.

snor·kel /ˈsnôrkəl/ ▶ **n.** a tube for a swimmer to breathe through while underwater. ■ **snor·kel·ing n.**

snort /snôrt/ ▶ **v. 1** make a loud explosive sound by forcing breath through the nose. **2** informal inhale cocaine. ▶ **n. 1** a snorting sound. **2** informal a small alcoholic drink.

snot /snät/ ▶ **n.** informal mucus in the nose.

snot·ty /ˈsnätē/ ▶ **adj.** informal **1** full of, or covered with, mucus from the nose. **2** superior or arrogant.

snout /snout/ ▶ **n. 1** the projecting nose and mouth of an animal. **2** the projecting front or end of something such as a pistol.

snow /snō/ ▶ **n. 1** frozen water vapor in the atmosphere that falls in light white flakes. **2** (**snows**) falls of snow. ▶ **v. 1** (**it snows, it is snowing, it snowed**) snow falls. **2** (**be snowed in**) be unable to leave a place because of heavy snow. **3** (**be snowed under**) be overwhelmed with a large quantity of something, especially work.

snow·ball /ˈsnōˌbôl/ ▶ **n.** a ball of packed snow. ▶ **v.** increase rapidly in size, strength, or importance.

snow·board /ˈsnōˌbôrd/ ▶ **n.** a board that resembles a short, broad ski, used for sliding downhill on snow. ■ **snow·board·er n. snow·board·ing n.**

snow·bound /ˈsnōˌbound/ ▶ **adj. 1** unable to travel or go out because of snow. **2** (of a place) cut off by snow.

snow·drift /ˈsnōˌdrift/ ▶ **n.** a bank of deep snow heaped up by the wind.

snow·drop /ˈsnōˌdräp/ ▶ **n.** a plant with drooping white flowers that appear during late winter.

snow·fall /ˈsnōˌfôl/ ▶ **n. 1** a fall of snow. **2** the quantity of snow falling within a certain area in a given time.

snow·flake /ˈsnōˌflāk/ ▶ **n.** each of the many ice crystals that fall as snow.

snow·line /ˈsnōˌlīn/ ▶ **n.** the altitude above which some snow remains on the ground throughout the year.

snow·man /ˈsnōˌman/ ▶ **n.** (plural **snowmen**) a model of a human figure made with compressed snow.

snow·mo·bile /ˈsnōmōˌbēl/ ▶ **n.** a motor vehicle for traveling over snow.

snow·plow /ˈsnōˌplou/ ▶ **n.** a device or vehicle for clearing roads of snow.

snow·shoe /ˈsnōˌsʜo͞o/ ▶ **n.** a flat device attached to the sole of a boot and used for walking on snow.

snow·storm /ˈsnōˌstôrm/ ▶ **n.** a heavy fall of snow accompanied by a high wind.

snow·y /ˈsnōē/ ▶ **adj.** (**snowier, snowiest**) **1** having a lot of snow. **2** pure white.

snub /snəb/ ▶ **v.** (**snubs, snubbing, snubbed**) **1** insult someone by ignoring them when you meet. **2** refuse to attend or accept something. ▶ **n.** an act of snubbing.

SYNONYMS ▶ **v. rebuff**, spurn, cold-shoulder, ignore, insult, slight; informal stiff, freeze out. ▶ **n. rebuff**, slap in the face; informal brush-off, put-down.

□ **snub nose** a nose that is short and turned up at the end.

snuck /snək/ informal past and past participle of SNEAK.

snuff¹ /snəf/ ▶ **v. 1** put out a candle. **2** (**snuff something out**) abruptly put an end to something.

snuff² ▶ **n.** powdered tobacco that is sniffed up the nostril. ▶ **v.** sniff at.

snuf·fle /ˈsnəfəl/ ▶ **v.** (**snuffles, snuffling, snuffled**) **1** breathe noisily through a partially blocked nose. **2** (of an animal) make repeated sniffing sounds. ▶ **n.** a snuffling sound.

snug /snəg/ ▶ **adj.** (**snugger, snuggest**) **1** warm and cozy. **2** close-fitting.

SYNONYMS **1 cozy**, comfortable, warm, sheltered, secure; informal comfy. **2 tight**, skintight, close-fitting, figure-hugging. ANTONYMS loose.

■ **snug·ly adv.**

snug·gle /ˈsnəgəl/ ▶ **v.** (**snuggles, snuggling, snuggled**) settle into a warm, comfortable position.

SYNONYMS **nestle**, curl up, huddle (up), cuddle up, nuzzle, settle.

so¹ /sō/ ▶ **adv. 1** to such a great extent. **2** extremely; very much. **3** to the same extent; as: *he isn't so bad as you'd think*. **4** that is the case. **5** similarly. **6** thus. ▶ **conj. 1** therefore. **2** (**so that**) with the result or aim that. **3** and then. **4** in the same way. □ **or so** approximately. **so-and-so** (plural **so-and-sos**) informal **1** a person whose name you do not know. **2** a person that you do not like. **so-called** wrongly or inappropriately called a particular thing. **so long!** informal goodbye. **so-so** neither very good nor very bad. **so to speak** indicating that you are not talking literally.

so² ▶ **n.** ⇒ SOL.

soak /sōk/ ▶ **v. 1** make something thoroughly wet by leaving it in liquid. **2** (of a liquid) spread completely throughout. **3** (**soak something up**) absorb a liquid. **4** (**soak something up**) expose yourself to something enjoyable. ▶ **n. 1** a period of soaking. **2** informal a heavy drinker.

SYNONYMS ▶ **v. 1 dip**, immerse, steep, submerge, douse, marinate, souse. **2 drench**, wet through, saturate. **3** *water soaked through the carpet* **permeate**, penetrate, impregnate, percolate, seep, spread. **4 absorb**, suck up, blot, mop up.

soak·ing /ˈsōkiɴɢ/ (also **soaking wet**) ▶ **adj.** very wet.

SYNONYMS **drenched**, wet (through), soaked (through), sodden, soggy, waterlogged, saturated, sopping, dripping, wringing. ANTONYMS parched.

soap /sōp/ ▶ **n. 1** a substance used with water for washing and cleaning. **2** informal a soap opera. ▶ **v.**

wash with soap. □ **soap opera** a television or radio serial that deals with the daily lives of a group of characters.

soap·box /'sōp,bäks/ ▶ **n.** a box that someone stands on to speak in public.

soap·stone /'sōp,stōn/ ▶ **n.** a soft rock used for making ornaments.

soap·y /'sōpē/ ▶ **adj.** (**soapier**, **soapiest**) **1** containing or covered with soap. **2** like soap.

soar /sôr/ ▶ **v. 1** fly or rise high into the air. **2** increase rapidly.

SYNONYMS **1 rise**, ascend, climb. **2 glide**, plane, float, hover. **3 increase**, escalate, shoot up, spiral, rocket; informal go through the roof, skyrocket. ANTONYMS plummet.

sob /säb/ ▶ **v.** (**sobs**, **sobbing**, **sobbed**) **1** cry with loud gasps. **2** say while sobbing. ▶ **n.** a sound of sobbing.

SYNONYMS ▶ **v. weep**, cry, snivel, whimper; informal blubber.

so·ber /'sōbər/ ▶ **adj.** (**soberer**, **soberest**) **1** not drunk. **2** serious. **3** (of a color) not bright or likely to attract attention. ▶ **v.** (**sobers**, **sobering**, **sobered**) **1** (**sober up**) make or become sober after being drunk. **2** make or become serious.

SYNONYMS ▶ **adj. 1 clear-headed**, teetotal, abstinent, dry; informal on the wagon. **2 serious**, solemn, sensible, staid, sedate, quiet, dignified, grave, levelheaded, down-to-earth. **3 somber**, subdued, restrained, austere, severe, drab, plain, dark. ANTONYMS drunk.

■ **so·ber·ly adv.**

so·bri·e·ty /sə'brīətē, sō-/ ▶ **n.** the state of being sober.

so·bri·quet /'sōbri,kā, -,ket/ (or **soubriquet**) ▶ **n.** a person's nickname.

soc·cer /'säkər/ ▶ **n.** a game played by two teams of eleven players with a round ball that may not be handled during play except by the goalkeepers.

so·cia·ble /'sōsʜəbəl/ ▶ **adj. 1** liking to talk to and do things with other people. **2** friendly and welcoming.

SYNONYMS **friendly**, amicable, affable, companionable, gregarious, cordial, warm, genial. ANTONYMS unfriendly.

■ **so·cia·bil·i·ty** /,sōsʜə'bilitē/ **n. so·cia·bly adv.**

so·cial /'sōsʜəl/ ▶ **adj. 1** having to do with society and its organization. **2** needing the company of other people. **3** (of an activity) in which people meet each other for pleasure. **4** (of animals) breeding or living in organized communities. ▶ **n.** an informal social gathering.

SYNONYMS ▶ **adj. 1 communal**, community, collective, general, popular, civil, public, civic. **2 recreational**, leisure, entertainment. ▶ **n. party**, gathering, function, get-together, celebration; informal do.

□ **social networking** the use of a dedicated website to communicate informally with other members of the site, by posting messages, photographs, etc. **social science 1** the study of human society and social relationships. **2** a subject within this field, such as economics. **Social Security** a federal insurance program that provides benefits to retired persons, the unemployed, and the disabled. **social services** services provided by the state such as education and medical care. **social worker** a person whose job is to help improve the conditions of the poor, the old, etc.
■ **so·cial·ly adv.**

so·cial·ism /'sōsʜə,lizəm/ ▶ **n.** the theory that a country's land, transport, industries, etc., should be owned or controlled by the community as a whole. ■ **so·cial·ist n. & adj.**

so·cial·ite /'sōsʜə,līt/ ▶ **n.** a person who mixes in fashionable society.

so·cial·ize /'sōsʜə,līz/ ▶ **v.** (**socializes**, **socializing**, **socialized**) **1** mix socially with other people. **2** make someone behave in a socially acceptable way.

SYNONYMS **interact**, converse, be sociable, mix, mingle, get together, meet, fraternize, consort; informal hobnob, hang out.

so·ci·e·ty /sə'sīətē/ ▶ **n.** (plural **societies**) **1** people living together in an ordered community. **2** a community of people. **3** (also **high society**) people who are fashionable, wealthy, and influential. **4** an organization formed for a particular purpose. **5** the situation of being in the company of other people.

SYNONYMS **1 the community**, the (general) public, the people, the population, civilization, humankind, mankind, the world at large. **2** *an industrial society* **culture**, community, civilization, nation. **3 high society**, polite society, the upper classes, the gentry, the elite, the smart set, the beau monde; informal the upper crust. **4 club**, association, group, circle, institute, guild, lodge, league, union, alliance. **5 company**, companionship, fellowship, friendship.

■ **so·ci·e·tal** /sə'sīitl/ **adj.**

so·ci·ol·o·gy /,sōsē'äləjē/ ▶ **n.** the study of human society. ■ **so·ci·o·log·i·cal** /,sōsēō'läjikəl/ **adj. so·ci·ol·o·gist n.**

sock /säk/ ▶ **n. 1** a knitted garment for the foot and lower part of the leg. **2** informal a hard blow. ▶ **v.** informal hit forcefully. □ **knock the socks off** informal **1** surpass or beat. **2** amaze or impress. **sock it to** informal make a forceful impression on.

sock·et /'säkit/ ▶ **n. 1** a hollow in which something fits or revolves. **2** an electrical device that a plug or light bulb fits into.

sod /säd/ ▶ **n. 1** grass-covered ground. **2** a piece of turf.

so·da /'sōdə/ ▶ **n. 1** (also **soda water** or **club soda**) carbonated water. **2** (also **soda pop**) a carbonated soft drink. **3** a compound of sodium. □ **soda fountain 1** a device dispensing soda water. **2** a counter at which soft drinks and ice cream are served.

sod·den /'sädn/ ▶ **adj. 1** soaked through. **2** having drunk too much alcohol: *whiskey-sodden.*

so·di·um /'sōdēəm/ ▶ **n.** a soft silver-white metallic element. □ **sodium bicarbonate** a white powder used in effervescent drinks, as a leavening agent in baking, and in fire extinguishers; baking soda. **sodium chloride** the chemical name for salt. **sodium hydroxide** a strongly alkaline white compound; caustic soda.

so·fa /'sōfə/ ▶ **n.** a long padded seat with a back and arms.

SYNONYMS **couch**, settee, divan, chaise longue, chesterfield.

soft /sôft/ ▶ **adj. 1** easy to mold, cut, compress, or fold. **2** not rough in texture. **3** quiet and gentle. **4** (of light or color) not harsh. **5** not strict enough.

6 informal not needing much effort. **7** informal foolish. **8** (**soft on**) informal having romantic feelings for. **9** (of a drink) not alcoholic. **10** (of a drug) not likely to cause addiction. **11** (of water) free from mineral salts.

SYNONYMS **1 mushy**, squashy, pulpy, squishy, doughy, spongy, springy, elastic, pliable, pliant; informal gooey. **2 swampy**, marshy, boggy, muddy, squelchy. **3 smooth**, velvety, fleecy, downy, furry, silky, silken. **4 dim**, low, faint, subdued, muted, subtle. **5 quiet**, low, gentle, faint, muted, subdued, muffled, hushed, whispered. **6 lenient**, easygoing, tolerant, forgiving, forbearing, indulgent, liberal, lax. ANTONYMS hard, firm, harsh.

□ **have a soft spot for** be fond of. **soft focus** deliberate slight blurring in a photograph or movie. **soft-pedal** play down the unpleasant aspects of. **soft sell** the selling of something in a gently persuasive way. **soft-soap** informal use flattery to persuade someone. **soft touch** informal a person who is easily persuaded. ■ **soft·ly** adv. **soft·ness** n.

soft·ball /ˈsôf(t)ˌbôl/ ▶ n. a form of baseball played with a larger, softer ball.

soft·cov·er /ˈsôf(t)ˌkəvər/ (or **softback** /ˈsôf(t)ˌbak/) ▶ n. ⇒ PAPERBACK.

soft·en /ˈsôfən/ ▶ v. **1** make or become soft or softer. **2** (**soften someone up**) make someone more likely to do or agree to something.

SYNONYMS *the compensation should soften the blow* **ease**, alleviate, relieve, soothe, take the edge off, cushion, lessen, diminish, blunt, deaden.

soft·en·er /ˈsôfənər/ ▶ n. a substance or device that softens something, especially fabric or water.

soft·heart·ed /ˈsôftˈhärtid/ ▶ adj. kind and sympathetic.

soft·ware /ˈsôftˌwe(ə)r/ ▶ n. programs and other operating information used by a computer.

soft·wood /ˈsôftˌwo͝od/ ▶ n. the wood from a conifer as opposed to that from a broadleaved tree.

sog·gy /ˈsägē/ ▶ adj. (**soggier**, **soggiest**) very wet and soft.

SYNONYMS **mushy**, squashy, pulpy, slushy, squelchy, swampy, marshy, boggy, soaking, wet, saturated, drenched.

soil /soil/ ▶ n. **1** the upper layer of earth, in which plants grow. **2** the territory of a particular nation. ▶ v. **1** make dirty. **2** bring discredit to.

SYNONYMS ▶ n. **1 earth**, dirt, clay, ground, loam. **2 territory**, land, region, country, domain, dominion. ▶ v. **dirty**, stain, smear, smudge, spoil, foul.

soi·rée /swäˈrā/ ▶ n. an evening social gathering.

so·journ /ˈsōjərn/ literary ▶ n. a temporary stay. ▶ v. stay temporarily.

SYNONYMS ▶ n. **stay**, visit, stop, stopover, vacation. ▶ v. **stay**, live, put up, stop (over), vacation, lodge, room, board.

sol /sōl/ (or **so** /sō/) ▶ n. Music the fifth note of a major scale.

sol·ace /ˈsälis/ ▶ n. comfort in a difficult time. ▶ v. (**solaces**, **solacing**, **solaced**) give comfort to.

SYNONYMS ▶ n. **comfort**, consolation, cheer, support, relief.

so·lar /ˈsōlər/ ▶ adj. having to do with the sun or its rays. □ **solar eclipse** an eclipse in which the sun is hidden by the moon. **solar panel** a panel designed to absorb the sun's rays as a source of energy for generating electricity or heating. **solar plexus** a network of nerves at the pit of the stomach. **solar system** the sun together with the planets, asteroids, comets, etc., in orbit around it.

so·lar·i·um /səˈle(ə)rēəm, sō-/ ▶ n. (plural **solariums** or **solaria** /-rēə/) **1** a room fitted with extensive areas of glass to admit sunlight; a sunroom. **2** a room equipped with sunlamps or sunbeds.

sold /sōld/ past and past participle of SELL.

sol·der /ˈsädər/ ▶ n. a soft alloy used for joining metals. ▶ v. (**solders**, **soldering**, **soldered**) join with solder. □ **soldering iron** an electrical tool for melting and applying solder.

sol·dier /ˈsōljər/ ▶ n. **1** a person who serves in an army. **2** a private in an army. ▶ v. (**soldiers**, **soldiering**, **soldiered**) **1** serve as a soldier. **2** (**soldier on**) informal keep trying or working.

SYNONYMS ▶ n. **fighter**, GI, trooper, serviceman, servicewoman, warrior.

□ **soldier of fortune** a mercenary. ■ **sol·dier·ly** adj.

sole¹ /sōl/ ▶ n. **1** the underside of the foot. **2** the underside of a piece of footwear. ▶ v. (**soles**, **soling**, **soled**) put a new sole on a shoe.

sole² ▶ adj. **1** one and only. **2** belonging or restricted to one person or group.

SYNONYMS **only**, one, single, solitary, lone, unique, exclusive.

sole³ ▶ n. (plural **sole**) a kind of edible flatfish.

sol·e·cism /ˈsäləˌsizəm, ˈsō-/ ▶ n. **1** a grammatical mistake. **2** an example of bad manners or incorrect behavior.

sole·ly /ˈsōl(l)ē/ ▶ adv. not involving anyone or anything else; only.

SYNONYMS **only**, simply, purely, just, merely, uniquely, exclusively, entirely, wholly, alone.

sol·emn /ˈsäləm/ ▶ adj. **1** formal and dignified. **2** serious. **3** deeply sincere.

SYNONYMS **1 dignified**, ceremonial, stately, formal, majestic, imposing, splendid, magnificent, grand. **2 serious**, grave, sober, somber, unsmiling, stern, grim, dour, humorless. **3 sincere**, earnest, honest, genuine, firm, heartfelt, wholehearted, sworn. ANTONYMS frivolous, lighthearted.

■ **sol·emn·ly** adv.

so·lem·ni·ty /səˈlemnitē/ ▶ n. (plural **solemnities**) **1** the quality of being solemn. **2** (**solemnities**) solemn rites or ceremonies.

sol·em·nize /ˈsäləmˌnīz/ ▶ v. (**solemnizes**, **solemnizing**, **solemnized**) **1** perform a ceremony. **2** mark an occasion with a ceremony.

so·le·noid /ˈsōləˌnoid/ ▶ n. a coil of wire that becomes magnetic when an electric current is passed through it.

so·lic·it /səˈlisit/ ▶ v. (**solicits**, **soliciting**, **solicited**) try to obtain something from someone.

SYNONYMS **1 ask for**, request, seek, apply for, put in for, call for, beg for, plead for. **2 ask**, approach, appeal to, lobby, petition, importune, call on, press.

■ **so·lic·i·ta·tion** /səˌlisəˈtāshən/ n.

so·lic·i·tor /sə'lisitər/ ▶ **n.** **1** a person who tries to obtain business orders, advertising, etc. **2** the chief law officer of a city, town, or government department.

so·lic·i·tous /sə'lisitəs/ ▶ **adj.** showing interest or concern about a person's well-being.

> SYNONYMS **concerned**, caring, considerate, attentive, mindful, thoughtful, interested, anxious, worried.

■ **so·lic·i·tous·ly** adv.

so·lic·i·tude /sə'lisi,t(y)o͞od/ ▶ **n.** care or concern.

sol·id /'sälid/ ▶ **adj.** (**solider**, **solidest**) **1** firm and stable in shape. **2** strongly built or made. **3** not hollow or having spaces or gaps. **4** consisting of the same substance throughout. **5** (of time) uninterrupted. **6** three-dimensional. ▶ **n.** **1** a solid substance or object. **2** (**solids**) food that is not liquid.

> SYNONYMS ▶ **adj.** **1** **hard**, rock-hard, rigid, firm, solidified, set, frozen, compact, compressed, dense. **2** *solid gold* **pure**, unadulterated, genuine. **3** **well-built**, sound, substantial, strong, sturdy, durable, stout. **4** **well-founded**, valid, sound, logical, authoritative, convincing, cogent. **5** *solid support* **unanimous**, united, consistent, undivided. ANTONYMS liquid, flimsy, untenable.

□ **solid-state** (of an electronic device) using solid semiconductors, e.g., transistors, as opposed to valves. ■ **so·lid·i·ty** /sə'liditē/ **n.** **sol·id·ly** adv.

sol·i·dar·i·ty /,sälə'de(ə)ritē/ ▶ **n.** agreement and support resulting from shared interests, feelings, or opinions.

> SYNONYMS **unanimity**, unity, agreement, team spirit, accord, harmony, consensus; formal concord.

so·lid·i·fy /sə'lidə,fī/ ▶ **v.** (**solidifies**, **solidifying**, **solidified**) make or become hard or solid.

> SYNONYMS **harden**, set, thicken, stiffen, congeal, cake, freeze, ossify, fossilize, petrify. ANTONYMS liquefy.

■ **so·lid·i·fi·ca·tion** /sə,lidəfi'kāsʜən/ **n.**

so·lil·o·quy /sə'liləkwē/ ▶ **n.** (plural **soliloquies**) a speech in a play in which a character speaks thoughts aloud when alone on stage.

sol·ip·sism /'sälip,sizəm/ ▶ **n.** the view that the self is all that can be known to exist. ■ **sol·ip·sist** **n.** **sol·ip·sis·tic** /,sälip'sistik/ **adj.**

sol·i·taire /'sälə,te(ə)r/ ▶ **n.** **1** any of various card games played by one person. **2** a single gem in a piece of jewelry.

sol·i·tar·y /'sälə,terē/ ▶ **adj.** **1** done or existing alone. **2** (of a place) secluded or isolated. **3** single.

> SYNONYMS **1** **lonely**, unaccompanied, by yourself, on your own, lonesome, alone, friendless, unsociable, withdrawn, reclusive. **2** **isolated**, remote, lonely, out of the way, in the back of beyond, outlying, off the beaten track, in the backwoods, secluded. **3** **single**, lone, sole, only, one, individual. ANTONYMS sociable.

□ **solitary confinement** the isolating of a prisoner in a separate cell as a punishment.

sol·i·tude /'sälə,t(y)o͞od/ ▶ **n.** the state of being alone.

> SYNONYMS **loneliness**, solitariness, isolation, seclusion, privacy, peace.

so·lo /'sōlō/ ▶ **n.** (plural **solos**) **1** a piece of music or dance for one performer. **2** a flight undertaken by a single pilot. ▶ **adj. & adv.** for or done by one person. ▶ **v.** (**soloes**, **soloing**, **soloed**) perform a solo.

> SYNONYMS ▶ **adj. & adv.** **1** *a solo performance* **unaccompanied**, single-handed, unescorted, unattended, alone, on your own, by yourself, independent, solitary. **2** *she was soon flying solo* **unaccompanied**, alone, on your own, single-handed(ly), by yourself, unescorted, unattended, unaided, independently. ANTONYMS accompanied.

■ **so·lo·ist** **n.**

sol·stice /'sōlstis/ ▶ **n.** each of the two times in the year when the sun reaches its highest or lowest point in the sky at noon, marked by the longest and shortest days.

sol·u·ble /'sälyəbəl/ ▶ **adj.** **1** (of a substance) able to be dissolved. **2** (of a problem) able to be solved. ■ **sol·u·bil·i·ty** /,sälyə'bilitē/ **n.**

so·lu·tion /sə'lo͞osʜən/ ▶ **n.** **1** a way of solving a problem. **2** the correct answer to a puzzle. **3** a mixture formed when a substance is dissolved in a liquid. **4** the process of dissolving.

> SYNONYMS **1** **answer**, result, resolution, key, explanation. **2** **mixture**, blend, emulsion, compound.

solve /sälv, sôlv/ ▶ **v.** (**solves**, **solving**, **solved**) find an answer to, or way of dealing with, a problem or mystery.

> SYNONYMS **answer**, resolve, work out, puzzle out, fathom, decipher, decode, clear up, straighten out, get to the bottom of, unravel, explain; informal figure out, crack.

sol·ven·cy /'sälvənsē/ ▶ **n.** the state of having more money than you owe.

sol·vent /'sälvənt/ ▶ **adj.** **1** having more money than you owe. **2** able to dissolve other substances. ▶ **n.** the liquid in which another substance is dissolved to form a solution.

So·ma·li /sə'mälē, sō-/ ▶ **n.** (plural **Somali** or **Somalis**) **1** a person from Somalia. **2** the language of the Somali. ▶ **adj.** relating to Somalia.

som·ber /'sämbər/ ▶ **adj.** **1** dark or dull. **2** very solemn or serious.

> SYNONYMS **1** **dark**, drab, dull, dingy, restrained, sober, funereal. **2** **solemn**, earnest, serious, grave, sober, unsmiling, gloomy, sad, mournful, melancholy, lugubrious, cheerless. ANTONYMS bright, cheerful.

■ **som·ber·ly** adv.

som·bre·ro /säm'bre(ə)rō/ ▶ **n.** (plural **sombreros**) a broad-brimmed felt or straw hat.

some /səm/ ▶ **determiner** **1** an unspecified amount or number of. **2** unknown or unspecified. **3** approximately. **4** a considerable amount or number of. **5** used to express admiration. ▶ **pron.** a certain amount or number of people or things.

some·bod·y /'səmbədē, 'səm,bädē/ ▶ **pron.** someone.

some·day /'səm,dā/ ▶ **adv.** at some time in the future.

some·how /'səm,hou/ ▶ **adv.** **1** by one means or another. **2** for an unknown or unspecified reason.

> SYNONYMS **one way or another**, no matter how, by hook or by crook, come what may, come hell or high water, by fair means or foul.

some·one /ˈsəmˌwən/ ▶ **pron.** **1** an unknown or unspecified person. **2** an important or famous person.

some·place /ˈsəmˌplās/ ▶ **adv. & pron.** informal somewhere.

som·er·sault /ˈsəmərˌsôlt/ ▶ **n.** a movement in which a person turns head over heels and finishes on their feet. ▶ **v.** perform a somersault.

some·thing /ˈsəmˌTHiNG/ ▶ **pron.** an unspecified or unknown thing or amount.

some·time /ˈsəmˌtīm/ ▶ **adv.** at some unspecified or unknown time. ▶ **adj.** former.

some·times /ˈsəmˌtīmz/ ▶ **adv.** occasionally.

> SYNONYMS **occasionally**, from time to time, now and then, every so often, once in a while, on occasion, at times, off and on.

some·what /ˈsəmˌ(h)wät/ ▶ **adv.** to some extent.

> SYNONYMS **1** *matters have improved somewhat* **a little**, a bit, to some extent, (up) to a point, in some measure; informal some, kind of, sort of. **2** *a somewhat longer book* **slightly**, relatively, comparatively, moderately, fairly, rather, quite, marginally. ANTONYMS greatly.

some·where /ˈsəmˌ(h)we(ə)r/ ▶ **adv.** in or to an unspecified or unknown place. ▶ **pron.** some unspecified place.

som·nam·bu·lism /sämˈnambyəˌlizəm/ ▶ **n.** formal sleepwalking. ■ **som·nam·bu·list** **n.**

som·no·lent /ˈsämnələnt/ ▶ **adj.** sleepy or drowsy. ■ **som·no·lence** **n.**

son /sən/ ▶ **n.** **1** a boy or man in relation to his parents. **2** a male descendant. **3** (**the Son**) Jesus. □ **son-in-law** (plural **sons-in-law**) the husband of a person's daughter.

so·nar /ˈsōˌnär/ ▶ **n.** a system for detecting objects underwater by giving out sound pulses.

so·na·ta /səˈnätə/ ▶ **n.** a piece of music for a solo instrument, sometimes with piano accompaniment.

song /sôNG/ ▶ **n.** **1** a set of words set to music. **2** singing. **3** the musical phrases uttered by some birds, whales, and insects. **4** literary a poem.

> SYNONYMS **air**, strain, ditty, chant, number, track, melody, tune.

□ **for a song** informal very cheaply. **a song and dance** informal a fuss.

song·bird /ˈsôNGˌbərd/ ▶ **n.** a bird with a musical song.

song·ster /ˈsôNGstər/ ▶ **n.** (feminine **songstress**) a person who sings.

song·writ·er /ˈsôNGˌrītər/ ▶ **n.** a writer of songs or the music for them.

son·ic /ˈsänik/ ▶ **adj.** relating to or using sound waves. □ **sonic boom** an explosive noise caused by the shock wave from an object traveling faster than the speed of sound. ■ **son·i·cal·ly** **adv.**

son·net /ˈsänit/ ▶ **n.** a poem of fourteen lines using a fixed rhyme scheme.

so·no·rous /ˈsänərəs/ ▶ **adj.** **1** (of a sound) deep and full. **2** (of speech) using powerful language.

> SYNONYMS **resonant**, rich, full, round, booming, deep, clear, mellow, strong, resounding, reverberant.

■ **so·nor·i·ty** /səˈnôritē/ **n.** **so·no·rous·ly** **adv.**

soon /so͞on/ ▶ **adv.** **1** in or after a short time. **2** early. **3** (**would sooner**) would rather.

> SYNONYMS **1 shortly**, presently, in the near future, before long, in a little while, in a minute, in a moment; informal in a sec. **2** (**sooner**) **earlier**, before now. **3** (**sooner**) **rather**, preferably, given the choice.

soot /so͝ot/ ▶ **n.** a black powdery substance produced when wood, coal, etc., is burned.

soothe /so͞oTH/ ▶ **v.** (**soothes**, **soothing**, **soothed**) **1** gently calm. **2** relieve pain or discomfort.

> SYNONYMS **1 calm** (**down**), pacify, comfort, hush, quiet (down), settle (down), appease, mollify. **2** (**soothing**) **relaxing**, restful, calm, calming, tranquil, peaceful. **3 ease**, alleviate, relieve, take the edge off, allay, lessen, reduce. ANTONYMS agitate, aggravate.

sooth·say·er /ˈso͞oTHˌsāər/ ▶ **n.** a person supposed to be able to foresee the future.

soot·y /ˈso͝otē/ ▶ **adj.** (**sootier**, **sootiest**) covered with or colored like soot.

sop /säp/ ▶ **n.** **1** a thing given or done to calm or please someone who is angry or disappointed. **2** a piece of bread dipped in gravy, soup, or sauce. ▶ **v.** (**sops**, **sopping**, **sopped**) (**sop something up**) soak up liquid.

soph·ism /ˈsäfizəm/ ▶ **n.** a false argument.

soph·ist /ˈsäfist/ ▶ **n.** a person who uses clever but false arguments. ■ **soph·ist·ry** /ˈsäfəstrē/ **n.**

so·phis·ti·cate /səˈfistəˌkit, -kāt/ ▶ **n.** a sophisticated person.

so·phis·ti·cat·ed /səˈfistiˌkātid/ ▶ **adj.** **1** having experience and taste in matters of culture or fashion. **2** highly developed and complex.

> SYNONYMS **1 advanced**, state-of-the-art, the latest, up-to-the-minute, cutting-edge, complex. **2 worldly**, worldly-wise, experienced, cosmopolitan, urbane, cultured, cultivated, polished, refined. ANTONYMS crude, naive.

so·phis·ti·ca·tion /səˌfistiˈkāSHən/ ▶ **n.** the quality or fact of having experience and taste in matters of fashion and culture.

> SYNONYMS **worldliness**, experience, urbanity, culture, polish, refinement, elegance, style, poise, finesse, savoir faire.

soph·o·more /ˈsäf(ə)ˌmôr/ ▶ **n.** a second-year university or high-school student.

sop·o·rif·ic /ˌsäpəˈrifik/ ▶ **adj.** causing drowsiness or sleep.

sop·ping /ˈsäpiNG/ ▶ **adj.** wet through.

so·pran·o /səˈpranō/ ▶ **n.** (plural **sopranos**) the highest singing voice.

sor·bet /sôrˈbā, ˈsôrbit/ ▶ **n.** a dessert consisting of frozen fruit juice or flavored water and sugar.

sor·cer·er /ˈsôrsərər/ ▶ **n.** (feminine **sorceress** /ˈsôrsəris/) a person who practices magic.

sor·cer·y /ˈsôrsərē/ ▶ **n.** the use of magic, especially black magic.

sor·did /ˈsôrdid/ ▶ **adj.** **1** dishonest or immoral. **2** very dirty and unpleasant.

> SYNONYMS **1 sleazy**, seedy, seamy, unsavory, tawdry, cheap, disreputable, discreditable, ignominious, shameful, wretched, despicable. **2 squalid**, slummy, dirty, filthy, shabby, scummy; informal scuzzy. ANTONYMS respectable.

■ **sor·did·ly** **adv.**

sore /sôr/ ▶ **adj.** **1** painful or aching. **2** urgent: *in sore need.* **3** informal upset and angry. ▶ **n.** a raw or painful place on the body. ▶ **adv.** old use very: *sore afraid.*

SYNONYMS ▶ **adj.** **1 painful**, hurting, aching, throbbing, smarting, stinging, inflamed, sensitive, tender, raw, wounded, injured. **2 upset**, angry, annoyed, cross, disgruntled, dissatisfied, irritated; informal aggravated, miffed, peeved, ticked off.

□ **sore point** an issue about which someone feels distressed or annoyed. ■ **sore·ness** n.

sore·ly /ˈsôrlē/ ▶ **adv.** extremely; badly.

sor·ghum /ˈsôrgəm/ ▶ **n.** a cereal plant found in warm regions, grown for grain and animal feed.

so·ror·i·ty /səˈrôritē, -ˈrä-/ ▶ **n.** (plural **sororities**) a society for female students in a university or college.

sor·rel /ˈsôrəl/ ▶ **n.** **1** an edible plant with a bitter flavor. **2** a light reddish-brown color.

sor·row /ˈsärō, ˈsôrō/ ▶ **n.** **1** deep distress caused by loss or disappointment. **2** a cause of sorrow.

SYNONYMS **1 sadness**, unhappiness, misery, despondency, regret, despair, desolation, heartache, grief. **2** *the sorrows of life* **trouble**, difficulty, problem, woe, affliction, trial, tribulation, misfortune. ANTONYMS joy.

sor·row·ful /ˈsärəfəl, ˈsôrō-/ ▶ **adj.** feeling or showing sorrow. ■ **sor·row·ful·ly** adv.

sor·ry /ˈsärē, ˈsô-/ ▶ **adj.** (**sorrier**, **sorriest**) **1** feeling sympathy for someone else's misfortune. **2** feeling or expressing regret. **3** in a bad or pitiful state. **4** unpleasant and regrettable.

SYNONYMS **1 regretful**, apologetic, remorseful, contrite, repentant, rueful, penitent, guilty, shamefaced, ashamed. **2** *he felt sorry for her* **full of pity**, sympathetic, compassionate, moved, concerned. **3** *I was sorry to hear about the accident* **sad**, sorrowful, distressed. ANTONYMS glad, unrepentant.

sort /sôrt/ ▶ **n.** **1** a category of people or things with a common feature or features. **2** informal a person: *a friendly sort.* ▶ **v.** **1** arrange systematically in groups. **2** (often **sort someone/thing out**) separate someone or something from a mixed group. **3** (**sort something out**) deal with a problem or difficulty.

SYNONYMS ▶ **n. type**, kind, variety, class, category, style, form, genre, species, breed, make, model, brand. ▶ **v.** **1 classify**, class, group, organize, arrange, order, grade, catalog. **2** *the problem was soon sorted out* **resolve**, settle, solve, fix, work out, straighten out, deal with, put right, set right, rectify, iron out.

□ **of a sort** (or **of sorts**) of a somewhat unusual or inferior kind. **out of sorts** slightly unwell or unhappy.

USAGE

Use **this sort of** to refer to a singular noun (e.g., *this sort of job*), and **these sorts of** to refer to a plural noun (e.g., *these sorts of questions*).

sort·ie /ˌsôrˈtē, ˈsôrtē/ ▶ **n.** **1** an attack made by troops from a position of defense. **2** a flight by an aircraft on a military operation. **3** a short trip.

SOS ▶ **n.** **1** an international signal sent when in great trouble. **2** an urgent appeal for help.

sot /sät/ ▶ **n.** old use a person who is regularly drunk. ■ **sot·tish** adj.

sot·to vo·ce /ˈsätō ˈvōCHē/ ▶ **adv. & adj.** in a quiet voice.

sou·bri·quet = **SOBRIQUET**.

souf·flé /so͞oˈflā/ ▶ **n.** a light, spongy dish made by mixing egg yolks with beaten egg whites.

sought /sôt/ past and past participle of **SEEK**. □ **sought after** in great demand.

souk /so͝ok/ ▶ **n.** an Arab market.

soul /sōl/ ▶ **n.** **1** the spiritual element of a person, believed by some to be immortal. **2** a person's inner nature. **3** emotional energy or power. **4** (**the soul of**) a perfect example of a particular quality. **5** an individual: *poor soul!* **6** a kind of music that expresses strong emotions, made popular by black Americans.

SYNONYMS **1 spirit**, psyche, (inner) self. **2 feeling**, emotion, passion, animation, intensity, warmth, energy, vitality, spirit.

□ **soul-destroying** unbearably dull and repetitive. **soul-searching** close examination of your emotions and motives.

soul·ful /ˈsōlfəl/ ▶ **adj.** expressing deep feeling. ■ **soul·ful·ly** adv.

soul·less /ˈsōlˌlis/ ▶ **adj.** **1** lacking character or interest. **2** lacking human feelings.

soul·mate /ˈsōlˌmāt/ ▶ **n.** a person ideally suited to another.

sound¹ /sound/ ▶ **n.** **1** vibrations that travel through the air and are sensed by the ear. **2** a thing that can be heard. **3** an impression given by words. ▶ **v.** **1** make sound. **2** make a sound to show or warn of something. **3** give a particular impression. **4** (**sound off**) express your opinions loudly or forcefully.

SYNONYMS ▶ **n.** **1 noise**, din, racket, resonance, reverberation. **2 utterance**, cry, word, noise, peep. ANTONYMS silence. ▶ **v.** **1 make a noise**, resonate, resound, reverberate, go off, ring, chime, ping. **2** *sound the horn* **blow**, blast, toot, ring, use, operate, activate, set off. **3 appear**, look (like), seem, give every indication of being, strike someone as.

□ **sound barrier** the point at which an aircraft approaches the speed of sound. **sound bite** a short, memorable extract from a speech or interview. **sound effect** a sound other than speech or music that is used in a play, movie, etc. **sound wave** a wave by which sound travels through water, air, etc. ■ **sound·less** adj.

sound² ▶ **adj.** **1** in good condition. **2** based on solid judgment. **3** financially secure. **4** competent or reliable. **5** (of sleep) deep and unbroken. **6** severe or thorough.

SYNONYMS **1 healthy**, in good condition/shape, fit, hale and hearty, in fine fettle, undamaged, unimpaired. **2 well-built**, solid, substantial, strong, sturdy, durable, stable, intact. **3 well-founded**, valid, reasonable, logical, weighty, authoritative, reliable. **4 reliable**, dependable, trustworthy, fair, good. **5 solvent**, debt-free, in the black, creditworthy, secure. **6 deep**, undisturbed, uninterrupted, untroubled, peaceful. ANTONYMS unhealthy, unsafe.

■ **sound·ly** adv.

sound³ ▶ **v.** **1** find out the depth of water using a line, pole, or sound echoes. **2** (**sound someone out**) question someone about their opinions or feelings.

sound⁴ ▶ n. a narrow stretch of water forming an inlet or connecting two larger areas of water.

sound·ing /ˈsoundiNG/ ▶ n. 1 a measurement of the depth of water. 2 (**soundings**) information found out before taking action. □ **sounding board** a person or group that you talk to in order to test out new ideas.

sound·proof /ˈsoun(d)ˌpro͞of/ ▶ adj. preventing sound getting in or out. ▶ v. make soundproof.

sound·track /ˈsoun(d)ˌtrak/ ▶ n. the sound accompaniment to a movie.

soup /so͞op/ ▶ n. a savory liquid dish made by boiling meat, fish, or vegetables. ▶ v. (**soup something up**) informal make a car more powerful. □ **soup kitchen** a place where free food is served to homeless or very poor people.

soup·çon /so͞opˈsôN/ ▶ n. a very small quantity of something.

sour /ˈsou(ə)r/ ▶ adj. 1 having a sharp taste like lemon or vinegar. 2 (especially of milk) stale and unpleasant. 3 resentful or angry. ▶ v. make or become sour.

> SYNONYMS ▶ adj. 1 **acid**, acidic, tart, bitter, sharp, vinegary, pungent. 2 **bad**, off, turned, curdled, rancid, fetid. 3 **embittered**, resentful, jaundiced, bitter, cross, crabby, crotchety, cantankerous, bad-tempered, disagreeable, unpleasant; informal grouchy. ANTONYMS sweet, fresh. ▶ v. **spoil**, mar, damage, harm, impair, upset, poison, blight.

□ **sour cream** cream that has been made sour by adding bacteria. **sour grapes** an attitude of pretending that something is worthless or undesirable because you cannot have it yourself. ■ **sour·ly** adv. **sour·ness** n.

source /sôrs/ ▶ n. 1 a place, person, or thing from which something originates. 2 a place where a river or stream starts. 3 a person, book, or document that provides information. ▶ v. (**sources, sourcing, sourced**) obtain from a particular source.

> SYNONYMS ▶ n. 1 **spring**, wellspring, wellhead, origin. 2 **origin**, derivation, starting point, start, beginning, fountainhead, root, author, originator.

sour·puss /ˈsou(ə)rˌpo͝os/ ▶ n. informal a bad-tempered or sulky person.

souse /sous/ ▶ v. (**souses, sousing, soused**) 1 soak in liquid. 2 (**soused**) pickled or marinated. 3 (**soused**) drunk.

south /souTH/ ▶ n. 1 the direction that is on your right-hand side when you are facing east. 2 the southern part of a place. ▶ adj. 1 lying toward or facing the south. 2 (of a wind) blowing from the south. ▶ adv. to or toward the south. □ **South American** 1 a person from South America. 2 relating to South America. ■ **south·ward** adj. & adv. **south·wards** adv.

south·east /ˌsouTHˈēst/ ▶ n. the direction or region halfway between south and east. ▶ adj. & adv. 1 toward or facing the southeast. 2 (of a wind) blowing from the southeast. ■ **south·east·ern** adj.

south·east·er·ly /ˌsouTHˈēstərlē/ ▶ adj. & adv. 1 in or toward the southeast. 2 (of a wind) blowing from the southeast.

south·er·ly /ˈsəT͟Hərlē/ ▶ adj. & adv. 1 facing or moving toward the south. 2 (of a wind) blowing from the south.

south·ern /ˈsəT͟Hərn/ ▶ adj. 1 situated in or facing the south. 2 coming from or characteristic of the south.

south·ern·er /ˈsəT͟Hərnər/ ▶ n. a person from the south of a region.

south·paw /ˈsouTHˌpô/ ▶ n. informal a left-handed person, especially a baseball pitcher who throws with the left hand.

south·west /ˌsouTHˈwest/ ▶ n. the direction or region halfway between south and west. ▶ adj. & adv. 1 toward or facing the southwest. 2 (of a wind) blowing from the southwest. ■ **south·west·ern** adj.

south·west·er·ly /ˌsouTHˈwestərlē/ ▶ adj. & adv. 1 in or toward the southwest. 2 (of a wind) blowing from the southwest.

sou·ve·nir /ˌso͞ovəˈni(ə)r/ ▶ n. a thing that is kept as a reminder of a person, place, or event.

> SYNONYMS **memento**, keepsake, reminder, memorial, trophy.

sou'·west·er /ˌsouˈwestər/ ▶ n. a waterproof hat with a brim that covers the back of the neck.

sov·er·eign /ˈsäv(ə)rən/ ▶ n. 1 a king or queen who is the supreme ruler of a country. 2 a former British gold coin worth one pound sterling. ▶ adj. 1 possessing supreme power. 2 (of a country) independent.

> SYNONYMS ▶ n. **ruler**, monarch, potentate, overlord, king, queen, emperor, empress, prince, princess. ▶ adj. **autonomous**, independent, self-governing, self-determining, nonaligned, free.

sov·er·eign·ty /ˈsäv(ə)rəntē/ ▶ n. (plural **sovereignties**) 1 supreme power or authority. 2 a self-governing state.

> SYNONYMS 1 **power**, rule, supremacy, dominion, jurisdiction, ascendancy, domination, authority, control. 2 **autonomy**, independence, self-rule, self-government, home rule, self-determination, freedom.

So·vi·et /ˈsōvēit, -ˌet/ ▶ n. 1 a citizen of the former Soviet Union. 2 (**soviet**) an elected council in the former Soviet Union. ▶ adj. having to do with the former Soviet Union.

sow¹ /sō/ ▶ v. (past **sowed**; past participle **sown** or **sowed**) 1 plant seed by scattering it on or in the earth. 2 spread or introduce something unwelcome.

> SYNONYMS **plant**, scatter, disperse, strew, broadcast, seed.

sow² /sou/ ▶ n. an adult female pig.

soy /soi/ ▶ n. the soybean. □ **soy sauce** a sauce made with fermented soybeans, used in Chinese and Japanese cooking.

soy·bean /ˈsoiˌbēn/ ▶ n. an edible bean that is high in protein.

spa /spä/ ▶ n. 1 a mineral spring considered to have health-giving properties. 2 a place with a mineral spring.

space /spās/ ▶ n. 1 unoccupied ground or area. 2 a blank between typed or written words or characters. 3 the dimensions of height, depth, and width within which all things exist and move. 4 (also **outer space**) the universe beyond the earth's atmosphere. 5 an interval of time. 6 freedom to live and develop as you wish. ▶ v. (**spaces, spacing, spaced**) 1 position items at a distance from one another. 2 (**be spaced out**) informal be confused or not completely conscious.

SYNONYMS ▶ n. 1 **room**, capacity, latitude, margin, leeway, play, elbow room, clearance. 2 **area**, expanse, stretch, sweep, tract. 3 **gap**, interval, opening, aperture, cavity, niche, interstice. 4 **blank**, gap, box. 5 **period**, span, time, duration, stretch, course, interval, gap. 6 **outer space**, deep space, the universe, the galaxy, the solar system. ▶ v. **position**, arrange, range, array, spread, lay out, set.

□ **space shuttle** a spacecraft used for journeys between earth and craft that are orbiting the earth. **space station** a large spacecraft used as a base for manned operations in space.

space·craft /ˈspāsˌkraft/ ▶ n. (plural **spacecraft** or **spacecrafts**) a vehicle used for traveling in space.

space·man /ˈspāsˌman, -mən/ ▶ n. (plural **spacemen**) a male astronaut.

space·ship /ˈspā(s)ˌshɪp/ ▶ n. a manned spacecraft.

space·suit /ˈspāsˌsōōt/ ▶ n. a pressurized suit covering the whole body that allows an astronaut to survive in space.

spa·cious /ˈspāshəs/ ▶ adj. (of a room or building) having plenty of space.

SYNONYMS **roomy**, capacious, commodious, voluminous, sizable, generous. ANTONYMS cramped.

spade /spād/ ▶ n. 1 a tool with a rectangular metal blade and a long handle, used for digging. 2 (**spades**) one of the four suits in a pack of playing cards, represented by a black heart-shaped figure with a small stalk. □ **call a spade a spade** speak plainly and frankly. **in spades** informal in large amounts or to a high degree.

spade·work /ˈspādˌwərk/ ▶ n. hard or routine work done to prepare for something.

spa·ghet·ti /spəˈgetē/ ▶ pl.n. pasta made in long, thin strands.

spake /spāk/ old use past of **SPEAK**.

spam /spam/ ▶ n. 1 (**Spam**) trademark a canned meat product made mainly from ham. 2 unwanted email sent to many Internet users.

span /span/ ▶ n. 1 the length of time for which something lasts. 2 width or extent from side to side. 3 a part of a bridge between the uprights supporting it. 4 the maximum distance between the tips of the thumb and little finger. ▶ v. (**spans**, **spanning**, **spanned**) extend across or over.

SYNONYMS ▶ n. 1 **extent**, length, width, reach, stretch, spread, distance, range. 2 **period**, space, time, duration, course, interval. ▶ v. 1 **bridge**, cross, traverse, pass over. 2 **last**, cover, extend, spread over.

Span·dex /ˈspandeks/ ▶ n. trademark a type of stretchy polyurethane fabric.

span·gle /ˈspaNGgəl/ ▶ n. 1 a small piece of decorative glittering material. 2 a spot of bright color or light. ■ **span·gled** adj. **span·gly** adj.

Span·iard /ˈspanyərd/ ▶ n. a person from Spain.

span·iel /ˈspanyəl/ ▶ n. a breed of dog with a long silky coat and drooping ears.

Span·ish /ˈspanish/ ▶ n. the main language of Spain and of much of Central and South America. ▶ adj. relating to Spain or Spanish.

spank /spaNGk/ ▶ v. slap someone on the buttocks with your hand or a flat object. ▶ n. a slap on the buttocks.

spank·ing /ˈspaNGkiNG/ ▶ adj. 1 brisk. 2 informal impressive or pleasing. ▶ n. a series of spanks.

spar¹ /spär/ ▶ n. 1 a thick, strong pole used to support the sails on a ship. 2 the main supporting structure of an aircraft's wing.

spar² ▶ v. (**spars**, **sparring**, **sparred**) 1 make the motions of boxing without landing heavy blows, as a form of training. 2 argue in a friendly way.

spare /spe(ə)r/ ▶ adj. 1 additional to what is required for ordinary use. 2 not being used or occupied. 3 thin. ▶ n. an item kept in case another is lost, broken, or worn out. ▶ v. (**spares**, **sparing**, **spared**) 1 let someone have something that you have enough of. 2 refrain from killing or harming. 3 protect from something unpleasant.

SYNONYMS ▶ adj. 1 **extra**, supplementary, additional, second, other, alternate, alternative, emergency, reserve, backup, relief, substitute. 2 **surplus**, superfluous, excess, leftover, redundant, unnecessary, unwanted; informal going begging. 3 *your spare time* **free**, leisure, unoccupied. 4 **slender**, lean, willowy, svelte, lissome, thin, skinny, gaunt, lanky, spindly. ▶ v. 1 **afford**, manage, part with, give, provide, do without. 2 **pardon**, let off, forgive, have mercy on, reprieve, release, free.

□ **spare no expense** be prepared to pay any amount. **spare tire** informal a roll of fat around a person's waist.

spare·ribs /ˈspe(ə)rˌribz/ ▶ pl.n. trimmed ribs of pork.

spar·ing /ˈspe(ə)riNG/ ▶ adj. not wasteful; economical.

SYNONYMS **thrifty**, economical, frugal, careful, prudent, cautious. ANTONYMS lavish, extravagant.

■ **spar·ing·ly** adv.

spark /spärk/ ▶ n. 1 a small fiery particle produced by burning or caused by friction. 2 a flash of light produced by an electrical discharge. 3 a small amount of a quality or feeling. 4 a sense of liveliness and excitement. ▶ v. 1 give out or produce sparks. 2 ignite a fire. 3 (usually **spark something off**) cause something.

SYNONYMS ▶ n. **flash**, glint, twinkle, flicker, flare. ▶ v. *their comments sparked immediate anger* **cause**, give rise to, occasion, bring about, start, precipitate, prompt, trigger, provoke, stimulate, stir up.

□ **spark plug** a device that produces a spark to ignite the fuel in a vehicle engine. ■ **spark·y** adj.

spar·kle /ˈspärkəl/ ▶ v. (**sparkles**, **sparkling**, **sparkled**) 1 shine brightly with flashes of light. 2 be attractively lively and witty. 3 (**sparkling**) (of a drink) fizzy. ▶ n. 1 a glittering flash of light. 2 attractive liveliness and wit.

SYNONYMS ▶ v. 1 **glitter**, glint, glisten, twinkle, flicker, flash, shimmer. 2 (**sparkling**) **brilliant**, dazzling, scintillating, exciting, exhilarating, stimulating, invigorating, vivacious, lively, vibrant. 3 (**sparkling**) **effervescent**, fizzy, carbonated, aerated. ▶ n. **glitter**, glint, glisten, twinkle, flicker, flash, shimmer.

■ **spar·kly** adj.

spar·kler /ˈspärk(ə)lər/ ▶ n. a hand-held firework that gives out sparks.

spar·row /ˈsparō/ ▶ n. a small bird with brown and gray feathers. □ **sparrow hawk** a small hawk that preys on small birds.

sparse /spärs/ ▶ **adj.** thinly scattered.

SYNONYMS **scant**, scanty, scattered, scarce, infrequent, few and far between, meager, paltry, limited, in short supply. ANTONYMS abundant.

■ **sparse·ly** **adv.** **spar·si·ty** **n.**

spar·tan /ˈspärtn/ ▶ **adj.** not comfortable or luxurious.

SYNONYMS **austere**, harsh, hard, frugal, rigorous, strict, severe, ascetic, self-denying, abstemious, bleak, bare, plain. ANTONYMS luxurious.

spasm /ˈspazəm/ ▶ **n.** **1** a sudden involuntary contraction of a muscle. **2** a sudden period of an activity or sensation.

SYNONYMS **1** *a muscle spasm* **contraction**, convulsion, cramp; twitch, jerk, tic, shudder, shiver, tremor. **2** *a spasm of coughing* **fit**, paroxysm, attack, burst, bout, seizure, outburst.

spas·mod·ic /spazˈmädik/ ▶ **adj.** happening or done in brief, irregular bursts. ■ **spas·mod·i·cal·ly** **adv.**

spas·tic /ˈspastik/ ▶ **adj.** **1** relating to or affected by muscle spasm. **2** offensive having to do with cerebral palsy. ▶ **n.** offensive a person with cerebral palsy. ■ **spas·tic·i·ty** /spaˈstisitē/ **n.**

USAGE

Say *person with cerebral palsy* rather than **spastic**, which many people find offensive.

spat¹ /spat/ past and past participle of SPIT¹.

spat² ▶ **n.** informal a quarrel about something unimportant.

spat³ ▶ **n.** a cloth covering formerly worn by men over their ankles and shoes.

spate /spāt/ ▶ **n.** **1** a large number of similar things coming quickly one after another. **2** a sudden flood in a river.

SYNONYMS **series**, succession, run, cluster, string, rash, epidemic, outbreak, wave, flurry.

spathe /spāt͟h/ ▶ **n.** a large sheath enclosing the flower cluster of certain plants.

spa·tial /ˈspāshəl/ ▶ **adj.** having to do with space. ■ **spa·tial·ly** **adv.**

spat·ter /ˈspatər/ ▶ **v.** (**spatters**, **spattering**, **spattered**) cover something with drops or spots of a liquid. ▶ **n.** a spray or splash.

spat·u·la /ˈspachələ/ ▶ **n.** an object with a broad, flat, blunt blade, used for mixing or spreading.

spawn /spôn/ ▶ **v.** **1** (of a fish, frog, etc.) release or deposit eggs. **2** give rise to. ▶ **n.** the eggs of fish, frogs, etc.

spay /spā/ ▶ **v.** sterilize a female animal by removing the ovaries.

speak /spēk/ ▶ **v.** (**speaks**, **speaking**, **spoke** /spōk/; past participle **spoken** /ˈspōkən/) **1** say something. **2** communicate, or be able to communicate, in a particular language. **3** (**speak up**) speak more loudly. **4** (**speak out** or **up**) express your opinions frankly and publicly.

SYNONYMS **1 talk**, converse, communicate, chat, have a word, gossip, commune, say something; informal chew the fat. **2 say**, utter, state, declare, voice, express, pronounce, articulate, enunciate, verbalize. **3 give a speech**, talk, lecture, hold forth; informal spout, sound off.

□ **speak in tongues** speak in an unknown language during religious worship. **speak volumes** convey a great deal without using words.

speak·eas·y /ˈspēkˌēzē/ ▶ **n.** (plural **speakeasies**) (in the United States during Prohibition) a secret illegal drinking club.

speak·er /ˈspēkər/ ▶ **n.** **1** a person who speaks. **2** (**Speaker**) the person who is in charge of proceedings in a legislature or parliament. **3** a loudspeaker.

SYNONYMS **speech-maker**, lecturer, talker, orator, spokesperson, spokesman, spokeswoman, reader, commentator, broadcaster, narrator.

spear /spi(ə)r/ ▶ **n.** **1** a weapon with a pointed metal tip and a long shaft. **2** a pointed stem of asparagus or broccoli. ▶ **v.** pierce with a spear or other pointed object.

spear·head /ˈspi(ə)rˌhed/ ▶ **v.** lead a campaign or attack. ▶ **n.** a person or group that leads a campaign or attack.

spear·mint /ˈspi(ə)rˌmint/ ▶ **n.** a type of garden mint, used in cooking.

spec /spek/ ▶ **n.** informal **1** (**on spec**) without any specific preparation or plan. **2** a detailed working description.

spe·cial /ˈspeshəl/ ▶ **adj.** **1** better or different from what is usual. **2** designed for or belonging to a particular person, place, or event. ▶ **n.** **1** something designed or organized for a particular occasion or purpose. **2** a dish not on the regular menu but served on a particular day.

SYNONYMS ▶ **adj.** **1 exceptional**, unusual, remarkable, out of the ordinary, outstanding, unique. **2 distinctive**, distinct, individual, particular, specific, peculiar. **3 momentous**, significant, memorable, important, historic, red-letter. ANTONYMS ordinary, general.

□ **special effects** illusions created for movies and television by camerawork, computer graphics, etc.

spe·cial·ist /ˈspeshəlist/ ▶ **n.** an expert in a particular subject, area of activity, etc. ▶ **adj.** involving detailed knowledge within a subject, area of activity, etc.

SYNONYMS ▶ **n.** **expert**, authority, pundit, professional, connoisseur, master, maestro; informal buff.

■ **spe·cial·ism** **n.**

spe·ci·al·i·ty /ˌspeshēˈalitē/ ▶ **n.** (plural **specialities**) ⇒ SPECIALTY.

SYNONYMS **strength**, strong point, forte, métier, strong suit, pièce de résistance, claim to fame.

spe·cial·ize /ˈspeshəˌlīz/ ▶ **v.** (**specializes**, **specializing**, **specialized**) **1** concentrate on and become expert in a particular skill or area. **2** (**specialized**) adapted or designed for a particular purpose or area of activity. ■ **spe·cial·i·za·tion** /ˌspeshəliˈzāshən/ **n.**

spe·cial·ly /ˈspeshəlē/ ▶ **adv.** **1** for a special purpose. **2** particularly.

spe·cial·ty /ˈspeshəltē/ (or **speciality** /ˌspeshēˈalitē/) ▶ **n.** (plural **specialties**) **1** a skill or area of study in which someone is an expert. **2** a product for which a person or region is famous. **3** a branch of medicine or surgery.

spe·cies /ˈspēsēz, -sHēz/ ▶ **n.** (plural **species**) **1** a group of animals or plants that are capable of breeding with each other. **2** a kind.

SYNONYMS **type**, kind, sort, breed, strain, variety, class, classification, category.

spe·cif·ic /spəˈsifik/ ▶ **adj.** **1** clearly defined or identified. **2** precise and clear. **3** (**specific to**) belonging or relating only to. ▶ **n.** (**specifics**) precise details.

SYNONYMS ▶ **adj.** **1 particular**, specified, fixed, set, determined, distinct, definite. **2 detailed**, explicit, express, clear-cut, unequivocal, precise, exact. ANTONYMS general, vague.

■ **spe·cif·i·cal·ly** **adv.**

spec·i·fi·ca·tion /ˌspesəfiˈkāsHən/ ▶ **n.** **1** the action of specifying. **2** (usually **specifications**) a detailed description of the design and materials used to make something. **3** the standard of workmanship and materials in a piece of work.

SYNONYMS *a shelter built to their specifications* **instruction**, guideline, parameter, stipulation, requirement, condition, order, detail.

spec·i·fy /ˈspesəˌfī/ ▶ **v.** (**specifies**, **specifying**, **specified**) state, identify, or require clearly and definitely.

SYNONYMS **state**, name, identify, define, set out, itemize, detail, list, enumerate, spell out, stipulate, lay down.

spec·i·men /ˈspesəmən/ ▶ **n.** **1** an example of an animal, plant, object, etc., used for study or display. **2** a sample for medical testing. **3** a typical example of something. **4** informal a person of a specific type: *a sorry specimen.*

SYNONYMS **sample**, example, model, instance, illustration, demonstration.

spe·cious /ˈspēsHəs/ ▶ **adj.** seeming right or reasonable, but actually wrong.

speck /spek/ ▶ **n.** a tiny spot or particle. ▶ **v.** mark with small spots.

speck·le /ˈspekəl/ ▶ **n.** a small spot or patch of color. ▶ **v.** (**speckles**, **speckling**, **speckled**) mark with speckles.

specs /speks/ ▶ **pl.n.** informal spectacles.

spec·ta·cle /ˈspektəkəl/ ▶ **n.** a visually striking performance or display.

SYNONYMS **1 display**, show, pageantry, performance, exhibition, pomp and circumstance, extravaganza, spectacular. **2 sight**, vision, scene, prospect, picture.

spec·ta·cles /ˈspektəkəlz/ ▶ **pl.n.** a pair of glasses.

spec·tac·u·lar /spekˈtakyələr/ ▶ **adj.** very impressive, striking, or dramatic. ▶ **n.** a spectacular performance or event.

SYNONYMS ▶ **adj.** **impressive**, magnificent, splendid, dazzling, sensational, stunning, dramatic, outstanding, memorable, unforgettable, striking, picturesque, eye-catching, breathtaking, glorious; informal out of this world. ANTONYMS dull, unimpressive.

■ **spec·tac·u·lar·ly** **adv.**

spec·tate /ˈspektāt/ ▶ **v.** (**spectates**, **spectating**, **spectated**) be a spectator.

spec·ta·tor /ˈspekˌtātər/ ▶ **n.** a person who is watching a show, game, etc.

SYNONYMS **watcher**, viewer, observer, onlooker, bystander, witness.

spec·ter /ˈspektər/ ▶ **n.** **1** a ghost. **2** a possible unpleasant or dangerous occurrence.

SYNONYMS **ghost**, phantom, apparition, spirit, wraith, presence; informal spook.

■ **spec·tral** **adj.**

spec·trom·e·ter /spekˈträmitər/ ▶ **n.** an apparatus used for recording and measuring spectra.

spec·trum /ˈspektrəm/ ▶ **n.** (plural **spectra** /-trə/) **1** a band of colors produced by separating light into elements with different wavelengths, e.g., in a rainbow. **2** the entire range of wavelengths of light. **3** a range of sound waves or different types of wave. **4** an entire range of beliefs, ideas, etc.: *the political spectrum.*

spec·u·late /ˈspekyəˌlāt/ ▶ **v.** (**speculates**, **speculating**, **speculated**) **1** form a theory without firm evidence. **2** invest in stocks, property, etc., in the hope of gain but with the risk of loss.

SYNONYMS **1 conjecture**, theorize, hypothesize, guess, surmise, wonder, muse. **2 gamble**, venture, wager, invest, play the market.

■ **spec·u·la·tion** /ˌspekyəˈlāsHən/ **n.** **spec·u·la·tor** **n.**

spec·u·la·tive /ˈspekyəˌlātiv, -lətiv/ ▶ **adj.** **1** based on theory or guesswork rather than knowledge. **2** (of an investment) risky.

SYNONYMS **1 conjectural**, suppositional, theoretical, hypothetical, tentative, unproven, unfounded, groundless, unsubstantiated. **2 risky**, hazardous, unsafe, uncertain, unpredictable; informal chancy.

■ **spec·u·la·tive·ly** **adv.**

speech /spēcH/ ▶ **n.** **1** the expression of thoughts and feelings using spoken language. **2** a formal talk given to an audience. **3** a sequence of lines written for one character in a play.

SYNONYMS **1 speaking**, talking, verbal communication, conversation, dialogue, discussion. **2 diction**, elocution, articulation, enunciation, pronunciation, delivery, words. **3 talk**, address, lecture, discourse, oration, presentation, sermon. **4 language**, parlance, tongue, idiom, dialect, vernacular; informal lingo.

□ **speech therapy** treatment to help people with speech problems.

speech·i·fy /ˈspēcHəˌfī/ ▶ **v.** (**speechifies**, **speechifying**, **speechified**) deliver a speech in a boring or pompous way.

speech·less /ˈspēcHlis/ ▶ **adj.** unable to speak because of shock or strong emotion.

SYNONYMS **lost for words**, dumbstruck, struck dumb, tongue-tied, inarticulate, mute, dumb, voiceless, silent.

speed /spēd/ ▶ **n.** **1** the rate at which someone or something moves or operates. **2** a fast rate of movement or action. **3** each of the possible gear ratios of a vehicle or bicycle. **4** the sensitivity of photographic film to light. **5** informal an amphetamine drug. ▶ **v.** (**speeds**, **speeding**, **speeded** or **sped** /sped/) **1** move quickly. **2** (**speed up**) move or work more quickly. **3** (of a motorist) travel at a speed greater than the legal limit. **4** old use make prosperous or successful.

SYNONYMS ▶ **n.** **1 rate**, pace, tempo, momentum, velocity; informal lick. **2 rapidity**, swiftness, promptness, alacrity, briskness, haste, hurry; old use celerity. ANTONYMS slowness. ▶ v. **1 hurry**, rush, dash, race, sprint, career, shoot, hurtle, fly, zoom, hasten; informal tear, belt, pelt. **2** *a vacation will speed his recovery* **hasten**, accelerate, advance, further, promote, boost, stimulate, aid, assist, facilitate. ANTONYMS slow, hinder.

speed·boat /'spēd,bōt/ ▶ n. a motorboat designed for high speed.

speed·om·e·ter /spə'dämitər/ ▶ n. an instrument that indicates a vehicle's speed.

speed·way /'spēd,wā/ ▶ n. a stadium or track used for automobile or motorcycle racing.

speed·y /'spēdē/ ▶ adj. (**speedier**, **speediest**) done, happening, or moving quickly.

SYNONYMS **fast**, swift, quick, rapid, expeditious, prompt, immediate, brisk, hasty, hurried, precipitate, rushed. ANTONYMS slow.

■ **speed·i·ly** adv.

spell¹ /spel/ ▶ v. (**spells**, **spelling**, **spelled** or **spelt**) **1** write or name the letters that form a word in correct sequence. **2** (of letters) form a word. **3** be a sign of. **4** (**spell something out**) explain something clearly and in detail.

SYNONYMS **signal**, signify, mean, amount to, add up to, constitute.

spell² ▶ n. **1** a form of words with magical power. **2** a state of enchantment caused by a spell. **3** an ability to control or influence other people.

SYNONYMS **1 charm**, incantation, magic formula, hex, curse; (**spells**) magic, sorcery, witchcraft. **2 influence**, charm, magnetism, charisma, magic.

spell³ ▶ n. a short period of time.

SYNONYMS **1 period**, time, interval, season, stretch, run, patch. **2 bout**, fit, attack.

spell·bound /'spel,bound/ ▶ adj. with your attention completely held by something.

SYNONYMS **enthralled**, fascinated, rapt, riveted, transfixed, gripped, captivated, bewitched, enchanted, mesmerized, hypnotized.

■ **spell·bind·ing** /'spel,bīndɪɴɢ/ adj.

spell·check·er /'spel,ᴄʜekər/ ▶ n. a computer program that checks the spelling of words in an electronic document.

spell·ing /'spelɪɴɢ/ ▶ n. **1** the process of spelling a word. **2** the way in which a word is spelled.

spend /spend/ ▶ v. (**spends**, **spending**, **spent**) **1** pay out money to buy or hire goods or services. **2** pass time in a particular way. **3** use up energy or resources.

SYNONYMS **1 pay out**, expend, disburse; informal lay out, blow, splurge. **2 pass**, occupy, fill, take up, while away. **3** (**spent**) **used up**, consumed, exhausted, finished, depleted, drained; informal burned/burnt out.

■ **spend·er** n.

spend·thrift /'spen(d),ᴛʜrift/ ▶ n. a person who spends too much money or wastes money.

SYNONYMS **1 profligate**, prodigal, squanderer, waster; informal big spender. **2** *the government's spendthrift ways* **profligate**, improvident, wasteful, extravagant, prodigal. ANTONYMS miser, frugal.

sperm /spərm/ ▶ n. (plural **sperm** or **sperms**) **1** informal semen. **2** a spermatozoon. □ **sperm whale** a toothed whale that feeds largely on squid.

sper·ma·to·zo·on /,spərmətə'zōən, spər,ma-/ ▶ n. (plural **spermatozoa** /-zōə/) the male sex cell of an animal, which fertilizes the egg.

spew /spyo͞o/ ▶ v. **1** pour out in large quantities. **2** informal vomit.

SYNONYMS **emit**, discharge, eject, expel, belch/pour out.

sphag·num /'sfagnəm, 'spag-/ ▶ n. a kind of moss that grows in boggy areas.

sphere /sfi(ə)r/ ▶ n. **1** a round solid figure in which every point on the surface is at an equal distance from the center. **2** an area of activity or interest.

SYNONYMS **1 globe**, ball, orb, bubble. **2** *his sphere of influence* **area**, field, compass, orbit, range, scope, extent. **3 domain**, realm, province, field, area, territory, arena, department.

spher·i·cal /'sfi(ə)rikəl, 'sfer-/ ▶ adj. shaped like a sphere. ■ **spher·i·cal·ly** adv.

sphinc·ter /'sfiɴɢktər/ ▶ n. a ring of muscle surrounding an opening such as the anus.

sphinx /sfiɴɢks/ ▶ n. an ancient Egyptian stone figure having a lion's body and a human or animal head.

spice /spīs/ ▶ n. **1** a strong-tasting substance used to flavor food. **2** an element that provides interest and excitement. ▶ v. (**spices**, **spicing**, **spiced**) **1** flavor with spice. **2** (**spice something up**) make something more exciting or interesting.

SYNONYMS ▶ n. **1 seasoning**, flavoring, condiment. **2 excitement**, interest, color, piquancy, zest, an edge.

spick-and-span /spik/ ▶ adj. neat, clean, and well looked after.

spic·y /'spīsē/ ▶ adj. (**spicier**, **spiciest**) **1** strongly flavored with spice. **2** mildly indecent.

SYNONYMS **hot**, tangy, peppery, piquant, spiced, highly seasoned, pungent. ANTONYMS bland.

■ **spic·i·ness** n.

spi·der /'spīdər/ ▶ n. a small insectlike creature (an arachnid) with eight legs.

spi·der·y /'spīdərē/ ▶ adj. long and thin, like a spider's legs: *spidery writing*.

spiel /spēl, sʜpēl/ ▶ n. informal an elaborate and insincere speech made in an attempt to persuade someone.

spiff·y /'spifē/ ▶ adj. (**spiffier**, **spiffiest**) informal neat or stylish in appearance.

spig·ot /'spigət/ ▶ n. **1** a small peg or plug. **2** a tap or a device for controlling the flow of liquid in a tap. **3** the end of a section of a pipe that fits into the socket of the next one.

spike /spīk/ ▶ n. **1** a thin, pointed piece of metal or wood. **2** each of several metal points set into the sole of a sports shoe to prevent slipping. **3** a cluster of flower heads attached directly to a long stem. ▶ v. (**spikes**, **spiking**, **spiked**) **1** impale on or pierce with a spike. **2** cover with sharp points. **3** informal secretly add alcohol or a drug to drink or food.

SYNONYMS ▶ n. **prong**, pin, barb, point, skewer, stake, spit.

spik·y /'spīkē/ ▶ adj. (**spikier**, **spikiest**) **1** like a spike or spikes or having many spikes: *short spiky* *hair*. **2** informal easily annoyed; irritable. ■ **spik·i·ly** adv. **spik·i·ness** n.

spill[1] /spil/ ▶ v. (**spills**, **spilling**, **spilt** or **spilled**) **1** flow, or allow to flow, over the edge of a container. **2** move or empty out from a place. ▶ n. **1** a quantity of liquid spilled. **2** informal a fall from a horse or bicycle.

SYNONYMS ▶ v. **1 knock over**, tip over, upset, overturn. **2 overflow**, brim over, run over, pour, slop, slosh, splash, leak.

□ **spill the beans** informal reveal confidential information. **spill blood** kill or wound people. ■ **spill·age** n.

spill[2] ▶ n. a thin strip of wood or paper used for lighting a fire.

spin /spin/ ▶ v. (**spins**, **spinning**, **spun** /spən/) **1** turn around quickly. **2** (of a person's head) have a dizzy sensation. **3** (of a ball) move through the air with a revolving motion. **4** draw out and twist the fibers of wool, cotton, etc., to convert them into yarn. **5** (of a spider, silkworm, etc.) produce silk or a web by forcing out a fine thread from a special gland. **6** (**spin something out**) make something last as long as possible. ▶ n. **1** a spinning motion. **2** informal a brief trip in a vehicle for pleasure. **3** a favorable slant given to a news story.

SYNONYMS ▶ v. **1 revolve**, rotate, turn, go around, whirl, twirl, gyrate. **2** *she spun around to face him* **whirl**, wheel, turn, swing, twist, swivel, pivot. ▶ n. **1 rotation**, revolution, turn, whirl, twirl, gyration. **2 slant**, angle, twist, bias. **3 trip**, jaunt, outing, excursion, journey, drive, ride, run, turn; informal tootle.

□ **spin doctor** informal a person employed by a political party to give a favorable interpretation of events to the media. **spinning wheel** a piece of equipment for spinning yarn or thread with a spindle driven by a wheel operated by hand or foot. **spin-off** something unexpected but useful resulting from an activity. ■ **spin·ner** n.

spi·na bif·i·da /ˈspīnə ˈbifidə/ ▶ n. a condition in which part of the spinal cord is exposed, sometimes causing paralysis.

spin·ach /ˈspinicн/ ▶ n. a plant with large dark green leaves that are eaten as a vegetable.

spi·nal /ˈspīnl/ ▶ adj. relating to the spine. □ **spinal column** the spine. **spinal cord** the nerve fibers enclosed in the spine and connected to the brain.

spin·dle /ˈspindl/ ▶ n. **1** a slender rod with tapered ends used for spinning wool, flax, etc., by hand. **2** a rod around which something revolves.

spin·dly /ˈspin(d)lē/ ▶ adj. long or tall and thin.

SYNONYMS **1 lanky**, thin, skinny, lean, spare, gangling, gangly, scrawny, bony, rangy, angular. **2** *spindly chairs* **rickety**, flimsy, wobbly, shaky. ANTONYMS stocky.

spin·drift /ˈspinˌdrift/ ▶ n. spray blown from the sea by the wind.

spine /spīn/ ▶ n. **1** a series of bones extending from the skull to the small of the back, enclosing the spinal cord; the backbone. **2** the part of a book that encloses the inner edges of the pages. **3** a hard pointed projection found on certain plants and animals.

SYNONYMS **1 backbone**, spinal column, back. **2 needle**, quill, bristle, barb, spike, prickle, thorn.

□ **spine-chiller** a story or movie that causes terror and excitement.

spine·less /ˈspīnlis/ ▶ adj. **1** lacking courage and determination. **2** having no backbone; invertebrate. **3** having no spines.

SYNONYMS **weak**, weak-willed, feeble, soft, ineffectual, cowardly, timid, faint-hearted, pusillanimous, craven, lily-livered, chicken-hearted; informal wimpish, wimpy, gutless. ANTONYMS bold, brave, strong-willed.

spin·et /ˈspinit/ ▶ n. **1** a type of small harpsichord. **2** a type of small upright piano.

spin·na·ker /ˈspinəkər/ ▶ n. a large three-cornered sail used on a racing yacht when the wind is coming from behind.

spin·ster /ˈspinstər/ ▶ n. a single woman beyond the usual age for marriage. ■ **spin·ster·hood** n.

spin·y /ˈspīnē/ ▶ adj. (**spinier**, **spiniest**) full of or covered with prickles. ■ **spin·i·ness** n.

spi·ral /ˈspīrəl/ ▶ adj. winding in a continuous curve around a central point or axis. ▶ n. **1** a spiral curve, shape, or pattern. **2** a continuous rise or fall of prices, wages, etc. ▶ v. (**spirals**, **spiraling**, **spiraled**) **1** follow a spiral course. **2** show a continuous increase or decrease.

SYNONYMS ▶ adj. **coiled**, helical, curling, winding, twisting. ▶ n. **coil**, curl, twist, whorl, scroll, helix, corkscrew. ▶ v. **coil**, wind, swirl, twist, snake.

■ **spi·ral·ly** adv.

spire /spī(ə)r/ ▶ n. a pointed structure, typically on the top of a church tower.

spir·it /ˈspirit/ ▶ n. **1** the part of a person that consists of their character and feelings rather than their body. **2** a supernatural being. **3** typical character, quality, or mood. **4** (**spirits**) a person's mood or state of mind. **5** courage, energy, and determination. **6** the real meaning of something as opposed to its strict interpretation. **7** (also **spirits**) strong alcoholic drink, e.g., rum. **8** purified distilled alcohol, e.g., methylated spirit. ▶ v. (**spirits**, **spiriting**, **spirited**) (**spirit someone/thing away**) take someone or something away quickly and secretly.

SYNONYMS ▶ n. **1 soul**, psyche, inner self, mind. **2 ghost**, phantom, specter, apparition, presence. **3 mood**, frame/state of mind, humor, temper, morale, esprit de corps. **4 ethos**, essence, atmosphere, mood, feeling, climate. **5 enthusiasm**, energy, verve, vigor, dynamism, dash, sparkle, exuberance, gusto, fervor, zeal, fire, passion; informal get-up-and-go. ANTONYMS body, flesh.

□ **spirit level** ⇒ LEVEL.

spir·it·ed /ˈspiritid/ ▶ adj. energetic and determined.

SYNONYMS **lively**, energetic, enthusiastic, vigorous, dynamic, passionate; informal peppy, feisty, gutsy. ANTONYMS apathetic, lifeless.

■ **spir·it·ed·ly** adv.

spir·it·u·al /ˈspiricнo͞oəl/ ▶ adj. **1** having to do with the human spirit as opposed to material or physical things. **2** having to do with religion or religious belief. ▶ n. a religious song of a kind associated with black Christians of the southern United States.

SYNONYMS ▶ adj. **1 inner**, mental, psychological, incorporeal, nonmaterial. **2 religious**, sacred, divine, holy, devotional. ANTONYMS physical, secular.

■ **spir·it·u·al·i·ty** /ˌspiricHo͞o'alitē/ n. **spir·it·u·al·ly** adv.

spir·it·u·al·ism /'spiricHo͞oəˌlizəm/ ▶ n. the belief that the spirits of the dead can communicate with the living. ■ **spir·it·u·al·ist** n.

spi·ro·gy·ra /ˌspīrə'jīrə/ ▶ n. a type of algae consisting of long green threads.

spit[1] /spit/ ▶ v. (**spits**, **spitting**, **spat** /spat/ or **spit**) **1** forcibly eject saliva, or food, liquid, etc., from the mouth. **2** say in a hostile way. **3** give out small bursts of sparks or hot fat. ▶ n. **1** saliva. **2** an act of spitting.

SYNONYMS ▶ v. **expectorate**, hawk. ▶ n. **spittle**, saliva, sputum, slobber, dribble.

□ **be the spitting image of** informal look exactly like. **spit it out** informal used to urge someone to say or confess something quickly.

spit[2] ▶ n. **1** a metal rod pushed through meat in order to hold and turn it while it is roasted. **2** a narrow point of land sticking out into the sea.

spit·ball /'spitˌbôl/ ▶ n. Baseball an illegal pitch made with a ball moistened with saliva or another substance to make it move erratically.

spite /spīt/ ▶ n. a desire to hurt, annoy, or offend someone. ▶ v. (**spites**, **spiting**, **spited**) deliberately hurt, annoy, or offend someone.

SYNONYMS ▶ n. **malice**, malevolence, ill will, vindictiveness, meanness, nastiness; informal bitchiness, cattiness. ▶ v. **upset**, hurt, wound. ANTONYMS please.

□ **in spite of** without being affected by.

spite·ful /'spītfəl/ ▶ adj. deliberately hurtful; malicious.

SYNONYMS **malicious**, malevolent, vindictive, vengeful, mean, nasty, hurtful, mischievous, cruel, unkind; informal bitchy, catty. ANTONYMS benevolent.

■ **spite·ful·ly** adv.

spit·fire /'spitˌfīr/ ▶ n. a person with a fierce temper.

spit·tle /'spitl/ ▶ n. saliva.

spit·toon /spi'to͞on/ ▶ n. a container for spitting into.

splash /splasH/ ▶ v. **1** (of a liquid) fall in scattered drops. **2** make wet with scattered drops. **3** move around in water, causing it to fly about. **4** (**splash down**) (of a spacecraft) land on water. **5** prominently display a story or photograph in a newspaper or magazine. ▶ n. **1** an instance of splashing. **2** a small quantity of liquid splashed on to a surface. **3** a small quantity of liquid added to a drink. **4** a bright patch of color. **5** informal a prominent news story.

SYNONYMS ▶ v. **1 sprinkle**, spatter, splatter, spray, shower, wash, squirt, slosh, slop. **2 wash**, break, lap, pound. **3 paddle**, wade, wallow.

□ **make a splash** informal attract a lot of attention.

splat /splat/ ▶ n. informal a sound of something soft and wet or heavy striking a surface.

splat·ter /'splatər/ ▶ v. (**splatters**, **splattering**, **splattered**) splash with a sticky or thick liquid. ▶ n. a splash of a sticky or thick liquid.

splay /splā/ ▶ v. spread out wide apart.

spleen /splēn/ ▶ n. **1** an organ involved in producing and removing blood cells. **2** bad temper.

splen·did /'splendid/ ▶ adj. **1** magnificent; very impressive. **2** informal excellent.

SYNONYMS **1 magnificent**, sumptuous, grand, imposing, superb, spectacular, resplendent, rich, lavish, ornate, gorgeous, glorious, dazzling, handsome, beautiful; informal plush, swish. **2 excellent**, wonderful, marvelous, superb, glorious, lovely, delightful, first-class; informal super, great, amazing, fantastic, terrific, tremendous. ANTONYMS simple, modest, inferior.

■ **splen·did·ly** adv.

splen·dor /'splendər/ ▶ n. magnificent and impressive appearance.

SYNONYMS **magnificence**, sumptuousness, grandeur, resplendence, richness, glory, majesty. ANTONYMS simplicity.

sple·net·ic /splə'netik/ ▶ adj. bad-tempered or spiteful.

splice /splīs/ ▶ v. (**splices**, **splicing**, **spliced**) **1** join ropes by weaving together the strands at the ends. **2** join pieces of film, tape, etc., at the ends. ▶ n. a spliced join.

splint /splint/ ▶ n. a rigid support for a broken bone.

splin·ter /'splin(t)ər/ ▶ n. a small, thin, sharp piece of wood, glass, etc., broken off from a larger piece. ▶ v. (**splinters**, **splintering**, **splintered**) break into splinters.

SYNONYMS ▶ n. **sliver**, chip, shard, fragment, shred. ▶ v. **shatter**, smash, break into smithereens, fracture, split, crack, disintegrate.

□ **splinter group** a small breakaway group.

split /split/ ▶ v. (**splits**, **splitting**, **split**) **1** break into parts by force. **2** divide into parts or groups. **3** (often **split up**) end a marriage or other relationship. **4** (**be splitting**) informal (of a person's head) be suffering from a bad headache. ▶ n. **1** a tear or crack. **2** an instance of splitting. **3** (**a split** or **the splits**) a leap or seated position with the legs straight and at right angles to the body.

SYNONYMS ▶ v. **1 break**, cut, burst, snap, crack, splinter, fracture, rupture, come apart. **2 tear**, rip, slash, slit. **3 share**, divide up, distribute, dole out, parcel out, carve up, slice up, apportion. **4 fork**, divide, branch, diverge. **5** *the band split up last year* **break up**, separate, part, part company, go their separate ways. ANTONYMS join, unite, converge. ▶ n. **1 crack**, fissure, cleft, crevice, break, fracture, breach. **2 rip**, tear, cut, rent, slash, slit. **3 division**, rift, breach, schism, rupture, separation, estrangement. **4 break-up**, split-up, separation, parting, estrangement, rift. ANTONYMS merger.

□ **split infinitive** Grammar an infinitive construction in which an adverb or other word is placed between *to* and the verb (e.g., *she used to secretly admire him*), traditionally regarded as bad English. **split-level** (of a room or building) having the floor divided into two levels. **split second** a very brief moment of time.

splosh /spläsH/ informal ▶ v. make a soft splashing sound. ▶ n. a splashing sound.

splurge /splərj/ informal ▶ v. (**splurges**, **splurging**, **splurged**) spend extravagantly. ▶ n. a sudden burst of extravagance.

splut·ter /'splətər/ ▶ v. (**splutters**, **spluttering**, **spluttered**) **1** make a series of short explosive spitting or choking sounds. **2** say in a rapid, unclear way. ▶ n. a spluttering sound.

spoil /spoil/ ▶ v. (**spoils**, **spoiling**, past and past participle **spoiled** or **spoilt**) **1** make something less good or enjoyable. **2** (of food) become unfit for eating. **3** harm the character of a child by not being strict enough. **4** treat with great or excessive kindness. **5** (**be spoiling for**) be very eager for. ▶ n. (**spoils**) stolen goods.

> SYNONYMS ▶ v. **1** **damage**, ruin, impair, blemish, disfigure, blight, deface, harm, destroy, wreck. **2** *rain spoiled my plans* **upset**, mess up, ruin, wreck, undo, sabotage, scotch, torpedo; informal muck up, screw up. **3** **overindulge**, pamper, indulge, mollycoddle, cosset, wait on someone hand and foot. **4** **go bad**, go rancid, turn, go sour, rot, decompose, decay, perish. ANTONYMS improve, enhance.

spoil·er /ˈspoilər/ ▶ n. **1** a flap on an aircraft wing that can be raised to create drag and slow it down. **2** a similar device on a car intended to improve roadholding at high speeds.

spoil·sport /ˈspoilˌspôrt/ ▶ n. a person who spoils the pleasure of other people.

> SYNONYMS **killjoy**, dog in the manger, misery; informal wet blanket, party pooper.

spoke[1] /spōk/ ▶ n. each of the rods connecting the center of a wheel to its rim.

spoke[2] past of SPEAK.

spo·ken /ˈspōkən/ past participle of SPEAK ▶ adj. speaking in a particular way: *a soft-spoken man.*

> SYNONYMS **verbal**, oral, vocal, unwritten, word-of-mouth.

□ **be spoken for** be already claimed.

spokes·man /ˈspōksmən/ (or **spokeswoman** /ˈspōksˌwo͝omən/) ▶ n. (plural **spokesmen** or **spokeswomen**) a person who makes statements on behalf of a group, company, organization, etc.

> SYNONYMS **representative**, voice, mouthpiece, agent, official; informal spin doctor.

spokes·per·son /ˈspōksˌpərsən/ ▶ n. (plural **spokespersons** or **spokespeople** /-ˌpēpəl/) a spokesman or spokeswoman.

> SYNONYMS **representative**, voice, mouthpiece, agent, official; informal spin doctor.

sponge /spənj/ ▶ n. **1** a simple sea creature with no backbone and a soft porous body. **2** a piece of a light, absorbent substance used for washing, as padding, etc. ▶ v. (**sponges**, **sponging** or **spongeing**, **sponged**) **1** wipe or clean with a wet sponge or cloth. **2** informal obtain money or food from other people without giving anything in return. □ **sponge cake** a cake of spongelike consistency, made with little or no fat. ■ **spong·er** n. **spon·gy** adj.

spon·sor /ˈspänsər/ ▶ n. **1** a person or organization that helps pays for an event in return for advertising. **2** a person who promises to give money to a charity if another person completes a task or activity. **3** a person who proposes a new law. ▶ v. be a sponsor for.

> SYNONYMS ▶ n. **backer**, patron, promoter, benefactor, supporter, contributor. ▶ v. **finance**, fund, subsidize, back, promote, support, contribute to; informal bankroll.

> **SPELLING**
>
> The word is spelled **-or**, not **-er**: sponsor.

spon·sor·ship /ˈspänsərˌsHip/ ▶ n. **1** financial support of a person, sports team, charity, or organization, provided in return for advertising. **2** support of an individual who is seeking citizenship, membership in a club, etc.

spon·ta·ne·ous /spänˈtānēəs/ ▶ adj. **1** done or happening as a result of an impulse. **2** open, natural, and relaxed. **3** happening without apparent external cause.

> SYNONYMS **1** **unplanned**, unpremeditated, impulsive, impromptu, spur-of-the-moment, unprompted; informal off-the-cuff. **2** **natural**, uninhibited, relaxed, unselfconscious, unaffected.

■ **spon·ta·ne·i·ty** /ˌspäntəˈnēitē, -ˈnā-/ n. **spon·ta·ne·ous·ly** adv.

spoof /spo͞of/ ▶ n. informal a humorous imitation of something.

spook /spo͞ok/ informal ▶ n. **1** a ghost. **2** a spy. ▶ v. frighten.

spook·y /ˈspo͞okē/ ▶ adj. (**spookier**, **spookiest**) informal sinister or ghostly.

> SYNONYMS **eerie**, sinister, ghostly, uncanny, weird, unearthly, mysterious; informal creepy, scary.

■ **spook·i·ly** adv.

spool /spo͞ol/ ▶ n. a cylindrical device on which thread, film, etc., can be wound. ▶ v. wind on to a spool.

spoon /spo͞on/ ▶ n. an implement consisting of a small, shallow bowl on a long handle, used for eating and serving food. ▶ v. transfer food with a spoon. □ **spoon-feed** **1** feed someone with a spoon. **2** provide someone with so much help that they do not need to think for themselves. ■ **spoon·ful** n.

spoon·bill /ˈspo͞onˌbil/ ▶ n. a tall wading bird that has a long bill with a very broad flat tip.

spoon·er·ism /ˈspo͞onəˌrizəm/ ▶ n. a mistake in speech in which the initial sounds or letters of two or more words are accidentally swapped around, as in *you have hissed the mystery lectures.*

spo·rad·ic /spəˈradik/ ▶ adj. happening at irregular intervals or only in a few places.

> SYNONYMS **occasional**, infrequent, irregular, periodic, scattered, patchy, isolated, odd, intermittent, spasmodic, fitful, desultory, erratic, unpredictable. ANTONYMS frequent, continuous.

■ **spo·rad·i·cal·ly** adv.

spore /spôr/ ▶ n. a tiny reproductive cell produced by fungi and plants such as mosses and algae.

spor·ran /ˈspärən, ˈspôr-/ ▶ n. a pouch worn around the waist as part of men's Scottish Highland dress.

sport /spôrt/ ▶ n. **1** a competitive activity involving physical effort and skill. **2** informal a person who behaves well when teased or defeated. ▶ v. **1** wear a distinctive item. **2** literary amuse yourself or play in a lively way.

> SYNONYMS ▶ n. **game**, physical recreation. ▶ v. **wear**, have on, dress in, show off, parade, flaunt.

□ **sports car** a small, fast car. **sports jacket** (or **sport coat**) a man's informal jacket resembling a suit jacket. **sport utility vehicle** a high performance four-wheel drive vehicle.

sport·ing /spôrtiNG/ ▶ **adj.** **1** connected with or interested in sports. **2** fair and generous.

SYNONYMS **sportsmanlike**, generous, considerate, fair.

□ **sporting chance** a reasonable chance of winning or succeeding. ■ **sport·ing·ly adv.**

spor·tive /'spôrtiv/ ▶ **adj.** playful; lighthearted.

sports·cast /'spôrts,kast/ ▶ **n.** a broadcast of sports news or a sports event. ■ **sports·cast·er n.** **sports·cast·ing n.**

sports·man /'spôrtsmən/ (or **sportswoman** /'spôrts,wo͝omən/) ▶ **n.** (plural **sportsmen** or **sportswomen**) **1** a person who takes part in a sport. **2** a person who behaves in a fair and generous way. ■ **sports·man·ship n.**

sport·y /'spôrtē/ ▶ **adj.** (**sportier**, **sportiest**) informal **1** fond of or good at sports. **2** (of clothing) suitable for sports or casual wear. **3** (of a car) compact and fast.

SYNONYMS **athletic**, fit, active, energetic.

spot /spät/ ▶ **n.** **1** a small round mark on a surface. **2** a pimple. **3** a particular place, point, or position. **4** a small amount of something. ▶ **v.** (**spots**, **spotting**, **spotted**) **1** notice or recognize, especially with difficulty or effort. **2** mark with spots.

SYNONYMS ▶ **n.** **1 mark**, patch, dot, fleck, smudge, smear, stain, blotch, splash; informal splotch. **2 pimple**, pustule, blackhead, boil, blemish; informal zit; (**spots**) acne, rash. **3 place**, site, position, situation, setting, location, venue. ▶ **v.** **1 see**, notice, observe, catch sight of, detect, make out, discern, recognize, identify, locate; literary espy, descry. **2** (**spotted**) **spotty**, dotted, polka-dot, freckled, mottled.

□ **on the spot 1** immediately. **2** at the scene of an action or event. **spot check** a test made without warning on a person or thing selected at random. **spot on** completely accurate. ■ **spot·ter n.**

spot·less /'spätlis/ ▶ **adj.** absolutely clean or pure.

SYNONYMS **clean**, pristine, immaculate, shining, shiny, gleaming, spick and span. ANTONYMS filthy.

■ **spot·less·ly adv.**

spot·light /'spät,līt/ ▶ **n.** **1** a lamp projecting a narrow, strong beam of light directly on to a place or person. **2** (**the spotlight**) intense public attention. ▶ **v.** (**spotlights**, **spotlighting**, past and past participle **spotlighted** or **spotlit** /-lit/) light up with a spotlight.

SYNONYMS ▶ **n.** **attention**, glare of publicity, limelight, public eye.

spot·ty /'spätē/ ▶ **adj.** (**spottier**, **spottiest**) **1** marked with or having spots. **2** of uneven quality.

spouse /spous/ ▶ **n.** a husband or wife.

SYNONYMS **partner**, husband, wife, mate, consort; informal other half, better half.

spout /spout/ ▶ **n.** **1** a projecting tube or lip through or over which liquid can be poured from a container. **2** a stream of liquid flowing out. ▶ **v.** **1** send out or flow in a stream. **2** express your views in a lengthy and forceful way.

SYNONYMS ▶ **n.** **nozzle**, lip. ▶ **v.** **1 spurt**, gush, spew, erupt, shoot, squirt, spray, discharge, emit, belch. **2** *he spouted about morality* **hold forth**, sound off, go on; informal mouth off.

sprain /sprān/ ▶ **v.** wrench a joint violently so as to cause pain and swelling. ▶ **n.** an instance of wrenching a joint.

sprang /spraNG/ past of **SPRING**.

sprat /sprat/ ▶ **n.** a small sea fish of the herring family.

sprawl /sprôl/ ▶ **v.** **1** sit, lie, or fall with your arms and legs spread out awkwardly. **2** spread out irregularly over a large area. ▶ **n.** **1** a sprawling position or movement. **2** the disorganized expansion of a town or city.

SYNONYMS ▶ **v.** **stretch out**, lounge, loll, slump, flop, slouch.

spray /sprā/ ▶ **n.** **1** liquid sent through the air in tiny drops. **2** a liquid that can be forced out of an aerosol or other container in a spray. **3** a stem or small branch with flowers and leaves. **4** a small bunch of cut flowers worn on clothing. ▶ **v.** **1** apply a spray of liquid to something. **2** scatter something over an area with great force.

SYNONYMS ▶ **n.** **1 shower**, sprinkle, jet, squirt, mist, spume, foam, froth, spindrift. **2 aerosol**, vaporizer, atomizer, sprinkler. ▶ **v.** **1 sprinkle**, dribble, drizzle, water, soak, douse, drench. **2 spout**, jet, gush, spurt, shoot, squirt.

spread /spred/ ▶ **v.** (**spreads**, **spreading**, **spread**) **1** open out fully. **2** stretch out hands, fingers, wings, etc. **3** extend over a wide area or a specified period of time. **4** apply a substance in an even layer. ▶ **n.** **1** the process of spreading. **2** the extent, width, or area covered by something. **3** the range of something. **4** a soft paste that can be spread on bread. **5** an article covering several pages of a newspaper or magazine. **6** informal a large and elaborate meal.

SYNONYMS ▶ **v.** **1 lay out**, open out, unfurl, unroll, roll out, straighten out, fan out, stretch out, extend. **2** *the landscape spread out below* **extend**, stretch, sprawl. **3 scatter**, strew, disperse, distribute. **4 circulate**, broadcast, put about, publicize, propagate, repeat. **5 travel**, move, be borne, sweep, diffuse, reproduce, be passed on, be transmitted. **6 smear**, daub, plaster, apply, rub. ▶ **n.** **1 expansion**, proliferation, dissemination, diffusion, transmission, propagation. **2 span**, width, extent, stretch, reach.

■ **spread·er n.**

spread·ea·gle /,spred'ēgəl/ ▶ **v.** (**be spreadeagled**) be stretched out with the arms and legs extended.

spread·sheet /'spred,SHēt/ ▶ **n.** **1** a paper or ledger page with rows and columns used for the presentation of numerical data. **2** a computer program in which figures are arranged in a grid and used in calculations.

spree /sprē/ ▶ **n.** a short period of time spent doing a lot of a particular thing: *a shopping spree*.

SYNONYMS **bout**, orgy; informal binge, splurge.

sprig /sprig/ ▶ **n.** a small stem with leaves or flowers, taken from a bush or plant.

spright·ly /'sprītlē/ ▶ **adj.** (**sprightlier**, **sprightliest**) (of an old person) lively; energetic.

SYNONYMS **spry**, lively, agile, nimble, energetic, active, vigorous, spirited, animated, vivacious, frisky. ANTONYMS doddery, lethargic.

■ **spright·li·ness n.**

spring /spriNG/ ▶ v. (**springs**, **springing**, **sprang** /spraNG/ or **sprung** /sprəNG/; past participle **sprung**) **1** move suddenly upward or forward. **2** (**spring from**) come or appear from. **3** (**spring up**) suddenly develop or appear. **4** (**sprung**) having springs. ▶ n. **1** the season after winter and before summer. **2** a spiral metal coil that returns to its former shape after being pressed or pulled. **3** a sudden jump upward or forward. **4** a place where water wells up from an underground source. **5** the quality of being elastic.

SYNONYMS ▶ v. **leap**, jump, bound, vault, hop. ▶ n. **springiness**, bounce, resilience, elasticity, flexibility, stretch, stretchiness, give.

□ **spring cleaning** a thorough cleaning of a house or building. **spring-loaded** containing a spring that presses one part against another. ■ **spring·y** adj.

spring·board /'spriNG,bôrd/ ▶ n. **1** a flexible board from which a diver or gymnast jumps in order to push off more powerfully. **2** something that starts off an activity or enterprise.

spring·bok /'spriNG,bäk/ ▶ n. a southern African gazelle that leaps when disturbed.

spring·er /'spriNGər/ (also **springer spaniel**) ▶ n. a small kind of spaniel.

spring·time /'spriNG,tīm/ ▶ n. **1** the season of spring. **2** the early part or first stage of something: *the springtime of their marriage.*

sprin·kle /'spriNGkəl/ ▶ v. (**sprinkles**, **sprinkling**, **sprinkled**) **1** scatter or pour small drops or particles over an object or surface. **2** distribute something randomly throughout. ▶ n. a small amount that is sprinkled.

SYNONYMS ▶ v. **splash**, trickle, drizzle, spray, shower, drip, scatter, strew, dredge, dust.

sprin·kler /'spriNGk(ə)lər/ ▶ n. **1** a device for watering lawns. **2** an automatic fire extinguisher installed in a ceiling.

sprint /sprint/ ▶ v. run at full speed over a short distance. ▶ n. **1** a period of sprinting. **2** a short, fast race.

SYNONYMS ▶ v. **run**, race, rush, dash, bolt, fly, charge, shoot, speed; informal hotfoot it, leg it. ANTONYMS stroll.

■ **sprint·er** n.

sprite /sprīt/ ▶ n. an elf or fairy.

spritz·er /'spritsər/ ▶ n. a mixture of wine and soda water.

sprock·et /'spräkit/ ▶ n. each of several projections on the rim of a wheel that engage with the links of a chain or with holes in film, paper, etc.

sprout /sprout/ ▶ v. produce shoots; begin to grow. ▶ n. **1** a shoot of a plant. **2** (**sprouts**) young shoots eaten as a vegetable, especially the shoots of alfalfa, mung beans, or soybeans. **3** a Brussels sprout.

SYNONYMS ▶ v. **1 germinate**, put/send out shoots, bud. **2 spring**, come up, grow, develop, appear.

spruce¹ /spro͞os/ ▶ adj. neat and well-groomed. ▶ v. (**spruces**, **sprucing**, **spruced**) (**spruce someone/thing up**) make someone or something neater, better-groomed, or better-dressed.

SYNONYMS ▶ adj. **neat**, well-groomed, well turned out, well-dressed, smart, trim, dapper; informal natty, snazzy. ANTONYMS disheveled.

spruce² ▶ n. an evergreen tree with hanging cones.

sprung /sprəNG/ past and past participle of **SPRING**.

spry /sprī/ ▶ adj. (of an old person) lively.

SYNONYMS **sprightly**, lively, agile, nimble, spirited, animated, vivacious, frisky, active. ANTONYMS doddery, lethargic.

spud /spəd/ ▶ n. informal a potato.

spume /spyo͞om/ ▶ n. literary froth or foam.

spun /spən/ past and past participle of **SPIN**.

spunk /spəNGk/ ▶ n. informal courage and determination.

spunk·y /'spəNGkē/ ▶ adj. (**spunkier**, **spunkiest**) informal brave and determined.

spur /spər/ ▶ n. **1** a spiked device worn on a rider's heel for urging a horse forward. **2** an encouragement. **3** an area of high ground that sticks out from a mountain. **4** a short branch road or railroad line. ▶ v. (**spurs**, **spurring**, **spurred**) **1** encourage someone to do something, or make something happen faster or sooner. **2** urge a horse forward with spurs.

SYNONYMS ▶ n. **stimulus**, incentive, encouragement, inducement, impetus, motivation. ANTONYMS disincentive. ▶ v. **stimulate**, encourage, prompt, prod, impel, motivate, move, galvanize, inspire, drive. ANTONYMS discourage.

□ **on the spur of the moment** on a sudden impulse; without planning in advance.

spu·ri·ous /'sp(y)o͝orēəs/ ▶ adj. **1** false or fake. **2** (of reasoning) apparently but not actually correct.

SYNONYMS **bogus**, fake, false, fraudulent, sham, artificial, imitation, simulated, feigned; informal phony. ANTONYMS genuine.

■ **spu·ri·ous·ly** adv.

spurn /spərn/ ▶ v. reject in a contemptuous way.

SYNONYMS **reject**, rebuff, scorn, turn down, treat with contempt, disdain, look down your nose at; informal turn your nose up at. ANTONYMS welcome, accept.

spurt /spərt/ ▶ v. **1** gush out in a stream. **2** move with a sudden burst of speed. ▶ n. **1** a gushing stream. **2** a sudden burst of activity or speed.

SYNONYMS ▶ v. **squirt**, shoot, jet, erupt, gush, pour, stream, pump, surge, spew, course, well, spring, burst, spout. ▶ n. **squirt**, jet, gush, stream, rush, surge, flood, cascade, torrent.

sput·ter /'spətər/ ▶ v. (**sputters**, **sputtering**, **sputtered**) make a series of soft explosive sounds. ▶ n. a sputtering sound.

spu·tum /'spyo͞otəm/ ▶ n. saliva and mucus that is coughed up.

spy /spī/ ▶ n. (plural **spies**) a person who secretly collects information about an enemy or competitor. ▶ v. (**spies**, **spying**, **spied**) **1** be a spy. **2** (**spy on**) watch secretly. **3** see or notice.

SYNONYMS ▶ n. **agent**, mole, plant; informal spook. ▶ v. **1 notice**, observe, see, spot, sight, catch sight of, glimpse, make out, discern, detect. **2** (**spying**) **espionage**, intelligence gathering, surveillance, infiltration.

spy·glass /'spī,glas/ ▶ n. a small telescope.

sq. ▶ abbr. square.

squab /skwäb/ ▶ **n.** a young pigeon that has not yet left the nest.

squab·ble /ˈskwäbəl/ ▶ **n.** a noisy quarrel about something unimportant. ▶ **v.** (**squabbles**, **squabbling**, **squabbled**) have a squabble.

> SYNONYMS ▶ **n. quarrel**, disagreement, row, argument, dispute, wrangle, clash, altercation; informal tiff, set-to, run-in, scrap. ▶ **v. quarrel**, row, argue, bicker, disagree; informal scrap.

squad /skwäd/ ▶ **n. 1** a division of a police force. **2** a group of sports players from which a team is chosen. **3** a small group of soldiers.

> SYNONYMS **1 team**, crew, gang, force. **2 detachment**, detail, unit, platoon, battery, troop, patrol, squadron, commando.

squad·ron /ˈskwädrən/ ▶ **n. 1** a unit of an air force. **2** a group of warships.

squal·id /ˈskwälid/ ▶ **adj. 1** very dirty and unpleasant. **2** immoral or dishonest.

> SYNONYMS **1 dirty**, filthy, dingy, grubby, grimy, wretched, miserable, mean, seedy, shabby, sordid, insalubrious. **2 improper**, sordid, unseemly, unsavory, sleazy, cheap, base, low, corrupt, dishonest, dishonorable, disreputable, discreditable, contemptible, shameful. ANTONYMS clean.

squall /skwôl/ ▶ **n. 1** a sudden violent gust of wind. **2** a loud cry. ▶ **v.** (of a baby) cry noisily and continuously.

squal·or /ˈskwälər/ ▶ **n.** the state of being squalid.

> SYNONYMS **dirt**, filth, grubbiness, grime, muck, foulness, poverty, wretchedness, shabbiness, neglect, decay, dilapidation, sordidness; informal scruffiness, crumminess, grunge. ANTONYMS cleanliness, pleasantness, smartness.

squan·der /ˈskwändər/ ▶ **v.** (**squanders**, **squandering**, **squandered**) waste time, money, etc., in a reckless or foolish way.

> SYNONYMS **waste**, throw away, misuse, misspend, fritter away, spend like water; informal blow, run through, splurge, pour down the drain. ANTONYMS save.

square /skwe(ə)r/ ▶ **n. 1** a flat shape with four equal straight sides and four right angles. **2** an open area surrounded by buildings. **3** the product of a number multiplied by itself. **4** an L-shaped or T-shaped instrument used for obtaining or testing right angles. **5** informal an old-fashioned or boring person. ▶ **adj. 1** having the shape of a square. **2** having or forming a right angle. **3** (of a unit of measurement) equal to the area of a square whose side is of the unit specified: *2,000 square feet*. **4** referring to the length of each side of a square shape or object: *ten meters square*. **5** level or parallel. **6** broad and solid in shape. **7** fair or honest. **8** informal old-fashioned or boringly conventional. ▶ **adv.** directly; straight. ▶ **v.** (**squares**, **squaring**, **squared**) **1** make something square or rectangular. **2** (**squared**) marked out in squares. **3** multiply a number by itself. **4** (**square with**) make or be consistent with. **5** settle a bill or debt. **6** make the score of a game even. **7** (**square up**) take up the position of a person about to fight.

> SYNONYMS ▶ **n. piazza**, plaza, quadrangle. ▶ **adj. level**, even, drawn, equal, tied; informal even-steven.

□ **square dance** a country dance that starts with four couples facing one another in a square. **square meal** a large and balanced meal. **square knot** a type of double knot that holds very securely but can be easily undone.

square·ly /ˈskwe(ə)rlē/ ▶ **adv. 1** not at an angle; directly. **2** without any doubt; firmly: *he put the blame squarely on your shoulders.*

squash¹ /skwäsн, skwôsн/ ▶ **v. 1** crush or squeeze something so that it becomes flat or distorted. **2** force into a restricted space. **3** stop something from continuing or developing. ▶ **n. 1** a state of being squashed. **2** (also **squash rackets**) a game in which two players use rackets to hit a small rubber ball against the walls of a closed court.

> SYNONYMS ▶ **v. 1 crush**, squeeze, mash, pulp, flatten, compress, distort, pound, trample. **2 force**, ram, thrust, push, cram, jam, stuff, pack, squeeze, wedge.

■ **squash·y adj.**

squash² ▶ **n.** an edible gourd, the flesh of which may be cooked and eaten as a vegetable.

squat /skwät/ ▶ **v.** (**squats**, **squatting**, **squatted**) **1** crouch or sit with the knees bent and the heels close to the thighs. **2** unlawfully occupy an uninhabited building or area of land. ▶ **adj.** short or low and wide. ▶ **n. 1** a squatting position. **2** a building occupied by squatters. ■ **squat·ter n.**

squaw /skwô/ ▶ **n.** offensive an American Indian woman or wife.

squawk /skwôk/ ▶ **v. 1** (of a bird) make a loud, harsh noise. **2** say something in a loud, ugly tone. ▶ **n.** a squawking sound.

> SYNONYMS **screech**, squeal, shriek, scream, croak, crow, caw, cluck, cackle, hoot, cry, call.

squeak /skwēk/ ▶ **n.** a short, high-pitched sound or cry. ▶ **v. 1** make a squeak. **2** say something in a high-pitched tone.

> SYNONYMS **peep**, cheep, squeal, tweet, yelp, whimper.

squeak·y /ˈskwēkē/▶ **adj.** (**squeakier**, **squeakiest**) having or making a high-pitched sound: *a high, squeaky voice.*

squeal /skwēl/ ▶ **n.** a long, high-pitched cry or noise. ▶ **v. 1** make a squeal. **2** say something in a high-pitched tone. **3** (**squeal on**) informal inform on.

squeam·ish /ˈskwēmisн/ ▶ **adj. 1** easily disgusted or made to feel sick. **2** having very strong moral views.

> SYNONYMS **easily nauseated**, nervous; (**be squeamish about**) **be put off by**, cannot stand the sight of, ... makes you feel sick.

squee·gee /ˈskwēˌjē/ ▶ **n.** a scraping tool with a rubber-edged blade, used for cleaning windows.

squeeze /skwēz/ ▶ **v.** (**squeezes**, **squeezing**, **squeezed**) **1** firmly press from opposite sides. **2** extract liquid from something by squeezing. **3** manage to get into or through a restricted space. ▶ **n. 1** an act of squeezing. **2** a hug. **3** a small amount of liquid extracted by squeezing. **4** a strong financial demand or pressure.

> SYNONYMS ▶ **v. 1 compress**, press, crush, squash, pinch, nip, grasp, grip, clutch. **2 extract**, press, force, express. **3 force**, thrust, cram, ram, jam, stuff, pack, wedge, press, push, squash, crush, crowd, force your way. ▶ **n. 1 press**, pinch, nip, grasp, grip, clutch, hug. **2 crush**, jam, squash, congestion.

squelch /skwelCH/ ▶ **v.** make a soft sucking sound, e.g., by treading in thick mud. ▶ **n.** a squelching sound. ■ **squelch·y adj.**

squib /skwib/ ▶ **n.** a small firework.

squid /skwid/ ▶ **n.** (plural **squid** or **squids**) a sea creature with a long body, eight arms, and two long tentacles.

squig·gle /ˈskwigəl/ ▶ **n.** a short line that curls and loops irregularly. ■ **squig·gly adj.**

squint /skwint/ ▶ **v. 1** look at someone or something with your eyes partly closed. **2** have a squint affecting one eye. ▶ **n. 1** a condition in which one eye looks in a different direction from the other. **2** informal a quick or casual look.

squire /skwīr/ ▶ **n. 1** a country gentleman. **2** (in the past) a young nobleman who acted as an attendant to a knight.

squirm /skwərm/ ▶ **v. 1** wriggle or twist the body from side to side. **2** be embarrassed or ashamed. ▶ **n.** a wriggling movement.

> SYNONYMS ▶ **v. 1 wriggle**, wiggle, writhe, twist, slither, fidget, twitch, toss and turn. **2 wince**, shudder.

squir·rel /ˈskwər(ə)l/ ▶ **n.** a bushy-tailed rodent that lives in trees. ▶ **v.** (**squirrels**, **squirreling**, **squirreled**) (**squirrel something away**) hide money or valuables in a safe place.

squir·rel·ly /ˈskwər(ə)lē/ ▶ **adj.** informal restless or nervous.

squirt /skwərt/ ▶ **v. 1** force liquid out in a thin jet from a small opening. **2** wet with a jet of liquid. ▶ **n. 1** a thin jet of liquid. **2** informal a weak or insignificant person.

> SYNONYMS ▶ **v. 1 spurt**, shoot, spray, jet, erupt, gush, rush, pump, surge, stream, spew, well, issue, emanate. **2 splash**, spray, shower, sprinkle.

squish /skwisH/ ▶ **v. 1** make a soft squelching sound. **2** informal squash. ▶ **n.** a soft squelching sound. ■ **squish·y adj.**

Sr. ▶ **abbr.** senior (in names): *E. T. Krebs, Sr.*

Sri Lan·kan /ˌsrē ˈläNGkən, ˌSHrē, ˈlaNGkən/ ▶ **n.** a person from Sri Lanka. ▶ **adj.** relating to Sri Lanka.

SS ▶ **abbr. 1** Saints. **2** steamship. ▶ **n.** the Nazi special police force.

St. ▶ **abbr. 1** Saint. **2** Street.

stab /stab/ ▶ **v.** (**stabs**, **stabbing**, **stabbed**) **1** thrust a knife or other pointed weapon into. **2** thrust a pointed object at. **3** (of a pain) cause a sudden sharp feeling. ▶ **n. 1** an act of stabbing. **2** a sudden sharp feeling or pain. **3** (**a stab at**) informal an attempt to do.

> SYNONYMS ▶ **v. knife**, run through, skewer, spear, gore, spike, impale. ▶ **n. 1** *a stab of pain* **twinge**, pang, throb, spasm, cramp, prick. **2 attempt**, try, endeavor, effort; informal go, shot, crack.

sta·bil·i·ty /stəˈbilitē/ ▶ **n.** the state of being stable.

> SYNONYMS **1 firmness**, solidity, steadiness. **2 balance** (**of mind**), (mental) health, sanity, reason. **3 strength**, durability, lasting nature, permanence.

sta·bi·lize /ˈstābəˌlīz/ ▶ **v.** (**stabilizes**, **stabilizing**, **stabilized**) make or become stable. ■ **sta·bi·li·za·tion** /ˌstābəliˈzāSHən/ **n.** **sta·bi·liz·er n.**

sta·ble[1] /ˈstābəl/ ▶ **adj. 1** not likely to give way or overturn; firmly fixed. **2** not worsening in health after an injury or operation. **3** emotionally well balanced. **4** not likely to change or fail.

> SYNONYMS **1 firm**, solid, steady, secure. **2 well-balanced**, well-adjusted, of sound mind, compos mentis, sane, normal, rational, reasonable, sensible. **3** *a stable relationship* **secure**, solid, strong, steady, firm, sure, steadfast, established, enduring, lasting.
> ANTONYMS unstable.

■ **sta·bly adv.**

sta·ble[2] ▶ **n. 1** a building in which horses are kept. **2** an establishment where racehorses are kept and trained. ▶ **v.** (**stables**, **stabling**, **stabled**) put or keep a horse in a stable.

sta·ble·mate /ˈstābəlˌmāt/ ▶ **n.** a horse from the same stable as another.

stac·ca·to /stəˈkätō/ ▶ **adj.** Music with each sound or note sharply separated from the others.

stack /stak/ ▶ **n. 1** a neat pile of objects. **2** a rectangular or cylindrical pile of hay, straw, etc. **3** informal a large quantity. **4** a chimney. ▶ **v. 1** arrange in a stack. **2** fill or cover with stacks of things. **3** cause aircraft to fly at different altitudes while waiting to land. **4** arrange a deck of cards dishonestly.

> SYNONYMS ▶ **n. heap**, pile, mound, mountain, pyramid, tower. ▶ **v. 1 heap** (**up**), pile (up), assemble, put together, collect. **2 load**, fill (up), pack, charge, stuff, cram, stock.

sta·di·um /ˈstādēəm/ ▶ **n.** (plural **stadiums** or **stadia** /-dēə/) a sports arena with rows of seats for spectators.

> SYNONYMS **arena**, field, ground, track, course, racetrack, racecourse, speedway, velodrome.

staff /staf/ ▶ **n. 1** the employees of an organization. **2** a group of military officers assisting an officer in command. **3** a long stick used as a support or weapon. **4** a rod or scepter held as a symbol of authority. **5** Music a stave. ▶ **v.** provide an organization with staff.

> SYNONYMS ▶ **n. 1 employees**, workers, workforce, personnel, human resources, manpower, labor. **2 stick**, stave, pole, rod. ▶ **v. man**, people, crew, work, operate.

stag /stag/ ▶ **n.** a fully adult male deer. □ **stag party** an all-male celebration held for a man who is about to get married.

stage /stāj/ ▶ **n. 1** a point or step in a process or development. **2** a raised platform on which actors, entertainers, or speakers perform. **3** (**the stage**) the acting profession. **4** a platform on to which passengers or cargo can be landed from a boat. ▶ **v.** (**stages**, **staging**, **staged**) **1** present a performance of a play. **2** organize an event.

> SYNONYMS ▶ **n. 1 phase**, period, juncture, step, point, level. **2 part**, section, portion, stretch, leg, lap, circuit. **3 platform**, dais, stand, rostrum, podium.

□ **stage fright** nervousness before or during a performance. **stage-manage** arrange something carefully to create a certain effect. **stage manager** the person responsible for lighting and other technical arrangements for a play. **stage-struck** having a strong desire to become an actor. **stage whisper** a loud whisper by an actor on stage, intended to be heard by the audience.

stage·coach /'stāj,kōCH/ ▶ **n.** a horse-drawn vehicle formerly used to carry passengers along a regular route.

stage·hand /'stāj,hand/ ▶ **n.** a person who deals with the scenery or props for a play.

stag·ger /'stagər/ ▶ **v.** (**staggers**, **staggering**, **staggered**) **1** walk or move unsteadily. **2** astonish. **3** spread over a period of time. ▶ **n.** an unsteady walk.

> SYNONYMS ▶ **v. 1 lurch**, reel, sway, teeter, totter, stumble. **2 amaze**, astound, astonish, surprise, stun, confound, daze, take aback; informal flabbergast, knock for a loop.

stag·nant /'stagnənt/ ▶ **adj. 1** (of water or air) not moving and having an unpleasant smell. **2** showing little activity.

> SYNONYMS **1 still**, motionless, standing, stale, dirty, brackish. **2 inactive**, sluggish, slow-moving, static, flat, depressed, moribund, dead, dormant. ANTONYMS flowing.

stag·nate /'stag,nāt/ ▶ **v.** (**stagnates**, **stagnating**, **stagnated**) become stagnant. ■ **stag·na·tion** /stag'nāSHən/ **n.**

stag·y /'stājē/ (or **stagey**) ▶ **adj.** very theatrical or exaggerated.

staid /stād/ ▶ **adj.** respectable and unadventurous.

> SYNONYMS **sedate**, respectable, serious, steady, conventional, traditional, unadventurous, set in your ways, sober, formal, stuffy, stiff; informal starchy, stick-in-the-mud. ANTONYMS frivolous.

stain /stān/ ▶ **v. 1** mark or discolor with something that is not easily removed. **2** damage someone's reputation. **3** color with a dye or chemical. ▶ **n. 1** a discolored patch or mark. **2** a thing that damages someone's reputation. **3** a dye or chemical used to color materials.

> SYNONYMS ▶ **v. 1 discolor**, soil, mark, spot, spatter, splatter, smear, splash, smudge, begrime. **2 color**, tint, dye, paint. ▶ **n. 1 mark**, spot, blotch, smudge, smear. **2 blemish**, taint, blot, smear, slur, stigma.

□ **stained glass** colored glass used to form pictures or designs. **stainless steel** a form of steel containing chromium, resistant to tarnishing and rust.

stain·less /'stānlis/ ▶ **adj.** unmarked by or resistant to stains.

stair /ste(ə)r/ ▶ **n. 1** each of a set of fixed steps. **2** (**stairs**) a set of steps leading from one floor of a building to another.

stair·case /'ste(ə)r,kās/ (or **stairway** /'ste(ə)r,wā/) ▶ **n.** a set of stairs and its surrounding structure.

stair·well /'ste(ə)r,wel/ ▶ **n.** a shaft in which a staircase is built.

stake¹ /stāk/ ▶ **n.** a strong post driven into the ground to support a tree, form part of a fence, etc. ▶ **v.** (**stakes**, **staking**, **staked**) **1** support with a stake. **2** (**stake something out**) mark an area with stakes to claim ownership. **3** (**stake someone/thing out**) informal keep a place or person under observation.

> SYNONYMS ▶ **n. post**, pole, stick, spike, upright, support, cane.

stake² ▶ **n. 1** a sum of money gambled. **2** a share or interest in a business or situation. **3** (**stakes**) prize money. **4** (**stakes**) a competitive situation. ▶ **v.** (**stakes**, **staking**, **staked**) gamble money or valuables.

> SYNONYMS ▶ **n. 1 bet**, wager, ante. **2 share**, interest, investment, involvement, concern. ▶ **v. bet**, wager, lay, put on, gamble, risk.

□ **at stake 1** at risk. **2** in question.

sta·lac·tite /stə'lak,tīt/ ▶ **n.** a tapering structure hanging from the roof of a cave, formed of calcium salts deposited by dripping water.

sta·lag·mite /stə'lag,mīt/ ▶ **n.** a tapering column rising from the floor of a cave, formed of calcium salts deposited by dripping water.

stale /stāl/ ▶ **adj. 1** (of food) no longer fresh. **2** no longer new and interesting. **3** no longer interested or motivated.

> SYNONYMS **1 old**, past its best, off, dry, hard, musty, moldy, rancid. **2 stuffy**, musty, fusty, stagnant. **3 overused**, hackneyed, tired, worn out, overworked, played out, threadbare, banal, clichéd, trite, unimaginative, uninspired, flat; informal old hat. ANTONYMS fresh.

■ **stale·ness n.**

stale·mate /'stāl,māt/ ▶ **n. 1** a situation in which further progress by opposing sides seems impossible. **2** Chess a position in which a player is not in check but can only move into check.

> SYNONYMS **deadlock**, impasse, standoff, gridlock.

stalk¹ /stôk/ ▶ **n. 1** the stem of a plant or support of a leaf, flower, or fruit. **2** a slender support or stem.

stalk² ▶ **v. 1** follow or approach stealthily. **2** obsessively follow, watch, or try to communicate with a particular person. **3** walk in a proud, stiff, or angry way.

> SYNONYMS **1 trail**, follow, shadow, track, go after, hunt; informal tail. **2 strut**, stride, march, flounce, storm, stomp, sweep.

■ **stalk·er n.**

stall /stôl/ ▶ **n. 1** a stand or booth where goods are sold in a market. **2** a compartment for an animal in a stable or cowshed. **3** a compartment in which a horse is held before the start of a race. **4** a compartment in a set of toilets. **5** a seat in the choir or chancel of a church. ▶ **v. 1** (of a vehicle's engine) suddenly stop running. **2** stop making progress. **3** be vague or indecisive so as to gain more time to deal with something. **4** (of an aircraft) be moving too slowly to be controlled effectively.

> SYNONYMS ▶ **n. 1 stand**, table, counter, booth, kiosk. **2 pen**, coop, sty, corral, enclosure, compartment. ▶ **v. 1 delay**, play for time, procrastinate, hedge, drag your feet, filibuster, stonewall. **2 hold off**, stave off, keep at bay, evade, avoid.

stal·lion /'stalyən/ ▶ **n.** an adult male horse that has not been castrated.

stal·wart /'stôlwərt/ ▶ **adj.** loyal, reliable, and hard-working. ▶ **n.** a stalwart supporter or member of an organization.

> SYNONYMS ▶ **adj. staunch**, loyal, faithful, committed, devoted, dedicated, dependable, reliable. ANTONYMS disloyal.

sta·men /'stāmin/ ▶ **n.** a male fertilizing organ of a flower.

stam·i·na /ˈstamənə/ ▶ **n.** the ability to keep up effort over a long period.

SYNONYMS **endurance**, staying power, energy, toughness, determination, tenacity, perseverance, grit.

stam·mer /ˈstamər/ ▶ **v.** (**stammers**, **stammering**, **stammered**) speak or say with difficulty, making sudden pauses and repeating the first letters of words. ▶ **n.** a tendency to stammer.

SYNONYMS ▶ **v.** **stutter**, stumble over your words, hesitate, falter, pause, splutter.

stamp /stamp/ ▶ **v.** **1** bring down your foot heavily. **2** walk with heavy, forceful steps. **3** (**stamp something out**) decisively put an end to something. **4** press with a device that leaves a mark or pattern. ▶ **n.** **1** a small piece of paper stuck to a letter or package to record payment of postage. **2** an instrument for stamping a pattern or mark. **3** a mark or pattern made by a stamp. **4** a characteristic impression or quality. **5** an act of stamping the foot.

SYNONYMS ▶ **v.** **1 trample**, step, tread, tramp, stomp, stump, clump, crush, squash, flatten. **2 imprint**, print, impress, punch, inscribe, emboss. ▶ **n.** **mark**, hallmark, sign, seal, sure sign, smack, savor, air.

□ **stamp duty** a tax on some legal documents. **stamping ground** a place you regularly visit or spend time in.

stam·pede /stamˈpēd/ ▶ **n.** **1** a sudden panicked rush of a number of horses, cattle, etc. **2** a sudden mass movement or reaction due to interest or panic. ▶ **v.** (**stampedes**, **stampeding**, **stampeded**) take part in a stampede.

SYNONYMS ▶ **n.** **charge**, panic, rush, flight, rout. ▶ **v.** **bolt**, charge, flee, take flight, race, rush, career, run.

stance /stans/ ▶ **n.** **1** the way in which someone stands. **2** an attitude or standpoint.

SYNONYMS **1 posture**, body position, pose, attitude. **2 attitude**, opinion, standpoint, position, approach, policy, line.

stanch /stôncʜ, stäncʜ/ (or **staunch**) ▶ **v.** stop or slow down a flow of blood.

SYNONYMS **stem**, stop, halt, check, curb.

stan·chion /ˈstancʜən/ ▶ **n.** an upright bar, post, or frame forming a support or barrier.

stand /stand/ ▶ **v.** (**stands**, **standing**, **stood** /sto͝od/) **1** be or become upright, supported by the feet. **2** place or be situated in a particular position. **3** remain stationary, undisturbed, or unchanged. **4** be in a particular state or condition. **5** tolerate or like. ▶ **n.** **1** an attitude toward an issue. **2** a determined effort to hold your ground or resist something. **3** a structure for holding or displaying something. **4** a large structure for spectators to sit or stand in. **5** a raised platform for a band, orchestra, or speaker. **6** a stall from which goods are sold or displayed. **7** (**the stand**) the witness box in a court of law. **8** a stopping of motion or progress.

SYNONYMS ▶ **v.** **1 rise**, get to your feet, get up, pick yourself up. **2 be situated**, be located, be positioned, be sited. **3 put**, set, erect, place, position, prop, install, arrange; informal park. **4 remain in force**, remain in operation, hold, hold good, apply, be the case, exist, prevail. **5 withstand**, endure, bear, put up with, take, cope with, handle, sustain, resist, stand up to. **6 put up with**, endure, tolerate, accept, take, abide, stand for, support, countenance; formal brook. ANTONYMS sit, lie down. ▶ **n.** **1 attitude**, stance, opinion, standpoint, position, approach, policy, line. **2 opposition**, resistance. **3 base**, support, platform, stage, dais, rest, plinth, tripod, rack, trivet. **4 stall**, counter, booth, kiosk.

□ **stand by 1** look on without becoming involved. **2** support or remain loyal to. **3** be ready to take action if needed. **stand down** (or **aside**) resign from a position or office. **stand for 1** be an abbreviation of or symbol for. **2** put up with. **stand in** deputize for someone. **stand-in** a substitute. **stand out 1** stick out or be easily noticeable. **2** be clearly better. **stand someone up** informal fail to keep a date with someone. **stand up for** speak or act in support of.

USAGE

Use **standing** rather than **stood** with the verb 'to be': say *we were standing in a line for hours* rather than *we were stood in a line for hours.*

stand·ard /ˈstandərd/ ▶ **n.** **1** a level of quality or achievement. **2** a measure or model used to make comparisons. **3** (**standards**) principles of good behavior. **4** a military or ceremonial flag. ▶ **adj.** used or accepted as normal or average.

SYNONYMS ▶ **n.** **1 quality**, level, caliber, merit, excellence. **2 guideline**, norm, yardstick, benchmark, gauge, measure, criterion, guide, touchstone, model, pattern. **3 principle**, ideal; (**standards**) morals, code of behavior, ethics. **4 flag**, banner, ensign, color(s). ▶ **adj.** **1 normal**, usual, average, typical, stock, common, ordinary, customary, conventional, established. **2 definitive**, classic, recognized, accepted, approved, authoritative. ANTONYMS unusual, special.

□ **standard-bearer 1** a leading figure in a cause or movement. **2** a soldier who carries a military or ceremonial flag. **standard English** the dialect of English used by most educated English speakers. **standard lamp** a floor lamp. **standard of living** the degree of comfort that a person or community has. **standard time** a uniform time for places in approximately the same longitude.

stand·ard·ize /ˈstandərˌdīz/ ▶ **v.** (**standardizes**, **standardizing**, **standardized**) make something fit in with a standard. ■ **stand·ard·i·za·tion** /ˌstandərdiˈzāsʜən/ **n.**

stand·by /ˈstan(d)ˌbī/ ▶ **n.** (plural **standbys**) **1** readiness for duty or action. **2** a person or thing ready to be used in an emergency. ▶ **adj.** (of tickets) sold only at the last minute.

stand·ee /stanˈdē/ ▶ **n.** a person who is standing rather than seated.

stand·ing /ˈstandiɴɢ/ ▶ **n.** **1** position, status, or reputation. **2** duration or length. ▶ **adj.** remaining in force or use: *a standing invitation.*

SYNONYMS ▶ **n.** **1 status**, ranking, position, reputation, stature. **2 prestige**, rank, eminence, seniority, repute, stature, esteem, importance, account.

□ **standing joke** something that regularly causes amusement. **standing order** any order or procedure permanently in effect unless specifically changed. **standing ovation** a long period of applause during which the members of the audience rise to their feet.

stand·off /'stand,ôf, -,äf/ ▶ **n.** a stalemate or deadlock between two equally matched opponents in a dispute or conflict.

stand·off·ish /,stand'ôfisн, -'äfisн/ ▶ **adj.** informal distant and cold in manner; unfriendly.

stand·point /'stan(d),point/ ▶ **n.** an attitude toward a particular issue.

stand·still /'stan(d),stil/ ▶ **n.** a situation or condition without movement or activity.

stank /stanɢk/ past of **STINK**.

stan·za /'stanzə/ ▶ **n.** a group of lines forming the basic unit in a poem.

sta·ple[1] /'stāpəl/ ▶ **n. 1** a small piece of wire used to fasten papers together. **2** a small U-shaped metal bar driven into wood to hold things in place. ▶ **v.** (**staples**, **stapling**, **stapled**) secure with a staple or staples. ■ **sta·pler n.**

sta·ple[2] ▶ **n. 1** a main item of trade or production. **2** a main or important element, especially of a diet. ▶ **adj.** main or important.

> SYNONYMS ▶ **adj. main**, principal, chief, major, primary, leading, foremost, first, most important, predominant, dominant, basic, prime; informal number-one.

star /stär/ ▶ **n. 1** a large ball of burning gas that appears as a glowing point in the night sky. **2** a simplified representation of a star with five or six points. **3** a famous entertainer or athlete. ▶ **v.** (**stars**, **starring**, **starred**) **1** have someone as a leading performer. **2** have a leading role in a movie, play, etc.

> SYNONYMS ▶ **n. 1 heavenly body**, celestial body. **2 principal**, leading lady/man, lead, hero, heroine. **3 celebrity**, superstar, famous name, household name, leading light, VIP, personality, luminary; informal celeb, big shot, megastar. **4** *a star pupil* **outstanding**, exceptional. **5** *the star attraction* **top**, leading, greatest, foremost, major, preeminent.

□ **star fruit** ⇒ **CARAMBOLA. star-spangled 1** covered or decorated with stars. **2** very successful. **Stars and Stripes** the national flag of the United States.

star·board /'stär,bôrd/ ▶ **n.** the side of a ship or aircraft that is on the right when you are facing forward.

starch /stärcн/ ▶ **n. 1** a carbohydrate that is obtained from potatoes, flour, rice, etc., and is an important part of the human diet. **2** powder or spray used to stiffen fabric. ▶ **v.** stiffen with starch.

starch·y /'stärcнē/ ▶ **adj.** (**starchier**, **starchiest**) **1** containing a lot of starch. **2** informal stiff and formal in manner.

star·dom /'stärdəm/ ▶ **n.** the state or status of being a famous or talented entertainer or athlete.

stare /ste(ə)r/ ▶ **v.** (**stares**, **staring**, **stared**) look with concentration and the eyes wide open. ▶ **n.** an act of staring.

> SYNONYMS ▶ **v. gaze**, gape, goggle, glare, ogle, peer; informal gawk.

star·fish /'stär,fisн/ ▶ **n.** (plural **starfish** or **starfishes**) a sea creature having five or more arms extending from a central point.

stark /stärk/ ▶ **adj. 1** severe or bare in appearance. **2** unpleasantly or sharply clear. **3** complete; sheer: *stark terror.*

> SYNONYMS **1 sharp**, sharply defined, crisp, distinct, clear, clear-cut. **2 desolate**, bare, barren, empty, bleak, dreary, depressing, grim. ANTONYMS indistinct, ornate.

□ **stark naked** completely naked. ■ **stark·ly adv.**

star·let /'stärlit/ ▶ **n.** informal a promising young actress or performer.

star·light /'stär,līt/ ▶ **n.** light coming from the stars.

star·ling /'stärlinɢ/ ▶ **n.** a bird with shiny dark speckled feathers.

star·lit /'stär,lit/ ▶ **adj.** lit by stars.

star·ry /'stärē/ ▶ **adj.** (**starrier**, **starriest**) full of or lit by stars. □ **starry-eyed** full of unrealistic hopes or dreams.

star·ship /'stär,sнip/ ▶ **n.** (in science fiction) a spaceship for travel between stars.

start /stärt/ ▶ **v. 1** begin to do or happen. **2** begin to operate or start working. **3** make something happen or start working. **4** begin to move or travel. **5** (**start out** or **up**) begin a project or undertaking. **6** jump or jerk from surprise. ▶ **n. 1** an act of beginning. **2** the point at which something begins. **3** an advantage given to a competitor at the beginning of a race. **4** a sudden movement of surprise.

> SYNONYMS ▶ **v. 1 begin**, commence, get under way, get going, go ahead, make a start; informal kick off, get the ball rolling, get the show on the road. **2 come into being**, begin, arise, originate, develop. **3 establish**, set up, found, create, bring into being, institute, initiate, inaugurate, introduce, open, launch. **4 activate**, switch/turn on, start up, fire up, boot up. **5 flinch**, jerk, jump, twitch, wince. ANTONYMS end, finish, stop. ▶ **n. 1 beginning**, commencement, inception, onset, inauguration, dawn, birth, emergence; informal kickoff. **2 lead**, head start, advantage. **3 jerk**, twitch, spasm, jump. ANTONYMS end.

start·er /'stärtər/ ▶ **n. 1** a person or thing that starts. **2** Baseball a pitcher who starts the game rather than coming in later as relief.

star·tle /'stärtl/ ▶ **v.** (**startles**, **startling**, **startled**) make someone feel sudden shock or alarm.

> SYNONYMS **surprise**, frighten, scare, alarm, shock, give someone a fright, make someone jump.

■ **star·tled adj.**

star·tling /'stärtl-inɢ/ ▶ **adj.** very surprising.

> SYNONYMS **surprising**, astonishing, amazing, unexpected, unforeseen, shocking, stunning; frightening, alarming, scary. ANTONYMS predictable, ordinary.

■ **star·tling·ly adv.**

starve /stärv/ ▶ **v.** (**starves**, **starving**, **starved**) **1** suffer or die from hunger. **2** make someone starve. **3** (**be starving** or **starved**) informal feel very hungry. **4** (**be starved of**) be deprived of.

> SYNONYMS (**starving** or **starved**) **hungry**, undernourished, malnourished, starved, ravenous, famished. ANTONYMS full.

■ **star·va·tion** /-'vāsнən/ **n.**

stash /stasн/ informal ▶ **v.** store safely in a secret place. ▶ **n.** a secret store.

> SYNONYMS ▶ **v. store**, stow, pack, load, cache, hide, conceal, secrete, hoard, save, stockpile.

▶ n. **cache**, hoard, stock, stockpile, store, supply, reserve.

sta·sis /ˈstāsis, ˈsta-/ ▶ n. formal a period or state when there is no activity or change.

state /stāt/ ▶ n. **1** the condition of someone or something at a particular time. **2** a country considered as an organized political community. **3** an area forming part of a federal republic. **4** (**the States**) the United States of America. **5** the government of a country. **6** the ceremonial procedures associated with monarchy or government. **7** (**a state**) informal an agitated, untidy, or dirty condition. ▶ v. (**states, stating, stated**) express definitely in speech or writing.

SYNONYMS ▶ n. **1 condition**, shape, position, situation, circumstances, state of affairs, predicament, plight. **2 country**, nation, land, kingdom, realm, power, republic. **3 government**, administration, parliament, regime. **4 state of anxiety**, panic, fluster; informal flap, tizzy. ▶ v. **express**, voice, utter, put into words, declare, announce, make known, put across/over, communicate, air.

□ **State Department** the US department of foreign affairs. **state-of-the-art** very up to date. **state's rights** the rights and powers held by individual US states rather than by the federal government. **state university** (or **school**) a university managed by the authorities of a particular US state. ■ **state·less** adj.

state·house /ˈstātˌhous/ ▶ n. the building where a state legislature meets.

state·ly /ˈstātlē/ ▶ adj. (**statelier, stateliest**) dignified, imposing, or grand.

SYNONYMS **dignified**, majestic, ceremonious, courtly, imposing, solemn, regal, grand. ANTONYMS undignified.

state·ment /ˈstātmənt/ ▶ n. **1** a clear expression of something in speech or writing. **2** an account of events given to the police or in court. **3** a list of amounts paid into and out of a bank account.

SYNONYMS **declaration**, expression, affirmation, assertion, announcement, utterance, communication, bulletin, communiqué.

state·side /ˈstātˌsīd/ ▶ adj. & adv. informal relating to or toward the United States.

states·man /ˈstātsmən/ (or **stateswoman** /ˈstātsˌwo͝omən/) ▶ n. (plural **statesmen** or **stateswomen**) an experienced and respected political leader.

state·wide /ˈstātˈwīd/ ▶ adj. & adv. extending throughout a particular US state.

stat·ic /ˈstatik/ ▶ adj. not moving, acting, or changing. ▶ n. **1** (also **static electricity**) an electric charge acquired by an object that is not a conductor of electricity. **2** crackling or hissing on a telephone, radio, etc.

SYNONYMS ▶ adj. **1 unchanged**, fixed, stable, steady, unchanging, unvarying, constant. **2 stationary**, motionless, immobile, unmoving, still, at a standstill. ANTONYMS variable, dynamic.

■ **stat·i·cal·ly** adv.

sta·tion /ˈstāshən/ ▶ n. **1** a place where passenger trains stop on a railroad line. **2** a place where an activity or service is based. **3** a broadcasting company. **4** the place where someone or something stands or is placed. **5** dated a person's social rank or position. ▶ v. put someone in a particular place or position.

SYNONYMS ▶ n. **1 establishment**, base, camp, post, depot, mission, site, facility, installation. **2 office**, depot, base, headquarters. **3 channel**, wavelength. ▶ v. **base**, post, establish, deploy, garrison.

□ **station wagon** a car with a large storage area behind the seats and an extra door at the rear.

sta·tion·ar·y /ˈstāshəˌnerē/ ▶ adj. not moving or changing.

SYNONYMS **static**, parked, motionless, immobile, still, stock-still, at a standstill, at rest. ANTONYMS moving.

USAGE

Don't confuse **stationary** and **stationery**: **stationary** means 'not moving or changing,' whereas **stationery** means 'paper and other writing materials.'

sta·tion·er /ˈstāsh(ə)nər/ ▶ n. a person who sells stationery.

sta·tion·er·y /ˈstāshəˌnerē/ ▶ n. paper and other materials needed for writing.

sta·tion·mas·ter /ˈstāshənˌmastər/ ▶ n. a person in charge of a railroad station.

sta·tis·tic /stəˈtistik/ ▶ n. **1** (**statistics**) the collection and analysis of large amounts of information shown in numbers. **2** a fact or piece of data obtained from a study of statistics. ■ **stat·is·ti·cian** /ˌstatiˈstishən/ n.

sta·tis·ti·cal /stəˈtistikəl/ ▶ adj. having to do with statistics. ■ **sta·tis·ti·cal·ly** adv.

stat·u·ar·y /ˈstacho͞oˌerē/ ▶ n. statues.

stat·ue /ˈstacho͞o/ ▶ n. a model of a person or animal made of stone, metal, etc.

stat·u·esque /ˌstacho͞oˈesk/ ▶ adj. (of a woman) attractively tall and dignified.

stat·u·ette /ˌstacho͞oˈet/ ▶ n. a small statue.

stat·ure /ˈstachər/ ▶ n. **1** a person's height when they are standing. **2** importance or reputation.

SYNONYMS **1 height**, size, build. **2 reputation**, repute, standing, status, position, prestige, distinction, eminence, prominence, importance.

sta·tus /ˈstātəs, ˈstatəs/ ▶ n. **1** a person's social or professional position. **2** high rank or social standing. **3** the situation at a particular time.

SYNONYMS **1 standing**, rank, position, level, place. **2 prestige**, kudos, cachet, standing, stature, esteem, image, importance, authority, fame.

□ **status symbol** a possession intended to show a person's wealth or high status.

sta·tus quo /ˈstātəs ˈkwō, ˈstatəs/ ▶ n. the existing situation.

stat·ute /ˈstacho͞ot/ ▶ n. **1** a written law. **2** a rule of an organization or institution.

SYNONYMS **law**, regulation, act, bill, decree, edict, rule, ruling, resolution, dictum, command, order, directive, bylaw; formal ordinance.

stat·u·to·ry /ˈstachəˌtôrē/ ▶ adj. **1** required or permitted by law. **2** done or happening regularly and therefore expected.

staunch[1] /stôncH, stäncH/ ▶ **adj.** very loyal and committed.

> SYNONYMS **stalwart**, loyal, faithful, committed, devoted, dedicated, reliable. ANTONYMS disloyal, unfaithful.

■ **staunch·ly adv.**

staunch[2] = STANCH.

stave /stāv/ ▶ **n. 1** any of the lengths of wood fixed side by side to make a barrel, bucket, etc. **2** a strong stick, post, or pole. **3** (also **staff** /staf/) Music a set of five parallel lines that notes are written on or between. ▶ **v.** (**staves, staving**, past and past participle **staved** or **stove** /stōv/) **1** (**stave something in**) break something by forcing it inward. **2** (past and past participle **staved**) (**stave something off**) stop or delay something bad or dangerous.

stay /stā/ ▶ **v. 1** remain in the same place. **2** remain in a particular state or position. **3** live somewhere temporarily as a visitor or guest. **4** stop, delay, or prevent. ▶ **n. 1** a period of staying somewhere. **2** a brace or support. **3** (**stays**) historical a corset stiffened by strips of whalebone.

> SYNONYMS ▶ **v. 1 remain** (**behind**), wait, linger, stick, be left, hold on, hang on; informal hang around; old use tarry. **2 continue** (**to be**), remain, keep, carry on being. **3 visit**, stop (off/over), vacation, lodge. ANTONYMS leave. ▶ **n. visit**, stop, stopover, break, vacation; literary sojourn.

□ **staying power** informal endurance or stamina. **stay of execution** a delay in carrying out the orders of a court of law.

stead /sted/ ▶ **n.** (**in someone's** or **something's stead**) instead of someone or something. □ **stand someone in good stead** be useful to someone over time.

stead·fast /'sted,fast/ ▶ **adj.** not changing in your attitudes or aims. ■ **stead·fast·ly adv.**

stead·y /'stedē/ ▶ **adj.** (**steadier, steadiest**) **1** firmly fixed, supported, or balanced. **2** not faltering or wavering. **3** sensible and reliable. **4** regular, even, and continuous. ▶ **v.** (**steadies, steadying, steadied**) make steady.

> SYNONYMS ▶ **adj. 1 stable**, firm, fixed, secure. **2 still**, motionless, static, stationary, unmoving. **3** *a steady gaze* **fixed**, intent, unwavering, unfaltering. **4** *steady breathing* **constant**, consistent, regular, even, rhythmic. **5 continuous**, continual, unceasing, ceaseless, perpetual, unremitting, endless. **6 regular**, settled, firm, committed, long-term. ANTONYMS unstable, shaky, fluctuating. ▶ **v. 1 stabilize**, hold steady, brace, support, balance, rest. **2 calm**, soothe, quiet, compose, settle, subdue, quell.

■ **stead·i·ly adv. stead·i·ness n.**

steak /stāk/ ▶ **n. 1** high-quality beef cut into thick slices for grilling or frying. **2** a thick slice of another meat or fish. **3** poorer-quality beef for stewing.

steal /stēl/ ▶ **v.** (**steals, stealing, stole** /stōl/; past participle **stolen** /'stōlən/) **1** take something without permission and without intending to return it. **2** move quietly or secretively. ▶ **n.** informal a bargain.

> SYNONYMS ▶ **v. 1 take**, thieve, help yourself to, pilfer, embezzle; informal swipe, lift, heist, filch. **2 plagiarize**, copy, pirate; informal rip off, lift, crib. **3 creep**, sneak, steal away, slink, slip, glide, tiptoe, **slope**.

□ **steal the show** attract the most attention and praise.

stealth /stelTH/ ▶ **n.** cautious and secretive action or movement.

> SYNONYMS **furtiveness**, secretiveness, secrecy, surreptitiousness.

stealth·y /'stelTHē/ ▶ **adj.** (**stealthier, stealthiest**) cautious and secretive.

> SYNONYMS **furtive**, secretive, secret, surreptitious, sneaky, sly. ANTONYMS open.

■ **stealth·i·ly adv.**

steam /stēm/ ▶ **n. 1** the hot vapor into which water is converted when heated. **2** power produced by steam under pressure. **3** momentum. ▶ **v. 1** give off or produce steam. **2** (**steam up**) mist over with steam. **3** cook food by heating it in steam from boiling water. **4** (of a ship or train) travel under steam power. **5** informal move quickly or forcefully.

steam·boat /'stēm,bōt/ ▶ **n.** a boat propelled by a steam engine.

steam·er /'stēmər/ ▶ **n. 1** a ship or boat powered by steam. **2** a type of saucepan in which food can be steamed. **3** (in full **steamer clam**) another term for **soft-shell clam**.

steam·roll·er /'stēm,rōlər/ ▶ **n.** a heavy, slow vehicle with a roller, used to flatten the surfaces of roads. ▶ **v.** (**steamrollers, steamrollering, steamrollered**) **1** force someone into doing or accepting something. **2** forcibly pass a law.

steam·y /'stēmē/ ▶ **adj.** (**steamier, steamiest**) producing or filled with steam.

> SYNONYMS **1 humid**, muggy, sticky, moist, damp, clammy, sultry, sweaty, steaming. **2** *a steamy love scene* **erotic**, sexually arousing, sexually stimulating, titillating, suggestive.

steed /stēd/ ▶ **n.** literary a horse.

steel /stēl/ ▶ **n. 1** a hard, strong metal that is a mixture of iron and carbon. **2** strength and determination. ▶ **v.** (**steel yourself**) mentally prepare yourself for something difficult.

> SYNONYMS ▶ **v.** (**steel yourself**) **brace yourself**, summon (up) your courage, screw up your courage, gear yourself up, prepare yourself, fortify yourself, harden yourself; informal psych yourself up; literary gird (up) your loins.

□ **steel band** a band that plays music on drums made from empty oil containers.

steel·works /'stēl,wərks/ ▶ **pl.n.** a factory where steel is produced.

steel·y /'stēlē/ ▶ **adj.** (**steelier, steeliest**) **1** like steel. **2** coldly determined.

> SYNONYMS **1** *his steely gaze* **piercing**, penetrating; merciless, ruthless, pitiless, severe, unrelenting, unpitying, unforgiving; literary adamantine. **2** *steely determination* **resolute**, firm, steadfast, unflinching, unswerving, unfaltering, untiring, unwavering, single-minded, ruthless, iron, grim, gritty. ANTONYMS halfhearted.

steep[1] /stēp/ ▶ **adj. 1** rising or falling sharply. **2** (of a rise or fall in an amount) very large or rapid. **3** informal (of a price or demand) too great.

> SYNONYMS **1 sheer**, precipitous, abrupt, sharp, perpendicular, vertical. **2** *a steep increase* **sharp**, sudden, dramatic, precipitate. ANTONYMS gentle, gradual.

■ **steep·en** v. **steep·ly** adv.

steep² ▶ v. **1** soak in water or other liquid. **2** (**be steeped in**) have a lot of a particular quality or atmosphere.

> SYNONYMS (**steeped in**) **imbued with**, filled with, permeated with, suffused with, soaked in, pervaded by.

stee·ple /ˈstēpəl/ ▶ n. a church tower and spire.

stee·ple·chase /ˈstēpəlˌCHās/ ▶ n. **1** a horse race with ditches and hedges as jumps. **2** a race in which runners must clear hurdles and water jumps. ■ **stee·ple·chas·er** n.

stee·ple·jack /ˈstēpəlˌjak/ ▶ n. a person who climbs tall structures such as chimneys and steeples to repair them.

steer¹ /sti(ə)r/ ▶ v. **1** guide or control the movement of a vehicle, ship, etc. **2** direct or guide.

> SYNONYMS **guide**, direct, maneuver, drive, pilot, navigate.

□ **steer clear of** take care to avoid. **steering wheel** a wheel that a driver turns in order to steer a vehicle.

steer² ▶ n. a male domestic bovine that has been castrated and is raised for beef.

steer·age /ˈsti(ə)rij/ ▶ n. (in the past) the cheapest accommodations in a ship.

steers·man /ˈsti(ə)rzmən/ ▶ n. (plural **steersmen**) a person who steers a boat or ship.

steg·o·saur /ˈstegəˌsôr/ (or **steg·o·sau·rus**) ▶ n. a plant-eating dinosaur with a double row of large bony plates along the back.

stel·lar /ˈstelər/ ▶ adj. having to do with a star or stars.

stem¹ /stem/ ▶ n. **1** the long, thin main part of a plant or shrub, or support of a fruit, flower, or leaf. **2** a long, thin supporting part of a wine glass, tobacco pipe, etc. **3** a vertical stroke in a letter or musical note. **4** the root or main part of a word. ▶ v. (**stems**, **stemming**, **stemmed**) (**stem from**) come from or be caused by.

> SYNONYMS ▶ n. **stalk**, shoot, trunk.

stem² ▶ v. (**stems**, **stemming**, **stemmed**) stop or slow down the flow or progress of something.

> SYNONYMS **stop**, stanch, halt, check, curb.

stench /stenCH/ ▶ n. a strong and very unpleasant smell.

> SYNONYMS **stink**, reek; informal **funk**; literary miasma.

sten·cil /ˈstensəl/ ▶ n. a thin sheet with a pattern or letters cut out of it, used to produce a design by applying ink or paint through the holes. ▶ v. (**stencils**, **stenciling**, **stenciled**) decorate or form something with a stencil.

ste·nog·ra·pher /stəˈnägrəfər/ ▶ n. a shorthand typist.

sten·to·ri·an /stenˈtôrēən/ ▶ adj. (of a person's voice) loud and powerful.

step /step/ ▶ n. **1** an act of lifting and putting down the foot or feet in walking. **2** the distance covered by a step. **3** a flat surface on which to place the feet when moving from one level to another. **4** a position or grade in a scale or ranking. **5** a measure or action taken to deal with something. ▶ v. (**steps**, **stepping**, **stepped**) lift and put down your foot or feet.

> SYNONYMS ▶ n. **1 pace**, stride, footstep, footfall, tread, tramp. **2 stair**, tread; (**steps**) stairs, staircase, flight of stairs. **3 action**, act, course of action, measure, move, operation, procedure. **4 advance**, development, move, movement, breakthrough. **5 stage**, level, grade, rank, degree, phase. ▶ v. **walk**, move, tread, pace, stride.

□ **step aerobics** a type of aerobics that involves stepping up on to and down from a block. **step down** resign from a job or position. **step in** become involved in a difficult situation. **step something up** increase the amount, speed, or strength of.

step·broth·er /ˈstepˌbrəT͟Hər/ ▶ n. a son of a person's stepfather or stepmother.

step·child /ˈstepˌCHīld/ ▶ n. (plural **stepchildren**) a child of a person's husband or wife from a previous marriage.

step·daugh·ter /ˈstepˌdôtər, ˈstepˌdätər/ ▶ n. a daughter of a person's husband or wife from a previous marriage.

step·family /ˈstepˌfam(ə)lē/ ▶ n. (plural **stepfamilies**) a family including one or more children that is formed when a divorced or widowed person remarries.

step·fa·ther /ˈstepˌfäT͟Hər/ ▶ n. a man who is married to a person's mother but is not his or her father.

step·lad·der /ˈstepˌladər/ ▶ n. a short free-standing folding ladder.

step·moth·er /ˈstepˌməT͟Hər/ ▶ n. a woman who is married to a person's father but is not his or her mother.

steppe /step/ ▶ n. a large area of flat unforested grassland in southeastern Europe and Siberia.

step·ping·stone /ˈstepiNGˌstōn/ ▶ n. **1** a raised stone on which to step when crossing a stream. **2** an action that helps you make progress toward a goal.

step·sis·ter /ˈstepˌsistər/ ▶ n. a daughter of a person's stepfather or stepmother.

step·son /ˈstepˌsən/ ▶ n. a son of a person's husband or wife from a previous marriage.

ster·e·o /ˈsterēˌō, ˈsti(ə)r-/ ▶ n. (plural **stereos**) **1** music or sound that comes from two or more speakers and seems to surround you. **2** a CD player, record player, etc., that has two or more speakers. ▶ adj. relating to this kind of sound.

ster·e·o·phon·ic /ˌsterēəˈfänik, ˌsti(ə)r-/ ▶ adj. (of sound reproduction) using two or more channels. Compare with MONOPHONIC.

ster·e·o·type /ˈsterēəˌtīp, ˈsti(ə)r-/ ▶ n. an oversimplified idea of the typical characteristics of a person or thing. ▶ v. (**stereotypes**, **stereotyping**, **stereotyped**) represent as a stereotype.

> SYNONYMS ▶ n. **conventional idea**, standard image, cliché, formula. ▶ v. **typecast**, pigeonhole, conventionalize, categorize, label, tag.

■ **ster·e·o·typ·i·cal** /ˌsterēəˈtipikəl/ adj.

ster·ile /ˈsterəl/ ▶ adj. **1** not able to produce children, young, crops, or fruit. **2** not imaginative, creative, or exciting. **3** free from bacteria.

> SYNONYMS **1 unproductive**, infertile, unfruitful, barren. **2 hygienic**, clean, pure, uncontaminated, sterilized, disinfected, germ-free, antiseptic. ANTONYMS fertile.

■ **ste·ril·i·ty** /stəˈrilitē/ n.

ster·i·lize /ˈsterəˌlīz/ ▶ **v.** (**sterilizes**, **sterilizing**, **sterilized**) make sterile.

> SYNONYMS **1 disinfect**, fumigate, decontaminate, sanitize, clean, cleanse, purify. **2 neuter**, castrate, spay, alter, geld. ANTONYMS contaminate.

■ **ster·i·li·za·tion** /ˌsterəl(ə)ˈzāsʜən/ **n.**

ster·ling /ˈstərlɪɴɢ/ ▶ **n.** British money. ▶ **adj.** **1** excellent. **2** (of silver) of at least $92^1/_4$ percent purity.

stern¹ /stərn/ ▶ **adj.** **1** grimly serious or strict. **2** severe.

> SYNONYMS **1 unsmiling**, frowning, serious, severe, forbidding, grim, unfriendly, austere, dour. **2 strict**, severe, stringent, harsh, drastic, hard, tough, extreme, draconian. ANTONYMS genial, lax.

■ **stern·ly** **adv.**

stern² ▶ **n.** the rear end of a ship or boat.

ster·num /ˈstərnəm/ ▶ **n.** the breastbone.

ste·roid /ˈsterˌoid, ˈsti(ə)r-/ ▶ **n.** **1** any of a class of substances that includes certain hormones and vitamins. **2** an anabolic steroid.

ster·to·rous /ˈstərtərəs/ ▶ **adj.** (of breathing) noisy and labored.

steth·o·scope /ˈsteᴛʜəˌskōp/ ▶ **n.** a device used by doctors for listening to the sound of a person's heart or breathing.

Stet·son /ˈstetsən/ ▶ **n.** trademark a hat with a high crown and a very wide brim, worn by cowboys and ranchers.

ste·ve·dore /ˈstēvəˌdôr/ ▶ **n.** a person employed at a dock to load and unload ships.

stew /st(y)o͞o/ ▶ **n.** **1** a dish of meat and vegetables cooked slowly in liquid. **2** informal a state of anxiety or agitation. ▶ **v.** **1** cook slowly in a liquid. **2** informal be anxious or agitated.

stew·ard /ˈst(y)o͞oərd/ ▶ **n.** **1** a person who looks after the passengers on a ship or aircraft. **2** an official who supervises arrangements at a large public event. **3** a person employed to manage a large house or estate. **4** a person responsible for supplies of food to a college, club, etc.
■ **stew·ard·ship** **n.**

stew·ard·ess /ˈst(y)o͞oərdis/ ▶ **n.** a woman who looks after the passengers on a ship or aircraft.

stick¹ /stik/ ▶ **n.** **1** a thin piece of wood that has fallen or been cut from a tree. **2** a piece of wood used for support in walking or as a weapon. **3** a long, thin implement used in hockey, polo, etc., to hit the ball or puck. **4** a long, thin object or piece. **5** (**the sticks**) informal remote country areas. **6** the threat of punishment as a means of persuasion. The opposite of CARROT (sense 2).

> SYNONYMS **1 branch**, twig, switch. **2 walking stick**, cane, staff, crutch. **3 post**, pole, cane, stake, rod.

□ **stick insect** a long, slender insect that resembles a twig. **stick shift** a nonautomatic or manual transmission in a motor vehicle.

stick² ▶ **v.** (**sticks**, **sticking**, **stuck** /stək/) **1** push something pointed into or through something. **2** be fixed with its point embedded in something. **3** protrude or extend. **4** informal put something somewhere quickly or carelessly. **5** cling firmly to a surface; adhere. **6** (**be stuck**) be fixed or unable to move. **7** (**be stuck**) be unable to complete a task. **8** (**be stuck with**) informal be unable to get rid of or escape from. **9** (**stick around**) informal remain in or near a place. **10** (**stick to**) continue doing or using. **11** (**stick up for**) informal support.

> SYNONYMS **1 thrust**, push, insert, jab, poke, dig, plunge. **2 pierce**, penetrate, puncture, prick, stab. **3 adhere**, cling. **4** *stick the stamp there* **attach**, fasten, affix, fix, paste, glue, gum, tape. **5 jam**, get jammed, catch, get caught, get trapped. **6** (**stuck**) *I'm stuck on this question* **baffled**, beaten, at a loss; informal stumped, up against a wall.

□ **stuck-up** informal having snobbish views and thinking that you are better than other people.

stick·er /ˈstikər/ ▶ **n.** a sticky label or notice.
□ **sticker price** the advertised retail price of an item, especially a new automobile. **sticker shock** dismay experienced by a potential buyer on discovering the high price of an item.

stick·le·back /ˈstikəlˌbak/ ▶ **n.** a small fish with sharp spines along its back.

stick·ler /ˈstik(ə)lər/ ▶ **n.** a person who insists on people behaving in a particular way.

stick·y /ˈstikē/ ▶ **adj.** (**stickier**, **stickiest**) **1** tending or designed to stick. **2** like glue in texture. **3** (of the weather) hot and humid.

> SYNONYMS **1 adhesive**, self-adhesive, gummed. **2 tacky**, gluey, gummy, treacly, glutinous, viscous; informal gooey. **3 humid**, muggy, close, sultry, steamy, sweaty, sweltering, oppressive. **4 awkward**, difficult, tricky, ticklish, delicate, embarrassing, sensitive; informal hairy. ANTONYMS dry, fresh, cool.

stiff /stif/ ▶ **adj.** **1** not easily bent. **2** difficult to turn or operate. **3** unable to move easily and without pain. **4** not relaxed or friendly. **5** severe or strong. ▶ **n.** informal a dead body.

> SYNONYMS ▶ **adj.** **1 rigid**, hard, firm, inelastic, unyielding, brittle. **2 thick**, firm, viscous, semisolid. **3 aching**, achy, painful, arthritic; informal creaky. **4 formal**, reserved, wooden, forced, strained, stilted; informal starchy, uptight. **5** *stiff penalties* **harsh**, severe, heavy, stringent, drastic, draconian. **6** *they put up a stiff resistance* **vigorous**, determined, strong, spirited, resolute, tenacious, dogged, stubborn. **7 difficult**, hard, arduous, tough, strenuous, laborious, exacting, tiring, demanding. **8 strong**, potent, alcoholic. ANTONYMS flexible, soft, limp.

□ **stiff upper lip** the tendency to hide your feelings and not complain. ■ **stiff·ly** **adv.** **stiff·ness** **n.**

stiff·en /ˈstifən/ ▶ **v.** **1** make or become stiff. **2** make or become stronger.

sti·fle /ˈstīfəl/ ▶ **v.** (**stifles**, **stifling**, **stifled**) **1** prevent from breathing freely; suffocate. **2** restrain or suppress.

> SYNONYMS **1 smother**, check, restrain, keep back, hold back, hold in, withhold, choke back, muffle, suppress, curb. **2 suppress**, quash, quell, put an end to, put down, stop, extinguish, stamp out, crush, subdue, repress. **3 suffocate**, smother, asphyxiate, choke.

sti·fling /ˈstīf(ə)lɪɴɢ/ ▶ **adj.** unpleasantly hot and stuffy.

> SYNONYMS **airless**, suffocating, oppressive; sweltering; humid, close, muggy; informal boiling. ANTONYMS fresh, airy, cold.

stig·ma /ˈstigmə/ ▶ **n.** (plural **stigmas** or **stigmata** /stigˈmätə, ˈstigmətə/) **1** a mark or sign of disgrace. **2** (**stigmata**) marks on a person's body believed by some Christians to correspond to those left on Jesus's body by the crucifixion. **3** the part of a plant that receives the pollen during pollination.

SYNONYMS **shame**, disgrace, dishonor, ignominy, humiliation, stain, taint. ANTONYMS honor.

stig·ma·tize /ˈstigməˌtīz/ ▶ **v.** (**stigmatizes**, **stigmatizing**, **stigmatized**) regard or treat as shameful.

SYNONYMS **condemn**, denounce, brand, label, mark.

stile /stīl/ ▶ **n.** an arrangement of steps in a fence or wall that allows people to climb over.

sti·let·to /stəˈletō/ ▶ **n.** (plural **stilettos**) **1** a thin, high heel on a woman's shoe. **2** a short dagger with a tapering blade.

still /stil/ ▶ **adj.** not moving. ▶ **n. 1** deep, quiet calm. **2** a photograph or a single shot from a movie. **3** a piece of equipment for distilling alcoholic drinks such as whiskey. ▶ **adv. 1** even now or at a particular time. **2** nevertheless. **3** even. ▶ **v.** make or become still.

SYNONYMS ▶ **adj. 1 motionless**, unmoving, stock-still, immobile, rooted to the spot, transfixed, static, stationary. **2 quiet**, silent, calm, peaceful, serene, windless, noiseless, undisturbed, flat, smooth, like a millpond. ANTONYMS moving, noisy. ▶ **adv. 1 even now**, yet. **2 nevertheless**, nonetheless, all the same, even so, but, however, despite that, in spite of that. ▶ **v. quiet**, silence, hush, calm, settle, pacify, quieten, subdue.

□ **still life** (plural **still lifes**) a painting or drawing of an arrangement of objects such as flowers or fruit. ■ **still·ness n.**

still·born /ˈstilˌbôrn/ ▶ **adj.** (of a baby) born dead. ■ **still·birth** /ˈstilˌbərTH/ **n.**

stilt /stilt/ ▶ **n. 1** either of a pair of upright poles that are used to walk raised above the ground. **2** each of a set of posts supporting a building.

stilt·ed /ˈstiltid/ ▶ **adj.** (of speech or writing) stiff and unnatural.

Stil·ton /ˈstiltn/ ▶ **n.** trademark a kind of strong, rich blue cheese.

stim·u·lant /ˈstimyələnt/ ▶ **n.** something that stimulates.

stim·u·late /ˈstimyəˌlāt/ ▶ **v.** (**stimulates**, **stimulating**, **stimulated**) **1** cause a reaction in the body. **2** make more active or interested.

SYNONYMS **1 encourage**, prompt, motivate, trigger, spark, spur on, galvanize, fire, inspire, excite, light a fire under. **2** (**stimulating**) **thought-provoking**, interesting, inspiring, inspirational, lively, exciting, provocative. ANTONYMS discourage.

■ **stim·u·la·tion** /ˌstimyəˈlāSHən/ **n.**

stim·u·lus /ˈstimyələs/ ▶ **n.** (plural **stimuli** /-ˌlī/) something that stimulates.

SYNONYMS **motivation**, encouragement, impetus, prompt, spur, inducement, incentive, inspiration, fillip; informal shot in the arm. ANTONYMS deterrent.

sting /stiNG/ ▶ **n. 1** a sharp-pointed part of an insect, capable of inflicting a wound by injecting poison. **2** a wound from a sting. **3** a sharp tingling sensation. ▶ **v.** (**stings**, **stinging**, **stung** /stəNG/) **1** wound with a sting. **2** produce a stinging sensation. **3** upset someone.

SYNONYMS ▶ **n. 1 prick**, wound, injury. **2 pain**, pricking, smarting, soreness, hurt, irritation. ▶ **v. 1 prick**, wound. **2 smart**, burn, hurt, be irritated, be sore. **3** *the criticism stung her* **upset**, wound, hurt, distress, pain, mortify.

sting·ray /ˈstiNGˌrā/ ▶ **n.** a ray (fish) with a poisonous spine at the base of the tail.

stin·gy /ˈstinjē/ ▶ **adj.** (**stingier**, **stingiest**) informal unwilling to give or spend money; ungenerous.

SYNONYMS **mean**, miserly, close-fisted, parsimonious, niggardly, penny-pinching; informal cheap, tight-fisted, tight, mingy. ANTONYMS generous, liberal.

stink /stiNGk/ ▶ **v.** (**stinks**, **stinking**, **stank** /staNGk/ or **stunk** /stəNGk/; past participle **stunk**) **1** have a strong, unpleasant smell. **2** informal be very bad or unpleasant. ▶ **n. 1** a strong, unpleasant smell. **2** informal a quarrel or fuss.

SYNONYMS ▶ **v. reek**, smell. ▶ **n. stench**, smell, reek; informal funk.

stink·er /ˈstiNGkər/ ▶ **n.** informal a very unpleasant person or thing.

stink·ing /ˈstiNGkiNG/ ▶ **adj. 1** foul-smelling. **2** informal very unpleasant or bad. ▶ **adv.** informal very: *stinking rich.*

stink·y /ˈstiNGkē/ ▶ **adj.** (**stinkier**, **stinkiest**) informal **1** having a strong or unpleasant smell. **2** very disagreeable and unpleasant: *a stinky job.*

stint /stint/ ▶ **v.** (**stint on**) be very economical or stingy about spending or providing something. ▶ **n.** a period of work.

SYNONYMS ▶ **n. spell**, stretch, turn, session, term, time, shift, tour of duty.

sti·pend /ˈstīˌpend, -pənd/ ▶ **n.** a fixed regular sum paid as a salary to a priest, teacher, or official.

sti·pen·di·ar·y /stīˈpendēˌerē/ ▶ **adj.** receiving a stipend; working for pay.

stip·ple /ˈstipəl/ ▶ **v.** (**stipples**, **stippling**, **stippled**) mark a surface with many small dots or specks.

stip·u·late /ˈstipyəˌlāt/ ▶ **v.** (**stipulates**, **stipulating**, **stipulated**) demand or specify as part of an agreement.

SYNONYMS **specify**, set out, lay down, demand, require, insist on.

■ **stip·u·la·tion** /ˌstipyəˈlāSHən/ **n.**

stir /stər/ ▶ **v.** (**stirs**, **stirring**, **stirred**) **1** move an implement around and around in a liquid or soft substance to mix it. **2** move slightly. **3** wake or get up. **4** (often **stir something up**) arouse a strong feeling in someone. ▶ **n. 1** an act of stirring. **2** a disturbance or commotion.

SYNONYMS ▶ **v. 1 mix**, blend, beat, whip, whisk, fold in, muddle. **2 move**, get up, get out of bed, rise, rouse yourself, bestir yourself. **3 disturb**, rustle, shake, move, agitate. **4** *the war stirred him to action* **spur**, drive, rouse, prompt, propel, motivate, encourage, urge, impel, provoke, goad. ▶ **n. commotion**, disturbance, fuss, excitement, sensation; informal to-do, hoo-ha.

□ **stir-crazy** informal psychologically disturbed as a result of being confined or imprisoned. **stir-fry** fry quickly over a high heat while stirring. ■ **stir·rer n.**

stir·ring /ˈstəriNG/ ▶ adj. causing great excitement or strong emotion.

SYNONYMS **exciting**, thrilling, rousing, stimulating, moving, inspiring, heady. ANTONYMS boring, pedestrian.

stir·rup /ˈstərəp, ˈstə-rəp, ˈstir-/ ▶ n. each of a pair of loops attached to a horse's saddle to support the rider's foot.

stitch /stiCH/ ▶ n. **1** a loop of thread made by a single pass of the needle in sewing or knitting. **2** a method of sewing or knitting that produces a particular pattern. **3** a sudden sharp pain in the side of the body, caused by strenuous exercise. ▶ v. make or mend with stitches. □ **in stitches** informal laughing uncontrollably.

stitch·ing /ˈstiCHiNG/ ▶ n. **1** a row of stitches sewn onto cloth. **2** the action or work of stitching or sewing.

stoat /stōt/ ▶ n. a small meat-eating animal of the weasel family.

stock /stäk/ ▶ n. **1** a supply of goods or materials available for sale or use. **2** farm animals; livestock. **3** money raised by selling shares in a company. **4** (**stocks**) shares in a company. **5** water in which bones, meat, fish, or vegetables have been simmered. **6** a person's ancestry. **7** a breed, variety, or population of an animal or plant. **8** the trunk or stem of a tree or shrub. **9** a plant with sweet-smelling lilac, pink, or white flowers. **10** (**the stocks**) (in the past) a wooden structure in which criminals were locked as a public punishment. ▶ adj. common or conventional: *stock characters*. ▶ v. **1** have or keep a stock of. **2** provide or fill with a stock of something. **3** (**stock up**) collect stocks of something.

SYNONYMS ▶ n. **1 merchandise**, goods, wares. **2 store**, supply, stockpile, reserve, hoard, cache, bank. **3 animals**, livestock, beasts, flocks, herds. **4 descent**, ancestry, origin(s), lineage, birth, extraction, family, blood, pedigree. ▶ adj. **usual**, routine, predictable, set, standard, staple, customary, familiar, conventional, traditional, stereotyped, clichéd, hackneyed, unoriginal, formulaic. ANTONYMS unusual, original. ▶ v. **sell**, carry, keep (in stock), offer, supply, provide, furnish.

□ **stock car** an ordinary car that has been modified for racing. **stock company** a repertory company that is largely based in one theater. **stock exchange** (or **stock market**) a place where stocks and shares are bought and sold. **stock-in-trade** the typical thing a person or company uses or deals in. **stock-still** completely still. **take stock** assess your situation.

stock·ade /stäˈkād/ ▶ n. a barrier or enclosure formed from wooden posts.

stock·brok·er /ˈstäk͵brōkər/ ▶ n. a person who buys and sells stocks and shares on behalf of clients.

stock·ing /ˈstäkiNG/ ▶ n. **1** either of a pair of women's close-fitting nylon garments covering the foot and leg. **2** a long sock. ■ **stock·inged** adj.

stock·pile /ˈstäk͵pīl/ ▶ n. a large stock of goods or materials. ▶ v. (**stockpiles**, **stockpiling**, **stockpiled**) gather together a large stock of.

SYNONYMS ▶ n. **stock**, store, supply, collection, reserve, hoard, cache; informal stash. ▶ v. **store up**, amass, accumulate, store (up), stock up on, hoard, cache, collect, lay in, put away, put/set aside, put by, stow away, save; informal salt away, stash away.

stock·tak·ing /ˈstäk͵tākiNG/ ▶ n. the process of listing all the stock held by a business.

stock·y /ˈstäkē/ ▶ adj. (**stockier**, **stockiest**) (of a person) short and sturdy.

SYNONYMS **thickset**, sturdy, heavily built, chunky, burly, strapping, brawny, solid, heavy, hefty, beefy. ANTONYMS slender.

stock·yard /ˈstäk͵yärd/ ▶ n. a large yard containing pens and sheds in which livestock is kept.

sto·gie /ˈstōgē/ ▶ n. a long, thin, inexpensive cigar.

sto·ic /ˈstō-ik/ ▶ n. a stoical person. ▶ adj. stoical.

sto·i·cal /ˈstō-ikəl/ ▶ adj. enduring pain and hardship without complaining.

SYNONYMS **long-suffering**, uncomplaining, patient, forbearing, accepting, tolerant, resigned, phlegmatic, philosophical. ANTONYMS complaining, intolerant.

■ **sto·i·cal·ly** adv. **sto·i·cism** n.

stoke /stōk/ ▶ v. (**stokes**, **stoking**, **stoked**) **1** add coal to a fire, furnace, etc. **2** encourage a strong emotion. ■ **stok·er** n.

stole[1] /stōl/ ▶ n. a woman's long scarf or shawl.

stole[2] past of STEAL.

sto·len /ˈstōlən/ past participle of STEAL.

stol·id /ˈstälid/ ▶ adj. calm, dependable, and unemotional. ■ **stol·id·ly** adv.

stom·ach /ˈstəmək/ ▶ n. **1** the internal organ in which the first part of digestion occurs. **2** the front part of the body below the chest; the belly. **3** inclination or desire. ▶ v. **1** consume food or drink without feeling ill. **2** accept or approve of something.

SYNONYMS ▶ n. **1 abdomen**, middle, belly, gut, paunch; informal tummy, insides, pot, spare tire. **2 appetite**, taste, inclination, desire, wish. ▶ v. **tolerate**, put up with, take, stand, endure, bear; informal hack, abide.

stomp /stämp, stômp/ ▶ v. **1** tread heavily and noisily. **2** dance with stamping steps.

stone /stōn/ ▶ n. **1** the hard material that rock is made of. **2** a small piece of stone found on the ground. **3** a piece of stone shaped as a memorial, a boundary marker, etc. **4** a gem. **5** the hard seed of certain fruits. ▶ v. (**stones**, **stoning**, **stoned**) **1** throw stones at. **2** remove the stone from a fruit. ▶ adv. extremely or totally: *stone cold*.

SYNONYMS ▶ n. **1 rock**, pebble, boulder. **2 gem**, gemstone, jewel; informal rock, sparkler. **3 kernel**, seed, pip, pit.

□ **Stone Age** the prehistoric period when tools were made of stone. **stone-faced** informal revealing no emotions through the expressions of the face. **a stone's throw** a short distance.

stoned /stōnd/ ▶ adj. informal strongly affected by drugs or alcohol.

stone·ma·son /ˈstōn͵māsən/ ▶ n. a person who prepares and builds with stone.

stone·wall /ˈstōn͵wôl/ ▶ v. refuse to answer questions, or give evasive replies.

ston·y /ˈstōnē/ ▶ adj. (**stonier**, **stoniest**) **1** full of stones. **2** made of or like stone. **3** cold and unfeeling.

SYNONYMS **1 rocky**, pebbly, gravelly, shingly, rough. **2** *a stony stare* **unfriendly**, hostile, unfeeling, uncaring, unsympathetic, indifferent, hard, flinty, steely, stern, severe, expressionless, blank, poker-faced. ANTONYMS smooth, friendly, sympathetic.

■ **ston·i·ly** adv.

stood /stŏŏd/ past and past participle of **STAND**.

stooge /stōōj/ ▶ n. **1** disapproving a less important person used by someone to do routine or unpleasant work. **2** a performer whose act involves being the butt of a comedian's jokes.

SYNONYMS **underling**, minion, lackey, henchman, subordinate, **puppet**, pawn, cat's paw; informal sidekick.

stool /stōōl/ ▶ n. **1** a seat without a back or arms. **2** Medicine a piece of feces. □ **stool pigeon** informal a police informer.

stoop /stōōp/ ▶ v. **1** bend the head or body forward and downward. **2** lower your standards to do something wrong. ▶ n. a stooping posture.

SYNONYMS ▶ v. **bend**, lean, crouch, bow, duck.

stop /stäp/ ▶ v. (**stops**, **stopping**, **stopped**) **1** come or bring to an end. **2** prevent from happening or from doing something. **3** no longer move or operate. **4** (of a bus or train) call at a place to pick up or let off passengers. **5** block up a hole or leak. ▶ n. **1** an act of stopping. **2** a place for a bus or train to stop at. **3** an object or part of a mechanism that prevents movement. **4** a set of organ pipes.

SYNONYMS ▶ v. **1 end**, halt, finish, terminate, wind up, bring to a stop/halt, discontinue, cut short, interrupt, nip in the bud, shut down. **2** *he stopped smoking* **cease**, refrain from, discontinue, desist from, break off, give up, abandon, cut out; informal quit, pack in. **3 pull up**, draw up, come to a stop/halt, come to (a) rest, pull in/over. **4** *the music stopped* **come to an end**, draw to a close, end, cease, halt, finish, be over, conclude. **5 prevent**, obstruct, impede, block, bar, preclude, dissuade from. ANTONYMS start, begin, continue. ▶ n. **1 halt**, end, finish, cessation, close, conclusion, termination, standstill. **2 break**, stopover, stop-off, stay, visit; literary sojourn. **3 stopping place**, station, halt.

□ **pull out all the stops** make a very great effort to achieve something.

stop·cock /ˈstäpˌkäk/ ▶ n. a valve that controls the flow of a liquid or gas through a pipe.

stop·gap /ˈstäpˌgap/ ▶ n. a temporary solution or substitute.

stop·page /ˈstäpij/ ▶ n. **1** an instance of being stopped. **2** an instance of industrial action. **3** a blockage.

stop·per /ˈstäpər/ ▶ n. a plug for sealing a hole. ▶ v. (**stoppers**, **stoppering**, **stoppered**) seal with a stopper.

stop·watch /ˈstäpˌwäCH/ ▶ n. a watch with buttons that start and stop the display, used to time races.

stor·age /ˈstôrij/ ▶ n. **1** the action of storing. **2** space available for storing.

store /stôr/ ▶ n. **1** a retail establishment selling items to the public. **2** an amount or supply kept to be used when needed. **3** (**stores**) equipment and food kept for use by an army, navy, etc. **4** a place where things are kept for future use or sale. ▶ v. (**stores**, **storing**, **stored**) **1** keep for future use. **2** enter information in the memory of a computer.

SYNONYMS ▶ n. **1 stock**, supply, stockpile, hoard, cache, reserve, bank, pool; informal stash. **2 storeroom**, storehouse, repository, stockroom, depot, depository, warehouse. **3** *ship's stores* **supplies**, provisions, stocks, food, rations, materials, equipment, hardware. **4** shop, market, grocery store, emporium, (retail) outlet, mart, boutique, department store, supermarket, superstore, megastore. ▶ v. **keep**, stockpile, stock up with, lay in, set aside, put aside, put away/by, save, collect, accumulate, amass, hoard; informal squirrel away, salt away, stash. ANTONYMS use, discard.

□ **in store** about to happen. **set store by** consider to be important. **store brand** a product manufactured specially for a retailer and bearing the retailer's name.

store·front /ˈstôrˌfrənt/ ▶ n. a commercial establishment occupying space facing the street on the ground floor of a building.

store·house /ˈstôrˌhous/ ▶ n. a building used for storing goods.

SYNONYMS **warehouse**, depository, repository, store, storeroom, depot.

store·keep·er /ˈstôrˌkēpər/ ▶ n. a person who owns or runs a store.

stork /stôrk/ ▶ n. a tall long-legged bird with a long, heavy bill.

storm /stôrm/ ▶ n. **1** a violent disturbance of the atmosphere with strong winds and rain, thunder, etc. **2** an uproar or controversy. ▶ v. **1** move angrily or forcefully. **2** (of troops) suddenly attack and capture a place. **3** shout angrily.

SYNONYMS ▶ n. **1 tempest**, squall, gale, hurricane, tornado, cyclone, typhoon, thunderstorm, rainstorm, monsoon, hailstorm, snowstorm, blizzard. **2 uproar**, outcry, fuss, furor, ruckus, rumpus, trouble; informal to-do, hoo-ha, ruction(s), stink. ▶ v. **1 stride**, march, stomp, stamp, stalk, flounce, fling. **2 attack**, charge, rush, swoop on.

storm·y /ˈstôrmē/ ▶ adj. (**stormier**, **stormiest**) **1** affected by a storm. **2** full of angry or violent outbursts of feeling.

SYNONYMS **1 blustery**, squally, windy, gusty, blowy, thundery, wild, violent, rough, foul. **2 angry**, heated, fierce, furious, passionate, acrimonious. ANTONYMS calm, peaceful.

sto·ry[1] /ˈstôrē/ ▶ n. (plural **stories**) **1** an account of imaginary or real events told for entertainment. **2** an item of news. **3** (also **storyline** /ˈstôrēˌlīn/) the plot of a novel, movie, etc. **4** informal a lie.

SYNONYMS **1 tale**, narrative, account, history, anecdote, saga; informal yarn. **2 plot**, storyline, scenario. **3 news**, report, item, article, feature, piece. **4 rumor**, whisper, allegation, speculation, gossip.

sto·ry[2] ▶ n. (plural **stories** or **storeys**) a particular level of a building.

sto·ry·board /ˈstôrēˌbôrd/ ▶ n. a sequence of drawings representing the shots planned for a movie or television production.

sto·ry·book /ˈstôrēˌbŏŏk/ ▶ n. a book containing a story or collection of stories intended for children. ▶ adj. absolutely perfect, as things typically are in storybooks: *it was a storybook finish to an illustrious career*.

stoup /stōōp/ ▶ n. a basin for holy water in a church.

stout /stout/ ▶ **adj. 1** rather fat or heavily built. **2** sturdy and thick. **3** brave and determined. ▶ **n.** a kind of strong, dark beer.

SYNONYMS ▶ **adj. 1 fat**, big, plump, portly, rotund, dumpy, corpulent, thickset, burly, bulky; informal tubby, pudgy, zaftig, corn-fed. **2 strong**, sturdy, solid, robust, tough, durable, hard-wearing. **3 determined**, vigorous, forceful, spirited, committed, brave, fearless, valiant, gallant, bold, plucky; informal gutsy. ANTONYMS thin, flimsy.

■ **stout·ly** adv.

stove¹ /stōv/ ▶ **n.** a device for cooking or heating.

stove² past and past participle of **STAVE**.

stove·pipe /ˈstōvˌpīp/ ▶ **n.** a pipe taking the smoke and gases from a stove up through a roof or to a chimney.

stow /stō/ ▶ **v. 1** pack or store an object tidily. **2** (**stow away**) hide on a ship, aircraft, etc., to travel secretly and without paying.

stow·a·way /ˈstōəˌwā/ ▶ **n.** a person who stows away.

strad·dle /ˈstradl/ ▶ **v.** (**straddles**, **straddling**, **straddled**) **1** sit or stand with one leg on either side of. **2** extend across both sides of.

strafe /strāf/ ▶ **v.** (**strafes**, **strafing**, **strafed**) attack with gunfire from a low-flying aircraft.

strag·gle /ˈstragəl/ ▶ **v.** (**straggles**, **straggling**, **straggled**) **1** trail slowly behind the person or people in front. **2** grow or spread out in an untidy way. ■ **strag·gler** n. **strag·gly** adj.

straight /strāt/ ▶ **adj. 1** extending in one direction only; without a curve or bend. **2** level, upright, or symmetrical. **3** in proper order or condition. **4** honest and direct. **5** in continuous succession. **6** (of an alcoholic drink) undiluted. **7** informal conventional or respectable. **8** informal heterosexual. **9** not addicted to drugs. ▶ **adv. 1** in a straight line or in a straight way. **2** without delay. **3** clearly and logically.

SYNONYMS ▶ **adj. 1 direct**, linear, unswerving, undeviating. **2 level**, even, in line, aligned, square, vertical, upright, perpendicular, horizontal. **3 in order**, tidy, neat, shipshape, spick and span, orderly, organized, arranged, sorted out, straightened out. **4 honest**, direct, frank, candid, truthful, sincere, forthright, straightforward, plain-spoken, blunt, unambiguous; informal upfront. **5 undiluted**, neat, pure; informal straight up. ANTONYMS winding, crooked. ▶ **adv. 1 right**, directly, squarely, full; informal smack, smack dab, (slam) bang. **2 frankly**, directly, candidly, honestly, forthrightly, plainly, point-blank, bluntly, flatly; informal straight up. **3 logically**, rationally, clearly, lucidly, coherently, cogently.

□ **straight-faced** having a serious expression. **straight-laced** = **STRAIT-LACED**.

straight·a·way /ˈstrātəˌwā/ ▶ **adv.** immediately. ▶ **adj.** extending or moving in a straight line. ▶ **n.** a straight section of a road or racetrack.

SYNONYMS ▶ **adv. at once**, right away, (right) now, this/that (very) minute, this/that instant, immediately, instantly, directly, forthwith, in short order, then and there, here and now; informal straight off, pronto, lickety-split.

straight·en /ˈstrātn/ ▶ **v.** make or become straight.

SYNONYMS **1 put straight**, adjust, put in order, arrange, rearrange, tidy, neaten. **2** *we must straighten things out with him* **put right**, sort out, clear up, settle, resolve, rectify, remedy; informal patch up.

straight·for·ward /ˌstrātˈfôrwərd/ ▶ **adj. 1** easy to do or understand. **2** honest and open.

SYNONYMS **1 uncomplicated**, easy, simple, elementary, undemanding. **2 honest**, frank, candid, open, truthful, sincere, on the level, forthright, plain-speaking, direct; informal on the up and up, upfront. ANTONYMS complicated, devious.

■ **straight·for·ward·ly** adv.

straight·jack·et = **STRAITJACKET**.

strain¹ /strān/ ▶ **v. 1** make an unusually great effort. **2** injure a muscle, limb, etc., by making it work too hard. **3** make great or excessive demands on. **4** pour a mainly liquid substance through a sieve to separate out solid matter. ▶ **n. 1** a force tending to strain something to an extreme degree. **2** an injury caused by straining a muscle, limb, etc. **3** a severe demand on strength or resources. **4** a state of tension or exhaustion. **5** the sound of a piece of music.

SYNONYMS ▶ **v. 1 overtax**, overwork, overextend, overreach, overdo it, exhaust, wear out; informal knock yourself out. **2 injure**, damage, pull, wrench, twist, sprain. **3 sieve**, sift, filter, screen. ▶ **n. 1 tension**, tightness, tautness. **2 injury**, sprain, wrench, twist. **3 pressure**, demands, burdens, stress; informal hassle. **4 stress**, (nervous) tension, exhaustion, fatigue, pressure, overwork.

strain² ▶ **n. 1** a breed or variety of an animal or plant. **2** a tendency in a person's character.

SYNONYMS **variety**, kind, type, sort, breed, genus.

strained /strānd/ ▶ **adj. 1** not relaxed or comfortable; showing signs of strain. **2** produced by deliberate effort; not graceful or spontaneous.

SYNONYMS **1 awkward**, tense, uneasy, uncomfortable, edgy, difficult, troubled. **2 forced**, unnatural, artificial, insincere, false, affected, put-on.

strain·er /ˈstrānər/ ▶ **n.** a device for straining liquids, having holes punched in it or made of wire mesh.

strait /strāt/ ▶ **n. 1** (also **straits**) a narrow passage of water connecting two other large areas of water. **2** (**straits**) trouble or difficulty: *in dire straits*.

SYNONYMS **1 channel**, sound, narrows, stretch of water. **2** (**straits**) **difficulty**, trouble, crisis, mess, predicament, plight; informal hot water, jam, hole, fix, scrape.

strait·ened /ˈstrātnd/ ▶ **adj.** without enough money; poor.

SYNONYMS **impoverished**, poverty-stricken, poor, destitute, penniless, dirt poor, in penury, impecunious, unable to make ends meet, in reduced circumstances.

strait·jack·et /ˈstrātˌjakət/ (or **straightjacket**) ▶ **n.** a strong garment with long sleeves that can be tied together to confine the arms of a violent person.

strait-laced (or **straight-laced**) ▶ **adj.** very strictly moral and conventional.

SYNONYMS **prim (and proper)**, prudish, puritanical, prissy, conservative, old-fashioned, stuffy, staid; informal starchy, square, fuddy-duddy. ANTONYMS broad-minded.

strand¹ /strand/ ▶ **v. 1** drive or leave a ship, whale, etc., aground on a shore. **2** leave someone or something without the means to move from a place. ▶ **n.** literary a beach or shore.

> SYNONYMS ▶ **v. 1** (**stranded**) **shipwrecked**, wrecked, marooned, grounded, aground, beached. **2** (**stranded**) **helpless**, abandoned, forsaken, left high and dry, left in the lurch.

strand² ▶ **n. 1** a single thin length of thread, wire, etc. **2** an element that forms part of a complex whole.

> SYNONYMS **thread**, filament, fiber, length.

strange /strānj/ ▶ **adj. 1** unusual or surprising. **2** not previously visited or encountered.

> SYNONYMS **1 unusual**, odd, curious, peculiar, funny, queer, bizarre, weird, uncanny, surprising, unexpected, anomalous, atypical; informal fishy. **2 unfamiliar**, unknown, new, novel. ANTONYMS ordinary, familiar.

■ **strange·ly** adv.

stran·ger /'strānjər/ ▶ **n. 1** a person that you do not know. **2** a person who does not know a particular place.

> SYNONYMS **newcomer**, new arrival, visitor, guest, outsider, foreigner.

stran·gle /'straNGgəl/ ▶ **v.** (**strangles**, **strangling**, **strangled**) **1** kill or injure someone by squeezing their neck. **2** prevent from growing or developing.

> SYNONYMS **throttle**, choke, garrote, asphyxiate.

■ **stran·gler** n.

stran·gle·hold /'straNGgəl,hōld/ ▶ **n. 1** a firm grip around a person's neck that deprives them of oxygen. **2** complete or overwhelming control.

stran·gu·la·tion /,straNGgyə'lāsHən/ ▶ **n.** the action of strangling.

strap /strap/ ▶ **n.** a strip of flexible material used for fastening, carrying, or holding on to. ▶ **v.** (**straps**, **strapping**, **strapped**) fasten or secure with a strap.

> SYNONYMS ▶ **n. belt**, tie, band, thong. ▶ **v. tie**, lash, secure, fasten, bind, make fast, truss.

■ **strap·less** adj. **strap·py** adj.

strapped /strapt/ ▶ **adj.** informal short of money: *I'm constantly strapped for cash.*

strap·ping /'strapiNG/ ▶ **adj.** (of a person) big and strong.

> SYNONYMS **big**, strong, well-built, brawny, burly, muscular; informal beefy.

strat·a·gem /'stratəjəm/ ▶ **n.** a plan or scheme intended to outwit an opponent.

> SYNONYMS **plan**, scheme, tactic, maneuver, ploy, device, trick, ruse, plot, machination, dodge; subterfuge, artifice.

stra·te·gic /strə'tējik/ ▶ **adj. 1** forming part of a long-term plan to achieve something. **2** relating to the gaining of long-term military advantage. **3** (of weapons) for use against enemy territory rather than in battle.

> SYNONYMS **planned**, calculated, deliberate, tactical, judicious, prudent, shrewd.

■ **stra·te·gi·cal·ly** adv.

strat·e·gy /'stratəjē/ ▶ **n.** (plural **strategies**) **1** a plan designed to achieve a long-term aim. **2** the planning and directing of military activity in a war or battle.

> SYNONYMS **plan**, grand design, game plan, policy, program, scheme, tactic.

■ **strat·e·gist** n.

strat·i·fy /'stratə,fī/ ▶ **v.** (**stratifies**, **stratifying**, **stratified**) form or arrange into strata.

■ **strat·i·fi·ca·tion** /,stratəfi'kāsHən/ n.

strat·o·sphere /'stratə,sfi(ə)r/ ▶ **n. 1** the layer of the earth's atmosphere above the lowest layer, extending to a height of about 30 miles (50 km). **2** informal the very highest levels of something.

■ **strat·o·spher·ic** /,stratə'sfi(ə)rik, -'sferik/ adj.

stra·tum /'strātəm, 'stra-/ ▶ **n.** (plural **strata** /-tə/) **1** a layer or series of layers of rock. **2** a level or class of society.

straw /strô/ ▶ **n. 1** dried stalks of grain. **2** a single dried stalk of grain. **3** a thin hollow tube used for sucking a drink from a container. **4** a pale yellow color. □ **clutch at straws** turn to something in desperation. **draw the short straw** be chosen to do something unpleasant. **the last** (or **final**) **straw** the final difficulty that makes a situation unbearable. **straw poll** an unofficial test of opinion.

straw·ber·ry /'strô,berē, -b(ə)rē/ ▶ **n.** (plural **strawberries**) a sweet red fruit with seeds on the surface. □ **strawberry blonde** (or **blond**) (of hair) light reddish-blonde.

stray /strā/ ▶ **v.** move away aimlessly from a group or from the right course or place. ▶ **adj. 1** not in the right place; separated from a group. **2** (of a domestic animal) having no home or having wandered away from home. ▶ **n.** a stray person or thing.

> SYNONYMS ▶ **v. 1 wander off**, go astray, get separated, get lost, drift away. **2 digress**, deviate, wander, get sidetracked, go off on a tangent, get off the subject. ▶ **adj. 1 homeless**, lost, abandoned, feral. **2** *a stray bullet* **random**, chance, freak, unexpected, isolated.

streak /strēk/ ▶ **n. 1** a long, thin mark. **2** an element in someone's character: *a ruthless streak.* **3** a period of success or luck of a certain kind: *a winning streak.* ▶ **v. 1** mark with streaks. **2** move very fast. **3** informal run naked in a public place to shock or amuse people.

> SYNONYMS ▶ **n. 1 band**, line, strip, stripe, vein, slash, ray, smear. **2 element**, vein, strain, touch. **3 period**, spell, stretch, run; informal patch. ▶ **v. 1 stripe**, band, fleck, smear, mark. **2 race**, speed, flash, shoot, dash, rush, hurtle, whiz, zoom, career, fly; informal belt, tear, zip, whip, barrel.

■ **streak·er** n. **streak·y** adj.

stream /strēm/ ▶ **n. 1** a small, narrow river. **2** a continuous flow of liquid, air, people, etc. ▶ **v. 1** move in a continuous flow. **2** run with tears, sweat, etc. **3** float out in the wind.

> SYNONYMS ▶ **n. 1 brook**, rivulet, tributary, creek. **2 jet**, flow, rush, gush, surge, torrent, flood, cascade. **3 succession**, series, string. ▶ **v. 1 flow**, pour, course, run, gush, surge, flood, cascade, spill. **2 pour**, surge, flood, swarm, pile, crowd.

□ **on stream** in operation or existence.

stream·er /'strēmər/ ▶ **n.** a long, narrow flag or strip of decorative material.

stream·line /ˈstrēmˌlīn/ ▶ v. (**streamlines, streamlining, streamlined**) **1** (**be streamlined**) have a shape that allows quick, easy movement through air or water. **2** make an organization or system more efficient.

> SYNONYMS (**streamlined**) **1** **aerodynamic**, smooth, sleek, elegant. **2** **efficient**, smooth-running, well-run, well-oiled, slick.

street /strēt/ ▶ n. a public road in a city, town, or village.

> SYNONYMS **road**, highway, thoroughfare, avenue, drive, boulevard, lane.

□ **street value** the price something, especially drugs, would fetch if sold illegally.

street·car /ˈstrētˌkär/ ▶ n. a passenger vehicle powered by electricity obtained from an overhead cable by means of a trolley wheel.

street·wise /ˈstrētˌwīz/ ▶ adj. informal able to deal with the difficulties and dangers of life in a big city.

strength /streNG(k)TH, strenTH/ ▶ n. **1** the quality or state of being strong. **2** a good or useful quality or attribute. **3** the number of people making up a group.

> SYNONYMS **1** **power**, muscle, might, brawn, muscularity, robustness, sturdiness, vigor, stamina. **2** **fortitude**, resilience, spirit, backbone, courage, bravery, pluck, grit; informal guts. **3** *strength of feeling* **intensity**, vehemence, force, depth. **4** *the strength of their argument* **force**, weight, power, persuasiveness, soundness, cogency, validity. **5** **strong point**, advantage, asset, forte, aptitude, talent, skill, specialty. ANTONYMS weakness.

□ **on the strength of** on the basis of.

> SPELLING
>
> Remember the **g** before the **-th**: stren**g**th.

strength·en /ˈstreNG(k)THən, ˈstren-/ ▶ v. make or become stronger.

> SYNONYMS **1** **make strong**, make stronger, build up, harden, toughen. **2** **grow strong**, grow stronger, gain strength, intensify, pick up. **3** **reinforce**, support, back up, bolster, authenticate, confirm, substantiate, corroborate. ANTONYMS weaken.

stren·u·ous /ˈstrenyo͞oəs/ ▶ adj. needing or using a lot of effort or exertion.

> SYNONYMS **1** **difficult**, arduous, hard, tough, taxing, demanding, exacting, exhausting, tiring, grueling, back-breaking. **2** **vigorous**, energetic, forceful, strong, spirited, intense, determined, resolute, dogged. ANTONYMS easy, halfhearted.

■ **stren·u·ous·ly** adv.

stress /stres/ ▶ n. **1** pressure or tension exerted on an object. **2** mental or emotional strain or tension. **3** particular emphasis. **4** emphasis given to a syllable or word in speech. ▶ v. **1** emphasize. **2** subject to pressure, tension, or strain.

> SYNONYMS ▶ n. **1** **strain**, pressure, (nervous) tension, worry, anxiety, trouble, difficulty; informal hassle. **2** **emphasis**, importance, weight, accent, accentuation. ▶ v. **1** **emphasize**, draw attention to, underline, underscore, point up, highlight, accentuate. **2** **overstretch**, overtax, pressurize, pressure, push to the limit, worry, harass; informal hassle. ANTONYMS play down.

stress·ful /ˈstresfəl/ ▶ adj. causing mental or emotional stress.

> SYNONYMS **demanding**, trying, taxing, difficult, hard, tough, fraught, traumatic, tense, frustrating. ANTONYMS relaxing.

stretch /strecH/ ▶ v. **1** be able to be made longer or wider without tearing or breaking. **2** extend something without tearing or breaking it. **3** extend part of the body to its full length. **4** extend over an area or period of time. **5** make demands on. ▶ n. **1** an act of stretching. **2** the capacity to stretch or be stretched; elasticity. **3** a continuous expanse or period.

> SYNONYMS ▶ v. **1** **expand**, give, be elastic, be stretchy, be tensile. **2** **pull** (**out**), draw out, extend, lengthen, elongate, expand. **3** **bend**, strain, distort, exaggerate, embellish. **4** *she stretched out her arm* **reach out**, hold out, extend, straighten (out). **5** *I stretched out on the sofa* **lie down**, recline, lean back, sprawl, lounge, loll. **6** **extend**, spread, continue, go on. ANTONYMS shorten, contract. ▶ n. **1** **expanse**, area, tract, belt, sweep, extent. **2** **period**, time, spell, run, stint, session, shift.

■ **stretch·y** adj.

stretch·er /ˈstrecHər/ ▶ n. a long framework covered with canvas, used for carrying sick, injured, or dead people. ▶ v. (**stretchers, stretchering, stretchered**) carry on a stretcher.

strew /stro͞o/ ▶ v. (**strews, strewing**, past participle **strewn** or **strewed**) **1** scatter untidily over a surface or area. **2** (**be strewn with**) be covered with untidily scattered things.

stri·at·ed /ˈstrīˌātid/ ▶ adj. marked with ridges or furrows. ■ **stri·a·tion** /strīˈāsHən/ n.

strick·en /ˈstrikən/ past participle of STRIKE ▶ adj. **1** seriously affected by something unpleasant. **2** showing great distress.

strict /strikt/ ▶ adj. **1** demanding that rules are obeyed. **2** following rules or beliefs exactly.

> SYNONYMS **1** **precise**, exact, literal, faithful, accurate, careful, scrupulous, meticulous, punctilious. **2** **stringent**, rigorous, severe, harsh, hard, stern, rigid, tough, uncompromising, authoritarian, firm. **3** *in strict confidence* **absolute**, utter, complete, total. ANTONYMS loose, liberal.

■ **strict·ly** adv. **strict·ness** n.

stric·ture /ˈstrikcHər/ ▶ n. **1** a rule restricting behavior or action. **2** a sternly critical remark.

stride /strīd/ ▶ v. (**strides, striding, strode** /strōd/; past participle **stridden** /ˈstridn/) walk with long, decisive steps. ▶ n. **1** a long, decisive step. **2** a step made toward an aim.

> SYNONYMS **step**, pace, march.

□ **take something in your stride** deal calmly with something difficult.

stri·dent /ˈstrīdnt/ ▶ adj. **1** loud and harsh. **2** presenting a point of view in a way that is too forceful.

> SYNONYMS **harsh**, raucous, rough, grating, jarring, loud, shrill, screeching, piercing, ear-piercing. ANTONYMS soft.

■ **stri·den·cy** n. **stri·dent·ly** adv.

strife /strīf/ ▶ n. angry or bitter disagreement.

SYNONYMS **conflict**, friction, discord, disagreement, dissension, dispute, argument, quarrelling. ANTONYMS peace.

strike /strīk/ ▶ v. (**strikes**, **striking**, **struck** /strək/) **1** hit someone or something with force. **2** attack suddenly. **3** (of a disaster) happen suddenly and have harmful effects on. **4** refuse to work as a form of organized protest. **5** discover gold, oil, etc., by digging or drilling. **6** light a match by rubbing it against a rough surface. **7** (of a clock) show the time by sounding a chime or stroke. **8** reach an agreement. ▶ n. **1** an act of striking by employees. **2** a sudden attack. **3** an act of hitting a ball. **4** Baseball a pitch that is counted against the batter, in particular one that the batter swings at and misses or that passes through the strike zone without the batter swinging.

SYNONYMS ▶ v. **1 hit**, slap, smack, thump, punch, beat, bang; informal clout, wallop, belt, whack, thwack, bash, clobber, bop. **2 crash into**, collide with, hit, run into, bump into, smash into, impact. **3 occur to**, come to (mind), dawn on someone, hit, spring to mind, enter your head. **4** ***you strike me as intelligent*** **seem to be**, appear to be, give someone the impression of being. **5 take industrial action**, go on strike, walk out. ▶ n. **1 industrial action**, walkout. **2 attack**, assault, bombing.

□ **strike out 1** start out on a new course. **2** Baseball put a batter out (or be put out) from play as a batter by means of three strikes. **3** informal fail or be unsuccessful. **strike up** begin to play a piece of music. **strike something up** begin a friendship or conversation with someone.

strike·out /ˈstrīkˌout/ ▶ n. Baseball an out called when a batter accumulates three strikes.

strik·er /ˈstrīkər/ ▶ n. **1** an employee who is on strike. **2** (in soccer) a forward.

strik·ing /ˈstrīkiNG/ ▶ adj. **1** noticeable. **2** dramatically good-looking.

SYNONYMS **1 noticeable**, obvious, conspicuous, visible, distinct, marked, unmistakable, strong, remarkable. **2 impressive**, imposing, magnificent, spectacular, breathtaking, marvelous, wonderful, stunning, sensational, dramatic. ANTONYMS unremarkable.

■ **strik·ing·ly** adv.

string /striNG/ ▶ n. **1** material consisting of threads twisted together to form a thin length. **2** a length of catgut or wire on a musical instrument, producing a note when it is made to vibrate. **3** (**strings**) the stringed instruments in an orchestra. **4** a sequence of similar items or events. ▶ v. (**strings**, **stringing**, **strung** /strəNG/) **1** thread things together on a string. **2** (**be strung** or **be strung out**) be arranged in a long line. **3** fit strings to a musical instrument, bow, etc.

SYNONYMS ▶ n. **1 twine**, cord, yarn, thread. **2 series**, succession, chain, sequence, run, streak. **3 line**, procession, queue, file, column, convoy, train, cavalcade. **4** (**strings**) **conditions**, qualifications, provisions, provisos, caveats, stipulations, riders, limitations, restrictions; informal catches. ▶ v. **hang**, suspend, sling, stretch, run, thread, loop, festoon.

□ **with no strings attached** informal with no special conditions or restrictions. **string someone along** informal deliberately mislead someone. **string bean** any of various beans eaten in their pods. **string quartet** a chamber music group consisting of two violinists and a viola and cello player.

stringed /striNGd/ ▶ adj. (of a musical instrument) having strings.

strin·gent /ˈstrinjənt/ ▶ adj. (of regulations or requirements) strict and precise.

SYNONYMS **strict**, firm, rigid, rigorous, severe, harsh, tough, tight, exacting, demanding. ANTONYMS lax.

■ **strin·gen·cy** n. **strin·gent·ly** adv.

string·y /ˈstriNGē/ ▶ adj. **1** like string. **2** (of meat) containing tough fibers that are difficult to chew.

SYNONYMS **1** *stringy hair* **straggly**, lank, thin. **2** *stringy meat* **fibrous**, gristly, sinewy, chewy, tough.

strip¹ /strip/ ▶ v. (**strips**, **stripping**, **stripped**) **1** remove all coverings or clothes from. **2** take off your clothes. **3** remove all the contents or fittings of a room, vehicle, etc. **4** remove paint from a surface. **5** (**strip someone of**) deprive someone of rank, power, or property. ▶ n. an act of undressing.

SYNONYMS ▶ v. **1 undress**, strip off, take your clothes off, disrobe. **2 dismantle**, disassemble, take to bits/pieces, take apart. **3 empty**, clear, clean out, plunder, rob, burgle, loot, pillage, ransack, sack.

strip² ▶ n. **1** a long, narrow piece of cloth, paper, etc. **2** a long, narrow area of land.

SYNONYMS (**narrow**) **piece**, band, belt, ribbon, slip, shred, stretch.

□ **strip mining** the extraction of coal or ore by way of the open-pit method.

stripe /strīp/ ▶ n. a long, narrow band or strip of a different color or texture from the areas next to it. ▶ v. (**stripes**, **striping**, **striped**) mark with stripes.

SYNONYMS ▶ n. **line**, band, strip, belt, bar, streak, vein, flash; technical stria, striation.

■ **strip·y** (or **stripey**) adj.

strip·ling /ˈstripliNG/ ▶ n. old use a young man.

strip·per /ˈstripər/ ▶ n. a device or substance for stripping paint, varnish, etc., off a surface.

strive /strīv/ ▶ v. (**strives**, **striving**, **strove** /strōv/ or **strived**; past participle **striven** /strivən/ or **strived**) try very hard to do or achieve something.

SYNONYMS **try** (**hard**), attempt, endeavor, aim, make an effort, exert yourself, struggle, do your best, do all you can, do your utmost, labor, work, toil, strain; informal go all out, give it your best shot.

strobe /strōb/ ▶ n. a bright light that shines at rapid intervals.

strode /strōd/ past of STRIDE.

stroke /strōk/ ▶ n. **1** an act of hitting. **2** a sound made by a striking clock. **3** an act of stroking with the hand. **4** a mark made by drawing a pen, pencil, etc., across paper or canvas. **5** a short diagonal line separating characters or figures. **6** each of a series of repeated movements, e.g., in rowing or swimming. **7** a style of moving the arms and legs in swimming. **8** a sudden disabling attack caused by an interruption in the flow of blood to the brain. ▶ v. (**strokes**, **stroking**, **stroked**) gently move your hand over.

SYNONYMS ▶ n. **1 blow**, hit, slap, smack, thump, punch. **2 movement**, action, motion. **3 mark**, line. **4 thrombosis**, embolism, seizure; dated apoplexy. ▶ v. **caress**, fondle, pat, pet, touch, rub, massage, soothe.

stroll /strōl/ ▶ v. walk in a leisurely way. ▶ n. a short leisurely walk.

SYNONYMS **walk**, amble, wander, meander, ramble, promenade, saunter; informal mosey.

stroll·er /ˈstrōlər/ ▶ n. a folding chair on wheels, in which a young child can be pushed along.

strong /strôNG, sträNG/ ▶ adj. (**stronger**, **strongest**) **1** physically powerful. **2** done with or supplying great force. **3** able to withstand great force or pressure. **4** secure or stable. **5** great in power, influence, or ability. **6** great in intensity or degree. **7** having a lot of flavor. **8** (of a solution or drink) containing a large proportion of a substance. **9** used after a number to indicate the size of a group.

SYNONYMS **1 powerful**, sturdy, robust, athletic, fit, tough, rugged, strapping, well-built, muscular, brawny, lusty, healthy. **2 forceful**, determined, spirited, assertive, self-assertive, tough, formidable, strong-minded, redoubtable; informal gutsy, feisty. **3 secure**, solid, well-built, durable, hard-wearing, heavy-duty, tough, sturdy, well-made, long-lasting. **4** *a strong supporter* **keen**, passionate, fervent, zealous, enthusiastic, eager, dedicated, loyal. **5** *strong feelings* **intense**, vehement, passionate, ardent, fervent, deep-seated. **6 forceful**, compelling, powerful, convincing, persuasive, sound, valid, cogent, well-founded. **7 intense**, bright, brilliant, vivid, vibrant, dazzling, glaring. **8 highly flavored**, mature, ripe, piquant, tangy, spicy. **9 concentrated**, undiluted. **10 alcoholic**, intoxicating, hard, stiff. ANTONYMS weak, gentle, mild.

□ **going strong** informal continuing to be healthy, active, or successful. ■ **strong·ly** adv.

strong·box /ˈstrôNG,bäks/ ▶ n. a small metal box in which valuables are kept.

strong·hold /ˈstrôNG,hōld/ ▶ n. **1** a place of strong support for a cause or political party. **2** a place that has been strengthened against attack.

SYNONYMS **1 fortress**, fort, castle, citadel, garrison. **2** *a Republican stronghold* **bastion**, center, hotbed.

strong·room /ˈstrôNG,ro͞om, -,ro͝om/ ▶ n. a room designed to protect valuable items against fire and theft.

stron·ti·um /ˈstränCHēəm, -tēəm/ ▶ n. a soft silver-white metallic element.

strove /strōv/ past of **STRIVE**.

struck /strək/ past and past participle of **STRIKE**.

struc·tur·al /ˈstrəkCHərəl/ ▶ adj. relating to or forming part of a structure. ■ **struc·tur·al·ly** adv.

struc·ture /ˈstrəkCHər/ ▶ n. **1** the putting together of different parts to form a whole. **2** a building or other object constructed from several parts. **3** good organization. ▶ v. (**structures**, **structuring**, **structured**) put parts together to form a whole.

SYNONYMS ▶ n. **1 building**, edifice, construction, erection. **2 construction**, organization, system, arrangement, framework, form, formation, shape, composition, anatomy, makeup. ▶ v. **arrange**, organize, design, shape, construct, build.

stru·del /ˈstro͞odl/ ▶ n. a dessert of thin pastry rolled up around a fruit filling and baked.

strug·gle /ˈstrəgəl/ ▶ v. (**struggles**, **struggling**, **struggled**) **1** make great efforts to get free. **2** try hard to do something. **3** make your way with difficulty. ▶ n. **1** an act of struggling. **2** a very difficult task.

SYNONYMS ▶ v. **1 strive**, try hard, endeavor, make every effort, exert yourself, do your best, do your utmost. **2 fight**, battle, grapple, wrestle, scuffle. ▶ n. **1 striving**, endeavor, effort, exertion, campaign, battle, drive, push. **2 fight**, scuffle, brawl, tussle, fracas; informal set-to. **3** *a power struggle* **contest**, competition, fight, clash, rivalry, friction, feuding, conflict.

■ **strug·gler** n.

strum /strəm/ ▶ v. (**strums**, **strumming**, **strummed**) play a guitar or similar instrument by sweeping the thumb or a plectrum up or down the strings. ▶ n. an instance of strumming.

strung /strəNG/ past and past participle of **STRING**.

strut /strət/ ▶ n. **1** a bar used to support or strengthen a structure. **2** a proud, confident walk. ▶ v. (**struts**, **strutting**, **strutted**) walk in a proud and confident way.

SYNONYMS ▶ v. **swagger**, prance, parade, stride, sweep, flounce; informal sashay.

strych·nine /ˈstrik,nīn, -,nēn/ ▶ n. a bitter and highly poisonous substance obtained from an Asian tree.

Stu·art /ˈst(y)o͞oərt/ (or **Stewart**) ▶ adj. relating to the royal family ruling Scotland 1371–1714 and Britain 1603–1714.

stub /stəb/ ▶ n. **1** the remaining part of a pencil, cigarette, etc., after use. **2** the part of a check, ticket, etc., that is torn off and kept as a record by the person issuing it. ▶ v. (**stubs**, **stubbing**, **stubbed**) **1** accidentally bump your toe against something. **2** (often **stub something out**) put out a cigarette by pressing the lighted end against something.

stub·ble /ˈstəbəl/ ▶ n. **1** short, stiff hairs growing on a man's face when he has not shaved for a while. **2** the cut stalks of cereal plants left in the ground after harvesting. ■ **stub·bly** adj.

stub·born /ˈstəbərn/ ▶ adj. **1** determined not to change your attitude or position. **2** difficult to move or remove.

SYNONYMS **1 obstinate**, headstrong, willful, strong-willed, pigheaded, mulish, inflexible, uncompromising, unbending, unyielding, obdurate, intractable, recalcitrant; informal stiff-necked. **2 indelible**, permanent, persistent, tenacious, resistant.

■ **stub·born·ly** adv. **stub·born·ness** n.

stub·by /ˈstəbē/ ▶ adj. (**stubbier**, **stubbiest**) short and thick.

stuc·co /ˈstəkō/ ▶ n. plaster used for coating wall surfaces or molding into decoration. ■ **stuc·coed** adj.

stuck /stək/ past participle of **STICK**[2].

stud[1] /stəd/ ▶ n. **1** a piece of metal with a large head that projects from a surface. **2** a small piece of jewelry that is pushed through a pierced ear or nostril. **3** a fastener consisting of two buttons joined with a bar. ▶ v. (**studs**, **studding**, **studded**) decorate with studs or similar small objects.

stud² ▶ **n.** **1** an establishment where horses are kept for breeding. **2** a stallion.

stu·dent /ˈst(y)o͞odnt/ ▶ **n.** **1** a person studying at a school, college, or university. **2** a person who takes an interest in a particular subject: *a student of the human psyche.*

SYNONYMS **1 scholar**, pupil, schoolchild, schoolboy, schoolgirl; freshman, sophomore, junior, senior, undergraduate. **2 trainee**, apprentice, probationer, novice, learner.

stu·di·o /ˈst(y)o͞odēˌō/ ▶ **n.** (plural **studios**) **1** a room from which television or radio programs are broadcast. **2** a place where movie or sound recordings are made. **3** a room where an artist works or where dancers practice.

SYNONYMS **workshop**, workroom, atelier; recording studio.

▫ **studio apartment** an apartment containing one main room.

stu·di·ous /ˈst(y)o͞odēəs/ ▶ **adj.** **1** spending a lot of time studying or reading. **2** done with careful effort.

SYNONYMS **scholarly**, academic, bookish, intellectual, erudite, learned, donnish; informal brainy.

▪ **stu·di·ous·ly** **adv.**

stud·y /ˈstədē/ ▶ **n.** (plural **studies**) **1** the reading of books or examination of other materials to gain knowledge. **2** a detailed investigation into a subject or situation. **3** a room used for reading and writing. **4** a piece of work done for practice or as an experiment. ▶ **v.** (**studies**, **studying**, **studied**) **1** learn about something. **2** investigate a subject or situation in detail. **3** look at something closely in order to observe or read it. **4** (**studied**) done with careful effort.

SYNONYMS ▶ **n.** **1 learning**, education, schooling, scholarship, tuition, research. **2 investigation**, inquiry, research, examination, analysis, review, survey. **3 office**, workroom, studio. ▶ **v.** **1 work**, review; informal cram. **2 learn**, read up on, be taught. **3 investigate**, research, inquire into, look into, examine, analyze, survey. **4 scrutinize**, examine, inspect, consider, regard, look at, observe, watch, survey.

stuff /stəf/ ▶ **n.** **1** material, articles, or activities of a particular kind, or of a mixed or unspecified kind. **2** basic characteristics. **3** (**your stuff**) informal the things that you are good at or responsible for. ▶ **v.** **1** fill a container or space tightly with something. **2** fill out the skin of a dead animal or bird with material to restore its original appearance.

SYNONYMS ▶ **n.** **1 material**, substance, fabric, matter. **2 items**, articles, objects, goods, belongings, possessions, effects, paraphernalia; informal gear, things, bits and pieces, odds and ends. ▶ **v.** **1 fill**, pack, pad, upholster. **2 shove**, thrust, push, ram, cram, squeeze, force, jam, pack, pile.

stuff·ing /ˈstəfiNG/ ▶ **n.** **1** a mixture used to stuff poultry or meat before cooking. **2** padding used to stuff cushions, furniture, or soft toys.

SYNONYMS **padding**, wadding, filling, packing.

stuff·y /ˈstəfē/ ▶ **adj.** (**stuffier**, **stuffiest**) **1** lacking fresh air or ventilation. **2** conventional and narrow-minded. **3** (of a person's nose) blocked up.

SYNONYMS **1 airless**, close, musty, stale, unventilated. **2 staid**, sedate, sober, priggish, strait-laced, conformist, conservative, old-fashioned; informal straight, starchy, square, fuddy-duddy. ANTONYMS airy.

stul·ti·fy /ˈstəltəˌfī/ ▶ **v.** (**stultifies**, **stultifying**, **stultified**) make someone feel bored or drained of energy.

stum·ble /ˈstəmbəl/ ▶ **v.** (**stumbles**, **stumbling**, **stumbled**) **1** trip and momentarily lose your balance. **2** walk unsteadily. **3** make a mistake in speaking. **4** (**stumble across** or **on**) find by chance. ▶ **n.** an act of stumbling.

SYNONYMS ▶ **v.** **1 trip**, lose your balance, lose your footing, slip. **2 stagger**, totter, blunder, hobble.

▫ **stumbling block** an obstacle.

stump /stəmp/ ▶ **n.** **1** the part of a tree trunk left sticking out of the ground after the rest has fallen or been cut down. **2** a remaining piece. **3** Cricket each of the three upright pieces of wood that form a wicket. ▶ **v.** informal baffle.

SYNONYMS ▶ **v.** **baffle**, perplex, puzzle, confound, defeat, put at a loss; informal flummox, throw, floor.

stump·y /ˈstəmpē/ ▶ **adj.** (**stumpier**, **stumpiest**) short and thick; squat.

stun /stən/ ▶ **v.** (**stuns**, **stunning**, **stunned**) **1** knock someone into a dazed or unconscious state. **2** greatly astonish or shock someone.

SYNONYMS **1 daze**, stupefy, knock out, lay out. **2 astound**, amaze, astonish, dumbfound, stupefy, stagger, shock, take aback; informal flabbergast, knock sideways.

stung /stəNG/ past and past participle of **STING**.

stunk /stəNGk/ past and past participle of **STINK**.

stun·ner /ˈstənər/ ▶ **n.** informal a strikingly attractive or impressive person or thing.

stun·ning /ˈstəniNG/ ▶ **adj.** very impressive or attractive.

SYNONYMS **beautiful**, lovely, glorious, wonderful, marvelous, magnificent, superb, sublime, spectacular, fine, delightful; informal fantastic, terrific, tremendous, sensational, heavenly, divine, gorgeous, fabulous, awesome. ANTONYMS ordinary.

▪ **stun·ning·ly** **adv.**

stunt¹ /stənt/ ▶ **v.** slow down the growth or development of.

SYNONYMS (**stunted**) **small**, undersized, underdeveloped, diminutive.

stunt² ▶ **n.** **1** an action displaying spectacular skill and daring. **2** something unusual done to attract attention.

SYNONYMS **feat**, exploit, trick.

stunt·man /ˈstəntˌman/ ▶ **n.** (plural **stuntmen**) a person taking an actor's place in performing dangerous stunts.

stu·pe·fy /ˈst(y)o͞opəˌfī/ ▶ **v.** (**stupefies**, **stupefying**, **stupefied**) make someone unable to think properly.

SYNONYMS **1 drug**, sedate, tranquilize, intoxicate, inebriate. **2** *his reply stupefied us* **shock**, stun, astound, dumbfound, overwhelm, stagger, amaze, astonish, take someone's breath away; informal flabbergast, knock sideways, knock for a loop, bowl over, floor.

■ **stu·pe·fac·tion** /ˌst(y)o͞opəˈfaksʜən/ **n.**

stu·pen·dous /st(y)o͞oˈpendəs/ ▶ **adj.** very impressive.

SYNONYMS **amazing**, astounding, astonishing, extraordinary, remarkable, phenomenal, staggering, breathtaking; informal fantastic, mind-boggling, awesome; literary wondrous. ANTONYMS ordinary.

■ **stu·pen·dous·ly** **adv.**

stu·pid /ˈst(y)o͞opid/ ▶ **adj. 1** lacking intelligence or common sense. **2** dazed and unable to think clearly.

SYNONYMS **1 unintelligent**, dense, obtuse, foolish, idiotic, slow, simpleminded, brainless, mindless; informal thick, dim, dumb, dopey, daft, moronic, cretinous. **2 foolish**, silly, senseless, idiotic, ill-advised, ill-considered, unwise, nonsensical, ludicrous, ridiculous, laughable, fatuous, asinine, lunatic; informal crazy, half-baked, cockeyed, harebrained, crackbrained. ANTONYMS intelligent, sensible.

■ **stu·pid·i·ty** /st(y)o͞oˈpiditē/ **n.** **stu·pid·ly** **adv.**

stu·por /ˈst(y)o͞opər/ ▶ **n.** a state of being very dazed or nearly unconscious.

SYNONYMS **daze**, torpor, insensibility, oblivion.

stur·dy /ˈstərdē/ ▶ **adj.** (**sturdier**, **sturdiest**) **1** strong and solidly built or made. **2** confident and determined.

SYNONYMS **1 strapping**, well-built, muscular, strong, hefty, brawny, powerful, solid, burly; informal beefy. **2 robust**, strong, well-built, solid, stout, tough, durable, long-lasting, hard-wearing. ANTONYMS feeble.

■ **stur·di·ly** **adv.** **stur·di·ness** **n.**

stur·geon /ˈstərjən/ ▶ **n.** a very large fish with bony plates on the body, from whose roe (eggs) caviar is made.

stut·ter /ˈstətər/ ▶ **v.** (**stutters**, **stuttering**, **stuttered**) **1** have difficulty talking because you are sometimes unable to stop repeating the first sounds of a word. **2** (of a machine or gun) produce a series of short, sharp sounds. ▶ **n.** a tendency to stutter while speaking.

SYNONYMS ▶ **v. stammer**, stumble, falter, hesitate.

■ **stut·ter·er** **n.**

sty[1] /stī/ ▶ **n.** (plural **sties**) a pigsty.

sty[2] (or **stye**) ▶ **n.** (plural **sties** or **styes**) an inflamed swelling on the edge of an eyelid.

Styg·i·an /ˈstijēən/ ▶ **adj.** literary very dark.

style /stīl/ ▶ **n. 1** a way of doing something. **2** a particular appearance, design, or arrangement. **3** a way of painting, writing, etc., characteristic of a particular period or person. **4** elegance and sophistication. **5** Botany a narrow extension of the ovary, carrying the stigma. ▶ **v.** (**styles**, **styling**, **styled**) **1** design, make, or arrange in a particular form. **2** give a particular name, description, or title to.

SYNONYMS ▶ **n. 1 manner**, way, technique, method, methodology, approach, system, mode. **2 flair**, elegance, stylishness, chic, taste, grace, poise, polish, sophistication, suavity, urbanity; informal class. **3 kind**, type, variety, sort, design, pattern, genre. **4 fashion**, trend, vogue, mode. ▶ **v. design**, fashion, tailor, cut.

styl·ish /ˈstīlisʜ/ ▶ **adj.** having a good sense of style; fashionably elegant.

SYNONYMS **fashionable**, modern, up to date, modish, smart, sophisticated, elegant, chic, dapper, dashing; informal trendy, natty, kicky, tony. ANTONYMS unfashionable.

■ **styl·ish·ly** **adv.**

styl·ist /ˈstīlist/ ▶ **n.** a person who designs fashionable clothes or cuts hair.

styl·is·tic /stīˈlistik/ ▶ **adj.** relating to style.
■ **styl·is·ti·cal·ly** **adv.**

styl·ized /ˈstīˌlīzd/ ▶ **adj.** represented in an artificial style.

sty·lus /ˈstīləs/ ▶ **n.** (plural **styli** /-ˌlī/) **1** a hard point that follows a groove in a phonograph record and transmits the recorded sound for reproduction. **2** a pointed implement used for scratching or tracing letters or engraving.

sty·mie /ˈstīmē/ ▶ **v.** (**stymies**, **stymying** or **stymieing**, **stymied**) informal prevent or slow down the progress of.

styp·tic /ˈstiptik/ ▶ **adj.** able to make bleeding stop.

suave /swäv/ ▶ **adj.** (of a man) charming, confident, and elegant.

SYNONYMS **charming**, sophisticated, debonair, urbane, smooth, polished, refined, poised, self-possessed, gallant. ANTONYMS unsophisticated.

■ **suave·ly** **adv.** **suav·i·ty** **n.**

sub /səb/ informal ▶ **n. 1** a submarine. **2** a subscription. **3** a substitute on a sports team. ▶ **v.** (**subs**, **subbing**, **subbed**) act as a substitute.

sub·a·tom·ic /ˌsəbəˈtämik/ ▶ **adj.** smaller than or occurring within an atom.

sub·con·scious /səbˈkänsʜəs/ ▶ **adj.** concerning the part of the mind that you are not aware of but that influences your actions and feelings. ▶ **n.** this part of the mind.

SYNONYMS ▶ **adj. unconscious**, latent, suppressed, repressed, subliminal, dormant, underlying, innermost. ▶ **n.** (**unconscious**) **mind**, imagination, inner(most) self, psyche.

■ **sub·con·scious·ly** **adv.**

sub·con·ti·nent /ˌsəbˈkäntənənt/ ▶ **n.** a large part of a continent considered as a particular area, such as the part of Asia including India.

sub·con·tract /ˌsəbkənˈtrakt/ ▶ **v.** employ a firm or person outside your company to do work.
■ **sub·con·trac·tor** /səbˈkänˌtraktər/ **n.**

sub·cul·ture /ˈsəbˌkəlcʜər/ ▶ **n.** a distinct group within a society or class, having beliefs or interests that are different from those of the larger group.

sub·cu·ta·ne·ous /ˌsəbkyo͞oˈtānēəs/ ▶ **adj.** situated or applied under the skin.

sub·di·vide /ˈsəbdəˌvīd/ ▶ **v.** (**subdivides**, **subdividing**, **subdivided**) divide a part into smaller parts. ■ **sub·di·vi·sion** /ˈsəbdəˌvizʜən/ **n.**

sub·due /səbˈd(y)o͞o/ ▶ **v.** (**subdues**, **subduing**, **subdued**) **1** overcome, quiet, or control. **2** bring a group or country under control by force.

SYNONYMS **conquer**, defeat, vanquish, overcome, overwhelm, crush, beat, subjugate, suppress.

sub·dued /ˌsəb'd(y)o͞od/ ▶ **adj. 1** quiet and thoughtful or depressed. **2** (of color or lighting) soft; muted.

SYNONYMS **1 somber**, downcast, sad, dejected, depressed, gloomy, despondent. **2 hushed**, muted, quiet, low, soft, faint, muffled, subtle, indistinct, dim, unobtrusive. ANTONYMS cheerful, loud, bright.

sub·hu·man /səb'(h)yo͞omən/ ▶ **adj.** not behaving like a human being.

sub·ject ▶ **n.** /'səbjəkt/ **1** a person or thing that is being discussed, studied, or dealt with. **2** a branch of knowledge that is studied or taught. **3** Grammar the word or words in a sentence that come before the verb and that the verb says something about, e.g., *Joe* in *Joe ran home*. **4** each of the people in a population ruled by a king or queen. ▶ **adj.** /'səbjəkt/ (**subject to**) **1** able to be affected by. **2** dependent or conditional on. **3** under the control or authority of. ▶ **adv.** /'səbjəkt/ (**subject to**) if certain conditions are fulfilled. ▶ **v.** /səb'jekt/ (**subject someone/thing to**) make someone or something undergo an unpleasant experience.

SYNONYMS ▶ **n. 1 theme**, subject matter, topic, issue, thesis, question, concern. **2 branch of study**, discipline, field. **3 citizen**, national, resident, taxpayer, voter. ▶ **v. expose to**, submit to, treat with, put through.

■ **sub·jec·tion** /səb'jeksHən/ **n.**

sub·jec·tive /səb'jektiv/ ▶ **adj.** based on or influenced by personal opinions.

SYNONYMS **personal**, individual, emotional, biased, intuitive. ANTONYMS objective.

■ **sub·jec·tive·ly adv. sub·jec·tiv·i·ty** /ˌsəbjek'tivitē/ **n.**

sub ju·di·ce /ˌso͝ob 'yo͞odiˌkā, ˌsəb 'jo͞odiˌsē/ ▶ **adj.** being considered by a court of law and therefore not to be publicly discussed elsewhere.

sub·ju·gate /'səbjəˌgāt/ ▶ **v.** (**subjugates, subjugating, subjugated**) bring someone under your control by force.

SYNONYMS **conquer**, vanquish, defeat, crush, quash, bring someone to their knees, enslave, subdue, suppress. ANTONYMS liberate.

■ **sub·ju·ga·tion** /ˌsəbjə'gāsHən/ **n.**

sub·junc·tive /səb'jəNG(k)tiv/ ▶ **adj.** Grammar (of a verb) expressing what is imagined or wished or possible.

sub·let /'səb'let/ ▶ **v.** (**sublets, subletting, sublet**) let a property or part of a property that you are already renting to someone else.

sub·lime /sə'blīm/ ▶ **adj. 1** of great beauty or excellence. **2** extreme: *sublime confidence*. ▶ **v.** (**sublimes, subliming, sublimed**) Chemistry (of a solid substance) change directly into vapor when heated.

SYNONYMS ▶ **adj. 1** *sublime music* **exalted**, elevated, noble, lofty, awe-inspiring, majestic, magnificent, glorious, superb, wonderful, marvelous, splendid; informal fantastic, fabulous, terrific, heavenly, divine, out of this world. **2** *the sublime confidence of youth* **supreme**, total, complete, utter, consummate.

■ **sub·lime·ly adv.**

sub·lim·i·nal /sə'blimənl/ ▶ **adj.** affecting your mind without your being aware of it.
■ **sub·lim·i·nal·ly adv.**

sub·ma·chine gun /ˌsəbmə'sHēn/ ▶ **n.** a hand-held lightweight machine gun.

sub·ma·rine /ˌsəbmə'rēn, 'səbməˌrēn/ ▶ **n. 1** a streamlined warship designed to operate completely submerged in the sea. **2** a hero sandwich. ▶ **adj.** existing, occurring, or used under the surface of the sea. ■ **sub·ma·rin·er** /səb'marənər, -mə'rēnər/ **n.**

sub·merge /səb'mərj/ ▶ **v.** (**submerges, submerging, submerged**) **1** push or hold something underwater. **2** go down below the surface of water. **3** completely cover or hide.

SYNONYMS **1 go under (water)**, dive, sink, plunge, plummet. **2 immerse**, dip, plunge, duck, dunk. **3** *the farmland was submerged* **flood**, deluge, swamp, overwhelm, inundate.

sub·merse /səb'mərs/ ▶ **v.** submerge.

sub·mers·i·ble /səb'mərsəbəl/ ▶ **adj.** designed to operate while submerged.

sub·mer·sion /səb'mərzHən, -sHən/ ▶ **n.** the action of submerging or the state of being submerged.

sub·mi·cro·scop·ic /ˌsəbmīkrə'skäpik/ ▶ **adj.** too small to be seen by a microscope.

sub·mis·sion /səb'misHən/ ▶ **n. 1** the action of submitting. **2** a proposal or application submitted for consideration.

SYNONYMS **1 yielding**, capitulation, surrender, resignation, acceptance, consent, compliance, acquiescence, obedience, subjection, subservience, servility. **2 proposal**, suggestion, proposition, tender, presentation. **3 argument**, assertion, contention, statement, claim, allegation. ANTONYMS defiance.

sub·mis·sive /səb'misiv/ ▶ **adj.** very obedient or passive.

SYNONYMS **compliant**, yielding, acquiescent, passive, obedient, dutiful, docile, pliant, tractable, biddable, malleable, meek, unassertive; informal under someone's thumb.

■ **sub·mis·sive·ly adv.**

sub·mit /səb'mit/ ▶ **v.** (**submits, submitting, submitted**) **1** give in to the authority, control, or greater strength of someone or something. **2** present a proposal or application for consideration. **3** subject to a particular process or treatment.

SYNONYMS **1 yield**, give in/way, back down, cave in, capitulate, surrender, acquiesce. **2** *he refused to **submit to** their authority* **be governed by**, abide by, comply with, accept, be subject to, agree to, consent to, conform to. **3 put forward**, present, offer, tender, propose, suggest, enter, put in, send in. **4 contend**, assert, argue, state, claim, allege. ANTONYMS resist.

sub·or·di·nate ▶ **adj.** /sə'bôrdnit/ **1** lower in rank or position. **2** of less importance. ▶ **n.** /sə'bôrdnit/ a person who is under the authority of someone else. ▶ **v.** /sə'bôrdnˌāt/ (**subordinates, subordinating, subordinated**) treat someone or something as less important than another.

SYNONYMS ▶ **adj. inferior**, junior, lower-ranking, lower, supporting. ▶ **n. junior**, assistant, second (in command), number two, deputy, aide, underling, minion. ANTONYMS superior, senior.

■ **sub·or·di·na·tion** /-ˌbôrdn'āsHən/ **n.**

sub·plot /'səbˌplät/ ▶ **n.** a secondary plot in a play, novel, etc.

sub·poe·na /sə'pēnə/ Law ▶ **n.** a written order instructing someone to attend a court. ▶ **v.** (**subpoenas**, **subpoenaing**, **subpoenaed**) summon someone with a subpoena.

sub·scribe /səb'skrīb/ ▶ **v.** (**subscribes**, **subscribing**, **subscribed**) **1** (often **subscribe to**) arrange to receive something regularly by paying in advance. **2** (**subscribe to**) contribute a sum of money to a project or cause. **3** (**subscribe to**) say you agree with an idea or proposal.

SYNONYMS **contribute**, donate, give, pay.

■ **sub·scrib·er** n.

sub·script /'səbˌskript/ ▶ **adj.** (of a letter, figure, or symbol) printed below the line.

sub·scrip·tion /səb'skripsHən/ ▶ **n. 1** money paid to subscribe to something. **2** the action of subscribing.

SYNONYMS **membership fee**, dues, annual payment, charge.

sub·sec·tion /'səbˌseksHən/ ▶ **n.** a division of a section.

sub·se·quent /'səbsəkwənt/ ▶ **adj.** coming after something.

SYNONYMS **following**, ensuing, succeeding, later, future, coming, to come, next. ANTONYMS previous.

sub·se·quent·ly /'səbsəkwəntlē/ ▶ **adv.** after something else.

SYNONYMS **later (on)**, at a later date, afterward, in due course, following this/that, eventually; formal thereafter.

sub·ser·vi·ent /səb'sərvēənt/ ▶ **adj.** too ready to obey other people.

SYNONYMS **1 submissive**, deferential, compliant, obedient, dutiful, docile, passive, subdued, downtrodden; informal under someone's thumb. **2** *individual rights are subservient to the interests of the state* **subordinate**, secondary, subsidiary. ANTONYMS independent.

■ **sub·ser·vi·ence** n.

sub·side /səb'sīd/ ▶ **v.** (**subsides**, **subsiding**, **subsided**) **1** become less strong, violent, or severe. **2** (of water) go down to a lower level. **3** (of a building) sink lower into the ground. **4** (of the ground) cave in; sink. **5** (**subside into**) give way to a strong feeling.

SYNONYMS **1 abate**, let up, quiet down, calm, slacken (off), ease (up), relent, die down, diminish, decline. **2 recede**, ebb, fall, go down, get lower. **3 sink**, settle, cave in, collapse, give way. ANTONYMS intensify, rise.

sub·sid·ence /səb'sīdns, 'səbsidns/ ▶ **n.** the gradual caving in or sinking of an area of land.

sub·sid·i·ar·y /səb'sidēˌerē/ ▶ **adj. 1** related but less important. **2** (of a company) controlled by another company. ▶ **n.** (plural **subsidiaries**) a subsidiary company.

SYNONYMS ▶ **adj. subordinate**, secondary, subservient, supplementary, peripheral, auxiliary. ANTONYMS principal. ▶ **n. branch**, division, subdivision, derivative, offshoot.

sub·si·dize /'səbsəˌdīz/ ▶ **v.** (**subsidizes**, **subsidizing**, **subsidized**) **1** support an organization or activity financially. **2** pay part of the cost of producing something to reduce its price.

SYNONYMS **finance**, fund, support, contribute to, give money to, underwrite, sponsor; informal shell out for, bankroll.

sub·si·dy /'səbsidē/ ▶ **n.** (plural **subsidies**) a sum of money given to help keep the price of a product or service low.

SYNONYMS **finance**, funding, backing, support, grant, sponsorship, allowance, contribution, handout.

sub·sist /səb'sist/ ▶ **v.** maintain or support yourself at a basic level.

SYNONYMS **survive**, live, stay alive, exist, eke out an existence/living, support yourself, manage, get along/by, make ends meet.

sub·sist·ence /səb'sistəns/ ▶ **n.** the action or fact of subsisting. ▶ **adj.** (of production) at a level that is enough only for your own use, without any surplus for trade.

sub·soil /'səbˌsoil/ ▶ **n.** soil lying under the surface soil.

sub·son·ic /ˌsəb'sänik/ ▶ **adj.** relating to or flying at a speed less than that of sound.

sub·stance /'səbstəns/ ▶ **n. 1** a type of solid, liquid, or gas that has particular qualities. **2** the real physical matter of which a person or thing consists. **3** solid basis in reality or fact. **4** the quality of being important, valid, or significant. **5** the most important or essential part or meaning.

SYNONYMS **1 material**, compound, matter, stuff. **2 significance**, importance, import, validity, foundation. **3 content**, subject matter, theme, message, essence. **4 wealth**, fortune, riches, affluence, prosperity, money, means.

sub·stand·ard /səb'standərd/ ▶ **adj.** below the usual or required standard.

SYNONYMS **inferior**, second-rate, poor, below par, imperfect, faulty, defective, shoddy, shabby, unsound, unsatisfactory; informal tenth-rate, crummy, lousy.

sub·stan·tial /səb'stancHəl/ ▶ **adj. 1** of considerable importance, size, or value. **2** strongly built or made. **3** concerning the essential points of something.

SYNONYMS **1 considerable**, real, significant, important, major, valuable, useful, sizable, appreciable. **2 sturdy**, solid, stout, strong, well-built, durable, long-lasting, hard-wearing. ANTONYMS insubstantial.

sub·stan·tial·ly /səb'stancHəlē/ ▶ **adv. 1** to a great extent. **2** for the most part; mainly.

sub·stan·ti·ate /səb'stancHēˌāt/ ▶ **v.** (**substantiates**, **substantiating**, **substantiated**) provide evidence to support or prove the truth of something.

SYNONYMS **prove**, show to be true, support, justify, vindicate, validate, corroborate, verify, authenticate, confirm. ANTONYMS disprove.

sub·stan·tive /'səbstəntiv/ ▶ **adj.** real and meaningful. ■ **sub·stan·tive·ly** adv.

sub·sti·tute /ˈsəbstiˌt(y)o͞ot/ ▶ **n.** a person or thing that does something in place of someone or something else. ▶ **v.** (**substitutes**, **substituting**, **substituted**) make someone or something act as a substitute for.

SYNONYMS ▶ **n.** **replacement**, deputy, relief, proxy, reserve, surrogate, cover, stand-in, understudy; informal sub. ▶ **v.** **1** **exchange**, swap, use instead of, use as an alternative to, use in place of, replace with. **2** *I found someone to substitute for for me* **deputize for**, stand in for, cover for, fill in for, take over from.

sub·sti·tu·tion /ˌsəbstiˈt(y)o͞oSHən/ ▶ **n.** the action of replacing someone or something with another person or thing.

sub·sume /səbˈso͞om/ ▶ **v.** (**subsumes**, **subsuming**, **subsumed**) include or absorb something in something else.

sub·ter·fuge /ˈsəbtərˌfyo͞oj/ ▶ **n.** secretive or dishonest actions.

SYNONYMS **1** **trickery**, intrigue, deviousness, deceit, deception, dishonesty, cheating, duplicity, guile, cunning, craftiness, chicanery, pretense, fraud, fraudulence. **2** *a disreputable subterfuge* **trick**, hoax, ruse, wile, ploy, stratagem, artifice, dodge, bluff, pretense, deception; informal con, scam.

sub·ter·ra·ne·an /ˌsəbtəˈrānēən/ ▶ **adj.** existing or happening under the earth's surface.

sub·text /ˈsəbˌtekst/ ▶ **n.** an underlying theme in a piece of writing or speech.

sub·ti·tle /ˈsəbˌtītl/ ▶ **n.** **1** (**subtitles**) words displayed at the bottom of a movie theater or television screen that translate what is being said. **2** a secondary title of a published work. ▶ **v.** (**subtitles**, **subtitling**, **subtitled**) provide something with a subtitle or subtitles.

sub·tle /ˈsətl/ ▶ **adj.** (**subtler**, **subtlest**) **1** so delicate or precise as to be difficult to analyze or describe. **2** capable of making fine distinctions. **3** making use of clever and indirect methods to achieve something.

SYNONYMS **1** **understated**, muted, subdued, delicate, soft, low-key, toned-down. **2** **gentle**, slight, gradual. **3** *a subtle distinction* **fine**, fine-drawn, nice, tenuous. ANTONYMS gaudy, crude.

■ **sub·tle·ty** **n.** **sub·tly** **adv.**

sub·to·tal /ˈsəbˌtōtl/ ▶ **n.** the total of one set within a larger set of figures.

sub·tract /səbˈtrakt/ ▶ **v.** take away a number or amount from another to calculate the difference.

sub·trac·tion /səbˈtrakSHən/ ▶ **n.** **1** the process or skill of taking one number or amount away from another. **2** Math the process of taking a matrix, vector, or other quantity away from another under specific rules to obtain the difference.

sub·urb /ˈsəbərb/ ▶ **n.** a residential district that is outside the central part of a city.

sub·ur·ban /səˈbərbən/ ▶ **adj.** **1** relating to or like a suburb. **2** boringly conventional.

SYNONYMS **1** **residential**, commuter, dormitory. **2** **dull**, boring, uninteresting, conventional, ordinary, unsophisticated, provincial, parochial, bourgeois, middle-class.

■ **sub·ur·ban·ize** **v.**

sub·ur·bi·a /səˈbərbēə/ ▶ **n.** suburbs, and the way of life of the people who live in them.

sub·ver·sive /səbˈvərsiv/ ▶ **adj.** trying to damage or weaken the power of an established system or institution. ▶ **n.** a subversive person.

SYNONYMS ▶ **adj.** **disruptive**, troublemaking, insurrectionary, seditious, dissident. ▶ **n.** **troublemaker**, dissident, agitator, renegade.

■ **sub·ver·sive·ly** **adv.**

sub·vert /səbˈvərt/ ▶ **v.** damage or weaken the power of an established system or institution.
■ **sub·ver·sion** /-ˈvərZHən, -SHən/ **n.**

sub·way /ˈsəbˌwā/ ▶ **n.** an underground railroad.

sub-zero ▶ **adj.** (of temperature) lower than zero; very cold.

suc·ceed /səkˈsēd/ ▶ **v.** **1** achieve an aim or purpose. **2** gain wealth or status. **3** take over a job, role, or title from someone else. **4** come after and take the place of.

SYNONYMS **1** **triumph**, achieve success, be successful, do well, flourish, thrive; informal make it, make the grade. **2** **be successful**, turn out well, work (out), be effective; informal come off, pay off. **3** **replace**, take over from, follow, supersede. ANTONYMS fail, precede.

suc·cess /səkˈses/ ▶ **n.** **1** the achievement of an aim or purpose. **2** the gaining of wealth or status. **3** a person or thing that achieves success.

SYNONYMS **1** **victory**, triumph. **2** **prosperity**, affluence, wealth, riches, opulence. **3** **best-seller**, sellout, winner, triumph; informal hit, smash, sensation. ANTONYMS failure.

SPELLING

Double **c** and double **s** in **success**, **successful**, **succession**, and **successive**.

suc·cess·ful /səkˈsesfəl/ ▶ **adj.** **1** having achieved an aim or purpose. **2** having gained wealth or status.

SYNONYMS **1** **prosperous**, affluent, wealthy, rich, famous, eminent, top, respected. **2** **flourishing**, thriving, booming, buoyant, profitable, moneymaking, lucrative.

■ **suc·cess·ful·ly** **adv.**

suc·ces·sion /səkˈseSHən/ ▶ **n.** **1** a number of people or things following one after the other. **2** the action, process, or right of inheriting a position or title.

SYNONYMS **sequence**, series, progression, chain, string, train, line, run.

suc·ces·sive /səkˈsesiv/ ▶ **adj.** following one another or following others.

SYNONYMS **consecutive**, in a row, sequential, in succession, running.

■ **suc·ces·sive·ly** **adv.**

suc·ces·sor /səkˈsesər/ ▶ **n.** a person or thing that succeeds another.

suc·cinct /sə(k)ˈsiNG(k)t/ ▶ **adj.** briefly and clearly expressed.

SYNONYMS **concise**, short (and sweet), brief, compact, condensed, crisp, laconic, terse, to the point, pithy. ANTONYMS verbose.

■ **suc·cinct·ly** **adv.**

suc·cor /ˈsəkər/ ▶ **n.** help and support in difficult times. ▶ **v.** give help and support to.

SYNONYMS ▶ **n.** **aid**, help, a helping hand, assistance, comfort, ease, relief, support.

suc·cu·lent /ˈsəkyələnt/ ▶ **adj. 1** (of food) tender, juicy, and tasty. **2** (of a plant) having thick fleshy leaves or stems that store water. ▶ **n.** a succulent plant.

SYNONYMS ▶ **adj. juicy**, moist, luscious, soft, tender, choice, mouthwatering, appetizing, flavorsome, tasty, delicious; informal scrumptious. ANTONYMS dry.

■ **suc·cu·lence n.**

suc·cumb /səˈkəm/ ▶ **v. 1** give in to pressure or temptation. **2** die from the effect of a disease or injury.

SYNONYMS **yield**, give in/way, submit, surrender, capitulate, cave in, fall victim. ANTONYMS resist.

such /səCH/ ▶ **determiner & pron. 1** of the type previously mentioned or about to be mentioned. **2** to so high a degree; so great. □ **such as 1** for example. **2** of a kind that; like.

such·like /ˈsəCHˌlīk/ ▶ **pron.** things of the type mentioned.

suck /sək/ ▶ **v. 1** draw something into your mouth by tightening your lip muscles to make a partial vacuum. **2** hold something in your mouth and draw at it by tightening your lip and cheek muscles. **3** draw something in a particular direction by creating a vacuum. **4** (**suck someone in** or **into**) involve someone in a situation or activity without their being able to choose or resist it. **5** (**suck up to**) informal do things to please someone in authority in order to gain advantage for yourself. **6** informal be very bad or unpleasant. ▶ **n.** an act of sucking.

SYNONYMS ▶ **v. sip**, sup, slurp, drink, siphon.

suck·er /ˈsəkər/ ▶ **n. 1** a rubber cup that sticks to a surface by suction. **2** an organ that allows an animal to cling to a surface by suction. **3** informal a person who is easily fooled. **4** (**a sucker for**) informal a person who is very fond of a particular thing. **5** a shoot springing from the base of a tree or other plant.

suck·le /ˈsəkəl/ ▶ **v.** (**suckles**, **suckling**, **suckled**) feed at the breast or a teat.

suck·ling /ˈsəkliNG/ ▶ **n.** a young child or animal that is still feeding on its mother's milk.

su·crose /ˈso͞oˌkrōs/ ▶ **n.** the main substance in cane or beet sugar.

suc·tion /ˈsəkSHən/ ▶ **n.** the force produced when a partial vacuum is created by the removal of air.

Su·da·nese /ˌso͞odnˈēz, -ˈēs/ ▶ **n.** (plural **Sudanese**) a person from Sudan. ▶ **adj.** relating to Sudan.

sud·den /ˈsədn/ ▶ **adj.** happening or done quickly and unexpectedly.

SYNONYMS **unexpected**, unforeseen, immediate, instantaneous, instant, precipitous, abrupt, rapid, swift, quick.

■ **sud·den·ness n.**

sud·den·ly /ˈsədnlē/ ▶ **adv.** quickly and unexpectedly.

SYNONYMS **all of a sudden**, all at once, abruptly, swiftly, unexpectedly, without warning, out of the blue. ANTONYMS gradually.

su·do·ku /so͞oˈdōko͞o/ ▶ **n.** a type of number puzzle.

suds /sədz/ ▶ **pl.n.** froth made from soap and water.

SYNONYMS **lather**, foam, froth, bubbles, soap.

sue /so͞o/ ▶ **v.** (**sues**, **suing**, **sued**) **1** start legal proceedings against someone that you claim has harmed you. **2** (**sue for**) formal appeal formally to a person for.

SYNONYMS **take legal action**, go to court, take to court, litigate.

suede /swād/ ▶ **n.** leather with the flesh side rubbed to give it a velvety surface.

su·et /ˈso͞oit/ ▶ **n.** hard white fat obtained from cattle, sheep, and other animals, used in cooking.

suf·fer /ˈsəfər/ ▶ **v.** (**suffers**, **suffering**, **suffered**) **1** experience something bad. **2** (**suffer from**) be affected by an illness or condition. **3** become worse in quality. **4** old use tolerate.

SYNONYMS **1 hurt**, ache, be in pain, be in distress, be upset, be miserable. **2** *he suffers from asthma* **be afflicted by**, be affected by, be troubled with, have. **3 undergo**, experience, be subjected to, receive, sustain, endure, face, meet with.

■ **suf·fer·er n.**

suf·fer·ance /ˈsəf(ə)rəns/ ▶ **n.** toleration, rather than genuine approval.

suf·fer·ing /ˈsəfəriNG/ ▶ **n.** pain or distress.

SYNONYMS **hardship**, distress, misery, adversity, pain, agony, anguish, trauma, torment, torture, hurt, affliction. ANTONYMS pleasure, joy.

suf·fice /səˈfīs/ ▶ **v.** (**suffices**, **sufficing**, **sufficed**) be enough or adequate.

suf·fi·cien·cy /səˈfiSHənsē/ ▶ **n.** (plural **sufficiencies**) **1** the quality of being enough or adequate. **2** an adequate amount.

suf·fi·cient /səˈfiSHənt/ ▶ **adj.** enough; adequate.

SYNONYMS **enough**, adequate, plenty of, ample. ANTONYMS inadequate.

■ **suf·fi·cient·ly adv.**

suf·fix /ˈsəfiks/ ▶ **n.** a part added on to the end of a word (e.g., *-ly*, *-ation*).

suf·fo·cate /ˈsəfəˌkāt/ ▶ **v.** (**suffocates**, **suffocating**, **suffocated**) die or cause to die from lack of air or being unable to breathe.
■ **suf·fo·ca·tion** /ˌsəfəˈkāSHən/ **n.**

suf·frage /ˈsəfrij/ ▶ **n.** the right to vote in political elections.

suf·fra·gette /ˌsəfrəˈjet/ ▶ **n.** (in the past, when only men could vote) a woman who campaigned for the right to vote in an election.

suf·fuse /səˈfyo͞oz/ ▶ **v.** (**suffuses**, **suffusing**, **suffused**) gradually spread through or over.

SYNONYMS **permeate**, spread over, cover, bathe, pervade, wash, saturate, imbue.

■ **suf·fu·sion n.**

sug·ar /ˈSHo͝ogər/ ▶ **n. 1** a sweet substance obtained from sugarcane or sugar beet. **2** a type of sweet soluble carbohydrate found in plant and animal tissue. ▶ **v.** sweeten, sprinkle, or coat with sugar. □ **sugar beet** a type of beet from which sugar is extracted. **sugar daddy** informal a rich older man who gives presents and money to a much younger woman. **sugar maple** a maple that yields the sap from which maple sugar and syrup are made.

sug·ar·cane /ˈSHo͝ogərˌkān/ ▶ **n.** a tropical grass with tall thick stems from which sugar is extracted.

sug·ar·coat·ed /ˈsʜo͝ogərˌkōtid/ ▶ **adj.** superficially attractive or excessively sentimental.

sug·ar·y /ˈsʜo͝ogərē/ ▶ **adj.** **1** containing much sugar. **2** coated in sugar. **3** too sentimental.

sug·gest /sə(g)ˈjest/ ▶ **v.** **1** put forward an idea or plan for people to consider. **2** make you think that something exists or is the case. **3** say or indicate something indirectly. **4** (**suggest itself**) (of an idea) come into your mind.

> SYNONYMS **1 propose**, put forward, recommend, advocate, advise. **2 indicate**, lead someone to the belief, give the impression, demonstrate, show. **3 hint**, insinuate, imply, intimate.

sug·gest·i·ble /sə(g)ˈjestəbəl/ ▶ **adj.** quick to accept other people's ideas or suggestions.

sug·ges·tion /sə(g)ˈjesᴄʜən/ ▶ **n.** **1** an idea or plan put forward for people to consider. **2** a thing that suggests that something is the case. **3** a slight trace or indication.

> SYNONYMS **1 proposal**, proposition, recommendation, advice, counsel, hint, tip, clue, idea. **2 hint**, trace, touch, suspicion, ghost, semblance, shadow, glimmer. **3 insinuation**, hint, implication.

sug·ges·tive /sə(g)ˈjestiv/ ▶ **adj.** making you think of a particular thing.

> SYNONYMS **1 redolent**, evocative, reminiscent, characteristic, indicative, typical. **2 provocative**, titillating, sexual, sexy, risqué, **indecent**, indelicate, improper, unseemly, smutty, dirty.

■ **sug·ges·tive·ly** **adv.**

su·i·cide /ˈso͞oiˌsīd/ ▶ **n.** **1** the action of killing yourself intentionally. **2** a person who commits suicide. ■ **su·i·cid·al** /ˌso͞oiˈsīdl/ **adj.** **su·i·cid·al·ly** **adv.**

suit /so͞ot/ ▶ **n.** **1** a set of clothes made of the same fabric, consisting of a jacket and trousers or a skirt. **2** a set of clothes for a particular activity. **3** any of the sets into which a pack of playing cards is divided (spades, hearts, diamonds, and clubs). **4** a lawsuit. ▶ **v.** **1** be right or good for. **2** (of clothes, colors, etc.) be right for someone's features or figure. **3** (**suit yourself**) do as you wish.

> SYNONYMS ▶ **n.** **1 outfit**, ensemble. **2 legal action**, lawsuit, (court) case, action, (legal/judicial) proceedings, litigation. ▶ **v.** **1 look attractive on**, look good on, become, flatter. **2 be convenient for**, be acceptable to, be suitable for, meet the requirements of; informal fit. **3** *recipes suited to students* **be appropriate for**, tailor to/for, fashion for, adjust to/for, adapt to/for, modify to/for, fit for, gear to, design for.

suit·a·ble /ˈso͞otəbəl/ ▶ **adj.** right or good for a particular person or situation.

> SYNONYMS **1 acceptable**, satisfactory, convenient. **2 appropriate**, apposite, apt, fitting, fit, suited, tailor-made, in keeping, ideal; informal right up someone's alley. **3 proper**, right, seemly, decent, appropriate, fitting, correct, due. ANTONYMS unsuitable.

■ **suit·a·bil·i·ty** /ˌso͞otəˈbilitē/ **n.** **suit·a·bly** **adv.**

suit·case /ˈso͞otˌkās/ ▶ **n.** a case with a handle and a hinged lid, used for carrying clothes and other possessions.

suite /swēt/ ▶ **n.** **1** a set of rooms. **2** a set of furniture. **3** (in music) a set of instrumental compositions to be played one after the other.

> SYNONYMS **apartment**, flat, rooms.

suit·or /ˈso͞otər/ ▶ **n.** dated a man who pays attention to a woman because he wants to marry her.

sul·fur /ˈsəlfər/ ▶ **n.** a chemical element in the form of yellow crystals, which easily catches fire. □ **sulfur dioxide** a poisonous gas formed by burning sulfur.

sul·fu·ric /səlˈfyo͝orik/ ▶ **adj.** containing sulfur. □ **sulfuric acid** a strong corrosive acid.

sul·fur·ous /ˈsəlfərəs/ ▶ **adj.** containing or obtained from sulfur.

sulk /səlk/ ▶ **v.** be quietly bad-tempered and resentful because you are annoyed. ▶ **n.** a period of sulking.

> SYNONYMS ▶ **v. mope**, brood, be in a bad mood, be in a huff. ▶ **n.** (**bad**) **mood**, fit of pique, pet, huff.

sulk·y /ˈsəlkē/ ▶ **adj.** quietly bad-tempered and resentful.

> SYNONYMS **sullen**, surly, petulant, disgruntled, put out, bad-tempered, grumpy, moody. ANTONYMS cheerful.

■ **sulk·i·ly** **adv.**

sul·len /ˈsələn/ ▶ **adj.** silent and bad-tempered.

> SYNONYMS **surly**, sulky, morose, resentful, moody, grumpy, bad-tempered, unsociable, uncommunicative, unresponsive. ANTONYMS cheerful.

■ **sul·len·ly** **adv.**

sul·ly /ˈsəlē/ ▶ **v.** (**sullies**, **sullying**, **sullied**) literary spoil the purity or cleanness of something.

> SYNONYMS **taint**, defile, soil, tarnish, stain, blemish, pollute, spoil, mar; literary besmirch.

sul·tan /ˈsəltn/ ▶ **n.** a Muslim king or ruler.

sul·tan·a /səlˈtanə/ ▶ **n.** **1** a light brown seedless raisin. **2** the wife of a sultan.

sul·try /ˈsəltrē/ ▶ **adj.** (of the weather) hot and humid.

> SYNONYMS **1 humid**, close, airless, stifling, oppressive, muggy, sticky, sweltering, hot, tropical, heavy; informal boiling, roasting. **2 passionate**, sensual, sexy, seductive. ANTONYMS refreshing.

sum /səm/ ▶ **n.** **1** a particular amount of money. **2** (also **sum total**) the total amount resulting from the addition of two or more numbers or amounts. **3** a calculation in arithmetic. ▶ **v.** (**sums**, **summing**, **summed**) (**sum someone/thing up**) **1** describe the nature or character of someone or something concisely. **2** summarize something briefly.

> SYNONYMS ▶ **n.** **1 amount**, quantity, price, charge, fee, cost. **2 total**, sum total, grand total, tally, aggregate. **3 entirety**, totality, total, whole, beginning and end. **4 calculation**, problem.

sum·mar·i·ly /səˈme(ə)rəlē, ˈsəmərəlē/ ▶ **adv.** in a summary way.

> SYNONYMS **immediately**, instantly, right away, straightaway, at once, on the spot, speedily, swiftly, rapidly, without delay, promptly, arbitrarily, without formality, peremptorily.

sum·ma·rize /ˈsəməˌrīz/ ▶ v. (**summarizes, summarizing, summarized**) give a summary of.

SYNONYMS **sum up**, abridge, condense, outline, put in a nutshell, précis.

sum·ma·ry /ˈsəmərē/ ▶ n. (plural **summaries**) a brief statement of the main points of something. ▶ adj. **1** not including many details; brief. **2** (of a legal process or judgment) done or made immediately and without following the normal procedures.

SYNONYMS ▶ n. **synopsis**, précis, résumé, abstract, outline, rundown, summing-up, overview.

sum·ma·tion /səˈmāsHən/ ▶ n. **1** the process of adding things together. **2** the action of summing up. **3** a summary.

sum·mer /ˈsəmər/ ▶ n. the season after spring and before autumn. ■ **sum·mer·y** adj.

sum·mer·house /ˈsəmərˌhous/ ▶ n. a small building in a garden or park, used for sitting in during the summer months.

sum·mer·time /ˈsəmərˌtīm/ ▶ n. the season or period of summer.

sum·mit /ˈsəmit/ ▶ n. **1** the highest point of a hill or mountain. **2** the highest possible level of achievement. **3** a meeting between heads of government.

SYNONYMS **1** (**mountain**) **top**, peak, crest, crown, apex, tip, cap, hilltop. **2 meeting**, conference, talk(s). ANTONYMS base.

sum·mon /ˈsəmən/ ▶ v. **1** order someone to be present. **2** urgently ask for help. **3** call people to attend a meeting. **4** make an effort to produce a quality or reaction from within yourself.

SYNONYMS **1 send for**, call for, request the presence of, ask, invite. **2 convene**, call, assemble, rally, muster, gather together. **3 summons**, subpoena.

sum·mons /ˈsəmənz/ ▶ n. (plural **summonses**) **1** an order to appear in a court of law. **2** an act of summoning.

SYNONYMS **writ**, subpoena, warrant, court order.

su·mo /ˈso͞omō/ ▶ n. a Japanese form of wrestling.

sump /səmp/ ▶ n. the base of an internal combustion engine, in which a reserve of oil is stored.

sump·tu·ous /ˈsəm(p)CHo͞oəs/ ▶ adj. splendid and expensive-looking.

SYNONYMS **lavish**, luxurious, opulent, magnificent, resplendent, gorgeous, splendid; informal plush, swish. ANTONYMS plain.

■ **sump·tu·ous·ly** adv.

sun /sən/ ▶ n. **1** (also **Sun**) the star around which the earth orbits. **2** any similar star. **3** the light or warmth received from the sun. ▶ v. (**suns, sunning, sunned**) (**sun yourself**) sit or lie outside in the heat of the sun.

SYNONYMS ▶ n. **sunshine**, sunlight, daylight, light, warmth.

sun·bathe /ˈsənˌbāT͟H/ ▶ v. (**sunbathes, sunbathing, sunbathed**) sit or lie outside in the sun to get a suntan.

sun·beam /ˈsənˌbēm/ ▶ n. a ray of sunlight.

Sun·belt /ˈsənˌbelt/ ▶ n. the southern US from California to Florida.

sun·block /ˈsənˌbläk/ ▶ n. a cream or lotion used on the skin for complete protection from sunburn.

sun·burn /ˈsənˌbərn/ ▶ n. redness and inflammation of the skin caused by too much exposure to the ultraviolet rays of the sun. ■ **sun·burned** adj.

sun·dae /ˈsənˌdā/ ▶ n. a dish of ice cream with added fruit, nuts, syrup, and whipped cream.

SPELLING
The word ends with **-ae**, not **-ay**: **sundae**.

Sun·day /ˈsəndā, -dē/ ▶ n. the day of the week before Monday and following Saturday, observed by Christians as a day of worship. □ **Sunday school** a class held on Sundays to teach children about Christianity or Judaism.

sun·der /ˈsəndər/ ▶ v. (**sunders, sundering, sundered**) literary split apart.

sun·di·al /ˈsənˌdīl/ ▶ n. an instrument showing the time by the shadow cast by a pointer.

sun·down /ˈsənˌdoun/ ▶ n. sunset.

sun·dress /ˈsənˌdres/ ▶ n. a light dress with shoulder straps instead of sleeves.

sun·dry /ˈsəndrē/ ▶ adj. of various kinds. ▶ n. (**sundries**) various items not important enough to be mentioned individually.

SYNONYMS ▶ adj. **various**, varied, miscellaneous, assorted, mixed, diverse, diversified, several, numerous, many, manifold, multifarious, multitudinous; literary divers.

sun·flow·er /ˈsənˌflou(-ə)r/ ▶ n. a tall plant with very large yellow flowers.

sung /səNG/ past participle of **SING**.

sun·glass·es /ˈsənˌglasiz/ ▶ pl.n. glasses tinted to protect the eyes from sunlight.

sunk /səNGk/ past participle of **SINK**.

sunk·en /ˈsəNGkən/ ▶ adj. **1** having sunk. **2** at a lower level than the surrounding area.

sun·lamp /ˈsənˌlamp/ ▶ n. a lamp giving off ultraviolet rays, under which you lie to get an artificial suntan.

sun·light /ˈsənˌlīt/ ▶ n. light from the sun. ■ **sun·lit** adj.

Sun·ni /ˈso͝onē/ ▶ n. (plural **Sunni** or **Sunnis**) **1** one of the two main branches of Islam. The other is **SHIA**. **2** a Muslim who follows the Sunni branch of Islam.

sun·ny /ˈsənē/ ▶ adj. (**sunnier, sunniest**) **1** bright with or receiving a lot of sunlight. **2** cheerful.

SYNONYMS **1 bright**, sunlit, clear, fine, cloudless. **2 cheerful**, cheery, happy, bright, merry, bubbly, jolly, good-natured, good-tempered, optimistic, upbeat. ANTONYMS dull, cloudy.

□ **sunny side up** (of an egg) fried on one side only.

sun·rise /ˈsənˌrīz/ ▶ n. **1** the time when the sun rises. **2** the colors and light visible in the sky at sunrise.

SYNONYMS **dawn**, crack of dawn, daybreak, sunup, break of day, first light, early morning.

sun·roof /ˈsənˌro͞of, -ˌro͝of/ ▶ n. a panel in the roof of a car that can be opened to let air in.

sun·screen /ˈsənˌskrēn/ ▶ n. a cream or lotion rubbed on to the skin to protect it from the sun.

sun·set /ˈsənˌset/ ▶ n. **1** the time when the sun sets. **2** the colors and light visible in the sky at sunset.

SYNONYMS **sundown**, nightfall, twilight, dusk, evening.

sun·shade /ˈsən,SHād/ ▶ **n.** a light umbrella or awning giving protection from the sun.

sun·shine /ˈsən,SHīn/ ▶ **n.** sunlight unbroken by cloud.

sun·spot /ˈsən,spät/ ▶ **n.** a temporary darker and cooler patch on the sun's surface.

sun·stroke /ˈsən,strōk/ ▶ **n.** heatstroke brought about by staying in the sun for too long.

sun·tan /ˈsən,tan/ ▶ **n.** a golden-brown coloring of the skin caused by spending time in the sun. ■ **sun·tanned adj.**

sun·up /ˈsən,əp/ ▶ **n.** sunrise.

sup¹ /səp/ ▶ **v.** (**sups, supping, supped**) dated take drink or liquid food by sips or spoonfuls. ▶ **n.** a sip.

sup² ▶ **v.** (**sups, supping, supped**) old use eat supper.

su·per /ˈso͞opər/ ▶ **adj.** informal excellent.

SYNONYMS **excellent**, superb, superlative, first-class, outstanding, marvelous, magnificent, wonderful, splendid, glorious; informal great, fantastic, fabulous, terrific, ace, divine, wicked, cool. ANTONYMS rotten.

su·per·an·nu·ate /,so͞opərˈanyo͞o,āt/ ▶ **v.** (**superannuates, superannuating, superannuated**) **1** arrange for someone to retire with a pension. **2** (**superannuated**) humorous too old to be effective or useful.

su·per·an·nu·a·tion /,so͞opər,anyo͞oˈāSHən/ ▶ **n.** regular payment made by an employee into a fund from which a future pension will be paid.

su·perb /so͞oˈpərb, sə-/ ▶ **adj. 1** very good; excellent. **2** magnificent or splendid.

SYNONYMS **excellent**, first-class, outstanding, marvelous, wonderful, splendid, admirable, fine, exceptional, glorious; informal great, fantastic, fabulous, terrific, super, awesome, ace. ANTONYMS poor, unimpressive.

■ **su·perb·ly adv.**

su·per·charg·er /ˈso͞opər,CHärjər/ ▶ **n.** a device that makes an engine more efficient by forcing extra air or fuel into it. ■ **su·per·charged adj.**

su·per·cil·i·ous /,so͞opərˈsilēəs/ ▶ **adj.** having a manner that shows you think you are better than other people.

SYNONYMS **arrogant**, haughty, conceited, disdainful, overbearing, pompous, condescending, superior, patronizing, imperious, proud, snobbish, smug, scornful, sneering; informal high and mighty, snooty, stuck-up.

su·per·com·put·er /ˈso͞opərkəm,pyo͞otər/ ▶ **n.** a particularly powerful mainframe computer.

su·per·cool /,so͞opərˈko͞ol/ ▶ **v.** Chemistry cool a liquid below its freezing point without solidification or crystallization.

su·per·fi·cial /,so͞opərˈfiSHəl/ ▶ **adj. 1** existing or happening at or on the surface. **2** apparent rather than real. **3** not thorough. **4** lacking the ability to think deeply about things.

SYNONYMS **1 surface**, exterior, external, outer, slight. **2 cursory**, perfunctory, casual, sketchy, desultory, token, slapdash, offhand, rushed, hasty, hurried. **3 apparent**, seeming, outward, ostensible, cosmetic, slight. **4 facile**, shallow, flippant, empty-headed, trivial, frivolous, silly, inane. ANTONYMS deep, thorough.

■ **su·per·fi·ci·al·i·ty** /-,fiSHēˈalitē/ **n. su·per·fi·cial·ly adv.**

su·per·flu·ous /so͞oˈpərflo͞oəs/ ▶ **adj.** more than what is needed.

SYNONYMS **surplus**, redundant, unneeded, unnecessary, excess, extra, (to) spare, remaining, unused, left over, waste. ANTONYMS necessary.

■ **su·per·flu·i·ty** /,so͞opərˈflo͞oitē/ **n.**

su·per·glue /ˈso͞opər,glo͞o/ ▶ **n.** a very strong quick-setting glue.

su·per·he·ro /ˈso͞opər,hirō/ ▶ **n.** (plural **superheroes**) a fictional hero with superhuman powers.

su·per·hu·man /,so͞opərˈ(h)yo͞omən/ ▶ **adj.** having exceptional ability or powers.

SYNONYMS **extraordinary**, phenomenal, prodigious, stupendous, exceptional, immense, heroic, Herculean.

su·per·im·pose /,so͞opərimˈpōz/ ▶ **v.** (**superimposes, superimposing, superimposed**) lay one thing over another. ■ **su·per·im·po·si·tion** /-,impəˈziSHən/ **n.**

su·per·in·tend /,so͞opərinˈtend/ ▶ **v.** manage or oversee.

su·per·in·tend·ent /,so͞opərinˈtendənt/ ▶ **n. 1** a person who supervises and controls a group or activity. **2** a senior police officer. **3** the caretaker of a building.

SYNONYMS **manager**, director, administrator, supervisor, overseer, controller, chief, head, governor; informal boss.

su·pe·ri·or /səˈpi(ə)rēər/ ▶ **adj. 1** higher in status, quality, or power. **2** of high quality. **3** arrogant and conceited. ▶ **n.** a person of higher rank or status.

SYNONYMS ▶ **adj. 1 senior**, higher-ranking, higher. **2 better**, finer, higher quality, top-quality, choice, select, prime, excellent. **3 condescending**, supercilious, patronizing, haughty, disdainful, lordly, snobbish; informal high and mighty, snooty. ANTONYMS junior, inferior. ▶ **n. manager**, chief, supervisor, senior, controller, foreman; informal boss. ANTONYMS subordinate.

su·pe·ri·or·i·ty /sə,pi(ə)rēˈôritē, -ˈäritē/ ▶ **n.** the state of being superior.

SYNONYMS **supremacy**, advantage, lead, dominance, primacy, ascendancy, eminence.

su·per·la·tive /səˈpərlətiv/ ▶ **adj. 1** of the highest quality or degree. **2** (of an adjective or adverb) expressing the highest degree of a quality (e.g., *bravest*). ▶ **n.** an exaggerated expression of praise.

su·per·man /ˈso͞opər,man/ ▶ **n.** (plural **supermen**) informal a man who is unusually strong or intelligent.

su·per·mar·ket /ˈso͞opər,märkit/ ▶ **n.** a large self-service store selling foods and household goods.

su·per·mod·el /ˈso͞opər,mädl/ ▶ **n.** a very successful and famous fashion model.

su·per·nat·u·ral /,so͞opərˈnaCH(ə)rəl/ ▶ **adj.** not able to be explained by the laws of nature. ▶ **n.** (**the supernatural**) supernatural events.

SYNONYMS ▶ **adj. 1 paranormal**, psychic, magic, magical, occult, mystic, mystical. **2 ghostly**, phantom, spectral, otherworldly, unearthly.

■ **su·per·nat·u·ral·ly adv.**

su·per·no·va /'so͞opər,nōvə/ ▶ **n.** (plural **supernovae** /-,nōvē/ or **supernovas**) a star that undergoes an explosion, becoming suddenly very much brighter.

su·per·nu·mer·ar·y /,so͞opər'n(y)o͞omə,rerē/ ▶ **adj.** **1** present in more than the required number. **2** not belonging to a regular staff but employed for extra work.

su·per·pow·er /'so͞opər,pouər/ ▶ **n.** a very powerful and influential country.

su·per·script /'so͞opər,skript/ ▶ **adj.** (of a letter, figure, or symbol) printed above the line.

su·per·sede /,so͞opər'sēd/ ▶ **v.** (**supersedes**, **superseding**, **superseded**) take the place of.

SYNONYMS **replace**, take the place of, take over from, succeed, supplant.

SPELLING

Super**sede** is not derived from the same root as words like **precede** and ends with **-sede**, not **-cede**.

su·per·son·ic /,so͞opər'sänik/ ▶ **adj.** involving or flying at a speed greater than that of sound.

su·per·star /'so͞opər,stär/ ▶ **n.** a very famous and successful performer or athlete.

su·per·sti·tion /,so͞opər'stishən/ ▶ **n.** a belief in the supernatural, especially that particular things bring good or bad luck.

su·per·sti·tious /,so͞opər'stishəs/ ▶ **adj.** believing in the supernatural and in the power of particular things to bring good or bad luck. ■ **su·per·sti·tious·ly** adv.

su·per·store /'so͞opər,stôr/ ▶ **n.** a retail store with more than the average amount of space and variety of stock.

su·per·struc·ture /'so͞opər,strəkchər/ ▶ **n.** **1** a structure built on top of something else. **2** the part of a structure that is built above a supporting base or foundation.

su·per·vene /,so͞opər'vēn/ ▶ **v.** happen so as to interrupt or change an existing situation.

su·per·vise /'so͞opər,vīz/ ▶ **v.** be in charge of the carrying out of a task or the work done by a person, ensuring that everything is done correctly.

SYNONYMS **oversee**, be in charge of, superintend, preside over, direct, manage, run, look after, be responsible for, govern, keep an eye on, observe, monitor, mind.

■ **su·per·vi·sion** /,so͞opər'vizhən/ **n.** **su·per·vi·so·ry** /,so͞opər'vīzərē/ **adj.**

su·per·vi·sor /'so͞opər,vīzər/ ▶ **n.** a person who supervises.

SYNONYMS **manager**, director, overseer, controller, superintendent, governor, chief, head, foreman; informal boss.

su·pine /'so͞o,pīn/ ▶ **adj.** **1** lying face upward. **2** failing to act as a result of laziness or weakness.

SYNONYMS **1 flat on your back**, face up, flat, stretched out. **2** *a supine media* **weak**, spineless, docile, acquiescent, submissive, passive. ANTONYMS prostrate, strong.

sup·per /'səpər/ ▶ **n.** a light or informal evening meal.

sup·plant /sə'plant/ ▶ **v.** take the place of.

SYNONYMS **1 replace**, supersede, displace, take over from. **2 oust**, usurp, overthrow, remove, topple, unseat, depose, dethrone, succeed.

sup·ple /'səpəl/ ▶ **adj.** (**suppler**, **supplest**) able to bend and move parts of your body easily; flexible.

SYNONYMS **1 lithe**, lissome, willowy, flexible, agile, acrobatic, nimble. **2 pliable**, flexible, soft, bendy, workable, stretchy, springy. ANTONYMS stiff, rigid.

sup·ple·ment /'səpləmənt/ ▶ **n.** **1** a thing added to something else to improve or complete it. **2** a substance taken to remedy the deficiencies in a person's diet. **3** a separate section added to a newspaper or magazine. **4** an additional charge payable for an extra service or facility. ▶ **v.** add an extra thing or amount to.

SYNONYMS ▶ **n.** **1 extra**, add-on, accessory, adjunct. **2 surcharge**, addition, increase, increment. **3 appendix**, addendum, postscript, addition, coda. **4 pullout**, insert. ▶ **v.** **add to**, augment, increase, boost, swell, amplify, enlarge, top off.

■ **sup·ple·men·tal** /,səplə'mentl/ **adj.**

sup·ple·men·ta·ry /,səplə'mentərē/ ▶ **adj.** completing or improving something.

SYNONYMS **additional**, supplemental, extra, more, further, add-on, subsidiary, auxiliary, ancillary.

sup·pli·ant /'səplēənt/ ▶ **n.** a person who makes a humble request. ▶ **adj.** making a humble request.

sup·pli·cate /'səpli,kāt/ ▶ **v.** (**supplicates**, **supplicating**, **supplicated**) humbly ask for something. ■ **sup·pli·cant** **n.** **sup·pli·ca·tion** /,səpli'kāshən/ **n.**

sup·ply /sə'plī/ ▶ **v.** (**supplies**, **supplying**, **supplied**) provide someone with something that is needed or wanted. ▶ **n.** (plural **supplies**) **1** a stock or amount of something supplied or available. **2** the action of supplying. **3** (**supplies**) provisions and equipment necessary for a large group of people or for an expedition.

SYNONYMS ▶ **v.** **1 provide**, give, furnish, equip, contribute, donate, grant, confer, dispense. **2 satisfy**, meet, fulfill. ▶ **n.** **1 stock**, store, reserve, reservoir, stockpile, hoard, cache, fund, bank. **2** (**supplies**) **provisions**, stores, rations, food, necessities.

■ **sup·pli·er** **n.**

sup·port /sə'pôrt/ ▶ **v.** **1** carry all or part of the weight of. **2** give help, encouragement, or approval to. **3** confirm or back up. **4** provide someone with a home and the things they need in order to live. **5** like a particular sports team and watch or go to their games. ▶ **n.** **1** help, encouragement, or approval. **2** a person or thing that supports. **3** the action of supporting.

SYNONYMS ▶ **v.** **1 hold up**, bear, carry, prop up, keep up, brace, shore up, underpin, buttress, reinforce. **2 provide for**, maintain, sustain, keep, take care of, look after. **3 stand by**, defend, back, stand/stick up for, take someone's side, side with. **4 back up**, substantiate, bear out, corroborate, confirm, verify. **5 help**, aid, assist, contribute to, back, subsidize, fund, finance; informal bankroll. **6 back**, champion, favor, be in favor of, advocate, encourage, promote, endorse, espouse. ANTONYMS contradict, oppose. ▶ **n.** **1 pillar**, post, prop, upright, brace, buttress, foundation, underpinning. **2 encouragement**, friendship, backing, endorsement, help, assistance, comfort. **3 contributions**, donations, money, subsidy, funding, funds, finance, capital.

sup·port·er /sə'pôrtər/ ▶ **n.** a person who supports a political party, etc.

SYNONYMS **1 advocate**, backer, adherent, promoter, champion, defender, upholder, campaigner. **2 contributor**, donor, benefactor, sponsor, backer, patron, subscriber, well-wisher. **3 fan**, follower, enthusiast, devotee, admirer.

sup·port·ive /sə'pôrtiv/ ▶ **adj.** providing encouragement or emotional help.

SYNONYMS **encouraging**, caring, sympathetic, reassuring, understanding, concerned, helpful.

sup·pose /sə'pōz/ ▶ **v.** (**supposes**, **supposing**, **supposed**) **1** think that something is true or likely, but lack proof. **2** consider something as a possibility. **3** (**be supposed to do**) be required or expected to do.

SYNONYMS **1 assume**, presume, surmise, expect, imagine, dare say, take it, suspect, guess, conjecture. **2 hypothesize**, postulate, posit. **3** (**supposed**) **alleged**, reputed, rumored, claimed, purported.

sup·pos·ed·ly /sə'pōzidlē/ ▶ **adv.** according to what is generally believed.

sup·po·si·tion /ˌsəpə'zisʜən/ ▶ **n.** a belief that something is likely to be true.

SYNONYMS **belief**, conjecture, speculation, assumption, presumption, inference, theory, hypothesis, feeling, idea, notion, guesswork.

sup·press /sə'pres/ ▶ **v. 1** forcibly put an end to. **2** prevent from acting or developing. **3** stop something from being stated or published.

SYNONYMS **1 subdue**, crush, quell, quash, squash, stamp out, crack down on, clamp down on, put an end to. **2 restrain**, repress, hold back, control, stifle, smother, check, keep in check, curb, contain, bottle up. **3 censor**, keep secret, conceal, hide, hush up, gag, withhold, cover up, stifle. ANTONYMS encourage, reveal.

■ **sup·pres·sant** **n.** **sup·pres·sion** **n.**

SPELLING

Two **p**s: su**pp**ress.

sup·pu·rate /'səpyəˌrāt/ ▶ **v.** (**suppurates**, **suppurating**, **suppurated**) form pus.
■ **sup·pu·ra·tion** /ˌsəpyə'rāsʜən/ **n.**

su·prem·a·cist /sə'preməsist, sōō-/ ▶ **n.** a person who believes that a particular group is superior to all others.

su·prem·a·cy /sə'preməsē, sōō-/ ▶ **n.** the state of being superior to all others.

SYNONYMS **control**, power, rule, sovereignty, dominance, superiority, predominance, primacy, dominion, authority, mastery, ascendancy.

su·preme /sə'prēm, sōō-/ ▶ **adj. 1** highest in authority or rank. **2** very great or greatest; most important.

SYNONYMS **1 highest**, chief, head, top, foremost, principal, superior, premier, first, prime. **2 extraordinary**, remarkable, phenomenal, exceptional, outstanding, incomparable, unparalleled. **3** *the supreme sacrifice* **ultimate**, greatest, highest, extreme, final, last. ANTONYMS subordinate.

□ **supreme court** the highest court of law in a country or state. ■ **su·preme·ly** **adv.**

sur·charge /'sərˌcʜärj/ ▶ **n.** an extra charge or payment.

surd /sərd/ ▶ **n.** Math a number that cannot be expressed as a ratio of two whole numbers.

sure /sʜŏŏr/ ▶ **adj. 1** completely confident that you are right. **2** (**sure of** or **to do**) certain to receive, get, or do. **3** undoubtedly true. **4** steady and confident. ▶ **adv.** informal certainly.

SYNONYMS ▶ **adj. 1 certain**, positive, convinced, confident, definite, satisfied, persuaded, assured, free from doubt. **2 guaranteed**, unfailing, infallible, unerring, foolproof, certain, reliable, dependable, trustworthy, trusty; informal surefire. ANTONYMS uncertain, unlikely.

■ **sure·ness** **n.**

sure·ly /'sʜŏŏrlē/ ▶ **adv. 1** it must be true that. **2** certainly.

sur·e·ty /'sʜŏŏritē/ ▶ **n.** (plural **sureties**) **1** a person who guarantees that somebody else will do something or pay a debt. **2** money given as a guarantee that someone will do something.

surf /sərf/ ▶ **n.** the breaking of large waves on a seashore or reef. ▶ **v. 1** stand or lie on a surfboard and ride on the crest of a wave toward the shore. **2** move from site to site on the Internet. ■ **surf·er** **n.** **surf·ing** **n.**

sur·face /'sərfis/ ▶ **n. 1** the outside or top layer of something. **2** outward appearance. ▶ **v.** (**surfaces**, **surfacing**, **surfaced**) **1** rise to the surface. **2** become apparent. **3** provide a road, floor, etc., with a top layer.

SYNONYMS ▶ **n. 1 outside**, exterior, top, side, finish. **2 outward appearance**, facade, veneer. ANTONYMS inside, interior. ▶ **v. 1 come to the surface**, come up, rise. **2 emerge**, arise, appear, come to light, crop up, materialize, spring up.

surf·board /'sərfˌbôrd/ ▶ **n.** a long, narrow board used in surfing.

sur·feit /'sərfət/ ▶ **n.** an amount that is more than is needed or wanted.

SYNONYMS **excess**, surplus, too much, abundance, oversupply, superabundance, superfluity, glut. ANTONYMS lack.

surge /sərj/ ▶ **n. 1** a sudden powerful movement forward or upward. **2** a sudden increase. **3** a powerful rush of an emotion or feeling. ▶ **v.** (**surges**, **surging**, **surged**) **1** move in a surge. **2** increase suddenly and powerfully.

SYNONYMS ▶ **n. 1 gush**, rush, outpouring, stream, flow. **2** *a surge in demand* **increase**, rise, growth, upswing, upsurge, escalation, leap. ▶ **v. 1 gush**, rush, stream, flow, burst, pour, cascade, spill, sweep, roll. **2 increase**, rise, grow, leap.

sur·geon /'sərjən/ ▶ **n.** a doctor who is qualified to practice surgery.

sur·ger·y /'sərjərē/ ▶ **n.** (plural **surgeries**) medical treatment that involves cutting open the body and repairing or removing parts.

sur·gi·cal /'sərjikəl/ ▶ **adj.** relating to or used in surgery. ■ **sur·gi·cal·ly** **adv.**

sur·ly /'sərlē/ ▶ adj. (**surlier**, **surliest**) bad-tempered and unfriendly.

SYNONYMS **sullen**, sulky, moody, morose, unfriendly, unpleasant, scowling, unsmiling, bad-tempered, grumpy, gruff, churlish, ill-humored. ANTONYMS friendly.

sur·mise /sər'mīz/ ▶ v. (**surmises**, **surmising**, **surmised**) suppose something without having evidence. ▶ n. a guess.

SYNONYMS ▶ v. **guess**, conjecture, suspect, deduce, infer, conclude, theorize, speculate, assume, presume, suppose, understand, gather.

sur·mount /sər'mount/ ▶ v. **1** overcome a difficulty or obstacle. **2** stand or be placed on top of.

SYNONYMS **overcome**, prevail over, triumph over, beat, vanquish, conquer, get the better of.

sur·name /'sərˌnām/ ▶ n. an inherited name used by all the members of a family.

sur·pass /sər'pas/ ▶ v. be greater or better than.

SYNONYMS **excel**, exceed, transcend, outdo, outshine, outstrip, outclass, eclipse, improve on, top, trump, cap, beat, better, outperform.

sur·plice /'sərplis/ ▶ n. a white robe worn over a cassock by Christian ministers and people singing in church choirs.

sur·plus /'sərpləs/ ▶ n. an amount left over. ▶ adj. more than what is needed or used.

SYNONYMS ▶ n. **excess**, surfeit, superfluity, oversupply, glut, remainder, residue, remains, leftovers. ANTONYMS dearth. ▶ adj. **excess**, leftover, unused, remaining, extra, additional, spare, superfluous, redundant, unwanted, unneeded, dispensable. ANTONYMS insufficient.

sur·prise /sə(r)'prīz/ ▶ n. **1** a feeling of mild astonishment or shock caused by something unexpected. **2** an unexpected or astonishing thing. ▶ v. (**surprises**, **surprising**, **surprised**) **1** make someone feel surprise. **2** attack or discover suddenly and unexpectedly.

SYNONYMS ▶ n. **1 astonishment**, amazement, wonder, bewilderment, disbelief. **2 shock**, bolt from the blue, bombshell, revelation, rude awakening, eye-opener. ▶ v. **1 astonish**, amaze, startle, astound, stun, stagger, shock, take aback; informal bowl over, knock for a loop, floor, flabbergast. **2 take by surprise**, catch unawares, catch off guard, catch red-handed.

sur·prised /sə(r)'prīzd/ ▶ adj. feeling mild astonishment or shock.

SYNONYMS **astonished**, amazed, astounded, startled, stunned, staggered, nonplussed, shocked, taken aback, dumbfounded, speechless, thunderstruck; informal bowled over, flabbergasted.

sur·pris·ing /sə(r)'prīziNG/ ▶ adj. causing mild astonishment or shock.

SYNONYMS **unexpected**, unforeseen, astonishing, amazing, startling, astounding, staggering, incredible, extraordinary.

sur·re·al /sə'rēəl/ ▶ adj. strange and having the qualities of a dream. ■ **sur·re·al·ly** adv.

sur·re·al·ism /sə'rēəˌlizəm/ ▶ n. an artistic movement that combined normally unrelated images in a bizarre way. ■ **sur·re·al·ist** n. & adj.

sur·ren·der /sə'rendər/ ▶ v. (**surrenders**, **surrendering**, **surrendered**) **1** give in to an opponent. **2** give up a right or possession. **3** (**surrender yourself to**) abandon yourself to a powerful emotion or influence. ▶ n. an act of surrendering.

SYNONYMS ▶ v. **1 give up**, give yourself up, give in, cave in, capitulate, concede (defeat), submit, lay down your arms/weapons. **2 give up**, relinquish, renounce, cede, abdicate, forfeit, sacrifice, hand over, turn over, yield. ANTONYMS resist. ▶ n. **1 capitulation**, submission, yielding. **2 relinquishing**, renunciation, abdication, resignation.

sur·rep·ti·tious /ˌsərəp'tisHəs/ ▶ adj. done secretly.

SYNONYMS **secret**, secretive, stealthy, clandestine, sneaky, sly, furtive, covert. ANTONYMS blatant.

■ **sur·rep·ti·tious·ly** adv.

sur·ro·gate /'sərəgit, -ˌgāt/ ▶ n. a person who stands in for someone else. □ **surrogate mother** a woman who carries and gives birth to a child on behalf of another woman. ■ **sur·ro·ga·cy** /'sərəgəsē/ n.

sur·round /sə'round/ ▶ v. **1** be all around someone or something. **2** be associated with. ▶ n. **1** a border or edging. **2** (**surrounds** or **surroundings**) the conditions or area around a person or thing.

SYNONYMS ▶ v. **1 encircle**, enclose, encompass, ring, hem in, confine, cut off, besiege, trap. **2** (**surrounding**) **neighboring**, enclosing, nearby, near, local, adjoining, adjacent. ▶ n. (**surroundings**) **environment**, setting, background, backdrop, vicinity, locality, habitat.

sur·tax /'sərˌtaks/ ▶ n. an extra tax on something already taxed.

sur·ti·tle /'sərˌtītl/ ▶ n. a caption projected on a screen above the stage in an opera, translating the words that are being sung.

sur·veil·lance /sər'vāləns/ ▶ n. close observation, especially of a suspected spy or criminal.

SYNONYMS **observation**, scrutiny, watch, view, inspection, supervision, spying, espionage.

sur·vey ▶ v. /sər'vā, 'sərˌvā/ (**surveys**, **surveying**, **surveyed**) **1** look carefully and thoroughly at. **2** examine and record the features of an area of land in order to produce a map or description. **3** question a group of people to find out their opinions. ▶ n. /'sərˌvā/ **1** an investigation into the opinions or experience of a group of people, based on a series of questions. **2** a general view, examination, or description. **3** an act of surveying. **4** a map or report obtained by surveying.

SYNONYMS ▶ v. **1 look at**, look over, view, contemplate, regard, gaze at, stare at, eye, scrutinize, examine, inspect, scan, study, assess, appraise, take stock of; informal size up. **2 interview**, question, canvass, poll, investigate, research. ▶ n. **1 study**, review, overview, examination, inspection, assessment, appraisal. **2 poll**, investigation, inquiry, study, probe, questionnaire, census, research.

■ **sur·vey·or** /sər'vāər/ n.

sur·viv·al /sər'vīvəl/ ▶ n. **1** the state or fact of surviving. **2** an object or practice that has survived from an earlier time.

sur·vive /sər'vīv/ ▶ **v.** (**survives**, **surviving**, **survived**) **1** continue to live or exist. **2** remain alive after an accident or ordeal. **3** remain alive after someone has died.

SYNONYMS **1 remain alive**, live, sustain yourself, pull through, hold out, make it. **2 continue**, remain, persist, endure, live on, persevere, abide, go on, carry on. **3 outlive**, outlast, remain alive after.

sur·vi·vor /sər'vīvər/ ▶ **n.** a person who survives, especially one who remains alive after an accident or ordeal.

sus·cep·ti·bil·i·ty /sə,septə'bilitē/ ▶ **n.** (plural **susceptibilities**) the quality of being easily influenced or hurt.

sus·cep·ti·ble /sə'septəbəl/ ▶ **adj.** **1** (**susceptible to**) likely to be influenced or harmed by. **2** easily influenced by feelings or emotions.

SYNONYMS **1** (**susceptible to**) **liable to**, prone to, subject to, inclined to, predisposed to, open to, vulnerable to, an easy target for. **2 impressionable**, credulous, gullible, innocent, ingenuous, naive, easily led, defenseless, vulnerable. ANTONYMS immune, resistant.

su·shi /'sōōshē/ ▶ **n.** a Japanese dish consisting of balls of cold rice with raw seafood, vegetables, etc.

sus·pect ▶ **v.** /sə'spekt/ **1** believe something to be likely or possible. **2** believe that someone is guilty of a crime or offense, without having definite proof. **3** feel that something may not be genuine or true. ▶ **n.** /'səs,pekt/ a person suspected of a crime or offense. ▶ **adj.** /'səs,pekt/ possibly dangerous or false.

SYNONYMS ▶ **v.** **1 have a suspicion**, have a feeling, feel, be inclined to think, fancy, reckon, guess, conjecture, surmise, have a hunch, fear. **2 doubt**, distrust, mistrust, have misgivings about, have qualms about, be suspicious of, be skeptical about. ▶ **adj.** **suspicious**, dubious, doubtful, untrustworthy; informal fishy, funny.

sus·pend /sə'spend/ ▶ **v.** **1** temporarily bring a stop to something. **2** temporarily stop someone from doing their job or attending school, as a punishment or during an investigation. **3** postpone or delay an action, event, or judgment. **4** (**suspended**) (of a sentence given by a court) not enforced as long as no further offense is committed. **5** hang something in the air.

SYNONYMS **1 adjourn**, table, interrupt, break off, cut short, discontinue. **2 exclude**, debar, remove, expel, eject, rusticate. **3 hang**, sling, string, swing, dangle.

sus·pend·ers /sə'spendərz/ ▶ **n.** a pair of straps that pass over the shoulders and fasten to the waistband of a pair of trousers or a skirt at the front and back to hold the trousers or skirt up.

sus·pense /sə'spens/ ▶ **n.** a state or feeling of excited or anxious uncertainty about what may happen.

SYNONYMS **tension**, uncertainty, doubt, anticipation, excitement, anxiety, strain.

sus·pen·sion /sə'spenshən/ ▶ **n.** **1** the action of suspending or the state of being suspended. **2** a system of springs and shock absorbers that supports a vehicle on its wheels and makes it more comfortable to ride in. **3** a mixture in which particles are spread throughout a fluid. □ **suspension bridge** a bridge that is suspended from cables running between towers.

sus·pi·cion /sə'spishən/ ▶ **n.** **1** an idea that something is possible or likely or that someone has done something wrong. **2** a feeling of distrust. **3** a very slight trace.

SYNONYMS **1 intuition**, feeling, impression, inkling, hunch, fancy, notion, idea, theory, premonition; informal gut feeling. **2 misgiving**, doubt, qualm(s), reservation, hesitation, skepticism. ANTONYMS trust.

sus·pi·cious /sə'spishəs/ ▶ **adj.** **1** having a feeling that someone has done something wrong. **2** making you feel that something is wrong. **3** not able to trust other people.

SYNONYMS **1 doubtful**, unsure, dubious, wary, chary, skeptical, mistrustful. **2 suspect**, dubious, unsavory, disreputable; informal shifty, shady. **3** *suspicious circumstances* **strange**, odd, questionable, irregular, funny, doubtful, mysterious; informal fishy. ANTONYMS trusting, innocent.

■ **sus·pi·cious·ly** **adv.**

sus·tain /sə'stān/ ▶ **v.** **1** strengthen or support someone physically or mentally. **2** keep something going over time or continuously. **3** experience something unpleasant. **4** carry the weight of an object.

SYNONYMS **1 comfort**, help, assist, encourage, support, give strength to, buoy up. **2 continue**, carry on, keep up, keep alive, maintain, preserve. **3** (**sustained**) **continuous**, ongoing, steady, continual, constant, prolonged, persistent, nonstop, perpetual, relentless. **4 nourish**, feed, nurture, keep alive. **5 suffer**, experience, undergo, receive. **6 confirm**, corroborate, substantiate, bear out, prove, authenticate, back up, uphold.

sus·tain·a·ble /sə'stānəbəl/ ▶ **adj.** **1** able to be sustained. **2** (of industry, development, or agriculture) avoiding using up natural resources. ■ **sus·tain·a·bil·i·ty** /sə,stānə'bilitē/ **n.** **sus·tain·a·bly** **adv.**

sus·te·nance /'səstənəns/ ▶ **n.** **1** the food needed to keep someone alive. **2** the process of keeping something going.

SYNONYMS **nourishment**, food, nutrition, provisions, rations; informal grub, chow, vittles; literary viands; dated victuals.

su·ture /'sōōchər/ ▶ **n.** a stitch holding together the edges of a wound or surgical cut. ▶ **v.** (**sutures**, **suturing**, **sutured**) stitch up a wound or cut.

SUV ▶ **abbr.** sport utility vehicle.

su·ze·rain·ty /'sōōzərəntē, 'sōōzə,rāntē/ ▶ **n.** the right of one country to rule over another country that has its own ruler but is not fully independent.

svelte /svelt, sfelt/ ▶ **adj.** slender and elegant.

SW ▶ **abbr.** southwest or southwestern.

swab /swäb/ ▶ **n.** **1** a pad used for cleaning a wound or taking liquid from the body for testing. **2** a sample of liquid taken with a swab. ▶ **v.** (**swabs**, **swabbing**, **swabbed**) **1** clean or take liquid from a wound or part of the body with a swab. **2** wash down a surface with water and a cloth or mop.

swad·dle /'swädl/ ▶ **v.** (**swaddles**, **swaddling**, **swaddled**) wrap in clothes or a cloth. □ **swaddling clothes** (in the past) strips of cloth wrapped around a baby to calm it.

swag /swag/ ▶ **n.** **1** a curtain hanging in a drooping curve. **2** informal property stolen by a burglar.

swag·ger /ˈswagər/ ▶ **v.** (**swaggers**, **swaggering**, **swaggered**) walk or behave in a very confident or arrogant way. ▶ **n.** a swaggering walk or way of behaving.

> SYNONYMS ▶ **v.** **strut**, parade, stride, prance; informal sashay.

swain /swān/ ▶ **n.** old use **1** a young male lover. **2** a country youth.

swal·low¹ /ˈswälō/ ▶ **v.** **1** contract the muscles of the mouth and throat so that food, drink, or saliva pass down the throat. **2** (**swallow someone/thing up**) surround or cover someone or something so that they disappear. **3** believe an untrue statement without question. ▶ **n.** an act of swallowing.

> SYNONYMS ▶ **v.** **eat**, drink, gulp down, consume, devour, put away, quaff, slug; informal swig, swill, down, scarf (down).

swal·low² ▶ **n.** a fast-flying bird with a forked tail.

swam /swam/ past of **SWIM**.

swamp /swämp/ ▶ **n.** an area of boggy or marshy land. ▶ **v.** **1** flood an area with water. **2** overwhelm with too much of something.

> SYNONYMS ▶ **n.** **marsh**, bog, fen, quagmire, morass. ▶ **v.** **1** **flood**, inundate, deluge, fill. **2** *fans swamped her message board* **overwhelm**, engulf, snow under, overload, inundate, deluge.

■ **swamp·y** **adj.**

swan /swän/ ▶ **n.** a large white waterbird with a long flexible neck.

swank /swaNGk/ informal ▶ **v.** show off your achievements, knowledge, or wealth. ▶ **n.** the act of showing off.

swank·y /ˈswaNGkē/ ▶ **adj.** (**swankier**, **swankiest**) informal stylishly luxurious and expensive.

swan·song /ˈswänˌsôNG/ ▶ **n.** the final performance or activity of a person's career.

swap /swäp/ (or **swop**) ▶ **v.** (**swaps**, **swapping**, **swapped**) exchange or substitute something for something else. ▶ **n.** an act of swapping.

> SYNONYMS ▶ **v.** **exchange**, trade, barter, switch, change, replace.

sward /swôrd/ ▶ **n.** literary an area of grass.

swarm /swôrm/ ▶ **n.** **1** a large group of insects flying closely together. **2** a large number of honeybees that leave a hive with a queen in order to form a new colony. **3** a large group of people or things. ▶ **v.** **1** move in or form a swarm. **2** (**swarm with**) be crowded or overrun with. **3** (**swarm up**) climb something rapidly by gripping with your hands and feet.

> SYNONYMS ▶ **n.** **1** **hive**, flock. **2** **crowd**, horde, mob, throng, mass, army, herd, pack. ▶ **v.** **flock**, crowd, throng, surge, stream.

swarth·y /ˈswôrT͟Hē/ ▶ **adj.** (**swarthier**, **swarthiest**) having a dark skin.

> SYNONYMS **dark-skinned**, olive-skinned, dusky, tanned. ANTONYMS pale.

swash·buck·ling /ˈswôsHˌbəkliNG, ˈswäsH-/ ▶ **adj.** having many daring and romantic adventures.
■ **swash·buck·ler** **n.**

swas·ti·ka /ˈswästikə/ ▶ **n.** an ancient symbol in the form of a cross with its arms bent at a right angle, used in the 20th century as the emblem of the Nazi party.

swat /swät/ ▶ **v.** (**swats**, **swatting**, **swatted**) hit or crush something with a sharp blow from a flat object.

swatch /swäcH/ ▶ **n.** a piece of fabric used as a sample.

swath /swäTH, swôTH/ ▶ **n.** **1** a broad strip or area. **2** a row or line of grass, grain, etc., as it falls when cut down.

swathe /swäT͟H, swāT͟H/ ▶ **v.** (**swathes** /swäT͟Hz, swāT͟Hz/, **swathing**, **swathed**) wrap in several layers of fabric.

> SYNONYMS **wrap**, envelop, bandage, cover, shroud, drape, wind, enfold.

SWAT team /swät/ ▶ **n.** a group of police marksmen who specialize in high-risk tasks such as hostage rescue.

sway /swā/ ▶ **v.** **1** move slowly and rhythmically backward and forward or from side to side. **2** make someone change their opinion. ▶ **n.** **1** a swaying movement. **2** influence or control over people.

> SYNONYMS ▶ **v.** **1** **swing**, shake, undulate, move to and fro. **2** **stagger**, wobble, rock, lurch, reel, roll. **3** **influence**, affect, manipulate, bend, mold. ▶ **n.** **1** **swing**, roll, shake, undulation. **2** **power**, rule, government, sovereignty, dominion, control, jurisdiction, authority.

□ **hold sway** have power or influence.

swear /swe(ə)r/ ▶ **v.** (**swears**, **swearing**, **swore** /swôr/; past participle **sworn** /swôrn/) **1** promise something solemnly or on oath. **2** use offensive or obscene language.

> SYNONYMS **1** **promise**, vow, pledge, give your word, undertake, guarantee. **2** **insist**, declare, proclaim, assert, maintain, emphasize, stress. **3** **curse**, blaspheme, use bad language; informal cuss. **4** (**swearing**) **bad language**, cursing, blaspheming, obscenities, expletives, swear words; informal four-letter words.

□ **swear by** informal have or express great confidence in. **swear someone in** admit someone to a new post by making them take a formal oath. **swear word** an offensive or obscene word.

sweat /swet/ ▶ **n.** moisture that comes out through the pores of the skin when you are hot, making a physical effort, or anxious. ▶ **v.** (**sweats**, **sweating**, past and past participle **sweated** or **sweat**) **1** give off sweat. **2** (**sweat over**) make a lot of effort in doing something: *I've sweated over this for six months.* **3** be very anxious: *I let her sweat for a while.* **4** cook vegetables very slowly.

> SYNONYMS ▶ **v.** **1** **perspire**, drip with sweat. **2** **work**, labor, toil, slave, work your fingers to the bone.

sweat·band /ˈswetˌband/ ▶ **n.** a band of absorbent material worn around the head or wrists to soak up sweat.

sweat·er /ˈswetər/ ▶ **n.** a knitted garment, usually with long sleeves, worn over the upper body.

sweat·pants /ˈswetˌpants/ ▶ **pl.n.** loose, warm trousers, often of fleece, with an elastic or drawstring waist.

sweat·shirt /ˈswetˌsHərt/ ▶ **n.** a loose, warm shirt, usually made of fleece.

sweat·shop /'swet,SHäp/ ▶ **n.** a factory or workshop employing workers for long hours in bad conditions.

sweat·y /'swetē/ ▶ **adj.** (**sweatier**, **sweatiest**) soaked in or causing sweat.

SYNONYMS **perspiring**, sweating, clammy, sticky, moist, damp.

■ **sweat·i·ly** **adv.** **sweat·i·ness** **n.**

Swede /swēd/ ▶ **n.** a person from Sweden.

Swed·ish /'swēdiSH/ ▶ **n.** the language of Sweden. ▶ **adj.** relating to Sweden.

sweep /swēp/ ▶ **v.** (**sweeps**, **sweeping**, **swept** /swept/) **1** clean an area by brushing away dirt or litter. **2** move quickly or forcefully. **3** (**sweep something away** or **aside**) remove or abolish something quickly and suddenly. **4** search an area. ▶ **n.** **1** an act of sweeping. **2** a long, swift, curving movement. **3** a long curved stretch of road, river, etc. **4** the range or scope of something. **5** (also **chimney sweep**) a person who cleans out the soot from chimneys.

SYNONYMS ▶ **v.** **brush**, clean (up), clear (up).

sweep·er /'swēpər/ ▶ **n.** **1** a person or device that cleans by sweeping. **2** Soccer a player stationed behind the other defenders, free to defend at any point across the field.

sweep·ing /'swēpiNG/ ▶ **adj.** **1** extending or performed in a long, continuous curve. **2** wide in range or effect. **3** (of a statement) too general.

SYNONYMS **1** **extensive**, wide-ranging, broad, comprehensive, far-reaching, thorough, radical. **2** **wholesale**, blanket, general, unqualified, indiscriminate, oversimplified. ANTONYMS limited.

sweep·stakes /'swēp,stāks/ (or **sweepstake**) ▶ **n.** a form of gambling in which the winner receives all the money bet by the other players.

sweet /swēt/ ▶ **adj.** **1** having the pleasant taste characteristic of sugar. **2** having a pleasant smell. **3** pleasing or satisfying. **4** charming and endearing: *a sweet little cat*. **5** kind and thoughtful.

SYNONYMS **1** **sugary**, sweetened, sugared, honeyed, syrupy, sickly, cloying. **2** **fragrant**, aromatic, perfumed. **3** **musical**, melodious, dulcet, tuneful, soft, harmonious, silvery, mellifluous. **4** **likable**, appealing, engaging, amiable, pleasant, agreeable, kind, nice, thoughtful, considerate, delightful, lovely. **5** **cute**, lovable, adorable, endearing, charming, winsome. ANTONYMS sour, savory, disagreeable.

□ **sweet-and-sour** cooked with both sugar and vinegar. **sweet pea** a climbing plant of the pea family with colorful, sweet-smelling flowers. **sweet pepper** a large pepper with a mild or sweet flavor. **sweet potato** the pinkish-orange tuber of a tropical climbing plant, eaten as a vegetable. **sweet-talk** informal use charming or flattering words to persuade someone to do something. **sweet tooth** a great liking for sweet-tasting foods. ■ **sweet·ly** **adv.**

sweet·bread /'swēt,bred/ ▶ **n.** an animal's pancreas, eaten as food.

sweet·en /'swētn/ ▶ **v.** **1** make or become sweet or sweeter. **2** make more pleasant or acceptable.

SYNONYMS **1** **make sweet**, add sugar to, sugar. **2** **mollify**, placate, soothe, soften up, pacify, appease, win over.

sweet·en·er /'swētn-ər, 'swētnər/ ▶ **n.** **1** a substance used to sweeten food or drink. **2** informal a bribe.

sweet·heart /'swēt,härt/ ▶ **n.** a person you are in love with.

SYNONYMS **lover**, love, girlfriend, boyfriend, beloved, beau; informal steady, squeeze; literary swain.

sweet·ie /'swētē/ ▶ **n.** informal used as a term of affection.

sweet·meat /'swēt,mēt/ ▶ **n.** old use a candy or other item of sweet food.

sweet·ness /'swētnis/ ▶ **n.** the quality of being sweet. □ **sweetness and light** good-natured benevolence or harmony.

swell /swel/ ▶ **v.** (**swells**, **swelling**, **swelled**; past participle **swollen** /'swōlən/ or **swelled**) **1** become larger or more rounded. **2** increase in strength, amount, or loudness. ▶ **n.** **1** a slow, regular, rolling movement of the sea. **2** a full or gently rounded form. **3** a gradual increase in strength, amount, or loudness. ▶ **adj.** informal, dated excellent.

SYNONYMS ▶ **v.** **1** **expand**, bulge, distend, inflate, dilate, bloat, blow up, puff up, balloon, fatten, fill out. **2** **grow**, enlarge, increase, expand, rise, escalate, multiply, proliferate, snowball, mushroom. **3** (**swollen**) **distended**, bulging, inflated, dilated, bloated, puffed up, puffy, tumescent, inflamed. ANTONYMS shrink, decrease.

swell·ing /'sweliNG/ ▶ **n.** a place on the body that has swollen as a result of illness or an injury.

SYNONYMS **bump**, lump, bulge, protuberance, protrusion, distension.

swel·ter /'sweltər/ ▶ **v.** (**swelters**, **sweltering**, **sweltered**) be uncomfortably hot.

SYNONYMS (**sweltering**) **hot**, stifling, humid, sultry, sticky, muggy, close, stuffy, tropical, torrid, searing, blistering; informal boiling (hot), baking, roasting, sizzling. ANTONYMS freezing.

swept /swept/ past and past participle of **SWEEP**.

swerve /swərv/ ▶ **v.** (**swerves**, **swerving**, **swerved**) abruptly go off from a straight course. ▶ **n.** an abrupt change of course.

SYNONYMS ▶ **v.** **veer**, deviate, diverge, weave, zigzag, change direction; Sailing tack.

swift /swift/ ▶ **adj.** **1** happening quickly or promptly. **2** moving or able to move very fast. ▶ **n.** a fast-flying bird with long, slender wings.

SYNONYMS ▶ **adj.** **fast**, rapid, quick, speedy, expeditious, prompt, brisk, immediate, instant, hasty, hurried, sudden, abrupt. ANTONYMS slow, leisurely.

■ **swift·ly** **adv.** **swift·ness** **n.**

swig /swig/ ▶ **v.** (**swigs**, **swigging**, **swigged**) drink deeply and quickly. ▶ **n.** a quick, deep drink.

swill /swil/ ▶ **v.** drink greedily or in large quantities. ▶ **n.** **1** waste food mixed with water for feeding to pigs. **2** inferior liquor.

swim /swim/ ▶ **v.** (**swims**, **swimming**, **swam** /swam/; past participle **swum** /swəm/) **1** move through water using your arms and legs. **2** be covered with liquid. **3** experience a dizzy, confusing feeling. ▶ **n.** a period of swimming. ■ **swim·mer** **n.**

swim·ming·ly /'swimiNGlē/ ▶ **adv.** informal smoothly and satisfactorily.

swim·suit /ˈswim,so͞ot/ ▶ **n.** a garment worn for swimming.

swin·dle /ˈswindl/ ▶ **v.** (**swindles**, **swindling**, **swindled**) cheat someone in order to get money from them. ▶ **n.** a dishonest scheme to get money from someone.

SYNONYMS ▶ **v.** **defraud**, cheat, trick, dupe, deceive, fool, hoax, hoodwink, bamboozle; informal fleece, do, con, stiff, rip off, take for a ride, pull a fast one on, put one over on. ▶ **n.** **fraud**, trick, deception, cheat, racket; informal con, con job, rip-off.

swin·dler /ˈswindlər/ ▶ **n.** a person who uses deception to obtain money or possessions from someone.

SYNONYMS **fraudster**, fraud, (confidence) trickster, cheat, rogue, charlatan, impostor, hoaxer; informal con man, shark, hustler, phony, crook.

swine /swīn/ ▶ **n.** **1** (plural **swine**) a pig. **2** (plural **swine** or **swines**) informal an unpleasant person. ▫ **swine flu** a form of influenza that affects pigs, or a form of human influenza caused by a related virus. ▪ **swin·ish** **adj.**

swing /swiNG/ ▶ **v.** (**swings**, **swinging**, **swung** /swəNG/) **1** move backward and forward or from side to side while suspended. **2** move by grasping a support and leaping. **3** move in a smooth, curving line. **4** (**swing at**) attempt to hit. **5** change from one opinion, mood, or situation to another. **6** have a decisive influence on a vote or opinion. **7** informal succeed in bringing something about. ▶ **n.** **1** a seat suspended by ropes or chains, on which you can sit and swing backward and forward. **2** an act of swinging. **3** a clear change in public opinion. **4** a style of jazz or dance music with an easy flowing rhythm.

SYNONYMS ▶ **v.** **1** **sway**, move back and forth, oscillate, wave, rock, swivel, pivot, turn, rotate. **2** **brandish**, wave, flourish, wield. **3** **curve**, bend, veer, turn, bear, wind, twist, deviate, slew. **4** **change**, fluctuate, waver, seesaw. ▶ **n.** **1** **oscillation**, sway, wave. **2** **change**, move, turnaround, turnabout, reversal, fluctuation, variation.

swing·ing /ˈswiNGiNG/ ▶ **adj.** informal lively, exciting, and fashionable.

swipe /swīp/ informal ▶ **v.** (**swipes**, **swiping**, **swiped**) **1** hit or try to hit something with a swinging blow. **2** steal. **3** pass a swipe card through an electronic reader. ▶ **n.** a swinging blow. ▫ **swipe card** a plastic card carrying coded information that is read when the card is slid through an electronic device.

swirl /swərl/ ▶ **v.** move in a twisting or spiraling pattern. ▶ **n.** a swirling movement or pattern.

SYNONYMS ▶ **v.** **whirl**, eddy, billow, spiral, twist, twirl, circulate, revolve, spin.

▪ **swirl·y** **adj.**

swish /swiSH/ ▶ **v.** move with a soft rushing sound. ▶ **n.** a soft rushing sound or movement.

Swiss /swis/ ▶ **adj.** relating to Switzerland. ▶ **n.** (plural **Swiss**) a person from Switzerland.

switch /swiCH/ ▶ **n.** **1** a device for making and breaking an electrical connection. **2** a change or exchange. **3** a flexible shoot cut from a tree. ▶ **v.** **1** change in position, direction, or focus. **2** exchange one thing for another. **3** (**switch something off** or **on**) turn an electrical device off or on. **4** (**switch off**) informal stop paying attention.

SYNONYMS ▶ **n.** **1** **button**, lever, control. **2** **change**, move, shift, transition, transformation, reversal, turnaround, U-turn, changeover, transfer, conversion. ▶ **v.** **1** **change**, shift. **2** **exchange**, swap, interchange, change around, rotate.

▫ **switch-hitter** Baseball a batter who can hit from either side of home plate. ▪ **switch·er** **n.**

switch·back /ˈswiCH,bak/ ▶ **n.** a 180-degree bend in a road or path, especially one leading up the side of a mountain.

switch·blade /ˈswiCH,blād/ ▶ **n.** a knife with a blade that springs out from the handle when a button is pressed.

switch·board /ˈswiCH,bôrd/ ▶ **n.** a device for putting phone calls made to an organization through to the right person.

switch·yard /ˈswiCH,yärd/ ▶ **n.** a large railroad yard in which freight cars are organized into trains.

swiv·el /ˈswivəl/ ▶ **v.** (**swivels**, **swiveling**, **swiveled**) turn around a central point. ▶ **n.** a connecting device between two parts enabling one to revolve without turning the other.

swol·len /ˈswōlən/ past participle of **SWELL**.

swoon /swo͞on/ literary ▶ **v.** faint, especially from strong emotion. ▶ **n.** an act of fainting.

swoop /swo͞op/ ▶ **v.** **1** move rapidly downward through the air. **2** carry out a sudden raid. ▶ **n.** an act of swooping.

SYNONYMS ▶ **v.** **dive**, descend, pounce, sweep down, plunge, drop down.

swoosh /swo͝osH, swo͞osH/ ▶ **n.** the sound produced by a sudden rush of air or liquid. ▶ **v.** move with such a sound.

swop /swäp/ = **SWAP**.

sword /sôrd/ ▶ **n.** a weapon with a long, sharp metal blade.

SYNONYMS **blade**, foil, épée, cutlass, rapier, saber, scimitar.

sword·fish /ˈsôrd,fiSH/ ▶ **n.** (plural **swordfish** or **swordfishes**) a large sea fish with a swordlike snout.

swords·man /ˈsôrdzmən/ ▶ **n.** (plural **swordsmen**) a man who fights with a sword.

swore /swôr/ past of **SWEAR**.

sworn /swôrn/ past participle of **SWEAR** ▶ **adj.** **1** made after having sworn to tell the truth. **2** determined to remain so: *sworn enemies*.

swum /swəm/ past participle of **SWIM**.

swung /swəNG/ past and past participle of **SWING**.

syb·a·rite /ˈsibə,rīt/ ▶ **n.** a person who is very fond of luxury. ▪ **syb·a·rit·ic** /,sibəˈritik/ **adj.**

syc·a·more /ˈsikə,môr/ ▶ **n.** **1** a tree with five-pointed leaves and seeds shaped like wings. **2** a plane tree.

syc·o·phant /ˈsikəfənt, -,fant/ ▶ **n.** a person who tries to gain favor with someone important by saying flattering things to them.

SYNONYMS **toady**, flatterer; informal bootlicker, yes-man.

syc·o·phan·tic /,sikəˈfantik/ ▶ **adj.** flattering and obsequious.

SYNONYMS **obsequious**, servile, subservient, groveling, toadying, fawning, ingratiating, unctuous; informal smarmy, bootlicking.

■ **syc·o·phan·cy** /ˈsikəfənsē, ˈsikəˌfansē/ n.

syl·la·ble /ˈsiləbəl/ ▶ n. a unit of pronunciation having one vowel sound and forming all or part of a word. ■ **syl·lab·ic** /səˈlabik/ adj.

syl·la·bus /ˈsiləbəs/ ▶ n. (plural **syllabuses** or **syllabi** /-ˌbī/) all the things covered in a course of study or teaching.

syl·lo·gism /ˈsiləˌjizəm/ ▶ n. a form of reasoning in which a conclusion is drawn from two propositions.

sylph /silf/ ▶ n. **1** a slender woman or girl. **2** an imaginary spirit of the air. ■ **sylph·like** adj.

syl·van /ˈsilvən/ ▶ adj. literary having to do with woods and trees.

sym·bi·o·sis /ˌsimbēˈōsis, -bī-/ ▶ n. (plural **symbioses**/ -ˌsēz/) Biology a situation in which two living things are connected with and dependent on each other to the advantage of both. ■ **sym·bi·ot·ic** adj.

sym·bol /ˈsimbəl/ ▶ n. **1** an object, person, or event that represents something else. **2** a letter, mark, or character used as a representation of something.

> SYNONYMS **1 representation**, token, sign, emblem, figure, image, metaphor, allegory. **2 sign**, character, mark, letter. **3 logo**, emblem, badge, stamp, trademark, crest, insignia, coat of arms, seal, device, monogram, hallmark, motif.

sym·bol·ic /simˈbälik/ ▶ adj. **1** acting as a symbol. **2** involving the use of symbols or symbolism.

> SYNONYMS **1 emblematic**, representative, typical, characteristic, symptomatic. **2 figurative**, metaphorical, allegorical. ANTONYMS literal.

■ **sym·bol·i·cal·ly** adv.

sym·bol·ism /ˈsimbəˌlizəm/ ▶ n. the use of symbols to represent ideas or qualities. ■ **sym·bol·ist** n. & adj.

sym·bol·ize /ˈsimbəˌlīz/ ▶ v. (**symbolizes**, **symbolizing**, **symbolized**) **1** be a symbol of. **2** represent something by means of symbols.

> SYNONYMS **represent**, stand for, be a sign of, denote, signify, mean, indicate, convey, express, embody, epitomize, encapsulate, personify.

sym·met·ri·cal /səˈmetrikəl/ ▶ adj. exactly the same on each side.

> SYNONYMS **regular**, uniform, consistent, even, equal, balanced, proportional.

■ **sym·met·ri·cal·ly** adv.

sym·me·try /ˈsimitrē/ ▶ n. (plural **symmetries**) **1** the exact match in size or shape between two halves, parts, or sides of something. **2** the quality of being exactly the same or very similar.

sym·pa·thet·ic /ˌsimpəˈᴛʜetik/ ▶ adj. **1** feeling or showing sympathy. **2** showing approval of an idea or action. **3** pleasing or likable.

> SYNONYMS **1 compassionate**, caring, concerned, understanding, sensitive, supportive, empathetic, kindhearted, warmhearted. **2 likable**, pleasant, agreeable, congenial, companionable. ANTONYMS unsympathetic.

■ **sym·pa·thet·i·cal·ly** adv.

sym·pa·thize /ˈsimpəˌᴛʜīz/ ▶ v. (**sympathizes**, **sympathizing**, **sympathized**) **1** feel or express sympathy. **2** agree with an opinion.

> SYNONYMS **commiserate**, show concern, offer condolences; (**sympathize with**) pity, feel sorry for, feel for, identify with, understand, relate to.

sym·pa·thy /ˈsimpəᴛʜē/ ▶ n. (plural **sympathies**) **1** the feeling of being sorry for someone. **2** support for or approval of something. **3** understanding between people.

> SYNONYMS **compassion**, care, concern, commiseration, pity, condolence. ANTONYMS indifference.

□ **in sympathy** fitting in; in keeping.

> USAGE
>
> Strictly, **sympathy** does not mean the same thing as **empathy**: if you have **sympathy** for someone you feel sorry for them, whereas if you have **empathy** for them you understand and share their feelings.

sym·phon·ic /simˈfänik/ ▶ adj. having the form of a symphony.

sym·pho·ny /ˈsimfənē/ ▶ n. (plural **symphonies**) a long, elaborate piece of music for a full orchestra.

sym·po·si·um /simˈpōzēəm/ ▶ n. (plural **symposia** /-zēə/ or **symposiums**) a conference to discuss a particular academic subject.

symp·tom /ˈsim(p)təm/ ▶ n. **1** a change in the body or mind that is the sign of a disease. **2** a sign of an undesirable situation.

> SYNONYMS **indication**, indicator, manifestation, sign, mark, feature, trait, clue, hint, warning, evidence, proof.

symp·to·mat·ic /ˌsim(p)təˈmatik/ ▶ adj. acting as a symptom or sign of something: *these difficulties are symptomatic of fundamental problems.*

> SYNONYMS **indicative**, characteristic, suggestive, typical, representative, symbolic.

syn·a·gogue /ˈsinəˌgäg/ ▶ n. a building where Jews meet for worship and teaching.

syn·apse /ˈsinˌaps/ ▶ n. a connection between two nerve cells. ■ **syn·ap·tic** /səˈnaptik/ adj.

sync /siɴɢk/ (or **synch**) ▶ n. informal synchronization. □ **in** (or **out of**) **sync** working well (or badly) together.

syn·chro·mesh /ˈsiɴɢkrōˌmesʜ/ ▶ n. a system of gear changing in which the gearwheels are made to revolve at the same speed during engagement.

syn·chro·nize /ˈsiɴɢkrəˌnīz/ ▶ v. (**synchronizes**, **synchronizing**, **synchronized**) make things happen or operate at the same time or rate. ■ **syn·chro·ni·za·tion** /ˌsiɴɢkrənəˈzāsʜən/ n.

syn·chro·nous /ˈsiɴɢkrənəs/ ▶ adj. existing or happening at the same time.

syn·co·pate /ˈsiɴɢkəˌpāt/ ▶ v. (**syncopates**, **syncopating**, **syncopated**) alter the beats or accents of music so that strong beats become weak and vice versa. ■ **syn·co·pa·tion** /ˌsiɴɢkəˈpāsʜən/ n.

syn·di·cate ▶ n. /ˈsindikit/ a group of people or organizations who get together to promote a common interest. ▶ v. /ˈsindiˌkāt/ (**syndicates**, **syndicating**, **syndicated**) **1** control or manage an operation through a syndicate. **2** publish or broadcast something in a number of different ways at the same time. ■ **syn·di·ca·tion** /ˌsindiˈkāsʜən/ n.

syn·drome /ˈsinˌdrōm/ ▶ n. a set of medical symptoms that tend to occur together.

syn·er·gy /'sinərjē/ ▶ n. the working together of two or more people or things to produce a combined effect that is greater than the sum of their separate effects.

syn·od /'sinəd/ ▶ n. an official meeting of church ministers and members.

syn·o·nym /'sinəˌnim/ ▶ n. a word or phrase that means the same as another word or phrase in the same language.

syn·on·y·mous /sə'nänəməs/ ▶ adj. **1** (of a word or phrase) having the same meaning as another word or phrase in the same language. **2** closely associated.

syn·op·sis /sə'näpsis/ ▶ n. (plural **synopses** /-ˌsēz/) a brief summary or survey.

> SYNONYMS **summary**, précis, abstract, outline, rundown, roundup, abridgment.

syn·tax /'sinˌtaks/ ▶ n. the way in which words and phrases are put together to form sentences. ■ **syn·tac·tic** /sin'taktik/ adj. **syn·tac·ti·cal** /sin'taktikəl/ adj.

syn·the·sis /'sinTHəsis/ ▶ n. (plural **syntheses** /-ˌsēz/) **1** the combination of parts to form a connected whole. **2** the production of chemical compounds from simpler materials.

> SYNONYMS **combination**, union, amalgam, blend, mixture, compound, fusion, composite, alloy.

syn·the·size /'sinTHiˌsīz/ ▶ v. (**synthesizes**, **synthesizing**, **synthesized**) **1** combine parts into a connected whole. **2** make something by chemical synthesis. **3** produce sound with a synthesizer.

syn·the·siz·er /'sinTHəˌsīzər/ ▶ n. an electronic musical instrument that produces sounds by generating and combining signals of different frequencies.

syn·thet·ic /sin'THetik/ ▶ adj. **1** made by chemical synthesis, especially to imitate a natural product. **2** not genuine.

> SYNONYMS **artificial**, fake, imitation, mock, simulated, man-made, manufactured; informal pretend. ANTONYMS natural.

■ **syn·thet·i·cal·ly** adv.

sy·phon = SIPHON.

Syr·i·an /'si(ə)rēən/ ▶ n. a person from Syria. ▶ adj. relating to Syria.

sy·ringe /sə'rinj, 'sirinj/ ▶ n. a tube with a nozzle and a piston that is fitted with a hollow needle for injecting drugs or withdrawing blood.

syr·up /'sirəp, 'sər-/ ▶ n. **1** a thick sweet liquid made by dissolving sugar in boiling water. **2** a thick sweet liquid derived from a sugar-rich plant, especially sugarcane, corn, or maple. **3** a thick sweet liquid containing medicine or diluted to make a drink.

syr·up·y /'sirəpē, 'sər-/ (or **sirupy**) ▶ adj. **1** like syrup. **2** too sentimental.

sys·tem /'sistəm/ ▶ n. **1** a set of things that are connected or that work together. **2** an organized scheme or method. **3** (**the system**) the laws and rules that govern society.

> SYNONYMS **1 structure**, organization, arrangement, order, network; informal setup. **2 method**, methodology, modus operandi, technique, procedure, means, way, scheme, plan, policy, program, formula, routine. **3** (**the system**) **the establishment**, the administration, the authorities, the powers that be, bureaucracy, officialdom.

sys·tem·at·ic /ˌsistə'matik/ ▶ adj. done according to a system.

> SYNONYMS **structured**, methodical, organized, orderly, planned, regular, routine, standardized, standard, logical, coherent, consistent. ANTONYMS disorganized.

■ **sys·tem·at·i·cal·ly** adv.

sys·tem·a·tize /'sistəməˌtīz/ ▶ v. (**systematizes**, **systematizing**, **systematized**) arrange things according to an organized system.

sys·tem·ic /sə'stemik/ ▶ adj. affecting the whole of a system.

Tt

T (or **t**) ▶ **n.** (plural **Ts** or **T's**) the twentieth letter of the alphabet. ▫ **to a T** informal to perfection. **T-bone** a large piece of steak containing a T-shaped bone. **T-shirt** (or **tee shirt**) a short-sleeved casual top, having the shape of a T when spread out flat. **T-square** a T-shaped instrument for drawing or testing right angles.

tab¹ /tab/ ▶ **n.** **1** a small flap or strip of material attached to something. **2** informal a restaurant bill. ▫ **keep tabs on** informal keep a watch on.

tab² ⇨ TABULATOR.

tab³ ▶ **n.** informal a tablet containing an illegal drug.

tab·by /'tabē/ ▶ **n.** (plural **tabbies**) a gray or brownish cat with dark stripes.

tab·er·nac·le /'tabər,nakəl/ ▶ **n.** **1** a place of worship for some religions. **2** (in the Bible) a tent in which the Israelites kept the Ark of the Covenant during the Exodus.

ta·ble /'tābəl/ ▶ **n.** **1** a piece of furniture with a flat top and legs, for eating, writing, or working at. **2** a set of facts or figures arranged in rows and columns. **3** (**tables**) multiplication sums arranged in sets. ▶ **v.** (**tables**, **tabling**, **tabled**) postpone consideration of.

> SYNONYMS ▶ **n.** **chart**, diagram, figure, graphic, graph, plan, list.

▫ **table tennis** a game played with small round paddles and a small hollow ball that is hit across a table over a net. **turn the tables** reverse a situation.

tab·leau /,ta'blō/ ▶ **n.** (plural **tableaux**) a group of models or motionless figures representing a scene.

ta·ble·cloth /'tābəl,klôTH, -,kläTH/ ▶ **n.** a cloth spread over a table.

ta·ble d'hôte /,täbəl 'dōt, ,täblə, ,tabəl/ ▶ **n.** a restaurant menu or meal offered at a fixed price and with limited choices.

ta·ble·land /'tābəl,(l)and/ ▶ **n.** a plateau

ta·ble·spoon /'tābəl,spo͞on/ ▶ **n.** **1** a large spoon for serving food. **2** a unit of measure equal to 15 milliliters or 1/2 fluid ounce.

tab·let /'tablit/ ▶ **n.** **1** a pill. **2** a slab of stone or other hard material on which an inscription is written.

> SYNONYMS **1** **slab**, stone, panel, plaque, plate, sign. **2** **pill**, capsule, lozenge, pastille, drop. **3** **bar**, cake, slab, brick, block.

tab·loid /'tab,loid/ ▶ **n.** a newspaper that has small pages and is written in a popular style.

ta·boo /tə'bo͞o, ta-/ ▶ **n.** (plural **taboos**) a social custom that prevents people from doing or talking about something. ▶ **adj.** banned or restricted by social custom.

> SYNONYMS ▶ **n.** **prohibition**, proscription, veto, ban, interdict. ▶ **adj.** **forbidden**, prohibited, vetoed, banned, proscribed, outlawed, off limits, beyond the pale, unmentionable, unspeakable; informal no go. ANTONYMS acceptable.

tab·u·lar /'tabyələr/ ▶ **adj.** (of facts or figures) arranged in columns or tables.

tab·u·late /'tabyə,lāt/ ▶ **v.** (**tabulates**, **tabulating**, **tabulated**) arrange facts or figures in columns or tables. ■ **tab·u·la·tion** /,tabyə'lāSHən/ **n.**

tab·u·la·tor /'tabyəlātər/ ▶ **n.** a facility in a word-processing program, or a device on a typewriter, used for moving to fixed positions in a document when creating tables or columns.

ta·chom·e·ter /ta'kämitər, tə-/ ▶ **n.** an instrument that measures the working speed of an engine.

tach·y·car·di·a /,taki'kärdēə/ ▶ **n.** an abnormally fast heart rate.

tac·it /'tasit/ ▶ **adj.** understood or meant without being stated.

> SYNONYMS **implicit**, understood, implied, inferred, hinted, suggested, unspoken, unstated, unsaid, unexpressed, unvoiced, taken for granted, taken as read. ANTONYMS explicit.

■ **tac·it·ly** **adv.**

tac·i·turn /'tasi,tərn/ ▶ **adj.** not saying very much.

> SYNONYMS **untalkative**, uncommunicative, reticent, unforthcoming, quiet, secretive, tight-lipped, close-mouthed; silent, mute, dumb, inarticulate. ANTONYMS talkative.

■ **tac·i·tur·ni·ty** /,tasi'tərnitē/ **n.**

tack¹ /tak/ ▶ **n.** **1** a small broad-headed nail. **2** a thumbtack. **3** a long stitch used to fasten fabrics together temporarily. **4** a course of action. **5** Sailing a sailboat's course relative to the direction of the wind. ▶ **v.** **1** fasten or fix with tacks. **2** (**tack something on**) casually add something to something else. **3** change course by turning a boat's head into and through the wind. **4** make a series of such changes of course while sailing.

> SYNONYMS ▶ **n.** **pin**, nail, staple, rivet. ▶ **v.** **pin**, nail, staple, fix, fasten, attach, secure.

tack² ▶ **n.** equipment used in horse riding.

tack·le /'takəl/ ▶ **v.** (**tackles**, **tackling**, **tackled**) **1** start to deal with a problem or task. **2** confront someone about a difficult issue. **3** (in soccer, rugby, etc.) try to take the ball from or prevent the movement of an opponent. **4** (in football) stop the forward progress of (the ball carrier) by seizing them and knocking them to the ground. ▶ **n.** **1** the equipment needed for a task or sport. **2** a mechanism consisting of ropes, pulley blocks, and hooks for lifting heavy objects. **3** (in sports) an act of tackling an opponent. **4** (in football) a player who lines up inside the end along the line of scrimmage.

> SYNONYMS ▶ **v. 1 deal with**, take care of, attend to, see to, handle, manage, come to grips with, address. **2 confront**, face up to, take on, challenge, attack, grab, struggle with, intercept, block, stop, bring down, floor, fell; informal take a shot at. ▶ **n. 1 equipment**, apparatus, kit, implements, paraphernalia; informal gear. **2 interception**, challenge, block, attack.

■ **tack·ler n.**

tack·y /ˈtakē/ ▶ **adj.** (**tackier**, **tackiest**) **1** (of glue, paint, etc.) not fully dry. **2** informal showing bad taste and quality.

> SYNONYMS **1 sticky**, wet, gluey, viscous, gummy; informal gooey. **2 tawdry**, tasteless, kitsch, vulgar, crude, garish, gaudy, trashy, cheap; informal cheesy.

ta·co /ˈtäkō/ ▶ **n.** (plural **tacos**) (in Mexican cooking) a folded tortilla filled with spicy meat or beans.

tact /takt/ ▶ **n.** sensitivity and skill in dealing with other people.

> SYNONYMS **diplomacy**, sensitivity, understanding, thoughtfulness, consideration, delicacy, discretion, prudence, judiciousness, subtlety; informal savvy.

tact·ful /ˈtak(t)fəl/ ▶ **adj.** having or showing tact.

> SYNONYMS **diplomatic**, discreet, considerate, sensitive, understanding, thoughtful, delicate, judicious, subtle.

■ **tact·ful·ly adv.**

tac·tic /ˈtaktik/ ▶ **n. 1** the method you use to achieve something. **2** (**tactics**) the art of organizing and directing the movement of soldiers and equipment during a war.

> SYNONYMS **1 scheme**, plan, maneuver, method, trick, ploy. **2** (**tactics**) **strategy**, policy, campaign, game plan, planning, maneuvers, logistics.

■ **tac·ti·cian** /takˈtisHən/ **n.**

tac·ti·cal /ˈtaktikəl/ ▶ **adj. 1** planned in order to achieve a particular end. **2** (of weapons) for use in direct support of military or naval operations.

> SYNONYMS **calculated**, planned, strategic, prudent, politic, diplomatic, judicious, shrewd.

■ **tac·ti·cal·ly adv.**

tac·tile /ˈtaktl, ˈtakˌtīl/ ▶ **adj. 1** having to do with the sense of touch. **2** liking to touch other people in a friendly way.

tact·less /ˈtaktləs/ ▶ **adj.** thoughtless and insensitive.

> SYNONYMS **insensitive**, inconsiderate, thoughtless, indelicate, undiplomatic, indiscreet, unsubtle, inept, gauche, blunt.

■ **tact·less·ly adv.**

tad /tad/ ▶ **adv.** (**a tad**) informal to a small extent.

tad·pole /ˈtadˌpōl/ ▶ **n.** the larva of a frog or toad, which lives in water and has gills, a large head, and a tail.

tae kwon do /ˌtī kwän ˈdō/ ▶ **n.** a modern Korean martial art similar to karate.

taf·fe·ta /ˈtafitə/ ▶ **n.** a crisp shiny fabric.

taf·fy /ˈtafē/ ▶ **n.** (plural **taffies**) a candy similar to toffee.

tag /tag/ ▶ **n. 1** a label giving information about something. **2** an electronic device attached to someone to monitor their movements. **3** a nickname or commonly used description. **4** a nickname or identifying mark written as the signature of a graffiti artist. **5** a frequently repeated phrase. **6** a metal or plastic point at the end of a shoelace. **7** a chasing game played by children. ▶ **v.** (**tags**, **tagging**, **tagged**) **1** attach a tag to. **2** (**tag something on**) add something to the end of something else as an afterthought. **3** (**tag along**) accompany someone without being invited.

> SYNONYMS ▶ **n. label**, ticket, badge, mark, tab, sticker, docket. ▶ **v. label**, mark, ticket, identify, flag, indicate.

ta·gli·a·tel·le /ˌtälyəˈtelē/ ▶ **pl.n.** pasta in narrow ribbons.

tail /tāl/ ▶ **n. 1** the part at the rear of an animal that sticks out and can be moved. **2** the rear part of an aircraft, with the horizontal stabilizer and rudder. **3** the final, more distant, or weaker part. **4** (**tails**) the side of a coin without the image of a head on it. **5** (**tails**) informal a tailcoat. ▶ **v. 1** informal secretly follow someone. **2** (**tail off** or **away**) gradually become smaller or weaker.

> SYNONYMS ▶ **n. rear**, end, back, extremity, bottom. ANTONYMS head, front. ▶ **v. follow**, shadow, stalk, trail, track, keep under surveillance.

tail·coat /ˈtālˌkōt/ ▶ **n.** a man's formal jacket with a long skirt divided at the back into tails and cut away in front.

tail·gate /ˈtālˌgāt/ ▶ **n. 1** a hinged flap at the back of a truck or wagon. **2** the door at the back of a station wagon or hatchback.

tai·lor /ˈtālər/ ▶ **n.** a person who makes men's clothing for individual customers. ▶ **v. 1** make clothes to fit individual customers. **2** make or adapt for a particular purpose or person.

> SYNONYMS ▶ **n. outfitter**, couturier, costumier, dressmaker, fashion designer. ▶ **v. customize**, adapt, adjust, modify, change, convert, alter, mold, gear, fit, shape, tune.

□ **tailor-made** made for a particular purpose.

tai·lored /ˈtālərd/ ▶ **adj.** (of clothes) neat, fitted, and well-cut.

tail·pipe /ˈtālˌpīp/ ▶ **n.** the rear section of the exhaust pipe of a motor vehicle.

tail·spin /ˈtālˌspin/ ▶ **n.** a fast spinning motion made by a rapidly descending aircraft.

tail·wind /ˈtālˌwind/ ▶ **n.** a wind blowing from behind.

taint /tānt/ ▶ **v. 1** contaminate or pollute. **2** affect with a bad or unpleasant quality. ▶ **n.** a trace of something bad or unpleasant.

> SYNONYMS ▶ **v. 1 contaminate**, pollute, adulterate, infect, blight, spoil, soil, ruin. **2 tarnish**, sully, blacken, stain, blot, damage.

Tai·wan·ese /ˌtīwəˈnēz, -wä-, -ˈnēs/ ▶ **n.** (plural **Taiwanese**) a person from Taiwan. ▶ **adj.** relating to Taiwan.

take /tāk/ ▶ **v.** (**takes**, **taking**, **took** /to͝ok/; past participle **taken**) **1** reach for and hold. **2** occupy a place or position. **3** gain possession of by force. **4** carry or bring with you. **5** remove from a place. **6** subtract. **7** consume. **8** bring into a particular state. **9** experience or be affected by. **10** use as a route or a means of transport. **11** accept or receive. **12** require or use up. **13** act on an opportunity. **14** see or deal with in a particular way. **15** tolerate or endure. **16** study a subject. **17** do an exam or test. ▶ **n. 1** a sequence of sound or vision photographed or recorded continuously. **2** a particular approach to something. **3** an amount gained.

SYNONYMS ▶ **v. 1** *she took his hand* **grasp**, get hold of, grip, clasp, clutch, grab. **2** *he took an envelope from his pocket* **remove**, pull, draw, withdraw, extract, fish. **3 capture**, seize, catch, arrest, apprehend, take into custody, carry off, abduct. **4 steal**, remove, appropriate, make off with, pilfer, purloin; informal filch, swipe. **5** *take four from the total* **subtract**, deduct, remove, discount; informal knock off, minus. **6 occupy**, use, utilize, fill, hold, reserve, engage. **7 write**, note (down), jot (down), scribble, scrawl, record, register, document, minute. **8 bring**, carry, bear, transport, convey, move, transfer, shift, ferry; informal cart, tote. **9 escort**, accompany, help, assist, show, lead, guide, see, usher, convey. **10 travel on/by**, journey on, go via, use. **11** *I can't take much more* **endure**, bear, tolerate, stand, put up with, abide, stomach, accept, allow, countenance, support, shoulder; formal brook. ANTONYMS give, add.

□ **take after** look or behave like a parent or ancestor. **take five** informal have a short break. **take someone/thing for granted 1** be too familiar with someone or something to appreciate them properly. **2** assume that something is true. **take someone/thing in 1** cheat or deceive someone. **2** make a garment tighter by altering its seams. **3** understand something. **take it out of** exhaust the strength of. **take off 1** become airborne. **2** leave hastily. **take someone/thing on 1** employ someone. **2** undertake a task. **3** begin to have a meaning or quality. **take over** begin to have control of or responsibility for something, in place of someone else. **take to 1** get into the habit of. **2** start liking. **3** go to a place to escape danger. **take something up 1** start to do something. **2** occupy time, space, or attention. **3** pursue a matter further. **take up with** begin to associate with.

take·off /ˈtākˌôf, -ˌäf/ ▶ **n. 1** the action of becoming airborne. **2** an act of mimicking someone or something.

take·out /ˈtākˌout/ ▶ **n.** food that is cooked and sold by a restaurant or store to be eaten elsewhere.

take·o·ver /ˈtākˌōvər/ ▶ **n.** an act of taking control of something from someone else.

SYNONYMS **buyout**, purchase, acquisition, amalgamation, merger.

tak·ings /ˈtākiNGz/ ▶ **pl.n.** money received by a store for goods sold.

SYNONYMS **proceeds**, returns, receipts, earnings, winnings, pickings, spoils, profit, gain, income, revenue.

talc /talk/ ▶ **n. 1** talcum powder. **2** a soft mineral.

tal·cum pow·der /ˈtalkəm/ ▶ **n.** a powder used to make the skin feel smooth and dry.

tale /tāl/ ▶ **n. 1** a story. **2** a lie.

SYNONYMS **story**, narrative, anecdote, account, history, legend, fable, myth, saga; informal yarn.

tal·ent /ˈtalənt/ ▶ **n. 1** natural ability or skill. **2** people possessing natural ability or skill. **3** an ancient weight and unit of currency.

SYNONYMS **flair**, aptitude, facility, gift, knack, technique, bent, ability, forte, genius, brilliance.

tal·ent·ed /ˈtaləntid/ ▶ **adj.** having a natural talent or skill for something: *a talented young musician.*

SYNONYMS **gifted**, skillful, accomplished, brilliant, expert, consummate, able, proficient; informal ace. ANTONYMS inept.

tal·is·man /ˈtalismən, -iz-/ ▶ **n.** (plural **talismans**) an object thought to have magic powers and to bring good luck. ■ **tal·is·man·ic** /ˌtalizˈmanik/ **adj.**

talk /tôk/ ▶ **v. 1** speak in order to give information or express ideas or feelings. **2** be able to speak. **3** (**talk something over** or **through**) discuss something thoroughly. **4** (**talk back**) reply in a defiant or impudent way. **5** (**talk down to**) speak to someone in a superior way. **6** (**talk someone around**) persuade someone to accept or agree to something. **7** (**talk someone into** or **out of**) persuade someone to do or not to do something. ▶ **n. 1** conversation. **2** a speech or lecture. **3** (**talks**) formal discussions.

SYNONYMS ▶ **v. 1 speak**, chat, chatter, gossip, jabber, prattle; informal yak. **2** *they were able to talk in peace* **converse**, communicate, speak (to one another), confer, consult, negotiate, parley; informal have a confab. ▶ **n. 1 conversation**, chat, discussion, tête-à-tête, heart-to-heart, dialogue; informal confab, gossip. **2 chatter**, gossip, prattle, jabbering; informal yak. **3 lecture**, speech, address, discourse, oration, presentation, report, sermon. **4** (**talks**) **negotiations**, discussions, conference, summit, meeting, consultation, dialogue.

□ **you should talk** informal used to convey that a criticism made applies equally well to the person making it. **look who's talking** ⇨ YOU SHOULD TALK. **now you're talking** informal expressing enthusiastic agreement or approval. **talking-to** informal a reprimand.

talk·a·tive /ˈtôkətiv/ ▶ **adj.** fond of talking.

SYNONYMS **chatty**, garrulous, loquacious, voluble, communicative; informal mouthy. ANTONYMS taciturn.

tall /tôl/ ▶ **adj. 1** of great or more than average height. **2** measuring a stated distance from top to bottom.

SYNONYMS **1** *a tall man* **big**, large, huge, giant, lanky, gangling. **2** *tall buildings* **high**, big, lofty, towering, sky-high, gigantic, colossal. ANTONYMS short, low.

□ **a tall order** a difficult challenge. **tall ship** a sailing ship with high masts. **a tall story** (or **tale**) an account of something that seems unlikely to be true.

tal·low /ˈtalō/ ▶ **n.** a hard substance made from animal fat, used in making candles and soap.

tal·ly /ˈtalē/ ▶ **n.** (plural **tallies**) **1** a current score or amount. **2** a record of a score or amount. ▶ **v.** (**tallies**, **tallying**, **tallied**) **1** agree or correspond. **2** calculate the total number of.

SYNONYMS ▶ **n. running total**, count, record, reckoning, register, account, roll. ▶ **v. correspond**, agree, accord, concur, coincide, match, fit, be consistent, conform, equate, parallel; informal square. ANTONYMS disagree.

□ **tally-ho** a huntsman's cry to the hounds on sighting a fox.

Tal·mud /'täl,mo͝od, 'talməd/ ▶ **n.** a collection of ancient writings on Jewish law and legend.

tal·on /'talən/ ▶ **n.** a curved claw.

tam·a·rind /'tamə,rind/ ▶ **n.** a fruit with sticky brown pulp used in Asian cooking.

tam·a·risk /'tamə,risk/ ▶ **n.** a small tree with tiny leaves on slender branches.

tam·bou·rine /,tambə'rēn/ ▶ **n.** a shallow drum with metal disks around the edge, which you play by shaking or hitting with your hand.

tame /tām/ ▶ **adj.** **1** (of an animal) not dangerous or frightened of people. **2** not exciting, adventurous, or controversial. ▶ **v.** (**tames**, **taming**, **tamed**) **1** make an animal tame. **2** make less powerful and easier to control.

> SYNONYMS ▶ **adj.** **1** **domesticated**, docile, trained, gentle, mild, pet. **2** **unexciting**, uninteresting, uninspiring, uninspired, dull, bland, flat, pedestrian, humdrum, boring. ANTONYMS wild. ▶ **v.** **1** **domesticate**, break in, train. **2** *she learned to tame her emotions* **subdue**, curb, control, calm, master, moderate, discipline, overcome.

■ **tame·ly** **adv.**

tamp /tamp/ ▶ **v.** firmly ram or pack a substance into something.

tam·per /'tampər/ ▶ **v.** (**tampers**, **tampering**, **tampered**) (**tamper with**) interfere with something without permission.

> SYNONYMS **interfere**, fool, meddle, monkey around, tinker, fiddle, play; informal mess around/about.

tam·pon /'tam,pän/ ▶ **n.** a plug of soft material that a woman puts into her vagina to absorb blood during a period.

tan /tan/ ▶ **n.** **1** a golden-brown shade of skin developed by pale-skinned people after being in the sun. **2** a yellowish-brown color. ▶ **v.** (**tans**, **tanning**, **tanned**) **1** become golden-brown from being in the sun. **2** convert animal skin into leather.

tan·dem /'tandəm/ ▶ **n.** a bicycle for two riders, one sitting behind the other. ▶ **adv.** one behind another. □ **in tandem** together or at the same time.

tan·door·i /tan'do͝orē, tän-/ ▶ **adj.** (of Indian food) cooked in a clay oven called a **tandoor**.

tang /taNG/ ▶ **n.** **1** a strong flavor or smell. **2** the projection on the blade of a tool that holds it firmly in the handle.

tan·gent /'tanjənt/ ▶ **n.** **1** a straight line that touches a curve but does not cross it at that point. **2** Math (in a right triangle) the ratio of the sides opposite and adjacent to a particular angle. **3** a completely different line of thought or action: *her mind went off at a tangent.*

tan·gen·tial /tan'jenCHəl/ ▶ **adj.** **1** only slightly relevant. **2** relating to or along a tangent.

tan·ge·rine /,tanjə'rēn/ ▶ **n.** a small citrus fruit with a loose skin.

tan·gi·ble /'tanjəbəl/ ▶ **adj.** **1** able to be perceived by touch. **2** real.

> SYNONYMS **real**, actual, physical, solid, palpable, material, substantial, concrete, visible, definite, perceptible, discernible, noticeable. ANTONYMS abstract, theoretical.

■ **tan·gi·bil·i·ty** /,tanjə'bilitē/ **n.** **tan·gi·bly** **adv.**

tan·gle /'taNGgəl/ ▶ **v.** (**tangles**, **tangling**, **tangled**) **1** twist together into a knotted mass. **2** (**tangle with**) informal come into conflict with. ▶ **n.** **1** a twisted, knotted mass. **2** a muddle.

> SYNONYMS ▶ **v.** **entangle**, snarl, catch, entwine, twist, knot, mat. ▶ **n.** **1** **snarl**, mass, knot, mesh. **2** **muddle**, mix-up, confusion, jumble, shambles.

tan·go /'taNGgō/ ▶ **n.** (plural **tangos**) a South American ballroom dance with abrupt pauses. ▶ **v.** (**tangoes**, **tangoing**, **tangoed**) dance the tango.

tang·y /'taNGē/ ▶ **adj.** (**tangier**, **tangiest**) having a strong, sharp flavor or smell.

> SYNONYMS **zesty**, sharp, tart, sour, bitter, piquant, spicy, tasty, flavorsome, pungent. ANTONYMS bland.

■ **tang·i·ness** **n.**

tank /taNGk/ ▶ **n.** **1** a large container for liquid or gas. **2** the container holding the fuel supply in a vehicle. **3** a clear container for keeping pet fish. **4** a heavy armored fighting vehicle that moves on a continuous metal track.

> SYNONYMS **container**, receptacle, vat, cistern, repository, reservoir, basin.

□ **tank top** a sleeveless top worn over a shirt or blouse.

tan·kard /'taNGkərd/ ▶ **n.** a large beer mug, sometimes with a hinged lid.

tank·er /'taNGkər/ ▶ **n.** a ship, road vehicle, or aircraft for carrying liquids in bulk.

tan·ner /'tanər/ ▶ **n.** a person employed to tan animal hides.

tan·nin /'tanin/ ▶ **n.** a bitter-tasting substance present in tea, grapes, etc.

tan·ta·lize /'tantl,īz/ ▶ **v.** (**tantalizes**, **tantalizing**, **tantalized**) tease someone by showing or promising them something that they cannot have.

> SYNONYMS **tease**, torment, torture, tempt, entice, lure, beguile, excite, fascinate, titillate, intrigue.

tan·ta·mount /'tantə,mount/ ▶ **adj.** (**tantamount to**) equivalent in seriousness to.

tan·trum /'tantrəm/ ▶ **n.** an uncontrolled outburst of anger and frustration.

> SYNONYMS **fit of temper**, fit of rage, outburst, pet, paroxysm, frenzy; informal hissy fit.

Tan·za·ni·an /,tanzə'nēən/ ▶ **n.** a person from Tanzania. ▶ **adj.** relating to Tanzania.

tap[1] /tap/ ▶ **n.** a device for controlling the flow of liquid or gas from a pipe or container. ▶ **v.** (**taps**, **tapping**, **tapped**) **1** make use of a supply or resource. **2** connect a device to a telephone so as to listen to conversations secretly. **3** draw liquid from a cask, barrel, etc. **4** draw sap from a tree by cutting into it.

> SYNONYMS ▶ **n.** **faucet**, spigot, valve, stopcock. ▶ **v.** **1** **draw on**, exploit, milk, mine, use, utilize, turn to account. **2** **bug**, wiretap, monitor, eavesdrop on.

□ **on tap** **1** ready to be poured from a tap. **2** informal freely available whenever needed.

tap[2] ▶ **v.** (**taps**, **tapping**, **tapped**) hit with a quick, light blow. ▶ **n.** a quick, light blow.

> SYNONYMS ▶ **v.** **knock**, rap, strike, beat, pat, drum.

▫ **tap-dancing** a style of dancing performed in shoes with metal pieces on the toes and heels.

ta·pas /ˈtäpəs/ ▶ **pl.n.** small Spanish savory dishes served with drinks at a bar.

tape /tāp/ ▶ **n. 1** light, flexible material in a narrow strip, used to hold, fasten, or mark off something. **2** tape with magnetic properties, used for recording sound, pictures, or computer data. **3** a cassette or reel containing magnetic tape. ▶ **v.** (**tapes**, **taping**, **taped**) **1** record sound or pictures on magnetic tape. **2** fasten, attach, or mark off with tape.

> SYNONYMS ▶ **n. 1 binding**, ribbon, string, braid, band. **2 cassette**, recording, video. ▶ **v. 1 bind**, stick, fix, fasten, secure, attach. **2 record**, tape-record, video.

▫ **tape measure** a strip of tape marked for measuring the length of things. **tape recorder** a device for recording and then reproducing sounds on magnetic tape.

ta·per /ˈtāpər/ ▶ **v.** (**tapers**, **tapering**, **tapered**) **1** reduce in thickness toward one end. **2** (**taper off**) gradually lessen. ▶ **n.** a thin candle.

> SYNONYMS ▶ **v. narrow**, thin (out), come to a point, attenuate. ANTONYMS thicken.

tap·es·try /ˈtapistrē/ ▶ **n.** (plural **tapestries**) a piece of thick fabric with a design woven or embroidered on it.

tape·worm /ˈtāpˌwərm/ ▶ **n.** a long ribbonlike worm that lives as a parasite in the intestines of a person or animal.

tap·i·o·ca /ˌtapēˈōkə/ ▶ **n.** hard white grains of cassava, used for making puddings.

ta·pir /ˈtāpər/ ▶ **n.** a piglike animal with a short flexible snout.

tap·pet /ˈtapit/ ▶ **n.** a moving part in a machine that transmits motion between a cam and another part.

tar /tär/ ▶ **n. 1** a dark, thick liquid distilled from wood or coal. **2** a similar substance formed by burning tobacco. ▶ **v.** (**tars**, **tarring**, **tarred**) cover with tar.

ta·ran·tu·la /təˈranCHələ/ ▶ **n. 1** a very large hairy spider found in warm parts of America. **2** a large black spider of southern Europe.

tar·dy /ˈtärdē/ ▶ **adj.** (**tardier**, **tardiest**) formal **1** late. **2** slow to act or respond. ■ **tar·di·ly adv. tar·di·ness n.**

tare /te(ə)r/ ▶ **n.** the weight of a vehicle without its fuel or load.

tar·get /ˈtärgit/ ▶ **n. 1** a person, object, or place that is aimed at in an attack. **2** a board marked with a series of circles that you aim at in archery or shooting. **3** something that you aim to achieve. ▶ **v.** (**targets**, **targeting**, **targeted**) **1** select as an object of attention or attack. **2** aim or direct.

> SYNONYMS ▶ **n. 1 objective**, goal, aim, mark, end, plan, intention, aspiration, ambition. **2 victim**, butt, recipient, focus, object, subject. ▶ **v. 1 pick out**, single out, earmark, fix on, attack, aim at, fire at. **2** ***a product targeted at women*** **aim at**, direct at, level at, intend for, focus on.

> **SPELLING**
>
> Note that **targeted** and **targeting** have a single **t** in the middle.

tar·iff /ˈtarif/ ▶ **n. 1** a tax to be paid on a particular class of imports or exports. **2** a list of the charges made by a hotel, restaurant, etc.

> SYNONYMS **tax**, duty, toll, excise, levy, charge, rate, fee.

> **SPELLING**
>
> One **r**, double **f**: tarif**f**.

Tar·mac /ˈtärˌmak/ ▶ **n. 1** trademark a mixture of broken stone and tar used for making road surfaces. **2** (**the tarmac**) a runway or other area with a tarmac surface. ▶ **v.** (**tarmacs**, **tarmacking**, **tarmacked**) give a road or runway a tarmac surface.

tarn /tärn/ ▶ **n.** a small mountain lake.

tar·nish /ˈtärnisH/ ▶ **v. 1** make metal lose its shine by exposure to air or damp. **2** make something less respected. ▶ **n.** a film or stain formed on the exposed surface of metal.

> SYNONYMS ▶ **v. 1 discolor**, rust, oxidize, corrode, stain, dull, blacken. **2 sully**, blacken, stain, blemish, ruin, disgrace, mar, damage, harm, drag through the mud. ▶ **n. discoloration**, oxidation, rust, verdigris.

ta·rot /ˈtarō, ˈte(ə)rō, təˈrō/ ▶ **n.** a set of cards used for fortune-telling.

tarp /tärp/ ▶ **n.** informal a tarpaulin sheet or cover.

tar·pau·lin /tärˈpôlən, ˈtärpə-/ ▶ **n.** a sheet of heavy waterproof cloth.

tar·ra·gon /ˈtarəˌgän, -gən/ ▶ **n.** an herb with narrow strong-tasting leaves.

tar·ry /ˈtarē/ ▶ **v.** (**tarries**, **tarrying**, **tarried**) literary stay longer than intended.

tar·sus /ˈtärsəs/ ▶ **n.** (plural **tarsi** /ˈtärsī, -sē/) the group of small bones in the ankle and upper foot.

tart¹ /tärt/ ▶ **n.** an open pastry case containing a sweet or savory filling.

> SYNONYMS **pastry**, flan, quiche, tartlet, vol-au-vent, pie.

■ **tart·let n.**

tart² informal ▶ **n.** disapproving a promiscuous woman. ■ **tart·y adj.**

tart³ ▶ **adj. 1** sharp or acid in taste. **2** (of a remark or tone of voice) sharp or hurtful.

> SYNONYMS **1 sour**, sharp, acidic, zesty, tangy, piquant. **2 scathing**, sharp, biting, cutting, sarcastic, hurtful, spiteful. ANTONYMS sweet, kind.

■ **tart·ly adv.**

tar·tan /ˈtärtn/ ▶ **n. 1** a pattern of colored checks and intersecting lines. **2** cloth with a tartan pattern.

tar·tar¹ /ˈtärtər/ ▶ **n.** a person who is fierce or difficult to deal with. ▫ **tartar** (or **tartare**) **sauce** a sauce consisting of mayonnaise mixed with chopped onions, sweet pickles, and capers.

tar·tar² ▶ **n. 1** a hard deposit that forms on the teeth. **2** a deposit formed during the fermentation of wine.

task /task/ ▶ **n.** a piece of work to be done.

> SYNONYMS **job**, duty, chore, charge, assignment, detail, mission, engagement, occupation, undertaking, exercise.

▫ **task force 1** an armed force organized for a special operation. **2** a group of people specially organized to deal with a particular problem. **take someone to task** criticize or reprimand someone.

task·mas·ter /ˈtask,mastər/ ▶ **n.** a person who gives someone a lot of difficult tasks.

tas·sel /ˈtasəl/ ▶ **n.** a tuft of threads that are knotted together at one end. ■ **tas·seled adj.**

taste /tāst/ ▶ **n. 1** the sensation of flavor perceived in the mouth when it comes into contact with a particular substance. **2** the sense by which taste is perceived. **3** a small sample of food or drink. **4** a brief experience of something. **5** a liking for something. **6** the ability to pick out things that are of good quality or appropriate. ▶ **v.** (**tastes**, **tasting**, **tasted**) **1** have a particular flavor. **2** perceive or recognize the flavor of. **3** test the flavor of. **4** have a brief experience of.

SYNONYMS ▶ **n. 1 flavor**, savor, relish, tang. **2 mouthful**, morsel, drop, bit, sip, nip, touch, soupçon, dash. **3** *a taste for adventure* **liking**, love, fondness, fancy, desire, penchant, partiality, inclination, appetite, stomach, palate, thirst, hunger. **4** *his first taste of opera* **experience with**, impression of, exposure to, contact with, involvement with. **5 judgment**, discrimination, discernment, refinement, elegance, grace, style. **6 sensitivity**, decorum, propriety, etiquette, nicety, discretion. ▶ **v. 1** *I tasted the wine* **sample**, test, try, savor. **2** *he could taste blood* **perceive**, discern, make out, distinguish.

□ **taste bud** any of the clusters of nerve endings on the tongue and in the mouth that provide the sense of taste. ■ **tast·er n.**

taste·ful /ˈtāstfəl/ ▶ **adj.** showing good judgment of quality, appearance, or appropriate behavior.

SYNONYMS **stylish**, refined, cultured, elegant, smart, chic, exquisite. ANTONYMS tasteless.

■ **taste·ful·ly adv.**

taste·less /ˈtāstlis/ ▶ **adj. 1** having little or no flavor. **2** not showing good judgment of quality, appearance, or appropriate behavior.

SYNONYMS **1 flavorless**, bland, insipid, unappetizing, watery, weak, thin. **2 vulgar**, crude, tawdry, garish, gaudy, loud, trashy, showy, ostentatious, cheap; informal flash, tacky, kitsch. **3 crude**, indelicate, uncouth, crass, tactless, undiplomatic, indiscreet, inappropriate, offensive. ANTONYMS tasty, tasteful.

■ **taste·less·ly adv.**

tast·y /ˈtāstē/ ▶ **adj.** (**tastier**, **tastiest**) (of food) having a pleasant flavor.

SYNONYMS **delicious**, palatable, luscious, mouthwatering, delectable, appetizing, tempting; informal yummy, scrumptious. ANTONYMS bland.

tat /tat/ ▶ **v.** make knotted lace by hand with a small shuttle.

ta·ter /ˈtātər/ ▶ **n.** informal a potato.

tat·tered /ˈtatərd/ ▶ **adj.** old and torn.

tat·ters /ˈtatərz/ ▶ **pl.n.** torn pieces of cloth, paper, etc. □ **in tatters 1** torn in many places. **2** destroyed; ruined.

tat·ting /ˈtatiNG/ ▶ **n. 1** a kind of knotted lace made by hand with a small shuttle. **2** the process of making such lace.

tat·tle /ˈtatl/ ▶ **n.** gossip. ▶ **v.** (**tattles**, **tattling**, **tattled**) engage in gossip.

tat·too¹ /taˈto͞o/ ▶ **n.** (plural **tattoos**) a permanent design made on the skin with a needle and ink. ▶ **v.** (**tattoos**, **tattooing**, **tattooed**) give someone a tattoo. ■ **tat·too·ist n.**

tat·too² ▶ **n.** (plural **tattoos**) **1** an evening drum or bugle signal recalling soldiers to quarters. **2** a rhythmic tapping or drumming.

tat·ty /ˈtatē/ ▶ **adj.** (**tattier**, **tattiest**) informal worn and shabby.

taught /tôt/ past and past participle of TEACH.

taunt /tônt/ ▶ **n.** a remark made in order to anger or upset someone. ▶ **v.** anger or upset with taunts.

SYNONYMS ▶ **n. jeer**, jibe, sneer, insult, barb; informal dig, put-down; (**taunts**) teasing, provocation, goading, derision, mockery. ▶ **v. jeer at**, sneer at, scoff at, poke fun at, make fun of, get at, insult, tease, torment, ridicule, deride, mock, ride; informal rib, needle.

taupe /tōp/ ▶ **n.** a gray tinged with brown.

Tau·rus /ˈtôrəs/ ▶ **n.** a sign of the zodiac (the Bull), April 21–May 20.

taut /tôt/ ▶ **adj. 1** stretched or pulled tight. **2** (of muscles or nerves) tense.

SYNONYMS **tight**, stretched, rigid, flexed, tensed. ANTONYMS slack.

■ **taut·en v. taut·ly adv.**

tau·tol·o·gy /tôˈtäləjē/ ▶ **n.** (plural **tautologies**) the saying of the same thing twice in different words. ■ **tau·to·log·i·cal** /,tôtlˈäjikəl/ **adj. tau·tol·o·gous** /-gəs/ **adj.**

tav·ern /ˈtavərn/ ▶ **n.** an establishment for the sale of beer and other drinks to be consumed on the premises, sometimes also serving food.

taw·dry /ˈtôdrē/ ▶ **adj. 1** showy but cheap and of bad quality. **2** sleazy or unpleasant.

SYNONYMS **gaudy**, flashy, showy, garish, loud, tasteless, vulgar, trashy, cheapjack, shoddy, shabby, gimcrack; informal rubbishy, tacky, kitsch. ANTONYMS tasteful.

■ **taw·dri·ness n.**

taw·ny /ˈtônē/ ▶ **adj.** of an orange-brown or yellowish-brown color.

tax /taks/ ▶ **n.** money that must be paid to the government, charged as a proportion of income, profits, and property values, or added to the cost of some goods and services. ▶ **v. 1** impose a tax on. **2** pay tax on a vehicle. **3** make heavy demands on. **4** accuse someone of doing something wrong.

SYNONYMS ▶ **n. duty**, excise, customs, dues, levy, tariff, toll, tithe, charge. ▶ **v. strain**, stretch, overburden, overload, overwhelm, try, wear out, exhaust, sap, drain, weary, weaken.

□ **tax-deductible** allowed to be deducted from income before the amount of tax to be paid is calculated. **tax exile** a rich person who chooses to live somewhere with low rates of taxation. **tax haven** a country or independent area where low rates of taxes are charged. **tax return** a form on which a person states their income, used to assess how much tax they should pay. ■ **tax·a·ble adj.**

tax·a·tion /takˈsāSHən/ ▶ **n. 1** the imposing of tax. **2** money paid as tax.

tax·i /ˈtaksē/ ▶ **n.** (plural **taxis**) a vehicle that takes fare-paying passengers to the place of their choice. ▶ **v.** (**taxies**, **taxiing** or **taxying**, **taxied**) (of an aircraft) move slowly along the ground before takeoff or after landing. ▫ **taxi stand** a place where taxis wait to be hired.

tax·i·cab /'taksē,kab/ ▶ **n.** a taxi.

tax·i·der·my /'taksə,dərmē/ ▶ **n.** the art of preparing and stuffing the skins of dead animals so that they look like living ones. ▪ **tax·i·der·mist** **n.**

tax·ing /'taksiNG/ ▶ **adj.** physically or mentally demanding.

> SYNONYMS **demanding**, exacting, challenging, burdensome, arduous, onerous, difficult, hard, tough, laborious, back-breaking, strenuous, rigorous, punishing; tiring, exhausting, enervating, wearing, stressful. ANTONYMS easy.

tax·on·o·my /tak'sänəmē/ ▶ **n.** **1** the branch of science concerned with classification. **2** a system of classifying things. ▪ **tax·o·nom·ic** /,taksə'nämik/ **adj.**

TB ▶ **abbr.** tuberculosis.

TBA ▶ **abbr.** to be announced.

tbsp. (or **tbs.**) ▶ **abbr.** tablespoonful.

tea /tē/ ▶ **n.** **1** a hot drink made by soaking the dried leaves of an evergreen Asian shrub in boiling water. **2** the dried leaves used to make tea. **3** a light afternoon meal of sandwiches, cakes, etc., with tea to drink. ▫ **tea bag** a small porous bag containing tea leaves or powdered tea, onto which boiling water is poured in order to make a drink of tea. **tea caddy** a small container for tea.

teach /tēCH/ ▶ **v.** (**teaches**, **teaching**, **taught** /tôt/) **1** give lessons in a particular subject to a class or student. **2** show someone how to do something. **3** make someone realize or understand something.

> SYNONYMS **educate**, instruct, school, tutor, inform, coach, train, drill.

teach·er /'tēCHər/ ▶ **n.** a person who teaches in a school.

> SYNONYMS **educator**, instructor, schoolteacher, professor, tutor, governess, coach, trainer, lecturer, guide, mentor, guru; old use schoolmarm.

tea·cup /'tē,kəp/ ▶ **n.** a cup from which you drink tea.

teak /tēk/ ▶ **n.** hard wood obtained from a tree native to India and Southeast Asia.

tea·ket·tle /'tē,ketl/ ▶ **n.** a container with a lid, spout, and handle used for boiling water.

teal /tēl/ ▶ **n.** (plural **teal** or **teals**) a small freshwater duck.

team /tēm/ ▶ **n.** **1** a group of players forming one side in a game or sport. **2** two or more people working together. **3** two or more horses harnessed together to pull something. ▶ **v.** **1** (**team up**) work together to achieve a shared goal. **2** (**team something with**) wear an item of clothing with another.

> SYNONYMS ▶ **n.** **group**, squad, company, party, crew, troupe, band, side, lineup; informal bunch, gang. ▶ **v.** *ankle boots teamed with jeans* **match**, coordinate, complement, pair up.

▫ **team spirit** trust and cooperation among the members of a team.

team·mate /'tē(m),māt/ ▶ **n.** a fellow member of a team.

team·ster /'tēmstər/ ▶ **n.** **1** a truck driver. **2** a driver of a team of animals.

team·work /'tēm,wərk/ ▶ **n.** organized effort as a group.

tea·pot /'tē,pät/ ▶ **n.** a pot with a handle, spout, and lid, in which tea is made.

tear[1] /te(ə)r/ ▶ **v.** (**tears**, **tearing**, **tore** /tôr/; past participle **torn** /tôrn/) **1** rip a hole or split in. **2** (usu. **tear something up**) pull something apart or to pieces. **3** damage a muscle or ligament by overstretching it. **4** (**tear something down**) demolish or destroy something. **5** (**be torn**) be unsure about which of two options to choose. **6** informal move very quickly. **7** (**tear into**) attack verbally. ▶ **n.** a hole or split caused by tearing.

> SYNONYMS ▶ **v.** **1** **rip**, split, slit, pull apart, pull to pieces, shred, rupture, sever. **2** **lacerate**, cut (open), gash, slash, scratch, hack, pierce, stab. **3** **snatch**, grab, seize, rip, wrench, wrest, pull, pluck; informal yank. **4** (**torn**) **wavering**, vacillating, irresolute, dithering, uncertain, unsure, undecided, of two minds. ▶ **n.** **rip**, hole, split, slash, slit, run, snag.

tear[2] /ti(ə)r/ ▶ **n.** a drop of clear salty liquid produced in a person's eye when they are crying or when the eye is irritated. ▫ **tear gas** gas that causes severe irritation to the eyes, used in warfare and riot control.

tear·drop /'ti(ə)r,dräp/ ▶ **n.** a single tear.

tear·ful /'ti(ə)rfəl/ ▶ **adj.** **1** crying or about to cry. **2** causing tears.

> SYNONYMS **1** **close to tears**, emotional, upset, distressed, sad, unhappy, in tears, crying, weeping, sobbing, sniveling; informal weepy, blubbering; formal lachrymose. **2** **emotional**, upsetting, distressing, sad, heartbreaking, sorrowful, poignant, moving, touching, tear-jerking. ANTONYMS laughing, merry.

▪ **tear·ful·ly** **adv.**

tear·jerk·er /'ti(ə)r,jərkər/ ▶ **n.** informal a very sad book, movie, or song.

tea·room /'tē,ro͞om/ ▶ **n.** a small restaurant or cafe where tea and other light refreshments are served.

tease /tēz/ ▶ **v.** (**teases**, **teasing**, **teased**) **1** playfully make fun of or attempt to provoke. **2** tempt sexually. **3** (**tease something out**) find out something by searching through a mass of information. **4** gently pull tangled wool, hair, etc., into separate strands. ▶ **n.** a person who teases.

> SYNONYMS ▶ **v.** **make fun of**, laugh at, deride, mock, ridicule, make a monkey (out) of, taunt, bait, goad, pick on; informal rag, pull someone's leg.

tea·sel /'tēzəl/ (or **teazle**) ▶ **n.** a tall prickly plant with spiny flower heads.

teas·er /'tēzər/ ▶ **n.** informal a tricky question or task.

tea·spoon /'tē,spo͞on/ ▶ **n.** **1** a small spoon for adding sugar to hot drinks. **2** a measurement used in cooking, equivalent to $^1/_6$ fluid ounce, $^1/_3$ tablespoon, or 4.9 milliliters.

teat /tēt/ ▶ **n.** a nipple on an animal's udder or similar organ.

tech /tek/ ▶ **n.** informal **1** a computer expert or other technician. **2** technology.

tech·ni·cal /'teknikəl/ ▶ **adj.** **1** having to do with the techniques of a particular subject, art, or craft. **2** needing specialized knowledge. **3** having to do with the practical use of machinery and methods in science and industry. **4** according to the law or rules when applied strictly.

SYNONYMS **1 practical**, scientific, technological, high-tech. **2 specialist**, specialized, scientific, complex, complicated, esoteric.

□ **technical college** a college specializing in applied sciences and other practical subjects. ■ **tech·ni·cal·ly** adv.

tech·ni·cal·i·ty /ˌtekniˈkalitē/ ▶ n. (plural **technicalities**) **1** a small formal detail in a set of rules. **2** (**technicalities**) small details of how something works or is done. **3** the use of technical terms or methods.

tech·ni·cian /tekˈnisʜən/ ▶ n. **1** a person who looks after equipment or does practical work in a laboratory. **2** a person skilled in the technique of an art, science, craft, or sport.

Tech·ni·col·or /ˈtekniˌkələr/ ▶ n. trademark a process of producing motion pictures in color.

tech·nique /tekˈnēk/ ▶ n. **1** a particular way of carrying out a task. **2** a person's level of skill in doing something.

SYNONYMS **1 method**, approach, procedure, system, way, manner, means, strategy. **2 skill**, ability, proficiency, expertise, artistry, craftsmanship, adroitness, deftness, dexterity.

tech·no /ˈteknō/ ▶ n. a style of fast, loud electronic dance music.

tech·nol·o·gy /tekˈnäləjē/ ▶ n. (plural **technologies**) **1** the application of scientific knowledge for practical purposes. **2** machinery or equipment developed from this knowledge. **3** the branch of knowledge concerned with applied sciences. ■ **tech·no·log·i·cal** /ˌteknəˈläjikəl/ adj. **tech·no·log·i·cal·ly** /ˌteknəˈläik(ə)lē/ adv. **tech·nol·o·gist** n.

tec·ton·ic /tekˈtänik/ ▶ adj. Geology having to do with the earth's crust.

ted·dy /ˈtedē/ (or **teddy bear**) ▶ n. (plural **teddies**) a soft toy bear.

te·di·ous /ˈtēdēəs/ ▶ adj. too long, slow, or dull.

SYNONYMS **boring**, dull, monotonous, repetitive, unrelieved, unvaried, uneventful, lifeless, uninteresting, unexciting, uninspiring, lackluster, dreary, soul-destroying; informal deadly, dullsville. ANTONYMS exciting.

■ **te·di·ous·ly** adv.

te·di·um /ˈtēdēəm/ ▶ n. the state of being tedious.

SYNONYMS **monotony**, boredom, ennui, uniformity, routine, dreariness, dryness, banality, vapidity, insipidity. ANTONYMS variety.

tee /tē/ ▶ n. **1** a place on a golf course from which the ball is struck at the beginning of each hole. **2** a small peg placed in the ground to support a golf ball before it is struck from a tee. **3** a mark aimed at in lawn bowling. ▶ v. (**tees**, **teeing**, **teed**) Golf **1** (**tee up**) place the ball on a tee ready to begin a round or hole. **2** (**tee off**) begin a round or hole. □ **tee shirt** a T-shirt.

teem /tēm/ ▶ v. **1** (**teem with**) be swarming with. **2** (of rain) fall heavily.

SYNONYMS *the pond was teeming with fish* **be full of**, be alive with, be brimming with, abound in, be swarming with; be packed with, be crawling with, be overrun by, bristle with, seethe with, be thick with; informal be jam-packed with, be chock-full of.

teen /tēn/ informal ▶ adj. having to do with teenagers. ▶ n. a teenager.

teen·age /ˈtēnˌāj/ ▶ adj. **1** (also **teenaged**) aged between 13 and 19 years. **2** having to do with teenagers.

teen·ag·er /ˈtēnˌājər/ ▶ n. a person aged between 13 and 19 years.

SYNONYMS **adolescent**, youth, young person, minor, juvenile; informal teen.

teens /tēnz/ ▶ pl.n. the years of a person's age from 13 to 19.

tee·ny /ˈtēnē/ (or **teensy** /ˈtēnsē/) ▶ adj. (**teenier**, **teeniest**) informal tiny.

tee·pee = **TEPEE**.

tee·ter /ˈtētər/ ▶ v. (**teeters**, **teetering**, **teetered**) move or sway unsteadily.

SYNONYMS **1 totter**, wobble, toddle, sway, stagger, stumble, reel, lurch, pitch. **2** *the situation teetered between tragedy and farce* **seesaw**, veer, fluctuate, oscillate, swing, alternate, waver.

teeth /tēᴛʜ/ plural of **TOOTH**.

teethe /tē<u>ᴛʜ</u>/ ▶ v. (**teethes**, **teething**, **teethed**) (of a baby) develop its first teeth.

tee·to·tal /ˈtēˌtōtl/ ▶ adj. choosing not to drink alcohol.

SYNONYMS **abstinent**, abstemious, sober, dry; informal on the wagon.

■ **tee·to·tal·er** n.

Tef·lon /ˈtefˌlän/ ▶ n. trademark a tough synthetic resin used to make seals and bearings and to coat nonstick cooking utensils.

tel·e·cast /ˈteləˌkast/ ▶ n. a television broadcast. ▶ v. transmit by television.

tel·e·com·mu·ni·ca·tions /ˌteləkəˌmyo͞oniˈkāsʜənz/ ▶ n. the technology concerned with long-distance communication by means of cable, telephone, broadcasting, satellite, etc.

tel·e·gram /ˈteləˌgram/ ▶ n. a message sent by telegraph and delivered in written or printed form.

tel·e·graph /ˈteləˌgraf/ ▶ n. a system or device for transmitting messages from a distance along a wire. ▶ v. send a message to someone by telegraph. ■ **tel·e·graph·ic** /ˌteləˈgrafik/ adj.

tel·e·ki·ne·sis /ˌteləkiˈnēsis/ ▶ n. the movement of objects supposedly as a result of using mental power. ■ **tel·e·ki·net·ic** /-ˈnetik/ adj.

te·lep·a·thy /təˈlepəᴛʜē/ ▶ n. the supposed communication of thoughts or ideas by means other than the known senses. ■ **tel·e·path·ic** /ˌteləˈpaᴛʜik/ adj.

tel·e·phone /ˈteləˌfōn/ ▶ n. **1** a system for transmitting voices over a distance using wire or radio. **2** an instrument used in a telephone system for speaking into. ▶ v. (**telephones**, **telephoning**, **telephoned**) contact someone by telephone.

SYNONYMS ▶ n. **phone**, handset, receiver, cellular phone, cell phone, cordless phone; informal blower, horn. ▶ v. **phone**, call, dial; informal call up, give someone a ring/buzz, get someone on the horn.

□ **telephone pole** a tall pole used to carry telephone wires and other utility lines above the ground.

te·leph·o·ny /tə'lefənē, 'telə,fōnē/ ▶ n. the working or use of telephones.

tel·e·pho·to lens /'telə,fōtō/ ▶ n. a lens that produces a magnified image of a distant object.

tel·e·play /'telə,plā/ ▶ n. a play written or adapted for television.

Tel·e·prompt·er /'telə,präm(p)tər/ ▶ n. trademark a device used to show an actor or broadcaster their script out of sight of the audience.

tel·e·sales /'telə,sālz/ ▶ pl.n. the selling of goods or services over the telephone.

tel·e·scope /'telə,skōp/ ▶ n. an instrument designed to make distant objects appear nearer. ▶ v. (**telescopes**, **telescoping**, **telescoped**) **1** (of an object made up of several tubes) slide into itself so as to become smaller. **2** condense or combine to occupy less space or time. ■ **tel·e·scop·ic** /,telə'skäpik/ adj.

tel·e·text /'telə,tekst/ ▶ n. an information service transmitted to televisions.

tel·e·thon /'telə,THän/ ▶ n. a long television program broadcast to raise money for a charity.

tel·e·van·ge·list /,telə'vanjəlist/ ▶ n. an evangelical preacher who appears regularly on television.

tel·e·vise /'telə,vīz/ ▶ v. (**televises**, **televising**, **televised**) show on television.

tel·e·vi·sion /'telə,vizHən/ ▶ n. **1** a system for transmitting visual images with sound and displaying them electronically on a screen. **2** (also **television set**) a device with a screen for receiving television signals. **3** the activity or medium of broadcasting on television.

SYNONYMS **TV**; informal the small screen, the tube; humorous the idiot box, boob tube.

■ **tel·e·vis·u·al** /,telə'vizHo͞oəl/ adj.

tell /tel/ ▶ v. (**tells**, **telling**, **told** /tōld/) **1** communicate information to. **2** say that someone must do something. **3** relate a story. **4** (**tell on**) informal inform someone about a person's wrongdoing. **5** (**tell someone off**) reprimand someone. **6** establish that something is the case. **7** have a noticeable effect on someone.

SYNONYMS **1** *why didn't you tell me?* **inform**, notify, let know, make aware, acquaint with, advise, put in the picture, brief, fill in, alert, warn; informal clue in. **2** *she told the story slowly* **relate**, recount, narrate, report, recite, describe, sketch. **3** **instruct**, order, command, direct, charge, enjoin, call on, require. **4** *it was hard to tell what he meant* **ascertain**, determine, work out, make out, deduce, discern, perceive, see, identify, recognize, understand, comprehend; informal figure out. **5** *he couldn't tell one from the other* **distinguish**, differentiate, discriminate. **6** *the strain began to* ***tell on*** *him* **take its toll on**, leave its mark on, affect.

tell time be able to find out the time from reading the face of a clock or watch. **there is no telling** it is not possible to know what has happened or will happen. **you're telling me** informal I am in complete agreement.

tell·er /'telər/ ▶ n. **1** a person who deals with customers' transactions in a bank. **2** a person who counts votes. **3** a person who tells something.

tell·ing /'teliNG/ ▶ adj. having a striking or revealing effect.

SYNONYMS **revealing**, significant, weighty, important, meaningful, influential, striking, potent, powerful, compelling. ANTONYMS insignificant.

■ **tell·ing·ly** adv.

tell·tale /'tel,tāl/ ▶ adj. revealing or betraying something: *telltale signs of stress*. ▶ n. informal a person who reports things that other people have done wrong.

te·mer·i·ty /tə'meritē/ ▶ n. very confident behavior that other people are likely to consider rude or disrespectful.

SYNONYMS **audacity**, nerve, effrontery, impudence, impertinence, cheek, gall, presumption; daring; informal face, front, brass, chutzpah.

temp /temp/ informal ▶ n. a person who is employed on a temporary basis. ▶ v. work as a temp.

tem·per /'tempər/ ▶ n. **1** a person's state of mind. **2** a tendency to become angry easily. **3** an angry state of mind. **4** the degree of hardness of a metal. ▶ v. (**tempers**, **tempering**, **tempered**) **1** make something less extreme. **2** harden metal by heating and then cooling it.

SYNONYMS ▶ n. **1** *he walked out in a temper* **rage**, fury, fit of pique, tantrum, bad mood, pet, sulk, huff; informal hissy fit. **2** *a display of temper* **anger**, fury, rage, annoyance, irritation, pique, petulance. **3** *she struggled to keep her temper* **composure**, self-control, self-possession, calm, good humor; informal cool. ▶ v. *their idealism is tempered with realism* **moderate**, modify, modulate, mitigate, alleviate, reduce, weaken, lighten, soften.

tem·per·a /'tempərə, tem'po͝orə/ ▶ n. a method of painting with powdered colors mixed with egg yolk.

tem·per·a·ment /'temp(ə)rəmənt/ ▶ n. a person's nature in terms of the way it affects their behavior.

SYNONYMS **character**, nature, disposition, personality, makeup, constitution, temper.

tem·per·a·men·tal /,temp(ə)rə'mentl/ ▶ adj. **1** tending to have sudden or unreasonable changes of mood. **2** relating to or caused by temperament.

SYNONYMS **volatile**, excitable, emotional, unpredictable, hotheaded, quick-tempered, impatient, touchy, moody, sensitive, highly strung. ANTONYMS placid.

■ **tem·per·a·men·tal·ly** adv.

tem·per·ance /'temp(ə)rəns/ ▶ n. moderation in drinking alcohol.

tem·per·ate /'temp(ə)rət/ ▶ adj. **1** (of a region or climate) having mild temperatures. **2** showing self-control.

SYNONYMS **1** *temperate climates* **mild**, clement, benign, gentle, balmy. **2** **self-restrained**, moderate, self-controlled, disciplined; abstemious, self-denying; teetotal, abstinent. ANTONYMS extreme.

tem·per·a·ture /'temp(ə)rəCHər, -,CHo͝or/ ▶ n. **1** the degree of heat in a place, substance, or object. **2** a body temperature above the normal.

SPELLING
Write **-era-** in the middle: temp**era**ture.

tem·pest /ˈtempist/ ▶ **n.** a violent windy storm.

tem·pes·tu·ous /temˈpeschōōəs/ ▶ **adj.** **1** very stormy. **2** full of strong and changeable emotions.

SYNONYMS **turbulent**, wild, stormy, violent, emotional, passionate, impassioned, fiery, intense, uncontrolled, unrestrained. ANTONYMS calm.

tem·plate /ˈtemplət/ ▶ **n.** **1** a shaped piece of rigid material used as a pattern for cutting out, shaping, or drilling. **2** a model for others to copy.

tem·ple¹ /ˈtempəl/ ▶ **n.** a building for the worship of a god or gods.

SYNONYMS **house/place of worship**, shrine, sanctuary, church, cathedral, mosque, synagogue, house of prayer.

tem·ple² ▶ **n.** the flat part either side of the head between the forehead and the ear.

tem·po /ˈtempō/ ▶ **n.** (plural **tempos** or **tempi** /-pē/) **1** the speed at which a passage of music is played. **2** the pace of an activity or process.

tem·po·ral /ˈtemp(ə)rəl/ ▶ **adj.** **1** relating to time. **2** having to do with the physical world rather than spiritual matters. ■ **tem·po·ral·ly** **adv.**

tem·po·rar·i·ly /ˌtempəˈre(ə)rəlē/ ▶ **adv.** for a short or limited time.

SYNONYMS **1 for the time being**, for the moment, for now, for the present, provisionally, pro tem, in the interim. **2 briefly**, for a short time, momentarily, fleetingly. ANTONYMS permanently.

tem·po·rar·y /ˈtempəˌrerē/ ▶ **adj.** lasting for only a limited period.

SYNONYMS **1 provisional**, short-term, interim, makeshift, stopgap, acting, fill-in, stand-in, caretaker. **2 brief**, short-lived, momentary, fleeting, passing, ephemeral. ANTONYMS permanent, lasting.

tem·po·rize /ˈtempəˌrīz/ ▶ **v.** (**temporizes**, **temporizing**, **temporized**) delay making a decision.

tempt /tem(p)t/ ▶ **v.** **1** try to persuade someone to do something appealing but wrong. **2** (**tempting**) appealing, even if wrong or unwise: *a tempting financial offer*. **3** (**be tempted to do**) have an urge or inclination to do.

SYNONYMS **1 entice**, persuade, convince, inveigle, induce, cajole, coax, lure, attract, appeal to, tantalize, whet the appetite of, seduce; informal sweet-talk. **2** (**tempting**) **enticing**, alluring, attractive, appealing, inviting, seductive, beguiling, fascinating, mouthwatering. ANTONYMS discourage, deter.

□ **tempt fate** do something risky or dangerous. ■ **tempt·ing·ly** **adv.**

temp·ta·tion /tem(p)ˈtāshən/ ▶ **n.** **1** the action of tempting. **2** a tempting thing.

SYNONYMS **1 desire**, urge, itch, impulse, inclination. **2 lure**, allure, enticement, attraction, draw, pull.

tempt·ress /ˈtem(p)tris/ ▶ **n.** a woman who sets out to make a man desire her.

SYNONYMS **seductress**, siren, femme fatale; informal vamp.

ten /ten/ ▶ **cardinal number** one more than nine; 10. (Roman numeral: **x** or **X**) □ **Ten Commandments** (in the Bible) the ten rules of conduct given by God to Moses. **ten to one** very probably. ■ **ten·fold** /ˈtenˌfōld/ **adj. & adv.**

ten·a·ble /ˈtenəbəl/ ▶ **adj.** **1** able to be defended against attack or objection. **2** (of an academic post, grant, etc.) able to be held or used for a stated period.

SYNONYMS **defensible**, justifiable, supportable, sustainable, arguable, able to hold water, reasonable, rational, sound, viable, plausible, credible, believable, conceivable. ANTONYMS untenable.

te·na·cious /təˈnāshəs/ ▶ **adj.** **1** firmly holding on to something. **2** continuing to exist or do something for longer than might be expected.

SYNONYMS **persevering**, persistent, determined, dogged, strong-willed, indefatigable, tireless, resolute, patient, purposeful, unflagging, staunch, steadfast, untiring, unwavering, unswerving, unshakable; formal pertinacious.

■ **te·na·cious·ly** **adv.** **te·nac·i·ty** /-ˈnasitē/ **n.**

ten·an·cy /ˈtenənsē/ ▶ **n.** (plural **tenancies**) possession of land or property as a tenant.

ten·ant /ˈtenənt/ ▶ **n.** a person who rents land or property from a landlord. ▶ **v.** occupy property as a tenant.

SYNONYMS ▶ **n. occupant**, resident, inhabitant, leaseholder, lessee, lodger.

tench /tench/ ▶ **n.** (plural **tench**) a Eurosian freshwater fish of the carp family.

tend¹ /tend/ ▶ **v.** **1** frequently behave in a particular way or have certain characteristics. **2** go or move in a particular direction.

SYNONYMS **be inclined**, be apt, be disposed, be prone, be liable, be likely, have a tendency.

tend² ▶ **v.** care for or look after.

SYNONYMS *who will **tend to** the children?* **look after**, take care of, minister to, attend to, see to, watch over, keep an eye on, mind, protect, guard. ANTONYMS neglect.

ten·den·cy /ˈtendənsē/ ▶ **n.** (plural **tendencies**) an inclination to act in a particular way.

SYNONYMS **inclination**, propensity, proclivity, proneness, aptness, likelihood, bent, leaning, liability.

ten·den·tious /tenˈdenshəs/ ▶ **adj.** formal expressing a strong, often controversial, opinion.

ten·der¹ /ˈtendər/ ▶ **adj.** (**tenderer**, **tenderest**) **1** gentle and sympathetic. **2** (of food) easy to cut or chew. **3** (of a part of the body) sensitive. **4** young and vulnerable. **5** (of a plant) easily damaged by severe weather.

SYNONYMS **1** *a gentle, tender man* **caring**, kind, kindhearted, softhearted, compassionate, sympathetic, warm, gentle, mild, benevolent. **2** *a tender kiss* **affectionate**, fond, loving, romantic, emotional; informal lovey-dovey. **3 soft**, succulent, juicy, melt-in-your-mouth. **4 sore**, sensitive, inflamed, raw, painful, hurting, aching, throbbing. **5** *the tender age*

others. **4** an area in which a person has special rights, responsibilities, or knowledge.

SYNONYMS **1 region**, area, enclave, country, state, land, dependency, colony, dominion. **2** *mountainous territory* **terrain**, land, ground, countryside.

ter·ror /'terər/ ▶ **n.** **1** extreme fear. **2** a cause of terror. **3** the use of terror to intimidate people. **4** informal a person causing trouble or annoyance.

SYNONYMS **fear**, dread, horror, fright, alarm, panic, shock.

ter·ror·ism /'terəˌrizəm/ ▶ **n.** the unofficial or unauthorized use of violence and intimidation in the attempt to achieve political aims. ■ **ter·ror·ist** **n. & adj.**

ter·ror·ize /'terəˌrīz/ ▶ **v.** (**terrorizes**, **terrorizing**, **terrorized**) threaten and frighten over a period of time.

SYNONYMS **persecute**, victimize, torment, tyrannize, intimidate, menace, threaten, bully, browbeat, scare, frighten, terrify, petrify.

ter·ry /'terē/ ▶ **n.** a toweling fabric.

terse /tərs/ ▶ **adj.** (**terser**, **tersest**) using few words.

SYNONYMS **brief**, short, to the point, concise, succinct, crisp, pithy, incisive, laconic, elliptical, brusque, abrupt, curt, clipped, blunt. ANTONYMS long-winded, polite.

■ **terse·ly** **adv.**

ter·ti·ar·y /'tərsHēˌerē, -sHərē/ ▶ **adj.** third in order or level.

tes·sel·lat·ed /'tesəˌlātid/ ▶ **adj.** decorated with mosaics. ■ **tes·sel·la·tion** /ˌtesə'lāsHən/ **n.**

test /test/ ▶ **n.** **1** a procedure intended to establish how reliable or good something is, or whether something is present. **2** a short examination of skill or knowledge. **3** a medical examination of part of the body. **4** a difficult situation. ▶ **v.** **1** subject someone or something to a test. **2** make great demands on someone's endurance or patience.

SYNONYMS ▶ **n.** **1 trial**, experiment, check, examination, assessment, evaluation, appraisal, investigation. **2 exam**, examination, quiz, questionnaire. ▶ **v.** **try out**, put through its paces, experiment with, check, examine, assess, evaluate, appraise, investigate, sample; informal run it up the flagpole (and see who salutes).

□ **test case** Law a case that sets an example for future cases. **test tube** a thin glass tube used to hold material in laboratory tests. **test-tube baby** informal a baby conceived by in vitro fertilization. ■ **test·er** **n.**

tes·ta·ment /'testəmənt/ ▶ **n.** **1** a person's will. **2** evidence or proof. **3** (**Testament**) each of the two divisions of the Bible. ■ **tes·ta·men·ta·ry** /ˌtestə'men(t)ərē/ **adj.**

tes·tate /'tesˌtāt/ ▶ **adj.** having made a valid will before dying.

tes·ti·cle /'testikəl/ ▶ **n.** either of the two oval organs that produce sperm in male mammals, enclosed in the scrotum. ■ **tes·tic·u·lar** /te'stikyələr/ **adj.**

tes·ti·fy /'testəˌfī/ ▶ **v.** (**testifies**, **testifying**, **testified**) **1** give evidence as a witness in a court of law. **2** (**testify to**) be evidence or proof of.

SYNONYMS **swear**, attest, give evidence, state on oath, declare, assert, affirm.

tes·ti·mo·ni·al /ˌtestə'mōnēəl/ ▶ **n.** **1** a formal statement of a person's good character and qualifications. **2** a public tribute to someone.

SYNONYMS **reference**, (letter of) recommendation, commendation.

tes·ti·mo·ny /'testəˌmōnē/ ▶ **n.** (plural **testimonies**) **1** a formal statement, especially one given in a court of law. **2** (**testimony to**) evidence or proof of.

SYNONYMS **evidence**, sworn statement, attestation, affidavit, statement, declaration, assertion.

□ **bear testimony to** testify to.

tes·tis /'testis/ ▶ **n.** (plural **testes** /-ˌtēz/) a testicle.

tes·tos·ter·one /te'stästəˌrōn/ ▶ **n.** a hormone that stimulates the development of male physical characteristics.

tes·ty /'testē/ ▶ **adj.** (**testier**, **testiest**) easily irritated. ■ **tes·ti·ly** **adv.**

tet·a·nus /'tetn-əs/ ▶ **n.** a disease that causes the muscles to stiffen and go into spasms.

tetch·y /'tecHē/ ▶ **adj.** (**tetchier**, **tetchiest**) bad-tempered and irritable. ■ **tetch·i·ly** **adv.** **tetch·i·ness** **n.**

tête-à-tête /'tāt ə 'tāt, 'tet ə 'tet/ ▶ **n.** a private conversation between two people. ▶ **adj. & adv.** happening privately between two people.

teth·er /'teTHər/ ▶ **v.** (**tethers**, **tethering**, **tethered**) tie an animal to a post with a rope or chain. ▶ **n.** a rope or chain used to tether an animal.

SYNONYMS ▶ **v.** **tie (up)**, hitch, rope, chain; fasten, secure. ANTONYMS unleash. ▶ **n.** **rope**, chain, cord, lead, leash; restraint; halter.

tet·ra·he·dron /ˌtetrə'hēdrən/ ▶ **n.** (plural **tetrahedrons** or **tetrahedra** /-drə/) a solid figure with four triangular faces.

Tex-Mex /'teks 'meks/ ▶ **adj.** (especially of food or music) having a blend of Mexican and southwestern US features. ▶ **n.** Tex-Mex food or music.

text /tekst/ ▶ **n.** **1** a book or other written or printed work. **2** the main part of a work as distinct from illustrations, notes, etc. **3** written or printed words or computer data. **4** a text message. **5** a passage from the Bible as the subject of a sermon. ▶ **v.** send someone a text message.

SYNONYMS ▶ **n.** **1 book**, work, textbook. **2** *the pictures relate well to the text* **words**, content, body, wording, script, copy.

□ **text message** an electronic message sent and received via cell phone. ■ **tex·tu·al** /'teksCHo͞oəl/ **adj.**

text·book /'teks(t)ˌbo͝ok/ ▶ **n.** a book used for the study of a subject. ▶ **adj.** done in exactly the recommended way.

tex·tile /'tekˌstīl/ ▶ **n.** any type of cloth.

SYNONYMS **cloth**, fabric, material.

tex·ture /'teksCHər/ ▶ **n.** the feel, appearance, or consistency of a surface, substance, or fabric. ▶ **v.** (**textures**, **texturing**, **textured**) give a rough or raised texture to.

SYNONYMS ▶ **n.** **feel**, touch, appearance, finish, surface, grain, consistency.

■ **tex·tur·al** **adj.**

Thai /tī/ ▶ **n.** (plural **Thai** or **Thais**) **1** a person from Thailand. **2** the official language of Thailand.

tha·lid·o·mide /THə'lidə,mīd/ ▶ **n.** a sedative drug that was found to cause abnormalities in the fetus when taken by pregnant women.

than /THan, THən/ ▶ **conj. & prep. 1** used to introduce the second part of a comparison. **2** used to introduce an exception or contrast. **3** used in expressions indicating one thing happening immediately after another.

thane /THān/ ▶ **n.** an Anglo-Saxon or medieval Scottish landowner or nobleman.

thank /THANGk/ ▶ **v. 1** express gratitude to. **2** ironic blame or hold responsible.

SYNONYMS **express your gratitude to**, say thank you to, show your appreciation to.

□ **thank your lucky stars** feel grateful for your good fortune. **thank you** a polite expression of gratitude.

SPELLING

Thank you is a two-word phrase: don't spell it as one word.

thank·ful /'THANGkfəl/ ▶ **adj.** pleased and relieved.

SYNONYMS **grateful**, relieved, pleased, glad.

■ **thank·ful·ness n.**

thank·ful·ly /'THANGkfəlē/ ▶ **adv. 1** in a thankful way. **2** fortunately.

thank·less /'THANGklis/ ▶ **adj. 1** (of a job or task) unpleasant and unlikely to be appreciated by other people. **2** not showing or feeling gratitude.

SYNONYMS **unenviable**, difficult, unpleasant, unrewarding, unappreciated, unrecognized, unacknowledged. ANTONYMS rewarding.

thanks /THANGks/ ▶ **pl.n. 1** an expression of gratitude. **2** ⇒ **THANK YOU**.

SYNONYMS **gratitude**, appreciation, acknowledgment, recognition, credit.

□ **thanks to** due to.

thanks·giv·ing /,THANGks'giviNG/ ▶ **n. 1** the expression of gratitude to God. **2** (**Thanksgiving**) (in North America) a national holiday held in November in the United States and October in Canada.

that /THat, THət/ ▶ **pron. & determiner** (plural **those** /THōz/) **1** used to refer to a person or thing seen or heard or already mentioned or known. **2** referring to the more distant of two things. ▶ **pron.** used instead of "which," "who," "when," etc., to introduce a clause that defines or identifies something. ▶ **adv.** to such a degree; so. ▶ **conj.** introducing a statement or suggestion.

thatch /THACH/ ▶ **n.** a roof covering of straw, reeds, etc. ▶ **v.** cover with thatch. ■ **thatch·er n.**

thaw /THô/ ▶ **v. 1** make or become liquid or soft after being frozen. **2** make or become friendlier. ▶ **n. 1** a period of warmer weather that thaws ice and snow. **2** an increase in friendliness.

SYNONYMS ▶ **v. melt**, unfreeze, defrost, soften, liquefy. ANTONYMS freeze.

the /THē, THə/ ▶ **determiner 1** used to refer to one or more people or things already mentioned or easily understood; the definite article. **2** used to refer to someone or something that is the only one of its kind. **3** used to refer to something in a general rather than specific way.

the·a·ter /'THēətər/ (also **theatre**) ▶ **n. 1** a building in which plays are performed. **2** the writing and production of plays. **3** the dramatic quality of a play or event. **4** a room where specific things are done: *an operating theater*. **5** the area in which something happens: *a theater of war*.

SYNONYMS **1 playhouse**, auditorium, amphitheater; **movie theater**, movie house, cineplex, multiplex. **2 acting**, the stage, drama, dramaturgy, show business; informal showbiz. **3** *a lecture theater* **hall**, room, auditorium.

the·at·ri·cal /THē'atrikəl/ ▶ **adj. 1** having to do with acting or the theater. **2** exaggerated and too dramatic. ▶ **n.** (**theatricals**) theatrical performances or behavior.

SYNONYMS ▶ **adj. 1 stage**, dramatic, thespian, show-business; informal showbiz. **2 exaggerated**, ostentatious, stagy, melodramatic, showy, affected, overdone; informal hammy.

■ **the·at·ri·cal·i·ty** /THē,atri'kalitē/ **n.** **the·at·ri·cal·ly adv.**

the·at·rics /THē'atriks/ ▶ **n.** theatricals.

thee /THē/ old use or dialect ⇒ **YOU** (as the singular object of a verb or preposition).

theft /THeft/ ▶ **n.** the action or crime of stealing.

SYNONYMS **robbery**, stealing, larceny, shoplifting, burglary, embezzlement, raid, holdup; informal heist.

their /THe(ə)r/ ▶ **possessive determiner 1** belonging to or associated with the people or things previously mentioned or easily identified. **2** belonging to or associated with a person whose sex is not specified.

USAGE

Don't confuse **their** with **there**, which means 'in or to that place,' or with **they're**, which is short for 'they are.'

theirs /THe(ə)rz/ ▶ **possessive pron.** used to refer to something belonging to or associated with two or more people or things previously mentioned.

SPELLING

No apostrophe: **theirs**.

them /THem, THəm/ ▶ **pron. 1** used as the object of a verb or preposition to refer to two or more people or things previously mentioned or easily identified. **2** referring to a person whose sex is not specified.

the·mat·ic /THi'matik/ ▶ **adj.** arranged according to subject, or connected with a subject.
■ **the·mat·i·cal·ly adv.**

theme /THēm/ ▶ **n. 1** a subject that a person speaks, writes, or thinks about. **2** a prominent or recurring melody in a piece of music. **3** an idea that is often repeated in a work of art or literature. **4** (also **theme music**) a piece of music played at the beginning and end of a movie or program.

SYNONYMS **1 subject**, topic, argument, idea, thrust, thread, motif, keynote. **2 melody**, tune, air, motif, leitmotif.

□ **theme park** a large amusement park based on a particular idea. ■ **themed adj.**

them·self /THəm'self, THem-/ ▶ **pron.** used instead of "himself" or "herself" to refer to a person whose sex is not specified: *it makes sense for a person to save themself*.

them·selves /THəm'selvz, THem-/ ▶ **pron.** **1** used as the object of a verb or preposition to refer to a group of people or things previously mentioned as the subject of the clause. **2** they or them personally. **3** used instead of "himself" or "herself" to refer to a person whose sex is not specified.

> USAGE
> It is standard practice to use **themselves** rather than **themself** to refer to a person whose sex is not specified, e.g., *helping someone to help themselves*, not *helping someone to help themself*.

then /THen/ ▶ **adv.** **1** at that time. **2** after that. **3** also. **4** therefore.

thence /THens/ (or **from thence**) ▶ **adv.** formal **1** from a place or source previously mentioned. **2** as a consequence.

thence·forth /THens'fôrTH/ (or **thenceforward**) ▶ **adv.** formal from that time, place, or point onward.

the·oc·ra·cy /THē'äkrəsē/ ▶ **n.** (plural **theocracies**) a system of government by priests. ■ **the·o·crat·ic** /THēə'kratik/ **adj.**

the·od·o·lite /THē'ädə,līt/ ▶ **n.** an instrument used in surveying for measuring horizontal and vertical angles.

the·o·lo·gian /THēə'lōjən/ ▶ **n.** a person who is an expert in or is studying theology.

the·ol·o·gy /THē'äləjē/ ▶ **n.** (plural **theologies**) **1** the study of God and religious belief. **2** a system of religious beliefs and theory. ■ **the·o·log·i·cal** /THēə'läjikəl/ **adj.** **the·ol·o·gist** **n.**

the·o·rem /'THēərəm, 'THi(ə)r-/ ▶ **n.** a scientific or mathematical rule or proposition that can be proved by reasoning.

the·o·ret·i·cal /THēə'retikəl/ ▶ **adj.** **1** concerned with the theory of a subject rather than its practical application. **2** based on theory rather than experience or practice.

> SYNONYMS **hypothetical**, speculative, academic, conjectural, suppositional, notional, unproven. ANTONYMS actual.

■ **the·o·ret·i·cal·ly** **adv.**

the·o·re·ti·cian /,THēərə'tisHən, ,THi(ə)rə-/ ▶ **n.** a person who develops or studies the theoretical framework of a subject.

the·o·rist /'THēərist, 'THi(ə)r-/ ▶ **n.** a theoretician.

the·o·rize /'THēə,rīz, 'THi(ə)r,īz/ ▶ **v.** (**theorizes**, **theorizing**, **theorized**) form a theory or theories about something.

the·o·ry /'THēərē, 'THi(ə)rē/ ▶ **n.** (plural **theories**) **1** an idea or system of ideas intended to explain something. **2** a set of principles on which an activity is based.

> SYNONYMS **1** **hypothesis**, thesis, conjecture, supposition, speculation, postulation, proposition, premise, opinion, view, belief, contention. **2** *modern economic theory* **ideas**, concepts, philosophy, ideology, thinking, principles.

ther·a·peu·tic /,THerə'pyo͞otik/ ▶ **adj.** **1** relating to the healing of disease. **2** having a good effect on the body or mind.

> SYNONYMS **healing**, curative, remedial, medicinal, restorative, health-giving.

■ **ther·a·peu·ti·cal·ly** **adv.**

ther·a·pist /'THerəpist/ ▶ **n.** a person who treats patients through physical or psychological therapy.

> SYNONYMS **psychologist**, psychotherapist, analyst, psychoanalyst, psychiatrist, counselor; informal shrink.

ther·a·py /'THerəpē/ ▶ **n.** (plural **therapies**) **1** treatment of a physical problem or illness. **2** treatment of mental or emotional problems using psychological methods.

> SYNONYMS **1** **treatment**, remedy, cure. **2** *he's currently in therapy* **psychotherapy**, psychoanalysis, counseling.

there /THe(ə)r/ ▶ **adv.** **1** in, at, or to that place or position. **2** on that issue. □ **there is** (or **there are**) used to indicate that something exists or is true.

> USAGE
> Don't confuse **there** with **their** or **they're**: see the note at **THEIR**.

there·a·bouts /'THe(ə)rə,bouts/ ▶ **adv.** near that place, time, or amount.

there·af·ter /THe(ə)r'aftər/ ▶ **adv.** after that time.

there·by /THe(ə)r'bī/ ▶ **adv.** by that means; as a result of that.

there·fore /'THe(ə)r,fôr/ ▶ **adv.** for that reason.

> SYNONYMS **consequently**, because of that, for that reason, that being the case, so, as a result, hence, accordingly.

there·in /THe(ə)r'in/ ▶ **adv.** formal in that place, document, or respect.

there·of /THe(ə)r'əv/ ▶ **adv.** formal of the thing just mentioned.

there's /THe(ə)rz/ ▶ **contr.** **1** there is. **2** there has.

there·up·on /'THe(ə)rə,pän/ ▶ **adv.** formal immediately or shortly after that.

there·with /THe(ə)r'wiTH, -'wiTH/ ▶ **adv.** old use or formal **1** with or in the thing mentioned. **2** soon or immediately after that.

ther·mal /'THərməl/ ▶ **adj.** **1** relating to heat. **2** (of a garment) designed to keep the body warm by stopping heat from escaping. ▶ **n.** an upward current of warm air. ■ **ther·mal·ly** **adv.**

ther·mo·dy·nam·ics /,THərmōdī'namiks/ ▶ **n.** the study of the relationship between heat and other forms of energy. ■ **ther·mo·dy·nam·ic** **adj.**

ther·mom·e·ter /THər'mämitər/ ▶ **n.** an instrument for measuring temperature, usually containing mercury or alcohol that expands when heated.

ther·mo·nu·cle·ar /,THərmō'n(y)o͞oklēər, -kli(ə)r/ ▶ **adj.** relating to or using nuclear fusion reactions that occur at very high temperatures.

ther·mo·plas·tic /,THərmə'plastik/ ▶ **adj.** (of a substance) becoming plastic when heated.

Ther·mos /'THərməs/ (also **thermos bottle**) ▶ **n.** trademark a container that keeps a drink or other fluid hot or cold by means of a double wall enclosing a vacuum.

ther·mo·stat /'THərmə,stat/ ▶ **n.** a device that automatically controls temperature or activates a device at a set temperature. ■ **ther·mo·stat·ic** /,THərmə'statik/ **adj.** **ther·mo·stat·i·cal·ly** /,THərmə'statik(ə)lē/ **adv.**

the·sau·rus /THəˈsôrəs/ ▶ **n.** (plural **thesauri** /-ˈsôrī/ or **thesauruses**) a book containing lists of words that have the same or a similar meaning.

these /THēz/ plural of **THIS**.

the·sis /ˈTHēsis/ ▶ **n.** (plural **theses** /-sēz/) **1** a statement or theory that is put forward to be supported or proved. **2** a long piece of work involving research, written by a candidate for a college degree.

> SYNONYMS **1 theory**, contention, argument, proposal, proposition, premise, assumption, supposition, hypothesis. **2 dissertation**, essay, paper, treatise, composition, theme (paper), study.

thes·pi·an /ˈTHespēən/ ▶ **n.** an actor or actress. ▶ **adj.** relating to drama and the theater.

they /THā/ ▶ **pron. 1** used to refer to two or more people or things previously mentioned or easily identified. **2** people in general. **3** used to refer to a person whose sex is not specified (in place of either "he" or "he or she").

they'd /THād/ ▶ **contr. 1** they had. **2** they would.

they'll /THāl/ ▶ **contr. 1** they shall. **2** they will.

they're /THe(ə)r/ ▶ **contr.** they are.

> USAGE
>
> Don't confuse **they're** with **their** or **there**: see the note at **THEIR**.

they've /THāv/ ▶ **contr.** they have.

thi·a·mine /ˈTHīəmin, -mēn/ (or **thiamin**) ▶ **n.** vitamin B_1, found in grains, nuts, beans, and liver.

thick /THik/ ▶ **adj. 1** with opposite sides or surfaces relatively far apart. **2** (of a garment or fabric) made of heavy material. **3** made up of a large number of things or people close together. **4** (**thick with**) filled or covered with. **5** (of the air or atmosphere) difficult to see through or breathe. **6** (of something liquid or semiliquid) relatively firm in consistency. **7** informal stupid. **8** (of a voice) hoarse or husky. **9** (of an accent) strong and difficult to understand. **10** informal having a very close, friendly relationship. ▶ **n.** (**the thick**) the middle or the busiest part.

> SYNONYMS ▶ **adj. 1 broad**, wide, deep, stout, bulky, hefty, chunky, solid, plump. **2 plentiful**, abundant, profuse, luxuriant, bushy, rich, riotous, exuberant, rank, rampant, dense; informal jungly. **3 semisolid**, firm, stiff, heavy, viscous, gelatinous. **4** *thick fog* **dense**, heavy, opaque, impenetrable, soupy, murky. ANTONYMS thin, slender, sparse.

□ **(as) thick as thieves** informal very close or friendly. **through thick and thin** in all circumstances. ■ **thick·ly adv.**

thick·en /ˈTHikən/ ▶ **v.** make or become thick or thicker.

> SYNONYMS **stiffen**, condense, solidify, set, gel, congeal, clot, coagulate.

thick·et /ˈTHikit/ ▶ **n.** a dense group of bushes or trees.

thick·ness /ˈTHiknis/ ▶ **n. 1** the distance through an object, as distinct from width or height. **2** the state or quality of being thick. **3** a layer of material.

thick·set /ˈTHikˌset/ ▶ **adj.** heavily built.

thief /THēf/ ▶ **n.** (plural **thieves** /THēvz/) a person who steals another person's property.

> SYNONYMS **robber**, burglar, housebreaker, shoplifter, pickpocket, mugger, kleptomaniac; informal crook.

> SPELLING
>
> Thief follows the rule **i** before **e**.

thieve /THēv/ ▶ **v.** (**thieves**, **thieving**, **thieved**) steal things.

> SYNONYMS **steal**, take, purloin, help yourself to, snatch, pilfer, embezzle, misappropriate; informal rob, swipe, nab, lift.

thiev·er·y /ˈTHēv(ə)rē/ ▶ **n.** the action of stealing another person's property.

thigh /THī/ ▶ **n.** the part of the leg between the hip and the knee.

thim·ble /ˈTHimbəl/ ▶ **n.** a small covering that you wear to protect the end of the finger and push the needle in sewing.

thin /THin/ ▶ **adj.** (**thinner**, **thinnest**) **1** having opposite surfaces or sides close together. **2** (of a garment or fabric) made of light material. **3** having little flesh or fat on the body. **4** having few parts or members in relation to the area covered or filled. **5** not dense or heavy. **6** containing a lot of liquid and not much solid substance. **7** (of a sound) faint and high-pitched. **8** weak and inadequate. ▶ **v.** (**thins**, **thinning**, **thinned**) (often **thin out**) make or become less thick or dense.

> SYNONYMS ▶ **adj. 1 narrow**, fine, attenuated. **2 lightweight**, light, fine, delicate, flimsy, diaphanous, gauzy, gossamer, sheer, filmy, transparent, see-through. **3 slim**, lean, slender, willowy, svelte, sylphlike, spare, slight, skinny, underweight, scrawny, scraggy, bony, gaunt, emaciated, skeletal, lanky, spindly, gangly; informal anorexic. **4 watery**, weak, runny, sloppy. ANTONYMS thick, broad, fat. ▶ **v. 1 dilute**, water down, weaken. **2** *the crowds thinned out* **disperse**, dissipate, scatter. ANTONYMS thicken.

■ **thin·ly adv. thin·ness n.**

thine /THīn/ ▶ **pron. & possessive determiner** old use your or yours.

thing /THiNG/ ▶ **n. 1** an inanimate object. **2** an unspecified object, action, activity, etc. **3** (**your things**) personal belongings. **4** (**the thing**) informal what is needed or required. **5** (**your thing**) informal your special interest.

> SYNONYMS **1 object**, article, item, artifact, commodity; informal doodad, whatsit. **2** (**things**) **belongings**, possessions, stuff, property, worldly goods, goods and chattels, effects, paraphernalia, bits and pieces, luggage, baggage; informal gear, junk. **3** (**things**) **equipment**, apparatus, gear, kit, tackle, stuff, implements, tools, utensils, impedimenta, accoutrements.

thing·a·ma·jig /ˈTHiNGəməˌjig/ (also **thing·a·ma·bob** /-ˌbäb/) ▶ **n.** informal a person or thing whose name you have forgotten or do not know.

think /THiNGk/ ▶ **v.** (**thinks**, **thinking**, **thought** /THôt/) **1** have a particular opinion, belief, or idea. **2** use or direct your mind. **3** (**think of** or **about**) take into account or consideration. **4** intend. **5** (**think something over**) consider something carefully. **6** (**think something up**) informal invent something. ▶ **n.** an act of thinking.

SYNONYMS ▶ v. **1 believe**, be of the opinion, be of the view, be under the impression, expect, imagine, anticipate, suppose, guess, fancy; informal reckon, figure. **2** *his family was thought to be rich* **consider to be**, judge to be, hold to be, reckon to be, deem to be, presume to be, estimate to be, regard as being, view as being. **3 ponder**, reflect, deliberate, consider, meditate, contemplate, muse, ruminate, brood; formal cogitate. **4** *she thought of all the visits she had made* **recall**, remember, recollect, call to mind, imagine, picture, visualize, envisage.

□ **think better of** reconsider and decide not to do. **think tank** a group of experts providing advice and ideas. **think twice** consider a course of action carefully before embarking on it.

think·er /ˈTHiNGkər/ ▶ n. a person who thinks deeply and seriously.

SYNONYMS **intellectual**, philosopher, scholar, sage, ideologist, theorist, intellect, mind; informal brain.

think·ing /ˈTHiNGkiNG/ ▶ adj. using thought or rational judgment; intelligent. ▶ n. a person's ideas or opinions.

SYNONYMS ▶ adj. **intelligent**, sensible, reasonable, rational, logical, analytical, thoughtful. ▶ n. **reasoning**, idea(s), theory, thoughts, philosophy, beliefs, opinion(s), view(s).

thin·ner /ˈTHinər/ ▶ n. a solvent used to thin paint or other solutions.

third /THərd/ ▶ ordinal number **1** that is number three in a sequence; 3rd. **2** (**a third** or **one third**) each of three equal parts into which something is divided. □ **third-degree** (of burns) of the most severe kind, affecting tissue below the skin. **the third degree** lengthy and harsh questioning. **third party** a person besides the two main ones involved in a situation. **Third World** the developing countries of Asia, Africa, and Latin America. ■ **third·ly** adv.

thirst /THərst/ ▶ n. **1** a feeling of needing or wanting to drink. **2** the state of not having enough water to drink. **3** (**thirst for**) a strong desire for. ▶ v. **1** (**thirst for** or **after**) have a strong desire for. **2** old use feel a need to drink.

SYNONYMS ▶ n. *a thirst for knowledge* **craving**, desire, longing, yearning, hunger, hankering, eagerness, lust, appetite; informal yen, itch.

thirst·y /ˈTHərstē/ ▶ adj. (**thirstier**, **thirstiest**) **1** feeling or causing thirst. **2** (**thirsty for**) having a strong desire for.

SYNONYMS **longing for a drink**, dry, dehydrated; informal parched, gasping.

■ **thirst·i·ly** adv.

thir·teen /ˌTHərˈtēn, ˈTHərˌtēn/ ▶ cardinal number one more than twelve; 13. (Roman numeral: **xiii** or **XIII**) ■ **thir·teenth** ordinal number.

thir·ty /ˈTHərtē/ ▶ cardinal number (plural **thirties**) ten less than forty; 30. (Roman numeral: **xxx** or **XXX**) ■ **thir·ti·eth** /-iTH/ ordinal number.

this /T͟His/ ▶ pron. & determiner (plural **these** /T͟Hēz/) **1** used to identify a specific person or thing close at hand, just mentioned, or being indicated or experienced. **2** referring to the nearer of two things close to the speaker. ▶ adv. to the degree or extent indicated.

this·tle /ˈTHisəl/ ▶ n. a plant with a prickly stem and leaves and purple flowers.

this·tle·down /ˈTHisəlˌdoun/ ▶ n. the light fluffy down of thistle seeds.

thith·er /ˈTHiT͟Hər, ˈT͟Hi-/ ▶ adv. old use to or toward that place.

tho' /T͟Hō/ (or **tho**) informal = **THOUGH**.

thong /THôNG, THäNG/ ▶ n. **1** a narrow strip used as a fastening or as the lash of a whip. **2** a skimpy bathing suit or pair of underpants like a G-string.

tho·rax /ˈTHôrˌaks/ ▶ n. (plural **thoraxes** or **thoraces** /ˈTHôrəˌsēz/) **1** the part of the body between the neck and the abdomen. **2** the middle section of an insect's body, to which the legs and wings are attached. ■ **tho·rac·ic** /THəˈrasik/ adj.

thorn /THôrn/ ▶ n. **1** a stiff sharp-pointed projection on a plant. **2** a thorny bush, shrub, or tree.

SYNONYMS **prickle**, spike, barb, spine.

□ **a thorn in someone's side** (or **flesh**) a source of continual annoyance or trouble.

thorn·y /ˈTHôrnē/ ▶ adj. (**thornier**, **thorniest**) **1** having many thorns. **2** causing difficulty.

SYNONYMS **1 prickly**, spiky, barbed, spiny, sharp. **2 problematic**, tricky, ticklish, delicate, controversial, awkward, difficult, knotty, tough, complicated, complex, involved, intricate, vexed; informal sticky.

thor·ough /ˈTHərō/ ▶ adj. **1** complete with regard to every detail. **2** very careful and complete. **3** absolute; utter.

SYNONYMS **1** *a thorough investigation* **rigorous**, in-depth, exhaustive, minute, detailed, close, meticulous, methodical, careful, complete, comprehensive. **2** *he's slow but thorough* **meticulous**, scrupulous, assiduous, conscientious, painstaking, punctilious, methodical, careful. **3 utter**, downright, absolute, complete, total, out-and-out, real, perfect, proper. ANTONYMS superficial, cursory.

■ **thor·ough·ly** adv.

thor·ough·bred /ˈTHərəˌbred/ ▶ adj. descended from animals that were all of the same breed. ▶ n. a thoroughbred animal.

thor·ough·fare /ˈTHərəˌfe(ə)r/ ▶ n. a road or path between two places.

thor·ough·go·ing /ˈTHərəˌgōiNG/ ▶ adj. **1** thorough. **2** complete; absolute.

those /T͟Hōz/ plural of **THAT**.

thou /T͟Hou/ ▶ pron. old use or dialect ⇨ **YOU** (as the singular subject of a verb).

though /T͟Hō/ ▶ conj. **1** despite the fact that; although. **2** however; but. ▶ adv. however.

thought[1] /THôt/ ▶ n. **1** an idea or opinion produced by thinking, or occurring suddenly in the mind. **2** the process of thinking. **3** (**thought of**) intention, hope, or idea of. **4** the forming of opinions, or the opinions so formed.

SYNONYMS **1 idea**, notion, opinion, view, impression, feeling, theory. **2 thinking**, contemplation, musing, pondering, consideration, reflection, rumination, deliberation, meditation; formal cogitation. **3** *have you no thought for others?* **consideration**, understanding, regard, sensitivity, care, concern, compassion, sympathy.

thought[2] past and past participle of **THINK**.

thought·ful /ˈTHôtfəl/ ▶ **adj. 1** absorbed in thought. **2** showing careful consideration. **3** showing consideration for other people.

SYNONYMS **1 pensive**, reflective, contemplative, musing, meditative, ruminative, introspective, philosophical, preoccupied, in a brown study. **2 considerate**, caring, attentive, understanding, sympathetic, solicitous, concerned, helpful, obliging, accommodating, kind, compassionate. ANTONYMS thoughtless.

■ **thought·ful·ly adv.**

thought·less /ˈTHôtləs/ ▶ **adj. 1** not showing consideration for other people. **2** without considering the consequences.

SYNONYMS **1 inconsiderate**, uncaring, insensitive, uncharitable, unkind, tactless, undiplomatic, indiscreet, careless. **2 unthinking**, heedless, careless, unmindful, absentminded, injudicious, ill-advised, ill-considered, imprudent, unwise, foolish, silly, stupid, reckless, rash, precipitate, negligent, neglectful, remiss. ANTONYMS thoughtful.

■ **thought·less·ly adv.**

thou·sand /ˈTHouzənd/ ▶ **cardinal number 1** the product of a hundred and ten; 1,000. (Roman numeral: **m** or **M**) **2** (**thousands**) informal an unspecified large number. ■ **thou·sandth** /ˈTHouzən(t)TH/ **ordinal number.**

thrall /THrôl/ ▶ **n.** the state of being in another person's power.

thrash /THrasH/ ▶ **v. 1** beat repeatedly with a stick or whip. **2** move in a violent or uncontrolled way. **3** informal defeat heavily. **4** (**thrash something out**) discuss an issue frankly and thoroughly.

SYNONYMS **1 hit**, beat, strike, batter, thump, hammer, pound; informal belt. **2** *he was thrashing about in pain* **flail**, writhe, thresh, jerk, toss, twist, twitch.

thread /THred/ ▶ **n. 1** a thin strand of cotton or other fibers used in sewing or weaving. **2** a spiral ridge on the outside of a screw or bolt or on the inside of a hole, to allow two parts to be screwed together. **3** a theme running through a situation or piece of writing. ▶ **v. 1** pass a thread through. **2** weave in and out of obstacles.

SYNONYMS ▶ **n. 1 cotton**, yarn, fiber, filament. **2 train of thought**, drift, direction, theme, tenor. ▶ **v.** *she threaded her way through the tables* **weave**, inch, squeeze, navigate, negotiate.

thread·bare /ˈTHredˌber/ ▶ **adj.** thin and tattered with age.

SYNONYMS **worn**, old, holey, moth-eaten, mangy, ragged, frayed, tattered, decrepit, shabby, scruffy; informal tatty, the worse for wear.

threat /THret/ ▶ **n. 1** a stated intention to inflict harm on someone. **2** a person or thing likely to cause harm. **3** the possibility of trouble or danger.

SYNONYMS **1 threatening remark**, warning, ultimatum. **2** *a possible threat to aircraft* **danger**, peril, hazard, menace, risk. **3** *the company faces the threat of liquidation* **possibility**, chance, probability, likelihood, risk.

threat·en /ˈTHretn/ ▶ **v. 1** make a threat to. **2** put at risk. **3** seem likely to produce an unwelcome result.

SYNONYMS **1 menace**, intimidate, browbeat, bully, terrorize. **2 endanger**, jeopardize, imperil, put at risk. **3 herald**, bode, warn of, presage, foreshadow, indicate, point to, be a sign of, signal.

■ **threat·en·ing adj. threat·en·ing·ly adv.**

three /THrē/ ▶ **cardinal number** one more than two; 3. (Roman numeral: **iii** or **III**) □ **three-dimensional** having or appearing to have length, breadth, and depth. ■ **three·fold** /ˈTHrēˌfōld/ **adj. & adv.**

three·some /ˈTHrēsəm/ ▶ **n.** a group of three people.

thren·o·dy /ˈTHrenədē/ ▶ **n.** (plural **threnodies**) a song, piece of music, or poem expressing grief or regret.

thresh /THresH/ ▶ **v. 1** separate grains of corn from the rest of the plant. **2** move in an uncontrolled way. ■ **thresh·er n.**

thresh·old /ˈTHresHˌ(h)ōld/ ▶ **n. 1** a strip of wood or stone forming the bottom of a doorway. **2** a level or point marking the start of something.

SYNONYMS **1 doorstep**, entrance, entry, gate, portal. **2 start**, beginning, commencement, brink, verge, dawn, inception, day one, opening, debut.

SPELLING

There is only one **h** in the middle: thres**h**old.

threw /THroo/ past of **THROW**.

USAGE

Don't confuse **threw** with **through**, which means 'in one side of an opening or place and out of the other.'

thrice /THrīs/ ▶ **adv.** old use three times.

thrift /THrift/ ▶ **n.** the quality of spending money very carefully, so that none is wasted. □ **thrift store** a store selling secondhand clothes and household goods.

thrift·y /ˈTHriftē/ ▶ **adj.** (**thriftier**, **thriftiest**) careful with money; economical.

SYNONYMS **frugal**, economical, sparing, careful with money, provident, prudent, abstemious, parsimonious, penny-pinching. ANTONYMS extravagant.

thrill /THril/ ▶ **n. 1** a sudden feeling of excitement and pleasure. **2** an exciting or enjoyable experience. **3** a wave of emotion or sensation. ▶ **v. 1** give someone a thrill. **2** (**thrill to**) experience something exciting.

SYNONYMS ▶ **n. excitement**, stimulation, pleasure, tingle; informal buzz, kick, charge. ANTONYMS boredom. ▶ **v. 1 excite**, stimulate, arouse, rouse, inspire, delight, exhilarate, intoxicate, stir, electrify, move; informal give someone a buzz/kick/charge. **2** (**thrilling**) **exciting**, stimulating, stirring, action-packed, rip-roaring, gripping, electrifying, riveting, fascinating, dramatic, hair-raising. ANTONYMS bore.

thrill·er /ˈTHrilər/ ▶ **n.** a novel, play, or movie with an exciting plot, typically involving crime or spying.

thrive /THrīv/ ▶ **v.** (**thrives**, **thriving**, **thrived** or **throve** /THrōv/; past participle **thrived** or **thriven**

/ˈTHrivən/) **1** grow or develop well. **2** be successful; flourish.

> SYNONYMS **flourish**, prosper, burgeon, grow, develop, bloom, blossom, do well, advance, succeed, boom; informal going strong; (**thriving**) healthy, successful, profitable. ANTONYMS decline, wither.

throat /THrōt/ ▶ **n. 1** the passage that leads from the back of the mouth to the lungs and stomach. **2** the front part of the neck.

throat·y /ˈTHrōtē/ ▶ **adj.** (**throatier**, **throatiest**) sounding deep and husky. ■ **throat·i·ly adv.**

throb /THräb/ ▶ **v.** (**throbs**, **throbbing**, **throbbed**) **1** beat or sound with a strong, regular rhythm. **2** feel pain in a series of pulsations. ▶ **n.** a strong, regular beat or sound.

> SYNONYMS ▶ **v. pulsate**, beat, pulse, palpitate, pound, thud, thump, drum, vibrate, quiver. ▶ **n. pulsation**, beat, pulse, palpitation, pounding, thudding, thumping, drumming, vibration, quivering.

throes /THrōz/ ▶ **pl.n.** severe or violent pain and struggle. □ **in the throes of** in the middle of doing or dealing with something difficult.

throm·bo·sis /THrämˈbōsis/ ▶ **n.** (plural **thromboses** /-ˌsēz/) the formation of a blood clot in a blood vessel or the heart.

throne /THrōn/ ▶ **n. 1** a chair for a king or queen, used during ceremonies. **2** (**the throne**) the power or rank of a king or queen.

throng /THrông, THräng/ ▶ **n.** a large, densely packed crowd. ▶ **v.** gather somewhere in large numbers.

> SYNONYMS ▶ **n. crowd**, horde, mass, army, herd, flock, drove, swarm, sea, troupe, pack; informal bunch, gaggle, gang. ▶ **v. 1** *pavements thronged with tourists* **fill**, crowd, pack, cram, jam. **2** *visitors thronged around him* **flock**, crowd, cluster, mill, swarm, congregate, gather.

throt·tle /ˈTHrätl/ ▶ **n.** a device controlling the flow of fuel or power to an engine. ▶ **v.** (**throttles**, **throttling**, **throttled**) **1** attack or kill by choking or strangling. **2** control an engine or vehicle with a throttle.

> SYNONYMS ▶ **v. choke**, strangle, garrotte.

through /THro͞o/ ▶ **prep. & adv. 1** in one side and out of the other side of an opening or place. **2** continuing in time toward. **3** from beginning to end. **4** by means of. ▶ **adj. 1** (of public transportation) continuing to the final destination. **2** (of traffic, roads, etc.) passing straight through a place. **3** having successfully reached the next stage of a competition. **4** informal having finished an activity, relationship, etc.

> SYNONYMS ▶ **prep. & adv. 1 by means of**, by way of, by dint of, via, using, thanks to, by virtue of, as a result of, as a consequence of, on account of, owing to. **2 throughout**, for the duration of, until/to the end of, all.

> USAGE
>
> Don't confuse **through** with **threw**, which is the past of throw.

through·out /THro͞oˈout/ ▶ **prep. & adv.** all the way through.

> SYNONYMS **1 all over**, in every part of, everywhere in. **2 all through**, for the duration of, for the whole of, until the end of, all.

through·put /ˈTHro͞oˌpo͝ot/ ▶ **n.** the amount of material or number of items passing through a process.

throve /THrōv/ past of **THRIVE**.

throw /THrō/ ▶ **v.** (**throws**, **throwing**, **threw** /THro͞o/; past participle **thrown**) **1** send through the air with a rapid movement of the arm and hand. **2** move or place hurriedly or roughly. **3** project, direct, or cast light, an expression, etc., in a particular direction. **4** send suddenly into a particular position or condition. **5** upset or confuse. ▶ **n. 1** an act of throwing. **2** a small rug or light cover for furniture.

> SYNONYMS ▶ **v. 1 hurl**, toss, fling, pitch, cast, lob, launch, bowl; informal chuck, heave, sling. **2** *he threw the door open* **push**, thrust, fling, bang. **3 cast**, send, give off, emit, radiate, project. **4 disconcert**, unnerve, fluster, ruffle, put off, throw off balance, unsettle, confuse; informal rattle, faze. ▶ **n. lob**, toss, pitch, bowl.

□ **throw something away** (or **out**) get rid of something. **throw up** informal vomit.

throw·a·way /ˈTHrōəˌwā/ ▶ **adj. 1** intended to be thrown away after use. **2** (of a remark) said without careful thought.

throw·back /ˈTHrōˌbak/ ▶ **n.** a person or thing that resembles someone or something that existed in the past.

thru /THro͞o/ informal = **THROUGH**.

thrum /THrəm/ ▶ **v.** (**thrums**, **thrumming**, **thrummed**) make a continuous rhythmic humming sound. ▶ **n.** a thrumming sound.

thrush[1] /THrəsh/ ▶ **n.** a bird with a brown back and spotted breast.

thrush[2] ▶ **n.** an infection of the mouth and throat or the genitals.

thrust /THrəst/ ▶ **v.** (**thrusts**, **thrusting**, **thrust**) **1** push suddenly or violently. **2** make your way forcibly. ▶ **n. 1** a sudden or violent lunge or attack. **2** the main point of an argument. **3** the force produced by an engine to push forward a jet, rocket, etc.

> SYNONYMS ▶ **v. 1 shove**, push, force, plunge, stick, drive, ram, lunge. **2** *fame had been thrust on him* **force**, foist, impose, inflict. ▶ **n. 1 shove**, push, lunge, poke. **2 advance**, push, drive, attack, assault, onslaught, offensive. **3 force**, propulsion, power, impetus. **4 gist**, substance, drift, message, import, tenor.

thrust·ing /ˈTHrəstiNG/ ▶ **adj.** aggressively ambitious.

thru·way /ˈTHro͞oˌwā/ (also **through·way**) ▶ **n.** a major road or highway.

thud /THəd/ ▶ **n.** a dull, heavy sound. ▶ **v.** (**thuds**, **thudding**, **thudded**) move, fall, or strike with a thud.

thug /THəg/ ▶ **n.** a violent man.

> SYNONYMS **ruffian**, hooligan, bully, hoodlum, gangster, villain; informal tough, hood, goon, bruiser, heavy.

■ **thug·ger·y n. thug·gish adj.**

thumb /THəm/ ▶ **n.** the short, thick first digit of the hand. ▶ **v. 1** turn over pages with your thumb. **2** ask for a free ride in a passing vehicle by signaling with your thumb. ▫ **thumb drive** ⇒ FLASH DRIVE. **thumb index** lettered notches cut into the side of a book to help you find the section you want. **thumbs up** (or **down**) informal an indication of approval (or disapproval). **under someone's thumb** under someone's control.

thumb·nail /ˈTHəmˌnāl/ ▶ n. the nail of the thumb. ▫ **thumbnail sketch** a brief, concise description.

thumb·screw /ˈTHəmˌskro͞o/ ▶ n. an instrument of torture that crushes the thumbs.

thumb·tack /ˈTHəmˌtak/ ▶ n. a short flat-headed pin, used for fastening paper to a wall or other surface.

thump /THəmp/ ▶ v. **1** hit heavily with your fist or a blunt object. **2** put down forcefully. **3** (of a person's heart) beat strongly. ▶ n. a dull, heavy blow or noise.

> SYNONYMS ▶ v. **1 hit**, beat, punch, strike, smack, batter, pummel; informal whack, wallop, slug, bash, clobber, clout. **2 throb**, pound, beat, thud, hammer.

thump·ing /ˈTHəmpiNG/ ▶ adj. informal very big.

thun·der /ˈTHəndər/ ▶ n. **1** a loud rumbling or crashing noise heard after a lightning flash due to the expansion of rapidly heated air. **2** a loud, deep noise. ▶ v. **1** (**it thunders**, **it is thundering**, **it thundered**) thunder is sounding. **2** make a loud, deep noise. **3** speak loudly and angrily.

> SYNONYMS ▶ n. **rumble**, boom, roar, pounding, crash, reverberation. ▶ v. **1 rumble**, boom, roar, pound, crash, resound, reverberate. **2** *"Answer me!" he thundered* **shout**, roar, bellow, bark.

thun·der·bolt /ˈTHəndərˌbōlt/ ▶ n. a flash of lightning with a crash of thunder at the same time.

thun·der·clap /ˈTHəndərˌklap/ ▶ n. a sudden crash of thunder.

thun·der·cloud /ˈTHəndərˌkloud/ ▶ n. a cloud charged with electricity and producing thunder and lightning.

thun·der·ous /ˈTHənd(ə)rəs/ ▶ adj. **1** very loud. **2** (of a person's expression) very angry or threatening.

thun·der·storm /ˈTHəndərˌstôrm/ ▶ n. a storm with thunder and lightning.

thun·der·struck /ˈTHəndərˌstrək/ ▶ adj. very surprised or shocked.

Thurs·day /ˈTHərzdā, -dē/ ▶ n. the day of the week before Friday and following Wednesday.

thus /T͟Həs/ ▶ adv. formal **1** as a result or consequence of this; therefore. **2** in this way. **3** to this point; so.

thwack /THwak/ ▶ v. hit with a sharp blow. ▶ n. a sharp blow.

thwart /THwôrt/ ▶ v. prevent someone from accomplishing something.

> SYNONYMS **foil**, frustrate, forestall, stop, check, block, prevent, defeat, impede, obstruct, derail, snooker; informal stymie. ANTONYMS help.

thy /T͟Hī/ (or (before a vowel) **thine** /T͟Hīn/) ▶ possessive determiner old use your.

thyme /tīm/ ▶ n. a low-growing, sweet-smelling plant used in cooking.

thy·mus /ˈTHīməs/ ▶ n. (plural **thymuses** or **thymi** /-mī/) a gland in the neck that produces white blood cells for the immune system.

thy·roid /ˈTHīˌroid/ ▶ n. a large gland in the neck that produces hormones regulating growth and development.

thy·self /T͟Hīˈself/ old form of YOURSELF.

ti /tē/ ▶ n. Music the seventh note of a major scale.

ti·ar·a /tēˈärə, -ˈarə, -ˈe(ə)rə/ ▶ n. a jeweled ornamental band worn above the forehead.

Ti·bet·an /təˈbetn/ ▶ n. a person from Tibet. ▶ adj. relating to Tibet.

tib·i·a /ˈtibēə/ ▶ n. (plural **tibiae** /ˈtibēˌē/ or **tibias**) the inner of the two bones between the knee and the ankle.

tic /tik/ ▶ n. a recurring spasm in the muscles of the face.

tick[1] /tik/ ▶ n. a regular short, sharp sound. ▶ v. **1** make regular ticking sounds. **2** (**tick away** or **by** or **past**) (of time) keep passing. **3** (of a mechanism) function. **4** (**tick someone off**) informal make someone annoyed or angry.

tick[2] ▶ n. a small arachnid that attaches itself to the skin and sucks blood.

tick·er /ˈtikər/ ▶ n. **1** informal a person's heart. **2** a machine that prints out data on a strip of paper. ▫ **ticker tape** strips of paper on which data is printed by a machine.

tick·et /ˈtikit/ ▶ n. **1** a piece of paper or small card giving you the right to travel on public transportation or letting you in to a place or an event. **2** an official notice that you have committed a parking or driving offense. **3** a label attached to a product, giving its price, size, etc.

> SYNONYMS **1 pass**, authorization, permit, token, coupon, voucher. **2 label**, tag, sticker, tab, slip, docket.

tick·ing /ˈtikiNG/ ▶ n. a hard-wearing material used to cover mattresses.

tick·le /ˈtikəl/ ▶ v. (**tickles**, **tickling**, **tickled**) **1** lightly touch in a way that causes itching or twitching and often laughter. **2** be appealing or amusing to. ▶ n. an act of tickling, or the sensation of being tickled.

> SYNONYMS ▶ v. **1 stroke**, pet. **2 stimulate**, interest, appeal to, amuse, entertain, divert, please, delight.

▪ **tick·ly** adj.

tick·lish /ˈtik(ə)liSH/ ▶ adj. **1** sensitive to being tickled. **2** needing care and tact.

tic-tac-toe /ˈtik ˌtak ˈtō/ ▶ n. a game in which each of two players tries to be the first to complete a row, column, or diagonal with either three O's or three X's on a nine-square grid.

tid·al /ˈtīdl/ ▶ adj. relating to or affected by tides. ▫ **tidal wave** a huge sea wave caused by an earthquake, storm, etc. ▪ **tid·al·ly** adv.

tid·bit /ˈtidˌbit/ ▶ n. **1** a small piece of tasty food. **2** a small item of very interesting information.

tid·dl·ywinks /ˈtidlēˌwiNGks/ ▶ pl.n. a game in which small plastic counters are flicked into a cup.

tide /tīd/ ▶ n. **1** the alternate rising and falling of the sea due to the attraction of the moon and sun. **2** a powerful surge of feeling or trend of events. ▶ v. (**tides**, **tiding**, **tided**) (**tide someone over**) help someone through a difficult period.

> SYNONYMS ▶ n. **1 current**, flow, stream, ebb. **2** *the tide of history* **course**, movement, direction, trend, current, drift, run.

ti·dings /ˈtīdiNGz/ ▶ pl.n. literary news; information.

ti·dy /ˈtīdē/ ▶ **adj.** (**tidier**, **tidiest**) **1** arranged neatly and in order. **2** liking to keep yourself and your possessions neat and in order. **3** informal (of a sum of money) large. ▶ **v.** (**tidies**, **tidying**, **tidied**) (often **tidy up**) make a place tidy. ▶ **n.** (plural **tidies**) **1** an act of tidying. **2** a container for holding small objects.

SYNONYMS ▶ **adj. 1** *a tidy room* **neat**, orderly, in good order, well-kept, in apple-pie order, shipshape, spick and span, spruce, uncluttered. **2** *a tidy person* **organized**, neat, methodical, meticulous, systematic. ANTONYMS untidy. ▶ **v. put in order**, clear up, sort out, straighten (up), clean up, spruce up, smarten up.

■ **ti·di·ly** **adv.** **ti·di·ness** **n.**

tie /tī/ ▶ **v.** (**ties**, **tying**, **tied**) **1** attach or fasten with string, cord, ribbon, etc. **2** form into a knot or bow. **3** restrict to a particular situation or place. **4** connect or link. **5** achieve the same score or ranking as another competitor. ▶ **n.** (plural **ties**) **1** a strip of material worn beneath a collar and tied in a knot at the front. **2** a thing that ties. **3** a result in a game or match in which two or more competitors are equal. **4** each of the wooden or concrete beams on which a railroad track rests.

SYNONYMS ▶ **v. 1** **bind**, tie up, tether, hitch, strap, truss, fetter, rope, make fast, moor, lash. **2** **do up**, lace, knot. **3** **restrict**, restrain, limit, tie down, constrain, cramp, hamper, handicap, hamstring, encumber, shackle. **4** **link**, connect, couple, relate, join, marry. **5** **draw**, be equal, be even. ▶ **n. 1** **lace**, string, cord, fastening. **2** **bond**, connection, link, relationship, attachment, affiliation. **3** **restriction**, constraint, curb, limitation, restraint, hindrance, encumbrance, handicap, obligation, commitment. **4** **draw**, dead heat.

□ **tie-dye** produce patterns on fabric by tying knots in it before it is dyed. **tie in** fit or be in harmony. **tie-in** **1** a connection or association. **2** a product produced to take commercial advantage of a related work in another medium. **tie someone/something up** **1** restrict someone's movement by tying their arms or legs. **2** bring something to a conclusion. **3** informal occupy someone so that they have no time for other activities.

tie·break·er /ˈtīˌbrākər/ (also **tiebreak** /ˈtīˌbrāk/) ▶ **n.** a means of deciding a winner from competitors who are equal at the end of a game or match.

tie·pin /ˈtīˌpin/ ▶ **n.** an ornamental pin for holding a tie in place.

tier /ti(ə)r/ ▶ **n.** one of a series of rows or levels placed one above and behind the other.

SYNONYMS **1** **row**, rank, bank, line, layer, level. **2** **grade**, gradation, echelon, rung on the ladder.

■ **tiered** **adj.**

tiff /tif/ ▶ **n.** informal a quarrel about something unimportant.

ti·ger /ˈtīgər/ ▶ **n.** a large cat with a yellow coat striped with black, native to the forests of Asia.

tight /tīt/ ▶ **adj.** **1** firmly fixed, closed, or fastened. **2** (of clothes) fitting very closely. **3** well-sealed against water or air. **4** (of a rope, fabric, or surface) stretched so as to leave no slack. **5** (of an area or space) allowing little room for movement. **6** closely packed together. **7** (of a form of control) very strict. **8** (of money or time) limited. ▶ **adv.** very closely or firmly.

SYNONYMS ▶ **adj. 1** **firm**, secure, fast. **2** **taut**, rigid, stiff, tense, stretched, strained, clenched. **3** **close-fitting**, narrow, figure-hugging, skintight; informal sprayed on. **4** *a tight mass of fibers* **compact**, compressed, dense, solid. **5** **small**, tiny, narrow, limited, restricted, confined, cramped, constricted. **6** *tight security* **strict**, rigorous, stringent, tough. ANTONYMS slack, loose.

□ **tight-fisted** informal not willing to spend your money. **tight-knit** (or **tightly knit**) (of a group of people) closely connected to each other through family or social relationships. **tight-lipped** unwilling to express emotion or give away information. ■ **tight·ly** **adv.** **tight·ness** **n.**

tight·en /ˈtītn/ ▶ **v.** make or become tight or tighter.

SYNONYMS **1** **stretch**, tauten, strain, stiffen, tense. **2** **strengthen**, increase, make stricter. ANTONYMS loosen, slacken.

tight·rope /ˈtītˌrōp/ ▶ **n.** a rope or wire stretched high above the ground, on which acrobats balance.

tights /tīts/ ▶ **pl.n.** a close-fitting garment made of stretchy material, covering the hips, legs, and feet.

tight·wad /ˈtītˌwäd/ ▶ **n.** informal a miserly person.

ti·gress /ˈtīgris/ ▶ **n.** a female tiger.

tik·ka /ˈtikə, ˈtē-/ ▶ **n.** an Indian dish of meat or vegetables marinated in spices.

til·de /ˈtildə/ ▶ **n.** an accent (~) placed over the Spanish *n* or Portuguese *a* or *o* to change the way they are pronounced.

tile /tīl/ ▶ **n.** a thin square or rectangular piece of fired clay, concrete, cork, etc., used for covering roofs, floors, or walls. ▶ **v.** (**tiles**, **tiling**, **tiled**) cover with tiles. ■ **til·er** **n.**

till[1] /til/ less formal way of saying **UNTIL**.

till[2] ▶ **n.** a cash register or drawer for money.

till[3] ▶ **v.** prepare and cultivate land for crops.

till·er /ˈtilər/ ▶ **n.** a horizontal bar fitted to a boat's rudder and used for steering.

tilt /tilt/ ▶ **v. 1** slip or move into a sloping position. **2** (**tilt at**) (in the past, in jousting) thrust at someone with a lance. ▶ **n. 1** a tilting position or movement. **2** a leaning or bias. **3** (in the past) a joust. **4** (**tilt at**) an attempt at winning something.

SYNONYMS ▶ **v.** **slope**, tip, lean, list, bank, slant, incline, pitch, cant, angle. ▶ **n.** **slope**, list, camber, gradient, grade, bank, slant, incline, pitch, cant, bevel, angle.

□ **(at) full tilt** with maximum speed or force.

tim·ber /ˈtimbər/ ▶ **n. 1** wood prepared for use in building and carpentry. **2** a wooden beam used in building.

SYNONYMS **1** **wood**, lumber. **2** **beam**, spar, plank, batten, lath, board, joist, rafter.

tim·ber·land /ˈtimbərˌland/ ▶ **n.** (also **timberlands**) land covered with forest suitable or managed for timber.

tim·ber·line /ˈtimbərˌlīn/ ▶ **n.** the height up a mountain above which trees do not grow.

tim·bre /ˈtambər, ˈtänbrə/ ▶ **n.** the quality of the sound in a voice or piece of music.

SYNONYMS **tone**, sound, voice, color, tonality.

time /tīm/ ▶ **n. 1** the continuing and unlimited progress of existence and events in the past, present, and future. **2** a point or period within this. **3** a point of time as measured in hours and minutes past midnight or noon. **4** the right or agreed moment to do something. **5** time as a resource to be used. **6** an instance of something happening or being done. **7** (**times**) (following a number) expressing multiplication. **8** the rhythmic pattern or tempo of a piece of music. ▶ **v.** (**times**, **timing**, **timed**) **1** arrange a time for. **2** do at a particular time. **3** measure the time taken by.

SYNONYMS ▶ **n. 1 moment**, point (in time), occasion, instant, juncture, stage. **2** *he worked there for a time* **while**, spell, stretch, stint, interval, period, length of time, duration, phase. **3 era**, age, epoch, eon, period, years, days. ▶ **v. schedule**, arrange, set, organize, fix, book, line up, slate, timetable, plan.

□ **behind the times** not using the latest ideas or techniques. **do time** informal spend a period of time in prison. **for the time being** until some other arrangement is made. **in time 1** not late. **2** eventually. **on time** punctual, or punctually. **time-honored** (of a custom or tradition) respected or valued because it has existed for a long time. **time off** time spent away from your usual work or studies. **time-server** a person who makes little effort at work because they are waiting to leave or retire. **time signature** a sign at the start of a piece of music showing the number of beats in a bar.

time·keep·er /ˈtīmˌkēpər/ ▶ **n. 1** a person who records the amount of time taken by a process or activity. **2** a person regarded in terms of their punctuality. ■ **time·keep·ing n.**

time·less /ˈtīmlis/ ▶ **adj.** not affected by the passing of time.

SYNONYMS **lasting**, enduring, classic, ageless, permanent, perennial, abiding, unchanging, unvarying, never-changing, eternal, everlasting. ANTONYMS ephemeral.

time·ly /ˈtīmlē/ ▶ **adj.** done or happening at a good or appropriate time.

SYNONYMS **opportune**, well-timed, convenient, appropriate, expedient, seasonable, propitious. ANTONYMS ill-timed.

■ **time·li·ness n.**

time·piece /ˈtīmˌpēs/ ▶ **n.** a clock or watch.

tim·er /ˈtīmər/ ▶ **n. 1** a device that records how long something is taking. **2** a device that stops or starts a machine at a preset time.

time·scale /ˈtīmˌskāl/ ▶ **n.** the time allowed for or taken by a process or events.

time·share /ˈtīmˌsнe(ə)r/ ▶ **n.** an arrangement in which joint owners use a property as a vacation home at different times.

time·ta·ble /ˈtīmˌtābəl/ ▶ **n.** a list or plan of times at which events are scheduled to take place. ▶ **v.** (**timetables**, **timetabling**, **timetabled**) schedule events to take place at particular times.

SYNONYMS ▶ **n. schedule**, program, agenda, calendar, diary.

tim·id /ˈtimid/ ▶ **adj.** not brave or confident.

SYNONYMS **fearful**, afraid, faint-hearted, timorous, nervous, scared, frightened, shy, diffident. ANTONYMS bold.

■ **ti·mid·i·ty** /təˈmiditē/ **n. tim·id·ly adv.**

tim·or·ous /ˈtimərəs/ ▶ **adj.** easily frightened.

tim·pa·ni /ˈtimpənē/ (or **tympani**) ▶ **pl.n.** kettledrums.

tin /tin/ ▶ **n. 1** a silvery-white metal. **2** an airtight container with a lid, made of tinplate or aluminum: *a cookie tin.* ▶ **v.** (**tins**, **tinning**, **tinned**) cover another metal with a thin layer of tin. □ **tin can** a tinplate or aluminum container for preserving food, especially an empty one. **tin whistle** a metal musical instrument like a small flute.

tinc·ture /ˈtiNGkCHər/ ▶ **n. 1** a medicine made by dissolving a drug in alcohol. **2** a slight trace.

tin·der /ˈtindər/ ▶ **n.** dry material used in lighting a fire.

tin·der·box /ˈtindərˌbäks/ ▶ **n.** (in the past) a box containing tinder, flint, and other items for lighting fires.

tine /tīn/ ▶ **n.** a prong or sharp point.

tin·foil /ˈtinˌfoil/ ▶ **n.** metal (usually aluminum) foil used for covering or wrapping food.

ting /tiNG/ ▶ **n.** a sharp, clear ringing sound.

tinge /tinj/ ▶ **n.** a slight trace of a color, feeling, or quality. ▶ **v.** (**tinges**, **tinging** or **tingeing**, **tinged**) give a tinge to.

SYNONYMS ▶ **n. 1 tint**, color, shade, tone, hue. **2 trace**, note, touch, suggestion, hint, flavor, element, streak, suspicion, soupçon. ▶ **v. tint**, color, stain, shade, wash.

tin·gle /ˈtiNGgəl/ ▶ **v.** (**tingles**, **tingling**, **tingled**) have a slight prickling or stinging feeling. ▶ **n.** a slight prickling or stinging sensation.

SYNONYMS ▶ **v. prickle**, prick, sting, itch, tickle. ▶ **n. prickle**, pricking, tingling, sting, itch, pins and needles.

■ **tin·gly adj.**

tin·horn /ˈtinˌhôrn/ informal ▶ **n.** a contemptible person, especially one pretending to have money, influence, or ability. ▶ **adj.** pretending to be more significant or influential than you really are.

tin·ker /ˈtiNGkər/ ▶ **n.** (in the past) a person who traveled from place to place mending pots, kettles, etc. ▶ **v.** (**tinkers**, **tinkering**, **tinkered**) (**tinker with**) casually try to repair or improve.

SYNONYMS ▶ **v. fiddle**, play around, mess about/around, adjust, try to mend.

tin·kle /ˈtiNGkəl/ ▶ **v.** (**tinkles**, **tinkling**, **tinkled**) make or cause to make a light, clear ringing sound. ▶ **n.** a tinkling sound.

tin·ni·tus /ˈtinitəs, tiˈnī-/ ▶ **n.** a ringing or buzzing in the ears.

tin·ny /ˈtinē/ ▶ **adj. 1** having a thin, metallic sound. **2** made of thin or poor-quality metal.

tin·plate /ˈtinˌplāt/ ▶ **n.** thin sheets of steel or iron coated with a layer of tin.

tin·pot /ˈtinˌpät/ ▶ **adj.** informal not important or effective.

tin·sel /ˈtinsəl/ ▶ **n.** thin strips of shiny metal foil attached to a length of thread, used to decorate a Christmas tree.

tint /tint/ ▶ **n. 1** a shade of a color. **2** a dye for coloring the hair. ▶ **v. 1** color something slightly. **2** dye hair with a tint.

SYNONYMS ▶ **n. 1 shade**, color, tone, hue, tinge, cast, flush, blush. **2 dye**, colorant, coloring, wash. ▶ **v. dye**, color, tinge.

tin·tin·nab·u·la·tion /ˌtintəˌnabyəˈlāsHən/ ▶ **n.** a ringing or tinkling sound.

ti·ny /ˈtīnē/ ▶ **adj.** (**tinier**, **tiniest**) very small.

SYNONYMS **minute**, minuscule, microscopic, very small, mini, diminutive, miniature, baby, toy, dwarf; informal teeny, teensy, teeny-weeny, teensy-weensy. ANTONYMS huge.

tip[1] /tip/ ▶ **n. 1** the pointed or rounded end of something slender or tapering. **2** a small part fitted to the end of an object.

SYNONYMS **1 point**, end, extremity, head, spike, prong, nib. **2 peak**, top, summit, apex, crown, crest, pinnacle.

□ **on the tip of your tongue** almost but not quite spoken or coming to mind. **tip-top** of the very best quality. ■ **tipped adj.**

tip[2] ▶ **v.** (**tips, tipping, tipped**) **1** overbalance so as to fall or turn over. **2** be or put in a sloping position. **3** empty out the contents of a container by holding it at an angle.

SYNONYMS **1 overturn**, turn over, topple (over), fall (over), keel over, capsize, roll over. **2 lean**, tilt, list, slope, bank, slant, incline, pitch, cant. **3 pour**, empty, drain, dump, discharge, decant.

tip[3] ▶ **n. 1** a small extra amount of money that you give to someone for their good service in a restaurant, taxi, etc. **2** a piece of practical advice. **3** a prediction about the likely winner of a race or contest. ▶ **v.** (**tips, tipping, tipped**) **1** give a tip to. **2** (**tip someone off**) informal give someone secret information.

SYNONYMS ▶ **n. 1 gratuity**, present, gift, reward, baksheesh. **2 piece of advice**, suggestion, word of advice, pointer, hint; informal wrinkle.

□ **tip-off** informal a piece of secret information.

tip·ple /'tipəl/ informal ▶ **n.** an alcoholic drink. ▶ **v.** (**tipples, tippling, tippled**) drink alcohol regularly. ■ **tip·pler n.**

tip·py-toe /'tipē/ ▶ **v.** informal tiptoe.

tip·ster /'tipstər/ ▶ **n.** a person who gives tips as to the likely winner of a race or contest.

tip·sy /'tipsē/ ▶ **adj.** slightly drunk. ■ **tip·si·ly adv.**

tip·toe /'tip,tō/ ▶ **v.** (**tiptoes, tiptoeing, tiptoed**) walk quietly and carefully with your heels raised. □ **on tiptoe** (or **tiptoes**) with your heels raised.

ti·rade /'tī,rād, ,tī'rād/ ▶ **n.** a long angry speech.

SYNONYMS **diatribe**, harangue, rant, attack, polemic, broadside, fulmination, tongue-lashing; informal blast.

tire[1] /tīr/ ▶ **v.** (**tires, tiring, tired**) **1** make or become in need of rest or sleep. **2** (**tire of**) become impatient or bored with.

SYNONYMS **1 get tired**, weaken, flag, droop. **2 fatigue**, tire out, exhaust, wear out, tax, drain, weary, enervate; informal knock out, take it out of; (**tiring**) hard, arduous, strenuous, onerous, grueling.

tire[2] ▶ **n.** a rubber covering, usually inflated, that fits around a wheel.

tired /tīrd/ ▶ **adj. 1** in need of sleep or rest. **2** (**tired of**) bored with. **3** (of a statement or idea) boring because it has been said or used too often.

SYNONYMS **1 exhausted**, worn out, weary, fatigued, ready to drop, drained, enervated; informal beat, all in, done in, pooped, tuckered out. **2** *I'm tired of him* **fed up with**, weary of, bored with/by, sick (and tired) of; informal (fed) up to here with. **3 hackneyed**, overused, stale, clichéd, predictable, unimaginative, unoriginal, dull, boring; informal corny. ANTONYMS energetic, fresh.

■ **tired·ness n.**

tire·less /'tīrlis/ ▶ **adj.** having or showing great effort or energy.

SYNONYMS **vigorous**, energetic, industrious, determined, enthusiastic, keen, zealous, spirited, dynamic, stout, untiring, unwearying, indefatigable, unflagging. ANTONYMS lazy.

■ **tire·less·ly adv.**

tire·some /'tīrsəm/ ▶ **adj.** making you feel impatient or bored.

SYNONYMS **1 wearisome**, laborious, wearing, tedious, boring, monotonous, dull, uninteresting, unexciting, humdrum, routine. **2 troublesome**, irksome, vexatious, irritating, annoying, exasperating, trying; informal aggravating, pesky. ANTONYMS interesting, pleasant.

■ **tire·some·ly adv.**

'tis ▶ **contr.** literary it is.

tis·sue /'tisHo͞o/ ▶ **n. 1** any of the distinct types of material of which animals or plants are made. **2** a disposable paper handkerchief. □ **a tissue of lies** a story that is full of lies. **tissue paper** a very thin, soft paper.

tit[1] /tit/ ▶ **n.** a small bird that searches for food among leaves and branches.

tit[2] ▶ **n.** (**tit for tat**) a situation in which you insult or hurt someone because they have done the same to you.

Ti·tan /'tītn/ ▶ **n. 1** any of a family of giant gods and goddesses in Greek mythology. **2** (**titan**) a person of very great strength, intelligence, or importance.

ti·tan·ic /tī'tanik/ ▶ **adj.** of exceptional strength, size, or power.

ti·ta·ni·um /tī'tānēəm/ ▶ **n.** a silver-gray metal used in making strong alloys.

tithe /tīTH/ ▶ **n.** (in the past) one tenth of what people produced or earned in a year, taken as a tax to support a church.

tit·il·late /'titl,āt/ ▶ **v.** (**titillates, titillating, titillated**) make someone feel interested or mildly excited, especially sexually.

SYNONYMS (**titillating**) **arousing**, exciting, stimulating, sexy, thrilling, provocative, tantalizing, interesting, fascinating; suggestive, salacious, lurid. ANTONYMS boring.

■ **tit·il·la·tion** /,titl'āsHən/ **n.**

SPELLING

One **t**, two **l**s: ti**t**i**ll**ate.

USAGE

Don't confuse **titillate** with **titivate**, which means 'make smarter or more attractive.'

tit·i·vate /'titə,vāt/ ▶ **v.** (**titivates, titivating, titivated**) informal make smarter or more attractive. ■ **tit·i·va·tion** /,titə'vāsHən/ **n.**

ti·tle /'tītl/ ▶ **n. 1** the name of a book, piece of music, or other work. **2** a name that describes someone's position or job. **3** a word, such as *Dr.*, *Mrs.*, or *Captain*, used before or instead of someone's name to indicate their rank or profession. **4** a descriptive name that someone has earned or chosen. **5** the position of being the champion of a major sports competition. **6** a caption or credit in a movie or broadcast. **7** a right or claim to the ownership of property or to a rank or throne. **8** ⇨ TITLE DEED. ▶ v. (**titles**, **titling**, **titled**) give a title to.

SYNONYMS ▶ n. **1 heading**, label, inscription, caption, subheading, legend. **2 name**, designation, form of address, rank, office, position; informal moniker, handle. **3** *an Olympic title* **championship**, crown, first place.

□ **title deed** a legal document giving evidence of someone's right to own a property. **title role** the part in a play, movie, or television show from which the title is taken.

ti·tled /'tītld/ ▶ adj. having a title indicating nobility, e.g., *Lord* or *Lady*.

ti·tra·tion /ˌtī'trāsʜən/ ▶ n. the calculation of the amount of a substance in a solution by measuring the volume of a reagent required to react with it.

tit·ter /'titər/ ▶ v. (**titters**, **tittering**, **tittered**) laugh quietly. ▶ n. a short, quiet laugh.

tit·tle-tat·tle /'titl ˌtatl/ ▶ n. gossip.

tit·u·lar /'ticʜələr/ ▶ adj. **1** holding a formal position or title without any real authority. **2** relating to a title.

tiz·zy /'tizē/ ▶ n. (plural **tizzies**) informal a state of nervous excitement or worry.

TM ▶ abbr. trademark.

TNT ▶ abbr. trinitrotoluene, a high explosive.

to /to͞o/ ▶ prep. **1** expressing direction or position in relation to a particular location, point, or condition: *we walked to school.* **2** (in telling the time) before the hour mentioned: *it is six minutes to nine.* **3** identifying the person or thing affected by an action: *you were unkind to her.* **4** identifying a particular relationship between one person or thing and another: *he is married to Emily.* **5** indicating a rate of return on something: *ten miles to the gallon.* **6** indicating that two things are attached: *he left his bike chained to a fence.* ▶ infinitive marker used with the base form of a verb to indicate that the verb is in the infinitive: *we want to go with you.* □ **to and fro** backward and forward or from side to side. **to-do** informal a commotion or fuss.

USAGE

Don't confuse **to** with **too** or **two**. **To** mainly means 'in the direction of' (as in *the next train to Boston*), while **too** means 'excessively' (as in *she was driving too fast*) or 'in addition,' and **two** is the number meaning 'one less than three.'

toad /tōd/ ▶ n. an amphibian with a short body, short legs, and no tail.

toad·stool /'tōdˌsto͞ol/ ▶ n. a fungus with a rounded cap on a stalk.

toad·y /'tōdē/ ▶ n. (plural **toadies**) a person who is too polite and respectful to someone in order to gain their favor. ▶ v. (**toadies**, **toadying**, **toadied**) act in a way that is too polite and respectful.

toast /tōst/ ▶ n. **1** sliced bread that has been held against a source of heat until it is brown and crisp. **2** an act of raising glasses at a gathering and drinking together in honor of a person or thing. **3** a person who is greatly respected or admired. ▶ v. **1** make bread brown and crisp by holding it against a source of heat. **2** drink a toast to.

SYNONYMS ▶ v. **drink (to) the health of**, salute, honor, pay tribute to; old use pledge.

toast·er /'tōstər/ ▶ n. an electrical device for making toast.

to·bac·co /tə'bakō/ ▶ n. (plural **tobaccos**) a preparation of the dried nicotine-rich leaves of an American plant, used for smoking or chewing.

to·bac·co·nist /tə'bakənist/ ▶ n. a store owner who sells cigarettes and tobacco.

to·bog·gan /tə'bägən/ ▶ n. a long narrow sled with no runners, and with its front curved upward, used for sliding downhill over snow or ice. ■ **to·bog·gan·ist** n.

toc·ca·ta /tə'kätə/ ▶ n. a piece of music for a keyboard instrument designed to show the performer's skill and technique.

to·day /tə'dā/ ▶ adv. **1** on or in the course of this present day. **2** at the present period of time. ▶ n. **1** this present day. **2** the present period of time.

tod·dle /'tädl/ ▶ v. (**toddles**, **toddling**, **toddled**) **1** (of a young child) move with short unsteady steps while learning to walk. **2** informal walk or go about in a leisurely way.

SYNONYMS **totter**, teeter, wobble, falter, waddle, stumble.

tod·dler /'tädlər/ ▶ n. a young child who is just beginning to walk.

tod·dy /'tädē/ ▶ n. (plural **toddies**) a drink made with liquor, hot water, sugar, and spices.

toe /tō/ ▶ n. **1** any of the five digits at the end of the foot. **2** the lower end, tip, or point of something. □ **on your toes** ready and alert. **toe the line** be obedient.

toe·cap /'tōˌkap/ ▶ n. a piece of steel or leather fitted over the front part of a boot or shoe.

toe·hold /'tōˌhōld/ ▶ n. a small foothold.

toe·nail /'tōˌnāl/ ▶ n. a nail on the upper surface of the tip of each toe.

tof·fee /'tôfē, 'täfē/ ▶ n. a kind of candy that softens when sucked or chewed, made by boiling together sugar and butter.

to·fu /'tōfo͞o/ ▶ n. a soft white substance made from mashed soybeans.

to·ga /'tōgə/ ▶ n. a loose outer garment made of a single piece of cloth, worn in ancient Rome.

to·geth·er /tə'ge<u>th</u>ər/ ▶ adv. **1** with or near to another person or people. **2** so as to touch, combine, or be united. **3** regarded as a whole. **4** (of two people) married or in a romantic relationship. **5** at the same time. **6** without interruption. ▶ adj. informal levelheaded and well-organized.

SYNONYMS ▶ adv. **1 with each other**, in conjunction, jointly, in cooperation, in collaboration, in partnership, in combination, in league, side by side; informal in cahoots. **2 simultaneously**, at the same time, at once, concurrently, as a group, in unison, in chorus. ANTONYMS separately. ▶ adj. **levelheaded**, well-adjusted, sensible, practical, realistic, mature, stable, full of common sense, well-organized, efficient, methodical, self-confident, self-assured; informal unflappable.

to·geth·er·ness /tə'ge<u>th</u>ərnis/ ▶ n. the state of being close to another person or other people: *the sense of family togetherness was strong.*

togs /tägz/ ▶ pl.n. informal clothes.

toil /toil/ ▶ v. **1** work very hard. **2** move somewhere slowly and with difficulty. ▶ n. exhausting work.

SYNONYMS ▶ v. **1 work**, labor, slave, strive; informal slog, beaver. **2 struggle**, drag yourself, trudge, slog, plod; informal schlep. ▶ n. **hard work**, labor, exertion, slaving, drudgery, effort; informal elbow grease; old use travail.

toi·let /'toilit/ ▶ n. **1** a large bowl for urinating or defecating into. **2** old use the process of washing yourself, dressing, brushing your hair, etc. □ **toilet-train** teach a young child to use the toilet. **toilet water** a diluted form of perfume.

toi·let·ries /'toilitrēz/ ▶ pl.n. articles used in washing and taking care of your body, such as soap and shampoo.

to·ken /'tōkən/ ▶ n. **1** a thing that represents a feeling, fact, or quality. **2** a voucher that can be exchanged for goods or services. **3** a disk used to operate a machine. ▶ adj. involving little effort or commitment and done only for show.

SYNONYMS ▶ n. **1 symbol**, sign, emblem, badge, representation, indication, mark, expression, demonstration. **2 memento**, souvenir, keepsake, reminder. **3 voucher**, coupon, note. ▶ adj. *token resistance* **symbolic**, nominal, perfunctory, slight, minimal, superficial.

told /tōld/ past and past participle of TELL.

tol·er·a·ble /'tälərəbəl/ ▶ adj. **1** able to be tolerated. **2** fairly good.

SYNONYMS **1 bearable**, endurable, supportable, acceptable. **2 fairly good**, fair, passable, adequate, all right, acceptable, satisfactory, average, run-of-the-mill, mediocre, middling, ordinary, unexceptional; informal OK, so-so, no great shakes. ANTONYMS intolerable.

■ **tol·er·a·bly** adv.

tol·er·ance /'täl(ə)rəns/ ▶ n. **1** the ability to accept things you do not like or agree with. **2** an allowable amount of variation in the dimensions of a machine or part.

SYNONYMS **1 toleration**, acceptance, open-mindedness, broad-mindedness, forbearance, patience, charity, understanding, lenience. **2 endurance**, resilience, resistance, immunity.

tol·er·ant /'tälərənt/ ▶ adj. **1** able to accept things you do not like or agree with. **2** able to cope with particular conditions.

SYNONYMS **open-minded**, forbearing, broad-minded, liberal, unprejudiced, unbiased, patient, long-suffering, understanding, charitable, lenient, easygoing, indulgent, permissive.

tol·er·ate /'tälə,rāt/ ▶ v. (**tolerates**, **tolerating**, **tolerated**) **1** allow someone to do something you do not like or agree with. **2** patiently accept something unpleasant. **3** be able to be exposed to a drug, toxin, etc., without a bad reaction.

SYNONYMS **1** *we do not tolerate tardiness* **allow**, permit, condone, accept, swallow, countenance; formal brook. **2** *he couldn't tolerate her moods any longer* **endure**, put up with, bear, take, stand, support, stomach, abide.

■ **tol·er·a·tion** /,tälə'rāsʜən/ n.

toll[1] /tōl/ ▶ n. **1** a charge you have to pay for the use of certain roads or bridges. **2** the number of deaths or casualties arising from an accident, war, etc. **3** the cost or damage resulting from something.

SYNONYMS **1 charge**, fee, payment, levy, tariff, tax. **2 number**, count, tally, total, sum. **3** *the toll on the environment has been high* **harm to**, damage to, injury to, detriment to, adverse effect on, cost to, loss to.

toll[2] ▶ v. (of a bell) sound with slow, even strokes, especially as a sign that someone has died. ▶ n. a single ring of a bell.

SYNONYMS ▶ v. **ring**, sound, clang, chime, strike, peal.

Tol·tec /'tōl,tek, 'täl-/ ▶ n. a member of an American Indian people living in Mexico before the Aztecs.

tom /täm/ (or **tomcat** /'täm,kat/) ▶ n. a male domestic cat.

tom·a·hawk /'tämə,hôk/ ▶ n. a light ax used in the past by American Indians.

to·ma·to /tə'mātō, -'mätō/ ▶ n. (plural **tomatoes**) a red fruit eaten as a vegetable or in salads.

SPELLING

No **e** on the end: tomat**o**.

tomb /to͞om/ ▶ n. **1** a burial place consisting of a stone structure built above ground, or an underground vault. **2** a monument to a dead person, built over their burial place.

SYNONYMS **burial chamber**, vault, crypt, catacomb, sepulcher, mausoleum, grave.

tom·boy /'täm,boi/ ▶ n. a girl who enjoys rough, noisy activities traditionally associated with boys. ■ **tom·boy·ish** adj.

tomb·stone /'to͞om,stōn/ ▶ n. a flat stone with an inscription, standing or laid over a grave.

tome /tōm/ ▶ n. a large, serious book.

tom·fool·er·y /täm'fo͞ol(ə)rē/ ▶ n. silly behavior.

to·mog·ra·phy /tə'mägrəfē/ ▶ n. a technique for seeing a cross section through a human body or other solid object using X-rays or ultrasound. ■ **to·mo·graph·ic** /,tōmə'grafik/ adj.

to·mor·row /tə'môrō, -'märō/ ▶ adv. on the day after today. ▶ n. **1** the day after today. **2** the future.

SPELLING

One **m**, two **r**s: tomorrow.

tom-tom ▶ n. a drum beaten with the hands.

ton /tən/ ▶ n. **1** (also **short ton**) a unit of weight equal to 2,000 pounds avoirdupois (907.19 kilograms). **2** (also **long ton**) a unit of weight equal to 2,240 pounds avoirdupois (1,016.05 kilograms). **3** a metric ton. **4** a unit of measurement of a ship's weight equal to 2,240 pounds or 35 cubic feet (0.99 cubic meters). **5** (also **tons**) informal a large number or amount.

ton·al /'tōnl/ ▶ adj. **1** relating to tone. **2** (of music) written using traditional keys and harmony. ■ **to·nal·i·ty** /tō'nalitē/ n. **ton·al·ly** adv.

tone /tōn/ ▶ n. **1** the quality of a musical sound. **2** the feeling or mood expressed in a person's voice. **3** general character. **4** a particular brightness, deepness, or shade in a color. **5** firmness in a resting muscle. **6** a basic interval in classical Western music, equal to two semitones. ▶ v. (**tones**, **toning**, **toned**) **1** (often **tone something up**) give greater strength or firmness to a part of your body. **2** (**tone something down**) make a statement or piece of writing less harsh, extreme, or strong.

SYNONYMS ▶ n. 1 **sound**, timbre, voice, color, tonality, intonation, inflection, modulation. 2 **mood**, air, feel, flavor, note, attitude, character, spirit, vein. 3 **shade**, color, hue, tint, tinge. ▶ v. **harmonize**, go, blend, coordinate, team, match, suit, complement.

□ **tone-deaf** unable to hear differences in musical pitch.

ton·er /'tōnər/ ▶ n. 1 a liquid applied to the skin to reduce oiliness. 2 a type of powder or ink used in photocopiers.

tongs /tôNGz, täNGz/ ▶ pl.n. a tool with two arms that are joined at one end, used for picking up and holding things.

tongue /təNG/ ▶ n. 1 the fleshy organ in the mouth, used for tasting, licking, swallowing, and speaking. 2 a person's way of speaking: *a sharp tongue*. 3 a language. 4 a strip of leather or fabric under the laces in a shoe. □ **hold your tongue** informal remain silent. **tongue and groove** wooden boards that are joined by means of interlocking ridges and grooves down their sides. **tongue-lashing** a loud or severe scolding. **tongue-tied** too shy or embarrassed to speak. **tongue-twister** a sequence of words that are difficult to pronounce. **with tongue in cheek** not seriously meaning what you are saying.

ton·ic /'tänik/ ▶ n. 1 a drink taken as a kind of medicine, to make you feel energetic and healthy. 2 something that makes you feel happier or healthier. 3 (also **tonic water**) a fizzy drink with a slightly bitter flavor, often mixed with gin.

SYNONYMS **stimulant**, boost, restorative, refresher, fillip; informal shot in the arm, pick-me-up, bracer.

to·night /tə'nīt/ ▶ adv. on the evening or night of the present day. ▶ n. the evening or night of the present day.

ton·nage /'tənij/ ▶ n. 1 weight in tons. 2 the size or carrying capacity of a ship measured in tons.

tonne /tən/ ▶ n. a metric ton.

ton·sil /'tänsəl/ ▶ n. each of two small masses of tissue in the throat.

ton·sil·lec·to·my /ˌtänsə'lektəmē/ ▶ n. (plural **tonsillectomies**) an operation to remove the tonsils.

ton·sil·li·tis /ˌtänsə'lītis/ ▶ n. inflammation of the tonsils.

ton·sure /'tänsHər/ ▶ n. a circular area on a monk's or priest's head where the hair is shaved off.

Ton·y /'tōnē/ ▶ n. an award given annually in the United States for outstanding achievement in the theater.

ton·y /'tōnē/ ▶ adj. (**tonier**, **toniest**) informal fashionable, stylish, or high-class.

too /to͞o/ ▶ adv. 1 to a higher degree than is desirable, allowed, or possible; excessively. 2 in addition.

SYNONYMS 1 **excessively**, overly, unduly, immoderately, inordinately, unreasonably, extremely, very. 2 **also**, as well, in addition, into the bargain, besides, furthermore, moreover.

USAGE

Don't confuse **too** with **to** or **two**: see the note at TO.

took /to͝ok/ past of TAKE.

tool /to͞ol/ ▶ n. 1 an object or device used to carry out a particular function. 2 a thing that helps you to do your job or achieve something. ▶ v. 1 impress a design on leather with a heated tool. 2 equip an organization with tools for industrial production.

SYNONYMS ▶ n. **implement**, utensil, instrument, device, apparatus, gadget, appliance, machine, contrivance, contraption; informal gizmo.

toon /to͞on/ ▶ n. informal 1 a cartoon film. 2 a character in a cartoon film.

toot /to͞ot/ ▶ n. a short sound made by a horn, trumpet, or similar instrument. ▶ v. make a toot.

tooth /to͞oTH/ ▶ n. (plural **teeth** /tēTH/) 1 each of the hard white projections in the mouth, used for biting and chewing. 2 a projecting part such as a cog on a gearwheel or a point on a saw or comb.

SYNONYMS **fang**, tusk; informal chopper.

■ **toothed** adj.

tooth·ache /'to͞oTHˌāk/ ▶ n. pain in a tooth.

tooth·brush /'to͞oTHˌbrəSH/ ▶ n. a small long-handled brush for cleaning your teeth.

tooth·less /'to͞oTHlis/ ▶ adj. 1 having no teeth. 2 lacking genuine power or effectiveness: *laws that are well-intentioned but toothless*.

tooth·paste /'to͞oTHˌpāst/ ▶ n. a paste for cleaning the teeth.

tooth·pick /'to͞oTHˌpik/ ▶ n. a thin, pointed piece of wood or plastic for removing bits of food from between your teeth.

tooth·some /'to͞oTHsəm/ ▶ adj. 1 (of food) appetizing or tasty. 2 informal attractive.

tooth·y /'to͞oTHē/ ▶ adj. having large or prominent teeth.

too·tle /'to͞otl/ ▶ v. (**tootles**, **tootling**, **tootled**) 1 make a series of sounds on a horn, trumpet, etc. 2 walk or drive somewhere without hurrying.

top¹ /täp/ ▶ n. 1 the highest or uppermost point, part, or surface. 2 a thing placed on, fitted to, or covering the upper part of something. 3 (**the top**) the highest or most important level or position. 4 the utmost degree. 5 a garment covering the upper part of the body. ▶ adj. highest in position, status, or degree. ▶ v. (**tops**, **topping**, **topped**) 1 be more, better, or taller than. 2 be at the highest place or rank in. 3 reach the top of a hill or rise. 4 provide with a top or topping.

SYNONYMS ▶ n. 1 **summit**, peak, pinnacle, crest, crown, brow, head, tip, apex, apogee. 2 **lid**, cap, cover, stopper, cork. 3 *he was at the top of his career* **height**, peak, pinnacle, zenith, culmination, climax, prime. ANTONYMS bottom, base. ▶ adj. 1 **highest**, topmost, uppermost. 2 **foremost**, chief, leading, principal, preeminent, greatest, best, finest, elite, premier, prime, superior, select, five-star, grade A. 3 **maximum**, greatest, utmost. ANTONYMS lowest, minimum. ▶ v. 1 **exceed**, surpass, go beyond, better, beat, outstrip, outdo, outshine, eclipse, transcend. 2 **lead**, head, be at the top of. 3 *mousse topped with whipped cream* **cover**, cap, coat, finish, garnish.

□ **on top of** 1 so as to cover. 2 in command or control of. 3 in addition to. **over the top** informal excessive or exaggerated. **top hat** a man's tall formal black hat. **top-heavy** too heavy at the top and therefore likely to fall. **top-notch** informal of the highest quality. **top something up** 1 add to a number or amount to bring it up to a certain level. **2** fill up a partly full container.

top² ▶ **n.** a toy shaped like a cone with a point at the base, that can be made to spin.

to·paz /ˈtōpaz/ ▶ **n.** a colorless, yellow, or pale blue precious stone.

top·coat /ˈtäpˌkōt/ ▶ **n.** **1** an overcoat. **2** an outer coat of paint.

to·pi·ar·y /ˈtōpēˌerē/ ▶ **n.** (plural **topiaries**) **1** the art of clipping evergreen shrubs into interesting shapes. **2** shrubs clipped in this way.

top·ic /ˈtäpik/ ▶ **n.** a subject that you talk, write, or learn about.

> SYNONYMS **subject**, theme, issue, matter, point, question, concern, argument, thesis.

top·i·cal /ˈtäpikəl/ ▶ **adj.** **1** relating to or dealing with current affairs. **2** relating to a particular subject.

> SYNONYMS **current**, up to date, up to the minute, contemporary, recent, relevant, in the news. ANTONYMS out of date.

■ **top·i·cal·i·ty** /ˌtäpəˈkalitē/ **n.** **top·i·cal·ly** **adv.**

top·knot /ˈtäpˌnät/ ▶ **n.** a knot of hair arranged on the top of the head.

to·pog·ra·phy /təˈpägrəfē/ ▶ **n.** **1** the arrangement of the physical features of an area of land. **2** the representation of these features on a map. ■ **top·o·graph·i·cal** /ˌtäpəˈgrafikəl/ (or **topographic** /ˌtäpəˈgrafik/) **adj.**

top·ple /ˈtäpəl/ ▶ **v.** (**topples**, **toppling**, **toppled**) **1** overbalance and fall down. **2** remove a government or leader from power.

> SYNONYMS **1 fall**, tumble, tip, overbalance, overturn, keel over, lose your balance. **2 knock over**, upset, push over, tip over, upend. **3 overthrow**, oust, unseat, overturn, bring down, defeat, get rid of, dislodge, eject.

top·soil /ˈtäpˌsoil/ ▶ **n.** the top layer of soil.

top·spin /ˈtäpˌspin/ ▶ **n.** a fast forward spin given to a moving ball.

top·sy-tur·vy /ˈtäpsē ˈtərvē/ ▶ **adj. & adv.** **1** upside down. **2** in a state of confusion.

tor /tôr/ ▶ **n.** a small steep hill or rocky peak.

torch /tôrch/ ▶ **n.** **1** (in the past) a piece of wood or cloth soaked in fat and set on fire. **2** a blowtorch. ▶ **v.** informal set fire to.

tore /tôr/ past of **TEAR¹**.

tor·e·a·dor /ˈtôrēəˌdôr/ ▶ **n.** a bullfighter.

tor·ment ▶ **n.** /ˈtôrment/ **1** great suffering. **2** a cause of suffering. ▶ **v.** /tôrˈment/ **1** make someone suffer very much. **2** annoy or tease in a cruel or unkind way.

> SYNONYMS ▶ **n.** **agony**, suffering, torture, pain, anguish, misery, distress, trauma. ▶ **v.** **1 torture**, afflict, rack, harrow, plague, haunt, distress, agonize. **2 tease**, taunt, bait, provoke, harass, bother, persecute; informal needle.

■ **tor·men·tor** /tôrˈmentər/ **n.**

torn /tôrn/ past participle of **TEAR¹**.

tor·na·do /tôrˈnādō/ ▶ **n.** (plural **tornadoes** or **tornados**) a violent rotating wind storm.

> SYNONYMS **whirlwind**, cyclone, storm; informal twister.

tor·pe·do /tôrˈpēdō/ ▶ **n.** (plural **torpedoes**) a long narrow underwater missile. ▶ **v.** (**torpedoes**, **torpedoing**, **torpedoed**) attack using torpedoes.

tor·pid /ˈtôrpid/ ▶ **adj.** inactive and having no energy. ■ **tor·pid·i·ty** /tôrˈpiditē/ **n.**

tor·por /ˈtôrpər/ ▶ **n.** the state of being inactive and having no energy.

torque /tôrk/ ▶ **n.** a force causing rotation.

tor·rent /ˈtôrənt, ˈtär-/ ▶ **n.** **1** a strong, fast-moving stream of water or other liquid. **2** a large outpouring.

> SYNONYMS **1** *a torrent of water* **flood**, deluge, spate, cascade, rush. **2** *a torrent of abuse* **outburst**, outpouring, stream, flood, volley, barrage, tide. ANTONYMS trickle.

tor·ren·tial /tôˈrenchəl, tə-/ ▶ **adj.** (of rain) falling rapidly and heavily.

tor·rid /ˈtôrəd, ˈtär-/ ▶ **adj.** **1** very hot and dry. **2** full of romantic passion. **3** full of difficulty.

> SYNONYMS **1** *a torrid summer* **hot**, dry, scorching, searing, blazing, blistering, sweltering, burning; informal boiling, baking. **2** *a torrid affair* **passionate**, ardent, lustful, amorous; informal steamy, sizzling. ANTONYMS cold.

tor·sion /ˈtôrshən/ ▶ **n.** the state of being twisted.

tor·so /ˈtôrsō/ ▶ **n.** (plural **torsos**) the trunk of the human body.

tort /tôrt/ ▶ **n.** Law a wrongful act or a violation of a right.

tor·tel·li·ni /ˌtôrtlˈēnē/ ▶ **pl.n.** stuffed pasta pieces rolled into small rings.

tor·til·la /tôrˈtē(y)ə/ ▶ **n.** **1** (in Mexican cooking) a thin, flat corn pancake. **2** (in Spanish cooking) an omelet.

tor·toise /ˈtôrtəs/ ▶ **n.** a slow-moving reptile with a hard, round shell into which it can draw its head and legs.

tor·toise·shell /ˈtôrtə(s)ˌshel/ ▶ **n.** **1** the semitransparent mottled yellow and brown shell of certain turtles, used to make jewelry or ornaments. **2** a domestic cat with markings resembling tortoiseshell. **3** a butterfly with mottled orange, yellow, and black markings.

tor·tu·ous /ˈtôrchōōəs/ ▶ **adj.** **1** full of twists and turns. **2** very long and complicated.

> SYNONYMS **1 twisting**, winding, zigzag, sinuous, snaky, meandering, serpentine. **2 convoluted**, complicated, complex, labyrinthine, involved, Byzantine, lengthy. ANTONYMS straight.

■ **tor·tu·ous·ly** **adv.**

> USAGE
> Don't confuse **tortuous** with **torturous**, which means 'characterized by pain or suffering.'

tor·ture /ˈtôrchər/ ▶ **n.** **1** severe pain inflicted on someone, especially to make them say something. **2** great suffering or anxiety. ▶ **v.** (**tortures**, **torturing**, **tortured**) subject someone to torture.

> SYNONYMS ▶ **n.** **1 abuse**, ill-treatment, mistreatment, maltreatment, persecution, cruelty, atrocity. **2 torment**, agony, suffering, pain, anguish, misery, distress, heartbreak, trauma. ▶ **v.** **1 abuse**, ill-treat, mistreat, maltreat, persecute. **2 torment**, rack, afflict, harrow, plague, distress, trouble.

■ **tor·tur·er** **n.**

tor·tur·ous /'tôrCHərəs/ ▶ **adj.** involving or causing pain or suffering.

To·ry /'tôrē/ ▶ **n.** (plural **Tories**) **1** a supporter of the British in the American Revolution. **2** a member or supporter of the British Conservative Party.

toss /tôs, täs/ ▶ **v. 1** throw lightly or casually. **2** move something from side to side or backward and forward. **3** jerk your head or hair backward. **4** throw a coin into the air and see which side is facing upward when it lands, using this to help decide something. **5** shake or turn food in a liquid to coat it lightly. ▶ **n.** an act of tossing.

SYNONYMS ▶ **v. 1 throw**, hurl, fling, sling, pitch, lob, launch; informal heave, chuck. **2** *he tossed a coin* **flip**, flick, spin. **3** *small boats tossing among the waves* **pitch**, lurch, rock, roll, plunge, reel, sway.

□ **toss-up 1** a situation in which any of two or more outcomes is equally possible. **2** the tossing of a coin to make a decision.

tos·ta·da /tō'städə/ ▶ **n.** a Mexican deep-fried tortilla topped with a mixture of beans, ground meat, and vegetables.

tot /tät/ ▶ **n.** a very young child.

to·tal /'tōtl/ ▶ **adj. 1** consisting of the whole number or amount. **2** complete. ▶ **n.** a total number or amount. ▶ **v.** (**totals**, **totaling**, **totaled**) **1** amount to a total number. **2** find the total of.

SYNONYMS ▶ **adj. 1 entire**, complete, whole, full, combined, aggregate, gross, overall. **2 utter**, complete, absolute, thorough, perfect, downright, out-and-out, outright, sheer, unmitigated, unqualified, unalloyed. ANTONYMS partial. ▶ **n. sum**, aggregate, whole, entirety, totality. ▶ **v. 1 add up to**, amount to, come to, run to, make. **2** *he totaled up his score* **add (up)**, count, reckon, tot up, compute, work out.

■ **to·tal·i·ty** /tō'talitē/ **n.**

to·tal·i·tar·i·an /tō,tali'te(ə)rēən/ ▶ **adj.** (of a system of government) consisting of only one leader or party and having complete power and control over the people.

SYNONYMS **autocratic**, undemocratic, one-party, dictatorial, tyrannical, despotic, fascist, oppressive, authoritarian, absolutist. ANTONYMS democratic.

■ **to·tal·i·tar·i·an·ism n.**

to·tal·ly /'tōtlē/ ▶ **adv.** completely; absolutely: *the building was totally destroyed by the fire.*

SYNONYMS **completely**, entirely, wholly, thoroughly, fully, utterly, absolutely, perfectly, unreservedly, unconditionally, downright. ANTONYMS partly.

tote[1] /tōt/ ▶ **n.** (**the tote**) informal a system of betting, in which winnings are calculated according to the amount staked rather than odds offered.

tote[2] ▶ **v.** (**totes**, **toting**, **toted**) informal carry. □ **tote bag** a large bag for carrying a number of items.

to·tem /'tōtəm/ ▶ **n.** a natural object or animal believed to have spiritual meaning and adopted as an emblem by a particular society. □ **totem pole** a pole on which totems are hung or on which images of totems are carved. ■ **to·tem·ic** /tō'temik/ **adj.**

tot·ter /'tätər/ ▶ **v.** (**totters**, **tottering**, **tottered**) **1** move in an unsteady way. **2** shake or rock as if about to collapse.

tou·can /'to͞o,kan, -,kän/ ▶ **n.** a tropical bird with a massive bill and brightly colored feathers.

tou·ch /təCH/ ▶ **v. 1** bring your fingers or another part of your body into contact with. **2** come into or be in physical contact with. **3** have an effect on. **4** (**be touched**) feel moved with gratitude or sympathy because of someone's actions or situation. **5** harm or interfere with. **6** use or consume. **7** (**touched**) informal mad. ▶ **n. 1** an act or way of touching. **2** the ability to become aware of something and learn what it is like through physical contact, especially with the fingers. **3** a small amount. **4** a distinctive detail or feature. **5** a distinctive or skillful way of dealing with something.

SYNONYMS ▶ **v. 1 contact**, meet, brush, graze, come up against, be in contact with, border, abut. **2 feel**, pat, tap, stroke, fondle, caress, pet, handle. **3** *sales touched $20,000* **reach**, attain, come to, make, rise to, soar to; informal hit. **4 compare with**, be on a par with, equal, match, rival, measure up to, better, beat; informal hold a candle to. **5 handle**, hold, pick up, move, use, meddle with, fiddle with, interfere with, tamper with, disturb. **6 affect**, move, stir, make an impression on. ▶ **n. 1 tap**, pat, contact, stroke, caress. **2 skill**, expertise, dexterity, deftness, adroitness, adeptness, ability, talent, flair, facility, proficiency, knack. **3 trace**, bit, suggestion, suspicion, hint, scintilla, tinge, dash, taste, spot, drop, dab, soupçon. **4** *the gas lights are a nice touch* **detail**, feature, point, element, addition. **5** *are you in touch with him?* **contact**, communication, correspondence.

□ **in touch 1** in or into communication. **2** having up-to-date knowledge. **out of touch** lacking up-to-date knowledge or awareness. **touch-and-go** (of a particular outcome) possible but very uncertain. **touch down** (of an aircraft or spacecraft) land. **touch on** deal briefly with. **touch-type** type using all of your fingers and without needing to look at the keys. **touch something up** make small improvements to something.

touch·down /'təCH,doun/ ▶ **n. 1** the moment at which an aircraft touches down. **2** (in football) a six-point score, usually made by carrying the ball across the opposing team's goal line.

tou·ché /to͞o'SHā/ ▶ **exclam.** used to acknowledge a good point made at your own expense.

touch·ing /'təCHiNG/ ▶ **adj.** making you feel gratitude or sympathy; moving.

SYNONYMS **moving**, affecting, heartwarming, emotional, emotive, poignant, sad, tear-jerking.

touch·line /'təCH,līn/ ▶ **n.** (in soccer) the boundary line on each side of the field.

touch·pad /'təCH,pad/ ▶ **n.** a computer input device in the form of a small touch-sensitive panel.

touch·stone /'təCH,stōn/ ▶ **n.** a standard by which something is judged.

touch·y /'təCHē/ ▶ **adj. 1** quick to take offense. **2** (of a situation or issue) needing careful treatment.

SYNONYMS **1 sensitive**, oversensitive, hypersensitive, easily offended, thin-skinned, highly strung, tense, irritable, tetchy, testy, crotchety, peevish, querulous, bad-tempered, petulant; informal snappy, cranky. **2 delicate**, sensitive, tricky, ticklish, embarrassing, awkward, difficult, contentious, controversial.

tough /təf/ ▶ **adj. 1** strong enough to withstand wear and tear. **2** able to deal with pain or difficulty. **3** strict. **4** involving problems or difficulties. **5** (of a person) rough or violent. ▶ **n.** informal a rough or violent man.

> SYNONYMS ▶ **adj. 1 durable**, strong, resilient, sturdy, rugged, solid, stout, robust, hard-wearing, long-lasting, heavy-duty, well-built, made to last. **2 chewy**, leathery, gristly, stringy, fibrous. **3 strict**, stern, severe, stringent, rigorous, hard, firm, hard-hitting, uncompromising. **4** *the training was pretty tough* **difficult**, hard, strenuous, onerous, grueling, exacting, arduous, demanding, taxing, tiring, exhausting, punishing. **5** *tough questions* **difficult**, hard, knotty, thorny, tricky. ANTONYMS weak, lenient, easy. ▶ **n. ruffian**, thug, hoodlum, hooligan, bully; informal heavy, bruiser.

■ **tough·ness n.**

tough·en /ˈtəfən/ ▶ **v.** make or become tough.

> SYNONYMS **1 strengthen**, fortify, reinforce, harden, temper, anneal. **2** *measures to* ***toughen up*** *discipline* **make stricter**, make more severe, stiffen, tighten up.

tou·pee /to͞oˈpā/ ▶ **n.** a small wig or hairpiece worn to cover a bald spot.

tour /to͝or/ ▶ **n. 1** a journey for pleasure in which several different places are visited. **2** a short trip to view or inspect something. **3** a series of plays, matches, etc., performed in several different places. **4** a period of military duty. ▶ **v.** make a tour of.

> SYNONYMS ▶ **n. 1 trip**, excursion, journey, expedition, jaunt, outing, trek. **2** *a tour of the factory* **visit**, inspection, walkabout. ▶ **v. travel around**, visit, explore, vacation in, go around.

tour de force /ˈto͝or də ˈfôrs/ ▶ **n.** (plural **tours de force**) a performance or achievement accomplished with great skill.

tour·ism /ˈto͝orˌizəm/ ▶ **n.** the business of organizing and operating vacations and visits to places of interest.

tour·ist /ˈto͝orist/ ▶ **n.** a person who travels for pleasure.

> SYNONYMS **sightseer**, traveler, vacationer, visitor, out-of-towner, backpacker, globetrotter, day tripper. ANTONYMS local.

tour·ist·y /ˈto͝oristē/ ▶ **adj.** informal visited by a lot of tourists.

tour·na·ment /ˈtərnəmənt, ˈto͝or-/ ▶ **n. 1** a series of contests between a number of competitors. **2** a medieval sporting event in which knights jousted with blunted weapons.

> SYNONYMS **competition**, contest, championship, meeting, event.

tour·ney /ˈtərnē, ˈto͝or-/ ▶ **n.** (plural **tourneys**) a tournament.

tour·ni·quet /ˈtərnikit, ˈto͝or-/ ▶ **n.** a cord or tight bandage tied round an arm or leg to stop the flow of blood through an artery.

tou·sle /ˈtouzəl/ ▶ **v.** (**tousles**, **tousling**, **tousled**) make someone's hair untidy.

tout /tout/ ▶ **v. 1** try to sell. **2** try to persuade people of something's value.

tow /tō/ ▶ **v.** use a vehicle or boat to pull another vehicle or boat along. ▶ **n.** an act of towing.

> SYNONYMS ▶ **v. pull**, haul, drag, draw, tug, lug.

□ **in tow 1** being towed. **2** accompanying or following someone. **tow rope** a rope, cable, etc., used in towing. **tow truck** a truck used to tow or pick up disabled vehicles.

to·ward /tôrd, t(ə)ˈwôrd/ (or **towards** /tôrdz, t(ə)ˈwôrdz/) ▶ **prep. 1** in the direction of: *they headed out toward California.* **2** getting nearer to: *it was another step toward freedom.* **3** in relation to: *she has always been kind toward animals.* **4** contributing to the cost of: *can you give us a few dollars toward the cost of the tickets?*

tow·el /ˈtoul/ ▶ **n.** a piece of absorbent cloth used for drying. ▶ **v.** (**towels**, **toweling**, **toweled**) dry someone or something with a towel.

tow·el·ing /ˈtouliNG/ ▶ **n.** absorbent cloth used for towels.

tow·er /ˈtou(ə)r/ ▶ **n. 1** a tall, narrow building or part of a building, especially of a church or castle. **2** a tall structure containing special equipment. ▶ **v.** (**towers**, **towering**, **towered**) **1** rise to or reach a great height. **2** (**towering**) very important or influential. **3** (**towering**) very great: *a towering rage.*

> SYNONYMS ▶ **v. soar**, rise, rear, overshadow, overhang, hang over, dominate.

town /toun/ ▶ **n. 1** a settlement larger than a village and generally smaller than a city. **2** the central part of a town or city containing its shopping area.

> SYNONYMS **municipality**, township, borough, village, hamlet; city, metropolis, conurbation.

□ **go to town** informal do something thoroughly or enthusiastically. **town crier** (in the past) a person employed to shout out public announcements in the streets. **town hall** the building where local government offices are located.

town·ship /ˈtounˌSHip/ ▶ **n.** an area that is part of a county and that has certain rights of local government.

tow·path /ˈtōˌpaTH/ ▶ **n.** a path beside a river or canal, originally used as a pathway for horses towing barges.

tox·ic /ˈtäksik/ ▶ **adj. 1** poisonous. **2** relating to or caused by poison.

> SYNONYMS **poisonous**, venomous, dangerous, harmful, injurious, noxious, pernicious, deadly, lethal. ANTONYMS harmless.

■ **tox·ic·i·ty** /täkˈsisitē/ **n.**

tox·i·col·o·gy /ˌtäksiˈkäləjē/ ▶ **n.** the branch of science concerned with how poisons work.
■ **tox·i·col·o·gist n.**

tox·in /ˈtäksin/ ▶ **n.** a poison caused by a germ, to which the body reacts by producing antibodies.

toy /toi/ ▶ **n.** an object for a child to play with. ▶ **v.** (**toy with**) **1** casually consider an idea. **2** play around or fiddle with something. ▶ **adj.** (of a breed of dog) very small.

> SYNONYMS ▶ **n. plaything**, game. ▶ **adj. model**, imitation, replica, miniature.

trace /trās/ ▶ **v.** (**traces**, **tracing**, **traced**) **1** find by careful investigation. **2** find or describe the origin or development of. **3** follow the course or position of something with your eye or finger. **4** copy something by drawing over its lines on a piece of transparent paper placed on top of it. **5** draw a pattern or outline. ▶ **n. 1** a mark or other sign of the existence or passing of something. **2** a very small amount. **3** a barely noticeable indication. **4** a line or pattern on paper or a screen showing information recorded by a machine.

> SYNONYMS ▶v. **1 track down**, find, discover, detect, unearth, turn up, hunt down, ferret out, run to ground. **2 draw**, outline, mark. ▶n. **1 sign**, mark, indication, evidence, clue, vestige, remains, remnant. **2 bit**, touch, hint, suggestion, suspicion, shadow, dash, tinge; informal smidgen, tad.

□ **trace element** a chemical element that is present in tiny amounts.

trac·er /ˈtrāsər/ ▶n. a bullet or shell whose course is made visible by a trail of flames or smoke.

trac·er·y /ˈtrāsərē/ ▶n. (plural **traceries**) **1** a decorative design of holes and outlines in stone. **2** a delicate branching pattern.

tra·che·a /ˈtrākēə/ ▶n. (plural **tracheae** /-kēˌē/ or **tracheas**) the tube carrying air between the larynx and the lungs; the windpipe.

tra·che·ot·o·my /ˌtrākēˈätəmē/ (or **tracheostomy**) ▶n. (plural **tracheotomies**) a surgical cut in the windpipe, made to enable someone to breathe when their windpipe is blocked.

track /trak/ ▶n. **1** a rough path or small road. **2** a course or circuit for racing. **3** a line of marks left on the ground by a person, animal, or vehicle as they move along. **4** a continuous line of rails on a railroad. **5** a recorded song or piece of music. **6** a strip or rail along which something may be moved. ▶v. **1** follow the trail or movements of. **2** (**track someone/thing down**) find someone or something after a thorough search. **3** follow a particular course. **4** (of a camera) move along with the subject being filmed.

> SYNONYMS ▶n. **1 path**, footpath, lane, trail, route, way. **2 course**, racecourse, racetrack, circuit, velodrome. **3** (**tracks**) *the tracks of a fox* **traces**, marks, prints, footprints, trail, spoor. **4** *the train tracks* **rail**, line. **5 song**, recording, number, piece. ▶v. **follow**, trail, pursue, shadow, stalk; informal tail.

□ **keep** (or **lose**) **track of** keep (or fail to keep) fully aware of or informed about. **on the right** (or **wrong**) **track** following a course that is likely to result in success (or failure). **track and field** athletic events that take place on a running track and a nearby field. **track record** someone's past achievements. ■ **track·er** n.

track·suit /ˈtrakˌso͞ot/ ▶n. an outfit consisting of a sweatshirt and loose pants.

tract[1] /trakt/ ▶n. **1** a large area of land. **2** a system of connected organs or tissues in the body along which something passes.

tract[2] ▶n. a short piece of religious writing in the form of a pamphlet.

trac·ta·ble /ˈtraktəbəl/ ▶adj. **1** (of a person) easy to control or influence. **2** (of a difficulty) easy to resolve.

trac·tion /ˈtrakSHən/ ▶n. **1** the action of pulling a thing along a surface. **2** the power used in pulling. **3** a way of treating a broken bone by gradually pulling it back into position. **4** the grip of a tire on a road or a wheel on a rail. □ **traction engine** a steam or diesel-powered road vehicle used for pulling heavy loads.

trac·tor /ˈtraktər/ ▶n. a powerful motor vehicle with large rear wheels, used for pulling farm machinery. □ **tractor-trailer** a large vehicle with an attached trailer for transport on roads.

trade /trād/ ▶n. **1** the buying and selling of goods and services. **2** a particular area of commercial activity. **3** a job requiring special skills and training. ▶v. (**trades**, **trading**, **traded**) **1** buy and sell goods and services. **2** exchange. **3** (**trade something in**) exchange a used article as part of the payment for another. **4** (**trade on**) take advantage of. **5** (**trade something off**) exchange something of value as part of a compromise.

> SYNONYMS ▶n. **1 dealing**, buying and selling, commerce, traffic, business. **2 occupation**, work, craft, job, career, profession, business, line (of work), métier. ▶v. **1 deal**, do business, bargain, negotiate, traffic, buy and sell, merchandise. **2** *I traded the car for a newer model* **swap**, exchange, barter.

□ **trade wind** a wind blowing steadily toward the equator from the northeast in the northern hemisphere or the southeast in the southern hemisphere. **trading post** a store or small settlement established for trading, typically in a remote place.

trade·mark /ˈtrādˌmärk/ ▶n. **1** a symbol, word, or words chosen to represent a company or product. **2** a distinctive characteristic.

trad·er /ˈtrādər/ ▶n. **1** a person who trades goods, currency, or shares. **2** a merchant ship.

> SYNONYMS **dealer**, merchant, buyer, seller, vendor, purveyor, supplier, trafficker.

trades·man /ˈtrādzmən/ ▶n. (plural **tradesmen**) a person involved in trading or a skilled trade.

tra·di·tion /trəˈdiSHən/ ▶n. **1** the passing on of customs or beliefs from generation to generation. **2** a long-established custom or belief passed on in this way. **3** a method or style established by an artist, writer, or movement, and followed by others.

> SYNONYMS **custom**, practice, convention, ritual, observance, way, usage, habit, institution, unwritten law; formal praxis.

tra·di·tion·al /trəˈdiSHənl/ ▶adj. having to do with or following tradition.

> SYNONYMS **customary**, long-established, time-honored, classic, wonted, accustomed, standard, regular, normal, conventional, habitual, ritual, age-old.

■ **tra·di·tion·al·ly** adv.

tra·di·tion·al·ism /trəˈdiSHənlˌizəm/ ▶n. the upholding of tradition, especially so as to resist change. ■ **tra·di·tion·al·ist** n. & adj.

tra·duce /trəˈd(y)o͞os/ ▶v. (**traduces**, **traducing**, **traduced**) formal say things about someone that are unpleasant or untrue.

traf·fic /ˈtrafik/ ▶n. **1** vehicles moving on public roads. **2** the movement of ships or aircraft. **3** the commercial transportation of goods or passengers. **4** the messages or signals that are sent through a communications system. **5** the action of trading in something illegal. ▶v. (**trafficks**, **trafficking**, **trafficked**) buy or sell something illegal. □ **traffic jam** a congestion in the flow of traffic so that it is at or almost at a standstill. **traffic lights** a set of automatically operated lights for controlling the flow of traffic. ■ **traf·fick·er** n.

tra·ge·di·an /trəˈjēdēən/ ▶n. **1** a person who writes tragedies for the theater. **2** a person who acts in tragedies.

trag·e·dy /ˈtrajidē/ ▶n. (plural **tragedies**) **1** a very sad event or situation. **2** a serious play with an unhappy ending.

SYNONYMS **disaster**, calamity, catastrophe, cataclysm, misfortune, adversity.

trag·ic /'trajik/ ▶ **adj.** **1** very sad. **2** relating to tragedy in a literary work.

SYNONYMS **1 disastrous**, calamitous, catastrophic, cataclysmic, devastating, terrible, dreadful, awful, appalling, horrendous, fatal. **2 sad**, unhappy, pathetic, moving, distressing, painful, harrowing, heart-rending, sorry. ANTONYMS fortunate, happy.

■ **trag·i·cal·ly adv.**

trag·i·com·e·dy /ˌtrajə'kämidē/ ▶ **n.** (plural **tragicomedies**) a play or novel containing elements of both comedy and tragedy.
■ **trag·i·com·ic adj.**

trail /trāl/ ▶ **n.** **1** a line of marks or signs left behind by someone or something as it moves along. **2** a track or scent used in following someone or hunting an animal. **3** a path through rough country. **4** a route planned or followed for a particular purpose. **5** a long thin part stretching behind or hanging down from something. ▶ **v.** **1** draw or be drawn along behind. **2** follow the trail of. **3** walk or move slowly or wearily. **4** (**trail away** or **off**) become gradually quieter and then stop. **5** be losing to an opponent in a contest. **6** (of a plant) grow along the ground or so as to hang down.

SYNONYMS ▶ **n.** **1** *a trail of clues* **series**, string, chain, succession, sequence. **2 track**, spoor, path, scent, traces, marks, signs, prints, footprints. **3 path**, way, footpath, track, route. ▶ **v.** **1 drag**, sweep, be drawn, dangle. **2** *roses trailed over the banks* **hang**, droop, fall, spill, cascade. **3 follow**, pursue, track, shadow, stalk, hunt; informal tail. **4 lose**, be down, be behind, lag behind.

trail·blaz·er /'trālˌblāzər/ ▶ **n.** **1** a person who is the first to do something new. **2** a person who finds a new way through wild country. ■ **trail·blaz·ing adj.**

trail·er /'trālər/ ▶ **n.** **1** an unpowered vehicle pulled by a car or truck, such as an open-platform trailer used for transporting a boat, or an enclosed trailer equipped for living in during vacations. **2** the rear section of a tractor-trailer. **3** an excerpt from a movie or television show used to advertise it. □ **trailer park** an area where house trailers are parked.

train /trān/ ▶ **v.** **1** teach a person or animal a particular skill or type of behavior. **2** be taught a particular skill. **3** make or become physically fit through a course of exercise. **4** (**train something on**) point something at. **5** make a plant grow in a particular direction or into a required shape. ▶ **n.** **1** a series of railroad cars moved by a locomotive. **2** a number of vehicles or animals moving in a line. **3** a series of connected events, thoughts, etc. **4** a long piece of trailing material attached to the back of a formal dress or robe.

SYNONYMS ▶ **v.** **1 instruct**, teach, coach, tutor, school, educate, prime, drill, ground. **2 study**, learn, prepare, take instruction. **3 exercise**, work out, get into shape, practice. **4 aim**, point, direct, level, focus. ▶ **n. chain**, string, series, set, sequence, succession, course.

train·ee /trā'nē/ ▶ **n.** a person undergoing training for a job or profession.

train·er /'trānər/ ▶ **n.** a person who trains people or animals.

SYNONYMS **coach**, instructor, teacher, tutor, handler.

train·ing /'trāniNG/ ▶ **n.** **1** the action of teaching a person or animal a particular skill or type of behavior. **2** the undertaking of a course of exercise in preparation for a sporting event. □ **in training** undergoing physical training for a sports event.

traipse /trāps/ ▶ **v.** (**traipses**, **traipsing**, **traipsed**) walk or move wearily or reluctantly. ▶ **n.** a boring walk.

trait /trāt/ ▶ **n.** a distinguishing quality or characteristic.

SYNONYMS **characteristic**, attribute, feature, quality, habit, mannerism, idiosyncrasy, peculiarity.

trai·tor /'trātər/ ▶ **n.** a person who betrays their country, an organization, or a cause.

SYNONYMS **betrayer**, backstabber, double-crosser, renegade, Judas, Benedict Arnold, quisling, fifth columnist, turncoat, defector; informal snake in the grass.

■ **trai·tor·ous adj.**

tra·jec·to·ry /trə'jektərē/ ▶ **n.** (plural **trajectories**) the path followed by a moving object.

tram /tram/ (or **tramcar** /'tramˌkär/) ▶ **n.** a cable car.

tram·lines /'tramˌlīnz/ ▶ **pl.n.** rails for a tram.

tram·mel /'traməl/ ▶ **n.** (**trammels**) literary restrictions on someone's freedom. ▶ **v.** (**trammels**, **trammeling**, **trammeled**) restrict or limit.

tramp /tramp/ ▶ **n.** **1** a homeless person who travels around and lives by begging or doing casual work. **2** the sound of heavy steps. **3** a long walk. ▶ **v.** **1** walk heavily or noisily. **2** walk over a long distance.

SYNONYMS ▶ **n.** **1 vagrant**, vagabond, homeless person, down-and-out, traveler, drifter, hobo; informal bum. **2 tread**, step, footstep, footfall. **3 trek**, walk, hike, slog, march, roam, ramble; informal schlep. ▶ **v. trudge**, plod, stamp, trample, lumber, trek, walk, slog, hike; informal traipse, schlep.

tram·ple /'trampəl/ ▶ **v.** (**tramples**, **trampling**, **trampled**) **1** tread on and crush. **2** (**trample on** or **over**) treat with contempt.

SYNONYMS **tread**, stamp, walk, squash, crush, flatten.

tram·po·line /'trampəˌlēn/ ▶ **n.** a strong fabric sheet connected by springs to a frame, used as a springboard and landing area in doing acrobatic or gymnastic exercises. ■ **tram·po·lin·ing n.**

trance /trans/ ▶ **n.** a half-conscious state in which someone does not respond to things happening around them.

SYNONYMS **daze**, stupor, hypnotic state, dream, reverie.

tranche /tränsh/ ▶ **n.** one of the parts into which something is divided, especially an amount of money.

tran·quil /'traNGkwəl/ ▶ **adj.** free from disturbance; calm.

SYNONYMS **peaceful**, calm, restful, quiet, still, serene, relaxing, undisturbed. ANTONYMS busy, excitable.

■ **tran·quil·i·ty** (or **tranquillity**) /ˌtraNG'kwilitē/ **n.** **tran·quil·ly adv.**

tran·quil·ize /'traNGkwə,līz/ ▶ v. (**tranquilizes, tranquilizing, tranquilized**) give a calming or sedative drug to someone.

tran·quil·iz·er /'traNGkwə,līzər/ ▶ n. a drug taken to reduce tension or anxiety.

> SYNONYMS **sedative**, barbiturate, calmative, narcotic, opiate; informal downer. ANTONYMS stimulant.

trans·act /tran'sakt, -'zakt/ ▶ v. conduct or carry out business.

trans·ac·tion /tran'saksHən, -'zak-/ ▶ n. **1** an act of buying or selling. **2** the process of carrying out business.

> SYNONYMS **deal**, bargain, agreement, undertaking, arrangement, negotiation, settlement.

trans·at·lan·tic /,tranzət'lantik, ,trans-/ ▶ adj. **1** crossing the Atlantic. **2** concerning countries on either side of the Atlantic.

tran·scend /tran'send/ ▶ v. **1** be or go beyond the range or limits of. **2** be superior to.

> SYNONYMS **go beyond**, rise above, exceed, surpass, excel, outstrip.

tran·scend·ent /tran'sendənt/ ▶ adj. **1** going beyond normal or physical human experience. **2** (of God) existing apart from the material world. ■ **tran·scend·ence** n.

tran·scen·den·tal /,transen'dentl/ ▶ adj. going beyond the limits of human knowledge in a religious or spiritual context. ■ **tran·scen·den·tal·ly** adv.

trans·con·ti·nen·tal /,tranzkäntə'nentl, ,trans-/ ▶ adj. crossing or extending across a continent or continents.

tran·scribe /tran'skrīb/ ▶ v. (**transcribes, transcribing, transcribed**) **1** put thoughts, speech, or data into written form, or into a different written form. **2** arrange a piece of music for a different instrument or voice.

tran·script /'tran,skript/ ▶ n. a written or printed version of material that was originally spoken or presented in another form.

tran·scrip·tion /tran'skripsHən/ ▶ n. **1** a transcript. **2** the process of transcribing. **3** a transcribed piece of music.

tran·sept /'tran,sept/ ▶ n. (in a cross-shaped church) either of the two parts extending at right angles from the nave.

trans·fer ▶ v. /trans'fər, 'transfər/ (**transfers, transferring, transferred**) **1** move someone or something from one place to another. **2** move to another department, job, etc. **3** change to another place, route, or means of transport during a journey. **4** pass a property, right, or responsibility to another person. ▶ n. /'transfər/ **1** an act of transferring. **2** a small colored picture or design on paper, which can be transferred to another surface by being pressed or heated.

> SYNONYMS ▶ v. **move**, take, bring, shift, convey, remove, carry, transport, relocate.

■ **trans·fer·ence** n.

trans·fig·ure /trans'figyər/ ▶ v. (**be transfigured**) be transformed into something more beautiful or spiritual. ■ **trans·fig·u·ra·tion** /trans,figyə'rāsHən/ n.

trans·fix /trans'fiks/ ▶ v. **1** make motionless with horror, wonder, or astonishment. **2** pierce with a sharp object.

> SYNONYMS *transfixed by the images* **mesmerize**, hypnotize, spellbind, bewitch, captivate, entrance, enthrall, fascinate, enrapture, grip, rivet.

trans·form /trans'fôrm/ ▶ v. **1** change or be changed in nature, form, or appearance. **2** change the voltage of an electric current.

> SYNONYMS **change**, alter, convert, revolutionize, overhaul, reconstruct, rebuild, reorganize, rearrange, rework.

trans·for·ma·tion /,transfər'māsHən/ ▶ n. a marked change in nature, form, or appearance.

> SYNONYMS **change**, alteration, conversion, metamorphosis, revolution, overhaul, reconstruction, rebuilding, reorganization, rearrangement, reworking.

■ **trans·for·ma·tion·al** adj.

trans·form·er /trans'fôrmər/ ▶ n. a device for changing the voltage of an electric current.

trans·fu·sion /trans'fyo͞ozHən/ ▶ n. a medical process in which someone is given a supply of someone else's blood.

trans·gen·der /tranz'jendər, trans-/ (also **trans·gen·dered**) ▶ adj. transsexual.

trans·gress /trans'gres, tranz-/ ▶ v. go beyond the limits of what is morally, socially, or legally acceptable. ■ **trans·gres·sor** n.

trans·gres·sion /trans'gresHən, tranz-/ ▶ n. the action or an act of transgressing.

> SYNONYMS **offense**, crime, sin, wrong, wrongdoing, misdemeanor, misdeed, lawbreaking; error, lapse; violation, defiance, disobedience, nonobservance; old use trespass.

tran·sient /'transHənt, -zHənt, -zēənt/ ▶ adj. **1** lasting only for a short time. **2** staying or working in a place for a short time only. ▶ n. a transient person.

> SYNONYMS ▶ adj. **transitory**, temporary, short-lived, short-term, ephemeral, impermanent, brief, short, momentary, fleeting, passing. ANTONYMS permanent.

■ **tran·sience** n. **tran·sient·ly** adv.

tran·sis·tor /tran'zistər/ ▶ n. **1** a silicon-based device that is able to amplify or rectify electric currents. **2** (also **transistor radio**) a portable radio using circuits containing transistors.

tran·sit /'tranzit/ ▶ n. **1** the carrying of people or things from one place to another. **2** an act of passing through or across a place.

tran·si·tion /tran'zisHən, -'sisHən/ ▶ n. **1** the process of changing from one state or condition to another. **2** a period of such change.

> SYNONYMS **change**, passage, move, transformation, conversion, metamorphosis, alteration, changeover, shift, switch.

tran·si·tion·al /tran'zisHənl, -'sisHənl/ ▶ adj. of, relating to, or featuring transition; temporary.

> SYNONYMS **1** *a transitional period* **intermediate**, interim, changeover, changing, fluid, unsettled. **2** *a transitional government* **interim**, temporary, provisional, pro tem, acting, caretaker.

tran·si·tive /'transitiv, 'tranz-/ ▶ adj. (of a verb) able to take a direct object, e.g., *saw* in *he saw the donkey*. ■ **tran·si·tiv·i·ty** /,transə'tivitē, -zə-/ n.

tran·si·to·ry /ˈtransi,tôrē, ˈtranzi-/ ▶ **adj.** lasting for only a short time.

SYNONYMS **transient**, temporary, brief, short, short-lived, short-term, impermanent, ephemeral, momentary, fleeting, passing. ANTONYMS permanent.

trans·late /transˈlāt, tranz-/ ▶ **v.** (**translates**, **translating**, **translated**) **1** express the sense of words or a piece of writing in another language. **2** (**translate into**) change or be changed into another form.

SYNONYMS **interpret**, convert, render, put, change, express, decipher, reword, decode, gloss, explain.

trans·la·tion /transˈlāshən, tranz-/ ▶ **n.** **1** the action of translating. **2** a piece of writing or word that is translated.

SYNONYMS **interpretation**, rendition, conversion, change, alteration, adaptation.

trans·la·tor /transˈlātər, tranz-/ ▶ **n.** a person who translates writing or speech from one language into another.

trans·lit·er·ate /transˈlitə,rāt, tranz-/ ▶ **v.** (**transliterates**, **transliterating**, **transliterated**) write a letter or word using the corresponding letters of a different alphabet or language. ■ **trans·lit·er·a·tion** /trans,litəˈrāshən, tranz-/ **n.**

trans·lu·cent /transˈlo͞osnt, tranz-/ ▶ **adj.** allowing light to pass through partially; semitransparent.

SYNONYMS **semitransparent**, pellucid, limpid, clear; diaphanous, gossamer, sheer. ANTONYMS opaque.

■ **trans·lu·cence** (or **translucency**) **n.**

trans·mis·sion /transˈmishən, tranz-/ ▶ **n.** **1** the passing of something from one place or person to another. **2** a transmitted program or signal. **3** the mechanism by which power is passed from an engine to the axle in a motor vehicle.

SYNONYMS **1 transfer**, communication, passing on, conveyance, dissemination, spread, circulation, relaying. **2 broadcasting**, televising, airing. **3 broadcast**, program, show.

trans·mit /tranzˈmit, trans-/ ▶ **v.** (**transmits**, **transmitting**, **transmitted**) **1** cause to pass from one place or person to another. **2** broadcast or send out an electrical signal or a radio or television program. **3** allow heat, light, etc., to pass through a material.

SYNONYMS **1 transfer**, communicate, pass on, hand on, convey, impart, channel, carry, relay, dispatch, disseminate, spread, circulate. **2 broadcast**, send out, air, televise.

trans·mit·ter /transˈmitər, tranz-/ ▶ **n.** a device used to produce and transmit electromagnetic waves carrying messages or signals, especially those of radio or television.

trans·mog·ri·fy /transˈmägrə,fī, tranz-/ ▶ **v.** (**transmogrifies**, **transmogrifying**, **transmogrified**) humorous change into something completely different.

trans·mute /transˈmyo͞ot, tranz-/ ▶ **v.** (**transmutes**, **transmuting**, **transmuted**) change in form, nature, or substance. ■ **trans·mu·ta·tion** /,transmyo͞oˈtāshən, ,tranz-/ **n.**

tran·som /ˈtransəm/ ▶ **n.** **1** the flat surface forming the stern of a boat. **2** a strengthening crossbar over a door or window.

trans·par·en·cy /tranˈsparənsē/ ▶ **n.** (plural **transparencies**) **1** the condition of being transparent. **2** a positive transparent photograph printed on plastic or glass, and viewed using a slide projector.

trans·par·ent /tranˈspe(ə)rənt, -ˈspar-/ ▶ **adj.** **1** allowing light to pass through so that objects behind can be distinctly seen. **2** obvious or evident.

SYNONYMS **1 clear**, translucent, limpid, crystal clear, crystalline, pellucid. **2 see-through**, sheer, filmy, gauzy, diaphanous. **3 obvious**, blatant, unambiguous, unequivocal, clear, plain, apparent, unmistakable, manifest, conspicuous, patent. ANTONYMS opaque, obscure.

■ **trans·par·ent·ly** **adv.**

tran·spire /tranˈspī(ə)r/ ▶ **v.** (**transpires**, **transpiring**, **transpired**) **1** come to be known. **2** take place; happen. **3** (of a plant or leaf) give off water vapor through pores in the surface layer. ■ **tran·spi·ra·tion** /-spəˈrāshən/ **n.**

trans·plant ▶ **v.** /transˈplant/ **1** take living tissue or an organ and implant it in another part of the body or in another body. **2** transfer to another place or situation. ▶ **n.** /ˈtrans,plant/ **1** an operation in which an organ or tissue is transplanted. **2** a person or thing that has been transplanted. ■ **trans·plan·ta·tion** /-,planˈtāshən/ **n.**

trans·port ▶ **v.** /transˈpôrt/ **1** carry people or goods from one place to another by means of a vehicle, aircraft, or ship. **2** (**be transported**) be overwhelmed with a strong emotion. **3** (in the past) send someone to a distant place as a punishment. ▶ **n.** /ˈtrans,pôrt/ **1** a system or method of carrying people or goods from one place to another. **2** the action of transporting. **3** a large vehicle, ship, or aircraft for carrying troops or stores. **4** (**transports**) very strong emotions.

SYNONYMS ▶ **v.** **convey**, carry, take, transfer, move, shift, send, deliver, bear, ship, ferry; informal cart. ▶ **n.** **conveyance**, carriage, delivery, shipping, freight, shipment, haulage.

■ **trans·por·ta·tion** /,transpərˈtāshən/ **n.**

trans·port·er /transˈpôrtər/ ▶ **n.** a large vehicle used to carry heavy objects.

trans·pose /transˈpōz/ ▶ **v.** (**transposes**, **transposing**, **transposed**) **1** cause two or more things to change places with each other. **2** move something to a different place or context. **3** write or play music in a different key from the original. ■ **trans·po·si·tion** /,transpəˈzishən/ **n.**

trans·sex·u·al /tran(s)ˈsekshо͞oəl/ (or **transexual** /tranˈsekshо͞oəl/) ▶ **n.** a person who emotionally and psychologically feels that they belong to the opposite sex. ▶ **adj.** relating to a transsexual person.

tran·sub·stan·ti·a·tion /,transəb,stanchēˈāshən/ ▶ **n.** (in Christian, especially Roman Catholic, thinking) the doctrine that the bread and wine served in the Eucharist become the actual body and blood of Jesus after they have been blessed.

trans·verse /transˈvərs, tranz-/ ▶ **adj.** placed or extending across something. ■ **trans·verse·ly** **adv.**

trans·ves·tite /transˈves,tīt, tranz-/ ▶ **n.** a person, especially a man, who likes to dress in clothes worn by the opposite sex. ■ **trans·ves·tism** **n.**

trap /trap/ ▶ **n.** **1** a device, pit, or enclosure designed to catch and hold animals. **2** an unpleasant situation from which you cannot escape. **3** a trick causing someone to say or do something that they do not intend. **4** a container or device used to collect a particular thing. **5** a light, two-wheeled carriage pulled by a horse or pony. ▶ **v.** (**traps**, **trapping**, **trapped**) **1** catch and hold in a trap. **2** trick into doing something.

> SYNONYMS ▶ **n. 1 snare**, net, mesh, gin. **2 trick**, ploy, ruse, deception, subterfuge; informal setup. ▶ **v. 1 snare**, entrap, capture, catch, ambush. **2 confine**, cut off, corner, shut in, pen in, hem in, imprison. **3 trick**, dupe, deceive, fool, hoodwink.

trap·door /ˈtrapˌdôr/ ▶ **n.** a hinged or removable panel in a floor, ceiling, or roof.

tra·peze /trəˈpēz, tra-/ ▶ **n.** a horizontal bar hanging on two ropes high above the ground, used by acrobats in a circus.

tra·pe·zi·um /trəˈpēzēəm/ ▶ **n.** (plural **trapezia** /-zēə/ or **trapeziums**) (in geometry) a quadrilateral with one pair of sides parallel.

trap·per /ˈtrapər/ ▶ **n.** a person who traps wild animals.

trap·pings /ˈtrapiNGz/ ▶ **pl.n. 1** the signs or objects associated with a particular situation or role. **2** a horse's ornamental harness.

Trap·pist /ˈtrapist/ ▶ **n.** a monk belonging to an order that speaks only at certain times.

trash /trasH/ ▶ **n. 1** waste material. **2** poor-quality writing, art, etc. **3** a person or people of very low social status. ▶ **v.** informal wreck or destroy.

> SYNONYMS ▶ **n. 1 rubbish**, garbage, refuse, waste, litter, junk. **2 nonsense**, rubbish, trivia, pulp fiction, pap; informal drivel.

□ **trash can** a garbage can .**trash-talking** (or **trash talk**) insulting or boastful speech intended to intimidate or humiliate someone. ■ **trash·y adj.**

trau·ma /ˈtroumə, ˈtrô-/ ▶ **n.** (plural **traumas**) **1** a deeply disturbing experience. **2** emotional shock following a stressful event. **3** (in medicine) physical injury.

> SYNONYMS **1 shock**, upheaval, distress, stress, strain, pain, anguish, suffering, upset, ordeal. **2 injury**, damage, wound.

trau·mat·ic /trəˈmatik, trou-, trô-/ ▶ **adj.** emotionally disturbing or distressing.

> SYNONYMS **disturbing**, shocking, distressing, upsetting, painful, agonizing, hurtful, stressful, devastating, harrowing.

■ **trau·mat·i·cal·ly adv.**

trau·ma·tize /ˈtroumәˌtīz, ˈtrô-/ ▶ **v.** (**be traumatized**) suffer lasting shock as a result of a disturbing experience or injury.

tra·vail /trəˈvāl, ˈtravˌāl/ (or **travails**) ▶ **n.** old use a situation involving a lot of hard work or difficulty.

trav·el /ˈtravəl/ ▶ **v.** (**travels**, **traveling**, **traveled**) **1** go from one place to another, especially over a long distance. **2** journey along a particular road or through a particular region. ▶ **n. 1** the action of traveling. **2** (**travels**) journeys over a long distance.

> SYNONYMS ▶ **v. journey**, tour, take a trip, voyage, go sightseeing, globetrot, backpack, trek. ▶ **n.** (**travels**) **traveling**, journeys, expeditions, trips, tours, excursions, voyages, treks, wanderings, jaunts.

□ **travel agent** a person or agency that makes the necessary arrangements for travelers.

trav·el·er /ˈtrav(ə)lər/ ▶ **n.** a person who is traveling or who often travels.

> SYNONYMS **tourist**, vacationer, out-of-towner, sightseer, day tripper, globetrotter, backpacker, passenger, commuter.

□ **traveler's check** a check for a fixed amount that can be exchanged for cash in foreign countries.

trav·e·logue /ˈtravəˌlôg, -ˌläg/ ▶ **n.** a film, book, or talk about a person's travels.

trav·erse /trəˈvərs/ ▶ **v.** (**traverses**, **traversing**, **traversed**) travel or extend across or through.

trav·es·ty /ˈtravistē/ ▶ **n.** (plural **travesties**) a ridiculous or shocking version of something.

> SYNONYMS *a travesty of justice* **misrepresentation**, distortion, perversion, corruption, mockery, parody; farce, charade, pantomime, sham; informal apology for.

trawl /trôl/ ▶ **v. 1** catch fish with a trawl net. **2** search through something thoroughly. ▶ **n. 1** an act of trawling. **2** a large wide-mouthed fishing net dragged by a boat along the bottom of the sea.

trawl·er /ˈtrôlər/ ▶ **n.** a fishing boat used for trawling.

tray /trā/ ▶ **n.** a flat container with a raised rim, used for carrying plates, cups, etc.

treach·er·ous /ˈtrecHərəs/ ▶ **adj. 1** guilty of or involving betrayal. **2** having hidden or unpredictable dangers.

> SYNONYMS **1 traitorous**, disloyal, unfaithful, duplicitous, deceitful, false, backstabbing, double-crossing, two-faced, untrustworthy, unreliable, apostate, renegade. **2 dangerous**, hazardous, perilous, unsafe, precarious, risky; informal dicey, hairy. ANTONYMS loyal, faithful.

■ **treach·er·ous·ly adv.**

treach·er·y /ˈtrecHərē/ ▶ **n.** (plural **treacheries**) behavior that involves betraying someone's trust.

trea·cle /ˈtrēkəl/ ▶ **n. 1** ⇨ MOLASSES. **2** cloying sentiment. ■ **trea·cly adj.**

tread /tred/ ▶ **v.** (**treads**, **treading**, **trod** /träd/; past participle **trodden** /ˈträdn/ or **trod**) **1** walk in a particular way. **2** press down or crush with your feet. **3** walk on or along. ▶ **n. 1** a way or the sound of walking. **2** the top surface of a step or stair. **3** the part of a vehicle tire that grips the road. **4** the part of the sole of a shoe that touches the ground.

> SYNONYMS ▶ **v. 1 walk**, step, stride, pace, march, tramp, plod, stomp, trudge. **2 crush**, flatten, press down, squash, trample on, stamp on. ▶ **n. step**, footstep, footfall, tramp.

□ **tread water 1** stay in an upright position in deep water by moving the feet with a walking movement. **2** fail to make progress.

trea·dle /ˈtredl/ ▶ **n.** a lever that you work with your foot to operate a machine.

tread·mill /ˈtredˌmil/ ▶ **n. 1** a job or situation that is tiring or boring and difficult to escape from. **2** a large wheel turned by the weight of people or animals treading on steps fitted into it, used in the past to drive machinery. **3** a device used for exercise consisting of a continuous moving belt on which you walk or run.

trea·son /ˈtrēzən/ (or **high treason**) ▶ **n.** the crime of betraying your country.

> SYNONYMS **treachery**, disloyalty, betrayal, sedition, subversion, mutiny, rebellion.

■ **trea·son·a·ble adj.**

treas·ure /ˈtrezHər/ ▶ **n. 1** a quantity of precious coins, gems, or other valuable objects. **2** a very valuable object. **3** informal a much loved or highly valued person. ▶ **v.** (**treasures**, **treasuring**, **treasured**) **1** look after carefully. **2** value highly.

SYNONYMS ▶ **n. 1 riches**, valuables, jewels, gems, gold, silver, precious metals, money, cash, wealth, fortune. **2 masterpiece**, gem, pearl, jewel. ▶ **v. cherish**, hold dear, prize, set great store by, value greatly.

□ **treasure hunt** a game in which players search for hidden objects by following a trail of clues. **treasure trove** a store of valuable or pleasant things.

treas·ur·er /'trezHərər/ ▶ **n.** a person appointed to manage the finances of a society, company, etc.

treas·ur·y /'trezHərē/ ▶ **n.** (plural **treasuries**) **1** the funds or revenue of a state, institution, or society. **2** (**Treasury**) (in some countries) the government department responsible for the overall management of the economy.

SYNONYMS **storehouse**, repository, treasure house, exchequer, fund, mine, bank, coffers, purse.

treat /trēt/ ▶ **v. 1** behave toward or deal with in a certain way. **2** give medical care or attention to. **3** use a substance or process to protect or preserve something, or give it particular properties. **4** present or discuss a subject. **5** (**treat someone to**) provide someone with food, drink, or entertainment that you have paid for. **6** (**treat yourself**) do or have something very enjoyable. ▶ **n.** a gift or event that gives someone great pleasure.

SYNONYMS ▶ **v. 1 behave toward**, act toward, use, deal with, handle. **2** *police are treating the fires as arson* **regard**, consider, view, look on, think of, put down. **3 deal with**, tackle, handle, discuss, explore, investigate. **4 tend**, nurse, attend to, give medical attention to. **5 cure**, heal, remedy. **6** *he treated her to lunch* **buy**, take out for, give, pay for; informal foot the bill for, pick up the tab for. **7** *the crowd was treated to a superb display* **entertain with**, regale with, fete with. ▶ **n. 1 celebration**, entertainment, amusement, surprise. **2 present**, gift, tidbit, delicacy, luxury, indulgence, extravagance; informal goody. **3 pleasure**, delight, thrill, joy.

trea·tise /'trētis/ ▶ **n.** a formal piece of writing on a subject.

treat·ment /'trētmənt/ ▶ **n. 1** a way of behaving toward someone or dealing with something. **2** medical care for an illness or injury. **3** the use of a substance or process to preserve or give particular properties to something. **4** the presentation or discussion of a subject.

SYNONYMS **1 behavior**, conduct, handling, management, dealings. **2 medical care**, therapy, nursing, ministrations, medication, medicament, drugs. **3 discussion**, handling, investigation, exploration, consideration, study, analysis.

trea·ty /'trētē/ ▶ **n.** (plural **treaties**) a formal agreement between states.

SYNONYMS **agreement**, settlement, pact, deal, entente, concordat, accord, protocol, compact, convention; formal concord.

tre·ble[1] /'trebəl/ ▶ **adj. 1** consisting of three parts. **2** multiplied or occurring three times. ▶ **pron.** an amount that is three times as large as usual. ▶ **v.** (**trebles**, **trebling**, **trebled**) make or become treble.

tre·ble[2] ▶ **n. 1** a high-pitched voice, especially a boy's singing voice. **2** the high-frequency output of a radio or audio system. □ **treble clef** (in music) a clef placing G above middle C on the second-lowest line of the stave.

tree /trē/ ▶ **n.** a plant consisting of a thick wooden stem and a number of branches, that can grow to a great height and live for many years. □ **tree diagram** a diagram with a structure of branching lines. **tree house** a structure built in the branches of a tree for children to play in.

tree·top /'trē,täp/ ▶ **n.** (usually **treetops**) the uppermost part of a tree.

tre·foil /'trē,foil, 'tref,oil/ ▶ **n. 1** a small plant with yellow flowers and cloverlike leaves. **2** a shape or design in the form of three rounded lobes like a clover leaf.

trek /trek/ ▶ **n.** a long, difficult journey, especially one made on foot. ▶ **v.** (**treks**, **trekking**, **trekked**) go on a trek.

SYNONYMS ▶ **n. journey**, trip, expedition, safari, hike, march, tramp, walk.

■ **trek·ker n.**

trel·lis /'trelis/ ▶ **n.** a framework of bars used as a support for climbing plants.

trem·ble /'trembəl/ ▶ **v.** (**trembles**, **trembling**, **trembled**) **1** shake in a way that you cannot control, usually as a result of fear, excitement, or weakness. **2** be in a state of great worry or fear. ▶ **n.** a trembling feeling, movement, or sound.

SYNONYMS ▶ **v. shake**, quiver, shudder, vibrate, wobble, rock, move, sway.

tre·men·dous /trə'mendəs/ ▶ **adj. 1** very great in amount, scale, or force. **2** informal very good or impressive.

SYNONYMS **1 huge**, enormous, immense, colossal, massive, prodigious, stupendous; informal whopping, astronomical, ginormous. **2 excellent**, first-class, outstanding, marvelous, wonderful, splendid, superb, admirable; informal great, fantastic, fabulous, terrific, super, awesome, ace.

■ **tre·men·dous·ly adv.**

trem·o·lo /'tremə,lō/ ▶ **n.** (plural **tremolos**) a wavering effect in singing or created in certain musical instruments.

trem·or /'tremər/ ▶ **n. 1** a quivering movement that cannot be controlled. **2** (also **earth tremor**) a slight earthquake. **3** a sudden feeling of fear or excitement.

SYNONYMS **1** *the sudden tremor of her hands* **tremble**, shake, quiver, twitch, tic. **2** *a tremor of fear ran through her* **shiver**, frisson, spasm, thrill, tingle, stab, dart, shaft; wave, surge, rush, ripple. **3** *the epicenter of the tremor* **earthquake**, shock; informal quake.

trem·u·lous /'tremyələs/ ▶ **adj. 1** shaking or quivering slightly. **2** nervous.

trench /trencH/ ▶ **n. 1** a long, narrow ditch. **2** a ditch dug by troops to provide shelter from enemy fire. **3** (also **ocean trench**) a long, deep depression in the ocean bed.

SYNONYMS **ditch**, channel, trough, excavation, furrow, rut, conduit.

□ **trench coat** a belted, double-breasted raincoat.

trench·ant /'trencHənt/ ▶ **adj.** (of something said or written) expressed strongly and clearly.

SYNONYMS **incisive**, penetrating, sharp, keen, acute, shrewd, razor-sharp, rapierlike, piercing. ANTONYMS vague.

■ **trench·ant·ly** adv.

trench·er /ˈtrenCHər/ ▶ n. (in the past) a flat piece of wood from which food was served or eaten.

trend /trend/ ▶ n. **1** a general direction in which something is developing or changing. **2** a fashion.

SYNONYMS **1 tendency**, movement, drift, swing, shift, course, current, direction, inclination, leaning. **2 fashion**, vogue, style, mode, craze, mania, rage; informal fad, thing.

trend·set·ter /ˈtren(d)ˌsetər/ ▶ n. a person who leads the way in fashion or ideas.

trend·y /ˈtrendē/ ▶ adj. (**trendier**, **trendiest**) informal very fashionable.

trep·i·da·tion /ˌtrepiˈdāSHən/ ▶ n. a feeling of fear or nervousness.

tres·pass /ˈtrespəs, -ˌpas/ ▶ v. **1** enter someone's land or property without their permission. **2** (**trespass on**) take advantage of someone's time, good nature, etc. **3** (**trespass against**) old use do wrong or harm to. ▶ n. **1** Law the entering of someone's land or property without their permission. **2** old use a bad or wrongful act.

SYNONYMS ▶ v. **intrude**, encroach, invade, enter without permission.

■ **tres·pass·er** n.

tress /tres/ ▶ n. literary a long lock of hair.

tres·tle /ˈtresəl/ ▶ n. a structure consisting of a horizontal bar on sloping legs, used in pairs to support a surface such as a table top.

tri·band /ˈtrīˌband/ (of a cell phone) having three frequencies enabling it to be used in different regions, such as the US and Europe.

tri·ad /ˈtrīˌad/ ▶ n. **1** a group of three people or things. **2** a musical chord of a note plus the third and fifth above it.

tri·al /ˈtrī(ə)l/ ▶ n. **1** a formal examination in a court of law to decide if someone is guilty. **2** a test of performance, qualities, or suitability. **3** (**trials**) an event in which horses or dogs compete or perform. **4** something that tests a person's endurance or patience. ▶ v. (**trials**, **trialing**, **trialed**) test something to assess its suitability or performance.

SYNONYMS ▶ n. **1 case**, lawsuit, hearing, tribunal, litigation, proceedings. **2 test**, experiment, pilot study, examination, check, assessment, audition, evaluation, appraisal; informal dry run. **3 trouble**, affliction, ordeal, tribulation, difficulty, problem, misfortune, mishap.

□ **on trial 1** being tried in a court of law. **2** undergoing tests. **trial and error** the process of trying out various methods until you find one that works well.

tri·an·gle /ˈtrīˌaNGgəl/ ▶ n. **1** a figure with three straight sides and three angles. **2** a musical instrument consisting of a steel rod bent into a triangle, sounded with a rod. **3** an emotional relationship involving a couple and a third person.

tri·an·gu·lar /trīˈaNGgyələr/ ▶ adj. **1** shaped like a triangle. **2** involving three people or groups. ■ **tri·an·gu·lar·i·ty** /trīˌaNGgyəˈlaritē/ n. **tri·an·gu·lar·ly** adv.

tri·an·gu·la·tion /ˌtrīˌaNGgyəˈlāSHən/ ▶ n. the division of an area into a series of triangles in order to determine distances and relative positions.

tri·ath·lon /trīˈaTHlən, -ˌlän/ ▶ n. an athletic contest involving three different events, typically swimming, cycling, and long-distance running. ■ **tri·ath·lete** n.

trib·al /ˈtrībəl/ ▶ adj. relating to or typical of a tribe or tribes. ■ **trib·al·ly** adv.

trib·al·ism /ˈtrībəˌlizəm/ ▶ n. behavior and attitudes that result from a system in which people belong to tribes.

tribe /trīb/ ▶ n. **1** a group of people within a traditional society sharing customs and beliefs and led by a chief. **2** informal a large number of people.

SYNONYMS **ethnic group**, people, family, clan, race, dynasty, house, nation.

tribes·man /ˈtrībzmən/ ▶ n. (plural **tribesmen**) a member of a tribe in a traditional society.

trib·u·la·tion /ˌtribyəˈlāSHən/ ▶ n. trouble, suffering, or difficulty.

SYNONYMS **1 trouble**, difficulty, problem, worry, anxiety, burden, cross to bear, ordeal, trial, adversity, hardship, tragedy, trauma; informal hassle. **2 suffering**, distress, trouble, misery, wretchedness, unhappiness, sadness, heartache, woe, grief, pain, anguish, agony.

tri·bu·nal /trīˈbyo͞onl, trə-/ ▶ n. **1** a group of people established to settle disputes. **2** a court of justice.

SYNONYMS **court**, board, panel, committee.

trib·une /ˈtribyo͞on, triˈbyo͞on/ ▶ n. (in ancient Rome) an official chosen by the ordinary people to protect their interests.

trib·u·tar·y /ˈtribyəˌterē/ ▶ n. (plural **tributaries**) a river or stream that flows into a larger river or lake.

trib·ute /ˈtribyo͞ot/ ▶ n. **1** an act, statement, or gift intended to show respect or admiration for someone. **2** historical payment made by a state to a more powerful one.

SYNONYMS **accolade**, praise, commendation, salute, testimonial, homage, congratulations, compliments, plaudits. ANTONYMS criticism.

trice /trīs/ ▶ n. (**in a trice**) in a moment.

tri·cen·ten·ni·al /ˌtrīsenˈtenēəl/ ▶ n. a three-hundredth anniversary.

tri·ceps /ˈtrīˌseps/ ▶ n. (plural **triceps**) the large muscle at the back of the upper arm.

tri·cer·a·tops /trīˈserəˌtäps/ ▶ n. a large plant-eating dinosaur with two large horns.

tri·chol·o·gy /triˈkäləjē/ ▶ n. the branch of medicine concerned with the hair and scalp. ■ **tri·chol·o·gist** n.

trick /trik/ ▶ n. **1** something intended to deceive or outwit someone. **2** a skillful act performed to entertain people. **3** an illusion. **4** a habit or mannerism. **5** (in card games) a single round of play. ▶ v. cunningly deceive or outwit someone.

SYNONYMS ▶ n. **1 stratagem**, ploy, ruse, scheme, device, maneuver, dodge, subterfuge, swindle, fraud; informal con, setup, scam, sting. **2 practical joke**, hoax, prank; informal leg-pulling, spoof, put-on. **3 knack**, skill, technique, secret, art. ▶ v. **deceive**, delude, hoodwink, mislead, take in, dupe, fool, gull, cheat, defraud, swindle; informal con, sucker, diddle, take for a ride, pull a fast one on.

□ **do the trick** informal achieve the required result. **trick or treat** a children's custom of calling at houses at Halloween with the threat of pranks if they are not given a small gift. ■ **trick·er·y** n.

trick·le /'trikəl/ ▶ v. (**trickles**, **trickling**, **trickled**) **1** (of a liquid) flow in a small stream. **2** come or go slowly or gradually. ▶ n. **1** a small flow of liquid. **2** a small number of people or things moving slowly.

SYNONYMS ▶ v. **dribble**, drip, ooze, leak, seep, spill, exude, percolate. ANTONYMS pour, gush. ▶ n. **dribble**, drip, thin stream, rivulet.

trick·ster /'trikstər/ ▶ n. a person who cheats or deceives people.

trick·y /'trikē/ ▶ adj. (**trickier**, **trickiest**) **1** difficult or awkward. **2** likely to deceive you; crafty.

SYNONYMS **1 difficult**, awkward, problematic, delicate, ticklish, sensitive; informal sticky. **2 cunning**, crafty, wily, devious, sly, scheming, calculating, deceitful. ANTONYMS straightforward.

tri·col·or /'trīˌkələr/ ▶ n. a flag with three bands of different colors, especially the French national flag.

tri·cy·cle /'trīsikəl, -ˌsikəl/ ▶ n. a vehicle similar to a bicycle but having three wheels.

tri·dent /'trīdnt/ ▶ n. a three-pronged spear.

tried /trīd/ past and past participle of **TRY**.

tri·en·ni·al /trī'enēəl/ ▶ adj. lasting for or happening every three years.

tri·er /tri(ə)r/ ▶ n. a person who always tries hard.

tri·fle /'trīfəl/ ▶ n. **1** something of little value or importance. **2** a small amount. ▶ v. (**trifles**, **trifling**, **trifled**) (**trifle with**) treat without seriousness or respect.

SYNONYMS ▶ n. **triviality**, thing of no consequence, bagatelle, inessential, nothing, technicality; (**trifles**) trivia, minutiae.

tri·fling /'trīf(ə)liNG/ ▶ adj. unimportant; trivial.

SYNONYMS **trivial**, unimportant, insignificant, inconsequential, petty, minor, of no account, incidental; informal piffling. ANTONYMS important.

trig·ger /'trigər/ ▶ n. **1** a small lever that sets off a gun or other mechanism when pulled. **2** an event that causes something to happen. ▶ v. (**triggers**, **triggering**, **triggered**) **1** cause a device to function. **2** make something happen.

SYNONYMS ▶ v. **start**, set off, initiate, spark, activate, touch off, provoke, precipitate, prompt, stir up, cause, give rise to, lead to, set in motion, bring about.

□ **trigger-happy** tending to fire a gun on the slightest provocation.

trig·o·nom·e·try /ˌtrigə'nämitrē/ ▶ n. the branch of mathematics concerned with the relationships between the sides and angles of triangles.

trike /trīk/ ▶ n. informal a tricycle.

trill /tril/ ▶ n. a high warbling sound. ▶ v. make a high warbling sound.

tril·lion /'trilyən/ ▶ cardinal number a million million (1,000,000,000,000 or 10^{12}). ■ **tril·lionth** ordinal number.

tri·lo·bite /'trīləˌbīt/ ▶ n. a fossil sea creature with a rear part divided into segments.

tril·o·gy /'triləjē/ ▶ n. (plural **trilogies**) a group of three related novels, plays, or films.

trim /trim/ ▶ v. (**trims**, **trimming**, **trimmed**) **1** cut away unwanted parts from something. **2** reduce the size, amount, or number of. **3** decorate something along its edges. **4** adjust a sail. ▶ n. **1** decoration along the edges of something. **2** the upholstery or interior lining of a car. **3** an act of trimming. **4** good condition. ▶ adj. (**trimmer**, **trimmest**) neat in appearance.

SYNONYMS ▶ v. **1 cut**, crop, bob, shorten, clip, snip, shear, dock, lop off, prune, shave, pare. **2 decorate**, adorn, ornament, embellish, edge, border, fringe. ▶ n. **1 decoration**, ornamentation, adornment, embellishment, border, edging, piping, fringe, frill. **2 haircut**, cut, clip, snip. ▶ adj. **1 neat**, tidy, orderly, uncluttered, well-kept, well-maintained, immaculate, spick and span, spruce, dapper. **2 slim**, slender, lean, sleek, willowy. ANTONYMS untidy.

□ **in trim** slim and fit.

tri·ma·ran /'trīməˌran/ ▶ n. a yacht with three hulls side by side.

trim·ming /'trimiNG/ ▶ n. **1** (**trimmings**) small pieces trimmed off. **2** decoration or accompaniments.

SYNONYMS **1 decoration**, ornamentation, adornment, borders, edging, piping, fringes, frills. **2** (**trimmings**) **accompaniments**, extras, frills, accessories, accoutrements, trappings, paraphernalia.

trin·i·ty /'trinitē/ ▶ n. (plural **trinities**) **1** (**the Trinity** or **the Holy Trinity**) (in Christian belief) the three persons (Father, Son, and Holy Spirit) that make up God. **2** a group of three people or things.

trin·ket /'triNGkit/ ▶ n. a small inexpensive ornament or item of jewelry.

tri·o /'trē-ō/ ▶ n. (plural **trios**) **1** a set or group of three. **2** a group of three musicians.

SYNONYMS **threesome**, three, triumvirate, triad, troika, trinity, trilogy.

trip /trip/ ▶ v. (**trips**, **tripping**, **tripped**) **1** catch your foot on something and stumble or fall. **2** (**trip up**) make a mistake. **3** walk, run, or dance with quick, light steps. **4** make a mechanism start working. **5** informal experience hallucinations as a result of taking a drug such as LSD. ▶ n. **1** a journey to a place and back again, especially for pleasure. **2** an instance of tripping or falling. **3** informal a period of hallucinations caused by taking a drug such as LSD. **4** a device that trips a mechanism.

SYNONYMS ▶ v. **1 stumble**, lose your footing, catch your foot, slip, fall (down), tumble. **2 skip**, dance, prance, bound, spring, scamper. ▶ n. **1 excursion**, outing, jaunt, vacation, break, visit, tour, journey, expedition, voyage, drive, run; informal spin. **2 stumble**, slip, fall, misstep.

tri·par·tite /trī'pärˌtīt/ ▶ adj. **1** consisting of three parts. **2** shared by or involving three parties.

tripe /trīp/ ▶ n. **1** the stomach of a cow or sheep used as food. **2** informal nonsense.

tri·plane /'trīˌplān/ ▶ n. an early type of aircraft with three pairs of wings, one above the other.

tri·ple /'tripəl/ ▶ adj. **1** consisting of three parts, things, or people. **2** having three times the usual size, quality, or strength. ▶ **n.** a thing that is three times as large as usual or is made up of three parts. ▶ **v.** (**triples**, **tripling**, **tripled**) make or become triple.

SYNONYMS ▶ **adj.** **threefold**, tripartite, three-way, three times, treble.

▫ **triple jump** an athletic event in which competitors perform a hop, a step, and a jump from a running start. **triple play** Baseball a play in which three players are put out. ■ **trip·ly adv.**

tri·plet /'triplit/ ▶ **n. 1** each of three children born at the same birth. **2** a group of three musical notes to be performed in the time of two or four.

trip·li·cate ▶ **adj.** /'triplikit/ existing in three copies or examples. ▶ **v.** /-ˌkāt/ (**triplicates**, **triplicating**, **triplicated**) **1** make three copies of. **2** multiply by three.

tri·pod /'trīpäd/ ▶ **n.** a three-legged stand for a camera or other device.

trip·tych /'triptik/ ▶ **n.** a picture or carving on three panels.

trip·wire /'tripˌwīr/ ▶ **n.** a wire that is stretched close to the ground and sets off a trap or alarm when disturbed.

trite /trīt/ ▶ **adj.** (of a remark or idea) unoriginal and dull.

SYNONYMS **banal**, hackneyed, clichéd, platitudinous, vapid, commonplace, stock, conventional, stereotyped, overused, overdone, overworked, timeworn, tired, stale, hoary, hack, unimaginative, unoriginal; informal old hat, corny, played out. ANTONYMS original, imaginative.

tri·ton /'trītn/ ▶ **n.** a large tropical mollusk with a spiral shell.

tri·umph /'trīəmf/ ▶ **n. 1** a great victory or achievement. **2** joy or satisfaction resulting from a success or victory. **3** a very successful example of something. ▶ **v.** be successful or victorious.

SYNONYMS ▶ **n. 1** **victory**, win, conquest, success, achievement. **2** **jubilation**, exultation, elation, delight, joy, happiness, glee, pride, satisfaction. ANTONYMS defeat, disappointment. ▶ **v.** **win**, succeed, come first, be victorious, carry the day, prevail. ANTONYMS lose.

■ **tri·um·phal** /trī'əmfəl/ **adj.**

tri·um·phant /trī'əmfənt/ ▶ **adj. 1** having won a battle or contest. **2** joyful after a victory or achievement.

SYNONYMS **1** **victorious**, successful, winning, conquering. **2** **jubilant**, exultant, celebratory, elated, joyful, delighted, gleeful, proud. ANTONYMS defeated, despondent.

■ **tri·um·phant·ly adv.**

tri·um·vi·rate /trī'əmvərit, -ˌrāt/ ▶ **n.** a group of three powerful or important people or things.

triv·et /'trivit/ ▶ **n.** a metal stand on which hot dishes are placed.

triv·i·a /'trivēə/ ▶ **pl.n.** unimportant details or pieces of information.

triv·i·al /'trivēəl/ ▶ **adj.** of little value or importance.

SYNONYMS **unimportant**, insignificant, inconsequential, minor, of no account, of no importance, petty, trifling, negligible; informal piffling. ANTONYMS important, significant.

■ **triv·i·al·i·ty** /ˌtrivē'alitē/ **n.** (plural **trivialities**) **triv·i·al·ly adv.**

triv·i·al·ize /'trivēəˌlīz/ ▶ **v.** (**trivializes**, **trivializing**, **trivialized**) make something seem less important or complex than it really is. ■ **triv·i·al·i·za·tion** /ˌtrivēəli'zāsʜən/ **n.**

trod /träd/ past and past participle of **TREAD**.

trod·den /'trädn/ past participle of **TREAD**.

trog·lo·dyte /'trägləˌdīt/ ▶ **n.** a person who lives in a cave.

troi·ka /'troikə/ ▶ **n. 1** a Russian vehicle pulled by a team of three horses side by side. **2** a group of three people working together.

Tro·jan /'trōjən/ ▶ **n.** an inhabitant of ancient Troy in Asia Minor (present-day Turkey). ▶ **adj.** relating to Troy. ▫ **Trojan Horse** something intended to weaken or defeat an enemy secretly.

troll[1] /trōl/ ▶ **n.** (in stories) an ugly giant or dwarf.

troll[2] ▶ **v.** fish by trailing a baited line along behind a boat.

trol·ley /'trälē/ ▶ **n.** (plural **trolleys**) **1** (in full **trolley wheel**) a wheel attached to a pole, used to carry current from an overhead electric wire to drive a streetcar. **2** (in full **trolley car**) ⇨ **STREETCAR**. **3** a small table on wheels.

trol·lop /'träləp/ ▶ **n.** dated or humorous a woman who has a lot of sexual partners.

trom·bone /träm'bōn, trəm-/ ▶ **n.** a large brass wind instrument with a sliding tube that you move to produce different notes. ■ **trom·bon·ist n.**

troop /tro͞op/ ▶ **n. 1** (**troops**) soldiers or armed forces. **2** a unit of troops. **3** a group of people or animals. ▶ **v.** come or go as a group.

SYNONYMS ▶ **n. 1** (**troops**) **soldiers**, armed forces, army, soldiery, servicemen, servicewomen. **2** **group**, party, band, gang, body, company, troupe, crowd, squad, unit. ▶ **v.** **walk**, march, file, flock, crowd, throng, stream, swarm.

troop·er /'tro͞opər/ ▶ **n. 1** a soldier in a cavalry or armored unit. **2** a state police officer.

tro·phy /'trōfē/ ▶ **n.** (plural **trophies**) **1** a cup or other object awarded as a prize. **2** a souvenir of an achievement.

SYNONYMS **1** **cup**, medal, prize, award. **2** **souvenir**, memento, keepsake, spoils, booty.

trop·ic /'träpik/ ▶ **n. 1** the line of latitude 23°26′ north (**tropic of Cancer**) or south (**tropic of Capricorn**) of the equator. **2** (**the tropics**) the region between the tropics of Cancer and Capricorn.

trop·i·cal /'träpəkəl/ ▶ **adj. 1** having to do with the tropics. **2** very hot and humid.

SYNONYMS **hot**, sweltering, humid, sultry, steamy, sticky, oppressive, stifling. ANTONYMS cold.

■ **trop·i·cal·ly adv.**

trot /trät/ ▶ **v.** (**trots**, **trotting**, **trotted**) **1** (of a horse) move at a pace faster than a walk. **2** run at a moderate pace with short steps. **3** (**trot something out**) informal repeat something that has been said many times before. ▶ **n. 1** a trotting pace. **2** a period of trotting.

SYNONYMS ▶ **v.** **run**, jog, scuttle, scurry, bustle, scamper.

troth /trôtʜ, trōtʜ/ ▶ **n.** (**plight your troth**) old use promise to marry.

trot·ter /ˈträtər/ ▶ **n.** a pig's foot.

trou·ba·dour /ˈtro͞obəˌdôr, -ˌdo͝or/ ▶ **n.** a traveling singer and poet in medieval France.

trou·ble /ˈtrəbəl/ ▶ **n. 1** difficulty or problems. **2** effort that you make to do something. **3** a cause of worry or inconvenience. **4** a situation in which you can be punished or blamed. **5** a situation in which people are angry or violent. ▶ **v.** (**troubles**, **troubling**, **troubled**) **1** cause distress or inconvenience to. **2** (**troubled**) feeling anxious or experiencing problems. **3** (**trouble to do**) make the effort required to do.

> SYNONYMS ▶ **n. 1 difficulty**, problems, bother, inconvenience, worry, anxiety, distress, stress, agitation, harassment, unpleasantness; informal hassle. **2** *she poured out all her troubles* **problem**, misfortune, difficulty, trial, tribulation, woe, grief, heartache, misery, affliction, suffering. **3** *he's gone to a lot of trouble* **bother**, inconvenience, fuss, effort, exertion, work, labor. **4 nuisance**, bother, inconvenience, irritation, problem, trial, pest; informal headache, pain, drag. **5** *you're too gullible, that's your trouble* **shortcoming**, weakness, failing, fault. **6 disease**, illness, sickness, ailment, complaint, problem, disorder, disability. **7 malfunction**, failure, breakdown. **8 disturbance**, disorder, unrest, fighting, scuffle, breach of the peace. ▶ **v. 1 worry**, bother, concern, disturb, upset, agitate, distress, perturb, annoy, nag, prey on someone's mind; informal bug. **2** (**troubled**) **anxious**, worried, concerned, perturbed, disturbed, bothered, uneasy, unsettled, agitated; distressed, upset, dismayed. **3** (**troubled**) *troubled times* **difficult**, problematic, unsettled, hard, tough, stressful, dark. **4 afflict**, burden, suffer from, be cursed with. **5** *I'm sorry to trouble you* **inconvenience**, bother, impose on, disturb, put out, disoblige; informal hassle.

trou·ble·mak·er /ˈtrəbəlˌmākər/ ▶ **n.** a person who regularly causes trouble.

> SYNONYMS **mischief-maker**, rabble-rouser, firebrand, agitator, agent provocateur, ringleader, incendiary; scandalmonger, gossipmonger, meddler.

trou·ble·shoot·er /ˈtrəbəlˌsʜo͞otər/ ▶ **n.** a person who investigates and solves problems or faults. ■ **trou·ble·shoot·ing n.**

trou·ble·some /ˈtrəbəlsəm/ ▶ **adj.** causing difficulty or problems.

> SYNONYMS **1 annoying**, irritating, exasperating, maddening, infuriating, bothersome, tiresome, nagging, difficult, awkward; informal pesky. **2 difficult**, awkward, uncooperative, rebellious, unmanageable, unruly, obstreperous, disruptive, disobedient, naughty, recalcitrant.

trough /trôf/ ▶ **n. 1** a long, narrow open container for animals to eat or drink out of. **2** (in weather forecasting) a long region of low atmospheric pressure. **3** a point of low activity or achievement.

trounce /trouns/ ▶ **v.** (**trounces**, **trouncing**, **trounced**) defeat heavily.

troupe /tro͞op/ ▶ **n.** a touring group of entertainers.

troup·er /ˈtro͞opər/ ▶ **n. 1** an entertainer with many years of experience. **2** a reliable and uncomplaining person.

trou·sers /ˈtrouzərz/ ▶ **pl.n.** pants.

trous·seau /ˈtro͞oˌsō, ˌtro͞oˈsō/ ▶ **n.** (plural **trousseaux** or **trousseaus**) clothes and other belongings collected by a bride for her marriage.

trout /trout/ ▶ **n.** (plural **trout** or **trouts**) an edible fish of the salmon family.

trove /trōv/ ▶ **n.** a store of valuable things.

trow·el /ˈtrouəl/ ▶ **n. 1** a small tool with a curved scoop for lifting plants or earth. **2** a small tool with a flat blade for applying mortar or plaster.

troy /troi/ ▶ **n.** a system of weights used mainly for precious metals and gems, with a pound of 12 ounces.

tru·ant /ˈtro͞oənt/ ▶ **n.** a student who stays away from school without permission or explanation. ▶ **v.** (also **play truant**) stay away from school without permission or explanation. ■ **tru·an·cy n.**

truce /tro͞os/ ▶ **n.** an agreement between enemies to stop fighting for a certain time.

> SYNONYMS **ceasefire**, armistice, cessation of hostilities, peace.

truck¹ /trək/ ▶ **n.** a large road vehicle for carrying goods. ▶ **v. 1** convey on or in a truck. **2** drive a truck. □ **truck farm** a farm that produces vegetables for the market. **truck stop** a roadside service station and restaurant for truckdrivers on highways. ■ **truck·er n.**

truck² ▶ **n.** (**have no truck with**) refuse to have any dealings or association with.

truc·u·lent /ˈtrəkyələnt/ ▶ **adj.** quick to argue or fight.

> SYNONYMS **defiant**, aggressive, antagonistic, belligerent, pugnacious, confrontational, obstreperous, argumentative, quarrelsome, uncooperative; bad-tempered, short-tempered, cross, snappish; informal feisty. ANTONYMS cooperative, amiable.

■ **truc·u·lence n. truc·u·lent·ly adv.**

trudge /trəj/ ▶ **v.** (**trudges**, **trudging**, **trudged**) walk slowly and with heavy steps. ▶ **n.** a difficult or long and tiring walk.

true /tro͞o/ ▶ **adj.** (**truer**, **truest**) **1** in accordance with fact or reality. **2** rightly so called: *true love.* **3** real or actual. **4** accurate and exact. **5** (**true to**) in keeping with what is usual or expected. **6** loyal or faithful. **7** upright or level.

> SYNONYMS **1 correct**, truthful, accurate, right, verifiable, the case; formal veracious. **2 genuine**, authentic, real, actual, bona fide, proper, legitimate; informal kosher. **3 sincere**, genuine, real, unfeigned, heartfelt. **4 loyal**, faithful, constant, devoted, trustworthy, reliable, dependable, staunch. **5** *a true reflection* **accurate**, faithful, telling it like it is, realistic, factual, lifelike. ANTONYMS false, untrue.

□ **true-blue** extremely loyal or traditional.

truf·fle /ˈtrəfəl/ ▶ **n. 1** an underground fungus that is eaten as a delicacy. **2** a soft chocolate candy.

tru·ism /ˈtro͞oˌizəm/ ▶ **n.** a statement that is obviously true and says nothing new or interesting.

tru·ly /ˈtro͞olē/ ▶ **adv. 1** in a truthful way. **2** genuinely or properly. **3** in actual fact; really. **4** absolutely or completely (used for emphasis): *a truly dreadful song.* □ **yours truly 1** used as a formula for ending a letter. **2** humorous used to refer to yourself.

SPELLING

Note that there's no **e** in **truly**.

trump /trəmp/ ▶ **n.** (in card games) a card of the suit chosen to rank above the others. ▶ **v. 1** play a trump on a card of another suit. **2** beat by saying or doing something better. **3** (**trump something up**) invent a false accusation or excuse.

trump·er·y /ˈtrəmpərē/ ▶ **adj.** old use showy but worthless.

trum·pet /ˈtrəmpit/ ▶ **n. 1** a brass musical instrument with a flared end. **2** the loud cry of an elephant. ▶ **v.** (**trumpets**, **trumpeting**, **trumpeted**) **1** announce widely or enthusiastically. **2** (of an elephant) make its characteristic loud cry. **3** play a trumpet.

SYNONYMS ▶ **v. proclaim**, announce, declare, noise abroad, shout from the rooftops.

□ **blow your own trumpet** talk boastfully about your achievements. ■ **trum·pet·er n.**

trun·cate /ˈtrəNGˌkāt/ ▶ **v.** (**truncates**, **truncating**, **truncated**) shorten by cutting off the top or end. ■ **trun·ca·tion** /ˌtrəNGˈkāSHən/ **n.**

trun·cheon /ˈtrənCHən/ ▶ **n.** a short, thick stick carried as a weapon by a police officer.

trun·dle /ˈtrəndl/ ▶ **v.** (**trundles**, **trundling**, **trundled**) move or roll slowly and heavily.

trunk /trəNGk/ ▶ **n. 1** the main woody stem of a tree. **2** a person's or animal's body apart from the limbs and head. **3** the long nose of an elephant. **4** a large box for storing or transporting articles. **5** the rear storage compartment of a car.

SYNONYMS **1 stem**, bole, stock, stalk. **2 torso**, body. **3 proboscis**, nose, snout. **4 chest**, box, crate, coffer, case, portmanteau.

trunks /trəNGks/ ▶ **pl.n.** men's shorts worn for swimming or boxing.

truss /trəs/ ▶ **n. 1** a framework that supports a roof, bridge, or other structure. **2** a padded belt worn to support a hernia. ▶ **v. 1** tie someone up tightly. **2** tie up the wings and legs of a bird before cooking.

trust /trəst/ ▶ **n. 1** firm belief in the truth, reliability, or ability of someone or something. **2** responsibility for someone or something. **3** an arrangement by which someone manages property for the benefit of another person or people. **4** an organization or company managed by trustees. ▶ **v. 1** have trust in. **2** (**trust someone with**) allow someone to have, use, or look after. **3** (**trust someone/thing to**) give someone or something to another person for safekeeping. **4** (**trust to**) rely on luck, fate, etc. **5** expect or hope.

SYNONYMS ▶ **n. confidence**, belief, faith, certainty, assurance, conviction, credence, reliance. ▶ **v. 1 have faith in**, have (every) confidence in, believe in, pin your hopes/faith on. **2 rely on**, depend on, bank on, count on, be sure of. **3** *I trust we shall meet again* **hope**, expect, take it, assume, presume. **4 entrust**, consign, commit, give, hand over, turn over, assign. ANTONYMS distrust, mistrust.

□ **trust fund** a fund of money or property that is held for someone by a trust. ■ **trust·ed adj.**

trust·ee /trəˈstē/ ▶ **n.** a person who is given legal powers to manage property for the benefit of others.

trust·ful /ˈtrəs(t)fəl/ ▶ **adj.** having total trust in someone. ■ **trust·ful·ly adv.**

trust·ing /ˈtrəstiNG/ ▶ **adj.** tending to trust other people; not suspicious.

SYNONYMS **trustful**, unsuspecting, unquestioning, naive, innocent, childlike, ingenuous, wide-eyed, credulous, gullible, easily taken in. ANTONYMS distrustful, suspicious.

■ **trust·ing·ly adv.**

trust·wor·thy /ˈtrəstˌwərT͟Hē/ ▶ **adj.** honest and reliable.

SYNONYMS **reliable**, dependable, honest, as good as your word, above suspicion; informal on the level, on the up and up. ANTONYMS unreliable.

■ **trust·wor·thi·ness n.**

trust·y /ˈtrəstē/ ▶ **adj.** (**trustier**, **trustiest**) old use or humorous reliable or faithful.

SYNONYMS **reliable**, dependable, trustworthy, unfailing; loyal, faithful, true, staunch, steadfast, constant. ANTONYMS unreliable.

truth /tro͞oTH/ ▶ **n.** (plural **truths** /tro͞oT͟HZ, tro͞oTHS/) **1** the quality or state of being true. **2** true facts. **3** a fact or belief that is accepted as true.

SYNONYMS **1 accuracy**, correctness, authenticity, veracity, verity, truthfulness. **2 fact(s)**, reality, real life, actuality. ANTONYMS lies, fiction, falsehood.

truth·ful /ˈtro͞oTHfəl/ ▶ **adj. 1** telling or expressing the truth. **2** accurate; true to life.

SYNONYMS **true**, accurate, correct, factual, faithful, reliable. ANTONYMS deceitful, untrue.

■ **truth·ful·ly adv. truth·ful·ness n.**

try /trī/ ▶ **v.** (**tries**, **trying**, **tried**) **1** make an attempt to do something. **2** (also **try something out**) test something new or different. **3** attempt to open a door. **4** (**try something on**) put on an item of clothing to see if it fits or looks good. **5** put someone on trial. ▶ **n.** (plural **tries**) **1** an attempt. **2** an act of testing something new or different. **3** Rugby an act of touching the ball down behind the opposing goal line to score points.

SYNONYMS ▶ **v. 1 attempt**, endeavor, make an effort, exert yourself, strive, do your best, do your utmost, aim, seek; informal have a go/shot/crack/stab, go all out. **2 test**, put to the test, sample, taste, inspect, investigate, examine, appraise, evaluate, assess; informal check out. **3** *she tried his patience* **tax**, strain, test, stretch, sap, drain, exhaust, wear out. ▶ **n. attempt**, effort, endeavor; informal go, shot, crack, stab.

□ **try your hand at** attempt to do for the first time. **try someone's patience** make someone feel irritated or annoyed.

USAGE

When writing, it is better to use **try to** rather than **try and** (*we should try to help them* rather than *we should try and help them*).

try·ing /ˈtrī-iNG/ ▶ **adj.** difficult or annoying.

SYNONYMS **1 stressful**, taxing, demanding, difficult, challenging, frustrating, tough, hard; informal hellish. **2 annoying**, irritating, exasperating, maddening, infuriating, tiresome, troublesome, irksome, vexatious.

tryst /trist/ ▶ n. literary a private, romantic meeting between lovers.

tsar /zär/ (or **czar** /zär, (t)sär/ or **tzar**) ▶ n. an emperor of Russia before 1917. ■ **tsar·ist** adj.

tse·tse fly /'(t)sētsē, '(t)set-/ ▶ n. an African bloodsucking fly that transmits diseases.

tsp. ▶ abbr. teaspoonful.

tsu·na·mi /(t)sōō'nämē/ ▶ n. a tidal wave caused by an underwater earthquake or other disturbance.

tub /təb/ ▶ n. **1** a low, wide, open container with a flat bottom. **2** a small plastic or cardboard container for food.

tu·ba /'t(y)ōōbə/ ▶ n. a large low-pitched brass wind instrument.

tub·by /'təbē/ ▶ adj. (**tubbier**, **tubbiest**) informal (of a person) short and rather fat.

tube /t(y)ōōb/ ▶ n. **1** a long, hollow cylinder for conveying or holding something. **2** a flexible container sealed at one end and having a cap at the other.

tu·ber /'t(y)ōōbər/ ▶ n. a thick underground part of the stem or root of some plants, from which new plants grow.

tu·ber·cu·lar /t(y)ōō'bərkyələr/ ▶ adj. relating to, or suffering from, tuberculosis.

tu·ber·cu·lo·sis /tə,bərkyə'lōsis, t(y)ōō-/ ▶ n. a serious infectious disease in which small swellings (**tubercles**) appear, especially in the lungs.

tu·bu·lar /'t(y)ōōbyələr/ ▶ adj. **1** long, round, and hollow like a tube. **2** made from a tube or tubes.

tuck /tək/ ▶ v. **1** push, fold, or turn between two surfaces. **2** put neatly into a small space. **3** (**tuck someone in** or **up**) settle someone in bed by pulling the edges of the bedclothes under the mattress. **4** (**tuck in** or **into**) informal eat food heartily. ▶ n. a flattened, stitched fold in a garment or material.

SYNONYMS ▶ v. **push**, insert, slip, thrust, stuff, stick, cram.

Tu·dor /'t(y)ōōdər/ ▶ adj. relating to the royal family that ruled England 1485–1603.

Tues·day /'t(y)ōōzdā, -dē/ ▶ n. the day of the week before Wednesday and following Monday.

tu·fa /'t(y)ōōfə/ ▶ n. **1** rock formed as a deposit from mineral springs. **2** rock formed from volcanic ash.

tuff /təf/ ▶ n. rock formed from volcanic ash.

tuf·fet /'təfit/ ▶ n. **1** a tuft or clump. **2** a footstool or low seat.

tuft /təft/ ▶ n. a bunch of threads, grass, or hair held or growing together at the base. ■ **tuft·ed** adj. **tuft·y** adj.

tug /təg/ ▶ v. (**tugs**, **tugging**, **tugged**) pull hard or suddenly. ▶ n. **1** a hard or sudden pull. **2** (also **tugboat** /'təg,bōt/) a small, powerful boat for towing larger boats and ships.

SYNONYMS ▶ v. **1** *he tugged at her sleeve* **pull**, pluck, tweak, twitch, jerk, catch hold of; informal yank. **2** **drag**, pull, lug, draw, haul, heave, tow, trail.

□ **tug of war** a contest in which two teams pull at opposite ends of a rope.

tu·i·tion /t(y)ōō'isHən/ ▶ n. teaching or instruction.

tu·lip /'t(y)ōōləp/ ▶ n. a plant with brightly colored cup-shaped flowers.

tulle /tōōl/ ▶ n. a soft, fine net material, used for making veils and dresses.

tum·ble /'təmbəl/ ▶ v. (**tumbles**, **tumbling**, **tumbled**) **1** fall suddenly or clumsily. **2** move in a headlong way. **3** decrease rapidly in amount or value. ▶ n. **1** a sudden or clumsy fall. **2** an untidy or confused arrangement.

SYNONYMS ▶ v. **1** **fall over**, fall down, topple over, go head over heels, lose your balance, take a spill, trip (up), stumble. **2** *housing prices tumbled* **plummet**, plunge, dive, nosedive, drop, slump, slide; informal crash. ANTONYMS rise.

□ **tumble dryer** a machine that dries washed clothes by turning them in hot air inside a revolving drum.

tum·ble·down /'təmbəl,doun/ ▶ adj. (of a building) ruined or falling into ruin.

tum·bler /'təmblər/ ▶ n. **1** a drinking glass with straight sides and no handle or stem. **2** an acrobat. **3** a part of a lock that holds the bolt until lifted by a key.

tum·ble·weed /'təmbəl,wēd/ ▶ n. an American and Australian plant of dry areas that breaks off near the ground and is blown about by the wind.

tum·bril /'təmbrəl/ ▶ n. an open cart of a kind used to take prisoners to the guillotine during the French Revolution.

tu·mes·cent /t(y)ōō'mesənt/ ▶ adj. swollen or becoming swollen.

tu·mid /'t(y)ōōmid/ ▶ adj. (of a part of the body) swollen.

tum·my /'təmē/ ▶ n. (plural **tummies**) informal a person's stomach or abdomen. □ **tummy button** the navel.

tu·mor /'t(y)ōōmər/ ▶ n. an abnormal growth of tissue in the body.

SYNONYMS **cancer**, growth, lump, malignancy; Medicine carcinoma, sarcoma.

tu·mult /'t(y)ōō,məlt/ ▶ n. **1** a loud, confused noise. **2** confusion or disorder.

SYNONYMS **1** **clamor**, din, noise, racket, uproar, commotion, ruckus, pandemonium, melee, frenzy; informal hullabaloo. **2** *years of political tumult* **turmoil**, confusion, disorder, disarray, unrest, chaos, turbulence, mayhem, havoc, upheaval. ANTONYMS tranquility.

tu·mul·tu·ous /t(y)ōō'məlcHōōəs, tə-/ ▶ adj. **1** very loud and showing strong feelings: *tumultuous applause*. **2** excited, confused, or disorderly.

SYNONYMS **1** *tumultuous applause* **loud**, deafening, thunderous, uproarious, noisy, clamorous, vociferous. **2** *a tumultuous crowd* **disorderly**, unruly, rowdy, turbulent, boisterous, excited, agitated, restless, wild, riotous. ANTONYMS soft, orderly.

tu·mu·lus /'t(y)ōōmyə,ləs/ ▶ n. (plural **tumuli** /-,lī/) an ancient burial mound.

tun /tən/ ▶ n. a large beer or wine cask.

tu·na /'t(y)ōōnə/ ▶ n. (plural **tuna** or **tunas**) a large edible fish of warm seas.

tun·dra /'təndrə/ ▶ n. the vast, flat, treeless regions of Europe, Asia, and North America in which the soil under the surface is permanently frozen.

tune /t(y)o͞on/ ▶ n. **1** a sequence of notes that form a piece of music; a melody. **2** correct musical pitch. ▶ v. (**tunes**, **tuning**, **tuned**) **1** adjust a musical instrument to the correct pitch. **2** adjust a radio or television to a particular frequency. **3** adjust an engine so that it runs smoothly and efficiently. **4** adjust or adapt to a purpose or situation.

SYNONYMS ▶ n. **melody**, air, strain, theme, song, jingle, ditty. ▶ v. **attune**, adapt, adjust, regulate.

□ **to the tune of** informal amounting to or involving (a sum of money). **tuning fork** a two-pronged steel device that produces a specific note when hit against a surface.

tune·ful /'t(y)o͞onfəl/ ▶ adj. having or producing a pleasing tune. ■ **tune·ful·ly** adv.

tune·less /'t(y)o͞onləs/ ▶ adj. not having or producing a pleasing tune. ■ **tune·less·ly** adv.

tun·er /'t(y)o͞onər/ ▶ n. **1** a person or device that tunes musical instruments. **2** a part of a stereo system that receives radio broadcasts.

tung·sten /'təNGstən/ ▶ n. a hard gray metal used to make electric light filaments.

tu·nic /'t(y)o͞onik/ ▶ n. **1** a loose sleeveless garment reaching to the thighs or knees. **2** a close-fitting short coat worn as part of a uniform.

Tu·ni·sian /t(y)o͞o'nēZHən/ ▶ n. a person from Tunisia. ▶ adj. relating to Tunisia.

tun·nel /'tənl/ ▶ n. a passage built underground for a road or railroad or by a burrowing animal. ▶ v. (**tunnels**, **tunneling**, **tunneled**) dig a tunnel.

SYNONYMS ▶ n. **underground passage**, underpass, subway, shaft, burrow, hole, warren, labyrinth. ▶ v. **dig**, burrow, mine, bore, drill.

□ **tunnel vision 1** a condition in which things cannot be seen properly if they are not straight ahead. **2** informal the tendency to focus only on a single aspect of a situation.

tur·ban /'tərbən/ ▶ n. a long length of material worn wound round the head by Muslim and Sikh men. ■ **tur·baned** (or **turbanned**) adj.

tur·bid /'tərbid/ ▶ adj. (of a liquid) cloudy or muddy; not clear.

tur·bine /'tər,bīn, -bin/ ▶ n. a machine in which a wheel or rotor is made to revolve by a fast-moving flow of water, air, etc.

tur·bo·charg·er /'tərbō,CHärjər/ (or **turbo**) ▶ n. a supercharger driven by a turbine powered by the engine's exhaust gases. ■ **tur·bo·charged** adj.

tur·bo·fan /'tərbō,fan/ ▶ n. a jet engine in which a turbine-driven fan provides additional thrust.

tur·bo·jet /'tərbō,jet/ ▶ n. a jet engine in which the exhaust gases also operate a device for compressing the air drawn into the engine.

tur·bo·prop /'tərbō,präp/ ▶ n. a jet engine in which a turbine is used to drive a propeller.

tur·bot /'tərbət/ ▶ n. (plural **turbot** or **turbots**) an edible flatfish.

tur·bu·lence /'tərbyələns/ ▶ n. **1** violent or unsteady movement of air or water. **2** conflict or confusion.

tur·bu·lent /'tərbyələnt/ ▶ adj. **1** involving a lot of conflict, disorder, or confusion. **2** (of air or water) moving unsteadily or violently.

SYNONYMS **tempestuous**, stormy, unstable, unsettled, tumultuous, chaotic, anarchic, lawless. ANTONYMS peaceful.

■ **tur·bu·lent·ly** adv.

tu·reen /t(y)o͝o'rēn/ ▶ n. a deep covered dish from which soup is served.

turf /tərf/ ▶ n. (plural **turfs** or **turves** /tərvz/) **1** grass and earth held together by its roots. **2** a piece of turf cut from the ground. **3** (**the turf**) horse racing. **4** (**your turf**) informal your territory. ▶ v. cover with turf.

tur·gid /'tərjid/ ▶ adj. **1** (of language) pompous and boring. **2** swollen or full.

Turk /tərk/ ▶ n. a person from Turkey.

tur·key /'tərkē/ ▶ n. (plural **turkeys**) a large game bird bred for food.

Turk·ish /'tərkiSH/ ▶ n. the language of Turkey. ▶ adj. relating to Turkey or its language. □ **Turkish bath** a period of sitting in a room filled with very hot air or steam, followed by washing and massage. **Turkish delight** a candy consisting of flavored gelatin coated in icing sugar.

tur·mer·ic /'tərmərik/ ▶ n. a bright yellow powder obtained from a plant, used in Asian cooking.

tur·moil /'tər,moil/ ▶ n. a state of great disturbance, confusion, or uncertainty.

SYNONYMS **confusion**, upheaval, turbulence, tumult, disorder, disturbance, ferment, chaos, mayhem. ANTONYMS peace, order.

turn /tərn/ ▶ v. **1** move around a central point. **2** move so as to face or go in a different direction. **3** make or become: *she turned pale*. **4** shape on a lathe. **5** twist or sprain an ankle. ▶ n. **1** an act of turning. **2** a bend in a road, river, etc. **3** a place where a road meets or branches off another. **4** the time when a member of a group must or is allowed to do something. **5** a time when one period of time ends and another begins. **6** a short walk or ride. **7** a brief feeling of illness. **8** a short performance.

SYNONYMS ▶ v. **1 go around**, revolve, rotate, spin, roll, circle, wheel, whirl, twirl, gyrate, swivel, pivot. **2 change direction**, change course, make a U-turn, turn around/about, wheel around. **3 bend**, curve, wind, twist, meander, snake, zigzag. **4** *he turned pale* **become**, go, grow, get. **5** (**go**) **sour**, curdle, become rancid, go bad, spoil. ▶ n. **1 rotation**, revolution, spin, whirl, twirl, gyration, swivel. **2 bend**, corner, junction, twist, dogleg, hairpin turn. **3 opportunity**, chance, say, stint, time, try; informal go, shot, stab, crack. **4** *she did me some good turns* **service**, deed, act, favor, kindness.

□ **be turned out** be dressed in a particular way. **do someone a good turn** do something that is helpful for someone. **out of turn** at a time when it is inappropriate or not your turn. **to a turn** to exactly the right degree. **turn someone away** refuse entry to someone. **turn someone/something down 1** reject an offer made by someone. **2** reduce the volume or strength of sound, heat, etc., produced by a device. **turn in** informal go to bed. **turn someone in** hand someone over to the authorities. **turning point** a time when a decisive change happens, especially one with good results. **turn something off** switch something off. **turn on** suddenly attack. **turn someone/something on 1** switch something on. **2** informal excite someone sexually. **turn out 1** prove to be the case. **2** be present at an event. **turn something out** switch off an electric light. **turn over** (of an engine) start to run. **turn signal** a flashing light on a vehicle to show that it is about to change lanes or turn. **turn up 1** be found.

2 arrive. **turn something up** increase the volume or strength of sound, heat, etc., produced by a device.

turn·coat /'tərn,kōt/ ▶ **n.** a person who deserts one party or cause in order to join an opposing one.

turn·ing /'tərniNG/ ▶ **n.** a place where a road branches off another.

> SYNONYMS **junction**, turnoff, side road, exit; turnout.

tur·nip /'tərnəp/ ▶ **n.** a round root that is eaten as a vegetable.

turn·key /'tərn,kē/ ▶ **n.** (plural **turnkeys**) old use a jailer.

turn·out /'tərn,out/ ▶ **n.** the number of people attending or taking part in an event.

> SYNONYMS **1 attendance**, audience, house, congregation, crowd, gate, gathering. **2 outfit**, clothing, dress, garb, attire, ensemble; informal getup.

turn·o·ver /'tərn,ōvər/ ▶ **n. 1** the amount of money taken by a business in a particular period. **2** the rate at which employees leave a workforce and are replaced. **3** the rate at which goods are sold and replaced in a shop. **4** a small pie made by folding a piece of pastry over on itself to enclose a filling.

> SYNONYMS **1 gross revenue**, income, yield, sales, business. **2** *staff turnover* **rate of replacement**, change, movement.

turn·pike /'tərn,pīk/ ▶ **n.** a road on which a toll is charged.

turn·stile /'tərn,stīl/ ▶ **n.** a gate with revolving arms allowing only one person at a time to pass through.

turn·ta·ble /'tərn,tābəl/ ▶ **n.** a circular revolving platform or support, e.g., for the record in a record player.

tur·pen·tine /'tərpən,tīn/ ▶ **n.** a liquid obtained from certain trees, used to thin paint and clean brushes.

tur·pi·tude /'tərpi,t(y)o͞od/ ▶ **n.** formal wickedness.

turps /tərps/ ▶ **n.** informal turpentine.

tur·quoise /'tər,k(w)oiz/ ▶ **n. 1** a greenish-blue or sky-blue semiprecious stone. **2** a greenish-blue color.

tur·ret /'tərit/ ▶ **n. 1** a small tower at the corner of a building or wall. **2** an armored tower for a gun in a ship, aircraft, or tank. ■ **tur·ret·ed adj.**

tur·tle /'tərtl/ ▶ **n.** a reptile with a bony or leathery shell, that lives in water. □ **turn turtle** (of a boat) turn upside down.

tur·tle·dove /'tərdl dōv/ ▶ **n.** a small dove with a soft purring call.

tur·tle·neck /'tərtl,nek/ ▶ **n.** a high, close-fitting, turned-over neck on a garment.

turves /tərvz/ plural of **TURF**.

tush /to͝osH/ ▶ **n.** informal a person's buttocks.

tusk /təsk/ ▶ **n.** a long, pointed tooth that protrudes from the closed mouth of an elephant, walrus, or wild boar. ■ **tusked adj.**

tus·sle /'təsəl/ ▶ **n.** a short struggle or scuffle. ▶ **v.** (**tussles, tussling, tussled**) be involved in a tussle.

tus·sock /'təsək/ ▶ **n.** a dense clump or tuft of grass.

tu·te·lage /'t(y)o͞otl-ij/ ▶ **n.** formal **1** protection or authority. **2** instruction.

tu·te·lar·y /'t(y)o͞otl,erē/ ▶ **adj.** formal acting as a protector, guardian, or patron.

tu·tor /'t(y)o͞otər/ ▶ **n.** a person who teaches a single student or a very small group. ▶ **v.** act as a tutor to.

> SYNONYMS ▶ **n. teacher**, instructor, coach, educator, lecturer, trainer, mentor. ▶ **v. teach**, instruct, educate, school, coach, train, drill.

tu·to·ri·al /t(y)o͞o'tôrēəl/ ▶ **n.** a period of teaching by a university or college tutor. ▶ **adj.** relating to a tutor.

tu·tu /'to͞o,to͞o/ ▶ **n.** a female ballet dancer's very short, stiff skirt that sticks out from the waist.

tux /təks/ ▶ **n.** informal a tuxedo.

tux·e·do /tək'sēdō/ ▶ **n.** (plural **tuxedos** or **tuxedoes**) a man's dinner jacket.

TV ▶ **abbr.** television.

twad·dle /'twädl/ ▶ **n.** informal silly talk or writing.

twain /twān/ dated ⇒ **TWO**.

twang /twaNG/ ▶ **n. 1** a strong ringing sound made by the plucked string of a musical instrument. **2** a distinctive nasal way of speaking. ▶ **v.** make a twang. ■ **twang·y adj.**

'twas ▶ **contr.** old use or literary it was.

tweak /twēk/ ▶ **v. 1** twist or pull with a small but sharp movement. **2** informal improve by making small adjustments. ▶ **n.** an act of tweaking.

tweed /twēd/ ▶ **n.** a rough woolen cloth flecked with mixed colors.

tweed·y /'twēdē/▶ **adj.** (**tweedier, tweediest**) **1** (of a garment) made of tweed cloth: *a tweedy suit*. **2** informal (of a person) tending to wear tweed clothes: *a stout, tweedy woman*.

tweet /twēt/ ▶ **n.** the chirp of a small or young bird. ▶ **v.** make a chirping noise.

tweet·er /'twētər/ ▶ **n.** a loudspeaker that reproduces high frequencies.

tweez·ers /'twēzərz/ ▶ **pl.n.** a small pair of pincers for plucking out hairs and picking up small objects.

twelfth /twelfTH/ ▶ **ordinal number** being number twelve in a sequence; 12th.

twelve /twelv/ ▶ **cardinal number** two more than ten; 12. (Roman numeral: **xii** or **XII**)

twen·ty /'twentē/ ▶ **cardinal number** (plural **twenties**) ten less than thirty; 20. (Roman numeral: **xx** or **XX**) □ **twenty-twenty vision** normal vision. ■ **twen·ti·eth** /'twentēiTH/ **ordinal number.**

24-7 (also **24/7**) ▶ **adv.** informal twenty-four hours a day, seven days a week; all the time.

twerp /twərp/ ▶ **n.** informal a silly person.

twice /twīs/ ▶ **adv. 1** two times. **2** double in degree or quantity.

twid·dle /'twidl/ ▶ **v.** (**twiddles, twiddling, twiddled**) fiddle with something in an aimless or nervous way. □ **twiddle your thumbs** have nothing to do. ■ **twid·dly adj.**

twig /twig/ ▶ **n.** a slender woody shoot growing from a branch or stem of a tree or shrub.

> SYNONYMS **stick**, sprig, shoot, offshoot, stem, branchlet.

twi·light /'twī,līt/ ▶ **n. 1** the soft glowing light from the sky when the sun is below the horizon. **2** a period or state of gradual decline.

> SYNONYMS **1 dusk**, sunset, sundown, nightfall, evening, close of day. **2 half-light**, semidarkness, gloom.

■ **twi·lit adj.**

twill /twil/ ▶ **n.** a fabric with a slightly ridged surface.

twin /twin/ ▶ **n. 1** each of two children born at the same birth. **2** a thing that is exactly like another. ▶ **adj.** forming or being one of a pair of twins. ▶ **v.** (**twins**, **twinning**, **twinned**) link or combine as a pair.

> SYNONYMS ▶ **n. duplicate**, double, carbon copy, likeness, mirror image, replica, lookalike, clone, match, pair; informal spitting image, dead ringer. ▶ **adj. 1 matching**, identical, paired. **2 twofold**, double, dual, related, linked, connected, parallel, complementary. ▶ **v. combine**, join, link, couple, pair.

twine /twīn/ ▶ **n.** strong string consisting of strands twisted together. ▶ **v.** (**twines**, **twining**, **twined**) wind round something.

twinge /twinj/ ▶ **n. 1** a sudden, sharp pain. **2** a brief, sharp pang of emotion.

> SYNONYMS **pain**, spasm, ache, throb, cramp, stitch, pang.

twin·kle /'twiNGkəl/ ▶ **v.** (**twinkles**, **twinkling**, **twinkled**) **1** shine with a gleam that changes constantly from bright to faint. **2** (of a person's eyes) sparkle with amusement or liveliness. ▶ **n.** a twinkling sparkle or gleam.

> SYNONYMS **glitter**, sparkle, shine, glimmer, shimmer, glint, gleam, glisten, flicker, flash, wink.

■ **twin·kly** **adj.**

twin·set /'twin,set/ ▶ **n.** a woman's matching cardigan and jumper.

twirl /twərl/ ▶ **v.** spin quickly and lightly round. ▶ **n.** an act of twirling.

> SYNONYMS ▶ **v. 1** *she twirled her parasol* **spin**, whirl, turn, gyrate, pivot, swivel, twist, revolve, rotate. **2** *she twirled her hair around her finger* **wind**, twist, coil, curl, wrap. ▶ **n. pirouette**, spin, whirl, turn, twist, rotation, revolution, gyration.

■ **twirl·y** **adj.**

twist /twist/ ▶ **v. 1** bend, curl, or distort. **2** force out of the natural position. **3** have a winding course. **4** deliberately change the meaning of. **5** (**twisted**) unpleasantly abnormal; perverted. ▶ **n. 1** an act of twisting. **2** a thing with a spiral shape. **3** a new or unexpected development or treatment. **4** (**the twist**) a dance with a twisting movement of the body, popular in the 1960s.

> SYNONYMS ▶ **v. 1 crumple**, crush, buckle, mangle, warp, deform, distort, contort. **2 sprain**, wrench, turn, crick. **3** *twist the ribbon around a pencil* **wind**, twirl, coil, curl, wrap. **4** *the wires were twisted together* **intertwine**, interlace, weave, plait, braid, coil, wind. **5** *the road twisted and turned* **wind**, bend, curve, turn, meander, weave, zigzag, snake. ▶ **n. bend**, curve, turn, zigzag, dogleg.

□ **twist someone's arm** informal forcefully persuade someone to do something. ■ **twist·er** **n.**

twit¹ /twit/ ▶ **n.** informal a silly or foolish person.

twit² ▶ **v.** (**twits**, **twitting**, **twitted**) informal tease someone in a good-humored way.

twitch /twicH/ ▶ **v.** make a short jerking movement. ▶ **n.** a twitching movement.

> SYNONYMS ▶ **v. jerk**, convulse, have a spasm, quiver, tremble, shiver, shudder. ▶ **n. spasm**, convulsion, quiver, tremor, shiver, shudder, tic.

twitch·y /'twicHē/ ▶ **adj.** informal nervous.

twit·ter /'twitər/ ▶ **v.** (**twitters**, **twittering**, **twittered**) **1** (of a bird) make a series of short, high sounds. **2** talk rapidly in a nervous or silly way. ▶ **n.** a twittering sound.

'twixt ▶ **contr.** old use or literary betwixt.

two /too/ ▶ **cardinal number** one less than three; 2. (Roman numeral: **ii** or **II**) □ **put two and two together** draw a conclusion from what is known or evident. **two-bit** insignificant, cheap, or worthless. **two-dimensional** having or appearing to have length and breadth but no depth. **two-faced** insincere and deceitful. **two-fisted** strong, virile, and straightforward. **two-step** a round dance with a sliding step in march or polka time. **two-time** be unfaithful to a husband, wife, or lover. ■ **two·fold** **adj. & adv.**

> USAGE
>
> Don't confuse **two** with **to** or **too**: see the note at **TO**.

two·some /'toosəm/ ▶ **n.** a set of two people or things.

ty·coon /tī'koon/ ▶ **n.** a wealthy, powerful person in business or industry.

> SYNONYMS **magnate**, mogul, businessman, captain of industry, industrialist, financier, entrepreneur; informal, disapproving fat cat.

ty·ing /'tī-iNG/ present participle of **TIE**.

tyke /tīk/ (or **tike**) ▶ **n.** informal a mischievous child.

tym·pa·ni = **TIMPANI**.

tym·pa·num /'timpənəm/ ▶ **n.** (plural **tympanums** or **tympana** /-nə/) the eardrum.

type /tīp/ ▶ **n. 1** a category of people or things that share particular qualities or features. **2** informal a person of a particular nature: *a sporty type*. **3** printed characters or letters. ▶ **v.** (**types**, **typing**, **typed**) write using a typewriter or computer.

> SYNONYMS ▶ **n. 1 kind**, sort, variety, class, category, set, genre, species, order, breed, ilk. **2 print**, typeface, characters, lettering, font.

type·cast /'tīp,kast/ ▶ **v.** (**be typecast**) (of an actor) always be cast in the same type of role.

type·face /'tīp,fās/ ▶ **n.** a particular design of printed letters or numbers.

type·script /'tīp,skript/ ▶ **n.** a typed copy of a written work.

type·set /'tīp,set/ ▶ **v.** (**typeset**, **typesetting**, **typeset**) arrange or generate the data or type for text to be printed. ■ **type·set·ter** **n.**

type·writ·er /'tīp,rītər/ ▶ **n.** a machine with keys that are pressed to produce characters similar to printed ones. ■ **type·writ·ing** **n.** **type·writ·ten** **adj.**

ty·phoid /'tī,foid/ ▶ **n.** an infectious fever that causes red spots on the chest and severe pain in the intestines.

ty·phoon /tī'foon/ ▶ **n.** a tropical storm with very high winds.

ty·phus /'tīfəs/ ▶ **n.** an infectious disease that causes a purple rash, headaches, fever, and usually delirium.

typ·i·cal /'tipikəl/ ▶ **adj. 1** having the distinctive qualities of a particular type of person or thing. **2** characteristic of a particular person or thing.

SYNONYMS **1 representative**, characteristic, classic, quintessential, archetypal. **2 normal**, average, ordinary, standard, regular, routine, run-of-the-mill, conventional, unremarkable. ANTONYMS unusual, exceptional.

■ **typ·i·cal·ly** adv.

typ·i·fy /'tipə,fī/ ▶ v. (**typifies**, **typifying**, **typified**) be typical of.

SYNONYMS **epitomize**, exemplify, characterize, embody, be representative of, personify, symbolize.

typ·ist /'tīpist/ ▶ n. a person skilled in typing and employed for this purpose.

ty·po /'tīpō/ ▶ n. (plural **typos**) informal a small error in typed or printed writing.

ty·pog·ra·phy /tī'pägrəfē/ ▶ n. **1** the setting and arrangement of printed characters. **2** the style and appearance of printed material. ■ **ty·pog·ra·pher** n. **ty·po·graph·i·cal** /,tīpə'grafikəl/ (or **typographic** /,tīpə'grafik/) adj.

ty·ran·ni·cal /tə'ranikəl/ ▶ adj. using power in a cruel or unfair way. ■ **ty·ran·ni·cal·ly** adv.

tyr·an·nize /'tirə,nīz/ ▶ v. (**tyrannizes**, **tyrannizing**, **tyrannized**) rule or dominate in a cruel or unfair way.

ty·ran·no·sau·rus /tə,ranə'sôrəs/ (or **tyrannosaurus rex** /reks/) ▶ n. a large meat-eating dinosaur that walked on its strong hind legs.

tyr·an·ny /'tirənē/ ▶ n. (plural **tyrannies**) cruel and oppressive government or rule.

SYNONYMS **despotism**, absolute power, autocracy, dictatorship, totalitarianism, fascism, oppression, repression, subjugation, enslavement.

SPELLING

One **r**, two **ns** : tyranny.

ty·rant /'tīrənt/ ▶ n. a cruel and oppressive ruler.

SYNONYMS **dictator**, despot, autocrat, authoritarian, oppressor, slave driver, martinet, bully.

ty·ro /'tīrō/ ▶ n. (plural **tyros**) a beginner or novice.

tzar = TSAR.

tza·tzi·ki /tsä'tsēkē/ ▶ n. a Greek side dish of yogurt with cucumber and garlic.

Uu

U (or **u**) ▶ n. (plural **Us** or **U's**) the twenty-first letter of the alphabet. ◻ **U-boat** a German submarine of World War I or II. **U-turn 1** the turning of a vehicle in a U-shaped course so as to face the opposite way. **2** a complete change of policy or behavior: *the government is doing a U-turn on road building.*

u·biq·ui·tous /yo͞oˈbikwətəs/ ▶ adj. appearing or found everywhere.

> SYNONYMS **everywhere**, omnipresent, all over the place, all-pervasive, universal, worldwide, global. ANTONYMS rare.

■ **u·biq·ui·tous·ly** adv. **u·biq·ui·ty** n.

ud·der /ˈədər/ ▶ n. the baglike milk-producing organ of female cattle, sheep, horses, etc.

UFO ▶ n. (plural **UFOs**) a mysterious object seen in the sky that some people believe is carrying beings from outer space (short for *unidentified flying object*).

U·gan·dan /yo͞oˈgandən/ ▶ n. a person from Uganda. ▶ adj. relating to Uganda.

ugh /əg, əKH, o͝oKH/ ▶ exclam. informal used to express disgust or horror.

ug·ly /ˈəglē/ ▶ adj. (**uglier**, **ugliest**) **1** unpleasant or unattractive in appearance. **2** hostile or threatening.

> SYNONYMS **1 unattractive**, unsightly, ill-favored, hideous, plain, unprepossessing, horrible, ghastly, repellent, grotesque, homely. **2 unpleasant**, nasty, disagreeable, alarming, dangerous, perilous, threatening, menacing, hostile, ominous, sinister. ANTONYMS beautiful.

◻ **ugly duckling** a person who unexpectedly turns out to be beautiful or talented. ■ **ug·li·ness** n.

uh-huh /ə ˈhə, əN ˈhəN/ ▶ exclam. used to express agreement or as a noncommittal response to a question or remark.

uh-oh /ˈə ˌō/ ▶ exclam. used to express alarm, dismay, or concern: *"uh-oh! Take cover!"*

UK ▶ abbr. United Kingdom.

u·ku·le·le /ˌyo͞okəˈlālē/ (or **ukelele**) ▶ n. a small four-stringed guitar.

ul·cer /ˈəlsər/ ▶ n. an open sore on the body or on an internal organ. ■ **ul·cer·at·ed** adj. **ul·cer·a·tion** /ˌəlsəˈrāSHən/ n.

ul·na /ˈəlnə/ ▶ n. (plural **ulnae** /-ˌnē, -ˌnī/ or **ulnas**) the thinner and longer of the two bones in the human forearm.

ul·te·ri·or /ˌəlˈti(ə)rēər/ ▶ adj. other than what is obvious or admitted: *she had an ulterior motive.*

> SYNONYMS **underlying**, undisclosed, undivulged, concealed, hidden, covert, secret, unapparent. ANTONYMS overt.

ul·ti·mate /ˈəltəmit/ ▶ adj. **1** happening at the end of a process. **2** being the best or most extreme example of its kind. **3** basic or fundamental. ▶ n. (**the ultimate**) the best of its kind that is imaginable.

> SYNONYMS ▶ adj. **1 eventual**, final, concluding, terminal, end. **2 fundamental**, basic, primary, elementary, absolute, central, crucial, essential. **3 best**, ideal, greatest, quintessential, supreme.

ul·ti·mate·ly /ˈəltəmitlē/ ▶ adv. **1** in the end; finally. **2** at the most basic level.

> SYNONYMS **1 eventually**, in the end, in the long run, at length, finally, in time, one day. **2 fundamentally**, basically, primarily, essentially, at heart, deep down.

ul·ti·ma·tum /ˌəltəˈmātəm, -ˈmät-/ ▶ n. a final warning that action will be taken against you if you do not agree to another party's demands.

ul·tra·ma·rine /ˌəltrəməˈrēn/ ▶ n. a brilliant deep blue color or pigment.

ul·tra·son·ic /ˌəltrəˈsänik/ ▶ adj. involving sound waves with a frequency above the upper limit of human hearing.

ul·tra·sound /ˈəltrəˌsound/ ▶ n. sound or other vibrations with an ultrasonic frequency, used in medical scans.

ul·tra·vi·o·let /ˌəltrəˈvī(ə)lət/ ▶ adj. (of electromagnetic radiation) having a wavelength just shorter than that of violet light.

ul·u·late /ˈəlyəˌlāt, ˈyo͞ol-/ ▶ v. (**ululates**, **ululating**, **ululated**) howl or wail. ■ **ul·u·la·tion** /ˌəlyəˈlāSHən, ˌyo͞ol-/ n.

um ▶ exclam. expressing hesitation or a pause in speech: *anyway, um, where was I?*

um·ber /ˈəmbər/ ▶ n. a dark brown or yellowish-brown color.

um·bil·i·cal /ˌəmˈbilikəl/ ▶ adj. relating to the navel or umbilical cord. ◻ **umbilical cord** a flexible tube that connects a developing fetus with the placenta while it is in the uterus.

um·bil·i·cus /ˌəmˈbilikəs/ ▶ n. the navel.

um·bra /ˈəmbrə/ ▶ n. (plural **umbras** or **umbrae** /-ˌbrē, -ˌbrī/) the shadow cast by the earth or the moon in an eclipse.

um·brage /ˈəmbrij/ ▶ n. (**take umbrage**) take offense; become annoyed.

um·brel·la /ˌəmˈbrelə/ ▶ n. a folding device used as protection against rain. ▶ adj. including or containing many different parts.

um·laut /ˈo͝omˌlout/ ▶ n. a mark (¨) placed over a vowel in some languages to indicate how it should sound.

ump /əmp/ ▶ n. & v. informal short for UMPIRE.

um·pire /ˈəmˌpī(ə)r/ ▶ **n.** (in certain sports) an official who supervises a game to make sure that players follow the rules. ▶ **v.** (**umpires**, **umpiring**, **umpired**) be the umpire of.

SYNONYMS ▶ **n.** **referee**, judge, line judge, linesman, adjudicator, arbitrator, moderator; informal ref.

ump·teen /ˈəm(p)ˌtēn/ ▶ **cardinal number** informal very many. ■ **ump·teenth** **ordinal number.**

UN ▶ **abbr.** United Nations.

un·a·bashed /ˌənəˈbasHt/ ▶ **adj.** not embarrassed or ashamed.

SYNONYMS **unashamed**, shameless, brazen, audacious, barefaced, blatant, flagrant, bold. ANTONYMS sheepish.

un·a·bat·ed /ˌənəˈbātid/ ▶ **adj.** not reduced in intensity or strength.

un·a·ble /ˌənˈābəl/ ▶ **adj.** not able to do something.

SYNONYMS **incapable**, powerless, impotent, inadequate, incompetent, unqualified, unfit.

un·ac·cept·a·ble /ˌənəkˈseptəbəl/ ▶ **adj.** not satisfactory or allowable.

SYNONYMS **unsatisfactory**, inadmissible, inappropriate, unsuitable, undesirable, unreasonable, insupportable, intolerable, objectionable, distasteful; informal out of line. ANTONYMS satisfactory.

■ **un·ac·cept·a·bly** **adv.**

un·ac·count·a·ble /ˌənəˈkountəbəl/ ▶ **adj.** **1** unable to be explained. **2** not having to explain your actions or decisions. ■ **un·ac·count·a·bly** **adv.**

un·ac·cus·tomed /ˌənəˈkəstəmd/ ▶ **adj.** **1** not usual. **2** (**unaccustomed to**) not familiar with or used to.

un·a·dul·ter·at·ed /ˌənəˈdəltəˌrātid/ ▶ **adj.** not mixed with any different or extra elements.

un·af·fect·ed /ˌənəˈfektid/ ▶ **adj.** **1** feeling or showing no effects. **2** sincere and genuine.

un·a·fraid /ˌənəˈfrād/ ▶ **adj.** feeling no fear.

un·aid·ed /ˌənˈādid/ ▶ **adj.** without any help.

un·al·loyed /ˌənəˈloid/ ▶ **adj.** **1** (of metal) not alloyed. **2** complete; total: *unalloyed delight.*

un·am·big·u·ous /ˌənamˈbigyo͞oəs/ ▶ **adj.** not open to more than one interpretation. ■ **un·am·big·u·ous·ly** **adv.**

un-A·mer·i·can /ˌənəˈmerikən/ ▶ **adj.** **1** not American in nature. **2** chiefly historical against the interests of the United States and therefore treasonable.

u·nan·i·mous /yo͞oˈnanəməs/ ▶ **adj.** **1** fully in agreement. **2** (of an opinion, decision, or vote) held or carried by everyone involved.

SYNONYMS **in agreement**, of one mind, in accord, united, undivided, with one voice. ANTONYMS split.

■ **u·na·nim·i·ty** /ˌyo͞onəˈnimətē/ **n.** **u·nan·i·mous·ly** **adv.**

un·an·nounced /ˌənəˈnounst/ ▶ **adj.** without warning or notice.

un·an·swered /ˌənˈansərd/ ▶ **adj.** not answered.

un·ap·pe·tiz·ing /ˌənˈapəˌtīziNG/ ▶ **adj.** not inviting or attractive.

SYNONYMS **unpalatable**, uninviting, unappealing, unpleasant, off-putting, distasteful, unsavory, insipid, flavorless; informal yucky, gross. ANTONYMS tempting.

un·ap·proach·a·ble /ˌənəˈprōCHəbəl/ ▶ **adj.** not welcoming or friendly.

SYNONYMS **aloof**, distant, remote, detached, reserved, withdrawn, uncommunicative, unforthcoming, unfriendly, unsympathetic; cool, frosty, stiff; informal standoffish. ANTONYMS friendly.

un·ar·gu·a·ble /ˌənˈärgyo͞oəbəl/ ▶ **adj.** not able to be disagreed with. ■ **un·ar·gu·a·bly** **adv.**

un·armed /ˌənˈärmd/ ▶ **adj.** not equipped with or carrying weapons.

SYNONYMS **defenseless**, unprotected, unguarded.

un·as·sail·a·ble /ˌənəˈsāləbəl/ ▶ **adj.** unable to be attacked, questioned, or defeated.

un·as·sum·ing /ˌənəˈso͞omiNG/ ▶ **adj.** not drawing attention to yourself or your abilities.

SYNONYMS **modest**, self-effacing, humble, meek, reserved, diffident, unobtrusive, unostentatious, unpretentious, unaffected, natural.

un·at·tached /ˌənəˈtacHt/ ▶ **adj.** without a husband or wife or established lover.

un·at·tend·ed /ˌənəˈtendid/ ▶ **adj.** not being supervised or looked after.

un·at·trac·tive /ˌənəˈtraktiv/ ▶ **adj.** not pleasing, appealing, or inviting. ■ **un·at·trac·tive·ly** **adv.**

un·au·thor·ized /ənˈôTHəˌrīzd/ ▶ **adj.** not having official permission or approval.

SYNONYMS **unofficial**, unsanctioned, unaccredited, unlicensed, unwarranted, unapproved, disallowed, prohibited, banned, forbidden, outlawed, illegal, illicit, proscribed. ANTONYMS official.

un·a·vail·a·ble /ˌənəˈvāləbəl/ ▶ **adj.** **1** not able to be used or obtained. **2** (of a person) not free to do something.

un·a·vail·ing /ˌənəˈvāliNG/ ▶ **adj.** achieving little or nothing.

un·a·void·a·ble /ˌənəˈvoidəbəl/ ▶ **adj.** not able to be avoided or prevented. ■ **un·a·void·a·bly** **adv.**

un·a·ware /ˌənəˈwe(ə)r/ ▶ **adj.** having no knowledge of a situation or fact.

SYNONYMS **ignorant**, oblivious, unconscious, unwitting, unsuspecting, uninformed, unenlightened, innocent; informal in the dark. ANTONYMS aware.

un·a·wares /ˌənəˈwe(ə)rz/ ▶ **adv.** so as to surprise someone; unexpectedly.

un·bal·anced /ˌənˈbalənst/ ▶ **adj.** emotionally or mentally disturbed.

SYNONYMS **1** **unstable**, mentally ill, deranged, demented, disturbed, unhinged, insane, mad; informal crazy, loopy, nuts, batty, bonkers. **2** *an unbalanced article* **biased**, prejudiced, one-sided, partisan, inequitable, unfair. ANTONYMS sane, unbiased.

un·bear·a·ble /ˌənˈbe(ə)rəbəl/ ▶ **adj.** not able to be endured.

SYNONYMS **intolerable**, insufferable, insupportable, unendurable, unacceptable, unmanageable, overpowering; informal too much. ANTONYMS tolerable.

■ **un·bear·a·bly** **adv.**

un·beat·a·ble /ˌənˈbētəbəl/ ▶ **adj.** not able to be bettered or beaten.

un·be·known /ˌənbiˈnōn/ (or **unbeknownst** /-ˈnōnst/) ▶ **adj.** (**unbeknown to**) without the knowledge of.

un·be·liev·a·ble /ˌənbəˈlēvəbəl/ ▶ **adj.** **1** unlikely to be true. **2** extraordinary.

> SYNONYMS **incredible**, inconceivable, unthinkable, unimaginable, unconvincing, far-fetched, implausible, improbable; informal hard to swallow.

■ **un·be·liev·a·bly** **adv.**

un·be·liev·er /ˌənbəˈlēvər/ ▶ **n.** a person without religious belief.

un·bend·ing /ˌənˈbendiNG/ ▶ **adj.** unwilling to compromise or change your mind.

> SYNONYMS **uncompromising**, inflexible, unyielding, hard-line, tough, strict, firm, resolute, determined, unrelenting, inexorable, intransigent, immovable.

un·bi·ased /ˌənˈbīəst/ (or **unbiassed**) ▶ **adj.** showing no prejudice.

> SYNONYMS **impartial**, unprejudiced, neutral, nonpartisan, disinterested, detached, dispassionate, objective, evenhanded, fair.

un·bid·den /ˌənˈbidn/ ▶ **adj.** without having been invited.

un·born /ˌənˈbôrn/ ▶ **adj.** not yet born.

> SYNONYMS **expected**, embryonic, fetal, in utero.

un·bound·ed /ˌənˈboundid/ ▶ **adj.** having no limits.

un·bowed /ˌənˈboud/ ▶ **adj.** not having given in or been defeated.

un·break·a·ble /ˌənˈbrākəbəl/ ▶ **adj.** not able to be broken.

> SYNONYMS **shatterproof**, indestructible, durable, toughened, laminated, sturdy, stout, hard-wearing, heavy-duty. ANTONYMS fragile.

un·bridge·a·ble /ˌənˈbrijəbəl/ ▶ **adj.** (of a gap or difference between people) not able to be made smaller or less significant.

un·bri·dled /ˌənˈbrīdld/ ▶ **adj.** uncontrolled: *unbridled ambition.*

un·bro·ken /ˌənˈbrōkən/ ▶ **adj.** **1** not broken, interrupted, or bettered. **2** (of a horse) not broken in.

> SYNONYMS **1 undamaged**, unharmed, unscathed, untouched, sound, intact, whole. **2 uninterrupted**, continuous, endless, constant, unremitting, ongoing. **3 unbeaten**, undefeated, unsurpassed, unrivaled, unmatched, supreme.

un·bur·den /ˌənˈbərdn/ ▶ **v.** (**unburden yourself**) confide in someone about your worries or problems.

un·called /ˌənˈkôld/ ▶ **adj.** (**uncalled for**) not fair or appropriate; unnecessary.

un·can·ny /ˌənˈkanē/ ▶ **adj.** (**uncannier**, **uncanniest**) strange or mysterious.

> SYNONYMS **1 eerie**, unnatural, unearthly, otherworldly, ghostly, strange, abnormal, weird; informal creepy, spooky. **2** *an uncanny resemblance* **striking**, remarkable, extraordinary, exceptional, incredible.

■ **un·can·ni·ly** **adv.**

un·ceas·ing /ˌənˈsēsiNG/ ▶ **adj.** not ceasing; continuous. ■ **un·ceas·ing·ly** **adv.**

un·cer·e·mo·ni·ous /ˌənserəˈmōnēəs/ ▶ **adj.** rude or abrupt. ■ **un·cer·e·mo·ni·ous·ly** **adv.**

un·cer·tain /ˌənˈsərtn/ ▶ **adj.** **1** not known, reliable, or definite. **2** not completely confident or sure.

> SYNONYMS **1** *the effects are uncertain* **unknown**, debatable, open to question, in doubt, in the balance, up in the air, unpredictable, unforeseeable, undetermined; informal iffy. **2** *he was uncertain about the decision* **unsure**, doubtful, dubious, undecided, irresolute, hesitant, vacillating, vague, unclear, ambivalent, of two minds. ANTONYMS certain, sure.

□ **in no uncertain terms** clearly and forcefully.
■ **un·cer·tain·ly** **adv.**

un·cer·tain·ty /ˌənˈsərtntē/ ▶ **n.** (plural **uncertainties**) **1** the state of being uncertain. **2** something that is uncertain or makes you feel uncertain.

un·chal·lenged /ˌənˈCHaləNjd/ ▶ **adj.** not questioned, opposed, or defeated.

un·changed /ˌənˈCHānjd/ ▶ **adj.** not changed.

un·char·ac·ter·is·tic /ˌənkariktəˈristik/ ▶ **adj.** not typical of a particular person or thing.
■ **un·char·ac·ter·is·ti·cal·ly** **adv.**

un·char·i·ta·ble /ˌənˈCHaritəbəl/ ▶ **adj.** unkind or unsympathetic to other people. ■ **un·char·i·ta·bly** **adv.**

un·chart·ed /ˌənˈCHärtid/ ▶ **adj.** (of an area of land or sea) not mapped or surveyed.

un·chris·tian /ˌənˈkrisCHən/ ▶ **adj.** **1** not in line with the teachings of Christianity. **2** not generous or fair.

un·civ·i·lized /ˌənˈsivəˌlīzd/ ▶ **adj.** **1** (of a place or people) not socially or culturally advanced. **2** bad-mannered.

> SYNONYMS **uncouth**, coarse, rough, boorish, vulgar, philistine, uneducated, uncultured, benighted, unsophisticated, ill-bred, barbarian, primitive, savage.

un·cle /ˈəNGkəl/ ▶ **n.** the brother of your father or mother or the husband of your aunt. □ **Uncle Sam** a personification of the federal government or citizens of the United States.

un·clean /ˌənˈklēn/ ▶ **adj.** **1** dirty. **2** immoral. **3** (of food) forbidden by a religion.

un·clear /ˌənˈkli(ə)r/ ▶ **adj.** not easy to see, hear, or understand.

> SYNONYMS **uncertain**, unsure, unsettled, up in the air, in doubt, ambiguous, equivocal, indefinite, vague, mysterious, obscure, hazy, nebulous. ANTONYMS clear, evident.

un·clog /ˌənˈklôg, -ˈkläg/ ▶ **v.** (**unclogs**, **unclogging**, **unclogged**) remove built-up matter from.

un·com·fort·a·ble/ ˌənˈkəmfərtəbəl, -ˈkəmftərbəl/ ▶ **adj.** **1** not physically comfortable. **2** uneasy or awkward.

> SYNONYMS **1 painful**, awkward, lumpy, confining, cramped. **2 uneasy**, ill at ease, awkward, nervous, tense, edgy, restless, embarrassed, anxious; informal rattled, twitchy. ANTONYMS comfortable, relaxed.

■ **un·com·fort·a·bly** **adv.**

un·com·mon /ˌənˈkämən/ ▶ **adj.** **1** out of the ordinary; unusual. **2** remarkably great.

SYNONYMS **unusual**, abnormal, rare, atypical, exceptional, unconventional, unfamiliar, strange, extraordinary, peculiar, scarce, few and far between, isolated, infrequent.

■ **un·com·mon·ly** adv.

un·com·mu·ni·ca·tive /ˌənkəˈmyo͞onəkətiv, -ˌkātiv/ ▶ adj. unwilling to talk or give out information.

SYNONYMS **taciturn**, quiet, unforthcoming, reserved, reticent, laconic, tongue-tied, silent, tight-lipped; guarded, secretive, close, private; distant, remote, aloof, withdrawn; informal mum, standoffish. ANTONYMS talkative.

un·com·pli·cat·ed /ˌənˈkämpləˌkātid/ ▶ adj. simple or straightforward.

SYNONYMS **simple**, straightforward, clear, accessible, undemanding, unchallenging, unsophisticated, trouble-free, painless, effortless, easy, elementary, idiot-proof; informal a piece of cake, child's play, a cinch, a breeze. ANTONYMS complex.

un·com·pre·hend·ing /ˌənˌkämpriˈhendiNG/ ▶ adj. unable to understand something.
■ **un·com·pre·hend·ing·ly** adv.

un·com·pro·mis·ing /ˌənˈkämprəˌmīziNG/ ▶ adj. unwilling to compromise.

SYNONYMS **inflexible**, unbending, unyielding, unshakable, resolute, rigid, hard-line, immovable, intractable, firm, determined, iron-willed, obstinate, stubborn, adamant, obdurate, intransigent, headstrong, pigheaded. ANTONYMS flexible.

■ **un·com·pro·mis·ing·ly** adv.

un·con·cern /ˌənkənˈsərn/ ▶ n. a lack of worry or interest.

un·con·cerned /ˌənkənˈsərnd/ ▶ adj. not concerned or interested. ■ **un·con·cern·ed·ly** /-ˈsərnədlē/ adv.

un·con·di·tion·al /ˌənkənˈdisHənl, -ˈdisHnəl/ ▶ adj. not subject to any conditions.

SYNONYMS **unquestioning**, unqualified, unreserved, unlimited, unrestricted, wholehearted, complete, total, entire, full, absolute, unequivocal.

■ **un·con·di·tion·al·ly** adv.

un·con·fined /ˌənkənˈfīnd/ ▶ adj. **1** not confined to a limited space. **2** (of joy or excitement) very great.

un·con·scion·a·ble /ˌənˈkänsH(ə)nəbəl/ ▶ adj. formal not right or reasonable. ■ **un·con·scion·a·bly** adv.

un·con·scious /ˌənˈkänsHəs/ ▶ adj. **1** not awake and aware of your surroundings. **2** done or existing without your realizing. **3** (**unconscious of**) unaware of. ▶ n. the part of the mind that you are not aware of but that affects behavior and emotions.

SYNONYMS ▶ adj. **1 knocked out**, senseless, comatose, inert, stunned; informal out cold, down for the count. **2 subconscious**, instinctive, involuntary, uncontrolled, subliminal; informal gut. **3 unaware**, oblivious, ignorant, in ignorance, heedless. ANTONYMS aware.

■ **un·con·scious·ly** adv. **un·con·scious·ness** n.

un·con·sti·tu·tion·al /ˌənˌkänstəˈt(y)o͞osHənl/ ▶ adj. not allowed by the constitution of a country or the rules of an organization.
■ **un·con·sti·tu·tion·al·ly** adv.

un·con·strained /ˌənkənˈstrānd/ ▶ adj. not restricted or limited.

un·con·trol·la·ble /ˌənkənˈtrōləbəl/ ▶ adj. not able to be controlled.

SYNONYMS **unmanageable**, ungovernable, wild, unruly, disorderly, irrepressible, unstoppable, recalcitrant, undisciplined; violent, frenzied, furious, mad, hysterical, passionate; formal refractory. ANTONYMS compliant.

■ **un·con·trol·la·bly** adv.

un·con·ven·tion·al /ˌənkənˈvensHənl/ ▶ adj. not fitting in with what is generally done or believed.

SYNONYMS **unusual**, irregular, unorthodox, unfamiliar, uncommon, unwonted, out of the ordinary, atypical, singular, alternative, different; new, novel, innovative, groundbreaking, pioneering, original, unprecedented; eccentric, idiosyncratic, quirky, odd, strange, bizarre, weird, outlandish, curious; extraordinary; nonconformist, bohemian, avant-garde; informal way out, far out, offbeat, wacky, madcap, zany, kooky. ANTONYMS orthodox.

■ **un·con·ven·tion·al·ly** adv.

un·con·vinced /ˌənkənˈvinst/ ▶ adj. not certain that something is true or can be relied on.

un·con·vinc·ing /ˌənkənˈvinsiNG/ ▶ adj. failing to convince or impress. ■ **un·con·vinc·ing·ly** adv.

un·cool /ˌənˈko͞ol/ ▶ adj. informal not fashionable or impressive.

un·co·op·er·a·tive /ˌənkōˈäp(ə)rətiv/ ▶ adj. unwilling to help other people or do what they ask.

SYNONYMS **unhelpful**, awkward, disobliging, recalcitrant, perverse, contrary, stubborn, willful, unyielding, unbending, inflexible, immovable, obstructive. ANTONYMS obliging.

un·co·or·di·nat·ed /ˌənkōˈôrdnˌātid/ ▶ adj. **1** clumsy. **2** badly organized.

un·couth /ˌənˈko͞oTH/ ▶ adj. lacking good manners.

SYNONYMS **uncivilized**, uncultured, rough, coarse, crude, loutish, boorish, rude, discourteous, disrespectful, bad-mannered, ill-bred. ANTONYMS civilized.

un·cov·er /ˌənˈkəvər/ ▶ v. (**uncovers**, **uncovering**, **uncovered**) **1** remove a cover or covering from. **2** discover something previously secret or unknown.

SYNONYMS **1 expose**, reveal, lay bare, unwrap, unveil, strip. **2 discover**, detect, come across, stumble on, chance on, find, turn up, unearth, dig up.

unc·tion /ˈəNG(k)sHən/ ▶ n. **1** formal the smearing of someone with oil or ointment as part of a religious ceremony. **2** excessive politeness or flattery.

unc·tu·ous /ˈəNG(k)CHo͞oəs/ ▶ adj. excessively polite or flattering. ■ **unc·tu·ous·ly** adv.

un·daunt·ed /ˌənˈdôntid, -ˈdänt-/ ▶ adj. not discouraged by difficulty or danger.

un·de·ceive /ˌəndiˈsēv/ ▶ v. tell someone that an idea or belief is mistaken.

un·de·cid·ed /ˌəndiˈsīdid/ ▶ adj. **1** not having made a decision. **2** not yet settled or resolved.

un·de·feat·ed /ˌəndiˈfētid/ ▶ adj. not defeated.

un·de·mand·ing /ˌəndəˈmandiNG, ˌəndēˈmandiNG/ ▶ adj. not demanding.

un·de·mon·stra·tive /ˌəndiˈmänstrətiv/ ▶ **adj.** not tending to express feelings openly.

un·de·ni·a·ble /ˌəndiˈnīəbəl/ ▶ **adj.** unable to be denied or disputed.

> SYNONYMS **indisputable**, indubitable, unquestionable, beyond doubt, undebatable, incontrovertible, irrefutable, unassailable; certain, sure, definite, positive, conclusive, self-evident, patent, unequivocal. ANTONYMS questionable.

■ **un·de·ni·a·bly** **adv.**

un·der /ˈəndər/ ▶ **prep.** **1** extending or directly below. **2** at a lower level or grade than. **3** expressing control by another person. **4** in accordance with rules. **5** used to express grouping or classification. **6** undergoing a process. ▶ **adv.** extending or directly below something.

> SYNONYMS ▶ **prep.** **1** **below**, beneath, underneath. **2** **less than**, lower than, below. **3** **subordinate to**, answerable to, responsible to, subject to, junior to, inferior to. ANTONYMS above, over.

□ **under way** **1** having started and making progress. **2** (of a boat) moving through the water.

un·der·a·chieve /ˌəndərəˈchēv/ ▶ **v.** (**underachieves**, **underachieving**, **underachieved**) do less well than is expected.

un·der·arm /ˈəndərˌärm/ ▶ **adj. & adv.** done with the arm or hand below shoulder level.

un·der·car·riage /ˈəndərˌkarij/ ▶ **n.** the wheeled structure that supports an aircraft when it is on the ground.

un·der·class /ˈəndərˌklas/ ▶ **n.** the lowest social class, consisting of very poor and unemployed people.

un·der·clothes /ˈəndərˌklō(th)z/ ▶ **pl.n.** underwear.

un·der·coat /ˈəndərˌkōt/ ▶ **n.** a layer of paint applied before the top layer.

un·der·cov·er /ˌəndərˈkəvər/ ▶ **adj. & adv.** involving secret work for police investigation or spying.

> SYNONYMS **secret**, covert, clandestine, underground, surreptitious, furtive, cloak-and-dagger, stealthy; informal hush-hush. ANTONYMS overt.

un·der·cur·rent /ˈəndərˌkərənt/ ▶ **n.** an underlying feeling or influence.

un·der·cut /ˌəndərˈkət/ ▶ **v.** (**undercuts**, **undercutting**, **undercut**) **1** offer products or services at a lower price than a competitor. **2** weaken or undermine.

un·der·dog /ˈəndərˌdôg, -ˌdäg/ ▶ **n.** a competitor thought to have little chance of winning a fight or contest.

un·der·done /ˌəndərˈdən/ ▶ **adj.** not cooked enough.

un·der·dressed /ˌəndərˈdrest/ ▶ **adj.** wearing clothes that are too plain or casual.

un·der·es·ti·mate ▶ **v.** /ˌəndərˈestəˌmāt/ (**underestimates**, **underestimating**, **underestimated**) **1** estimate something to be smaller or less important than it really is. **2** think of someone as less capable than they really are. ▶ **n.** /-mit/ an estimate that is too low.

> SYNONYMS ▶ **v.** **underrate**, undervalue, miscalculate, misjudge, do an injustice to. ANTONYMS overestimate.

■ **un·der·es·ti·ma·tion** /-ˌestəˈmāshən/ **n.**

un·der·foot /ˌəndərˈfo͝ot/ ▶ **adv.** **1** on the ground. **2** constantly present and in the way.

un·der·gar·ment /ˈəndərˌgärmənt/ ▶ **n.** a piece of underwear.

un·der·go /ˌəndərˈgō/ ▶ **v.** (**undergoes**, **undergoing**, **underwent** /ˌəndərˈwent/; past participle **undergone** /ˌəndərˈgôn/) experience something unpleasant or difficult.

> SYNONYMS **experience**, go through, submit to, face, be subjected to, receive, endure, brave, bear, withstand, weather.

un·der·grad·u·ate /ˌəndərˈgrajəwit/ ▶ **n.** a student at a university who has not yet earned a bachelor's or equivalent degree.

un·der·ground /ˌəndərˈground/ ▶ **adj. & adv.** **1** beneath the surface of the ground. **2** in secrecy or hiding. ▶ **n.** a secret group working against the government or an enemy.

> SYNONYMS ▶ **adj. & adv.** **1** **subterranean**, buried, sunken. **2** **secret**, clandestine, surreptitious, covert, undercover, closet, cloak-and-dagger, resistance, subversive.

un·der·growth /ˈəndərˌgrōth/ ▶ **n.** a mass of shrubs and other plants growing closely together.

un·der·hand·ed /ˌəndərˈhandəd/ ▶ **adj.** done in a secret or dishonest way.

un·der·lay /ˌəndərˈlā/ ▶ **n.** material laid under a carpet.

un·der·lie /ˌəndərˈlī/ ▶ **v.** (**underlies**, **underlying**, **underlay** /ˌəndərˈlā/; past participle **underlain**) **1** lie or be situated under. **2** (**underlying**) basic or fundamental.

> SYNONYMS (**underlying**) **fundamental**, basic, primary, central, essential, principal, elementary, initial.

un·der·line /ˈəndərˌlīn/ ▶ **v.** (**underlines**, **underlining**, **underlined**) **1** draw a line under. **2** emphasize.

> SYNONYMS **1** **underscore**, mark, point out, emphasize, highlight. **2** **emphasize**, stress, highlight, accentuate, accent, focus on, spotlight.

un·der·ling /ˈəndərliNG/ ▶ **n.** disapproving a person of lower status.

un·der·mine /ˌəndərˈmīn, ˈəndərˌmīn/ ▶ **v.** (**undermines**, **undermining**, **undermined**) **1** damage or weaken. **2** wear away the base or foundation of.

> SYNONYMS **weaken**, diminish, reduce, impair, mar, spoil, ruin, damage, sap, shake, threaten, subvert, compromise, sabotage. ANTONYMS strengthen.

un·der·neath /ˌəndərˈnēth/ ▶ **prep. & adv.** **1** situated directly below. **2** so as to be concealed by. ▶ **n.** the part or side facing toward the ground.

un·der·nour·ished /ˌəndərˈnərisht, -ˈnə-risht/ ▶ **adj.** having insufficient food for good health and condition.

un·der·pants /ˈəndərˌpan(t)s/ ▶ **pl.n.** a piece of underwear covering the lower part of the torso and having two holes for the legs.

un·der·part /ˈəndərˌpärt/ ▶ **n.** a lower part.

un·der·pass /ˈəndərˌpas/ ▶ **n.** a road or tunnel passing under another road or a railroad.

un·der·pin /ˌəndərˈpin/ ▶ **v.** (**underpins**, **underpinning**, **underpinned**) **1** support or form the basis for an argument, claim, etc. **2** support a structure from below.

un·der·play /ˌəndərˈplā, ˈəndərˌplā/ ▶ **v.** represent something as being less important than it really is.

un·der·priv·i·leged /ˌəndərˈpriv(ə)lijd/ ▶ **adj.** not having the same rights or standard of living as the majority of the population.

un·der·rat·ed /ˌəndə(r)ˈrātid/ ▶ **v.** rated less highly than is deserved.

un·der·score /ˈəndərˌskôr, ˌəndərˈskôr/ ▶ **v.** underline.

un·der·sea /ˌəndərˈsē/ ▶ **adj.** found or situated below the surface of the sea.

un·der·sec·re·tar·y /ˌəndərˈsekriˌterē/ ▶ **n.** (plural **undersecretaries**) a subordinate official, in particular (in the US) the principal assistant to a member of the cabinet.

un·der·sell /ˌəndərˈsel/ ▶ **v.** (**undersells**, **underselling**, **undersold** /ˌəndərˈsōld/) sell something at a lower price than a competitor.

un·der·side /ˈəndərˌsīd/ ▶ **n.** the bottom or lower side or surface of something.

un·der·signed /ˈəndərˌsīnd/ ▶ **n.** formal the person or people who have signed the document in question.

un·der·sized /ˌəndərˈsīzd/ (or **undersize**) ▶ **adj.** of less than the usual size.

un·der·staffed /ˌəndərˈstaft/ ▶ **adj.** having too few members of staff.

un·der·stand /ˌəndərˈstand/ ▶ **v.** (**understands**, **understanding**, **understood** /ˌəndərˈsto͝od/) **1** know or realize the real or intended meaning or cause of. **2** know how someone feels or why they behave in a particular way. **3** interpret or view in a particular way. **4** believe that something is the case because of information that you have received.

SYNONYMS **1 comprehend**, grasp, take in, see, apprehend, follow, make sense of, fathom; informal work out, figure out, make heads or tails of, get. **2 know**, realize, recognize, acknowledge, appreciate, be aware of, be conscious of. **3 believe**, gather, take it, hear (tell), notice, see, learn.

un·der·stand·a·ble /ˌəndərˈstandəbəl/ ▶ **adj.** **1** able to be understood. **2** natural, reasonable, or forgivable.

SYNONYMS **1 comprehensible**, intelligible, clear, plain, unambiguous, transparent, straightforward, explicit, coherent. **2 unsurprising**, expected, predictable, inevitable, reasonable, acceptable, logical, rational, normal, natural, justifiable, excusable, pardonable, forgivable. ANTONYMS incomprehensible.

■ **un·der·stand·a·bly** **adv.**

un·der·stand·ing /ˌəndərˈstandiNG/ ▶ **n.** **1** the ability to understand something. **2** a person's intellect. **3** the way in which a person looks at a situation. **4** sympathetic awareness or tolerance. **5** an informal or unspoken agreement or arrangement. ▶ **adj.** sympathetically aware of other people's feelings.

SYNONYMS ▶ **n.** **1 comprehension**, grasp, mastery, appreciation, knowledge, awareness, skill, expertise, proficiency; informal know-how. **2 intellect**, intelligence, brainpower, judgment, insight, intuition, acumen, sagacity, wisdom. **3 belief**, perception, view, conviction, feeling, opinion, intuition, impression. **4 sympathy**, compassion, pity, feeling, concern, consideration, kindness, sensitivity, decency, goodwill. **5 agreement**, arrangement, deal, bargain, settlement, pledge, pact. ANTONYMS ignorance. ▶ **adj.** **sympathetic**, compassionate, sensitive, considerate, kind, thoughtful, tolerant, patient, forbearing, lenient, forgiving.

■ **un·der·stand·ing·ly** **adv.**

un·der·state /ˌəndərˈstāt/ ▶ **v.** (**understates**, **understating**, **understated**) represent something as being smaller or less significant than it really is.

SYNONYMS **play down**, underrate, underplay, trivialize, minimize, diminish, downgrade, brush aside, gloss over. ANTONYMS exaggerate.

un·der·stat·ed /ˌəndərˈstātid/ ▶ **adj.** pleasingly subtle.

un·der·state·ment /ˈəndərˌstātmənt/ ▶ **n.** the description of something as being smaller, worse, or less important than it actually is.

un·der·stud·y /ˈəndərˌstədē/ ▶ **n.** (plural **understudies**) an actor who learns another's role in order to take their place if necessary. ▶ **v.** (**understudies**, **understudying**, **understudied**) be an understudy for.

un·der·take /ˌəndərˈtāk/ ▶ **v.** (**undertake**, **undertaking**, **undertook** /ˌəndərˈto͝ok/; past participle **undertaken**) **1** begin an activity. **2** formally guarantee or promise.

SYNONYMS **1 set about**, embark on, go about, engage in, take on, be responsible for, get down to, tackle, attempt; informal have a go at. **2 promise**, pledge, vow, give your word, swear, guarantee, contract, give an assurance, commit yourself.

un·der·tak·er /ˈəndərˌtākər/ ▶ **n.** a person whose job is preparing dead bodies for burial or cremation and making arrangements for funerals.

SYNONYMS **funeral director**, mortician.

un·der·tak·ing /ˈəndərˌtākiNG, ˌəndərˈtā-/ ▶ **n.** **1** a formal promise to do something. **2** a task.

SYNONYMS **1 enterprise**, venture, project, campaign, scheme, plan, operation, endeavor, effort, task. **2 promise**, pledge, agreement, oath, covenant, vow, commitment, guarantee, assurance.

un·der·tone /ˈəndərˌtōn/ ▶ **n.** **1** a subdued or muted tone. **2** an underlying quality or feeling.

un·der·tow /ˈəndərˌtō/ ▶ **n.** a current under the surface of water.

un·der·used /ˌəndərˈyo͞ozd/ ▶ **adj.** not used as much as it could or should be. ■ **un·der·use** /ˌəndərˈyo͞os/ **n.**

un·der·wa·ter /ˌəndərˈwôtər, -ˈwätər/ ▶ **adj. & adv.** situated, happening, or used beneath the surface of the water.

SYNONYMS **submerged**, sunken, undersea, submarine.

un·der·way /ˌəndərˈwā/ ▶ **adj.** = **UNDER WAY**.

USAGE

The spelling **underway** is best avoided in formal writing: use **under way** instead.

un·der·wear /ˈəndərˌwer/ ▶ **n.** clothing worn under other clothes next to the skin.

SYNONYMS **underclothes**, undergarments, underthings, lingerie; informal undies.

un·der·weight /ˈəndərˌwāt, ˌəndərˈwāt/ ▶ **adj.** below a normal or desirable weight.

un·der·went /ˌəndərˈwent/ past of **UNDERGO**.

un·der·whelmed /ˌəndərˈ(h)welmd/ ▶ **v.** humorous not very impressed.

un·der·world /ˈəndərˌwərld/ ▶ **n.** **1** the world of criminals or of organized crime. **2** (in myths and legends) the home of the dead, imagined as being under the earth.

un·der·write /ˈəndə(r)ˌrīt, ˌəndə(r)ˈrīt/ ▶ **v.** (**underwrites**, **underwriting**, **underwrote** /ˈəndə(r)ˌrōt/; past participle **underwritten** /ˈəndə(r)ˌritn/) **1** accept legal responsibility for an insurance policy. **2** accept financial responsibility for an undertaking.

SYNONYMS **sponsor**, support, back, insure, indemnify, subsidize, pay for, finance, fund; informal bankroll.

■ **un·der·writ·er** **n.**

un·de·serv·ing /ˌəndiˈzərviNG/ ▶ **adj.** not deserving or worthy of something good.

un·de·sir·a·ble /ˌəndiˈzīrəbəl/ ▶ **adj.** harmful, offensive, or unpleasant. ▶ **n.** an unpleasant or offensive person.

SYNONYMS ▶ **adj.** **unpleasant**, disagreeable, nasty, unwelcome, unwanted, unfortunate. ANTONYMS pleasant.

un·de·terred /ˌəndiˈtərd/ ▶ **adj.** persevering despite setbacks.

un·de·vi·at·ing /ˌənˈdēvēˌātiNG/ ▶ **adj.** constant and steady.

un·dies /ˈəndēz/ ▶ **pl.n.** informal pieces of underwear.

un·dis·cov·ered /ˌəndisˈkəvərd/ ▶ **adj.** not discovered.

un·dis·put·ed /ˌəndiˈspyo͞otid/ ▶ **adj.** not disputed or called into question.

un·dis·tin·guished /ˌəndiˈstiNGgwisHt/ ▶ **adj.** not particularly good or successful.

un·di·vid·ed /ˌəndəˈvīdid/ ▶ **adj.** **1** not divided or broken into parts. **2** complete; total: *my undivided attention.*

SYNONYMS **complete**, full, total, whole, entire, absolute, unqualified, unreserved, unmitigated, unbroken, consistent, thorough, exclusive, dedicated; focused, engrossed, absorbed, attentive, committed.

un·do /ˌənˈdo͞o/ ▶ **v.** (**undoes** /ˌənˈdəs/, **undoing**, **undid** /ˌənˈdid/; past participle **undone** /ˌənˈdən/) **1** unfasten or loosen. **2** reverse the effects of something previously done. **3** formal cause the downfall or ruin of.

SYNONYMS **1 unfasten**, unbutton, unhook, untie, unlace, unlock, unbolt, loosen, detach, free, open. **2 cancel**, reverse, overrule, overturn, repeal, rescind, countermand, revoke, annul, invalidate, negate. **3 ruin**, undermine, overturn, scotch, sabotage, spoil, impair, mar, destroy, wreck; informal blow. ANTONYMS fasten.

un·do·ing /ˌənˈdo͞o-iNG/ ▶ **n.** formal a person's ruin or downfall.

un·doubt·ed /ˌənˈdoutid/ ▶ **adj.** not questioned or doubted.

un·doubt·ed·ly /ˌənˈdoutidlē/ ▶ **adv.** without doubt: *they are undoubtedly guilty.*

SYNONYMS **doubtless**, indubitably, unquestionably, indisputably, undeniably, incontrovertibly, without (a) doubt, clearly.

un·dreamed /ˌənˈdrēmd/ (or **undreamt** /ˌənˈdremt/) ▶ **adj.** (**undreamed of**) not previously thought to be possible.

un·dress /ˌənˈdres/ ▶ **v.** **1** (also **get undressed**) take off your clothes. **2** take the clothes off someone else. ▶ **n.** formal the state of being naked or only partially clothed.

un·due /ˌənˈd(y)o͞o/ ▶ **adj.** more than is reasonable or necessary.

SYNONYMS **excessive**, immoderate, intemperate, inordinate, disproportionate, uncalled for, unnecessary, unwarranted, unjustified, unreasonable, inappropriate, unmerited, unsuitable, improper. ANTONYMS appropriate.

■ **un·du·ly** **adv.**

un·du·late /ˈənjəˌlāt, ˈəndyə-/ ▶ **v.** (**undulates**, **undulating**, **undulated**) **1** move with a smooth wavelike motion. **2** have a wavy form or outline.
■ **un·du·la·tion** /ˌənjəˈlāsHən, ˌəndyə-/ **n.**

un·dy·ing /ˌənˈdī-iNG/ ▶ **adj.** lasting forever.

un·earth /ˌənˈərTH/ ▶ **v.** **1** find in the ground by digging. **2** discover by investigation or searching.

SYNONYMS **1 dig up**, excavate, exhume, disinter, root out. **2** *I unearthed an interesting fact* **discover**, find, come across, hit on, bring to light, expose, turn up.

un·earth·ly /ˌənˈərTHlē/ ▶ **adj.** **1** unnatural or mysterious. **2** informal very early and therefore inconvenient or annoying.

un·ease /ˌənˈēz/ ▶ **n.** anxiety or discontent.

un·eas·y /ˌənˈēzē/ ▶ **adj.** (**uneasier**, **uneasiest**) anxious or uncomfortable.

SYNONYMS **1 worried**, anxious, troubled, disturbed, nervous, nervy, tense, edgy, on edge, apprehensive, fearful, uncomfortable, unsettled, ill at ease; informal jittery. **2** *an uneasy peace* **tense**, awkward, strained, fraught, precarious, unstable, insecure. ANTONYMS calm.

■ **un·eas·i·ly** **adv.** **un·eas·i·ness** **n.**

un·ed·i·fy·ing /ˌənˈedəˌfī-iNG/ ▶ **adj.** distasteful or unpleasant.

un·em·bar·rassed /ˌənemˈbarəst/ ▶ **adj.** not feeling or showing embarrassment.

un·em·ploy·a·ble /ˌənimˈploi-əbəl/ ▶ **adj.** not having enough skills or qualifications to obtain paid employment.

un·em·ployed /ˌənimˈploid/ ▶ **adj.** without a paid job but available to work.

SYNONYMS **jobless**, out of work, laid off.

un·em·ploy·ment /ˌənimˈploimənt/ ▶ **n.** **1** the state of being unemployed. **2** the number or proportion of unemployed people.

un·en·cum·bered /ˌənenˈkəmbərd/ ▶ **adj.** not burdened or held back.

un·end·ing /ˌənˈendiNG/ ▶ **adj.** seeming to last forever.

un·en·thu·si·as·tic /ˌənenˌTHo͞ozēˈastik/ ▶ **adj.** not having or showing enthusiasm.
■ **un·en·thu·si·as·ti·cal·ly** **adv.**

un·en·vi·a·ble /ˌənˈenvēəbəl/ ▶ **adj.** difficult, undesirable, or unpleasant.

un·e·qual /ˌənˈēkwəl/ ▶ **adj.** **1** not equal. **2** not fair or even. **3** (**unequal to**) not having the ability to meet a challenge. ■ **un·e·qual·ly adv.**

un·e·qualed /ˌənˈēkwəld/ ▶ **adj.** better or greater than all others.

un·e·quiv·o·cal /ˌəniˈkwivəkəl/ ▶ **adj.** leaving no doubt; unambiguous. ■ **un·e·quiv·o·cal·ly adv.**

un·err·ing /ˌənˈəriNG, -ˈer-/ ▶ **adj.** always right or accurate. ■ **un·err·ing·ly adv.**

un·eth·i·cal /ˌənˈeTHikəl/ ▶ **adj.** not morally correct. ■ **un·eth·i·cal·ly adv.**

un·e·ven /ˌənˈēvən/ ▶ **adj.** **1** not level or smooth. **2** not regular or equal.

> SYNONYMS **1 bumpy**, rough, lumpy, stony, rocky, rutted. **2 irregular**, crooked, lopsided, askew, asymmetrical. **3 inconsistent**, variable, fluctuating, irregular, erratic, patchy, fitful. ANTONYMS flat, regular.

■ **un·e·ven·ly adv. un·e·ven·ness n.**

un·e·vent·ful /ˌəniˈventfəl/ ▶ **adj.** not marked by interesting or exciting events. ■ **un·e·vent·ful·ly adv.**

un·ex·cep·tion·a·ble /ˌənikˈsepSH(ə)nəbəl/ ▶ **adj.** not able to be objected to, but not particularly new or exciting.

un·ex·cep·tion·al /ˌənikˈsepSHənl/ ▶ **adj.** not out of the ordinary; usual. ■ **un·ex·cep·tion·al·ly adv.**

un·ex·pect·ed /ˌənikˈspektid/ ▶ **adj.** not expected or thought likely to happen. ■ **un·ex·pect·ed·ly adv.**

un·ex·plored /ˌənikˈsplôrd/ ▶ **adj.** not explored, investigated, or evaluated.

un·ex·pur·gat·ed /ˌənˈekspərˌgātid/ ▶ **adj.** (of a written work) complete and containing all the original material.

un·fail·ing /ˌənˈfāliNG/ ▶ **adj.** reliable or never changing. ■ **un·fail·ing·ly adv.**

un·fair /ˌənˈfe(ə)r/ ▶ **adj.** not fair or just.

> SYNONYMS **1 unjust**, prejudiced, biased, discriminatory, one-sided, unequal, uneven, unbalanced, partisan. **2 undeserved**, unmerited, unreasonable, unjustified; informal out of line. **3 unsporting**, dirty, underhanded/underhand, dishonorable, dishonest. ANTONYMS just, justified.

■ **un·fair·ly adv. un·fair·ness n.**

un·faith·ful /ˌənˈfāTHfəl/ ▶ **adj.** **1** having an intimate relationship with someone who is not your husband, wife, or usual partner. **2** disloyal.

un·fa·mil·iar /ˌənfəˈmilyər/ ▶ **adj.** **1** not known or recognized. **2** (**unfamiliar with**) not having knowledge or experience of. ■ **un·fa·mil·i·ar·i·ty** /-ˌmilēˈe(ə)ritē, -fəmilˈyer-/ **n.**

un·fas·ten /ˌənˈfasən/ ▶ **v.** open the fastening of something.

> SYNONYMS **undo**, open, disconnect, untie, unbutton, unzip, loosen, free, unlock, unbolt.

un·fath·om·a·ble /ˌənˈfaTHəməbəl/ ▶ **adj.** incapable of being fully understood.

un·fa·vor·a·ble /ˌənˈfāv(ə)rəbəl/ ▶ **adj.** **1** not approving. **2** not good or likely to lead to success. ■ **un·fa·vor·a·bly adv.**

un·fazed /ˌənˈfāzd/ ▶ **adj.** informal not worried or confused by something unexpected.

un·fea·si·ble /ˌənˈfēzəbəl/ ▶ **adj.** not able to be done or achieved. ■ **un·fea·si·bly adv.**

un·feel·ing /ˌənˈfēliNG/ ▶ **adj.** unsympathetic, harsh, or callous.

> SYNONYMS **uncaring**, unsympathetic, unemotional, uncharitable; heartless, hard-hearted, harsh, austere, cold. ANTONYMS compassionate.

un·fin·ished /ˌənˈfinisht/ ▶ **adj.** not finished.

un·fit /ˌənˈfit/ ▶ **adj.** **1** unsuitable. **2** not in good physical condition.

> SYNONYMS **1** *a movie unfit for children* **unsuitable**, inappropriate, not designed. **2** unfit for *duty* **incapable of**, not up to, not equal to, unequipped for, inadequate for, unprepared for; informal not cut out for. **3 unhealthy**, out of condition/shape, debilitated. ANTONYMS suitable, healthy.

un·flag·ging /ˌənˈflagiNG/ ▶ **adj.** not becoming weak or tired.

un·flap·pa·ble /ˌənˈflapəbəl/ ▶ **adj.** informal calm in a crisis.

un·flinch·ing /ˌənˈflinCHiNG/ ▶ **adj.** not afraid or hesitant. ■ **un·flinch·ing·ly adv.**

un·fold /ˌənˈfōld/ ▶ **v.** **1** open or spread out from a folded position. **2** reveal or be revealed.

> SYNONYMS **1 open out**, spread out, flatten, straighten out, unroll, unfurl. **2 develop**, evolve, happen, take place, occur.

un·fore·seen /ˌənfôrˈsēn, -fər-/ ▶ **adj.** not anticipated or predicted; unexpected.

> **SPELLING**
> Remember the **e** after the **r**: unforeseen.

un·for·get·ta·ble /ˌənfərˈgetəbəl/ ▶ **adj.** very memorable. ■ **un·for·get·ta·bly adv.**

un·for·giv·a·ble /ˌənfərˈgivəbəl/ ▶ **adj.** so bad as to be unable to be forgiven. ■ **un·for·giv·a·bly adv.**

un·for·giv·ing /ˌənfərˈgiviNG/ ▶ **adj.** **1** not willing to forgive. **2** (of conditions) harsh.

un·forth·com·ing /ˌənfôrTHˈkəmiNG/ ▶ **adj.** **1** not willing to give out information. **2** not available when needed.

un·for·tu·nate /ˌənˈfôrCHənət/ ▶ **adj.** **1** unlucky. **2** regrettable or inappropriate. ▶ **n.** a person who suffers bad luck.

> SYNONYMS ▶ **adj. 1 unlucky**, hapless, ill-starred, star-crossed, wretched, poor, pitiful; informal down on your luck. **2 unwelcome**, disadvantageous, unfavorable, unlucky, adverse, unpromising, inauspicious. **3 regrettable**, inappropriate, unsuitable, tactless, injudicious. ANTONYMS lucky.

un·for·tu·nate·ly /ˌənˈfôrCHənətlē/ ▶ **adv.** it is unfortunate that: *unfortunately, we do not have the time to interview every applicant.*

un·found·ed /ˌənˈfoundid/ ▶ **adj.** having no basis in fact.

un·friend·ly /ˌənˈfren(d)lē/ ▶ **adj.** (**unfriendlier**, **unfriendliest**) not friendly.

> SYNONYMS **hostile**, disagreeable, antagonistic, aggressive, unpleasant, surly, uncongenial, inhospitable, unneighborly, unwelcoming, unsociable, cool, cold, aloof, distant; informal standoffish.

■ **un·friend·li·ness n.**

un·ful·filled /ˌənfo͝o(l)ˈfild/ ▶ **adj.** not fulfilled. ■ **un·ful·fill·ing adj.**

un·furl /ˌənˈfərl/ ▶ **v.** open something that is rolled or folded.

un·gain·ly /ˌənˈgānlē/ ▶ **adj.** clumsy; awkward.

> SYNONYMS **awkward**, clumsy, graceless, inelegant, gawky, gauche, uncoordinated. ANTONYMS graceful.

■ **un·gain·li·ness n.**

un·gen·tle·man·ly /ˌənˈjentlmənlē/ ▶ **adj.** not appropriate to or behaving like a gentleman.

un·god·ly /ˌənˈgädlē/ ▶ **adj. 1** immoral or disrespectful to God. **2** informal very early or late, and therefore annoying.

un·gov·ern·a·ble /ˌənˈgəvərnəbəl/ ▶ **adj.** impossible to control or govern.

un·gra·cious /ˌənˈgrāsʜəs/ ▶ **adj.** not gracious. ■ **un·gra·cious·ly adv.**

un·grate·ful /ˌənˈgrātfəl/ ▶ **adj.** not grateful. ■ **un·grate·ful·ly adv.**

un·guard·ed /ˌənˈgärdid/ ▶ **adj. 1** without protection. **2** not well-considered; careless: *an unguarded remark.*

un·guent /ˈəɴɢgwənt/ ▶ **n.** a soft greasy or thick substance used as ointment or for lubrication.

un·gu·late /ˈəɴɢgyələt, -ˌlāt/ ▶ **n.** the name in zoology for a hoofed mammal.

un·hap·pi·ly /ˌənˈhapəlē/ ▶ **adv. 1** in an unhappy manner. **2** unfortunately: *unhappily, such days do not come too often.*

un·hap·py /ˌənˈhapē/ ▶ **adj.** (**unhappier, unhappiest**) **1** not happy. **2** unfortunate.

> SYNONYMS **1 sad**, miserable, sorrowful, dejected, despondent, disconsolate, morose, heartbroken, down, dispirited, downhearted, depressed, melancholy, mournful, gloomy, glum; informal down in the mouth, blue. **2** *unhappy with the service* **dissatisfied**, displeased, discontented, disappointed, disgruntled. **3 unfortunate**, unlucky, ill-starred, ill-fated, doomed; informal jinxed. ANTONYMS happy, pleased.

■ **un·hap·pi·ness n.**

un·harmed /ˌənˈhärmd/ ▶ **adj.** not harmed.

un·health·y /ˌənˈhelᴛʜē/ ▶ **adj.** (**unhealthier, unhealthiest**) **1** not having good health. **2** not good for your health.

> SYNONYMS **1 harmful**, detrimental, destructive, injurious, damaging, noxious, poisonous. **2 sick**, poorly, ill, unwell, unfit, ailing, weak, frail, infirm, washed out, rundown. **3 abnormal**, morbid, macabre, twisted, unwholesome, warped, depraved, unnatural; informal sick.

■ **un·health·i·ly adv.**

un·heard /ˌənˈhərd/ ▶ **adj. 1** not heard or listened to. **2** (**unheard of**) previously unknown.

un·help·ful /ˌənˈhelpfəl/ ▶ **adj.** not helpful. ■ **un·help·ful·ly adv.**

un·her·ald·ed /ˌənˈherəldid/ ▶ **adj.** not previously announced, expected, or recognized.

un·hes·i·tat·ing /ˌənˈheziˌtātiɴɢ/ ▶ **adj.** without doubt or hesitation. ■ **un·hes·i·tat·ing·ly adv.**

un·hinged /ˌənˈhinjd/ ▶ **adj.** mentally ill or unbalanced.

un·ho·ly /ˌənˈhōlē/ ▶ **adj. 1** sinful; wicked. **2** unnatural and likely to be harmful. **3** informal dreadful.

un·hur·ried /ˌənˈhərēd, -ˈhə-rēd/ ▶ **adj.** moving or doing things in a leisurely way. ■ **un·hur·ried·ly adv.**

un·hurt /ˌənˈhərt/ ▶ **adj.** not hurt or harmed.

u·ni·cam·er·al /ˌyo͞onəˈkam(ə)rəl/ ▶ **adj.** (of a legislature or parliament) consisting of only one main part.

u·ni·corn /ˈyo͞onəˌkôrn/ ▶ **n.** a mythical creature like a horse with a single long horn on its forehead.

u·ni·cy·cle /ˈyo͞onəˌsīkəl/ ▶ **n.** a cycle with a single wheel. ■ **u·ni·cy·clist n.**

un·i·den·ti·fi·a·ble /ˌənīˈdentəˌfīəbəl/ ▶ **adj.** unable to be identified.

un·i·den·ti·fied /ˌənīˈdentəˌfīəd/ ▶ **adj.** not recognized or identified.

u·ni·fi·ca·tion /ˌyo͞onəfiˈkāsʜən/ ▶ **n.** the process of uniting or of being united.

u·ni·form /ˈyo͞onəˌfôrm/ ▶ **n.** the distinctive clothing worn by members of the same organization or school. ▶ **adj.** not varying; the same in all cases and at all times.

> SYNONYMS ▶ **n. costume**, outfit, suit, ensemble, livery, regalia; informal getup, rig, gear. ▶ **adj. 1 constant**, consistent, steady, invariable, unchanging, stable, static, regular, fixed, even. **2 identical**, matching, similar, equal, same, like, consistent. ANTONYMS variable.

■ **u·ni·formed adj. u·ni·form·i·ty** /ˌyo͞onəˈfôrmətē/ **n. u·ni·form·ly adv.**

u·ni·fy /ˈyo͞onəˌfī/ ▶ **v.** (**unifies, unifying, unified**) make or become united.

> SYNONYMS **unite**, combine, bring together, join, merge, fuse, amalgamate, coalesce, consolidate. ANTONYMS separate.

u·ni·lat·er·al /ˌyo͞onəˈlatərəl, -ˈlatrəl/ ▶ **adj.** done by or affecting only one person or group. ■ **u·ni·lat·er·al·ly adv.**

un·im·ag·i·na·ble /ˌənəˈmaj(ə)nəbəl/ ▶ **adj.** impossible to imagine or understand. ■ **un·im·ag·i·na·bly adv.**

un·im·ag·i·na·tive /ˌənəˈmaj(ə)nətiv/ ▶ **adj.** not using or showing imagination or new ideas; dull. ■ **un·im·ag·i·na·tive·ly adv.**

un·im·peach·a·ble /ˌənimˈpēcʜəbəl/ ▶ **adj.** not able to be doubted or criticized.

un·im·por·tant /ˌənimˈpôrtnt/ ▶ **adj.** not important. ■ **un·im·por·tance n.**

un·im·pressed /ˌənimˈprest/ ▶ **adj.** not impressed.

un·im·pres·sive /ˌənimˈpresiv/ ▶ **adj.** not impressive.

un·in·hab·it·ed /ˌəninˈhabitid/ ▶ **adj.** having no people living there. ■ **un·in·hab·it·a·ble adj.**

un·in·hib·it·ed /ˌəninˈhibitid/ ▶ **adj.** saying or doing things without concern about what other people think.

un·in·i·ti·at·ed /ˌənəˈnisʜēˌātid/ ▶ **adj.** without knowledge or experience of something.

un·in·jured /ˌənˈinjərd/ ▶ **adj.** not hurt or injured.

un·in·spired /ˌəninˈspīrd/ ▶ **adj. 1** not original or exciting; dull. **2** feeling no excitement. ■ **un·in·spir·ing adj.**

un·in·tel·li·gi·ble /ˌəninˈteləjəbəl/ ▶ **adj.** impossible to understand. ■ **un·in·tel·li·gi·bil·i·ty** /ˌəninˌteləjəˈbilətē/ **n. un·in·tel·li·gi·bly adv.**

un·in·ten·tion·al /ˌəninˈtencʜənl/ ▶ **adj.** not done on purpose. ■ **un·in·ten·tion·al·ly adv.**

un·in·ter·est·ed /ˌənˈintəˌrestid, ˌənˈintristid/ ▶ **adj.** not interested or concerned.

> USAGE
> Don't confuse **uninterested** and **disinterested**. **Disinterested** means 'impartial,' while **uninterested** means 'not interested.'

un·in·ter·est·ing /ˌənˈintəˌrestiNG, ˌənˈintristiNG/ ▶ **adj.** not interesting; dull.

> SYNONYMS **boring**, dull, unexciting, tiresome, tedious, dreary, lifeless, humdrum, colorless, bland, insipid, banal, dry. ANTONYMS exciting.

un·in·ter·rupt·ed /ˌənˌintəˈrəptid/ ▶ **adj.** not interrupted; continuous.

un·in·vit·ed /ˌəninˈvītid/ ▶ **adj.** arriving or doing things without being invited.

un·ion /ˈyo͞onyən/ ▶ **n. 1** the act of uniting two or more things. **2** a labor union. **3** a club, society, or association. **4** (also **Union**) a political unit consisting of a number of states or provinces with the same central government. **5** the United States, especially from its founding to the beginning of the Civil War in 1861, or the northern states that opposed the Confederacy during the Civil War. **6** a state of harmony or agreement. **7** a marriage.

> SYNONYMS **1 unification**, joining, merger, fusion, amalgamation, coalition, combination, synthesis, blend. **2 association**, league, guild, confederation, federation. ANTONYMS separation.

□ **Union Jack** (or **Union Flag**) the national flag of the United Kingdom.

un·ion·ist /ˈyo͞onyənist/ ▶ **n. 1** a member of a labor union. **2** (**Unionist**) a person who opposed secession in the Civil War.

un·ion·ize /ˈyo͞onyəˌnīz/ ▶ **v.** (**unionizes**, **unionizing**, **unionized**) make or become members of a labor union. ■ **un·ion·i·za·tion** /ˌyo͞onyəniˈzāSHən, -ˌnīˈzā-/ **n.**

u·nique /yo͞oˈnēk/ ▶ **adj. 1** being the only one of its kind. **2** (**unique to**) belonging or connected to one particular person, group, or place. **3** very special or unusual.

> SYNONYMS **1 distinctive**, individual, special, particular, specific, idiosyncratic, single, sole, lone, unrepeated, solitary, exclusive. **2 remarkable**, special, notable, unequaled, unparalleled, unmatched, unsurpassed, incomparable. ANTONYMS common.

■ **u·nique·ly** **adv.**

u·ni·sex /ˈyo͞onəˌseks/ ▶ **adj.** designed to be suitable for both sexes.

u·ni·son /ˈyo͞onəsən, -zən/ ▶ **n.** (**in unison**) at the same time; together.

u·nit /ˈyo͞onit/ ▶ **n. 1** a single thing or group that is complete in itself but can also form part of something larger. **2** a device, part, or item of furniture with a particular function: *a sink unit*. **3** a self-contained section of a building or group of buildings. **4** a subdivision of a larger military grouping. **5** a quantity used as a standard measure.

> SYNONYMS **1 component**, part, section, segment, element, module, constituent, subdivision. **2 quantity**, measure, denomination. **3 group**, detachment, contingent, division, cell, faction, department, office, branch.

U·ni·tar·i·an /ˌyo͞oniˈte(ə)rēən/ ▶ **n.** a member of a Christian church that believes that God is one being and rejects the idea of the Trinity.

u·ni·tar·y /ˈyo͞oniˌterē/ ▶ **adj. 1** forming a single unit or entity. **2** relating to a unit or units.

u·nite /yo͞oˈnīt/ ▶ **v.** (**unites**, **uniting**, **united**) **1** join together with others in order to do something as a group. **2** bring people or things together to form a unit or whole.

> SYNONYMS **1 unify**, join, link, connect, combine, amalgamate, fuse, weld, bond, bring together. **2 join together**, join forces, combine, band together, ally, cooperate, collaborate, work together, team up. **3 merge**, mix, blend, mingle, combine. ANTONYMS divide.

u·nit·ed /yo͞oˈnītid/ ▶ **adj.** joined together politically or for a shared purpose.

u·ni·ty /ˈyo͞onətē/ ▶ **n.** (plural **unities**) **1** the state of being united or forming a whole. **2** a thing forming a complex whole. **3** Math the number one.

> SYNONYMS **1 union**, unification, integration, amalgamation, coalition, federation, confederation. **2 harmony**, accord, cooperation, collaboration, agreement, consensus, solidarity. **3 oneness**, singleness, wholeness, uniformity, homogeneity. ANTONYMS disunity.

u·ni·ver·sal /ˌyo͞onəˈvərsəl/ ▶ **adj. 1** affecting or done by all people or things in the world or in a particular group. **2** true or right in all cases.

> SYNONYMS **general**, common, widespread, ubiquitous, comprehensive, global, worldwide, international.

■ **u·ni·ver·sal·i·ty** /-vərˈsalətē/ **n.**

u·ni·ver·sal·ly /ˌyo͞onəˈvərsəlē/ ▶ **adv.** by everyone; in every case.

> SYNONYMS **always**, without exception, by everyone, in all cases, everywhere, worldwide, globally, internationally, commonly, generally.

u·ni·verse /ˈyo͞onəˌvərs/ ▶ **n.** the whole of space and everything in it.

> SYNONYMS **cosmos**, macrocosm, space, infinity, nature, all existence.

u·ni·ver·si·ty /ˌyo͞onəˈvərsətē/ ▶ **n.** (plural **universities**) an institution where students study for a degree and where academic research is done.

un·just /ˌənˈjəst/ ▶ **adj.** not just; unfair. ■ **un·just·ly** **adv.**

un·jus·ti·fi·a·ble /ˌənˈjəstəˌfīəbəl, -jəstəˈfī-/ ▶ **adj.** impossible to justify. ■ **un·jus·ti·fi·a·bly** **adv.**

un·jus·ti·fied /ˌənˈjəstəˌfīd/ ▶ **adj.** not justified; unfair.

un·kempt /ˌənˈkem(p)t/ ▶ **adj.** having an untidy appearance.

un·kind /ˌənˈkīnd/ ▶ **adj.** not caring or kind.

> SYNONYMS **unpleasant**, disagreeable, nasty, mean, cruel, vicious, spiteful, malicious, callous, unsympathetic, uncharitable, harsh, hard-hearted, heartless, cold-hearted; informal bitchy, catty.

■ **un·kind·ly** **adv.** **un·kind·ness** **n.**

un·know·ing /ˌənˈnōiNG/ ▶ **adj.** not knowing or aware. ■ **un·know·ing·ly** **adv.**

un·known /ˌənˈnōn/ ▶ **adj.** not known or familiar. ▶ **n.** an unknown person or thing.

SYNONYMS ▶ adj. **1 undisclosed**, unrevealed, secret, undetermined, undecided. **2 unexplored**, uncharted, unmapped, undiscovered, untraveled. **3 unidentified**, unnamed, anonymous, nameless. **4 obscure**, unfamiliar, unheard of, unsung, minor, undistinguished. ANTONYMS familiar.

□ **unknown quantity** a person or thing that is not known about and whose actions or effects are unpredictable. **Unknown Soldier** an unidentified member of a country's armed forces killed in war, buried in a national memorial to represent all those killed but unidentified.

un·la·dy·like /ˌənˈlādēˌlīk/ ▶ adj. not typical of a well-mannered woman or girl.

un·latch /ˌənˈlacʜ/ ▶ v. unfasten the latch of.

un·law·ful /ˌənˈlôfəl/ ▶ adj. not obeying or allowed by law or rules. ■ **un·law·ful·ly** adv.

un·lead·ed /ˌənˈledid/ ▶ adj. (of gas) without added lead.

un·leash /ˌənˈlēsʜ/ ▶ v. release something from a leash or restraint; set free.

un·leav·ened /ˌənˈlevənd/ ▶ adj. (of bread) flat because made without yeast.

un·less /ənˈles, ˌən-/ ▶ conj. except when; if not.

un·like /ˌənˈlīk/ ▶ prep. **1** different from; not like. **2** in contrast to. **3** not characteristic of. ▶ adj. different from each other.

un·like·ly /ˌənˈlīklē/ ▶ adj. (**unlikelier**, **unlikeliest**) **1** not likely to happen. **2** not what you would expect.

SYNONYMS **improbable**, doubtful, dubious, questionable, unconvincing, implausible, far-fetched, unrealistic, incredible, unbelievable, inconceivable. ANTONYMS probable, likely.

■ **un·like·li·hood** n.

un·lim·it·ed /ˌənˈlimitid/ ▶ adj. not limited or restricted.

un·load /ˌənˈlōd/ ▶ v. remove goods from a vehicle, ship, aircraft, or container.

SYNONYMS **unpack**, empty, clear, remove, offload.

un·lock /ˌənˈläk/ ▶ v. undo the lock of a door, container, etc., using a key.

un·looked /ˌənˈlo͝okt/ ▶ adj. (**unlooked for**) not planned or expected.

un·loose /ˌənˈlo͞os/ (or **unloosen** /ˌənˈlo͞osən/) ▶ v. (**unlooses**, **unloosing**, **unloosed**) release something.

un·luck·y /ˌənˈləkē/ ▶ adj. (**unluckier**, **unluckiest**) having, bringing, or resulting from bad luck.

SYNONYMS **1 unfortunate**, hapless, luckless, down on your luck, unsuccessful, ill-fated, ill-starred, jinxed. **2 unfavorable**, inauspicious, unpropitious, ominous. ANTONYMS lucky, fortunate.

■ **un·luck·i·ly** adv.

un·made /ˌənˈmād/ ▶ adj. (of a bed) not having the bedclothes arranged tidily, ready for sleeping in.

un·man·age·a·ble /ˌənˈmanijəbəl/ ▶ adj. difficult or impossible to manage or control.

un·manned /ˌənˈmand/ ▶ adj. not having or needing a crew or staff.

un·marked /ˌənˈmärkt/ ▶ adj. **1** not marked. **2** not noticed.

un·mar·ried /ˌənˈmarēd/ ▶ adj. not married.

un·mask /ˌənˈmask/ ▶ v. reveal the true character of.

un·matched /ˌənˈmacʜt/ ▶ adj. not matched or equaled.

un·men·tion·a·ble /ˌənˈmencʜənəbəl/ ▶ adj. too embarrassing or shocking to be spoken about.

un·mer·ci·ful /ˌənˈmərsəfəl/ ▶ adj. showing no mercy. ■ **un·mer·ci·ful·ly** adv.

un·mind·ful /ˌənˈmīn(d)fəl/ ▶ adj. (**unmindful of**) not conscious or aware of.

un·miss·a·ble /ˌənˈmisəbəl/ ▶ adj. that should not or cannot be missed.

un·mis·tak·a·ble /ˌənməˈstākəbəl/ ▶ adj. not able to be mistaken for anything else. ■ **un·mis·tak·a·bly** adv.

un·mit·i·gat·ed /ˌənˈmitəˌgātid/ ▶ adj. complete: *an unmitigated disaster.*

un·moved /ˌənˈmo͞ovd/ ▶ adj. not affected by emotion or excitement.

un·name·a·ble /ˌənˈnāməbəl/ ▶ adj. too bad or frightening to mention.

un·nat·u·ral /ˌənˈnacʜ(ə)rəl/ ▶ adj. **1** different from what is found in nature or what is normal in society. **2** not spontaneous.

SYNONYMS **1 abnormal**, unusual, uncommon, extraordinary, strange, unorthodox, exceptional, irregular, untypical. **2 artificial**, man-made, synthetic. **3 affected**, artificial, stilted, forced, false, fake, insincere, contrived, mannered, self-conscious; informal put on, phony. ANTONYMS natural.

■ **un·nat·u·ral·ly** adv.

un·nec·es·sar·y /ˌənˈnesəˌserē/ ▶ adj. not necessary, or more than is necessary.

SYNONYMS **unneeded**, inessential, not required, uncalled for, unwarranted, dispensable, optional, extraneous, expendable, redundant.

■ **un·nec·es·sar·i·ly** /ˌənˌnesəˈse(ə)rəlē/ adv.

un·nerve /ˌənˈnərv/ ▶ v. (**unnerves**, **unnerving**, **unnerved**) make someone feel fearful or lacking in confidence.

SYNONYMS **demoralize**, discourage, dishearten, dispirit, alarm, frighten, disconcert, perturb, upset, discomfit, take aback, unsettle, disquiet, fluster, shake, ruffle, throw off balance; informal rattle, faze, shake up, discombobulate. ANTONYMS hearten.

■ **un·nerv·ing** adj.

un·no·tice·a·ble /ˌənˈnōtisəbəl/ ▶ adj. not easily seen or noticed.

un·no·ticed /ˌənˈnōtist/ ▶ adj. not being or having been seen or noticed.

un·ob·served /ˌənəbˈzərvd/ ▶ adj. not seen.

un·ob·tain·a·ble /ˌənəbˈtānəbəl/ ▶ adj. not able to be obtained.

un·ob·tru·sive /ˌənəbˈtro͞osiv/ ▶ adj. not conspicuous or attracting attention. ■ **un·ob·tru·sive·ly** adv.

un·of·fi·cial /ˌənəˈfisʜəl/ ▶ adj. not officially authorized or confirmed. ■ **un·of·fi·cial·ly** adv.

un·o·pened /ˌənˈōpənd/ ▶ adj. not opened.

un·op·posed /ˌənəˈpōzd/ ▶ adj. not opposed or challenged.

un·o·rig·i·nal /ˌənəˈrijənl/ ▶ adj. lacking originality.

un·or·tho·dox /ˌənˈôrᴛʜəˌdäks/ ▶ **adj.** different from what is usual, traditional, or accepted.

un·pack /ˌənˈpak/ ▶ **v.** take things out of a suitcase, bag, or package.

un·paid /ˌənˈpād/ ▶ **adj. 1** (of a debt) not yet paid. **2** done without payment. **3** not receiving payment for work done.

un·pal·at·a·ble /ˌənˈpalətəbəl/ ▶ **adj. 1** not pleasant to taste. **2** difficult to accept.

un·par·al·leled /ˌənˈparəˌleld/ ▶ **adj.** having no equal; exceptional.

un·par·don·a·ble /ˌənˈpärdn-əbəl, -ˈpärdnəbəl/ ▶ **adj.** (of a fault or offense) unforgivable. ■ **un·par·don·a·bly adv.**

un·per·turbed /ˌənpərˈtərbd/ ▶ **adj.** not concerned or worried about something.

un·pick /ˌənˈpik/ ▶ **v. 1** undo the sewing of stitches or a garment. **2** carefully analyze the different elements of something.

un·pleas·ant /ˌənˈplezənt/ ▶ **adj. 1** not pleasant or comfortable. **2** not friendly or kind.

> SYNONYMS **1** *an unpleasant situation* **disagreeable**, distressing, nasty, horrible, terrible, awful, dreadful, invidious, objectionable. **2** *an unpleasant man* **unlikable**, unlovable, disagreeable, bad-tempered, unfriendly, rude, impolite, obnoxious, nasty, spiteful, mean, objectionable, annoying, irritating. **3 unappetizing**, unpalatable, unsavory, unappealing, disgusting, revolting, nauseating, sickening. ANTONYMS pleasant, agreeable.

■ **un·pleas·ant·ly adv. un·pleas·ant·ness n.**

un·plug /ˌənˈpləg/ ▶ **v.** (**unplugs**, **unplugging**, **unplugged**) disconnect an electrical device from a socket.

un·pop·u·lar /ˌənˈpäpyələr/ ▶ **adj.** not liked or popular.

> SYNONYMS **disliked**, friendless, unloved, unwelcome, avoided, ignored, rejected, shunned, out of favor.

■ **un·pop·u·lar·i·ty** /-ˌpäpyəˈlaritē/ **n.**

un·prec·e·dent·ed /ˌənˈpresəˌdentid/ ▶ **adj.** never done or known before.

un·pre·dict·a·ble /ˌənpriˈdiktəbəl/ ▶ **adj.** not able to be predicted; changeable. ■ **un·pre·dict·a·bil·i·ty** /-ˌdiktəˈbilətē/ **n. un·pre·dict·a·bly adv.**

un·prej·u·diced /ˌənˈprejədist/ ▶ **adj.** without prejudice; unbiased.

un·pre·med·i·tat·ed /ˌənpriˈmedəˌtātid, -prē-/ ▶ **adj.** not planned beforehand.

un·pre·pared /ˌənpriˈpe(ə)rd/ ▶ **adj.** not ready or able to deal with something.

un·pre·pos·ses·sing /ˌənˌprēpəˈzesiɴɢ/ ▶ **adj.** not attractive or interesting.

un·prin·ci·pled /ˌənˈprinsəpəld/ ▶ **adj.** without moral principles.

un·print·a·ble /ˌənˈprintəbəl/ ▶ **adj.** (of words or comments) too improper or offensive to be published.

un·pro·duc·tive /ˌənprəˈdəktiv/ ▶ **adj. 1** not able to produce the required quantity of goods or crops. **2** not achieving much; not very useful.

un·pro·fes·sion·al /ˌənprəˈfesʜənl/ ▶ **adj.** not in accordance with professional standards or behavior. ■ **un·pro·fes·sion·al·ly adv.**

un·prof·it·a·ble /ˌənˈpräfitəbəl/ ▶ **adj. 1** not making a profit. **2** not helpful or useful.

un·prompt·ed /ˌənˈpräm(p)tid/ ▶ **adj.** without being prompted; spontaneous.

un·pro·nounce·a·ble /ˌənprəˈnounsəbəl/ ▶ **adj.** too difficult to pronounce.

un·prov·en /ˌənˈpro͞ovən/ (or **unproved**) ▶ **adj.** not proved or tested.

un·pro·voked /ˌənprəˈvōkt/ ▶ **adj.** (of an attack or crime) not directly provoked.

un·pun·ished /ˌənˈpənisʜt/ ▶ **adj.** (of an offense or offender) not receiving any punishment or penalty.

un·qual·i·fied /ˌənˈkwäləˌfīd/ ▶ **adj. 1** not having the necessary qualifications or requirements. **2** complete.

un·quan·ti·fi·a·ble /ˌənˈkwäntəˌfīəbəl, -ˌkwäntəˈfī-/ ▶ **adj.** impossible to express or measure in terms of quantity.

un·ques·tion·a·ble /ˌənˈkwesᴄʜənəbəl/ ▶ **adj.** not able to be denied or doubted. ■ **un·ques·tion·a·bly adv.**

un·ques·tioned /ˌənˈkwesᴄʜənd/ ▶ **adj.** not denied or doubted.

un·rav·el /ˌənˈravəl/ ▶ **v.** (**unravels**, **unraveling**, **unraveled**) **1** undo twisted, knitted, or woven threads. **2** (of threads) become undone. **3** solve a mystery or puzzle.

> SYNONYMS **1 untangle**, disentangle, separate out, unwind, untwist. **2 solve**, resolve, clear up, puzzle out, get to the bottom of, explain, clarify; informal figure out. ANTONYMS entangle.

un·reach·a·ble /ˌənˈrēᴄʜəbəl/ ▶ **adj.** unable to be reached or contacted.

un·read /ˌənˈred/ ▶ **adj.** not having been read.

un·read·a·ble /ˌənˈrēdəbəl/ ▶ **adj. 1** not clear enough to read. **2** too dull or difficult to be worth reading.

un·re·al /ˌənˈrē(ə)l/ ▶ **adj. 1** strange and not seeming real. **2** not related to reality; unrealistic.

> SYNONYMS **imaginary**, fictitious, pretend, make-believe, made-up, dreamed-up, mock, false, illusory, mythical, fanciful, hypothetical, theoretical; informal phony.

■ **un·re·al·i·ty** /-rēˈalətē/ **n.**

un·re·al·is·tic /ˌənrēəˈlistik/ ▶ **adj. 1** not showing things in a way that is accurate and true to life. **2** not having a sensible understanding of what can be achieved. ■ **un·re·al·is·ti·cal·ly adv.**

un·rea·son·a·ble /ˌənˈrēz(ə)nəbəl/ ▶ **adj. 1** not based on good sense. **2** beyond what is achievable or acceptable. ■ **un·rea·son·a·bly adv.**

un·rec·og·niz·a·ble /ˌənˈrekəgˌnīzəbəl/ ▶ **adj.** not able to be recognized.

un·re·lent·ing /ˌənriˈlentiɴɢ/ ▶ **adj. 1** not stopping or becoming less severe. **2** not giving in to requests.

> SYNONYMS **1** *the unrelenting heat* **continual**, constant, unremitting, unabating, unrelieved, incessant, unceasing, endless, persistent. **2** *an unrelenting opponent* **implacable**, inflexible, uncompromising, unyielding, unbending, determined, dogged, tireless, unswerving, unwavering. ANTONYMS intermittent.

■ **un·re·lent·ing·ly adv.**

un·re·li·a·ble /ˌənriˈlīəbəl/ ▶ **adj.** not able to be relied on. ■ **un·re·li·a·bil·i·ty** /ˌənriˌlīəˈbilətē/ **n.** **un·re·li·a·bly** **adv.**

un·re·lieved /ˌənriˈlēvd/ ▶ **adj.** lacking variation or change.

un·re·mark·a·ble /ˌənriˈmärkəbəl/ ▶ **adj.** not particularly interesting or surprising.

un·re·mit·ting /ˌənriˈmitiNG/ ▶ **adj.** never stopping or easing.

un·re·peat·a·ble /ˌənriˈpētəbəl/ ▶ **adj.** **1** not able to be repeated. **2** too offensive or shocking to be said again.

un·re·pent·ant /ˌənriˈpentənt/ ▶ **adj.** showing no shame or regret for your actions.

un·re·quit·ed /ˌənriˈkwītid/ ▶ **adj.** (of love) not given in return.

un·re·served /ˌənriˈzərvd/ ▶ **adj.** **1** without any doubts or reservations. **2** not set apart or booked in advance. ■ **un·re·serv·ed·ly** **adv.**

un·re·solved /ˌənriˈzälvd, -ˈzôlvd/ ▶ **adj.** (of a problem, dispute, etc.) not resolved.

un·rest /ˌənˈrest/ ▶ **n.** **1** a situation in which people are feeling discontented and rebellious. **2** a state of uneasiness.

> SYNONYMS **disturbance**, trouble, turmoil, disruption, disorder, chaos, anarchy, dissatisfaction, dissent, strife, agitation, protest, rebellion, uprising, rioting. ANTONYMS peace.

un·ri·valed /ˌənˈrīvəld/ ▶ **adj.** greater or better than all others.

un·roll /ˌənˈrōl/ ▶ **v.** open out something that is rolled up.

un·ruf·fled /ˌənˈrəfəld/ ▶ **adj.** calm and undisturbed.

un·ru·ly /ˌənˈrōōlē/ ▶ **adj.** (**unrulier**, **unruliest**) difficult to control; disorderly.

> SYNONYMS **disorderly**, rowdy, wild, unmanageable, uncontrollable, disobedient, disruptive, undisciplined, wayward, willful, headstrong, obstreperous, difficult, intractable, out of hand, recalcitrant; formal refractory. ANTONYMS disciplined.

■ **un·ru·li·ness** **n.**

un·safe /ˌənˈsāf/ ▶ **adj.** not safe; dangerous.

> SYNONYMS **1 dangerous**, risky, hazardous, high-risk, treacherous, insecure, unsound, harmful, injurious, toxic. **2 unreliable**, open to doubt, questionable, doubtful, dubious, suspect; informal iffy. ANTONYMS safe.

un·sat·is·fac·to·ry /ˌənˌsatəsˈfakt(ə)rē/ ▶ **adj.** not good enough.

> SYNONYMS **disappointing**, displeasing, inadequate, unacceptable, poor, bad, substandard, weak, mediocre, not up to par, defective, deficient; informal leaving a lot to be desired.

■ **un·sat·is·fac·to·ri·ly** **adv.**

un·sat·u·rat·ed /ˌənˈsaCHəˌrātid/ ▶ **adj.** Chemistry (of fats) having double or triple bonds between carbon atoms in their molecules and therefore being more easily processed by the body.

un·sa·vor·y /ˌənˈsāv(ə)rē/ ▶ **adj.** **1** unpleasant to taste, smell, or look at. **2** not respectable.

un·scathed /ˌənˈskā*TH*d/ ▶ **adj.** without suffering any injury, damage, or harm.

un·sched·uled /ˌənˈskejōōld, -əld/ ▶ **adj.** not scheduled.

un·schooled /ˌənˈskōōld/ ▶ **adj.** lacking schooling or training.

un·sci·en·tif·ic /ˌənˌsīənˈtifik/ ▶ **adj.** not using proper scientific methods. ■ **un·sci·en·tif·i·cal·ly** **adv.**

un·screw /ˌənˈskrōō/ ▶ **v.** unfasten something by twisting it or undoing screws.

un·scru·pu·lous /ˌənˈskrōōpyələs/ ▶ **adj.** without moral principles; dishonest or unfair.

> SYNONYMS **dishonest**, deceitful, devious, underhanded/underhand, unethical, immoral, shameless, exploitative, corrupt, unprincipled, dishonorable, disreputable; informal crooked, shady.

■ **un·scru·pu·lous·ly** **adv.**

un·sea·son·a·ble /ˌənˈsēzənəbəl/ ▶ **adj.** (of weather) unusual for the time of year. ■ **un·sea·son·a·bly** **adv.**

un·sea·son·al /ˌənˈsēzənəl/ ▶ **adj.** unusual or inappropriate for the time of year.

un·seat /ˌənˈsēt/ ▶ **v.** **1** make someone fall from a saddle or seat. **2** remove someone from a position of power.

un·see·ing /ˌənˈsēiNG/ ▶ **adj.** having your eyes open but not noticing anything.

un·seem·ly /ˌənˈsēmlē/ ▶ **adj.** (of behavior or actions) not proper or appropriate.

un·seen /ˌənˈsēn/ ▶ **adj.** not seen or noticed.

un·self·con·scious /ˌənˌselfˈkänSHəs/ ▶ **adj.** not self-conscious; not shy or embarrassed. ■ **un·self·con·scious·ly** **adv.**

un·sel·fish /ˌənˈselfiSH/ ▶ **adj.** putting other people's needs before your own. ■ **un·self·ish·ly** **adv.**

un·ser·vice·a·ble /ˌənˈsərvəsəbəl/ ▶ **adj.** not in working order; unfit for use.

un·set·tle /ˌənˈsetl/ ▶ **v.** (**unsettles**, **unsettling**, **unsettled**) make someone anxious or uneasy.

> SYNONYMS **disturb**, disconcert, unnerve, upset, disquiet, perturb, alarm, dismay, trouble, bother, agitate, fluster, ruffle, shake (up), throw; informal rattle, faze.

■ **un·set·tling** **adj.**

un·set·tled /ˌənˈsetld/ ▶ **adj.** **1** frequently changing, or likely to change. **2** anxious or uneasy. **3** not yet resolved.

un·shak·a·ble /ˌənˈSHākəbəl/ ▶ **adj.** (of a belief or feeling) firm and unable to be changed.

un·shav·en /ˌənˈSHāvən/ ▶ **adj.** not having shaved.

un·sight·ly /ˌənˈsītlē/ ▶ **adj.** unpleasant to look at; ugly.

> SYNONYMS **unattractive**, ugly, unprepossessing, hideous, horrible, repulsive, revolting, offensive, grotesque. ANTONYMS attractive.

un·signed /ˌənˈsīnd/ ▶ **adj.** **1** not bearing a person's signature. **2** not having signed a contract.

un·skilled /ˌənˈskild/ ▶ **adj.** not having or needing special skill or training.

un·smil·ing /ˌənˈsmīliNG/ ▶ **adj.** not smiling; serious or unfriendly.

un·so·cia·ble /ˌənˈsōSHəbəl/ ▶ **adj.** not enjoying the company of other people.

SYNONYMS **unfriendly**, uncongenial, unneighborly, unapproachable, introverted, reserved, withdrawn, retiring, aloof, distant, remote, detached; informal standoffish.

un·so·cial /ˌənˈsōSHəl/ ▶ **adj.** **1** not seeking the company of others. **2** causing annoyance and disapproval in others; antisocial.

un·sold /ˌənˈsōld/ ▶ **adj.** (of an item) not sold.

un·so·lic·it·ed /ˌənsəˈlisitid/ ▶ **adj.** not asked for.

un·solved /ˌənˈsälvd, -ˈsôlvd/ ▶ **adj.** not solved.

un·so·phis·ti·cat·ed /ˌənsəˈfistəˌkātid/ ▶ **adj.** **1** not having much experience in matters of culture or fashion. **2** not complicated or highly developed; basic.

SYNONYMS **1 unworldly**, naive, simple, innocent, green, immature, callow, inexperienced, childlike, artless, guileless, ingenuous, natural, unaffected, unassuming, unpretentious. **2** *unsophisticated software* **simple**, crude, basic, rudimentary, primitive, rough and ready.

un·sound /ˌənˈsound/ ▶ **adj.** **1** not safe or strong; in bad condition. **2** not based on reliable evidence or reasoning.

SYNONYMS **1** *structurally unsound* **rickety**, flimsy, wobbly, unstable, crumbling, damaged, rotten, ramshackle, insubstantial, unsafe, dangerous. **2** *unsound evidence* **untenable**, flawed, defective, faulty, ill-founded, flimsy, unreliable, questionable, dubious, tenuous, suspect, fallacious; informal iffy. **3** *of unsound mind* **disordered**, deranged, disturbed, demented, unstable, unbalanced, unhinged, insane; informal touched. ANTONYMS strong.

un·spar·ing /ˌənˈspe(ə)riNG/ ▶ **adj.** **1** very severe or harsh. **2** giving generously.

un·speak·a·ble /ˌənˈspēkəbəl/ ▶ **adj.** too bad or horrific to express in words. ■ **un·speak·a·bly adv.**

un·spoiled /ˌənˈspoild/ (or **unspoilt** /ˌənˈspoilt/) ▶ **adj.** (of a place) beautiful because it has not been changed or built on.

un·spo·ken /ˌənˈspōkən/ ▶ **adj.** understood without being expressed in speech.

SYNONYMS **unstated**, unexpressed, unuttered, unsaid, unvoiced, unarticulated, undeclared, not spelled out; tacit, implicit, implied, understood. ANTONYMS explicit.

un·sta·ble /ˌənˈstābəl/ ▶ **adj.** **1** likely to fall or collapse. **2** likely to change; unsettled. **3** tending to experience mental health problems or sudden changes of mood.

SYNONYMS **1 unsteady**, rocky, wobbly, rickety, shaky, unsafe, insecure, precarious. **2 changeable**, volatile, variable, fluctuating, irregular, unpredictable, erratic. **3 unbalanced**, of unsound mind, mentally ill, deranged, demented, disturbed, unhinged. ANTONYMS steady, firm.

un·stead·y /ˌənˈstedē/ ▶ **adj.** **1** liable to fall or shake; not firm. **2** not uniform or even. ■ **un·stead·i·ly adv.**

un·stick /ˌənˈstik/ ▶ **v.** (**unsticks**, **unsticking**, **unstuck** /ˌənˈstək/) separate things that have been stuck together. □ **come unstuck** informal fail.

un·stint·ing /ˌənˈstintiNG/ ▶ **adj.** given or giving freely or generously.

un·stop·pa·ble /ˌənˈstäpəbəl/ ▶ **adj.** impossible to stop or prevent.

un·suc·cess·ful /ˌənsəkˈsesfəl/ ▶ **adj.** not successful.

SYNONYMS **1 failed**, abortive, ineffective, fruitless, profitless, unproductive, vain, futile. **2 unprofitable**, loss-making.

■ **un·suc·cess·ful·ly adv.**

un·suit·a·ble /ˌənˈsōōtəbəl/ ▶ **adj.** not right or appropriate for a particular purpose or occasion.

SYNONYMS **1 inappropriate**, ill-suited, inapposite, inapt, unacceptable, unfitting, incompatible, out of place, out of keeping, incongruous, unseemly. **2** *an unsuitable moment* **inopportune**, badly timed, unfortunate, difficult, infelicitous. ANTONYMS appropriate.

■ **un·suit·a·bil·i·ty** /ˌənˌsōōtəˈbilətē/ **n.** **un·suit·a·bly adv.**

un·sung /ˌənˈsəNG/ ▶ **adj.** not celebrated or praised.

un·su·per·vised /ˌənˈsōōpərˌvīzd/ ▶ **adj.** not done or acting under supervision.

un·sure /ˌənˈSHŏŏr/ ▶ **adj.** having doubts about something; not certain.

SYNONYMS **1 undecided**, uncertain, irresolute, dithering, of two minds, in a quandary, dubious, doubtful, skeptical, unconvinced. **2 unconfident**, unassertive, insecure, hesitant, diffident, anxious, apprehensive. ANTONYMS sure, certain.

un·sur·passed /ˌənsərˈpast/ ▶ **adj.** better or greater than any other.

un·sur·pris·ing /ˌənsə(r)ˈprīziNG/ ▶ **adj.** expected and so not causing surprise. ■ **un·sur·pris·ing·ly adv.**

un·sus·pect·ed /ˌənsəˈspektid/ ▶ **adj.** **1** not known or thought to exist. **2** not regarded with suspicion.

un·sus·pect·ing /ˌənsəˈspektiNG/ ▶ **adj.** not aware of the presence of danger.

un·sus·tain·a·ble /ˌənsəˈstānəbəl/ ▶ **adj.** **1** not able to be maintained at the current level. **2** upsetting the ecological balance by using up natural resources.

un·swerv·ing /ˌənˈswərviNG/ ▶ **adj.** not changing or becoming weaker; steady and constant.

un·sym·pa·thet·ic /ˌənˌsimpəˈTHetik/ ▶ **adj.** **1** not sympathetic. **2** not showing approval of an idea or action. **3** not likable. ■ **un·sym·pa·thet·i·cal·ly adv.**

un·sys·tem·at·ic /ˌənˌsistəˈmatik/ ▶ **adj.** not done or acting according to a fixed plan. ■ **un·sys·tem·at·i·cal·ly adv.**

un·tan·gle /ˌənˈtaNGgəl/ ▶ **v.** (**untangles**, **untangling**, **untangled**) **1** free from tangles. **2** free from complications or confusion.

SYNONYMS **disentangle**, unravel, unsnarl, straighten out, untwist, unknot, sort out.

un·tapped /ˌənˈtapt/ ▶ **adj.** (of a resource) available but not yet used.

un·ten·a·ble /ˌənˈtenəbəl/ ▶ **adj.** (of a theory or view) not able to be defended against criticism or attack.

un·think·a·ble /ˌənˈTHiNGkəbəl/ ▶ **adj.** too unlikely or unpleasant to be considered a possibility.

SYNONYMS **unimaginable**, inconceivable, unbelievable, incredible, implausible, out of the question, impossible, unconscionable, unreasonable.

un·think·ing /ˌənˈTHiNGkiNG/ ▶ **adj.** not thinking about the effects of what you do or say. ■ **un·think·ing·ly adv.**

un·ti·dy /ˌənˈtīdē/ ▶ **adj.** (**untidier**, **untidiest**) **1** not arranged tidily. **2** not inclined to be neat.

SYNONYMS **1 disordered**, messy, disorganized, cluttered, in chaos, haywire, in disarray, disorderly, topsy-turvy, at sixes and sevens, jumbled; informal higgledy-piggledy. **2 scruffy**, disheveled, unkempt, messy, rumpled, bedraggled. ANTONYMS neat, tidy.

■ **un·ti·di·ly adv. un·ti·di·ness n.**

un·tie /ˌənˈtī/ ▶ **v.** (**unties**, **untying**, **untied**) undo or unfasten something that is tied.

un·til /ˌənˈtil, ən-/ ▶ **prep. & conj.** up to the time or event mentioned.

SPELLING

Just one l at the end: until.

un·time·ly /ˌənˈtīmlē/ ▶ **adj. 1** happening or done at an unsuitable time. **2** (of a death or end) happening too soon or sooner than normal.

un·to /ˈəntoo/ ▶ **prep.** old use **1** to. **2** until.

un·told /ˌənˈtōld/ ▶ **adj. 1** too much or too many to be counted. **2** (of a story) not told to anyone.

un·touch·a·ble /ˌənˈtəCHəbəl/ ▶ **adj. 1** not able to be touched. **2** not able to be criticized or rivaled. ▶ **n.** offensive a member of the lowest Hindu caste (social class).

USAGE

The official term today for the lowest Hindu social class is **scheduled caste**.

un·touched /ˌənˈtəCHt/ ▶ **adj. 1** not handled, used, or consumed. **2** not affected, changed, or damaged.

un·to·ward /ˌənˈtôrd, -t(ə)ˈwôrd/ ▶ **adj.** unexpected and unwanted.

SYNONYMS **unexpected**, unforeseen, surprising, unusual, inappropriate, inconvenient, unwelcome, unfavorable, adverse, unfortunate, infelicitous.

un·trained /ˌənˈtrānd/ ▶ **adj.** not having been trained in a particular skill.

un·tram·meled /ˌənˈtraməld/ ▶ **adj.** not restricted or hampered.

un·true /ˌənˈtroo/ ▶ **adj. 1** false. **2** not faithful or loyal.

SYNONYMS **false**, invented, made up, fabricated, concocted, trumped up, erroneous, wrong, incorrect, inaccurate. ANTONYMS true, correct.

un·trust·wor·thy /ˌənˈtrəstˌwərTHē/ ▶ **adj.** unable to be trusted.

un·truth·ful /ˌənˈtrooTHfəl/ ▶ **adj.** not truthful. ■ **un·truth·ful·ly adv.**

un·used ▶ **adj. 1** /ˌənˈyoozd/ not used. **2** /ˌənˈyoost/ (**unused to**) not accustomed to.

un·u·su·al /ˌənˈyooZHooəl/ ▶ **adj. 1** not often done or happening. **2** exceptional.

SYNONYMS **1** *an unusual sight* **uncommon**, abnormal, atypical, unexpected, surprising, unfamiliar, different, strange, odd, curious, extraordinary, unorthodox, unconventional, peculiar, queer, unwonted; informal weird, offbeat. **2** *a man of unusual talent* **remarkable**, extraordinary, exceptional, particular, outstanding, notable, noteworthy, distinctive, striking, significant, special, unique, unparalleled, prodigious. ANTONYMS common.

■ **un·u·su·al·ly adv.**

un·ut·ter·a·ble /ˌənˈətərəbəl/ ▶ **adj.** too great or bad to describe. ■ **un·ut·ter·a·bly adv.**

un·var·nished /ˌənˈvärnisHt/ ▶ **adj. 1** not varnished. **2** plain and straightforward.

un·veil /ˌənˈvāl/ ▶ **v. 1** show or announce something publicly for the first time. **2** remove a veil or covering from.

un·want·ed /ˌənˈwäntid, ˌənˈwôntid/ ▶ **adj.** not wanted.

un·war·rant·a·ble /ˌənˈwôrəntəbəl, -ˈwär-/ ▶ **adj.** not reasonable or justifiable.

un·war·rant·ed /ˌənˈwôrəntid, -ˈwär-/ ▶ **adj.** not justified.

SYNONYMS **1 unjustified**, indefensible, inexcusable, unforgivable, unpardonable, uncalled for, unnecessary, unjust, groundless. **2 unauthorized**, unsanctioned, unapproved, uncertified, unlicensed, illegal, unlawful, illicit, illegitimate, criminal, actionable. ANTONYMS justified.

un·war·y /ˌənˈwe(ə)rē/ ▶ **adj.** not cautious.

un·washed /ˌənˈwôsHt, -ˈwäsHt/ ▶ **adj.** not washed. □ **the** (**great**) **unwashed** disapproving the multitude of ordinary people.

un·wa·ver·ing /ˌənˈwāvəriNG/ ▶ **adj.** not changing or becoming weaker; constant.

un·wel·come /ˌənˈwelkəm/ ▶ **adj.** not wanted.

un·well /ˌənˈwel/ ▶ **adj.** ill.

un·whole·some /ˌənˈhōlsəm/ ▶ **adj. 1** harmful to health. **2** unpleasant or unnatural.

un·wield·y /ˌənˈwēldē/ ▶ **adj.** hard to move or manage because of its size, shape, or weight.

SYNONYMS **awkward**, unmanageable, unmaneuverable, cumbersome, clumsy, massive, heavy, hefty, bulky.

un·will·ing /ˌənˈwiliNG/ ▶ **adj.** not willing.

SYNONYMS **1 reluctant**, unenthusiastic, hesitant, resistant, grudging, involuntary, forced. **2** *he was unwilling to go* **disinclined**, reluctant, averse, loath, not in the mood; (**be unwilling to do something**) balk at, demur at, shy away from, flinch from, shrink from, have qualms about, have misgivings about, have reservations about. ANTONYMS willing.

■ **un·will·ing·ly adv. un·will·ing·ness n.**

un·wind /ˌənˈwīnd/ ▶ **v.** (**unwinds**, **unwinding**, **unwound** /ˌənˈwound/) **1** undo something that has been wound or twisted. **2** relax after a period of work or tension.

un·wise /ˌənˈwīz/ ▶ **adj.** foolish. ■ **un·wise·ly adv.**

un·wit·ting /ˌənˈwitiNG/ ▶ **adj. 1** not aware of the full facts. **2** unintentional. ■ **un·wit·ting·ly adv.**

un·wont·ed /ˌənˈwôntid/ ▶ **adj.** not usual or expected.

un·world·ly /ˌənˈwərldlē/ ▶ **adj. 1** having little awareness of the realities of life. **2** not seeming to belong to this world.

un·wor·ried /ˌənˈwərēd/ ▶ **adj.** not worried.

un·wor·thy /ˌənˈwərTHē/ ▶ **adj.** not deserving effort, attention, or respect. ■ **un·wor·thi·ness n.**

un·wrap /ˌənˈrap/ ▶ **v.** (**unwraps**, **unwrapping**, **unwrapped**) remove the wrapping from.

un·writ·ten /ˌənˈritn/ ▶ **adj.** (of a rule or law) generally known about and accepted, although not made official.

un·yield·ing /ˌənˈyēldiNG/ ▶ **adj. 1** not bending or breaking; firm. **2** (of a person) not changing their mind.

SYNONYMS **resolute**, inflexible, uncompromising, unbending, unshakable, unwavering, immovable, intractable, intransigent, determined, dogged, obstinate, stubborn, tenacious, relentless, implacable, single-minded.

un·zip /ˌənˈzip/ ▶ **v.** (**unzips**, **unzipping**, **unzipped**) **1** unfasten the zipper of. **2** Computing decompress a file.

up /əp/ ▶ **adv. 1** toward a higher place or position. **2** to the place where someone is. **3** at or to a higher level or value. **4** into the desired condition or position. **5** out of bed. **6** (of the sun) visible in the sky. ▶ **prep. 1** from a lower to a higher point of. **2** from one end of a street to another. ▶ **adj. 1** directed or moving toward a higher place or position. **2** at an end. ▶ **v.** (**ups**, **upping**, **upped**) increase a level or an amount. □ **up against 1** close to or touching. **2** informal confronted with. **up and down** in various places throughout. **up to 1** as far as. **2** (also **up until**) until. **3** indicating a maximum amount. **up-and-coming** likely to be successful. **up to date** using or aware of the latest developments and trends.

up·beat /ˈəpˌbēt/ ▶ **adj.** positive and cheerful or enthusiastic.

SYNONYMS **cheerful**, optimistic, cheery, positive, confident, hopeful, sanguine, bullish, buoyant. ANTONYMS pessimistic.

up·braid /ˌəpˈbrād/ ▶ **v.** scold or criticize.

up·bring·ing /ˈəpˌbriNGiNG/ ▶ **n.** the way in which a person is taught and looked after as a child.

SYNONYMS **childhood**, early life, formative years, teaching, instruction, rearing.

UPC ▶ **abbr.** Universal Product Code.

up·chuck /ˈəpˌCHək/ informal ▶ **v.** vomit. ▶ **n.** matter vomited from the stomach.

up·com·ing /ˈəpˌkəmiNG/ ▶ **adj.** forthcoming.

up·date ▶ **v.** /ˌəpˈdāt, ˈəpˌdāt/ (**updates**, **updating**, **updated**) **1** make something more modern. **2** give someone the latest information on something. ▶ **n.** /ˈəpˌdāt/ an act of updating, or an updated version of something.

SYNONYMS ▶ **v. 1 modernize**, upgrade, improve, overhaul. **2 brief**, bring up to date, inform, fill in, tell, notify, keep posted; informal clue in, put in the picture, bring/keep up to speed.

up·end /ˌəpˈend/ ▶ **v.** set something on its end or upside down.

up·front /ˌəpˈfrənt/ informal ▶ **adj. 1** not trying to hide your thoughts or intentions; frank. **2** (of a payment) made in advance. ▶ **adv.** (usually **up front**) (of a payment) in advance.

up·grade /ˈəpˌgrād, ˌəpˈgrād/ ▶ **v.** (**upgrades**, **upgrading**, **upgraded**) raise something to a higher standard or rank. ▶ **n.** an act of upgrading, or an upgraded version of something.

SYNONYMS ▶ **v. improve**, modernize, update, reform. ANTONYMS downgrade.

up·heav·al /ˌəpˈhēvəl/ ▶ **n.** a big change that causes a lot of upset or disruption.

SYNONYMS **disturbance**, disruption, trouble, turbulence, disorder, confusion, turmoil.

up·hill /ˌəpˈhil/ ▶ **adv.** toward the top of a slope. ▶ **adj. 1** sloping upward. **2** difficult: *an uphill struggle*.

SYNONYMS ▶ **adj. 1 upward**, rising, ascending, climbing. **2 difficult**, hard, tough, demanding, arduous, taxing, exacting, stiff, grueling, onerous. ANTONYMS downhill.

up·hold /ˌəpˈhōld/ ▶ **v.** (**upholds**, **upholding**, **upheld** /ˌəpˈheld/) **1** confirm or support something that has been questioned. **2** maintain a custom or practice.

SYNONYMS **1 confirm**, endorse, sustain, approve, support, back (up). **2 maintain**, sustain, continue, preserve, protect, keep, hold to, keep alive, keep going. ANTONYMS oppose.

up·hol·ster /əpˈhōlstər, əˈpōl-/ ▶ **v.** (**upholsters**, **upholstering**, **upholstered**) provide an armchair, sofa, etc., with a soft, padded covering. ■ **up·hol·ster·er n.**

up·hol·ster·y /əpˈhōlst(ə)rē, əˈpōl-/ ▶ **n. 1** the soft, padded covering on an armchair, sofa, etc. **2** the art of upholstering furniture.

up·keep /ˈəpˌkēp/ ▶ **n.** the process or cost of keeping something in good condition or of supporting a person.

SYNONYMS **1 maintenance**, repair(s), servicing, care, preservation, conservation, running. **2 (financial) support**, maintenance, keep, subsistence, care.

up·land /ˈəplənd/ (or **uplands**) ▶ **n.** an area of high or hilly land.

up·lift /ˌəpˈlift/ ▶ **v.** make someone feel hope or happiness. ▶ **n. 1** an act of lifting or raising something. **2** a feeling of hope or happiness.

SYNONYMS ▶ **n.** (**uplifting**) **inspiring**, stirring, inspirational, rousing, moving, touching, affecting, cheering, heartening, encouraging.

up·load /ˈəpˌlōd, ˌəpˈlōd/ ▶ **v.** transfer data to a larger computer system.

up·mar·ket /ˌəpˈmärkit, ˈəpˌmär-/ ▶ **adj.** expensive or of high quality.

up·on /əˈpän, əˈpôn/ ▶ **prep.** more formal term for *on*.

up·per /ˈəpər/ ▶ **adj. 1** higher in position or status. **2** (in place names) situated on higher land, further from the sea, or to the north. ▶ **n.** the part of a boot or shoe above the sole.

SYNONYMS ▶ **adj. 1 higher**, superior, top. **2 senior**, superior, higher-level, higher-ranking, top. ANTONYMS lower.

□ **have the upper hand** have an advantage or control over someone. **upper class** the social group with the highest status. **upper house** the smaller body of a bicameral legislature or parliament, e.g., the Senate of the US Congress.

up·per·case /ˈəpərˈkās/ ▶ **n.** capital letters.

up·per·class·man /ˌəpərˈklasmən/ ▶ **n.** (plural **upperclassmen**) a junior or senior in high school or college.

up·per·cut /'əpər,kət/ ▶ **n.** a punch delivered with an upward motion and the arm bent.

up·per·most /'əpər,mōst/ ▶ **adj. & adv.** highest in place, rank, or importance.

up·pi·ty /'əpətē/ ▶ **adj.** informal behaving as if you are more important than you really are.

up·right /'əp,rīt/ ▶ **adj. 1** in a vertical position. **2** greater in height than breadth. **3** strictly honest and respectable. **4** (of a piano) having vertical strings. ▶ **adv.** in or into an upright position. ▶ **n.** a vertical post, structure, or line.

> SYNONYMS ▶ **adj. 1 vertical**, perpendicular, plumb, straight (up), erect, on end, on your feet. **2 honest**, honorable, upstanding, respectable, high-minded, law-abiding, worthy, righteous, decent, good, virtuous, principled. ANTONYMS flat, horizontal.

up·ris·ing /'əp,rīzing/ ▶ **n.** a rebellion.

> SYNONYMS **rebellion**, revolt, insurrection, mutiny, revolution, insurgence, rioting, coup.

up·riv·er /,əp'rivər/ = **UPSTREAM**.

up·roar /'əp,rôr/ ▶ **n. 1** a loud noise or disturbance made by people who are angry or upset about something. **2** a public expression of outrage.

> SYNONYMS **1 commotion**, disturbance, rumpus, disorder, confusion, chaos, tumult, mayhem, pandemonium, bedlam, noise, din, clamor, hubbub, racket; informal hullabaloo. **2 outcry**, furor, fuss, commotion, hue and cry, rumpus; informal stink. ANTONYMS calm.

up·roar·i·ous /,əp'rôrēəs/ ▶ **adj. 1** very noisy and lively. **2** very funny. ■ **up·roar·i·ous·ly** **adv.**

up·root /,əp'ro͞ot, -'ro͝ot/ ▶ **v. 1** pull a tree or other plant out of the ground. **2** move someone from their home or usual surroundings.

up·scale /,əp'skāl, 'əp,skāl/ ▶ **adj.** relating to the more expensive or affluent sector of the market.

up·set ▶ **v.** /,əp'set/ (**upsets**, **upsetting**, **upset**) **1** make someone unhappy, disappointed, or worried. **2** knock something over. **3** disrupt or disturb a situation or arrangement. ▶ **n.** /'əp,set/ **1** a difficult or unexpected result or situation. **2** a state of being upset. ▶ **adj.** /,əp'set/ **1** unhappy, disappointed, or worried. **2** (of a person's stomach) not digesting food normally; feeling nauseous or unwell.

> SYNONYMS ▶ **v. 1 distress**, trouble, perturb, dismay, sadden, grieve, disturb, unsettle, disconcert, disquiet, worry, bother, agitate, fluster, throw, ruffle, unnerve, shake. **2 knock over**, overturn, upend, tip over, topple, spill. **3 disrupt**, interfere with, disturb, throw into confusion, mess up. ANTONYMS calm. ▶ **n. 1 distress**, trouble, dismay, disquiet, worry, bother, agitation, hurt, grief. **2** *a stomach upset* **disorder**, complaint, ailment, illness, sickness; informal bug. ▶ **adj. 1 distressed**, troubled, perturbed, dismayed, disturbed, unsettled, disconcerted, worried, bothered, anxious, agitated, flustered, ruffled, unnerved, shaken, saddened, grieved; informal cut up, choked up. **2** *an upset stomach* **disturbed**, unsettled, queasy, bad, poor. ANTONYMS calm.

■ **up·set·ting** /,əp'seting/ **adj.**

up·shot /'əp,shät/ ▶ **n.** the eventual outcome or conclusion of something.

up·side /'əp,sīd/ ▶ **n.** the positive aspect of something. □ **upside down** with the upper part where the lower part should be.

up·stage /,əp'stāj/ ▶ **v.** (**upstages**, **upstaging**, **upstaged**) draw attention away from someone so that people notice you instead. ▶ **adv. & adj.** at or toward the back of a stage.

up·stairs /,əp'ste(ə)rz/ ▶ **adv. & adj.** on or to an upper floor. ▶ **n.** an upper floor.

up·stand·ing /,əp'standing, 'əp,stan-/ ▶ **adj.** very respectable and responsible.

up·start /'əp,stärt/ ▶ **n.** disapproving a person who thinks they are more important than they really are.

up·state /'əp'stāt/ ▶ **adj. & adv.** in or to the northern part of a state, especially a part remote from large cities.

up·stream /,əp'strēm/ (or **upriver** /,əp'rivər/) ▶ **adv. & adj.** at or to a point nearer the source of a stream or river.

up·surge /'əp,sərj/ ▶ **n.** an increase.

up·take /'əp,tāk/ ▶ **n.** the action of taking up or making use of something. □ **be quick** (or **slow**) **on the uptake** informal be quick (or slow) to understand something.

up·tight /,əp'tīt/ ▶ **adj.** informal nervously tense or angry, and unable to express your feelings.

up·town /,əp'toun/ ▶ **adj. & adv.** of, in, or into the residential area of a town or city.

up·turn /'əp,tərn/ ▶ **n.** an improvement or upward trend. ▶ **v.** (**be upturned**) be turned upward or upside down.

up·ward /'əpwərd/ ▶ **adj. & adv.** toward a higher level. ■ **up·wards** **adv.**

up·wind /,əp'wind/ ▶ **adv. & adj.** against the direction of the wind.

u·ra·ni·um /yo͝o'rānēəm/ ▶ **n.** a radioactive metallic element used as a fuel in nuclear reactors.

U·ran·us /'yo͝orənəs, yo͝o'rā-/ ▶ **n.** the seventh planet from the sun in the solar system.

ur·ban /'ərbən/ ▶ **adj.** having to do with a city or large town.

> SYNONYMS **town**, city, municipal, metropolitan, built-up, inner-city, suburban. ANTONYMS rural.

ur·bane /,ər'bān/ ▶ **adj.** (of a man) confident, polite, and sophisticated. ■ **ur·ban·i·ty** /,ər'banitē/ **n.**

ur·chin /'ərchin/ ▶ **n.** a poor child dressed in ragged clothes.

Ur·du /'o͝ordo͞o, 'ər-/ ▶ **n.** a language of Pakistan and India.

u·re·ter /'yo͝oritər, yo͝o'rētər/ ▶ **n.** the duct by which urine passes from the kidney to the bladder.

u·re·thra /yo͝o'rēthrə/ ▶ **n.** the duct by which urine passes out of the body, and which in males also carries semen. ■ **u·re·thral** **adj.**

urge /ərj/ ▶ **v.** (**urges**, **urging**, **urged**) **1** encourage or earnestly ask someone to do something. **2** strongly recommend. ▶ **n.** a strong desire or impulse.

> SYNONYMS ▶ **v. 1 encourage**, exhort, press, entreat, implore, call on, appeal to, beg, plead with. **2 advise**, counsel, advocate, recommend. ▶ **n.** *his urge to travel* **desire**, wish, need, compulsion, longing, yearning, hankering, craving, hunger, thirst; informal yen, itch.

ur·gent /'ərjənt/ ▶ **adj.** needing immediate action or attention.

SYNONYMS **pressing**, acute, dire, desperate, critical, serious, grave, intense, crying, burning, compelling, extreme, high-priority, life-and-death.

■ **ur·gen·cy** n. **ur·gent·ly** adv.

u·ri·nal /ˈyo͝orənl/ ▶ n. a container into which men urinate, attached to the wall in a public bathroom.

u·ri·nate /ˈyo͝orəˌnāt/ ▶ v. (**urinates**, **urinating**, **urinated**) pass urine out of the body. ■ **u·ri·na·tion** /ˌyo͝orəˈnāsʜən/ n.

u·rine /ˈyo͝orən/ ▶ n. a yellowish liquid that is stored in the bladder and that contains waste substances that are passed with it out of the body. ■ **u·ri·nar·y** adj.

URL ▶ abbr. uniform (or universal) resource locator, the address of a World Wide Web page.

urn /ərn/ ▶ n. **1** a container for storing a cremated person's ashes. **2** a metal container with a tap, in which tea or coffee is made and kept hot.

ur·sine /ˈərˌsīn/ ▶ adj. having to do with bears.

U·ru·guay·an /ˌ(y)o͝orəˈgwīən, -ˈgwā-/ ▶ n. a person from Uruguay. ▶ adj. relating to Uruguay.

US ▶ abbr. United States.

us /əs/ ▶ pron. used by a speaker to refer to himself or herself and one or more other people as the object of a verb or preposition.

USA ▶ abbr. **1** United States Army. **2** United States of America.

us·a·ble /ˈyo͞ozəbəl/ (or **useable**) ▶ adj. able to be used. ■ **us·a·bil·i·ty** /ˌyo͞ozəˈbilətē/ n.

USAF ▶ abbr. United States Air Force.

us·age /ˈyo͞osij, -zij/ ▶ n. the using of something.

SYNONYMS **1** *energy usage* **consumption**, use. **2** *the usage of equipment* **use**, utilization, operation, manipulation, running, handling. **3** **language**, expression, phraseology, parlance, idiom.

USB ▶ abbr. Computing universal serial bus, a connector that enables any of a variety of peripheral devices to be plugged into a computer.

use ▶ v. /yo͞oz/ (**uses**, **using**, **used**) **1** do something with an object or adopt a method in order to achieve a purpose. **2** (**use something up**) consume all of something. **3** take unfair advantage of a person or situation. **4** (**used to**) did something repeatedly in the past, or existed or happened in the past. **5** (**be** or **get used to**) be or become familiar with something through experience. **6** (**used**) secondhand. ▶ n. /yo͞os/ **1** the using of something. **2** the ability to use a part of the body. **3** a purpose for something, or a way in which something can be used. **4** value.

SYNONYMS ▶ v. **1** **utilize**, employ, avail yourself of, work, operate, wield, ply, apply, put into service. **2** **exercise**, employ, bring into play, practice, apply. **3** **take advantage of**, exploit, manipulate, take liberties with, impose on, abuse, capitalize on, profit from, trade on, milk; informal cash in on, walk all over. **4** *we have* **used up** *our funds* **consume**, go through, exhaust, deplete, expend, spend. **5** (**used to**) **accustomed to**, no stranger to, familiar with, at home with, in the habit of, experienced in, versed in, conversant with, acquainted with. **6** (**used**) **secondhand**, pre-owned, nearly new, old, worn, hand-me-down, castoff. ▶ n. **1** **utilization**, application, employment, operation, manipulation. **2** **exploitation**, manipulation, abuse. **3** *what is the use of that?* **advantage**, benefit, good, point, object, purpose, sense, reason, service, utility, help, gain, avail, profit, value, worth.

use·ful /ˈyo͞osfəl/ ▶ adj. able to be used for a practical purpose or in several ways.

SYNONYMS **1** *a useful tool* **functional**, practical, handy, convenient, utilitarian, serviceable, of service; informal nifty. **2** *a useful experience* **beneficial**, advantageous, helpful, worthwhile, profitable, rewarding, productive, constructive, valuable, fruitful. ANTONYMS useless.

■ **use·ful·ly** adv. **use·ful·ness** n.

use·less /ˈyo͞osləs/ ▶ adj. **1** serving no purpose. **2** informal having no ability or skill.

SYNONYMS **1** **futile**, pointless, to no avail, vain, to no purpose, unavailing, hopeless, ineffectual, fruitless, unprofitable, unproductive, abortive. **2** **incompetent**, inept, ineffective, incapable, inadequate, hopeless, bad. ANTONYMS useful, beneficial.

■ **use·less·ly** adv.

us·er /ˈyo͞ozər/ ▶ n. a person who uses or operates something. □ **user-friendly** easy for people to use or understand.

ush·er /ˈəsʜər/ ▶ n. **1** a person who shows people to their seats in a theater or at a wedding. **2** an official in a court of law who swears in jurors and generally keeps order. ▶ v. (**ushers**, **ushering**, **ushered**) guide someone somewhere.

SYNONYMS ▶ n. **guide**, attendant, escort. ▶ v. **escort**, accompany, take, show, see, lead, conduct, guide.

ush·er·ette /ˌəsʜəˈret/ ▶ n. a woman who shows people to their seats in a theater or church.

USMC ▶ abbr. United States Marine Corps.

USN ▶ abbr. United States Navy.

USPS ▶ abbr. United States Postal Service.

USS ▶ abbr. United States Ship.

USSR ▶ abbr. historical Union of Soviet Socialist Republics.

u·su·al /ˈyo͞ozʜo͞oəl/ ▶ adj. happening or done typically, regularly, or frequently.

SYNONYMS **normal**, customary, accustomed, wonted, habitual, routine, regular, standard, typical, established, set, stock, conventional, traditional, expected, familiar. ANTONYMS exceptional.

u·su·al·ly /ˈyo͞ozʜ(o͞o)əlē/ ▶ adv. **1** in a way that is usual or normal. **2** generally speaking; as a rule.

SYNONYMS **normally**, generally, habitually, customarily, routinely, typically, ordinarily, commonly, as a rule, in general, more often than not, mainly, mostly.

SPELLING

Remember that usually is spelled with a double l.

u·surp /yo͞oˈsərp, yo͞oˈzərp/ ▶ v. take over someone's position or power without having the right to do so. ■ **u·surp·er** n.

u·su·ry /ˈyo͞ozʜ(ə)rē/ ▶ n. formal the practice of lending money at unreasonably high rates of interest. ■ **u·su·rer** n.

u·ten·sil /yo͞oˈtensəl/ ▶ **n.** a tool or container, especially for household use.

> SYNONYMS **implement**, tool, instrument, device, apparatus, gadget, appliance, contrivance, contraption; informal gizmo.

u·ter·us /ˈyo͞otərəs/ ▶ **n.** the organ in the lower part of a woman's or female mammal's body where offspring are conceived and in which they gestate before birth; the womb. ■ **u·ter·ine** /ˈyo͞otərin, -ˌrīn/ **adj.**

u·til·i·tar·i·an /yo͞oˌtiliˈte(ə)rēən/ ▶ **adj.** useful or practical rather than attractive.

u·til·i·tar·i·an·ism /yo͞oˌtiləˈte(ə)rēəˌnizəm/ ▶ **n.** the doctrine that the right course of action is the one that will lead to the greatest happiness of the greatest number of people.

u·til·i·ty /yo͞oˈtilətē/ ▶ **n.** (plural **utilities**) **1** the state of being useful or profitable. **2** an organization supplying electricity, gas, water, or sewage removal to the public.

> SYNONYMS **usefulness**, use, benefit, value, advantage, help, practicality, effectiveness, service.

□ **utility knife** a knife with a short, strong, replaceable blade. **utility room** a room where a washing machine and other domestic equipment are kept.

u·ti·lize /ˈyo͞otlˌīz/ ▶ **v.** (**utilizes**, **utilizing**, **utilized**) make practical and effective use of.

> SYNONYMS **use**, employ, avail yourself of, press into service, bring into play, deploy, draw on, exploit.

■ **u·ti·li·za·tion** /ˌyo͞otl-əˈzāsʜən/ **n.**

ut·most /ˈətˌmōst/ ▶ **adj.** most extreme; greatest. ▶ **n.** (**the utmost**) the greatest or most extreme extent or amount.

> SYNONYMS ▶ **adj. greatest**, highest, maximum, most, extreme, supreme, paramount.

U·to·pi·a /yo͞oˈtōpēə/ ▶ **n.** an imagined world or society where everything is perfect.

u·to·pi·an /yo͞oˈtōpēən/ ▶ **adj.** idealistic.

ut·ter[1] /ˈətər/ ▶ **adj.** complete; absolute.

> SYNONYMS **complete**, total, absolute, thorough, perfect, downright, out-and-out, outright, sheer, positive, prize, pure, unmitigated, unadulterated, unqualified, unalloyed; dated arrant

■ **ut·ter·ly** **adv.**

ut·ter[2] ▶ **v.** (**utters**, **uttering**, **uttered**) make a sound, or say something.

> SYNONYMS **say**, speak, voice, mouth, express, articulate, pronounce, enunciate, emit, let out, give, produce.

ut·ter·ance /ˈətərəns/ ▶ **n.** **1** a word, statement, or sound uttered. **2** the action of saying or uttering something.

> SYNONYMS **remark**, comment, statement, observation, declaration, pronouncement.

ut·ter·most /ˈətərˌmōst/ ⇨ **UTMOST**.

u·vu·la /ˈyo͞ovyələ/ ▶ **n.** (plural **uvulae** /-ˌlē, -ˌlī/) a small piece of flesh that hangs down at the top of the throat.

ux·o·ri·ous /ˌəkˈsôrēəs, ˌəgˈzôr-/ ▶ **adj.** (of a man) very fond of his wife.

Vv

V (or **v**) ▶ n. (plural **Vs** or **V's**) **1** the twenty-second letter of the alphabet. **2** the Roman numeral for five. ▶ abbr. **1** (**V**) volt(s). **2** (**v.**) versus. ◻ **V-sign** a gesture made with the first two fingers pointing up and the palm of the hand facing outward, used as a symbol of victory.

va·can·cy /'vākənsē/ ▶ n. (plural **vacancies**) **1** a job or position that is available. **2** an available room in a hotel, guest house, etc. **3** empty space.

> SYNONYMS **opening**, position, post, job, opportunity.

va·cant /'vākənt/ ▶ adj. **1** empty. **2** (of a job or position) available. **3** showing no intelligence or interest.

> SYNONYMS **1 empty**, unoccupied, not in use, free, available, unfilled, uninhabited, untenanted; informal up for grabs. **2 blank**, expressionless, unresponsive, emotionless, impassive, vacuous, empty, glazed. ANTONYMS full, occupied.

■ **va·cant·ly** adv.

va·cate /'vā,kāt/ ▶ v. (**vacates, vacating, vacated**) **1** go out of a place, leaving it empty. **2** give up a position.

> SYNONYMS **1 leave**, move out of, evacuate, quit, depart from. **2 resign from**, leave, stand down from, give up, bow out of, relinquish, retire from; informal quit. ANTONYMS occupy.

va·ca·tion /vā'kāsнən, və-/ ▶ n. **1** an extended period of recreation, especially one spent away from home or traveling. **2** the action of vacating a place. ▶ v. take a vacation.

> SYNONYMS ▶ n. **break**, time off, recess, leave, holiday, trip, tour.

■ **va·ca·tion·er** n.

vac·ci·nate /'vaksə,nāt/ ▶ v. (**vaccinates, vaccinating, vaccinated**) give a person or animal an injection of a vaccine to protect them against a disease. ■ **vac·ci·na·tion** /,vaksə'nāsнən/ n.

vac·cine /vak'sēn/ ▶ n. a substance injected into the body that causes the production of antibodies and so provides immunity against a disease.

vac·il·late /'vasə,lāt/ ▶ v. (**vacillates, vacillating, vacillated**) keep changing your mind about something. ■ **vac·il·la·tion** /,vasə'lāsнən/ n.

vac·u·ous /'vakyəwəs/ ▶ adj. showing a lack of thought or intelligence.

> SYNONYMS **silly**, inane, unintelligent, foolish, stupid, brainless, vapid, vacant, empty-headed; informal moronic, brain-dead. ANTONYMS intelligent.

■ **va·cu·i·ty** /va'kyo͞oətē, və-/ n.

vac·u·um /'vak,yo͞o(ə)m, -yəm/ ▶ n. (plural **vacuums** or **vacua** /-yəwə) **1** a completely empty space in which there is no air or other matter. **2** a gap left by the loss of someone or something important. ▶ v. clean a surface using a vacuum cleaner. ◻ **vacuum cleaner** an electrical machine that collects dust by means of suction. **vacuum flask** a container with a double wall enclosing a vacuum, used for keeping liquids hot or cold.

vag·a·bond /'vagə,bänd/ ▶ n. a person who has no settled home or job.

va·gar·y /'vāgərē/ ▶ n. (plural **vagaries**) a change that is difficult to predict or control.

va·gi·na /və'jīnə/ ▶ n. (in a woman or girl) a tube leading from an outer opening to the uterus. ■ **vag·i·nal** adj.

va·grant /'vāgrənt/ ▶ n. a person who has no settled home or job. ▶ adj. having no settled home or job.

> SYNONYMS ▶ n. **tramp**, drifter, hobo, down-and-out, beggar, itinerant, wanderer; informal bum.

■ **va·gran·cy** n.

vague /vāg/ ▶ adj. **1** not certain or definite. **2** saying things or thinking in a way that is not clear.

> SYNONYMS **1 indistinct**, indefinite, indeterminate, unclear, ill-defined, hazy, fuzzy, misty, blurry, out of focus, shadowy, obscure. **2 imprecise**, rough, approximate, inexact, nonspecific, ambiguous, hazy, uncertain. **3 absentminded**, forgetful, dreamy, abstracted; informal with your head in the clouds, not with it. ANTONYMS clear, definite.

■ **vague·ness** n.

vague·ly /vāglē/ ▶ adv. in a vague way.

> SYNONYMS **1 slightly**, a little, a bit, somewhat, rather, in a way, faintly, obscurely; informal sort of, kind of. **2 absentmindedly**, abstractedly, vacantly.

vain /vān/ ▶ adj. **1** having too high an opinion of yourself. **2** useless or meaningless.

> SYNONYMS **1 conceited**, narcissistic, proud, arrogant, boastful, cocky, egotistical, immodest; informal bigheaded. **2 futile**, useless, pointless, ineffective, unavailing, fruitless, unproductive, unsuccessful, failed, abortive. ANTONYMS modest, successful.

◻ **in vain** without success. ■ **vain·ly** adv.

vain·glo·ri·ous /,vān'glôrēəs/ ▶ adj. literary boastful or vain. ■ **vain·glo·ry** /'vān,glôrē, ,vān'glôrē/ n.

val·ance /'valəns, 'vāləns/ ▶ n. **1** a length of decorative drapery attached to the canopy or frame of a bed in order to screen the structure or the space beneath it. **2** a length of decorative drapery hung above a window to screen the curtain fittings. **3** a dust ruffle.

vale /vāl/ ▶ n. literary a valley.

val·e·dic·tion /ˌvaləˈdiksʜən/ ▶ **n. 1** the action of saying farewell. **2** a farewell statement.

val·e·dic·to·ry /ˌvaləˈdikt(ə)rē/ ▶ **adj.** (especially of a speech) saying farewell. ▶ **n.** (plural **valedictories**) a farewell speech delivered by the highest-ranked student (**valedictorian**) at an academic graduation.

va·lence /ˈvāləns/ (or **valency** /ˈvālənsē/ (plural **valencies**)) ▶ **n.** Chemistry the combining power of an element, especially as measured by the number of hydrogen atoms it can displace or combine with.

val·en·tine /ˈvalənˌtīn/ ▶ **n. 1** a card that you send to a person you love on St. Valentine's Day (February 14). **2** a person to whom you send such a card.

va·le·ri·an /vəˈli(ə)rēən/ ▶ **n. 1** a plant with small pink, red, or white flowers. **2** a sedative drug obtained from valerian roots.

val·et /vaˈlā, ˈvalā, ˈvalit/ ▶ **n. 1** a person who looks after a man's clothes and other personal needs. **2** a person employed to clean or park cars. ▶ **v.** (**valets**, **valeting**, **valeted**) **1** clean a car as a professional service. **2** act as a valet to.

val·e·tu·di·nar·i·an /ˌvaləˌt(y)o͞odnˈe(ə)rēən/ ▶ **n.** a person who is in bad health, or who worries too much about their health.

val·iant /ˈvalyənt/ ▶ **adj.** showing courage or determination.

SYNONYMS **brave**, courageous, plucky, intrepid, heroic, gallant, bold, fearless, daring, unflinching, unafraid, undaunted, doughty, indomitable, stouthearted; informal game, gutsy. ANTONYMS cowardly.

■ **val·iant·ly** adv.

val·id /ˈvalid/ ▶ **adj. 1** (of a reason, argument, etc.) sound or logical. **2** legally binding or acceptable.

SYNONYMS **1 well-founded**, sound, reasonable, rational, logical, justifiable, defensible, cogent, credible, forceful. **2 legally binding**, lawful, official, in force, in effect.

■ **va·lid·i·ty** /vəˈlidətē/ **n.**

val·i·date /ˈvaləˌdāt/ ▶ **v.** (**validates**, **validating**, **validated**) make valid, or show to be valid.

SYNONYMS **ratify**, endorse, approve, agree to, accept, authorize, legalize, legitimize, warrant, license, certify, recognize.

■ **val·i·da·tion** /ˌvaləˈdāsʜən/ **n.**

va·lise /vəˈlēs/ ▶ **n.** a small traveling bag or suitcase.

Val·i·um /ˈvalēəm/ ▶ **n.** trademark a tranquilizing drug used to relieve anxiety.

val·ley /ˈvalē/ ▶ **n.** (plural **valleys**) a low area between hills or mountains.

SYNONYMS **dale**, vale, glen, hollow, gully, gorge, ravine, canyon, rift.

val·or /ˈvalər/ ▶ **n.** great courage in the face of danger.

SYNONYMS **bravery**, courage, pluck, nerve, daring, fearlessness, audacity, boldness, stoutheartedness, heroism; informal guts. ANTONYMS cowardice.

■ **val·or·ous** adj.

val·u·a·ble /ˈvaly(o͞o)əbəl/ ▶ **adj. 1** worth a lot of money. **2** very useful or important. ▶ **n.** (**valuables**) valuable items.

SYNONYMS ▶ **adj. 1 precious**, costly, high-priced, expensive, dear, priceless. **2 useful**, helpful, beneficial, advantageous, invaluable, productive, worthwhile, worthy, important. ANTONYMS worthless. ▶ **n. precious items**, costly items, prized possessions, treasures.

val·u·a·tion /ˌvalyo͞oˈāsʜən/ ▶ **n.** an estimation of how much something is worth.

val·ue /ˈvalyo͞o/ ▶ **n. 1** the importance or usefulness of something. **2** the amount of money that something is worth. **3** (**values**) standards of behavior. **4** Math the amount represented by a letter or symbol. **5** the relative length of the sound represented by a musical note. ▶ **v.** (**values**, **valuing**, **valued**) **1** estimate how much something is worth. **2** consider something to be important or useful.

SYNONYMS ▶ **n. 1 worth**, usefulness, advantage, benefit, gain, profit, good, help. **2 price**, cost, worth, market price. **3** (**values**) **principles**, ethics, morals, standards, code of behavior. ▶ **v. 1 evaluate**, assess, estimate, appraise, price. **2 think highly of**, have a high opinion of, rate highly, esteem, set great store by, respect. ANTONYMS despise.

valve /valv/ ▶ **n. 1** a device for controlling the flow of a liquid or gas through a pipe or duct. **2** a mechanism that varies the length of the tube in a brass musical instrument. **3** a structure in the heart or a vein that allows blood to flow in one direction only.

vamp[1] /vamp/ ▶ **v.** (**vamp something up**) informal improve something by adding something more interesting to it.

vamp[2] ▶ **n.** informal a woman who uses her physical attractiveness to control men. ■ **vamp·ish** adj.

vam·pire /ˈvamˌpī(ə)r/ ▶ **n. 1** (in stories) a dead person that leaves their grave at night to drink the blood of living people. **2** (also **vampire bat**) a bloodsucking bat found mainly in tropical America. ■ **vam·pir·ism** n.

van[1] /van/ ▶ **n.** a motor vehicle used for moving goods or a group of people.

van[2] ▶ **n.** (**the van**) the leading part of an advancing group of people.

va·na·di·um /vəˈnādēəm/ ▶ **n.** a hard gray metallic chemical element, used to make some types of steel.

van·dal /ˈvandl/ ▶ **n.** a person who deliberately destroys or damages property. ■ **van·dal·ism** n.

van·dal·ize /ˈvandlˌīz/ ▶ **v.** (**vandalizes**, **vandalizing**, **vandalized**) deliberately destroy or damage property.

vane /vān/ ▶ **n.** a broad blade that is moved by wind or water, forming part of a windmill, propeller, or turbine.

van·guard /ˈvanˌgärd/ ▶ **n. 1** the leading part of an advancing army. **2** a group of people leading the way in new developments or ideas.

va·nil·la /vəˈnilə/ ▶ **n.** a substance obtained from the pods of a tropical plant, used as a flavoring or scent.

van·ish /ˈvanisʜ/ ▶ **v. 1** disappear suddenly and completely. **2** gradually cease to exist.

SYNONYMS **disappear**, be lost to sight, become invisible, recede from view, fade (away), evaporate, melt away, end, cease to exist. ANTONYMS appear.

■ **van·ish·ing** adj. & n.

van·i·ty /ˈvanətē/ ▶ **n.** (plural **vanities**) **1** too much pride in your own appearance or achievements.

2 the quality of being pointless or futile.

SYNONYMS **conceit**, narcissism, self-love, self-admiration, egotism, pride, arrogance, boastfulness, cockiness; informal bigheadedness. ANTONYMS modesty.

van·quish /ˈvaNGkwisH/ ▶ **v.** literary defeat completely.

van·tage /ˈvantij/ (or **vantage point**) ▶ **n.** a place or position giving the best view.

vap·id /ˈvapid/ ▶ **adj.** offering no stimulation or challenge. ■ **va·pid·i·ty** /vaˈpidətē/ **n.**

va·por /ˈvāpər/ ▶ **n.** **1** moisture suspended in the air. **2** Physics a gaseous substance that can be made into liquid by pressure alone.

va·por·ize /ˈvāpəˌrīz/ ▶ **v.** (**vaporizes**, **vaporizing**, **vaporized**) convert something into vapor. ■ **va·por·i·za·tion** /ˌvāpərəˈzāsHən, -ˌrīˈzā-/ **n.** **va·por·iz·er** **n.**

var·i·a·ble /ˈve(ə)rēəbəl/ ▶ **adj.** **1** not consistent or having a fixed pattern. **2** able to be changed or adapted. ▶ **n.** a variable element, feature, or quantity.

SYNONYMS ▶ **adj.** **changeable**, shifting, fluctuating, irregular, inconstant, inconsistent, fluid, unstable; informal up and down. ANTONYMS constant.

■ **var·i·a·bil·i·ty** /ˌve(ə)rēəˈbilitē/ **n.** **var·i·a·bly** **adv.**

var·i·ance /ˈve(ə)rēəns/ ▶ **n.** **1** the fact or quality of being different or inconsistent. **2** the state of disagreeing or quarreling. **3** Statistics a quantity equal to the square of the standard deviation.

var·i·ant /ˈve(ə)rēənt/ ▶ **n.** a version that varies from other forms of the same thing.

SYNONYMS **1 variation**, version, form, alternative, adaptation, alteration, modification. **2** *there are two variant spellings* **alternative**, other, different, divergent.

var·i·a·tion /ˌve(ə)rēˈāsHən/ ▶ **n.** **1** a change or slight difference in condition, amount, or level. **2** a different or distinct form or version. **3** a new but still recognizable version of a musical theme.

SYNONYMS **1** *regional variations* **difference**, dissimilarity, disparity, contrast, discrepancy, imbalance. **2** *there was little variation from the pattern* **deviation**, variance, divergence, departure, fluctuation, change, alteration, modification.

var·i·cose /ˈvarəˌkōs/ ▶ **adj.** (of a vein) swollen, twisted, and lengthened, as a result of bad circulation.

var·ied /ˈve(ə)rēd/ ▶ **adj.** involving a number of different types or elements.

SYNONYMS **diverse**, assorted, miscellaneous, mixed, sundry, wide-ranging, disparate, heterogeneous, motley.

var·i·e·gat·ed /ˈver(ē)əˌgātid/ ▶ **adj.** having irregular patches or streaks of a different color or colors. ■ **var·i·e·ga·tion** /ˌver(ē)iˈgāsHən/ **n.**

SPELLING

Remember the **e** in the middle: variegated.

va·ri·e·ty /vəˈrīətē/ ▶ **n.** (plural **varieties**) **1** the quality of being varied. **2** (**a variety of**) a number of things of the same type that are distinct in character. **3** a thing that differs in some way from others of the same general class. **4** a form of entertainment involving singing, dancing, and comedy.

SYNONYMS **1 diversity**, variation, diversification, change, difference. **2 assortment**, miscellany, range, array, collection, selection, mixture, medley. **3 sort**, kind, type, class, category, style, form, make, model, brand, strain, breed. ANTONYMS uniformity.

var·i·ous /ˈve(ə)rēəs/ ▶ **adj.** of different kinds or sorts. ▶ **determiner & pron.** more than one; individual and separate.

SYNONYMS ▶ **adj.** **diverse**, different, differing, varied, assorted, mixed, sundry, miscellaneous, disparate, heterogeneous, motley.

■ **var·i·ous·ly** **adv.**

var·mint /ˈvärmənt/ ▶ **n.** dated, informal or dialect a troublesome or mischievous person or wild animal.

var·nish /ˈvärnisH/ ▶ **n.** a liquid applied to wood to give a hard, clear, shiny surface when dry. ▶ **v.** put varnish on.

SYNONYMS **lacquer**, shellac, japan, enamel, glaze, polish.

var·si·ty /ˈvärsətē/▶ **n.** (plural **varsities**) a sports team representing a school or college.

var·y /ˈve(ə)rē/ ▶ **v.** (**varies**, **varying**, **varied**) **1** differ in size, degree, or nature from something else of the same general class. **2** change from one form or state to another. **3** alter something to make it less uniform.

SYNONYMS **1 differ**, be dissimilar, disagree, be at variance. **2 fluctuate**, rise and fall, go up and down, change, alter, shift, swing.

vas·cu·lar /ˈvaskyələr/ ▶ **adj.** referring to the system of vessels for carrying blood or (in plants) the tissues carrying sap, water, and nutrients.

vas de·fe·rens /ˌvas ˈdefərənz, -ˌrenz/ ▶ **n.** (plural **vasa deferentia** /ˌvāsə ˌdefəˈrensH(ē)ə, ˌvāzə/) the duct carrying sperm from a testicle to the urethra.

vase /vās, vāz, väz/ ▶ **n.** a container for displaying cut flowers.

vas·ec·to·my /vəˈsektəmē, va-/ ▶ **n.** (plural **vasectomies**) the surgical cutting and sealing of part of each vas deferens as a means of sterilization.

Vas·e·line /ˌvasəˈlēn, ˈvasəˌlēn/ ▶ **n.** trademark a type of petroleum jelly used as an ointment and lubricant.

vas·sal /ˈvasəl/ ▶ **n.** (in the feudal system) a man who promised to support and fight for a king or lord in return for holding a piece of land.

vast /vast/ ▶ **adj.** of very great extent or quantity; immense.

SYNONYMS **huge**, extensive, broad, wide, boundless, enormous, immense, great, massive, colossal, gigantic, mammoth, giant, mountainous; informal mega, whopping. ANTONYMS tiny.

■ **vast·ly** **adv.** **vast·ness** **n.**

VAT /vat/ ▶ **abbr.** value-added tax.

vat /vat/ ▶ **n.** a large tank or tub used to hold liquid.

Vat·i·can /ˈvatikən/ ▶ **n.** the official residence of the pope in Rome.

vaude·ville /ˈvôd(ə)ˌvil, -vəl/ ▶ **n.** a type of entertainment featuring a mixture of musical and comedy acts.

vault¹ /vôlt/ ▶ n. **1** a large room used for storage, especially in a bank. **2** a chamber beneath a church or in a graveyard, used for burials. **3** a roof in the form of an arch or a series of arches.

SYNONYMS **1 safe**, strongroom, repository, wall safe. **2 cellar**, basement, crypt, undercroft, catacomb, burial chamber.

■ **vault·ed** adj.

vault² ▶ v. leap or spring using your hands or a pole to push yourself. ▶ n. an act of vaulting.

SYNONYMS ▶ v. **jump**, leap, spring, bound, clear.

vaunt /vônt, vänt/ ▶ v. (usu. **vaunted**) boast about or praise: *his vaunted gift for spotting talent.*

SYNONYMS **boast about**, brag about, make much of, crow about, parade, flaunt; informal show off about; formal laud.

VCR ▶ abbr. videocassette recorder.

veal /vēl/ ▶ n. meat from a young calf.

vec·tor /'vektər/ ▶ n. **1** Math a quantity having direction as well as magnitude. **2** the carrier of a disease or infection.

Ve·da /'vādə, 'vēdə/ ▶ n. the most ancient Hindu scriptures.

veer /vi(ə)r/ ▶ v. (**veers**, **veering**, **veered**) **1** change direction suddenly. **2** (of the wind) change direction clockwise around the points of the compass.

SYNONYMS **turn**, swerve, swing, weave, wheel, change direction, change course, deviate.

veg·an /'vēgən, 'vejən/ ▶ n. a person who does not eat or use any animal products.

veg·e·ta·ble /'vejtəbəl, 'vəjətə-/ ▶ n. **1** a plant used as food. **2** offensive a person who is incapable of normal mental or physical activity as a result of brain damage.

SPELLING

Write **vege-**, not **vega-**: vegetable.

veg·e·tal /'vejətl/ ▶ adj. relating to plants.

veg·e·tar·i·an /ˌveji'te(ə)rēən/ ▶ n. a person who does not eat meat or fish. ▶ adj. eating or including no meat or fish. ■ **veg·e·tar·i·an·ism** n.

veg·e·tate /'vejəˌtāt/ ▶ v. (**vegetates**, **vegetating**, **vegetated**) spend your time in a dull way that involves little mental stimulation.

veg·e·ta·tion /ˌvejə'tāsʜən/ ▶ n. plants.

veg·e·ta·tive /'vejəˌtātiv/ ▶ adj. **1** relating to vegetation. **2** Medicine alive but showing no sign of brain activity or responsiveness.

veg·gie /'vejē/ (also **vegie**) ⇨ VEGETARIAN or VEGETABLE.

ve·he·ment /'vēəmənt/ ▶ adj. showing strong feeling.

SYNONYMS **passionate**, forceful, ardent, impassioned, heated, spirited, urgent, fervent, fierce, strong, forcible, powerful, emphatic, vigorous, intense, earnest, keen, enthusiastic, zealous. ANTONYMS mild.

■ **ve·he·mence** n. **ve·he·ment·ly** adv.

ve·hi·cle /'vēəkəl, 'vēˌhikəl/ ▶ n. a car, truck, etc., used for transporting people or goods on land.

SYNONYMS **1 means of transport**, transportation, conveyance; motor vehicle, automobile, car, truck. **2 channel**, medium, means, agent, instrument, mechanism, organ, apparatus.

■ **ve·hic·u·lar** /vē'hikyələr/ adj.

veil /vāl/ ▶ n. **1** a piece of thin material worn to protect or hide the face. **2** the part of a nun's headdress that covers the head and shoulders. **3** a thing that hides or disguises. ▶ v. **1** cover with a veil. **2** (**veiled**) partially hidden or disguised.

SYNONYMS ▶ n. **covering**, screen, curtain, mantle, cloak, mask, blanket, shroud, canopy, cloud, pall. ▶ v. **cover**, surround, swathe, enfold, envelop, conceal, hide, obscure, screen, shield, cloak, blanket, shroud.

vein /vān/ ▶ n. **1** any of the tubes that carry blood from all parts of the body toward the heart. **2** a blood vessel. **3** (in plants) a thin rib running through a leaf. **4** (in insects) a hollow rib forming part of the supporting framework of a wing. **5** a streak of a different color in wood, marble, cheese, etc. **6** a fracture in rock containing a deposit of minerals or ore. **7** a source of a particular quality: *a vein of humor.*

SYNONYMS **1 blood vessel**, capillary. **2 layer**, seam, lode, stratum, deposit.

■ **veined** adj.

Vel·cro /'velkrō/ ▶ n. trademark a fastener consisting of two strips of fabric covered with tiny hooks.

veld /velt/ (or **veldt**) ▶ n. open uncultivated country or grassland in southern Africa.

vel·lum /'veləm/ ▶ n. fine parchment made from animal skin.

ve·loc·i·rap·tor /və'läsəˌraptər/ ▶ n. a small meat-eating dinosaur.

ve·loc·i·ty /və'läsətē/ ▶ n. (plural **velocities**) speed in a particular direction.

SYNONYMS **speed**, pace, rate, tempo, rapidity.

ve·lour /və'lo͝or/ ▶ n. a thick, soft fabric resembling velvet.

vel·vet /'velvət/ ▶ n. a fabric with a soft, short pile on one side. ■ **vel·vet·y** adj.

vel·vet·een /'velvəˌtēn, ˌvelvə'tēn/ ▶ n. a cotton fabric resembling thin velvet.

ve·nal /'vēnl/ ▶ adj. open to bribery. ■ **ve·nal·i·ty** /vē'nalətē, və-/ n.

vend /vend/ ▶ v. sell small items. □ **vending machine** a machine from which you can buy drinks, snacks, etc., by inserting coins.

ven·det·ta /ven'detə/ ▶ n. **1** a feud in which the family of a murdered person seeks vengeance on the murderer or the murderer's family. **2** a long and bitter quarrel.

ven·dor /'vendər, -ˌdôr/ (or **vender**) ▶ n. **1** a person selling small items. **2** Law a person who is selling a property.

ve·neer /və'ni(ə)r/ ▶ n. **1** a thin covering of fine wood applied to a cheaper wood or other material. **2** an outward appearance that hides the true nature of a person or thing.

SYNONYMS **1 surface**, lamination, layer, overlay, facing, covering, finish, exterior. **2 facade**, front, show, outward display, appearance, impression, semblance, guise, mask, pretense, cover, camouflage.

■ **ve·neered** adj.

ven·er·a·ble /'venərəbəl, 'venrə-/ ▶ adj. given great respect because of age, wisdom, or character.

ven·er·ate /ˈvenəˌrāt/ ▶ v. (**venerates**, **venerating**, **venerated**) respect someone highly. ■ **ven·er·a·tion** /ˌvenəˈrāsʜən/ n.

ve·ne·re·al /vəˈni(ə)rēəl/ ▶ adj. **1** relating to venereal disease. **2** formal relating to sexual desire or sexual intercourse. ◻ **venereal disease** a disease caught by having sex with an infected person.

Ve·ne·tian /vəˈnēsʜən/ ▶ adj. relating to Venice. ◻ **venetian blind** a window blind consisting of horizontal slats that can be turned to control the amount of light that passes through.

Ven·e·zue·lan /ˌvenəz(ə)ˈwālən/ ▶ n. a person from Venezuela. ▶ adj. relating to Venezuela.

venge·ance /ˈvenjəns/ ▶ n. an act of harming or punishing someone in return for what they have done to you or someone close to you.

> SYNONYMS **revenge**, retribution, retaliation, requital, reprisal, an eye for an eye. ANTONYMS forgiveness.

◻ **with a vengeance** with great intensity.

venge·ful /ˈvenjfəl/ ▶ adj. wanting to punish or harm someone in return for something they have done.

ve·ni·al /ˈvēnēəl, ˈvēnyəl/ ▶ adj. (of a fault or offense) slight and able to be forgiven.

ven·i·son /ˈvenəsən, -zən/ ▶ n. meat from a deer.

Venn di·a·gram /ven/ ▶ n. a diagram representing mathematical sets as circles, with overlapping sections representing elements shared between sets.

ven·om /ˈvenəm/ ▶ n. **1** the poisonous liquid produced by some animals that bite or sting, such as snakes and scorpions. **2** a strong feeling of hatred or bitterness.

ven·om·ous /ˈvenəməs/ ▶ adj. **1** producing venom. **2** full of hatred or bitterness.

> SYNONYMS **poisonous**, toxic, dangerous, deadly, lethal, fatal. ANTONYMS harmless.

■ **ven·om·ous·ly** adv.

ve·nous /ˈvēnəs/ ▶ adj. relating to a vein or the veins.

vent[1] /vent/ ▶ n. an opening that allows air, gas, or liquid to pass out of or into a confined space. ▶ v. **1** allow yourself to express a strong emotion. **2** let air, gas, or liquid pass through a vent.

> SYNONYMS ▶ n. **outlet**, **inlet**, opening, aperture, hole, gap, orifice, space, duct, flue, shaft, well, passage, airway. ▶ v. **let out**, release, pour out, utter, express, air, voice.

vent[2] ▶ n. a slit in a garment.

ven·ti·late /ˈventəˌlāt/ ▶ v. (**ventilates**, **ventilating**, **ventilated**) cause air to enter and circulate freely in a room or building.

> SYNONYMS **air**, aerate, oxygenate, freshen, cool.

■ **ven·ti·la·tion** /ˌventəˈlāsʜən/ n.

ven·ti·la·tor /ˈventəˌlātər/ ▶ n. **1** an opening or a machine for ventilating a room or building. **2** a machine that pumps air in and out of a person's lungs to help them breathe.

ven·tral /ˈventrəl/ ▶ adj. having to do with the underside or abdomen.

ven·tri·cle /ˈventrəkəl/ ▶ n. each of the two larger and lower cavities of the heart.

ven·tril·o·quist /venˈtriləˌkwist/ ▶ n. an entertainer who can make their voice seem to come from elsewhere. ■ **ven·tril·o·quism** n.

ven·ture /ˈvencʜər/ ▶ n. **1** a business enterprise involving considerable risk. **2** a risky or daring journey or undertaking. ▶ v. (**ventures**, **venturing**, **ventured**) **1** dare to do something dangerous or risky. **2** dare to say something.

> SYNONYMS ▶ n. **enterprise**, undertaking, project, scheme, operation, endeavor, speculation. ▶ v. **1 put forward**, advance, proffer, offer, air, suggest, volunteer, submit, propose. **2 dare**, be so bold as, presume, have the audacity, have the nerve, take the liberty.

ven·ture·some /ˈvencʜərsəm/ ▶ adj. literary willing to take on something risky or difficult.

ven·ue /ˈvenˌyo͞o/ ▶ n. the place where an event or meeting is held.

Ve·nus /ˈvēnəs/ ▶ n. the second planet from the sun in the solar system. ◻ **Venus flytrap** a plant with hinged leaves that spring shut on and digest insects that land on them.

ve·ra·cious /vəˈrāsʜəs/ ▶ adj. formal truthful.

ve·rac·i·ty /vəˈrasətē/ ▶ n. the quality of being truthful and accurate.

ve·ran·da /vəˈrandə/ (or **verandah**) ▶ n. a roofed structure with an open front along the outside of a house.

verb /vərb/ ▶ n. a word expressing an action or occurrence.

ver·bal /ˈvərbəl/ ▶ adj. **1** relating to or in the form of words. **2** spoken rather than written. **3** relating to a verb.

> SYNONYMS **oral**, spoken, word-of-mouth, stated, said, unwritten.

■ **ver·bal·ly** adv.

ver·bal·ize /ˈvərbəˌlīz/ ▶ v. (**verbalizes**, **verbalizing**, **verbalized**) express something in words.

ver·ba·tim /vərˈbātəm/ ▶ adv. & adj. in exactly the same words as were used originally.

ver·bi·age /ˈvərbē-ij/ ▶ n. speech or writing that is too long or detailed.

ver·bose /vərˈbōs/ ▶ adj. using more words than are needed.

> SYNONYMS **wordy**, loquacious, garrulous, talkative, voluble, long-winded, lengthy, prolix, circumlocutory, rambling. ANTONYMS succinct.

■ **ver·bos·i·ty** /-ˈbäsətē/ n.

ver·dant /ˈvərdnt/ ▶ adj. green with grass or other lush vegetation.

ver·dict /ˈvərdikt/ ▶ n. **1** a decision made by a jury or judge in a court of law about whether someone is innocent or guilty. **2** an opinion or judgment formed after trying or testing something.

> SYNONYMS **judgment**, adjudication, decision, finding, ruling, sentence.

ver·di·gris /ˈvərdəˌgrēs, -ˌgris, -ˌgrē/ ▶ n. a bright bluish-green substance formed on copper or brass by oxidation.

ver·dure /ˈvərjər/ ▶ n. literary lush green vegetation.

verge /vərj/ ▶ n. **1** an edge or border. **2** a limit beyond which a particular thing will happen: *I was on the verge of tears.* ▶ v. (**verges**, **verging**, **verged**) (**verge on**) be very close or similar to.

> SYNONYMS ▶ n. **1 edge**, border, margin, side, brink, rim, lip, fringe, boundary, perimeter. **2** *I was on the verge of tears* **brink**, threshold, edge, point.

verg·er /ˈvərjər/ ▶ **n.** an official in a church who acts as a caretaker and attendant.

ver·i·fy /ˈverəˌfī/ ▶ **v.** (**verifies, verifying, verified**) make sure or show that something is true and accurate.

> SYNONYMS **confirm**, prove, substantiate, corroborate, back up, bear out, justify, support, uphold, testify to, validate, authenticate. ANTONYMS refute.

■ **ver·i·fi·a·ble** adj. **ver·i·fi·ca·tion** /ˌverəfiˈkāsʜən/ n.

ver·i·ly /ˈverəlē/ ▶ **adv.** old use truly; certainly.

ver·i·si·mil·i·tude /ˌverəsəˈmiliˌt(y)o͞od/ ▶ **n.** the appearance of being true or real.

ver·i·ta·ble /ˈveritəbəl/ ▶ **adj.** genuine.
■ **ver·i·ta·bly** adv.

ver·i·ty /ˈveritē/ ▶ **n.** (plural **verities**) formal truthfulness, or a truth.

ver·mi·cel·li /ˌvərməˈcʜelē, -ˈselē/ ▶ **pl.n.** pasta made in long thin threads.

ver·mil·ion /vərˈmilyən/ ▶ **n.** a bright red color.

ver·min /ˈvərmən/ ▶ **n.** wild animals or birds that carry disease or harm crops. ■ **ver·min·ous** adj.

ver·mouth /vərˈmo͞otʜ/ ▶ **n.** a red or white wine flavored with herbs.

ver·nac·u·lar /vərˈnakyələr/ ▶ **n.** the language or dialect spoken by the ordinary people of a country or region.

ver·nal /ˈvərnl/ ▶ **adj.** relating to the season of spring.

ver·ru·ca /vəˈro͞okə/ ▶ **n.** a contagious wart on the sole of the foot.

ver·sa·tile /ˈvərsətl/ ▶ **adj.** able to adapt or be adapted to many different functions or activities.

> SYNONYMS **1** *a versatile player* **adaptable**, flexible, all-around, multitalented, resourceful. **2** *a versatile device* **adjustable**, adaptable, multipurpose, all-purpose.

■ **ver·sa·til·i·ty** /ˌvərsəˈtilətē/ n.

verse /vərs/ ▶ **n. 1** writing arranged with a metrical rhythm. **2** a group of lines that form a unit in a poem or song. **3** each of the short numbered divisions of a chapter in the Bible.

> SYNONYMS **1 poetry**, lyrics. **2 poem**, lyric, rhyme, ditty, limerick. **3 stanza**, canto.

versed /vərst/ ▶ **adj.** (**versed in**) experienced or skilled in.

ver·si·fy /ˈvərsəˌfī/ ▶ **v.** (**versifies, versifying, versified**) write verse, or turn a piece of writing into verse. ■ **ver·si·fi·ca·tion** /ˌvərsəfiˈkāsʜən/ n.

ver·sion /ˈvərzʜən/ ▶ **n. 1** a particular form of something that differs from other forms of the same type of thing. **2** an account of something told from a particular person's point of view.

> SYNONYMS **1 account**, report, statement, description, record, story, rendering, interpretation, explanation, understanding, reading, impression, side. **2 edition**, translation, impression. **3 type**, sort, kind, form, equivalent, variety, variant, design, model, style.

ver·so /ˈvərsō/ ▶ **n.** (plural **versos**) a left-hand page of an open book, or the back of a loose document.

ver·sus /ˈvərsəs, -səz/ ▶ **prep. 1** against. **2** as opposed to.

ver·te·bra /ˈvərtəbrə/ ▶ **n.** (plural **vertebrae** /-ˌbrē, -ˌbrā/) each of the series of small bones forming the backbone.

ver·te·brate /ˈvərtəbrət, -ˌbrāt/ ▶ **n.** an animal having a backbone, e.g., a mammal, bird, reptile, amphibian, or fish.

ver·tex /ˈvərˌteks/ ▶ **n.** (plural **vertices** /-təˌsēz/ or **vertexes**) **1** the highest point. **2** a meeting point of two lines that form an angle.

ver·ti·cal /ˈvərtikəl/ ▶ **adj.** going straight up or down, at a right angle to a horizontal line or surface. ▶ **n.** a vertical line or surface.

> SYNONYMS ▶ **adj. upright**, erect, perpendicular, plumb, on end, standing. ANTONYMS flat, horizontal.

■ **ver·ti·cal·ly** adv.

ver·tig·i·nous /vərˈtijənəs/ ▶ **adj.** very high or steep.

ver·ti·go /ˈvərtəgō/ ▶ **n.** a feeling of giddiness caused by looking down from a great height.

verve /vərv/ ▶ **n.** energy, spirit, and style.

ver·y /ˈverē/ ▶ **adv.** in a high degree. ▶ **adj. 1** actual; precise. **2** extreme. **3** mere.

> SYNONYMS ▶ **adv. extremely**, exceedingly, exceptionally, extraordinarily, tremendously, immensely, acutely, singularly, decidedly, highly, remarkably, really; informal real, awfully, terribly, seriously, mega, mighty, ultra. ANTONYMS slightly.

ves·pers /ˈvespərz/ ▶ **n.** a Christian service of evening prayer.

ves·sel /ˈvesəl/ ▶ **n. 1** a ship or large boat. **2** a tube or duct carrying a liquid within the body, or within a plant. **3** old use a bowl, cup, or other container for liquids.

> SYNONYMS **1 boat**, ship, craft. **2 container**, receptacle, basin, bowl, pan, pot, jug.

vest /vest/ ▶ **n.** a close-fitting waist-length garment with no sleeves or collar, usually buttoning down the front. ▶ **v.** (**vest something in**) give someone power or property, or the legal right to hold power or own property. □ **vested interest** a personal reason for wanting something to happen.

ves·ti·bule /ˈvestəˌbyo͞ol/ ▶ **n.** a room or hall just inside the outer door of a building.

ves·tige /ˈvestij/ ▶ **n. 1** a last remaining trace of something. **2** the smallest amount.

> SYNONYMS **remnant**, fragment, relic, echo, trace, mark, legacy, reminder.

■ **ves·tig·i·al** /veˈstij(ē)əl/ adj.

vest·ment /ˈves(t)mənt/ ▶ **n.** a robe worn by ministers or members of the choir during church services.

ves·try /ˈvestrē/ ▶ **n.** (plural **vestries**) a small room in a church, used as an office and for changing into ceremonial robes.

vet[1] /vet/ ▶ **n.** short for **VETERINARIAN**. ▶ **v.** (**vets, vetting, vetted**) find out about someone's background and past before employing them.

> SYNONYMS ▶ **v. check up on**, screen, investigate, examine, scrutinize, inspect, look over, assess, evaluate, appraise; informal check out.

vet[2] ▶ **n.** informal a veteran.

vetch /vecʜ/ ▶ **n.** a plant of the pea family grown as food for farm animals.

vet·er·an /ˈvet(ə)rən/ ▶ **n. 1** a person who has had many years of experience in a particular field. **2** a person who used to serve in the armed forces.

SYNONYMS **1 old hand**, past master, doyen, doyenne; informal vet, old-timer. **2** *a veteran campaigner* **long-serving**, seasoned, old, hardened, practiced, experienced; informal battle-scarred. ANTONYMS novice.

□ **Veterans Day** a US holiday held on November 11 to commemorate military veterans.

vet·er·i·nar·i·an /ˌvet(ə)rəˈne(ə)rēən/ ▶ **n.** a person qualified to treat diseased or injured animals.

vet·er·i·nar·y /ˈvet(ə)rəˌnerē/ ▶ **adj.** relating to the treatment of diseases and injuries in animals.

SPELLING

Note the **-er-** before the **-in-**: vet**er**inary.

ve·to /ˈvētō/ ▶ **n.** (plural **vetoes**) **1** the right or power to reject a ruling or decision made by others. **2** a refusal to allow something. ▶ **v.** (**vetoes**, **vetoing**, **vetoed**) use a veto against, or refuse to allow.

SYNONYMS ▶ **n. rejection**, dismissal, prohibition, proscription, embargo, ban, interdict. ▶ **v. reject**, turn down, throw out, dismiss, prohibit, forbid, proscribe, disallow, embargo, ban, rule out; informal kill, give the thumbs down to. ANTONYMS approve.

vex /veks/ ▶ **v.** make someone annoyed or worried. ■ **vex·a·tion** /vekˈsāsʜən/ **n.** **vex·a·tious** /vekˈsāsʜəs/ **adj.**

vexed /vekst/ ▶ **adj. 1** (of an issue) difficult to deal with and causing a lot of debate. **2** annoyed or worried.

VHF ▶ **abbr.** very high frequency.

VHS ▶ **abbr.** trademark video home system.

vi·a /ˈvīə, ˈvēə/ ▶ **prep. 1** traveling through a particular place on the way to a destination. **2** by way of; through. **3** by means of.

vi·a·ble /ˈvīəbəl/ ▶ **adj. 1** capable of working successfully. **2** (of a plant, animal, or cell) able to live.

SYNONYMS **feasible**, workable, practicable, practical, realistic, achievable, attainable; informal doable. ANTONYMS impracticable.

■ **vi·a·bil·i·ty** /ˌvīəˈbilətē/ **n.**

vi·a·duct /ˈvīəˌdəkt/ ▶ **n.** a long bridgelike structure carrying a road or railroad across a valley or other low ground.

vi·al /ˈvī(ə)l/ ▶ **n.** a small cylindrical glass bottle for medicines etc.

vi·ands /ˈvīəndz/ ▶ **pl.n.** old use food.

vibe /vīb/ (or **vibes**) ▶ **n.** informal the atmosphere of a place, or a feeling passing between people.

vi·brant /ˈvībrənt/ ▶ **adj. 1** full of energy and enthusiasm. **2** (of sound) strong or resonant. **3** (of color) bright.

SYNONYMS **1 spirited**, lively, energetic, vigorous, dynamic, passionate, fiery; informal feisty. **2 vivid**, bright, striking, brilliant, glowing, strong, rich. ANTONYMS lifeless, pale.

■ **vi·bran·cy n. vi·brant·ly adv.**

vi·bra·phone /ˈvībrəˌfōn/ ▶ **n.** an electrical percussion instrument giving a vibrato effect.

vi·brate /ˈvīˌbrāt/ ▶ **v.** (**vibrates**, **vibrating**, **vibrated**) **1** move with rapid small movements to and fro. **2** (of a sound) resonate.

SYNONYMS **shake**, tremble, shiver, quiver, shudder, throb, pulsate.

■ **vi·bra·tion** /vīˈbrāsʜən/ **n.**

vi·bra·to /vəˈbrätō, vī-/ ▶ **n.** a rapid, slight variation in pitch in singing or playing some musical instruments.

vic·ar /ˈvikər/ ▶ **n.** (in the Church of England) a minister in charge of a parish.

vic·ar·age /ˈvikərij/ ▶ **n.** a vicar's house.

vi·car·i·ous /vīˈkerēəs, vi-/ ▶ **adj.** experienced in the imagination rather than directly: *a vicarious thrill*. ■ **vi·car·i·ous·ly adv.**

vice /vīs/ ▶ **n. 1** immoral or wicked behavior. **2** criminal activities that involve sex or drugs. **3** a bad personal characteristic. **4** a bad habit.

SYNONYMS **1 immorality**, wrongdoing, wickedness, evil, iniquity, villainy, corruption, misconduct, sin, depravity. **2 fault**, failing, flaw, defect, shortcoming, weakness, deficiency, foible, frailty. ANTONYMS virtue.

vice pres·i·dent ▶ **n.** a person serving as deputy to a president.

vice·roy /ˈvīsˌroi/ ▶ **n.** a person sent by a king or queen to govern a colony.

vice ver·sa /ˈvīs ˈvərsə, ˈvīsə/ ▶ **adv.** reversing the order of the items just mentioned.

vi·cin·i·ty /vəˈsinətē/ ▶ **n.** (plural **vicinities**) the area near or surrounding a place.

vi·cious /ˈvisʜəs/ ▶ **adj. 1** cruel or violent. **2** (of an animal) wild and dangerous.

SYNONYMS **1 brutal**, ferocious, savage, violent, ruthless, merciless, heartless, callous, cruel, cold-blooded, inhuman, barbaric, bloodthirsty. **2 malicious**, spiteful, vindictive, venomous, cruel, bitter, acrimonious, hostile, nasty; informal catty. ANTONYMS gentle.

□ **vicious circle** a situation in which one problem leads to another, which then makes the first one worse. ■ **vi·cious·ly adv. vi·cious·ness n.**

SPELLING

No **s** in the middle: vi**c**ious.

vi·cis·si·tudes /vəˈsisəˌt(y)o͞odz/ ▶ **pl.n.** the ups and downs and changes in your life.

vic·tim /ˈviktəm/ ▶ **n.** a person who is harmed or killed as a result of a crime, injustice, or accident.

SYNONYMS **sufferer**, injured party, casualty, fatality, loss, survivor.

vic·tim·ize /ˈviktəˌmīz/ ▶ **v.** (**victimizes**, **victimizing**, **victimized**) single someone out for cruel or unfair treatment.

SYNONYMS **persecute**, pick on, bully, abuse, discriminate against, exploit, take advantage of; informal have it in for.

■ **vic·tim·i·za·tion** /ˌviktəməˈzāsʜən/ **n.**

vic·tor /ˈviktər/ ▶ **n.** a person who defeats an opponent in a battle, game or competition.

Vic·to·ri·an /vikˈtôrēən/ ▶ **adj.** relating to the reign of Queen Victoria (1837–1901) of Great Britain.

vic·to·ri·ous /vikˈtôrēəs/ ▶ **adj.** having won a victory.

SYNONYMS **triumphant**, conquering, vanquishing, winning, champion, successful. ANTONYMS unsuccessful.

vic·to·ry /'vikt(ə)rē/ ▶ **n.** (plural **victories**) an act of defeating an opponent.

> SYNONYMS **success**, triumph, conquest, win, coup; informal walkover. ANTONYMS defeat, loss.

vict·uals /'vitlz/ ▶ **pl.n.** old use food and provisions.

vid·e·o /'vidē,ō/ ▶ **n.** (plural **videos**) **1** a system of recording and reproducing moving images using magnetic tape. **2** a movie or other recording on magnetic tape or in a digital format. ▶ **v.** (**videoes**, **videoing**, **videoed**) film or make a video recording of. ▫ **video game** a computer game played on a television screen. **video recorder** a device that records videos on magnetic tape or in a digital format.

vid·e·o·cas·sette /,vidēōkə'set/ ▶ **n.** a cassette of videotape.

vid·e·o·link /'vidēō,liNGk/ ▶ **n.** a connection used to convey a video signal.

vid·e·o·tape /'vidēō,tāp/ ▶ **n.** **1** magnetic tape for recording and reproducing visual images and sound. **2** a cassette on which this magnetic tape is held. ▶ **v.** (**videotapes**, **videotaping**, **videotaped**) record on videotape.

vie /vī/ ▶ **v.** (**vies**, **vying**, **vied**) compete eagerly with others in order to do or achieve something.

> SYNONYMS **compete**, contend, struggle, fight, battle, jockey.

Vi·et·nam·ese /vē,etnə'mēz, ,vyet-, ,vēət-, -'mēs/ ▶ **n.** (plural **Vietnamese**) **1** a person from Vietnam. **2** the language of Vietnam. ▶ **adj.** relating to Vietnam.

view /vyo͞o/ ▶ **n.** **1** the ability to see something or to be seen from a particular position. **2** something seen from a particular position, especially natural scenery. **3** an attitude or opinion. ▶ **v.** **1** look at or inspect. **2** have a particular attitude toward.

> SYNONYMS ▶ **n.** **1 outlook**, prospect, panorama, vista, scene, scenery, landscape. **2 opinion**, viewpoint, belief, judgment, thinking, notion, idea, conviction, persuasion, attitude, feeling, sentiment. **3** *the church came into view* **sight**, perspective, vision, visibility. ▶ **v.** **1 look at**, observe, eye, gaze at, contemplate, regard, scan, survey, inspect, scrutinize; informal check out, eyeball. **2 consider**, regard, look on, see, perceive, judge, deem, reckon.

▫ **in view of** because or as a result of. **with a view to** with the intention of.

view·er /'vyo͞oər/ ▶ **n.** **1** a person who views something. **2** a device for looking at film transparencies or similar photographic images.

> SYNONYMS **watcher**, spectator, onlooker, observer; (**viewers**) audience, crowd.

view·find·er /'vyo͞o,fīndər/ ▶ **n.** a device on a camera that you look through to see what will appear in the picture.

view·point /'vyo͞o,point/ ▶ **n.** an opinion.

vig·il /'vijəl/ ▶ **n.** a period of staying awake through the night to keep watch or pray.

vig·i·lant /'vijələnt/ ▶ **adj.** keeping careful watch for possible danger or difficulties.

> SYNONYMS **watchful**, observant, attentive, alert, eagle-eyed, on the lookout, on your guard. ANTONYMS inattentive.

▪ **vig·i·lance** **n.** **vig·i·lant·ly** **adv.**

vig·i·lan·te /,vijə'lantē/ ▶ **n.** a member of a group of people who take it on themselves to prevent crime or punish criminals without legal authority. ▪ **vig·i·lan·tism** **n.**

vi·gnette /vin'yet/ ▶ **n.** **1** a brief, vivid description or episode. **2** a small illustration or photograph that fades into its background without a definite border.

vig·or /'vigər/ ▶ **n.** **1** physical strength and good health. **2** effort, energy, and enthusiasm.

> SYNONYMS **health**, strength, robustness, energy, life, vitality, spirit, passion, determination, dynamism, drive; informal oomph, get-up-and-go. ANTONYMS lethargy.

vig·or·ous /'vig(ə)rəs/ ▶ **adj.** **1** strong, healthy, and full of energy. **2** involving physical strength, effort, or energy.

> SYNONYMS **1 robust**, healthy, hale and hearty, strong, sturdy, fit, hardy, tough, energetic, lively, active. **2 strenuous**, powerful, forceful, spirited, determined, aggressive, passionate; informal feisty. ANTONYMS weak, feeble.

vig·or·ous·ly /'vig(ə)rəslē/ ▶ **adv.** with vigor.

> SYNONYMS **strenuously**, strongly, powerfully, forcefully, energetically, heartily, all out, fiercely, hard; informal like mad.

Vi·king /'vīkiNG/ ▶ **n.** a member of the Scandinavian people who settled in parts of Britain and elsewhere in northwestern Europe between the 8th and 11th centuries.

vile /vīl/ ▶ **adj.** **1** very unpleasant. **2** wicked.

> SYNONYMS **foul**, nasty, unpleasant, bad, horrid, repulsive, disgusting, hateful, nauseating; informal gross. ANTONYMS pleasant.

▪ **vile·ly** **adv.**

vil·i·fy /'vilə,fī/ ▶ **v.** (**vilifies**, **vilifying**, **vilified**) speak or write about someone in a very unpleasant way. ▪ **vil·i·fi·ca·tion** /,viləfi'kāSHən/ **n.**

vil·la /'vilə/ ▶ **n.** **1** (especially in southern Europe) a large country house in its own grounds. **2** a rented vacation home abroad. **3** a large house in ancient Rome.

vil·lage /'vilij/ ▶ **n.** **1** a small community of streets and houses in a country area. **2** a small municipality.

vil·lain /'vilən/ ▶ **n.** **1** a bad person. **2** a bad character in a novel or play whose actions are important to the plot.

> SYNONYMS **criminal**, lawbreaker, offender, felon, miscreant, wrongdoer, rogue, scoundrel, reprobate; informal crook, bad guy.

▪ **vil·lain·ous** **adj.**

vil·lain·y /'vilənē/ ▶ **n.** (plural **villainies**) wicked or criminal behavior.

vil·lein /'vilən, -,ān/ ▶ **n.** (in medieval England) a poor man who had to work for a lord in return for a small piece of land on which to grow food.

vim /vim/ ▶ **n.** informal energy; enthusiasm.

vin·ai·grette /,vinə'gret/ ▶ **n.** a salad dressing consisting of oil mixed with vinegar.

vin·di·cate /'vində,kāt/ ▶ **v.** (**vindicates**, **vindicating**, **vindicated**) **1** clear someone of blame or suspicion. **2** show something to be right or justified.

> SYNONYMS **1 acquit**, clear, absolve, exonerate; informal let off. **2 justify**, warrant, substantiate, confirm, corroborate, prove, defend, support, back, endorse. ANTONYMS incriminate.

■ **vin·di·ca·tion** /ˌvindəˈkāsHən/ n.

vin·dic·tive /vinˈdiktiv/ ▶ adj. having or showing a strong or inappropriate desire for revenge.

SYNONYMS **vengeful**, unforgiving, resentful, acrimonious, bitter; spiteful, mean, rancorous, venomous, malicious, malevolent, nasty, cruel. ANTONYMS forgiving.

■ **vin·dic·tive·ness** n.

vine /vīn/ ▶ n. a climbing plant, especially one that produces grapes.

vin·e·gar /ˈvinəgər/ ▶ n. a sour liquid made from wine, cider, or beer, used as a seasoning, a condiment, or for pickling. ■ **vin·e·gar·y** adj.

vine·yard /ˈvinyərd/ ▶ n. a plantation of grapevines producing grapes used in winemaking.

vin·tage /ˈvintij/ ▶ n. **1** the year or place in which wine was produced. **2** a wine of high quality made from the crop of a single identified district in a good year. **3** the harvesting of grapes for winemaking. **4** the grapes or wine of a particular season. **5** the time that something was produced. ▶ adj. **1** referring to vintage wine. **2** referring to something from the past of high quality.

SYNONYMS ▶ adj. **1 high-quality**, quality, choice, select, superior. **2 classic**, ageless, timeless, old, antique, historic.

vint·ner /ˈvintnər/ ▶ n. a wine merchant.

vi·nyl /ˈvīnl/ ▶ n. a type of strong flexible plastic, used in making floor coverings, paints, and phonograph records.

vi·ol /ˈvīəl/ ▶ n. an early instrument like a violin, but with six strings.

vi·o·la[1] /vēˈōlə, vī-/ ▶ n. an instrument of the violin family, larger than the violin and tuned to a lower pitch.

vi·o·la[2] /ˈvīələ, vīˈōlə/ ▶ n. a plant of a group that includes pansies and violets.

vi·o·late /ˈvīəˌlāt/ ▶ v. (**violates**, **violating**, **violated**) **1** break a rule or formal agreement. **2** treat something with disrespect.

SYNONYMS **1 contravene**, breach, infringe, break, transgress, disobey, defy, flout, disregard, ignore. **2 desecrate**, profane, defile, degrade, debase, damage, vandalize, deface, destroy. ANTONYMS respect.

vi·o·la·tion /ˌvīəˈlāsHən/ ▶ n. **1** the breaking of a rule or agreement. **2** disrespectful treatment of something.

SYNONYMS **1 contravention**, breach, infringement, transgression, defiance, flouting, disregard. **2 desecration**, defilement, damage, vandalism, destruction.

vi·o·lence /ˈvī(ə)ləns/ ▶ n. **1** actions using physical force and intended to hurt or kill someone or to cause damage. **2** an unpleasant or destructive natural force. **3** strength of emotion.

SYNONYMS **1 brutality**, savagery, cruelty, barbarity. **2 force**, power, strength, might, ferocity, intensity, vehemence.

vi·o·lent /ˈvī(ə)lənt/ ▶ adj. **1** using or involving violence. **2** very forceful or powerful.

SYNONYMS **1 brutal**, vicious, savage, rough, aggressive, threatening, fierce, ferocious, bloodthirsty. **2 powerful**, forceful, hard, sharp, smart, strong, vigorous, mighty, hefty. **3 intense**, extreme, strong, powerful, fierce, unbridled, uncontrollable, ungovernable, consuming, passionate. ANTONYMS gentle, mild.

■ **vi·o·lent·ly** adv.

vi·o·let /ˈvī(ə)lət/ ▶ n. **1** a small plant with purple or blue flowers. **2** a bluish-purple color.

vi·o·lin /ˌvīəˈlin/ ▶ n. a musical instrument with four strings, that you play with a bow. ■ **vi·o·lin·ist** n.

vi·o·lon·cel·lo /ˌvīələnˈcHelō, ˌvē-/ formal ⇒ CELLO.

VIP ▶ n. a very important person.

vi·per /ˈvīpər/ ▶ n. a poisonous snake with large fangs and a patterned body.

vi·ra·go /vəˈrägō, -ˈrā-/ ▶ n. (plural **viragos** or **viragoes**) a domineering, violent, or bad-tempered woman.

vi·ral /ˈvīrəl/ ▶ adj. having to do with a virus or viruses.

vir·gin /ˈvərjən/ ▶ n. **1** a person who has never had sex. **2** (**the Virgin**) the Virgin Mary, mother of Jesus. ▶ adj. **1** having had no sexual experience. **2** not yet used, touched, or spoiled: *virgin forest*. **3** (of olive oil) made from the first pressing of olives. ■ **vir·gin·al** adj. **vir·gin·i·ty** /vərˈjinətē/ n.

Vir·go /ˈvərgō/ ▶ n. a sign of the zodiac (the Virgin), August 23–September 22.

vir·ile /ˈvirəl/ ▶ adj. (of a man) having strength, energy, and a strong sex drive.

SYNONYMS **manly**, masculine, male; strong, tough, vigorous, robust, muscly, brawny; red-blooded, fertile; informal macho. ANTONYMS effeminate.

■ **vi·ril·i·ty** /vəˈrilitē/ n.

vir·tu·al /ˈvərcHo͞oəl/ ▶ adj. **1** almost or nearly the thing described, but not completely. **2** not existing in reality but made by computer software to appear to do so.

SYNONYMS **effective**, near (enough), essential, practical, to all intents and purposes, in all but name, implied, unacknowledged.

□ **virtual reality** a system in which images that look like real objects are created by computer.

vir·tu·al·ly /ˈvərcHə(wə)lē/ ▶ adv. **1** nearly; almost. **2** Computing by means of virtual reality techniques.

SYNONYMS **effectively**, all but, more or less, practically, almost, nearly, close to, verging on, just about, as good as, essentially, to all intents and purposes.

vir·tue /ˈvərcHo͞o/ ▶ n. **1** behavior showing high moral standards. **2** a good or useful quality. **3** old use virginity or chastity.

SYNONYMS **1 goodness**, righteousness, morality, integrity, dignity, rectitude, honor, probity. **2 good point**, good quality, strong point, asset, forte, attribute, strength, merit, advantage, benefit; informal plus. ANTONYMS vice.

□ **by virtue of** because or as a result of.

vir·tu·o·so /ˌvərcHo͞oˈōsō/ ▶ n. (plural **virtuosi** /-sē/ or **virtuosos**) a person highly skilled in music or another art. ■ **vir·tu·os·i·ty** /-ˈäsitē/ n.

vir·tu·ous /ˈvərcHəwəs/ ▶ adj. **1** having high moral standards. **2** old use chaste.

SYNONYMS **righteous**, good, moral, ethical, upright, upstanding, high-minded, principled, exemplary; irreproachable, honest, honorable, reputable, decent, respectable, worthy; pure, whiter than white, saintly, angelic; informal squeaky clean.

■ **vir·tu·ous·ly** adv.

vir·u·lent /'vir(y)ələnt/ ▶ adj. **1** (of a disease or poison) very harmful in its effects. **2** bitterly hostile or critical. ■ **vir·u·lence** n. **vir·u·lent·ly** adv.

vi·rus /'vīrəs/ ▶ n. **1** a submicroscopic organism that can cause disease. **2** an infection or disease caused by a virus. **3** a piece of code introduced secretly into a computer system in order to damage or destroy data.

vi·sa /'vēzə/ ▶ n. a note on your passport indicating that you are allowed to enter, leave, or stay in a country.

vis·age /'vizij/ ▶ n. literary a person's facial features or expression.

vis-à-vis /'vēz ə 'vē/ ▶ prep. in relation to.

vis·cer·a /'visərə/ ▶ pl.n. the internal organs of the body.

vis·cer·al /'vis(ə)rəl/ ▶ adj. **1** relating to deep inward feelings rather than to the intellect. **2** relating to the viscera. ■ **vis·cer·al·ly** adv.

vis·cose /'vis,kōs, -,kōz/ ▶ n. a smooth synthetic fabric made from cellulose.

vis·cos·i·ty /,vi'skäsitē/ ▶ n. the state of being viscous.

vis·count /'vī,kount/ ▶ n. a British nobleman ranking above a baron and below an earl. ■ **vis·count·ess** n.

vis·cous /'viskəs/ ▶ adj. having a thick, sticky consistency between solid and liquid.

vise /vīs/ ▶ n. a metal tool with movable jaws that are used to hold an object firmly in place while work is done on it.

vis·i·bil·i·ty /,vizə'bilitē/ ▶ n. **1** the state of being able to see or be seen. **2** the distance you can see, as determined by light and weather conditions.

vis·i·ble /'vizəbəl/ ▶ adj. able to be seen or noticed.

SYNONYMS **observable**, perceptible, noticeable, detectable, discernible, in sight, in view, on display, evident, apparent, manifest, plain.

■ **vis·i·bly** adv.

vi·sion /'vizHən/ ▶ n. **1** the ability to see. **2** the ability to think about the future with imagination or wisdom. **3** an experience of seeing something in a dream, trance, etc. **4** the images seen on a television screen. **5** a person or sight of unusual beauty.

SYNONYMS **1 eyesight**, sight, observation, eyes, view, perspective. **2 apparition**, specter, phantom, ghost, wraith, manifestation, hallucination, illusion, mirage. **3 dream**, reverie, plan, hope, fantasy, pipe dream. **4 imagination**, creativity, inventiveness, inspiration, intuition, perception, insight.

vi·sion·ar·y /'vizHə,nerē/ ▶ adj. **1** thinking about the future with imagination or wisdom. **2** relating to supernatural or dreamlike visions. ▶ n. (plural **visionaries**) a person with imaginative and original ideas about the future.

vis·it /'vizit/ ▶ v. (**visits**, **visiting**, **visited**) **1** go to spend time with a person or in a place. **2** view a website or web page. **3** (**visit with**) chat with someone. **4** (**visit something on**) literary cause something harmful or unpleasant to affect someone. ▶ n. an act of visiting.

SYNONYMS ▶ v. **call on**, go to see, look in on, stay with, stop by, drop by; informal pop/drop in on, look up. ▶ n. **(social) call**, stay, stopover, trip, vacation; literary sojourn.

vis·it·a·tion /,vizə'tāsHən/ ▶ n. **1** an official or formal visit. **2** the appearance of a god, goddess, etc. **3** a disaster or difficulty seen as a punishment from God.

vis·i·tor /'vizitər/ ▶ n. **1** a person visiting a person or place. **2** a bird that migrates to a particular area for only part of the year.

SYNONYMS **1 guest**, caller, company. **2 tourist**, traveler, daytripper, vacationer, sightseer.

vi·sor /'vīzər/ (or **vizor**) ▶ n. **1** a movable part of a helmet that can be pulled down to cover the face. **2** a screen for protecting the eyes from light.

vis·ta /'vistə/ ▶ n. a pleasing view.

SYNONYMS **view**, scene, prospect, panorama, sight, scenery, landscape.

vis·u·al /'vizHo͞oəl/ ▶ adj. relating to seeing or sight. ▶ n. a picture, piece of film, or display used to illustrate or accompany something.

SYNONYMS ▶ adj. **1 optical**, ocular. **2 visible**, observable, perceptible, discernible.

■ **vis·u·al·ly** adv.

vis·u·al·ize /'vizH(ə)wə,līz/ ▶ v. (**visualizes**, **visualizing**, **visualized**) form an image of something in the mind.

SYNONYMS **envisage**, conjure up, picture, call to mind, see, imagine, dream up.

■ **vis·u·al·i·za·tion** /,vizH(ə)wələ'zāsHən/ n.

vi·tal /'vītl/ ▶ adj. **1** absolutely necessary. **2** essential for life. **3** full of energy. ▶ n. (**vitals**) the body's important internal organs.

SYNONYMS ▶ adj. **1 essential**, critical, crucial, indispensable, all-important, imperative, mandatory, high-priority, key, life-and-death. **2 lively**, energetic, active, sprightly, spirited, vivacious, exuberant, dynamic, vigorous; informal full of beans. ANTONYMS unimportant.

□ **vital statistics 1** quantitative data concerning a population, such as the number of births, marriages, and deaths. **2** informal the measurements of a woman's bust, waist, and hips. ■ **vi·tal·ly** adv.

vi·tal·i·ty /vī'talitē/ ▶ n. the state of being strong and active.

SYNONYMS **life**, energy, spirit, vivacity, exuberance, dynamism, vigor, passion, drive; informal get-up-and-go.

vi·tal·ize /'vītl,īz/ ▶ v. (**vitalizes**, **vitalizing**, **vitalized**) give strength and energy to.

vi·ta·min /'vītəmən/ ▶ n. any of a group of natural substances that are present in many foods and are essential for normal nutrition.

vi·ti·ate /'visHē,āt/ ▶ v. (**vitiates**, **vitiating**, **vitiated**) formal make something less good or effective.

vit·i·cul·ture /'viti,kəlcHər/ ▶ n. the cultivation of grapevines.

vit·re·ous /'vitrēəs/ ▶ adj. containing or like glass. □ **vitreous humor** the transparent jellylike tissue that fills the eyeball.

vit·ri·fy /'vitrə,fī/ ▶ v. (**vitrifies**, **vitrifying**, **vitrified**) convert into glass or a glasslike substance by exposure to heat.

vit·ri·ol /ˈvitrēəl, -ˌôl/ ▶ **n. 1** very cruel or bitter remarks. **2** old use sulfuric acid. ■ **vit·ri·ol·ic** /ˌvitrēˈälik/ **adj.**

vi·tu·per·a·tion /vəˌt(y)o͞opəˈrāshən, vī-/ ▶ **n.** bitter and abusive language. ■ **vi·tu·per·a·tive** /vəˈt(y)o͞opəˌrātiv, vī-, -p(ə)rətiv/ **adj.**

vi·va /ˈvēvə/ ▶ **exclam.** long live!

vi·va·cious /vəˈvāshəs, vī-/ ▶ **adj.** attractively lively.

> SYNONYMS **lively**, spirited, bubbly, ebullient, buoyant, merry, happy, jolly, full of fun, cheery, perky, sunny, breezy, enthusiastic, vibrant, dynamic; informal peppy, bouncy, upbeat, chirpy. ANTONYMS dull.

■ **vi·va·cious·ly adv. vi·vac·i·ty** /vəˈvasitē, vī-/ **n.**

vi·var·i·um /vīˈve(ə)rēəm/ ▶ **n.** (plural **vivaria** /-rēə/) a place for keeping animals in natural conditions for study or as pets.

vi·va vo·ce /ˌvēvə ˈvōchā, ˌvīvə ˈvōsē/ ▶ **adj.** (especially of an examination) oral rather than written. ▶ **adv.** orally rather than in writing.

viv·id /ˈvivid/ ▶ **adj. 1** producing powerful feelings or strong, clear images in the mind. **2** (of a color) very deep or bright.

> SYNONYMS **1 bright**, colorful, brilliant, radiant, vibrant, strong, bold, deep, intense, rich, warm. **2 graphic**, realistic, lifelike, faithful, authentic, striking, evocative, arresting, colorful, dramatic, memorable, powerful, stirring, moving, haunting. ANTONYMS dull, vague.

■ **viv·id·ly adv. viv·id·ness n.**

viv·i·fy /ˈvivəˌfī/ ▶ **v.** (**vivifies**, **vivifying**, **vivified**) formal make more lively or interesting; enliven.

vi·vip·a·rous /vīˈvip(ə)rəs, vi-/ ▶ **adj.** (of an animal) giving birth to live young.

viv·i·sec·tion /ˌvivəˈsekshən/ ▶ **n.** the performance of operations on live animals for scientific research.

vix·en /ˈviksən/ ▶ **n. 1** a female fox. **2** a spirited or hot-tempered woman.

viz. /viz/ ▶ **adv.** namely; in other words.

vi·zier /vəˈzi(ə)r/ ▶ **n.** historical a high official in some Muslim countries.

vi·zor = **VISOR**.

V-neck ▶ **n.** a neckline having straight sides meeting at a point to form a V-shape. ■ **V-necked adj.**

vo·cab·u·lar·y /vōˈkabyəˌlerē, və-/ ▶ **n.** (plural **vocabularies**) **1** all the words used in a particular language or activity. **2** all the words known to a person. **3** a list of words and their meanings, provided with a piece of technical or foreign writing.

vo·cal /ˈvōkəl/ ▶ **adj. 1** relating to the human voice. **2** expressing opinions or feelings freely or loudly. **3** (of music) consisting of or including singing. ▶ **n.** (also **vocals**) a part of a piece of music that is sung.

> SYNONYMS ▶ **adj. 1 spoken**, said, voiced, uttered, articulated, oral. **2 vociferous**, outspoken, forthright, plain-spoken, blunt, frank, candid, passionate, vehement, vigorous.

□ **vocal cords** strips of muscle in the throat that vibrate to produce the voice. ■ **vo·cal·ly adv.**

vo·cal·ist /ˈvōkəlist/ ▶ **n.** a singer.

vo·cal·ize /ˈvōkəˌlīz/ ▶ **v.** (**vocalizes**, **vocalizing**, **vocalized**) **1** make a sound or say a word. **2** express something with words. ■ **vo·cal·i·za·tion** /ˌvōkələˈzāshən/ **n.**

vo·ca·tion /vōˈkāshən/ ▶ **n. 1** a strong feeling that you ought to pursue a particular career or occupation. **2** a person's career or occupation.

> SYNONYMS **calling**, life's work, mission, purpose, profession, occupation, career, job, employment, trade, craft, line (of work).

■ **vo·ca·tion·al adj.**

voc·a·tive /ˈväkətiv/ ▶ **n.** Grammar the case of nouns, pronouns, and adjectives used in addressing a person or thing.

vo·cif·er·ous /vəˈsifərəs, vō-/ ▶ **adj.** expressing opinions in a loud and forceful way. ■ **vo·cif·er·ous·ly adv.**

vod·ka /ˈvädkə/ ▶ **n.** a clear alcoholic spirit, originally from Russia.

vogue /vōg/ ▶ **n.** the fashion or style current at a particular time.

> SYNONYMS **fashion**, trend, fad, fancy, craze, rage, enthusiasm, passion.

■ **vogu·ish adj.**

voice /vois/ ▶ **n. 1** the sound produced in a person's larynx and uttered through the mouth, as speech or song. **2** the ability to speak or sing. **3** a vocal part in a piece of music. **4** Grammar a form of a verb showing the relation of the subject to the action. ▶ **v.** (**voices**, **voicing**, **voiced**) express something in words.

> SYNONYMS ▶ **n. opinion**, view, feeling, wish, desire, vote. ▶ **v. express**, communicate, declare, state, vent, utter, say, speak, articulate, air; informal come out with.

□ **voice box** the larynx. **voice-over** a piece of speech in a movie or broadcast that is spoken by a person who is not seen on the screen. ■ **voice·less adj.**

voice·mail /ˈvoisˌmāl/ ▶ **n.** an electronic system that can store messages from telephone callers.

void /void/ ▶ **adj. 1** not valid or legally binding. **2** completely empty. **3** (**void of**) free from; lacking. ▶ **n.** a completely empty space. ▶ **v. 1** empty waste matter from the bladder or bowels. **2** declare to be not valid or legally binding.

> SYNONYMS ▶ **adj. 1 empty**, vacant, blank, bare, clear, free. **2 invalid**, null (and void), ineffective, worthless. ANTONYMS full, valid. ▶ **n. vacuum**, emptiness, nothingness, blankness, (empty) space, gap, cavity, chasm, gulf.

voile /voil/ ▶ **n.** a thin, semitransparent fabric.

vol·a·tile /ˈvälətl/ ▶ **adj. 1** liable to change rapidly and unpredictably. **2** (of a substance) easily evaporated at normal temperatures.

> SYNONYMS **1 unpredictable**, temperamental, capricious, fickle, impulsive, emotional, excitable, turbulent, erratic, unstable. **2** *a volatile situation* **tense**, strained, fraught, uneasy, uncomfortable, charged, explosive, inflammatory, turbulent. ANTONYMS stable.

■ **vol·a·til·i·ty** /ˌväləˈtilitē/ **n.**

vol-au-vent /ˌvôl ō ˈvän/ ▶ **n.** a small round case of puff pastry filled with a savory mixture.

vol·ca·no /välˈkānō, vôl-/ ▶ **n.** (plural **volcanoes** or **volcanos**) a mountain with an opening through which lava, rock, and gas are forced from the earth's crust. ■ **vol·can·ic** /välˈkanik, vôl-/ **adj.**

vole /vōl/ ▶ **n.** a small mouselike rodent.

vo·li·tion /vəˈlishən, vō-/ ▶ **n.** a person's will or power of independent action.

vol·ley /ˈvälē/ ▶ **n.** (plural **volleys**) **1** a number of bullets, arrows, etc., fired at one time. **2** a series of questions, insults, etc., directed rapidly at someone. **3** (in sports) an act of hitting the ball before it touches the ground. ▶ **v.** (**volleys**, **volleying**, **volleyed**) hit the ball before it touches the ground.

> SYNONYMS ▶ **n. barrage**, cannonade, battery, bombardment, salvo, burst, storm, hail, shower, deluge, torrent.

vol·ley·ball /ˈväleˌbôl/ ▶ **n.** a team game in which a ball is hit by hand over a net and must be kept from touching the ground.

volt /vōlt/ ▶ **n.** the basic unit of electric potential.

volt·age /ˈvōltij/ ▶ **n.** an electrical force expressed in volts.

volte-face /ˌvält(ə) ˈfäs, ˌvōlt(ə), ˌvôlt(ə)/ ▶ **n.** an abrupt and complete change of attitude or policy.

vol·u·ble /ˈvälyəbəl/ ▶ **adj.** talking easily and at length. ■ **vol·u·bil·i·ty** /ˌvälyəˈbilətē/ **n.** **vol·u·bly** **adv.**

vol·ume /ˈvälyəm, -ˌyo͞om/ ▶ **n.** **1** the amount of space occupied by something or enclosed within a container. **2** the amount or quantity of something. **3** degree of loudness. **4** a book, especially one forming part of a larger work or series.

> SYNONYMS **1 book**, publication, tome, work, title. **2 capacity**, mass, bulk, extent, size, dimensions. **3 quantity**, amount, mass, bulk, measure. **4 loudness**, sound, amplification.

vo·lu·mi·nous /vəˈlo͞omənəs/ ▶ **adj.** **1** (of clothing) loose and full. **2** (of writing) very lengthy.

vol·un·tar·i·ly /ˌvälənˈte(ə)rəlē, ˈvälənˌter-/ ▶ **adv.** of your own free will: *they agreed to leave the country voluntarily.*

> SYNONYMS **of your own free will**, of your own volition, by choice, by preference, spontaneously, willingly, readily, freely.

vol·un·tar·y /ˈvälənˌterē/ ▶ **adj.** **1** done or acting of your own free will. **2** working or done without payment. ▶ **n.** (plural **voluntaries**) an organ solo played before, during, or after a church service.

> SYNONYMS ▶ **adj. 1 optional**, discretionary, at your discretion, elective, noncompulsory. **2 unpaid**, unsalaried, for free, honorary. ANTONYMS compulsory.

vol·un·teer /ˌvälənˈtir/ ▶ **n.** **1** a person who freely offers to do something. **2** a person who does work without being paid. **3** a person who freely joins the armed forces. ▶ **v.** (**volunteers**, **volunteering**, **volunteered**) **1** freely offer to do something. **2** say or suggest something without being asked.

> SYNONYMS ▶ **v. 1 offer**, tender, proffer, put forward, put up, venture. **2 offer your services**, present yourself, make yourself available, come forward.

vo·lup·tu·ar·y /vəˈləpcHo͞oˌerē/ ▶ **n.** (plural **voluptuaries**) a person who loves luxury and pleasure.

vo·lup·tu·ous /vəˈləpcHəwəs/ ▶ **adj.** **1** (of a woman) curvaceous and physically attractive. **2** giving sensual pleasure. ■ **vo·lup·tu·ous·ly** **adv.**

vom·it /ˈvämət/ ▶ **v.** (**vomits**, **vomiting**, **vomited**) **1** bring up food from the stomach through the mouth. **2** send out in an uncontrolled stream. ▶ **n.** food vomited from the stomach.

> SYNONYMS ▶ **v. be sick**, spew, heave, retch, gag; informal throw up, puke, barf.

voo·doo /ˈvo͞oˌdo͞o/ ▶ **n.** a religious cult practiced mainly in the Caribbean and involving sorcery and possession by spirits.

vo·ra·cious /vəˈrāsHəs/ ▶ **adj.** **1** wanting or eating great quantities of food. **2** doing something eagerly and enthusiastically. ■ **vo·ra·cious·ly** **adv.** **vo·rac·i·ty** /-ˈrasitē/ **n.**

vor·tex /ˈvôrˌteks/ ▶ **n.** (plural **vortexes** or **vortices** /-təˌsēz/) a whirling mass of water or air.

vo·ta·ry /ˈvōtərē/ ▶ **n.** (plural **votaries**) **1** a person who has dedicated themselves to God or religious service. **2** a devoted follower or supporter.

vote /vōt/ ▶ **n.** **1** a formal choice made between two or more candidates or courses of action. **2** (**the vote**) the right to take part in an election. ▶ **v.** (**votes**, **voting**, **voted**) give or register a vote.

> SYNONYMS ▶ **n. 1 ballot**, poll, election, referendum, plebiscite, show of hands. **2** (**the vote**) **suffrage**, franchise, voting rights.

■ **vot·er** **n.**

vo·tive /ˈvōtiv/ ▶ **adj.** offered to a god as a sign of thanks.

vouch /voucH/ ▶ **v.** (**vouch for**) **1** state that something is true or accurate. **2** state that someone is who they claim to be, or that they are of good character.

vouch·er /ˈvoucHər/ ▶ **n.** a piece of paper that entitles you to a discount, or that may be exchanged for goods or services.

> SYNONYMS **coupon**, token, ticket, pass, chit, slip, stub.

vouch·safe /voucHˈsāf, ˈvoucHˌsāf/ ▶ **v.** (**vouchsafes**, **vouchsafing**, **vouchsafed**) formal give or say in a gracious or superior way.

vow /vou/ ▶ **n.** a solemn promise. ▶ **v.** solemnly promise to do something.

> SYNONYMS ▶ **n. promise**, pledge, oath, bond, covenant, commitment, word (of honor). ▶ **v. promise**, pledge, swear, undertake, make a commitment, give your word, guarantee.

vow·el /ˈvou(ə)l/ ▶ **n.** a letter of the alphabet representing a sound in which the mouth is open and the tongue is not touching the top of the mouth, the teeth, or the lips (in English *a*, *e*, *i*, *o*, and *u*).

vox pop·u·li /ˈväks ˈpäpyəˌlī, -ˌlē/ ▶ **n.** the opinions or beliefs of the majority.

voy·age /ˈvoi-ij/ ▶ **n.** a long journey by sea or in space. ▶ **v.** (**voyages**, **voyaging**, **voyaged**) go on a voyage.

> SYNONYMS ▶ **n. journey**, trip, cruise, passage, sail, crossing, expedition, odyssey.

■ **voy·ag·er** **n.**

vo·yeur /voiˈyər, vwä-/ ▶ **n.** **1** a person who gains sexual pleasure from watching other people when they are naked or having sex. **2** a person who enjoys seeing the pain or distress of other people. ■ **vo·yeur·ism** /ˈvoiyəˌrizəm, voiˈyərˌizəm, vwäˈyər-/ **n.** **voy·eur·is·tic** /ˌvoiyəˈristik, ˌvwäyə-/ **adj.**

VP ▶ **abbr.** vice president.

vs. ▶ **abbr.** versus.

vul·can·ized /ˈvəlkəˌnīzd/ ▶ **adj.** (of rubber) hardened by being treated with sulfur at a high temperature.

vul·gar /ˈvəlgər/ ▶ **adj.** **1** lacking sophistication or good taste. **2** referring to sex or bodily functions in an offensive or inappropriate way.

SYNONYMS **1** *vulgar decor* **tasteless**, crass, tawdry, ostentatious, flamboyant, showy, gaudy, garish; informal flashy, tacky. **2** *vulgar online videos* **obscene**, smutty, indecent, crude, dirty, filthy, naughty, coarse, risqué; informal blue. **3** **impolite**, ill-mannered, boorish, uncouth, unsophisticated, unrefined. ANTONYMS tasteful.

■ **vul·gar·i·ty** /ˌvəlˈgaritē/ **n.** **vul·gar·ly** **adv.**

vul·gar·ize /ˈvəlgəˌrīz/ ▶ **v.** (**vulgarizes**, **vulgarizing**, **vulgarized**) spoil something by making it less refined or exclusive.

vul·ner·a·bil·i·ty /ˌvəln(ə)rəˈbilitē/ ▶ **n.** the quality of being vulnerable; likely to be attacked or harmed.

vul·ner·a·ble /ˈvəln(ə)rəbəl/ ▶ **adj.** able to be attacked or harmed.

SYNONYMS **1** **in danger**, in peril, in jeopardy, at risk, unprotected, undefended, unguarded, open to attack, exposed, defenseless, an easy target. **2** **helpless**, weak, sensitive, thin-skinned. ANTONYMS invulnerable.

■ **vul·ner·a·bly** **adv.**

vul·pine /ˈvəlˌpīn/ ▶ **adj.** having to do with foxes, or like a fox.

vul·ture /ˈvəlCHər/ ▶ **n.** a large bird of prey that feeds mainly on dead animals.

vul·va /ˈvəlvə/ ▶ **n.** the female external genitals.

vy·ing /ˈvī-iNG/ present participle of **VIE**.

Ww

W (or **w**) ▶ **n.** (plural **Ws** or **W's**) the twenty-third letter of the alphabet. ▶ **abbr.** **1** (**W**) watt(s). **2** (**W**) West or Western.

wack·o /ˈwakō/ ▶ **adj.** informal mad; insane.

wack·y /ˈwakē/ (or **whacky**) ▶ **adj.** (**wackier**, **wackiest**) informal funny or amusing in a slightly odd way.

wad /wäd/ ▶ **n.** **1** a lump or bundle of a soft material. **2** a bundle of paper or banknotes. ▶ **v.** (**wads**, **wadding**, **wadded**) **1** press a soft material into a wad. **2** line or fill with soft material.

wad·dle /ˈwädl/ ▶ **v.** (**waddles**, **waddling**, **waddled**) walk with short steps and a clumsy swaying motion. ▶ **n.** a waddling way of walking.

SYNONYMS ▶ **v.** **toddle**, totter, wobble, shuffle.

wade /wād/ ▶ **v.** (**wades**, **wading**, **waded**) **1** walk through water or mud. **2** (**wade through**) read or deal with something that is boring or takes a long time. **3** (**wade in** or **into**) informal attack or intervene in a forceful way.

wad·er /ˈwādər/ ▶ **n.** **1** a long-legged bird that feeds in shallow water. **2** (**waders**) high waterproof boots.

wa·fer /ˈwāfər/ ▶ **n.** **1** a very thin, light, sweet biscuit. **2** a thin disc of unleavened bread used in the Christian service of Holy Communion.

waf·fle[1] /ˈwäfəl, ˈwô-/ ▶ **n.** a small, crisp batter cake, eaten hot with butter or syrup.

waf·fle[2] informal ▶ **v.** (**waffles**, **waffling**, **waffled**) speak or write at length without saying anything interesting or important, especially to be evasive or misleading. ▶ **n.** lengthy talk or writing that does not say anything interesting or important.

waft /wäft, waft/ ▶ **v.** pass easily or gently through the air. ▶ **n.** a gentle movement of air.

wag /wag/ ▶ **v.** (**wags**, **wagging**, **wagged**) move rapidly to and fro. ▶ **n.** **1** a wagging movement. **2** informal a person who likes making jokes.

SYNONYMS ▶ **v.** **1** **swing**, swish, switch, sway, shake; informal waggle. **2** **shake**, wave, wiggle, flourish, brandish.

■ **wag·gish** **adj.**

wage /wāj/ ▶ **n.** (also **wages**) a fixed regular payment for work. ▶ **v.** (**wages**, **waging**, **waged**) carry on a war or campaign.

SYNONYMS ▶ **n.** **pay**, salary, stipend, fee, remuneration, income, earnings. ▶ **v.** **engage in**, carry on, conduct, execute, pursue, prosecute, proceed with.

wa·ger /ˈwājər/ formal ⇨ **BET**.

wag·gle /ˈwagəl/ ▶ **v.** (**waggles**, **waggling**, **waggled**) move with short, quick movements from side to side or up and down.

wag·on /ˈwagən/ ▶ **n.** a vehicle, especially a horse-drawn one, for transporting goods. ◻ **on the wagon** informal not drinking alcohol.

wag·tail /ˈwagˌtāl/ ▶ **n.** a slender bird with a long tail that it frequently wags up and down.

waif /wāf/ ▶ **n.** **1** a poor, helpless person, especially a child. **2** a person who is thin and pale.

wail /wāl/ ▶ **n.** **1** a long high-pitched cry of pain, grief, or anger. **2** a sound resembling this. ▶ **v.** make a wail.

SYNONYMS **howl**, cry, bawl, moan, groan, yowl, whine, lament.

wain /wān/ ▶ **n.** old use a wagon or cart.

wain·scot /ˈwānskət, -ˌskät, -skōt/ ▶ **n.** an area of wooden paneling on the lower part of the walls of a room.

waist /wāst/ ▶ **n.** **1** the part of the human body below the ribs and above the hips. **2** a narrow part in the middle of something.

waist·band /ˈwās(t)ˌband/ ▶ **n.** a strip of cloth forming the waist of a skirt or pair of trousers.

waist·line /ˈwās(t)ˌlīn/ ▶ **n.** the measurement around a person's body at the waist.

wait /wāt/ ▶ **v.** **1** stay in a particular place or delay doing anything until a particular time or event. **2** be delayed or postponed. **3** (**wait on**) act as an attendant to. **4** serve people at a meal or in a restaurant. ▶ **n.** a period of waiting.

SYNONYMS ▶ **v.** **1** *we waited in the airport* **stay** (**put**), remain, rest, stop, linger, loiter; informal stick around; old use tarry. **2** *she had to wait until her bags arrived* **stand by**, hold back, bide your time, mark time, kill time, waste time, twiddle your thumbs; informal hold on, hang around, sit tight. ▶ **n.** **delay**, holdup, interval, interlude, pause, break, suspension, stoppage, halt, interruption, lull, gap.

wait·er /ˈwātər/ (or **waitress** /ˈwātris/) ▶ **n.** a person whose job is to serve customers at their tables in a restaurant.

SYNONYMS **server**, waitperson, waitron, steward, stewardess, attendant, butler, servant.

wait·per·son /ˈwātˌpərsən/ ▶ **n.** a waiter or waitress.

waive /wāv/ ▶ **v.** (**waives**, **waiving**, **waived**) choose not to insist on a claim or right.

SYNONYMS **1** **give up**, abandon, renounce, relinquish, surrender, sacrifice, turn down. **2** **disregard**, ignore, overlook, set aside, forgo.

waiv·er /ˈwāvər/ ▶ **n.** an instance of waiving a right or claim, or a document recording this.

wake[1] /wāk/ ▶ **v.** (**wakes**, **waking**, **woke** /wōk/; past participle **woken** /ˈwōkən/) **1** (often **wake up**) stop sleeping. **2** bring to life, or make more alert.

3 (**wake up to**) become aware of. ▶ n. **1** a party held after a funeral. **2** a gathering held beside the body of someone who has died.

SYNONYMS ▶ v. **awake**, waken, wake up, stir, come to, come round, rouse. ▶ n. **vigil**, watch, funeral.

wake² ▶ n. a trail of disturbed water or air left by a ship or aircraft.

SYNONYMS **backwash**, slipstream, trail, path, track.

□ **in the wake of** following as a result of.

wake·ful /ˈwākfəl/ ▶ adj. **1** not sleeping. **2** alert and aware of possible dangers. ■ **wake·ful·ness** n.

wak·en /ˈwākən/ ▶ v. wake from sleep.

walk /wôk/ ▶ v. **1** move fairly slowly using the legs. **2** travel over a route or area on foot. **3** accompany someone on foot. **4** take a dog out for exercise. ▶ n. **1** a journey on foot. **2** a fairly slow rate of movement on foot. **3** a person's way of walking. **4** a path for walking.

SYNONYMS ▶ v. **1 stroll**, saunter, amble, trudge, plod, hike, tramp, trek, march, stride, troop, wander, ramble, promenade, traipse; informal mosey, hoof it. **2 accompany**, escort, guide, show, see, take, usher. ▶ n. **1 ramble**, hike, tramp, march, stroll, promenade, constitutional, turn. **2 gait**, step, stride, tread. **3 path**, pathway, footpath, track, walkway, promenade, footway, pavement, trail, towpath.

□ **walk-in** (of a storage area) large enough to walk into. **walking papers** informal notice of dismissal from a job. **walk off with** (or **away with**) informal **1** steal. **2** win. **walking stick** a stick used for support when walking. **walk of life** the position in society that someone holds.

walk·er /ˈwôkər/ ▶ n. **1** a person who walks, especially for exercise or enjoyment. **2** a frame used by disabled or infirm people for support while walking.

SYNONYMS **pedestrian**, hiker, stroller, rambler, trekker.

walk·ie-talk·ie /ˈwôkē ˈtôkē/ ▶ n. a portable two-way radio.

walk·out /ˈwôkˌout/ ▶ n. a sudden angry departure as a protest or strike.

walk·o·ver /ˈwôkˌōvər/ ▶ n. an easy victory.

walk·way /ˈwôkˌwā/ ▶ n. a raised passageway or a wide path.

wall /wôl/ ▶ n. **1** a continuous upright structure forming a side of a building or room, or enclosing or dividing an area of land. **2** a barrier. **3** the outer layer or lining of an organ or cavity in the body. ▶ v. enclose or block with walls.

SYNONYMS ▶ n. **fortification**, rampart, barricade, bulwark, partition.

□ **go to the wall** informal (of a business) fail. **off the wall** informal unconventional.

wal·la·by /ˈwäləbē/ ▶ n. (plural **wallabies**) an Australian animal like a small kangaroo.

wal·let /ˈwälit, ˈwô-/ ▶ n. a small flat, folding holder for money and plastic cards.

SYNONYMS **purse**, billfold, case, pouch, pocketbook.

wall·eye /ˈwôlˌī/ ▶ n. an eye directed abnormally outward. ■ **wall·eyed** adj.

wall·flow·er /ˈwôlˌflou(-ə)r/ ▶ n. **1** a plant with sweet-smelling flowers that bloom in early spring. **2** informal a girl who has no one to dance with at a party.

wal·lop /ˈwäləp/ informal ▶ v. (**wallops**, **walloping**, **walloped**) hit very hard. ▶ n. a heavy blow.

wal·low /ˈwälō/ ▶ v. **1** roll about or lie in mud or water. **2** (of a boat or aircraft) roll from side to side. **3** (**wallow in**) indulge in. ▶ n. **1** an act of wallowing. **2** an area of mud or shallow water where animals go to wallow.

SYNONYMS ▶ v. **1 roll**, loll about, lie around, splash about. **2 luxuriate**, bask, take pleasure, take satisfaction, indulge (yourself), delight, revel, glory.

wall·pa·per /ˈwôlˌpāpər/ ▶ n. **1** paper pasted in strips over the walls of a room as decoration. **2** a background pattern or picture on a computer screen.

wal·nut /ˈwôlˌnət/ ▶ n. an edible nut with a wrinkled shell.

wal·rus /ˈwôlrəs, ˈwä-/ ▶ n. a large sea mammal with downward-pointing tusks.

waltz /wôlts/ ▶ n. a ballroom dance in triple time performed by a couple. ▶ v. **1** dance a waltz. **2** move in a casual or inconsiderate way.

waltz·er /ˈwôltsər/ ▶ n. a fairground ride in which cars are carried round a track that moves up and down.

wam·pum /ˈwämpəm/ ▶ n. historical a string of small beads made by North American Indians from shells, worn as a decorative belt or used as money.

wan /wän/ ▶ adj. **1** (of a person) pale and appearing ill or exhausted. **2** (of light) pale or weak. **3** (of a smile) lacking enthusiasm; strained.

SYNONYMS **pale**, ashen, white, gray, anemic, colorless, waxen, pasty, peaked, sickly, washed out, ghostly.

■ **wan·ly** adv.

wand /wänd/ ▶ n. a long, thin rod, especially one used in casting magic spells or performing tricks.

wan·der /ˈwändər/ ▶ v. (**wanders**, **wandering**, **wandered**) **1** move in a leisurely, casual, or aimless way. **2** move slowly away from the correct place. ▶ n. a period of wandering.

SYNONYMS ▶ v. **1 stroll**, amble, saunter, walk, ramble, meander, roam, range, drift; informal traipse, mosey. **2 stray**, depart, diverge, deviate, digress, drift, get sidetracked.

■ **wan·der·er** n.

wan·der·lust /ˈwändərˌləst/ ▶ n. a strong desire to travel.

wane /wān/ ▶ v. (**wanes**, **waning**, **waned**) **1** (of the moon) appear to decrease in size day by day. **2** become weaker.

SYNONYMS **decline**, diminish, decrease, dwindle, shrink, tail off, ebb, fade, lessen, peter out, fall off, recede, slump, weaken, wither, evaporate, die out. ANTONYMS grow.

□ **on the wane** becoming weaker.

wan·gle /ˈwaNGgəl/ ▶ v. (**wangles**, **wangling**, **wangled**) informal get something by using persuasion or a clever plan.

wan·na·be /ˈwänəbē, ˈwô-/ ▶ n. informal, disapproving a person who tries to be like someone else or to fit in with a particular group of people.

want /wänt, wônt/ ▶ **v.** **1** have a desire to possess or do. **2** (**be wanted**) (of a suspected criminal) be searched for by the police. **3** (also **want for**) lack or be short of. **4** feel sexual desire for. ▶ **n.** **1** lack or shortage. **2** poverty. **3** a desire for something.

> SYNONYMS ▶ **v.** **desire**, wish for, hope for, fancy, care for, like, long for, yearn for, crave, hanker after, hunger for, thirst for, cry out for, covet; informal have a yen for, be dying for. ▶ **n.** **1 lack**, absence, nonexistence, dearth, deficiency, inadequacy, insufficiency, paucity, shortage, scarcity. **2 need**, austerity, privation, deprivation, poverty, destitution. **3** *her wants would be taken care of* **wish**, desire, demand, longing, fancy, craving, need, requirement; informal yen.

want·ing /ˈwäntiɴɢ, wônt-/ ▶ **adj.** **1** not having something required or desired. **2** not good enough.

> SYNONYMS **deficient**, inadequate, lacking, insufficient, imperfect, flawed, unsound, substandard, inferior, second-rate.

wan·ton /ˈwäntn/ ▶ **adj.** **1** (of a cruel or violent action) deliberate and unprovoked. **2** having many sexual partners.

> SYNONYMS **deliberate**, willful, malicious, gratuitous, unprovoked, motiveless, arbitrary, unjustifiable, senseless.

■ **wan·ton·ly** **adv.**

WAP /wap/ ▶ **abbr.** Wireless Application Protocol, a means of enabling a cell phone to browse the Internet.

wap·i·ti /ˈwäpitē/ ▶ **n.** ⇨ **ELK.**

war /wôr/ ▶ **n.** **1** a state of armed conflict between different nations, states, or groups. **2** a long contest between rivals or campaign against something. ▶ **v.** (**wars**, **warring**, **warred**) be involved in a war.

> SYNONYMS ▶ **n.** **1 conflict**, warfare, combat, fighting, action, bloodshed, fight, campaign, hostilities. **2 campaign**, crusade, battle, fight, struggle. ANTONYMS peace. ▶ **v.** **fight**, battle, combat, wage war, take up arms, feud, quarrel, struggle, contend, wrangle, cross swords.

□ **be on the warpath** be very angry with someone. **war crime** an action that breaks accepted international rules of war.

war·ble /ˈwôrbəl/ ▶ **v.** (**warbles**, **warbling**, **warbled**) sing in a trilling or quavering voice.

war·bler /ˈwôrb(ə)lər/ ▶ **n.** a small songbird with a warbling song.

ward /wôrd/ ▶ **n.** **1** a room in a hospital for one or more patients. **2** a division of a city or borough that is represented by a councilor or councillors. **3** a young person looked after by a guardian appointed by their parents or a court. **4** a ridge or bar in a lock that engages with grooves on a key. ▶ **v.** (**ward someone/thing off**) prevent someone or something from harming you.

> SYNONYMS ▶ **n.** **1 room**, department, unit, area. **2 district**, constituency, division, quarter, zone, parish. **3 dependent**, charge, protégé.

war·den /ˈwôrdn/ ▶ **n.** **1** a person supervising a place or procedure. **2** the head official in a prison.

> SYNONYMS **1 guard**, prison officer, jailer, warder, keeper; informal screw. **2 superintendent**, caretaker, porter, steward, custodian, watchman, concierge, doorman, commissionaire.

ward·er /ˈwôrdər/ ▶ **n.** a guard or caretaker.

ward·robe /ˈwôrˌdrōb/ ▶ **n.** **1** a large, tall cupboard for hanging clothes in. **2** a person's entire collection of clothes. **3** the costume department of a theater or film company.

ward·room /ˈwôrdˌro͞om, -ˌro͝om/ ▶ **n.** the room on a warship where the officers eat.

ware /we(ə)r/ ▶ **n.** **1** pottery of a particular type. **2** manufactured articles. **3** (**wares**) articles offered for sale.

> SYNONYMS (**wares**) **goods**, merchandise, products, produce, stock, commodities.

ware·house /ˈwe(ə)rˌhous/ ▶ **n.** **1** a large building for storing raw materials or manufactured goods. **2** a large wholesale or retail store.

> SYNONYMS **storeroom**, depot, depository, stockroom.

war·fare /ˈwôrˌfe(ə)r/ ▶ **n.** the activity of fighting a war.

> SYNONYMS **fighting**, war, combat, conflict, action, hostilities.

war·head /ˈwôrˌhed/ ▶ **n.** the explosive head of a missile, torpedo, etc.

war·horse /ˈwôrˌhôrs/ ▶ **n.** informal a very experienced soldier, politician, etc.

war·like /ˈwôrˌlīk/ ▶ **adj.** **1** hostile. **2** intended for war.

war·lock /ˈwôrˌläk/ ▶ **n.** a man who practices witchcraft.

war·lord /ˈwôrˌlôrd/ ▶ **n.** a military commander, especially one controlling a region.

warm /wôrm/ ▶ **adj.** **1** at a fairly high temperature. **2** helping the body to stay warm. **3** enthusiastic, affectionate, or kind. **4** (of a color) containing red, yellow, or orange tones. **5** (of a scent or trail) fresh and easy to follow. ▶ **v.** **1** make or become warm. **2** (**warm to** or **towards**) become more interested in or enthusiastic about. ▶ **n.** (**the warm**) a warm place or area.

> SYNONYMS ▶ **adj.** **1** *a warm kitchen* **hot**, cozy, snug. **2** *a warm day* **balmy**, summery, sultry, hot, mild, temperate. **3** *warm water* **tepid**, lukewarm, heated. **4** *a warm sweater* **thick**, chunky, thermal, woolly. **5** *a warm welcome* **friendly**, cordial, amiable, genial, kind, pleasant, fond, welcoming, hospitable, hearty. ANTONYMS cold, chilly.

□ **warm-blooded** (of animals) keeping a constant body temperature by their body's chemical processes. **warm up** prepare for physical exertion by doing gentle stretches and exercises. **warm something up** entertain an audience before the arrival of the main act. ■ **warm·ly** **adv.**

war·mon·ger /ˈwôrˌməɴɢgər, -ˌmäɴɢ-/ ▶ **n.** a person who tries to bring about war.

warmth /wôrmᴛʜ/ ▶ **n.** **1** the quality of being warm. **2** enthusiasm, affection, or kindness. **3** strength of emotion.

> SYNONYMS **1 heat**, coziness, snugness. **2 friendliness**, amiability, geniality, cordiality, kindness, tenderness, fondness.

warn /wôrn/ ▶ **v.** **1** tell someone of a possible danger or problem. **2** advise someone not to do something. **3** (**warn someone off**) order someone to keep away.

SYNONYMS **1 inform**, notify, tell, alert, apprise, make someone aware, remind; informal tip off. **2 advise**, exhort, urge, counsel, caution.

warn·ing /'wôrniNG/ ▶ **n. 1** a statement or event that indicates a possible danger or problem. **2** advice against wrong or foolish behavior. **3** advance notice.

SYNONYMS **1** (**advance**) **notice**, alert, hint, signal, sign, alarm; informal tip-off. **2 caution**, notification, information, exhortation, advice. **3 omen**, premonition, foreboding, prophecy, prediction, forecast, token, portent, signal, sign. **4** *his sentence is a warning to other drunk drivers* **example**, deterrent, lesson, caution, message, moral. **5 reprimand**, caution, remonstrance, admonition, censure; informal dressing-down, talking-to, telling-off.

warp /wôrp/ ▶ **v. 1** make or become bent or twisted. **2** make abnormal or strange. ▶ **n. 1** a distortion or twist in shape. **2** the lengthwise threads on a loom over and under which the weft threads are passed to make cloth.

SYNONYMS ▶ **v. 1 buckle**, twist, bend, distort, deform, curve, bow, contort. **2 corrupt**, twist, pervert, deprave.

□ **warp speed** informal an extremely high speed.

war·rant /'wôrənt, 'wä-/ ▶ **n. 1** an official authorization allowing police, soldiers, etc., to make an arrest, search premises, etc. **2** a document that entitles you to receive goods, money, or services. **3** justification or authority. ▶ **v. 1** justify or make necessary. **2** officially state or guarantee.

SYNONYMS ▶ **n. 1 authorization**, order, writ, mandate, license, permit, summons. **2 voucher**, chit, slip, ticket, coupon, pass. ▶ **v. 1 justify**, deserve, vindicate, call for, sanction, permit, authorize, excuse, account for, legitimize, support, license, merit, qualify for, rate. **2 guarantee**, promise, affirm, swear, vouch, vow, pledge, undertake, declare, testify.

□ **warrant officer** a rank of military officer below the commissioned officers.

war·ran·ty /'wôrəntē, 'wä-/ ▶ **n.** (plural **warranties**) a written guarantee promising to repair or replace an article if necessary within a stated period.

SYNONYMS **guarantee**, assurance, promise, commitment, undertaking, pledge, agreement, covenant.

war·ren /'wôrən, 'wä-/ ▶ **n. 1** a network of interconnecting rabbit burrows. **2** a complex network of paths or passages.

war·ri·or /'wôrēər/ ▶ **n.** a brave or experienced soldier or fighter.

SYNONYMS **fighter**, soldier, serviceman, combatant.

war·ship /'wôr,SHip/ ▶ **n.** an armed ship designed to take part in warfare at sea.

wart /wôrt/ ▶ **n.** a small, hard growth on the skin. ■ **wart·y adj.**

wart·hog /'wôrt,häg/ ▶ **n.** an African wild pig with warty lumps on the face.

war·y /'we(ə)rē/ ▶ **adj.** (**warier**, **wariest**) cautious about possible dangers or problems.

SYNONYMS **1 cautious**, careful, circumspect, on your guard, chary, alert, on the lookout, attentive, heedful, watchful, vigilant, observant. **2** *we are wary of strangers* **suspicious**, chary, leery, careful, distrustful. ANTONYMS inattentive, trustful.

■ **war·i·ly adv. war·i·ness n.**

was /wəz/ 1st and 3rd person singular past of **BE**.

wash /wäSH, wôSH/ ▶ **v. 1** clean with water and usually soap or detergent. **2** (of water) flow freely in a particular direction. **3** (**wash over**) happen all around someone without affecting them very much. **4** informal seem convincing or genuine. ▶ **n. 1** an act of washing. **2** a quantity of clothes needing to be washed. **3** the water or air disturbed by a moving boat or aircraft. **4** a medicinal or cleansing solution. **5** a thin coating of paint.

SYNONYMS ▶ **v. 1 clean yourself**, bathe, shower. **2 clean**, cleanse, scrub, wipe, shampoo, launder, lather, douse, swab, disinfect. **3** *she washed off the blood* **remove**, expunge, eradicate, sponge off, scrub off, wipe off, rinse off. **4 splash**, lap, break, beat, surge, ripple, roll. ▶ **n. 1 laundry**, washing. **2 backwash**, wake, trail, path.

□ **be washed out 1** be postponed or canceled because of rain. **2** (**washed out**) pale and tired. **wash your hands of** take no further responsibility for. **washed up** informal no longer effective or successful.

wash·ba·sin /'wäSH,bāsən, 'wôSH-/ ▶ **n.** a basin for washing your hands and face.

wash·board /'wäSH,bôrd, 'wôSH-/ ▶ **n.** a ridged or corrugated board formerly used for scrubbing clothes when washing them.

wash·cloth /'wäSH,klôTH, 'wôSH-/ ▶ **n.** a small cloth for washing your face.

wash·er /'wäSHər, 'wôSH-/ ▶ **n. 1** a person or device that washes. **2** a small flat ring fixed between a nut and bolt.

wash·er·wom·an /'wäSHər,wo͝omən, 'wôSH-/ ▶ **n.** (plural **washerwomen**) a woman whose occupation is washing clothes.

wash·ing /'wäSHiNG, 'wôSH-/ ▶ **n.** clothes, sheets, towels, etc., that need washing or have just been washed.

wash·out /'wäSH,out, 'wôSH-/ ▶ **n.** informal a disappointing failure.

wash·room /'wäSH,ro͞om, 'wôSH-, -,ro͝om/ ▶ **n.** a room with washing and toilet facilities.

wash·stand /'wäSH,stand, 'wôSH-/ ▶ **n.** a piece of furniture formerly used to hold a bowl or basin for washing the hands and face.

was·n't /'wəzənt/ ▶ **contr.** was not.

WASP /wäsp/ (or **Wasp**) ▶ **n.** an upper- or middle-class American white Protestant, seen as a member of the most powerful social group.

wasp /wäsp/ ▶ **n.** a stinging winged insect with a black and yellow striped body. □ **wasp waist** a very narrow waist.

wasp·ish /'wäspiSH/ ▶ **adj.** sharply irritable. ■ **wasp·ish·ly adv.**

was·sail /'wäsəl, -,sāl/ old use ▶ **n.** lively festivities involving the drinking of a lot of alcohol. ▶ **v. 1** celebrate with a lot of alcohol. **2** go carol-singing at Christmas.

wast·age /'wāstij/ ▶ **n. 1** the process of wasting. **2** an amount wasted.

waste /wāst/ ▶ **v.** (**wastes**, **wasting**, **wasted**) **1** use more of something than is necessary. **2** fail to make good use of. **3** (**be wasted on**) not be appreciated by. **4** (often **waste away**) gradually become weaker and thinner. **5** (**wasted**) informal under the influence of alcohol or illegal drugs. ▶ **adj.** **1** discarded because no longer useful or required. **2** (of land) not used, cultivated, or built on. ▶ **n.** **1** an instance of wasting. **2** material that is not wanted or useful. **3** a large area of barren, uninhabited land.

SYNONYMS ▶ **v.** **1** **squander**, misspend, misuse, fritter away, throw away, lavish, dissipate; informal blow, splurge. **2** *she is wasting away* **grow weak**, grow thin, wilt, fade, deteriorate. ANTONYMS conserve. ▶ **adj.** **1** **unwanted**, excess, superfluous, left over, scrap, unusable, unprofitable. **2** **uncultivated**, barren, desert, arid, bare, desolate. ▶ **n.** **1** **misuse**, misapplication, abuse, extravagance, lavishness. **2** **refuse**, garbage, trash, rubbish, litter, debris, junk, sewage, effluent.

□ **lay waste to** completely destroy. ■ **wast·er** **n.**

waste·ful /ˈwāstfəl/ ▶ **adj.** using more of something than is necessary.

SYNONYMS **prodigal**, profligate, uneconomical, extravagant, lavish, excessive, imprudent, improvident, spendthrift. ANTONYMS frugal.

■ **waste·ful·ly** **adv.**

waste·land /ˈwāstˌland/ ▶ **n.** a barren or empty area of land.

wast·rel /ˈwāstrəl/ ▶ **n.** literary a lazy person who spends their time or money wastefully.

watch /wäCH/ ▶ **v.** **1** look at attentively. **2** keep under careful observation. **3** be cautious about. **4** (**watch for**) look out for. **5** (**watch out**) be careful. ▶ **n.** **1** a small clock worn on a strap on your wrist. **2** an instance of watching. **3** a period of keeping watch during the night. **4** a shift worked by firefighters or police officers.

SYNONYMS ▶ **v.** **1** **observe**, view, look at, eye, gaze at, peer at, contemplate, inspect, scrutinize, scan; informal check out, get a load of, eyeball. **2** **spy on**, keep in sight, keep under surveillance, track, monitor, tail; informal keep tabs on, stake out. **3** **guard**, mind, protect, look after, keep an eye on, take care of, shield, defend. ANTONYMS ignore. ▶ **n.** **1** **wristwatch**, timepiece, chronometer. **2** **guard**, vigil, lookout, observation, surveillance.

□ **keep watch** be alert for danger or trouble. ■ **watch·a·ble** **adj.** **watch·er** **n.**

watch·dog /ˈwäCHˌdôg/ ▶ **n.** **1** a dog kept to guard property. **2** a person or group that monitors the practices of companies providing a particular service.

SYNONYMS **ombudsman**, monitor, scrutineer, inspector, supervisor.

watch·ful /ˈwäCHfəl/ ▶ **adj.** alert to possible difficulty or danger.

SYNONYMS **observant**, alert, vigilant, attentive, aware, sharp-eyed, eagle-eyed, on the lookout, wary, cautious, careful.

■ **watch·ful·ly** **adv.** **watch·ful·ness** **n.**

watch·man /ˈwäCHmən/ ▶ **n.** (plural **watchmen**) a man employed to look after an empty building.

watch·tow·er /ˈwäCHˌtou(-ə)r/ ▶ **n.** a tower built as a high observation point.

watch·word /ˈwäCHˌwərd/ ▶ **n.** a word or phrase expressing a central aim or belief.

wa·ter /ˈwôtər, ˈwä-/ ▶ **n.** **1** the liquid that forms the seas, lakes, rivers, and rain. **2** (**waters**) an area of sea under the authority of a particular country. **3** (**waters**) fluid that passes from a woman's body shortly before she gives birth. ▶ **v.** (**waters**, **watering**, **watered**) **1** pour water over a plant. **2** give a drink of water to an animal. **3** (of the eyes or mouth) produce tears or saliva. **4** dilute a drink with water. **5** (**water something down**) make something less forceful or controversial.

SYNONYMS ▶ **v.** **1** **sprinkle**, moisten, dampen, wet, spray, splash, hose, douse. **2** **salivate**, become wet, moisten.

□ **hold water** (of a theory) seem valid or reasonable. **water buffalo** a kind of Asian buffalo used for carrying heavy loads. **water cannon** a device that sends out a powerful jet of water, used to make a crowd disperse. **water closet** dated a flush toilet. **watering can** a portable container with a long spout, used for watering plants. **watering hole** informal a bar or pub. **water lily** a plant that grows in water, with large round floating leaves. **water meadow** a meadow that is periodically flooded by a stream or river. **water polo** a game played by swimmers in a pool, who try to throw the ball into their opponents' net. **water table** the level below which the ground is saturated with water. **water tower** a tower that raises up a water tank to create enough pressure to distribute the water through pipes. **water under the bridge** (or **over the dam**) past events that are over and done with. ■ **wa·ter·less** **adj.**

wa·ter·bed /ˈwôtərˌbed, ˈwä-/ ▶ **n.** a bed with a water-filled mattress.

wa·ter·board·ing /ˈwôtərˌbôrdiNG, ˈwä-/ ▶ **n.** a torture in which a person is strapped on their back to a sloping board, head downward, with their face covered by a cloth over which water is poured, nearly drowning them.

wa·ter·col·or /ˈwôtərˌkələr, ˈwä-/ ▶ **n.** **1** artists' paint that is thinned with water. **2** a picture painted with watercolors.

wa·ter·course /ˈwôtərˌkôrs, ˈwä-/ ▶ **n.** a stream or artificial water channel.

wa·ter·cress /ˈwôtərˌkres, ˈwä-/ ▶ **n.** a kind of cress that grows in running water.

wa·ter·fall /ˈwôtərˌfôl, ˈwä-/ ▶ **n.** a place where a stream of water falls from a height.

SYNONYMS **falls**, cascade, cataract, rapids.

wa·ter·fowl /ˈwôtərˌfoul, ˈwä-/ ▶ **pl.n.** ducks, geese, or other large birds living in water.

wa·ter·front /ˈwôtərˌfrənt, ˈwä-/ ▶ **n.** a part of a town or city alongside an area of water.

wa·ter·hole /ˈwôtərˌhōl, ˈwä-/ ▶ **n.** a water-filled hollow where animals drink.

wa·ter·line /ˈwôtərˌlīn, ˈwä-/ ▶ **n.** the level normally reached by the water on the side of a ship.

wa·ter·logged /ˈwôtərˌlôgd, ˈwä-/ ▶ **adj.** saturated with water.

wa·ter·mark /ˈwôtərˌmärk, ˈwä-/ ▶ **n.** a faint design made in some paper that can be seen when held against the light.

wa·ter·mel·on /ˈwôtərˌmelən, ˈwä-/ ▶ **n.** a very large fruit with smooth green skin, red pulp, and watery juice.

wa·ter·mill /ˈwôtərˌmil, ˈwä-/ ▶ **n.** a mill worked by a waterwheel.

wa·ter·proof /ˈwôtərˌpro͞of, ˈwä-/ ▶ **adj.** unable to be penetrated by water. ▶ **v.** make waterproof.

wa·ter·shed /ˈwôtərˌsнed, ˈwä-/ ▶ **n.** **1** an area of land that separates waters flowing to different rivers, seas, etc. **2** a turning point in a situation.

wa·ter·ski /ˈwôtərˌskē, ˈwä-/ ▶ **n.** (plural **waterskis**) each of a pair of skis that let you skim the surface of the water when towed by a motorboat. ▶ **v.** (**waterskis**, **waterskiing**, **waterskied**) travel on waterskis. ■ **wa·ter·ski·er n.**

wa·ter·spout /ˈwôtərˌspout, ˈwä-/ ▶ **n.** a column of water formed by a whirlwind over the sea.

wa·ter·tight /ˈwôtərˌtīt, ˈwä-/ ▶ **adj.** **1** not allowing any water to pass through. **2** unable to be called into question.

> SYNONYMS **1 impermeable**, impervious, (hermetically) sealed, waterproof. **2 indisputable**, unquestionable, incontrovertible, irrefutable, unassailable, foolproof, sound, flawless, conclusive. ANTONYMS leaky.

wa·ter·way /ˈwôtərˌwā, ˈwä-/ ▶ **n.** a river, canal, or other route for travel by water.

wa·ter·wheel /ˈwôtərˌ(h)wēl, ˈwä-/ ▶ **n.** a large wheel driven by flowing water, used to work machinery or to raise water to a higher level.

wa·ter·works /ˈwôtərˌwərks, ˈwä-/ ▶ **n.** a place with equipment for managing a water supply.

wa·ter·y /ˈwôtərē, ˈwä-/ ▶ **adj.** **1** consisting of, containing, or resembling water. **2** (of food or drink) thin or tasteless as a result of containing too much water. **3** weak or pale: *watery sunlight*.

watt /wät/ ▶ **n.** the basic unit of power.

watt·age /ˈwätij/ ▶ **n.** an amount of electrical power expressed in watts.

wat·tle¹ /ˈwätl/ ▶ **n.** rods interlaced with twigs or branches, used for making fences, walls, etc. ▫ **wattle and daub** wattle covered with mud or clay, formerly used in building walls.

wat·tle² ▶ **n.** a fleshy part hanging from the head or neck of the turkey and some other birds.

wave /wāv/ ▶ **v.** (**waves**, **waving**, **waved**) **1** move your hand, or something held in it, to and fro, especially when greeting someone. **2** move to and fro with a swaying motion. ▶ **n.** **1** a ridge of water moving along the surface of the sea or breaking on the shore. **2** a sudden increase in a phenomenon or emotion. **3** a gesture made by waving your hand. **4** a slightly curling lock of hair. **5** a regular to-and-fro motion of particles of matter involved in transmitting sound, light, heat, etc.

> SYNONYMS ▶ **v.** **1 flap**, wag, shake, swish, swing, brandish, flourish, wield. **2 ripple**, flutter, undulate, stir, flap, sway, shake, quiver. **3 gesture**, signal, beckon, motion. ▶ **n.** **1 signal**, sign, motion, gesture. **2 breaker**, roller, comber, boomer, ripple; (**waves**) swell, surf. **3** *a wave of planning applications* **spate**, surge, flow, flood, stream, torrent. **4** *a wave of emotion* **surge**, rush, tide, upsurge, sudden feeling.

wave·band /ˈwāvˌband/ ▶ **n.** a range of wavelengths used in radio transmission.

wave·length /ˈwāvˌleng(k)тн/ ▶ **n.** **1** the distance between successive crests of a wave of sound, light, radio, etc. **2** a person's way of thinking.

wave·let /ˈwāvlit/ ▶ **n.** a small wave.

wa·ver /ˈwāvər/ ▶ **v.** (**wavers**, **wavering**, **wavered**) **1** move in a quivering way; flicker. **2** begin to weaken; falter. **3** be indecisive.

> SYNONYMS **1** *the candlelight wavered* **flicker**, quiver. **2** *his voice wavered* **falter**, wobble, tremble, quaver. **3 hesitate**, dither, be irresolute, be undecided, vacillate, blow hot and cold, hem and haw; informal shilly-shally, sit on the fence.

wav·y /ˈwāvē/ ▶ **adj.** (**wavier**, **waviest**) having a series of wavelike curves.

wax¹ /waks/ ▶ **n.** **1** a soft solid substance used for making candles or polishes. **2** a substance produced by bees to make honeycombs; beeswax. ▶ **v.** polish or treat with wax. ■ **wax·en adj. wax·y adj.**

wax² ▶ **v.** **1** (of the moon) gradually appear to increase in size. **2** literary become larger or stronger. **3** literary speak or write in a particular way: *they waxed lyrical.*

wax·work /ˈwaksˌwərk/ ▶ **n.** **1** a lifelike dummy made of wax. **2** (**waxworks**) an exhibition of waxworks.

way /wā/ ▶ **n.** **1** a method, style, or manner of doing something. **2** a road, track, or path. **3** a route or means taken in order to reach, enter, or leave a place. **4** a direction. **5** the distance in space or time between two points. **6** condition or state. **7** (**ways**) parts into which something divides. ▶ **adv.** informal at or to a considerable distance or extent.

> SYNONYMS ▶ **n.** **1 method**, process, procedure, technique, system, plan, strategy, scheme, means, mechanism, approach. **2 manner**, style, fashion, mode. **3** *I've changed my ways* **practice**, wont, habit, custom, convention, routine, trait, attribute, peculiarity, idiosyncrasy, conduct, behavior. **4 route**, course, direction, track, path, access, gate, exit, entrance, door. **5 distance**, length, stretch, journey. **6** *April is a long way away* **time**, stretch, term, span, duration. **7 direction**, bearing, course, orientation, line, tack. **8** *in some ways, he may be better off* **respect**, regard, aspect, facet, sense, detail, point, particular. **9** *the country is in a bad way* **state**, condition, situation, circumstances, position, predicament, plight; informal shape.

▫ **by the way** used to introduce a comment that is not connected to the current subject of conversation. **come your way** happen or become available to you. **get** (or **have**) **your**(**own**) **way** get or do what you want in spite of opposition. **give way 1** yield. **2** collapse or break under pressure. **3** (**give way to**) be replaced by. **go your way** (of events, circumstances, etc.) be favorable to you. **have a way with** have a particular talent for dealing with or ability in. **have your way with** humorous have sexual intercourse with. **in the way** obstructing someone's progress. **make way** allow room for someone or something else. **on the** (or **its**) **way** about to arrive or happen. **on the** (or **your**) **way out** informal **1** going out of fashion or favor. **2** dying. **way-out** informal very unconventional.

way·far·er /ˈwāˌfe(ə)rər/ ▶ **n.** literary a person who travels on foot.

way·lay /ˈwāˌlā/ ▶ **v.** (**waylays**, **waylaying**, **waylaid**) **1** intercept someone in order to attack them. **2** stop someone and talk to them.

> SYNONYMS **1 ambush**, hold up, attack, pounce on. **2 accost**, detain, intercept; informal buttonhole.

way·side /ˈwāˌsīd/ ▶ **n.** the edge of a road.

way·ward /ˈwāwərd/ ▶ **adj.** unpredictable and hard to control.

SYNONYMS **willful**, headstrong, stubborn, obstinate, perverse, contrary, disobedient, undisciplined, rebellious, defiant, recalcitrant, unruly, wild; formal refractory.

we /wē/ ▶ **pron.** **1** used by a speaker to refer to himself or herself and one or more other people considered together. **2** people in general.

weak /wēk/ ▶ **adj.** **1** lacking strength and energy. **2** likely to break or give way under pressure. **3** not secure or stable. **4** lacking power, influence, or ability. **5** (of a liquid or solution) heavily diluted.

SYNONYMS **1 feeble**, frail, delicate, fragile, infirm, ailing, debilitated, decrepit, exhausted, enervated. **2 inadequate**, poor, defective, faulty, deficient, imperfect, substandard. **3 unconvincing**, tenuous, implausible, unsatisfactory, poor, inadequate, lame, feeble, flimsy, hollow; informal pathetic. **4** *a weak bridge* **fragile**, rickety, insubstantial, wobbly, unstable, ramshackle, jerry-built, shoddy. **5 spineless**, craven, cowardly, timid, irresolute, indecisive, ineffectual, meek, tame, soft, faint-hearted; informal yellow, gutless. **6** *a weak voice* **indistinct**, muffled, muted, hushed, faint, low. **7 watery**, dilute, diluted, watered down, thin, tasteless. ANTONYMS strong.

□ **weak at the knees** helpless with emotion.

weak·en /ˈwēkən/ ▶ **v.** make or become weak.

SYNONYMS **1 enfeeble**, debilitate, incapacitate, sap, tire, exhaust. **2 decrease**, dwindle, diminish, wane, ebb, subside, peter out, fizzle out, tail off, decline, falter. **3 impair**, undermine, compromise, lessen. ANTONYMS strengthen, bolster.

weak·ling /ˈwēkliNG/ ▶ **n.** a weak person or animal.

SYNONYMS **milksop**, namby-pamby, pushover; informal wimp, sissy, wuss, doormat.

weak·ly /ˈwēklē/ ▶ **adv.** in a weak way. ▶ **adj.** (**weaklier**, **weakliest**) weak or sickly.

weak·ness /ˈwēknis/ ▶ **n.** **1** the state of being weak. **2** a fault. **3** (**weakness for**) a liking for something that you find difficult to resist.

SYNONYMS **1 frailty**, feebleness, fragility, delicacy, debility, incapacity, decrepitude. **2 fault**, flaw, defect, deficiency, failing, shortcoming, imperfection, Achilles heel. **3** *a weakness for champagne* **fondness**, liking, partiality, love, penchant, predilection, inclination, taste. **4 timidity**, cravenness, cowardliness, indecision, irresolution, ineffectuality, ineffectiveness, impotence.

weal /wēl/ ▶ **n.** a red swollen mark left on flesh by a blow or pressure.

wealth /welTH/ ▶ **n.** **1** a large amount of money, property, or possessions. **2** the state of being rich. **3** a large amount of something desirable.

SYNONYMS **1 affluence**, prosperity, riches, means, fortune, money, cash, capital, treasure, finance; informal wherewithal, dough, bread. **2 abundance**, profusion, plethora, mine, store; informal lot, load, mountain, stack, ton. ANTONYMS poverty, dearth.

wealth·y /ˈwelTHē/ ▶ **adj.** (**wealthier**, **wealthiest**) rich.

SYNONYMS **rich**, affluent, moneyed, well off, well-to-do, prosperous; informal well-heeled, rolling in it, made of money, loaded, flush. ANTONYMS poor.

wean /wēn/ ▶ **v.** **1** make a young mammal used to food other than its mother's milk. **2** (**wean someone off**) make someone give up a habit or addiction. **3** (**be weaned on**) be strongly influenced by something from an early age.

weap·on /ˈwepən/ ▶ **n.** **1** a thing used to cause physical harm or damage. **2** a means of gaining an advantage or defending yourself.

weap·on·ry /ˈwepənrē/ ▶ **n.** weapons regarded collectively.

wear /we(ə)r/ ▶ **v.** (**wears**, **wearing**, **wore** /wôr/; past participle **worn** /wôrn/) **1** have something on your body as clothing, decoration, or protection. **2** have a particular facial expression. **3** damage something by continuous use or rubbing. **4** (**wear off**) stop being effective or strong. **5** (**wear someone out**) exhaust someone. **6** (**wearing**) mentally or physically tiring. **7** (**wear on**) (of time) pass in a slow or boring way. ▶ **n.** **1** clothing of a particular type. **2** damage caused by continuous use.

SYNONYMS ▶ **v.** **1 be dressed in**, be clothed in, have on, sport. **2 bear**, show, display, exhibit, give, put on, assume. **3 erode**, abrade, rub away, grind away, wash away, crumble (away), eat away (at). **4** (**wearing**) **tiring**, exhausting, wearying, fatiguing, enervating, draining, sapping, demanding, exacting, taxing, grueling, punishing. **5 last**, endure, hold up, bear up. ▶ **n.** **1 use**, service, value; informal mileage. **2 clothes**, garments, dress, attire, garb, wardrobe; informal getup, gear, togs. **3 damage**, friction, abrasion, erosion.

■ **wear·er** **n.**

wear·i·some /ˈwi(ə)rēsəm/ ▶ **adj.** making you feel tired or bored.

wear·y /ˈwi(ə)rē/ ▶ **adj.** (**wearier**, **weariest**) **1** tired. **2** causing tiredness. **3** (**weary of**) bored with. ▶ **v.** (**wearies**, **wearying**, **wearied**) **1** make someone weary. **2** (**weary of**) grow bored with.

SYNONYMS ▶ **adj.** **1 tired**, worn out, exhausted, fatigued, sapped, spent, drained; informal done in, ready to drop, bushed, pooped. **2 tiring**, exhausting, fatiguing, enervating, draining, sapping, demanding, taxing, arduous, grueling. ANTONYMS energetic.

■ **wea·ri·ly** **adv.** **wea·ri·ness** **n.**

wea·sel /ˈwēzəl/ ▶ **n.** **1** a small, slender meat-eating animal with reddish-brown fur. **2** informal a deceitful or treacherous person. ■ **wea·sel·ly** **adj.**

weath·er /ˈweT͟Hər/ ▶ **n.** the state of the atmosphere in terms of temperature, wind, rain, etc. ▶ **v.** (**weathers**, **weathering**, **weathered**) **1** wear something away by long exposure to the weather. **2** come safely through a difficult or dangerous situation.

SYNONYMS ▶ **n.** **conditions**, climate, elements, forecast, outlook. ▶ **v.** **survive**, come through, ride out, pull through, withstand, endure, rise above; informal stick out.

□ **make heavy weather of** informal have unnecessary difficulty in dealing with. **under the weather** informal slightly unwell. **weather-beaten** damaged, worn, or tanned through being exposed to the weather.

weath·er·cock /ˈweT͟Hərˌkäk/ ▶ **n.** a weathervane in the form of a rooster.

weath·er·man /ˈweT͟Hərˌman/ ▶ **n.** (plural **weathermen**) a man who gives a description and forecast of weather conditions on television or radio.

weath·er·vane /ˈweT͟Hərˌvān/ ▶ **n.** a revolving pointer that shows the direction of the wind.

weave[1] /wēv/ ▶ **v.** (**weaves**, **weaving**, **wove** /wōv/; past participle **woven** /ˈwōvən/ or **wove**) **1** make fabric by interlacing long threads with others. **2** make facts, events, etc., into a story. ▶ **n.** a particular way in which fabric is woven.

SYNONYMS ▶ **v.** **1** **entwine**, lace, twist, knit, braid, plait. **2** **invent**, make up, fabricate, construct, create, spin.

■ **weav·er** **n.**

weave[2] ▶ **v.** (**weaves**, **weaving**, **weaved**) move from side to side to get around obstructions.

SYNONYMS *he had to weave his way through the crowds* **thread**, wind, wend, dodge, zigzag.

web /web/ ▶ **n.** **1** a network of fine threads made by a spider to catch its prey. **2** a complex system of interconnected elements. **3** (**the Web**) the World Wide Web. **4** the skin between the toes of a bird or animal living in water.

SYNONYMS **1** **mesh**, net, lattice, lacework, gauze, gossamer. **2** **network**, nexus, complex, tangle, chain.

□ **web page** a document that can be accessed via the Internet.

webbed /webd/ ▶ **adj.** (of an animal's feet) having the toes connected by a web.

web·bing /ˈwebiNG/ ▶ **n.** strong fabric used for making straps, belts, etc.

Web·cam /ˈwebˌkam/ ▶ **n.** trademark a video camera connected to a computer, so that the film produced may be viewed on the Internet.

web·log /ˈwebˌlôg, -ˌläg/ ▶ **n.** ⇒ **BLOG**.

web·site /ˈwebˌsīt/ ▶ **n.** a location on the Internet that maintains one or more web pages.

wed /wed/ ▶ **v.** (**weds**, **wedding**, **wedded** or **wed**) **1** formal or literary marry. **2** (**wedded**) having to do with marriage. **3** combine two desirable factors or qualities. **4** (**be wedded to**) be entirely devoted to a particular activity or belief.

SYNONYMS (**wedded**) **1** **married**, matrimonial, marital, conjugal, nuptial. **2** *he is wedded to his work* **dedicated**, devoted, attached, fixated.

we'd /wēd/ ▶ **contr.** **1** we had. **2** we should or we would.

wed·ding /ˈwediNG/ ▶ **n.** a marriage ceremony.

SYNONYMS **marriage** (**service**), nuptials, union.

wedge /wej/ ▶ **n.** **1** a piece of wood, metal, etc., with a thick end that tapers to a thin edge. **2** a golf club for hitting the ball as high as possible into the air. **3** a shoe with a fairly high heel forming a solid block with the sole. ▶ **v.** (**wedges**, **wedging**, **wedged**) **1** fix in position using a wedge. **2** force into a narrow space.

SYNONYMS ▶ **n.** **triangle**, segment, slice, section, chunk, lump, slab, hunk, block, piece. ▶ **v.** **squeeze**, cram, jam, ram, force, push, shove; informal stuff.

□ **the thin end of the wedge** informal something unimportant in itself that is likely to lead to a more serious or unpleasant situation.

wed·lock /ˈwedˌläk/ ▶ **n.** formal the state of being married.

Wednes·day /ˈwenzdā, -dē/ ▶ **n.** the day of the week before Thursday and following Tuesday.

SPELLING

Remember the **d** before the **n**: Wed**n**esday.

wee /wē/ ▶ **adj.** little.

weed /wēd/ ▶ **n.** **1** a wild plant growing where it is not wanted. **2** informal cannabis. **3** (**the weed**) informal tobacco. **4** (**weeds**) old use black clothes worn by a widow in mourning for her husband. ▶ **v.** **1** remove weeds from. **2** (**weed someone/thing out**) remove unwanted members or items.

weed·kill·er /ˈwēdˌkilər/ ▶ **n.** a substance used to destroy weeds.

weed·y /ˈwēdē/ ▶ **adj.** (**weedier**, **weediest**) containing or covered with many weeds.

week /wēk/ ▶ **n.** **1** a period of seven days. **2** the five days from Monday to Friday, when many people work.

week·day /ˈwēkˌdā/ ▶ **n.** a day of the week other than Saturday or Sunday.

week·end /ˈwēkˌend/ ▶ **n.** the period from Friday evening through Sunday evening.

week·ly /ˈwēklē/ ▶ **adj. & adv.** happening or produced once a week.

weep /wēp/ ▶ **v.** (**weeps**, **weeping**, **wept** /wept/) **1** shed tears; cry. **2** (of a wound) produce liquid. ▶ **n.** a period of shedding tears.

SYNONYMS ▶ **v.** **cry**, shed tears, sob, snivel, whimper, wail, bawl, keen; informal boohoo, blubber.

weep·y /ˈwēpē/ ▶ **adj.** (**weepier**, **weepiest**) informal **1** tearful. **2** sentimental.

wee·vil /ˈwēvəl/ ▶ **n.** a small beetle that eats crops or stored food.

weft /weft/ ▶ **n.** (in weaving) the threads that are passed over and under the warp threads to make cloth.

weigh /wā/ ▶ **v.** **1** find out how heavy someone or something is. **2** have a particular weight. **3** (**weigh something out**) measure and take out a portion of a particular weight. **4** (**weigh someone down**) be a burden to someone. **5** (**weigh on**) be depressing or worrying to. **6** (**weigh in**) (of a boxer or jockey) be officially weighed before or after a contest. **7** (often **weigh something up**) consider something carefully. **8** (often **weigh against**) influence a decision or action. **9** (**weigh in**) informal join in something enthusiastically or forcefully.

SYNONYMS **1** **measure the weight of**, put on the scale(s). **2** **have a weight of**, tip the scales at. **3** *he weighed the possibilities* **consider**, contemplate, think about, mull over, chew over, reflect on, ruminate about, muse on, assess, examine, review, explore, take stock of. **4** *they need to weigh benefit against risk* **balance**, evaluate, compare, juxtapose, contrast.

weigh·bridge /ˈwāˌbrij/ ▶ **n.** a machine on to which vehicles are driven to be weighed.

weight /wāt/ ▶ **n.** **1** the heaviness of a person or thing. **2** the quality of being heavy. **3** a unit used for expressing how much something weighs. **4** a piece of metal known to weigh a definite amount and used on scales to find out how heavy something is. **5** a heavy object. **6** ability to influence decisions. **7** the importance attached to something. ▶ **v. 1** make heavier or keep in place with a weight. **2** (**be weighted**) be arranged so as to give one party an advantage.

> SYNONYMS ▶ **n. 1 mass**, heaviness, load, burden. **2 influence**, force, leverage, sway, pull, power, authority; informal clout. **3 burden**, load, millstone, trouble, worry. **4** *the weight of the evidence is against him* **most**, bulk, majority, preponderance, body, lion's share.

■ **weight·less adj.**

weight·ing /ˈwātiNG/ ▶ **n.** adjustment made to take account of special circumstances.

weight·lift·ing /ˈwātˌliftiNG/ ▶ **n.** the sport or activity of lifting heavy weights. ■ **weight·lift·er n.**

weight·y /ˈwātē/ ▶ **adj.** (**weightier**, **weightiest**) **1** heavy. **2** very serious and important. **3** very influential.

weir /wi(ə)r/ ▶ **n.** a low dam built across a river to control its flow.

weird /wi(ə)rd/ ▶ **adj. 1** informal very strange. **2** mysterious or strange in a frightening way; eerie.

> SYNONYMS **1 uncanny**, eerie, unnatural, supernatural, unearthly, otherworldly, ghostly, mysterious, strange, abnormal, unusual; informal creepy, spooky, freaky. **2 bizarre**, odd, curious, strange, quirky, outlandish, eccentric, unconventional, unorthodox, idiosyncratic, surreal, crazy, absurd, grotesque, peculiar; informal wacky, wacko, freaky. ANTONYMS normal, conventional.

■ **weird·ly adv. weird·ness n.**

> SPELLING
>
> Weird does not follow the rule of **i** before **e** because the sound is not ee.

weird·o /ˈwi(ə)rdō/ ▶ **n.** (plural **weirdos**) informal a strange or eccentric person.

welch = **WELSH**.

wel·come /ˈwelkəm/ ▶ **n. 1** an instance or way of greeting someone. **2** a pleased or approving reaction. ▶ **v.** (**welcomes**, **welcoming**, **welcomed**) **1** greet someone in a polite or friendly way when they arrive somewhere. **2** be glad to receive or hear of. ▶ **adj. 1** gladly received. **2** very pleasing because much needed or wanted. **3** allowed or invited to do a particular thing.

> SYNONYMS ▶ **n. greeting**, salutation, reception, hospitality, the red carpet. ▶ **v. 1 greet**, salute, receive, meet, usher in. **2 be pleased by**, be glad about, approve of, applaud, appreciate, embrace. ANTONYMS resent. ▶ **adj. pleasing**, good, agreeable, encouraging, gratifying, heartening, promising, favorable, pleasant.

weld /weld/ ▶ **v. 1** join together metal parts by heating the surfaces and pressing or hammering them together. **2** make two things combine into a whole. ▶ **n.** a welded joint.

> SYNONYMS ▶ **v. fuse**, bond, stick, join, attach, seal, splice, melt, solder.

■ **weld·er n.**

wel·fare /ˈwelˌfe(ə)r/ ▶ **n. 1** the general health, happiness, and safety of a person or group. **2** organized help given to people in need.

> SYNONYMS **1 well-being**, health, comfort, security, safety, protection, success, interest, good. **2 social security**, benefit, public assistance, pension, credit, support, sick pay, unemployment benefit; informal the dole.

□ **welfare state** a system under which the state provides pensions, health care, etc.

well[1] /wel/ ▶ **adv. 1** in a good way. **2** thoroughly. **3** to a great extent or degree. **4** very probably. **5** without difficulty. **6** with good reason. ▶ **adj. 1** in good health. **2** in a satisfactory state or position. **3** sensible; advisable. ▶ **exclam.** used to express surprise, anger, resignation, etc.

> SYNONYMS ▶ **adv. 1 satisfactorily**, nicely, correctly, properly, fittingly, suitably, appropriately. **2 skillfully**, ably, competently, proficiently, adeptly, deftly, expertly, excellently. **3** *they speak well of him* **admiringly**, highly, approvingly, favorably, appreciatively, warmly, enthusiastically, in glowing terms. ANTONYMS badly. ▶ **adj. 1 healthy**, fine, fit, robust, strong, vigorous, blooming, thriving, in fine fettle; informal in the pink. **2 satisfactory**, all right, fine, in order, as it should be, acceptable; informal OK, okay, hunky-dory. ANTONYMS unwell, unsatisfactory.

□ **as well 1** in addition. **2** with equal reason or an equally good result. **well-advised** sensible; wise. **well-appointed** having a high standard of equipment or furnishing. **well-being** the state of being comfortable, healthy, or happy. **well-disposed** having a sympathetic or friendly attitude. **well-heeled** informal wealthy. **well nigh** almost. **well off 1** wealthy. **2** in a good situation. **well-read** having read widely. **well-spoken** having an educated and refined voice. **well-to-do** wealthy. **well-wisher** a person who wants someone else to be happy or successful.

> USAGE
>
> **Well** is often used with a past participle such as *known* or *dressed* to form adjectives such as **well-known, well-dressed**, etc., Write these adjectives with a hyphen when they come directly in front of a noun (*a well-known writer*), but when they come after a noun or pronoun, they can be written with or without a hyphen (*she is well-known* or *she is well known*).

well[2] ▶ **n. 1** a shaft sunk into the ground to obtain water, oil, or gas. **2** a hollow made to hold liquid. **3** a space in the middle of a building for stairs, a lift, etc. ▶ **v.** (often **well up**) **1** (of a liquid) rise up to the surface. **2** (of an emotion) develop and become stronger.

> SYNONYMS ▶ **n. borehole**, spring, waterhole, shaft. ▶ **v. flow**, spill, stream, gush, roll, cascade, flood, spout, burst, issue.

we'll /wēl/ ▶ **contr.** we shall or we will.

wel·ling·ton /ˈweliNGtən/ ▶ **n.** a knee-length waterproof rubber or plastic boot.

Welsh /welsH/ ▶ **n.** the language of Wales. ▶ **adj.** relating to Wales. □ **Welsh rarebit** (or **Welsh rabbit**) a dish of melted cheese on toast.

welsh /welsH/ (or **welch**) ▶ **v.** (**welsh on**) fail to repay a debt or fulfill an obligation.

welt /welt/ ▶ **n. 1** a leather rim to which the sole of a shoe is attached. **2** a red swollen mark left on the skin by a blow or pressure.

wel·ter /ˈweltər/ ▶ **n.** a large and confused or disorganized number of items.

wel·ter·weight /ˈweltərˌwāt/ ▶ **n.** a weight in boxing between lightweight and middleweight.

wen /wen/ ▶ **n.** a boil or other swelling or growth on the skin.

wench /wencн/ ▶ **n.** old use or humorous a girl or young woman.

wend /wend/ ▶ **v.** (**wend your way**) go slowly or by an indirect route.

went /went/ past of **GO**.

wept /wept/ past and past participle of **WEEP**.

were /wər/ 2nd person singular past, plural past, and past subjunctive of **BE**.

we're /wi(ə)r/ ▶ **contr.** we are.

weren't /wər(ə)nt/ ▶ **contr.** were not.

were·wolf /ˈwe(ə)rˌwo͝olf/ ▶ **n.** (plural **werewolves**) (in stories) a person who periodically changes into a wolf, especially when there is a full moon.

west /west/ ▶ **n. 1** the direction in which the sun sets. **2** the western part of a place. **3** (**the West**) the western part of the US. **4** (**the West**) Europe and North America. ▶ **adj. & adv. 1** toward or facing the west. **2** (of a wind) blowing from the west. ■ **west·ward adj. & adv. west·wards adv.**

west·er·ly /ˈwestərlē/ ▶ **adj. & adv. 1** facing or moving toward the west. **2** (of a wind) blowing from the west.

west·ern /ˈwestərn/ ▶ **adj. 1** situated in or facing the west. **2** (**Western**) having to do with the west, in particular Europe and North America. ▶ **n.** a movie or novel about cowboys in western North America.

west·ern·er /ˈwestərnər/ ▶ **n.** a person from the west of a region.

west·ern·ize /ˈwestərˌnīz/ ▶ **v.** (**westernizes**, **westernizing**, **westernized**) bring under the influence of Europe and North America.

wet /wet/ ▶ **adj.** (**wetter**, **wettest**) **1** covered or soaked with liquid. **2** (of the weather) rainy. **3** not yet having dried or hardened. ▶ **v.** (**wets**, **wetting**, **wet** or **wetted**) **1** cover or touch with liquid. **2** urinate in or on. ▶ **n. 1** (**the wet**) rainy weather. **2** liquid that makes something damp.

> SYNONYMS ▶ **adj. 1 damp**, moist, soaked, drenched, saturated, sopping, dripping, soggy, waterlogged. **2 rainy**, pouring, teeming, showery, drizzly. **3 sticky**, tacky. ▶ **v. dampen**, moisten, sprinkle, spray, splash, soak, saturate, flood, douse, drench. ANTONYMS dry.

□ **wet behind the ears** informal lacking experience. **wet blanket** informal a person who spoils other people's enjoyment by being disapproving or unenthusiastic. **wet nurse** a woman employed to breastfeed another woman's child. ■ **wet·ly adv. wet·ness n.**

wet·back /ˈwetˌbak/ ▶ **n.** informal, disapproving a Mexican living in the US, especially one who is an illegal immigrant.

weth·er /ˈweт͟нər/ ▶ **n.** a castrated ram.

wet·suit /ˈwetˌso͞ot/ ▶ **n.** a close-fitting rubber garment covering the entire body, worn in water sports or diving.

we've /wēv/ ▶ **contr.** we have.

whack /(h)wak/ informal ▶ **v. 1** hit forcefully. **2** murder. ▶ **n.** a sharp blow. □ **have a whack at** attempt. **out of whack** out of order; malfunctioning.

whack·y = **WACKY**.

whale /(h)wāl/ ▶ **n.** (plural **whales**) a very large sea mammal with a blowhole on top of the head for breathing. □ **have a whale of a time** informal enjoy yourself very much.

whale·bone /ˈ(h)wālˌbōn/ ▶ **n.** a hard substance growing in plates in the upper jaw of some whales, used by them to strain plankton from the seawater.

whal·er /ˈ(h)wālər/ ▶ **n. 1** a ship used for hunting whales. **2** a sailor who hunts and kills whales.

whal·ing /ˈ(h)wāliɴɢ/ ▶ **n.** the practice of hunting and killing whales.

wham /(h)wam/ ▶ **exclam.** informal used to express the sound of a hard impact or the idea of a sudden and dramatic occurrence.

wham·my /ˈ(h)wamē/ ▶ **n.** (plural **whammies**) informal an event with a powerful and unpleasant effect.

wharf /(h)wôrf/ ▶ **n.** (plural **wharves** /(h)wôrvz/ or **wharfs**) a level area where ships are moored to load and unload.

> SYNONYMS **quay**, pier, dock, berth, landing, jetty, harbor, dockyard.

what /(h)wət, (h)wät/ ▶ **pron. & determiner 1** asking for information about something. **2** whatever. **3** used to emphasize something surprising or remarkable. ▶ **pron. 1** asking someone to repeat something. **2** (used in specifying something) the thing or things that: *what we need is a broom.* ▶ **adv.** to what extent?

what·ev·er /(h)wətˈevər, ˌ(h)wät-/ (or **whatsoever** /ˌ(h)wətsōˈevər, ˌ(h)wät-/) ▶ **pron. & determiner** everything or anything that; no matter what. ▶ **pron.** used for emphasis instead of "what" in questions. ▶ **adv.** at all; of any kind.

what·not /ˈ(h)wətˌnät, ˈ(h)wät-/ ▶ **n.** informal an unspecified item or items.

whats·his·name /ˈ(h)wətsizˌnām, ˈ(h)wät-/ (also **whatshisface** /-ˌfās/ or **whatshername** /-sərˌnām/) ▶ **n.** informal used to refer to a person whose name you cannot recall or do not know.

wheat /(h)wēt/ ▶ **n.** a cereal crop whose grain is ground to make flour.

wheat·ear /ˈ(h)wētˌir/ ▶ **n.** a small songbird.

wheat·germ /ˈ(h)wētˌjərm/ ▶ **n.** a nutritious food consisting of the center parts of grains of wheat.

whee·dle /ˈ(h)wēdl/ ▶ **v.** (**wheedles**, **wheedling**, **wheedled**) try to persuade someone to do something by flattering them or saying nice things that you do not mean.

wheel /(h)wēl/ ▶ **n. 1** a revolving circular object that is fixed below a vehicle to enable it to move along, or that forms part of a machine. **2** (**the wheel**) a steering wheel. **3** a turn or rotation. ▶ **v. 1** push or pull a vehicle with wheels. **2** carry on a vehicle with wheels. **3** fly or turn in a wide curve. **4** turn around quickly. **5** (**wheel something out**) informal resort to something that has been frequently seen or heard before.

> SYNONYMS ▶ **v. 1 push**, trundle, roll. **2** *gulls wheeled overhead* **turn**, go around, circle, orbit.

□ **wheel and deal** take part in commercial or political scheming.

wheel·bar·row /ˈ(h)wēlˌbarō/ ▶ **n.** a small cart with a wheel at the front and two handles at the rear.

wheel·base /ˈ(h)wēlˌbās/ ▶ **n.** the distance between the front and rear axles of a vehicle.

wheel·chair /ˈ(h)wēlˌcнe(ə)r/ ▶ **n.** a chair on wheels for a person who is ill or disabled.

wheel·er-deal·er /ˈ(h)wēlər/ ▶ **n.** a person who takes part in commercial or political scheming.

wheel·ie /ˈ(h)wēlē/ ▶ **n.** informal a maneuver whereby a bicycle or motorcycle is ridden for a short distance with the front wheel raised off the ground.

wheeze /(h)wēz/ ▶ **v.** (**wheezes**, **wheezing**, **wheezed**) **1** breathe with a whistling or rattling sound in the chest. **2** make a rattling or spluttering sound. ▶ **n.** a sound of wheezing.

> SYNONYMS ▶ **v.** **gasp**, whistle, hiss, rasp, croak, pant, cough.

wheez·y /ˈ(h)wēzē/ ▶ **adj.** making the sound of a person wheezing: *a wheezy laugh.* ■ **wheez·i·ly adv.** **wheez·i·ness n.**

whelk /(h)welk/ ▶ **n.** a shellfish with a pointed spiral shell.

whelp /(h)welp/ ▶ **n.** old use **1** a puppy. **2** disapproving a boy or young man. ▶ **v.** give birth to a puppy.

when /(h)wen/ ▶ **adv.** **1** at what time? **2** in what circumstances? **3** at which time or in which situation. ▶ **conj.** **1** at or during the time that. **2** at any time that; whenever. **3** in view of the fact that. **4** although; whereas.

whence /(h)wens/ (or **from whence**) ▶ **adv.** formal **1** from what place or source? **2** from which or from where. **3** to the place from which. **4** as a consequence of which.

when·ev·er /(h)wənˈevər/ or formal (**whensoever** /ˌ(h)wensōˈevər/) ▶ **conj.** **1** at whatever time or on whatever occasion. **2** every time that. ▶ **adv.** used for emphasis instead of "when" in questions.

where /(h)we(ə)r/ ▶ **adv.** **1** in or to what place or position? **2** in what direction or respect? **3** at, in, or to which. **4** in or to a place or situation in which.

where·a·bouts /ˈ(h)we(ə)rəˌbouts/ ▶ **adv.** where or approximately where? ▶ **n.** the place where someone or something is.

> SYNONYMS ▶ **n.** **location**, position, site, situation, spot, point, home, address, neighborhood.

where·as /(h)we(ə)rˈaz/ ▶ **conj.** **1** in contrast or comparison with the fact that. **2** taking into consideration the fact that.

where·by /(h)we(ə)rˈbī/ ▶ **adv.** by which.

where·fore /ˈ(h)we(ə)rˌfôr/ old use ▶ **adv.** for what reason? ▶ **adv. & conj.** as a result of which.

where·in /(h)we(ə)rˈin/ ▶ **adv.** formal **1** in which. **2** in what place or respect?

where·of /(h)weˈräv, -ˈəv/ ▶ **adv.** formal of what or that.

where·up·on /ˌ(h)we(ə)rəˈpän, -ˈpôn/ ▶ **conj.** immediately after that.

wher·ev·er /(h)we(ə)rˈevər/ or formal (**wheresoever** /ˌ(h)we(ə)rsōˈevər/) ▶ **adv.** **1** in or to whatever place. **2** used for emphasis instead of "where" in questions. ▶ **conj.** in every case when.

where·with·al /ˈ(h)we(ə)rwiTHˌôl, -wiTH-/ ▶ **n.** the money or other resources needed for something.

wher·ry /ˈ(h)werē/ ▶ **n.** (plural **wherries**) a light rowboat or barge.

whet /(h)wet/ ▶ **v.** (**whets**, **whetting**, **whetted**) **1** sharpen a blade. **2** stimulate someone's interest or appetite.

wheth·er /ˈ(h)weTHər/ ▶ **conj.** **1** expressing a doubt or choice between alternatives. **2** indicating that a statement applies whichever of the alternatives mentioned is the case.

whet·stone /ˈ(h)wetˌstōn/ ▶ **n.** a stone used for sharpening cutting tools.

whew /hyo͞o, hwyo͞o/ ▶ **exclam.** used to express surprise, relief, or a feeling of being very hot or tired: *whew—and I thought it was serious!*

whey /(h)wā/ ▶ **n.** the watery part of milk that remains after curds have formed.

which /(h)wiCH/ ▶ **pron. & determiner** **1** asking for information specifying one or more people or things from a set. **2** used to refer to something previously mentioned when introducing a clause giving further information.

which·ev·er /ˌ(h)wiCHˈevər/ ▶ **determiner & pron.** **1** any that; that or those that. **2** regardless of which.

whiff /(h)wif/ ▶ **n.** **1** a smell that is smelled only briefly or faintly. **2** a trace or hint of something bad or exciting. **3** a puff or breath of air or smoke.

Whig /(h)wig/ ▶ **n.** historical **1** a member of a British political party that became the Liberal Party. **2** a member of an American political party in the 19th century, succeeded by the Republicans. **3** an American colonist who supported the American Revolution.

while /(h)wīl/ ▶ **n.** **1** (**a while**) a period of time. **2** (**a while**) for some time. **3** (**the while**) meanwhile. ▶ **conj.** **1** at the same time as. **2** whereas. **3** although. ▶ **adv.** during which. ▶ **v.** (**whiles**, **whiling**, **whiled**) (**while something away**) pass time in a leisurely way.

> SYNONYMS ▶ **n.** *we chatted for a while* **time**, spell, stretch, stint, span, interval, period. ▶ **v.** *tennis helped to **while away** the time* **pass**, spend, occupy, use up, kill.

□ **worth your while** worth the time or effort spent.

whilst /(h)wīlst/ ▶ **conj. & adv.** while.

whim /(h)wim/ ▶ **n.** a sudden desire or change of mind.

> SYNONYMS **impulse**, urge, notion, fancy, inclination, caprice, vagary.

whim·per /ˈ(h)wimpər/ ▶ **v.** (**whimpers**, **whimpering**, **whimpered**) make low, feeble sounds expressing fear, pain, or discontent. ▶ **n.** a whimpering sound.

> SYNONYMS ▶ **v.** **whine**, cry, sob, moan, snivel, wail, groan.

whim·si·cal /ˈ(h)wimzikəl/ ▶ **adj.** **1** playfully unusual. **2** showing sudden changes of mood or behavior.

> SYNONYMS **fanciful**, playful, mischievous, waggish, quaint, curious, droll, eccentric, quirky, idiosyncratic, unconventional.

■ **whim·si·cal·ly adv.**

whim·sy /ˈ(h)wimzē/ ▶ **n.** (plural **whimsies**) **1** playfully unusual behavior or humor. **2** an odd or unusual thing. **3** a whim.

whine /(h)wīn/ ▶ **n.** **1** a long, high-pitched complaining cry. **2** a long, high-pitched sound. ▶ **v.** (**whines**, **whining**, **whined**) give or make a whine.

> SYNONYMS ▶ **v.** **1** **wail**, whimper, cry, mewl, moan, howl, yowl. **2** **complain**, grouse, grouch, grumble, moan, carp; informal gripe, bellyache.

■ **whin·y adj.**

whin·ny /'(h)winē/ ▶ **n.** (plural **whinnies**) a gentle, high-pitched neigh. ▶ **v.** (**whinnies**, **whinnying**, **whinnied**) (of a horse) make a whinny.

whip /(h)wip/ ▶ **n. 1** a length of leather or cord fastened to a handle, used for beating a person or urging on an animal. **2** an official of a political party appointed to maintain discipline among its members in Congress or Parliament. **3** a dessert made from cream or eggs beaten into a light fluffy mass. ▶ **v.** (**whips**, **whipping**, **whipped**) **1** hit a person or animal with a whip. **2** beat or move violently. **3** move or take out fast or suddenly. **4** beat cream, eggs, etc., into a froth.

SYNONYMS ▶ **n.** **lash**, scourge, strap, belt. ▶ **v.** **1 flog**, lash, flagellate, cane, belt, thrash, beat; informal tan someone's hide. **2 whisk**, beat. **3 rouse**, stir up, excite, galvanize, electrify, stimulate, inspire, fire up, inflame, provoke.

□ **the whip hand** a position of power or control over someone. **whipping boy** a person who is blamed or punished for other people's faults. **whip something up** make or prepare something very quickly.

whip·lash /'(h)wip,lash/ ▶ **n. 1** injury caused by a severe jerk to the head. **2** the flexible part of a whip.

whip·per·snap·per /'(h)wipər,snapər/ ▶ **n.** informal a young and inexperienced but overconfident person.

whip·pet /'(h)wipit/ ▶ **n.** a small, slender, fast-running breed of dog.

whip·poor·will /'(h)wipər,wil/ ▶ **n.** an American bird with a distinctive call.

whip·saw /'(h)wip,sô/ ▶ **n.** a saw with a narrow blade and a handle at both ends.

whir /(h)wər/ ▶ **v.** (**whirs**, **whirring**, **whirred**) (of something rapidly rotating or moving) make a low, continuous, regular sound. ▶ **n.** a whirring sound.

whirl /(h)wərl/ ▶ **v. 1** move rapidly around and around. **2** (of the head or mind) seem to spin around. ▶ **n. 1** a rapid movement around and around. **2** busy or hurried activity.

SYNONYMS ▶ **v.** **rotate**, circle, wheel, turn, revolve, orbit, spin, twirl, pirouette, gyrate.

whirl·i·gig /'(h)wərlē,gig/ ▶ **n. 1** a toy that spins around. **2** a merry-go-round at a fair.

whirl·pool /'(h)wərl,po͞ol/ ▶ **n.** a current of water that whirls in a circle.

SYNONYMS **eddy**, vortex, maelstrom.

whirl·wind /'(h)wərl,wind/ ▶ **n. 1** a column of air moving rapidly around and around. **2** a situation in which many things happen very quickly. ▶ **adj.** very quick and unexpected: *a whirlwind romance*.

SYNONYMS ▶ **n.** **tornado**, hurricane, typhoon, cyclone, vortex; informal twister. ▶ **adj.** **rapid**, lightning, headlong, impulsive, breakneck, meteoric, sudden, swift, fast, quick, speedy.

whisk /(h)wisk/ ▶ **v. 1** beat eggs, cream, etc., with a light, rapid movement. **2** move or take suddenly and quickly. ▶ **n. 1** a device for whisking eggs, cream, etc. **2** a bunch of grass, twigs, etc., for flicking away dust or flies.

SYNONYMS ▶ **v. 1 speed**, hurry, rush, sweep, hurtle, shoot. **2 pull**, snatch, pluck, tug, jerk; informal whip, yank. **3 whip**, beat, mix. ▶ **n.** **beater**, mixer, blender.

□ **whisk broom** a small, stiff broom used especially to brush clothing.

whis·ker /'(h)wiskər/ ▶ **n. 1** each of the long hairs or bristles growing from the face of an animal. **2** (**whiskers**) the hair growing on a man's face. **3** (**a whisker**) informal a very small amount.

whis·key /'(h)wiskē/ (Canadian & British **whisky**) ▶ **n.** (plural **whiskeys** or **whiskies**) a strong alcoholic drink distilled from malted grain.

SPELLING

Kentucky bourbon whis**key** but Scotch and Canadian whis**ky**.

whis·per /'(h)wispər/ ▶ **v.** (**whispers**, **whispering**, **whispered**) **1** speak very softly. **2** literary rustle or murmur softly. ▶ **n. 1** something whispered. **2** a very soft voice. **3** literary a soft rustling or murmuring. **4** a rumor or piece of gossip. **5** a slight trace.

SYNONYMS ▶ **v.** **murmur**, mutter, mumble, speak softly, breathe, say sotto voce. ▶ **n.** **1 murmur**, mutter, mumble, low voice, undertone. **2 rumor**, story, report, gossip, speculation, suggestion, hint; informal buzz. ANTONYMS shout.

■ **whis·per·er n. whis·per·y adj.**

whist /(h)wist/ ▶ **n.** a card game in which points are scored according to the number of tricks won.

whis·tle /'(h)wisəl/ ▶ **n. 1** a clear, high-pitched sound made by forcing breath between the lips or teeth. **2** any similar high-pitched sound. **3** a device used to produce a whistling sound. ▶ **v.** (**whistles**, **whistling**, **whistled**) **1** give out a whistle. **2** move rapidly with a whistling sound. **3** blow a whistle. □ (**as**) **clean as a whistle** extremely clean or clear. **whistle-stop** very fast and with only brief pauses. ■ **whis·tler n.**

whit /(h)wit/ ▶ **n.** a very small part or amount.

white /(h)wīt/ ▶ **adj. 1** having the color of milk or fresh snow. **2** very pale. **3** relating to people with light-colored skin. **4** (of wine) yellowish in color. **5** innocent and pure. ▶ **n. 1** white color. **2** the visible pale part of the eyeball around the iris. **3** the outer part that surrounds the yolk of an egg; the albumen. **4** a white person.

SYNONYMS ▶ **adj.** **pale**, pallid, wan, ashen, chalky, pasty, peaked, washed out, ghostly, deathly.

□ **white blood cell** (or **white cell**) a cell in the blood or lymph that acts against foreign substances and disease. **white-bread** informal belonging to or representative of the white middle class. **white chocolate** a whitish candy made with cocoa butter. **white-collar** relating to work in an office or other professional environment. **white dwarf** Astronomy a small very dense star that is typically the size of a planet. **white elephant** a useless or troublesome possession. **white flag** a white flag waved as a symbol of surrender or truce. **white goods 1** household linen. **2** large household appliances. **white heat** the temperature or state of something that is so hot that it gives out white light. **white-hot** so hot that it glows white. **White House** the official residence of the US president, and the offices of the executive branch of government, in Washington, DC. **white lie** a harmless lie told to avoid hurting someone's feelings. **white lightning** illegal homemade whiskey; moonshine. **white magic** magic used only for good purposes. **white meat** meat that is pale when cooked, such as poultry, veal, and rabbit.

white noise noise containing many frequencies with equal intensities. **white pages** the part of the telephone book that lists residential and business telephone numbers in alphabetical order by name. **white paper** a government or corporate report giving information or proposals on an issue. **white sale** a store's special sale of household linen. **white sauce** a sauce made with flour, butter, and milk or stock. **white tie** a man's white bow tie and full evening dress. **white-tie** requiring full evening dress. ■ **white·ness** n.

white·bait /ˈ(h)wīt,bāt/ ▶ n. the young of various sea fish used as food.

white·fish /ˈ(h)wīt,fisн/ ▶ n. a mainly freshwater fish of the salmon family, widely used as food.

whit·en /ˈ(h)wītn/ ▶ v. make or become white. ■ **whit·en·er** n.

white·wash /ˈ(h)wīt,wäsн, -,wôsн/ ▶ n. 1 a solution of lime or chalk and water, used for painting walls or fences white. 2 a deliberate concealment of mistakes or faults. ▶ v. 1 paint with whitewash. 2 conceal mistakes or faults.

whitewa·ter /(h)wītˈwôtər, -ˈwä-/ (also **white water**) ▶ n. a fast shallow stretch of water in a river.

whith·er /ˈ(h)wiтнər/ ▶ adv. formal or old use 1 to what place or state. 2 what is the likely future of?

whit·ing /ˈ(h)wītiNG/ ▶ n. (plural **whiting**) a sea fish with white flesh eaten as food.

Whit·sun /ˈ(h)witsən/ (or **Whitsuntide** /ˈ(h)witsən,tīd/) ▶ n. the weekend or week including Whitsunday.

Whit·sun·day /,(h)witˈsəndā/ ▶ n. ⇨ PENTECOST.

whit·tle /ˈ(h)witl/ ▶ v. (**whittles**, **whittling**, **whittled**) 1 carve wood by cutting small slices from it. 2 (**whittle something away** or **down**) gradually reduce something.

whiz /(h)wiz/ (also **whizz**) ▶ v. (**whizzed**, **whizzing**) 1 move quickly through the air with a whistling or whooshing sound. 2 move or go fast. 3 (**whiz through**) do or deal with quickly. ▶ n. 1 a whistling or whooshing sound made by something moving fast through the air. 2 (also **wiz** /wiz/) informal a person who is extremely clever at something: *a computer whiz*. □ **whiz kid** informal a young person who is very successful or skillful.

who /ho͞o/ ▶ pron. 1 what or which person or people? 2 introducing a clause giving further information about a person or people previously mentioned.

USAGE

The rule is that you should use **who** as the subject of a verb (*who decided this?*) and **whom** as the object of a verb or preposition (*whom do you think we should support?*). When speaking, however, it's acceptable to use **who** instead of **whom**, as in *who do you think we should support?*.

whoa /wō/ ▶ exclam. used as a command to a horse to stop or slow down.

who'd /ho͞od/ ▶ contr. 1 who had. 2 who would.

who·dun·it /ho͞oˈdənit/ ▶ n. informal a crime story in which the identity of the murderer is not revealed until the end.

who·ev·er /ho͞oˈevər/ (or formal **whosoever** /,ho͞osōˈevər/) ▶ pron. 1 the person or people who; any person who. 2 regardless of who. 3 used for emphasis instead of "who" in questions.

whole /hōl/ ▶ adj. 1 complete; entire. 2 in one piece. ▶ n. 1 a thing that is complete in itself. 2 (**the whole**) all of something.

SYNONYMS ▶ adj. 1 **entire**, complete, full, unabridged, uncut. 2 **intact**, in one piece, unbroken, undamaged, flawless, unmarked, perfect. ANTONYMS incomplete. ▶ n. 1 **entity**, unit, body, ensemble. 2 *the whole of the year* **all**, every part, the lot, the sum.

□ **on the whole** taking everything into account; in general. **whole note** Music a note having the time value of two half notes or four quarter notes. ■ **whole·ness** n.

whole·heart·ed /ˈhōlˈhärtid/ ▶ adj. completely sincere and committed.

SYNONYMS **unqualified**, unreserved, unconditional, complete, full, total, absolute. ANTONYMS halfhearted.

■ **whole·heart·ed·ly** adv.

whole·sale /ˈhōl,sāl/ ▶ n. the selling of goods in large quantities to be sold to the public by others. ▶ adj. & adv. 1 being sold in such a way. 2 done to a very large number of people or things. ▶ v. (**wholesales**, **wholesaling**, **wholesaled**) sell goods wholesale.

SYNONYMS ▶ adj. & adv. **extensive**, widespread, large-scale, wide-ranging, comprehensive, total, mass, indiscriminate, sweeping. ANTONYMS partial.

■ **whole·sal·er** n.

whole·some /ˈhōlsəm/ ▶ adj. 1 good for health or well-being. 2 morally good.

SYNONYMS 1 **healthy**, health-giving, good, nutritious, nourishing, natural, organic. 2 **moral**, ethical, good, clean, virtuous, pure, innocent, chaste, uplifting, edifying.

whol·ly /ˈhōl(l)ē/ ▶ adv. entirely; fully.

SYNONYMS **completely**, totally, absolutely, entirely, fully, thoroughly, utterly, downright, in every respect; informal one hundred percent.

SPELLING

Two **l**s, no **e**: who**ll**y, not who**lely**.

whom /ho͞om/ ▶ pron. used instead of "who" as the object of a verb or preposition.

whom·ev·er /ho͞omˈevər/ ▶ pron. chiefly formal used instead of "whoever" as the object of a verb or preposition.

whom·so·ev·er /,ho͞omsōˈevər/ ▶ relative pron. formal used instead of "whosoever" as the object of a verb or preposition.

whoop /(h)wo͝op, ho͞op/ ▶ n. a loud cry of joy or excitement. ▶ v. give or make a whoop. □ **whooping cough** an illness that mainly affects children, marked by coughs followed by a noisy drawing in of breath.

whoop·ee /ˈ(h)wo͝opē, ˈ(h)wo͞oˈpē/ ▶ exclam. informal expressing excitement or joy.

whoosh /(h)wo͞osн, (h)wo͝osн/ ▶ v. move quickly with a rushing sound. ▶ n. a whooshing movement.

whop·per /ˈ(h)wäpər/ ▶ n. informal 1 something that is very large. 2 a blatant lie.

whop·ping /ˈ(h)wäpiNG/ ▶ adj. informal very large.

whore /hôr/ ▶ **n.** **1** a prostitute. **2** disapproving a woman who has many sexual partners.

whorl /(h)wôrl/ ▶ **n.** **1** each of the turns in a spiral or coil. **2** a spiral or coil. **3** a coil of leaves, flowers, or branches encircling a stem.

who's /ho͞oz/ ▶ **contr.** **1** who is. **2** who has.

USAGE

Don't confuse **who's** with **whose**. **Who's** is short for either **who is** or **who has**, as in *he has a son who's a doctor* or *who's done the reading?*, whereas **whose** means 'belonging to which person' or 'of whom or which,' as in *whose is this?* or *he's a man whose opinion I respect*.

whose /ho͞oz/ ▶ **possessive determiner & pron.** **1** belonging to or associated with which person. **2** of whom or which.

whump /(h)wəmp/ ▶ **n.** a dull thud. ▶ **v.** make a whump.

whup /(h)wo͝op/ ▶ **v.** (**whups**, **whupping**, **whupped**) informal or dialect beat or whip.

why /(h)wī/ ▶ **adv.** **1** for what reason or purpose? **2** on account of which; the reason that. ▶ **exclam.** expressing surprise, annoyance, etc.

wick /wik/ ▶ **n.** a length of cord in a candle, lamp, or lighter that carries liquid fuel to the flame.

wick·ed /'wikid/ ▶ **adj.** **1** very bad; evil. **2** playfully mischievous. **3** informal excellent; wonderful.

SYNONYMS **1 evil**, sinful, immoral, wrong, bad, iniquitous, corrupt, base, vile, villainous, criminal, nefarious; informal crooked. **2 mischievous**, playful, naughty, impish, roguish, puckish, cheeky. ANTONYMS virtuous.

■ **wick·ed·ly** adv. **wick·ed·ness** n.

wick·er /'wikər/ ▶ **n.** twigs plaited or woven to make items such as furniture and baskets. ■ **wick·er·work** n.

wick·et /'wikit/ ▶ **n.** **1** Cricket each of the two sets of three stumps with two bails across the top that are defended by a batsman. **2** a small door or gate.

wide /wīd/ ▶ **adj.** (**wider**, **widest**) **1** of great or more than average width. **2** having a particular width. **3** open to the full extent. **4** including a great variety of people or things. **5** spread among a large number or over a large area. **6** at a distance from a point or mark. **7** (in soccer) at or near the side of the field. ▶ **adv.** **1** to the full extent. **2** far from the target.

SYNONYMS ▶ **adj.** **1 broad**, extensive, spacious, vast, spread out. **2 comprehensive**, ample, broad, extensive, wide-ranging, large, exhaustive, all-inclusive, expansive, all-embracing, encyclopedic, catholic. **3 off target**, off the mark, inaccurate. ANTONYMS narrow.

□ **wide awake** fully awake. **wide-eyed** **1** having your eyes wide open in amazement. **2** inexperienced; innocent. **wide of the mark** **1** a long way from the target. **2** inaccurate. ■ **wide·ly** adv.

wid·en /'wīdn/ ▶ **v.** make or become wider.

SYNONYMS **broaden**, open up/out, expand, extend, enlarge.

wide·spread /'wīd'spred/ ▶ **adj.** spread among a large number or over a large area.

SYNONYMS **general**, extensive, universal, common, global, worldwide, omnipresent, ubiquitous, across the board, predominant, prevalent, rife, broad. ANTONYMS limited.

widg·eon = **WIGEON**.

widg·et /'wijit/ ▶ **n.** informal a small gadget or mechanical device.

wid·ow /'widō/ ▶ **n.** a woman whose husband has died and who has not married again. ▶ **v.** (**be widowed**) become a widow or widower.

wid·ow·er /'widō-ər/ ▶ **n.** a man whose wife has died and who has not married again.

width /widTH, witTH/ ▶ **n.** **1** the measurement or extent of something from side to side. **2** wide range or extent.

SYNONYMS **breadth**, thickness, span, diameter, girth.

width·wise /'widTH,wīz, 'witTH-/ (or **widthways** /-,wāz/) ▶ **adv.** in a direction parallel with a thing's width.

wield /wēld/ ▶ **v.** **1** hold and use a weapon or tool. **2** have power or influence.

SYNONYMS **1 brandish**, flourish, wave, swing, use, employ, handle. **2** *he wields enormous power* **exercise**, exert, hold, maintain, command, control.

SPELLING

Remember, the usual rule is **i** before **e**, when the sound is *ee*, except after **c**: w**ie**ld.

wie·ner /'wēnər/ ▶ **n.** a frankfurter or similar sausage.

wife /wīf/ ▶ **n.** (plural **wives** /wīvz/) the woman a man is married to.

SYNONYMS **spouse**, partner, mate, consort, bride; informal better half, missus.

■ **wife·ly** adj.

Wi-Fi /'wī 'fī/ ▶ **abbr.** Wireless Fidelity, a group of technical standards used for sending data over wireless networks.

wig /wig/ ▶ **n.** a covering for the head made of real or artificial hair.

wig·eon /'wijən/ (or **widgeon**) ▶ **n.** a duck with mainly reddish-brown and gray feathers.

wig·gle /'wigəl/ ▶ **v.** (**wiggles**, **wiggling**, **wiggled**) move with short movements up and down or from side to side. ▶ **n.** a wiggling movement. ■ **wig·gly** adj.

wig·wam /'wig,wäm/ ▶ **n.** a tent consisting of animal skins fixed over a framework of poles, formerly lived in by some North American Indian peoples.

wild /wīld/ ▶ **adj.** **1** (of animals or plants) living or growing in their natural environment. **2** (of scenery or a region) not lived in or changed by people. **3** lacking discipline or control. **4** not based on reason or evidence. **5** informal very enthusiastic or excited. ▶ **n.** **1** (**the wild**) a natural state. **2** (**the wilds**) a remote area.

SYNONYMS ▶ **adj.** **1 untamed**, undomesticated, feral, fierce, ferocious, savage. **2 uncultivated**, native, indigenous. **3 uninhabited**, unpopulated, uncultivated, rugged, rough, inhospitable, desolate, barren. **4 stormy**, squally, tempestuous, turbulent, blustery. **5 uncontrolled**, unrestrained, undisciplined, unruly, rowdy, disorderly, riotous, out of control, unbridled. **6** *a wild scheme* **foolish**, ridiculous, ludicrous, stupid, foolhardy, idiotic, madcap, absurd, silly, impractical, impracticable, unworkable; informal crazy, crackpot. **7** *a wild guess* **random**, arbitrary, haphazard, uninformed. ANTONYMS tame, cultivated, calm, disciplined.

□ **wild card 1** a playing card that can take on any value, suit, or color that the player holding it needs. **2** Computing a character that will match any character or sequence of characters in a search. **3** an opportunity to enter a sports competition without having qualified in the usual way, or a player or team given such an opportunity. **wild goose chase** a hopeless search for something that you will never find. **Wild West** the western US during its lawless early history. ■ **wild·ly** adv. **wild·ness** n.

wild·cat /'wīld,kat/ ▶ n. a bobcat or other smaller member of the cat family. ▶ adj. (of a strike) sudden and unofficial.

wil·de·beest /'wildə,bēst/ ▶ n. a gnu (a kind of antelope).

wil·der·ness /'wildərnis/ ▶ n. a wild, uninhabited, and unwelcoming region.

SYNONYMS **wilds**, desert, wasteland.

wild·fire /'wīld,fīr/ ▶ n. (**spread like wildfire**) spread very fast.

wild·fowl /'wīld,foul/ ▶ pl.n. birds that are hunted for sport or food.

wild·life /'wīld,līf/ ▶ n. all the animals, birds, and insects that naturally inhabit a particular region.

wiles /wīlz/ ▶ pl.n. cunning methods used by someone to get what they want.

SYNONYMS **tricks**, ruses, ploys, schemes, dodges, maneuvers, subterfuges, guile, artfulness, cunning.

will¹ /wil/ ▶ modal v. (3rd singular present **will**; past **would** /wo͝od/) **1** expressing the future tense. **2** expressing a request. **3** expressing desire or consent. **4** expressing facts about ability or capacity.

USAGE

The traditional rule is that you should use **shall** when forming the future tense with **I** and **we** (*I shall be late*) and **will** with **you**, **he**, **she**, **it**, and **they** (*he will not be there*). Nowadays, people do not follow this rule so strictly and are more likely to use the shortened forms **I'll**, **she'll**, etc.

will² ▶ n. **1** the power you have to decide on something and take action. **2** (also **willpower** /'wil,pou(ə)r/) the ability to control your thoughts and actions in order to achieve something. **3** a desire or intention. **4** a legal document in which someone gives instructions about what should be done with their money and property after their death. ▶ v. **1** intend or desire that something should happen. **2** bring something about by using your mental powers. **3** leave money or property to someone in a will.

SYNONYMS ▶ n. **1 determination**, strength of character, resolve, single-mindedness, drive, commitment, dedication, doggedness, tenacity, staying power. **2** *they stayed against their will* **desire**, wish, preference, inclination, intention. **3** *it was God's will* **wish**, desire, decision, choice, decree, command. ▶ v. **1 want**, wish, please, see fit, think best/fit, like, choose, prefer. **2 decree**, order, ordain, command.

□ **at will** whenever or in whatever way you like.

will·ful /'wilfəl/ ▶ adj. **1** (of a bad act) deliberate. **2** stubborn and determined.

SYNONYMS **1 deliberate**, intentional, premeditated, planned, conscious, calculated. **2 headstrong**, strong-willed, obstinate, stubborn, pig-headed, recalcitrant. ANTONYMS accidental.

■ **will·ful·ly** adv.

will·ing /'wiliNG/ ▶ adj. **1** ready, eager, or prepared to do something. **2** given or done readily.

SYNONYMS **1 ready**, prepared, disposed, inclined, minded, happy, glad, pleased, agreeable, amenable; informal game. **2 readily given**, ungrudging. ANTONYMS reluctant.

will·ing·ly /'wiliNGlē/ ▶ adv. of your own free will.

SYNONYMS **voluntarily**, of your own free will, of your own accord, readily, without reluctance, ungrudgingly, cheerfully, happily, gladly, with pleasure. ANTONYMS reluctantly.

will·ing·ness /'wiliNGnis/ ▶ n. the state of being ready, eager, or prepared to do something: *we appreciate your willingness to help.*

SYNONYMS **readiness**, inclination, will, wish, desire. ANTONYMS reluctance.

will-o'-the-wisp /'wil ə T͟Hə 'wisp/ ▶ n. **1** a thing that is impossible to obtain. **2** a faint flickering light seen at night over marshy ground, thought to result from natural gases burning.

wil·low /'wilō/ ▶ n. a tree that has narrow leaves and produces catkins.

wil·low·y /'wilōē/ ▶ adj. tall and slim.

wil·ly-nil·ly /'wilē 'nilē/ ▶ adv. **1** whether you like it or not. **2** without any direction or plan.

wilt /wilt/ ▶ v. **1** (of a plant) become limp through heat or lack of water. **2** feel tired and weak.

SYNONYMS **1 droop**, sag, become limp, flop. **2 languish**, flag, droop, become listless, fade. ANTONYMS flourish.

wil·y /'wīlē/ ▶ adj. clever in a cunning or crafty way.

SYNONYMS **shrewd**, clever, sharp, astute, canny, smart, crafty, cunning, artful, sly, scheming, calculating, devious; informal foxy. ANTONYMS naive.

wimp /wimp/ ▶ n. informal a person who is not strong, brave, or confident. ■ **wimp·ish** adj. **wimp·y** adj.

wim·ple /'wimpəl/ ▶ n. a cloth headdress covering the head, neck, and sides of the face, worn in the past by women and still today by some nuns.

win /win/ ▶ v. (**wins**, **winning**, **won** /wən/) **1** be the most successful in a contest or conflict. **2** gain something as a result of success in a contest or conflict. **3** gain someone's attention, support, or love. **4** (**win someone over**) gain someone's agreement or support by persuading them that you are right. ▶ n. a victory in a game or contest.

SYNONYMS ▶ v. **1 come first**, be victorious, carry/win the day, come out on top, succeed, triumph, prevail. **2 earn**, gain, secure, collect, pick up, walk away/off with, carry off; informal land, net, bag, scoop. ANTONYMS lose. ▶ n. **victory**, triumph, conquest. ANTONYMS defeat.

wince /wins/ ▶ v. (**winces**, **wincing**, **winced**) flinch slightly on feeling pain or distress. ▶ n. an act of wincing.

SYNONYMS ▶ v. **grimace**, pull a face, flinch, blench, start.

winch /winCH/ ▶ n. a hauling or lifting device consisting of a rope or chain winding around a rotating drum. ▶ v. hoist or haul something with a winch.

wind¹ /wind/ ▶ n. **1** a natural movement of the air. **2** breath needed to play an instrument or do exercise. **3** wind or woodwind instruments forming a band or section of an orchestra. **4** air or gas in the stomach or intestines. ▶ v. make someone unable to breathe easily for a short time.

SYNONYMS ▶ n. **1 breeze**, current of air, gale, hurricane, gust, draft; informal blow; literary zephyr. **2 breath**; informal puff.

□ **get wind of** informal hear a rumor of. **wind farm** an area containing a group of energy-producing windmills or wind turbines. **wind instrument** **1** a musical instrument that you play by blowing into it. **2** a woodwind instrument as distinct from a brass instrument. **wind tunnel** a tunnel-like structure in which a strong current of air is created, to test the effect of wind and air flow on vehicles.

wind² /wīnd/ ▶ v. (**winds**, **winding**, **wound** /wound/) **1** move in or take a twisting or spiral course. **2** pass something around a thing or person so as to encircle or enfold them. **3** (with reference to something long) twist or be twisted around itself or a central thing. **4** make a clockwork device work by turning a key or handle. **5** turn a key or handle repeatedly. **6** move an audiotape, videotape, or film backward or forward.

SYNONYMS **1 twist (and turn)**, bend, curve, loop, meander, zigzag, weave, snake; (**winding**) serpentine, sinuous. **2 wrap**, furl, entwine, lace. **3 coil**, roll, twist, twine.

□ **wind down 1** (of a clockwork mechanism) gradually lose power. **2** (also **wind something down**) draw or bring something gradually to an end. **3** informal relax. **wind up** informal end up in a particular situation or place. **wind someone/something up** gradually bring something to an end.

wind·bag /'wind,bag/ ▶ n. informal a person who talks a lot but without saying anything interesting or important.

wind·break /'wind,brāk/ ▶ n. a screen providing shelter from the wind.

wind·break·er /'wind,brākər/ ▶ n. a wind-resistant jacket with a close-fitting neck and cuffs.

wind·fall /'wind,fôl/ ▶ n. **1** a piece of unexpected good fortune. **2** an apple or other fruit blown from a tree by the wind.

SYNONYMS **bonanza**, jackpot, pennies from heaven, godsend.

wind·lass /'windləs/ ▶ n. a winch used on a ship or in a harbor.

wind·mill /'wind,mil/ ▶ n. a building with sails or vanes that turn in the wind and generate power to grind corn, generate electricity, or draw water.

win·dow /'windō/ ▶ n. **1** an opening in a wall, fitted with glass to let in light and allow people to see out. **2** a framed area on a computer screen for viewing information. □ **window dressing** **1** the arrangement of a display in a store window. **2** the presentation of something in a superficially attractive way to give a good impression. **window-shop** spend time looking at the goods displayed in store windows.

win·dow·pane /'windō,pān/ ▶ n. a pane of glass in a window.

win·dow·sill /'windō,sil/ ▶ n. a ledge or sill at the bottom of a window.

wind·pipe /'wind,pīp/ ▶ n. the tube carrying air down the throat and into the lungs; the trachea.

wind·shield /'win(d),SHēld/ ▶ n. a window at the front of the passenger compartment of a motor vehicle. □ **windshield wiper** a device consisting of a rubber blade on an arm that moves in an arc, for keeping a windshield clear of rain.

wind·sock /'wind,säk/ ▶ n. a light, flexible cone mounted on a mast to show the direction and strength of the wind.

wind·storm /'wind,stôrm/ ▶ n. a storm with very strong wind but little or no rain or snow.

wind·surf·ing /'wind,sərfiNG/ ▶ n. the sport of riding on a sailboard on water. ■ **wind·surf** v. **wind·surf·er** n.

wind·swept /'wind,swept/ ▶ adj. exposed to strong winds.

wind·ward /'windwərd/ ▶ adj. & adv. facing the wind, or on the side facing the wind.

wind·y /'windē/ ▶ adj. (**windier**, **windiest**) **1** marked by or exposed to strong winds: *a windy day*. **2** informal (of speaking or writing) using many words that sound impressive but mean little.

SYNONYMS **breezy**, blowy, fresh, blustery, gusty, wild, stormy, squally. ANTONYMS still.

wine /wīn/ ▶ n. an alcoholic drink made from fermented grape juice.

win·er·y /'wīnərē/ ▶ n. (plural **wineries**) an establishment where wine is made.

wing /wiNG/ ▶ n. **1** a kind of limb used by a bird, bat, or insect for flying. **2** a rigid structure projecting from both sides of an aircraft and supporting it in the air. **3** a part of a large building. **4** a group or faction within an organization. **5** (**the wings**) the sides of a theater stage out of view of the audience. **6** the part of a soccer or rugby field close to the sidelines. **7** an air force unit of several squadrons. ▶ v. **1** fly, or move quickly as if flying. **2** shoot a bird so as to wound it in the wing. **3** (**wing it**) informal speak or act without preparation.

SYNONYMS ▶ n. **1 part**, section, side, annex, extension. **2 faction**, camp, caucus, arm, branch, group, section, set. ▶ v. **1 fly**, glide, soar. **2 wound**, graze, hit.

□ **wing nut** a nut with a pair of projections for the fingers to turn it on a screw.

winged /wiNGd/ ▶ adj. **1** having wings. **2** literary fast and graceful; seeming to have wings.

wing·er /'wiNGər/ ▶ n. an attacking player on the wing in soccer, hockey, etc.

wing·span /'wiNG,span/ ▶ n. the full extent from tip to tip of the wings of an aircraft, bird, etc.

wink /wiNGk/ ▶ v. **1** close and open one eye quickly as a private signal. **2** shine with an unsteady light; flash on and off. ▶ n. an act of winking.

SYNONYMS ▶ v. **1 blink**, flutter, bat. **2 sparkle**, twinkle, flash, glitter, gleam, shine, scintillate.

win·ner /'winər/ ▶ n. **1** a person or thing that wins. **2** informal a successful or highly promising thing.

SYNONYMS **victor**, champion, conqueror, medalist; informal champ, top dog. ANTONYMS loser.

win·ning /'winiNG/ ▶ adj. attractive. ▶ n. (**winnings**) money won by gambling.

SYNONYMS ▶ **adj.** **engaging**, charming, appealing, endearing, sweet, cute, winsome, attractive, prepossessing, fetching, disarming, captivating. ▶ **n.** (**winnings**) **prize money**, gains, booty, spoils, proceeds, profits, takings, purse.

■ **win·ning·ly** adv.

win·now /'winō/ ▶ **v.** **1** remove people or things from a group until only the best ones are left. **2** blow air through grain in order to remove the chaff.

win·o /'wīnō/ ▶ **n.** (plural **winos**) informal a person who sits all day in the streets drinking alcohol.

win·some /'winsəm/ ▶ **adj.** appealing.

win·ter /'wintər/ ▶ **n.** the coldest season of the year, after autumn and before spring. ▶ **v.** (**winters, wintering, wintered**) spend the winter in a particular place.

win·ter·ize /'wintə,rīz/ ▶ **v.** adapt or prepare something for use in cold weather.

win·try /'wintrē/ ▶ **adj.** cold or bleak.

SYNONYMS **bleak**, cold, chilly, frosty, freezing, icy, snowy, arctic, glacial, bitter, raw; informal nippy. ANTONYMS warm.

wipe /wīp/ ▶ **v.** (**wipes, wiping, wiped**) **1** clean or dry something by rubbing it with a cloth or your hand. **2** remove something from a surface in this way. **3** erase data from a computer, tape, etc. ▶ **n.** **1** an act of wiping. **2** an absorbent cleaning cloth.

SYNONYMS ▶ **v.** **1** **rub**, mop, sponge, swab, clean, dry, polish. **2** *he wiped off the marks* **rub off**, clean off, remove, erase, efface.

□ **wipe someone/something out** **1** remove or eliminate something. **2** kill a large number of people. ■ **wip·er** n.

wire /wīr/ ▶ **n.** **1** metal in the form of a thin flexible strand. **2** a length of wire used for fencing, to carry an electric current, etc. **3** a concealed listening device. **4** informal a telegram. ▶ **v.** (**wires, wiring, wired**) **1** install electric circuits or wires in a room or building. **2** fasten or reinforce with wire. **3** informal send a telegram to.

wire·less /'wīrlis/ ▶ **adj.** using radio, microwaves, etc., (as opposed to wires) to transmit signals. ▶ **n.** **1** computer networking, etc., using radio signals. **2** dated a radio.

wire·tap·ping /'wīr,tapiNG/ ▶ **n.** the secret tapping of telephone lines in order to listen to other people's conversations.

wir·ing /'wīriNG/ ▶ **n.** a system of wires providing electric circuits for a device or building.

wir·y /'wī(ə)rē/ ▶ **adj.** **1** resembling wire. **2** lean, tough, and sinewy.

SYNONYMS **1** *a wiry man* **sinewy**, tough, athletic, strong; lean, spare, thin, skinny. **2** *wiry hair* **coarse**, rough, strong. ANTONYMS flabby, smooth.

wis·dom /'wizdəm/ ▶ **n.** **1** the quality of being wise. **2** the knowledge that a particular society or culture has gained over a period of time.

SYNONYMS **1** **understanding**, intelligence, sagacity, sense, common sense, shrewdness, astuteness, judgment, prudence, circumspection, logic, rationale, soundness, advisability. **2** **knowledge**, learning, erudition, scholarship, philosophy, lore. ANTONYMS folly.

□ **wisdom tooth** each of the four molars at the back of the mouth that usually appear at about the age of eighteen.

wise /wīz/ ▶ **adj.** **1** having or showing experience, knowledge, and good judgment. **2** (**wise to**) informal aware of. ▶ **v.** (**wises, wising, wised**) (**wise up**) informal become aware of something.

SYNONYMS ▶ **adj.** **sage**, sagacious, intelligent, clever, learned, knowledgeable, enlightened, astute, smart, shrewd, sharp-witted, canny, knowing, sensible, prudent, discerning, perceptive. ANTONYMS foolish.

□ **wise guy** **1** a person who makes sarcastic or sassy remarks to demonstrate their cleverness. **2** a member of the Mafia. ■ **wise·ly** adv.

wise·a·cre /'wīz,ākər/ ▶ **n.** a person who affects wisdom or knowledge.

wise·crack /'wīz,krak/ informal ▶ **n.** a witty remark or joke. ▶ **v.** make a wisecrack.

wish /wisH/ ▶ **v.** **1** feel a strong desire for something. **2** silently express a hope that something will happen. **3** say that you hope that someone will be happy, successful, etc. ▶ **n.** **1** a desire or hope. **2** (**wishes**) an expression of hope that someone will be happy, successful, etc. **3** a thing wished for.

SYNONYMS ▶ **v.** **want**, desire, feel inclined, feel like, care, choose, please, think fit. ▶ **n.** **1** **desire**, longing, yearning, whim, craving, hunger, hope, aspiration, aim, ambition, dream; informal hankering, yen. **2** *her parents' wishes* **request**, requirement, bidding, instruction, direction, demand, order, command, want, desire, will.

wish·bone /'wisH,bōn/ ▶ **n.** a forked bone between the neck and breast of a bird.

wish·ful /'wisHfəl/ ▶ **adj.** wishing for something to happen. □ **wishful thinking** expectations that are based on optimistic wishes rather than facts.

wish·y-wash·y /'wisHē 'wäsHē, -'wôsHē/ ▶ **adj.** not firm or forceful; feeble.

wisp /wisp/ ▶ **n.** a small, thin bunch or strand of something.

wisp·y /wispē/ ▶ **adj.** consisting of or resembling a wisp or wisps; having thin strands.

wis·te·ri·a /wi'sti(ə)rēə/ ▶ **n.** a climbing plant with hanging clusters of bluish-lilac flowers.

wist·ful /'wistfəl/ ▶ **adj.** having a feeling of vague or regretful longing.

SYNONYMS **nostalgic**, yearning, longing, forlorn, melancholy, sad, mournful, pensive, reflective, contemplative.

■ **wist·ful·ly** adv. **wist·ful·ness** n.

wit /wit/ ▶ **n.** **1** (also **wits**) the ability to think quickly and make good decisions. **2** a natural talent for using words and ideas in a quick and funny way. **3** a witty person.

SYNONYMS **1** *he needed all his wits to escape* **intelligence**, shrewdness, astuteness, cleverness, canniness, sense, judgment, acumen, insight, brains, mind. **2** **wittiness**, humor, drollery, repartee, badinage, banter, wordplay, jokes, witticisms, quips, puns. **3** **comedian**, humorist, comic, joker; informal wag.

□ **at your wits' end** not knowing what to do.

witch /wicH/ ▶ **n.** a woman believed to have evil magic powers.

SYNONYMS **sorceress**, enchantress, hex.

□ **witch doctor** a person believed to have magic powers that cure illness. **witch hazel** a lotion made from the bark and leaves of a shrub, used for treating injuries on the skin. **witch-hunt** a campaign against a person who holds unpopular views.

witch·craft /'wicH,kraft/ ▶ **n.** the use of evil magic powers.

SYNONYMS **sorcery**, (black) magic, wizardry, spells, incantations, necromancy, Wicca.

with /wiTH, wiTH/ ▶ **prep.** **1** accompanied by. **2** in the same direction as. **3** possessing; having. **4** indicating the instrument used to perform an action or the material used for a purpose. **5** in opposition to or competition with. **6** indicating the way or attitude in which a person does something. **7** in relation to. □ **with it** informal **1** up to date or fashionable. **2** alert and able to understand.

with·draw /wiTH'drô, wiTH-/ ▶ **v.** (**withdraws**, **withdrawing**, **withdrew** /-'dro͞o/; past participle **withdrawn**) **1** remove or take away. **2** leave or cause to leave a place. **3** stop taking part in an activity. **4** take back something you have said. **5** take money out of an account. **6** go away to another place in search of quiet or privacy. **7** stop taking an addictive drug. **8** (**withdrawn**) very shy or reserved.

SYNONYMS **1 remove**, extract, pull out, take out, take back. **2 abolish**, cancel, lift, set aside, end, stop, remove, reverse, revoke, rescind, repeal, annul. **3 retract**, take back, go back on, recant, repudiate, renounce, back down, climb down, backtrack, back-pedal, do a U-turn, eat your words. **4 retreat**, pull out of, evacuate, quit, leave. **5 retire**, retreat, adjourn, decamp, leave, depart, absent yourself; formal repair. **6** (**withdrawn**) **introverted**, unsociable, inhibited, uncommunicative, unforthcoming, quiet, reticent, reserved, retiring, private, reclusive, distant, shy, timid. ANTONYMS insert, enter.

with·draw·al /wiTH'drôl, wiTH-/ ▶ **n.** **1** the action of withdrawing. **2** the process of giving up an addictive drug.

SYNONYMS **1 removal**, abolition, cancellation, discontinuation, termination, elimination. **2 departure**, pullout, exit, exodus, evacuation, retreat.

with·er /'wiTHər/ ▶ **v.** (**withers**, **withering**, **withered**) **1** (of a plant) become dry and shriveled. **2** become shrunken or wrinkled from age or disease. **3** become weaker; decline. **4** (**withering**) scornful.

SYNONYMS **1 shrivel** (**up**), dry up, wilt, droop, go limp, fade, perish. **2 waste** (**away**), shrivel (up), shrink, atrophy. **3 diminish**, dwindle, shrink, lessen, fade, wane, evaporate, disappear. **4** (**withering**) **scornful**, contemptuous, scathing, stinging. ANTONYMS thrive.

with·ers /'wiTHərz/ ▶ **pl.n.** the highest part of a horse's back, at the base of the neck.

with·hold /wiTH'hōld, wiTH-/ ▶ **v.** (**withholds**, **withholding**, **withheld** /'held/) **1** refuse to give. **2** hold back an emotion or reaction.

SYNONYMS **1 hold back**, keep back, refuse to give, retain, hold on to, hide, conceal, keep secret; informal sit on. **2 suppress**, repress, hold back, fight back, choke back, control, check, restrain, contain. ANTONYMS release.

SPELLING

Remember to double the **h**: with**h**old.

with·in /wiTH'in, wi'TH-/ ▶ **prep.** **1** before a particular period of time has passed. **2** inside the range or bounds of something. **3** inside something. ▶ **adv.** inside.

with·out /wiTH'out, wiTH-/ ▶ **prep.** not accompanied by, using, or having. ▶ **adv.** old use outside.

with·stand /wiTH'stand, wiTH-/ ▶ **v.** (**withstands**, **withstanding**, **withstood** /'sto͝od/) remain undamaged by; resist.

SYNONYMS **resist**, weather, survive, endure, cope with, stand, tolerate, bear, defy, brave, hold out against.

wit·less /'witlis/ ▶ **adj.** foolish; stupid.

wit·ness /'witnis/ ▶ **n.** **1** a person who sees an event take place. **2** a person who gives evidence in a court of law. **3** a person who is present at the signing of a document and signs it themselves to confirm this. ▶ **v.** **1** be a witness to. **2** be the place, period, etc., in which an event takes place.

SYNONYMS ▶ **n.** **observer**, onlooker, eyewitness, spectator, viewer, watcher, bystander, passerby. ▶ **v.** **1 see**, observe, watch, view, notice, spot, be present at, attend. **2 countersign**, sign, endorse, validate.

□ **bear witness to** testify to.

wit·ti·cism /'witi,sizəm/ ▶ **n.** a witty remark.

wit·ty /'witē/ ▶ **adj.** (**wittier**, **wittiest**) able to say clever and amusing things.

SYNONYMS **humorous**, amusing, droll, funny, comic, jocular, sparkling, scintillating, entertaining, clever, quick-witted.

■ **wit·ti·ly** **adv.**

wives /wīvz/ plural of **WIFE**.

wiz·ard /'wizərd/ ▶ **n.** **1** a man who has magical powers. **2** a person who is very skilled in something.

SYNONYMS **1 sorcerer**, warlock, magus, (black) magician, enchanter. **2 genius**, expert, master, virtuoso, maestro, marvel; informal hotshot, whiz/wiz, whiz kid, maven.

■ **wiz·ard·ry** **n.**

wiz·ened /'wizənd, 'wē-/ ▶ **adj.** shriveled or wrinkled with age.

WMD ▶ **abbr.** weapon (or weapons) of mass destruction.

woad /wōd/ ▶ **n.** a plant whose leaves were used in the past to make blue dye.

wob·ble /'wäbəl/ ▶ **v.** (**wobbles**, **wobbling**, **wobbled**) **1** move unsteadily from side to side. **2** (of the voice) tremble. ▶ **n.** a wobbling movement or sound.

SYNONYMS ▶ **v.** **1 rock**, sway, seesaw, teeter, jiggle, shake. **2 teeter**, totter, stagger, lurch, waddle. **3** *her voice wobbled* **tremble**, shake, quiver, quaver, waver.

wob·bly /'wäb(ə)lē/ ▶ **adj.** (**wobblier**, **wobbliest**) **1** tending to wobble. **2** weak and unsteady from illness, tiredness, or anxiety. **3** uncertain or insecure: *the evening got off to a wobbly start.*

SYNONYMS **1 unsteady**, unstable, shaky, rocky, rickety, unsafe, precarious; informal wonky. **2 shaky**, quivery, weak, unsteady; informal like jelly. ANTONYMS stable.

woe /wō/ ▶ **n.** literary **1** great sadness or distress. **2** (**woes**) troubles.

SYNONYMS **1 misery**, sorrow, distress, sadness, unhappiness, heartache, heartbreak, despair, adversity, misfortune, disaster, suffering, hardship. **2** *financial woes* **trouble**, difficulty, problem, trial, tribulation, misfortune, setback, reverse. ANTONYMS joy.

□ **woe betide someone** a person will be in trouble if they do a particular thing.

woe·be·gone /ˈwōbiˌgôn, -ˌgän/ ▶ **adj.** looking sad or miserable.

woe·ful /ˈwōfəl/ ▶ **adj. 1** very sad. **2** very bad.

SYNONYMS **1 sad**, unhappy, sorrowful, miserable, gloomy, doleful, plaintive, wretched. **2 dreadful**, awful, terrible, atrocious, disgraceful, deplorable, hopeless, lamentable; informal rotten, appalling, pathetic, pitiful, lousy, abysmal, dire. ANTONYMS cheerful, excellent.

■ **woe·ful·ly adv.**

wok /wäk/ ▶ **n.** a bowl-shaped frying pan used in Chinese cooking.

woke /wōk/ past of **WAKE**[1].

wok·en /ˈwōkən/ past participle of **WAKE**[1].

wolf /wo͝olf/ ▶ **n.** (plural **wolves** /wo͝olvz/) a wild animal of the dog family, that lives and hunts in packs. ▶ **v.** (**wolfs**, **wolfing**, **wolfed**) eat food quickly and greedily. □ **cry wolf** keep raising false alarms, so that when you really need help you are ignored. **wolf whistle** a whistle with a rising and falling note, used by a man to show that he finds a woman attractive. ■ **wolf·ish adj.**

wolf·hound /ˈwo͝olfˌhound/ ▶ **n.** a large breed of dog originally used to hunt wolves.

wolf·ram /ˈwo͝olfrəm/ ▶ **n.** tungsten or its ore.

wol·ver·ine /ˌwo͝olvəˈrēn, ˈwo͝olvəˌrēn/ ▶ **n.** a heavily built meat-eating animal found in cold northern areas.

wolves /wo͝olvz/ plural of **WOLF**.

wom·an /ˈwo͝omən/ ▶ **n.** (plural **women** /ˈwimin/) an adult human female.

SYNONYMS **lady**, female; informal chick, sister, dame, broad; literary damsel.

■ **wom·an·hood n.**

wom·an·ize /ˈwo͝oməˌnīz/ ▶ **v.** (**womanizes**, **womanizing**, **womanized**) (of a man) have a lot of casual affairs with women. ■ **wom·an·iz·er n.**

wom·an·kind /ˈwo͝omənˌkīnd/ ▶ **n.** women as a whole.

wom·an·ly /ˈwo͝omənlē/ ▶ **adj. 1** relating to or having the characteristics of a woman or women. **2** (of a girl's or woman's body) fully developed and curvaceous.

SYNONYMS **1 feminine**, female. **2 voluptuous**, curvaceous, shapely, ample, buxom, full-figured; informal curvy, busty. ANTONYMS manly, boyish.

womb /wo͞om/ ▶ **n.** the organ in a woman's body in which a baby develops before it is born.

wom·bat /ˈwämˌbat/ ▶ **n.** an Australian animal resembling a small bear with short legs.

won /wən/ past and past participle of **WIN**.

won·der /ˈwəndər/ ▶ **v.** (**wonders**, **wondering**, **wondered**) **1** be interested to know about something. **2** feel doubt. **3** feel amazement and admiration. ▶ **n. 1** a feeling of amazement and admiration. **2** a person or thing that causes such a feeling.

SYNONYMS ▶ **v. 1** *I wonder what she is thinking* **ponder** (**over**), think about, meditate on, reflect on, muse on, speculate about, be curious about. **2** *they wondered at the spectacle* **marvel**, be amazed, be astonished, stand in awe, be dumbfounded; informal be flabbergasted. ▶ **n. 1 awe**, admiration, fascination, surprise, astonishment, amazement. **2** *the wonders of nature* **marvel**, miracle, phenomenon, sensation, spectacle, beauty, curiosity.

□ **no wonder** it is not surprising.

won·der·ful /ˈwəndərfəl/ ▶ **adj.** very good or remarkable.

SYNONYMS **marvelous**, magnificent, superb, glorious, sublime, lovely, delightful; informal super, great, fantastic, terrific, tremendous, sensational, fabulous, awesome, neat, magic, wicked, peachy, dandy.

■ **won·der·ful·ly adv.**

won·der·land /ˈwəndərˌland/ ▶ **n.** a place full of wonderful things.

won·drous /ˈwəndrəs/ ▶ **adj.** literary inspiring wonder.

wonk /wäNGk/ ▶ **n.** informal, disapproving **1** a studious, hard-working person. **2** a person who takes an excessive interest in minor details of an issue or subject.

won·ky /ˈwäNGkē/ ▶ **adj.** informal **1** crooked. **2** unsteady or faulty.

wont /wônt, wōnt/ ▶ **n.** (**your wont**) formal your normal behavior. ▶ **adj.** (**wont to**) literary in the habit of doing something.

won't /wōnt/ ▶ **contr.** will not.

wont·ed /ˈwôntid, ˈwōn-/ ▶ **adj.** literary usual.

woo /wo͞o/ ▶ **v.** (**woos**, **wooing**, **wooed**) **1** (of a man) try to make a woman love him. **2** try to get someone's support or custom.

SYNONYMS **1 romantically pursue**, pursue, chase (after); dated court, pay court to, romance, seek the hand of. **2 seek**, pursue, curry favor with, try to win, try to attract, try to cultivate. **3 entice**, tempt, coax, persuade, wheedle, seduce; informal sweet-talk.

wood /wo͝od/ ▶ **n. 1** the hard material forming the trunk and branches of a tree. **2** (also **woods**) a small forest.

SYNONYMS **1 lumber**, timber, logs, planks, boards. **2 forest**, woodland, trees, copse, coppice, grove.

■ **wood·y adj.**

wood·chuck /ˈwo͝odˌCHək/ ▶ **n.** a burrowing rodent with a heavy body and short legs; a groundhog.

wood·cut /ˈwo͝odˌkət/ ▶ **n.** a print made with a block of wood in which a design has been cut.

wood·cut·ter /ˈwo͝odˌkətər/ ▶ **n.** a person who cuts down trees for wood.

wood·ed /ˈwo͝odid/ ▶ **adj.** (of land) covered with woods.

SYNONYMS **forested**, afforested, tree-covered; literary sylvan.

wood·en /ˈwo͝odn/ ▶ **adj. 1** made of wood. **2** acting or speaking in a stiff and awkward way.

SYNONYMS **1 wood**, timber. **2 stilted**, stiff, unnatural, awkward, flat, clumsy, graceless, inelegant. **3 expressionless**, impassive, poker-faced, emotionless, blank, vacant, unresponsive, lifeless.

■ **wood·en·ly adv.**

wood·land /ˈwo͝odlənd/ (or **woodlands**) ▶ **n.** land covered with trees.

wood·louse /ˈwo͝od,lous/ ▶ **n.** (plural **woodlice**) a small insect-like creature with a gray segmented body.

wood·peck·er /ˈwo͝od,pekər/ ▶ **n.** a bird with a strong bill that pecks at tree trunks to find insects.

woods·y /ˈwo͝odzē/ ▶ **adj.** (**woodsier**, **woodsiest**) relating to or characteristic of wood or woodlands.

wood·turn·ing /ˈwo͝od,tərniNG/ ▶ **n.** the activity of shaping wood with a lathe.

wood·wind /ˈwo͝od,wind/ ▶ **n.** wind instruments other than brass instruments forming a section of an orchestra.

wood·work /ˈwo͝od,wərk/ ▶ **n. 1** the wooden parts of a room, building, or other structure. **2** the activity of making things from wood. ■ **wood·work·er n.**

wood·worm /ˈwo͝od,wərm/ ▶ **n.** the larva of a kind of beetle, which bores into wood.

woof¹ /wo͝of/ ▶ **n.** the barking sound made by a dog. ▶ **v.** bark.

woof² ▶ **n.** (in weaving) the weft (see **WEFT**).

woof·er /ˈwo͝ofər/ ▶ **n.** a loudspeaker that reproduces low frequencies.

wool /wo͝ol/ ▶ **n.** the fine, soft hair forming the coat of a sheep.

SYNONYMS **fleece**, hair, coat.

wool·en /ˈwo͝olən/ ▶ **adj. 1** made of wool. **2** relating to the production of wool. ▶ **n.** (**woolens**) woolen clothes.

wool·ly /ˈwo͝olē/ ▶ **adj. 1** made of wool. **2** covered with wool or hair resembling wool. **3** resembling wool. **4** confused or unclear.

SYNONYMS **1 woolen**, wool. **2 fleecy**, shaggy, hairy, fluffy. **3 vague**, ill-defined, hazy, unclear, fuzzy, indefinite, confused, muddled.

wooz·y /ˈwo͞ozē/ ▶ **adj.** informal unsteady, dizzy, or dazed. ■ **wooz·i·ly adv.**

word /wərd/ ▶ **n. 1** a unit of language that has meaning and is used with others to form sentences. **2** a remark or statement. **3** (**words**) angry talk. **4** (**the word**) a command, slogan, or signal. **5** (**your word**) your account of the truth of something that happened. **6** (**your word**) a thing that you promise. **7** news. ▶ **v.** express something in particular words.

SYNONYMS ▶ **n. 1 term**, name, expression, designation. **2 remark**, comment, observation, statement, utterance. **3 script**, lines, lyrics, libretto. **4** *I give you my word* **promise**, assurance, guarantee, undertaking, pledge, vow, oath, bond. **5 talk**, conversation, chat, tête-à-tête, heart-to-heart, one-to-one, discussion; informal confab. **6** *there's no word from the hospital* **news**, information, communication, intelligence, message, report, communiqué, dispatch, bulletin; literary tidings. ▶ **v. phrase**, express, put, couch, frame, formulate, style.

□ **in so many words** precisely in the way mentioned. **in a word** briefly. **word of mouth** talking as a way of passing on information. **word processor** a computer or program for creating and printing a document or piece of text. **word class** a category in which a word is placed according to its function in grammar; a part of speech. ■ **word·less adj.**

word·ing /ˈwərdiNG/ ▶ **n.** the way in which something is worded.

SYNONYMS **phrasing**, phraseology, language, words, expression, terminology.

word·play /ˈwərd,plā/ ▶ **n.** the witty exploitation of the meanings of words.

word·y /ˈwərdē/ ▶ **adj.** using too many words.

SYNONYMS **long-winded**, verbose, lengthy, rambling, garrulous, voluble; informal windy.
ANTONYMS succinct.

wore /wôr/ past of **WEAR**.

work /wərk/ ▶ **n. 1** activity involving mental or physical effort done in order to achieve a result. **2** the activity or job that a person does in order to earn money. **3** a task or tasks to be done. **4** a thing or things done or made. **5** (**works**) a place where industrial or manufacturing processes are carried out. **6** (**works**) activities involving the building or repair of something. **7** (**works**) the mechanism of a clock or other machine. ▶ **v. 1** do work as your job. **2** make someone do work. **3** (of a machine or system) function properly. **4** (of a machine) be in operation. **5** have the desired result. **6** bring a material or mixture to a desired shape or consistency. **7** cultivate land, or extract materials from a mine or quarry. **8** move something gradually or with difficulty into another position.

SYNONYMS ▶ **n. 1 labor**, toil, drudgery, exertion, effort, industry; informal grind, sweat; old use travail. **2 employment**, job, post, position, situation, occupation, profession, career, vocation, calling. **3 tasks**, jobs, duties, assignments, projects, chores. **4 composition**, piece, creation, opus; (**works**) oeuvre, canon.
ANTONYMS leisure. ▶ **v. 1 labor**, toil, exert yourself, slave (away); informal slog (away), beaver away. **2 be employed**, have a job, earn your living, do business. **3 function**, go, run, operate. **4 operate**, use, handle, control, run, manipulate. **5 succeed**, turn out well, go as planned, get results, be effective; informal come off, pay off, do the trick. **6 achieve**, accomplish, bring about, produce, perform.
ANTONYMS rest, fail.

□ **get worked up** become stressed or angry. **work out 1** develop in the desired way. **2** do energetic physical exercise. **work something out 1** solve something. **2** plan something in detail. **work permit** an official document giving a foreigner permission to take a job in a country. **work up to** proceed gradually toward something more demanding or advanced.

work·a·ble /ˈwərkəbəl/ ▶ **adj. 1** able to be worked. **2** capable of producing the desired result.

work·a·day /ˈwərkə,dā/ ▶ **adj.** ordinary.

work·bench /ˈwərk,benCH/ ▶ **n.** a bench at which carpentry and other work is done.

work·er /ˈwərkər/ ▶ **n.** **1** a person who works. **2** a neuter or undeveloped female bee, wasp, ant, etc., large numbers of which perform the basic work of a colony.

SYNONYMS **employee**, member of staff, workman, laborer, hand, operator, operative, agent, wage-earner, breadwinner, proletarian.

work·force /ˈwərkˌfôrs/ ▶ **n.** the people working or available for work in a particular area, firm, or industry.

work·ing /ˈwərkiNG/ ▶ **adj.** **1** having paid employment. **2** doing manual work. **3** functioning or able to function. **4** used as a basis for work or discussion and likely to be changed later. ▶ **n.** **1** a mine from which minerals are being extracted. **2** (**workings**) the way in which a machine, organization, or system operates. ▫ **working class** the social group consisting mainly of people who do manual or industrial work.

work·load /ˈwərkˌlōd/ ▶ **n.** the amount of work to be done by someone or something.

work·man /ˈwərkmən/ ▶ **n.** (plural **workmen**) a man employed to do manual work.

work·man·like /ˈwərkmənˌlīk/ ▶ **adj.** showing efficient skill.

work·out /ˈwərkˌout/ ▶ **n.** a session of energetic physical exercise.

work·sheet /ˈwərkˌSHēt/ ▶ **n.** **1** a paper listing questions or tasks for students. **2** a paper recording work done or in progress.

work·shop /ˈwərkˌSHäp/ ▶ **n.** **1** a room or building in which things are made or repaired. **2** a meeting for discussion and activity on a particular subject or project.

SYNONYMS **1 workroom**, studio, factory, works, plant, industrial unit. **2 study group**, discussion group, seminar, forum, class.

work·space /ˈwərkˌspās/ ▶ **n.** **1** an area rented or sold for commercial purposes. **2** Computing a memory storage facility for temporary use.

work·sta·tion /ˈwərkˌstāSHən/ ▶ **n.** a desktop computer that is part of a network.

world /wərld/ ▶ **n.** **1** (**the world**) the earth with all its countries and peoples. **2** all that belongs to a particular region, period, or area of activity.

SYNONYMS **1 earth**, globe, planet, sphere. **2** (**the world**) **everyone**, people, mankind, humankind, humanity, the public, all and sundry. **3 sphere**, society, circle, arena, milieu, province, domain, preserve, realm, field.

▫ **out of this world** informal extremely enjoyable or impressive. **world-class** of or among the best in the world. **World Series** the championship for North American major league baseball. **world-weary** bored with or cynical about life. **World Wide Web** an information system on the Internet that allows documents to be connected to each other using hypertext links.

world·ly /ˈwərldlē/ ▶ **adj.** **1** relating to material things rather than spiritual ones. **2** experienced and sophisticated.

SYNONYMS **1 earthly**, terrestrial, temporal, mundane, mortal, human, material, physical. **2 sophisticated**, experienced, worldly-wise, knowledgeable, knowing, enlightened, mature, seasoned, cosmopolitan, urbane, cultured. ANTONYMS spiritual, naive.

▫ **worldly-wise** having a lot of experience of life.

world·wide /ˈwərldˈwīd/ ▶ **adj. & adv.** throughout the world.

SYNONYMS **global**, international, intercontinental, universal, ubiquitous. ANTONYMS local.

worm /wərm/ ▶ **n.** **1** an earthworm or other creeping or burrowing creature with a long, thin body and no limbs. **2** (**worms**) long, thin creatures that live as parasites in a person's or animal's intestines. ▶ **v.** **1** move by crawling or wriggling. **2** (**worm your way into**) gradually move into. **3** (**worm something out of**) cleverly obtain information from someone who is reluctant to give it. ▫ **worm cast** a small spiral of earth or sand thrown up at the surface by a burrowing worm.

worm·wood /ˈwərmˌwo͝od/ ▶ **n.** a plant with a bitter flavor, used in drinks such as vermouth.

worn /wôrn/ past participle of **WEAR** ▶ **adj.** thin or damaged as a result of wear.

SYNONYMS **shabby**, worn out, threadbare, in tatters, falling to pieces, ragged, frayed, moth-eaten, scruffy, having seen better days. ANTONYMS new, smart.

▫ **worn out 1** exhausted. **2** damaged by wear, and no longer usable.

wor·ried /ˈwərēd/ ▶ **adj.** feeling anxiety or concern.

SYNONYMS **anxious**, troubled, bothered, concerned, uneasy, fretful, agitated, nervous, edgy, tense, apprehensive, fearful, afraid, frightened; informal in a stew, in a tizzy, in a sweat, a bundle of nerves. ANTONYMS carefree.

▪ **wor·ried·ly** **adv.**

wor·ri·some /ˈwərēˌsəm/ ▶ **adj.** causing anxiety or concern.

wor·ry /ˈwərē/ ▶ **v.** (**worries**, **worrying**, **worried**) **1** feel or cause to feel troubled over unwelcome things that have happened or may happen. **2** annoy or disturb. **3** (of a dog) repeatedly push at and bite something. **4** (of a dog) chase and attack livestock. ▶ **n.** (plural **worries**) **1** the state of being worried. **2** a source of anxiety.

SYNONYMS ▶ **v.** **1 be anxious**, be concerned, fret, agonize, brood, panic, lose sleep, get worked up; informal get in a tizzy, get in a state. **2 trouble**, bother, make anxious, disturb, distress, upset, concern, unsettle, perturb, scare, prey on someone's mind; informal bug, get to. ▶ **n.** **1 anxiety**, distress, concern, unease, disquiet, nerves, agitation, edginess, tension, apprehension, fear, misgiving. **2 problem**, cause for concern, nuisance, pest, trial, trouble, bane, bugbear; informal pain, headache, hassle.

▪ **wor·ri·er** **n.** **wor·ry·ing** **adj.**

worse /wərs/ ▶ **adj.** **1** less good, satisfactory, or pleasing. **2** more serious or severe. **3** more ill or unhappy. ▶ **adv.** **1** less well. **2** more seriously or severely. ▶ **n.** a worse event or circumstance.

wors·en /ˈwərsən/ ▶ **v.** make or become worse.

SYNONYMS **1 aggravate**, add to, intensify, increase, compound, magnify, heighten, inflame, exacerbate. **2 deteriorate**, degenerate, decline; informal go downhill. ANTONYMS improve.

wor·ship /ˈwərSHəp/ ▶ **n.** **1** the practice of praising and praying to God or a god or goddess. **2** religious rites and ceremonies. **3** a strong feeling of admiration and respect for someone. ▶ v. (**worships**, **worshiping**, **worshiped**) **1** offer praise and prayers to God or a god or goddess. **2** feel great admiration and respect for.

SYNONYMS ▶ n. **1 reverence**, veneration, adoration, glorification, exaltation, devotion, praise, thanksgiving, homage, honor. **2 service**, rite, prayer, praise, devotion, observance. ▶ v. **1 revere**, pray to, pay homage to, honor, adore, venerate, praise, glorify, exalt. **2 love**, cherish, treasure, hold dear, esteem, adulate, idolize, deify, hero-worship, lionize; informal put on a pedestal.

■ **wor·ship·er** n.

wor·ship·ful /ˈwərsʜəpfəl/ ▶ adj. feeling or showing great respect and admiration.

worst /wərst/ ▶ adj. most bad, severe, or serious. ▶ adv. **1** most severely or seriously. **2** least well. ▶ n. the worst part, event, or circumstance.

wor·sted /ˈwo͝ostid, ˈwərstid/ ▶ n. a smooth woolen fabric of good quality.

worth /wərᴛʜ/ ▶ adj. **1** equivalent in value to a particular sum or item. **2** deserving to be treated in a particular way. ▶ n. **1** the value of someone or something. **2** an amount of something that is equivalent to a particular sum of money.

SYNONYMS ▶ n. **1 value**, price, cost, valuation, estimate. **2 benefit**, good, advantage, use, value, virtue, desirability, sense.

worth·less /ˈwərᴛʜlis/ ▶ adj. **1** having no practical or financial value. **2** having no good qualities.

SYNONYMS **1 valueless**, of no value; informal trashy. **2 useless**, pointless, meaningless, senseless, inconsequential, ineffective, ineffectual, fruitless, unproductive, unavailing, valueless. **3 good-for-nothing**, ne'er-do-well, useless, despicable, contemptible, degenerate; informal no-good, lousy. ANTONYMS valuable, useful.

worth·while /ˈwərᴛʜˈ(h)wīl/ ▶ adj. worth the time, money, or effort spent.

SYNONYMS **valuable**, useful, of service, beneficial, rewarding, advantageous, positive, helpful, profitable, gainful, fruitful, productive, constructive, effective.

wor·thy /ˈwər<u>ᴛʜ</u>ē/ ▶ adj. (**worthier**, **worthiest**) **1** deserving effort, attention, or respect. **2** (**worthy of**) deserving or good enough for. **3** well-intended but too serious and dull. ▶ n. (plural **worthies**) humorous an important person.

SYNONYMS ▶ adj. **good**, righteous, virtuous, moral, ethical, upright, respectable, upstanding, high-minded, principled, reputable, decent. ANTONYMS disreputable. ▶ n. **dignitary**, personage, grandee, VIP, notable, pillar of society, luminary, leading light; informal bigwig.

■ **wor·thi·ly** adv. **wor·thi·ness** n.

would /wo͝od/ ▶ modal v. (3rd singular present **would**) **1** past of WILL[1]. **2** indicating the consequence of an imagined event. **3** expressing a desire or inclination. **4** expressing a polite request. **5** expressing an opinion or assumption. **6** literary expressing a wish or regret. □ **would-be** often disapproving wishing to be a particular type of person: *a would-be actress.*

would·n't /ˈwo͝odnt/ ▶ contr. would not.

wound[1] /wo͞ond/ ▶ n. **1** an injury to the body caused by a cut, blow, or bullet. **2** an injury to a person's feelings. ▶ v. **1** inflict a wound on. **2** injure someone's feelings.

SYNONYMS ▶ n. **1 injury**, cut, gash, laceration, graze, scratch, abrasion, puncture, lesion; Medicine trauma. **2 insult**, blow, slight, offense, affront, hurt, damage, injury. ▶ v. **1 injure**, hurt, harm, lacerate, cut, graze, gash, stab, slash. **2** *her words wounded him* **hurt**, offend, affront, distress, grieve, pain.

wound[2] /wound/ past and past participle of WIND[2].

wove /wōv/ past of WEAVE[1].

wo·ven /ˈwōvən/ past participle of WEAVE[1].

wow /wou/ informal ▶ exclam. expressing great surprise or admiration. ▶ v. impress someone very much.

wrack[1] /rak/ = RACK.

wrack[2] ▶ n. a brown seaweed.

wraith /rāᴛʜ/ ▶ n. a ghost.

wran·gle /ˈraɴɢɡəl/ ▶ n. a long dispute or argument. ▶ v. (**wrangles**, **wrangling**, **wrangled**) **1** have a long and complicated dispute or argument. **2** round up or take charge of livestock. ■ **wran·gler** n.

wrap /rap/ ▶ v. (**wraps**, **wrapping**, **wrapped**) **1** enclose something in paper or soft material. **2** encircle or wind around. ▶ n. **1** a loose outer garment or piece of material. **2** paper or material used for wrapping.

SYNONYMS ▶ v. **1 enclose**, enfold, envelop, encase, cover, fold, wind, swathe, bundle, swaddle. **2 pack**, package, parcel up, bundle (up), gift-wrap. ▶ n. **shawl**, stole, cloak, cape, mantle, scarf.

□ **under wraps** kept secret. **wrap someone/something up 1** (also **wrap up**) dress someone in or put on warm clothes. **2** bring a meeting or deal to a close. ■ **wrap·ping** n.

wrap·per /ˈrapər/ ▶ n. a piece of paper or other material used for wrapping something.

wrasse /ras/ ▶ n. (plural **wrasse** or **wrasses**) a brightly colored sea fish with thick lips and strong teeth.

wrath /raᴛʜ/ ▶ n. extreme anger.

SYNONYMS **anger**, rage, temper, fury, outrage, spleen, resentment, (high) dudgeon, indignation; literary ire. ANTONYMS happiness.

■ **wrath·ful** adj.

wreak /rēk/ ▶ v. **1** cause a lot of damage or harm. **2** take revenge on someone.

wreath /rēᴛʜ/ ▶ n. (plural **wreaths**) **1** an arrangement of flowers or leaves fastened in a ring. **2** a curl or ring of smoke or cloud.

SYNONYMS **garland**, circlet, chaplet, crown, festoon, lei, ring, loop, circle.

wreathe /rē<u>ᴛʜ</u>/ ▶ v. (**wreathes**, **wreathing**, **wreathed**) **1** (**be wreathed**) be surrounded or encircled. **2** move with a curling motion.

SYNONYMS **1 festoon**, garland, drape, cover, deck, decorate, ornament, adorn. **2 spiral**, coil, loop, wind, curl, twist, snake.

wreck /rek/ ▶ n. **1** the destruction of a ship at sea. **2** a ship destroyed at sea. **3** a building, vehicle, etc., that has been destroyed or badly damaged. **4** a road or rail crash. **5** a person in a very bad state.

▶ **v.** **1** destroy or badly damage. **2** spoil a plan. **3** cause a ship to sink or break up.

> SYNONYMS ▶ **n.** **1 shipwreck**, sunken ship, hull. **2 wreckage**, debris, ruins, remains, burned-out shell. ▶ **v.** **1 destroy**, break, demolish, crash, smash up, write off; informal trash, total. **2 ruin**, spoil, disrupt, undo, put a stop to, frustrate, blight, crush, dash, destroy, scotch, shatter, devastate, sabotage; informal mess up, screw up, put paid to, stymie.

wreck·age /'rekij/ ▶ **n.** the remains of something that has been badly damaged.

wreck·er /'rekər/ ▶ **n.** **1** a person or thing that wrecks something. **2** a person who breaks up damaged vehicles to obtain usable spares or scrap. **3** a tow truck.

wren /ren/ ▶ **n.** a very small bird with a cocked tail.

wrench /rencH/ ▶ **v.** **1** pull or twist something suddenly and violently. **2** twist and injure a part of the body. ▶ **n.** **1** a sudden violent twist or pull. **2** a feeling of sadness on leaving a place or person. **3** an adjustable tool used for gripping and turning nuts or bolts.

> SYNONYMS ▶ **v.** **1 tug**, pull, jerk, wrest, heave, twist, force, pry, prize; informal yank. **2 sprain**, twist, turn, strain, crick.

wrest /rest/ ▶ **v.** **1** forcibly pull something from someone's grasp. **2** succeed in taking power or control from someone after a struggle.

wres·tle /'resəl/ ▶ **v.** (**wrestles**, **wrestling**, **wrestled**) **1** take part in a fight or contest that involves close grappling with your opponent. **2** struggle with a difficulty or problem. **3** struggle to move an object. ▶ **n.** **1** a wrestling bout or contest. **2** a hard struggle.

> SYNONYMS ▶ **v.** **grapple**, fight, struggle, scuffle, tussle, brawl; informal scrap.

■ **wres·tler** **n.**

wres·tling /'reslinG/ ▶ **n.** the sport of grappling with an opponent and trying to throw or hold them down on the ground.

wretch /recH/ ▶ **n.** **1** an unfortunate person. **2** informal an unpleasant person.

wretch·ed /'recHid/ ▶ **adj.** **1** in a very unhappy or unfortunate state. **2** of bad quality.

> SYNONYMS **1 miserable**, unhappy, sad, heartbroken, grief-stricken, distressed, desolate, devastated, disconsolate, downcast, dejected, depressed, melancholy, forlorn. **2 harsh**, hard, grim, difficult, poor, pitiful, piteous, pathetic, tragic, miserable, bleak, cheerless, hopeless, sorry, sordid; informal crummy. ANTONYMS cheerful, comfortable.

■ **wretch·ed·ly** **adv.**

wrig·gle /'rigəl/ ▶ **v.** (**wriggles**, **wriggling**, **wriggled**) **1** twist and turn with quick short movements. **2** (**wriggle out of**) use excuses to avoid doing something. ▶ **n.** a wriggling movement.

> SYNONYMS ▶ **v.** **squirm**, writhe, wiggle, thresh, flounder, flail, twitch, twist and turn, snake, worm.

■ **wrig·gly** **adj.**

wring /rinG/ ▶ **v.** (**wrings**, **wringing**, **wrung** /rənG/) **1** squeeze and twist something to force water out of it. **2** twist and break an animal's neck. **3** squeeze someone's hand tightly. **4** (**wring something from** or **out of**) obtain something from someone with difficulty. ■ **wring·er** **n.**

wring·ing /'rinGinG/ ▶ **adj.** very wet.

wrin·kle /'rinGkəl/ ▶ **n.** a slight line or fold, especially in fabric or a person's skin. ▶ **v.** (**wrinkles**, **wrinkling**, **wrinkled**) make or become covered with wrinkles.

> SYNONYMS ▶ **n.** **crease**, fold, pucker, line, crinkle, furrow, ridge, groove; informal crow's feet. ▶ **v.** **crease**, pucker, gather, crinkle, crumple, rumple, scrunch up.

■ **wrin·kly** **adj.**

wrist /rist/ ▶ **n.** the joint connecting the hand with the lower part of the arm.

wrist·band /'rist,band/ ▶ **n.** a band worn around the wrist.

wrist·watch /'rist,wäcH/ ▶ **n.** a watch worn on a strap around the wrist.

writ[1] /rit/ ▶ **n.** an official document from a court or other legal authority, ordering someone to do or not do something.

writ[2] old use past of WRITE. □ **writ large** in an obvious or exaggerated form.

write /rīt/ ▶ **v.** (**writes**, **writing**, **wrote** /rōt/; past participle **written** /'ritn/) **1** mark letters, words, or other symbols on a surface with a pen, pencil, etc. **2** write and send a letter to someone. **3** compose a written or musical work. **4** fill out a check or similar document.

> SYNONYMS **1 put in writing**, put down, jot down, note (down), take down, record, inscribe, sign, scribble, scrawl, pen, pencil. **2 compose**, draft, think up, formulate, compile, pen, dash off, produce. **3 correspond**, communicate, get in touch, keep in contact; informal drop someone a line.

□ **write-in** a vote cast for a candidate whose name is not listed, by writing their name on a ballot paper. **write something off 1** decide that something is useless or a failure. **2** decide not to pursue a debt. **write-off** a thing written off, such as a worthless investment or a canceled debt. **write-up** a newspaper review of a recent event, performance, etc.

writ·er /'rītər/ ▶ **n.** **1** a person who has written a particular work, or who writes books, stories, or articles as an occupation. **2** Computing a device that writes data to a storage medium.

> SYNONYMS **author**, wordsmith; informal scribbler, scribe, pen-pusher, hack.

□ **writer's block** the condition of being unable to think of what to write. **writer's cramp** pain or stiffness in the hand caused by excessive writing.

writhe /rīTH/ ▶ **v.** (**writhes**, **writhing**, **writhed**) twist or squirm in pain or embarrassment.

> SYNONYMS **squirm**, wriggle, thrash, flail, toss, twist.

writ·ing /'rītinG/ ▶ **n.** **1** the activity or skill of writing. **2** a sequence of letters or symbols forming words. **3** (**writings**) books or other written works.

> SYNONYMS **1 handwriting**, hand, script, calligraphy, lettering, print, printing; informal scribble, scrawl. **2 written work**, compositions, books, publications, papers, articles, essays, oeuvre.

wrong /rônG/ ▶ **adj.** **1** not correct or true; mistaken or in error. **2** unjust, dishonest, or immoral. **3** in a bad or abnormal condition. ▶ **adv.** **1** in a mistaken or unwelcome way or direction. **2** with an incorrect result. ▶ **n.** an unjust, dishonest, or immoral action. ▶ **v.** treat someone unfairly.

SYNONYMS ▶ **adj. 1 incorrect**, mistaken, erroneous, inaccurate, wide of the mark, inexact, imprecise; informal off beam, out. **2 inappropriate**, unsuitable, ill-advised, ill-considered, ill-judged, unwise, infelicitous; informal out of order. **3 bad**, dishonest, illegal, unlawful, illicit, criminal, corrupt, unethical, immoral, wicked, sinful, iniquitous, nefarious, reprehensible; informal crooked. **4 amiss**, awry, out of line, not right, defective, faulty. ANTONYMS right, correct. ▶ **adv. incorrectly**, wrongly, inaccurately, erroneously, mistakenly. ▶ **n. 1 immorality**, sin, wickedness, evil, illegality, unlawfulness, crime, corruption, villainy, dishonesty, injustice, misconduct, transgression. **2 misdeed**, offense, injury, crime, transgression, sin, injustice, outrage, atrocity. ANTONYMS right. ▶ **v. mistreat**, ill-use, ill-treat, do an injustice to, abuse, harm, hurt, injure.

□ **in the wrong** responsible for a mistake or offense. **on the wrong side of 1** out of favor with. **2** somewhat more than (a specified age). ■ **wrong·ly** adv. **wrong·ness** n.

wrong·do·er /ˈrôNG,do͞oər/ ▶ **n.** a person who behaves in an illegal or dishonest way.

SYNONYMS **offender**, lawbreaker, criminal, felon, delinquent, villain, culprit, evildoer, sinner, transgressor, malefactor, miscreant, rogue, scoundrel; informal crook.

■ **wrong·do·ing** n.

wrong·ful /ˈrôNGfəl/ ▶ **adj.** not fair, just, or legal. ■ **wrong·ful·ly** adv.

wrong·head·ed /ˈrôNG,hedid/ ▶ **adj.** having bad judgment.

wrote /rōt/ past tense of WRITE.

wrought /rôt/ old use past and past participle of WORK ▶ **adj. 1** (of metals) beaten out or shaped by hammering. **2** made in a particular way: *well-wrought*. □ **wrought iron** tough iron suitable for forging or rolling.

wrung /rəNG/ past and past participle of WRING.

wry /rī/ ▶ **adj.** (**wryer**, **wryest** or **wrier**, **wriest**) **1** using dry, mocking humor. **2** (of a person's face) twisted into an expression of disgust, disappointment, or annoyance. **3** bending or twisted to one side.

SYNONYMS **1** *his wry humor* **ironic**, sardonic, satirical, mocking, sarcastic; dry, droll, witty, humorous. **2** *a wry expression* **unimpressed**, displeased, annoyed, irritated, irked, vexed, piqued, disgruntled, dissatisfied; informal peeved.

■ **wry·ly** adv.

wun·der·kind /ˈwo͝ondər,kind/ ▶ **n.** a person who is very successful at a young age.

Wur·litz·er /ˈwərlitsər/ ▶ **n.** trademark a large pipe organ or electric organ.

WWI ▶ **abbr.** World War I.

WWII ▶ **abbr.** World War II.

WWW ▶ **abbr.** World Wide Web.

wy·vern /ˈwīvərn/ ▶ **n.** Heraldry a winged two-legged dragon with a barbed tail.

X (or **x**) ▶ **n.** (plural **Xs** or **X's**) **1** the twenty-fourth letter of the alphabet. **2** an X-shaped written symbol, used to show that an answer is wrong, or to symbolize a kiss. **3** the Roman numeral for ten. □ **X chromosome** a sex chromosome, two of which are normally present in female cells and one in male cells. **X-rated** pornographic or indecent. **X-ray 1** an electromagnetic wave of very short wavelength, which is able to pass through many solids and so make it possible to see into or through them. **2** an image of the internal structure of an object produced by passing X-rays through it.

xe·non /'zē,nän, 'zen,än/ ▶ **n.** an inert gaseous element, present in small amounts in the air.

xen·o·pho·bi·a /,zēnə'fōbēə, ,zenə-/ ▶ **n.** dislike or fear of people from other countries. ■ **xen·o·pho·bic adj.**

Xer·ox /'zi(ə)r,äks/ ▶ **n.** trademark **1** a process for copying documents using an electric charge and dry powder. **2** a copy made using such a process. ▶ **v.** (**xerox**) copy a document by such a process.

Xmas /'krisməs, 'eksməs/ ▶ **n.** informal Christmas.

xy·lem /'zīləm/ ▶ **n.** Botany the woody tissue in plants that carries water and nutrients upward from the root.

xy·lo·phone /'zīlə,fōn/ ▶ **n.** a musical instrument consisting of a row of bars that you hit with small hammers.

Yy

Y (or **y**) ▶ **n.** (plural **Ys** or **Y's**) the twenty-fifth letter of the alphabet. □ **Y chromosome** a sex chromosome that is normally present only in male cells.

yacht /yät/ ▶ **n. 1** a medium-sized sailboat. **2** a boat with an engine, equipped for cruising. ■ **yacht·ing n. yachts·man n.** (plural **yachtsmen**) **yachts·wom·an n.** (plural **yachtswomen**).

ya·hoo /'yä,hōō, yä'hōō/ ▶ **n.** informal a rude or bad-mannered person.

yak¹ /yak/ ▶ **n.** a large ox with shaggy hair and large horns, found in Tibet and central Asia.

yak² (or **yack**) ▶ **v.** (**yaks**, **yakking**, **yakked**) informal talk continuously about something unimportant.

y'all /yôl/ ▶ **contr.** dialect you all.

yam /yam/ ▶ **n.** the tuber of a tropical plant, eaten as a vegetable.

yam·mer /'yamər/ informal ▶ **v.** (**yammers**, **yammering**, **yammered**) **1** talk loudly and without pausing. **2** make a loud, constant noise. ▶ **n.** loud and sustained noise.

yang /yaNG, yäNG/ ▶ **n.** (in Chinese philosophy) the active male force in the universe.

Yank /yaNGk/ ▶ **n.** informal an American.

yank /yaNGk/ informal ▶ **v.** pull quickly and hard. ▶ **n.** a sudden hard pull.

SYNONYMS **jerk**, pull, tug, wrench.

Yan·kee /'yaNGkē/ ▶ **n.** informal **1** an American. **2** a person from New England or one of the northern states. **3** historical a Federal soldier in the Civil War.

yap /yap/ ▶ **v.** (**yaps**, **yapping**, **yapped**) give a sharp, high-pitched bark. ▶ **n.** a sharp, high-pitched bark.

yard¹ /yärd/ ▶ **n. 1** a unit of length equal to 3 feet (0.9144 meter). **2** a square or cubic yard. **3** a long piece of wood slung across a ship's mast for a sail to hang from.

yard² ▶ **n. 1** a piece of enclosed ground next to a building. **2** the lawn and garden area of a house. □ **yard sale** a sale of secondhand items held on the grounds of the seller's home.

yard·age /'yärdij/ ▶ **n.** a number of yards of material, etc.

yard·arm /'yärd,ärm/ ▶ **n.** either end of a ship's yard supporting a sail.

yard·man /'yärd,man/ ▶ **n.** (plural **yardmen**) **1** a person working in a railroad yard or lumberyard. **2** a person who does various outdoor jobs.

yard·stick /'yärd,stik/ ▶ **n.** a standard used for judging how good or successful something is.

SYNONYMS **standard**, measure, gauge, scale, guide, guideline, indicator, test, touchstone, barometer, criterion, benchmark.

yar·mul·ke /'yäməl)kə, 'yärmə(l)kə/ (or **yarmulka**) ▶ **n.** a skullcap worn by Jewish men.

yarn /yärn/ ▶ **n. 1** thread used for knitting, weaving, or sewing. **2** informal a long story.

SYNONYMS **thread**, cotton, wool, fiber, filament.

yash·mak /yäsH'mäk, 'yasH,mak/ ▶ **n.** a veil concealing all of the face except the eyes, worn by some Muslim women.

yaw /yô/ ▶ **v.** (of a moving ship or aircraft) turn unsteadily from side to side. ▶ **n.** a yawing movement.

yawl /yôl/ ▶ **n.** a kind of sailboat with two masts.

yawn /yôn/ ▶ **v. 1** open your mouth wide and take a deep breath, usually when tired or bored. **2** (**yawning**) wide open. ▶ **n.** an act of yawning.

SYNONYMS ▶ **v.** (**yawning**) **gaping**, wide, cavernous, deep, huge, vast.

yd. ▶ **abbr.** yard.

ye¹ /yē/ plural of **THOU**.

ye² ▶ **determiner** old use the.

yea /yā/ ▶ **adv.** old use yes.

yeah /ye(ə), ya(ə)/ (or **yeh** /ye/) nonstandard ⇨ **YES**.

year /yi(ə)r/ ▶ **n. 1** the period of 365 days (or 366 days in leap years) starting from January 1. **2** a period of this length starting at a different point. **3** the time taken by the earth to go around the sun. **4** (**your years**) your age or time of life. **5** (**years**) informal a very long time. **6** a set of students who enter and leave a school or college at the same time. □ **year-round** happening or continuing throughout the year.

year·book /'yi(ə)r,bo͝ok/ ▶ **n. 1** an annual publication giving current information about and listing events of the previous year. **2** an annual publication of the graduating class in a school or university, giving photographs of students and details of school activities in the previous year.

year·ling /'yi(ə)rliNG/ ▶ **n.** an animal between one and two years old.

year·ly /'yi(ə)rlē/ ▶ **adj. & adv.** happening or produced once a year or every year.

SYNONYMS **annually**, once a year, per annum, each/every year.

yearn /yərn/ ▶ **v.** have a strong feeling of longing for something.

SYNONYMS **long**, pine, crave, desire, want, wish, hanker, covet, hunger, thirst, ache; informal itch.

■ **yearn·ing n. & adj.**

yeast /yēst/ ▶ **n. 1** a fungus that can convert sugar into alcohol and carbon dioxide. **2** a substance formed from this, used to make bread dough rise and to ferment beer and wine. ■ **yeast·y adj.**

yell /yel/ ▶ **n.** a loud, sharp call or cry. ▶ **v.** shout loudly.

SYNONYMS ▶ **v.** **shout**, cry out, howl, wail, scream, shriek, screech, yelp, squeal, roar, bawl; informal holler.

yel·low /ˈyelō/ ▶ **adj.** **1** of the color of egg yolks or ripe lemons. **2** informal cowardly. ▶ **n.** a yellow color. ▶ **v.** (of paper, fabric, etc.) become slightly yellow with age.

SYNONYMS ▶ **adj.** golden, gold, blonde, fair, flaxen, lemon, primrose, mustard.

□ **yellow card** (in soccer) a yellow card shown by the referee to a player being cautioned. **yellow fever** a tropical disease that causes fever and jaundice and often death. **Yellow Pages** (or **yellow pages**) a telephone directory of classified business listings and display ads, on yellow paper. ■ **yel·low·ish** **adj.**

yelp /yelp/ ▶ **n.** a short, sharp cry. ▶ **v.** give a yelp or yelps.

yen¹ /yen/ ▶ **n.** (plural **yen**) the basic unit of money of Japan.

yen² ▶ **n.** informal a strong desire to have or do something.

yeo·man /ˈyōmən/ ▶ **n.** (plural **yeomen**) (in the past) a man having his own house and small area of farming land.

yes /yes/ ▶ **exclam.** **1** used to give a response in favor of something. **2** used to respond to someone who is talking to you. ▶ **n.** (plural **yeses** or **yesses**) a decision or vote in favor of something.

SYNONYMS ▶ **exclam.** **certainly**, very well, of course, by all means, sure, all right, absolutely, indeed, affirmative, agreed, roger; old use or dialect aye; informal yeah, yep. ANTONYMS no.

□ **yes-man** a person who always agrees with people in authority.

yes·ter·day /ˈyestərˌdā, -dē/ ▶ **adv.** on the day before today. ▶ **n.** **1** the day before today. **2** the recent past.

yes·ter·year /ˈyestərˌyir/ ▶ **n.** literary last year or the recent past.

yet /yet/ ▶ **adv.** **1** up until now or then. **2** as soon as this. **3** from now into the future. **4** referring to something that will or may happen. **5** still; even. **6** in spite of that. ▶ **conj.** but at the same time.

yet·i /ˈyetē, ˈyātē/ ▶ **n.** a large hairy creature like a bear or a man, said to live in the highest part of the Himalayas.

yew /yo͞o/ ▶ **n.** an evergreen tree with poisonous red fruit.

Yid·dish /ˈyidisн/ ▶ **n.** a language used by Jews from central and eastern Europe. ▶ **adj.** relating to Yiddish.

yield /yēld/ ▶ **v.** **1** produce or provide a natural or industrial product. **2** produce a result or financial gain. **3** give way to demands or pressure; give in. **4** give up possession of. **5** give way under force or pressure; be broken down. ▶ **n.** an amount or result yielded.

SYNONYMS ▶ **v.** **1** **produce**, bear, give, provide, afford, return, bring in, earn, realize, generate, deliver, pay out. **2** **surrender**, capitulate, submit, admit defeat, back down, give in, cave in, raise the white flag, throw in the towel, give up the struggle. ANTONYMS withhold, resist. ▶ **n.** **profit**, gain, return, dividend, earnings.

SPELLING

Remember, **i** before **e**, when the sound is *ee*, except after **c**: y**ie**ld.

yikes /yīks/ ▶ **exclam.** informal, humorous expressing shock and alarm.

yin /yin/ ▶ **n.** (in Chinese philosophy) the passive female presence in the universe.

yo·del /ˈyōdl/ ▶ **v.** (**yodels**, **yodeling**, **yodeled**) sing or call in a style that alternates rapidly between a normal voice and a very high voice. ▶ **n.** a song or call of this type. ■ **yo·del·er** **n.**

yo·ga /ˈyōgə/ ▶ **n.** a system involving breathing exercises and the holding of particular body positions, followed for fitness and relaxation and based on Hindu philosophy. ■ **yo·gic** **adj.**

yo·gi /ˈyōgē/ ▶ **n.** (plural **yogis**) a person who is skilled in yoga.

yo·gurt /ˈyōgərt/ (or **yoghurt**) ▶ **n.** a thick liquid food made from milk with bacteria added.

yoke /yōk/ ▶ **n.** **1** a piece of wood fastened over the necks of two animals and attached to a plow or cart in order for them to pull it. **2** a frame fitting over a person's neck and shoulders, used for carrying buckets or baskets. **3** something that limits freedom or is difficult to bear. **4** a part of a garment that fits over the shoulders and to which the main part of the garment is attached. ▶ **v.** (**yokes**, **yoking**, **yoked**) join together or attach to a yoke.

yo·kel /ˈyōkəl/ ▶ **n.** an unsophisticated country person.

SYNONYMS **rustic**, bumpkin, peasant, provincial; informal hayseed, hillbilly, hick.

yolk /yōk/ ▶ **n.** the yellow part in the middle of an egg.

Yom Kip·pur /ˈyôm kiˈpo͝or, ˈyōm, ˈyäm, ˈkipər/ ▶ **n.** an important day in the Jewish religion in which people pray and fast.

yon /yän/ old use or dialect ▶ **determiner & adv.** that. ▶ **pron.** that person or thing.

yon·der /ˈyändər/ old use or dialect ▶ **adv.** over there. ▶ **determiner** that or those.

yore /yôr/ ▶ **n.** (**of yore**) literary in the past; long ago.

you /yo͞o/ ▶ **pron.** **1** used to refer to the person or people that the speaker is talking to. **2** used to refer to any person in general.

you'd /yo͞od/ ▶ **contr.** **1** you had. **2** you would.

you'll /yo͞ol/ ▶ **contr.** you will or you shall.

young /yənɢ/ ▶ **adj.** (**younger**, **youngest**) **1** having lived or existed for only a short time. **2** relating to or characteristic of young people. ▶ **pl.n.** young children or animals; offspring.

SYNONYMS ▶ **adj.** **1** **youthful**, juvenile, junior, adolescent, teenage, in your salad days. **2** **immature**, childish, inexperienced, naive, green, wet behind the ears. **3** *a young industry* **new**, fledgling, developing, budding, in its infancy, emerging, in the making. ANTONYMS old, mature. ▶ **pl.n.** **offspring**, progeny, family, babies, litter, brood.

young·ster /ˈyənɢstər/ ▶ **n.** a young person.

SYNONYMS **child**, teenager, adolescent, youth, juvenile, minor, junior, boy, girl; informal teen, kid, lad, whippersnapper.

your /yôr, yŏŏr/ ▶ **possessive determiner 1** belonging to or associated with the person or people that the speaker is talking to. **2** belonging to or associated with any person in general.

USAGE

Don't confuse **your** meaning 'belonging to you' (as in *let me talk to your daughter*) with the form **you're**, which is short for **you are** (as in *you're a good cook*).

you're /yŏŏr, yôr/ ▶ **contr.** you are.

yours /yôrz, yŏŏrz/ ▶ **possessive pron.** used to refer to something belonging to or associated with the person or people that the speaker is talking to.

SPELLING

No apostrophe: **yours**.

your·self /yər'self, yôr-, yŏŏr-/ ▶ **pron.** (plural **yourselves**) **1** used as the object of a verb or preposition when this is the same as the subject of the clause and the subject is the person or people being spoken to. **2** you personally.

youth /yo͞oTH/ ▶ **n.** (plural **youths**) **1** the period between childhood and adult age. **2** the qualities of energy, freshness, etc., associated with being young. **3** a young man. **4** young people.

SYNONYMS **1 early years**, teens, adolescence, boyhood, girlhood, childhood, minority. **2 young man**, boy, juvenile, teenager, adolescent, junior, minor; informal lad, kid.

□ **youth club** a club where young people can meet and take part in various activities. **youth hostel** a place providing cheap overnight accommodations, especially for young people.

youth·ful /'yo͞oTHfəl/ ▶ **adj. 1** young or seeming young. **2** characteristic of young people.

SYNONYMS **young**, boyish, girlish, fresh-faced, young-looking, spry, sprightly, vigorous, active. ANTONYMS elderly.

■ **youth·ful·ly adv. youth·ful·ness n.**

you've /yo͞ov/ ▶ **contr.** you have.

yowl /youl/ ▶ **n.** a loud wailing cry of pain or distress. ▶ **v.** make such a cry.

yo-yo /'yō ˌyō/ ▶ **n.** (plural **yo-yos**) a toy consisting of a pair of joined discs with a groove between them in which string is attached and wound, which can be spun down and up as the string unwinds and rewinds. ▶ **v.** (**yo-yoes**, **yo-yoing**, **yo-yoed**) move up and down repeatedly.

yuc·ca /'yəkə/ ▶ **n.** a plant with long, stiff pointed leaves, native to the southern United States and Mexico.

yuck /yək/ (or **yuk**) informal ▶ **exclam.** used to express disgust.

yuck·y /'yəkē/ (also **yukky**)▶ **adj.** (**yuckier**, **yuckiest**) informal messy or disgusting.

Yu·go·slav /'yo͞ogōˌsläv, ˌyo͞ogō'släv, -gə-/ ▶ **n.** a person from any of the states of the former Yugoslavia. ■ **Yu·go·sla·vi·an** /ˌyo͞ogō'slävēən, -gə-/ **n. & adj.**

Yule /yo͞ol/ (or **Yuletide**) ▶ **n.** old use Christmas.

yum·my /'yəmē/ ▶ **adj.** (**yummier**, **yummiest**) informal delicious.

yup·pie /'yəpē/ (or **yuppy**) ▶ **n.** (plural **yuppies**) informal a young middle-class professional person who earns a lot of money.

Zz

Z (or **z**) ▶ **n.** (plural **Zs** or **Z's**) the twenty-sixth letter of the alphabet.

za·ny /'zānē/ ▶ **adj.** (**zanier**, **zaniest**) amusingly unconventional or unusual.

SYNONYMS **eccentric**, odd, unconventional, bizarre, weird, mad, crazy, comic, madcap, quirky, idiosyncratic; informal wacky, oddball, off the wall, daft, kooky. ANTONYMS conventional.

zap /zap/ informal ▶ **v.** (**zaps**, **zapping**, **zapped**) **1** destroy completely. **2** move very fast. **3** use a remote control to change television channels.

zeal /zēl/ ▶ **n.** great energy and enthusiasm for a cause or aim.

SYNONYMS **enthusiasm**, passion, ardor, fervor, fervency, fire, devotion, gusto, vigor, energy, vehemence, intensity, eagerness, fanaticism. ANTONYMS apathy.

zeal·ot /'zelət/ ▶ **n.** a person who follows a religion, cause, or policy very strictly and enthusiastically.

SYNONYMS **fanatic**, enthusiast, extremist, radical, diehard, activist, militant.

■ **zeal·ot·ry** **n.**

zeal·ous /'zeləs/ ▶ **adj.** showing great energy and enthusiasm for a cause or aim.

SYNONYMS **ardent**, fervent, passionate, impassioned, enthusiastic, devoted, committed, dedicated, eager, keen, avid, vehement, intense, fierce, fanatical. ANTONYMS apathetic.

■ **zeal·ous·ly** **adv.**

ze·bra /'zēbrə/ ▶ **n.** an African wild horse with black and white stripes.

zeit·geist /'tsīt,gīst, 'zīt-/ ▶ **n.** the general spirit or mood of a particular period of history.

Zen /zen/ ▶ **n.** a type of Buddhism that emphasizes the value of meditation and intuition.

ze·nith /'zēniTH/ ▶ **n.** **1** the time at which someone or something is most powerful or successful. **2** the point in the sky directly overhead. **3** the highest point in the sky reached by the sun or moon.

SYNONYMS **high point**, crowning point, height, top, acme, peak, pinnacle, apex, apogee, crown, crest, summit, culmination, climax. ANTONYMS nadir.

zeph·yr /'zefər/ ▶ **n.** literary a soft, gentle breeze.

zep·pe·lin /'zep(ə)lən/ ▶ **n.** a large German airship of the early 20th century.

ze·ro /'zi(ə)rō, 'zē,rō/ ▶ **cardinal number** (plural **zeros**) **1** the figure 0; naught. **2** a temperature of 0°C (32°F), marking the freezing point of water. **3** a point on a scale of measurement from which a positive or negative quantity is reckoned. ▶ **v.** (**zeroes**, **zeroing**, **zeroed**) (**zero in on**) take aim at or focus attention on.

SYNONYMS ▶ **cardinal number** **nothing**, nil, 0, naught, nothing at all; informal zilch, zip, nada, diddly-squat.

□ **size zero** a very small size of women's clothing. **zero hour** the time at which a military operation or important event is set to begin.

zest /zest/ ▶ **n.** **1** great enthusiasm and energy. **2** excitement or stimulation. **3** the outer colored part of the peel of an orange or lemon.

SYNONYMS **enthusiasm**, gusto, relish, appetite, eagerness, keenness, zeal, passion, energy, liveliness.

zig·zag /'zig,zag/ ▶ **n.** a line or course having sharp alternate right and left turns. ▶ **adj. & adv.** veering to right and left alternately. ▶ **v.** (**zigzags**, **zigzagging**, **zigzagged**) move in a zigzag.

SYNONYMS ▶ **v.** **twist**, meander, snake, wind, weave, swerve.

zilch /zilCH/ ▶ **pron.** informal nothing.

zil·lion /'zilyən/ ▶ **cardinal number** informal a very large number of people or things. ■ **zil·lionth** **ordinal number.**

Zim·bab·we·an /zim'bäbwāən, -wēən/ ▶ **n.** a person from Zimbabwe. ▶ **adj.** relating to Zimbabwe.

zinc /ziNGk/ ▶ **n.** a silvery-white metallic element used in making brass and to coat iron and steel.

zing /ziNG/ ▶ **n.** informal energy, enthusiasm, or liveliness. ■ **zing·y** **adj.**

Zi·on·ism /'zīə,nizəm/ ▶ **n.** a movement for the development of a Jewish nation in Israel. ■ **Zi·on·ist** **n. & adj.**

zip /zip/ ▶ **n.** informal energy; liveliness. ▶ **v.** (**zips**, **zipping**, **zipped**) **1** (often **zip up**) fasten with a zipper. **2** informal move quickly. **3** Computing compress a file so that it takes up less space.

SYNONYMS ▶ **n.** **energy**, liveliness, vivacity, verve, zest; informal pep, zing, pizzazz. ▶ **v.** **hurry**, rush, speed, dart, dash, shoot, fly; informal tear, belt, zoom, whizz.

□ **zip code** (or **ZIP code**) a numerical postal code for sorting mail by destination.

zip·per /'zipər/ ▶ **n.** a zip fastener.

zip·py /'zipē/ ▶ **adj.** informal **1** speedy. **2** bright, fresh, or lively.

zir·con /'zər,kän/ ▶ **n.** a brown or semitransparent mineral.

zir·co·ni·um /,zər'kōnēəm/ ▶ **n.** a hard silver-grey metallic element.

zit /zit/ ▶ **n.** informal a spot on the skin.

zith·er /ˈziTHər, ˈziTH-/ ▶ **n.** a musical instrument with numerous strings stretched across a flat box, which you hold horizontally and play with your fingers and a plectrum.

zo·di·ac /ˈzōdē,ak/ ▶ **n.** an area in the sky in which the sun, moon, and planets appear to lie, divided by astrologers into twelve equal divisions or signs. ■ **zo·di·a·cal** /zōˈdīəkəl/ **adj.**

zom·bie /ˈzämbē/ ▶ **n. 1** informal a person who seems to be only partly alive. **2** (in stories) a dead body that has been brought back to life by magic.

zone /zōn/ ▶ **n. 1** an area that has particular characteristics or a particular use. **2** (also **time zone**) an area where a common standard time is used. ▶ **v.** (**zones**, **zoning**, **zoned**) divide something into zones.

SYNONYMS ▶ **n. area**, sector, section, belt, stretch, region, territory, district, quarter, neighborhood.

■ **zon·al adj.**

zoo /zo͞o/ ▶ **n.** a place where wild animals are kept for study, conservation, or display to the public.

zoo·keep·er /ˈzo͞o,kēpər/ ▶ **n.** a person employed to look after the animals in a zoo.

zo·ol·o·gy /zōˈäləjē, zo͞o-/ ▶ **n. 1** the scientific study of animals. **2** the animal life of a particular area or time. ■ **zo·o·log·i·cal** /,zōəˈläjikəl, ,zo͞oə-/ **adj.** **zo·ol·o·gist n.**

zoom /zo͞om/ ▶ **v. 1** move or travel very quickly. **2** (of a camera) change smoothly from a long shot to a close-up or vice versa.

SYNONYMS **hurry**, rush, dash, race, speed, sprint, career, shoot, hurtle, fly; informal tear, belt, whiz.

□ **zoom lens** a lens allowing a camera to zoom.

zuc·chi·ni /zo͞oˈkēnē/ ▶ **n.** (plural **zucchini** or **zucchinis**) a green variety of smooth-skinned summer squash.

Zu·lu /ˈzo͞olo͞o/ ▶ **n. 1** a member of a South African people. **2** the language of the Zulus.

zy·gote /ˈzī,gōt/ ▶ **n.** Biology a cell resulting from the joining of two gametes.

THE FRUGAL GOURMET COOKS THREE ANCIENT CUISINES

CHINA • GREECE • ROME

JEFF SMITH

"THE LEO BUSCAGLIA OF COOKING!"
Newsweek

"ANOTHER FINE OFFERING FROM JEFF SMITH . . . This internationally flavored and well-illustrated cookbook provides a new appreciation of the three ancient cuisines."
The Atlanta Journal

"A rich variety of Chinese, Greek and Roman gustatory delights."
Los Angeles Herald Examiner

Other **FRUGAL GOURMET** *Books by*
Jeff Smith
from Avon Books

THE FRUGAL GOURMET COOKS AMERICAN
THE FRUGAL GOURMET COOKS WITH WINE

Coming Soon

THE FRUGAL GOURMET ON OUR IMMIGRANT ANCESTORS

THE FRUGAL GOURMET COOKS THREE ANCIENT CUISINES

CHINA • GREECE • ROME

JEFF SMITH

Craig Wollam, Culinary Consultant

Terrin Haley, Research Assistant

Illustrations by Chris Cart

AVON BOOKS NEW YORK

TO MRS. MARY YOUNG
*my adopted Chinese Auntie
who remains convinced that I was
Chinese in a previous life...
I hope it is true!*

AND TO
COLONEL JOHN YOUNG,
whose memory is on every page.

Permissions, constituting a continuation of the copyright page, are listed on page 614.

AVON BOOKS
A division of
The Hearst Corporation
105 Madison Avenue
New York, New York 10016

Cover photograph by Mark Ricketts
Published by arrangement with William Morrow and Company, Inc.
Library of Congress Catalog Card Number: 89-33238
ISBN: 0-380-71217-2

The William Morrow and Company edition contains the following Library of Congress Cataloging in Publication Data:
Smith, Jeff.
The Frugal gourmet cooks three ancient cuisines : China, Greece, and Rome / Jeff Smith ; Craig Wollam, culinary consultant ; Terrin Haley, research assistant ; illustrations by Chris Cart.
p. cm.
Bibliography: p.
Includes index.
1. Cookery, Chinese. 2. Cookery, Greek. 3. Cookery, Roman. 4. China—Social life and customs. 5. Greece—Social life and customs. 6. Italy—Social life and customs. I. Title. II. Title: Frugal gourmet cooks 3 ancient cuisines.
TX724.5.C5S597 1989
641.59—dc20 89-33238

First Avon Books Printing: March 1991

Printed in the U.S.A.

OPM 10 9 8 7 6 5 4 3 2 1

Acknowledgments

I must offer thanks to so many people who helped in the preparation of this book. All three ancient cuisines were equally giving. A cookbook, like the history of the cuisines of the world, is never a private matter. Never!

CHINA

Mrs. Mary Young, of San Francisco, the woman to whom this book is dedicated, has patiently taught me for years about the meaning of the world's oldest cuisine. I am so thankful.

Ken Hom, TV chef and author of several terrific books on Chinese cooking, took my assistant and me through Hong Kong. Ken is a kind and giving person, as are his Hong Kong friends, Willy Mark, Grace and Kendle Oei, and Justice and Mrs. Power. Thank you all.

The restaurant people of Hong Kong, particularly Frank Yuen and Pierre Tang of Maxim's, were most gracious to us, as were the people in the fine hotels of the city. Thanks to the Peninsula, the Regent Li Ching Heen Restaurant, and the Rainbow Room at Lee Gardens.

My thanks must go to Brenda Poon and the Hong Kong Tourist Association. This is a fine company that will make your stay in Hong Kong just a delight. The people in Hong Kong are even nice in the subway!

To my American Chinese friends I must also say thank you. Martin Yan and Bruce Cost (he is Chinese by decision) and to Sharon Jay, in Chicago.

SONG HAY! Hsieh, hsieh.

GREECE

The whole citizenry of Athens seemed to be helpful to us. The Greeks are so gracious that it is embarrassing, and yet you keep going back for more. Particularly helpful was the staff at the National Archeological Museum and my friends at the King Minos Hotel.

The many restaurants that welcomed us are listed among the recipes, but I must offer particular thanks to the characters at Taverna Sigalas, a great spot.

My Greek friends in Tacoma, Mrs. Koustela Stergachis and Mrs. Marie Arger, introduced themselves to me twenty-five years ago, and they have been teaching me ever since.

Finally, the people of Delphi were willing to share their Easter with us. Thanks to all of you, including the staff at the wonderful Hotel Amalia.

YASOU! Efharisto.

ROME

I met Roberto and Micaela Bolzoni in Chicago and we became fast friends. He is with the American Embassy in Rome and I asked Micaela to act as our tour guide while in the Eternal City. Her sense of history, her grace and beauty, and the fact that she can talk anyone out of anything made our work delightful.

Carlo Middione, dear friend and the author of *The Food of Southern Italy,* told me about the markets and about some of his friends. Mrs. Jo Bettoja of Rome, and the Nasi family of Bologna, were just a blessing.

Ms. June di Schino, a beautiful woman who has become an authority on ancient Roman eating practices, was giving beyond belief, as was the Museo Nazionale Romano.

Finally, the restaurants and markets of Rome were most patient with us. Each of the restaurants is mentioned somewhere in the recipes. And to Prince Ugo of Rome, descendant of the caesars, thank you.

ALLA SALUTE! Grazie, grazie.

HOME

My crew from WTTW Television, Chicago, have always been patient and kind to me. The trips we made together to Rome, Athens, and Hong Kong stretched all of our bunch to the breaking point, I am sure. But I received nothing but support from Tim, my producer/director, Cynthia, my assistant producer, Bob, our sound man, and Roy, a cameraman who can get anything. And could this crowd eat!

Bill Adler, my book agent, has become a serious source of strength and insight. And my friends at William Morrow. Five years ago I would never have believed that I would become so attached to my editor, Maria Guarnaschelli, and the boss man, Al Marchioni. Chris Cart, my illustrator, has the most wonderful ability to understand what I am up to . . . and to put it into a drawing. He is charming and gifted, and I am thankful.

I will put my office crew in Seattle up against any crew in the country. Jim Paddleford, my business manager, Dawn Sparks, my secretary, and Terrin Haley, my research assistant, are committed to what I am trying to do and terribly skilled in their fields. Such a help!

Finally, thanks to Craig Wollam, my cooking assistant. His labors and insights have made an indelible impression on this book, and I thank him for his skill and commitment, and for his friendship.

HERE'S TO YOU! And thanks a million!

Contents

Introduction: Credit Must Be Given!

I cannot understand it! How can you call a dish ''new'' or ''nouvelle'' if you do not know the old dishes? The whole idea of calling something new before you have understood the history of a dish is totally inconsistent. Most people in our culture have not yet tasted the old cuisines so it is difficult to know what is new. The basic and wonderful flavors of the past belong to us as a culture, and these flavors have come from many sources. It is through the examination of the sources that one realizes what is new and what is simply repetition on a plate, along with a slice of kiwi fruit.

Do not misunderstand my concern here. I am very taken by the willingness of young chefs to try almost anything and any combination. I remain convinced, however, that a tasting of the creativity of the past would be very helpful in the quest for something new in the present. Chinese artists, for instance, are not expected to try to develop their own styles until they have mastered all the styles in painting that have preceded them. This takes many years, and the result is an artist with insight, with history. He knows what is new and what is not, and therefore he really does understand the meaning of innovation. Anything less is like a junior high student who rebels against all of the rules before he has even considered why the rules came into being. Therefore, duck with grapefruit and coffee-extract sauce is, for me, bizarre! Please learn to cook the duck first, cook it so that I know it is a duck. Learn to cook a duck Chinese style, or Greek style, or Roman style, and then try out some new recipes. Incidentally, Duck à l'Orange goes back to the first century in Rome. It was invented by an Italian! And credit must be given.

The necessity for giving credit to previous cuisines, thereby helping you understand your own cuisine, is the reason behind this book. The three ancient cuisines that most influenced the West were those of China, Greece, and Rome. The Chinese did it first. Everything from the first cooked meat to the first domesticated animals to the first metal cooking pot must be credited to the Chinese. And the Greeks! They taught us to make mayonnaise, baked pasta, basic white sauce (Béchamel), fancy breads, the frying pan as we know it today, the stewing pot brought to perfection, the Dutch oven, and the packed lunch. They even taught us to dip our bread in wine, though the Italians and French think it is their custom. Finally, the Romans took a whole style of cuisine from the Greeks, made some wonderful improvements upon it, and then, through their wild and warring travels, took this cuisine to the rest of Europe. When Catherine de Médicis moved to Paris in 1533 to marry Henri II she brought her Florentine cooks with her. The cooking of Paris was radically changed. Credit must be given.

Many other cuisines have influenced the West, the French being one of these. But French cooking, as we know it, is not ancient. It is excellent, but it is not ancient. The French really did not learn to cook until the beginning of the seventeenth century, and they are not embarrassed by that fact. They admit that the Greeks taught the Romans to cook and the Romans taught the French. Even the *Larousse Gastronomique* admits this! The French are wonderful cooks in our time, but the influences of the past must be shared with the young cooks, the sources must be acknowledged. Did you know that bouillabaisse is actually a Greek dish that came from Marseilles when the city was a Greek shipping port? Credit must be given.

This collection of recipes and comments is aimed at giving credit to the Chinese, Greeks, and Romans. The Chinese had great influence on the Western world, though we seem to have had little influence on them. The Chinese have always preferred their own ways and thus they have kept a rather closed house. But the Greek and Romans have had great influence on one another, and for me it has been fascinating trying to study some of these influences, and to taste the results.

Some of the bits of food history included in this volume will sound unimportant until you take time to consider the consequences of a particular event. The discovery of dried food, for instance, a process perfected by the Chinese, allowed trade routes to become established between the East and the West. And toast. This one sounds absurd, but Paxamos, a Greek of two thousand years ago, discovered that toasted bread will keep a long time in your pack, and thus the Greeks were able to carry an interesting diet with them while trading. Credit must be given.

Rome and China were linked in the pre-Christian era. The trade routes meant that silk and spices could flow into Rome, and with these items came stories of every culture encountered between Rome and the Orient. Feasting was changed, eating habits were modified, and diet was given wonderful variations.

Some of these recipes are included simply as nighttime reading material. I doubt that you will want to prepare them. Others have been included as a blatant attempt on my part to help you understand that Chinese, Greek, and Roman cooking are very different when prepared in their own lands. So I want you to travel to Hong Kong, to Athens, and to Rome. You will be much better prepared to judge whether or not a dish that you have found in America is really "new." After all, credit must be given.

Eat well!

—JEFF SMITH
Chinese New Year, 1989
The Year of the Snake

Glossary

Hints

Kitchen Equipment

Knives

Knives are the most important pieces of equipment in your kitchen. When purchasing such equipment you should be mindful of the following points:

1. Please do not buy knives that are cheaply made and designed to go into a dishwasher. (No good knife should *ever* be put into a dishwasher. They are made of stainless steel so that they are hard enough to take a dishwasher, but they cannot be sharpened.)
2. I prefer the standard old French chef's knife, not a designer gadget. The old model is hard to improve upon, and I have seen no improvement in function with the new "modern"-looking knives. Form follows function. A knife is for cutting. Buy one that does just that. My favorite knives are made in Germany by Der Messermeister company.
3. Buy good-quality knives of high carbon steel. They are now made to be nonstaining but are *not* stainless steel. Use a sharpening steel on them often to keep a good edge. If a sharpening steel makes you a bit nervous, use a Chantry knife sharpener. It is safe and works very well.
4. There is no such thing as a knife that never needs to be sharpened, any more than there is a plate that never needs to be washed. Good knives need sharpening and care, so never just throw them in a drawer. Keep them in a rack, and in good repair. A dull knife is very dangerous since you have to work harder and thus are more apt to let the knife slip and cut yourself.

5. I use the following knives constantly, but you may wish some other sizes. (I own about fifty knives. You don't need that many. Neither do I but I love good knives!)

   10-inch-blade chef's knife
   8-inch-blade chef's knife
   Boning knife
   Paring knife
   Long slicing knife (thin)
   Sharpening steel

Chinese cleaver: There are several thicknesses available. A thin one is used for vegetables and a thicker one for cutting meat and hacking poultry. Do not bother buying a stainless-steel cleaver. You cannot sharpen it.

Pots and Pans

Good pots and pans make good cooking easy. Pans that are thin and flimsy can offer only burning, sticking, and lumps. Buy good equipment that is heavy. You will not be sorry.

Tips for Buying Good Equipment

1. Don't buy pots and pans with wooden or plastic handles. You can't put them in the oven or under a broiler.
2. Buy pans that fit your life-style, that are appropriate for the way you cook. They should be able to perform a variety of purposes in the kitchen. Avoid pans that can be used only for one dish or one particular style of cooking, such as upside-down crepe pans.
3. I do not buy sets of pans but rather a selection of several different materials that work in different ways. Most of my frying pans are aluminum with SilverStone lining. I have aluminum stockpots and saucepans. No, I do not worry about cooking in aluminum since I never cook acids such as eggs or tomatoes or lemon juice in that metal . . . and I always keep aluminum well cleaned, remembering never to store anything in aluminum pots or pans.

I have copper saucepans for special sauces and some stainless-steel saucepans as well. These are heavy stainless with plain metal handles, with an aluminum core sandwiched into the bottom. I also have a selection of porcelain-enameled cast-iron pans, Le Creuset being my favorite brand for that type of thing.

4. The pots and pans I use the most:

20-quart aluminum stockpot with lid
12-quart aluminum stockpot with lid
12-quart stainless-steel heavy stockpot with lid
4-quart aluminum *sauteuse,* with lid
10-inch aluminum frying pan, lined with SilverStone, with lid
Several cast-iron porcelain-coated casseroles, with lids
Copper saucepans in varying sizes, with lids
Chinese wok—I own six of them. See page 12 for descriptions.

Machines and Appliances

Please do not fill your kitchen with appliances that you will rarely use. I do not own an electric deep-fryer or an electric slow-cooking ceramic pot or an electric egg cooker or . . . you know what I am saying. Other pieces of equipment will work for these jobs, and have many other functions as well.

I do have:

Food mixer: Choose a heavy machine, one that will sit in one spot and make bread dough, grind meat, mix cake batters. I prefer a KitchenAid and have the large model with the five-quart bowl.

Food processor: While I use this machine less than my mixer, it is helpful. I have the medium-sized model.

Food blender: I have a heavy-duty model that will take a beating. Don't skimp on this machine.

Electric coffee grinder, small size: I use this for grinding herbs and spices, not for coffee. It is from Germany.

Espresso/cappuccino machine: A good one is expensive, but since my heart surgery I have been allowed only one cup of coffee per day. Caffeine is hard on the heart. A regular espresso has less caffeine in it than a regular cup of coffee, due to the way in which it is roasted and brewed. Since I am allowed only one cup I do a real deal on it! I own a Baby Gaggia, which is a professional-quality machine from Italy. It is expensive, but I have tried many and this is the best one.

SPECIAL EQUIPMENT

Pick and choose among these.
Most of them are just terribly helpful:

Flavor injector: This is a strange-looking plastic device that resembles a hypodermic needle and is used for injecting flavors and juices into meats.

Garlic press: I cannot abide garlic in any form except fresh. Buy a Susi garlic press. Be careful in purchase as there are now many impersonators and they just do not work.

Lemon reamer, wooden: This is a great device, but since I began using it on television many companies have been producing copies that are just not the right size and shape for proper use. Buy a good one, even if you have seen a cheaper model.

Heat diffuser or tamer: This is an inexpensive gadget that you place on your gas or electric burner to even out or reduce the heat. It will save you from a lot of burned sauces.

Tomato Shark: This little gadget takes the stem out of a tomato in nothing flat. Be careful—there is a phony one on the market that doesn't work half as well.

Wooden spoons and spatulas: I never put metal spoons or gadgets into my frying pans or saucepans. Metal will scratch the surface, causing food to stick. Buy wooden gadgets and avoid that problem. I have grown very fond of tools made from olive wood as it is very hard and will last for years, even with regular use and washing. They cost more to start with but they will outlast the others by three times, at least.

Wok: I use my Chinese wok constantly. It is an ingenious device that is made of steel. Do not buy an aluminum or copper wok. The idea is to have a "hot spot" at the bottom of the wok, thus quickly cooking small amounts of food by moving them about in the pan. Aluminum and copper woks heat too evenly and the advantage of wok cooking is lost. Electric woks do not heat quickly enough, nor do they cool quickly enough. You can use your steel wok on an electric burner, though I prefer gas. If cooking with electricity, simply keep the burner always on high and control the temperature of the wok by moving it off and on the burner.

Bamboo steamers from China: These stackable steamers, usually three or four in a set, allow you to steam several dishes at once. The advantage that these have over metal steamers stems from the fact that bamboo will not cause moisture to condense and drip on your food, as metal will. I use bamboo steamers for cooking Chinese foods and for warming up leftovers. I could not run a kitchen without them.

Sand pots: While these are not a necessity, they are fun to have. Great for use in the oven or on top of the stove. Find them in Chinatown.

Stove-top smoker: This is a wonderful device put out by Cameron and it is made entirely of stainless steel. The idea is to place it on the top of your stove with a bit of alder or hickory sawdust in the bottom and you can smoke things in just a moment in your kitchen. These are an investment, but you will find yourself smoking all kinds of things. Instructions for use are found on page 23. Other sawdusts come with the device and can also be purchased in additional quantities. I remain partial to alder and hickory.

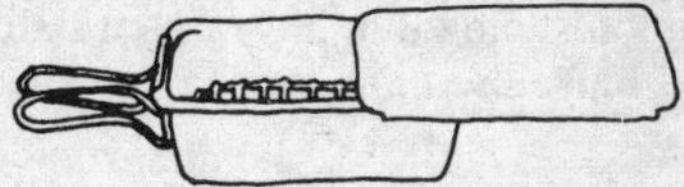

Stove-top grill: This is great for grilling peppers, bread, and other things right on top of the burner. It is called an *asador*, and it works very well.

Grill racks: Choose one or two sizes of these racks for grilling on the top of a griddle or on the barbecue. They are especially helpful in holding a fish together while you grill it Greek style.

Tortilla press: This is very helpful in rolling out dough for Chinese dumplings. Buy a good one that is smoothly polished and you will have less trouble with sticking.

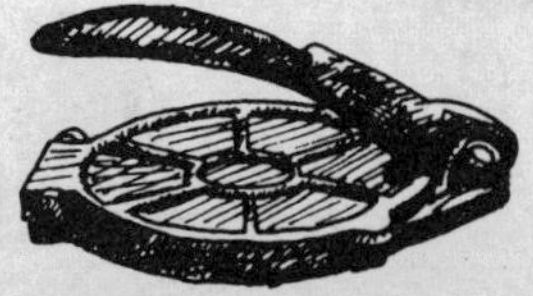

Dumpling maker, Chinese: This plastic gadget is cheap but clever. Helps you make Chinese filled dumplings in nothing flat.

Truffle cutter for cheese: A very fancy gadget . . . but it does a great job on slicing thin bits of hard Italian cheeses. Great for pasta! I also use mine for shaving chocolate bars.

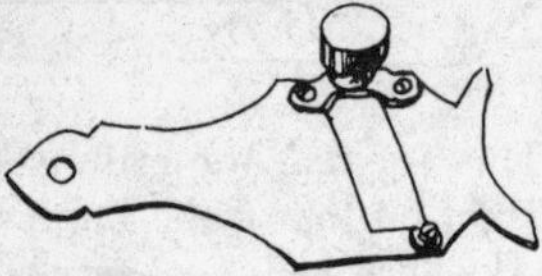

Cheese grater, hand-held: This little stainless-steel grater is wonderful for grating cheese on top of pasta. I use mine right at the table.

Ginger grater: This little porcelain piece works like a scrubboard to grate fresh ginger very quickly and very fine. From Japan.

Chopper/noodle cutter/breadstick maker: A German cutting device that I find just great for noodles and making thin Italian breadsticks.

Noodle bird-nest fryer: This two-basket device presses the fresh noodles together for deep frying. Also used for grated potatoes. The result is a fried "bird nest" basket.

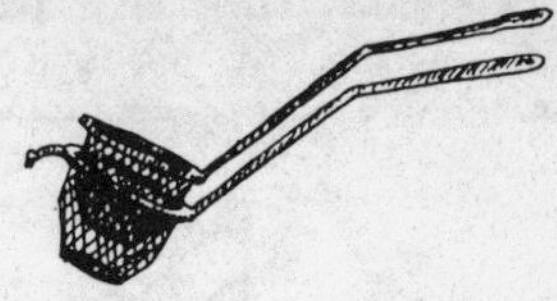

Meat skewers: All kinds are available for making souvlaki and barbecued meat cubes. I prefer those made of stainless steel. These are easily found. The wide thick ones for ground meat will probably have to be made for you.

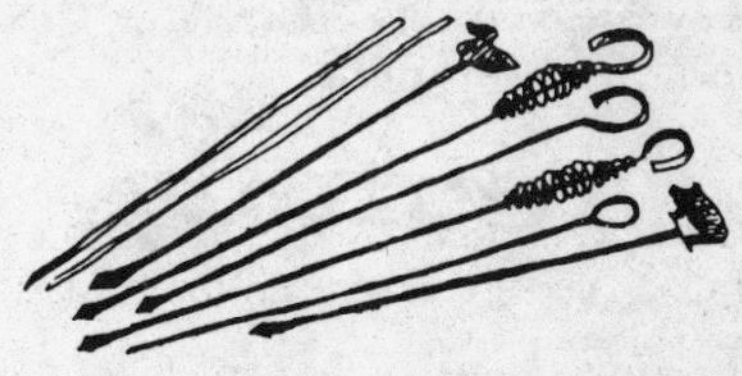

Apple parer/slicer: This is a great device for peeling and slicing apples. I use mine for making the best thin-cut potato fries that you can imagine. Great for shoestring potatoes, as well.

Apple parer/wedger: This little device cores and cuts an apple into wedges. Perfect for desserts, appetizers, or baking.

Pepper mill: The flavor of freshly ground black pepper is very different from that of the preground. Find a good mill and grind your own. I have several mills, but my favorite is a Turkish coffee grinder. These are expensive, but if you are a pepper lover you will love this device. Be careful that the one you buy comes with a guarantee that it can be adjusted for pepper.

Meat pounder: This device will flatten out slices of meat so that they are very thin. Great for Greek and Italian chicken, beef, and veal dishes.

Plastic sheeting: Sheeting is very helpful when you are pounding meat thin. It is inexpensive and available at most large lumberyards or hardware stores. Ask for clear vinyl sheeting 8 millimeters thick.

Fire extinguisher: A must for your kitchen. Buy one that will work on electrical fires as well as stove fires. Talk to the salesperson. You will sleep better at night.

Marble pastry board: These can be purchased in several sizes. I could not make pastry, bread, or pasta without one.

Stainless-steel steamer basket: This is a great help. I have two sizes, and they will adjust themselves to fit different pans. Great for steaming vegetables and not expensive.

Steamer stand: This aluminum stand sits in the bottom of your kettle. A plate of food is placed on top and the pan becomes a steamer. You can also use this as a rack for a double boiler.

Fine strainer for skimming oil: If you do get into deep-frying, this very thin mesh strainer will help you keep the oil clean. From Japan.

Baking tiles: These will help you get a good crust on your bread. Whether or not you use a pan the tiles keep your oven temperature even. Salday makes these.

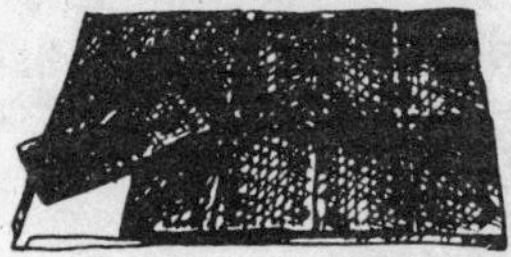

Pasta-rolling machine: This is the easiest way to make good pasta. I prefer rolled pasta to extruded, and this machine can also be used for making other thin doughs.

Ravioli cutters: These stamp forms are helpful if you decide to become a ravioli freak.

Wooden pasta fork: I love this old device. The metal or plastic mockeries of this gadget tear up the pasta.

Roasting racks, nonstick: At last a roasting rack for a serious chicken lover. These work very well as the bird or roast does not stick to the rack.

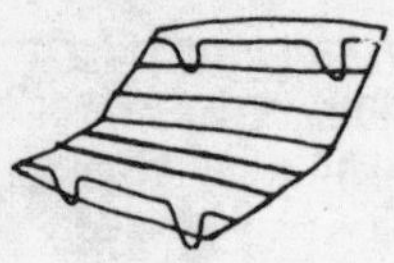

Kitchen scale: Buy something that is fairly accurate. It will be helpful in baking perfect breads and in judging the size of roasts.

Mandoline: This is a wonderful device for cutting vegetables into thin slices or into julienne-style matchstick cuts. Be sure that you get a good one and be careful with it. You can cut yourself unless you use the guards properly. You can also cut french fries or vegetables with this.

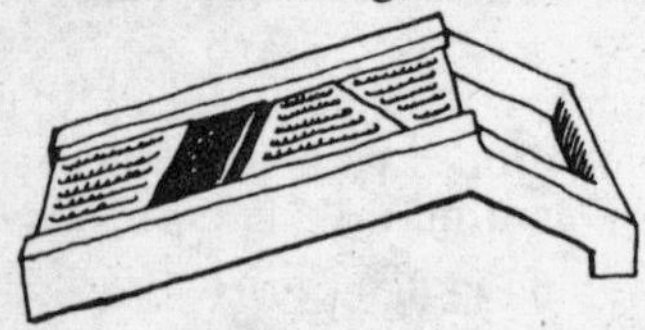

Big dinner and serving plates: A dinner is much more exciting if served on large platters. Loneoak, in California, makes my favorite large white plates and serving platters. You can also find wonderful old serving platters in antique and junk shops.

Big wooden salad bowl: A good one will cost you some money, but if you like salad, you know that the greens will just not taste as good in metal or glass bowls as they will in wood.

Cooking Methods and Terms

AL DENTE
This is a wonderful Italian term that means to cook "to the teeth." It means nobody wants soggy pasta. Cook pasta to the teeth, or until it is barely tender, still a bit firm. It is much better that way . . . and the way Italians intended same to be eaten.

BLANCHING
Plunging a food product into boiling water for a very few minutes (the time varies and will be explained in each recipe). The food is then removed and generally placed in cold water to stop the cooking process. The purpose is to loosen the skin of a vegetable or fruit, to set the color of a vegetable, or to cook a food partially in preparation for later completion of the dish.

CHOW (stir-fry)
A basic cooking method in the Chinese kitchen. Generally a wok is used, but you can also do this in a frying pan. The food is tossed about in a hot pan with very little oil, in a process not unlike sautéing.

CORRECT THE SEASONING
When a dish is completed, a cook should always taste before serving. To correct the seasoning simply means to check for salt, pepper, or herbs to make sure that the dish has turned out as expected. A little correction at the last minute may be necessary.

DASH
Generally means "to taste." Start with less than 1/16 teaspoon.

DEGLAZING A PAN
After meats or vegetables have been browned, wine or stock is added to the pan over high heat, and the rich coloring that remains in the pan is gently scraped with a wooden spoon and combined with the wine or stock.

DEVELOP
Developing a food product means that you have allowed it to sit for a time before serving so that the flavors might have a chance to blend or brighten.

DICE
This means to cut into small cubes; the size of the cube is generally stated in the recipe. For instance, a ¼-inch dice means a cube of that size. It is accomplished very quickly and easily with a good vegetable knife.

DREDGING IN FLOUR
Meats and fish, generally sliced thin, are rolled about in flour in preparation for frying or sautéing. The flour is usually seasoned.

DUSTING WITH FLOUR
Most often a fillet of fish or some type of shellfish (shrimps, scallops, etc.) is rolled in flour, and the excess flour is patted or shaken off. The idea is to have a very light coating on the food.

GRILLING
An ancient method whereby the food is cooked on a rack or skewer over hot coals or an open flame.

HACK
When cutting up chickens or thin-boned meats, one "hacks" with a cleaver, thus cutting the meat into large bite-size pieces and retaining the bone. The presence of the

bone will help keep the meat moist during cooking. Do this hacking carefully.

LOOING

To gently cook a piece of meat (beef, pork, a whole chicken or fowl) in a broth composed of water, soy sauce, and spices. This is also known as "master sauce."

MARINATING

Meats or vegetables are soaked for a time in a flavoring liquid, such as soy sauce, wine, oil, or vinegar. The time of the marinating varies with the recipe.

MATCHSTICK OR JULIENNE CUT

Cut vegetable into thin slices, stack the slices, and then cut the slices into thin sticks, like matchsticks.

MINCE

A minced vegetable or herb is one that is chopped very fine. It is fine enough to be of a very coarse, granular nature. This pertains especially to garlic, onion, and herbs. The process is done by hand with a knife or a food processor.

PINCH OF HERBS OR SPICES

Usually means "to taste." Start with less than 1/16 teaspoon, and then increase if you wish.

POACHING

Gently cooking fish, meat, or eggs in stock or water at just below a simmer. The liquid should just barely move during the poaching process. When fish or eggs are poached, a little vinegar or lemon juice is added to the liquid to help keep the food product firm.

PURÉE

When you wish to make a sauce or soup that is free of all lumps of any sort, purée the stock. This means that you put it in a food processor and mill it until it is free of all lumps, or run it through a strainer or sieve.

RECONSTITUTING
A procedure used for preparing dried foods, whereby the product is soaked in fresh water for a time. The food absorbs the water, so that its "life" is restored and it can be used properly in a given recipe. The process of drying food concentrates flavor and changes the texture, giving it a unique quality in the dish.

REDUCING
Boiling a sauce or liquid over high heat until it is reduced in volume, generally by half. The result is a very rich concentration of flavors.

ROUX
A blend of oil or butter and flour used to thicken sauces and gravies. The fat and flour are mixed together in equal amounts over heat. If a white roux is desired, the melting and blending are done over low heat for a few minutes. If a brown roux is desired, the flour is cooked in the fat until it is lightly browned.

RUBBED
When whole-leaf herbs, such as sage or bay leaves, are crushed in the hands so that their oils are released, the herbs are then referred to as having been rubbed.

SAND-POT COOKING
Using a ceramic lidded vessel originally designed to rest directly in an ash fire, thus cooking or stewing its contents. It can be used on the stove top, quite often with torn lettuce under the food inside. When the lettuce begins to cook, it creates a steaming action; then, as it begins to burn, it adds a unique flavor to the contents of the pot.

SAUTÉ
This term comes from a French word that means "to jump." In cooking, sauté means to place food in a very hot pan with a bit of butter or oil and to shake the pan during the cooking process so that the food jumps about. Thus one can cook very quickly over high heat without burning the food. It is not unlike Chinese chowing, or stir-frying.

SCALDED
Generally this term applies to milk in recipes and it simply means to heat the milk to just under simmering. The milk is scalded when it becomes very hot. It is not a boil at all.

SHOT
A liquid measurement that amounts to very little or to taste. A shot of wine is about an ounce, but a shot of Tabasco is less than 1/16 teaspoon.

SMOKING AND TEA SMOKING
To cook or flavor food with smoldering wood. This can be done on the stove top with the Cameron smoker, providing there is a strong out-of-the-house exhaust system. Chinese black teas such as oolong or po nay can be added to the wood chips to enhance the flavor of the food you are smoking.

STEAMING
Cooking with steam as the heat source. See page 106 for a full discussion. This method is not to be confused with pressure cooking.

STIR-FRY
See Chow.

VELVETING
Deep-frying a food in oil at a temperature of about 280°F. This procedure is commonly used for shellfish. The shrimp, et cetera, is first marinated in a cornstarch and egg-white mixture. When deep-fried, a pale light coating is formed. This process also has a very tenderizing effect.

Ingredients, Condiments, and Food Definitions

Chinese Ingredients

ABALONE
Shellfish that can be found in Chinese markets in cans. Very expensive! It is also eaten fresh on the west coast of the United States.

BEAN CURD
Cheeselike product made from soybean milk. Buy fresh in cakes at Oriental markets or in produce sections of most supermarkets. It can also be purchased in cans, but the flavor is far inferior. Fresh bean curd looks very much like a five-inch rectangular block of soft but firmly shaped white cheese.

BEAN SPROUTS
You will find these fresh in most produce sections. The canned variety is so tasteless that you should omit them if you cannot find fresh ones.

BOK CHOY
A vegetable resembling Swiss chard in shape, but much lighter in color and flavor. A member of the mustard family, it can be found fresh in most supermarket produce sections and Oriental markets.

CELERY, CHINESE
Looks like common celery but has much thinner stalks and a brighter flavor. Find fresh in Oriental markets.

CELLOPHANE NOODLES
Noodles from China made from the mung bean, the same bean from which bean sprouts grow. Find in Oriental markets and some supermarkets. Also called glass noodles, *sai fun,* or bean threads.

CHESTNUTS, CHINESE DRIED
Find in Oriental markets already peeled and dried. Chinese chestnuts are slightly smaller than the Western variety.

DUCK, DRIED
Find in Chinese markets. These ducks have been cut down the breastbone, flattened out, and dried. Soak in water before using.

DOW SEE
See Fermented Black Beans

EGGPLANT, CHINESE
There are many types. The most common is purple in color, thin and long in shape compared to the varieties in the West. Also called Japanese eggplant. Can be found in Oriental markets and some supermarkets.

FERMENTED BLACK BEANS
Fermented black beans are a classic condiment in Chinese cuisine. Buy in Oriental markets, and keep in tightly sealed glass jars. No need to refrigerate.

FOO YEE
Fermented bean curd. Find in any Chinese market.

FUNGUS, BLACK
Chinese dried fungus, also known as ''cloud ears'' or ''tree ears.'' Find in any Oriental market.

FUNGUS, WHITE
Related to black fungus, but white in color and very delicate. Found in Chinese markets.

GARLIC AND RED CHILI PASTE
Very hot Chinese sauce made of red peppers and garlic. Find in Oriental markets, or substitute garlic and Tabasco. It is worth the effort to find this delicious sauce.

GARLIC CHIVES
Light green in color, long thin stalks with a small bud on the tip. Find fresh in some Chinese markets.

GLASS NOODLES
See Cellophane Noodles

HOG MAWS
The actual stomach lining of the pig. Sometimes called pork tripe. Find in Oriental markets.

HOISIN
A soybean and pepper sauce common to Chinese recipes. Find in some supermarkets and in any Oriental market.

HOT BEAN SAUCE
Found canned or in jars in Oriental markets. It is *mein see* with hot pepper oil. That blend would be a good substitute.

HOT PEPPER OIL
May be purchased in Oriental markets.

JELLYFISH, DRIED
Also known as salted jellyfish. Packaged in folded sheets or already sliced. Find in Oriental markets.

LILY BUDS, DRIED
Dried lily flowers that have not blossomed. Look like little golden strands when dried. Buy in small packages in Oriental markets.

LOP CHONG
Chinese sweet pork sausage. Find in any Chinese market.

LOTUS ROOT
Found fresh in many Chinese markets, or in cans. Starchy, and when sliced displays a beautiful hollow pattern.

MEIN SEE
The remains of the process of making soy sauce. Very rich soybean condiment used in many Chinese dishes. Can be found in Oriental markets under this name or soybean jam or condiment. Refrigerate after opening.

MUSHROOMS, CHINESE
Find in Oriental markets. Soak in water before cooking. Trim the stems and save for chicken soup.

NAPA CABBAGE
Sometimes called Chinese celery cabbage, it can be found in many supermarket produce sections and Oriental markets.

OLIVES, SALTY AND SWEET (LAM SEE)
Dried olives, pitted, found in Chinese markets. Substitute dried Italian olives.

OYSTERS, DRIED
Removed from the shell and dried. Reconstitute in water for use. Found in small packages in Chinese markets.

OYSTER SAUCE
Classic cooking sauce from China. While actually made from oysters, it has no strong fishy taste. Found in Oriental markets. Refrigerate after opening.

PICKLED SHALLOTS (KUE TAO)
Shallots pickled in vinegar, sugar, and salt. Can be purchased in Oriental markets in bottles or cans.

POTATO STARCH
Starch made from diced potatoes ground into flour.

RED CHILI PASTE WITH GARLIC
See Garlic and Red Chili Paste. Same product.

RED DATES
Dark red in color, found in Chinese markets in the dried form. Use in double-boiled soups (page 137) and other dishes.

RED VINEGAR, CHINESE
Rice vinegar with spices and color added. Can be found in any Chinese market.

RICE WINE
Called *shao hsing* in Chinese markets. Basic to Chinese cooking. A good dry sherry is fine for a substitute.

RICE WINE VINEGAR
Delicious vinegar used in Chinese cooking. Find it in Oriental markets.

SAI FUN
See Cellophane Noodles

SCALLOPS, DRIED
Air-dried, resemble the common sea scallop. Reconstitute in water to use. Also called *conpoy*. Find in Chinese markets. Expensive.

SEAWEED SHEETS, DRIED
Also known as *nori*. Used in Chinese Seaweed Soup (page 131). Find in Oriental markets.

SESAME OIL
Used as a flavoring in Oriental cooking, not a cooking oil. Find this at an Oriental market. Used for flavoring a dish at the last minute. The health-food store version is not made from toasted sesame seeds, so the flavor will be very bland.

SESAME PASTE
Ground sesame seeds, oil, and salt. Purchase in any Oriental market. Used in sauces and dressings. Make your own (page 248).

SESAME SEEDS
Buy in bulk in Oriental markets. Roast them by stirring them in a hot frying pan until lightly browned, or on a baking sheet in a hot oven.

SESAME SEEDS, BLACK
Purchase in small packages in Oriental markets.

SHRIMP, DRIED
Tiny bay shrimp that have been dried. Any Chinese market will carry them.

SHU-MEI WRAPPERS OR GYOZA SKINS
A round flat noodle used to make dumplings and dim sum. Quite often used for Pork Shu-Mei (page 108). Find in any Chinese market.

SOUTHERN HAM
See Virginia Ham

SOYBEAN CONDIMENT
See Mein See

SOY SAUCE
Light, Chinese: To be used when you don't want to color a dish with caramel coloring, which is what dark soy contains. Do not confuse this with ''Lite'' soy sauce, which is lower in salt and flavor. Find in Oriental markets. I prefer Wing Nien brand. It is the very best quality and made by the company founded by my adopted Chinese uncle, Colonel John Young. This book is dedicated to his wife and to his memory.

Dark, Chinese: Used in dishes in which you wish to color the meat and sweeten the flavor with caramel sugar. Most common soy sauce. Buy good quality. I prefer Wing Nien brand. See explanation above.

SQUID, DRIED
Has a flat appearance when dried. Much larger than the familiar "calamari." Reconstitute in water to use. Find in Chinese markets; sometimes it can be found already soaking in water.

STICKY SWEET RICE
Very starchy rice, used in the making of Pearl Meatballs (page 344) and other dishes. Found in any Oriental market.

SWEET BEAN SAUCE
Find canned in any Chinese market. Use *mein see* with a bit of sugar for a substitute.

SWEET RED BEAN PASTE
Thick starchy paste used in Eight-Treasure Rice Pudding (page 569). Find in Oriental markets.

SWEET PICKLED RED GINGER (SUERN GEUNG)
Ginger packed in sugar syrup with red food color. Can be purchased in Oriental markets in bottles or cans. Very sweet.

SWEET PICKLED WHITE CUCUMBER (CHA GWA)
Chinese white cucumber packed in sugar syrup and salt. Can be purchased in Oriental markets in bottles or cans. Very sweet.

TARO ROOT
A starchy vegetable from China. Its shape and size are similar to that of a russet potato. Found fresh in most Oriental or Chinese markets.

TEA, OOLONG AND JASMINE
Oolong, a dark tea from China. Jasmine, a lighter tea with a flower-blossom flavor. Both are great for "smoked" dishes as well as for drinking. Can be found in any Oriental market.

TURNIP BALL, DRIED
A preserved vegetable from China used in the making of a good Chinese Chicken Soup (page 126) and other dishes. Found in Oriental markets.

VIRGINIA HAM
Also known as Southern ham or by the brand name Smithfield. A salty dry cured ham resembling the Chinese Yunnan ham. Used in very small amounts for flavoring dishes. Find these hanging in Chinese markets and meat shops or fancy delicatessens.

WATER-CHESTNUT FLOUR
A starch ground from dried water chestnuts. Find in any Chinese market.

Greek Ingredients

BÉCHAMEL SAUCE
Basic white sauce made of milk or stock and thickened with a roux of flour and butter; also known as cream sauce (page 234).

BRINE-CURED OLIVES
Sometimes called Greek olives or Calamata olives. Imported. Find in Italian markets, delicatessens, and supermarkets. California black olives are a very poor substitute.

BULGUR WHEAT
Coarse-ground processed wheat. Buy in bulk in health-food shops and good delicatessens.

CALAMATA OLIVES
See Brine-Cured Olives

FETA CHEESE
Soft white Greek cheese made from goat's milk. Buy in delicatessens. Domestic varieties made from cow's milk are available but not as good as imported feta from Greece.

GRAPE LEAVES
The leaves of the grapevine. Find in supermarkets and delicatessens packed in jars in brine.

KEFALOTYRI CHEESE
Hard cheese from Greece, made from sheep's milk. Purchase in good delicatessens. Good grating cheese.

KASSERI CHEESE
Hard cheese from Greece, good for grating. Find in delicatessens and cheese shops.

MIZITHRA CHEESE
Hard cheese from Greece, made from sheep's milk. Purchase in good delicatessens. Good grating cheese.

ORZO PASTA
Pasta shaped like rice. Great for pilaf. Find in Middle Eastern or Italian shops or in a good delicatessen.

PHYLLO DOUGH (FILLO)
Thin sheets of dough for Middle Eastern baking. Can be found in most delicatessens. Also called fillo dough.

PITA BREAD
Middle Eastern flat bread. Also known as pocket bread. Purchase in any supermarket, deli, or Middle Eastern shop.

SALT COD, DRIED
Codfish that has been cured with salt. Also known as *baccalà*. Must be soaked in water a long time before use. Buy in good delicatessens and seafood shops. This is common in both Greek and Roman cooking.

TARAMAS
Fish eggs from the carp. Purchase in small jars in Greek shops and good delicatessens.

Italian Ingredients

ANCHOVIES
Used for salads and pasta dishes in Italian cooking. Buy in cans from Portugal or Spain. Very salty.

ARBORIO RICE
Special rice from Italy used in making Risotto (page 441).

BACCALÀ
See Salt Cod, Dried, above.

CAPERS
Pickled buds used in salads and dressings. Found in any good supermarket.

CHESTNUTS, ITALIAN DRIED
These have been peeled and dried. Buy in Italian markets and delicatessens. Expensive.

FONTINA CHEESE
Rich semisoft cheese from Italy. Purchase in Italian markets or good delicatessens.

MORTADELLA
Famous sausage made in Bologna, Italy. Domestic brands can be found in Italian markets and delicatessens.

MUSHROOMS, DRIED EUROPEAN
Cepe, boletus, or porcini. These are delicious, but if they come from Europe they will be terribly expensive. Find an Italian market that brings them in from South America, and you will pay about $15 to $20 a pound. The real Italian dried mushrooms will cost you a fortune! You may also find some that are domestic. In any case, keep them in a tightly sealed jar at the back of your refrigerator, where they will keep for a year.

PANCETTA
Italian-style bacon with a flavor all its own. Find in Italian markets and good delicatessens. Regular bacon can be substituted, but it is not as good.

PARMESAN CHEESE
Hard cheese from Italy, made from cow's milk. Generally used for grating on salads and pasta dishes. Find in Italian markets, delicatessens, or supermarkets. Not as expensive as Pecorino Romano (see below).

PECORINO ROMANO CHEESE
Hard cheese from Italy made from sheep's milk. Rich flavor; common in Italian cooking. Buy in good delicatessens and Italian markets. Parmesan cheese is the best substitute.

PESTO
A sauce of northern Italian origin, made from fresh basil, olive oil, garlic, cheese, and pine nuts. Great on pasta or in soups and on vegetable dishes. Best to make your own. For recipe see page 240. You can purchase this frozen or in glass jars at Italian markets.

PINE NUTS
Expensive little treasures that actually come from the large pinecone of Italy. Find in Italian markets, or substitute slivered almonds.

POLENTA
Coarse cornmeal used in Italy. You can find this in any Italian market.

PORCINI
See Mushrooms, Dried European

PROSCIUTTO
A very firm and salty ham from Italy. The imported version is illegal in America but you can find fine domestic versions in Italian markets. Primo brand from Canada is quite good. Buy very little at a time, as it is very rich. Have the butcher slice it thin. You may substitute sliced Virginia ham or, in some recipes, a fully cured uncooked ham will do.

RADICCHIO
Resembles our purple cabbage, but smaller in size and has a bitter taste. Find in most supermarkets. Expensive.

RICOTTA CHEESE
White curd-type cheese. Find in delicatessens or in the dairy section of any supermarket.

SEMOLINA
A very coarse-ground flour made from hard durum wheat. Buy in an Italian grocery. Ideal for making fresh pasta, and the flavor is superior to farina, which may be used as a substitute.

Herbs and Spices

Chinese Herbs and Spices

CORIANDER
The dry, whole seed is common in Mediterranean cooking. The fresh plant, which looks like parsley, is common in Chinese, Indian, and Mexican cuisines. You may see the fresh form in your supermarket listed as cilantro or Chinese parsley.

FIVE-SPICE POWDER
A Chinese blend of spices. Find in any Oriental market, or blend equal amounts of powdered cinnamon, ginger, anise, fennel, and clove. Some blends contain a bit of black pepper.

GARLIC
The bulb, of course. Use only fresh. I like mine from the garlic capital of the world, Gilroy, California. My friends at Christopher Ranch weave garlic braids that hang in the kitchen for up to a year. Just pull off a bulb as needed. This is a common and important ingredient in all three ancient cuisines. And buy a good garlic press (page 11).

GINGER, FRESH
Very common in Chinese dishes. Buy by the "hand," or whole stem, at the supermarket. Keep in the refrigerator, uncovered and unwrapped. Grate when needed. Also used in ancient Rome.

MALT SUGAR
Necessary ingredient in making a true Peking Roast Duck. Can be purchased dry or in liquid form. Easy to find in Chinese markets.

MSG
A powder made from seaweed or soybeans. Used as a natural flavor enhancer. Some people seem to be allergic to it and talk of Chinese Restaurant Syndrome, in which they have a headache or light chest pains when eating food containing too much monosodium glutamate (MSG). Few are bothered by this natural chemical and I use it now and then. IT SHOULD BE USED SPARINGLY, JUST AS YOU USE SALT.

MUSTARD, DRY
Absolute necessity if you love salad dressings. And when mixed with water, makes Chinese hot mustard dip. I buy Colman's, from Britain.

PEPPERCORNS, BLACK
Buy whole, and always grind fresh.

RED PEPPER FLAKES, HOT, CRUSHED
Also labeled "crushed red pepper flakes." Buy in bulk, and use sparingly. The seeds make this a very hot product. Common in both Chinese and Roman cuisines.

STAR ANISE
Anise seeds in whole form in the shape of five-pointed stars. Wonderful flavor. Buy whole in any Chinese or Oriental market.

SZECHUAN PEPPERCORNS
A wild peppercorn from China, sometimes called *fagara*. Not hot but very flavorful. No substitute. Find in any Chinese market.

WHITE PEPPER, GROUND
White peppercorns in the powder form. Important ingredient in good Chinese cooking.

GREEK HERBS AND SPICES

ALLSPICE
Not a blend of spices at all, but a single one. Very common in the Greek kitchen. Buy it ground because it is hard to grind yourself.

CARAWAY SEED
This ancient dried seed used by the Greeks and the Romans is excellent for baking fresh breads.

CINNAMON
Very common in Greek cooking. Hard to grind your own, so buy it in the powder form. Also used by the Romans.

CLOVES, WHOLE AND GROUND
I use both the ground and the whole. Common in Greece and Rome.

DILLWEED
Both fresh and dried are used in Greece and Rome. The fresh is a great addition to a tossed salad.

GARLIC (Page 35)

MAHLEB
Small seed that is ground fresh for wonderful Greek breads. Hard to find. Try Greek shops as it is worth the search. No substitute.

MINT
The dried form is common in both ancient Greek and Roman dishes; it also makes great tea. Fresh mint can be grown in the backyard; when cooking with it, use twice the amount in recipes calling for dried mint. Fresh mint is also good in salads.

OREGANO
Basic to the kitchen. For salads, meats, sauces. You can grow your own, but the best comes from Greece. Buy whole, dried.

PARSLEY, DRIED AND FRESH
I rarely use dried because fresh is better. However, dried holds up better in salad dressings. Buy whole. Fresh parsley can be purchased in the supermarket or you can grow your own. I like the Italian variety, which has a flat leaf and a bright flavor. Basic to Greek and Roman cooking.

PEPPERCORNS, BLACK (Page 36)

Roman Herbs and Spices

BASIL
Common in Italian cooking. Buy it fresh or dried, whole at the supermarket. You can also grow your own.

BAY LEAVES
Basic to the kitchen for good soups, stews, et cetera. Buy whole, dried, or if your area is not too cold, grow a bay laurel tree. I have one in Tacoma.

CARAWAY SEED (Page 37)

CINNAMON (Page 37)

CLOVES, WHOLE AND GROUND (Page 37)

CORIANDER, LEAF AND SEEDS (Page 35)

CUMIN
An ancient Roman spice. Can be purchased by the can in powder form, or buy the whole seed and grind it. The flavor is much brighter with the whole seed.

FENNEL SEED
Resembles anise or licorice in flavor. Produces that special flavor in Italian sausage. Buy it whole or grind it as you need it. Common in Ancient Rome.

GARLIC (Page 35)

JUNIPER BERRIES
These are to be found dried in good spice shops. They will remind you of the flavor of English gin. Used in ancient Rome. There is no substitute.

LOVAGE
Ancient Roman herb that resembles celery, with thin stalks and a leafy top. Common celery leaves can be substituted, but the flavor is not as bright. Similar to Chinese celery (page 25).

MARJORAM
Common kitchen herb, light in flavor. Used in Roman cooking. Buy whole, dried.

MINT, FRESH AND DRIED (Page 37)

PARSLEY, DRIED AND FRESH (Page 38)

PEPPERCORNS, BLACK (Page 36)

RED PEPPER FLAKES, HOT, CRUSHED (Page 36)

ROSEMARY
Basic to the cooking of Italy. Grow your own or buy it whole, dried.

THYME
An ancient Roman herb used extensively in soups, stews, and sauces and for seasoning meats. Buy it whole, dried, or grow your own.

Television Shows and Recipes

Show Number and Title

Bean Curd Soup *(page 127)*
Peas and Egg Soup *(page 128)*
Seaweed Soup *(page 131)*
Double-Boiled Soups *(page 137)*
Tripe Soup with Egg-Lemon Sauce *(page 373)*
Roman "Rag" Soup *(page 149)*

505 SAUCES
Greek Tomato Sauce *(page 232)*
Okra in Greek Tomato Sauce (refer to Artichokes in Greek Tomato Sauce, *page 468)*
Egg-Lemon Sauce *(page 233)*
Italian Tomato Sauce *(page 237)*
Basic Brown Sauce *(page 236)*
Sauce Bolognese *(page 238)*
Green Sauce for Boiled Meats *(page 239)*
Chinese Dip Sauces *(page 229)*

506 MUSHROOMS
Dried Abalone with Mushrooms *(page 385)*
Pork and Egg with Tree Fungus in Pancakes *(page 531)*
Mushrooms Stuffed with Feta Cheese *(page 534)*
Pasta with Mushrooms Natalie *(page 536)*
White Fungus Soup *(page 532)*
Double-Boiled Soups *(page 137)*
Mushroom Omelet Apicius *(page 537)*
Pizza with Two Mushrooms *(page 564)*

507 EGGS
Baby Corn and Quail Eggs *(page 257)*
Tea Eggs *(page 255)*
Salted Eggs *(page 256)*
Steamed Pork with Salted Eggs *(page 258)*
Asparagus with Cheese and Eggs, Italian Style *(page 477)*
Egg, Artichoke, and Tuna Pizza *(page 564)*

508 HONG KONG
Pork Shu-Mei *(page 108)*
Ha Gow *(page 104)*
Fried Dumplings (see Rolled Dumplings, *page 451)*
Chinese Roast Duck *(page 291)*
Wonton Dumplings *(page 451)*
Chow Mein, Cantonese Style *(page 398)*
Looed Goose *(page 287)*
Chinese Fish Salad *(page 158)*

509 LEEKS
Chinese Lamb and Leeks *(page 519)*

Chicken with Leek Belts *(page 521)*
Boiled Leeks with Cabbage Apicius *(page 524)*
Beans and Leeks Apicius *(page 523)*
Artichokes and Leeks *(page 522)*
Fava Beans with Leeks *(page 524)*
Leeks and Juniper Berries *(page 525)*
Leek Cakes *(page 522)*

510 LAMB
Roast Lamb, Italian Style *(page 328)*
Roast Lamb, Greek Style *(page 323)*
Lamb and Tomato Sauce, Greek Style *(page 320)*
Lamb with Orzo Pasta, Greek Style *(page 321)*
Greek Lamb and Pasta Salad *(page 162)*
Lamb Hot Pot, Mongolian Style *(page 317)*
Chinese Dip Sauces *(page 229)*
Chinese Lamb and Leeks *(page 519)*

511 PORK
Crispy Roast Pork *(page 334)*
Barbecued Pork Strips *(page 331)*
Barbecued Spareribs *(page 333)*
Slow-Simmered Pork Roast *(page 336)*
Bird's Nest Meatballs *(page 344)*
Pearl Meatballs *(page 344)*
Pork with Celery, Greek Style *(page 347)*
Roast Pork, Roman Style *(page 348)*

512 BREAD
Ancient Roman Bread *(page 555)*
Old Greek Bread *(page 550)*
Focaccia Romana *(page 558)*
Chinese Steamed Bread *(page 546)*
Chinese Fried Bread Strips *(page 545)*
Peking Pancakes *(page 548)*
Corn Crepes, Chinese Style *(page 547)*
Onion Cakes *(page 549)*
Greek Sesame Bread *(page 552)*
Sesame Circles *(page 553)*
Greek Easter Bread *(page 553)*

513 ATHENS
Stuffed Grape Leaves with Egg-Lemon Sauce *(page 438)*
Barley Pudding with Lamb *(page 325)*

514 CHESTNUTS
Roasted Chestnuts *(page 498)*
Chestnuts Soaked in Wine *(page 499)*

Chestnuts Soaked in Ouzo *(page 498)*
Chestnut Focaccia *(page 563)*
Chestnut Pasta *(page 499)*
Chestnut Polenta *(page 500)*
Chestnuts and Lentils Apicius *(page 500)*
Sweet Chestnut Purée *(page 579)*
Italian Chestnut Jam Cake *(page 580)*
Chinese Beef and Chestnut Stew *(page 493)*
Chinese Chicken with Chestnuts *(page 495)*
Peking Dust *(page 574)*
Water Chestnuts and Green Beans *(page 496)*
Shrimp Chowed with Water-Chestnut Flour and Gin *(page 497)*

515 FISH

Fish with Celery in a Hot Plate *(page 175)*
Steamed Fish with Soybean Condiment and Bean Curd *(page 178)*
Braised Fish Oi Mann *(page 178)*
Steamed Fish with Black Beans *(page 180)*
Small Fish Deep-Fried in Olive Oil *(page 182)*
Baked Fish Archestratus *(page 184)*
Greek Fish Chowder *(page 183)*
Assorted Fried Seafood *(page 186)*

516 DUCKS

Peking Duck *(page 292)*
Duck Like a Mandolin *(page 294)*
Stewed Duck with Mushrooms *(page 295)*
Chinese Roast Duck *(page 291)*
Steamed Dried Duck and Pork *(page 296)*
Tea-Smoked Duck *(page 297)*
Looed Duck Feet *(page 299)*
Greek Duck with Olives *(page 300)*

517 ROME

Pasta Carbonara, Roman Style *(page 421)*
Deep-Fried Vegetables Piperno *(page 539)*
Celery and Mushroom Salad Savini *(page 166)*
Italian Flag Salad *(page 167)*

518 DESSERTS

Eight-Treasure Rice Pudding *(page 569)*
Fried Custard *(page 570)*
Cherries in Almond *(page 572)*
Sweet Almond Cream Soup *(page 573)*
Peking Dust *(page 574)*
Halvah Cake *(page 575)*
Strawberry Yogurt with Honey *(page 576)*

524 PASTA
Chow Mein, Cantonese Style *(page 398)*
Chow Fun Noodles *(page 402)*
Cold Chow Fun and Pork Roll *(page 403)*
Meat-Stuffed Chow Fun Rolls *(page 405)*
Noodles in Oyster Sauce *(page 406)*

525 OLIVES AND OLIVE OIL
Deep-Fried Squid, Italian Style *(page 216)*
Olive and Pepper Salad *(page 168)*
Olive Bread *(page 559)*
Green Olive Soup *(page 150)*
Fish with Olives and Bean Curd *(page 181)*
Steamed Pork with Chinese Olives *(page 345)*
Rice Congee *(page 436)*
Chinese Fried Bread Strips *(page 545)*

526 ASPARAGUS
Blanching Asparagus Apicius *(page 476)*
Asparagus Custard Apicius *(page 476)*
Asparagus with Beef and Black Beans *(page 471)*
Cold Asparagus, Chinese Style *(page 471)*
Pickled Asparagus, Greek Style *(page 474)*
Cold Asparagus, Greek Style *(page 473)*
Asparagus with Oil and Tomato, Greek Style *(page 473)*

527 BEANS
Smoked Bean Curd *(page 480)*
Bean Curd with Pork *(page 481)*
Long Beans with Beef *(page 482)*
Fresh Fava Beans, Roman Style *(page 488)*
Beans, Artichokes, and Peas *(page 489)*
Lima Beans with Greek Tomato Sauce *(page 484)*
Black-Eyed Pea Salad Sigalas *(page 485)*
White Beans, Greek Style *(page 485)*
Pasta and Bean Soup *(page 486)*

528 CHICKEN AND GOOSE
Chinese Poached Chicken *(page 265)*
Beggar's Chicken *(page 267)*
Chicken with Two Onions in Sand Pot *(page 269)*
Chicken Baked with Honey and Soy Sauce *(page 266)*
Looed Goose *(page 287)*
Goose Chiu Chow Style *(page 288)*
Fricassee of Chicken, Roman Style *(page 280)*

Chicken with Sweet Bell Peppers *(page 282)*
Devil's Chicken *(page 281)*
Roasted Chicken, Greek Style *(page 279)*
Chicken Roll, Greek Style *(page 279)*

529 RICE
Fried Rice *(page 432)*
Rice Congee *(page 436)*
Sticky Sweet Rice with Meats *(page 434)*
Chinese Sausage on Steamed Rice *(page 437)*
Risotto with Mushrooms *(page 441)*
Risotto with Mushrooms and Herbs *(page 442)*
Risotto with Champagne *(page 443)*
Stuffed Grape Leaves with Egg-Lemon Sauce *(page 438)*
Stuffed Tomatoes Hydra *(page 440)*
Squid Pilaf *(page 217)*

530 ARTICHOKES
Cleaning Artichokes *(page 463)*
Artichokes Sautéed in Wine *(page 464)*
Artichokes, Jewish Style *(page 463)*
Artichokes Chilled, Roman Style *(page 465)*
Artichokes Stuffed, Roman Style *(page 466)*
Artichokes in Greek Tomato Sauce *(page 468)*

531 BEEF
Poached Meatballs in Egg and Lemon Sauce *(page 359)*
Fried Meatballs *(page 360)*
Meatballs in Tomato Sauce *(page 361)*
Beef Slices with Rosemary *(page 363)*
Pepper Onion Beef *(page 353)*
Smoked Meatballs *(page 356)*
Looed Beef *(page 358)*
Looed Beef in Sand Pot *(page 358)*

532 UNUSUAL FOODS
Jellyfish Salad *(page 153)*
Duck and Jellyfish Salad *(page 155)*
Spareribs with Lotus Root *(page 346)*
Bird's Nest Soup *(page 139)*
Looed Duck Feet *(page 299)*
Looed Chicken Feet (Refer to Looed Duck Feet, *page 299)*

533 TAKE-OUT FOODS
Barbecued Spareribs *(page 333)*
Barbecued Pork Strips *(page 331)*
Chinese Roast Duck *(page 291)*
Quick Chinese Roast Chicken *(page 277)*
The Antipasti Bar *(page 97)*

Headcheese Appetizer (*page 100)*
Focaccia Romana (*page 558)*
Souvlaki (*page 324)*
Pita Bread with Olive Oil, Grilled (*page 554)*
Cheese Pies (*page 95)*
Spinach Pies (*page 96)*
Strawberry Yogurt with Honey (*page 576)*

534 DRIED FOODS
Jellyfish Salad (*page 153)*
Dried Abalone with Mushrooms (*page 385)*
Dried Scallop and Chive Soup (*page 387)*
Dried Oysters and Pork in Lettuce (*page 388)*
Chinese Sausage, Dried Duck, and Roast Pork Sand Pot (*page 390)*
Steamed Pork with Mushroom and Dried Squid (*page 389)*
Steamed Dried Duck and Pork (*page 296)*
Salted Cod in Cream Sauce (*page 392)*
Salted Cod, Greek Style (*page 391)*
Garlic Sauce (*page 235)*

535 GRILLING
Ground Meat on Skewers (*page 326)*
Grilled Lamb Cubes, Greek Style (*page 327)*
Firebrick Grill (*page 327)*
Fish Grilled Greek Style (*page 185)*
Pita Bread with Olive Oil, Grilled (*page 554)*
Mongolian Lamb (*page 319)*
Grilled Sweet Red Peppers (*HINTS page 168)*

536 INNARDS
Looed Beef Tongue (*page 369)*
Looed Pork Tripe (*page 370)*
Pork Tripe in Hot Sauce (*page 370)*
Stewed Oxtail, Chinese Style (*page 372)*
Tripe, Roman Style (*page 377)*
Oxtails, Roman Style (*page 379)*
Fried Innards, Roman Style, Edmondo (*page 380)*
Tongue in Sweet and Sour Sauce, Roman Style (*page 381)*
Lamb Innard Soup for Easter (*page 375)*

537 PASTA II
Pasta with Sweet Red Peppers and Anchovies (*page 419)*
Pasta Ears with Cauliflower (*page 419)*
Pasta Ties with Cabbage (*page 423)*
Pappardelle with Pesto (*page 425)*
Pastitsio (*page 412)*
Pastitsio Baked with Phyllo (*page 414)*

The Three Ancient Cuisines

China and Its Inventions

There is no culture in the world that is more obsessed with food than the Chinese, and it seems to have always been that way. When the Chinese are not involved in the actual preparation of a meal, they are talking about the next meal. The sense of anticipation that centers around the family table is like nothing that I have ever seen in other cultures. Further, in their quest for the proper celebration of food, the Chinese have invented or discovered nearly every kind of cooking piece and cooking process, and they were probably the first in history to use them. Yet many books on food history begin with Sumeria, pass through Greece and Rome, and head for Paris, with China receiving a minor mention. That is an absurd way to do history.

The Chinese Mind-set

"A man cannot be too serious about his eating,
for food is the force that binds
society together."
—Confucius

The Chinese preoccupation with food is not due to the fact that they have known starvation. Many cultures have passed through starving times but have never reached the culinary heights attained by the Chinese. Nor is their fascination with food due to their willingness to try anything and everything, though they have. Rather, the Chinese see themselves as a part of nature and its processes, and the celebration of food is a very matter-of-fact event. It is not a *part* of living, it *is* living. The sharing of a meal is what seems to hold the culture together, and even their common greeting to one another, *"Chi fan le mei you?"* actually translates as "Have you eaten yet?" It is close to our "How are you?" but of course it centers around food.

In order to better understand the integral role that food plays in the culture, we need to admit that a culture cooks in a particular way because of the way it thinks. That is true in the West, but I have come to believe that the Chinese also think in a particular way because of the way they cook. The meal passes on to the members of the family a certain insight into history, family ties, holidays, celebrations—in short, into one's place in the scheme of things.

The concept of the Tao is important here. It refers to the belief that there is a natural order and flow to things, a place for all and each in the cosmos, and everything is somehow tied to this proper order or Way. When one is in tune with the Way, things go as they are intended to go. It is very different from the Western belief that we must be at odds with creation, be in charge, remake or reshape everything.

The Way of the Tao means that those who understand it try to get into the flow of things rather than make things into something else. For instance, in Western art we generally use oil paints when preparing a portrait. The oil remains wet for weeks and we can keep pushing it about until we get what we want, which is usually a bust, the person from the waist up, on his own, alone in the frame. The Chinese artist uses ink on rice paper, and he has one chance to catch what he sees or feels, only one chance. The Chinese portrait of a man will more often show a mountainside, with trees and rivers, great cloud formations, and mystical beauty. And there, down in one corner, stands the man. He is in the midst of the flow of the Way, of the cosmos, of the order of things. And he seems to be content to stand there.

Chuang-tze, a classic writer on the Way of the Tao, tells of the life of a chef. A chef who does not understand must always be sharpening his cleaver since he is always hacking away at reality. A Taoist chef rarely sharpens his cleaver since he knows where to place the blade effortlessly and thus separate the joints and meat from the bone. It appears as work without effort, but it amounts to work based on insight.

In terms of cooking this means that you do not force foods into becoming something that they are not. The covering over of one food with the sharp or overwhelming flavor of another is therefore considered very bad taste among the

Chinese. For them a sauce must support, not cover over, a flavor. It also means that in order to bring each food product in a particular dish to its own point of fulfillment, you must cook several ingredients separately, and then join them together in the wok at the last moment. In this way you have contrast in both flavor and texture, all in the same dish. In our culture we are fond of a certain blending and equalizing, consistency and smoothness, a sort of democratic method of cooking. Thus, we are fond of stews, not contrasts.

The doctrine of contrasts in China, Yin/Yang, means that things are defined by other things. Woman is not the opposite of man, since she is woman only when a man is present. And man is only man when a woman is present. Otherwise he is just a person. Each defines the other; they do not battle one another.

These philosophical concepts give rise to all sorts of eating and cooking habits. Americans like to value privacy so we use separate plates for each person and we sit at square tables, thus showing our independence. The Chinese, understanding themselves in a much more communal way, eat from a common bowl in the center of the table, a table that is always enormous and round so that each person may always see the others, face to face. That is probably the only way that such a culture, one in which everyone has always lived so close to everyone else, could possibly work.

One further observation, this one about chopsticks. The idea that chopsticks are primitive is about as astute as the wisecrack about being hungry an hour after eating Chinese food. American-Chinese food, which is filled with celery and bean sprouts and little else, might leave you with hunger, but not real Chinese cooking. Nor are the chopsticks primitive. Willie Mark, a serious gourmet in Hong Kong, claims that the Chinese knew of the knife and fork before they settled on the use of chopsticks. That was news to me, but it is obvious that the Chinese do not use knives and forks at the table because they think butchering food at the table is somewhat barbaric. Better for the chef to chop everything in the kitchen so that it can be eaten by the guest without effort, and with delight. No, the chopping is not done so that one may eat faster. The Chinese spend more time at table than any other people I know, and it is not a matter of efficiency here. It is a matter of philosophy and courtesy and taste.

Finally, the above philosophical concepts allow the Chinese to enjoy their food unabashedly. They do not seem to be burdened with the guilt that is associated with food in our Puritan culture. Enjoy! That's the message. And enjoy food to your good health; the Chinese use food to prevent illness and to heal illness. They are the oldest nutritionists and herb doctors in the world. So, to the table!

The First Cooks and First Restaurants

The first person to cook meat, according to the anthropologists, was Peking Man. That was about 250,000 B.C. Meat sitting on a rock near a fire was probably discovered to be more flavorful than raw meat, and then it happened. Peking Man put some meat on the end of a stick, the first cooking device, and roasted it over the fire. Since it was probably a good-sized piece of meat, he shared it with his associates. There! First Chinese restaurant!

Actually, the first restaurant did appear in China. Prior to the T'ang dynasty (618 B.C.) the Chinese enjoyed the old custom of stopping off for rest and food at a Buddhist or Taoist monastery during a pilgrimage to the holy temples. Later, the Emperor came forth with an edict that these institutions should be kept in good condition for receiving secular guests, since an important goal of both religions was the welfare of all living beings. Thus was born the restaurant.

It is true that Rome had street shops, but these really must be considered take-out houses. The Romans picked the idea up from the Greeks, the inventors of take-out food, it seems to me. But the Romans provided no place to sit and you were expected to take the food to your residence, if you had one. The Chinese, on the other hand, had complete eating houses where you might even stay overnight. These predated anything else that could possibly be called a restaurant.

The Chinese also had take-out houses. The lack of fuel in the Old World meant that few homes could have kitchens, and those that did generally had the fire in the middle of the room. It was out of the question to have two fires going at once, one for cooking and one for heating the house. There was no central heating aside from the cooking fire, so the whole family gathered about that flame. The frugality of the Chinese meant that they would go often to take-out shops that had meat already cooked. Baked goods could be purchased across the street. And, finally, as the last stop, one could visit the special shop for boiling water for your teapot. We find this system strange, but please consider that we are terribly inefficient and burn incredible amounts of fuel all for the sake of privacy. The Chinese just do not think that way.

By the Sung dynasty (A.D. 960–1279) great restaurants were common in China. Marco Polo, who came a bit later, was amazed at the restaurants, hotels, taverns, and tea-houses. All of these ventures were operated with paper money, something that Mr. Polo had never seen. The Chinese invented that, too!

The restaurants of China served meals that are hard to believe. It was not at all uncommon for the wealthy classes to go to an evening meal that consisted of forty courses. Many of the first dishes would simply be brought into the dining room in order to show the skill of the chef, and no one was expected to eat these decorative delights. They were returned to the kitchen, where the staff consumed the food. And since the rule was to serve the best dishes as the last, one had to know how many courses were being served so that one might know when to begin eating in earnest. While the number of courses is no longer so great, I have eaten in Hong Kong with older gentlemen who sit through a feast of many courses with little interest. Finally, near the end of the meal they begin eating everything in sight . . . the best dishes, of course. And I, I am too full to eat anything since I lack the discipline and insight and training to eat in a formal Chinese restaurant. I simply cannot wait, and the old men knew it!

It is still possible to find banquets of twenty-eight courses in Hong Kong, but they are three-day meals. I have eaten in Beijing and I have eaten in Chinese restaurants all over the Western world. The best Chinese food in our time is not to be found on the mainland since the government is so desperate for money that the quality food is shipped out to Hong Kong, and that is exactly where you will find the most profound and exciting Chinese food available... anywhere.

Be prepared to taste many schools of Chinese cooking in Hong Kong. The nation of China has many different ethnic and cultural groups within its borders, so I suppose we should not even use the term "Chinese food." It makes no more sense than the term "American food." What region are you talking about? Boston is certainly different from Dallas, which is different from Seattle. The schools of cuisine in China are many and run from lighter dishes in the south to western dishes that are so hot you are shocked.

The Oldest Chinese Cookbook

We don't know if it is the first Chinese cookbook, but it is certainly the oldest one we have. We have all kinds of claims as to the oldest cookbook, some going back to clay tablets from southern Babylonia around 1700 B.C. Other claims are based on references to earlier volumes that we no longer have. Such is the case with the oldest Chinese cookbook.

My friend Bruce Cost, the fine author of *Ginger East to West* and *Bruce Cost's Asian Ingredients,* has found a jewel. He has a manuscript that goes back to A.D. 535 in China. A government official from the Shandong Province, one Jai Sixie, offered a book that contained recipes from earlier books that we do not have, but the recipes go back to the sixth century B.C. Bruce is beside himself and busily translating the text. It will be called *How to Steam a Bear*.

Many recipes in the book are just as we see them today. Chinese eggplant braised in soy, ginger, and scallions with Szechwan peppercorns. I had the dish the other night in Chinatown. Bruce also claims that this book proves that the Chinese invented prepared mustard, not the French; *sashimi* and *sushi,* not the Japanese; and yeast breads, things that we did not know the Chinese appreciated prior to the time of Christ. All of the current methods of Chinese cooking are explained in this ancient text, and the roasting sections are just wonderful. They were into grilling—we call it barbecuing—long before we expected it. They even invented the meatloaf!

I have already ordered my copy of the book.

The Chinese Kitchen

In the old days the kitchen of a wealthy family was out in back of the house. The smoke from the fire and the noise of the kitchen could not be contained in the house. If you were very wealthy the kitchen was attended by a large staff. But as far as I can understand the method, the basic plan and equipment were always pretty much the same.

The wok, or large round frying pan, was placed over a small burner of charcoal or over a large ceramic stove that could take several woks at once. The pan itself, the wok, originally developed as a result of Chinese inventiveness and a sense of frugality. There is probably some connection between the helmet used by the invading Mongols during the Bronze Age and the pan itself. Food could be cooked in the helmet over the fire. It was also a very frugal use of fuel since the heat is concentrated in a small area in the bottom of the pan, or helmet. In my opinion a good carbon-steel wok, well seasoned, is a must for cooking Chinese food. It is one of the oldest devices we have for the kitchen and I can see no way of improving it.

The kitchen also had a series of clay pots, called sand pots because of the crude method used in casting them, and the bamboo steamers, of course. Ovens for roasting were found only in the houses of the wealthy. The old cleaver and usual cutting boards were also present.

The quality of the porcelain soup bowls and dishes would depend on the wealth of the family.

The methods of cooking have changed little:

Stir-frying or Chowing: Food is tossed about in the wok over high heat. Little oil is needed and the heat is kept high, thus sealing in the flavors of the ingredients.

Steaming or Jing: Food is placed in bowls in bamboo steaming racks, or on the racks themselves. The result is very tender and moist food.

Deep-frying or Jow: Food is quickly deep-fried in peanut oil. This seals the food and offers a wonderful crusty coating.

Pan-frying or Jin: Just as in our system.

Red Cooking or Loo Soey: The meats are simmered slowly in soy sauce, ginger, spices, and wine until tender and close to heaven.

Roasting or Shew: Meats and birds are oven-roasted.

In addition, foods are smoked, barbecued, and grilled, much as we do in our culture.

The Food Products

You will not need to find terribly special ingredients for the recipes in this book. Oh, the Chinese do enjoy some food products that appear strange to us, and I have tasted most of them. I enjoy sea slug or sea cucumber, bird's nest soup, shark fin, and eggs preserved in lime. The only dish I have ever been offered by a Chinese chef that I did not like was sour bamboo. I still cannot get into that one.

The ingredients for all the Chinese recipes are explained in the recipe itself or in the glossary.

A Final Observation

Westerners seem to think that Chinese table manners are a bit different. Please understand that, as I said above, the Chinese enjoy food unabashedly and without hesitation. Therefore they do not pretend that they are *not* eating when they are. That is our game in the West. The Chinese meal celebration may feature everything from burping at the table to reaching clear across the table in order to reach some special tidbit. So, they admit that they are eating . . . and everyone will be eating with their mouths open. However, you will never see a Chinese blow his nose at the table. That is a gross deed, according to the Chinese, that only Westerners would do.

Relax and enjoy this most profound and most ancient cuisine of the world.

When in Hong Kong

Hong Kong is one of the great cities of the world, and it certainly does not act like the rest of China. The mainland Chinese have always kept to themselves, preferring their own culture and habits to those of the outsiders who attempted to break into the Chinese life-style. This provincial attitude was common even during the days of the silk routes that ran from Rome to central China prior to the Christian era. The Romans wanted to talk and gossip but the Chinese kept to themselves. Not so with Hong Kong. Not at all!

Hong Kong's history is bound up with the pirates and smugglers who founded the city two hundred years ago. The Opium Wars, the trade with Great Britain, the relationships established with every other major country in the world, make Hong Kong Island a very different and more open culture than the one you will find on the mainland of China. I think it is the best food city in the world and I urge you to go there. The city population is five and a half million, and another four and a half million visit each year. It is about time you got in on it. Traveling in Hong Kong is just a delight!

The following restaurants and markets will interest you.

Hong Kong Markets

I owe the discovery of these markets to my dear friend, Ken Hom, Chinese cooking instructor and cookbook author. He knows Hong Kong!

The food markets are most unusual and exciting. Go to the Central Market in Hong Kong, in the Central District. Live ducks are being freshly killed, fish are being cleaned, and it is a little much if you have a weak stomach.

Graham Street in the Central District has some of the most beautiful produce you have ever seen. Noodles, eggs, bean curd, everything. Be prepared to hike uphill for three or four blocks.

Dried-food markets on Des Voeux Road in downtown Hong Kong. Dried snakes, fish, mushrooms, almost everything you can imagine.

Yaumati District in Kowloon. Open street stalls, butchers, produce, poultry, and color. Tons of color. Don't miss the pots and pans shops on Canton Road and upper Shanghai Street.

You will enjoy the Tin Hau Temple in the same neighborhood.

Hong Kong Restaurants

The Maxim's Restaurants are all very good. For fine dim sum go to Maxim's Palace in Causeway Bay. The Sichuan Garden in Central Hong Kong is excellent, as is the Peking Garden and the Chiu Chow Garden. You will be happy in any of these places. Your hotel staff can give you instructions as to location.

Spring Deer Restaurant in Kowloon. Wonderful Peking duck and not very expensive.

Great Shanghai in Kowloon. This place is big, friendly, and very authentic. Want to try looed duck tongues? Moderate in price.

King Heung Restaurant in Causeway Bay. Some of the best food I had in Hong Kong. Peking style, moderate in price.

Wu Kong Shanghai in Kowloon near the Peninsula Hotel. Great food and moderate in price. Have their vegetarian goose. Tell Mr. Kong that I sent you.

City Chiu Chow Restaurant, Ocean Center, Kowloon. It is a madhouse but the food is great. Moderate in price.

Carriana Chiu Chow in Causeway Bay. Elegant, delicious, and expensive.

Capitol Dim Sum Restaurant on Nathan Street, Kowloon. Good dim sum and inexpensive.

I am sorry to report that the King Bun Dim Sum House, the one that you saw on my television show, has closed. Problems with a lease. What a pain!

Sun Tung Lok, Kowloon, specializes in dried seafoods. Very delicious, very elegant, and verrrrry expensive.

Li Ching Heen, at the Regent Hotel in Kowloon. Real class, rather nouvelle Chinese, and expensive. Great for a special party.

Rainbow Room at the Lee Gardens Hotel, Hong Kong Island. Fine food, pricy and classy. Great Peking duck and roast suckling pig.

Oi Mann Seafood Restaurant in the Lau Fau Shan fishing village outside of Kowloon. A day trip you will never forget. Moderate in price and all of the fish is alive when you arrive. Ask at hotel for directions. You must go. Tell Mr. Mann I sent you.

Greece and Its Insights

History

It is impossible to discuss the food of Greece without discussing history, art, and philosophy . . . then food. In the early days, during the time of Sophocles (400 B.C.), it was common for poets and philosophers to sit about talking, or writing, about food. It was, and it remains, an integral part of the culture. Food and cooking were listed among the arts, and entertaining with food was another way of understanding and celebrating Greek life and culture.

Plato, Homer, Aristotle, Demosthenes, Aristophanes, Aesop, all discussed food as they discussed history and the rest of the arts. Since the cooks of the day were also priests (they alone knew how to prepare and butcher meats for the sacrificial rites that gave rise to the Greek banquet), it is easy to see why cooking was the prerogative of men. Dining in Greece has always been both a religious and artistic celebration. Even the term *gastronomy* is an ancient Greek word meaning the art and science of good eating. And did they eat! Homer records banquets involving enough meat and wine to take care of people for weeks, and it was done to honor both the gods and a hero of some sort.

Greek culinary art became highly sophisticated during the period of Alexander the Great (fourth century B.C.) when the Greeks spread their culture as far east as the heart of Asia and along the shores of the entire Mediterranean basin. As a result of their travels they came in contact with just about all the foods that we are familiar with in our time. Foods came in from all over the Mediterranean world, as well as from Persia and India.

Food and Eating Habits

We have some interesting recipes and menus from that time through the goodness of one Archestratus, who traveled and wrote, and certainly ate, during the fourth century B.C.

While his original series of articles—a cookbook, really—has been lost, we do have many references to them through such scholars as Athenaeus, a Greek writer of the third century A.D., who quoted Archestratus's works extensively. For instance, we know from these writings that the early Greeks preferred their meat boiled first; then it was roasted, if desired. They seemed to think that only peasants consumed rare meat as we do now. Further, they were fond of cooking with wine, gratinéeing with cheese, making meat broths and gravy stews, and stuffing birds. They also stuffed meats, fish, and fig and grape leaves. So many sauces contained cheese that I expect we must also credit the Greeks with the invention of cheese sauce. Archestratus also was firm on the number of persons who should eat at a table, the number being no more than five. How could you talk if you had more than five people at the table? So we should salute this writer not only for his wisdom but for his timing. He offered one of the first real cookbooks in the Western world, certainly the largest collection of recipes to survive those early times.

One of the principles of the table that was celebrated in the early days of Greece was that of moderation. All went well until the Greeks came in contact with the Persians, serious cooks and eaters, all. The ideals of the Spartans, whose name we still use today, who were very careful and moderate at table, were dumped when the peoples of Athens and Sparta began to understand the lushness of a Persian banquet. Thus began the change from the old habits to a newer form of celebration among the powerful and wealthy Greeks.

A Greek breakfast in the early days consisted of bread soaked in wine, a practice that the French still enjoy. Wonderful breads were available, better than any others to be found in the Mediterranean world. And the wines! Wines were cultivated in Greece, of course, but they were also imported from the rest of what we now call Western Europe.

The Greeks seem to have invented the practice of four meals a day, a practice we still continue, if you count the evening snack. They also developed the sack lunch. When one attended the theater in the old days it was outdoors, of course. Since there was no electric lighting, the plays would begin at the first sign of dawn. Greek theater fans would come armed with their breakfast of bread to be dipped in wine, and of course some olives, and cheese, and oil for the bread. We are talking about a serious meal here, not just a breakfast snack. When the players first noticed the sunlight they would cry, "Hail, rising orb!" and the Grecians would nod approvingly, all the time spitting out olive pits and happily munching on wonderful breads. Thus, the first packed lunch. It became a custom to ask guests in to share dinner and urge them to bring their own wine and food. "Bring your pitcher and supper chest!"

In the time of Homer meat was a major part of the diet. But with the growth of agriculture, the raising of animals for food became grossly expensive, and the whole culture turned to eating breads and grains. They realized that feeding the animals valuable grain was simply not feasible in terms of space and resources. The animals would eat up everything! That has happened throughout much of the world, though we Americans have gone back to meat, refusing to admit that it is not an ecologically sound practice. Meat must be for flavoring, as it is in the Greek diet today, and it should not be used as the basis of the whole diet.

One never saw butter in the ancient Greek diet. You still don't see much of it. The blessed olive offered oil that would provide flavor and lubrication in cooking, so butter was looked down upon. The Greek navy developed as a result of the desire of the Greeks for their beloved oil. Shipping lanes had to remain open, and thus the navy.

The movement of the olive-oil shippers throughout the Mediterranean gave the Greeks the chance to further influence the eating habits of the Western world. Each of the established ports was to feel the influence of the Grecian kitchen. Marseilles, in southern France, was to learn about the original fish stew, *kakkavi,* which the French simply renamed *bouillabaisse*. White sauce, bread for breakfast, which was later to become pizza, toast, and baked pasta. All of these Greek inventions began to influence Western cuisines.

Cooks were highly respected in Greece, and they were not brought in as slaves, as later in Rome. The cook was highly paid and he could be hired in the marketplace. For a special dinner he would bring his staff as well as the pots and pans. A good cook could become quite wealthy since he was allowed a kind of copyright on a new dish, a copyright that was not to be broken for one full year. Famous cooks thus were very much in demand. Everyone wanted to taste the chef's latest dish. They could also pick up some extra cash in the marketplace by selling the leftovers from a feast! It was all perfectly understood and acceptable.

When the Byzantine Empire fell to the Turks in 1453 the respected chefs fled to the monasteries. After all, they had always been associated with food and butchering as a religious rite. While in the monastery they wore clothes like those of the monk, complete with the tall black hat with a puff in the top. Eventually they changed the color of their uniforms to mark them from the priests, and we have the birth of the chef's cap. Even that is Greek!

From the Persians the Greeks picked up the practice of lying on a couch while eating. Food was generally eaten with the fingers since silverware was not popular nor was it used until the seventeenth century. Bread accompanied every course, both for the sake of eating and for the sake of wiping one's mouth, the used piece of bread then being thrown to the dogs. A small and necessary finger bowl was served with the meals as well.

One of the great Greek contributions to the art of dining was the symposium. Following the evening meal the climax of the night centered around the finishing of the wine and the discussion to follow. When the guests were sufficiently intoxicated, and the conversations and hymns completed, the party was finished.

The Kitchen

The Greek kitchen of the old days absolutely fascinates me. They had most of the pots and pans that we use now, but they were instrumental in developing the frying pan. The pot fork was a Greek invention as well, and remember that forks were never used at the table. They were simply used to remove boiled meat from the great pots. I am also convinced that the Greeks invented the concept of the Dutch oven, theirs being an enclosed clay baking dish on three feet. A fire was placed underneath the device and more coals heaped on the flat top. Food was put into the oven through a small door in the side. I saw one of these in the wonderful National Museum in Athens, and it was dated 1500 B.C.! I also found a grill, probably the original barbecue, and it was made at the same time. You can see page 327 for instructions for your own.

Further, we know that the kitchens had to be large since the records list so many kitchen helpers and cooks. Be mindful, now, of the fact that only the wealthy had such kitchens, but these centers did influence the eating habits of the Western world at that time.

Some Conclusions

You must go to Greece. I have traveled there three times so far, and I would leave tonight if it were not for the deadline on this book. American tourists tell me that the food is boring, but that is because they eat in the hotels, agencies of the government destined to serve mediocre food at government-controlled prices. Greece has been in the forefront of creative cooking since Athena called forth the olive tree in Athens. Don't put up with poor food! Go to the restaurants and the tavernas. Taste the wines and talk to the people. Tour the islands and the ancient cities such as Corinth and Athens. I expect that you will better understand why Theresa Yianilos, author of the wonderful *The Complete Greek Cookbook,* offers this profound remark:

"The Greeks' fierce pride in their heritage has kept the basic culture intact. Whether a slave under Roman rule, a captive under Turkish domination, or a newly arrived immigrant, the Greek is always aware that he is the direct descendant of men like Plato, Homer, Aristotle, Demosthenes, Aristophanes. The Greek who begins life in a new land on the bottom step of society as a dishwasher needs only to remember how Aesop left a legacy of poetry while cooking as a slave."

Such confidence. She is Greek!

Chronological Table

A brief chronological table will help you understand the various influences that the Greeks encountered. Yianilos was helpful in preparing this list of events.

900 to 158 B.C. Greece became a powerful military force in the Mediterranean, with bases or colonies on the coast of Asia Minor, Cyprus, Egypt, Gaza, Italy, France, Spain, Sardinia, Persia, and India. The Greeks brought to the colonists their foods, such as olives and olive oil, cheese, figs, wheat, barley, wine, and honey, as well, of course, as Greek cuisine. In return they were influenced by all with whom they came in contact. Foods from foreign lands poured into Greece through the agency of the Greek navy, a navy necessary to the protection of the olive-oil trade routes that Greece had established all over the Mediterranean.

600 B.C. Already the Greeks knew how to bake dozens of different kinds of raised breads. The Egyptians, who were fine bakers, having learned to make leavened bread from the Jews, offered the bread secrets to the Greeks. They in turn began baking breads that contained seeds and spices and herbs and flowers, even wine. This was the beginning of what you and I know as bread.

150 B.C. Rome became the major power in the Mediterranean and it conquered Greece. The Romans loved Greek culture and took on Greek teachers for their children and Greek cooks for their kitchens . . . all as slaves.

A.D. 330 Greeks and Christian Romans overpowered the Roman state and moved the seat of culture from Rome to Byzantium, which they renamed Constantinople. The Byzantine world had the blessings of Greek art, language, and literature, plus Roman laws and government.

500. The barbarian Huns invaded Corinth. The Huns disgusted the Greeks—they used knives to cut their food at the table, a gross practice, and they preferred a fat called "butter," which the Greeks considered a body salve, not a substitute for fine Greek olive oil.

800. Crete became Muslim and the *Kritiki* had to abstain from their favorite meat: pork.

The Bulgars (Bulgarians) crossed over the border and taught the Greek mountaineers the secret of making yogurt.

1000. Romanian nomads invaded and taught the Greeks how to make a hot spiced preserved beef called *pastourma*, "pastrami."

1200. The Venetians settled in coastal regions of Greece.

Crusaders brought in new ways of making wines, and the lemon seed, which they had discovered in Palestine.

1300–1400. Serbs, Italians, and Franks came to Greece bringing pasta.

1453. Constantinople fell to the Ottoman Turks. They changed the name of the Byzantine Christian city to Istanbul and ordered the Turkish language to be spoken. Greek dishes thus took on Turkish names. Greek cooks began to add great amounts of garlic to meat and vegetable dishes to please the Turkish palate.

1821. The Turks began to lose control over Greece, but Turkish cooking left a distinct impression on the Greek cuisine.

New influences moved in. The British brought potatoes, tea, beef, margarine, and ginger beer. The French returned the recipes that they had borrowed hundreds of years before, most of them greatly improved.

1945. Americans entered Greece after World War II and brought new methods of agriculture . . . and such questionable gifts as ham and eggs, bacon, hamburgers, hot dogs, french-fried potatoes, sodas, and milk shakes. And corn on the cob, a dish that you now see roasted on charcoal braziers in the city squares of Athens.

Modern Greece

The Athens Market

Athens is a most wonderful city for touring. The cabs are cheap and generally honest and the markets are fascinating. After you have seen the National Archeological Museum and the Parthenon, you must visit the open food markets on Athinas Street. It is located between Monastiraki Square and Omonia Square. Believe me, you cannot miss it. Go in the morning so that the great hallway of butchers is open. Don't miss the fish stalls, the sausage peddlers, or the produce stalls, either.

The second market area that will astound you is the Flea Market just off Monastiraki Square. You can buy stuff in these backstreets that will tickle them back home.

The Restaurants

When you visit Athens you might want to try some of the following restaurants. I have eaten well at each of these. Just remember The Frugal Gourmet's Rule for Eating in Greece: *Don't eat in the hotels.*

Taverna Sigalas. Right behind the old church in Monastiraki Square. Good food at very reasonable prices. You can eat out in the square if you wish. Be sure and see the kitchen.

Keunan Souvlaki is located around the corner from Taverna Sigalas near the entrance to the Flea Market. Wonderful grilled lamb sandwich in pita bread.

Pelopenese Grill offers wonderful grilled pork, chicken, and lamb. All cooked over charcoal the old way. Dinner is cheap. Just behind Omonia Square.

Fast Food Tunnel. Channing and Jason's favorite place in Athens. Real Greek food in take-out places. Omonia Square.

Taverna Ideal. Near Omonia Square. Good for lunch or dinner. Moderate prices and good food. The hotel desk man will know the place.

Taverna Delphi. Near Syntagma Square, NIKIS 13. Very good food and you are welcome to look at the kitchen.

Vasilenas. ETOLIKOU 72, Piraeus. This place is a joy! Eighteen courses and the price is fixed. Eat till you pop, moderate price. Worth the trip to Piraeus. Watch the cabbie on this one as he might try and take you for too much money. Piraeus is a tourist trap. This place, however, is legit.

Taverna Anna. This is a wonderful, more formal restaurant in North Filotheh, a suburb of Athens. It is worth the cab ride. Opens for dinner at about 9:00 in the evening. Beautiful buffet.

There are several restaurants along the waterfront in Piraeus. It is a notorious tourist trap, but if you insist on going you can trust the food at Kokkini Varka. Be sure you see the prices before you sit down.

Rome and Its Travels

Rome is filled with history and wonderful food. It is the birthplace of many sophisticated forms of art, architecture, and government, forms that we now take for granted, and it is the center of some of the most historically profound uses of food in the world. But while the ancient Romans proudly recorded their accomplishments in every field that you could imagine, including architecture, philosophy, war and conquering techniques, political and governmental systems, and art history, there is very little written about their food and daily diet. What we do have, however, is fascinating. June di Schino, a wonderful South African woman who adopted Rome—or Rome adopted her—has offered the most helpful and insightful material for Roman food history.

The History

The Eternal City was founded around 700 B.C. with the union of several villages and tribes. Romulus, who, legend has it, was raised along with his brother by a she-wolf, became the first king, thus the name of the city. Kings ruled the area until 509 B.C. when the Roman Republic was founded, and the government was run by elected officials until 44 B.C. During this time the Roman armies conquered most of Europe and a good part of the Mediterranean, and their food and diet were very much influenced by the nations that they conquered, especially Greece. It became very "in" to enjoy Hellenistic or Greek art and values, and certainly Greek food. Greek cooks were brought into Roman households and with the cook came the food. Many of these cooks were slaves, others were hired by the house. The vast majority of the cooks of the day were nevertheless Greek. I must also note that the majority of the Greeks had no slaves. In Rome even the most humble householder went around with a train of eight slaves in attendance. Slaves were considered a necessity in Rome, not a luxury, close to the mindset of our South during the nineteenth century. The more nations the Romans conquered, the more slaves poured into Rome, and the cheaper the price per person became.

In 44 B.C. the warring Romans called for a new governmental form and Roman democracy fell before the head of the heroic soldiers, a man who then declared himself emperor. His name was Julius Caesar. You will remember that he kept siding with the peasants rather than the wealthy class and he was finally assassinated by members of the Senate. Interestingly enough, the site of the theater in which Caesar was murdered is now a restaurant. Perfect for my business! This murder marked the end of the Roman Republic and the beginning of the Roman Empire. The emperors who followed became incredibly powerful and the Empire very wealthy. For the next two hundred years Rome lived high, high indeed. The time of the Pax Romana eventually lapsed into a time of gross excesses at the table, excesses that lasted until, and probably contributed to, the Fall of Rome in the fifth century A.D.

The Diet

The very early Romans lived primarily on grains. They ground many different types of seeds and grains and cooked them into an ancient form of polenta, *puls*. In other words, they lived on mush. When wheat flour was introduced during the third century B.C. a much more palatable type of bread was produced.

Vegetables have always been important to Romans. They still are! Onions, garlic, cabbage, and turnips were common, and wild mushrooms were very much appreciated, especially by the wealthy classes. Asparagus, wild in those times, and artichokes, remain two vegetables popular with Romans since the very early days.

Fish among the early Romans was rare, as was beef. Up until the fourth century B.C. cattle were considered primarily as work animals, and they were rarely eaten. Pork seems to have been fairly common, but it generally was reserved for some sort of religious holiday. Goats, sheep, pigs, and poultry were the most common domesticated animals, and these seem to have been eaten more often than fish, even though Rome is only thirty miles from the sea. They just were not fond of fish.

The early Romans were fond of olives, having learned about them from the Greeks. Olive oil became a regular part of the diet, as did Greek wines. As the Romans became more interested in growing grapes and olives, the lands reserved for grains began to diminish. The eventual popularity of cattle for meat also changed the whole agricultural structure, and the Romans finally suffered great grain shortages. Many scholars contend that this was a contributing factor in the Fall of Rome.

While bread was reserved for the wealthy classes in the early days, the peasants living on *puls,* the introduction of flour and Greek bakers brought bread to everyone during the early days of the Republic.

With the importing of the Greek chefs things began to look up for Roman diners. The wealthy classes could afford kitchens and chefs, but the peasants generally bought cooked meat from shops, street shops of great filth. Cheeses were both made locally and imported, and cooked pork was readily available in the street markets. Lamb became more popular, but it has always remained expensive.

The goose was very popular in Rome, a popularity that has been maintained. The Romans developed a method of feeding a goose with figs in order to fatten the livers for rich pâtés. Chickens were kept for eggs, and the birds seldom eaten. Eggs were very popular and we can probably thank the Romans for the invention of the omelet.

Fish gained popularity in later days and the Romans are to be credited with the first fish farms in the Western world. The Romans also prized oysters and raised them in private ponds and lakes or had them imported.

The average Roman ate quite well during the days between the late Republic and the early Empire.

Meals and Tableware

The first meal of the day for the average Roman was simply bread dipped in wine, a custom picked up from the Greeks. One might also include an egg, some cheese, or perhaps a garlic sauce with olives and figs. Doesn't that sound like an eye-opener? A snack was consumed before noon and the biggest meal of the day was offered in the late afternoon.

The wealthy Romans did not recline on couches at dinner until they had met the Greeks, and the Greeks picked up the habit from the Persians. The practice became very popular for two reasons. First, the position allowed the eater to consume more food, and second, it was a comfortable position for falling asleep. This is hardly the way in which we now judge the comfort of our guests!

Since the Roman spent his dinnertime on one elbow, reclining on the couch, it was impossible to use a knife and fork. The meal was eaten with the fingers and the only piece of tableware that was used was the spoon. Among the middle class each person brought his own spoon to the dinner party. The host was not expected to provide them. Among the very wealthy, during the days of the decline of the Empire, the host would often give away gold spoons as a sign of his wealth and importance. The guests were obligated to take the gold spoon with them following the meal. Can you imagine the hosts talking after the meal and making that terribly important and insulting discovery? "Oh, no. They didn't take all of the tableware!"

If you were not invited to one of these meals you could always eat in the many taverns that provided wine, food, and . . . whatever. "Whatever" was generally a bit more expensive. And, further, you would not have a spoon in a tavern, only a knife. No, you did not recline but ate sitting upright on a stool or bench.

The eating position of free citizens was very important in the ancient world. The practice of reclining at meals was also common in the Holy Land, which means that our typical picture of the Last Supper of Jesus is historically wrong. The group would not have been at table but in a room of couches, probably heavy stone couches. You might want to read an essay on this very topic called *Now I Lay Me Down to Eat,* by Bernard Rudofsky (see Bibliography).

The equipment to be found in a Roman kitchen was creative and not far from what we use now. Please remember that only the wealthy had such kitchens, but they were filled with pots and pans, frying pans and portable ovens, many of these items coming from Greece. The Romans took the crude Greek pot fork, a device for removing boiled meats from a pot, and embellished it until it became a thing of great beauty. The Romans had a wonderful ability to take an idea from another culture and improve upon both the functionality of the item and its aesthetic value. They still do this!

The Roman kitchen had just about everything we see in the kitchen nowadays with the exception of gas and electricity. The kitchen was run instead on slave power. Slaves were so cheap at the time that one could afford an enormous kitchen staff, and the chief cook, or chef, was very often able to make a fortune from presents and wages and thus buy his freedom.

As interest in food grew with the growth of the Republic, so did the need for a special room for cooking. The Greeks had special rooms for dining and cooking in their homes and the Romans decided that these were necessary for their life-style as well. Prior to this time, during the time of the first kings, every activity in the house took place in one room, a room with an open hearth where the food was cooked. Smoke from the fire escaped through a hole in the ceiling, but only after blackening the walls. Thus the main room of the house was called the atrium, for *ater,* meaning "coal black."

The Roman Cookbook

We really do not know who this fellow was, this Apicius. We do know that there were at least three different fellows with the same name and all seemed capable of adding something to a cookbook. What we have from the first century A.D. in Rome is probably a compilation of recipes attributed to this Apicius character, later authors adding a few recipes here and there with the recipes gaining a bit of authority since they were attributed to the famous Roman cook. In any case, the collection of recipes comes to us intact and they are fascinating.

The man himself, if we stick to the most famous of the three, must have been a character. He loved to cook and eat, and it was the custom in those days for the men to be the cooks. Women were not expected to appear in the kitchen during formal parties. Often they were not even invited to the banquets, unless they were expected to perform special functions such as dancing, or whatever. (For an explanation of "whatever," please see above.) In any case, Apicius loved his dinner parties and spent a great deal of money setting them up. Remember, now, that this was during the first century A.D. He once heard about some shrimp that were larger than anything that could be found near Rome, these shrimp being in Africa. He immediately called for a ship and set off to sail for his dinner. Days later, when he approached the shores of Africa, he was shown samples of the fabled crawfish or shrimp. "Why," he yelled, "they are no bigger than those of my Rome!" whereupon he pulled up anchor and returned to Rome, having neither set foot on the soil nor tasted the shrimp. Years later he realized that he was down to just a million dollars or so and he had just spent ten million on feasts. He was so terrified of starving to death that he had a final feast and then drank poison. Now, this is the kind of cookbook author who should have met my editor, Maria Guarnaschelli. She could have straightened him out!

The cookbook remains a fascinating document. Several translations are available today (see Bibliography) and we gain an interesting bit of insight into the flavors favored at that time.

Seasonings were used with a heavy hand, seasonings that included salt and pepper, saffron, ginger, laser (an aromatic resin), myrtle berries, cloves, cardamom, poppyseed, laurel, anise, celery, fennel, cumin, parsley, and the ever-present *garum,* a solution of salt and fermented fish which is probably close to what we now call *nuc moom* from the Vietnamese kitchen. The above list certainly would not have been found in the Greek kitchen; they still do not use much in the way of herbs and spices. But the Romans, that was something else. The *garum* sauce probably came from the Middle East through Greece, and then the Romans took it with them on the road. It went with them into India where tamarind and ginger were added and then the Romans brought it into England. The sauce that we now know as Worcestershire is the result of such a journey.

Given the recipes, we can make some general observations about the food of the time. The Romans had a tendency to mix sweet with salty, much like our pickled peaches. Their chief meat, pork, was usually salted and often cured, such as our hams. Red meats were boiled first, and then roasted. They disliked rare meats. They were also fond of casseroles, something taught them by the Greeks, and pies filled with all sorts of things. Many different types of birds were eaten, including figpeckers, chicken, goose, duck, partridge, pheasant, peacock, swan, crane, and flamingo, though the latter birds were seen only on the tables of the extremely wealthy.

We must give credit to the Romans for developing a wonderful menu of sausages and forcemeats, though it appears that they learned about the dishes originally from the Greeks. The Romans ate with fingers and perhaps a spoon, since they were always lying on one side. The finger foods that sausages and forcemeats could provide were perfect for such a meal.

The Excesses

We must remember that most of the Roman peasants and middle class lived not on the fancy foods mentioned above but on gruels, *puls,* and bread. Innards were almost given away by the butchers and these became popular with the lower classes. The menu for the aristocracy was something else.

The first century A.D. saw the appearance of the formal banquet and the use of many slaves in serving. During a time of relative peace and prosperity I suspect that the Roman wealthy classes became bored and thus turned the banquet into the most lavish and gross exercise of excess that we have ever seen at table. The first emperors, Julius, Augustus, and Tiberius, seemed to have rather modest dining habits, but after Tiberius the emperors and their friends just went crazy at banquets. Claudius ate and drank until he fell asleep in front of his guests and Domitian once called the entire Senate together to determine how best to cook an enormous turbot. Heliogabalus had menus embroidered onto the tablecloths. Caligula and Cleopatra used to drink expensive pearls crushed and dissolved in vinegar, and they served their guests loaves and meats of gold. And then, there was Heliogabalus.

Heliogabalus was not a small, informal party man. He loved eels and kept tubs of them at his residence. Food for the eels was provided by the flesh of Christians from the gross displays at the Colosseum. He would eat the brains of six hundred ostriches at a single dinner, and the themes of the banquets were just unbelievable. Artificial ceilings were built into the dining rooms, and when they were opened, gifts would rain on the guests. One such affair featured tons of flowers petals that fell when the ceiling was pulled back . . . and four guests suffocated to death. Such nice evenings! The greater the waste, the more absurd the extravagance, the more successful the dinner was deemed. And if the evening got to be too much for you it was expected that you would make a dash to the "vomitorium." It was all part of the evening's entertainment, and it marked the beginning of the decline and fall of the Empire.

The Fall

The Empire of Rome began around 700 B.C. and lasted until about A.D. 450. During that time the Romans experienced every form of good cooking that we now know, and they knew of almost every food product that we now know. They took these cooking practices and food products to the rest of the world through their travels and conquering efforts, and the world was changed.

The early kings of Rome tended their own gardens, and the final Emperors of Rome simply consumed themselves to death. The motto of Rome, Senatus Populusque Romanus, S.P.Q.R., referred to the Senate and People of Rome only during the Republic. By the end, the citizens were driven to eating anything they could get their hands on since the government ceased to provide for the citizenry.

At this point we must ask the question, Who conquered whom? The Romans swept into Greece and took back to Rome food products, eating methods, cooking methods, chefs, teachers for their children, art forms—in short, a whole new mind-set. The Greeks believe that indeed *they* conquered Rome, not the reverse. I can understand how they feel.

Rome at Present

Rome is one of the most wonderful cities for touring. The food is superb and the city is quite ready for your visit. Just remember to bring your walking shoes and assume that many taxi drivers are dishonest. With that, plan a trip to Rome.

The Markets

You must go to the Campo de' Fiori. This is a great city square jammed with food and flower stalls. Be prepared to spend a few hours.

The market at Piazza Vittorio Emanuele is the biggest in Rome. If you can't buy it there, you don't need it. Wonderful open food displays. Plan to spend several hours.

Neighborhood markets are fun, too. There is a good one each morning on Via Metauro, near Villa Borghese.

Restaurants

Da Franco is a seafood house. All courses are seafood, and the price is fixed. Very informal joint that is strictly for the Romans. Just great and inexpensive for what you get. Via dei Falisci and Via degli Equi.

Edmondo, an old Roman-style house that specializes in innards. Not expensive, filled with locals, and tons of color. Circonvallazione Clodia 90. Tell Edmondo that I sent you. Wonderful place!

Da Pancrazio is on the site of the assassination of Julius Caesar. Really! Campo de' Fiori. Very nice, a little formal, good food, somewhat expensive. Great for your visit to Rome.

La Carbonara, Campo de' Fiori market square. A fine eating house with one of the best antipasti tables I have ever seen. Moderate in price by Roman standards. Have the Pasta La Carbonara.

Romolo, with a wonderful Roman garden in the back. Good food, a little more than moderate. Via di Porta Settimiana 8.

Piperno is a very famous restaurant in the Jewish Ghetto. Ask directions and bring lots of money. The food is just terrific. If during artichoke season you must have artichoke, Jewish style.

Da Giggetto al Portico d'Ottavia. The name is also the address. Good food in the middle of the fascinating Jewish Ghetto. Moderate in price.

Vecchia Roma, near the Jewish Ghetto, Piazza Campitelli 18. One of the best restaurants you will find in Rome. Good staff, nice garden for eating, very fresh food. Expensive but worth it.

Cesarina serves Bolognese food. Wonderful grilled meats and *bollito,* boiled-meat dinners. Via Piemonte 109, medium expensive.

Er Moccoletto is near the American Embassy. Wonderful food and a charming atmosphere. Great antipasti table. Fairly expensive but worth the price. Via Lucania 35.

THE RECIPES

Appetizers

It is hard for Americans to understand the meaning of an appetizer because we see the meal as a single unit. In all three of our ancient cultures, the meal was always viewed as a series of courses. The idea was to come together and eat with friends, family—and perhaps a few politicians that you had to include. The meal *was* the evening, not an event prior to it.

For two thousand years the Chinese have been famous for banquets of many courses. In early times the feasting was expected to continue for two or three days, the first day being just a sort of enticement and celebration of that which was to come. Great dishes would be prepared and brought into the dining room only to be smelled, gazed upon, admired, and finally passed to the servants. Why fill up on the early dishes when one knows that the best dishes are served last? The Chinese still enjoy this sense of anticipation, and these appetizer dishes from China are very typical of modern banquets, though some of the dishes go back hundreds of years.

The Greeks held lavish banquets and the guests could certainly tell what was coming just from gazing upon the first courses. The Romans, of course, who later brought the concept of the formal banquet to its high point and its downfall, had as many as fifteen early courses before the main table was offered. I use the word "downfall" since the Romans really did eat to excess on the strangest things, things that could only be eaten by a people who had come to a point of boredom with food . . . and art . . . and life. However, in our time, one of the greatest treats you can enjoy in Rome is the first dishes, the *antipasti,* literally, the plates "before the meal."

When you read these recipes, some of which are very old, think of the table, the people you wish to entertain, and the fact that it is still possible to enjoy a meal for the evening, and I mean the entire evening. That is how it was done in each of our three ancient cuisines.

China

CHINESE COLD PLATE

The first course in a formal Chinese meal is always to be seen as an anticipation of what is to come. Thus, an elaborate opening dish, made up of a wonderful assortment of delicacies, is a great compliment to the guests, and a signal to "get serious." The only problem is that you must discipline yourself so that you do not fill up on these first creations. They are meant to prepare the palate for at least ten other dishes that will follow.

You may think up your own cold-plate variations, and some ideas might come from the chapter on Dim Sum. Barbecued Pork would be good as an opening course. However, most of the opening dishes would traditionally be served cold or lukewarm. Place each variation on its own plate in the center of the table. Each of your guests can help themselves, eating from their own small private plates. Fresh plates are then offered and the meal is on its way! You can make a very elaborate display of this opening course.

I would suggest the following:

Cold Looed Beef *(page 358)*
Walnuts Fried with Sugar *(page 92)*
Shredded Chicken Sesame *(page 91)*
Glass Noodles with Peanut Sauce *(page 410)*
Bean Sprouts and Szechwan Pepper Salad *(page 155)*
Chinese Brine Pickles *(page 90)*

CHINESE BRINE PICKLES
(Dragon Kiln)
MAKES 4 CUPS OF PICKLES

These pickles are so easy to make that it is almost embarrassing. While the recipe is common, this one comes from the Dragon Kiln people, who import wonderful and inexpensive cooking pieces from China. This recipe comes with their Chinese pickling jar.

- **2 tablespoons salt**
- **1 tablespoon Szechwan peppercorns (page 36)**
- **2 to 4 small dried red chili peppers**
- **½ cup boiling water**
- **3½ cups cold water**
- **4 to 5 slices fresh ginger, each the size of a 25-cent piece**
- **1 tablespoon vodka or dry sherry**
- **4 cups *total* of any combination of the following, cut into bite-size pieces: Broccoli stems, Napa or Chinese celery cabbage, Carrots, Cauliflower, Daikon, Green string beans, Red sweet bell peppers**

In a mixing bowl combine the salt, peppercorns, chile peppers, and boiling water, and stir until the salt dissolves. Stir in the cold water, fresh ginger, and vodka or sherry. Put the vegetables of your choice into a Chinese pickling jar or 2-quart glass jar. If using a Chinese pickling jar, seal with water according to the instructions. If using a regular glass jar, simply cover with plastic wrap. Do not wrap tightly as gas must escape. Allow the pickles to sit, unrefrigerated, for 24 hours and serve.

The pickles will keep for several days if sealed and in the refrigerator.

SHREDDED CHICKEN SESAME

SERVES 6–8 AS AN APPETIZER

This dish can be served as a salad course with a garnish of lettuce or served on crackers as an appetizer. Be careful or your guests will fill up on this dish before the main courses are served!

- 1 chicken, 2¾ pounds, lightly boiled, skin removed and discarded, boned and shredded. Use the bones and skin for later soup stock (See Chinese Poached Chicken, page 265)

THE SESAME GARLIC DRESSING

- 1 teaspoon sugar
- ½ teaspoon MSG (optional)
- 2 tablespoons light soy sauce
- 2½ tablespoons sesame paste (page 248) (tahini works fine)
- 1 tablespoon sesame oil
- 1 tablespoon cider vinegar or Chinese red vinegar
- 1 tablespoon chopped green onion
- ½ teaspoon grated fresh ginger
- 2 cloves garlic, crushed
- ¼ tablespoon Chinese hot pepper oil, or to taste

Place the shredded chicken in a bowl. Mix the remaining ingredients together to form a salad dressing. Toss with the chicken and arrange on a platter. Garnish with more chopped green onion, if desired.

WALNUTS FRIED WITH SUGAR

SERVES 8 AS AN APPETIZER

A delightful appetizer from China. Ken Hom, a fine Chinese cooking teacher, who appears on television, and a dear friend, taught me this one. It is great with cocktails or may be served as a part of the first appetizer course. Remember, in the ancient world nuts of any kind were very expensive, so the host would show off by serving something like this.

1 pound walnut meats, halved

THE SYRUP

2 cups water
1 cup sugar
2 star anise, whole
1 cinnamon stick
3 tablespoons honey
4 cups peanut oil for deep frying

Preheat the oven to its lowest temperature and then switch it off.

Bring a 2-quart saucepan filled ¾ full of water to a boil. Add the walnuts and blanch for 2 minutes. Remove the nuts from the pan and drain, discarding all water.

Mix the syrup ingredients together in the same saucepan. Bring to a simmer and add the nuts. Lightly boil, uncovered, for 10 minutes, or until the syrup begins to thicken. Remove the nuts with a slotted spoon and place on a baking pan and dry in the warmed oven for at least 2 hours.

Heat the oil in a deep fryer or wok to about 360°. Fry the nuts in small batches for about 2 minutes or until the nuts turn dark brown. Do not allow them to burn. Remove to a tray and allow to cool.

Greece

TZATZIKI

SERVES 10–12 AS A FIRST COURSE

You will find this dish in every taverna, or eating house, in Greece. Our whole family loved the dish and we have learned to make it here at home. It goes back a long way into Greek history, along with the habit of eating all sorts of food hand-dipped into wonderfully thick mixtures such as this one. Channing, my oldest son, tasted this variation in my test kitchen. He turned to my assistant and told him that I did not really know how to make a good tzatziki. "Put in more garlic!" he howled. This version is his, and it *is* better than mine.

This Greek appetizer is just delicious served as a dip with small wedges of pita bread.

4 cups fresh yogurt, unflavored
1 medium cucumber, peeled and coarsely grated
4 cloves garlic, crushed
2 tablespoons olive oil
½ teaspoon dried dillweed
Salt and freshly ground black pepper to taste
Additional olive oil for garnish

Place a piece of cheesecloth in a colander and pour in the yogurt. I always make my own so that it will be good and tart. Allow the yogurt to drain for several hours. Use the whey in a soup or in baking.

Place the grated cucumber in another colander and allow to drain for 2 hours.

Mix together all ingredients except the additional olive oil and chill. Place in serving dishes and drizzle additional olive oil on top. Serve as a spread for bread or as a dip for vegetables. This is generally served as a first course.

NOTE: Store this dish covered in the refrigerator and it will keep well for 2 or 3 days. Add to salad dressings for an unusual and delicious flavor. Or smear it on a slice of dark rye bread for a late-night snack.

TARAMASALATA

SERVES 6–8 AS A FIRST COURSE

You will find this dish everywhere in Greece. It is a delicious spread for bread or a wonderful dip for a first course. The basis for this mixture is a cod roe that is whipped with other ingredients until it is lighter than mayonnaise.

By the way, did you know that the Greeks invented mayonnaise?

4 ounces taramas (Find this in any Greek or Middle Eastern deli. It comes in 8- or 10-ounce jars and keeps well under refrigeration. Do not buy taramasalata that has already been mixed. You want to make your own!)
5 slices fresh white bread, crust removed
Juice of 2 lemons
1 cup olive oil
½ yellow onion, peeled and coarsely chopped
1 cup mashed potatoes

Place all ingredients in a food processor and blend until all is smooth.

Serve as a dip with bread and vegetables.

TAHINI BEAN DIP

MAKES 4 CUPS

This paste is common throughout Greece and the whole of the Middle East. I love the stuff, having been introduced to it by my Lebanese Uncle Vic when I was a child. This Greek version is a bit different from the Middle Eastern version in that it includes vinegar and cayenne pepper.

2 cans (15½-ounce size) garbanzo beans
¼ cup olive oil
1 tablespoon white wine vinegar
¼ cup peeled and coarsely chopped yellow onion
2 cloves garlic, chopped coarsely
Pinch of cayenne pepper
½ cup tahini
Salt to taste

Open both cans of garbanzos and drain the juice from *one*. Pour the contents of both cans into a food processor and add all other ingredients. Process until very smooth. Serve as a dip for crackers, olives, pita bread, cucumber slices.

CHEESE PIES

MAKES 8–10 PIES

This is not only a wonderful appetizer but it does very well as a luncheon dish. In Athens you can purchase these in the street and munch as you walk about the city during lunchtime.

FILLING
1 pound feta cheese, crumbled
3 eggs, beaten
1 tablespoon olive oil
1 tablespoon chopped parsley
½ pound butter, melted but not hot
1-pound package of prepared phyllo dough

Mix the ingredients for the filling.

Now, calm down! These are really easy to make. Put a couple of sheets of waxed paper on your counter. Open the phyllo package and unwrap the dough. Now you must work quickly as the dough will dry out in very little time. Place a sheet of dough on the counter and quickly brush it with some of the melted butter. Place another sheet on top of the first and brush it with a little more butter. Place 2 tablespoons of filling at the narrow end of the dough and begin to roll it up in the dough. Use wide rolls rather than narrow ones.

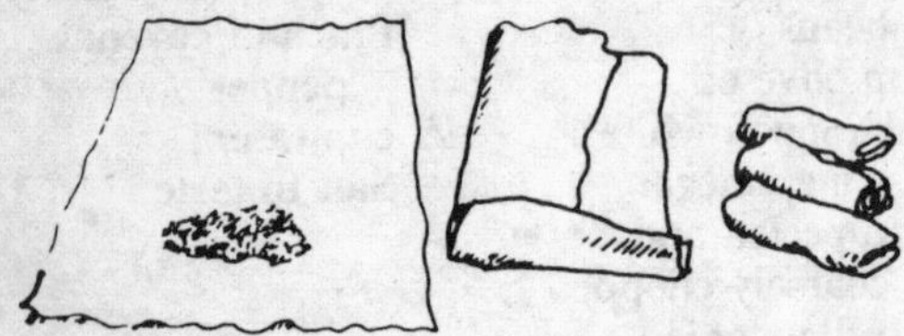

After two rolls, fold one side to the center. Roll one more time and fold the other side to the center, thus giving you a neat package. Continue rolling and place the package, seam side down, on an oiled baking sheet. Brush the top with more butter and continue with the next one.

Bake at 400° for 25 to 30 minutes, or until the pies are a light golden brown. Serve warm.

SPINACH PIES

MAKES 8–10 PIES

This is a very famous dish in Greece. Spinach and dill, along with the cheese, make a superb filling for the phyllo bundle.

FILLING

- 2 packages frozen chopped spinach, defrosted and squeezed dry
- 4 eggs
- ½ pound feta cheese, crumbled
- 1 bunch green onions, chopped
- ¼ cup chopped parsley
- ¼ cup chopped fresh dill or 1 tablespoon dried dill
- ½ pound butter
- 1-pound package prepared phyllo dough

Prepare the filling and roll and bake the pies just as in the recipe on previous page.

Italy

THE ANTIPASTI BAR

In the old days of Rome several courses were brought to your couch. While we don't generally have time to lie about on a couch, we do have time to calm down and open the Italian meal with an assortment of little things *antipasti,* "before the main part of the meal." In Rome you can wander into wonderful shops and just fill up a plate with tasty morsels. It is almost enough to satisfy you for the evening.

The Antipasti Bar would contain any of the following, and you can use these for your own antipasti course at home.

Cold veal, sliced thin with lemon and olive-oil dressing
Cold pasta salad
Artichokes, cooked and chilled
White bean salad
Garbanzo salad
Olives of all kinds
Salami, thin-sliced
Prosciutto, thin-sliced
Headcheese Appetizer *(page 100)*
Smelt Antipasti *(page 98)*
Peperonata *(page 99)*
Mortadella *(page 100)*

SMELT ANTIPASTI
(Vecchia Roma)
SERVES 8 AS AN APPETIZER

I found a dish very close to this one in the Vecchia Roma restaurant near the Jewish Ghetto in Rome. Its history probably goes back to ancient Roman times since it uses raisins and pine nuts, two favorite food products during the first century.

This dish can be served with crackers or as an antipasti course.

1 cup flour, seasoned with salt and pepper
1 pound fresh smelts
1 cup olive oil
2 cloves garlic, crushed
1 teaspoon crushed whole dry rosemary
1 teaspoon crushed whole dry sage
¼ teaspoon dried hot red-pepper flakes
¼ cup red-wine vinegar
½ medium yellow onion, sliced thin
¼ cup white seedless raisins
¼ cup pine nuts, toasted for a few minutes in a 350° oven
Chopped parsley for garnish

Dredge the smelts in the seasoned flour. Pan-fry in ¼ cup of the olive oil. Do not overcook; 1½ minutes per side should be ample. Remove to a cooling rack or paper towels.

In a pan sauté the garlic, rosemary, sage, and red-pepper flakes in ½ cup olive oil for just a few moments. Add the wine vinegar and reduce for a couple of minutes. Set aside.

In another pan sauté the onion slices in the remaining ¼ cup oil until they are limp. Do not brown the onion.

When the smelts are cool, remove the heads and cut lengthwise to debone. Arrange on a platter with the skin side down. Add the sautéed onion, raisins, and pine nuts to the vinegar and herb reduction. Pour all of this over the smelts.

Garnish with parsley.

PEPERONATA

SERVES 8 AS AN APPETIZER

This makes a very attractive appetizer when served with crackers or tiny slices of French bread. Allow each person to place a bit of the mixture on the fresh bread. If the bread is covered ahead of time, the dish will be soggy.

- **6 flat anchovy fillets**
- **2 cloves garlic, crushed**
- **5 tablespoons olive oil**
- **4 red sweet bell peppers, each cut into 8 long strips**
- **4 ripe tomatoes, medium, coarsely chopped**
- **1 medium yellow onion, peeled and sliced thin**
- **2 tablespoons red wine vinegar**
- **6 green olives, pitted and sliced**
- **2 tablespoons capers, small or chopped**
- **Salt and freshly ground black pepper to taste**

Sauté the anchovies and garlic in the oil until the anchovies turn to a paste. Add the pepper strips and sauté, covered, for about 15 minutes.

Add the remaining ingredients and simmer until the tomatoes become tender.

MORTADELLA

Mortadella is the ancestor of what we call bologna, but it is far superior to the salty but flavorless product we know. It comes from the city of Bologna, and there they eat mortadella as a first course regularly. It is sliced thin and offered with wonderful bread, or I have even had it cut into good-sized cubes that you can simply eat with your fingers. Find a good brand of this sausage in an Italian delicatessen. I am fond of Primo brand from Canada.

HEADCHEESE APPETIZER

Place slices of Italian headcheese on a large platter and splash with a dressing of olive oil, lemon juice, and a tad of good red-wine vinegar. Salt and pepper will also be needed. This is a wonderful first course, but you must buy good headcheese to start with.

Dim Sum

The celebration of dim sum is one of the most civilized events I know. It is not a breakfast meal, nor is it lunch, though it can function as either of these. It is more of a brunch that is enjoyed among friends who take one another to enormous dim sum houses that will seat up to one thousand persons. The staff in the restaurant wheels carts about, chanting out the names of the items on their carts as they pass by. The patrons simply point to what they want on the cart and the dishes are placed on the table. When the meal is finished the dishes are counted and you are charged accordingly. Tea is a must with the meal, of course, and it is assumed that you will take a great deal of time to eat and talk and drink tea . . . and choose the various dim sum. The restaurant may offer four hundred different kinds, which means you would have to go back several times in order just to see the varieties pass your table, let alone eat them all.

The name of this style of food, "dim sum," literally means "little jewels that tug at the heart." The Chinese, however, do not see this as snack food. It is far from that. The selection includes meat-filled dumplings, steamed or deep-fried, shrimp in tiny noodle bags, round meatballs of pork or beef. Little plates of spareribs and spicy squid will be found on the carts, and beautiful one-bite pastries made of rice flour and stuffed with a hundred different fillings. The "tug at the heart" is supposed to come from the beauty of the delicacies, but the tug that comes at my heart stems from the pain of not being able to taste everything in the place!

The history of some of these dishes goes back two thousand years and many have wonderful symbolic meanings. For instance, during the New Year Festival dumplings that look like little money bags are served in order to wish wealth for the New Year upon the guest. One emperor in the early days was so fond of dumplings that the staff made them and froze them in crocks in the ground so that they could be ready to serve him whenever he hungered for his favorite food. Did the Chinese invent frozen foods? I think there is some good evidence for this.

You can make these tasty jewels at home with only a little practice. The shouts and cheers that you will receive when you serve this food will make the time involved very much worth it. Or you can just read about these dishes and then go to a major Chinatown in this country and enjoy. I think my recipes are very good, so you might just offer your own dim sum parties and be the happier for it.

I love these dishes . . . and I have to confess that once when I finished lunch with my cousin David in San Francisco, we counted seventeen plates on the table. Eating it all took some doing, but I have never forgotten that meal.

You might also consider:

Barbecued Spareribs *(page 333)*
Chicken Wings in Five Spices *(page 271)*
Chinese Boiled Dumplings with Hot Sauce *(page 449)*
Pot Stickers *(page 450)*
Looed Chicken Feet *(page 299)*
Looed Duck Feet *(page 299)*
Fried Wontons *(page 118)*
Hot and Spicy Squid *(page 119)*
Steamed Meat-Stuffed Buns *(page 120)*

Shrimp

HA GOW

MAKES 24 HA GOW

This is my favorite dim sum. I have eaten them in Hong Kong, San Francisco, Seattle, New York, Vancouver, B.C., and I can never get enough. My love for shrimp is brought to fulfillment in this wonderful delicacy, the name of which refers to the shape and is translated as "cat's paw." Any cat would go crazy over these things.

NOTE: The Ha Gow Filling can be used for several other dim sum, recipes for which follow.

HA GOW FILLING

- ½ pound raw shrimp, peeled and chopped very coarsely
- ¼ pound precooked salad shrimp, chopped coarsely
- 2 ounces pork fat, chopped fine
- ¼ cup coarsely chopped bamboo shoots
- ¼ teaspoon ground white pepper
- ¼ teaspoon grated fresh ginger
- ½ teaspoon salt
- ½ teaspoon sesame oil
- 1 tablespoon finely chopped green onion, white part only
- 1 egg white
- 1 tablespoon dry sherry
- 1 tablespoon cornstarch

Place all in a bowl and mix well, by hand. I mean, use your hand! Keep stirring and whipping with your fingers until the ingredients form a smooth and rather firm stuffing. This will take about 2 minutes.

From *Favorite Dim Sum*. I have made changes only in the amount of water.

HA GOW DOUGH

2 tablespoons potato starch*
1 cup wheat starch†
¼ teaspoon salt
½ cup plus 3 tablespoons boiling water
1 teaspoon lard
Additional wheat starch for dusting

Measure both starches and salt into a small mixing bowl. Quickly pour the boiling water into the starches while stirring with chopsticks until you get a partially cooked dough. Do not overwork the dough. Quickly add the lard in little pinches and then knead until smooth. A marble board is great for this. When the dough is smooth, after about 2 minutes' kneading, cover it with the mixing bowl and allow it to rest for 15 minutes before shaping.

To shape the dumplings, pull just a tad more than 1 teaspoon of dough from the ball. Keep the remainder of the dough covered with the bowl. Roll the small amount into a ball and place onto the floured marble board. Roll out into a circle about 3 inches in diameter. Place 1 teaspoon of the shrimp filling in the center of the circle of dough and fold over into a half-moon. Use a tiny bit of water for sealing the edges. Be sure to gently press out all the air. If you wish, you can form little pleats in the dough for added decoration.

Steam on an oiled bamboo steaming rack (see next page) for 12 minutes.

*Available in most fine groceries and delicatessens
†Can be purchased in any Chinese market

HINT: A TORTILLA PRESS FOR MAKING DIM SUM WRAPPERS. Try using a lightly oiled tortilla press to press the ball of dough out to an initial stage. Then dust with flour and quickly finish the rolling by hand. This works great!

HINT: A BAMBOO STEAMER FOR PROPERLY STEAMED FOOD. These can be found in most gourmet shops or Oriental markets. The steamer racks are placed in a wok with water in the bottom. Several dishes can be steamed at once since steam does not carry flavors. So clever! The advantage of bamboo over metal is that bamboo will not cause water to condense on your food. A metal lid will.

SHRIMP TOAST

Trim the crust from slices of white bread and cut each slice into 2 rectangles. Add ½ cup chopped water chestnuts to 1 cup of Ha Gow Filling and smear a bit on each slice of bread. Press in raw sesame seeds. Deep-fry in oil at 360° until golden brown. Delicious!

SHRIMP BOATS

Cut a green sweet bell pepper in half and remove the seeds and stem part. Cut each half into 4 little boats or shells. Fill each with some of the Ha Gow Filling and gently fry each boat, shrimp side down, in a very little oil in a covered frying pan. Cook just until the shrimp begins to brown, about 3 minutes. The pepper should still be a bit crisp.

SHRIMP BALL WITH PINE NUTS

Make small 1½-inch balls of Ha Gow Filling. Roll in raw pine nuts. Deep-fry in peanut oil at 360° until golden. These are very beautiful snacks.

SHRIMP-STUFFED MUSHROOMS

MAKES 12 DIM SUM

Soak 12 Chinese dried mushrooms in water for 3 hours. Trim away the stems and, using paper towels, pat the mushrooms dry. Place the mushrooms top side down and place a bit of Ha Gow Filling paste on each. Place them on a plate in a steamer and steam for 15 minutes.

EGGPLANT STUFFED WITH SHRIMP

SERVES 6 AS PART OF A DIM SUM MEAL

In the Hong Kong dim sum houses, a cart with propane burner is circulated about the restaurant. As she moves along, the server fries these great delicacies so that they are very hot when she comes to your table. This is another great dim sum dish.

- ½ pound Chinese or Japanese eggplant (the long gorgeous kind available in Chinese markets)
- 2 tablespoons peanut oil
- 1 clove garlic, crushed or chopped fine
- 2 tablespoons chopped green onions
- 1 teaspoon sesame oil
- 1 teaspoon sweet bean sauce (page 30)
- ½ teaspoon hot bean sauce (page 26)
- 1 cup Ha Gow Filling (see page 104)

Do not peel the eggplant but cut the vegetable into small rounds, on an angle, about 1 inch thick.

Heat 1 tablespoon of the oil in a wok and add the garlic. Chow for just a moment and then add the green onions and the eggplant slices. Add the remaining ingredients, except for the Ha Gow Filling, and chow until the eggplant is tender but not soggy, about 5 minutes. Remove the pieces of eggplant to a tray to cool.

When cool, put a bit of the Ha Gow Filling on each. When completed, pan-fry them with the remaining 1 tablespoon oil in a SilverStone-lined frying pan. Cook them, uncovered, just until the shrimp filling is cooked, about 4 minutes.

Pork

PORK SHU-MEI

When I was a very young boy I used to save my allowance and travel down to Chinatown, in Seattle, to have pork shu-mei for brunch. These are easy to make and are probably the most popular dim sum that I know. They resemble little money bags and are offered at Chinese New Year since they help anticipate wealth.

THE FILLING

- 1 pound lean ground pork, finely chopped
- 2 tablespoons light soy sauce
- 2 tablespoons dry sherry
- 1 teaspoon freshly grated ginger
- ½ teaspoon ground white pepper
- 1 tablespoon sesame oil
- ½ teaspoon MSG (optional)
- Pinch of sugar
- 1 tablespoon chopped green onion
- 1 egg white
- 1 tablespoon cornstarch
- 1 teaspoon salt
- 4 tablespoons medium chopped bamboo shoots or water chestnuts (optional)
- 2 cloves garlic, crushed

THE WRAPPER

- 1 package shu-mei skins or Gyoza skins, available at the supermarket

Mix all of the ingredients for the filling together, and mix them well. Place about ¾ tablespoon of filling in the center of each noodle wrapper and bring up the corners so that you have a little money bag. Leave the top open so that you can see some of the meat. For fun you might put 1 frozen green pea on the top of each for added color.

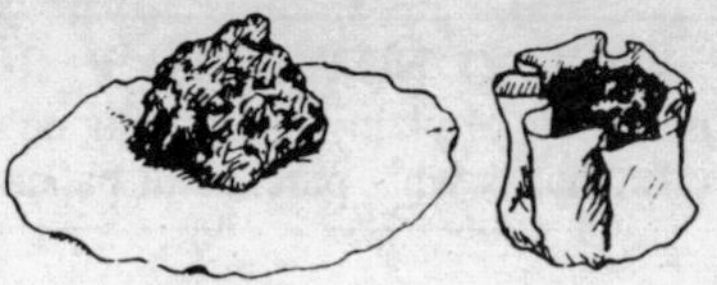

Steam in an oiled bamboo steamer for 15 minutes, on high heat.

NOTE: You can also add a bit of shrimp to this dish. It adds a great deal of flavor. Try about ½ cup of chopped fresh shrimp.

DEEP-FRIED SHU-MEI

Prepare the recipe as above and deep-fry the dumplings in peanut oil at 360° until golden brown and the inside is cooked to your taste.

QUAIL EGG SHU-MEI

Prepare Pork Shu-Mei and place 1 cooked quail egg on the top of each dumpling. Push it down a bit into the meat and steam as instructed.

Cooked quail eggs, all peeled and ready to go, can be purchased in the can at any Chinese grocery.

PORK AND TARO MEATBALLS

Prepare a batch of Pork Shu-Mei Filling (page 108). Roll 1½-inch balls of the mixture in finely grated taro root. Deep-fry these at 360° for a very attractive and delicious treat.

Taro root can be found in any Oriental market.

STEAMED POT STICKERS

Prepare a batch of Pot Stickers (page 450) and steam them on tiny pieces of parchment paper so that they do not stick to the bamboo steamer. Steam for about 20 minutes and serve.

HINT: IF YOU DO NOT HAVE PARCHMENT PAPER, use sheets of plain white typing paper and rub them with oil. That is what parchment paper is!

FUN GOR

MAKES 24 DIM SUM

The dough, or wrapper, on this one has a light and transparent look since you use cake flour and boiling water. When steamed the dough has a rather ''pearly'' look and it is delicious.

THE DOUGH
(From *Favorite Dim Sum*)

- 1 cup Swans Down cake flour
- ¼ teaspoon salt
- ½ cup boiling water
- ½ teaspoon lard
- Additional flour for dusting

THE FILLING

- ¾ pound pork, coarsely ground
- 1 tablespoon light soy sauce
- 1 tablespoon dry sherry
- ¼ teaspoon freshly grated ginger
- 1 clove garlic, crushed
- 6 water chestnuts, coarsely chopped
- 2 tablespoons grated carrot
- 2 tablespoons coarsely chopped Napa cabbage
- 2 tablespoons chopped fresh cilantro
- ¼ cup dry roasted peanuts, coarsely chopped
- 2 tablespoons coarsely chopped Western-style cabbage
- 1 egg white
- 1 tablespoon cornstarch
- Pinch of sugar
- ½ teaspoon salt
- ¼ teaspoon ground white pepper

Mix well all of the ingredients for the filling.

Prepare the wrappers in the same way that you prepare Ha Gow wrappers (page 105). Try to use Swans Down cake flour for best results.

Shape the dumplings and fill them just as you do the Ha Gow. When you have filled and sealed the dumpling, set it down, seam straight up, and put a few finger pleats in the seam. Place in an oiled bamboo steaming rack (page 106) and steam for 15 minutes over high heat. They should sit right up in the rack.

STUFFED BEAN CURD SKIN, PAN-FRIED

You may have trouble finding fresh bean curd skin unless you live in a large city with a bustling Chinatown. Seattle, New York, Chicago, San Francisco, Los Angeles, Boston, and Washington, D.C., will have this product in the Chinese markets.

Prepare a batch of Shu-Mei Filling (page 108), adding some chopped garlic chives or regular chives. Chopped cabbage is good in this dish as well.

Soak the sheets of bean curd skin in tepid water for just a few moments until they soften a bit.

Place a portion of soaked bean curd skin, about 6 inches by 8 inches, on the counter and put 2 tablespoons of filling on one end of the skin. Roll it up like a spring roll or burrito, folding the sides in so that you have a neat package. Pat the rolls dry on a kitchen towel. Dip each in an egg wash made of whole eggs, 1 tablespoon of water for each egg, and a dash of sesame oil. Dust each with cornstarch and pan-fry on medium heat in a bit of peanut oil until they are golden brown. Flatten them out a bit and pan-fry slowly on both sides.

Try deep-frying these in order to warm them up just before serving.

STUFFED BEAN CURD

MAKES 20 DIM SUM

These are especially appropriate for a larger dim sum celebration because they can be made ahead and then simply steamed to finish the cooking. I love these little pillows of goodness.

- 1 cake bean curd, firm style
- 1 batch Pork Shu-Mei Filling (page 108)
- Oil for deep frying

OYSTER GRAVY

- ¾ cup water
- 2 tablespoons oyster sauce
- 1 teaspoon sesame oil
- Pinch of sugar
- 1 tablespoon cornstarch mixed with 1 tablespoon cold water

Cut the bean curd into 2 pieces, the long way. Then cut into ¾-inch slices and cut each slice into 2 triangles. Place in a colander and allow to drain for 1 hour. Pat dry with paper towels and deep-fry at 320°, in two batches, until they are a light golden brown and they float. Drain on paper towels.

Cut a deep slash in the long side of each triangle. Do not go through to the edges. Fill the pocket with the meat filling. Go ahead and leave a bit overflowing from the pocket. Place in a glass pie plate or dish and steam for 30 minutes.

In the meantime, prepare the oyster gravy by bringing the water to a boil and stirring in the rest of the ingredients. Stir carefully over medium heat until thick.

Drain the water from the steaming dish and top the bean-curd pockets with the oyster gravy.

SPICY PORK TRIPE

SERVES 6–8 AS A DIM SUM COURSE

Some things come by on the dim sum cart and only the Chinese will order them. What a shame it is that most other Americans will not try the very best dishes. This is a favorite of mine, but you must cook it for a long time.

- 1½ pounds pork tripe (hog maws)
- 2 green onions cut into 3-inch pieces
- 1 dried turnip ball (page 30), chopped and rinsed well
- 2 tablespoons peanut oil
- 1 tablespoon finely chopped garlic
- 1 teaspoon freshly grated ginger
- 1 tablespoon fermented black beans (*dow see*), rinsed
- 2 green onions, chopped
- 2 tablespoons light soy sauce
- 2 tablespoons Chinese rice wine or dry sherry
- ½ tablespoon garlic and red chili paste (page 26)
- ½ tablespoon sesame oil
- 2 tablespoons cornstarch mixed with 3 tablespoons water (optional)

Cut the tripe into strips about 4 inches long and ½ inch wide. Blanch in boiling water for 5 minutes and discard the water.

Cover the tripe with fresh water and add the green onions cut in 3-inch pieces and the dried turnip. Cover and simmer until the tripe is tender, about 1 hour. Longer if you prefer, of course.

Drain the tripe well, discarding the water. Heat a wok and add the peanut oil, garlic, and ginger. Chow for a moment and add the tripe. Toss in the oil and then add the remaining ingredients, except the cornstarch solution. Cook to your taste and then thicken the sauce, if you wish, with the cornstarch and water, stirring as you add.

To reheat for a dim sum party, simply steam in small bowls.

SPARERIBS WITH BLACK BEANS AND PEPPER SAUCE

SERVES 6 AS A DIM SUM COURSE

This is another dish that causes traffic jams among the dim sum carts in Hong Kong. Everyone wants an order and the chaos is infectious. Easy to prepare, they will just make a dim sum party.

- 1 pound pork spareribs, cut into 1-inch pieces (Have the butcher cut them for you on his band saw)

MARINADE

- 3 tablespoons light soy sauce
- 2 tablespoons Chinese rice wine or dry sherry
- 1 teaspoon ginger, freshly grated

- 2 tablespoons peanut oil
- 3 cloves garlic, chopped fine
- ½ teaspoon salt
- 1 tablespoon fermented black beans (*dow see*), rinsed
- Pinch of sugar
- 1 teaspoon garlic and red chili paste (page 26)

Blanch the ribs in boiling water for 1 minute. Drain well. Mix soy sauce, rice wine, and ginger. Soak ribs in the marinade for 20 minutes. Heat a wok and chow the ribs until lightly browned. Remove from wok and drain the oil. Add the fresh peanut oil, garlic, and salt to wok. Chow until the garlic browns just a bit and then add the remaining ingredients. Return the ribs to the wok and toss in the sauce. Place in a steaming dish and steam for 45 minutes to an hour, or until the ribs are very tender.

VARIATION: You can also avoid browning the ribs. Just add 1 tablespoon cornstarch to the marinade and continue with the dish. When steamed the cornstarch will form a wonderful gravy on the ribs.

GARLIC RIBS WITH GREEN PEPPER AND BLACK BEANS

Use the same recipe as previous page but omit the garlic and red chili paste and add ½ green sweet bell pepper, cored and diced into ½-inch pieces. Add the pepper just before steaming the dish.

Chicken

CHICKEN SHU-MEI

Use the same recipe as for the Pork Shu-Mei (page 108) but substitute ground chicken for the pork. The chicken product can be found frozen in your supermarket and the result will please everyone at your table. It will also contain less fat.

CHICKEN AND CHINESE CHIVE SHU-MEI

You can use regular chives for this but the Chinese chive has a much brighter garlic flavor. As a matter of fact, it is sometimes found in the Chinese markets listed as "garlic chives." It is worth the search . . . but then you know me and garlic!

- **1 pound ground chicken (page 115)**
- **½ cup finely chopped Chinese garlic chives**
- **1 clove garlic, crushed**
- **1 tablespoon dry sherry or Chinese rice wine**
- **1 tablespoon light soy sauce**
- **½ teaspoon freshly grated ginger**
- **½ teaspoon MSG (optional)**
- **Pinch of sugar**
- **1½ teaspoons sesame oil**
- **1 tablespoon cornstarch**
- **1 teaspoon salt**
- **½ teaspoon ground white pepper**
- **Additional whole chives for "belts"**

- **24 Shu-Mei wrappers (page 108)**

Mix all ingredients together, except the chives for the "belts." Whip by hand, using your hand, until the mixture holds together very well. Form into shu-mei just as in the pork recipe (page 108). Blanch the whole chives in very hot tap water just for a moment. Tie one chive around the neck of each chicken-chive dumpling so that it looks like it is wearing a little green belt. Steam in an oiled bamboo steamer for 15 minutes (page 106).

> **HINT: USE LETTUCE CIRCLES FOR STEAMING SMALL DUMPLINGS.** Simply cut iceberg lettuce into small circles using a small cookie cutter. Place a little circle of lettuce under each dumpling or shu-mei. No stick and lots of flavor.

Beef

BEEF MEATBALLS

MAKES ABOUT 20 DIM SUM

This is a quicky. Buy good hamburger and do something very special in almost no time at all. I love these meatballs and they can be used in Hoko Pot soup (page 129) or chowed with vegetables . . . should you ever have any left over. I really doubt that you will have this problem.

- 1 pound lean ground beef
- 1 tablespoon dark soy sauce
- 1 tablespoon Chinese rice wine or dry sherry
- ¼ teaspoon ginger, freshly grated
- 1 teaspoon sugar
- 2 green onions, chopped
- 1 egg, beaten
- 1 tablespoon cornstarch
- 1 teaspoon sesame oil
- 2 cloves garlic, crushed
- 1 teaspoon soybean condiment (*mein see*)
- 2 teaspoons finely grated orange peel
- ¼ teaspoon MSG (optional)
- 1 bunch spinach or mustard greens, fresh, for garnish

Mix all ingredients together, with the exception of the garnish. You need to whip this dish to make it smooth, so I suggest an electric mixer . . . but it must be a good one. Otherwise, do it by hand and beat the blazes out of this stuff.

Roll into small meatballs about 1¼ inches in diameter. Press some of the greens into a steaming bowl and top with the meatballs. Steam the meatballs in several dishes, steaming each, or all together, for that matter, for about 15 minutes. It is best to use your bamboo steaming racks for these dishes (page 106).

HINT: TO KEEP MEATBALLS FROM STICKING TO YOUR HANDS simply moisten your hands in between each molding of a meatball. Works great!

Additional Dim Sum

FRIED WONTONS

I don't really care for these but they seem to be common fare on American/Chinese restaurant menus. So here is the recipe.

Deep-fry some prepared Wonton Dumplings (page 451) in fat at 360° until golden brown. Drain.

Prepare a dip of plum sauce (purchased in the can) thinned with a bit of hot water or Chinese Chicken Soup Stock (page 126).

Dip the hot wontons into the sauce. That's it. I apologize for my lack of enthusiasm but I will admit that these are much better than those you find in restaurants.

HOT AND SPICY SQUID

SERVES 4–6 AS A DIM SUM COURSE

When the dim sum cart passes me and I see Hot and Spicy Squid I am a wreck. No matter how much I have already eaten I always order a plate of this wonderful seafood.

- 1 pound squid, cleaned and cut into ⅓-inch circles (page 212)
- 2 tablespoons peanut oil
- 1 tablespoon finely chopped garlic
- 1 teaspoon freshly grated ginger
- 2 green onions, chopped
- 2 tablespoons light soy sauce
- 2 tablespoons Chinese rice wine or dry sherry
- Shot of hot pepper sauce such as Tabasco or 1 teaspoon garlic and red chili paste (page 26) (This is more legit!)
- 1 teaspoon sesame oil
- 2 tablespoons cornstarch mixed with 3 tablespoons water

Prepare the squid and set aside. Heat a wok and chow the oil, garlic, and ginger for about 1 minute over high heat. Add the green onions and the soy, along with the squid. Chow just until hot and add the remaining ingredients, adding the cornstarch mixture last and stirring until the mixture is thick.

Remove from heat and serve immediately, or cool and place in small dishes. Reheat for serving by steaming for about 4 minutes.

STEAMED MEAT-STUFFED BUNS
(Ham Bow)
MAKES 24 HAM BOW

This is certainly one of the most popular dim sum dishes in Chinese restaurants, whether they be in Hong Kong, Beijing, or San Francisco. The buns take a bit of time to prepare but they are delicious and fun to eat.

BREAD DOUGH

- 2 packages fast-rising yeast
- ½ cup lukewarm water
- 1 tablespoon sugar
- 1 cup milk, heated to lukewarm
- 4¼ cups regular flour

FILLING

- ½ pound Chinese Barbecued Strips (page 331), chopped into medium-small dice
- 2 green onions, chopped
- ¼ cup fairly finely chopped Chinese celery cabbage (Napa)
- 1 tablespoon hoisin sauce
- ½ tablespoon oyster sauce
- ½ teaspoon sesame oil
- Pinch of salt
- 1 tablespoon light soy sauce
- 1 teaspoon sugar
- 1 tablespoon cornstarch dissolved in 1 tablespoon water or cold chicken stock

THE DOUGH

Sprinkle the yeast over the lukewarm water and then add the sugar. Allow to stand and then stir in the yeast. Add the warm milk. Be careful that this is only lukewarm or tepid, about 90°. Stir in the flour and knead until smooth. I do all of this with my KitchenAid mixer. Place the dough on a plastic countertop and cover with a large metal bowl. Allow to rise until double in bulk, around an hour. When properly risen, punch the dough down and allow to rise another 30 minutes.

THE FILLING

While the dough is rising, prepare the filling. Combine all ingredients in a wok, except for the dissolved cornstarch, and chow just until the mixture is hot. Thicken with the cornstarch and allow the filling to cool.

THE CONSTRUCTION

Punch the dough down and knead for 1 minute. Roll the dough into a snake about 1 foot long and divide the dough into 24 pieces. Roll each into a ball and then roll out into a 4-inch circle. I do this on a marble board so that I do not have to use too much additional flour.

Fill each bun as you roll it. Place a little more than a teaspoon of filling in the center of the dough circle. With your fingers, gather the sides of the dough up around the filling in loose folds, meeting at the top. Pinch the dough together so that it will hold. Place the filled bun upside down on a 2-inch square of waxed paper and place in a bamboo steamer. When all the buns are finished, cover the steamer with the lid and allow the dough to rise until not quite double in size. In about 30 minutes the dough should spring back slowly when pushed gently with your finger. Steam them for 15 minutes. Serve with a bit of Chinese mustard (page 36).

Soups

Who invented soup? This most glorious of dishes, a dish that seems to transcend all cultures and all geographical barriers, has been with us since ancient peoples discovered that they could heat things in water held in the stomach lining of an animal. What an amazing technological step forward that was!

And the grass basket, if tightly woven, could be made waterproof. Foods were boiled in these baskets by adding hot rocks from the fire. Then the great advance called "The Clay Pot," and the soup was on! Copper, bronze, and iron cooking pots soon offered a whole new means of cooking by boiling in a liquid, and everyone knew that the liquid left in the pot was the best part. It would warm the heart, relax the body, and calm the spirit.

The peasants of our three ancient cuisines must be credited with wonderful discoveries once they had a pot in which to cook. Boiling foods was the simplest way of cooking and it eventually became one of the most sophisticated methods of food preparation. The peasants have always taught the upper classes how to eat. Soup was invented out of sheer hunger and frugal necessity . . . and now it is a dish in its own right.

In ancient China soup was often served as the last course, not the first as in our culture. And it did not need to be complex. A few chicken bones and a dried mushroom or two and you have a soup that is thousands of years old. Or perhaps you use the water in which the rest of the dinner has been cooked, a practice that the frugal Chinese still observe. With a light and simple stock, great dishes are prepared, such as the famous sharkfin or even bird's nest soups . . . these being two of the most expensive soups that I know of anywhere in the world. The recipes follow, of course.

The Greeks must be credited with the invention of "Fish in the Pot," which they call simply "The Pot," *kakavia*.

They taught the French to make such a soup when Marseilles was a Greek shipping town, though the French name for "pot" gave the dish the title of *bouillabaisse*. And the Greeks taught the Romans to make the same soup. Greek soups are heavy and rich, just like the Greek mind. The Greek recipes in this section go back so far that some cannot be traced. I love the tripe soup!

The Romans took on the Greek cooks and learned a great deal from them. In Rome in our time you can find soups that are so old that one soup actually has the name "As Old as Adam." The range in Roman soups, and in Italian soups in general, is much wider than in either of our two earlier cultures. The Romans took the task of making soup very seriously and you can have anything from a simple bread soup to a vegetable soup, a minestrone, that will bring you to tears.

These were all peasant soups in the beginning. The people of the region of Liguria claim that they invented minestrone. During the time of the Crusades the soldiers from Genoa attempted to provide their leader with soup for a meal. They asked all the peasants in town to contribute herbs and vegetables, and the soldiers provided the stock. The soup became known as minestrone and do you know the name of their leader? It was Godfrey of Bouillon.

Enjoy the soups!

You might also like to consider:

Tripe Soup with Egg-Lemon Sauce *(page 373)*
Pasta and Bean Soup *(page 486)*
White Fungus Soup *(page 532)*
Clear Mushroom Soup *(page 533)*

China

CHINESE CHICKEN SOUP STOCK

MAKES 4½ QUARTS

This is basic to the Chinese kitchen. It is easy to prepare and wonderfully versatile. One batch of this and you have a thousand possibilities for filling the soup bowl with wonderful things.

You will notice the practice of properly blanching the chicken pieces first. This is the way that a clear and light Chinese soup stock is made.

5 pounds chicken backs and necks
2 slices fresh ginger, each the size of a 25-cent piece
2 Chinese dried turnip balls (preserved turnip or preserved radish) (page 30), coarsely chopped and rinsed with fresh water

Place the bones in a 12-quart stockpot and cover with water. On high heat bring the bones barely to a simmer. We do not want to cook the soup yet so do not let it do more than just simmer. Foam and scum will form on the top of the pot. You do not want this to boil. Drain the bones, discarding the water, and rinse well with cold water. Add 1 quart of fresh water for each pound of bones, along with the ginger and rinsed dried turnip. Bring to a simmer and cook 1 hour, uncovered.

Strain the soup stock and discard the solids. Remove the fat by using a plastic tube (see below) or simply chill the stock overnight and remove the fat when it has congealed.

HINT: TO REMOVE FAT FROM SOUP STOCK use a plastic tube and siphon the strained stock from beneath the layer of fat. The tube can be purchased at a hardware store and should be ½-inch diameter. Wash and use regularly with your soup stocks.

BEAN CURD SOUP

SERVES 4

This should probably be called "peasant style" since it is so very common in China, but I love the stuff and make it often.

1 quart Chinese Chicken Soup Stock (page 126)
½ pound pork, trimmed and cut julienne
1 cake bean curd, firm Chinese style (page 24), cut into ½-inch cubes and drained
1 cup bok choy (page 24) or mustard greens, chopped
Salt and ground white pepper to taste
1 fresh egg

GARNISH

Green onion, chopped
Sesame oil

Bring the stock to a simmer and add the pork. Cook for 6 minutes and add the bean curd and the bok choy or mustard greens. Bring to a boil and add salt and white pepper. Pour into a serving bowl and crack the raw egg into the bowl. It will cook on the way to the table. Garnish with the sesame oil and chopped green onions. Stir the egg into the soup at the table and serve.

PEAS AND EGG SOUP

SERVES 4

This is the common "egg flower" soup that you find in Chinese/American restaurants. It is a good dish if you use good soup stock.

1 quart Chinese Chicken Soup Stock (page 126)
1 10-ounce package frozen peas
¼ cup sliced water chestnuts
3 eggs, beaten
1 teaspoon Chinese red vinegar
Salt and white pepper to taste

GARNISH

Green onions, chopped
Sesame oil

Bring the stock to a simmer and add the peas and water chestnuts. When all is hot, add the beaten eggs very slowly in a stream. Count to ten and stir the pot slowly. You should have lovely thin streams of egg. Add the remaining seasonings and garnishes and serve.

ABALONE SOUP

SERVES 8–10

This is a great favorite of mine. When I was thirteen years old I used to save my allowance and travel to the old Tai Tung restaurant in Seattle. They would prepare this dish for me and I have never forgotten it. Now canned abalone is terribly expensive, something like $15 a can . . . but the soup is just wonderful. Prepare this for some kind of a state occasion such as your birthday or your lover's birthday . . . or maybe it should be served on a slow Monday.

6 cups Chinese Chicken Soup Stock (page 126)
1 16-ounce can abalone (available in Chinese markets), sliced thin, the liquid reserved
¼ pound pork, cut in a medium dice
4 Chinese dried mushrooms, soaked for 6 hours, drained and sliced julienne
¼ cup sliced water chestnuts
1 cup thinly sliced bok choy or Chinese celery cabbage (Napa)
Salt and white pepper to taste

GARNISH
Green onion, chopped
Sesame oil
1 egg

Bring the stock to a heavy simmer and add the juice from the canned abalone. Add the pork and mushrooms. Simmer for 10 minutes and add the water chestnuts, abalone, vegetable, and salt and pepper. Bring to a simmer again, being careful not to let this boil. You do not want to toughen the abalone. Place in a serving bowl and add the garnishes. The raw egg is cracked into the bowl just before serving. It will cook on the way to the table. Stir in the egg when you present this absolutely smashing soup.

HOKO POT

The fun of cooking soup at the table is increased if you own a Hoko Pot. This device is much like an angel-food-cake pan on a stand. The pan is filled with soup stock and glowing hot charcoal pieces are dumped into the center tube. The soup is cooked in this way and everyone simply helps him/herself to the pot.

This is probably a very old method of cooking going back three thousand years to the Shang Dynasty in China. Metal helmets were an invention of the time and soldiers would cook soup in them by simply placing them in the fire. The wok also is no doubt connected with this history.

The ingredients depend on what you have on hand.

Fill the Hoko Pot with hot Chinese Chicken Soup Stock. Heat the stock in a pan on the stove and pour it into the table device. Or you can use an electric hot plate and a soup pot, right on the table. Add one thin slice of fresh ginger for each quart of stock.

Have the charcoal already burning, just before dinner. *Remember that this can be done only in a well-ventilated room*. Place the Hoko Pot on a deep tray and set it on a mat in the middle of the table. Add several cups of water to the tray so that the table is not damaged by the heat. The water should run inside the bottom chamber of the Hoko Pot. After you have poured the stock into the pot, cover the container with the lid. Using metal tongs and a heavy protective metal tray, drop several burning charcoal briquets into the chimney of the cooker. Do this with the windows open so that you do not get sick from the charcoal fumes.

Now you are ready for the feast!

Place any or all of the ingredients on the next page in the pot. Remember that anything goes, but you must first put in the things that take the longest to cook. Put in a few things, have a glass of wine with your guests, and then put in a few others. Eventually all will be finished at the right time and your guests may serve themselves from the pot. You may go on cooking more, if you wish, and the remaining soup is served as the last course.

Control the heat of the pot by placing a Chinese teacup filled with water over the top of the vent or chimney. The fire will calm down immediately.

POSSIBLE INGREDIENTS

Cook in this order.

Pork, lean and cut julienne style
Chinese mushrooms, soaked first for 3 hours and cut julienne
Beefsteak, cut julienne
Chicken, boneless, cut julienne
Bean curd, cut into ½-inch cubes
Beef Meatballs left over (page 356)
Deep-Fried Pork Balls left over (page 343)
Cooked ham, cut julienne
Green onions, cut Chinese style (page 158)
Sugar-pea pods
Shrimp, large and peeled
Chinese greens of any kind, sliced
Anything else that you can think of . . .

Garnish the soup with a bit of sesame oil and perhaps some white pepper as it cooks.

Remember to wait a bit for the pot to heat up between additions. The wait is worth it!

NOTE: You might also wish to serve one or even several dip sauces. Several possibilities are offered on pages 229–230.

SEAWEED SOUP

SERVES 6

This is a wonderful soup and certainly a very old one. Both the Chinese and the Japanese enjoy seaweed in their soups, though the Chinese are much more likely to make a meal of this saltwater vegetable instead of using it just for flavoring.

- 6 cups Chinese Chicken Soup Stock (page 126)
- 1 slice fresh ginger, the size of a 25-cent piece, cut julienne
- 2 tablespoons peanut oil
- 1 teaspoon salt
- ¼ pound lean pork, diced medium
- 3 dried Chinese mushrooms, soaked for 3 hours, drained, and cut julienne
- 6 water chestnuts, peeled and sliced
- ¾ ounce dried seaweed sheets (commonly called *nori* in Oriental markets)
- ¼ cup cooked ham, cut into thin slivers
- Salt and white pepper to taste

GARNISH

- Green onion, chopped
- Sesame oil to taste
- 1 teaspoon white vinegar
- 1 raw egg

Bring the stock to a simmer. In the meantime, chow the ginger with the oil and salt in a hot wok. Cook just until the ginger begins to brown and add this mixture to the soup stock. Add the pork and mushrooms and simmer for 15 minutes. Add remaining ingredients, except the garnishes and egg, and simmer for 6 minutes. Place in the serving bowl and add the garnishes. Stir the raw egg into the soup at the table.

FISH AND LETTUCE SOUP

SERVES 4–5

Fish and iceberg lettuce sound too simple to be attractive. Here is one of the secrets of fine Chinese cuisine, simplicity.

You can throw this soup together in nothing flat, and you will relish the delicate flavors.

- ½ pound very fresh white fish, boneless fillet sliced thin (cod or snapper will do well)

MARINADE

- 1 tablespoon light soy sauce
- ¼ teaspoon MSG (optional)
- 1 tablespoon peanut oil
- Pinch of ground white pepper

- 3 cups iceberg lettuce, sliced taco style
- 1 slice fresh ginger, the size of a 25-cent piece, cut julienne
- 1 tablespoon peanut oil
- ¼ teaspoon salt
- 4 cups Chinese Chicken Soup Stock (page 126)
- 1 tablespoon Chinese rice wine or dry sherry

GARNISH

- Sesame oil, few drops
- White pepper, ground, to taste

Slice the boneless fish and soak in the marinade.

Prepare the lettuce and set aside. Chow the ginger, oil, and salt just until the ginger begins to brown a bit. Add this to the soup stock and bring to a heavy simmer. When you are *actually ready to serve,* drain the marinade from the fish and add the fish to the pot, all at once, along with the lettuce and the rice wine or sherry. Bring back to a simmer and remove from the stove. You do not want to overcook this soup. Add the sesame oil and pepper for garnish and serve immediately.

HOT AND SOUR SOUP

SERVES 8–10

This is a classic coming from the northern regions. You will be surprised at how simple this is to prepare . . . and better than what you find in most of the American/Chinese neighborhood restaurants. I make this for my sons on occasion, and it is always a great hit.

- 6 cups Chinese Chicken Soup Stock (page 126)
- 2 tablespoons light soy sauce
- ¼ pound lean pork, cut into ¼-inch dice
- 6 dried Chinese mushrooms, soaked for 3 hours, drained, and cut julienne
- ¾ teaspoon ground white pepper or more to taste
- ¼ cup white vinegar, more or less to taste
- 5 tablespoons cornstarch mixed with 5 tablespoons water
- Salt, if necessary
- ½ cup bamboo shoots, cut thin julienne
- ¼ cup dried black fungus (cloud ears, page 25), soaked for 1 hour, drained, and shredded
- 1 cake bean curd, cut into ¼-inch cubes
- 4 eggs, beaten

GARNISH

- Cooked ham, cut into slivers
- Green onions, chopped
- Sesame oil to taste, a few drops
- Grated carrot
- Fresh-ground black pepper to taste

Bring the stock to a simmer and add the soy, pork, and mushrooms. Simmer for 10 minutes, add the pepper and vinegar, and thicken with the cornstarch mixed with water. Taste for seasonings and add the bamboo, fungus, and bean curd. Bring to a simmer again and pour in the eggs in a very thin stream over the surface of the soup. Count to ten and stir a few times very slowly. Egg threads will have formed. Add the garnishes to the pot and serve. You may wish to add additional vinegar.

You may wish to add more fresh-ground black pepper as well.

VARIATION: If you really want this to be "hot," try adding some garlic and red chili paste (page 26). That will make them sit up at the table!

SCALLOP, ASPARAGUS, AND MUSHROOM SOUP

SERVES 6–8

This one blends a bit from the East and a bit from the West. It is very light and unusually good.

6 cups Chinese Chicken Soup Stock (page 126)
4 dried Chinese mushrooms, soaked for 3 hours, drained, and cut julienne
½ pound fresh or frozen asparagus, cut into ½-inch pieces
2 tablespoons peanut oil
2 cloves garlic, chopped fine
¼ teaspoon salt
2 tablespoons light soy sauce
½ pound bay scallops or small scallops
2 eggs, beaten
White pepper, ground, to taste

GARNISH
Green onions, chopped
Chinese parsley, chopped
Sesame oil, a few drops

Bring the stock to a simmer and add the mushrooms. Cut the asparagus and set aside. Heat a wok and chow the peanut oil, garlic, and salt until the garlic barely begins to brown. Add the asparagus and chow just until it is hot and not quite tender. Add this mixture to the soup along with the soy and scallops. Bring to a simmer and add the beaten eggs in a thin stream over the top of the soup. Count to ten and stir slowly a couple of times. Add the white pepper and garnish, and serve.

Do not overcook this soup. The asparagus should taste fresh and still be quite green in color.

> **HINT: ADD ICEBERG LETTUCE TO YOUR CHINESE SOUPS.** The flavor of cooked lettuce, and the texture that it imparts, will surprise you. Try it in any kind of Chinese soup.

VELVET CHICKEN AND SWEET CORN SOUP

SERVES 4–6

This is a very popular soup at formal banquets in China. Corn, which came from America, became a mainstay in the diet of many of the peoples from the north, and Chinese ingenuity certainly has given us some new ways to appreciate our native grain. This one should become a family favorite.

- ½ pound chicken breasts, boneless, cut into ¼-inch-thick strips

MARINADE

- 2 egg whites, beaten
- 2 tablespoons cornstarch
- ⅛ teaspoon salt

- 3 cups peanut oil for deep frying

THE SOUP

- 1 17-ounce can creamed corn
- 3 cups Chinese Chicken Soup Stock (page 126)
- 1 tablespoon light soy sauce
- Salt and ground white pepper to taste
- Sesame oil, a few drops, for garnish

Cut the chicken and pat dry on paper towels. Mix with the egg-white marinade and refrigerate for ½ hour. Heat the oil in a saucepan or wok to between 280° and 300°, no hotter. Deep-fry the chicken strips in the oil just until they are barely tender. They will not brown.

Heat the creamed corn along with the soup stock and light soy. When hot add the chicken and season to taste with the salt and pepper. Add the sesame garnish and serve.

HINT: ADD VIRGINIA HAM TO CHINESE SOUPS. Our Southern dry-cured ham is very close to Chinese ham. Use just a tiny bit and slice it into very thin sticks. It adds depth and flavor as a garnish.

DOUBLE-BOILED SOUPS

This style of cooking soup sounds confusing until you remind the Westerner what a double boiler looks like. Our prepared Chinese Chicken Soup Stock (page 126) is cooked and then placed in a porcelain double-boil soup container. You can find these pots under the Dragon Kiln Brand from China and they are sold in Chinatowns or some gourmet equipment shops.

Special ingredients are added to the pot, along with the soup, and the pot is covered and placed in a pan of boiling water, thus making a double boiler. The soup is cooked for the second time very slowly so that the flavors are rich and warming.

Try your skill at some of the following double-boiled soups. You do not need recipes since the ingredients are actually up to you.

Chicken with Mushrooms
Small pieces of chicken and dried mushrooms
Ginseng Chicken
A piece of dried ginseng root and chicken
Chicken Feet, Red Dates, Peanuts, and Dried Mushroom
This one is supposed to be very good for curing all sorts of diseases. Yes, I said chicken feet, not legs.

SHARK FIN SOUP

SERVES 6–8, AS IT IS VERY RICH

When you see this on a fine Chinese menu you will also see a very high price. Shark sounds cheap to you but it is prepared in a very costly way. If you wish to buy a whole fin, skin and bone intact, be prepared to work with it for about 5 days before it is ready to serve. That is a bit much! Purchase prepared shark fin at any good Chinese grocery. Simply tell the clerk what you want to make and he will show you shark fin that is ready for the soup pot.

¼ pound refined shark fin, prepared shredded type, soaked in water overnight
2 green onions, cut into several pieces
2 pieces fresh ginger, each the size of a 25-cent piece
6 cups Chinese Chicken Soup Stock (page 126)
¼ pound lean pork, cut julienne
¼ cup bamboo shoots, cut thin julienne
5 Chinese dried mushrooms, soaked for 3 hours, cut julienne
2 tablespoons Chinese rice wine or dry sherry
Salt to taste
¼ teaspoon MSG (optional)
2 egg whites, beaten until fluffy and double in bulk

GARNISH

Ham slivers
Sesame oil, a few drops

Soak the shark fin overnight. Drain and place in fresh water to cover, along with the green onion and the ginger. Bring to a boil and turn off the heat. Cover and allow to cool. Drain and remove the onion and ginger. Place in a 4-quart soup pot and add the soup stock and simmer, covered, until tender, about 20 minutes.

Add the pork, bamboo shoots, and mushrooms. Simmer for 10 minutes and then add the wine and taste for salt. Add the optional MSG and pour the fluffy egg whites over the top of the soup. Very gently stir in the egg whites. Add the garnishes and serve.

BIRD'S NEST SOUP

SERVES 4–5

This is one of the most famous soups in China. A small bird lives on an island just off the coast of the land of the Emperors. The island has little natural vegetation so the sparrow gathers twigs and grass at the tideline on the beach. With these pieces a nest is made. Mother Nature has endowed the bird with the ability to regurgitate a gelatinous liquid with which to glue the nest together. The nests are gathered, after the birds have left, and meticulously cleaned. What remains is simply gelatin with a very light flavor of fish. It is really very wonderful.

You can buy nests for soup all cleaned and ready for the pot. Any good Chinese market will have them for you. When you see the price on the bird's nests you will understand that this soup is served only on special occasions . . . very special occasions. The cost for enough nest to make *two* batches of this soup will be somewhere between $30 and $40. Calm down and at least *read* the recipe; it is a very interesting dish.

- 1¾ ounces cleaned bird's nest
- 2 cups water
- 2 slices fresh ginger, each the size of a 25-cent piece
- 4 cups Chinese Chicken Soup Stock (page 126)
- 2 tablespoons cornstarch mixed with 2 tablespoons water
- Salt to taste
- 2 eggs, beaten
- Ham, cut julienne, very fine, for garnish

Soak the bird's nest overnight in fresh water. Using a fine mesh strainer drain and rinse the nest. Place in a saucepan and add 2 cups of water and the ginger slices. Simmer for 5 minutes and drain in the strainer, discarding the ginger. Pick out any impurities and add to the soup stock and simmer for ½ hour.

Stir in the cornstarch mixed with water and cook to thicken. Add salt to taste and pour the beaten eggs in a thin stream over the top of the soup. Count to ten and gently stir the eggs into the soup.

The shredded-ham garnish will go nicely on the top of this very delicately flavored soup.

Greece

FISH STOCK

You really don't need a recipe for such a thing. It is so easy to make that you will read this once and never refer to it again, but I hope you make it often. It is great to have a fine fish stock in your refrigerator so that you can create soups, sauces, and fish stews without any pain at all. This will freeze well in 1-quart plastic containers.

Pick up fresh fish bones, skin, heads, and tails. Just tell your fishmonger what you are preparing and he will take good care of you. Be sure that everything is very fresh.

Rinse the bones in fresh water and then place in a soup pot. Add 1 quart of water for each pound of bones and a few chopped carrots, yellow onions, celery ribs, and a bit of salt and pepper. Do not oversalt as you may wish to reduce the stock. Bring to a boil and then turn to a simmer. Cover and cook for 1 hour. Strain the stock and discard the solid material. Chill.

AVGOLEMONO SOUP

SERVES 10–12

This soup is a classic. The lemon has been common in Greece for a thousand years and when they go to the market to buy lemons they do not buy them one or two at a time. They buy them in big bags the way we buy potatoes! I cannot even think of Greek cooking without the cleansing flavor of lemon. The flavor of lemon and egg, *Avgolemono,* is found in sauces, baked dishes, and soups.

This must be considered one of the classic soups of the world.

2 cups milk
2 tablespoons cornstarch
6 egg yolks, beaten
2 quarts Basic Chicken Stock (page 144)
½ cup long-grain rice
½ stick (⅛ pound) butter
Chopped parsley to taste
1 cup fresh lemon juice
Grated lemon peel to taste (optional)
Salt and pepper to taste

Stir the milk and cornstarch together and then beat in the egg yolks. Set aside. Bring the stock to boil in a 4-quart soup pot and add the rice. Cook, covered, until the rice is puffy and tender, about 25 minutes. Remove the soup from the heat and add the milk and egg mixture, stirring carefully. Continue to cook for a moment until all thickens. Remove from the heat again and add the butter, chopped parsley, and lemon juice. You may wish to add some grated lemon peel as well. Add salt and pepper to serve.

FISH SOUP AVGOLEMONO

SERVES 10

The Greeks invented the fish stew. This version, and there are many versions of this dish, is heavy and rich with the flavor of egg and lemon. During the summer months when eggs were scarce in the old days, a version was served minus the eggs. I prefer this one.

2 quarts Fish Stock (page 141)
1 medium yellow onion, peeled and coarsely chopped
1½ cups coarsely chopped ripe tomatoes
1 cup coarsely chopped celery tops
1 cup olive oil
½ pound cod fillets, boneless, cut into 1½-inch-square pieces
½ pound mussels, trimmed of their beards, soaked in cold water for 1 hour, and drained
½ pound medium prawns, shelled
8 egg yolks
Juice of 2 lemons
Chopped parsley for garnish

Prepare the fish stock.

In a heavy 6-quart stockpot sauté the onions, tomatoes, and celery tops in the olive oil until the onions are transparent, about 15 minutes. Add the fish stock to the pot and bring to a simmer. Add the cod and simmer for 3 minutes. Add the mussels and simmer for 3 minutes more. Just as the mussels begin to open add the shrimp and continue cooking for about 2 more minutes, or until the shrimp have changed color and are a bit opaque. Strain the seafood from the pot. Mix the egg yolks and lemon juice together, beating until a froth is formed. Stir into the hot stock and cook gently, stirring all the time, until the soup is thickened. Return the seafood to the pot and bring up to serving temperature. Season with salt and pepper. Garnish with parsley and serve.

BASIC LAMB STOCK

MAKES ABOUT 3 QUARTS

This stock is another basic in the Greek household, and it has been for a long time. The Greeks have been eating lamb for thousands of years and they rarely waste any part of the animal. The recipe is simple and it is necessary to several other recipes in the Greek portions of this book. You cannot buy a commercial lamb stock in any form. Don't let anyone tell you that you can!

3 pounds lamb bones, cut into 1-inch pieces (You may use up to ½ of this weight in pork neck bones)
1 yellow onion, peeled and quartered
3 ribs of celery, coarsely chopped
2 carrots, unpeeled, chopped
1 handful parsley, stems and all
8 black peppercorns, whole

Place the bones in a large stockpot and rinse with very hot tap water. Drain and just cover with fresh *cold* water. Add vegetables and peppercorns and bring to a simmer. Skim the froth that forms on the top of the soup. Simmer, covered, for 3 to 4 hours. You may need to add additional water.

Note that the stock will taste a bit flat to you since we have not added salt. Salt will be added when you use the stock in a soup, sauce, or stew.

BASIC CHICKEN STOCK

There is no way that you can run a proper kitchen without having fresh stocks on hand. If you buy commercially prepared products you are generally getting little more than salt, and in a very expensive form. I know it sounds like lots of work but to tell the truth stocks are very easy to make, and they are not expensive. Cook one day a week and fill the refrigerator and freezer with the blessed liquids that free you to be creative and comforting when cooking. Chicken stock is one of those necessary and comforting fluids.

- 3 pounds chicken backs and necks
- 4 ribs celery, coarsely chopped
- 6 carrots, unpeeled, sliced thick
- 2 yellow onions, peeled and quartered
- 8 peppercorns

Place the chicken backs and necks in a soup pot and rinse with very hot tap water. Drain and add 3 quarts of fresh *cold* water to the pot, along with the other ingredients. Bring to a simmer and cook for 2 hours. Be sure to skim the froth that forms when the pot first comes to a simmer.

The stock will taste a bit flat to you since it has no salt. Salt will be added when you use the stock in the preparation of soups, sauces, or stews.

ZUPPA IMPERIALE
(Bologna)
SERVES 8

Some dishes are just simply fun to cook. This is such a dish. It was given to me by my friend Mrs. Nasi in Bologna, Italy. The pasta shops there sell this "cubed noodle" ready to go . . . but I think you can do better on your own. It is very simple and provides a most hearty meal.

THE CUBED NOODLE

- 4 eggs
- 4 tablespoons semolina flour (page 34)
- 6 tablespoons freshly grated Parmesan cheese
- 3 tablespoons butter, melted

Additional oil and butter for frying:

- 1 tablespoon butter
- 2 tablespoons olive oil

Mix all ingredients for the cubed noodle together. Heat a large frying pan and add the additional butter and olive oil. Fry the mixture very lightly on both sides. It should not be discolored. Allow to cool and cut into tiny cubes.

THE SOUP

6 cups Basic Chicken Stock (page 144)
The Cubed Noodle
Parmesan cheese, freshly grated
Salt and freshly ground black pepper to taste
Parsley for garnish, chopped

When ready to serve, heat the stock to a simmer. Add the cubed noodles, a bit of cheese to taste, salt and pepper, and garnish with the parsley. Serve very hot and enjoy a very old-world food product.

ITALIAN FISH SOUP

SERVES 8

This wonderful soup from Italy looks like a bouillabaisse from France . . . but it is not. The Greeks taught the Romans to make this dish . . . though it did not contain tomatoes, of course. Tomatoes were brought to Europe from the Americas during the fifteenth century.

This version is quick and easy since I use Italian Tomato Sauce that I have prepared ahead.

½ cup olive oil
3 leeks, cleaned and sliced, white part only
2 cloves of garlic, diced fine
1 yellow onion, peeled and chopped
1 cup chopped celery
1 cup fresh mushrooms, sliced
6 cups Fish Stock (page 141), clam nectar, or water
1 cup Italian Tomato Sauce (page 237)
1 cup dry white wine
Cayenne pepper to taste
Salt to taste
1 pound white fish, boneless fillet, cut into small pieces (seabass, cod)
2 pounds, combined, of any or all of the following:
Clams, soaked in fresh water 1 hour and drained;
Crab; Shrimp in the shell;
Mussels, cleaned and prepared as in Fish Soup Avgolemono (page 142);
Squid, cleaned and cut into ½-inch circles (page 212);
Baby octopus, cleaned (page 224)
Chopped parsley, for garnish

Heat a large heavy soup pot and add the olive oil. Sauté the leeks, garlic, onion, celery, and mushrooms until the onions are clear. Add the stock or nectar, Italian Tomato Sauce, and white wine. Bring to a heavy simmer and taste. Add the cayenne pepper and salt to taste.

Prepare the seafood and add to the pot, remembering to add first those things that take the longest to cook. Clams and mussels would go in first. When they are almost cooked add the remaining seafood and simmer until all is tender.

Garnish with the parsley and serve.

BASIC BROWN SOUP STOCK

MAKES 5 QUARTS OF STOCK

The Old World has always had basic soup stocks on hand. The frugal cook was not about to throw out anything since he could not afford our luxury of waste. The bones of any and every creature were used for stock, and the stock eventually became the basis of another meal, in the form of either a soup, a sauce, or a gravy. You will need to make a batch of this now and then. It freezes well and it has a much better flavor than the only other possible substitute, canned beef stock. Please do not even think of using a bouillon cube. It is nothing but salt!

5 pounds bare beef rendering bones, sawed into 2-inch pieces
1 bunch carrots, unpeeled and chopped
3 yellow onions, unpeeled and chopped
1 bunch of celery, chopped

Tell your butcher that you need bare rendering bones. They should not have any meat on them at all, so they should be cheap. Have him saw them up into 2-inch pieces.

Roast the bones in an uncovered pan at 400° for 2 hours. Be careful with this, because your oven may be a bit too hot. Watch the bones, which you want to be toasty brown, not black.

Place the roasted bones in a soup pot and add 1 quart water for each pound of bones. For 5 pounds of bones, add 1 bunch carrots, 1 bunch of celery, chopped, and 3 yellow onions, chopped with peel and all. (The peel will give lovely color to the stock.)

Bring to a simmer, uncovered, and cook for 12 hours. You may need to add water to keep soup up to the same level. Do not salt the stock.

Strain the stock, and store in the refrigerator. Allow the fat to stay on the top of the stock when you refrigerate it; the fat will seal the stock and allow you to keep it for several days.

ROMAN "RAG" SOUP
(Stracciatella)
SERVES 8 AS A FIRST COURSE

I love the often amusing names that we put upon food products. The "rags" in this soup come about when you pour an egg batter into the hot broth. As you gently stir, the little pieces of torn egg appear. The Chinese would call this "egg flower," but I will bet that your kids will get a bigger kick out of "rags" in their soup.

This is a very popular soup in Rome and has been so for hundreds of years.

THE SOUP

- 4 cups Basic Chicken Stock (page 144)
- 4 cups Basic Brown Soup Stock (page 148) or canned
- Salt and freshly ground black pepper

THE "RAGS"

- 3 eggs, beaten
- 4 tablespoons semolina or regular flour
- 4 tablespoons freshly grated Parmesan cheese
- 1 teaspoon finely grated lemon peel
- Pinch of salt

GARNISH

- Italian parsley, chopped
- Parmesan cheese, freshly grated

Mix the stocks for the soup in a large soup pot. Bring to a simmer and season to taste with the salt and pepper.

Beat the eggs, flour, and cheese together. Add the lemon peel and salt and ¼ cup of the mixed soup stock.

Move the simmering pot from the heat and pour the rag batter into the soup in a thin stream, pouring carefully all over the surface of the soup. Return to the heat and stir with a wooden spoon as the tatters and rags cook. Simmer for about 2 minutes. Serve very hot with the parsley and cheese garnish.

GREEN OLIVE SOUP

SERVES 6–8 AS A FIRST COURSE

I cannot claim this dish as either Roman or Greek. I tasted it in a restaurant in this country and fell in love with it. All I can say is that a Greek or Roman would love this dish. It is a serious celebration of the olive!

2 cups green olives, pitted
3 tablespoons olive oil
½ medium yellow onion, peeled and sliced
2 cloves garlic, crushed
1 quart Basic Chicken Stock (page 144)
1 cup whipping cream
6 tablespoons flour cooked with 3 tablespoons olive oil to make a roux (page 22)
Black pepper, freshly ground, to taste (No salt will be necessary due to the olives)
4 shots Tabasco
⅓ cup dry sherry

GARNISH

Sliced pimento-stuffed green olives
Garlic-bread croutons

Soak the olives in cold water for 1 hour. Drain and coarsely chop the olives. Heat a frying pan and add the oil, onion, and garlic, along with ⅔ of the olives. Sauté until the onions are transparent. Puree this mixture in a food processor along with 1 cup of the stock. Place this mixture in a 4-quart saucepan and add the remaining stock. Simmer for 20 minutes and add the cream. Whisk in the roux and simmer, stirring constantly, until thickened. Add pepper to taste and the remaining chopped olives, Tabasco, and dry sherry. Heat to serving temperature and serve with the sliced olive and crouton garnish.

Salads

What we call a salad in our time is a long way from the first leaves and roots that were eaten by our ancestors. What has developed in our three cultures is just amazing.

The Chinese have traditionally used almost anything and everything as a food product. This openness was due partly to creativity and partly to necessity. Starvation is no fun . . . and finding wonderful new things to eat is! Please do not be put off by the salads from China. If you have never tried dried-jellyfish salad you are in for a fabulous treat, and the raw-fish salad is one of my favorite dishes in the whole world.

The Greek salads that follow all reflect the fact that the Greeks traveled a great deal and were willing to try all sorts of things. It is interesting that the Greeks have never been terribly concerned about admitting that they had received a dish from another culture . . . contrary to some Western European cultures who claim to have invented everything but the light bulb. You will love the Greek Village Salad with Cabbage, and the Salad Mykonos is just the most simple and delicious green dish that you can imagine.

Our American love for mixed salads probably came from the Romans. Since the time of the Emperor Domitian, who ruled Rome during the first century A.D., the people of the Eternal City have enjoyed a salad at the beginning of their meal. I have not bothered to offer you a simple green Roman salad, but I can tell you that the wonderful markets in Rome carry tiny lettuce leaves of all kinds, each picked leaf by leaf. None of this chopping and hacking at lettuce; the leaves are delicate and lovely just as they are. You can see from the Italian recipes I have selected that a salad can also function as an antipasto.

You might also consider:

Peperonata *(page 99)*
Chinese Duck Salad *(page 298)*

China

JELLYFISH SALAD

This is a bit unusual, I will admit. One wonders how destitute you have to be in order to catch jellyfish, salt them, and then dry them in the sun. Later, the dried fish is sliced thin, refreshed in water, and made into many dishes, this salad being the most famous. I can only say that I am glad for that first person who tried such a thing because this is one of the *great* dishes in Chinese cuisine—I promise. The texture is a bit firm and tender at the same time, and the Chinese love that sort of confusion in the mouth and tastebuds.

It will take some doing to find the dried jellyfish, but if you are near a big Chinatown you should have no problem.

I love this stuff, and so do my sons. Jason named this "rubber-band salad" and, when he was little, he used to get a kick out of serving this to his very young friends. "It's rubber-band salad," he would say. Only after the kids had eaten several helpings would he tell them what it was. That night I would get calls from parents asking me to explain what their child was talking about.

It may be an unusual salad for Westerners, but it is not unusual in China.

- 1 pound dried jellyfish (to be found in Chinatown)

DRESSING

- ¼ teaspoon salt
- ½ teaspoon MSG (optional)
- 2 tablespoons sesame oil
- 2 tablespoons light soy sauce
- ½ teaspoon sugar
- 1 teaspoon garlic and red chili paste (page 26) or hot mustard *or* horseradish
- 1 tablespoon rice wine vinegar

- 1 cup fresh bean sprouts

Cut the jellyfish into ⅛-inch-thin strips. Rinse with water and place in a stainless-steel or glass bowl. Cover with water and refrigerate. Change the water every 30 minutes for a total soaking time of 2½ hours. Drain.

Heat 2 quarts of water to boiling and remove the pan from the heat. Allow to cool for 5 minutes and then plunge the drained jellyfish into the water. Wait 5 seconds and drain and rinse in ice-cold water. I put ice cubes in the bowl at this point. This is the critical step. Do this whole step in a hurry or your jellyfish will not be tender and tasty. Drain well.

Mix the dressing and toss with the jellyfish and bean sprouts.

VARIATION: You may wish to add Chinese mustard (page 36) or even hot horseradish to this dish. I will follow you anywhere for jellyfish salad with hot horseradish!

DUCK AND JELLYFISH SALAD

I had this dish for the first time in San Francisco. I was so taken by it that I have worked out a method of duplication. This is very serious eating, which means it is also very serious cooking.

Prepare a batch of Jellyfish Salad (page 153). Also prepare a batch of Duck Salad (page 298) using regular roast duck, not smoked duck. (Leftover Peking Duck is just great with this dish . . . but then, who has leftover Peking Duck?) Also, omit the bean sprouts in the Duck Salad.

Toss the two salads together and then serve over a head of thinly sliced iceberg lettuce, sliced "taco style." This is just outstanding!

BEAN SPROUT AND SZECHWAN PEPPER SALAD

SERVES 4 AS PART OF A CHINESE MEAL

The wonderful pinelike flavor of the Szechwan peppercorns gives this salad its depth. Actually it is a warm salad and very easy to prepare.

3 tablespoons peanut oil
1 teaspoon whole Szechwan peppercorns
1 pound fresh bean sprouts
1 green sweet bell pepper, cored and cut julienne
1 teaspoon salt
½ teaspoon sugar
½ teaspoon MSG (optional)
2 teaspoons white vinegar

Heat a wok and add the oil. When the oil barely begins to smoke add the peppercorns and chow for just a moment.

Remove the pan from the heat and allow the oil to cool a few minutes. Remove the peppercorns, leaving the oil in the wok. Heat the wok and oil again and lightly chow the sprouts and green pepper, and remaining ingredients. Toss and serve. Or you may chill this and serve it later.

CHICKEN WITH BLACK BEAN SALAD

This is so easy that I will just describe it for you. Use leftover Chicken Chowed with Black Beans (page 270). Debone it and chop it up. Toss with shredded lettuce, cucumbers cut julienne, and Sesame Oil Salad Dressing (below). I like to add a shot of hot sauce such as Tabasco.

SESAME OIL SALAD DRESSING

MAKES APPROXIMATELY ¾ CUP

Your enjoyment of this light and tasty dressing need not be restricted to Chinese salads. It is good on just about any kind of vegetable salad, and will certainly give your dinner party an unusual twist.

2 tablespoons light soy sauce
3 tablespoons sesame oil
3 tablespoons light salad oil
¼ cup rice wine vinegar
½ teaspoon sugar
Black pepper, freshly ground, to taste

Blend all ingredients together and toss with fresh salad greens. You will not need to add salt to this dressing, though you might wish to put a bit of salt on the salad, depending on the ingredients.

MING'S CHICKEN SALAD

SERVES 6 AS A MAIN LUNCHEON COURSE OR 8–10 AS A CHINESE DINNER COURSE

Chicken salad is not an uncommon dish in fancy Chinese restaurants in San Francisco. Ming's Restaurant, in Palo Alto, serves a dish very close to this one. It is perfect for a summer meal or a meeting at which you wish to feed a good-size group of people but do not want to do any cooking.

This dish is prepared in several stages and then thrown together at the last minute.

CHICKEN SESAME DEEP-FRIED

8 chicken thighs (about 1 pound)

MARINADE

2 tablespoons light soy sauce
½ teaspoon freshly grated ginger
2 tablespoons Chinese rice wine or dry sherry
¼ teaspoon ground white pepper
1 egg white, beaten

½ cup flour
½ cup cornstarch
½ cup sesame seeds
6 cups peanut oil for frying

THE NOODLES

2 ounces cellophane (*sai fun*) noodles (page 25)

THE DRESSING

3 tablespoons light soy sauce
½ tablespoon dry mustard (I prefer Colman's English)
3 tablespoons sesame oil
Juice of ½ lemon
¼ cup rice wine vinegar
½ teaspoon five-spice powder
1 teaspoon salt
½ teaspoon freshly ground black pepper
4 tablespoons peanut oil
½ teaspoon sugar

THE SALAD

12 green onions, slivered (see HINT next page)
1 bunch Chinese parsley, chopped
½ cup thinly sliced water chestnuts
2 quarts shredded iceberg lettuce

Prepare the marinade and marinate the chicken thighs for 20 minutes. Drain and mix with the egg white. Mix the flour, cornstarch, and sesame seeds together and dredge the thighs in this coating mix.

Using a pair of kitchen shears cut the dry noodles into 2-inch lengths. Deep-fry at 360° for just a moment. Be sure to have tray covered with paper towels ready for draining the noodles. They will cook in just a second or two and will puff up greatly. Fry them in 3 different batches and drain them well. Set aside.

Deep-fry the chicken thighs at 360° until golden brown and crunchy, about 14 minutes.

Prepare the dressing and chop the vegetables. Debone the chicken thighs and julienne the meat. Toss all together except the noodles. They should go in last, just before serving. They are the source of the crunchiness that makes this salad so fresh and appealing.

VARIATION: Try substituting a couple of handfuls of crushed potato chips for the crunchiness of the deep-fried chicken. Use Chinese Poached Chicken (page 265) instead of frying the chicken. I know it sounds strange but it is a delicious variation.

HINT: TO SLIVER GREEN ONIONS simply cut the onions in half the long way. Lay the halves flat side down on the cutting board and cut lengthwise into long thin strands. Cut these strands, on an angle, into 1-inch-long pieces.

CHINESE FISH SALAD

SERVES 6–8 AS PART OF A CHINESE MEAL

The first time I ever tasted this dish I was shocked. I had no idea that the Chinese had been enjoying raw fish prepared in this way and I began to wonder if they were behind Japanese sashimi and Mexican ceviche. No matter. This salad is so totally unusual and delicious that your guests will cheer you on. It does take a bit of time to chop and slice everything, but you will surely become converted and see it as a simple and outstanding dish.

Be sure the fish is very fresh. The salad dressing and lemon juice firm up the fish a bit so that it really does not taste raw at all. It is almost "cooked" by the lemon juice.

This dish was a gift to me from my beloved friend Mrs. Mary Young. I served it one night at a formal party at my first restaurant, and I told no one what it was. They ate it, loved it, and begged for more. Only at the second serving did I tell them what it was. "Raw fish salad," said I. One woman, whose plate had been absolutely licked clean, yelled, "I didn't like it!" Such a loss. Don't let the thought of raw fish soaked in lemon put you off. What do you think pickled herring is?

- **1½ pounds fresh fish fillet, such as cod or sea bass, completely skinless and boneless**
- **Juice of 1 lemon**
- **½ cup dry-roasted unsalted shelled peanuts, chopped medium coarse**
- **2 tablespoons sesame seeds, roasted**
- **1 bunch Chinese parsley, chopped coarsely**
- **6 green onions, cut julienne**
- ***3 tablespoons Chinese sweet pickled scallions (*kue tao*), cut julienne**
- ***2 tablespoons Chinese sweet pickled red ginger (*suern geung*), cut julienne**
- ***3 tablespoons Chinese sweet pickled white cucumber (*cha gwa*), cut julienne**

DRESSING

- **½ teaspoon dry mustard (Colman's English)**
- **½ teaspoon ground cinnamon**
- **1 teaspoon sugar**
- **½ teaspoon salt**
- **3 tablespoons light soy sauce**
- **½ tablespoon sesame oil**
- **2 tablespoons *hot* peanut oil (I heat mine in the microwave in a glass measuring cup)**
- **1 cup crushed potato chips**

*Can be purchased in any Chinese market.

Cut the fish into very thin slices. Be sure that you have removed or cut away all bone. Marinate the fish in the lemon juice while you prepare the rest of the ingredients.

Mix the dressing. Be sure that the oil is quite hot. It helps blend and brighten the flavors in the dressing.

Toss all ingredients, except for the crushed potato chips, in a salad bowl with the dressing. Add the chips just as you are serving and toss again.

Greece

GREEK SALAD DRESSING

The flavor of this simple dressing is common throughout Greece. The quality of the wonderful Greek olive oil, that from Sparta being my favorite, and the common use of fresh lemons, makes this dressing a natural. I will give you a recipe but all you really need is an explanation. Try it on any salad, and on fish, on meat, on shellfish, on . . . who knows.

¾ cup good Greek olive oil
¼ cup fresh lemon juice
Salt and pepper to taste

That is it! Just mix the oil and lemon 3 to 1 and season. It is great on any kind of salad. You might like to add a bit of oregano now and then. The very best oregano in the world comes from my beloved Greece.

GREEK VILLAGE SALAD WITH CABBAGE

I dislike coleslaw. No, let me be honest. I hate coleslaw! I know that this sounds un-American but I have never learned to like chopped raw cabbage—until I had this dish at Taverna Sigalas in Athens. It is simply the old Greek salad that you find in any really good Greek restaurant, but it is made with cabbage instead of lettuce. It is terrific!

Use any amount of the following, according to your taste.

White or yellow onions, peeled and sliced very thin
Green sweet bell peppers, cored and sliced thin
Feta cheese, cut up into tiny pieces
Greek olives
Greek Salad Dressing (previous page)
Oregano, whole and crushed by hand, to taste
Cabbage, cut as for coleslaw
Cherry tomatoes, or regular tomatoes (very ripe, *please*), cut or sliced to salad size
Cucumber, peeled and sliced thin
Salt and freshly ground black pepper to taste

Place the onions, peppers, feta cheese, and olives in a bowl and add enough Greek Salad Dressing, along with some oregano to taste, for your entire salad. Let this marinate for 1 hour.

Toss all remaining ingredients together with the marinated vegetables and dressing. Taste for salt and pepper and serve.

VARIATION: Of course you can use green lettuce instead of the cabbage. That would be the more traditional way and it is always a refreshing change from plain green salads.

SARDINE AND MACARONI SALAD

SERVES 6 AS A FIRST COURSE

I tasted this in a Greek village. It is common village food, I suppose, since canned sardines are always on hand and it is a wonderful change from normal summer pasta salads.

- 1 pound dry pasta, cooked just until barely tender, rinsed, drained, and chilled. Shells are great for this dish.
- 2 3¾-ounce cans of sardines, drained on paper towels

DRESSING

- 1 cup mayonnaise
- 1 cup olive oil
- 2 tablespoons chopped capers
- 1 teaspoon oregano
- Salt and freshly ground black pepper to taste

Lettuce leaves for garnish

Prepare the pasta and chill. Mix the dressing and toss with the pasta and drained sardines. Serve in lettuce-leaf cups.

GREEK LAMB AND PASTA SALAD

SERVES 6–8 AS A LUNCHEON COURSE OR 8–10 AS A DINNER SALAD

This is not a dish that I found in Greece . . . but it certainly tastes Greek. Craig, my cooking assistant, and I developed this dish one night when unexpected visitors called and announced their coming. The dish is a great way to use up good roast lamb, provided that the meat has not been overcooked. Overdone lamb should be fed to the cat! (Unless you have a Greek cat. In that case he wouldn't eat overcooked lamb.)

- 1 pound dry penne pasta, cooked just until firm, rinsed, and chilled
- 1 pound medium-rare lamb, cut julienne
- 2 medium yellow onions, peeled and sliced thin
- 3 tablespoons olive oil for frying the onions
- ½ cup chopped green onions
- ¼ cup pitted and chopped green olives
- ½ cup crumbled feta cheese
- 1 cup ripe tomatoes, cut into large dice
- 3 tablespoons chopped parsley

DRESSING

- 1 cup olive oil
- 2 tablespoons mayonnaise
- 2 cloves garlic, crushed
- ½ tablespoon dillweed
- Salt and freshly ground black pepper to taste

Prepare the pasta and the lamb. Sauté the onions in the oil just until clear. Toss all ingredients together with the mixed dressing. Taste for salt and pepper and chill.

RUSSIAN SALAD, GREEK STYLE

SERVES 8–10 AS A SALAD COURSE

This is very popular in Greece and you will find it in all the large restaurants in downtown Athens. It is a milder form of the famous Salad Olivier offered in Russia. It is actually just a potato salad with peas and carrots added. I am convinced that the Greeks are to be credited with the invention of mayonnaise, given their affection for and early use of lemon whipped with olive oil. It is no wonder that this dish is common in the tavernas of Athens. No mustard is used in this dish and very little chopped pickle. I do add hard-boiled eggs to mine.

- 3 pounds potatoes, cooked, peeled, cut, and chilled for salad
- 8 green onions, chopped
- 4 eggs, hard-boiled, chilled, and peeled
- 1 10-ounce package frozen peas and carrots, defrosted and drained

DRESSING

- 1 cup mayonnaise
- ½ cup olive oil
- 1 dill pickle, chopped
- 1 tablespoon drained and chopped capers
- Salt and freshly ground black pepper to taste

GARNISH

- Additional mayonnaise for a decorative garnish
- Parsley or celery leaves, whole

Place all the salad ingredients in a large mixing bowl. In a small bowl blend the dressing. Toss with the salad and then place in a smooth mound on a serving dish. Pipe the mound with a bit of mayonnaise in an interesting pattern and garnish with whole parsley or celery leaves.

POTATO SALAD, GREEK STYLE

When in Athens you must eat at Monastiraki Square in a taverna called Sigalas. It is a wonderful old joint that serves everything in the classic Greek kitchen buffet. This salad is often on the menu. Note that it is typical of regular Greek potato salad in that it contains no mayonnaise and the main flavor is provided by good olive oil and celery leaves.

The quantity of the ingredients is simply decided according to your taste.

- Potatoes, cooked and cut for salad, chilled
- Green onions, chopped
- Parsley, chopped
- Celery leaves, chopped (I like lots!)
- Greek Salad Dressing (page 160)
- Oregano, whole, hand-crushed, to taste

Toss all with the mixed dressing. At Sigalas they just heap it on a plate. It is delicious and simple.

VEGETABLE SALAD, GREEK STYLE

Since eating in Greece I have taken to offering salads in this wonderful style. Cold, cooked vegetables, such as green beans, asparagus, artichoke hearts, cabbage, cauliflower, okra, spinach, tomatoes, are tossed with olive oil, fresh lemon juice, oregano, and salt and pepper. That's it! You prepare any mixture you like and it will hold up well on your buffet.

SALAD MYKONOS

I spent a few days on the island of Mykonos, and it was in the middle of February, a rather cold time of the year. There were no tourists about and most of the hotels and restaurants, which catered to the tourists, were closed. A resident, a bricklayer that I met in one of the back streets, took me to a tiny eating place that stayed open all year round for the local fishermen. It is called Kouneli or "The Rabbit." There is no menu but fish is always served. The cook is charming, though she speaks no English at all. This is the salad that comes with dinner. It is simple, elegant, and just wonderful.

Lettuce: green-leaf, red-leaf, or butterhead
Green onions, chopped
Dillweed, fresh, chopped
Greek Salad Dressing (page 160)
Salt and freshly ground black pepper to taste

Toss and serve. To tell the truth I think she also throws in a shot of good white wine vinegar.

VARIATION: You might just try a shot of crushed garlic in this salad. Though my friend in Mykonos did not use it, I think the blend of garlic and dill is basic and you should try it!

Italy

CELERY AND MUSHROOM SALAD SAVINI

Savini's is a very fancy restaurant in the Galleria in Milan. Yes, it is expensive, but you must at least have coffee in the middle of the most beautiful shopping ''mall'' you have ever seen. It has been there for one hundred years. Savini's serves a salad very close to this one. The secret is the cheese. Don't use cheap cheese or cheap olive oil in this dish.

8–10 ribs celery, cleaned and sliced as thin as possible
¼ pound fresh white mushrooms, sliced thin
½ cup thinly shaved Pecorino cheese
¾ cup good olive oil
Juice of 1 lemon
Salt and freshly ground black pepper to taste

Toss all together and marinate 1 hour before serving. See next page for a hint on shaving cheese.

FENNEL SALAD, ROMAN STYLE

This is a common item on Roman restaurant menus, but you must not think it is common food. It raises a green salad to new heights.

Prepare a green salad of lettuce, cucumbers, celery, and thinly sliced fresh fennel bulb. Toss with a dressing of olive oil, lemon juice, salt and pepper, and perhaps a bit of grated Parmesan or Romano cheese. Wonderful, and you can tell the children that you are making "Licorice Salad" since fennel does have that wonderful light licorice flavor.

ITALIAN FLAG SALAD
(Insalata alla Bandiera)

This one is fun to prepare. For each guest, cut a few ripe tomato wedges, a few sweet green bell pepper wedges, and some white onion wedges. Use just a few leaves of the onion wedges on each plate and arrange a circle of the three colors of the Italian flag. The dressing is just good olive oil, lemon juice or wine vinegar, and salt and pepper. This is fun to serve and very colorful.

HINT: USE A TRUFFLE SLICER FOR SHAVING HARD WHITE CHEESES. This sounds very extravagant but they are not expensive and they will make tiny shavings for salads and garnish.

ROASTED PEPPER SALAD, ROMAN STYLE

One of the most refreshing salads that you can find in Rome consists simply of roasted red sweet bell peppers, peeled and dressed with lemon juice, olive oil, a pinch of oregano, and salt and pepper.

Sweet bell peppers are easily roasted and peeled. The process is the same for red, green, yellow, or orange sweet peppers. Place them on a baking sheet and broil in your electric oven, close to the top element, watching closely until small black and brown spots appear on the skin. Turn the peppers to roast them evenly. Place the peppers in a baking pan and place in a preheated 375° oven uncovered. Bake for about 35 minutes. Remove from the oven and cover the pan with a kitchen towel, thus allowing the peppers to cool in the midst of their own steam. When cool enough to handle, the skin will come right off. Seed and core the peppers and proceed with the production of your pepper appetizer salad.

You also might try the roasting method in the hint on the next page.

HINT: ROASTING SWEET BELL PEPPERS on an *asador* grill (page 13) is simple. Place the grill over your burner and roll the peppers on the top of the heated grill. Watch closely so that they do not burn. This method gives you a much more "toasted" flavor than the oven-broiler method.

OLIVE AND PEPPER SALAD

SERVES 6–8 AS A FIRST COURSE

This is the kind of dish that you will find in a good trattoria in Rome. I have put together a version that is a compilation of various similar salads I tasted in the Eternal City. This is simple to prepare and terribly rich.

- 1 cup olive oil
- 3 cloves garlic, crushed
- 5 anchovies, flat fillets
- 1 medium yellow onion, peeled and sliced
- 3 red sweet bell peppers, cut into large julienne strips
- 3 green sweet bell peppers, cut into large julienne strips
- 1 cup pimiento-stuffed small green olives, drained
- Juice of 1 lemon
- 1 teaspoon dry oregano, crushed by hand
- ¼ cup chopped parsley
- Salt and pepper to taste

Heat a large frying pan and add 4 tablespoons of the oil. Add garlic and anchovies, and mash the anchovies to form a paste. Add onion, peppers, olives. Sauté just until the peppers are barely tender but still bright in color. Allow mixture to cool. Make a dressing with the remaining oil, lemon juice, oregano, parsley, and salt and pepper to taste. Toss with the cooled olive and pepper mixture. Allow to marinate 1 hour before serving.

I like to serve this on a bed of iceberg lettuce or in a lettuce cup.

Seafood

Fish

Someday it would be fun to have a food anthropologist answer my question. Have more people in the world been kept alive on fish or on meat? I think the answer is fish. The Chinese have always been great fish eaters, with fresh fish being the primary protein source in the southern regions and dried and salted fish being a major food source in the northern regions.

Two thousand years ago, at the time of the Roman Empire, the Chinese were raising fish in ponds and tanks, some right outside the kitchen window. Carp, a member of the goldfish family, will eat almost anything, and it does not need a lot of fresh water. You could throw leftover food or scraps right out the window and into the tank . . . and a few weeks later harvest a wonderful big fish. The Chinese must be credited with the invention of the fish farm, a method of raising food that is just beginning to become popular in our culture.

The Chinese insist on fresh fish, and I mean alive, whenever possible. I have seen women in Hong Kong reject a fish because they can tell that it was killed several hours ago. And they waste nothing; even the bones can be steamed over bean curd or the cheeks and heads used in a fine casserole. To this day the fish as a symbol means plenty and fulfillment. That is why I wear an antique Chinese jade fish around my neck.

The peoples of the Mediterranean have always enjoyed fish, from the beginning of recorded history. In the fourth century B.C. Aristotle, the great Greek philosopher, wrote exhaustive biological studies on fish that overshadowed any other work done on fish until the sixteenth or seventeenth century. Even the art of the time used fish in common daily decoration, a time that predated the Roman Christian use of the fish symbol. There is good evidence to prove that the Greeks actually taught the Romans how to catch and appreciate fish. The Romans had shown little interest in fish until their armies returned to Italy from Greece in 185 B.C. Eventually, Apicius, the great Roman gourmet of the first century, learned to love fish so much that he offered an entire chapter on sauces for fish in his ancient cookbook.

When you go to Rome remember that one of the reasons the Italians have always loved fish is that there is no single spot in all of Italy that is more than one hundred miles from the seacoast. You will eat very well in the Roman fish houses.

You may also wish to consider:

Shrimp Chowed with Water-Chestnut Flour and Gin *(page 497)*
Hot and Spicy Squid *(page 119)*
Steamed Pork with Mushrooms and Dried Squid *(page 389)*

China

FISH WITH CELERY IN A HOT PLATE

The history of certain foods is *so* interesting. In ancient Rome an herb called lovage was used constantly. It is a member of the celery family and celery leaves can be used in place of the older herb. In China a special type of celery has always been appreciated, and it looks and tastes very much like the Roman version. Who got which from whom?

We simply do not know, but the following recipe will show how the celery leaf is used to flavor something as delicate as a very fresh fish. I will simply give the ingredients and method for this dish. It is really quite simple and yet it makes a very grand presentation in Hong Kong restaurants such as the Chiu Chow Garden. Frank Yuen, one of the managers of Maxim's, the group that owns this restaurant, gave me one of the special pans that they use in the final cooking of this dish. You can use a simple pan, though in Hong Kong a fish-shaped aluminum pan is placed on a burner at your table. The result is simple and terribly elegant.

A whole fish is cleaned and marinated in light soy, dry sherry or Chinese rice wine, and a tiny bit of grated ginger. The fish is then steamed (page 12) until it is just barely tender, about 20 minutes. A small amount of chicken broth is seasoned with sherry, white pepper, and salt and placed in the fish-shaped cooking pan. The pan is placed on a burner at your table and filled with the fish and the seasoned broth. Celery leaves are heaped about the fish and it is allowed to cook while you watch and anticipate. The time of cooking at the table is only about 10 minutes, but the resulting meal will be remembered for years.

FISH FILLETS STIR-FRIED WITH CELERY

SERVES 4 AS PART OF A CHINESE MEAL

I tasted this dish for the first time in Hong Kong. The utter simplicity and the refreshing flavor of the celery make for a blend that we seldom see in Chinese restaurants in this country. We Americans always seem to go for fish dishes that are much more complicated than they need be.

Chinese celery looks very much like thick parsley and the leaves are the source of the flavor. If you use American celery in this dish be sure to find stalks with lots of leaves.

½ pound whitefish fillets, boneless and sliced thin (cod, sea bass, or flounder will work well)

MARINADE

2 egg whites, beaten
2 tablespoons cornstarch
⅛ teaspoon salt

4 cups peanut oil for deep-frying
1 tablespoon peanut oil
1 large clove garlic, crushed
⅛ teaspoon salt
½ teaspoon fresh ginger, cut into paper-thin slices and then into sticks
1 cup celery, cut julienne, very fine, leaves and all
¼ cup chicken broth or Chinese Chicken Soup Stock (page 126)
Pinch of ground white pepper
Pinch of sugar
1 tablespoon cornstarch mixed with 1 tablespoon water

GARNISH

Carrot, finely grated
Green onion, chopped

Cut the fish and mix the marinade. Mix it well. Soak the fish in the marinade for 20 minutes, or longer, in the refrigerator.

In the meantime, cut up and prepare all other ingredients.

Heat the peanut oil to between 280° and 300°, no hotter. Deep-fry the drained fish just until it turns white—a couple of minutes. It will not brown.

Heat a wok and add the tablespoon of fresh peanut oil, garlic, salt, and ginger. Chow for a moment over high heat and add the celery. Cook just until hot and add the chicken broth, pepper, and sugar. Bring the sauce to a boil and thicken with the cornstarch and water mixture. Add the drained fish fillets and stir-fry just until hot. Garnish and serve.

This delicate dish is great with rice.

VARIATION: You may wish to dip the fresh pieces in a dipping sauce. See pages 229-230 for some possibilities. Soy and vinegar are very good with this dish.

STEAMED FISH WITH SOYBEAN CONDIMENT AND BEAN CURD

SERVES 4 AS PART OF A CHINESE MEAL

In this simple and profound dish the bean curd picks up the wonderful flavors of fish, ginger, and the soybean condiment. It is a favorite among the Chinese and if you enjoy bean curd as I do, it will be a favorite with you as well.

- **½ pound whitefish, boneless fillet, cut into thin slices (cod or sea bass will be fine)**
- **1 cake bean curd, cut into ½-inch slices**

SAUCE

- **1 clove garlic, crushed**
- **¼ teaspoon finely grated fresh ginger**
- **2 tablespoons peanut oil**
- **1 tablespoon Chinese rice wine or dry sherry**
- **2 tablespoons light soy sauce**
- **Pinch of sugar**
- **Pinch of MSG (optional)**
- **1 tablespoon soybean condiment (*mein see*)**

- **3 green onions, sliced Chinese style (page 158), for garnish**

So simple. Cut the bean curd and arrange on a large steaming plate. Arrange the fish on the top of the bean curd. Mix the sauce and pour over the top. Garnish with the green onions and place in a bamboo steamer (page 12). Steam for 20 minutes or to your taste.

BRAISED FISH OI MANN

SERVES 4 AS PART OF A CHINESE MEAL

Oi Mann is a wonderful restaurant in the Lau Fau Shan fishing village. It is in the New Territories, on the mainland just west of Hong Kong. You can make the trip for just a day and you will find a superb meal in this restaurant. The fish for sale is arranged in tanks in front of a long alleyway of restaurants and peddlers. You pick out what you want and the owner carries it, live, into his restaurant. The place is rather plain but the food will be unforgettable.

½ pound whitefish fillets, boneless and cut into 1-inch-square pieces

FRYING BATTER

1 egg
1 teaspoon baking powder
¾ cup cornstarch
4 cups peanut oil for deep frying

SAUCE

1 tablespoon peanut oil
1 large clove garlic, diced very fine
½ teaspoon fresh ginger, cut into fine julienne twigs
1 teaspoon soybean condiment (*mein see*)
1 tablespoon oyster sauce
1 tablespoon light soy sauce
1 tablespoon Chinese rice wine or dry sherry
¼ cup Chinese Chicken Soup Stock (page 126)
Pinch of sugar
1 tablespoon cornstarch dissolved in 1½ tablespoons water

GARNISH

Green onion, sliced, *or* celery leaves, chopped

Heat the oil for deep frying in a wok to 360°.

Mix the egg with the baking powder and add the fish to the batter. Put the cornstarch on a plate and remove the fish pieces from the batter and dredge each in the cornstarch. Deep-fry, in two batches, until the fish is golden brown, about 5 minutes. Be sure to keep your oil up to temperature. Drain the fish pieces on paper towels.

Heat another wok and add the 1 tablespoon of fresh peanut oil. Chow the garlic and ginger together for a moment and then add the soybean condiment. Chow for a moment and add the remaining ingredients for the sauce. Thicken with the cornstarch. Add the fish to the sauce and toss just until all is hot. Garnish and serve.

HINT: IF YOUR DEEP-FRYING OIL SMELLS OF FISH simply deep-fry a few slices of fresh ginger in the oil for a few minutes. You will be amazed at how the ginger will clean up the flavor and odor of the oil.

STEAMED FISH WITH BLACK BEANS

SERVES 6 AS PART OF A CHINESE MEAL

I never tire of the flavor of fermented black beans, *dow see*. Black beans and garlic are just the thing for fish of any kind, and I think you will be surprised at how easy this classic Chinese dish really is.

1 pound whitefish or other fish fillets *or* 1 pound of fish cut into steaks

SAUCE

1 tablespoon peanut oil
2 cloves garlic, chopped very fine or crushed
¼ teaspoon fresh grated ginger
1 tablespoon fermented black beans (*dow see*)
2 green onions, cut Chinese style (page 158)
Pinch of sugar
1 tablespoon Chinese rice wine or dry sherry
2 tablespoons light soy sauce
Pinch of MSG (optional)

Place the fish in a steaming plate. Heat a wok and add the oil, garlic, and ginger. Rinse the black beans in a bit of water and add to the wok. Chow for just a moment, then add the rest of the sauce ingredients, and pour this sauce over the fish. Place in a bamboo steamer (page 106) and cook for about 15 minutes, or until the fish flakes and is done to your taste.

FISH WITH OLIVES AND BEAN CURD

SERVES 4–6

The heavy sweet flavor of dried Chinese olives gives this dish a most interesting richness. This is not for lovers of Chinese Dinner #1 on the menu. The flavors are strictly Chinese!

- **4 tablespoons peanut oil**
- **1 teaspoon salt**
- **2 pounds fish fillets, cut into 1-inch-square pieces (whitefish, cod, salmon, or a mixture of these)**
- **⅓ cup dried olives (*lom see*), soaked in water for 2 hours, drained, and rinsed in fresh water**
- **¼ pound bean cake, deep-fried (page 24)**

SAUCE

- **4 slices fresh ginger root, cut julienne**
- **2 tablespoons light soy sauce**
- **2 teaspoons dry sherry or Chinese rice wine**

GARNISH

- **2 green onions, chopped**
- **1 tablespoon Chinese parsley (cilantro), coarsely chopped**

Heat a wok and add the oil and salt. Stir-fry the fish fillets for a few minutes. Add the sauce mixture and stir until hot. Add the drained olives and bean curd, cover, and cook a few more moments, stirring occasionally. Garnish with the green onions and Chinese parsley.

FISH FILLETS WITH SESAME

SERVES 6–8 AS A CHINESE MEAL

This is a very tasty way of preparing fish, a way that even your children will enjoy. It is not uncommon to see whole families in Hong Kong restaurants enjoying this dish late in the evening.

- 1½ pounds whitefish fillets, boneless, cut into pieces 1 inch by 3 inches
- Salt and pepper to taste
- 1 tablespoon light soy sauce
- 1 tablespoon sesame oil
- 1 cup flour for dredging
- 2 egg whites, beaten
- 4 tablespoons white sesame seeds
- 4 tablespoons black sesame seeds
- 4 cups peanut oil for deep frying
- Soy, Ginger, and Vinegar Dip Sauces (page 229)

Marinate the fish pieces in the salt and pepper, soy, and sesame oil for about 15 minutes. Drain. Dust each piece with flour, then dip into the egg white, then sesame seeds.

Deep-fry the fish pieces in oil at 360° until done to taste, about 5 minutes. Serve with the dip sauce.

Greece

SMALL FISH DEEP-FRIED IN OLIVE OIL

I had never thought of deep-frying fish in olive oil until the family and I had lunch at a wonderful restaurant in Piraeus, the waterfront of Greece. The place has been taken over by the son now and is inferior to the old man's version, but you might like to visit Kokkina Varka, "The Red Boat," nevertheless.

The old cook would dust small fish in flour seasoned with salt and pepper. Then he would deep-fry the fish in a big frying pan of hot olive oil on the top of the stove. The result was just delightful. Try the same thing at home. Buy decent olive oil by the gallon at any Middle Eastern or Italian market and use it for deep-frying. Keep it refrigerated in between fryings and keep it clean. Strain it after each use and remove the sediment from the container before the next use.

Olive oil is much better for you for deep-frying than most other vegetable oils, with the exception of peanut oil. Either of those two oils will do you well.

GREEK FISH CHOWDER

The proper name for this Greek dish is *kakkavi,* meaning "pot."

- ¼ cup olive oil
- 3 medium yellow onions, peeled and chopped
- 2 cloves garlic, chopped fine
- 2 1-pound cans peeled tomatoes, coarsely chopped
- 4 ribs of celery, chopped
- 2 teaspoons salt
- ⅛ teaspoon cayenne pepper
- 1 bay leaf
- ½ cup dry red wine
- 4 cups water
- 1 pound whitefish, boneless fillets
- ½ pound each of any or all of the following: Clams, rinsed; Mussels, scrubbed clean and rinsed; Crabs; Scallops; Shrimp; Squid, cleaned and cut into ½-inch circles (page 212)

Heat a 6-quart heavy stockpot and add the oil, onion, and garlic. Sauté until they are clear, about 5 minutes. Add the remaining ingredients, except the seafood, and simmer, uncovered, until the sauce is rich and full-flavored, about ½ hour. Add the fish and shellfish in the order given, giving each variety a moment to cook. The clams will take longer than the squid.

Serve in bowls with Old Greek Bread (page 550) or French bread, and a Greek Village Salad (page 161).

NOTE: In some Greek communities the *kakkavi* is served with *avgolemono* sauce stirred in. The older dishes, however, are plain, as above, with the exception of the tomatoes. I like this version.

BAKED FISH ARCHESTRATUS

SERVES 4–5

Archestratus was a Greek from Syracuse who wrote one of the earliest known cookbooks about 330 B.C. His recipe for baked fish gives the following advice:

"Buy the best fish you can find, preferably from Byzantium. Sprinkle with marjoram. Wrap the fish in fig leaves and bake. Have slaves serve it on silver platters."

1 pound whitefish
½ teaspoon marjoram
Salt and pepper
Juice of 1 lemon
4 green onions, sliced the long way into 2-inch pieces
12 fig leaves or 1 small jar grape leaves, drained and rinsed
1 cup dry white wine

Cut fish into 1-inch-square pieces. Sprinkle with marjoram, salt and pepper, and lemon juice. Pour hot water over the fig leaves to soften, or rinse the canned grape leaves in cold water.

Spread leaves out one by one. Place a piece of fish and a bit of green onion on a leaf and wrap it up, tucking in the sides as you roll. Place the rolls side by side in an oiled baking pan and pour the wine over all. Bake in a preheated over at 350° for 20 minutes, uncovered.

FISH GRILLED GREEK STYLE

I was so amazed by this simple process that when I returned to Tacoma from Greece I immediately learned to duplicate the equipment. Since the equipment is the critical matter here, I shall just explain the process. The ingredients are easy.

In Piraeus, the waterfront in Athens, a chef used to heat up a piece of sheet steel, about ¼-inch thick, until it was very hot indeed. The long and narrow metal grill would cover 2 burners of his restaurant gas range. He would then place a whole cleaned fish, head on, in a wire fish-shaped grilling rack, brush it with an olive oil and garlic mixture, and place the rack *on top of* the murderously hot piece of sheet steel. The fish oil, combined with the garlic and olive oil, would drip onto the sheet steel and smoke like mad. He would turn the fish now and then and check for doneness by simply poking it with his finger. When the fish was served at the table the skin was removed and the whole doused with fresh lemon juice. The flavor was just spectacular.

I do this on my commercial gas range in my restaurant, with all the fans going. *I do not suggest* that you try this on your home gas range as it cannot take the terrific heat buildup under the sheet steel. Instead, try this process on your barbecue. Put the steel on the barbecue rack and get it as close to the coals as possible. Heat it until it is very hot and then proceed as above. By the way, this method does cause wonderful little dark-brown toasty spots to form on the fish . . . causing one to call this the earliest version of "blackened fish."

Italy

ASSORTED FRIED SEAFOOD
(Fritto Misto di Mare)

MAKES 2½ CUPS BATTER, ENOUGH FOR 3 POUNDS OF FOOD

You will see this dish all over Rome. The Romans eat less seafood than you might expect, given the fact they are only thirty miles from the sea. But they do love *Fritto Misto di Mare*. You can make an excellent one at home, far better than you will find in most American restaurants. I picked up this recipe in Rome. It is very typical.

THE DEEP-FRYING BATTER

- 3 eggs, beaten
- 1 cup water
- 1 teaspoon baking powder
- 1 cup flour
- 1 teaspoon salt

- Ample oil for deep-frying
- Whitefish fillets of any kind
- Shrimp, cleaned of their shells
- Squid, cleaned and cut into ½-inch circles (page 212)
- Artichoke hearts (page 463) (optional)
- Zucchini sticks (optional)
- Lots of lemon wedges for garnish

Mix all for the batter and let it rest for a few minutes while you bring the cooking oil up to 400°. The secret to this dish and to having a coating that is not greasy or soggy is the temperature of the oil. Fry just a few things at a time and keep the oil up to 400°. It is very easy to do, but remember, deep-frying is dangerous. Be sure you use every safety precaution.

Garnish with lots of lemon wedges.

FISH STEW FOR CHRISTMAS EVE

SERVES 6 AS A MAIN COURSE

Christmas Eve in Italy is very much like Lent in America in that you are not expected to eat meat. To solve the problems of this difficult red-meat-abstinence rule, the Italians invented a wonderful fish stew for the eve of the birth of the Christ. It calls for up to eight or nine different kinds of fish and seafood put together in a wonderful stew. The result makes abstinence a blessing!

- ½ cup olive oil
- 3 cloves garlic, chopped fine
- 1 quart Fish Stock (page 141)
- 1 cup dry white wine
- 2 cups Italian Tomato Sauce (page 237)

THE EIGHT OR NINE DIFFERENT KINDS OF FISH:

- ½ pound *baccalà*, soaked for 2 days as per instructions (page 392)
- 2 pounds of either or a combination of both: Clams, rinsed Mussels, scrubbed clean
- 2 pounds of any one or a combination of all: Shrimp; Squid, cleaned and cut into ½-inch circles (page 212); Baby octopus, cleaned (page 224); Crab, in the shell; Lobster; Cod, fresh fillets
- Salt and freshly ground black pepper to taste

GARNISH

- Italian bread, sliced and toasted
- Italian parsley, chopped

You had best prepare the fish before you do much more with this recipe as the salt cod (*baccalà*) must soak for 2 days.

Heat a 12-quart heavy stockpot and add the olive oil and garlic. Barely brown the garlic and then add the Fish Stock, wine, and Italian Tomato Sauce. Bring to a simmer and cook for about 15 minutes, uncovered. Begin adding the seafood, in the order listed. It is important not to overcook or undercook the various kinds of fish.

When the clams are open and the fish barely tender, the stew is ready to serve. Taste the stew first to see if you desire salt and pepper.

Serve with a toast slice in each bowl and a bit of parsley garnish.

PAN-FRIED FISH WITH OIL AND LEMON JUICE

The simplest method of frying fish is used throughout Rome, and I expect this has been going on for a long time. We do too much to our fish in this country. Sometimes the simple method is the best one.

Pan-fry any fish fillet you wish in olive oil. Use no salt or pepper until you serve it at the table. Garnish the fish with a great deal of fresh lemon juice and you will need little salt or anything else, for that matter.

Shellfish

Shellfish have been popular with all three of our ancient cultures for hundreds of years. You simply cannot think of the cuisine of China without thinking of shellfish, even in those areas inland where fresh fish is impossible to obtain. The shrimp, scallops, abalone, and oysters are dried and relished by people far from the sea.

Shellfish were of particular importance to the Greeks in ancient times, but not just for eating. In democratic Greece the shells of oysters or mussels, called *ostraka,* were used as ballots. Voters would inscribe their choice of candidates in the mother-of-pearl lining of the shell and then cast their ballots. And a purple dye, the imperial color, was made from a sea snail.

Apicius, the great Roman gourmet, loved shellfish and advised pickling them in a vinegar brine, a dish that we still enjoy today. Certainly the Seafood Salad, Roman Style (page 207) is a descendant of Apicius's ingenuity.

The Shrimp and Oyster Sauce (page 194) and the Shrimp in Greek Tomato Sauce with Feta (page 205) will become favorites for you, I am sure.

You might also consider:

Shrimp Chowed with Water-Chestnut Flour and Gin *(page 497)*

China

LIVE DRUNKEN SHRIMP

I hesitate to tell you about this dish, but I have decided I can chance it with you. By this time we understand one another and you know that I will try anything, any food anywhere at any time, at least once.

In Hong Kong a very strange dish is offered. I do not think it really worth the effort, but it is good. A large glass casserole is brought to your table with quite a bit of Chinese rice wine in the bottom of the dish. The lid is removed and live shrimp are dumped into the heavy wine. They sit still for a moment and then, as the wine intoxicates them, they begin jumping about. They then begin banging themselves on the lid, jumping about in such a violent manner that it is amusing. They are drunk! The shellfish are then removed from the wine bath and dropped into rapidly boiling Chinese Chicken Soup Stock. They die instantly, of course, but when they are served you can certainly taste the wine that they imbibed. A light dipping sauce accompanies this very Hong Kong dish.

There are two reasons why I expect that you will not try this dish in this country. First, your children will think you heartless, though they will eat a hamburger, never having met the cow. Second, it is very difficult to find fresh lively shrimp in this country. So . . . go to Hong Kong. It is one of the most fascinating cities in the world.

VELVET PRAWNS

SERVES 3–4 AS PART OF A CHINESE MEAL

The process of "velveting" a food is a Chinese invention of great importance. The flavor of the food is preserved, the texture is enhanced by the process, and the end result will just blow your socks off! It is very easy to do.

½ pound large prawns, 30–35 count per pound

THE BATTER
2 egg whites
2 tablespoons cornstarch
⅛ teaspoon salt

4 cups peanut oil for deep-frying

Peel the shrimp, leaving the tail attached. Cut the shrimp down the back side so that they can be opened and "butterflied."

Mix well the ingredients for the batter. Marinate the prawns in this mixture, refrigerated, for ½ hour. Heat the oil to between 280° and 300° and deep-fry the shrimp. When the shrimp turn white and float they are cooked. Do not overcook them as they will not turn the least bit brown at this temperature. Drain well and serve or quickly chow with a favorite sauce.

PRAWNS WITH CHILI SAUCE

SERVES 4 AS PART OF A CHINESE MEAL

The seafood in Hong Kong is just unbelievable. Craig, my cooking assistant, and I tried a new restaurant every night for two weeks and took our camera crew with us most of the time. It is hard to get a bad meal in this city since the competition is so severe and the seafood so fresh.

This dish is from the Peking Garden in Hong Kong.

½ pound large prawns, 30–35 count per pound

MARINADE
3 eggs, beaten
⅛ teaspoon baking powder
¾ cup cornstarch

4 cups peanut oil for deep-frying

THE SAUCE
1 tablespoon fresh peanut oil
1 large clove garlic, diced very fine
1 teaspoon garlic and red chili paste (page 26)
Pinch of sugar
1 teaspoon rice wine vinegar or Chinese red vinegar
2 tablespoons Chinese rice wine or dry sherry
1 tablespoon light soy sauce

Peel the prawns and slice them halfway through down the back in order to butterfly them. Mix the marinade and add the shrimp. Refrigerate for 15 minutes.

Heat the oil for deep-frying to 360° and deep-fry the shrimp for 3 to 4 minutes. Drain and set aside.

Heat another wok and add the fresh peanut oil for the sauce. Chow the garlic for a moment and then add all remaining ingredients. Toss until the sauce is hot and then add the shrimp. Toss until all is hot again and serve.

STEAMED SHRIMP WITH SPECIAL SAUCE

SERVES 6–8 AS PART OF A CHINESE MEAL

The shrimp used in this dish at the Oi Mann restaurant in Lau Fau Shan, Hong Kong, are fresh, of course. You can see them alive in a tank outside as you go in to enjoy your meal. In this country shrimp are hard to find live but do not pass up this dish simply because you must use frozen shrimp. Just be sure that they smell fresh and still have the shell on.

1 pound large prawns or shrimp, shell on, 30–35 count per pound

THE SAUCE (THIS IS WHAT DOES IT!)

2 small red or green fresh hot peppers, *or both*, seeded and sliced *very* thin
2 tablespoons light soy sauce
1 tablespoon *hot* peanut oil

Place the shrimp, shell still intact, in a bamboo steamer rack (page 12). Have the water in the steamer boiling before you put the shrimp rack in the steamer. Steam until the shrimp change color and are hot all the way through, about 6 minutes.

In the meantime, clean the peppers for the sauce by removing the seeds and slicing the pods. Place the slices in a small dish and add the soy. Heat the peanut oil in a wok until it is just smoking hot. Pour the oil into the peppers. Be careful with this as it will spit at you!

Serve the shrimp on a large platter with the sauce in a dipping dish in the center of the platter. Each guest will shell the shrimp and dip them in the sauce. Then each guest will give you a hug! This is powerful stuff.

SHRIMP AND OYSTER SAUCE

SERVES 4–5 AS PART OF A CHINESE MEAL

This is a regular dish on the menu of really good Chinese restaurants in this country, and it is just as popular in Hong Kong. You may have seen this dish with the title "Shrimp and Lobster Sauce,'' since the sauce can also be used on lobster. Who can afford lobster? Try this one with good shrimp or prawns.

1 pound shrimp, 30–40 count per pound
1 tablespoon dry sherry or Chinese rice wine
1 tablespoon light soy sauce
1 tablespoon peanut oil for chowing
¼ pound pork, coarsely ground
2 cloves garlic, chopped fine or crushed
2 slices fresh ginger, each the size of a 25-cent piece, cut julienne
2 teaspoons fermented black beans (*dow see*), rinsed
3 green onions, chopped
Dash of MSG (optional)
¼ teaspoon sugar
2 tablespoons oyster sauce
½ cup Chinese Chicken Soup Stock (page 126) or canned chicken stock
1 teaspoon cornstarch mixed with 1 tablespoon water
1 egg, beaten

Peel the shrimp and marinate in the soy and wine for 15 minutes.

In the meantime, heat a wok and add ½ tablespoon of the oil. Chow the pork and remove the meat to the serving dish, leaving the oil in the wok. Heat the wok again and add the rest of the oil. Chow the garlic, ginger, and black beans for a moment and then add the shrimp, drained of the marinade. Chow on high heat until the shrimp have changed color and are just barely tender, about 3 minutes. Add all remaining ingredients, including the cooked pork, with the exception of the egg. Stir until a sauce forms and then stir in the egg. Serve immediately.

SHRIMP AND PEPPERS ON AN IRON PLATE

SERVES 6 AS PART OF A CHINESE MEAL

The rage, it's the rage, in Hong Kong, New York, and San Francisco. Actually, sometimes the rage is quite delicious. The principle behind this dish is a round iron plate that is heated and brought to the table; then the cooked food is dumped on this murderously hot plate. The steam, the sizzling of the food on the metal, the hot oil from the peppers now in the air . . . the whole production is very dramatic. This is a delicious seafood version of the Hong Kong "in" dish.

- 1 pound whole shrimp, 25 to 35 per pound, peeled

MARINADE

- 2 tablespoons Chinese rice wine or dry sherry
- 2 tablespoons light soy sauce
- ¼ teaspoon ground white pepper
- 1 egg white, beaten
- 1 teaspoon cornstarch

- 2 tablespoons peanut oil for chowing
- ¼ teaspoon salt
- 2 cloves garlic, chopped fine or crushed
- 1 slice ginger, the size of a 25-cent piece, cut julienne
- 4 small green or red hot peppers, seeded and sliced
- Hot red crushed pepper flakes to taste *or* hot red pepper oil
- 4 green onions, chopped Chinese style (page 158)
- 8 water chestnuts, sliced
- Sesame oil for garnish

Mix the marinade and soak the shrimp in this for 20 minutes.

Put the iron plate on the stove to get very hot. (You can use a black frying pan for this and later just set it on a piece of wood on the table.)

Heat the wok and add the oil, salt, garlic, and ginger. Add the peppers and pepper flakes or oil, and chow for a moment. Throw the shrimp, drained, into the wok. Chow until the shrimp are done to taste and then add the green onions and water chestnuts. Garnish with the sesame oil and remove to a serving plate. Quickly take the serving plate to the dining room while someone else brings in the iron plate or frying pan. Pour the shrimp into the pan *after* warning everyone to hold up their cloth napkins in front of them to prevent the hot gases from the oil from getting in their eyes. Hold the napkins high and peek over the top so that all can see the shrimp sizzle on the iron plate.

This is fun to serve!

SCALLOPS WITH GARLIC CHIVES

SERVES 5–6 AS PART OF A CHINESE MEAL

I love scallops and I love garlic chives. When I tasted this dish in Hong Kong I decided that I was in heaven. You may have trouble finding garlic chives in this country unless you live in a city with a large Chinatown. Otherwise, use regular chives, or even green onions, and the dish will still be most delightful.

- 2 tablespoons peanut oil
- 2 cloves garlic, diced very fine
- 1 slice fresh ginger the size of a 25-cent piece, cut very thin julienne
- ¾ pound large scallops, cut in half through the middle
- 1 cup garlic chives, cut into ½-inch pieces, or regular American chives or green onions

THE SAUCE

- 1 teaspoon rice wine vinegar or Chinese red vinegar
- ½ teaspoon salt
- 2 tablespoons Chinese rice wine or dry sherry
- ¼ teaspoon ground white pepper
- ¼ cup Chinese Chicken Soup Stock (page 126)
- 1 tablespoon cornstarch mixed with 1 tablespoon water

Unless you are really fast in the kitchen I suggest you cut the scallops and mix the sauce before you do anything else. You must not overcook this dish. Cut the chives as well.

Heat a wok and add the oil. Chow the garlic and ginger for just a moment and then add the scallops. Chow for 2 minutes or so and add the chives. Stir the sauce and then add it to the wok. Stir-fry until all is thick and hot.

This light and flavorful dish is great as the focal point of a Chinese meal, or it is delicious served with rice as a regular Chinese meal.

VELVETED SCALLOPS IN CELERY

SERVES 4–6 AS PART OF A CHINESE MEAL

We tasted this dish in Hong Kong, and I cannot remember where. It sounds complex, but, as is typical of most Chinese cooking, it is not. The rules are always the same. Have the wok hot and do not overcook.

MARINADE

2 egg whites
2 tablespoons cornstarch
⅛ teaspoon salt

¾ pound large scallops, cut in half through the middle

SAUCE

⅛ teaspoon salt
2 tablespoons Chinese rice wine or dry sherry
¼ cup Chinese Chicken Soup Stock (page 126)
1 tablespoon cornstarch mixed with 1 tablespoon water

4–5 cups peanut oil for deep frying
1 tablespoon peanut oil
1 clove garlic, chopped very fine
⅛ teaspoon grated fresh ginger
3 green onions, chopped
1 cup chopped Chinese celery leaves, or regular celery leaves

Mix the ingredients for the marinade and add the scallops. Refrigerate for 20 minutes while preparing the other ingredients.

Mix the ingredients for the sauce and set aside.

Heat the oil to between 280° and 300°. Deep-fry the drained scallops for just a few minutes, until they turn white and begin to float. Drain and set aside.

Heat a wok and add the oil, garlic, and ginger. Chow for a moment and then add the green onions and celery leaves. Stir-fry for just a moment and then add the drained scallops. Toss for a moment until all is hot and add the mixed sauce. Stir until all is thickened and hot. Serve immediately.

SCALLOPS IN SZECHWAN SPICY SAUCE

SERVES 4–5 AS PART OF A CHINESE MEAL

The Maxim's restaurants in Hong Kong just amaze me. Normally, when you find out that a restaurant is a part of a chain, you are prepared for a rather "chain" meal. This is not so with this company. I can recommend them over and over again, though they have restaurants offering several different kinds of Chinese cuisine.

This dish is from the Szechwan Garden in Hong Kong.

4–5 cups peanut oil for deep-frying
¾ pound large scallops, cut in half through the middle

SAUCE
1 *or* 2 dried red chile peppers, seeded, soaked for 1 hour in water, then drained and chopped
2 tablespoons light soy sauce
Pinch of sugar
½ tablespoon rice wine vinegar or Chinese red vinegar
1 tablespoon dry sherry or Chinese rice wine

2 tablespoons fresh peanut oil
½ teaspoon finely grated fresh ginger
2 cloves garlic, chopped fine
6 green onions, cut Chinese style (page 158)

Heat the deep-frying oil to 360° and deep-fry the scallops for just a few minutes. Drain and set aside.

Mix the ingredients for the sauce and set aside. Heat a wok and add the oil, ginger, and garlic and chow for a moment. Add the green onions and the scallops. Toss for a few seconds and add the sauce mixture. Stir-fry until all is hot and serve immediately.

CRAB IN BLACK BEAN SAUCE

SERVES 3–5 AS PART OF A CHINESE MEAL, DEPENDING ON THE SIZE OF THE CRAB

Jason will not eat most shellfish. When he was very little he told me that he was not interested in shellfish, not interested at all. So I cooked this dish for him one day and I had him hooked. He is convinced that this is the best crab dish possible. I think I agree.

- 1 large fresh Dungeness crab

THE SAUCE

- 2 tablespoons peanut oil
- 2 cloves garlic, chopped fine
- 1 tablespoon fermented black beans (*dow see*)
- 2 tablespoons Chinese rice wine or dry sherry
- 2 tablespoons light soy sauce
- Pinch of sugar
- 1 tablespoon sesame oil
- 6 green onions, sliced Chinese style (page 158)
- 1 egg, beaten

If the crab is alive, plunge it into boiling water and simmer for 15 minutes. If the crab has been precooked, you may omit this step.

Remove the shell and clean out the crab by removing the long spongy gray gills. Leave the rest of the roe and liquid in the crab. Break the legs off the crab, leaving them whole, and then break the body into 4 pieces.

Heat a wok and add the oil and the garlic. Rinse the black beans quickly and add them to the wok. Chow this for just a moment and then add the rest of the sauce ingredients. Chow until all is hot and then add the crab pieces. Stir-fry for a couple of minutes and add the green onions. Chow until all is hot and stir in the egg. Stir until the sauce thickens a bit. Serve immediately.

HINT: FOR FINELY CHOPPED GARLIC simply clean 20 or so cloves and put them in a medium-sized food processor. Using short pulses of power, chop the garlic finely. Remove to a covered jelly jar and add a few tablespoons of peanut oil to the top of the garlic. It will keep well in your refrigerator for several days and it will save you a good deal of time when you come home from work late and want to cook a good, quick meal.

GARLIC-STEAMED LOBSTER OR CRAB

This is a dish that I can only describe. It is just wonderful and terribly simple, and comes from the Oi Mann restaurant in the Lau Fau Shan fishing village that I described earlier.

The dish is easy to prepare and the results are spectacular. One need simply have a very fresh or a live lobster. Plunge it into boiling water to kill it quickly. Remove and drain. Cut the lobster in half the long way and drench it with peanut oil mixed with as much garlic as you wish, or can stand. Place the halves in a bamboo steamer (page 12) and steam until very tender, about 15 minutes.

Garnish with green onion slivers and chopped Chinese parsley.

CRAB WITH SOYBEAN CONDIMENT

SERVES 3–5 AS PART OF A CHINESE MEAL, DEPENDING ON THE SIZE OF THE CRAB

I found this recipe in San Francisco. The Chinese food in San Francisco rivals any Chinese food anywhere, except Hong Kong. And that includes mainland China, as far as I can tell.

This is a simple dish to prepare and therefore "frugal." I simply will not discuss the cost of Dungeness crab. Whatever it is when you go to get one, it will be worth it.

1 large Dungeness crab

SAUCE

1 tablespoon peanut oil
1 clove garlic, chopped fine
½ teaspoon grated fresh ginger
2 tablespoons soybean condiment (*mein see*)
3 green onions, cut Chinese style (page 158)
Pinch of sugar
2 tablespoons light soy sauce
2 tablespoons Chinese rice wine or dry sherry
1 teaspoon cornstarch mixed with 1 tablespoon water, for thickening

Prepare the crab for chowing just as you would for the recipe for Crab in Black Bean Sauce (page 200).

Heat a wok and add the peanut oil, garlic, and ginger. Stir-fry for just a moment or two and then add the remaining ingredients for the sauce. Add the crab pieces and chow until all is hot. Thicken with the cornstarch and water mixture and serve.

FRIED MILK WITH CRABMEAT

SERVES 4 AS PART OF A CHINESE MEAL

I cannot tell you enough about the glories of Hong Kong. On my first visit a few years ago, I wandered into the Jade Palace Restaurant, at the Star Ferry Dock Terminal. I could not imagine what they could do with fried milk and crab, so I ordered the dish. This is as close as I can come to this great delicacy, and my rendition is pretty close. You will enjoy this.

- 5 egg whites
- ½ teaspoon salt
- 1½ tablespoons cornstarch
- ¾ cup cold milk
- ½ pound fresh crabmeat, cleaned
- ¼ cup peanut oil for cooking

SAUCE

- 1 teaspoon sesame oil
- 1 teaspoon light soy sauce
- Pinch of ground white pepper

GARNISH

- 1 tablespoon Virginia ham slivers or Italian ham slivers
- 1 tablespoon chopped Chinese parsley

Whip the egg whites by hand until they are frothy. Add the salt. Blend the milk and cornstarch together and combine with the crabmeat. Gently fold in the egg whites.

Heat the oil in a SilverStone-lined 12-inch frying pan to normal scrambled-egg cooking temperature. Pour in the crab and egg mixture and cook over a medium flame, stirring gently until the mixture sets up. Add the sauce ingredients as the dish comes to completion. Do not brown.

Put on a serving platter and add the garnishes.

Greece

SHRIMP ANANIUS

SERVES 2 FOR DINNER OR 4 AS A FIRST COURSE

In about 550 B.C. there lived in Greece a poet named Ananius. He was a great lover of shrimp and he described a recipe he called his favorite. Theresa Karas Yianilos, in her wonderful little book, *The Complete Greek Cookbook,* has worked out the directions. It is interesting to see what the Greeks were eating 2,500 years ago. It sounds to me very much like yuppie food from the Upper East Side of Manhattan.

1 pound large shrimp, unpeeled, 30–35 count per pound
1 cup water
1 cup dry white wine or beer
½ teaspoon marjoram
½ teaspoon salt

Bring the water, wine or beer, and seasonings to a full rolling boil. Plunge in the shrimp. Allow the liquid to come to a boil again and boil the shrimp for 2 minutes. Drain the liquid and serve.

SHRIMP IN GREEK TOMATO SAUCE WITH FETA

SERVES 4–6

When I first saw the old cook preparing this dish in Athens I was fascinated. He used small Greek clay casseroles and placed them directly on a high gas burner. The flames would leap about the casserole and thus bring everything to temperature in just a short time. It is one of the finest shrimp dishes that I know, and it is actually very easy to prepare.

By the way, I think you need to know that the term "casserole" comes from the Greek word *katsarola,* which simply refers to a baking pot. The Greeks invented the concept of the casserole . . . another one of the things for which they have not been given proper credit.

You will like this dish. I demonstrated this method of cooking shrimp before two thousand chefs and eaters in New Orleans. Coals to Newcastle! They loved it . . . and we were doing the demonstration in order to raise funds for a wonderful school for retarded children. Sister Lillian runs St. Michael's School, and I am convinced she must be one of God's favorite people. So, when you eat this dish think of St. Michael's . . . or just send them a check. They need it.

2 cups Greek Tomato Sauce (page 232)
½ cup clam juice or Fish Stock (page 141)
1½ pounds large shrimp in the shell, 30–35 count per pound
½ pound imported feta cheese, sliced ¼ inch thick

Mix the clam juice with the tomato sauce. Place the shrimp, shells intact, in the bottom of a 12-inch SilverStone-lined frying pan or casserole. Cover with the sauce and top with the sliced cheese. Place the pan on high heat and bring to a rapid simmer, covered. Reduce the heat and cook until the shrimp are done to your liking, about 7 to 10 minutes. Stir in the cheese and serve. Many people eat the shell and all!

NOTE: If you are preparing this dish on an electric stove rather than gas, have the burner preheated to High before placing the pan on the burner.

VARIATION: You may also bake this dish in a 475° oven, uncovered, for about 15 minutes or until all is very hot and bubbly.

BABY SNAILS IN GREEK TOMATO SAUCE

The Greeks call them snails but we call them periwinkles, or tiny snails. They are served as a first course in Greece and they are wonderful. Don't worry about the distressing sound that you must make in order to suck them out of the shell. Everyone else will either understand or be jealous!

Buy the tiny snails in a good fish market or in Chinatown. The Chinese love these as well. Rinse them several times by rubbing them together a bit in order to get rid of the mud. Place some Greek Tomato Sauce (page 232) in a saucepan and bring it to a simmer. Add a few tablespoons of olive oil and pour in the drained snails. Simmer until they are tender, about 6 minutes.

This is a first course that will stop your guests in their tracks, though it is a bit of an effort to eat. Just suck out the meat and have a sip of good Greek wine.

FRIED SHRIMP PIRAEUS

This is how they do it at the famous harbor in Athens. It is so simple that it is embarrassing, but you must remember that olive oil is the secret. Do not substitute vegetable oil. Blah!

Dust whole shrimp with flour. Fry in deep pan with 2 inches of olive oil for 3 minutes. Drain and serve.

That is it. Cook as much as you like and you will certainly compliment your guests.

BABY SNAILS IN ITALIAN TOMATO SAUCE

When you go to Rome you must eat at the Da Franco seafood restaurant. Every course is fish and the price is fixed. It is not at all expensive and the place is delightful. You might have such a dish on your visit there.

Cook small snails just as you do in the Greek recipe on previous page, but use Italian Tomato Sauce (page 237) instead. And NO, don't put grated cheese on fish of any kind, at least not for me.

SEAFOOD SALAD, ROMAN STYLE
(Vecchia Roma)

SERVES 8–10 AS A FIRST COURSE FOR AN ITALIAN MEAL

When the owner of the wonderful Vecchia Roma restaurant near the Jewish Ghetto of Rome told me that he put mayonnaise in his seafood salad, I was a bit curious. But when Antonio Palladino told me that I would love it, I watched closely. He makes his own mayonnaise and uses just a touch. This recipe is superb!

- 2½ pounds octopus, pounded, washed, simmered until tender (about 2 hours and 15 minutes, covered)
- 24 mussels
- ½ pound bay scallops
- ½ pound medium shrimp
- 1½ pounds squid, cleaned and cut into ½-inch circles (page 212)
- 1 white onion, peeled and sliced
- 1 cup chopped celery
- ½ cup chopped parsley

DRESSING

- ½ cup olive oil
- ⅓ cup white wine vinegar
- 3 tablespoons mayonnaise
- 1 teaspoon whole, crushed oregano
- Freshly ground black pepper to taste
- Salt to taste, if necessary

Cook the octopus in water to cover. Remove from the water and let cool, reserving the liquid. Clean the tentacles by washing off the membranes. Save the suction cups for the salad. Then slice the tentacles and set aside.

In the same liquid simmer the mussels until they just open. Remove and cool, then take them from the shells. Set aside.

To the same pot add enough water to poach the scallops, shrimp, and cleaned squid. Poach these separately, using the same water. Remove and allow to cool. Peel the shrimp.

Allow all seafood ingredients to cool and then place in a large bowl with the onion, celery, and parsley. Toss with the mixed salad dressing.

Squid

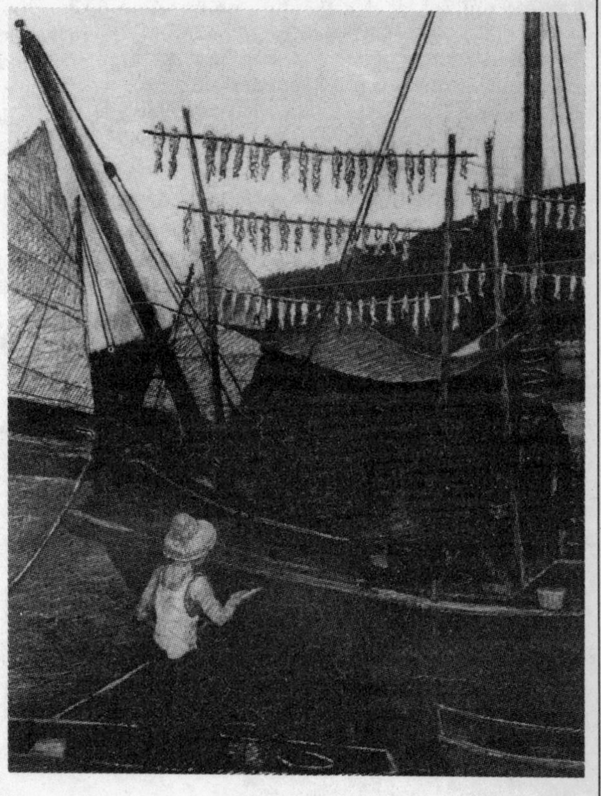

Yes, I will admit that they are ugly. Squid do not look attractive on the plate if you are serving them whole, but please understand that squid has been extremely popular in all three of our ancient cuisines since the seventh century. If you had been raised eating these creatures you would cease to call them ugly. They are delicious!

The Chinese dry them and then restore the meat during the wintertime. The Greeks stew them, make salad with them, and deep-fry them. When fried squid come to the table with Garlic Sauce (page 235) I am overjoyed. And when I have a cold squid salad in Rome I begin to feel sorry for Americans who demean this unattractive cephalopod.

Squid is probably the most underutilized seafood in American waters. But there seems to be some hope for us as we, as a people, are beginning to enjoy this creature, an enjoyment that our three ancient cuisines have celebrated for as long as they can remember.

You might also like to consider:

Hot and Spicy Squid *(page 119)*
Steamed Pork with Mushrooms and Dried Squid *(page 389)*

China

SQUID BALLS

SERVES 6–8 AS PART OF A CHINESE MEAL

Squid is a marvelously versatile food product, and it is not expensive. Americans feel a bit squeamish about eating one of the great denizens of the deep but we are being silly. Squid, like shrimp, may not look attractive when they are live in a basket, but they certainly are when cooked and ready to eat.

This is a wonderful way of getting into squid. It takes little time to prepare and it will certainly convince your squid skeptics that they must convert and join us squid lovers.

- **1 pound squid, cleaned and drained**
- **1 tablespoon pork fat, chopped**
- **¼ teaspoon freshly grated ginger**
- **1 teaspoon Chinese rice wine or dry sherry**
- **½ teaspoon salt**
- **¼ teaspoon MSG (optional)**
- **1 egg white**
- **1 tablespoon cornstarch**
- **4–6 cups peanut oil for frying**

Place all of the ingredients except the cooking oil in a food processor and work to a smooth paste. Form into small balls ¾ inch in diameter. Heat oil to 350° and fry the balls in 3 batches, cooking them until they float. Remove and drain in a colander and bowl. Increase the temperature of the oil to 375° and fry all of the balls a second time, all at once, until light and golden.

These may be served with Szechwan Pepper and Salt Dip (page 230) or with the following sauce:

THE SAUCE

1 tablespoon peanut oil
1 teaspoon fresh ginger, cut julienne
Pinch of sugar
3 tablespoons light soy sauce
1 tablespoon rice wine vinegar or Chinese red vinegar
½ teaspoon garlic and red chili paste **(page 26)**

Chow all of the above ingredients together and then throw in the squid balls. Chow until the balls are hot. Serve immediately.

HINT: HOW TO CLEAN SQUID. Squid is probably the most maligned creature from the sea. You remember the great stories from Jules Verne's classics about gigantic squid that swim under the sea. What a horrible fright to put upon the squid lovers of the world. While it is true that squid grow to great length, the kind that you and I buy in a fish market, either frozen or fresh, are little rascals, being about 5 or 6 inches long total. They are easy to clean. You simply cut the head off each and remove the filling from the tube, or body. Don't forget the plasticlike backbone of the squid. You will find it within the tube of the fish while digging around. Rinse the tubes, and you are ready to begin. I also save the tentacles, though not the head, for other dishes.

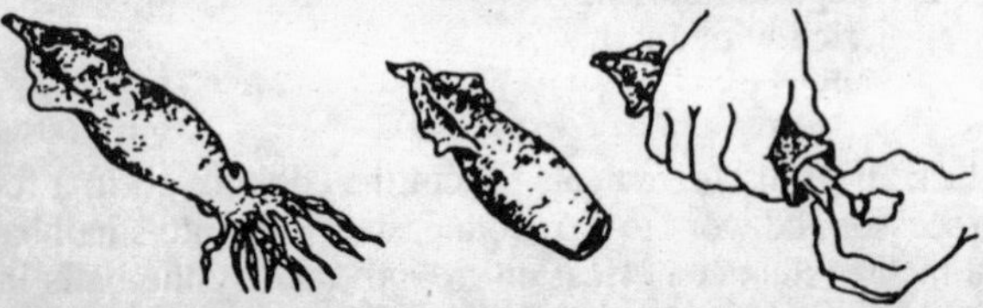

HINT: ON COOKING SQUID. The rule is simple. Never sauté the squid *more* than three minutes . . . and never stew or simmer the fish *less* than twenty minutes.

TWO SQUID, CHOWED

SERVES 6–8 AS PART OF A CHINESE MEAL

You see dried squid waving in the breeze all over the harbor in Aberdeen, in Hong Kong. It is a staple for the wintertime but it can be enjoyed at other seasons, of course. In this case you cook dried squid along with fresh squid, thus giving the name to the dish.

- ¼ pound dried squid, soaked for 24 hours (Change the water at least twice)
- 1 pound fresh squid, cleaned but not cut (page 212)
- 2 tablespoons peanut oil
- ½ teaspoon salt
- 2 cloves garlic, chopped fine
- 1 teaspoon finely grated fresh ginger
- 2 tablespoons light soy sauce
- 3 green onions, cut Chinese style (page 158)
- ½ teaspoon garlic and red chili paste (page 26)
- 1 teaspoon sesame oil
- 2 tablespoons Chinese rice wine or dry sherry
- Pinch of sugar
- ½ teaspoon MSG (optional)
- White pepper, ground, to taste
- ½ tablespoon cornstarch mixed with 1 tablespoon water

Rinse the soaked dried squid and clean. Be sure to remove the cuttlebone in the bag. Remove the head and score the back side of the squid by cutting just into the skin with a cleaver. Make long cuts and then angled cuts so that you have a trellis pattern cut into the skin. Do not cut all the way through. Cut the squid into 1-inch-wide pieces, cutting across the squid body. Set aside.

Clean the fresh squid and slit the creature down the belly so that you can open it into one piece. Cut a trellis pattern as above and then into 1-inch-wide pieces. Set aside.

Heat a wok and chow the oil, salt, garlic, and ginger. Chow for just a moment and then add the dried squid pieces. Chow for 2 minutes and add the fresh squid. Chow for 2 minutes and add the remaining ingredients except the cornstarch and water. Chow until all is hot and then thicken with the cornstarch mixed with water.

This is great served with a vegetable course and lots of rice. You can make it much hotter by adding more garlic and red chili paste.

DEEP-FRIED SQUID WITH SPICED SALT

This is a terrific dish and a bit different from the usual deep-fried squid that everyone is eating in the Greek restaurants.

Clean the squid and cut it into ½-inch circles (page 212). Dust with flour and deep-fry at 360° until barely golden. Do not overcook as it will get tough.

Serve with Szechwan Pepper and Salt Dip (page 230).

SQUID SALAD

SERVES 6 AS A FIRST COURSE

The secret to this great delicacy is not to cook the squid too long. If it is undercooked it is rubbery, and if it is overcooked it is rubbery. So, either quickly blanch it or cook it for 20 minutes. There is no middle road.

Many Americans say that they do not like squid. I had this dish in several places in Rome, as well as in San Francisco, and I still contend that anyone who likes seafood will love this dish.

I picked up the allspice addition from the Plaza Café on the corner of Thirty-fourth Street and Eighth Avenue in New York. A very nice place for lunch!

- 1½ pounds fresh squid, cleaned and cut into ½-inch circles (page 212)
- 1 cup chopped celery
- 1 yellow onion, medium, peeled and sliced

DRESSING

- ⅓ cup olive oil
- ¼ cup white wine vinegar
- 1 teaspoon whole oregano, crushed
- ¼ teaspoon allspice
- ½ cup chopped parsley
- Salt and freshly ground black pepper to taste

Lemon wedges for garnish

Clean and cut the squid. Blanch in ample boiling water just until the circles curl, about 30 to 60 seconds. Drain and place the squid, along with the celery and onion, in a salad bowl. Mix the dressing and toss. Garnish with the lemon wedges and chill for a short time before serving.

SEAFOOD SALAD DA FRANCO

Da Franco restaurant in Rome is a scene! All the courses are seafood and the price is set. Not at all expensive and you will have one of the most enjoyable meals in Rome.

Why am I telling you this when I probably will never be able to get into the place again!

The seafood salad consists of the following:

Octopus, cooked and sliced
Squid, cleaned and blanched
Shrimp, peeled and cooked

The flavors that make this salad so wonderful come from fresh fennel bulb, yellow onion, and celery, all sautéed in olive oil and chilled. These are tossed with the chilled seafood along with a good deal of parsley and a nice olive oil and lemon juice dressing, with just a shot of wine vinegar. The result is delicious.

DEEP-FRIED SQUID, ITALIAN STYLE
(Calamari Fritti)

Clean the squid and cut into ½-inch circles. Dust with seasoned flour and deep-fry at 360° until the pieces are barely golden, about 3 minutes. Serve with ample fresh lemon wedges and you have the dish, Roman style. They have been eating it this way for a long time.

SQUID IN ITALIAN TOMATO SAUCE

The ease with which you can prepare this dish will amaze you. Just remember that you must not overcook this dish. Taste often!

Clean and cut the squid into ½-inch circles (page 212). Place the squid in a saucepan and add a bit of Italian Tomato Sauce (page 237) and a few shots of dry red wine. Bring to a simmer and cook for a few minutes until tender. Taste regularly so that you do not overcook this dish.

Greece

SQUID PILAF
(Kalamaria Pilafi)
SERVES 6 AS A DINNER

This is a wonderful dish that is common throughout the Greek Islands. It is easy to prepare and the results are just short of spectacular.

- **1½ pounds squid, cleaned and cut into ½-inch circles (page 212)**
- **½ cup olive oil**
- **3 cloves garlic, crushed**
- **½ cup chopped yellow onion**
- **¼ cup finely chopped celery**
- **¼ cup dry red wine**
- **½ cup Greek Tomato Sauce (page 232)**
- **¼ cup chopped parsley**
- **¼ cup finely chopped green onion**
- **1 teaspoon salt**
- **Freshly ground black pepper to taste**
- **2¼ cups boiling water**
- **1 cup long-grain rice**

Clean and cut the squid and chop the tentacles into small pieces. Heat a 12-inch frying pan and add the oil, garlic, onion, and celery, and sauté until the onion is clear. Add the prepared squid and the remaining ingredients except the water and rice. Bring to a simmer and cook for 20 minutes, covered.

Stir in the rice. Add the water, bring to a boil, and turn to a simmer. Cook, covered, for 25 minutes or until the rice is done. Additional salt may be added if needed.

SQUID WITH LEMON AND OIL

It is very common for Greek cooks to simply clean squid and cook it, unsliced, in a hot frying pan with a bit of olive oil. Salt and pepper are added when served, along with a good deal of fresh lemon juice. This is the easiest of favorites!

SQUID AND SPINACH

How easy can a dish be? This is a common way of serving squid in Greece and I enjoyed it several times. The recipe need only be described.

Clean the squid and cut into ½-inch circles (page 212). Wash 2 bunches of spinach and chop. Drain well.

Cook squid in olive oil and garlic for just a few minutes. Add spinach, cover pot, and cook down. Add lemon juice and salt before serving.

STUFFED SQUID, GREEK STYLE

SERVES 4–6 AS A REGULAR MEAL

After eating so much squid in Greece one has to ask what the Greeks would eat if squid did not exist. I am flabbergasted by the variations on a common theme that the Greek cook has managed to create. This one is a jewel.

- 12 squid, cleaned (page 212), with tentacles removed
- 3 tablespoons olive oil
- 2 cloves garlic, chopped fine
- 1 medium yellow onion, peeled and chopped medium fine
- ⅔ cup long-grain rice
- 2 medium tomatoes, ripe, chopped medium fine
- 1 bunch spinach, carefully washed and chopped medium
- ½ cup Fish Stock (page 141) or Basic Chicken Stock (page 144)

SAUCE

- ½ cup additional Fish Stock or Basic Chicken Stock
- ¼ teaspoon oregano
- ⅛ teaspoon dried mint
- Juice of 1 lemon
- Salt and freshly ground black pepper to taste

Clean the squid and chop the tentacles (page 212). Heat a large frying pan and add the olive oil, garlic, and onion. Sauté until the onion is clear, and stir in the rice. Add the chopped tomatoes, spinach, and tentacles, and the ½ cup stock, and simmer, covered, for 8 minutes. Allow this mixture to cool a bit. Stuff the squid tubes with the rice mixture and place them in a stove-top casserole.

Mix the sauce and pour over the squid. Cover and bring to a simmer. Cook until tender, about 20 minutes.

VARIATION: You might try adding a bit of dill to this dish as well. It is typical of the Islands.

Octopus

I am always amused by the look on the face of a person who is tasting octopus for the first time. It is a wonderful food, if it is cooked properly, and it is not difficult to prepare.

The Chinese seem to ignore these creatures, except in a dried form, but the Romans and Greeks have eaten them fresh since ancient times. The Greeks pound the meat on a rock in order to tenderize it a bit and then grill it. It is wonderful. And the Romans still make wisecracks about the octopus being an aphrodisiac . . . a belief they have held since the first century.

Try these recipes and you will be converted into an octopus lover. If you have trouble finding the meat, come and see me in Seattle. I have scuba-diving friends who love to "wrestle" octopus in the bay in front of my office. What some people will do for kicks!

Greece

OCTOPUS SPAGHETTI ZORBA

SERVES 4–6 AS A MAIN COURSE

There is a restaurant in Delphi run by a strange fellow named Niki. His mother is behind most of the recipes in the place but he does a very decent job. This dish is excellent.

- 1¾ pounds octopus tentacles
- ½ teaspoon salt
- ½ cup olive oil
- 1 yellow onion, peeled and chopped
- 2 cloves garlic, chopped fine
- 2 cups Greek Tomato Sauce (page 232)
- ¼ cup dry red wine
- Salt and pepper to taste
- ½ pound dry pasta (I like fettucini for this dish)
- Juice of 1 lemon

Place the octopus in a stockpot along with about 3½ cups of water. Add the teaspoon of salt and bring to a simmer, covered. Cook for about 1 hour. You may need to add more water as it cooks away. When the octopus is tender, remove from the pot, reserving the broth. Allow the tentacles to cool and wash off the purple membrane. Cut the tentacles up into pieces about ½ inch thick. Chop the suction cups and return the meat to the broth and add the remaining ingredients, except the pasta and lemon juice. Simmer for an additional hour. Drain the broth from the pot and measure to be sure that you have 4 cups of liquid. If not, make up the difference with water. Return the liquid to the pot and add the pasta and cook, covered, just until tender. Add the fresh lemon juice and serve immediately.

OCTOPUS IN WINE AND TOMATO SAUCE

SERVES 6–8

This is the easy way to enjoy a dish that is very common, but very much appreciated, in the Greek tavernas. It is rich and tender, none of that rubbery texture that you are so nervous about.

¼ cup olive oil
2 cloves garlic, chopped fine
1 medium yellow onion, peeled and chopped
3 pounds octopus tentacles, washed and sliced into ½-inch pieces
1 cup dry red wine
4 very ripe tomatoes, chopped
½ cup Greek Tomato Sauce (page 232)
1 cup water
Salt and freshly ground black pepper to taste

Heat an 8-quart covered stove-top casserole and add the oil and garlic. Sauté for a few minutes and then add the onions and cook until they are transparent. Add all remaining ingredients and cover. Simmer until the octopus is tender, about 2 hours or so. You may need to add additional water during the cooking process.

Check for salt and pepper before serving.

Generally this is served over rice and it makes a fine meal.

OCTOPUS SALAD, GREEK STYLE

This is a colorful and delicious dish, and it will shock guests who think they do not like octopus.

Cold cooked octopus, sliced thin (Simmer in salted water for 1½ hours and cool)
Cucumber, sliced
Ripe tomatoes, ½-inch dice
Greek olives
Greek Salad Dressing (page 160)
Parsley for garnish

I think the best dressing for this dish is made simply from good olive oil, lemon juice, a shot of white wine vinegar, and some oregano. A little salt and pepper will help, of course.

Serve this as a main course in the summertime and as a first course during the winter.

Italy

BABY OCTOPUS SALAD

This is one for those strong of stomach and dull of eye. These little creatures are rather cute if you are into that sort of thing, but for many they might be a little too much. This is a common salad in both Rome and Greece.

You can find the baby version of the great octopus in very large fish markets or in markets that cater to people from the Far East. Clean by pinching out the little beak that is to be found in the mouth, surrounded by the legs. Also, if you wish, you can make a tiny slit in the back of the head and squeeze out the insides. Generally this is already done on the frozen variety.

Simmer them in salted water for about 30 to 45 minutes, or until done to your taste. Drain and cool them a bit and then serve lukewarm with a good olive oil and lemon juice dressing. You might add some parsley and fresh basil as well. This is a delicious dish and I do hope you will try it.

Sauces and Condiments

Sauces

When most Americans think of a sauce, they think of a heavy topping that often covers the food, thus dramatically changing the flavor of the main ingredient. That is not the case with our three ancient cuisines. In each of these cultures a sauce is seen as a supporter of flavor, not the flavor itself. Our habit of saucing has certainly given rise to our use of much too much sauce on pasta. We seem to think that more is better so we heap it on, thus covering the delicate flavor of the pasta itself. Not so in Rome, China, or Greece.

China

The Chinese do not use sauces in the way that the Greeks or Romans, and eventually the French, used them. In good Chinese cooking you bring each food to its own point of fulfillment, and then blend it, if you wish, with other foods. Thus, each food should taste like what it is. To put it bluntly, it is considered almost immoral to cover the flavor of a food with the flavor of something else. Sauces therefore support, they do not flavor.

DIP SAUCES

One of the most common ways sauces are used in Chinese cuisine is for dipping. A food, most often meat or fish, is completed and brought to the table and one may choose to dip it in any one of the following.

These sauces are not used for actual cooking, though they could be. Instead, they are placed in little dishes on the table.

SOY AND GINGER

Just that. Grate some ginger into light soy.

JULIENNED GINGER, SOY, AND VINEGAR

The vinegar adds a wonderful touch. Try a rice vinegar or a red Chinese vinegar.

GINGER, SOY, VINEGAR, AND SESAME OIL

The sesame oil adds a great deal of depth and would therefore be used with foods stronger in flavor.

GREEN ONION SAUCE

I tasted this sauce for the first time at the Peking Garden in Hong Kong. It is a fine place and this sauce is light and delicious.

6 green onions, chopped
1 clove garlic, chopped fine
¼ teaspoon salt and ¼ teaspoon pepper cooked together (Pan-fry for a moment or two until it just begins to smoke)
2 tablespoons very hot peanut oil poured over the whole

Coriander, chopped, might be a nice addition.

PEPPER SAUCE FOR SEAFOOD

This is one from the wonderful Oi Mann seafood restaurant in the Lau Fau Shan fishing village.

2 small red or green hot peppers, seeded and sliced thin
1 tablespoon light soy sauce and 1 tablespoon dark soy sauce
3 tablespoons hot peanut oil poured over the whole

SZECHWAN PEPPER AND SALT DIP

This is not actually a sauce but a dry dip. It is delicious with meats, particularly fowl.

2 tablespoons salt
1 teaspoon coarsely ground black pepper
1 teaspoon Szechwan peppercorns (page 36)

Heat all in a frying pan until it barely begins to smoke, shaking the pan as you heat the mixture. Remove and cool and then grind in a small electric coffee grinder or with mortar and pestle.

CHOWING SAUCE

A real Chinese chef would probably not approve of what I am offering here since the Chinese would be more apt to mix the sauce at the last minute, and every time. This sauce holds up well, however, and you can keep it in the refrigerator. Just give it a shake and slosh some into the wok when you are chowing. Mix as much as you wish, given these proportions, and keep it sealed and refrigerated.

I was given this sauce by Sharon at the wonderful Mandar-Inn in Chicago's Chinatown. She would always mix it fresh, for each dish, of course, but you and I can get away with this.

1 tablespoon dark soy sauce
1 tablespoon light soy sauce
1 tablespoon oyster sauce
1 tablespoon dry sherry
½ teaspoon white pepper
½ tablespoon sugar

LOOING SAUCE

This is often called a "master sauce" since it is used in one of the major methods of cooking in China, simmering in a very rich sauce. This sauce can be used over and over again, as long as you keep it refrigerated and bring it up to boiling temperature before each use. As the flavors change and mellow you can add more of this or that and thus develop your own special master sauce.

4 cups water
1 cup light soy sauce
1 cup dark soy sauce
1 star anise
½ cup Chinese rice wine or dry sherry
5 tablespoons sugar
4 slices fresh ginger

GARNISH

Sesame oil
Green onion, chopped

Mix all together in a stainless-steel pot and bring to a boil. You can simmer any kind of meat in this that you wish, and the sauce just gets better with each use. Do not put fish of any kind in this sauce as it will be ruined, but chicken, duck, goose, quail, pork, beef, and even lamb will do nicely. A bit of sesame oil and green onion garnish are added just as the dish is served.

Remember that now and then you must add more of the ingredients to the sauce.

Greece

The Greeks love good sauces and use them often, but they are generally cooked into the dish rather than put on top. The most famous sauce is Egg-Lemon, or *Avgolemono*. You will see it with meats, vegetables, even with pasta. The other important cooking sauces are a good tomato sauce, and of course, Basic White Sauce.

GREEK TOMATO SAUCE

MAKES ABOUT 6 CUPS OF SAUCE

This wonderful sauce is basic to the Greek kitchen. It is used with vegetables, fish, meats, shellfish, and even with rice. The cinnamon and allspice certainly point to the Middle Eastern or Turkish influence on Greek cooking. Make a batch of this and have it in the refrigerator at all times and you will always be ready for Greek cooking.

3 tablespoons olive oil
1 yellow onion, peeled and coarsely chopped
1 clove garlic, chopped fine
5 very ripe tomatoes, cored and coarsely chopped (about 4½ cups)
2 tablespoons chopped parsley
2 teaspoons whole oregano
1 cup dry red wine
1 8-ounce can tomato sauce
¼ teaspoon ground cinnamon
Pinch of ground allspice
Salt and freshly ground black pepper to taste

Heat a large SilverStone-lined frying pan and add the olive oil. Sauté the onion and garlic until clear. Add the tomatoes, parsley, and oregano. Simmer, covered, until the tomatoes are very tender, about 25 minutes. Add remaining ingredients and cook an additional 20 minutes.

NOTE: The sauce will keep well in the refrigerator for several days. Use it for any of the foods mentioned in the explanation to this recipe.

EGG-LEMON SAUCE
(Avgolemono)

I love this stuff and it is a great invention of the Greeks. It probably is the ancestor of mayonnaise and is very useful in the kitchen. Use fresh lemon juice, always . . . always.

1 cup Basic Lamb Stock (page 143) or Basic Chicken Stock (page 144)
2 tablespoons butter and 2 tablespoons flour cooked to form a roux
2 eggs
Juice of 1 lemon
2 tablespoons water
Salt and pepper to taste

Heat the Lamb or Chicken Stock and prepare the roux. Thicken the stock with the roux.

In a separate bowl whip the eggs, lemon juice, and water together until frothy. Add the egg to the thickened stock, stirring constantly. Bring to temperature but do not boil, stirring all the time until thick. Salt and pepper.

BASIC WHITE SAUCE

The more common term for this sauce is Béchamel, named for a Frenchman. However, this sauce was in use in Greece 150 years before it appeared in France so I hesitate to use the French name. One Greek writer claims that this sauce was invented in Greece three thousand years ago by a chef named Orion. In any case, the Greeks have received so little credit for what they have given the food world that even *they* call this sauce by the French name. Enough of this!

2 cups milk
3 tablespoons peeled and chopped yellow onion
1 bay leaf
Cayenne pepper to taste
½ stock (⅛ pound) butter
3 tablespoons flour
Salt to taste

Bring the milk to a simmer. Add the yellow onion, bay leaf, and cayenne. Simmer for a few minutes and then strain the onion and bay from the milk. In another pan melt the butter, and stir in the flour. Cook for just a moment and stir this into the hot milk. Return the milk to the heat, stirring constantly until it is thick, about 10 minutes. Add salt to taste.

VARIATION: The Greeks very often add just a touch of cinnamon and/or allspice to this sauce. It is just great for meats, vegetables, or even fish.

GARLIC SAUCE
(Skorthalia)

MAKES ABOUT 2½ CUPS

This is not a cooking sauce but a dipping sauce, and believe me, when you dip into this you will know that you have eaten some garlic. It is great with fish, especially fish that has been deep-fried. I also enjoy it on vegetables, such as Eggplant Slices Baked (page 513).

1 large head garlic
10 slices white bread
1 cup olive oil
½ cup white vinegar
2 tablespoons lemon juice
3 tablespoons water

Peel and crush the garlic, the entire head. Remove the crusts from the white bread, and place the crustless bread in a mixing bowl. Add the garlic along with the olive oil and vinegar. Let this soften for 1 hour.

Beat with an electric mixer until all is smooth. Don't try this with a food processor as it will be *too* smooth. I use my KitchenAid mixer with the wire whisk. Add the lemon juice, and slowly add the water while the mixer is running so that you will have a thick and fluffy sauce.

Italy

BASIC BROWN SAUCE

MAKES 1 QUART

Many Americans think only of tomato sauce when they think of Italian food. Not so! The tomato did not arrive in Italy until the 1600s and it came from the Americas. Cheeses and oils were commonly used for sauces in Italy prior to the tomato, and they still are. A good brown sauce is also common in many regions, though this sauce will look a bit French to you. The use of thyme goes back to the early Roman Empire.

This sauce takes some doing but it is well worth it and it will keep several days in your refrigerator.

- 1 stick (¼ pound) butter or ½ cup olive oil
- 1 cup peeled and chopped yellow onion
- 1 cup unpeeled and chopped carrots
- ⅓ cup chopped parsley
- 1 bay leaf
- 1 teaspoon whole, dried thyme
- ½ cup flour
- 2 cups dry red wine
- 2 quarts Basic Brown Soup Stock (page 148)
- 2 tablespoons tomato paste
- ¼ teaspoon freshly ground black pepper
- ¼ cup dry sherry
- Salt to taste

Heat a 4-quart heavy stockpot and add ½ of the butter or olive oil. Add the onions, carrots, and parsley. Sauté until the vegetables begin to lightly brown. Add the bay leaf and thyme and turn to a low simmer.

In a small frying pan melt the remaining butter or oil. Add the flour and cook, stirring, until it is light brown. Stir this roux into the vegetables. Add the remaining ingredients to the pot, except for the sherry and salt. Bring to a boil, turn to a heavy simmer, and cook the sauce, uncovered, for about 2 hours, or until it has reduced by half. Add the sherry and simmer for 5 minutes. Add salt to taste. Strain before serving or using.

ITALIAN TOMATO SAUCE

MAKES 3 QUARTS

This one is easy to prepare and very versatile in your kitchen. You will be surprised at how quickly you will use up this flavorful sauce.

This one is made without meat so that you can use it in all sorts of dishes, meat dishes included.

- 2 28-ounce cans tomato purée
- 1 6-ounce can tomato paste
- 1 quart Basic Chicken Stock (page 144) or 1 quart Basic Brown Soup Stock (page 148)
- 2 cups dry red wine
- ¼ cup olive oil
- 2 yellow onions, peeled and minced
- 6 large cloves garlic, chopped fine
- 2 ribs of celery, with leaves, minced
- 1 carrot, unpeeled, grated
- ½ cup chopped parsley
- ½ pound fresh mushrooms, chopped
- ½ teaspoon crushed red pepper flakes
- 1 tablespoon oregano
- 1 teaspoon dried rosemary
- 2 bay leaves, whole
- 1 tablespoon dried basil or 2 tablespoons fresh basil
- 2 cloves, whole
- ½ tablespoon freshly ground black pepper
- 2 tablespoons salt, or to taste
- 1 teaspoon sugar

Place the tomato purée, tomato paste, chicken or beef stock, and wine in a large pot. Heat a frying pan and add the olive oil. Sauté the onions, garlic, celery, and carrot until they just begin to brown a bit. Add to the pot along with all remaining ingredients. Bring to a light boil and then turn to a simmer. Simmer for 2 hours, partly covered. Store in the refrigerator in plastic, glass, or stainless steel containers . . . *never aluminum* as the acid in the tomato will "eat" the aluminum. The sauce will keep for a week in the refrigerator.

SAUCE BOLOGNESE

MAKES 3 CUPS

This is a cheater's method, I suppose, but it is just terrific. I tasted a pasta dish with a sauce very close to this one at dinner one night in Bologna and I was totally content. You prepare this sauce from two other sauces that you already have in your refrigerator . . . and I contend the result will be better than the usual recipes for such a dish.

- **1 cup Italian Tomato Sauce (page 237)**
- **1 cup Basic Brown Sauce (page 236)**
- **¼ cup whipping cream**
- **¼ cup freshly grated Parmesan or Romano cheese**
- **Salt and pepper to taste**
- **1 cup Pot Roast Shredded (page 365)**

Mix all ingredients together and simmer for a few minutes. Serve over pasta, gnocchi, or polenta.

GREEN SAUCE FOR BOILED MEATS

MAKES ABOUT 2½ CUPS

The Cesarina Restaurant in Rome serves some wonderful food. It is actually not Roman style at all, but Bolognese. This sauce is served with the boiled meat cart, a heated trolley filled with *bollito*. It is just a wonderful event, what with six or seven boiled meats heaped on your plate . . . and then this sauce.

I have omitted the cooked tongue that is usually used in this dish in this particular restaurant.

3 cups chopped Italian parsley, clean but very dry
1 small yellow onion, coarsely chopped
3 cloves garlic, crushed
2 stalks celery, coarsely chopped
½ cup drained *giardiniera* (These Italian pickled vegetables can be found in any Italian market)
¼ cup capers
3 flat anchovies
¼ teaspoon dry red pepper flakes
½ lemon peel, grated
1½ cups olive oil
3 tablespoons white wine vinegar
Salt and pepper to taste

Place all of the ingredients in a food processor and process just until it is rather coarsely ground. It should not be smooth.

Serve with boiled meats such as beef, chicken, tongue, pig's feet, pork, and sausages.

TUNA SAUCE FOR MEATS

(Tonnata)

MAKES 1½ CUPS

This is the famous *tonnata* sauce of Italy. It is really quite simple and I found an interesting variation in Rome. The chef put a shot of brandy in the sauce and it took on a whole new possibility. This is very close to a tuna mayonnaise, and since it keeps for several days sealed in the refrigerator, you are ready to use leftover meats or precooked meats in a very creative way.

1 7-ounce can of tuna, drained
8 flat anchovies, drained on a paper towel
¼ cup fresh lemon juice
2 tablespoons brandy
¾ cup olive oil, at room temperature
1 tablespoon chopped capers

Place the tuna, anchovies, and lemon juice in a food blender. Blend for a few moments and add the brandy. Slowly pour in the olive oil as the machine runs. Remove the sauce from the container and stir in the capers.

Serve over meats and salads. Traditionally this is served with cold veal but I love it over chicken.

PESTO SAUCE

MAKES ABOUT 2 CUPS

This uncooked sauce originally came from Genoa, where it is still prized. You will find it useful in Italian cooking and it keeps for several days in the refrigerator. Or you can buy a prepared sauce, but buy one packed in glass, not in a tin. Christopher Ranch in California makes a fairly decent pesto.

4 cups tightly packed fresh basil leaves
½ cup olive oil
2 cloves garlic, crushed
6 sprigs parsley
Salt and freshly ground black pepper to taste
¼ cup pine nuts, walnuts, or almonds
½ cup freshly grated Parmesan or Romano cheese

Place the basil in a food blender, not a processor. (Don't bother trying this with dried basil; it won't work.) Add the oil, garlic, parsley, salt, pepper, and nuts. Blend until all are chopped very fine but not smooth. Remove from the blender and stir in the grated cheese.

Use in soups and on pasta.

Condiments

The proper definition of a condiment is simply a seasoning for food, such as mustard or spices. Each of our three ancient cuisines uses condiments in a very different way and the background of some of these differences is most interesting.

The most famous condiment in China, and the most common, is soy sauce. This is made from fermented soybeans, a bit of wheat, and salt. The time of the invention of this luscious liquid was probably during the Chou dynasty, which means the sauce is at the very least 2,600 years old. It is one of the oldest condiments we have in the world.

The Romans were very fond of a heavy condiment made of fermented anchovies and salt, along with water. It is called *garum,* and I expect that it was very close to what the Vietnamese call *nuc moom,* or fish sauce. The Romans mixed this with reduced wine, making *oenogarum,* and used this to flavor many dishes . . . too many as far as I am concerned. The flavor does not go well with our contemporary palates. It is interesting to note, however, that the Romans took this sauce with them to India via the spice and silk route. The Indians added a bit of tamarind and some additional spices. The sauce became very popular with the British when they hit India during the nineteenth century. The sauce was taken back to England and we know this ancient Roman banquet sauce, with some changes, as Lea & Perrins or Worcestershire. Funny how far this sauce traveled before we tasted it in America!

The Greeks do not really have a special mixed condiment but we must mention the use of lemons in Greece. The lemon came to Greece during pre-Christian times, probably from Babylonia. The shape of the lemon appeared in the art of the time though the Greeks did not seem to use them much in food preparation. By the fifth century A.D. the Greek cook began using the fruit in the kitchen and in our time it is impossible to think of the cuisine of Greece without thinking of the lemon. People buy them in Athens in great bags, just as we buy five or ten pounds of potatoes. The lemon is now a most serious condiment in the land of Athena.

I have listed some of the condiments that are common in each of our cuisines. A more detailed explanation of the more complex items will be found in the glossary.

These lists are to help you in your planning and shopping.

China

- Soy sauce *(page 29)*
- Fermented black beans *(dow see) (page 25)*
- Soybean condiment *(mein see) (page 27)*
- Rice vinegar *(page 28)*
- Red vinegar *(page 28)*
- Chinese rice wine *(page 28)*
- Sugar
- MSG *(page 36)*
- Pickles
- Foo yee *(page 25)*
- Oyster sauce *(page 27)*
- Ginger, fresh
- Garlic
- Five-spice powder *(page 35)*
- Star anise *(page 36)*
- Szechwan peppercorns *(page 36)*
- Dried hot chili peppers
- Chinese parsley *(page 35)*

Greece

- Mint and oregano
- Cinnamon and allspice
- Dill
- Olive oil
- Tomato sauce
- Onions
- Garlic
- Wine
- Lemon juice
- Vinegars
- Cheeses *(pages 31–32)*

Rome

- Garlic
- Olive oil
- Lemons
- Mint
- Basil
- Tomato sauce
- Wine
- Vinegars
- Onions
- Dried hot chili peppers
- Cheeses

Ancient Rome

- Garum (Try *nuc moom* from the Vietnamese grocery)
- Reduced wines (boiled)
- Lovage (Use celery leaves)
- Coriander, both fresh and in seed form

PINZIMONIO

This is a contemporary bit that is common in Rome.

Salt and pepper, mixed with a little good olive oil. Eaten with raw vegetables such as fava beans or fresh fennel.

OENOGARUM

I doubt that you will enjoy this in your food but the old Romans thought it was great!

1 cup red wine, reduced to ¾ cup

2 tablespoons fish sauce (*nuc moom* from Vietnam or Thailand)

Sesame

The sesame seed is an Old World wonder, and it is a common food in all three of our ancient cuisines.

The seed probably originated in the subtropics of Asia, and it has been important there as a food and oil for thousands of years. The Chinese were using the plant as early as the third millennium B.C. and the Greeks and Romans used it very early in their cooking. The Greek soldiers considered the seeds so typical of their culture that they carried little bags of the product with them to battle so that they might have a small reminder of home when they were far away.

The seeds come from a rough and gummy sort of plant. When the pod dries in the fall it pops open with such force that the tiny explosion scatters the seeds all over the place. This is probably what Ali Baba was referring to in the Arabian Nights when he stood before the locked door at the cave and shouted, "Open sesame!" He was literally saying, "Open up like an exploding sesame pod!" Oh, where do I get this stuff?

The seed offers 55 percent of its weight in oil, an oil that has been used in cooking since Biblical times. The seeds and oil are used in cooking candy, salads, breads, seasoning, coatings, and a thousand other dishes.

You might also consider:

Shredded Chicken Sesame *(page 91)*
Fish Fillets with Sesame *(page 181)*
Sesame Dragon Mouths *(page 546)*
Sesame Almond Chicken Wings *(page 276)*
Chinese Sesame Chicken *(page 278)*
Chinese Sesame Cookies *(page 573)*
Greek Sesame Bread *(page 552)*
Sesame Circles *(page 553)*
Breadsticks, Italian Sesame *(page 557)*
Tahini Bean Dip *(page 95)*

Greece and China

TAHINI, HOMEMADE

MAKES 1½ CUPS

If you cannot find tahini or sesame paste in a Middle Eastern grocery or a Chinese grocery, you can certainly make your own. It is very simple, but I think that you should remember that in ancient times there was no such thing as a food processor. This paste was ground by hand with a mortar and pestle, both in China and in Greece.

¾ pound sesame seeds
2 teaspoons plus 3 tablespoons peanut oil
Salt, very little (optional)

Place seeds on baking sheet and toast in 350° oven for 20 minutes or until lightly roasted. Process in medium-sized food processor for 3 minutes. Add 2 teaspoons peanut oil and process on high for 30 seconds. Add 3 tablespoons peanut oil and process until very smooth, about 2 minutes. Add the optional salt.

Olives and Olive Oil

The olive is a holy symbol, one of the most ancient foods in the world, and it is delicious! Archaeological evidence indicates that the earliest use of olives dates as far back as 6000 B.C., and this was probably in what is now called Syria, Palestine, and Crete. And it was an olive branch that was brought to Noah by the dove, signaling his deliverance from the Flood. For all of the peoples of the Mediterranean region, the olive branch is a superb symbol of life, of cuisine, of joy.

While the Chinese have eaten olives since ancient times, they did not seem to get into olive oil. Greece, on the other hand, has lived by the olive since the olive tree thrives in difficult terrains, as does the other symbolic biblical plant, the grape. The goddess Athena bestowed the olive on the city of Athens, and the people of Greece have been making use of the tree ever since. They had markets for their wonderful olive oil all about the Mediterranean, and thus they had to develop a navy to protect their sea-lanes, a navy that became the greatest sea power in its day. And the Romans are to be credited with the invention of the screw press, which meant that the rich oil could be more easily extracted from the fruit. The oil of the olive has been basic to life in Rome since before the Christian era.

There are many types of olives in the world, as the following list will show. Green olives are simply that, olives picked before they ripen.

California black olives
Calamata, Greek
Greek: several varieties and qualities
Dried Italian
Tiny French Niçoises
Green Spanish
Green stuffed
Chinese dried olives *(lam see)*
Preserved Chinese olives, sweet
Licorice-flavored salty Chinese olives
Licorice-flavored sweet Chinese olives

Olive oils vary a great deal in their richness, color, and flavor. The reason the Chinese have never used olive oil in their cooking is because the oil has a bright flavor all its own and it will impart that flavor to any dish. The Chinese traditionally used lard since it adds less flavor to the food. They now use peanut oil. The Greeks and Romans, however, used the oil not only as a cooking lubricant but as a flavoring in itself.

Don't be confused by the grades of olive oil. There is really quite a simple system.

The first pressing of the olive gives us an "Extra Virgin" grade, one that was not produced with undue pressure or heat. The oil is light and flavorful, the kind you want for your very best salad dressings.

"Superfine Virgin Olive Oil" is next in quality, with "Fine Virgin Olive Oil" being next. "Virgin Olive Oil" is still a very good product and certainly suitable for most of your kitchen needs.

Products labeled simply as "Pure Olive Oil" are just that, and generally the oil comes from the last of the pressings, which means heat has been applied in order to get the last drop out of the pulp and seed. Generally the oil is a bit more bitter but certainly fine for cooking. Buy it by the gallon. You can find some very good brands from Greece that are very reasonable.

The country of origin also has something to do with the flavor. Generally the Italian, Spanish, and Greek oils are bright in flavor and usually affordable. I love oil from Sparta, in Greece, since it has a flavor that reminds me of herbs and of the Greek sun. This is strictly for salads since it is expensive.

Do not worry about buying large amounts of olive oil; it will keep better than any other oil you can buy. I keep a quart each of two or three different kinds on my cooking counter. The rest of the gallon can I store in the refrigerator, though some people tell me that even that is not necessary.

We now know that olive oil is really quite good for us. It contains no cholesterol, of course, since it is not an animal fat. As a matter of fact, the heart people now believe that olive oil helps break down cholesterol that has already built up in your system. That's the best news I've had all year!

You will find many recipes in this book that include olive oil. Among them are:

Greek Salad Dressing *(page 160)*
Greek Duck with Olives *(page 300)*
Olive and Pepper Salad *(page 168)*
Olive Rolls *(page 559)*
Olive Bread *(page 559)*
Green Olive Soup *(page 150)*
Fish with Olives and Bean Curd *(page 181)*
Steamed Pork with Chinese Olives *(page 345)*
Rice Congee *(page 436)*
Chinese New Year Noodles with Olives *(page 409)*

HINT: WHEN BUYING OLIVE OIL consider the use. You should probably buy a good extra virgin oil for salads, and a medium grade for pasta. For deep-frying and normal cooking buy the stuff by the gallon at a good Italian or Greek grocery. The merchant will help you so that you do not feel obligated to use the wrong oil at any time. Oil by the gallon for pan-frying is not at all expensive. On the other hand, fine extra virgin for salads is expensive. Boy, is it expensive! But it makes the difference between making a really fine salad and just playing around with lettuce.

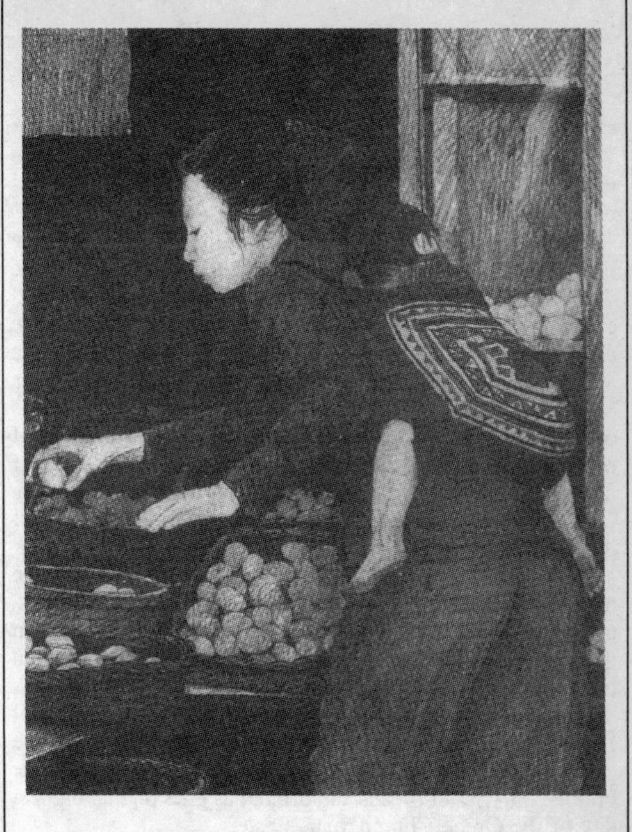

Eggs

The egg is a most ingenious package. Architecturally it is a near miracle, and in terms of food content and flavor it is a great gift to the cook. It is also one of the most versatile foods that we have.

While the fact that the egg is a religious symbol of new life is well known to most of us, we are not aware of the many kinds of eggs that are eaten. The Chinese domesticated chickens around 2000 B.C. and thus we have enjoyed the chicken egg. But the duck egg is also very common in China and these are the eggs that are preserved in mud and ashes and called "100-year-old eggs." They are only a few weeks old, at the most. The Chinese also salt eggs, a method of preservation that results in a wonderful concentration of flavors. While the egg has always been a common food in China, it is nevertheless associated with wealth because of its richness.

The Romans ate all kinds of eggs, and the more exotic they were, the more they were desired. Peacock eggs, ostrich eggs, and quail eggs, as well as the more common duck and chicken eggs, were all enjoyed by the Roman citizen.

The Greeks are probably responsible for our image of Easter eggs, though they have always dyed their eggs one color, red, for the blood of the Christ. The colored eggs are braided into Easter breads and offered as gifts on that highest day of the Greek Church year, Easter.

You might also want to consider:

Egg, Artichoke, and Tuna Pizza *(page 564)*
Asparagus with Cheese and Eggs, Italian Style *(page 477)*

China

TEA EGGS

MAKES 12 EGGS

This is one of the most beautiful food products that I know. The process leaves the egg looking like alabaster, a very rich and old alabaster. Your guests will be delighted with both the appearance and the taste since the anise is very plain. Channing and Jason used to call these "Licorice Eggs."

12 eggs
2 tablespoons salt
2 tablespoons dark soy sauce
3 star anise, whole
2 tablespoons dark tea such as oolong or black tea

Using an egg poker put a hole in the *large* end of 12 eggs. Place in a stainless-steel pan and cover with water. Add 1 tablespoon salt. Bring to a simmer and cook for 20 minutes, the lid off. Cool the eggs under running water. Using the back of a dinner spoon, gently crack the eggs so that there are many hairline cracks in the shell.

Replace the eggs in the pan. Add 1 tablespoon salt, the dark soy sauce, star anise, and the very dark tea. Bring to a simmer, uncovered, and cook for 2 to 3 hours. Let cool in the broth for 8 hours. Gently peel the shells from the eggs and serve whole or wedged.

You might like to serve these with a splash of light soy and sesame oil.

SALTED EGGS

This is obviously a very old method of preserving eggs and giving additional flavor, all in the same operation. What you will have is an uncooked pickled egg and the eggs must be cooked eventually. Do not be concerned about the fact that they are not refrigerated. The salt solves the problem of preservation.

4 cups water
1¼ cups kosher salt
1 dozen eggs
⅛ cup black tea, such as po nay or dark oolong

Boil the water and add the salt, stirring until it dissolves. Allow the water to cool completely. Place the eggs in a bowl and add the tea. Cover with the salt solution, being careful not to add any salt that did not dissolve. Place a saucer on top of the eggs so that they remain under the solution at all times. Cover and allow to sit for 20 days. Then refrigerate. They can actually be used after the first ten days, but a brighter flavor will develop if you wait the longer time.

The eggs can be hard-boiled, peeled, and served just as they are, along with a little light soy sauce and some sesame oil. Or they can be used in cooking other dishes such as the Steamed Pork with Salted Eggs (page 258).

Do not be alarmed when you break the shell of the uncooked egg and find that the yolk is firm, almost as if cooked. The salt does that and preserves the egg for a long time.

BABY CORN AND QUAIL EGGS

SERVES 6–8 AS PART OF A CHINESE MEAL

This dish is fun, and very easy. Both of the main ingredients come from China canned. The blending offers a dish of color, texture, and excellent flavor.

- 2 tablespoons peanut oil
- 1 slice ginger, the size of a 25-cent piece, cut julienne
- 1 clove garlic, chopped fine
- 1 15-ounce can baby corn, drained
- 1 15-ounce can quail eggs, drained
- ¼ cup Chinese Chicken Soup Stock (page 126) or ¼ cup Basic Chicken Stock (page 144)
- 2 tablespoons oyster sauce
- 1 teaspoon cornstarch mixed with 1 tablespoon water
- Pinch of sugar
- ½ tablespoon sesame oil

GARNISH

- Chinese parsley
- Shredded iceberg lettuce for a bed

Heat the wok and add the oil. Chow the ginger and garlic for just a moment and add the drained corn. Chow just until the corn is hot and add the drained eggs. Be careful from here on that you do not break or tear up the eggs. Add the remaining ingredients, except the garnishes, and chow until the dish is hot and thick. Place on a bed of shredded iceberg lettuce and garnish with the Chinese parsley.

STEAMED PORK WITH SALTED EGGS

SERVES 6 AS PART OF A CHINESE MEAL

This is a favorite of mine. Chinese friends tell me that they remember the days of their youth, when their parents were short on money, and Mama would have to divide the salted yolk very carefully to see that each was served the fair amount. Such is the history of this dish.

- **1 pound pork, finely ground**
- **10 water chestnuts, coarsely chopped**
- **2 tablespoons dry sherry or Chinese rice wine**
- **2 tablespoons light soy sauce**
- **½ teaspoon grated fresh ginger**
- **1 tablespoon cornstarch**
- **1 fresh egg**
- **1 teaspoon sesame oil**
- **½ teaspoon freshly ground black pepper**
- **1 green onion, chopped**
- **2 Salted Eggs (page 256)**

Place all ingredients, except the salted eggs, in a mixing bowl and mix vigorously until smooth. Place the meat in a 9-inch-square stainless-steel cake pan or dish. Make two indentations in the top of the meat and break the salted eggs over the meat, placing the yolks in the indentations. Steam in a bamboo steamer (page 106) for 20 minutes. Be sure the steamer is hot before beginning to time the cooking process.

Italy

RICOTTA FRITTATA

SERVES 6

The omelet goes back to ancient times. The Greeks loved eggs, but I think that the classic frittata, an omelet partially cooked and then broiled, must be credited to the Romans. Apicius had several dishes that he called "custards," which were really closer to a frittata. This is a good one, and it is rich and filling.

- **1 pound ricotta**
- **Salt and freshly ground black pepper to taste**
- **6 eggs**
- **3 tablespoons grated Parmesan or Romano cheese**
- **2 tablespoons olive oil**

Using an electric mixer, cream the ricotta with the salt and pepper until smooth and fluffy. In a separate bowl beat the eggs with the grated cheese. Add eggs to the ricotta and blend well.

Heat a 10-inch SilverStone-lined frying pan and add the oil. Add the egg and cheese mixture and cook over low heat until the bottom is golden and the eggs begin to set. Place under a heated broiler until lightly browned on top.

Place on a serving platter and cut into wedges to serve.

Poultry and Game

Chicken

Chicken is so common to our Western table that we think the chicken is ours. It is not. What we know as the common fowl is probably the descendant of the wild red jungle fowl of South Asia and we should most likely credit the Chinese with domesticating the bird around 200 B.C. And what a job of domestication! There are now more chickens in the world than human beings and the meat of the old hen is the most universally eaten by humans. This is due to the fact that the chicken is willing to acclimate to all but the coldest regions on earth. Only the dog can live in a wider range of climates.

Actually I should not give all of the credit for spreading the bird to the Chinese. The Greeks also raised chickens for their eggs, and by the time the Chinese were commonly raising the fowl for food, the Greeks began to eat them as well. The Greeks spread the good word of the good bird and the Romans, who had eaten chickens during their tours in Asia Minor, went to Greece to learn new techniques for breeding and raising the flavorful and versatile creature. The bird increased in popularity in Rome, with both poor and wealthy citizens, and some of the high-class crowd did strange things with chickens. Horace loved the taste of a chicken that had been drowned in wine prior to cooking!

All three of our ancient cultures still enjoy this ancient bird, but you must go to a Chinese community to understand which of the three cultures is the most concerned about freshness. The Chinese buy the creatures live, and you witness a great deal of poking and pushing at the bird so that one can be sure the chicken is young. I saw one old woman pick up the live chicken, turn him over, and blow on his tail! My Chinese friend, Ken Hom, later explained that she simply wanted to see how large the tail oil sack was, since the younger the bird, the smaller the sack. Oh!

You might also like to consider:

Chicken with Leek Belts *(page 521)*
Chinese Chicken with Chestnuts *(page 495)*

China

CHINESE POACHED CHICKEN

I did this dish for you a few years ago when we first began the shows in Chicago. It is the most simple chicken recipe I know. It is so simple that some people have called to say that they doubt it will work. Everyone who has tried it, however, loves it. The final product is moist and flavorful. Since there is no salt in this dish you must add whatever seasoning you like when serving.

Read the instructions carefully and you will be very pleased. The dish was given to me by my adopted Chinese aunt, Mrs. Mary Young. Please try it.

Fill a 12-quart kettle almost full of water and bring it to a boil. Place 1 whole chicken, about 3 pounds, in the boiling water. The water will stop boiling in just a moment or so. Using wooden spoons so that you do not tear the skin, remove the chicken from the water and place it on a tray. Cover the pot and bring the water back to the boiling point. Put the chicken back into the pot, cover, and turn off the heat. Leave the bird in the pot and the pot on the burner, but you will need no more heat. The water will be hot enough to cook the bird. After 1 hour the chicken is done. Remove, cool, and debone the chicken.

I save the skin and bones for a later soup stock. I use some of the poaching water for covering the meat, which is then refrigerated. Some of the poaching water can be used for the soup stock. It has no flavor of its own.

This chicken can be used in the preparation of several other dishes. It is also great for chicken salads, chicken with pasta, etc.

ROAST SALT CHICKEN

SERVES 4–6 AS PART OF A CHINESE MEAL

I know, I know. This is too much salt. But, strangely enough, the juices from the chicken are sealed in the chicken by the salt. The result is not as salty as you might think. It is a classic method of preparation and it is certainly easy. The salt falls right off!

1 3-pound chicken

MARINADE

3 tablespoons dark soy sauce
3 tablespoons sesame oil
3 cloves garlic, crushed

2¼ cups rock salt (for pickling)
1 green onion, chopped
Aluminum foil

Mix the marinade and rub the chicken inside and out. Put ¼ cup of the salt inside the bird, along with the chopped onion. Place 1 cup of the salt on a large piece of aluminum foil and set the bird in the salt. Cup the foil up around the bird and pour the remaining cup of salt on top. Seal up with more foil if necessary and place on a baking pan. Bake at 375° for 1 hour, or until done to your taste.

Brush the salt from the chicken before serving. Hack (page 20) the chicken up into small serving pieces. Serve warm or cold.

CHICKEN BAKED WITH HONEY AND SOY SAUCE

SERVES 4–6 AS PART OF A CHINESE MEAL

The point behind this book has something to do with the interesting connections among the "old cuisines"—China, Greece, and Rome. This recipe was given to me one evening while eating at an informal Roman fish house, Da Franco. I was eating dinner with . . . I hope you understand and believe this story . . . a prince of Rome, one Prince Ugo. He traces his ancestry back to the Caesars, and I found him fascinating. He has an old family castle right in the middle of the city of Rome. The man has been everywhere and knows everybody, and we began to talk food. When I told him about this book, he blurted out this recipe. I say "blurted out" because we both had had too much Roman wine. The dish is simple. The dish is delicious. The dish should be cooked by your children while *you* drink the Roman wine.

1 3-pound chicken, whole

MARINADE

2 tablespoons honey

2 tablespoons dark soy sauce

2 tablespoons sesame oil

Mix the marinade ingredients and rub the chicken inside and out. Allow the bird to marinate for about ½ hour, turning now and then. Save the marinade for basting. Tie the legs and place the chicken on a roasting rack and pan. Bake at 350° for 15 minutes and then 325° for 20 minutes. Then, turn the heat down to 300° for 30 minutes. Baste with the remaining marinade a few times during cooking.

Watch the bird closely as it cooks. You want it to be golden brown and certainly not burned.

BEGGAR'S CHICKEN

SERVES 6–8 AS PART OF A CHINESE MEAL

There are many legends behind this famous Chinese dish. The most common story claims that a famished pauper stole a chicken and wrapped the feathered bird in wet clay and placed it in a fire. He certainly did not have any cooking equipment! When the clay had dried out, the bird was removed from the fire. The feathers stuck to the clay so the final result was a moist and lovely dish. One story goes so far as to claim that a beggar brought this dish to the Empress during a famine in China. She was so impressed that she declared it one of the great dishes of China. You can make up any story you like when you serve this dish, and we will assume that your creativity will add to the joy of the evening.

No, I do not use a feathered chicken for this dish. One cleaned at the supermarket will do just fine.

1 3½ pound chicken, washed and patted dry

MARINADE

2 tablespoons dark soy sauce
1 tablespoon sesame oil
1 tablespoon dry sherry or Chinese rice wine
1½ teaspoons five-spice powder (page 35)
1 teaspoon freshly grated ginger
1 teaspoon salt
2 cloves garlic, crushed

Parchment paper (or make your own, page 110)
1 paper lunch bag
12 pounds clay from a local potter

Mix all of the marinade ingredients together and rub the bird with this mixture, inside and out. Tie the legs together and place the bird on a roasting rack in a pan. Roast in a 450° oven, breast side up, for 20 minutes, or until the bird browns a bit. Remove from the oven and allow to cool slightly. Place the chicken, breast side up, on a large piece of parchment paper and wrap up. Slip the wrapped bird into the paper lunch sack and fold up the ends of the bag.

Roll out the clay on a dish towel on a breadboard to about ⅜ inch thick, 16 inches wide, and 21 inches long.

Place the bagged chicken in the middle of the clay and bring the sides of the clay slab up to meet across the top, shaping close to the bird. Press the ends down and secure by pinching the clay. Do this carefully so that you have a kind of clay envelope with about a 1-inch edge of clay on the top and the ends. Trim off the excess. Pinch together decoratively if you like.

Place the clay-covered chicken in a large baking pan and bake at 350° for about 2½ hours. Transfer the bird to a large shallow tray or basket and invite your guests to watch the cracking of the clay. Use a wooden mallet. The clay will crack readily and you can lift off the pieces. Return the chicken to the kitchen and remove all the clay. Pull off the paper bag and hack (page 20) the chicken into serving pieces.

CHICKEN WITH TWO ONIONS IN SAND POT

SERVES 4–6 AS PART OF A CHINESE MEAL

This dish will have an unusual flavor due to the use of the wonderful five-spice powder. If you do not have a sand pot (page 12), you can certainly use a stove-top casserole.

- 1 3-pound chicken, hacked (page 20) into 2-inch pieces

MARINADE

- 2 tablespoons light soy sauce
- 2 tablespoons dry sherry or Chinese rice wine
- 1 teaspoon ginger, either cut julienne or grated

- 4 tablespoons peanut oil
- 2 cloves garlic, finely chopped
- ¼ teaspoon salt
- 1 cup Chinese Chicken Soup Stock (page 126)
- 2 yellow onions, peeled and cut into 8 wedges each; divide the wedges into leaves
- 6 green onions, cut Chinese style (page 158)
- Pinch of brown sugar
- ¼ teaspoon five-spice powder (page 35)
- ½ head iceberg lettuce, torn up

Cut the chicken and mix with the marinade. Allow to sit for 15 minutes.

Heat the wok and add ½ of the oil. Chow the garlic and salt for just a moment. Add the chicken, drained of the marinade. Reserve the marinade.

Brown the chicken well on all sides and add the broth. Cover and cook until the chicken is done to your taste. Remove the cover and allow the broth to reduce a bit. Remove all from the wok and set aside.

Heat the wok again and add the remaining 2 tablespoons of oil. Chow the garlic for a moment and add the onions and the *dow see* mashed with the sherry. Chow for a moment and add the green peppers. Return the chicken to the wok along with the reserved marinade. Add the ingredients for the final sauce. Stir well and cover. Simmer the dish until the chicken is tender but not overcooked, about 20 minutes.

CHICKEN CHOWED WITH BLACK BEANS

SERVES 4–6 AS PART OF A CHINESE MEAL

This is a favorite of all serious Chinese food freaks. If the chicken is not overcooked the result will be spectacular. It looks like a lot of work but it is not.

1 3-pound chicken, hacked (page 20) into 2-inch pieces

MARINADE

2 tablespoons light soy sauce
2 tablespoons cornstarch
1 egg white
1 teaspoon salt
2 tablespoons peanut oil

4 tablespoons peanut oil
3 cloves garlic, chopped fine
1 yellow onion, peeled and cut into 1-inch pieces
3 tablespoons fermented black beans *(dow see)* rinsed in plain water and mashed with 2 tablespoons dry sherry or Chinese rice wine
2 green sweet bell peppers, cored and cut julienne

FINAL SAUCE

1 tablespoon light soy sauce
2 tablespoons dry sherry or Chinese rice wine
1 cup Chinese Chicken Soup Stock (page 126)
1 teaspoon brown sugar

Cut the chicken and soak in the marinade for 15 minutes. Heat a wok and add 2 tablespoons of the oil. Drain the marinade from the chicken and reserve. Brown the chicken pieces well in the wok, then remove and set aside. Drain the oil from the wok and discard. (Too much chicken fat in it!)

Heat the wok again and add the remaining 2 tablespoons of oil. Chow the garlic for a moment and add the onions and the *dow see* mashed with the sherry. Chow for a moment and add the green peppers. Return the chicken to the wok along with the reserved marinade. Add the ingredients for the final sauce. Stir well and cover. Simmer the dish until the chicken is tender but not overcooked, about 20 minutes.

VARIATION: You may wish to thicken this dish with 1 tablespoon of cornstarch mixed with an equal amount of water. Add it after the final sauce is hot. Stir well and serve.

CHICKEN WINGS IN FIVE SPICE

MAKES 24 PIECES

The Chinese have always been fond of chicken wings. The reason is that the wing is very moist and filled with gelatin, thus creating a wonderful bite, but only a bite. It takes a pile of these to fill a family but they make a wonderful addition to a Chinese meal of several courses.

12 chicken wings, whole

MARINADE

½ teaspoon freshly grated ginger
⅛ cup light soy sauce
⅛ cup dry sherry or Chinese rice wine
½ teaspoon five-spice powder

1 cup water-chestnut flour (page 31)
4 cups peanut oil for deep-frying

Cut each wing into 3 logical pieces. Save the tips for soup and use only the 2 meatier parts for this recipe.

Prepare the marinade and marinate the wing pieces for ½ hour. Drain and toss in the water-chestnut flour. Deep-fry at 360° until golden brown, about 5 minutes.

FRIED GARLIC CHICKEN BALLS

SERVES 8–10 AS PART OF A CHINESE MEAL

Ground chicken is now available in most supermarkets. It is a good product and these chicken balls put a good product to good use. The kids will prefer these to chicken nuggets, I'm sure.

2 pounds ground chicken meat
½ teaspoon white pepper
½ teaspoon salt
2 tablespoons cornstarch
1 tablespoon dark soy sauce
2 egg whites
½ teaspoon freshly grated ginger
2 tablespoons dry sherry or Chinese rice wine vinegar
4 cloves garlic, crushed

COATING

1 cup cornstarch
1 cup water-chestnut flour (page 31)

4 cups peanut oil for deep-frying

Mix the chicken with all of the seasonings and egg whites. Mix it very well. Form into balls about the size of large walnuts and set on waxed paper. When all are formed, mix the cornstarch with the water-chestnut flour and roll each ball in this mixture. Deep-fry, in several batches, in 360° oil until the balls float and are golden brown in color, about 5 minutes. Taste one to be sure they are done to your liking.

CHICKEN STEAMED WITH CHINESE SAUSAGE

SERVES 4–6 AS PART OF A CHINESE MEAL

The sweetness of wonderful Chinese sausage, *lop chong,* adds a most interesting dimension to this dish. It is easy to prepare since there is no browning of meat involved. The only problem you will have is finding the sausage, unless you are in a large city that has Chinese markets. If you cannot find the *lop chong,* try the dish using julienned ham instead.

1 3-pound chicken, hacked (page 20) into 2-inch pieces

MARINADE

1½ teaspoons salt
2 tablespoons light soy sauce
1 tablespoon cornstarch
1 tablespoon dry sherry or Chinese rice wine

1 tablespoon peanut oil

6 large Chinese mushrooms, soaked for 3 hours and sliced; drain, but save the liquid
3 Chinese sausages *(lop chong)*, diagonally sliced into thin pieces

Hack the chicken and place in a bowl with the marinade ingredients. Mix well and let marinate for 2 hours.

Slice the mushrooms and sausages and add to the bowl. Also add 2 tablespoons of the mushrooms' soaking water.

Place in a steamer pan or bowl and steam for 45 minutes or until the chicken is tender but not dry.

CHICKEN AND PORK IN LETTUCE

SERVES 6 AS PART OF A CHINESE MEAL

This dish is akin to mu-shu pork, though the addition of chicken pleases my palate. If you have never had such a dish in lettuce leaves you are in for a treat. Of course you can use Peking Pancakes (page 548) or even wheat tortillas, but for me the lettuce does the job!

- ½ pound pork, coarsely chopped
- ½ pound chicken, skinless and boneless, coarsely chopped

MARINADE

- 2 tablespoons light soy sauce
- 1 egg white, beaten
- 1 tablespoon cornstarch
- 1 tablespoon dry sherry or Chinese rice wine
- ½ teaspoon freshly grated ginger
- 3 tablespoons peanut oil
- 1 teaspoon salt
- 2 tablespoons peanut oil for chowing
- 3 eggs, beaten
- 1 ounce black tree-ear fungus (page 25), soaked in fresh water for 1 hour
- 1 tablespoon oyster sauce
- 1 tablespoon sesame oil
- 3 green onions, chopped
- 1 head iceberg lettuce, separated into whole leaves

Chop the meats and marinate *only the pork* in the marinade mixture for 15 minutes.

Heat the wok and add the oil and salt. Chow the chicken first, just until barely done, and remove. Add the pork, along with the marinade, and chow until done to taste. Remove.

Heat the wok again and add the oil for the eggs. Beat the eggs and chow over medium heat so that they become scrambled but not dry. Chop them up in the wok with the wok paddle and remove to a plate.

Add the remaining ingredients, except the lettuce, to the wok and chow until the fungus is hot. Add the pork, chicken, and eggs to the mixture and toss until all is hot. Remove to a serving bowl.

Serve by wrapping a few tablespoons of the meat mixture in a lettuce leaf, just like a burrito.

VARIATIONS:

1. Add some garlic and red chili paste (page 26) to this dish. Serve as above. Wonderful!
2. Substitute Peking Pancakes (page 548) for the lettuce leaves.
3. See the Dried Oysters and Pork in Lettuce recipe (page 388) for another version of this dish.

ROAST "LUNG KONG" CHICKEN

SERVES 4–6 FOR A CHINESE DINNER

The wonderful Peninsula Hotel in Hong Kong makes a dish very much like this. At least this is as close as I can come to the dish that I had there. It is not complicated and the results are moist and delicious.

1 3-pound chicken, cut in half the long way

Looing Sauce (page 231)

6 cups peanut oil for deep-frying

Blanch the chicken halves in boiling water for 2 minutes. Drain. Place the bird halves in a pot of Looing Sauce and bring to a boil. They should be covered with the sauce. Turn the heat to a simmer and cook lightly for 15 minutes, then allow the halves to cool in the sauce.

Remove and place on a rack on the counter. Pat dry with paper towels and dry the meat using an electric fan. Aim the fan at the bird halves for about 3 hours, or until the skin is dry to the touch.

Deep-fry one half at a time in oil at 350°. Be very careful when sliding the half into the hot oil. A wok lid will be helpful in protecting your hands and face in case the oil should pop and spit at you.

Deep-fry each half until the skin is crispy and golden. Drain on paper towels before cutting up to serve.

LOOED CHICKEN

SERVES 6 AT A CHINESE-STYLE DINNER

Prepare a basic Looing Sauce (page 231) or use one that you have reserved in your refrigerator. Place enough of the sauce in a 6-quart stove-top covered casserole to cover 1 whole chicken. Bring the sauce to a boil and add the chicken. Cover and turn to a simmer. Cook for 30 minutes and turn off the heat, allowing the chicken to cool in the sauce for 1 hour.

My favorite method of serving this simple and tasty peasant dish is to simply hack up the bird (page 20) and arrange on a platter. Garnish with a bit of sesame oil and chopped green onions.

SESAME ALMOND CHICKEN WINGS

SERVES 6 AS PART OF A CHINESE MEAL

I love chicken wings, and so do the Chinese. The wing has a great deal of flavor so it is moist and wonderful eating. This is a quickie recipe using the ancient sesame seed as well as the almond.

12 chicken wings

MARINADE

1 tablespoon light soy sauce

1 tablespoon Chinese rice wine or dry sherry

½ teaspoon freshly grated ginger

2 egg whites, beaten

COATING MIXTURE

2 tablespoons ground almonds

2 tablespoons rice flour

2 tablespoons cornstarch

½ tablespoon wheat flour

2 tablespoons sesame seeds

4 cups peanut oil for deep-frying

Chinese Dip Sauce (page 229) (Choose your favorite)

Cut each of the wings into 3 logical pieces, setting the wing tips aside for soup stock. Prepare the marinade and soak the wing pieces in this for 15 minutes. In the meantime, blend the coating mixture and heat the oil. Drain the marinade from the wings and dip each in the egg whites. Then dredge in the coating mixture. Deep-fry at 360° until each piece is golden brown, about 5 minutes. Serve hot with any of the dip sauces.

QUICK CHINESE ROAST CHICKEN

You can throw this recipe together in nothing flat, and it really does taste very much like the roast chicken you will find in a good Chinese takeout house.

1 3½-pound chicken, whole, cleaned

MARINADE

2 tablespoons dark soy sauce

2 tablespoons Chinese rice wine or dry sherry

¼ teaspoon grated fresh ginger

½ teaspoon five-spice powder (page 35)

2 tablespoons honey

Salt and freshly ground black pepper to taste

Mix marinade and rub chicken inside and out. Allow to marinate in bowl for 1 hour. Place on a poultry rack and bake at 375° for about 1 hour, or to taste.

CHINESE SESAME CHICKEN

SERVES 8 AS PART OF A CHINESE MEAL

This is so simple that you must not tell anyone about it. Just prepare the dish and let them compliment you . . . and leave it at that.

8 chicken thighs

MARINADE

2 tablespoons light soy sauce
2 tablespoons Chinese rice wine or dry sherry
½ teaspoon freshly grated ginger
¼ teaspoon ground white pepper

1 egg white, beaten
½ cup flour
½ cup cornstarch
½ cup sesame seeds
6 cups peanut oil for deep-frying

Marinate the thighs in the marinade mixture for 15 minutes. Dip each thigh into the egg white and then dredge in the flour and cornstarch mixed with the sesame seeds. Deep-fry at 360° until golden and tender, about 15 minutes. You will have better luck with this dish if you fry 4 pieces at a time and keep your oil up to temperature.

Greece

ROASTED CHICKEN, GREEK STYLE

SERVES 4

The wonderful thing about Greek cooking is that it is rarely complex. You can bake this chicken or cut it in half to place on the barbecue. Either way is most enjoyable and the olive oil helps keep it moist.

- **1 3-pound chicken**
- **½ cup olive oil**
- **Juice of 2 lemons**
- **1 tablespoon oregano**
- **Salt and pepper to taste**

Marinate the chicken in the above mixture for 1 hour, being sure to rub some inside the chicken. Bake at 375° for 1 hour or until done. If you wish to do this on a barbecue, it is best to cut the bird in half the long way and then marinate. Cook to your liking over medium-hot coals.

CHICKEN ROLL, GREEK STYLE

SERVE 6–8

Prepare two chickens just as for the Chicken Roll, Roman Style (page 283) but omit the marjoram and parsley and substitute 1 tablespoon whole oregano. Roast, and serve with a good Greek salad (pages 160–165) and a dry white wine.

Italy

FRICASSEE OF CHICKEN, ROMAN STYLE

SERVES 4

This has got to be one of the best Italian chicken dishes I know. I added a bit with the artichokes and the result is delightful. It is a chicken stew that has a sauce so rich that you can save the sauce and get another entire meal out of it. Just serve it over pasta. Period!

- 2 tablespoons olive oil
- 1 3-pound chicken, cut into 8 pieces
- 3 cloves garlic, chopped
- 1 cup red wine
- 2 cups Basic Brown Soup Stock (page 148)
- ½ cup coarsely chopped pancetta or bacon
- 1 cup coarsely chopped ripe tomatoes
- 2 teaspoons whole marjoram
- 1 14-ounce can artichoke hearts, quartered, drained well
- 1 tablespoon *each* butter and flour, cooked together to form a roux (page 22)
- Salt and freshly ground black pepper to taste

Heat a large frying pan and add the oil. Brown the chicken pieces well. Remove to a 6-quart covered stove-top casserole. Add the garlic to the pan and sauté just a moment. Deglaze (page 20) the pan with the red wine and add to the casserole. Add all remaining ingredients except the artichokes, roux, and salt and pepper. Bring to a boil and cover. Turn to a simmer and cook for 40 minutes. Add the artichokes and simmer another 10 minutes, uncovered. Stir in the roux and taste for seasoning. Careful with the salt as the pancetta is salty itself.

DEVIL'S CHICKEN
(Pollo alla Diavola)

SERVES 4

This dish has a wonderful name that will tickle your children. The dish will probably also tickle their throats since chicken of the devil is supposed to be *very hot!* You can calm it down for the kids and spice it up for your mate. Either way it is easy and delicious. I like this dish cooked on the charcoal barbecue.

- **1 3–4-pound chicken**
- **½ cup olive oil**
- **2 tablespoons hot pepper sauce (Tabasco) or to taste**
- **Juice of 2 lemons**
- **1 tablespoon freshly ground black pepper to taste**
- **1 teaspoon salt**

Using poultry shears, cut the bird open by cutting down the backbone. Flatten a bit by pounding with your hand so that the chicken is "butterflied."

Mix the remaining ingredients in a large bowl and marinate the bird for 2 hours.

Grill on a medium-hot charcoal barbecue, skin side down, for 25 minutes. Turn and cook until the juices run clear, about another 20 minutes. Keep basting with the remaining marinade.

CHICKEN WITH SWEET BELL PEPPERS

SERVES 4

Please don't use canned pimientos for this dish. Find good fresh peppers and you will have a wonderful meal.

- **1 3-pound chicken, cut into serving pieces**
- **½ cup olive oil**
- **Salt and freshly ground black pepper to taste**
- **3 cloves garlic, diced fine**
- **6 flat anchovies, rinsed**
- **4 sweet red bell peppers, cored and cut into 2-inch squares**
- **3 large ripe tomatoes, cored and chopped very coarsely**
- **3 tablespoons chopped parsley**
- **1 cup dry white wine**
- **1 teaspoon whole marjoram**

Cut up the chicken. Pan-brown in ½ of the oil. Place in stove-top casserole. Add salt and pepper to taste.

Sauté the garlic and anchovies in remaining oil. After about 2 minutes you can mash the anchovies and mix with the oil. Add peppers and sauté a bit. Put all in a casserole along with remaining ingredients. Cover and simmer until tender, 40 minutes.

CHICKEN ROLL, ROMAN STYLE

SERVES 6–8

No, you do not prepare this after you have gotten home late from the office and have a friend to entertain. On the other hand, if you made this dish in front of your friend, he/she would certainly be entertained! It is a bit more difficult than a stew but not as tough as you think.

- **2 chickens, each 3 pounds**
- **4 tablespoons olive oil**
- **Juice of 1 lemon**
- **3 cloves garlic, crushed**
- **2 teaspoons whole marjoram**
- **1 tablespoon chopped parsley**
- **Salt and freshly ground black pepper to taste**

Debone one chicken, leaving the skin and meat intact. This is not as difficult as it sounds. Simply use a very sharp paring knife and start at the neck of the bird. Gently pull the skin back and begin cutting the meat from the bone and carcass, being careful not to puncture the skin. Remove the wings and the legs, just where they join the thigh. Once you have cut the meat away from the carcass halfway down the bird, do the same from the other end. The carcass will come right out! Remove any meat from the bones that you may have missed. Skin and remove the meat from the second chicken, this time in large pieces. Do the same with the legs from both birds. Save the bones from both birds for soup stock. You can throw in the skin from the second bird as well.

Mix the meat from the second chicken with the remaining ingredients. Stuff the whole boneless bird with the seasoned meat and tie with string into a long, round loaf. You will need some help with the tying; someone needs to hold the thing as you wrap it.

COOKING: You may either poach the chicken roll in Basic Chicken Stock (page 144) made from the bones or you can bake it at 350° until the center registers 180° on a meat thermometer. This will take about 1 hour 30 minutes, or less.

Cool and slice. I like to serve this with Tuna Sauce (page 239) and a pasta dish such as Pappardelle (pages 425 or 426). A green salad is a necessity.

Goose

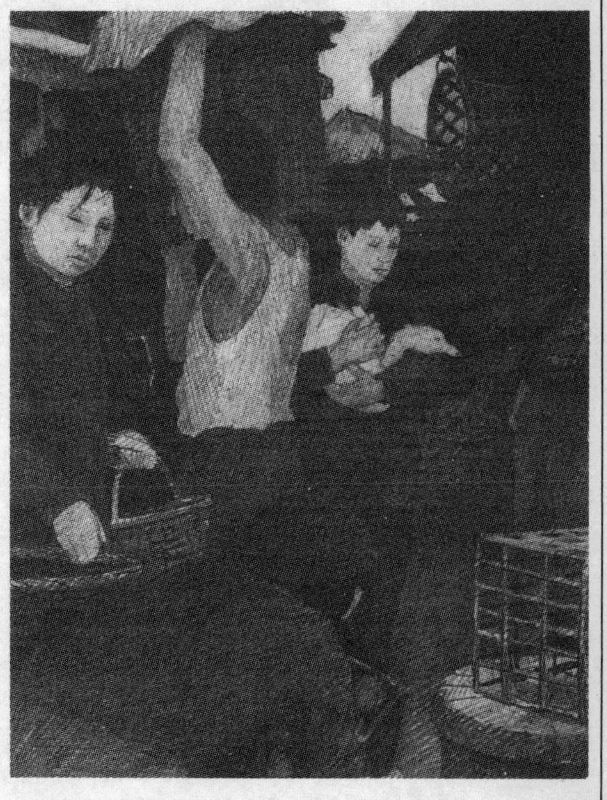

I wish Americans better understood the goose. He is easy to cook and I think he is the greatest of the fowl for feasting.

We know that people have been enjoying goose for thousands of years. It is believed that geese have been domesticated since neolithic times and we know that the ancient Egyptians loved goose. In classical Greece geese were treated to special diets of moistened grain to fatten them up and the people of Gaul did the same for the geese marketed in Rome.

Geese are mentioned in early Chinese texts and were highly valued through the ages. Marco Polo reported that the Chinese were raising huge geese! They still do. And while the bird is seen on the tables of the rest of Europe and America, I believe that the most creative uses of the bird come from China. You will love these two recipes, as they are neither fatty nor difficult to prepare.

LOOED GOOSE

SERVES 10–12 AS PART OF A CHINESE MEAL

I love the name of the dish . . . and the flavor of the dish is even better. ''Looing'' refers to simmering in a soy-based sauce, so cut the wisecracks about this bird being lewd! It is tender and moist, and actually very simple to prepare. The fattiness of the goose can be removed easily since it cooks into the sauce. When you chill the sauce prior to the next use, the fat can be removed.

1 8–9-pound goose

BASIC LOOING SAUCE

1½ cups dark soy sauce
1½ cups light soy sauce
2 star anise, whole
½ cup sugar
½ cup dry sherry or Chinese rice wine
6 slices fresh ginger, each the size of a 25-cent piece
3 quarts water

Cut the goose into quarters. Rinse well and drain.

Place all the ingredients for the looing sauce in a 12-quart kettle and bring to a boil. Add the goose pieces and add additional water just so that the pieces are barely covered. Bring to a simmer, cover, and gently cook for 30 minutes. Allow the bird to cool in the broth, covered, for 1 hour. Remove and slice for dinner.

You can serve the meat as it is with a bit of sauce or try it with Roasted Salt and Pepper (page 305).

SAVE THE LOOING SAUCE FOR ANOTHER USE. REFRIGERATE.

GOOSE, CHIU CHOW STYLE

This is just a wonderful mixture of flavors . . . and very rich flavors indeed. I had this dish the first time in a Chiu Chow restaurant in Hong Kong. It is in the Ocean City Building in Kowloon and called Ocean City Chiu Chow. You would do well to try the original version. The following is simply a guess, and it is delicious.

Use the full breast of a Looed Goose (page 287). Pan-fry the breast until the skin is golden brown. Place the meat, sliced thin, on a platter. Debone the breast before slicing.

PEPPER SAUCE

1 tablespoon Szechwan peppercorns (page 36)
1 teaspoon black peppercorns
3 tablespoons peanut oil
1 clove garlic, crushed
1 tablespoon sesame oil
Pinch of salt

Prepare the pepper sauce by crushing both types of peppercorns with a mortar and pestle or in a small electric coffee grinder. Do not pound or grind too fine. Heat the peanut oil in a small frying pan and add the peppercorns. Stir a bit until the oil barely begins to smoke. Remove from the heat and add the remaining ingredients.

Pour the pepper sauce over the sliced goose and serve.

Servings depend on how much goose you slice! Prepare plenty as this will be very popular at your Chinese table.

Duck

In 1873 one of the famed Yankee Clippers delivered a cargo of nine Peking ducks to Long Island, New York. From these nine creatures have descended all the millions and millions of domestic ducks of this species in the United States. Known today as "Long Island Duckling," they remain in this country an underrated and underconsumed food, despite their rich and distinctive flavor. In contrast, our three ancient cuisines have always appreciated ducks, and have eaten them in great numbers.

Duck is particularly prized in China and has been for centuries. After pork, duck and chicken are considered the most important meats in China. I am amused by the fact that the duck is respected by the Chinese not just because he is delicious to eat but because he can take care of himself! You let him out in the morning and he returns home having fed himself . . . though you do not, of course, ask him what he has been eating. Most of the recipes in this section are indeed Chinese, as they are the wisest of cooks when it comes to duckling.

Although their preparations were far more mundane and straightforward, the ancient Greeks and Romans were very fond of duck. As a matter of fact the famous French dish Duck à l'Orange was actually invented in ancient Rome . . . and Apicius was very fond of the dish.

Read these recipes and maybe I will be able to convince you that you should enjoy duck much more often. You might also wish to consider:

Duck and Jellyfish Salad (page 155)

China

CHINESE ROAST DUCK

SERVES 6 AS PART OF A CHINESE MEAL

When I was a boy of about fourteen I began to hang around Seattle's Chinatown. Roast duck was expensive and I decided that I should learn to make my own. Some arrogance! I asked a woman in a Chinese grocery, Wa Sang Market, to help me. Florence has been a friend ever since and I still ask her advice on recipes.

- **1 duck, approximately 4 pounds in size, completely defrosted if frozen, washed and dried with paper towels**
- **1 tablespoon salt**
- **2 cups water**
- ***2 packages George Washington Brown Broth**
- **2 pieces orange peel—1 inch wide, the length of the orange**
- **2 teaspoons five-spice powder**
- **2 teaspoons MSG (optional)**
- **2 star anise flowers**
- **1 tablespoon sugar**
- **1½ tablespoons soybean condiment *(mein see)***
- **2 cloves garlic, sliced thin**
- **2 tablespoons dry sherry or Chinese rice wine**
- **1 medium-size onion, peeled**
- **½ cup honey**
- **1 tablespoon vinegar**
- **¼ teaspoon ground dry ginger**
- **Chinese plum sauce for dipping (can be purchased in a can in any Chinese grocery)**

*George Washington Brown Broth is available in most fancy grocery stores and delicatessens. It is an excellent product.

Salt the duck completely inside and out. Allow the duck to sit for 1 hour and then, using paper towels, wipe the bird down completely.

Bring the water to a boil and add the Brown Broth, orange peel, five-spice powder, optional MSG, star anise, sugar, soybean condiment, garlic, and the sherry or rice wine. Boil for a few minutes and allow the sauce to cool to lukewarm.

Put the onion inside the bird and sew up the neck and open body cavity, leaving just an opening into which you pour the sauce. Then, close up the opening completely. We do not want the sauce to run out of the bird during the baking. Tie the legs together and place, breast side up, on an oiled roasting rack. Put the rack in a roasting pan and roast the bird, uncovered, at 400° for 20 minutes. Lower the heat to 375° and continue roasting, allowing 25 minutes per pound total roasting time. Include the first 20 minutes in the total time. Do not overcook the bird. You may have to turn the heat down to 350° during the last ⅓ of the total roasting time so that he does not brown too quickly.

Mix the honey, vinegar, and ground ginger together and baste the bird with this mixture about every 20 minutes during the roasting process.

NOTE: I have good luck using small poultry wires for the closing-up process. You can find them in almost any kitchen-gadget store.

Cut the duck up into serving pieces and serve the plum sauce on the side as a condiment.

PEKING DUCK

SERVES 8 AS PART OF A CHINESE MEAL

The Lee Gardens Hotel in Hong Kong has a duck oven on the roof! It is still heated with charcoal in contrast to most restaurants, which now use gas. The chef, head of the Rainbow Dining Room, was most gracious in showing me the whole process involved in the proper preparation of this dish, the most famous duck recipe in the world. It is not at all complicated, nor will you need any special equipment.

1 4½-pound duck, defrosted and patted dry

INSIDE SEASONING

¼ tablespoon salt
½ teaspoon Chinese five-spice powder
¼ teaspoon MSG (optional)
½ teaspoon sugar

2 quarts boiling water for blanching

BASTING SYRUP

*1 cup malt sugar (dry or liquid) (page 36)
1 cup hot water
2 tablespoons Chinese red vinegar or red wine vinegar
3 slices lemon, peel and all

GARNISH

Peking Pancakes (page 548) or wheat tortillas
Hoisin sauce (page 26)
Green onions or scallions

Mix the inside seasoning together and rub the mixture into the inside of the duck. Sew up the duck, both head and end. You might use poultry pins for this.

Make a large loop of string and place it under the wings of the bird so that you can hang him over a very large bowl. Use a kitchen-cabinet knob for the hanger. Pour the boiling water over the duck and continue ladling the hot water over the bird—about eight times. Allow to drain 10 minutes.

In the meantime, mix the ingredients for the basting syrup together. Drain the bowl beneath the duck of the water. Now, repeat the pouring process, this time using the basting syrup. Allow the duck to dry for about 3 hours. I use an electric fan for this process.

Place the duck on an oiled poultry rack and place the rack in a pan. Roast at 400° for 20 minutes. Then, turn the oven down to 375° and cook 25 minutes per pound, total cooking time. Include the first 20 minutes in the total time.

*Malt sugar or syrup can be found in any Chinese grocery.

Serve the thinly sliced duck, along with the skin, which is the best part, in the pancakes, along with a bit of hoisin and green onions. Make "brushes" of the onions or simply slice them the long way into nice slivers.

DUCK LIKE A MANDOLIN

SERVES 8 AS PART OF A CHINESE MEAL

This recipe is basically the same as the Peking Duck (page 292), but it is a bit easier. The duck will actually look like a mandolin only if you can find a bird that still has the head on. The head is left on the bird to resemble the top of the neck of the mandolin.

Cut the bird down the breastbone, using poultry shears. Open, or "butterfly," the duck and pat dry. Season with the inside seasoning just as in the preceding recipe. Place the bird, inside down, on a roasting rack and allow to sit while you boil 2 quarts of water and prepare the basting sauce, as in the above recipe. Place the broiling-pan rack, along with the bird, over the sink. I put mine on a large bowl in the sink. Using a ladle, gently pour the boiling water over the skin side of the bird only. Allow to dry for 20 minutes and then pour the sauce over the bird. Return the rack to the broiling pan. Discard the boiling water and basting syrup that flowed into the bowl in the sink.

Allow the bird to dry on the rack for 3 hours. I use an electric fan for this, just as in the preceding recipe.

Bake 20 minutes at 400° and then turn down the heat to 350° and bake 1 hour. Serve as Peking Duck, above, or simply cut up into serving pieces and then restore the shape of the "mandolin" on a large platter for serving.

STEWED DUCK WITH MUSHROOMS

SERVES 6 AS PART OF A CHINESE MEAL

When you prepare a Chinese meal you want to have several courses, and often cooking too many at the last minute can be a chore. This one is a casserole dish and it waits on the top of the stove or in the oven until you are ready to serve. Easy and a mushroom lover's paradise.

- **1 4-pound duck cut into 6 pieces**
- **3 tablespoons peanut oil for pan-frying**
- **3 cloves garlic, sliced thin**
- **2 slices fresh ginger, size of a 25-cent piece, cut julienne**
- **2 whole green onions, cleaned**
- **8–10 whole dried Chinese mushrooms, soaked for 3 hours**
- **3 cups Chinese Chicken Soup Stock (page 126) or regular Basic Chicken Stock (page 144)**
- **½ cup Chinese rice wine or dry sherry**
- **¼ cup light soy sauce**
- **½ tablespoon sugar**
- **½ tablespoon soybean condiment *(mein see)* or 1 star anise (I prefer the soybean condiment in this dish)**

Pan-brown the duck pieces in a few tablespoons of oil in a large frying pan. Remove the pieces to a 6-quart covered stove-top casserole. In the same frying pan sauté the garlic and ginger for a few moments. Add the green onion and sauté for just a moment. Place *all* ingredients in the casserole and mix well. Bring to a boil and lower the heat. Simmer, covered, until the duck is very tender, about 1¼ hours.

STEAMED DRIED DUCK AND PORK

SERVES 6 AS PART OF A CHINESE MEAL

The richness of the dried duck invades the pork in this dish. It is common food in Hong Kong, but very uncommon in this country. You might have to get used to the "cured" flavor of the dried duck.

- ¼ dried duck, hacked (page 20) into ¼-inch-wide pieces
- 1 pound lean ground pork
- 8–10 water chestnuts, coarsely chopped
- 2 tablespoons Chinese rice wine or dry sherry
- 2 tablespoons light soy sauce
- ½ teaspoon grated fresh ginger
- 1 tablespoon cornstarch
- 1 egg
- 1 teaspoon sesame oil
- ⅛ teaspoon freshly ground black pepper
- 1 green onion, chopped fine

Cut the duck and soak it in fresh water for 2 hours. Change the water and bring to a simmer. Immediately turn off the stove and leave the duck, covered, in the water for ½ hour. Drain and discard the water.

Place all ingredients, except the duck, into a bowl and mix well. Place in a steaming bowl or glass pie plate. Top with the duck slices. Steam in a bamboo steamer (page 106) for 30 minutes.

TEA-SMOKED DUCK

SERVES 6–8 AS PART OF A CHINESE MEAL

This is probably the second most famous Chinese method of preparing duck. In terms of Hong Kong popularity it stands right behind the famous Peking Duck.

1 4-pound duck, split in half
1 teaspoon salt
¼ teaspoon freshly ground black pepper
3 tablespoons dry sherry or Chinese rice wine
2 tablespoons sesame oil

FOR SMOKING
½ cup alder or hickory sawdust
¼ cup black tea leaves
2 teaspoons sugar

4 cups peanut oil for deep-frying

Split the duck, using poultry shears and a cleaver, and pat dry. Marinate the halves in the salt, pepper, wine, and sesame oil for 2 hours. Blanch in boiling water for 2 minutes. Allow to dry on a rack for 1 hour.

Smoke in a wok or a Cameron smoker (page 13) using the wood, tea, and sugar. If you use a wok simply line the bottom with heavy aluminum foil and put the wood, tea, and sugar on the foil. Place a cake rack or steaming rack into the wok and put the duck on the rack. Bring the temperature up until you get some smoke, then turn it down a bit and watch it carefully, whether using the Cameron or the wok. Smoke for 20 minutes.

Place each half in a glass pie plate or steaming dish and steam for 45 minutes. Allow to cool and deep-fry in peanut oil until golden brown and crispy.

NOTE: This dish may also be done with chicken.

CHINESE DUCK SALAD

SERVES 4 AS PART OF A CHINESE MEAL

I developed this dish one night since I had a bit of roast duck left over. That does not happen very often. This salad is so good, however, that it would be worth your time to roast a duck just for this dish.

- ½ pound cooked boneless duck meat, cut julienne (I prefer the smoked duck)
- ¾ pound bean sprouts
- ¼ cup fresh chopped coriander

DRESSING

- ¼ cup rice wine vinegar (Japanese)
- 2 tablespoons light soy sauce
- 2 tablespoons sesame oil
- ½ teaspoon sugar
- 2 tablespoons freshly toasted sesame seeds
- Black pepper, freshly ground, to taste

- Iceberg lettuce, shredded, for base

Place the ingredients for the salad in a bowl. Mix the dressing separately and toss with the salad. Serve over shredded iceberg lettuce.

DUCK SOUP, CHINESE STYLE

SERVES 8 AS PART OF A CHINESE MEAL

This sounds like an old Groucho Marx movie, I know. Realize, however, that the Chinese are very frugal cooks. Little or nothing is wasted. When the Peking Duck is finished, the bones go into soup and it is not uncommon to see a restaurant advertise its Peking Duck "Cooked Three Ways." This means that the duck skin and pancakes are served first. The meat of the duck is then served with vegetables, and finally, the carcass comes back as soup.

This is easy and delicious, so don't throw out those duck bones.

2 quarts Chinese Chicken Soup Stock (page 126)
6 dried Chinese mushrooms, soaked in 1 cup warm water, the water reserved
Pinch of ground white pepper
1 cup Chinese greens (bok choy, Napa)
Bones from 1 roast duck
3 green onions, chopped
1 teaspoon sesame oil
1 cup cooked duck meat, cut julienne
Salt to taste
1 ounce cellophane noodles *(sai fun)* (page 25)

GARNISH
1 raw egg
1 tablespoon chopped Chinese parsley

Bring the stock to a simmer and add the mushrooms and the water in which they were soaked. Add the pepper, greens, and bones. Simmer for 1 hour.

Drain the stock and discard all solids except the mushrooms. Cut the mushrooms julienne and return to the stockpot. Add the green onions, sesame oil, and cooked duck meat and taste for salt. Drop the noodles into the pot and simmer until they are just tender, about 5 minutes.

Place the soup in a tureen and add the shelled raw egg, whole. It will cook on the way to the table. Add the parsley garnish. Stir the egg into the soup at the table.

LOOED DUCK FEET

SERVES 8, AT LEAST, AS PART OF A CHINESE MEAL

I told you that the Chinese never waste food. The feet of the duck are blanched and peeled. You can buy them in Chinatown all ready to be cooked. When Mary Young, my adopted Chinese aunt, and I go to a dim sum lunch in San Francisco, we always have this great delicacy. You simply chew the gelatinous meat off the bone and spit out the toes. Are you still with me?

8 duck feet, peeled
2 cups Looing Sauce (page 231)
1 teaspoon sesame oil for garnish

Soak the duck feet overnight in water in the refrigerator. Prepare the feet for cooking by cutting off the toenails, if this has not already been done. Blanch the feet in boiling water for 3 minutes and drain. Place in a stove-top casserole and add the looing sauce. Bring to a simmer and cook, covered, until the feet are very tender, about 2 hours. Remove from the sauce to a serving plate and garnish with the sesame oil.

NOTE: You can prepare these ahead of time and simply reheat them either in the sauce or put them in a bowl with very little sauce and reheat them in your bamboo steamer (page 106).

Greece

GREEK DUCK WITH OLIVES

SERVES 6

Duck is not as common in Greece or Rome as it is in China. This dish, however, is a smash. I tasted it the first time in a fine restaurant on the outskirts of Athens and the recipe is simple to duplicate. You will have no problems with this one.

1 4-pound duck, cut into 6 pieces
3 tablespoons olive oil
1 yellow onion, peeled and sliced
2 cups Greek Tomato Sauce (page 232)
½ cup dry red wine
1 cup green olives
Salt and freshly ground black pepper to taste

Heat a 6-quart stove-top casserole and add the oil. Brown the duck pieces and remove from the pan. Sauté the onion and then add all ingredients to the pot. Cover and bring to a simmer. You may need to add a bit of water. Simmer until tender, about 1½ hours. Watch that it does not dry out, in which case you must add a bit more water.

DUCK GRILLED GREEK STYLE

This one is typical of the whole concept of Greek grilling. You split a duck down the middle, rub it with olive oil, garlic, oregano, and salt and pepper, and put it on the grill. Or you can broil it carefully in the oven.

Do not overcook the duck. The inside should be very moist and tender. Garnish the duck with fresh lemon juice just prior to serving.

Italy

In Roman times the duck was prized by the wealthy, who thought up all kinds of ways to serve this bird.

DUCK WITH TURNIPS APICIUS

The most interesting duck dish that I found in early Western recipes comes from Apicius, around the first century. Craig, my cooking assistant, tried one of these and we both thought it was interesting, but you have to be a serious lover of turnips to get into this one.

The recipe is described in this way:

The duck is simmered in water and aniseed for 30 minutes. It is then stuffed with a bread dressing seasoned with leeks and coriander. Turnips are boiled, mashed, and spread over the stuffed duck, which is then roasted for 1½ hours. A sauce is made, using the popular herbs of that time, mixed with a bit of wine vinegar and the pan gravy. The herbs were cumin, coriander, pepper, and fennel.

The result is rather strange-looking by contemporary standards, but it is moist and tasty.

Give me a Peking Duck any day!

Small Birds

In the ancient world small birds were considered great delicacies. They were enjoyed in China, and still are, a fried quail, Chinese style, being one of the finest bird dishes I know.

We Americans do not relish small birds much since we seem to think that they are too much work to eat. We want big chunks of meat so we will enjoy a chicken or turkey more than a pigeon or squab. But we are missing a flavor, albeit in a small quantity, that was celebrated at the great banquets of ancient Rome. Apicius, the first-century cookbook author, loved figpeckers, small birds with a very funny name, and squabs and pigeons of all kinds. His Roman friends loved them as well and went from these small birds to a great deal of ostentatious nonsense, serving flamingo tongues and brains with eggs, and even roasted canary. How many of those creatures would you have to kill before you had a luncheon platter? And the ancient Greeks used to enjoy roasted peacock!

I prepared and taped a whole show on small birds in ancient cuisines . . . but you will never see it. I realized after the taping that even though we raise all kinds of quails, pigeons, squabs, and game hens for public consumption, I would never get away with chopping up little birds on the air. I have too many children in my audience who would think me evil. I wish I could make them understand that we all must subsist on the resources of the world, and there is little difference between enjoying a small bird and a hamburger. The cow felt no better about the meal than did the bird. I hope you will try these dishes; they are some of the finest foods that I have ever found.

China

BROWNED SQUAB WITH ROASTED SALT AND PEPPER

SERVES 4 AS PART OF A CHINESE MEAL

Squab, a fancy name for pigeon, is very popular with the Chinese. The meat is dark and moist and will respond to several methods of cooking. In ancient China these birds were eaten by rich and poor alike.

- **2 squabs**
- **Salt and freshly ground black pepper to taste**
- **1 teaspoon dark soy sauce**
- **3–4 cups peanut oil for deep-frying**

Cut each squab in half. Rub with the salt, pepper, and soy. Deep-fry in the hot oil, at 375°, until lightly browned, about 15 minutes. Do not overcook.

Hack (page 20) the squab into bite-sized slices and arrange on a heated platter.

Serve with Roasted Salt and Pepper (below). The pieces of bird are lightly dipped into the salt and pepper mixture.

ROASTED SALT AND PEPPER

Heat a wok and add 3 tablespoons kosher salt, 2 tablespoons freshly ground coarse black pepper, and 1 tablespoon Szechwan peppercorns. Heat until the aroma is bright and the salt begins to brown a tiny bit, stirring all the time. Cool and grind in a food blender. Serve with poultry.

FRIED QUAIL, CHINESE STYLE

SERVES 6–8 AS PART OF A CHINESE MEAL

This is a delicious dish. Since the bird is simmered first in the looing sauce, it is very moist, even after a quick deep-frying.

3 cups Looing Sauce (page 231)
4 quails, split in half
4 cups peanut oil for deep-frying

Bring the looing sauce to a boil and put in the quails. Bring back to a simmer and cook for 4 minutes. Remove from the sauce, drain, and pat dry with paper towels. Deep-fry in oil at 375° until golden, about 3 minutes. Do not overcook.

BROWNED QUAIL, CHINESE STYLE

The quail is generally a bit smaller than the squab, but each responds to cooking in the same way. This is a delicious dish, though given the price of quail it is a tad expensive.

Prepare the quail just as you do the squab in the recipe on page 305. Serve with Roasted Salt and Pepper (page 305) and a lemon squeeze.

FRIED SQUAB, CHINESE STYLE

The squab is cooked in exactly the same manner as the quail above, but it will need a bit more time at each step since the bird is a little larger. Simmer in the looing sauce for 8 minutes and then deep-fry for 5 minutes.

TEA-SMOKED GAME HEN

SERVES 3–4 AS PART OF A CHINESE MEAL

Game hens are a relatively recent bird, a development of modern agricultural science. However, in old China similar birds were common and this method of cooking remains a classic.

1 1½-pound game hen
Salt and freshly ground black pepper to taste
2 tablespoons dry sherry or Chinese rice wine
2 tablespoons sesame oil
3 tablespoons jasmine tea leaves
4 tablespoons alder or hickory sawdust
6 cups peanut oil for deep-frying

Cut the bird in half, using poultry shears or a Chinese cleaver.

Rub the halves with the salt and pepper, wine, and sesame oil. Allow to marinate for 2 hours.

Dip the halves into boiling water for 1 minute. Remove and place on a rack for drying.

Smoke the halves in a Cameron smoker (page 13) for 15 minutes using the tea leaves and the alder or hickory sawdust.

Place the halves on a plate and steam in a bamboo steamer (page 106) for 20 minutes. Allow the pieces to cool and then deep-fry in hot peanut oil, at 375°, until golden brown and crispy, about 4–5 minutes.

Greece

QUAIL IN TOMATO SAUCE, GREEK STYLE

The great thing about always having a bit of Greek Tomato Sauce in your refrigerator is that you can prepare Greek meals in a hurry. This is a simple method of cooking quail that is common in the tavernas of Athens.

- **6 quails, each split in half**
- **¼ cup olive oil**
- **1½ cups Greek Tomato Sauce (page 232)**
- **½ cup dry red wine**
- **Salt and freshly ground black pepper to taste**

Heat a large covered frying pan or *sauteuse*. Cut the quails in half and pan-brown in the olive oil. Add the tomato sauce and wine. Cover and simmer 45 minutes to 1 hour, or until the legs move easily. Add salt and pepper to taste.

ROASTED QUAIL APPETIZERS HOMER

SERVES 6

In ancient Greece small birds were very popular at a formal feast. Homer, the great poet, was particularly fond of thrushes and he sang an epic poem about them, a poem entitled "Epikichlides." This recipe is probably as close as we can come to the object of his affection.

- ¼ pound butter
- 6 quails
- 2 slices toasted bread, cut into cubes
- ½ pound crumbled feta cheese
- ½ teaspoon thyme
- ½ teaspoon oregano
- Salt and freshly ground black pepper to taste
- 1 clove garlic, crushed

Heat the butter in a large frying pan. Roll the birds in the hot butter. Butter a baking dish with some of the melted butter and spread the bread cubes in the dish. Stuff the birds with the feta and place them on top of the bread. Stir the herbs, seasonings, and garlic into the remaining butter and baste each bird. Bake, uncovered, in a preheated oven at 375° for 40 minutes to 1 hour, depending on your taste.

GRILLED SQUAB, GREEK STYLE

SERVES 3–6, DEPENDING ON HOW YOU WISH TO FINALLY CUT THE BIRDS!

Another example of the brilliant background of Greek grilling. Remember that the Greeks invented the grill as we know it and they still use rather simple and basic ingredients. The results are always delicious.

- 3 squabs, ¾ to 1 pound each, split down the back and "butterflied" or flattened out
- 3 tablespoons olive oil
- 2 cloves garlic, crushed
- ½ teaspoon whole oregano, crushed by hand
- Juice of 1 lemon
- Salt and freshly ground black pepper to taste

Mix all the ingredients together in a large bowl. Allow the birds to marinate for 1 hour. Place the birds on a barbecue grill, at low heat, and grill 15 minutes bone side down. Turn each and grill 20 minutes on the skin side.

Be careful not to allow fires to start when the fat begins to drip on the charcoal.

Cook a total of 35 minutes or until the juice of the bird is clear and not pink or bloody.

Italy

ROAST QUAIL EDMONDO

Trattoria Edmondo is a wonderful place to eat. To say it is informal is putting it mildly! The place is a collection of people who look like character actors for wild Italian movies and the owner, Edmondo, stands beside your table and slices the bread on his chest. Plates of olives, sausages, and pepperoni come as you sit down. It is in the style of a very old Roman establishment. His quail is just outstanding and this recipe is somewhat close to what he does. The treatment is really quite simple.

The birds are split in half and pan-browned in olive oil and garlic, along with a bit of salt and pepper. A small amount of dry red wine is added to the pan along with some Italian Tomato Sauce (page 237). The pan is then covered and gently simmered until the birds are tender.

They can be served with a side of pasta, the sauce becoming the glory of the evening.

GAME HENS WITH ROSEMARY AND GARLIC

The smell of rosemary and garlic in the air always makes me think of the back streets of the villages on the edge of Rome. You can have a fine Roman party with this dish and you can even urge your guests to place themselves on their sides on cushions and eat only with their fingers. Slaves had to eat sitting upright in Rome, but free citizens reclined. This would be a great dish for such an eating method.

3 game hens, split in half
¾ cup olive oil
4 cloves garlic, crushed
3 tablespoons dry sherry
3 dashes Tabasco
1 tablespoon finely chopped fresh rosemary
Juice of 1 lemon
Salt and freshly ground black pepper to taste

Split each bird in half, using either a Chinese cleaver or poultry shears. Set aside.

Using a very large bowl mix the remaining ingredients together. Marinate the bird halves in this mixture for 1 hour, turning often.

Broil in an electric oven, 7 or 8 minutes on a side, or on a charcoal barbecue. I prefer the charcoal, but be sure not to have the coals too hot. Cook to your preference.

VARIATION: You can use this same recipe for squab or quail. Just remember to cut down on the cooking time according to the size of the bird.

HINT: WHEN CUTTING POULTRY OR LARGE FISH with a Chinese cleaver, save your hand by placing a piece of rubber garden hose, cut along one side, over the top of the cleaver. In this way you can use your hand for pounding on the cleaver without hurting yourself.

QUAIL OR SQUAB IN CREAMED ITALIAN SAUCE

This dish is done in the same style as Roast Quail Edmondo (page 310). Instead of the red wine use a little white wine along with the Italian Tomato Sauce. Just before serving remove the halves to a serving platter and add a few tablespoons of whipping cream to the sauce remaining in the pan. Bring to a simmer and pour over the birds. This is just delicious!

Meats

Lamb

We are talking ancient food here. Men and women have eaten lamb for thousands and thousands of years. Sheep bones have been found in the caves Peking Man inhabited half a million years ago, although domestication of the sheep probably did not begin until about 12,000 years ago. At that time wild goats and sheep were attracted to the fields of wild grain that began to grow as the world climate changed. Domestication eventually followed as the villagers moved to protect this generous grain supply. The first hard evidence of sheep raising dates from 8920 B.C. in Iraq and Romania, and sheep appear to have been raised in prehistoric China on the loess plateau, a region where the ancient winds had deposited rich soils.

Italy and Greece still have their own ancient traditions of eating lamb. Lamb was raised in Greece from prehistoric times and remains the favorite meat of its people. Today about three million lambs are eaten annually in Greece, and they are cooked according to recipes that go back to the earliest days of recorded history. I spent time in Greece during the Eastertide and feasted on lamb that was cooked the way the Greeks have always cooked it, and I do mean always. Olive oil, lemon juice, oregano, and thyme. The result is just wonderful.

Lamb in the Roman kitchen has always been important. To this day the Romans claim that they have the best pastureland in Italy, and thus the best lamb. I shall not argue. Every part of the animal is celebrated in the Eternal City, and the innards seem to have an especially high place in the celebration. The Romans would rather eat a slice of lamb than a piece of fish, though they are only thirty miles from the sea.

I expect the Chinese were the first to couple lamb with its best seasoning, garlic. In the *Book of Songs,* a volume from around 600 B.C., lamb is offered with garlic, and to this day in the northern regions of China the dish is made the same way . . . the very same.

I wish Americans would stop overcooking lamb so that it could be enjoyed more in our culture. We still seem to be suffering from the argument common in the Old West. It was the cattleman against the sheepherder. Lamb is, I believe, the finest of the red meats.

You might also wish to consider the following recipes:

Greek Lamb and Pasta Salad *(page 162)*
Chinese Lamb and Leeks *(page 519)*

China

LAMB HOT POT, MONGOLIAN STYLE

The first time I tasted this dish was in Beijing. I enjoyed my time there but I was surprised . . . no, I was somewhat hurt by the quality of the food. I tried to get into good restaurants, but that is hard for a Westerner unless you have a local with you. I finally managed to get into the most famous Lamb Hot Pot restaurant in Beijing. When I left I was filled, content, and yet still disappointed. I believe the problem with quality stems from the fact that there is very little refrigeration in China and to make matters worse, much of the good-quality food is shipped out of China to Hong Kong and America. China needs the money, and Chinese eaters suffer for it. I think you can get the best Chinese food in Hong Kong and, secondly, in San Francisco. New York and Seattle do very well, too.

In any case, here is the dish. You can do it at home with little effort as long as you have a Hoko or Hot Pot.

Lamb, boneless and lean, sliced into strips, very thin
Chinese Chicken Soup Stock *(page 126) or* Basic Lamb Stock *(page 143)* for the Hoko Pot
Napa cabbage, chopped as for coleslaw, *or* bok choy, chopped
Bean curd, cut into ½-inch cubes
Bean thread or cellophane noodles, soaked for 20 minutes

The lamb is sliced very thin and cooked in a Hot Pot filled with bubbling chicken or lamb broth. Each guest is to have his own plate of thinly sliced lamb. Napa and bean curd may also be added to the pot and removed when you will. The noodles can be added at any time, but they are generally added as one of the last ingredients. Small brass strainers can be provided for each person to use in claiming his/her portion of the pot.

Each guest cooks his lamb and then dips it into a sauce. The dip sauces vary and several recipes are given on page 229. You may wish to create your own, given any of the following ingredients:

Light soy sauce
Sesame oil
Ginger, freshly grated
Hot pepper oil
Chinese rice wine or dry sherry
Worcestershire sauce
Sugar, just a pinch
Green onions, chopped
Chinese parsley, chopped

The meal is concluded with the consumption of the soup. For full instructions on using the Hoko Pot, see page 129.

MONGOLIAN LAMB

SERVES 6 AS PART OF A CHINESE MEAL

Great grills are used for this dish in famous Mongolian restaurants in China. You may want to use a tabletop grill of some sort and cook this at the table in front of your guests. I think the dish is just fine straight from the kitchen wok. It is rich!

- 1 pound lean, boneless lamb shoulder, sliced thin in 1-inch-wide strips

MARINADE

- 2 tablespoons oyster sauce
- 3 green onions, chopped
- 1 tablespoon chili sauce (from catsup department)
- Freshly ground black pepper to taste (I like lots)

FOR CHOWING

- 2 tablespoons peanut oil
- ½ teaspoon salt
- 3 cloves garlic, diced fine

GARNISH

- 2 cups iceberg lettuce, shredded as for tacos
- 3 green onions, chopped
- 1 tablespoon sesame oil

I often freeze the lamb just a bit so that I can slice it very thin. Mix the marinade and soak the meat in same for 30 minutes.

Heat a wok and add the oil, salt, and garlic. Chow just until the garlic begins to change color and then add ½ of the marinated meat. Chow over very high heat until done to your taste. Remove to a warm plate and chow the second half. Serve over the lettuce and add the onion and sesame oil garnish.

VARIATION: You might want to serve the meat along with lettuce leaves that can be rolled like burritos instead of the chopped lettuce. Peking Pancakes (page 548) are also just delicious filled with the meat and shredded lettuce.

LAMB AND TOMATO SAUCE, GREEK STYLE

SERVES 6–8

This is a very common way of serving the favorite meat of Greece. Since it uses tomato, we can assume the recipe is rather recent, only about four hundred years old, but this same dish can be found throughout Greece.

- **3 tablespoons olive oil**
- **3 pounds lean lamb shoulder, bone in, cut into serving pieces**
- **Salt and freshly ground black pepper to taste**
- **2 cups Basic Lamb Stock (page 143) Basic Chicken Stock (page 144)**
- **1 cup dry red wine**
- **3 cloves garlic, finely chopped**
- **2 yellow onions, peeled and coarsely chopped**
- **1 cup chopped parsley**
- **¼ teaspoon allspice**
- **¼ teaspoon cinnamon**
- **½ teaspoon oregano**
- **2 cups coarsely chopped ripe tomatoes**
- **Salt and freshly ground black pepper to taste**

Heat a large frying pan and add the olive oil. Brown the cut-up pieces of lamb, in 2 batches, on both sides. Season with the salt and pepper. Place the meat in a 6-quart casserole, along with the broth and wine, leaving the oil in the frying pan. Reheat the frying pan and sauté the garlic and onions until clear. Add the remaining ingredients, except the final salt and pepper, and sauté just until the tomatoes cook down a bit. Add this mixture to the casserole, along with salt and pepper to taste. Bring to a simmer, cover, and cook until the meat is very tender, about 1½ hours.

LAMB WITH CHEESE AND PASTA

SERVES 4 AS A MAIN COURSE

This is a tasty way to use up a little leftover lamb, providing you have not overcooked the lamb in the first place.

- ½ pound fettucine (dry)
- ½ cup olive oil
- 3 cloves garlic
- ¾ to 1 pound medium-rare lamb, cut julienne
- 1 cup grated kefalotyri cheese (page 31)
- ¼ cup chopped parsley
- Salt and pepper to taste

Bring a pot of water to boil for the pasta.

Heat a frying pan and sauté the garlic in the oil. Just as the pasta is finishing, add the cooked lamb to the hot garlic oil and sauté for just a moment. Toss the meat with the drained pasta, along with all other ingredients.

LAMB WITH ORZO PASTA, GREEK STYLE

SERVES 6–8 AS A MAIN COURSE

This is another dish that I first tasted at Taverna Sigalas, in Monastiraki Square, in Athens. The food that they serve is not complex, and while it is typical of taverna food it is of very good quality and seasoned nicely. I think it is better than most of the fancier eating houses in the city.

This is an exceptionally good dish that is just great for entertaining.

3 pounds boneless lamb shoulder
3 tablespoons olive oil for pan-browning
Salt and freshly ground black pepper to taste
6 cups Basic Lamb Stock (page 143) or Basic Chicken Stock (page 144)
½ cup olive oil
2 cups orzo pasta (page 32)
1½ cups peeled and chopped yellow onion
2 large ripe tomatoes, chopped
2 teaspoons dried dillweed
¼ cup chopped parsley
Juice of 1 lemon for garnish

In a stove-top Dutch oven brown the boneless lamb shoulder in the olive oil. Add the salt and pepper. Add enough stock to come halfway up the side of the meat, and simmer, covered, until very tender, about 2 hours.

Remove the meat from the pot and set aside, covered to keep warm. Remove the fat from the stock in the pan and add additional stock, if necessary, to make up a total of 4 cups. Remove the stock from the pan and set aside.

Heat the Dutch oven again and add ½ cup olive oil. Add the orzo pasta and toss for a minute. Add the chopped yellow onion and sauté until the onion is clear. Stir in the tomatoes, dillweed, and parsley.

Return the meat to the pot, along with the 4 cups of stock. Cover and simmer until the broth is absorbed and the pasta is tender, about 30 minutes. Add the juice of 1 lemon just before serving.

NOTE: If the dish is too wet when the pasta is tender, continue to cook for a few more minutes with the lid off to reduce the sauce.

Serve with the lamb on top of the pasta.

ROAST LAMB, GREEK STYLE

SERVES 4–6

Nothing can equal the scent of a lamb roasting on Easter Day in the back streets of a Greek village. I suppose that lamb on Easter is the annual culinary highlight of the Greek diet. I have added a bit of olive oil to keep this roast moist, but you would not have to do this with a whole lamb.

1 5–6-pound leg of lamb
½ cup olive oil
3 cloves garlic, crushed
1 teaspoon whole oregano, crushed by hand
Salt and freshly ground black pepper to taste

FOR RARE LAMB: Allow the lamb to come to room temperature. Heat your oven to 400°. Mix the oil, garlic, and oregano together and rub the leg completely. Season with salt and pepper and place on baking rack in a pan. Insert a meat thermometer in the thickest part of the leg, being careful not to touch the bone. Bake at 400° for 40 minutes, so that the meat can brown. Turn the oven down to 325° and bake for an additional 40 to 50 minutes, or until the thermometer registers 140°.

Remove the meat from the oven and allow it to sit ½ hour before slicing. It will continue to cook during this time.

FOR MEDIUM LAMB: Follow the above instructions but cook a bit longer so that the thermometer registers 145° to 150°.

Slice thin and serve with some of the pan juices.

LAMB RIB CHOPS, BROILED GREEK STYLE

Lamb recipes do not have to take long to prepare. This recipe is very quick, and flavorful as well. Just don't overcook the meat.

Remove the bone from lamb rib chops or lamb shoulder steak. I prefer the shoulder steak as it is a bit more moist.

Pound the meat fairly thin, using a metal meat pounder (page 16). Brush with olive oil and garlic, and sprinkle with salt and pepper, and oregano. Grill or broil quickly so that the meat remains tender. Use high heat for this.

SOUVLAKI

MAKES 8 SANDWICHES

This is an old Athenian dish that will make you wonder about who invented the first takeout food. These lamb-laden skewers are for sale all over the major Greek cities, and the flavor is made even more exciting by the grilled bread with the yogurt dripping down the sides.

- 2 pounds of lean lamb cut into 1- inch-square cubes

MARINADE

- ½ cup olive oil
- 1 cup red wine
- 1 teaspoon salt
- Freshly ground black pepper to taste
- 1 teaspoon oregano
- 1 teaspoon whole dried mint, crushed by hand
- 3 cloves garlic, crushed

- 8 loaves of Pita Bread with Olive Oil, Grilled (page 554)

GARNISHES

- Purple onions, sliced paper thin
- Tomatoes, ripe and sliced thin
- Plain yogurt

Marinate cubes of meat in a large bowl. Mix two or three times during a 2-hour period.

Place on wooden skewers and broil, turning once, until tender but still a bit pink on the inside.

Serve in a grilled pita loaf with onions, tomatoes, and yogurt on top.

NOTE: This dish is also just great with pork.

BARLEY PUDDING WITH LAMB

SERVES 6 AS A MAIN COURSE

This dish goes back to the second century B.C. The flavors are unusual for us but this kind of food was evidently very common in ancient times. I have added a bit of garlic to the old recipe and I think that you will love the result.

6 cups water
2 teaspoons salt
2 pounds boneless lamb, cut into serving chunks
3 cloves garlic, crushed
1 cup barley
2 tablespoons olive oil

Place the water, salt, lamb, and garlic in a 4-quart heavy covered saucepan. Bring to a boil, turn to a simmer, cover, and cook for 2 hours. Remove all from the pots, reserving the broth. Remove the fat from the broth and add enough additional water to make 6 cups.

Place the barley in a grain grinder and grind very coarsely. You want something like groats or bulgur wheat, in terms of texture. Stir the olive oil into the barley groats and place in the pan. Return the meat and measured broth to the pan and bring to a light boil. Simmer, covered, for 25 minutes, or until the barley is soft and tasty and the liquid is absorbed.

Serve this with crusty Italian bread or with pita bread. Eat the pudding with the bread for a rather heavy but simply delicious meal.

GROUND MEAT ON SKEWERS

SERVES 8

This is a very creative version of meat on a stick. Just off Monastiraki Square in Athens is a place that puts ground meat on metal skewers and then broils it. The result is delicious, very close to the famous "gyros" sandwiches that are made from ground meat that is grilled upright on a rotating spit. This is just great for a party as you can prepare everything ahead of time and then cook these for your guests at the last minute. Use the firebrick grill (page 327).

1 pound ground pork
1 pound ground lamb
1 teaspoon each salt and pepper
3–6 cloves garlic, crushed, to taste
Juice of 1 lemon
1 teaspoon whole oregano, hand-crushed
2 tablespoons ouzo
4 loaves Pita Bread with Olive Oil, Grilled (page 554)

GARNISHES

Tzatziki (page 93)
Purple onions, peeled and sliced paper thin
Parsley, chopped
Cherry tomatoes, broiled on metal skewers until tender

Mix all and mold on flat metal skewers. The skewers will have to be about ⅜ inch wide and 18 inches long in size. You may have to have these made for you at a sheet-metal shop. Thin skewers just will not work as the meat will fall off. Put about ¼ pound of meat on each oiled skewer and sort of press it until it is the shape of a sausage. Place the meat sticks on an oiled baking sheet and bake for 20 minutes at 375°. Brush with olive oil and garlic for final grilling over the firebrick grill.

Pull the metal skewers from the meat as you serve them in the grilled pita bread. Fill each loaf with the garnishes of tzatziki, sliced purple onions, parsley, and tiny broiled tomatoes.

GRILLED LAMB CUBES, GREEK STYLE

This is a simple dish that one sees in the villages outside of Athens and on the islands. It is easy to prepare, and the flavors will be very close to what you would find in beautiful Greece.

Lamb cubes, about 1 inch square, are marinated in olive oil, garlic, oregano, and fresh lemon juice for about 3 hours. The meat cubes are then put on sticks and grilled over charcoal fires. Your barbecue will do well. Add a bit of salt and pepper before serving. Do not overcook the meat. This can be avoided by not creating too hot a fire. Just cut down a bit on the number of charcoal briquets that you use.

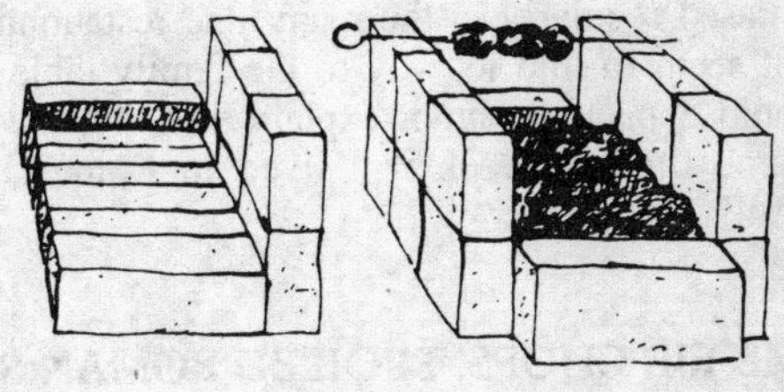

ROAST LAMB, ITALIAN STYLE

Young roast lamb is the expected dish for Easter in Rome. While the Romans have loved lamb since the time of the Empire it still seems to be most popular on holidays. It can be purchased regularly in the many fine restaurants, but it does not seem to find its way to the family table as often as I would expect. I cannot explain this, but I would eat lamb three times a week if I lived in Rome. It is just wonderful!

LAMB RIB CHOPS, BROILED ROMAN STYLE

The Romans have loved mint since ancient times. A typical bit of grilling genius can be accomplished by using the Lamb Rib Chops, Broiled Greek Style (page 324), and using dried mint in the recipe instead of oregano. The flavor is refreshing . . . and now you know why the rest of us began using mint sauce or jelly on our lamb. It is an old Roman custom.

Pork

The story is absurd! When Charles Lamb was asked how people first came to realize that roast pork is delicious, he spun a charming tale—though historically it is out of whack. He told of a child in ancient China who returned to his home after a serious fire. The family's pet pig had been burned in the blaze and the boy tasted roast pork for the first time. Come now . . . are you going to tell me that architecture, the building of houses, developed before the discovery of cooking? It could not be, since people were roasting meat while living in caves. No, the simple truth is that pork has been popular since ancient times, and each of our three cultures learned to cook the piggy in the early days.

To this day pork is so prized in China that it is listed among the "Eight Marvels" of food, and it is listed not once but *twice,* as pork and as ham. In Italy there is an old phrase that refers to the pig as having "thirteen flavors," simply because the animal is so versatile in the kitchen.

Please remember that everything on or in the pig is used. Nearly every morsel is turned into food or some other product. The skin becomes leather and can be used for skin grafts for human burn victims. The glands go into pharmaceuticals, the stomach for pepsin, and the inedible fat for lubricants. The hair goes into hairbrushes, paintbrushes, insulation, and upholstery. No wonder 400 million pigs live on this good earth. We need them!

The pig was probably the second animal to be domesticated, the dog being the first. The meat is easy to preserve and the results are delicious. It is no wonder that the ancient Chinese began to domesticate pigs as early as 5000 B.C., and while a pork taboo began in ancient Egypt and Israel, the Chinese and Greeks have never wavered from their culinary commitment to the porker.

While you enjoy the following recipes you might also consider:

Pork with Leeks and Black Beans *(page 520)*
Spareribs with Black Beans and Pepper Sauce *(page 114)*
Garlic Ribs with Green Pepper and Black Beans *(page 115)*
Steamed Pork with Salted Eggs *(page 258)*

China

BARBECUED PORK STRIPS
(Cha Shao)

SERVES 6–8 FOR A DIM SUM SNACK OR A COURSE IN A CHINESE DINNER

This is the most commonly known Chinese pork dish in America, and I do not know why. Usually American-Chinese restaurants use very lean cuts of pork and the result is a dry and tasteless version of the real Chinese delight. That's why you put all that mustard and sesame seed on the pork. It is too dry to eat otherwise. (Boy, am I talking American heresy here!) A little fat in the meat is necessary for good flavor, according to the Chinese.

For this version choose pork butt that has little streaks of fat in it and the result will be juicy and flavorful.

2 pounds boneless pork butt

MARINADE

2 tablespoons Chinese Chicken Soup Stock (page 126)
2 tablespoons dark soy sauce
1 tablespoon soybean condiment *(mein see)*
1 tablespoon Chinese rice wine or dry sherry
1½ tablespoons honey
¾ teaspoon salt
1 large clove garlic, crushed
2 tablespoons hoisin sauce (page 26)
A few drops of red food coloring

Cut the pork into long strips 1½ to 2 inches square. Mix all for the marinade and marinate the meat for 3 hours, unrefrigerated, or 6 hours in the refrigerator. Turn the strips every hour or so.

Preheat the oven to 350°. Place a large cake pan half filled with water on the lowest shelf of your oven. This will catch drips from the meat and prevent smoking. Place the meat strips directly on an oven rack and put in the top position of the oven. Be sure that all of the meat is over the dripping pan. Roast for 45 minutes without disturbing the meat. Then, turn the heat up to 450° and roast for an additional 15 minutes or until the pork strips are crisp and a rich brown color. Slice the meat and serve it hot or cold . . . or use in other dishes as directed.

HINT: TO MAKE HOT CHINESE MUSTARD simply purchase a can of Colman's English dry mustard. Boil a bit of water and allow it to cool. Mix the water with dry mustard to the desired consistency. Keep stirring the mustard until it is as hot as you like it. The longer you stir the hotter it will get!

BARBECUED SPARERIBS

SERVES 4–6 AS A COURSE IN A CHINESE DINNER

In Hong Kong you can purchase these ribs already prepared, and still warm, just as you have been able to do for one thousand years in China. Since pork has been popular almost since the beginning of Chinese history we can bet that a lot of these ribs have been consumed.

MARINADE

- **2 cloves garlic, crushed**
- **3 tablespoons dark soy sauce**
- **2 tablespoons dry sherry or Chinese rice wine**
- **1 teaspoon freshly grated ginger**
- **½ tablespoon brown sugar**
- **½ tablespoon sesame oil**
- **½ teaspoon five-spice powder (page 35)**
- **1 tablespoon hoisin sauce**
- **1 teaspoon pepper sauce, such as Tabasco or Mexican Hot Sauce**
- **1 tablespoon catsup**

- **1 2-pound side of pork spareribs, cut into 2 or 3 pieces**

Mix all for the marinade and pour in a bowl over the ribs. Coat the ribs well by rubbing in the sauce and marinate, turning now and then, for 3 hours, unrefrigerated.

Bake on a preheated roasting pan in a 400° oven for 35–40 minutes. Serve hot or at room temperature.

If you wish to have a bit more "crunch" on the ribs broil them a bit after baking. Broil them just until they are nicely browned.

CRISPY ROAST PORK

SERVES 8–10 AS PART OF A CHINESE MEAL

This is the richest pork dish I know in terms of the Chinese table. It is rich because it is very fatty. I love this meat, sometimes called *litchen,* though I do not allow myself this fatty luxury very often. I hope, once you taste this, that you will be as disciplined. It may be hard to stop eating!

I found this recipe in a cookbook published in the Chinese community in Seattle. It is called *Flavors of China* and has many recipes that are very typical of Chinese home cooking.

2–2½ pounds fresh side of pork, lean, with skin
1 teaspoon salt

MARINADE

1 tablespoon soybean condiment *(mein see)*
1 tablespoon dark soy sauce
¼ teaspoon salt
1 teaspoon sugar
1 clove garlic, crushed
1 teaspoon fresh ginger, grated

Lay pork on a board, skin side up, and pierce it all over with an ice pick. Rub salt into the pork on both sides. Mix all of the ingredients for the marinade together. Place the meat on a broiling-pan rack, skin side down, and rub the meaty side with the marinade. Let stand for 1 hour.

Heat the oven to 350°. Turn the meat skin side up and place the pan on the middle rack in the oven. Roast, uncovered, for 1½ hours, piercing the skin in many places with an ice pick. Do this 3 or 4 times during the baking. Then, turn the oven on broil and broil the meat for 15 to 20 minutes, or until the skin is crisp. Be careful that you do not burn the meat at this point. You want it to be a dark golden brown.

Chop into bite-size pieces and garnish with green onions. Or use the meat in other recipes.

SMOKED SIDE OF PORK

Smoke the raw side of pork in a Cameron smoker (page 13) for about 20 minutes and then proceed as below. The results are absolutely delicious! The meat is eaten as is or it can be chowed with other ingredients as in the recipe below.

SMOKED SIDE OF PORK WITH HOT BLACK BEAN SAUCE

SERVES 6 AS PART OF A CHINESE MEAL

The Smoked Side of Pork can be sliced and chowed Hunan style. Your guests will probably consider this one of the best Chinese dishes that you have learned to prepare. Yes, it takes some time, as you must smoke it, roast it, and then chow it. The flavors are so delectable that you will not mind the work.

2 tablespoons peanut oil
1 tablespoon fermented black beans *(dow see)*, rinsed in warm water and drained
1 tablespoon finely chopped garlic
1¼ pounds Smoked Side of Pork (above), cooked and cut into ¼-inch slices, and then into ½-inch pieces
1 green sweet bell pepper, cored and seeded, cut into ½-inch squares
2 tablespoons light soy sauce
½ teaspoon garlic and red chili paste (page 26)
½ cup Chinese Chicken Soup Stock (page 126) or regular chicken soup
3 green onions, cut Chinese style (page 158)
½ teaspoon salt

Heat a wok and add the oil, black beans, and garlic. Chow for a moment, mashing them together, and then add the pork slices. Chow for a moment and add the remaining ingredients. Chow until all is very hot.

SLOW-SIMMERED PORK ROAST

SERVES 8 AS PART OF A CHINESE MEAL

I have not seen Ann Gelow for years. She is a charming woman from Taiwan who married a fellow who was running our University Church draft-counseling center, years ago, when I was a college chaplain. She worked during the day and offered me this dish for dinner one evening. It had been slowly cooking all the time she had been at work. It is simple to make and just heaven to eat.

- **3 green onions, cut Chinese style (page 158)**
- **1 teaspoon fresh ginger, cut julienne**
- **2 star anise, whole**
- **2 tablespoons soybean condiment *(mein see)***
- **2 tablespoons light soy sauce**
- **2 teaspoons brown sugar**
- **½ cup dry sherry or Chinese rice wine**
- **2 cloves garlic, sliced thin**
- **½ teaspoon ground white pepper**
- **2 cups water (More may be needed)**
- **2¼ pounds boneless pork roast (I prefer pork butt)**

Mix all the ingredients together, except the pork. Place the meat in an ovenproof casserole that is just large enough to hold it. Pour the sauce over the top, cover the dish, and bake at 275° for anywhere from 5 to 8 hours, depending on your taste.

PORK AND GARLIC CHIVES

SERVES 3–4 AS PART OF A CHINESE MEAL

There is a vegetable in China that looks like pale green chives but has the wonderful flavor of garlic. If you are near a Chinatown you can find this ingredient; otherwise try this tasty dish with regular chives.

- 2 tablespoons peanut oil
- 2 cloves garlic, chopped fine
- 1 slice fresh ginger, cut into tiny julienne sticks
- 2 green onions, sliced Chinese style (page 158)
- 1 tablespoon light soy sauce
- ⅛ teaspoon ground white pepper
- Pinch of MSG (optional)
- 1 tablespoon Chinese rice wine or dry sherry
- ½ pound lean pork cut into julienne strips
- 1 cup chopped garlic chives or regular chives
- Sesame oil, just a splash, for garnish

Heat a wok and add 1 tablespoon of the oil, the garlic, and ginger. Chow for a moment and add the green onions, soy, pepper, the optional MSG, and the wine. Chow for a minute and remove from the wok.

Reheat the wok to smoking. Add the remaining tablespoon of oil and the pork. Chow just until the pork is tender and remove from the wok, leaving the oil in the wok. Add the chives and chow until tender, then return the sauce and the pork. Toss for a moment until all is hot. Add the sesame oil, toss, and serve.

HINT: FOR PROPER CHINESE CHOWING remember these simple rules.

1. Always have everything totally prepared, chopped, mixed, sliced, before you turn on the wok.
2. Heat the wok first, and then add the oil and ingredients. "Hot wok, cold oil, foods won't stick." If using an electric stove rather than gas leave the burner on high and control the heat by moving the wok off and on the burner.
3. Use fresh ingredients as much as possible.
4. Do not overcook the food.
5. Serve the dish the moment it is done, no matter what is going on at the table. An old Chinese proverb says, "A man should wait for the dish. The dish should never wait for the man."

PORK AND PEPPERS ON IRON PLATE

SERVES 3–4 AS PART OF A CHINESE MEAL

This type of dish is the current rage in Hong Kong. It hit San Francisco a few years ago and everyone seems to get a bang out of a dish coming to the table that positively spews hot pepper oil all over the guests. The iron plate, which can be purchased in large Chinese communities, is heated on the stove and then placed on a wooden plank and brought to the table. The server pours the cooked dish, hot from the wok and filled with hot peppers, on the hot iron plate. Everything sizzles and bubbles and brings out a most marvelous flavor. Of course, most of the guests have to hide behind a big cloth napkin in order to protect their eyes and clothing from the pepper oil. You can try this with a black frying pan that has been heated very hot and placed on a board. Great fun and very dramatic! The taste of this dish can also be very hot. Adjust it to your own taste.

- **¾ pound boneless pork butt, cut julienne**
- **1 tablespoon dark soy**
- **1 tablespoon dry sherry or Chinese rice wine**
- **½ teaspoon julienne-cut ginger**
- **3 tablespoons peanut oil**
- **3 cloves garlic, finely chopped**
- **½ teaspoon salt**
- **½ cup green onions, cut Chinese style (page 158)**
- **½ cup julienne-cut green sweet bell peppers**
- **6 dried small red peppers, soaked in ¼ cup water**
- **½ cup julienne-cut bamboo shoots**
- **1 teaspoon ground white pepper**
- **1 tablespoon sesame oil**
- **1 teaspoon garlic and red chili paste or to taste**

Marinate the cut pork in the soy, wine, and ginger for about 15 minutes. Heat the wok and add 2 tablespoons of the oil, along with the garlic, and salt. Chow the pork over high heat just until barely done to taste. Remove. Heat the remaining tablespoon of oil and add the vegetables and pepper to the wok and chow for a moment. Add the remaining ingredients and return the pork to the wok. Toss until all is hot and bring to the table. Pour on the preheated iron plate or black frying pan and stand back!!!

SIDE OF PORK AND OYSTERS IN SAND POT

SERVES 4 AS PART OF A CHINESE MEAL

While this dish takes some doing, it is a classic. You will need to have some leftover Crispy Roast Pork for an opener, and then you are on your way.

The sand pot is explained on page 12 and can be found in Chinatown. Otherwise, use any good stove-top casserole.

½ cake firm bean curd
4 cups peanut oil for deep-frying
1 tablespoon peanut oil
Pinch of salt
¼ teaspoon freshly grated ginger
1 clove garlic, chopped fine or crushed
½ tablespoon light soy sauce
3 green onions, cut Chinese style (page 158)
⅛ teaspoon sugar
1 tablespoon oyster sauce
Pinch of MSG (optional)
Pinch of ground white pepper
1 cup of Crispy Roast Pork (page 334) sliced ¼ inch thick and then into 1-inch pieces
½ cup Chinese Chicken Soup Stock (page 126) or Basic Chicken Stock (page 144)
1 teaspoon cornstarch mixed with 1½ teaspoons water
1 medium head iceberg lettuce, torn up
1 cup small oysters

Slice the bean curd into squares ½ inch thick, and then cut each square into 2 triangles. Place bean curd slices on paper towels to drain a bit of the moisture.

Heat the deep-frying oil to 360° and deep-fry the bean curd slices until golden, about 10 minutes. Be careful with this as the bean curd will "spit" at you when you put it in the hot oil. Remove and drain the slices.

Heat a wok and add the tablespoon of peanut oil. Chow the salt, ginger, and garlic for just a moment. Add the soy sauce, green onions, sugar, oyster sauce, the optional MSG, and the white pepper. Stir for just a moment and add the cooked pork. Chow just until the pork is hot and then add the chicken broth. When the broth begins to boil, stir in the cornstarch and water. Cook until thickened. Place the lettuce in the bottom of a sand pot or stove-top casserole. Stir the oysters into the pork and sauce and pour all over the lettuce. Cover and place on high heat until all is hot. Serve from the casserole.

SIDE OF PORK WITH COD AND BEAN CURD IN SAND POT

SERVES 4–6 AS PART OF A CHINESE MEAL

This one is similar to the dish above in that it uses seafood, bean curd, and Crispy Roast Pork. A dish that is similar to this one, but superior, I am afraid, is served at the wonderful Sea Garden Restaurant in Seattle's Chinatown. This is as close as I can come to the delicate flavors that they can create in this fine Hong Kong-style seafood house.

- ½ cake firm bean curd
- 4 cups peanut oil for deep-frying
- 1 cup Crispy Roast Pork (page 334), sliced ¼ inch thick and then into 1-inch pieces

THE FISH

- ½ pound codfish fillets, skinless and boneless, cut into 1-inch by 1-inch pieces
- ½ tablespoon Chinese rice wine or dry sherry

½ tablespoon light soy sauce
⅛ teaspoon baking powder
1 egg white, beaten
¼ cup *each* cornstarch and flour, mixed

FOR CHOWING
1 tablespoon peanut oil
1 clove garlic, chopped fine
⅛ teaspoon freshly grated ginger
3 green onions, cut Chinese style (page 158)
½ tablespoon light soy sauce
Pinch of sugar
1 tablespoon oyster sauce
Pinch of MSG (optional)
Pinch of ground white pepper
½ cup Chinese Chicken Soup Stock (page 126) or Basic Chicken Stock (page 144)
1 teaspoon cornstarch mixed with 1½ teaspoons water
1 medium head iceberg lettuce, torn up

Slice the bean curd into squares ½ inch thick, and then cut each square into 2 triangles. Place bean curd slices on paper towels to drain a bit of the moisture.

Heat the deep-frying oil to 360° and deep-fry the bean curd slices until golden, about 10 minutes. Be careful with this as the bean curd will "spit" at you when you put it in the hot oil. Remove and drain the slices.

Prepare the cod and marinate in the sherry and soy for 10 minutes. Heat the deep-frying oil again to 360°. Mix the baking powder with the egg white. Drain the fish of the marinade and mix with the egg white. Dredge each piece of fish in the cornstarch/flour mixture and deep-fry until golden, about 5 minutes or less. Drain and set aside.

Heat the wok and add the oil for chowing. Chow the garlic and ginger for a moment and add the green onions. Add the soy, sugar, oyster sauce, optional MSG, and white pepper. Chow for a moment and add the chicken stock. Bring to a quick boil and stir in the cornstarch/water mixture. Stir to thicken. Add the bean curd, pork, and fish to the wok.

Put the torn lettuce in the bottom of a sand pot (page 12) or stove-top casserole. Pour the sauce and meat mixture over the top. Heat on a high burner until all is steaming hot.

SPARERIBS WITH BLACK BEANS

SERVES 6 AS PART OF A CHINESE MEAL

I suppose all of us love to chew on bones when we can get away with it. This dish, popular even at formal Chinese dinners, *must* be chewed on, and the flavor is wonderful. You cannot make too much of this dish for me!

- 1 pound pork spareribs, cut into 1-inch-long individual pieces (Have your butcher run them through his bandsaw!)
- 3 tablespoons light soy sauce
- 2 tablespoons dry sherry or Chinese rice wine
- 3 cloves garlic, chopped fine
- 1 tablespoon fermented black beans *(dow see)*, rinsed and mashed
- Pinch of brown sugar
- ½ teaspoon MSG (optional)
- 1 teaspoon sesame oil
- 1 teaspoon garlic and red chili paste (page 26), or to taste
- 2 tablespoons cornstarch
- 2 green onions, chopped
- ½ green pepper, cut into julienne strips

Place the sparerib pieces in a colander and pour 2 quarts of boiling water over them. Do this in the sink. Drain them well and chow, or pan-fry, until lightly browned. Drain the fat and place them in a bowl. Add all other ingredients except the onions and green pepper. Mix well and then add the onions and pepper. Place in a steaming dish and steam for 1 hour 15 minutes. They will be very tender and delicious.

SPARERIBS WITH BLACK BEANS IN SAND POT

SERVES 2–3 AS A MAIN COURSE,
4 AS PART OF A CHINESE MEAL

The secret behind sand-pot cooking is to put the casserole on a very high burner and almost burn the lettuce, which is used as a base in the dish. The almost smoky flavor that results will completely change the nature of the spareribs. It is luscious!

Prepare the above recipe. Place a medium-sized head of iceberg lettuce, torn up, in a 2-quart sand pot (page 12) or stove-top casserole. Place the cooked ribs on top of the lettuce. Cover and place on high heat. When the whole is hot and bubbling, serve. This is great on rice, and yes, I eat the lettuce as well.

DEEP-FRIED PORK BALLS

SERVES 4–6 AS PART OF A CHINESE MEAL

These are easy! Even the kids will love to make them, and yet they are a real delicacy. This same meat mixture can be used for other dishes as well, as you will see from the following recipes.

- 1 pound lean pork, finely ground
- 1 green onion, finely chopped
- 1 teaspoon freshly grated ginger
- 1 teaspoon light soy sauce
- 1 tablespoon dry sherry or Chinese rice wine
- 1 egg, beaten
- ¼ teaspoon salt
- Pinch of MSG (optional)
- 2 tablespoons cornstarch
- 1 teaspoon sesame oil
- ¼ teaspoon ground white pepper
- 6 cups peanut oil for deep-frying

Mix all of the ingredients together and stir, using your hand, until the mixture is smooth and holds together. Moisten your hands with a bit of water and form the meat into balls about the size of large walnuts. Fry ½ of the meatballs in oil at 360° until they float. Remove and fry the other half. Allow the oil to return to temperature and fry the whole batch a second time, just until they are nicely browned and crispy, about 5 more minutes.

Drain and set aside.

These can be served just as they are, or with Szechwan Pepper and Salt Dip (page 230). You can also simply chow them with a bit of garlic and red chili paste along with a bit of soup stock.

BIRD'S NEST MEATBALLS

SERVES 4–6 AS PART OF A CHINESE MEAL

No, there is no bird's nest in this dish. However, these are easy to prepare and great fun to eat. The noodle fries and curls up a bit to resemble the tiny twigs of a bird's nest. Great flavor is imparted by the noodle.

Prepare a batch of meatballs as directed on page 343 and 344, adding some chopped yellow onion and some grated carrot to the meat mixture. Do not cook. Cut 3 ounces of *sai fun* noodles (page 28) into 1-inch lengths. I use kitchen scissors for this. Roll the meatballs in the small noodle pieces and then deep-fry ½ the batch at 375° for 4 seconds, or until the noodles puff up. Remove and do the other half. Let the oil cool to 325° and cook the whole batch a second time until done to taste, about 6 minutes. Drain and serve hot.

PEARL MEATBALLS

SERVES 4–6 AS PART OF A CHINESE MEAL

The wonderful name for this dish comes from the fact that the sticky-sweet rice in which you roll the meatballs takes on a pearly color and appearance when steamed. This dish is great served right from the steamer. It certainly adds some class to meatballs! Yes, you can do this with lean ground beef. It will work well.

⅔ cup sticky sweet rice
1 pound pork, ground fine
2 tablespoons light soy sauce
1 tablespoon dry sherry or Chinese rice wine
1 clove garlic, crushed
6 water chestnuts, peeled and chopped coarsely
½ ounce dried Chinese mushrooms, soaked in water 2 hours, drained and chopped coarsely
1 teaspoon salt
1 teaspoon sugar
3 tablespoons cornstarch
1 green onion, chopped
¼ teaspoon MSG (optional)
¼ teaspoon ground white pepper
Lettuce leaves for steaming *or* waxed paper (3-inch squares) for steaming

Rinse the rice until the water is clear and soak in cold water for 6 hours. Place rice in colander and drain very well.

Mix all together except the rice and lettuce. Form into 1-inch meatballs and roll each to cover in the soaked rice.

Cut the lettuce leaves into 2-inch squares or circles and place a meatball on each, then into the steamer. Or, you can use waxed paper. Steam for 30 minutes or until the rice is glossy and tender.

STEAMED PORK WITH CHINESE OLIVES

The flavor of the dried Chinese olive, *lam see,* is very rich and rather heavy. The *lam see* resemble dried Italian olives, though when you buy them in Chinatown they will be pitted.

Soak ½ cup *lam see* olives in warm water for 1 hour. Drain. Prepare a batch of Steamed Pork with Salted Eggs (page 258), omitting the salted eggs. Mix the olives with the meat and steam as directed. Be prepared for a very interesting but rather strong flavor.

SPARERIBS WITH LOTUS ROOT

SERVES 6–8 AS PART OF A CHINESE MEAL

The lotus plant, a wonderful waterlily, provides China with leaves in which to wrap and cook food, a starch for thickening dishes that is much older than cornstarch, and a root vegetable that is simply a piece of art. As you slice the root or tuber you find a lovely lace pattern in the vegetable. Since it is so attractive, the Chinese love to use it in special dishes. This is such a dish.

2 pounds pork spareribs, cut into 1-inch pieces (Have the butcher do this for you)

MARINADE

2 tablespoons light soy sauce
2 tablespoons Chinese rice wine or dry sherry
½ teaspoon freshly grated ginger
¼ teaspoon sugar
¼ teaspoon ground white pepper

1 tablespoon peanut oil for chowing
2 cloves garlic, chopped fine or crushed
3 green onions, chopped
1 cup lotus root, sliced thin (Fresh is best, but hard to find; canned will do nicely)

Bring 3 quarts of water to a boil and dump in cut ribs. Blanch for 1 minute. Drain the ribs well and soak in the marinade for ½ hour.

Heat a wok and add the oil and garlic. Chow for a second and add half the ribs, drained. Chow until lightly browned and remove to a steaming bowl. Chow the second half of the ribs in the same oil. Place in another steaming bowl. Top each with the onions and sliced lotus root. Steam in a bamboo steamer (page 106) until tender, about 1 hour.

Greece

PORK WITH CELERY, GREEK STYLE

SERVES 4–6 AS A MAIN COURSE

Taverna Sigalas, on Monastiraki Square in Athens, served this dish one night to Craig, my cooking assistant, and me. We were both very taken by the utter simplicity of the dish and the brightness of the flavors.

Celery leaves have been common in cooking since the very early days of all three of our cultures, China, Greece, and Rome. In Rome, during the first century, lovage would have been used in such a dish. It is a member of the celery family and the flavor is very sharp. In our time you can simply use celery leaves.

Don't be cool to this dish just because it is so simple. The best of Greek cuisine is not necessarily complex.

- 2 tablespoons olive oil for browning
- 2 pounds boneless pork roast, cut into several large pieces

COOKING LIQUID

- 2 cups Basic Chicken Stock (page 144)
- ½ cup dry white wine
- 5 tablespoons olive oil
- 2 cloves garlic, chopped fine
- Salt and freshly ground black pepper to taste
- 4 cups chopped celery leaves and stalks (The more leaves, the better)

In a 6-quart Dutch oven, heat the oil for browning and brown the meat on both sides. Add all of the ingredients for the cooking liquid. It should come up about halfway on the side of the meat. If it does not, add more chicken stock or wine. Bring to a simmer and cover. Cook for 1¾ hours or until tender. Add the celery and simmer ½ hour more until the celery is very tender. Uncover the pot for the last 15 minutes to reduce the sauce.

This can be served with rice pilaf or pasta, but I love it just plain in a bowl with crunchy Greek bread and a good glass of retsina wine.

PORK SOUVLAKI

The Greeks have been cooking meat on little sticks for thousands of years. You can make Pork Souvlaki, an old dish, just the same way you make lamb Souvlaki (page 324). The pork makes a wonderful change.

Italy

ROAST PORK, ROMAN STYLE

SERVES 5–6 FOR DINNER

In Italy, particularly in Rome and Bologna, you can find stands that sell pork roast already cooked. It is roasted in such a beautiful way that it is very hard to resist the urge to simply buy a chunk and eat it on the street, the crunchy pork fat sticking to your beard and fingers. This is as close to the Roman style as I can come. It sounds like a lot of work when you read the recipe but it is really quite simple.

1 2-pound piece fresh side of pork, skin left on
1 2-pound boneless pork butt roast
Salt and freshly ground black pepper to taste
1 tablespoon dried, whole rosemary
1 tablespoon olive oil
2 cloves garlic, crushed

Place the side of pork skin side down on the counter and, using a good butcher knife, cut off enough meat so that only ¾ inch remains attached to the skin. Place the knife parallel to the counter and do this carefully. It is not a big job at all. Reserve the removed meat and fat for another dish.

Cut the boneless roast open so that you can add all of the additional seasonings and then roll up the roast. Encase it in the side of pork, skin side out, and tie with several pieces of string. You should wind up with a nice long, shaped roast encased by the pork skin. The ends will be open, of course.

Place the meat in a roasting rack, skin side up. Prick the skin thoroughly, using an ice pick. Place in the upper third of an oven preheated to 325°. Place a meat thermometer in the roast and roast until the thermometer hits 170°. Then, turn the oven on to BROIL and cook until the skin is bubbly and crunchy. Be careful, as this should take only a few minutes. You need to watch this.

The whole cooking process will take about 35 minutes per pound, total time.

Remove and slice the roast for serving. The skin is the best part . . . although I think that the roast served cold the next day is almost as good. What decisions!

Beef

We can understand why beef was not popular in the ancient world if we understand that beef is the most costly meat in the world. That is to say, it costs more to produce a pound of beef than of any other meat that we normally eat. More grain, more grass, more fresh water, more space, more of everything. So, in the old days it was simply not popular. We Americans still insist on our beef, each of us eating nearly eighty pounds a year. We have the room to raise the animal, but the rest of the world does not.

The Greeks did raise oxen, but they were roasted only on very special occasions. One occasion, in 400 B.C., called for the public roasting of three hundred oxen. Some barbecue! But in general Greece was simply not suited to keeping those animals on the little land that they had. And as the development of agriculture moved from raising meat to growing more grain, the land available for cattle shrank. By A.D. 1000 the developments in food and diet due to the advancement of agriculture had converted men and women from a diet in which meat was dominant to one in which grains were dominant. In the days of Peking Man, about 300,000 years ago, people lived on a diet that was about 70 percent meat. That is not the case now, and it can never be again. Nevertheless, our three ancient cultures do enjoy beef, but it is generally used as a flavoring rather than as a whole course, as the following recipes will show.

You may also wish to see:

Chinese Beef and Chestnut Stew *(page 493)*

China

MONGOLIAN BEEF

SERVES 4 AS PART OF A CHINESE MEAL

Channing and Jason, my sons, always order this dish when we go to a favorite Chinese restaurant. It is not a complex dish but it uses both the deep-frying method of cooking and the chowing method, and all of this for beef. You would think that after the meat is cooked twice, it would be dead. It is not, and you will love the flavors that these two cooking methods create.

1 pound beef flank steak, sliced thin across the grain

MARINADE

1 tablespoon light soy sauce
1 tablespoon dry sherry or Chinese rice wine
½ teaspoon freshly grated ginger

4 cups peanut oil for deep-frying

FOR CHOWING

1 tablespoon peanut oil
2 cloves garlic, sliced thin
4 green onions, sliced Chinese style (page 158)
1 teaspoon hoisin sauce (page 26)
Pinch of MSG, (optional)
¼ teaspoon ground white pepper

Marinate the cut meat in the soy, wine, and ginger. Mix well and let sit for 15 minutes. Drain the marinade well. Separate the meat into individual pieces.

In a wok or deep pan heat the deep-frying oil to 375°. Add the meat all at once and stir a bit to separate. Remove after 1 minute and allow the meat to drain in a colander.

Heat the wok again and add the oil for chowing. Add the garlic and green onions and chow for just a moment. Add the hoisin, optional MSG, and the pepper. Add the meat. Stir-fry until all is hot, and serve.

VARIATION: You may wish to serve this dish over deep-fried cellophane *(sai fun)* noodles (page 25). It is very dramatic.

> **HINT: USE THE SERVING PLATE WHEN CHOWING** Chinese food. It is silly to dirty lots of little dishes when you are simply organizing the chopped meat and vegetables for a chowed dish. Since some ingredients must be cooked separately, you can just arrange these on the platter, cook them as you go, return them to the platter, and then finish the dish. In the end the whole works goes on the same plate anyhow!

PEPPER ONION BEEF

SERVES 4 AS PART OF A CHINESE MEAL

Your mouth should burn a bit from all of the black pepper that you are to put in this dish. I know that nothing but green onions and black pepper sounds strange to you . . . but the flavor is just wonderful.

1 pound beef flank steak, sliced thin across the grain

MARINADE

1 tablespoon light soy sauce
1 tablespoon dry sherry or Chinese rice wine
½ teaspoon freshly grated ginger

4 cups peanut oil for deep-frying

FOR CHOWING

1 tablespoon peanut oil
2 cloves garlic, sliced thin
8 green onions, cut Chinese style (page 158)
Pinch of MSG (optional)
Pinch of sugar
Freshly ground black pepper to taste (Use lots of pepper for this dish. That is what makes it so terrific!)

Marinate the cut meat in the soy, wine, and ginger. Mix well and let sit for 15 minutes. Drain the marinade well and separate the meat into individual pieces.

In a wok or deep pan heat the oil for deep-frying to 375°. Add the meat all at once and stir a bit to separate. Remove after 1 minute and drain the meat in a colander.

Heat the wok again and add the oil for chowing. Add the garlic and green onions and chow for just a moment. Add the drained meat and all remaining ingredients, using plenty of black pepper. Chow until the meat is hot, and serve.

HINT: AVOID THE HIGH COST OF FLANK STEAK for Chinese cooking by purchasing lean chuck roast. Remove any large chunks of fat. Cut it into thick strips and place it in a freezer until it is very firm. Slice thin and proceed with the recipes.

OYSTER BEEF

SERVES 4 AS PART OF A CHINESE MEAL

This is a fine beef dish, and the lettuce cooked with the meat makes an interesting change from the normal restaurant version.

- 1 pound beef flank steak, sliced thin across the grain
- 1 tablespoon light soy sauce
- 1 tablespoon Chinese rice wine or dry sherry
- Pinch of sugar
- Black pepper, freshly ground, to taste
- 2 tablespoons oyster sauce
- 3 tablespoons peanut oil
- ½ teaspoon sesame oil
- 2 green onions, sliced Chinese style (page 158)
- ½ head iceberg lettuce, shredded
- ⅛ cup Chinese Chicken Soup Stock (page 126)

Marinate the beef in the soy sauce, wine, sugar, black pepper, and oyster sauce for 15 minutes. Heat a wok and add 1½ tablespoons of the peanut oil. Chow the meat quickly on high heat, about 3 minutes. Remove from the pan to a serving bowl. Heat the wok again and add another 1½ tablespoons peanut oil. Add the sesame oil and green onions, and chow for a moment. Add the lettuce and return the meat to the wok. Add the chicken stock and cook for a moment while a sauce forms.

GINGER BEEF

SERVES 4 AS PART OF A CHINESE MEAL

Some people claim they dislike the flavor of fresh ginger in Chinese food. Generally that is because the cook is using too much ginger. In this dish it is impossible to put in too much of that wonderful root. Go to it and enjoy!

- **1 pound beef flank steak, sliced thin across the grain**
- **1 tablespoon dry sherry or Chinese rice wine**
- **1 tablespoon light soy sauce**
- **Pinch of sugar**
- **2 tablespoons peanut oil**
- **2 cloves garlic, chopped fine**
- **5–6 thin slices fresh ginger, cut julienne (page 21)**
- **2 teaspoons oyster sauce**
- **⅛ cup Chinese Chicken Soup Stock (page 126)**
- **2 green onions, cut Chinese style (page 158)**
- **2 eggs, well beaten**

Marinate the meat in the wine, soy sauce, and sugar for 15 minutes. Heat a wok and add the oil. Chow the garlic and the ginger for 1 minute. Remove the garlic and ginger from the wok, reserving them, and leaving the oil in the pan. Chow the beef on one side for 1 minute and then add the removed ginger and garlic. Add the oyster sauce, chicken broth, and green onions and chow for a moment. Stir in the beaten eggs and cook just for a moment, until the mixture thickens.

SMOKED MEATBALLS

SERVES 10–12 AS PART OF A CHINESE MEAL

These are very flavorful little numbers that can be served in several ways. They are also rich and therefore go a long way at the table.

- **1¼ pounds ground beef**
- **1¼ pounds ground pork**
- **1 egg**
- **1 teaspoon freshly grated ginger**
- **2 tablespoons dry sherry or Chinese rice wine**
- **2 tablespoons dark soy sauce**
- **1 tablespoon sesame oil**
- **3 tablespoons chopped green onion**
- **2 tablespoons cornstarch**

I place all of the ingredients above in my KitchenAid and then let the machine beat it into a smooth mixture. If you do not have such a machine you will need to mix this by hand very well.

Form meatballs just a bit bigger than 1 inch in diameter. Place them on plates and steam them in your bamboo steamer (page 106) for about 20 minutes. Then place them in a Cameron smoker (page 13), or some other smoker, and smoke them for about 15 minutes, using either alder or hickory sawdust.

The meatballs can be served just as they are or you can offer Szechwan Pepper and Salt Dip (page 230) as a dip. You might also try one of the various dip sauces on page 229. They can also be chowed with a sauce or with vegetables, as in the next recipe.

NOTE: These meatballs freeze very well, either cooked or raw.

MEATBALLS WITH BLACK BEANS AND GREEN PEPPER

SERVES 5 AS PART OF A CHINESE MEAL

If you have some leftover smoked meatballs, try serving them in this manner. This is the kind of food that keeps the Hunan farmers alive during those bitterly cold winters. The hot chili paste keeps the system aware of reality!

1 tablespoon peanut oil
2 cloves garlic, chopped fine
2 teaspoons fermented black beans *(dow see)* (page 25), rinsed
½ green sweet bell pepper
½ teaspoon garlic and red chili paste (page 26)
1 teaspoon light soy sauce
½ cup Chinese Chicken Soup Stock (page 126) or Basic Chicken Stock (page 144)
1 teaspoon cornstarch mixed with 1 tablespoon water
½ batch cooked smoked meatballs (above)
4 green onions, cut Chinese style (page 158)

Heat a wok and add the oil, garlic, and black beans. Smash them together a bit as you chow for a moment. Add the bell pepper, chili paste, soy, and soup stock. Bring to a quick boil and stir in cornstarch and water mixture. Cook until thick. Add the cooked meatballs and green onions and chow until all is hot.

LOOED BEEF

SERVES 4–6 AS PART OF A CHINESE MEAL AND 6–8 AS AN APPETIZER COURSE

I just love the name of this dish, and you can be assured that your kids will have fun throwing the name around the neighborhood. The name refers to a style of cooking, a slow simmering in a dark sauce or looing sauce. The result is delightful and a wonderful way to do a pot roast.

- **2 tablespoons peanut oil**
- **2–3 pounds boneless chuck roast**
- **5 cups Looing Sauce (page 231)**

Heat a large frying pan and add the oil. Brown the meat on both sides, and brown it well. Place the meat in a heavy stove-top covered casserole and add enough looing sauce to cover. Bring to a boil and turn to a simmer. Simmer covered for 1 hour and 20 minutes, or until the meat is tender. Serve the meat hot with a bit of the sauce or turn off the heat and allow the meat to cool in the sauce and then slice it for an appetizer course.

Save the sauce for other uses.

LOOED BEEF IN SAND POT

SERVES 4 AS PART OF A CHINESE MEAL

This is a typical winter casserole dish in China. The cooked lettuce adds a nice refreshing flavor to the meat.

- **2 cups iceberg lettuce**
- **1 pound Looed Beef (above), cooked and cut into ½-inch cubes**
- **½ cup Looing Sauce from the meat**
- **2 tablespoons thinly sliced yellow onion**

GARNISH

- **2 green onions, chopped**

Place the lettuce in the bottom of a 2-quart sand pot (page 12) and top with the meat and sauce. Place the yellow onions on top and place the dish on a heat diffuser over high heat. When all is hot serve with the green-onion garnish.

You can do this dish in any kind of stove-top casserole.

Greece

POACHED MEATBALLS IN EGG AND LEMON SAUCE
(Youvarlakia)

SERVES 6

Every taverna in Athens has a variation on this dish, but the version offered at Taverna Sigalas, in Monastiraki Square, is particularly delicious. The restaurant is behind an Orthodox Church, which is one thousand years old, at least. Somehow this adds to the delight of a lunch in the courtyard.

- 1½ pounds lean ground beef
- ½ cup long-grain rice (uncooked)
- ½ cup finely chopped yellow onion
- 2 eggs, separated
- 3 tablespoons chopped parsley
- ¼ teaspoon allspice
- Salt and freshly ground black pepper to taste
- ½ cup olive oil
- Juice of 2 lemons

Place the meat in a mixing bowl and mix in the rice, onion, eggs (whites only), parsley, allspice, and salt and pepper. Mix very well and form into small meatballs, about 1 inch in diameter. Place the oil in a large covered frying pan and add the meatballs in a single layer. Barely cover with water and put on the lid. Simmer the meatballs until the rice is tender, about 40 minutes. Remove the meatballs to a heated plate.

Leave ¾ cup of the remaining liquid in the pan and discard the rest. (If you are short of liquid, add chicken broth to make up the difference.) Beat the egg yolks in a bowl and add the lemon juice. While stirring, add the broth from the pan. Return this mixture to the pan and heat and stir until it is thick. Return the meatballs to the sauce and gently heat for serving.

FRIED MEATBALLS
(Keftedes)
SERVES 6

If you are tired of hamburger dishes, American style—and who isn't?—then try these Greek meatballs. They are simple to make and just wonderful served cold—with yogurt, of course.

- ¾ cup bread crumbs, soaked in ½ cup water
- 1½ pounds lean ground beef
- 1 large yellow onion, peeled and chopped fine
- 3 tablespoons chopped parsley
- 1 teaspoon mint leaves
- 1 teaspoon oregano
- 2 cloves garlic, peeled and crushed
- 1 tablespoon olive oil
- 2 eggs
- 1 tablespoon fresh lemon juice
- Salt and freshly ground black pepper to taste
- Flour for dredging
- 1 cup olive oil for frying

Squeeze the water from the bread crumbs and place in a mixing bowl along with the beef. Add all other ingredients except the flour and oil for frying. Mix well and form into small oblong meatballs. Dredge each in flour and pan-fry in the olive oil until lightly browned and done to your taste. Do not dry them out!

These are great hot or cold.

MEATBALLS IN TOMATO SAUCE

(Keftedes me Saltsa)

Prepare the meatballs as above. Reheat them in a bit of Greek Tomato Sauce (page 232).

HAMBURGERS, GREEK STYLE

This is for Channing, my hamburger lover, but I will share it with you as well. Niki, the owner and cook at Zorba's Taverna in Delphi, told me that he makes a terrific hamburger and he used to sell them from a canteen truck in the States. He gave me the recipe, a recipe that only a crazed Greek could think up. It is delicious.

Try adding a bit of dried mint and oregano, along with crushed garlic and olive oil, to your hamburger meat, along with some salt and pepper, of course. Now, here is the crazed part. Add a stiff shot of ouzo, that wonderful Greek anise liquor, to the meat as well. Mix this all up and grill or pan-fry just as you normally do. You may become crazed as well!

Italy

BEEF, ROMAN JEWISH STYLE

SERVES 6

The Jewish Ghetto in Rome, a place you must visit, still has a few restaurants that serve food that has been typical of these people for the last few hundred years. You will find kosher bakers and kosher butchers. And you will find a few dishes like the following.

- **2 pounds boneless beef pot roast, cut into 1-inch cubes**
- **4 tablespoons olive oil**
- **3 cloves garlic, chopped fine**
- **Salt and freshly ground black pepper to taste**
- **½ cup Basic Brown Soup Stock (page 148)**
- **½ cup dry red wine**
- **2 cups Italian Tomato Sauce (page 237)**

In a large frying pan brown the meat pieces very well in the olive oil and garlic. You may have to do this in 2 or 3 batches. See the **HINT** on page 363.

Place the meat in a suitable stove-top covered casserole and add the remaining ingredients. Simmer, covered, until the meat is very tender, about 2 hours. You may have to add some water to the pot now and then. Do not let the dish dry out.

This can be served in a bowl with a great deal of bread or with pasta.

BEEF SLICES WITH ROSEMARY

SERVES 6 AS PART OF AN ITALIAN MEAL

Beef is quite expensive in Rome, at least by our standards. I expect this has always been the case, given the fact that Rome was literally at the crossroads of the world for so long. Foods came in from all over the Mediterranean, but meat had to be local. If you were not a free citizen, I expect you saw few dishes like the following.

The butcher in Rome, who may very well operate from a mobile truck shop in the middle of the market square, will slice meat for you very thin. You buy just a few slices for the family and grill them in this way.

3 tablespoons olive oil
2 cloves garlic, chopped medium
1 pound lean beef roast, sliced quite thin
Salt and freshly ground black pepper to taste
1 tablespoon chopped fresh rosemary
¼ cup dry white wine

Heat a large heavy frying pan and add the oil and garlic. Pan-fry the meat on both sides quickly over medium-high heat. Salt and pepper the meat and remove it to a heated serving platter. Add the rosemary to the pan along with the white wine. Deglaze the pan (page 20) and pour the sauce over the meat.

HINT: WHEN BROWNING MEATS use a very heavy frying pan and small batches of meat. If you put all the meat in a thin pan at once, the little heat available in the thin metal of the pan will be absorbed quickly and you cannot sear the meat, only slowly cook it, thus toughening the meat. Proper browning means that you sear the meat quickly, thus sealing in the flavorful juices and coloring the natural sugar that is in the meat.

MEATBALLS, ROMAN STYLE

MAKES 20 MEATBALLS; SERVES 6–8 PERSONS

I suppose I could live on meatballs: Swedish meatballs, Chinese meatballs, German meatballs, Polish meatballs, Hungarian meatballs, Jewish meatballs, and certainly Italian meatballs. This version from Rome has a very deep flavor due to the pancetta and prosciutto that are added to the beef. You can substitute our bacon and ham, if you must, but the flavor will not be as rich.

THE MEATBALLS

- 2 pounds lean ground beef
- ½ pound ground pork
- 6 ounces pancetta, diced very small
- 6 ounces prosciutto, sliced thin and chopped
- 3 eggs
- 1 cup chopped parsley
- 3 cloves garlic, crushed
- 1 cup bread crumbs, soaked in 1 cup milk
- Salt and freshly ground black pepper to taste (Careful with the salt as the pancetta and prosciutto will also add salt to the dish)
- ¼ cup olive oil for browning

THE SAUCE

- 1 cup dry red wine
- 2 cups Italian Tomato Sauce (page 237)
- 1 cup Basic Brown Sauce (page 236) or substitute brown gravy
- 1 ounce dried mushrooms, soaked in 2 cups water (Reserve the water)
- Additional parsley for garnish

Mix the meatball ingredients together, with the exception of the oil for browning. Form into 20 balls and pan-brown in the olive oil. Do this in 2 or 3 batches.

Place the meatballs, along with the oil, in a 6-quart stove-top casserole. Deglaze (page 20) with the wine in the frying pan in which you cook the meatballs. Add the wine to the pot along with the 2 sauces and the mushroom water. Chop the mushrooms and add to the pot.

Cover and bring to a simmer. Leave the lid ajar so that the sauce will reduce a bit. Cook for about ½ hour. Place meatballs on a platter and serve the gravy separately. It is great on pasta or polenta.

POT ROAST SHREDDED

I cannot figure out any other way of getting a fresh-tasting beef flavor into a dish, as they do in Rome. The beef must be cooked separately and then blended with the sauce at the last minute so that it does not have that "cooked forever" flavor. In any case you will find it helpful to have a cooked and shredded pot roast sitting in your refrigerator. It will add depth to many dishes such as a Bolognese sauce or a meat salad.

- **1 boneless pot roast, 3 to 4 pounds**
- **1 tablespoon olive oil**
- **1 cup dry white wine**
- **2 cups water**
- **Salt and freshly ground black pepper to taste**

Pan-brown the roast in a large frying pan with the olive oil. Place in a stove-top covered casserole and add the wine and water. Cover and simmer for about 2½ hours. It should be very tender. Add the salt and pepper to taste. Cool and shred the meat, saving the juice. Store in the refrigerator with the juice on the meat.

BEEF ON A STICK, ROMAN STYLE

The fancy meat shops in Rome are just astoundingly beautiful. Many meats are prepared, seasoned, tied, put on sticks, rolled into special shapes . . . and put in a butcher's case that becomes a mosaic of tidbits all ready to take home and quickly finish in your broiler or oven. It is important to note that none of these offerings contains a great deal of meat, at least not by American standards. Meat is expensive in Rome and the dishes are prepared in a careful, artistic, and frugal manner.

An example of such shop preparation is a stick of beef cubes separated alternately by whole, fresh bay leaves, onion wedges, and sliced mushrooms. Dress this with a bit of olive oil and salt and pepper, perhaps some basil and thyme, and dinner is ready for the broiler.

Innards

From prehistoric times innards have been an important part of mankind's diet. In America we have largely rejected these meats since we seem to feel that they are symbols of poverty. In our three ancient cuisines, however, they were symbols of delight and joy at the table.

In classic Rome innards were offered at the most exclusive banquets. To this day the Romans love innards and they are served in the oldest of the city's trattorias. My favorite, Trattoria Edmondo, serves pasta with lamb intestines and deep-fried lamb brains along with vegetables. Now be careful with your rejection of these dishes as they are just delicious. *Frattagli,* or innards, have been enjoyed since the early days of the empire when these cheap cuts of meat were all that the lower classes could afford. They were sold, already cooked, in stalls in the streets of Rome. The peasants rarely got their hands on the better cuts of meat and thus the affection for innards lingers on in Rome as a profound culinary memory.

You will find some wonderful Greek dishes for innards in this section as well. When you have been raised on tripe soup, or on innard soup that is served after the Easter Mass at midnight, then you continue to long for these dishes for the rest of your life. Liver cooked Greek style may very well change your opinion of liver!

Finally, the most experienced cooks in the world, the Chinese, have prized tripe and tongue since before recorded history. I had wonderful innards in Hong Kong, and I shall never forget a big plate of braised duck tongues that was served me at the Great Shanghai Restaurant.

Please calm down and give me a chance to convince you that Americans are going without some of the best flavors in the animal. We prefer our innards ground up and stuffed into a hot dog so that we cannot tell the contents. Enough! Cook tripe, tongue, and lamb brains and taste flavors that go "back to the beginning" of cooking.

You might also wish to consider:

Spicy Pork Tripe *(page 112)*
Headcheese Appetizer *(page 100)*

China

LOOED BEEF TONGUE
(Ngow Lay)

SERVES 8–10 AS A FIRST COURSE AT A CHINESE MEAL

If you do not care for tongue, so be it. For those of us who do, it is a premium food. This recipe is great served warm, sliced thin, as a part of a Chinese appetizer plate. Served cold, with a bit of hot mustard and horseradish sauce, it is even better.

1 fresh beef tongue, around 3 pounds

SEASONINGS

2 teaspoons salt
½ cup light soy sauce
¼ cup sugar
2 slices ginger, each the size of a 25-cent piece
2 cloves garlic, sliced thin
3 star anise, whole

Place the tongue in a 4-quart stove-top casserole and add water just to cover. Bring to a boil and discard the water. Add the ingredients for the seasonings and enough fresh water to come halfway up the tongue. Bring to a boil, turn to a simmer, cover, and cook for 1 hour and 15 minutes, turning 3 times during the process. Remove the tongue from the pot but save the juices. Allow the meat to cool and remove the skin. Just pull it off! Put the tongue back in the pot and simmer again for about 45 minutes more. Remove, cool a bit, and slice.

LOOED PORK TRIPE
(Hog Maws)

This is very popular as a dim sum or as a first course. John Young, my beloved adopted Chinese uncle in San Francisco, brought this dish home one evening for a snack before our dinner. It was served at room temperature along with a glass of Scotch. The flavor was mild and a bit sweet, and I was surprised at the difference between pork tripe and beef tripe, which is much tougher and takes much longer to cook. Colonel Young smiled at my appreciation. He always seemed to enjoy exposing me to a new and wonderful Chinese delicacy. How I wish he could sit with me now and review this book.

Clean the tripe by removing all fat. Just pull it off. Rinse well and cut the tripe into ¼-inch strips. Drain well and place in a saucepan or stove-top casserole. Add Looing Sauce (page 231) just to cover. Simmer until tender, about 1 hour.

Steam to reheat, if you wish. Garnish with sesame oil and chopped Chinese parsley.

Serve as a first course or at a dim sum feast.

PORK TRIPE IN HOT SAUCE
SERVES 4 AS A FIRST COURSE

While this is commonly served as a dim sum course it is just great for dinner, if you have the right crowd. Pork tripe is very mild in flavor, not like beef tripe at all. Please try this one. Please. And write me and tell me what you think. I love it!

- 2 pounds pork tripe (hog maws)
- 3 tablespoons peanut oil for chowing
- 3 cloves garlic, chopped fine
- 1 teaspoon salt

SAUCE

- 3 tablespoons light soy sauce
- 2 slices ginger, the size of a 25-cent piece, cut julienne
- ¼ cup Chinese rice wine or dry sherry
- 2 teaspoons chili sauce with fermented black beans (page 25)
- ½ teaspoon ground white pepper
- 6 green onions, cut Chinese style (page 158)

- 1 tablespoon cornstarch mixed with 1 table-spoon water for thickening

Remove as much fat as possible from the tripe. Blanch the tripe in boiling water for 2 minutes. Drain. Cut the meat into ¼-inch-wide strips.

Heat a wok and add the oil, garlic, and salt. Chow the tripe for a few minutes and add the ingredients for the sauce. Cover and simmer until all is very tender, about 15 minutes. If you wish to thicken this dish, stir in the cornstarch mixed with water.

A favorite trick in the restaurant dim sum business is to make a large batch of this and keep it in the refrigerator. When someone orders a bit simply steam it and serve. So easy . . . and just delicious.

STEWED OXTAIL, CHINESE STYLE

SERVES 5–6

This is a very rich dish. I prefer to make a batch of this the day ahead and then chill it so that I can remove much of the fat. It is then easy to reheat for a dinner. I do hope you like oxtail. No, of course it is not from an ox. Oxtail in our time comes from a steer.

- **3 pounds oxtails, cut at each joint**
- **4 tablespoons peanut oil**
- **2 cloves garlic, sliced thin**
- **1 teaspoon salt**
- **2 tablespoons fermented black beans *(dow see)*, rinsed and drained**
- **½ yellow onion, peeled and coarsely chopped**
- **3 slices ginger, the size of a 25-cent piece, cut julienne**
- **2 tablespoons dark soy sauce**
- **2 tablespoons Chinese rice wine or dry sherry**
- **1 teaspoon sugar**

Trim the oxtail pieces of excess fat. Heat a large wok or frying pan and add the peanut oil. Add the garlic and salt and chow for just a moment. Add the oxtails and brown on both sides. Remove the oxtails from the wok and drain the oil, reserving the oil. Set the oxtails aside.

Heat the wok again and add 2 tablespoons of the oil. Add the black beans and chow for a moment. Add the remaining ingredients on the list and then add the reserved oxtails. Toss and remove the whole to a stove-top casserole. Add water to not quite cover. Cover the pot and simmer until the meat is very tender, about 2 hours, or longer to taste. The pieces should be very tender and certainly flavorful.

Serve with rice or noodles as a main course for a Chinese dinner.

Greece

GRILLED LIVER, GREEK STYLE

While we were in Delphi for Greek Easter, friends we had just met served us this dish in the streets, along with much too much wine. It is simple and will give you a new image of liver.

Lamb or beef liver, cut thin

MARINADE

Olive oil
Garlic, crushed
Oregano, crushed
Salt and freshly ground black pepper to taste

Marinate the slices of liver and then cook them on a hot grill, turning once. Do not overcook liver as it will be tough.

TRIPE SOUP WITH EGG-LEMON SAUCE
(Skembe Avgolemono)

SERVES 4–6

The first time I ever tasted this wonderful soup I was in the home of Mrs. Koustela Stergachis. She came to America from the Isle of Rhodes, and she is a wonderful cook. While making pastries for my delicatessen she offered me a bowl of *skembe* or *patsas*. It is just superb. And if you are too lazy to make it, you can have it at the Parthenon Restaurant in Chicago, but "only on Sundays." I make my own.

1 pound tripe, lamb or beef
1 medium yellow onion, peeled and quartered
2 bay leaves
2 cloves garlic, peeled and cut in half
4 cups Basic Chicken Stock (page 144) *or* Basic Lamb Stock (page 143)
½ pound boneless lamb, trimmed and cut into very small pieces
½ cup dry white wine
1 rib celery, chopped medium fine
Salt and freshly ground black pepper to taste

EGG-LEMON SAUCE
3 eggs, at room temperature
½ cup fresh lemon juice

Rinse the tripe and place in a 6-quart kettle. Add the onion, bay leaves, and garlic. Barely cover with water and bring to a boil. Cover and simmer for 2 hours. Drain and discard the broth. Cut the tripe into small sticklike pieces and return to the kettle. Add the remaining ingredients, except the eggs and lemon juice, and bring to a boil. Cover and simmer until both meats are tender, about 45 minutes.

Whip the eggs well and stir in the lemon juice. Add 1 cup of the broth from the kettle to this mixture and stir well again. Remove the kettle from the burner and stir in the egg-lemon sauce. We do not want the eggs to curdle. Check for seasoning and serve immediately.

LAMB INNARDS ON A SPIT
(Kokoretsi)

I do not expect you to run out and buy the makings for this dish for two reasons. You are not used to eating a whole dish of innards and you would have a very difficult time buying them even if you wanted to. We use innards in "meat products," but they are often hard to find on the fresh market.

I just want to describe this dish for you because it is very old and, as far as I am concerned, a classic dish.

The liver, heart, kidneys, sweetbreads, and spleen of the lamb are cut into pieces and placed on a large skewer. The whole is wrapped with the intestines of the lamb and then seasoned with salt and pepper, olive oil, and a bit of oregano. This is roasted, turning the skewer over a charcoal fire, until the whole thing is wonderfully golden and crunchy. The skewer is removed and the dish served in thick slices.

When you are in Athens you can go to the Pelopenese Grill just behind Omonia Square. They have this traditional dish all the time, and I hope you will try it. Buy a beer and a side of roast pork or chicken, and eat until you cannot move. The bill will be tiny.

HINT: PUT FRESH ANISE OR FENNEL IN INNARDS. When you are cooking a boiled tongue, or perhaps a tripe dish, just add the cut-up fresh vegetable to the pot. It has a wonderfully cleansing and flavoring effect.

LAMB INNARD SOUP FOR EASTER

(Mageiritsa)

SERVES 10

This is a bowl of memories, of traditions, more than it is a soup. The Easter lamb, the Paschal lamb, is purchased by each Greek family just a day or so before Easter. The head is removed, along with all of the innards, and with these a special soup is made for midnight on Easter Eve. It is the moment of the breaking of the Lenten fast, the moment of the Resurrection, the moment of excitement and joy in every city in Greece. Christmas Eve is the closest thing we have to the great Easter celebration of the Orthodox Church, and we do very little with Easter. Just as a turkey or ham is necessary to the Western Christmas, so this soup is necessary to the midnight meal on Easter Eve.

I have eliminated the use of the lamb head for stock as I am quite sure you will have a tough time finding one in any case.

- 2 quarts Basic Lamb Stock (page 143)
- ½ cup olive oil
- 1 medium yellow onion, peeled and chopped
- 1 bunch green onions, cleaned and chopped
- ½ cup chopped parsley
- 2 or 3 lamb hearts, cut in half
- 2 lamb kidneys, cleaned of extra fat and cut in half
- 3 or 4 lamb tongues, whole
- ½ pound boneless lamb (shoulder steak, etc.), diced
- 1 tablespoon flour
- ½ cup white wine
- ¼ pound lamb liver
- 1 tablespoon dried dillweed
- Salt and pepper to taste
- ½ cup rice

EGG-LEMON SAUCE

- 3 eggs, at room temperature
- ½ cup fresh lemon juice

- Parsley, chopped, for garnish

Prepare the stock.

Heat a large frying pan or stove-top casserole and add the olive oil. Sauté the onions and parsley for just a moment and then add the heart, kidneys, and tongues, along with the boneless lamb. Sauté for 15 minutes or so and stir in the flour. Stir it well. Add the white wine and stock, stirring all the time, and cook until the mixture thickens a bit. Cover and simmer until the meats are tender, about 2 hours. Add additional water now and then to keep the soup up to the same level.

When the meats are tender add the liver, dillweed, salt and pepper to taste, and the rice. Simmer, covered, for 20 minutes or until the rice is tender. Turn off the heat and remove the meats from the pot. Peel the tongue and dice fine. Chop the heart, kidney, and liver as well. Return to the pot and bring to a simmer once again.

Whip the eggs with the lemon juice in a 2-cup measuring glass. Quickly stir in 1 cup of the broth. Add this mixture to the pot and stir until it thickens a bit. Taste to see if salt and pepper are needed. Garnish with the parsley and serve.

TRIPE, ROMAN STYLE
(Trippa alla Romana)
SERVES 6 AS A MAIN COURSE ON PASTA

I gave you a recipe like this in my first cookbook, years ago. This one is much better. But I must tell you that a man once approached me in a large airport, just after I had published the first book . . . in 1984. He did not introduce himself . . . he did not tell me he watches the shows . . . he just said, "Hey, Frugal! How long do you have to cook that damn tripe before you eat it. Mine is now at a week on the stove." I laughed very hard but you understand that cooking tripe is not at all difficult. Just be patient. This is a very good recipe, and typical of Rome.

- 3 pounds beef tripe
- 6 tablespoons olive oil
- 3 cloves garlic, sliced thin
- 1 yellow onion, peeled and coarsely chopped
- ½ pound boneless pork, cut into medium dice
- 1 cup red wine
- 2 cups Basic Brown Soup Stock (page 148) or canned stock, not bouillon cubes!
- 2 cups Italian Tomato Sauce (page 237)
- Peel of ¼ fresh lemon in very large pieces
- 1 tablespoon fresh rosemary needles *or* 1 teaspoon dried rosemary needles
- ¼ cup chopped parsley
- Salt and freshly ground black pepper to taste (I like LOTS of black pepper in this dish)
- ½ cup freshly grated Parmesan cheese
- 1 cup whipping cream

Rinse the tripe and place in a 12-quart pot. Cover with water and bring to a boil. Drain and rinse the tripe in cold water. Cut the tripe into small pieces about ½ inch wide and 2 inches long. Set aside.

In a large frying pan heat the oil and add the garlic. Sauté for just a moment and then add the onion and pork. Cook until the onion is clear.

Return the tripe to the pot. Add all other ingredients except the cheese and cream and simmer until the meat is very tender, about 2 hours. You may wish to leave the lid off the pot for part of this time so that the sauce will reduce a bit. Watch carefully that the liquids do not evaporate too quickly. If this should happen, simply add a bit of water so that all can continue to cook properly.

Just before serving stir in the cheese and cream. Reheat, test for seasonings, and serve.

This is great with polenta, rice, or pasta. I just eat it from a bowl with French bread and some dry red wine.

OXTAILS, ROMAN STYLE

SERVES 6–8, ALONG WITH PASTA, FOR A MAIN DISH

Simple is the word and wonderful is the dish. The Jews in Rome, who still live around the Jewish Ghetto, love meat cooked in this way. The secret is to brown the meat severely and then simmer it slowly in tomato sauce and wine. There is a wonderful restaurant in the Ghetto that serves food in this manner, but it has no name and is known only to the locals. I don't know how to explain the location since an address will not help you. The locals won't tell you where the place is located!

- **4 pounds oxtails, cut at the joint**
- **Salt and freshly ground black pepper to taste**
- **2 tablespoons olive oil**
- **2 cloves garlic, sliced thin**
- **1 cup dry red wine**
- **2 cups Italian Tomato Sauce (page 237)**

Season the oxtails with salt and pepper. Heat a 6-quart stove-top covered casserole and add the oil and garlic. Sauté for just a moment and add one third of the meat. Brown well on both sides and remove. Brown the next third and then the last. Drain the fat from the pot and return all of the meat, along with all other ingredients. Cover and simmer until very tender, about 2½ hours. You may need to add a bit of water now and then if the mixture dries out.

Serve with pasta as a main course. Salad and bread will complete a very "old-fashioned" Roman meal. The sauce is so rich you won't believe it!

NOTE: See **HINT: WHEN BROWNING MEATS** (page 363)

PASTA WITH LAMB INTESTINES
(Rigatoni con Pagliata Edmondo)

Now, I ask you. Are you not surprised that I would include such a dish in this collection? I have already explained in the opening section to this chapter that Romans traditionally have eaten and enjoyed innards. This one, however, threw me. The lamb intestines are to be from a young lamb, thus they are not available at all seasons. I did have a chance to taste this Roman classic at Edmondo's, in Rome. He simmers the lamb intestines very gently and then cooks them a second time in a light Italian tomato sauce with a bit of cream. This mixture is served over rigatoni, along with cheese and pepper on top. I really was not sure what to expect, but I can tell you now that when you are in Rome you must go to his restaurant and try this dish. It is unusually good and certainly Roman!

Try this dish using the beef tripe recipe on page 377 instead of the lamb intestines. It will work well.

FRIED INNARDS, ROMAN STYLE EDMONDO
(Fritto Misto)

I love this restaurant, really a trattoria, a wonderful neighborhood joint. Edmondo specializes in Roman innards and his deep-fried dishes, a mixture of lamb brains, lamb cutlets, artichokes, and vegetables, are just the best imaginable. This is his method of frying these wonders, as far as I can understand it.

THE BATTER

See the recipe for Assorted Fried Seafood (page 186)

Ample peanut oil for deep-frying

THE MEATS

Lamb brains, cut into 3-inch lengths

Lamb cutlets (I use thin pieces of boneless lamb steak)

Lamb heart, boiled in broth a bit until it is tender, then cut into strips

THE VEGETABLES

Artichoke hearts (page 463)

Zucchini sticks

Prepare everything completely before you begin. Be sure that your deep-frying oil is at 400° before you start frying. Fry the assorted foods in small batches so that the oil stays hot. Be sure to reheat the oil to 400° between batches. Drain the food well on paper towels before serving.

HEADCHEESE SALAD

SERVES 6 AS A FIRST COURSE

You will enjoy this excellent dish only if you can buy headcheese from a good Italian delicatessen. Don't buy that inferior product that is sold in a plastic container in your supermarket. It is not the genuine article. If you have an Italian deli in your town, you will find yourself making this easy dish often.

- **1 pound Italian headcheese, cut into julienne strips**
- **1 cup Pot Roast Shredded (page 365)**
- **1 tablespoon of the broth in which the beef was cooked**
- **1 medium yellow onion, peeled and sliced thin**
- **¼ cup olive oil**
- **Juice of 1 lemon**
- **Salt and freshly ground black pepper to taste**
- **1 tablespoon parsley**
- **6 lettuce-leaf "cups" for garnish**

Julienne the headcheese and place in a bowl along with the beef and broth. Sauté the onion in a bit of the oil just until it is limp, not discolored. Add all ingredients, except the lettuce, to the meat bowl and toss. Marinate for 1 hour and serve at room temperature in the lettuce cups.

TONGUE IN SWEET AND SOUR SAUCE, ROMAN STYLE

(Lingua in Agrodolce alla Romana)

SERVES 6–8

This is another wonderful dish from my friend in Rome, Mrs. Jo Bettoja. She reminded me that the presence of the raisins and pine nuts, along with the sweet dressing, points directly back to earlier times in Rome. I think this is one of the best tongue dishes I have ever tasted . . . and I thank her for it. You will too!

1 beef tongue, about 2 pounds
2 bay leaves
1 medium yellow onion, peeled and quartered
1 clove, whole
10 black peppercorns, whole
1 tablespoon kosher salt
3½ tablespoons sugar
3 tablespoons white wine vinegar
Juice of 2 fresh lemons
⅓ cup white raisins
3 cloves garlic, crushed
¼ teaspoon dried red pepper flakes
3 tablespoons finely chopped parsley
¼ cup pine nuts, lightly toasted (page 34)

Clean the tongue by trimming off a bit of the part where the tongue was attached. Wash and place in a 4-quart kettle with lid. Cover with water and add the bay leaves, onion, clove, peppercorns, and salt. Bring to a boil and simmer, covered, for 2 hours. Drain, cool enough to handle, and peel the tongue.

Dissolve the sugar in the vinegar over low heat, stirring. Add all the remaining ingredients except the pine nuts.

Slice the tongue thinly and arrange on a serving dish. Pour over the sauce, taking care to cover all the meat. Sprinkle over the pine nuts. Leave for a night to marinate in a cool place, preferably not in the refrigerator.

NOTE: I would suggest that you make this dish early in the day and allow it to marinate a few hours before serving.

Garnish with additional parsley, if you wish.

Dried Foods

Sometimes a discovery becomes so commonplace in our lives that we forget about its implications. Consider how life was changed with the realization that foods could be dried. This oldest method of preserving food was probably discovered during the arid windstorms some 30,000 years ago. Preservation of food for the winter was the most important result of this process, but consider that this discovery also allowed people to travel with a food supply in their bags. Finally, dried food gave us possibilities for trade since the food would not spoil en route. Life was seriously changed when we learned to dry foods.

The first food to be dried was probably fish. Why do we continue to dry it when freezing and refrigeration now allow us to keep the fish for a time and yet still maintain fresh flavor? We continue to dry certain foods because the process changes and enriches the flavor. The Chinese still dry fish and enjoy the concentration of the original taste even though fresh fish is sold in the same shop.

Almost any food product can be dried, and many actually improve in flavor during the process. Chinese black mushrooms are a good example. Fresh Chinese mushrooms, now available in many American supermarkets, simply do not have that wonderful rich flavor that you find in the dried ones. And leave it to the Chinese to continue to enjoy the flavors of the Old World. They dry almost every vegetable and fish product available and then reconstitute them in dishes that are hardly to be considered peasant style. They are the wisest of the food driers, and perhaps the oldest.

The Greeks were fond of drying fruits of all kinds and they brought this appreciation with them when they were taken into Rome as cooks. The Romans enjoyed the dried figs and citrus fruits from Greece to such an extent that they gave their traveling armies a fruit allotment when they went off to conquer. Is it too farfetched to believe that they took these delights with them on their invasions of England, and that we now credit the English with the invention of fruitcake when it is actually a very old Roman dish? Go to the Jewish Ghetto in Rome and buy some fruit bars. And you thought English fruitcake was heavy! Craig, my assistant, saw the clerks selling the cakes by weight, and I replied that it was just like selling pound cake. After tasting one he exclaimed, "This is no pound cake. This is ton cake!"

You might also wish to consider:

Two Squid, Chowed *(page 213)*
Steamed Dried Duck and Pork *(page 296)*
Jellyfish Salad *(page 153)*
Duck and Jellyfish Salad *(page 155)*

China

DRIED ABALONE WITH MUSHROOMS

SERVES 4–6 AS PART OF A CHINESE MEAL— A VERY EXPENSIVE PART

The flavor of dried abalone is heavy and rich . . . absolutely delicious. However, it is not what you would call "tender" in the normal sense. The richness makes up for the nice, rather chewy, texture.

Don't put this book back on the shelf just because this dish takes several hours to cook and dried abalone costs over $30 a pound. Hey, I didn't ask you to buy a whole pound! Just look at this as one of those dishes that you do once . . . for very important guests. I expect that for those of you who are closet cookbook readers, this is the only taste you will have of this dish . . . just reading about it. That is fine with me, but you must know that such a thing exists.

6 ounces dried abalone (available in good Chinese markets), soaked for 24 hours
3 green onions
2 ginger slices, each the size of a 25-cent piece
Chinese dried mushrooms, soaked for 2 hours
1 tablespoon peanut oil
2 cloves garlic, chopped fine
2 tablespoons light soy sauce
1 tablespoon Chinese rice wine or dry sherry
Pinch of sugar
2 tablespoons oyster sauce
½ cup Chinese Chicken Soup Stock (page 126) or Basic Chicken Stock (page 144)
¼ teaspoon sesame oil
Pinch of ground white pepper
1 teaspoon cornstarch and 1 tablespoon water mixed together (optional)

Soak the dried abalone in warm water for 24 hours, changing the water several times. Drain, and place in a 1-quart saucepan. Add the green onions and ginger slices and cover with water. Simmer, covered, until tender, about 5 or 6 hours. You will need to add a little more water now and then. Test for tenderness by poking with a skewer. Slice thinly and set aside in the cooking broth.

Soak the mushrooms, remove the stems, and slice the caps into ¼-inch-wide pieces. Set aside.

Heat the wok and add the oil. Chow the garlic for just a moment and add the drained abalone and mushroom slices. Chow until they are hot and add the remaining ingredients. Thicken if you wish with the cornstarch and water mixture.

DRIED SCALLOP AND CHIVE SOUP

SERVES 8–10

I tried a dish close to this one at the wonderful Sun Tung Lok Restaurant, in Kowloon, Hong Kong. The place is terribly expensive but they serve wonderful food, and many are fancy variations on old dried foods. This is such a dish.

- **4 ounces dried scallops, soaked**
- **8 cups Chinese Chicken Soup Stock (page 126)**
- **2 dried Chinese mushrooms**
- **2 tablespoons Chinese rice wine or dry sherry**
- **1 tablespoon light soy sauce**
- **Salt to taste**
- **¼ cup Chinese Poached Chicken (page 265), shredded**
- **Pinch of ground white pepper**
- **1 tablespoon sesame oil**
- **1 tablespoon Chinese garlic chives or Western chives**
- **3 egg whites, beaten**
- **Slivers of Chinese or Southern ham for garnish (Substitute boiled ham if necessary)**

Soak the dried scallops overnight, changing the water twice. Place the chicken stock, along with the mushrooms and the drained scallops, in a Chinese double boiler (page 137) or regular double boiler, and cook, covered, for 3 hours.

Remove the soup from the double boiler and place it in a 4-quart saucepan. Bring to a light boil and add the remaining ingredients, except the chives, egg whites, and ham-sliver garnish, and cook for 10 minutes. Stir in the chives and the beaten egg whites and garnish with a few slivers of ham. Serve immediately.

DRIED OYSTERS AND PORK IN LETTUCE

SERVES 4 AS PART OF A CHINESE MEAL

This is wonderful fun to prepare and even more fun to eat. You will begin to wonder if the Chinese also invented the burrito! I think they did!

- **4 ounces dried oysters, rinsed and soaked for 2 hours**
- **6 Chinese dried mushrooms, soaked for 2 hours**
- **½ pound lean pork coarsely ground**
- **1 tablespoon light soy sauce**
- **⅛ teaspoon freshly grated ginger**
- **1 tablespoon Chinese rice wine or dry sherry**
- **2 cloves garlic, crushed**
- **1 teaspoon cornstarch**
- **2 tablespoons peanut oil for chowing**
- **8 water chestnuts, chopped coarsely**
- **1 tablespoon oyster sauce**
- **½ teaspoon sesame oil**
- **6 green onions, chopped**
- **8 lettuce-leaf cups (iceberg lettuce)**

Soak the oysters and mushrooms, drain, and grind together, coarsely. Mix with the ground pork. Add the soy sauce, ginger, rice wine, garlic, and cornstarch. Mix well and place in a steaming dish. Steam for 20 minutes (page 106).

When ready to serve dinner, add the peanut oil to a hot wok. Chow the steamed mixture, along with the water chestnuts, oyster sauce, sesame oil, and green onions, breaking up the mixture as it cooks for about 3 minutes.

Drain any excess fat from the cooked meats and serve in

a bowl along with the lettuce cups on the side. Place a bit of meat in each cup and roll up and eat like a burrito.

HINT: TO PREPARE LETTUCE CUPS simply remove the core of the iceberg lettuce by banging the bottom core of the head on the counter. The core can then be easily and quickly removed. Hold the head under running cold water and remove the leaves gently, letting the water do much of the work. Drain and chill.

STEAMED PORK WITH MUSHROOM AND DRIED SQUID

SERVES 4–5 AS PART OF A CHINESE MEAL

In the early days of the Chinatowns in America, many staff members of a shop or market would eat at least 2 meals a day in the shop itself. Kitchens were built in the back of the store and the boss would often do the cooking. In a few places in Seattle and San Francisco, Chicago and New York, you can still see such a practice. This recipe was given me by my friend Mr. George Foo Yee of the Wah Young Company, located in Seattle's Chinatown. He recited the ingredients *after* he had fed his staff.

- 2 ounces dried squid, soaked overnight, drained and chopped
- 4 Chinese dried mushrooms, soaked for 2 hours
- 1 pound lean pork coarsely chopped
- 8 dried red dates, soaked for 4 hours
- 2 cloves garlic, crushed
- ¼ teaspoon freshly grated ginger
- 2 tablespoons light soy sauce
- 1 tablespoon Chinese rice wine or dry sherry
- ½ tablespoon cornstarch
- 1 tablespoon peanut oil
- White pepper, ground, to taste
- Pinch of MSG (optional)

Drain all the soaked items well. Mix all together and place in a steaming dish. Steam in a bamboo steamer (page 106) for 30 minutes.

Serve as a course in a Chinese meal. The liquid remaining in the steaming dish is just great over rice.

CHINESE SAUSAGE, DRIED DUCK, AND ROAST PORK SAND POT

SERVES 4 AS PART OF A CHINESE MEAL

The flavors of these meats, each already very rich because they are dried, combine in this dish to offer a distinct and wonderful blend. It is very typical of the "hot sand pot" dishes that you find in Hong Kong.

- ½ pound dried duck, cut into 1-inch-square pieces (Use a cleaver for this), soaked in ample water overnight
- 3 Chinese sausages *(lop chong)*, whole
- 1 tablespoon peanut oil
- 1 clove garlic, chopped fine
- 1 medium yellow onion, peeled and sliced
- ⅛ teaspoon freshly grated ginger
- ½ pound Crispy Roast Pork (page 334), sliced, *or* ½ pound Barbecued Pork Strips (page 331)
- 4 green onions, cut Chinese style (page 158)
- 1 tablespoon light soy sauce
- Pinch of brown sugar
- ½ teaspoon sesame oil
- White pepper, ground, to taste
- 1 medium head iceberg lettuce, torn

Simmer the soaked dried duck, along with the sausage, for 20 minutes. Cut the sausage into 1-inch pieces. Chow the duck and sausage quickly in the wok along with the remaining ingredients except the lettuce. Drain the fat. Place in a sand pot (page 12) over the lettuce and place on a heat diffuser over a hot burner. When all is piping hot, serve.

Greece

SALTED COD, GREEK STYLE
(Bakaliaros)

It is interesting to note how common dried fish was in the ancient world. Many early citizens knew only this kind of fish, as they lived inland and shipment of fresh fish was impossible. For an old-timer these flavors bring forth wonderful memories of a youth in Greece.

During the holidays that call for fasting beforehand, such as Christmas and Easter, this dried cod becomes a major menu item. I have talked with so many young Greeks who say, "No, I don't really care for the stuff. My mother practically raised us on *bakaliaros!*" Then I asked them what they now eat on Christmas Eve or during the fasting times in Lent. Well, it is *bakaliaros,* of course. There is something to remembering who you are through certain foods. The Romans also loved this dish and Italian variations follow in the next series of recipes.

Soak the salted cod just as in the recipe for Salted Cod in Cream Sauce (page 392). Cook in just the same manner but omit the cream sauce and serve the hot fish with any of the following:

- Greek Salad Dressing (page 160)
- Yogurt, plain or with dillweed
- Garlic Sauce (page 235)

Italy

SALTED COD IN CREAM SAUCE
(Baccalà)

SERVES 4–6 AS A FISH COURSE FOR AN ITALIAN MEAL

The secret to refreshing this dried salt cod is lots of water. It is soaked for days and you can find it ready to go in Roman fish markets. They use wonderful old marble tanks that sit out on the street, filled with *baccalà* and with a stream of fresh water running into the tank all the time. You can find this dried fish in any Italian market. Don't buy the stuff imported from Canada in tiny boxes. It is much too expensive.

I should also tell you that there is a restaurant in Rome, between Campo de' Fiori and the Jewish Ghetto, that has this on its menu . . . and it is the *only* item on the menu. You cannot get into the place!

1 pound dried salt cod fillets, soaked and refreshed for 2 days
1 yellow onion, peeled and chopped
1 carrot, unpeeled, sliced
1 bay leaf, whole
6 peppercorns

CREAM SAUCE

1½ tablespoons butter
1½ tablespoons olive oil
3 tablespoons flour
½ cup dry white wine
1 cup milk
½ cup cream
1 teaspoon capers, rinsed and chopped
Salt and freshly ground black pepper to taste
1 tablespoon pine nuts, toasted (page 34), for garnish

Buy pieces of salt cod that are fairly thick and fresh-looking. Cut them into 1½-inch pieces, across the grain of the fish. Rinse well and place in a large bowl. Cover with water and allow to soak, changing the water 2 or 3 times each day, for 48 hours. You do not have to refrigerate.

Drain the cod and place in a 4-quart soup pot. Add fresh water to cover and the onion, carrot, bay leaf, and peppercorns. Bring to a simmer and cook for 20 minutes or until the fish is tender.

While the fish is cooking, prepare the sauce. Heat the oil and butter in a small frying pan and add the flour. Cook just a few minutes to prepare a roux. Do not discolor. In a saucepan heat the wine, milk, and cream. Add the roux, stirring constantly. When the sauce thickens, remove from the heat and add the capers. Taste, and adjust pepper. I doubt that you will want any salt.

Drain the pieces of cod well and place on a serving platter. Top with the sauce and garnish with the pine nuts.

SALTED COD IN TOMATO SAUCE

SERVES 4–5 AS A FIRST COURSE

This one is easy, providing you are keeping some Italian Tomato Sauce in the house.

Soak 1 pound of salt cod fillets as instructed above. Drain and simmer in Italian Tomato Sauce (page 237) just to cover. You may need to add a little water as it cooks. It should be tender in about 20 minutes.

Serve with pasta or salad, and a very dry white wine. This is also great for a first course, chopped and served directly over spaghetti.

Pasta

Who did it? Who invented pasta? Food lovers have argued about this issue for hundreds of years, and I certainly intend to get in on the debate.

The Italians claim that pasta was invented in Italy. The Chinese claim that they invented pasta and prove their case by pointing out that Marco Polo brought pasta or noodles from China back to his beloved Venice. He also brought back coal and gunpowder, but there is good evidence that indicates pasta was being enjoyed in other areas of Italy prior to Polo's trip, though the dish was not known in Venice at the time. There is an ancient macaroni maker depicted on the frescoes of an Etruscan tomb. There are other references to pasta dishes, including that of a Greek, one Hesychius, who wrote during the eighth century. All of these events predate the trip by Mr. Polo.

Reay Tannahill, in her terrific volume, *Food in History* (see Bibliography), points out that prior to Polo's trip people in both India and the Arab lands were eating noodles. They called them *sevika* or *righta,* meaning "threads." Tannahill hypothesizes that pasta was introduced to Italy via the Arab–Venice/Florence/Genoa trade connections and then spread gradually throughout Italy. In support of this theory she notes that the word *spaghetti* is derived from *spago,* "string," a word and item not dissimilar to the "thread" noodles of the Arabs.

It appears that the argument as to who invented which is not an argument at all. The Chinese and the peoples of Arabia and Italy knew of pasta quite independently of one another, though the Chinese probably had it first. So much for that!

Grains were cooked into pastes or pulses in ancient Rome, and the term "polenta" probably comes from *puls*. The mush was eaten with a sauce of some sort and was enjoyed by both the peasants and the city dwellers. The trip that the grain took from a mush to noodles of a thousand different shapes was a profound trip, indeed. My dear friend Carlo Middione says in his wonderful book, *The Food of Southern Italy* (see Bibliography), that for southern Italians in our time "pasta is as necessary as water and air for survival." After tasting some of the following recipes you will understand why.

The Greeks have some wonderful pasta dishes, though they are not as complicated or as varied as the Italian ones. There are some theories that the Italians introduced pasta into Greece during the fourteenth century, but I think it is just as likely that the Middle Eastern peoples brought pasta into Greece at a much earlier date. In any case, you must make *pastitsio*. And when you prepare such a dish, you will realize that the Greeks invented what the Italians call *lasagne*.

There are major differences between Italy and China when it comes to the celebration of the noodle. Italy has at least one hundred shapes of pasta, but all are made from wheat. China, on the other hand, has only two shapes, long noodles and flat noodles, but they are made from all kinds of foods such as wheat, rice, beans, tapioca, and buckwheat, thus giving us few shapes but many textures. Some cook up to look like glass; others have a rich dark brown color with a flavor to match. The importance of the noodle for the meal is also different in the two cultures. In China the meal can consist of noodles, long thin noodles to symbolize longevity, or noodles with fish to represent plenteousness. In Italy pasta is never a main course but rather one part of the whole meal.

China has always been a hungry nation, and the invention of the noodle was a great blessing. We know that noodles were commercially prepared as early as A.D. 100 and sold on the streets. The peasants seemed to enjoy them from the first, with the upper classes not catching up until the sixteenth century. After all, the noodle provided the peasant kitchen with good nutrition and endless possibilities for variation, and the noodle cooked quickly, not a small matter for a people short on fuel.

There is one more difference between the noodle makers of China and those of Italy. In Italy pasta is either rolled and then cut, or it is extruded from machines. The Chinese use both of these methods, but they also "pull" noodles. A large piece of dough is pulled and then floured, pulled again and floured, and each time the number of strands doubles. Finally, and in just a minute or two, the noodle maker has a thousand strands in his hands. It is one of the most fascinating food-preparation techniques that I know of anywhere in the world. You can see it done when you go to Hong Kong. Wonderful fun!

You might also wish to consider:

Lamb with Orzo Pasta, Greek Style *(page 321)*
Greek Lamb and Pasta Salad *(page 162)*
Octopus Spaghetti Zorba *(page 221)*
Pasta with Mushrooms Natalie *(page 536)*

China

CHOW MEIN, CANTONESE STYLE

SERVES 6 AS PART OF A CHINESE MEAL

This is surely the most famous Chinese noodle dish in America. The only problem is that the deep-fried noodle dish most Caucasians think of as Chinese is not a Chinese dish at all. Real chow mein is not deep-fried. *Chow* means "to pan-fry," and *mein* means "noodle." Pan-fried is what is going on here. So, here is my favorite version. Your kids will think you are a genius, though you may have to call this something other than its real name . . . otherwise your children will probably be expecting the old deep-fried noodle bit.

- ⅜ pound Chinese dried egg noodles
- 1 cup pork, cut julienne
- ½ cup sliced water chestnuts
- 3 ribs bok choy (page 24), sliced

MARINADE

- 1 tablespoon dry sherry or Chinese rice wine
- 2 tablespoons light soy sauce
- ½ teaspoon freshly grated ginger

- 6 tablespoons peanut oil for pan-frying
- 1 yellow onion, peeled and sliced
- 2 ribs celery, chopped thin
- 3 Chinese dried mushrooms, soaked (page 27), drained, and chopped

SAUCE

- 1 tablespoon light soy sauce
- ⅛ teaspoon sugar
- ¼ teaspoon salt
- Pinch of MSG (optional)
- 1 tablespoon sesame oil
- 1 cup Chinese Chicken Soup Stock (page 126) or Basic Chicken Stock (page 144)
- 1 tablespoon cornstarch
- 2 cups fresh bean sprouts

THE NOODLES

Bring an 8-quart pot of water to a boil and add the noodles. Carefully stir. When they begin to float freely, drain and rinse in cold water. Drain well again. Spread the noodles out on a large oiled broiling rack and allow them to dry for two hours. I use an electric fan to help them along.

Heat a large wok and add 3 tablespoons of peanut oil. Place the noodles in the wok, all in a big nest, and gently pan-brown them on one side. Get them good and brown. Turn the nest and brown it a bit on the other side. Remove from the wok and allow to cool.

THE MEAT AND VEGETABLES

Marinate the cut pork for 15 minutes. Drain the marinade and reserve. Heat the wok and add 1 tablespoon oil. Chow the meat for a few minutes until tender. Remove to the serving plate.

Heat the wok again and add 2 tablespoons oil. Chow the onion, celery, and mushrooms until the onions are clear. Add the water chestnuts and bok choy. Remove all to the serving plate.

Mix the sauce, adding the reserved marinade. Place the noodles in the heated wok and add the sauce. Toss just to cover the noodles and add the meat and vegetable mixture. Gently toss and stir-fry all together until the noodles are tender but still a bit firm.

Add the bean sprouts and toss just until they are hot, not cooked. Serve immediately.

HINT: TO FREEZE CHOW MEIN NOODLES you need simply boil, dry, and then pan-fry them. This is a lot to do on a day when you want chow mein. Do a double or triple batch one day and freeze the rest in seal-tight freezer bags. They defrost in a very short time and you simply refresh them with a bit of oil in a hot wok. Then, add the soup stock and vegetables as per your recipe.

CHOWED NOODLES WITH PORK AND SESAME SAUCE

SERVES 4 AS PART OF A CHINESE MEAL

This dish is old, popular, easy, and frugal. If you have put some chowed noodles in the freezer you can prepare this dish in very little time and everyone will love it. It is just the perfect blend of pork and sesame!

- ½ pound dried Chinese egg noodles, chowed or pan-fried (page 399)
- 2 tablespoons peanut oil
- 1 clove garlic, crushed
- ⅛ teaspoon salt
- ½ pound lean pork, cut julienne
- ½ cup Chinese Chicken Soup Stock (page 126) or Basic Chicken Stock (page 144)

THE SAUCE

Prepare 1 batch of Sesame Garlic Dressing from Chicken Shredded with Sesame Garlic Paste (page 91)

Green onions, chopped, *or* Chinese parsley, chopped, for garnish

Pan-fry or chow the noodles as instructed. Remove them from the wok. Reheat the wok and add the oil, garlic, and salt. Chow for a moment and add the pork. Chow the pork to your taste and remove from the wok. Return the noodles to the wok and heat them for a few moments, tossing all the time. Add the broth and cooked pork and chow until the noodles absorb the liquid. Remove from the heat and add the sesame sauce. Toss and place in a bowl. Add the garnish and serve.

CHOW FUN NOODLES

MAKES 8–10 10-INCH-ROUND NOODLES

This is one of the most wonderful and versatile noodles that I know, but I cannot tell you how to make it of rice. This one is made with wheat flour—strictly a home version of a Chinese classic—but it is very close to the original. The actual rice noodle involves grinding rice flour while trickling water onto the mill. The batter simply dribbles out the bottom of the mill. You can see this being made in San Francisco and New York, but once you see the enormous old stone mill needed for this dish you will trust me and try this wheat-flour version. Make a few batches and then use them in the recipes that follow.

1¼ cups *cold* water
2 tablespoons peanut oil
1 cup unsifted Swans Down cake flour
1 tablespoon cornstarch
1 teaspoon salt

Place the above ingredients, *in the order given,* in a food blender. The order is important as you must have the liquids in the blender first. Blend for a moment and then scrape down the sides of the blender with a rubber spatula. Blend again at high speed for 30 seconds. Pour into a small bowl and cook.

TO COOK THE NOODLES

I use 10-inch stainless-steel cake pans. They work beautifully. Oil each pan with a bit of peanut oil and a paper towel. Place 2 ounces of batter in each pan and steam (see page 106) for 3 minutes. Remove from the steamer and allow the pans to cool a bit. Pull the noodles from the bottoms of the pans and place on waxed paper. Oil the pans again and continue. I do 3 at a time.

Be very careful to see that your steamer is level so that the noodles will be even all the way across. Also, remember that the steamer must be good and hot, with a great deal of boiling going on. A quiet steamer will not do the job!

You will need to make more than one batch of this if you are serving more than 2 people. You will catch on to this very quickly.

NOTE: You will have poor luck with this recipe if you use a cake flour other than Swans Down. I have tried several others but they are not milled as fine as is this particular product. Stick to this flour and you will have good luck with all of the noodle and dumpling recipes in this book.

VARIATION: You can also just go ahead and buy these noodles premade in any city that has a large Chinatown. I know they are available in New York, San Francisco, Seattle, Chicago, Portland, Vancouver, B.C., Los Angeles, and Boston.

COLD CHOW FUN AND PORK ROLL

SERVES 8 AS A DIM SUM OR APPETIZER COURSE

This is just a delicious cold dish. It can be served as part of a dim sum meal or as an appetizer for a formal Chinese meal. In either situation everyone will love this one.

4 Chow Fun Noodles (page 402)
¾ cup Barbecued Pork Strips (page 331), cut in julienne strips
1 cup fresh bean sprouts
3 tablespoons chopped Chinese parsley

DRESSING
2 tablespoons light soy sauce
2 tablespoons sesame oil
⅛ teaspoon sugar
1 teaspoon rice vinegar

Prepare a batch of Chow Fun Noodles.

Mix the pork, bean sprouts, and parsley in a bowl. Prepare the dressing and toss with the vegetable and meat mixture. Divide the filling among the 4 noodles and roll up. Chill a bit before serving. Cut each roll into 4 pieces.

BEEF CHOW FUN

SERVES 6 AS PART OF A CHINESE MEAL

The first time I ever tasted this dish I was with my friend Mary Young. It was 1967, in San Francisco, and this dish was very popular there. I don't believe that at that time you could get it anywhere else in the country . . . but San Francisco, yes. Mary took me to a particular restaurant and we enjoyed this dish. When I returned to San Francisco I asked her to take me to the same restaurant for the same dish. No, we had to go to a different restaurant to get the same version. The chef had moved to a different restaurant and his fans moved with him. Such is San Francisco . . . and, I suppose, the restaurant business.

1 batch Chow Fun Noodles (page 402)
1 pound beef flank steak, sliced thin across the grain

MARINADE
1 tablespoon dark soy sauce
1 tablespoon cornstarch
1 egg white
1 tablespoon peanut oil

7 tablespoons peanut oil for pan-frying
2 cloves garlic, chopped fine
1 slice ginger, the size of a 25-cent piece, cut julienne
1 tablespoon fermented black beans *(dow see)*, rinsed
1 tablespoon Chinese rice wine or dry sherry
½ medium yellow onion, peeled and sliced
½ green sweet bell pepper, cored and cut julienne

SAUCE
¼ teaspoon MSG (optional)
1 tablespoon dark soy sauce
¼ teaspoon sugar
1 tablespoon Chinese rice wine or dry sherry
Pinch of white pepper
1 tablespoon oyster sauce

1 cup fresh bean sprouts
Chinese parsley for garnish (optional)

Prepare the Chow Fun and slice into noodles about ½ inch wide. I usually oil the noodle a bit before cutting it so that the strands will not stick together.

Slice the meat and mix the marinade. Marinate the meat for 15 minutes.

Heat the wok and add 2 tablespoons of the peanut oil. Toss the noodles about in the oil until they are very hot and begin to color just a bit on the edges. Remove to the serving platter and set aside.

Heat the wok again and add 3 tablespoons of the peanut oil, along with the garlic and ginger. Chow for a moment and add the rinsed black beans and the sherry. In this chow the onion and green pepper, just until very hot. Remove to the serving platter.

Heat the wok a third time and add 2 tablespoons of the peanut oil and the meat. Chow on one side only until it begins to brown. Return the vegetables, the noodles, and the sauce to the wok and toss with the meat until hot. Add the bean sprouts, toss just a minute or so, and serve.

You might like to offer a Chinese parsley garnish.

MEAT-STUFFED CHOW FUN ROLLS

This dish is usually served in a formal dim sum house. I have seen patrons get up from their chairs and simply march across the dining room to take this dish from a cart. They do not want to miss out should the cart be empty by the time it gets to their table. The dish is that popular.

Prepare a batch of Chow Fun Noodles (page 402).

Choose a cooked meat filling, such as chopped barbecued pork, chowed beef, or chowed shrimp. Roll a bit of the meat filling into each noodle and place on a small oiled plate. Steam until the noodle is heated through and then add a bit of the following sauce just as you serve.

SAUCE FOR CHOW FUN ROLLS

- 2 tablespoons dark soy sauce
- ⅛ teaspoon sugar
- ¼ teaspoon freshly grated ginger
- ¼ teaspoon crushed garlic
- Pinch of MSG (optional)
- 2 tablespoons peanut oil
- ½ teaspoon Worcestershire sauce
- 2 green onions, chopped

Blend all together in a small saucepan and warm a bit. Allow to cool before serving over the rolled chow fun.

NOODLES IN OYSTER SAUCE
(Gon Lo Mein)
SERVES 4 AS A LUNCHEON DISH OR 6 AS PART OF A CHINESE MEAL

My friend Mary Young first explained this dish to me because she knew I was feeding a goodly number of college students during my days as a chaplain. "You can't afford to feed students unless you know about this dish. It is delicious and cheap!" She was right . . . as she always has been.

2 chicken breasts, skinned, boned, and cut julienne

MARINADE
1 tablespoon light soy sauce
1 tablespoon dry sherry or Chinese rice wine
½ teaspoon freshly grated ginger

2 tablespoons peanut oil
1 ounce Chinese dried mushrooms, soaked (page 27), drained, and cut julienne
½ pound dried Chinese egg noodles
1 tablespoon sesame oil
3 tablespoons oyster sauce
3 green onions, chopped
Chinese parsley, chopped, for garnish

Have all prepared before starting this dish. Bring a pot of water to boil for the noodles. Cut the chicken and marinate for 15 minutes. Heat a wok and add the peanut oil. Chow the chicken and mushrooms together just until the chicken is tender. Remove to a plate. Boil the noodles in the salted water just until they float and are soft but still quite firm, about 4 minutes. Drain. Heat the wok again and add the chicken, noodles, and remaining ingredients, except the parsley. Gently toss and stir-fry until the dish is hot throughout.

Top with the parsley and serve immediately.

CHINESE NEW YEAR NOODLES
(Jai)

SERVES 6 AS PART OF A CHINESE MEAL

Jai is a classic method of preparing *sai fun* (mung bean noodles). This vegetarian dish is eaten on the New Year to remind all of the necessity of a simpler and more contemplative life-style. The Buddhist monks still practically live on this dish, and I love it. My dear friend John Young, my adopted Chinese uncle, used to eat this dish with so much garlic and red chili paste (page 26) that I was amazed. His theory was: "The hotter, the better." You adjust this dish to your own desired level of heat.

2 tablespoons peanut oil
½ teaspoon salt
3 cloves garlic, chopped very fine or crushed
¼ teaspoon freshly grated ginger

VEGETABLES

6 Chinese dried mushrooms, soaked for 2 hours, cut julienne
1 cup Chinese celery cabbage (Napa), sliced as for coleslaw
*¼ cup dried lily buds, soaked for 1 hour (optional)
2 ounces dried bean-curd skin, soaked for 1 hour (optional)
½ cup bamboo shoots, cut julienne

THE SAUCE

2 tablespoons *foo yee* (page 25)
1 tablespoon light soy sauce
⅛ teaspoon sugar
2 teaspoons sesame oil
½ teaspoon ground white pepper
1 teaspoon garlic and red chili paste (page 26), to taste

4 ounces cellophane *(sai fun)* noodles, soaked for 1 hour
2 cups Chinese Chicken Soup Stock (page 126) or Basic Chicken Stock (page 144)
Green onions, chopped, *or* Chinese parsley, chopped, for garnish

*Lily buds, dried, can be found in Chinese markets. They offer a fragrant blessing to the dish.

Remember the basic rule for chowing: Have everything ready before you light the wok. Soak and prepare the vegetables, mix the sauce, and then go to it.

Heat the wok and add the oil, salt, garlic, and ginger. Chow for a moment and then add the vegetables. Chow until hot and tender and then add the sauce, the drained noodles, and the chicken stock to the wok. Stir and simmer uncovered until the noodles are clear and tender and have absorbed most of the broth. Taste for salt and place in a serving bowl. Garnish and serve.

CHINESE NEW YEAR NOODLES WITH OLIVES

Most of us in this country are surprised to hear that the Chinese enjoy dried olives, and have for a long time. The olives are called *lam see* and can be purchased in most Chinese markets. They are similar to an Italian dried olive, and very rich. Soak them in water for an hour or so, drain them, and then add them along with your vegetables during the preparation of *jai* for the New Year. This makes the dish very special but you may be surprised by the taste as it is a bit sharp.

GLASS NOODLES WITH PEANUT SAUCE

SERVES 4–6 AS AN APPETIZER COURSE, 4 AS PART OF A CHINESE MEAL

Sai fun, the thin noodles made from mung beans, are often called "cellophane" or "glass" noodles since they become almost transparent when cooked. This is a very tasty cold salad that will tickle your youngsters. When Channing and Jason were little we called this dish "Peanut Butter and Worms." Such fun!

- 1 4-ounce package of *sai fun* noodles
- 2 cups Chinese Chicken Soup Stock (page 126) or Basic Chicken Stock (page 144)

THE SAUCE

- 2 tablespoons peanut butter
- 4 tablespoons hot tap water
- 3 tablespoons light soy sauce
- Pinch of sugar
- ½ teaspoon sesame oil
- Shot of Tabasco or garlic and red chili paste (page 26) to taste

GARNISH

- Green onions, chopped
- 1 tablespoon dry roasted peanuts, chopped

Soak the noodles for 1 hour and drain. Place in a saucepan with the soup stock and simmer until they are tender but not mushy, about 10 minutes. Drain the stock from the noodles, reserving it for another use. Place the noodles on a tray and refrigerate them for 1 hour.

Mix the sauce by putting the peanut butter in a 2-cup measuring glass and adding the hot water. Stir with a fork until it is the consistency of whipping cream. Add the remaining ingredients for the sauce and mix with the chilled noodles. Place the noodles on a serving dish and garnish with the green onions and peanuts.

Greece

PASTA WITH MIZITHRA

SERVE 6 AS A FIRST COURSE OR SIDE DISH

This is a very basic dish. It can be found on the menu of most tavernas in Athens and it makes a wonderful side dish for just about anything. It is simply macaroni and cheese, Greek style. The flavor of the Mizithra cheese is what makes you remember beautiful Greece.

- ½ cup olive oil
- 4 cloves garlic, chopped fine
- 1 pound dry pasta, cooked and drained
- ½ cup freshly grated Parmesan cheese
- ½ cup freshly grated Mizithra cheese
- Salt and freshly ground black pepper to taste
- ¼ cup chopped parsley for garnish

Bring the water for the pasta to boil and prepare everything else. It is important never to overcook pasta.

Heat the olive oil in a small frying pan and add the chopped garlic. Sauté for just a moment and set aside. Boil the pasta until just barely tender. Drain and toss with all ingredients. Serve as a side dish in the place of another starch.

PASTITSIO

SERVES 6–8

The Greeks seem to have been into baking things long before the rest of us. I think they are to be given credit for the invention of baked pastas, this particular dish being the most famous of the many regional varieties. It is a splendid invention, and predates what the Italians were later to call *lasagne*.

When you see this dish in Greece it is not made with what we call macaroni. The hollow tubes of pasta are very long and very thin and much closer to what an American Italian would call long ziti. In any case, do not use elbow macaroni. The Greeks think that would verge on heresy!

You must prepare this dish in 3 different stages. It will go together beautifully and is not as complicated as a properly made lasagne. This version is from the women at St. Demetrios Greek Orthodox Church in Seattle. Their terrific cookbook is called *Greek Cooking in an American Kitchen* (see Bibliography).

THE MEAT MIXTURE

- 6 tablespoons butter
- ¾ cup peeled and finely chopped yellow onion
- 2 cloves garlic, crushed
- 1¼ pounds lean ground beef
- 1 16-ounce can peeled tomatoes, mashed
- ½ cup canned tomato sauce
- ½ cup water
- 1 teaspoon salt
- ⅛ teaspoon freshly ground black pepper
- ½ teaspoon cinnamon
- ⅛ teaspoon cloves

THE MACARONI

- 4 quarts water
- Salt
- ¾ pound Greek macaroni or Italian ziti (Use long, medium size, not elbow or short pasta)
- ¼ cup butter, melted
- 6 eggs, beaten
- 1 cup grated Parmesan or Romano cheese

THE WHITE SAUCE

- 6 tablespoons butter
- 6 tablespoons flour
- 2 cups warm milk
- 3 eggs, beaten

- 2 tablespoons dry sherry (optional)
- ½ teaspoon nutmeg
- ½ cup grated Parmesan cheese
- ½ teaspoon salt
- Dash of white pepper

Prepare the meat mixture by heating a large skillet and adding 2 tablespoons of the butter. Sauté the onion and garlic until golden. Add remaining butter and the crumbled ground beef. Add remaining ingredients for the meat mixture and simmer, uncovered, for 20 minutes, or until most of the liquid has been absorbed. Mixture should be thick. Set aside.

Prepare the macaroni by bringing the water to a boil in a large stockpot. Add the salt and the macaroni. Stir gently and cook uncovered until tender, about 7 to 8 minutes. Drain and rinse with cool water. Drain well and place in a large bowl. Add the melted butter, beaten eggs, and grated cheese. Put half of this mixture into a greased 9 × 9 × 2-inch baking pan and top with the meat mixture. Cover the meat with the remaining half of the pasta.

NOTE: I like to arrange the pasta in straight rows so that when you cut and serve the dish the pasta is even and beautiful. That is how they do it in Greece!

Prepare the white sauce by melting the butter in a medium saucepan. Stir in the flour and cook for a moment. Gradually add the heated milk, stirring constantly, and cook until thickened and smooth. Beat the eggs in a separate bowl and stir in ½ cup of the sauce. Blend and stir the egg mixture into the saucepan. Continue to stir and cook over low heat until all is thickened. Add remaining ingredients for the sauce. Pour the sauce over the macaroni and bake at 350° for 25 minutes, or until the top is delicately browned.

PASTITSIO BAKED WITH PHYLLO

SERVES 6–8

Generally I stay away from hotel dining rooms when I travel. I find the food neither good nor bad . . . it just sits there on the plate and bores me. However, the Amalia Hotels in Greece offer good quality in terms of service and the food is most often quite good. The Hotel Amalia in Delphi, a well-run hotel indeed, offered this dish to us on Easter Day, along with the roast lamb, of course. It makes a smashing presentation since it looks like a beautiful baked cake but it is really filled with pastitsio.

Prepare all of the ingredients for a Pastitsio (page 412) but do not construct the final dish.

Brush an 11-inch-diameter tube pan (3 inches deep) with melted butter. Brush 5 or 6 sheets of phyllo (page 32) with butter and line the pan with the sheets, leaving a bit to hang over the edges so that you can fold the excess over the top when the construction is completed.

Mix the meat sauce and the pasta together and lay this in the pan, with a bit of the white sauce, in 2 or 3 layers. Fold the excess phyllo over the top and brush with a bit more butter. Bake at 350° until the phyllo is golden brown, about 50 minutes or so. To serve, place a large serving plate over the top of the pan. Turn both pan and plate over at once so that the pastitsio comes out upside down on the serving platter.

Italy

PASTA WITH ZUCCHINI

SERVES 6 AS A DINNER COURSE
OR 8 AS A PASTA COURSE

This dish is not supposed to save you from the neighbors who will leave that eighteen-pound zucchini on your porch. You will not need that much for this recipe. However, during the winter you will begin to long for this dish . . . once you have tried it . . . and once zucchini has risen high in cost. This is all a Roman plot!

- **½ cup pancetta (Bacon will work, but the flavor is very different)**
- **¼ cup olive oil**
- **3 cloves garlic, chopped fine**
- **1½ pounds zucchini, cut julienne and *well drained***
- **½ cup whipping cream**
- **⅓ cup freshly grated Parmesan cheese**
- **Salt and pepper to taste**
- **1 pound dry pasta (I prefer penne with this dish)**

Heat a large frying pan and sauté the pancetta until clear. Remove the meat and fat from the pan. Drain and discard the fat and set the meat aside. Add the olive oil to the pan and sauté the garlic for just a moment. Add the well-drained zucchini and sauté over high heat until the zucchini is hot but not mushy. Add the cream and stir.

Toss the above with the cooked pasta (page 422), adding the pancetta, cheese, and salt and pepper to taste.

PASTA ALL' AMATRICIANA

SERVES 4 AS A FIRST COURSE

The name sounds so complicated . . . but this is simply pasta with tomatoes and Italian bacon. It is very popular in Rome and has been for many generations. It is simple to prepare and obviously one of those dishes that Romans depend upon when in a hurry.

SAUCE

- **⅓ pound pancetta, coarsely chopped**
- **1 medium yellow onion, coarsely chopped**
- **2 tablespoons olive oil**
- **¼ teaspoon dried red pepper flakes, or to taste**
- **1 cup Italian Tomato Sauce (page 237)**
- **Salt and pepper to taste**
- **½ pound dry pasta (I prefer penne with this dish)**
- **4 tablespoons freshly grated Pecorino or Parmesan cheese for garnish**

Sauté the pancetta and onion until transparent. Add the oil, red pepper, Italian Tomato Sauce, and salt and pepper to taste. Simmer for a few minutes and toss with the cooked pasta. Top with the cheese.

CANNELLONI

SERVES 8 FOR A PASTA COURSE, 4 FOR A MAIN DISH

I have made this dish before, of course. It is a classic in the pasta world. However, I was not prepared for the delicious version served in Bologna. I was invited to the home of friends of Carlo Middione, the chef at Vivande Porta Via, in San Francisco. The couple have lived in Bologna for many years and they are just charming. Mrs. Nasi prepared a dish very close to this one for lunch. I have attempted to duplicate her wonderful flavors and I think the presence of mortadella, the wonderful cold prepared meat of Bologna, will change your mind about any previous versions of this dish that you may have tasted.

NOODLES

3 eggs
1 cup water
1 cup flour
Salt to taste
Olive oil for oiling the pan

FILLING

2 tablespoons olive oil
½ pound lean pork, coarsely ground
½ pound lean veal or beef, coarsely ground
½ pound mortadella, coarsely ground
1 egg
2 tablespoons chopped parsley
2 tablespoons freshly grated Parmesan cheese
Fresh chopped basil or dried basil to taste
Salt and freshly ground black pepper to taste

SAUCE

2 cups Sauce Bolognese (page 238)
1 cup Basic White Sauce (page 234)

GARNISH

3 tablespoons freshly grated Parmesan cheese

Prepare the noodles. Place the eggs in a food blender. Add the water, flour, and salt. Blend until smooth, scraping down the sides of the blender once, using a rubber spatula. Heat a 10-inch SilverStone-lined crepe or omelet pan and oil with a tiny bit of olive oil. I use a small paper towel for this. Add 2 ounces of batter to the hot pan and turn the pan to spread out the batter evenly. Cook on one side only until the noodle is dry on top. These should not be at all browned or too dry, so the pan should not be too hot. Separate the cooked noodles with waxed paper. You should have 8 noodles.

Prepare the filling. Heat a frying pan and add the olive oil. Sauté the pork for a few minutes and then add the beef or veal. Cook until the meat falls apart. Remove from the pan and drain the fat. Allow the meat to cool and then add the remaining filling ingredients. Mix well.

To finish: Lay out a noodle on waxed paper, cooked side up. Place filling in the center and roll it up. Place seam side down in a baking dish and top with the two sauces. Just pour one on top of the other. Sprinkle the cheese on top and bake at 375° until the dish browns and all is hot, about 15 to 20 minutes.

VARIATION: You might want to mix the white sauce with the meat filling and proceed as above.

PASTA WITH GARLIC AND EGGS

SERVES 4–6 AS A FIRST COURSE

Garlic, eggs, and cheese. It is not a complex dish to prepare but the flavors simply belong together. Another dish that is very typical of the Roman trattorias, and if you have not been there yet you must go. You will eat *so* well!

- **½ pound dry pasta of your choice**
- **2 eggs, beaten**
- **½ cup olive oil**
- **4 cloves garlic, crushed**
- **2 tablespoons freshly grated Parmesan cheese**
- **Salt and pepper to taste**

Put the pasta on to boil in plenty of salted water. In the meantime, heat the oil in a small frying pan and add the garlic. Sauté just for a moment. Drain the pasta and toss all ingredients together. Salt and pepper to taste.

PASTA WITH SWEET RED PEPPERS AND ANCHOVIES

SERVES 6

When I think of the pasta dishes of Rome I rarely think of a tomato sauce. Peppers and anchovies are really more typical. This dish can be found in many fine trattorias and it is a snap to prepare. No, the anchovy flavor will not be too strong for you since you are going to soak the salty little fishes in milk first.

- **1 2-ounce can anchovies, rinsed and drained**
- **¼ cup milk**
- **3 cloves garlic, diced fine or crushed**
- **¾ cup olive oil**
- **2 sweet red bell peppers, cut in a ¼-inch dice**
- **1 pound dry penne pasta, cooked**
- **Freshly ground black pepper to taste**
- **Salt to taste**
- **Parsley, chopped, for garnish**

Drain the anchovies and soak them in the milk for 15 minutes. Drain and discard the milk.

Sauté the garlic and the anchovies in the olive oil. Cook just for a few minutes so that you can mash the anchovies into a paste. Add the chopped peppers and sauté just until they are tender but not soft. Toss with hot pasta. Add salt and pepper to taste. Careful with that salt as the anchovies will probably add enough. Top with the parsley garnish. No cheese with fish, please.

PASTA EARS WITH CAULIFLOWER

SERVES 6–8 AS A FIRST COURSE

I had so much fun with the kids when I did this show. I told my younger fans—and we have a wonderful flock of children watching the shows—that this dish had a funny name. Well, they remembered the time that I cooked tortellini and claimed that the noodle was modeled after Venus de Milo's belly button. Actually, that is supposed to be true. I showed them this dish, a dish made with tiny little balls of pasta pressed into ear shapes, and served it with cauliflower, thus giving us cauliflower ears! They booed and hissed and ate the whole works.

This dish comes from Sicily, where the grandmas still stand about and press out the tiny pasta ears. You can buy them already prepared in any Italian grocery. Ask for *orecchiette,* "little pasta ears."

1 1½-pound head of cauliflower, broken into little flowerets
½ cup olive oil
¾ pound dry pasta ears *(orecchiette)*
3 cloves garlic, chopped fine or crushed
16 anchovies, flat, soaked in ½ cup milk for 1 hour and then drained, discarding the milk
½ teaspoon dried red pepper flakes or to taste
Salt and freshly ground black pepper to taste (Careful with that salt!)

Bring a pot of 4 quarts of water to a boil and blanch the flowerets of cauliflower for just a few minutes. Add 1 tablespoon of the olive oil to the water during this process. Drain the vegetable, reserving the water, and plunge the flowerets into cold water. Set aside.

Bring the water in which the cauliflower was cooked to a boil again and cook the pasta, just until it is barely tender.

In the meantime, heat the remaining oil and sauté the garlic, drained anchovies, and pepper flakes until the anchovies can be mashed with a wooden fork. Drain the pasta and the cauliflower and mix all together, heating until the dish is hot. Serve *without* cheese. They tell me that's how they do it in Sicily.

PASTA CARBONARA, ROMAN STYLE

SERVES 8–10 AS A FIRST COURSE

Pasta Carbonara is one of the great inventions of the food world. It is an old dish and reminds us of times when people had to live on a few pieces of dried Italian bacon and an egg or two . . . but with pasta you could survive, and survive very well.

I had this dish one night at Trattoria Edmondo, a wonderful and basic Roman joint. The dish was filled with pancetta, that great Italian bacon that is not smoked at all but hung to age until it has a musty and heavy flavor. Talk about flavors of the Old World! We want everything fresh and therefore lose those ancient tastes. Drying and curing were terribly important not just for preservation but also for flavor. Our American bacon will just not do in this dish.

¼ pound pancetta (You can use regular bacon for this dish but it is just not the same, nor as good)
¼ pound butter
1 cup milk
2 tablespoons white wine vinegar
1 pound pasta, dry
2 eggs, whipped
⅓ cup grated Parmesan or Romano cheese
Salt and pepper to taste

Cut the pancetta into little pieces ¼ inch square and sauté in the butter until the bacon is clear. Heat the milk in a small saucepan and add the bacon and butter. Add the vinegar; this will turn the milk to cheese. Simmer gently for about 15 minutes, or until the sauce cooks smooth.

Boil your favorite pasta al dente. Drain and return to the pan. Immediately throw in the eggs, the bacon sauce, and the grated cheese. Add salt and pepper, toss, and serve immediately.

PASTA CARBONARA WITH MUSTARD

Add 1 tablespoon of Dijon mustard to the above sauce, just as you are tossing the pasta. A very delicious addition!

PENNE CARBONARA
(La Carbonara Restaurant)

SERVES 6–8 AS A FIRST COURSE

I don't know if they named this restaurant after this dish but both the restaurant and its version of this pasta are classics!

The eating house is located on the edge of the market square in Rome, Campo de' Fiori. You will be treated very well and you will have trouble passing up their exceptionally beautiful antipasto table. Try this dish as well.

- **½ pound pancetta, chopped**
- **1 pound penne pasta, dry**
- **4 eggs, beaten**
- **⅓ cup grated Pecorino cheese**
- **⅓ cup grated Parmesan cheese**
- **Salt and freshly ground black pepper to taste**

Sauté the pancetta until transparent. Set aside. Cook the pasta al dente. Drain and return to the pot. Add the bacon, along with its fat, the eggs, both cheese, and pepper. Cook over very low heat, stirring constantly. Keep the pasta moving in the pot so that the eggs do not scramble. You may have to take the pot off the heat now and then. A thin sauce should form on the noodles. Serve immediately.

HINT: ON COOKING PASTA AHEAD OF TIME. If you have a large party and intend to serve pasta, you may want to consider cooking the pasta before and heating it up at the last minute. This can be done, if you are careful, by boiling the pasta until it is not quite done to your taste and then draining it and plunging it *immediately* into cold water. Drain the pasta and keep it cold until dinner. Heat it up by throwing it into a pot of boiling water for just a moment and then draining it and serving it immediately. This will work only if you do not overcook the pasta in the first place!

FRESH PASTA

Now, away with the fancy shapes of pasta and let us get down to serious eating. I do not believe that fresh pasta is necessarily superior to the dried product. Some is better, some is not. When you desire a very thin pasta, however, as I do in these next few dishes, it must be made fresh. It is worth the effort and if you have a hand-crank pasta machine it is little effort. I do not care for pasta from those electric "extruder" machines. Pasta must be rolled for me.

1½ cups unbleached white flour
1 cup semolina flour
½ teaspoon salt
3 eggs
1 tablespoon olive oil
1 tablespoon water

Place the flours and salt in a large bowl. Mix well and form a well in the center. Add the remaining ingredients and pinch all together with your fingers to form a dough. Knead for a few minutes until the dough is smooth and elastic. Place the dough on the counter and cover with the bowl. Let rest ½ hour.

Knead a few times again and form into any shape desired.

Remember to allow your pasta to dry for about an hour before cooking. Or, most pasta forms freeze very well. Dry a bit first and then freeze on covered trays or in boxes.

PASTA TIES WITH CABBAGE

SERVES 6 AS A FIRST COURSE

The Italians have done a wonderful thing with pasta. The shapes they have thought up are just fascinating, what with the wheels, ears, corkscrews, tubes, pens, angel hair, ribbons, horns, conchs, stars, snails, little hats, little tubes, rice shapes, butterflies, and bow ties. We are talking about a culture that has fun with pasta!

You will like this dish. I stole it from a street restaurant in Rome.

- ½ pound pasta ties
- ½ cup olive oil
- 3 tablespoons butter
- 3 cloves garlic, crushed
- 6 anchovies, flat
- ⅛ teaspoon dried red pepper flakes
- ¾ cup peeled and chopped yellow onions
- 3 cups thinly sliced green cabbage
- 2 cups thinly sliced radicchio or 2 cups thinly sliced red cabbage
- ¾ cup cream
- Salt to taste
- ¼ cup grated Parmesan or Romano cheese

Heat a large frying pan and add the oil, butter, garlic, anchovies, and red pepper flakes. Sauté for a few minutes so that you can mash up the anchovies.

Add the onions and sauté until transparent. Add the cabbage and sauté over low heat just until tender. Add the radicchio and continue cooking until all is tender and the water cooked out.

In the meantime, cook the pasta to taste.

Add the cream to the vegetable sauce and simmer lightly. Salt to taste.

Toss this mixture with the cooked and drained pasta and stir in the cheese.

HINT: ON COOKING PASTA "AL DENTE." Most Americans have traditionally cooked pasta until is too tender to really enjoy. You want to cook pasta "to the tooth," which is what "al dente" means. Pasta should be tender but still be a bit firm to the tooth. If the pot is boiling too fast and you seem to be losing control, just calm down, throw in a glass of cold water, and gently stir the pot and regain control. I have done that during dinner parties many times.

PAPPARDELLE WITH PESTO

SERVES 4 AS A FIRST COURSE

Felidia's, on the corner of East Fifty-eighth Street and Second Avenue in New York, makes wonderful pappardelle. This version that Lydia, the charming owner, served me on my last visit was simply prepared but with very fine ingredients. Oh, recording this recipe for you is making me hungry for my friends at Felidia's. Call ahead for a table or you'll never get near the place. It is very fine.

- ½ batch Fresh Pasta (page 423), rolled into very thin sheets and cut into 1-inch-wide noodles
- 1 cup coarsely diced tomatoes, very ripe
- 3 tablespoons Pesto Sauce (page 240)
- 3 tablespoons freshly grated Parmesan or Romano cheese
- Salt and freshly ground black pepper to taste

Boil pasta until barely tender. Toss with remaining ingredients, but toss gently. You don't want to tear the noodles. Heat to table temperature and serve immediately.

GARBANZO POLENTA

SERVES 6 AS A SIDE DISH AT AN ITALIAN MEAL

Normally, polenta is made with cornmeal, corn that came from America. In the very old days a polenta was made from garbanzo beans, sometimes called chick-peas, *ceci* to the Italians. They also made a lovely sweet polenta out of dried chestnut flour. Try this dish. It is unusually good, and you will have no trouble finding garbanzo flour in any Italian market.

- 1 quart water
- 2 teaspoons salt
- 1½ cups garbanzo flour
- Freshly ground black pepper to taste
- ½ teaspoon whole thyme
- 1 cup freshly grated Parmesan or Romano cheese

Bring the water to a boil and add the salt. Remove the pan from the heat and stir in the garbanzo flour, using a wire whip. Work fast and stir hard or you will get lumps. Return the pan to the burner and cook, stirring with a wooden spoon, until it is very thick, about 15 minutes. It should be as thick as hot breakfast cereal. Add the remaining ingredients and pour the mixture into an oiled bread pan. Chill overnight, covered. Slice the polenta ¼ inch thick and pan-fry in olive oil, just before dinner.

PAPPARDELLE WITH TELEPHONE WIRES

SERVES 4 AS A FIRST COURSE

The "telephone wires" in the name of this dish come from the strings that will form between your fork and the plate. They are from the mozzarella cheese, of course. This is fun to prepare for your children but you must be fair and tell them that all normal rules of polite eating are to be disregarded that night.

- **½ batch Fresh Pasta (page 423), rolled into very thin sheets and cut into 1-inch-wide noodles**

SAUCE

- **2 cups fresh tomatoes**
- **4 tablespoons olive oil**
- **1 tablespoon finely chopped garlic**
- **2 tablespoons butter**
- **1 teaspoon oregano**
- **Salt and freshly ground black pepper to taste**
- **3 tablespoons cream**
- **2 cups coarsely grated mozzarella cheese**

Prepare the pasta and let it dry for about ½ hour.

Place all the ingredients for the sauce in a pan and simmer until all is tender, about 15 minutes. Cook the pasta al dente and toss all ingredients together, beginning with the sauce and adding the cheese last. Be careful that you do not tear the pasta when stirring it.

GREEN TUBES WITH MEAT SAUCE
(Bologna)

SERVES 8–10 AS A FIRST COURSE

This is too rich to believe, but I urge you cook it nevertheless. The use of mortadella in the dish indicates the source of the dish: Bologna. I ate so well in that city that I cannot wait to go back. No tomato in this dish, just heaven.

- **1 cup Basic White Sauce (page 234)**
- **⅛ teaspoon freshly ground nutmeg**
- **2 tablespoons olive oil**
- **3 cloves garlic, finely chopped or crushed**
- **¼ pound pancetta, coarsely chopped**
- **½ pound veal or very lean beef, coarsely ground**
- **½ pound mortadella, coarsely ground**
- **¼ cup freshly grated Parmesan or Romano cheese**
- **1 pound green penne pasta**
- **Salt and freshly ground black pepper to taste**

Prepare the white sauce and stir in the nutmeg. Set aside.

Bring 4 quarts of salted water to boil for the pasta.

Heat a large frying pan and add the olive oil. Sauté the garlic for just a moment and then add the pancetta, cooking it until it is clear. Add the veal and cook until done to your taste. Add the mortadella, cheese, and the white sauce. Keep the sauce warm.

Boil the pasta, drain, and toss with the sauce. Check for salt and pepper, though you will probably not need any salt at all due to the pancetta.

Rice

The Chinese have been eating rice for the past four thousand years, and they each eat nearly a pound a day. Approximately three out of five people in this world live on rice, the main item in their diet, and the ways in which they have learned to cook it, especially in China, are wonderfully creative. It is served in the form of noodles, made into soup, rolled in leaves and vegetables, fried, steamed, made into sausages, and finally into sweet desserts. You can eat rice three meals a day. In China they do just that. In the ancient writings of 2000 B.C. rice is listed as one of the "five sacred crops," the others being soybeans, wheat, barley, and millet.

Our other two ancient cultures did not see rice until they encountered the soldiers of Alexander the Great, and rice was not cultivated in Italy until the fifteenth century. While the Greeks and Romans do enjoy rice, especially in the regions around Milan, they do not eat nearly as much of this grain as do the Chinese. The Greeks roll it in grape leaves, and the Italians prepare creamy risotto, but the rice is generally seen as a side dish, even though the Italians do eat more rice than any other European nation.

In China a meal without rice is inconceivable. The term for *rice* literally means "food," and even a common greeting involves mention of the food product. In our culture we say "Hello, how are you?" The Chinese say, "*Chi fan le mei you?*" which is literally translated, "Have you eaten rice yet today?" Rice, or *fan,* is so much a part of the Chinese mind-set that it has become a symbol of plenteousness, which explains why we throw rice at a newlywed couple. We wish for them rice and plenty forever.

There are several types of rice used in the following recipes. It is best not to attempt to replace one with another in a recipe. All can be found in supermarkets, Italian groceries, or Chinese groceries:

Long grain—Chinese common rice
Short-grain or pearl rice—Japanese. A bit more sticky than long-grain
Sticky sweet rice—Japanese. A fat round Chinese rice that becomes very sticky when cooked
Arborio—Italian rice that is rich in flavor and absolutely necessary to a good risotto

HINT: TO COOK RICE PROPERLY simply measure out 1 cup of long-grain, short-grain, or converted rice, and place it in a 2-quart heavy stovetop pot with a tight-fitting lid. Add 2 cups of water for each cup of rice, along with a pinch of salt. (Japanese short-grain or pearl rice should be washed first. Do not wash other forms of rice.) Bring the water to a boil with the lid off. When the rice begins to expand, cover the pot, turn the heat to low, and cook for 15 minutes. Do not disturb the rice during this time. Turn off the heat and allow the pot to sit on the burner, undisturbed, for another 10 minutes. Stir and serve the rice. It will be perfect and it will not taste like the cardboard box in which "instant" rice is packed!

China

FRIED RICE

SERVES 6 AS PART OF A CHINESE MEAL

I did not think that I would see much fried rice in Hong Kong since the versions that we get in Chinese restaurants in this country are so poor. It is usually used as ''filler'' in Dinner No. 1. But in Hong Kong, even at a formal meal, the last course is very often a wonderful fried rice. The Chinese must be sure that you are absolutely stuffed before you leave the table. If by chance you should still have the least bit of room left in your tummy you are to fill it with fried rice. This is a most gracious and wonderful way of caring for your guests.

½ pound pork steak, chopped

MARINADE

1 teaspoon light soy sauce
1 teaspoon Chinese rice wine or dry sherry
⅛ teaspoon freshly grated ginger

3 tablespoons peanut oil for chowing
Additional meats, all optional: Add any or all of these in any amount you wish: *lop chong* sausage, sliced; cooked chicken; cooked shrimp; ham, cut julienne
2 eggs, beaten
1 cup dry long-grain rice, cooked and cooled
2 cloves garlic, chopped fine
2 ribs celery, sliced thin
1 medium yellow onion, peeled and chopped
1 cup chopped bok choy or Chinese celery cabbage
8 water chestnuts, sliced thin
1 cup defrosted frozen peas
3 Chinese mushrooms, soaked for 2 hours, drained and sliced thin
4 green onions, cut Chinese style (page 158)

SAUCE

1 tablespoon light soy sauce
¼ teaspoon MSG (optional)
¼ teaspoon salt
Pinch of sugar

1 cup fresh bean sprouts

Marinate the pork for 15 minutes. Heat a wok and add ½ tablespoon of the peanut oil. Chow the pork until done to your taste and then add the remaining cooked meats. Chow all for a few minutes and remove to a large serving bowl.

Heat the wok again and add another ½ tablespoon of peanut oil. Pour the beaten eggs into the wok and tilt the wok in circles over the heat causing a thin egg pancake to form in the wok. Using the metal wok paddle, cut the pancake into pieces and chow for just a moment. Remove to the serving bowl.

Add a tablespoon of the peanut oil and chow the cooked cold rice until hot. Remove to the serving bowl.

Add the last tablespoon of the peanut oil and chow the garlic. Add all the vegetables, except the bean sprouts, in the order given, chowing the celery and onions a moment before you add the remaining items. Add the mixed sauce and chow until all is hot. Return the ingredients in the serving bowl to the wok and chow until very hot. Stir in the bean sprouts, test for salt, and serve.

STICKY SWEET RICE WITH MEATS

SERVES 6–8 AS PART OF A CHINESE MEAL

This is a very flavorful rice dish, and a great way to use up meats left over from your Chinese dinner party. In Hong Kong, and in many American Chinatowns, you will see lotus leaves or bamboo leaves stuffed with this rice mixture and then tied into neat little bundles. Another common way to serve this dish is steamed, in a bowl. It is nice and filling.

All meats must be cooked ahead of time. Use 1 cup total of any or all of the following:

Chinese Poached Chicken (page 265)
Chicken Baked with Honey and Soy Sauce (page 266)
Roast "Lung Kong" Chicken (page 275)
Chinese Sesame Chicken (page 278)
Quick Chinese Roast Chicken (page 277)
Crispy Roast Pork (page 334)
Barbecued Pork Strips (page 331)

- ½ cup sticky sweet rice (page 30)
- 1 cup long-grain rice
- ½ tablespoon peanut oil
- 2 *lop chong* sausages, sliced
- 1 tablespoon dried shrimp (page 29), soaked for 1 hour and drained
- 3 Chinese dried mushrooms, soaked for 2 hours, drained and sliced
- ½ tablespoon light soy sauce
- ½ tablespoon Chinese rice wine or dry sherry
- 1 tablespoon oyster sauce
- ½ teaspoon sugar
- 1 tablespoon chopped green onions, *white part only*

Place the 2 kinds of rice in a heavy pot with a tight-fitting lid and add 3 cups of water. Cover and bring to a boil. Turn down to a low simmer and cook for 40 minutes. Watch that you do not burn this.

In the meantime, heat the oil in a wok and chow the *lop chong* slices and the dried shrimp for just a moment. Add the mushrooms and chow for a moment. Stir this mixture into the cooked rice, along with the cup of cooked meats, chopped into bite-size pieces. Stir in all remaining ingredients and place in a suitable steaming bowl. Steam in a bamboo steamer (page 106) for 20 minutes and serve.

VARIATION: You can also wrap this mixture in lotus leaves or bamboo leaves. These leaves are found in Chinatown. Soak them for 1 hour in warm tap water and then wrap up about ½ cup of the above mixture in each leaf. Make a nice little bundle and tie with string in several places. Steam in a bamboo steamer (page 106) for 20 minutes and serve. This is the traditional method of serving but you might not be impressed with the work in tying and wrapping.

RICE CONGEE
(Jook)
SERVES 8–10

Westerners are often surprised to find that citizens in the south of China eat rice at three meals a day. Why should that surprise us? We eat bread at three meals a day! In any case, this is a very warming soup made by cooking rice until it simply turns to a thick liquid. It is most often served for breakfast, and the flavor can be different each time, depending on what kind of meats you add to the soup. I love this stuff and Mary Young, my adopted Chinese aunt, brews up a batch of it that will just amaze you.

- **1 cup long-grain rice**
- **12 cups water**
- **½ teaspoon MSG (optional)**
- **1 pound chicken bones or pork neck bones, or a bit of each**
- **½ roll preserved Chinese turnip, chopped and rinsed**
- **1 slice fresh ginger**
- **2 eggs, beaten (optional)**
- **1 teaspoon sesame oil**
- **1 teaspoon white wine vinegar**
- **Pinch of white pepper to taste**
- **2 green onions, chopped, for garnish**

This is very simple to prepare. Put the rice in a 6-quart heavy-lidded saucepan and add the water, optional MSG, bones, preserved turnips, and ginger. Bring to a boil and turn down to a low simmer, covered. Stir often and cook for 2 hours or more, until the mixture is thick and fairly smooth. Remove the bones and ginger slice. Pour the beaten eggs over the top of the soup in a thin stream and count to 10. Gently stir in the eggs, thus forming "egg flowers." Mix the sesame oil, vinegar, and white pepper together and add to the pot. Garnish with the green onions.

VARIATIONS: You can add almost any kind of cooked meat or fish to this. Mary Young's favorite addition is abalone. Try any of the following:

- Abalone, canned, drained, and sliced thin (but very expensive)
- Pork, chopped, and dried oysters, soaked for 2 hours, drained and chopped a bit. Add to the pot during the last 15 minutes of cooking.
- Chicken, cooked, chopped
- Chinese Roast Duck (page 291), chopped into bite-size pieces
- Seafood: shrimp, scallops, etc. added during last 10 or 15 minutes of cooking
- Olives, Chinese dried, called *lam see* (page 27). Add during last couple of minutes of cooking.

GARNISHES

Chopped iceberg lettuce
Chinese parsley
Green onions, additional
Chinese Fried Bread Strips (page 545)

CHINESE SAUSAGE ON STEAMED RICE
(Lop Chong)

This is a simple and delicious lunch. Cook 1 cup of rice according to the instructions in the hint on page 431. Just before you cover the rice with a lid, set 2 *lop chong* sausages on top of the rice. Cover and cook according to instructions. The flavor is wonderful and the sausages provide another course along with the rice.

Lop chong can be purchased in any Chinese market.

Greece

STUFFED GRAPE LEAVES WITH EGG-LEMON SAUCE

SERVES 6–8 AS AN APPETIZER COURSE

I cannot think of a more frugal dish . . . providing you understand that "frugal" means that you waste nothing. There was a time in Greek history when certain people were so hungry that they took to eating the leaves from the grape vines. From that time of destitution comes this dish, one of the most famous dishes in Greece. It is flavorful beyond belief!

- 1 16-ounce jar grape leaves (California leaves are fine; they are not quite as sharp as the imported Greek variety)

FILLING

- 1 cup raw long-grain rice
- ½ cup olive oil
- 1 cup chopped yellow onions
- ¼ cup chopped Italian parsley
- 1 tablespoon dried dillweed
- Juice of 1 lemon
- 1 pound lean lamb, coarsely ground or chopped
- 1 teaspoon allspice
- 2 cloves garlic, crushed
- Salt and freshly ground black pepper to taste

BROTH

- 2 cups Basic Chicken Stock (page 144) or canned chicken broth
- Juice of 1 lemon

SAUCE

- 1 batch Egg-Lemon Sauce (page 233)

Mix all the ingredients for the filling.

Pick out the smallest leaves in the jar and set aside. Use some of these leaves to place a single layer on the bottom of the pot.

Cut the stems off the grape leaves. Spread a leaf on the counter, bottom side up, stem side toward you. Place 1 teaspoon of the filling in the center of the leaf. Fold the stem end over the filling, then fold the sides over to secure the filling, then roll from you toward the tip of the leaf, forming a small cigar or cylinder. The size should be approximately 2½ inches long and ¾ inch wide.

Do not wrap these too tightly as the rice needs room for expansion when it cooks.

Using a 2-quart heavy-lidded kettle, place the rolled leaves on top of the single layer in the bottom. Place the rolls up against each other rather tightly so that they will not come undone while cooking. Cover them with a layer of unrolled leaves and then add another layer of rolled leaves. Continue until all rolled leaves are in the pot. Top with the remaining unrolled leaves.

Place a medium plate over the top of the leaves, as a weight. Mix the chicken stock and lemon juice for the broth and pour over the leaves in the pot. Cover and bring to a light simmer. I use a heat diffuser (page 11) for this. Cook 1 hour. Remove the pan from the heat and allow it to cool for 1 more hour. *Do not remove the lid* or the leaves will darken.

Serve warm with Egg-Lemon Sauce on top.

STUFFED TOMATOES HYDRA

SERVES 6

The day I tasted this dish was memorable because our family was drenched during bad weather in Greece. We were cold and hungry and on a boat trip to the island of Hydra. As we approached the island of white domed houses and *no cars* anywhere in the village, the sun broke forth and polished all the buildings, right before our eyes. "Look, Dad," young Channing shouted, "this is the *real* Greece!" It was, too, as this recipe, which I found in a local restaurant, will prove.

6 large ripe tomatoes
½ pound lean lamb, coarsely chopped
4 tablespoons olive oil
2 cloves garlic, crushed
1 medium yellow onion, peeled and coarsely chopped
1½ cups raw long-grain rice
1 tablespoon chopped parsley
2 teaspoons fresh chopped mint *or* 1 teaspoon dried mint
¼ teaspoon allspice
Salt and freshly ground black pepper to taste
½ teaspoon sugar (optional)
2¼ cups water

Core the tomatoes and remove the center pulp, leaving a bowl for stuffing. I use a grapefruit spoon for this. Save the pulp and juice.

Heat a 4-quart stove-top covered casserole and add the lamb, olive oil, garlic, and onion. Cook until the onion is transparent. Add the rice, the pulp from the tomatoes, parsley, mint, allspice, salt and pepper, optional sugar, and water. Bring the mixture to a boil, cover with a lid, turn to low heat, and cook until the rice is just barely tender, about 15 to 20 minutes.

Salt the insides of the tomatoes and stuff with the rice mixture. Place them in a oiled baking dish and bake at 375°

for about 20 minutes, or until the tomatoes are hot and tender, but not soggy.

Use the remaining filling to stuff green sweet bell peppers or zucchini, or simply serve it a day or two later as a side dish.

VARIATION: These can be prepared ahead of time, up to the baking point. Baking is no problem when your guests arrive.

Italy

We most often think of pasta when we think of the starchy part of an Italian meal. Rice, however, is very popular in Italy and has been since ancient times. In Milan the rice dishes are so spectacular that they are more popular than the pasta!

The method of cooking rice in Italy is very different from the Chinese method, and certainly different from our own. It takes a bit of time and care and the rice must be served immediately, but the results will make you proud. Just be sure and always use Arborio rice for these Italian dishes. Everything else will just turn to mush.

RISOTTO WITH MUSHROOMS
(Risotto con Funghi)
SERVES 4–6 AS A FIRST COURSE

This is a classic and a favorite of the Milanese. I had a plate of rice with mushrooms in a rather inexpensive garden restaurant on a May day in Milan. I kept closing my eyes and relishing the flavor. The waiter finally told me I would have to order lunch as this dish was simply considered a pasta course. I really could have sat there for days eating *risotto con funghi*. Even the name is fun to say!

- 1 ounce dried mushrooms (page 33), soaked in 1 cup water, the water reserved
- 3 tablespoons butter
- 2 tablespoons olive oil
- ¼ medium yellow onion, peeled and coarsely chopped
- 1½ cups raw Italian Arborio rice
- 2 cups Basic Brown Soup Stock (page 147)
- 3 cups water (Include in this the water from soaking mushrooms)
- ¼ cup freshly grated Parmesan cheese
- Salt and freshly ground black pepper to taste

Soak the mushrooms until very soft, about 1 hour. Drain, reserving the water for the dish, and chop the mushrooms.

Heat a 4-quart heavy saucepan and add the butter, oil, onions, and mushrooms. Cook until the onions are clear and then add the rice. Stir carefully so that each grain is coated with the oil. In a separate pan bring the stock and water, including the mushroom water, to a simmer and add 1 cup of this liquid to the rice. Stir as it cooks to ensure a nice creamy dish. Continue adding broth as it is absorbed until the rice is tender but still a bit chewy. Stir in the cheese and salt and pepper to taste. Serve immediately.

RISOTTO WITH MUSHROOMS AND HERBS
(Risotto con Funghi ed Erbe)

Follow the recipe above but add ¼ cup chopped, drained, cooked spinach. I use frozen. Also, add a bit of oregano and rosemary or basil, to taste. This makes a lovely change from your usual starches at dinner.

RISOTTO WITH CHAMPAGNE
(Risotto con Sciampagna)
SERVES 4–6 AS A FIRST COURSE

Shall we talk about rich foods? In Italy cream and champagne belong together, as this recipe proves. You can find such a dish in fancy Roman eating houses such as the wonderful Er Moccoletto.

- **1 ounce dried mushrooms (page 33), soaked in 1 cup water**
- **3 tablespoons butter**
- **2 tablespoons olive oil**
- **¼ yellow onion, peeled and coarsely chopped**
- **1½ cups Italian Arborio rice, raw or precooked (page 32)**
- **3 cups Basic Chicken Stock (page 144) or canned chicken soup**
- **1 cup champagne or dry white wine**
- **½ cup whipping cream**
- **Salt**

Soak the mushrooms until soft, about 1 hour. Drain and use the liquid for some other purpose, perhaps a soup stock. Do not use the mushroom water in the risotto as it will cover the flavor of the cream and wine. Chop the mushrooms.

Heat a 4-quart heavy saucepan and add the butter, oil, onions, and mushrooms. Cook until the onions are clear and then add the rice. Stir carefully so that each grain is coated with the oil. In a separate pan bring the chicken stock to a simmer. Add 1 cup of the stock to the rice, stirring to ensure a nice creamy dish. Continue adding broth as it is absorbed. When the stock is absorbed, add the champagne and continue to cook, stirring gently. When the rice is beginning to become tender, add the cream and cook until the rice is tender but still a bit chewy. Taste for salt and serve immediately.

RISOTTO WITH SEAFOOD
(Risotto con Frutti di Mare)
SERVES 6 AS A FIRST COURSE

This is a common dish in the great seaports of Italy. No, I should not use the word "common." It is anything but that, though the dish is not difficult to find. I had one in Venice that was just unbelievable. This is as close as I can come to the recipe.

- 2 tablespoons olive oil
- 3 tablespoons butter
- ¼ medium yellow onion, peeled and coarsely chopped
- 2 cloves garlic, chopped fine
- 1 pound small clams or mussels, scrubbed clean
- ¼ pound large shrimp, peeled
- 1 pound squid, cleaned and cut into ½-inch circles (page 212)
- 1 cup dry white wine
- 1½ cups Italian Arborio rice, raw or precooked (page 32)
- Chicken broth to make up 5 cups, including the broth from the cooked seafood
- 1 tablespoon tomato paste
- 1 tablespoon chopped parsley
- Salt and freshly ground black pepper to taste

Heat a large heavy-bottomed covered saucepan and add 1 tablespoon of the oil and the butter. Sauté the garlic and onion for a moment or two and add the cleaned seafood, along with the wine. Cover and cook until the seafood is barely tender. Drain the broth from the pot and set aside both the seafood and the broth.

Heat a heavy 6-quart stove-top covered casserole. Add the rice and the remaining tablespoon of olive oil. Stir to coat each grain of rice. Heat the 5 cups chicken stock and seafood broth combined and add 1 cup to the rice pot. Cook until almost absorbed and add a second cup, stirring constantly to ensure a creamy consistency. Add the tomato paste and continue to add the broth as it is absorbed until the rice is just tender but still a bit chewy. Return the seafood to the pot, and add the parsley and salt and pepper to taste. Serve immediately.

FRIED RISOTTO CAKES

Make small patties of leftover mushroom or herb risotto and fry them in a bit of olive oil. Serve in a puddle of Basic Brown Sauce (page 236). This will be a hit, I promise!

Dumplings

I have a dumpling addiction. I always have had. I have no intention of ever attempting to rid myself of this burden. Just the thought of a Chinese dumpling, filled with ginger, or an Italian ravioli sitting in truffle butter, or a Greek rice-filled grape leaf, sends me to the kitchen with the shakes! I am addicted, I confess it.

The dumpling was probably first seen in China, though at that time it was a crude food product. Around three thousand years ago grains were pounded coarsely and roasted before being mixed with tea or water to make a primitive type of dumpling. This may be the oldest surviving form of pasta. The dumpling, a ball of dough with some sort of filling, certainly predates cut pasta, and the Chinese seem to be the most creative at preparing these gems. They are used at celebrations of all kinds and seasons, and at regular daily meals as well. The flavorings and fillings, as well as the types of flour used for the casings, seem endless in China.

In Italy dumplings do not have such a wide range. Ravioli and tortellini seem to be the most popular, and that is enough for me. The Greeks use few stuffed-dough dumplings though I suppose that the stuffed grape leaf, and maybe even the phyllo dough filled pies must also be called dumplings.

Don't put these recipes aside due to the time involved in preparation. Chinese, Greek, and Italian grandmas have always known that a good dumpling will cure one thousand ills.

China

CHINESE BOILED DUMPLINGS

MAKES ABOUT 36 DUMPLINGS

These are fun to prepare and, believe me, they stay with you. I always eat too many of these when I make them . . . and so does everyone else at the table.

DOUGH

2½ cups unsifted flour
½ teaspoon salt
1 cup boiling water
1 tablespoon lard, cut up into little pieces

Mix the flour and salt. Add the boiling water and stir with chopsticks. Add the lard. Knead all and let rest on a plastic counter under a bowl for 20 minutes.

THE FILLING

Prepare a batch of Pork Shu-Mei Filling (page 108) and add 1 cup finely chopped cabbage, squeezed dry in a potato ricer. Also add a stiff shot of garlic and red chili paste (page 26) the amount to your taste. Careful, this stuff is hot!

THE CONSTRUCTION

Break off a piece of the dough the size of 1 teaspoon. Keep the rest of the dough under the bowl. Roll the dough into a ball and then roll out into a 3-inch circle. You may need extra flour for this. Or, use a tortilla press that has been very lightly oiled with peanut oil on a paper towel. This gets you going and the rest of the rolling is easy.

Place 1 teaspoon of filling in the middle of each dough circle and brush a tiny bit of water on the edge of half of each circle. Seal up into half-moons, being careful to work the air out as you go.

Drop into boiling water and simmer until they float. Cook another 5 minutes after they rise. Drain and place in a bowl.

THE GARNISH

Garnish with chopped Chinese parsley, sesame oil, and red pepper oil.

VARIATION: These may also be served in soup broth or they can be steamed in oiled bamboo racks just as you cook Pork Shu-Mei (page 108).

POT STICKERS

You know you are in an American-Chinese restaurant that is popular with the young and sophisticated set when you see these dumplings marked on the menu as a "House Special." They are also very popular in China and Hong Kong.

The name comes, I suppose, from the fact that they always stick a bit to the pan. They always stick to me, as well!

Prepare a batch of dumplings from the recipe on page 449 but do not cook them. Heat a large lidded frying pan (I prefer SilverStone lined for this one) and add 2 tablespoons of peanut oil. Place half the dumplings in the pan and lightly brown them, over medium heat, on one side. Pour in 1 cup of Chinese Chicken Soup Stock (page 126) or Basic Chicken Stock (page 144) and put the cover on the pan. Turn up the heat and cook for 5 to 10 minutes. When the liquid has been absorbed, the dumplings are done. Repeat, using the other half of the dumplings.

Do not overcook these as you do not want them to be soggy. Check the pan carefully as they cook so that they are still a bit firm and delicious.

Serve with the garnish as in the recipe on the previous page or with any of the Dip Sauces on pages 229–230.

ROLLED DUMPLINGS

A quick version of dumplings can be made by using wonton skins. Buy them at the supermarket, though you can probably get the thin skins down in Chinatown.

Place a teaspoon of Shu-Mei Filling in the center of the wonton skin and roll it up, starting with one corner and rolling it over the meat. Fold in the other two corners on each side and finish the roll. You will have a neat little sealed package. Moisten the final corner to seal. You can boil these or prepare them as in the pot-sticker recipe on page 450. They are much easier than using the homemade fresh dough . . . but they will not taste quite as good. So what! Some nights you just have to cut down on kitchen time and give yourself a good meal as well as a break. I understand.

WONTON DUMPLINGS

MAKES ABOUT 50 WONTONS, ENOUGH FOR 8 HUNGRY PEOPLE

This is the basis of a very famous and simply delicious soup, but I have certainly had some cheap and disgusting versions of this classic little Cantonese dumpling. American-Chinese restaurants serve a cheap and precooked mess with this name, and always with Dinner No. 1, a sin which must be avoided at all cost. Make your own and then you will understand me. They are simple and the kids will get a bang out of the construction.

THE FILLING

- 1 pound fresh-ground lean pork or beef (I prefer the pork, but you can try a mixture of both)
- 2 tablespoons light soy sauce
- 1 tablespoon Chinese rice wine or dry sherry
- ½ teaspoon sugar
- 2 green onions, chopped
- ½ teaspoon freshly grated ginger
- 2 cloves garlic, crushed
- 8 water chestnuts, chopped very coarsely
- 1 teaspoon sesame oil
- 1 egg
- 1 tablespoon cornstarch

THE NOODLE

- 1 pound fresh wonton wrappers from the Chinese market (I prefer the thin ones)

THE SOUP

- 8 cups Chinese Chicken Soup Stock (page 126)
- ¼ cup chopped Chinese bok choy *or* mustard green from the supermarket *or* 1 10-ounce package frozen peas
- Leftover sliced barbecued pork or roast side of pork (optional)

GARNISH

- 1 tablespoon sesame oil
- 2 green onions, chopped
- Pinch ground white pepper

For the filling mix all together, and mix well! Place a teaspoon of the filling on each noodle and lightly moisten 2 joining edges of the noodle. Fold over on the wet edges, forming a triangle. Be sure to press out all the air so that there is a good seal on the noodle. Place the dumplings on waxed paper until all are filled. Do not stack them on top of one another.

Bring the soup stock to a boil and drop in the wontons. Boil for about 10 minutes, uncovered, or until they float and look a bit wrinkled on the outside. They should be tender but not mushy. Add the remaining ingredients to the pot, bring up to heat, and place in a serving bowl. Add the garnishes and serve.

VARIATION: You may wish to add some fresh shrimp, chopped, to the filling. That is a classic form found in Hong Kong.

CHICKEN AND SPINACH RAVIOLI

MAKES 60 RAVIOLI

I don't suppose that any dumplings from Italy are more famous than the wonderful ravioli. They can be made in any size, stuffed with any filling, and covered with just about any sauce. In Italy these dumplings form a first course . . . but I can make a whole meal of these little pillows of delight.

THE RAVIOLI DOUGH

3 eggs
Equal amount of water
4 cups regular flour
1 teaspoon salt

Crack the eggs into a 2-cup measuring glass and add an equal amount of water. Place the flour in a mixing bowl, stir in the salt, and mix in the egg-water mixture and flour, pinching and stirring until you have a dough that can be kneaded. Knead this for about 5 minutes. This is very easy to do in a good mixer such as KitchenAid. It will do the work.

Roll out the dough and prepare 2 sheets, each of the same size. The thickness of the dough is up to you, but I like mine rather light and thin. Don't worry about rerolling the dough that needs to be cut away in this process. It will work fine. Use about ¼ of the dough for this step and thus prepare 4 batches of ravioli for cutting. If using a ravioli press just follow the instructions. I always use a small watercoloring brush to brush a bit of water around the filling so that the dumpling will seal properly. I remind you that if you don't press the air out of the ravioli before sealing, they will blow up like the *Hindenburg* when you cook them. Dust each with flour and set on a cookie sheet while you prepare the rest of the dinner.

THE FILLING

- 2 cups poached chicken (see Chinese Poached Chicken page 265), skinless and boneless
- 1 10-ounce package frozen chopped spinach, thawed and the water carefully squeezed out (I use a potato ricer for this!)
- 2 eggs, beaten
- ⅔ cup freshly grated Parmesan cheese
- 2 tablespoons finely chopped Italian parsley
- ⅛ teaspoon freshly ground nutmeg
- ¼ teaspoon whole marjoram
- Salt and freshly ground black pepper to taste (I like lots of pepper in this filling)

TOPPING

Toss with as much melted butter and grated Parmesan cheese as you like. Italian parsley, chopped, is great on top. Or, you may use a tomato-based sauce.

Using the fine blade on your meat grinder, grind the chicken and spinach, which has been squeezed well to drain moisture. Add the remaining ingredients and mix well.

Fill the ravioli as above and seal. Boil for about 8 minutes in ample water and toss with the melted butter and cheese.

HINT: FREEZE YOUR OWN RAVIOLI. It is simple and makes the next meal a breeze. Freeze them raw and use self-sealing freezer bags.

CHEESE AND SPINACH RAVIOLI

In the recipe on page 453 substitute 2 cups drained ricotta cheese for the chicken. Omit the marjoram and nutmeg and add the grated peel of ½ lemon. Mix and fill the ravioli. Serve with a bit of butter, grated Parmesan cheese, cream, salt, and black pepper. Garnish with toasted pine nuts (page 34).

BEEF-FILLED RAVIOLI, ROMAN-JEWISH STYLE

This is a simple recipe, a simple explanation, and a wonderful dish. It is typical of the food that has been served in the Jewish Ghetto in Rome for hundreds of years.

Mix salt and pepper with good lean ground beef. Fill the ravioli, as on page 454, and boil. Drain and serve with olive oil and grated Parmesan cheese and a little more salt and pepper. That is it! An easy recipe, and one that the children will enjoy.

COTEGHINO-FILLED RAVIOLI

Prepare the ravioli dough as on page 453 and stuff with coteghino sausage, a spicy pork sausage available in Italian delicatessens. Since the meat is raw, be sure that you give the ravioli ample time to cook.

Top with Italian Tomato Sauce (page 237) or with butter and grated Parmesan cheese, a little cream, and salt with lots of black pepper.

GNOCCHI WITH CHEESE

SERVES 8–10 AS PART OF A REGULAR MEAL OR AS A PASTA APPETIZER

This dish sounds so simple but it takes time to prepare. It reminds us again that in the Old World the cook spent a great deal of time preparing even the most basic and inexpensive dishes. This one is worth the time and the rest of your household crowd can certainly help. Then it will take very little time.

- **2 pounds baking potatoes, washed but *unpeeled***
- **1 egg yolk**
- **3 cups regular flour**
- **3 tablespoons semolina flour**
- **½ teaspoon salt**

SAUCE

- **¼ pound butter, melted**
- **1 cup freshly grated Parmesan or Romano cheese**

Boil the potatoes, skin on, until they are fork tender. Drain them well and allow to cool just so that you can touch them. Peel and run through a potato ricer.

Place the potatoes in the bowl from your electric mixer and beat in the egg yolk. Add the flour, semolina, and salt and mix just until you have a smooth dough.

Roll the dough into long cylinders the thickness of your finger. Cut into ½-inch-thick slices. Roll each piece a bit on the rough side of a vegetable grater to give the dumpling some texture. Roll each piece quickly and set on a tray to dry a bit. You can forget about the rolling if you wish and just allow the dumplings to dry a bit before you boil them.

Flouring the dumplings before you put each on a tray will help keep them separated when they cook.

Bring 8 quarts of water to a boil and add about ¼ of the batch. Boil gently until the gnocchi float to the top. Continue to boil for one minute and then, using a strainer, remove them from the pot to a warm bowl. Continue cooking until all are done and then toss the dumplings with the butter and cheese.

Serve as a pasta or starch dish with almost any meal.

HINT: FREEZE A BATCH OF GNOCCHI in preparation for your dinner party. Just roll them and flour them. Place them in a plastic self-sealing bag and freeze. Boil them without even defrosting.

GNOCCHI WITH SAUCE BOLOGNESE

Prepare the gnocchi as on page 456 and serve with Sauce Bolognese (page 238). Wonderful!

GNOCCHI FRIED

Try deep-frying a batch of gnocchi. Fry them in oil at 360° until they are golden brown and float on the oil. You will need to cook them in several batches. These are delicious with Italian Tomato Sauce (page 237) or with butter and cheese.

Vegetables

Artichokes

What a wonder this old thistle is. The artichoke, a wild perennial herb of the thistle family, seems to have been first discovered in the Mediterranean region, more specifically, Sicily or Carthage. It has been popular ever since.

Apicius, the great Roman gourmet, reported that artichokes were all the rage during the first century A.D. Like so many vegetables, this lovely thistle disappeared from view in Europe during the Dark Ages only to make a spectacular reappearance in the late nineteenth century. It was reintroduced into Italy and traveled from Venice to Naples and on to Florence in the company of one Stozza family. During the sixteenth century Catherine de Médicis went from Florence to Paris to marry Henry II, and she brought with her not only her favorite Florentine chefs but also her beloved artichokes. The French were scandalized by her actions since all considered the vegetable to be a very powerful aphrodisiac, and Catherine's fondness for large quantities of this sensuous plant enhanced her notoriety—and, I might add, it certainly did not hurt the reputation of the artichoke.

We Americans are small-time artichoke eaters. Since the artichoke became familiar in America in the 1920s we have hardly made it a commonplace vegetable. About 70 million pounds of artichokes are raised each year, primarily in California, where Castroville is king in the artichoke kingdom, which means we eat about three quarters of an artichoke each year. In Rome everyone eats at least 175 artichokes a year. The Roman markets are just filled with them during the height of the season and you will see from the following recipes that the celebration of this vegetable is a grand feast.

The Greeks enjoy the artichoke in several ways and I was always surprised to see that the markets had this vegetable in its freshest form possible. If our markets did a better job at getting the thistle to us while it was still fresh I am sure we would consume more. The Greeks and Romans would simply not put up with artichokes in the condition in which we find them. One more dish from Greece . . . an artichoke moussaka. Place cleaned and sliced artichokes in your Moussaka (page 510) and cut down on the meat. This is just delicious.

You will want to remember that you should never cook artichokes in aluminum or iron; the metal will cause them to discolor. Use stainless steel or glass for best results.

You might also wish to consider:

Beans, Artichokes, and Peas *(page 489)*
Artichokes and Leeks *(page 522)*

HINT: CLEANING AN ARTICHOKE, ROMAN STYLE, is simple. Break off the first two or three rows of the lower outer leaves. Using a paring knife, cut off the top half of the remaining leaves. Do this by holding the artichoke on its side, cutting down on an angle away from the stem. Turn the choke as you cut until the purple thistle center is exposed. Using a grapefruit spoon, remove the purple center, exposing the meaty artichoke bottom. Cut off the stem, leaving about an inch. Trim off the tough exterior skin of the stem. Rub the whole choke with fresh lemon juice to prevent discoloring.

ARTICHOKES, JEWISH STYLE

I had read about this dish but I could not quite understand what it would be. The first time that I tasted such a thing was at a restaurant called Trattoria "Da Giggetto," in the Roman Jewish Ghetto. The recipe itself is not complex, though you will find slight variations on the dish. If you have lots of money to spare, try this same dish at Piperno, in the same neighborhood. Be prepared to sell your luggage, your jewelry, and your mate in order to pay the bill.

The home version can be made in this way, and it is very good indeed.

6 artichokes, cleaned Roman style (see page 463)
Olive oil for deep-frying (Several cups will be necessary. Buy a brand in a large container. It need not be of expensive quality)
1 lemon
Salt to taste

In a heavy pot or wok heat the oil to 375°. Deep-fry the artichokes 2 or 3 at a time for 3 to 4 minutes. Remove from the oil and set aside. Restore the temperature of the oil and fry the chokes a second time until nicely browned, another 3 to 4 minutes. Remove and drain on paper towels. Season with a squeeze of lemon juice and a bit of salt to taste.

ARTICHOKES SAUTÉED IN WINE

SERVES 4–6 AS A VEGETABLE COURSE

This is the simplest of cooking methods, though you will have to catch on to how easily a choke can be cleaned. The flavor of this dish is clean and pure, and typical of the artichoke season in Rome.

6 artichokes, cleaned Roman style (page 463)
Lemon juice
3 tablespoons olive oil
3 cloves garlic, peeled and crushed
1 cup dry white wine
Salt and pepper to taste

Cut the cleaned artichokes in half lengthwise. With the flat side down slice the halves into ½-inch pieces. Place in a bowl and toss with lemon juice to prevent discoloring. Heat a large frying pan and add the oil and garlic. Sauté for just a moment and then add the artichoke slices. Sauté until very lightly browned, about 5 minutes. Add the wine, cover and simmer until tender, about 15 minutes. Salt and pepper to taste.

ARTICHOKES, CHILLED, ROMAN STYLE

SERVES 6 AS A FIRST COURSE

I saw artichokes cooked in this fashion all over Rome . . . and I ate them every chance I got. The methods that the Romans have thought up for cooking artichokes are just amazing, as is their affection for this blessed thistle.

- 6 artichokes, cleaned Roman style (page 463)
- 2 tablespoons olive oil for cooking
- 1 cup water

DRESSING

- ¾ cup olive oil
- ½ tablespoon whole oregano, crushed
- ¼ teaspoon salt
- Juice of 1 fresh lemon
- Black pepper, freshly ground, to taste

Place the cleaned artichokes upside down in a stove-top covered casserole. Add the 2 tablespoons of olive oil and about 1 cup of water. Cover and bring to a simmer. Cook for about 30 to 40 minutes, or until the chokes are tender. Chill, and pour the dressing over the dish. Serve with the stem upright, just as they were cooked.

ARTICHOKES STEAMED WITH PESTO

SERVES 6 AS A FIRST COURSE

I saw this dish on an antipasti table in Rome. I knew right away what it was and how it is to be prepared. This method is simple and the concept inspired.

6 artichokes, cleaned and trimmed **(page 463)**
2 tablespoons olive oil
6 tablespoons Pesto Sauce **(page 240)**
1 cup water

Cut the stems from the cleaned artichokes so that they will sit up in a *sauteuse* or deep SilverStone-lined frying pan. Add the oil to the pan. Rub a tablespoon of Pesto Sauce into the leaves of each choke and place it in the pan, along with a cup of water on the bottom. Cover and bring to a simmer. Cook until tender, about 45 to 50 minutes, or to your taste.

ARTICHOKES, STUFFED ROMAN STYLE

SERVES 6 AS A FIRST COURSE

The owner of Er Moccoletto, Hilda Bergonzi, is very proud of her excellent kitchens. When I was invited into these wonderfully clean and heavenly-smelling rooms, the cooks were preparing this dish. They were only too happy to tell me how to make it. The use of mint has been common in Rome since ancient times.

The Er Moccoletto restaurant is near the American Embassy in Rome. You can have a wonderful meal there.

6 artichokes, cleaned Roman style **(page 463)**
3 tablespoons chopped fresh mint
3 tablespoons chopped fresh parsley
2 cloves garlic, crushed
Salt and pepper to taste
½ cup olive oil
1 cup water

Cut the stems from the bottoms of the cleaned artichokes so that they will sit upright in a stove-top casserole or *sauteuse*. Mix mint, parsley, and garlic, along with salt and pepper to taste, with half of the olive oil. Place the remaining oil in the casserole and arrange the artichokes. Rub the leaves of each artichoke with the herb mixture. Cook over a low flame for a few minutes. Add the water and cover. Simmer until tender, about 45 to 50 minutes.

ARTICHOKES WITH HAM ON TOAST
(Crostini con Carciofi)

This elegant bit was served us in the midst of a Roman garden, in a restaurant not far from the great ruins of the old market. It is just lovely and a perfect dish for a light lunch.

Toasted bread slice
Italian Tomato Sauce (page 237)
Ham slice, boiled
Artichokes Sautéed in Wine (page 464), chopped or sliced very thin
1 slice mozzarella or Swiss cheese
Romano cheese for garnish

Put a bit of the tomato sauce on the toast. Add the ham slice and cover with the chopped or sliced artichokes. Top with the sliced cheese and then the grated cheese. Lightly broil until barely browned.

Greece

ARTICHOKES WITH POTATOES, GREEK STYLE
SERVES 6 AS A VEGETABLE COURSE

When you walk into a Greek restaurant kitchen to look at the food, and you *are* expected to do this, you will very often find a great pan of artichokes and potatoes sitting in a steam table. The olive oil used is rich and aromatic, and the artichokes are fresh and tender. You cannot help but point at the pan and yell, "Yes!"

This dish is too good to limit to artichoke season. I make them with frozen chokes and the results are not bad.

- **1 medium yellow onion, peeled and sliced**
- **3 cloves garlic, peeled and crushed**
- **3 tablespoons olive oil**
- **½ cup coarsely chopped parsley**
- **1 pound new potatoes, unpeeled and quartered**
- **2 cups Basic Chicken Stock (page 144) or canned broth**
- **3 cups frozen artichokes, defrosted**
- **Salt and freshly ground black pepper to taste**

Sauté the onions and garlic in the oil until almost transparent. Add the parsley, potatoes, and chicken stock and cook, covered, for 10 to 15 minutes, or until the potatoes are just barely tender. Add the artichokes and simmer, covered, for another 10 minutes. Add salt and pepper to taste.

ARTICHOKES IN GREEK TOMATO SAUCE

This common taverna dish need only be described. Cleaned artichokes (page 463) are sliced and sautéed for a moment in olive oil and a bit of garlic. A little Greek Tomato Sauce (page 232), along with a touch of dry white wine, is added to the pan. The pan is covered and brought to a simmer. Cook just until tender and serve.

Asparagus

How our three ancient cuisines have loved asparagus, this distinguished and royal member of the lily family. The vegetable grows in so many places now that it is hard to decide just where it first began. We do know that it was commonly enjoyed in ancient Egypt, Greece, and Rome. The Greeks loved the wild asparagus and the Romans began to cultivate it around 100 B.C.

Apicius, the first-century Roman gourmet, loved asparagus and claims that it was enjoyed in Rome as early as 400 B.C. He took great care in the preparation of this vegetable and people who overcook it in our time would do well to read Apicius's recipe from two thousand years ago. We assume, from his and other writings, that asparagus remained a food of the wealthy until the fall of the Roman Empire in the fifth century. Julius Caesar, for instance, loved the stuff.

Following the fall of Rome, the vegetable disappeared from Europe. In China, however, mention was made of asparagus as early as the seventh century, and the food was finally reintroduced into Europe during the sixteenth century.

HINT: ON CLEANING ASPARAGUS. The old European method of peeling the stems in order to make them tender takes too much time for me. Besides, nothing is wasted if we save the broken ends for soup. Hold the bottom end of the stem in one hand and gently bend the stalk with the other. The stalk will break where it is tender, thus giving you a piece of asparagus that is entirely edible. With a little practice you will know exactly where to try to break the vegetable. Save the broken-off ends for soup. Slice and add to the soup stock and then drain well and discard the coarse stalks before serving.

COLD ASPARAGUS, CHINESE STYLE

This is a lovely dish for a first course or a real hit when served later in the meal.

Clean the asparagus (see previous page) and leave it whole. Bring a pan of water to boil and add a tablespoon or so of peanut oil to help keep the color. Blanch the vegetable for about 4 or 5 minutes and then plunge into cold water. Drain and chill. When ready to serve, dress with Sesame Oil Salad Dressing (page 156).

ASPARAGUS WITH BEEF AND BLACK BEANS

SERVES 4–5 AS PART OF A CHINESE MEAL

People are always asking me about my favorite recipe. I have too many! This one, however, is surely my favorite asparagus recipe.

- 1½ pounds asparagus, cleaned (page 470)
- ½ pound beef flank steak, sliced thin across the grain
- 3 tablespoons light soy sauce
- ½ teaspoon grated fresh ginger
- 2 tablespoons dry sherry or Chinese rice wine
- 1 tablespoon cornstarch
- 3 tablespoons peanut oil
- 2 cloves garlic, sliced thin
- 1 tablespoon fermented black beans *(dow see)*, rinsed (page 25)
- Pinch of salt
- Pinch of sugar
- ¼ cup Chinese Chicken Soup Stock (page 126)

Slice the cleaned asparagus diagonally into ¼-inch pieces. Set aside.

In a small bowl marinate the sliced beef in 2 tablespoons of the light soy sauce, ginger, sherry or rice wine, and the cornstarch. Mix well and let sit for 15 minutes.

Heat a wok or large frying pan and add the oil. The oil should just begin to smoke. Quickly lay the meat on one side in the pan. Do not turn but cook over high heat for a moment until the one side begins to brown. Toss-stir the meat for a moment and remove from the pan, allowing the oil to drain back into the pan.

Heat the pan again and add the garlic. Chow for just a moment and add the rinsed fermented black beans. Chow for another moment and add the asparagus. Toss for a few seconds and then add the remaining soy sauce, salt, and sugar. Chow just until tender, about 5 minutes. Add the meat and chicken broth. Stir to make a sauce. Serve immediately.

Greece

COLD ASPARAGUS, GREEK STYLE

This is so refreshing and so delicious and so utterly Greek! Asparagus is cleaned, blanched, and chilled, just as you do for the Cold Asparagus, Chinese Style (page 471). A dressing is prepared of 2 parts good Greek olive oil and 1 part lemon juice. Add a bit of salt and pepper to taste. The created sauce is called "Ladolemono." Dress the asparagus in plenty of this sauce and serve.

Please, don't be too Greek with this. I think both the Greeks and the Italians tend to overcook this wonderful vegetable. Don't you commit the same crime!

ASPARAGUS WITH OIL AND TOMATO, GREEK STYLE

SERVES 4 AS A VEGETABLE COURSE

You are probably beginning to think that the Greeks cook everything in tomato sauce. Well, that is not far from the truth. The rule is simple. Don't use much tomato sauce and you will have wonderful dishes, and dishes that are typical of the glorious and flavor-filled tavernas of Athens. In this case you will be making a fresh tomato sauce.

- **½ cup olive oil**
- **2 cloves garlic, chopped fine**
- **1 medium yellow onion, peeled and chopped**
- **¼ cup chopped Italian parsley**
- **1 cup chopped very ripe tomatoes**
- **Salt and freshly ground black pepper to taste**
- **1 pound asparagus, cleaned 470)**
- **¼ cup dry white wine**

Heat a 3-quart heavy stainless-steel or porcelain-lined stove-top casserole and add the olive oil. Sauté the garlic and onion until clear. Add the parsley and tomatoes and simmer for about 25 to 30 minutes, or until the tomatoes are very soft. Add salt and pepper to taste.

Cut the cleaned asparagus into 1-inch pieces and add to the pot, along with the white wine. Cook until done to your taste, which I hope will be a short time, just until tender and still a bit crunchy.

NOTE: I am convinced that the Greeks and the Italians both cook asparagus too long. Please do not be guilty of this crime!

PICKLED ASPARAGUS, GREEK STYLE

MAKES ABOUT 5 QUARTS

Theresa Karas Yainilos has written *The Complete Greek Cookbook* (see Bibliography). I hope you can find a copy as she loves pickles and vegetables. The basis for the following recipe came from her book, though I weighted the salad toward asparagus.

This is a good example of the taste of the Greek islands. As this recipe makes quite a bit, you should plan on preparing it when asparagus is cheap and you have some nice neighbors with whom you would like to share this delicious salad. It will keep for about 6 days in the refrigerator.

- 2 tablespoons salt
- 3 cups olive oil
- 2 carrots, peeled and sliced
- ½ pound small pearl onions, peeled
- ½ pound radishes, cleaned and cut in half
- 5 pounds asparagus, cleaned (page 470) and cut into 2-inch pieces
- 1 cup drained Calamata olives
- 1 cup drained green olives
- 8 cloves garlic, peeled and sliced
- 2 tablespoons mixed pickling spices
- 5 cups white wine vinegar (approximately)

Bring 3 quarts of water to a boil in a large stainless-steel or porcelain-lined kettle. Add the salt, 3 tablespoons of the olive oil, the carrot slices, and onions. Blanch for about 2 minutes and add the radishes and asparagus. Bring to a simmer and drain the liquid. Refresh the vegetables in cold water and drain again. Mix the olives with the vegetables.

Put the vegetable mixture in five 1-quart glass canning jars and divide the remaining ingredients among the jars, starting with the remaining olive oil and ending with the vinegar. Cap the jars and shake a bit to mix all. Store in the refrigerator for 2 days before serving, turning the jars upside down now and then to mix all. This will keep in the refrigerator for about 6 days, but it is best served on the second or third day.

Italy

BLANCHING ASPARAGUS APICIUS

Apicius must have been some asparagus lover. He talks about this vegetable in the most tender manner and he urges us, in his cookbook from the first century, not to overcook the asparagus. His method is the one that we use today. He would peel the stems, though I just break them off (see **HINT: ON CLEANING ASPARAGUS,** page 470). They were then tied into bunches and cooked standing up in salted water, with the tender tips sticking out of the water. In this way the stem, the tougher part of the vegetable, is cooked without overcooking the tender top. There is no way that this ancient Roman method can be improved upon. Try it.

ASPARAGUS CUSTARD APICIUS

SERVES 3–4 AS A SIDE DISH AT DINNER

It is exciting to realize that the Romans ate so well, at least some of them ate well. This dish goes back 2,000 years and needs little improvement, though you may find the flavoring from the fresh herbs a bit strange. Change them to suit your palate.

- ½ pound asparagus, cleaned (page 470), blanched, and coarsely chopped
- ½ cup chopped lovage (page 39) or chopped celery leaves
- ¼ cup medium-chopped fresh coriander
- 1 teaspoon savory
- ¼ medium yellow onion, peeled and chopped medium
- Black pepper to taste
- ⅛ cup white wine
- ⅛ cup Basic Chicken Stock (page 144)
- 2 tablespoons olive oil
- 6 eggs, beaten

Chop the blanched asparagus, along with the fresh herbs and the onion. Mix this with the pepper, wine, chicken broth, and ½ tablespoon of the olive oil.

Heat a large frying pan or wok and add the remaining oil and the asparagus and herb mixture. Cook for a minute over high heat and then add the beaten eggs. Lower the heat and continue cooking, stirring occasionally, until the mixture begins to set up. Do not overcook. This should be very much like moist scrambled eggs.

ASPARAGUS WITH CHEESE AND EGGS, ITALIAN STYLE

SERVES 3–4 AS PART OF A REGULAR MEAL

So what is new? If you will read the preceding recipe you will recognize the source of this contemporary dish, a dish from Florence and therefore called *Asparagi alla Fiorentina*. This is just a stupendous dish!

- **1 pound asparagus, cleaned (page 470) and cut into 2-inch pieces**
- **½ stick (⅛ pound) butter, melted**
- **½ cup freshly grated Parmesan cheese**
- **Salt and freshly ground black pepper to taste**
- **6 eggs, beaten**

Blanch and drain the asparagus, being careful not to overcook it. In a bowl toss the asparagus with the butter, cheese, and salt and pepper. Remove to a platter and keep warm.

Scramble the eggs (do not overcook) and cover the asparagus with the eggs. Serve quickly!

Beans

In terms of subsistence the bean is almost as important in this world as is bread. From prehistoric times, beans, in one form or another, have kept people alive, and I suppose this is as true today as it was in early times.

There are three beans that lead the world: the soybean, the haricot bean, and the broad or fava bean. The soybean goes back to Asia about four thousand years ago and it is still a major food source there, though most soybeans are now grown in America. The fava bean is now popular everywhere, as is the haricot. There are many other types of beans, of course, and the following recipes will offer you a few new ideas for their use in your kitchen.

There were other uses for beans in earlier times. The Romans used beans as voting tokens in certain elections, giving rise to the saying, "Abstain from beans," meaning, stay out of politics. However, the primary use for beans in the Mediterranean has always been for food, and they are served with soup, rice, fish, as antipasto, with meat, and in many other ways.

The Chinese rarely serve a bean as a bean. They are the most accomplished among our three ancient cuisines at using the bean in some other profound way as a food or flavoring source. Soybean curd, *dow foo,* is called "meat without bones" in China, since it is so nutritious and can be prepared in so many ways. Trish, a flight attendant on United Airlines, told me that she even made a bean-curd lasagne. Boy, I can hear you running to the kitchen for that one! It is best, in my opinion, to cook bean curd in the Chinese manner, and a few recipes follow.

The Chinese also use beans to make bean sprouts, soy sauce, soybean condiment, fermented bean cheese *(foo yee)*, bean-curd skin, and MSG, a natural derivative of the soybean. Beans are made into noodles, fermented for black-bean flavorings, and cooked into heavy sauces, both hot and sweet. In short, the Chinese serve beans in every way imaginable—except as beans.

You may also wish to consider:

Beans and Leeks Apicius *(page 523)*

SMOKED BEAN CURD

I offer this in an effort to show you how this food can be made to taste like many meat products, though it has no meat or animal-fat content whatsoever.

Cut a cake of firm bean curd, Chinese style, into ¾-inch slices. Drain them well on paper towels. Rub the rack of your smoker (I prefer a Cameron, page 13), with a bit of peanut oil and place the drained slices on the rack. Smoke them, according to instructions for your smoker, for about 15 minutes. Serve the slices with the following sauce for a terrific vegetarian dish.

Use any of the ingredients in any amount you wish. It is a matter of your personal taste. The amounts given are for my taste.

SAUCE
- 2 green onions, chopped
- ¼ teaspoon grated fresh ginger
- ⅛ teaspoon sugar
- 2 tablespoons light soy sauce
- 1 tablespoon rice wine vinegar
- 1 teaspoon sesame oil
- Shot of Tabasco to taste

BEAN CURD WITH PORK

SERVES 4 AS PART OF A CHINESE MEAL

Tai Tung restaurant, a Seattle institution, has been operating in Chinatown since the thirties. I have eaten there since I was about thirteen, and that is some thirty-seven years ago. Through the years the food has been inconsistent sometimes, but it is still a fine eating house. When one of the old crew is on duty in the kitchen, this dish is prepared in such a delicious manner that you think you could live on bean curd flavored with soybean condiment. Beans with beans, that's what this one is!

- 1 pound bean curd, cut into ½-inch cubes and drained
- 2 tablespoons peanut oil
- 3 cloves garlic
- 1 slice fresh ginger root, size of a 25-cent piece, cut julienne
- ½ pound pork, sliced into thin julienne strips
- 1 tablespoon soybean condiment *(mein see)*
- 3 green onions, cut Chinese style (page 158)
- 2 tablespoons dry sherry or Chinese rice wine
- 1 tablespoon light soy sauce
- ½ teaspoon sugar
- ⅛ teaspoon salt
- Freshly ground white pepper to taste
- Pinch of MSG (optional)
- ¼ cup Chinese Chicken Soup Stock (page 126)
- 1 tablespoon each cornstarch and water, mixed together

Cut the bean curd and allow it to drain for one half hour.

Heat a wok and add the oil. Chow the garlic and ginger for a moment and then add the pork. Cook for a couple of minutes over high heat and remove the meat to the serving bowl, leaving the oil in the wok. Add the soybean condiment and green onions to the hot wok and chow for a moment. Add the bean curd along with all remaining ingredients, except the cornstarch mixed with water, and the meat. Chow the bean curd until all is very hot and then add the pork and, finally, stir in the cornstarch mixture.

This dish is great over rice. It is versatile in that you can brighten the flavor simply by increasing the amount of garlic or soybean condiment.

LONG GREEN BEANS WITH BEEF

SERVES 4 AS PART OF A CHINESE MEAL

If you have never seen the long variety of Chinese string beans you are in for a surprise. They are over a foot long and can be found in large Chinatowns. The flavor is close to the bean we know but the texture is completely different as this long bean holds its crunchiness when cooked. You must find some of these legumes . . . though the substitution of our green bean still makes for a delicious dish.

1 pound Chinese long green beans, cut into 1-inch pieces (You can substitute fresh green beans)
½ pound beef flank steak, sliced thin

MARINADE
½ tablespoon light soy sauce
½ tablespoon dry sherry or Chinese rice wine
¼ teaspoon grated fresh ginger
2 teaspoons cornstarch

3 teaspoons peanut oil for chowing
1 quart peanut oil for deep-frying
2 cloves garlic, chopped fine
½ tablespoon fermented black beans *(dow see)*, rinsed, *or* soybean condiment *(mein see)*
¼ cup Basic Brown Soup Stock (page 148)
Pinch of sugar
1 teaspoon sesame oil

Cut and rinse beans and pat dry with kitchen towel.

Marinate the beef and chow on one side, using 1 tablespoon of the peanut oil. Chowing on one side on high heat prevents the overcooking of the beef. Remove from the pan and set aside.

Deep-fry beans quickly at 360°. These should cook for only a minute or so. Be careful of the spitting fat if the beans have not been dried properly. Drain well.

Place 2 tablespoons peanut oil in *hot* wok and add garlic and black beans. Chow for just a moment and add the green beans, beef, and remaining ingredients, stirring to form a light sauce.

Greece

LIMA BEANS WITH GREEK TOMATO SAUCE

SERVES 4 AS A SIDE DISH

Yes, your child will eat lima beans if you cook them this way. This recipe is common in the tavernas in Greece and it is really very delicious. The tomato and onion seem to remove the bitterness from the bean, that bitterness that children so "bitterly" dislike.

- ½ pound dried lima beans, soaked overnight
- 4 tablespoons olive oil
- 3 cloves garlic, sliced thin
- 1 yellow onion, peeled and sliced thin
- 1 tomato, large and ripe, cut in ¼-inch dice
- 3 tablespoons tomato paste
- 1 cup Greek Tomato Sauce (page 232)
- ½ cup dry red wine
- Salt and freshly ground black pepper to taste
- ½ cup chopped parsley
- ¼ teaspoon *each* cinnamon and allspice (optional)

Soak the beans overnight and drain.

Heat a 4-quart stove-top casserole and add the oil. Sauté the garlic and onion just until clear. Add tomato, tomato paste, and tomato sauce and sauté 5 minutes.

Add all remaining ingredients, including the beans, cover, and simmer until the beans are tender but not soggy, about 30 to 40 minutes.

NOTE: The addition of the cinnamon and allspice is up to you.

BLACK-EYED PEA SALAD SIGALAS

SERVES 6 AS A SALAD OR SIDE COURSE

The taverna called Sigalas, in Monastiraki Square, Athens, has all of the dishes out on display for you to see. It is typical of a good taverna in that they want you to check out everything before you order. Craig, my cooking assistant, and I, found this dish on their buffet and we were somewhat surprised. Beans are American, and certainly black-eyed peas are from this country. In Greece they are very popular.

2 cups dried black-eyed peas
4 green onions, chopped
1 cup olive oil
Juice of 1½ lemons
½ cup chopped parsley
Salt and freshly ground black pepper to taste

Place peas in saucepan and cover with ample water. Bring to a boil, cover, and turn off the heat. Let sit for 1 hour.

Drain the peas, add fresh water and simmer 10 minutes, or until tender. Do not overcook. Drain and allow to cool.

Blend remaining ingredients together to form a dressing and toss with the beans.

WHITE BEANS, GREEK STYLE

SERVES 6 AS A SALAD OR SIDE DISH

This dish is not to be confused with a hot bean dish for your dinner. In Greece dried-bean dishes are often served cold, as in the case above. This is close to the dish above but the flavor of the beans is a bit lighter. It is a very good salad course.

- 2 cups small white beans
- ½ cup peeled and chopped shallots
- ½ white onion, peeled and sliced thin
- ½ cup lovage, coarsely chopped, *or* substitute celery leaves
- 1 cup olive oil
- Juice of 1 lemon
- Salt and freshly ground black pepper to taste

Place the beans in a saucepan and cover with ample water. Bring to a boil, cover, and turn off the heat. Allow to sit for 1 hour. Drain and add fresh water. Simmer for about 35 to 45 minutes, or until the beans are just barely tender. Drain and cool.

Mix remaining ingredients together to form a dressing and toss with the beans.

PASTA AND BEAN SOUP

(Pasta e Fagioli)

SERVES 8–10 AS A VERY HEARTY SOUP

Everyone has heard the name of this soup, I am sure, but few of us have eaten a good version of it. This is a very decent recipe based on the dish that has been common in Italy for the last few hundred years. It is hearty, to say the least.

- 2 cups small white beans
- 1 pound pork neck bones
- 1 or 2 drops liquid smoke *or* use smoked pork neck bones. Great for the soup, but hard to find. Smoked pork hocks are easier to find. Use about 1¾ pounds.
- 1 cup Basic Chicken Stock (page 144)
- Salt and freshly ground black pepper to taste
- 1 bay leaf
- 2 cloves garlic, peeled and chopped
- ½ medium yellow onion, peeled and diced
- 1 carrot, unpeeled and diced medium fine
- ¼ cup chopped lovage or celery leaves
- ½ cup Italian Tomato Sauce (page 237)
- 6 cups water
- 1 cup small shaped pasta such as stars or shells

Place the beans in a 4-quart pot and add ample water for cooking. Bring to a boil, cover, turn off the heat and let sit for 1 hour. Drain the beans and discard the cooking water. Add all ingredients to the pot, except the salt and pepper and pasta. Cover and simmer lightly for 1½ hours or until the beans are very tender.

Remove the pork bones and the bay leaf. Take the meat off the bones and set aside. Remove ⅔ of the contents of the pot and purée in a food processor or food blender. Return to the pot, along with the meat, and restore to a simmer. Add salt and pepper to taste. Add the pasta and cook until the pasta is just tender, about 15 minutes.

FRESH FAVA BEANS, ROMAN STYLE

This is the strangest practice, but a practice loved by the Romans. When the fresh fava beans arrive in springtime, people come to the market and purchase them, shell them, and eat them raw, some of them eating these right in the middle of the market. They dip them in a bit of salt and pepper mixed with olive oil. This delicacy is eaten with a fine Pecorino cheese along with a good red wine.

Yes, I tried it at Er Moccoletto restaurant, and I really cannot understand the excitement. You might want to try it sometime and see if your tongue is really Roman.

LIMA BEANS WITH LETTUCE AND ONION

SERVES 4 AS A VEGETABLE COURSE

You will find this dish in both Roman and Greek cuisines. It is usually made with fava beans in Rome, but frozen baby limas will work very well.

- **1 tablespoon olive oil**
- **1 clove garlic, chopped fine or crushed**
- **3 ribs of celery, sliced thin**
- **1 medium yellow onion, peeled and sliced**
- **1 10-ounce box frozen baby lima beans, defrosted**
- **¼ cup Basic Chicken Stock (page 144) or canned broth**
- **¼ cup dry white wine**
- **½ head iceberg lettuce, torn into ½-inch pieces**
- **Salt and pepper to taste**

Heat a 3-quart stove-top lidded casserole and add the oil. Sauté the garlic, celery, and onion until the onion is clear. Add the beans, chicken broth, and wine, cover, and bring to a simmer. Cook the beans to taste and then add the lettuce. Cook covered for just a moment or two so that the lettuce collapses. Add salt and pepper to taste and serve.

BEANS, ARTICHOKES, AND PEAS
(Frittella)

SERVES 8 AS A VEGETABLE COURSE OR AN ANTIPASTO COURSE

When I saw this dish on the antipasti counter of La Carbonara restaurant in Rome, it was in the middle of the artichoke season, of course. This is as close as I can come to their version, which is just terrific, and I am pleased to tell you that it is served at room temperature. It can therefore be used as an antipasto, salad, or vegetable course. It sounds unusual but it is one of the best dishes that I found in Rome.

- **2 artichokes, cleaned and cored (page 463)**
- **Juice of 1 lemon**
- **4 tablespoons olive oil**
- **¼ cup diced pancetta**
- **¼ cup water**
- **1½ cups peeled and thinly sliced yellow onion**
- **4 tablespoons olive oil**
- **1 10-ounce package frozen baby lima beans, defrosted, *or* use fresh fava or broad beans**
- **1 10-ounce package frozen peas, defrosted**
- **¼ cup Basic Chicken Stock (page 144)**
- **3 cups sliced iceberg lettuce**
- **¼ cup dry white wine**
- **Salt and freshly ground black pepper to taste**
- **Additional olive oil if desired**

Clean the artichokes and chop them into bite-size pieces. Toss in the lemon juice. Heat a frying pan and add 4 tablespoons olive oil. Sauté the artichokes, along with the lemon juice, covered, until tender, about 15 minutes. Do not overbrown them. Set aside.

Heat a large covered frying pan and add the pancetta. Sauté for a moment and add ¼ cup water. Turn down the heat, cover the pan, and simmer for about 10 minutes. This will render the wonderful fat from the bacon. Turn up the heat to medium high and add the onions and 4 tablespoons olive oil. Sauté until the onions are transparent and then add beans and peas. Cook for a few minutes and add the chicken broth and lettuce, along with the cooked artichokes. When the lettuce is tender but not soggy, add the wine and salt and pepper to taste.

You may wish additional olive oil in this dish. In Rome it is served with a great deal of oil.

Chestnuts

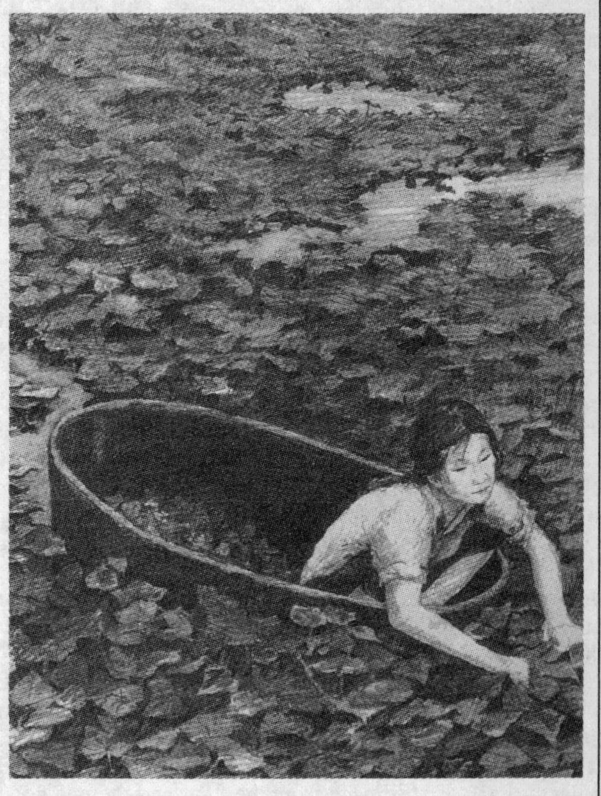

There was a time not long ago when chestnut trees covered the United States. And we knew what to do with them. In 1904 a blight hit our trees and by 1940 few remained. We think of chestnuts now as a specialty food, but in the Old World they were a staple.

It is doubtful that we will ever get back to an appreciation of the chestnut since the trees offer the best nuts at age sixty, and the great trees live for hundreds of years. An 1850 volcanic eruption at the foot of Mount Etna, in Sicily, destroyed a tree that had been planted there by the Romans two thousand years before.

Affection for chestnuts as food is still common in all three of our ancient cuisines. They have never been considered food for the wealthy, except, perhaps, in China, since in early times they were so plentiful. The hunter-gatherer tribes could collect them easily since they simply fall from the tree when they are ripe. In ancient Rome the nut was crucial to the diet of the lower classes; it offered both starch and sweetness, and it was cheap. However, the Roman gourmet of the first century, Apicius, took great delight in chestnuts and suggested that they be cooked with wild greens in order to cut the sharpness of flavor found in the green vegetable. Further, the Roman legionnaires spread the chestnut throughout Europe. Wherever they went they planted the nut so that troops following behind them would have something to eat. Talk about long-range planning!

Originally the chestnuts were dried and ground to make a cheap flour substitute. Wheat flour was very expensive in the old days but chestnut flour could be had for little money. It could be made into breads, cakes, puddings, sauces, and polenta. Pasta is still made from the flour and there is good evidence that one of the ancestors of what we call the pizza was actually made from chestnut flour. In addition, the whole nut served as a vegetable, which explains why I have placed it in this section.

The Chinese have enjoyed the nut since the Han dynasty (210 B.C.) and I have included a dish or two showing its use in both the great kitchens and the peasant kitchens of China.

You can find chestnut flour in most Italian delicatessens. You will have a grand time experimenting with this sweet and flavorful substance, and you can help your children learn something more about the history of Rome. When Rome collapsed, nearly everyone was reduced to a diet of chestnuts.

You may also wish to consider:

Peking Dust *(page 574)*
Sweet Chestnut Purée *(page 579)*
Italian Chestnut Jam Cake *(page 580)*
Focaccia Romana *(page 558)*

China

CHINESE BEEF AND CHESTNUT STEW

SERVES 6–8 AS PART OF A CHINESE MEAL

Ken Hom taught me about this recipe. I hope you know who he is—he should be declared a national treasure on public television. He was born in Arizona of American–Chinese parents and was raised in Chicago's Chinatown. He has a wonderful sense of who he is . . . and it is a bit complex, I can tell you. This fine chef uses chestnuts in the following Chinese stew. The nuts add a wonderful sweetness to the meat.

- 4 tablespoons peanut oil
- 3 pounds stewing beef, cut into ¾-inch cubes

SAUCE

- 1 tablespoon hoisin sauce (page 26)
- 4 tablespoons Chinese rice wine or dry sherry
- 4 tablespoons light soy sauce
- 1 tablespoon finely minced or crushed garlic
- 1 whole star anise
- 1 teaspoon roasted and crushed Szechwan peppercorns (page 36)
- 4 cups water

- ½ pound dried chestnuts, soaked overnight and drained

Heat a wok or large frying pan and add the oil. Brown the meat and place in a stove-top casserole. Mix all ingredients for the sauce and add to the pot, along with the browned meat. Add the drained chestnuts and cover. Simmer for about 1½ hours, or until all is very tender.

CHINESE CHICKEN WITH CHESTNUTS

SERVES 5–6 AS PART OF A CHINESE MEAL

This is a simple recipe that will confuse your guests since they will think that you have been working for days on one dish. It is surprisingly rich because you are using both the richest part of the chicken—the thigh—and the sweet chestnuts. A little will go a long way.

10 chicken thighs

MARINADE

3 tablespoons light soy sauce
2 tablespoons Chinese rice wine or dry sherry
1 teaspoon grated ginger
3 green onions, chopped Chinese style (page 158)
Pinch of salt
Pinch of white pepper
4 tablespoons peanut oil for chowing

2 cups Chinese Chicken Soup Stock (page 126)
5 Chinese dried mushrooms, soaked for 1 hour and drained
½ pound dried chestnuts, soaked overnight and drained

GARNISH

½ tablespoon sesame oil
Chopped green onions

Prepare the marinade and soak the chicken in this for ½ hour. Drain and reserve the marinade. Heat a wok and add the peanut oil. Brown the chicken in 2 batches. Remove to a sand-pot casserole (page 12) or covered stove-top casserole. Add to the pot the remaining marinade, chicken broth, mushrooms, and soaked dried chestnuts. Cover and bring to a simmer. Cook for about 40 minutes or until the chestnuts are tender. Top with the garnish before serving.

NOTE: You might wish to thicken this dish with a mixture of 2 tablespoons each cornstarch and water. Stir it into the dish when all is tender. Cook and stir until the sauce is thick and clear. Then top with the garnish and serve.

WATER CHESTNUTS AND GREEN BEANS

SERVES 4–5 AS PART OF A CHINESE MEAL

While water chestnuts are not actually of the same family as the regular chestnut they do have a very important place in Chinese cuisine. This dish is quite simple and can be served with any number of main dishes that need not be Chinese.

- **1 10-ounce package frozen green beans**
- **1 tablespoon peanut oil**
- **1 clove garlic, crushed**
- **½ cup sliced water chestnuts**
- **¼ cup Chinese Chicken Soup Stock (page 126) or Basic Chicken Stock (page 144)**
- **1 teaspoon light soy sauce**
- **Pinch of ground white pepper**
- **1 teaspoon cornstarch mixed with 1 tablespoon water**

Defrost the green beans. Heat a wok and add the oil. Add the garlic and chow for just a moment. Add the beans and chow until they are hot and barely tender. Add the remaining ingredients, in the order given, and stir until a sauce forms. Serve immediately.

SHRIMP CHOWED WITH WATER-CHESTNUT FLOUR AND GIN

SERVES 2–3 AS PART OF A CHINESE MEAL

Water-chestnut flour, which can be found in any Chinese market, has the wonderful ability to provide thick and rich coating on foods . . . or a very crunchy one if you are deep-frying. This dish is a favorite at our house and certainly easy on the cook who is short of time after work.

- **½ pound raw shrimp in the shell (headless)**
- **1 tablespoon water-chestnut flour**
- **2 tablespoons peanut oil**
- **⅛ teaspoon salt**
- **2 cloves garlic, chopped fine or crushed**
- **1 slice fresh ginger, the size of a 25-cent piece, cut julienne**
- **3 tablespoons gin**

Toss the shrimp in the water-chestnut flour and set aside.

Heat a wok and add the oil. When it smokes a bit add the salt, garlic, and ginger. Chow for just a few seconds and add the shrimp. Chow on high heat until they change color, about 2 minutes. Have a lid in your hand and pour in the gin. Cover immediately and cook for just a moment until the wonderful noise stops. Stir quickly over high heat. Garnish with the green onions and serve.

Greece

ROASTED CHESTNUTS

I do not know why I was so surprised to find peddlers offering roasted chestnuts in the streets of Athens. I thought to myself, "Just like New York!" No, Greece had them first and shared them with the rest of us.

To roast fresh chestnuts, cut a small cross in the top of each. You can roast them in a hot oven but they taste best if roasted over a small charcoal fire in your barbecue. Roast them just until they are very hot and begin to brown a bit on the outside. Peel and eat an Old World treat. You can find a chestnut roasting pan to use in your fireplace. Now we are talking a very romantic evening!

CHESTNUTS SOAKED IN OUZO

Cut a cross in the chestnuts and soak them overnight in ouzo. Roast as above and serve. This is totally Greek!

Italy

CHESTNUTS SOAKED IN WINE

Cut a cross in the top of each chestnut and soak them overnight in dry red wine. Roast as in the Greek Roasted Chestnuts recipe and serve. This is considered a great winter treat in Rome . . . and has been so considered for hundreds of years.

WILD GREENS AND CHESTNUTS

In the early days of Rome it was very common for the peasants to cook chestnuts with wild greens. The sweetness of the chestnuts cut the harshness of the vegetables. Try this with collard greens or mustard greens.

CHESTNUT PASTA

MAKES ABOUT 6 SERVINGS OF PASTA

This sounds a bit strange, or at least "very nouvelle." It is neither. In the old days, when wheat flour was so expensive, pasta was commonly made from chestnut flour, since the chestnuts could be gathered free by just about anybody. The pasta has a bit of a sweet flavor and is very delicious. I am told by people who know that in Genoa, where pesto sauce developed and is still very prized, the best places serve their pesto sauce on chestnut pasta, not the plain wheat variety. I have tried it and it is wonderful.

1 cup unbleached white flour
1 cup semolina flour
½ cup chestnut flour
Pinch of salt
3 eggs
1 tablespoon olive oil
1 tablespoon water

Combine all dry ingredients in a large bowl. Make a well in the flour and add the wet ingredients. Stir together and pinch into a dough. Knead until it all holds together and is smooth. Let rest, covered, ½ hour. Roll into sheets and let dry 20 minutes. Cut into noodles.

CHESTNUT POLENTA

SERVES 8–10 AS PART OF AN ITALIAN MEAL

This again sounds a bit strange to our ears. Corn was not commonly used in Italy until the 1600s, and prior to that time garbanzo flour or chestnut flour was used to make polenta. Many other grains were used as well, but this dish is particularly interesting because it is a bit sweet and when fried forms a wonderful crust.

1 quart water
1½ teaspoons salt
3½ cups chestnut flour
Olive oil for pan-frying

Bring the water to boil in a 2-quart saucepan and add the salt. Remove the pan from the heat and stir in the flour, using a wire whip. Work hard at this as you do not want lumps. Return to low heat and continue stirring and cooking until the mixture becomes very thick, about 10 to 15 minutes. Pour into an oiled loaf pan and chill overnight. Unmold and slice into ⅓-inch pieces. Pan-fry in olive oil over medium heat until golden brown and a bit crispy.

CHESTNUTS AND LENTILS APICIUS

SERVES 6 AS A VEGETABLE COURSE

I should like to chat with Apicius. He was so far ahead of his time, in terms of our standards, that I think he would have made a great dinner guest. Too bad he is not around for an informal chat. He died sometime during the first century A.D. but that does not stop me from fantasizing about a dinner party with Apicius, Mozart, Henry VIII, and Bach. I would do the cooking, of course.

This is a favorite dish of Apicius that is really quite contemporary.

- 2½ cups Basic Brown Soup Stock (page 148)
- ½ pound dried chestnuts, soaked overnight and drained
- 2 cups chopped and rinsed leeks
- 2 tablespoons chopped fresh coriander
- ½ teaspoon freshly ground black pepper
- ½ teaspoon coriander seed, crushed with a mortar and pestle
- 1 teaspoon dried mint
- ⅛ teaspoon crushed whole rosemary
- 1 tablespoon red wine vinegar
- 1 cup dried lentils
- Salt to taste
- 2 tablespoons good olive oil

Place the stock and chestnuts in a 4-quart covered saucepan and simmer until tender, about 1 hour. Drain the liquid and measure it. Add enough water to make a total of 2½ cups liquid. Return to the pan and add all ingredients except the lentils, salt, and olive oil. Cover and bring to a boil. Add the lentils and simmer, covered, for about 20 minutes, or until the lentils are tender and the liquid is absorbed. Add the salt to taste and place the whole in a serving dish. Garnish with the olive oil and serve hot.

NOTE: The old recipe also calls for the addition of honey. I find the dish already very sweet. You can certainly do as you wish.

Eggplant

A junior high school viewer asked me why eggplant is so called. "Eggs are not purple!" he claimed. Well, he is right on that point, but he is talking about a vegetable that is very old and has appeared in many forms. It goes back about four thousand years, and in South and Southeast Asia, where it originated, it shows up globular and white (as well as purple and palest green and oblong and cigar-shaped too) and does live up to its name. It has been used as a popular food in the East for thousands of years. The West is another story.

The wonderful eggplant, which the Greeks and Romans now love dearly, did not reach Italy until the fourteenth century. It arrived with a rather bad reputation and was dubbed *mela insana,* which means "bad apple" (any strange or new vegetable seems to have been called an apple in those days), and the superstitious people of the Middle Ages claimed the vegetable was poison and would cause severe fevers! It took a while to catch on.

The Chinese, however, during the Sung dynasty (tenth to thirteenth centuries), made the plant very popular and it was considered proper for the rich households to nab the first eggplants of the season. The popularity of the vegetable has not decreased in China since that time.

Remember a few basic rules about cooking the eggplant. First, whether you are going to deep-fry it, grill it, bake it, sauté it, or pickle it, remember that the smaller the eggplant, the fewer the seeds and the less oil it will absorb. Eggplant is like a sponge when it comes to good olive oil and in the Middle East people joke about a man's wealth in terms of his ability to provide enough olive oil when his wife is cooking eggplant. I cook my eggplant with ample olive oil, and good oil at that.

The second rule is simple: Always slice and then salt the eggplant before cooking. Let it sit in a colander for an hour or so with ample salt, and then rinse it in fresh water and pat dry. This process will get rid of the bitter flavor that you remember from your childhood when your mother first decided to try eggplant on you. Prepared properly, it is one of the most delicious vegetables I know . . . in all three ancient cuisines.

You may also wish to consider:

Eggplant Stuffed with Shrimp *(page 107)*

China

EGGPLANT WITH PORK, CHINESE STYLE

SERVES 4–5 AS PART OF A CHINESE MEAL

I wish Americans could appreciate the eggplant more. In China it has been revered for so long, and this particular recipe is so good, and so simple, and so delicious, and so . . . make it!

- 1 pound long Chinese or Japanese eggplant
- 1 teaspoon salt

MARINADE

- ½ tablespoon light soy sauce
- ½ tablespoon Chinese rice wine or dry sherry
- ¼ teaspoon grated fresh ginger

- ½ pound lean pork, chopped into ¼-inch dice
- 2 tablespoons peanut oil for chowing
- 2 cloves garlic, chopped fine or crushed
- 6 green onions, cut Chinese style (page 158)
- Pinch of sugar
- 1 teaspoon sesame oil
- Pinch of MSG (optional)
- 2 green onions, chopped for garnish

Cut the eggplant into long sticks, about ½-inch square. Sprinkle them with the salt and place in a colander to drain for ½ hour. Rinse and pat dry.

Mix the marinade and soak the meat for 20 minutes. Drain and set aside.

Heat the wok and add 1 tablespoon of the oil. Chow the pork just until tender and remove from the wok to a serving plate. Add the remaining oil to the hot wok and add the garlic. Chow for just a moment and add the green onions and the eggplant sticks. Chow until the eggplant is tender. Return the meat to the wok and add the sugar, sesame oil, and the optional MSG. Chow until all is hot and place on the serving platter. Garnish with the green onions and serve.

EGGPLANT WITH SOYBEAN CONDIMENT AND HOISIN SAUCE

SERVES 3–4 AS PART OF A CHINESE MEAL

This dish has a bit of a bright flavor due to the added sauces. It is quick and just filled with flavor.

- ½ pound lean pork, cut julienne
- 1 teaspoon cornstarch
- 1 teaspoon light soy sauce
- 1 teaspoon dry sherry or Chinese rice wine
- 1 pound eggplant, cut into ½-inch cubes
- 1 teaspoon salt
- 2 tablespoons peanut oil for chowing
- 2 cloves garlic, chopped fine or crushed
- 1 slice fresh ginger, the size of a 25-cent piece, cut into slivers
- 4 green onions, cut Chinese style (page 158)
- 1 teaspoon sesame oil
- ¼ teaspoon hot pepper sauce (such as Tabasco), or more to taste
- 1 teaspoon soybean condiment *(mein see)*
- 1 tablespoon hoisin sauce
- Pinch of sugar
- 1 tablespoon chopped Chinese parsley for garnish

Mix the pork with the cornstarch, soy, and wine and set aside.

Mix the cut-up eggplant with the salt and set in a colander to drain for 15 minutes. Rinse and pat dry.

Heat a wok and add 1 tablespoon of the peanut oil. Chow the pork just until tender and remove from the wok. Set aside.

Heat the wok again and add the remaining oil and the garlic and ginger. Chow for a moment and add the green onions and drained eggplant. Chow over high heat until the eggplant is tender but not soggy. Add the remaining ingredients, except the parsley, return the pork to the wok and chow until all is hot and done to your liking. Place in a serving bowl and add the garnish.

EGGPLANT AND PORK MANDAR-INN

SERVES 3–4 AS PART OF A CHINESE MEAL

When I first tasted this dish at the Mandar-Inn restaurant, located in Chicago's Chinatown, I was ready to grovel in order to get the recipe. I went in several times and tasted it over and over again. Though the owner, and the one who directs the cooks, is a charming woman, I did not have the nerve to ask her for the recipe. You just don't do that with people who make their living feeding the rest of us. I finally got up my nerve. I brought Craig, my cooking assistant, along for moral support. I was ready for anything. Then . . . I did it. "Sharon, will you give me the recipe for this wonderful dish?" She replied, "Sure, but I have to explain my secrets." Only a truly kind person would "explain her secrets." Such is the nature of this restaurateur. Sharon Jay offered the following recipe, and since it is very detailed, you may think it is complicated. It is not. Chinese cooking seldom is. Just read the thing through once and you will realize that it is very simple and just heaven!

This dish will be simple for you if you have everything ready, including the mixed sauce, before you turn on the wok!

MARINADE

½ tablespoon cornstarch
1 egg white
½ tablespoon peanut oil
Pinch of salt

½ pound pork, cut julienne
4 cups of peanut oil for deep-frying
1 pound eggplant, cut into ½-inch-square sticks, 2½ inches long (I prefer the long, thin Oriental eggplant for this dish)
1 teaspoon grated fresh ginger
3 cloves garlic, chopped fine or crushed
1 tablespoon minced celery
1 tablespoon garlic and red chili paste

MIXED SAUCE

1 tablespoon dark soy sauce
1 tablespoon light soy sauce
1 tablespoon oyster sauce
1 tablespoon dry sherry
1 teaspoon white pepper powder
½ tablespoon sugar

⅔ cup Chinese Chicken Soup Stock (page 126)
1 tablespoon cornstarch mixed with 1½ tablespoons water

GARNISH

1 tablespoon Chinese red vinegar or cider vinegar
½ tablespoon sesame oil
2 green onions, chopped

Mix the marinade and soak the pork in this for 10 minutes.

Heat the oil in a wok to 375° and deep-fry the marinated pork for 1 minute. Remove from the wok and drain.

Deep-fry the eggplant pieces for 2 minutes, or until soft. Remove, drain, and set aside.

In another wok heat 2 tablespoons peanut oil and stir-fry the ginger, garlic, celery, and chili paste with garlic for about 1 minute. Return eggplant to the pan and add the cooked pork. Chow for about 1 minute. Add mixed sauce and soup stock and bring to a boil.

Thicken sauce with cornstarch and water mixture. Cook until the sauce clears and becomes a glaze, about 1 minute.

Sprinkle eggplant with the vinegar, sesame oil, and chopped green onions.

EGGPLANT STUFFED GREEK STYLE

SERVES 6–8

This makes a nice individual eggplant dish; each serving looks like a little pie. Since there is no white sauce on the top, as in a moussaka, the dish is also a bit lower in calories.

2 medium eggplants, about 1 pound each, sliced ½ inch thick
½ tablespoon salt for the eggplant
¾ cup olive oil
1 pound lean beef or lamb, or a mixture of both, ground
Salt and freshly ground black pepper to taste
1 yellow onion, peeled and chopped
2 cloves garlic, chopped fine or crushed
1 teaspoon dried oregano, crushed by hand
1½ cups Greek Tomato Sauce (page 232)
1 cup grated kefalotyri cheese (page 31)

Slice the eggplants and sprinkle with the salt. Arrange in a colander and allow the vegetables to drain for ½ hour. Rinse off and pat dry.

Heat a large frying pan and add 2 tablespoons of the oil.

Sauté the meat, along with the salt and pepper, onion, garlic, and oregano. Cook until the meat is browned and the onions clear. Add ½ cup of the tomato sauce and simmer for 15 minutes longer. Set aside.

Pan-fry the eggplant slices in a bit of the olive oil, reserving ½ cup oil for the final step. Brown on both sides. Place some of the meat mixture between two slices of eggplant and arrange on an oiled baking sheet. Drizzle the top of each serving with the remaining olive oil and the remaining tomato sauce. Top with the cheese and bake at 350° until all is hot and very tender.

MOUSSAKA

SERVES 10–12 AS A MAIN COURSE

This is a classic dish of Greece. The origins are probably Turkish, though the white sauce used on top is certainly Greek. In any case, it is a very old and beloved eggplant dish to be found in every taverna in Athens.

- **2 medium eggplants, about 1 pound each, sliced ¼ inch thick**
- **½ tablespoon salt**
- **1 cup freshly grated Parmesan or Romano cheese**
- **½ cup olive oil**

MEAT SAUCE

- **2 yellow onions, peeled and chopped**
- **2 tablespoons olive oil**
- **2½ pounds lean ground beef or lamb**
- **1 teaspoon salt**
- **3 cups Greek Tomato Sauce (page 232)**
- **Cinnamon to taste (optional)**

TOPPING

- **⅓ cup butter**
- **½ cup flour**
- **1 quart milk**
- **1 teaspoon salt**
- **¼ teaspoon nutmeg**
- **½ cup freshly grated Parmesan or Romano cheese**
- **6 eggs, beaten**
- **Extra cheese for garnish**

Slice the eggplants and sprinkle with the salt. Place in a colander to drain for ½ hour.

Prepare the meat sauce by heating a large SilverStone frying pan or porcelain-lined stove-top casserole and add the onions and 2 tablespoons olive oil. Sauté until the onions are clear and then add the meat. Sauté until the meat begins to brown. Add the salt and Greek Tomato Sauce and simmer for 30 minutes, uncovered. Taste for optional cinnamon and stir in the cheese. Set aside.

Rinse the eggplant slices and pat dry with paper towels. Pour the ½ cup olive oil onto a large baking sheet and dip the slices in it, coating both sides. Arrange the slices on the sheet and bake at 425° for 30 minutes, turning once during this time. The slices should be tender.

Prepare the topping by melting the butter in a small frying pan and stirring in the flour, making a roux. Cook for a few moments. Heat the milk in a saucepan and stir in the butter-flour mixture, using a wire whip. Stir over medium heat until it thickens. Stir in the salt, nutmeg, and cheese. Stir 1 cup of the hot sauce into the beaten eggs, using the wire whip. Stir this mixture back into the saucepan and stir the whole over medium heat until it is thick and rich.

THE CONSTRUCTION

Arrange ½ of the eggplant in the bottom of a 9 × 13-inch baking pan and top with the meat mixture. Place the remaining eggplant slices on the meat and pour the topping over the whole. Sprinkle the cheese for garnish on top and bake at 350° for 1 hour.

Cut into squares at serving time.

EGGPLANT SHOES

MAKES 6 SERVINGS

This is a wonderfully rich dish, and the name is a riot! They do look like shoes, shoes filled with a flavor that your whole family will love, even those supposed to be eggplant haters. You will find this dish in the tavernas all over Greece. If you have the good fortune to get outside the city and into the villages the versions of this dish that you will find there will be even better.

3 medium eggplants, each about 1 pound
2 tablespoons salt
2 yellow onions, peeled and sliced
5 tablespoons olive oil
3 cloves garlic, crushed
Freshly ground black pepper to taste
2 cups Greek Tomato Sauce (page 232)

Cut the eggplants in half the long way. Salt them and allow to drain in a colander for 1 hour. Rinse and pat dry.

Dig out the eggplant meat to form boats with a ⅜-inch layer of eggplant, reserving the removed eggplant. Chop the reserved eggplant and set aside to drain.

Sauté the onions in 3 tablespoons of the olive oil until browned or even caramelized. Remove from the pan and set aside.

Sauté, in the remaining oil, the garlic, chopped eggplant, and pepper to taste. Place this mixture in the boats. Top with 2 tablespoons of the tomato sauce and then top with the onions. Place the remaining tomato sauce in a baking dish large enough to take the "shoes." You may need to use two pans. Set the shoes on top of the sauce and bake at 350° for 1 hour or until the eggplant is very tender.

HINT: TASTE BEFORE SALTING, always, and consider what other sources of salt you already have in the dish. Cheese, pancetta, olives, dried foods, anchovies—all are examples of foods that need to be seen as salts. Be careful!

EGGPLANT SLICES BAKED

SERVES 6 AS A SALAD OR VEGETABLE COURSE

This is a very common way of serving eggplant in Greece. Since the dish can be served cold or warm, it is also very versatile. I enjoy the utter simplicity of this dish.

2 medium eggplants, each about 1 pound
1 tablespoon salt
¾ cup olive oil
Juice of 1 lemon
½ teaspoon dried oregano, crushed by hand
Freshly ground black pepper to taste
Salt if needed

With a fork, score the eggplant lengthwise. Cut into slices ¼ inch thick and sprinkle with the salt. Drain in a colander for 1 hour and then rinse with water and pat dry with paper towels.

Pan-brown the slices using ¼ cup of the olive oil. When lightly browned place on a baking sheet and bake at 375° until very tender. Remove and allow to cool a bit.

Mix the remaining ½ cup oil with the lemon juice, oregano, and pepper. Dress the slices with this sauce and test for needed salt.

VARIATION: This eggplant is also terrific with garlicky Skorthalia Sauce (page 235).

EGGPLANT SALAD
(Melitzanosalata)

SERVES 6–8 AS A FIRST COURSE OR SALAD COURSE

This is a relish/salad/sauce/type thing . . . and I cannot do better at describing it than that. You must try this. It has a smoky flavor because the eggplant is charred over a burner. There is an obvious connection between this dish and a similar salad found in Turkey.

3 medium eggplants, about 1 pound each
5 cloves garlic, crushed
½ medium yellow onion, chopped fine
⅓ cup parsley
2 medium tomatoes, chopped
1 teaspoon marjoram
1 teaspoon oregano
¼ cup of olive oil
Juice of 1 lemon
Salt and freshly ground black pepper to taste

Grill the eggplants over an open gas flame or under the broiler until the skin is a bit blackened and charred. I use a long barbecue fork and do this over my gas burner. Or, you can simply set them on a hot *asador* grill (page 13). When evenly charred, place them on a baking sheet and bake at 350° for 45 minutes. Allow to cool and then peel, discarding the peel, and chop the eggplant. Place in a bowl with the remaining ingredients and toss. Chill before serving.

Italy

BROILED EGGPLANT BOLOGNA

This is a simple dish—very common food, but delicious. My friend Mrs. Nasi, in Bologna, served this for lunch one afternoon. I need only describe the dish for you as you will certainly have no trouble in making it.

Slice the eggplant thin and sprinkle with a bit of salt. Do not peel. Drain the slices in a colander for ½ hour. Rinse with water and pat dry with paper towels.

Pan-fry the slices slowly in a bit of olive oil until they are brown. Arrange them on a baking sheet and sprinkle bread crumbs, which have been mixed with olive oil and fresh garlic, on top. Place under a broiler until the crumbs are browned and all is hot. Serve immediately.

BROILED EGGPLANT WEDGES

In Rome the antipasti tables often offer this dish. It makes a wonderful first course or salad and can be made ahead, so it is helpful at dinner parties, besides.

Pick out small eggplants and cut them into wedges, about 8 pieces from each vegetable. Do not peel. Salt them and allow them to drain in a colander for ½ hour. Rinse with water and pat dry with paper towels. Arrange the wedges on a baking sheet, skin side down. Brush each with ample olive oil and broil until each is brown and tender. Allow to cool and dress with your favorite Italian dressing. I simply use olive oil, lemon juice, salt and pepper, and oregano. Delicious served at room temperature.

EGGPLANT, ROMAN STYLE
(Melanzane alla Romana)

This is a common lunch dish in Rome and it is simply a quick and easy form of Eggplant Parmesan. It is nice for a party because you can make it ahead and pop it into an oven at the last minute.

The eggplants are sliced ⅓ inch thick and salted. Allow to drain in a colander for ½ hour. Rinse with water and pat dry with paper towels. Pan-brown the slices on both sides, in a little olive oil. Arrange on a baking sheet.

Brown a bit of hamburger, along with some chopped yellow onion, crushed garlic, and salt and pepper. Place a bit of the cooked meat on top of each eggplant slice. Top with a bit of Italian Tomato Sauce (page 237) along with a sprinkle of grated Parmesan or Romano cheese. Place a slice of mozzarella cheese on top of each and sprinkle with a bit of oregano. Bake in a 375° oven until all is hot and bubbly. You may wish to broil at the last minute, thus browning the cheese.

GRILLED EGGPLANT AND FONTINA

I saw this dish in a quick takeout joint in a very fashionable district of Rome. You can wander in that city for days and eat from wonderful shops. I hope you can find this dish. Or make it now.

Slice eggplants the long way, about ¼ inch thick. Salt each slice and allow to drain in a colander for ½ hour. Rinse with water and pat dry with paper towels. Grill the slices on the charcoal barbecue with a bit of olive oil on each. Be sure to keep the heat low so that you do not burn them. Allow to cool. Roll each up with a thin slice of fontina cheese and secure with a toothpick. Drizzle a dressing of olive oil, lemon juice, salt and pepper, and oregano over each. Serve at room temperature.

Leeks

Leeks are a mild and delightful member of the onion and lily family. They have been with us since the Early Bronze Age (3000 B.C.) and they were cultivated and loved in the gardens of Ur in Babylonia around 2100 B.C. The Bible mentions the vegetable when it says that the Israelites, after fleeing Egypt, lamented the fact that they had to leave leeks behind. The leeks had been cultivated in ancient Egypt, where they were a part of the ration package distributed to the pyramid workers. Further, they are mentioned in a 1500 B.C. Chinese guide to good eating.

The Greeks and the Romans all enjoyed this lovely long-stemed lily. The Emperor Nero made sure he had a bowl of leek soup every day in order to keep his voice clear and sonorous so that he might deliver even more stirring orations. And our favorite Roman gourmet, Apicius, offered several wonderful recipes for the enjoyment of the leek during the first century.

The leek has been popular since ancient days, and only now are we Americans beginning to appreciate this vegetable. The Chinese use of the leek in the following recipes remains my favorite.

HINT: ON CLEANING LEEKS. Leeks are often full of mud. To clean, cut off the roots and slice the leek in half lengthwise. Then, cut into pieces 1 inch long and remove those outer pieces that are too tough to eat. The white part will be fine, but as you go up the stalk into the greener part, the outer layers are tough. Remove them and use the inner pieces. Separate the layers and rinse well in a sink full of water. Drain well before cooking.

China

CHINESE LAMB AND LEEKS

SERVES 4 AS PART OF A CHINESE MEAL

This is a most wonderful dish, and even those in your house who claim that they dislike lamb will enjoy this. It is a common winter dish in China.

- ¾ pound lean boneless lamb, sliced and cut into strips
- 4 cups leeks, cleaned and cut (see **HINT** on page 518)

MARINADE

- 1 tablespoon light soy sauce
- 1 tablespoon Chinese rice wine or dry sherry
- ½ teaspoon grated fresh ginger
- 1 teaspoon cornstarch

- 2 tablespoons peanut oil for pan-frying
- ½ teaspoon salt
- 2 cloves garlic, chopped fine or crushed

SAUCE

- 1 teaspoon light soy sauce
- 1 teaspoon Chinese rice wine or dry sherry
- 2 teaspoons rice vinegar
- ½ teaspoon sugar
- ¼ teaspoon ground white pepper

GARNISH

- 1 teaspoon sesame oil
- Hot pepper oil or hot sauce to taste

Cut the meat and soak in the marinade for 15 minutes. Heat the wok and add 1 tablespoon of the oil. Drain the marinade from the meat and chow the meat on high heat until tender. Remove to the serving plate. Heat the wok again and add the remaining peanut oil, salt, and garlic. Chow for just a moment and add the leeks. Chow until they are tender, just a few minutes. Return the meat to the wok along with the sauce. Chow until all is hot and garnish with the sesame oil and hot pepper oil.

PORK WITH LEEKS AND BLACK BEANS

SERVES 4–5 AS PART OF A CHINESE MEAL

This is another winter dish in China. The flavor of the winter leeks mingled with the fermented black beans will warm anyone, and it gets cold in the northern regions.

- ¾ pound lean pork, cut julienne

MARINADE
- 1 tablespoon light soy sauce
- 1 tablespoon Chinese rice wine or dry sherry
- ½ teaspoon grated fresh ginger

- 2 tablespoons peanut oil for chowing
- 2 cloves garlic, chopped fine or crushed
- ½ tablespoon fermented black beans *(dow see)*, rinsed
- 4 cups leeks, cleaned and cut (page 518)
- 1 teaspoon sesame oil
- ⅛ teaspoon sugar
- Pinch of MSG (optional)

Cut the meat and soak in the marinade for 15 minutes. Heat the wok and add 1 tablespoon of the oil, along with the garlic and the rinsed black beans. Chow for a moment and add the drained pork. Chow over high heat until the pork is tender and remove to a serving plate. Add the remaining peanut oil to the hot wok, along with the leeks. Chow until they are tender. Return the meat to the pan along with the remaining ingredients. Chow for a moment and serve.

CHICKEN WITH LEEK BELTS

SERVES 3–4 AS PART OF A CHINESE MEAL

This is fun to make and a good one for your children. Tying the belt is a bit complicated for a child but he or she can have a good time trying.

This is formal banquet food in China.

- 2 leeks, cut into ribbons ½ inch wide, the long way
- 8 chicken thighs, cut in half

MARINADE

- 1 tablespoon light soy sauce
- 1 tablespoon Chinese rice wine or dry sherry
- ½ teaspoon grated fresh ginger

- 2 tablespoons peanut oil for chowing
- 2 cloves garlic, chopped fine or crushed
- ⅛ teaspoon sugar

Rinse the leek ribbons and dip into boiling water for just a moment in order to soften them. Set aside.

Hack each thigh in two, across the bone. I use my cleaver for this. Marinate the chicken for 15 minutes. Heat a wok and add 1 tablespoon of the oil. Brown half the drained chicken pieces and remove from the wok. Add the remaining peanut oil and garlic. Brown the second half of the chicken pieces. Return the first chicken pieces to the wok, add the sugar, and chow for a moment. Remove from the wok and allow the pieces to cool enough to handle.

Tie a ribbon of leek around each piece of chicken, as if it is a little package. Place the pieces in a steaming dish and steam in a bamboo steamer (page 106) for about 20 minutes.

Italy

LEEK CAKES

SERVES 6 AS A FIRST COURSE

I tasted these in Rome, and they were used as a first course. It is so simple and so very good . . . and obviously a peasant dish that the cook learned from his grandmother.

- **4 cups leeks, cleaned (page 518) and chopped in food processor or chopped medium fine by hand**

BATTER

- **2 eggs, beaten**
- **1½ cups milk**
- **1 cup flour**
- **½ teaspoon baking powder**
- **Pinch of sugar**
- **Salt and freshly ground black pepper to taste**

- **Olive oil for pan-frying**

Cut up the leeks and prepare the batter. Mix the leeks into the batter and fry like little pancakes in a bit of olive oil.

ARTICHOKES AND LEEKS

I was impressed with the touch of leeks in sautéed artichokes. The leeks are not heavy enough to burden the artichokes. Simply prepare a batch of Artichokes Sautéed in Wine (page 464) and add a cup of cleaned and cut leeks (page 518) when you sauté the dish. It is very delicious.

SAUTÉED LEEKS

SERVES 3–4 AS A VEGETABLE COURSE

Americans do not often think of a plate of sautéed leeks as a vegetable course. In Italy they are enjoyed throughout the winter and they are easy to prepare.

8 cups leeks, cleaned and cut (page 518)
1 clove garlic, crushed or chopped fine
2 tablespoons olive oil
¼ cup dry white wine
¼ cup Basic Chicken Stock (page 144) or canned broth
Salt and freshly ground black pepper to taste

Clean the leeks and drain well. Heat a large stove-top casserole and sauté the garlic in the olive oil. Add the leeks and sauté until they begin to collapse. Add the remaining ingredients and cook, uncovered, until the leeks are tender.

BEANS AND LEEKS APICIUS

SERVES 4–6 AS A VEGETABLE COURSE

During the first century leeks appeared on Roman tables quite often. They are one of those vegetables that will hold well into the winter and so they were prized, both by the aristocracy and the peasants. Apicius gave us this recipe, and although you may not be terribly fond of the heavy use of herbs in these old Roman dishes, they are interesting nevertheless.

4 tablespoons olive oil
6 cups leeks, cleaned and cut (page 518)
1 pound green beans, preferably fresh, cleaned and cut into 2-inch pieces
Pinch of crushed coriander seed
½ cup dry white wine
¼ teaspoon dried rosemary
1 cup Basic Chicken Stock (page 144) or canned broth
Salt and freshly ground black pepper to taste

Heat a large stove-top covered casserole and add the oil. Put the leeks, beans, coriander seed, and wine in the pot and cover. Simmer until not quite tender and then add the remaining ingredients. Cook, uncovered, until all is tender and the stock is rich.

FAVA BEANS WITH LEEKS

You may use the same recipe as on page 523, substituting fresh shelled fava beans or baby limas. Frozen baby limas beans work well in this dish.

BOILED LEEKS WITH CABBAGE APICIUS

SERVES 8 AS A FUN VEGETABLE COURSE

The only reason that you would go to all this work for a vegetable course would be a Roman party. Maybe that is reason enough, but when you prepare this, please remember that Apicius had slaves. This dish takes a bit of doing but it is fun to eat. Those old Romans must have had wild dinner parties!

- **16 medium leeks, cleaned (page 518) and cut in half and then into 4-inch-long pieces**
- **½ teaspoon salt**
- **8 large cabbage leaves**
- **3 tablespoons olive oil**
- **½ cup Basic Chicken Stock (page 144) or canned broth**
- **¼ teaspoon dried rosemary**
- **Salt and freshly ground black pepper to taste**

Trim the leeks and cut them as directed. Wash them well while trying to keep the pieces intact. Place in a saucepan and barely cover with water. Add the salt and cook until the leeks are barely tender. Drain and allow to cool.

Bring a pot of water to boil and blanch the cabbage leaves for just a moment so that they will be pliable. Cool them quickly in cold water. Drain and set aside.

Divide the leeks into 8 little batches and place each batch in the center of a cabbage leaf. Roll the leaf up, folding in the ends of the roll so that you have a neat bundle. Tie with string in 2 or 3 places.

Place the bundles in a stove-top casserole and add the remaining ingredients. Bring to a simmer, cover, and cook until tender. Serve hot.

LEEKS AND JUNIPER BERRIES

SERVES 3–4 AS A VEGETABLE COURSE

This is another one of the dishes that the servants might have brought you had you been invited to a dinner party at the home of Apicius. The herbs and spices can always change but juniper seems to go nicely with leeks. However, as was the Roman custom, some Liquamen, a salty sauce made of fermented anchovies, would probably be added. You can get a similar effect if you add a shot of *nuc moom,* available in Vietnamese stores. I cannot take the flavor myself, but then maybe you want to be authentic.

1 tablespoon whole juniper berries
3 tablespoons olive oil
3 cups leeks, cleaned and cut (page 518)
Salt and pepper to taste
½ cup Basic Chicken Stock (page 144)

Crush juniper berries with a mortar and pestle or coarsely grind in a small electric coffee mill. Sauté the juniper berries in oil for a moment. Add the leeks and sauté, uncovered, for 2 minutes. Add broth, cover, and simmer just until tender. Salt and pepper to taste.

Mushrooms

Who ate the first mushroom? We can only guess that it was a prehistoric character and he was hungry. There have always been a thousand varieties of this wonderful fungus about, and many are poisonous—deadly poisonous. How did the first person learn which mushrooms were edible and which were not? We can only guess that it was by trial and error. And the error! The Great Buddha died of mushroom poisoning about 500 B.C. and one of the caesars died in ancient Rome of the same malady.

Since ancient times all three of our cultures have enjoyed mushrooms, though in China they were considered food for the poor and in Rome they were food for the rich. We have no records of Chinese peasants dying of mushroom poisoning, but a wild record of royal deaths in Rome. Apicius, the cookbook author of first-century Rome, lists some fifteen recipes for his beloved mushrooms and some are still used today. For instance, I expect he should be given credit for pickled mushrooms.

I think the Chinese have been the most creative with their recipes for mushrooms . . . and we have to admit that Americans really did not begin to enjoy fresh mushrooms until very recently. In Greece and Rome the mushroom has always been considered necessary to a good table.

You can find many varieties of mushrooms on the market. Some are dried and some can be purchased fresh.

White meadow mushroom: The common mushroom found in the American supermarket.

Oyster mushroom: Wide and white, these are delicious fresh.

Chanterelle: A wild forest mushroom very popular in my Pacific Northwest.

Portobello: Large Italian mushroom. Delicious and found fresh in very fancy food shops.

Cremini: A smaller Italian brown mushroom. Very rich and wonderful flavor. Find fresh in fancy food shops.

Porcini: Dried Italian mushrooms. The genuine imported will cost you about $60 a pound . . . so look for the South American variety. They will cost about $15 a pound and they are almost as good.

Chinese black mushroom: Fresh in the markets as *shiitake* (Japanese name) or *tong ku*. They can be purchased dried in any Chinese market. I prefer the dried since they have a much richer flavor.

Straw mushrooms: Imported from China in a tin. Very delicate and delicious.

Black fungus: Two types are brought in from China—Jew's-ears, and the smaller tree ears. Both are just wonderful.

White fungus: These round wooly balls of fungus are dried and can be found in any Chinese market. White fungus soup is very famous in China.

A note about cleaning mushrooms. All you need do is wipe them with a damp cloth. Do not wash them or soak them or splash them about. Just rub clean and slice. Nothing to it!

See also Pizza with Two Mushrooms *(page 564)*

Chinese

ABALONE AND MUSHROOMS

SERVES 6 AS PART OF A CHINESE MEAL

When I was a boy I could afford this dish. Abalone was not expensive and I could go to Tai Tung Restaurant, in Seattle's Chinatown, and enjoy myself. Now the price has risen to something like fifteen dollars for a one-pound can . . . and that is a little much. However, if you are feeling grand and have a special event to celebrate, this is one of the finest mushroom dishes in the world. In Hong Kong you would pay a fortune for this dish.

- **1 16-ounce can abalone, drained (reserve the juice) and sliced *very* thin**
- **1 tablespoon peanut oil**
- **1 clove garlic, chopped fine or crushed**
- **16 Chinese dried mushrooms, soaked for 2 hours, drained and sliced**
- **2 tablespoons oyster sauce**
- **1 teaspoon sesame oil**
- **⅛ teaspoon sugar**
- **Pinch of MSG (optional)**
- **½ cup Chinese Chicken Soup Stock (page 126)**
- **1 teaspoon cornstarch mixed with 1 tablespoon water**
- **2 or 3 cups of shredded iceberg lettuce for garnish**

Very carefully slice the canned abalone and set aside in the juice.

Heat a wok and add the oil and garlic. Chow for a moment and add the drained mushrooms. Chow on high heat for a minute or two and add the remaining ingredients, except the abalone, cornstarch, and lettuce garnish. When all is very hot, add the cornstarch mixture and stir until a sauce is formed. Add the abalone, drained (the juice discarded), and cook for a moment. When all is hot pour over the bed of lettuce and serve immediately.

NOTE: Do not cook the abalone too long. Since it is canned it is already cooked and all you need do is to warm it. Further cooking will toughen this precious seafood.

MUSHROOM SHREDDED CHICKEN

SERVES 4–5 AS PART OF A CHINESE MEAL

Mary Young, my adopted Chinese aunt, taught me this dish. It is simple if you have some leftover cooked chicken, and the flavors of the mushrooms and chicken simply belong together.

2 tablespoons peanut oil
12 Chinese dried mushrooms, soaked for 2 hours, drained, and sliced julienne
2 cups Chinese Poached Chicken (page 265), shredded
¼ cup ham or barbecued pork, sliced julienne

SAUCE

½ cup Chinese Chicken Soup Stock (page 126) or Basic Chicken Stock (page 144)
⅛ teaspoon grated fresh ginger
1 tablespoon oyster sauce
Pinch of sugar
Pinch of MSG (optional)
½ teaspoon sesame oil
1 teaspoon cornstarch

GARNISH

3 green onions, chopped
1 tablespoon pine nuts, toasted (page 34)

Have everything mixed and ready to go before you start this dish. It will take only a few minutes to cook.

Heat the wok and add the oil. Chow the mushroom slices for a few moments and add the chicken and ham. As soon as these are hot, add the sauce ingredients, all mixed. Chow until all is hot and the sauce thickens a bit. Remove from the wok and top with the garnishes.

PORK AND EGG WITH TREE FUNGUS IN PANCAKES

SERVES 6 AS PART OF A CHINESE MEAL

This is the ever-popular Mu-shu Pork that seems to be on so many menus these days. It is not difficult to make and the wonderful flavor of the tree fungus will set your dish apart from those in restaurants that do not wish to serve the real thing.

- 1 batch Peking Pancakes (page 548)
- 2 tablespoons peanut oil for chowing
- 3 eggs, beaten
- ½ pound lean pork, coarsely ground
- 2 egg whites
- 1 tablespoon cornstarch
- Pinch of sugar
- 2 cloves garlic, chopped fine or crushed
- 1 ounce dried tree fungus (page 25), soaked for ½ hour and drained

SAUCE

- Pinch of MSG (optional)
- ¼ teaspoon salt
- 1 tablespoon light soy sauce
- ½ tablespoon Chinese rice wine or dry sherry
- ½ tablespoon cornstarch mixed with 2 tablespoons water
- White pepper, ground, to taste

GARNISHES

- 3 green onions, chopped
- 1 tablespoon sesame oil

Prepare the pancakes and set aside. They can be reheated in a bamboo steamer (page 106) just before serving.

Heat the wok and add 1 tablespoon of the oil. Chow the beaten eggs just as you would scrambled eggs, over medium heat. Do not allow them to cook dry, and chop them up a bit. Remove and set aside.

Mix the pork with the egg whites, cornstarch, and sugar. Wash the wok and heat again. Add ½ tablespoon of the peanut oil and chow the meat until it falls apart but is not dry. Remove from the wok and set aside.

Heat the wok a third time and add the remaining oil. Chow the garlic for a moment and add the drained tree fungus. Chow for a moment and return the pork to the wok. Add the mixed sauce and chow until the mixture thickens. Add the eggs to the dish, stir, and top with the garnishes. Serve in the pancakes rolled up like burritos.

WHITE FUNGUS SOUP

This is a very delicate matter, and one of the five most famous soups of China. It is simple to prepare if you have some Chinese Chicken Soup Stock on hand. The fungus can be found in any good Chinese market.

Soak a small amount of white fungus, remembering that it will swell up. Cut the fungus into soup-size bits and cook in Chinese Chicken Soup Stock (page 126). It will take a very short time for the fungus to become very tender. Garnish with a bit of sesame oil and a tiny bit of chopped green onions. This is to be a very delicate soup. Add salt sparingly.

CLEAR MUSHROOM SOUP

This soup is used as a first course in a Chinese banquet because it will excite the palate. It is used as a middle course because it will cleanse the palate and as a last course almost as a dessert. It is very refreshing and quite easy to prepare.

Place 8 or 10 dried Chinese mushrooms in a double boiler and add 1 quart of Chinese Chicken Soup Stock (page 126). Cook in the double boiler for about 2 hours, thus giving you an extract of mushroom. This clear soup is served in very small bowls or teacups at any point in the meal. Be careful with the salt, but you might need some.

Greece

The Greeks did not seem to get into mushrooms the way the other two cultures did. Very few recipes from the old Greek world even *consider* mushrooms. I don't know why. Seems to me all that traveling around the Mediterranean would have caused everyone to eat mushrooms. The Romans loved them!

MUSHROOMS STUFFED WITH FETA CHEESE

MAKES 15 APPETIZERS

This first course is from the excellent cookbook prepared by the women of St. Demetrios Greek Orthodox Parish in Seattle. The feta cheese is great with mushrooms.

15 large fresh white mushrooms
¼ cup melted butter
Salt and freshly ground black pepper to taste
2 tablespoons butter
3 tablespoons chopped green onions
1 tablespoon flour
¼ cup milk
3 tablespoons finely chopped parsley
1 clove garlic, crushed
Salt and pepper to taste
3 tablespoons crumbled feta cheese
¼ cup grated kasseri cheese
2 tablespoons butter

Brush the mushrooms clean. Remove the stems and reserve them. Brush caps with melted butter; arrange hollow side up in a baking dish. Sprinkle with salt and pepper.

Mince reserved mushroom stems. Heat small frying pan and add the butter. Add stems and onions and sauté until the liquid has been absorbed.

To the frying pan add the flour and mix well. Add the milk, stirring until thickened a bit. Add the parsley, garlic, and salt and pepper to taste. Mix well. Add feta cheese to mixture and fill mushroom caps.

Top with kasseri and a few dots of butter. Bake at 375° 15 to 20 minutes, or until stuffing has browned lightly and cheese has melted.

GRILLED MUSHROOMS, ROMAN STYLE

The mushrooms used for this dish might be a bit hard to find. In Italy they use great big brown mushrooms, and the flavor is just heavenly. When you go to Milan you must go to Peck's Market, not far from the Grand Galleria. They have wonderful mushrooms, porcini, arranged like fancy tiles, but they sell them like gold. If you cannot get the large brown ones, use large meadow mushrooms.

The stems of the mushrooms are removed and reserved for another purpose. The mushrooms are then basted with a mixture of olive oil, chopped garlic, and parsley. A bit of salt and pepper is added and then they are grilled on a hot steel grill or over charcoal. Be careful not to overcook these and don't bother to try this in a frying pan as they will get mushy.

Serve them as a first dish or a side vegetable dish.

PASTA WITH MUSHROOMS NATALIE

SERVES 6 AS A PASTA COURSE

Natalie is the concierge at the Halloran House Hotel on Forty-eighth and Lexington, in Manhattan. It is not a great hotel but a very nice one. She, however, is a great concierge. She can find you anything in New York. Since Alitalia crews stay in the hotel all the time she must speak Italian, and she is Italian. She told me of this dish from her childhood. If you can read this recipe and not immediately run to the kitchen, you have much more willpower than I!

- 2 ounces dried Italian mushrooms (page 33), soaked in water for 2 hours, drained and chopped
- 1 medium yellow onion, peeled and chopped
- 3 tablespoons olive oil
- 2 cloves garlic, chopped fine or crushed
- ¼ cup whipping cream
- 1 teaspoon tomato paste
- Salt and freshly ground black pepper to taste
- 1 pound favorite dried pasta, cooked al dente

GARNISH

- Parmesan or Romano cheese, grated

MUSHROOMS IN WINE AND CORIANDER APICIUS

Evidently mushrooms were boiled for Roman banquets during the first century. All we have is a description of the process and I have tried it. If you do not overcook these morsels and do not use much water at all, they are quite good. I think Apicius was talking about a kind of steaming process.

A very small amount of salted water is heated, and to this is added olive oil and a bit of white wine. When all is boiling, the mushroom caps are set in the pan and blanched for just a few moments. The garnish for this Roman dish is fresh coriander leaves, slightly chopped. It is quite good . . . but you are supposed to have your slaves serve it on silver trays. So much for that part of the recipe!

MUSHROOM OMELET APICIUS

Old Apicius, whoever he was, was certainly a mushroom lover. In this description of a dish the mushrooms are covered with scrambled eggs. It is really very good, though a bit sweet with the honey. Here is the description.

Mushrooms are sautéed with a bit of olive oil, dry white wine, and salt. They are placed on a formal platter and covered with very moist scrambled eggs. The whole is then topped with a sauce made with black pepper, celery leaves, honey, chicken broth, and olive oil. Heat the sauce, of course, before pouring it on the eggs and mushrooms.

Additional Vegetables

SPINACH WITH OLIVE OIL, GARLIC, AND LEMON JUICE, GREEK STYLE

Sauté fresh spinach with olive oil and garlic and add fresh lemon juice just before serving. It is that simple and it is that delicious.

LETTUCE WITH FOO YEE

SERVES 3–4 AS A VEGETABLE DISH AT A CHINESE MEAL

Try chowing iceberg lettuce. It is simple and wonderful in flavor.

Heat a wok and add a bit of peanut oil and 2 cloves of garlic, chopped fine. Then add 1 head of iceberg lettuce, torn up. Chow for a moment and add 1 tablespoon of *foo yee* (page 25) mixed with 1 tablespoon of dry sherry. Chow until the lettuce is tender but not soggy. It is rich and surprisingly satisfying.

DEEP-FRIED VEGETABLES PIPERNO
(Fritto Misto)

The Piperno restaurant in the Jewish Ghetto in Rome is a fine eating house, though the bill will astound you. They serve a plate of assorted deep-fried vegetables that is just wonderful. This is as close as I can come to figuring out what it is that they do.

ARTICHOKES, FRIED JEWISH STYLE (page 463)

MOZZARELLA

The cheese is dipped in beaten egg and then rolled in bread crumbs. When you deep-fry this, be sure the oil is about 360°.

POTATO GNOCCHI

Use our recipe on page 456, but add a good deal of lemon peel and nutmeg. The gnocchi are then dipped in beaten egg and rolled in bread crumbs, then deep-fried.

RICE BALLS *(Arancini)*

Cooked rice is placed in a bowl with a bit of Italian Tomato Sauce (page 237), just enough to color the rice. Salt and pepper are added and the mixture is rolled into golf-ball-sized balls. These are rolled in beaten egg and then in bread crumbs. Deep-fried, they make the finishing touch on the platter.

HINT: KEEP YOUR DEEP-FRYING OIL FRESH AND CLEAN BY straining it through cheesecloth often. Keep it refrigerated so that it cannot become rancid. And you can freshen the oil by deep-frying a piece of fresh ginger in it now and then. Always use peanut oil or an inexpensive grade of olive oil (page 251) for deep-frying. Neither of these oils contains any cholesterol since they are pure vegetable oils, not animal fats. Remember, fresh, clean oil is much less likely to be absorbed by the food you are cooking.

Breads and Pizza

Breads

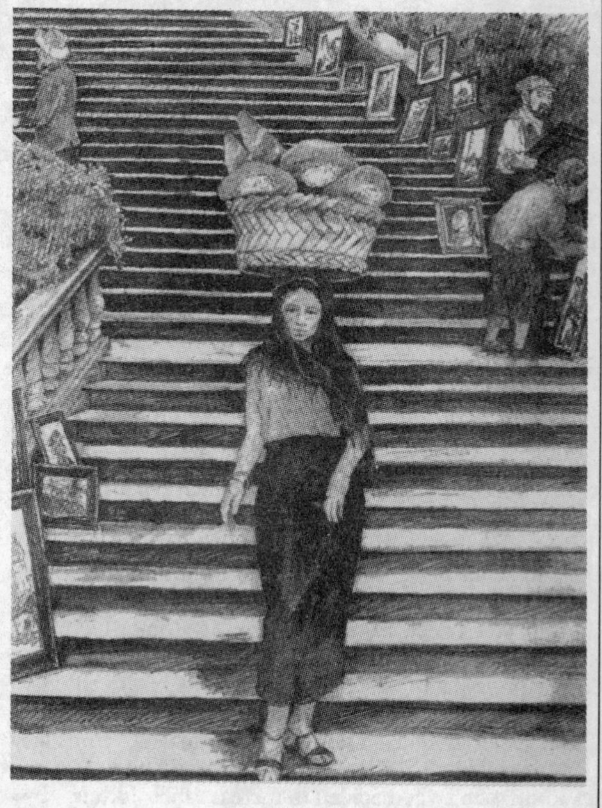

Bread from its earliest days has symbolized life. It is one of the most common and necessary forms of food in the world, and always has been. The bread of early times, however, was very different from that which we call bread.

Our primate ancestors ate wild grass seeds and wild grains. We have no idea when someone discovered that the seeds could be ground between two rocks and then dried on a hot rock by the fire . . . but that was the discovery of a crude form of bread. By 7000 B.C. we see bread ovens in the Middle East, though the rock-hard loaves, which contained no leavening, had to be soaked in water, soaked into a gruel, before they could be eaten. Yeast was to come much later.

Credit for the breads of Continental Europe must go in large part to Greece. By the seventh century B.C. the Greeks had added poppyseeds to some of their breads and by the fifth century B.C. an enormous variety of breads was available in Greece, both leavened and unleavened. Loaves, rolls, cakes made with whole wheat, rice, and barley were all baked, enriched, and enlivened with suet, lard, honey, cheese, milk, or oil, cooked in ovens, on griddles, roasted in coals, baked in ashes or on a spit.

By 170 B.C. Greek bakers appeared in Rome, typically as slaves. They taught their art of bread baking to the conquering Romans and bread became the staff of life all over the Mediterranean. One of the reasons for the fall of Rome seems to center around the fact that the Roman government, which controlled all the land, rented the agricultural properties to the rich, who decided to increase their fortunes by growing olives or grapes rather than the necessary grain for bread. The small farmers were forced off the land and grain had to be imported. The end of the Roman wheat supply coincided almost precisely with the fall of the Empire and its subsequent dismemberment by the barbarians. A government unable to feed its people is on very shaky ground.

Thus did wheat and bread influence the history and destiny of the great Roman Empire.

The Chinese have enjoyed bread since early times as well. The northern regions of China began producing wheat as early as 1400 B.C., and it was baked along with other grains such as millet and, later, corn. Steaming is the most popular way of cooking bread in the north and the recipe for steamed bread that follows will please your family. It is very old, going back to about 220 B.C.

When you are in Rome you must go to the Forno Campo de' Fiori bakery. You will not believe the bread that is offered there. It is right next door to La Carbonara restaurant.

China

CHINESE FRIED BREAD STRIPS
(You Tiau)

This is a very delicious bread that is often served for breakfast along with Rice Congee *(Jook)* (page 436). It is not difficult to make but I find that frozen white bread dough works great for this dish and certainly saves a lot of time.

Defrost a loaf of frozen bread dough and let it rise as per the instructions. When risen cut the dough into strips, each about ½ inch in diameter. Cut the strips into pieces about 5 inches long. Stretch out the strips of frozen bread dough just a bit and put two strips together, one on top of the other. Press the two strips together with a chopstick, pushing down right in the middle of the dough, the long way, and pull or stretch it just a bit. Deep-fry in oil at 375° until golden brown, turning once or twice.

The bread is cut into 1-inch-long pieces and served in Rice Congee for breakfast or brunch.

The bread can be made a few hours ahead of time and quickly warmed up in the oven.

CHINESE STEAMED BREAD
(Bow)

Plain steamed bread is very popular in the northern regions of China. We Westerners seem to forget that northern China grows a great deal of wheat and these people live on wheat noodles and breads such as this one.

Use the bread dough recipe for the Steamed Meat-Stuffed Buns on page 120. Let the dough rise once and punch it down. Roll the dough out to about ⅓ inch thick and cut into strips 2 inches wide. Cut the strips into pieces each 5 inches long. Brush each with sesame oil and fold it over, making a little bun 2 inches wide and 2½ inches long. Top with toasted sesame seeds and put on small pieces of parchment paper. Place in bamboo steamers and allow to rise for a bit. Steam for 15 minutes over high heat.

These can be eaten along with any number of Chinese meat dishes and they are commonly eaten with vegetables as well.

SESAME DRAGON MOUTHS
MAKES 18 ROLLS

The name is for the kids, but the Chinese do have a habit of naming foods after wonderful concepts.

Prepare a batch of dough as in the Chinese Steamed Bread above. Oil and fold the dough as instructed and place on an oiled baking sheet. Brush the top of each with a bit of milk and sprinkle with raw sesame seeds. Allow to rise until double in bulk and bake in a 400° oven for 20 minutes, or until golden. Cool on cake racks.

CORN CREPES, CHINESE STYLE
(Jian Bin)

MAKES 5 LARGE PANCAKES

This is a fine recipe from our *Sunset Magazine*, certainly one of the best regional magazines in the country.

When corn was taken to China it became a great hit. Sweet potatoes and peanuts were other gifts brought from the New World to the peoples of the Far East. These corn pancakes are thin and just perfect for eating with many Chinese meat dishes.

1⅞ cups water
1 cup yellow cornmeal
½ cup all-purpose white flour
½ teaspoon salt
Peanut oil for pan-frying

In a food blender combine the water, cornmeal, flour, and salt. Whirl until well blended. Preheat an electric griddle to 400° or place a heavy griddle on medium-high heat. When hot, brush the griddle with a bit of oil. For each pancake pour ½ cup batter all at once onto the hot griddle. Spread about with a ladle or spatula to form a thin, even round. Cook until the bottom is dry. With a wide spatula, turn the cake over and cook until the bottom feels dry to the touch and the sides are crisp, 3 to 4 minutes total time. Remove and repeat the process. You should have about 5 large thin pancakes.

Stack them to keep them warm or reheat before dinner in aluminum foil in a 350° oven for about 10 minutes.

PEKING PANCAKES

MAKES ABOUT 24 PANCAKES

These wonderfully thin wheat pancakes are most often served with Peking Duck. However, with any imagination you can think up all kinds of uses for them. Put meat and vegetable dishes in these pancakes and roll them up like burritos. The package is really very good.

Prepare one batch of Chinese Boiled Dumpling Dough (page 449) and let the dough rest the prescribed time.

Roll the dough into a snake about 1 inch in diameter and cut into pieces 1 inch long. Roll each into a ball and then press out flat to make a small pancake. Brush the top of one pancake with sesame oil and place another pancake on top of the first. Using a rolling pin, and additional flour if needed, roll out the two pancakes together until they are about 5 inches in diameter. Roll all and keep under plastic wrap.

To cook the pancakes, place them, one pair at a time, in a hot SilverStone-lined pan. Cook until tiny brown spots form on the bottom and then turn the pancake over, cooking the second side in the same way. When the pancakes are done they can be separated into individual Peking Pancakes. To reheat them simply warm them in a bamboo steamer (page 106).

NOTE: You can save a bit of work in this process if you use a tortilla press. Roll the cut dough into balls and flatten them with the press. Oil one, put another on top, and press the two. Then, using the rolling pin, finish the rolling-out process.

ONION CAKES

MAKES 6 ONION CAKES

This is a most unusual dish. I gave you a version of this dish in my first cookbook, but I used a cheater's method. I told you that when I urged you use tortillas for this dish. This is the legit method and it comes from a very fine cookbook by Pei Mei, the first in a three-volume set. If you are really serious about Chinese cooking you will look for these books (see Bibliography).

3 cups flour
1 cup boiling water
⅓ cup cold water
6 tablespoons lard
3 tablespoons chopped green onions
3 teaspoons salt
1 cup peanut oil for pan-frying

Place the flour in a bowl and add the boiling water. Mix with chopsticks. Cover with plate and wait 3 minutes. Add cold water. Knead and let rest for 15 minutes.

Roll dough into a thick snake and cut into 6 pieces. Roll out each piece to 6 inches round. Place ½ tablespoon of lard on the pancake and smear around. Add salt and ½ tablespoon green onions. Roll up like a jelly roll and into a snail shape. Press flat and then roll out to about ⅛-inch thickness. Fry in 2 tablespoons oil. Turn. Add more oil as you go along. These should be very flaky.

Greece

OLD GREEK BREAD

MAKES 2 OR 3 LARGE LOAVES

I had the most wonderful experience on the Isle of Mykonos. It was February, off tourist season, and the little island was just going along for the sake of the regular inhabitants. A fellow took me to see a sight that tourists seldom see, the oldest bakery on the island. After a difficult search through the very narrow and wonderfully winding streets we stepped through a door and into a room so dark it took me several minutes to realize that the only light in the place was coming from the door of the wood-fired oven. The baker loads the oven twice a day and sells out twice a day. His ancestors built the ovens five hundred years ago, and there has not been a break in the family line.

Barley flour has been used by the Greeks since ancient times, and the windmills on Mykonos were originally used to power the grain-grinding mills. Grain would be shipped in from other ports in the Mediterranean and ground into flour on the windy Isle of Mykonos. This bread is as close as I can come to the wonderful bread of the Isle.

- 2½ cups tepid water (90°)
- 2 packages dry yeast (I prefer a quick-rising yeast)
- 2 cups barley flour
- ¼ cup rye flour
- Unbleached white flour to make up total flour weight of 2 pounds 3 ounces
- 1 tablespoon honey
- 2 tablespoons olive oil
- 2 teaspoons salt, mixed with 2 teaspoons water
- Cornmeal for the baking sheets

In a mixing bowl, dissolve the yeast in the tepid water.

Place a paper lunch sack on a scale and put in the barley and rye flour. Add enough additional unbleached flour to make up the 2 pounds 3 ounces.

Put the yeast water in an electric mixer bowl and add 4 cups of the flour mixture. (I simply use my KitchenAid for this whole process.) Add the honey and olive oil and mix to form a sponge, or very soft dough. Mix by hand or by machine until the dough begins to pull away from the side of the bowl, about 10 minutes. Mix in the salt mixed with water and finally the remaining flour. If you are using a hand mixer the last of the flour will have to be stirred in by hand. If you are using a powerful mixer use the dough hook.

Knead the dough until it is smooth and elastic. Place on a plastic counter and cover with a large bowl. Allow to rise until double in bulk, and then punch down and cover; allow to rise a second time.

Punch down and mold 2 or 3 loaves. Place on a baking sheet that has been sprinkled with a little cornmeal. Dust the loaves with a little flour and allow to rise again until double in size. Bake in a 450° oven for about 25 to 35 minutes, or until the bread is a rich dark brown and the loaf sounds hollow when you thump it on the bottom with your finger. Allow the loaves to cool on cake racks.

GREEK SESAME BREAD

MAKES 2 LOAVES

This is served all over Greece; the sesame seed has been popular there since ancient times. The Greeks were the ones who first started putting unusual seeds and flavorings into their baking. They taught the Romans to do the same.

- 1 cup tepid water
- 1 cup tepid milk
- 2 envelopes fast-rising dry yeast
- 2 tablespoons sugar
- 2 tablespoons salad oil
- 2 pounds 3 ounces unbleached white flour
- 1 teaspoon salt dissolved in 1 tablespoon water

TOPPING

- ¼ cup milk
- ½ cup raw sesame seeds

Cornmeal for the baking sheets

Mix the warm water and milk in your electric mixer bowl. Dissolve the yeast. Add the sugar, oil, and 4 cups of the total flour. Whip for 10 minutes and add the salted water. If you have a very strong mixer, such as a KitchenAid, you can use the dough hook to blend in the remaining flour. If not, you must do it by hand. Knead the dough for several minutes so that it is smooth and elastic. Place the dough on a plastic counter, and cover with a large inverted metal bowl. Allow to rise double in bulk and punch down. Allow to rise a second time and punch down. Divide into 2 halves. Roll each into a ball and punch a hole in the center. Work with the dough until you have a round circle about 13 inches in diameter. Place each loaf on a greased baking sheet that has been dusted with cornmeal. Brush the tops of the loaves with a bit of milk and top with the sesame seeds.

Bake at 400° until golden and light, about 25 to 30 minutes.

SESAME CIRCLES

These are sold in the streets of Athens. Wagons and little carts park on the sidewalk around the great squares of the city and sell these tasty bread circles by the hundreds.

Make a batch of Greek Sesame Bread (page 552) and form only one loaf. With the other half of the dough make sesame circles in this way. Roll the dough out to about ¼ inch thick and cut it into strips ½ inch wide. Using a strip of dough 18 inches long make a circle. It will be about 4 inches in diameter. Place the strips on an oiled baking sheet and allow to rise. Brush with milk and top with sesame seeds. Bake at 425° until golden brown, about 15 minutes.

GREEK EASTER BREAD

MAKES 2 LOAVES

Easter is the most holy of the holidays in Greece, and certainly the most involved. The special meals go on for days and the Great Paschal Feast of Easter Day cannot be celebrated without this bread. It is great fun to make and it will wow the kids on Easter morning.

1 cup warm milk
***2 teaspoons Mahleb, ground (optional)**
2 packages fast-acting yeast
1¼ cups tepid water
2 tablespoons salad oil
2 tablespoons sugar
2 raw eggs
2 pounds 3 ounces unbleached white flour
1 teaspoon salt dissolved in 1 teaspoon water
5 hard-boiled eggs, dyed a very bright red
1 egg, beaten, for a glaze

Heat the milk, along with the Mahleb, and allow it to cool until tepid. In your electric mixing bowl, dissolve the yeast in the water. Add the warm milk, salad oil, sugar, and eggs. Measure out 4 cups of the total flour and add to the bowl. Mix for about 10 minutes. Stir in the salt and water. The rest of the flour must be added by hand unless you have a

*Available in Greek markets.

powerful mixer such as a KitchenAid. Use the dough hook and blend in the rest of the flour. Knead until smooth. Place the dough on a plastic counter and cover with a large inverted bowl. Allow to rise until double in bulk, punch down, and allow to rise again. (See, it *is* Easter Bread!)

Divide the dough into 2 pieces. Cover one half with the bowl and divide the other half into 3 equal parts. Roll each into a snake about 25 inches long. Lay the pieces side by side and pinch one end together. Braid the three pieces and form into a round loaf. Place the Easter eggs in the braid and allow the bread to rise until double in bulk. Brush with the beaten egg and bake at 375° for about 30 minutes, or until golden brown.

PITA BREAD WITH OLIVE OIL, GRILLED

The ancient Greek grill is a wonderful device. From it came our barbecue and a hundred gadgets in between. You can grill pita bread as they do in Greece and you can grill it on your gas or electric stove. Buy fresh pita bread at your market and brush a loaf on both sides with a small amount of olive oil. Place the loaf on a hot asador grill (page 13) and heat, turning once. You will be amazed at the difference in flavor.

PAXIMADI

This is not a recipe but a qualified commercial for the ingenious early Greeks. The Greeks invented toast! A baker in ancient times realized that bread sliced and cooked a second time, or toasted, would keep well on the road. He gave us a whole new possibility for travel, since his invention could feed us on long journeys. His name was Paxamos, and to this day you can find, in every bakery in Greece, sweet toasts called *paximadi*. You will also find signs outside coffee shops advertising the product. It is a funny sign, according to my sons, because it is translated into English and simply advertises "Toast." "Wow!" Jason laughed. "Let's get some!"

You probably have never thought about the fact that the invention of toast changed travel patterns in the ancient world. Neither had I!

Italy

ANCIENT ROMAN BREAD

MAKES 2 OR 3 LOAVES

We are quite sure that when the Romans invaded Greece they had their eating habits changed drastically. The Greeks were better bakers, for one thing, and the Greek slaves who were taken back to Rome taught the Romans to use several different flours in a single loaf instead of the one common flour that was used in Rome. I think this recipe is about as close as we can come to the flavors that were enjoyed during the early days.

- **2 envelopes fast-rising dry yeast**
- **2½ cups tepid water**
- **1 cup whole-wheat flour**
- **½ cup rye flour**
- **Unbleached white flour to make up 2 pounds 3 ounces of total flour weight**
- **1 teaspoon salt dissolved in 1 tablespoon water**
- **Cornmeal for dusting the baking sheets**

Put the tepid water in your electric mixer bowl and dissolve the yeast.

Use a paper lunch sack for weighing out the flour. Put the whole-wheat and rye flour in the bag first, and then make up the weight with the white flour. Put 4 cups from the bag into the mixer and whip it for 10 minutes. Add the salted water. If you have a heavy mixing machine such as a KitchenAid, allow the dough hook to do the rest of the work. If not, you need to add the remaining flour by hand. Knead until the dough is smooth and elastic.

Put the dough on a plastic counter and cover with an inverted steel bowl. Allow it to rise once, punch it down, and allow it to rise a second time. Punch down and form into 2 or 3 loaves. I never use bread pans for this, as they will ruin the crust. Place the loaves on baking sheets that have been dusted with cornmeal and allow the loaves to rise until double in bulk.

Bake in a 450° oven about 25 minutes, or until the crust is golden and the loaf light to the touch. It should make a hollow sound when you thump your finger on the bottom of the loaf.

ROMAN BREAD

MAKES 2 OR 3 LOAVES

The bakeries in Rome produce a bread that has a crust so dark it looks almost burned. It has wonderful flavor and I think this method will produce something close to the crusty Roman version.

Prepare a batch of Ancient Roman Bread (page 555), but use only unbleached white flour. The total weight should be *only* white flour. Prepare the loaves and allow them to rise on pans dusted with cornmeal.

Preheat the oven to 450° 1 hour prior to baking. Place a sheet of baking tiles (page 17) on the middle rack of the oven. These will even out the heat. Place a 9 × 13-inch cake pan filled with water on the bottom rack of the oven. Add more water as needed. Bake the risen loaves in the oven at 450° for 20 minutes. Then turn the heat to 500° and bake another 10 minutes or until the crust is very dark.

BREADSTICKS, ITALIAN SESAME

These are simple to make and far superior to the fat, thick, pasty, flavorless things that we call breadsticks in this country. The Roman variety is very thin, closer to the size of a pencil. They are found on every restaurant table and they have a nutty, toasted flavor that goes beautifully with a glass of wine.

To make them, prepare a batch of dough using only unbleached white flour, as in the recipe on the previous page. Allow the dough to rise twice and then punch down. Roll it out into rectangles about ¼ inch thick. Cut into ¼-inch-wide strips and then cut these to the desired length for your breadsticks. Twist each strand of dough as you place it on a baking sheet dusted with cornmeal. Simply hold the strand of dough between two hands and turn the ends in opposite directions. Set on the baking sheet. Allow to rise for a short time and bake at 425° for 15 minutes or until golden brown.

VARIATION: If you wish to brush some of these with a bit of milk and then top them with raw sesame seeds, you will have a serious treat for the kids.

HINT: FOR MAKING BREADSTICKS you might try using a noodle cutter. There is one on the market that has five large stainless blades, each ¼ inch apart. It is used for chopping noodles, but it also works great for cutting breadsticks. See page 14.

CRUSTULUM

I could not resist telling you about this delight. It is garlic toast, but made as in the days of the Roman Empire. I am quite sure that they learned the trick from the Greeks (see Paximadi, page 554). In our time the Italians call this *bruschetta,* but in the early days it was called *crustulum,* and from it we have our word "crust."

To make Crustulum simply toast good Roman bread on both sides over charcoal. None of this electric pop-toaster jazz! Rub the toast with an entire clove of garlic, and rub until the clove disappears. Drizzle extra virgin olive oil on the toast and enjoy. This is great with any Italian meal, and with a salad and a good wine it makes a meal in itself.

FOCACCIA ROMANA

Marion, who helps me in my studio kitchen in Chicago, does not eat a lot when she is working. None of us have time! But when I made this dish she ate as if I would never make it again for her. This recipe is for her.

Craig, my cooking assistant, and I tasted this version at the Forno Campo de' Fiori, the bakery in the great market center in Rome. People line up to buy this fabulous bread, and they bake throughout the day. They gave us the recipe . . . though it was just a description. We have worked out the following simple formula, and I think it is superb. It is a very old form of bread in Rome, going back hundreds of years. It is great for sandwiches and eating with dinner, and it forms the background of what was later to be called "Pizza."

- **2 packages fast-rising dry yeast**
- **2 cups tepid water (90°)**
- **2 tablespoons sugar**
- **4 tablespoons olive oil**
- **½ cup salad oil**
- **1 teaspoon table salt**
- **5½ cups unbleached white flour**
- **3 cloves garlic, crushed**
- **¼ cup olive oil for topping**
- **1 tablespoon whole rosemary**
- **1 tablespoon kosher salt for topping**

Dissolve the yeast in the tepid water. Add the sugar, olive oil, salad oil, and regular salt. Mix in 3 cups of the flour and whip until the dough begins to leave the sides of the mixing bowl, about 10 minutes. I use my KitchenAid mixer for this whole process.

Mix in remaining flour by hand or with a dough hook and knead the dough until it is smooth. Allow the dough to rise twice, right in the bowl, and punch down after each rising.

Oil 2 baking sheets, each 13 inches by 18 inches, and divide the dough between the 2 pans. Using your fingers, press the dough out to the edges of each pan. Allow to rise for about 30 minutes and brush with the crushed garlic mixed with the oil for topping. Sprinkle the rosemary and kosher salt on top.

Bake at 375° for about 30 minutes.

VARIATION: Top with green onions instead of rosemary. Delicious.

OLIVE BREAD

This is a popular Roman treat that an olive lover cannot resist. Prepare a batch of Roman Bread (page 555) and knead in some stuffed green olives. Bake per instructions and get ready to surprise your guests when you slice the beautiful loaf.

OLIVE ROLLS

This is the same as above but you simply prepare rolls instead of loaves. Bake at 425° for about 20 minutes, or until golden brown.

Pizza

We cannot date the first pizza, but we do know that flat, round loaves of bread go back to prehistoric times. It was peasant food from the beginning, and it has been raised to glory with a few wonderful toppings. Pizza is now the second most popular fast food in America.

The Greeks are credited with originating the concept of pizza in a refined form. They developed the "edible plate," for that is what pizza is, by topping the bread with an assortment of "relishes," here meaning anything that was put on the bread. A rim was put on the loaf so that it could hold the garnishes, and the pizza was born. It was actually a trencher! The Greeks took this with them into southern Italy and it became very popular there.

In the northern portion of Italy the Etruscans ate a *puls* or thick gruel made of grains. They customarily baked this on stones beneath the ashes of the household fires, seasoning these cakes with oil and herbs. The Romans adopted this ash cake and called it *focaccia* (from the Latin *panis focacius,* "bread from the floor of the fireplace"). *Focaccia* survives today and is certainly one of the ancestors of what we call pizza.

It is easy to see how the Greek idea of flat bread with relishes combined with the Etruscan bread on ashes to produce pizza. The word "pizza" is derived from the Latin word *picea,* meaning the black ashes on the floor of the fireplace. This is still the way pizza should be made today. Two wandering peoples, the Greeks and the Etruscans, thus armed the Italian immigrant with a great treasure when he came to America. Our contribution to the cause was tomato sauce, of course. Since the tomato is a product of the New World, we can claim credit for the introduction of the sauce, which was first brought to Italy during the 1500s. Naples remains the center of great tomato-topped pies. Thus pizza has come full circle.

I understand that some character is planning on opening a pizza parlor in Beijing. Won't the Chinese be in for a surprise!

Ancestors of Wheat-Flour Pizza

GARBANZO PIZZA, OLD ROMAN STYLE
(Cecina)

SERVES 6 AS A VERY INTERESTING HISTORICAL LESSON AND SNACK

Garbanzo beans, or chick-peas, are a very old food product. Apicius lists them in his first-century cookbook and we know they were used for common food long before wheat became popular. When wheat did become available in the Mediterranean it was very expensive, so people continued to eat the less-expensive garbanzo bean and the chestnut. Polenta and a kind of pizza were made from these products a thousand years ago. It had no yeast, nor tomatoes, of course.

This recipe is from Bugialli's wonderful book, *Classic Techniques of Italian Cooking* (see Bibliography). I am not sure that you are going to love this dish, but I do want you to know something about the history of pizza.

1½ cups dried garbanzo beans, soaked in water overnight
1 teaspoon salt
4 tablespoons olive oil
1 tablespoon fresh rosemary leaves
Salt and freshly ground black pepper to taste

Rinse the soaked beans and place them in a saucepan. Cover with fresh water, along with the salt. Bring to a simmer and cook, covered, for 1½ hours. You will need to add more water during the process. Cook until they are soft. Drain, reserving the liquid, and place the beans in a food processor. Grind them up using the pulse button—you do not want a fine mush. Add a bit of the reserved cooking liquid, about 1 cup, so that you have a nice thick paste. Stir in 2 tablespoons of the olive oil and add more salt to taste, if necessary. Use another tablespoon of the oil to grease a 14-inch pizza pan and spread the batter out in the pan. Top with the last portion of the oil, the rosemary leaves, and the black pepper to taste. Bake at 375° for 35 minutes. Slice up the pie and serve it while it is hot.

CHESTNUT FOCACCIA

This is also an interesting bit of history. When chestnuts were near free, the locals in the Old World used them to make flour. The flour was not suitable for what we call bread but it did make a flavorful baked pulse, or a flat polenta. That is the background of this very early pizza. The chestnut flour also made a good pasta (page 499).

1¼ cups chestnut flour
1¼ cups water
Olive oil for greasing the baking pan
2 tablespoons pine nuts
¼ teaspoon whole rosemary
1 tablespoon olive oil

Beat water and flour to a batter consistency. Oil a 12-inch-round pizza tray and pour batter on the tray. Spread out evenly and top with the pine nuts and herbs, and sprinkle the olive oil over the top. Bake at 380° for 25 minutes or until golden on top.

NOTE: In the oldest versions of this dish, golden raisins were also used, thus marking it as a favorite of the Roman palate. However, I think the raisins make it much too sweet.

PIZZA DOUGH

The best pizza dough that I have ever come across is the bread dough for Focaccia Romana (page 558). Make a batch and then choose your topping. A single batch of dough will make 2 pizzas, each 13 inches by 18 inches. Follow the instructions for pressing out the dough but do not use the toppings for Focaccia. Use other creative toppings instead.

PIZZA TOPPINGS

Most of these call for an Italian Tomato Sauce topping (page 237). Just brush a bit on the dough and then go ahead and create any of the following pizzas. In Rome the items are generally not mixed but only a single item used on a pizza. However, don't let that stop your creativity.

Once the topping is on and you are ready to bake, drizzle some good olive oil over the whole thing. Then, into the oven!

Zucchini, sliced thin, and arranged like tiles over a bit of Italian Tomato Sauce and grated cheese.

Tomatoes, sliced thin, and arranged like tiles on top of sauce and cheese. Add lots of black pepper.

Onions, sliced thin and arranged like tiles on sauce with grated cheese.

Potato, sliced thin and arranged like tiles on sauce with grated cheese.

Eggs, hard-boiled and sliced, artichokes, sliced, and tuna. These items are placed on top of a tomato-sauce pizza while it is still hot. They are not baked.

Pancetta, sliced thin on top of tomato sauce and grated cheese.

Green olives, stuffed, sliced thin, arranged on a tomato-sauce pizza with grated cheese.

Mushrooms, sliced thin and arranged like tiles on a tomato-sauce pizza with grated cheese.

Two Mushrooms. Dried mushrooms (page 33) are soaked, drained, chopped, and spread on the tomato sauce. Fresh mushrooms are then sliced and arranged on top.

Anchovies, arranged in a neat pattern on a tomato pizza. No cheese on this one.

Old Roman. Olive oil, garlic, pine nuts, fresh rosemary, kosher salt. No cheese or tomato on this.

RUSTIC PIZZA

SERVES 4–6 AS A MAIN DISH

This is the original deep-dish pizza, I suppose, and it comes from southern Italy. It is not difficult to prepare and the presentation is just smashing. If you can eat more than 2 wedges of this I will give up on you!

CRUST

Use Focaccia dough pressed into a 10-inch-round cake pan.

FILLING

- ½ cup chopped ham
- ½ cup freshly grated Parmesan cheese
- ½ cup cream cheese
- 2 hard-boiled eggs, chopped
- 2 cups Basic White Sauce (page 234), enriched with 2 egg yolks
- Salt and pepper to taste
- 2 stiffly beaten egg whites

Mix all of the above except the egg whites. Taste for salt and pepper and then gently fold in the beaten egg whites. Pour this mixture into the crust and bake in a 375° oven for 30 minutes. Then turn down the oven to 350° and bake 10 more minutes or until the pie sets and is golden on top.

Desserts

Our Western desire for a sweet at the close of the meal was certainly not celebrated in our three ancient cuisines. There were exceptions, of course, particularly for special occasions and festivals, but the Greeks and the Romans most often ended their meals with a bit of fresh fruit. The Chinese have a bit of fruit, an orange perhaps, at the end of the meal, but even that practice is uncommon. Sweets were reserved for festivals and this practice continues in China even today.

The Greeks and the Romans make wonderful pastries, but even these are offered at some other time of the day, rarely after a meal. I offer these recipes with the understanding that I never serve desserts to my family, although I love each of the following recipes. My idea of a fine dessert is a good cup of Italian coffee, or perhaps a glass of fine wine. Just remember that we Americans eat much too much sugar, and we need to cut down. Diabetes was practically unknown in China until very recently. The Chinese have never been that concerned about consuming sugar, but now, with the invasion of Western tastes, soda pop and all of the evils that go with it are common in China. Diabetes in Beijing cannot be far behind.

China

EIGHT-TREASURE RICE PUDDING

SERVES 8–10 AS CHINESE DESSERT

Boy, does this one take some doing. Rice is served here as a dessert, and I can just hear you commenting on the fact that the Chinese eat rice three meals a day and in all forms. Don't forget that rice pudding is very popular in America, too.

You will have fun making an attractive arrangement of the fruits. This dessert is served only on special occasions, and after making one I am sure you will know why.

2 cups sticky sweet rice (page 30)
1 tablespoon peanut oil for greasing the bowl

THE EIGHT TREASURES

1 tablespoon white raisins, soaked in water for 1 hour
1 tablespoon black raisins, soaked in water for 1 hour
6 Chinese dried red dates, soaked in water for 1 hour
3 dates, sliced into quarters the long way
6 candied red cherries, sliced in half
½ tablespoon diced candied lemon peel
1 tablespoon green candied peel or green pineapple, cut into diamond shapes or wedges
½ tablespoon pine nuts

1¾ cups water
2 tablespoons lard
3 tablespoons sugar
4 ounces sweet red bean paste (page 30)

THE SYRUP

1 cup water
3 tablespoons sugar
1 tablespoon cornstarch mixed with 1 tablespoon water

Rinse the rice several times in cold running water and then cover with water and allow to soak for 3 hours.

While the rice is soaking, select a 7-inch-diameter bowl, 3 inches deep. Oil the bowl with the peanut oil and arrange the soaked and drained fruits and nuts in an interesting pattern in the bottom of the bowl. You can make quite a production of this if you wish to take the time. Place things in circles, lines, wheel-spoke patterns. . . .

After the rice has soaked, drain and add 1¾ cups fresh water. Bring to a boil with the lid off and boil for 3 minutes. Turn the heat to low, cover the pot, and cook for an additional 7 minutes. Remove from the heat and stir in the lard and 3 tablespoons sugar. Very carefully place half of this mixture in the bowl, being careful not to mess up your colorful fruit arrangement. Place the sweet bean paste in a ball in the center of the bowl and top with the rest of the rice. Pat it down so that it will all stick together when it cooks.

Place the bowl in a bamboo steamer (page 106) and cook for 1 hour 15 minutes. Remove the dish from the steamer and place a plate upside down on top of the rice bowl and invert. Tap very gently so that the rice and fruit come out in one piece.

Prepare the syrup by bringing the water and sugar to a boil. Stir in the cornstarch and water and stir until thick. Pour over the pudding and serve.

FRIED CUSTARD

SERVES 4–5 AS A DESSERT

The cook who thought this one up has got to be credited with being very, very clever. The dish goes back many generations in China and it is popular at formal banquets in Hong Kong, since Westerners are so used to having a sweet dessert. It is not complex to prepare and it is a great deal of fun to serve.

3 egg yolks, beaten
1 cup cold water
½ teaspoon almond extract
½ cup flour
6 tablespoons cornstarch
4 tablespoons sugar
4 cups peanut oil for deep-frying
3 tablespoons sesame seeds, toasted and ground (page 29)

In a 1-quart saucepan place the yolks, water, almond extract, flour, and 3 tablespoons of cornstarch. Add 1 tablespoon of the sugar. Mix thoroughly and cook over medium heat, stirring constantly, until the mixture thickens into a heavy custard. Remove to a flat dish that has been greased with a bit of vegetable oil and spread the custard out to a ½-inch thickness. Place in the refrigerator to cool. When cooled and firm, cut the custard into diamond shapes about 1½ inches long. Dust with the remaining 3 tablespoons of cornstarch. Deep-fry the coated diamonds in 360° oil until golden brown. Do this in 2 batches. Mix the remaining 3 tablespoons of sugar with the ground sesame seeds and sprinkle over the fried custard. Serve hot.

CANDIED BANANA FRITTERS

SERVES 6–8 FOR DESSERT

When the Chinese finally decide to serve a sweet dessert it is spectacular. Be careful with this classic as the sugar syrup is very hot and will burn.

BATTER

1 egg, beaten
3 tablespoons flour
3 tablespoons cornstarch
1 tablespoon water
3 medium bananas (not too ripe)

Oil for deep-frying

SYRUP

1 tablespoon peanut oil
½ cup sugar

In a small bowl mix the beaten egg, flour, cornstarch, and water to form a smooth batter. Slice the bananas into ½-inch-thick pieces and coat with the batter. Deep-fry at 360° for 20 seconds, in 2 batches, and remove and drain. Allow the oil to return to temperature and fry the slices, all at once, a second time just until golden brown.

While the slices are frying, heat the oil and sugar in a small saucepan. Cook on medium heat until the sugar dissolves and turns a very light golden color. Coat the bananas in the syrup and then plunge into a serving bowl of cold water and ice cubes. Serve at once so that the bananas are still hot and the syrup crystallized. Remove from the water with chopsticks for each serving.

CHERRIES IN ALMOND

SERVES 6 AS PART OF A CHINESE MEAL

This dish is actually from Taiwan. It was given me by the same woman who gave me the Slow Simmered Pork Roast, Ann Gelow. We shared meals in my days as university chaplain in Tacoma, and my students had little money in the sixties. This was her clever Chinese solution to an inexpensive dessert. It cleans the tongue of the richness of the meal since it contains no sugar.

1 16-ounce can unsweetened pie cherries (not pie-filling mix)

1 teaspoon almond extract

Heat the cherries in their juice and stir in the almond extract. Serve just a few cherries, along with some juice, in tiny bowls to each guest.

CHINESE SESAME COOKIES
(Heung Yun Beng)
MAKES 100 COOKIES

These are very rich because of the heavy use of lard. They are a favorite with Chinese children, but they are generally reserved for special occasions and holidays. After you eat one, you will know why. They are delicious.

- **¾ cup brown sugar**
- **1½ cups granulated sugar**
- **1½ tablespoons powdered milk**
- **1 tablespoon ice water**
- **1 pound lard**
- **2 eggs**
- **3 teaspoons baking soda**
- **5 teaspoons cream of tartar**
- **5½ cups flour**
- **2 cups raw white sesame seeds**

In an electric mixer mix all but the flour and sesame together. Then add the flour and do not overmix. Mix just until it holds together. Roll dough into walnut-sized balls and then roll in the sesame seeds. Place on a cookie sheet about 2 inches apart. Bake at 350° for 15 minutes until cookies have irregular cracks on the surface.

SWEET ALMOND CREAM SOUP

This is most unusual and very simple. You can buy the Sweet Almond Soup already prepared in a tin. Add one can of milk to each can of soup and heat. Serve small amounts to each person at the end of the meal.

PEKING DUST

SERVES 8–10 AS A DESSERT

This wonderful dish includes whipping cream, so I doubt that this version was served in early times in Peking. Cream was simply not used as we use it. As a matter of fact, the Chinese have never really gotten into dairy products. The cream is obviously a much more recent addition.

This is best made with fresh chestnuts, either roasted or boiled, peeled of course. If you wish to use fresh, use about 2½ pounds in order to prepare this elaborate dish.

THE CHESTNUTS

- 1 pound dried chestnuts, soaked overnight and drained
- 1 cup water
- 1 cup regular sugar
- 1 teaspoon salt
- ½ cup powdered or confectioner's sugar
- 1 teaspoon vanilla

WHIPPED CREAM

- 2 cups whipping cream
- 3 tablespoons powdered or confectioner's sugar
- 1 teaspoon vanilla

GARNISH

- 3 tablespoons dark brown sugar
- Glacéed or candied fruit (optional)

Place the drained chestnuts in a saucepan and add 1 cup of water, along with the 1 cup sugar. Bring to a boil, cover, and simmer until the nuts are barely tender, about 1 hour. Drain, reserving the syrup. Place the nuts in a food processor and process, in 2 batches, just until grainy. Remove to a bowl and stir in the remaining ingredients for the chestnuts. Set aside.

Whip the cream and add the sugar and vanilla. Gently fold *half* of the whipped cream into the chestnut mixture and mound this on a serving plate. Make it look like a mountain. Cover the mountain with the remaining whipped cream and garnish with the brown sugar and optional dried fruits.

Greece

HALVAH CAKE

SERVES 12–15 PEOPLE

This cake is unusual in that it has no flour in it at all. The farina soaks up the syrup that is poured on after baking and the result is very close to the sweet moist cakes that you find in the street cafés in Athens. This is truly a wonderful dessert.

BATTER

- 1 cup sugar
- 2 sticks (½ pound) butter
- 2 cups semolina flour or regular cream of wheat cereal
- ½ cup almonds, peeled, coarsely chopped in food processor
- 6 eggs, beaten
- 1 teaspoon baking powder
- 1 teaspoon cinnamon
- ½ cup whole pine nuts

SYRUP

- 2 cups sugar
- 3 cups water
- 1 whole clove
- 2 ounces brandy
- Juice of 2 lemons

Using an electric mixer, cream the butter and sugar. Add the remaining ingredients, except the pine nuts, and blend to form a smooth batter. Spread the batter evenly in a greased 9 × 13-inch cake pan. Sprinkle the pine nuts on the top of the batter. Bake in a preheated 350° oven for 30 to 35 minutes.

In a small pan heat all of the ingredients for the syrup. Boil the syrup until it begins to thicken a bit, about 6 minutes. Remove from the heat and cool until just very warm to touch. Hold a saucer over the cake and drizzle the warm syrup onto the saucer and thus onto the cake. This will prevent your marring the surface of the cake.

Cover the cake pan with plastic wrap and allow the cake to sit for 2 hours so that the syrup will be absorbed.

BAKLAVA

It seems silly for me to give you a recipe for baklava when I know that you are not going to make the phyllo dough from scratch. It takes years to learn to do this, and I have tried several times. Mrs. Stergachis, my Greek friend in Tacoma, makes all of her phyllo by hand, and she supplies me with baklava for my restaurants. I could not believe the work involved, and she is still making the pastries for our Greek Orthodox Church.

Buy 2 pounds of phyllo dough from your Greek market or delicatessen. A recipe for baklava will be on the side of the box and you can bake the dish yourself. Pulling your own phyllo? Forget it.

STRAWBERRY YOGURT WITH HONEY

This is a classic dessert in Athens. There are shops just off Omonia Square that specialize in this very thing. It is great to sit in the Greek sun and enjoy a cool dish of yogurt made very sweet with fine Greek honey.

In the States one can simply purchase strawberry yogurt in the supermarket. Place a bit in a small bowl and drizzle a bit of good honey over the top.

Greek Heaven!

HALVAH

Sesame halvah can be purchased in fancy food stores and in Middle Eastern markets and delicatessens. It is a wonderful candy that is simply eaten at the close of the meal, as a dessert. It goes great with strong coffee. You will see it in several flavors, including vanilla and chocolate marbled.

COFFEE FRAPPÉ

The street cafés around the great Omonia Square in Athens serve a coffee drink that is very refreshing, and a great summer dessert. They call it a frappé, and it is served in tall glasses. You can make one with little effort.

Make some strong espresso coffee and chill it. Put 1 cup of whole milk, plus 2 tablespoons whipping cream, in a food blender and whip it a bit. Add coffee to taste, along with a bit of sugar, and whip again. Serve in a tall chilled glass.

Italy

RICOTTA PIE, ROMAN STYLE
(Crostata di Ricotta alla Romana)

SERVES 8–10

I met the most wonderful woman in Rome. Her name is Jo Bettoja and she is married to a very famous Italian hotel owner. She has lived in Rome for more than twenty years but she was born in Georgia! She teaches Roman women how to cook American, Southern style, and she is good. She offered me this dish as being typical of old Roman eating. The dried fruits and pine nuts certainly bear out her case. This kind of baking is very old indeed. Mrs. Bettoja also teaches Americans how to cook Italian and she does know her history.

THE PASTRY

- 2½ cups all-purpose flour
- ½ cup plus 1 tablespoon sugar
- 3 egg yolks, beaten
- Grated zest (outer peel) of ½ lemon
- 10 tablespoons unsalted butter, at cool room temperature

THE FILLING

- 1 pound ricotta cheese
- 1 cup sugar
- 2 eggs
- 2 ounces white raisins, soaked in rum to cover for 2 hours, and drained
- 2 ounces citron or green candied lemon peel, cut in a small dice
- ⅓ cup pine nuts, toasted in a 375° oven until just barely browned

Butter and dust with flour a 10-inch cheesecake pan with removable sides.

Place the flour for the crust in a large mixing bowl and make a well in the center. Add the sugar, egg yolks, lemon zest, and butter, cut into small pieces. Mix by pinching and rubbing the ingredients together until the consistency of coarse meal. Add a tablespoon of water, or perhaps 2, in order to form a dough. Knead just a couple of times.

NOTE: If using a food processor for this step, use well-chilled butter and just throw all of the ingredients into the machine. Process and add the water if you need it.

Cut the pastry into two pieces, one a little larger for the bottom crust. Roll out to about ⅛-inch thickness. (I find that a marble sheet and marble rolling pin work well for this.) Detach the pastry from the surface with a spatula or long knife and drape over the rolling pin. Unroll over the cake pan, leaving some overhang.

Cream the ricotta with the sugar, add all the other ingredients for the filling, and mix well. Pour this into the prepared cake pan. Roll out the remaining pastry and cut into ¾-inch-wide strips. Lay the strips across the pie in a lattice. Pinch or crimp the edges of the strips to the crust to seal.

Bake in a preheated 375° oven for 45 minutes or until lightly browned. Cool on a rack for 15 minutes before turning out. Serve warm or at room temperature.

SWEET CHESTNUT PURÉE

MAKES 2 CUPS FOR USE IN DESSERTS

You can buy this product already made from fresh chestnuts . . . and it costs a fortune. This version will do you nicely for desserts and cake sauces and it will cost much less.

1 pound dried chestnuts, soaked overnight
1 cup sugar
⅛ teaspoon lemon extract
1 teaspoon salt
½ cup brandy

Drain the soaked chestnuts and rinse. Place in a 2-quart pot and cover with water. Bring to a boil, covered, and simmer for 1 hour or until tender. Drain, reserving the water.

Grind the chestnuts in a medium-size food processor until smooth. This will have to be done in 2 batches. Use some of the reserved liquid to get a smooth and very thick paste. Remove to a saucepan and add the remaining ingredients, along with enough of the reserved water to make a purée of desired consistency. Heat gently for about 5 minutes to dissolve the sugar.

WINE AND COOKIES

This old Roman custom is a delight. No preparation, no pain, and all of your guests will be delighted.

At the end of a heavy Roman meal, serve glasses of Vin Santo, available at Italian specialty shops, or you can use a good dry Marsala. A plate of *ghiottini,* almond cookies, are passed with the glasses. The fun comes when you instruct everyone to dip their cookies in the wonderful dessert wine. The flavor is ancient and contemporary, all at once.

ITALIAN CHESTNUT JAM CAKE

SERVES 8–10

This is a very dramatic presentation, though I have taken some gross liberties with this recipe. The older versions are just too complex to bother with and this one is both simple and delicious.

- 1 pound cake, sliced horizontally into 3 equal layers

SYRUP

- Rind of one lemon, grated
- 1 teaspoon vanilla
- ½ cup brandy
- ½ cup sugar

- 2 cups Sweet Chestnut Purée (page 579)

BUTTERCREAM FROSTING

- 2 sticks soft butter
- 2½ cups powdered or confectioner's sugar
- 1 teaspoon vanilla
- 1 egg white

GARNISH:

- 1 cup sliced almonds, toasted
- 2 milk-chocolate bars

Mix the ingredients for the syrup together and heat for a moment on the stove or in the microwave. Dribble this mixture on all 3 slices of cake. Spread the chestnut purée on 2 of the slices and place on top of each other, the bare slice going on top.

Mix all of the ingredients for the icing with an electric mixer. Whip until light and smooth. Ice the cake and top with the toasted almonds. Melt the chocolate bars in a glass measuring cup in the microwave. Then stir in enough very hot water to make a very thick syrup. Dribble this over the top of the cake and allow to cool.

Epilogue: The Earth Is Too Small for Private Dinner Parties

I am always concerned when I see a person in the supermarket with a basket filled with private food. You know what I mean by private food, of course. Little packages of instant and prepared foods that indicate that this person intends to eat alone again tonight. We see a lot of this among the older members of our culture, and we always mumble something about being pleased with their sense of independence. It may not be independence. It may be simple loneliness.

The three ancient cultures that we have looked at in this volume did not, and do not, understand private eating. For one thing it was economically impossible to eat by yourself in the early days. The fuel for the kitchen was too expensive, and the idea of living by yourself was unheard of. In America we claim that we value privacy and independence, and have therefore put a whole life-style on the market based on the ability to get along without anyone else. That is what private foods mean. We have sought a time of independence for everyone in our culture . . . and I am convinced that the result has not been pride in privacy, but rather an insight into the fact that privatude, in the end, offers only one thing—and that is loneliness.

Great food is not to be eaten by oneself. Eating privately is simply learning to sustain yourself, but dining is always done with other people. Please reconsider the plight of the people you know who live by themselves. Invite them in for a Roman dinner party, or for a Chinese or Greek dinner party. You and your children will be richer for it and your children will understand that the table is the proper place for sharing. And your guest? He or she, at the end of the evening, will give you a hug and say, "When can I come back?" That is what the ancient table was for . . . and what the table should be for in our time.

I bid you Peace.

Bibliography

*Indicates books of which I am particularly fond. You should look at them.

Allen, Jana, and Margaret Gin. *Innards and Other Variety Meats* (San Francisco: 101 Productions, 1974).

Bianchini, Francesco, and Francesco Corbetta. *The Complete Book of Fruits and Vegetables* (New York: Crown Publishers, Inc., 1973).

Boni, Ada. *Italian Regional Cooking* (New York: Bonanza Books, 1969).

Boni, Ada. *The Talisman Italian Cookbook* (New York: Crown Publishers, 1950).

Brennen, Jennifer. *The Cuisines of Asia: Nine Great Oriental Cuisines by Technique* (New York: Martin's/Marek, 1984).

Buehr, Wendy, editor in charge. *The Horizon Cookbook and Illustrated History of Eating and Drinking Through the Ages* (New York: American Heritage Publishing Company, 1968).

Bugialli, Giuliano. *Classic Techniques of Italian Cooking* (New York: Simon and Schuster, 1982).

Bugialli, Giuliano. *Foods of Italy* (New York: Stewart, Tabori, and Chang, 1984).

Burum, Linda. *Asian Pasta* (New York: Aris Books, 1985).

*Chang, K. C., ed. *Food in Chinese Culture* (New Haven: Yale University Press, 1977).

Chantiles, Vilma Liacouras. *The Food of Greece* (New York: Dodd, Mead, and Co., 1975).

Chinese American Women's Club of Santa Clara County. *Chinese Cooking Our Way* (Campbell, Calif.: Phoenix Press, 1971).

Chinese Parents Service Organization. *Flavors of China* (Seattle: Trinity Printing, 1975).
Address: Trinity Printing, P.O. Box 68922, Seattle, Washington 98188.

Coyle, L. Patrick. *World Encyclopedia of Food* (New York: Facts on File, 1982).

Cronin, Israel. *The International Squid Book* (New York: Aris Books, 1981).

Davidson, Alan. *Mediterranean Seafood* (New York: Penguin, 1981).

Defenbacher, D. S. (based on exhibition prepared by the Walker Art Center, Minneapolis). *Knife, Fork and Spoon* (Colwell Press, 1951).

di Schino, June. *L'Eterno Banchetto* (Rome: Commune di Roma, Assessorato alla Cultura, 1987).

Dosi, A., and F. Schnell. *Le Abitudini Alimentari dei Romani* (Rome: Edizioni Quasar, 1986).

Dosi, A., and F. Schnell. *Pasti e Vasellame da Tavola* (Rome: Edizioni Quasar, 1986).

Dosi, A., and F. Schnell. *I Romani in Cucina* (Rome: Edizioni Quasar, 1986).

*Edwards, John. *The Roman Cookery of Apicius* (Point Roberts, Wash.: Hartley and Marks, 1984).

Elegant, Robert, and the editors of Time-Life Books. *Hong Kong* (Alexandria, Va.: Time-Life Books, 1977).

Ellwanger, George. *The Pleasures of the Table* (New York: Doubleday Page, 1902).

Field, Carol. *The Italian Baker* (New York: Harper and Row, 1985).

Grist, D. H. *Rice* (London: Longman, Green, and Co., 1955).

Gunther, John. *Twelve Cities* (New York: Harper & Row, 1976).

Hale, William Harlan, editor in charge. *The Horizon Book of Ancient Greece* (New York: American Heritage Publishing Co., 1965).

Hazan, Marcella. *The Classic Italian Cookbook* (New York: Alfred A. Knopf, 1980).

Hazan, Marcella. *Marcella's Italian Kitchen* (New York: Alfred A. Knopf, 1986).

*Hom, Ken. *Asian Vegetarian Feast* (New York: William Morrow, 1988).

Kubly, Herbert. *Italy* (New York: Time-Life Books, 1965).

Lassen, Erik. *Knives, Forks, and Spoons* (Copenhagen: Host and Son, 1960).

Liebman, Malvina W. *From Caravan to Casserole: Herbs and Spices in Legend, History and Recipes* (Miami: Seemann 1977).

*Lin, Florence. *Florence Lin's Complete Book of Chinese Noodles, Dumplings and Bread* (New York: William Morrow, 1986).

Lin, Hsiang Ju, and Tsui Feng Lin. *Chinese Gastronomy* (New York: Hastings House, 1969).

McNeil, William H. *History of Western Civilization* (Chicago: University of Chicago Press, 1986).

McNeil, William H. *The Rise of the West* (Chicago: University of Chicago Press, 1963).

*Mark, Willy. *Chinese Cookery Masterclass* (London: Macdonald & Co., 1984).

*Middione, Carlo. *The Food of Southern Italy* (New York: William Morrow, 1987).

Mock, Lonnie. *Favorite Dim Sum* (Walnut Creek, Calif.: Alpha Gamma Arts, 1979). Address: P.O. Box 4671, Walnut Creek, CA 94596.

Montagne, Prosper. *The New Larousse Gastronomique* (New York: Crown Publishers, 1960).

*Norman, Barbara. *Tales of the Table* (Englewood Cliffs, N.J.: Prentice-Hall, 1972).

Passmore, Jacki, and Daniel P. Reid. *The Complete Chinese Cookbook* (Los Angeles: Exeter Books, 1982).

*Pei Mei. *Pei Mei's Chinese Cook Book,* Volumes I, II, and III (Taipei, Taiwan, R.O.C.: Industrial Company, Ltd., P.O. Box 53-319).

Perl, Lila. *Rice, Spice and Bitter Oranges*. (Cleveland: World Publishing Co., 1967).

Revel, Jean-Francois. *Culture and Cuisine* (Jersey City, N.J.: Da Capo Press, 1982).

Richards, Ersie, and Maria-Daphne Mavrelli. *The Tastes of Greece* (Athens: United Travel Press, Ltd., 1985).

Root, Waverly. *Food* (New York: Simon & Schuster, Inc., 1980).

*Root, Waverly. *The Food of Italy* (New York: Vintage Books, 1977).

Rudofsky, Bernard. *Now I Lay Me Down to Eat* (New York: Anchor Books, 1980).

*St. Demetrios Cookbook Committee. *Greek Cooking in an American Kitchen* (Seattle: 1982).
Address: St. Demetrios Cookbook, 2100 Boyer Avenue East, Seattle, Washington 98122; cost is $20.00.

Seranne, Ann, and John Tebbel. *The Epicure's Companion* (New York: David McKay Co., Inc., 1962).

Sheraton, Mimi. *Time,* November 19, 1984, p. 143.

Simon, Andre L., and Robin Howe. *Dictionary of Gastronomy* (New York: McGraw-Hill, 1970).

Slomon, Evelyn. *The Pizza Book* (New York: Times Books, 1984).

Spoerri, Daniel. *Mythology and Meatballs* (New York: Aris, 1982).

Editors of Sunset Books and Sunset Magazine. *Sunset Chinese Cookbook* (Menlo Park, Calif.: Lane Publishing Company, 1979).

*Tannahill, Reay. *Food in History* (New York: Stein and Day, 1973).

Trager, James. *Foodbook* (New York: Grossman Publishers, 1970).

*Tselementes, Nicholas. *Greek Cookery* (New York: D.C. Divry, Inc., 1967).

Von Welanetz, Paul and Diana. *The Von Welanetz Guide to Ethnic Ingredients* (Los Angeles: J. P. Tarcher, Inc., 1982).

*Yianilos, Theresa Karas. *The Complete Greek Cookbook: The Best From Three Thousand Years of Greek Cooking* (New York: Funk and Wagnalls, 1970).

Encyclopedia Americana (Danbury, Conn.: Grolier, Inc., 1987).

Index

D

E

H

I

J

K

L

Permissions

Permission to reprint has been kindly granted as follows:

Chinese Brine Pickles from Dragon Kiln.

Ha Gow Dough and Fun Gor Dough from *Favorite Dim Sum* by Lonnie Mock, Alpha Gamma Arts, P.O. Box 4671, Walnut Creek, CA 94596, 1979.

Egg-Lemon Soup and Garlic Sauce both appeared originally in *The Frugal Gourmet*, copyright © 1984 by Jeff Smith.

Basic Brown Soup Stock, Basic Brown Sauce, and Pesto Sauce all appeared originally in *The Frugal Gourmet Cooks with Wine*, copyright © 1986 by Frugal Gourmet, Inc.

Baked Fish Archestratus, Shrimp Ananius, Roasted Quail Appetizers Homer, Barley Pudding with Lamb, and Pickled Asparagus, Greek Style, all adapted from recipes in *The Complete Greek Cookbook* by Theresa Karas Yianilos, Avenel Books, New York, 1970.

Crispy Roast Pork from *Flavors of China*, Chinese Parents Service Organization, Trinity Printing, Seattle, 1975.

Pastitsio from *Greek Cooking in an American Kitchen*, St. Demetrios Cookbook Committee, 2100 Boyer Avenue East, Seattle, WA 98122.

Corn Crepes, Chinese Style, from *Sunset Magazine*, October 1985.

Onion Cakes from *Pei Mei's Chinese Cook Book, Volume I* by Pei Mei, T & S Industrial Co., Ltd., P.O. Box 53-319, Taipei, Taiwan.

Garbanzo Pizza from *Giuliano Bugialli's Classic Techniques in Italian Cooking*, copyright © 1982 by Giuliano Bugialli, reprinted by permission of Simon & Schuster, Inc.

Chinese Sesame Cookies adapted from *Chinese Cooking Our Way*, Chinese American Women's Club of Santa Clara County, Phoenix Press, Campbell, CA, 1971.